CW00616660

Longman
Compact
English
Dictionary

Longman

Longman Group Limited,
Longman House, Burnt Mill, Harlow,
Essex CM20 2JE, England
and Associated Companies throughout the world.

© Longman Group Limited 1985

First published 1985

Set in Monophoto Times New Roman

Printed in Great Britain
by Hazell Watson & Viney Ltd, Aylesbury.

British Library Cataloguing in Publication Data

Longman compact dictionary.
  1. English—Dictionaries
  423   PE1625
  ISBN 0-582-89290-2

Preface

People consult dictionaries for many reasons, some of them so specialized that they call for the heaviest and most expensive volumes. But research shows that the most common uses of a dictionary are to find the meaning, spelling, and pronunciation of a word or phrase encountered in everyday reading or conversation. The *Longman Compact English Dictionary* has been planned to answer these needs by providing a convenient, uncluttered guide to the main vocabulary of contemporary English. Compiled by experts from the vast resources of the Longman dictionary database, it includes extensive coverage of scientific, technical, colloquial, and idiomatic language, and terms as up to date as 'breakdance' and 'nuclear winter'. The pronunciations are particularly easy to understand, since the system is based almost entirely on English spelling and avoids unfamiliar symbols or marks.

Abbreviations used in this Dictionary

A

A ampere
abbr abbreviation
AD Anno Domini
adj adjective
adv adverb
am ante meridiem
apprec appreciative
approx approximate,
 approximately
arch archaic
attrib attributive
Austr Australian

B

BC before Christ
Br British
Btu British thermal unit

C

c century
C Celsius, centigrade
Can Canadian
cap capital, capitalized
cgs centimetre-gram-
 second
cm centimetre
conj conjunction
constr construction
cwt hundredweight

D

derog derogatory
dial dialect
dr dram

E

E East, Eastern
eg for example
Eng English, England
esp especially
etc etcetera
euph euphemistic

F

F Fahrenheit
fem feminine
fl oz fluid ounce
fml formal
ft foot

G

gall gallon
gr grain

H

h hour
ha hectare
hp horsepower
humor humorous
Hz hertz

I

ie that is
imper imperative
in inch
Ind Indian
indic indicative
infin infinitive
infml informal

interj interjection
interrog interrogative

J

J joule
journ journalistic

K

kg kilogram
km kilometre

L

l litre
lb pound

M

M metre
masc masculine
MHz megahertz
ml mile
Mid Eng Midlands
Mid US Mid United
 States
mil military
min minute
ml millilitre
mm millimetre
mph miles per hour
Mt Mount

N

n noun
N North, Northern
N Newton

NAm North American
naut nautical
neg negative
NZ New Zealand

O

obs obsolete
occas occasionally
orig original, originally
oz ounce

P

p pence
part participle
pass passive
perf perfect
phr(s) phrase(s)
pl plural
pm post meridiem
prep preposition
pres present
prob probably
pron pronoun
pt pint

Q

qr quarter
qt quart

S

s second
S South, Southern
SAfr South Africa, South African
sby somebody
Scot Scotland, Scottish
SI Système International d'Unités
sing singular
specif specifically
st stone
St Saint
sthg something
substand substandard

T

tech technical

U

UK United Kingdom
US United States
USA United States of America
usu usually

V

v verb
V volt
vulg vulgar

W

W watt
W West, Western
WWI World War 1
WWII World War 2

Y

yd yard

How to use this Dictionary

1   Order of entries

1.1   Main entries

All main entries appear in letter-by-letter alphabetical order. Words that have the same spelling but differ in pronunciation, history, or grammatical function are distinguished from one another by small numbers in front of them; see, for example, the entries at **lead**.

1.2   Undefined words

Words whose meaning can easily be guessed, because they consist of a base form plus an added ending, are not given definitions. They follow the main entry and are shown in these ways:

a Where the undefined word is the same as the main entry, but has a different part of speech, it appears in full

b Where the main entry forms a stem to which an ending is added to form the undefined word, the stem is represented by ~, and the ending follows:

   content *adj* . . . ~**ment** *n*

c Where any part of the main entry forms the stem of an undefined word, the unchanged part is represented by – :

   indifferent *adj* . . . -**ence** *n*

Occasionally no shortening of the undefined entry is possible, and it is given in full.

1.3   Idiomatic phrases

Idioms are fixed phrases whose meaning cannot be guessed from the meanings of the individual words of which they are composed. Idioms are shown here at the end of an entry, after any derived undefined words. They are generally entered at the first meaningful word they contain: **live it up** appears at **live**, **on the ball** at **ball**, and **in spite of** at **spite**.

2   Alternative versions of words

Many words come in pairs, or even trios, that differ only in spelling (eg **judgment, judgement**), in their ending (eg **consistency, consistence**), or in the presence or absence of a complete word in a compound (eg **prime**, **prime number**). In this dictionary, common variant forms of a word are shown immediately after the main entry. When the variant is preceded by a comma, it is about as common as the main entry in current standard usage; when the variant is preceded by *also*, it is rather less common.

Variant spellings of the **-ize/-ise** type are shown in abbreviated form at the main entry:

real·ize, **-ise** *v*

This means that **realize** can also be spelt **realise**.

Variant forms that are entirely or partially restricted to British or American English are labelled *Br* or *NAm*:

jail, *Br also* **gaol** . . . *n* . . .
gaol . . . *v or n, chiefly Br* (to) jail

This means that the spelling **jail** is used everywhere in the English-speaking world, but British English also uses **gaol** (see 7.2).

3 Inflections

3.1 Nouns

Regular plurals of nouns (eg **cats, matches, spies**) are not shown. All other plurals (eg **louse, lice; sheep, sheep**) are given.

Nouns that are always plural (eg **environs**) are labelled *n pl*. Plural nouns that take a singular verb ('Genetics is . . . .') are labelled '*n pl but sing in constr*'; those that take either a singular or plural verb ('Politics is . . .' or 'Politics are . . .') are labelled '*n pl but sing or pl in constr*'. Likewise, nouns in apparently singular form can be '*pl in constr*' ('Several police are . . .') or '*sing or pl in constr*' ('The crew is . . .' or 'The crew are . . .'). Nouns that can be used in the plural with the same meaning as the singular (eg **latitude/ latitudes**) are labelled '*often pl with sing meaning*'.

3.2 Verbs

Regular verb forms (eg **halted, cadged, carrying**) are not shown. All other verb inflections (eg **ring, rang, rung**) are shown, including those for verbs which keep a final *-e* before inflections, and for verbs having alternative inflections.

Inflections are shown in the following order:

present: 1st, 2nd, and 3rd person singular; plural; present subjunctive; present participle; past: 1st, 2nd and 3rd person singular; plural; past subjunctive; past participle.

Only the irregular inflections are shown.

3.3 Adjectives and adverbs

Adjectives and adverbs whose comparative and superlative are formed with **more** and **most**, or by adding **-(e)r** and **-(e)st** (eg **nicer, fastest, happier**), are not shown.

All other inflections (eg **good** ... **better** ... **best**) are shown.

3.4 Pronouns

Inflections of pronouns are entered at their alphabetical place and cross-referred to their main form:

²her *pron, objective case of* **she**

4   Capitalization

Some words, or meanings of words, can be used with or without a capital letter, and this is shown by the notes *often cap* and *often not cap*. In the case of compound words, the note specifies which parts are capitalized:

pop art *n, often cap P&A* ...

5   How the meaning of words is shown

5.1 The numbering of meanings

The main meanings of a word are numbered (**1, 2, 3**, etc) where there is more than one sense. Subdivisions of the senses are distinguished by lower-case letters, and further subdivisions by bracketed numbers.

When a definition is followed by a colon and two or more subsenses, this indicates that the meaning of the subsenses is covered by the introductory definition.

Sometimes an introductory definition is simply the common element shared by the following subsenses:

cheapen ... *v* to make or become **a** cheap in price or value **b** lower in esteem **c** tawdry, vulgar, or inferior

This indicates that **cheapen** means 'to make or become cheap in price and value', 'to make or become lower in esteem', and 'to make or become tawdry, vulgar, or inferior'.

When two meanings of a word are very closely related, they are not separated off with numbers or letters, but run together, with the word *esp*, *specif*, *also*, or *broadly* between them to show the way in which they are related.

5.2 The order in which senses are shown

Those meanings that would be understood anywhere in the English-speaking world are shown first, in their historical order: the older senses before the newer. After these come the meanings whose usage is restricted in some way (eg because they are used in only one area, or have gone out of current use).

5.3 Brackets

Round brackets are used in four main ways in definitions:
They enclose the object of a verb:

²**contract** *v* . . . **2a** to catch (an illness)

They give extra information:

³**nap** *n* a hairy or downy surface (eg on a woven fabric)

They separate the parts of a combined definition that relate to different parts of speech:

cheep . . . *v or n* (to utter) a faint shrill sound characteristic of a young bird

They enclose optional wording:

afloat . . . *adj or adv* **1a** borne (as if) on the water or air

This indicates that **afloat** means both 'borne on the water or air' and 'borne as if on the water or air'.

6   Examples

Phrases illustrating a typical use of a word in context are used to clarify the definitions of some words, like **in** and **up**. These examples appear in round brackets.

7   Usage

Many words have peculiarities of usage that a dictionary must take account of. They may be restricted to a particular geographical area; they may be colloquial or slang, or felt to be 'incorrect'; they may have fallen out of use; and there may be limitations on the sort of context they can be used in.

This dictionary shows such restrictions in two different ways.

Words, or meanings, that are limited to a particular period or area are identified by an italic label. When an italic label comes between the main entry and the first definition it refers to all meanings of the word; otherwise, it applies to all subsenses of the number or letter it follows.

All other information on usage is given in a note at the end of a definition. When such a note applies to all or several meanings of a word, it follows the last definition, and is introduced by the word *USE*.

7.1 Words that are no longer in current use

The label *obs* for 'obsolete' means there is no evidence of use for a word or meaning since 1755.

The label *archaic* means that a word or meaning once in common use is found today only in special contexts, such as poetry or historical fiction.

Comparatively modern terms which have become old-fashioned are treated in a note:

matron ... *n* ... 3 a woman in charge of the nursing in a hospital – not now used technically

groovy ... *adj* fashionably attractive or exciting – infml: no longer in vogue

7.2 Words that are not used throughout the English-speaking world

A word or sense limited in use to one or more of the countries of the English-speaking world is labelled accordingly:

tuxedo ... *n, NAm* a dinner jacket

The label *Br* indicates that a word or meaning is used in Britain and also usually in the Commonwealth countries of Australasia. The label *NAm* indicates the use of a word or meaning in both the USA and Canada.

The label *dial* for 'dialect' indicates that a word or meaning belongs to the common local speech of several different places.

7.3 Words that suggest a particular style, attitude, or level of formality

Most English words can be generally used in both speech and writing, but some would be traditionally described as 'colloquial' or 'slang', and others, perhaps, as 'formal'.

The note '– infml' is used for words or senses that are characteristic of conversational speech and casual writing rather than of official or 'serious' speech or writing.

The note '– slang' is used for words or meanings usually found in contexts of extreme informality. Such words may be, or may have been until recently, used by a particular social group such as criminals or drug users. They often refer to topics that are thought of as risqué or 'low'.

The note '– fml', for 'formal', is used for words or meanings characteristic of written rather than spoken English, and particularly of official or academic writings.

Other notes describe the attitude or tone of the user of a word, eg 'derog' (derogatory) or 'euph' (euphemistic).

7.4 Words that are not 'correct'

Many people disapprove of the use of some of the words we have described as 'slang' or 'informal', and there are contexts in which their use would be inappropriate; but there is a further distinct class of words that are generally felt to be 'incorrect'.

The note '– nonstandard' is used for words or meanings that are quite commonly used in English but are considered incorrect by many speakers.

Certain highly controversial words or meanings have the warning note '– disapproved of by some speakers'.

The note '– substandard' is used for words or meanings that are widely used but are not part of standard English.

7.5   The context in which a word can appear

Many words or meanings can be used only in certain contexts within a sentence: some verbs are used only in the passive; some words can appear only in the negative, along with **not**, **never**, etc; others are always used with particular prepositions or adverbs, or in certain fixed phrases. Such restrictions are shown in a note following a definition:

abide ... *v* **1** to bear patiently; tolerate – used negatively
agree ... *v* ... **4** to give assent; accede – often + *to*

Sometimes a word that is commonly used with the main entry word in a sentence is printed in italic within the definition:

allude ... *v* to make indirect or implicit reference *to*
²**altogether** *n the* nude – infml

This means that **allude** is almost always used in the phrase **allude to**, and that the noun **altogether** is almost always used with **the**.

8   Pronunciation

8.1   Symbols used

Pronunciations, enclosed within slash marks / /, use the following symbols:

Vowels

a	as in	b*a*d, f*a*t	oh	„	n*o*te, J*oa*n
ah	„	f*a*ther, oomp*ah*	oo	„	p*u*t, c*oo*k
aw	„	s*aw*, *aw*ful	ooh	„	b*oo*t, l*u*te
ay	„	m*a*ke, h*ay*	ooə	„	j*u*ry, c*u*re
e	„	b*e*d, h*ea*d	ow	„	n*ow*, b*ou*gh
ee	„	sh*ee*p, k*ey*	owə	„	*ou*r, p*ow*er
eə	„	th*ere*, h*air*	oy	„	b*oy*, l*oi*ter
i	„	sh*i*p, l*i*ck	oyə	„	l*awyer*, s*awyer*
ie	„	b*i*te, l*ie*d	u	„	c*u*t, l*u*ck
ie·ə	„	f*ire*, l*iar*	uh	„	b*ir*d, abs*ur*d
iə	„	h*ere*, f*ear*	ə	„	moth*er*, *a*bout
o	„	p*o*t, cr*o*p			

Consonants

b	as in	*bad*	ng	„	su*ng*
ch	„	*cheer*	nh	„	restaura*nt*
d	„	*day*	p	„	*pot*
dh	„	*they*	r	„	*red*
f	„	*few*	s	„	*soon*
g	„	*gay*	sh	„	*fish*
h	„	*hot*	t	„	*tea*
j	„	*jump*	th	„	*thing*
k	„	*king*	v	„	*view*
kh	„	*loch*	w	„	*wet*
l	„	*led*	y	„	*yet*
m	„	*man*	z	„	*zero*
n	„	*sun*	zh	„	*pleasure*

8.2   Stress

In all English words of 2 or more syllables, one syllable is more prominent
that the others; the sign ' is placed before this syllable on which the main
stress falls. Some longer words have a secondary stress on another syllable;
the sign , is placed before this syllable.

    Pronunciations are not usually given for entries which are compounds of
words listed individually, or which have (wholly or partly) the same
pronunciation as the preceding entry. Only part of their pronunciation may
be shown; or they may merely be marked with the signs showing stress; or
the pronunciation may be shown simply as a stress pattern, in which each
syllable is represented by a hyphen.

8.3   Special symbols

The symbol (ə) is used where the sound /ə/ may be either pronounced or
omitted.

    A centred dot (·) separates pairs of letters that might otherwise be
wrongly read as one sound.

    A swung dash (~) indicates that a plural form is pronounced in the same
way as the singular.

    A hyphen indicates an identical part of two pronunciations which has not
been repeated.

8.4   Variant pronunciations

Alternative pronunciations separated by a comma may be taken as equally
acceptable; alternatives preceded by '*also*' are less common, or considered
incorrect by some speakers, while those preceded by '*often*' are generally
considered incorrect.

    Pronunciations labelled '*naut*' and '*tech*' are specialized forms used by experts within the field to which the word belongs.

Specifically American pronunciations (labelled '*NAm*') are shown only when a word is pronounced in such a way that it might not be recognized by British speakers (eg **clerk**, **lieutenant**).

A

¹**a** /ay/ *n, pl* **a's, as,** *often cap* **1 a** (a graphic representation of or device for reproducing) the 1st letter of the English alphabet **b** a speech counterpart of written *a* **2** one designated *a*, esp as the 1st in order or class

²**a** /ə/; *strong* /ay/ *indefinite article* **1** one – used before singular nouns when the referent is unspecified (e g *a* sheep) and before number collectives and some numbers (e g *a* great many) **2** the same (e g birds of *a* feather) **3a(1)** any (e g *a* bike has 2 wheels) **a(2)** one single (e g can't see *a* thing) **b** one particular (e g health is *a* good thing) **c** – used before the gerund or infinitive of a verb to denote a period or occurrence of the activity concerned (e g *a* good cry) **4** – used before a proper name to denote (1) membership of a class (e g born *a* Romanov) (2) resemblance (e g *a* little Hitler) (3) one named but not otherwise known (e g *a* Dr Smith) *USE* used before words or letter sequences with an initial consonant sound

³**a** /ə/ *prep* **1** per **2** *chiefly dial* on, in, at *USE* used before words or letter sequences with an initial consonant sound

A1 *adj* **1** *of a ship* having the highest possible classification of seaworthiness for insurance purposes **2** of the finest quality; first-rate

abacus /'abəkəs/ *n, pl* **abaci** /-kie, -sie/, **abacuses 1** a slab that forms the uppermost part of the capital of a column **2** an instrument for performing calculations by sliding counters along rods or in grooves

abandon /ə'band(ə)n/ *v* **1** to give up completely, esp with the intention of never resuming or reclaiming **2** to leave, often in the face of danger **3** to forsake or desert (e g a responsibility) **4** to give (oneself) over to an emotion or activity – ~ment *n*

abase /ə'bays/ *v* to bring lower in rank or esteem – ~ment *n*

abash /ə'bash/ *v* to destroy the self-possession or self-confidence of – usu pass

abate /ə'bayt/ *v* **1** to put an end to; abolish **2** to reduce in amount, intensity, or degree; moderate **3** to decrease in force or intensity – ~ment *n*

abattoir /'abə,twah/ *n* a slaughterhouse

abbess /'abes/ *n* the female superior of a convent of nuns

abbey /'abi/ *n* **1** a religious community governed by an abbot or abbess **2** the buildings, esp the church, of a (former) monastery

abbot /'abət/ *n* the superior of an abbey of monks

abbreviate /ə'breeviayt/ *v* to reduce to a shorter form – **-ation** *n*

ABC *n, pl* **ABC's, ABCs 1** the alphabet **2** the first principles of a subject

abdicate /'abdikayt/ *v* **1** to relinquish (e g sovereign power) formally **2** to renounce a throne, dignity, etc – **-cation** *n*

abdomen /'abdəmən, ab'dohmən/ *n* **1** (the cavity of) the part of the body between the thorax and the pelvis that contains the liver, gut, etc **2** the rear part of the body behind the thorax in an insect, spider, etc – **-dominal** *adj*

abduct /əb'dukt/ *v* to carry off secretly or by force – ~ion *n*

aberrant /ə'berənt/ *adj* **1** deviating from the right or normal way **2** diverging from the usual or natural type

aberration /,abə'raysh(ə)n/ *n* **1** being aberrant, esp with respect to a moral standard or normal state **2** (an instance of) unsoundness or disorder of the mind

abet /ə'bet/ *v* **-tt-** to give active encouragement or approval to – ~tor, ~ter *n*

abeyance /ə'bayəns/ *n* temporary inactivity; suspension

abhor /əb'(h)aw/ *v* **-rr-** to loathe

abhorrent /əb'(h)orənt, əb'(h)awrənt/ *adj* **1** opposed, contrary to **2** causing horror; repugnant – **-rence** *n*

abide /ə'bied/ *v* **abode** /ə'bohd/, **abided 1** to bear patiently; tolerate – used negatively **2** to remain stable or fixed in a state **3** *archaic* to dwell **4** to comply with – usu + *by*

abiding /ə'bieding/ *adj* enduring

ability /ə'biləti/ *n* **1** being able; *esp* physical, mental, or legal power to perform **2** natural or acquired competence in doing; skill

abject /'abjekt/ *adj* **1** showing utter hopelessness; wretched, miserable **2** despicable, degraded **3** very humble, esp to the point of servility – ~ly *adv* – ~ion *n*

abjure /əb'jooə/ *v* to renounce on oath or reject formally (e g a claim, opinion, or allegiance) – **-ration** *n*

ablative /'ablətiv/ *n* (a form in) a grammatical case expressing typically separation, source, cause, or instrument

ablaze /ə'blayz/ *adj or adv* **1** on fire **2** radiant with light or bright colour

able /'aybl/ *adj* **1** having sufficient power, skill, resources, or qualifications *to* **2** marked by intelligence, knowledge, skill, or competence

able-'bodied *adj* physically strong and healthy; fit

abnormal /,ab'nawməl, əb-/ *adj* deviating from the normal or average – ~ly *adv* – ~ity *n*

aboard /ə'bawd/ *adv or prep* **1** on, onto, or within (a ship, aircraft, train, or road vehicle) **2** alongside

abolish /ə'bolish/ *v* to do away with (e g a law or custom) wholly; annul – **-ition** *n*

'**A-, bomb** /ay/ *n* an atom bomb

abominable /ə'bominəbl/ *adj* worthy of or causing disgust or hatred – **-bly** *adv*

abominate /ə'bominayt/ *v* to hate or loathe intensely and unremittingly; abhor

abomination /ə,bomi'naysh(ə)n/ *n* **1** sthg abominable; *esp* a detestable or shameful action **2** extreme disgust and hatred; loathing

aboriginal /,abə'rijin(ə)l/ *adj* **1** indigenous **2** of esp Australian aborigines

aborigine /,abə'rijinee/ *n* an indigenous inhabitant, esp as contrasted with an invading or colonizing people; *specif, often cap* a member of the indigenous people of Australia

abort /ə'bawt/ *v* **1** to (cause to) expel a premature foetus **2** to fail to develop completely **3** to end prematurely – ~ **ion** *n* – ~ **ionist** *n*

abortive /ə'bawtiv/ *adj* **1** fruitless, unsuccessful **2** imperfectly formed or developed – ~ **ly** *adv*

abound /ə'bownd/ *v* **1** to be present in large numbers or in great quantity **2** to be amply supplied – + *in* **3** to be crowded or infested *with*

'**about** /ə'bowt/ *adv* **1** round **2** in succession or rotation; alternately **3** approximately **4** almost **5** in the vicinity

²**about** *prep* **1** on every side of; surrounding **2a** in the vicinity of **b** on or near the person of **c** in the make-up of **d** at the command of **3a** engaged in **b** on the verge of – + *to* **4a** with regard to, concerning **b** intimately concerned with **5** over or in different parts of **6** *chiefly NAm* – used with the negative to express intention or determination

³**about** *adj* **1** moving from place to place; *specif* out of bed **2** in existence, evidence, or circulation

'**above** /ə'buv/ *adv* **1a** in the sky overhead **b** in or to heaven **2a** in or to a higher place **b** higher on the same or an earlier page **c** upstairs **3** in or to a higher rank or number **4** upstage

²**above** *prep* **1** higher than the level of **2** over **3** beyond, transcending **4a** superior to (e g in rank) **b** too proud or honourable to stoop to **5** upstream from — **above oneself** excessively self-satisfied

³**above** *n, pl* **above 1a** sthg (written) above **b** a person whose name is written above **2a** a higher authority **b** heaven

⁴**above** *adj* written higher on the same, or on a preceding, page

a,bove'board /-'bawd/ *adj* free from all traces of deceit or dishonesty

abracadabra /,abrəkə'dabrə/ *n* a magical charm or incantation – used interjectionally as an accompaniment to conjuring tricks

abrade /ə'brayd/ *v* to roughen, irritate, or wear away, esp by friction

abrasion /ə'brayzh(ə)n/ *n* **1** a wearing, grinding, or rubbing away by friction **2** an abraded area

'**abrasive** /ə'braysiv, -ziv/ *adj* tending to abrade; causing irritation – ~ **ly** *adv*

²**abrasive** *n* a substance (e g emery) that may be used for grinding away, smoothing, or polishing

abreast /ə'brest/ *adv* or *adj* **1** side by side and facing in the same direction **2** up-to-date in attainment or information

abridge /ə'brij/ *v* **1** to reduce in scope; curtail **2** to shorten by omission of words without sacrifice of sense; condense – **-gment** *n*

abroad /ə'brawd/ *adv* or *adj* **1** over a wide area; widely **2** away from one's home; out of doors **3** beyond the boundaries of one's country **4** in wide circulation; about

abrogate /'abrəgayt/ *v* to abolish by authoritative action; annul, repeal – **-gation** *n*

abrupt /ə'brupt/ *adj* **1** ending as if sharply cut off; truncated **2a** occurring without warning; unexpected **b** unceremoniously curt **3** rising or dropping sharply; steep – ~ **ly** *adv* – ~ **ness** *n*

abscess /'abses, -sis/ *n* a pocket of pus surrounded by inflamed tissue

abscond /əb'skond/ *v* to depart secretly, esp so as to evade retribution

absence /'absəns/ *n* **1** being absent **2** the period of time that one is absent **3** a lack

absence of 'mind *n* inattention to present surroundings or occurrences

'**absent** /'absənt/ *adj* **1** not present or attending; missing **2** not existing; lacking **3** preoccupied – ~ **ly** *adv*

²**absent** /əb'sent/ *v* to take or keep (oneself) away – usu + *from*

absentee /,abz(ə)n'tee/ *n* one who is absent or who absents him-/herself

absen'tee,ism /-,iz(ə)m/ *n* persistent and deliberate absence from work or duty

absent'minded /-'miendid/ *adj* lost in thought and unaware of one's surroundings or actions – ~ **ly** *adv* – ~ **ness** *n*

absinth, absinthe /'absinth/ *n* a green liqueur flavoured with wormwood and aniseed

absolute *adj* **1a** perfect **b** (relatively) pure or unmixed **c** outright, unmitigated **2** completely free from constitutional or other restraint **3** having no restriction, exception, or qualification **4** positive, unquestionable – ~ **ness** *n*

abso'lutely /-li/ *adv* totally, completely – often used to express emphatic agreement

absolute 'zero *n* the lowest temperature theoretically possible at which there is a complete absence of heat and which is equivalent to about –273.16°C or 0°K

absolution /,absə'loohsh(ə)n, -bz-, -ps-/ *n* the act of absolving; *specif* a declaration of forgiveness of sins pronounced by a priest

absolutism /,absə'loohtiz(ə)m, -bz-, -ps-, '---,-/ *n* (the theory favouring) government by an absolute ruler or authority

absolve /əb'zolv/ v 1 to set free *from* an obligation or the consequences of guilt 2 to declare (a sin) of (a person) forgiven by absolution

absorb /əb'zawb; *also* -bs-/ v 1 to take in and make part of an existing whole; incorporate 2a to suck up or take up b to assimilate; take in 3 to engage or occupy wholly – ~ent *adj*

absorbing /əb'zawbing; *also* -bs-/ *adj* engaging one's full attention; engrossing

absorption /əb'zawpsh(ə)n; *also* əb'sawpsh(ə)n/ n 1 absorbing or being absorbed 2 total involvement of the mind

abstain /əb'stayn/ v 1 to refrain deliberately, and often with an effort of self-denial, *from* 2 to refrain from using one's vote

abstemious /əb'steemi-əs/ *adj* sparing, esp in eating or drinking – ~ly *adv* – ~ness n

abstention /əb'stensh(ə)n/ n 1 abstaining – often + *from* 2 an instance of withholding a vote

abstinence /'abstinəns/ *also* **abstinency** /-si/ n 1 voluntary forbearance, esp from indulgence of appetite or from eating some foods – often + *from* 2 habitual abstaining from intoxicating beverages – esp in *total abstinence* – **-nent** *adj*

¹**abstract** /'abstrakt/ *adj* 1a detached from any specific instance or object b difficult to understand; abstruse 2 *of a noun* naming a quality, state, or action rather than a thing; not concrete 3 theoretical rather than practical 4 having little or no element of pictorial representation

²**abstract** n 1 a summary of points (e g of a piece of writing) 2 an abstract concept or state 3 an abstract composition or creation

³**abstract** /əb'strakt/ v 1 to remove, separate 2 to consider in the abstract 3 to make an abstract of; summarize

ab'stracted *adj* preoccupied, absentminded – ~ly *adv*

abstraction /əb'straksh(ə)n/ n 1 an abstract idea or term stripped of its concrete manifestations 2 absentmindedness 3 an abstract composition or creation

abstruse /əb'stroohs/ *adj* difficult to understand; recondite – ~ly *adv* – ~ness n

absurd /əb'suhd, -bz-/ *adj* 1 ridiculously unreasonable or incongruous; silly 2 lacking order or value; meaningless – ~ly *adv* – ~ity n

abundance /ə'bund(ə)ns/ n 1 an ample quantity; a profusion 2 affluence, wealth

abundant /ə'bund(ə)nt/ *adj* 1a marked by great plenty (e g of resources) b amply supplied *with*; abounding *in* 2 occurring in abundance – ~ly *adv*

¹**abuse** /ə'byoohz/ v 1 to attack in words; revile 2 to put to a wrong or improper use 3 to use so as to injure or damage; maltreat – **-sive** *adj*

²**abuse** /ə'byoohs/ n 1 a corrupt practice or custom 2 improper use or treatment; misuse 3 vehemently expressed condemnation or disapproval 4 physical maltreatment

abut /ə'but/ v -tt- 1 to border on; touch 2 to lean *on* for support

abysmal /ə'bizməl/ *adj* 1 deplorably great 2 immeasurably bad

abyss /ə'bis/ n an immeasurably deep gulf

¹**academic** /,akə'demik/ *also* **academical** /-kl/ *adj* 1a of an institution of higher learning b scholarly c very learned but inexperienced in practical matters 2 conventional, formal 3 theoretical with no practical or useful bearing

²**academic** n a member (of the teaching staff) of an institution of higher learning

academy /ə'kadəmi/ n 1 *cap* the school for advanced education founded by Plato 2a a secondary school; *esp* a private high school – now only in names b a college in which special subjects or skills are taught 3 a society of learned people organized to promote the arts or sciences

accede /ək'seed/ v 1 to become a party (e g to a treaty) 2 to express approval or give consent, often in response to urging 3 to enter on an office or position; *esp* to become monarch *USE* usu + *to*

accelerate /ək'selərayt/ v 1 to bring about at an earlier time 2 to increase the speed of 3 to hasten the progress, development, or growth of 4 to move faster; gain speed 5 to increase more rapidly

acceleration /ək,selə'raysh(ə)n/ n (the rate of) change, specif increase, of velocity

accelerator /ək'seləraytə/ n a pedal in a motor vehicle that controls the speed of the motor

¹**accent** /'aksənt/ n 1 a distinctive pattern in inflection, tone, or choice of words, esp as characteristic of a regional or national area 2a prominence given to 1 syllable over others by stress or a change in pitch b greater stress given to 1 musical note c rhythmically significant stress on the syllables of a verse 3a accent, accent mark a mark added to a letter (e g in à, ñ, ç) to indicate how it should be pronounced b a symbol used to indicate musical stress 4 special concern or attention; emphasis

²**accent** /ək'sent/ v 1 to pronounce (a vowel, syllable, or word) with accent; stress 2 to make more prominent; emphasize

accentuate /ək'sentyoo-ayt, -choo-ayt/ v to accent, emphasize – **-ation** n

accept /ək'sept/ v 1a to agree to receive; *also* to agree to b to be able or designed to take or hold (sthg applied or inserted) 2 to give admittance or approval to 3a to endure without protest; accommodate oneself to b to regard as proper, normal, or inevitable c to recognize as true, factual, or adequate 4 to undertake the responsibility of 5 to receive favourably sthg offered

acceptable /ək'septəbl/ *adj* 1 capable or worthy of being accepted; satisfactory 2 welcome or pleasing to the receiver 3 tolerable – **-ability** n – **-bly** *adv*

acc

acceptance /əkˈsept(ə)ns/ *n* **1** accepting, approval **2** acceptability **3** agreement to the act or offer of another so that the parties become legally bound

access /ˈakses, -səs/ *n* **1** freedom to approach, reach, or make use of sthg **2** a means (e g a doorway or channel) of access **3** the state of being readily reached or obtained

accessible /əkˈsesəbl/ *adj* **1** capable of being reached **2** of a form that can be readily grasped intellectually **3** able to be influenced – **-ibility** *n*

accession /əkˈsesh(ə)n/ *n* **1** becoming joined **2** the act by which a nation becomes party to an agreement already in force **3a** an increase due to sthg added **b** acquisition of property by addition to existing property **4** the act of entering on a high office **5** assent, agreement – *fml*

¹**accessory** /əkˈsesəri/ *n* an inessential object or device that adds to the beauty, convenience, or effectiveness of sthg else

²**accessory** *adj* supplementary, subordinate

accident /ˈaksid(ə)nt/ *n* **1a** an event occurring by chance or arising from unknown causes **b** lack of intention or necessity; chance **2** an unexpected happening causing loss or injury **3** a nonessential property or condition of sthg

¹**accidental** /ˌaksiˈdentl/ *adj* **1** arising incidentally; nonessential **2a** occurring unexpectedly or by chance **b** happening without intent or through carelessness and often with unfortunate results – **~ly** *adv*

²**accidental** *n* **1** a nonessential property or condition **2** (a sign indicating) a note altered to sharp, flat, or natural and foreign to a key indicated by a key signature

accident-prone *adj* having personality traits that predispose to accidents

¹**acclaim** /əˈklaym/ *v* **1** to applaud, praise **2** to hail or proclaim by acclamation

²**acclaim** *n* acclamation

acclamation /ˌakləˈmaysh(ə)n/ *n* **1** a loud expression of praise, goodwill, or assent **2** an overwhelming affirmative vote by cheers or applause rather than by ballot

acclimat·ize, -ise /əˈklīmətīz/ *v* to adapt to a new climate or situation – **-tization** *n*

accolade /ˈakəlayd/ *n* **1** a mark of acknowledgment or honour; an award **2** an expression of strong praise

accommodate /əˈkomədayt/ *v* **1** to make fit or suitable *to* **2** to bring into agreement or concord; reconcile **3a** to give help to; oblige *with* **b** to provide with lodgings; house **4** to have or make adequate room for **5** to give consideration to; allow for

accommodating /əˈkomədayting/ *adj* helpful, obliging – **~ly** *adv*

accommodation /əˌkoməˈdaysh(ə)n/ *n* **1a** lodging, housing **b** space, premises **2a** sthg needed or desired for convenience; a facility **b** an adaptation, adjustment **c** a settlement, agreement **d** the (range of) automatic adjustment of the eye for seeing at different distances

accompaniment /əˈkumpənimənt/ *n* **1** a subordinate instrumental or vocal part supporting or complementing a principal voice or instrument **2** an addition intended to give completeness; a complement

accompany /əˈkumpəni/ *v* **1** to go with as an escort or companion **2** to perform an accompaniment (to or for) **3a** to make an addition to; supplement *with* **b** *of a thing* to happen, exist, or be found with

accomplice /əˈkumplis, -ˈkom-/ *n* sby who collaborates with another, esp in wrongdoing

accomplish /əˈkumplish, -ˈkom-/ *v* **1** to bring to a successful conclusion; achieve **2** to complete, cover (a measure of time or distance)

ac·complished *adj* **1** fully effected; completed **2a** skilled, proficient **b** having many social accomplishments

ac·complishment /-mənt/ *n* **1** completion, fulfilment **2** an achievement **3** an acquired ability or esp social skill

¹**accord** /əˈkawd/ *v* **1** to grant, concede **2** to give, award **3** to be consistent *with*

²**accord** *n* **1a** accordance **b** a formal treaty of agreement **2** balanced relationship (e g of colours or sounds); harmony — **of one's own accord** of one's own volition; unbidden — **with one accord** with the consent or agreement of all

accordance /əˈkawd(ə)ns/ *n* **1** agreement, conformity **2** the act of granting

accordingly /əˈkawdingli/ *adv* **1** as suggested; appropriately **2** consequently, so

accordion /əˈkawdi·ən/ *n* a portable keyboard wind instrument in which the wind is forced past free reeds by means of a hand-operated bellows

accost /əˈkost/ *v* **1** to approach and speak to, esp boldly or challengingly **2** *of a prostitute* to solicit

¹**account** /əˈkownt/ *n* **1** a record of debits and credits relating to a particular item, person, or concern **2** a list of items of expenditure to be balanced against income – usu pl **3** a periodically rendered calculation listing purchases and credits **4** a business arrangement whereby money is deposited in, and may be withdrawn from, a bank, building society, etc **5** a commission to carry out a particular business operation (e g an advertising campaign) given by one company to another **6** value, importance **7a** a statement explaining one's conduct **b** a statement of facts or events; a relation — **on account of** due to; because of — **on no account** *or* **not on any account** under

no circumstances — **on one's own account 1** on one's own behalf **2** at one's own risk — **on somebody's account** for sby's sake

²**account** v to think of as; consider — **account for 1** to give an explanation or reason for **2** to be the sole or primary explanation for **3** to bring about the defeat, death, or destruction of

accountable /ə'kowntəbl/ adj **1** responsible, answerable **2** explicable

accountancy /ə'kownt(ə)nsi/ n the profession or practice of accounting

accountant /ə'kownt(ə)nt/ n one who practises and is usu qualified in accounting

accredit /ə'kredit/ v **1a** to give official authorization to or approval of **b** to recognize or vouch for as conforming to a standard **2** to credit with, attribute to

accretion /ə'kreesh(ə)n/ n **1a** an increase in size caused by natural growth or the external adhesion or addition of matter **b** sthg added or stuck extraneously **2** the growth of separate particles or parts (e g of a plant) into one

accrue /ə'krooh/ v **1** to come as a (periodic) increase or addition to sthg; arise as a growth or result **2** to collect, accumulate

accumulate /ə'kyoohmyoo,layt/ v **1** to collect together gradually; amass **2** to increase in quantity or number

accumulation /ə,kyoohmyoo'laysh(ə)n/ n **1** increase or growth caused by esp repeated or continuous addition **2** sthg that has accumulated

accumulative /ə'kyoohmyoolətiv/ adj **1** cumulative **2** tending or given to accumulation, esp of money – **ly** adv

accumulator /ə'kyoohmyoo,laytə/ n **1** a part (e g in a computer) where numbers are added or stored **2** Br a rechargeable secondary electric cell; also a connected set of these **3** Br a bet whereby the winnings from one of a series of events are staked on the next event

accurate /'akyoorət/ adj **1** free from error, esp as the result of care **2** conforming precisely to truth or a measurable standard; exact – **-acy** n – **-ly** adv

accursed /ə'kuhst, ə'kuhsid/, **accurst** /ə'kuhst/ adj **1** under a curse; ill-fated **2** damnable, detestable – **-ly** adv

accusative /ə'kyoohzətiv/ n (a form (e g me) in) a grammatical case expressing the direct object of a verb or of some prepositions

accuse /ə'kyoohz/ v to charge with a fault or crime; blame – **-sation** n – **-singly** adv

ac'cused n, pl accused the defendant in a criminal case

accustom /ə'kust(ə)m/ v to make used to through use or experience; habituate

ac'customed adj **1** customary, habitual **2** in the habit of; used to

¹**ace** /ays/ n **1** a die face, playing card, or domino marked with 1 spot or pip; also the single spot or pip on any of these **2** (a point scored by) a shot, esp a service in tennis, that an opponent fails to touch **3** a combat pilot who has brought down at least 5 enemy aircraft **4** an expert or leading performer in a specified field — **ace in the hole** an effective argument or resource held in reserve — **within an ace of** on the point of; very near to

²**ace** v to score an ace against (an opponent)

³**ace** adj great, excellent – infml

acetate /'asitayt/ n a salt or ester of acetic acid

a,cetic 'acid n a pungent liquid acid that is the major acid in vinegar

¹**ache** /ayk/ v **1a** to suffer a usu dull persistent pain **b** to feel anguish or distress **2** to yearn, long

²**ache** n a usu dull persistent pain

achieve /ə'cheev/ v **1** to carry out successfully; accomplish **2** to obtain by effort; win – **achievable** adj

a'chievement /-mənt/ n **1** successful completion; accomplishment **2** sthg accomplished, esp by resolve, persistence, or courage; a feat **3** performance in a test or academic course

A,chilles' 'heel /ə'kileez, -liz/ n a person's only vulnerable point

¹**acid** /'asid/ adj **1a** sour or sharp to the taste **b** sharp, biting, or sour in speech, manner, or disposition; caustic **2** of, like, containing, or being an acid; specif having a pH of less than 7

²**acid** n **1** a sour substance; specif any of various typically water-soluble and sour compounds having a pH of less than 7 that are capable of giving up a hydrogen ion to or accepting an unshared pair of electrons from a base to form a salt **2** LSD – infml

acidify /ə'sidifie/ v to make or convert into (an) acid

'acid ,rain n rain containing high levels of acid substances (e g sulphuric and nitric acid), caused by the release of effluent into the atmosphere

,acid 'test n a severe or crucial test (e g of value or suitability)

ack-ack /'ak,ak/ adj antiaircraft

acknowledge /ək'nolij/ v **1** to admit knowledge of; concede to be true or valid **2** to recognize the status or claims of **3a** to express gratitude or obligation for **b** to show recognition of (e g by smiling or nodding) **c** to confirm receipt of – **-gment** n

acme /'akmi/ n the highest point or stage; esp a perfect representative of a specified class or thing

acne /'akni/ n a skin disorder found esp among adolescents, characterized by inflammation of the skin glands and hair follicles and causing red pustules, esp on the face and neck

acorn /'ay,kawn/ n the nut of the oak, usu seated in a hard woody cup

¹acoustic /ə'koohstik/ *also* **acoustical** /-kl/ *adj* of or being a musical instrument whose sound is not electronically modified – ~ **ally** *adv*

²acoustic *n* **1** *pl but sing in constr* the science of sound **2** the properties of a room, hall, etc that govern the quality of sound heard – usu pl with sing. meaning

acquaint /ə'kwaynt/ *v* to make familiar *with*

acquaintance /ə'kwayntəns/ *n* **1** personal knowledge; familiarity **2a** *sing or pl in constr* the people with whom one is acquainted **b** a person whom one knows but who is not a particularly close friend — **make the acquaintance of** to come to know; meet

acquiesce /ˌakwee'es/ *v* to submit or comply tacitly or passively – often + *in* – **-escence** *n*

acquire /ə'kwie-ə/ *v* **1** to gain or come into possession of, often by unspecified means; *also* to steal – euph **2** to gain as a new characteristic or ability, esp as a result of skill or hard work

acquisition /ˌakwi'zish(ə)n/ *n* **1** acquiring, gaining **2** sby or sthg acquired or gained

acquisitive /ə'kwizətiv/ *adj* keen or tending to acquire and possess – ~**ly** *adv* – ~**ness** *n*

acquit /ə'kwit/ *v* **-tt-** **1** to free from responsibility or obligation; *specif* to declare not guilty **2** to conduct (oneself) in a specified, usu favourable, manner

acquittal /ə'kwitl/ *n* a judicial release from a criminal charge

acre /'aykə/ *n* **1** *pl* lands, fields **2** a unit of area equal to 4840yd² (4046.86m²) **3** *pl* great quantities – infml

acrid /'akrid/ *adj* **1** unpleasantly pungent in taste or smell **2** violently bitter in manner or language; acrimonious

acrimony /'akriməni/ *n* caustic sharpness of manner or language resulting from anger or ill nature – **-nious** *adj* – **-niously** *adv*

acrobat /'akrəbat/ *n* one who performs gymnastic feats requiring skilful control of the body – ~**ic** *adj* – ~**ically** *adv*

acro'batics *npl* **1** *sing or pl in constr* the art, performance, or activity of an acrobat **2a** spectacular performance involving great agility

acronym /'akrənim/ *n* a word (e g *radar*) formed from the initial letters of other words

¹across /ə'kros/ *adv* **1** from one side to the other crosswise **2** to or on the opposite side **3** so as to be understandable, acceptable, or successful

²across *prep* **1a** from one side to the other of **b** on the opposite side of **2** so as to intersect at an angle **3** into transitory contact with

acrostic /ə'krostik/ *n* a composition, usu in verse, in which sets of letters (e g the first of each line) form a word or phrase

¹act /akt/ *n* **1** a thing done; a deed **2** a statute; *also* a decree, edict **3** the process of doing **4** *often cap* a formal record of sthg done or transacted **5a** any

of the principal divisions of a play or opera **b** any of the successive parts or performances in an entertainment (e g a circus) **6a** a display of affected behaviour; a pretence – **be/get in on the act** to be or deliberately become involved in a situation or undertaking, esp for one's own advantage

²act *v* **1** to represent by action, esp on the stage **2** to feign, simulate **3** to play the part of (as if) in a play **4** to behave in a manner suitable to **5** to perform on the stage; engage in acting **6** to behave insincerely **7** to function or behave in a specified manner **8** to perform a specified function; serve *as* **9** to be a substitute or representative *for* **10** to produce an effect

¹acting /'akting/ *adj* holding a temporary rank or position

²acting *n* the art or practice of representing a character in a dramatic production

action /'aksh(ə)n/ *n* **1** a civil legal proceeding **2** the process of acting or working, esp to produce alteration by force or through a natural agency **3** the mode of movement of the body **4** a voluntary act; a deed **5a** the state of functioning actively **b** practical, often militant, activity, often directed towards a political end **c** energetic activity; enterprise **6a** combat (e g in a war) **b** the unfolding (of) the events in a play or work of fiction **7** an operating mechanism (e g of a gun or piano); *also* the manner in which it operates **8** (the most) lively or productive activity – infml

activate /'aktivayt/ *v* to make (more) active or reactive, esp in chemical or physical properties – **-ation** *n*

¹active /'aktiv/ *adj* **1** characterized by practical action rather than by contemplation or speculation **2** quick in physical movement; lively **3a** marked by or requiring vigorous activity **b** full of activity; busy **4** having practical operation or results; effective **5** of a *volcano* liable to erupt; not extinct **6** of a *verb form or voice* having as the subject the person or thing doing the action **7** of, in, or being full-time service, esp in the armed forces **8** capable of acting or reacting; activated – ~**ly** *adv*

²active *n* **1** an active verb form **2** the active voice of a language

activity /ak'tivəti/ *n* **1** the quality or state of being active **2** vigorous or energetic action; liveliness **3** a pursuit in which a person is active – usu pl

actor /'aktə/, *fem* **actress** /'aktris/ *n* one who represents a character in a dramatic production; *esp* one whose profession is acting

act out *v* **1** to represent in action **2** to translate into action

actual /'aktyooəl, -chooəl/ *adj* **1** existing in fact or reality; real **2** existing or occurring at the time; current

actuality /ˌaktyoo'aləti, ˌakchoo-/ *n* an existing circumstance; a real fact – often pl

'actually /-li/ *adv* 1 really; in fact 2 at the present moment 3 strange as it may seem; even

actuary /'aktyoo(ə)ri, 'akchoo-/ *n* sby who calculates insurance risks and premiums – **-arial** *adj*

act up *v* 1 to behave in an unruly manner; play up 2 to give pain or trouble *USE* infml

acuity /ə'kyooh-əti/ *n* keenness of mental or physical perception – fml

acumen /'akyoomən/ *n* keenness and depth of discernment or discrimination, esp in practical matters

acupuncture /'ak(y)oo,pungkchə/ *n* an orig Chinese practice of puncturing the body at particular points with needles to cure disease, relieve pain, produce anaesthesia, etc

acute /ə'kyooht/ *adj* 1 *of an angle* measuring less than 90° 2a marked by keen discernment or intellectual perception, esp of subtle distinctions b responsive to slight impressions or stimuli 3 intensely felt or perceived 4 *esp of an illness* having a sudden severe onset and short course – contrasted with *chronic* 5 demanding urgent attention; severe 6 marked with, having the pronunciation indicated by, or being an accent mark written '– **~ly** *adv* – **~ness** *n*

ad /ad/ *n* an advertisement – infml

adage /'adij/ *n* a maxim or proverb that embodies a commonly accepted observation

'adagio /ə'dahjioh/ *adv or adj* in an easy slow graceful manner – used in music

'adagio *n, pl* **adagios** 1 a musical composition or movement in adagio tempo 2 ballet dancing, esp a pas de deux, involving difficult feats of balance

'adamant /'adəmənt/ *n* a stone formerly believed to be of impenetrable hardness and sometimes identified with the diamond; *broadly* any very hard unbreakable substance

'adamant *adj* unshakable in determination; unyielding – **~ly** *adv*

,Adam's 'apple *n* the projection in the front of the neck formed by the largest cartilage of the larynx

adapt /ə'dapt/ *v* to make or become fit, often by modification

adaptation /,adap'taysh(ə)n/ *n* 1 adjustment to prevailing or changing conditions 2 a composition rewritten in a new form or for a different medium

adapter *also* **adaptor** /ə'daptə/ *n* 1 a device for converting a tool, piece of apparatus, etc to some new use 2 a plug or connector for joining several pieces of electrical apparatus to a single power point

add /ad/ *v* 1 to join so as to bring about an increase or improvement 2 to say or write further 3 to combine (numbers) into a single number – often + *up* 4a to perform addition b to come together or unite by addition 5 to make or serve as an addition *to*

addendum /ə'dendəm/ *n, pl* **addenda** /-də/ a supplement to a book – often pl with sing. meaning but sing. in constr

'adder /'adə/ *n* the common European venomous viper or other ground-living viper

'adder *n* a device (e g in a computer) that performs addition

'addict /ə'dikt/ *v* 1 to devote or surrender (oneself) to sthg habitually or obsessively – usu pass 2 to cause (an animal or human) to become physiologically dependent upon a habit-forming drug – **~ion** *n* – **~ive** *adj*

'addict /'adikt/ *n* 1 one who is addicted to a drug 2 a devotee, fan

addition /ə'dish(ə)n/ *n* 1 sthg or sby added, esp as an improvement 2 the act or process of adding, esp adding numbers — **in addition** also, furthermore

additional /ə'dish(ə)nl/ *adj* existing by way of addition; supplementary – **~ly** *adv*

additive /'adətiv/ *n* a substance added to another in relatively small amounts to impart desirable properties or suppress undesirable ones

addle /'adl/ *v* **addling** /'adling, 'adl-ing/ 1 to throw into confusion 2 *of an egg* to become rotten 3 to become confused or muddled

'address /ə'dres/ *v* 1 to direct the efforts or attention of (oneself) 2a to communicate directly b to speak or write directly to; *esp* to deliver a formal speech to 3 to mark directions for delivery on 4 to greet by a prescribed form 5 to take one's stance and adjust the club before hitting (a golf ball)

'address /ə'dres/ *n* 1 a formal communication; *esp* a prepared speech delivered to an audience 2 a place of residence (where a person or organization may be communicated with); *also* a detailed description of its location (e g on an envelope)

add up *v* 1 to amount to *in* total or substance 2 to come to the expected total 3 to be internally consistent; make sense

adept /'adept, ə'dept/ *adj or n* (being) a highly skilled expert *at* – **~ly** *adv*

adequate /'adikwət/ *adj* (barely) sufficient for a specific requirement – **~ly** *adv* – **-quacy** *n*

adhere /əd'(h)iə/ *v* 1 to give continued support, observance, or loyalty 2 to hold or stick fast (as if) by glueing, suction, grasping, or fusing – **adherence** *n*

adherent /əd'(h)iərənt/ *n* a supporter of a leader, faction, etc

adhesion /əd'(h)eezh(ə)n, ad'hee-/ *n* the action or state of adhering

'adhesive /əd'(h)eeziv, -siv/ *adj* sticky

'adhesive *n* an adhesive substance (e g glue or cement)

ad hoc /,ad 'hok/ *adj or adv* with respect to the particular purpose at hand

adieu /ə'dyooh, ə'dyuh/ *n, pl* **adieus, adieux** /ə'-dyooh(z), ə'dyuh(z)/ a farewell – often used interjectionally; usu poetic

ad infinitum /,ad infi'nietəm/ *adv or adj* without end or limit

adipose /'adipohs, -pohz/ *adj* of animal fat; fatty

adjacent /ə'jays(ə)nt/ *adj* having a common border; *broadly* neighbouring, nearby

adjective /'ajiktiv/ *n* a word that modifies a noun or pronoun by describing a particular characteristic of it – **-tival** *adj* – **-tivally** *adv*

adjoin /ə'joyn/ *v* to be next to or in contact with (one another)

adjourn /ə'juhn/ *v* to suspend (a session) until a later stated time – ~**ment** *n*

adjudicate /ə'joohdikayt/ *v* **1** to make a judicial decision on **2** to act as judge (e g in a competition) – **-cation** *n*

adjunct /'ajungkt/ *n* **1** sthg joined to another thing as an incidental accompaniment **2** a person assisting another to perform some duty or service

adjure /ə'jooə/ *v* **1** to charge or command solemnly (as if) under oath or penalty of a curse **2** to entreat or advise earnestly *USE* fml

adjust /ə'just/ *v* **1** to bring to a more satisfactory or conformable state by minor change or adaptation; regulate, correct, or modify **2** to determine the amount to be paid under an insurance policy in settlement of (a loss) **3** to adapt or conform oneself (e g to climate) – ~**able** *adj* – ~**ment** *n*

adjutant /'ajoot(ə)nt/ *n* an officer who assists the commanding officer

ad-lib /,ad 'lib/ *v* **-bb-** to say (e g lines in a speech) spontaneously and without preparation; improvise – **ad-lib** *n, adj*

ad lib *adv* without restraint or limit

administer /əd'ministə/ *v* **1** to manage, supervise **2a** to mete out; dispense **b** to give or perform ritually **3** to perform the office of administrator; manage affairs – **-tration** *n*

administrative /əd'ministrətiv/ *adj* of (an) administration – ~**ly** *adv*

administrator /əd'mini,straytə/ *n* sby who administers esp business, school, or governmental affairs

admirable /'admərəbl/ *adj* deserving the highest respect; excellent – **-bly** *adv*

admiral /'admərəl/ *n* the commander in chief of a navy

'admiralty /-ti/ *n* **1** *sing or pl in constr, cap* the executive department formerly having authority over naval affairs **2** the court having jurisdiction over maritime questions

admiration /,admə'raysh(ə)n/ *n* a feeling of delighted or astonished approval

admire /əd'mie·ə/ *v* to think highly of; express admiration for – ~**r** *n*

admissible /əd'misəbl/ *adj, esp of legal evidence* capable of being allowed or conceded; permissible – **-bility** *n*

admission /əd'mish(ə)n/ *n* **1** acknowledgment that a fact or allegation is true **2a** allowing or being allowed to enter sthg (e g a secret society) **b** a fee paid at or for admission

admit /əd'mit/ *v* **-tt- 1a** to allow scope for; permit **b** to concede as true or valid **2** to allow to enter sthg (e g a place or fellowship) **3** to give entrance or access

admittance /əd'mit(ə)ns/ *n* **1** permission to enter a place **2** access, entrance

admittedly /əd'mitidli/ *adv* as must reluctantly be admitted

admixture /əd'miksche, 'admiksche/ *n* an ingredient added by mixing, or the resulting mixture

admonish /əd'monish/ *v* **1** to warn about remissness or error, esp gently **2** to give friendly earnest advice or encouragement to – ~**ing** *adj* – ~**ingly** *adv*

admonition /,admə'nish(ə)n/ *n* (a) gentle friendly reproof, counsel, or warning – **-tory** *adj*

ad nauseam /,ad 'nawzi·əm, -si·əm/ *adv* in an extremely tedious manner; enough to make one sick

ado /ə'dooh/ *n* fussy bustling excitement, esp over trivia; to-do

adolescent /,adə'les(ə)nt/ *n* sby in the period of life between puberty and maturity – **-cence** *n*

adopt /ə'dopt/ *v* **1** to take by choice into a new relationship; *specif* to bring up voluntarily (a child of other parents) as one's own child **2** to take up and practise; take to oneself **3** to vote to accept **4** *of a constituency* to nominate as a Parliamentary candidate **5** *Br, of a local authority* to assume responsibility for the maintenance of (e g a road) – ~**ion** *n*

adoptive /ə'doptiv/ *adj* made or acquired by adoption

adorable /ə'dawrəbl/ *adj* sweetly lovable; charming

adore /ə'daw/ *v* **1** to worship or honour as a deity **2** to regard with reverent admiration and devotion **3** to like very much – infml – **adoration** *n*

adorn /ə'dawn/ *v* **1** to decorate, esp with ornaments **2** to add to the pleasantness or attractiveness of – ~**ment** *n*

adrenalin, adrenaline /ə'drenəlin/ *n* a hormone that stimulates the heart and causes constriction of blood vessels and relaxation of smooth muscle

adrift /ə'drift/ *adv or adj* **1** afloat without motive power or mooring and at the mercy of winds and currents **2** in or into a state of being unstuck or unfastened; loose – esp in *come adrift* **3** astray – infml

adroit /ə'droyt/ *adj* 1 dexterous, nimble 2 marked by shrewdness, readiness, or resourcefulness in coping with difficulty or danger – **~ly** *adv* – **~ness** *n*

adsorb /əd'zawb/ *v* to become absorbed – **adsorption** *n*

¹**adult** /'adult, ə'dult/ *adj* 1 fully developed and mature; grown-up 2 of or befitting adults 3 suitable only for adults; *broadly* salacious, pornographic

²**adult** *n* a grown-up person or creature; *esp* a human being after an age specified by law (in Britain, 18)

adulterate /ə'dultərayt/ *v* to corrupt or make impure by the addition of a foreign or inferior substance

adulterer /ə'dultərə/, *fem* **adulteress** /-ris/ *n* sby who has sex with someone other than his/her spouse – **adultery** *n* – **-terous** *adj*

¹**advance** /əd'vahns/ *v* 1 to bring or move forwards in position or time 2 to accelerate the growth or progress of; further 3 to raise in rank; promote 4 to supply (money or goods) ahead of time or as a loan 5 to bring (an opinion or argument) forward for notice; propose 6 to go forwards; proceed 7 to make progress 8 to rise in rank, position, or importance

²**advance** *n* 1a a moving forward b (a signal for) forward movement (of troops) 2a progress in development; an improvement b advancement; promotion 3 a friendly or *esp* an amorous approach – usu pl 4 (a provision of) money or goods supplied before a return is received — **in advance** beforehand

³**advance** *adj* 1 made, sent, or provided ahead of time 2 going or situated ahead of others

advanced *adj* 1 far on in time or course 2 beyond the elementary; more developed

ad'vancement /-mənt/ *n* 1a (a) promotion or elevation to a higher rank or position b furtherance towards perfection or completeness 2 an advance of money or value

advantage /əd'vahntij/ *n* 1 superiority of position or condition – often + of or over 2 a benefit, gain; *esp* one resulting from some course of action 3 (the score of) the first point won in tennis after deuce — **to advantage** so as to produce a favourable impression or effect

advantageous /,advə(ə)n'tayjəs/ *adj* furnishing an advantage; favourable – **~ly** *adv*

Advent /'advent, -vənt/ *n* 1 the 4-week period before Christmas 2 the coming of Christ to earth as a human being 3 *not cap* a coming into being; an arrival

adventitious /,advən'tishəs, -ven-/ *adj* 1 coming accidentally or casually from another source; extraneous 2 occurring sporadically or in an unusual place – **~ly** *adv*

¹**adventure** /əd'venchə/ *n* an undertaking involving danger, risks, uncertainty of outcome, or excitement – **-rous** *adj*

²**adventure** *v* 1 to hazard oneself; dare to go or enter 2 to take a risk

adventurer /əd'venchərə/, *fem* **adventuress** /-ris/ *n* 1 sby who takes part in an adventure 2 sby who seeks wealth or position by unscrupulous means

adverb /'advuhb/ *n* a word that modifies a verb, an adjective, another adverb, a preposition, a phrase, a clause, or a sentence, and that answers such questions as how?, when?, where?, etc – **~ial** *n, adj* – **~ially** *adv*

adversary /'advəs(ə)ri/ *n* an enemy, opponent, or opposing faction

adverse /'advuhs, əd'vuhs/ *adj* 1 acting against or in a contrary direction 2 unfavourable – **~ly** *adv*

adversity /əd'vuhsəti/ *n* a condition of suffering, affliction, or hardship

¹**advert** /əd'vuht/ *v* to make a (glancing) reference or refer casually *to* – *fml*

²**advert** /'advuht/ *n, chiefly Br* an advertisement

advertise /'advətiez/ *v* 1 to make publicly and generally known 2 to announce (e g an article for sale or a vacancy) publicly, esp in the press 3 to encourage sales or patronage (of), esp by emphasizing desirable qualities, or by description in the mass media 4 to seek *for* by means of advertising – **~r** *n*

advertisement /əd'vuhtismənt, -tiz-, 'advətiezmənt/ *n* a notice published, broadcast, or displayed publicly to advertise a product, service, etc

advertising /'advə,tiezing/ *n* 1 the action of calling sthg to the attention of the public, esp by paid announcements 2 advertisements 3 the profession of preparing advertisements for publication or broadcast

advice /əd'vies/ *n* 1 recommendation regarding a decision or course of conduct 2 communication, esp from a distance; intelligence – usu pl 3 an official notice concerning a business transaction

advisable /əd'viezəbl/ *adj* fitting to be advised or done; prudent – **-sability** *n*

advise /əd'viez/ *v* 1a to give advice (to) b to caution, warn 2 to give information or notice to; inform

advisory /əd'viez(ə)ri/ *adj* 1 having or exercising power to advise 2 containing or giving advice

advocacy /'advəkasi/ *n* 1 active support or pleading 2 the function of an advocate

¹**advocate** /'advəkət/ *n* 1 a professional pleader before a tribunal or court 2 one who defends or supports a cause or proposal

²**advocate** /'advəkayt/ *v* to plead in favour of

adze, *NAm chiefly* **adz** /adz/ *n* a tool that has the blade at right angles to the handle for cutting or shaping wood

aegis /'eejis/ *n* sponsorship, backing

aeon, eon /'ee-ən, 'ee,on/ *n* an immeasurably long period of time; *also* a geological unit of time equal to 1000 million years

aerate /'eərayt, -'-/ *v* 1 to combine, supply, charge, or impregnate with a gas, esp air, oxygen, or carbon dioxide 2 to make fizzy or effervescent – **-ation** *n*

¹**aerial** /'eəri-əl/ *adj* 1a of or occurring in the air or atmosphere b consisting of air c growing in the air rather than in the ground or water d operating overhead on elevated cables or rails 2 lacking substance; thin – ~**ly** *adv*

²**aerial** *n* a conductor (e g a wire) or arrangement of conductors designed to radiate or receive radio waves

aerobatics /,eərə'batiks/ *n pl but sing or pl in constr* the performance of feats (e g rolls) in an aircraft – **aerobatic** *adj*

aerobics /eə'rohbikz/ *n pl but sing or pl in constr* a system of physical exercises, usu performed to music, intended to improve respiration and circulation

aerodrome /'eərə,drohm/ *n, chiefly Br* an airfield

aerodynamics /,eərohdie'namiks, -di-/ *n pl but sing or pl in constr* the dynamics of the motion of (solid bodies moving through) gases (e g air) – **aerodynamic** *adj* – **-ically** *adv*

aeronautics /,eərə'nawtiks/ *n pl but sing in constr* the art or science of flight – **-ic, -ical** *adj*

aeroplane /'eərəplayn/ *n, chiefly Br* an aircraft that is heavier than air, has nonrotating wings from which it derives its lift, and is mechanically propelled (e g by a propeller or jet engine)

aerosol /'eərəsol/ *n* (a container of) a substance dispersed from a pressurized container as a suspension of fine solid or liquid particles in gas – **aerosol** *v*

aerospace /'eəroh,spays/ *n* (a branch of physical science dealing with) the earth's atmosphere and the space beyond – **aerospace** *adj*

aesthete, *NAm also* **esthete** /'ees,theet/ *n* one who has or professes a developed sensitivity to the beautiful in art or nature

aesthetic /ees'thetik, es-, əs-/ *also* **aesthetical** /-kl/, *NAm also* **esthetic** *also* **esthetical** *adj* 1a of or dealing with aesthetics or the appreciation of the beautiful b artistic 2 having a developed sense of beauty – ~**ally** *adv*

aesthetics /ees'thetiks/, *NAm also* **esthetics** /ees-, es-/ *n pl but sing or pl in constr* a branch of philosophy dealing with the nature of the beautiful, with judgments concerning beauty and taste, and with theories of criticism in the arts

afar /ə'fah/ *adv or n* (from, to, or at) a great distance

affable /'afəbl/ *adj* 1 being pleasant and relaxed in talking to others 2 characterized by ease and friendliness; benign – **-bility** *n* – **-bly** *adv*

affair /ə'feə/ *n* 1a *pl* commercial, professional, or public business or matters b a particular or personal concern 2a a procedure, action, object, or occasion only vaguely specified b a social event; a party 3 *also* **affaire, affaire de coeur** a romantic or passionate attachment between 2 people who are not married to each other 4 a matter causing public anxiety, controversy, or scandal

¹**affect** /ə'fekt/ *v* 1 to be given to 2 to put on a pretence of (being); feign

²**affect** *v* 1 to have a material effect on or produce an alteration in 2 to act on (e g a person or his/her mind or feelings) so as to effect a response

affectation /,afek'taysh(ə)n/ *n* 1 an insincere display (e g of a quality not really possessed) 2 a deliberately assumed peculiarity of speech or conduct; an artificiality

affected /ə'fektid/ *adj* 1 inclined, disposed *towards* – chiefly in combination, **ill-affected** 2a given to affectation b assumed artificially or falsely; pretended – ~**ly** *adv* – ~**ness** *n*

affection /ə'feksh(ə)n/ *n* 1 emotion as compared with reason – often pl with sing. meaning 2 tender and lasting attachment; fondness

affectionate /ə'feksh(ə)nət/ *adj* 1 showing affection or warm regard; loving 2 proceeding from affection; tender – ~**ly** *adv*

affidavit /,afi'dayvit/ *n* a sworn written statement for use as judicial proof

affiliate /ə'filiayt/ *v* 1 to attach as a member or branch – + *to* or *with* 2 to connect or associate oneself *with* another

affinity /ə'finəti/ *n* 1 sympathy of thought or feeling 2 resemblance based on relationship or causal connection

affirm /ə'fuhm/ *v* 1a to confirm; make valid b to state positively 2 to assert (e g a judgment of a lower court) as valid; ratify – ~**ation** *n*

¹**affirmative** /ə'fuhmətiv/ *adj* 1 asserting or answering that the fact is so 2 favouring or supporting a proposition or motion – ~**ly** *adv*

²**affirmative** *n* 1 an expression (e g the word *yes*) of agreement or assent 2 an affirmative proposition

¹**affix** /ə'fiks/ *v* 1 to attach (physically); *esp* to add in writing 2 to impress (e g a seal)

²**affix** /'afiks/ *n* 1 an addition to the beginning or end of or an insertion in a word or root to produce a derivative word or inflectional form 2 an appendage

afflict /ə'flikt/ *v* 1 to distress so severely as to cause persistent suffering 2 to trouble

affliction /ə'fliksh(ə)n/ *n* 1 great suffering 2 a cause of persistent pain or distress

affluent /'afloo-ənt/ *adj* 1 flowing in abundance 2 wealthy – **-ence** *n*

afford /ə'fawd/ *v* 1a to be able to do or to bear without serious harm – esp + *can* b to be able to bear the cost of 2 to provide, supply

afforest /ə'forist/ *v* to establish or plant forest cover on – ~**ation** *n*

affray /ə'fray/ *n* a (public) brawl

affront /ə'frunt/ *v* to insult by openly insolent or disrespectful behaviour or language; give offence to

Afghan /'afgan/ *n* **1** a native or inhabitant of Afghanistan **2** the language of Afghanistan; Pashto **3** *not cap* a blanket or shawl of coloured wool knitted or crocheted in strips or squares **4** **Afghan, Afghan hound** a tall hunting dog with a coat of silky thick hair

aficionado /ə,fishyə'nahdoh/, *fem* **aficionada** /-' nahdə/ *n*, *pl* **aficionados**, *fem* **aficionadas** a devotee, fan

afield /ə'feeld/ *adv* **1** to, in, or on the field **2** (far) away from home; abroad **3** out of the way; astray

afloat /ə'floht/ *adj or adv* **1a** borne (as if) on the water or air **b** at sea or on ship **2** free of debt **3** circulating about; rumoured **4** flooded with or under water

afoot /ə'foot/ *adv or adj* **1** on foot **2** (in the process of) happening; astir

aforesaid /ə'faw,sed/ *adj* previously mentioned

aforethought /ə'faw,thawt/ *adj* premeditated, deliberate – *fml*; esp in *with malice aforethought*

afraid /ə'frayd/ *adj* **1** filled with fear or apprehension **2** regretfully of the opinion – in apology for an utterance

afresh /ə'fresh/ *adv* anew, again

African /'afrikan/ *n or adj* (a native or inhabitant) of Africa

Afrikaans /,afri'kahnz/ *n* a language of S Africa developed from 17th-c Dutch

Afrikaner /,afri'kahnə/ *n* an Afrikaans-speaking S African of European, esp Dutch, descent

¹**aft** /ahft/ *adv* near, towards, or in the stern of a ship or the tail of an aircraft

²**aft** *adj* rearward

¹**after** /'ahftə/ *adv* **1** behind **2** afterwards

²**after** *prep* **1** behind in place or order – used in yielding precedence or in asking for the next turn (e g *after* you with the map) **2a** following in time; later than **b** continuously succeeding **c** in view of or in spite of (sthg preceding) **3** – used to indicate the goal or purpose of an action (e g go *after* trout) **4** so as to resemble: e g **4a** in accordance with **b** in allusion to the name of **c** in the characteristic manner of **d** in imitation of **5** about, concerning

³**after** *conj* later than the time when

⁴**after** *adj* later, subsequent

after all *adv* **1** in spite of everything **2** it must be remembered

afterbirth /-,buhth/ *n* the placenta and foetal membranes expelled after delivery of a baby, young animal, etc

aftereffect /-i,fekt/ *n* an effect that follows its cause after an interval of time

afterglow /-,gloh/ *n* **1** a glow remaining (e g in the sky) where a light source has disappeared **2** a vestige of past splendour, success, or happy emotion

afterlife /-,lief/ *n* **1** an existence after death **2** a later period in one's life

aftermath /-,mahth, -,math/ *n* **1** a consequence, result **2** the period immediately following a usu ruinous event

afternoon /,ahftə'noohn/ *n* the time between noon and sunset

afters /'ahftəz/ *n pl*, *Br* a dessert – *infml*

aftertaste /-,tayst/ *n* persistence of a flavour or impression

afterthought /-,thawt/ *n* **1** an idea occurring later **2** sthg added later

afterwards /-,woodz/ *adv* after that; subsequently, thereafter

again /ə'gayn, ə'gen/ *adv* **1** so as to be as before **2** another time; once more **3** on the other hand **4** further; in addition

¹**against** /ə'gaynst, ə'genst/ *prep* **1a** in opposition or hostility to **b** unfavourable to **c** as a defence or protection from **2** compared or contrasted with **3a** in preparation or provision for **b** with respect to; towards **4** (in the direction of and) in contact with **5** in a direction opposite to the motion or course of; counter to **6** in exchange for

²**against** *adj* **1** opposed to a motion or measure **2** unfavourable to a specified degree; *esp* unfavourable to a win

agape /ə'gayp/ *adj* **1** wide open; gaping **2** in a state of wonder

agate /'agət, 'agayt/ *n* a mineral used as a gem composed of quartz of various colours, often arranged in bands

¹**age** /ayj/ *n* **1a** the length of time a person has lived or a thing existed **b** the time of life at which some particular qualification, power, or capacity arises **c** a stage of life **2** a generation **3** a period of time dominated by a central figure or prominent feature **4** a division of geological time, usu shorter than an epoch **5** a long time – usu pl with sing. meaning; *infml* — **of age** of legal adult status

²**age** *v* **aging, ageing** /'ayjing/ **1** to become old; show the effects of increasing age **2** to become mellow or mature; ripen **3** to cause to seem old, esp prematurely **4** to bring to a state fit for use or to maturity

aged /'ayjid; *sense 'b* ayjd/ *adj* **1** grown old: e g **1a** of an advanced age **b** having attained a specified age **2** typical of old age

ageless /'ayjlis/ *adj* **1** never growing old or showing the effects of age **2** timeless, eternal – ~**ness** *n*

agency /'ayjənsi/ *n* **1** a power or force through which a result is achieved; instrumentality **2** the function or place of business of an agent or representative **3** an establishment that does business for another

agenda /ə'jendə/ *n* **1** a list of items to be discussed or business to be transacted (e g at a meeting) **2** a plan of procedure; a programme

agent /'ayjənt/ *n* **1** sthg or sby that produces an effect or that acts or exerts power **2** a person who acts for or in the place of another by authority from him/her: e g **2a** a business representative **b** one employed by or controlling an agency **3a** a representative of a government **b** a spy

agent provocateur /,ahzhonh provokə'tuh, ,ayjənt / *n*, *pl* **agents provocateurs** /~/ a person employed to incite suspected people to some open action that will make them liable to punishment

,age of con'sent *n* the age at which one is legally competent to give consent; *specif* that at which a person, esp a female, may consent to sexual intercourse

[1]**agglomerate** /ə'glomərayt/ *v* to (cause to) gather into a cluster or disorderly mass – **-ation** *n*

[2]**ag'glomerate** /-rət/ *adj* gathered into a ball, mass, or cluster

[3]**ag'glomerate** /-rət/ *n* **1** a disorderly mass or collection **2** a rock composed of irregular volcanic fragments

aggrand·ize, -ise /ə'grandiez, 'agrən-/ *v* **1** to give a false air of greatness to **2** to advance the power, position, etc of – **-izement** *n*

aggravate /'agrəvayt/ *v* **1** to make worse or more severe **2** to annoy, irritate – **-tion** *n*

[1]**aggregate** /'agri,gayt/ *v* **1** to bring together into a mass or whole **2** to amount to (a specified total)

[2]**aggregate** /'agrigət/ *n* **1** a mass of loosely associated parts; an assemblage **2** the whole amount; the sum total

aggression /ə'greshən/ *n* **1** a hostile attack; *esp* one made without just cause **2** hostile, injurious, or destructive behaviour or outlook – **-ssor** *n*

aggressive /ə'gresiv/ *adj* **1a** tending towards or practising aggression **b** ready to attack **2** forceful, dynamic – **~ly** *adv* – **~ness** *n*

ag'grieved *adj* showing or expressing resentment; hurt

aggro /'agroh/ *n*, *chiefly Br* **1** provocation, hostility **2** deliberate aggression or violence *USE* infml

aghast /ə'gahst/ *adj* suddenly struck with terror or amazement; shocked

agile /'ajiel/ *adj* **1** quick, easy, and graceful in movement **2** mentally quick and resourceful – **~ly** *adv* – **-ility** *n*

agitate /'ajitayt/ *v* **1** to move, shake **2** to excite and often trouble the mind or feelings of; disturb **3** to work to arouse public feeling for or against a cause – **-tation** *n*

agitator /'ajitaytə/ *n* **1** sby who stirs up public feeling on controversial issues **2** a device or apparatus for stirring or shaking

aglow /ə'gloh/ *adj* radiant with warmth or excitement

[1]**agnostic** /ag'nostik, əg-/ *n* sby who holds the view that any ultimate reality is unknown and prob unknowable; *also* one who doubts the existence of God – **~ism** *n*

[2]**agnostic** *adj* of or being an agnostic or the beliefs of agnostics

ago /ə'goh/ *adj or adv* earlier than now

agog /ə'gog/ *adj* eager

agony /'agoni/ *n* intense and often prolonged pain or suffering of mind or body; anguish – **-nize** *v* – **-nized** *adj* – **-nizing** *adj*

agoraphobia /,agrə'fohbi-ə/ *n* abnormal dread of being in open spaces – **-bic** *n*, *adj*

agrarian /ə'greəri-əbl/ *adj* **1** of or relating to (the tenure of) fields **2** (characteristic) of farmers or agricultural life or interests – **agrarian** *n*

agree /ə'gree/ *v* **1** to admit, concede – usu + a clause **2** to bring into harmony **3** *chiefly Br* to come to terms on, usu after discussion; accept by mutual consent **4** to give assent; accede – often + *to* **5a** to be of one mind – often + *with* **b** to decide together **6a** to correspond **b** to be consistent **7** to suit the health – + *with*

agreeable /ə'gree-əbl/ *adj* **1** to one's liking; pleasing **2** willing to agree or consent

a'greement /-mənt/ *n* **1a** harmony of opinion or feeling **b** correspondence **2a** an arrangement laying down terms, conditions, etc **b** a treaty **3** (the language or document embodying) a legally binding contract

agriculture /'agri,kulchə/ *n* the theory and practice of cultivating and producing crops from the soil and of raising livestock – **-tural** *adj* – **-turally** *adv* – **-tur(al)ist** *n*

aground /ə'grownd/ *adv or adj* on or onto the shore or the bottom of a body of water

ah /ah *often prolonged*/ *interj* – used to express delight, relief, regret, or contempt

ahead /ə'hed/ *adv or adj* **1a** in a forward direction **b** in front **2** in, into, or for the future **3** in or towards a better position

[1]**aid** /ayd/ *v* **1** to give assistance to; help – **2** to bring about the accomplishment of; facilitate

[2]**aid** *n* **1** help; assistance; *specif* tangible means of assistance (e g money or supplies) **2a** a helper **b** sthg that helps or supports; *specif* a hearing aid — **in aid of 1** in order to aid; for the use of **2** *Br* for the purpose of — infml

aide /ayd, ed/ *n* **1** an aide-de-camp **2** *chiefly NAm* an assistant

,aide-de-'camp /də 'kamp/ *n*, *pl* **aides-de-camp** /~/ an officer in the armed forces acting as a personal assistant to a superior officer

AIDS /aydz/ *n* acquired immune deficiency syndrome; an often fatal disease caused by a virus attacking cells that normally stimulate the production of antibodies to fight infection

ail /ayl/ *v* **1** to give pain, discomfort, or trouble to **2** to be unwell

aileron /'aylərɒn, -rən/ *n* a movable control surface of an aircraft wing or a movable flap external to the wing at the trailing edge for giving a rolling motion and providing lateral control

ailment /'aylmənt/ *n* a bodily disorder or chronic disease

¹**aim** /aym/ *v* 1 to direct a course; *specif* to point a weapon at an object 2 to channel one's efforts; aspire 3 to have the intention; mean 4 to direct or point (e g a weapon) at a target 5 to direct at or towards a specified goal; intend

²**aim** *n* 1a the pointing of a weapon at a mark b the ability to hit a target c a weapon's accuracy or effectiveness 2 a clear intention or purpose – ~**less** *adj*

¹**air** /eə/ *n* 1a the mixture of invisible odourless tasteless gases, containing esp nitrogen and oxygen, that surrounds the earth b a light breeze 2 the supposed medium of transmission of radio waves; *also* radio, television 3a the appearance or bearing of a person; demeanour b *pl* an artificial or affected manner; haughtiness c outward appearance of a thing d a surrounding or pervading influence; an atmosphere 4 a tune, melody — **in the air 1** not yet settled; uncertain 2 being generally spread round or hinted at

²**air** *v* 1 to expose to the air for drying, freshening, etc; ventilate 2 to expose to public view

air bed *n*, *chiefly Br* an inflatable mattress

air brick *n* a building brick or brick-sized metal box perforated to allow ventilation

aircraft /-,krahft/ *n*, *pl* **aircraft** a weight-carrying structure that can travel through the air and is supported either by its own buoyancy or by the dynamic action of the air against its surfaces

aircraft carrier *n* a warship designed so that aircraft can be operated from it

aircraftman /-mən/ *n* (a person who holds) the lowest rank in the Royal Air Force

Airedale /'eə,dayl/, **Airedale 'terrier** *n* any of a breed of large terriers with a hard wiry coat that is dark on the back and sides and tan elsewhere

airfield /-,feeld/ *n* an area of land maintained for the landing and takeoff of aircraft

air force *n* the branch of a country's armed forces for air warfare

air gun *n* 1 a gun from which a projectile is propelled by compressed air 2 any of various hand tools that work by compressed air

airing cupboard *n* a heated cupboard in which esp household linen is aired and kept dry

air lane *n* a path customarily followed by aeroplanes

airless /-lis/ *adj* 1 still, windless 2 lacking fresh air; stuffy

airlift /-,lift/ *n* the transport of cargo or passengers by air, usu to an otherwise inaccessible area – **airlift** *v*

airline /-,lien/ *n* an organization that provides regular public air transport

air lock *n* 1 an airtight intermediate chamber (e g in a spacecraft) which allows movement between 2 areas of different pressures or atmospheres 2 a stoppage of flow caused by air being in a part where liquid ought to circulate

airmail /-,mayl/ *n* (the postal system using) mail transported by aircraft

airplane /-,playn/ *n*, *chiefly NAm* an aeroplane

air pocket *n* a region of down-flowing or rarefied air that causes an aircraft to drop suddenly

airport /-,eə,pawt/ *n* a fully-equipped airfield that is used as a base for the transport of passengers and cargo by air

air raid *n* an attack by armed aircraft on a surface target

airship /-,ship/ *n* a gas-filled lighter-than-air self-propelled aircraft that has a steering system

airspace /-,spays/ *n* the space lying above the earth or a certain area of land or water; *esp* the space lying above a nation and coming under its jurisdiction

airstrip /-,strip/ *n* a runway without airport facilities

airtight /-,tiet/ *adj* 1 impermeable to air 2 unassailable

airway /-,way/ *n* 1 a passage for air in a mine 2 a designated route along which aircraft fly

airy /'eəri/ *adj* 1 not having solid foundation; illusory b showing lack of concern; flippant 2 being light and graceful in movement or manner 3 delicately thin in texture 4 open to the free circulation of air; breezy 5 high in the air; lofty – poetic – **airily** *adv*

aisle /iel/ *n* 1 the side division of a church separated from the nave by columns or piers 2 *chiefly NAm* a gangway

ajar /ə'jah/ *adj or adv*, *esp of a door* slightly open

akimbo /ə'kimboh/ *adj or adv* having the hands on the hips and the elbows turned outwards

akin /ə'kin/ *adj* 1 descended from a common ancestor 2 essentially similar, related, or compatible *USE* often + *to*

alabaster /'aləbastə, -bah-/ *n* a fine-textured usu white and translucent chalky stone often carved into ornaments

à la carte /,ah lah 'kaht/ *adv or adj* according to a menu that prices each item separately

alacrity /ə'lakrəti/ *n* promptness or cheerful readiness – *fml*

à la mode /,ah lah 'mod, 'mohd/ *adj* fashionable, stylish

¹**alarm** /ə'lahm/ *n* 1 a signal (e g a loud noise or flashing light) that warns or alerts; *also* an automatic device that alerts or rouses 2 the fear resulting from the sudden sensing of danger

²**alarm** *v* 1 to give warning to 2 to strike with fear

alas /ə'las, ə'lahs/ *interj* – used to express unhappiness, pity, or disappointment

albatross /'albatros/ *n* any of various (very) large web-footed seabirds related to the petrels

albeit /awl'bee-it/ *conj* even though – *fml*

albino /al'beenoh/ *n, pl* **albinos** a human being or other animal with a (congenital) lack of pigment resulting in a white or translucent skin, white or colourless hair, and eyes with a pink pupil

album /'albəm/ *n* 1 a book with blank pages used for making a collection (e g of stamps or photographs) 2 a recording or collection of recordings issued on 1 or more long-playing gramophone records or cassettes

albumen /'albyoomin, al'byoomin/ *n* the white of an egg

alchemy /'alkəmi/ *n* 1 a medieval chemical science and philosophical doctrine aiming to achieve the transformation of the base metals into gold, a cure for disease, and immortality 2 the transformation of sthg common into sthg precious – **-mist** *n*

alcohol /'alkəhol/ *n* 1 a colourless volatile inflammable liquid that is the intoxicating agent in fermented and distilled drinks and is used also as a solvent 2 any of various organic compounds, specif derived from hydrocarbons, containing the hydroxyl group 3 intoxicating drink containing alcohol; *esp* spirits

alcoholic /,alkə'holik/ *adj* affected with alcoholism – ~ **ally** *adv* – **alcoholic** *n*

alcoholism /'alkəho,liz(ə)m/ *n* (a complex chronic psychological and nutritional disorder associated with) excessive and usu compulsive use of alcoholic drinks

alcove /'alkohv/ *n* 1a a nook or recess off a larger room 2 a niche or arched opening (e g in a wall or hedge)

alder /'awldə/ *n* any of a genus of trees or shrubs of the birch family that grow in moist ground

alderman /'awldəmən/ *n pl* **aldermen** /-mən/ 1 a person governing a kingdom, district, or shire as viceroy for an Anglo-Saxon king 2 a senior member of a county or borough council elected by the other councillors – not used officially in Britain after 1974

ale /ayl/ *n* a malted and hopped alcoholic drink that is usually more bitter, stronger, and heavier than beer

¹**alert** /ə'luht/ *adj* 1 watchful, aware 2 active, brisk – ~ **ly** *adv* – ~ **ness** *n*

²**alert** *n* 1 an alarm or other signal that warns of danger (e g from hostile aircraft) 2 the danger period during which an alert is in effect — **on the alert** on the lookout, esp for danger or opportunity

³**alert** *v* 1 to call to a state of readiness; warn 2 to cause to be aware (e g of a need or responsibility)

alfalfa /al'falfə/ *n, NAm* lucerne

algebra /'aljibrə/ *n* a branch of mathematics in which letters, symbols, etc representing various entities are combined according to special rules of operation – ~ **ic(al)** *adj* – ~ **ically** *adv*

algorithm /'algə,ridhəm/ *n* a systematic procedure for solving a (mathematical) problem or accomplishing some end – ~ **ic** *adj*

¹**alias** /'ayli·əs/ *adv* otherwise called or known as

²**alias** *n* an assumed name

alibi /'aləbie/ *n* 1 (evidence supporting) the plea of having been elsewhere when a crime was committed 2 a plausible excuse, usu intended to avert blame or punishment

¹**alien** /'ayli·ən/ *adj* 1a of or belonging to another person, place, or thing; strange b foreign 2 differing in nature or character, esp to the extent of being opposed – + **to**

²**alien** *n* 1 a person from another family, race, or nation; *also* an extraterrestrial being 2 a foreign-born resident who has not been naturalized; *broadly* a foreign-born citizen

alienate /'ayli·ə,nayt, 'aylyə-/ *v* 1 to make hostile or indifferent, esp in cases where attachment formerly existed 2 to cause to be withdrawn or diverted

alienation /,ayli·ə'naysh(ə)n, ,aylyə-/ *n* (a feeling of) withdrawal from or apathy towards one's former attachments or whole social existence

¹**alight** /ə'liet/ *v* **alighted** *also* **alit** /ə'lit/ 1 to come down from sthg: e g 1a to dismount b to disembark 2 to descend from the air and settle; land

²**alight** *adj* 1 animated, alive 2 *chiefly Br* on fire; ignited

align *also* **aline** /ə'lien/ *v* 1 to bring into proper relative position or state of adjustment; *specif* to bring three or more points into line 2 to join with others in a common cause – ~ **ment** *n*

¹**alike** /ə'liek/ *adj* showing close resemblance without being identical

²**alike** *adv* in the same manner, form, or degree; equally

ali,mentary ca'nal *n* the tubular passage that extends from the mouth to the anus and functions in the digestion and absorption of food

alimony /'aliməni/ *n* 1 means of living; maintenance 2 *chiefly NAm* maintenance paid to a spouse during legal separation or after divorce

alive /ə'liev/ *adj* 1 having life 2 still in existence, force, or operation; active 3 realizing the existence of sthg; aware of sthg 4 marked by alertness 5 showing much activity or animation; swarming

alkali /'alkəlie/ *n, pl* **alkalies, alkalis** any of various chemical bases, esp a hydroxide or carbonate of an alkali metal – ~ **ic** *adj*

alkaloid /'alkə,loyd/ *n* any of various plant-derived substances often used as drugs (e g morphine)

¹**all** /awl/ *adj* **1** the whole amount or quantity of (e g awake *all* night) **2** every one of (more than 2) **3** the whole number or sum of (e g *all* cats like milk) **4** every (e g *all* manner of hardship) **5** any whatever (e g beyond *all* hope) — **all there** not mentally subnormal; *esp* shrewd — infml — **all very well** — used in rejection of advice or sympathy

²**all** *adv* **1** wholly, altogether (e g sitting *all* alone) **2** to a supreme degree – usu in combination (e g *all*-powerful) **3** for each side (e g a score of 3 *all*)

³**all** *pron, pl* **all 1** the whole amount, quantity, or amount (e g it was all we could afford) **2** everybody, everything (e g give up *all* for love) — **all in all 1** generally; on the whole **2** supremely important — **all of** fully; at least — **all the same** just the same

⁴**all** *n* one's total resources (e g gave his *all* for the cause) — **in all** all told

Allah /'alah, 'alə/ *n* God – used by Muslims or in reference to the Islamic religion

allay /ə'lay/ *v* **1** to reduce the severity of; alleviate **2** to make quiet; pacify

,**all 'clear** *n* a signal that a danger has passed or that it is safe to proceed

allege /ə'lej/ *v* to assert without proof or before proving – **-gation** *n*

allegedly /ə'lejidli/ *adv* according to allegation

allegiance /ə'leejəns/ *n* **1** the obligation of a subject or citizen to his/her sovereign or government **2** dedication to or dutiful support of a person, group, or cause

allegory /'alig(ə)ri/ *n* **1** (an instance of) the expression by means of symbolic figures and actions of truths or generalizations about human existence **2** a symbolic representation; an emblem – **-rical** *adj* – **-rically** *adv*

allegretto /,ali'gretoh/ *adv or adj* faster than andante but not so fast as allegro – used in music

allegro /ə'legroh/ *n, adv, or adj, pl* **allegros** (a musical composition or movement to be played) in a brisk lively manner

alleluia /,ali'looh·yə/ *interj* – used as a joyous exclamation in praise of God

allergy /'aləji/ *n* **1** exaggerated reaction by sneezing, itching, skin rashes, etc to substances that have no such effect on the average individual **2** a feeling of antipathy or aversion – infml – **-gic** *adj*

alleviate /ə'leevi,ayt/ *v* to relieve (a troublesome situation, state of mind, etc) – **-ation** *n*

alley /'ali/ *n* **1** a bowling alley **2** a narrow back street or passageway between buildings

,**all 'fours** *n pl* hands and knees

alliance /ə'lie·əns/ *n* **1** a union of families by marriage **2** a uniting of nations by formal treaty **3** a tie, connection

allied /'alied, ə'lied/ *adj* **1** in close association; united **2** joined in alliance by agreement or treaty **3a** related by resemblance or common properties; associated **b** related genetically

alligator /'ali,gaytə/ *n* either of 2 reptiles related to the crocodiles, with broad heads that do not taper towards the snout

,**all-'in** *adj, chiefly Br* all-inclusive; *esp* including all costs

all in *adj* tired out; exhausted – infml

alliteration /ə,litə'raysh(ə)n/ *n* the repetition of usu initial consonant sounds in neighbouring words or syllables (e g *threatening throngs of threshers*) – **-tive** *adj* – **-tively** *adv*

allocate /'aləkayt/ *v* **1a** to apportion and distribute (e g money or responsibility) in shares **b** to assign (sthg limited in supply) to as a share **2** to earmark, designate – **-tion** *n*

allot /ə'lot/ *v* **-tt-** to allocate

allotment /ə'lotmənt/ *n, Br* a small plot of land let out to an individual (e g by a town council) for cultivation

,**all-'out** using maximum effort and resources

,**all 'out** *adv* with maximum determination and effort; flat out – chiefly in *go all out*

,**all'over** /-'ohvə/ *adj* covering the whole extent or surface

,**all 'over 1** over the whole extent or surface **2** in every respect

allow /ə'low/ *v* **1a(1)** to assign as a share or suitable amount (e g of time or money) **a(2)** to grant as an allowance **b** to reckon as a deduction or an addition **2a** to admit as true or valid; acknowledge **b** to admit the possibility (of) **3a** to make it possible for; enable **b** to fail to prevent; let **4** to make allowance *for*

allowable /ə'lowəbl/ *adj* **1** permissible **2** assigned as an allowance – **-bly** *adv*

allowance /ə'lowəns/ *n* **1a** a (limited) share or portion allotted or granted; a ration **b** a sum granted as a reimbursement or bounty or for expenses **2** a handicap (e g in a race) **3a** permission, sanction **b** acknowledgment **4** the taking into account of mitigating circumstances – often pl with sing. meaning

¹**alloy** /'aloy/ *n* **1** a solid substance composed of a mixture of metals or a metal and a nonmetal thoroughly intermixed **2** a metal mixed with a more valuable metal

²**alloy** /ə'loy/ *v* **1** to reduce the purity or value of by adding sthg **2** to mix so as to form an alloy **3a** to impair or debase by addition **b** to temper, moderate

,**all-'purpose** *adj* suited for many purposes or uses

¹,**all 'right** *adv* **1** well enough **2** beyond doubt; certainly

²,**all 'right** *adj* **1** satisfactory, acceptable **2** safe, well **3** agreeable, pleasing – used as a generalized term of approval

³,**all 'right** *interj* **1** – used for giving assent **2** – used in indignant or menacing response

,all-'round *adj* 1 competent in many fields 2 having general utility 3 encompassing all aspects; comprehensive – ~er *n*

,all 'round *adv* 1 by, for, or to everyone present 2 in every respect

'all-,time *adj* exceeding all others yet known

allude /ə'l(y)oohd/ *v* to make indirect or implicit reference *to*

¹**allure** /ə'l(y)ooə/ *v* to entice by charm or attraction

²**allure** *n* power of attraction or fascination; charm

allusion /ə'lyooh-zh(ə)n, -'looh-/ *n* 1 alluding or hinting 2 (the use of) implied or indirect reference, esp in literature – **-sive** *adj* – **-sively** *adv*

al'luvium /-vi-əm/ *n, pl* **alluviums, alluvia** /-vi-ə/ clay, silt, or similar material deposited by running water – **-vial** *adj*

¹**ally** /ə'lie; *also* ə'lie/ *v* 1 to join, unite *with/to* 2 to relate *to* by resemblance or common properties 3 to form or enter into an alliance *with*

²**ally** /'alie/ *n* 1 a sovereign or state associated with another by treaty or league 2 a helper, auxiliary

alma mater /,almə 'mahtə, 'maytə/ *n* a school, college, or university which one has attended

almanac, almanack /'awlmənak/ *n* 1 a usu annual publication containing statistical, tabular, and general information 2 *chiefly Br* a publication containing astronomical and meteorological data arranged according to the days, weeks, and months of a given year

¹**almighty** /awl'mieti/ *adj* 1 *often cap* having absolute power over all 2 having relatively unlimited power 3 great in extent, seriousness, force, etc – infml

²**almighty** *adv* to a great degree; mighty – infml

Almighty *n* God – + *the*

almond /'ahmənd; *also* 'awl-; *NAm* al-/ *n* (the edible oval nut of) a small tree of the rose family

almoner /'ahmənə, 'al-/ *n* 1 one who distributes alms 2 a social worker attached to a British hospital – not now used technically

almost /'awlmohst/ *adv* very nearly but not exactly or entirely

alms /'ahmz/ *n sing or pl in constr* money, food, etc given to help the poor

'**alms,house** /-,hows/ *n, Br* a privately endowed house in which a poor person can live

aloft /ə'loft/ *adv* 1 at or to a great height 2 on, or to the masthead or the upper rigging of a ship

alone /ə'lohn/ *adj or adv* 1 considered without reference to any other; *esp* unassisted 2 separated from others; isolated 3 exclusive of other factors 4 free from interference

¹**along** /ə'long/ *prep* 1 in a line parallel with the length or direction of 2 in the course of (a route or journey) 3 in accordance with

²**along** *adv* 1 forward, on (e g move *along*) 2 as a necessary or pleasant addition; with one (e g bring the picnic *along*) 3 in company and simultaneously *with* (e g caught flu *along* with the others) 4 on hand, there (e g I'll be *along* soon) — **all along** all the time

¹**a,long'side** /-'sied/ *adv* along or at the side

²**alongside, alongside of** *prep* 1 side by side with; *specif* parallel to 2 concurrently with

¹**aloof** /ə'loohf/ *adv* at a distance; out of involvement

²**aloof** *adj* distant in interest or feeling; reserved, unsympathetic – ~**ly** *adv* – ~**ness** *n*

aloud /ə'lowd/ *adv* with the speaking voice

alpaca /al'pakə/ *n* 1 (the fine long woolly hair of) a type of domesticated llama found in Peru 2 a cloth made of or containing this wool

¹**alpha** /'alfə/ *n* 1 the 1st letter of the Greek alphabet 2 sthg that is first; a beginning 3 – used to designate the chief or brightest star of a constellation

²**alpha, α-** *adj* alphabetical

alphabet /'alfəbet/ *n* a set of characters, esp letters, used to represent 1 or more languages, esp when arranged in a conventional order; *also* a system of signs and signals that can be used in place of letters – ~**ical** *adj* – ~**ically** *adv*

alpha particle *n* a positively charged nuclear particle identical with the nucleus of a helium atom ejected at high speed by some radioactive substances

alpine /'alpien/ *n* an (ornamental) plant native to alpine or northern parts of the northern hemisphere

Alpine *adj* 1 *often not cap* of, growing in, or resembling the Alps; *broadly* of or resembling any mountains 2 *often not cap* of or growing in the elevated slopes above the tree line 3 of or being competitive ski events comprising slalom and downhill racing

already /awl'redi/ *adv* 1 no later than now or then; even by this or that time 2 before, previously

alright /awl'riet/ *adv, adj, or interj* all right – nonstandard

Alsatian /al'saysh(ə)n/ *n* (any of) a breed of large intelligent dogs often used as guard dogs

also /'awlsoh/ *adv* as an additional circumstance; besides

'**also-,ran** *n* 1 an entrant, esp a horse, that finishes outside the first 3 places in a race 2 a person of little importance

altar /'awltə/ *n* 1 a usu raised structure or place on which sacrifices are offered or incense is burnt in worship 2 a table on which the bread and wine used at communion are consecrated or which serves as a centre of worship or ritual

alter /'awltə/ *v* 1 to make different without changing into sthg else 2 to become different – ~**able** *adj* – ~**ation** *n*

altercation /ˌawltəkaysh(ə)n/ n a heated quarrel

alter 'ego /ˈaltə/ n a second self; esp a trusted friend

¹**alternate** /awl'tuhnət/ adj 1 occurring or succeeding each other by turns 2 arranged one above or alongside the other 3 every other; every second – **~ly** adv

²**alternate** /ˈawltəˌnayt/ v 1 to interchange with sthg else in turn 2 of 2 things to occur or succeed each other by turns 3 to undergo or consist of repeated change from one thing to another – **~nation** n

alternating current n an electric current that reverses its direction at regularly recurring intervals

¹**alternative** /awl'tuhnətiv/ adj 1 affording a choice, esp between 2 mutually exclusive options 2 constituting an alternative – **~ly** adv

²**alternative** n 1 an opportunity or need for deciding between 2 or more possibilities 2 either of 2 possibilities between which a choice is to be made; also any of more than 2 such possibilities

alternator /ˈawltəˌnaytə/ n an electric generator for producing alternating current

although also **altho** /awl'dhoh/ conj in spite of the fact or possibility that

altimeter /ˈaltiˌmeetə/ n an instrument for measuring altitude

altitude /ˈaltityoohd/ n 1 the angular elevation of a celestial object above the horizon 2 the height of an object (e g an aircraft), esp above sea level

alto /ˈaltoh/ n, pl **altos** 1a a countertenor b a contralto 2 the second highest part in 4-part harmony 3 a member of a family of instruments having a range between the treble or soprano and the tenor – **alto** adj

¹**altogether** /ˌawltə'gedhə/ adv 1 wholly, thoroughly 2 all told 3 in the main; on the whole 4 in every way

²**altogether** n the nude – infml

altruism /ˈaltrooh,iz(ə)m/ n unselfish regard for or devotion to the welfare of others – **altruist** n – **-istic** adj – **-istically** adv

aluminium /ˌalyooh'mini·əm, -yoo-/ n a bluish silver-white malleable light metallic element with good electrical and thermal conductivity and resistance to oxidation

always /ˈawlwayz, -wiz/ adv 1a at all times b in all cases 2 on every occasion; repeatedly 3 forever, perpetually 4 as a last resort; at any rate

am /əm, m; strong am/ pres 1 sing of be

amalgam /əˈmalgəm/ n a mixture of different elements

amalgamate /əˈmalgəmayt/ v to combine into a single body – **-ation** n

amass /əˈmas/ v 1 to collect for oneself; accumulate 2 to bring together into a mass; gather

amateur /ˈamətə, -chə/ n 1 one who engages in a pursuit as a pastime rather than as a profession; esp a sportsman who has never competed for money 2 one who practises an art or science unskilfully; a dabbler – **amateur** adj

amatory /ˈamət(ə)ri/ adj of or expressing sexual love

amaze /əˈmayz/ v to fill with wonder; astound – **~ment** n

amazing /əˈmayzing/ adj – used as a generalized term of approval – **~ly** adv

amazon /ˈamaz(ə)n/ n, often cap a tall strong athletic woman – **~ian** adj

ambassador /amˈbasədə/ n 1 a top-ranking diplomat accredited to a foreign government or sovereign as a temporary or resident representative 2 a representative, messenger – **~ship** n – **~ial** adj

amber /ˈambə/ n 1 a hard yellowish to brownish translucent fossil resin used chiefly for ornaments and jewellery 2 the colour of amber 3 a yellow traffic light meaning 'caution'

amber gris /-ˌgrees, -ˌgris/ n a waxy substance found floating in tropical waters, that originates in the intestines of the sperm whale, and is used in perfumery as a fixative

ambidextrous /ˌambi'dekstrəs/ adj 1 able to use either hand with equal ease 2 unusually skilful; versatile 3 characterized by deceitfulness and double-dealing – **~ly** adv

ambience, ambiance /ˈambi·əns · ˈ/ n a surrounding or pervading atmosphere; an environment, milieu

ambiguous /amˈbigyoo·əs/ adj vague, indistinct, or difficult to interpret 2 capable of 2 or more interpretations – **-guity** n – **~ly** adv – **~ness** n

ambition /amˈbish(ə)n/ n 1a a strong desire for status, wealth, or power b a desire to achieve a particular end 2 an object of ambition

ambitious /amˈbishəs/ adj 1a having, resulting from, or showing ambition b desirous of, aspiring 2 elaborate – **~ly** adv – **~ness** n

¹**amble** /ˈambl/ v **ambling** /ˈambling, 'ambl·ing/ to move at an amble

²**amble** n 1 an easy gait 2 a leisurely stroll

ambrosia /amˈbrohzi·ə, -zh(y)ə/ n 1 the food of the Greek and Roman gods 2 sthg extremely pleasing to the taste or smell

ambulance /ˈambyoolans/ n a vehicle equipped to transport the injured or ill

¹**ambush** /ˈamboosh/ v to attack from an ambush; waylay

²**ambush** n the concealment of soldiers, police, etc in order to carry out a surprise attack from a hidden position

ameliorate /əˈmeelyərayt/ v to make or become better or more tolerable – **-ration** n

amen /ˌah'men, ˌay-, -ˌ-/ interj – used to express solemn confirmation (e g of an expression of faith) or hearty approval (e g of an assertion)

amenable /ə'meenəbl/ *adj* 1 capable of submission (e g to judgment or test) 2 readily persuaded to yield or agree; tractable

amend /ə'mend/ *v* 1 to put right; *specif* to make corrections in (e g a text) 2 to change or modify for the better; improve

a'mendment /-mənt/ *n* 1 the act of amending, esp for the better 2 an alteration proposed or effected by amending

a'mends *n pl but sing or pl in constr* compensation for a loss or injury; recompense

amenity /ə'menəti, ə'mee-/ *n* 1 sthg (e g a public facility) conducive to material comfort – often pl 2 sthg (e g a conventional social gesture) conducive to ease of social intercourse – usu pl

¹**American** /ə'merikən/ *n* 1 a N or S American Indian 2 a native or inhabitant of N or S America 3 a citizen of the USA 4 English as typically spoken and written in the USA

²**American** *adj* 1 (characteristic) of N or S America 2 (characteristic) of the USA 3 of the N and S American Indians

American Indian *n* a member of any of the indigenous peoples of N, S, or central America excluding the Eskimos

Americanism /ə'merikəniz(ə)m/ *n* 1 a characteristic feature (e g a custom or belief) of Americans or American culture 2 adherence or attachment to America, its culture, or its policies

amethyst /ə'məthist/ *n* a semiprecious gemstone of clear purple or violet quartz

amiable /'aymi-əbl/ *adj* 1 (seeming) agreeable and well-intentioned; inoffensive 2 friendly, congenial – **-bility** *n* – **-bly** *adv*

amicable /'amikəbl/ *adj* characterized by friendly goodwill; peaceable – **-bility** *n* – **-bly** *adv*

amid /ə'mid/ *prep* in or to the middle of – poetic

amidships /ə'mid,ships/ *adv* in or towards the middle part (of a ship)

a,mino 'acid *n* any of various organic acids occurring esp in linear chains as the chief components of proteins

amiss /ə'mis/ *adv or adj* 1 astray 2 out of order; at fault 3 out of place in given circumstances – usu + a negative

amity /'amiti/ *n* friendship

ammeter /'ameetə/ *n* an instrument for measuring electric current in amperes

ammonia /ə'mohnyə, -ni-ə/ *n* a pungent colourless gas that is a compound of nitrogen and hydrogen

ammunition /,amyoo'nish(ə)n/ *n* 1 the projectiles, together with their propelling charges, used in the firing of guns; *also* bombs, grenades, etc containing explosives 2 material used to defend or attack a point of view

amnesia /am'neezyə, -zh(y)ə/ *n* a (pathological) loss of memory

amnesty /'amnəsti/ *n* the act of pardoning a large group of individuals, esp for political offences

amoeba, *chiefly NAm* **ameba** /ə'meebə/ *n, pl* **amoebas, amoebae** /-bi/ any of various protozoans that are widely distributed in water and wet places – **-bic** *adj*

amok, amuck /ə'muk/ *adv* in a murderous frenzy; raging violently

among /ə'mung/ *prep* 1 in or through the midst of; surrounded by 2 by or through the whole group of 3 in the number or class of 4 between – used for more than 2 (e g fight *among* themselves)

amoral /a(y)'morəl, ə-/ *adj* 1 being neither moral nor immoral; *specif* lying outside the sphere of ethical judgments 2 having no understanding of, or unconcerned with, morals – **~ity** *n*

amorous /'amərəs/ *adj* 1 of or relating to love 2 moved by or inclined to love or desire – **~ly** *adv* – **~ness** *n*

amorphous /ə'mawfəs/ *adj* 1 having no definite form; shapeless 2 without definite character; unclassifiable – **~ly** *adv* – **~ness** *n*

¹**amount** /ə'mownt/ *v* to be equal in number, quantity, or significance *to*

²**amount** *n* 1 the total quantity 2 the quantity at hand or under consideration

amp /amp/ *n* an ampere *USE* infml

ampere /'ampeə/ *n* the basic unit of electrical current

ampersand /'ampə,sand/ *n* a sign, typically &, standing for the word *and*

amphibian /am'fibi-ən/ *n, pl* **amphibians**, (1) **amphibians**, *esp collectively* **amphibia** /-bi-ə/ 1 an amphibious organism; *esp* a frog, toad, newt, or other member of a class of cold-blooded vertebrates intermediate in many characteristics between fishes and reptiles 2 an aeroplane, tank, etc adapted to operate on or from both land and water

amphibious /am'fibi-əs/ *adj* 1 able to live both on land and in water 2a relating to or adapted for both land and water b involving or trained for coordinated action of land, sea, and air forces organized for invasion

'amphi,theatre /-,thiətə/ *n* an oval or circular building with rising tiers of seats ranged about an open space

amphora /'amfərə/ *n, pl* **amphorae** /-ri,-rie/, **amphoras** a 2-handled oval jar or vase with a narrow neck and base

ample /'ampl/ *adj* 1 generous in size, scope, or capacity 2 abundant, plentiful – **-ply** *adv*

amplify /'ampli,fie/ *v* 1 to expand (e g a statement) by the use of detail, illustration, etc 2 to make larger or greater; increase 3 to increase the magnitude of (a signal or other input of power) 4 to expand *on* one's remarks or ideas – **-fication** *n*

amplitude /'amplityoohd, -choohd/ *n* largeness of a dimensions b scope; abundance

ampoule, *chiefly NAm* **ampul, ampule** /'ampoohl/ *n* a hermetically sealed small bulbous glass vessel

amputate /'ampyootayt/ *v* to cut or lop off; *esp* to cut (e g a damaged or diseased limb) from the body – **-tation** *n*

amuck /ə'muk/ *adv* amok

amulet /'amyoolit/ *n* a small object worn as a charm against evil

amuse /ə'myoohz/ *v* 1 to entertain or occupy in a light or pleasant manner 2 to appeal to the sense of humour of

a'musement /-mənt/ *n* a means of entertaining or occupying; a pleasurable diversion

¹**an** /(ə)n; *strong* an/ *indefinite article* **a** – used (1) before words with an initial vowel sound (2) frequently, esp formerly or in the USA, before words whose initial /h/ sound is often lost before the *an*

²**an, an'** *conj* and – *infml*

³**an** *prep* a – used under the same conditions as ¹**an**

anachronism /ə'nakrə,niz(ə)m/ *n* 1 an error in chronology; *esp* a chronological misplacing of people, events, objects, or customs 2 sby who or sthg that seems chronologically out of place – **-nistic** *adj* – **-nistically** *adv*

anaconda /,anə'kondə/ *n* a large semiaquatic S American snake of the boa family that crushes its prey in its coils

anaemia, *chiefly NAm* **anemia** /ə'neemyə, -mi-ə/ *n* 1 a condition in which the blood is deficient in red blood cells, haemoglobin, etc 2 lack of vitality – **anaemic** *adj* – **-ically** *adv*

anaesthesia, *chiefly NAm* **anesthesia** /,anəs'theezh(y)ə, -zyə/ *n* 1 loss of sensation, esp loss of sensation of pain, resulting either from injury or a disorder of the nerves or from the action of drugs – **-thetist** *n* – **-thetize** *v*

anaesthetic, *chiefly NAm* **anesthetic** /,anəs'the-tik/ *n* a substance that produces anaesthesia, e g so that surgery can be carried out painlessly – **anaesthetic** *adj*

anagram /'anə,gram/ *n* a word or phrase made by rearranging the letters of another

anal /'aynl/ *adj* of or situated near the anus

analogue, *NAm chiefly* **analog** /'analog/ *n* sthg similar or parallel to sthg else

analogy /ə'naləji/ *n* 1 inference from a parallel case 2 resemblance in some particulars; similarity – **-gous** *adj*

analyse, *NAm chiefly* **analyze** /'anəliez/ *v* 1 to subject to analysis 2 to determine by analysis the constitution or structure of 3 to psychoanalyse

analysis /ə'nalisis/ *n, pl* **analyses** /-seez/ **1a** examination and identification of the components of a whole **b** a statement of such an analysis 2 psychoanalysis – **-lytic, -lytical** *adj* – **-lytically** *adv*

analyst /'anəlist/ *n* 1 a person who analyses or is skilled in analysis 2 a psychoanalyst

anarchism /'anə,kiz(ə)m/ *n* 1 a political theory holding all forms of governmental authority to be undesirable 2 the attacking of the established social order or laws; rebellion – **-chist** *n* – **-chistic** *adj* – **-chistically** *adv*

anarchy /'anəki/ *n* **1a** absence of government **b** lawlessness; (political) disorder **c** a utopian society with complete freedom and no government 2 anarchism – **-chic, -chical** *adj* – **-chically** *adv*

anatomy /ə'natəmi/ *n* 1 dissection 2 structural make-up, esp of (a part of) an organism 3 an analysis 4 the human body – **-ist** *n* – **-ical** *adj* – **-ically** *adv*

ancestor /'ansestə, -səs-/, *fem* **ancestress** /-tris/ *n* 1 one from whom a person is descended, usu more distant than a grandparent 2 a progenitor of a more recent species or organism – *-tral* *adj*

ancestry /'ansestri, -səs-/ *n* a line of esp noble descent; a lineage

¹**anchor** /'angkə/ *n* **1a** a usu metal device dropped to the bottom from a ship or boat to hold it in a particular place 2 sby or sthg providing support and security; a mainstay 3 sthg that serves to hold an object firmly

²**anchor** *v* 1 to hold in place in the water by an anchor 2 to secure firmly; fix 3 to become fixed; settle

anchorage /'angkərij/ *n* 1 a place (suitable) for vessels to anchor 2 a source of reassurance 3 sthg that provides a secure hold or attachment

anchorite /'angkə,riet/, *fem* **anchoress** /'angk(ə)ris/, **anchress** /'angkris/ *n* one who lives in seclusion, usu for religious reasons

anchovy /'an,chəvi/ *n* a common small Mediterranean fish resembling a herring

¹**ancient** /'aynsh(ə)nt, -chənt/ *adj* 1 having existed for many years 2 of (those living in) a remote period, specif that from the earliest known civilizations to the fall of the western Roman Empire in AD 476 3 old-fashioned, antique

²**ancient** *n* 1 sby who lived in ancient times 2 *pl the* members of a civilized, esp a classical, nation of antiquity

¹**ancillary** /an'siləri; *NAm usu* 'ansə,leri/ *adj* 1 subordinate, subsidiary 2 auxiliary, supplementary

²**ancillary** *n, Br* one who assists; a helper

and /(ə)n, (ə)nd; *strong* and/ *conj* 1 – used to join coordinate sentence elements of the same class or function expressing addition or combination (e g cold *and* tired) 2 – used, esp in Br speech, before the numbers 1–99 after the number 100 3 plus 4 – used to introduce a second clause expressing temporal sequence, consequence, contrast, or supplementary explanation 5 – used to join repeated words expressing continuation or progression (e g for miles *and* miles) 6 – used to join words expressing contrast of type or quality (e g fair, fat *and* forty) — **and all that, and all** and so forth —

and how — used to emphasize the preceding idea; infml — **and so forth, and so on 1** and others or more of the same kind **2** and further in the same manner **3** and the rest **4** other things — **and that** *chiefly Br* and so forth — nonstandard

andante /an'danti/ *n, adv, or adj* (a musical composition or movement to be played) moderately slow

android /'androyd/ *n* an automaton externally indistinguishable from a human

anecdote /'anik‚doht/ *n* a usu short narrative about an interesting or amusing person or incident – **-dotal** *adj*

anemone /ə'neməni/ *n* **1** any of a large genus of plants of the buttercup family with lobed or divided leaves and showy flowers **2** a sea anemone

anew /ə'nyooh/ *adv* **1** again, afresh **2** in a new form or way

angel /'aynj(ə)l/ *n* **1** a spiritual being, usu depicted as being winged, serving as God's intermediary or acting as a heavenly worshipper **2** an attendant spirit or guardian **3** a very kind or loving person, esp a woman or girl **4** a financial backer of a theatrical venture or other enterprise – chiefly infml – **~ic** *adj* – **~ically** *adv*

angelica /an'jelikə/ *n* (the candied stalks, used esp as a decoration on cakes and desserts, of) a biennial plant of the carrot family

Angelus /'anjələs/ *n* (a bell rung to mark) a devotion of the Western church said at morning, noon, and evening to commemorate the Incarnation

¹anger /'ang·gə/ *n* a strong feeling of displeasure and usu antagonism

²anger *v* to make or become angry

¹angle /'ang·gl/ *n* **1** a corner **2a** the figure formed by 2 lines extending from the same point or by 2 surfaces diverging from the same line **b** a measure of the amount of turning necessary to bring one line of an angle to coincide with the other at all points **3a** a precise viewpoint; an aspect **b** a special approach or technique for accomplishing an objective **4** a divergent course or position; a slant – esp in *at an angle*

²angle *v* **angling** /'ang·gling/ **1** to place, move, or direct obliquely **2** to present (e g a news story) from a particular or prejudiced point of view; slant **3** to turn or proceed at an angle

³angle *v* **angling** /'ang·gling/ to use artful means to attain an objective

Anglican /'ang·glikən/ *adj* of the body of churches including the established episcopal Church of England and churches of similar faith in communion with it – **~ism** *n*

anglicism /'angli‚siz(ə)m/ *n, often cap* **1** a characteristic feature of English occurring in another language **2** adherence or attachment to England, English culture, etc

angling /'ang·gling/ *n* (the sport of) fishing with hook and line – **-gler** *n*

‚Anglo-A'merican /‚ang·gloh-/ *n or adj* (a) N American, esp of the USA, of English origin or descent

‚Anglo-'Indian /n **1** a British person domiciled for a long time in India **2** a Eurasian of mixed British and Indian birth or descent

anglophile /'ang·gləfiel, -fil/ *also* **anglophil** /-fil/ *n, often cap* a foreigner who is greatly interested in and admires England and things English

anglophobe /'ang·glə‚fohb/ *n, often cap* a foreigner who is averse to England and things English

‚Anglo-'Saxon *n* **1** a member of the Germanic peoples who conquered England in the 5th c AD and formed the ruling group until the Norman conquest **2** sby of English, esp Anglo-Saxon, descent

angora /ang'gawrə/ *n* **1** the hair of the Angora rabbit or goat **2** a fabric or yarn made (in part) of Angora rabbit hair, used esp for knitting **3** *cap* an Angora cat, goat, or rabbit

An‚gora 'cat *n* a long-haired domestic cat

An‚gora 'goat *n* (any of) a breed of the domestic goat raised for its long silky hair which is the true mohair

An‚gora 'rabbit *n* a long-haired usu white domestic rabbit

angry /'ang·gri/ *adj* **1** feeling or showing anger **2** seeming to show or typify anger **3** painfully inflamed – **angrily** *adv*

angst /angst/ *n* anxiety and anguish, caused esp by considering the state of the world and the human condition

anguish /'ang·gwish/ *n* extreme physical pain or mental distress – **~ed** *adj*

angular /'ang·gyoolə/ *adj* **1a** having 1 or more angles **b** forming an angle; sharp-cornered **2a** stiff in character or manner; awkward **b** lean, bony – **~ity** *n*

animadvert /‚animad'vuht/ *v* to comment critically or adversely *on* – fml – **-version** *n*

¹animal /'animəl/ *n* **1** any of a kingdom of living things typically differing from plants in their capacity for spontaneous movement, esp in response to stimulation **2a** any of the lower animals as distinguished from human beings **b** a mammal – not in technical use **3** a person considered as a purely physical being; a creature

²animal *adj* **1** of or derived from animals **2** of the body as opposed to the mind or spirit – chiefly derog

¹animate /'animət/ *adj* **1** possessing life; alive **2** of animal life **3** lively

²animate /'animayt/ *v* **1** to give spirit and support to; encourage **2** to give life or vigour to **3** to produce in the form of an animated cartoon

animated cartoon *n* a film that creates the illusion of fmovement by photographing successive positional changes of drawings, models, etc

animation /,ani'maysh(ə)n/ n 1 vigorous liveliness 2 (the preparation of) an animated cartoon

animism /'animiz(ə)m/ n attributing conscious life, spirits, or souls to nature or natural objects or phenomena – **animist** n, adj

animosity /,ani'mositi/ n powerful often active ill will or resentment

aniseed /'anəseed/ n a pep̣ ̣erminty seed used esp as a flavouring

ankle /'angkl/ n the (region of the) joint between the foot and the leg; the tarsus

annals /'anlz/ n pl 1 a record of events, activities, etc, arranged in yearly sequence 2 historical records; chronicles

anneal /ə'neel/ v to temper, toughen

¹**annex** /ə'neks/ v 1 to append 2 to take possession of; esp to incorporate (a country or other territory) within the domain of a state – ~**ation** n

²**annex**, chiefly Br **annexe** /'aneks/ n 1 sthg, esp an addition to a document, annexed or appended 2 a separate or attached extra structure; esp a building providing extra accommodation

annihilate /ə'nie-ə,layt/ v 1 to destroy (almost) entirely 2 to defeat conclusively; rout – **-lation** n

anniversary /,ani'vuhs(ə)ri/ n (the celebration of) a day marking the annual recurrence of the date of a notable event

anno Domini /,anoh 'dominie/ adv, often cap A – used to indicate that a year or century comes within the Christian era

annotate /'anətayt, 'anoh-/ v to provide (e g a literary work) with notes – **-tation** n

announce /ə'nowns/ v 1 to make known publicly; proclaim 2a to give notice of the arrival, presence, or readiness of b to indicate in advance; foretell 3 to give evidence of; indicate by action or appearance – ~**r** n – ~**ment** n

annoy /ə'noy/ v 1 to disturb or irritate, esp by repeated acts; vex – often pass + with or at 2 to harass 3 to be a source of annoyance – ~**ance** n

¹**annual** /'anyoo(ə)l/ adj 1 covering or lasting for the period of a year 2 occurring or performed once a year; yearly 3 of a plant completing the life cycle in 1 growing season – ~**ly** adv

²**annual** n 1 a publication appearing yearly 2 sthg lasting 1 year or season; specif an annual plant

annuity /ə'nyooh-əti/ n 1 an amount payable at a regular (e g yearly) interval 2 (a contract embodying) the right to receive or the obligation to pay an annuity

annul /ə'nul/ v -ll- 1 to reduce to nothing; obliterate, cancel 2 to declare (e g a marriage) legally invalid – **annulment** n

annular /'anyoolə/ adj of or forming a ring

Annunciation /ə,nunsi'aysh(ə)n/ n (March 25 observed as a church festival commemorating) the announcement of the Incarnation to the Virgin Mary

anode /'anohd/ n 1 the electrode by which electrons leave a device and enter an external circuit; specif the negative terminal of a primary or secondary cell that is delivering current 2 a positive electrode used to accelerate electrons in an electron gun

anoint /ə'noynt/ v 1 to smear or rub with oil or a similar substance 2a to apply oil to as a sacred rite, esp for consecration b to designate (as if) through the rite of anointment; consecrate – ~**ment** n

anomalous /ə'noməs/ adj 1 irregular, abnormal 2 incongruous – ~**ly** adv

anomaly /ə'noməli/ n 1 deviation from the common rule; an irregularity, incongruity 2 sthg anomalous

anon /ə'non/ adv, archaic 1 soon, presently 2 at another time

anonymous /ə'nonəməs/ adj 1 having or giving no name 2 of unknown or unnamed origin or authorship 3 nondescript – **-mity** n – ~**ly** adv

anorak /'anarak/ n, chiefly Br a short weatherproof coat with a hood

anorexia /,anə'reksi-ə/ n (prolonged) loss of appetite; specif a pathological aversion to food – ~**exic** adj

¹**another** /ə'nudhə/ adj 1 being a different or distinct one 2 some other 3 being one additional (e g another baby) 4 patterned after (e g another Picasso)

²**another** pron, pl **others** 1 an additional one; one more 2 a different one

¹**answer** /'ahnsə/ n 1 a spoken or written reply to a question, remark, etc 2 an esp correct solution to a problem 3 a response or reaction 4 sby or sthg intended to be a close equivalent or rival of another

²**answer** v 1 to speak, write, or act in reply (to) 2a to be responsible or accountable for b to make amends; atone for 3 to correspond to 4 to reply to in justification or explanation 5 to act in response to (a sound or other signal) 6 to offer a solution for; esp to solve

answerable /'ahns(ə)rəbl/ adj 1 responsible 2 capable of being answered or refuted – **-bly** adv

ant /ant/ n any of a family of insects that live in large social groups having a complex organization and hierarchy

antacid /ant'asid/ adj that corrects excessive acidity, esp in the stomach

antagonism /an'tagəniz(ə)m/ n hostility or antipathy, esp when actively expressed

antagonist /an'tagənist/ n an opponent, adversary – ~**ic** adj – ~**ically** adv

antagon·ize, -ise /an'tagəniez/ v to provoke the hostility of

antarctic /an'tahktik/ adj, often cap of the South Pole or surrounding region

'ant,eater /-,eeta/ *n* any of several mammals that feed (chiefly) on ants and termites

¹antecedent /,anti'seed(a)nt/ *n* **1** a word, phrase, or clause functioning as a noun and referred to by a pronoun **2** a preceding thing, event, or circumstance **3** *pl* family origins; parentage

²antecedent *adj* **1** prior in time or order **2** causally or logically prior

antechamber /'anti,chaymba/ *n* an anteroom

'ante,date /-,dayt/ *v* **1** to attach or assign a date earlier than the true one to (e g a document), esp with intent to deceive **2** to precede in time

,antedi'luvian /-di'loohvi-an/ *adj* of the period before the flood described in the Bible **2** completely out-of-date; antiquated

antelope /'antilohp/ *n* any of various Old World ruminant mammals that are lighter and more graceful than the true oxen

ante meridiem /,anti ma'ridi-am/ *adj* being before noon – abbr *am*

,ante'natal /-'naytl/ *adj* of or concerned with an unborn child, pregnancy, or a pregnant woman

antenna /an'tena/ *n, pl* antennae /-ni/, antennas **1** a movable segmented sense organ on the head of insects, crustaceans, etc **2** an aerial

anterior /an'tiari-a/ *adj* **1** before in time **2** situated before or towards the front

anteroom /'anti,roohm/ *n* an outer room that leads to another usu more important one

anthem /'anthəm/ *n* **1** a piece of church music for voices usu set to a biblical text **2** a song or hymn of praise or gladness

anther /'antha/ *n* the part of a stamen that contains and releases pollen

'ant,hill /-,hil/ *n* **1** a mound thrown up by ants digging their nest **2** a place (e g a city) that is overcrowded and constantly busy

anthology /an'tholəji/ *n* a collection of selected (literary) passages or works

anthracite /'anthrə,siet/ *n* a hard slow-burning coal

anthrax /'anthraks/ *n* an often fatal infectious disease of warm-blooded animals (e g cattle, sheep, or human beings) caused by a spore-forming bacterium

anthropoid /'anthrə,poyd/ *adj* resembling human beings or the apes (e g in form or behaviour); apelike

anthropology /,anthrə'poləji/ *n* the scientific study of human beings, esp in relation to physical characteristics, social relations and culture, and the origin and distribution of races – **-gist** *n* – **-gical** *adj* – **-gically** *adv*

anthropomorphism /,anthrəpə'mawfiz(ə)m/ *n* the ascribing of human behaviour, form, etc to what is not human (e g a god or animal) – **-phic** *adj*

anti'biotic /-bie'otik/ *n* a substance produced by a microorganism and able in dilute solution to inhibit the growth of or kill another microorganism – ~ **ally** *adv*

'anti,body /-,bodi/ *n* a protein that is produced by the body in response to a specific antigen and that counteracts its effects (e g by neutralizing toxins or grouping bacteria into clumps)

antic /'antik/ *n* a ludicrous act or action; a caper – usu *pl*

anticipate /an'tisipayt/ *v* **1** to give advance thought, discussion, or treatment to **2** to foresee and deal with in advance; forestall **3** to act before (another) often so as to thwart **4** to look forward to as certain; expect **5** to speak or write in knowledge or expectation of sthg due to happen – **-pation** *n*

,anti'climax /-'kliemaks/ *n* **1** (an instance of) the usu sudden and ludicrous descent in writing or speaking from a significant to a trivial idea **2** an event (e g at the end of a series) that is strikingly less important or exciting than expected

,anti'clockwise /-'klokwiez/ *adj or adv* in a direction opposite to that in which the hands of a clock rotate when viewed from the front

,anti'cyclone /-'sieklohn/ *n* (a system of winds that rotates about) a centre of high atmospheric pressure

antidote /'anti,doht/ *n* **1** a remedy that counteracts the effects of poison **2** sthg that relieves or counteracts

'anti,freeze /-,freez/ *n* a substance added to a liquid (e g the water in a car radiator) to lower its freezing point

antigen /'antijən/ *n* a protein, carbohydrate, etc that stimulates the production of an antibody when introduced into the body

'anti-,hero, *fem* 'anti-,heroine *n* a protagonist who lacks traditional heroic qualities (e g courage)

,anti'logarithm /-'logə,ridhəm/ *n* the number corresponding to a given logarithm

,antima'cassar /-mə'kasə/ *n* a usu protective cover put over the backs or arms of upholstered seats

'anti,matter /-,matə/ *n* matter composed of antiparticles (e g antiprotons instead of protons, positrons instead of electrons, and antineutrons instead of neutrons)

antimony /'antiməni; *NAm* 'anti,mohni/ *n* a metal-like element used esp as a constituent of alloys

antipathy /an'tipəthi/ *n* a fixed aversion or dislike; a distaste – **-thetic** *adj*

antipodes /an'tipə,deez/ *n pl the* region of the earth diametrically opposite; *specif, often cap* Australasia

¹antiquarian /,anti'kweəri-ən/ *n* one who collects or studies antiquities

²antiquarian *adj* **1** of antiquarians or antiquities **2** of books or prints old (and rare)

antiquary /'antikwəri/ *n* an antiquary

antiquated /'anti,kwaytid/ *adj* **1** out-of-date **2** advanced in age

¹antique /an'teek/ *adj* **1** belonging to or surviving from earlier, esp classical, times; ancient **2** old-fashioned **3** made in an earlier period and therefore valuable

²antique *n* **1** *the* the ancient Greek or Roman style in art **2** a relic or object of ancient times **3** a work of art, piece of furniture, or decorative object made at an earlier period and sought by collectors

antiquity /an'tikwəti/ *n* **1** ancient times; esp the period before the Middle Ages **2** the quality of being ancient **3** *pl* relics or monuments of ancient times

antirrhinum /,anti'rienəm/ *n* any of a large genus of plants (e g the snapdragon or a related plant) with bright-coloured 2-lipped flowers

anti-'Semitism *n* hostility towards Jews – **Semitic** *adj* – **Semite** *n*

¹anti,septic /-'septik/ *adj* **1a** opposing sepsis (in living tissue), specif by arresting the growth of microorganisms, esp bacteria **b** of, acting or protecting like, or using an antiseptic **2a** scrupulously clean **b** extremely neat or orderly, esp to the point of being bare or uninteresting **3** impersonal, detached

²antiseptic *n* an antiseptic substance; *also* a germicide

anti,social /-'sohsh(ə)l/ *adj* **1** hostile or harmful to organized society **2a** averse to the society of others; unsociable **b** *Br* unsocial

antithesis /an'tithəsis/ *n*, *pl* **antitheses** /-seez/ **1a** a contrast of ideas expressed by a parallel arrangement of words (e g in 'action, not words') **b** opposition, contrast **c** the direct opposite **2** the second stage of a reasoned argument, in contrast to the thesis

antler /'antlə/ *n* (a branch of) the solid periodically shed horn of an animal of the deer family

antonym /'antənim/ *n* a word having the opposite meaning

anus /'aynəs/ *n* the rear excretory opening of the alimentary canal

anvil /'anvil/ *n* **1** a heavy, usu steel-faced, iron block on which metal is shaped **2** a bone in the inner ear

anxiety /ang'zie-əti/ *n* **1** apprehensive uneasiness of mind, usu over an impending or anticipated ill **2** a cause of anxiety

anxious /'ang(k)shəs/ *adj* **1** troubled, worried **2** causing anxiety; worrying **3** ardently or earnestly wishing *to* – **~ly** *adv*

¹any /'eni/ *adj* **1** one or some indiscriminately; whichever is chosen **2** one, some, or all; whatever: e g **2a** of whatever number or quantity; being even the smallest number or quantity of (e g

there's never *any* salt) **b** no matter how great (e g make *any* sacrifice) **c** no matter how ordinary or inadequate (e g *any* old card will do) **3** being an appreciable number, part, or amount of – not in positive statements (e g not for *any* length of time)

²any *pron*, *pl* **any 1** any person; anybody **2a** any thing **b** any part, quantity, or number

³any *adv* to any extent or degree; at all

anybody /'eni,bodi, -bodi/ *pron* any person

'any,how /-,how/ *adv* **1** in a haphazard manner **2** anyway

'any,road /-,rohd/ *adv*, *Br* anyway – nonstandard

¹'any,thing /-,thing/ *pron* any thing whatever — **anything but** not at all; far from

²anything *adv* in any degree; at all

'any,way /-,way/ *adv* **1** in any case, inevitably **2** – used when resuming a narrative (e g *anyway*, the moment we arrived...)

¹'any,where /-,weə/ *adv* **1** in, at, or to any place **2** to any extent; at all **3** – used to indicate limits of variation (e g *anywhere* between here and London)

²anywhere *n* any place

aorta /ay'awtə/ *n*, *pl* **aortas, aortae** /-ti/ the great artery that carries blood from the left side of the heart to be distributed by branch arteries throughout the body

apace /ə'pays/ *adv* at a quick pace; swiftly

apart /ə'paht/ *adv* **1a** at a distance (from one another in space or time) **b** at a distance in character or opinions **2** so as to separate one from another **3** excluded from consideration or in or into 2 or more parts

apartheid /ə'paht-(h)ayt, -(h)iet/ *n* racial segregation; *specif* a policy of segregation and discrimination against non-Europeans in the Republic of S Africa

apartment /ə'pahtmənt/ *n* **1** a single room in a building **2** a suite of rooms used for living quarters **3** *chiefly NAm* a flat

apathetic /,apə'thetik/ *adj* **1** having or showing little or no feeling; spiritless **2** lacking interest or concern; indifferent – **~ally** *adv*

apathy /'apəthi/ *n* **1** lack of feeling or emotion; impassiveness **2** lack of interest or concern; indifference

¹ape /ayp/ *n* **1** a chimpanzee, gorilla, or any similar primate **2a** a mimic **b** a large uncouth person

²ape *v* to imitate closely but often clumsily and ineptly

aperitif /ə,perə'teef, -'---/ *n* an alcoholic drink taken before a meal to stimulate the appetite

aperture /'apəchə/ *n* an open space; a hole, gap

apex /'aypeks/ *n*, *pl* **apexes, apices** /'aypə,seez/ **1a** the uppermost peak; the vertex **b** the narrowed or pointed end; the tip **2** the highest or culminating point

aphid /'ayfid/ *n* a greenfly or related small sluggish insect that sucks the juices of plants

aphorism /'afəriz(ə)m/ n an adage

aphrodisiac /ˌafrə'diziak/ n or adj (a substance) that stimulates sexual desire

apiary /'aypiˌori/ n a place where bees are kept, esp for their honey – **-rist** n

apiece /ə'pees/ adv for each one; individually

apish /'aypish/ adj resembling an ape: e g a slavishly imitative **b** extremely silly or affected – ~**ly** adv – ~**ness** n

aplomb /ə'plom, ə'plom/ n complete composure or self-assurance; poise

apocalypse /ə'pokəlips/ n 1 cap the biblical Book of Revelation which describes the end of the world 2 sthg viewed as a prophetic revelation

apocalyptic /əˌpokə'liptik/ also **apocalyptical** /-kl/ adj 1 of or resembling an apocalypse 2 forecasting the ultimate destiny of the world; prophetic 3 foreboding imminent disaster; terrible – **~ally** adv

apocrypha /ə'pokrifə/ n 1 (a collection of) writings or statements of dubious authenticity 2 sing or pl in constr, cap books included in the Septuagint and Vulgate but excluded from the Jewish and Protestant canons of the Old Testament – usu + the

apocryphal /ə'pokrif(ə)l/ adj 1 often cap of or resembling the Apocrypha 2 of doubtful authenticity

apogee /'apəjee/ n 1 the point farthest from a planet or other celestial body reached by any object orbiting it 2 the farthest or highest point; the culmination

apologetic /əˌpolə'jetik/ adj 1 offered in defence or apology 2 regretfully acknowledging fault or failure; contrite – ~**ally** adv

apologize, -ise /ə'poləjiez/ v to make an apology

apology /ə'polji/ n 1 a excuse 2 an admission of error or discourtesy accompanied by an expression of regret 3 a poor substitute for

apoplectic /ˌapə'plektik/ adj violently excited (e g from rage) – infml – ~**ally** adv

apoplexy /'apəˌpleksi/ n a seizure caused by rupture or blockage of a blood artery

apostle /ə'pos(ə)l/ n 1 one sent on a mission; esp any of an authoritative New Testament group sent out to preach the gospel and made up esp of Jesus's original 12 disciples and Paul 2a one who first advocates an important belief or system **b** an ardent supporter; an adherent

apostolic /ˌapə'stolik/ adj 1 of an apostle or the New Testament apostles 2a of the divine authority vested in the apostles held (e g by Roman Catholics, Anglicans, and Eastern Orthodox) to be handed down through the successive ordinations of bishops **b** of the pope as the successor to the apostolic authority vested in St Peter – ~**ally** adv

apostrophe /ə'postrəfi/ n a mark ' used to indicate the omission of letters or figures, the possessive case, or the plural of letters or figures

apothecary /ə'pothək(ə)ri/ n, archaic or NAm a pharmacist, chemist

appal, NAm chiefly **appall** /ə'pawl/ v -ll- to overcome with consternation, horror, or dismay

apparatus /ˌapə'raytəs, --'--; NAm also -'ratəs/ n, pl **apparatuses, apparatus** 1 (a piece of) equipment designed for a particular use, esp for a scientific operation 2 the administrative bureaucracy of an organization, esp a political party

apparel /ə'parəl/ n 1 garments, clothing – chiefly fml 2 sthg that clothes or adorns – chiefly poetic – **apparel** v

apparent /ə'parənt/ adj 1 easily seen or understood; plain, evident 2 seemingly real but not necessarily so 3 having an absolute right to succeed to a title or estate – ~**ly** adv

apparition /ˌapə'rish(ə)n/ n 1a an unusual or unexpected sight; a phenomenon **b** a ghostly figure 2 the act of becoming visible; appearance

¹**appeal** /ə'peel/ n 1 a legal proceeding by which a case is brought to a higher court for review 2a(1) an application (e g to a recognized authority) for corroboration, vindication, or d...sion a(2) a call by members of the fielding side in cricket, esp by the bowler, for the umpire to decide whether a batsman is out **b** an earnest plea for aid or mercy; an entreaty 3 the power of arousing a sympathetic response; attraction

²**appeal** v 1 to take (a case) to a higher court 2a to call on another for corroboration, vindication, or decision **b** to make an appeal in cricket 3 to make an earnest plea or request 4 to arouse a sympathetic response USE often + to

appealing /ə'peeling/ adj 1 having appeal; pleasing 2 marked by earnest entreaty; imploring – ~**ly** adv

appear /ə'piə/ v 1a to be or become visible **b** to arrive 2 to come formally before an authoritative body 3 to give the impression of being; seem 4 to come into public view

appearance /ə'piərəns/ n 1 the coming into court of a party in an action or his/her lawyer 2a a visit or attendance that is seen or noticed by others 3a an outward aspect; a look **b** an external show; a semblance **c** pl an outward or superficial indication that hides the real situation

appease /ə'peez/ v to pacify, calm, or conciliate – ~**ment** n

appellation /ˌapə'laysh(ə)n/ n an identifying name or title

append /ə'pend/ v to attach or add, esp as a supplement or appendix

appendage /ə'pendij/ n sthg appended to sthg larger or more important

appendicitis /əˌpendi'sietəs/ n inflammation of the vermiform appendix

appendix /ə'pendiks/ *n, pl* **appendixes, appendices** /-di,seez/ **1** a supplement (e g containing explanatory or statistical material), usu attached at the end of a piece of writing **2** the vermiform appendix or similar bodily outgrowth

appertain /,apə'tayn/ *v* to belong or be connected *to*

appetite /'apətiet/ *n* **1** a desire to satisfy an internal bodily need; *esp* an (eager) desire to eat **2** a strong desire demanding satisfaction; an inclination

appet·izer, -iser /'apətiezə/ *n* a food or drink that stimulates the appetite and is usu served before a meal

appet·izing, -ising /'apətiezing/ *adj* appealing to the appetite, esp in appearance or aroma – ~ly *adv*

applaud /ə'plawd/ *v* to express approval (of), esp by clapping the hands

applause /ə'plawz/ *n* **1** approval publicly expressed (e g by clapping the hands) **2** praise

apple /'apl/ *n* **1** (the fleshy, edible, usu rounded, red, yellow, or green fruit of) a tree of the rose family **2** a fruit or other plant structure resembling an apple — **apple of someone's eye** sby or sthg greatly cherished — **she's apples** *Austr* everything's fine — *infml*

appliance /ə'plie·əns/ *n* an instrument or device designed for a particular use; *esp* a domestic machine or device powered by gas or electricity (e g a food mixer, vacuum cleaner, or cooker)

applicable /'aplikəbl/ *adj* appropriate

applicant /'aplikənt/ *n* one who applies

application /,apli'kaysh(ə)n/ *n* **1a** an act of applying **b** a use to which sthg is put **c** close attention; diligence **2** a request, petition **3** a lotion **4** capacity for practical use; relevance

applied /ə'plied/ *adj* put to practical use; *esp* applying general principles to solve definite problems

appliqué /ə'pleekay, ,aplee'kay/ *n* a cutout decoration fastened (e g by sewing) to a larger piece of material – **appliqué** *v*

apply /ə'plie/ *v* **1a** to bring to bear; put to use, esp for some practical purpose **b** to lay or spread on **2** to devote (e g oneself) with close attention or diligence – usu + *to* **3** to have relevance – usu + *to* **4** to make a request, esp in writing

appoint /ə'poynt/ *v* **1** to fix or name officially **2** to select for an office or position **3** to declare the disposition of (an estate) to sby

ap'pointed *adj* equipped, furnished

ap'pointment /-mənt/ *n* **1** an act of appointing; a designation **2** an office or position held by sby who has been appointed to it rather than voted into it **3** an arrangement for a meeting **4** *pl* equipment, furnishings

apportion /ə'pawsh(ə)n/ *v* to divide and share out in just proportion or according to a plan; allot – ~ment *n*

apposite /'apəzit/ *adj* highly pertinent or appropriate; apt

appraisal /ə'prayz(ə)l/ *n* an act or instance of appraising; *specif* a valuation of property by an authorized person

appraise /ə'prayz/ *v* to evaluate the worth, significance, or status of; *esp* to give an expert judgment of the value or merit of – **appraiser** *n*

appreciable /ə'preesh(y)əbl/ *adj* **1** capable of being perceived or measured **2** fairly large – **-bly** *adv*

appreciate /ə'preeshiayt, -siayt/ *v* **1a** to understand the nature, worth, quality, or significance of **b** to recognize with gratitude; value or admire highly **2** to increase in value

appreciation /ə,preeshi'aysh(ə)n, -si-/ *n* **1a** a sensitive awareness; *esp* recognition of aesthetic values **b** a judgment, evaluation; *esp* a favourable critical estimate **c** an expression of admiration, approval, or gratitude **2** an increase in value

apprehend /,apri'hend/ *v* **1** to arrest, seize **2** to understand, perceive

apprehension /,apri'hensh(ə)n/ *n* **1** the act or power of comprehending **2** arrest, seizure – used technically in Scottish law **3** anxiety or fear, esp of future evil; foreboding

apprehensive /,apri'hensiv, -ziv/ *adj* viewing the future with anxiety, unease, or fear – often + *for* or *of* – ~ly *adv*

¹**apprentice** /ə'prentis/ *n* **1** one who is learning an art or trade **2** an inexperienced person; a novice

²**apprentice** *v* to set at work as an apprentice

apprise /ə'priez/ *v* to give notice to; tell – usu + *of*; fml

¹**approach** /ə'prohch/ *v* **1a** to draw closer (to) **b** to come very near to in quality, character, etc **2a** to make advances to, esp in order to create a desired result **b** to begin to consider or deal with

²**approach** *n* **1a** an act or instance of approaching **b** an approximation **2** a manner or method of doing sthg, esp for the first time **3** a means of access **4** the final part of an aircraft flight before landing **5** an advance made to establish personal or business relations – usu pl

approachable /ə'prohchəbl/ *adj* easy to meet or deal with

approbation /,aprə'baysh(ə)n/ *n* formal or official approval; sanction

¹**appropriate** /ə'prohpriayt/ *v* **1** to take exclusive possession of **2** to set apart (*specif* money) for a particular purpose or use **3** to take or make use of without authority or right

²**appropriate** /ə'prohpri·ət/ *adj* especially suitable or compatible; fitting – ~ly *adv* – ~ness *n*

appropriation /ə,prohpri'aysh(ə)n/ *n* sthg appropriated; *specif* money set aside by formal action for a particular use

approval /ə'proohvl/ *n* 1 a favourable opinion or judgment 2 formal or official permission — **on approval** *of goods supplied commercially* to be returned without payment if found unsatisfactory

approve /ə'proohv/ *v* 1 to have or express a favourable opinion (of) 2a to accept as satisfactory b to give formal or official sanction to; ratify – **approvingly** *adv*

¹**approximate** /ə'proksimət/ *adj* nearly correct or exact – **~ly** *adv*

²**approximate** /ə'proksimayt/ *v* 1 to bring or come near or close – often + *to* 2 to come near to; approach, esp in quality or number

apricot /'ayprikot/ *n* 1 (the oval orange-coloured fruit of) a temperate-zone tree of the rose family closely related to the peach and plum 2 an orange pink colour

April /'ayprəl/ *n* the 4th month of the Gregorian calendar

,**April 'fool** *n* the victim of a joke or trick played on April 1st

apron /'ayprən/ *n* 1 a garment usu tied round the waist and used to protect clothing 2 sthg that suggests or resembles an apron in shape, position, or use 3 the part of a stage that projects in front of the curtain

'**apron ,strings** *n pl* dominance, esp of a man by his mother or wife

¹**apropos** /,aprə'poh/ *adv* 1 at an opportune time 2 by the way

²**apropos** *adj* both relevant and opportune

³**apropos** *prep* concerning; with regard to

apse /aps/ *n* a projecting part of a building (e g a church) that is usu semicircular or polygonal and vaulted

apt /apt/ *adj* 1 ordinarily disposed; likely – usu + *to* 2 suited to a purpose; relevant – **~ly** *adv* – **~ness** *n*

aptitude /'aptityoohd, -choohd/ *n* 1 a natural ability; a talent, esp for learning 2 general fitness or suitability – usu + *for*

aqualung /'akwə,lung/ *n* cylinders of compressed air, oxygen, etc carried on the back and connected to a face mask for breathing underwater

aquamarine /,akwəmə'reen/ *n* 1 a transparent blue to green beryl used as a gemstone 2 a pale blue to light greenish blue colour

aquarium /ə'kweəri·əm/ *n, pl* **aquariums, aquaria** /-ri·ə/ a glass tank, artificial pond, etc in which living aquatic animals or plants are kept

Aquarius /ə'kweəri·əs/ *n* (sby born under) the 11th sign of the zodiac in astrology, which is pictured as a man pouring water

aquatic /ə'kwotik, -kwa-/ *adj* 1 growing, living in, or frequenting water 2 taking place in or on water – **~ally** *adv*

aqueduct /'akwə,dukt/ *n* a conduit, esp an arched structure over a valley, for carrying water

aqueous /'akwi·əs, 'ay-/ *adj* of, resembling, or made from, with, or by water – **~ly** *adv*

aquiline /'akwilien/ *adj* 1 of or like an eagle 2 of the human nose hooked

Arab /'arəb/ *n* 1 a member of a Semitic people orig of the Arabian peninsula and now widespread throughout the Middle East and N Africa b a member of an Arabic-speaking people 2 a typically intelligent, graceful, and swift horse of an Arabian stock – **~ian** *adj*

arabesque /,arə'besk/ *n* 1 a decorative design or style that combines natural motifs (e g flowers or foliage) to produce an intricate pattern 2 a posture in ballet in which the dancer is supported on one leg with one arm extended forwards and the other arm and leg backwards

¹**Arabic** /'arəbik/ *adj* 1 (characteristic) of Arabia, Arabians, or the Arabs 2 of or being Arabic

²**Arabic** *n* a Semitic language, now the prevailing speech of Arabia, Jordan, Lebanon, Syria, Iraq, Egypt, and parts of N Africa

,**Arabic 'numeral** *n, often not cap A* any of the number symbols 0, 1, 2, 3, 4, 5, 6, 7, 8, 9

arable /'arəbl/ *n or adj* (land) being or fit to be farmed for crops

arachnid /ə'raknid/ *n* any of a class (e g spiders, mites, ticks, and scorpions) of arthropods whose bodies have 2 segments of which the front bears 4 pairs of legs

arbiter /'ahbitə/ *n* a person or agency with absolute power of judging and determining

arbitrary /'ahbitrəri/ *adj* 1 depending on choice or discretion 2a arising from unrestrained exercise of the will b selected at random and without reason – **-rily** *adv* – **-riness** *n*

arbitrate /'ahbitrayt/ *v* 1 to settle differences between 2 parties in dispute 2 to act as arbiter upon – **-trator** *n* – **-tration** *n*

arboreal /,ah'bawri·əl/ *adj* of, resembling, inhabiting, or frequenting a tree or trees

arboretum /,ahbə'reetəm, ,ah'boritəm/ *n, pl* **arboretums, arboreta** /-tə/ a place where trees and shrubs are cultivated for study and display

arbour, *NAm chiefly* **arbor** /'ahbə/ *n* a bower of (latticework covered with) shrubs, vines, or branches

arc /ahk/ *n* 1 the apparent path described by a celestial body 2 sthg arched or curved

arcade /ah'kayd/ *n* 1 a long arched gallery or building 2 a passageway or avenue (e g between shops)

¹**arch** /ahch/ *n* **1** a typically curved structural member spanning an opening **2** sthg (e g the vaulted bony structure of the foot) resembling an arch in form or function **3** an archway

²**arch** *v* **1** to span or provide with an arch **2** to form or bend into an arch **3** to form an arch

³**arch** *adj* **1** principal, chief **2a** cleverly sly and alert **b** playfully saucy – ~**ly** *adv*

archaeology /,ahki'olǝji/ *n* the scientific study of material remains (e g tools or dwellings) of past human life and activities – -**gical** *adj* – -**gically** *adv* – -**gist** *n*

archaic /ah'kayik/ *adj* **1** (characteristic) of an earlier or more primitive time; antiquated **2** no longer used in ordinary speech or writing – ~**ally** *adv*

archaism /ah'kayiz(ǝ)m/ *n* **1** (an instance of) the use of archaic diction or style **2** sthg outmoded or old-fashioned

archangel /,ahk'aynjǝl, '-,--/ *n* a chief angel

archbishop /,ahch'bishǝp/ *n* a bishop at the head of an ecclesiastical province, or one of equivalent honorary rank

,**arch'deacon** /-'deekǝn/ *n* a clergyman having the duty of assisting a bishop, esp in administrative work

,**arch'duke** /-'dyoohk/ *n* a sovereign prince

archer /'ahchǝ/ *n* one who practises archery

archery /'ahchǝri/ *n* the art, practice, skill, or sport of shooting arrows from a bow

archetype /'ahki,tiep/ *n* **1** an original pattern or model; a prototype **2** a transcendent entity of which existing things are imperfect realizations – -**typal** *adj* – -**typical** *adj* – -**typically** *adv*

archipelago /,ahki'pelǝgoh, ,ahchi-/ *n, pl* **archipelagoes, archipelagos** (an expanse of water with) a group of scattered islands

architect /'ahkitekt/ *n* **1** sby who designs buildings and superintends their construction **2** sby who devises, plans, and achieves a difficult objective

architecture /'ahki,tekchǝ/ *n* **1** the art, practice, or profession of designing and erecting buildings; *also* a method or style of building **2** product or work of architecture – -**tural** *adj* – -**turally** *adv*

archway /'ahch,way/ *n* (an arch over) a way or passage that runs beneath arches

arctic /'ahktik/ *adj* **1** *often cap* of the N Pole or the surrounding region **2a** extremely cold; frigid **b** cold in temper or mood

ardent /'ahd(ǝ)nt/ *adj* characterized by warmth of feeling; eager, zealous – ~**ly** *adv*

ardour, *NAm chiefly* **ardor** /'ahdǝ/ *n* **1** (transitory) warmth of feeling **2** extreme vigour or intensity; zeal

arduous /'ahdyoo·ǝs/ *adj* **1** hard to accomplish or achieve; difficult, strenuous **2** hard to climb; steep – ~**ly** *adv* – ~**ness** *n*

are /ǝ; *strong* ah/ *pres* **2** *sing or pres pl of* **be**

area /'eǝri·ǝ/ *n* **1** a level piece of ground **2** a particular extent of space or surface, or one serving a special function **3** the extent, range, or scope of a concept, operation, or activity; a field

arena /ǝ'reenǝ/ *n* **1** (a building containing) an enclosed area used for public entertainment **2** a sphere of interest or activity; a scene

argon /'ahgon/ *n* a noble gaseous element found in the air and volcanic gases and used esp as a filler for vacuum tubes and electric light bulbs

argot /'ahgoh/ *n a* (more or less secret) vocabulary peculiar to a particular group

argue /'ahgyooh/ *v* **1** to give reasons for or against (sthg); reason, discuss **2** to contend or disagree in words **3** to give evidence of; indicate **4** to (try to) prove by giving reasons; maintain

argument /'ahgyoomǝnt/ *n* **1** a reason given in proof or rebuttal **2a** the act or process of arguing; debate **b** a coherent series of reasons offered **c** a quarrel, disagreement **3** an abstract or summary, esp of a literary work

argumentative /,ahgyoo'mentǝtiv/ *adj* given to argument – ~**ly** *adv*

aria /'ahri·ǝ/ *n pl* **arias** an accompanied melody sung (e g in an opera) by **1** voice

arid /'arid/ *adj* **1** excessively dry; *specif* having insufficient rainfall to support agriculture **2** lacking in interest and life – ~**ity** *n* – ~**ly** *adv*

Aries /'eǝriz, -reez/ *n* (sby born under) the 1st sign of the zodiac in astrology, which is pictured as a ram

aright /ǝ'riet/ *adv* rightly, correctly

arise /ǝ'riez/ *v* **arose** /ǝ'rohz/; **arisen** /ǝ'riz(ǝ)n/ **1a** to originate from a source – often + *from* **b** to come into being or to attention **2** to get up, rise – chiefly *fml*

aristocracy /,ari'stokrǝsi/ *n* **1** (a state with) a government in which power is vested in a small privileged usu hereditary noble class **2** *sing or pl in constr* a (governing) usu hereditary nobility **3** *sing or pl in constr* the whole group of those believed to be superior (e g in wealth, rank, or intellect)

aristocrat /'aristǝkrat, ǝ'ri-/ *n* **1** a member of an aristocracy; *esp* a noble **2** one who has the bearing and viewpoint typical of the aristocracy – ~**ic** *adj* – ~**ically** *adv*

arithmetic /ǝ'rithmǝtik/ *n* **1** a branch of mathematics that deals with real numbers and calculations with them **2** computation, calculation – ~**al** *adj* – ~**ally** *adv*

ark /ahk/ *n* **1** a ship; *esp* (one like) the one built by Noah to escape the Flood **2a** the sacred chest representing to the Hebrews the presence of God among them **b** a repository for the scrolls of the Torah

¹**arm** /ahm/ *n* **1** (the part between the shoulder and the wrist of) the human upper limb **2** sthg like or corresponding to an arm: e g **2a** the forelimb of a vertebrate animal **b** a limb of an invertebrate

animal **3** an inlet of water (e g from the sea) **4** might, authority **5** a support (e g on a chair) for the elbow and forearm **6** a sleeve **7** a functional division of a group or activity – ~**less** *adj* — **at arm's length** far enough away to avoid intimacy

²arm *v* **1** to supply or equip with weapons **2** to provide with sthg that strengthens or protects **3** to equip for action or operation **4** to prepare oneself for struggle or resistance – ~**ed** *adj*

³arm *n* **1a** a weapon; *esp* a firearm – usu pl **b** a combat branch (e g of an army) **2** *pl* the heraldic insignia of a group or body (e g a family or government) **3** *pl* **3a** active hostilities **b** military service or profession — **up in arms** angrily rebellious and protesting strongly

armada /ah'mahda/ *n* a fleet of warships; *specif*, *cap* that sent against England by Spain in 1588

armadillo /,ahma'diloh/ *n, pl* **armadillos** any of several burrowing chiefly nocturnal S American mammals with body and head encased in an armour of small bony plates

armament /'ahmamant/ *n* **1** a military or naval force **2** the military strength, esp in arms and equipment, of a ship, fort, or combat unit, nation, etc **3** the process of preparing for war

armature /'ahmacha/ *n* **1** the central rotating part of an electric motor or generator **2** a framework on which a modeller in clay, wax, etc builds up his/her work

¹armchair /'ahm,chea/ *n* a chair with armrests

²armchair *adj* **1** remote from direct dealing with practical problems **2** sharing vicariously in another's experiences

'arm,hole /-,hohl/ *n* an opening for the arm in a garment

armistice /'ahmistis/ *n* a temporary suspension of hostilities; a truce

armour, *NAm chiefly* **armor** /'ahma/ *n* **1a** a defensive covering for the body; *esp* a covering (e g of metal) worn in combat **b** a usu metallic protective covering (e g for a ship, fort, aircraft, or car) **2** armoured forces and vehicles (e g tanks)

armoured /'ahmad/ *adj* consisting of or equipped with vehicles protected with armour plate

armourer /'ahmara/ *n* **1** sby who makes or looks after armour or arms **2** sby who repairs, assembles, and tests firearms

,armour 'plate *n* a defensive covering of hard metal plates for combat vehicles and vessels – **armour-plated** *adj*

armoury /'ahmari/ *n* (a collection of or place for storing) arms and military equipment

'arm,pit /-,pit/ *n* the hollow beneath the junction of the arm and shoulder

army /'ahmi/ *n* **1a** a large organized force for war on land **b** *often cap* the complete military organization of a nation for land warfare **2** a great multitude **3** a body of people organized to advance a cause

aroma /a'rohma/ *n* **1** a distinctive and usu pleasant or savoury smell **2** a distinctive quality or atmosphere – ~**tic** *adj* – ~**tically** *adv*

arose /a'rohz/ *past of* **arise**

¹around /a'rownd/ *adv, prep* **1** round **2** about

²around *adj* **1** about **2** in existence, evidence, or circulation

arouse /a'rowz/ *v* **1** to waken from sleep **2** to rouse to action; excite, esp sexually

arpeggio /ah'pejioh/ *n, pl* **arpeggios** (the sounding of) a chord whose notes are played in succession, not simultaneously

arraign /a'rayn/ *v* **1** to charge before a court **2** to accuse of wrong, inadequacy, or imperfection – ~**ment** *n*

arrange /a'raynj/ *v* **1** to put in order or into sequence or relationship **2** to make preparations (for); plan **3** to bring about an agreement concerning; settle **4** to adapt (a musical composition) by scoring for different voices or instruments

ar'rangement /-mant/ *n* **1a** a preliminary measure; a preparation **b** an adaptation of a musical composition for different voices or instruments **c** an informal agreement or settlement, esp on personal, social, or political matters **2** sthg made by arranging constituents or things together

arrant /'arant/ *adj* notoriously without moderation; extreme

¹array /a'ray/ *v* **1** to set or place in order; marshal **2** to dress or decorate, esp in splendid or impressive clothes; adorn

²array *n* **1** military order **2a** clothing, garments **b** rich or beautiful apparel; finery **3** an imposing group; a large number

¹arrest /a'rest/ *v* **1a** to bring to a stop **b** to make inactive **2** to seize, capture; *specif* to take or keep in custody by authority of law **3** to catch and fix or hold

²arrest *n* **1** the act of stopping **2** the taking or detaining of sby in custody by authority of law **3** a device for arresting motion — **under arrest** in legal custody

arrival /a'rievl/ *n* **1** the attainment of an end or state **2** sby or sthg that has arrived **3** the act of arriving

arrive /a'riev/ *v* **1** to reach a destination **2** to come **3** to achieve success — **arrive at** to reach by effort or thought

arrogant /'aragant/ *adj* aggressively conceited – ~**ly** *adv* – **ance** *n*

arrogate /'aragayt/ *v* to claim or seize without justification

¹arrow /'aroh/ *n* **1** a projectile shot from a bow, usu having a slender shaft, a pointed head, and feathers at the end **2** sthg shaped like an arrow; *esp* a mark to indicate direction

²arrow *v* to indicate with an arrow

'arrow,head /-,hed/ *n* **1** the pointed front part of an arrow **2** sthg shaped like an arrowhead

'arrow,root /-,rooht/ *n* (a tropical American plant whose roots yield) a starch used esp as a thickening agent in cooking

arse /ahs/ *n* 1 the buttocks 2 the anus *USE* vulg

arsenal /'ahsnl, 'ahsnəl/ *n* 1 an armoury 2 a store, repertory

arsenic /'ahsnik/ *n* a semimetallic steel-grey poisonous element – **arsenic, arsenical** *adj*

arson /'ahsən/ *n* the criminal act of setting fire to property in order to cause destruction – **ist** *n*

¹art /aht/ *archaic pres 2 sing of* be

²art *n* 1 a skill acquired by experience, study, or observation 2 *pl* the humanities as contrasted with science 3a the conscious use of skill and creative imagination, esp in the production of aesthetic objects; *also* works so produced b (any of) the fine arts or graphic arts

³art *adj* 1 composed, designed, or created with conscious artistry 2 designed for decorative purposes

arterial /ah'tiəri·əl/ *adj* 1 of or (being the bright red blood) contained in an artery 2 of or being a main road

arteriosclerosis /ah,tiəriohsklə'rohsis/ *n* abnormal thickening and hardening of the arterial walls

artery /'ahtəri/ *n* 1 any of the branching elastic-walled blood vessels that carry blood from the heart to the lungs and through the body 2 an esp main channel (e g a river or road) of transport or communication

artful /'ahtf(ə)l/ *adj* crafty – **~ly** *adv* – **~ness** *n*

arthritis /ah'thrietəs/ *n, pl* arthritides /ah'thrieti-,deez/ usu painful inflammation of 1 or more joints – **tic** *adj, n*

arthropod /'ahthrə,pod/ *n* any of a group of backboneless animals (e g insects, spiders, lobsters, etc) with a jointed body and hard outer skin

artichoke /'ahti,chohk/ *n* 1a a tall composite plant like a thistle b the partly edible flower head of the artichoke, used as a vegetable 2 jerusalem artichoke the edible tuber of a plant of the sunflower family

¹article /'ahtikl/ *n* 1a(1) a separate clause, item, provision, or point in a document a(2) *pl* a written agreement specifying conditions of apprenticeship b a piece of nonfictional prose, usu forming an independent part of a magazine, newspaper, etc 2 an item of business; a matter 3 a word or affix (e g a, an, and the) used with nouns to give indefiniteness or definiteness 4a a particular or separate object or thing, esp viewed as a member of a class of things b a thing of a particular and distinctive kind

²article *v* to bind by articles (e g of apprenticeship)

¹articulate /ah'tikyoolət/ *adj* 1a divided into syllables or words meaningfully arranged b having the power of speech c expressing oneself readily, clearly, or effectively; *also* expressed in this manner 2 jointed – **~ly** *adv* – **~ness** *n*

²articulate /ah'tikyoolayt/ *v* 1a to utter distinctly b to give clear and effective utterance to 2 to unite with a joint 3 to utter articulate sounds 4 to become united or connected (as if) by a joint – **-lation** *n*

artifact /'ahtifakt/ *n* a product of human workmanship; *esp* one characteristic of a (primitive) civilization

artifice /'ahtifis/ *n* 1 an artful device, expedient, or stratagem; a trick 2 clever or artful skill; ingenuity

artificial /,ahti'fish(ə)l/ *adj* 1 man-made 2a lacking in natural quality; affected b imitation, sham – **~ly** *adv* – **~ity** *n*

,arti,ficial insemi'nation *n* introduction of semen into the uterus or oviduct by other than natural means

,arti,ficial respi'ration *n* the rhythmic forcing of air into and out of the lungs of sby whose breathing has stopped

artillery /ah'tiləri/ *n* 1 large-calibre mounted firearms (e g guns, howitzers, missile launchers, etc) 2 *sing or pl in constr* a branch of an army armed with artillery

artisan /'ahti,zan, ,--', 'ahtiz(ə)n/ *n* 1 a skilled manual worker (e g a carpenter, plumber, or tailor) 2 a member of the urban proletariat

artist /'ahtist/ *n* 1a one who professes and practises an imaginative art b a person skilled in a fine art 2 a skilled performer; *specif* an artiste 3 one who is proficient in a specified and usu dubious activity; an expert – *infml*

artiste /ah'teest/ *n* a skilled public performer; *specif* a musical or theatrical entertainer

artistic /ah'tistik/ *adj* 1 concerning or characteristic of art or artists 2 showing imaginative skill in arrangement or execution – **~ally** *adv*

artistry /'ahtistri/ *n* artistic quality or ability

'artless /-lis/ *adj* 1 free from artificiality; natural 2 free from deceit, guile, or craftiness; sincerely simple – **~ly** *adv* – **~ness** *n*

art nouveau /,ah(t) nooh'voh/ *n, often cap A&N* a decorative style of late 19th-c origin, characterized esp by curved lines and plant motifs

arty /'ahti/ *adj* showily or pretentiously artistic – **artiness** *n*

¹as /əz; *strong* az/ *adv* 1 to the same degree or amount; equally 2 when considered in a specified form or relation - usu used before a preposition or participle (e g blind *as* opposed to stupid)

²as *conj* 1a to the same degree that – usu used as a correlative after *as* or *so* to introduce a comparison or as a result b - used after *same* or *such* to introduce an example or comparison c - used after *so* to introduce the idea of purpose (e g hid so *as* to escape) 2 in the way that – used before *so* to introduce a parallel 3 in accordance with what (e g late *as* usual) 4 while, when 5 regardless of the fact that; though (e g late *as* it was, I phoned her)

6 for the reason that; seeing (e g *as* it's wet, we'll stay at home) **— as is** in the present condition without modification – *infml* **— as it is** in reality **— as it were** so to speak **— as often as not** at least half the time

³as *pron* **1** a fact that; and this (e g which, *as* history relates, was a bad king) **2** which also; and so (e g he's a doctor, *as* was his mother)

⁴as *prep* **1** in the capacity, character, role, or state of (e g works *as* an actor)

asbestos /ə'spestos, -zb-, -sb-/ *n* either of 2 minerals composed of thin flexible fibres, used to make noncombustible, nonconducting, or chemically resistant materials

ascend /ə'send/ *v* **1** to move or slope gradually upwards; rise **2a** to rise from a lower level or degree **b** to go back in time or in order of genealogical succession **3** to go or move up **4** to succeed to; begin to occupy – esp in *ascend the throne* – ~ancy *n* – ~ant *adj*

ascension /ə'sensh(ə)n/ *n* the act or process of ascending

A'scension ,Day *n* the Thursday 40 days after Easter observed in commemoration of Christ's ascension into Heaven

ascent /ə'sent/ *n* **1a** the act of going, climbing, or travelling up **b** a way up; an upward slope or path **2** an advance in social status or reputation; progress

ascertain /,asə'tayn/ *v* to find out or learn with certainty – ~able *adj*

ascetic /ə'setik/ *also* **ascetical** /-kl/ *adj* **1** practising strict self-denial as a spiritual discipline **2** austere in appearance, manner, or attitude – **ascetic** *n* – ~ally *adv* – ~ism *n*

ascribe /ə'skrieb/ *v* to refer or attribute something *to* a supposed cause or source

asexual /ay'seksyooəl, -'seksh(ə)l, ə-/ *adj* **1** lacking sex (organs) **2** produced without sexual action or differentiation **3** without expression of or reference to sexual interest – ~ly *adv* – ~ity *n*

¹ash /ash/ *n* (the tough elastic wood of) any of a genus of tall trees of the olive family

²ash *n* **1** the solid residue left when material is thoroughly burned or oxidized

ashamed /ə'shaymd/ *adj* **1** feeling shame, guilt, or disgrace **2** restrained by fear of shame – ~ly *adv*

¹ashen /'ash(ə)n/ *adj* of or made from the wood of the ash tree

²ashen *adj* **1** consisting of or resembling ashes **2** deadly pale; blanched

ashore /ə'shaw/ *adv* on or to the shore

'ash ,tray /-,tray/ *n* a (small) receptacle for tobacco ash and cigar and cigarette ends

,Ash 'Wednesday *n* the first day of Lent

Asian /'aysh(ə)n, 'ayzh(ə)n/ *adj* (characteristic) of the continent of Asia or its people – **Asian** *n*

Asiatic /,ayzi'atik, ,ayzhi-/ *adv or n* Asian

¹aside /ə'sied/ *adv or adj* **1** to or towards the side **2** out of the way **3** apart; in reserve **4** apart

²aside *n* **1** an utterance meant to be inaudible; *esp* an actor's speech supposedly not heard by other characters on stage **2** a digression

as 'if *conj* **1** as it would be if **2** as one would do if **3** that **4** – used in emphatic rejection of a notion (e g *as if* he would ever do a thing like that!)

asinine /'asinien/ *adj* stupid

ask /ahsk/ *v* **1a** to call on for an answer **b** to put a question about **c** to put or frame (a question) **2** to make a request of or for **3** to behave in such a way as to provoke (an unpleasant response) **4** to set as a price **5** to invite **6** to seek information

askance /ə'skahns/ *adv* with disapproval or distrust – esp in *look askance*

askew /ə'skyooh/ *adv or adj* awry

'asking ,price /'ahsking/ *n* the price set by the seller

aslant /ə'slahnt/ *prep, adv, or adj* (over or across) in a slanting direction

asleep /ə'sleep/ *adj* **1** in a state of sleep **2** dead – euph **3** lacking sensation; numb

as 'long as *conj* providing, while; so long as

asparagus /ə'sparəgəs/ *n* (any of a genus of Old World perennial plants of the lily family including) a tall plant widely cultivated for its edible young shoots

aspect /'aspekt/ *n* **1a** the position of planets or stars with respect to one another, held by astrologers to influence human affairs **b** a position facing a particular direction **2a** appearance to the eye or mind **b** a particular feature of a situation, plan, or point of view

aspen /'aspən/ *n* any of several poplars with leaves that flutter in the lightest wind

asperity /ə'sperəti/ *n* **1** rigour, hardship **2** roughness of surface; unevenness **3** roughness of manner or temper; harshness

aspersion /ə'spuhsh(ə)n/ *n* **1** a sprinkling with water, esp in religious ceremonies **2** an unwarranted doubt

asphalt /'asfalt, -felt, ash-; *NAm* 'asfawlt/ *n* **1** a brown to black bituminous substance found in natural beds and also obtained as a residue in petroleum or coal tar refining **2** an asphaltic composition used for surfacing roads and footpaths

asphyxia /ə'sfiksi-ə/ *n* a lack of oxygen in the body, usu caused by interruption of breathing, and resulting in unconsciousness or death – -xiate *v*

aspic /'aspik/ *n* a clear savoury jelly (e g of fish or meat stock) used as a garnish or to make a meat, fish, etc mould

aspidistra /,aspi'distrə/ *n* any of various Asiatic plants of the lily family with large leaves, often grown as house plants

¹aspirate /'aspirayt/ *v* to pronounce (a vowel, consonant, or word) with an *h*-sound

²aspirate /'aspirət/ *n* 1 (a character, esp *h*, representing) an independent /h/ sound 2 an aspirated consonant (e g the *p* of *pit*)

aspiration /ˌaspi'raysh(ə)n/ *n* 1 a strong desire to achieve sthg high or great 2 an object of such desire

aspire /ə'sayl/ *v* to seek to attain or accomplish a particular goal – usu + *to*

aspirin /'asprin/ *n*, *pl* **aspirin**, **aspirins** (a tablet containing) a derivative of salicylic acid used for relief of pain and fever

¹ass /as/ *n* 1 the donkey or a similar long-eared hardy gregarious mammal related to and smaller than the horse 2 a stupid, obstinate, or perverse person or thing

²ass *n*, *chiefly NAm* the arse

assail /ə'sayl/ *v* 1 to attack violently with blows or words 2 to prey on – ~ **ant** *n*

assassin /ə'sasin/ *n* 1 *cap* any of a secret order of Muslims who at the time of the Crusades committed secret murders 2 a murderer; *esp* one who murders a politically important person, for money or from fanatical motives

assassinate /ə'sasinayt/ *v* to murder suddenly or secretly, usu for political reasons – **-ation** *n*

¹assault /ə'sawlt/ *n* 1 a violent physical or verbal attack 2a an attempt to do or immediate threat of doing unlawful personal violence b rape 3 an attempt to attack a fortification by a sudden rush

²assault *v* 1 to make an (indecent) assault on 2 to rape

assay /ə'say/ *v* 1a to analyse (e g an ore) for 1 or more valuable components b to judge the worth or quality of 2 to try, attempt – fml – **assay** *n*

assegai, assagai /'asigie/ *n* a slender iron-tipped hardwood spear used in southern Africa

assemblage /ə'semblij/ *n* 1 a collection of people or things; a gathering

assemble /ə'sembl/ *v* **assembling** /ə'sembling/ 1 to bring or gather together (e g in a particular place or for a particular purpose) 2 to fit together the parts

assembly /ə'sembli/ *n* 1 a company of people gathered for deliberation and legislation, entertainment, or worship 2 *cap* a legislative body 3a an assemblage b assembling or being assembled 4 (a collection of parts assembled by) the fitting together of manufactured parts into a complete machine, structure, etc

¹assent /ə'sent/ *v* to agree to sthg

²assent *n* acquiescence, agreement

assert /ə'suht/ *v* 1 to state or declare positively and often forcefully 2 to demonstrate the existence of — **assert oneself** to compel recognition of esp one's rights

assertion /ə'suhsh(ə)n/ *n* a declaration, affirmation

assertive /ə'suhtiv/ *adj* characterized by bold assertion; dogmatic – ~**ly** *adv* – ~**ness** *n*

assess /ə'ses/ *v* 1a to determine the rate or amount of (e g a tax) b to impose (e g a tax) according to an established rate 2 to make an official valuation of (property) for the purposes of taxation 3 to determine the importance, size, or value of – ~**ment** *n*

assessor /ə'sesə/ *n* 1 a specialist who advises a court 2 an official who assesses property for taxation 3 *chiefly Br* sby who investigates and values insurance claims

asset /'aset/ *n* 1a *pl* the total property of a person, company, or institution; *esp* that part which can be used to pay debts b a single item of property 2 an advantage, resource 3 *pl* the items on a balance sheet showing the book value of property owned

asseverate /ə'sevərayt/ *v* to affirm solemnly – fml – **-ation** *n*

assiduous /ə'sidyoo·əs/ *adj* diligent – ~**ly** *adv* – **-duity** *n*

assign /ə'sien/ *v* 1 to transfer (property) to another, esp in trust or for the benefit of creditors 2 to appoint to a post or duty 3 to fix authoritatively; specify, designate – ~**able** *adj*

assignation /ˌasig'naysh(ə)n/ *n* 1 the act of assigning; *also* the assignment made 2 a meeting, esp a secret one with a lover

assignment /ə'sienmənt/ *n* 1a a position, post, or job to which one is assigned b a specified task or amount of work assigned by authority 2 (a document effecting) the legal transfer of property

assimilate /ə'similayt/ *v* 1a to take in or absorb into the system (as nourishment) b to absorb; *esp* to take into the mind and fully comprehend 2a to make similar – usu + *to* or with b to absorb into a cultural tradition – **-lation** *n*

assist /ə'sist/ *v* 1 to give support or aid 2 to be present as a spectator 3 to give support or aid to – ~**ance** *n*

¹associate /ə'sohs(h)iayt/ *v* 1 to join as a friend, companion, or partner in business 2 to bring together in any of various ways (e g in memory, thought, or imagination) 3 to combine or join with other parts; unite *USE* often + *with*

²associate /ə'sohs(h)i·ət/ *adj* 1 closely connected (e g in function or office) with another 2 having secondary or subordinate status

³associate /ə'sohs(h)i·ət, -ayt/ *n* 1 a fellow worker; partner, colleague 2 a companion, comrade 3 sthg closely connected with or usu accompanying another 4 one admitted to a subordinate degree of membership

association /ə,sohs(h)i'aysh(ə)n/ *n* 1 an organization of people having a common interest; a society, league 2 sthg linked in memory, thought, or imagination with a thing or person 3 the formation of mental connections between sensations, ideas, memories, etc

ass

assonance /'asɒnəns/ n 1 resemblance of sound in words or syllables 2 repetition of esp only the vowel sounds (e g in *stony* and *holy*) or only the consonant sounds, as an alternative to rhyme – **assonant** *adj*

as'sorted *adj* 1 consisting of various kinds 2 suited by nature, character, or design; matched

as'sortment /-mənt/ n a collection of assorted things or people

assuage /ə'swayj/ v to lessen the intensity of (pain, suffering, desire, etc); ease

assume /ə'syoohm/ v 1a to take to or upon oneself; undertake b to invest oneself formally with (an office or its symbols) 2 to seize, usurp 3 to pretend to have or be; feign 4 to take as granted or true; suppose – often + *that*

assumption /ə'sum(p)sh(ə)n/ n 1a the taking up of a person into heaven b *cap* August 15 observed in commemoration of the assumption of the Virgin Mary 2 the act of laying claim to or taking possession of sthg 3a the supposition that sthg is true b a fact or statement (e g a proposition, axiom, or postulate) taken for granted

assurance /ə'shawrəns, -'shooə-/ n 1a a pledge, guarantee b *chiefly Br* (life) insurance 2a the quality or state of being sure or certain; freedom from doubt b confidence of mind or manner; *also* excessive self-confidence; brashness 3 sthg that inspires or tends to inspire confidence

assure /ə'shaw, -'shooə/ v 1 to make safe; insure (esp life or safety) 2 to give confidence to; reassure 3 to inform positively 4 to guarantee the happening or attainment of; ensure

¹as'sured *adj* 1 characterized by self-confidence 2 satisfied as to the certainty or truth of a matter; convinced – ~ly *adv*

²assured *n pl* assured, assureds an insured person

aster /'astə/ n any of various chiefly autumn-blooming leafy-stemmed composite plants with often showy heads

asterisk /'astərisk/ n a sign * used as a reference mark, esp to denote the omission of letters or words or to show that sthg is doubtful or absent

astern /ə'stuhn/ *adv or adj* 1 behind the stern; to the rear 2 at or towards the stern of a ship 3 backwards

asteroid /'astəroyd/ n any of thousands of small planets mostly between Mars and Jupiter

asthma /'as(th)mə/ n (an allergic condition marked by attacks of) laboured breathing with wheezing and usu coughing, gasping, and a sense of constriction in the chest – **-tic** *adj*, n – ~**tically** *adv*

astir /ə'stuh/ *adj* 1 in a state of bustle or excitement 2 out of bed; up

astonish /ə'stonish/ v to strike with sudden wonder or surprise – ~**ment** n

astound /ə'stownd/ v to fill with bewilderment and wonder

astray /ə'stray/ *adv or adj* 1 off the right path or route 2 in error; away from a proper or desirable course or development

¹astride /ə'stried/ *adv* with the legs wide apart

²astride *prep* 1 on or above and with 1 leg on each side of 2 extending over or across; spanning

astringent /ə'strinj(ə)nt/ *adj* 1 capable of making firm the soft tissues of the body; styptic 2 rigidly severe; austere – ~**gency** n – ~**ly** *adv*

astrology /ə'stroləji/ n the art or practice of determining the supposed influences of the planets on human affairs – **-ger** n – **-gical** *adj* – **-gically** *adv*

astronaut /'astrə,nawt/ n sby who travels beyond the earth's atmosphere

astronomical /,astrə'nomikl/, astronomic /-'nomik/ *adj* 1 of astronomy 2 enormously or inconceivably large – *infml* – ~**ly** *adv*

astronomy /ə'stronəmi/ n a branch of science dealing with the celestial bodies – **-nomer** n

astrophysics /,astrōh'fiziks/ n pl but sing or pl in constr a branch of astronomy dealing with the physical and chemical constitution of the celestial bodies – **-ical** *adj* – **-icist** n

astute /ə'styooht, ə'schooht/ *adj* shrewdly perspicacious – ~**ly** *adv* – ~**ness** n

asunder /ə'sundə/ *adv or adj* 1 into parts 2 apart from each other in position

asylum /ə'sieləm/ n 1 a place of retreat and security; a shelter 2a the protection from the law or refuge afforded by an asylum b protection from arrest and being returned home given by a nation to political refugees 3 an institution for the care of the destitute or afflicted, esp the insane

asymmetric /aysi'metrik/, asymmetrical /-kl/ *adj* not symmetrical – ~**ally** *adv*

at /ət; *strong at*/ *prep* 1 – used to indicate presence or occurrence in, on, or near a place imagined as a point (e g *sick at* heart) 2 – used to indicate the goal or direction of an action or motion (e g aim *at* the goal) 3a – used to indicate occupation or employment (e g *at* tea) b when it comes to (an occupation or employment) (e g an expert *at* chess) 4 – used to indicate situation or condition (e g *at* risk) 5 in response to (e g shudder *at* the thought) 6 – used to indicate position on a scale (e g of cost, speed, or age) (e g *at* 80 mph) 7 – used to indicate position in time (e g *at* midday) — **at all** as a result of only 1; by or during only 1 — **at it** doing it; *esp* busy — **at that** 1 at that point and no further 2 which makes it more surprising; in addition

at 'all *adv* to the least extent or degree; under any circumstances — **not at all** — used in answer to thanks or to an apology

ate /et, ayt/ *past of* eat, -ated

atheist /'aythi·ist/ n a person who disbelieves in the existence of a deity – **atheism**

athlete /'athleet/ *n* sby who is trained in, skilled in, or takes part in exercises, sports, etc that require physical strength, agility, or stamina

athlete's 'foot *n* ringworm of the feet

athletic /ath'letik/ *adj* 1 of athletics or athletics 2 characteristic of an athlete; *esp* vigorous, active

ath'letics *n pl but sing or pl in constr, Br* competitive walking, running, throwing, and jumping sports collectively

¹**athwart** /ə'thwawt/ *adv* 1 across, esp in an oblique direction 2 in opposition to the right or expected course

²**athwart** *prep* 1 across 2 in opposition to

atlas /'atlas/ *n* a bound collection of maps, charts, or tables

atmosphere /'atmosfiə/ *n* 1 a mass of gas enveloping a celestial body (e g a planet); *esp* all the air surrounding the earth 2 the air of a locality 3 a surrounding influence or environment 4 a dominant aesthetic or emotional effect or appeal

atmospheric /ˌatmə'sferik/ *adj* 1 of, occurring in, or like the atmosphere 2 having, marked by, or contributing aesthetic or emotional atmosphere

atmo'spherics *n pl* (the electrical phenomena causing) audible disturbances produced in a radio receiver by electrical atmospheric phenomena (e g lightning)

atoll /'atol, ə'tol/ *n* a coral reef surrounding a lagoon

atom /'atəm/ *n* 1 any of the minute indivisible particles of which according to ancient materialism the universe is composed 2 a tiny particle; a bit 3 the smallest particle of an element that can exist either alone or in combination, consisting of various numbers of electrons, protons, and neutrons

'atom ˌbomb *n* a bomb whose violent explosive power is due to the sudden release of atomic energy derived from the splitting of the nuclei of plutonium, uranium, etc by neutrons in a very rapid chain reaction; *also* a hydrogen bomb

atomic /ə'tomik/ *adj* 1 of or concerned with atoms, atom bombs, or atomic energy 2 *of a chemical element* existing as separate atoms – ~ally *adv*

atomic energy *n* energy liberated in an atom bomb, nuclear reactor, etc by changes in the nucleus of an atom

atomic pile *n* a nuclear reactor

atom·ize, -ise /'atəmiez/ *v* to break up a liquid into a fine mist or spray

atonal /a'tohnl, ay-/ *adj* organized without reference to a musical key and using the notes of the chromatic scale impartially – ~ly *adv* – ~ity *n*

atone /ə'tohn/ *v* to supply satisfaction *for*; make amends *for* – ~ment *n*

atrium /'atri·əm, 'ay-/ *n, pl* **atria** /'atri·ə, 'ay-/ *also* **atriums** 1 an inner courtyard open to the sky (e g in a Roman house) 2 a chamber of the heart that receives blood from the veins and forces it into a ventricle or ventricles

atrocious /ə'trohshəs/ *adj* 1 extremely wicked or cruel; barbaric 2 of very poor quality – ~city *n*

atrophy /'atrəfi/ *n* 1 (sometimes natural) decrease in size or wasting away of a body part or tissue 2 a wasting away or progressive decline; degeneration – **atrophy** *v*

attach /ə'tach/ *v* 1 to seize by legal authority 2 to bring (oneself) into an association 3 to appoint to serve with an organization for special duties or for a temporary period 4 to fasten 5 to ascribe, attribute 6 to become attached; stick *USE* often + *to*

attaché /ə'tashay/ *n* a technical expert on a diplomatic staff

at'taché ˌcase *n* a small thin case used esp for carrying papers

at'tachment /-mənt/ *n* 1 a seizure by legal process 2a fidelity – often + *to* b an affectionate regard 3 a device attached to a machine or implement 4 the physical connection by which one thing is attached to another

¹**attack** /ə'tak/ *v* 1 to set upon forcefully in order to damage, injure, or destroy 2 to take the initiative against in a game or contest 3 to assail with unfriendly or bitter words 4 to set to work on, esp vigorously 5 to make an attack

²**attack** *n* 1 the act of attacking; an assault 2 a belligerent or antagonistic action or verbal assault – often + *on* 3 the beginning of destructive action (e g by a chemical agent) 4 the setting to work on some undertaking 5 a fit of sickness or (recurrent) disease 6a an attempt to score or to gain ground in a game b *sing or pl in constr* the attacking players in a team or the positions occupied by them; *specif* the bowlers in a cricket team

attain /ə'tayn/ *v* 1 to reach as an end; achieve 2 to come or arrive by motion, growth, or effort – + *to* – ~able *adj*

attainment /ə'taynmənt/ *n* sthg attained; an accomplishment

¹**attempt** /ə'tempt/ *v* to make an effort to do, accomplish, solve, or effect, esp without success

²**attempt** *n* 1 the act or an instance of attempting; *esp* an unsuccessful effort 2 an attack, assault – often + *on*

attend /ə'tend/ *v* 1 to take charge of; look after 2 to go or stay with as a companion, nurse, or servant 3 to be present with; accompany, escort 4 to be present at 5 to deal with 6 to apply the mind or pay attention; heed *USE* – often + *to*

attendance /ə'tend(ə)ns/ *n* 1 the number of people attending 2 the number of times a person attends, usu out of a possible maximum

¹**attendant** /ə'tend(ə)nt/ *adj* accompanying or following as a consequence

²**attendant** *n* one who attends another to perform a service; *esp* an employee who waits on customers

attention /ə'tensh(ə)n/ *n* **1** attending, esp through application of the mind to an object of sense or thought **2** consideration with a view to action **3a** an act of civility or courtesy, esp in courtship – usu pl **b** sympathetic consideration of the needs and wants of others **4** a formal position of readiness assumed by a soldier – usu as a command

attentive /ə'tentiv/ *adj* **1** mindful, observant **2** solicitous **3** paying attentions (as if) in the role of a suitor – ~**ly** *adv* – ~**ness** *n*

attenuate /ə'tenyooayt/ *v* **1** to make thin **2** to lessen the amount, force, or value of; weaken **3** to become thin or fine; diminish

attest /ə'test/ *v* **1** to affirm to be true, authenticate **2** to be proof of; bear witness to **3** to put on oath **4** to bear witness, testify – often + *to*

attic /'atik/ *n* a room or space immediately below the roof of a building

Attic *adj* (characteristic) of Attica or Athens

¹**attire** /ə'tie-ə/ *v* to put garments on; dress, array; *esp* to clothe in fancy or rich garments

²**attire** *n* dress, clothes; *esp* splendid or decorative clothing

attitude /'atityoohd/ *n* **1** the arrangement of the parts of a body or figure; a posture **2** a feeling, emotion, or mental position with regard to a fact or state **3** a manner assumed for a specific purpose

attorney /ə'tuhni/ *n* **1** sby with legal authority to act for another **2** *NAm* a lawyer

at,torney 'general *n, pl* **attorneys general, attorney generals** *often cap A&G* the chief legal officer of a nation or state

attract /ə'trakt/ *v* **1** to pull to or towards oneself or itself **2** to draw by appeal to interest, emotion, or aesthetic sense **3** to possess or exercise the power of attracting sthg or sby – ~**ive** *adj*

attraction /ə'traksh(ə)n/ *n* **1** a characteristic that elicits interest or admiration – usu pl **2** the action or power of drawing forth a response (e g interest or affection); an attractive quality **3** a force between unlike electric charges, unlike magnetic poles, etc, resisting separation **4** sthg that attracts or is intended to attract people by appealing to their desires and tastes

¹**attribute** /'atribyooht/ *n* **1** an inherent characteristic **2** an object closely associated with a usu specified person, thing, or office

²**attribute** /ə'tribyooht/ *v* to reckon as originating in an indicated fashion – usu + *to* – **table** *adj* – **tion** *n* — **attribute to 1** to explain by indicating as a cause **2** to regard as a characteristic of (a person or thing)

attrition /ə'trish(ə)n/ *n* **1** sorrow for one's sins arising from fear of punishment **2** the act of rubbing together; friction; *also* the act of wearing or grinding down by friction **3** the act of weakening or exhausting by constant harassment or abuse

attune /ə'tyoohn/ *v* to cause to become used or accustomed *to*

atypical /,ay'tipikl/ *adj* not typical; irregular – ~**ly** *adv*

aubergine /'ohbəzheen, -jeen/ **1** (the edible usu smooth dark purple ovoid fruit of) the eggplant **2** a deep reddish purple colour

auburn /'awbən/ *adj or n* (of) a reddish brown colour

¹**auction** /'awksh(ə)n/ *n* **1** a public sale of property to the highest bidder **2** the act or process of bidding in some card games

²**auction** *v* to sell at an auction – often + *off* – ~**eer** *n*

audacious /aw'dayshəs/ *adj* **1a** intrepidly daring; adventurous **b** recklessly bold; rash **2** insolent – **audacity** *n* – ~**ly** *adv*

audible /'awdəbl/ *adj* heard or capable of being heard – **bility** *n* – **bly** *adv*

audience /'awdi-əns/ *n* **1a** a formal hearing or interview **b** an opportunity of being heard **2** *sing or pl in constr* a group of listeners or spectators

audio /'awdioh/ *adj* **1** of or being acoustic, mechanical, or electrical frequencies corresponding to those of audible sound waves, approx 20 to 20,000Hz **2a** of sound or its reproduction, esp high-fidelity reproduction **b** relating to or used in the transmission or reception of sound – **audio** *n*

audiovisual /,awdioh'viz(h)yoool/ *adj* of (teaching methods using) both hearing and sight

¹**audit** /'awdit/ *n* (the final report on) a formal or official examination and verification of an account book

²**audit** *v* to perform an audit on

¹**audition** /aw'dish(ə)n/ *n* **1** the act of hearing; *esp* a critical hearing **2** a trial performance to appraise an entertainer's abilities

²**audition** *v* **1** to test (e g for a part) in an audition **2** to give a trial performance – usu + *for*

auditorium /,awdi'tawri-əm/ *n, pl* **auditoria** /-ri-ə/, **auditoriums** the part of a public building where an audience sits

auditory /'awdit(ə)ri/ *adj* of or experienced through hearing

au fait /,oh 'fay/ *adj* **1** fully competent; capable **2** fully informed; familiar *with*

auger /'awgə/ *n* a tool for boring holes in wood

aught /awt/ *pron* all

augment /awg'ment/ *v* to make or become greater, more numerous, larger, or more intense

¹**augur** /'awgə/ *n* one held to foretell events by omens; a soothsayer; *specif* an official diviner of Ancient Rome

²augur *v* **1** to foretell or predict the future, esp from omens **2** to give promise of; presage

augury /'awgyoori/ *n* **1** predicting the future from omens or portents **2** an omen, portent

august /aw'gust/ *adj* marked by majestic dignity or grandeur – **~ly** *adv*

August /'awgəst/ *n* the 8th month of the Gregorian calendar

auk /awk/ *n* a puffin, guillemot, razorbill, or related short-necked diving seabird of the northern hemisphere

aunt /ahnt/ *n* **1a** the sister of one's father or mother **b** the wife of one's uncle **2** – often used as a term of affection for a woman who is a close friend of a young child or its parents

Aunt 'Sally /'sali/ *n* **1** an effigy of a woman at which objects are thrown at a fair **2** *Br* an easy target of criticism or attack

au pair /,oh 'peə/ *n* a foreign girl who does domestic work for a family in return for room and board and the opportunity to learn the language of the family

aura /'awrə/ *n* **1** a distinctive atmosphere surrounding a given source **2** a luminous radiation; a nimbus

aural /'awrəl/ *adj* of the ear or the sense of hearing – **~ly** *adv*

au revoir /,oh rə'vwah ./ *n* goodbye – often used interjectionally

auricle /'awrikl/ *n* **1** the projecting portion of the outer ear **2** an atrium of the heart – not now in technical use

aurora /aw'rawrə/ *n*, *pl* **auroras, aurorae** /-ri/ dawn

auspicious /aw'spish(ə)s/ *adj* **1** affording a favourable omen; propitious **2** attended by good omens; prosperous – **~ly** *adv*

Aussie /'ozi/ *n* an Australian – infml

austere /aw'stiə, o'stiə/ *adj* **1** stern and forbidding in appearance and manner **2** rigidly abstemious; self-denying **3** unadorned, simple – **~ly** *adv* – **~rity** *n*

Australasian /,ostrə'layzh(y)ən; *also* ,aw-/ *n or adj* (a native or inhabitant) of Australasia

¹Australian /o'straylyən; *also* aw-/ *n* **1** a native or inhabitant of Australia **2** the speech of the aboriginal inhabitants of Australia **3** English as spoken and written in Australia

²Australian *adj* (characteristic) of Australia

authentic /aw'thentik/ *adj* **1** trustworthy **2** genuine – **~ally** *adv* – **~ity** *n*

authenticate /aw'thentikayt/ *v* (to serve) to prove the authenticity of – **-ation** *n*

author /'awthə/, *fem* **authoress** /-res, -ris/ *n* **1a** the writer of a literary work **b** (the books written by) sby whose profession is writing **2** sby or sthg that originates or gives existence; a source

authoritarian /aw,thori'teəri·ən/ *adj* of or favouring submission to authority rather than personal freedom

authoritative /aw'thoritətiv/ *adj* **1a** having or proceeding from authority; official **b** entitled to credit or acceptance; conclusive **2** dictatorial, peremptory – **~ly** *adv*

authority /aw'thorəti/ *n* **1a** a book, quotation, etc referred to for justification of one's opinions or actions **b** a conclusive statement or set of statements **c** an individual cited or appealed to as an expert **2a** power to require and receive submission; the right to expect obedience **b** power to influence or command **c** a right granted by sby in authority; authorization **3a** *pl* the people in command **b** persons in command; *specif* government **c** *often cap* a governmental administrative body **4a** grounds, warrant **b** convincing force; weight

author·ize, -ise /'awthoriez/ *v* **1** to empower **2** to sanction – **-ization** *n*

'authorship /-ship/ *n* **1** the profession or activity of writing **2** the identity of the author of a literary work

autism /'awtiz(ə)m/ *n* a disorder of childhood development marked esp by inability to form relationships with other people – **-istic** *adj* – **-istically** *adv*

autobiography /,awtəbie'ogrəfi/ *n* the biography of a person written by him-/herself; *also* such writing considered as a genre – **-graphic** *adj* – **-graphically** *adv*

autocracy /aw'tokrəsi/ *n* government by an autocrat

autocrat /'awtəkrat/ *n* **1** one who rules with unlimited power **2** a dictatorial person – **~ic** *adj* – **~ically** *adv*

autocue /'awtoh,kyooh/ *n* a device that enables a person (e g a newsreader) being televised to read a script without averting his/her eyes from the camera

¹autograph /'awtə,grahf, -,graf/ *n* an identifying mark, *specif* a person's signature, made by the individual him-/herself

²autograph *v* to write one's signature in or on

automate /'awtəmayt/ *v* **1** to operate by automation **2** to convert to largely automatic operation

¹automatic /,awtə'matik/ *adj* **1a** acting or done spontaneously or unconsciously **b** resembling an automaton; mechanical **2** having a self-acting or self-regulating mechanism **3** *of a firearm* repeatedly ejecting the empty cartridge shell, introducing a new cartridge, and firing it – **~ally** *adv*

²automatic *n* an automatic machine or apparatus; *esp* an automatic firearm or vehicle

automation /,awtə'maysh(ə)n/ *n* **1** the technique of making an apparatus, process, or system operate automatically **2** automatic operation of an apparatus, process, or system by mechanical or electronic devices that take the place of human operators

automaton /aw'tomət(ə)n/; *also* ,awtə'mayt(ə)n/ *n, pl* **automatons, automata** /-tə/ **1** a mechanism having its own power source; *also* a robot **2** a person who acts in a mechanical fashion

automobile /'awtəmə,beel/ *n, NAm* a motor car

autonomy /aw'tonəmi/ *n* **1** self-determined freedom and esp moral independence **2** self-government; *esp* the degree of political independence possessed by a minority group, territorial division, etc – **mous** *adj* – **mously** *adv*

autopsy /'awtopsi/ *n* a postmortem examination

autumn /'awtəm/ *n* **1** the season between summer and winter, extending, in the northern hemisphere, from the September equinox to the December solstice **2** a period of maturity or the early stages of decline – ~ **al** *adj* – ~ **ally** *adv*

¹**auxiliary** /awg'zilyəri/ *adj* **1** subsidiary **2** being a verb (e g *be, do,* or *may*) used typically to express person, number, mood, voice, or tense, usu accompanying another verb **3** supplementary

²**auxiliary** *n* **1** an auxiliary person, group, or device **2** an auxiliary verb **3** a member of a foreign force serving a nation at war

¹**avail** /ə'vayl/ *v* to be of use or advantage (to) — **avail oneself of** to make use of; take advantage of

²**avail** *n* benefit, use – chiefly after *of* or *to* and in negative contexts

available /ə'vaylbbl/ *adj* **1** present or ready for immediate use **2** accessible, obtainable **3** qualified or willing to do sthg or to assume a responsibility – **ability** *n* – **ably** *adv*

avalanche /'avəlahnch/ *n* **1** a large mass of snow, rock, ice, etc falling rapidly down a mountain **2** a sudden overwhelming rush or accumulation of sthg

¹**avant-garde** /,avong'gahd/ *n* the group of people who create or apply new ideas and techniques in any field, esp the arts

²**avant-garde** *adj* of the avant-garde or artistic work that is new and experimental

avarice /'avəris/ *n* excessive or insatiable desire for wealth or gain; cupidity – **cious** *adj* – **ciously** *adv*

avenge /ə'venj/ *v* **1** to take vengeance on behalf of **2** to exact satisfaction for (a wrong) by punishing the wrongdoer – ~ **r** *n*

avenue /'avənyooh/ *n* **1** a line of approach **2** a broad passageway bordered by trees **3** an often broad street or road

aver /ə'vuh/ *v* **-rr- 1** to allege, assert **2** to declare positively – *fml*

¹**average** /'avərij, 'avrij/ *n* **1** a single value representative of a set of other values; *esp* an arithmetic mean **2** a level (e g of intelligence) typical of a group, class, or series **3** a ratio expressing the average performance of a sports team or sportsman as a fraction of the number of opportunities for successful performance

²**average** *adj* **1** equalling an arithmetic mean **2a** about midway between extremes **b** not out of the ordinary; common

³**average** *v* **1** to be or come to an average **2** to do, get, or have on average or as an average sum or quantity **3** to find the arithmetic mean of **4** to bring towards the average **5** to have an average value of

averse /ə'vuhs/ *adj* having an active feeling of repugnance or distaste – + *to* or *from*

aversion /ə'vuhsh(ə)n/ *n* **1** a feeling of settled dislike for sthg; antipathy **2** *chiefly Br* an object of aversion; a cause of repugnance

avert /ə'vuht/ *v* **1** to turn away or aside (e g the eyes) in avoidance **2** to see coming and ward off; avoid, prevent

aviary /'ayvyəri/ *n* a place for keeping birds

aviation /,ayvi'aysh(ə)n/ *n* **1** the operation of heavier-than-air aircraft **2** aircraft manufacture, development, and design

aviator /'ayviaytə/, *fem* **aviatrix** /-triks/ *n* the pilot of an aircraft

avid /'avid/ *adj* urgently or greedily eager; keen *n* – ~ **ly** *adv* – **-ity** *n*

avocado /,avə'kahdoh/ *n, pl* **avocados** *also* **avocadoes** (a tropical American tree of the laurel family bearing) a pulpy green or purple pear-shaped edible fruit

avocation /,avə'kaysh(ə)n/ *n* a subordinate occupation pursued in addition to one's vocation, esp for enjoyment; a hobby

avoid /ə'voyd/ *v* **1a** to keep away from; shun **b** to prevent the occurrence or effectiveness of **c** to refrain from **2** to make legally void – ~ **able** *adj* – ~ **ance** *n*

avoirdupois /,avwahdooh'pwah, ,avədə'poyz/, **avoirdupois weight** *n* the series of units of weight based on the pound of 16 ounces and the ounce of 16 drams

avow /ə'vow/ *v* **1** to declare assuredly **2** to acknowledge openly, bluntly, and without shame – ~ **al** *n*

avuncular /ə'vungkyoolə/ *adj* **1** of an uncle **2** kindly, genial – ~ **ly** *adv*

await /ə'wayt/ *v* **1** to wait for **2** to be in store for

¹**awake** /ə'wayk/ *v* **awoke** /ə'wohk/ *also* **awaked; awoken** /ə'wohkən/ **1** to emerge or arouse from sleep or a sleeplike state **2** to become conscious or aware of sthg – usu + *to* **3** to make active; stir up

²**awake** *adj* **1** roused (as if) from sleep **2** fully conscious; aware – usu + *to*

¹**award** /ə'wawd/ *v* **1** to give by judicial decree **2** to confer or bestow as being deserved or needed

²**award** n 1 a final decision; esp the decision of arbitrators in a case submitted to them 2 sthg that is conferred or bestowed, esp on the basis of merit or need

aware /ə'weə/ adj having or showing realization, perception, or knowledge; conscious – often + of – ~**ness** n

awash /ə'wosh/ adj 1 covered with water; flooded 2 marked by an abundance

¹**away** /ə'way/ adv 1 on the way; along (e g get away early) 2 from here or there; hence, thence 3a in a secure place or manner (e g locked away) b in another direction; aside (e g looked away) 4 out of existence; to an end (e g glaze away an afternoon) 5 from one's possession (e g gave the car away) 6 on, uninterruptedly (e g chatted away)

²**away** adj 1 absent from a place; gone 2 distant (e g a town some way away) 3 played on an opponent's grounds

awe /aw/ v or n (to inspire with) an emotion compounded of dread, veneration, and wonder

¹**awe·struck** /-,struk/ also **awe·stricken** /-,strikən/ adj filled with awe

awful /'awf(ə)l/ adj 1 extremely disagreeable or objectionable 2 exceedingly great – used as an intensive; chiefly infml – ~**ly** adv

awkward /'awkwəd/ adj 1 lacking dexterity or skill, esp in the use of hands; clumsy 2 lacking ease or grace (e g of movement or expression) 3a lacking social grace and assurance b causing embarrassment 4 poorly adapted for use or handling 5 requiring caution 6 deliberately thwarting or obstructive – ~**ly** adv – ~**ness** n

awl /awl/ n a pointed instrument for marking surfaces or making small holes (e g in leather)

awning /'awning/ n 1 an often canvas rooflike cover, used to protect sthg (e g a shop window or a ship's deck) from sun or rain 2 a shelter resembling an awning

awoken /ə'wohkən/ past part of **awake**

awry /ə'rie/ adv or adj 1 in a turned or twisted position or direction; askew 2 out of the right or hoped-for course; amiss

¹**axe**, NAm chiefly **ax** /aks/ n 1 a tool that has a cutting edge parallel to the handle and is used esp for felling trees and chopping and splitting wood 2 drastic reduction or removal (e g of personnel) — **axe to grind** an ulterior often selfish purpose to further

²**axe**, NAm chiefly **ax** v 1a to hew, shape, dress, or trim with an axe b to chop, split, or sever with an axe 2 to remove abruptly (e g from employment or from a budget)

axiom /'aksi-əm/ n a principle, rule, or maxim widely accepted on its intrinsic merit; a generally recognized truth – ~**atic** adj – ~**atically** adv

axis /'aksis/ n, pl **axes** /-seez/ 1 a straight line about which a body or a geometric figure rotates or may be supposed to rotate 2 a straight line with respect to which a body or figure is symmetrical 3 any of the reference lines of a coordinate system

axle /'aksl/ n 1 a shaft on or with which a wheel revolves 2 a rod connecting a pair of wheels of a vehicle

axon /'akson/ n a usu long projecting part of a nerve cell that usu conducts impulses away from the cell body

¹**aye** also **ay** /ay/ adv ever, always

²**aye** also **ay** /ie/ adv yes – used as the correct reply to a naval order

azalea /ə'zaylyə/ n any of a group of rhododendrons with funnel-shaped flowers and usu deciduous leaves

azimuth /'aziməth/ n an arc of the horizon expressed as the clockwise angle measured between a fixed point (e g true N or true S) and the vertical circle passing through the centre of an object

azure /'azyooə, 'ay-, -zhə/ n sky blue

B

b /bee/ n, pl **b's**, **bs** often cap 1a (a graphic representation of or device for reproducing) the 2nd letter of the English alphabet b a speech counterpart of written b 2 one designated b, esp as the 2nd in order or class

baa, **ba** /bah/ v or n (to make) the bleat of a sheep

babble /'babl/ v **babbling** /'babling, 'babl·ing/ 1a to utter meaningless or unintelligible sounds b to talk foolishly; chatter 2 to make a continuous murmuring sound 3 to reveal by talk that is too free

babe /bayb/ n 1 a naive inexperienced person 2a an infant, baby – chiefly poetic b a girl, woman – slang; usu as a noun of address

Babel /'baybl/ n, often not cap 1 a confusion of sounds or voices 2 a scene of noise or confusion

baboon /bə'boohn/ n any of several large African and Asiatic primates having doglike muzzles and usu short tails

¹**baby** /'baybi/ n 1a(1) an extremely young child; esp a newborn child a(2) an unborn child a(3) an extremely young animal b the youngest of a group 2 an infantile person 3a a person or thing for which one feels special responsibility or pride 4 a person; esp a girl, woman – slang; usu as a noun of address

²**baby** adj very small

³baby *v* to tend or indulge with often excessive or inappropriate care

'baby-,minder *n, chiefly Br* sby who minds babies or preschool children

'baby-,sit *v* **-tt-; baby-sat** to care for a child, usu for a short period while the parents are out – **~ter** *n*

bacchanal /'bakənl/ *n* **1a** a devotee of Bacchus, the Greek and Roman god of wine; *esp* one who takes part in a festival devoted to his riotous worship **b** a reveller **2** drunken revelry or carousal

baccy /'baki/ *n, chiefly Br* tobacco – infml

bachelor /'bachələ, 'bachlə/ *n* **1** a recipient of what is usu the lowest degree conferred by a college or university **2** an unmarried man – **~hood** *n*

¹back /bak/ *n* **1a** the rear part of the human body, esp from the neck to the end of the spine **b** the corresponding part of a quadruped or other lower animal **2a** the side or surface behind the front or face; the rear part; *also* the farther or reverse side **b** sthg at or on the back for support **3** (the position of) a primarily defensive player in some games (e g soccer) — **with one's back to the wall** in a situation from which one cannot retreat and must either fight or be defeated

²back *adv* **1a(1)** to, towards, or at the rear **a(2)** away (e g from the speaker) **b** in or into the past or nearer the beginning; ago **c** in or into a reclining position **d** in or into a delayed or retarded condition **2a** to, towards, or in a place from which sby or sthg came **b** to or towards a former state **c** in return or reply — **back and forth** backwards and forwards repeatedly

³back *adj* **1a** at or in the back **b** distant from a central or main area; remote **2** being behindhand or in arrears **3** not current

⁴back *v* **1a** to support by material or moral assistance – often + *up* **b** to substantiate – often + *up* **c(1)** to countersign, endorse **c(2)** to assume financial responsibility for **2** to cause to go back or in reverse **3a** to provide with a back **b** to be at the back of **4** to place a bet on (e g a horse) **5** to move backwards **6** *of the wind* to shift anticlockwise **7** to have the back in the direction of sthg

,back 'bench *n* any of the benches in Parliament on which rank and file members sit – usu pl – **~er** *n*

'back,bite /-,biet/ *v* **backbit** /-,bit/; **backbitten** /-,bit(ə)n/ to say mean or spiteful things about (sby) – **-biting** *n*

'back,bone /-,bohn/ *n* **1** the spinal column **2a** a chief mountain ridge, range, or system **b** the foundation or most substantial part of sthg **3** a firm and resolute character

'back,chat /-,chat/ *n, chiefly Br* impudent or argumentative talk made in reply, esp by a subordinate – infml

'back,cloth /-,kloth/ *n, Br* **1** a painted cloth hung across the rear of a stage **2** a background or setting

'back,comb /-,kohm/ *v* to comb (the hair) against the direction of growth starting with the short underlying hairs in order to produce a bouffant effect

'back,date /-,dayt/ *v* to apply (e g a pay rise) from a date in the past

back down *v* to retreat from a commitment or position

'back,drop /-,drop/ *n* a backcloth

backer /'bakə/ *n* **1** one who supports, esp financially **2** *Br* one who has placed a bet

¹'back,fire /-,fie·ə/ *n* a premature explosion in the cylinder or an explosion in the exhaust system of an internal-combustion engine

²,back'fire *v* **1** to make or undergo a backfire **2** to have the reverse of the desired or expected effect

'back,gammon /-,gamən/ *n* a board game played with dice and counters in which each player tries to move his/her counters along the board and at the same time to block or capture his/her opponent's counters

'back,ground /-,grownd/ *n* **1a** the scenery or ground behind sthg **b** the part of a painting or photograph that depicts what lies behind objects in the foreground **2** an inconspicuous position **3a** the conditions that form the setting within which sthg is experienced **b** information essential to the understanding of a problem or situation **c** the total of a person's experience, knowledge, and education

'back,hand /-,hand/ *n* a stroke in tennis, squash, etc made with the back of the hand turned in the direction of movement; *also* the side of the body on which this is made

,back'handed /-'handid/ *adj* **1** using or made with a backhand **2** indirect, devious; *esp* sarcastic

'back,hander /-,handə/ *n* **1** a backhanded blow or stroke **2** *Br* a backhanded remark **3** a bribe – infml

backing /'baking/ *n* **1** sthg forming a back **2a** support, aid **b** endorsement

'back,lash /-,lash/ *n* **1** a sudden violent backward movement or reaction **2** a strong adverse reaction

'back,log /-,log/ *n* **1** a reserve **2** an accumulation of tasks not performed, orders unfulfilled, or materials not processed

'back,most /-,mohst/ *adj* farthest back

'back ,number *n* sby or sthg that is out of date; *esp* an old issue of a periodical or newspaper

back out *v* to withdraw, esp from a commitment or contest

'back,pedal /-,pedl/ *v* **1** to move backwards (e g in boxing) **2** to back down from or reverse a previous opinion or stand

,back'side /-'sied/ *n* the buttocks

'back,slide /-,slied/ v -slid /-,slid/; -slid, -slidden /-,slid(ə)n/ to lapse morally or in the practice of religion – **-slider** n

¹back'stage /-'stayj/ adv 1 in or to a backstage area 2 in private, secretly

²back'stage adj 1 of or occurring in the parts of a theatre that cannot be seen by the audience 2 of the inner working or operation (e g of an organization)

'back,street /-,street/ adj made, done, or acting illegally or surreptitiously

'back,stroke /-,strohk/ n a swimming stroke executed on the back

'back,track /-,trak/ v 1 to retrace a path or course 2 to reverse a position or stand

'back,up /-,up/ n 1 sby or sthg that serves as a substitute, auxiliary, or alternative 2 sby or sthg that gives support

back up v to support (sby), esp in argument or in playing a team game

'backward /-wood/ adj 1a directed or turned backwards b done or executed backwards 2 retarded in development 3 of or occupying a fielding position in cricket behind the batsman's wicket – ~ly adv – ~ness n

'backwards, chiefly NAm backward adv 1 towards the back 2 with the back foremost 3 in a reverse direction; towards the beginning 4 perfectly; by heart 5 towards the past 6 towards a worse state – **bend/fall/lean over backwards** to make extreme efforts, esp in order to please or conciliate

'back,wash /-,wosh/ n 1a a backward movement in air, water, etc produced by a propelling force (e g the motion of oars) b the backward movement of a receding wave 2 a usu unwelcome consequence or by-product of an event; an aftermath

'back,water /-,wawtə/ n 1 a stagnant pool or inlet kept filled by the opposing current of a river; broadly a body of water turned back in its course 2 a place or condition that is isolated or backward, esp intellectually

'backwoods /-woodz/ n, pl but sing or pl in constr a remote or culturally backward area – usu + the

bacon /'baykən/ n (the meat cut from) the cured and often smoked side of a pig

bacteriology /bak,tiəri'oluhj/ n 1 a science that deals with bacteria 2 bacterial life and phenomena – **-ologist** n

bacterium /bak'tiəri·əm/ n, pl bacteria /-ri·ə/ pl bacteria a small, often disease-causing microorganism – **-rial** adj

bad /bad/ adj worse /wuhs/; worst /wuhst/ 1a failing to reach an acceptable standard; poor, inadequate b unfavourable c no longer acceptable, because of decay or disrepair 2a morally objectionable b mischievous, disobedient 3

unskilful, incompetent – often + at 4 disagreeable, unpleasant 5a injurious, harmful b worse than usual; severe 6 incorrect, faulty 7a suffering pain or distress; unwell b unhealthy, diseased 8 sorry, unhappy 9 invalid, worthless 10 of a debt not recoverable – ~ness n – ~ly adv – **in someone's bad books** out of favour with sby

,bad 'blood n ill feeling; bitterness

bade /bed, bad/ past of bid

badge /baj/ n 1 a device or token, esp of membership in a society or group 2 a characteristic mark 3 an emblem awarded for a particular accomplishment

¹badger /'bajə/ n any of several sturdy burrowing nocturnal mammals widely distributed in the northern hemisphere

²badger v to harass or annoy persistently

badinage /'badi,nahzh, -nij/ n banter

badminton /'badmint(ə)n/ n a court game played with light long-handled rackets and a shuttle volleyed over a net

¹baffle /bafl/ v baffling /'bafling, 'bafl·ing/ to perplex – **-ling** adj – **-lingly** adv – ~ment n

²baffle n a structure that reduces the exchange of sound waves between the front and back of a loudspeaker

¹bag /bag/ n 1 a usu flexible container for holding, storing, or carrying sthg 2 sthg resembling a bag; esp a sagging in cloth 3 spoils, loot 4 pl chiefly Br lots, masses – infml 5 a slovenly unattractive woman – slang — **bag and baggage** 1 with all one's belongings 2 entirely, wholesale — **in the bag** as good as achieved; already certain before the test — infml

²bag v -gg- 1 to swell out; bulge 2 to hang loosely 3 to put into a bag 4a to take (animals) as game b to get possession of, seize; also to steal

bagatelle /,bagə'tel/ n 1 a trifle; an unimportant matter 2 a game in which balls must be put into or through cups or arches at one end of an oblong table

baggage /'bagij/ n 1 portable equipment, esp of a military force 2 superfluous or useless things, ideas, or practices 3 luggage, esp for travel by sea or air 4 a good-for-nothing woman; a pert girl – infml

baggy /'bagi/ adj loose, puffed out, or hanging like a bag

bags /bagz/ n pl in constr pl bags wide trousers

¹bail /bayl/ n 1 security deposited as a guarantee that sby temporarily freed from custody will return to stand trial 2 temporary release on bail 3 one who provides bail

²bail v 1 to deliver (property) in trust to another for a special purpose and for a limited period 2 to release on bail 3 to procure the release of (a person in custody) by giving bail – often + out

³**bail** n 1 either of the 2 crosspieces that lie on the stumps from the wicket in cricket 2 *chiefly Br* a device for confining or separating animals

⁴**bail**, *Br also* **bale** n a container used to remove water from a boat

⁵**bail**, *Br also* **bale** v 1 to clear (water) from a boat by collecting in a bail, bucket etc and throwing over the side 2 to parachute from an aircraft *USE* usu + *out*

bailey /'bayli/ n (the space enclosed by) the outer wall of a castle or any of several walls surrounding the keep

'**Bailey** ,**bridge** n a prefabricated bridge built from interchangeable latticed steel panels

bailiff /'baylif/ n 1 an official employed by a sheriff to serve writs, make arrests, etc 2 *chiefly Br* one who manages an estate or farm

bail out, *Br also* **bale out** v to help from a predicament; release from difficulty

bairn /bean/ n, *chiefly Scot & N Eng* a child

¹**bait** /bayt/ v 1 to provoke, tease, or exasperate with unjust, nagging, or persistent remarks 2 to harass (e g a chained animal) with dogs, usu for sport 3 to provide with bait

²**bait** n 1a sthg used in luring, esp to a hook or trap b a poisonous material placed where it will be eaten by pests 2 a lure, temptation

baize /bayz/ n a woollen cloth, resembling felt, used chiefly for covering and lining sthg (e g table tops or drawers)

bake /bayk/ v 1 to dry or harden by subjecting to heat 2 to cook (food) by baking 3 to become baked 4 to become extremely hot – ~r n

Bakelite /'baykəliet/ *trademark* – used for any of various synthetic resins and plastics

,**baker's** '**dozen** /'baykəz/ n thirteen

bakery /'bayk(ə)ri/ n a place for baking or selling baked goods, esp bread and cakes

'**baking** ,**powder** /'bayking/ n a powder that consists of a bicarbonate and an acid substance used in place of yeast as a raising agent in making scones, cakes, etc

baksheesh /'bak,sheesh, -'-/ n pl **baksheesh** money given as a tip

balaclava / ,balə'klahvə/, **balaclava helmet** n, *often cap B* a knitted pull-on hood that covers the ears, neck, and throat

balalaika / ,balə'lieka/ n a stringed musical instrument of Russian origin

¹**balance** /'baləns/ n 1 an instrument for weighing 2 a counterbalancing weight, force, or influence 3 stability produced by even distribution of weight on each side of a vertical axis 4a equilibrium between contrasting, opposing, or interacting elements b equality between the totals of the 2 sides of an account 5 an aesthetically pleasing integration of elements 6 the ability to retain one's physical equilibrium 7 the weight or force of one side in

excess of another 8a (a statement of) the difference between credits and debits in an account b sthg left over; a remainder c an amount in excess, esp on the credit side of an account 9 mental and emotional steadiness — **in the balance** in an uncertain critical position; with the fate or outcome about to be determined — **on balance** all things considered

²**balance** v 1a(1) to compute the difference between the debits and credits of (an account) a(2) to pay the amount due on b to arrange so that one set of elements exactly equals another 2a to counterbalance, offset b to equal or equalize in weight, number, or proportion 3 to compare the relative importance, value, force, or weight of; ponder 4 to bring to a state or position of balance 5 to become balanced or established in balance 6 to be an equal counterweight – often + *with*

,**balance of** '**payments** n the difference over a period of time between a country's payments to and receipts from abroad

balcony /'balkəni/ n 1 a platform built out from the wall of a building and enclosed by a railing or low wall 2 a gallery inside a building (e g a theatre)

bald /bawld/ adj 1a lacking a natural or usual covering (e g of hair, vegetation, or nap) b having little or no tread 2 unadorned, undisguised 3 *of an animal* marked with white, esp on the head or face – ~ness n

balderdash /'bawldədash/ n nonsense – often as a generalized expression of disagreement

¹**bale** /bayl/ n a large bundle of goods; *specif* a closely pressed package of merchandise bound and usu wrapped for storage or transportation

²**bale** n or v, Br ⁴/⁵**bail**

baleful /'baylf(ə)l/ adj 1 deadly or pernicious in influence 2 gloomily threatening – -**fully** adv

bale out v, Br bail out

balk, *chiefly Br* **baulk** /bawlk, bawk/ v 1 to stop short and refuse to continue 2 to refuse or turn down abruptly – usu + *at*

¹**ball** /bawl/ n 1 a round or roundish body or mass: 1a a solid or hollow spherical or egg-shaped body used in a game or sport b a spherical or conical projectile; *also* projectiles used in firearms c the rounded slightly raised fleshy area at the base of a thumb or big toe 2 a delivery or play of the ball in cricket, baseball, etc 3 a game in which a ball is thrown, kicked, or struck; *specif, NAm* baseball 4a a testis – usu pl; vulg b pl nonsense – often used interjectionally; vulg — **on the ball** marked by being knowledgeable and competent; alert — infml — **start/set/keep the ball rolling** to begin/continue sthg

²**ball** v 1 to form or gather into a ball 2 to have sexual intercourse (with) – vulg

³**ball** n 1 a large formal gathering for social dancing 2 a very pleasant experience; a good time – infml

ballad /'balǝd/ n 1 a narrative composition in rhythmic verse suitable for singing 2 a (slow, romantic or sentimental) popular, esp narrative, song

ballast /'balǝst/ n **1a** heavy material carried in a ship to improve stability **b** heavy material that is carried on a balloon or airship to steady it and can be jettisoned to control the rate of descent 2 sthg that gives stability, esp in character or conduct 3 gravel or broken stone laid in a bed for railway lines or the lower layer of roads

,**ball 'bearing** n a bearing having minimal friction in which hardened steel balls roll easily in a groove between a shaft and a support; *also* any of the balls in such a bearing

'**ball ,cock** n an automatic valve (e g in a cistern) controlled by the rise and fall of a float at the end of a lever

ballerina /,balǝ'reenǝ/ n a female, esp principal, ballet dancer

ballet /'balay; *NAm also* ba'lay/ n 1 (a group that performs) artistic dancing in which the graceful flowing movements are based on conventional positions and steps 2 a theatrical art form using ballet dancing, music, and scenery to convey a story, theme, or atmosphere

bal'listics n pl *but sing or pl in constr* 1 the science dealing with the motion of projectiles in flight 2 (the study of) the individual characteristics of and firing processes in a firearm or cartridge – **ballistic** adj

¹**balloon** /bǝ'loohn/ n 1 an envelope filled with hot air or a gas lighter than air so as to rise and float in the atmosphere 2 an inflatable usu brightly coloured rubber bag used as a toy 3 a line enclosing words spoken or thought by a character, esp in a cartoon

²**balloon** v 1 to inflate, distend 2 to ascend or travel in a balloon 3 to swell or puff out; expand – often + *out* 4 to increase rapidly

³**balloon** adj relating to, resembling, or suggesting a balloon

ballooning /bǝ'loohning/ n the act or sport of riding in a balloon – **-ist** n

¹**ballot** /'balǝt/ n 1 (a sheet of paper, or orig a small ball, used in) secret voting 2 the right to vote 3 the number of votes cast

²**ballot** v 1 to vote by ballot 2 to ask for a vote from

'**ball,point** /-,poynt/, ,**ballpoint 'pen** n a pen having as the writing point a small rotating metal ball that inks itself by contact with an inner magazine

'**balls-,up**, *NAm* **ball-up** n a state of muddled confusion caused by a mistake – slang

balls up, *NAm* **ball up** v to make or become badly muddled or confused – slang

ballyhoo /,bali'hooh/ n pl **ballyhoos** flamboyant, exaggerated, or sensational advertising or propaganda

balm /bahm/ n 1 an aromatic preparation (e g a healing ointment) 2 any of various aromatic plants of the mint family 3 sthg that soothes, relieves, or heals physically or emotionally

balmy /'bahmi/ adj **1a** having the qualities of balm; soothing **b** mild 2 barmy

baloney /bǝ'lohni/ n nonsense – often used interjectionally

balsa /'bawlsǝ, 'bolsǝ/ n (the strong very light wood of) a tropical American tree

balsam /'bals(ǝ)m, 'bol-/ n 1 (a preparation containing) an oily and resinous substance flowing from various plants **2a** any of several trees yielding balsam **b** any of a widely distributed genus of watery-juiced annual plants (e g touch-me-not) 3 sthg soothing

balustrade /,balǝ'strayd, 'balǝ,strayd/ n a row of low pillars topped by a rail; *also* a usu low parapet or barrier

bamboo /bam'booh/ n pl **bamboos** any of various chiefly tropical giant grasses including some with strong hollow stems used for building, furniture, or utensils

bamboozle /bam'boohzl/ v to deceive by trickery

¹**ban** /ban/ v **-nn-** to prohibit, esp by legal means or social pressure

²**ban** n 1 an ecclesiastical curse; excommunication 2 a legal or social prohibition

banal /bǝ'nahl/ adj lacking originality, freshness, or novelty; trite, hackneyed – ~ **ity** n

banana /bǝ'nahnǝ/ n (a tropical tree that bears) an elongated usu tapering fruit with soft pulpy flesh enclosed in a soft usu yellow rind that grows in bunches

ba'**nana re,public** n a small tropical country that is politically unstable and usu economically underdeveloped – derog

¹**band** /band/ n 1 a strip or belt serving to join or hold things together 2 a ring of elastic 3 a more or less well-defined range of wavelengths, frequencies, or energies of light waves, radio waves, sound waves, etc 4 a narrow strip serving chiefly as decoration: e g **4a** a narrow strip of material applied as trimming to an article of dress **b** pl 2 cloth strips sometimes worn at the front of the neck as part of clerical, legal, or academic dress 5 a strip distinguishable in some way (e g by colour, texture, or composition) 6 *Br* a group of pupils assessed as being of broadly similar ability

²**band** v 1 to fasten a band to or tie up with a band 2 *Br* to divide (pupils) into bands 3 to unite for a common purpose; confederate – often + *together*

³**band** n *sing or pl in constr* a group of people, animals, or things; *esp* a group of musicians organized for ensemble playing and using chiefly woodwind, brass, and percussion instruments

bandage /'bandij/ n a strip of fabric used esp to dress and bind up wounds

bandanna, bandana /ban'danə/ *n* a large coloured and patterned handkerchief

bandit /'bandit/ *n, pl* **bandits** *also* **banditti** /ban 'deeti/ **1** an outlaw; *esp* a member of a band of marauders **2** a political terrorist – ~**ry** *n*

bandoleer, bandolier /ˌbandə'liə/ *n* a cartridge belt usu worn over the shoulder and across the chest

'bandsman /-mən/ *n* a member of a musical band

'band,stand /-ˌstand/ *n* a usu roofed stand or platform for a band to perform on outdoors

'band,wagon /-ˌwagən/ *n* a party, faction, or cause that attracts adherents by its timeliness, momentum, etc — **jump/climb on the bandwagon** to attach oneself to a successful cause or enterprise in the hope of personal gain

¹bandy /'bandi/ *v* **1** to exchange (words) in an argumentative, careless, or lighthearted manner **2** to use in a glib or offhand manner – often + *about*

²bandy *adj* **1** *of legs* bowed **2** bowlegged

bane /bayn/ *n* **1** poison – esp in combination **2** a cause of death, ruin, or trouble – ~**ful** *adj* – ~**fully** *adv*

¹bang /bang/ *v* **1** to strike sharply; bump **2** to knock, beat, or strike hard, often with a sharp noise **3** to have sexual intercourse with – vulg **4** to strike with a sharp noise or thump **5** to produce a sharp often explosive noise or noises

²bang *n* **1** a resounding blow; a thump **2** a sudden loud noise – often used interjectionally **3** an act of sexual intercourse – vulg

³bang *adv* **1** right, directly **2** exactly *USE* infml

⁴bang *n* a short squarely-cut fringe of hair – usu pl with sing. meaning

banger /'bang-ə/ *n, Br* **1** a firework that explodes with a loud bang **2** a sausage **3** an old usu dilapidated car *USE* (2&3) infml

bangle /'bang-gl/ *n* a bracelet or anklet

,bang-'on *adj or adv, Br* just what is needed; first-rate – infml

banish /'banish/ *v* **1** to require by authority to leave a place, esp a country **2** to dispel – ~**ment** *n*

banister *also* **bannister** /'banistə/ *n* a handrail with its upright supports guarding the edge of a staircase – often pl with sing. meaning

banjo /'banjoh, -'-/ *n, pl* **banjos** *also* **banjoes** a stringed instrument with a drumlike body that is strummed with the fingers

¹bank /bangk/ *n* **1a** a mound, pile, or ridge (e g of earth or snow) **b** a piled up mass of cloud or fog **c** an undersea elevation rising esp from the continental shelf **2** the rising ground bordering a lake or river or forming the edge of a cut or hollow **3** the lateral inward tilt of a surface along a curve or of a vehicle when following a curved path

²bank *v* **1** to surround with a bank **2** to keep *up* to ensure slow burning **3** to build (a road or railway) with the outer edge of a curve higher than the

inner **4** to rise in or form a bank – often + *up* **5** to incline an aircraft sideways when turning **6** to follow a curve or incline, specif in racing

³bank *n* a bench for the rowers of a galley

⁴bank *n* **1** an establishment for the custody, loan, exchange, or issue of money and for the transmission of funds **2** a person conducting a gambling house or game; *specif* the banker in a game of cards **3** a supply of sthg held in reserve: e g **3a** the money, chips, etc held by the bank or banker for use in a gambling game **b** the pool of pieces belonging to a game (e g dominoes) from which the players draw **4** a place where data, human organs, etc are held available for use when needed

⁵bank *v* **1** to deposit (money) or have an account in a bank **2** to rely or count *on* — **bank on** to depend or rely on; COUNT ON

banker /'bangkə/ *n* **1** one who engages in the business of banking **2** the player who keeps the bank in various games

'banker's ,card *n, Br* a cheque card

,bank 'holiday *n often cap B&H* a public holiday in the British Isles on which banks and most businesses are closed by law

banking /'bangking/ *n* the business of a bank or a banker

¹bankrupt /'bangkrupt/ *n* **1** an insolvent person whose estate is administered under the bankruptcy laws for the benefit of his/her creditors **2** one who is destitute of a usu specified quality or thing

²bankrupt *v* **1** to reduce to bankruptcy **2** to impoverish

³bankrupt *adj* **1** reduced to a state of financial ruin; *specif* legally declared a bankrupt **2a** broken, ruined **b** destitute – + *of* or *in* – ~**cy** *n*

banner /'banə/ *n* **1** a usu square flag bearing heraldic arms; *broadly* a flag **2** a headline in large type running across a newspaper page **3** a strip of cloth on which a sign is painted **4** a name, slogan, or goal associated with a particular group or ideology – often + *under*

banns /banz/ *n pl* the public announcement, esp in church, of a proposed marriage

banquet /'bangkwit/ *n, v* (to provide with or partake of) an elaborate ceremonial meal for numerous people often in honour of a person; (to have) a feast

banshee /'banshee *also* -'-/ *n* a female spirit in Gaelic folklore whose wailing warns of approaching death in a household

bantam /'bantəm/ *n* any of numerous small domestic fowl

'bantam,weight /-ˌwayt/ *n* a boxer who weighs not more than 8st 6lb (about 53.5kg) if professional or more than 51kg (about 8st) but not more than 54kg (about 8st 7lb) if amateur

¹banter /'bantə/ *v* to speak or act playfully or wittily

²banter *n* good-natured repartee; badinage

baptism /'baptiz(ə)m/ *n* 1 the ritual use of water for purification, esp in the Christian sacrament of admission to the church 2 an act, experience, or ordeal by which one is purified, sanctified, initiated, or named – ~**al** *adj* – **-tize** *v*

baptist /'baptist/ *n* 1 one who baptizes 2 *cap* a member of a Protestant denomination which reserves baptism for full believers

¹bar /bah/ *n* 1 a straight piece (e g of wood or metal), that is longer than it is wide and has any of various uses (e g as a lever, support, barrier, or fastening) 2a the extinction of a claim in law b an intangible or nonphysical impediment c a submerged or partly submerged bank (e g of sand) along a shore or in a river, often obstructing navigation 3a the dock in a law court; *also* the railing that encloses the dock b *often cap* b(1) *sing or pl in constr* the whole body of barristers b(2) the profession of barrister 4a a stripe or chevron b a strip of metal attached to a military medal to indicate an additional award of the medal 5a(1) a counter at which food or esp alcoholic drinks are served a(2) a room or establishment whose main feature is a bar for the serving of alcoholic drinks b a place where goods, esp a specified commodity, are sold or served across a counter 6 (a group of musical notes and rests that add up to a prescribed time value, bounded on each side on the staff by) a bar line

²bar *v* -**rr**- 1a to fasten with a bar b to place bars across to prevent movement in, out, or through 2 to mark with stripes 3a to shut in or out (as if) by bars b to set aside the possibility of; rule out 4a to interpose legal objection to b to prevent, forbid

³bar *prep* except

⁴bar *adv, of odds in betting* being offered for all the unnamed competitors

¹barb /bahb/ *n* 1a a sharp projection extending backwards from the point of an arrow, fishhook, etc, and preventing easy extraction b a biting or pointedly critical remark or comment 2 any of the side branches of the shaft of a feather 3 a plant hair or bristle ending in a hook

²barb *v* to provide (e g an arrow) with a barb

barbarian /bah'beəri·ən/ *adj* 1 of a land, culture, or people alien and usu believed to be inferior to and more savage than one's own 2 lacking refinement, learning, or culture – **barbarian** *n*

barbaric /bah'barik/ *adj* 1 (characteristic of) barbarians; *esp* uncivilized 2 savage, barbarous – **-barize** *v* – **-barism** *n* – ~**ally** *adv*

barbarity /bah'barəti/ *n* 1 barbarism 2 (an act or instance of) barbarous cruelty; inhumanity

barbarous /'bahb(ə)rəs/ *adj* 1 uncivilized 2 lacking culture or refinement 3 mercilessly harsh or cruel – ~**ly** *adv*

¹barbecue /'bahbi,kyooh/ *n* 1 a (portable) fireplace over which meat and fish are roasted 2 meat roasted over an open fire or barbecue pit 3 a social gathering, esp in the open air, at which barbecued food is served

²barbecue *v* to roast or grill on a rack over hot coals or on a revolving spit in front of or over a source of cooking heat, esp an open fire

barbed /bahbd/ *adj* 1 having barbs 2 characterized by pointed and biting criticism

,barbed 'wire *n* twisted wires armed at intervals with sharp points

barbel /'bahbl/ *n* a European freshwater fish with 4 barbels on its upper jaw

²barbel *n* a slender tactile projecting organ on the lips of certain fishes (e g catfish) used in locating food

barber /'bahbə/ *n* sby, esp a man, whose occupation is cutting and dressing men's hair and shaving

barber's pole *n* a red and white striped pole fixed to the front of a barber's shop

barbiturate /bah'bityoorət/ *n* any of several drugs that are used esp in the treatment of epilepsy and were formerly much used in sleeping pills

¹bard /bahd/ *n* 1 sby, specif a Celtic poet-singer, who composed, sang, or recited verses on heroes and their deeds 2 a poet; *specif* one recognized or honoured at an eisteddfod 3 *cap* – used as an epithet for Shakespeare; + *the*

²bard, barde *n* a strip of pork fat, bacon, etc for covering lean meat before roasting

¹bare /beə/ *adj* 1 lacking a natural, usual, or appropriate covering, esp clothing 2 open to view; exposed – often in *lay bare* 3a unfurnished, empty b destitute *of* 4a having nothing left over or added; scant, mere b undisguised, unadorned – ~**ness** *n*

²bare *v* to make or lay bare; uncover, reveal

'bare,back /-,bak/, **'bare,backed** *adv or adj* on the bare back of a horse without a saddle

,bare'faced /-'fayst/ *adj* lacking scruples; shameless – ~**ly** *adv*

barely /'beəli/ *adv* 1 scarcely, hardly 2 in a meagre manner; scantily

¹bargain /'bahgən/ *n* 1 an agreement between parties concerning the terms of a transaction between them or the course of action each pursues in respect to the other 2 an advantageous purchase — **into the bargain** also

²bargain *v* 1 to negotiate over the terms of a purchase, agreement, or contract 2 to come to terms; agree 3 to be prepared *for* — **bargain for** to be at all prepared for; expect

¹barge /bahj/ *n* 1a a flat-bottomed boat used chiefly for the transport of goods on inland waterways or between ships and the shore b a flat-bottomed coastal sailing vessel **2a** a large naval motorboat used by flag officers **b** an ornate carved vessel used on ceremonial occasions

²**barge** v **1** to move in a headlong or clumsy fashion **2** to intrude *in* or *into*

bargee /bah'jee/ *n, Br* sby who works on a barge

baritone /'baritohn/ *n* **1** (a person with) a male singing voice between bass and tenor **2** a member of a family of instruments having a range next below that of the tenor

barium /'beeri·əm/ *n* a soft bivalent metallic element of the alkaline-earth group

¹**bark** /bahk/ *v* **1** to make (a sound similar to) the short loud cry characteristic of a dog **2** to speak or utter in a curt, loud, and usu angry tone; snap — **bark up the wrong tree** to proceed under a misapprehension

²**bark** *n* **1** (a sound similar to) the sound made by a barking dog **2** a short sharp peremptory utterance

³**bark** *n* the tough exterior covering of a woody root or stem

⁴**bark** *v* to abrade the skin of

⁵**bark** *n* a boat – poetic

barley /'bahli/ *n* a widely cultivated cereal grass whose seed is used to make malt and in foods and stock feeds

,**barley 'wine** *n* a strong ale

¹**barman** /-mən/, *fem* '**bar,maid** /-,mayd/ *n* one who serves drinks in a bar

bar mitzvah /,bah 'mitsvə/ *n, often cap B&M* (the initiatory ceremony of) a Jewish youth of 13 who assumes adult religious duties and responsibilities

barmy /'bahmi/ *adj* slightly mad; foolish – infml

barn /bahn/ *n* **1** a usu large farm building for storage, esp of feed, cereal products, etc **2** an unusually large and usu bare building

barnacle /'bahnəkl/ *n* any of numerous marine crustaceans that are free-swimming as larvae but fixed to rocks or floating objects as adults

¹**barn ,dance** *n* a type of country dance, esp a round dance or a square dance with called instructions; *also* a social gathering for such dances

²**barn ,yard** /-,yahd/ *n* a farmyard

barometer /bə'romitə/ *n* **1** an instrument for determining the pressure of the atmosphere and hence for assisting in predicting the weather or measuring the height of an ascent **2** sthg that serves to register fluctuations (e g in public opinion) – **-metric** *adj* – **-metrically** *adv*

baron /'barən/ *n* **1** a lord of the realm **2a** a member of the lowest rank of the peerage in Britain **b** a European nobleman **3** a man of great power or influence in a specified field of activity **4** a joint of meat consisting of 2 loins or sirloins joined by the backbone – ~ **ial** *adj*

baroness /,barə'nes/ *n* **1** the wife or widow of a baron **2** a woman having in her own right the rank of a baron

baronet /,barə'net, 'barənit/ *n* the holder of a rank of honour below a baron and above a knight – ~ **cy** *n*

barony /'barəni/ *n* the domain or rank of a baron

baroque /bə'rok/ *adj* (typical) of a style of artistic expression prevalent esp in the 17th c that is marked by extravagant forms and elaborate and sometimes grotesque ornamentation

barque *NAm chiefly* **bark** /bahk/ *n* a sailing vessel with the rearmost of usu 3 masts fore-and-aft rigged and the others square-rigged

¹**barrack** /'barək/ *n* **1** (a set or area of) buildings for lodging soldiers in garrison – often pl with sing. meaning but sing. or pl in constr **2** a large building characterized by extreme plainness or dreary uniformity with others – usu pl with sing. meaning but sing. or pl in constr

²**barrack** *v* to lodge in barracks

³**barrack** *v, chiefly Br* to jeer, scoff (at)

barrage /'barahzh/ *n* **1** a barrier, esp of intensive artillery fire, to hinder enemy action **2** a rapid series (e g of questions) – **barrage** *v*

barrel /'barəl/ *n* **1** an approximately cylindrical vessel with bulging sides and flat ends constructed from wooden staves bound together with hoops; *also* any similar vessel **2** a drum or cylindrical part: e g **2a** the discharging tube of a gun **b** the part of a fountain pen or pencil containing the ink or lead — **over a barrel** at a disadvantage; in an awkward situation so that one is helpless — infml

'**barrel ,organ** *n* a musical instrument consisting of a revolving cylinder studded with pegs that open a series of valves to admit air from a bellows to a set of pipes

barren /'barən/ *adj* **1a** *of a female or mating* incapable of producing offspring **b** habitually failing to fruit **2** not productive; *esp* producing inferior or scanty vegetation **3** lacking, devoid of **4** lacking interest, information, or charm – ~ **ness** *n*

¹**barricade** /'barikayd, --'-/ *v* **1** to block off, stop up, or defend with a barricade **2** to prevent access to by means of a barricade

²**barricade** *n* **1** an obstruction or rampart thrown up across a way or passage to check the advance of the enemy **2** a barrier, obstacle

barrier /'bari·ə/ *n* **1** a material object (e g a stockade, fortress, or railing) or set of objects that separates, demarcates, or serves as a barricade **2** sthg immaterial that impedes or separates **3** a factor that tends to restrict the free movement, mingling, or interbreeding of individuals or populations

barring /'bahring/ *prep* excepting

barrister /'baristə/, ,**barrister-at-'law** *n* a lawyer who has the right to plead as an advocate in an English or Welsh superior court

¹**barrow** /'baroh/ *n* a large mound of earth or stones over the remains of the dead

²barrow *n* a cart with a shallow box body, 2 wheels, and shafts for pushing it

¹barter /'bahtə/ *v* to trade by exchanging one commodity for another without the use of money

²barter *n* the carrying on of trade by bartering

basalt /'ba(y)sawlt, bə'sawlt/ *n* a dense to fine-grained dark igneous rock

¹base /bays/ *n* **1a** the bottom of sthg; a foundation **b** the lower part of a wall, pier, or column considered as a separate architectural feature **c** that part of an organ by which it is attached to another structure nearer the centre of a living organism **2** a main ingredient **3** the fundamental part of sthg; a basis **4a** a centre from which a start is made in an activity or from which operations proceed **b** a line in a survey which serves as the origin for computations **c** the locality or installations on which a military force relies for supplies or from which it starts operations **d** the basis from which a word is derived **5a** the starting place or goal in various games **b** any of the stations at each of the 4 corners of the inner part of a baseball field to which a batter must run in turn in order to score a run **6** any of various typically water-soluble and acrid or brackish tasting chemical compounds that are capable of taking up a hydrogen ion from or donating an unshared pair of electrons to an acid to form a salt

²base *v* **1** to make, form, or serve as a base for **2** to use as a base or basis for; establish, found – usu + *on* or *upon*

³base *adj* constituting or serving as a base

⁴base *adj* **1** of a metal of comparatively low value and having relatively inferior properties (e g resistance to corrosion) **2** lacking higher values; degrading **3** of relatively little value – ~**ly** *adv* – ~**ness** *n*

'base,ball /-,bawl/ *n* (the ball used in) a game played with a bat and ball between 2 teams of 9 players each on a large field

'base,born /-,bawn/ *adj* of humble or illegitimate birth

'base ,line /-,lien/ *n* the back line at each end of a court in tennis, badminton, etc

'basement /-mənt/ *n* the part of a building that is wholly or partly below ground level

¹bash /bash/ *v* **1** to strike violently; *also* to injure or damage by striking; smash – often + *in* or *up* **2** to make a violent attack on *USE* infml

²bash *n* **1** a forceful blow **2** *chiefly Br* a try, attempt **3** a festive social gathering; a party *USE* infml

bashful /'bashf(ə)l/ *adj* socially shy or timid – **-fully** *adv* – **-fulness** *n*

¹basic /'baysik, -zik/ *adj* **1** of forming the base or essence; fundamental **2** constituting or serving as the minimum basis or starting point **3** of, containing, or having the character of a chemical base

²basic *n* sthg basic; a fundamental

BASIC /'baysik/ *n* a high-level computer language for programming and interacting with a computer in a wide variety of applications

basilica /bə'zilika, bə'si-/ *n* **1** an oblong building used in ancient Rome as a place of assembly or as a lawcourt and usu ending in an apse **2** an early Christian church similar to a Roman basilica **3** a Roman Catholic church given certain ceremonial privileges

basin /'bays(ə)n/ *n* **1a** a round open usu metal or ceramic vessel with a greater width than depth and sides that slope or curve inwards to the base, used typically for holding water for washing **b** a bowl with a greater depth than width esp for holding, mixing, or cooking food **c** the contents of a basin **2a** a dock built in a tidal river or harbour **b** a (partly) enclosed water area, esp for ships **3a** a depression in the surface of the land or ocean floor **b** the region drained by a river and its tributaries

basis /'baysis/ *n, pl* **bases** /'bayseez/ **1** a foundation **2** the principal component of sthg **3** a basic principle or way of proceeding

bask /bahsk/ *v* **1** to lie in, or expose oneself to, a pleasant warmth or atmosphere **2** to enjoy sby's favour or approval – usu + *in*

basket /'bahskit/ *n* **1a** a receptacle made of interwoven material (e g osiers, cane, wood, or metal) **b** any of various lightweight usu wood containers **c** the contents of a basket **2** sthg that resembles a basket, esp in shape or use **3** a net open at the bottom and suspended from a metal ring that constitutes the goal in basketball

'basket,ball /-,bawl/ *n* (the ball used in) an indoor court game between 2 teams of 5 players each who score by tossing a large ball through a raised basket

basketry /'bahskitri/ *n* (the art or craft of making) baskets or objects woven like baskets

bas-relief /,bas ri'leef, ,bah, ,bahs, '- -,-/ *n* sculptural relief in which the design projects very slightly from the surrounding surface

¹bass /bas/ *n*, *any of* numerous edible spiny-finned fishes

²bass /bays/ *adj* **1** deep or grave in tone **2a** of low pitch **b** of or having the range or part of a bass

³bass /bays/ *n* **1** the lowest part in 4-part harmony **2a** (a person with) the lowest adult male singing voice **b** a member of a family of instruments having the lowest range; *esp* a double bass or bass guitar

bass clef /bays/ *n* a clef placing the F below middle C on the fourth line of the staff

basset /'basit/, **'basset ,hound** *n* (any of) a breed of short-legged hunting dogs with very long ears

bassoon /bə'soohn/ *n* a double-reed woodwind instrument with a usual range 2 octaves lower than the oboe

¹**bastard** /'bahstəd, 'ba-/ n 1 an illegitimate child 2 sthg spurious, irregular, inferior, or of questionable origin 3a an offensive or disagreeable person b a fellow of a usu specified type – infml

²**bastard** adj 1 illegitimate 2 of an inferior or less typical type, stock, or form 3 lacking genuineness or authority; false – ~ize v

¹**baste** /bayst/ v to tack (fabric, etc)

²**baste** v to moisten (e g meat) at intervals with melted butter, dripping, etc during cooking, esp roasting

bastion /'basti·ən/ n 1 a projecting part of a fortification 2 a fortified area or position 3 sthg considered a stronghold

¹**bat** /bat/ n 1 a stout solid stick; a club 2 a sharp blow; a stroke 3 a (wooden) implement used for hitting the ball in cricket, baseball, table tennis, etc 4a a batsman b a turn at batting in cricket, baseball, etc — **off one's own bat** through one's own efforts, esp without being prompted

²**bat** v -tt- 1 to strike or hit (as if) with a bat 2 to strike a ball with a bat 3 to take one's turn at batting, esp in cricket – **batter** n

³**bat** n any of an order of nocturnal flying mammals with forelimbs modified to form wings

⁴**bat** v -tt- to blink, esp in surprise or emotion

batch /bach/ n 1 the quantity baked at 1 time 2 the quantity of material produced at 1 operation or for use at 1 time 3 a group of people or things; a lot

¹**bath** /bahth/ n pl **baths** /bahths; sense 3 often bahdhz/ 1 a washing or soaking (e g in water or steam) of all or part of the body 2a water used for bathing b a vessel for bathing in; esp one that is permanently fixed in a bathroom c (a vat, tank, etc holding) a specified type of liquid used for a special purpose (e g to keep samples at a constant temperature) 3a a building containing an apartment or a series of rooms designed for bathing b a swimming pool – usu pl with sing. meaning but sing. or pl in constr c a spa USE (3a&3c) usu pl with sing meaning

²**bath** v, Br 1 to give a bath to 2 to take a bath

'**bath ,chair** n, often cap B a usu hooded wheelchair

¹**bathe** /baydh/ v 1 to wash or soak in a liquid (e g water) 2 to moisten 3 to apply water or a liquid medicament to 4 to suffuse, esp with light 5 to take a bath 6 to swim (e g in the sea or a river) for pleasure

²**bathe** n, Br an act of bathing, esp in the sea

bathos /'baythos/ n a sudden descent from the sublime to the commonplace or absurd; an anticlimax

'**bath ,robe** /-,rohb/ n a loose usu absorbent robe worn before and after having a bath

'**bathroom** /-,roohm, -room/ n 1 a room containing a bath or shower and usu a washbasin and toilet 2 a toilet – chiefly euph

bathyscaphe /'bathiskayf, -skaf/ n a navigable submersible ship for deep-sea exploration

batman /'batman/ n a British officer's servant

baton /'bat(ə)n, 'ba,ton, bo'ton ʹ   / n 1 a cudgel, truncheon 2 a staff borne as a symbol of office 3 a wand with which a conductor directs a band or orchestra 4 a stick or hollow cylinder passed by each member of a relay team to the succeeding runner

bats /bats/ adj, chiefly Br batty – infml

'**batsman** /-mən/ n sby who bats or is batting, esp in cricket

battalion /bə'talyən/ n sing or pl in constr 1 a large body of organized troops 2 a military unit composed of a headquarters and 2 or more companies 3 a large group

¹**batten** /'bat(ə)n/ n 1 a thin narrow strip of squared timber 2a a thin strip of wood, plastic, etc inserted into a sail to keep it flat and taut b a slat used to secure the tarpaulins and hatch covers of a ship 3 a strip holding a row of floodlights 2 to seize on (an excuse, argument, etc)

²**batten** v 1 to provide or fasten (e g hatches) with battens – often + down 2 to make oneself selfishly dependent on 3 to seize on (an excuse, argument, etc)

¹**batter** /'batə/ v 1 to beat persistently or hard so as to bruise, shatter, or demolish 2 to wear or damage by hard usage or blows

²**batter** n a mixture that consists essentially of flour, egg, and milk or water and is thin enough to pour or drop from a spoon

'**battering ,ram** /'batəring/ n an ancient military siege engine consisting of a large wooden beam with a head of iron used for beating down walls

battery /'bat(ə)ri/ n 1a the act of battering b the unlawful application of any degree of force to a person without his/her consent 2 sing or pl in constr a tactical and administrative army artillery unit equivalent to an infantry company 3 one or more cells connected together to provide an electric current 4a a number of similar articles, items, or devices arranged, connected, or used together; a set, series b(1) a large number of small cages in which egg-laying hens are kept b(2) a series of cages or compartments for raising or fattening animals, esp poultry c an impressive or imposing group; an array

¹**battle** /'batl/ n 1 a general hostile encounter between armies, warships, aircraft, etc 2 a combat between 2 people 3 an extended contest, struggle, or controversy

²**battle** v battling /'batling, 'batl·ing/ 1 to engage in battle; fight against 2 to contend with full strength, craft, or resources; struggle 3 to force (e g one's way) by battling

'**battle-,axe** n a quarrelsome domineering woman

'battle ,cruiser *n* a large heavily-armed warship faster than a battleship

,battle 'royal *n, pl* battles royal, battle royals a violent struggle or heated dispute

'battle,ship /-,ship/ *n* the largest and most heavily armed and armoured type of warship

batty /'bati/ *adj* mentally unstable; crazy – infml

bauble /'bawbl/ *n* 1 a trinket or trifle 2 a jester's staff

baulk /baw(l)k/ *v or n, chiefly Br* (to) balk

bauxite /'bawksiet/ *n* the principal ore of aluminium

¹bawdy /'bawdi/ *adj* boisterously or humorously indecent

²bawdy *n* suggestive, coarse, or obscene language

bawl /bawl/ *v* 1 to yell, bellow 2 to cry, wail

¹bay /bay/ *n* 1 a horse with a bay-coloured body and black mane, tail, and points 2 a reddish brown colour

²bay *n* 1 any of several shrubs or trees resembling the laurel 2 an honorary garland or crown, esp of laurel, given for victory or excellence

³bay *n* 1 a division of a part of a building (e g the walls or roof) or of the whole building 2 a main division of a structure; *esp* a compartment in the fuselage of an aircraft

⁴bay *v* to bark with prolonged tones

⁵bay *n* the position of one unable to retreat and forced to face a foe or danger

⁶bay *n* (a land formation resembling) an inlet of a sea, lake, etc, usu smaller than a gulf

'bay ,leaf *n* the leaf of the European laurel used dried in cooking

¹bayonet /,baya'net, '---/ *n* a blade attached to the muzzle of a firearm used in hand-to-hand combat

²bayonet *v* to stab or drive (as if) with a bayonet

,bay 'window *n* a window or series of windows projecting outwards from the wall

bazaar /bə'zah/ *n* 1 an (Oriental) market consisting of rows of shops or stalls selling miscellaneous goods 2 a fair for the sale of miscellaneous articles, esp for charitable purposes

bazooka /bə'zoohkə/ *n* an individual infantry antitank rocket launcher

be /bi, bee; strong bee/ *v, pres* 1 *sing* am /əm, m; strong am/; 2 *sing* are /ə; strong ah/; 3 *sing* is /z, strong iz/; *pl* are; *pres subjunctive* be; *pres part* being; *past* 1&3 *sing* was /wəz; strong woz/; 2 *sing* were /wə; strong wuh/; *pl* were; *past subjunctive* were; *past part* been /bin, been/ **1a** to equal in meaning; have the same connotation as (e g Venus *is* the evening star) **b** to represent, symbolize **c** to have identity with **d** to belong to the class of **e** to occupy a specified position in space (e g Dundee *is* in Scotland) **f** to take place at a specified time; occur (e g that concert *was* yesterday) **g** to have a specified qualification, destination, origin, occupation, function or purpose,

cost or value, or standpoint **2** to have reality or actuality; exist **3** – used with the past participle of transitive verbs as a passive-voice auxiliary **4** – used as the auxiliary of the present participle in progressive tenses expressing continuous action or arrangement in advance **5** – used with *to* and an infinitive to express destiny, arrangement in advance, obligation or necessity, or possibility

¹beach /beech/ *n* a (gently sloping) seashore or lakeshore usu covered by sand or pebbles; *esp* the part of this between the high and low water marks

²beach *v* to run or drive ashore

'beach,comber /-,kohmə/ *n* one who searches along a shore for useful or salable flotsam and jetsam

'beach,head /-,hed/ *n* an area on a hostile shore occupied to secure further landing of troops and supplies

beacon /'beekən/ *n* 1 a signal fire commonly on a hill, tower, or pole; *also, Br* a high conspicuous hill suitable for or used in the past for such a fire 2a a signal mark used to guide shipping b a radio transmitter emitting signals for the guidance of aircraft 3 a source of light or inspiration

¹bead /beed/ *n* 1 a small ball (e g of wood or glass) pierced for threading on a string or wire 2 *pl* (a series of prayers and meditations made with) a rosary 3 a small ball-shaped body: e g 3a a drop of liquid b a small metal knob on a firearm used as a front sight 4 a projecting rim, band, or moulding

²bead *v* 1 to adorn or cover with beads or beading 2 to string together like beads 3 to form into a bead

beading /'beeding/ *n* 1 material adorned with or consisting of beads 2a a narrow moulding of rounded often semicircular cross section b a moulding that resembles a string of beads 3 a narrow openwork insertion or trimming (e g on lingerie)

beadle /'beedl/ *n* a minor parish official whose duties include ushering and preserving order at services

beady /'beedi/ *adj, esp of eyes* small, round, and shiny with interest or greed

beagle /'beegl/ *n* (any of) a breed of small short-legged smooth-coated hounds

beak /beek/ *n* 1 the bill of a bird; *also* any similar structure on another creature 2a the pouring spout of a vessel b a projection suggesting the beak of a bird 3 the human nose – infml 4 *chiefly Br* 4a a magistrate – slang b a schoolmaster – slang

beaker /'beekə/ *n* 1 a large drinking cup with a wide mouth; a mug 2 a cylindrical flat-bottomed vessel usu with a pouring lip that is used esp by chemists and pharmacists

,be-all and 'end-all *n* the chief factor; the essential element – often derog

¹**beam** /'beem/ *n* **1a** a long piece of heavy often squared timber suitable for use in construction **b** the bar of a balance from which scales hang **c** any of the principal horizontal supporting members of a building or across a ship **d** the width of a ship at its widest part **2a** a ray or shaft of radiation, esp light **b** (the course indicated by) a radio signal transmitted continuously in one direction as an aircraft navigation aid — **off (the) beam** wrong, irrelevant — **on the beam** proceeding or operating correctly

²**beam** *v* **1** to emit in beams or as a beam, esp of light **2** to aim (a broadcast) by directional aerials **3** to smile with joy

bean /been/ *n* **1a** (the often edible seed of) any of various erect or climbing leguminous plants **b** a bean pod used when immature as a vegetable **c** (a plant producing) any of various seeds or fruits that resemble beans or bean pods **2a** a valueless item **b** the smallest possible amount of money *USE* (2) *infml*

¹**bear** /bea/ *n pl* **bears**, (1) **bears** or *esp collectively* **bear 1** any of a family of large heavy mammals that have long shaggy hair and a short tail and feed largely on fruit and insects as well as on flesh **2** a surly, uncouth, or shambling person **3** one who sells securities or commodities in expectation of a fall in price

²**bear** *v* **bore** /baw/; **borne** *also* **born** /bawn/ **1a** to carry, transport – often in combination **b** to entertain mentally **c** to behave, conduct **d** to have or show as a feature **e** to give as testimony **2a** to give birth to **b** to produce as yield **c** to contain – often in combination **3a** to support the weight of **b** to accept the presence of; tolerate; *also* show patience *with* **c** to sustain, incur **d** to admit of; allow **4a** to become directed **b** to go or extend in a usu specified direction **5** to apply, have relevance **6** to support weight or strain — **bear fruit** to come to satisfying fruition or production — **bear in mind** to think of, esp as a warning; remember — **bear with** to show patience or indulgence towards

¹**beard** /biad/ *n* **1** the hair that grows on the lower part of a man's face, usu excluding the moustache **2** a hairy or bristly appendage or tuft (e g on a goat's chin)

²**beard** *v* to confront and oppose with boldness, resolution, and often effrontery; defy

bear down *v* **1** to overcome, overwhelm **2** to exert full strength and concentrated attention **3** *of a woman in childbirth* to exert concentrated downward pressure in an effort to expel the child from the womb **4** to come near threateningly – usu + *on* **5** to weigh heavily down *on*

bearer /'beara/ *n* **1** a porter **2** a plant bearing fruit **3** a pallbearer **4** one holding an order for payment, esp a bank note or cheque

¹**bear ,hug** *n* a rough tight embrace

bearing /'bearing/ *n* **1** the manner in which one bears or conducts oneself **2** the act, power, or time of bringing forth offspring or fruit **3a** an object, surface, or point that supports **b** a machine part in which another part turns or slides – often pl with sing. meaning **4a** the compass direction of one point (with respect to another) **b** a determination of position **c** *pl* comprehension of one's position, environment, or situation **d** a relation, connection, significance – usu + *on*

bear out *v* to confirm, substantiate

¹**bear ,skin** /-,skin/ *n* an article made of the skin of a bear; *esp* a tall black military hat worn by the Brigade of Guards

bear up *v* **1** to support, encourage **2** to summon up courage, resolution, or strength

beast /beest/ *n* **1a** an animal as distinguished from a plant **b** a 4-legged mammal as distinguished from human beings, lower vertebrates, and invertebrates **2** a contemptible person

¹**beastly** /'beestli/ *adj* **1** bestial **2** abominable, disagreeable – **-liness** *n*

²**beastly** *adv* very – *infml*

¹**beat** /beet/ *v* **beat**; **beaten** /'beet(ə)n/, **beat 1** to strike repeatedly: **1a** to hit repeatedly so as to inflict pain – often + *up* **b** to strike directly against (sthg) forcefully and repeatedly **c** to flap or thrash (at) vigorously **d** to strike at or range over (as if) in order to rouse game **e** to mix (esp food) by stirring; whip **f** to strike repeatedly in order to produce music or a signal **2a** to drive or force by blows **b** to pound into a powder, paste, or pulp **c** to make by repeated treading or driving over **d** to shape by beating; *also* to flatten thin by blows **3** to overcome, defeat; *also* to surpass **4** to leave dispirited, irresolute, or hopeless **5** to act ahead of, usu so as to forestall – chiefly in *beat someone to it* **6** to bewilder, baffle – *infml* **7** to glare or strike with oppressive intensity **8a** to pulsate, throb **b** to sound on being struck **9** to progress with much difficulty; *specif, of a sailing vessel* to make way at sea against the wind by a series of alternate tacks across the wind — **beat about the bush** to fail to come to the point in conversation by talking indirectly or evasively — **beat it** to hurry away; scram – *infml* — **beat one's brains out** to try intently to resolve sthg difficult by thinking

²**beat** *n* **1a** a single stroke or blow, esp in a series; *also* a pulsation, throb **b** a sound produced (as if) by beating **2a** (the rhythmic effect of) a metrical or rhythmic stress in poetry or music **b** the tempo indicated to a musical performer **3** an area or route regularly patrolled, esp by a policeman

³**beat** *adj* **1** of or being beatniks **2** exhausted – *infml*

⁴**beat** *n* a beatnik

beaten /'beet(ə)n/ *adj* **1** hammered into a desired shape **2** defeated

beater /'beetə/ n **1a** any of various hand-held implements for whisking or beating **b** a rotary blade attached to an electric mixer **c** a stick for beating a gong **2** one who strikes bushes or other cover to rouse game

beatific /ˌbee-ə'tifik/ adj **1** of, possessing, or imparting blessedness **2** having a blissful or benign appearance; saintly, angelic – ~**ally** adv

beating /'beeting/ n **1** injury or damage inflicted by striking with repeated blows **2** a throbbing **3** a defeat

beatnik /'beetnik/ n a person, esp in the 1950s and 1960s, who rejected the moral attitudes of established society (e g by unconventional behaviour and dress)

beau /boh/ n, pl **beaux, beaus** /bohz/ **1** a lover **2** archaic a dandy

Beaujolais /'bohzhəlay/ n a chiefly red table wine made in southern Burgundy in France

beauteous /'byoohti-əs, -tyəs/ adj, archaic beautiful – ~**ly** adv

beautician /byooh'tish(ə)n/ n sby who gives beauty treatments

beautiful /'byoohtif(ə)l/ adj **1** having qualities of beauty; exciting aesthetic pleasure or keenly delighting the senses **2** generally pleasing; excellent – ~**ly** adv

beautify /'byoohtifie/ v to make beautiful; embellish

beauty /'byoohti/ n **1** the qualities in a person or thing that give pleasure to the senses or pleasurably exalt the mind or spirit; loveliness **2** a beautiful person or thing; esp a beautiful woman **3** a brilliant, extreme, or conspicuous example or instance **4** a particularly advantageous or excellent quality

beauty spot n a beautiful scenic area

¹beaver /'beevə/ n pl **beavers, (1a) beavers** or esp collectively **beaver 1a** a large semiaquatic rodent mammal that has webbed hind feet, a broad flat tail, and builds dams and underwater lodges **b** the fur or pelt of the beaver **2** an energetic hard-working person

²beaver v to work energetically

because /bi'koz, bə-, -kəz/ conj **1** for the reason that; since **2** and the proof is that

beckon /'bekən/ v **1** to summon or signal, typically with a wave or nod **2** to appear inviting

become /bi'kum/ v **became** /bi'kaym/; **become 1** to come into existence **2** to come to be **3** to suit or be suitable for **4** to happen to – usu + of — **become of** to happen to

becoming /bi'kuming/ adj suitable, fitting; esp attractively suitable – ~**ly** adv

¹bed /bed/ n **1a** a piece of furniture on or in which one may lie and sleep and which usu includes bedstead, mattress, and bedding **b** a place of sexual relations; also lovemaking **c** a place for sleeping or resting **d** sleep; also a time for sleeping **2** a flat or level surface: e g **2a** (plants grown in) a plot of ground, esp in a garden, prepared for plants **b** the bottom of a body of water; also an area of sea or lake bottom supporting a heavy growth of a specified organism **3** a supporting surface or structure; esp the foundation that supports a road or railway **4** a stratum or layer of rock **5** a mass or heap resembling a bed; esp a heap on which sthg else is laid — **in bed** in the act of sexual intercourse

²bed v **-dd- 1a** to provide with a bed or bedding; settle in sleeping quarters **b** to go to bed with, usu for sexual intercourse **2a** to embed **b** to plant or arrange (garden plants, vegetable plants, etc) in beds – often + out **c** to base, establish **3** to lay flat or in a layer **4** to find or make sleeping accommodation **5** to form a layer

'bed,bug /-ˌbug/ n a wingless bloodsucking bug that sometimes infests beds

'bed,clothes /-ˌklohdhz/ n pl the covers (e g sheets and blankets) used on a bed

¹bedding /'beding/ n **1** bedclothes **2** a bottom layer; a foundation **3** material to provide a bed for livestock

²bedding adj, of a plant appropriate or adapted for culture in open-air beds

bedeck /bi'dek/ v to clothe with finery; deck out

bedevil /bi'devl/ v **1** to possess (as if) with a devil; bewitch **2** to change for the worse; spoil, frustrate **3** to torment maliciously; harass – ~**ment** n

'bed,fellow /-ˌfeloh/ n **1** one who shares a bed **2** a close associate; an ally

bedlam /'bedlam/ n a place, scene, or state of uproar and confusion

bedouin, beduin /'bedwin, 'bedooh-in/ n pl **bedouins, esp collectively bedouin** often cap a nomadic Arab of the Arabian, Syrian, or N African deserts

'bed,pan /-ˌpan/ n a shallow vessel used by a person in bed for urination or defecation

'bed,post /-ˌpohst/ n a usu turned or carved post of a bedstead

be'draggled adj **1** left wet and limp (as if) by rain **2** soiled and stained (as if) by trailing in mud

'bed,ridden /-ˌrid(ə)n/ adj confined (e g by illness) to bed

'bed,rock /-ˌrok/ n **1** the solid rock underlying less compacted surface materials (e g soil) **2** the basis of sthg

bedroom /-ˌroohm, -room/ n a room furnished with a bed and intended primarily for sleeping

ˌbedside 'manner n the manner with which a medical doctor deals with his/her patients

ˌbed-'sitter n, Br a single room serving as both bedroom and sitting room

'bed,spread /-ˌspred/ n a usu ornamental cloth cover for a bed

'bed,stead /-ˌsted/ n the framework of a bed

bee

bee /bee/ *n* **1** a social 4-winged insect often kept in hives for the honey that it produces **2** a gathering of people for a usu specified purpose — **bee in one's bonnet** an obsession about a specified subject or idea

beech /beech/ *n pl* **beeches, beech** (the wood of) any of a genus of hardwood deciduous trees with smooth grey bark and small edible triangular nuts

¹**beef** /beef/ *n pl* **beefs, (2a) beeves** /beevz/, **beef,** *NAm chiefly* **beefs 1** the flesh of a bullock, cow, or other adult domestic bovine animal **2** an ox, cow, or bull in a (nearly) full-grown state; *esp* a bullock or cow fattened for food **3** muscular flesh; brawn **4** a complaint – *infml*

²**beef** *v* **1** to add weight, strength, or power to – usu + *up* **2** to complain – *infml*

'**beef,eater** /-,eeta/ *n* a yeoman of the guard – not used technically

beefy /'beefi/ *adj* **1** full of beef **2** brawny, powerful

'**bee,line** /-,lien/ *n* a straight direct course

been /bin, been; *strong* been/ *past part of* **be**; *specif* paid a visit

beer /bia/ *n* **1** an alcoholic drink brewed from fermented malt flavoured with hops **2** a carbonated nonalcoholic or fermented slightly alcoholic drink flavoured with roots or other plant parts

beeswax /'beez,waks/ *n* a yellowish plastic substance secreted by bees that is used by them for constructing honeycombs and is used as a wood polish

beet /beet/ *n* any of various plants with a swollen root used as a vegetable, as a source of sugar, or for forage

¹**beetle** /'beetl/ *n* any of an order of insects that have 4 wings of which the front pair are modified into stiff coverings that protect the back pair at rest

²**beetle** *v* **beetling** /'beetling/ *Br* to move swiftly – *infml*

³**beetle** *n* a heavy wooden tool for hammering or ramming

beetroot /'beetrooht/ *n, pl* **beetroot, beetroots** *chiefly Br* a cultivated beet with a red edible root that is a common salad vegetable

befall /bi'fawl/ *v* **befell** /bi'fel/, **befallen** /bi-'fawln/ *v* to happen (to), esp as if by fate

befit /bi'fit/ *v* **-tt-** to be proper or becoming to – ~ **ting** *adj* – ~ **tingly** *adv*

¹**before** /bi'faw/ *adv* **1** so as to be in advance of others; ahead **2** earlier in time; previously

²**before** *prep* **1a** in front of **b** under the jurisdiction or consideration of **2** preceding in time; earlier than **3** in a higher or more important position than **4** under the onslaught of

³**before** *conj* **1** earlier than the time when **2** rather than

beforehand /bi'faw,hand/ *adv or adj* in anticipation **2** ahead of time

befriend /bi'frend/ *v* to become a friend of purposely; show kindness and understanding to

befuddle /bi'fudl/ *v* **befuddling** /bi'fudling/ to muddle or stupefy (as if) with drink

beg /beg/ *v* **-gg- 1** to ask for alms or charity **2** to ask earnestly (for); entreat **3a** to evade, sidestep **b** to assume as established or proved without justification **4** to ask permission – usu + an infinitive

beget /bi'get/ *v* **-tt-; begot** /bi'got/, *archaic* **begat** /bi'gat/; **begotten** /bi'gotn/, **begot 1** to procreate as the father; sire **2** to produce an effect; cause

¹**beggar** /'begə/ *n* **1** one who lives by asking for gifts **2** a pauper **3** a person; *esp* a fellow – *infml*

²**beggar** *v* **1** to reduce to beggary **2** to exceed the resources or abilities of

'**beggarly** /-li/ *adj* **1** marked by extreme poverty **2** contemptibly mean, petty, or paltry – **-liness** *n*

beggary /'begəri/ *n* poverty, penury

begin /bi'gin/ *v* **-nn-; began** /bi'gan/; **begun** /bi-'gun/ **1a** to do the first part of an action; start **b** to undergo initial steps **2a** to come into existence; arise **b** to have a starting point **3** to call into being; found **4** to come first in

beginning /bi'gining/ *n* **1** the point at which sthg begins; the start **2** the first part **3** the origin, source **4** a rudimentary stage or early period – usu *pl*

beg off *v* to ask to be released from sthg

begone /bi'gon/ *v* to go away; depart – usu in the infin or esp the imperative

begonia /bi'gohni-ə/ *n* any of a large genus of tropical plants that are widely cultivated as ornamental garden and house plants

begrudge /bi'gruj/ *v* **1** to give or concede reluctantly **2** to envy the pleasure or enjoyment of

beguile /bi'giel/ *v* **1** to deceive, hoodwink **2** to please or persuade by the use of deceit; charm – **-ling** *adj* – **-lingly** *adv* – ~ **ment** *n*

behalf /bi'hahf/ *n* representative interest – usu in *on someone's behalf* — **on behalf of,** *NAm* **in behalf of** in the interest of; as a representative of

behave /bi'hayv/ *v* **1** to conduct (oneself) in a specified way **2** to conduct (oneself) properly

behaviour, *NAm chiefly* **behavior** /bi'hayvyə/ *n* **1a** anything that an organism does involving action and response to stimulation **b** the response of an individual, group, or species to its environment **2** the way in which sthg (e g a machine) functions – ~ **al** *adj*

behead /bi'hed/ *v* to cut off the head of; decapitate

behest /bi'hest/ *n* an urgent prompting or insistent request

¹**behind** /bi'hiend/ *adv* **1a** in the place, situation, or time that is being or has been departed from **b** in, to, or towards the back **2a** in a secondary or inferior position **b** unpaid, overdue **c** slow

²**behind** *prep* **1a(1)** at or to the back or rear of **a(2)** remaining after (sthg who has departed) **b** obscured by **2** – used to indicate backwardness, delay, or deficiency (e g he's always a long way

behind the rest) **3a** in the background of **b** in a supporting position at the back of — **behind the times** old-fashioned, out-of-date

³**behind** *n* the buttocks – slang

behindhand /bi'hiend,hand/ *adj* **1** behind schedule; in arrears **2** lagging behind the times; backward

behold /bi'hohld/ *v* **beheld** /bi'held/ to see, observe – ~ **er** *n*

beholden /bi'hohldn/ *adj* under obligation for a favour or gift; indebted *to*

behove /bi'hohv/ *v* to be incumbent (on), or necessary, proper, or advantageous (for)

beige /bayzh, bayj/ *n* a yellowish grey colour

¹**being** /'bee·ing/ *n* **1a** the quality or state of having existence **b** conscious existence; life **2** the qualities that constitute an existent thing; the essence; *esp* personality **3** a living thing; *esp* a person

²**being** *adj* — **for the time being** for the moment

belabour /bi'laybə/ *v* **1** to work on or at to absurd lengths **2a** to beat soundly **b** to assail, attack

belated /bi'laytid/ *adj* delayed beyond the usual time – ~**ly** *adv*

¹**belay** /bi'lay/ *v* **1** to secure or make fast (e g a rope) by turns round a support, post, etc **2** to stop **3** to secure (by or to) a rope **4** to stop; leave off – in the *imper*

²**belay** *n* **1** a method or act of belaying a rope or person in mountain climbing **2** (sthg to which is attached) a mountain climber's belayed rope

belch /belch/ *v* **1** to expel gas suddenly from the stomach through the mouth **2** to erupt, explode, or detonate violently **3** to issue forth spasmodically; gush **4** to eject or emit violently

belfry /'belfri/ *n* (a room in which a bell is hung in) a bell tower, esp when associated with a church

belie /bi'lie/ *v* **belying 1** to give a false impression of **2** to show (sthg) to be false

belief /bi'leef/ *n* **1** trust or confidence in sby or sthg **2** sthg believed; *specif* a tenet or body of tenets held by a group **3** conviction of the truth of some statement or the reality of some being, thing, or phenomenon, esp when based on examination of evidence

believe /bi'leev/ *v* **1a** to have a firm religious faith **b** to accept sthg trustfully and on faith **2** to have a firm conviction as to the reality or goodness of sthg **3** to consider to be true or honest **4** to hold as an opinion; think – **believable** *adj* – **believably** *adv* – ~ **s** *n*

Be,lisha 'beacon /bə'leeshə/ *n* a flashing light in an amber globe mounted on a pole that marks a zebra crossing

belittle /bi'litl/ *v* **belittling** /bi'litling, -'litl·ing/ to undermine the value of

¹**bell** /bel/ *n* **1** a hollow metallic device that vibrates and gives forth a ringing sound when struck **2** *the* sound of a bell as a signal; *specif* one to mark the

start of the last lap in a running or cycling race or the start or end of a round in boxing, wrestling, etc **3a** a bell rung to tell the hour **b** a half-hour subdivision of a watch on shipboard indicated by the strokes of a bell **4** *sthg* bell-shaped: e g **4a** the corolla of any of many flowers **b** the flared end of a wind instrument

²**bell** *v* **1** to provide with a bell **2** to make or take the form of a bell; flare

³**bell** *v, of a stag or hound* to make a resonant bellowing or baying sound

'**bell-,bottoms** *n pl* trousers with wide flaring bottoms

'**bell,boy** /-,boy/ *n, chiefly NAm* a hotel page

belle /bel/ *n* a popular and attractive girl or woman

bellicose /'belikohs/ *adj* disposed to or fond of quarrels or wars – **-cosity** *n*

bel'ligerent /-rənt/ *adj* **1** engaged in war **2** aggressive, hostile

bellow /'beloh/ *v* **1** to make the loud deep hollow sound characteristic of a bull **2** to shout in a deep voice – **bellow** *n*

bellows /'belohz/ *n, pl* **bellows 1** a device that by alternate expansion and contraction supplies a current of air – often pl with sing. meaning **2** a pleated expandable part in a camera

¹**belly** /'beli/ *n* **1a** the undersurface of an animal's body **b** a cut of pork consisting of this part of the body **c** the stomach and associated organs **2** an internal cavity; the interior **3** a surface or object curved or rounded like a human belly

²**belly** *v* to swell, fill

¹·**belly,ache** /-,ayk/ *n* colic

²**bellyache** *v* to complain whiningly or peevishly; find fault – infml

'**belly ,button** *n* the navel – infml

'**bellyful** /-f(ə)l/ *n* an excessive amount – infml

'**belly-,land** *v* to land an aircraft on its undersurface without the use of landing gear – **belly landing** *n*

'**belly ,laugh** *n* a deep hearty laugh

belong /bi'long/ *v* **1** to be in a proper situation (e g according to ability or social qualification), position, or place **2** to be attached or bound *to* by birth, allegiance, dependency, or membership **3** to be an attribute, part, or function of a person or thing — **belong to** to be the property of

belongings /bi'longingz/ *n pl* (personal) possessions

beloved /bi'luvid, bi'luvd/ *n or adj pl* **beloved** (sby) dearly loved – usu in fml or religious contexts

¹**below** /bi'loh/ *adv* **1** in, on, or to a lower place, floor, or deck; *specif* on earth or in or to Hades or hell **2** under **3** under the surface of the water or earth

bel

²below *prep* **1** in or to a lower place than; under **2** inferior to (e g in rank) **3** not suitable to the rank of; beneath **4** covered by; underneath **5** downstream from **6** under

³below *n pl* **below** the thing or matter written or discussed lower on the same page or on a following page

¹belt /belt/ *n* **1** a strip of material worn round the waist or hips or over the shoulder for decoration or to hold sthg (e g clothing or a weapon) **2** an endless band of tough flexible material for transmitting motion and power or conveying materials **3** an area characterized by some distinctive feature (e g of culture, geology, or life forms); *esp* one suited to a specified crop — **below the belt** in an unfair way — **under one's belt** as part of one's experience; having been attained

²belt *v* **1a** to encircle or fasten with a belt **b** to strap on **2a** to beat (as if) with a belt; thrash **b** to strike, hit – *infml* **3** to sing in a forceful manner or style – usu + *out*; *infml* **4** to move or act in a vigorous or violent manner – *infml*

³belt *n* a jarring blow; a whack – *infml*

belt up *v, Br* shut up – *infml*

bemoan /bi'mohn/ *v* to lament

bench /bench/ *n* **1** a long usu backless seat (e g of wood or stone) for 2 or more people **2** *often cap* **2a** a judge's seat in court **b** the office of judge or magistrate **3** any of the long seats on which members sit in Parliament **4** a long worktable

'bench,mark /-,mahk/ *n* a point of reference from which measurements or judgments may be made

¹bend /bend/ *n* any of various knots for fastening one rope to another or to an object

²bend *v* **bent** /bent/ **1** to force into or out of a curve or angle **2** to make submissive; subdue **3a** to cause to turn from a course; deflect **b** to guide or turn towards sthg; direct **4** to direct strenuously or with interest; apply **5** to alter or modify to make more acceptable, esp to oneself **6** to move or curve out of a straight line or position **7** to incline the body, esp in submission; bow **8** to yield, compromise — **bend over backwards** to make extreme efforts

³bend *n* **1** bending or being bent **2** a curved part, esp of a road or stream **3** *pl but sing or pl in constr* pain or paralysis caused by the release of gas bubbles in body tissue occurring typically when a diver returns to the surface too quickly — **round the bend** mad, crazy — *infml*

¹beneath /bi'neeth/ *adv* **1** in or to a lower position; below **2** directly under; underneath

²beneath *prep* **1a** in or to a lower position than; below **b** directly under, esp so as to be close or touching **2** not suitable to; unworthy of **3** under the control, pressure, or influence of

benediction /,beni'diksh(ə)n/ *n* **1** the invocation of a blessing; *esp* the short blessing with which public worship is concluded **2** *often cap* a Roman Catholic or Anglo-Catholic devotion including the exposition of the Host and the blessing of the people

benefactor /'beni,faktə/, *fem* **benefactress** /-tris/ *n* one who gives aid; *esp* one who makes a gift or bequest to a person, institution, etc – **-tion** *n*

beneficent /bi'nefis(ə)nt/ *adj* doing or producing good; *esp* performing acts of kindness and charity – **-cence** *n* – ~**ly** *adv*

beneficial /,beni'fish(ə)l/ *adj* conferring benefits – ~**ly** *adv*

beneficiary /,beni'fish(ə)ri/ *n* one who benefits from sthg, esp the income or proceeds of a trust, will, or insurance policy

¹benefit /'benifit/ *n* **1a** an advantage **b** good, welfare **2a** financial help in time of need (e g sickness, old age, or unemployment) **b** a payment or service provided for under an annuity, pension scheme, or insurance policy **3** an entertainment, game, or social event to raise funds for a person or cause

²benefit *v* **-t-** (*NAm* **-t-**, **-tt-**) **1** to be useful or profitable to **2** to receive benefit

,benefit of the 'doubt *n* the assumption of innocence in the absence of complete proof of guilt

benevolent /bi'nevələnt/ *adj* having, showing, or motivated by a desire to do good – **-ence** *n*

benighted /bi'nietid/ *adj* intellectually, morally, or socially unenlightened – ~**ly** *adv*

benign /bi'nien/ *adj* **1** gracious **2** mild **3** *of a tumour* not malignant – ~**ly** *adv*

¹bent /bent/ *adj* **1** changed from an original straight or even condition by bending; curved **2** set *on* (doing something) **3** *Br* homosexual – *slang* **4** *Br* corrupt; crooked – *slang*

²bent *n* **1** a strong inclination or interest; a bias **2** a special ability or talent

benzene /'benzeen/ *n* an inflammable poisonous liquid hydrocarbon used in the manufacture of organic chemical compounds and as a solvent

bequeath /bi'kweeth, bi'kweedh/ *v* **1** to give or leave (sthg, esp personal property) by will **2** to transmit; hand down – **bequest** *n*

berate /bi'rayt/ *v* to scold or condemn vehemently

bereave /bi'reev/ *vt* **bereaved**, **bereft** /bi'reft/ to rob or deprive of sby or sthg held dear, esp through death – ~**ment** *n*

beret /'beray/ *n* a cap with a tight headband, a soft full flat top, and no peak

berk /buhk/ *n, Br* a stupid person; a fool – *slang*

berry /'beri/ *n* **1** a small, pulpy, and usu edible fruit (e g a strawberry or raspberry) **2** an egg of a fish or lobster

berserk /bə'zuhk, buh-/ *adj* frenzied, esp with anger; crazed – usu in **go berserk**

¹**berth** /buhth/ *n* **1** safe distance for manoeuvring maintained between a ship and another object **2** an allotted place for a ship when at anchor or at a wharf **3** a place for sleeping (e g a bunk), esp on a ship or train **4** a job, post – *infml* — **give a wide berth to** to remain at a safe distance from; avoid

²**berth** *v* to dock

beryl /'beril/ *n* a mineral that is a silicate of beryllium and aluminium, occurs as green, yellow, pink, or white crystals, and is used as a gemstone

beseech /bi'seech/ *v* **besought** /-sawt/, **beseeched** **1** to beg for urgently or anxiously **2** to implore

besetting /bi'seting/ *adj* constantly causing temptation or difficulty; continuously present

beside /bi'sied/ *prep* **1a** by the side of **b** in comparison with **c** on a par with **2** besides — **beside oneself** in a state of extreme agitation or excitement

¹**be·sides** *adv* **1** as an additional factor or circumstance **2** moreover, furthermore

²**besides** *prep* **1** other than; unless we are to mention **2** as an additional circumstance to

besiege /bi'seej/ *v* **1** to surround with armed forces **2** to press with questions, requests, etc; importune

besmirch /bi'smuhch/ *v* to sully, soil

besotted /bi'sotid/ *adj* **1** made dull or foolish, esp by infatuation **2** drunk, intoxicated

bespeak /bi'speek/ *v* **bespoke** /-'spohk/; **bespoken** /-'spohkən/ **1** to hire, engage, or claim beforehand **2** to indicate, signify *USE fml*

bespoke /bi'spohk/ *adj*, *Br* made-to-measure

¹**best** /best/ *adj*, *superlative of* GOOD **1** excelling all others (e g in ability, quality, integrity, or usefulness) **2** most productive of good **3** most, largest **4** reserved for special occasions

²**best** *adv*, *superlative of* WELL **1** in the best manner; to the best extent or degree **2** better — **as best in** the best way

³**best** *n, pl* **best 1** the best state or part **2** sby or sthg that is best **3** the greatest degree of good or excellence **4** one's maximum effort **5** best clothes **6** a winning majority — **at best** even under the most favourable circumstances; seen in the best light — **make the best of** to cope with an unfavourable situation in the best and most optimistic manner possible

bestial /'besti·əl/ *adj* marked by brutal or inhuman instincts or desires; *specif* sexually depraved – ∼ly *adv* – ∼ity *n*

bestir /bi'stuh/ *v* to stir up; rouse to action

‚**best 'man** *n* the principal attendant of a bridegroom at a wedding

bestow /bi'stoh/ *v* to present as a gift – usu + *on* or *upon* – ∼al *n*

bestrew /bi'strooh/ *v* **bestrewed**; **bestrewed**, **bestrewn** /-'stroohn/ to lie scattered over

bestride /bi'stried/ *v* **bestrode** /-'strohd/; **bestridden** /-'stridən/ **1** to straddle **2** to tower over; dominate

‚**best-'seller** *n* **1** sthg which has sold in very large numbers **2** an author or performer whose works sell in very large numbers

¹**bet** /bet/ *n* **1a** the act of risking a sum of money or other stake on the forecast outcome of a future event (e g a race or contest), esp in competition with a second party **b** a stake so risked **2** an opinion, belief **3** a plan of action; course – usu in *best bet*; *infml*

²**bet** *v* **bet** *also* **betted; -tt- 1** to stake as a bet – usu + *on* or *against* **2** to make a bet with (sby) **3** to be convinced that – *infml* — **bet one's bottom dollar** to be virtually certain – *infml* — **you bet** you may be sure; certainly — *slang*

beta /'beetə/ *n, NAm usu* /'baytə/ *n* **1a** the 2nd letter of the Greek alphabet **b** a second-class mark or grade **2** — used to designate the second brightest star of a constellation

'**beta ‚particle** *n* an electron or positron ejected from the nucleus of an atom during radioactive decay

'**betel ‚nut** *n* the astringent seed of an Asiatic palm

bête noire /‚bet 'nwah/ *n, pl* **bêtes noires** /∼/ a person or thing strongly detested

betide /bi'tied/ *v* to happen, esp as if by fate *USE fml* or *poetic*

betray /bi'tray/ *v* **1** to deceive, lead astray **2** to deliver to an enemy by treachery **3** to disappoint the hopes, expectation, or confidence of **4a** to be a sign of (sthg one would like to hide) **b** to disclose, deliberately or unintentionally, in violation of confidence – ∼er *n* – ∼al *n*

betroth /bi'trohth, -'trohdh/ *v* **betrothed** /-dhd/, **betrothing** /-dhing/ to promise to marry or give in marriage – ∼al *n*

¹**better** /'betə/ *adj, comparative of* GOOD *or of* WELL **1** improved in health; recovered **2** of greater quality, ability, integrity, usefulness, etc

²**better** *adv, comparative of* WELL **1** in a better manner; to a better extent or degree **2a** to a higher or greater degree **b** more wisely or usefully

³**better** *n, pl* **better, (1b) betters 1a** sthg better **b** one's superior, esp in merit or rank – usu pl **2** the advantage, victory — **for better or for worse** whatever the outcome

⁴**better** *v* **1** to make better: e g **1a** to make more tolerable or acceptable **b** to make more complete or perfect **2** to surpass in excellence; excel – ∼ment *n*

¹**between** /bi'tween/ *prep* **1a** through the common action of; jointly engaging **b** in shares to each of **2a** in or into the time, space, or interval that separates **b** in intermediate relation to **3a** from

bet

one to the other of **b** serving to connect or separate **4** in point of comparison of **5** taking together the total effect of; what with — **between you and me** in confidence

²between *adv* in or into an intermediate space or interval

be,twixt and be'tween *adv or adj* in a midway position; neither one thing nor the other

¹bevel /'bevl/ *n* the angle or slant that one surface or line makes with another when they are not at right angles

²bevel *v* **-ll-** (*NAm* **-l-, -ll-**), /'bevl-ing/ **1** to cut or shape to a bevel **2** to incline, slant

beverage /'bev(ə)rij/ *n* a liquid for drinking; *esp* one that is not water

bevy /'bevi/ *n* a group or collection, esp of girls

beware /bi'weə/ *v* to be wary (of) – usu in imper and infin

bewilder /bi'wildə/ *v* to perplex or confuse – ~**ment** *n*

bewitch /bi'wich/ *v* **1** to influence or affect by witchcraft **2** to enchant

¹beyond /bee'ond/ *adv* **1** on or to the farther side; farther **2** as an additional amount; besides

²beyond *prep* **1** on or to the farther side of; at a greater distance than **2a** out of the reach or sphere of **b** in a degree or amount surpassing **c** out of the comprehension of **3** besides **4** later than; past

³beyond *n* **1** sthg that lies beyond **2** sthg that lies outside the scope of ordinary experience; *specif* the hereafter

¹bias /'bie·əs/ *n* **1** a line diagonal to the grain of a fabric, often used in the cutting of garments for smoother fit – usu + *the* **2a** a personal prejudice **b** a bent, tendency **3** (the property of shape or weight causing) the tendency in bowls for a bowl to take a curved path when rolled — **on the bias** askew, obliquely

²bias *v* **1** to give a prejudiced outlook to **2** to influence unfairly

bib /bib/ *n* **1** a covering (e g of cloth or plastic) placed over a child's front to protect his/her clothes **2** a small rectangular section of a garment (e g an apron or dungarees) extending above the waist

bible /'biebl/ *n* **1a** *cap* the sacred book of Christians comprising the Old Testament and the New Testament **b** any book containing the sacred writings of a religion **2** an authoritative book – **-lical** *adj*

bibliography /bibli'ogrəfi/ *n* a list of writings relating to a particular topic, written by a particular author, referred to in a text or consulted by the author in its production, etc – **-pher** *n*

bibulous /'bibyooləs/ *adj* prone to alcoholic over-indulgence

bicarbonate /bie'kahbənət/ *n* an acid carbonate; *esp* sodium bicarbonate used in baking or as a treatment for indigestion

bicentenary /,biesen'teenəri, -'te-/ *n or adj* (the celebration) of a 200th anniversary

biceps /'biseps/ *n* the large muscle at the front of the upper arm that bends the arm at the elbow when it contracts

bicker /'bikə/ *v* to engage in petulant or petty argument

bicycle /'biesikl/ *v or n* **bicycling** /'biesikling/ (to ride) a 2 wheeled pedal-driven vehicle with handlebars and a saddle – **bicyclist** *n*

¹bid /bid/ *v* **bade** /bad, bed/, **bid**, (3) **bid; bidden** /'bidn/, **bid** *also* **bade; -dd-** **1a** to issue an order to; tell **b** to invite to come **2** to give expression to **3a** to offer (a price) for payment or acceptance (e g at an auction) **b** to make a bid of or in (a suit at cards) – ~**der** *n* — **bid fair** to seem likely; show promise

²bid *n* **1a** the act of one who bids **b** a statement of what one will give or take for sthg; *esp* an offer of a price **2** an opportunity to bid **3** (an announcement of) the amount of tricks to be won, suit to be played in, etc in a card game **4** an attempt to win or achieve sthg

biddable /'bidəbl/ *adj* **1** easily led or controlled; docile **2** capable of being reasonably bid

bidding /'biding/ *n* order, command

bide /bied/ *v* **bode** /bohd/, **bided** /'biedid/; **bided** *archaic or dial* to remain awhile; stay — **bide one's time** to wait until the appropriate time comes to initiate action or to proceed

bidet /'beeday/ *n* a bathroom fixture used esp for bathing the external genitals and the anus

biennial /bie'eni·əl/ *adj* **1** occurring every 2 years **2** *of a plant* fruiting and dying during the second year of growth – ~**ly** *adv*

bier /biə/ *n* a stand on which a corpse or coffin is placed; *also* a coffin together with its stand

biff /bif/ *n* a whack, blow – *infml*

bi'focals *n pl* glasses with the upper and lower parts of the lenses ground to different prescriptions – **bifocal** *adj*

¹big /big/ *adj* **1** of great force **2a** large in bulk or extent, number or amount **b** large-scale **c** important in influence, standing, or wealth **3a** advanced in pregnancy **b** full to bursting; swelling **4** *of the voice* loud and resonant **5** older, grown-up **6** of great importance or significance **7a** pretentious, boastful **b** magnanimous, generous **8** popular – *infml* – ~**ness** *n*

²big *adv* **1a** outstandingly **b** on a grand scale **2** pretentiously *USE infml*

bigamy /'bigəmi/ *n* the crime of going through a marriage ceremony with one person while legally married to another – **-mist** *n* – **-mous** *adj* – **-mously** *adv*

,big 'bang ,theory *n* a theory in cosmology: the universe originated from the explosion of a single mass of material so that the components are still flying apart

,**big 'end** *n* the end of an engine's connecting rod nearest the crankpin

,**big 'game** *n* large animals hunted or fished for sport

'**big head** /-,hed/ *n* a conceited person – infml

'**big head** *n* an exaggerated opinion of one's importance – infml

bigot /'bigət/ *n* one who is obstinately or intolerantly devoted to his/her own religion, opinion, etc – ~**ed** *adj* – ~**edly** *adv* – ~**ry** *n*

,**big 'top** *n* the main tent of a circus

'**big,wig** /-,wig/ *n* an important person – infml

bike /biek/ *v or n* (to ride) **1** a bicycle **2** a motorcycle

bikini /bi'keeni/ *n* a woman's brief 2-piece garment resembling bra and pants worn for swimming or sunbathing

bilateral /bie'lat(ə)rəl/ *adj* **1** having 2 sides **2** bipartite – ~**ly** *adv* /biel/ *n* **1** a yellow or greenish fluid secreted by the liver into the intestines to aid the digestion of fats **2** inclination to anger – **bilious** *adj* – **biliousness** *n*

bilge /bilj/ *n* **1** the (space inside the) lowest usu rounded part of a ship's hull between the keel and the vertical sides **2** stale or worthless remarks or ideas – infml

bilingual /bie'ling-gwəl/ *adj* of, containing, using or expressed in 2 languages

¹**bill** /bil/ *n* **1** (a mouthpart resembling) the jaws of a bird together with variously shaped and coloured horny coverings **2** a projection of land like a beak

²**bill** *v* to caress affectionately – chiefly in *bill and coo*

³**bill** *n* **1** a long staff with a hook-shaped blade used as a weapon up to the 18th c **2** a billhook

⁴**bill** *n* **1** a draft of a law presented to a legislature **2** (an itemized account of) charges due for goods or services **3a** a written or printed notice advertising an event of interest to the public (e g a theatrical entertainment) **b** an item (e g a film or play) in a programme entertainment

⁵**bill** *v* **1** to submit a bill of charges to **2a** to advertise, esp by posters or placards **b** to arrange for the presentation of as part of a programme

'**bill,board** /-,bawd/ *n* an advertising hoarding

¹**billet** /'bilit/ *n* **1a** an official order directing that a member of a military force be provided with board and lodging (e g in a private home) **b** quarters assigned (as if) by a billet **2** a position, job

²**billet** *n* **1** a small thick piece of wood (e g for firewood) **2** a usu small bar of iron, steel, etc

billiards /'bilyədz/ *n pl but sing in constr* any of several games played on an oblong table by driving small balls against one another or into pockets with a cue – **billiard** *adj*

billion /'bilyən/ *n* **1** *Br* a million millions (10¹²) **2** *chiefly NAm* a thousand millions (10⁹) **3** an indefinitely large number – often pl with sing. meaning – ~**th** *adj, n, pron, adv*

¹**billow** /'biloh/ *n* **1** a great wave, esp in the open sea **2** a rolling swirling mass (e g of flame or smoke) – ~**y** *adj*

²**billow** *v* to (cause to) rise, roll, bulge, or swell out (as if) in billows

billy ,goat *n* a male goat – infml

bimonthly /,bie'munthli/ *adj or adv* (occurring) every 2 months or twice a month

bin /bin/ *n* **1** a container used for storage (e g of flour, grain, bread, or coal) **2** a partitioned case or stand for storing and aging bottles of wine **3** *Br* a wastepaper basket, dustbin, or similar container for rubbish

binary /'bienəri/ *adj* **1** consisting of or marked by 2 things or parts **2** of, being, or belonging to a system of numbers having 2 as its base

¹**bind** /biend/ *v* **bound** /bownd/ **1a** to make secure by tying (e g with cord) or tying together **b** to put under a (legal) obligation **2** to wrap round with sthg (e g cloth) so as to enclose or cover **3** to encircle, gird **4** to cause to stick together **5** to cause to be attached (e g by gratitude or affection) **6** to form a cohesive mass

²**bind** *n* a nuisance, bore – infml — **in a bind** *chiefly NAm* in trouble or difficulty — infml

binder /'biendə/ *n* **1** a person who binds books **2** a usu detachable cover (e g for holding sheets of paper) **3** sthg (e g tar or cement) that produces or promotes cohesion in loosely assembled substances

¹**binding** /'biending/ *n* a material or device used to bind: e g **a** a covering that fastens the leaves of a book **b** a narrow strip of fabric used to finish raw edges

²**binding** *adj* imposing an obligation

bind over *v* to impose a specific legal obligation on

'**bind,weed** /-,weed/ *n* any of various twining plants with usu large showy trumpet-shaped flowers

binge /binj/ *n* an unrestrained indulgence in sthg, esp drink – infml

¹**bingo** /'bing-goh/ *interj* **1** – used to express the suddenness or unexpectedness of an event **2** – used as an exclamation to show that one has won a game of bingo

²**bingo** *n* a game of chance played with cards having numbered squares corresponding to numbers drawn at random and won by covering or marking off all or a predetermined number of such squares

binnacle /'binəkl/ *n* a case, stand, etc containing a ship's compass

binocular /bi'nokyoolə/ *adj* of, using, or adapted to the use of both eyes

bin

bi'noculars *n pl, pl* **binoculars** field glasses or opera glasses

biochemistry /ˌbie-oh'keməstri/ *n* chemistry that deals with the chemical compounds and processes occurring in organisms

biodegradable /ˌbie-ohdee'graydəbl/ *adj* capable of being broken down, esp into simpler harmless products, by the action of living beings (e g microorganisms)

biography /bie'ografi/ *n* **1** a usu written account of a person's life **2** biographical writing as a literary genre – **-phic, -phical** *adj* – **-phically** *adv* – **-pher** *n*

biology /bie'oləji/ *n* a science that deals with the structure, growth, development, distribution, and life processes of organisms – **-gical** *adj* – **-gically** *adv* – **-gist** *n*

bionic /bie'onik/ *adj* having exceptional abilities or powers – *infml*

biosphere /'bie·ə‚sfiə/ *n* the part of the world in which life exists

bipartisan /ˌbie'pahtizn/ *adj* of or involving 2 parties

bipartite /ˌbie'pahtiet/ *adj* **1** being in 2 parts *of a treaty, contract, etc between 2 parties* **2a** having 2 correspondent parts, one for each party **b** affecting both parties in the same way

biped /'bieped/ *n* a 2-footed animal

biplane /'bieplayn/ *n* an aeroplane with 2 pairs of wings placed one above and usu slightly forward of the other

¹**birch** /buhch/ *n* **1** (the hard pale close-grained wood of) any of a genus of deciduous usu short-lived trees or shrubs typically having a layered outer bark that peels readily **2** a birch rod or bundle of twigs for flogging

²**birch** *v* to whip (as if) with a birch

bird /buhd/ *n* **1** any of a class of warm-blooded vertebrates with the body more or less completely covered with feathers and the forelimbs modified as wings **2a** a (peculiar) fellow – chiefly infml **b** chiefly *Br* a girl – infml **3** a hissing or jeering expressive of disapproval or derision – chiefly in *give somebody the bird/get the bird* infml **4** *Br* a spell of imprisonment – slang — **for the birds** trivial, worthless – infml

birdie /'buhdi/ *n* **1** a (little) bird – used esp by or to children **2** a golf score of 1 stroke less than par on a hole

bird's-eye 'view *n* **1** an aerial view **2** a brief and general summary

Biro /'bieroh/ *trademark* – used for a ballpoint pen

birth /buhth/ *n* **1** the act or process of bringing forth young from within the body **2** being born, esp at a particular time or place **3** (noble) lineage or extraction **4** a beginning, start

'**birth con‚trol** *n* contraception

birthday /'buhthday, -di/ *n* **1a** the day of a person's birth **b** a day of origin **2** an anniversary of a birth

'**birth‚right** /-‚riet/ *n* sthg (e g a privilege or possession) to which a person is entitled by birth

biscuit /'biskit/ *n* **1** earthenware or porcelain after the first firing and before glazing **2** a light yellowish brown colour **3** *Br* any of several variously-shaped small usu unleavened thin dry crisp bakery products that may be sweet or savoury **4** *NAm* a soft cake or bread (e g a scone) made without yeast

bisect /ˌbie'sekt/ *v* **1** to divide into 2 (equal) parts **2** to cross, intersect – **~ion** *n*

bisexual /bie'seksyoo(ə)l, -sh(ə)l/ *adj* **1** possessing characteristics of both sexes **2** sexually attracted to both sexes – **~ity** *n* – **~ly** *adv*

bishop /'bishəp/ *n* **1** a clergyman ranking above a priest, having authority to ordain and confirm, and typically governing a diocese **2** either of 2 chess pieces of each colour allowed to move diagonally across any number of consecutive unoccupied squares

bismuth /'bizməth/ *n* a heavy metallic element

bison /'biesn/ *n, pl* **bison 1** a large shaggy-maned European bovine mammal that is now nearly extinct **2** the American buffalo

bistro /'beestroh/ *n pl* **bistros** a small bar, restaurant, or tavern

¹**bit** /bit/ *n* **1** a bar of metal or occas rubber attached to the bridle and inserted in the mouth of a horse **2** the biting, boring, or cutting edge or part of a tool

²**bit** *n* **1a** a small piece or quantity of anything (e g food) **b(1)** a usu specified small coin **b(2)** a money unit worth $1/8$ of a US dollar e g part, section **2** sthg small or unimportant of its kind: e g **2a** a brief period; a while **b** an indefinite usu small degree, extent, or amount — **a bit 1** somewhat, rather – infml **2** the smallest or an insignificant amount or degree – infml — **a bit much** a little more than one wants to endure — **a bit of all right** *Br* sby or sthg very pleasing; *esp* a sexually attractive person – infml — **bit by bit** little by little — **bit on the side** (a person with whom one has) occasional sexual intercourse usu outside marriage — **to bits** to pieces

³**bit** *n* a unit of computer information equivalent to the result of a choice between 2 alternatives (e g *on* or *off*)

¹**bitch** /bich/ *n* **1** the female of the dog or similar flesh-eating animals **2** a malicious, spiteful, and domineering woman

²**bitch** *v* to complain – infml

bitchy /'bichi/ *adj* characterized by malicious, spiteful, or arrogant behaviour – **bitchily** *adv* – **bitchiness** *n*

¹**bite** /biet/ *v* **bit** /bit/; **bitten** /'bit(ə)n/ *also* **bit 1a** to seize or sever with teeth or jaws **b** to sting with a fang or other specialized part **2** *of a weapon or tool*

bla

to cut, pierce **3** to cause sharp pain or stinging discomfort **4** to take strong hold of; grip **5** *of fish* to take a bait — **bite off more than one can chew** to undertake more than one can perform — **bite the dust 1** to fall dead, esp in battle **2** to be finished or defeated

²**bite** *n* **1** the amount of food taken with 1 bite; *also* a snack **2** a wound made by biting **3** the hold or grip by which friction is created or purchase is obtained **4** a sharp incisive quality or effect

biting /'bieting/ *adj* sharp, cutting – ~**ly** *adv*

¹**bitter** /'bitə/ *adj* **1a** being or inducing an acrid, astringent, or disagreeable taste similar to that of quinine that is one of the 4 basic taste sensations **b** distressing, galling **2a** intense, severe **b** very cold **c** cynical; full of ill-will – ~**ly** *adv* – ~**ness** *n*

²**bitter** *n* **1** *pl but sing or pl in constr* a usu alcoholic solution of bitter and often aromatic plant products used esp in preparing mixed drinks or as a mild tonic **2** *Br* a very dry beer heavily flavoured with hops

bittern /'bitən/ *n* any of various small or medium-sized herons with a characteristic booming cry

bitty /'biti/ *adj* scrappy, disjointed – **-tiness** *n*

bitumen /'bityoomin/ *n* any of various mixtures of hydrocarbons (e g tar) that occur naturally or as residues after heating petroleum, coal, etc – **-minous** *adj*

bivalent /bie'vaylənt/ *adj* having a valency of 2

bivalve /'bie,valv/ *n or adj* (a mollusc) having a shell composed of 2 valves

biweekly /,bie'weekli/ *n, adj, or adv* (a publication) issued or occurring **a** every 2 weeks **b** twice a week

bizarre /bi'zah/ *adj* **1** odd, extravagant, eccentric **2** involving sensational contrasts or incongruities – ~**ly** *adv*

blab /blab/ *v* **-bb-** to talk indiscreetly or thoughtlessly

blabber /'blabə/ *v* **1** to babble **2** to say indiscreetly

¹**black** /blak/ *adj* **1a** of the colour black **b** very dark in colour **2** *often cap* **2a** having dark pigmentation; *esp* of the Negro race **b** of black people or culture **3** having or reflecting little or no light **4** *of coffee* served without milk or cream **5** thoroughly sinister or evil **6** very dismal or disastrous **7** characterized by grim, distorted, or grotesque humour **8** bought, sold, or operating illegally and esp in violation of official economic regulations – ~**ness** *n*

²**black** *n* **1** the colour of least lightness that belongs to objects that neither reflect nor transmit light **2** sthg black; *esp* black clothing **3** one who belongs wholly or partly to a dark-skinned race; *esp* a Negro **4** (the player playing) the dark-coloured pieces in a board game (e g chess) for 2 players **5** the condition of being financially in credit or solvent or of making a profit – usu + *in the*

³**black** *v chiefly Br* to declare (e g a business or industry) subject to boycott by trade-union members

,**black-and-'white** *adj* **1** reproducing visual images in tones of grey rather than in colours **2** evaluating things as either all good or all bad

,**black and 'white** *n* writing, print

'**black,ball** /-,bawl/ *v* **1** to vote against (esp a candidate for membership of a club) **2** to ostracize

'**black ,belt** *n* (one who has) a rating of expert in judo, karate, etc

'**black,berry** /-b(ə)ri/ *n* (the usu black seedy edible fruit of) any of various prickly shrubs of the rose family

'**black,bird** /-,buhd/ *n* a common Old World thrush the male of which is black with an orange beak and eye rim

'**black,board** /-,bawd/ *n* a hard smooth usu dark surface for writing or drawing on with chalk

blackcurrant /'blak,kurənt, ,-'--/ *n* (the small black edible fruit of) a widely cultivated European currant

,**black 'death** *n, often cap B&D* a form of plague epidemic in Europe and Asia in the 14th c

blacken /'blakən/ *v* **1** to make dark or black **2** to defame, sully

blackguard /'blagəd, -,gahd/ *n* a coarse or unscrupulous person; a scoundrel – now often humor

'**black,head** /-,hed/ *n* a small usu dark-coloured oily plug blocking the duct of a sebaceous gland, esp on the face

,**black 'hole** *n* a celestial body, prob formed from a collapsed star, with a very high density and an intense gravitational field, from which no radiation can escape

,**black 'ice** *n, Br* transparent slippery ice (e g on a road)

blacking /'blaking/ *n* a paste, polish, etc applied to an object to make it black

'**black,leg** /-,leg/ *n, chiefly Br* a worker hostile to trade unionism or acting in opposition to union policies

'**black,list** /-,list/ *n, v* (to put on) a list of people or organizations who are disapproved of or are to be punished or boycotted

,**black 'magic** *n* magic performed with the aim of harming or killing sby or sthg

'**black,mail** /-,mayl/ *v* to extort or obtain money by threats, esp of exposure of secrets that would lead to loss of reputation, prosecution, etc – **blackmail** *n* – ~**er** *n*

Black Maria /,blak mə'rie-ə/ *n* an enclosed motor vehicle used by police to carry prisoners

,**black 'market** *n* illicit trade in commodities or currencies in violation of official regulations (e g rationing) – ~**eer** *n* '**black,out** /-,owt/ *n* **1** a period of darkness enforced as a precaution against air raids, or caused by a failure of electrical power **2** a temporary loss or dulling of vision, consciousness, or memory **3** a usu temporary loss of radio signal (e g during the reentry of a spacecraft)

black out *v* **1** to faint **2** to suppress, esp by censorship

,**black 'pudding** *n, chiefly Br* a very dark sausage made from suet and a large proportion of pig's blood

,**black 'sheep** *n* a disreputable member of a respectable group, family, etc

'**Black,shirt** /-,shuht/ *n* a member of a fascist organization having a black shirt as part of its uniform

'**black,smith** /-,smith/ *n* one who works iron, esp at a forge

'**black ,spot** *n, Br* a stretch of road on which accidents occur frequently

'**black,thorn** /-,thawn/ *n* a European spiny shrub of the rose family with hard wood and small white flowers

,**black-'tie** *adj* characterized by or requiring the wearing of semiformal evening dress by men including a dinner jacket and a black bow tie

bladder /'bladə/ *n* **1a** a membranous sac in animals that serves as the receptacle of a liquid or contains gas; *esp* the urinary bladder **2** a bag filled with a liquid or gas (e g the air-filled rubber one inside a football)

blade /blayd/ *n* **1** (the flat expanded part, as distinguished from the stalk, of) a leaf, esp of a grass, cereal, etc **2a** the broad flattened part of an oar, paddle, bat, etc **b** an arm of a screw propeller, electric fan, steam turbine, etc **c** the broad flat or concave part of a machine (e g a bulldozer) that comes into contact with material to be moved **3a** the cutting part of a knife, razor, etc **b** the runner of an ice skate **4** *archaic* a dashing lively man – now usu humor

'**blame** /blaym/ *v* **1** to find fault with; hold responsible for **2** to place responsibility for (sthg reprehensible) – + *on*

²**blame** *n* **1** an expression of disapproval or reproach **2** responsibility for sthg reprehensible – ~**worthy** *adj* – ~**worthiness** *n*

blanch /blahnch/ *v* **1** to take the colour out of **2** to scald or parboil (e g almonds or food for freezing) in water or steam

blancmange /blə'monj, -'monzh/ *n* a usu sweetened and flavoured dessert made from cornflour and milk

bland /bland/ *adj* **1a** smooth, soothing **b** unperturbed **2a** not irritating or stimulating; mild **b** dull, insipid – ~**ly** *adv* – ~**ness** *n*

'**blank** /blangk/ *adj* **1a** dazed; taken aback **b** expressionless **2a** lacking interest, variety, or change **b** free from writing; not filled in **3** absolute, unqualified **4** having a plain or unbroken surface where an opening is usual – ~**ly** *adv* – ~**ness** *n*

²**blank** *n* **1** an empty space **2a** a void **b** a vacant or uneventful period **3** a piece of material prepared to be made into sthg (e g a key or coin) by a further operation **4** a cartridge loaded with powder but no bullet

³**blank** *v* **1** to make blank – usu + *out* **2** to block – usu + *off*

'**blanket** /'blangkit/ *n* **1** a large thick usu rectangular piece of fabric (e g woven from wool or acrylic yarn) used esp as a bed covering or a similar piece of fabric used as a body covering (e g for a horse) **2** a thick covering or layer

²**blanket** *v* to cover (as if) with a blanket

³**blanket** *adj* applicable in all instances or to all members of a group or class

,**blank 'verse** *n* unrhymed verse, esp in iambic pentameters

blare /bleə/ *v* **1** to emit loud and harsh sound **2** to proclaim loudly or sensationally

blarney /'blahni/ *n* **1** smooth wheedling talk **2** nonsense

blasé /'blahzay, -'-/ *adj* indifferent to pleasure or excitement as a result of excessive indulgence or enjoyment; *also* sophisticated

blaspheme /blas'feem/ *v* to speak of or address (God or sthg sacred) with impiety – ~**r, -my** *n* – **-mous** *adj* – **-mously** *adv*

'**blast** /blahst/ *n* **1** a violent gust of wind **2** the sound produced by air blown through a wind instrument or whistle **3** a stream of air or gas forced through a hole **4** (a violent wave of increased atmospheric pressure followed by a wave of decreased atmospheric pressure produced in the vicinity of) an explosion or violent detonation **5** the utterance of the word *blast* as a curse

²**blast** *v* **1** to injure (as if) by the action of wind; blight **2** to shatter, remove, or open (as if) with an explosive **3** to apply a forced draught to **4** to denounce vigorously **5** to curse, damn **6** to hit vigorously and effectively – ~**ed** *adj*

³**blast** *interj, Br* – used to express annoyance; slang

'**blast ,furnace** *n* a furnace, esp for converting iron ore into iron, in which combustion is forced by a current of air under pressure

blast off *v, esp of rocket-propelled missiles and vehicles* to take off – **blast-off** *n*

blatant /'blayt(ə)nt/ *adj* completely obvious, conspicuous, or obtrusive, esp in a crass or offensive manner – ~**ly** *adv*

¹blaze /blayz/ *n* **1a** an intensely burning flame or sudden fire **b** intense direct light, often accompanied by heat **2** a sudden outburst **3** *pl* hell – usu as an interjection or as a generalized term of abuse

²blaze *v* **1a** to burn intensely **b** to flare up **2** to be conspicuously brilliant or resplendent **3** to shoot rapidly and repeatedly

³blaze *n* **1** a broad white mark on the face of an animal, esp a horse **2** a trail marker; *esp* a mark made on a tree by cutting off a piece of the bark

⁴blaze *v* to lead or pioneer in (some direction or activity) – chiefly in *blaze the trail*

blazer /'blayzə/ *n* a jacket, esp with patch pockets, that is for casual wear or is part of a school uniform

¹bleach /bleech/ *v* **1** to remove colour or stains from **2** to make whiter or lighter, esp by physical or chemical removal of colour

²bleach *n* a chemical preparation used in bleaching

bleak /bleek/ *adj* **1** barren and windswept **2** cold, raw **3a** lacking in warmth or kindness **b** not hopeful or encouraging **c** severely simple or austere

bleary /'bliari/ *adj* **1** of the eyes or vision dull or dimmed, esp from fatigue or sleep **2** poorly outlined or defined – **blearily** *adv* – **bleariness** *n*

bleat /bleet/ *v* **1** to make (a sound like) the cry characteristic of a sheep or goat **2** to talk complainingly or with a whine – **bleat** *n*

bleed /bleed/ *v* **bled** /bled/ **1** to emit or lose blood **2** to feel anguish, pain, or sympathy **3** to lose some constituent (e g sap or dye) by exuding it or by diffusion **4** to extort money from **5** to extract or drain the vitality or lifeblood from

bleeding /'bleeding/ *adj or adv* bloody – slang

bleep /bleep/ *n* a short high-pitched sound (e g from electronic equipment)

blemish /'blemish/ *v or n* (to spoil the perfection of by) a noticeable imperfection

blench /blench/ *v* to draw back or flinch from lack of courage

¹blend /blend/ *v* **blended** *also* **blent** /blent/ **1** to mix; *esp* to combine or associate so that the separate constituents cannot be distinguished **2** to produce a harmonious effect

²blend *n* **1** an act or product of blending **2** a word (e g *brunch*) produced by combining other words or parts of words

blender /'blendə/ *n* an electric appliance for grinding or mixing; *specif* a liquidizer

bless /bles/ *v* **blessed** *also* **blest** /blest/ **1** to hallow or consecrate, esp by making the sign of the cross **2** to invoke divine favour for **3a** to praise, glorify **b** to speak gratefully of **4** to confer prosperity or happiness on **5** – used in exclamations chiefly to express mild or good-humoured surprise

blessed /'blesid/ *adj* **1** *often cap* holy; venerated **2** – used as an intensive – **~ly** *adv* – **~ness** *n*

blessing /'blesing/ *n* **1a** the invocation of God's favour upon a person **b** approval **2** sthg conducive to happiness or welfare

blew /blooh/ *past of* **blow**

¹blight /bliet/ *n* **1** (an organism that causes) a disease or injury of plants resulting in withering, cessation of growth, and death of parts without rotting **2** sthg that impairs, frustrates, or destroys **3** a condition of disorder or decay

²blight *v* **1** to affect (e g a plant) with blight **2** to impair, frustrate

blighter /'blietə/ *n*, *chiefly Br* a fellow; *esp* one held in low esteem – *infml*

blimey /'bliemi/ *interj*, *chiefly Br* – used for expressing surprise; slang

¹blind /bliend/ *adj* **1** unable to see; sightless **2a** unable or unwilling to discern or judge **b** not based on reason, evidence, or knowledge **3** without sight or knowledge of anything that could serve for guidance beforehand **4** performed solely by the use of instruments within an aircraft **5** hidden from sight; concealed **6** having only 1 opening or outlet – **~ly** *adv* – **~ness** *n*

²blind *v* **1** to make blind **2** to rob of judgment or discernment **3** to dazzle — **blind with science** to impress or overwhelm with a display of usu technical knowledge

³blind *n* **1** sthg to keep out light: e g **1a** *chiefly Br* an awning **b** a flexible screen (e g a strip of cloth) usu mounted on a roller for covering a window **2** a cover, subterfuge

⁴blind *adv* **1** to the point of insensibility – usu in *blind drunk* **2** without seeing outside an aircraft

‚blind 'alley *n* a fruitless or mistaken course or direction

‚blind 'date *n* a date between people who have not previously met

'blind‚fold /-‚fohld/ *v or n* **1** (to cover the eyes of with) a piece of material (e g a bandage) for covering the eyes to prevent sight **2** (to hinder from seeing or esp understanding with) sthg that obscures vision or mental awareness

blindman's buff /‚bliend‚manz 'buf/ *n* a group game in which a blindfolded player tries to catch and identify another player

'blind ‚spot *n* **1a** the point in the retina where the optic nerve enters that is not sensitive to light **b** a part of a visual field that cannot be seen or inspected **2** an area in which one lacks knowledge, understanding, or discrimination

¹blink /blingk/ *v* **1** to close and open the eyes involuntarily **2** to shine intermittently **3a** to wink *at* **b** to look with surprise or dismay *at*

²blink *n* **1** a glimmer, sparkle **2** a usu involuntary shutting and opening of the eye — **on the blink** not working properly — *infml*

blinking /'blingking/ *adj or adv*, *Br* bloody – euph

blip /blip/ *n* an image on a radar screen

bliss /blis/ n 1 complete happiness 2 paradise, heaven – ~**ful** adj – ~**fully** adv – ~**fulness** n

blister /'blistə/ n 1 a raised part of the outer skin containing watery liquid 2 an enclosed raised spot (e g in paint) resembling a blister

blithe /bliedh/ adj 1 lighthearted, merry, cheerful 2 casual, heedless – ~**ly** adv

blitz /blits/ v or n 1 (to make) an intensive aerial bombardment 2 (to mount) an intensive nonmilitary campaign – chiefly journ

blizzard /'blizəd/ n 1 a long severe snowstorm 2 an intensely strong cold wind filled with fine snow 3 an overwhelming rush or deluge

bloated /'blohtid/ adj 1 unpleasantly swollen 2 much larger than is warranted

bloater /'blohtə/ n a large herring or mackerel lightly salted and briefly smoked

blob /blob/ n 1 a small drop of liquid or of sthg viscous or thick 2 sthg ill-defined or amorphous

bloc /blok/ n a (temporary) combination of individuals, parties, or nations for a common purpose

¹**block** /blok/ n 1 a mould or form on which articles are shaped or displayed 2 a rectangular building unit that is larger than a brick 3 a wooden or plastic building toy that is usu provided in sets 4 the metal casting that contains the cylinders of an internal-combustion engine 5 a head – slang 6 an obstacle 7 a wooden or metal case enclosing 1 or more pulleys 8 (a ballet shoe with) a solid toe on which a dancer can stand on points 9 a part of a building or set of buildings devoted to a particular use 10 chiefly NAm (the distance along 1 side of) a usu rectangular space (e g in a town) enclosed by streets and usu occupied by buildings 11 a piece of engraved or etched material (e g wood or metal) from which impressions are printed

²**block** v 1a to hinder the passage, progress, or accomplishment of (as if) by interposing an obstruction b to shut off from view c to prevent or interfere usu legitimately with (e g an opponent) in various games or sports d to prevent normal functioning of 2 to arrange (e g a school timetable) in long continuous periods – ~**age** n

blockade /blo'kayd, blo–/ n the surrounding or blocking of a particular enemy area to prevent passage of people or supplies – **blockade** v

block and 'tackle n an arrangement of pulley blocks with associated rope or cable for hoisting or hauling

block,buster /-,bustə/ n 1 a huge high-explosive demolition bomb 2 sby or sthg particularly outstanding or effective **USE** infml

bloke /blohk/ n, chiefly Br a man – infml

¹**blond** /blond/ adj 1a (having hair) of a flaxen, golden, light auburn, or pale yellowish brown colour b of a pale white or rosy white colour 2 of a light colour

²**blond** n 1 sby with blond hair and often a light complexion and blue or grey eyes 2 a light yellowish brown to dark greyish yellow colour

blonde /blond/ n or adj (a) blond – used esp for or in relation to women

¹**blood** /blud/ n 1a the usu red fluid that circulates in the heart, arteries, capillaries, and veins of a vertebrate animal, carrying nourishment and oxygen to, and bringing away waste products from, all parts of the body b a comparable fluid of an invertebrate animal 2a human lineage; esp the royal lineage b kinship 3 temper, passion 4 archaic a dashing lively esp young man; a rake – now usu humor

²**blood** v to stain or wet with blood; esp to mark the face of (an inexperienced fox hunter) with the blood of the fox 2 to give an initiating experience to (sby new to a particular field of activity)

¹**blood,bath** /-,bahth/ n a great slaughter; a massacre

¹**blood,curdling** /-,kuhdling/ adj arousing horror

¹**blood ,heat** n a temperature approximating to that of the human body; about 37°C or 98°F

¹**blood,hound** /-,hownd/ n 1 a large powerful hound of European origin remarkable for its acuteness of smell and poor sight 2 a person (e g a detective) who is keen in pursuing or tracking sby or sthg down

¹**bloodless** /-lis/ adj 1 deficient in or free from blood 2 not accompanied by the shedding of blood 3 lacking in spirit, vitality, or human feeling – ~**ly** adv – ~**ness** n

¹**blood,letting** /-,leting/ n bloodshed

¹**blood ,pressure** n pressure that is exerted by the blood on the walls of the blood vessels, esp arteries, and that varies with the age and health of the individual

¹**blood,shed** /-,shed/ n the taking of life

¹**blood,shot** /-,shot/ adj, of an eye having the white part tinged with red

¹**blood ,sport** n a field sport (e g fox hunting or beagling) in which animals are killed

¹**blood,sucker** /-,sukə/ n a person who extorts sthg, esp money, from another

¹**blood,thirsty** /-,thuhsti/ adj eager for bloodshed – ~**tily** adv – ~**tiness** n

bloody /'bludi/ adj 1 smeared, stained with, or containing blood 2 accompanied by or involving bloodshed 3a murderous, bloodthirsty b merciless, cruel 4 – used as an intensive; slang – **bloodily** adv – **bloodiness** n

,**Bloody 'Mary** /'meəri/ n pl **Bloody Marys** a cocktail consisting chiefly of vodka and tomato juice

,**bloody-'minded** adj deliberately obstructive or unhelpful – ~**ness** n

¹**bloom** /bloohm/ *n* **1a** a flower **b** the flowering state **2** a time of beauty, freshness, and vigour **3a** a delicate powdery coating on some fruits and leaves **b** cloudiness on a film of varnish or lacquer **4** a rosy or healthy appearance

²**bloom** *v* **1** to produce or yield flowers **2a** to flourish **b** to reach maturity; blossom

bloomer /'bloohmə/ *n* a st ,pid blunder – *infml*

bloomers /'bloohmaz/ *n pl* a woman's undergarment with full loose legs gathered at the knee

blooming /'blooming, 'blooh-/ *adj, chiefly Br* – used as a generalized intensive

¹**blossom** /'blosəm/ *n* **1a** the flower of a plant **b** the mass of bloom on a single plant **2** a high point or stage of development

²**blossom** *vi* **1** to bloom **2** to come into one's own; develop

¹**blot** /blot/ *n* **1** a soiling or disfiguring mark; a spot **2** a mark of reproach; a blemish

²**blot** *v* **-tt-** **1** to spot, stain, or spatter with a discolouring substance **2** to dry or remove with an absorbing agent (e g blotting paper) — **blot one's copybook** to mar one's previously good record or standing

blotch /bloch/ *n* **1** an imperfection, blemish **2** an irregular spot or mark (e g of colour or ink) – ~y *adj*

blotter /'blotə/ *n* a piece of blotting paper

'**blotting ,paper** /'bloting/ *n* a spongy unsized paper used to absorb ink

blotto /'blotoh/ *adj, Br* extremely drunk – *slang*

blouse /blowz/ *n* a usu loose-fitting woman's upper garment that resembles a shirt or smock

¹**blow** /bloh/ *v* **blew** /blooh/; **blown** /blohn/ **1** of air to move with speed or force **2** to act on with a current of gas or vapour **3** to make a sound by blowing **4a** to pant **b** of a whale to eject moisture-laden air from the lungs through the blowhole **5** of an electric fuse to melt when overloaded **6a** to shatter, burst, or destroy by explosion **b** of a tyre to lose the contained air through a spontaneous puncture – usu + out **7** to produce or shape by the action of blown or injected air **8** to damn, disregard – *infml* **9** to squander (money or an advantage) – *slang* **10** to leave hurriedly – *slang* — **blow hot and cold** to act changeably by alternately favouring and rebuffing — **blow off steam** to release pent-up emotions — **blow one's own trumpet** to praise oneself; boast — **blow one's top** to become furious; explode with anger — *infml* — **blow the gaff** *Br* to let out a usu discreditable secret — **blow someone's mind 1** to cause sby to hallucinate – *slang* **2** to amaze sby – *infml* — **blow the whistle on 1** to bring (sthg secret) into the open – *slang* **2** to inform against — *slang*

²**blow** *n* **1** an instance of (the wind) blowing **2** a walk or other outing in the fresh air – *infml*

³**blow** *v* **blew** /blooh/; **blown** /blohn/ to cause (e g flowers or blossom) to open out, usu just before dropping

⁴**blow** *n* **1** a hard stroke delivered with a part of the body or with an instrument **2** *pl* a hostile or aggressive state – esp in **come to blows 3** a shock or misfortune

,**blow-by-'blow** *adj* minutely detailed

blower /'bloh-ə/ *n* **1** a device for producing a current of air or gas **2** *Br* the telephone – *infml*

'**blow,fly** /-,flie/ *n* any of various 2-winged flies that deposit their eggs or maggots esp on meat or in wounds

'**blow,hole** /-,hohl/ *n* **1** a nostril in the top of the head of a whale, porpoise, or dolphin **2** a hole in the ice to which aquatic mammals (e g seals) come to breathe

blow in *v* to arrive casually or unexpectedly – *infml*

'**blow,lamp** /-,lamp/ *n* a small portable burner that produces an intense flame and has a pressurized fuel tank

'**blow,out** /-,owt/ *n* **1** a large meal – *infml* **2** a bursting of a container (e g a tyre) by pressure of the contents on a weak spot **3** an uncontrolled eruption of an oil or gas well

blow out *v, of an oil or gas well* to erupt out of control

'**blow,pipe** /-,piep/ *n* **1** a small tube for blowing air, oxygen, etc into a flame to direct and increase the heat **2** a tube for propelling a projectile (e g a dart) by blowing

blowsy also **blowzy** /'blowzi/ *adj, esp of a woman* slovenly in appearance and usu fat

'**blow,up** /-,up/ *n* **1** an outburst of temper **2** a photographic enlargement

blow up *v* **1** to explode or be exploded **2** to build up or exaggerate to an unreasonable extent **3** to fill up with a gas, esp air **4** to make a photographic enlargement of **5** to become violently angry **6** to come into being; arise

blowy /'bloh-i/ *adj* windy

¹**blubber** /'blubə/ *n* the fat of large marine mammals, esp whales

²**blubber** *v* to weep noisily – *infml*

¹**bludgeon** /'blujən/ *n* a short club used as a weapon

²**bludgeon** *v* to overcome by aggressive argument

¹**blue** /blooh/ *adj* **1** of the colour blue **2** discoloured through cold, anger, bruising, or fear **3** low in spirits **4** Conservative **5a** obscene, pornographic **b** off-colour, risqué – *slang* — **~ness** *n* – **bluish** *adj* — **once in a blue moon** very rarely — **until one is blue in the face** unsuccessfully for ever

²**blue** *n* **1** a colour whose hue is that of the clear sky and lies between green and violet in the spectrum **2** a blue preparation used to whiten clothes in laundering **3a** the sky **b** the far distance **4** any of numerous small chiefly blue butterflies **5** often

cap, Br a usu notional award given to sby who has played in a sporting contest between Oxford and Cambridge universities; also sby who has been given such an award — **out of the blue** without warning; unexpectedly

³**blue** v, **blueing, bluing** /'blooh·ing/ Br to spend lavishly and wastefully – infml

'**blue·bell** /-ˌbel/ n 1 the wild hyacinth 2 chiefly Scot the harebell

'**blueberry** /-b(ə)ri; NAm -ˌberi/ n (the edible blue or blackish berry of) any of several shrubs of the heath family

ˌ**blue 'blood** n high or noble birth

'**blue·bottle** /-ˌbotl/ n any of several blowflies of which the abdomen or the whole body is iridescent blue, that make a loud buzzing noise in flight

ˌ**blue-'collar** adj of or being the class of manual wage-earning employees

'**blue·print** /-ˌprint/ n 1 a photographic print in white on a bright blue ground, used esp for copying maps and plans 2 a detailed programme of action

blues /bloohz/ n pl **blues** 1 sing or pl in constr low spirits; melancholy – + the 2 (a song in) a melancholy style of music characterized by flattened thirds or sevenths where a major interval would be expected in the melody and harmony

'**blue·stocking** /-ˌstoking/ n a woman with intellectual or literary interests – derog

¹**bluff** /bluf/ adj 1 rising steeply with a broad, flat, or rounded front 2 good-naturedly frank and outspoken – **~ly** adv – **~ness** n

²**bluff** v to deceive by pretence or an outward appearance of strength, confidence, etc – **bluff** n

¹**blunder** /'blundə/ v 1 to move unsteadily or confusedly 2 to make a blunder – **~er** n

²**blunder** n a gross error or mistake

blunderbuss /'blundəˌbus/ n an obsolete short firearm with a large bore and usu a flaring muzzle

¹**blunt** /blunt/ adj 1 having an edge or point that is not sharp 2a aggressively outspoken b direct, straightforward – **~ness** n – **~ly** adv

²**blunt** v to make less sharp or definite

¹**blur** /bluh/ n 1 a smear or stain 2 sthg vague or indistinct

²**blur** v -rr- 1 to obscure or blemish by smearing 2 to become vague, indistinct, or confused

blurb /bluhb/ n a short publicity notice, esp on a book cover

blurt out /bluht/ v to utter abruptly and impulsively

¹**blush** /blush/ v to become red in the face, esp from shame, modesty, or embarrassment – **~ingly** adv

²**blush** n a reddening of the face, from shame, embarrassment, etc 2 a red or rosy tint

¹**bluster** /'blustə/ v to talk or act in a noisily self-assertive or boastful manner

²**bluster** n a violent blowing of 1 loudly boastful or threatening talk – **~ous, ~y** adj

BO /ˌbee 'oh/ n a disagreeable smell, esp of stale perspiration, given off by a person's body

boa /'boh·ə/ n 1 a large snake (e g the boa constrictor, anaconda, or python) that crushes its prey 2 a long fluffy scarf of fur, feathers, or delicate fabric

boar /baw/ n 1a an uncastrated male pig b the male of any of several mammals (e g a guinea pig or badger) 2 the Old World wild pig from which most domestic pigs derive

¹**board** /bawd/ n 1a a usu long thin narrow piece of sawn timber b pl the stage 2 daily meals, esp when provided in return for payment 3 sing or pl in constr 3a a group of people having managerial, supervisory, or investigatory powers b an official body 4 a flat usu rectangular piece of material designed or marked for a special purpose (e g for playing chess, ludo, backgammon, etc or for use as a blackboard or surfboard) 5 any of various wood pulps or composition materials formed into stiff flat rectangular sheets (e g cardboard) — **on board** aboard

²**board** v 1 to come up against or alongside (a ship), usu to attack 2 to go aboard (e g a ship, train, aircraft, or bus) 3 to cover with boards – + over or up 4 to take one's meals, usu as a paying customer

boarder /'bawdə/ n 1 a lodger 2 a resident pupil at a boarding school

boardinghouse /'bawding,hows/ n a lodging house that supplies meals

'**boarding ˌschool** n a school at which meals and lodging are provided

'**boardroom** /-ˌroohm, -room/ n a room in which board meetings are held

'**boardsailing** n wind-surfing – -**sailor** n

boast /bohst/ v 1 to praise oneself 2 to speak of or assert with excessive pride – **boast** n – **boaster** n – **~ful** adj

¹**boat** /boht/ n 1 a usu small ship 2 a boat-shaped utensil or dish — **in the same boat** in the same situation or predicament

²**boat** v to use a boat, esp for recreation

boater /'bohtə/ n a stiff straw hat with a shallow flat crown and a brim 2 a pole with a hook at one end, used esp for fending off or holding boats alongside

boatswain /'bohz(ə)n, 'bohs(ə)n/ n a petty officer or warrant officer responsible for the supervision of all work done on deck and for routine maintenance of the ship's structure

¹**bob** /bob/ v -bb- 1 to move down and up briefly or repeatedly 2 to curtsy briefly 3 to try to seize a suspended or floating object with the teeth

²**bob** n 1 a short quick down-and-up motion 2 (a method of bell ringing using) a modification of the order in change ringing

³**bob** *n* **1a** a knot or twist (e g of ribbons or hair) **b** a haircut for a woman or girl in which the hair hangs loose just above the shoulders **2** a float **3** *pl* a small insignificant item – in *bits and bobs*

⁴**bob** *v* **-bb-** to cut (hair) shorter; crop

⁵**bob** *n, pl* **bob** *Br* a shilling; *also* the sum of 5 new pence – *infml*

bobbin /'bobin/ *n* a cylinder or spindle on which yarn or thread is wound (e g for use in spinning, sewing, or lacemaking)

'**bob,sleigh** /-,slay/ *n* a large usu metal sledge for 2 or 4 people used in racing

bod /bod/ *n* a person – *infml*

bode /bohd/ *v* to augur, presage

bodice /'bodis/ *n* the part of a dress that is above the waist

bodily /'bodəli/ *adv* **1** in the flesh, in person **2** as a whole; altogether

bodkin /'bodkin/ *n* a blunt thick needle with a large eye

body /'bodi/ *n* **1a(1)** the organized physical substance of a living animal or plant **a(2)** a corpse **b** a human being; a person **2** the main, central, or principal part: e g **2a** the main part of a plant or animal body, esp as distinguished from limbs and head **b** the part of a vehicle on or in which the load is placed **3** the part of a garment covering the body or trunk **4a** a mass of matter distinct from other masses **b** sthg that embodies or gives concrete reality to a thing; *specif* a material object in physical space **5** *sing or pl in constr* a group of people or things: e g **5a** a fighting unit **b** a group of individuals organized for some purpose **6a** compactness or firmness of texture **b** comparative richness of flavour in wine – **bodily** *adj*

'**body,guard** /-,gahd/ *n* an escort whose duty it is to protect a person from bodily harm

,**body 'politic** *n* a group of people under a single government

'**body,work** /-,wuhk/ *n* the structure or form of a vehicle body

Boer /'baw·ə, 'boh·ə/ *n* a S African of Dutch descent

boffin /'bofin/ *n, chiefly Br* a scientific or technical expert – *infml*

bog /bog/ *n* **1** (an area of) wet spongy poorly-drained ground **2** *Br* a toilet – slang – ~**gy** *adj*

bog down *v* **-gg-** to cause to sink (as if) into a bog; impede

bogey *also* **bogy, bogie** /'bohgi/ *n pl* **bogeys** *also* **bogies 1** a monstrous imaginary figure used to frighten children **2** a golf score of 1 stroke over par on a hole

bogie *also* **bogey, bogy** /'bohgi/ *n pl* **bogies** *also* **bogeys** a swivelling framework with 1 or more pairs of wheels to carry and guide one end of a railway vehicle

bogus /'bohgəs/ *adj* spurious, sham

Bohemian /boh'heemyən, -mi·ən/ *n* **1** a native or inhabitant of Bohemia **2** a person (e g a writer or artist) living an unconventional life

¹**boil** /boyl/ *n* a localized pus-filled swelling of the skin resulting from infection in a skin gland

²**boil** *v* **1a** *of a fluid* to change into (bubbles of) a vapour when heated **b** to come to the boiling point **2** to bubble or foam violently; churn **3** to be excited or stirred **4** to subject to the action of a boiling liquid (e g in cooking)

³**boil** *n* the boiling point

boil down *v* **1** to condense or summarize **2** to amount *to*

boiler /'boylə/ *n* **1** a vessel used for boiling **2** the part of a steam generator in which water is converted into steam under pressure **3** a tank in which water is heated or hot water is stored

'**boiler ,suit** *n, chiefly Br* a one-piece outer garment combining shirt and trousers, worn chiefly to protect clothing

'**boiling ,point** *n* **1** the point at which a liquid boils **2** the point at which a person loses his/her self-control

boil over *v* **1** to overflow as a result of boiling **2** to lose one's temper

boisterous /'boyst(ə)rəs/ *adj* **1** noisily and cheerfully rough **2** stormy, wild – ~**ly** *adv* – ~**ness** *n*

bold /bohld/ *adj* **1** showing or requiring a fearless adventurous spirit **2** impudent, presumptuous **3** standing out prominently; conspicuous – ~**ly** *adv* – ~**ness** *n*

bole /bohl/ *n* the trunk of a tree

bolero /bə'leəroh; *sense 2* 'boləroh/ *n, pl* **boleros 1** (music for) a type of Spanish dance **2** a loose waist-length jacket open at the front

boll /bohl/ *n* the seed pod of cotton or similar plants

bollard /'bolahd, -ləd/ *n* **1** a post on a wharf or on a ship's deck round which to fasten mooring lines **2** *Br* a short post (e g on a kerb or traffic island) to guide vehicles or forbid access

bollock /'bolək/ *n, Br* **1** a testicle – usu pl **2** *pl* nonsense – often used interjectionally *USE* vulg

Bolshevik /'bolshəvik/ *n, pl* **Bolsheviks** *also* **Bolsheviki** /,bolshə'veeki/ **1** a member of the more radical wing of the Russian Social Democratic party that seized power in Russia in 1917 **2** a communist – derog – -**vism** *n*

¹**bolster** /'bolstə/ *n* **1** a long pillow or cushion placed across the head of a bed, usu under other pillows **2** a structural part (e g in machinery) that eliminates friction or provides support

²**bolster** *v* to give support to; reinforce

bol

¹**bolt** /bolt, bohlt/ *n* **1a** a short stout usu blunt-headed arrow shot from a crossbow **b** a thunderbolt **2a** a sliding bar or rod used to fasten a door **b** the part of a lock that is shot or withdrawn by the key **3** a roll of cloth or wallpaper of a standard length **4a** a metal rod or pin for fastening objects together **b** a screw-bolt with a head suitable for turning with a spanner **5** a rod or bar that closes the breech of a breech-loading firearm

²**bolt** *v* **1** to move rapidly; dash **2a** to dart off or away; flee **b** to break away from control **3** to produce seed prematurely **4** to swallow (e g food) hastily or without chewing

³**bolt** *adv* in a rigidly erect position

⁴**bolt** *n* a dash, run

⁵**bolt** *v* to sift (e g flour)

'**bolt-,hole** *n* **1** a hole into which an animal runs for safety **2** a means of rapid escape or place of refuge

¹**bomb** /bom/ *n* **1a** any of several explosive or incendiary devices usu dropped from aircraft and detonated by impact **b** nuclear weapons – + *the* **2** a rounded mass of lava exploded from a volcano **3** *Br* a large sum of money – infml **4** *NAm* a failure, flop – infml — **a bomb** *Br* very successfully — infml

²**bomb** *v* **1** to attack with bombs; bombard **2** to fail; fall flat – infml

bombard /bom'bahd, '--'/ *v* **1** to attack with heavy artillery or with bombers **2** to attack vigorously or persistently (e g with questions)

bombardier /,bombə'diə/ *n* **1** a noncommissioned officer in the British artillery **2** a US bomber-crew member who aims and releases the bombs

bombast /'bombast/ *n* pretentious inflated speech or writing – **~ic** *adj* – **~ically** *adv*

bomber /'bomə/ *n* **1** an aircraft designed for bombing **2** sby who throws or places bombs

'**bomb,shell** /-,shel/ *n* sby or sthg that has a stunning or devastating effect

bona fide /,bohnə 'fiedi/ *adj* genuine, sincere

bonanza /bə'nanzə/ *n* sthg (unexpectedly) considered valuable, profitable, or rewarding

bonbon /'bon,bon/ *n* a sweet; *specif* a fondant

¹**bond** /bond/ *n* **1** sthg (e g a fetter) that binds or restrains **2** a binding agreement **3** an adhesive or cementing material **4** sthg that unites or binds **5a** a legally enforceable agreement to pay **b** a certificate of intention to pay the holder a specified sum, with or without other interest, on a specified date **6** the system of overlapping bricks in a wall **7** the state of imported goods retained by customs authorities until duties are paid **8** a strong durable paper, now used esp for writing and typing

²**bond** *v* **1** to overlap (e g bricks) for solidity of construction **2** to put (goods) in bond until duties and taxes are paid **3** to cause to stick firmly

bondage /'bondij/ *n* **1** the tenure or service of a villein, serf, or slave **2a** slavery, serfdom **b** a form of sexual gratification involving the physical restraint of one partner

bonded /'bondid/ *adj* **1** used for or being goods in bond **2** composed of 2 or more layers of fabric held together by an adhesive

bone /bohn/ *n* **1a** (the material that makes up) any of the hard body structures of which the adult skeleton of most vertebrate animals is chiefly composed **b** (a structure made of) ivory or another hard substance resembling bone **2** *the* essential or basic part or level; *the* core **3** *pl* the core of one's being **4** a subject or matter of dispute – **~less** *adj* — **bone to pick** a matter to argue or complain about

²**bone** *v* **1** to remove the bones from **2** to try to find out about, esp hurriedly; revise – usu + *up* – **~d** *adj*

³**bone** *adv* absolutely, utterly – chiefly in **bone dry, bone idle**

,**bone 'china** *n* a type of translucent and durable white porcelain made from a mixture of bone ash and kaolin

'**bone ,meal** *n* fertilizer or feed made of crushed or ground bone

bonfire /'bonfie-ə/ *n* a large fire ouilt in the open air

¹**bongo** /'bong·goh/ *n pl* **bongos,** *esp collectively* **bongo** any of 3 large striped antelopes of tropical Africa

²**bongo** *n, pl* **bongos** *also* **bongoes** either of a pair of small tuned drums played with the hands

bonhomie /,bono'mee, bo'nomi/ *n* good-natured friendliness

bonkers /'bongkəz/ *adj, chiefly Br* mad, crazy – infml

bonnet /'bonit/ *n* **1** a cloth or straw hat tied under the chin, now worn chiefly by children **2** *Br* the hinged metal covering over the engine of a motor vehicle

bonny /'boni/ *adj, chiefly Br* attractive, comely – **bonnily** *adv*

bonsai /bon'sie/ *n pl* **bonsai** (the art of growing) a potted plant dwarfed by special methods of culture

bonus /'bohnəs/ *n* sthg given in addition to what is usual or strictly due

bony, boney /'bohni/ *adj* **1** consisting of or resembling bone **2** having large or prominent bones **3** skinny, scrawny

¹**boo** /booh/ *interj* – used to express contempt or disapproval or to startle or frighten

²**boo** *n, pl* **boos** a shout of disapproval or contempt

³**boo** *v* to show scorn or disapproval (of) by uttering 'boo'

¹**boob** /boohb/ *n* **1** a stupid mistake; a blunder – infml **2** a breast – slang

²**boob** *v* to make a stupid mistake – infml

¹booby /'boohbi/ n **1** an awkward foolish person **2** any of several small gannets of tropical seas **3** the poorest performer in a group

²booby n a breast – vulg

'booby ,prize n an award for the poorest performance in a contest

'booby ,trap n **1** a trap for the unwary or unsuspecting **2** a harmless-looking object concealing an explosive device that is set to explode by remote control or if touched

¹book /book/ n **1a** a set of written, printed, or blank sheets bound together into a volume **b** a long written or printed literary composition **c** a major division of a treatise or literary work **d** a record of business transactions – usu pl **2** the bets registered by a bookmaker — **by/according to the book** by following previously laid down instructions and not using personal initiative — **in one's book** in one's own opinion — **one for the book** an act or occurrence worth noting

²book v **1a** to reserve or make arrangements for in advance **b** chiefly Br to register in a hotel **2a** to take the name of with a view to prosecution **b** to enter the name of (a player) in a book for a violation of the rules usu involving foul play – used with reference to a rugby or soccer player – **~able** adj – **~ing** n

³book adj **1** derived from books; theoretical **2** shown by books of account

'book,case /-,kays/ n a piece of furniture consisting of a set of shelves to hold books

'book,end /-,end/ n a support placed at the end of a row of books

bookish /'bookish/ adj **1** relying on theoretical knowledge rather than practical experience **2** literary as opposed to colloquial – **~ly** adv – **~ness** n

'book,keeper /-,keepə/ n sby who records the financial dealings of a business – **-ping** n

'book,maker /-,maykə/ n sby who determines odds and receives and pays off bets

'book,mark /-,mahk/, **'book,marker** /-,mahkə/ n sthg used to mark a place in a book

'book,stall /-,stawl/ n a stall where books, magazines, and newspapers are sold

'book,worm /-,wuhm/ n a person unusually fond of reading and study

¹boom /boohm/ n **1** a spar at the foot of the mainsail in fore-and-aft rig that is attached at its fore end to the mast **2a** a long movable arm used to manipulate a microphone **b** a barrier across a river or enclosing an area of water to keep logs together; also the enclosed logs **4** a cable or line of spars extended across a river or the mouth of a harbour as a barrier to navigation

²boom /boom, boohm/ v **1** to make a deep hollow sound or cry **2** to experience a rapid increase in activity or importance

³boom /boom, boohm/ n **1** a booming sound or cry **2a** a rapid growth or increase in a specified area **b** a rapid widespread expansion of economic activity

boomerang /'boohmə,rang/ n **1** a bent piece of wood shaped so that it returns to its thrower and used by Australian aborigines as a hunting weapon **2** an act or utterance that backfires on its originator

¹boon /boohn/ n a benefit or favour

²boon adj close, intimate, and convivial – esp in **boon companion**

boor /booə, baw/ n a coarse, ill-mannered, or insensitive person – **~ish** adj – **~ishly** adv – **~ishness** n

¹boost /boohst/ v **1** to push or shove up from below **2** to increase, raise **3** to encourage, promote **4** to raise the voltage of or across (an electric circuit)

²boost n **1** a push upwards **2** an increase in amount **3** an act that promotes or encourages

booster /'boohstə/ n **1** an auxiliary engine which assists (e g at take-off) by providing a large thrust for a short time **2** a supplementary dose of a medicament

¹boot /booht/ n **1** a high stout shoe; also a shoe for certain sports (e g football) **2** a blow or kick delivered (as if) by a booted foot **3** Br the major luggage compartment of a motor car **4** summary discharge or dismissal – slang; chiefly in give/get the boot — **put/stick the boot in 1** chiefly Br to cause added distress to one who is already defeated – infml **2** to act with brutal decisiveness – infml

²boot v to kick

bootee, bootie /'booh,tee, -'-/ n **1** a short boot **2** an infant's sock worn in place of a shoe

booth /boohth/ n pl **booths** /boohths, boohdhz/ **1** a stall or stand for the sale or exhibition of goods **2** a small enclosure affording privacy (e g for telephoning, dining, etc)

'boot,leg /-,leg/ v, chiefly NAm to manufacture, sell, or transport for sale (esp alcoholic drink) contrary to law – **-legger** n

booty /'boohti/ n **1** plunder taken (e g in war) **2** a rich gain or prize

¹booze /boohz/ v to drink intoxicating liquor to excess – slang

²booze n intoxicating drink USE slang

boozer /'boohzə/ n **1** a public house **2** sby who boozes – slang

¹bop /bop/ v or n -pp- (to strike with) a blow (e g of the fist) – infml

²bop n jazz characterized by unusual chord structures, syncopated rhythm, and harmonic complexity and innovation

³bop v -pp- to dance (e g in a disco) in a casual and unrestricted manner, esp to popular music – infml

borage /'borij, 'burij/ n a coarse hairy blue-flowered European herb

Bordeaux /baw'doh/ n pl **Bordeaux** /baw'doh(z)/ a red or white wine of the Bordeaux region of France

¹**border** /'bawdə/ n 1 an outer part or edge 2 a boundary, frontier 3 a narrow bed of planted ground (e g beside a path) 4 an ornamental design at the edge of sthg

²**border** v 1 to put a border on 2 to adjoin at the edge or boundary — **border on 1** to adjoin & **2** to resemble closely

'**border line** /-,lien/ adj 1 verging on one or other place or state without being definitely assignable to either 2 not quite meeting accepted standards (e g of morality or good taste)

¹**bore** /baw/ v 1 to make a hole with a rotary tool 2 to drill a mine or well – ~**r** n

²**bore** n 1 a hole made (as if) by boring 2 a barrel (e g of a gun) 3a the interior diameter of a tube b the diameter of an engine cylinder

³**bore** past of **bear**

⁴**bore** n a tidal flood that moves swiftly as a steep-fronted wave in a channel, estuary, etc

⁵**bore** n a tedious person or thing

⁶**bore** v to weary by being dull or monotonous – ~**dom** n

born /bawn/ adj 1a brought into existence (as if) by birth b by birth; native 2 having a specified character or situation from birth

borne /bawn/ past part of **bear**

borough /'burə/ n a British urban constituency; also a similar political unit in the USA

borrow /'boroh/ v 1 to take or receive with the intention of returning 2a to appropriate for one's own use b to copy or imitate – ~**er** n – ~**ing** n

borscht /bawsht/ n beetroot soup

borstal /'bawstl/ n, often cap, Br a penal institution for young offenders

bosh /bosh/ n nonsense – infml

¹**bosom** /'boozəm/ n 1 the front of the human chest; esp the female breasts 2a the breast considered as the centre of secret thoughts and emotions b close relationship

²**bosom** adj close, intimate

bosomy /'boozəmi/ adj having large breasts

¹**boss** /bos/ n 1 a protuberant part or body 2 a raised ornamentation 3 a carved ornament concealing the intersection of the ribs of a vault or panelled ceiling

²**boss** n 1 one who exercises control or authority; specif one who directs or supervises workers 2 a politician who controls a party organization (e g in the USA)

³**boss** v to order – often + about or around USE infml

'**boss-'eyed** adj, Br having a squint; cross-eyed – infml

bossy /'bosi/ adj domineering, dictatorial – infml – **bossiness** n

bosun /'bohz(ə)n, 'bohs(ə)n/ n a boatswain

botany /'botəni/ n a branch of biology dealing with plant life – -**anist** n – -**anic, -anical** adj – -**anize** v

¹**botch** /boch/ v 1 to repair, patch, or assemble in a makeshift or inept way 2 to foul up hopelessly; bungle USE infml

²**botch** n 1 sthg botched; a mess 2 a clumsy patch-work USE infml

¹**both** /bohth/ adj being the 2; affecting or involving the one as well as the other

²**both** pron pl in constr the one as well as the other

³**both** conj – used to indicate and stress the inclusion of each of 2 or more things specified by coordinated spoken or word groups

¹**bother** /'bodhə/ v 1 to cause to be troubled or perplexed 2a to annoy or inconvenience b – used as a mild interjection of annoyance 3 to take pains; take the trouble

²**bother** n 1 (a cause of) mild discomfort, annoyance, or worry 2 unnecessary fussing 3 a minor disturbance – ~**some** adj

¹**bottle** /'botl/ n 1a a rigid or semirigid container, esp for liquids, usu of glass or plastic, with a comparatively narrow neck or mouth b the contents of a bottle 2a intoxicating drink – slang b bottled milk used to feed infants 3 Br nerve; guts – slang

²**bottle** v **bottling** /'botling/ 1 to put into a bottle 2 Br to preserve (e g fruit) by storage in glass jars

'**bottle-feed** v **bottle-fed** /fed/ to feed (e g an infant) by means of a bottle

bottle green adj or n very dark green

'**bottleneck** /-,nek/ n a narrow point or situation where free movement or progress is held up

bottle up v to confine, restrain

¹**bottom** /'botəm/ n 1a the underside of sthg b a surface on which sthg rests c the buttocks, rump 2 the ground below a body of water 3 the part of a ship's hull lying below the water 4a the lowest, deepest, or farthest part or place b the lowest or last place in order of precedence c the transmission gear of a motor vehicle giving lowest speed of travel d the lower part of a two-piece garment – often pl with sing. meaning — **at bottom** really, basically

,**bottom 'drawer** n, Br a young woman's collection of clothes and esp household articles, kept in anticipation of her marriage

'**bottomless** /-lis/ adj 1 extremely deep 2 boundless, unlimited

botulism /'botyoo,liz(ə)m, -chə-/ n acute often fatal bacterial food poisoning

boudoir /'boohdwah/ n a woman's dressing room, bedroom, or private sitting room

bouffant /'boohfong/ adj puffed out

bough /bow/ n a (main) branch of a tree

bought /bawt/ *past of* **buy**

bouillon /'booh·yong / *n* a thin clear soup made usu from lean beef

boulder /'bohldǝ/ *n* a large stone or mass of rock

boulevard /'boohlǝ,vahd, -,vah/ *n* a broad avenue, usu lined by trees

¹**bounce** /bowns/ *v* 1 to cause to rebound 2 to return (a cheque) as no good because of lack of funds in the payer's account – *infml*

²**bounce** *n* 1a a sudden leap or bound b a rebound 2 verve, liveliness – **bouncy** *adj* – **-cily** *adv* – **-ciness** *n*

bounce back *v* to recover quickly from a blow or defeat

bouncer /'bownsǝ/ *n* 1 a man employed in a public place to restrain or remove disorderly people 2 a fast intimidatory short-pitched delivery of a cricket ball that passes or hits the batsman at above chest height after bouncing

bouncing /'bownsing/ *adj* enjoying good health; robust

¹**bound** /bownd/ *adj* going or intending to go

²**bound** *n* 1 a limiting line; a boundary 2 sthg that limits or restrains *USE* usu pl with sing. meaning

³**bound** *v* 1 to set limits to 2 to form the boundary of *USE* usu pass

⁴**bound** *adj* 1 confined 2 certain, sure *to* 3 placed under legal or moral obligation

⁵**bound** *n* 1 a leap, jump 2 a bounce

⁶**bound** *v* 1 to move by leaping 2 to rebound, bounce

boundary /'bownd(ǝ)ri/ *n* 1 sthg, esp a dividing line, that indicates or fixes a limit or extent 2a the marked limits of a cricket field b (the score of 4 or 6 made by) a stroke in cricket that sends the ball over the boundary

bounder /'bowndǝ/ *n* a cad – not now in vogue

'**boundless** /-lis/ *adj* limitless – ~ **ly** *adv* – ~ **ness** *n*

bounteous /'bowntyǝs, -ti·ǝs/ *adj* giving or given freely – ~ **ly** *adv* – ~ **ness** *n*

bountiful /'bowntif(ǝ)l/ *adj* 1 generous, liberal 2 abundant, plentiful – ~ **ly** *adv*

bounty /'bownti/ *n* 1 generosity 2 sthg given generously 3 a financial inducement or reward, esp when offered by a government for some act or service

bouquet /booh'kay/ *n* 1 a bunch of flowers fastened together 2 a distinctive and characteristic fragrance (e g of wine)

bouquet garni /'gahni/ *n* a small bunch of herbs (e g thyme, parsley, and a bay leaf) for use in flavouring stews and soups

¹**bourgeois** /'boozhwah, 'baw-/ *n, pl* **bourgeois** 1 a middle-class person 2 one whose behaviour and views are influenced by bourgeois values or interests

²**bourgeois** *adj* 1 middle-class 2 marked by a narrow-minded concern for material interests and respectability 3 capitalist

bourgeoisie /,boozhwah'zee/ *n sing or pl in constr* the middle class

bout /bowt/ *n* 1 a spell of activity 2 an athletic match (e g of boxing) 3 an outbreak or attack of illness, fever, etc

boutique /booh'teek/ *n* a small fashionable shop selling specialized goods

bouzouki *also* **bousouki** /boo'zoohki/ *n* a long-necked Greek stringed instrument that resembles a mandolin

bovine /'bohvien/ *adj* 1 of oxen or cows 2 like an ox or cow (e g in being slow, stolid, or dull)

¹**bow** /bow/ *v* 1 to submit, yield 2 to bend the head, body, or knee in respect, submission, or greeting – ~ **ed** *adj* — **bow and scrape** to act in an obsequious manner

²**bow** /bow/ *n* a bending of the head or body in respect, submission, or greeting

³**bow** /boh/ *n* 1 a bend, arch 2 a strip of wood, fibreglass, etc held bent by a strong cord and used to shoot an arrow 3 an often ornamental slipknot (e g for tying a shoelace) 4 (a stroke made with) a resilient wooden rod with horsehairs stretched from end to end, used in playing an instrument of the viol or violin family

⁴**bow** /boh/ *v* 1 to (cause to) bend into a curve 2 to play (a stringed instrument) with a bow

⁵**bow** /bow/ *n* 1 the forward part of a ship – often pl with sing. meaning 2 the rower in the front end of a boat

bowdler·ize, -ise /'bowdlǝriez/ *v* to remove unseemly or offensive passages from a book

bowels /'bowǝlz/ *n* 1 the gut, intestines 2 the innermost parts

bower /'bowǝ/ *n* 1 an attractive dwelling or retreat 2 a (garden) shelter made with tree boughs or vines twisted together 3 a boudoir – *poetic*

¹**bowl** /bohl/ *n* 1 any of various round hollow vessels used esp for holding liquids or food or for mixing food 2 the contents of a bowl 3a the hollow of a spoon or tobacco pipe b the receptacle of a toilet 4a a bowl-shaped geographical region or formation b *NAm* a bowl-shaped structure; *esp* a sports stadium – ~ **ful** *n*

²**bowl** *n* 1 a ball used in bowls that is weighted or shaped to give it a bias 2 *pl but sing in constr* a game played typically outdoors on a green, in which bowls are rolled at a target jack in an attempt to bring them nearer to it than the opponent's bowls

³**bowl** *v* 1 to play or roll a ball in bowls or bowling 2a to play as a bowler in cricket b to deliver (a ball) to a batsman in cricket c to dismiss (a batsman in cricket) by breaking the wicket – used with reference to a bowled ball or a bowler 3 to travel in a vehicle smoothly and rapidly – often + *along*

bow·legged /-'leg(i)d/ *adj* having legs that are bowed outwards at the knees

¹**bowler** /'bohlə/ n the person who bowls in a team sport; *specif* a member of the fielding side who bowls (as a specialist) the ball in cricket

²**bowler, bowler 'hat** n a stiff felt hat with a rounded crown and a narrow brim

bowling /'bohling/ n any of several games in which balls are rolled at 1 or more objects

bowl over v 1 to strike with a swiftly moving object 2 to overwhelm with surprise

bow out /bow/ v to retire, withdraw

bow 'window /boh/ n a curved bay window

¹**box** /boks/ n pl **box, boxes** any of several evergreen shrubs or small trees used esp for hedges

²**box** n **1a** a rigid container having 4 sides, a bottom, and usu a cover **b** the contents of a box **2a** a small compartment (e g for a group of spectators in a theatre) **b**(1) the penalty area **b**(2) the penalty box **3a** a shield to protect the genitals, worn esp by batsmen and wicketkeepers in cricket **b** a structure that contains a telephone for use by members of a specified organization **4** a small simple sheltering or enclosing structure **5** *Br* a gift given to tradesmen at Christmas **6** *Br* television; *specif* a television set – + *the; infml*

³**box** v 1 to enclose (as if) in a box – + *in* or *up* 2 to hem in (e g an opponent in soccer) – usu + *in* — **box the compass** 1 to name the 32 points of the compass in their order 2 to make a complete reversal

⁴**box** v 1 to slap (e g the ears) with the hand 2 to engage in boxing

Box and Cox /koks/ *adv* or *adj, Br* alternating; in turn

¹**boxer** /'boksə/ n one who engages in the sport of boxing

²**boxer** n a compact medium-sized short-haired dog of a breed originating in Germany

boxing /'boksing/ n the art of attack and defence with the fists practised as a sport

'**Boxing ,Day** n December 26, observed as a public holiday in Britain (apart from Scotland)

'**box ,number** n the number of a box or pigeon hole at a newspaper or post office where arrangements are made for replies to advertisements or other mail to be sent

'**box ,office** n an office (e g in a theatre) where tickets of admission are sold

¹**boy** /boy/ n **1a** a male child from birth to puberty **b** a son **c** an immature male; a youth **d** a boyfriend **2** a fellow, person **3** a male servant – sometimes taken to be offensive – ~**hood** n – ~**ish** adj – ~**ishly** adv – ~**ishness** n

²**boy** interj, chiefly NAm – used to express excitement or surprise

boycott /'boykot/ v to refuse to have dealings with (e g a person, shop, or organization), usu to express disapproval or to force acceptance of certain conditions – **boycott** n

'**boy,friend** /-,frend/ n 1 a frequent or regular male companion of a girl or woman 2 a male lover

bra /brah/ n, pl **bras** a woman's closely fitting undergarment with cups for supporting the breasts

¹**brace** /brays/ n pl **braces**, (1) **braces**, *after a determiner* **brace** 1 two of a kind; a pair 2 sthg (e g a clasp) that connects or fastens 3 a crank-shaped instrument for turning a drilling bit **4a** a diagonal piece of structural material that serves to strengthen **b** a rope attached to a yard on a ship that swings the yard horizontally to trim the sail **c** pl straps worn over the shoulders to hold up trousers **d** an appliance for supporting a weak leg or other body part **e** a dental fitting worn to correct irregular teeth **5a** a mark { or } used to connect words or items to be considered together **b** (this mark connecting) 2 or more musical staves the parts of which are to be performed simultaneously

²**brace** v **1a** to prepare for use by making taut **b** to prepare, steel 2 to provide or support with a brace

bracelet /'brayslit/ n 1 an ornamental band or chain worn round the wrist 2 pl handcuffs – infml

bracing /'braysing/ adj refreshing, invigorating

bracken /'brakən/ n a common large coarse fern of esp moorland

¹**bracket** /'brakit/ n 1 an overhanging projecting fixture or member that is designed to support a vertical load or strengthen an angle **2a** a parenthesis **b** either of a pair of marks [ ] used in writing and printing to enclose matter 3 (the distance between) a pair of shots fired usu in front of and beyond a target to aid in range-finding 4 any of a graded series of income groups

²**bracket** v 1 to place (as if) within brackets 2 to put in the same category; associate – usu + *together* **3a** to get a range by firing in front of and behind (a target) **b** to establish a margin on either side of (e g an estimation)

brackish /'brakish/ adj slightly salty – ~**ness** n

bract /brakt/ n a usu small leaf near a flower or floral axis

bradawl /'brad,awl/ n an awl; esp one used by a woodworker

¹**brag** /brag/ n a card game resembling poker

²**brag** v **-gg-** to talk or assert boastfully

braggart /'bragət/ n a loud arrogant boaster

Brahman /'brahmən/ n **1a** a Hindu of the highest caste traditionally assigned to the priesthood **b** the impersonal ground of all being in Hinduism 2 any of an Indian breed of humped cattle

¹**braid** /brayd/ v 1 chiefly NAm to plait 2 to ornament, esp with ribbon or braid

²**braid** n 1 a narrow piece of fabric, esp plaited cord or ribbon, used for trimming 2 chiefly NAm a length of plaited hair

braille /brayl/ *n, often cap* a system of writing or printing for the blind that uses characters made up of raised dots

¹**brain** /brayn/ *n* **1a** the portion of the vertebrate central nervous system enclosed within the skull, that constitutes the organ of thought and neural coordination **b** a nervous centre in invertebrates comparable to the vertebrate brain **2a** intelligence – often *pl* with sing. meaning **b(1)** a very intelligent or intellectual person **b(2)** the chief planner of an organization or enterprise – usu *pl* with sing. meaning but sing. in constr — **on the brain** as an obsession; continually in mind

²**brain** *v* **1** to kill by smashing the skull **2** to hit hard on the head – infml

'**brain,child** /-,chield/ *n* a product of one's creative imagination

'**brain ,drain** *n the* loss of highly qualified workers and professionals through emigration

'**brainless** /-lis/ *adj* stupid, foolish – ~**ly** *adv*

'**brain,storm** /-,stawm/ *n* **1** a fit of insanity **2** *chiefly NAm* a sudden good idea

'**brain ,wave** *n* **1** a rhythmic fluctuation of voltage between parts of the brain **2** a sudden bright idea

brainy /'brayni/ *adj* intelligent, clever – infml – **braininess** *n*

braise /brayz/ *v* to cook (e g meat) slowly by first sautéing in hot fat and then simmering gently in a closed container

¹**brake** /brayk/ *n* **1** a device for arresting usu rotary motion, esp by friction **2** sthg that slows down or stops movement or activity

²**brake** *v* to slow or stop by a brake

³**brake** *n* an estate car

bramble /'brambl/ *n* a rough prickly shrub, esp a blackberry

bran /bran/ *n* the broken husk of cereal grain separated from the flour or meal by sifting

¹**branch** /brahnch/ *n* **1** a secondary shoot or stem (e g a bough) arising from a main axis (e g of a tree) **2a** a tributary **b** a side road or way **3** a distinct part of a complex whole: e g **3a** a division of a family descending from a particular ancestor **b** a distinct area of knowledge **c** a division or separate part of an organization

²**branch** *v* **1** to put forth branches **2** to spring out (e g from a main stem)

¹**brand** /brand/ *n* **1** a charred piece of wood **2a** a mark made by burning with a hot iron, or with a stamp or stencil, to identify manufacture or quality or to designate ownership (e g of cattle) **b** a mark formerly put on criminals with a hot iron **3a** a class of goods identified by name as the product of a single firm or manufacturer **b** a characteristic or distinctive kind **4** a sword – poetic

²**brand** *v* **1** to mark with a brand **2** to stigmatize **3** to impress indelibly

brandish /'brandish/ *v* to shake or wave (e g a weapon) menacingly or ostentatiously

,**brand-'new** *adj* conspicuously new and unused

brandy /'brandi/ *n* a spirit distilled from wine or fermented fruit juice

brash /brash/ *adj* **1** impetuous, rash **2** uninhibitedly energetic or demonstrative **3** aggressively self-assertive; impudent

brass /brahs/ *n* **1** an alloy of copper and zinc **2** *sing or pl in constr* the brass instruments of an orchestra or band **3** brazen self-assurance **4 brass, brass hats** *sing or pl in constr* senior military personnel **5** *chiefly N Eng* money *USE* (3, 4, & 5) infml

,**brass 'band** *n* a band consisting (chiefly) of brass and percussion instruments

brassiere /'brazi-ə/ *n* a bra – fml

,**brass 'tacks** *n pl* details of immediate practical importance

brassy /'brahsi/ *adj* **1** shamelessly bold; brazen **2** resembling brass, esp in colour

brat /brat/ *n* an (ill-mannered) child

bravado /brə'vahdoh/ *n pl* **bravadoes, bravados** blustering swaggering conduct

¹**brave** /brayv/ *adj* **1** courageous, fearless **2** excellent, splendid – ~**ly** *adv* – ~**ry** *n*

²**brave** *v* to face or endure with courage

³**brave** *n* a N American Indian warrior

¹**bravo** /'brahvoh/ *n, pl* **bravos, bravoes** a villain, desperado; *esp* a hired assassin

²**bravo** /brah'voh/ *n, pl* **bravos** a shout of approval – often used interjectionally in applauding a performance

¹**brawl** /brawl/ *v* **1** to quarrel or fight noisily **2** *of water* to make a loud confused bubbling sound

²**brawl** *n* a noisy quarrel or fight

brawn /brawn/ *n* **1a** strong muscles **b** muscular strength **2** pork trimmings, esp the meat from a pig's head, boiled, chopped, and pressed into a mould

brawny /'brawni/ *adj* muscular, strong – -**niness** *n*

bray /bray/ *v* **1** to utter the loud harsh cry characteristic of a donkey **2** to utter or play loudly, harshly, or discordantly – **bray** *n*

¹**brazen** /'brayz(ə)n/ *adj* **1** resembling or made of brass **2** sounding harsh and loud like struck brass **3** contemptuously bold

²**brazen** *v* to face with defiance or impudence – esp in *brazen it out*

¹**brazier** /'brayzi-ə, 'brayzhə/ *n* one who works in brass

²**brazier** *n* a receptacle or stand for holding burning coals

¹**breach** /breech/ *n* **1** infraction or violation (e g of a law, obligation, or standard) **2** a gap (e g in a wall) made by battering **3** a break in customarily friendly relations

²**breach** *v* **1** to make a breach in **2** to break, violate

¹**bread** /bred/ *n* **1** a food consisting essentially of flour or meal which is baked and usu leavened, esp with yeast **2** food, sustenance **3a** livelihood **b** money – *slang* — **bread upon the waters** resources chanced or charitable deeds performed without expectation of return

²**bread** *v* to cover with breadcrumbs

'**bread,crumb** /-,krum/ *n* a small fragment of bread

'**bread,line** /-,lien/ *n* **1** *Br* the level of income required for subsistence **2** *chiefly NAm* a queue of people waiting to receive food given in charity

breadth /bret·th, bredth/ *n* **1** distance from side to side **2a** sthg of full width **b** a wide expanse **3** liberality of views or taste

'**bread,winner** /-,wina/ *n* one whose wages are a family's livelihood

¹**break** /brayk/ *v* **broke** /brohk/; **broken** /'brohkən/ **1a** to separate into parts with suddenness or violence **b** to come apart or split into pieces; burst, shatter **2** to violate, transgress **3a** to force a way through or into **b** to escape with sudden forceful effort – often + *out* or *away* **c** to make a sudden dash **4** to make or effect by cutting or forcing through **5** to disrupt the order or compactness of **6a** to defeat utterly; destroy **b** to give way in disorderly retreat **c** to crush the spirit of **d**(1) to train (an animal, esp a horse) for the service of human beings **d**(2) to inure, accustom **e**(1) to exhaust in health, strength, or capacity **e**(2) to fail in health, strength, or control **7a** to ruin financially **b** to reduce in rank **8a** to reduce the force or intensity of **b** to cause failure and discontinuance of (a strike) by measures outside bargaining processes **9** to exceed, surpass **10** to ruin the prospects of **11a** to stop or interrupt **b** to destroy the uniformity of **12a** to end a relationship, agreement, etc *with* **b** to cause to discontinue a habit **13a** to come to pass; occur **b** to make known; tell **14a** to solve or crack (a code or cipher system) **b** to demonstrate the falsity of (an alibi) **15** to split into smaller units, parts, or processes; divide – often + *up* or *down* **16** to become inoperative because of damage, wear, or strain **17** to open the operating mechanism of (a gun) **18** to separate after a clinch in boxing **19** *of a wave* to curl over and disintegrate in surf or foam **20** *of weather* to change suddenly, esp after a fine spell **21** *esp of a ball bowled in cricket* to change direction of forward travel on bouncing **22** *of a voice* to alter sharply in tone, pitch, or intensity; *esp* to shift abruptly from one register to another **23** to interrupt one's activity for a brief period **24** to make the opening shot of a game of snooker, billiards, or pool **25** *of cream* to separate during churning into liquid and fat — **break a leg** to be successful in a performance – used in the theatre to wish another luck — **break cover** to emerge abruptly from a hiding place — **break even** to achieve a balance between expenditure and income; *esp* to recover precisely what one spends — **break into 1a** to begin abruptly **b** to give voice or expression to abruptly **2** to enter by force **3** to make entry or entrance into **4** to interrupt — **break new ground** to make or show new discoveries; pioneer — **break service/break someone's service** to win a game against the server (e g in tennis) — **break someone's heart** to cause sby heartbreak — **break the back** to do or overcome the largest or hardest part — **break the ice** to overcome initial reserve — **break wind** to expel gas from the intestine through the anus

²**break** *n* **1** an act or action of breaking **2a** a condition produced (as if) by breaking; a gap **b** a rupture in previously good relations **3** the action or act of breaking in, out, or forth **4** a dash, rush **5a** a change or interruption in a continuous process or trend **b** a respite from work or duty; *specif* a daily pause for play and refreshment at school or a planned interruption in a radio or television programme **6a** the opening shot in a game of snooker, billiards, or pool **b** a slow ball bowled in cricket that deviates in a specified direction on bouncing **c** the act or an instance of breaking an opponent's service in tennis **d** a sequence of successful shots or strokes (e g in snooker) **7** a notable variation in pitch, intensity, or tone in the voice **8a** the point where one musical register changes to another **b** a short ornamental passage inserted between phrases in jazz **9a** a stroke of esp good luck; an opportunity, chance

breakage /'braykij/ *n* **1** sthg broken – usu pl **2** allowance for things broken (e g in transit)

¹**breakaway** /'brayka,way/ *n* a breaking away (e g from a group or tradition); a withdrawing

²**breakaway** *adj* **1** favouring independence from an association; withdrawing **2** *chiefly NAm* made to break or bend easily

breakdance /'brayk,dahns/ *v* or *n* (to perform) an acrobatic freestyle dance, usu to the accompaniment of rock music, featuring spins on the performer's head and shoulders – ~ **r** *n*

'**break,down** /-,down/ *n* **1** a failure to function **2** a physical, mental, or nervous collapse **3** failure to progress or have effect **4** a division into categories; a classification **5** an account in which the transactions are recorded under various categories

break down *v* **1a** to divide into (simpler) parts or categories **b** to undergo decomposition **2** to take apart, esp for storage or shipment **3** to become inoperative through breakage or wear **4** to lose one's composure completely

¹**breaker** /'brayka/ *n* a wave breaking into foam

²**breaker** *n* a small water cask

,**break-'even** *adj* or *n* (of or being) the point at which profit equals loss

breakfast /'brekfəst/ n (food prepared for) the first meal of the day, esp when taken in the morning

break in v 1 to enter a house or building by force 2a to interrupt a conversation b to intrude 3 to accustom to a certain activity 4 to use or wear until comfortable or working properly

'**break,neck** /-,nek/ adj extremely dangerous

break out v 1 to become affected with a skin eruption 2 to develop or emerge with suddenness and force 3 to escape 4 to take from shipboard stowage ready for use 5 to unfurl (a flag) at the mast

'**break,through** /-,throoh/ n 1 an act or point of breaking through an obstruction 2 an attack that penetrates enemy lines 3 a sudden advance, esp in knowledge or technique

'**break,up** /-,up/ n 1 a dissolution, disruption 2 a division into smaller units 3 chiefly Can the spring thaw

break up v 1 to disrupt the continuity of 2 to decompose 3 to come or bring to an end 4a to break into pieces (e g for salvage); scrap b to crumble 5 to (cause to) lose morale or composure; also to give way to laughter 6 Br, of a school to disband for the holidays

'**break,water** /-,wawtə/ n an offshore structure (e g a wall) used to protect a harbour or beach from the force of waves

bream /breem/ n any of various European freshwater fishes related to the carps and minnows

¹**breast** /brest/ n 1 either of 2 milk-producing organs situated on the front of the chest in the human female and some other mammals 2 the fore part of the body between the neck and the abdomen 3 sthg (e g a swelling or curve) resembling a breast 4 the seat of emotion and thought; the bosom – fml

²**breast** v 1 to contend with resolutely; confront 2 to meet, lean, or thrust against with the breast or front 3 chiefly Br to climb, ascend

'**breast,bone** /-,bohn/ n the sternum

'**breast-,feed** v to feed (a baby) with milk from the breast rather than a bottle

'**breast,plate** /-,playt/ n a metal plate worn as defensive armour for the chest

'**breast,stroke** /-,strohk/ n a swimming stroke executed on the front by thrusting the arms forwards while kicking outwards and backwards with the legs, then sweeping the arms backwards

breath /breth/ n 1 a slight indication; a suggestion 2a breathing b opportunity or time to breathe; respite 3 spirit, animation — **out of breath** breathing very rapidly (e g from strenuous exercise) — **under one's breath** in a whisper

breathalyse also **breathalyze** /'bretha,liez/ v to test (e g a driver) for the level of alcohol in exhaled breath

'**breatha,lyser** also **breathalyzer** /-,liezə/ n a device used to test the alcohol content in the blood of a motorist

breathe /breedh/ v 1a to draw air into and expel it from the lungs b to send out by exhaling 2 to live 3a to pause and rest before continuing b to allow (e g a horse) to rest after exertion 4 of wine to be exposed to the beneficial effects of air after being kept in an airtight container (e g a bottle) 5 to utter, express — **breathe down someone's neck** to keep sby under constant or too close surveillance — **breathe easily/freely** to enjoy relief (e g from pressure or danger)

breather /'breedhə/ n 1 a small vent in an otherwise airtight enclosure (e g a crankcase) 2 a break in activity for rest or relief – infml

'**breathing ,space** n a pause in a period of activity, esp for rest

breathless /'brethlis/ adj 1 not breathing; esp holding one's breath due to excitement or suspense 2a gasping; out of breath b gripping, intense – ~**ly** adv – ~**ness** n

'**breath,taking** /-,tayking/ adj making one breathless; exciting, thrilling – ~**ly** adv

breathy /'brethi/ adj characterized or accompanied by the audible passage of breath – **breathily** adv – **breathiness** n

breech /breech/ n 1 the buttocks 2 the part of a firearm at the rear of the barrel

breeches /'brichiz, 'breechiz/ n pl 1 knee-length trousers, usu closely fastened at the lower edges 2 jodhpurs that are baggy at the thigh and close fitting and fastened with buttons from the knee to the ankle

breeches buoy n a seat in the form of a pair of canvas breeches hung from a life buoy running on a rope leading to a place of safety for use in rescue at sea

¹**breed** /breed/ v **bred** /bred/ 1 to rear; bring up 2 to produce, engender 3 to propagate (plants or animals) sexually and usu under controlled conditions – ~**er** n

²**breed** n 1 a group of animals or plants, often specially selected, visibly similar in most characteristics 2 race, lineage 3 class, kind

breeding /'breeding/ n 1 ancestry 2 behaviour; esp that showing good manners 3 the sexual propagation of plants or animals

¹**breeze** /breez/ n 1 a light gentle wind 2 a slight disturbance or quarrel – infml 3 chiefly NAm sthg easily done; a cinch – infml

²**breeze** v 1 to come in or into, or move along, swiftly and airily 2 to make progress breezily and easily – infml

'**breeze-,block** n a rectangular building block made of coke ash mixed with sand and cement

breezy /'breezi/ adj 1 windy, fresh 2 brisk, lively 3 off-hand, airy – **breezily** adv – **breeziness** n

bre

brethren /'breðhrin/ *pl of* **brother** – chiefly in fml address or in referring to the members of a profession, society, or sect

breve /breev/ *n* a note equal in time value to 2 semibreves or 4 minims

brevity /'brevəti/ *n* **1** shortness of duration; the quality of being brief **2** expression in few words; conciseness

¹brew /brooh/ *v* **1** to prepare (e g beer or ale) by steeping, boiling, and fermentation or by infusion and fermentation **2a** to contrive, plot – often + *up* **b** to be in the process of formation – often + *up* **3** to prepare (e g tea) by infusion in hot water

²brew *n* **1** a brewed beverage **2a** an amount brewed at once **b** the quality of what is brewed

brewery /'brooh-əri/ *n* an establishment in which beer or ale is brewed

¹briar /'brie-ə/ *n* a plant with a prickly stem (e g a blackberry)

²briar *n* **1** a plant of the heather family; a brier **2** a tobacco pipe made from the root of a brier

¹bribe /brieb/ *v* to induce or influence (as if) by a bribe – ~**ry** *n*

²bribe *n* sthg, esp money, given or promised to influence the judgment or conduct of a person

bric-a-brac /'brik ə ˌbrak/ *n* miscellaneous small articles, usu of ornamental or sentimental value; curios

¹brick /brik/ *n* **1** a usu rectangular unit for building or paving purposes, typically about 8in × 3³/₄in × 2¹/₄in made of moist clay hardened by heat **2** a rectangular compressed mass (e g of ice cream) **3** a reliable stout-hearted person; a stalwart – infml

²brick *v* to close, face, or pave with bricks – usu + *up*

¹brick.bat /-ˌbat/ *n* **1** a fragment of a hard material (e g a brick); *esp* one used as a missile **2** a critical remark

bride /bried/ *n* a woman at the time of her wedding – **dal** *adj*

¹bride.groom /-ˌgroohm, -ˌgroom/ *n* a man at the time of his wedding

¹brides.maid /-ˌmayd/ *n* an unmarried girl or woman who attends a bride

¹bridge /brij/ *n* **1a** a structure spanning a depression or obstacle and supporting a roadway, railway, canal, or path **b** a time, place, or means of connection or transition **2a** the upper bony part of the nose **b** an arch serving to raise the strings of a musical instrument **c** a raised platform on a ship from which it is directed **d** the support for a billiards or snooker cue formed esp by the hand **3a** sthg (e g a partial denture permanently attached to adjacent natural teeth) that fills a gap

²bridge *v* to make a bridge over or across; *also* to cross (e g a river) by a bridge

³bridge *n* any of various card games for usu 4 players in 2 partnerships in which players bid for the right to name a trump suit, and in which the hand of the declarer's partner is exposed and played by the declarer

¹bridge.head /-ˌhed/ *n* an advanced position (to be) seized in hostile territory as a foothold for further advance

¹bridle /'briedl/ *n* a framework of leather straps buckled together round the head of a draught or riding animal, including the bit and reins, used to direct and control it

²bridle *v* **bridling** /'briedling/ **1** to restrain or control (as if) with a bridle **2** to show hostility or resentment (e g because of an affront), esp by drawing back the head and chin

¹bridle.path *n* a track or right of way suitable for horseback riding

Brie /bree/ *n* a large round cream-coloured soft cheese

¹brief /breef/ *adj* **1** short in duration or extent **2** in few words; concise – ~**ly** *adv*

²brief *n* **1a** a statement of a client's case drawn up for the instruction of counsel **b** a case, or piece of employment, given to a barrister **c** a set of instructions outlining what is required, and usu setting limits to one's powers (e g in negotiating) **2** *pl* short close-fitting pants — **in brief** in a few words; briefly

³brief *v* **1** to provide with final instructions or necessary information **2** *Br* to retain (a barrister) as legal counsel – ~**ing** *n*

¹brief.case /-ˌkays/ *n* a flat rectangular case for carrying papers or books

¹brier, briar /'brie-ə/ *n* a plant with a thorny, prickly stem

²brier, briar *n* a S European plant of the heather family with a root used for making pipes

¹brig /brig/ *n* a 2-masted square-rigged sailing vessel

²brig *n* a prison in the US Navy

brigade /bri'gayd/ *n* **1** a large section of an army usu composed of a headquarters, several fighting units (e g infantry battalions or armoured regiments), and supporting units **2** an organized or uniformed group of people (e g firemen)

brigadier /ˌbrigə'diə/ *n* an officer commanding a brigade in the British army

brigand /'brigand/ *n* one who lives by plunder, usu as a member of a group; a bandit – ~**age** *n*

bright /briet/ *adj* **1a** radiating or reflecting light; shining **b** radiant with happiness **2** *of a colour* of high saturation or brilliance **3a** intelligent, clever **b** lively, charming **c** promising, talented – ~**ly** *adv* – ~**ness** *n*

brighten /'brietn/ *v* to make or become bright or brighter – often + *up*

bro

brilliant /'brilyənt, -li·ənt/ adj 1 very bright; glittering 2 of high quality; good – infml – **-liance, -liancy** n

¹**brim** /brim/ n 1 the edge or rim of a hollow vessel, a natural depression, or a cavity 2 the projecting rim of a hat

²**brim** v **-mm-** to be full

brimstone /'brim,stohn/ n sulphur

brindled /'brind(ə)ld/ adj having obscure dark streaks or flecks on a grey or tawny ground

brine /brien/ n water (almost) saturated with common salt

bring /bring/ v **brought** /brawt/ **1a** to convey (sth) to a place or person; come with or cause to come **b** to cause to achieve a particular condition **2a** to cause to occur, lead to **b** to offer, present **3** to prefer (a charge or legal case) **4** to sell for (a price) — **bring home** to make unmistakably clear to — **bring to bear 1** to put to use **2** to apply, exert — **bring to book 1** to put in a position in which one must answer for one's acts **2** to cause to be reproved — **bring to light** to disclose, reveal — **bring to mind** to cause to be recalled — **bring up the rear** to come last

bring down v 1 to cause to fall or come down 2 to kill by shooting 3 to reduce — **bring the house down** to win the enthusiastic approval of the audience

bring forth v 1 to give birth to; produce 2 to offer, present

bring forward v 1 to produce to view; introduce 2 to carry (a total) forward (e g to the top of the next page)

bring in v 1 to produce as profit or return 2 to introduce 3 to pronounce (a verdict) in court 4 to earn

bring off v to carry to a successful conclusion; achieve, accomplish

bring on v 1 to cause to appear or occur 2 to improve, help

bring out v 1 to make clear **2a** to publish **b** to introduce (a young woman) formally to society 3 to utter 4 to cause (sby) to be afflicted with a rash, spots, etc – usu + in 5 to encourage to be less reticent – esp in *bring somebody out of him-/herself* 6 *chiefly Br* to instruct or cause (workers) to go on strike

bring round v 1 to cause to adopt a particular opinion or course of action; persuade 2 to restore to consciousness; revive

bring up v 1 to educate, rear 2 to cause to stop suddenly 3 to bring to attention; introduce 4 to vomit

brink /bringk/ n 1 an edge; *esp* the edge at the top of a steep place 2 *the* verge, onset

brisk /brisk/ adj 1 keenly alert; lively 2 fresh, invigorating 3 energetic, quick – ~**ly** adv – ~**ness** n

brisket /'briskit/ n a joint of beef cut from the breast

¹**bristle** /'brisl/ n a short stiff coarse hair or filament

²**bristle** v **bristling** /'brisling, 'brisl·ing/ 1 to rise and stand stiffly erect 2 to take on an aggressive attitude or appearance (e g in response to a slight) 3 to be filled or thickly covered (*with* sth suggestive of bristles)

bristly /'brisli/ adj 1 thickly covered with bristles 2 tending to bristle easily; belligerent

British /'british/ n 1 *pl in constr the* people of Britain 2 *chiefly NAm* English as typically spoken and written in Britain – **British** adj

Briton /'brit(ə)n/ n 1 a member of any of the peoples inhabiting Britain before the Anglo-Saxon invasions 2 a native, inhabitant, or subject of Britain

brittle /'britl/ adj 1 easily broken or cracked; frail 2 easily hurt or offended; sensitive

¹**broach** /brohch/ n any of various pointed or tapered tools: e g **a** a tool for tapping casks **b** a spit for roasting meat

²**broach** v 1 to open up or break into (e g a bottle or stock of sth) and start to use 2 to open up (a subject) for discussion

¹**broad** /brawd/ adj 1 having ample extent from side to side 2 extending far and wide; spacious 3 open, full – esp in *broad daylight* 4 marked by lack of restraint or delicacy; coarse 5 liberal, tolerant 6 relating to the main points; general – ~**ly** adv – ~**ness** n

²**broad** n 1 the broad part 2 *often cap, Br* a large area of fresh water formed by the broadening of a river – usu pl 3 *chiefly NAm* a woman – slang

broad 'bean n (the large flat edible seed of) a widely cultivated Old World leguminous plant

¹**broadcast** /'brawd,kahst/ adj cast or scattered in all directions

²**broadcast** n 1 the act of transmitting by radio or television 2 a single radio or television programme

³**broadcast** v **broadcast** *also* **broadcasted** 1 to scatter or sow (seed) broadcast 2 to make widely known 3 to transmit as a broadcast, esp for widespread reception 4 to speak or perform on a broadcast programme – ~**er** n – ~**ing** n

broaden /'brawdn/ v to make or become broad

broad,loom /-,loohm/ n or adj (a carpet) woven on a wide loom

broad-'minded adj tolerant of varied views, unconventional behaviour, etc; liberal – ~**ly** adv – ~**ness** n

broad,sheet /-,sheet/ n a large sheet of paper printed on 1 side only; *also* sth (e g an advertisement) printed on a broadsheet

¹**broad,side** /-,sied/ n 1 a broadsheet **2a** (the simultaneous firing of) all the guns on 1 side of a ship **b** a forceful verbal or written attack

²**broadside** *adv* with the broader side towards a given object or point

'**broad,sword** /-,sawd/ *n* a sword for cutting rather than thrusting

brocade /brə'kayd/ *n* a rich (silk) fabric woven with raised patterns

broccoli /'brokali/ *n* a branching form of cauliflower whose young shoots are used for food

brochure /'brohshə, broh'shooə/ *n* a small pamphlet

'**brogue** /brohg/ *n* a stout walking shoe

²**brogue** *n* a dialect or regional pronunciation; *esp* an Irish accent

broil /broyl/ *v* 1 to cook by direct exposure to radiant heat (e g over a fire); *specif*, *NAm* to grill 2 to become extremely hot

'**broke** /brohk/ *past of* **break**

²**broke** *adj* penniless – *infml*

broken /'brohkan/ *adj* 1 violently separated into parts; shattered 2a having undergone or been subjected to fracture **b** *of a land surface* irregular, interrupted, or full of obstacles **c** not fulfilled; violated **d** discontinuous, interrupted 3a made weak or infirm **b** subdued completely; crushed **c** not working; defective 4 affected by separation or divorce – **~ly** *adv* – **~ness** *n*

broker /'brohkə/ *n* an intermediary; *specif* an agent who negotiates contracts of purchase and sale (e g of securities)

brolly /'broli/ *n*, *chiefly Br* an umbrella – *infml*

bromine /'brohmeen, -min/ *n* a nonmetallic element, usu occurring as a deep red corrosive toxic liquid

bronchitis /brong'kietas/ *n* (a disease marked by) acute or chronic inflammation of the tubes of the lungs accompanied by a cough and catarrh – **-tic** *adj*

bronco /'brongkoh/ *n*, *pl* **broncos** an unbroken or imperfectly broken horse of western N America

brontosaurus /,brontə'sawros/ *n* any of various large 4-legged and prob plant-eating dinosaurs – no longer used technically

'**bronze** /bronz/ *v* to make brown or tanned

²**bronze** *n* 1 any of various copper-base alloys; *esp* one containing tin 2 a sculpture or artefact made of bronze 3 a yellowish-brown colour 4 **bronze, bronze medal** an award for coming third in a competition

'**Bronze ,Age** *n* the period of human culture characterized by the use of bronze or copper tools and weapons

brooch /brohch/ *n* an ornament worn on clothing and fastened by means of a pin

'**brood** /broohd/ *n* 1 young birds, insects, etc hatched or cared for at one time 2 the children of one family – humor

²**brood** *v* 1 *of a bird* to sit on eggs in order to hatch them 2a to dwell gloomily *on*; worry *over* or *about* **b** to be in a state of depression – **~er** *n*

³**brood** *adj* kept for breeding

broody /'broohdi/ *adj* 1 *of fowl* ready to brood eggs 2 contemplative; moody 3 *of a woman* feeling a strong desire or urge to be a mother – *infml* – **-dily** *adv* – **-diness** *n*

'**brook** /brook/ *v* to tolerate; stand for

²**brook** *n* a usu small freshwater stream

broom /broohm, broom/ *n* 1 any of various leguminous shrubs with long slender branches, small leaves, and usu showy yellow flowers 2 a long-handled brush; *esp* one made of a bundle of twigs

'**broom,stick** /-,stik/ *n* the long thin handle of a broom

broth /broth/ *n* (a thin soup made from) stock

brothel /'broth(ə)l, 'brodh(ə)l/ *n* a house of prostitution

brother /'brudhə/ *n*, *pl* **brothers**, (3, 4, & 5) **brothers** *also* **brethren** /'bredhrin/ 1 a male having the same parents as another person; *also* a half brother or stepbrother 2 a kinsman 3 a fellow member 4 one, esp a male, who is related to another by a common tie or interest 5 a member of a men's religious order who is not in holy orders

'**brotherhood** /-hood/ *n* 1 being brothers 2a an association (e g a religious body) for a particular purpose **b** (an idea of) fellowship between all human beings

'**brother-in-,law** *n*, *pl* **brothers-in-law** 1 the brother of one's spouse 2 the husband of one's sister

brought /brawt/ *past of* **bring**

brow /brow/ *n* 1a an eyebrow **b** the forehead 2 the top or edge of a hill, cliff, etc

'**brow,beat** /-,beet/ *v* **browbeat**; **browbeaten** to intimidate, coerce, or bully by a persistently threatening or dominating manner

'**brown** /brown/ *adj* 1 of the colour brown; *esp* of dark or tanned complexion 2 (made with ingredients that are) partially or wholly unrefined or unpolished – **~ish** *adj*

²**brown** *n* any of a range of dark colours between red and yellow in hue

³**brown** *v* to make or become brown (e g by sautéing)

brownie /'browni/ *n* 1 **brownie guide, brownie** a member of the most junior section of the (British) Guide movement for girls aged from 7 to 10 2 *chiefly NAm* a small square or rectangle of rich chocolate cake containing nuts

,**brown 'study** *n* a state of serious absorption or abstraction; a reverie

'**browse** /browz/ *n* a period of time spent browsing

²**browse** *v* 1 *of animals* to nibble at leaves, grass, or other vegetation 2 to read or search idly *through* a book or a mass of things (e g in a shop), in the hope of finding sthg interesting

brucellosis /ˌbroohsəˈlohsis, -siz/ *n* a serious long-lasting disease, esp of human beings and cattle, caused by a bacterium

¹**bruise** /broohz/ *v* 1 to inflict a bruise on 2 to crush (e g leaves or berries) by pounding 3 to wound, injure; *esp* to inflict psychological hurt on

²**bruise** *n* 1 an injury involving rupture of small blood vessels and discoloration without a break in the skin; *also* a similar plant injury 2 an injury to the feelings

bruiser /ˈbroohzə/ *n* a large burly man; *specif* a prizefighter

brunch /brunch/ *n* a meal, usu taken in the middle of the morning, that combines a late breakfast and an early lunch

brunette *NAm also* **brunet** /broohˈnet/ *n or adj* (sby, esp a young adult woman,) having dark hair and usu a relatively dark complexion

brunt /brunt/ *n* the principal force or stress (e g of an attack)

¹**brush** /brush/ *n* scrub vegetation

²**brush** *n* 1 an implement composed of bristles set into a firm piece of material and used for grooming hair, painting, sweeping, etc 2 a bushy tail, esp of a fox 3 an act of brushing 4 a quick light touch or momentary contact in passing

³**brush** *v* 1 to apply a brush to **b** to apply with a brush 2 to remove with sweeping strokes (e g of a brush) – usu + *away* or *off* 3 to pass lightly over or across 4 to move lightly, heedlessly, or rudely – usu + *by* or *past*

⁴**brush** *n* a brief encounter or skirmish

'**brush-,off** *n* a quietly curt or disdainful dismissal; a rebuff – *infml*

brush up *v* 1 to tidy one's clothes, hair, etc 2 to renew one's skill in; refresh one's memory of – **brush-up** *n*

brusque /brusk, broosk, broohsk/ *adj* curt – ~**ly** *adv* – ~**ness** *n*

,**brussels 'sprout** *n, often cap B* (any of the many edible small green buds that grow on the stem of) a plant of the cabbage family

brutal /ˈbroohtl/ *adj* 1 grossly ruthless or unfeeling 2 cruel, cold-blooded 3 harsh, severe – **-tality** *n* – **-tally** *adv*

¹**brute** /brooht/ *adj* 1 characteristic of an animal in quality, action, or instinct: e g 1a cruel, savage **b** not working by reason; mindless 2 purely physical

²**brute** *n* 1 a beast 2 a brutal person – **brutish** *adj* – **brutishly** *adv*

¹**bubble** /ˈbubl/ *v* **bubbling** /ˈbubling, ˈbubl·ing/ 1 to form or produce bubbles 2 to make a sound like the bubbles rising in liquid 3 to be highly excited or overflowing (with a feeling)

²**bubble** *n* **1a** a usu small body of gas within a liquid or solid **b** a thin spherical usu transparent film of liquid inflated with air or vapour 2 sthg

that lacks firmness or reality; *specif* an unreliable or speculative scheme 3 a sound like that of bubbling

¹**bubbly** /ˈbubli/ *adj* 1 full of bubbles 2 overflowing with good spirits or liveliness; vivacious

²**bubbly** *n* champagne; *broadly* any sparkling wine – *infml*

bu,bonic 'plague /byooˈbonik, byooh-/ *n* plague characterized by swellings in the groin and armpits

buccaneer /ˌbukəˈniə/ *n* 1 a pirate esp in the W Indies in the 17th c 2 an unscrupulous adventurer, esp in politics or business

¹**buck** /buk/ *n pl* **bucks**, (1) **bucks**, *esp collectively* **buck 1a** a male animal, esp a male deer, antelope, rabbit, rat, etc **b** an antelope 2 a dashing fellow; a dandy 3 *NAm* a dollar – *slang*

²**buck** *v* 1 *of a horse or mule* to spring into the air with the back curved and come down with the forelegs stiff and the head lowered 2 to fail to comply with; run counter to

³**buck** *n* the responsibility – esp in *pass the buck*

bucked /bukt/ *adj* pleased, encouraged

bucket /ˈbukit/ *n* 1 a large open container used esp for carrying liquids 2 the scoop of an excavating machine 3 *pl* large quantities – *infml*

¹**buckle** /ˈbukl/ *n* a fastening consisting of a rigid rim, usu a hinged pin, used to join together 2 loose ends (e g of a belt or strap) or for ornament

²**buckle** *v* **buckling** /ˈbukling, ˈbukl·ing/ 1 to fasten with a buckle 2 to bend, give way, or crumple

buckle down *v* to apply oneself vigorously

buckshee /ˈbukshee, -ˈ-/ *adj or adv*, *Br* without charge; free – *slang*

buckshot /ˈbuk,shot/ *n* a coarse lead shot used esp for shooting large animals

'**buck,skin** /-,skin/ *n* a soft pliable usu suede-finished leather

,**buck'tooth** /-ˈtoohth/ *n* a large projecting front tooth

buck up *v* 1 to become encouraged 2 to hurry up

bucolic /byoohˈkolik/ *adj* 1 of shepherds or herdsmen; pastoral 2 (typical) of rural life – ~**ally** *adv*

¹**bud** /bud/ *n* 1 a small protuberance on the stem of a plant that may develop into a flower, leaf, or shoot 2 sthg not yet mature or fully developed: e g **2a** an incompletely opened flower **b** an outgrowth of an organism that becomes a new individual

²**bud** *v* **-dd-** 1 *of a plant* to put forth buds 2 to reproduce asexually by forming and developing buds 3 to graft a bud into (a plant of another kind), usu in order to propagate a desired variety

Buddhism /ˈboodiz(ə)m/ *n* an eastern religion teaching that one can be liberated from the suffering inherent in life by mental and moral self-purification – **Buddhist** *n or adj*

budding /ˈbuding/ *adj* being in an early and usu promising stage of development

buddy /'budi/ n, *chiefly NAm* a companion, partner *N infml*

budge /buj/ v 1 to (cause to) move or shift 2 to (force or cause to) change an opinion or yield

budgerigar /'buj(ə)ri,gah/ n a small Australian bird that belongs to the same family as the parrots and is often kept in captivity

¹budget /'bujit/ n 1 a statement of a financial position over a definite period of time 2 a plan of how money will be spent or allocated 3 the amount of money available for, required for, or assigned to a particular purpose – ~ ary *adj*

²budget v to plan or provide for the use of (e g money, time, or manpower) in detail

¹buff /buf/ n 1 *the* bare skin – chiefly in *in the buff* 2 (a) pale yellowish brown 3 a device (e g a stick or pad) with a soft absorbent surface used for polishing sthg 4 one who has a keen interest in and wide knowledge of a specified subject; an enthusiast

²buff v to polish, shine *up*

buffalo /'bufəloh/ n pl **buffaloes** *also* **buffalos**, *esp collectively* **buffalo** 1 **buffalo, water buffalo** an often domesticated Asian ox 2 a large N American wild ox with short horns, heavy forequarters, and a large muscular hump

¹buffer /'bufə/ n an (ineffectual) fellow – chiefly in *old buffer*, infml

²buffer n 1 a spring-loaded metal disc on a railway vehicle or at the end of a railway track 2 a device that serves to protect sthg, or to cushion against shock 3 a person who shields another, esp from annoying routine matters

³buffer v to lessen the shock of; cushion

¹buffet /'bufit/ n 1 a blow, esp with the hand 2 sthg that strikes with telling force

²buffet /'bufit/ v 1 to strike sharply, esp with the hand; cuff 2 to strike repeatedly; batter 3 to treat roughly; treat unpleasantly

³buffet /'boofay/ n 1 a meal set out on tables or a sideboard for diners to help themselves 2 *chiefly Br* a self-service restaurant or snack bar

buffoon /bo'foohn/ n 1 a ludicrous figure; a clown 2 a rough and noisy fool – ~ **ery** n

¹bug /bug/ n 1 any of several insects commonly considered obnoxious; *esp* a bedbug 2 an unexpected defect or imperfection 3 a disease-producing germ; *also* a disease caused by it – not used technically 4 a concealed listening device 5 a temporary enthusiasm; a craze – infml

²bug v -gg- 1 to plant a concealed listening device in 2 to bother, annoy – infml

bugbear /'bug,beə/ n an object or (persistent) source of fear, concern, or difficulty

¹bugger /'bugə/ n 1 a sodomite 2 a (worthless or contemptible) person, esp male 3 *Br* a cause of annoyance or difficulty *USE (except* 1) vulg

²bugger v 1 to practise sodomy on 2 – used interjectionally to express contempt or annoyance 3 to damage or ruin – often + *up* 4 to fool *around* or *about USE (except* 1) vulg

buggery /'bugəri/ n sodomy

buggy /'bugi/ n a light one-horse carriage

¹bugle /'byoohgl/ n a European annual plant of the mint family that has spikes of blue flowers

²bugle n a valveless brass instrument that is used esp for military calls

¹build /bild/ v **built** /bilt/ 1 to construct by putting together materials gradually into a composite whole 2 to develop according to a systematic plan, by a definite process, or on a particular base 3a to increase in intensity b to develop in extent – ~ **er** n

²build n the physical proportions of a person or animal; *esp* a person's figure of a usu specified type

build in v to construct or develop as an integral part

building /'bilding/ n 1 a permanent structure (e g a school or house) usu having walls and a roof 2 the art, business, or act of assembling materials into a structure

'building so,ciety n any of various British organizations in which the public can invest money, and which advance money for house purchase

'build,up /-,up/ n praise or publicity, esp given in advance

build up v 1 to accumulate or develop appreciably 2 to promote the esteem of; praise

bulb /bulb/ n 1a a short stem base of a plant (e g the lily, onion, or hyacinth), with 1 or more buds enclosed in overlapping membranous or fleshy leaves, that is formed underground as a resting stage in the plant's development b a tuber, corm, or other fleshy structure resembling a bulb in appearance c a plant having or developing from a bulb 2 a glass globe containing a filament that produces light when electricity is passed through it – ~ **ous** *adj*

¹bulge /bulj/ n 1 a swelling or convex curve on a surface, usu caused by pressure from within or below 2 a sudden and usu temporary expansion (e g in population) – **bulgy** *adj* – **bulgily** *adv* – **bulginess** n

²bulge v to jut out; swell

¹bulk /bulk/ n 1a a spatial dimension; also volume b roughage 2 voluminous or ponderous mass – often used with reference to the shape or size of a corpulent person 3 the main or greater part of — **in bulk** in large amounts or quantities; *esp, of goods bought and sold* in amounts or quantities much larger than as usu packaged or purchased

²bulk v 1 to cause to swell or to be thicker or fuller; pad – often + *out* 2 to gather into a mass 3 to appear as a factor; loom

³bulk *adj* (of materials) in bulk

'**bulk,head** /-,hed/ n a partition or wall separating compartments (e g in an aircraft or ship)

bulky /'bulki/ adj 1 having too much bulk; esp unwieldy 2 corpulent – chiefly euph – **-kily** adv – **-kiness** n

[1]**bull** /bool/ n 1a an adult male bovine animal b an adult male elephant, whale, or other large animal 2 one who buys securities or commodities in expectation of a price rise or who acts to effect such a rise 3 a bull's eye – ~**ish** adj

[2]**bull** n a papal edict on a subject of major importance

[3]**bull** n 1 empty boastful talk; nonsense 2 Br unnecessary or irksome fatigues or discipline, esp in the armed forces USE slang

'**bull,dog** /-,dog/ n a thickset muscular short-haired dog

bulldoze /'bool,dohz/ v 1 to move, clear, gouge out, or level off with a bulldozer 2 to force insensitively or ruthlessly

'**bull,dozer** /-,dohzə/ n a tractor-driven machine with a broad blunt horizontal blade that is used for clearing land, building roads, etc

bullet /'boolit/ n a small round or elongated missile designed to be fired from a firearm; broadly a cartridge – ~**proof** adj

bulletin /'boolətin/ n a brief public notice; specif a brief news item

'**bull,fight** /-,fiet/ n a spectacle (in an arena) in which bulls are ceremonially excited, fought with, and killed, for public entertainment – ~**ing** n – ~**er** n

'**bull,finch** /-,finch/ n a European finch, the male of which has a rosy red breast and throat

'**bull,frog** /-,frog/ n a heavy-bodied deep-voiced frog

bullion /'boolyən/ n gold or silver (in bars) that has not been minted

bullock /'boolək/ n a young or castrated bull

'**bull,ring** /-,ring/ n an arena for bullfights

'**bull's-,eye** n 1 a small thick disc of glass inserted (e g in a ship's deck) to let in light 2 a very hard round usu peppermint sweet 3a (a shot that hits) the centre of a target b sthg that precisely attains a desired end

[1]**bully** /'booli/ n 1 a browbeating person; esp one habitually cruel to others weaker than him-/herself 2 a hired ruffian

[2]**bully** v to treat abusively; intimidate — **bully for** — used to congratulate a specified person, sometimes ironically

[3]**bully** v or n (to perform) a procedure for starting play in a hockey match in which 2 opposing players face each other and alternately strike the ground and the opponent's stick 3 times before attempting to gain possession of the ball

bulrush /'bool,rush/ n 1 any of a genus of annual or perennial sedges 2 Br either of 2 varieties of reed

bulwark /'boolək/ n 1a a solid wall-like structure raised for defence; a rampart b a breakwater, seawall 2 a strong support or protection 3 the side of a ship above the upper deck – usu pl with sing. meaning

[1]**bum** /bum/ n the buttocks – slang

[2]**bum** v -mm- 1 to spend time idly and often travelling casually – usu + around; slang 2 to obtain by begging; cadge – slang

[3]**bum** n, NAm 1 a vagrant, tramp 2 an incompetent worthless person USE slang

[4]**bum** adj, chiefly NAm 1 inferior, worthless 2 disabled USE slang

bumble /'bumbl/ v **bumbling** /'bumbling/ 1 to speak in a faltering manner 2 to proceed unsteadily; stumble – often + along

'**bumble,bee** /-,bee/ n any of numerous large robust hairy bees

bumf, bumph /bumf/ n (boring or unnecessary) paperwork – infml

[1]**bump** /bump/ v to knock against sthg with a forceful jolt – often + into — **bump into** to encounter, esp by chance

[2]**bump** n 1 a sudden forceful blow or jolt 2 a rounded projection from a surface; esp a swelling of tissue

[1]**bumper** /'bumpə/ n a brimming cup or glass

[2]**bumper** adj unusually large

[3]**bumper** n a metal or rubber bar, usu at either end of a motor vehicle, for absorbing shock or minimizing damage in collision

bumpkin /'bum(p)kin/ n an awkward and unsophisticated rustic

bump off v to murder – slang

bumptious /'bum(p)shəs/ adj self-assertive in a presumptuous, obtuse, and often noisy manner – ~**ly** adv – ~**ness** n

bumpy /'bumpi/ adj 1 having or covered with bumps; uneven 2 marked by jolts – **-pily** adv – **-piness** n

bun /bun/ n 1 any of various usu sweet and round small rolls or cakes 2 a usu tight knot of hair worn esp on the back of the head

[1]**bunch** /bunch/ n 1 a compact group formed by a number of things of the same kind, esp when growing or held together; a cluster 2 sing or pl in constr the main group (e g of cyclists) in a race 3 pl, Br a style in which the hair is divided into 2 lengths and tied, usu one on each side of the head 4 sing or pl in constr a group of people – infml

[2]**bunch** v to form (into) a group or cluster – often + up

[1]**bundle** /'bundl/ n 1a a collection of things held loosely together b a package c a collection, conglomerate 2 a great deal; mass 3 a sizable sum of money – slang

²**bundle** v **bundling** /'bundling, 'bundl·ing/ **1** to make into a bundle or package **2** to hustle or hurry unceremoniously **3** to hastily deposit or stuff *into* a suitcase, box, drawer, etc

¹**bung** /bung/ n the stopper of a cask; *broadly* sthg used to plug an opening

²**bung** v **1** to plug, block, or close (as if) with a bung – often + *up* **2** *chiefly Br* to throw, toss – *infml*

bungalow /'bung·gəloh/ n a usu detached or sem-idetached 1-storied house

bungle /'bung·gl/ v **bungling** /'bung·gling, bung·gl·ing/ to perform clumsily; mishandle, botch – ~**r** n

bunion /'bunyən/ n an inflamed swelling at the side of the foot on the first joint of the big toe

¹**bunk** /bungk/ n a built-in bed (e g on a ship) that is often one of a tier of berths

²**bunk** v to sleep or bed *down*, esp in a makeshift bed

³**bunk** n nonsense, humbug

bunker /'bungkə/ n **1** a bin or compartment for storage; *esp* one on a ship for storing fuel **2a** a fortified chamber mostly below ground **b** a golf course hazard that is an area of sand-covered bare ground with 1 or more embankments

bunkum /'bungkəm/ n insincere or foolish talk; nonsense

bunny /'buni/ n a rabbit – usu used by or to children

Bunsen 'burner /'buns(ə)n/ n a gas burner with an intensely hot blue flame

¹**bunting** /'bunting/ n any of various birds that have short strong beaks and are related to the finches

²**bunting** n (flags or decorations made of) a light-weight loosely woven fabric

¹**buoy** /boy/ n a distinctively shaped and marked float moored to the bottom **a** as a navigational aid to mark a channel or hazard **b** for mooring a ship

²**buoy** v **1** to mark (as if) with a buoy **2a** to keep afloat **b** to support, sustain **3** to raise the spirits of *USE* (2 & 3) usu + *up* – ~**ancy** n – ~**ant** adj – ~**antly** adv

burble /'buhbl/ v **burbling** /'buhbling, 'buhbl·ing/ **1** to make a bubbling sound; gurgle **2** to babble, prattle

¹**burden** /'buhd(ə)n/ n **1a** sthg that is carried; a load **b** a duty, responsibility **2** sthg oppressive or wearisome; an encumbrance

²**burden** v to load, oppress

³**burden** n **1** a chorus, refrain **2** a central topic; a theme

'**burdensome** /-səm/ adj oppressive – ~**ness** n

bureau /'byooaroh/ n, pl **bureaus** also **bureaux** /-rohz/ **1a** a specialized administrative unit; *esp* a government department **b** an establishment for exchanging information, making contacts, or coordinating activities **2** *Br* a writing desk; *esp* one with drawers and a sloping top

bureaucracy /byooə'rokrəsi/ n government characterized by specialization of functions, adherence to fixed rules, and a hierarchy of authority; *also* the body of appointed government officials

bureaucrat /'byooərə,krat/ n a government offi-cial who follows a rigid routine – ~**ic** adj – ~**ically** adv

burgeon /'buhj(ə)n/ v **1** to send forth new growth (e g buds or branches) **2** to grow and expand rapidly

burgh /'burə/ n a borough; *specif* a town in Scot-land that has a charter – ~**er** n

burglar /'buhglə/ n sby who unlawfully enters a building (e g to steal) – ~**y** n – **burgle** v

Burgundy /'buhgəndi/ n a red or white table wine from the Burgundy region of France

burial /'beri·əl/ n the act, process, or ceremony of burying esp a dead body

burlesque /buh'lesk/ n **1** a literary or dramatic work that uses exaggeration or imitation to ridi-cule **2** mockery, usu by caricature **3** a US stage show usu consisting of short turns, comic sketches, and striptease acts

burly /'buhli/ adj strongly and heavily built – **liness** n

¹**burn** /buhn/ n, *chiefly Scot* a small stream

²**burn** v **burnt** /buhnt/, **burned** /buhnd, buhnt/ **1a** to consume fuel and give off heat, light, and gases **b** to undergo combustion **c** to destroy by fire **d** to use as fuel **2a** *of the ears or face* to become very red and feel uncomfortably hot **b** to produce or undergo a painfully stinging or smarting sensa-tion **c** to be filled *with*; experience sthg strongly **3a** to injure or damage by exposure to fire, heat, radiation, caustic chemicals, or electricity **b** to execute by burning **c** to char or scorch by expos-ing to fire or heat — **burn one's bridges/boats** to cut off all means of retreat — **burn the candle at both ends** to use one's resources or energies to excess; *esp* to be active at night as well as by day — **burn the midnight oil** to work or study far into the night

³**burn** n **1** injury or damage resulting (as if) from burning **2** a burned area **3** a burning sensation

burner /'buhnə/ n the part of a fuel-burning device (e g a stove or furnace) where the flame is produced

burning /'buhning/ adj **1a** on fire **b** ardent, intense **2a** affecting (as if) with heat **b** resembling that produced by a burn **3** of fundamental impor-tance; urgent

burnish /'buhnish/ v to make shiny or lustrous, esp by rubbing; polish

burnous /,buh'noohs/ n a hooded cloak tradi-tionally worn by Arabs

burnt-out adj exhausted or worn out by too much activity or use

burn up v to drive along extremely fast – *infml*

burp /buhp/ v to (cause to) belch – infml

burr, bur /buh/ n 1 a rough or prickly fruit or seed that sticks or clings 2 a thin rough edge left after cutting or shaping metal, plastic, etc 3 the pronunciation of /r/ in a W country or Northumberland accent

¹**burrow** /'buroh/ n a hole or excavation in the ground made by a rabbit, fox, etc for shelter and habitation

²**burrow** v **1a** to make a burrow **b** to progress (as if) by digging 2 to make a motion suggestive of burrowing; snuggle, nestle 3 to make a search as if by digging

bursar /'buhsə/ n an officer (e g of a monastery or college) in charge of funds

bursary /'buhs(ə)ri/ n 1 a bursar's office 2 a grant of money to a needy student

¹**burst** /buhst/ v **burst** 1 to break open, apart, or into pieces, usu from impact or because of pressure from within 2a to give way from an excess of emotion **b** to give vent suddenly to a repressed emotion 3a to emerge or spring suddenly **b** to launch, plunge 4 to be filled to breaking point or to the point of overflowing

²**burst** n 1 an explosion, eruption 2 a sharp temporary increase (of speed, energy, etc) 3 a volley of shots

burst out v 1 to begin suddenly 2 to exclaim suddenly

bury /'beri/ v 1 to dispose of by depositing (as if) in the earth; esp to (ceremonially) dispose of a dead body thus 2 to conceal, hide 3 to put completely out of mind 4 to submerge, engross – usu + in – **bury the hatchet** to settle a disagreement; become reconciled

¹**bus** /bus/ n pl **-s-**, chiefly NAm **-ss-** a large motor-driven passenger vehicle operating usu according to a timetable along a fixed route

²**bus** v **-s-**, **-ss-** to transport by bus; specif, chiefly NAm to transport (children) by bus to a school in another district where the pupils are of a different race, in order to create integrated classes

busby /'buzbi/ n 1 a military full-dress fur hat worn esp by hussars 2 the bearskin worn by the Brigade of Guards – not used technically

¹**bush** /boosh/ n **1a** (low densely branched) shrub **b** a close thicket of shrubs 2 a large uncleared or sparsely settled area (e g in Africa or Australia), usu scrub-covered or forested 3 a bushy tuft or mass

²**bush** v to extend like or resemble a bush

'**bush ,baby** n a member of either of 2 genera of small active nocturnal tree-dwelling African primates

bushed adj 1 perplexed, confused 2 tired, exhausted – infml

bushel /'booshl/ n 1 any of various units of dry capacity 2 a container holding a bushel

bush telegraph n the rapid unofficial communication of news, rumours, etc by word of mouth

bushy /'booshi/ adj 1 full of or overgrown with bushes 2 growing thickly or densely – **bushiness** n

business /'biznis/ n **1a** a role, function **b** an immediate task or objective **2a** a usu commercial or mercantile activity engaged in as a means of livelihood **b** one's regular employment, profession, or trade **c** a commercial or industrial enterprise; also such enterprises **d** economic transactions or dealings 3 an affair, matter 4 movement or action performed by an actor **5a** personal concern **b** proper motive; justifying right 6 serious activity – **~ man**, **– ~ woman** n — **like nobody's business** extraordinarily well

'**business,like** /-,liek/ adj 1 (briskly) efficient 2 serious, purposeful

busk /busk/ v to sing or play an instrument in the street (e g outside a theatre) in order to earn money – **~er** n

,**busman's 'holiday** n a holiday spent doing one's usual work

'**bus-,stop** n a place, usu marked by a standardized sign, where people may board and alight from buses

¹**bust** /bust/ n 1 a sculpture of the upper part of the human figure including the head, neck, and usu shoulders 2 the upper part of the human torso between neck and waist; esp (the size of) the breasts of a woman

²**bust** v **busted** also **bust 1a** to break, smash; also to make inoperative **b** to bring to an end; break up – often + up **c** to burst **d** to break down **2a** to arrest **b** to raid 3 to lose a game or turn by exceeding a limit (e g the count of 21 in pontoon) — **bust a gut** to exert oneself; make a great effort — infml

³**bust** adj 1 broken – chiefly infml 2 bankrupt – chiefly in go bust; infml

¹**bustle** /'busl/ v **bustling** /'busling, 'busl·ing/ to move briskly and often ostentatiously

²**bustle** n noisy and energetic activity

³**bustle** n a pad or framework worn to expand and support fullness at the back of a woman's skirt

'**bust-,up** n 1 a breaking up or apart 2 a quarrel USE infml

¹**busy** /'bizi/ adj 1 engaged in action; occupied 2 full of activity; bustling 3 foolishly or intrusively active; meddlesome 4 full of detail – **busily** adv – **busyness** n

²**busy** v to make (esp oneself) busy; occupy

'**busy,body** /-,bodi/ n an officious or inquisitive person

¹**but** /bət/, strong but/ conj **1a** were it not for **b** without the necessary accompaniment that – used after a negative **2a** on the contrary; on the other hand – used to join coordinate sentence elements of the same class or function expressing contrast **b** and nevertheless; and yet

but

²but *prep* **1a** with the exception of; barring **b** other than **c** not counting **2** *Scot* without, lacking

³but *adv* **1** only, merely **2** to the contrary **3** – used for emphasis **4** *NE Eng & Aust* however, though

butane /'byoohtayn/ *n* an inflammable gas used esp as a fuel (e g in cigarette lighters)

butch /booch/ *adj* aggressively masculine in appearance – used, often disparagingly, of both women and (esp homosexual) men

¹butcher /'boocha/ *n* **1** sby who slaughters animals or deals in meat **2** sby who kills ruthlessly or brutally

²butcher *v* **1** to slaughter and prepare for market **2** to kill in a barbarous manner **3** to spoil, ruin – ~ y *n*

butler /'butlə/ *n* **1** a manservant in charge of the wines and spirits **2** the chief male servant of a household

¹butt /but/ *n* a blow or thrust, usu with the head or horns – **butt** *v*

²butt *n* **1a** a target **b** *pl* a range, specif for archery or rifle practice **c** a low mound, vault, etc from behind which sportsmen shoot at game birds **2** an object of abuse or ridicule; a victim

³butt *v* to abut – usu + *against* or *onto*

⁴butt *n* **1** the end of a plant or tree nearest the roots **2** the thicker or handle end of a tool or weapon **3** the unsmoked remnant of a cigar or cigarette

⁵butt *n* a large cask, esp for wine, beer, or water

butter /'butə/ *n* **1** a pale yellow solid emulsion made by churning milk or cream and used as food **2** any of various food spreads made with or having the consistency of butter

'butter ,bean *n* a large flat usu dried bean

'butter,cup /-,kup/ *n* any of many plants with usu bright yellow flowers that commonly grow in fields and as weeds

'butter,fingers /-,fing·gəz/ *n pl* **butterfingers** sby clumsy and bad at catching – *infml*

'butter,fly /-,flie/ *n* **1** any of numerous slender-bodied day-flying insects with large broad often brightly coloured wings **2** a swimming stroke executed on the front by moving both arms together forwards out of the water and then sweeping them back through the water **3** *pl* a feeling of sickness caused esp by nervous tension – *infml*

'butter,milk /-,milk/ *n* **1** the liquid left after butter has been churned from milk or cream **2** cultured milk made by the addition of suitable bacteria to milk

'butter,scotch /-,skoch/ *n* (the flavour of) a brittle toffee made from brown sugar, syrup, butter, and water

butter up *v* to charm with lavish flattery; cajole – *infml*

¹buttery /'but(ə)ri/ *n* a room (e g in a college) in which food and drink are served or sold

²buttery *adj* similar to or containing butter

butt in *v* to intrude or interrupt

buttock /'butək/ *n* the back of a hip that forms one of the 2 fleshy parts on which a person sits

¹button /'but(ə)n/ *n* **1** a small knob or disc secured to an article (e g of clothing) and used as a fastener by passing it through a buttonhole or loop **2** an immature whole mushroom **3** a guard on the tip of a fencing foil

²button *v* to close or fasten (as if) with buttons – often + *up*

¹button,hole /-,hohl/ *n* **1** a slit or loop through which a button is passed **2** *chiefly Br* a flower worn in a buttonhole or pinned to the lapel

²buttonhole *v* to detain in conversation

buttress /'butris/ *n* **1** a structure built against a wall or building to provide support or reinforcement **2** a projecting part of a mountain **3** sthg that supports or strengthens

buxom /'buks(ə)m/ *adj* attractively or healthily plump; *specif* full-bosomed

¹buy /bie/ *v* **bought** /bawt/ **1** to purchase **2** to obtain, often by some sacrifice **3** to bribe, hire **4** to believe, accept – *slang* — **buy time** to delay an imminent action or decision; stall

²buy *n* an act of buying; a purchase

buyer /'bie·ə/ *n* one who selects and buys stock to be sold in an esp large shop

buy off *v* to make a payment to in order to avoid some undesired course of action (e g prosecution)

buy out *v* **1** to purchase the share or interest of **2** to free (e g from military service) by payment – usu + *of*

buy up *v* **1** to purchase a controlling interest in (e g a company), esp by acquiring shares **2** to buy the entire available supply of

¹buzz /buz/ *v* **1** to make a low continuous vibratory sound like that of a bee **2** to be filled with a confused murmur **3** to fly over or close to in order to threaten or warn **4** to summon or signal with a buzzer

²buzz *n* **1** a persistent vibratory sound **2a** a confused murmur or flurry of activity **b** rumour, gossip **3** a telephone call – *infml* **4** a pleasant stimulation; a kick – *infml*

buzzard /'buzəd/ *n* **1** a common large European hawk with soaring flight **2** *chiefly NAm* a (large) bird of prey (e g the turkey buzzard)

buzzer /'buzə/ *n* an electric signalling device that makes a buzzing sound

buzz off *v* to go away quickly

¹by /bie/ *prep* **1a** in proximity to; near **b** on the person or in the possession of **2a** through (the medium of); via **c** up to and then beyond; past **3a** in the circumstances of; during (e g slept *by* day) **b** not later than (e g home *by* dark) **4a**(1) through the instrumentality or use of (e g by bus) **a**(2) through the action or creation of (e g a song *by* Wolf) **b**(1) sired by **b**(2) with the participation of (the other parent) (e g a son *by* an earlier marriage) **5** with the witness or sanction of **6a** in conformity with (e g done *by* the rules) **b** in terms of (e g paid *by* the dozen) **c** from the evidence of (e g judge *by* appearances) **7** with respect to **8** to the amount or extent of **9** in successive units or increments of **10** – used in division as the inverse of *into*, in multiplication, and in measurements **11** *chiefly Scot* in comparison with; beside — **by oneself 1** alone, unaccompanied **2** unaided

²**by** *adv* **1a** close at hand; near **b** at or to another's home (e g *by* sometime) **2** past **3** aside, away; *esp* in or into reserve

,**by and 'by** *adv* soon

,**by and 'large** *adv* on the whole, in general

¹**bye, by** /bie/ *n* **1** the passage to the next round of a tournament allowed to a competitor without an opponent **2** a run scored in cricket off a ball that passes the batsman without striking the bat or body — **by the bye** by the way

²**bye, by** *interj* – used to express farewell

'**by-e,lection** *also* '**bye-e,lection** *n* a special election to fill a vacancy

bygone /'bie,gon/ *adj* earlier, past; *esp* outmoded — **let bygones be bygones** to forgive and forget past quarrels

bylaw, byelaw /'bie,law/ *n* a local or secondary law or regulation

'**by-,line** *n* **1** a secondary line; a sideline **2** the author's name printed with a newspaper or magazine article

¹**by,pass** /-,pahs/ *n* a road built so that through traffic can avoid a town centre

²**bypass** *v* to neglect or ignore, usu intentionally; · circumvent

'**by-,product** *n* sthg produced (e g in manufacturing) in addition to a principal product

byre /'bie·ə/ *n*, *dial* a cow shed

bystander /'bie,standə/ *n* one present but not involved in a situation or event

byte /biet/ *n* a string of adjacent binary digits that is processed by a computer as a unit; *esp* one that is 8 bits long

'**by,way** /-,way/ *n* **1** a little-used road **2** a secondary or little known aspect

'**by,word** /-,wuhd/ *n* (the name of) sby or sthg taken as representing some usu bad quality

C

c /see/ *n*, *pl* **c's, cs 1a** (a graphic representation of or device for reproducing) the 3rd letter of the English alphabet **b** a speech counterpart of written *c* **2** one designated *c*, esp as the 3rd in order or class **3** one hundred

cab /kab/ *n* **1** a taxi **2** the part of a locomotive, lorry, crane, etc that houses the driver and controls

cabal /kə'bal/ *v or n* **-ll-** (to unite in or form) a clandestine or unofficial faction.

cabaret /'kabəray/ *n* a stage show or series of acts provided at a nightclub, restaurant, etc

cabbage /'kabij/ *n* **1** a cultivated plant that has a short stem and a dense globular head of usu green leaves used as a vegetable **2a** one who has lost control of his/her esp mental and physical faculties as the result of illness or accident **b** an inactive and apathetic person *USE* (2) infml

cabby, cabbie /'kabi/ *n* a taxi driver

caber /'kaybə/ *n* a roughly trimmed tree trunk that is tossed for distance in a Scottish sport

cabin /'kabin/ *n* **1a** a room or compartment on a ship or boat for passengers or crew **b** a compartment in an aircraft for cargo, crew, or passengers **2** a small usu single-storied dwelling of simple construction

'**cabin ,boy** *n* a boy employed as a servant on board a ship

'**cabin ,cruiser** *n* a private motorboat with living accommodation

cabinet /'kab(i)nit/ *n* **1a** a case for storing or displaying articles **2** *sing or pl in constr, often cap* a body of advisers of a head of state, who formulate government policy – **cabinet** *adj*

¹**cable** /'kaybl/ *n* **1** a strong thick (wire) rope **2** an assembly of electrical conductors insulated from each other and surrounded by a sheath **3** a telegram **4** a nautical unit of length equal to about **4a** *Br* 185m (202yd) **b** *NAm* 219m (240yd)

²**cable** *v* **cabling** /'kaybl·ing, 'kaybling/ to communicate by means of a telegram

'**cable ,car** *n* a carriage made to be moved on a cable railway or along an overhead cable

cable railway *n* a railway along which the carriages are pulled by an endless cable operated by a stationary motor

'**cable ,stitch** *n* a knitting stitch that produces a twisted rope-like pattern

caboodle /kə'boohdl/ *n* a collection, lot – infml

cacao /kə'kahòh, -'kayoh/ *n* a S American tree bearing fatty seeds which are used in making cocoa and chocolate

cache /kash/ n a hiding place, esp for provisions or weapons

cachet /'kashay, kə'shay/ n (a characteristic feature or quality conferring) prestige

cackle /'kakl/ v **cackling** /'kakl·ing, 'kakling/ **1** to make the sharp broken noise or cry characteristic of a hen, esp after laying **2** to laugh in a way suggestive of a hen's cackle **3** to chatter – **cackle** n – **cackler** n

cacophony /kə'kofəni/ n harsh or discordant sound – **-onous** adj

cactus /'kaktəs/ n, pl **cacti** /-tie/, **cactuses** any of a family of plants that have fleshy stems and scaly or spiny branches instead of leaves and are found esp in dry areas (e g deserts)

cad /kad/ n an unscrupulous or dishonourable man – derog; not now in vogue – ~ **dish** adj

cadaver /kə'davə, -'dahvə, -'dayvə/ n a corpse, usu intended for dissection

cadaverous /kə'dav(ə)rəs/ adj **1** (suggestive of) a corpse **2** unhealthily pale or thin

caddie, caddy /'kadi/ n one who assists a golfer, esp by carrying clubs

cadence /'kayd(ə)ns/, **'cadency** /-si/ n **1** a falling inflection of the voice **2** a concluding strain; specif a musical chord sequence giving the sense of harmonic completion **3** the modulated and rhythmic recurrence of a sound

cadenza /kə'denzə/ n a technically showy sometimes improvised solo passage in a concerto

cadet /kə'det/ n **1** a younger brother or son; a younger branch of a family **2** sby receiving basic military or police training

cadge /kaj/ v to get (sthg) by asking and usu imposing on sby's hospitality or good nature – infml – **cadger** n

cadmium /'kadmi·əm/ n a bluish-white soft toxic metallic element

cadre /'kahdə/ n **1** a permanent nucleus of an esp military organization, capable of rapid expansion if necessary **2** (a member of) a group of activists working for the Communist party cause

caecum /'seekəm/ n a cavity open at one end; esp the pouch in which the large intestine begins

Caerphilly /keə'fili, kah-, kə-/ n a mild white moist cheese

caesura /si'zyooərə, -'zhooərə/ n, pl **caesuras**, **caesurae** /-ri/ a break or pause in usu the middle of a line of verse

café /'kafay/ n a small restaurant serving snacks, tea, coffee etc

cafeteria /,kafə'tiəri·ə/ n a restaurant in which the customers serve themselves or are served at a counter and take the food to tables to eat

caffeine /'kafeen/ n an alkaloid found esp in tea and coffee that acts as a stimulant and diuretic

caftan, kaftan /'kaftan/ n a long loose garment traditionally worn by Arabs

¹cage /kayj/ n **1** a box or enclosure of open construction for animals **2** a barred cell or fenced area for prisoners **3** a framework serving as a support

²cage v to put or keep (as if) in a cage

cagey also **cagy** /'kayji/ adj **1** hesitant about committing oneself **2** wary of being trapped or deceived; shrewd USE infml – **cagily** adv – **caginess** n

cagoule /'kagoohl/ n a long waterproof anorak

cairn /keən/ n a pile of stones built as a memorial or landmark

cajole /kə'johl/ v to persuade or deceive with deliberate flattery, esp in the face of reluctance

¹cake /kayk/ n **1** (a shaped mass of) any of various sweet baked foods made from a basic mixture of flour and sugar, usu with fat, eggs, and a raising agent **2** a block of compressed or congealed matter

²cake v to encrust

calamity /kə'laməti/ n **1** a state of deep distress caused by misfortune or loss

calcify /'kalsifie/ v to make or become hardened by deposition of calcium salts, esp calcium carbonate

calcium /'kalsi·əm/ n a silver-white metallic element that occurs only in combination

calculate /'kalkyoolayt/ v **1** to determine by mathematical processes **2** to forecast consequences **3** to count, rely – + on or upon

calculating /'kalkyoolayting/ adj marked by shrewd consideration of self-interest; scheming

calculation /,kalkyoo'laysh(ə)n/ n **1** (the result of) the process or an act of calculating **2** studied care in planning, esp to promote self-interest

calculator /'kalkyoolaytə/ n an electronic or mechanical machine for performing mathematical operations

calculus /'kalkyooləs/ n, pl **calculi** /-lie/ also **calculuses** the mathematical methods comprising differential and integral calculus

caldron /'kawldrən/ n a cauldron

calendar /'kaləndə/ n **1** a system for fixing the beginning, length, and divisions of the civil year and arranging days and longer divisions of time (e g weeks and months) in a definite order **2** a usu printed display of the days of 1 year **3** a chronological list of events or activities

calends, kalends /'kalindz/ n pl but sing or pl in constr the first day of the ancient Roman month

¹calf /kahf/ n, pl **calves** /kahvz/ also **calfs**, (2) **calfs 1a** the young of the domestic cow or a closely related mammal (e g a bison) **b** the young of some large animals (e g the elephant and whale) **2** calf-skin – **calve** v – **in calf** of a cow pregnant

²calf n, pl **calves** the fleshy back part of the leg below the knee

'calf,skin /-,skin/ n a high-quality leather made from the skin of a calf

calibrate /'kali,brayt/ v to determine the correct reading of (an arbitrary or inaccurate scale or instrument) by comparison with a standard – **-ation** n

calibre, *NAm chiefly* **caliber** /'kalibə/ n **1** the diameter of a round body (e g a bullet or other projectile) or a hollow cylinder (e g a gun barrel) **2a** degree of mental capacity or moral quality **b** degree of excellence or importance

calico /'kalikoh/ n, pl **calicoes, calicos** white unprinted cotton cloth of medium weight

caliph, calif /'kalif, 'kay-/ n an Islamic leader claiming descent from Mohammad

¹**call** /kawl/ v **1a** to speak loudly or distinctly so as to be heard at a distance **b** to utter or announce in a loud distinct voice – often + *out* c *of an animal* to utter a characteristic noise or cry **2a** to command or request to come or be present **b** to summon to a particular activity, employment, or office **3** to rouse from sleep **4** to make a brief visit – often + *in* or *by* **5** to (try to) get into communication by telephone – often + *up* **6a** to make a demand in bridge for (a card or suit) **b** to require (a player) to show the hand in poker by making an equal bet **7** to speak of or address by a specified name; give a name to **8a** to regard or characterize as a certain kind; consider **b** to consider for purposes of an estimate or for convenience **9** to predict, guess — **call a spade a spade** to speak frankly and usu bluntly — **called to the bar** admitted as a barrister — **call for 1** to get; collect **2** to require as necessary or appropriate **3** to demand, order — **call in/into question** to cast doubt upon — **call it a day** to stop whatever one has been doing at least for the present — **call it quits 1** call it a day **2** to acknowledge that the advantage is now even — **call on/upon 1** to require, oblige **2** to appeal to; invoke — **call someone's bluff** to challenge and expose an empty pretence or threat — **call the shots/the tune** to be in charge or control; determine the policy or procedure — **call to account** to hold responsible; reprimand — **call to order** to order (a meeting) to observe the customary rules

²**call** n **1a** calling with the voice **b** the cry of an animal (e g a bird); *also* an imitation of an animal's cry made to attract the animal **2a** a request or command to come or assemble **b** a summons or signal on a drum, bugle, or pipe **3a** a divine vocation or stronger inner prompting **b** the attraction or appeal of a particular activity or place **4a** a demand, request **b** need, justification **5** a short usu formal visit **6** calling in a card game **7** telephoning **8** a direction or succession of directions for a square dance rhythmically called to the dancers – ~ **er** n — **on call 1** available for use **2** ready to respond to a summons or command — **within call** within hearing or reach of a call or summons

'**call box** n a public telephone box

'**call girl** n a prostitute who accepts appointments by telephone

calligraphy /kə'ligrəfi/ n (beautiful or elegant) handwriting – **-pher, -phist** n

calling /'kawling/ n **1** a strong inner impulse towards a particular course of action, esp when accompanied by conviction of divine influence **2** a vocation, profession

call off v **1** to draw away; divert **2** to cancel

callous /'kaləs/ adj **1** hardened and thickened **2** unfeeling; *esp* unsympathetic – ~ **ly** adv – ~ **ness** n

call out v **1** to summon into action **2** to challenge to a duel **3** to order a strike

callow /'kaloh/ adj lacking adult attitudes; immature

'**call-,up** n an order to report for military service

call up v **1** to bring to mind; evoke **2** to summon together or collect (e g for a united effort) **3** to summon for active military duty

callus /'kaləs/ n **1** a hard thickened area on skin or bark **2** soft tissue that forms over a cut plant surface

¹**calm** /kahm; *NAm* kah(l)m/ n **1a** the absence of winds or rough water; stillness **b** a state in which the wind has a speed of less than 1km/h (about $^5/_8$mph) **2** a state of repose free from agitation

²**calm** adj **1** marked by calm; still **2** free from agitation or excitement

³**calm** v to make or become calm

calorie *also* **calory** /'kaləri/ n **1a** the quantity of heat required to raise the temperature of 1g of water by 1°C under standard conditions **b** a kilocalorie; *also* an equivalent unit expressing the energy-producing value of food when oxidized **2** an amount of food having an energy-producing value of 1 kilocalorie

calumniate /kə'lumniayt/ v to slander – fml

calumny /'kaləmni/ n slander

calves pl of **calf**

Calvinism /'kalviniz(ə)m/ n the theological system of Calvin and his followers, marked esp by the doctrine of predestination – **-ist** adj, n

calypso /kə'lipsoh/ n, pl **calypsos** *also* **calypsoes** an improvised ballad, usu satirizing current events, in a style originating in the W Indies

calyx /'kaliks, 'kay-/ n, pl **calyxes, calyces** /-li,seez/ the outer usu green or leafy part of a flower or floret, consisting of sepals

cam /kam/ n a mechanical device (e g a wheel attached to an axis at a point other than its centre) that transforms circular motion into intermittent or back-and-forth motion

camaraderie /,kamə'rahdəri, -'radəri/ n friendly good humour amongst comrades

¹**camber** /'kambə/ v to curve upwards in the middle

²**camber** n a slight convexity or arching (e g of a beam or road)

cambium /'kambi·əm/ *n pl* **cambiums, cambia** /-bi·ə/ a thin layer of cells between the xylem and phloem of most plants that divides to form more xylem and phloem

cambric /'kambrik/ *n* a fine thin white linen or cotton fabric

came /kaym/ *past of* **come**

camel /'kaməl/ *n* **1** either of 2 large ruminants used as draught and saddle animals in (African and Asian) desert regions: **1a** the 1-humped Arabian camel **b** the 2-humped Bactrian camel **2** a light yellowish brown colour

'camel hair *n* cloth, usu of a light tan colour with a soft silky texture, made from the hair of a camel or a mixture of this and wool

camellia *also* **camelia** /kə'meelyə/ *n* an ornamental shrub with glossy evergreen leaves and rose-like flowers

Camembert /'kaməmbeə (*Fr* kamãbɛːr)/ *n* a round thin-rinded soft rich cheese

cameo /'kamioh/ *n pl* **cameos 1a** a gem cut in relief in one layer with another contrasting layer serving as background **b** a small medallion with a profiled head in relief **2** a usu brief part in literature or film that reveals or highlights character, plot, or scene **3** a small dramatic role often played by a well-known actor

camera /'kamrə/ *n* a lightproof box having an aperture, and esp a lens, for recording the image of an object on a light-sensitive material: e g **a** one containing photographic film for producing a permanent record **b** one containing a device which converts the image into an electrical signal (e g for television transmission)

camiknickers /'kami,nikəz/ *n pl in constr, pl* **camiknickers** *Br* a one-piece close-fitting undergarment worn by women, that combines a camisole and knickers

camisole /'kami,sohl/ *n* a short bodice worn as an undergarment by women

camomile, chamomile /'kaməmiel/ *n* a plant whose flower heads are often used in herbal remedies

camouflage /'kamə,flahzh, -,flahj/ *n* **1** the disguising of esp military equipment or installations with nets, paint, etc **2** concealment by means of disguise

¹camp /kamp/ *n* **1a** a temporary shelter (e g a tent) or group of shelters **b** a new settlement (e g in a lumbering or mining region) **2** *sing or pl in constr* a group of people engaged in promoting or defending a theory or position **3** a place where troops are housed or trained

²camp *v* **1** to pitch or occupy a camp **2** to live temporarily in a camp or outdoors – **~er** *n*

³camp *adj* **1** exaggeratedly effeminate **2** deliberately and outrageously artificial, affected, or inappropriate, esp to the point of tastelessness *USE* infml

⁴camp *v* to behave in a camp style, manner, etc – usu + *up*; infml — **camp it up** to act or behave in an affected or esp exaggeratedly effeminate manner — infml

campaign /,kam'payn/ *n* a connected series of (military) operations designed to bring about a particular result – **campaign** *v* – **~er** *n*

campanology /,kampə'noləji/ *n* the art of bell ringing – **-gist** *n*

camp'bed *n* a small collapsible bed, usu of fabric stretched over a frame

camphor /'kamfə/ *n* a tough gummy volatile fragrant compound obtained esp from the wood and bark of an evergreen tree – **~ated** *adj*

campus /'kampəs/ *n* the grounds and buildings of a university or college

camshaft /'kam,shahft/ *n* a shaft to which a cam is fastened

¹can /kən; *strong* kan/ *verbal auxiliary, pres sing & pl* **can;** *past* **could** /kəd; *strong* kood/ **1a** know how to **b** to be physically or mentally able to **c** may perhaps – chiefly in questions **d** be logically inferred or supposed to – chiefly in negatives **e** be permitted by conscience or feeling to **f** be inherently able or designed to **g** be logically able to **h** be enabled by law, agreement, or custom to **2** have permission to – used interchangeably with *may* **3** will – used in questions with the force of a request — **can keep it** — used in rejection of sthg distasteful

²can /kan/ *n* **1** a usu cylindrical receptacle: **1a** a vessel for holding liquids **b** a tin: *esp* a tin containing a beverage (e g beer) **2** *NAm* the toilet – infml — **in the can** *of a film or videotape* completed and ready for release

³can *v* **-nn- 1** to pack or preserve in a tin **2** *chiefly NAm* to put a stop or end to – slang

Canadian /kə'naydi·ən/ *n or adj* (a native or inhabitant) of Canada

canal /kə'nal/ *n* **1** a tubular anatomical channel **2** an artificial waterway for navigation, drainage, or irrigation

canal·ize, -ise /'kanəliez/ *v* to direct into (preferred) channels

canapé /'kanəpay, -pi/ *n* an appetizer consisting of a piece of bread, biscuit, etc, topped with a savoury spread

canary /kə'neəri/ *n* a small usu green to yellow finch, widely kept as a cage bird

canasta /kə'nastə/ *n* a form of rummy usu for 4 players using 2 full packs plus jokers

cancan /'kan,kan/ *n* a high-kicking dance performed by women

cancel /'kansl/ *v* **-ll-** (*NAm* **-l-, -ll-**), /'kansl·ing/ **1** to mark or strike out for deletion **2a** to make void; countermand, annul **b** to bring to nothingness; destroy **c** to match in force or effect; counterbalance – usu + *out* **3** to call off, usu without intending to reschedule to a later time **4** to deface (a stamp), usu with a set of parallel lines, so as to invalidate reuse

cancellation, *NAm also* **cancelation** /ˌkansə'laysh(ə)n/ *n* **1** sthg cancelled, esp a seat in an aircraft, theatre performance, etc **2** a mark made to cancel sthg (e g a postage stamp)

cancer /'kansə/ *n* **1** *cap* (sby born under) the 4th zodiacal constellation, pictured as a crab **2** (a condition marked by) a malignant tumour of potentially unlimited growth **3** a source of evil or anguish – ~**ous** *adj* – ~**ously** *adv*

candelabrum /ˌkandl'ahbrəm/, *n, pl* **candelabra** /-brə/ *also* **candelabrums** a branched candlestick or lamp with several lights

candid /'kandid/ *adj* **1** indicating or suggesting complete sincerity **2** disposed to criticize severely; blunt – ~**ly** *adv*

candidate /'kandidayt, -dət/ *n* **1** one who is nominated or qualified for, or aspires to an office, membership, or award **2** one who is taking an examination **3** sthg suitable for a specified action or process – **-ature** *n*

candle /'kandl/ *n* a usu long slender cylindrical mass of tallow or wax enclosing a wick that is burnt to give light — **not worth the candle** *chiefly Br* not worth the effort; not justified by the result

'candle,stick /-ˌstik/ *n* a holder with a socket for a candle

'candle,wick /-ˌwik/ *n* a very thick soft cotton yarn; *also* fabric with a raised tufted pattern, used esp for bedspreads

candour, *NAm chiefly* **candor** /'kandə/ *n* unreserved and candid expression; forthrightness

'candy /'kandi/ *n* **1** crystallized sugar formed by boiling down sugar syrup **2** *chiefly NAm* a sweet

'candy *v* to encrust or glaze (e g fruit or fruit peel) with sugar

'candy ,floss /flos/ *n* a light fluffy mass of spun sugar, usu wound round a stick as a sweet

'cane /kayn/ *n* **1a** a hollow or pithy usu flexible jointed stem (e g of bamboo) **b** an elongated flowering or fruiting stem (e g of a raspberry) **c** any of various tall woody grasses or reeds; *esp* sugarcane **2a** a walking stick made of cane **b** (the use of) a cane or rod for flogging **c** a length of split cane for use in basketry

'cane *v* to beat with a cane; *broadly* to punish

'canine /'kaynien/ *adj* of or resembling a dog or (members of) the dog family

'canine *n* any of the 4 conical pointed teeth on each side of both the top and bottom jaws

canister *also* **cannister** /'kanistə/ *n* a small usu metal box or tin for holding a dry product (e g tea or shot)

'canker /'kangkə/ *n* **1a** an area of local tissue death in a plant **b** any of various inflammatory animal diseases **2** a source of corruption or debasement – ~**ous** *adj*

'canker *v* **1** to corrupt with evil intentions **2** to become infested with canker

cannabis /'kanəbis/ *n* the dried flowering spikes of the female hemp plant, sometimes smoked in cigarettes for their intoxicating effect

cannibal /'kanibl/ *n* **1** a human being who eats human flesh **2** an animal that eats its own kind – ~**ism** *n* – ~**istic** *adj*

cannibal·ize, **-ise** /'kanibl,iez/ *v* to dismantle a machine to provide spare parts for others

'cannon /'kanən/, *n, pl* **cannons, cannon 1** a usu large gun mounted on a carriage **2** an automatic shell-firing gun mounted esp in an aircraft

'cannon *n, Br* a shot in billiards in which the cue ball strikes each of 2 object balls

'cannon *v* **1** to collide – usu + *into* **2** to collide with and be deflected *off* sthg

'cannon,ball /-ˌbawl/ *n* a round solid missile made for firing from an old type of cannon

cannot /'kanot, -nɒt, kə'not/ *can not* — **cannot but/cannot help but** to be bound to; must

canny /'kani/ *adj* **1** cautious and shrewd; *specif* thrifty **2** *Scot & NE Eng* careful, steady **3** *NE Eng* agreeable, comely – **cannily** *adv*

canoe /kə'nooh/ *n* **1** a long light narrow boat with sharp ends and curved sides usu propelled by paddling **2** *chiefly Br* a kayak

'canon /'kanən/ *n* **1** the series of prayers forming the unvarying part of the Mass **2a** an authoritative list of books accepted as Holy Scripture **b** the authentic works of a writer **3** an accepted principle, rule, or criterion **4** a musical composition for 2 or more voice parts in which the melody is repeated by the successively entering voices

'canon *n* a clergyman belonging to the chapter of a cathedral or collegiate church

canon·ize, **-ise** /'kanəniez/ *v* to recognize officially as a saint

canopy /'kanəpi/ *n* **1a** a cloth covering suspended over a bed **b** an awning, marquee **2** an ornamental rooflike structure **3a** the transparent enclosure over an aircraft cockpit **b** the lifting or supporting surface of a parachute

canst /kanst; *strong* kanst/ *archaic pres* **2** *sing of* **can**

'cant /kant/ *n* an oblique or slanting surface; a slope

'cant *v* **1** to set at an angle; tip or tilt up or over **2** to pitch to one side; lean

'cant *n* **1** jargon; *specif* the argot of the underworld **2** a set or stock phrase **3** the insincere expression of platitudes or sentiments, esp those suggesting piety

can't /kahnt/ *can not*

cantaloup, cantaloupe /'kantəˌloohp/ *n* a melon with a hard rough rind and reddish orange flesh

cantankerous /ˌkan'tangkərəs/ *adj* ill-natured, quarrelsome – ~**ly** *adv* – ~**ness** *n*

cantata /kan'tahtə/ *n* a usu religious choral composition comprising choruses, solos, recitatives, and interludes

canteen /kan'teen/ *n* **1** a dining hall **2** a partitioned chest or box for holding cutlery **3** a usu cloth-covered flask carried by a soldier, traveller, etc and containing a liquid, esp drinking water

[1]**canter** /'kantə/ *v* to progress or ride at a canter

[2]**canter** *n* **1** a 3-beat gait of a horse, resembling but smoother and slower than the gallop **2** a brisk ride

cantilever /'kanti,leevə/ *n* a projecting beam or member supported at only 1 end:

canto /'kantoh/ *n, pl* **cantos** a major division of a long poem

cantor /'kantaw/ *n* a singer who leads liturgical music (e g in a synagogue)

canvas *also* **canvass** /'kanvəs/ *n* **1** a firm closely woven cloth usu of linen, hemp, or cotton used for clothing, sails, tents etc **2** a set of sails; sail **3** a cloth surface suitable for painting on in oils; *also* the painting on such a surface **4** a coarse cloth so woven as to form regular meshes as a basis for embroidery or tapestry **5** the floor of a boxing or wrestling ring — **under canvas** living in a tent

canvass *also* **canvas** /'kanvəs/ *v* to seek orders or votes; solicit

canyon, cañon /'kanyən/ *n* a deep valley or gorge

[1]**cap** /kap/ *n* **1a** a soft usu flat head covering with a peak and no brim **b** (one who has gained) selection for an esp national team; *also* a cap awarded as a mark of this **2a** a usu unyielding overlying rock or soil layer **b** (a patch of distinctively coloured feathers on) the top of a bird's head **3** sthg that serves as a cover or protection, esp for the end or top of an object **4** the uppermost part; the top **5** a small container holding an explosive charge (e g for a toy pistol or for priming the charge in a firearm)

[2]**cap** *v* **-pp-** to follow with sthg more noticeable or significant; outdo

capability /,kaypə'biləti/ *n* **1** being capable **2** the capacity for an indicated use or development; potential

capable /'kaypəbl/ *adj* **1** susceptible **2** having the attributes or traits required to perform a specified deed or action **3** able *USE (except 3)* + *of* – **-bly** *adv*

capacious /kə'payshəs/ *adj* able to hold a great deal – **~ly** *adv* – **~ness** *n*

capacitance /kə'pasit(ə)ns/ *n* **1** the ability of a conductor or system of conductors and insulators to store electric charge **2** the measure of capacitance equal to the ratio of the charge induced to the potential difference

capacity /kə'pasəti/ *n* **1a** the ability to accommodate or deal with sthg **b** an ability to contain **c** the maximum amount that can be contained or produced **2** legal competence or power **3a** ability, calibre **b** potential **4** a position or role assigned or assumed

[1]**cape** /kayp/ *n* a peninsula or similar land projection jutting out into water

[2]**cape** *n* a sleeveless outer (part of a) garment that fits closely at the neck and hangs loosely from the shoulders

[1]**caper** /'kaypə/ *n* a greenish flower bud or young berry pickled and used as a seasoning, garnish, etc

[2]**caper** *v* to prance

[3]**caper** *n* **1** a joyful leap **2** a high-spirited escapade; a prank **3** an illegal enterprise; a crime

[1]**capillary** /kə'piləri/ *adj* **1** resembling a hair, esp in slender elongated form **2** of a tube, passage, etc having a very fine bore

[2]**capillary** *n* a capillary tube; *esp* any of the smallest blood vessels connecting arteries with veins and forming networks throughout the body

[1]**capital** /'kapitl/ *adj* **1a** punishable by death **b** involving execution **2** of a letter of or conforming to the series (e g A, B, C rather than a, b, c) used to begin sentences or proper names **3a** of the greatest importance or influence **b** being the seat of government **4** excellent – not now in vogue

[2]**capital** *n* **1a** (the value of) a stock of accumulated goods, esp at a particular time and in contrast to income received during a particular period **b** accumulated possessions calculated to bring in income **c** *sing or pl in constr* people holding capital **d** a sum of money saved **2** an esp initial capital letter **3** a city serving as a seat of government — **make capital of/out of** to turn (a situation) to one's advantage

[3]**capital** *n* the top part or piece of an architectural column

capital 'assets *n pl* tangible or intangible long-term assets

capitalism /'kapitl,iz(ə)m/ *n* an economic system characterized by private ownership and control of the means of production, distribution, and exchange and by the profit motive

capitalist /'kapitl-ist/, **capitalistic** /-'istik/ *adj* **1** owning capital **2** practising, advocating, or marked by capitalism – **capitalist** *n*

capital·ize, -ise /'kapitl,iez/ *v* **1** to write in capital letters **2** to convert assets into capital **3** to gain by turning sthg to advantage – usu + *on*

capitol /'kapitl/ *n* **1** a building in which a US legislative body meets **2** *cap* the building in which Congress meets at Washington

capitulate /kə'pityoolayt, -choo-/ *v* to surrender, often after negotiation of terms – **-tion** *n*

capon /'kaypon, -pən/ *n* a castrated male chicken

caprice /kə'prees/ *n* a sudden and seemingly unmotivated change of mind or behaviour

capricious /kə'prishəs/ *adj* apt to change suddenly or unpredictably – ~**ly** *adv* – ~**ness** *n*

Capricorn /'kaprikawn/ *n* (sby born under) the 10th zodiacal constellation, pictured as a creature resembling a goat with the tail of a fish

capsicum /'kapsikəm/ *n* a sweet pepper

capsize /kap'siez/ *v* to (cause to) overturn

capstan /'kapstən/ *n* a mechanical device consisting of an upright drum round which a rope, hawser, etc is fastened, used for moving or raising heavy weights

capsule /'kapsyoohl, -yool/ *n* 1 a closed plant receptacle containing spores or seeds 2 a usu gelatin shell enclosing a drug for swallowing 3 a detachable pressurized compartment, esp in a spacecraft or aircraft, containing crew and controls; *also* a spacecraft

captain /'kaptin/ *n* 1a a middle-ranking military or naval officer b an officer in charge of a ship c a pilot of a civil aircraft 2 a distinguished military leader 3 a leader of a team, esp a sports team 4 a dominant figure 5 *Br* the head boy or girl at a school

caption /'kapshən/ *n* 1 a heading or title, esp of an article or document 2 a comment or description accompanying a pictorial illustration 3 a film subtitle

captivate /'kaptivayt/ *v* to fascinate or charm irresistibly – **-ation** *n*

captive /'kaptiv/ *adj* 1a taken and held as prisoner, esp by an enemy in war b kept within bounds 2 in a situation that makes departure or inattention difficult – **captive** *n* – **-vity** *n*

captor /'kaptə/ *n* one who or that which holds another captive

capture /'kapchə/ *v* 1 to take captive; win, gain 2 to preserve in a relatively permanent form 3 to remove (e g a chess piece) from the playing board according to the rules of a game – **capture** *n*

car /kah/ *n* 1a a railway carriage; *esp* one used for a specific purpose b a motor car 2 the passenger compartment of an airship or balloon 3 *NAm* the cage of a lift

carafe /kə'rahf, -'raf, 'karəf/ *n* a (glass) bottle used to hold water or wine, esp at table

caramel /'karəməl, -mel/ *n* 1 a brittle brown somewhat bitter substance obtained by heating sugar and used as a colouring and flavouring agent 2 a chewy usu quite soft caramel-flavoured toffee

carapace /'karə,pays/ *n* a hard case over the back of a turtle, crab, etc

carat /'karət/ *n* 1 a unit of weight for precious stones equal to 200mg 2 *NAm chiefly* **karat** a unit of fineness for gold equal to $\frac{1}{24}$ part of pure gold in an alloy

caravan /'karə,van/ *n* 1a *sing or pl in constr* a company of travellers on a journey through desert or hostile regions; *also* a train of pack animals b a group of vehicles travelling together 2 *Br* a covered vehicle designed to be towed by a motor car or horse and to serve as a dwelling when parked

caraway /'karəway/ *n* an aromatic plant with pungent seeds used as a flavouring

carbohydrate /,kahbə'hiedrayt, -boh-/ *n* any of various compounds of carbon, hydrogen, and oxygen (e g sugars, starches, and celluloses) formed by green plants and constituting a major class of energy-providing animal foods

carbon /'kahb(ə)n/ *n* 1 a nonmetallic element occurring as diamond, graphite, charcoal, coke, etc and as a constituent of coal, petroleum, carbonates (e g limestone), and organic compounds 2a a sheet of carbon paper b a copy (e g of a letter) made with carbon paper – ~**ize** *v*

carbonate /'kahbənət, -nayt/ *n* a salt or ester containing a metal and carbon and oxygen

carbonated /'kahbənaytid/ *adj* made fizzy by having carbon dioxide gas added

carbon di'oxide *n* a heavy colourless gas that is formed esp by the combustion and decomposition of organic substances and is absorbed from the air by plants in photosynthesis

carboniferous /,kahbə'nif(ə)rəs/ *adj* producing or containing carbon or coal

carbon mo'noxide *n* a colourless odourless very toxic gas formed as a product of the incomplete combustion of carbon

'carbon ,paper *n* thin paper coated on one side with a dark pigment used to make copies of letters, etc by pressure

carbuncle /'kah,bungkl/ *n* 1 a red gemstone, usu a garnet, cut in a domed shape without facets 2 a painful local inflammation of the skin and deeper tissues with multiple openings for the discharge of pus

carburettor, *NAm* **carburetor** /,kahbyoo'retə, ,kahbə'retə/ *n* a device for supplying an internal combustion engine with vaporized fuel mixed with air in an explosive mixture

carcass, *Br also* **carcase** /'kahkəs/ *n* a dead body; *esp* the dressed body of a meat animal

carcinogen /'kahsinəjən/ *n* sthg that causes cancer

card /kahd/ *n* 1 a playing card 2 *pl but sing or pl in constr* a game played with cards 3 a valuable asset or right for use in negotiations 4 a flat stiff usu small and rectangular piece of paper or thin cardboard: e g 4a a postcard b a visiting card c a programme; *esp* one for a sporting event d a greeting card 5 *pl, Br* the National Insurance and other papers of an employee, held by his/her employer — **on the cards** quite possible; likely to occur — **get/ask for one's cards** to be dismissed/resign from employment

'card,board /-,bawd/ *n* material of similar composition to paper but thicker and stiffer

²cardboard *adj* **1** made (as if) of cardboard **2** unreal, insubstantial

'card-,carrying *adj* being a fully paid-up member, esp of the Communist party

cardiac /'kahdiak/ *adj* of, situated near, or acting on the heart

cardigan /'kahdigən/ *n* a knitted garment for the upper body that opens down the front

¹cardinal /'kahdinl/ *adj* of primary importance; fundamental

²cardinal *n* a member of a body of high officials of the Roman Catholic church whose powers include the election of a new pope

cardinal number *n* a number (e g 1, 2, 3) that is used in simple counting and that indicates how many elements there are in a collection

'card,sharp /-,shahp/, **'card,sharper** /-,shahpə/ *n* one who habitually cheats at cards

¹care /keə/ *n* **1** a cause for anxiety **2** close attention; effort **3** change, supervision; *specif, Br* guardianship and supervision of children by a local authority

²care *v* **1** to feel interest or concern – often + *about* **2** to give care – often + *for* **3** to have a liking or taste *for*

¹career /kə'riə/ *n* a field of employment in which one expects to remain; *esp* such a field which requires special qualifications and training

²career *v* to move swiftly in an uncontrolled fashion

carefree /'keə,free/ *adj* free from anxiety or responsibility

'careful /-f(ə)l/ *adj* **1** exercising or taking care **2a** marked by attentive concern **b** cautious, prudent – often + *to* and an infinitive – ~**ly** *adv* – ~**ness** *n*

'careless /-lis/ *adj* **1** not taking care **2a** negligent, slovenly **b** unstudied, spontaneous **3a** free from care; untroubled **b** indifferent, unconcerned – ~**ly** *adv* – ~**ness** *n*

¹caress /kə'res/ *n* **1** a kiss **2** a caressing touch or stroke

²caress *v* **1** to touch or stroke lightly and lovingly **2** to touch or affect gently or soothingly

'care,taker /-,taykə/ *n* **1** one who takes care of the house or land of an owner, esp during his/her absence **2** one who keeps clean a large and/or public building (e g a school or office), looks after the heating system, and carries out minor repairs **3** sby or sthg temporarily installed in office

'care,worn /-,wawn/ *adj* showing the effects of grief or anxiety

cargo /'kahgoh/ *n, pl* **cargoes, cargos** the goods conveyed in a ship, aircraft, or vehicle

caribou /'kari,booh/ *n pl* **caribous**, *esp collectively* **caribou** any of several large N American deer

caricature /'karikəchə, -chooə, -tyooə/ *n* **1** exaggeration of features or characteristics, often to a ludicrous or grotesque degree **2** a comic or satirical representation, esp in literature or art, that has the qualities of caricature – **caricature** *v*

caries /'keəreez, -riz/ *n, pl* **caries** progressive decay of a tooth or sometimes a bone, caused by microorganisms – **-ious** *adj*

Carmelite /'kahmə,liet/ *n* a member of the Roman Catholic mendicant Order of Our Lady of Mount Carmel

carmine /'kahmin/ *n* a vivid red (pigment)

carnage /'kahnij/ *n* great slaughter (e g in battle)

carnal /'kahnl/ *adj* **1** given to or marked by physical and esp sexual pleasures and appetites **2** temporal, worldly – ~**ly** *adv* – ~**ity** *n*

carnation /kah'naysh(ə)n/ *n* **1** light red or pink **2** any of numerous cultivated usu double-flowered pinks

carnival /'kahnivl/ *n* **1** an instance of merrymaking or feasting **2** an exhibition or organized programme of entertainment; a festival

carnivore /'kahni,vaw/ *n* a flesh-eating animal – **-rous** *adj*

¹carol /'karəl/ *n* a Christmas song or hymn

²carol *v* **-ll-** (*NAm* **-l-**, **-ll-**) to sing (joyfully)

carotid /kə'rotid/ *adj or n* (of or being) the chief artery or pair of arteries that supply the head with blood

carouse /kə'rowz/ *v* **1** to drink alcoholic beverages heavily or freely **2** to take part in a drinking bout – **carouse, carousal** *n*

¹carp /kahp/ *v* to find fault or complain querulously and often unreasonably – *infml*; usu + *at*

²carp *n* a large soft-finned freshwater fish often farmed for food

carpel /'kahpl/ *n* any of the structures of a flowering plant that constitute the female (innermost) part of a flower and usu consist of an ovary, style, and stigma

carpenter /'kahpintə/ *n* a woodworker; *esp* one who builds or repairs large-scale structural woodwork – **-try** *n*

¹carpet /'kahpit/ *n* a heavy woven or felted material used as a floor covering; *also* a floor covering made of this fabric — **on the carpet** before an authority for censure or reprimand

²carpet *v* **1** to cover (as if) with a carpet **2** to reprimand – *infml*

'carpet,bag /-,bag/ *n* a bag made of carpet fabric, common in the 19th c

'car,port /-,pawt/ *n* a usu open-sided shelter for cars

carriage /'karij/ *n* **1** the manner of bearing the body; posture **2** (the price or cost of) carrying **3** a wheeled vehicle; *esp* a horse-drawn passenger-carrying vehicle designed for private use **4** a movable part of a machine that supports some other part **5** a railway passenger vehicle; a coach

'carriage ,way /-,way/ *n* the part of a road used by traffic

carrier /'kari·ə/ *n* **1** an individual or organization that contracts to transport goods, messages, etc **2** a container for carrying **3** a bearer and transmitter of something that causes a disease; *esp* one who is immune to the disease **4** a radio or electrical wave of relatively high frequency that can be modulated by a signal (e g representing sound or vision information), esp in order to transmit that signal **5** an aircraft carrier

carrier bag /'---,-,---'-/ *n* a bag of plastic or thick paper used for carrying goods, esp shopping

'carrier ,pigeon *n* a homing pigeon (used to carry messages)

carrion /'kari·ən/ *n* dead and putrefying flesh

carrot /'karət/ *n* **1** (a biennial plant with) a usu orange spindle-shaped root eaten as a vegetable **2** a promised and often illusory reward or advantage

carroty /'karəti/ *adj* bright orange-red in colour

'carry /'kari/ *v* **1** to support and move (a load); transport **2** to convey, conduct **3** to lead or influence by appeal to the emotions **4** to transfer from one place to another; *esp* to transfer (a digit corresponding to a multiple of 10) to the next higher power of 10 in addition **5a** to bear on or within oneself **b** to have as a mark, attribute, or property **6** to have as a consequence, esp in law; involve **7** to hold (e g one's person) in a specified manner **8** to keep in stock for sale **9** to maintain through financial support or personal effort **10** to extend or prolong in space, time, or degree **11** to gain victory for **12a** to broadcast or publish **b** to reach or penetrate to a distance **c** to convey itself to a reader or audience **13** to perform with sufficient ability to make up for the poor performance of (e g a partner or teammate) — **carry a torch** to be in love, esp without reciprocation; cherish a longing or devotion — **carry the can** to bear the responsibility; accept the blame — *infml* — **carry the day** to win, prevail

²carry *n* the range of a gun or projectile

carry forward *v* to transfer (e g a total) to the succeeding column, page, or book relating to the same account

carry off *v* **1** to cause the death of **2** to perform easily or successfully **3** to gain possession or control of; capture

'carry-,on *n* an instance of rowdy, excited, or improper behaviour; a to-do – *infml*

carry on *v* **1** to conduct, manage **2** to behave in a rowdy, excited, or improper manner **3** to continue one's course or activity, esp in spite of obstacles or discouragement **4** to flirt; *also* to have a love affair – *usu* + *with*

'carry,out /-,owt/ *n, chiefly Scot* (an item of) food or esp alcoholic drink bought to be consumed off the premises

carry out *v* **1** to put into execution **2** to bring to a successful conclusion; complete, accomplish

carry over *v* to persist from one stage or sphere of activity to another

carry through *v* carry out

'cart /kaht/ *n* **1** a heavy 2-wheeled or 4-wheeled vehicle used for transporting bulky or heavy loads (e g goods or animal feed) **2** a lightweight 2-wheeled vehicle drawn by a horse or pony **3** a small wheeled vehicle

²cart *v* to take or drag away without ceremony or by force – infml; usu + *off*

cartel /kah'tel/ *n* a combination of independent commercial enterprises designed to limit competition

cartilage /'kahtilij/ *n* a translucent elastic tissue that is mostly converted into bone in adult higher vertebrates – **-ginous** *adj*

cartography /kah'togrəfi/ *n* map making – **-pher** *n*

carton /'kaht(ə)n/ *n* a box or container made of plastic, cardboard, etc

cartoon /kah'toohn/ *n* **1** a preparatory design, drawing, or painting (e g for a fresco) **2a** a satirical drawing commenting on public and usu political matters **b** a series of drawings (e g in a magazine) telling a story **3** a film using animated drawings – ~ **ist** *n*

cartridge /'kahtrij/ *n* **1** a tube of metal, paper, etc containing a complete charge, a primer, and often the bullet or shot for a firearm **2** the part of the arm of a record player holding the stylus and the mechanism that converts movements of the stylus into electrical signals

cartwheel /-,weel/ *n* a sideways handspring with arms and legs extended – **cartwheel** *v*

carve /kahv/ *v* **1** to cut so as to shape **2** to make or acquire (a career, reputation, etc) through one's own efforts – often + *out* **3** to cut (food, esp meat) into pieces or slices

carving /'kahving/ *n* a carved object or design

caryatid /'kari·ə,tid, ,kari'atid, kə'rie·atid/ *n, pl* **caryatids, caryatides** /,kari'atideez, kə,rie·ə'teediz/ a draped female figure used as a column

cascade /kas'kayd/ *n* **1** a steep usu small fall of water; *esp* one of a series of such falls **2a** sthg arranged in a series or in a succession of stages so that each stage derives from or acts on the product of the preceding stage **b** an arrangement of fabric (e g lace) that falls in a wavy line **3** sthg falling or rushing forth in profusion – **cascade** *v*

'case /kays/ *n* **1** a situation (requiring investigation or action) **2** an (inflectional) form of a noun, pronoun, or adjective indicating its grammatical relation to other words **3a** a suit or action that reaches a court of law **b**(1) the evidence supporting a conclusion **b**(2) an argument; *esp* one that is convincing **4a** an instance of disease or injury; *also* a patient suffering from a specific illness **b** an

example **5** a peculiar person; a character – infml
— **in any case** without regard to or in spite of other considerations; whatever else is done or is the case — **in case 1** as a precaution; as a precaution against the event that **2** *chiefly NAm* if — **in case of 1** in the event of **2** for fear of; as a precaution against

²**case** *n* **1** a box or receptacle for holding sthg: e g **1a** a glass-panelled box for the display of specimens (e g in a museum) **b** a suitcase **2** an outer covering (e g of a book)

³**case** *v* to inspect or study (e g a house), esp with intent to rob – slang

¹**cash** /kash/ *n* **1** ready money **2** money or its equivalent paid promptly at the time of purchase

²**cash** *v* to pay or obtain cash for **2** to lead and win a bridge trick with (the highest remaining card of a suit)

,**cash-and-'carry** *adj* sold for cash and collected by the purchaser

'**cash ,crop** *n* a crop (e g cotton or sugar beet) produced for sale rather than for use by the grower

cashew /'kashooh, kə'shooh, ka'shooh/ *n* an edible kidney-shaped nut

¹**cashier** /ka'shiə/ *v* to dismiss, usu dishonourably, esp from service in the armed forces

²**cashier** *n* **1** one employed to receive cash from customers, esp in a shop **2** one who collects and records payments (e g in a bank)

cash in *v* **1** to convert into cash **2** to exploit a financial or other advantage – usu + *on*

cashmere /'kashmiə, -'-/ *n* fine wool from the undercoat of the Kashmir goat

'**cash ,register** *n* a machine that has a drawer for cash and is used to record and display the amount of each purchase and the money received

casing /'kaysing/ *n* sthg that encases; material for encasing

casino /kə'seenoh/ *n*, *pl* **casinos** a building or room used for gambling

cask /kahsk/ *n* a barrel-shaped container, usu for holding liquids

casket /'kahskit/ *n* **1** a small usu ornamental chest or box (e g for jewels) **2** *NAm* a coffin

casserole /'kasərohl/ *n* **1** a heatproof dish with a cover in which food may be baked and served **2** the savoury food cooked and served in a casserole

cassette, casette /kə'set/ *n* **1** a lightproof container for holding film or plates that can be inserted into a camera **2** a small case containing magnetic tape that can be inserted into a tape recorder

cassock /'kasək/ *n* an ankle-length garment worn by the Roman Catholic and Anglican clergy or by laymen assisting in services

¹**cast** /kahst/ *v* **cast 1a** to cause to move (as if by throwing) **b** to place as if by throwing **c** to deposit (a vote) formally **d**(1) to throw off or away **d**(2) to

shed, moult **d**(3) *of an animal* to give birth to (prematurely) **2** to calculate (a horoscope) by means of astrology **3a** to arrange into a suitable form or order **b** to assign a part for (e g a play) or to (e g an actor) **4** to shape (e g metal or plastic) by pouring into a mould when molten **5** to throw out a line and lure with a fishing rod **6** to look round; seek – + *about* or *around* — **cast anchor** to lower the anchor; to anchor

²**cast** *n* **1** a throw of a (fishing) line or net **2** *sing or pl in constr* the set of performers in a dramatic production **3** a slight squint in the eye **4a** a reproduction (e g of a statue) formed by casting **b** an impression taken from an object with a molten or plastic substance **c** a plaster covering and support for a broken bone **5** a tinge, suggestion **6** the excrement of an earthworm

castaway /'kahstə,way/ *n* a person who is cast adrift or ashore as a result of a shipwreck or as a punishment

caste /kahst/ *n* **1** any of the hereditary social groups in Hinduism that restrict the occupations of their members and their association with members of other castes **2** a social class; *also* the prestige conferred by this

castellated /'kasti,laytid/ *adj* having battlements like a castle

caster sugar *n* finely granulated white sugar

castigate /'kastigayt/ *v* to punish or reprimand severely – fml – **-gation** *n*

casting /'kahsting/ *n* **1** sthg cast in a mould **2** sthg cast out or off

,**cast-'iron** *adj* **1** capable of withstanding great strain; strong, unyielding **2** impossible to disprove or falsify

,**cast 'iron** *n* a hard brittle alloy of iron, carbon, and silicon cast in a mould

¹**castle** /kahsl/ *n* **1** a large fortified building or set of buildings **2** a stronghold **3** a rook in chess

²**castle** *v* **castling** /'kahsl·ing/ to move (a chess king) 2 squares towards a rook and then place the rook on the square on the other side of the king

,**cast-'off** *adj* thrown away or discarded, esp because outgrown or no longer wanted – **castoff** *n*

cast off *v* **1** to unfasten or untie (a boat or line) **2a** to remove (a stitch or stitches) from a knitting needle in such a way as to prevent unravelling **b** to finish a knitted article by casting off all the stitches **3** to get rid of; discard

cast on *v* to take up (a stitch or stitches) on a knitting needle for beginning or enlarging a knitted article

castor, caster /'kahstə/ *n* **1** a small wheel set in a swivel mounting on the base of a piece of furniture, machinery, etc **2** a container with a perforated top for sprinkling powdered or granulated foods, esp sugar

,**castor 'oil** *n* a pale viscous oil from the beans of a tropical Old World plant, used esp as a purgative

castrate /ˈkaˈstrayt/ *v* **1a** to remove the testes of; geld **b** to remove the ovaries of; spay **2** to deprive of vitality or vigour; emasculate – **-tration** *n*

casual /ˈkazh(y)oοəl, kazyoοəl/ *adj* **1** subject to, resulting from, or occurring by chance **2a** occurring without regularity; occurring for irregular periods **3a** feeling or showing little concern; nonchalant **b** informal, natural; *also* designed for informal wear – **~ly** *adv* – **~ness** *n*

casualty /ˈkazh(y)oοəlti, -zyοοəl-/ *n* **1** a member of a military force killed or wounded in action **2** a person or thing injured, lost, or destroyed

¹**cat** /kat/ *n* **1a** a small domesticated flesh-eating mammal kept as a pet or for catching rats and mice **b** any of a family of carnivores that includes the domestic cat, lion, tiger, leopard, jaguar, cougar, lynx, and cheetah **2** a malicious woman **3** a cat-o'-nine-tails **4** a (male) person – *slang*

²**cat** *n* a catamaran – *infml*

cataclysm /ˈkatəˌkliz(ə)m/ *n* **1** a flood, deluge **2** a violent geological change of the earth's surface **3** a momentous event marked by violent upheaval and destruction – **~ic** *adj*

catacomb /ˈkatəˌkoohm/ *n* **1** a galleried subterranean cemetery with recesses for tombs **2** an underground passageway or group of passageways; a labyrinth *USE* often pl with sing. meaning

catalogue, *NAm chiefly* **catalog** /ˈkatəlog/ **1** (a pamphlet or book containing) a complete list of items arranged systematically with descriptive details **2** a list, series – **catalogue** *v*

catalyst /ˈkatəlist/ *n* **1** a substance that changes, esp increases, the rate of a chemical reaction but itself remains chemically unchanged **2** sby or sthg whose action inspires further and usu more important events – **-lytic** *adj* – **-lysis** *n*

catamaran /ˈkatəməˌran, -rahn, ˌ---'-/ *n* **1** a raft made of logs or pieces of wood lashed together **2** a boat with two hulls side by side

cat-and-mouse *adj* consisting of continuous chasing and near captures and escapes

¹**catapult** /ˈkatəpoolt, -pult/ *n* **1** an ancient military device for hurling missiles **2** *Br* a Y-shaped stick with a piece of elastic material fixed between the 2 prongs, used for shooting small objects (e g stones)

²**catapult** *v* **1** to throw or launch (a missile) by means of a catapult **2** to (cause to) move suddenly or abruptly

cataract /ˈkatərakt/ *n* **1** clouding of (the enclosing membrane of) the lens of the eye; *also* the clouded area **2** steep rapids in a river; *also* a waterfall

catarrh /kəˈtah/ *n* (the mucus resulting from) inflammation of a mucous membrane, esp in the human nose and air passages – **~al** *adj*

catastrophe /kəˈtastrəfi/ *n* a momentous, tragic, and unexpected event of extreme gravity – **-phic** *adj* – **-phically** *adv*

¹**cat burglar** *n*, *Br* a burglar who enters buildings by climbing up walls, drainpipes, etc

¹**cat call** /-ˌkawl/ *n* a loud or raucous cry expressing disapproval

¹**catch** /kach/ *v* **caught** /kawt/ **1a** to capture or seize, esp after pursuit **b** to discover unexpectedly; surprise **c** to become entangled, fastened, or stuck **2a** to seize; *esp* to intercept and keep hold of (a moving object), esp in the hands **b** to dismiss (a batsman in cricket) by catching the ball after it has been hit and before it has touched the ground **3a** to contract; become infected with **b** to hit, strike **c** to receive the force or impact of **4** to attract, arrest **5** to take or get quickly or for a moment **6** to be in time for **7** to grasp with the senses or the mind **8** *of a fire* to start to burn — **catch a crab** to make a faulty stroke in rowing — **catch it** to incur blame, reprimand, or punishment — *infml* — **catch one's breath 1** to rest long enough to restore normal breathing **2** to stop breathing briefly, usu under the influence of strong emotion — **catch someone on the hop** to find sby unprepared — *infml*

²**catch** *n* **1** sthg caught; *esp* the total quantity caught at one time **2** a game in which a ball is thrown and caught **3** sthg that retains or fastens **4** an often humorous or coarse round for 3 or more voices **5** a concealed difficulty; a snag **6** an eligible marriage partner – *infml*

catching /ˈkaching/ *adj* **1** infectious, contagious **2** alluring, attractive

catchment area /ˈkatʃmənt/ *n* **1** the area from which a lake, reservoir, etc gets its rainwater **2** a geographical area from which people are drawn to attend a particular school, hospital, etc

catch on *v* **1** to become popular **2** to understand, learn – often + *to*; *infml*

catch out *v* to expose or detect in wrongdoing or error – usu passive

catchpenny /ˈkach peni/ *adj also* ˈkachpəni/ *n or adj* (sthg) worthless but designed to appear attractive, esp by being showy – *derog*

catch phrase /-ˌfrayz/ *n* an arresting phrase that enjoys short-lived popularity

catchup /ˈkachəp/ *n*, *chiefly NAm* ketchup

catch up *v* **1** to act or move fast enough to draw level *with* **2** to acquaint oneself or deal with sthg belatedly – + *on* or *with*

catch word /-ˌwuhd/ *n* a word or expression associated with some school of thought or political movement; a slogan

catchy /ˈkachi/ *adj* **1** tending to attract the interest or attention **2** easy to remember and reproduce – **catchily** *adv*

catechism /ˈkatəˌkiz(ə)m/ *n* **1** a summary of religious doctrine, often in the form of questions and answers **2** a set of formal questions put as a test – **catechist** *n*

categorical /ˌkatə'gorikl/ *also* ˌcate'goric /-' gorik/ *adj* absolute, unqualified – ~ ly *adv*

category /'katəg(ə)ri/ *n* **1** a general or fundamental form or class of terms, things, or ideas (e g in philosophy) **2** a division within a system of classification – **-orize** *v*

cater /'kaytə/ *v* **1** to provide and serve a supply of usu prepared food **2** to supply what is required or desired – usu + *for* or *to* – ~ **er** *n*

caterpillar /'katə,pilə/ *n* a wormlike larva, specif of a butterfly or moth

caterwaul /'katə,wawl/ *v* to cry noisily – **caterwaul** *n*

'**cat,fish** /-,fish/ *n* any of numerous large-headed fishes with long barbels

'**cat,gut** /-,gut/ *n* a tough cord usu made from sheep intestines and used esp for the strings of musical instruments and tennis rackets and for surgical sutures

catharsis /kə'thahsis/ *n, pl* **catharses** /-seez/ **1** purification or purgation of the emotions through drama **2** the process of bringing repressed ideas and feelings to consciousness and expressing them, esp during psychoanalysis – **-artic** *adj*

cathedral /kə'theedrəl/ *n* a church that is the official seat of a bishop

'**catherine ,wheel** /'kath(ə)rin/ *n, often cap C* a firework in the form of a wheel that spins as it burns

catheter /'kathətə/ *n* a tubular device for insertion into a hollow body part (e g a blood vessel), usu to inject or draw off fluids or to keep a passage open

cathode /'ka,thohd/ *n* the electrode by which electrons leave an external circuit and enter a device; *specif* the positive terminal of a primary cell or of a storage battery that is delivering current

cathode-ray tube *n* a vacuum tube in which a beam of electrons is projected onto a fluorescent screen to provide a visual display (e g a television picture)

catholic /'kath(ə)lik/ *adj* **1** comprehensive, universal; *esp* broad in sympathies or tastes **2** *cap* **2a** of or forming the entire body of worshippers that constitutes the Christian church **b** of or forming the ancient undivided Christian church or a church claiming historical continuity from it; *specif* Roman Catholic

Catholic *n* a member of a Catholic church; *specif* a Roman Catholic

catkin /'kat,kin/ *n* a hanging spike-shaped densely crowded group of flowers without petals (e g in a willow)

'**cat,nap** /-,nap/ *n* a brief period of sleep, esp during the day

ˌ**cat-o'-'nine-,tails** *n, pl* **cat-o'-nine-tails** a whip made of usu 9 knotted cords fastened to a handle

'**cat's-,eye** *n, pl* **cat's-eyes** a small reflector set in a road, usu in a line with others, to reflect vehicle headlights

'**cat's-,paw** *n, pl* **cat's-paws 1** a light breeze that ruffles the surface of water in irregular patches **2** sby used by another as a tool or dupe

cattle /'katl/ *n, pl* bovine animals kept on a farm, ranch, etc

'**cattle ,grid** *n, Br* a shallow ditch in a road covered by parallel bars spaced far enough apart to prevent livestock from crossing

catty /'kati/ *adj* slyly spiteful; malicious – **cattiness** *n* – **cattily** *adv*

'**cat,walk** /-,wawk/ *n* **1** a narrow walkway (e g round a machine) **2** a narrow stage in the centre of a room on which fashion shows are held

caucus /'kawkəs/ *n* a closed political meeting to decide on policy, select candidates, etc

caught /kawt/ *past of* **catch**

caul /kawl/ *n* **1** the large fatty fold of membrane covering the intestines **2** the inner foetal membrane of higher vertebrates, esp when covering the head at birth

cauldron, caldron /'kawldrən/ *n* a large open metal pot for cooking over an open fire

cauliflower /'koli,flowə/ *n* (a plant closely related to the cabbage with) a compact head of usu white undeveloped flowers eaten as a vegetable

caulk, calk /kawk/ *v* to stop up and make watertight (e g the seams of a boat, cracks in wood, etc) by filling with a waterproof material

causal /'kawzl/ *adj* **1** expressing or indicating cause; causative **2** of or being a cause – ~ **ly** *adv*

¹**cause** /kawz/ *n* **1a** sby or sthg that brings about an effect **b** a reason for an action or condition; a motive **2** a ground for legal action **3** a principle or movement worth defending or supporting

²**cause** *v* to serve as the cause or occasion of

'**cause** /kəz; *strong* koz/ *conj* because – nonstandard

cause célèbre /ˌkohz say'leb(rə) (*Fr* kozˈselebr)/ *n, pl* **causes célèbres** /~ ~/ **1** a legal case that excites widespread interest **2** a notorious incident or episode

causeway /'kawz,way/ *n* a raised road or path, esp across wet ground or water

caustic /'kostik, 'kaw-/ *adj* **1** capable of destroying or eating away by chemical action; corrosive **2** incisive, biting

cauter·ize, -ise /'kawtə,riez/ to sear or burn (e g a wound) with a hot iron or caustic chemical, esp to get rid of infection

¹**caution** /'kawsh(ə)n/ *n* **1** a warning, admonishment; *specif* an official warning given to sby who has committed a minor offence **2** prudent forethought intended to minimize risk; care **3** sby or sthg that causes astonishment or amusement – *infml*

²**caution** v **1a** to advise caution to; warn; specif to warn (sby under arrest) that his/her words will be recorded and may be used in evidence **b** to admonish, reprove; specif to give an official warning to **2** of a soccer referee to book

cautious /'kawshəs/ adj careful, prudent – ~ly adv – ~ness n

cavalcade /,kavl,kayd, ,--'-/ n **1** a procession; esp one of riders or carriages **2** a dramatic sequence or procession; a series

¹**cavalier** /,kavə'liə/ n **1** a gallant gentleman of former times; esp one in attendance on a lady **2** cap an adherent of Charles I of England, esp during the Civil War

²**cavalier** adj **1** debonair **2** given to or characterized by offhand dismissal of important matters

cavalry /'kavəlri/ n, sing or pl in constr **1** a branch of an army consisting of mounted troops **2** a branch of a modern army consisting of armoured vehicles – ~man n

¹**cave** /kayv/ n a natural chamber (e g underground or in the side of a hill or cliff) having a usu horizontal opening on the surface

²**cave** interj, Br – used as a warning call among schoolchildren, esp at public school

cave in v **1** to fall in or collapse **2** to cease to resist; submit – **cave-in** n

'**cave,man** /-,man/ n **1** a cave dweller, esp of the Stone Age **2** a man who acts in a rough primitive manner, esp towards women

cavern /'kavən/ n a large usu underground chamber or cave

caviar, caviare /'kaviah/ n salted fish (esp sturgeon) roe usu considered a delicacy

cavil /'kavil, -vl/ v -ll- (NAm -l-, -ll-), /'kavl·ing/ to raise trivial and frivolous objections – ~ler n

cavity /'kavəti/ n an empty or hollowed-out space within a mass; specif a decaying hollow in a tooth

cavort /kə'vawt/ v **1** to prance **2** to engage in extravagant behaviour

cavy /'kayvi/ n a guinea pig or related short-tailed S American rodent

caw /kaw/ v to utter (a sound like) the harsh raucous cry of the crow

,cayenne 'pepper /kay'en/ n a pungent red condiment consisting of the ground dried pods and seeds of hot peppers

cease /sees/ v to bring to an end; terminate, discontinue – **cease** n

,**cease-'fire** n (a military order) for a cessation of firing or of active hostilities

'**ceaseless** /-lis/ adj continuing endlessly; constant – ~ly adv

cedar /'seedə/ n (the fragrant wood of) any of a genus of usu tall evergreen coniferous trees of the pine family

cede /seed/ v to yield or surrender (e g territory), usu by treaty

cedilla /sə'dilə/ n a mark , placed under a letter (e g ç in French) to indicate an alteration or modification of its usual phonetic value

ceiling /'seeling/ n **1** the overhead inside surface of a room **2** the height above the ground of the base of the lowest layer of clouds **3** an upper usu prescribed limit

celebrant /'selibrənt/ n the priest officiating at the Eucharist

celebrate /'selibrayt/ v **1** to perform (a sacrament or solemn ceremony) publicly and with appropriate rites **2a** to mark (a holy day or feast day) ceremonially **b** to mark (a special occasion) with festivities or suspension of routine activities – **-ation** n – **-atory** adj

'**cele,brated** adj widely known and often referred to

celebrity /sə'lebrəti/ n **1** the state of being famous **2** a well-known and widely acclaimed person

celerity /sə'lerəti/ n rapidity of motion or action – fml

celery /'seləri/ n a European plant of the carrot family with leafstalks eaten cold or hot as a vegetable

celestial /sə'lesti·əl/ adj **1** of or suggesting heaven or divinity; divine **2** of or in the sky or visible heavens

celibate /'selibət/ n one who is unmarried and does not have sexual intercourse, esp because of a religious vow – **-bacy** n

cell /sel/ n **1** a 1-room dwelling occupied esp by a hermit **2** a small room for a prisoner, monk, etc **3** a small compartment (e g in a honeycomb), receptacle, cavity (e g one containing seeds in a plant ovary), or bounded space **4** the smallest structural unit of living matter consisting of nuclear and cytoplasmic material bounded by a membrane and capable of functioning either alone or with others in all fundamental life processes **5** a vessel (e g a cup or jar) containing electrodes and an electrolyte either for generating electricity by chemical action or for use in electrolysis **6** the primary unit of a political, esp Communist, organization

cellar /'selə/ n **1** an underground room; esp one used for storage **2** an individual's stock of wine

cello /'cheloh/ n, pl **cellos** a large stringed instrument of the violin family tuned an octave below the viola – **cellist** n

cellophane /'selə,fayn/ n regenerated cellulose in the form of thin transparent sheets, used esp for wrapping goods

cellular /'selyoolə/ adj **1** of, relating to, or consisting of cells **2** containing cavities; porous

celluloid /'selyoo,loyd/ n film for the cinema; also film as a medium

Celluloid trademark – used for a tough inflammable plastic composed essentially of cellulose nitrate and camphor

cellulose /'selyoo͵lohs/ n 1 a sugar made up of glucose units that constitutes the chief part of plant cell walls, occurs naturally in cotton, kapok, etc, and is the raw material of many manufactured goods (e g paper, rayon, and cellophane) 2 paint or lacquer of which the main constituent is cellulose nitrate or acetate

Celsius /'selsi-əs/ adj relating to, conforming to, or being a scale of temperature on which water freezes at 0° and boils at 100° under standard conditions

¹**Celtic, Keltic** /'keltik/ adj (characteristic) of the Celts or their languages

²**Celtic, Keltic** n a branch of Indo-European languages comprising Welsh, Cornish, Breton, Irish, Scots Gaelic, and Manx, which is now confined to Brittany and parts of the British Isles

¹**cement** /si'ment/ n 1 a powder consisting of ground alumina, silica, lime, iron oxide, and magnesia burnt in a kiln, that is used as the binding agent in mortar and concrete 2 a substance (e g a glue or adhesive) used for sticking objects together 3 sthg serving to unite firmly 4 concrete – not used technically

²**cement** v 1 to unite or make firm (as if) by the application of cement 2 to overlay with concrete

cemetery /'semətri/ n a burial ground; esp one not in a churchyard

cenotaph /'senə͵tahf/ n a tomb or monument erected in honour of a person or group of people whose remains are elsewhere; specif, cap that standing in Whitehall in London in memory of the dead of WWs I and II

censor /'sensə/ n an official who examines publications, films, letters, etc and has the power to suppress objectionable (e g obscene or libellous) matter – ~**ship** n – ~**ious** adj – **censor** v

censure /'senshə/ n 1 a judgment involving condemnation 2 the act of blaming or condemning sternly 3 an official reprimand – **censure** v

census /'sensəs/ n 1 a periodic counting of the population and gathering of related statistics (e g age, sex, or social class) carried out by government 2 a usu official count or tally

cent /sent/ n (a coin or note representing) a unit worth ¹/₁₀₀ of the basic money unit of certain countries (e g the American dollar)

centaur /'sen͵taw/ n any of a race of mythological creatures having the head, arms, and upper body of a man, and the lower body and back legs of a horse

centenarian /͵sentə'neəri-ən/ n sby who is (more than) 100 years old

centenary /sen'teenəri, -'tenəri/ n (the celebration of) a 100th anniversary

centigrade /'senti͵grayd/ adj Celsius

centigram /'senti͵gram/ n one hundredth of a gram

centimetre /'senti͵meetə/ n one hundredth of a metre (about 0.4in)

centipede /'senti͵peed/ n any of a class of many-segmented arthropods with each segment bearing 1 pair of legs

central /'sentrəl/ adj 1 containing or constituting a centre 2 of primary importance; principal 3 at, in, or near the centre 4 having overall power or control 5 of, originating in, or comprising the central nervous system – ~**ly** adv – ~**ize** v

͵central 'heating n a system of heating whereby heat is produced at a central source (e g a boiler) and carried by pipes to radiators or air vents throughout a building

͵central 'nervous ͵system n the part of the nervous system which in vertebrates consists of the brain and spinal cord and which coordinates the activity of the entire nervous system

¹**centre,** NAm chiefly **center** /'sentə/ n 1 the point round which a circle or sphere is described; broadly the centre of symmetry 2a a place, esp a collection of buildings, round which a usu specified activity is concentrated b sby or sthg round which interest is concentrated c a source from which sthg originates d a region of concentrated population 3 the middle part (e g of a stage) 4 often cap a group, party, etc holding moderate political views 5 a player occupying a middle position in the forward line of a team (e g in football or hockey) 6 a temporary wooden framework on which an arch is supported during construction

²**centre,** NAm chiefly **center** v 1 to place, fix, or move in, into, or at a centre or central area 2 to gather to a centre; concentrate 3 to adjust (e g lenses) so that the axes coincide

'centre͵board /-͵bawd/ n a retractable keel used esp in small yachts

͵centre-'forward n (the position of) a player in hockey, soccer, etc positioned in the middle of the forward line

͵centre of 'gravity n the point at which the entire weight of a body may be considered as concentrated so that if supported at this point the body would remain in equilibrium in any position

centrifugal /͵sentri'fyoohg(ə)l, sen'trifyoog(ə)l/ adj proceeding or acting in a direction away from a centre or axis

centripetal /'sentri͵petl, sen'tripitl/ adj 1 proceeding or acting in a direction towards a centre or axis 2 tending towards centralization; unifying

centurion /sen'tyooəri-ən/ n an officer commanding a Roman century

century /'senchəri/ n 1 a subdivision of the ancient Roman legion orig consisting of 100 men 2 a group, sequence, or series of 100 like things; specif 100 runs made by a cricketer in 1 innings 3 a period of 100 years; *esp* any of the 100-year periods reckoned forwards or backwards from the conventional date of the birth of Christ

ceramic /sə'ramik/ *adj* of or relating to pots and pottery

cereal /'siəri·əl/ *n* 1 (a grass or other plant yielding) grain suitable for food 2 a food made from grain and usu eaten with milk and sugar at breakfast

cerebellum /,serə'beləm/ *n, pl* **cerebellums, cerebella** /-lə/ a large part of the back of the brain which projects outwards and is concerned esp with coordinating muscles and maintaining equilibrium

cerebral /'serəbrəl/ *adj* 1 of the brain or the intellect 2a appealing to the intellect b primarily intellectual in nature – ~**ly** *adv*

ceremonial /,serə'mohnyəl, -ni·əl/ *n* 1 a usu prescribed system of formalities or rituals 2 (a book containing) the order of service in the Roman Catholic church

ceremony /'serəməni/ *n* 1 a formal act or series of acts prescribed by ritual, protocol, or convention 2 (observance of) established procedures of civility or politeness – **-nial** *adj* – **-nious** *adj*

cerise /sə'rees, -'reez/ *n or adj* (a) light purplish red

cert /suht/ *n, Br* a certainty; *esp* a horse that is sure to win a race – *infml*

certain /'suhtn/ *adj* 1a of a particular but unspecified character, quantity, or degree b named but not known 2a established beyond doubt or question; definite b unerring, dependable 3a inevitable b incapable of failing; sure – + *infinitive* 4 assured in mind or action – ~**ly** *adv* — **for certain** as a certainty; assuredly

certainty /-ti/ *n* 1 sthg certain 2 the quality or state of being certain

¹**certificate** /sə'tifikət/ *n* a document containing a certified statement; *esp* one declaring the status or qualifications of the holder

²**certificate** /sə'tifikayt/ *v* to testify to with a certificate – **-ation** *n*

certify /'suhtifie/ *v* 1a to declare officially as being true or as meeting a standard b to declare officially the insanity of 2 to certificate, license 3 to guarantee the payment or value of (a cheque) by endorsing on the front – **-fiable** *adj* – **-fiably** *adv*

certitude /'suhti,tyoohd/ *n* the state of being or feeling certain

cervix /'suhviks/ *n, pl* **cervices** /-viseez/, **cervixes** the narrow outer end of the uterus – **-ical** *adj*

cessation /si'saysh(ə)n/ *n* a temporary or final stop; an ending

cesspit /'ses,pit/ *n* 1 a pit for the disposal of refuse (e g sewage) 2 a corrupt or squalid place

cetacean /si'taysh(ə)n/ *n* any of an order of aquatic, mostly marine, mammals that includes the whales, dolphins, and porpoises – **cetacean** *adj*

cha-cha /'chah ,chah/, **,cha-cha-'cha** *n* (a piece of music for performing) a fast rhythmic ballroom dance of Latin American origin

chafe /chayf/ *v* 1 to feel irritation or discontent; fret 2 to warm (part of the body) by rubbing 3 to rub so as to wear away or make sore

¹**chaff** /chaf, chahf/ *n* 1 the seed coverings and other debris separated from the seed in threshing grain 2 worthless matter – esp in *separate the wheat from the chaff* 3 chopped straw, hay, etc used for animal feed

²**chaff** *n* light jesting talk; banter

³**chaff** *v* to tease good-naturedly

chaffinch /'chafinch/ *n* a European finch with a reddish breast, a bluish head, and white wing bars

chagrin /'shagrin/ *v or n* (to subject to) mental distress caused by humiliation, disappointment, or failure

¹**chain** /chayn/ *n* 1a a series of usu metal links or rings connected to or fitted into one another and used for various purposes (e g support or restraint) b a unit of length equal to 66ft (about 20.12m) 2 sthg that confines, restrains, or secures – usu *pl* 3a a series of linked or connected things b a group of associated establishments (e g shops or hotels) under the same ownership

²**chain** *v* to fasten, restrict, or confine (as if) with a chain – often + *up* or *down*

'chain ,gang *n, sing or pl in constr* a gang of convicts chained together, usu while doing hard labour outside prison

'chain ,mail *n* flexible armour of interlinked metal rings

chain reaction *n* 1 a series of events so related to each other that each one initiates the next 2 a self-sustaining chemical or nuclear reaction yielding energy or products that cause further reactions of the same kind

'chain ,saw *n* a portable power saw that has teeth linked together to form a continuous revolving chain

'chain ,store *n* any of several usu retail shops under the same ownership and selling the same lines of goods

¹**chair** /cheə/ *n* 1 a seat for 1 person, usu having 4 legs and a back and sometimes arms 2a an office or position of authority or dignity; *specif* a professorship b a chairman 3 a sedan chair

²**chair** *v* 1 to install in office 2 to preside as chairman of 3 *chiefly Br* to carry shoulder-high in acclaim

'chairman /-mən/, *fem* **'chair,lady, 'chair ,woman** *n* 1 one who presides over or heads a meeting, committee, organization, or board of directors 2 a radio or television presenter; *esp* one who coordinates unscripted or diverse material – ~**ship** *n* a light carriage, usu having 2 wheels and a folding top

,chaise 'longue /long·g/ n, pl chaise longues also chaises longues /~ long·g(z)/ a low sofa with only 1 armrest, on which one may recline

chalet /'shalay/ n 1 a usu wooden house or hut with a steeply sloping roof and widely overhanging eaves, common esp in Switzerland 2 a small house or hut used esp for temporary accommodation (e g at a holiday camp)

chalice /'chalis/ n a drinking cup or goblet; esp one used to hold the wine at communion

¹chalk /chawk/ n 1 a soft white, grey, or buff limestone composed chiefly of the shells of small marine organisms 2 a short stick of chalk or chalky material used esp for writing and drawing – ~ y adj

²chalk v to set down or add up (as if) with chalk – usu + up

chalk up v 1 to ascribe, credit; specif to charge to sby's account 2 to attain, achieve

¹challenge /'chalinj/ v 1 to order to halt and prove identity 2 to dispute, esp as being unjust, invalid, or outmoded; impugn 3a to defy boldly; dare b to call out to duel, combat, or competition 4 to stimulate by testing the skill of (sby or sthg) – ~ r n

²challenge n 1a a command given by a sentry, watchman, etc to halt and prove identity b a questioning of right or validity 2a a summons that is threatening or provocative; specif a call to a duel b an invitation to compete 3 (sthg having) the quality of being demanding or stimulating

chamber /'chaymbə/ n 1 a natural or artificial enclosed space or cavity 2 a room 2a(1) where a judge hears private cases – usu pl with sing. meaning a(2) pl used by a oup of barristers b with an official or state function 3 (a hall used by) a legislative or judicial body; esp either of 2 houses of a legislature 4 the part of a gun that holds the charge or cartridge

chamberlain /'chaymbəlin/ n 1 a chief officer of a royal or noble household 2 a treasurer (e g of a corporation)

'chamber,maid /-,mayd/ n a maid who cleans bedrooms and makes beds (e g in a hotel)

'chamber ,music n music written for a small group of instruments

'chamber ,pot n a bowl-shaped receptacle for urine and faeces, used chiefly in the bedroom

chameleon /shə'meelyən, kə-/ n 1 any of a group of Old World lizards with a long tongue, a prehensile tail, and the ability to change the colour of the skin 2 sby or sthg changeable; specif a fickle person

chamois /'shamwah/ n, pl chamois also chamoix /'shamwah(z)/ 1 a small goatlike antelope of Europe and the Caucasus 2 a soft pliant leather prepared from the skin of the chamois or sheep, used esp as a cloth for polishing

¹champ /champ/ v 1 to make biting or gnashing movements 2 to eat noisily 3 to show impatience or eagerness – usu in champ at the bit

²champ n a champion – infml

champagne /sham'payn/ n a white sparkling wine made in the old province of Champagne in France

¹champion /'champi·ən/ n 1 a militant supporter of, or fighter for, a cause or person 2 one who shows marked superiority; specif the winner of a competitive event

²champion v to protect or fight for as a champion

³champion adj, chiefly N Eng superb, splendid

'champion,ship /-,ship/ n a contest held to determine a champion

¹chance /chahns/ n 1 the incalculable (assumed) element in existence; that which determines unaccountable happenings 2 a situation favouring some purpose; an opportunity 3a the possibility of a specified or favourable outcome in an uncertain situation b pl the more likely indications 4 a risk – chance adj

²chance v 1 to take place or come about by chance; happen 2 to come or light on or upon by chance 3 to accept the hazard of; risk

chancel /'chahnsl/ n the part of a church containing the altar and seats for the clergy and choir

chancellery, chancellory /'chahns(ə)ləri/ n 1 the position or department of a chancellor 2 the office or staff of an embassy or consulate

chancellor /'chahns(ə)lə/ n 1 the Lord Chancellor 2 the titular head of a British university 3 a usu lay legal officer of an Anglican diocese 4 the chief minister of state in some European countries

chancery /'chahnsəri/ n 1 Chancery Division, Chancery a division of the High Court having jurisdiction over causes in equity 2 a record office for public archives or those of ecclesiastical, legal, or diplomatic proceedings 3 a chancellor's court, office, etc

chancy /'chahnsi/ adj uncertain in outcome or prospect; risky – -ciness n

chandelier /,shandə'liə/ n a branched often ornate lighting fixture suspended from a ceiling

¹change /chaynj/ v 1a to make or become different b to exchange, reverse – often + over or round 2a to replace with another b to move from one to another c to exchange for an equivalent sum or comparable item d to put on fresh clothes or covering 3 to go from one vehicle of a public transport system to another 4 of the (male) voice to shift to a lower register; break 5 to undergo transformation, transition, or conversion — change hands to pass from the possession of one person to that of another

²**change** n **1a** a (marked) alteration **b** a substitution **2** an alternative set, esp of clothes **3a** money returned when a payment exceeds the amount due **b** coins of low denominations **4** an order in which a set of bells is struck in change ringing

changeable /'chaynjəbl/ adj **1** able or apt to vary **2** capable of being altered or exchanged **3** fickle – **-bly** adv – **~ness** n

changeling /'chaynjling/ n a child secretly exchanged for another in infancy; specif an elf-child left in place of a human child by fairies

change of 'life n the menopause

'**change-,over** n a conversion to a different system or function

¹**channel** /'chanl/ n **1a** the bed where a stream of water runs **b** the deeper part of a river, harbour, or strait **c** a narrow region of sea between 2 land masses **d** a path along which information passes or can be stored (e g on a recording tape) **e** a course or direction of thought, action, or communication – often pl with sing. meaning **f** a television station **2** a usu tubular passage, esp for liquids **3** a long gutter, groove, or furrow

²**channel** v **-ll-** (NAm **-l-**, **-ll-**), **channelling** /' chanl·ing/ to convey into or through a direct channel;

chant /chahnt/ n **1** (the music or performance of) a repetitive melody used for liturgical singing in which as many syllables are assigned to each note as required **2** a rhythmic monotonous utterance or song – **chant** v

chaos /'kayos/ n **1** often cap the confused unorganized state of primordial matter before the creation of distinct forms **2** a state of utter confusion – **chaotic** adj – **chaotically** adv

¹**chap** /chap/ n a man, fellow – infml

²**chap** v **-pp-** to (cause to) open in slits or cracks

³**chap** n a crack in the skin caused by exposure to wind or cold

⁴**chap** n (the fleshy covering of) a jaw

chapel /'chapl/ n **1a** a place of worship serving a residence, institution, or a Christian group other than an established church **b** a room or bay in a church for prayer or minor religious services **2** a chapel service or assembly **3** sing or pl in constr the members of a trade union, esp in a printing office

chaperone, chaperon /'shapə,rohn/ n an older woman who accompanies a younger woman on social occasions to guard against impropriety

chaplain /'chaplin/ n a clergyman officially attached to a branch of the armed forces, an institution, or a family or court – **~cy** n

chaps /chaps/ n pl leather leggings worn over the trousers, esp by N American ranch hands

chapter /'chaptə/ n **1a** a major division of a book **b** sthg resembling a chapter in being a significant specified unit **2** (a regular meeting of) the canons of a cathedral or collegiate church, or the members of a religious house **3** a local branch of a society or fraternity

¹**char, charr** /chah/ n pl **chars**, esp collectively **char** any of a genus of small-scaled trouts

²**char** v **-rr-** **1** to convert to charcoal or carbon, usu by heat; burn **2** to burn slightly; scorch

³**char** v or n **-rr-** to (work as) a cleaning woman

⁴**char** n, Br tea – infml

character /'karəktə/ n **1a** a distinctive mark, usu in the form of a stylized graphic device **b** a graphic symbol (e g a hieroglyph or alphabet letter) used in writing or printing **2** (any of) qualities that make up and distinguish the individual **3a** a person, esp one marked by notable or conspicuous traits **b** any of the people portrayed in a novel, film, play, etc **4** (good) reputation **5** moral strength; integrity — **in/out of character** in/not in accord with a person's usual qualities, traits, or behaviour

¹**characteristic** /,karəktə'ristik/ adj serving to reveal and distinguish the individual character; typical – **~ally** adv

²**characteristic** n a distinguishing trait, quality, or property

character-ize, -ise /'karəktə,riez/ v **1** to describe the character of **2** to be a characteristic of – **-ization** n

charade /shə'rahd/; NAm -'rayd/ n **1** pl a game in which one team acts out each syllable of a word or phrase while the other tries to guess it **2** a ridiculous pretence

charcoal /'chah,kohl/ n **1** a dark or black porous carbon prepared by partly burning vegetable or animal substances (e g wood or bone) **2** fine charcoal used in pencil form for drawing

¹**charge** /chahj/ v **1a** to load or fill to capacity **b(1)** to restore the active materials in (a storage battery) by the passage of a direct current in the opposite direction to that of discharge **b(2)** to give an electric charge to **c** to imbue with (passionate) emotion, feeling, etc **2** to command or exhort with right or authority **3** to blame or accuse **4** to rush violently at; attack; also to rush into (an opponent), usu illegally, in soccer, basketball, etc **5a** to fix or ask as fee or payment **b** to ask payment of (a person) **c** to record (an item) as an expense, debt, obligation, or liability — **charge with** to impose (a task or responsibility) on

²**charge** n **1** the quantity that an apparatus is intended to receive and fitted to hold; esp the quantity of explosive for a gun or cannon **2a** power, force **b** a definite quantity of electricity; esp the charge that a storage battery is capable of yielding **3a** an obligation, requirement **b** control, supervision **c** sby or sthg committed to the care of another **4** the price demanded or paid for sthg **5** an accusation, indictment, or statement of complaint **6** a violent rush forwards (e g in attack)

chargé d'affaires /ˌshahzhay daˈfeə/ n, pl **chargés d'affaires** /~ daˈfeə(z)/ a diplomatic representative inferior in rank to an ambassador

¹**charger** /ˈchahjə/ n a large flat meat dish

²**charger** n a horse for battle or parade

chariot /ˈchari-ət/ n 1 a light 4-wheeled pleasure or state carriage 2 a 2-wheeled horse-drawn vehicle of ancient times used in warfare and racing – ~ **eer** n

charisma /kəˈrizmə/ n the special magnetic appeal of an individual that inspires popular loyalty and enthusiasm – ~ **tic** adj – ~ **tically** adv

charitable /ˈcharitəbl/ adj 1a liberal in giving to the poor; generous b of or giving charity 2 merciful or kind in judging others; lenient – **-bly** adv

charity /ˈcharəti/ n 1 benevolent goodwill towards or love of humanity 2a kindly generosity and helpfulness, esp towards the needy or suffering; also aid given to those in need b an institution engaged in relief of the poor, sick, etc 3a a gift for public benevolent purposes b an institution (e g a hospital) funded by such a gift 4 lenient judgment of others

charlatan /ˈshahlət(ə)n/ n 1 a quack doctor 2 one who pretends, usu ostentatiously, to have special knowledge or ability; a fraud

Charleston /ˈchahlstən/ v or n (to dance) a lively ballroom dance in which the heels are swung sharply outwards on each step

¹**charm** /chahm/ n 1 an incantation 2 sthg worn to ward off evil or to ensure good fortune 3a a quality that fascinates, allures, or delights b pl physical graces or attractions, esp of a woman 4 a small ornament worn on a bracelet or chain

²**charm** v 1a to affect (as if) by magic; bewitch b to soothe or delight by compelling attraction 2 to control (esp a snake) by the use of rituals (e g the playing of music)– ~ **ing** adj – ~ **ingly** adv – ~ **er** n

¹**chart** /chaht/ n 1a an outline map showing the geographical distribution of sthg (e g climatic or magnetic variations) b a navigator's map 2a a sheet giving information in the form of a table; esp, pl the list of best-selling popular gramophone records (produced weekly) b a graph c a schematic, usu large, diagram

²**chart** v 1 to make a chart of 2 to lay out a plan for

¹**charter** /ˈchahtə/ n 1 a document that creates and defines the rights of a city, educational institution, or company 2 a constitution 3 a special privilege, immunity, or exemption 4 a total or partial lease of a ship, aeroplane, etc for a particular use or group of people

²**charter** v 1a to establish or grant by charter b to certify as qualified 2 to hire or lease for usu exclusive and temporary use

charwoman /ˈchahˌwoomən/ n a cleaning woman

chary /ˈcheəri/ adj 1 cautious; esp wary of taking risks 2 slow to grant or accept – **charily** adv

¹**chase** /chays/ v 1a to follow rapidly or persistently; pursue b to rush, hasten 2 to cause to depart or flee; drive 3 chiefly Br to investigate (a matter) or contact (a person, company, etc) in order to obtain information or (hasten) results – usu + up

²**chase** n 1a chasing, pursuit b the hunting of wild animals 2 sthg pursued; a quarry 3 a tract of unenclosed land set aside for the breeding of animals for hunting and fishing 4 a steeplechase

³**chase** v to ornament (metal) by indenting with a hammer and tools that have no cutting edge – ~ **r** n

⁴**chase** n a groove cut in a surface for a pipe, wire, etc

chaser /ˈchaysə/ n 1 a glass or swallow of a mild drink (e g beer) taken after spirits; also a drink of spirits taken after a mild drink (e g beer) 2 a horse for steeplechases

chasm /ˈkaz(ə)m/ n 1 a deep cleft in the earth 2 an apparently unbridgeable gap

chassis /ˈshasi/ n, pl **chassis** /ˈshasiz/ 1 a supporting framework for the body of a vehicle (e g a car) 2 the frame on which the electrical parts of a radio, television, etc are mounted

chaste /chayst/ adj 1 abstaining from (unlawful or immoral) sexual intercourse; celibate 2 pure in thought and act; modest 3 severely simple in design or execution; austere – ~ **ly** adv – ~ **ness** n – **chastity** n

chasten /ˈchays(ə)n/ v 1 to correct by punishment or suffering; discipline 2 to subdue, restrain

chastise /chasˈtiez/ v 1 to inflict punishment on, esp by whipping 2 to subject to severe reproof or criticism – ~ **ment** n

¹**chat** /chat/ v -tt- to talk in an informal or familiar manner

²**chat** n (an instance of) light familiar talk; esp (a) conversation

chattel /ˈchatl/ n an item of personal property – usu in goods and chattels

chatter /ˈchatə/ v 1 to talk idly, incessantly, or fast; jabber 2a esp of teeth to click repeatedly or uncontrollably (e g from cold) b of a cutting tool (e g a drill) to vibrate rapidly while cutting – ~ **er** n – **chatter** n

chatterbox /-ˌboks/ n one who engages in much idle talk – infml

chatty /ˈchati/ adj 1 fond of chatting; talkative 2 having the style and manner of light familiar conversation

chat up v to engage (sby) in friendly conversation for an ulterior motive, esp with amorous intent – infml

chauffeur /ˌshohˈfuh, ˈshohfə/ n a person employed to drive a car

chauvinism /'shohvə,niz(ə)m/ *n* blind attachment to one's group, cause, or country – **-ist** *n, adj* – **-istic** *adj* – **-istically** *adv*

cheap /cheep/ *adj* **1a** (relatively) low in price **b** charging a low price **2** gained with little effort; *esp* gained by contemptible means **3a** of inferior quality or worth; tawdry, sleazy **b** contemptible because of lack of any fine or redeeming qualities – **~ly** *adv* – **~ness** *n*

cheapen /'cheep(ə)n/ *v* to make or become **a** cheap in price or value **b** lower in esteem **c** tawdry, vulgar, or inferior

¹**cheap-jack** /jak/ *n* sby, esp a pedlar, who sells cheap wares

²**cheap-jack** *adj* **1** inferior, cheap, or worthless **2** characterized by unscrupulous opportunism

¹**cheat** /cheet/ *n* **1** a fraudulent deception; a fraud **2** one who cheats; a pretender, deceiver

²**cheat** *v* **1a** to practise fraud or deception **b** to violate rules dishonestly (e g at cards or in an exam) **2** to be sexually unfaithful – usu + *on* **3** to defeat the purpose or blunt the effects of

¹**check** /chek/ *n* **1** exposure of a chess king to an attack from which it must be protected or moved to safety – often used interjectionally **2** a sudden stoppage of a forward course or progress; an arrest **3** one who or that which arrests, limits, or restrains; a restraint **4** a criterion **5** an inspection, examination, test, or verification **6a** (a square in) a pattern of squares (of alternating colours) **b** a fabric woven or printed with such a design **7** *NAm* a cheque **8a** *chiefly NAm* a ticket or token showing ownership or identity **b** *NAm* a bill, esp for food and drink in a restaurant — **in check** under restraint or control

²**check** *v* **1** to put (a chess opponent's king) in check **2a** to slow or bring to a stop; brake **b** to block the progress of **3** to restrain or diminish the action or force of **4a** to compare with a source, original, or authority; verify **b** to inspect for satisfactory condition, accuracy, safety, or performance – sometimes + *out* or *over* **c** *chiefly NAm* to correspond point for point; tally – often + *out* **5** to note or mark with a tick – often + *off* **6** *chiefly NAm* to leave or accept for safekeeping in a cloakroom or left-luggage office – often + *in* — **check into** to check in at — **check up on 1** to examine for accuracy or truth, esp in order to corroborate information **2** to make thorough inquiries about

checkers /'chekəz/ *n pl but sing in constr, NAm* the game of draughts

check in *v* to report one's presence or arrival; *esp* to arrive and register at a hotel or airport

checkmate /'chek'mayt/ *v* **1** to thwart or counter completely **2** to check (a chess opponent's king) so that escape is impossible

checkout /'chek,owt/ *n* a cash desk equipped with a cash register in a self-service shop

check out *v* to complete the formalities for leaving, esp at a hotel

checkup /'chek,up/ *n* a (routine) general medical examination

Cheddar /'chedə/ *n* a hard smooth-textured cheese

cheek /cheek/ *n* **1** the fleshy side of the face below the eye and above and to the side of the mouth **2** either of 2 paired facing parts (e g the jaws of a vice) **3** insolent boldness; impudence **4** a buttock – *infml*

cheeky /'cheeki/ *adj* impudent, insolent – **cheekily** *adv* – **cheekiness** *n*

cheep /cheep/ *v or n* (to utter) a faint shrill sound characteristic of a young bird

¹**cheer** /chiə/ *n* **1** happiness, gaiety **2** sthg that gladdens **3** a shout of applause or encouragement

²**cheer** *v* **1a** to instil with hope or courage; comfort **b** to make glad or happy – usu + *up* **2** to urge *on*, encourage, or applaud esp by shouts

cheerful /-f(ə)l/ *adj* **1a** full of good spirits; merry **b** ungrudging **2** conducive to good cheer; likely to dispel gloom – **~ly** *adv* – **~ness** *n*

cheerio /,chiəri'oh/ *interj, chiefly Br* – used to express farewell

cheers /chiəz/ *interj* – used as a toast and sometimes as an informal farewell or expression of thanks

cheery /'chiəri/ *adj* marked by or causing good spirits; cheerful – **cheerily** *adv* – **cheeriness** *n*

¹**cheese** /cheez/ *n* **1** (an often cylindrical cake of) a food consisting of coagulated, compressed, and usu ripened milk curds **2** a fruit preserve with the consistency of cream cheese

²**cheese** *n* an important person; a boss – *slang*; chiefly in **big cheese**

cheesecake /-,kayk/ *n* **1** a baked or refrigerated dessert consisting of a soft filling, usu containing cheese, in a biscuit or pastry case **2** titillating photography of women

cheesecloth /-,kloth/ *n* a very fine unsized cotton gauze

cheeseparing /'cheez,peəring/ *n* miserly or petty economizing; stinginess

cheetah /'cheetə/ *n* a long-legged spotted swift-moving African cat

chef /shef/ *n* a skilled cook; *esp* the chief cook in a restaurant or hotel

¹**chemical** /'kemikl/ *adj* **1** of, used in, or produced by chemistry **2** acting, operated, or produced by chemicals – **~ly** *adv*

²**chemical** *n* a substance (e g an element or chemical compound) obtained by a chemical process or used for producing a chemical effect

chemise /shə'meez/ *n* **1** a woman's one-piece undergarment **2** a usu loose straight-hanging dress

chemist /'kemist/ n **1** one who is trained in chemistry **2** Br (a pharmacist, esp in) a retail shop where medicines and miscellaneous articles (e g cosmetics and films) are sold

chemistry /'kemistri/ n **1** a science that deals with the composition, structure, and properties of substances and of the transformations they undergo **2a** the composition and chemical properties of a substance **b** chemical processes and phenomena (e g of an organism)

cheque /chek/ n, chiefly Br a written order for a bank to pay money as instructed;

'cheque ,card n a card issued to guarantee that the holder's cheques up to a specific amount will be honoured by the issuing bank

chequer, chiefly NAm **checker** /'chekə/ v **1** to mark with different colours or shades; esp to mark with squares of (2) alternating colours **2** to vary with contrasting elements or situations USE usu in past part

cherish /'cherish/ v **1a** to hold dear; feel or show affection for **b** to keep or cultivate with care and affection; nurture **2** to keep in the mind deeply and with affection

cheroot /shə'rooht/ n a cigar cut square at both ends

cherry /'cheri/ n **1** (the wood or small pale yellow to deep red or blackish fruit of) any of numerous trees and shrubs of the rose family, often cultivated for their fruit or ornamental flowers **2** light red

cherub /'cherəb/ n, pl **cherubs**, (1) **cherubim** /'cherəbim/ **1** a biblical attendant of God or of a holy place, often represented as a being with large wings, a human head, and an animal body **2a** a beautiful usu winged child in painting and sculpture **b** an innocent-looking usu chubby and pretty person – ~**ic** adj – ~**ically** adv

chess /ches/ n a game for 2 players each of whom moves his/her 16 chessmen according to fixed rules across a chessboard and tries to checkmate his/her opponent's king

chessman /-,man/ n, pl **chessmen** /-mən, -,men/ any of the pieces used by each side in playing chess

chest /chest/ n **1a** a box with a lid used esp for the safekeeping of belongings **b** a usu small cupboard used esp for storing medicines or first-aid supplies **2** the part of the body enclosed by the ribs and breastbone

¹chestnut /'ches(t),nut/ n **1** (the nut or wood of) a tree or shrub of the beech family **2** reddish brown **3** a horse chestnut **4** a chestnut-coloured animal, specif a horse **5** an often repeated joke or story; broadly anything repeated excessively

²chestnut adj of the colour chestnut

chevron /'shevrən/ n a figure, pattern, or object having the shape of an (inverted) V; esp a sleeve badge that usu consists of 1 or more chevron-shaped stripes and indicates the wearer's rank

chew /chooh/ v to crush, grind, or gnaw (esp food) (as if) with the teeth

chic /sheek, shik/ adj or n (having or showing) elegance and sophistication, esp of dress or manner – ~**ly** adv

chicanery /shi'kaynə)ri/ n **1** deception by the use of fallacious or irrelevant arguments **2** a piece of sharp practice or legal trickery

chichi /'shee,shee/ adj or n **1** showy, frilly, or elaborate (ornamentation) **2** unnecessarily elaborate or affected (behaviour, style, etc)

chick /chik/ n **1** a young bird; esp a (newly hatched) chicken **2** a young woman – slang

¹chicken /'chikin/ n **1** the common domestic fowl, esp when young; also its flesh used as food **2** a young person – chiefly in he/she is no chicken – slang

²chicken adj scared – infml

'chicken ,feed n a small and insignificant amount, esp of money – infml

,chicken'hearted /-'hahtid/ adj timid, cowardly – ~**ness** n

chicken out v to lose one's nerve – infml

'chicken ,pox /poks/ n an infectious virus disease, esp of children, that is marked by mild fever and a rash of small blisters

chick-pea /'chik ,pee/ n (the hard edible seed of) an Asiatic leguminous plant

chicory /'chik(ə)ri/ n a usu blue-flowered European perennial composite plant widely grown for its edible thick roots and as a salad plant; also the ground roasted root used as a coffee additive

chide /chied/ v **chid** /chid/, **chided**; **chid**, **chidden** /'chid(ə)n/, **chided** to rebuke (sby) angrily; scold

¹chief /cheef/ n the head of a body of people or an organization; a leader

²chief adj **1** accorded highest rank or office **2** of greatest importance or influence

chiefly /'cheefli/ adv **1** most importantly; principally, especially **2** for the most part; mostly, mainly

,chief of 'staff n the senior officer of an armed forces staff that serves a commander

chieftain /'cheeftən/, fem **chieftainess** /-'nes/ n a chief, esp of a band, tribe, or clan

chiffchaff /'chif,chaf/ n a small greyish European warbler

chiffon /'shifon, -'-/ n a sheer (silk) fabric

chignon /'shi'nyon, '-nə/ n a usu large smooth knot of hair worn esp at the nape of the neck

Chihuahua /chi'wah·wə/ n a very small dog of Mexican origin

chilblain /'chil,blayn/ n an inflammatory sore, esp on the feet or hands, caused by exposure to cold

child /chield/ n, pl **children** /'childrən/ **1** an unborn or recently born person **2a** a young person, esp between infancy and youth **b** sby under the age of 14 – used in English law **3a** a son or daughter **b** a descendant **4** one strongly influenced by another or by a place or state of affairs **5** a product, result — **with child** of a woman pregnant

'**child** ,**birth** /-,buhth/ n parturition

childhood /'chield,hood/ n **1** the state or period of being a child **2** an early period in the development of sthg

childish /'chieldish/ adj **1** of or befitting a child or childhood **2** marked by or suggestive of immaturity – ~**ly** adv – ~**ness** n

childlike /'chield,liek/ adj marked by innocence and trust

'**child's** ,**play** n an extremely simple task or act

¹**chill** /chil/ v **1a** to make cold or chilly **b** to make (esp food or drink) cool, esp without freezing **2** to affect as if with cold; dispirit

²**chill** adj chilly

³**chill** n **1** a cold **2** a moderate but disagreeable degree of cold **3** coldness of manner

chilli, chili /'chili/ n pl **chillies, chilies** the pod of a hot pepper used either whole or ground as a pungent condiment

chilly /'chili/ adj **1** noticeably (unpleasantly) cold **2** lacking warmth of feeling; distant, unfriendly **3** tending to arouse fear or apprehension – **chilliness** n

¹**chime** /chiem/ n (the sound of) a set of bells or other objects producing a similar sound – often pl with sing. meaning

²**chime** v **1** to cause to chime **2** to signal or indicate by chiming **3** to be or act in accord

chime in v **1** to break into a conversation or discussion, esp in order to express an opinion **2** to combine harmoniously – often + with

chimera /ki'miərə, kie-/ n **1** a mythological monster with a lion's head, a goat's body and a serpent's tail **2** an illusion or fabrication of the mind; also an imaginary terror – **-rical** adj

chimney /'chimni/ n **1** a flue or flues for carrying off smoke; esp the part of such a structure extending above a roof **2** a structure through which smoke and gases (e g from a furnace or steam engine) are discharged **3** a tube, usu of glass, placed round a flame (e g of an oil lamp) to serve as a shield

'**chimney** ,**breast** n the wall that encloses a chimney and projects into a room

'**chimney** ,**pot** n a usu earthenware pipe at the top of a chimney

'**chimney** ,**stack** n **1** a masonry, brickwork, etc chimney rising above a roof and usu containing several flues **2** a tall chimney, typically of circular section, serving a factory, power station, etc

'**chimney** ,**sweep** n one whose occupation is cleaning soot from chimney flues

chimpanzee /,chimpan'zee/ n a tree-dwelling anthropoid ape of equatorial Africa

chin /chin/ n the lower portion of the face lying below the lower lip; the lower jaw

china /'chienə/ n **1** porcelain; also vitreous porcelain ware (e g dishes and vases) for domestic use **2** crockery **3** chiefly Br bone china

'**china** ,**clay** n kaolin

chinaman /'chienəmən/ n **1** a delivery by a left-handed bowler in cricket that is an off break as viewed by a right-handed batsman **2** cap a native of China – derog

Chinese /,chie'neez/ n, pl **Chinese 1** a native or inhabitant of China **2** a group of related Sino-Tibetan tone languages used by the people of China; specif Mandarin – **Chinese** adj

¹**chink** /chingk/ n **1** a small slit or fissure **2** a means of evasion or escape; a loophole

²**chink** n a short sharp sound

chinless /'chinlis/ adj lacking firmness of purpose; ineffectual – infml

chintz /chints/ n a (glazed) printed plain-weave fabric, usu of cotton

'**chin-**,**wag** n a conversation, chat – infml

¹**chip** /chip/ n **1** a small usu thin and flat piece (e g of wood or stone) cut, struck, or flaked off **2** a counter used as a token for money in gambling games **3** a flaw left after a chip is removed **4** (the small piece of semiconductor, esp silicon, on which is constructed) an integrated circuit **5a** chiefly Br a strip of potato fried in deep fat **b** NAm & Austr a potato crisp — **chip off the old block** a child that resembles either of his/her parents — **chip on one's shoulder** a challenging, belligerent, or embittered attitude — **when the chips are down** when the crucial or critical point has been reached

²**chip** v **-pp- 1a** to cut or hew with an edged tool **b** to cut or break a fragment from **2** to kick or hit a ball, pass, etc in a short high arc

'**chip** ,**board** /-,bawd/ n an artificial board made from compressed wood chips

chip in v **1** to contribute **2** to interrupt or add a comment to a conversation between other people

chipmunk /'chip,mungk/ n any of numerous small striped American squirrels graceful outline and fine ornamentation

chiropody /ki'ropədi, shi-/ n the care and treatment of the human foot in health and disease – **-dist** n

chirp /chuhp/ v or n (to make or speak in a tone resembling) the characteristic short shrill sound of a small bird or insect

chirpy /'chuhpi/ *adj* lively, cheerful – *infml* – **chirpily** *adv* – **chirpiness** *n*

¹**chisel** /'chizl/ *n* a metal tool with a cutting edge at the end of a blade used in dressing, shaping, or working wood, stone, metal, etc

²**chisel** *v* **-ll-** (*NAm* **-l-, -ll-**), /'chizl·ing/ **1** to cut or work (as if) with a chisel **2** to trick, cheat, or obtain (sthg) by cheating – *slang* – ~**ler** *n*

¹**chit** /chit/ *n* an immature often disrespectful young woman

²**chit** *n* a small slip of paper with writing on it; *esp* an order for goods

chitchat /'chit,chat/ *v or n* **-tt-** (to make) small talk; gossip – *infml*

chivalrous /'shiv(ə)lrəs/ *adj* having the characteristics (e g valour or gallantry) of a knight **2a** honourable, generous **b** graciously courteous and considerate, esp to women – ~**ly** *adv*

chivalry /'shiv(ə)lri/ *n* **1** the system, spirit, or customs of medieval knighthood **2** the qualities (e g courage, integrity, and consideration) of an ideal knight; chivalrous conduct

chive /chiev/ *n* a perennial plant related to the onion and used esp to flavour and garnish food – usu *pl* with sing. meaning

chivvy, chivy /'chivi/ *v* **1** to harass **2** to rouse to activity – usu + *up or along*

chloride /'klawried/ *n* a compound of chlorine with another element or radical; *esp* a salt or ester of hydrochloric acid

chlorine /'klawreen/ *n* a highly reactive element that is isolated as a pungent heavy greenish yellow gas

chloroform /'klorə,fawm/ *v or n* (to anaesthetize with) a colourless volatile liquid used esp as a solvent and formerly as a general anaesthetic

chlorophyll /'klorəfil/ *n* the green colouring matter found in the stems and leaves of plants

¹**chock** /chok/ *n* a wedge or block placed under a door, barrel, wheel, etc to prevent movement

²**chock** *v* to raise or support on blocks

³**chock** *adv* as closely or as completely as possible

chock-a-block /,chok ə 'blok/ *adj or adv* tightly packed; in a very crowded condition

chocolate /'choklət/ *n* **1** a paste, powder, or solid block of food prepared from (sweetened or flavoured) ground roasted cacao seeds **2** a beverage made by mixing chocolate with usu hot water or milk **3** a sweet made or coated with chocolate **4** a dark brown colour

¹**choice** /choys/ *n* **1** the act of choosing; selection **2** the power of choosing; an option **3** sby or sthg chosen **4** a sufficient number and variety to choose among

²**choice** *adj* **1** selected with care; well chosen **2** of high quality – ~**ly** *adv* – ~**ness** *n*

choir /kwie·ə/ *n* **1** *sing or pl in constr* an organized company of singers **2** the part of a church occupied by the singers or the clergy; *specif* the part of the chancel between the sanctuary and the nave

¹**choke** /chohk/ *v* **1** to check the normal breathing esp by compressing or obstructing the windpipe **2a** to stop or suppress expression of or by; silence – often + *back* or *down* **b** to become obstructed or checked **c** to become speechless or incapacitated, esp from strong emotion – usu + *up* **3a** to restrain the growth or activity of **b** to obstruct by filling up or clogging; jam

²**choke** *n* sthg that obstructs passage or flow: e g **a** a valve in the carburettor of a petrol engine for controlling the amount of air in a fuel air mixture **b** a narrowing towards the muzzle in the bore of a gun

³**choke** *n* the fibrous (inedible) central part of a globe artichoke

choker /'chohkə/ *n* a short necklace or decorative band that fits closely round the throat

cholera /'kolərə/ *n* an often fatal infectious epidemic disease caused by a bacterium and marked by severe gastrointestinal disorders

choleric /'kolərik/ *adj* **1** irascible **2** angry *USE* *fml* – ~**ally** *adv*

cholesterol /kə'lestərol/ *n* a substance present in animal and plant cells that is a possible factor in artery and heart disease

choose /choohz/ *v* **chose** /chohz/; **chosen** /'chohz(ə)n/ **1a** to select freely and after consideration **b** to decide on; *esp* to elect **2a** to decide **b** to wish

choosy, choosey /'choohzi/ *adj* fastidiously selective

¹**chop** /chop/ *v* **-pp-** **1a** to cut into or sever, usu by a blow or repeated blows of a sharp instrument **b** to cut into pieces – often + *up* **2** to make a quick stroke or repeated strokes (as if) with a sharp instrument

²**chop** *n* **1** a forceful blow (as if) with an axe **2** a small cut of meat often including part of a rib **3** an uneven motion of the sea, esp when wind and tide are opposed **4** abrupt removal; *esp* the sack – *infml* to keep changing one's mind, plans, etc — **chop logic** to argue with minute oversubtle distinctions

chopper /'chopə/ *n* **1** a short-handled axe or cleaver **2** a helicopter – *infml*

choppy /'chopi/ *adj*, of the sea or other expanse of water rough with small waves – **choppiness** *n*

'**chop,stick** /-,stik/ *n* either of 2 slender sticks held between thumb and fingers, used chiefly in oriental countries to lift food to the mouth

chopsuey /,chop'sooh·i/ *n* a Chinese dish of shredded meat or chicken with bean sprouts and other vegetables, usu served with rice

choral /'kawrəl/ *adj* accompanied with or designed for singing (by a choir)

chorale *also* **choral** /ko'rahl/ *n* (music composed for) a usu German traditional hymn or psalm for singing in church

¹**chord** /kawd/ *n* a combination of notes sounded together

²**chord** *n* 1 a strand-like anatomical structure 2 a straight line joining 2 points on a curve 3 an individual emotion or disposition

chore /chaw/ *n* 1 a routine task or job 2 a difficult or disagreeable task

choreography /,kori'ografi/ *n* the composition and arrangement of a ballet or other dance for the stage – **-grapher** *n*

chorister /'korista/ *n* a singer in a choir; *specif* a choirboy

chortle /'chawtl/ *v* **chortling** /'chawtl·ing, 'chawtling/ to laugh or chuckle, esp in satisfaction or exultation

chorus /'kawras/ *n* 1 a character (e g in Elizabethan drama) or group of singers and dancers (e g in Greek drama) who comment on the action 2 *sing or pl in constr* 2a a body of singers who sing the choral parts of a work (e g in opera) b a group of dancers and singers supporting the featured players in a musical or revue 3 a part of a song or hymn recurring at intervals 4 sthg performed, sung, or uttered simultaneously by a number of people or animals – **in chorus** in unison

chose /chohz/ *past of* **choose**

chosen /'chohz(a)n/ *adj* selected or marked for favour or special privilege

chowder /'chowda/ *n* a thick (clam or other seafood) soup or stew

chow mein /,chow 'mayn/ *n* a Chinese dish of fried noodles usu mixed with shredded meat or poultry and vegetables

Christ /kriest/ *n* the Messiah; Jesus

christen /'kris(ə)n/ *v* **1a** to baptize **b** to name esp at baptism **2** to name or dedicate (e g a ship or bell) by a ceremony suggestive of baptism **3** to use for the first time – *infml* – **~ing** *n*

Christendom /'kris(ə)ndəm, 'krist-/ *n* the community of people or nations professing Christianity

¹**Christian** /'kristi·an/ *n* **1a** an adherent of Christianity **b** a member of a Christian denomination, esp by baptism **2** a good or kind person regardless of religion

²**Christian** *adj* **1** of or consistent with Christianity or Christians **2** commendably decent or generous

Christianity /,kristi'anati/ *n* **1** the religion based on the life and teachings of Jesus Christ and the Bible **2** conformity to (a branch of) the Christian religion

Christian ,name *n* **1** a name given at christening (or confirmation) **2** a forename

Christian 'Science *n* a religion founded by Mary Baker Eddy in 1866 that includes a practice of spiritual healing

Christmas /'krismas/ *n* **1** a festival of the western Christian churches on December 25 that commemorates the birth of Christ and is usu observed as a public holiday **2 Christmas, Christmastide** the festival season from Christmas Eve till the Epiphany (January 6)

chromatic /kroh'matik/ *adj* **1a** of colour sensation or (intensity of) colour **b** highly coloured **2a** *of a scale* having an interval of a semitone between each note **b** characterized by frequent use of intervals or notes outside the diatonic scale – **~ally** *adv*

chrome /krohm/ *n* **1** (a pigment formed from) chromium **2** (sthg with) a plating of chromium

chromium /'krohmyam, -mi·am/ *n* a blue-white metallic element found naturally only in combination and used esp in alloys and in electroplating

chromosome /'krohma,sohm, -,zohm/ *n* any of the gene-carrying bodies that contain DNA and protein and are found in the cell nucleus

chronic /'kronik/ *adj* **1** *esp of an illness* marked by long duration or frequent recurrence **2a** always present or encountered; *esp* constantly troubling **b** habitual, persistent **3** *Br* bad, terrible – *infml* – **~ally** *adv*

¹**chronicle** /'kronikl/ *n* **1** a usu continuous and detailed historical account of events arranged chronologically without analysis or interpretation **2** a narrative

²**chronicle** *v* **chronicling** /'kronikl·ing/ **1** to record (as if) in a chronicle **2** to list, describe – **~r** *n*

chronology /kra'nolaji/ *n* (a method for) setting past events in order of occurrence – **-gical** *adj*

chronometer /kra'nomita/ *n* an instrument for measuring time

chrysalis /'krisalis/ *n, pl* **chrysalides** /kri'sala,deez/, **chrysalises** **1** (the case enclosing) a pupa, esp of a butterfly or moth **2** a sheltered state or stage of being or growth

chrysanthemum /kri'zanthimam/ *n* any of various (cultivated) composite plants with brightly coloured often double flower heads

chubby /'chubi/ *adj* of large proportions; plump – **chubbiness** *n*

¹**chuck** /chuk/ *n* – used as a term of endearment

²**chuck** *v* **1** to pat, tap **2a** to toss, throw **b** to discard – often + *out* or *away* **3** to leave; give up – often + *in* or *up* *USE* (*except* 1) *infml*

³**chuck** *n* **1** a pat or nudge under the chin **2** a throw – *infml*

⁴**chuck** *n* **1** a cut of beef that includes most of the neck and the area about the shoulder blade **2** a device for holding a workpiece (e g for turning on a lathe) or tool (e g in a drill)

chuckle /'chukl/ *v* **chuckling** /'chukling/ to laugh inwardly or quietly – **chuckle** *n*

chuck out *v* to eject (a person) from a place or an office; dismiss – *infml*

chug /chug/ *v or n* **-gg-** (to move or go with) a usu repetitive dull explosive sound made (as if) by a labouring engine

¹**chum** /chum/ *n* a close friend; a mate – *infml; no longer in vogue*

²**chum** *v* **-mm-** to form a friendship, esp a close one – usu + (*up*) *with; no longer in vogue*

chump /chump/ *n* **1** a cut of meat taken from between the loin and hindleg **2** a fool, duffer – *infml*

chunk /chungk/ *n* **1** a lump; esp one of a firm or hard material (e g wood) **2** a (large) quantity – *infml*

chunky /'chungki/ *adj* **1** stocky **2** *of materials, clothes, etc* thick and heavy

church /chuhch/ *n* **1** a building for public (Christian) worship; *esp* a place of worship used by an established church **2** *often cap* institutionalized religion; *esp* the established Christian religion of a country **3** *cap* a body or organization of religious believers: e g **3a** the whole body of Christians **b** a denomination **c** a congregation **4** an occasion for public worship **5** the clerical profession

church,warden /'-wawd(ə)n/ *n* either of 2 lay parish officers in Anglican churches with responsibility esp for parish property and alms

church,yard /-,yahd/ *n* an enclosed piece of ground surrounding a church; esp one used as a burial ground

churl /chuhl/ *n* **1a** a rude ill-bred person **b** a mean morose person **2** *archaic* a rustic, countryman

churlish /'chuhlish/ *adj* **1** lacking refinement or sensitivity **2** rudely uncooperative; surly – ~**ly** *adv* – ~**ness** *n*

¹**churn** /chuhn/ *n* **1** a vessel used in making butter in which milk or cream is agitated to separate the oily globules from the watery medium **2** *Br* a large metal container for transporting milk

²**churn** *v* **1** to agitate (milk or cream) in a churn in order to make butter **2** to produce or be in violent motion

churn out *v* to produce prolifically and mechanically, usu without great concern for quality – *chiefly infml*

chute /shooht/ *n* **1** a waterfall, rapid, etc **2** an inclined plane, channel, or passage down which things may pass **3** a parachute – *infml*

chutney /'chutni/ *n* a thick condiment or relish of Indian origin that contains fruits, sugar, vinegar, and spices

cicada /si'kahdə, -'kaydə/ *n* any of a family of insects that have large transparent wings and whose males produce a shrill singing noise

cider, *Br also* **cyder** /'siedə/ *n* an alcoholic drink made from apples

cigar /si'gah/ *n* a small roll of tobacco leaf for smoking

cigarette, *NAm also* **cigaret** /,sigə'ret/ *n* a narrow cylinder of tobacco enclosed in paper for smoking

¹**cinch** /sinch/ *n* **1** a task performed with ease **2** sthg certain to happen

²**cinch** *v* to make certain of; assure

cinder /'sində/ *n* **1** a fragment of ash **2** a piece of partly burned material (e g coal) that will burn further but will not flame

cinema /'sinimə/ *n* **1a** films considered esp as an art form, entertainment, or industry – usu + *the* **b** the art or technique of making films **2** a theatre where films are shown – ~**tic** *adj*

cinematography /,sinimə'tografi/ *n* the art or science of cinema photography – **-phic** *adj*

cinnamon /'sinəmən/ *n* **1** (any of several trees of the laurel family with) an aromatic bark used as a spice **2** a light yellowish brown colour

circa /'suhkə/ *prep* at, in, or of approximately – *used esp with dates*

circadian /suh'kaydiən/ *adj* of approximately day-long periods or cycles (e g of biological activity or function)

¹**circle** /'suhkl/ *n* **1a** a closed plane curve every point of which is equidistant from a fixed point within the curve **b** the plane surface bounded by such a curve **2** sthg in the form of (an arc of) a circle **3** a balcony or tier of seats in a theatre **4** cycle, round **5** *sing or pl in constr* a group of people sharing a common interest, activity, or leader

²**circle** *v* **circling** /'suhkling, 'suhkl·ing/ **1** to enclose or move (as if) in a circle **2** to move or revolve round

circuit /'suhkit/ *n* **1** a closed loop encompassing an area **2a** a course round a periphery **b** a racetrack **3** a regular tour (e g by a judge) round an assigned area or territory **4a** the complete path of an electric current, usu including the source of energy **b** an array of electrical components connected so as to allow the passage of current **5a** an association or league of similar groups **b** a chain of theatres at which productions are presented successively

circuitous /suh'kyooh·itəs/ *adj* indirect in route or method; roundabout – ~**ly** *adv*

¹**circular** /'suhkyoolə/ *adj* **1** having the form of a circle **2** moving in or describing a circle or spiral **3** marked by the fallacy of assuming sthg which is to be demonstrated **4** marked by or moving in a cycle **5** intended for circulation – ~**ity** *n* – ~**ly** *adv*

²**circular** *n* a paper (e g a leaflet or advertisement) intended for wide distribution

circulate /'suhkyoo,layt/ *v* **1** to move in a circle, circuit, or orbit; *esp* to follow a course that returns to the starting point **2a** to flow without obstruction **b** to become well known or widespread **c** to go from group to group at a social gathering **d** to come into the hands of readers; *specif* to become sold or distributed **3** to cause to circulate

circulation /,suhkyoo'laysh(ə)n/ *n* **1** a flow **2** orderly movement through a circuit; *esp* the movement of blood through the vessels of the body induced by the pumping action of the heart **3a** passage or transmission from person to person or place to place; *esp* the interchange of currency **b** the average number of copies (e g of a newspaper) of a publication sold over a given period

circumcise /'suhkəm,siez/ *v* to cut off the foreskin of (a male) or the clitoris of (a female) – **-ision** *n*

circumference /suh'kumfərəns/ *n* 1 the perimeter of a circle 2 the external boundary or surface of a figure or object – **-ential** *adj*

circumflex /'suhkəm,fleks/ *n* an accent mark ^, ~ **circumflex** *adj*

circumlo'cution /-lə'kyoohsh(ə)n/ *n* 1 the use of an unnecessarily large number of words to express an idea 2 evasive speech – **-tory** *adj*

circum'navigate /-'navigayt/ *v* to go round; *esp* to travel completely round (the earth), esp by sea – **-gation** *n*

'circum,scribe /-,skrieb/ *v* 1 to surround by a physical or imaginary line 2 to restrict the range or activity of definitely and clearly

'circum,spect /-,spekt/ *adj* careful to consider all circumstances and possible consequences; prudent – ~**ly** *adv* – ~**ion** *n*

circumstance /'suhkəm,stahns, -stans, -stəns/ *n* 1 a condition or event that accompanies, causes, or determines another; *also* the sum of such conditions or events **2a** a state of affairs; an occurrence – often pl with sing. meaning **b** *pl* situation with regard to material or financial welfare **3** attendant formalities and ceremony — **in/under the circumstances** because of the conditions; considering the situation

circumstantial /,suhkəm'stansh(ə)l, -'stahnsh(ə)l/ *adj* 1 belonging to, consisting in, or dependent on circumstances 2 pertinent but not essential; incidental – ~**ly** *adv*

,circum'vent /-'vent/ *v* to check or evade, esp by ingenuity or stratagem – usu *n* – **ion** *n*

circus /'suhkəs/ *n* **1a** a large circular or oval stadium used esp for sports contests or spectacles **b** a public spectacle **2a** the (usu covered arena housing) an entertainment in which a variety of performers (e g acrobats and clowns) and performing animals are involved in a series of unrelated acts **b** an activity suggestive of a circus (e g in being a busy scene of noisy or frivolous action) **3** *Br* a road junction in a town partly surrounded by a circle of buildings – usu in proper names

cirque /suhk/ *n* a deep steep-walled basin on a mountain

cirrhosis /si'rohsis/ *n pl* **cirrhoses** /-,seez/ hardening of the liver

cirrus /'sirəs/ *n, pl* **cirri** /-rie/ 1 a slender usu flexible (invertebrate) animal appendage 2 a wispy white cloud formation usu of minute ice crystals formed at high altitudes

cissy, sissy /'sisi/ *n, Br* 1 an effeminate boy or man 2 a cowardly person *USE* infml

cistern /'sist(ə)n/ *n* an artificial reservoir for storing liquids, esp water

citadel /'sitədl, -,del/ *n* 1 a fortress; *esp* one that commands a city 2 a stronghold

citation /sie'taysh(ə)n/ *n* **1a** an act of citing or quoting **b** a quotation **2** a mention; *specif* specific reference in a military dispatch to meritorious conduct

cite /siet/ *v* 1 to call upon to appear before a court 2 to quote by way of example, authority, precedent, or proof 3 to refer to or name; *esp* to mention formally in commendation or praise

citizen /'sitiz(ə)n/ *n* an inhabitant of a city or town; *esp* a freeman 2 a (native or naturalized) member of a state – ~**ship** *n*

'citizenry /-ri/ *n sing or pl in constr* the whole body of citizens

,citric 'acid /'sitrik/ *n* an acid occurring in lemons, limes, etc and used as a flavouring

citron /'sitrən/ *n* 1 a (tree that bears) fruit like the lemon but larger and with a thicker rind 2 the preserved rind of the citron, used esp in cakes and puddings

citrus /'sitrəs/ *n pl* **citrus, citruses** any of several shrubs or trees with edible thick-rinded juicy fruit (e g the orange or lemon) – **citrus** *adj*

city /'siti/ *n* **1a** a large town **b** an incorporated British town that has a cathedral or has had civic status conferred on it **c** a usu large chartered municipality in the USA 2 a city-state **3a** *the* financial and commercial area of London **b** *cap, sing or pl in constr* the influential financial interests of the British economy

civic /'sivik/ *adj* of a citizen, a city, or citizenship

'civics *n pl but sing or pl in constr* a social science dealing with the rights and duties of citizens

civil /'sivl/ *adj* 1 of citizens 2 adequately courteous and polite; not rude 3 relating to private rights as distinct from criminal proceedings 4 of or involving the general public as distinguished from special (e g military or religious) affairs

,civil de'fence *n, often cap C&D* protective measures organized by and for civilians against hostile attack, esp from the air, or natural disaster

civilian /si'vilyən/ *n* one who is not in the army, navy, air force, or other uniformed public body

civility /si'viləti/ *n* 1 courtesy, politeness 2 a polite act or expression – usu pl

civil·ization, -isation /,sivilie'zaysh(ə)n, -li-/ *n* 1 a relatively high level of development of culture and technology 2 the culture characteristic of a time or place

civil·ize, -ise /'siv(ə)l,iez/ *v* 1 to cause cultural development, esp along Western or modern lines 2 to educate, refine – ~**d** *adj*

civ

,civil 'law n, *often cap C&L* **1** the body of private law developed from Roman law as distinct from common law **2** the law established by a nation or state for its own jurisdiction (e g as distinct from international law) **3** the law of private rights

,civil 'liberty n a right or freedom of the individual citizen in relation to the state (e g freedom of speech); *also* such rights or freedoms considered collectively

,civil 'rights n pl civil liberties; *esp* those of status equality between races or groups

,civil 'servant n a member of a civil service

,civil 'service n sing or pl in constr the administrative service of a government or international agency, exclusive of the armed forces

,civil 'war n a war between opposing groups of citizens of the same country

¹clack /klak/ v **1** to clatter – infml **2** to make an abrupt striking sound or sounds **3** to cause to make a clatter

²clack n **1** rapid continuous talk; chatter – infml **2** a sound of clacking

clad /klad/ adj being covered or clothed

¹claim /klaym/ v **1a** to ask for, esp as a right **b** to require, demand **c** to take; account for **2** to take as the rightful owner **3** to assert in the face of possible contradiction; maintain

²claim n **1** a demand for sthg (believed to be) due **2a** a right or title to sthg **b** an assertion open to challenge **3** sthg claimed; *esp* a tract of land staked out

claimant /'klaymənt/ n one who asserts a right or entitlement

clairvoyance /kleə'voyəns/ n **1** the power or faculty of discerning objects not apparent to the physical senses **2** the ability to perceive matters beyond the range of ordinary perception – **-ant** n, adj

clam /klam/ n **1** any of numerous edible marine molluscs (e g a scallop) living in sand or mud **2** a freshwater mussel

clamber /'klambə/ v to climb awkwardly or with difficulty – **clamber** n

clammy /'klami/ adj being damp, clinging, and usu cool – **-mily** adv – **-miness** n

clamour, *NAm chiefly* clamor /'klamə/ v or n **1** (to engage in) noisy shouting **2** (to make) a loud continuous noise **3** (to make) insistent public expression (e g of support or protest)

¹clamp /klamp/ n **1** a device that holds or compresses 2 or more parts firmly together **2** a heap of wooden sticks or bricks for burning, firing, etc

²clamp v **1** to fasten (as if) with a clamp **2** to hold tightly

clamp down v to impose restrictions; *also* to make restrictions more stringent

clam up v to become silent – infml

clan /klan/ n **1a** a (Highland Scots) Celtic group of households descended from a common ancestor **b** a group of people related by family **2** a usu close-knit group united by a common interest or common characteristics

clandestine /klan'destin, 'klandəstin/ adj surreptitious – ~**ly** adv – ~**ness** n

clang /klang/ v to cause to make a loud metallic ringing sound – **clang** n

clanger /'klangə/ n, Br a blunder – infml

clank /klangk/ n a sharp brief metallic sound

clannish /'klanish/ adj tending to associate only with a select group of similar background, status, or interests – ~**ly** adv – ~**ness** n

¹clap /klap/ v **-pp- 1** to strike (e g 2 flat hard surfaces) together so as to produce a loud sharp noise **2a** to strike (the hands) together repeatedly, usu in applause **b** to applaud **3** to strike with the flat of the hand in a friendly way **4** to place, put, or set, esp energetically – infml

²clap n **1** a loud sharp noise, specif of thunder **2** a friendly slap **3** the sound of clapping hands; *esp* applause

³clap n venereal disease; *esp* gonorrhoea – slang

,clapped 'out adj, *chiefly Br, esp of machinery* (old and) worn-out – infml

clapper /'klapə/ n the tongue of a bell — **like the clappers** Br as fast as possible — infml; + run or go

'clapper-,board n a hinged board containing identifying details of the scene to be filmed that is held before the camera and banged together to mark the beginning and end of each take

claptrap /'klap,trap/ n pretentious nonsense; rubbish – infml

claret /'klarit/ n **1** a dry red Bordeaux **2** a dark purplish red colour

clarify /'klari,fie/ v **1** to make (e g a liquid) clear or pure, usu by freeing from suspended matter **2** to make free from confusion **3** to make understandable – **-ification** n

clarinet /,klari'net/ n a single-reed woodwind instrument – ~**(t)ist** n

¹clarion /'klari-ən/ n (the sound of) a medieval trumpet

²clarion adj brilliantly clear

clarity /'klarəti/ n the quality or state of being clear

¹clash /klash/ v **1** to make a clash **2a** to come into conflict **b** to form a displeasing combination; not match

²clash n **1** a noisy usu metallic sound of collision **2a** a hostile encounter **b** a sharp conflict

¹clasp /klahsp/ n **1** a device for holding objects or parts of sthg together **2** a holding or enveloping (as if) with the hands or arms

²clasp v **1** to fasten (as if) with a clasp **2** to enclose and hold with the arms; *specif* to embrace **3** to seize (as if) with the hand; grasp

cle

¹**class** /klahs/ n **1a** sing or pl in constr a group sharing the same economic or social status in a society consisting of several groups with differing statuses – often pl with sing. meaning **b** the system of differentiating society by classes **c** high quality; elegance **2** sing or pl in constr a body of students meeting regularly to study the same subject **3** a group, set, or kind sharing common attributes **4a** a division or rating based on grade or quality **b** Br a level of university honours degree awarded to a student according to merit

²**class** v to classify **2** taking part in class war – ~**ness** n

¹**classic** /'klasik/ adj **1a** of recognized value or merit; serving as a standard of excellence **b** both traditional and enduring **2** classical **3a** authoritative, definitive **b** being an example that shows clearly the characteristics of some group of things or occurrences

²**classic** n **1a** a literary work of ancient Greece or Rome **b** pl Greek and Latin literature, history, and philosophy considered as an academic subject **2a** (the author of) a work of lasting excellence **b** an authoritative source **3** a classic example; archetype **4** an important long-established sporting event; specif, Br any of 5 flat races for horses (e g the Epsom Derby)

classical /'klasikl/ adj **1** standard, classic **2** of the (literature, art, architecture, or ideals of the) ancient Greek and Roman world **3** of or being music in the educated European tradition that includes such forms as chamber music, opera, and symphony as distinguished from folk, popular music, or jazz **4a** both authoritative and traditional **b** of or being systems or methods that constitute an accepted although not necessarily modern approach to a subject – ~**ly** adv – ~**ity** n

classicism /'klasi,siz(ə)m/, **classicalism** /'klasikl ,iz(ə)m/ n **1a** the principles or style embodied in classical literature, art, or architecture **b** a classical idiom or expression **2** adherence to traditional standards (e g of simplicity, restraint, and proportion) that are considered to have universal and lasting worth – -**icist** n

classification /,klasifi'kaysh(ə)n/ n **1** classifying **2a** systematic arrangement in groups according to established criteria; specif taxonomy **b** a class, category

classified /'klasi,fied/ adj withheld from general circulation for reasons of national security

classify /'klasi,fie/ v **1** to arrange in classes **2** to assign to a category

classless /'klahslis/ adj **1** free from class distinction **2** belonging to no particular social class – ~**ness** n

'**class mate** /-,mayt/ n a member of the same class in a school or college

'**classroom** /-room, -,roohm/ n a room where classes meet

classy /'klahsi/ adj elegant, stylish – infml

¹**clatter** /'klatə/ v (to cause) to make a clatter

²**clatter** n **1** a rattling sound (e g of hard bodies striking together) **2** a commotion

clause /klawz/ n **1** a distinct article or condition in a formal document **2** a phrase containing a subject and predicate capable of functioning either in isolation or as part of a sentence

claustrophobia /,klostrə'fohbi-ə, ,klaw-/ n abnormal dread of being in closed or confined spaces – -**phobic** n, adj

clavichord /'klavi,kawd/ n an early usu rectangular keyboard instrument

clavicle /'klavikl/ n a bone of the vertebrate shoulder typically linking the shoulder blade and breastbone; the collarbone

¹**claw** /klaw/ n **1** (a part resembling or limb having) a sharp usu slender curved nail on an animal's toe **2** any of the pincerlike organs on the end of some limbs of a lobster, scorpion, or similar arthropod **3** sthg (e g the forked end of a claw hammer) resembling a claw

²**claw** v to rake, seize, dig, pull, or make (as if) with claws

clay /klay/ n **1a** (soil composed chiefly of) an earthy material that is soft when moist but hard when fired and is used for making brick, tile, and pottery **b** thick and clinging earth or mud **2a** a substance that resembles clay and is used for modelling **b** the human body as distinguished from the spirit – ~**ey** adj

,**clay 'pigeon** n a saucer-shaped object usu made of baked clay and hurled into the air as a target for shooting at with a shotgun

¹**clean** /kleen/ adj **1** (relatively) free from dirt or pollution **2** unadulterated, pure **3a** free from illegal, immoral, or disreputable activities or characteristics **b** observing the rules; fair **4** thorough, complete **5** relatively free from error or blemish; clear; specif legible **6a** characterized by clarity, precision, or deftness **b** not jagged; smooth – ~**ness** n – ~**ly** adv

²**clean** adv **1a** so as to leave clean **b** in a clean manner **2** all the way; completely

³**clean** v **1** to make clean – often + up **2a** to strip, empty **b** to deprive of money or possessions – often + out; infml **3** to undergo cleaning

⁴**clean** n an act of cleaning away dirt

,**clean-'cut** adj **1** sharply defined **2** of wholesome appearance

cleaner /'kleenə/ n **1** sby whose occupation is cleaning rooms or clothes **2** a substance, implement, or machine for cleaning – **to the cleaners** to or through the experience of being deprived of all one's money – infml

cleanliness /'klenlinis/ n fastidiousness in keeping things or one's person clean – **cleanly** adj

cleanse /klenz/ v to clean – ~**r** n

,clean-'shaven *adj* with the hair, specif of the beard and moustache, shaved off

clean up *v* to make a large esp sweeping gain (e g in business or gambling)

¹clear /klia/ *adj* 1a bright, luminous b free from cloud, mist, haze, or dust c untroubled, serene 2 clean, pure: e g 2a free from blemishes b easily seen through; transparent 3 easily heard, visible or understood 4a capable of sharp discernment; keen b free from doubt; sure 5 free from guilt 6a net b unqualified, absolute c free from obstruction or entanglement d full – ~ness *n* – ~ly *adv*

²clear *adv* 1 clearly 2 *chiefly NAm* all the way

³clear *v* 1a to make transparent or translucent b to free from unwanted material – often + *out* 2a to free from accusation or blame; vindicate b to certify as trustworthy 3a to rid (the throat) of phlegm; *also* to make a rasping noise in (the throat) b to erase accumulated totals or stored data from (e g a calculator or computer memory) 4 to authorize or cause to be authorized 5a to free from financial obligation b(1) to settle, discharge b(2) to deal with unfinished or settled c to gain without deduction d to put or pass through a clearinghouse 6a to get rid of; remove – often + *off*, *up*, or *away* b to kick or pass (the ball) away from the goal as a defensive measure in soccer 7 to go over without touching 8a to become clear – often + *up* b to go away; vanish – sometimes + *off*, *out*, or *away* — **clear the air** to remove elements of hostility, tension, confusion, or uncertainty from the mood or temper of the time — **clear the decks** to get things ready for action

clearance /'kliarans/ *n* 1a an authorization b a sale to clear out stock c the removal of buildings, people, etc from the space they previously occupied d a clearing of the ball in soccer 2 the distance by which one object clears another, or the clear space between them

,clear-'cut *adj* 1 sharply outlined; distinct 2 free from ambiguity or uncertainty

,clear'headed /-'hedid/ *adj* 1 not confused; sensible, rational 2 having no illusions about a state of affairs; realistic

clearing /'kliaring/ *n* an area of land cleared of wood and brush

'clearing,house /-,hows/ *n* an establishment maintained by banks for settling mutual claims and accounts

,clear-'sighted *adj* clearheaded; *esp* having perceptive insight – ~ly *adv* – ~ness *n*

clear up *v* 1 to tidy up 2 to explain

'clear,way /-,way/ *n*, *Br* a road on which vehicles may stop only in an emergency

cleavage /'kleevij/ *n* 1 (a) division 2 (the space between) a woman's breasts, esp when exposed by a low-cut garment

¹cleave /kleev/ *v* cleaved, clove /klohv/ to stick firmly and closely or loyally and steadfastly – usu + *to*

²cleave *v* cleaved *also* cleft /kleft/, clove /klohv/; cleaved *also* cleft, cloven /'klohv(a)n/ to divide or pass through (as if) by a cutting blow; split, esp along the grain

cleaver /'kleeva/ *n* a butcher's implement for cutting animal carcasses into joints or pieces

clef /klef/ *n* a sign placed on a musical staff to indicate the pitch represented by the notes following it

cleft /kleft/ *n* 1 a space or opening made by splitting; a fissure 2 a usu V-shaped indented formation; a hollow between ridges or protuberances

,cleft 'palate *n* a congenital fissure of the roof of the mouth

clematis /kla'maytis, 'klematis/ *n* a vine usu climbing or scrambling plant of the buttercup family

clement /'klemant/ *adj* 1 inclined to be merciful; lenient 2 *of weather* pleasantly mild – ~ly *adv* – ~ency *n*

clench /klench/ *v* 1 to clinch 2 to hold fast; clutch 3 to set or close tightly

clerestory, clearstory /'klia,stawri/ *n* the part of an outside wall of a room or building that rises above an adjoining roof

clergy /'kluhji/ *n sing or pl in constr* a group performing pastoral or liturgical functions in an organized religion, esp a Christian church

'clergyman /-man/ *n* an ordained minister

¹clerical /'klerikl/ *adj* 1 (characteristic) of the clergy or a clergyman 2 of a clerk or office worker

²clerical *n* 1 a clergyman 2 *pl* clerical clothes

clerk /klahk/ *NAm* kluhk/ *n* sby whose occupation is keeping records or accounts or doing general office work

clever /'kleva/ *adj* 1 skilful or adroit *with* the hands or body; nimble b mentally quick and resourceful; intelligent 2 marked by wit or ingenuity; *also* thus marked but lacking depth or soundness – ~ly *adv* – ~ness *n*

,clever-'dick /dik/ *n*, *Br* a know-all – *infml*

cliché /'klee,shay/ *n* a hackneyed phrase, theme, or situation – ~d *adj*

¹click /klik/ *n* 1 a slight sharp sound 2 a sharp speech sound in some languages made by the sudden inrush of air at the release of an obstruction or narrowing in the mouth

²click *v* 1 to strike, move, or produce with a click 2 to operate with or make a click 3a to strike up an immediately warm friendship, esp with sby of the opposite sex b to succeed c *Br* to cause sudden insight or recognition – sometimes in *click into place USE* – *infml*

client /'klie-ant/ *n* 1 sby who engages or receives the advice or services of a professional person or organization 2 a customer

clientele /ˌklee·on'tel/ *n sing or pl in constr* a body of clients

cliff /klif/ *n* a very steep high face of rock, earth, ice, etc

¹**cliff-ˌhanger** *n* **1** an adventure serial or melodrama, usu presented in instalments each ending in suspense **2** a contest or situation whose outcome is in doubt to the very end

climacteric /ˌklie'maktərik, ˌklie·mək'terik/ *n* **1** a major turning point or critical stage **2** the menopause; *also* a corresponding period in the male during which sexual activity and competence are reduced – **climacteric** *adj*

climactic /klie'maktik/ *adj* of or being a climax

climate /'kliemət/ *n* **1** (a region of the earth having a specified) average course or condition of the weather over a period of years as shown by temperature, wind, rain, etc **2** the prevailing state of affairs or feelings of a group or period; a milieu – **-atic** *adj*

climatology /ˌkliemə'toləji/ *n* a branch of meteorology dealing with climates

¹**climax** /'klie·maks/ *n* **1** the highest point; a culmination **2** the point of highest dramatic tension or a major turning point in some action (e g of a play) **3** an orgasm

²**climax** *v* to come to a climax

climb /kliem/ *v* **1a** to go gradually upwards; rise **b** to slope upwards **2a** to go *up, down,* etc on a more or less vertical surface using the hands to grasp or give support **b** *of a plant* to ascend in growth (e g by twining) **3** to get *into* or *out of* clothing, usu with some haste or effort **4** to go upwards on or along, to the top of, or over **5** to draw or pull oneself up, over, or to the top of, by using hands and feet **6** to grow up or over – **~er** *n*

climb down *v* to back down – **climb-down** *n*

clinch /klinch/ *v* **1** to turn over or flatten the protruding pointed end of (e g a driven nail) **2** to fasten in this way **3** to hold an opponent (e g in boxing) at close quarters – **clinch** *n*

clincher /'klincho/ *n* a decisive fact, argument, act, or remark

cling /kling/ *v* **clung** /klung/ **1a** to stick as if glued firmly **b** to hold (on) tightly or tenaciously **2a** to have a strong emotional attachment or dependence **b** *esp of a smell* to linger

clinic /'klinik/ *n* **1** a meeting held by an expert or person in authority, to which people bring problems for discussion and resolution **2a** a facility (e g of a hospital) for the diagnosis and treatment of outpatients **b** a usu private hospital

clinical /'klinikl/ *adj* detached; unemotional – **~ly** *adv*

¹**clink** /klingk/ *v* to (cause to) give out a slight sharp short metallic sound – **clink** *n*

²**clink** *n* prison – *slang*

clinker /'klingkə/ *n* stony matter fused by fire; slag

¹**clip** /klip/ *v* **-pp-** to clasp or fasten with a clip

²**clip** *n* **1** any of various devices that grip, clasp, or hold **2** (a device to hold cartridges for charging) a magazine from which ammunition is fed into the chamber of a firearm

³**clip** *v* **-pp- 1a** to cut (off) (as if) with shears **b** to excise **2** to abbreviate in speech or writing **3** to hit with a glancing blow; *also* to hit smartly – *infml*

⁴**clip** *n* **1a** the product of (a single) shearing (e g of sheep) **b** a section of filmed material **2a** an act of clipping **b** the manner in which sthg is clipped **3** a sharp blow **4** a rapid rate of motion *USE* (3&4) *infml*

¹**clipboard** /-ˌbawd/ *n* a small writing board with a spring clip for holding papers

clipper /'klipə/ *n* **1** an implement for cutting or trimming hair or nails – usu pl with sing. meaning **2** a fast sailing ship

clippie /'klipi/ *n*, *Br* a female bus conductor – *infml*

clipping /'kliping/ *n* a (newspaper) cutting

clique /kleek/ *n sing or pl in constr* a highly exclusive and often aloof group of people – **~y, cliquish** *adj* – **cliquishness** *n*

clitoris /'klitəris, 'klie-/ *n* a small erectile organ at the front or top part of the vulva that is a centre of sexual sensation in females

¹**cloak** /klohk/ *n* **1** a sleeveless outer garment that usu fastens at the neck and hangs loosely from the shoulders **2** sthg that conceals; a pretence, disguise

²**cloak** *v* to cover or hide (as if) with a cloak

cloak-and-ˌdagger *adj* dealing in or suggestive of melodramatic intrigue and action usu involving espionage

¹**cloakroom** /-room, -ˌroohm/ *n* **1** a room in which outdoor clothing or luggage may be left during one's stay **2** *chiefly Br* a room with a toilet – *euph*

¹**clobber** /'klobə/ *n*, *Br* gear, paraphernalia – *infml*

²**clobber** *v* **1** to hit with force **2** to defeat overwhelmingly *USE infml*

cloche /klosh/ *n* **1** a translucent cover used for protecting outdoor plants **2** a woman's usu soft close-fitting hat

¹**clock** /klok/ *n* **1** a device other than a watch for indicating or measuring time **2** a recording or metering device with a dial and indicator attached to a mechanism **3** *Br* a face – *slang* — **round the clock 1** continuously for 24 hours; day and night without cessation **2** without relaxation and heedless of time

²**clock** *v* **1a** to register on a mechanical recording device **b** *Br* to attain a time, speed, etc, of – often + *up*; *infml* **2** to hit – *infml*

³**clock** *n* an ornamental pattern on the outside ankle or side of a stocking or sock

clock in *v* to record the time of one's arrival or commencement of work by punching a card in a time clock

clock out v to record the time of one's departure or stopping of work by punching a card in a time clock n

clock,wise /-,wiez/ adj, adv in the direction in which the hands of a clock rotate as viewed from in front

clock,work /-,wuhk/ n machinery that operates in a manner similar to that of a mechanical clock; specif machinery powered by a coiled spring — **like clockwork** smoothly and with no hitches

clod /klod/ n 1 a lump or mass, esp of earth or clay 2 an oaf, dolt

clodhopper /'klod,hopə/ n 1 an awkward, boorish person – infml 2 a large heavy shoe – chiefly humor

¹**clog** /klog/ n a shoe, sandal, or overshoe with a thick typically wooden sole

²**clog** v -gg- 1 to obstruct so as to hinder motion in or through 2 to block or become blocked up

cloister /'kloystə/ n 1 a monastic establishment 2 a covered passage on the side of an open court, usu having one side walled and the other an open arcade

clone /klohn/ n an individual that is asexually produced and is therefore identical to its parent – **clone** v

clop /klop/ n a sound made (as if) by a hoof or shoe against a hard surface

¹**close** /klohz/ v 1a to move so as to bar passage b to deny access to c to suspend or stop the operations of; also to discontinue or dispose of (a business) permanently – often + down 2a to bring to an end b to conclude discussion or negotiation about; also to bring to agreement or settlement 3 to bring or bind together the parts or edges of 4a to contract, swing, or slide so as to leave no opening b to cease operation; specif, Br to stop broadcasting – usu + down 5 to draw near, esp in order to fight – usu + with 6 to come to an end — **close one's doors** 1 to refuse admission 2 to go out of business — **close one's eyes to** to ignore deliberately — **close ranks** to unite in a concerted stand, esp to meet a challenge — **close the door** to be uncompromisingly obstructive

²**close** /klohz/ n a conclusion or end in time or existence

³**close** /klohs; sense 2 also klohz/ n 1 a road closed at one end 2 Br the precinct of a cathedral

⁴**close** /klohs/ adj 1 having no openings; closed 2 confined, cramped 3 restricted, closed 4 secretive, reticent 5 strict, rigorous 6 hot and stuffy 7 having little space between items or units; compact, dense 8 very short or near to the surface 9 near; esp adjacent 10 intimate, familiar 11a searching, minute b faithful to an original 12 evenly contested or having a (nearly) even score – ~ly adv – ~ness n — **close to home** within one's personal interests so that one is strongly affected

⁵**close** /klohs/ adv in or into a close position or manner; near — **close on** almost

close 'call /klohs/ n a narrow escape

close-'cropped /klohs/ adj clipped short

closed /klohzd/ adj 1a not open b enclosed 2 forming a self-contained unit allowing no additions 3a confined to a few b rigidly excluding outside influence

closed 'circuit n a television installation in which the signal is transmitted by wire to a limited number of receivers, usu in 1 location

closedown /'klohz,down/ n the act or result of closing down; esp the end of a period of broadcasting

closed 'shop n an establishment which employs only union members

close in /klohz/ v 1 to gather in close all round with an oppressing effect 2 to approach from various directions to close quarters, esp for an attack or arrest 3 to grow dark

close-'knit /klohs/ adj bound together by close ties

'close ,season /klohs/ n, Br a period during which it is illegal to kill or catch certain game or fish

¹**closet** /'klozit/ n 1 a small or private room 2 chiefly NAm a cupboard

²**closet** v 1 to shut (oneself) up (as if) in a closet 2 to take into a closet for a secret interview

'close-,up /klohs/ n 1 a photograph or film shot taken at close range 2 a view or examination of sthg from a small distance away

closure /'klohzhə/ n 1 closing or being closed 2 the ending of a side's innings in cricket by declaration 3 the closing of debate in a legislative body, esp by calling for a vote

¹**clot** /klot/ n 1 a viscous lump formed by coagulation of a liquid 2 Br a stupid person – infml

²**clot** v -tt- to form clots

cloth /kloth/ n pl **cloths** /klodhz, kloths/ 1 a pliable material made usu by weaving, felting, or knitting natural or synthetic fibres and filaments 2 a piece of cloth adapted for a particular purpose 3 (the distinctive dress of) a profession or calling distinguished by its dress; specif the clergy

clothe /klohdh/ v **clothed**, **clad** /klad/ to cover (as if) with clothing; dress

clothes /klohdhz/ n pl 1 articles of material (e g cloth) worn to cover the body, for warmth, protection, or decoration 2 bedclothes

'clothes,horse /-,haws/ n a frame on which to hang clothes, esp for drying or airing indoors

clothing /'klohdhing/ n clothes

¹**cloud** /klowd/ n 1a a visible mass of particles of water or ice at a usu great height in the air b a light filmy, puffy, or billowy mass seeming to float in the air 2 any of many masses of opaque matter in interstellar space 3 a swarm, esp of insects 4 sthg that obscures or blemishes

²**cloud** v 1 to grow cloudy – usu + *over* or *up* 2a *of facial features* to become troubled, apprehensive, etc b to become blurred, dubious, or ominous 3a to envelop or obscure (as if) with a cloud b to make opaque or murky by condensation, smoke, etc 4 to make unclear or confused 5 to taint, sully 6 to cast gloom over

'**cloud burst** /-,buhst/ n a sudden very heavy fall of rain

cloudy /'klowdi/ adj 1 (having a sky) overcast with clouds 2 not clear or transparent – **cloudiness** n

¹**clout** /klowt/ n 1 a blow or lusty hit 2 influence; *esp* effective political power *USE* infml

²**clout** v to hit forcefully – infml

¹**clove** /klohv/ n any of the small bulbs (e g in garlic) developed as parts of a larger bulb

²**clove** *past of* **cleave**

³**clove** n (a tree of the myrtle family that bears) a flower bud that is used dried as a spice

cloven /'klohv(ə)n/ *past part of* **cleave**

clover /'klohvə/ n any of a genus of leguminous plants having leaves with 3 leaflets and flowers in dense heads — **in clover** in prosperity or in pleasant circumstances

clown /klown/ n 1 a jester in an entertainment (e g a play); *specif* a grotesquely dressed comedy performer in a circus 2 one who habitually plays the buffoon; a joker – **clown** v

cloy /kloy/ v to (cause) surfeit with an excess, usu of sthg orig pleasing

¹**club** /klub/ n 1a a heavy stick thicker at one end than the other and used as a hand weapon b a stick or bat used to hit a ball in golf and other games 2a a playing card marked with 1 or more black figures in the shape of a cloverleaf b *pl but sing or pl in constr* the suit comprising cards identified by this figure 3 *sing or pl in constr* 3a an association of people for a specified object, usu jointly supported and meeting periodically b an often exclusive association of people that has premises available as a congenial place of retreat or temporary residence or for dining at

²**club** v -**bb**- 1 to beat or strike (as if) with a club 2 to combine to share a common expense or object – usu + *together*

'**club foot** /-'foot/ n a misshapen foot

¹**cluck** /kluk/ v 1 to make or call with a cluck 2 to express fussy interest or concern – usu + *over*; infml

²**cluck** n the characteristic guttural sound made by a hen

clue /klooh/ n sthg that guides via intricate procedure to the solution of a problem

'**clueless** /-lis/ adj, Br hopelessly ignorant or lacking in sense – infml

¹**clump** /klump/ n 1 a compact group of things of the same kind, esp trees or bushes; a cluster 2 a compact mass 3 a heavy tramping sound

²**clump** v 1 to tread clumsily and noisily 2 to arrange in or (cause to) form clumps

clumsy /'klumzi/ adj 1a awkward and ungraceful in movement or action b lacking tact or subtlety 2 awkwardly or poorly made; unwieldy – **clumsily** adv – **clumsiness** n

clung /klung/ *past of* **cling**

¹**cluster** /'klustə/ n a compact group formed by a number of similar things or people

²**cluster** v to grow or assemble in or collect into a cluster

¹**clutch** /kluch/ v 1 to grasp or hold (as if) with the hand or claws, esp tightly or suddenly 2 to seek to grasp and hold – often + *at*

²**clutch** n 1 (the claws or a hand in) the act of grasping or seizing firmly 2 (a lever or pedal operating) a coupling used to connect and disconnect a driving and a driven part of a mechanism

³**clutch** n a nest of eggs or a brood of chicks; *broadly* a group, bunch

¹**clutter** /'klutə/ v to fill or cover with scattered or disordered things – often + *up*

²**clutter** n 1 a crowded or confused mass or collection 2 scattered or disordered material

¹**coach** /kohch/ n 1a a large usu closed four-wheeled carriage b a railway carriage c a usu single-deck bus used esp for long-distance or charter work 2a a private tutor b sby who instructs or trains a performer, sportsman, etc

²**coach** v 1 to train intensively by instruction, demonstration, and practice 2 to act as coach to

'**coachman** /-mən/ n a man who drives a coach or carriage

coagulate /koh'agyoolayt/ v to (cause to) become viscous or thickened into a coherent mass – **lation** n – **lant** adj

coal /kohl/ n 1 a piece of glowing, burning, or burnt carbonized material (e g partly burnt wood) 2 a (small piece or broken up quantity of) black or blackish solid combustible mineral consisting chiefly of carbonized vegetable matter and widely used as a natural fuel

coalesce /,koh-ə'les/ v to unite into a whole; fuse – **coalescence** n

coalition /,koh-ə'lish(ə)n/ n 1a an act of coalescing; a union b a body formed by the union of orig distinct elements 2 *sing or pl in constr* a temporary alliance (e g of political parties) for joint action (e g to form a government)

coarse /kaws/ adj 1 of ordinary or inferior quality or value; common 2a(1) composed of relatively large particles a(2) rough in texture or tone b adjusted or designed for heavy, fast, or less delicate work c not precise or detailed with respect to adjustment or discrimination **3** crude or unrefined in taste, manners, or language – ~**ly** *adv* – ~**ness** *n*

'**coarse** ,**fish** *n*, *chiefly Br* any freshwater fish not belonging to the salmon family

coarsen /'kaws(ə)n/ *v* to make or become coarse

¹**coast** /kohst/ *n* the land near a shore; the seashore – ~**al** *adj*

²**coast** *v* **1** to sail along the shore (of) **2a** to slide, glide, etc downhill by the force of gravity **b** to move along (as if) without further application of driving power **c** to proceed easily without special application of effort or concern

coaster /'kohstə/ *n* **1** a small vessel trading from port to port along a coast **2a** a tray or stand, esp of silver, for a decanter **b** a small mat used, esp under a drinks glass, to protect a surface

'**coast**,**guard** /-,gahd/ *n* (a member of) a force responsible for maintaining lookout posts round the coast of the UK for mounting rescues at sea, preventing smuggling, etc

¹**coat** /koht/ *n* **1** an outer garment that has sleeves and usu opens the full length of the centre front **2** the external covering of an animal **3** a coating

²**coat** *v* to cover or spread with a protective or enclosing layer

coating /'kohting/ *n* a layer of one substance covering another

,**coat of** '**arms** *n pl* **coats of arms** a set of distinctive heraldic shapes or representations, usu depicted on a shield, that is the central part of a heraldic achievement

coax /kohks/ *v* **1** to influence or gently urge by caresses or flattery **2** to obtain by persuading gently – ~**ingly** *adv*

cob /kob/ *n* **1** a male swan **2** a corncob **3** (any of) a breed of short-legged stocky horses **4** *Br* a small rounded usu crusty loaf

cobalt /'koh,bawlt/ *n* a tough silver-white magnetic metallic element

cobber /'kobə/ *n*, *Austr* a man's male friend; a mate – *infml*

¹**cobble** /'kobl/ *v* **cobbling** /'kobling, 'kobl·ing/ **1** to repair (esp shoes); *also* to make (esp shoes) **2** to make or assemble roughly or hastily – usu + *together*

²**cobble** *n* a naturally rounded stone of a size suitable for paving a street

cobbler /'koblə/ *n* **1** a mender or maker of leather goods, esp shoes **2** *pl*, *Br* nonsense, rubbish – *infml*

cobra /'kobrə, 'kohbrə/ *n* any of several venomous Asiatic and African hooded snakes that have grooved fangs

cobweb /'kob,web/ *n* a web or thread spun by a spider

cocaine /,koh'kayn, kə-/ *n* an alkaloid that is obtained from coca leaves, has been used as a local anaesthetic, and is a common drug of abuse that can result in psychological dependence

cochineal /,kochi'neel/ *n* a red dyestuff consisting of the dried bodies of female cochineal insects

cochlea /'kokli·ə/ *n*, *pl* **cochleas**, **cochleae** /-li,ee/ a coiled part of the inner ear of higher vertebrates that is filled with liquid through which sound waves are transmitted to the auditory nerve

¹**cock** /kok/ *n* **1a** the (adult) male of various birds, specif the domestic fowl **b** the male of fish, crabs, lobsters, and other aquatic animals **2** a device (e g a tap or valve) for regulating the flow of a liquid **3** the hammer of a firearm or its position when cocked ready for firing **4** *Br* – used as a term of infml address to a man **5** the penis – *vulg* **6** nonsense, rubbish – *slang*

²**cock** *v* **1a** to draw back and set the hammer of (a firearm) for firing **b** to draw or bend back in preparation for throwing or hitting **2a** to set erect **b** to turn, tip, or tilt, usu to one side **3** to turn up (e g the brim of a hat) – **cock a snook** to react with disdain or defiance

³**cock** *n* a small pile (e g of hay)

cockade /ko'kayd/ *n* an ornament (e g a rosette or knot of ribbon) worn on the hat as a badge

cock-a-hoop /,kok ə 'hoohp/ *adj* triumphantly boastful; exulting – *infml*

cockatoo /,koka'tooh/ *n pl* **cockatoos** any of numerous large noisy usu showy and crested chiefly Australasian parrots

cockchafer /'kok,chayfə/ *n* a large European beetle destructive to vegetation

'**cock**,**crow** /-,kroh/ *n* dawn

,**cocked** '**hat** *n* a hat with brim turned up at 3 places to give a 3-cornered shape

cockerel /'kok(ə)rəl/ *n* a young male domestic fowl

,**cocker** '**spaniel** /'kokə/ *n* a small spaniel with long ears and silky coat

,**cock**,**eyed** /-'ied/ *adj* **1** having a squint **2a** askew, awry **b** somewhat foolish or mad – *USE infml*

cockle /'kokl/ *n* (the ribbed shell of) a (common edible) bivalve mollusc

'**cockle**,**shell** /-,shel/ *n* **1** the shell of a cockle, scallop, or similar mollusc **2** a light flimsy boat

cockney /'kokni/ *n* a native or the dialect of London and now esp of the E End of London

'**cock**,**pit** /-,pit/ *n* **1** a pit or enclosure for cock-fights **2a** a recess below deck level from which a small vessel (e g a yacht) is steered **b** a space in the fuselage of an aeroplane for the pilot (and crew) **c** the driver's compartment in a racing or sports car

'**cock**,**roach** /-,rohch/ *n* any of numerous omnivorous usu dark brown chiefly nocturnal insects that include some that are domestic pests

,**cock**,**sure** /-'shooə, -'shaw/ *adj* cocky – *infml*

cocktail /'kok,tayl/ *n* 1 a drink of mixed spirits or of spirits mixed with flavourings 2 sthg resembling or suggesting such a drink; *esp* a mixture of diverse elements

cocky /'koki/ *adj* marked by overconfidence or presumptuousness – *infml*

cocoa /'koh,koh/ *n* 1 the cacao tree 2a powdered ground roasted cacao seeds from which some fat has been removed b a beverage made by mixing cocoa with usu hot milk

coconut *also* **cocoanut** /'kohkə,nut/ *n* the large oval fruit of the coconut palm whose outer fibrous husk yields coir and whose nut contains thick edible meat and a thick sweet milk

'**coconut shy** /-/ *n* a stall at a funfair where one throws balls at coconuts on stands

¹**cocoon** /kə'koohn/ *n* 1 (an animal's protective covering similar to) a (silk) envelope which an insect larva forms about itself and in which it passes the pupa stage 2 a (protective) covering like a cocoon (e g for an aeroplane in storage) 3 a sheltered or insulated state of existence

²**cocoon** *v* to wrap or envelop, esp tightly, (as if) in a cocoon

¹**cod** /kod/, '**cod,fish** *n*, *pl* **cod** (the flesh of) a soft-finned N Atlantic food fish or related Pacific fish

²**cod** *n*, *Br* nonsense – *slang*

coda /'kohdə/ *n* 1 a concluding musical section that is formally distinct from the main structure 2 sthg that serves to round out or conclude sthg, esp a literary or dramatic work, and that has an interest of its own

coddle /'kodl/ *v* **coddling** /'kodling, 'kodl·ing/ 1 to cook (esp eggs) slowly in a liquid just below the boiling point 2 to treat with extreme care; pamper

¹**code** /kohd/ *n* 1 a systematic body of laws, esp with statutory force 2 a system of principles or maxims 3a a system of signals for communication b a system of symbols used to represent assigned and often secret meanings

²**code** *v* to put into the form or symbols of a code

codeine /'koh,deen/ *n* a derivative of morphine that is given orally to relieve pain and coughing

codger /'kojə/ *n* an old and mildly eccentric man – *infml*

codicil /'kohdisil/ *n* 1 a modifying clause added to a will 2 an appendix, supplement

codify /'kohdi,fie/ *v* 1 to reduce to a code 2 to express in a systematic form – **fication** *n*

'**cod,piece** /-,pees/ *n* a flap or bag concealing an opening in the front of men's breeches, esp in the 15th and 16th c

codswallop /'kodz,woləp/ *n*, *chiefly Br* nonsense – *slang*

coed /,koh'ed/ *n* a coeducational school

coeducation /,koh-edyoo'kaysh(ə)n, -ejoo-/ *n* the education of students of both sexes at the same institution – ~**al** *adj*

coefficient /,koh-i'fish(ə)nt/ *n* 1 any of the factors, esp variable quantities, that are multiplied together in a mathematical product considered in relation to a usu specified factor 2 a number that serves as a measure of some property or characteristic (e g of a device or process)

coerce /koh'uhs/ *v* 1 to compel to an act or choice 2 to enforce or bring about by force or threat – ~**cion** *n* – ~**cive** *adj* – ~**cively** *adv*

coexist /,koh-ig'zist/ *v* 1 to exist together or at the same time 2 to live in peace with each other – ~**ence** *n* – ~**ent** *adj*

coffee /'kofi/ *n* 1 a beverage made from the roasted seeds of a coffee tree; *also* these seeds either green or roasted 2 a cup of coffee

'**coffee-,table** *adj*, *of a publication* outsize and lavishly produced as if for display rather than use

coffer /'kofə/ *n* 1 a chest, box; *esp* a strongbox 2 a treasury, exchequer; *broadly* a store of wealth – usu pl with sing. meaning 3 a recessed decorative panel in a vault, ceiling, etc

coffin /'kofin/ *n* 1 a box or chest for the burial of a corpse 2 the horny body forming the hoof of a horse's foot

cog /kog/ *n* 1 a tooth on the rim of a wheel or gear 2 a subordinate person or part

cogent /'kohj(ə)nt/ *adj* convincing – **ency** *n* – ~**ly** *adv*

cogitate /'koji,tayt/ *v* to meditate on – **ation** *n*

cognac /'konyak/ *n* a French brandy, specif one from W France distilled from white wine

¹**cognate** /'kog,nayt/ *adj* 1 related by blood, esp on the mother's side 2 of the same or similar nature

²**cognate** *n* sthg (e g a word) having the same origin as another

cognition /kog'nish(ə)n/ *n* (a product of) the act or process of knowing that involves the processing of sensory information and includes perception, awareness, and judgment – **ive** *adj* – **ively** *adv*

cognizant, -isant /'kogniz(ə)nt/ *adj* having special or certain knowledge, often from firsthand sources – *fml* or *technical*

cohabit /koh'habit/ *v* to live or exist together, specif as if husband and wife – ~**ation** *n*

cohere /koh'hiə/ *v* 1 to hold together firmly as parts of the same mass; *broadly* to stick, adhere 2a to become united in ideas or interests b to be logically or aesthetically consistent

coherent /koh'hiərənt/ *adj* 1 having the quality of cohering 2a logically consistent b showing a unity of thought or purpose – ~**ly** *adv* – **ence, -ency** *n*

cohesion /koh'heezh(ə)n/ *n* the act or process of cohering – **ive** *adj* – **ively** *adv*

cohort /'koh,hawt/ *n* **1a** a group of soldiers; *esp, sing or pl in constr* a division of a Roman legion **b** a band, group **2** *chiefly NAm* a companion, accomplice

coiffure /kwah'f(y)ooə (*Fr* kwafy:r)/ *n* a hairstyle – **-fured** *adj*

¹**coil** /koyl/ *v* **1** to wind into rings or spirals **2** to move in a circular, spiral, or winding course **3** to form or lie in a coil

²**coil** *n* **1a** (a length of rope, cable, etc gathered into) a series of loops; a spiral **b** a single loop of a coil **2** a number of turns of wire, esp in spiral form, usu for electromagnetic effect or for providing electrical resistance **3** a series of connected pipes in rows, layers, or windings

¹**coin** /koyn/ *n* **1** a usu thin round piece of metal issued as money **2** metal money

²**coin** *v* **1a** to make (a coin), esp by stamping; mint **b** to convert (metal) into coins **2** to create, invent **3** to make or earn (money) rapidly and in large quantity – often in *coin it* – **~er** *n*

coinage /'koynij/ *n* **1** coining or (a large number of) coins **2** sthg (e g a word) made up or invented

coincide /,koh·in'sied/ *v* **1** to occupy the same place in space or time **2** to correspond in nature, character, function, or position **3** to be in accord or agreement; concur – **-dent** *adj*

coincidence /koh'insid(ə)ns; *sense 1 also* ,koh·in'sied(ə)ns/ *n* **1** the act or condition of coinciding; a correspondence **2** (an example of) the chance occurrence at the same time or place of 2 or more events – **-ental** *adj* – **-entally** *adv*

coir /'koyə/ *n* a stiff coarse fibre from the husk of a coconut

coitus /'koytəs, 'koh·itəs/ *n* sexual intercourse – **coital** *adj*

coitus inter'ruptus /intə'ruptəs/ *n* coitus which is purposely interrupted in order to prevent ejaculation of sperm into the vagina

¹**coke** /kohk/ *n* a solid porous fuel that remains after gases have been driven from coal by heating

²**coke** *n* cocaine – slang

col /kol/ *n* a depression or pass in a mountain ridge or range

cola *also* **kola** /'kohlə/ *n* a carbonated soft drink flavoured with extract from coca leaves, sugar, caramel, etc

colander /'koləndə; *also* 'ku-/, **cullender** /'kuləndə/ *n* a perforated bowl-shaped utensil for washing or draining food

¹**cold** /kohld/ *adj* **1** having a low temperature, often below some normal temperature or below that compatible with human comfort **2a** marked by lack of warm feeling; unemotional; *also* unfriendly **b** marked by deliberation or calculation **3** previously cooked but served cold **4a** depressing, cheerless **b** producing a sensation of cold; chilling **5a** dead **b** unconscious **6a** retaining only faint scents, traces, or clues **b** far from a goal,

object, or solution sought **7** presented or regarded in a straightforward way; impersonal **8** unprepared – **~ly** *adv* – **~ness** *n* — **in cold blood** with premeditation; deliberately

²**cold** *n* **1a** a condition of low temperature **b** cold weather **2** bodily sensation produced by relative lack of heat; chill **3** a bodily disorder popularly associated with chilling; *specif* an inflammation of the mucous membranes of the nose, throat, etc **4** a state of neglect or deprivation – esp in *come/bring out of the cold*

³**cold** *adv* with utter finality; absolutely

,**cold-'blooded** *adj* **1a** done or acting without consideration or compunction; ruthless **b** concerned only with the facts; emotionless **2** having a body temperature not internally regulated but approximating to that of the environment

,**cold 'cream** *n* a thick oily often perfumed cream for cleansing and soothing the skin of the neck, face, etc

,**cold 'shoulder** *n* intentionally cold or unsympathetic treatment – usu + *the*

'**cold ,war** *n* a conflict carried on by methods short of military action

coleslaw /'kohl,slaw/ *n* a salad of raw sliced or chopped white cabbage

coley /'kohli/ *n, pl* **coley**, *esp for different types* **coleys** *Br* an important N Atlantic food fish closely related to the cod

colic /'kolik/ *n* a paroxysm of abdominal pain localized in the intestines or other hollow organ and caused by spasm, obstruction, or twisting – **~ky** *adj*

collaborate /kə'labərayt/ *v* **1** to work together or with another (e g in an intellectual endeavour) **2** to cooperate with an enemy of one's country – **-ration** *n* – **-rator** *n*

collage /'kolahzh/ *n* **1** an (abstract) composition made of pieces of paper, wood, cloth, etc fixed to a surface **2** an assembly of diverse fragments

¹**collapse** /kə'laps/ *v* **1** to break down completely; disintegrate **2** to fall in or give way abruptly and completely (e g through compression) **3** to lose force, value, or effect suddenly **4** to break down in energy, stamina, or self-control through exhaustion or disease; *esp* to fall helpless or unconscious **5** to fold down into a more compact shape **6** to cause to collapse

²**collapse** *n* **1a** an (extreme) breakdown in energy, strength, or self-control **b** an airless state of (part of) a lung **2** the act or an instance of collapsing

¹**collar** /'kolə/ *n* **1a** a band that serves to finish or decorate the neckline of a garment; *esp* one that is turned over **b** a band fitted about the neck of an animal **c** a part of the harness of draught animals that fits over the shoulders and takes the strain when a load is drawn **d** a protective or supportive device worn round the neck **2** any of various

animal structures or markings similar to a collar in appearance or form **3** a cut of bacon from the neck of a pig

²**collar** *v* **1** to seize by the collar or neck; *broadly* to apprehend **2** to buttonhole *USE infml*

'**collar,bone** /-,bohn/ *n* the clavicle

collate /kə'layt/ *v* **1** to collect and compare carefully in order to verify and often to integrate or arrange in order **2** to assemble in proper order – **-ation** *n*

¹**collateral** /kə'lat(ə)rəl/ *adj* **1** accompanying as secondary or subordinate **2** belonging to the same ancestral stock but not in a direct line of descent – usu contrasted with *lineal* **3** parallel or corresponding in position, time, or significance **4** of or being collateral

²**collateral** *n* **1** a collateral relative **2** property pledged by a borrower to protect the interests of the lender

colleague /'koleeg/ *n* a fellow worker, esp in a profession

¹**collect** /'kolikt/ *n* a short prayer; *specif, often cap* one preceding the Epistle read at Communion

²**collect** /kə'lekt/ *v* **1a** to bring together into **1** body or place; *specif* to assemble a collection of **b** to gather or exact from a number of sources **2** to accumulate, gather **3** to claim as due and receive possession or payment of **4** to come together in a band, group, or mass; gather **5a** to assemble a collection **b** to receive payment – ~ *or n*

collected /kə'lektid/ *adj* exhibiting calmness and composure – ~ **ly** *adv*

collection /kə'leksh(ə)n/ *n* sthg collected; *esp* an accumulation of objects gathered for study, comparison, or exhibition

¹**collective** /kə'lektiv/ *adj* **1** denoting a number of individuals considered as 1 group **2** of, made, or held in common by a group of individuals **3** collectivized – ~ **ly** *adv*

²**collective** *n* **1** *sing or pl in constr* a collective body; a group **2** a cooperative organization; *specif* a collective farm

col,lective 'bargaining *n* negotiation between an employer and union representatives usu over wages, hours, and working conditions

collectivism /kə'lekti,viz(ə)m/ *n* a political or economic theory advocating collective control, esp over production and distribution

collectiv·ize, -ise /kə'lektiviez/ *v* to organize under collective control

colleen /ko'leen/ *n* **1** an Irish girl **2** *Irish* a girl

college /'kolij/ *n* **1** a building used for an educational or religious purpose **2a** a self-governing endowed constituent body of a university offering instruction and often living quarters but not granting degrees **b** an institution offering vocational or technical instruction **3** an organized body of people engaged in a common pursuit **4**

chiefly Br a public school or private secondary school; *also* a state school for older pupils *USE* (except 1) sing. or pl in constr

collegiate /kə'leeji·ət/ *adj* of or comprising a college

collide /kə'lied/ *v* **1** to come together forcibly **2** to come into conflict

collie /'koli/ *n* a large dog of any of several varieties of a breed developed in Scotland, esp for use in herding sheep and cattle

collier /'kolyə/ *n* **1** a coal miner **2** a ship for transporting coal

colliery /'kolyəri/ *n* a coal mine and its associated buildings

collision /kə'lizh(ə)n/ *n* an act or instance of colliding; a clash

colloquial /kə'lohkwi·əl/ *adj* used in, characteristic of, or using the style of familiar and informal conversation; conversational – ~ **ism** *n* – ~ **ly** *adv*

collude /kə'loohd/ *v* to conspire, plot – **-lusion** *n*

collywobbles /'koli,woblz/ *n pl* **1** stomachache **2** qualms, butterflies *USE* + *the; infml*

cologne /kə'lohn/ *n* toilet water

¹**colon** /'koh,lon/ *n, pl* **colons, cola** /-lə/ the part of the large intestine that lies in front of the rectum

²**colon** *n, pl* **colons, cola** /-lə/ **1** a punctuation mark : used chiefly to direct attention to matter that follows **2** the sign : used in a ratio where it is usu read as 'to' (e g in 4:1)

colonel /'kuhnl/ *n* an officer of middle rank in the army or American air force

Colonel 'Blimp /blimp/ *n* a pompous person with out-of-date or ultraconservative views; *broadly* a reactionary

¹**colonial** /kə'lohnyəl, -ni·əl/ *adj* **1** (characteristic of) a colony **2** *often cap* made or prevailing in America before 1776 **3** possessing or composed of colonies

²**colonial** *n* a member or inhabitant of a (British Crown) colony

colonialism /kə'lohni·ə,liz(ə)m/ *n* (a policy based on) control by a state over a dependent area or people – **-ist** *n, adj*

colonist /'kolənist/ *n* **1** a member or inhabitant of a colony **2** one who colonizes or settles in a new country

colony /'koləni/ *n* **1** a body of settlers living in a new territory but subject to control by the parent state; *also* their territory **2** (the area occupied by) a group of individuals with common interests living close together **3** a group of people segregated from the general public – **-nize** *v*

coloration, *Br also* **colouration** /,kulə'raysh(ə)n/ *n* **1** colouring, complexion **2** use or choice of colours (e g by an artist) **3** an arrangement or range of colours

colossal /kə'los(ə)l/ *adj* of or like a colossus; *esp* of very great size or degree – ~ **ly** *adv*

colossus /kə'losəs/ n, pl **colossuses, colossi** /-sie/ 1 a statue of gigantic size 2 sby or sthg remarkably preeminent

colostrum /kə'lostrəm/ n the milk that is secreted for a few days after giving birth

¹**colour,** NAm chiefly **color** /'kulə/ n 1 a hue, esp as opposed to black, white, or grey 2 an identifying badge, pennant, or flag (e g of a ship or regiment) 3 character, nature 4 the use or combination of colours (e g by painters) 5 vitality, interest 6 a pigment 7 tonal quality in music 8 skin pigmentation other than white, characteristic of race 9 Br the award made to a regular member of a team

²**colour,** NAm chiefly **color** v 1a to give colour to b to change the colour of 2 to change as if by dyeing or painting: e g 2a to misrepresent, distort b to influence, affect 3 to take on or impart colour; specif to blush

'**colour-,blind** adj (partially) unable to distinguish 1 or more colours – **colour blindness** n

¹'**coloured** adj 1 having colour 2 marked by exaggeration or bias 3a of a race other than the white; esp black b often cap of mixed race – esp of S Africans of mixed descent

²**coloured** n pl **coloureds, coloured** often cap a coloured person

colourfast /'kulə,fahst/ adj having colour that will not fade or run – ~**ness** n

'**colourful** /-f(ə)l/ adj 1 having striking colours 2 full of variety or interest – ~**ly** adv – ~**ness** n

colouring /'kuləring/ 1a (the effect produced by combining or) applying colours b sthg that produces colour c(1) natural colour c(2) complexion 2 an influence, bias 3 a timbre, quality

colourless /'kulə,lis/ adj lacking colour: e g a pallid b dull, uninteresting – ~**ly** adv – ~**ness** n

colt /kohlt, kolt/ n a young male horse that is either sexually immature or has not attained an arbitrarily designated age

coltish /'kohltish, 'kol-/ adj frisky, playful 2 of or resembling a colt – ~**ly** adv – ~**ness** n

¹**column** /'koləm/ n 1a a vertical arrangement of items or a vertical section of printing on a page b a special and usu regular feature in a newspaper or periodical 2 a pillar that usu consists of a round shaft, a capital, and a base 3 sthg resembling a column in form, position, or function 4 a long narrow formation of soldiers, vehicles, etc in rows – ~**ar** adj

columnist /'koləmnist/ n one who writes a newspaper or magazine column

coma /'kohmə/ n a state of deep unconsciousness caused by disease, injury, etc

comatose /'kohmə,tohs, -,tohz/ adj characterized by lethargy and sluggishness; torpid

¹**comb** /kohm/ n 1a a toothed instrument used esp for adjusting, cleaning, or confining hair b a structure resembling such a comb; esp any of several toothed devices used in handling or ordering textile fibres 2 a fleshy crest on the head of a domestic fowl or a related bird 3 a honeycomb

²**comb** v 1 to draw a comb through for the purpose of arranging or cleaning 2 to pass across with a scraping or raking action 3 to search or examine systematically 4 to use with a combing action 5 of a wave to roll over or break into foam

¹**combat** /'kombat, kəm'bat/ v -**tt**- (NAm -**t**-, -**tt**-) 1 to fight with; battle 2 to struggle against; esp to strive to reduce or eliminate

²**combat** /'kombat/ n 1 a fight or contest between individuals or groups 2 a conflict, controversy 3 active fighting in a war

combatant /'kombətənt, kəm'bat(ə)nt/ n a person, nation, etc that is (ready to be) an active participant in combat

combative /'kombətiv/ adj marked by eagerness to fight or contend – ~**ly** adv – ~**ness** n

combination /,kombi'naysh(ə)n/ n 1a a result or product of combining b a group of people working as a team 2 pl any of various 1-piece undergarments for the upper and lower parts of the body and legs 3 a (process of) combining, esp to form a chemical compound

¹**combine** /kəm'bien/ v 1a to bring into such close relationship as to obscure individual characters; merge b to (cause to) unite into a chemical compound 2 to cause to mix together 3 to possess in combination 4 to become one 5 to act together

²**combine** /'kombien/ n 1 a combination of people or organizations, esp in industry or commerce, to further their interests 2 **combine, combine harvester** a harvesting machine that cuts, threshes, and cleans grain while moving over a field

combustible /kəm'bustəbl/ adj 1 capable of (easily) being set on fire 2 easily excited

combustion /kəm'buschən/ n a chemical reaction, esp an oxidation, in which light and heat are evolved

¹**come** /kum/ v **came** /kaym/; **come 1a** to move towards sthg nearer, esp towards the speaker; approach b to move or journey nearer, esp towards or with the speaker, with a specified purpose c(1) to reach a specified position in a progression c(2) to arrive, appear, occur d(1) to approach, reach, or fulfil a specified condition – often + to d(2) – used with a following infinitive to express arrival at a condition or chance occurrence 2a to happen, esp by chance b(1) to extend, reach b(2) to amount c to originate, arise, or be the result of d to fall within the specified limits, scope, or jurisdiction e to issue from f to be available or turn out, usu as specified g to be or belong in a specified place or relation; also take place 3 to become; esp to reach a culminating state 4 to experience orgasm – infml 5a to move nearer by traversing b to reach some state after traversing 6 to take on the aspect of; play the

of – *infml* — **as it comes** without stipulated additions — **come a cropper 1** *chiefly Br* to have a fall or an accident **2** to fail completely — *slang* — **come across** to meet with or find by chance — **come by** to get possession of; acquire — **come clean** to tell the whole story; confess — *infml* — **come home to roost** to rebound upon the perpetrator — **come into** to acquire as a possession or inheritance — **come it** *chiefly Br* to act with bold disrespect — *slang* — **come off it** to cease foolish or pretentious talk or behaviour — *usu used imperatively*; *infml* — **come one's way** to fall to one's lot — **come over** to seize suddenly and strangely — **come through** to survive (e g an illness) — **come to** to be a question of — **come to a head** to arrive at a culminating point or crisis — **come to grief** to fail badly; fail — **come round 1** COME TO **2** to regain self-control — **come to pass** HAPPEN **2** — *fml* — **come unstuck** COME TO GRIEF — *infml* — **come upon** to meet with or find by chance — **to come** in the future; coming — **whether one is coming or going** — used to suggest frenetic disorder and bewilderment

²**come** *interj* – used to express encouragement or to urge reconsideration

comedian /kə'meedi·ən/, *fem* **comedienne** /kə‚meedi'en/ *n* **1** an actor who plays comic roles **2** one, esp a professional entertainer, who aims to be amusing

'**come‚down** /-‚down/ *n* a striking descent in rank or dignity – *infml*

comedy /'komədi/ *n* **1a** a drama of light and amusing character, typically with a happy ending **b** (a work in) the genre of (dramatic) literature dealing with comic or serious subjects in a light or satirical manner **2** a ludicrous or farcical event or series of events **3** the comic aspect of sthg

‚**come-'hither** *adj* sexually inviting

comely /'kumli/ *adj* of pleasing appearance – **comeliness** *n*

'**come-‚on** *n* **1** *chiefly NAm* an attraction or enticement (e g in sales promotion) to induce an action **2** an instance of sexually provocative enticement – *infml*

comet /'komit/ *n* a celestial body that follows a usu highly elliptical orbit round the sun and consists of an indistinct head usu surrounding a bright nucleus, often with a long tail which points away from the sun

‚**come 'to** *v* to recover consciousness

‚**come-'uppance** /'up(ə)ns/ *n* a deserved rebuke or penalty

'**comfort** /'kumfət/ *n* **1** (sby or sthg that provides) consolation or encouragement in time of trouble or worry **2** contented well-being

²**comfort** *v* **1** to cheer up **2** to ease the grief or trouble of; console – ~**er** *n*

comfortable /'kumftəbl/ *adj* **1a** providing or enjoying contentment and security **b** providing or enjoying physical comfort **2a** causing no worry or doubt **b** free from stress or tension – **-bly** *adv*

'**comic** /'komik/ *adj* **1** of or marked by comedy **2** causing laughter or amusement; funny

²**comic** *n* **1** a magazine consisting mainly of strip-cartoon stories

comical /'komikl/ *adj* of a kind to excite laughter, esp because of a startlingly or unexpectedly humorous impact – **-ly** *adv*

'**comic ‚strip** *n* a cartoon story

'**coming** /'kuming/ *n* an act or instance of arriving

²**coming** *adj* **1** immediately due in sequence or development; next **2** gaining in importance; up-and-coming

comma /'komə/ *n* **1** a punctuation mark , used esp as a mark of separation within the sentence **2** a butterfly with a silvery comma-shaped mark on the underside of the hind wing

'**command** /kə'mahnd/ *v* **1** to direct authoritatively; order **2a** to have at one's immediate disposal **b** to be able to ask for and receive **c** to overlook or dominate (as if) from a strategic position **d** to have military command of as senior officer **3** to be commander; be supreme

²**command** *n* **1** an order given **2a** the ability or power to control; the mastery **b** the authority or right to command **c** facility in use **3** *sing or pl in constr* the unit, personnel, etc under a commander

³**command** *adj* done on command or request

commandant /‚komən'dant, -'dahnt/ *n* a commanding officer

commandeer /‚komən'dia/ *v* **1** to seize for military purposes **2** to take arbitrary or forcible possession of

commander /kə'mahndə/ *n* a middle-ranking officer in the navy; *also* an officer of any rank who is in charge of a group of soldiers

com‚mander-in-'chief *n* one who is in supreme command of an armed force

commanding /kə'mahnding/ *adj* **1** having command; being in charge **2** dominating or having priority **3** deserving or expecting respect and obedience

com'mandment /-mənt/ *n* sthg commanded; *specif* any of the biblical Ten Commandments

commando /kə'mahndoh/ *n*, *pl* **commandos**, **commandoes** (a member of) a usu small military unit for surprise raids

commemorate /kə'memərayt/ *v* **1** to call to formal remembrance **2** to mark by some ceremony or observation; observe **3** to serve as a memorial of – **-ration** *n* – **-rative** *adj*

commence /kə'mens/ *v* to start, begin – *fml* – ~**ment** *n*

commend /kə'mend/ v 1 to entrust for care or preservation 2 to recommend as worthy of confidence or notice – ~ **able** adj – ~ **ably** adv

commendation /ˌkɒmən'daysh(ə)n/ n sthg (e g a formal citation) that commends

commensurate /kə'menshərət/ adj 1 (approximately) equal in measure or extent; coextensive 2 corresponding in size, extent, amount, or degree; proportionate

¹**comment** /'kɒment/ n 1 a note explaining or criticizing the meaning of a piece of writing 2 an observation or remark expressing an opinion or attitude b a judgment expressed indirectly

²**comment** v to explain or interpret sthg by comment; broadly to make a comment

commentary /'kɒmənt(ə)ri/ n 1 a systematic series of explanations or interpretations (e g of a piece of writing) 2 a series of spoken remarks and comments used as a broadcast description of some event

commentate /'kɒməntayt/ v to give a broadcast commentary – **-tator** n

commerce /'kɒmuhs/ n the exchange or buying and selling of commodities, esp on a large scale

¹**commercial** /kə'muhsh(ə)l/ adj 1a(1) engaged in work designed for the market a(2) (characteristic) of commerce a(3) having or being a good financial prospect b producing work to a standard determined only by market criteria 2a viewed with regard to profit b designed for a large market 3 supported by advertisers – ~ **ize** v

²**commercial** n an advertisement broadcast on radio or television

com‚mercial 'traveller n, Br a sales representative

commie /'kɒmi/ n a communist – chiefly derog

commiserate /kə'mizərayt/ v to feel or express sympathy with sby

commissar /ˌkɒmi'sah/ n 1 a Communist party official assigned to a military unit to teach party principles and ideals 2 the head of a government department in the USSR until 1946

¹**commission** /kə'mish(ə)n/ n 1a a formal warrant granting various powers b (a certificate conferring) military rank above a certain level 2 an authorization or command to act in a prescribed manner or to perform prescribed acts; a charge 3 authority to act as agent for another; also sthg to be done by an agent 4a sing or pl in constr a group of people directed to perform some duty b often cap a government agency 5 an act of committing sthg 6 a fee, esp a percentage, paid to an agent or employee for transacting a piece of business or performing a service — **in/into commission** 1 of a ship ready for active service 2 in use or in condition for use — **on commission** with commission serving as partial or full pay for work done — **out of commission** 1 out of active service or use 2 out of working order

²**commission** v 1a to confer a formal commission on b to order, appoint, or assign to perform a task or function 2 to put (a ship) in commission

commissionaire /kəˌmishə'neə/ n, chiefly Br a uniformed attendant at a cinema, theatre, office, etc

commissioner /kə'mishənə/ n 1 a member or the head of a commission 2 the government representative in a district, province, etc

commit /kə'mit/ v -tt- 1a to entrust b to place in a prison or mental institution c to consign, consign 2 to carry out (a crime, sin, etc) 3a to obligate, bind b to assign to some particular course or use

com'mitment /-mənt/ n 1 an act of committing to a charge or trust; esp a consignment to an institution 2a an agreement or pledge to do sthg in the future b sthg pledged c loyalty to a system of thought or action

committal /kə'mitl/ n commitment or consignment (e g to prison or the grave)

committee /kə'miti/ n sing or pl in constr a body of people delegated a to report on, investigate, etc some matter b to organize or administrate a society, event, etc

commode /kə'mohd/ n 1 a low chest of drawers 2 a boxlike structure or chair with a removable seat covering a chamber pot

commodious /kə'mohdi-əs/ adj comfortably or conveniently spacious; roomy – fml – ~ **ly** adv

commodity /kə'mɒdəti/ n 1 sthg useful or valuable 2a a product possessing utility; sthg that can be bought and sold b an article of trade or commerce

commodore /'kɒmədaw/ n 1 a middle-ranking officer in the navy 2 the senior captain of a merchant shipping line 3 the chief officer of a yacht club

¹**common** /'kɒmən/ adj 1 of the community at large; public 2 belonging to or shared by 2 or more individuals or by all members of a group 3 occurring or appearing frequently; familiar 4 characterized by a lack of privilege or special status 5 lacking refinement – ~ **ness** n – ~ **ly** adv

²**common** n 1 pl but sing or pl in constr, often cap 1a the political group or estate made up of commoners b the House of Commons 2 a piece of land open to use by all: e g 2a undivided land used esp for pasture b a more or less treeless expanse of undeveloped land available for recreation — **in common** shared together — used esp of shared interests, attitudes, or experience

commoner /'kɒmənə/ n a member of the common people; sby not of noble rank

‚**common-'law** adj 1 of the common law 2 recognized in law without formal marriage

‚**common 'law** n the body of uncodified English law that forms the basis of the English legal system

,common 'market n an economic unit formed to remove trade barriers among its members; *specif, often cap C&M the* European economic community

[1]'common,place /-,plays/ n 1 an obvious or trite observation 2 sthg taken for granted

[2]'commonplace *adj* routinely found; ordinary, unremarkable

'common ,room n a room or set of rooms in a school, college, etc for the recreational use of the staff or students

,common 'sense n sound and prudent (but often unsophisticated) judgment

'common,wealth /-,welth/ n 1 a political unit: e g 1a one founded on law and united by agreement of the people for the common good b one in which supreme authority is vested in the people 2 *cap* the English state from 1649 to 1660 3 a state of the USA 4 *cap* a federal union of states – used officially of Australia 5 *often cap* a loose association of autonomous states under a common allegiance; *specif* an association consisting of Britain and states that were formerly British colonies

commotion /kə'mohsh(ə)n/ n 1 a state of civil unrest or insurrection 2 a disturbance, tumult 3 noisy confusion and trouble

communal /'komyoonl/ *adj* 1 of a commune or communes 2 of a community 3 shared

[1]commune /kə'myoohn/ v 1 to receive Communion 2 to communicate intimately

[2]commune /'ko,myoohn/ n 1 the smallest administrative district of many (European) countries 2 *sing or pl in constr* an often rural community of unrelated individuals or families organized on a communal basis

communicable /kə'myoohnikəbl/ *adj, esp of a disease* transmittable – **-bly** *adv*

communicant /kə'myoohnikənt/ n 1 a church member who receives or is entitled to receive Communion 2 an informant

communicate /kə'myoohni,kayt/ v 1 to convey knowledge of or information about; make known 2 to receive Communion 3 to transmit information, thought, or feeling so that it is satisfactorily received or understood 4 to give access to each other; connect

communication /kə,myoohni'kaysh(ə)n/ n 1 a verbal or written message 2 (the use of a common system of symbols, signs, behaviour, etc for the) exchange of information 3 *pl* a system (e g of telephones) for communicating 4 *pl but sing or pl in constr* techniques for the effective transmission of information, ideas, etc

com,muni'cation ,cord n, *Br* a device (e g a chain or handle) in a railway carriage that may be pulled in an emergency to sound an alarm

communicative /kə'myoohnikətiv/ *adj* 1 tending to communicate; talkative 2 of communication

communion /kə'myoohnyən, -ni·ən/ n 1a *often cap* the religious service celebrating the Eucharist in Protestant churches b the act of receiving the Eucharist 2 intimate fellowship or rapport 3 a body of Christians having a common faith and discipline

communiqué /kə'myoohni,kay/ n a bulletin

communism /'komyooniz(ə)m/ n 1a a theory advocating elimination of private property b a system in which goods are held in common and are available to all as needed 2 *cap* 2a a doctrine based on revolutionary Marxian socialism and Marxism-Leninism that is the official ideology of the USSR b a totalitarian system of government in which a single party controls state-owned means of production – **-ist** n – **-istic** *adj*

community /kə'myoohnəti/ n 1 *sing or pl in constr* 1a a group of people living in a particular area b a group of individuals or a body of people or nations with some common characteristic 2 society in general 3a joint ownership or participation b common character; likeness c social ties; fellowship d the state or condition of living in a society

commutation /,komyoo'taysh(ə)n/ n 1 a replacement; *specif* a substitution of one form of payment or charge for another 2 an act or process of commuting 3 the process of converting an alternating current to a direct current – **-tative** *adj*

commutator /'komyoo,taytə/ n a device for reversing the direction of an electric current; *esp* a device on a motor or generator that converts alternating current to direct current

commute /kə'myooht/ v 1 to convert (e g a payment) into another form 2 to exchange (a penalty) for another less severe 3 to travel back and forth regularly (e g between home and work) – **-muter** n

[1]compact /kəm'pakt/ *adj* 1 having parts or units closely packed or joined 2 succinct, terse 3 occupying a small volume because of efficient use of space – ~ly *adv* – ~ness n – **-ed** *adj*

[2]compact v 1a to knit or draw together; combine, consolidate b to press together; compress 2 to make up by connecting or combining; compose

[3]compact /'kom,pakt/ n 1 a small slim case for face powder 2 a medium-sized US motor car

[4]compact /'kom,pakt/ n an agreement, contract

compact disk n a small plastic aluminium-coated disk on which sound is stored in digital form in microscopic pits and read by a laser beam mounted in a special record player

companion /kəm'panyən/ n one who accompanies another; a comrade – ~ship n

companionable /kəm'panyənəbl/ *adj* marked by, conducive to, or suggestive of companionship; sociable

com'panion,way /-,way/ n a ship's stairway from one deck to another

company /'kump(ə)ni/ *n* **1a** friendly association with another; fellowship **b** companions, associates *c sing or pl in constr* visitors, guests **2** *sing or pl in constr* **2a** a group of people or things **b** a unit of soldiers composed usu of a headquarters and 2 or more platoons **c** an organization of musical or dramatic performers **d** the officers and men of a ship **3** *sing or pl in constr* an association of people for carrying on a commercial or industrial enterprise

comparable /'komp(ə)rəbl/ *adj* **1** capable of or suitable for comparison **2** approximately equivalent; similar – **~bly** *adv*

comparative /kəm'parətiv/ *adj* **1** considered as if in comparison to sthg else as a standard; relative **2** characterized by the systematic comparison of phenomena – **~ly** *adv*

¹**compare** /kəm'peə/ *v* **1** to represent as similar; liken **2** to examine the character or qualities of, esp in order to discover resemblances or differences **3** to bear being compared **4** to be equal or alike – + *with*

²**compare** *n* comparison

comparison /kəm'paris(ə)n/ *n* **1a** the representing of one thing or person as similar to or like another **b** an examination of 2 or more items to establish similarities and dissimilarities **2** identity or similarity of features

compartment /kəm'pahtmənt/ *n* **1** any of the parts into which an enclosed space is divided **2** a separate division or section – **~alize** *v*

¹**compass** /'kumpəs/ *v* **1** to encompass **2** to travel entirely round *USE* fml

²**compass** *n* **1a** a boundary, circumference **b** range, scope **2a** an instrument that indicates directions, typically by means of a freely-turning needle pointing to magnetic north **b** an instrument for drawing circles or transferring measurements that consists of 2 legs joined at 1 end by a pivot – usu pl with sing. meaning

compassion /kəm'pash(ə)n/ *n* sympathetic consciousness of others' distress together with a desire to alleviate it – **~ate** *adj* – **~ately** *adv*

compatible /kəm'patəbl/ *adj* capable of existing together in harmony – **-bility** *n* – **-bly** *adv*

compatriot /kəm'patri·ət/ *n* a fellow countryman

compel /kəm'pel/ *v* **-ll- 1** to drive or force irresistibly *to* do sthg **2** to cause to occur by overwhelming pressure – **compelling** *adj* – **compellingly** *adv*

compendious /kəm'pendi·əs/ *adj* comprehensive but relatively brief – **~ly** *adv*

compendium /kəm'pendi·əm/ *n, pl* **compendiums, compendia** /-di·ə/ **1** a brief summary of a larger work or of a field of knowledge; an abstract **2** a collection of indoor games and puzzles

compensate /'kompənsayt/ *v* **1** to have an equal and opposite effect to; counterbalance **2** to make amends for, esp by appropriate payment **3** to supply an equivalent *for* – **-sation** *n* – **-satory** *adj*

compere /'kompeə/ *n, Br* the presenter of a radio or television programme, esp a light entertainment programme – **compere** *v*

compete /kəm'peet/ *v* to strive consciously or unconsciously for an objective; *also* to be in a state of rivalry

competence /'kompit(ə)ns/ *also* **competency** /-si/ *n* **1** the quality or state of being competent **2** a sufficiency of means for the necessities and conveniences of life – fml

competent /'kompit(ə)nt/ *adj* **1a** having requisite or adequate ability **b** showing clear signs of production by a competent agent (e g a workman or writer) **2** legally qualified – **~ly** *adv*

competition /,kompə'tish(ə)n/ *n* **1** the act or process of competing; rivalry **2** a usu organized test of comparative skill, perf...ance, etc; *also, sing or pl in constr* the others competing with one – **-itive** *adj* – **-itively** *adv* – **-itiveness** *n*

competitor /kəm'petitə/ *n* sby who or sthg that competes; a rival

compile /kəm'piel/ *v* **1** to collect into 1 work **2** to compose out of materials from other documents – **~r** *n* – **-lation** *n*

complacency /kəm'plays(ə)nsi/ *also* **complacence** *n* self-satisfaction – **complacent** *adj* – **complacently** *adv*

complain /kəm'playn/ *v* **1** to express feelings of discontent **2** to make a formal accusation or charge – **~ing** *adj* – **~ingly** *adv*

complaint /kəm'playnt/ *n* **1** an expression of discontent **2a** sthg that is the cause or subject of protest or outcry **b** a bodily ailment or disease

complaisant /kəm'plays(ə)nt/ *adj* marked by an inclination to please or comply – **~ly** *adv*

¹**complement** /'komplimənt/ *n* **1** sthg that fills up or completes **2** the quantity required to make sthg complete **3** either of 2 mutually completing parts; a counterpart

²**complement** *v* to be complementary to

complementary /,kompli'ment(ə)ri/ *adj* **1** serving to fill out or complete **2** mutually supplying each other's lack **3** of or constituting either of a pair of contrasting colours that produce a neutral colour when combined

¹**complete** /kəm'pleet/ *adj* **1** having all necessary parts, elements, or steps **2** whole or concluded **3** thoroughly competent; highly proficient **4a** fully carried out; thorough **b** total, absolute – **~ness** *n*

²**complete** *v* **1** to bring to an end; *esp* to bring to a perfected state **2a** to make whole or perfect **b** to mark the end of **c** to execute, fulfil – **~ly** *adv* – **-tion** *n*

¹**complex** /'kompleks/ *adj* 1 composed of 2 or (many) more parts 2 hard to separate, analyse, or solve – ~ **ity** *n*

²**complex** *n* 1 a whole made up of complicated or interrelated parts 2 a group of repressed related desires and memories that usu adversely affects personality and behaviour

complexion /kəm'pleksh(ə)n/ *n* 1 the appearance of the skin, esp of the face 2 overall aspect or character

compliance /kəm'plie·əns/ *n* 1 the act or process of complying (readily) with the wishes of others 2 a disposition to yield to others

complicate /'komplikayt/ *v* 1 to combine, esp in an involved or inextricable manner 2 to make complex or difficult

complicated /'kompli,kaytid/ *adj* 1 consisting of parts intricately combined 2 difficult to analyse, understand, or explain – ~ **ly** *adv* – ~ **ness** *n*

complication /,kompli'kaysh(ə)n/ *n* 1a intricacy, complexity b an instance of making difficult, involved, or intricate c a complex or intricate feature or element d a factor or issue that occurs unexpectedly and changes existing plans, methods, or attitudes – often pl 2 a secondary disease or condition developing in the course of a primary disease

complicity /kəm'plisəti/ *n* (an instance of) association or participation (as if) in a wrongful act

¹**compliment** /'komplimənt/ *n* 1 an expression of esteem, affection, or admiration; *esp* a flattering remark 2 *pl* best wishes; regards

²**compliment** /'kompli,ment/ *v* 1 to pay a compliment to 2 to present with a token of esteem

complimentary /,kompli'ment(ə)ri/ *adj* 1 expressing or containing a compliment 2 given free as a courtesy or favour

comply /kəm'plie/ *v* to conform or adapt one's actions to another's wishes or to a rule – **-liant** *adj*

¹**component** /kəm'pohnənt/ *n* a constituent part; an ingredient

²**component** *adj* serving or helping to constitute; constituent

compose /kəm'pohz/ *v* 1a to form by putting together b to form the substance of; make up – chiefly passive 2a to create by mental or artistic labour; produce b to formulate and write (a piece of music) 3 to free from agitation; calm, settle

composer /kəm'pohzə/ *n* a person who writes music

¹**composite** /'kompəzit/ *adj* 1 made up of distinct parts 2 combining the typical or essential characteristics of individuals making up a group

²**composite** *n* sthg composite; a compound

composition /,kompə'zish(ə)n/ *n* 1 the act or process of composing; *specif* arrangement into proper proportion or relation and esp into artistic form 2 the factors or parts which go to make sthg; *also* the way in which the factors or parts make up

the whole 3 a product of mixing or combining various elements or ingredients 4 an intellectual creation: e g 4a a piece of writing; *esp* a school essay b a written piece of music

compositor /kəm'pozitə/ *n* sby who sets type

compost /'kompost/ *n* a mixture of decayed organic matter used for fertilizing and conditioning land

composure /kəm'pohzhə/ *n* calmness or repose, esp of mind, bearing, or appearance

¹**compound** /kəm'pownd/ *v* 1 to put together (parts) so as to form a whole; combine 2 to form by combining parts 3 to add to; augment 4 to become joined in a compound

²**compound** /'kompownd/ *adj* 1 composed of or resulting from union of (many similar) separate elements, ingredients, or parts 2 involving or used in a combination

³**compound** /'kompownd/ *n* 1 a word consisting of components that are words or affixes (e g *houseboat, anthropology*) 2 sthg formed by a union of elements or parts; *specif* a distinct substance formed by combination of chemical elements in fixed proportion by weight

⁴**compound** /'kompownd/ *n* a fenced or walled-in area containing a group of buildings, esp residences

,**compound 'interest** *n* interest computed on the original principal plus accumulated interest

comprehend /,kompri'hend/ *v* 1 to grasp the nature, significance, or meaning of; understand 2 to include – *fml* – ~ **hensible** *adj* – ~ **hensibility** *n*

comprehension /,kompri'hensh(ə)n/ *n* 1a grasping with the intellect; understanding b knowledge gained by comprehending c the capacity for understanding fully 2 a school exercise testing understanding of a passage

¹**comprehensive** /,kompri'hensiv/ *adj* 1 covering completely or broadly; inclusive 2 having or exhibiting wide mental grasp 3 *chiefly Br* of or being the principle of educating in 1 unified school nearly all children above the age of 11 from a given area regardless of ability – ~ **ly** *adv* – ~ **ness** *n*

²**comprehensive** *n, Br* a comprehensive school

¹**compress** /kəm'pres/ *v* 1 to press or squeeze together 2 to reduce in size or volume as if by squeezing 3 to be compressed – ~ **ible** *adj* – ~ **ibility** *n* – ~ **ion** *n*

²**compress** /'kompres/ *n* a pad pressed on a body part (e g to ease the pain and swelling of a bruise)

compressor /kəm'presə/ *n* a machine for compressing gases

comprise /kəm'priez/ *v* 1 to include, contain 2 to be made up of 3 to make up, constitute

¹**compromise** /'komprəmiez/ *n* 1a the settling of differences through arbitration or through consent reached by mutual concessions b a settlement

reached by compromise **c** sthg blending qualities of 2 different things **2** a concession to sthg disreputable or prejudicial

²**compromise** *v* **1** to adjust or settle by mutual concessions **2** to expose to discredit or scandal **3** to come to agreement by mutual concession

compulsion /kəm'pulsh(ə)n/ *n* **1a** compelling or being compelled **b** a force or agency that compels **2** a strong impulse to perform an irrational act

compulsive /kəm'pulsiv/ *adj* of, caused by, like, or suffering from a psychological compulsion or obsession – ~**ly** *adv* – ~**ness** *n*

compulsory /kəm'puls(ə)ri/ *adj* **1** mandatory, enforced **2** involving compulsion or obligation; coercive – **-rily** *adv*

compunction /kəm'pungksh(ə)n/ *n* **1** anxiety arising from awareness of guilt; remorse **2** a twinge of misgiving; a scruple

computation /ˌkompyoo'taysh(ə)n/ *n* **1** the use or operation of a computer **2** (a system of) calculating; *also* the amount calculated

compute /kəm'pyooht/ *v* **1** to determine, esp by mathematical means; *also* to determine or calculate by means of a computer **2** to make calculation; reckon **3** to use a computer

computer /kəm'pyoohtə/ *n* a programmable electronic device that can store, retrieve, and process data

comrade /'komrid, -rayd/ *n* **1a** an intimate friend or associate; a companion **b** a fellow soldier **2** a communist – ~**ship** *n*

¹**con**, *NAm chiefly* **conn** /kon/ *v* **-nn-** to conduct or direct the steering of (e g a ship) – **con** *n*

²**con**, *NAm chiefly* **conn** *adv* on the negative side; in opposition

³**con** *n* (sby holding) the opposing or negative position

⁴**con** *v* **1** to swindle, trick **2** to persuade, cajole *USE* slang

⁵**con** *n* a convict – slang

concave /ˌkon'kayv, '--/ *adj* hollowed or rounded inwards like the inside of a bowl – **-cavity** *n*

conceal /kən'seel/ *v* **1** to prevent disclosure or recognition of **2** to place out of sight – ~**ment** *n*

concede /kən'seed/ *v* **1** to grant as a right or privilege **2a** to accept as true, valid, or accurate **b** to acknowledge grudgingly or hesitantly **3** to allow involuntarily – chiefly journ **4** to make concession; yield

conceit /kən'seet/ *n* **1** excessively high opinion of oneself **2a** a fanciful idea **b** an elaborate, unusual, and cleverly expressed figure of speech – ~**ed** *adj*

conceivable /kən'seevəbl/ *adj* imaginable – **-bly** *adv*

conceive /kən'seev/ *v* **1** to become pregnant (with) **2a** to cause to originate in one's mind **b** to form a conception of; evolve mentally; visualize **3** to be of the opinion – *fml*

¹**concentrate** /'kons(ə)ntrayt/ *v* **1a** to bring or direct towards a common centre or objective; focus **b** to gather into 1 body, mass, or force **2a** to make less dilute **b** to express or exhibit in condensed form **3** to draw towards or meet in a common centre **4** to gather, collect **5** to concentrate one's powers, efforts, or attention

²**concentrate** *n* sthg concentrated; *esp* a feed for animals rich in digestible nutrients

concentration /ˌkonsən'traysh(ə)n/ *n* **1** direction of attention to a single object **2** a concentrated mass or thing **3** the relative content of a (chemical) component; strength

concentration camp *n* a camp where political prisoners, refugees, etc are confined; *esp* any of the Nazi camps for the internment or mass execution of (Jewish) prisoners during WW II

concentric /kən'sentrik, kon-/ *adj* having a common centre

concept /'konsept/ *n* **1** sthg conceived in the mind; a thought, notion **2** a generic idea abstracted from particular instances – ~**ual** *adj* – ~**ually** *adv* – ~**ualize** *v*

conception /kən'sepsh(ə)n/ *n* **1** conceiving or being conceived **2** a general idea; a concept **3** the originating of sthg in the mind

¹**concern** /kən'suhn/ *v* **1** to relate to; be about **2** to have an influence on; involve; *also* to be the business or affair of **3** to be a care, trouble, or distress to **4** to engage, occupy

²**concern** *n* **1** sthg that relates or belongs to one **2** matter for consideration **3** marked interest or regard, usu arising through a personal tie or relationship **4** a business or manufacturing organization or establishment – ~**ed** *adj* – ~**edly** *adv*

concerning /kən'suhning/ *prep* relating to; with reference to

concert /'konsuht, -sət; *sense 2 usu* 'konsət/ *n* **1** an instance of working together; an agreement – esp in *in concert* (*with*) **2** a public performance of music or dancing; *esp* a performance, usu by a group of musicians, that is made up of several individual compositions

concerted /kən'suhtid/ *adj* **1a** planned or done together; combined **b** performed in unison **2** arranged in parts for several voices or instruments – ~**ly** *adv*

¹**concertina** /ˌkonsə'teenə/ *n* a small hexagonal musical instrument of the accordion family

²**concertina** *v*, **concertinaed** /-nad/; **concertinaing** /-nə·ing/ *Br* to become compressed in the manner of a concertina being closed, esp as a result of a crash

concerto /kən'cheətoh, -'chuh-/ *n, pl* **concerti** /-ti/, **concertos** a piece for 1 or more soloists and orchestra, usu with 3 contrasting movements

concession /kən'sesh(ə)n/ *n* **1** the act or an instance of conceding **2** a grant of land, property, or a right made, esp by a government, in return for services or for a particular use **3** a reduction of demands or standards made esp to accommodate shortcomings

conch /konch, kongk/ *n, pl* **conches** /'konchiz/, **conchs** (the spiral shell of) any of various large marine snails

conciliate /kən'sili·ayt/ *v* **1** to reconcile **2** to appease – **-tion** *n* – **-tory** *adj*

concise /kən'sies/ *adj* marked by brevity of expression or statement – ~**ly** *adv* – ~**ness**, ~**ision** *n*

conclude /kən'kloohd/ *v* **1** to bring to an end, esp in a particular way or with a particular action **2a** to arrive at as a logically necessary inference **b** to decide **c** to come to an agreement on; effect **3** to end – **-clusion** *n*

conclusive /kən'kloohsiv, -ziv/ *adj* putting an end to debate or question, esp by reason of irrefutability – ~**ly** *adv*

concoct /kən'kokt/ *v* to prepare (e g a meal, story, etc) by combining diverse ingredients – ~**ion** *n*

concord /'kongkawd, 'kon-/ *n* **1a** a state of agreement; harmony **b** a harmonious combination of simultaneously heard notes **2** a treaty, covenant

concordance /kəng'kawd(ə)ns, kon-/ *n* **1** an alphabetical index of the principal words in a book or an author's works **2** agreement

¹**concrete** /'kongkreet, 'kon-/ *adj* **1a** characterized by or belonging to immediate experience of actual things or events **b** specific, particular **c** real, tangible – ~**ly** *adv* – ~**ness** *n*

²**concrete** *n* a hard strong building material made by mixing a cementing material (e g portland cement) and a mineral aggregate (e g sand and gravel) with sufficient water to cause the cement to set and bind the entire mass

³**concrete** /kong'kreet, kən-; *sense 2 usu* 'kongkreet, 'kon-/ *v* **1** to form into a solid mass; solidify **2** to cover with, form of, or set in concrete

concubine /'kongkyoobien, 'kon-/ *n* a woman who lives with a man as his wife; a mistress; *esp* a woman who lives with a man in addition to his lawful wife or wives

concur /kən'kuh/ *v* **-rr- 1** to happen together; coincide **2** to act together to a common end or single effect **3** to express agreement – ~**rence** *n*

concurrent /kən'kurənt/ *adj* **1** meeting or intersecting in a point **b** running parallel **2** operating or occurring at the same time – ~**ly** *adv*

concuss /kən'kus/ *v* to affect with concussion

concussion /kən'kush(ə)n/ *n* a jarring injury to the brain, often resulting in unconsciousness, caused by a hard blow

condemn /kən'dem/ *v* **1** to declare to be utterly reprehensible, wrong, or evil, usu after considering evidence **2a** to prescribe punishment for;

specif to sentence to death **b** to sentence, doom **3** to declare unfit for use or consumption – ~**ation** *n*

condensation /,kondən'saysh(ə)n, -den-/ *n* **1** a change to a denser form (e g from vapour to liquid) **2** a product of condensing; *specif* an abridgment of a literary work

condense /kən'dens/ *v* **1** to make denser or more compact; *esp* to subject to or to undergo condensation

condenser /kən'densə/ *n* **1** an apparatus for condensing gas or vapour **2** a device for storing electrical charge – now used chiefly in the motor trade

condescend /,kondi'send/ *v* to waive the privileges of rank; *broadly* to descend to less formal or dignified action or speech – **-cension** *n*

condiment /'kondimənt/ *n* sthg used to enhance the flavour of food; *esp* seasoning

¹**condition** /kən'dish(ə)n/ *n* **1** sthg essential to the appearance or occurrence of sthg else; a prerequisite **2** a favourable or unfavourable state of sthg **3a** a state of being **b** a usu defective state of health or appearance **c** a state of physical fitness or readiness for use **d** *pl* attendant circumstances

²**condition** *v* **1** to put into a proper or desired state for work or use **2** to give a certain condition to **3a** to adapt to a surrounding culture **b** to modify so that an act or response previously associated with one stimulus becomes associated with another

conditional /kən'dish(ə)nl/ *adj* **1** subject to, implying, or dependent on a condition **2** expressing, containing, or implying a supposition – ~**ly** *adv*

condole /kən'dohl/ *v* to express sympathetic sorrow – **-ence** *n*

condom /'kondəm/ *n* a sheath, usu of rubber, worn over the penis (e g to prevent conception or venereal infection during sexual intercourse)

condone /kən'dohn/ *v* to pardon or overlook voluntarily; tacitly accept; *esp* to treat as if harmless or of no importance

condor /'kondaw/ *n* a very large vulture of the high Andes with bare head and neck

¹**conduct** /'kondukt/ *n* **1** the act, manner, or process of carrying on; management **2** a mode or standard of personal behaviour, esp as based on moral principles

²**conduct** /kən'dukt/ *v* **1** to bring (as if) by leading; guide **2** to carry on or out, usu from a position of command or control **3** to convey in a channel, pipe, etc **4** to behave in a specified manner **5** to direct the performance or execution of (e g a musical work or group of musicians) **6** to act as leader or director, esp of an orchestra **7** to have the property of transmitting (heat, sound, electricity, etc)

conduction /kən'duksh(ə)n/ *n* **1** the act of conducting or conveying **2** the transmission of an electrical impulse through (nerve) tissue – **-tive** *adj*

conductor /kən'duktə/ *n* **1** a collector of fares on a public conveyance, esp a bus **2** one who directs the performance of musicians **3** a substance or body capable of transmitting electricity, heat, sound, etc

conduit /'kondit, 'kondwit, 'kondyoo-it/ *n* **1** a channel through which sthg (e g a fluid) is conveyed **2** a pipe, tube, or tile for protecting electric wires or cables

cone /kohn/ *n* **1** a mass of overlapping woody scales that, esp in trees of the pine family, are arranged on an axis and bear seeds between them; *broadly* any of several similar flower or fruit clusters **2a** a solid generated by rotating a right-angled triangle about a side other than its hypotenuse **b** a solid figure tapering evenly to a point from a circular base **3** any of the relatively short light receptors in the retina of vertebrates that are sensitive to bright light and function in colour vision **4** a crisp cone-shaped wafer for holding a portion of ice cream

confection /kən'feksh(ə)n/ *n* a fancy or rich dish (e g a cream cake or preserve) or sweetmeat

confectioner /kən'fekshənə/ *n* a manufacturer of or dealer in confectionery

confectionery /kən'fekshənri/ *n* **1** confections, sweets **2** the confectioner's art, business, or shop

confederacy /kən'fed(ə)rəsi/ *n* **1** a league or compact for mutual support or common action; an alliance **2a** an unlawful association; a conspiracy **3** a league or alliance for common action; *esp, cap* the 11 states withdrawing from the USA in 1860 and 1861 – **-ate** *n, adj*

confer /kən'fuh/ *v* **-rr-** **1** to bestow (as if) from a position of superiority **2** to come together to compare views or take counsel; consult – **~ment** *n*

conference /'konf(ə)rəns/ *n* **1a** a usu formal interchange of views; a consultation **b** a meeting of 2 or more people for the discussion of matters of common concern **2** a representative assembly or administrative organization of a denomination, organization, association, etc

confess /kən'fes/ *v* **1** to make known (e g sthg wrong or damaging to oneself); admit **2a** to acknowledge (one's sins or the state of one's conscience) to God or a priest **b** to hear a confession **3** to declare faith in or adherence to

confession /kən'fesh(ə)n/ *n* **1** a disclosure of one's sins **2** a statement of what is confessed: e g **2a** a written acknowledgment of guilt by a party accused of an offence **b** a formal statement of religious beliefs **3** an organized religious body having a common creed

confessional /kən'fesh(ə)nl/ *n* **1** a place where a priest hears confessions **2** *the* practice of confessing to a priest

confetti /kən'feti/ *n* small bits of brightly coloured paper meant to be thrown (e g at weddings)

confide /kən'fied/ *v* **1** to show confidence *in* by imparting secrets **2** to tell confidentially

confidence /'konfid(ə)ns/ *n* **1** faith, trust **2** a feeling or consciousness of one's powers being sufficient, or of reliance on one's circumstances **3** the quality or state of being certain **4a** a relationship of trust or intimacy **b** reliance on another's discretion **5** sthg said in confidence; a secret

'confidence ,trick *n* a swindle performed by a person who pretends to be sthg that he/she is not

confident /'konfid(ə)nt/ *adj* **1** characterized by assurance; *esp* self-reliant **2** full of conviction; certain – **~ly** *adv*

confidential /,konfi'densh(ə)l/ *adj* **1** private, secret **2** marked by intimacy or willingness to confide – **~ity** *n* – **~ly** *adv*

configuration /kən,figoo'raysh(ə)n, -,figyoo-/ *n* **1** (relative) arrangement of parts **2** sthg (e g a figure, pattern, or apparatus) produced by such arrangement

'confine /kən'fien/ *v* **1** to keep within limits; restrict **2a** to shut up; imprison **b** to keep indoors or in bed, esp just before childbirth – usu passive

'confine /'konfien/ *n* **1** bounds, borders **2** outlying parts; limits *USE* usu pl with sing. meaning

con'finement /-mənt/ *n* confining or being confined, esp in childbirth

confirm /kən'fuhm/ *v* **1** to make firm or firmer; strengthen **2** to give approval to; ratify **3** to administer the rite of confirmation to **4** to make certain of; remove doubt about by authoritative act or indisputable fact – **~ation** *n*

confirmed /kən'fuhmd/ *adj* **1a** made firm; strengthened **b** being so fixed in habit as to be unlikely to change **2** having received the rite of confirmation

confiscate /'konfiskayt/ *v* to seize (as if) by authority – **-cation** *n*, **-catory** *adj*

conflagration /,konflə'graysh(ə)n/ *n* a (large disastrous) fire

'conflict /'konflikt/ *n* **1** a sharp disagreement or clash (e g between divergent ideas, interests, or people) **2** (distress caused by) mental struggle resulting from incompatible impulses **3** a hostile encounter (e g a fight, battle, or war)

'conflict /kən'flikt/ *v* to be in opposition (to another or each other); disagree

confluence /'konflooəns/, **confluency** /-si/ *n* **1** a coming or flowing together; a meeting or gathering at 1 point **2** the (place of) union of 2 or more streams

conform /kən'fawm/ *v* **1** to give the same shape, outline, or contour to; bring into harmony or accord **2** to be similar or identical **3** to be obedient or compliant; *esp* to adapt oneself to prevailing standards or customs – ~**ist** *adj*, n – ~**ism** *n*

conformity /kən'fawməti/ *n* **1** correspondence in form, manner, or character; agreement **2** an act or instance of conforming **3** action in accordance with a specified standard or authority; obedience

confound /kən'fownd/ *v* **1** to refute **2** to damn – used as a mild interjection of annoyance **3** to throw into confusion or perplexity

con'founded *adj* damned

confront /kən'frunt/ *v* **1** to face, esp in challenge; oppose **2a** to cause to meet; bring face to face *with* **b** to be faced with – ~**ation** *n*

confuse /kən'fyoohz/ *v* **1a** to make embarrassed; abash **b** to disturb or muddle in mind or purpose **2a** to make indistinct; blur **b** to mix indiscriminately; jumble **c** to fail to differentiate from another often similar or related thing – ~**d** *adj* – ~**dly** *adv* – **-fusing** *adj* – **-fusingly** *adv*

confusion /kən'fyoohzh(ə)n/ *n* **1** an instance of confusing or being confused **2** (a) disorder, muddle

conga /'kong·gə/ *n* a dance involving 3 steps followed by a kick and performed by a group, usu in single file

congeal /kən'jeel/ *v* **1** to bring from a fluid to a solid state (as if) by cold; to coagulate **2** to make rigid, inflexible, or immobile **3** to become congealed

congenial /kən'jeenyəl, -ni·əl/ *adj* **1** existing or associated together harmoniously – often + *with* **2** pleasant; *esp* agreeably suited to one's nature, tastes, or outlook – ~**ly** *adv*

congenital /kən'jenitl/ *adj* **1a** existing at or dating from birth **b** constituting an essential characteristic; inherent **2** being such by nature – ~**ly** *adv*

congest /kən'jest/ *v* **1** to cause an excessive fullness of the blood vessels of (e g an organ) **2** to clog – ~**ion** *n*

¹conglomerate /kən'glomərət/ *adj* made up of parts from various sources or of various kinds

²conglomerate /kən'glomərayt/ *v* **1** to accumulate **2** to gather into a mass or coherent whole

³conglomerate /kən'glomərət/ *n* **1** a composite mixture; *specif* (a) rock composed of variously-sized fragments in a cement **2** a widely diversified business company

conglomeration /kən,glomə'raysh(ə)n/ *n* a mixed coherent mass

congratulate /kən'gratyoolayt, -choo-/ *v* to express pleasure to (a person) on account of success or good fortune – **-lation** *n* – **-latory** *adj*

congregate /'kong·gri,gayt/ *v* to (cause to) gather together

congregation /,kong·gri'gaysh(ə)n/ *n* **1** assembly of people; *esp* such an assembly for religious worship **2** a religious community; *esp* an organized body of believers in a particular locality – ~**al** *adj*

congress /'kong·gres, -gris/ *n* **1** a formal meeting of delegates for discussion and usu action on some question **2** the supreme legislative body of a nation; *esp*, *cap* that of the USA **3** an association, usu made up of delegates from constituent organizations **4** the act or action of coming together and meeting – *fml*

congressman /'kong·gresmən, -gris-/, *fem* **'con·gress,woman** *n* a member of a congress

congruent /'kong·grooənt/ *adj* **1** in harmony or correspondent; appropriate **2** being exactly the same in size and shape – ~**ly** *adv* – **-ence, -uity** *n* – **-uous** *adj*

conical /'konikl/, **conic** /'konik, 'kohnik/ *adj* of or resembling a cone – ~**ly** *adv*

conifer /'konifə, 'koh-/ *n* any of an order of mostly evergreen cone-bearing trees and shrubs including pines, cypresses, and yews – ~**ous** *adj*

¹conjecture /kən'jekchə/ *n* **1** the drawing of conclusions from inadequate evidence **2** a conclusion reached by surmise or guesswork – **-tural** *adj*

²conjecture *v* **1** to arrive at by conjecture **2** to make conjectures as to

conjugal /'konjoogl/ *adj* of the married state or married people and their relationship

conjugate /'konjoogayt/ *v* **1** to give in prescribed order the various inflectional forms of (a verb) **2** to become joined together – **-ation** *n*

conjunction /kən'jungksh(ə)n/ *n* **1** joining together; being joined together **2** occurrence together in time or space; concurrence **3** the apparent meeting or passing of 2 or more celestial bodies **4** a word (e g *and* or *when*) that joins together sentences, clauses, phrases, or words

conjunctiva /kən'jungktivə/ *n*, *pl* **conjunctivas, conjunctivae** /-vi/ the mucous membrane that lines the inner surface of the eyelids and is continued over part of the eyeball

conjunctivitis /kən,jungkti'vietəs/ *n* inflammation of the conjunctiva

conjure /'konjə, 'kun-;   / *v* **1a** to summon by invocation or by uttering a spell, charm, etc **b(1)** to affect or effect (as if) by magical powers **b(2)** to imagine, contrive – often + *up* **2** to make use of magical powers **3** to use a conjurer's tricks – **-rer, -ror** *n*

¹conk /kongk/ *n* (a punch on) the nose – *infml*

²conk *v* **1** to break down; *esp* to stall **2** to faint USE usu + *out*; *infml*

conker /'kongkə/ *n* **1** *pl but sing in constr* a British game in which each player in turn swings a conker on a string to try to break one held on its string by his/her opponent **2** the large seed of the horse chestnut, esp as used in playing conkers

con

connect /kə'nekt/ v 1 to join or fasten together, usu by some intervening thing 2 to place or establish in relationship 3 to be or become joined 4 to make a successful hit or shot – ~**ed** *adj* – ~**ion**, **connexion** *n*

con'necting rod /kə'nekting/ *n* a rod that transmits power from a part of a machine in reciprocating motion (e g a piston) to another that is rotating (e g a crankshaft)

'conning ,tower /'koning/ *n* a raised observation tower and usu entrance on the deck of a submarine

connive /kə'niev/ v 1 to pretend ignorance of or fail to take action against sthg one ought to oppose 2a to be indulgent or in secret sympathy **b** to cooperate secretly or have a secret understanding; conspire *USE* often *+ at* – **-vance** *n*

connoisseur /,konə'suh, -'sooə/ *n* an expert judge in matters of taste or appreciation (e g of art)

connote /kə'noht/ v 1 to convey in addition to exact explicit meaning 2 to be associated with or inseparable from as a consequence or accompaniment – **-tation** *n*

connubial /kə'nyoohbi-əl/ *adj* conjugal

conquer /'kongkə/ v 1 to acquire or overcome by force of arms; subjugate 2 to gain mastery over 3 to be victorious – ~**or** *n*

conquest /'kon(g)kwest/ *n* 1 conquering 2a sthg conquered; *esp* territory appropriated in war – often pl **b** a person who has been won over, esp by love or sexual attraction

conquistador /kon'k(w)istədaw/ *n*, *pl* **conquistadores** /-'dawrays, -reez/, **conquistadors** one who conquers; *specif* any of the Spanish conquerors of America

conscience /'konsh(ə)ns/ *n* 1 the consciousness of the moral quality of one's own conduct or intentions, together with a feeling of obligation to refrain from doing wrong 2 conformity to the dictates of conscience; conscientiousness — **in all conscience** by any standard of fairness

conscientious /,konshi'enshəs/ *adj* 1 governed by or conforming to the dictates of conscience; scrupulous 2 meticulous or careful, esp in one's work; *also* hard-working – ~**ly** *adv* – ~**ness** *n*

consci,entious ob'jector *n* one who refuses to serve in the armed forces or bear arms, esp on moral or religious grounds – **conscientious objection** *n*

¹conscious /'konshəs/ *adj* 1 perceiving with a degree of controlled thought or observation 2 personally felt 3 capable of or marked by thought, will, intention, or perception 4 having mental faculties undulled by sleep, faintness, or stupor; awake 5 done or acting with critical awareness 6 marked by awareness of or concern for sthg specified – ~**ness** *n* – ~**ly** *adv*

²conscious *n* consciousness – used in Freudian psychology

¹conscript /'konskript/ *n or adj* (sby) conscripted

²conscript /kən'skript/ v to enlist compulsorily, esp for military service – ~**ion** *n*

consecrate /'konsikrayt/ v 1 to ordain to a religious office, esp that of bishop 2a to make or declare sacred by a solemn ceremony **b** to prepare (bread and wine used at communion) to be received as Christ's body and blood **c** to devote to a purpose with deep solemnity or dedication 3 to make inviolable or venerable – **-ration** *n*

consecutive /kən'sekyootiv/ *adj* following one after the other in order without gaps – ~**ly** *adv*

consensus /kən'sensəs/ *n* 1 general agreement; unanimity 2 the judgment arrived at by most of those concerned

¹consent /kən'sent/ v to give assent or approval; agree *to*

²consent *n* compliance in or approval of what is done or proposed by another; acquiescence

consequence /'konsikwəns/ *n* 1 sthg produced by a cause or necessarily following from a set of conditions 2 a conclusion arrived at by reasoning 3a importance in terms of power to produce an effect; moment **b** social importance — **in consequence** as a result; consequently

consequent /'konsikwənt/ *adj* following as a result or effect

consequential /,konsi'kwensh(ə)l/ *adj* 1 consequent 2 of the nature of a secondary result; indirect 3 having significant consequences; important

consequently /'konsikwəntli/ *adv* as a result; in view of the foregoing

conservancy /kən'suhv(ə)nsi/ *n* 1 conservation 2 (an area protected by) an organization with powers to conserve and protect the environment

conservation /,konsə'vaysh(ə)n/ *n* careful preservation and protection, esp of a natural resource, the quality of the environment, or plant or animal species

conservatism /kən'suhvətiz(ə)m/ *n* 1 (a political philosophy based on) the disposition to preserve what is established 2 *cap* the principles and policies of a Conservative party 3 the tendency to prefer an existing situation to change

¹conservative /kən'suhvətiv/ *adj* 1a of or being a philosophy of conservatism; traditional **b** *cap* advocating conservatism; *specif* of or constituting a British political party associated with support of established institutions and opposed to radical change 2a moderate, cautious **b** marked by or relating to traditional norms of taste, elegance, style, or manners – **-tively** *adv*

²conservative *n* 1 *cap* a supporter of a Conservative party 2 one who keeps to traditional methods or views

conservatory /kən'suhvət(ə)ri/ *n* a greenhouse, usu forming a room of a house, for growing or displaying ornamental plants

¹conserve /kən'suhv/ *v* **1a** to keep in a state of safety or wholeness **b** to avoid wasteful or destructive use of **2** to preserve, esp with sugar **3** to maintain (mass, energy, momentum, etc) constant during a process of chemical or physical change

²conserve /kən'suhv, 'konsuhv/ *n* a preserve of fruit boiled with sugar that is used like jam

consider /kən'sidə/ *v* **1** to think about with care or caution **2** to gaze on steadily or reflectively **3** to think of as specified; regard as being **4** to have as an opinion **5** to reflect, deliberate

considerable /kən'sid(ə)rəbl/ *adj* **1** worth consideration; significant **2** large in extent or degree – **-bly** *adv*

considerate /kən'sid(ə)rət/ *adj* marked by or given to consideration of the rights and feelings of others – ~**ly** *adv* – ~**ness** *n*

consideration /kən,sidə'raysh(ə)n/ *n* **1** continuous and careful thought **2a** sthg considered as a basis for thought or action; a reason **b** a taking into account **3** thoughtful and sympathetic or solicitous regard

con'sidered *adj* matured by extended thought

¹considering /kən'sid(ə)ring/ *prep* taking into account

²considering *conj* in view of the fact that

consign /kən'sien/ *v* **1** to give over to another's care **2** to give, transfer, or deliver into the hands or control of another; *also* to assign *to* sthg as a destination or end

consignee /,konsie'nee/ *n* one to whom sthg is consigned

consignment /kən'sienmənt/ *n* sthg consigned, esp in a single shipment

consist /kən'sist/ *v* **1** to lie, reside *in* **2** to be made up or composed *of*

consistency /kən'sist(ə)nsi/ *also* **consistence** *n* **1** internal constancy of constitution or character **2** degree of resistance of **2a** a liquid to movement **b** a soft solid to deformation **3a** agreement or harmony of parts or features to one another or a whole; *specif* ability to be asserted together without contradiction **b** harmony of conduct or practice with past performance or stated intent

consistent /kən'sist(ə)nt/ *adj* free from irregularity, variation, or contradiction – ~**ly** *adv*

¹console /kən'sohl/ *v* to alleviate the grief or sense of loss of – **-lation** *n* – **-latory** *adj*

²console /'konsohl, 'konsl/ *n* **1** a carved bracket projecting from a wall to support a shelf or cornice **2** the desk containing the keyboards, stops, etc of an organ **3** a control panel; *also* a cabinet in which a control panel is mounted **4** a cabinet (e g for a radio or television set) designed to rest directly on the floor

consolidate /kən'solidayt/ *v* **1** to join together into 1 whole; unite **2** to make firm or secure; strengthen **3** to form into a compact mass **4** to become consolidated; *specif* to merge – **-dation** *n*

consommé /kən'somay, ,konsə'may/ *n* a thin clear meat soup made from meat broth

consonance /'konsənəns/ *n* **1** an agreeable combination of musical notes in harmony **2** harmony or agreement among components – *fml*

¹consonant /'kons(ə)nənt/ *n* (a letter or other symbol representing) any of a class of speech sounds (e g /p/, /g/, /n/, /l/, /s/, /r/) characterized by constriction or closure at 1 or more points in the breath channel

²consonant *adj* **1** marked by musical consonances **2** in agreement or harmony; free from elements making for discord – *fml*

¹consort /'konsawt/ *n* **1** an associate **2** a spouse

²consort *n* **1** a group of musicians performing esp early music **2** a set of musical instruments (e g viols or recorders) of the same family played together

³consort /kən'sawt/ *v* **1** to keep company *with* **2** to accord, harmonize *with USE fml*

consortium /kən'sawti·əm/ *n, pl* **consortia** /-ti·ə/ *also* **consortiums** a business or banking agreement or combination

conspicuous /kən'spikyoo·əs/ *adj* **1** obvious to the eye or mind **2** attracting attention; striking – ~**ly** *adv* – ~**ness** *n*

conspiracy /kən'spirəsi/ *n* **1** (the offence of) conspiring together **2a** an agreement among conspirators **b** *sing or pl in constr* a group of conspirators

conspire /kən'spie·ə/ *v* **1a** to join in a plot **b** to scheme **2** to act together – **-rator** *n* – **-ratorial** *adj* – **-ratorially** *adv*

constable /'konstəbl, 'kun-/ *n* **1** a high officer of a medieval royal or noble household **2** the warden or governor of a royal castle or a fortified town **3** *Br* a policeman; *specif* one ranking below sergeant

constabulary /kən'stabyoolari/ *n, sing or pl in constr* **1** the police force of a district or country **2** an armed police force organized on military lines

constancy /'konstansi/ *n* **1** fidelity, loyalty **2** freedom from change

¹constant /'konstant/ *adj* **1** marked by steadfast resolution or faithfulness **2** invariable, uniform **3** continually occurring or recurring; regular – ~**ly** *adv*

²constant *n* sthg invariable or unchanging: e g **a** a number that has a fixed value in a given situation or universally or that is characteristic of some substance or instrument **b** a number that is assumed not to change value in a given mathematical discussion **c** a term in logic with a fixed designation

constellation /ˌkɒnstəˈlaysh(ə)n/ n 1 any of many arbitrary configurations of stars supposed to fill the outlines of usu mythical figures 2 a cluster, group, or configuration; *esp* a large or impressive one

consternation /ˌkɒnstəˈnaysh(ə)n/ n amazed dismay that hinders or throws into confusion

constipate /ˈkɒnstipayt/ v to cause constipation in

constipation /ˌkɒnstiˈpaysh(ə)n/ n 1 abnormally delayed or infrequent passage of faeces 2 impairment or a blocking of proper functioning

constituency /kənˈstityoo·ənsi, -ˈstichoo-/ n (the residents in) an electoral district

¹**constituent** /kənˈstityoo·ənt, -choo-/ n 1 an essential part; a component 2 a resident in a constituency

²**constituent** adj 1 serving to form, compose, or make up a unit or whole; component 2 having the power to frame or amend a constitution

constitute /ˈkɒnstityooht, -chooht/ v 1 to appoint to an often specified office, function, or dignity 2 to establish; set up: e g 2a to establish formally b to give legal form to 3 to form, make, be

constitution /ˌkɒnstiˈtyoohsh(ə)n/ n 1 the act of establishing, making, or setting up 2a the physical and mental structure of an individual b the factors or parts which go to make sthg; composition; *also* the way in which these parts or factors make up the whole 3 the way in which a state or society is organized 4 (a document embodying) the fundamental principles and laws of a nation, state, or social group

¹**constitutional** /ˌkɒnstiˈtyoohsh(ə)nl/ adj 1 relating to, inherent in, or affecting the constitution of body or mind 2 being in accordance with or authorized by the constitution of a state or society 3 regulated according to a constitution 4 of a constitution – ∼ly adv

²**constitutional** n a walk taken for one's health

constrain /kənˈstrayn/ v 1 to force by imposed stricture or limitation 2 to force or produce in an unnatural or strained manner 3 to hold within narrow confines; *also* to clasp tightly – ∼t n

constrict /kənˈstrikt/ v 1a to make narrow b to compress, squeeze 2 to set or keep within limits – ∼ion n – ∼ive adj

construct /kənˈstrukt/ v 1 to make or form by combining parts; build 2 to set in logical order – ∼ion n – ∼or n – ∼ional adj

constructive /kənˈstruktiv/ adj 1 (judicially) implied rather than explicit 2 of or involved in construction 3 suggesting improvement or development – ∼ly adv – ∼ness n

construe /kənˈstrooh/ v 1 to analyse the syntax of (e g a sentence or sentence part) 2 to understand or explain the sense or intention of 3 to construe a sentence or sentence part, esp in connection with translating

consubstantiation /ˌkɒnsəbˌstanshiˈaysh(ə)n, -si'aysh(ə)n/ n (the Anglican doctrine of) the actual presence and combination of the body and blood of Christ with the bread and wine used at Communion

consul /ˈkɒns(ə)l/ n 1a either of 2 elected chief magistrates of the Roman republic b any of 3 chief magistrates of France from 1799 to 1804 2 an official appointed by a government to reside in a foreign country to look after the (commercial) interests of citizens of the appointing country – ∼ar adj – ∼ship n

consulate /ˈkɒnsyoolət/ n 1 a government by consuls 2 the residence, office, or jurisdiction of a consul

consult /kənˈsult/ v 1 to ask the advice or opinion of 2 to refer to 3 to deliberate together; confer 4 to serve as a consultant – ∼ation n – ∼ative adj

consultant /kənˈsult(ə)nt/ n 1 one who consults sby or sthg 2 an expert who gives professional advice or services 3 the most senior grade of British hospital doctor – **-ancy** n

consulting /kənˈsulting/ adj 1 providing professional or expert advice 2 of a (medical) consultation or consultant

consume /kənˈsyoohm/ v 1 to do away with completely; destroy 2a to spend wastefully; squander b to use or use up 3 to eat or drink, esp in great quantity or eagerly 4 to engage fully; engross 5 to waste or burn away; perish

consumer /kənˈsyoohmə/ n a customer for goods or services

¹**consummate** /kənˈsumət, ˈkɒnsyoomət, -sə-, -su-/ adj 1 extremely skilled and accomplished 2 of the highest degree

²**consummate** /ˈkɒnsyoomayt, -sə-, -su-/ v to make (a marriage) complete by sexual intercourse

consumption /kənˈsumsh(ə)n, -ˈsumpsh(ə)n/ n 1 the act or process of consuming 2 the making use of economic goods for the satisfaction of wants or in the process of production, resulting chiefly in their destruction, deterioration, or transformation 3 (a progressive wasting of the body, esp from) lung tuberculosis

consumptive /kənˈsum(p)tiv/ adj of or affected with consumption (of the lungs) – **consumptive** n

¹**contact** /ˈkɒntakt/ n 1a (an instance of) touching b (a part made to form) the junction of 2 electrical conductors through which a current passes 2a association, relationship b connection, communication c the act of establishing communication with sby or observing or receiving a significant signal from a person or object 3 one serving as a carrier or source

²**contact** /'kontakt, kon'takt, kən-/ *v* 1 to bring into contact 2a to enter or be in contact with; join b to get in communication with

'**contact ˌlens** *n* a thin lens designed to fit over the cornea of the eye, esp for the correction of a visual defect

contagion /kən'tayj(ə)n, -jyən/ *n* 1 the transmission of a disease by (indirect) contact 2 corrupting influence or contact

contagious /kən'tayjəs, -jyəs/ *adj* 1 communicable by contact; catching 2 exciting similar emotions or conduct in others – ~**ly** *adv* – ~**ness** *n*

contain /kən'tayn/ *v* 1 to keep within limits; hold back or hold down: e g 1a to restrain, control b to check, halt c to prevent (an enemy, opponent, etc) from advancing or attacking 2a to have within; hold b to comprise, include

container /kən'taynə/ *n* 1 a receptacle 2 a metal packing case, standardized for mechanical handling, usu forming a single lorry or rail-wagon load – ~**ize** *v*

contaminate /kən'taminayt/ *v* 1a to soil, stain, or infect by contact or association b to make inferior or impure by adding sthg 2 to make unfit for use by the introduction of unwholesome or undesirable elements – **nation** *n*

contemplate /'kontəmplayt/ *v* 1 to view or consider with continued attention; meditate on 2 to have in view as contingent or probable or as an end or intention – **lation** *n* – **lative** *adj*

contemporaneous /kənˌtempə'raynyəs, kon-, -ni·əs/ *adj* contemporary – ~**ly** *adv*

¹**contemporary** /kən'temp(ə)rəri, -pri/ *adj* 1 happening, existing, living, or coming into being during the same period of time 2 modern

²**contemporary** *n* sby or sthg contemporary with another; *specif* one of about the same age as another

contempt /kən'tem(p)t/ *n* 1a the act of despising; the state of mind of one who despises b lack of respect or reverence for sthg 2 the state of being despised 3 obstruction of the administration of justice in court; *esp* wilful disobedience to or open disrespect of a court – ~**ible** *adj* – ~**ibly** *adv*

contemptuous /kən'tem(p)choo·əs, -tyoo·əs/ *adj* manifesting, feeling, or expressing contempt – ~**ly** *adv*

contend /kən'tend/ *v* 1 to strive or vie in contest or rivalry or against difficulties 2 to strive in debate; argue 3 to maintain, assert – **tention** *n* – ~**er** *n*

¹**content** /kən'tent/ *adj* happy, satisfied – ~**ment** *n* – ~**ed** *adj*

²**content** /kən'tent/ *v* 1 to appease the desires of; satisfy 2 to limit (oneself) in requirements, desires, or actions – usu + *with*

³**content** /kən'tent/ *n* freedom from care or discomfort; satisfaction

⁴**content** /'kontent/ *n* 1a that which is contained – usu pl with sing. meaning b *pl* the topics or matter treated in a written work 2a the substance, gist b the events, physical detail, and information in a work of art 3 the matter dealt with in a field of study 4 the amount of specified material contained; proportion

contentious /kən'tenshəs/ *adj* 1 argumentative 2 likely to cause strife – ~**ly** *adv* – ~**ness** *n* – **tion** *n*

¹**contest** /kən'test/ *v* 1 to make the subject of dispute, contention, or legal proceedings 2 to strive, vie – ~**ant** *n*

²**contest** /'kontest/ *n* 1 a struggle for superiority or victory 2 a competitive event; *esp* one adjudicated by a panel of specially chosen judges

context /'kontekst/ *n* 1 the parts surrounding a written or spoken word or passage that can throw light on its meaning 2 the interrelated conditions in which sthg exists or occurs – ~**ual** *adj* – ~**ually** *adv*

contiguous /kən'tigyoo·əs/ *adj* 1 in actual contact; touching along a boundary or at a point 2 next or near in time or sequence – **-guity** *n* – ~**ly** *adv*

continence /'kontinəns/ *n* 1 self-restraint from yielding to impulse or desire 2 ability to refrain from a bodily activity

¹**continent** /'kontinənt/ *adj* 1 exercising continence 2 not suffering from incontinence of the urine or faeces

²**continent** *n* 1 any of the (7) great divisions of land on the globe 2 *cap the* continent of Europe as distinguished from the British Isles

ˌconti'nental 'shelf *n* the gently sloping part of the ocean floor that borders a continent and ends in a steeper slope to the ocean depths

contingency /kən'tinj(ə)nsi/ *n* 1 an event that may occur; *esp* an undesirable one 2 an event that is liable to accompany another event

¹**contingent** /kən'tinj(ə)nt/ *adj* 1 happening by chance or unforeseen causes 2 dependent *on* or conditioned by sthg else 3 not logically necessary; *esp* empirical – ~**ly** *adv*

²**contingent** *n* a quota or share, esp of people supplied from or representative of an area, group, or military force

continual /kən'tinyoo·əl, -yool/ *adj* 1 continuing indefinitely without interruption 2 recurring in steady rapid succession – ~**ly** *adv*

continue /kən'tinyooh/ *v* 1 to maintain (a condition, course, or action) without interruption; carry on 2 to remain in existence; endure 3 to remain in a place or condition; stay 4 to resume (an activity) after interruption 5 to cause to continue 6 to say further – **-uation** *n* – ~**uance** *n*

continuity /ˌkonti'nyooh·əti/ *n* 1a uninterrupted connection, succession, or union b persistence without essential change c uninterrupted duration in time 2 sthg that has, displays, or provides continuity: e g **2a** a script or scenario in the performing arts; *esp* one giving the details of the sequence of individual shots **b** speech or music used to link parts of an entertainment, esp a radio or television programme

continuous /kən'tinyoo-əs/ *adj* marked by uninterrupted extension in space, time, or sequence – ~**ly** *adv*

continuum /kən'tinyoo-əm/ *n, pl* **continua** /-nyoo-ə/, **continuums 1** sthg (e g duration or extension) absolutely continuous and homogeneous that can be described only by reference to sthg else (e g numbers) **2a** sthg in which a fundamental common character is discernible amid a series of imperceptible or indefinite variations **b** an uninterrupted ordered sequence

contort /kən'tawt/ *v* to twist in a violent manner; deform – ~**ion** *n*

contortionist /kən'tawsh(ə)nist/ *n* **1** an acrobat who specializes in unnatural body postures **2** one who extricates him-/herself from a dilemma by complicated but doubtful arguments

¹**contour** /'kon,tooə/ *n* **1** (a line representing) an outline, esp of a curving or irregular figure **2 contour, contour line** a line (e g on a map) connecting points of equal elevation or height

²**contour** *v* **1a** to shape the contour of **b** to shape or construct so as to fit contours

contraband /'kontrə,band/ *n* goods or merchandise whose import, export, or possession is forbidden; *also* smuggled goods – **contraband** *adj*

contra'bass /-'bays/ *n* a double bass

contraceptive /,kontrə'septiv/ *n* a method or device used in preventing conception – **-tion** *n* – **-tive** *adj*

¹**contract** /'kontrakt/ *n* **1a** (a document containing) a legally binding agreement between 2 or more people or parties **b** a betrothal **2** an undertaking to win a specified number of tricks in bridge

²**contract** /kən'trakt; *sense ' and ' usu* 'kontrakt/ *v* **1** to undertake by contract **2a** to catch (an illness) **b** to incur as an obligation **3** to knit, wrinkle **4** to reduce to a smaller size (as if) by squeezing or forcing together **5** to shorten (e g a word) **6** to make a contract **7** to draw together so as to become smaller or shorter

contract 'bridge /'kontrakt/ *n* a form of bridge in which tricks made in excess of the contract do not count towards game bonuses

contractile /kən'traktiel/ *adj* having the power or property of contracting

contraction /kən'traksh(ə)n/ *n* **1** the shortening and thickening of a muscle (fibre) **2** (a form produced by) shortening of a word, syllable, or word group

contractor /kən'traktə, 'kontraktə/ *n* one who contracts to perform work, esp building work, or to provide supplies, usu on a large scale

contract out *v* to agree to exclusion (of) from a particular scheme

contractual /kən'traktyoo-əl, -choo-əl/ *adj* of or constituting a contract – **contractually** *adv*

contradict /,kontrə'dikt/ *v* **1** to state the contrary of (a statement or speaker) **2** to deny the truthfulness of (a statement or speaker) – ~**ion** *n* – ~**ory** *adj*

contralto /kən'traltoh, kən'trahltoh/ *n pl* **contraltos 1** (a person with) the lowest female singing voice **2** the part sung by a contralto

contraption /kən'trapsh(ə)n/ *n* a newfangled or complicated device; a gadget

contrapuntal /,kontrə'puntl/ *adj* of counterpoint – ~**ly** *adv*

contrariwise /'kontrəri,wiez, kən'treə-/ *adv* conversely; vice versa

¹**contrary** /'kontrəri/ *n* **1** a fact or condition incompatible with another **2** either of a pair of opposites — **on the contrary** ju' 'he opposite; no — **to the contrary** to the opposite effect **2** notwithstanding

²**contrary** /'kontrəri; *sense 4 often* kən'treəri/ *adj* **1** completely different or opposed **2** opposite in position, direction, or nature *of wind or weather* unfavourable **4** obstinately self-willed; inclined to oppose the wishes of others – **-arily** *adv* – **-ariness** *n*

¹**contrast** /'kontrahst/ *n* **1a** juxtaposition of dissimilar elements (e g colour, tone, or emotion) in a work of art **b** degree of difference between the lightest and darkest parts of a painting, photograph, television picture, etc **2** comparison of similar objects to set off their dissimilar qualities **3** a person or thing against which another may be contrasted

²**contrast** /kən'trahst/ *v* **1** to exhibit contrast **2** to put in contrast **3** to compare in respect to differences

contravene /,kontrə'veen/ *v* to go or act contrary to – **-vention** *n*

contribute /kən'tribyooht, 'kontri-/ *v* **1** to give in common with others **2** to supply (e g an article) for a publication **3** to help bring about an end or result – **-bution** *n*

contributory /kən'tribyoot(ə)ri/ *adj* **1** contributing to a common fund or enterprise **2** of or forming a contribution **3** financed by contributions; *specif, of an insurance or pension plan* contributed to by both employers and employees

contrite /kən'triet/ *adj* penitent – ~**ly** *adv*

contrition /kən'trish(ə)n/ *n* repentance

contrive /kən'triev/ *v* **1a** to devise, plan **b** to create in an inventive or resourceful manner **2** to bring about; manage – **-vance** *n*

con'trived *adj* unnatural and forced

¹**control** /kən'trohl/ v **-ll- 1** to check, test, or verify **2a** to exercise restraining or directing influence over **b** to have power over; rule – **~ ler** n – **~ lable** adj – **~ lably** adv

²**control** n **1** power to control, direct, or command **2a** (an organism, culture, etc used in) an experiment in which the procedure or agent under test in a parallel experiment is omitted and which is used as a standard of comparison in judging experimental effects **b** a mechanism used to regulate or guide the operation of a machine, apparatus, or system – often pl **c** an organization that directs a space flight

controversy /'kontrə,vuhsi; *also* kən'trovəsi/ n (a) debate or dispute, esp in public or in the media – **-sial** adj – **-sially** adv

contuse /kən'tyoohz/ v to bruise (tissue) – **-sion** n

conundrum /kə'nundrəm/ n **1** a riddle; esp one whose answer is or involves a pun **2** an intricate problem

conurbation /,konuh'baysh(ə)n/ n a grouping of several previously separate towns to form 1 large community

convalesce /,konvə'les/ v to recover gradually after sickness or weakness – **~ nce** n – **~ nt** adj, n

convection /kən'veksh(ə)n/ n (the transfer of heat by) the circulatory motion that occurs in a gas or liquid at a nonuniform temperature owing to the variation of density with temperature

convector /kən'vektə/ n a heating unit from which heated air circulates by convection

convene /kən'veen/ v **1** to come together in a body **2** to summon before a tribunal **3** to cause to assemble – **~ r, -enor** n

convenience /kən'veenyəns, -ni-əns/ n **1** fitness or suitability **2** an appliance, device, or service conducive to comfort **3** a suitable time; an opportunity **4** personal comfort or advantage **5** Br a public toilet

convenient /kən'veenyənt, -ni-ənt/ adj **1** suited to personal comfort or to easy use **2** suited to a particular situation **3** near at hand; easily accessible – **~ ly** adv

convent /'konv(ə)nt, -vent/ n a local community or house of a religious order or congregation; esp an establishment of nuns

convention /kən'vensh(ə)n/ n **1** an agreement or contract, esp between states or parties **2** a generally agreed principle, technique, or practice **3** an assembly

conventional /kən'vensh(ə)nl/ adj **1a** conforming to or sanctioned by convention **b** lacking originality or individuality **2** of warfare not using atom or hydrogen bombs – **~ ly** adv – **~ ize** v

converge /kən'vuhj/ v **1** to move together towards a common point; meet **2** to come together in a common interest or focus – **~ nt** adj – **~ nce** n

conversant /kən'vuhs(ə)nt/ adj having knowledge or experience; familiar with

conversation /,konvə'saysh(ə)n/ n (an instance of) informal verbal exchange of feelings, opinions, or ideas – **~ al** adj – **~ ally** adv – **~ alist** n

¹**converse** /kən'vuhs/ v to talk

²**converse** /'kon,vuhs/ n conversation – fml

³**converse** /'kon,vuhs/ adj reversed in order, relation, or action; opposite – **~ ly** adv

⁴**converse** /'kon,vuhs/ n sthg converse to another

¹**convert** /kən'vuht/ v **1a** to win over from one persuasion or party to another **b** to win over to a particular religion or sect **2a** to alter the physical or chemical nature or properties of, esp in manufacturing **b** to change from one form or function to another; esp to make (structural) alterations to (a building or part of a building) **c** to exchange for an equivalent **3** to gain extra points for a try in rugby by kicking the ball between the uprights of the goal above the cross-bar – **-version** n

²**convert** /'konvuht/ n a person who has experienced an esp religious conversion

¹**convertible** /kən'vuhtəbl/ adj **1** capable of being converted **2** of a motor vehicle having a top that may be lowered or removed **3** capable of being exchanged for a specified equivalent (e g another currency) – **-bility** n

²**convertible** n a convertible motor car

convex /,kon'veks; not attrib 'kon'veks/ adj curved or rounded outwards like the outside of a bowl – **~ ity** n – **~ ly** adv

convey /kən'vay/ v **1** to take or carry from one place to another **2** to impart or communicate (e g feelings or ideas) **3** to transmit, transfer; specif to transfer (property or the rights to property) to another – **~ er, ~ or** n

conveyance /kən'vayəns/ n **1** a document by which rights to property are transferred **2** a means of transport; a vehicle

conveyancing /kən'vayənsing/ n the act or business of transferring rights to property

¹**convict** /kən'vikt/ v **1** to find or prove to be guilty **2** to convince of error or sinfulness

²**convict** /'konvikt/ n a person serving a (long-term) prison sentence

conviction /kən'viksh(ə)n/ n **1** convicting or being convicted, esp in judicial proceedings **2a** a strong persuasion or belief **b** the state of being convinced

convince /kən'vins/ v to cause to believe; persuade – **~ d** adj

convincing /kən'vinsing/ adj having the power to overcome doubt or disbelief; plausible – **~ ly** adv

convivial /kən'vivi-əl/ adj relating to or fond of eating, drinking, and good company – **~ ly** adv – **~ ity** n

convocation /,konvə'kaysh(ə)n, -voh-/ n **1** an assembly of people called together **2** the act of calling together

convoke /kən'vohk/ *v* to call together to a formal meeting

convolution /ˌkonvə'loohsh(ə)n/ *n* sthg intricate or complicated – **-ted** *adj*

convolvulus /kən'volvyooləs/ *n, pl* **convolvuluses, convolvuli** /-lie/ any of a genus of usu twining plants (e g bindweed)

¹**convoy** /'konvoy/ *v* to accompany or escort, esp for protection

²**convoy** *n* **1** convoying or being convoyed **2** *sing or pl in constr* a group of ships, military vehicles, etc moving together, esp with a protective escort; *also* such an escort

convulse /kən'vuls/ *v* **1** to shake or agitate violently, esp (as if) with irregular spasms **2** to cause to laugh helplessly – **-sion** *n* – **-sive** *adj* – **-sively** *adv*

cony, coney /'kohni/ *n* a rabbit; *also* its fur, esp when prepared to imitate some other fur

coo /kooh/ *v* **cooed, coo'd 1** to make (a sound similar to) the low soft cry characteristic of a dove or pigeon **2** to talk lovingly or appreciatively – **coo** *n*

¹**cook** /kook/ *n* sby who prepares food for eating

²**cook** *v* **1** to prepare food for eating, esp by subjection to heat **2** to undergo the process of being cooked **3** to subject to the action of heat or fire — **cook someone's goose** to ruin sby irretrievably — **cook the books** to falsify financial accounts in order to deceive

cooker /'kookə/ *n* **1** an apparatus, appliance, etc for cooking; *esp* one typically consisting of an oven, hot plates or rings, and a grill fixed in position **2** a variety, esp of fruit, not usu eaten raw

cookery /'kook(ə)ri/ *n* the art or practice of cooking

cookie, cooky /'kooki/ *n* **1a** *Scot* a plain bun **b** *NAm* a sweet flat or slightly leavened biscuit **2** *chiefly NAm* a person, esp of a specified type – *infml*

¹**cool** /koohl/ *adj* **1** moderately cold; lacking in warmth **2a** dispassionately calm and self-controlled **b** lacking friendliness or enthusiasm **c** of or being an understated, restrained, and melodic style of jazz **3** bringing or suggesting relief from heat **4** showing sophistication by a restrained or detached manner – ~**ish** *adj* – ~**ly** *adv* – ~**ness** *n*

²**cool** *v* **1** to become cool; lose heat or warmth **2** to lose enthusiasm or passion **3** to make cool; impart a feeling of coolness to – often + *off* or *down* **4** to moderate the excitement, force, or activity of — **cool it** to become calm or quiet; relax — *infml* — **cool one's heels** to wait or be kept waiting for a long time, esp (as if) from disdain or discourtesy

³**cool** *n* **1** a cool atmosphere or place **2** poise, composure – *infml*

⁴**cool** *adv* in a casual and nonchalant manner – *infml*

coolant /'koohlənt/ *n* a liquid or gas used in cooling, esp in an engine

coolie /'koohli/ *n* an unskilled labourer or porter, usu in or from the Far East, known for low or subsistence wages

¹**coop** /koohp/ *n* **1** a cage or small enclosure or building, esp for housing poultry **2** a confined space

²**coop** *v* **1** to confine in a restricted space – usu + *up* **2** to place or keep in a coop – often + *up*

co-op /'koh ˌop/ *n* a cooperative

cooper /'koohpə/ *n* a maker or repairer of barrels, casks, etc

cooperate /koh'opərayt/ *v* to act or work with others for a common purpose – **-ation** *n* – **-ative** *adj*

cooperative /koh'op(ə)rətiv/ *n* an enterprise (e g a shop) or organization (e g a society) owned by and operated for the benefit of those using its services

co-opt /ˌkoh 'opt/ *v* to choose or elect as a member; *specif, of a committee* to draft onto itself as an additional member

¹**coordinate** /koh'awd(ə)nət, -di-/ *adj* **1** equal in rank, quality, or significance **2** relating to or marked by coordination – ~**ly** *adv*

²**coordinate** *n* **1** any of a set of numbers used in specifying the location of a point on a line, on a surface, or in space **2** *pl* outer garments, usu separates, in harmonizing colours, materials, and pattern

³**coordinate** /koh'awd(ə)nayt, -di-/ *v* **1** to combine in a common action; harmonize **2** to be or become coordinate, esp so as to act together harmoniously – **-ation** *n* – **-ative** *adj* – **-ator** *n*

coot /kooht/ *n* **1** any of various slaty-black water birds of the rail family that somewhat resemble ducks **2** a foolish person – *infml*

¹**cop** /kop/ *v* **-pp-** to get hold of; catch; *specif, Br* to arrest – *slang* — **cop it** *Br* to be in serious trouble — *slang*

²**cop** *n, Br* a capture, arrest – esp in *a fair cop*; *slang* — **not much cop** *chiefly Br* fairly bad; worthless — *slang*

³**cop** *n* a policeman – *infml*

¹**cope** /kohp/ *n* a long ecclesiastical vestment resembling a cape, worn on special occasions (e g processions)

²**cope** *v* to supply or cover with a cope or coping

³**cope** *v* to deal with a problem or task effectively – usu + *with*

copier /'kopi·ə/ *n* a machine for making copies, esp by photocopying or xeroxing

co-ˌpilot /koh/ *n* a qualified aircraft pilot who assists or relieves the pilot but is not in command

coping /'kohping/ *n* the final, usu sloping, course of brick, stone, etc on the top of a wall

copious /'kohpi-əs, 'kohpyəs/ *adj* **1** plentiful, lavish **2** profuse in words or expression – **~ly** *adv* – **~ness** *n*

cop out *v* to avoid an unwanted responsibility or commitment – *infml* – **cop-out** *n*

¹copper /'kopə/ *n* **1** a common reddish metallic element that is ductile and malleable and one of the best conductors of heat and electricity **2** a coin or token made of copper or bronze and usu of low value **3** any of various small butterflies with usu copper-coloured wings **4** *chiefly Br* a large metal vessel used, esp formerly, for boiling clothes – **copper, ~y** *adj*

²copper *n* a policeman – *infml*

'copper,plate /-,playt/ *n* handwriting modelled on engravings in copper and marked by lines of sharply contrasting thickness; *broadly* formal and ornate handwriting

coppice /'kopis/ *n* a thicket, grove, etc of small trees

copulate /'kopyoolayt/ *v* to engage in sexual intercourse – **-lation** *n*

¹copy /'kopi/ *n* **1** an imitation, transcript, or reproduction of an original work **2** any of a series of esp mechanical reproductions of an original impression **3** (newsworthy) material ready to be printed

²copy *v* **1** to make a copy (of) **2** to model oneself on **3** to undergo copying

'copy,book /-,book/ *n* a book formerly used in teaching writing and containing models for imitation

'copy-,book *adj, Br* completely correct; proper

'copy,cat /-,kat/ *n* one who slavishly imitates the behaviour or practices of another – used chiefly by children

'copy,right /-,riet/ *v or n* (to secure) the exclusive legal right to reproduce, publish, and sell a literary, musical, or artistic work

'copy,writer /-,rietə/ *n* a writer of advertising or publicity copy

coquetry /'kokətri, 'koh-/ *n* flirtatious behaviour or attitude

coquette /ko'ket, kə-, koh-/ *n* a woman who tries to gain the attention and admiration of men without sincere affection – **coquettish** *adj*

coracle /'korəkl/ *n* a small (nearly) circular boat of a traditional Welsh or Irish design made by covering a wicker frame with waterproof material

coral /'korəl/ *n* **1** (the hard esp red deposit produced as a skeleton chiefly by) a colony of smart marine animals **2** a piece of (red) coral **3a** a bright reddish mass of ovaries (e g of a lobster or scallop) **b** deep orange-pink – **coral** *adj*

cor anglais /,kawr 'ong·glay, -·'-/ (*Fr* kɔr ãglɛ/ *n* a double-reed woodwind instrument similar to, and with a range a fifth lower than, the oboe

¹cord /kawd/ *n* **1** (a length of) long thin flexible material consisting of several strands (e g of thread or yarn) woven or twisted together **2** a moral, spiritual, or emotional bond **3** an electric flex **4** a unit of cut wood usu equal to 128ft³ (about 3.63m³); *also* a stack containing this amount of wood **5a** a rib like a cord on a textile **b(1)** a fabric made with such ribs **b(2)** *pl* trousers made of corduroy

²cord *v* to provide, bind, or connect with a cord

¹cordial /'kawdi-əl/ *adj* **1** warmly and genially affable **2** sincerely or deeply felt – **~ity** *n* – **~ly** *adv*

²cordial *n* **1** a stimulating medicine **2** a nonalcoholic sweetened fruit drink; a fruit syrup

¹cordon /'kawd(ə)n/ *n* **1a** *sing or pl in constr* a line of troops, police, etc enclosing an area **b** a line or ring of people or objects **2** a plant, esp a fruit-tree, trained to a single stem by pruning off all side shoots

²cordon *v* to form a protective or restrictive cordon round – often + *off*

cordon bleu /,kawdonh 'bluh /·/ *adj or n* (typical of or being) sby with great skill or distinction in (classical French) cookery

corduroy /'kawd(ə)roy/ *n* a durable usu cotton pile fabric with lengthways ribs

¹core /kaw/ *n* **1** a central or interior part, usu distinct from an enveloping part: e g **1a** the usu inedible central part of an apple, pineapple, etc **b** the portion of a foundry mould that shapes the interior of a hollow casting **c** a cylindrical portion removed from a mass for inspection; *specif* such a portion of rock got by boring **d** a piece of ferromagnetic material (e g iron) serving to concentrate and intensify the magnetic field resulting from a current in a surrounding coil **e** the central part of a planet, esp the earth **f** a subject which is central in a course of studies **2** the essential, basic, or central part (e g of an individual, class, or entity)

²core *v* to remove a core from

co-respondent /,koh ri'spond(ə)nt/ *n* a person claimed to have committed adultery with the respondent in a divorce case

corgi /'kawgi/ *n, pl* **corgis** (any of) either of 2 varieties of short-legged long-backed dogs with fox-like heads, orig developed in Wales

¹cork /kawk/ *n* **1a** the elastic tough outer tissue of the cork oak used esp for stoppers and insulation **b** a layer of similar tissue in other plants **2** a usu cork stopper, esp for a bottle **3** an angling float

²cork *v* to fit or close with a cork

'cork,screw /-,skrooh/ *n* an implement for removing corks from bottles

²corkscrew *v* **1** to twist into a spiral **2** to move in a winding course

³corkscrew *adj* spiral

corm /kawm/ *n* a rounded thick underground plant stem base with buds and scaly leaves

cormorant /'kawmərənt/ n a common dark-coloured web-footed European seabird with a long neck and hooked bill

¹**corn** /kawn/ n 1 a small hard seed 2 (the seeds of) the important cereal crop of a particular region (e g wheat and barley in Britain) 3 sweet corn, maize 4 sthg corny – infml

²**corn** v to preserve or season with salt or brine

³**corn** n a local hardening and thickening of skin (e g on the top of a toe)

'**corn,cob** /-,kob/ n 1 the axis on which the edible kernels of sweet corn are arranged 2 an ear of sweet corn

cornea /kaw'nee·ə, 'kawni·ə/ n the hard transparent part of the coat of the eyeball that covers the iris and pupil – ~l adj

cornelian /kaw'neelyən/ n a hard reddish gem stone

¹**corner** /'kawnə/ n 1a the point where converging lines, edges, or sides meet; an angle b the place of intersection of 2 streets or roads c a piece designed to form, mark, or protect a corner (e g of a book) 2 the angular space between meeting lines, edges, or borders: e g 2a the area of a playing field or court near the intersection of the sideline and the goal line or baseline b any of the 4 angles of a boxing ring; esp that in which a boxer rests between rounds 3 sing or pl in constr a contestant's group of supporters, adherents, etc 4 a corner kick; also a corner hit 5a a private, secret, or remote place b a difficult or embarrassing situation 6 control or ownership of enough of the available supply of a commodity or security to permit manipulation of esp the price 7 a point at which significant change occurs – often in turn a corner — **round the corner** imminent; at hand

²**corner** v 1a to drive into a corner b to catch and hold the attention of, esp so as to force into conversation 2 to get a corner on 3 to turn a corner

'**corner,stone** /-,stohn/ n 1 a block of stone forming a part of a corner or angle in a wall; specif a foundation stone 2 the most basic element; a foundation

cornet /'kawnit/ n 1 a valved brass instrument resembling a trumpet but with a shorter tube and less brilliant tone 2 sthg shaped like a cone: e g 2a a piece of paper twisted for use as a container b an ice cream cone

'**corn,flakes** /-,flayks/ n pl toasted flakes of maize eaten as a breakfast cereal

'**corn,flour** /-,flowə/ n a finely ground flour made from maize, rice, etc and used esp as a thickening agent in cooking

'**corn,flower** /-,flowə/ n a usu bright-blue-flowered European composite (garden) plant

cornice /'kawnis/ n 1a the ornamental projecting piece that forms the top edge of a building, pillar, etc b an ornamental plaster moulding between wall and ceiling 2 a decorative band of metal or wood used to conceal curtain fixtures 3 an overhanging mass of snow, ice, etc on a mountain

¹**Cornish** /'kawnish/ adj (characteristic) of Cornwall

²**Cornish** n the ancient Celtic language of Cornwall

cornucopia /,kawnyoo'kohpi·ə/ n 1 a goat's horn overflowing with fruit and corn used to symbolize abundance 2 an inexhaustible store; an abundance 3 a vessel shaped like a horn or cone

corny /'kawni/ adj 1 tiresomely simple and sentimental; trite 2 hackneyed – infml

corolla /kə'rolə/ n the petals of a flower constituting the inner floral envelope

corollary /kə'roləri/ n 1 a direct conclusion from a proved proposition 2 sthg that naturally follows or accompanies

corona /kə'rohnə/ n 1a a usu coloured circle of usu diffracted light seen round and close to a luminous celestial body (e g the sun or moon) b the tenuous outermost part of the atmosphere of the sun and other stars appearing as a halo round the moon's black disc during a total eclipse of the sun 2 a long straight-sided cigar with a roundly blunt sealed mouth end

¹**coronary** /'korən(ə)ri/ adj (of or being the arteries or veins) of the heart

²**coronary** n coronary thrombosis

,**coronary throm'bosis** /throm'bohsis/ n the blocking of a coronary artery of the heart by a blood clot, usu causing death of heart muscle tissue

coronation /,korə'naysh(ə)n/ n the act or ceremony of investing a sovereign or his/her consort with the royal crown

coroner /'korənə/ n a public officer whose principal duty is to inquire into the cause of any death which there is reason to suppose might not be due to natural causes

coronet /'korənit/ n 1 a small crown 2 an ornamental wreath or band for the head

¹**corporal** /'kawp(ə)rəl/ adj of or affecting the body

²**corporal** n a low-ranking non-commissioned officer in the army or British air force

corporate /'kawp(ə)rət/ adj 1a incorporated b of a company 2 of or formed into a unified body of individuals – ~ly adv

corporation /,kawpə'raysh(ə)n/ n 1 sing or pl in constr the municipal authorities of a town or city 2 a body made up of more than 1 person which is formed and authorized by law to act as a single person with its own legal identity, rights, and duties **3** an association of employers and employees or of members of a profession in a corporate state **4** a potbelly – humor

corps /kaw/ n, pl **corps** /kawz/ **1** sing or pl in constr an army unit usu consisting of 2 or more divisions (organized for a particular purpose) **2** any of various associations of people united for some common purpose

corps de ballet /ˌkaw də 'balay, NAm ba'lay/ n, pl **corps de ballet** /~/ the ensemble of a ballet company

corpse /kawps/ n a dead (human) body

corpuscle /'kawpəsl, -pu-, kaw'pusl/ n **1** a minute particle **2** a living (blood) cell

¹**corral** /kə'rahl, ko-, kaw-, -ral/ n **1** a pen or enclosure for confining livestock **2** an enclosure made with wagons for defence of an encampment

²**corral** v **-ll- 1** to enclose in a corral **2** to arrange (wagons) so as to form a corral

¹**correct** /kə'rekt/ v **1** to alter or adjust so as to counteract some imperfection or failing **2a** to punish (e g a child) with a view to reforming or improving **b** to point out the faults of – ∼**ion** n – ∼**ive** adj, n

²**correct** adj **1** conforming to an approved or conventional standard **2** true, right – ∼**ly** adv – ∼**ness** n

correlate /'korilayt/ v to have a mutual or reciprocal relationship; correspond – **-ation** n – **-ative** adj

correspond /ˌkori'spond/ v **1a** to be in conformity or agreement; suit, match – usu + to or with **b** to be equivalent or parallel to **2** to communicate with a person by exchange of letters – ∼**ence** n

¹**correspondent** /ˌkori'spond(ə)nt/ adj **1** corresponding **2** fitting, conforming USE + with or to

²**correspondent** n **1** one who communicates with another by letter **2** one who has regular commercial relations with another **3** one who contributes news or comment to a publication or radio or television network

corresponding /ˌkori'sponding/ adj **1a** agreeing in some respect (e g kind, degree, position, or function) **b** related, accompanying **2** participating at a distance and by post – ∼**ly** adv

corridor /'koridaw, -də/ n, **1** a passage (e g in a hotel or railway carriage) onto which compartments or rooms open **2** a usu narrow passageway or route: e g **2a** a narrow strip of land through foreign-held territory **3** a strip of land that by geographical characteristics is distinct from its surroundings

corrigendum /ˌkori'jendəm/ n, pl **corrigenda** /-də/ an error in a printed work, shown with its correction on a separate sheet

corroborate /kə'robərayt/ v to support with evidence or authority; make more certain – **-rator** n – **-rative** adj – **-ration** n

corrode /kə'rohd/ v **1** to eat or wear (esp metal) away gradually, esp by chemical action **2** to weaken or destroy (as if) by corrosion **3** to undergo corroding – **-rosion** n – **-rosive** adj – **-rosively** adv

corrugate /'korəgayt, -roo-/ v to shape or become shaped into alternating ridges and grooves; furrow – **-tion** n

¹**corrupt** /kə'rupt/ v **1a** to change from good to bad in morals, manners, or actions; also to influence by bribery **b** to degrade with unsound principles or moral values **2** to alter from the original or correct form or version **3** to become corrupt – ∼**ible** adj – ∼**ibility** n

²**corrupt** adj **1a** morally degenerate and perverted **b** characterized by bribery **2** having been vitiated by mistakes or changes – ∼**ly** adv – ∼**ness** n

corruption /kə'rupsh(ə)n/ n **1** impairment of integrity, virtue, or moral principle **2** decay, decomposition **3** inducement by bribery to do wrong **4** a departure from what is pure or correct

corsair /'kawseə/ n a pirate; esp a privateer of the Barbary coast

¹**corset** /'kawsit/ n a boned supporting undergarment for women, extending from beneath the bust to below the hips, and designed to give shape to the figure; also a similar garment worn by men and women, esp in cases of injury

²**corset** v to restrict closely

cortege /kaw'tayzh, -'teazh/ also **cortège** /kaw'tezh/ n a funeral procession

cortex /'kawteks/ n, pl **cortices** /'kawtiseez/, **cortexes 1** the outer part of the kidney, adrenal gland, a hair, etc; esp the outer layer of grey matter of the brain **2** the layer of tissue between the inner vascular tissue and the outer epidermal tissue of a green plant

coruscate /'korəskayt/ v to sparkle, flash

corvette /kaw'vet/ n **1** a small sailing warship with a flush deck **2** a highly manoeuvrable armed escort ship

¹**cos** /kəz; strong koz/ conj because – used in writing to represent a casual or childish pronunciation

²**cos** /koz/, '**cos** lettuce n a long-leaved variety of lettuce

cosh /kosh/ v or n, chiefly Br (to strike with) a short heavy rod often enclosed in a softer material and used as a hand weapon

cosine /'koh,sien/ n the trigonometric function that for an acute angle in a right-angled triangle is the ratio between the side adjacent to the angle and the hypotenuse

¹**cosmetic** /koz'metik/ n a cosmetic preparation for external use

²**cosmetic** adj of or intended to improve beauty (e g of the hair or complexion); broadly intended to improve the outward appearance – ∼**ian** n

cosmic /'kozmik/ *also* **cosmical** /-kl/ *adj* 1 of the universe in contrast to the earth alone 2 great in extent, intensity, or comprehensiveness – **~ally** *adv*

cosmic 'ray *n* a stream of highly energetic radiation reaching the earth's atmosphere from space – usu pl with sing. meaning

cosmology /koz'moləji/ *n* 1 a theoretical account of the nature of the universe 2 astronomy dealing with the origin, structure, and space-time relationships of the universe

cosmonaut /'kozmə,nawt/ *n* a usu Soviet astronaut

¹cosmopolitan /,kozmə'polit(ə)n/ *adj* 1 having worldwide rather than provincial scope or bearing 2 marked by a sophistication that comes from wide and often international experience 3 composed of people, constituents, or elements from many parts of the world

²cosmopolitan *n* a cosmopolitan person

cosmos /'kozmos/ *n* 1 an orderly universe 2 a complex and orderly system that is complete in itself 3 any of a genus of tropical American composite plants grown for their yellow or red flower heads

cosset /'kosit/ *v* to treat as a pet; pamper

¹cost /kost/ *n* 1a the price paid or charged for sthg **b** the expenditure (e g of effort or sacrifice) made to achieve an object 2 the loss or penalty incurred in gaining sthg 3 *pl* expenses incurred in litigation — **at all costs** regardless of the price or difficulties — **to one's cost** to one's disadvantage or loss

²cost *v* cost, (*vt* 2) costed 1 to require a specified expenditure 2 to require the specified effort, suffering, or loss 3 to cause to pay, suffer, or lose 4 to estimate or set the cost of

'co-,star /koh/ *n* a star who has equal billing with another leading performer in a film or play – **co-star** *v*

costermonger /'kostə,mung·gə/ *n, Br* a seller of articles, esp fruit or vegetables, from a street barrow or stall

costly /'kostli/ *adj* 1 valuable, expensive 2 made at great expense or with considerable sacrifice – **-liness** *n*

¹costume /'kostyoohm, 'kostyoom/ *n* 1 a distinctive fashion in coiffure, jewellery, and apparel of a period, country, class, or group 2 a set of garments suitable for a specified occasion, activity, or season 3 a set of garments belonging to a specific time, place, or character, worn in order to assume a particular role (e g in a play or at a fancy-dress party)

²costume *v* 1 to provide with a costume 2 to design costumes for

³costume *adj* characterized by the use of costumes

¹cosy, *NAm chiefly* **cozy** /'kohzi/ *adj* 1 enjoying or affording warmth and ease; snug 2a marked by the intimacy of the family or a close group **b** self-satisfied, complacent – **cosily** *adv* – **cosiness** *n*

²cosy, *NAm chiefly* **cozy** *n* a covering, esp for a teapot, designed to keep the contents hot

¹cot /kot/ *n* a small house; a cottage – poetic

²cot *n* 1 a lightweight bedstead 2 a small bed with high enclosing sides, esp for a child

cottage /'kotij/ *n* a small house, esp in the country

,cottage 'cheese *n* a soft white bland cheese made from the curds of skimmed milk

,cottage 'pie *n* a shepherd's pie esp made with minced beef

¹cotton /'kot(ə)n/ *n* 1 (a plant producing or grown for) a soft usu white fibrous substance composed of the hairs surrounding the seeds of various tropical plants of the mallow family 2a fabric made of cotton **b** yarn spun from cotton

²cotton *v* to come to understand; catch on – usu + *on* or *onto*; infml

,cotton 'wool *n* raw cotton; *esp* cotton pressed into sheets used esp for lining, cleaning, or as a surgical dressing

cotyledon /,koti'leed(ə)n/ *n* the first leaf or either of the first pair or whorl of leaves developed by the embryo of a seed plant

¹couch /kowch/ *v* 1 to phrase in a specified manner 2 *of an animal* to lie down to sleep; *also* to lie in ambush

²couch *n* 1 a piece of furniture for sitting or lying on 1a with a back and usu armrests **b** with a low back and raised head-end 2 a long upholstered seat with a headrest for patients to lie on during medical examination or psychoanalysis 3 the den of an animal (e g an otter)

'couch ,grass /'kowch, 'koohch/ *n* any of several grasses that spread rapidly by long creeping underground stems and are difficult to eradicate

cougar /'koohgə/ *n, pl* **cougars**, *esp collectively* **cougar** *chiefly NAm* a puma

cough /kof/ *v* 1 to expel air from the lungs suddenly with an explosive noise 2 to make a noise like that of coughing – **cough** *n*

cough up *v* to produce or hand over (esp money or information) unwillingly

could /kəd; *strong* kood/ *verbal auxiliary* 1 *past of* **can** – used in the past, in the past conditional, as an alternative to *can* suggesting less force or certainty, as a polite form in the present, as an alternative to *might* expressing purpose in the past, and as an alternative to *ought* or *should* 2 feel impelled to

council /'kownsl, -sil/ *n sing or pl in constr* an elected or appointed body with administrative, legislative, or advisory powers; *esp* a locally-elected body having power over a parish, district, county, etc

councillor /'kowns(ə)lə, -silə/, *NAm also* **councilor** *n* a member of a council – ~**ship** *n*

¹**counsel** /'kownsl/ *n pl* **counsels,** (4) **counsel 1** advice; consultation **2** thoughts or intentions – chiefly in *keep one's own counsel* **3a** a barrister engaged in the trial of a case in court **b** a lawyer appointed to advise a client

²**counsel** *v* -**ll**- (*NAm* -**l**, -**ll**-), /'kownsl·ing/ to advise

counsellor, *NAm chiefly* **counselor** /'kownsl·ə/ *n* **1** an adviser **2** *NAm* a lawyer; *specif* a counsel

¹**count** /kownt/ *v* **1a** to reckon by units so as to find the total number of units involved – often + *up* **b** to name the numbers in order **c** to include in a tallying and reckoning **2** to include or exclude (as if) by counting **3** to rely *on* or *upon* sby or sthg **4** to have value or significance – ~**able** *adj* — **count on** to look forward to as certain; anticipate

²**count** *n* **1** a total obtained by counting **2a** an allegation in an indictment **b** a specific point under consideration; an issue **3** the total number of individual things in a given unit or sample **4** the calling out of the seconds from 1 to 10 when a boxer has been knocked down during which he must rise or be defeated

³**count** *n* a European nobleman corresponding in rank to a British earl

'**count,down** /-,down/ *n* a continuous counting backwards to zero of the time remaining before an event, esp the launching of a space vehicle

¹**countenance** /'kownt(ə)nəns/ *n* **1** composure of a face; *esp* the face as an indication of mood, emotion, or character

²**countenance** *v* to extend approval or support to – fml

¹**counter** /'kowntə/ *n* **1** a small disc of metal, plastic, etc used in counting or in games **2** sthg of value in bargaining; an asset **3** a level surface (e g a table) over which transactions are conducted or food is served or on which goods are displayed — **over the counter** without a prescription — **under the counter** by surreptitious means; in an illicit and private manner

²**counter** *v* **1** to nullify the effects of; offset **2** to meet attacks or arguments with defensive or retaliatory steps

³**counter** *adv* in an opposite, contrary, or wrong direction

⁴**counter** *n* **1** the contrary, opposite **2** an overhanging stern of a vessel **3a** the blow resulting from (a) making of an attack while parrying (e g in boxing or fencing) **b** an agency or force that offsets; a check

⁵**counter** *adj* **1** marked by or tending towards an opposite direction or effect **2** showing opposition, hostility, or antipathy

counteract /,kowntə'rakt/ *v* to lessen or neutralize the usu ill effects of by an opposing action – ~**ion** *n*

,**counterat'tack** /-ə'tak/ *v* to make an attack (against) in reply to an enemy's attack – **counterattack** *n*

'**counter,balance** /-,baləns/ *v* to oppose or balance with an equal weight or force – **counterbalance** *n*

,**counter'clockwise** /-'klokwiez/ *adj or adv,* chiefly *NAm* anticlockwise

,**counter'espionage** /-'espi·ənahzh/ *n* espionage directed towards detecting and thwarting enemy espionage

'**counterfeit** /'kowntəfit, -feet/ *v* to imitate or copy (sthg) closely, esp with intent to deceive or defraud – ~**er** *n*

²**counterfeit** *adj* **1** made in imitation of sthg else with intent to deceive or defraud **2** insincere, feigned

³**counterfeit** *n* a forgery

'**counter,foil** /-,foyl/ *n* a detachable part of a cheque, ticket, etc usu kept as a record or receipt

,**counter'telligence** /-in'telij(ə)ns/ *n* organized activity of an intelligence service designed to block an enemy's sources of information

countermand /,kowntə'mahnd/ /,---/ *v* **1** to revoke (a command) by a contrary order **2** to order back (e g troops) by a superseding contrary order

'**counter,measure** /-,mezhə/ *n* a measure designed to counter another action or state of affairs

,**counterof'fensive** /-ə'fensiv/ *n* a military offensive undertaken from a previously defensive position

'**counter,pane** /-,payn/ *n* a bedspread

'**counter,part** /-,paht/ *n* **1** sthg that completes; a complement **2** one having the same function or characteristics as another; an equivalent, duplicate

¹**counter,point** /-,poynt/ *n* **1a** one or more independent melodies added above or below a given melody **b** the combination of 2 or more independent melodies into a single harmonic texture **2** (use of) contrast or interplay of elements in a work of art

²**counterpoint** *v* to set off or emphasize by contrast or juxtaposition

,**counter,revo'lution** /-,revə'loohsh(ə)n/ *n* a revolution directed towards overthrowing the system established by a previous revolution – ~**ary** *n, adj*

'**counter,sign** /-,sien/ *n* a password or secret signal given by one wishing to pass a guard

²**countersign** *v* to add one's signature to (a document) as a witness of another signature

'**counter,tenor** /-,tenə/ *n* (a person with) an adult male singing voice higher than tenor

countess /'kowntis, -tes/ *n* **1** the wife or widow of an earl or count **2** a woman having in her own right the rank of an earl or count

countinghouse /'kownting,hows/ *n* a building, room, or office used for keeping account books and transacting business

countless /-lis/ *adj* too numerous to be counted; innumerable

countrified *also* **countryfied** /'kuntrified/ *adj* 1 rural, rustic 2 unsophisticated

country /'kuntri/ *n* 1 an indefinite usu extended expanse of land; a region 2a the land of a person's birth, residence, or citizenship b a political state or nation or its territory 3 *sing or pl in constr* 3a *the* populace b *the* electorate 4 rural as opposed to urban areas

country 'dance *n* any of various native or folk dances for several pairs of dancers

'countryman /-mən/, *fem* **'country,woman** *n* 1 a compatriot 2 one living in the country or having country ways

'country ,music *n* music derived from or imitating the folk style of the southern USA or the Western cowboy

,country 'seat *n* a mansion or estate in the country that is the hereditary property of 1 family

'country,side /-,sied/ *n* a rural area

¹county /'kownti/ *n* any of the territorial divisions of Britain and Ireland constituting the chief units for administrative, judicial, and political purposes; *also* a local government unit in various countries (e g the USA)

²county *adj* characteristic of or belonging to the English landed gentry

,county 'court *n*, *often cap 1st C* a local civil court in England which is presided over by a judge and deals with relatively minor claims

coup /kooh/ *n* 1 a brilliant, sudden, and usu highly successful stroke or act 2 **coup, coup d'état** an overthrowing of a government, esp by a small group

coupé /'koohpay; *sense 2 also* koohp/, **coupe** /koohp/ *n* 1 a 4-wheeled horse-drawn carriage for 2 passengers with an outside seat for the driver 2 a closed 2-door motor car for usu 2 people

¹couple /'kupl/ *v* **coupling** /'kupling/ 1 to unite or link 2 to fasten together; connect 3 to copulate

²couple *n* 1 *sing or pl in constr* 2 people paired together; *esp* a married or engaged couple 2a 2 things considered together; a pair b an indefinite small number; a few – *infml*

³couple *adj* two

couplet /'kuplit/ *n* a unit of 2 successive, usu rhyming, lines of verse

coupling /'kupling/ *n* a device that serves to connect the ends of adjacent parts or objects

coupon /'koohpon/ *n* 1 a detachable ticket or certificate that entitles the holder to sthg 2 a voucher given with a purchase that can be

exchanged for goods 3 a part of a printed advertisement to be cut off for use as an order form or enquiry form 4 a printed entry form for a competition, esp the football pools

courage /'kurij/ *n* mental or moral strength to confront danger, fear, etc; bravery – **-ageous** *adj* – **-ageously** *adv*

courgette /kaw'zhet, kooə-/ *n* (the plant that bears) a variety of small vegetable marrow cooked and eaten as a vegetable

courier /'koori·ə/ *n* 1a a member of a diplomatic service who carries state or embassy papers b one who carries secret information, contraband, etc 2 a tourist guide employed by a travel agency

¹course /kaws/ *n* 1 the moving in a path from point to point 2 the path over which sthg moves: e g 2a a racecourse b the direction of travel, usu measured as a clockwise angle from north c a golf course 3a usual procedure or normal action b progression through a series of acts or events or a development or period 4a a series of educational activities relating to a subject, esp when constituting a curriculum b a particular medical treatment administered over a designated period 5 a part of a meal served at one time 6 a continuous horizontal layer of brick or masonry throughout a wall — **of course** 1 as might be expected; naturally 2 admittedly; to be sure

²course *v* 1 to hunt or pursue (e g hares) with dogs that follow by sight 2 *of a liquid* to run or pass rapidly (as if) along an indicated path

¹court /kawt/ *n* 1a the residence or establishment of a dignitary, esp a sovereign b *sing or pl in constr* the sovereign and his officers and advisers who are the governing power c a reception held by a sovereign 2a a manor house or large building (e g a block of flats) surrounded by usu enclosed grounds – archaic except in proper names b a space enclosed wholly or partly by a building c (a division of) a rectangular space walled or marked off for playing lawn tennis, squash, basketball, etc d a yard surrounded by houses, with only 1 opening onto a street 3a (a session of) an official assembly for the transaction of judicial business b *sing or pl in constr* judicial officers in session

²court *v* 1 to act so as to invite or provoke 2a to seek the affections of; woo b *of a man and woman* to be involved in a relationship that may lead to marriage c *of an animal* to perform actions to attract (a mate) 3 to seek to win the favour of

courteous /'kuhtyəs, -ti·əs, *also* 'kaw-/ *adj* showing respect and consideration for others – ~**ly** *adv* – ~**ness** *n*

courtesan /,kawti'zan, '--,-/ *n* a prostitute with a courtly, wealthy, or upper-class clientele

¹courtesy /'kuhtəsi/ *n* courteous behaviour; a courteous act — **by courtesy of** through the kindness, generosity, or permission granted by (a person or organization)

²**courtesy** /adj granted, provided, or performed by way of courtesy

courtier /'kawtyə/ n one in attendance at a royal court

courtly /'kawtli/ adj of a quality befitting the court; elegant, refined – **-liness** n

¹**court-'martial** n pl **courts-martial** also **court-martials** (a trial by) a court of commissioned officers that tries members of the armed forces

²**court-martial** v **-ll-** (NAm **-l-**, **-ll-**) to try by court-martial

'**court,ship** /-,ship/ n the act, process, or period of courting

'**court,yard** /-,yahd/ n an open court or enclosure adjacent to a building

cousin /'kuzn/ n **1** a child of one's uncle or aunt **2** a relative descended from one's grandparent or more remote ancestor in a different line

couture /,kooh'tyooə/ n the business of designing and making fashionable women's clothing – **couturier** n

¹**cove** /kohv/ n **1** a small sheltered area; esp an inlet or bay **2** a concave moulding, esp at the point where a wall meets a ceiling or floor

²**cove** n, Br a man, fellow – slang; no longer in vogue

coven /'kuvn, 'kovn/ n sing or pl in constr an assembly or band of witches

covenant /'kuv(ə)nant, 'kov-/ n **1** a solemn agreement **2** a written promise

Coventry /'kov(ə)ntri; also 'ku-/ n a state of social exclusion – chiefly in send to Coventry

¹**cover** /'kuvə/ v **1a** to guard from attack **b** to have within the range of one's guns **c** to insure **d** to make sufficient provision for (a demand or charge) by means of a reserve or deposit **2a** to hide from sight or knowledge; conceal – usu + up **b** to lie or spread over; envelop **3** to lay or spread sthg over **4** to extend thickly or conspicuously over the surface of **5** to include, consider, or take in **6a** to have as one's territory or field of activity **b** to report news about **7** to pass over; traverse **8** to conceal sthg illicit, blameworthy, or embarrassing from notice – usu + up **9** to act as a substitute or replacement during an absence – chiefly in cover for someone — **cover one's tracks** to conceal evidence of one's past actions in order to elude pursuit or investigation — **cover the ground 1** to cover a distance with adequate speed **2** to deal with an assignment or examine a subject thoroughly

²**cover** n **1a** natural shelter for an animal **b(1)** a position affording shelter from attack **b(2)** (the protection offered by) a force supporting a military operation **2** sthg that is placed over or above another thing **e.g 2a** a lid, top **b** (the front or back part of) a binding or jacket of a book **c** a cloth (e g a blanket) used on a bed **d** sthg (e g vegetation or snow) that covers the ground **e** the extent to which clouds obscure the sky **3a** sthg that conceals or obscures **b** a masking device; a pretext **4** an envelope or wrapper for postal use **5a** cover-point, extra cover, or a cricket fielding position between them **b** pl the fielding positions in cricket that lie between point and mid-off

coverage /'kuv(ə)rij/ n **1** the act or fact of covering **2** inclusion within the scope of discussion or reporting **3** the total range of risks covered by the terms of an insurance contract

'**cover ,charge** n a charge (e g for service) made by a restaurant or nightclub in addition to the charge for food and drink

¹**covering** /'kuv(ə)ring/ n sthg that covers or conceals

²**covering** adj containing an explanation of an accompanying item

'**coverlet** /-lit/ n a bedspread

'**cover ,note** n, Br a provisional insurance document providing cover between acceptance of a risk and issue of a full policy

'**cover-,point** n a fielding position in cricket further from the batsman than point and situated between mid-off and point

¹**covert** /'kuvət, -vuht, 'ko-/ adj not openly shown; secret – **~ly** adv

²**covert** n **1** a hiding place; a shelter **2** a thicket affording cover for game

covet /'kovit, 'ku-/ v to desire what belongs to another

covetous /'kovitas, 'ku-/ adj showing an inordinate desire for esp another's wealth or possessions – **~ly** adv – **~ness** n

¹**cow** /kow/ n **1** the mature female of cattle or of any animal the male of which is called bull **2** a domestic bovine animal regardless of sex or age **3** a woman; esp one who is unpleasant — **till the cows come home** forever

²**cow** v to intimidate with threats or a show of strength

coward /'kowəd/ n one who lacks courage or resolve – **~ly** adj – **~ice** n – **~liness** n

'**cow,bell** /-,bel/ n a bell hung round the neck of a cow

'**cow,boy** /-,boy/, fem '**cow,girl** n **1** a cattle ranch hand in N America **2** one who employs irregular or unscrupulous methods, esp in business

cower /'kowə/ v to crouch down or shrink away (e g in fear) from sthg menacing

cowl /kowl/ n **1a** a hood or long hooded cloak, esp of a monk **b** a draped neckline on a garment resembling a folded-down hood **2** a chimney covering designed to improve ventilation

cowling /'kowling/ n a removable metal covering over an engine, esp in an aircraft

'**cow,pat** /-,pat/ n a small heap of cow dung

¹**cow,pox** /-,poks/ *n* a mild disease of the cow that when communicated to humans gives protection against smallpox

cowrie, cowry /'kowri/ a rounded often glossy and brightly coloured sea shell with a long thin opening

¹**cow,slip** /-,slip/ *n* a common European plant of the primrose family with fragrant yellow or purplish flowers

cox /koks/ *v* to steer esp a rowing boat – **cox** *n*

coxcomb /'koks,kohm/ *n* a conceited foolish person; a fop

coy /koy/ *adj* **1a** (affectedly) shy **b** provocatively playful or coquettish **2** showing reluctance to make a definite commitment or face unpleasant facts – ~**ly** *adv* – ~**ness** *n*

coyote /'koyoht, -'-, -'ohti, kie'ohti/ *n pl* **coyotes**, *esp collectively* **coyote** a small N American wolf

coypu /'koyp(y)ooh/ *n pl* **coypus**, *esp collectively* **coypu** a S American aquatic rodent with webbed feet now commonly found in E Anglia

¹**crab** /krab/ *n* any of numerous chiefly marine crustaceans usu with the front pair of limbs modified as grasping pincers and a short broad flattened carapace; *also* the flesh of this cooked and eaten as food

²**crab** *v* -**bb**- to (cause to) move sideways or in an indirect or diagonal manner

³**crab** *v* -**bb**- **1** to make sullen; sour **2** to carp, grouse

⁴**crab** *n* an ill-tempered person – *infml*

'**crab ,apple** /a tree that bears) a small usu wild sour apple

crabbed /'krabid/ *adj* **1** morose, peevish **2** difficult to read or understand – ~**ly** *adv* – ~**ness** *n*

'**crab,wise** /-,wiez/ *adv* **1** sideways **2** in a sidling or cautiously indirect manner

¹**crack** /krak/ *v* **1** to make a sudden sharp explosive noise **2** to break or split (apart) esp so that fissures appear **3** to lose control or effectiveness under pressure – often – *up* **4a** *esp of hydrocarbons* to break up into simpler chemical compounds when heated, usu with a catalyst **b** to produce (e g petrol) by cracking **5** to tell (a joke) **6a** to puzzle out and expose, solve, or reveal the mystery of **b** to break into **7** to open (e g a can or bottle) for drinking – *infml*

²**crack** *n* **1** a sudden sharp loud noise **2** a narrow break or opening; a chink, fissure **3** a sharp resounding blow **4** a witty remark; a quip – *infml* **5** an attempt, try *at* – *infml*

³**crack** *adj* of superior quality or ability

crack down *v* to take regulatory or disciplinary action – usu + *on*

cracked *adj* **1** marked by harshness, dissonance, or failure to sustain a tone **2** mentally disordered; crazy – *infml*

cracker /'krakə/ *n* **1** a brightly coloured paper and cardboard tube that makes an explosive crack when pulled sharply apart and usu contains a toy,

paper hat, or other party item **2** *pl* a tool for cracking nuts **3** a thin often savoury biscuit **4** *Br* an outstandingly attractive girl or woman – *infml*

'**crackers** *adj, chiefly Br* mad, crazy – *infml*

¹**crackle** /'krakl/ *v* **crackling** /'krakling, 'krakl·ing/ to crush or crack with a snapping sound

²**crackle** *n* **1** the noise of repeated small cracks or reports **2** a network of fine cracks on an otherwise smooth surface

crackling /'krakling/ *n* the crisp skin of roast meat, esp pork

'**crack,pot** /-,pot/ *n* sby with eccentric ideas; a crank – *infml*

¹**cradle** /'kraydl/ *n* **1a** a baby's bed or cot, usu on rockers **b** a framework of wood or metal used as a support, scaffold, etc **2a** the earliest period of life; infancy **b** a place of origin

²**cradle** *v* **cradling** /'kraydling/ **1** to place or keep (as if) in a cradle **2** to shelter or hold protectively

¹**craft** /krahft/ *n pl* **crafts**, (5) **craft** *also* **crafts 1** skill in planning, making, or executing; dexterity – often in combination **2** an activity or trade requiring manual dexterity or artistic skill; *broadly* a trade, profession **3** skill in deceiving to gain an end **4a** a (small) boat **b** an aircraft **c** a spacecraft

²**craft** *v* to make (as if) using skill and dexterity

'**craftsman** /-mən/, *fem* '**crafts,woman** *n* **1** a workman who practises a skilled trade or handicraft **2** one who displays a high degree of manual dexterity or artistic skill – ~**ship** *n*

crafty /'krahfti/ *adj* showing subtlety and guile – **craftily** *adv* – **craftiness** *n*

crag /krag/ *n* a steep rugged rock or cliff

craggy /'kragi/ *adj* rough, rugged

cram /kram/ *v* -**mm**- **1** to pack tight; jam **2** to thrust forcefully **3** to study hastily and intensively for an examination **4** to eat greedily or until uncomfortably full – *infml*

¹**cramp** /kramp/ *n* **1** a painful involuntary spasmodic contraction of a muscle **2** *pl* severe abdominal pain

²**cramp** *n* **1** a usu metal device bent at the ends and used to hold timbers or blocks of stone together **2** a clamp

³**cramp** *v* **1a** to confine, restrain **b** to restrain from free expression – esp in *cramp someone's style* **2** to fasten or hold with a clamp

crampon /'krampon/ *n* a metal frame with downward- and forward-pointing spikes that is fixed to the sole of a boot for climbing slopes of ice or hard snow

cranberry /'kranb(ə)ri/ *n* any of various plants of the heath family; *also* the red acid berry of such plants used in making sauces and jellies

¹**crane** /krayn/ n 1 any of a family of tall wading birds 2 a machine for moving heavy weights by means of a projecting swinging arm or a hoisting apparatus supported on an overhead track

²**crane** v to stretch one's neck, esp in order to see better

'**crane ,fly** n any of numerous long-legged slender two-winged flies that resemble large mosquitoes but do not bite

cranium /'kraynyəm, -ni·əm/ n, pl **craniums, crania** /-nyə, -ni·ə/ the skull; specif the part that encloses the brain – **ial** adj – **ially** adv

¹**crank** /krangk/ n 1 a part of an axle or shaft bent at right angles by which reciprocating motion is changed into circular motion or vice versa 2 an eccentric person; also one who is excessively enthusiastic or fastidious about sthg

²**crank** v 1 to move or operate (as if) by a crank 2 to start by use of a crank – often + up

'**crank,shaft** /-,shahft/ n a shaft driven by or driving a crank

cranky /'krangki/ adj 1 of machinery working erratically; unpredictable 2 eccentric, mad

cranny /'krani/ n a small crack or slit; a chink – **-nied** adj

crap /krap/ n 1a excrement b an act of defecation 2 nonsense, rubbish – slang; sometimes used as an interjection USE (1) vulg

¹**crash** /krash/ v 1a to break violently and noisily; smash b to damage (an aircraft) in landing c to damage (a vehicle) by collision 2a to make a crashing noise b to force one's way with loud crashing noises 3 to enter without invitation or payment – infml 4 to spend the night in a (make-shift) place; go to sleep – sometimes + out; slang 5 esp of a computer system or program to become (suddenly) completely inoperative

²**crash** n 1 a loud noise (e g of things smashing) 2 a breaking to pieces (as if) by collision; also an instance of crashing 3 a sudden decline or failure (e g of a business)

³**crash** adj designed to achieve an intended result in the shortest possible time

'**crash ,helmet** n a helmet that is worn (e g by motorcyclists) to protect the head in the event of an accident

crass /kras/ adj 1 insensitive, coarse 2 deplorably stupid – **-ly** adv – **-ness** n

¹**crate** /krayt/ n a usu wooden framework or box for holding goods, esp during transit

²**crate** v to pack in a crate

crater /'kraytə/ n 1 a hole in the ground made (as if) by an explosion 2 a jar or vase with a wide mouth used in classical antiquity for mixing wine and water

cravat /krə'vat/ n a decorative band or scarf worn round the neck, esp by men

crave /krayv/ v 1 to have a strong or urgent desire for 2 to ask for earnestly; beg – fml – **-ving** n

craven /'krayv(ə)n/ adj completely lacking in courage; cowardly – **cravenness** n – **cravenly** adv

¹**crawl** /krawl/ v 1 to move slowly in a prone position (as if) without the use of limbs 2 to move or progress slowly or laboriously 3 to be alive or swarming (as if) with creeping things 4 to behave in a servile manner – infml

²**crawl** n 1a crawling b slow or laborious motion 2 the fastest swimming stroke, executed lying on the front and consisting of alternating overarm strokes combined with kicks with the legs

crayfish /'kray,fish/ n any of numerous usu fresh-water crustaceans resembling the lobster but usu much smaller

crayon /'krayon, -ən/ v or n (to draw or colour with) a stick of coloured chalk or wax used for writing or drawing

¹**craze** /krayz/ v 1 to produce minute cracks on the surface or glaze of 2 to make (as if) insane

²**craze** n 1 an exaggerated and often short-lived enthusiasm; a fad 2 fine cracks in a surface or coating of glaze, enamel, etc

crazy /'krayzi/ adj 1 mad, insane 2 impractical, eccentric 3 extremely enthusiastic about; very fond – **-zily** adv – **-ziness** n — **like crazy** to an extreme degree – infml

,**crazy 'paving** n a paved surface made up of irregularly shaped paving stones

creak /kreek/ v or n (to make) a prolonged grating or squeaking noise

¹**cream** /kreem/ n 1 the yellowish part of milk that forms a surface layer when milk is allowed to stand 2a a food (e g a sauce or cake filling) pre-pared with or resembling cream in consistency, richness, etc b basic, chocolate, etc filled with (a soft preparation resembling) whipped cream c sthg with the consistency of thick cream; esp a usu emulsified medicinal or cosmetic preparation 3 the choicest part 4 a pale yellowish white colour – **creamy** adj – **-iness** n

²**cream** v 1 to take away (the choicest part) – usu + off 2 to break into a creamy froth 3 to form a surface layer of or like cream

,**cream 'cheese** n a mild white soft unripened cheese made from whole milk enriched with cream

,**cream of 'tartar** /'tahtə/ n a white powder used esp in baking powder

¹**crease** /krees/ n 1 a line or mark made (as if) by folding a pliable substance 2a an area surround-ing the goal in lacrosse, hockey, etc into which an attacking player may not precede the ball or puck b the bowling crease, popping crease, or return crease of a cricket pitch

²**crease** v 1 to make a crease in or on; wrinkle 2 chiefly Br to cause much amusement to – often + up

create /kri'ayt/ *v* 1 to bring into existence 2a to invest with a new form, office, or rank b to produce, cause 3 to design, invent 4 to make a loud fuss about sthg – *infml* – **-tively** *adv* – **-tiveness** *n* – **-tivity** *n*

creation /kri'aysh(ə)n/ *n* 1 *often cap* the act of bringing the world into ordered existence 2 sthg created: e g 2a creatures singly or collectively b an original work of art c a product of some minor art or craft (e g dressmaking or cookery) showing unusual flair or imagination – often *derog* – **-tive** *adj*

creator /kri'aytə/ *n* a person who creates, usu by bringing sthg new or original into being; *esp, cap* God

creature /'kreechə/ *n* 1 a lower animal 2a an animate being; *esp* a non-human one b a human being; a person 3 one who is the servile dependant or tool of another

crèche /kresh/ *n* 1 a representation of the Nativity scene 2 *chiefly Br* a centre where children under school age are looked after while their parents are at work

credence /'kreedəns/ *n* acceptance of sthg as true or real

credible /'kredəbl/ *adj* offering reasonable grounds for belief – **-ibility** *n* – **-bly** *adv*

¹**credit** /'kredit/ *n* 1a the balance in a person's favour in an account b a sum loaned by a bank to be repaid with interest c time given for payment for goods or services provided but not immediately paid for 2 credence 3 influence derived from enjoying the confidence of others; standing 4 a source of honour or repute 5 acknowledgment, approval 6 an acknowledgment of a contributor by name that appears at the beginning or end of a film or television programme 7a recognition that a student has fulfilled a course requirement b the passing of an examination at a level well above the minimum though not with distinction — **on credit** with the cost charged to one's account and paid later

²**credit** *v* 1 to believe 2 to place to the credit of 3 to ascribe some usu favourable characteristic to – + **with**

creditable /'kreditəbl/ *adj* 1 worthy of esteem or praise 2 *NAm* capable of being attributed *to* – **-bly** *adv*

credit card *n* a card provided by a bank, agency, or business allowing the holder to obtain goods and services on credit

creditor /'kreditə/ *n* one to whom a debt is owed

credo /'kreedoh, 'kray-/ *n, pl* **credos** 1 a creed 2 *cap* a musical setting of the creed in a sung mass

credulity /kri'dyoohləti/ *n* undue willingness to believe; gullibility – **-lous** *adj* – **-lously** *adv* – **-lousness** *n*

creed /kreed/ *n* 1 a brief statement of religious belief; *esp* such a statement said or sung as part of Christian worship 2 a set of fundamental beliefs

creek /kreek/ *n* 1 *chiefly Br* a small narrow inlet of a lake, sea, etc 2 *chiefly NAm & Austr* a brook — **up the creek 1** in trouble — *infml* **2** wrong, mistaken — *infml*

¹**creep** /kreep/ *v* **crept** /krept/ **1** to move along with the body prone and close to the ground **2a** to go very slowly b to go timidly or cautiously so as to escape notice **3a** to crawl b *of a plant* to spread or grow over a surface by clinging with tendrils, roots, etc or rooting at intervals

²**creep** *n* **1** a movement of or like creeping **2** *Br* an obnoxious or ingratiatingly servile person – *infml*

creeper /'kreepə/ *n* **1** a creeping plant **2** a bird (e g a tree creeper) that creeps about on trees or bushes

creepy /'kreepi/ *adj* producing a sensation of shivery apprehension – **creepily** *adv* – **creepiness** *n*

creepy-'crawly /'krawli/ *n, Br* a small creeping or scuttling creature (e g a spider) – *infml*

cremate /kri'mayt/ *v* to reduce (a dead body) to ashes by burning – **cremation** *n*

crematorium /,kremə'tawri·əm/ *n, pl* **crematoriums, crematoria** /-ri·ə/ a place where cremation is carried out

crème de 'menthe /də 'mont (*Fr* də mã:t)/ *n* a sweet green or white mint-flavoured liqueur

Creole *n* **1** a person of European descent in the W Indies or Spanish America **2** a person of mixed French or Spanish and Negro descent **3** *not cap* a language based on 2 or more languages that serves as the native language of its speakers

creosote /'kree·ə,soht/ *n* a brownish oily liquid obtained from tar and used esp as a wood preservative – **creosote** *v*

crepe, crêpe /krayp/ *n* **1** a light crinkled fabric **2** a thin pancake

crepe 'paper *n* thin paper with a crinkled or puckered texture

crept /krept/ *past of* **creep**

crepuscular /kri'puskyoolə/ *adj* of or resembling twilight

¹**crescendo** /krə'shendoh/ *n, pl* **crescendos, crescendoes** a gradual increase; *esp* a gradual increase in volume in a musical passage

²**crescendo** *adv or adj* with an increase in volume – used in music

crescent /'krez(ə)nt/ *n* **1** the figure of the moon at any stage between new moon and first quarter and last quarter and the succeeding new moon **2** sthg shaped like a crescent and consisting of a concave and a convex curve

cress /kres/ *n* any of numerous plants of the mustard family that have mildly pungent leaves and are used in salads and as a garnish

crest /krest/ *n* **1a** a showy tuft or projection on the head of an animal, esp a bird **b** the plume, emblem, etc worn on a knight's helmet **c** coat of arms – not used technically in heraldry **2** the ridge or top, esp of a wave, roof, or mountain **3** *the* climax, culmination – ~**ed** *adj*

crestfallen /'krest,fawlən/ *adj* disheartened, dejected

cretin /'kretin/ *n* sby physically stunted and mentally retarded as the result of a glandular deficiency; *broadly* an imbecile, idiot

crevasse /krə'vas/ *n* a deep fissure, esp in a glacier

crevice /'krevis/ *n* a narrow opening resulting from a split or crack

¹**crew** /krooh/ *chiefly Br past of* **crow**

²**crew** *n sing or pl in constr* **1** a company of men working on 1 job or under 1 foreman **2a** the personnel of a ship or boat (excluding the captain and officers) **b** the people who man an aircraft in flight **3** a number of people temporarily associated – infml

'**crew ,cut** *n* a very short bristly haircut, esp for a man

¹**crib** /krib/ *n* **1** a manger for feeding animals **2** a cradle **3** cribbage **4** a literal translation; *esp* one used surreptitiously by students

²**crib** *v* **-bb-** to pilfer, steal; *esp* to copy from the work of another

cribbage /'kribij/ *n* a card game for 2 to 4 players each attempting to form various counting combinations of cards

¹**crick** /krik/ *n* a painful spasmodic condition of the muscles of the neck, back, etc

²**crick** *v* to cause a crick in

¹**cricket** /'krikit/ *n* a leaping insect noted for the chirping sounds produced by the male

²**cricket** *n* a game played with a bat and ball on a large field with 2 wickets near its centre by 2 sides of 11 players each – ~**er** *n* — **not cricket** against the dictates of fair play; not honourable

crime /kriem/ *n* **1** (a) violation of law **2** a grave offence, esp against morality **3** criminal activity **4** sthg deplorable, foolish, or disgraceful – infml

¹**criminal** /'kriminl/ *adj* **1** involving or being a crime **2** relating to crime or its punishment **3** guilty of crime **4** disgraceful, deplorable – infml – ~**ly** *adv*

²**criminal** *n* one who has committed or been convicted of a crime

criminology /,krimi'noləji/ *n* the study of crime, criminals, and penal treatment – **-gist** *n*

crimp /krimp/ *v* **1** to make wavy, or curly **2** to pinch or press together in order to seal or join

crimson /'krimz(ə)n/ *adj or n* (a) deep purplish red

cringe /krinj/ *v* **1** to shrink or wince, esp in fear or servility **2** to behave with fawning self-abasement

¹**crinkle** /'kringkl/ *v* **crinkling** /'kringkling/ to wrinkle

²**crinkle** *n* a wrinkle – **-kly** *adj*

crinoline /'krinəlin/ *n* (a padded or hooped petticoat supporting) a full skirt as worn by women in the 19th c

¹**cripple** /'kripl/ *n* a lame or partly disabled person or animal

²**cripple** *v* **crippling** /'kripling/ **1** to make a cripple; lame **2** to deprive of strength, efficiency, wholeness, or capability for service

crisis /'kriesis/ *n, pl* **crises** /-seez/ **1** the turning point for better or worse in an acute disease (e g pneumonia) **2** an unstable or crucial time or situation; *esp* a turning point

¹**crisp** /krisp/ *adj* **1a** easily crumbled; brittle **b** desirably firm and fresh **c** newly made or prepared **2** sharp, clean-cut, and clear **3** decisive, sharp **4** *of weather* briskly cold; fresh; *esp* frosty – ~**ly** *adv* – ~**ness** *n*

²**crisp** *n, chiefly Br* a thin slice of (flavoured or salted) fried potato, usu eaten cold

¹**crisscross** /'kris,kros/ *adj or n* (marked or characterized by) crisscrossing or a crisscrossed pattern

²**crisscross** *v* **1** to mark with intersecting lines **2** to pass back and forth through or over

criterion /krie'tiəri·ən/ *n, pl* **criteria** /-ri·ə/ *also* **criterions** a standard on which a judgment or decision may be based

critic /'kritik/ *n* **1** one who evaluates works of art, literature, or music, esp as a profession **2** one who tends to judge harshly or to be over-critical of minor faults

critical /'kritikl/ *adj* **1a** inclined to criticize severely and unfavourably **b** involving careful judgment or judicious evaluation **2a** of a measurement, point, etc at which some phenomenon undergoes a marked change **b** crucial, decisive **c** being in or approaching a state of crisis **3** *of a nuclear reactor* sustaining an energy-producing chain reaction – ~**ly** *adv*

criticism /'kriti,siz(ə)m/ *n* **1** criticizing, usu unfavourably **2** the art or act of analysing and evaluating esp the fine arts, literature, or literary documents

critic·ize, -ise /'kriti,siez/ *v* **1** to judge the merits or faults of **2** to stress the faults of

critique /kri'teek/ *n* a critical estimate or discussion (e g an article or essay)

¹**croak** /krohk/ *v* **1** to utter (gloomily) in a hoarse raucous voice **2** to die – slang

²**croak** *n* a deep hoarse cry characteristic of a frog or toad

¹**crochet** /'krohshay/ *n* crocheted work

²**crochet** *v* to form (e g a garment or design) by drawing a single continuous yarn or thread into a pattern of interlocked loops using a hooked needle

¹**crock** /krok/ n 1 a thick earthenware pot or jar 2 a piece of broken earthenware used esp to cover the bottom of a flowerpot

²**crock** n 1 an old (broken-down) vehicle 2 an (elderly) disabled person

crockery /'krokəri/ n earthenware or china tableware, esp for everyday domestic use

crocodile /'krokədiel/ n 1 any of several tropical or subtropical large voracious thick-skinned long-bodied aquatic reptiles 2 (leather prepared from) the skin of a crocodile 3 a line of people (e g schoolchildren) walking in pairs

'**crocodile ,tears** n pl false or affected tears; hypocritical sorrow

crocus /'krohkəs/ n, pl **crocuses** any of a large genus of usu early-flowering plants of the iris family bearing a single usu brightly-coloured long-tubed flower

croft /kroft/ n a small farm on often poor land, esp in Scotland, worked by a tenant – ~**er** n

croissant /'kwahsong (Fr krwas̃)/ n a usu flaky rich crescent-shaped roll of bread or yeast-leavened pastry

crone /krohn/ n a withered old woman

crony /'krohni/ n a close friend, esp of long standing; a chum – infml; often derog

crook /krook/ n 1 a shepherd's staff 2 a bend, curve 3 a person given to criminal practices; a thief, swindler – infml

crooked /'krookid/ adj 1 having a crook or curve; bent 2 not morally straightforward; dishonest – ~**ly** adv – ~**ness** n

croon /kroohn/ v to sing usu sentimental popular songs in a low or soft voice

¹**crop** /krop/ n 1 (the stock or handle of) a riding whip 2 a pouched enlargement of the gullet of many birds in which food is stored and prepared for digestion 3 a short haircut 4 (the total production of) a plant or animal product that can be grown and harvested extensively

²**crop** v -pp- 1a to harvest b to cut short; trim 2 to grow as or to cause (land) to bear a crop

cropper /'kropə/ n 1 a severe fall 2 a sudden or complete disaster *USE* chiefly in *come a cropper*; infml

crop up v to happen or appear unexpectedly or casually – infml

croquet /'krohkay/ n a game in which wooden balls are driven by mallets through a series of hoops set out on a lawn

croquette /kroh'ket/ n a small (rounded) piece of minced meat, vegetable, etc coated with egg and breadcrumbs and fried in deep fat

¹**cross** /kros/ n 1a an upright stake with a transverse beam used, esp by the ancient Romans, for execution b *often cap* the cross on which Jesus was crucified; *also* the Crucifixion 2 an affliction, trial 3 a design of an upright bar intersected by a horizontal one used esp as a Christian emblem 4 a

monument surmounted by a cross 5 a mark formed by 2 intersecting lines crossing at their midpoints that is used as a signature, to mark a position, to indicate that sthg is incorrect, or to indicate a kiss in a letter 6 sby who or sthg that combines characteristics of 2 different types or individuals 7 a hook delivered over the opponent's lead in boxing 8 crossing the ball in soccer — **on the cross** on the bias; diagonally

²**cross** v 1 to make the sign of the cross on or over 2a to intersect b to move, pass, or extend across sthg – usu + *over* 3 to run counter to; oppose 4 to go across 5 to draw 2 parallel lines across (a cheque) so that it can only be paid directly into a bank account 6 to kick or pass (the ball) across the field in soccer, specif from the wing into the goal area 7 of letters, travellers, etc to meet and pass 8 to interbreed, hybridize — **cross the floor** *of a member of parliament* to transfer allegiance to the opposing party — **cross swords** to come into conflict — **cross one's mind** to occur to one

³**cross** adj 1 lying or moving across 2 mutually opposed 3 involving mutual interchange; reciprocal 4a irritable, grumpy b angry, annoyed 5 crossbred, hybrid – ~**ly** adv – ~**ness** n

'**cross,bar** /-,bah/ n a transverse bar (e g between goalposts)

crossbow /'kros,boh/ n a short bow mounted crosswise near the end of a wooden stock and used to fire bolts and stones

'**cross,breed** v '**cross,bred** to hybridize or cross (esp 2 varieties or breeds of the same species) – **crossbreed** n

,**cross-'check** v to check (information) for validity or accuracy by reference to more than 1 source

¹,**cross-'country** adj proceeding over countryside and not by roads – **cross-country** adv

²,**cross-'country** n cross-country running, horse riding, etc

'**cross,current** /-,kurənt/ n a conflicting tendency – usu pl

,**cross-ex'amine** v to question closely (esp a witness in a law court) in order to check answers or elicit new information – -**ination** n – -**iner** n

,**cross-'eyed** adj having a squint towards the nose

,**cross-'fertilize** v 1 to fertilize with pollen or sperm from a different individual 2 to interreact, esp in a productive or useful manner – -**lization** n

'**cross,fire** /-,fie·ə/ n 1 firing from 2 or more points in crossing directions 2 rapid or heated interchange

crossing /'krosing/ n 1 a place or structure (e g on a street or over a river or railway) where pedestrians or vehicles may cross 2 a place where railway lines, roads, etc cross each other

'**cross,piece** /-,pees/ n a horizontal part (e g of a structure)

crossply /'kros,plie/ *n or adj* (a tyre) with the cords arranged crosswise to strengthen the tread

cross-re'fer *v* **-rr- 1** to direct (a reader) from one page or entry (e g in a book) to another **2** to refer from (a secondary entry) to a main entry – **-reference** *n*

'**cross-,section** *n* **1** (a drawing of) a surface made by cutting across sthg, esp at right angles to its length **2** a representative sample

'**cross-,talk** *n* rapid exchange of repartee (e g between comedians)

'**cross,wise** /-,wiez/ *adv* so as to cross sthg; across

crotch /kroch/ *n* **1** an angle formed where 2 branches separate off from a tree trunk **2** the angle between the inner thighs where they meet the human body

crotchet /'krochit/ *n* a musical note with the time value of half a minim or 2 quavers

crotchety /'krochiti/ *adj* bad-tempered – infml

crouch /krowch/ *v* to lower the body by bending the legs – **crouch** *n*

croup *n* a spasmodic laryngitis, esp in infants, marked by periods of difficult breathing and a hoarse cough – **croupy** *adj*

croupier /'kroohpi-ə, -ay/ *n* an employee of a gambling casino who collects and pays out bets at the gaming tables

crouton /'kroohton/ *n* a small cube of crisp toasted or fried bread served with soup or used as a garnish

¹**crow** /kroh/ *n* **1** the carrion or hooded crow or a related large usu entirely glossy black bird **2** a crowbar — **as the crow flies** in a straight line

²**crow** *v* **crowed,** (1) **crowed** *also* **crew** /krooh/ **1** to make the loud shrill cry characteristic of a cock **2** *esp of an infant* to utter sounds of happiness or pleasure **3** to exult gloatingly, esp over another's misfortune

³**crow** *n* **1** the characteristic cry of the cock **2** a triumphant cry

crowbar /'kroh,bah/ *n* an iron or steel bar for use as a lever that is wedge-shaped at the working end

¹**crowd** /krowd/ *v* **1a** to collect in numbers; throng **b** to force or thrust into a small space **2** to hoist more (sail) than usual for greater speed – usu + **on 3** to press close to; jostle

²**crowd** *n sing or pl in constr* **1** a large number of people gathered together without order; a throng **2** people in general – + **the 3** a large number of things close together and in disorder

crowded /'krowdid/ **1** filled with numerous people, things, or events **2** pressed or forced into a small space – **~ness** *n*

¹**crown** /krown/ *n* **1** a reward of victory or mark of honour; *esp* the title representing the championship in a sport **2** a (gold and jewel-encrusted) headdress worn as a symbol of sovereignty **3a** the topmost part of the skull or head **b** the summit of a slope, mountain, etc **c** the upper part of the

foliage of a tree or shrub **d** the part of a hat or cap that covers the crown of the head **e** (an artificial substitute for) the part of a tooth visible outside the gum **4** *often cap* the sovereign as head of state; *also* sovereignty **5** the high point or culmination **6** a British coin worth 25 pence (formerly 5 shillings)

²**crown** *v* **1** to invest with a crown **2** to surmount, top **3** to bring to a successful conclusion **4** to put an artificial crown on (a tooth)

Crown 'Court *n* a local criminal court in England and Wales having jurisdiction over serious offences

,**crown 'prince** *n* an heir apparent to a crown or throne

,**crown prin'cess** *n* **1** the wife of a crown prince **2** a female heir apparent or heir presumptive to a crown or throne

'**crow's ,nest** *n* a partly enclosed high lookout platform (e g on a ship's mast)

crucial /'kroohshəl/ *adj* **1** essential to the resolving of a crisis; decisive **2** of the greatest importance or significance – **~ly** *adv*

crucible /'kroohsibl/ *n* **1** a vessel for melting a substance at a very high temperature **2** a severe test

crucifix /'kroohsifiks/ *n* a representation of Christ on the cross

crucifixion /,kroohsi'fiksh(ə)n/ *n cap* the crucifying of Christ

crucify /'kroohsi,fie/ *v* to execute by nailing or binding the hands and feet to a cross and leaving to die

¹**crude** /kroohd/ *adj* **1** existing in a natural state and unaltered by processing **2** vulgar, gross **3** rough or inexpert in plan or execution – **~ly** *adv* – **~ness, crudity** *n*

²**crude** *n* a substance, esp petroleum, in its natural unprocessed state

cruel /'kroohəl/ *adj* **-ll-** (*NAm* **-l-, -ll-**) **1** liking to inflict pain or suffering; pitiless **2** causing suffering; painful – **~ly** *adv* – **~ness** *n*

'**cruelty** /-ti/ *n* **1** being cruel **2** (an instance of) cruel behaviour

cruet /'krooh-it/ *n* a small container (e g a pot, shaker or jug) for holding a condiment, esp salt, pepper, oil, vinegar, or mustard, at table

¹**cruise** /kroohz/ *v* **1** to travel by sea for pleasure **2** to go about or patrol the streets without any definite destination **3a** *of an aircraft* to fly at the most efficient operating speed **b** *of a vehicle* to travel at an economical speed that can be maintained for a long distance **4** to make progress easily **5** to search (e g in public places) for an esp homosexual partner – slang

²**cruise** *n* an act or instance of cruising; *esp* a sea voyage for pleasure

'**cruise ,missile** *n* a long-distance low-flying guided missile with small wings

cruiser /'kroohzə/ n 1 a cabin cruiser 2 a large fast lightly armoured warship

crumb /krum/ n 1 a small fragment, esp of bread 2 a small amount 3 (loose crumbly soil or other material resembling) the soft part of bread inside the crust 4 a worthless person – slang

¹**crumble** /'krumbl/ v **crumbling** /'krumbling/ to break or fall into small pieces; disintegrate – often + away – **ly** adj

²**crumble** n a dessert of stewed fruit topped with a crumbly mixture of fat, flour, and sugar

crummy, crumby /'krumi/ adj 1 miserable, filthy 2 of poor quality; worthless USE slang

crumpet /'krumpit/ n 1 a small round cake made from an unsweetened leavened batter that is cooked on a griddle and usu toasted before serving 2 Br women collectively as sexual objects – slang

crumple /'krumpl/ v **crumpling** /'krumpling/ 1 to press, bend, or crush out of shape 2 to collapse – often + up

¹**crunch** /krunch/ v 1 to chew or bite (sthg) with a noisy crushing sound 2 to make (one's way) with a crushing sound – **crunchy** adj

²**crunch** n 1 an act or sound of crunching 2 the critical or decisive situation or moment – infml

crusade /krooh'sayd/ n 1 cap any of the medieval Christian military expeditions to win the Holy Land from the Muslims 2 a reforming enterprise undertaken with zeal and enthusiasm – **crusade** v

¹**crush** /krush/ v 1 to alter or destroy by pressure or compression 2 to subdue, overwhelm 3 to crowd, push

²**crush** n 1 a crowding together, esp of many people 2 (the object of) an intense usu brief infatuation – infml

crust /krust/ n 1 the hardened exterior of bread 2 the pastry cover of a pie 3a the outer rocky layer of the earth b a deposit built up on the inside of a wine bottle during long aging

crustacean /kru'staysh(ə)n/ n, pl **crustaceans, crustacea** /-shə/ any of a large class of mostly aquatic arthropods including the lobsters, crabs and woodlice

crusty /'krusti/ adj 1 having a hard well-baked crust 2 surly, uncivil – **tily** adv – **tiness** n

crutch /kruch/ n 1a a staff of wood or metal typically fitting under the armpit to support a disabled person in walking b a prop, stay 2 the crotch of an animal or human 3 the part of a garment that covers the human crotch

crux /kruks, krooks/ n, pl **cruxes** also **cruces** /'krooh,seez/ 1 a puzzling or difficult problem 2 an essential or decisive point

¹**cry** /krie/ v 1 to call loudly; shout (e g in fear or pain) 2 to weep, sob 3 of a bird or animal to utter a characteristic sound or call 4 to require or suggest strongly a remedy – usu + out for; infml — **cry over spilt milk** to express vain regrets for what

cannot be recovered or undone — **cry wolf** to raise a false alarm and risk the possibility that a future real need will not be taken seriously — **for crying out loud** used to express exasperation and annoyance; infml

²**cry** n 1 an inarticulate utterance of distress, rage, pain, etc 2 a loud shout 3 a watchword, slogan 4 a general public demand or complaint 5 a spell of weeping 6 the characteristic sound or call of an animal or bird 7 pursuit – in **in full cry**

,crying /'krie·ing/ adj calling for notice

,cry off v to withdraw; back out

crypt /kript/ n a chamber (e g a vault) wholly or partly underground; esp a vault under the main floor of a church

cryptic /'kriptik/ adj 1 intended to be obscure or mysterious 2 making use of cipher or code – **~ally** adv

cryptogram /'kriptə,gram/ n a communication in cipher or code

cryptography /krip'togrəfi/ n 1 secret writing; cryptic symbolization 2 the preparation of cryptograms, ciphers, or codes – **-pher** n – **-phic** adj – **-phically** adv

crystal /'kristl/ n 1 a chemical substance in a form that has a regularly repeating internal arrangement of atoms and often regularly arranged external plane faces 2 (an object made of) a clear colourless glass of superior quality 3 sthg resembling crystal in transparency and colourlessness – **~line** adj – **~lize** v

'**crystal ,gazing** n the attempt to predict future events, esp without adequate data – **crystal gazer** n

cub /kub/ n 1 the young of a flesh-eating mammal (e g a bear or lion) 2 an inexperienced newspaper reporter

¹**cube** /kyoohb/ n 1a the regular solid of 6 equal square sides b a block of anything so shaped 2 the product got by multiplying together 3 equal numbers

²**cube** v 1 to raise to the third power 2 to cut into cubes

cubic /'kyoohbik/ adj 1 cube-shaped 2 three-dimensional 3 being the volume of a cube whose edge is a specified unit

cubicle /'kyoohbikl/ n a small partitioned space or compartment

cubism /'kyooh,biz(ə)m/ n a 20th-c art movement that stresses abstract form – **cubist** n

cubit /'kyoohbit/ n any of various ancient units of length based on the length of the forearm from the elbow to the tip of the middle finger

¹**cuckoo** /'kookooh/ n, pl **cuckoos** (any of a large family of birds including) a greyish brown European bird that lays its eggs in the nests of other birds which hatch them and rear the offspring

²**cuckoo** adj deficient in sense or intelligence; silly – infml

'cuckoo ,spit *n* (a frothy secretion exuded on plants by the larva of) a small insect

cucumber /'kyoohkumbə/ *n* (a climbing plant with) a long green edible fruit cultivated as a garden vegetable and eaten esp in salads

cud /kud/ *n* food brought up into the mouth by a ruminating animal from its first stomach to be chewed again

cuddle /'kudl/ *v* **cuddling** /'kudling, 'kudl·ing/ to hold close for warmth or comfort or in affection – **cuddle** *n*

cudgel /'kuj(ə)l/ *n* a short heavy club

¹cue /kyooh/ *n* **1** a signal to a performer to begin a specific speech or action **2** sthg serving a comparable purpose; a hint

²cue *n* a leather-tipped tapering rod for striking the ball in billiards, snooker, etc

¹cuff /kuf/ *n* a fold or band at the end of a sleeve which encircles the wrist — **off the cuff** without preparation

²cuff *v* to strike, esp (as if) with the palm of the hand

³cuff *n* a blow with the hand, esp when open; a slap

'cuff ,link *n* a usu ornamental device consisting of 2 linked parts used to fasten a shirt cuff

cuisine /kwi'zeen/ *n* a manner of preparing or cooking food; *also* the food prepared

cul-de-sac /'kul di ,sak/ *n*, *pl* **culs-de-sac** / ~ /*also* **cul-de-sacs** /saks/ a street, usu residential, closed at 1 end

culinary /'kulin(ə)ri/ *adj* of the kitchen or cookery

cull /kul/ *v* **1** to select from a group; choose **2** to identify and remove the rejects from (a flock, herd, etc) **3** to control the size of a population of (animals) by killing a limited number

culminate /'kulminayt/ *v* to reach the highest or a decisive point – often + *in* – **-ation** *n*

culottes /koo'lots/ *n pl* short trousers having the appearance of a skirt and worn by women

culpable /'kulpəbl/ *adj* meriting condemnation or blame – **-bility** *n* – **-bly** *adv*

culprit /'kulprit/ *n* one guilty of a crime or a fault

cult /kult/ *n* **1a** a system of religious beliefs and ritual **b** a religion regarded as unorthodox or spurious **2** great devotion, often regarded as a fad, to a person, idea, or thing

cultivate /'kultivayt/ *v* **1** to prepare or use (land, soil, etc) for the growing of crops; *also* to break up the soil about (growing plants) **2a** to foster the growth of (a plant or crop) **b** to improve by labour, care, or study; refine **3** to further, encourage – **-ation** *n* – **-ator** *n*

'cultivated *adj* refined, educated

¹culture /'kulchə/ *n* **1** enlightenment and excellence of taste acquired by intellectual and aesthetic training **2a** the socially transmitted pattern of human behaviour that includes thought, speech, action, institutions, and man-made objects **b** the customary beliefs, social forms, etc

of a racial, religious, or social group **3** (a product of) the cultivation of living cells, tissue, viruses, etc in prepared nutrient media – **-ral** *adj* – **-rally** *adv*

²culture *v* **1** to cultivate **2** to grow (bacteria, viruses, etc) in a culture

cultured /'kulchəd/ *adj* cultivated

culvert /'kulvət/ *n* a construction that allows water to pass over or under an obstacle (e g a road or canal)

'cumbersome /-s(ə)m/ *adj* unwieldy because of heaviness and bulk

cummerbund /'kumə,bund/ *n* a broad waistsash worn esp with men's formal evening wear

cumulative /'kyoohmyoolətiv/ *adj* **1a** made up of accumulated parts **b** increasing by successive additions **2** formed by adding new material of the same kind – **~ly** *adv*

cumulonimbus /,kyoohmyoolooh'nimbəs/ *n* a cumulus cloud formation often in the shape of an anvil, extending to great heights and characteristic of thunderstorm conditions

cumulus /'kyoohmyooləs/ *n*, *pl* **cumuli** /-lie, -li/ a massive cloud formation with a flat base and rounded outlines often piled up like a mountain

¹cunning /'kuning/ *adj* **1** dexterous, ingenious **2** devious, crafty – **~ly** *adv*

²cunning *n* craft, slyness

cunt /kunt/ *n* **1** the female genitals **2** sexual intercourse – used by men **3** *Br* an unpleasant person *USE* vulg

cup /kup/ *n* **1** a small open drinking vessel that is usu bowl-shaped and has a handle on 1 side **2** (a competition or championship with) an ornamental usu metal cup offered as a prize **3** sthg resembling a cup **4** any of various usu alcoholic and cold drinks made from mixed ingredients — **in one's cups** intoxicated

cupboard /'kubəd/ *n* a shelved recess or freestanding piece of furniture with doors, for storage of utensils, food, clothes, etc

'cupboard ,love *n* insincere love professed for the sake of gain

Cupid /'kyoohpid/ *n* **1** the Roman god of erotic love **2** *not cap* a representation of Cupid as a winged naked boy often holding a bow and arrow

cupidity /kyooh'pidəti/ *n* avarice, greed

cupola /'kyoohpələ/ *n* a small domed structure built on top of a roof

cuppa /'kupə/ *n*, *chiefly Br* a cup of tea – *infml*

'cup-,tie *n* a match in a knockout competition for a cup

cur /kuh/ *n* **1** a mongrel or inferior dog **2** a surly or cowardly fellow

curate /'kyoorət/ *n* a clergyman serving as assistant (e g to a rector) in a parish – **-acy** *n*

curator /kyoo'raytə/ *n* sby in charge of a place of exhibition (e g a museum or zoo) – **~ship** *n*

¹**curb** /kuhb/ *n* **1a** a chain or strap that is used to restrain a horse and is attached to the sides of the bit and passes below the lower jaw **b** a bit used esp with a curb chain or strap, usu in a double bridle **2** a check, restraint **3** an edge or margin that strengthens or confines

²**curb** *v* to check, control

curd /kuhd/ *n* **1** the thick part of coagulated milk used as a food or made into cheese **2** a rich thick fruit preserve made with eggs, sugar, and butter

curdle /'kuhdl/ *v* **curdling** /'kuhdling/ **1** to form curds (in); *specif* to separate into solid curds and liquid **2** to spoil, sour

¹**cure** /kyooə/ *n* **1** spiritual or pastoral charge **2** (a drug, treatment, etc that gives) relief or esp recovery from a disease **3** sthg that corrects a harmful or troublesome situation; a remedy **4** a process or method of curing

²**cure** *v* **1a** to restore to health, soundness, or normality **b** to bring about recovery from **2a** to rectify **b** to free (sby) from sthg objectionable or harmful **3** to prepare by chemical or physical processing; *esp* to preserve (meat, fish, etc) by salting, drying, smoking, etc – **-rable** *adj*

'cure-,all *n* a remedy for all ills; a panacea

curfew /'kuhfyooh/ *n* **1** a regulation imposed esp during times of civil disturbance, requiring people to withdraw from the streets by a stated time **2** a signal (e g the sounding of a bell) announcing the beginning of a time of curfew

curio /'kyooərioh/ *n pl* **curios** sthg considered novel, rare, or bizarre

curiosity /,kyooəri'osəti/ *n* **1** inquisitiveness; nosiness **2** a strange, interesting, or rare object, custom, etc

curious /'kyooəri-əs/ *adj* **1** eager to investigate and learn **2** inquisitive, nosy **3** strange, novel, or odd – **~ly** *adv*

¹**curl** /kuhl/ *v* **1a** to grow in coils or spirals **b** to form curls or twists **2** to move or progress in curves or spirals

²**curl** *n* **1** a curled lock of hair **2** sthg with a spiral or winding form; a coil **3** a (plant disease marked by the) rolling or curling of leaves

curler /'kuhlə/ *n* a small cylinder on which hair is wound for curling

curlew /'kuhlyooh/ *n pl* **curlews,** *esp collectively* **curlew** any of various largely brownish (migratory) wading birds with long legs and a long slender down-curved bill

curling /'kuhling/ *n* a game in which 2 teams, of 4 players each, slide heavy round flat-bottomed stones over ice towards a target circle marked on the ice

curly /'kuhli/ *adj* tending to curl; having curls – **curliness** *n*

curmudgeon /kə'mujən/ *n* a crusty ill-tempered (old) man

currant /'kurənt/ *n* **1** a small seedless type of dried grape used in cookery **2** a redcurrant, blackcurrant, or similar acid edible fruit

currency /'kurənsi/ *n* **1** (the state of being in) general use, acceptance, or prevalence **2** sthg (e g coins and bank notes) that is in circulation as a medium of exchange

¹**current** /'kurənt/ *adj* **1** occurring in or belonging to the present time **2** used as a medium of exchange **3** generally accepted, used, or practised at the moment – **~ly** *adv*

²**current** *n* **1a** the part of a body of gas or liquid that moves continuously in a certain direction **b** the swiftest part of a stream **c** a (tidal) movement of lake, sea, or ocean water **2** a flow of electric charge; *also* the rate of such flow

current account *n, chiefly Br* a bank account against which cheques may be drawn and on which interest is not payable

curriculum /kə'rikyooləm/ *n, pl* **curricula** /-lə/ *also* **curriculums** the courses offered by an educational institution or followed by an individual or group

cur,riculum 'vitae /'veetie/ *n, pl* **curricula vitae** /-lə/ a summary of sby's career and qualifications, esp as relevant to a job application

¹**curry** /'kuri/ *v* to dress tanned leather — **curry favour** to seek to gain favour by flattery or attention

²**curry** *also* **currie** /'kuri/ *n* a food or dish seasoned with a mixture of spices or curry powder

³**curry** *v* to flavour or cook with curry powder or sauce

'curry ,powder *n* a condiment consisting of several pungent ground spices

¹**curse** /kuhs/ *n* **1** an utterance (of a deity) or a request (to a deity) that invokes harm or injury **2** an evil or misfortune that comes (as if) in response to cursing or as retribution **3** a cause of misfortune **4** menstruation – + *the*; *infml*

²**curse** *v* **1** to call upon divine or supernatural power to cause harm or injury to **2** to use profanely insolent language against **3** to bring great evil upon; afflict

cursed /kuhsid, kuhst/ *also* **curst** /kuhst/ *adj* under or deserving a curse – **~ly** *adv*

cursive /'kuhsiv/ *adj* written in flowing, usu slanted, strokes with the characters joined in each word – **~ly** *adv*

cursory /'kuhsəri/ *adj* rapid and often superficial; hasty – **-rily** *adv*

curt /kuht/ *adj* marked by rude or peremptory shortness; brusque – **~ly** *adv* – **~ness** *n*

curtail /kuh'tayl/ *v* to cut short, limit – **~ment** *n*

curtain /'kuht(ə)n/ *n* **1** a hanging fabric screen (at a window) that can usu be drawn back **2** a device or agency that conceals or acts as a barrier **3** an exterior wall that carries no load **4a** the movable screen separating the stage from the auditorium of a theatre **b** the ascent or opening (e g at the beginning of a play) of a stage curtain; *also* its descent or closing **c** *pl* the end; *esp* death – *infml*

'curtain ,call *n* an appearance by a performer after the final curtain of a play in response to the applause of the audience

curtsy, curtsey /'kuhtsi/ *n* an act of respect, made by a woman, by bending at the knees and bowing the head – **curtsy** *v*

curvaceous *also* **curvacious** /kuh'vayshəs/ *adj*, *of a woman* having an attractively well-developed figure

curvature /'kuhvəchə/ *n* **1** (a measure or amount of) curving or being curved **2** an abnormal curving (e g of the spine)

'curve /kuhv/ *v* to have or make a turn, change, or deviation from a straight line without sharp breaks or angularity

'curve *n* **1** a curving line or surface **2** sthg curved (e g a curving line of the human body) **3** a representation on a graph of a varying quantity (e g speed, force, or weight)

'cushion /'kooshn/ *n* **1** a soft pillow or padded bag; *esp* one used for sitting, reclining, or kneeling on **2** a bodily part resembling a pad **3** a pad of springy rubber along the inside of the rim of a billiard table off which balls bounce **4** sthg serving to mitigate the effects of disturbances or disorders

'cushion *v* **1** to mitigate the effects of **2** to protect against force or shock

cushy /'kooshi/ *adj* entailing little hardship or effort; easy – *infml* – **cushiness** *n*

cusp /kusp/ *n* a point, apex: e g **a** either horn of a crescent moon **b** a pointed projection formed by or arising from the intersection of 2 arcs or foils **c** a point on the grinding surface of a tooth

'cuss /kus/ *n* **1** a curse **2** a fellow *USE* infml

'cuss *v* to curse – *infml*

cussed /'kusid/ *adj* **1** cursed **2** obstinate, cantankerous *USE* infml – **~ly** *adv* – **~ness** *n*

custard /'kustəd/ *n* **1** a semisolid usu sweetened and often baked mixture made with milk and eggs **2** a sweet sauce made with milk and eggs or a commercial preparation of coloured cornflour

custodian /ku'stohdi·ən/ *n* the curator of a public building – **~ship** *n*

custody /'kustədi/ *n* **1a** the state of being cared for or guarded **b** imprisonment, detention **2** the act or right of caring for a minor, esp when granted by a court of law; guardianship – **-dial** *adj*

'custom /'kustəm/ *n* **1a** an established socially accepted practice **b** the usual practice of an individual **c** the usages that regulate social life **2a** *pl* duties or tolls imposed on imports or exports **b** *pl but sing or pl in constr* the agency, establishment, or procedure for collecting such customs **3** business patronage

'custom *adj*, *chiefly NAm* made or performed according to personal order

customary /'kustəm(ə)ri/ *adj* established by or according to custom; usual – **-rily** *adv*

customer /'kustəmə/ *n* **1** one who purchases a commodity or service **2** an individual, usu having some specified distinctive trait

'cut /kut/ *v* **-tt-; cut 1a** to penetrate (as if) with an edged instrument **b** to hurt the feelings of **2a** to trim, pare **b** to shorten by omissions **c** to reduce in amount **3a** to mow or reap **b**(1) to divide into parts with an edged instrument **b**(2) to fell, hew **c** to make a stroke with a whip, sword, etc **4a** to divide into segments **b** to intersect, cross **c** to break, interrupt **d** to divide (a pack of cards) into 2 portions **5a** to refuse to recognize (an acquaintance) **b** to stop (a motor) by opening a switch **c** to terminate the filming of (a scene in a film) **6a** to make or give shape to (as if) with an edged tool **b** to record sounds on (a gramophone record) **c** to make an abrupt transition from one sound or image to another in film, radio, or television **7a** to perform, make **b** to give the appearance or impression of **8a** to stop, cease – *infml* **b** to absent oneself from (e g a class) – *infml* – **cut corners** to perform some action in the quickest, easiest, or cheapest way – **cut no ice** to fail to impress; have no importance or influence – *infml* – **cut short 1** to abbreviate **2** to interrupt

'cut *n* **1a** (a slice cut from a) piece from a meat carcass or a fish **b** a share **2a** a canal, channel, or inlet made by excavation or worn by natural action **b**(1) an opening made with an edged instrument **b**(2) a gash, wound **c** a passage cut as a roadway **3a** a gesture or expression that hurts the feelings **b** a stroke or blow with the edge of sthg sharp **c** a lash (as if) with a whip **d** the act of reducing or removing a part **e** (the result of) a cutting of playing cards **4** an attacking stroke in cricket played with the bat held horizontally and sending the ball on the off side **5** an abrupt transition from one sound or image to another in film, radio, or television **6a** the shape and style in which a thing is cut, formed, or made **b** a pattern, type **c** a haircut – **a cut above** superior (to); of higher quality or rank (than)

,cut-and-'dried *adj* completely decided; not open to further discussion

'cut,back /-,bak/ *n* a reduction

cute /kyooht/ *adj* attractive or pretty, esp in a dainty or delicate way – *infml* – **~ly** *adv* – **~ness** *n*

,cut 'glass *n* glass ornamented with patterns cut into its surface by an abrasive wheel and then polished

cuticle /'kyoohtikl/ *n* a skin or outer covering: e g **a** the (dead or horny) epidermis of an animal **b** a thin fatty film on the external surface of many higher plants

cutlass *also* **cutlas** /'kutləs/ *n* a short curved sword, esp as used formerly by sailors

cutler /'kutlə/ n one who deals in, makes, or repairs cutlery

cutlery /'kutləri/ n edged or cutting tools; *esp* implements (e g knives, forks, and spoons) for cutting and eating food

cutlet /'kutlit/ n 1 (a flat mass of minced food in the shape of) a small slice of meat from the neck of lamb, mutton, or veal 2 a cross-sectional slice from between the head and centre of a large fish

'cut,out /-,owt/ n a device that is automatically switched off by an excessive electric current

¹**cut out** v 1 to form or remove by cutting, erosion, etc 2 to supplant 3 to desist from

²**cut 'out** *adj* naturally fitted or suited

,cut-'price *adj* selling or sold at a discount

cutter /'kutə/ n 1 one whose work is cutting or involves cutting (e g of cloth or film) 2a a ship's boat for carrying stores or passengers b a fore-and-aft rigged sailing boat with a single mast and 2 foresails c a small armed boat in the US coastguard

¹**'cut,throat** /-,throht/ n a murderous thug

²**cutthroat** *adj* 1 murderous, cruel 2 ruthless, unprincipled

¹**cutting** /'kuting/ n 1 a part of a plant stem, leaf, root, etc capable of developing into a new plant 2 *chiefly Br* an excavation or cut, esp through high ground, for a canal, road, etc 3 *chiefly Br* an item cut out of a publication

²**cutting** *adj* 1 designed for cutting; sharp, edged 2 *of wind* marked by sharp piercing cold 3 likely to wound the feelings of another; *esp* sarcastic – **~ly** *adv*

cuttlefish /'kutl,fish/ n a 10-armed marine animal differing from the related squids in having a hard internal shell

cwm /koohm/ n a cirque

cyanide /'sie·ənied/ n an extremely poisonous chemical with a smell of bitter almonds

cybernetics /,siebə'netiks/ n pl but sing or pl in constr the comparative study of the automatic control systems formed by the nervous system and brain and by mechanical-electrical communication systems – **~ic** *adj* – **~ally** *adv*

cyclamate /'sieklə,mayt, -,mat, 'siklə-/ n a synthetic compound used, esp formerly, as an artificial sweetener

¹**cycle** /'siekl/ n 1a (the time needed to complete) a series of related events happening in a regularly repeated order b one complete performance of a periodic process (e g a vibration or electrical oscillation) 2 a group of poems, plays, novels, or songs on a central theme 3 a bicycle, motorcycle, tricycle, etc

²**cycle** v cycling /'siekling/ to ride a bicycle – **-list** n

cyclic /'siklik, 'sieklik/, **'cyclical** /-kl/ *adj* 1 of or belonging to a cycle 2 of or containing a ring of atoms – **~ally** *adv*

cyclone /'sieklohn/ n a storm or system of winds that rotates about a centre of low atmospheric pressure, advances at high speeds, and often brings abundant rain

cyclopedia, cyclopaedia /,sieklə'peedi·ə/ n an encyclopedia

cygnet /'signit/ n a young swan

cylinder /'silində/ n 1a a surface traced by a straight line moving in a circle or other closed curve round and parallel to a fixed straight line b a hollow or solid object with the shape of a cylinder and a circular cross-section 2a the piston chamber in an engine b any of various rotating parts (e g in printing presses) – **-drical** *adj*

cymbal /'simbl/ n a concave brass plate that produces a clashing tone when struck – **~ist** n

cynic /'sinik/ n 1 cap an adherent of an ancient Greek school of philosophers who held that virtue is the highest good and that its essence lies in mastery over one's desires and wants 2 one who sarcastically doubts the existence of human sincerity or of any motive other than self-interest; *broadly* a pessimist – **~al** *adj* – **~ism** n – **~ally** *adv*

cynosure /'sinə,zyooə, 'sie-, -,shooə/ n a centre of attraction or attention

cypher /'siefə/ v or n, *chiefly Br* (to) cipher

cypress /'sieprəs/ n (the wood of) any of a genus of evergreen trees with aromatic overlapping leaves resembling scales

cyst /sist/ n a closed sac (e g of watery liquid or gas) with a distinct membrane, developing (abnormally) in a plant or animal

cystitis /si'stietəs/ n inflammation of the urinary bladder

cytology /sie'toləji/ n the biology of (the structure, function, multiplication, pathology, etc of) cells – **-gist** n

cytoplasm /'sietə,plaz(ə)m/ n the substance within a plant or animal cell excluding the nucleus – **~ic** *adj*

czar /zah/ n a former ruler of Russia

Czech /chek/ n 1 a native or inhabitant of Czechoslovakia; *specif* a Slav of W Czechoslovakia 2 the Slavonic language of the Czechs – **Czech** *adj*

D

d /dee/ n, pl **d's, ds** *often cap* 1 (a graphic representation of or device for reproducing) the 4th letter of the English alphabet 2 five hundred 3 one designated d, esp as the 4th in order or class

¹dab /dab/ *n* **1** a sudden feeble blow or thrust; a poke **2** a gentle touch or stroke (e g with a sponge); a pat

²dab *v* **-bb-** **1** to touch lightly, and usu repeatedly; pat **2** to apply lightly or irregularly; daub

³dab *n* **1** a daub, patch **2** *pl, Br* fingerprints – *infml*

⁴dab *n* a flatfish; *esp* any of several flounders

dabble /'dabl/ *v* **dabbling** /'dabling/ **1** to paddle, splash, or play (as if) in water **2** to work or concern oneself superficially **3** to wet slightly or intermittently by dipping in a liquid

dachshund /'daksənd/ *n* (any of) a breed of dogs of German origin with a long body, short legs, and long drooping ears

dad /dad/ *n* a father – *infml*

daddy 'longlegs /'long,legz/ *n, pl* **daddy longlegs** a crane fly

daemon /'deemən/ *n* **1** an attendant power or spirit **2** a supernatural being of Greek mythology **3** a demon – ~**ic** *adj* – ~**ically** *adv*

daffodil /'dafədil/ *n* any of various plants with flowers that have a large typically yellow corona elongated into a trumpet shape

daft /dahft/ *adj* **1** silly, foolish **2** *chiefly Br* fanatically enthusiastic *USE infml* – ~**ly** *adv* – ~**ness** *n*

dagger /'dagə/ *n* a short sharp pointed weapon for stabbing — **at daggers drawn** in bitter conflict

dahlia /'dayli-ə, 'dah-/ *n* any of an American genus of composite (garden) plants with showy flower heads and roots that form tubers

¹daily /'dayli/ *adj* **1a** occurring, made, or acted on every day **b** *of a newspaper* issued every weekday **c** of or providing for every day **2** covering the period of or based on a day

²daily *adv* every day; every weekday

³daily *n* **1** a newspaper published daily from Monday to Saturday **2** *Br* a charwoman who works on a daily basis

¹dainty /'daynti/ *n* a delicacy

²dainty *adj* **1** attractively prepared and served **2** delicately beautiful **3a** fastidious **b** showing avoidance of anything rough – **-tily** *adv* – **-tiness** *n*

dairy /'deəri/ *n* **1** a room, building, etc where milk is processed and butter or cheese is made **2** farming concerned with the production of milk, butter, and cheese **3** an establishment for the sale or distribution of milk and milk products – ~**ing** *n*

dairyman /-mən/, *fem* **dairy,maid** /-,mayd/ *n* one who operates or works for a dairy (farm)

dais /'day·is/ *n* a raised platform; *esp* one at the end of a hall

daisy /'dayzi/ *n* a usu white composite plant with a yellow disc and well-developed ray flowers in its flower head

dally /'dali/ *v* **1a** to act playfully; *esp* to flirt **b** to deal lightly; toy **2** to waste time; dawdle – **dalliance** *n*

dalmatian /dal'maysh(ə)n/ *n, often cap* (any of) a breed of medium-sized dogs with a white short-haired coat with black or brown spots

¹dam /dam/ *n* a female parent – used esp with reference to domestic animals

²dam *n* a barrier preventing the flow of a fluid; *esp* a barrier across a watercourse

³dam *v* **-mm-** to stop up; block

¹damage /'damij/ *n* **1** loss or harm resulting from injury to person, property, or reputation **2** *pl* compensation in money imposed by law for loss or injury

²damage *v* to cause damage to

damask /'daməsk/ *n* a reversible lustrous fabric (e g of linen, cotton, or silk) having a plain background woven with patterns

dame /daym/ *n* **1a** the wife or daughter of a lord **b** a female member of an order of knighthood – used as a title preceding the Christian name **2a** an elderly woman; *specif* a comic one in pantomime played usu by a male actor **b** *chiefly NAm* a woman – *infml*

¹damn /dam/ *v* **1** to condemn to a punishment or fate; *esp* to condemn to hell **2** to condemn as a failure by public criticism **3** to bring ruin on **4** to curse – often used as an interjection to express annoyance — **I'll be damned** – used to express astonishment — **I'll be damned if** I emphatically do not or will not

²damn *n* **1** the utterance of the word *damn* as a curse **2** the slightest bit – chiefly in negative phrases

³damn *adj or adv* – used as an intensive — **damn well** beyond doubt or question; certainly

damnation /dam'naysh(ə)n/ *n* damning or being damned

damning /'daming/ *adj* causing or leading to condemnation or ruin

¹damp /damp/ *n* moisture, humidity

²damp *v* **1a** to diminish the activity or intensity of – often + *down* **b** to reduce progressively the vibration or oscillation of (e g sound waves) **2** to make damp

³damp *adj* slightly or moderately wet – ~**ly** *adv*

damper /'dampə/ *n* **1a** a valve or plate (e g in the flue of a furnace) for regulating the draught **b** a small felted block which prevents or stops the vibration of a piano string **c** a device (e g a shock absorber) designed to bring a mechanism to rest with minimum oscillation **2** a dulling or deadening influence

damsel /'damzəl/ *n, archaic* a young woman; a girl

damson /'damzən/ *n* (the small acid purple fruit of) an Asiatic plum

¹dance /dahns/ *v* **1** to engage in or perform a dance **2** to move quickly up and down or about – **dancer** *n*

²**dance** n **1** (an act or instance or the art of) a series of rhythmic and patterned bodily movements usu performed to music **2** a social gathering for dancing **3** a piece of music for dancing to

dandelion /'dandi,lie·ən/ n any of a genus of yellow-flowered composite plants including one that occurs virtually worldwide as a weed

dandle /'dandl/ v **dandling** /'dandling, 'dandl·ing/ to move (e g a baby) up and down in one's arms or on one's knee in affectionate play

dandruff /'dandruf, -drəf/ n a scurf that comes off the scalp in small white or greyish scales

dandy /'dandi/ n a man who gives exaggerated attention to dress and demeanour

danger /'daynjə/ n **1** exposure to the possibility of injury, pain, or loss **2** a case or cause of danger – ~**ous** adj – ~**ously** adv

dangle /'dang·gl/ v **dangling** /'dang·gling/ to hang or swing loosely

¹**Danish** /'daynish/ adj (characteristic) of Denmark

²**Danish** n the Germanic language of the people of Denmark

,**Danish** '**pastry** n (a piece of) confectionery made from a rich yeast dough with a sweet filling

dank /dangk/ adj unpleasantly moist or wet – ~**ness** n

dapper /'dapə/ adj, esp of a small man neat and spruce

Darby and Joan /,dahbi ənd 'john/ n a happily married elderly couple

¹**dare** /deə/ v **dared**, archaic **durst** /duhst/ **1** to have sufficient courage or impudence (to) **2a** to challenge to perform an action, esp as a proof of courage **b** to confront boldly; defy

²**dare** n a challenge to a bold act

daredevil /'deə,devl/ n or adj (sby) recklessly bold

¹**daring** /'deəring/ adj adventurously bold in action or thought

²**daring** n venturesome boldness

¹**dark** /dahk/ adj **1** (partially) devoid of light **2a** (partially) black **b** of a colour of (very) low lightness **3a** arising from or showing evil traits or desires; evil **b** dismal, sad **c** lacking knowledge or culture **4** not fair; swarthy – ~**ly** adv – ~**ness** n

²**dark** n a place or time of little or no light; night, nightfall — **in the dark** in ignorance

'**Dark Ages** n pl the period from about AD 476 to about 1000

darken /'dahkən/ v to make or become dark or darker

,**dark** '**horse** n sby or sthg (e g a contestant) little known, but with a potential much greater than the evidence would suggest

'**darkroom** /-,roohm, -room/ n a room for handling and processing light-sensitive photographic materials

¹**darling** /'dahling/ n **1a** a dearly loved person **b** a dear **2** a favourite

²**darling** adj **1** dearly loved; favourite **2** charming – used esp by women

¹**darn** /dahn/ v to mend (sthg) with interlacing stitches woven across a hole or worn part

²**darn** n a place that has been darned

³**darn** v to damn

⁴**darn** adj or adv damned

¹**dart** /daht/ n **1a** a small projectile with a pointed shaft at one end and flights of feather, plastic, etc at the other **b** pl but sing in constr a game in which darts are thrown at a dartboard **2** sthg with a slender pointed shaft or outline; specif a stitched tapering fold put in a garment to shape it to the figure **3** a quick movement; a dash

²**dart** v to move suddenly or rapidly

'**dart,board** /-,bawd/ n a circular target used in darts that is divided, usu by wire, into different scoring areas

¹**dash** /dash/ v **1** to move with sudden speed **2a** to strike or knock violently **b** to break by striking or knocking **3** to destroy, ruin **4** Br to damn – euph

²**dash** n **1** (the sound produced by) a sudden burst or splash **2a** a stroke of a pen **b** a punctuation mark – used esp to indicate a break in the thought or structure of a sentence **3** a small but significant addition **4** liveliness of style and action; panache **5** a sudden onset, rush, or attempt **6** a signal (e g a flash or audible tone) of relatively long duration that is one of the 2 fundamental units of Morse code

dashboard /'dash,bawd/ n a panel extending across a motor car, aeroplane, etc below the windscreen and usu containing dials and controls

dashing /'dashing/ adj **1** vigorous, spirited **2** smart in dress and manners – ~**ly** adv

data /'dahtə, 'daytə/ n pl but sing or pl in constr factual information (e g measurements or statistics) used as a basis for reasoning, discussion, or calculation

,**data** '**processing** n the conversion (e g by computer) of crude information into usable or storable form

¹**date** /dayt/ n (the oblong edible fruit of) a tall palm

²**date** n **1** the time reckoned in days or larger units at which an event occurs **2** the period of time to which sthg belongs **3a** an appointment for a specified time; esp a social engagement between 2 people of opposite sex – infml **b** NAm a person of the opposite sex with whom one has a date – infml — **to date** up to the present moment

³**date** v **1** to determine or record the date of **2a** to have been in existence – usu + from **b** to become old-fashioned **3** to mark with characteristics typical of a particular period **4** chiefly NAm to make or have a date with (a person of the opposite sex) – infml – **datable, dateable** adj

'**dated** adj out-of-date, old-fashioned

dea

'date,line /-,lien/ n 1 a line in a written document or publication giving the date and place of composition or issue 2 an arbitrary line east and west of which the date differs by 1 calendar day

dative /'daytiv/ n (a form in) a grammatical case expressing typically the indirect object of a verb, the object of some prepositions, or a possessor – dative adj

'daub /dawb/ v 1 to coat with a dirty substance 2 to paint without much skill

²daub n 1 sthg daubed on; a smear 2 a crude picture

daughter /'dawta/ n 1a a human female having the relation of child to parent 1b a female descendant – often pl 2a a human female having a specified origin, loyalties, etc 1b sthg considered as a daughter

'daughter-in-,law n, pl daughters-in-law the wife of one's son

daunt /dawnt/ v to lessen the courage of; inspire awe in

dauphin /'dohfanh (Fr dofẽ)/ n, often cap the eldest son of a king of France

davit /'davit/ n any of 2 or more projecting arms on a vessel used esp for lowering boats

dawdle /'dawdl/ v dawdling /'dawdling/ 1 to spend time idly 2 to move lackadaisically – ~r n

'dawn /dawn/ v 1 to begin to grow light as the sun rises 2 to begin to be perceived or understood

²dawn n 1 the first appearance of light in the morning 2 a first appearance; a beginning

day /day/ n 1 the time of light when the sun is above the horizon between one night and the next 2 the time required by a celestial body, specif the earth, to turn once on its axis 3 the solar day of 24 hours beginning at midnight 4 a specified day or date 5 a specified time or period 6 the time established by usage or law for work, school, or business

'day,break /-,brayk/ n dawn

'day,dream /-,dreem/ v or n (to have) a visionary, usu wish-fulfilling, creation of the waking imagination – ~er n

'day,light /-,liet/ n 1 dawn 2 knowledge or understanding of sthg that has been obscure 3 pl mental soundness or stability; wits – infml

,day-to-'day adj 1 taking place, made, or done in the course of successive days 2 providing for a day at a time with little thought for the future

daze /dayz/ v to stupefy, esp by a blow; stun – daze n – ~dly adv

dazzle /'dazl/ v dazzling /'dazling/ 1 to overpower or temporarily blind (the sight) with light 2 to impress deeply, overpower, or confound with brilliance – dazzle n

'D-,day /dee/ n a day set for launching an operation; specif June 6, 1944, on which the Allies began the invasion of France in WW II

DDT n a synthetic insecticide that tends to accumulate in food chains and is poisonous to many vertebrates

deacon /'deekan/ n 1 a clergyman ranking below a priest and, in the Anglican and Roman Catholic churches, usu a candidate for ordination as priest 2 any of a group of laymen with administrative and sometimes spiritual duties in various Protestant churches

'dead /ded/ adj 1 deprived of life; having died 2a(1) having the appearance of death; deathly a(2) lacking power to move, feel, or respond; numb b grown cold; extinguished 3 inanimate, inert 4a no longer having power or effect, interest or significance b no longer used; obsolete c lacking in activity d lacking elasticity or springiness 5a absolutely uniform b exact c abrupt d complete, absolute – ~ness n

²dead n 1 pl in constr dead people or animals 2 the time of greatest quiet or inactivity

³dead adv 1 absolutely, utterly 2 suddenly and completely 3 directly, exactly 4 Br very, extremely – infml

deaden /'dedan/ v 1 to deprive of liveliness, brilliance, sensation, or force 2 to make (e g a wall) impervious to sound

,dead 'heat n an inconclusive finish to a race or other contest, in which the fastest time, highest total, etc is achieved by more than one competitor

,dead 'letter n a law that has lost its force without being formally abolished

deadline /'dedlien/ n a date or time before which sthg (e g the presentation of copy for publication) must be done

deadlock /'dedlok/ n 1 inaction or neutralization resulting from the opposition of equally powerful and uncompromising people or factions; a standstill 2 a tied score

'deadly /'dedli/ adj 1 capable of producing death 2a implacable b unerring c marked by determination or extreme seriousness 3 lacking animation; dull 4 intense, extreme – -liness n

²deadly adv 1 suggesting death 2 extremely

,deadly 'night,shade /'niet,shayd/ n a European poisonous nightshade that has dull purple flowers and black berries

deadpan /ded'pan/ adj impassive, expressionless

,dead 'reckoning n the calculation without celestial observations of the position of a ship or aircraft, from the record of the courses followed, the distance travelled, etc

'dead,weight /-,wayt/ n 1 the unrelieved weight of an inert mass 2 a ship's total weight including cargo, fuel, stores, crew, and passengers

deaf /def/ adj 1 (partially) lacking the sense of hearing 2 unwilling to hear or listen to; not to be persuaded – ~ness n

deafen /'defan/ v to make deaf

,deaf-'mute n or adj (one who is) deaf and dumb

dea

¹**deal** /deel/ n 1 a usu large or indefinite quantity or degree; a lot 2 the act or right of distributing cards to players in a card game; *also* the hand dealt to a player

²**deal** v **dealt** /delt/ 1 to distribute the cards in a card game 2 to concern oneself or itself 3a to trade b to sell or distribute sthg as a business 4 to take action with regard to sby or sthg – ~**er** n

³**deal** n 1 a transaction 2 treatment received 3 an arrangement for mutual advantage

⁴**deal** n (a sawn piece of) fir or pine timber

dealing /'deeling/ n 1 pl friendly or business interactions 2 a method of business; a manner of conduct

dean /deen/ n 1 the head of a cathedral chapter or of part of a diocese – often used as a title 2 the head of a university division, faculty, or school

deanery /'deenəri/ n the office, jurisdiction, or official residence of a clerical dean

¹**dear** /diə/ adj 1 highly valued; much loved – often used in address 2 expensive 3 heartfelt – ~**ness** n – ~**ly** adv

²**dear** n 1a a loved one; a sweetheart b – used as a familiar or affectionate form of address 2 a lovable person

³**dear** interj – used typically to express annoyance or dismay

dearth /duhth/ n an inadequate supply; a scarcity

death /deth/ n 1 a permanent cessation of all vital functions; the end of life 2 the cause or occasion of loss of life 3 cap death personified, usu represented as a skeleton with a scythe 4 the state of being dead 5 extinction, disappearance — **at death's door** seriously ill — **to death** beyond all acceptable limits; excessively

'**death ,blow** /-,bloh/ n a destructive or killing stroke or event

'**deathless** /-lis/ adj immortal, imperishable – ~**ly** adv

'**death's-,head** n a human skull symbolic of death

'**death ,trap** n a potentially lethal structure or place

'**death,watch** /-,woch/ n 1 a vigil kept with the dead or dying 2 **deathwatch beetle, deathwatch** a small wood-boring beetle common in old buildings

debacle /di'bahkəl/ n 1 a violent disruption (e g of an army); a rout 2 a complete failure; a fiasco

debar /,dee'bah/ v -rr- to bar or ban *from* having, doing, or undergoing sthg

debase /di'bays/ v 1 to lower in status, esteem, quality, or character 2 to reduce the intrinsic value of (a coin) by increasing the content of low-value metal – ~**ment** n

¹**debate** /di'bayt/ n the usu formal discussion of a motion a in parliament b between 2 opposing sides

²**debate** v 1 to argue about 2 to consider – -**table** adj – ~**r** n

¹**debauch** /di'bawch/ v 1 to lead away from virtue or excellence 2 to make excessively intemperate or sensual

²**debauch** n an orgy

debauchery /di'bawchəri/ n excessive indulgence in the pleasures of the flesh

debenture /di'benchə/ n, Br a loan secured on the assets of a company in respect of which the company must pay a fixed interest before any dividends are paid to its own shareholders

debilitate /di'bilitayt/ v to impair the strength of; enfeeble – **debility** n

¹**debit** /'debit/ n 1 a record of money owed 2 a charge against a bank account

²**debit** v to charge to the debit of

debonair /,debə'neə/ adj 1 suave, urbane 2 lighthearted, nonchalant

debouch /di'bowch/ v to emerge or issue, esp from a narrow place into a wider place

debris /'debri/ n 1 the remains of sthg broken down or destroyed 2a an accumulation of fragments of rock b accumulated rubbish or waste

debt /det/ n 1 a state of owing 2 sthg owed; an obligation — **in someone's debt** owing sby gratitude; indebted to sby

debtor /'detə/ n one who owes a debt

debut /'dayb(y)ooh/ n 1 a first public appearance 2 a formal entrance into society

debutante /'debyoo,tont/ n a young woman making her formal entrance into society

decade /'dekayd; also di'kayd/ n 1 a period of 10 years 2 a division of the rosary containing 10 Hail Marys

decadence /'dekədəns/ n 1 the gratification of ones desires, whims, etc in an excessive or unrestrained manner 2 a (period of) decline in moral or cultural standards – -**ent** adj – -**ently** adv

decamp /,dee'kamp/ v 1 to break up a camp 2 to depart suddenly; abscond

decant /di'kant/ v to pour from one vessel into another, esp without disturbing the sediment – ~**er** n

decapitate /di'kapitayt/ v to cut off the head of – -**tation** n

decathlon /di'kathlon/ n a men's athletic contest in which each competitor competes in 10 events

¹**decay** /di'kay/ v 1 to decline from a sound or prosperous condition 2 to decrease gradually in quantity, activity, or force; *specif* to undergo radioactive decay 3 to decline in health, strength, or vigour 4 to undergo decomposition

²**decay** n 1 a gradual decline in strength, soundness, prosperity, or quality 2 a wasting or wearing away; ruin 3 (a product of) rot; *specif* decomposition of organic matter chiefly by bacteria in the

presence of oxygen **4** decrease in quantity, activity, or force; *esp* spontaneous disintegration of an atom or particle usu with the emission of radiation

decease /di'sees/ *n* death – *fml* – **~d** *adj, n*

deceit /di'seet/ *n* **1** the act or practice of deceiving; deception **2** the quality of being deceitful

de·ceitful /-f(ə)l/ *adj* having a tendency or disposition to deceive: as not honest **b** deceptive, misleading – **~ly** *adv* – **~ness** *n*

deceive /di'seev/ *v* to cause to accept as true or valid what is false or invalid; delude – **deceiver** *n*

decelerate /,dee'seləraytt/ *v* to (cause to) move at decreasing speed – **-ation** *n*

December /di'sembə/ *n* the 12th month of the Gregorian calendar

decent /'dees(ə)nt/ *adj* **1** conforming to standards of propriety, good taste, or morality; *specif* clothed according to standards of propriety **2** adequate, tolerable **3** *chiefly Br* obliging, considerate – *infml* – **decency** *n* – **~ly** *adv*

decentral·ize, -ise /,dee'sentrəliez/ *v* to shift governmental powers from central to regional or local authorities – **-ization** *n*

deception /di'sepsh(ə)n/ *n* **1** deceiving or being deceived **2** sthg that deceives; a trick

deceptive /di'septiv/ *adj* tending or having power to deceive; misleading – **~ly** *adv* – **~ness** *n*

decibel /'desibel/ *n* a unit for expressing the intensity of sounds on a scale from zero for the average least perceptible sound to about 130 for the average pain level

decide /di'sied/ *v* **1** to arrive at a solution that ends uncertainty or dispute about **2** to bring to a definitive end **3** to make a choice or judgment

de·cided *adj* **1** unquestionable **2** free from doubt or hesitation – **~ly** *adv*

deciduous /di'sidyoo·əs/ *adj* (having parts) that fall off or are shed seasonally or at a particular stage in development

¹decimal /'desiml/ *adj* numbered or proceeding by tens: **1a** based on the number 10 **b** subdivided into units which are tenths, hundredths, etc of another unit **2** using a decimal system (e g of coinage) – **~ly** *adv*

²decimal, decimal 'fraction *n* a fraction that is expressed as a sum of integral multiples of powers of ¹/₁₀ by writing a dot followed by 1 digit for the number of tenths, 1 digit for the number of hundredths, and so on (e g 0.25 = ²⁵/₁₀₀)

decimal·ize, -ise /'desiməliez/ *v* to convert (currency, weights and measures, etc) to a decimal system

decimal 'point *n* the dot at the left of a decimal fraction

decimate /'desimaytt/ *v* **1** to kill every tenth man of (e g mutinous soldiers) **2** to destroy a large part of – **-mation** *n*

decipher /di'siefə/ *v* **1** to decode **2** to make out the meaning of despite obscurity

decision /di'sizh(ə)n/ *n* **1a** deciding **b** a conclusion arrived at after consideration **2** a report of a conclusion **3** promptness and firmness in deciding

decisive /di'siesiv/ *adj* **1** conclusive, final **2** firm, resolute **3** unmistakable, unquestionable – **~ly** *adv* – **~ness** *n*

¹deck /dek/ *n* **1** a platform in a ship serving usu as a structural element and forming the floor for its compartments **2a** a level or floor of a bus with more than 1 floor **b** the part of a record player or tape recorder on which the record or tape is mounted when being played **3** *NAm* a pack of playing cards **4** *the* ground – *infml*; chiefly in *hit the deck*

²deck *v* to array, decorate – often + *out*

'deck ,chair *n* an adjustable folding chair made of canvas stretched over a wooden frame

'deck ,hand /-,hand/ *n* a seaman who performs manual duties

declaim /di'klaym/ *v* to speak rhetorically, pompously, or bombastically – **declamation** *n* – **declamatory** *adj*

declaration /,deklə'raysh(ə)n/ *n* **1** sthg declared **2** a document containing such a declaration

declare /di'kleə/ *v* **1** to make known formally or explicitly **2** to make evident; show **3** to state emphatically; affirm **4** to make a full statement of (one's taxable or dutiable income or property) **5** *of a captain or team* to announce one's decision to end one's side's innings in cricket before all the batsmen are out – **declarable** *adj* – **declaratory** *adj* — **declare war** to commence hostilities; *specif* to make a formal declaration of intention to go to war

declination /,dekli'naysh(ə)n/ *n* **1** angular distance (e g of a star) N or S from the celestial equator **2** the angle between a compass needle and the geographical meridian, equal to the difference between magnetic and true north

¹decline /di'klien/ *v* **1** to slope or bend down **2a** *of a celestial body* to sink towards setting **b** to draw towards a close; wane **3a** to refuse to undertake, engage in, or comply with **b** to refuse courteously

²decline *n* **1a** a gradual physical or mental decay **b** a change to a lower state or level **2** the period during which sthg is approaching its end **3** a downward slope

decode /,dee'kohd/ *v* to convert (a coded message) into intelligible language

decolon·ize, -ise /,dee'koləniez/ *v* to free from colonial status; grant self government

decompose /,deekəm'pohz/ *v* to undergo chemical breakdown; decay, rot – **-position** *n*

decompress /,deekəm'pres/ *v* to release from pressure or compression – **~ion** *n*

decontaminate /,deekən'taminaytt/ *v* to rid of (radioactive) contamination – **-nation** *n*

dec

decor, décor /'dekaw/ n the style and layout of interior decoration and furnishings

decorate /'dekərayt/ v **1a** to add sthg ornamental to b to apply new coverings of paint, wallpaper, etc to the interior or exterior surfaces of **2** to award a mark of honour to – **-ation** n

decorative /'dek(ə)rətiv/ adj purely ornamental rather than functional – ~**ly** adv

decorator /'dekə,raytə/ n one who designs or executes interior decoration and furnishings

decorous /'dekərəs/ adj marked by propriety and good taste; correct – ~**ly** adv

decorum /di'kawrəm/ n propriety and good taste in conduct or appearance

decoy /'deekoy, di'koy/ n **1** a pond into which wild fowl are lured for capture **2** sthg used to lure or lead another into a trap b sby or sthg used to distract or divert the attention (e g of an enemy) – **decoy** v

¹**decrease** /di'krees/ v to (cause to) grow progressively less (e g in size, amount, number, or intensity)

²**decrease** /'dee,krees, di'krees/ n **1** the process of decreasing **2** the amount by which sthg decreases

¹**decree** /di'kree/ n **1** an order usu having legal force **2** a judicial decision, esp in a equity, probate, or divorce court

²**decree** v to command or impose by decree

decree nisi /di,kree 'neezi, -zie, 'niesie/ n a provisional decree of divorce that is made absolute after a fixed period unless cause to the contrary is shown

decrepit /di'krepit/ adj **1** wasted and weakened e g by old age **2a** worn-out b fallen into ruin or disrepair – ~**ude** n

decry /di'krie/ v to express strong disapproval of

dedicate /'dedikayt/ v **1** to consecrate **2a** to set apart to a definite use b to assign permanently to a goal or way of life **3** to inscribe or address (a book, song, etc) to somebody or something as a mark of esteem or affection

'**dedicated** adj **1** devoted to a cause, ideal, or purpose; zealous **2** given over to a particular purpose – ~**ly** adv

dedication /,dedi'kaysh(ə)n/ n **1** a devoting or setting aside for a particular, specif religious, purpose **2** a phrase or sentence that dedicates **3** self-sacrificing devotion

deduce /di'dyoohs/ v to infer from a general principle – **-ducible** adj – **-duction** n – **-ductive** adj

deduct /di'dukt/ v to subtract (an amount) from a total – ~**ible** adj – ~**ion** n

deed /deed/ n **1** an illustrious act or action; a feat, exploit **2** the act of performing **3** a signed (and sealed) written document containing some legal transfer, bargain, or contract

deem /deem/ v to judge, consider – fml

---

¹**deep** /deep/ adj **1a** extending far downwards b (extending) far from the surface of the body c extending well back from a front surface d near the outer limits of the playing area **2** having a specified extension in an implied direction **3a** difficult to understand b capable of profound thought c engrossed, involved d intense, extreme **4a** of a colour high in saturation and low in lightness b having a low musical pitch or pitch range – ~**ly** adv – ~**ness** n — **in deep water** in difficulty or distress; unable to manage

²**deep** adv **1a(1)** to a great depth **a(2)** deep to a specified degree – usu in combination b well within the boundaries **2** far on; late **3** in a deep position

³**deep** n **1** a vast or immeasurable extent; an abyss **2** the sea

deepen /'deep(ə)n/ v to make or become deeper or more profound

,**deep-'freeze** v **-froze** /frohz/; **-frozen** /'frohz(ə)n/ to freeze or store (e g food) in a freezer

deep freeze n a freezer

,**deep-'fry** v to fry (food) by complete immersion in hot fat or oil

,**deep-'rooted** adj firmly established

,**deep-'seated** adj **1** situated far below the surface **2** firmly established

deer /diə/ n, pl **deer** also **deers** any of several ruminant mammals of which most of the males and some of the females bear antlers

'**deer,stalker** /-,stawkə/ n a close-fitting hat with peaks at the front and the back and flaps that may be folded down as coverings for ears

deface /di'fays/ v to mar the external appearance of – ~**ment** n

defame /di'faym/ v to injure the reputation of by libel or slander – **defamatory** adj – **defamation** n

¹**default** /di'fawlt/ n failure to act, pay, appear, or compete — **in default of** in the absence of

²**default** v to fail to meet an esp financial obligation – ~**er** n

¹**defeat** /di'feet/ v **1a** to nullify b to frustrate **2** to win victory over

²**defeat** n **1** an overthrow, esp of an army in battle **2** the loss of a contest

defeatism /di'feetiz(ə)m/ n acceptance of or resignation to defeat – **-ist** n

defecate /'defikayt/ v to discharge (esp faeces) from the bowels – **-cation** n

¹**defect** /'deefekt/ n an imperfection that impairs worth or usefulness – ~**ive** n

²**defect** /di'fekt/ v to desert a cause or party, often in order to espouse another – ~**or** n – ~**ion** n

defence, NAm chiefly **defense** /di'fens/ n **1** the act or action of defending **2a** a means or method of defending; also, pl a defensive structure b an argument in support or justification c a defendant's denial, answer, or strategy **3** sing or pl in constr **3a** a defending party or group (e g in a court of law) b defensive players, acts, or moves in a game or sport 4 the military resources of a country – ~less adj

defend /di'fend/ v **1a** to protect from attack **b** to maintain by argument or be in the face of opposition or criticism **2a** to play or be in defence **b** to attempt to prevent an opponent from scoring (e g a goal) **3** to act as legal representative in court for

defendant /di'fend(ə)nt/ n a person, company, etc against whom a criminal charge or civil claim is made

defensible /di'fensəbl/ adj capable of being defended – **-bly** adv

¹**defensive** /di'fensiv/ adj **1** serving to defend **2a** disposed to ward off expected criticism or critical inquiry **b** of or relating to the attempt to keep an opponent from scoring

²**defensive** n — **on the defensive** being prepared for expected aggression, attack, or criticism

¹**defer** /di'fuh/ v **-rr-** to delay; put off – ~ment n

²**defer** v **-rr-** to submit to another's opinion, usu through deference or respect

deference /'def(ə)rəns/ n respect and esteem due a superior or an elder – **-ential** adj – **-entially** adv — **in deference to** because of respect for

defiance /di'fie-əns/ n a disposition to resist; contempt of opposition – **defiant** adj – **defiantly** adv — **in defiance of** despite; contrary to

deficient /di'fish(ə)nt/ adj **1** lacking in some necessary quality or element **2** not up to a normal standard or complement – ~ly adv – **-iency** n

deficit /'defəsit/ n **1** a deficiency in amount or quality **2** an excess of expenditure over revenue

¹**defile** /di'fiel/ v to make unclean or (sexually) impure – ~r n – ~ment n

²**defile** v to march off in a file

³**defile** n a narrow passage or gorge

define /di'fien/ v **1** to fix or mark the limits of; demarcate **2a** to be the essential quality or qualities of; identify **b** to set forth the meaning of

definite /'definət/ adj **1** having distinct or certain limits **2a** free of all ambiguity, uncertainty, or obscurity **b** unquestionable, decided **3** designating an identified or immediately identifiable person or thing – ~ly adv

definition /,defi'nish(ə)n/ n **1** a word or phrase expressing the essential nature of a person, word, or thing; a meaning **2a** the action or power of making definite and clear **b**(1) distinctness of outline or detail (e g in a photograph) **b**(2) clarity, esp of musical sound in reproduction

definitive /di'finətiv/ adj authoritative and apparently exhaustive – ~ly adv

deflate /di'flayt, ,dee-/ v **1** to release air or gas from **2a** to reduce in size or importance **b** to reduce in self-confidence or self-importance, esp suddenly **3** to reduce (a price level) or cause (the availability of credit or the economy) to contract

deflation /di'flaysh(ə)n, ,dee-/ n **1** a contraction in the volume of available money and credit, and thus in the economy, esp as a result of government policy **2** a decline in the general level of prices

deflect /di'flekt/ v to turn from a straight course or fixed direction

deflection, Br also **deflexion** /di'fleksh(ə)n/ n (the amount or degree of) deflecting

deflower /,dee'flowə/ v to deprive of virginity; ravish

deform /di'fawm/ v **1** to spoil the form or appearance of **2** to make hideous or monstrous **3** to alter the shape of by stress – ~**ation** n

deformity /di'fawməti/ n a physical blemish or distortion; a disfigurement

defraud /di'frawd/ v to cheat of sth

defray /di'fray/ v to provide for the payment of

defrost /,dee'frost/ v **1** to thaw out, esp from a deep-frozen state **2** to free from ice – ~er n

deft /deft/ adj marked by facility and skill – ~ly adv – ~ness n

defunct /di'fungkt/ adj no longer existing or in use; esp dead

defuse /,dee'fyoohz/ v **1** to remove the fuse from (a mine, bomb, etc) **2** to make less harmful, potent, or tense

defy /di'fie/ v **1** to challenge to do sth considered impossible; dare **2** to show no fear of nor respect for **3** to resist attempts at

¹**degenerate** /di'jen(ə)rət/ n sth g or esp sby degenerate; esp one showing signs of reversion to an earlier cultural or evolutionary stage

²**degenerate** /di'jenərayt/ v **1** to pass from a higher to a lower type or condition; deteriorate **2** to sink into a low intellectual or moral state **3** to decline from a former thriving or healthy condition – **-ration** n – **-rative** adj – **-racy** n

degrade /di'grayd/ v **1a** to demote **b** to impair with respect to some physical property **2** to bring to low esteem or into disrepute – **-dation** n

degree /di'gree/ n **1** a step or stage in a process, course, or order of classification **2a** the extent or measure of an action, condition, or relation **b** a legal measure of guilt or negligence **c** a positive and esp considerable amount **3** the civil condition or status of a person **4** an academic title conferred: **4a** on students in recognition of proficiency **b** honorarily **5** a division or interval of a scale of measurement; specif any of various units for measuring temperature **6** a 360th part of the circumference of a circle — **to a degree 1** to a remarkable extent **2** in a small way

dehuman·ize, -ise /,dee'hyoohmaniez/ v to divest of human qualities

dehydrate /,deehie'drayt/ v to remove (bound) water from (a chemical compound, foods, etc) – ~d adj – **-dration** n

deify /'dee·ifie, 'day-/ v to make a god or an object of worship of – **deification** n

deign /dayn/ *v* to condescend to give or offer

deity /'dee-əti, 'day-/ *n 1 cap the* Supreme Being; God **2** a god or goddess

déjà vu /ˌdayzhah 'vooh/ *n* the illusion of remembering scenes and events when they are experienced for the first time

dejected /di'jektid/ *adj* cast down in spirits; depressed – **~ly** *adv*

dejection /di'jeksh(ə)n/ *n* lowness of spirits

¹**delay** /di'lay/ *n 1* delaying or (an instance of) being delayed **2** the time during which sthg is delayed

²**delay** *v 1a* to postpone **b** to move or act slowly **2a** to pause momentarily **b** to stop, detain, or hinder for a time

delectable /di'lektəbl/ *adj 1* highly pleasing; delightful **2** delicious – **-bly** *adv* – **-tation** *n*

¹**delegate** /'deligət/ *n* a person delegated to act for another; *esp* a representative to a conference

²**delegate** /'deligayt/ *v 1* to assign responsibility or authority **2** to appoint as one's representative

delegation /ˌdeli'gaysh(ə)n/ *n sing or pl in constr* a group of people chosen to represent others

delete /di'leet/ *v* to eliminate, esp by blotting out, cutting out, or erasing – **-tion** *n*

deleterious /ˌdeli'tiəri-əs/ *adj* harmful, detrimental – fml – **~ly** *adv*

¹**deliberate** /di'lib(ə)rət/ *adj 1* of or resulting from careful and thorough consideration **2** characterized by awareness of the consequences **3** slow, unhurried – **~ly** *adv* – **~ness** *n*

²**deliberate** /di'librayt/ *v* to ponder issues and decisions carefully – **-ative** *adj*

deliberation /di,libə'raysh(ə)n/ *n 1* deliberating or being deliberate **2** a discussion and consideration of pros and cons

delicacy /'delikəsi/ *n 1* sthg pleasing to eat that is considered rare or luxurious **2** the quality or state of being dainty **3** frailty, fragility **4** precise and refined perception or discrimination **5** refined sensibility in feeling or conduct

delicate /'delikət/ *adj 1* pleasing to the senses in a subtle way; dainty, charming **2a** marked by keen sensitivity or subtle discrimination **b** fastidious, squeamish **3** marked by extreme precision or sensitivity **4** calling for or involving meticulously careful treatment **5a** very finely made **b(1)** fragile **b(2)** weak, sickly **c** marked by or requiring tact – **~ly** *adv*

delicatessen /ˌdelikə'tes(ə)n/ *n 1 pl in constr* (delicacies and foreign) foods ready for eating (e g cooked meats) **2** a shop where delicatessen are sold

delicious /di'lishəs/ *adj 1* affording great pleasure; delightful **2** highly pleasing to one of the bodily senses, esp of taste or smell – **~ly** *adv* – **~ness** *n*

¹**delight** /di'liet/ *n 1* great pleasure or satisfaction; joy **2** sthg that gives great pleasure

²**delight** *v* to take great pleasure *in* doing sthg

de'lightful /-f(ə)l/ *adj* highly pleasing – **~ly** *adv*

delineate /di'liniayt/ *v 1* to show by drawing lines in the shape of **2** to describe in usu sharp or vivid detail – **-ation** *n*

delinquency /di'lingkwənsi/ *n* (the practice of engaging in) antisocial or illegal conduct – used esp when emphasis is placed on maladjustment rather than criminal intent – **-quent** *n*

delinquent /di'lingkwənt/ *adj 1* guilty of wrongdoing or of neglect of duty **2** marked by delinquency

delirium /di'liəri-əm/ *n 1* confusion, frenzy, disordered speech, hallucinations, etc occurring as a (temporary) mental disturbance **2** frenzied excitement – **-rious** *adj* – **-riously** *adv*

de lirium 'tremens /'tremənz/ *n* a violent delirium with tremors induced by chronic alcoholism

deliver /di'livə/ *v 1* to set free **2** to hand over **3a** to aid in the birth of **b** to give birth to **4** to utter **5** to aim or guide (e g a blow) to an intended target or destination **6** to produce the promised, desired, or expected results – *infml*

deliverance /di'liv(ə)rəns/ *n* liberation, rescue

delivery /di'liv(ə)ri/ *n 1* handing over **2a** a physical or legal transfer **b** sthg delivered at **1** time or in **1** unit **3** the act of giving birth **4** the manner or style of uttering in speech or song **5** the act or manner or an instance of sending forth, throwing, or bowling

dell /del/ *n* a small secluded hollow or valley, esp in a forest

delphinium /del'fini-əm/ *n* any of a genus of plants of the buttercup family with deeply cut leaves and flowers in showy spikes

delta /'deltə/ *n 1* the 4th letter of the Greek alphabet **2** a triangular deposit (e g of silt) at the mouth of a river

'**delta ,wing** *n* an approximately triangular aircraft wing with a (nearly) straight rearmost edge

delude /di'loohd/ *v* to mislead the mind or judgment of; deceive, trick

¹**deluge** /'delyoohj, -yoohzh/ *n 1a* a great flood; *specif, cap the* Flood recorded in the Old Testament (Gen 6:8) **b** a drenching fall of rain **2** an overwhelming amount or number

²**deluge** *v 1* to overflow with water; inundate **2** to overwhelm, swamp

delusion /di'loohzh(ə)n/ *n* (a mental state characterized by) a false belief (about the self or others) that persists despite the facts – **-sive** *adj*

de luxe /di 'luks/ *adj* notably luxurious or elegant

delve /delv/ *v 1* to dig or work (as if) with a spade **2** to make a careful or detailed search for information

159   den

demagogue, *NAm also* **demagog** /'deməgog/ *n* **1** a leader of the common people in ancient times **2** an agitator who makes use of popular prejudices in order to gain power – **~ry** *n* – **gogic** *adj* – **gogically** *adv*

¹demand /di'mahnd/ *n* **1** demanding or asking, esp with authority; a claim **2a** an expressed desire for ownership or use **b** willingness and ability to purchase a commodity or service **c** the quantity of a commodity or service wanted at a specified price and time **3** a desire or need *for*; the state of being sought after — **on demand** whenever the demand is made

²demand *v* **1** to make a demand; ask **2** to call for urgently, abruptly, or insistently

demanding /di'mahnding/ *adj* exacting

demarcate /'deemah,kayt/ *v* **1** to mark the limits of **2** to set apart; separate – **tion** *n*

demean /di'meen/ *v* to degrade, debase

demeanour, *NAm chiefly* **demeanor** /di'meenə/ *n* behaviour towards others; outward manner

demented /di'mented/ *adj* insane; *also* crazy – **~ly** *adv*

demerara sugar /,demə'reərə/ *n* brown crystallized unrefined cane sugar from the W Indies

demesne /di'mayn, -'meen/ *n* **1** land actually occupied by the owner and not held by tenants **2a** the land attached to a mansion **b** landed property; an estate

demise /di'miez/ *n* **1** the conveyance of an estate or transfer of sovereignty by will or lease **2a** death – technical, euph, or humor **b** a cessation of existence or activity – fml or humor

demist /,dee'mist/ *v* to remove mist from (e g a car windscreen) – **~er** *n*

demo /'demoh/ *n pl* **demos** a (political) demonstration

demobilize, -ise /,dee'mohbiliez/ *v* to discharge from military service – **ization** *n*

democracy /di'mokrəsi/ *n* **1a** government by the people **b** (a political unit with) a government in which the supreme power is exercised by the people directly or indirectly through a system of representation usu involving free elections **2** the absence of class distinctions or privileges

democrat /'deməkrat/ *n* **1a** an adherent of democracy **b** one who practises social equality **2** *cap* a member of the Democratic party of the USA

democratic /,demə'kratik/ *adj* **1** of or favouring democracy or social equality **2** *often cap* of or constituting a political party of the USA associated with policies of social reform and internationalism – **~ally** *adv* – **ratization** *n*

demography /di'mogrəfi/ *n* the statistical study of human populations, esp with reference to size and density, distribution, and vital statistics – **pher** *n* – **phic** *adj*

demolish /di'molish/ *v* **1** to destroy, smash, or tear down **2** to eat up – infml – **~er** *n* – **ition** *n*

demon /'deemən/ *n* **1** an evil spirit **2** one who has unusual drive or effectiveness – **ic** *adj* – **ically** *adv*

demonstrate /'demənstrayt/ *v* **1** to show clearly **2** to illustrate and explain, esp with many examples **3** to show or prove the application, value, or efficiency of to a prospective buyer **4** to take part in a (political) demonstration – **tion** *n* – **strable** *adj*

demonstrative /di'monstrətiv/ *adj* given to or marked by display of feeling

demonstrator /'demən,straytə/ *n* **1** a junior staff member who demonstrates experiments in a university science department **2** sby who participates in a demonstration

demoralize, -ise /di'morə,liez/ *v* to discourage; dispirit

demote /di'moht/ *v* to reduce to a lower grade or rank – **tion** *n*

demur /di'muh/ *v* **-rr-** to take exception; (mildly) object

demure /di'myooə/ *adj* **1** reserved, modest **2** affectedly modest, reserved, or serious; coy – **~ly** *adv* – **~ness** *n*

den /den/ *n* **1** the lair of a wild, usu predatory, animal **2** a centre of secret, esp unlawful, activity **3** a comfortable usu secluded room

denial /di'nie-əl/ *n* **1** a refusal to satisfy a request or desire **2a** a refusal to admit the truth or reality (e g of a statement or charge) **b** an assertion that an allegation is false **3** a refusal to acknowledge sby or sthg; a disavowal

denier /'deeni-ə, 'deenyə/ *n* a unit of fineness for silk, rayon, or nylon yarn

denigrate /'denigrayt/ *v* **1** to cast aspersions on; defame **2** to belittle – **gration** *n* – **gratory** *adj*

denim /'denəm/ *n* **1** a firm durable twilled usu blue cotton fabric used esp for jeans **2** *pl* denim trousers; *esp* blue jeans

denizen /'deniz(ə)n/ *n* **1** an inhabitant **2** a naturalized plant or animal

denomination /di,nomi'naysh(ə)n/ *n* **1** a religious organization or sect **2** a grade or degree in a series of values or sizes (e g of money)

denominator /di'nomi,naytə/ *n* the part of a vulgar fraction that is below the line and that in fractions with 1 as the numerator indicates into how many parts the unit is divided

denote /di'noht/ *v* **1** to indicate **2** to be a sign or mark for **3** to mean – **denotation** *n*

denouement /day'noohmonh/ *n* **1** the resolution of the main complication in a literary work **2** the outcome of a complex sequence of events

denounce /di'nowns/ *v* **1** to condemn, esp publicly, as deserving censure or punishment **2** to inform against; accuse

dense /dens/ *adj* 1 marked by high density, compactness, or crowding together of parts 2 sluggish of mind; stupid 3 demanding concentration to follow or comprehend – ~ **ly** *adv* – ~ **ness** *n*

density /'densəti/ *n* 1 the mass of a substance or distribution of a quantity per unit of volume or space 2 the degree of opaqueness of sthg translucent

dent /dent/ *n* 1 a depression or hollow made by a blow or by pressure 2 an adverse effect – **dent** *v*

dental /'dentl/ *adj* of the teeth or dentistry

dentifrice /'denti,fris/ *n* a powder, paste, or liquid for cleaning the teeth

dentine /'denteen/ *n* a calcium-containing material, similar to but harder and denser than bone, of which the principal mass of a tooth is composed

dentist /'dentist/ *n* one who treats diseases, injuries, etc of the teeth, and mouth and who makes and inserts false teeth – ~ **ry** *n*

denture /'denchə, -chooə/ *n* an artificial replacement for 1 or more teeth; *esp, pl* a set of false teeth

denude /di'nyoohd/ *v* **1a** to strip of all covering **b** to lay bare by erosion 2 to remove an important possession or quality from; strip

denunciation /di,nunsi'aysh(ə)n/ *n* a (public) condemnation

deny /di'nie/ *v* 1 to declare to be untrue or invalid; refuse to accept **2a** to give a negative answer to **b** to refuse to grant 3 to restrain (oneself) from self-indulgence

deodorant /dee'ohdərənt/ *n* a preparation that destroys or masks unpleasant smells – **orize** *v*

depart /di'paht/ *v* 1 to leave; go away (from) 2 to turn aside; deviate *from* – ~ **ed** *adj* – ~ **ure** *v*

department /di'pahtmənt/ *n* **1a** a division of an institution or business that provides a specified service or deals with a specified subject **b** a major administrative subdivision (e g in France) **c** a section of a large store 2 a distinct sphere (e g of activity or thought) – infml – ~ **al** *adj*

depend /di'pend/ *v* 1 to be determined by or based on some condition or action **2a** to place reliance or trust **b** to be dependent, esp for financial support *USE* (1&2) + *on* or *upon*

dependable /di'pendəbl/ *adj* reliable – **bly** *adv* – **bility** *n*

dependant, *NAm chiefly* **dependent** /di'pendənt/ *n* a person who relies on another for esp financial support

dependence *also* **dependance** /di'pendəns/ *n* 1 being influenced by or subject to another 2 reliance, trust 3 psychological need for a drug after a period of use; habituation

dependency /di'pend(ə)nsi/ *n* a territorial unit under the jurisdiction of a nation but not formally annexed to it

dependent /di'pend(ə)nt/ *adj* 1 determined or conditioned by another; contingent 2 relying on another for support 3 subject to another's jurisdiction *USE* (1&2) + *on* or *upon*

depict /di'pikt/ *v* 1 to represent by a picture 2 to describe – **depiction** *n*

deplete /di'pleet/ *v* to reduce in amount by using up; exhaust, esp of strength or resources – **depletion** *n*

deplore /di'plaw/ *v* to regret or disapprove of strongly – **rable** *adj* – **rably** *adv*

deploy /di'ploy/ *v* 1 to spread out (e g troops or ships), esp in battle formation 2 to utilize or arrange as if deploying troops – ~ **ment** *n*

depopulate /,dee'popyoolayt/ *v* to greatly reduce the population of – **lation** *n*

¹deport /di'pawt/ *v* to expel (e g an alien or convicted criminal) legally from a country – ~ **ation** *n*

deport 2 *v* to behave or conduct (oneself) in a specified manner – fml

de'portment /-mənt/ *n* 1 the manner in which one stands, sits, or walks; posture 2 behaviour, conduct

depose /di'pohz/ *v* 1 to remove from a position of authority (e g a throne) 2 to testify under oath or by affidavit

¹deposit /di'pozit/ *v* 1 to place, esp for safekeeping or as a pledge; *esp* to put in a bank 2 to lay down; place – ~ **or** *n*

²deposit *n* 1 depositing or being deposited **2a** money deposited in a bank **b** money given as a pledge or down payment 3 a depository 4 sthg laid down; *esp* (an accumulation of) matter deposited by a natural process

de'posit ac,count *n, chiefly Br* an account (e g in a bank) on which interest is usu payable and from which withdrawals can be made usu only by prior arrangement

deposition /,depə'zish(ə)n, ,dee-/ *n* 1 removal from a position of authority 2 a (written and sworn) statement presented as evidence

depository /di'pozit(ə)ri/ *n* a place where sthg is deposited, esp for safekeeping

depot /'depoh/ *n* 1 a place for the reception and training of military recruits; a regimental headquarters **2a** a place for storing goods **b** a store, depository 3 *Br* an area (e g a garage) in which buses or trains are stored, esp for maintenance

deprave /di'prayv/ *v* to corrupt morally; pervert – **depravation** *n*

depravity /di'pravəti/ *n* (an instance of) moral corruption

deprecate /'deprikayt/ *v* to express disapproval of, esp mildly or regretfully – **catingly** *adv* – **cation** *n*

deprecatory /'deprikayt(ə)ri/ *adj* 1 apologetic 2 disapproving

depreciate /di'prees(h)iayt/ *v* to lessen in value – **atory** *adj* – **depreciation** *n*

depress /di'pres/ *v* **1** to push or press down **2** to lessen the activity or strength of **3** to sadden, dispirit – **depressing** *adj* – **depressingly** *adv* – **depressed** *adj*

depression /di'presh(ə)n/ *n* **1a** a pressing down; a lowering **b** (a mental disorder marked by inactivity, difficulty in thinking and concentration, and esp by) sadness or dejection **2** a depressed place or part; a hollow **3** an area of low pressure in a weather system **4** a period of low general economic activity marked esp by rising levels of unemployment

deprivation /,depri'vaysh(ə)n/ *n* **1** an act of depriving; a loss **2** being deprived; privation

deprive /di'priev/ *v* **1** to take sthg away from **2** to withhold sthg from *USE + of*

de'prived *adj* lacking the necessities of life or a good environment

depth /depth/ *n* **1a** a part that is far from the outside or surface **b(1)** a profound or intense state (e g of thought or feeling) **b(2)** the worst, most intensive, or severest part **2a** the perpendicular measurement downwards from a surface **b** the distance from front to back **3** the degree of intensity *USE* (1) often pl with sing. meaning — **in depth** with great thoroughness — **out of one's depth 1** in water that is deeper than one's height **2** beyond one's ability to understand

'**depth ,charge** *n* an explosive projectile for use underwater, esp against submarines

deputation /,depyoo'taysh(ə)n/ *n sing or pl in constr* a group of people appointed to represent others

depute /di'pyooht/ *v* to delegate

deputy /'depyooti/ *n* **1** a person (e g a second-in-command) appointed as a substitute with power to act for another **2** a member of the lower house of some legislative assemblies – **-tize** *v*

derail /,dee'rayl/ *v* to cause (e g a train) to leave the rails – ~**ment** *n*

derange /di'raynj/ *v* to disturb the operation or functions of – ~**ment** *n*

derby /'dahbi/ *n* **1** *cap* a flat race for 3-year-old horses over 1 ^{1}/$_2$mi (about 2.9km) held annually at Epsom in England **2** a usu informal race or contest for a specified category of contestant **3** a sporting match against a major local rival **4** *chiefly NAm* a bowler hat

'**derelict** /'derəlikt/ *adj* left to decay

²**derelict** *n* **1** sthg voluntarily abandoned; *specif* a ship abandoned on the high seas **2** a down-and-out

dereliction /,derə'liksh(ə)n/ *n* **1** (intentional) abandonment or being abandoned **2a** conscious neglect **b** a fault, shortcoming

deride /di'ried/ *v* to mock, scorn – **derision** *n* – **derisive** *adj* – **derisively** *adv*

derisory /di'riez(ə)ri/ *adj* worthy of derision; ridiculous; *specif* contemptibly small – **-rily** *adv*

derivative /di'rivətiv/ *adj* made up of derived elements; not original – **derivative** *n*

derive /di'riev/ *v* **1** to obtain or receive, esp *from* a specified source **2** to infer, deduce *from* – **-vation** *n*

dermatitis /,duhmə'tietəs/ *n* a disease or inflammation of the skin

dermatology /,duhmə'toləji/ *n* a branch of medicine dealing with (diseases of) the skin – **-ogist** *n*

derogatory /di'rogət(ə)ri/ *adj* expressing a low opinion; disparaging – **-rily** *adv*

derrick /'derik/ *n* **1** a hoisting apparatus employing a tackle rigged at the end of a beam **2** a framework over an oil well or similar hole, for supporting drilling tackle

derring-do /,dering 'dooh/ *n* daring action

derv /duhv/ *n* fuel oil for diesel engines

dervish /'duhvish/ *n* a member of a Muslim religious order noted for devotional exercises (e g bodily movements leading to a trance)

descant /'des,kant/ *n* a counterpoint superimposed on a simple melody and usu sung by some or all of the sopranos

descend /di'send/ *v* **1** to pass from a higher to a lower level **2** to pass by inheritance **3** to incline, lead, or extend downwards **4** to come down or make a sudden attack – usu + *on* or *upon* **5** to sink in status or dignity; stoop

descendant, *NAm also* **descendent** /di'send(ə)nt/ *n* sby or sthg descended or deriving from another

de'scended *adj* having as an ancestor; sprung *from*

descent /di'sent/ *n* **1** the act or process of descending **2** a downward step (e g in status or value) **3a** derivation from an ancestor **b** a transmission from a usu earlier source; a derivation **4** a downward inclination; a slope

describe /di'skrieb/ *v* **1** to give an account of in words **2** to trace the outline of

description /di'skripsh(ə)n/ *n* **1** an account **2** kind, sort – **-tive** *adj* – **-tively** *adv* – **-tiveness** *n*

descry /di'skrie/ *v* to notice or see, esp at a distance – *fml*

desecrate /'desikrayt/ *v* to violate the sanctity of; profane – **-cration** *n*

desensit·ize, -ise /,dee'sensətiez/ *v* to cause to become less sensitive, or insensitive

'**desert** /'dezət/ *n* (a desolate region like) a dry barren region incapable of supporting much life

²**desert** /di'zuht/ *n* deserved reward or punishment – usu pl with sing. meaning

³**desert** /di'zuht/ *v* **1** to quit one's post, (military) service, etc without leave or justification **2** to abandon or forsake, esp in time of need – **deserter** *n* – **desertion** *n*

Desert /'dezət/ *trademark* – used for an ankle-high laced suede boot with a rubber sole

deserve /di'zuhv/ v to be worthy of or suitable for (some recompense or treatment) – ~**ly** adv – **deserving** adj

deshabille /,dayza'beel, dis-/, **déshabillé** /,dayza'bee,ay/ n the state of being only partially or carelessly dressed

desiccate /'desikayt/ v 1 to dry up 2 to preserve (a food) by drying to dehydrate – **-cant** n – **-ation** n

¹design /di'zien/ v 1 to conceive and plan out in the mind 2a to draw the plans for b to create or execute according to a plan; devise – ~**er** n

²design n 1 a mental plan or scheme 2 pl dishonest, hostile, or acquisitive intent – + **on** 3 (the act of producing) a drawing, plan, or pattern showing the details of how sthg is to be constructed 4 the arrangement of the elements of a work of art or article 5 a decorative pattern

¹designate /'dezignət, -nayt/ adj chosen for an office but not yet installed

²designate /'dezignayt/ v 1 to indicate 2 to call by a distinctive name or title 3 to nominate for a specified purpose, office, or duty – **-nation** n

designing /di'ziening/ adj crafty, scheming

desirable /di'zie·ərəbl/ adj 1 causing (sexual) desire; attractive 2 worth seeking or doing as advantageous, beneficial, or wise – **-bility** n – **-bly** adv

¹desire /di'zie·ə/ v 1 to long or hope for 2 to express a wish for; request 3 to wish to have sexual relations with – **desirous** adj

²desire n 1 a conscious impulse towards something promising enjoyment or satisfaction 2 a (sexual) longing or craving

desist /di'zist/ v to cease to proceed or act – fml

desk /desk/ n 1a a table with a sloping or horizontal surface and often drawers and compartments, that is designed esp for writing and reading b a music stand 2 a division of an organization specializing in a usu specified phase of activity

desolate /'dezələt/ adj 1 deserted, uninhabited 2 forsaken, forlorn 3 barren, lifeless – ~**ly** adv – **-lation** n

¹despair /di'speə/ v to lose all hope or confidence

²despair n 1 utter loss of hope 2 a cause of hopelessness

despatch /di'spach/ v or n (to) dispatch

desperado /,despə'rahdoh/ n pl **desperadoes, desperados** a bold, reckless, or violent person, esp a criminal

desperate /'desp(ə)rət/ adj 1 being (almost) beyond hope 2a reckless because of despair b undertaken as a last resort 3 suffering extreme need or anxiety – ~**ly** adv – **-ation** n

despicable /di'spikəbl/ adj morally contemptible – **bly** adv

despise /di'spiez/ v 1 to regard with contempt or distaste 2 to regard as negligible or worthless

despite /di'spiet/ prep notwithstanding; in spite of

despondent /di'spond(ə)nt/ adj dejected – ~**ly** adv – **-dency** n

despot /'despot/ n 1 a ruler with absolute power 2 a person exercising power abusively or tyrannically – ~**ic** adj – ~**ically** adv – ~**ism** n

dessert /di'zuht/ n a usu sweet course or dish served at the end of a meal

des'sert,spoon /-,spoohn/ n a spoon intermediate in size between a teaspoon and a tablespoon and used for eating dessert

destination /,desti'naysh(ə)n/ n a place which is set for the end of a journey or to which sthg is sent

destine /'destin/ v 1 to designate or dedicate in advance 2 to direct or set apart for a specified purpose or goal

destiny /'destini/ n 1 the power or agency held to determine the course of events 2 sthg to which a person or thing is destined; fortune 3 a predetermined course of events

destitute /'destityooht/ adj 1 lacking sthg necessary or desirable – + **of** 2 lacking the basic necessities of life; extremely poor – **-tution** n

destroy /di'stroy/ v 1 to demolish, ruin 2 to put an end to; kill

destroyer /di'stroyə/ n a fast multi-purpose warship smaller than a cruiser

destruction /di'struksh(ə)n/ n 1 destroying or being destroyed 2 a cause of ruin or downfall

destructive /di'struktiv/ adj 1 causing destruction 2 designed or tending to destroy; negative – ~**ly** adv – ~**ness** n

desultory /'desəlt(ə)ri, 'dez-/ adj passing aimlessly from one subject or activity to another – **-rily** adv

detach /di'tach/ v to separate, esp from a larger mass and usu without causing damage – ~**able** adj

de'tached adj 1 standing by itself; specif not sharing any wall with another building 2 free from prejudice or emotional involvement; aloof – ~**ly** adv

de'tachment /-mənt/ n 1 a detaching, separation 2 sing or pl in constr a body of troops, ships, etc separated from the main body for a special mission 3 freedom from bias

¹detail /'dee,tayl/ n 1 a small and subordinate part; specif part of a work of art considered or reproduced in isolation 2 an individual relevant part or fact – usu pl 3 sing or pl in constr a small military detachment selected for a particular task — **in detail** item by item; thoroughly

²detail v 1 to report in detail 2 to assign to a particular task or place

detain /di'tayn/ v 1 to hold or retain (as if) in custody 2 to delay; hold back

detainee /,deetay'nee/ n a person held in custody, esp for political reasons

detect /di'tekt/ v to discover the existence or presence of – **detector** n – **-ive** adj

detective /di'tektiv/ n a policeman or other person engaged in investigating crimes, detecting lawbreakers, or getting information that is not readily accessible

détente, detente /day'tonht/ n a relaxation of strained relations (e g between ideologically opposed nations)

detention /di'tensh(ə)n/ n 1 detaining or being detained, esp in custody 2 the keeping in of a pupil after school hours as a punishment

deter /di'tuh/ v -rr- to discourage or prevent from acting

detergent /di'tuhj(ə)nt/ n a cleansing agent (e g washing-up liquid)

deteriorate /di'tiəri-ə,rayt/ v to grow or make or worse – -ration n

determinant /di'tuhminənt/ n sthg that determines, fixes, or conditions

determination /di,tuhmi'naysh(ə)n/ n 1 firm intention 2 the ability to make and act on firm decisions; resoluteness

determine /di'tuhmin/ v 1 to settle, decide 2a to fix beforehand b to regulate 3 to ascertain the intent, nature, or scope of

de'termined adj 1 decided, resolved 2 firm, resolute

determinism /di'tuhmi,niz(ə)m/ n 1 a doctrine that all phenomena are determined by preceding occurrences 2 a belief in predestination

deterrent /di'terənt/ n sthg that deters; esp a (nuclear) weapon that is held in readiness by one nation or alliance in order to deter another from attacking – -rence n

detest /di'test/ v to feel intense dislike for; loathe – ~able adj – ~ably adv – ~ation n

detonate /'detə,nayt/ v to (cause to) explode with sudden violence – -ation n

detonator /'detə,naytə/ n a device used for detonating a high explosive

detour /'dee,tooə/ n a deviation from a course or procedure; specif a way that is an alternative to a shorter or planned route – **detour** v

detract /di'trakt/ v to take away something desirable from – ~ion n

detractor /di'traktə/ n one who belittles sby or his/her ideas or beliefs

detriment /'detrimənt/ n (a cause of) injury or damage – ~al adj – ~ally adv

detritus /di'trietəs/ n, pl **detritus** /~/ debris caused by disintegration

deuce /dyoohs/ n 1 a playing card or the face of a dice representing the number 2 2 a tie in a game (e g tennis) after which a side must score 2 consecutive clear points to win 3a the devil, the dickens – formerly used as an interjection or intensive

devalue /,dee'valyooh/, **devaluate** /dee'valyoo,ayt/ v 1 to reduce the exchange value of (money) 2 to lessen the value or reputation of – **-uation** n

devastate /'devəstayt/ v 1 to reduce to ruin; lay waste 2 to have a shattering effect on; overwhelm – **-station** n

develop /di'veləp/ v 1a to show signs of b to subject (exposed photograph material) esp to chemicals, in order to produce a visible image 2 to bring out the possibilities of 3a to promote the growth of b to make more available or usable 4 to acquire gradually 5a to go through a process of natural growth, differentiation, or evolution by successive changes b to evolve; broadly to grow

developer /di'veləpə/ n 1 a chemical used to develop exposed photographic materials 2 sby who buys land and builds and sells houses on it

de'velopment /-mənt/ n 1 the act, process, or result of developing; esp economic growth 2 being developed

deviant /'deevi·ənt/ adj deviating, esp from a norm

deviate /'deevi,ayt/ v to stray, esp from a topic, principle, or accepted norm or from a straight course – **-ation** n

device /di'vies/ n 1a sthg elaborate or intricate in design b sthg (e g a figure of speech or a dramatic convention) designed to achieve a particular artistic effect c a piece of equipment or a mechanism designed for a special purpose or function 2 pl desire, will

devil /'devl/ n 1 often cap the supreme spirit of evil in Jewish and Christian belief 2 a malignant spirit 3 an extremely cruel or wicked person 4 a high-spirited, reckless, or energetic person 5a a person of the specified type b sthg provoking, difficult, or trying – ~ish adj – ~ishly adv – ~ry n

devilment /'devlmənt/ n wild mischief

,devil's 'advocate n 1 the Roman Catholic official who presents the possible objections to claims to canonization 2 a person who champions the less accepted or approved cause, esp for the sake of argument

devious /'deevi·əs, -vyəs/ adj 1 deviating from a straight or usual course 2 not straightforward or wholly sincere – ~ly adv – ~ness n

devise /di'viez/ v 1 to formulate in the mind; invent 2 to give or leave (real property) by will

devoid /di'voyd/ adj not having or using; lacking – + of

devolution /,deevə'loohsh(ə)n/ n 1 the passage of rights, property, etc to a successor 2 the surrender of functions and powers to regional authorities by a central government

devolve /di'volv/ v 1 to pass by transmission or succession 2 to fall or be passed, usu as an obligation or responsibility USE + on

devote /di'voht/ v 1 to set apart for a special purpose; dedicate to 2 to give (oneself) over wholly to

de'voted adj loyally attached – ~ly adv

devotee /ˌdevə'tee/ n a keen follower or supporter; an enthusiast

devotion /di'vohsh(ə)n/ n 1 a special act of prayer – usu pl 2a devoting or being devoted b ardent love, affection, or dedication

devour /di'vowə/ v 1 to eat up greedily or ravenously 2 to swallow up; consume 3 to take in eagerly through the mind or senses

devout /di'vowt/ adj devoted to religion; pious – **ly** adv – **ness** n

dew /dyooh/ n moisture that condenses on the surfaces of cool bodies, esp at night – **dewy** adj – **dewily** adv – **dewiness** n

dexterous, dextrous /'dekstrəs/ adj 1 skilful with the hands 2 mentally adroit – **ly** adv – **rity** n

dextrose /'dekstrohz, 'dekstrohs/ n the form of glucose found in fruit and honey

dhow /dow/ n an Arab boat, usu having a large 4-sided sail, a long overhanging bow and a high poop

diabetes /ˌdie-ə'beetis, -teez/ n any of various abnormal conditions characterized by an excess of sugar in the blood – **betic** adj

diabolic /ˌdie-ə'bolik/ adj 1 (characteristic of) the devil; fiendish 2 dreadful, appalling – **ally** adv

diadem /'die-ə,dem/ n a crown; specif a headband worn as a badge of royalty

diagnosis /ˌdie-əg'nohsis/ n, pl **diagnoses** /-seez/ 1 the art or act of identifying a disease from its signs and symptoms 2 (a statement resulting from) the investigation of the cause or nature of a problem or phenomenon – **nostic** adj – **nose** v

diagonal /die'ag(ə)nl/ adj 1 joining 2 nonadjacent angles of a polygon or polyhedron 2 running in an oblique direction from a reference line (e g the vertical) – **ly** adv

diagram /'die-ə,gram/ n 1 a line drawing made for mathematical or scientific purposes 2 a drawing or design that shows the arrangement and relations (e g of parts) – **matic** adj

¹dial /die·əl/ n 1 the graduated face of a timepiece 2a a face on which some measurement is registered, usu by means of numbers and a pointer b a disc-shaped control on an electrical or mechanical device 3 Br a person's face – slang

²dial v **-ll-** (NAm **-l-, -ll-**) to make a call on the telephone

dialect /'die-əlekt/ n a regional, social, or subordinate variety of a language – **al** adj

dialectic /ˌdie-ə'lektik/ n a systematic reasoning, exposition, or argument that juxtaposes opposed or contradictory ideas and usu seeks to resolve their conflict – **al** adj – **ally** adv – **ian** n

dialogue, NAm also dialog /'die-əlog/ n 1a a conversation between 2 people or between a person and sthg else (e g a computer) b an exchange of ideas and opinions 2 the conversational element of literary or dramatic composition

diameter /die'amitə/ n the length of a straight line through the centre of an object (e g a circle)

¹diamond /'die-əmənd/ n 1 a (piece of) very hard crystalline carbon that is highly valued as a precious stone and is used industrially as an abrasive and in rock drills 2 a square or rhombus orientated so that the diagonals are horizontal and vertical 3a a playing card marked with 1 or more red diamond-shaped figures b pl but sing or pl in constr the suit comprising cards identified by this figure

²diamond adj of, marking, or being a 60th or 75th anniversary

diaper /'diepə, 'die-əpə/ n, chiefly NAm a nappy

diaphanous /die'afənəs/ adj so fine as to be almost transparent

diaphragm /'die-ə,fram/ n 1 the partition separating the chest and abdominal cavities in mammals 2 a device that limits the aperture of a lens or optical system 3 a thin flexible disc that is free to vibrate (e g in an earphone) 4 a Dutch cap

diarist /'die-ərist/ n one who keeps a diary

diarrhoea, NAm chiefly diarrhea /ˌdie-ə'riə/ n abnormally frequent intestinal evacuations with more or less fluid faeces

diary /'die-əri/ n 1 (a book containing) a daily record of personal experiences or observations 2 chiefly Br a book with dates marked in which memoranda can be noted

diatom /'die-ətəm, -,tom/ n any of a class of minute single-celled plants with hard shell-like skeletons

diatonic /ˌdie-ə'tonik/ adj of a musical scale of 8 notes to the octave

diatribe /'die-ə,trieb/ n a (lengthy) piece of bitter and abusive criticism

¹dibble /'dibl/ n a small pointed hand implement used to make holes in the ground for plants, seeds, or bulbs

²dibble v 1 to plant with a dibble 2 to make holes in (soil) (as if) with a dibble

¹dice /dies/ n, pl **dice** /~/ 1a a small cube that is marked on each face with from 1 to 6 spots so that spots on opposite faces total 7 and that is used to determine arbitrary values in various games b a gambling game played with dice 2 a small square piece (e g of food)

²dice v 1 to cut (e g food) into small cubes 2 to take a chance

dicey /'diesi/ adj risky, unpredictable – infml

dichotomy /die'kotəmi/ n a division into 2 groups

dickens /'dikinz/ n devil, deuce – used as an interjection or intensive

dicky /'diki/ adj, Br in a weak or unsound condition – infml

¹**dictate** /dik'tayt/ *v* **1** to speak or read for a person to transcribe or for a machine to record **2** to impose, pronounce, or specify with authority – **-tation** *n*

²**dictate** /'diktayt/ *n* **1** an authoritative rule, prescription, or command **2** a ruling principle – usu *pl*

dictator /dik'taytə/ *n* an absolute ruler – **~ial** *adj*

dic'tator,ship /-,ship/ *n* **1** total or absolute control; leadership, rule **2** a state or form of government where absolute power is concentrated in one person or a small clique

diction /'diksh(ə)n/ *n* **1** choice of words, esp with regard to correctness or clearness **2** pronunciation and enunciation of words in speaking or singing

dictionary /'dikshən(ə)ri/ *n* **1** a reference book containing the meanings of words or terms often together with information about their pronunciations, etymologies, etc **2** a reference book giving for words of one language equivalents in another

dictum /'diktəm/ *n, pl* **dicta** /-tə/ *also* **dictums** an authoritative statement on some topic; a pronouncement

did /did/ *past of* **do**

didactic /die'daktik/ *adj* **1** intended to teach sthg, esp a moral lesson **2** having a tendency to teach in an authoritarian manner – **~ally** *adv*

diddle /'didl/ *v* **diddling** /'didl·ing, 'didling/ to cheat, swindle – *infml*

didst /didst/ *archaic past 2 sing of* **do**

¹**die** /die/ *v* **dying 1** to stop living; suffer the end of physical life **2** to pass out of existence, cease **3** to long keenly or desperately

²**die** *n pl* (1) **dice** /dies/, (2) **dies** /diez/ **1** a dice **2** any of various tools or devices for giving a desired shape, form, or finish to a material or for impressing an object or material — **the dice are loaded** all the elements of a situation are combined to work — usu + *against* or *in favour of* — **the die is cast** the irrevocable decision or step has been taken

'die-,hard *n or adj* (one) strongly resisting change

'diesel ,engine *n* an internal-combustion engine in which fuel is ignited by air compressed to a sufficiently high temperature

¹**diet** /'die·ət/ *n* **1** the food and drink habitually taken by a group or individual **2** the kind and amount of food prescribed for a special purpose (eg losing weight) – **~ary** *adj*

²**diet** *v* to eat and drink sparingly or according to prescribed rules

³**diet** *n* any of various national or provincial legislatures

differ /'difə/ *v* **1** to be unlike; be distinct *from* **2** to disagree

difference /'difrəns/ *n* **1a** unlikeness between 2 or more people or things **b** the degree or amount by which things differ **2** a disagreement, dispute; dissension **3** a significant change in or effect on a situation

different /'difrənt/ *adj* **1** partly or totally unlike; dissimilar – + *from*, chiefly Br *to*, or chiefly NAm *than* **2a** distinct **b** various **c** another **3** unusual, special – **~ly** *adv*

¹**differential** /,difə'rensh(ə)l/ *adj* **1a** of or constituting a difference **b** based on or resulting from a differential **c** functioning or proceeding differently or at a different rate **2** of or involving a differential or differentiation **3** of quantitative differences

²**differential** *n* **1** the amount of a difference between comparable individuals or classes; *specif* the amount by which the remuneration of distinct types of worker differs **2** (a case covering) a differential gear

diffe,rential 'calculus *n* a branch of mathematics dealing chiefly with the rate of change of functions with respect to their variables

differential gear *n* an arrangement of gears in a vehicle that allows one of the wheels imparting motion to turn (e g in going round a corner) faster than the other

differentiate /,difə'renshiayt/ *v* **1** to obtain the mathematical derivative of **2** to mark or show a difference in **3** to express the specific difference of – **-ation** *n*

difficult /'difik(ə)lt/ *adj* **1** hard to do, make, carry out, or understand **2a** hard to deal with, manage, or please **b** puzzling

difficulty /'difik(ə)lti/ *n* **1** being difficult **2** an obstacle or impediment **3** a cause of (financial) trouble or embarrassment – usu *pl* with sing. meaning

diffident /'difid(ə)nt/ *adj* **1** lacking in self-confidence **2** reserved, unassertive – **~ly** *adv* – **-dence** *n*

diffract /di'frakt/ *v* to cause a beam of light to become a set of light and dark or coloured bands in passing by the edge of an opaque body, through narrow slits, etc – **~ion** *n*

¹**diffuse** /di'fyoohs/ *adj* **1** not concentrated or localized; scattered **2** lacking conciseness; verbose – **~ly** *adv* – **~ness** *n*

²**diffuse** /di'fyoohz/ *v* **1** to spread out freely in all directions **2** to break up and distribute (incident light) by reflection – **-fusion** *n*

¹**dig** /dig/ *v* **-gg-;** **dug** /dug/ **1** to break up, turn, or loosen earth with an implement **2** to bring to the surface (as if) by digging; unearth **3** to hollow out by removing earth; excavate **4** to drive down into; thrust **5** to poke, prod **6** to understand, appreciate – slang – **~ger** *n*

²dig n **1a** a thrust, poke **b** a cutting or snide remark **2** an archaeological excavation (site) **3** pl, chiefly Br lodgings

¹digest /'diejest/ n **1** a systematic compilation of laws **2** a shortened version (e g of a book)

²digest /di'jest, die-/ v **1** to convert (food) into a form the body can use **2** to assimilate mentally **3** to compress into a short summary – ~**ible** adj – ~**ibility** n

digestion /di'jeschən/ n the process or power of digesting sthg, esp food – **-tive** n

digestive /di'jestiv/ adj of, causing, or promoting digestion

digit /'dijit/ n **1a** any of the Arabic numerals from 1 to 9, usu also including 0 **b** any of the elements that combine to form numbers in a system other than the decimal system **2** a finger or toe – ~**al** adj

dignify /'dignifie/ v to confer dignity or distinction on – **-fied** adj

dignitary /'dignit(ə)ri/ n a person of high rank or holding a position of dignity or honour

dignity /'dignəti/ n **1** being worthy, honoured, or esteemed **2** high rank, office, or position **3** stillness of manner; gravity

digress /di'gres, die-/ v to turn aside, esp from the main subject in writing or speaking – ~**ion** n – ~**ive** adj

dike /diek/ n a dyke

dilapidated /di'lapidaytid/ adj decayed or fallen into partial ruin – **-dation** n

dilate /di'layt, die-/ v **1** to comment at length on or upon **2** to become wide – **-lation** n

dilatory /'dilət(ə)ri/ adj **1** causing delay **2** slow, tardy

dilemma /di'lemə, die-/ n a situation involving choice between 2 equally unsatisfactory alternatives

diligent /'dilij(ə)nt/ adj showing steady application and effort – ~**ly** adv – **-gence** n

dill /dil/ n a European plant with aromatic foliage and seeds, both of which are used in flavouring foods (e g pickles)

dillydally /'dili,dali/ v to waste time by loitering; dawdle – infml

¹dilute /die'looht, -'lyooht/ v **1** to make thinner or more liquid by adding another liquid **2** to diminish the strength or brilliance of by adding more liquid, light, etc – **-tion** n

²dilute adj weak, diluted

¹dim /dim/ adj **-mm-** **1** giving out a weak or insufficient light **2a** seen or seeing indistinctly **b** characterized by an unfavourable or pessimistic attitude – esp in take a dim view of **3** lacking intelligence; stupid – infml – ~**ly** adv – ~**ness** n

²dim v **-mm-** to make or become dim

dime /diem/ n a coin worth $^1/_{10}$ of a US dollar

dimension /di'mensh(ə)n, die-/ n **1a** (the size of) extension in 1 or all directions **b** the range over which sthg extends; the scope – usu pl with sing. meaning **c** an aspect **2** any of the fundamental quantities, specif mass, length, and time, which combine to make a derived unit – usu pl – ~**al** adj

diminish /di'minish/ v **1** to become gradually less; dwindle **2** to lessen the reputation of; belittle – **-nution** n

di'minished adj, of a musical interval made a semitone less than perfect or minor

diminuendo /di,minyoo'endoh/ n, adv, or adj, pl **diminuendos** (a musical passage played) with a decrease in volume

diminutive /di'minyootiv/ adj **1** of a word or affix indicating small size and sometimes lovableness or triviality **2** exceptionally small; tiny – ~**ly** adv – ~**ness** n

dimple /'dimpl/ n **1** a slight natural indentation in the cheek or another part of the human body **2** a depression or indentation on a surface

dimwit /'dim,wit/ n a stupid or mentally slow person – infml – **dim-witted** adj

din /din/ n a loud continued discordant noise

dine /dien/ v to eat dinner – **diner** n — **dine off/on/upon** to eat (sthg) as one's meal, esp one's dinner

¹dingdong /'ding,dong/ n **1** the ringing sound produced by repeated strokes, esp on a bell **2** a rapid heated exchange of words or blows – infml

²dingdong adj **1** of or resembling the sound of a bell **2** with the advantage (e g in an argument or race) passing continually back and forth from one participant, side, etc to the other – infml

dinghy /'ding·gi/ n **1** a small boat often carried on a ship and used esp as a lifeboat or to transport passengers to and from shore **2** a small open sailing boat

dingo /'ding·goh/ n, pl **dingoes** a wild dog of Australia

dingy /'dinji/ adj **1** dirty, discoloured **2** shabby, squalid – **dingily** adv – **dinginess** n

dinner /'dinə/ n **1** (the food eaten for) the principal meal of the day taken either in the evening or at midday **2** a formal evening meal or banquet

'dinner jacket n a usu black jacket for men's semiformal evening wear

dinosaur /'dienə,saw/ n **1** any of a group of extinct, typically very large flesh- or plant-eating reptiles, most of which lived on the land **2** something that is unwieldy and outdated

diocese /'die·əsis/ n the area under the jurisdiction of a bishop – **-cesan** adj

diode /'die,ohd/ n **1** an electronic valve having only an anode and a cathode **2** a semiconductor device having only 2 terminals

¹dip /dip/ v **-pp-** **1a(1)** to plunge or immerse in a liquid (e g in order to moisten or dye) **a(2)** to plunge into a liquid and quickly emerge **b(1)** to immerse sthg in a processing liquid or finishing material **b(2)** to immerse a sheep in an antiseptic or parasite-killing solution **2a** to lower and then raise again **b** to drop down or decrease suddenly **3** to reach inside or below sthg, esp so as to take out part of the contents – usu + *in* or *into* **4** to lower (the beam of a vehicle's headlights) so as to reduce glare **5** to incline downwards from the plane of the horizon — **dip into 1** to make inroads into for funds **2** to read superficially or in a random manner

²**dip** *n* **1** a brief bathe for sport or exercise **2** a sharp downward course; a drop **3** a hollow, depression **4a** a sauce or soft mixture into which food is dipped before being eaten **b** a liquid preparation into which an object or animal may be dipped (e g for cleaning or disinfecting)

diphtheria /dif'thiəri·ə, dip-/ *n* an acute infectious disease marked by the formation of a false membrane in the throat, causing difficulty in breathing

diphthong /'difthong, 'dip-/ *n* a gliding monosyllabic vowel sound (e g /oy/ in *toy*) combining 2 vowels

diploma /di'plohmə/ *n* **1** a document conferring some honour or privilege **2** (a certificate of) a qualification, usu in a more specialized subject or at a lower level than a degree

diplomacy /di'plohməsi/ *n* **1** the art and practice of conducting international relations **2** skill and tact in handling affairs – **-mat** *n* – **-matic** *adj* – **-matically** *adv*

dipsomania /,dipsoh'maynyə, -ni·ə, ,dipsə-/ *n* an uncontrollable craving for alcoholic drinks – ~ **c** *n*

dipstick /'dip,stik/ *n* a graduated rod for measuring the depth of a liquid (e g the oil in a car's engine)

dire /die·ə/ *adj* **1** dreadful, awful **2** warning of disaster; ominous **3** desperately urgent

¹**direct** /di'rekt, die-/ *v* **1** to address or aim a remark **2** to cause to turn, move, point, or follow a straight course **3** to show or point out the way for **4a** to supervise **b** to order or instruct with authority **c** to produce a play **d** *NAm* to conduct an orchestra

²**direct** *adj* **1** going from one point to another in time or space without deviation or interruption; straight **2** stemming immediately from a source, cause, or reason **3** frank, straightforward **4a** operating without an intervening agency **b** effected by the action of the people or the electorate and not by representatives **5** consisting of or reproducing the exact words of a speaker or writer – ~ **ness** *n*

³**direct** *adv* **1** from point to point without deviation; by the shortest way **2** without an intervening agency or stage

direct current *n* an electric current flowing in 1 direction only

direction /di'reksh(ə)n, die-/ *n* **1** guidance or supervision of action **2a** the act, art, or technique of directing an orchestra, film, or theatrical production **b** a word, phrase, or sign indicating the appropriate tempo, mood, or intensity of a passage or movement in music **3** *pl* explicit instructions on how to do sthg or get to a place **4a** the line or course along which sby or sthg moves or is aimed **b** the point towards which sby or sthg faces **5a** a tendency, trend **b** a guiding or motivating purpose

directional /di'reksh(ə)nl, die-/ *adj* **1a** of or indicating direction in space **b** of or being a device that operates more efficiently in one direction than in others **2** relating to direction or guidance, esp of thought or effort

¹**directive** /di'rektiv, die-/ *adj* **1** serving to direct, guide, or influence **2** serving to provide a direction

²**directive** *n* an authoritative instruction issued by a high-level body or official

¹**directly** /-li/ *adv* **1** in a direct manner **2a** without delay; immediately **b** soon, shortly

²**directly** *conj* immediately after; as soon as – *infml*

direct object *n* a grammatical object representing the primary goal or the result of the action of its verb (e g *me* in 'he hit me' and *house* in 'we built a house')

director /di'rektə, die-/ *n* **1** the head of an organized group or administrative unit **2** a member of a governing board entrusted with the overall direction of a company **3** sby who has responsibility for supervising the artistic and technical aspects of a film or play – ~ **ship** *n*

directory /di'rekt(ə)ri, die-/ *n* an alphabetical or classified list (e g of names, addresses, telephone numbers, etc)

dirge /duhj/ *n* **1** a song or hymn of grief or lamentation **2** a slow mournful piece of music

¹**dirigible** /'dirijəbl, -'---/ *adj* capable of being steered

²**dirigible** *n* an airship

dirk /duhk/ *n* a long straight-bladed dagger, used esp by Scottish Highlanders

dirndl /'duhndl/ *n* a full skirt with a tight waistband

dirt /duht/ *n* **1a** a filthy or soiling substance (e g mud or grime) **b** sby or sthg worthless or contemptible **2** soil **3a** obscene or pornographic speech or writing **b** scandalous or malicious gossip

dirty /'duhti/ *adj* **1a** not clean or pure **b** causing sby or sthg to become soiled or covered with dirt **2a** base, sordid **b** unsportsmanlike, unfair **c** low, despicable **3a** indecent, obscene **b** sexually illicit – **dirtily** *adv*

dis

disability /ˌdisəˈbiləti/ n **1a** inability to do sthg (e g pursue an occupation) because of physical or mental impairment **b** a handicap **2** a legal disqualification

disable /disˈaybl/ v **1** to deprive of legal right, qualification, or capacity **2** to cripple – ~**ment** n

disadvantage /ˌdisədˈvahntij/ n **1** an unfavourable, inferior, or prejudicial situation **2** a handicap

disaffected adj discontented and resentful – **-tion** n

disagree /ˌdisəˈgree/ v **1** to be unlike or at variance **2** to differ in opinion – usu + with **3** to have a bad effect – usu + with – ~**ment** n

disagreeable /ˌdisəˈgree-əbl/ adj **1** unpleasant, objectionable **2** peevish, ill-tempered – ~**ness** n – **-ably** adv

disappear /ˌdisəˈpiə/ v **1** to pass from view **2** to cease to be or to be known **3** to leave or depart, esp secretly – infml – ~**ance** n

disappoint /ˌdisəˈpoynt/ v to fail to meet the expectation or hope of; also to sadden by so doing – ~**ed** adj – ~**edly** adv – ~**ing** adj – ~**ingly** adv – ~**ment** n

disapprobation /ˌdisˌaprəˈbaysh(ə)n/ n disapproval – fml

disapprove /ˌdisəˈproohv/ v to have or express an unfavourable opinion of – **-proval** n – **-provingly** adv

disarm /disˈahm/ v **1a** to deprive of a weapon or weapons **b** to make (e g a bomb) harmless, esp by removing a fuse or warhead **2** to reduce or abolish weapons and armed forces **3** to dispel the hostility or suspicion of – ~**ament** n

disarray /ˌdisəˈray/ n a lack of order

disassociate /ˌdisəˈsohs(h)iayt/ v to dissociate

disaster /diˈzahstə/ n **1** a sudden event bringing great damage, loss, or destruction **2** a failure – **-trous** adj – **-trously** adv

disavow /ˌdisəˈvow/ v to deny knowledge of or responsibility for; repudiate – fml – ~**al** n

disband /disˈband/ v to (cause to) break up and separate; disperse – ~**ment** n

disbar /disˈbah/ v to deprive (a barrister) of the right to practise; expel from the bar – ~**ment** n

disbelief /ˌdisbiˈleef/ n mental rejection of sthg as untrue

disbelieve /ˌdisbiˈleev/ v to reject or withhold belief (in) – **-liever** n

disburse /disˈbuhs/ v to pay out, esp from a fund – ~**ment** n

disc, NAm chiefly **disk** /disk/ n **1** a thin flat circular object **2** any of various round flat anatomical structures; esp any of the cartilaginous discs between the spinal vertebrae **3** a gramophone record **4** a disk

discard /disˈkahd/ v to get rid of as useless or superfluous

discern /diˈsuhn/ v **1** to detect with one of the senses, esp vision **2** to perceive or recognize mentally – ~**ible,** also **-able** adj – ~**ibly** adv – ~**ment** n

discerning /diˈsuhning/ adj showing insight and understanding; discriminating

¹**discharge** /disˈchahj/ v **1** to unload **b** to release from an obligation **2a** to shoot **b** to release from custody or care **c** to send or pour out; emit **3a** to dismiss from employment or service **b** to fulfil (e g a debt or obligation) by performing an appropriate act **4** to remove an electric charge from or reduce the electric charge of

²**discharge** /ˈdischahj, -ˈ-/ n **1** the relieving of an obligation, accusation, or penalty **2** the act of discharging or unloading **3** legal release from confinement; also an acquittal **4** a flowing or pouring out **5** release or dismissal, esp from an office or employment **6** the conversion of the chemical energy of a battery into electrical energy

disciple /diˈsiepl/ n one who assists in spreading another's doctrines; esp any of Christ's 12 appointed followers – ~**ship** n

disciplinarian /ˌdisipliˈneəri·ən/ n one who enforces or advocates (strict) discipline or order

¹**discipline** /ˈdisiplin/ n **1** a field of study **2** training of the mind and character designed to produce obedience and self-control **3** punishment, chastisement **4** order obtained by enforcing obedience (e g in a school or army) – **-plinary** adj

²**discipline** v **1** to punish or penalize for the sake of discipline **2** to train by instruction and exercise, esp in obedience and self-control **3** to bring (a group) under control

'**disc jockey** n one who introduces records of popular usu contemporary music (e g on a radio programme or at a discotheque)

disclaim /disˈklaym/ v **1** to renounce a legal claim to **2** to deny, disavow

disclaimer /disˈklaymə/ n **1** a denial of legal responsibility **2** a denial, repudiation

disclose /disˈklohz/ v **1** to expose to view **2** to reveal to public knowledge

disclosure /disˈklohzhə/ n **1** (an instance of) disclosing; an exposure **2** sthg disclosed; a revelation

disco /ˈdiskoh/ n, pl **discos 1** a collection of popular records together with the equipment for playing them **2** a discotheque – infml

discolour /disˈkulə/ v to (cause to) change colour for the worse; stain – **discoloration** n

discomfit /disˈkumfit/ v **1** to frustrate the plans of; thwart **2** to cause perplexity and embarrassment to; disconcert – ~**ure** n

¹**discomfort** /disˈkumfət/ v to make uncomfortable or uneasy

²**discomfort** n (sthg causing) mental or physical unease

discompose /ˌdiskəmˈpohz/ v to destroy the composure of – fml – **-posure** n

disconcert /ˌdiskən'suht/ v to disturb the composure of; fluster – ~**ingly** adv

disconnect /ˌdiskə'nekt/ v to cut off (e g an electricity supply)

discon'nected adj disjointed, incoherent – ~**ly** adv – **-nection** n

disconsolate /dis'konsələt/ adj dejected, downcast – ~**ly** adv

discontent /ˌdiskən'tent/ n 1 lack of contentment; dissatisfaction 2 one who is discontented; a malcontent – ~**ed** adj – ~**edly** adv – **discontent** v

discontinue /ˌdiskən'tinyooh/ v to cease, stop; specif to cease production of – **-tinuance** n

discontinuous /ˌdiskən'tinyoo-əs/ adj lacking sequence, coherence, or continuity – ~**ly** adv – **-tinuity** n

discord /'diskawd/ n 1 lack of agreement or harmony; conflict 2 a harsh unpleasant combination of sounds – ~**ant** adj – ~**antly** adv – ~**ance** n

discotheque /'diskə,tek/ n a nightclub for dancing to usu recorded music

¹**discount** /'diskownt/ n 1 a reduction in the price of goods, accorded esp to special or trade customers 2 a reduction in the amount due on a bill of exchange, debt, etc when paid promptly or before the specified date — **at a discount** below the usual price

²**discount** /'diskownt; sense 2 dis'kownt/ v 1a to make a deduction from, usu for cash or prompt payment b to sell or offer for sale at a discount 2a to leave out of account as unimportant, unreliable, or irrelevant b to underestimate the importance of

discountenance /dis'kownt(ə)nəns/ v 1 to abash, disconcert 2 to discourage by showing disapproval – fml

discourage /dis'kurij/ v 1 to deprive of confidence; dishearten 2a to hinder, deter from b to attempt to prevent, esp by showing disapproval – **-agingly** adv – ~**ment** n

¹**discourse** /'diskaws/ n 1 a talk, conversation 2 (orderly expression of ideas in) a formal speech or piece of writing

²**discourse** /'--, -'-/ v 1 to express one's ideas in speech or writing 2 to talk, converse USE usu + on or upon

discourteous /dis'kuhtyəs, -'kaw-, -ti-əs/ adj rude, impolite – ~**ly** adv – ~**ness** n

discourtesy /dis'kuhtəsi, -'kaw-/ n (an instance of) rudeness; (an) incivility

discover /di'skuvə/ v 1 to obtain sight or knowledge of for the first time 2 to make known or visible – fml – ~**able** adj – ~**er** n – ~**y** n

¹**discredit** /dis'kredit/ v 1 to refuse to accept as true or accurate 2 to cast doubt on the accuracy, authority, or reputation of

²**discredit** n 1 (sby or sthg causing) loss of credit or reputation 2 loss of belief or confidence; doubt

discreditable /dis'kreditəbl/ adj bringing discredit or disgrace – **-bly** adv

discreet /di'skreet/ adj 1 capable of maintaining a prudent silence 2 unpretentious, modest – ~**ly** adv

discrete /di'skreet/ adj 1 individually distinct 2 consisting of distinct or unconnected elements – ~**ly** adv – ~**ness** n

discretion /di'skresh(ə)n/ n 1 the ability to make responsible decisions 2a individual choice or judgment b power of free decision within legal bounds – in age of discretion – ~**ary** adj

discriminate /di'skrimi,nayt/ v 1a to make a distinction between b to show good judgment or discernment 2 to treat sby differently and esp unfavourably on the grounds of race, sex, religion, etc – **-ation** n

discriminatory /di'skriminət(ə)ri/ adj showing esp unfavourable discrimination

discursive /di'skuhsiv, -ziv/ adj 1 passing usu unmethodically from one topic to another; digressive 2 proceeding by logical argument or reason – ~**ly** adv – ~**ness** n

discus /'diskəs/ n, pl **discuses** (the athletic field event involving the throwing of) a solid disc, between 180mm and 219mm (about 7 to 9in) in diameter, that is thicker in the centre than at the edge

discuss /di'skus/ v to consider or examine (a topic) in speech or writing – ~**ion** n

disdain /dis'dayn/ n contempt for sthg regarded as worthless or insignificant; scorn – **disdain** v

dis'dainful /-f(ə)l/ adj feeling or showing disdain – ~**ly** adv

disease /di'zeez/ n 1 a condition of (a part of) a living animal or plant body that impairs the performance of a vital function; (a) sickness, malady 2 a harmful or corrupt development, situation, condition, etc – ~**d** adj

disembark /ˌdisim'bahk/ v to (cause to) alight from a ship, plane, etc – ~**ation** n

disembowel /ˌdisim'bowəl/ v to remove the bowels or entrails of; eviscerate

disembroil /ˌdisim'broyl/ v to free from a confused or entangled state or situation

disenchant /ˌdisin'chahnt/ v to rid of an illusion – ~**ment** n

disencumber /ˌdisin'kumbə/ v to free from a burden or impediment

disengage /ˌdising'gayj/ v to detach or release (oneself) specif, esp of troops to withdraw – ~**ment** n

disentangle /ˌdisin'tang-gl/ v to (cause to) become free from entanglements: unravel – ~**ment** n

disfavour /dis'fayvə/ n 1 disapproval, dislike 2 the state of being disapproved of

disfigure /dis'figə/ v to spoil the appearance or quality of; mar – ~**ment** n

disfranchise /dis'frahnchiez, -'fran-/ v to deprive of the right to select an elected representative – ~ment n

disgorge /dis'gawj/ v 1 to discharge the contents of with force; *specif* to vomit 2 to give up on request or under pressure

¹**disgrace** /dis'grays/ v 1 to bring reproach or shame to 2 to cause to lose favour or standing

²**disgrace** n 1a loss of favour, honour, or respect; shame b the state of being out of favour 2 sby or sthg shameful

dis'graceful /-f(ə)l/ adj shameful, shocking – ~ly adv

disgruntled /dis'gruntld/ adj aggrieved and dissatisfied

¹**disguise** /dis'giez/ v 1 to change the appearance or nature of in order to conceal identity 2 to hide the true state or character of

²**disguise** n 1a (the use of) sthg (e g clothing) to conceal one's identity 2 an outward appearance that misrepresents the true nature of sthg

disgust /dis'gust/ n strong aversion aroused by sby or sthg physically or morally distasteful – **disgust** v

¹**dish** /dish/ n 1a a shallow open often circular or oval vessel used esp for holding or serving food; *broadly* any vessel from which food is eaten or served b pl the utensils and tableware used in preparing, serving, and eating a meal 2 a type of food prepared in a particular way 3a a directional aerial, esp for receiving radio or television transmissions or microwaves, having a concave usu parabolic reflector b a hollow or depression 4 an attractive person – infml

²**dish** v 1 to make concave like a dish 2 *chiefly Br* to ruin or spoil (e g a person or his/her hopes) – infml

dishabille /,disə'beel/ n deshabille

disharmony /dis'hahməni/ n lack of harmony; discord – **-monious** adj

dishcloth /-,kloth/ n a cloth for washing or drying dishes

dishearten /dis'haht(ə)n/ v to cause to lose enthusiasm or morale; discourage – ~ment n

di'shevelled, *NAm chiefly* **disheveled** adj, *esp of a person's hair or appearance* unkempt, untidy

dishonest /dis'onist/ adj not honest, truthful, or sincere – ~ly adv – ~y n

dishonour /dis'onə/ n 1 (sby or sthg causing) loss of honour or reputation 2 a state of shame or disgrace – **dishonour** v – ~able adj – ~ably adv

dish out v to give or distribute freely – infml

dish up v 1 to put (a meal, food, etc) onto dishes; serve 2 to produce or give (e g facts) – infml

'**dish,washer** /-,woshə/ n a person or electrical machine that washes dishes

dishy /'dishi/ adj, *chiefly Br, of a person* attractive – infml

disillusion /,disi'loohzh(ə)n, -'lyooh-/ v to reveal the usu unpleasant truth (e g about sby or sthg admired) to; disenchant – **disillusion**, ~ment n

disincentive /,disin'sentiv/ n sthg that discourages action or effort; a deterrent

disinclined /,disin'kliend/ adj unwilling – **-clination** n

disinfect /,disin'fekt/ v to cleanse of infection, esp by destroying harmful microorganisms – ~ion n

disinfectant /,disin'fekt(ə)nt/ n a chemical that destroys harmful microorganisms

disingenuous /,disin'jenyoo·əs/ adj insincere; *also* falsely frank or naive in manner – ~ly adv – ~ness n

disinherit /,disin'herit/ v to deprive (an heir) of the right to inherit – ~ance n

disintegrate /dis'intigrayt/ v 1 to break into fragments or constituent elements 2 to lose unity or cohesion – **-gration** n

disinter /,disin'tuh/ v 1 to remove from a grave or tomb 2 to bring to light; unearth – ~ment n

dis'interested adj 1 uninterested – disapproved of by some speakers 2 free from selfish motive or interest; impartial – ~ly adv – ~ness n

dis'jointed adj lacking orderly sequence; incoherent – ~ly adv – ~ness n

disk, *Br also* **disc** /disk/ n a round flat plate coated with a magnetic substance on which data for a computer is stored

¹**dislike** /dis'liek/ v to regard with dislike

²**dislike** n (an object of) a feeling of aversion or disapproval

dislocate /'dislə,kayt/ v 1 to put out of place; *esp* to displace (e g a bone or joint) 2 to put (plans, machinery, etc) out of order – **-cation** n

dislodge /dis'loj/ v to force out of or remove from a fixed or entrenched position – ~ment n

disloyal /dis'loyəl/ adj untrue to obligations or ties; unfaithful – ~ly adv – ~ty n

dismal /'dizm(ə)l/ adj causing or expressing gloom or sadness – ~ly adv

dismantle /dis'mantl/ v to take to pieces

dismay /di'smay, diz-/ v or n (to fill with) sudden consternation or apprehension

dis'member v 1 to cut or tear off the limbs or members of 2 to divide up (e g a territory) into parts – ~ment n

dismiss /dis'mis/ v 1 to remove or send away, esp from employment or service 2 to put out of one's mind; reject as unworthy of serious consideration 3 to refuse a further hearing to (e g a court case) 4 to bowl out (a batsman or side) in cricket – ~al n

dismount /dis'mownt/ v 1 to alight from a horse, bicycle, etc 2 to remove from a mounting

disobedient /,disə'beedi·ənt/ adj refusing or failing to obey – ~ly adv – **-ience** n

disobey /,disə'bay/ v to fail to obey

disorder /dis'awdə/ n 1 lack of order; confusion 2 breach of the peace or public order 3 an abnormal physical or mental condition; an ailment – **disorder** v

dis·orderly /-li/ adj 1a untidy, disarranged b unruly, violent 2 offensive to public order – **~liness** n

disorgan·ize, -ise /dis'awgəniez/ v to throw into disorder or confusion – **-ization** n

disorientate /dis'awri·ən,tayt/ v to confuse – **-tation** n

disown /dis'ohn/ v 1 to refuse to acknowledge as one's own 2 to repudiate any connection with

disparage /di'sparij/ v to speak slightingly of; belittle – **-agingly** adv – **~ment** n

disparate /'dispərət/ adj markedly distinct in quality or character – **~ly** adv

disparity /di'sparəti/ n (a) difference or inequality

dispassionate /dis'pash(ə)nət/ adj not influenced by strong feeling; esp calm, impartial – **~ly** adv – **~ness** n

¹**dispatch** /di'spach/ v 1 to send off or away promptly, esp on some last task 2 to get through or carry out quickly 3 to kill, esp with quick efficiency – euph

²**dispatch** n 1 an important diplomatic or military message 2 a news item sent into a newspaper by a correspondent 3 promptness and efficiency

dispel /di'spel/ v **-ll-** 1 to drive away; disperse

dispensable /di'spensəbl/ adj inessential

dispensary /di'spens(ə)ri/ n a part of a hospital or chemist's shop where drugs, medical supplies, etc are dispensed

dispensation /,dispen'saysh(ə)n/ n 1 a usu specified religious system, esp considered as controlling human affairs during a particular period 2a an exemption from a law, vow, etc; specif permission to disregard or break a rule of Roman Catholic church law b a formal authorization

dispense /di'spens/ v 1a to deal out, distribute b to administer (e g law or justice) 2 to prepare and give out (drugs, medicine, etc on prescription) 3 to do without – usu + with – **dispenser** n

disperse /di'spuhs/ v 1 to break up in random fashion; scatter 2 to evaporate or vanish – **dispersal** n – **dispersion** n

dispirit /di'spirit/ v to dishearten, discourage

displace /dis'plays/ v 1a to remove from or force out of the usual or proper place b to remove from office 2 to take the place of (e g an atom) in a chemical reaction

dis·placement /-mənt/ n 1 the volume or weight of a fluid (e g water) displaced by a body (e g a ship) of equal weight floating in it 2 the difference between the initial position of a body and any later position

¹**display** /di'splay/ v 1 to expose to view; show 2 to exhibit, esp ostentatiously

²**display** n 1a a presentation or exhibition of sthg in open view b an esp ostentatious show or demonstration c an eye-catching arrangement of sthg (e g goods for sale) 2 a pattern of behaviour exhibited esp by male birds in the breeding season

displease /dis'pleez/ v to cause annoyance or displeasure (to)

displeasure /dis'plezhə/ n disapproval, annoyance

disposable /di'spohzəbl/ adj 1 available for use; specif remaining after deduction of taxes 2 designed to be used once and then thrown away

disposal /di'spohzl/ n 1a orderly arrangement or distribution b bestowal c the act or action of getting rid of sthg; specif the destruction or conversion of waste matter 2 the power or right to use freely

dispose /di'spohz/ v 1 to incline to 2 to put in place; arrange 3 to cause to have a specified attitude towards 4 to settle a matter finally; also get rid of 1

disposition /,dispə'zish(ə)n/ n 1a final arrangement; settlement b orderly arrangement 2a natural temperament b a tendency, inclination

dispossess /,dispə'zes/ v to deprive of possession or occupancy – **~ed** adj – **~ion** n

disproportion /,disprə'pawsh(ə)n/ n (a) lack of proportion, symmetry, or proper relation

disproportionate /,disprə'pawsh(ə)nət/ adj out of proportion – **~ly** adv

disprove /dis'proohv/ v to prove to be false; refute

disputant /di'spyooht(ə)nt, 'dispyoot(ə)nt/ n one engaged in a dispute

¹**dispute** /di'spyooht/ v 1a to discuss angrily b to call into question 2a to struggle against; resist b to struggle over; contest – **disputation** n – **disputable** adj – **disputably** adv

²**dispute** n 1 controversy, debate 2 a quarrel, disagreement

disqualification /dis,kwolifi'kaysh(ə)n, ,---'--/ n 1 disqualifying or being disqualified 2 sthg that disqualifies

disqualify /dis'kwolifie/ v 1 to make or declare unfit or unsuitable to do sthg 2 to declare ineligible (e g for a prize) because of violation of the rules

disquiet /dis'kwie·ət/ v or n (to cause) anxiety or worry

disregard /,disri'gahd/ v 1 to pay no attention to 2 to treat as not worthy of regard or notice – **disregard** n

disrepair /,disri'peə/ n the state of being in need of repair

disreputable /dis'repyootəbl/ adj 1 having a bad reputation; not respectable 2 dirty or untidy in appearance – **~ness** n – **-tably** adv

disrepute /,disri'pyooht/ n lack of good reputation or respectability

disrespect /ˌdisriˈspekt/ n lack of respect or politeness – **~ful** adj – **~fully** adv

disrobe /disˈrohb/ v to take off (esp ceremonial outer) clothing – fml or humor

disrupt /disˈrupt/ v **1** to throw into disorder **2** to interrupt the continuity of – **~ion** n – **~ive** adj – **~ively** adv

dissatisfy /diˈsatisfie, disˈsa-/ v to make displeased, discontented, or disappointed – **-faction** n

dissect /diˈsekt, die-/ v **1** to cut (e g an animal or plant) into pieces, esp for scientific examination **2** to analyse and interpret in detail – **~ion** n

dissemble /diˈsembl/ v to conceal facts, intentions, or feelings under some pretence – **~r** n

disseminate /diˈseminayt/ v to spread about freely or widely – **-nation** n

dissension /diˈsensh(ə)n/ n disagreement in opinion; discord

¹**dissent** /diˈsent/ v **1** to withhold assent **2** to differ in opinion; specif to reject the doctrines of an established church

²**dissent** n religious or political nonconformity

dissertation /ˌdisəˈtaysh(ə)n/ n a long detailed treatment of a subject; specif one submitted for a (higher) degree

disservice /diˈsuhvis, disˈsuh-/ n an action or deed which works to sby's disadvantage

dissident /ˈdisid(ə)nt/ n or adj (sby) disagreeing strongly or rebelliously with an established opinion, group, government, etc – **-dence** n

dissimilar /diˈsimilə, disˈsi-/ adj not similar; unlike – **~ly** adv – **~ity** n

dissimulate /diˈsimyoolayt, disˈsi-/ v to dissemble – **-lation** n

dissipate /ˈdisipayt/ v **1** to cause to disappear or scatter; dispel **2** to spend or use up (money, energy, etc) aimlessly or foolishly – **-pation** n

¹**dissipated** adj dissolute

dissociate /diˈsohs(h)i,ayt/ v to separate from association or union with sby or sthg else; disconnect – **-ation** n

dissolute /ˈdisalooht, -lyooht/ adj loose in morals; debauched – **~ly** adv – **~ness** n

dissolution /ˌdisəˈloohsh(ə)n, -ˈlyooh, ˌdis-sə-/ n **1** the termination of an association, union, etc **2** the breaking up or dispersal of a group, assembly, etc

dissolve /diˈzolv/ v **1a** to terminate officially **b** to cause to break up; dismiss **2a** to pass into solution **b** to melt, liquefy **3** to fade away; disperse **4** to fade out (one film or television scene) while fading into another

dissonance /ˈdisənəns/ n **1** a combination of discordant sounds **2** lack of agreement **3** (the sound produced by playing) an unresolved musical note or chord – **-nant** adj – **-nantly** adv

dissuade /diˈswayd/ v to deter or discourage from a course of action by persuasion – **-suasion** n

distaff /ˈdistahf/ n **1** a staff for holding the flax, wool, etc in spinning **2** woman's work or domain

¹**distance** /ˈdist(ə)ns/ n **1a** (the amount of) separation in space or time between 2 points or things **b** a distant point or place **2a** remoteness in space **b** reserve, coldness **c** difference, disparity

²**distance** v to place or keep physically or mentally at a distance

distant /ˈdist(ə)nt/ adj **1a** separated in space or time by a specified distance **b** far-off or remote in space or time **2** not closely related **3** different in kind **4** reserved, aloof **5** coming from or going to a remote place – **~ly** adv

distaste /disˈtayst/ n (a) dislike, aversion

dis'tasteful /-f(ə)l/ adj showing or causing distaste; offensive – **~ly** adv – **~ness** n

¹**distemper** /diˈstempə/ n any of various animal diseases; esp a highly infectious virus disease of dogs

²**distemper** n **1** a method of painting in which pigments are mixed with white or yolk of egg or size, esp for mural decoration **2** the paint used in the distemper process; broadly any of numerous water-based paints for general, esp household, use – **distemper** v

distend /diˈstend/ v to (cause to) swell from internal pressure – **-tension** n

distil, NAm chiefly **distill** /diˈstil/ v **-ll- 1** to subject to or transform by heating and condensing the resulting vapour **2a** to obtain or separate out or off (as if) by distilling **b** to obtain spirits by distilling the products of fermentation **c** to extract the essence of (e g an idea or subject) – **~lation** n

distiller /diˈstilə/ n a person or company that makes alcohol, esp spirits, by distilling

distinct /diˈstingkt/ adj **1** different, separate from **2** readily perceptible to the senses or mind; clear – **~ly** adv – **~ness** n

distinction /diˈstingksh(ə)n/ n **1** a difference made or marked; a contrast **2** a distinguishing quality or mark **3a** outstanding merit, quality, or worth **b** special honour or recognition

distinctive /diˈstingktiv/ adj clearly marking sby or sthg as different from others; characteristic – **~ly** adv – **~ness** n

distinguish /diˈsting-gwish/ v **1a** to mark or recognize as separate or different – often + from **b** to recognize the difference between **c** to make (oneself) outstanding or noteworthy **d** to mark as different; characterize **2** to discern; make out – **~able** adj

di'stinguished adj **1** marked by eminence, distinction, or excellence **2** dignified in manner, bearing, or appearance

distort /diˈstawt/ v **1** to alter the true meaning of; misrepresent **2** to cause to take on an unnatural or abnormal shape – **~ion** n

distract /diˈstrakt/ v to draw (e g one's attention) to a different object

distraction /di'straksh(ə)n/ *n* **1** extreme agitation or mental confusion **2** sthg that distracts; *esp* an amusement

distraught /di'strawt/ *adj* mentally agitated; frantic

distress /di'stres/ *n* **1** mental or physical anguish **2** a state of danger or desperate need – **distress** *v*

distribute /di'stribyooht/ *v* **1** to divide among several or many **2a** to disperse or scatter over an area **b** to give out, deliver – **-bution** *n* – **-butional,-butive** *adj*

distributor /di'stribyootə/ *n* **1** sby employed to manage the distribution of goods **2** an apparatus for directing current to the various sparking plugs of an internal-combustion engine

district /'distrikt/ *n* **1** a territorial division made esp for administrative purposes **2** an area or region with a specified character or feature

distrust /dis'trust/ *v or n* (to view with) suspicion or lack of trust – ~**ful** *adj* – ~**fully** *adv*

disturb /di'stuhb/ *v* **1a** to break in upon; interrupt **b** to alter the position or arrangement of **2a** to destroy the peace of mind or composure of **b** to throw into disorder **c** to put to inconvenience – ~**ance** *n*

di'sturbed *adj* having or showing symptoms of emotional or mental instability

disunite /,disyoo'niet/ *v* to divide, separate

disuse /dis'yoohs/ *n* the state of no longer being used – ~**d** *adj*

¹ditch /dich/ *n* a long narrow excavation dug in the earth for defence, drainage, irrigation, etc

²ditch *v* **1** to make a forced landing of (an aircraft) on water **2** to get rid of; abandon

¹dither /'didhə/ *v* to act nervously or indecisively; vacillate

²dither *n* a state of indecision or nervous excitement

ditto /'ditoh/ *n* **1** a thing mentioned previously or above; the same – used to avoid repeating a word **2** *also* **ditto mark** a mark ,, or " used as a sign indicating repetition usu of a word directly above in a previous line

ditty /'diti/ *n* a short simple song

diuretic /,dieyoo'retik/ *n or adj* (a drug) acting to increase the flow of urine

diurnal /die'uhnl/ *adj* **1** having a daily cycle **2a** occurring during the day or daily **b** opening during the day and closing at night **c** active during the day – ~**ly** *adv*

divan /di'van, 'dievan; *sense* 3 di'van/ *n* **1** a council chamber in some Muslim countries, esp Turkey **2a** a long low couch, usu without arms or back, placed against a wall **b** a bed of a similar style without a head or foot board

¹dive /diev/ *v* **dived**, *NAm also* **dove** /dohv/ **1a** to plunge into water headfirst **b** to submerge **2a** to descend or fall steeply **b** to plunge one's hand quickly *into* **3** to lunge or dash headlong

²dive *n* **1a(1)** a headlong plunge into water; *esp* one executed in a prescribed manner **a(2)** submerging (e g by a submarine) **2** a sharp decline **2** a disreputable bar, club, etc – *informal*

diver /'dievə/ *n* **1** a person who works or explores underwater for long periods, either carrying a supply of air or having it sent from the surface **2** any of various diving birds

diverge /die'vuhj/ *v* **1a** to move in different directions from a common point **b** to differ in character, form, or opinion – often + *from* **2** to turn aside from a path or course – often + *from* – ~**gence, -gency** *n* – ~**gent** *adj*

divers /'dievəz/ *adj, archaic* various

diverse /'die,vuhs, -'-/ *adj* **1** different, unlike **2** varied, assorted – ~**ly** *adv*

diversify /die'vuhsi,fie/ *v* **1** to make diverse; vary **2** to engage in varied business operations in order to reduce risk

diversity /di'vuhsəti, die-/ *n* **1** the condition of being different or having differences **2** a variety, assortment

divert /die'vuht/ *v* **1a** to turn aside from one course or use to another **b** to distract **2** to entertain, amuse – **diversion** *n* – **diversionary** *adj*

divest /die'vest/ *v* **1** to rid or free oneself *of* **2** to take away (e g property or vested rights)

¹divide /di'vied/ *v* **1** to separate into 2 or more parts, categories, divisions, etc **2** to give out in shares; distribute **3a** to cause to be separate; serve as a boundary between **b** to separate into opposing sides or parties **4** to determine how many times a number contains another number by means of a mathematical operation – **divisible** *adj* — **divide into** to use as a divisor of

²divide *n* **1** a watershed **2** a point or line of division

dividend /'dividend, -dənd/ *n* **1a** (a pro rata share in) the part of a company's profits payable to shareholders **2** a reward, benefit **3** a number to be divided by another

divination /,divi'naysh(ə)n/ *n* **1** the art or practice that seeks to foresee the future or discover hidden knowledge (e g by using supernatural powers) **2** (an instance of) unusual insight or perception

¹divine /di'vien/ *adj* **1a** of, being, or proceeding directly from God or a god **b** devoted to the worship of God or a god; sacred **2** delightful, superb – *infml* – ~**ly** *adv*

²divine *n* a clergyman; *esp* one skilled in theology

³divine *v* **1** to discover, perceive, or foresee intuitively or by supernatural means **2** to discover or locate (e g water or minerals) by means of a divining rod – **diviner** *n*

di'vining ,rod /di'viening/ *n* a forked rod (e g a twig) believed to dip downwards when held over ground concealing water or minerals

divinity /di'vinəti/ *n* **1** the quality or state of being divine **2** a male or female deity **3** theology

division /di'vizh(ə)n/ *n* **1** dividing or being divided **2** any of the parts or sections into which a whole is divided **3** *sing or pl in constr* a military unit having the necessary tactical and administrative services to act independently **4** an administrative or operating unit of an organization **5** a group of organisms forming part of a larger group **6** a competitive class or category (e g of a soccer league) **7** sthg that divides, separates, or marks off **8** disagreement, disunity **9** the physical separation into different lobbies of the members of a parliamentary body voting for and against a question **10** the mathematical operation of dividing one number by another

divisive /di'viesiv, -ziv/ *adj* tending to cause disunity or dissension — ~**ly** *adv* — ~**ness** *n*

divisor /di'viezə/ *n* the number by which another number or quantity is divided

divorce /di'vaws/ *v* **1a** to end marriage with (one's spouse) by divorce **b** to dissolve the marriage between **2** to end the relationship or union of; separate – usu + *from* – **divorce** *n*

divot /'divət/ *n* a piece of turf dug out in making a golf shot

divulge /die'vulj, di-/ *v* to make known (e g a confidence or secret); reveal – ~**nce** *n*

dixie land /-,land/ *n* traditional jazz

¹**dizzy** /'dizi/ *adj* **1** experiencing a whirling sensation in the head with a tendency to lose balance **2** causing or feeling giddiness or mental confusion **3** foolish, silly – infml – **dizzily** *adv* – **dizziness** *n*

²**dizzy** *v* to make dizzy; bewilder

DJ /'dee,jay/ *n* **1** a disc jockey **2** a dinner jacket

DNA *n* any of various acids that are found esp in cell nuclei, are constructed of a double helix and are responsible for transmitting genetic information

¹**do** /dooh/ *v* **does** /daz; *strong* duz/; **did** /did/; **done** /dun/ **1a** to carry out the task of; effect, perform (e g *do* some washing) **b** to act, behave (e g *do* as I say) **2** to put into a specified condition (e g *do* him to death) **3** to have as a function (e g what's that book *doing* on the floor?) **4** to cause, impart (e g sleep will *do* you good) **5** to bring to an esp unwanted conclusion; finish – used esp in the past participle (e g that's *done* it) **6a** to fare; get along (e g *do* well at school) **b** to carry on business or affairs; manage (e g we can *do* without you) **7** to be in progress; happen (e g there's nothing *doing*) **8** to provide or have available (e g they *do* teas here) **9** to bring into existence; produce (e g *did* a portrait of his mother) **10** to put on; perform (e g *do* a Shakespearean comedy) **11** to come to or make an end; finish – used in the past participle; (e g have you *done* with the newspaper?) **12** to suffice, serve (e g half of that will *do*) **13** to be fitting; conform to custom or propriety (e g won't *do* to be late) **14a** to put in order, arrange, clean (e g *do* the garden) **b** to cook (e g likes her steak

well *done*) **15** to perform the appropriate professional service or services for (e g the barber will *do* you now) **16a** to work at, esp as a course of study or occupation (e g *do* classics) **b** to solve; work out (e g *do* a sum) **17** to travel at a (maximum) speed of (e g *do* 70 on the motorway) **18** to serve out, esp as a prison sentence (e g *did* 3 years) **19** to suffice, suit (e g that will *do* nicely) **20** – used as a substitute verb to avoid repetition (e g if you must make a noise; *do* it elsewhere) **21** – used to form present and past tenses expressing emphasis (e g *do* be quiet) **22a** *chiefly Br* to arrest, convict – slang (e g get *done* for theft) **b** to treat unfairly; *esp* to cheat, deprive (e g *did* him out of his inheritance) – infml **c** to rob – slang (e g *do* a shop) — **do away with 1** to put an end to; abolish **2** to put to death; kill — **do by** to deal with; treat — **do duty for** to act as a substitute for; serve as — **do for 1** *chiefly Br* to keep house for **2a** to wear out, exhaust **b** to bring about the death or ruin of — **do justice (to) 1a** to treat fairly or adequately **b** to show due appreciation for **2** to show in the best light — **do one's bit** *Br* to make one's personal contribution, esp to a cause — **do one's nut** to become frantic or angry — infml — **do proud** to treat or entertain splendidly — **do the dirty on** to play a sly trick on — **do something for** to improve the appearance of — **do the trick** to achieve the desired result — infml — **to do with** concerned with; of concern to

²**do** *n, pl* **dos, do's** /doohz/ **1** sthg one ought to do – usu pl **2** *chiefly Br* a festive party or occasion – infml

³**do, doh** /doh/ *n* the 1st note of the diatonic scale in solmization

docile /'doh,siel/ *adj* easily led or managed; tractable – ~**lity** *n*

¹**dock** /dok/ *n* any of a genus of coarse weeds whose leaves are used to alleviate nettle stings

²**dock** *v* **1** to cut (e g a tail) short **2** to make a deduction from (e g wages) **3** to take away (a specified amount) from

³**dock** *n* **1** a usu artificially enclosed body of water in a port or harbour, where a ship can moor (e g for repair work to be carried out) **2** *pl* the total number of such enclosures in a harbour, together with wharves, sheds, etc

⁴**dock** *v* **1** to come or go into dock **2** *of spacecraft* to join together while in space

⁵**dock** *n* the prisoner's enclosure in a criminal court

docker /'dokə/ *n* sby employed in loading and unloading ships, barges, etc

¹**docket** /'dokit/ *n* **1** a label attached to goods bearing identification or instructions **2** (a copy of) a receipt

²**docket** *v* to put an identifying statement or label on

dock yard /-,yahd/ *n* a place or enclosure in which ships are built or repaired

¹**doctor** /'doktə/ n 1 a holder of the highest level of academic degree conferred by a university 2 one qualified to practise medicine; a physician or surgeon 3 sby skilled in repairing or treating a usu specified type of machine, vehicle, etc

²**doctor** v 1a to give medical treatment to b to repair, mend 2a to adapt or modify for a desired end b to alter in a dishonest way 3 to castrate or spay – euph

doctrinaire /,doktri'neə/ n or adj (one) concerned with abstract theory to the exclusion of practical considerations – chiefly derog

doctrine /'doktrin/ n 1 sthg that is taught 2 a principle or the body of principles in a branch of knowledge or system of belief – **inal** adj

¹**document** /'dokyoomənt/ n an original or official paper that gives information about or proof of sthg – **~ary** adj

²**document** /'dokyoo,ment/ v 1 to provide documentary evidence of 2 to support with factual evidence, references, etc 3 to provide (a ship) with papers required by law recording ownership, cargo, etc

documentary /,dokyoo'ment(ə)ri/ n a broadcast or film that presents a factual account of a person or topic using a variety of techniques (e g narrative and interview)

dodder v 1 to tremble or shake from weakness or age 2 to walk feebly and unsteadily – **~ er** n, **~ing** adj

doddle /'dodl/ n, chiefly Br a very easy task – infml

¹**dodge** /doj/ v 1 to shift position suddenly (e g to avoid a blow or a pursuer) 2 to evade (e g a duty) usu by trickery

²**dodge** n 1 a sudden movement to avoid sthg 2 a clever device to evade or trick

dodgem /'dojəm/, **'dodgem ,car** n, Br any of a number of small electric cars designed to be steered about and bumped into one another as a fun-fair amusement

dodgy /'doji/ adj, chiefly Br 1 shady, dishonest 2 risky, dangerous 3 liable to collapse, fail, or break down

dodo /'doh,doh/ n, pl **dodoes, dodos** an extinct heavy flightless bird

doe /doh/ n, pl **does**, esp collectively **doe** the adult female fallow deer; broadly the adult female of any of various mammals (e g the rabbit) or birds (e g the guinea fowl) of which the male is called a buck

doer /'dooh-ə/ n one who takes action or participates actively in sthg, rather than theorizing

does /daz/ strong duz/ pres 3rd sing of **do**

doff /dof/ v to take off (one's hat) in greeting or as a sign of respect

¹**dog** /dog/ n **1a** a 4-legged flesh-eating domesticated mammal occurring in a great variety of breeds and prob descended from the common wolf b any of a family of carnivores to which the dog belongs c a male dog 2 any of various usu simple mechanical devices for holding, fastening, etc that consist of a spike, rod, or bar 3 chiefly NAm sthg inferior of its kind 4 an esp worthless man or fellow 5 pl ruin

²**dog** v **-gg-** to pursue closely like a dog; hound

³**dog** adj male

'dog ,collar n a narrow collar without points worn by clergymen – infml

'dog ,days n pl the hottest days in the year

'dog-,eared adj worn, shabby

,dog-eat-'dog adj marked by ruthless self-interest; cutthroat

'dog,fight /-,fiet/ n 1 a viciously fought contest 2 a fight between aircraft, usu at close quarters

'dog,fish /-,fish/ n any of various small sharks

dogged /'dogid/ adj stubbornly determined – **~ly** adv – **~ness** n

doggerel /'dog(ə)rəl/ n (an example of) verse that is loosely styled and irregular in measure, esp for comic effect

doggo /'dogoh/ adv, Br in hiding and without moving – infml; chiefly in **lie doggo**

'dog,house /-,hows/ n a dog kennel — **in the doghouse** in a state of disfavour — infml

'dog,leg /-,leg/ n 1 a sharp bend (e g in a road) 2 an angled fairway on a golf course

dogma /'dogmə/ n 1 an authoritative tenet or principle 2 a doctrine or body of doctrines formally and authoritatively stated by a church 3 a point of view or tenet put forth as authoritative without adequate grounds – chiefly derog – **~ tic** adj – **~ tically** adv – **~ tism** n

do-gooder /,dooh 'goodə/ n an earnest often naive and ineffectual humanitarian or reformer

'dogs,body /-,bodi/ n, chiefly Br a person who carries out routine or menial work – infml

,dog-'tired adj extremely tired – infml

doh /doh/ n the note of do

doily, doyley, doyly /'doyli/ n a small decorative mat, esp of paper, often placed under cakes on a plate or stand

do in v 1 to kill 2 to wear out, exhaust **USE** infml

doing /'dooh-ing/ n 1 the act or result of performing; action (e g this must be your doing) 2 effort, exertion (e g it will take a great deal of doing) 3 pl things that are done or that occur; activities

doings /'dooh-ings/ n, pl **doings** also **doinges** /-ziz/, chiefly Br a small object, esp one whose name is forgotten or not known – infml

doldrums /'doldramz/ n pl 1 a depressed state of mind; the blues 2 an equatorial ocean region where calms, squalls, and light shifting winds prevail 3 a state of stagnation or slump

dole /dohl/ n 1 a distribution of food, money, or clothing to the needy 2 the government unemployment benefit

doleful /'dohlf(ə)l/ adj sad, mournful – **~ly** adv – **~ness** n

dole out v to give, distribute, or deliver, esp in small portions

doll /dol/ n 1 a small-scale figure of a human being used esp as a child's toy 2a a (pretty but often silly) young woman – infml b an attractive person – slang

dollar /'dolə/ n (a coin or note representing) the basic money unit of the USA, Canada, Australia, etc

¹**dollop** /'doləp/ n a soft shapeless blob; esp a serving of mushy or semiliquid food

²**dollop** v to serve *out* carelessly or clumsily

'**doll's ,house** n a child's small-scale toy house

doll up v to dress prettily or showily – infml

¹**dolly** /'doli/ n 1 a doll – used chiefly by or to children 2 a wooden-pronged instrument for beating and stirring clothes while washing them in a tub 3a a platform on a roller or on wheels or castors for moving heavy objects b a wheeled platform for a film or television camera

²**dolly** v to move a film or television camera on a dolly towards or away from a subject – usu + *in* or *out*

'**dolly ,bird** n, *chiefly Br* a pretty young woman, esp one who is a slavish follower of fashion and not regarded as intelligent

dolmen /'dolmen/ n a prehistoric monument consisting of 2 or more upright stones supporting a horizontal slab

dolorous /'doloəs/ adj causing or expressing misery or grief – ~**ly** adv

dolphin /'dolfin/ n any of various small toothed whales with the snout elongated into a beak to varying extents

dolt /dohlt/ n an extremely dull or stupid person – ~**ish** adj – ~**ishly** adv

domain /də'mayn/ n 1 a territory over which control is exercised 2 a sphere of influence or activity

¹**dome** /dohm/ n a (nearly) hemispherical roof or vault – ~**d** adj

²**dome** v to cover with or form into a dome

'**Domesday ,Book** /'doohmz,day, -di/ n a record of a survey of English lands made by order of William I about 1086

¹**domestic** /də'mestik/ adj 1 of or devoted to the home or the family 2 of one's own or some particular country; not foreign 3a living near or about the habitations of human beings b tame; *also* bred by human beings for some specific purpose (e g food, hunting, etc) – ~**ally** adv

²**domestic** n a household servant

domesticate /də'mestikayt/ v 1 to bring (an animal or species) under human control for some specific purpose (e g for carrying loads, hunting, food, etc) 2 to cause to be fond of or adapted to household duties or pleasures – **cation** n

domesticity /,dome'stisəti/ n (devotion to) home or family life

¹**domicile** /'domisiel/ *also* **domicil** /-s(i)l/ n a home; *esp* a person's permanent and principal home for legal purposes

²**domicile** v to establish in or provide with a domicile

¹**dominant** /'dominənt/ adj 1 commanding, controlling, or prevailing over all others 2 overlooking and commanding from a superior height 3 being the one of a pair of (genes determining) contrasting inherited characteristics that predominates – **nance** n

²**dominant** n the fifth note of a diatonic scale

dominate /'dominayt/ v 1 to exert controlling influence or power over 2 to overlook from a superior height 3 to occupy a commanding or preeminent position in 4 to have or exert mastery or control – **nation** n

domineer /,domi'niə/ v to exercise arbitrary or overbearing control

Dominican /də'minikən/ n or adj (a member) of a preaching order of mendicant friars

dominion /də'minyən, -ni-ən/ n 1 the power or right to rule; sovereignty 2 absolute ownership 3 *often cap* a self-governing nation of the Commonwealth other than the United Kingdom

domino /'dominoh/ n, pl **dominoes, dominos** 1a a long loose hooded cloak worn with a mask as a masquerade costume b a half mask worn with a masquerade costume 2a a flat rectangular block whose face is divided into 2 equal parts that are blank or bear from 1 to usu 6 dots arranged as on dice faces b pl but usu sing in constr any of several games played with a set of usu 28 dominoes

¹**don** /don/ n 1 a Spanish nobleman or gentleman – used as a title preceding the Christian name 2 a head, tutor, or fellow in a college of Oxford or Cambridge university; *broadly* a university teacher

²**don** v -**nn**- to put on (clothes, etc)

donate /doh'nayt/ v to make a gift (of), esp to a public or charitable cause – **ion** n

¹**done** /dun/ 1 past part of do 2 *chiefly dial & NAm* past of do

²**done** adj 1 socially conventional or accepted (e g it's not *done* to eat peas off your knife) 2 arrived at or brought to an end; completed 3 physically exhausted; spent 4 no longer involved; through (e g I'm *done* with the Army) 5 doomed to failure, defeat, or death 6 cooked sufficiently 7 arrested, imprisoned – slang

³**done** interj – used in acceptance of a bet or transaction

Don Juan /don 'jooh-ən, 'hwahn/ n a promiscuous man; *broadly* a lady-killer

donkey /'dongki/ n 1 the domestic ass 2 a stupid or obstinate person

'**donkey ,jacket** n a thick hip-length hard-wearing jacket, usu blue and with a strip of (imitation) leather across the shoulders

'**donkey's ,years** n pl, chiefly Br a very long time – infml

'**donkey,work** /-,wuhk/ n hard, monotonous, and routine work – infml

donnish /'donish/ adj pedantic – ~ **ly** adv

donor /'dohnə/ n 1 a person who gives, donates, or presents 2 sby used as a source of biological material

doodle /'doohdl/ v or n **doodling** /'doohdling,' doohdl·ing/ (to make) an aimless scribble or sketch

¹**doom** /doohm/ n 1 God's judgment of the world 2a an (unhappy) destiny b unavoidable death or destruction; also environmental catastrophe – often in combination

²**doom** v to destine, esp to failure or destruction

doomsday /'doohmz,day, -di/ n, often cap judgment day; broadly some remote point in the future

door /daw/ n 1 a usu swinging or sliding barrier by which an entry is closed and opened; also a similar part of a piece of furniture 2 a doorway 3 a means of access — **at someone's door** as a charge against sby as being responsible

'**door,keeper** /-,keepə/ n a person who guards the main door to a building and lets people in and out

'**doorman** /-mən/ n a (uniformed) person who tends the entrance to a hotel, theatre, etc and assists people (e g in calling taxis)

'**door,mat** /-,mat/ n a mat (e g of bristles) placed before or inside a door for wiping dirt from the shoes 2 a person who submits to bullying and indignities – infml

'**door,step** /-,step/ n 1 a step in front of an outer door 2 Br a very thick slice of bread – infml

'**door,way** /-,way/ n an entrance into a building or room that is closed by means of a door

¹**dope** /dohp/ n 1 a coating (e g a cellulose varnish) applied to a surface or fabric (e g of an aeroplane or balloon) to improve strength, impermeability, or tautness 2 absorbent or adsorbent material used in various manufacturing processes (e g the making of dynamite) 3a marijuana, opium, or another drug b a preparation given illegally to a racing horse, greyhound, etc to make it run faster or slower 4 a stupid person – infml 5 information, esp from a reliable source – infml

²**dope** v to treat or affect with dope; esp to give a narcotic to

dopey, dopy /'dohpi/ adj 1 dulled, doped, or stupefied (e g by drugs, alcohol, or sleep) 2 dull, stupid

doppelgänger /'dopl,gengə/, **doppelganger** /-, gangə/ n a ghostly counterpart of a living person

'**Doppler ef,fect** n a change in the apparent frequency of sound, light, or other waves when there is relative motion between the source and the observer

dormant /'dawmənt/ adj 1 marked by a suspension of activity: e g **1a** temporarily devoid of external activity b temporarily in abeyance 2 (appearing to be) asleep or inactive, esp throughout winter – **-ancy** n

dormer /'dawmə/ n a window set vertically in a structure projecting through a sloping roof

dormitory /'dawmət(ə)ri/ n 1 a large room containing a number of beds 2 a residential community from which the inhabitants commute to their places of employment

dormouse /'daw,mows/ n any of numerous small Old World rodents having a long bushy tail

dorsal /'dawsl/ adj relating to or situated near or on the back or top surface

dose /dohs/ n 1 the measured quantity of medicine to be taken at one time 2 a part of an experience to which one is exposed 3 an infection with a venereal disease – slang

²**dose** v to give a dose, esp of medicine, to

doss /dos/ n, chiefly Br 1 a crude or makeshift bed, esp one in a cheap lodging house 2 a short sleep USE slang

doss down v, chiefly Br to sleep or bed down in a makeshift bed – infml

dosser /'dosə/ n, chiefly Br a down-and-out

dossier /'dosi-ə, 'dosiay/ n a file of papers containing a detailed report or information

dost /dust/ archaic pres 2 sing of **do**

¹**dot** /dot/ n 1 a small spot; a speck **2a**(1) a small point made with a pointed instrument **a**(2) a small round mark used in spelling or punctuation **b**(1) a point after a note or rest in music indicating lengthening of the time value by one half **b**(2) a point over or under a note indicating that it is to be played staccato 3 a precise point, esp in time **4** a signal (e g a flash or audible tone) of relatively short duration that is one of the 2 fundamental units of Morse code

²**dot** v **-tt-** 1 to mark with a dot 2 to intersperse with dots or objects scattered at random

dotage /'dohtij/ n a state or period of senile mental decay resulting in feeblemindedness

doth /duth/ archaic pres 3 sing of **do**

dotty /'doti/ adj 1 crazy, mad 2 pleasantly eccentric or absurd USE infml – **dottiness** n – **dottily** adv

¹**double** /'dubl/ adj 1 twofold, dual 2 consisting of 2, usu combined, similar members or parts 3 being twice as great or as many 4 marked by duplicity; deceitful 5 folded in 2 6 of twofold or extra size, strength, or value

²**double** n 1 a double amount; esp a double measure of spirits **2a** a living person who closely resembles another living person b a ghostly counterpart of a living person **c**(1) an understudy **c**(2) one who resembles an actor and takes his/her place in scenes calling for special skills 3 a sharp turn or twist **4a** a bet in which the winnings and

stake from a first race are bet on a second race **b** two wins or on horse races, esp in a single day's racing **5** an act of doubling in a card game **6** the outermost narrow ring on a dartboard counting double the stated score; *also* a throw in darts that lands there — **at the double** at a fast rate between running and walking; *specif, of a military order to move* in double time

³**double** *adv* **1** to twice the extent or amount **2** two together

⁴**double** *v* **doubled; doubling** /'dubling, 'dubl·ing/ **1a** to increase by adding an equal amount **b** to make a call in bridge that increases the value of tricks won or lost on (an opponent's bid) **2a** to make into 2 thicknesses; fold **b** to clench **c** to cause to stoop or bend over – usu + *up* or *over* **3** to become twice as much or as many **4** to turn back on one's course – usu + *back* **5** to become bent or folded, usu in the middle – usu + *up* or *over* **6** to serve an additional purpose – usu + *as*

,**double-'barrelled** *adj* **1** *of a firearm* having 2 barrels **2** having a double purpose **3** *of a surname* having 2 parts

,**double 'bass** *n* the largest instrument in the violin family tuned a fifth below the cello

,**double-'breasted** *adj* having a front fastening with one half of the front overlapping the other and usu a double row of buttons and a single row of buttonholes

,**double 'cream** *n* thick heavy cream suitable for whipping

,**double-'cross** *v or n* (to deceive by) an act of betraying or cheating – **double-crosser** *n*

,**double-'decker** /'dekə/ *n* sthg that has 2 decks, levels, or layers; *esp* a bus with seats on 2 floors

,**double 'dutch** *n, often cap 2nd D* unintelligible or nonsensical speech or writing; gibberish – infml

,**double-'edged** *adj* having 2 purposes or possible interpretations; *specif, of a remark* seeming innocent, but capable of a malicious interpretation

,**double-'jointed** *adj* having or being a joint that permits an exceptional degree of flexibility of the parts joined

,**double-'park** *v* to park beside a row of vehicles already parked parallel to the kerb

,**double-'quick** *adj* very quick

doubles /'dublz/ *n* a game between 2 pairs of players

doublet /'dublit/ *n* a man's close-fitting jacket, with or without sleeves, worn in Europe, esp in the 15th to 17th c

'**double ,take** *n* a delayed reaction to a surprising or significant situation – esp in *do a double take*

'**double-,talk** *n* involved and often deliberately ambiguous language – **double-talk** *v* – **double-talker** *n*

doubloon /dub'loohn/ *n* a former gold coin of Spain and Spanish America

doubly /'dubli/ *adv* **1** to twice the degree **2** in 2 ways

¹**doubt** /dowt/ *v* **1** to be in doubt about **2a** to lack confidence in; distrust **b** to consider unlikely – ~ **er** *n*

²**doubt** *n* **1** (a state of) uncertainty of belief or opinion **2** a lack of confidence; distrust **3** an inclination not to believe or accept; a reservation — **in doubt** uncertain — **no doubt** doubtless

'**doubtful** /-f(ə)l/ *adj* **1** causing doubt; open to question **2a** lacking a definite opinion; hesitant **b** uncertain in outcome; not settled **3** of questionable worth, honesty, or validity – ~ **ly** *adv*

'**doubtless** /-lis/ *adv* **1** without doubt **2** probably

douche /doohsh/ *n* (a device for giving) a jet or current of fluid, directed against a part or into a cavity of the body, esp the vagina

dough /doh/ *n* **1** a mixture that consists essentially of flour or meal and milk, water, or another liquid and is stiff enough to knead or roll **2** money – slang

doughnut /'doh,nut/ *n* a small round or ring-shaped cake that is often made with a yeast dough, filled with jam, and deep-fried

doughty /'dowti/ *adj* valiant, bold – poetic

doughy /'doh·i/ *adj* unhealthily pale; pasty

do up *v* **1** to repair, restore **2** to wrap up **3** to fasten (clothing or its fastenings) together **4** to make more beautiful or attractive – infml

dour /dowə/ *adj* **1** stern, harsh **2** gloomy, sullen – ~ **ly** *adv*

douse , dowse /dows/ *v* **1** to plunge into or drench with water **2** to extinguish (e g lights)

dove /duv/ *n* **1** any of various (smaller and slenderer) types of pigeon **2** an advocate of negotiation and compromise; *esp* an opponent of war – usu contrasted with *hawk*

¹**dovetail** /'duv,tayl/ *n* a tenon like a dove's tail and the mortise into which it fits to form a joint

²**dovetail** *v* **1** to join (as if) by means of dovetails **2** to fit skilfully together to form a whole

dowager /'dowajə/ *n* **1** a widow holding property or a title received from her deceased husband **2** a dignified elderly woman

dowdy /'dowdi/ *adj* **1** not neat or smart in appearance **2** old-fashioned, frumpy – **-dily** *adv* – **-diness** *n*

dowel /'dowəl/ *n* a usu metal or wooden pin fitting into holes in adjacent pieces to preserve their relative positions; *also* rods of wood or metal for sawing into such pins

¹**down** /down/ *n* (a region of) undulating treeless usu chalk uplands, esp in S England – usu pl with sing. meaning

²**down** *adv* **1a** at or towards a relatively low level (e g *down* into the cellar) **b** in or into a lying or sitting position (e g lie *down*) **c** to or on the

ground, surface, or bottom (e g telephone wires are *down*) **2** on the spot *esp* as an initial payment (e g paid £10 *down*) **3a(1)** in or into a relatively low condition or status (e g family has come *down* in the world) – sometimes used interjectionally to express opposition (e g *down* with the oppressors!) **a(2)** to prison – often + *go* or *send* **b(1)** in or into a state of relatively low intensity or activity (e g calm *down*) **b(2)** into a slower pace or lower gear (e g changed *down* into second) **c** lower in amount, price, figure, or rank (e g prices are *down*) **d** behind an opponent (e g we're 3 points *down*) **4a** so as to be known, recognized, or recorded, esp on paper (e g scribbled it *down*; you're *down* to speak next) **b** so as to be firmly held in position (e g stick *down* the flap of the envelope **c** to the moment of catching or discovering (e g track the criminal *down*) **5** in a direction conventionally the opposite of up: e g **5a** to leeward **b** in or towards the south **c** *chiefly Br* away from the capital of a country or from a university city

³**down** *adj* **1** directed or going downwards (e g the *down* escalator) **2a** depressed, dejected **b** ill (e g *down* with flu) **3** having been finished or dealt with (e g eight *down* and two to go) **4** with the rudder to windward – used with reference to a ship's helm **5** *chiefly Br* bound in a direction regarded as down; *esp* travelling away from a large town, *esp* London

⁴**down** *prep* **1a** down along, round, through, towards, in, into, or on **b** at the bottom of (e g the bathroom is *down* those stairs) **2** *Br* down to; to (e g going *down* the shops) – nonstandard

⁵**down** *n* a grudge, prejudice – often in *have a down on*

⁶**down** *v* **1** to cause to go or come down **2** to drink down; swallow quickly – infml **3** to defeat – infml — **down tools** *chiefly Br* to stop working; *esp* to go on strike

⁷**down** *n* a covering of soft fluffy feathers

,**down-and-'out** *n or adj* (sby) destitute or impoverished

¹'**down,beat** /-,beet/ *n* the principally accented (e g the first) note of a bar of music

²**downbeat** *adj* **1** pessimistic, gloomy **2** relaxed, informal

'**down,cast** /-,kahst/ *adj* **1** dejected, depressed **2** directed downwards

'**down,fall** /-,fawl/ *n* **1** (a cause of) a sudden fall (e g from high rank or power) **2** an often heavy fall of rain or esp snow

,**down'grade** /-'grayd/ *v* to lower in rank, value, or importance

,**down'hearted** /-'hahtid/ *adj* downcast, dejected – **~ly** *adv*

¹'**down,hill** /-,hil/ *n* a skiing race downhill against time

²,**down'hill** *adv* **1** towards the bottom of a hill **2** towards a lower or inferior state or level – in *go downhill*

³**down'hill** *adj* sloping downhill

'**Downing ,Street** /'downing/ *n* the British government; *also* (a spokesman for) the British prime minister

'**down ,payment** *n* a deposit paid at the time of purchase or delivery

'**down,pour** /-,paw/ *n* a heavy fall of rain

¹,**down'right** /-,riet/ *adv* thoroughly, outright

²**downright** *adj* **1** absolute, thorough **2** plain, blunt

'**Down's ,syndrome** /downz/ *n* a form of congenital mental deficiency in which a child is born with slanting eyes, a broad short skull, and broad hands with short fingers

,**down'stage** /-'stayj/ *adv or adj* at the front of a theatrical stage; *also* towards the audience or camera

¹,**down'stairs** /-'steaz/ *adv* down the stairs; on or to a lower floor

²**downstairs** *adj* situated on the main, lower, or ground floor of a building

³**downstairs** *n, pl* **downstairs** the lower floor of a building

,**down'stream** /-'streem/ *adv or adj* in the direction of the flow of a stream

,**down-to-'earth** *adj* practical, realistic

'**down,trodden** /-,trod(ə)n/ *adj* oppressed by those in power

downward /'downwood/ *adj* **1** moving or extending downwards (e g the *downward* path) **2** descending to a lower pitch **3** descending from a head, origin, or source

'**downwards** /-woodz/ *adv* **1a** from a higher to a lower place or level; in the opposite direction from up **b** downstream *c* so as to conceal a particular surface (e g turned it face *downwards*) **2a** from a higher to a lower condition **b** going down in amount, price, figure, or rank **3** from an earlier time **4** from an ancestor or predecessor

,**down'wind** /-'wind/ *adv or adj* in the direction that the wind is blowing

downy /'downi/ *adj* **1** resembling or covered in down **2** made of down

dowry /'dowri/ *n* the money, goods, or estate that a woman brings to her husband in marriage

¹**dowse** /dows/ *v* to douse

²**dowse** /dowz/ *v* to search for hidden water or minerals with a divining rod – **~ r** *n* – **dowsing** *n*

'**dowsing ,rod** /'dowzing/ *n* a divining rod

doyen /'doyan (*Fr* dwajĕ)/, *fem* **doyenne** /doy'en (*Fr* dwajen)/ *n* the senior or most experienced member of a body or group

doze /dohz/ *v* **1** to sleep lightly **2** to fall into a light sleep – usu + *off* – **doze** *n*

dozen /'duzən/ n, pl **dozens, dozen 1** a group of 12 **2** an indefinitely large number – usu pl with sing. meaning – **dozen** adj

dozy /'dohzi/ adj **1** drowsy, sleepy **2** chiefly Br stupid and slow-witted – infml – **-zily** adv – **-ziness** n

drab /drab/ adj **1** of a dull brown colour **2** dull, cheerless – ~ **ly** adv – ~ **ness** n

drachma /'drakmə/ n pl **drachmas, drachmae** /-mi/, **drachmai** /-mie/ the standard unit of currency of Greece

draconian /dray'kohnyən, -ni·ən, drə-/, **draconic** /dray'konik, drə-/ adj, often cap, esp of a law extremely severe; drastic

¹draft /drahft/ n **1** the act, result, or plan of drawing out or sketching: e g **1a** a construction plan **b** a preliminary sketch, outline, or version **2a** a group of individuals selected for a particular job **b** (the group of individuals resulting from) the selecting of certain animals from a herd or flock **3a** an order for the payment of money drawn from one person or bank on another **b** (an instance of) drawing from or making demands on sthg **4** chiefly NAm conscription – usu + the

²draft adj, esp of livestock chosen from a group

³draft v **1** to draw the preliminary sketch, version, or plan of **2** NAm to conscript for military service

draftsman /'drahftsmən/ n sby who draws up legal documents or other writings

¹drag /drag/ n **1** a device for dragging under water to search for objects **2** sthg that retards motion, action, or progress; a burden **3a** a drawing along or over a surface with effort or pressure **b** motion effected with slowness or difficulty **c** a drawing into the mouth of pipe, cigarette, or cigar smoke – infml **4a** woman's clothing worn by a man – slang; often in in drag **b** clothing – slang **5** a dull or boring person or experience – slang

²drag v **-gg- 1a** to draw slowly or heavily; haul **b** to cause to move with painful or undue slowness or difficulty **2a** to search (a body of water) with a drag **b** to catch with a dragnet or trawl **3** to bring by force or compulsion – infml **4** to hang or lag behind **5** to trail along on the ground **6** to move or proceed laboriously or tediously – infml **7** to draw tobacco smoke into the mouth – usu + on; infml – **drag one's feet/heels** to act in a deliberately slow, dilatory, or ineffective manner

'drag,net /-,net/ n **1** a net drawn along the bottom of a body of water or the ground to catch fish or small game **2** a network of measures for apprehension (e g of criminals)

dragon /'dragən/ n **1** a mythical winged and clawed monster, often breathing fire **2** a fierce, combative, or very strict person

'dragon,fly /-,flie/ n any of various long slender-bodied often brightly coloured insects that live near water

¹dragoon /drə'goohn/ n a member of a European military unit formerly composed of mounted infantrymen armed with carbines

²dragoon v **1** to reduce to subjection by harsh use of troops **2** to (attempt to) force into submission by persecution

¹drain /drayn/ v **1a** to draw off (liquid) gradually or completely **b** to exhaust physically or emotionally **2a** to make gradually dry **b** to carry away the surface water of **c** to deplete or empty (as if) by drawing off gradually **d** to empty by drinking the contents of **3** to flow off gradually **4** to become gradually dry

²drain n **1** a means (e g a pipe) by which usu liquid matter is drained away **2** a gradual outflow or withdrawal **3** sthg that causes depletion; a burden — **down the drain** being used wastefully or brought to nothing

drainage /'draynij/ n **1a** draining **b** sthg drained off **2** a system of drains

'drain,pipe /-,piep/ n a pipe that carries waste, liquid sewage, excess water, etc away from a building

,drain,pipe 'trousers, 'drain,pipes n pl tight trousers with narrow legs

drake /drayk/ n a male duck

dram /dram/ n **1** a unit of mass equal to ¹/₁₆oz avoirdupois (about 1.77g) **2** chiefly Scot a tot of spirits, usu whisky

drama /'drahmə/ n **1** a composition in verse or prose intended to portray life or character or to tell a story through action and dialogue; specif a play **2** dramatic art, literature, or affairs **3** a situation or set of events having the qualities of a drama – ~ **tize** v

dramatic /drə'matik/ adj **1** of drama **2a** suitable to or characteristic of drama; vivid **b** striking in appearance or effect – ~ **ally** adv

dramatis personae /,drahmatis puh'sohnie/ n pl (a list) of the characters or actors in a play

dramatist /'drahmatist, 'dra-/ n a playwright

drank /drangk/ past of **drink**

¹drape /drayp/ v **1** to cover or decorate (as if) with folds of cloth **2** to hang or stretch loosely or carelessly **3** to arrange in flowing lines or folds

²drape n a piece of drapery; esp, chiefly NAm a curtain

draper /'draypə/ n, chiefly Br a dealer in cloth and sometimes also in clothing, haberdashery, and soft furnishings

drapery /'draypə(ə)ri/ n **1a** (a piece of) cloth or clothing arranged or hung gracefully, esp in loose folds **b** cloth or textile fabrics used esp for clothing or soft furnishings **2** Br the trade of a draper

drastic /'drastik/ adj radical in effect or action; severe – ~ **ally** adv

drat /drat/ v **-tt-** to damn – euph; used as a mild oath

¹draught, *NAm chiefly* **draft** /drahft/ *n* **1** a team of animals together with what they draw **2** the act or an instance of drinking; *also* the portion drunk in such an act **3** the act of drawing (e g from a cask); *also* a quantity of liquid so drawn **4** the depth of water a ship requires to float in, esp when loaded **5** a current of air in a closed-in space — **on draught** *of beer or cider* ready to be served from the cask or barrel with or without the use of added gas in serving

²draught, *NAm chiefly* **draft** *adj* **1** used for drawing loads **2** served from the barrel or cask

'draught,board /-,bawd/ *n* a chessboard

draughts /drahfts/ *n pl but sing or pl in constr,* *Br* a game for 2 players each of whom moves his/her usu 12 draughtsmen according to fixed rules across a chessboard usu using only the black squares

draughtsman /'drahtsman/ *n* **1a** an artist skilled in drawing **b** *fem* **draughtswoman** sby who draws plans and sketches (e g of machinery or structures) **2** *Br* a disc-shaped piece used in draughts

draughty /'drahfti/ *adj* having a cold draught blowing through

¹draw /draw/ *v* **drew** /drooh/; **drawn** /drawn/ **1** to pull, haul **2** to cause to go in a certain direction **3a** to attract **b** to bring in, gather, or derive from a specified source **c** to bring on oneself; provoke **d** to bring out by way of response; elicit **4** to inhale **5a** to bring or pull out, esp with effort **b** to disembowel **c** to cause (blood) to flow **6a** to accumulate, gain **b** to take (money) from a place of deposit – often + *out* **c** to use in making a cash demand **d** to receive regularly, esp from a particular source **7a** to take (cards) from a dealer or pack **b** to receive or take at random **8** to strike (a ball) so as to impart a curved motion or backspin **9** to produce a likeness of (e g by making lines on a surface); portray, delineate **10** to formulate or arrive at by reasoning **11** to pull together and close (e g curtains) **12** to stretch or shape (esp metal) by pulling through dies; *also* to produce (e g a wire) thus **13** to come or go steadily or gradually **14** to advance as far as a specified position **15a** to pull back a bowstring **b** to bring out a weapon **16** to produce or allow a draught **17** to sketch **18** to finish a competition or contest without either side winning **19** to obtain resources (e g of information) **20** *chiefly NAm* to suck in sthg, esp tobacco smoke – usu + *on* — **draw a blank** to fail to gain the desired object (e g information sought) — **draw lots** to decide an issue by lottery in which objects of unequal length or with different markings are used — **draw on/upon** to use as source of supply — **draw rein** to bring a horse to a stop while riding — **draw stumps** to end play in a cricket match — **draw the/a line** to fix an arbitrary boundary between things that tend to merge **2** to fix a boundary beyond which one will not tolerate or engage in — usu + *at*

²draw *n* **1a** a sucking pull on sthg held between the lips *b* the removing of a handgun from its holster in order to shoot **2** a drawing of lots; a raffle **3** a contest left undecided; a tie **4** sthg that draws public attention or patronage **5** the usu random assignment of starting positions in a competition, esp a competitive sport

'draw,back /-,bak/ *n* an objectionable feature; a disadvantage

draw back *v* to avoid an issue or commitment; retreat

'draw,bridge /-,brij/ *n* a bridge made to be raised up, let down, or drawn aside so as to permit or hinder passage

drawer /*sense* 1 'draw·ə; *senses* 2, 3 draw/ *n* **1** one who draws a bill of exchange or order for payment or makes a promissory note **2** an open-topped box in a piece of furniture which to open and close slides back and forth in its frame **3** *pl* an undergarment for the lower body – now usu humor

drawing /'draw·ing/ *n* **1** the art or technique of representing an object, figure, or plan by means of lines **2** sthg drawn or subject to drawing: e g **2a** an amount drawn from a fund **b** a representation formed by drawing

'drawing ,pin *n, Br* a pin with a broad flat head for fastening esp sheets of paper to boards

'drawing ,room *n* **1** a formal reception room **2** a living room – *fml*

¹drawl /drawl/ *v* to speak or utter slowly and often affectedly, with vowels greatly prolonged

²drawl *n* a drawling manner of speaking

draw on *v* **1** to approach **2** to cause; bring on **3** to put on

draw out *v* **1** to remove, extract **2** to extend beyond a minimum in time; prolong **3** to cause to speak freely

'draw,string /-,string/ *n* a string or tape threaded through fabric, which when pulled closes an opening (e g of a bag) or gathers material (e g of curtains or clothes)

draw up *v* **1** to bring (e g troops) into array **2** to draft **3** to straighten (oneself) to an erect posture, esp as an assertion of dignity or resentment **4** to bring or come to a halt

¹dray /dray/ *n* a strong low cart or wagon without sides, used esp by brewers

²dray *n* a squirrel's nest

¹dread /dred/ *v* to fear greatly

²dread *n* (the object of) great fear, uneasiness, or apprehension

³dread *adj* causing or inspiring dread

'dreadful /-f(ə)l/ *adj* **1** inspiring dread **2** extremely unpleasant or shocking – ~ness *n* – ~ly *adv*

¹**dream** /dreem/ *n* **1** a series of thoughts, images, or emotions occurring during sleep **2** sthg notable for its beauty, excellence, or enjoyable quality **3** a strongly desired goal; an ambition; *also* a realization of an ambition – often used attributively

²**dream** *v* **dreamed** /dreemd, dremt/, **dreamt** /dremt/ **1** to have a dream (of) **2** to indulge in daydreams or fantasies **3** to consider as a possibility; imagine **4** to pass (time) in reverie or inaction – usu + *away* — **dream of** to consider even the possibility of — in neg constructions

'**dream,boat** /-,boht/ *n* a highly attractive person of the opposite sex – infml; no longer in vogue

dreamy /'dreemi/ *adj* **1** pleasantly abstracted from immediate reality **2** given to dreaming or fantasy **3a** suggestive of a dream in vague or visionary quality **b** delightful, pleasing; *esp, of a man* sexually attractive – infml **--mily** *adv* **--miness** *n*

dreary /'driəri/ *adj* causing feelings of cheerlessness or gloom; dull – **-arily** *adv* **-ariness** *n*

¹**dredge** /drej/ *n* **1** an oblong frame with an attached net for gathering fish, shellfish, etc from the bottom of the sea, a river, etc **2** a machine for removing earth, mud, etc usu by buckets on an endless chain or suction tube

²**dredge** *v* **1a** to dig, gather, or pull out with a dredge – often + *up* or *out* **b** to deepen (e g a waterway) with a dredging machine **2** to bring to light by thorough searching – usu + *up*; infml **3** to use a dredge

³**dredge** *v* to coat (e g food) by sprinkling (e g with flour)

dredger /'drejə/ *n* a barge with an apparatus for dredging harbours, waterways, etc

dregs /dregz/ *n pl* **1** sediment **2** the most undesirable part

¹**drench** /drench/ *n* a poisonous or medicinal drink, esp put down the throat of an animal

²**drench** *v* **1** to administer a drench to (an animal) **2** to make thoroughly wet (e g with falling water or by immersion); saturate

¹**dress** /dres/ *v* **1a** to put clothes on **b** to provide with clothing **2** to add decorative details or accessories to; embellish **3** to prepare for use or service; *esp* to prepare (e g a chicken) for cooking or eating **4a** to apply dressings or medicaments to (e g a wound) **b(1)** to arrange (the hair) **b(2)** to groom and curry (an animal) **c** to kill and prepare for market **d** to cultivate, esp by applying manure or fertilizer **e** to finish the surface of (e g timber, stone, or textiles) **f** to arrange goods on a display in (e g a shop window) **5a** to put on clothing **b** to put on or wear formal, elaborate, or fancy clothes **6** *of a man* to have one's genitals lying on a specified side of the trouser crutch

²**dress** *n* **1** utilitarian or ornamental covering for the human body; *esp* clothing suitable for a particular purpose or occasion **2** a 1-piece outer garment including both top and skirt usu for a woman or girl **3** covering, adornment, or appearance appropriate or peculiar to a specified time

dressage /'dresahzh, -'-/ *n* the execution by a trained horse of precise movements in response to its rider

'**dress ,circle** *n* the first or lowest curved tier of seats in a theatre

dress down *v* to reprove severely – **dressing-down** *n*

¹**dresser** /'dresə/ *n* a piece of kitchen furniture resembling a sideboard with a high back and having compartments and shelves for holding dishes and cooking utensils

²**dresser** *n* a person who looks after stage costumes and helps actors to dress

dressing /'dresing/ *n* **1** a seasoning, sauce, or stuffing **2** material applied to cover a wound, sore, etc **3** manure or compost to improve the growth of plants

'**dressing ,gown** *n* a loose robe worn esp over nightclothes or when not fully dressed

'**dressing ,table** *n* a table usu fitted with drawers and a mirror for use while dressing and grooming oneself

'**dress re,hearsal** *n* **1** a full rehearsal of a play in costume and with stage props shortly before the first performance **2** a full-scale practice

dressy /'dresi/ *adj* **1** showy in dress or appearance **2** *of clothes* stylish, smart

drew /drooh/ *past of* **draw**

¹**dribble** /'dribl/ *v* **dribbled; dribbling** /'dribling/ **1** to fall or flow in drops or in a thin intermittent stream; trickle **2** to let saliva trickle from the mouth; drool **3** to come or issue in piecemeal or disconnected fashion **4** to propel (a ball or puck) by successive slight taps or bounces with hand, foot, or stick **5** to proceed by dribbling

²**dribble** *n* **1** a small trickling stream or flow **2** a tiny or insignificant bit or quantity **3** an act or instance of dribbling

drier *also* **dryer** /'drie-ə/ *n* any of various machines for drying sthg (e g the hair or clothes)

¹**drift** /drift/ *n* **1a** a mass of sand, snow, etc deposited (as if) by wind or water **b** rock debris deposited by natural wind, water, etc; *specif* a deposit of clay, sand, gravel, and boulders transported by (running water from) a glacier **2** a general underlying tendency or meaning, esp of what is spoken or written **3** the motion or action of drifting: e g **3a** a ship's deviation from its course caused by currents **b** a slow-moving ocean current **c** an easy, moderate, more or less steady flow along a spatial course **d** a gradual shift in attitude, opinion, or emotion **e** an aimless course, with no attempt at direction or control **4** a nearly horizontal mine passage on or parallel to a vein or rock stratum

²**drift** v **1a** to become driven or carried along by a current of water or air **b** to move or float smoothly and effortlessly **2a** to move in a random or casual way **b** to become carried along aimlessly **3** to pile up under the force of wind or water **4** to pile up in a drift

drifter /'driftə/ n **1** sby or sthg that travels or moves about aimlessly **2** a coastal fishing boat equipped with drift nets

'**drift,wood** /-,wood/ n wood cast up on a shore or beach

¹**drill** /dril/ v **1a** to bore or drive a hole in (as if) by the piercing action of a drill **b** to make (e g a hole) by piercing action **2a** to instruct and exercise by repeating **b** to train or exercise in military drill

²**drill** n **1** (a device or machine for rotating) a tool with an edged or pointed end for making a hole in a solid substance by revolving or by a succession of blows **2** training in marching and the manual of arms **3** a physical or mental exercise aimed at improving facility and skill by regular practice **4** a marine snail that bores through oyster shells and eats the flesh **5** chiefly Br the approved or correct procedure for accomplishing sthg efficiently – infml

³**drill** n **1a** a shallow furrow into which seed is sown **b** a row of seed sown in such a furrow **2** a planting implement that makes holes or furrows, drops in the seed and sometimes fertilizer, and covers them with earth

⁴**drill** v to sow (seeds) by dropping along a shallow furrow

⁵**drill** n a durable cotton fabric in twill weave

drily /'drieli/ adv dryly

¹**drink** /dringk/ v **drank** /drangk/, **drunk** /drungk/, **drank 1a** to swallow (a liquid); also to swallow the liquid contents of (e g a cup) **b** to take in or suck up; absorb **c** to take in or receive avidly – usu + in **2** to join in (a toast) **3** to take liquid into the mouth for swallowing **4** to drink alcoholic beverages, esp habitually or to excess — **drink like a fish** to habitually drink alcohol to excess — **drink to** to drink a toast to

²**drink** n **1a** liquid suitable for swallowing **b** alcoholic drink **2** a draught or portion of liquid for drinking **3** excessive consumption of alcoholic beverages **4** the ocean; broadly any large body of water – + the; infml

drinkable /'dringkəbl/ adj suitable or safe for drinking

drinker /'dringkə/ n one who drinks alcoholic beverages to excess

¹**drip** /drip/ v **-pp- 1a** to let fall drops of moisture or liquid **b** to overflow (as if) with moisture or liquid **2** to fall or let fall (as if) in drops

²**drip** n **1a** the action or sound of falling in drops **b** liquid that falls, overflows, or is forced out in drops **2** a projection for throwing off rainwater **3** a device for the administration of a liquid at a slow rate, esp into a vein **4** a dull or inconsequential person – infml

¹**drip-'dry** v to dry with few or no wrinkles when hung dripping wet

²**drip-'dry** adj made of a washable fabric that drip-dries

dripping /'driping/ n the fat that runs out from meat during roasting

¹**drive** /driev/ v **drove** /drohv/; **driven** /'driv(ə)n/ **1a** to set in motion by physical force **b** to force into position by blows **c** to repulse or cause to go by force, authority, or influence **d** to set or keep in motion or operation **2a** to control and direct the course of (a vehicle or draught animal) **b** to convey or transport in a vehicle **3** to carry on or through energetically **4a** to exert inescapable or persuasive pressure on; force **b** to compel to undergo or suffer a change (e g in situation, awareness, or emotional state) **c** to urge relentlessly to continuous exertion **5** to cause (e g game or cattle) to move in a desired direction **6a** to propel (an object of play) swiftly **b** to play a drive in cricket at (a ball) or at the bowling of (a bowler) **7** to rush or dash rapidly or with force against an obstruction **8** to imply as an ultimate meaning or conclusion – + at — **drive at** to imply as an ultimate meaning or conclusion — **drive up the wall** to infuriate or madden (sby)

²**drive** n **1** a trip in a carriage or motor vehicle **2** a private road giving access from a public way to a building on private land **3** a (military) offensive, aggressive, or expansionist move **4** a strong systematic group effort; a campaign **5a** a motivating instinctual need or acquired desire **b** great zeal in pursuing one's ends **6a** the means for giving motion to a machine (part) **b** the means by or position from which the movement of a motor vehicle is controlled or directed **7** the act or an instance of driving an object of play; esp an attacking cricket stroke played conventionally with a straight bat and designed to send the ball in front of the batsman's wicket

'**drive-,in** adj or n (being) a place (e g a bank, cinema, or restaurant) that people can use while remaining in their cars

¹**drivel** /'drivl/ v **-ll-** (NAm **-l-, -ll-**), /'drivl·ing/ **1** to let saliva dribble from the mouth or mucus run from the nose **2** to talk stupidly and childishly or carelessly

²**drivel** n foolish or childish nonsense

driver /'drievə/ n **1** a coachman **2** the operator of a motor vehicle **3** a golf club with a wooden head used in hitting the ball long distances, esp off the tee

driving /'drieving/ adj **1** that communicates force **2a** having great force **b** acting with vigour; energetic

drizzle /'driz(ə)l/ v drizzling /'drizl·ing/ to rain in very small drops or very lightly – **drizzle** n – **drizzly** adj

droll /drohl/ adj humorous, whimsical, or odd – **drolly** adv – **~ness** n

drollery /'drohləri/ n the act or an instance of jesting or droll behaviour

dromedary /'dromǝd(ǝ)ri, 'drum-/ n a (1-humped) camel bred esp for riding

¹**drone** /drohn/ n 1 the male of a bee (e g the honeybee) that has no sting and gathers no honey 2 sby who lives off others 3 a remotely-controlled pilotless aircraft, missile, or ship

²**drone** v 1 to make a sustained deep murmuring or buzzing sound 2 to talk in a persistently monotonous tone

³**drone** n 1 any of the usu 3 pipes on a bagpipe that sound fixed continuous notes 2 a droning sound 3 an unvarying sustained bass note

drool /droohl/ v 1 to secrete saliva in anticipation of food 2 to make a foolishly effusive show of pleasure 3 to express sentimentally or effusively

¹**droop** /droohp/ v 1 to (let) hang or incline downwards 2 to become depressed or weakened; languish

²**droop** n the condition or appearance of drooping

¹**drop** /drop/ n 1a(1) the quantity of fluid that falls in 1 spherical mass a(2) pl a dose of medicine measured by drops b a minute quantity 2a an ornament that hangs from a piece of jewellery (e g an earring) b a small globular often medicated sweet or lozenge 3a the act or an instance of dropping; a fall b a decline in quantity or quality 4 the distance from a higher to a lower level or through which sthg drops 5 sthg that drops, hangs, or falls: e g 5a an unframed piece of cloth stage scenery b a hinged platform on a gallows 6 a small quantity of drink, esp alcohol; broadly an alcoholic drink – infml

²**drop** v -pp- 1 to fall in drops 2a(1) to fall, esp unexpectedly or suddenly a(2) to descend from one level to another b to fall in a state of collapse or death 3a to cease to be of concern; lapse b to become less 4 to let fall; cause to fall 5a to lower from one level or position to another b to cause to lessen or decrease; reduce 6 to set down from a ship or vehicle; unload; also to airdrop 7a to give up (e g an idea) b to leave incomplete; cease c to break off an association or connection with; also to leave out of a team or group 8a to utter or mention in a casual way b to send through the post 9 to lose – infml — **drop a brick/clanger** to make an embarrassing error or mistaken remark — infml

'**drop·kick** /-,kik/ n a kick made (e g in rugby) by dropping a football to the ground and kicking it at the moment it starts to rebound – **drop-kick** v

'**drop-,off** n a marked dwindling or decline

drop off v 1 to fall asleep 2 to decline, slump

'**drop,out** /-,owt/ n 1 one who rejects or withdraws from participation in conventional society 2 a student who fails to complete or withdraws from a course, usu of higher education 3 a dropkick awarded to the defending team in rugby (e g after an unconverted try)

drop out v 1 to withdraw from participation 2 to make a dropout in rugby

dropper /'dropǝ/ n a short usu glass tube fitted with a rubber bulb and used to measure or administer liquids by drops

droppings /'dropingz/ n pl animal dung

dropsy /'dropsi/ n abnormal accumulation of liquid in the body tissues causing painful swelling – **-sical** adj

dross /dros/ n waste, rubbish, or foreign matter; impurities

drought /drowt/ n 1 a prolonged period of dryness 2 a prolonged shortage of sthg

¹**drove** /drohv/ n 1 a group of animals driven or moving in a body 2 a crowd of people moving or acting together

²**drove** past of drive

drover /'drohvǝ/ n one who drives cattle or sheep

drown /drown/ v 1a to suffocate by submergence, esp in water b to wet thoroughly; drench 2 to engage (oneself) deeply and strenuously 3 to blot out (a sound) by making a loud noise 4 to destroy (e g a sensation or an idea) as if by drowning

drowse /drowz/ v to doze – **drowse** n

drowsy /'drowzy/ adj 1a sleepy b tending to induce sleepiness c indolent, lethargic 2 giving the appearance of peaceful inactivity – **-sily** adv – **-siness** n

drub /drub/ v **-bb-** 1 to beat severely 2 to defeat decisively

drudge /druj/ v to do hard, menial, routine, or monotonous work – **drudge** n – **~ry** n

¹**drug** /drug/ n 1 a substance used as (or in the preparation of) a medication 2 a substance that causes addiction or habituation

²**drug** v **-gg-** 1 to administer a drug to 2 to lull or stupefy (as if) with a drug

'**drug,store** /-,staw/ n, chiefly NAm a chemist's shop; esp one that also sells sweets, magazines, and refreshments

druid /'drooh·id/, fem **druidess** /-dis/ n, often cap a member of a pre-Christian Celtic order of priests associated with a mistletoe cult

¹**drum** /drum/ n 1 a percussion instrument usu consisting of a hollow cylinder with a drumhead stretched over each end, that is beaten with a stick or a pair of sticks in playing 2 the tympanic membrane of the ear 3 the sound made by striking a drum; also any similar sound 4 a cylindrical container; specif a large usu metal container for liquids

²**drum** v **-mm-** 1 to beat a drum 2 to make a succession of strokes, taps, or vibrations that produce drumlike sounds 3 to throb or sound rhythmically 4 to summon or enlist (as if) by beating a drum 5 to instil (an idea or lesson) by constant repetition – usu + *into* or *out of* 6 to strike or tap repeatedly 7 to produce (rhythmic sounds) by such action

'**drum,head** /-,hed/ n the material stretched over the end of a drum

drummer /'drumə/ n one who plays a drum

drum out v to dismiss in disgrace; expel

'**drum,stick** /-,stik/ n 1 a stick for beating a drum 2 the part of a fowl's leg below the thigh when cooked as food

drum up v 1 to bring about by persistent effort 2 to invent, originate

¹**drunk** /drungk/ *past part of* **drink**

²**drunk** adj 1 under the influence of alcohol 2 dominated by an intense feeling

drunkard /'drungkəd/ n a person who is habitually drunk

drunken /'drungkən/ adj 1 drunk 2a given to habitual excessive use of alcohol b of, characterized by, or resulting from alcoholic intoxication – ~ly adv – ~ness n

¹**dry** /drie/ adj 1a (relatively) free from a liquid, esp water b not in or under water c lacking precipitation or humidity 2a characterized by exhaustion of a supply of water or liquid b devoid of natural moisture; *also* no longer sticky or damp d *of a mammal* not giving milk e lacking freshness; stale 3 not shedding or accompanied by tears 4 prohibiting the manufacture or distribution of alcoholic beverages 5 lacking sweetness 6 functioning without lubrication 7 built or constructed without a process which requires water 8a not showing or communicating warmth, enthusiasm, or feeling; impassive b uninteresting c lacking embellishment, bias, or emotional concern; plain 9 not yielding what is expected or desired; unproductive 10 marked by a matter-of-fact, ironic, or terse manner of expression – ~ly, drily adv – ~ness n

²**dry** v to make or become dry – often + *out*

dryad /'drie·ad, -od/ n a nymph of the woods in Greek mythology

,**dry-'clean** v to subject to or undergo dry-cleaning – ~er n

,**dry-'cleaning** n 1 the cleaning of fabrics or garments with organic solvents and without water 2 that which is dry-cleaned

dry dock n a dock from which the water can be pumped to allow ships to be repaired

dry 'ice n solidified carbon dioxide

dry out v to undergo treatment for alcoholism or drug addiction

,**dry 'rot** n (a fungus causing) a decay of seasoned timber in which the cellulose of wood is consumed leaving a soft skeleton which is readily reduced to powder

,**dry-'shod** adj having or keeping dry shoes or feet

dry up v 1 to disappear or cease to yield (as if) by evaporation, draining, or the cutting off of a source of supply 2 to wither or die through gradual loss of vitality 3 to wipe dry dishes, cutlery, etc by hand after they have been washed 4 to stop talking; shut up – infml 5 to cause to dry up

dt's /,dee 'teez/ n pl, *often cap* D&T delirium tremens

dual /'dyooh·əl/ adj 1 consisting of 2 (like) parts or elements 2 having a double character or nature

,**dual 'carriage,way** n, *chiefly Br* a road that has traffic travelling in opposite directions separated by a central reservation

¹**dub** /dub/ v **-bb-** 1 to confer knighthood on 2 to call by a descriptive name or epithet; nickname

²**dub** v **-bb-** 1 to make alterations to the original sound track of (a film): e g **1a** to provide with a sound track in which the voices are not those of the actors on the screen b to provide with a sound track in a new language 2 to transpose (a previous recording) to a new record 3 *chiefly Br* to mix (a recording)

dubbin /'dubin/ *also* **dubbing** /'dubing/ n a dressing of oil and tallow for leather – **dubbin** v

dubious /'dyoohbi·əs/ adj 1 giving rise to doubt; uncertain 2 unsettled in opinion; undecided 3 of uncertain outcome 4 of questionable value, quality, or origin – ~ly adv – ~ness n

ducal /'dyoohkl/ adj of or relating to a duke or duchy

ducat /'dukət/ n a usu gold coin formerly used in many European countries

duchess /'duchis/ n 1 the wife or widow of a duke 2 a woman having in her own right the rank of a duke

duchy /'duchi/ n a dukedom

¹**duck** /duk/ n pl **ducks**, (1a) **ducks**, *esp collectively* **duck** 1a any of various swimming birds in which the neck and legs are short, the bill is often broad and flat, and the sexes are almost always different from each other in plumage b the flesh of any of these birds used as food 2a female duck 3 *chiefly Br* dear – often pl with sing. meaning but sing. in constr; infml

²**duck** v 1 to plunge (something) under the surface of water 2 to move or lower the head or body suddenly, esp as a bow or to avoid being hit 3 to avoid, evade (a duty, question, or responsibility) – *infml*

³**duck** n a durable closely woven usu cotton fabric

⁴**duck** n a score of nought, esp in cricket

duckling /'dukling/ n a young duck

'duck,weed /-,weed/ *n* any of several small free-floating stemless plants that often cover large areas of the surface of still water

duct /dukt/ *n* **1** a bodily tube or vessel, esp when carrying the secretion of a gland **2** a pipe, tube, or channel that conveys a substance **3** a continuous tube in plant tissue

ductile /'duktiel/ *adj* **1** capable of being easily fashioned into a new form **2** *of metals* capable of being drawn out or hammered thin **3** easily led or influenced; tractable – infml – -**tility** *n*

'dud /dud/ *n* **1** a bomb, missile, etc that fails to explode **2** *pl* personal belongings; *esp* clothes **3** a failure **4** a counterfeit, fake *USE* (2, 3, & 4) infml

²dud *adj* valueless – infml

dudgeon /'dujən/ *n* indignation, resentment – esp in *in high dudgeon*

'due /dyooh/ *adj* **1** owed or owing as a debt **2a** owed or owing as a natural or moral right (e g got his *due* reward) **b** appropriate (e g after *due* consideration) **3a** (capable of) satisfying a need, obligation, or duty **b** regular, lawful (e g *due* proof of loss) **4** ascribable – + *to* **5** payable **6** required or expected in the prearranged or normal course of events (e g *due* to arrive soon) — **in due course** after a normal passage of time; in the expected or allocated time

²due *n* sthg due or owed: e g **a** sthg esp nonmaterial that rightfully belongs to one **b** *pl* fees, charges

³due *adv* directly, exactly – used before points of the compass

'duel /'dyooh·əl/ *n* **1** a formal combat with weapons fought between 2 people in the presence of witnesses in order to settle a quarrel **2** a conflict between usu evenly matched antagonistic people, ideas, or forces

²duel *v* -**ll-** (*NAm* -**l-**, -**ll-**) to fight a duel

duenna /dyooh'enə/ *n* **1** an older woman serving as governess and companion to the younger ladies in a Spanish or Portuguese family **2** a chaperone

duet /dyooh'et/ *n* a (musical) composition for 2 performers

'duffel ,bag *n* a fabric bag, usu closed with a drawstring

'duffel ,coat *n* a usu thigh or knee-length coat with a hood and fastened with toggles

duffer /'dufə/ *n* an incompetent, ineffectual, or clumsy person

'dug /dug/ *past of* **dig**

²dug /dug/ *n* an udder; *also* a teat – usu used with reference to animals

dugout /'dug,owt/ *n* **1** a boat made by hollowing out a large log **2** a shelter dug in the ground or in a hillside, esp for troops

duke /dyoohk/ *n* **1** a sovereign ruler of a European duchy **2** a nobleman of the highest hereditary rank; *esp* a member of the highest rank of the British peerage – ~**dom** *n*

dulcimer /'dulsimə/ *n* a stringed instrument having strings of graduated length stretched over a sounding board and played with light hammers

'dull /dul/ *adj* **1** mentally slow; stupid **2a** slow in perception or sensibility; insensible **b** lacking zest or vivacity; listless **3** lacking sharpness of cutting edge or point; blunt **4** not resonant or ringing **5** cloudy, overcast **6** boring, uninteresting – ~**y** *adv* – ~**ness** *n*

²dull *v* to make or become dull

dullard /'dulad/ *n* a stupid or insensitive person

duly /'dyoohli/ *adv* in a due manner, time, or degree; properly

dumb /dum/ *adj* **1** (temporarily) devoid of the power of speech **2** not expressed in uttered words **3** not willing to speak **4** stupid – ~**ly** *adv* – ~**ness** *n*

dumbfound, dumfound /dum'fownd/ *v* to strike (as if dumb) with amazement

,dumb 'waiter *n* **1** a movable table or stand often with revolving shelves for holding food or dishes **2** a small lift for conveying food and dishes (e g from the kitchen to the dining area of a restaurant)

dumdum /'dum,dum/ *n* a bullet that expands on impact and inflicts a severe wound

'dummy /'dumi/ *n* **1** the exposed hand in bridge played by the declarer in addition to his/her own hand; *also* the player whose hand is a dummy **2** an imitation or copy of sthg used to reproduce some of the attributes of the original; e g **2a** *chiefly Br* a rubber teat given to babies to suck in order to soothe them **b** a large puppet in usu human form, used by a ventriloquist **c** a model of the human body, esp the torso, used for fitting or displaying clothes **3** a person or corporation that seems to act independently but is in reality acting for or at the direction of another **5** an instance of dummying an opponent in sports **6** a dull or stupid person – infml

²dummy *adj* resembling or being a dummy: e g **a** sham, artificial **b** existing in name only; fictitious

³dummy *v* to deceive an opponent (e g in rugby or soccer) by pretending to pass or release the ball while still retaining possession of it

'dummy ,run *n* a rehearsal; trial run

'dump /dump/ *v* **1a** to unload or let fall in a heap or mass **b** to get rid of unceremoniously or irresponsibly; abandon **2** to sell in quantity at a very low price; *specif* to sell abroad at less than the market price at home

²dump *n* **1a** an accumulation of discarded materials (e g refuse) **b** a place where such materials are dumped **2** a quantity of esp military reserve materials accumulated in 1 place **3** a disorderly, slovenly, or dilapidated place – infml

dumpling /'dumpling/ n 1 a small usu rounded mass of leavened dough cooked by boiling or steaming often in stew 2 a short round person – humor

dumps /dumps/ n pl a gloomy state of mind; despondency – esp in *in the dumps*; infml

dumpy /'dumpi/ adj short and thick in build; squat – **-piness** n

¹**dun** /dun/ adj 1 of the colour dun 2 *of a horse* having a greyish or light brownish colour

²**dun** n 1 a dun horse 2 a slightly brownish dark grey colour

³**dun** v **-nn-** to make persistent demands upon for payment

⁴**dun** n an urgent request; *esp* a demand for payment

dunce /duns/ n a dull or stupid person

dunderhead /'dundə,hed/ n a dunce, blockhead

dune /dyoohn/ n a hill or ridge of sand piled up by the wind

dung /dung/ n the excrement of an animal

dungarees /,dungə'reez/ n pl a 1-piece outer garment consisting of trousers and a bib with shoulder straps fastened at the back

dungeon /'dunjən/ n a dark usu underground prison or vault, esp in a castle

dunk /dungk/ v to dip (e g a piece of bread) into liquid (e g soup) before eating

duo /'dyooh,oh/ n, pl **duos** a pair (of performers); *also* a piece (e g of music) written for 2 players

duodecimal /,dyooh·oh'desim(ə)l/ adj proceeding by or based on the number of 12

duodenum /,dyooh·ə'deenəm/ n, pl **duodena** /-nə/, **duodenums** the first part of the small intestine – **-nal** adj

¹**dupe** /dyoohp/ n one who is easily deceived or cheated

²**dupe** v to make a dupe of; deceive

¹**duplicate** /'d(y)oohplikət/ adj 1 consisting of or existing in 2 corresponding or identical parts or examples 2 being the same as another

²**duplicate** n 1 either of 2 things that exactly resemble each other; *specif* an equally valid copy of a legal document 2 a copy — **in duplicate** with an original and 1 copy; *also* with 2 identical copies

³**duplicate** /'d(y)oohpli,kayt/ v to make an exact copy of – **-cation** n

duplicator /'d(y)oohpli,kaytə/ n a machine for making copies, esp by means other than photocopying or xeroxing

duplicity /dyooh'plisəti/ n malicious deception in thought, speech, or action

durable /'dyoorəbl; *also* j-/ adj able to exist or be used for a long time without significant deterioration – **-bly** adv – **-bility** n

duration /dyoo(ə)'raysh(ə)n/ n 1 a continuing in time 2 the time during which sthg exists or lasts

duress /dyoo(ə)'res; *also* j-/ n 1 forcible restraint or restriction 2 compulsion by threat, violence, or imprisonment

Durex /'dyooəreks/ trademark – used for a condom

during /'dyooəring; *also* j-/ prep 1 throughout the whole duration of 2 at some point in the course of

dusk /dusk/ n (the darker part of) twilight

dusky /'duski/ adj 1 somewhat dark in colour; *esp* dark-skinned 2 shadowy, gloomy – **-kiness** n

¹**dust** /dust/ n 1 fine dry particles of any solid matter, esp earth; *specif* the fine particles of waste that settle esp on household surfaces 2 the particles into which sthg, esp the human body, disintegrates or decays 3 sthg worthless 4 the surface of the ground 5a a cloud of dust b confusion, disturbance – esp in *kick up/raise a dust* – ~ **less** adj

²**dust** v 1 to make free of dust (e g by wiping or beating) 2 to prepare to use again – usu + *down* or *off* 3a to sprinkle with fine particles b to sprinkle in the form of dust 4 *of a bird* to work dust into the feathers 5 to remove dust (e g from household articles), esp by wiping or brushing

'**dust bin** /-,bin/ n, Br a container for holding household refuse until collection

'**dust bowl** n a region that suffers from prolonged droughts and dust storms

'**dust cart** /-,kaht/ n, Br a vehicle for collecting household waste

duster /'dustə/ n sthg that removes dust; *specif* a cloth for removing dust from household articles

'**dust jacket** n a removable outer paper cover for a book

'**dustman** /-mən/ n, Br one employed to remove household refuse

'**dust pan** /-,pan/ n a shovel-like utensil with a handle into which household dust and litter is swept

'**dust sheet** /-,sheet/ n a large sheet (e g of cloth) used as a cover to protect sthg, esp furniture, from dust

'**dust-up** n a quarrel, row – infml

dusty /'dusti/ adj 1 covered with or full of dust 2 consisting of dust; powdery 3 resembling dust, esp in consistency or colour 4 lacking vitality; dry

¹**dutch** /duch/ adv, *often cap* with each person paying for him/herself

²**dutch** n, Br one's wife – slang

Dutch n 1 the Germanic language of the Netherlands 2 pl in constr the people of the Netherlands

Dutch auction n an auction in which the auctioneer gradually reduces the bidding price until a bid is received

Dutch barn n a large barn with open sides used esp for storage of hay

Dutch cap n a moulded cap, usu of thin rubber, that fits over the cervix to act as a contraceptive barrier

,Dutch 'courage *n* courage produced by drink rather than inherent resolution

,Dutch 'elm di,sease *n* a fatal disease of elms caused by a fungus, spread from tree to tree by a beetle

,Dutch 'uncle *n* one who admonishes sternly and bluntly

dutiable /'dyoohti·əbl, -tyəbl/ *adj* subject to a duty

dutiful /'dyoohtif(ə)l/ *adj* 1 filled with or motivated by a sense of duty 2 proceeding from or expressive of a sense of duty – ~ly *adv*

duty /'dyoohti/ *n* 1 conduct due to parents and superiors; respect 2a tasks, conduct, service, or functions that arise from one's position, job, or moral obligations b assigned (military) service or business 3a a moral or legal obligation b the force of moral obligation 4 a tax, esp on imports

,duty-'free *adj* exempted from duty

duvet /'doohvay/ *n* a large quilt filled with insulating material (e g down, feathers, or acrylic fibre), usu placed inside a removable fabric cover and used in place of bedclothes

¹dwarf /dwawf/ *n, pl* dwarfs, dwarves /dwawvz/ 1 a person of unusually small stature 2 an animal or plant much below normal size 3 a small manlike creature in esp Norse and Germanic mythology who was skilled as a craftsman

²dwarf *v* 1 to stunt the growth of 2 to cause to appear smaller

dwell /dwel/ *v* dwelt /dwelt/, dwelled /dweld, dwelt/ 1 to remain for a time 2 to keep the attention directed, esp in speech or writing; linger – + *on* or *upon* 3 to live as a resident; reside – fml

dwelling /'dweling/ *n* a place (e g a house or flat) in which people live – fml or humor

dwindle /'dwindl/ *v* dwindling /'dwindling/ to become steadily less in quantity; shrink, diminish

¹dye /die/ *n* a soluble or insoluble colouring matter

²dye *v* dyeing to impart a new and often permanent colour to, esp by dipping in a dye – dyer *n*

,dyed-in-the-'wool *adj* thoroughgoing, uncompromising

dying /'die·ing/ *pres part of* die

dyke, dike /diek/ *n* 1 a bank, usu of earth, constructed to control or confine water 2 *dial Br* a wall or fence of turf or stone

dynamic /die'namik, di-/ *adj* 1a of physical force or energy in motion b of dynamics 2a marked by continuous activity or change b energetic, forceful – ~ally *adv* – ~ism *n*

dy'namics *n pl but sing or pl in constr* 1 a branch of mechanics that deals with forces and their relation to the motion of bodies 2 a pattern of change or growth 3 variation and contrast in force or intensity (e g in music)

dynamite /'dienə,miet/ *n* 1 a blasting explosive that is made of nitroglycerine absorbed in a porous material 2 sby or sthg that has explosive force or effect – infml

dynamo /'dienəmoh/ *n, pl* dynamos 1 a machine by which mechanical energy is converted into electrical energy; *specif* such a device that produces direct current (e g in a motor car) 2 a forceful energetic person

dynasty /'dinasti/ *n* a succession of hereditary rulers; *also* the time during which such a dynasty rules – -tic *adj*

dysentery /'dis(ə)ntri/ *n* any of several infectious diseases characterized by severe diarrhoea, usu with passing of mucus and blood

dys'lexia /-'leksi·ə/ *n* a failure in children to learn to read and write – -lexic *adj*

dys'pepsia /-'pepsi·ə/ *n* indigestion – -peptic *adj, n*

E

e /ee/ *n, pl* e's, e's *often cap* 1a (a graphic representation of or device for reproducing) the 5th letter of the English alphabet b a speech counterpart of written *e* 2 one designated *e* (e g the 5th in order or class)

¹each /eech/ *adj* being one of 2 or more distinct individuals considered separately

²each *pron* each one

³each *adv* to or for each; apiece

,each 'other *pron* each of 2 or more in reciprocal action or relation

,each 'way *adj or adv, Br, of a bet* backing a horse, dog, etc to finish in the first two, three, or four in a race as well as to win

eager /'eegə/ *adj* marked by keen, enthusiastic, or impatient desire or interest – ~ly *adv* – ~ness *n*

eagle /'eegl/ *n* 1 any of various large birds of prey noted for their strength, size, gracefulness, keenness of vision, and powers of flight 2 a golf score for 1 hole of 2 strokes less than par

,eagle-'eyed *adj* 1 having very good eyesight 2 good at noticing details; observant

¹ear /iə/ *n* 1 (the external part of) the characteristic vertebrate organ of hearing and equilibrium 2 the sense or act of hearing 3 sthg resembling an ear in shape or position; *esp* a projecting part (e g a lug or handle) — by ear from memory of the sound without having seen the written music — in one

ear and out the other through one's mind without making an impression — **up to one's ears** deeply involved; heavily implicated

²**ear** n the fruiting spike of a cereal, including both the seeds and protective structures

'**ear,drum** /-,drum/ n a thin membrane separating the outer ear from the middle ear and transmitting sound to the organs of hearing

'**earful** /-f(ə)l/ n 1 an outpouring of news or gossip 2 a sharp verbal reprimand *USE* infml

earl /uhl/ n a member of the British peerage ranking below a marquess and above a viscount – ~**dom** n

'**ear,lobe** /-,lohb/ n the pendent part of the ear of humans or of some fowls

¹**early** /'uhli/ adv 1 at or near the beginning of a period of time, a development, or a series 2 before the usual time or proper time

²**early** adj 1a at or occurring near the beginning of a period of time, a development, or a series **b(1)** distant in past time **b(2)** primitive 2a occurring before the usual time **b** occurring in the near future – ~**liness** n

¹**earmark** /'iə,mahk/ n 1 a mark of identification on the ear of an animal 2 a distinguishing or identifying characteristic

²**ear,mark** v 1 to mark (livestock) with an earmark 2 to designate (e g funds) for a specific use or owner

earn /uhn/ v 1 to receive (e g money) as return for effort, esp for work done or services rendered 2 to bring in as income 3a to gain or deserve because of one's behaviour or qualities **b** to make worthy of or obtain for – ~**er** n

¹**earnest** /'uhnist/ n a serious and intent mental state – esp in *in earnest*

²**earnest** adj determined and serious – ~**ly** adv – ~**ness** n

³**earnest** n 1 stg of value, esp money, given by a buyer to a seller to seal a bargain 2 a token of what is to come; a pledge

earnings /'uhningz/ n pl money earned; esp gross revenue

earphone /'iə,fohn/ n a device that converts electrical energy into sound waves and is worn over or inserted into the ear

'**ear,ring** /-,ring/ n an ornament for the ear

'**ear,shot** /-,shot/ n the range within which stg, esp the unaided voice, may be heard

¹**earth** /uhth/ n 1 soil 2 the sphere of mortal or worldly existence as distinguished from spheres of spiritual life 3a areas of land as distinguished from sea and air **b** the solid ground 4 *often cap* the planet on which we live that is third in order from the sun 5 the people of the planet earth 6 the lair of a fox, badger, etc 7 *chiefly Br* an electrical connection to earth — **on earth** — used to intensify an interrogative pronoun

²**earth** v 1 to drive (e g a fox) to hiding in its earth 2 to draw soil about (plants) – usu + *up* 3 *chiefly Br* to connect electrically with earth

'**earth,bound** /-,bownd/ adj 1a restricted to the earth **b** heading or directed towards the planet earth 2a bound by worldly interests **b** unimaginative

earthen /'uhdh(ə)n, -th(ə)n/ adj made of earth or baked clay

'**earthen,ware** /-,weə/ n ceramic ware made of slightly porous opaque clay fired at a low temperature

'**earthly** /-li/ adj 1a characteristic of or belonging to this earth **b** worldly 2 possible – usu + neg or interrog

'**earth,quake** /-,kwayk/ n a (repeated) usu violent earth tremor caused by volcanic action or processes within the earth's crust

'**earth,shaking** /-,shayking/ adj having tremendous importance or a widespread often violent effect – chiefly infml – ~**ly** adv

'**earth,worm** /-,wuhm/ n any of numerous widely distributed worms that live in the soil

earthy /'uhthi/ adj 1 consisting of, resembling, or suggesting earth 2 crude, coarse – -**thiness** n

earwig /'iə,wig/ n any of numerous insects that have slender many-jointed antennae and a pair of appendages resembling forceps

¹**ease** /eez/ n 1 being comfortable: e g **1a** freedom from pain, discomfort, or anxiety **b** freedom from labour or difficulty **c** freedom from embarrassment or constraint 2 effortlessness 3 easing or being eased — **at ease 1** free from pain or discomfort 2 free from restraint or formality 3 standing with the feet apart and usu 1 or both hands behind the body — used esp as a military command

²**ease** v 1 to free from stg that pains, disquiets, or burdens – + *of* 2 to alleviate 3 to lessen the pressure or tension of 4 to make less difficult 5 to manoeuvre gently or carefully in a specified way 6 to decrease in activity, intensity, or severity – often + *off* or *up*

easel /'eezl/ n a frame for supporting stg (e g an artist's canvas)

easily /'eezali/ adv 1 without difficulty 2 without doubt; by far

¹**east** /eest/ adj or adv towards, at, belonging to, or coming from the east

²**east** n 1 (the compass point corresponding to) the direction 90° to the right of north that is the general direction of sunrise 2a *often cap* regions or countries lying to the east of a specified or implied point of orientation **b** *cap* regions lying to the east of Europe 3 the altar end of a church 4 sby (e g a bridge player) occupying a position designated east

Easter /'eestə/ n a feast that commemorates Christ's resurrection and is observed on the first Sunday after the first full moon following March 21

'Easter ,egg n a (chocolate or painted and hard-boiled) egg given as a present and eaten at Easter

¹'easterly /-li/ adj or adv east

²'easterly n a wind from the east

eastern /'eest(ə)n/ adj 1 often cap (characteristic) of a region conventionally designated east 2 east 3 **Eastern, Eastern Orthodox** of the Russian or Greek Orthodox churches

¹easy /'eezi/ adj 1 causing or involving little difficulty or discomfort 2a not severe; lenient b readily prevailed on; compliant: e g b(1) not difficult to deceive or take advantage of b(2) readily persuaded to have sexual relations – infml 3a plentiful in supply at low or declining interest rates b less in demand and usu lower in price 4a marked by peace and comfort b not hurried or strenuous c free from pain, annoyance, or anxiety 5 marked by social ease – **easiness** n

²easy adv 1 easily 2 slowly, cautiously

¹'easy ,chair n a large usu upholstered armchair designed for comfort and relaxation

,easy'going /-goh·ing/ adj taking life easily: e g a placid and tolerant b indolent and careless

eat /eet/ v ate /et, ayt/; **eaten** /'eet(ə)n/ 1 to take in through the mouth and swallow as food 2 to consume gradually; corrode 3 to vex, bother – infml 4 to take food or a meal — **eat humble pie** to apologize or retract under pressure — **eat one's heart out** to grieve bitterly, esp for sthg desired but unobtainable — **eat one's words** to retract what one has said — **eat out of someone's hand** to accept sby's domination

eats /eets/ n pl food – infml

eau de cologne /,oh də kə'lohn/ n, pl **eaux de cologne** /~/ toilet water

eaves /eevz/ n pl the lower border of a roof that overhangs the wall

eavesdrop /'eevz,drop/ v to listen secretly to what is said in private – **dropper** n

¹ebb /eb/, **'ebb ,tide** n 1 the flowing out of the tide towards the sea 2 a point or condition of decline

²ebb v 1 of tidal water to recede from the flood state 2 to decline from a higher to a lower level or from a better to a worse state

¹ebony /'ebəni/ n (any of various tropical trees that yield) a hard heavy black wood

²ebony adj 1 made of or resembling ebony 2 black, dark – usu apprec

ebullience /i'buli·əns, -yəns/, **ebulliency** /-si/ n the quality of being full of liveliness and enthusiasm; exuberance – **-ient** adj – **-iently** adv

¹eccentric /ik'sentrik/ adj 1 deviating from established convention; odd 2a deviating from a circular path b located elsewhere than at the geometrical centre; also having the axis or support so located – **~ally** adv – **~ity** n

²eccentric n an eccentric person

ecclesiastical /i,kleezi'astikl/ adj of a church or religion

echelon /'eshəlon, 'ay-/ n 1 an arrangement of units (e g of troops or ships) resembling a series of steps 2 a particular division of a headquarters or supply organization in warfare 3 any of a series of levels or grades (e g of authority or responsibility) in some organized field of activity

echinoderm /i'kienoh,duhm/ n any of a phylum of radially symmetrical marine animals consisting of the starfishes, sea urchins, and related forms

¹echo /'ekoh/ n, pl **echoes** 1 the repetition of a sound caused by the reflection of sound waves 2 sby or sthg that repeats or imitates another 3 a repercussion, result

²echo v 1 to resound with echoes 2 to produce an echo 3 to repeat, imitate

éclair /i'kleə, ay-/ n a small light oblong cake that is split and filled with cream and usu topped with (chocolate) icing

¹eclectic /e'klektik, i-/ adj 1 selecting or using elements from various doctrines, methods, or styles 2 composed of elements drawn from various sources – **~ally** adv – **~ism** n

²eclectic n one who uses an eclectic method or approach

¹eclipse /i'klips/ n 1a the total or partial obscuring of one celestial body by another b passage into the shadow of a celestial body 2 a falling into obscurity or decay; a decline

²eclipse v to cause an eclipse of: e g a to obscure, darken b to surpass

ecliptic /i'kliptik/ n the plane of the earth's orbit extended to meet the celestial sphere – **ecliptic** adj

ecology /i'koləji, ee-/ n (a science concerned with) the interrelationship of living organisms and their environments – **-gist** n – **-gical** adj

economic /,ekə'nomik, ,ee-/ adj 1 of economics 2 of or based on the production, distribution, and consumption of goods and services 3 of an economy 4 having practical or industrial significance or uses 5 profitable

economical /,ekə'nomikl, ,ee-/ adj thrifty – **~ly** adv

,eco'nomics n pl but sing or pl in constr 1 a social science concerned chiefly with the production, distribution, and consumption of goods and services 2 economic aspect or significance – **-mist** n

econom·ize, -ise /i'konə,miez/ v to be frugal – often + on

economy /i'konəmi/ n 1 thrifty and efficient use of material resources; frugality in expenditure; *also* an instance or means of economizing 2 efficient and sparing use of nonmaterial resources (e g effort, language, or motion) 3 the structure of economic life in a country, area, or period; *specif* an economic system

ecstasy /'ekstəsi/ n 1 a state of very strong feeling, esp of joy or happiness 2 a (mystic or prophetic) trance

ecstatic /ik'statik, ek-/ adj subject to, causing, or in a state of ecstasy – ~ally adv

ecumenical *also* **oecumenical** /ˌekyoo'menikl, ˌeek-/ adj promoting worldwide Christian unity or cooperation

eczema /'eksi)mə/ n an inflammatory condition of the skin characterized by itching and oozing blisters

Edam /'eedam/ n a yellow mild cheese of Dutch origin usu made in flattened balls coated with red wax

¹**eddy** /'edi/ n 1 a current of water or air running contrary to the main current; *esp* a small whirlpool 2 sthg (e g smoke or fog) moving in the manner of an eddy or whirlpool

²**eddy** v to (cause to) move in or like an eddy

Eden /'eedn/ n 1 the garden where, according to the account in Genesis, Adam and Eve lived before the Fall 2 paradise

¹**edge** /ej/ n 1a the cutting side of a blade b the (degree of) sharpness of a blade c penetrating power; keenness 2a the line where an object or area begins or ends; a border b the narrow part adjacent to a border; the brink, verge c a point that marks a beginning or transition; a threshold – esp in *on the edge of* d a favourable margin; an advantage 3 a line where 2 planes or 2 plane faces of a solid object meet or cross — **on edge** anxious, nervous

²**edge** v 1 to give or supply an edge to 2 to move or force gradually in a specified way 3 to hit (a ball) or the bowling of (a bowler) in cricket with the edge of the bat

¹**edgeways** /-ˌwayz, -wiz/, **edgewise** /-ˌwiez/ adv with the edge foremost; sideways

edging /'ejing/ n sthg that forms an edge or border

edgy /'eji/ adj tense, irritable – **edgily** adv

edible /'edəbl/ adj fit to be eaten – **edibility** n – ~s n

edict /'eedikt/ n 1 an official public decree 2 the order or command of an authority

edification /ˌedifi'kaysh(ə)n/ n the improvement of character or the mind – fml

edifice /'edifis/ n 1 a building; *esp* a large or massive structure 2 a large abstract structure or organization

edify /'ediˌfie/ v to instruct and improve, esp in moral and spiritual knowledge

edit /'edit/ v 1a to prepare an edition of b to assemble (e g a film or tape recording) by deleting, inserting, and rearranging material c to alter or adapt (e g written or spoken words), esp to make consistent with a particular standard or purpose 2 to direct the publication of 3 to delete – usu + out

edition /i'dish(ə)n/ n 1a the form in which a text is published b the whole number of copies published at one time c the issue of a newspaper or periodical for a specified time or place 2 the whole number of articles of one style put out at one time 3 a copy, version

editor /'editə/ n 1 one who edits written material, films, etc, esp as an occupation 2 a person responsible for the editorial policy and content of a (section of a) newspaper or periodical – ~ship n

¹**editorial** /ˌedi'tawri-əl/ adj of or written by an editor – ~ly adv

²**editorial** n a newspaper or magazine article that gives the opinions of the editors or publishers

educate /'edyoo,kayt, 'ejoo,-/ v 1 to provide schooling for 2 to develop mentally or morally, esp by instruction 3 to train or improve (faculties, judgment, skills, etc) – **-ator** n

education /ˌedyoo'kaysh(ə)n, -joo-/ n 1 educating or being educated 2 the field of study that deals with methods of teaching and learning – ~al adj – ~ally adv

educe /i'dyoohs; *also* ij-/ v 1 to elicit, develop 2 to arrive at through a consideration of the facts or evidence; infer *USE* fml

eel /eel/ n any of numerous long snakelike fishes with a smooth slimy skin and no pelvic fins

eerie *also* **eery** /'iəri/ adj frighteningly strange or gloomy; weird – **eerily** adv – **eeriness** n

efface /i'fays/ v 1 to eliminate or make indistinct (as if) by wearing away a surface; obliterate 2 to make (oneself) modestly or shyly inconspicuous – ~ment n

¹**effect** /i'fekt/ n 1a the result of a cause or agent b the result of purpose or intention 2 the basic meaning; intent – esp in *to that effect* 3 power to bring about a result 4 pl personal movable property; goods 5a a distinctive impression on the human senses b the creation of an often false desired impression c sthg designed to produce a distinctive or desired impression – often pl 6 the quality or state of being operative; operation — **in effect** for all practical purposes; actually although not appearing so — **to the effect** with the meaning

²**effect** v 1 to bring about; accomplish 2 to put into effect; carry out

effective /i'fektiv/ adj 1a producing a decided, decisive, or desired effect b impressive, striking 2 ready for service or action 3 actual, real 4 being in effect; operative – ~ly adv – ~ness n

effectual /i'fektyooɔl, -chooɔl/ *adj* producing or able to produce a desired effect; adequate, effective – ~**ness** *n* – ~**ly** *adv*

effeminate /i'feminət/ *adj* **1** *of a man* having qualities usu thought of as feminine; not manly in appearance or manner **2** marked by an unbecoming delicacy or lack of vigour – ~**ly** *adv* – **-acy** *n*

effervesce /ˌefə'ves/ *v* **1** *of a liquid* to bubble, hiss, and foam as gas escapes **2** to show liveliness or exhilaration – **-vescence** *n* – **-vescent** *adj* – **-vescently** *adv*

effete /i'feet/ *adj* **1** worn out; exhausted **2** marked by weakness or decadent overrefinement – ~**ness** *n*

efficacious /ˌefi'kayshəs/ *adj* effectual – ~**ly** *adv* – **-acy** *n* – ~**ness** *n*

efficient /i'fish(ə)nt/ *adj* **1** *of a person* able and practical; briskly competent **2** productive of desired effects, esp with minimum waste – ~**ly** *adv* – **-ency** *n*

effigy /'efəji/ *n* an image or representation, esp of a person; *specif* a crude figure representing a hated person

¹**effluent** /'efloo·ənt/ *adj* flowing out; emanating

²**effluent** *n* sthg that flows out: e g **a** an outflowing branch of a main stream or lake **b** smoke, liquid industrial refuse, sewage, etc discharged into the environment, esp when causing pollution

effort /'efət/ *n* **1** conscious exertion of physical or mental power **2** a serious attempt; a try **3** sthg produced by exertion or trying **4** the force applied (e g to a simple machine) as distinguished from the force exerted against the load

effrontery /i'frunt(ə)ri/ *n* the quality of being shamelessly bold; insolence

effusion /i'fyoozhzh(ə)n/ *n* **1** unrestrained expression of words or feelings **2** the escape of a fluid from a containing vessel; *also* the fluid that escapes

effusive /i'fyoohsiv/ *adj* unduly emotionally demonstrative; gushing – ~**ly** *adv* – ~**ness** *n*

egalitarian /iˌgali'teəri·ən/ *adj* marked by or advocating social, political, and economic equality between human beings – **egalitarian** *n* – ~**ism** *n*

¹**egg** /eg/ *v* to incite to action – usu + *on*

²**egg** *n* **1** the hard-shelled reproductive body produced by a bird; *esp* that produced by domestic poultry and used as a food **2** an animal reproductive body consisting of an ovum together with its nutritive and protective envelopes that is capable of developing into a new individual **3** an ovum

'**egg,cup** /-ˌkup/ *n* a small cup without a handle used for holding a boiled egg

'**egg,head** /-ˌhed/ *n* an intellectual, highbrow – derog or humor

'**egg,nog** /-ˌnog/ *n* a drink consisting of eggs beaten up with sugar, milk or cream, and often spirits

'**egg,plant** /-ˌplahnt/ *n* a widely cultivated plant of the nightshade family; *also, chiefly NAm* its fruit, the aubergine

¹'**egg,shell** /-ˌshel/ *n* the hard exterior covering of an egg

²'**egg,shell** *adj* **1** *esp of china* thin and fragile **2** *esp of paint* having a slight sheen

ego /'eegoh, 'egoh/ *n pl* **egos 1** the self, esp as contrasted with another self or the world **2** self-esteem **3** the one of the 3 divisions of the mind in psychoanalytic theory that serves as the organized conscious mediator between the person and reality, esp in the perception of and adaptation to reality

ˌ**ego'centric** /-'sentrik/ *adj* self-centred, selfish – ~**ally** *adv* – ~**ity** *n*

'**ego,ism** /-ˌiz(ə)m/ *n* **1** (conduct based on) a doctrine that individual self-interest is or should be the foundation of morality **2** egotism – **-ist** *n* – **-istic** *adj* – **-istical** *adj* – **-istically** *adv*

'**egotism** /'eegəˌtiz(ə)m, 'egə-/ *n* **1** the practice of talking about oneself too much **2** an extreme sense of self-importance – **-ist** *n* – **-istic** *adj* – **-istical** *adj* – **-istically** *adv*

egregious /i'greej(y)əs/ *adj* conspicuously or shockingly bad; flagrant – *fml* – ~**ly** *adv*

egress /'eegres/ *n* **1** going or coming out; *specif* the emergence of a celestial object from eclipse, transit, etc **2** a place or means of going out; an exit – *fml*

Egyptian /ee'jipsh(ə)n/ *adj* (characteristic) of Egypt – **Egyptian** *n*

'**eider,down** /-ˌdown/ *n* **1** the down of the eider duck **2** a thick warm quilt filled with eiderdown or other insulating material

'**eider ,duck** *n* any of several large northern sea ducks having fine soft down

eight /ayt/ *n* **1** the number 8 **2** the eighth in a set or series **3** sthg having 8 parts or members or a denomination of 8; *esp* (the crew of) an 8-person racing boat – **eighth** *adj, n, pron, adv*

eighteen /ˌay'teen/ *n* the number 18 – ~**th** *adj, n, pron, adv*

18 *n* or **adj** (a film that is) certified in Britain as suitable only for people over 18

eighty /'ayti/ *n* **1** the number 80 **2** *pl* the numbers 80 to 89; *specif* a range of temperatures, ages, or dates within a century characterized by those numbers – **eightieth** *adj, n, pron, adv*

eisteddfod /ie'stedhvod/ *n, pl* **eisteddfods, eisteddfodau** /-ˌdie/ a Welsh-language competitive festival of the arts, esp music and poetry

¹**either** /'iedhə, 'iedh-/ *adj* **1** being the one and the other of 2 (e g flowers blooming on *either* side of the path) **2** being the one or the other of 2 (e g take *either* road)

²**either** *pron* the one or the other (e g could be happy with *either* of them)

³**either** *conj* – used before 2 or more sentence elements of the same class or function joined usu by *or* to indicate that what immediately follows is the first of 2 or more alternatives (e g *either* sink or swim)

⁴**either** *adv* for that matter, likewise – used for emphasis after a negative or implied negation (e g not wise or handsome *either*)

ejaculate /i'jakyoo,layt/ *v* **1** to eject (semen) in orgasm **2** to utter suddenly and vehemently – *fml* – **-lation** *n*

eject /i'jekt/ *v* **1** to drive out, esp by physical force **2** to evict from property **3** to escape from an aircraft by using the ejector seat – **~ion**, **~or** *n*

e'jector ,seat *n* an emergency escape seat that propels an occupant out and away from an aircraft by means of an explosive charge

,**eke 'out** /eek/ *v* **1a** to make up for the deficiencies of; supplement **b** to make (a supply) last by economy **2** to make (e g a living) by laborious or precarious means

¹**elaborate** /i'lab(ə)rət/ *adj* **1** planned or carried out with great care and attention to detail **2** marked by complexity, wealth of detail, or ornateness; intricate – **~ly** *adv* – **~ness** *n*

²**elaborate** /i'labə,rayt/ *v* to work out or go into in detail; develop – often + *on* or *upon* – **-tion** *n*

elapse /i'laps/ *v*, *of a period of time* to pass by

¹**elastic** /i'lastik, i'lah-/ *adj* **1** buoyant, resilient **2** capable of being easily stretched or expanded and resuming its former shape **3** capable of ready change; flexible, adaptable – **~ity** *n*

²**elastic** *n* **1** an elastic fabric usu made of yarns containing rubber **2** easily stretched rubber, usu prepared in cords, strings, or bands

e,lastic 'band *n*, *Br* a rubber band

elate /i'layt/ *v* to fill with joy or pride; put in high spirits – **~d** *adj* **-tion** *n*

elbow /'elboh/ *n* **1** the joint between the human forearm and upper arm **2** the part of a garment that covers the elbow — **out at elbows 1** shabbily dressed **2** impoverished — **up to the elbows in/with** busily engaged in

²**elbow** *v* to push or shove aside (as if) with the elbow; jostle

'**elbow ,grease** *n* hard physical effort – *infml*

'**elbowroom** /-,roohm, -room/ *n* adequate space or scope for movement, work, or operation

¹**elder** /'eldə/ *n* any of several shrubs or small trees of the honeysuckle family

²**elder** *adj* of earlier birth or greater age, esp than another related person or thing

³**elder** *n* **1** one who is older; a senior **2** one having authority by virtue of age and experience **3** an official of the early church or of a Presbyterian congregation

'**elderly** /-li/ *adj* rather old

eldest /'eldist/ *adj* of the greatest age or seniority; oldest

¹**elect** /i'lekt/ *adj* **1** chosen for salvation through divine mercy **2** chosen for office or position but not yet installed

²**elect** *v* **1** to select by vote for an office, position, or membership **2** to choose, decide – *fml* – **~ion** *n*

electioneer /i,leksh(ə)n'iə/ *v* to work for a candidate or party in an election – **~ing** *n*

elective /ilektiv/ *adj* **1a** chosen or filled by popular election **b** of election **2** permitting a choice; optional

elector /i'lektə/ *n* **1** sby qualified to vote in an election **2** sby entitled to participate in an election: e g **2a** *often cap* any of the German princes entitled to elect the Holy Roman Emperor **b** a member of the electoral college in the USA

electoral /i'lekt(ə)rəl/ *adj* of (an) election or electors

electorate /i'lekt(ə)rət/ *n* **1** *often cap* the territory, jurisdiction, etc of a German elector **2** *sing or pl in constr* a body of electors

electric /i'lektrik/ *adj* **1a** of, being, supplying, producing, or produced by electricity **b** operated by or using electricity **2** producing an intensely stimulating effect; thrilling **3** *of a musical instrument* electronically producing or amplifying sound

electrical /i'lektrikl/ *adj* **1** of or connected w¹th electricity **2** producing, produced, or operated by electricity – **~ly** *adv*

e,lectric 'chair *n* **1** a chair used in legal electrocution **2** *the* penalty of death by electrocution

electricity /i,lek'trisəti, ,ee-/ *n* **1** (the study of) the phenomena due to (the flow or accumulation of) positively and negatively charged particles (e g protons and electrons) **2** electric current; *also* electric charge

electrify /i'lektrifie/ *v* **1a** to charge (a body) with electricity **b** to equip for use of or supply with electric power **2** to excite, thrill – **-fication** *n*

electrocardiogram /i,lektroh'kahdi·ə,gram/ *n* the tracing made by an electrocardiograph

,**electro'cardio,graph** /-,grahf, -,graf/ *n* an instrument for recording the changes of electrical potential difference occurring during the heartbeat

electrocute /i'lektrə,kyooht/ *v* to execute or kill by electricity – **-cution** *n*

electrode /i'lektrohd/ *n* a conductor used to establish electrical contact with a nonmetallic part of a circuit (e g the acid in a car battery)

e,lectroen'cephalo,gram /-in'sef(ə)lə,gram/ *n* the tracing made by an electroencephalograph

e,lectroen'cephalo,graph /-in'sef(ə)lə,grahf, -,graf/ *n* an instrument for detecting and recording brain waves

electrolysis /,elek'troləsis, ,i,lek-/ *n* **1** the passage of an electric current through an electrolyte to generate a gas, deposit a metal on (an object serving as) an electrode, etc **2** the destruction of hair roots, warts, moles etc by means of an electric current

electrolyte /i'lektrə,liet/ n a nonmetallic electric conductor (e g a salt solution) in which current is carried by the movement of ions

electromagnetic /i,lektrohmag'netik/ adj of or relating to magnetic effects produced by the flowing of an electric current

electron /i'lektron/ n a negatively charged elementary particle that occurs in atoms outside the nucleus and the mass movement of which constitutes an electric current in a metal

electronic /i,lek'tronik, ,eelek-/ adj of, being, or using devices constructed or working by the methods or principles of electronics – ~ ally adv

elec'tronics n pl but sing in constr physics or technology dealing with the emission, behaviour, and effects of electrons in valves, transistors, or other electronic devices

e,lectron 'micro,scope n an instrument in which a beam of electrons is used to produce an enormously enlarged image of a minute object

electroplate /i'lektroh,playt/ v to plate with a continuous metallic coating by electrolysis

elegant /'elig(ə)nt/ adj **1** gracefully refined or dignified **2** tastefully rich or luxurious, esp in design or ornamentation – ~ ly adv -ance n

elegy /'eləji/ n a song, poem, or other work expressing sorrow or lamentation, esp for one who is dead – -giac adj – -giacally adv

element /'elamant/ n **1a** any of the 4 substances air, water, fire, and earth formerly believed to constitute the physical universe b pl forces of nature; esp violent or severe weather c the state or sphere natural or suited to sby or sthg **2** a constituent part: e g **2a** pl the simplest principles of a subject of study; the rudiments b a constituent of a mathematical set c any of the factors determining an outcome d a distinct part of a composite device; esp a resistor in an electric heater, kettle, etc **3** any of more than 100 fundamental substances that consist of atoms of only one kind

elemental /,eli'mentl/ adj of or resembling a great force of nature

elementary /,eli'ment(ə)ri/ adj of or dealing with the basic elements or principles of sthg; simple

ele,mentary 'particle n any of the constituents of matter and energy (e g the electron, proton, or photon) whose nature has not yet been proved to be due to the combination of other more fundamental entities

elephant /'elifant/ n a very large nearly hairless mammal having the snout prolonged into a muscular trunk and 2 upper incisors developed into long tusks which provide ivory

elephantine /,eli'fantien/ adj **1a** huge, massive b clumsy, ponderous **2** of an elephant

elevate /'eli,vayt/ v **1** to lift up; raise **2** to raise in rank or status; exalt **3** to improve morally, intellectually, or culturally **4** to raise the spirits of; elate

'elevated adj **1** raised, esp above a surface (e g the ground) **2** morally or intellectually on a high plane; lofty **3** exhilarated in mood or feeling

elevation /,eli'vaysh(ə)n/ n **1** the height to which sthg is elevated: e g **1a** the angle to which a gun is aimed above the horizon b the height above sea level **2** (the ability to achieve) a ballet dancer's or a skater's leap and seeming suspension in the air **3** an elevated place **4** being elevated **5** a geometrical projection (e g of a building) on a vertical plane

elevator /'eli,vaytə/ n **1** sby or sthg that raises or lifts sthg up: e g **1a** an endless belt or chain conveyer for raising grain, liquids, etc b chiefly NAm a lift **2** a movable horizontal control surface, usu attached to the tailplane of an aircraft for controlling climb and descent

eleven /i'lev(ə)n/ n **1** the number 11 **2** the eleventh in a set or series **3** sing or pl in constr sthg having 11 parts or members or a denomination of 11; esp a cricket, soccer, or hockey team – ~ th adj, n, pron, adv

e,leven-'plus, 11-plus n an examination taken, esp formerly, at the age of 10–11 to determine which type of British state secondary education a child should receive

e'levenses n pl but sometimes sing in constr, Br light refreshment taken in the middle of the morning

e,leventh 'hour n the latest possible time

elf /elf/ n, pl elves /elvz/ a (mischievous) fairy – ~ in, ~ ish adj

elicit /i'lisit/ v **1** to draw forth or bring out (sthg latent or potential) **2** to call forth or draw out (a response or reaction); evoke – ~ ation n

eligible /'elijəbl/ adj **1** qualified to be chosen; also entitled **2** worthy or desirable, esp as a marriage partner – -bility n – -bly adv

eliminate /i'limi,nayt/ v **1a** to cast out or get rid of completely; eradicate b to set aside as unimportant; ignore **2** to expel (e g waste) from the living body **3a** to kill (a person), esp so as to remove as an obstacle b to remove (a competitor, team, etc) from a competition, usu by defeat – -nation n

élite, elite /i'leet, ay-/ n sing or pl in constr a small superior group

é'li,tism, elitism /-,tiz(ə)m/ n (advocacy of) leadership by an élite

elixir /i'liksə, -siə/ n **1** an alchemist's substance supposedly capable of changing base metals into gold **2a** elixir, elixir of life a substance held to be capable of prolonging life indefinitely b a cure-all **3** a sweetened liquid (e g a syrup) containing a drug or medicine

Elizabethan /i,lizə'beeth(ə)n/ adj (characteristic) of (the age of) Elizabeth I

elk /elk/ *n pl* **elks,** *esp collectively* **elk 1** the largest existing deer of Europe and Asia **2** *NAm* a large N American deer

ellipse /i'lips/ *n* a curve generated by a point that moves in such a way that the sum of its distances from 2 fixed points is constant – **elliptical** *adj*

elm /elm/ *n* (the wood of) any of a genus of large graceful trees

elocution /ˌelə'kyoohsh(ə)n/ *n* the art of effective public speaking, esp of good diction – ~**ary** *adj* – ~**ist** *n*

¹**elongate** /'elong,gayt, 'ee-/ *v* **1** to extend the length of **2** to grow in length – **-ation** *n*

²**elongate, elongated** *adj* long in proportion to width – used esp in botany and zoology

elope /i'lohp/ *v* to run away secretly with the intention of getting married or cohabiting, usu without parental consent – ~**ment** *n*

eloquent /'eləkwənt/ *adj* **1** characterized by fluent, forceful, and persuasive use of language **2** vividly or movingly expressive or revealing – ~**quence** *n* – ~**ly** *adv*

else /els/ *adv* **1** apart from the person, place, manner, or time mentioned or understood (e g how *else* could he have acted) **2** also, besides **3** if not, otherwise – used absolutely to express a threat (e g do what I tell you or *else*)

ˌelse'**where** /-'weə/ *adv* in or to another place

elucidate /i'loohsi,dayt/ *v* to make (sthg) lucid, esp by explanation – **-dation** *n*

elude /i'loohd/ *v* **1** to avoid cunningly or adroitly **2** to escape the memory, understanding, or notice of

elusive /i'loohsiv/ *adj* tending to elude – ~**ly** *adv* – ~**ness** *n*

elver /'elvə/ *n* a young eel

elves /elvz/ *pl of* elf

elvish /'elvish/ *adj* elfish

Elysium /i'lizi-əm/ *n, pl* **Elysiums, Elysia** /-zi-ə/ **1** the home of the blessed after death in Greek mythology **2** paradise – **sian** *adj*

emaciate /i'maysi,ayt/ *v* to make or become excessively thin or feeble – **-ation** *n*

emanate /'emə,nayt/ *v* to come out *from* a source – **-ation** *n*

emancipate /i'mansi,payt/ *v* to free from restraint, control, or esp slavery – **-pator** *n* – **-pation** *n*

emasculate /i'maskyoo,layt/ *v* **1** to castrate **2** to deprive of strength, vigour, or spirit; weaken – **-lation** *n*

embalm /im'bahm/ *v* **1** to treat (a dead body) so as to give protection against decay **2** to preserve from oblivion – ~**er** *n*

embankment /im'bangkmənt/ *n* a raised structure to hold back water or to carry a roadway or railway

embargo /im'bahgoh/ *n, pl* **embargoes 1** an order of a government prohibiting the departure or entry of commercial ships **2** a legal prohibition on commerce **3** a stoppage, impediment; *esp* a prohibition

embark /im'bahk/ *v* **1** to go on board a boat or aircraft **2** to make a start; commence – usu + *on* or *upon* – ~**ation** *n*

embarrass /im'barəs/ *v* **1** to involve in financial difficulties, esp debt **2** to cause to experience a state of self-conscious distress; disconcert – ~**ingly** *adv* – ~**ment** *n*

embassy /'embəsi/ *n* **1a** the position of an ambassador **b** an ambassador's official mission abroad **2** (the residence of) a diplomatic body headed by an ambassador

em'battled *adj* involved in battle or conflict

embed /im'bed/ *v* **-dd-** to place or fix firmly (as if) in surrounding matter

embellish /im'belish/ *v* **1** to make beautiful by adding ornaments; decorate **2** to make (speech or writing) more interesting by adding fictitious or exaggerated detail – ~**ment** *n*

ember /'embə/ *n* **1** a glowing fragment (e g of coal or wood) in a (dying) fire **2** *pl* the smouldering remains of a fire **3** *pl* slowly fading emotions, memories, ideas, or responses

embezzle /im'bezl/ *v* **embezzling** /im'bezling, imˌbezl·ing/ to appropriate (e g property entrusted to one's care) fraudulently to one's own use – ~**ment** *n* – **-zler** *n*

embitter /im'bitə/ *v* **1** to make bitter **2** to excite bitter feelings in – ~**ment** *n*

emblazon /im'blayz(ə)n/ *v* **1** to display conspicuously **2** to inscribe, adorn, or embellish (as if) with heraldic bearings or devices

emblem /'embləm/ *n* **1** an object or a typical representation of an object symbolizing another object or idea **2** a device, symbol, or figure adopted and used as an identifying mark – ~**atic** *adj* – ~**atically** *adv*

embody /im'bodi/ *v* **1** to give a body to (a spirit); incarnate **2** to make (e g ideas or concepts) concrete and perceptible **3** to make (e g connected ideas or principles) a part of a body or system; incorporate, include – usu + *in* **4** to represent in human or animal form; personify – **-diment** *n*

embolden /im'bohld(ə)n/ *v* to make bold or courageous

embolism /'embəliz(ə)m/ *n* (the sudden obstruction of a blood vessel by) a clot, air bubble, or other particle

emboss /im'bos/ *v* **1** to ornament with raised work **2** to raise in relief from a surface

¹**embrace** /im'brays/ *v* **1** to take and hold closely in the arms as a sign of affection; hug **2** to encircle, enclose **3a** to take up, esp readily or eagerly;

emb

adopt **b** to avail oneself of; welcome **4** to include as a part or element of a more inclusive whole **5** to join in an embrace; hug one another

²**embrace** *n* an act of embracing or gripping

embrocation /ˌembrɔˈkaysh(ə)n/ *n* a liniment

embroider /imˈbroydə/ *v* **1** to ornament (e g cloth or a garment) with decorative stitches made by hand or machine **2** to elaborate on (a narrative); embellish with exaggerated or fictitious details – ~**y** *n*

embroil /imˈbroyl/ *v* **1** to throw (e g a person or affairs) into disorder or confusion **2** to involve in conflict or difficulties

embryo /ˈembrioh/ *n pl* **embryos 1** an animal in the early stages of growth before birth or hatching **2** a rudimentary plant within a seed **3a** sthg as yet undeveloped **b** a beginning or undeveloped state of sthg – *in embryo* – ~**nic** *adj*

emend /iˈmend/ *v* to correct, usu by textual alterations – ~**ation** *n*

emerald /ˈem(ə)rəld/ *adj or n* (of the bright green colour of) a beryl used as a gemstone

emerge /iˈmuhj/ *v* **1** to rise (as if) from an enveloping fluid; come out into view **2** to become manifest or known **3** to rise from an obscure or inferior condition – ~**gence** *n*

emergency /iˈmuhj(ə)nsi/ *n* an unforeseen occurrence or combination of circumstances that calls for immediate action

emergent /iˈmuhj(ə)nt/ *adj* emerging; *esp* in the early stages of formation or development

emery /ˈem(ə)ri/ *n* a dark granular mineral used for grinding and polishing

emetic /iˈmetik/ *n or adj* (sthg) that induces vomiting

emigrant /ˈemigrənt/ *n* one who emigrates

emigrate /ˈemiˌgrayt/ *v* to leave one's home or country for life or residence elsewhere – ~**tion** *n*

émigré, emigré /ˈemigray/ (*Fr* emigre)/ *n* a (political) emigrant

eminence /ˈeminəns/ *n* **1** a position of prominence or superiority – used as a title for a cardinal **2** sby or sthg high, prominent, or lofty: e g **2a** a person of high rank or attainments **b** a natural geographical elevation; a height

eminent /ˈeminənt/ *adj* **1** conspicuous, notable **2** exhibiting eminence, esp in position, fame, or achievement

emir /ˈemiə, -ˈ-/ *n* **1** a ruler of any of various Muslim states **2** a high-ranking Turkish official of former times **3** a male descendant of Muhammad

emirate /ˈemirət/ *n* the position, state, power, etc of an emir

emissary /ˈemis(ə)ri/ *n* one sent on an often secret mission as the agent of another

emission /iˈmish(ə)n/ *n* **1** an act or instance of emitting **2** an unpleasant discharge of waste

emit /iˈmit/ *v* **-tt- 1a** to throw or give off or out (e g light) **b** to send out; eject **2** to give utterance or voice to

emollient /iˈmohli-ənt, iˈmo-, -yənt/ *n or adj* (a substance) that makes soft or gives relief

emolument /iˈmolyoomənt/ *n* the returns arising from office or employment; a salary

emotion /iˈmohsh(ə)n/ *n* **1** excitement **2** a mental and physical reaction (e g anger, fear, or joy) marked by strong feeling and often physiological changes that prepare the body for immediate vigorous action – ~**less** *adj*

emotional /iˈmohsh(ə)nl/ *adj* **1** of the emotions **2** inclined to show (excessive) emotion **3** emotive – ~**ly** *adv*

emotive /iˈmohtiv/ *adj* **1** emotional **2** appealing to, expressing, or arousing emotion rather than reason – ~**ly** *adv*

empathy /ˈempathi/ *n* **1** the imaginative projection of a subjective state into an object, esp a work of art, so allowing it to be better understood and appreciated **2** the capacity for participation in another's feelings or ideas – **-thize** *v* – **-thic** *adj*

emperor /ˈemp(ə)rə/ *n* the supreme ruler of an empire

emphasis /ˈemfəsis/ *n, pl* **emphases** /-ˌseez/ special consideration of or stress on sthg – **-atic** *adj* – **-atically** *adv* – **-asize** *v*

empire /ˈempie-ə/ *n* **1a** (the territory of) a large group of countries or peoples under **1** authority **b** sthg resembling a political empire; *esp* an extensive territory or enterprise under single domination or control **2** imperial sovereignty

empirical /emˈpirikl/ *also* **empiric** *adj* originating in, based, or relying on observation or experiment rather than theory – ~**ly** *adv* – **-cism** *n*

¹**employ** /imˈploy/ *v* **1a** to use in a specified way or for a specific purpose **b** to spend (time) **c** to use **2a** to engage the services of **b** to provide with a job that pays wages or a salary – ~**er** *n*

²**employ** *n* the state of being employed, esp for wages or a salary – *fml*

employee, *NAm also* **employe** /ˌemployˈee, imˌemployˈee/ *n* one employed by another, esp for wages or a salary and in a position below executive level

employment /imˈploymənt/ *n* (an) activity in which one engages or is employed

em'ployment ex,change *n* a labour exchange

emporium /imˈpawri-əm/ *n, pl* **emporiums, emporia** /-ri-ə/ a place of trade; *esp* a commercial centre or large shop

empower /imˈpowə/ *v* to give official authority or legal power to

empress /ˈempris/ *n* **1** the wife or widow of an emperor **2** a woman having in her own right the rank of emperor

¹**empty** /'empti/ *adj* **1a** containing nothing; *esp* lacking typical or expected contents **b** not occupied, inhabited, or frequented **2a** lacking reality or substance; hollow **b** lacking effect, value, or sincerity **c** lacking sense; foolish **3** hungry – *infml* – **emptily** *adv* – **emptiness** *n*

²**empty** *v* **1a** to make empty; remove the contents of **b** to deprive, divest **c** to discharge (itself) of contents **2** to remove from what holds, encloses, or contains **3** to transfer by emptying **4** to become empty

³**empty** *n* a bottle, container, vehicle, etc that has been emptied

,empty-'handed *adj* having or bringing nothing, esp because nothing has been gained or obtained

,empty-'headed *adj* foolish, silly

emu /'eemyooh/ *n* a swift-running Australian flightless bird

emulate /'emyoo,layt/ *v* **1** to rival **2** to imitate closely; approach equality with – -**tion** *n*

emulsion /i'mulsh(ə)n/ *n* **1** (the state of) a substance (e g fat in milk) consisting of one liquid dispersed in droplets throughout another liquid **2** a suspension; *esp* a suspension of a silver compound in a gelatin solution or other solid medium for coating photographic plates, film, etc

enable /in'aybl/ *v* **1** to provide with the means or opportunity **2** to make possible, practical, or easy

enact /in'akt/ *v* **1** to make into law **2** to act out, play – ~**ment** *n*

enamel /i'naml/ *n* -**ll**- (*NAm* -**l**-, -**ll**-), /i'naml'ing/ **1** a usu opaque glassy coating applied to the surface of metal, glass, or pottery **2** a substance composed of calcium phosphate that forms a thin hard layer capping the teeth **3** a paint that dries with a glossy appearance

encamp /in'kamp/ *v* to place or establish (in) a camp – ~**ment** *n*

encapsulate /in'kapsyoo,layt/ *v* **1** to enclose (as if) in a capsule **2** to epitomize, condense – -**ation** *n*

encase /in'kays/ *v* to enclose (as if) in a case

enchant /in'chahnt/ *v* **1** to bewitch **2** to attract and move deeply; delight – ~**ment** *n*

enchanter /in'chahntə/ *n* a sorcerer

enchanting /in'chahnting/ *adj* charming – ~**ly** *adv*

encircle /in'suhkl/ *v* **1** to form a circle round; surround **2** to move or pass completely round – ~**ment** *n*

enclave /'enklayv/ *n* a territorial or culturally distinct unit enclosed within foreign territory

enclose *also* **inclose** /in'klohz/ *v* **1a(1)** to close in completely; surround **a(2)** to fence off (common land) for individual use **b** to hold in; confine **2** to include in a package or envelope, esp along with sthg else – -**sure** *n*

encomium /en'kohmi-əm, -myəm/ *n, pl* **encomiums, encomia** /-mi-ə, -myə/ a usu formal expression of warm or high praise; a eulogy

encompass /in'kumpəs/ *v* **1** to form a circle about; enclose **2** to include

encore /'ong,kaw/ *n* (an audience's appreciative demand for) a performer's reappearance to give an additional or repeated performance – **encore** *interj*

¹**encounter** /in'kowntə/ *v* **1a** to meet as an adversary or enemy **b** to engage in conflict with **2** to meet or come across, esp unexpectedly

²**encounter** *n* **1** a meeting or clash between hostile factions or people **2** a chance meeting

encourage /in'kurij/ *v* **1** to inspire with courage, spirit, or hope **2** to spur on **3** to give help or patronage to (e g a process or action); promote – -**agingly** *adv* – ~**ment** *n*

encroach /in'krohch/ *v* **1** to enter gradually or by stealth into the possessions or rights of another; intrude, trespass **2** to advance beyond the usual or proper limits *USE* usu + *on* or *upon* – ~**ment** *n*

encrust *also* **incrust** /in'krust/ *v* **1** to cover, line, or overlay with a crust, esp of jewels or precious metal **2** to form a crust

encumber /in'kumbə/ *v* **1** to weigh down, burden **2** to impede or hamper the function or activity of **3** to burden with a legal claim – -**brance** *n*

encyclical /en'siklikl/ *n* a papal letter to the bishops of the church as a whole or to those in 1 country

encyclopedia, encyclopaedia /in,sieklə'peedi-ə, -dyə/ *n* a reference book containing information on all branches of knowledge or comprehensive information on 1 branch

encyclopedic, encyclopaedic /in,sieklə'peedik/ *adj* very comprehensive

¹**end** /end/ *n* **1a** the part of an area that lies at the boundary; *also* the farthest point from where one is **b(1)** the point that marks the extent of sthg in space or time; the limit **b(2)** the point where sthg ceases to exist **c** either of the extreme or last parts lengthways of an object that is appreciably longer than it is broad **2a** (the events, sections, etc immediately preceding) the cessation of action, activity, or existence **b** the final condition; *esp* death **3** sthg left over; remnant **4** an aim or purpose **5** sthg or sby extreme of a kind; the ultimate **6a** either half of a games pitch, court, etc **b** a period of action or turn to play in bowls, curling, etc **7** a particular part of an undertaking or organization *USE* (5 & 7) *infml* — **in the end** ultimately — **no end 1** exceedingly **2** an endless amount; a huge quantity — **on end 1** upright **2** without a stop or letup

²**end** *v* **1** to bring or come to an end **2** to destroy **3** to reach a specified ultimate situation, condition, or rank – often + *up*

³**end** *adj* final, ultimate

endanger /in'daynjə/ *v* to bring into or expose to danger or peril

endear /in'diə/ v to cause to become beloved or admired – usu + *to*

en'dearment /-mənt/ n a word or act (e g a caress) expressing affection

¹**endeavour** /in'devə/ *NAm chiefly* **endeavor** /in'devə/ v to attempt by exertion or effort; try – usu + infin; *fml*

²**endeavour,** *NAm chiefly* **endeavor** n serious determined effort ; *also* an instance of this – fml

endemic /en'demik/ adj 1 belonging or native to a particular people or region; not introduced or naturalized 2 regularly occurring in or associated with a particular topic or sphere of activity

ending /'ending/ n 1 the last part of a book, film, etc 2 one or more letters or syllables added to a word base, esp as an inflection

endless /'endlis/ adj 1 (seeming) without end 2 extremely numerous 3 of a belt, chain, *etc* that is joined to itself at its ends – ~ly *adv*

¹**endocrine** /'endəhkrin, -krien, -də-/ adj 1 producing secretions that are discharged directly into the bloodstream 2 of or being an endocrine gland or its secretions

²**endocrine** n the thyroid, pituitary, or other gland that produces an endocrine secretion

endorse /in'daws/ v 1a to write on the back of b to write (one's signature) on a cheque, bill, or note 2 to express approval of; support; *specif, chiefly NAm* to express support for (e g a political candidate) publicly 3 *Br* to record on (e g a driving licence) particulars of an offence committed by the holder – ~**ment** n

endow /in'dow/ v 1 to provide with a continuing source of income 2 to provide *with* an ability or attribute – ~**ment** n

endurance /in'dyooorəns/ n the ability to withstand hardship, adversity, or stress

endure /in'dyoo/ v 1 to continue in the same state; last 2 to undergo (e g a hardship), esp without giving in 3 to tolerate, permit – **-durable** *adj* – **ring** *adj* – **-ringly** *adv*

'**end,ways** /-,wayz/, '**end,wise** /-,wiez/ *adv or adj* 1 with the end forwards (e g towards the observer) 2 in or towards the direction of the ends; lengthways 3 upright; on end 4 end to end

enema /'enimə/ n, pl **enemas** *also* **enemata** /,eni'mahtə/ 1 injection of liquid into the intestine by way of the anus (e g to ease constipation) 2 material for injection as an enema

enemy /'enəmi/ n 1 one who is antagonistic to another; *esp* one seeking to injure, overthrow, or confound an opponent 2 sthg harmful or deadly 3 a hostile military unit or force

energetic /,enə'jetik/ adj 1 marked by energy, activity, or vigour 2 operating with power or effect; forceful – ~**ally** *adv*

energy /'enəji/ n 1 the capacity of acting or being active 2 natural power vigorously exerted 3 the capacity for doing work

enervate /'enə,vayt/ v to lessen the mental or physical strength or vitality of; weaken – **-ation** n

en famille /on fa'mee/ *adv* all together as a family

enfeeble /in'feebl/ v to make feeble – ~**ment** n

enfold /in'fohld/ v 1 to wrap up; envelop 2 to clasp in the arms; embrace

enforce /in'faws/ v 1 to give greater force to (e g an argument); reinforce 2 to impose, compel 3 to cause (a rule or law) to be carried out effectively – ~**able** *adj* – ~**ment** n

enfranchise /in'franchiez/ v 1 to set free (e g from slavery) 2a to admit to the right of voting b to admit (a municipality) to political privileges, esp the right of Parliamentary representation – ~**ment** n

engage /in'gayj/ v 1a to attract and hold (sby's thoughts, attention, etc) b to interlock or become interlocked with; cause to mesh 2a to arrange to employ (sby) b to arrange to obtain the services of c to order (a room, seat, etc) to be kept for one; reserve 3a to hold the attention of; engross b to induce to participate, esp in conversation 4a to enter into contest with b to bring together or interlock (e g weapons) 5 to pledge oneself; promise 6 to occupy one's time; participate 7 to enter into conflict

engagé /,ong·ga'zhay (*Fr* ᾱgaʒe)/ adj actively involved or committed (politically)

engaged /in'gayjd/ adj 1 involved in activity; occupied 2 pledged to be married 3 *chiefly Br* 3a in use b reserved, booked

en'gagement /-mənt/ n 1 an agreement to marry; a betrothal 2 a pledge 3a a promise to be present at a certain time and place b employment, esp for a stated time 4 a hostile encounter between military forces

engaging /in'gayjing/ adj attractive, pleasing – ~**ly** *adv*

engender /in'jendə/ v to cause to exist or develop; produce

engine /'enjin/ n 1 a mechanical tool 2 a machine for converting any of various forms of energy into mechanical force and motion 3 a railway locomotive

¹**engineer** /,enji'niə/ n 1a a designer or builder of engines b a person who is trained in or follows as a profession a branch of engineering c a person who starts or carries through an enterprise, esp by skilful or artful contrivance 2 a person who runs or supervises an engine or apparatus

²**engineer** v 1 to lay out, construct, or manage as an engineer 2 to contrive, plan, or guide, usu with subtle skill and craft

engineering /,enji'niəring/ n 1 the art of managing engines 2 the application of science and mathematics by which the properties of matter and the sources of energy in nature are made useful to human beings

¹**English** /'ing·glish/ *adj* (characteristic) of England

²**English** *n* **1a** the Germanic language of the people of Britain, the USA, and most Commonwealth countries **b** English language, literature, or composition as an academic subject **2** *pl in constr* the people of England

engrave /in'grayv/ *v* **1a** to cut (a design or lettering) on a hard surface (e g metal or stone) with a sharp tool **b** to impress deeply, as if by engraving **2a** to cut a design or lettering on (a hard surface) for printing; *also* to print from an engraved plate **b** to produce a plate for printing by photographic methods, photoengrave – ~ **r** *n*

engraving /in'grayving/ *n* (a print made from) an engraved printing surface

engross /in'grohs/ *v* to occupy fully the time and attention of; absorb

engulf /in'gulf/ *v* to flow over and enclose; overwhelm

enhance /in'hahns/ *v* to improve (e g in value, desirability, or attractiveness); heighten – ~ **ment** *n*

enjoin /in'joyn/ *v* **1** to order (sby) to do sthg; command **2** to impose (a condition or course of action) on sby **3** to forbid by law; prohibit *USE* fml

enjoy /in'joy/ *v* **1** to take pleasure or satisfaction in **2a** to have the use or benefit of **b** to experience – ~ **ment** *n*

enlarge /in'lahj/ *v* **1** to make larger **2** to reproduce in a larger form; *specif* to make a photographic enlargement of **3** to grow larger **4** to speak or write at length; elaborate – often + *on* or *upon*

en'largement /-mənt/ *n* a photographic print that is larger than the negative

enlighten /in'liet(ə)n/ *v* to cause to understand; free from false beliefs – ~ **ment** *n*

enlist /in'list/ *v* **1** to engage (a person) for duty in the armed forces **2** to secure the support and aid of – ~ **ment** *n*

enliven /in'liev(ə)n/ *v* to give life, action, spirit, or interest to; animate

en masse /,om 'mas/ *adv* in a body; as a whole

enmesh /in'mesh/ *v* to catch or entangle (as if) in a net or mesh

enmity /'enmiti/ *n* (a state of) hatred or ill will

ennoble /i'nohbl/ *v* to make noble; elevate to the rank of the nobility – ~ **ment** *n*

ennui /on'wi/ *n* weariness and dissatisfaction resulting from lack of interest

enormity /i'nawməti/ *n* **1** great wickedness **2** a terribly wicked or evil act **3** the quality or state of being enormous

enormous /i'nawməs/ *adj* marked by extraordinarily great size, number, or degree – ~ **ness** *n*

¹**enough** /i'nuf/ *adj* fully adequate in quantity, number, or degree

²**enough** *adv* **1** to a fully adequate degree; sufficiently **2** to a tolerable degree

³**enough** *pron, pl* **enough** a sufficient quantity or number

en passant /,on pa'sonh (Fr ã pasã)/ *adv* in passing

enquire /in'kwie·ə/ *v* to inquire

enquiry /in'kwie·əri/ *n* an inquiry

enrage /in'rayj/ *v* to fill with rage; anger – ~ **d** *adj*

enrapture /in'rapchə/ *v* to fill with delight – ~ **d** *adj*

enrich /in'rich/ *v* **1** to make rich or richer, esp in some desirable quality **2** to adorn, ornament – ~ **ment** *n*

enrol, NAm also enroll /in'rohl/ *v* **-ll-** to enter (oneself) on a list (e g for a course of study)

en route /,on 'rooht (Fr ã rut)/ *adv or adj* on or along the way

ensconce /in'skons/ *v* to settle (e g oneself) comfortably or snugly – ~ **d** *adj*

ensemble /on'sombl (Fr ãsã:bl)/ *n* **1a** concerted music of 2 or more parts **b** a complete outfit of matching garments **c** the musicians engaged in the performance of a musical ensemble **2** the quality of togetherness in performance

enshrine /in'shrien/ *v* **1** to enclose (as if) in a shrine **2** to preserve or cherish, esp as sacred – ~ **d** *adj*

enshroud /in'shrowd/ *v* to shroud – ~ **d** *adj*

ensign /'ensien; *sense* ¹ *naval* 'ensən/ *n* **1** a flag that is flown (e g by a ship) as the symbol of nationality **2a** a standard-bearer **b** (in Britain before 1871) an officer of the lowest rank in the army **c** an officer of the lowest rank in the US navy

enslave /in'slayv/ *v* to reduce (as if) to slavery; subjugate – ~ **ment** *n*

ensnare /in'sneə/ *v* to take (as if) in a snare

ensue /in'syooh/ *v* to take place afterwards or as a result

ensure /in'shooə, -'shaw/ *v* to make sure, certain, or safe; guarantee

entail /in'tayl/ *v* **1** to settle (property) so that sale or gift is not permitted and inheritance is limited to (a specified class of) the owner's lineal descendants **2** to involve or imply as a necessary accompaniment or result – **entail** *n*

entangle /in'tang·gl/ *v* **entangling** /in'tang·gling; *also* -gl·ing/ **1** to make tangled, complicated, or confused **2** to involve in a tangle

en'tanglement /-mənt/ *n* **1** sthg that entangles, confuses, or ensnares **2** the condition of being deeply involved

entente /on'tont/ *n* a friendly relationship between 2 or more countries

enter /'entə/ *v* **1** to go or come in or into **2** to register as candidate in a competition **3** to make a beginning **4** to inscribe, register **5** to cause to be received, admitted, or considered – often + *for* **6** to put in; insert **7** to become a member of or an active participant **in 8** to put on record **9a** to make oneself a party to – + *into* **b** to participate or share in – + *into*

enteritis /,entə'rietəs/ *n* inflammation of the intestines usu marked by diarrhoea

enterprise /'entə,priez/ *n* **1** a (difficult or complicated) project or undertaking **2** a unit of economic organization or activity; *esp* a business organization **3** readiness to engage in enterprises

enterprising /'entə,priezing/ *adj* marked by initiative and readiness to engage in enterprises – **~ly** *adv*

entertain /,entə'tayn/ *v* **1** to show hospitality to **2** to be ready and willing to think about (an idea, doubt, suggestion, etc) **3** to hold the attention of, usu pleasantly or enjoyably; divert **4** to invite guests to sup one's home – **~er** *n*

enter'tainment /-mənt/ *n* **1** sthg entertaining, diverting, or engaging **2** a public performance

enthral, *NAm also* **enthrall** /in'thrawl/ *v* -**ll-** to captivate

enthrone /in'throhn/ *v* to seat, esp ceremonially, (as if) on a throne – **~ment** *n*

enthuse /in'thyoohz/ *v* **1** to make enthusiastic **2** to show enthusiasm

enthusiasm /in'thyoohzi,az(ə)m/ *n* **1** keen and eager interest and admiration – usu + *for* or *about* **2** an object of enthusiasm – **-ast** *n* – **-astic** *adj*

entice /in'ties/ *v* to tempt or persuade by arousing hope or desire – **~ment** *n* – **-ticing** *adj*

entire /in'tie-ə/ *adj* **1** having no element or part left out **2** complete in degree; total **3a** consisting of 1 piece; homogeneous **b** intact – **~ly** *adv*

entirety /in'tie-ərəti/ *n* **1** the state of being entire or complete **2** the whole or total

entitle /in'tietl/ *v* **1** to title **2** to give (sby) the right *to* (do or have) sthg – **~ment** *n*

entity /'entəti/ *n* **1a** being, existence; *esp* independent, separate, or self-contained existence **b** the existence of a thing as contrasted with its attributes **2** sthg that has separate and distinct existence

entomb /in'toohm/ *v* to deposit (as if) in a tomb; bury – **~ment** *n*

entomology /,entə'moləji/ *n* zoology that deals with insects – **-gist** *n* – **-gical** *adj*

entourage /'ontoo,rahzh/ *n sing or pl in constr* a group of attendants or associates, esp of sby of high rank

entrails /'entraylz/ *n pl* internal parts; *esp* the intestines

¹**entrance** /'entrəns/ *n* **1** the act of entering **2** the means or place of entry **3** power or permission to enter; admission **4** an arrival of a performer onto the stage or before the cameras

²**entrance** /in'trahns/ *v* to fill with delight, wonder, or rapture – **~d** *adj*

entrant /'entrənt/ *n* sby or sthg that enters or is entered; *esp* one who enters a contest

entrap /in'trap/ *v* -**pp-** **1** to catch (as if) in a trap **2** to lure into a compromising statement or act – **~ment** *n*

entreat /in'treet/ *v* to ask urgently or plead with (sby) *for* (sthg); beg – **~ingly** *adv*

entreaty /in'treeti/ *n* an act of entreating; a plea

entrée, **entree** /'ontray (*Fr* ãtre)/ *n* **1** freedom of entry or access **2a** *chiefly Br* a dish served between the usual (fish and meat) courses of a dinner **b** *chiefly NAm* the principal dish of a meal

entrench /in'trench/ *v* to establish solidly, esp so as to make dislodgement difficult – **~ed** *adj*

entrepreneur /,ontrəprə'nuh (*Fr* ãtrəprənœːr)/ *n* one who organizes, manages, and assumes the risks of a business or enterprise

entropy /'entrəpi/ *n* **1** a measure of the unavailable energy in a closed thermodynamic system **2** the degradation of the matter and energy in the universe to an ultimate state of inert uniformity

entrust /in'trust/ *v* to commit *to* the trust of another; to confer another *with* the trust of

entry /'entri/ *n* **1** the act of entering; entrance **2** the right or privilege of entering **3** a door, gate, hall, vestibule, or other place of entrance **4a** a record made in a diary, account book, index, etc **b** a dictionary headword, often with its definition **5** a person, thing, or group entered in a contest; an entrant **6** the total of those entered or admitted

entwine /in'twien/ *v* to twine together or round

enumerate /i'nyoohmərayt/ *v* **1** to count **2** to specify one after another; list – **-ration** *n*

enunciate /i'nunsi,ayt/ *v* **1a** to make a definite or systematic statement of; formulate **b** to announce, proclaim **2** to articulate, pronounce – **-tion** *n*

envelop /in'veləp/ *v* **1** to enclose or enfold completely (as if) with a covering **2** to surround so as to cut off communication or retreat – **~ment** *n*

envelope /'envəlohp, 'on-/ *n* **1** sthg that envelops; a wrapper, covering **2** a flat container, usu of folded and gummed paper (e g for a letter) **3** a membrane or other natural covering that encloses

enviable /'envi-əbl/ *adj* highly desirable – **-bly** *adv*

envious /'envi-əs/ *adj* feeling or showing envy – **~ly** *adv*

en'vironment /-mənt/ *n* **1** the circumstances, objects, or conditions by which one is surrounded **2** the complex of climatic, soil, and biological factors that acts upon an organism or an ecological community – **~al** *adj* – **~ally** *adv*

en,viron'mentalist /-ist/ *n* sby concerned about the quality of the human environment – **-ism** *n*

environs /in'vie(ə)rənz/ *n pl* the neighbourhood surrounding sthg, esp a town

envisage /in'vizij/ *v* to have a mental picture of; visualize, esp in advance of an expected or hoped-for realization

envoy /'envoy/ n 1 a diplomatic agent, esp one who ranks immediately below an ambassador 2 a messenger, representative

¹**envy** /'envi/ n painful, resentful, or admiring awareness of an advantage enjoyed by another, accompanied by a desire to possess the same advantage; also an object of such a feeling

²**envy** v to feel envy towards or on account of

enzyme /'enziem/ n any of numerous complex proteins that are produced by living cells and catalyse specific biochemical reactions at body temperatures

eon /'eeon, 'ee-ən/ n an aeon

epaulette, NAm chiefly **epaulet** /,epə'let/ n an ornamental (fringed) pad or strip attached to the shoulder of a uniform

épée /'epay (Fr epe)/ n (the sport of fencing with) a sword having a bowl-shaped guard and a rigid tapering blade of triangular cross-section with no cutting edge

ephemeral /i'femərəl/ adj 1 lasting 1 day only 2 lasting a very short time – ~**ly** adv – ~**ity** n

¹**epic** /'epik/ adj 1 (having the characteristics) of an epic 2a extending beyond the usual or ordinary, esp in size or scope b heroic – ~**ally** adv

²**epic** n 1 a long narrative poem recounting the deeds of a legendary or historical hero 2 a series of events or body of legend or tradition fit to form the subject of an epic

epicentre /'epi,sentə/ n the centre from which an earthquake spreads

epicure /'epikyooo/ n sby with sensitive and discriminating tastes, esp in food or wine – ~ **an** adj, n

epidemic /,epi'demik/ n or adj (an outbreak of a disease) affecting many individuals within a population, community, or region at the same time

epidermis /,epi'duhmis/ n 1 the thin outer layer of the skin of the animal body 2 a thin surface layer of tissue in higher plants

epigram /'epi,gram/ n 1 a short often satirical poem 2 a neat, witty, and often paradoxical remark or saying – ~**matic** adj

epilepsy /'epi,lepsi/ n any of various disorders marked by disturbed electrical rhythms of the brain and spinal chord and typically manifested by convulsive attacks often with clouding of consciousness – **-ptic** adj, n

epilogue /'epi,log/ n 1 a concluding section of a literary or dramatic work that comments on or summarizes the main action or plot 2 a speech or poem addressed to the audience by an actor at the end of a play

epiphany /i'pifəni/ n 1 cap (January 6 observed as a church festival in commemoration of the coming of the Magi 2 a usu sudden manifestation or perception of the essential nature or meaning of sthg

episcopal /i'piskəpl/ adj 1 of a bishop 2 of, having, or constituting government by bishops 3 cap Anglican; esp of an Anglican church that is not established (e g in the USA or Scotland)

episode /'episohd/ n 1a a developed situation or incident that is integral to but separable from a continuous narrative (e g a play or novel) b the part of a serial presented at 1 performance 2 an event that is distinctive and separate although part of a larger series (e g in history or in sby's life)

epistle /i'pisl/ n 1 cap (a liturgical reading from) any of the letters (e g of St Paul) adopted as books of the New Testament 2 an esp formal letter

epitaph /'epi,tahf, -taf/ n 1 a commemorative inscription on a tombstone or monument 2 a brief statement commemorating a deceased person or past event

epithet /'epithet/ n 1 a descriptive word or phrase accompanying or occurring in place of the name of a person or thing 2 a disparaging or abusive word or phrase

epitome /i'pitəmi/ n 1 a condensed account or summary, esp of a literary work 2 a typical or ideal example; an embodiment

epoch /'eepok/ n 1 a memorable event or date; esp a turning point 2 an extended period of time, usu characterized by a distinctive development or by a memorable series of events

equable /'ekwəbl/ adj uniform, even; esp free from extremes or sudden changes – **-bly** adv

¹**equal** /'eekwəl/ adj 1a of the same quantity, amount, or number as another b identical in value; equivalent 2a like in quality, nature, or status b like for each member of a group, class, or society 3 evenly balanced or matched 4 capable of meeting the requirements of sthg (e g a situation or task) – + to – ~**ity** n – ~**ize** v

²**equal** v -ll- 1 to be equal to; esp to be identical in value to 2 to make or produce sthg equal to

equalitarian /i,kwoli'teəri·ən/ n or adj (an) egalitarian

equanimity /,eekwə'niməti, ,ekwə-/ n evenness of mind or temper, esp under stress

equate /i'kwayt/ v 1 to make or set equal 2 to treat, represent, or regard as equal, equivalent, or comparable

equation /i'kwayzh(ə)n; sense ' i'kwaysh(ə)n/ n a statement of the equality of 2 mathematical expressions

equator /i'kwaytə/ n 1 the great circle of the celestial sphere whose plane is perpendicular to the rotational axis of the earth 2 a great circle; specif the one that is equidistant from the 2 poles of the earth and divides the earth's surface into the northern and southern hemispheres – ~**ial** adj – ~**ially** adv

equerry /i'kweri, 'ekwəri/ n 1 an officer of a prince or noble charged with the care of horses 2 an officer of the British royal household in personal attendance on a member of the royal family

equestrian /i'kwestri·ən/ adj 1a of or featuring horses, horsemen, or horsemanship b representing a person on horseback 2 (composed) of knights

equidistant /ˌeekwi'dist(ə)nt, ˌekwi-/ adj equally distant

equilateral /ˌeekwi'lat(ə)rəl, ˌekwi-/ adj having all sides equal

equilibrium /ˌeekwi'libri·əm, ˌekwi-/ n pl **equilibriums, equilibria** /-bri·ə/ 1 a state of balance between opposing forces, actions, or processes (e g in a reversible chemical reaction) 2a a state of adjustment between opposing or divergent influences or elements b a state of intellectual or emotional balance 3 the normal state of the animal body in respect to its environment that involves adjustment to changing conditions

equine /'ekwien/ adj of or resembling the horse (family)

equinox /'ekwi,noks/ n 1 either of the 2 times each year that occur about March 21st and September 23rd when the sun crosses the equator and day and night are of equal length everywhere on earth 2 either of the 2 points on the celestial sphere where the celestial equator intersects the ecliptic – **-noctial** adj

equip /i'kwip/ v **-pp-** 1 to make ready for service, action, or use; provide with appropriate supplies 2 to dress, array

equipage /'ekwipij/ n 1 material or articles used in equipment 2 trappings 3 a horse-drawn carriage (with its servants)

equipment /i'kwipmənt/ n 1 the set of articles, apparatus, or physical resources serving to equip a person, thing, enterprise, expedition, etc 2 mental or emotional resources

equipoise /'ekwi,poyz, 'eekwi-/ n 1 a state of equilibrium 2 a counterbalance

equitable /'ekwitəbl/ adj 1 fair and just 2 valid in equity as distinguished from law – **-bly** adv

equity /'ekwiti/ n 1 justice according to natural law or right; fairness 2 a system of justice originally developed in the Chancery courts on the basis of conscience and fairness to supplement or override the more rigid common law 3a a right, claim, or interest existing or valid in equity b the money value of a property or of an interest in a property in excess of claims against it 4 a share that does not bear fixed interest – usu pl

equivalent /i'kwivəl(ə)nt/ adj 1 equal in force, amount, or value 2 corresponding or virtually identical, esp in effect, function, or meaning

equivocal /i'kwivokl/ adj 1 ambiguous 2 questionable, suspicious – **~ly** adv

equivocate /i'kwivə,kayt/ v to use equivocal language, esp with intent to deceive or avoid committing oneself – **-tion** n

era /'iərə/ n 1 a system of chronological notation computed from a given date as a basis 2 an epoch 3 a usu historical period set off or typified by some distinctive figure or characteristic feature

eradicate /i'radi,kayt/ v 1 to pull up by the roots 2 to eliminate; do away with – **-cation** n

erase /i'rayz/ v to obliterate or rub out – **~r** n

¹**erect** /i'rekt/ adj 1a vertical in position; upright b standing up or out from the body c characterized by firm or rigid straightness (e g in bodily posture) 2 in a state of physiological erection – **~ly** adv – **~ness** n

²**erect** v 1a to put up by the fitting together of materials or parts; build b to fix in an upright position 2 to elevate in status 3 to establish; set up

erectile /i'rektiel/ adj, of animal tissue capable of becoming swollen with blood to bring about the erection of a body part esp the penis

erection /i'reksh(ə)n/ n 1 (an occurrence in the penis or clitoris of) the filling with blood and resulting firmness of a previously flaccid body part 2 sthg erected

erg /uhg/ n the cgs unit of work or energy; 10^{-7}J

ergo /'uhgoh/ adv therefore, hence

ergonomics /ˌuhgə'nomiks/ n pl but sing or pl in constr a science concerned with the relationship between human beings, the machines they use, and the working environment

ermine /'uhmin/ n pl **ermines**, esp collectively **ermine** (the winter fur of) a stoat or related weasel that has a white winter coat usu with black on the tail

erode /i'rohd/ v 1 to diminish or destroy by degrees 2 to eat into or away by slow destruction of substance; corrode 3 to wear away by the action of water, wind, glacial ice, etc – **erosion** n

erogenous /i'rojənəs/ also **erogenic** /ˌerə'jenik/ adj of or producing sexual excitement (when stimulated)

erotic /i'rotik/ adj 1 of, concerned with, or tending to arouse sexual desire 2 strongly affected by sexual desire – **~ism** n – **~ally** adv

err /uh/ v 1a to make a mistake b to do wrong; sin 2 to be inaccurate or incorrect

errand /'erənd/ n (the object or purpose of) a short trip taken to attend to some business, often for another

errant /'erənt/ adj 1 (given to) travelling, esp in search of adventure 2 going astray ; esp doing wrong; erring

erratic /i'ratik/ adj 1 having no fixed course 2 characterized by lack of consistency, regularity, or uniformity, esp in behaviour – **~ally** adv

erratum /i'rahtəm/ n, pl **errata** /-tə/ a corrigendum

erroneous /i'rohnyəs, -ni·əs/ *adj* containing or characterized by error; incorrect – ~**ly** *adv*

error /'erə/ *n* **1** a mistake or inaccuracy in speech, opinion, or action **2** the state of being wrong in behaviour or beliefs **3** an act that fails to achieve what was intended

ersatz /'eazatz, 'uh-/ *adj* being a usu artificial and inferior substitute; imitation

erudite /'eroodiet/ *adj* learned – ~**ly** *adv* – **-dition** *n*

erupt /i'rupt/ *v* **1a** *esp of a volcano* to release lava, steam, etc suddenly and usu violently **b** to burst violently from limits or restraint **c** to become suddenly active or violent; explode **2** to break out (e g in a rash) – ~**ion** *n*

escalate /'eskəlayt/ *v* **1** to expand **2** to rise – **-lation** *n*

escalator /'eskəlaytə/ *n* a power-driven set of stairs arranged like an endless belt that ascend or descend continuously

escalope /'eskə,lop/ *n* a thin boneless slice of meat; *esp* a slice of veal from the leg

escapade /'eskəpayd/ *n* a wild, reckless, and often mischievous adventure, esp one that flouts rules or convention

¹escape /i'skayp/ *v* **1a** to get away, esp from confinement or restraint **b** to leak out gradually; seep **2** to avoid a threatening evil **3** to get or stay out of the way of; avoid **4** to fail to be noticed or recallable by **5** to be produced or made by (esp a person), usu involuntarily

²escape *n* **1** an act or instance of escaping **2** a means of escape **3** a cultivated plant run wild

³escape *adj* **1** providing a means of escape **2** providing a means of evading a regulation, claim, or commitment

escapism /i'skay,piz(ə)m/ *n* habitual diversion of the mind to purely imaginative activity or entertainment as an escape from reality or routine – **escapist** *adj, n*

escarpment /i'skahpmənt/ *n* a long cliff or steep slope separating 2 more gently sloping surfaces

eschew /is'chooh/ *v* to shun – *fml*

¹escort /'eskawt/ *n* **1** a person, group of people, ship, aircraft, etc accompanying shy or that by to give protection or show courtesy **2** one who accompanies another socially

²escort /i'skawt/ *v* to accompany as an escort

escutcheon /i'skuchən/ *n* a protective or ornamental shield or plate (e g round a keyhole)

Eskimo *also* **Esquimau** /'eskimoh/ *n pl* **Eskimos**, *esp collectively* **Eskimo** (a member or the language of) any of a group of peoples of N Canada, Greenland, Alaska, and E Siberia

esoteric /ˌeesə'terik, ˌesoh-/ *adj* **1** designed for, understood by, or restricted to a small group, esp of the specially initiated **2** private, confidential – ~**ally** *adv*

ESP *n* awareness or perception taking place without the use of any of the known senses

espadrille /ˌespə'dril/ *n* a flat sandal that usu has a canvas upper and a rope sole and is tied round the ankle or leg with laces

especial /i'spesh(ə)l/ *adj* (distinctively or particularly) special

Esperanto /ˌespə'rantoh/ *n* an artificial international language

espionage /'espi·ənahzh, ˌ---'-, -nij, i'spie-/ *n* spying or the use of spies to obtain information

esplanade /'esplə'nahd, -nayd/ *n* a level open stretch of paved or grassy ground, esp along a shore

espouse /i'spowz/ *v* **1** to marry – *fml* **2** to take up and support as a cause; become attached to

espresso /i'spresoh/ *n pl* **espressos** (an apparatus for making) coffee brewed by forcing steam through finely ground coffee beans

e‚sprit de 'corps /də 'kaw/ *n* the common spirit and loyalty existing among the members of a group

espy /i'spie/ *v* to catch sight of

esquire /i'skwie·ə/ *n* – used as a title equivalent to Mr and placed after the surname

¹essay /e'say/ *v* to attempt – *fml*

²essay /'esay/ *n* **1** a short piece of prose writing on a specific topic **2** an (initial tentative) effort or attempt – *fml* – ~**ist** *n*

essence /'es(ə)ns/ *n* **1a** the real or ultimate nature of an individual being or thing **b** the properties or attributes by means of which sthg can be categorized or identified **2** sthg that exists, esp in an abstract form; an entity **3a** (an alcoholic solution or other preparation of) an extract, essential oil, etc possessing the special qualities of a plant, drug, etc in concentrated form **b** an odour, perfume **c** one who or that which resembles an extract in possessing a quality in concentrated form — **in essence** in or by its very nature; essentially — **of the essence** of the utmost importance; essential

¹essential /i'sensh(ə)l/ *adj* **1** of or being (an) essence; inherent **2** of the utmost importance; basic, necessary – ~**ly** *adv*

²essential *n* sthg basic, indispensable, or fundamental

establish /i'stablish/ *v* **1** to make firm or stable **2** to enact permanently **3** to bring into existence; found **4a** to set on a firm basis; place (e g oneself) in a permanent or firm usu favourable position **b** to gain full recognition or acceptance of **5** to make (a church or religion) a national institution supported by civil authority **6** to put beyond doubt; prove **7** to cause (a plant) to grow and multiply in a place where previously absent

e'stablishment /-mənt/ *n* **1** sthg established: e g **1a** a usu large organization or institution **b** a place of business or residence with its furnishings and staff **2** an established order of society: e g **2a** *sing or pl in constr, often cap the* entrenched social, economic, and political leaders of a nation **b** *often cap* a controlling group

estate /i'stayt/ *n* **1** a social or political class (e g the nobility, clergy, or commons) **2a(1)** the whole of sby's real or personal property **a(2)** the assets and liabilities left by sby at death **b** a large landed property, esp in the country, usu with a large house on it **3** *Br* a part of an urban area devoted to a particular type of development ; *specif* one devoted to housing

e'state ˌagent *n, Br* **1** an agent who is involved in the buying and selling of land and property (e g houses) **2** one who manages an estate; a steward – **estate agency** *n*

e'state ˌcar *n, Br* a relatively large motor car with a nearly vertical rear door and 1 compartment in which both passengers and bulky luggage can be carried

[1]esteem /i'steem/ *n* favourable regard

[2]esteem *v* **1** to consider, deem **2** to set a high value on; regard highly and prize accordingly

ester /'estə/ *n* a (fragrant) compound formed by the reaction between an acid and an alcohol

estimable /'estiməbl/ *adj* worthy of esteem

[1]estimate /'estimayt/ *v* **1a** to judge approximately the value, worth, or significance of **b** to determine roughly the size, extent, or nature of **c** to produce a statement of the approximate cost of **2** to judge, conclude – **-tor** *n*

[2]estimate /'estimət/ *n* **1** the act of appraising or valuing; a calculation **2** an opinion or judgment of the nature, character, or quality of sby or sthg **3** a statement of the expected cost of a job

estimation /ˌesti'maysh(ə)n/ *n* **1** an opinion of the worth or character of sby or sthg **2** esteem

estrange /i'straynj/ *v* to alienate – usu + *from* – **~ment** *n*

estuary /'estyooəri/ *n* a water passage where the tide meets a river; *esp* a sea inlet at the mouth of a river

et al /ˌet 'al/ *adv* and others

et cetera /it 'setrə/ *adv* and other things, esp of the same kind; *broadly* and so forth

etch /ech/ *v* **1** to produce (e g a picture or letters), esp on a plate of metal or glass, by the corrosive action of an acid **2** to delineate or impress clearly – **~er** *n*

etching /'eching/ *n* **1** the art of producing pictures or designs by printing from an etched metal plate **2** an impression from an etched plate

eternal /i'tuhnl/ *adj* **1** having infinite duration; everlasting **2** incessant, interminable **3** timeless

eternal triangle *n* a conflict that results from the sexual attraction between 2 people of one sex and 1 person of the other

eternity /i'tuhnəti/ *n* **1** the quality or state of being eternal **2** infinite time **3** the eternal life after death **4** a (seemingly) endless or immeasurable time

ether /'eethə/ *n* **1** a medium formerly held to permeate all space and transmit electromagnetic waves (e g light and radio waves) **2** a volatile inflammable liquid used esp as a solvent and formerly as a general anaesthetic

ethereal /i'thiəri·əl; *sense 3* ˌethə'ree·əl/ *adj* **1** lacking material substance; light, delicate **2** of, resembling, or containing chemical ether – **~ly** *adv*

ethic /'ethik/ *n* **1** *pl but sing or pl in constr* inquiry into the nature and basis of moral principles and judgments **2** a set of moral principles or values **3** *pl but sing or pl in constr* the principles of conduct governing an individual or a group

ethical /'ethikl/ *also* **ethic** *adj* conforming to accepted, esp professional, standards of conduct or morality – **~ly** *adv*

[1]ethnic /'ethnik/ *adj* **1** of or being human races or large groups classed according to common traits **2** of an exotic, esp peasant, culture

[2]ethnic *n, chiefly NAm* a member of an ethnic (minority) group

ethnography /eth'nografi/ *n* ethnology; *specif* descriptive anthropology – **-pher** *n* – **-phic** *adj*

ethnology /eth'noləji/ *n* a science that deals with the various forms of social relationships (e g kinship, law, religion, etc) found in esp preliterate human societies – **-gist** *n* – **-gical** *adj*

ethyl alcohol *n* the main alcoholic component of beers, wines, spirits, etc

ethylene /'ethi,leen/ *n* an inflammable gaseous unsaturated hydrocarbon, found in coal gas and used esp in organic chemical synthesis

etiolate /'eeti·ə,layt, -tioh-/ *v* **1** to bleach and alter the natural development of (a green plant) by excluding sunlight **2** to make weak, pale, or sickly – **-lation** *n*

etiquette /'eti,ket/ *n* the conventionally accepted standards of proper social or professional behaviour

etymology /ˌeti'moləji/ *n* the history of the origin and development of a word or other linguistic form – **-gical** *adj* – **-gically** *adv* – **-gist** *n*

eucalyptus /ˌyoohkə'liptəs/ *n, pl* **eucalyptuses, eucalypti** /-'liptie/ any of a genus of mostly Australian evergreen trees of the myrtle family that are widely cultivated for their gums, resins, oils, and wood

Eucharist /'yoohkərist/ *n* (the bread and wine consecrated in) the Christian sacrament in which bread and wine, being or representing the body and blood of Christ, are ritually consumed in accordance with Christ's injunctions at the Last Supper – **~ic** *adj*

eu'genics *n pl but sing in constr* a science dealing with the improvement (e g by control of human mating) of the hereditary qualities of a race or breed – **eugenic** *adj* – **-ically** *adv*

eulogy /'yoohləji/ *n* 1 a (formal) speech or piece of writing in praise of a person or thing 2 high praise – **-gist** *n* – **-gistic** *adj* – **-gize** *v*

eunuch /'yoohnək/ *n* 1 a castrated man employed, esp formerly, in a harem or as a chamberlain in a palace 2 a man or boy deprived of the testes or external genitals

euphemism /'yoohfə,miz(ə)m/ *n* the substitution of a mild, indirect, or vague expression for an offensive or unpleasant one; *also* the expression so substituted – **-istic** *adj* – **-istically** *adv*

euphonious /yooh'fohnyəs, -ni·əs/ *adj* pleasing to the ear

euphonium /yooh'fohnyəm, -ni·əm/ *n* a brass instrument smaller than but resembling a tuba

euphony /'yoohfəni/ *n* a pleasing or sweet sound, esp in speech

euphoria /yooh'fawri·ə/ *n* an (inappropriate) feeling of well-being or elation – **euphoric** *adj* – **-ically** *adv*

euphuism /'yoohfyooh,iz(ə)m/ *n* an artificial and ornate style of writing or speaking

Eurasian /yooə'rayzh(ə)n, yoo'ray-/ *adj* 1 of, growing in, or living in Europe and Asia 2 of mixed European and Asian origin

eureka /yoo(ə)'reekə/ *interj* – used to express triumph at a discovery

¹European /,yooərə'pee·ən/ *adj* 1 native to Europe 2 of European descent or origin 3 concerned with or affecting (the whole of) Europe

²European *n* a native or inhabitant of (the mainland of) Europe

eu,stachian 'tube /yooh'stayshyən, -shən/ *n*, *often cap E* a tube connecting the middle ear with the pharynx that equalizes air pressure on both sides of the eardrum

euthanasia /,yoohthə'nayzyə, -zhə, -zi·ə/ *n* the act or practice of killing (hopelessly sick or injured) individuals for reasons of mercy

evacuate /i'vakyoo,ayt/ *v* 1a to empty 2a to remove, esp from a dangerous area b to vacate 3 to withdraw from a place in an organized way, esp for protection 4 to pass urine or faeces from the body – **-ation** *n*

evacuee /i,vakyoo'ee/ *n* a person evacuated from a dangerous place

evade /i'vayd/ *v* 1 to get away from or avoid, esp by deception 2a to avoid facing up to b to fail to pay 3 to baffle, foil

evaluate /i'valyoo,ayt/ *v* to determine the amount, value, or significance of – **-ation** *n*

evanescent /,evə'nes(ə)nt/ *adj* tending to dissipate or vanish like vapour – **-cence** *n*

evangelical /,eevan'jelikl/ *also* **evangelic** /-'jelik/ *adj* 1 of or in agreement with the Christian message as presented in the 4 Gospels 2 *often cap* Protestant; *specif* of the German Protestant church 3 *often cap* (of or being a usu Protestant denomination) emphasizing salvation by faith in the atoning death of Jesus Christ, personal conversion, and the authority of Scripture 4a of, adhering to, or marked by fundamentalism b low church 5 evangelistic, zealous

evangelist /i'vanjəlist/ *n* 1 *often cap* a writer of any of the 4 Gospels 2 one who evangelizes; *specif* a Protestant minister or layman who preaches at special services – **-lism** *n* – **-listic** *adj*

evangel·ize, -ise /i'vanjə,liez/ *v* to preach the Christian gospel, esp in order to make converts to Christianity

evaporate /i'vapərayt/ *v* 1a to pass off in vapour b to pass off or away; disappear, fade 2 to give out vapour 3 to convert into vapour – **-ration** *n*

evasion /i'vayzh(ə)n/ *n* an act, instance, or means of evading

evasive /i'vaysiv, -ziv/ *adj* tending or intended to evade; equivocal – ~**ly** *adv* – ~**ness** *n*

eve /eev/ *n* 1 the evening or the day before a special day, esp a religious holiday 2 the period immediately preceding an event 3 the evening – *chiefly poetic*

¹even /'eev(ə)n/ *n*, *archaic* the evening – poetic

²even *adj* 1a having a horizontal surface; flat, level b without break or irregularity; smooth c in the same plane or line – + **with** 2a without variation; uniform b level 3a equal; *also* fair b being in equilibrium 4 exactly divisible by 2 5 exact, precise – ~**ly** *adv* – ~**ness** *n*

³even *adv* 1 at the very time – + *as* 2a – used as an intensive to emphasize the contrast with a less strong possibility (e g can't *even* walk, let alone run) b – used as an intensive to emphasize the comparative degree — **even if** in spite of the possibility or fact that — **even now** 1 at this very moment 2 in spite of what has happened — **even so** in spite of that

⁴even *v* to make or become even – often + *up* or *out*

even'handed /-'handid/ *adj* fair, impartial

evening /'eevning/ *n* 1 the latter part of the day and the early part of the night; the time between sunset and bedtime 2 a late period (e g of time or life); the end

'evening ,dress *n* clothes for formal or semiformal evening occasions

'even,song /-,song/ *n*, *often cap* 1 vespers 2 an evening service of worship esp in the Church of England

event /i'vent/ *n* 1a a (noteworthy or important) happening or occurrence b a social occasion or activity 2 a contingency, case – esp in *in the event of* and *in the event that* 3 any of the contests in a sporting programme or tournament

eventual /i'ventyoo­əl, -chəl, -chooəl/ *adj* taking place at an unspecified later time; ultimately resulting

eventuality /i,ventyoo'aləti, -choo-/ *n* a possible, esp unwelcome, event or outcome

ever /'evə/ *adv* **1** always – now chiefly in certain phrases and in combination (e g an *ever*-growing need) **2** at any time – chiefly in negatives and questions (e g he won't *ever* do it) **3** – used as an intensive (e g looks *ever* so angry) — **ever so/such** *chiefly Br* very much — *infml*

¹**ever,green** /-,green/ *adj* **1** having leaves that remain green and functional through more than 1 growing season **2** always retaining freshness, interest, or popularity

²**evergreen** *n* an evergreen plant; *also* a conifer

everlasting /-'lahsting/ *adj* **1** lasting or enduring through all time **2a** continuing long or indefinitely; perpetual **b** *of a plant* retaining its form or colour for a long time when dried **3** lasting or wearing for a long time; durable

ever,more /-'maw/ *adv* **1** always, forever **2** in the future

every /'evri/ *adj* **1** being each member without exception, of a group larger than 2 (e g *every* word counts) **2** being each or all possible (e g was given *every* chance) **3** being once in each (e g go *every* third day) — **every now and then/again, every so often** at intervals; occasionally

every,body /-,bodi/ *pron* every person

every,day /-,day/ *adj* encountered or used routinely or typically; ordinary

every,thing /-,thing/ *pron* **1a** all that exists **b** all that is necessary or that relates to the subject **2** sthg of the greatest importance; all that counts

every,where /-,wea/ *adv or n* (in, at, or to) every place or the whole place

evict /i'vikt/ *v* **1a** to recover (property) from a person by a legal process **b** to remove (a tenant) from rented accommodation or land by a legal process **2** to force out — **~ion** *n*

¹**evidence** /'evid(ə)ns/ *n* **1** an outward sign; an indication **2** sthg, esp a fact, that gives proof or reasons for believing or agreeing with sthg; *specif* information used (by a tribunal) to arrive at the truth — **in evidence** to be seen; conspicuous

²**evidence** *v* to offer evidence of; show

evident /'evid(ə)nt/ *adj* clear to the vision or understanding — **~ly** *adv*

¹**evil** /'eevl/ *adj* **-ll-** (*NAm* **-l-, -ll-**) **1a** not good morally; sinful, wicked **b** arising from bad character or conduct **2a** causing discomfort or repulsion; offensive **b** disagreeable **3a** pernicious, harmful **b** marked by misfortune — **evilly** *adv*

²**evil** *n* **1** sthg evil; sthg that brings sorrow, distress, or calamity **2a** the fact of suffering, misfortune, or wrongdoing **b** wickedness, sin

evil 'eye *n* (a spell put on sby with) a look believed to be capable of inflicting harm

evince /i'vins/ *v* to show clearly; reveal – *fml*

eviscerate /i'visərayt/ *v* **1** to disembowel **2** to deprive of vital content or force – *fml* – **-ation** *n*

evoke /i'vohk/ *v* to call forth or up: e g **a** to conjure **b** to cite, esp with approval or for support; invoke **c** to bring to mind or recollection – **evocation** *n*

evolution /,eevə'loohsh(ə)n/ *n* **1a** a process of change and development, esp from a lower or simpler state to a higher or more complex state **b** a process of gradual and relatively peaceful social, political, economic, etc advance **2** the process of working out or developing **3a** the historical development of a biological group (e g a race or species) **b** a theory that the various types of animals and plants derived from preexisting types and that the distinguishable differences are due to natural selection – **~ary** *adj*

evolve /i'volv/ *v* **1a** to work out, develop **b** to produce by natural evolutionary processes **2** to undergo evolutionary change

ewe /yooh/ *n* the female of the (mature) sheep or a related animal

ewer /'yooh-ə/ *n* a wide-mouthed pitcher or jug; *esp* one used to hold water for washing or shaving

exacerbate /ek'sasəbayt, ig'za-/ *v* to make (sthg bad) worse; aggravate – **-bation** *n*

¹**exact** /ig'zakt/ *v* to demand and obtain by force, threats, etc; require – **~ion** *n*

²**exact** *adj* **1** exhibiting or marked by complete accordance with fact **2** marked by thorough consideration or minute measurement of small factual details – **~ness, ~itude** *n*

exacting /ig'zakting/ *adj* making rigorous demands; *esp* requiring careful attention and precise accuracy – **~ly** *adv*

exactly /ig'zaktli/ *adv* **1** altogether, entirely **2** quite so – used to express agreement

exaggerate /ig'zajərayt/ *v* **1** to say or believe more than the truth about **2** to make greater or more pronounced than normal; overemphasize – **~d** *adj* – **~dly** *adv* – **-ation** *n*

exalt /ig'zawlt/ *v* **1** to raise high, esp in rank, power, or character **2** to praise highly; glorify

exaltation /,egzawl'taysh(ə)n/ *n* an excessively intensified sense of well-being, power, or importance

examination /ig,zami'naysh(ə)n/ *n* **1** (an) examining **2** (the taking by a candidate for a university degree, Advanced level, Ordinary level, etc of) a set of questions designed to test knowledge **3** a formal interrogation (in a law court)

examine /ig'zamin/ *v* **1** to inspect closely; investigate **2a** to interrogate closely **b** to test (e g a candidate for a university degree) by an examination in order to determine knowledge – **-iner** *n*

example /ig'zahmpl/ *n* 1 sthg representative of all of the group or type to which it belongs 2 sby or sthg that may be copied by other people 3 (the recipient of) a punishment inflicted as a warning to others — **for example** as an example

exasperate /ig'zahspə,rayt/ *v* to anger or irritate (sby) – **-ration** *n* – **-ratedly** *adv* – **-ratingly** *adv*

excavate /'ekskəvayt/ *v* 1 to form by hollowing 2 to dig out and remove – **-vation** *n*

exceed /ik'seed/ *v* 1 to extend beyond 2 to be greater than or superior to 3 to act or go beyond the limits of

exceedingly /ik'seedingli/, **exceeding** *adv* very, extremely

excel /ik'sel/ *v* **-ll-** to be superior (to); surpass (others) in accomplishment or achievement – often + *at* or *in*

excellent /'eksəl(ə)nt/ *adj* outstandingly good – **-ence** *n* – **~ly** *adv*

[1]**except** /ik'sept/ *v* to take or leave out from a number or a whole; exclude

[2]**except** *also* **excepting** *prep* with the exclusion or exception of

[3]**except** *also* **excepting** *conj* 1 only, but (e g would go *except* it's too far) 2 unless (e g *except* you repent) – fml

exception /ik'sepsh(ə)n/ *n* 1 excepting or excluding 2 sby or sthg excepted; *esp* a case to which a rule does not apply 3 question, objection

ex'ceptionable /-əbl/ *adj* likely to cause objection; objectionable

exceptional /ik'sepsh(ə)nl/ *adj* 1 forming an exception; unusual 2 not average; *esp* superior – **~ly** *adv*

[1]**excerpt** /ek'suhpt/ *v* 1 to select (a passage) for quoting, copying, or performing 2 to take excerpts from (e g a book)

[2]**excerpt** /'ek,suhpt/ *n* a passage taken from a book, musical composition, etc

[1]**excess** /ik'ses/ *n* 1a the exceeding of usual, proper, or specified limits b the amount or degree by which one thing or quantity exceeds another 2 (an instance of) undue or immoderate indulgence; intemperance – **~ive** *adj* – **~ively** *adv* — **in excess of** more than

[2]**excess** /'ekses, ik'ses/ *adj* more than the usual, proper, or specified amount; extra

[1]**exchange** /iks'chaynj/ *n* 1 the act of exchanging one thing for another; a trade b a usu brief interchange of words or blows 2 sthg offered, given, or received in an exchange 3a (the system of settling, usu by bills of exchange rather than money) debts payable currently, esp in a foreign country b(1) change or conversion of one currency into another b(2) **exchange, exchange rate** the value of one currency in terms of another 4 a place where things or services are exchanged: e g 4a an organized market for trading in securities

or commodities b a centre or device controlling the connection of telephone calls between many different lines

[2]**exchange** *v* 1a to part with, give, or transfer in return for sthg received as an equivalent b *of* 2 *parties* to give and receive (things of the same type) 2 to replace by other goods 3 to engage in an exchange – **-able** *adj*

exchequer /iks'chekə/ *n* 1 *cap* a former civil court having jurisdiction primarily over revenue and now merged with the Queen's Bench Division 2 *often cap* the department of state in charge of the national revenue 3 the (national or royal) treasury

[1]**excise** /'ek,siez, ,-'-/ *n* 1 an internal tax levied on the manufacture, sale, or consumption of a commodity within a country 2 any of various taxes on privileges, often levied in the form of a licence that must be bought

[2]**excise** /ek'siez/ *v* to impose an excise on

[3]**excise** *v* to remove (as if) by cutting out – **-sion** *n*

excitable /ik'sietəbl/ *adj* capable of being readily activated or roused into a state of excitement or irritability; *specif* capable of being activated by and reacting to stimuli – **-bility** *n*

excite /ik'siet/ *v* 1 to provoke or stir up (action) 2 to rouse to strong, esp pleasurable, feeling 3 to arouse (e g an emotional response) – **~ment** *n*

exclaim /ik'sklaym/ *v* to cry out or speak in strong or sudden emotion

exclamation /,eksklə'maysh(ə)n/ *n* exclaiming or the words exclaimed

,**excla'mation ,mark** *n* a punctuation mark ! used esp after an interjection or exclamation

exclude /ik'skloohd/ *v* 1a to shut out b to bar from participation, consideration, or inclusion 2 to expel, esp from a place or position previously occupied – **-usion** *n*

[1]**exclusive** /ik'skloohsiv, -ziv/ *adj* 1a excluding or having power to exclude b limiting or limited to possession, control, use, etc by a single individual, group, etc 2a excluding others (considered to be inferior) from participation, membership, or entry b snobbishly aloof 3 stylish and expensive 4a sole b whole, undivided 5 not inclusive – **~ly** *adv* – **~ness** *n*

[2]**exclusive** *n* 1 a newspaper story printed by only 1 newspaper 2 an exclusive right (e g to sell a particular product in a certain area)

excommunicate /,ekskə'myoohni,kayt/ *v* 1 to deprive officially of the rights of church membership 2 to exclude from fellowship of a group or community – **excommunicate** *n*, *adj* – **-ation** *n*

excoriate /ik'skawriayt/ *v* 1 to wear away the skin of; abrade 2 to censure scathingly – fml – **-ation** *n*

excrement /'ekskrəmənt/ *n* faeces or other waste matter discharged from the body

excrescence /ik'skres(ə)ns/, **excrescency** /-si/ n an excessive or abnormal outgrowth or enlargement

excreta /ik'skreetə/ n pl excrement

excrete /ik'skreet/ v to separate and eliminate or discharge (waste) from blood or living tissue – **-tion** n

excruciating /ik'skroohshi,ayting/ adj agonizing, tormenting – **-ly** adv

exculpate /'ekskul,payt, ik'skul,payt/ v to clear from alleged fault, blame, or guilt – **-pation** n

excursion /ik'skuhsh(ə)n/ n 1 a (brief) pleasure trip, usu at reduced rates 2 a deviation from a direct, definite, or proper course; esp a digression

¹**excuse** /ik'skyoohz/ v 1a to make apology for b to try to remove blame from 2 to forgive entirely or overlook as unimportant 3 to allow to leave; dismiss 4 to be an acceptable reason for; justify – usu neg 5 Br to free from (a duty) – usu pass

²**excuse** /ik'skyoohs/ n 1 sthg offered as grounds for being excused 2 pl an expression of regret for failure to do sthg or esp for one's absence

ex-di'rectory adj, Br intentionally not listed in a telephone directory

execrable /'eksikrəbl/ adj detestable, appalling – chiefly fml – **-bly** adv

execrate /'eksi,krayt/ v 1 to declare to be evil or detestable; denounce 2 to detest utterly; abhor USE chiefly fml – **-cration** n

execute /'eksi,kyooht/ v 1 to carry out fully; put completely into effect 2 to put to death (legally) as a punishment 3 to make or produce (e g a work of art), esp by carrying out a design 4 to (do what is required to) make valid 5 to play, perform

execution /,eksi'kyoohsh(ə)n/ n 1 a putting to death as a punishment 2 a judicial writ directing the enforcement of a judgment 3 the act, mode, or result of performance

executioner /,eksi'kyoohsh(ə)nə/ n one who puts to death; specif one legally appointed to perform capital punishment

¹**executive** /ig'zekyootiv/ adj 1 concerned with making and carrying out laws, decisions, etc; specif, Br of or concerned with the detailed application of policy or law rather than its formulation 2 of, for, or being an executive

²**executive** n 1 the executive branch of a government 2 an individual or group that controls or directs an organization 3 one who holds a position of administrative or managerial responsibility

executor /'eksi,kyoohtə, ig'zekyoota/, fem **executrix** /ig'zekyoo,triks/ n pl **executors**, fem **executrices** /-,trieseez/ one appointed to carry out the provisions of a will

exemplary /ig'zempləri/ adj 1 deserving imitation; commendable 2 serving as a warning 3 serving as an example, instance, or illustration

exemplify /ig'zemplifie/ v 1 to show or illustrate by example 2 to be an instance of or serve as an example of; typify, embody – **-fication** n

¹**exempt** /ig'zempt/ adj freed from some liability or requirement to which others are subject – ~**ion** n

²**exempt** v to make exempt; excuse

¹**exercise** /'eksə,siez/ n 1 the use of a specified power or right 2 bodily exertion for the sake of developing and maintaining physical fitness 3 sthg performed or practised in order to develop, improve, or display a specific power or skill

²**exercise** v 1 to make effective in action; use, exert 2a to use repeatedly in order to strengthen or develop b to train (e g troops) by drills and manoeuvres 3 to engage the attention and effort of

exert /ig'zuht/ v 1 to bring (e g strength or authority) to bear 2 to take upon (oneself) the effort of doing sthg – ~**ion** n

exeunt /'eksi,oont/ – used as a stage direction to specify that all or certain named characters leave the stage

ex gratia /,eks 'graysh(i)ə/ adj or adv as a favour; not compelled by legal right

exhale /eks'hayl, ig'zayl/ v to breathe out – **-lation** n

¹**exhaust** /ig'zawst/ v 1 to empty by drawing off the contents; specif to create a vacuum in 2a to consume entirely; use up b to tire out 3 to develop or deal with to the fullest possible extent

²**exhaust** n 1 (the escape of) used gas or vapour from an engine 2 the conduit or pipe through which used gases escape

exhaustion /ig'zawschən/ n extreme tiredness

exhaustive /ig'zawstiv/ adj comprehensive, thorough – ~**ly** adv – ~**ness** n

¹**exhibit** /ig'zibit/ v 1 to reveal, manifest 2 to show publicly, esp for purposes of competition or demonstration – ~**or** n

²**exhibit** n 1 sthg exhibited 2 sthg produced as evidence in a lawcourt

exhibition /,eksi'bish(ə)n/ n 1 a public showing (e g of works of art or objects of manufacture) 2 Br a grant drawn from the funds of a school or university to help to maintain a student

exhi'bitionism /-iz(ə)m/ n 1 a perversion marked by a tendency to indecent exposure 2 behaving so as to attract attention to oneself – ~**ist** n – **-istic** adj

exhilarate /ig'zilərayt/ v 1 to make cheerful 2 to enliven, invigorate – **-ration** n

exhort /ig'zawt/ v to urge or advise strongly – ~**ation** n

exhume /eks'hyoohm, ek'syoohm, ik-/ v 1 to dig up again after burial 2 to bring back from neglect or obscurity – **exhumation** n

exigency /'eksij(ə)nsi, ig'zij(ə)nsi/, **exigence** /' eksij(ə)ns, 'egz-/ *n* such need or necessity as belongs to the occasion; a requirement – usu pl with sing meaning *USE* fml – **exigent** *adj* – **exigently** *n*

exiguous /ig'zigyoo·əs/ *adj* excessively scanty; inadequate, meagre – fml – ~**ly** *adv* – ~**ness** *n*

exile /'eksiel/ *n* 1 enforced or voluntary absence from one's country or home 2 a person who is exiled – **exile** *v*

exist /ig'zist/ *v* 1 to have being esp in specified conditions 2 to continue to be 3a to have life b to live at an inferior level or under adverse circumstances

existence /ig'zist(ə)ns/ *n* 1a the totality of existent things b the state or fact of existing; life 2 manner of living or being

existent /ig'zist(ə)nt/ *adj* 1 having being; existing 2 extant

existential /,egzi'stensh(ə)l/ *adj* 1 of or grounded in existence 2 existentialist

existentialism /-,iz(ə)m/ *n* a philosophical movement characterized by inquiry into human beings' experience of themselves in relation to the world, esp with reference to their freedom, responsibility, and isolation – **list** *adj*, *n*

¹**exit** /'eksit, 'egzit/ – used as a stage direction to specify who goes off stage

²**exit** *n* 1 a departure of a performer from a scene 2 the act of going out or away 3 a way out of an enclosed place or space

Exocet /'eksoh,set/ *trademark* – used for an air- or ground-launched radar-guided missile, deployed esp in attacks on ships

exodus /'eksədəs/ *n* a mass departure; an emigration

exonerate /ig'zonərayt/ *v* to free from blame *USE* usu + *from* – **ration** *n*

exorbitant /ig'zawbit(ə)nt/ *adj*, *of prices, demands, etc* much greater than is reasonable; excessive – **tance** *n* – ~**ly** *adv*

exorcise, -ize /'eksaw,siez/ *v* to free a place, person , etc from an evil spirit; *also* to expel an evil spirit – **ism** *n* – **ist** *n*

exoskeleton /,eksoh'skelitn/ *n* an external supportive (hard or bony) covering of an animal

exotic /ig'zotik/ *adj* 1 introduced from another country; not native to the place where found 2 strikingly or excitingly different or unusual – ~**ally** *adv* – ~**ism** *n*

expand /ik'spand/ *v* 1 to increase the size, extent, number, volume, or scope of 2 to express in detail or in full 3 to grow easier, more benign; become more sociable – ~**able** *adj* – **expansion** *n*

expanse /ik'spans/ *n* 1 sthg spread out, esp over a wide area 2 the extent to which sthg is spread out

expansive /ik'spansiv/ *adj* 1 having a capacity or tendency to expand or cause expansion 2 genial, effusive 3 having wide expanse or extent – ~**ly** *adv* – ~**ness** *n*

¹**expatriate** /eks'patriayt/ *v* 1 to exile, banish 2 to withdraw (oneself) from residence in or allegiance to one's native country

²**expatriate** /,eks'patri·ət/ *n* one who lives in a foreign country

expect /ik'spekt/ *v* 1 to anticipate or look forward to 2 to be pregnant 3a to consider an event probable or certain b to consider reasonable, due, or necessary 4 to suppose, think

expectant /ik'spekt(ə)nt/ *adj* 1 characterized by expectation 2 *of a pregnant woman* expecting the birth of a child

expectation /,ekspek'taysh(ə)n/ *n* 1 expecting or sthg expected 2 prospects of inheritance – usu pl with sing meaning

expectorate /ik'spektərayt/ *v* to spit (e g saliva) – **ation** *n* – **ant** *n or adj*

expediency /ik'speedi·ənsi, -dyənsi/ *n* 1 suitability, fitness 2 use of expedient means and methods 3 an expedient

¹**ex'pedient** /-ənt/ *adj* 1 suitable for achieving a particular end 2 concerned with what is opportune rather than with what is moral – ~**ly** *adv*

²**expedient** *n* a means to an end; *esp* one devised or used in case of urgent need

expedite /'ekspi,diet/ *v* to hasten the process or progress of; facilitate

expedition /,ekspi'dish(ə)n/ *n* 1 a journey or excursion undertaken for a specific purpose (e g for war or exploration) 2 efficient promptness; speed

expeditionary /-ri/ *adj* sent on military service abroad

expeditious /-shəs/ *adj* speedy – ~**ly** *adv*

expel /ik'spel/ *v* -**ll**- 1 to drive or force out 2 to drive away; *esp* to deport 3 to cut off from membership

expend /ik'spend/ *v* 1 to pay out 2 to consume (e g time, care, or attention)

ex'pendable /-dəbl/ *adj* 1 normally used up in service; not intended to be kept or reused 2 regarded as available for sacrifice or destruction in order to accomplish an objective

expenditure /ik'spendichə/ *n* 1 the act or process of expending 2 the amount expended

expense /ik'spens/ *n* 1a financial burden or outlay b *pl* the charges incurred by an employee in performing his/her duties c an item of business outlay chargeable against revenue in a specific period 2 a cause or occasion of usu high expenditure — **at somebody's expense** in a manner that causes sby to be ridiculed — **at the expense of** to the detriment of

expensive /ik'spensiv/ *adj* **1** involving great expense **2** commanding a high price; dear – ~**ly** *adv*

experience /ik'spiəri·əns/ *n* **1** the usu conscious perception or apprehension of reality or of an external, bodily, or mental event **2** (the knowledge, skill, or practice derived from) direct participation or observation **3** sthg personally encountered or undergone – **experience** *v*

ex'perienced *adj* skilful or wise as a result of experience

experiment /ik'sperimənt/ *n* **1** a tentative procedure or policy that is on trial **2** an operation carried out under controlled conditions in order to test or establish a hypothesis or to illustrate a known law – ~**al** *adj*

expert /'ekspuht/ *n or adj* (sby or sthg) having or showing special skill or knowledge derived from training or experience – ~**ly** *adv* – ~**ness** *n*

expertise /ˌekspuh'teez/ *n* skill in or knowledge of a particular field; know-how

expiate /'ekspi·ayt/ *v* **1** to eradicate the guilt incurred by (e g a sin) **2** to make amends for – ~**ation** *n*

expiration /ˌekspiə·ə'raysh(ə)n, -spi-/ *n* **1** the release of air from the lungs through the nose or mouth **2** expiry, termination

expire /ik'spie·ə/ *v* **1** to come to an end **2** to emit the breath **3** to die – **expiry** *n*

explain /ik'splayn/ *v* **1** to make sthg plain or understandable **2** to give the reason for or cause of – ~**er** *n* — **explain oneself** to clarify one's statements or the reasons for one's conduct

explanation /ˌekspls'naysh(ə)n/ *n* the act or process of explaining; sthg, esp a statement, that explains

explanatory /ik'splanət(ə)ri/ *adj* serving to explain

expletive /ek'spleetiv/ *n* a usu meaningless exclamatory word or phrase; *specif* one that is obscene or profane

explicable /'eksplikəbl, ek'splikəbl/ *adj* capable of being explained – **bly** *adv*

explicate /'eksplikayt/ *v* **1** to give a detailed explanation of **2** to analyse logically – **ation** *n* – **atory, -ative** *adj*

explicit /ik'splisit/ *adj* clear, unambiguous ; *also* graphically frank – ~**ly** *adv* – ~**ness** *n*

explode /ik'splohd/ *v* **1** to give expression to sudden, violent, and usu noisy emotion **2** to burst or expand violently as a result of pressure, or a rapid chemical reaction **3** to bring (e g a belief or theory) into discredit by demonstrating falsity

[1]**exploit** /'eksployt/ *n* a deed, act; *esp* a notable or heroic one

[2]**exploit** /ik'sployt/ *v* **1** to turn to economic account ; *also* to utilize **2** to take unfair advantage of for financial or other gain – ~**ation** *n* – ~**er** *n*

explore /ik'splaw/ **1** to make or conduct a search **2** to travel into or through for purposes of geographical discovery – ~**r** *n* – **-ration** *n*

explosion /ik'splohzh(ə)n/ *n* **1** (a noise caused by something) exploding **2** a rapid large-scale expansion, increase, or upheaval **3** a sudden violent outburst of emotion

[1]**explosive** /ik'splohsiv, -ziv/ *adj* **1** threatening to burst forth with sudden violence or noise **2** tending to arouse strong reactions – ~**ly** *adv* – ~**ness** *n*

[2]**explosive** *n* an explosive substance

exponent /ik'spohnənt/ *n* **1** a symbol written above and to the right of a mathematical expression to indicate the operation of raising to a power **2a** sby or sthg that expounds or interprets **b** sby who advocates or exemplifies *USE* (2) usu + *of*

export /ik'spawt/ *v* to carry or send a commodity to another country for purposes of trade – ~**able** *adj* – ~**ation** *n* – ~**er** *n* – **export** *n*

expose /ik'spohz/ *v* **1** to submit or subject to an action or influence; *specif* to subject (a photographic film, plate, or paper) to the action of radiant energy **2a** to exhibit for public veneration **b** to engage in indecent exposure of (oneself) **3** to bring (sthg shameful) to light

exposé, expose /ek'spohzay (*Fr* ɛkspoze)/ *n* **1** a formal recital or exposition of facts; a statement **2** an exposure of sthg discreditable

exposition /ˌekspo'zish(ə)n/ *n* **1a** a detailed explanation or elucidation, esp of sthg difficult to understand **b** the first part of a musical composition in which the theme is presented **2** a usu international public exhibition or show (e g of industrial products)

expostulate /ik'spostyoolayt, -chəlayt/ *v* to reason earnestly *with* sby in order to dissuade or remonstrate – **-lation** *n*

exposure /ik'spohzh(ə)/ *n* **1a** a disclosure, esp of a weakness or sthg shameful or criminal **b(1)** the act of exposing a sensitized photographic film, plate, or paper; *also* the duration of such an exposure **b(2)** a section of a film with 1 picture on it **2a** being exposed, specif to the elements **b** the specified direction in which a building, room, etc faces

expound /ik'spownd/ *v* to set forth, esp in careful or elaborate detail

[1]**express** /ik'spres/ *adj* **1** firmly and explicitly stated **2a** travelling at high speed **b** to be delivered without delay by special messenger

[2]**express** *n* **1** an express vehicle **2** express mail

[3]**express** *v* **1** to state **2** to make known the opinions, feelings, etc of (oneself) **3** to represent by a sign or symbol

expression /ik'spresh(ə)n/ *n* **1a** expressing, esp in words **b** a significant word or phrase **2a** a means or manner of expressing sthg; *esp* sensitivity and feeling in communicating or performing **b** facial aspect or vocal intonation indicative of feeling – ~**less** adj

ex·pression·ism /-,iz(ə)m/ n a mode of artistic expression that attempts to depict the artist's subjective emotions and responses to objects and events – **expressionist** n, adj

expressive /ik'spresiv/ adj **1** of expression **2** serving to express or represent **3** full of expression; significant – ~**ly** adv – ~**ness** n

expressly /ik'spresli/ adv **1** explicitly **2** for the express purpose; specially

expropriate /ek'sprohpri,ayt/ v **1** to dispossess **2** to transfer to one's own possession – **-ation** n – **-ator** n

expulsion /ik'spulsh(ə)n/ n expelling or being expelled

expunge /ik'spunj/ v to strike out; obliterate, erase

expurgate /'ekspuh,gayt/ v to remove objectionable parts from, before publication or presentation – **-gation** n

exquisite /ik'skwizit, 'ekskwizit/ adj **1a** marked by flawless delicate craftsmanship **b** keenly sensitive, esp in feeling **2a** extremely beautiful; delightful **b** acute, intense – ~**ly** adv – ~**ness** n

extant /ek'stant/ adj still or currently existing

extemporaneous /ik,stempə'raynyəs, -ni·əs/ adj **1** done, spoken, performed, etc on the spur of the moment **2** makeshift – ~**ly** adv – ~**ness** n

extempore /ik'stempəri/ adj or adv (spoken or done) in an extemporaneous manner

ex·tempor·ize, -ise /ik'stempə,riez/ v to speak, perform, etc without prior preparation; improvise

extend /ik'stend/ v **1** to stretch out in distance, space, or time **2** to exert (e g a horse or oneself) to full capacity **3** to give or offer, usu in response to need; proffer **4a** to reach in scope or application **b** to prolong in time **c** to advance, further **5** to increase the scope, meaning, or application of

extension /ik'stensh(ə)n/ n **1a** extending or being extended **b** sthg extended **2** extent, scope **3a** a straightening of (a joint between the bones of) a limb **4** an increase in length of time **5a** a part added (e g to a building) **b** an extra telephone connected to the principal line

extensive /ik'stensiv, -ziv/ adj having wide or considerable extent – ~**ly** adv – ~**ness** n

extent /ik'stent/ n **1** the range or distance over which sthg extends **2** the point or limit to which sthg extends

extenuate /ik'stenyoo,ayt/ v to (try to) lessen the seriousness or extent of (e g a crime) by giving excuses – **-tion** n

¹**exterior** /ik'stiari·ə/ adj **1** on the outside or an outside surface; external **2** suitable for use on outside surfaces

²**exterior** n **1** an exterior part or surface; outside **2** an outward manner or appearance

exterminate /ik'stuhmi,nayt/ v to destroy completely; esp to kill all of – **-nation** n

¹**external** /ik'stuhnl/ adj **1a** superficial **b** not intrinsic or essential **2** of, connected with, or intended for the outside or an outer part **3a(1)** situated outside, apart, or beyond **a(2)** arising or acting from outside **b** of dealings with foreign countries **c** having existence independent of the mind – ~**ly** adj

²**external** n an external feature or aspect – usu pl

extinct /ik'stingkt/ adj no longer active, alive, or in operation

extinction /ik'stingksh(ə)n/ n making or being extinct or (causing to be) extinguished

extinguish /ik'sting·gwish/ v **1a** to cause to cease burning; quench **b** to bring to an end **2** to make void

extirpate /'ekstuh,payt/ v to destroy completely (as if) by uprooting; annihilate – **-pation** n

extol, NAm also **extoll** /ik'stohl, -'stol/ v **-ll-** to praise highly; glorify

extort /ik'stawt/ v to obtain from sby by force or threats

extortion /ik'stawsh(ə)n/ n the unlawful extorting of money – ~**er**, ~**ist** n

extortionate /ik'stawsh(ə)nət/ adj excessive, exorbitant – ~**ly** adv

¹**extra** /'ekstrə/ adj **1** more than is due, usual, or necessary; additional **2** subject to an additional charge

²**extra** n sthg or sby extra or additional: e g **a** an added charge to a specified edition of a newspaper **c** a run in cricket (e g a bye, leg bye, no-ball, or wide) that is not credited to a batsman's score **d** an additional worker; specif one hired to act in a group scene in a film or stage production

³**extra** adv beyond or above the usual size, extent, or amount

¹**extract** /ik'strakt/ v **1** to draw forth or pull out, esp with effort **2** to withdraw (e g a juice or fraction) by physical or chemical process **3** to separate (a metal) from an ore **4** to excerpt

²**extract** /'ekstrakt/ n an excerpt

extraction /ik'straksh(ə)n/ n **1** ancestry, origin **2** sthg extracted

extracurricular /,ekstrəkə'rikyoolə/ adj **1** not falling within the scope of a regular curriculum **2** lying outside one's normal activities

extradite /'ekstrə,diet/ v to return (someone accused of a crime) to the country in which the crime took place for trial – **-dition** n

extramural /,ekstrə'myooərəl/ adj **1** outside (the walls or boundaries of) a place or organization **2** chiefly Br of courses or facilities offered by a university or college to those who are not regular full-time students

extraneous /ik'straynyəs, -ni-əs/ *adj* 1 on or coming from the outside 2 not forming an essential or vital part; irrelevant – ~**ly** *adv*

extraordinary /ik'strawdin(ə)ri/ *adj* 1 exceptional; remarkable 2 on or for a special function or service – **rily** *adv*

extrapolate /ek'strapə,layt/ *v* to use or extend (known data or experience) in order to surmise or work out sthg unknown – ~**ation** *n*

extraterrestrial /,ekstrətə'restri-əl/ *adj* originating, existing, or occurring outside the earth or its atmosphere

ex'travagant /-gənt/ *adj* 1 excessive 2a wasteful, esp of money b profuse – ~**ance** *n* – ~**ly** *adv*

extravaganza /ik,stravə'ganzə/ *n* a lavish or spectacular show or event

extravert /'ekstrə,vuht/ *n or adj* (an) extrovert

¹**extreme** /ik'streem/ *adj* 1a existing in a very high degree b not moderate c exceeding the usual or expected 2 situated at the farthest possible point from a centre or the nearest to an end 3 most advanced or thoroughgoing – ~**ly** *adv*

²**extreme** *n* 1 sthg situated at or marking one or other extreme point of a range 2 a very pronounced or extreme degree 3 an extreme measure or expedient — **in the extreme** to the greatest possible extent

extremism /ik'stree,miz(ə)m/ *n* advocacy of extreme political measures; radicalism – **extremist** *n, adj*

extremity /ik'streməti/ *n* 1a the most extreme part, point, or degree b a (human) hand, foot, or other limb 2 a drastic or desperate act or measure

extricate /'ekstri,kayt/ *v* to disentangle, esp with considerable effort – **cable** *adj* – **cation** *n*

extrinsic /ek'strinsik, -zik/ *adj* 1 not forming part of or belonging to a thing; extraneous 2 originating from or on the outside – ~**ally** *adv*

extrovert *also* **extravert** /'ekstrə,vuht/ *n* one whose interests are directed outside the self; *broadly* an outgoing boisterous person

extrude /ik'stroohd/ *v* 1 to force or push out 2 to shape (e g metal or plastic) by forcing through a die – **extrusion** *n*

exuberant /ig'zyoohb(ə)rənt/ *adj* 1 joyously unrestrained; flamboyant 2 abundant, luxuriant – **ance** *n* – ~**ly** *adv*

exude /ig'zyoohd/ *v* 1 to ooze out 2 to radiate an air of

exult /ig'zult/ *v* to be extremely joyful; rejoice openly – usu + *at, in,* or *over* – ~**ant** *adj* – ~**antly** *adv* – ~**ation** *n*

¹**eye** /ie/ *n* 1a any of various usu paired organs of sight b the faculty of seeing c a gaze, glance 2a the hole through the head of a needle b a loop; *esp* one of metal or thread into which a hook is inserted c an undeveloped bud (e g on a potato) d a calm area in the centre of a tropical cyclone e the (differently coloured or marked) centre of a flower 3 the direction from which the wind is blowing – ~**less** *adj* — **in the eye/eyes of** in the judgment or opinion of — **my eye** — used to express mild disagreement or sometimes surprise; *infml* — **set/clap eyes on** to catch sight of — **with an eye to** having as an aim or purpose

²**eye** *v* **eyeing, eying** to watch closely

'**eye,ball** *n* the capsule of the eye of a vertebrate together with the structures it contains

'**eye,brow** *n* (hair growing on) the ridge over the eye

'**eye,lash** *n* (a single hair of) the fringe of hair edging the eyelid

'**eyelet** /-lit/ *n* a small usu reinforced hole designed so that a cord, lace, etc may be passed through it

'**eye,lid** *n* a movable lid of skin and muscle that can be closed over the eyeball

'**eye,liner** *n* a cosmetic for emphasizing the contours of the eyes

'**eye-,opener** *n* sthg surprising and esp revelatory – *infml*

'**eye,piece** *n* the lens or combination of lenses at the eye end of an optical instrument

'**eye ,shadow** *n* a coloured cream or powder applied to the eyelids to accentuate the eyes

'**eye,sore** *n* sthg offensive to the sight

,**eye'tooth** *n* a canine tooth of the upper jaw

'**eye,wash** *n* deceptive statements or actions; rubbish, claptrap – *infml*

'**eye,witness** *n* one who sees an occurrence and can bear witness to it (e g in court)

eyrie /'iəri, 'eəri, 'ie-əri/ *n* the nest of a bird of prey on a cliff or mountain top

F

f /ef/ *n, pl* **f's, fs** *often cap* 1 (a graphic representation or device for reproducing) the 6th letter of the English alphabet 2 a speech counterpart of written *f*

fa, fah /fah/ *n* the 4th note of the diatonic scale in solmization

fable /'faybl/ *n* 1 a legendary story of supernatural happenings 2 a fictitious account 3 a story conveying a moral; *esp* one in which animals speak and act like human beings

fabric /'fabrik/ *n* 1a the basic structure of a building b an underlying structure; a framework 2 cloth

'**fabricate** /-kayt/ *v* 1 to construct or manufacture from many parts 2 to invent or create, esp in order to deceive – **tion** *n*

fabulous /'fabyoolas/ adj 1 extraordinary, incredible 2 told in or based on fable 3 marvellous, great – infml

facade also **façade** /fə'sahd/ n 1 a face, esp the front or principal face, of a building given special architectural treatment 2 a false or superficial appearance

¹**face** /fays/ n 1 the front part of the (human) head including the chin, mouth, nose, eyes, etc and usu the forehead 2 a facial expression; specif a grimace 3a an outward appearance b effrontery, impudence c dignity, reputation 4a a front, upper, or outer surface b an exposed surface of rock c the right side (e g of cloth or leather) 5 the exposed working surface of a mine or excavation — **in the face of/in face of** in opposition to; despite — **to someone's face** candidly in sby's presence and to his/her knowledge

²**face** v 1 to meet or deal with firmly and without evasion 2 to cover the front or surface of 3 to have the face towards; also to turn the face in a specified direction — **face the music** to confront and endure the unpleasant consequences of one's actions — **face up to** to confront without shrinking — **face with** to confront with

'**face,cloth** n a flannel

faceless /-lis/ adj lacking identity; anonymous

'**face-,lift** n 1 plastic surgery to remove facial defects (e g wrinkles) typical of aging 2 an alteration intended to improve appearance or utility

face out v to confront defiantly or impudently

facet /'fasit/ n 1 a small plane surface (e g of a cut gem or an insect's eye) 2 any of the aspects from which sthg specified may be considered

facetious /fə'seeshas/ adj flippant – **~ly** adv – **~ness** n

¹**facial** /'faysh(a)l/ adj of the face – **~ly** adv

²**facial** n a facial beauty treatment

facile /'fasiel/ adj 1 easily or readily accomplished or performed 2 specious, superficial – **~ly** adv – **~ness** n

facilitate /fə'silitayt/ v to make easier – fml – **-tation** n

facility /fə'silati/ n 1 the ability to perform sthg easily; aptitude 2 sthg (e g equipment) that promotes the ease of an action or operation – usu pl

facing /'faysing/ n 1a a lining at the edge of sthg, esp a garment, for stiffening or ornament b pl the collar, cuffs, and trimmings of a uniform coat 2 an ornamental or protective layer

facsimile /fak'simali/ n an exact copy, esp of printed material

fact /fakt/ n 1a a thing done; esp a criminal act 2 the quality of having actual existence in the real world; also sthg having such existence 3 an event, esp as distinguished from its legal effect 4 a piece of information presented as having objective reality — **in fact** 1 really 2 briefly

faction /'faksh(a)n/ n 1 a party or minority group within a party or group 2 dissension with a party or group

fact of 'life n, pl **facts of life** pl the processes and behaviour involved in (human) sex and reproduction

factor /'fakta/ n 1 one who acts for another; an agent 2 a condition, force, or fact that actively contributes to a result 3 any of the numbers or symbols that when multiplied together form a product – **~ize** v

factory /'fakt(a)ri/ n a building or set of buildings with facilities for manufacturing

factotum /fak'tohtam/ n a servant employed to carry out many types of work

factual /'faktyooal, -chooal/ adj 1 of facts 2 restricted to or based on fact – **~ly** adv

faculty /'fakalti/ n 1 an inherent capability, power, or function of the body 2 a group of related subject departments in a university

fad /fad/ n 1 a usu short-lived but enthusiastically pursued practice or interest; a craze 2 an personal or eccentric taste or habit – **~dish** adj – **~dishly** adv

fade /fayd/ v 1 to lose freshness or vigour; wither 2 of a brake to lose braking power gradually, esp owing to prolonged use 3 to lose freshness or brilliance of colour 4 to disappear gradually; vanish – often + **away**

faeces, NAm chiefly **feces** /'feeseez/ n pl bodily waste discharged through the anus – **faecal** adj

¹**fag** /fag/ n 1 a British public-school pupil who acts as servant to an older schoolmate 2 chiefly Br a tiring or boring task – infml

²**fag** n a cigarette – infml

'**fag ,end** n 1 a poor or worn-out end; a remnant 2 the extreme end USE infml

faggot /'fagat/ n 1 NAm chiefly **fagot** 1a a bundle of sticks b a round mass of minced meat (e g pig's liver) mixed with herbs and usu breadcrumbs 2 chiefly NAm a usu male homosexual – derog

Fahrenheit /'faran,hiet/ adj relating to, conforming to, or being a scale of temperature on which water freezes at 32° and boils at 212° under standard conditions

¹**fail** /fayl/ v 1a to lose strength; weaken b to fade or die away c to stop functioning 2a to fall short b to be unsuccessful (e g in passing a test) c to become bankrupt or insolvent 3a to disappoint the expectations or trust of b to prove inadequate for 4 to leave undone; neglect

²**fail** n 1 failure – chiefly in without fail 2 an examination failure

¹**failing** /'fayling/ n a usu slight or insignificant defect in character; broadly a fault, imperfection

²**failing** prep in absence or default of

'**fail ,safe** /-,sayf/ adj designed so as to counteract automatically the effect of an anticipated possible source of failure

fai
214

failure /'faylya/ *n* **1** a failing to perform a duty or expected action **2** lack of success **3a** a falling short; a deficiency **b** deterioration, decay **4** sby or sthg unsuccessful

¹**faint** /faynt/ *adj* **1** cowardly, timid – chiefly in *faint heart* **2** weak, dizzy, and likely to faint **3** feeble **4** lacking distinctness; *esp* dim – **~ly** *adv* – **~ness** *n*

²**faint** *v* to lose consciousness because of a temporary decrease in the blood supply to the brain (e g through exhaustion or shock) – **faint** *n*

¹**fair** /fea/ *adj* **1** attractive, beautiful **2** superficially pleasing **3** clean, clear **4** not stormy or foul; fine **5a** free from self-interest or prejudice; honest **b** conforming with the established rules; allowed **6** light in colour; blond **7** moderately good or large; adequate – **~ness** *n* – **in a fair way** to likely to

²**fair** *n* **1** a periodic gathering of buyers and sellers at a particular place and time for trade or a competitive exhibition, usu accompanied by entertainment and amusements **2** *Br* a fun fair

,**fair 'game** *n* sby or sthg open to legitimate pursuit, attack, or ridicule

¹**fair,ground** /-,grownd/ *n* an area where outdoor fairs, circuses, or exhibitions are held

¹**fairly** /-li/ *adv* **1** completely, quite **2** properly, impartially, or honestly **3** to a full degree or extent **4** for the most part

¹**fair,way** /-,way/ *n* **1** a navigable channel in a river, bay, or harbour **2** the mowed part of a golf course between a tee and a green

fairy /'feari/ *n* a small mythical being having magic powers and usu human form

¹**fairy-,tale** *adj* marked by **a** unusual grace or beauty **b** apparently magical success or good fortune

¹**fairy ,tale** *n* **1** a story which features supernatural or imaginary forces and beings **2** a made-up story, usu designed to mislead – **fairy-tale** *adj*

fait accompli /,fayt ə'kompli, ,fet əkom'pli (*Fr* fεt akɔ̃pli)/ *n, pl* **faits accomplis** /~/ sthg already accomplished and considered irreversible

faith /fayth/ *n* **1a** allegiance to duty or a person; loyalty – chiefly in *good/ bad faith* **b** fidelity to one's promises – chiefly in *keep/ break faith* **2a** belief and trust in and loyalty to God or the doctrines of a religion **b** complete confidence **3** sthg believed with strong conviction; *esp* a system of religious beliefs

¹**faithful** /-f(ə)l/ *adj* **1** showing faith; loyal; *specif* loyal to one's spouse in having no sexual relations outside marriage **2** firm in adherence to promises or in observance of duty **3** true to the facts; accurate – **~ness** *n* – **~ly** *adv*

²**faithful** *n pl* **1** the full church members **2** the body of adherents of a religion (e g Islam) **3** loyal followers or members

¹**faithless** /-lis/ *adj* **1a** lacking esp religious faith **b** disloyal **2** untrustworthy – **~ly** *adv* – **~ness** *n*

¹**fake** /fayk/ *n* any of the loops of a coiled rope or cable

²**fake** *v* **1** to alter or treat so as to impart a false character or appearance; falsify **2a** to counterfeit, simulate **b** to feign

³**fake** *n* a worthless imitation passed off as genuine **2** a hypocrite, charlatan

⁴**fake** *adj* counterfeit, phoney

fakir /'faykiə, fə'kiə, 'fahkiə, -kə/ *n* **1** a Muslim mendicant **2** a wandering Hindu ascetic holy man

falcon /'faw(l)kən/ *n* any of various hawks distinguished by long wings

¹**falconer** /-nə/ *n* one who hunts with hawks or who breeds or trains hawks for hunting – **falconry** *n*

¹**fall** /fawl/ *v* fell /fel/; **fallen** /'fawlən/ **1a** to descend freely (as if) by the force of gravity **b** to hang freely **2a** to become less or lower in degree, rank, pitch, or volume **b** to be uttered; issue **c** to look down **3a** to come down from an erect to a usu prostrate position suddenly and esp involuntarily **b** to enter an undesirable state, esp unavoidably or unwittingly **c** to drop because wounded or dead; *esp* to die in battle – *euph* **d** to lose office **4a** to yield to temptation; sin **b** *of a woman* to lose one's virginity, esp outside marriage **5a** to move or extend in a downward direction – often + *off* or *away* **b** to decline in quality or quantity; abate, subside – often + *off* or *away* **c** to assume a look of disappointment or dismay **d** to decline in financial value **6a** to occur at a specified time or place **b** to come (as if) by chance – + *in* or *into* **c** to come or pass by lot, assignment, or inheritance; devolve – usu + *on, to,* or *upon* **7** to come within the limits, scope, or jurisdiction of sthg **8** to begin heartily or actively – usu + *to* **9** to fall in love with – + *for* **10** to be deceived by – + *for* — **fall behind** to fail to keep up (with) — **fall between two stools** to fail because of inability to choose between or reconcile **2** alternative or conflicting courses of action — **fall flat** to produce no response or result — **fall for 1** to fall in love with **2** to be deceived by — **fall foul of** to arouse aversion in; clash with — **fall on/upon 1** to descend upon; attack **2** to meet with **3** to hit on — **fall over oneself** to display almost excessive eagerness — **fall short** to fail to attain a goal or target

²**fall** *n* **1** the act of falling by the force of gravity **2a** a falling out, off, or away; a dropping **b** sthg or a quantity that falls or has fallen **3a** a loss of greatness or power; a collapse **b** the surrender or capture of a besieged place *c often cap* mankind's loss of innocence through the disobedience of Adam and Eve **4a** a downward slope **b** a cataract – usu pl with sing. meaning but sing. or pl in constr **5** a decrease in size, quantity, degree, or value **6** *chiefly NAm* autumn

fallacy /'faləsi/ *n* **1** deceptive appearance or nature; deception, delusiveness **2** a false idea **3** an argument failing to satisfy the conditions of valid inference – **-acious** *adj*

fallible /'faləbl/ *adj* capable of being or likely to be wrong – **-bility** *n*

fall in *v* **1** to sink or collapse inwards **2** to take one's proper place in a military formation **3** to concur with – **fall in with** to concur with

fal,lopian 'tube /fə'lohpi·ən, -pyən/ *n, often cap F* either of the pair of tubes conducting the egg from the ovary to the uterus in mammals

'fall,out /-,owt/ *n* **1** (the fall of) polluting particles, esp radioactive particles resulting from a nuclear explosion **2** secondary results or products

fall out *v* **1** to have a disagreement; quarrel **2** to leave one's place in the ranks of a military formation **3** to happen; come about – *fml or poetic*

¹fallow /'faloh/ *adj* light yellowish brown

²fallow *n* (ploughed and harrowed) land that is allowed to lie idle during the growing season

³fallow *v* to plough, harrow, etc (land) without seeding, esp so as to destroy weeds

⁴fallow *adj* **1** *of land* left unsown after ploughing **2** dormant, inactive – chiefly in *to lie fallow*

fallow deer *n* a small European deer with broad antlers and a pale yellow coat spotted with white in the summer

fall through *v* to fail to be carried out

fall to *v* to begin doing sthg (e g working or eating), esp vigorously – often imper

false /fawls/ *adj* **1** not genuine **2a** intentionally untrue; lying **b** adjusted or made so as to deceive **3** not based on reality; untrue **4** disloyal, treacherous **5** resembling or related to a more widely known kind **6** imprudent, unwise – **~ly** *adv* – **~ness** *n* – **falsity** *n*

'falsehood /-hood/ *n* **1** an untrue statement; a lie **2** absence of truth or accuracy; falsity

falsetto /fawl'setoh/ *n, pl* **falsettos** (a singer who uses) an artificially high singing voice, specif an artificially produced male singing voice that extends above the range of the singer's natural voice

falsify /'fawlsi,fie/ *v* **1** to prove or declare false **2a** to make false by alteration **b** to represent falsely; misrepresent – **-fication** *n*

falter /'fawltə/ *v* **1** to walk or move unsteadily or hesitatingly; stumble **2** to speak brokenly or weakly; stammer **3** to lose strength, purpose, or effectiveness; waver – **~ingly** *adv*

fame /faym/ *n* **1** public estimation; reputation **2** popular acclaim; renown – **~d** *adj*

familial /fə'mili·əl, -yəl/ *adj* (characteristic) of a family or its members

¹familiar /fə'mili·ə, -yə/ *n* an intimate associate; a companion

²familiar *adj* **1** closely acquainted; intimate **2a** casual, informal **b** too intimate and unrestrained; presumptuous **3** frequently seen or experienced; common – **~ize** *v* – **~ly** *adv*

familiarity /fə,mili'arəti/ *n* **1a** absence of ceremony; informality **b** an unduly informal act or expression **2** close acquaintance with or knowledge of sthg

¹family /'faməli/ *n sing or pl in constr* **1** a group of people of common ancestry or common convictions **2a** a group of people living under 1 roof; *esp* a set of 2 or more adults living together and rearing their children **2** a group of related languages descended from a single ancestral language **4** a category in the biological classification of living things ranking above a genus and below an order

²family *adj* of or suitable for a family or all of its members

,family 'planning *n* a system of achieving planned parenthood by contraception

,family 'tree *n* (a diagram of) a genealogy

famine /'famin/ *n* an extreme scarcity of food; *broadly* any great shortage

famish /'famish/ *v* to cause to suffer severely from hunger – usu pass – **~ed** *adj*

famous /'fayməs/ *adj* well-known

¹fan /fan/ *n* **1** a folding circular or semicircular device that consists of material (e g paper or silk) mounted on thin slats that is waved to and fro by hand to produce a cooling current of air **2** a device, usu a series of vanes radiating from a hub rotated by a motor, for producing a current of air

²fan *v* **-nn-** **1** to eliminate (e g chaff) by winnowing **2** to move or impel (air) with a fan **3** to stir up to activity as if by fanning a fire; stimulate **4** to spread *out* like a fan

³fan *n* an enthusiastic supporter or admirer (e g of a sport, pursuit, or celebrity)

fanatic /fə'natik/ *n or adj* (one who is) excessively and often uncritically enthusiastic – **~al** *adj* – **~ally** *adv* – **~ism** *n*

'fan ,belt *n* an endless belt driving a cooling fan for a car radiator

fancier /'fansi·ə/ *n* one who breeds or grows a usu specified animal or plant for points of excellence

fanciful /'fansif(ə)l/ *adj* **1** given to or guided by fancy or imagination rather than by reason and experience **2** existing in fancy only; imaginary **3** marked by fancy or whim – **~ly** *adv*

¹fancy /'fansi/ *n* **1** an inclination **2** a notion, whim **3a** imagination, esp of a capricious or misleading sort **b** the power of mental conception and representation, used in artistic expression (e g by a poet)

²fancy *v* **1** to believe without knowledge or evidence **2a** to have a fancy for; like, desire **b** to consider likely to do well **3** to form a conception of; imagine

³**fancy** *adj* **1** based on fancy or the imagination; whimsical **2a** not plain or ordinary; *esp* fine, quality **b** ornamental – **fancily** *adv*

,**fancy** '**dress** *n* unusual or amusing dress (e g representing a historical or fictional character) worn for a party or other special occasion

fanfare /'fan,feə/ *n* **1** a flourish of trumpets **2** a showy outward display

fang /fang/ *n* a projecting tooth or prong: e g **a** a tooth by which an animal's prey is seized and held or torn **b** any of the long hollow or grooved teeth of a venomous snake

'**fan,light** /-,liet/ *n* an esp semicircular window with radiating divisions over a door or window

fanny /'fani/ *n* **1** *Br* the female genitals – vulg **2** *NAm* the buttocks – infml

fantasia /fan'tayzyə, -zh(y)ə/ *n* a free instrumental or literary composition not in strict form

fantastic /fan'tastik/ *adj* **1a** unreal, imaginary **b** so extreme as to challenge belief; *specif* exceedingly large or great **2** marked by extravagant fantasy or eccentricity **3** – used as a generalized term of approval – ~ **ally** *adv*

fantasy /'fantəsi/ *n* **1** unrestricted creative imagination; fancy **2** imaginative fiction or drama characterized esp by strange, unrealistic, or grotesque elements **3** (the power or process of creating) a usu extravagant mental image or daydream

¹**far** /fah/ *adv* **farther** /'fahdhə/, **further** /'fuhdhə/, **farthest** /'fahdhist/, **furthest** /'fuhdhist/ **1** to or at a considerable distance in space (e g wandered *far* into the woods) **2** in total contrast (e g a *far* from criticizing you, I'm delighted) – + *from* **3** to or at an extent or degree (e g as *far* as I know) **4a** to or at a considerable distance or degree (e g a bright student will go *far*) **b** much (e g *far* too hot) **5** to or at a considerable distance in time (e g worked *far* into the night) — **by far** far and away — **far and away** by a considerable margin — **how far** to what extent, degree, or distance — **so far 1** to a certain extent, degree, or distance **2** up to the present

²**far** *adj* **farther** /'fahdhə/, **further** /'fuhdhə/, **farthest** /'fahdhist/, **furthest** /'fuhdhist/ **1** remote in space, time, or degree (e g in the *far* distance) **2** long **3** being the more distant of 2 (e g the *far* side of the lake) **4** *of a political position* extreme

faraway /,fahrə'way/ *adj* **1** lying at a great distance; remote **2** dreamy, abstracted

farce /fahs/ *n* **1** forcemeat **2** a comedy with an improbable plot **3** a ridiculous or meaningless situation or event – **farcical** *adj* – **farcically** *adv*

¹**fare** /feə/ *v* to get along; succeed, do

²**fare** *n* **1a** the price charged to transport sby **b** a paying passenger **2** food provided for a meal

¹**farewell** /feə'wel/ *interj* goodbye

²**farewell** *n* an act of departure or leave-taking

,**far'fetched** /-'fecht/ *adj* not easily or naturally deduced; improbable

,**far-'flung** *adj* **1** widely spread or distributed **2** remote

¹**farm** /fahm/ *n* an area of land devoted to growing crops or raising (domestic) animals

²**farm** *v* **1** to collect and take the proceeds of (e g taxation or a business) on payment of a fixed sum **2** to produce crops or livestock

farmer /'fahmə/ *n* **1** sby who pays a fixed sum for some privilege or source of income **2** sby who cultivates land or crops or raises livestock

'**farm,hand** /-,hand/ *n* a farm worker

'**farm,house** /-,hows/ *n* a dwelling house on a farm

farm out /-,sted, -stid/ *v* **1** to turn over for performance or use, usu on contract **2** to put (e g children) into sby's care in return for a fee

'**farm,yard** /-,yahd/ *n* the area round or enclosed by farm buildings

,**far-'out** *adj* extremely unconventional; weird

farrago /fə'rahgoh/ *n, pl* **farragoes** a confused collection; a hotchpotch

farrier /'fari-ə/ *n* a blacksmith who shoes horses

¹**farrow** /'faroh/ *v* to give birth to (pigs) – often + *down*

²**farrow** *n* (farrowing) a litter of pigs

,**far'sighted** /-'sietid/ *adj* **1a** seeing or able to see to a great distance **b** having foresight or good judgment; sagacious **2** long-sighted – ~ **ness** *n*

¹**farther** /'fahdhə/ *adv* **1** at or to a greater distance or more advanced point (e g *farther* down the corridor) **2** to a greater degree or extent

²**farther** *adj* **1a** more distant; remoter **b** far (e g the *farther* side) **2** additional

¹**farthest** /'fahdhist/ *adj* most distant in space or time

²**farthest** *adv* **1** to or at the greatest distance in space, time, or degree **2** by the greatest distance or extent; most

farthing /'fahdhing/ *n* **1** (a coin representing) a former British money unit worth ¼ of an old penny **2** sthg of small value

fascia /'faysho; *med* 'fashi-ə/ *n, pl* **fasciae** /-i,ee, -i, ie/, **fascias 1** a flat horizontal piece (e g of stone or board) under projecting eaves **2** *Br* the dashboard of a motor car

fascinate /'fasinayt/ *v* **1** to transfix by an irresistible mental power **2** to attract strongly, esp by arousing interest; captivate – **-ting** *adj* – **-tingly** *adv*

fascism /'fashiz(ə)m/ *n* **1** a political philosophy, movement, or regime that is usu hostile to socialism, exalts nation and race, and stands for a centralized government headed by a dictatorial leader **2** brutal dictatorial control – **fascist** *n, adj*

¹**fashion** /'fash(ə)n/ *n* **1** a manner, way **2a** a prevailing and often short-lived custom or style **b** the prevailing style or custom, esp in dress — **after a fashion** in an approximate or rough way

²**fashion** v 1 to give shape or form to, esp by using ingenuity; mould, construct 2 to mould into a particular character by influence or training; transform, adapt

fashionable /'fash(ə)nəbl/ adj 1 conforming to the latest custom or fashion 2 used or patronized by people of fashion – **-ably** adv

¹**fast** /fahst/ adj 1a firmly fixed or attached b tightly closed or shut 2a(1) moving or able to move rapidly; swift a(2) taking a comparatively short time a(3) accomplished quickly a(4) quick to learn b conducive to rapidity of play or action or quickness of motion c of a clock indicating in advance of what is correct 3 of a colour permanently dyed; not liable to fade 4 dissipated, wild; also promiscuous

²**fast** adv 1 in a firm or fixed manner 2 sound, deeply 3a in a rapid manner; quickly b in quick succession 4 in a reckless or dissipated manner 5 ahead of a correct time or posted schedule

³**fast** v to abstain from some or all foods or meals

⁴**fast** n an act or time of fasting

fasten /'fahs(ə)n/ v 1 to attach or secure, esp by pinning, tying, or nailing 2 to fix or direct steadily 3 to attach, impose on — **~er** n — **fasten on/upon/onto** 1 to take a firm grip or hold on 2 to focus attention on

fastening /'fahs(ə)ning/ n a fastener

fastidious /fa'stidi·əs, -dyəs/ adj 1 excessively difficult to satisfy or please 2 showing or demanding great delicacy or care – **~ly** adv – **~ness** n

fastness /'fahstnis/ n 1a the quality of being fixed b colourfast quality 2 a fortified, secure, or remote place

¹**fat** /fat/ adj -tt- 1a plump b obese 2a well filled out; thick, big b prosperous, wealthy 3 richly rewarding or profitable; substantial 4 productive, fertile – **~ness** n

²**fat** n 1 (animal tissue consisting chiefly of cells distended with) greasy or oily matter 2 the best or richest part

fatal /'faytl/ adj 1 fateful, decisive 2a of fate b like fate in proceeding according to a fixed sequence; inevitable 3a causing death b bringing ruin

'**fatal,ism** /-,iz(ə)m/ n the belief that all events are predetermined and outside the control of human beings – **-ist** n – **-istic** adj

fatality /fə'taləti/ n 1a the quality or state of causing death or destruction b the quality or condition of being destined for disaster 2 death resulting from a disaster

fatally /'faytl-i/ adv 1 mortally 2 as is or was fatal

¹**fate** /fayt/ n 1 the power beyond human control that determines events; destiny 2a a destiny b a disaster; esp death 3 an outcome, end; esp one that is adverse and inevitable

²**fate** v to destine; also to doom – usu pass

'**fateful** /-f(ə)l/ adj 1 having an ominous quality 2a having momentous and often unpleasant consequences b deadly, catastrophic – **~ly** adv

Fates /fayts/ n pl the 3 goddesses of classical mythology who determine the course of human life

'**fat,head** /-,hed/ n a slow-witted or stupid person; a fool – infml

¹**father** /'fahdhə/ n 1a a male parent of a child; also a sire b cap God; the first person of the Trinity 2 a man receiving filial respect from another 3 often cap an early Christian writer accepted by the church as authoritative 4 a source, origin 5 a priest of the regular clergy – used esp as a title in the Roman Catholic church

²**father** v 1a to beget b to give rise to; initiate 2 to fix the paternity of on

'**father-in-,law** n, pl **fathers-in-law** the father of one's spouse

¹**fathom** /'fadhəm/ n a unit of length equal to 6ft used esp for measuring the depth of water

²**fathom** v to penetrate and come to understand – often + out

¹**fatigue** /fə'teeg/ n 1 physical or nervous exhaustion 2a manual or menial military work b pl the uniform or work clothing worn on fatigue 3 the tendency of a material to break under repeated stress

²**fatigue** v to weary, exhaust

fatten /'fat(ə)n/ v to make fat, fleshy, or plump; esp to feed (e g a stock animal) for slaughter – often + up

¹**fatty** /'fati/ adj 1 containing (large amounts of) fat; also corpulent 2 greasy – **-tiness** n

²**fatty** n a fat person – infml

fatuous /'fatyoo·əs/ adj complacently or inanely foolish; idiotic – **-tuity** n – **~ly** adv – **~ness** n

¹**fault** /fawlt/ n 1a a failing; a defect b a service that does not land in the prescribed area in tennis, squash, etc 2a a misdemeanour b a mistake 3 responsibility for wrongdoing or failure 4 a fracture in the earth's crust accompanied by displacement (e g of the strata) along the fracture line – **~y** adj – **-ily** adv – **-iness** n — **at fault** in the wrong; liable for blame

²**fault** v 1 to commit a fault; err 2 to produce a geological fault (in)

fauna /'fawnə/ n pl **faunas** also **faunae** /-ni, -nie/ the animals or animal life of a region, period, or special environment

faux pas /,foh 'pah/ n, pl **faux pas** /,foh 'pah(z)/ an esp social blunder

¹**favour**, NAm chiefly **favor** /'fayvə/ n 1a friendly or approving regard shown towards another; approbation b popularity 2 (an act of) kindness beyond what is expected or due 3 a token of allegiance or love (e g a ribbon or badge), usu worn conspicuously 4 consent to sexual activities, esp given by a woman – usu pl with sing. meaning;

euph — **in favour of 1** in agreement or sympathy with; on the side of **2** to the advantage of **3** in order to choose; out of preference for — **in someone's favour** I liked or esteemed by sby **2** to sby's advantage — **out of favour** unpopular, disliked

²**favour**, *NAm chiefly* **favor** *v* **1a** to regard or treat with favour **b** to do a favour or kindness for; oblige – usu + *by* or *with* **2** to show partiality towards; prefer **3** to sustain; facilitate

favourable /'fayv(ə)rəbl/ *adj* **1a** disposed to favour; partial **b** giving a result in one's favour **2a** helpful, advantageous **b** successful – **-rably** *adv*

'**favoured** *adj* **1** endowed with special advantages or gifts **2** having an appearance or features of a specified kind – usu in combination **3** receiving preferential treatment

¹**favourite** /'fayv(ə)rit/ *n* **1** sby or sthg favoured or preferred above others; *specif* one unduly favoured **2** the competitor judged most likely to win, esp by a bookmaker

²**favourite** *adj* constituting a favourite

favouritism /'fayv(ə)ri,tiz(ə)m/ *n* the showing of unfair favour; partiality

¹**fawn** /fawn/ *v* to court favour by acting in a servilely flattering manner *USE* usu + *on* or *upon*

²**fawn** *n* **1** a young (unweaned) deer **2** a light greyish brown colour

fealty /'fee-əlti/ *n* fidelity or allegiance, esp to a feudal lord

¹**fear** /fiə/ *n* **1** (an instance of) an unpleasant often strong emotion caused by anticipation or awareness of (a specified) danger **2** anxiety, solicitude **3** profound reverence and awe, esp towards God **4** reason for alarm; danger – ~**less** *adj* – ~**lessly** *adv* – ~**lessness** *n* – **for fear of** because of anxiety about

²**fear** *v* **1** to have a reverential awe of **2** to be afraid of; consider or expect with alarm

'**fearful** /-f(ə)l/ *adj* **1** causing or likely to cause fear **2a** showing or arising from fear **b** timid, timorous **3** extremely bad, large, or intense – infml – ~**ly** *adv* – ~**ness** *n*

'**fearsome** /-s(ə)m/ *adj* fearful – ~**ly** *adv* – ~**ness** *n*

feasible /'feezəbl/ *adj* **1** capable of being done or carried out **2** reasonable, likely; *also* suitable – **-sibility** *n* – **-sibly** *adv*

¹**feast** /feest/ *n* **1a** an elaborate often public meal; a banquet **b** sthg that gives abundant pleasure **2a** a periodic religious observance commemorating an event or honouring a deity, person, or thing

²**feast** *v* **1** to take part in a feast; give a feast for **2** to delight, gratify

feat /feet/ *n* **1** a notable and esp courageous act or deed **2** an act or product of skill, endurance, or ingenuity

¹**feather** /'fedhə/ *n* **1a** any of the light outgrowths forming the external covering of a bird's body **b** the vane of an arrow **2** plumage **3** the act of

feathering an oar — **a feather in one's cap** a deserved honour or mark of distinction in which one can take pride

²**feather** *v* **1** to cover, clothe, adorn, etc with feathers **2a** to turn (an oar blade) almost horizontal when lifting from the water **b** to change the angle at which (a propeller blade) meets the air so as to have the minimum wind resistance — **feather one's nest** to provide for oneself, esp dishonestly, through a job in which one is trusted

'**feather,weight** /-,wayt/ *n* **1** a boxer weighing not more than 9st **2** sby or sthg of limited importance or effectiveness

¹**feature** /'feechə/ *n* **1** a part of the face; *also*, *pl* the face **2** a prominent or distinctive part or characteristic **3a** a full-length film **b** a distinctive article or story, in a newspaper, magazine, or on radio

²**feature** *v* **1** to give special prominence to (e g in a performance or newspaper) **2** to play an important part; be a feature – usu + *in*

febrile /'feebriel/ *adj* of fever; feverish

February /'febrooəri, -,eri/ *n* the 2nd month of the Gregorian calendar

feckless /'feklis/ *adj* worthless, irresponsible – ~**ly** *adv* – ~**ness** *n*

fecund /'feekənd, 'fekənd/ *adj* **1** fruitful in offspring or vegetation; prolific **2** very intellectually productive or inventive to a marked degree *USE* fml – ~**ity** *n*

federal /'fed(ə)rəl/ *adj* **1** formed by agreement between political units that surrender their individual sovereignty to a central authority but retain limited powers of government; *also* of or constituting a government so formed **2** of or loyal to the federal government of the USA in the American Civil War

federation /,fedə'raysh(ə)n/ *n* sthg formed by federating: e g **a** a country formed by the federation of separate states **b** a union of organizations

fed 'up *adj* discontented, bored – infml

fee /fee/ *n* **1** a sum of money paid esp for entrance or for a professional service **2** money paid for education – usu pl with sing. meaning — **in fee** in absolute and legal possession

feeble /'feebl/ *adj* **1** lacking in strength or endurance; weak **2** deficient in authority, force, or effect – **feebly** *adv* – ~**ness** *n*

¹**feed** /feed/ *v* **fed** /fed/ **1a** to give food to **b** to give as food **2** to provide sthg essential to the growth, sustenance, maintenance, or operation of **3** to produce or provide food for **4** to supply for use, consumption, or processing, esp in a continuous manner

²**feed** *n* **1** an act of eating **2** (a mixture or preparation of) food for livestock **3** a mechanism by which the action of feeding is effected **4** one who supplies cues for another esp comic performer's lines or actions

'feed,back /-,bak/ n 1 the return to the input of a part of the output of a machine, system, or process 2 (the return to a source of) information about the results of an action or process, usu in response to a request

feed up v to fatten by plentiful feeding

'feel /feel/ v **felt** /felt/ 1a to handle or touch in order to examine or explore b to perceive by a physical sensation coming from discrete end organs (e g of the skin or muscles) 2 to experience actively or passively; be affected by 3 to ascertain or explore by cautious trial – often + *out* 4a to be aware of by instinct or by drawing conclusions from the evidence available b to believe, think 5 to have sympathy or pity *for* — **feel like** 1 to resemble or seem to be on the evidence of touch 2 to wish for; be in the mood for

²feel n 1 the sense of feeling; touch 2a the quality of a thing as imparted through touch b typical or peculiar quality or atmosphere 3 intuitive skill, knowledge, or ability – usu + *for*

feeler /'feelə/ n 1 a tactile appendage (e g a tentacle) of an animal 2 sthg (e g a proposal) ventured to ascertain the views of others

feeling /'feeling/ n 1 (a sensation experienced through) the one of the 5 basic physical senses 2a an emotional state or reaction b *pl* susceptibility to impression; sensibility 3 a conscious recognition; a sense 4a an opinion or belief, esp when unreasoned b a presentiment 5 capacity to respond emotionally, esp with the higher emotions – **feeling** *adj*

feign /fayn/ v to deliberately give a false appearance or impression of; *also* to pretend

'feint /faynt/ n a mock blow or attack directed away from the point one really intends to attack

²feint *adj, of rulings on paper* faint, pale

feldspar /'fel(d)spah/, **felspar** /'felspah/ n any of a group of minerals that are an essential constituent of nearly all crystalline rocks

felicitate /fə'lisitayt/ v to offer congratulations or compliments to – usu + *on* or *upon*; fml – **-tation** n

felicitous /fə'lisitəs/ adj 1 very well suited or expressed; apt; *also* marked by or given to such expression 2 pleasant, delightful *USE* fml – ~**ly** adv

felicity /fə'lisiti/ n 1 (sthg causing) great happiness 2 a felicitous faculty or quality, esp in art or language; aptness 3 a felicitous expression *USE* fml

feline /'feelien/ adj 1 of cats or the cat family 2 resembling a cat

'fell /fel/ v 1 to cut, beat, or knock down 2 to kill

²fell *past of* **fall**

³fell n a steep rugged stretch of high moorland, esp in northern England – often *pl* with sing. meaning

⁴fell adj 1 fierce, cruel 2 very destructive; deadly *USE* poetic — **at one fell swoop** all at once; *also* with a single concentrated effort

'fellow /'feloh/ n 1 a comrade, associate – usu *pl* 2a an equal in rank, power, or character; a peer b either of a pair; a mate 3 a member of an incorporated literary or scientific society 4 a man; *also* a boy 5 an incorporated member of a collegiate foundation 6 a person appointed to a salaried position allowing for advanced research

²fellow adj being a companion or associate; belonging to the same group – used before a noun

fellow feeling n a feeling of mutual understanding; *specif* sympathy

fellowship /-ship/ n 1 the condition of friendly relations between people; companionship 2a community of interest, activity, feeling, or experience b the state of being a fellow or associate 3 *sing* or *pl in constr* a group of people with similar interests; an association 4 the position of a fellow (e g of a university)

fellow traveller n a nonmember who sympathizes with and often furthers the ideals and programme of an organized group, esp the Communist party – chiefly derog

felon /'felən/ n sby who has committed a felony

felony /'feləni/ n a grave crime (e g murder or arson) that was formerly regarded in law as more serious than a misdemeanour – **-nious** adj

felspar /'fel,spah/ n feldspar

'felt /felt/ n a nonwoven cloth made by compressing wool or fur often mixed with natural or synthetic fibres

²felt v 1 to make into or cover with felt 2 to cause to stick and mat together

³felt *past of* **feel**

female /'feemayl/ adj, n 1 an individual that bears young or produces eggs; *esp* a woman or girl as distinguished from a man or boy 2 a plant or flower with an ovary but no stamens – **female** adj

'feminine /'feminin/ adj 1 of or being a female person 2 characteristic of, appropriate to, or peculiar to women; womanly 3 of or belonging to the gender that normally includes most words or grammatical forms referring to females – **-nity** n

²feminine n 1 the feminine principle in human nature – esp in *eternal feminine* 2 (a word of) the feminine gender

feminism /'feminiz(ə)m/ n the advocacy or pursuit of women's rights, interests, and equality with men in political, economic, and social spheres – **-ist** n

femme fatale /,fam fa'tahl, 'femi (Fr fam fatal)/ n, *pl* **femmes fatales** /fatahl(z) (Fr ~)/ a seductive and usu mysterious woman

femur /'feemə/ n, *pl* **femurs**, **femora** /'femərə/ 1 the bone of the hind or lower limb nearest the body; the thighbone 2 the third segment of an insect's leg counting from the base – **femoral** adj

fen /fen/ n an area of low wet or flooded land

¹**fence** /fens/ n 1 a barrier (e g of wire or boards) intended to prevent escape or intrusion or to mark a boundary 2 a receiver of stolen goods — **on the fence** in a position of neutrality or indecision

²**fence** v 1a to enclose with a fence – usu + in b to separate *off* or keep *out* (as if) with a fence 2a to practise fencing b to use tactics of attack and defence (e g thrusting and parrying) resembling those of fencing 3 to receive or sell stolen goods

fencing /'fensing/ n 1 the art of attack and defence with a sword (e g the foil, épeé, or sabre) 2 (material used for building) fences

fender /'fendə/ n a device that protects: e g a a cushion (e g of rope or wood) hung over the side of a ship to absorb impact b a low metal guard for a fire used to confine the coals

fend off v to keep or ward off; repel

feral /'fiərəl/ adj 1 (suggestive) of a wild beast; savage 2a not domesticated or cultivated; wild b having escaped from domestication and become wild

¹**ferment** /fə'ment/ v 1 to (cause to) undergo fermentation 2 to (cause to) be in a state of agitation or intense activity

²**ferment** /'fuhment/ n a state of unrest or upheaval; agitation, tumult

fermentation /,fuhmen'taysh(ə)n/ n 1 a chemical change with effervescence 2 a transformation of an organic compound that is controlled by an enzyme (e g a carbohydrate to carbon dioxide and alcohol)

fern /fuhn/ n any of a class of flowerless seedless lower plants; *esp* any of an order resembling flowering plants in having a root, stem, and leaflike fronds but differing in reproducing by spores – **ferny** adj

ferocious /fə'rohshəs/ adj extremely fierce or violent – ~**ly** adv – ~**ness** n

ferocity /fə'rosəti/ n the quality or state of being ferocious

¹**ferret** /'ferit/ n 1 a partially domesticated usu albino European polecat used esp for hunting small rodents (e g rats) 2 an active and persistent searcher

²**ferret** v 1 to hunt with ferrets 2 to search *about, around* or *out* – infml

ferrite /'feriet/ n any of several highly magnetic substances consisting mainly of an iron oxide

ferrous /'ferəs/ adj of, containing, or being (bivalent) iron

ferrule /'feroohl, -rəl/ n 1 a ring or cap, usu of metal, strengthening a cane, tool handle, etc 2 a short tube or bush for making a tight joint (e g between pipes)

¹**ferry** /'feri/ v 1 to carry by boat over a body of water 2 to convey (e g by car) from one place to another

²**ferry** n (a boat used at) a place where people or things are carried across a body of water (e g a river)

fertile /'fuhtiel/ adj 1a (capable of) producing or bearing fruit (in great quantities); productive b characterized by great resourcefulness and activity; inventive 2a capable of sustaining abundant plant growth b affording abundant possibilities for development c capable of breeding or reproducing – **-lity** n – **-lize** v

'fertil,izer, -iser /-zə/ n a substance (e g manure) used to make soil more fertile

fervent /'fuhv(ə)nt/ adj ardent – **-vency** n – ~**ly** adv

fervid /'fuhvid/ adj ardent – ~**ly** adv

fervour, *NAm chiefly* **fervor** /'fuhvə/ n the quality or state of being fervent or fervid

fester /'festə/ v 1 to generate pus 2 to putrefy, rot 3 to rankle

¹**festival** /'festivl/ adj of, appropriate to, or set apart as a festival

²**festival** n 1a a time marked by special (e g customary) celebration b a religious feast 2 a usu periodic programme or season of cultural events or entertainment 3 gaiety, conviviality

festive /'festiv/ adj 1 of or suitable for a feast or festival 2 joyous, gay

festivity /fe'stivəti/ n festive activity – often pl with sing. meaning

¹**festoon** /fe'stoohn/ n a decorative chain or strip hanging between 2 points; *also* a carved, moulded, or painted ornament representing this

²**festoon** v 1 to hang or form festoons on 2 to cover profusely and usu gaily

fetch /fech/ v 1 to go or come after and bring or take back 2a to cause to come; bring b to produce as profit or return; realize 3 to reach by sailing, esp against the wind or tide and without having to tack 4 to strike or deal (a blow, slap, etc) – infml

fetch up v to come to a specified standstill, stopping place, or result; arrive

¹**fete, fête** /fayt, fet/ n 1 a festival 2 Br a usu outdoor bazaar or other entertainment held esp to raise money for a particular purpose

²**fete, fête** v to honour or commemorate (sby or sthg) with a fete or other ceremony

fetid, foetid /'feetid/ adj having a heavy offensive smell; stinking

fetish *also* **fetich** /'fetish/ n 1 an object believed among a primitive people to have magical power 2 an object of irrational reverence or obsessive devotion 3 an object or bodily part whose presence in reality or fantasy is psychologically necessary for sexual gratification

fetishism *also* **fetichism** /'fetishiz(ə)m/ n 1 belief in magical fetishes 2 the displacement of erotic interest and satisfaction to a fetish – **-ist** n

fetlock /'fet,lok/ n 1 a projection bearing a tuft of hair on the back of the leg above the hoof of an animal of the horse family 2 the joint of the limb or tuft of hair at the fetlock

¹**fetter** /'fetə/ n 1 a shackle for the feet 2 sthg that confines; a restraint – usu pl with sing. meaning

²**fetter** v 1 to put fetters on 2 to bind (as if) with fetters; shackle, restrain

fettle /'fetl/ n fettling /'fetling/ a state of physical or mental fitness or order; condition

feud /fyoohd/ n a lasting state of hostilities, esp between families or clans, marked by violent attacks for the purpose of revenge – **feud** v

feudal /'fyoohdl/ adj of or resembling the system of social relations (e g lord to vassal) characteristic of the Middle Ages – ~**ism** n

fever /'feevə/ n 1 a rise of body temperature above the normal; also a disease marked by this 2a a state of intense emotion or activity b a contagious usu transient enthusiasm; a craze

feverish /'feevərish/ also **feverous** /-rəs/ adj 1a having the symptoms of a fever b indicating, relating to, or caused by (a) fever 2 marked by intense emotion, activity, or instability

¹**few** /fyooh/ adj 1 amounting to only a small number (e g one of his few pleasures) 2 at least some though not many – + a (e g caught a few more fish)

²**few** n pl in constr 1 not many (e g few of his stories were true) 2 at least some though not many – + a (e g a few of them) 3 a select or exclusive group of people; an élite

fey /fay/ adj 1 marked by an otherworldly and irresponsible air 2 chiefly Scot 2a fated to die; doomed b marked by an excited or elated state

fez /fez/ n, pl -**zz**- also -**z**- a brimless hat shaped like a truncated cone, usu red and with a tassel, which is worn by men in southern and eastern Mediterranean countries

fiancé, fem **fiancée** /fi'onsay/ n sby engaged to be married

fiasco /fi'askoh/ n pl **fiascoes** a complete and ignominious failure

fiat /'fie·ət, -at/ n an authoritative and often arbitrary order; a decree

fib /fib/ v or n -**bb**- (to tell) a trivial or childish lie – infml – ~**ber** n

fibre, NAm chiefly **fiber** /'feebə/ n 1 a slender natural or man-made thread or filament (e g of wool, cotton, or asbestos) 2 material made of fibres 3 essential structure or character; also strength, fortitude

'**fibre,glass** /-,glahs/ n 1 glass in fibrous form used in making various products (e g textiles and insulation materials) 2 a combination of synthetic resins and fibreglass

fibrous /'fiebrəs/ adj 1a containing, consisting of, or resembling fibres b capable of being separated into fibres 2 tough, stringy

fibula /'fibyoolə/ n, pl **fibulae** /-li/, **fibulas** the (smaller) outer of the 2 bones of the hind limb of higher vertebrates between the knee and ankle

fickle /'fikl/ adj lacking steadfastness or constancy; capricious – ~**ness** n

fiction /'fiksh(ə)n/ n 1 an invented story 2 literature (e g novels or short stories) describing imaginary people and events – ~**al** adj – ~**alize** v – ~**alization** n

fictitious /fik'tishəs/ adj 1 (characteristic) of fiction 2 of a name false, assumed 3 not genuinely felt; feigned – ~**ly** adv – ~**ness** n

¹**fiddle** /'fidl/ n 1 a violin 2 a device to keep objects from sliding off a table on board ship 3 a dishonest practice; a swindle – infml 4 an activity involving intricate manipulation – infml

²**fiddle** v fiddling /'fidling, 'fidl·ing/ 1 to play on a fiddle 2a to move the hands or fingers restlessly b to spend time in aimless or fruitless activity – often + about or around 3 to falsify (e g accounts), esp so as to gain financial advantage 4 to get or contrive by cheating or deception – ~**r** n — **fiddle with** to tamper or meddle with – infml

fiddlesticks /ı/ˈfɪdlˌɒstɪks/ n pl nonsense – used as an interjection; infml

fiddling /'fidling/ adj trifling, petty

fidelity /fi'deləti/ n 1a the quality or state of being faithful; loyalty b accuracy in details; exactness 2 the degree of similarity between some reproduced (e g recorded) material and its original source

¹**fidget** /'fijit/ n 1 uneasiness or restlessness shown by nervous movements – usu pl with sing. meaning 2 sby who fidgets USE infml

²**fidget** v to move or act restlessly or nervously – ~**y** adj

fief /feef/ n 1 a feudal estate 2 sthg over which one has rights or exercises control

¹**field** /feeld/ n 1a an (enclosed) area of land free of woods and buildings (used for cultivation or pasture) b an area of land containing a natural resource c (the place where) a battle is fought; also a battle 2a an area or division of an activity b the sphere of practical operation outside a place of work (e g a laboratory) c an area in which troops are operating (e g in an exercise or theatre of war) 3 the participants in a sports activity, esp with the exception of the favourite or winner 4 a region or space in which a given effect (e g magnetism) exists 5 also **field of view** the area visible through the lens of an optical instrument

²**field** v 1a to stop and pick up a hit ball b to deal with by giving an impromptu answer 2 to put into the field of play or battle

'**field ,day** n a day for military exercises or manoeuvres

fielder /'feeldə/ n any of the players whose job is to field the ball (e g in cricket)

'**field ,event** n an athletic event (e g discus, javelin, or jumping) other than a race

'field ,glasses *n pl* an optical instrument usu consisting of 2 telescopes on a single frame with a focussing device

field marshal *n* the top-ranking officer in the British army

'field,work /-,wuhk/ *n* 1 a temporary fortification 2 work done in the field (e g by students) to gain practical experience through firsthand observation 3 the gathering of data in anthropology, sociology, etc through the observation or interviewing of subjects in the field

fiend /feend/ *n* 1a *the* devil b a demon c a person of great wickedness or cruelty 2 sby excessively devoted to a specified activity or thing; a fanatic, devotee

fiendish /'feendish/ *adj* 1 perversely diabolical 2 extremely cruel or wicked 3 excessively bad, unpleasant, or difficult – ~ **ness** *n* – ~ **ly** *adv*

fierce /fias/ *adj* 1 violently hostile or aggressive; combative, pugnacious 2a lacking restraint or control; violent, heated b extremely intense or severe 3 furiously active or determined 4 wild or menacing in appearance – ~ **ly** *adv* – ~ **ness** *n*

fiery /'fie·əri/ *adj* 1a consisting of fire b burning, blazing 2 very hot 3 of the colour of fire; *esp* red 4a full of or exuding strong emotion or spirit; passionate b easily provoked; irascible

fiesta /fi'estə/ *n* a saint's day in Spain and Latin America, often celebrated with processions and dances

fife /fief/ *n* a small flute used chiefly to accompany the drum

fifteen /fif'teen/ *n* 1 the number 15 2 the fifteenth in a set or series 3 *sing or pl in constr* sthg having 15 parts or members or a denomination of 15; *esp* a Rugby Union football team – ~ **th** *adj, n, pron, adv*

15 *n or adj* (a film that is) certified in Britain as suitable for people of 15 or over

fifth /fith; *also* fifth/ *n* 1 number five in a countable series b (the combination of 2 notes at) a musical interval of 5 diatonic degrees – **fifth** *adj* – **ly** *adv*

,fifth 'column *n* a group within a nation or faction that sympathizes with and works secretly for an enemy or rival – ~ **ist** *n*

fifty /'fifti/ *n* 1 the number 50 2 *pl* the numbers 50 to 59; *specif* a range of temperatures, ages, or dates within a century characterized by those numbers – **-tieth** *adj, n, pron, adv*

¹fifty-'fifty *adv* evenly, equally

²fifty-fifty *adj* half favourable and half unfavourable; even

¹fig /fig/ *n* 1 (any of a genus of trees that bear) a many-seeded fleshy usu pear-shaped or oblong edible fruit 2 a contemptibly worthless trifle

²fig *n* dress, array

¹fight /fiet/ *v* **fought** /fawt/ 1a to contend in battle or physical combat b to attempt to prevent the success, effectiveness, or development of 2 to

stand as a candidate for (e g a constituency) in an election 3 to struggle to endure or surmount 4 to resolve or control by fighting – + *out* or *down* — **fight shy of** to avoid facing or meeting

²fight *n* 1a a battle, combat b a boxing match c an argument 2 a usu protracted struggle for an objective 3 strength or disposition for fighting; pugnacity

fighter /'fietə/ *n* 1 a pugnacious or boldly determined individual 2 a fast manoeuvrable aeroplane designed to destroy enemy aircraft

figment /'figmənt/ *n* sthg fabricated or imagined

figurative /'figyoorətiv/ *adj* 1a representing by a figure or likeness b representational 2 characterized by or using figures of speech, esp metaphor – ~ **ly** *adv*

¹figure /'figə/ *n* 1a an (Arabic) number symbol b *pl* arithmetical calculations c value, esp as expressed in numbers 2 bodily shape or form, esp of a person 3 a diagram or pictorial illustration 4 an intentional deviation from the usual form or syntactic relation of words 5 an often repetitive pattern in a manufactured article (e g cloth) or natural substance (e g wood) 6a a series of movements in a dance b an outline representation of a form traced by a series of evolutions (e g by a skater on an ice surface) 7 a personage, personality 8 a short musical phrase

²figure *v* 1 to decorate with a pattern 2 to take an esp important or conspicuous part – often + *in* 3 to seem reasonable or expected – infml; esp in *that figures* 4a *chiefly NAm* to conclude, decide b *chiefly NAm* to regard, consider — **figure on** *NAm* to take into consideration (e g in planning)

'figure,head /-,hed/ *n* 1 an ornamental carved figure on a ship's bow 2 a head or chief in name only

,figure of 'speech *n* a form of expression (e g a hyperbole or metaphor) used to convey meaning or heighten effect

figure out *v* 1 to discover, determine 2 to solve, fathom

filament /'filamənt/ *n* a single thread or a thin flexible threadlike object or part: e g a a slender conductor (e g in an electric light bulb) made incandescent by the passage of an electric current b the anther-bearing stalk of a stamen

filch /filch/ *v* to steal (sthg of small value); pilfer

¹file /fiel/ *n* a tool, usu of hardened steel, with many cutting ridges for shaping or smoothing objects or surfaces

²file *v* to rub, smooth, or cut away (as if) with a file

³file *v* 1 to arrange in order (e g alphabetically) for preservation and reference 2 to submit or record officially

⁴file *n* 1 a folder, cabinet, etc in which papers are kept in order 2 a collection of papers or publications on a subject, usu arranged or classified

⁵**file** *n* 1 a row of people, animals, or things arranged one behind the other 2 any of the rows of squares that extend across a chessboard from white's side to black's side

⁶**file** *v* to march or proceed in file

filial /'fili·əl, -yəl/ *adj* 1 of or befitting a son or daughter, esp in his/her relationship to a parent 2 having or assuming the relation of a child or offspring

filibuster /'fili,bustə/ *v or n*, chiefly NAm (to engage in) the use of extreme delaying tactics in a legislative assembly

filigree /'filigree/ *v or n* (to decorate with) **a** ornamental openwork of delicate or intricate design **b** a pattern or design resembling such openwork

¹**fill** /fil/ *v* 1a to put into as much as can be held or conveniently contained **b** to supply with a full complement **c** to repair the cavities of (a tooth) **d** to stop up; obstruct, plug 2a to feed, satiate **b** to satisfy, fulfil 3a to occupy the whole of **b** to spread through 4 to possess and perform the duties of; hold — **fill somebody's shoes** to take over sby's job, position, or responsibilities — **fill the bill** to suffice

²**fill** *n* 1 as much as one can eat or drink 2 as much as one can bear

¹**fillet**, chiefly NAm **filet** /'filit/ *n* 1 a ribbon or narrow strip of material used esp as a headband 2a a fleshy boneless piece of meat cut from the hind loin or upper hind leg **b** a long slice of boneless fish

²**fillet** *v* 1a to cut (meat or fish) into fillets **b** to remove the bones from (esp fish) 2 to remove inessential parts from

fill in *v* 1 to give necessary or recently acquired information to 2 to add what is necessary to complete 3 to take sby's place, usu temporarily; substitute

filling /'filing/ *n* 1 sthg used to fill a cavity, container, or depression 2 a food mixture used to fill cakes, sandwiches, etc

fillip /'filip/ *n* sthg that arouses or boosts; a stimulus

²**fillip** *v* to stimulate

fill out *v* to put on flesh

filly /'fili/ *n* 1 a young female horse, usu of less than 4 years 2 a young woman; a girl – infml

¹**film** /film/ *n* 1a a thin skin or membranous covering **b** an abnormal growth on or in the eye 2a a thin layer or covering **b** a roll or strip of cellulose acetate or cellulose nitrate coated with a light-sensitive emulsion for taking photographs 3a a series of pictures recorded on film for the cinema and projected rapidly onto a screen so as to create the illusion of movement **b** a representation (e g of an incident or story) on film **c** cinema – often pl with sing. meaning

²**film** *v* to make a film of or from

¹**filter** /'filtə/ *n* 1 a porous article or mass (e g of paper, sand, etc) through which a gas or liquid is passed to separate out matter in suspension 2 an apparatus containing a filter medium

²**filter** *v* 1 to remove by means of a filter 2 to move gradually 3 to become known over a period of time 4 Br, of traffic to turn left or right in the direction of the green arrow while the main lights are still red

filter 'tip *n* (a cigar or cigarette with) a tip of porous material that filters the smoke before it enters the smoker's mouth – **filter-tipped** *adj*

filth /filth/ *n* 1 foul or putrid matter, esp dirt or refuse 2 sthg loathsome or vile; esp obscene or pornographic material – ~y *adj* – ~ily *adv* – ~iness *n*

fin /fin/ *n* 1 an external membranous part of an aquatic animal (e g a fish or whale) used in propelling or guiding the body 2a an appendage of a boat (e g a submarine) **b** a vertical control surface attached to an aircraft for directional stability

¹**final** /'fienl/ *adj* 1 not to be altered or undone; conclusive 2 being the last; occurring at the end 3 of or relating to the ultimate purpose or result of a process – ~ize *v* – ~ly *adv*

²**final** *n* 1 a deciding match, game, trial, etc in a sport or competition; also, pl a sound made up of these 2 the last examination in a course – usu pl

finalist /'fienl·ist/ *n* a contestant in the finals of a competition

finality /fi'naləti, fie-/ *n* 1 the condition of being at an ultimate point, esp of development or authority 2 a fundamental fact, action, or belief

¹**finance** /'fienans/ *n* 1 pl resources of money 2 the system that includes the circulation of money and involves banking, credit, and investment 3 the science of the management of funds 4 the obtaining of funds – **-cial** *adj* – **-cially** *adv*

²**finance** *v* to raise or provide money for

financier /fi'nansi·ə, fie-/ *n* one skilled in dealing with finance or investment

finch /finch/ *n* any of numerous songbirds with a short stout beak adapted for crushing seeds

¹**find** /fiend/ *v* **found** /fownd/ 1a to come upon, esp accidentally; encounter **b** to meet with (a specified reception) 2a to come upon or discover by searching, effort, or experiment; obtain **b** to obtain by effort or management 3a to experience, feel **b** to perceive (oneself) to be in a specified place or condition **c** to gain or regain the use or power of **d** to bring (oneself) to a realization of one's powers or of one's true vocation 4 to provide, supply 5 to determine and announce — **find fault** to criticize unfavourably

²**find** *n* 1 an act or instance of finding sthg, esp sthg valuable 2 sby or sthg found; esp a valuable object or talented person discovered

finding /'fiending/ n 1 the result of a judicial inquiry 2 the result of an investigation – usu pl with sing. meaning

find out v 1 to learn by study, observation, or search; discover 2a to detect in an offence b to ascertain the true character or identity of; unmask

¹**fine** /fien/ n 1 a sum payable as punishment for an offence 2 a forfeiture or penalty paid to an injured party in a civil action

²**fine** v to punish by a fine – **finable, fineable** adj

³**fine** adj 1 free from impurity 2a very thin in gauge or texture b consisting of relatively small particles c very small d keen, sharp 3a subtle or sensitive in perception or discrimination b performed with extreme care and accuracy 4a superior in quality, conception, or appearance; excellent b bright and sunny 5 marked by or affecting often excessive elegance or refinement 6 very well 7 awful – used as an intensive – ~ly adv – ~ness n

⁴**fine** v 1 to purify, clarify – often + down 2 to make finer in quality or size – often + down

finery /'fienəri/ n dressy or showy clothing and jewels

¹**finesse** /fi'nes/ n 1 skilful handling of a situation; adroitness 2 the withholding of one's highest card in the hope that a lower card will take the trick because the only opposing higher card is in the hand of an opponent who has already played

²**finesse** v to make a finesse in playing cards

¹**finger** /'fing·gə/ n 1 any of the 5 parts at the end of the hand or forelimb; esp one other than the thumb 2a sthg that resembles a finger, esp in being long, narrow, and often tapering in shape b a part of a glove into which a finger is inserted — **have a finger in the/every pie** to be involved or have an interest in sthg/everything — infml — **pull/take one's finger out** Br to start working hard; get cracking — slang

²**finger** v 1 to play (a musical instrument) with the fingers 2 to touch or feel with the fingers; handle

'**finger,board** /-,bawd/ n the part of a stringed instrument against which the fingers press the strings to vary the pitch

fingering /'fing·gəring/ n (the marking indicating) the use or position of the fingers in sounding notes on an instrument

'**finger,print** /-,print/ n 1 the impression of a fingertip on any surface; esp an ink impression of the lines upon the fingertip taken for purposes of identification 2 unique distinguishing characteristics (e g of a recording machine or infrared spectrum)

'**finger,stall** /-,stawl/ n a protective cover for an injured finger

'**finger,tip** /-,tip/ adj readily accessible; being in close proximity

finicky /'finiki/ adj 1 fussy 2 requiring delicate attention to detail

finis /'finis/ n the end, conclusion – used esp to mark the end of a book or film

¹**finish** /'finish/ v 1a to end, terminate; also to end a relationship with b to eat, drink, or use entirely – often + off or up 2a to bring to completion or issue; complete, perfect – often + off b to complete the schooling of (a girl), esp in the social graces 3a to bring to an end the significance or effectiveness of b to bring about the death of 4 to arrive, end, or come to rest in a specified position or manner – often + up

²**finish** n 1a the final stage; the end b the cause of one's ruin; downfall 2 the texture or appearance of a surface, esp after a coating has been applied 3 the result or product of a finishing process 4 the quality or state of being perfected, esp in the social graces

'**finishing ,school** /'finishing/ n a private school for girls that prepares its students esp for social activities

finite /'fieniet/ adj 1a having definite or definable limits b subject to limitations, esp those imposed by the laws of nature 2 completely determinable in theory or in fact by counting, measurement, or thought – ~ly adv

¹**Finnish** /'finish/ adj (characteristic) of Finland

²**Finnish** n a language of Finland, Karelia, and parts of Sweden and Norway

fiord, fjord /fjawd, 'fee,awd/ n a narrow inlet of the sea between cliffs (e g in Norway)

fir /fuh/ n (the wood of) any of various related evergreen trees of the pine family that have flattish leaves and erect cones

¹**fire** /fie·ə/ n 1a the phenomenon of combustion manifested in light, flame, and heat b(1) burning passion or emotion b(2) inspiration 2 fuel in a state of combustion (e g in a fireplace or furnace) 3a a destructive burning (e g of a building or forest) b a severe trial or ordeal 4 brilliance, luminosity 5 the discharge of firearms 6 Br a small usu gas or electric domestic heater — **on fire** eager, burning — **under fire** under attack

²**fire** v 1a to ignite b(1) to inspire b(2) to inflame 2 to dismiss from a position 3 to discharge a firearm

'**fire,arm** /-,ahm/ n a weapon from which a shot is discharged by gunpowder – usu used only with reference to small arms

'**fire,ball** /-,bawl/ n 1 a large brilliant meteor 2 ball lightning 3 a highly energetic person – infml

'**fire,brand** /-,brand/ n 1 a piece of burning material, esp wood 2 one who creates unrest or strife; an agitator, troublemaker

'**fire,break** /-,brayk/ n a strip of cleared or unplanted land intended to check a forest or grass fire

'**fire,brick** /-,brik/ n a brick that is resistant to high temperatures and is used in furnaces, fireplaces, etc 'fire bri,gade n an organization for preventing or extinguishing fires; *esp* one maintained in Britain by local government

'fire,bug /-,bug/ n a pyromaniac, fire-raiser – *infml*

'fire,damp /-,damp/ n (the explosive mixture of air with) a combustible mine gas that consists chiefly of methane

'fire,fly /-,flie/ n any of various night-flying beetles that produce a bright intermittent light

'fire,guard /-,gahd/ n a protective metal framework placed in front of an open fire

'fire ,irons n pl utensils (e g tongs, poker, and shovel) for tending a household fire

'fire,light /-,liet/ n the light of a fire, esp of one in a fireplace

'fire ,lighter n a piece of inflammable material used to help light a fire (e g in a grate)

'fireman /-mən/, n, pl firemen 1 sby employed to extinguish fires 2 sby who tends or feeds fires or furnaces

'fire,place /-,plays/ n a usu framed opening made in a chimney to hold a fire; a hearth

'fire,proof /-,proohf/ v or adj (to make) proof against or resistant to fire; *also* heatproof

'fire-,raising n, Br arson – **fire-raiser** n

'fire,side /-,sied/ n 1 a place near the fire or hearth 2 home

'fire ,station n a building housing fire apparatus and usu firemen

'fire,trap /-,trap/ n a building difficult to escape from in case of fire

'fire,water /-,wawtə/ n strong alcoholic drink – *infml*

'fire,work /-,wuhk/ n 1 a device for producing a striking display (e g of light or noise) by the combustion of explosive or inflammable mixtures 2 pl **2a** a display of temper or intense conflict **b** pyrotechnics

'firing ,line n the forefront of an activity, esp one involving risk or difficulty – esp in *in the firing line*

'firing ,squad n a detachment detailed to fire a salute at a military burial or carry out an execution

firkin /'fuhkin/ n a small wooden vessel or cask of usu 9 gall capacity

¹firm /fuhm/ adj **1a** securely or solidly fixed in place **b** not weak or uncertain; vigorous **c** having a solid or compact structure that resists stress or pressure **2** not subject to change, unsteadiness, or disturbance; steadfast **3** indicating firmness or resolution – **~ly** adv – **~ness** n

²firm v 1 to make solid, compact, or firm 2 to put into final form; settle 3 to support, strengthen *USE* often + *up*

³firm n a business partnership not usu recognized as a legal person distinct from the members composing it; *broadly* any business unit or enterprise

firmament /'fuhməmənt/ n the vault or arch of the sky; the heavens

¹first /fuhst/ adj **1** preceding all others in time, order, or importance: e g **1a** earliest **b** being the lowest forward gear or speed of a motor vehicle **c** relating to or having the (most prominent and) usu highest part among a group of instruments or voices **2** least, slightest (e g hasn't the first idea what to do) – **at first hand** directly from the original source

²first adv 1 before anything else; at the beginning 2 for the first time 3 in preference to sthg else

³first n sthg or sby that is first: e g **a** the first occurrence or item of a kind **b** the first and lowest forward gear or speed of a motor vehicle **c** the winning place in a contest **d** *first, first class often cap* the highest level of an honours degree — **at first** at the beginning; initially — **from the first** from the beginning

,first 'aid n emergency care or treatment given to an ill or injured person before proper medical aid can be obtained

,first'born n born before all others; eldest

,first 'class n the first or highest group in a classification: e g **a** the highest of usu 3 classes of travel accommodation **b** the highest level of an honours degree – **first-class** adj

,first'fruits n pl **1** agricultural produce offered to God in thanksgiving **2** the earliest products or results of an enterprise

,first'hand adj of or coming directly from the original source

,firstly /-li/ adv in the first place; first

,first 'person n (a member of) a set of linguistic forms (e g verb forms and pronouns) referring to the speaker or writer of the utterance in which they occur

,first-'rate adj of the first or greatest order of size, importance, or quality

¹fiscal /'fiskl/ adj of taxation, public revenues, or public debt

²fiscal n a procurator-fiscal

¹fish /fish/ n, pl fish, fishes **1a** an aquatic animal – usu in combination **b** (the edible flesh of) any of numerous cold-blooded aquatic vertebrates that typically have gills and an elongated scaly body **2** a person; *esp* a fellow – usu derog — **fish out of water** a person who is out of his/her proper sphere or element

²fish v **1** to try to catch fish **2** to seek sthg by roundabout means **3a** to search for sthg underwater **b** to search (as if) by groping or feeling

'fisherman /-mən/ n 1 fem **fisherwoman** one who engages in fishing as an occupation or for pleasure **2** a ship used in commercial fishing

fishery /'fishəri/ n **1** the activity or business of catching fish and other sea animals **2** a place or establishment for catching fish and other sea animals

fish 'finger *n* a small oblong of fish coated with breadcrumbs

fishing /'fishing/ *n* the sport or business of or a place for catching fish

'fish,monger /-,mung·gə/ *n*, *chiefly Br* a retail fish dealer

'fish ,slice *n* **1** a broad-bladed knife for cutting and serving fish at table **2** a kitchen implement with a broad blade and long handle used esp for turning or lifting food in frying

'fish,wife /-,wief/ *n* **1** a woman who sells or guts fish **2** a vulgar abusive woman

fishy /'fishi/ *adj* **1** of or like fish, esp in taste or smell **2** creating doubt or suspicion; questionable – *infml*

fission /'fish(ə)n/ *n* **1** a splitting or breaking up into parts **2** reproduction by spontaneous division into 2 or more parts each of which grows into a complete organism **3** the splitting of an atomic nucleus with the release of large amounts of energy

fissure /'fishə/ *n* a narrow, long, and deep opening, usu caused by breaking or parting

fist /fist/ *n* the hand clenched with the fingers doubled into the palm and the thumb across the fingers

fisticuffs /'fisti,kufs/ *n pl* the act or practice of fighting with the fists – no longer in vogue; *humor*

¹fit /fit/ *n* **1a** a sudden violent attack of a disease (e g epilepsy), esp when marked by convulsions or unconsciousness **b** a sudden but transient attack of a specified physical disturbance **2** a sudden outburst or flurry, esp of a specified activity or emotion – **by/in fits and starts** in a jerky, impulsive, or irregular manner

²fit *adj* **1a** adapted or suited to an end or purpose **b** acceptable from a particular viewpoint (e g of competence, morality, or qualifications) **2a** in a suitable state; ready **b** in such a distressing state as to be ready to do or suffer sthg specified **3** healthy – ~**ness** *n*

³fit *v* **-tt-** **1** to be suitable for or to; harmonize with **2a** to be of the correct size or shape for **b** to insert or adjust until correctly in place **c** to try on (clothes) in order to make adjustments in size **d** to make a place or room for **3** to be in agreement or accord with **4** to cause to conform to or suit sthg **5** to supply, equip –often + *out*

⁴fit *n* **1** the manner in which clothing fits the wearer **2** the degree of closeness with which surfaces are brought together in an assembly of parts

fitful /'fitf(ə)l/ *adj* having a spasmodic or intermittent character; irregular – ~**ly** *adv*

fitment /'fitmənt/ *n* **1** a piece of equipment; *esp* an item of built-in furniture **2** *pl* fittings

fitter /'fitə/ *n* sby who assembles or repairs machinery or appliances

¹fitting /'fiting/ *adj* appropriate to the situation

²fitting *n* **1** a trying on of clothes which are in the process of being made or altered **2** a small often standardized part

fit up *v* **1** to fix up **2** *Br* to frame (e g for a crime) – *slang*

five /fiev/ *n* **1** the number 5 **2** the fifth in a set or series **3** sthg having 5 parts or members or a denomination of 5 **4** *pl but sing in constr* any of several games in which players hit a ball with their hands against the front wall of a 3- or 4-walled court

fiver /'fievə/ *n* a £5 or $5 note; *also* the sum of £5 – *infml*

¹fix /fiks/ *v* **1a** to make firm, stable, or stationary **b(1)** to kill, harden, and preserve for microscopic study **b(2)** to make the image of (a photographic film) permanent by removing unused sensitive chemicals **c** to fasten, attach **2** to hold or direct steadily **3a** to set or place definitely; establish **b** to assign **4** to set in order; adjust **5** to repair, mend **6** *chiefly NAm* to get ready or prepare (esp food or drink) **7a** to get even with – *infml* **b** to influence by illicit means – *infml*

²fix *n* **1** a position of difficulty or embarrassment; a trying predicament **2** (a determination of) the position (e g of a ship) found by bearings, radio, etc **3** a shot of a narcotic – *slang*

fixation /fik'saysh(ə)n/ *n* an (obsessive or unhealthy) attachment or preoccupation

fixative /'fiksətiv/ *n* sthg that fixes or sets: e g **a** a substance added to a perfume, esp to prevent too rapid evaporation **b** a varnish used esp to protect crayon drawings **c** a substance used to fix living tissue

fixed /fikst/ *adj* **1a** securely placed or fastened; stationary **b** not subject to or capable of change or fluctuation **c** intent **2** supplied with sthg needed or desirable (e g money) – *infml* – **no fixed abode** no regular home

fixity /'fiksəti/ *n* the quality or state of being fixed or stable

fixture /'fikschə/ *n* **1** fixing or being fixed **2** sthg fixed (e g to a building) as a permanent appendage or as a structural part **3** (an esp sporting event held on) a settled date or time

fix up *v* to provide *with*; make the arrangements for – *infml*

¹fizz /fiz/ *v* to make a hissing or sputtering sound

²fizz *n* **1a** a fizzing sound **b** spirit, liveliness **2** an effervescent beverage (e g champagne) – *infml* – ~**y** *adj*

fizzle /'fizl/ *v or n* fizzling /'fizling/ (to make) a weak fizzing sound

fizzle out *v* to fail or end feebly, esp after a promising start – *infml*

fjord /fyawd, 'fee,awd/ *n* a fiord

flabbergast /'flabə,gahst/ *v* to overwhelm with shock or astonishment – *infml*

flabby /'flabi/ *adj* **1** (having flesh) lacking resilience or firmness **2** ineffective, feeble – **bily** *adv* – **biness** *n*

flaccid /'flaksid/ *adj* **1a** lacking normal or youthful firmness; flabby **b** limp **2** lacking vigour or force – ~**ity** *n*

¹**flag** /flag/ *n* a (wild) iris or similar plant of damp ground with long leaves

²**flag** *n* a (slab of) hard evenly stratified stone that splits into flat pieces suitable for paving – **flag** *v*

³**flag** *n* **1** a usu rectangular piece of fabric of distinctive design that is used as a symbol (e g of a nation) or as a signalling device **2** the nationality of registration of a ship, aircraft, etc

⁴**flag** *v* -**gg- 1** to put a flag on (e g for identification) **2a** to signal to (as if) with a flag **b** to signal to stop – usu + *down*

⁵**flag** *v* -**gg-** to become feeble, less interesting, or less active; decline

¹**flagellate** /'flajilayt/ *v* to whip or flog, esp as a religious punishment or for sexual gratification – **lation** *n*

²**flagellate** /'flajilat/, **flagellated** /-laytid/ *adj* **1** having flagella **2** shaped like a flagellum

flagellum /flə'jelam/ *n, pl* **flagella** /-lə/ *also* **flagellums** any of various elongated filament-shaped appendages of plants or animals

flag of con'venience *n* the flag of a country in which a ship is registered in order to avoid the taxes and regulations of the ship-owner's home country

flagon /'flagon/ *n* a large squat short-necked bottle, often with 1 or 2 ear-shaped handles, in which cider, wine, etc are sold

flagrant /'flaygront/ *adj* conspicuously scandalous; outrageous – **ancy** *n* – ~**ly** *adv*

'flag,ship /-,ship/ *n* **1** the ship that carries the commander of a fleet or subdivision of a fleet and flies his flag **2** the finest, largest, or most important one of a set

'flag-,waving *n* passionate appeal to patriotic or partisan sentiment; jingoism

¹**flail** /flayl/ *n* a threshing implement consisting of a stout short free-swinging stick attached to a wooden handle

²**flail** *v* **1** to strike (as if) with a flail **2** to wave, thrash – often + *about*

flair /fleə/ *n* **1** intuitive discernment, esp in a specified field **2** natural aptitude; talent **3** sophistication or smartness *USE* (1 & 2) usu + *for*

flak /flak/ *n* **1** the fire from antiaircraft guns **2** heavy criticism or opposition – infml

flake /flayk/ *n* a platform, tray, etc for drying fish or produce

¹**flake** *n* **1** a small loose mass or particle **2** a thin flattened piece or layer; a chip **3** a pipe tobacco of small irregularly cut pieces

²**flake** *v* to form or separate into flakes; chip

flake out *v* to collapse or fall asleep from exhaustion – infml

flaky /'flayki/ *adj* **1** consisting of flakes **2** tending to flake – **flakiness** *n*

flamboyant /flam'boyont/ *adj* **1** ornate, florid; *also* resplendent **2** given to dashing display; ostentatious – **boyance** *n*

¹**flame** /flaym/ *n* **1** (a tongue of) the glowing gaseous part of a fire **2a** a state of blazing usu destructive combustion – often pl with sing. meaning **b** a condition or appearance suggesting a flame, esp in having red, orange, or yellow colour **c** a bright reddish orange colour **3** a sweetheart – usu in *old flame*

²**flame** *v* **1** to burn with a flame; blaze **2** to break out violently or passionately **3** to shine brightly like flame; glow

flamenco /flə'mengkoh/ *n, pl* **flamencos** (music suitable for) a vigorous rhythmic dance (style) of the Andalusian gypsies

'flame,thrower /-,throh·ə/ *n* a weapon that expels a burning stream of liquid

flaming /'flayming/ *adj* **1** being in flames or on fire; blazing **2** resembling or suggesting a flame in colour, brilliance, or shape **3** ardent, passionate **4** bloody, blooming – slang

flamingo /flə'ming·goh/ *n, pl* **flamingos** *also* **flamingoes** any of several web-footed broad-billed aquatic birds with long legs and neck and rosy-white plumage

flan /flan/ *n* a pastry or cake case containing a sweet or savoury filling

flange /flanj/ *n* a rib or rim for strength, for guiding, or for attachment to another object

¹**flank** /flangk/ *n* **1** the (fleshy part of the) side, esp of a quadruped, between the ribs and the hip **2a** a side **b** the right or left of a formation

²**flank** *v* to be situated at the side of; border

¹**flannel** /'flanl/ *n* **1a** a twilled loosely woven wool or worsted fabric with a slightly napped surface **b** a stout cotton fabric usu napped on 1 side **2** *pl* garments of flannel; *esp* men's trousers **3** *Br* a cloth used for washing the skin, esp of the face **4** *chiefly Br* flattering talk; *also* nonsense – infml

²**flannel** *v*, -**ll-** (*NAm* -**l-**, -**ll-**) /'flanl·ing/ *chiefly Br* to speak or write flannel, esp with intent to deceive *USE* infml

flannelette /,flanl'et/ *n* a napped cotton flannel

¹**flap** /flap/ *n* **1** sthg broad or flat, flexible or hinged, and usu thin, that hangs loose or projects freely: e g **1a** an extended part forming a closure (e g of an envelope or carton) **b** a movable control surface on an aircraft wing for increasing lift or lift and drag **2** the motion of sthg broad and flexible (e g a sail); *also* an instance of the up-and-down motion of a wing (e g of a bird) **3** a state of excitement or panicky confusion; an uproar – infml

fla

²flap *v* **-pp-** **1** to sway loosely, usu with a noise of striking and esp when moved by the wind **2** to beat (sthg suggesting) wings **3** to be in a flap or panic – infml

'flap,jack /-ˌjak/ *n* **1** a thick pancake **2** a biscuit made with oats and syrup

¹flare /fleə/ *v* **1a** to shine or blaze with a sudden flame – usu + *up* **b** to become suddenly and often violently excited, angry, or active – usu + *up* **2** to open or spread outwards; *esp* to widen gradually towards the lower edge

²flare *n* **1a** (a device or substance used to produce) a fire or blaze of light used to signal, illuminate, or attract attention **b** a temporary outburst of energy from a small area of the sun's surface **3** a sudden outburst (e g of sound, excitement, or anger) **4** a spreading outwards; *also* a place or part that spreads

'flare-ˌup *n* an instance of sudden activity, emotion, etc

¹flash /flash/ *v* **1a** to cause the sudden appearance or reflection of (esp light) **b(1)** to cause (e g a mirror) to reflect light **b(2)** to cause (a light) to flash **c** to convey by means of flashes of light **2a** to make known or cause to appear with great speed **b** to display ostentatiously **c** to expose to view suddenly and briefly

²flash *n* **1** a sudden burst of light **2** a sudden burst of perception, emotion, etc **3** a short time **4** an esp vulgar or ostentatious display **5a** a brief look; a glimpse **b** a brief news report, esp on radio or television **c** flashlight photography **6** a thin ridge on a cast or forged article, resulting from the hot metal, plastic, etc penetrating between the 2 parts of the mould **7** an indecent exposure of the genitals – slang

³flash *adj* **1** of sudden origin or onset and usu short duration; *also* carried out very quickly **2** flashy, showy – infml

'flash,back /-ˌbak/ *n* **1** (an) interruption of chronological sequence in a book, play, or film by the evocation of earlier events **2** a burst of flame back or out to an unwanted position (e g in a furnace)

'flash,bulb /-ˌbulb/ *n* an electric flash lamp in which metal foil or wire is burned

flasher /'flashə/ *n* **1** a device for automatically flashing a light **2** one who commits the offence of indecent exposure – slang

'flash,gun /-ˌgun/ *n* a device for holding and operating a photographic flashlight

'flash,light /-ˌliet/ *n* **1** a usu regularly flashing light used for signalling (e g in a lighthouse) **2** (a photograph taken with) a sudden bright artificial light used in taking photographic pictures **3** an electric torch

'flash ,point *n* the temperature at which vapour from a volatile substance ignites

flashy /'flashi/ *adj* **1** superficially attractive; temporarily brilliant or bright **2** ostentatious or showy, esp beyond the bounds of good taste – **-hily** *adv* – **-hiness** *n*

flask /flahsk/ *n* **1** a broad flat bottle, usu of metal or leather-covered glass, used to carry alcohol or other drinks on the person **2** any of several conical, spherical, etc narrow-necked usu glass containers used in a laboratory **3** a vacuum flask

¹flat /flat/ *adj* **-tt-** **1** having a continuous horizontal surface **2a** lying at full length or spread out on a surface; prostrate **b** resting with a surface against sthg **3** having a broad smooth surface and little thickness; *also* shallow **4a** clearly unmistakable; downright **b(1)** fixed, absolute **b(2)** exact **5a** lacking animation; dull, monotonous; *also* inactive **b** having lost effervescence or sparkle **6a** *of a tyre* lacking air; deflated **b** *of a battery* completely or partially discharged **7a** *of a musical note* lowered a semitone in pitch **b** lower than the proper musical pitch **8** having a low trajectory **9a** uniform in colour **b** *of a painting* lacking illusion of depth **c** *esp of paint* having a matt finish – **~ness** *n*

²flat *n* **1** a flat part or surface **2** (a character indicating) a musical note 1 semitone lower than a specified or particular note **3** a flat piece of theatrical scenery **4** a flat tyre **5** *often cap* horse racing over courses without jumps; *also* the season for this

³flat *adv* **1** positively, uncompromisingly **2** on or against a flat surface **b** so as to be spread out; at full length **3** below the proper musical pitch **4** wholly, completely – infml

⁴flat *n* **-tt-** a self-contained set of rooms used as a dwelling

'flat,fish /-ˌfish/ *n* any of an order of marine fishes (e g the flounders and soles) that swim on one side of the flattened body and have both eyes on the upper side

,flat 'out *adv* at maximum speed, capacity, or performance

flat spin *n* **1** an aerial manoeuvre or flight condition consisting of a spin in which the aircraft is roughly horizontal **2** a state of extreme agitation – infml

flatten /'flat(ə)n/ *v* **1** to lower in pitch, esp by a semitone **2** to beat or overcome utterly – infml **3** to become flat or flatter: e g **3a** to extend in or into a flat position or form – often + *out* **b** to become uniform or stabilized, often at a new lower level – usu + *out*

flatter /'flatə/ *v* **1** to praise excessively, esp from motives of self-interest or in order to gratify another's vanity **2** to raise the hope of or gratify, often groundlessly or with intent to deceive **3** to portray or represent (too) favourably – **~er** *n* – **~y** *n*

flaunt /flawnt/ *v* **1** to display ostentatiously or impudently; parade **2** to flout – nonstandard

flautist /'flawtist/ *n* one who plays a flute

¹**flavour**, *NAm chiefly* **flavor** /'flayvə/ n 1 the blend of taste and smell sensations evoked by a substance in the mouth; *also* a distinctive flavour 2 characteristic or predominant quality – ~**less** *adj*

²**flavour**, *NAm chiefly* **flavor** v to give or add flavour to

flaw /flaw/ n 1 a blemish, imperfection 2 a usu hidden defect (e g a crack) that may cause failure under stress – **flaw** v

flax /flaks/ n 1 (a plant related to or resembling) a slender erect blue-flowered plant cultivated for its strong woody fibre and seed 2 the fibre of the flax plant, esp when prepared for spinning into linen

flaxen /'flaks(ə)n/ adj 1 made of flax 2 resembling flax, esp in being a pale soft straw colour

flay /flay/ v 1 to strip off the skin or surface of; *also* to whip savagely 2 to criticize or censure harshly

flea /flee/ n any of an order of wingless bloodsucking jumping insects that feed on warm-blooded animals — **with a flea in one's ear** with a usu embarrassing reprimand

'**flea bite** /-ˌbiet/ n a trifling problem or expense – infml

'**flea pit** /-ˌpit/ n, *chiefly Br* a shabby cinema or theatre – infml or humor

¹**fleck** /flek/ v to mark or cover with flecks; streak

²**fleck** n 1 a small spot or mark, esp of colour 2 a grain, particle

fledgling, fledgeling /'flejling/ n 1 a young bird just fledged 2 an inexperienced person

flee /flee/ v **fled** /fled/ 1 to run away from danger, evil, etc 2 to pass away swiftly; vanish

¹**fleece** /flees/ n the coat of wool covering a sheep or similar animal

²**fleece** v to strip of money or property, usu by fraud or extortion; *esp* to overcharge – infml

¹**fleet** /fleet/ n 1 a number of warships under a single command 2 *often cap* a country's navy – usu + *the* 3 a group of ships, aircraft, lorries, etc owned or operated under one management

²**fleet** adj swift in motion; nimble – ~**ly** adv – ~**ness** n

fleeting /'fleeting/ adj passing swiftly; transitory – ~**ly** adv

'**Fleet Street** n the national London-based press

¹**flesh** /flesh/ n 1a the soft, esp muscular, parts of the body of a (vertebrate) animal as distinguished from visceral structures, bone, hide, etc **b** excess weight; fat 2 the edible parts of an animal 3a the physical being of humans **b** the physical or sensual aspect of human nature 4a human beings; humankind – esp in *all flesh* **b** kindred, stock 5 a fleshy (edible) part of a plant or fruit – ~**y** adj — **in the flesh** in bodily form; in person

²**flesh** v to clothe or cover (as if) with flesh; *broadly* to give substance to – usu + *out*

'**flesh wound** n an injury involving penetration of body muscle without damage to bones or internal organs

fleur-de-lis, fleur-de-lys /ˌfluh də 'lee/ n, pl **fleurs-de-lis, fleur-de-lis, fleurs-de-lys, fleur-de-lys** /lee(z)/ a conventionalized iris in heraldry usu associated with France

flew /flooh/ *past of* **fly**

¹**flex** /fleks/ v 1 to bend 2 to move (a muscle or muscles) so as to flex a limb or joint

²**flex** n a length of flexible insulated electrical cable used in connecting a portable electrical appliance to a socket

flexible /'fleksəbl/ adj 1 capable of being bent; pliant 2 yielding to influence; tractable 3 capable of changing in response to new conditions; versatile – ~**ibly** adv – ~**ibility** n

flibbertigibbet /ˌflibəti'jibit/ n a flighty or garrulous woman – infml

¹**flick** /flik/ n a light jerky movement or blow

²**flick** v 1a to strike lightly with a quick sharp motion **b** to remove with flicks – usu + *away* or *off* 2 to cause to move with a flick

³**flick** n 1 a film, movie 2 (a showing of a film at) a cinema – + *the*; usu pl *USE* infml

¹**flicker** /'flikə/ v 1 to move irregularly or unsteadily; quiver 2a to burn fitfully or with a fluctuating light **b** *of a light* to fluctuate in intensity

²**flicker** n 1 a flickering (movement or light) 2 a momentary quickening or stirring

'**flick-knife** n a pocket knife with a blade that flicks open when required

flier, flyer /'flie-ə/ n 1 sby or sthg that moves very fast 2 an airman

¹**flight** /fliet/ n 1 a passage through the air using wings 2a a passage or journey through air or space; *specif* any such flight scheduled by an airline **b** swift movement 3 a group of similar creatures or objects flying through the air 4 a brilliant, imaginative, or unrestrained exercise or display 5 (a series of locks, hurdles, etc resembling) a continuous series of stairs from one landing or floor to another 6 any of the vanes or feathers at the tail of a dart, arrow, etc that provide stability 7 a small unit of (military) aircraft or personnel in the Royal Air Force

²**flight** n an act or instance of fleeing

'**flight deck** n 1 the deck of a ship used for the takeoff and landing of aircraft 2 the compartment housing the controls and those crew who operate them in an aircraft

flighty /'flieti/ adj 1 easily excited or upset; skittish 2 irresponsible, silly; *also* flirtatious – ~**tiness** n

flimsy /'flimzi/ adj 1a lacking in strength or substance **b** of inferior materials or workmanship; easily destroyed or broken 2 having little worth or plausibility – ~**sily** adv – ~**siness** n

flinch /flinch/ v to shrink (as if) from physical pain; *esp* to tense the muscles involuntarily in fear

¹**fling** /fling/ *v* **flung** /flung/ **1** to throw or cast (aside), esp with force or recklessness **2** to place or send suddenly and unceremoniously **3** to cast or direct (oneself or one's efforts) vigorously or unrestrainedly

²**fling** *n* **1** a period devoted to self-indulgence **2** a casual attempt – chiefly infml

flint /flint/ *n* **1** a hard quartz found esp in chalk or limestone **2** a flint implement used by primitive human beings **3** a material used for producing a spark (e g in a cigarette lighter) – **~y** *adj*

¹**flip** /flip/ *v* **-pp- 1** to toss or cause to move with a sharp movement, esp so as to be turned over in the air **2** to flick **3** to turn *over* **4** to lose one's sanity or self-control

²**flip** *n* **1** a (motion used in) flipping or a flick **2** a somersault, esp when performed in the air **3** a mixed drink usu consisting of a sweetened spiced alcoholic drink to which beaten eggs have been added

³**flip** *adj* **-pp-** flippant, impertinent – infml

flip-flop /'flip ,flop/ *n* **1** a backward handspring **2** a rubber sandal consisting of a sole and a strap fixed between the toes

flippant /'flip(ə)nt/ *adj* lacking proper respect or seriousness, esp in the consideration of grave matters – **-pancy** *n* – **~ly** *adv*

flipper /'flipə/ *n* **1** a broad flat limb (e g of a seal) adapted for swimming **2** a flat rubber shoe with the front expanded into a paddle used for underwater swimming

flipping /'fliping/ *adj or adv*, *Br* damned, bloody – euph

'**flip ,side** *n* the side of a gramophone record which is not the principal marketing attraction

¹**flirt** /flɜːt/ *v* **1** to behave amorously without serious intent **2** to slow superficial interest in – + *with* – **~ation** *n* – **~atious** *adj* – **~atiously** *adv*

²**flirt** *n* **1** an act or instance of flirting **2** one, esp a woman, who flirts

flit /flit/ *v* **-tt- 1** to pass lightly and quickly or irregularly from one place or condition to another; *esp* to fly in this manner **2** to move house, esp rapidly and secretly – **flit** *n*

¹**float** /fləʊt/ *n* **1a** a cork or other device used to keep the baited end of a fishing line afloat **b** sthg (e g a hollow ball) that floats at the end of a lever in a cistern, tank, or boiler and regulates the liquid level **c** a watertight structure enabling an aircraft to float on water **2** a tool for smoothing a surface of plaster, concrete, etc **3** (a vehicle with) a platform supporting an exhibit in a parade **4** a sum of money available for day-to-day use (e g for expenses or for giving change)

²**float** *v* **1** to rest on the surface of or be suspended in a fluid **2a** to drift (as if) on or through a liquid **b** to wander aimlessly **3** to lack firmness of purpose; vacillate **4** *of a currency* to find a level in the international exchange market in response to the

law of supply and demand and without artificial support or control **5** to present (e g an idea) for acceptance or rejection – **~er** *n*

¹**flock** /flok/ *n sing or pl in constr* **1** a group of birds or mammals assembled or herded together **2** a church congregation, considered in relation to its pastor **3** a large group

²**flock** *v* to gather or move in a crowd

³**flock** *n* **1** a tuft of wool or cotton fibre **2** woollen or cotton refuse used for stuffing furniture, mattresses, etc **3** very short or pulverized fibre used esp to form a velvety pattern on cloth or paper or a protective covering on metal

floe /fləʊ/ *n* (a sheet of) floating ice, esp on the sea

flog /flog/ *v* **-gg- 1** to beat severely with a rod, whip, etc **2** to force into action; drive **3** to repeat (sthg) so frequently as to make uninteresting – esp in *flog something to death*; infml **4** *Br* to sell – slang — **flog a dead horse** to waste time or energy on worn-out or previously settled subjects

¹**flood** /flʌd/ *n* **1** an overflowing of a body of water, esp onto normally dry land **2** an overwhelming quantity or volume **3** a floodlight

²**flood** *v* **1** to cover with a flood; inundate **2** to fill abundantly or excessively **3** to drive *out* of a house, village, etc by flooding

'**flood ,gate** /-,gaɪt/ *n* sthg serving to restrain an outburst

'**flood ,light** /-,liet/ *n* (a source of) a broad beam of light for artificial illumination – **floodlight** *v*

¹**floor** /flaw/ *n* **1** the level base of a room **2a** the lower inside surface of a hollow structure (e g a cave or bodily part) **b** a ground surface **3** a structure between 2 storeys of a building; *also* a storey **4a** the part of an assembly in which members sit and speak **b** the members of an assembly **c** the right to address an assembly **5** a lower limit

²**floor** *v* **1** to knock to the floor or ground **2** to reduce to silence or defeat; nonplus

¹**flop** /flop/ *v* **-pp- 1** to swing or hang loosely but heavily **2** to fall, move, or drop in a heavy, clumsy, or relaxed manner **3** to relax completely; slump **4** to fail completely

²**flop** *n* **1** (the dull sound of) a flopping motion **2** a complete failure – infml

³**flop** *adv* with a flop

floppy /'flopi/ *adj* tending to hang loosely; *esp* being both soft and flexible – **floppily** *adv* – **floppiness** *n*

,**floppy 'disk** *n* a flexible disk that is coated with a magnetic substance and is used to store data for a computer

flora /'flawrə/ *n pl* **floras** *also* **florae** /'flawri/ **1** a treatise on, or a work used to identify, the plants of a region **2** plant life (of a region, period, or special environment)

floral /'flawrəl, 'florəl/ *adj* of flowers or a flora

florid /'florid/ *adj* **1** excessively flowery or ornate in style **2** tinged with red; ruddy – **~ly** *adv*

flu

florin /'florin/ *n* **1** any of various former gold coins of European countries **2** a former British or Commonwealth silver coin worth 2 shillings **3** the major unit of currency of the Netherlands and Surinam

florist /'florist/ *n* one who deals in or grows flowers and ornamental plants for sale

floss /flos/ *n* **1** waste or short silk or silky fibres, esp from the outer part of a silkworm's cocoon **2** soft thread of silk or cotton for embroidery

flotilla /fla'tila/ *n* a small fleet of ships, esp warships

flotsam and 'jetsam /'jets(a)m/ *n* **1** vagrants **2** unimportant miscellaneous material

¹**flounce** /flowns/ *v* **1** to move in a violent or exaggerated fashion **2** to go in such a way as to attract attention, esp when angry

²**flounce** *n* a wide gathered strip of fabric attached by the gathered edge (e g to the hem of a skirt or dress) – ~**d** *adj*

¹**flounder** /'flowndə/ *n, pl* **flounder**, *esp for different types* **flounders** any of various flatfishes including some marine food fishes

²**flounder** *v* **1** to struggle to move or obtain footing **2** to proceed or act clumsily or feebly

flour /flowə/ *n* **1** finely ground meal, esp of wheat **2** a fine soft powder – ~**y** *adj*

¹**flourish** /'flurish/ *v* **1** to grow luxuriantly; thrive **2a** to prosper **b** to be in good health **3** to wave or wield with dramatic gestures; brandish – ~**ingly** *adv*

²**flourish** *n* a showy or flowery embellishment (e g in literature or handwriting) or passage (e g in music) **2a** an act of brandishing **b** an ostentatious or dramatic action

flout /flowt/ *v* to treat with contemptuous disregard; scorn

¹**flow** /floh/ *v* **1a** to issue or move (as if) in a stream **b** to circulate **2** *of the tide* to rise **3** to abound **4a** to proceed smoothly and readily **b** to have a smooth graceful continuity **5** to hang loose or freely

²**flow** *n* **1** a flowing **2a** a smooth uninterrupted movement or supply; the motion characteristic of fluids **b** a stream or gush of fluid **c** the direction of (apparent) movement **3** the quantity that flows in a certain time

¹**flower** /flowə/ *n* **1a** a blossom **b** a plant cultivated for its blossoms **2a** the finest or most perfect part or example **b** the finest most vigorous period; prime **c** a state of blooming or flourishing – esp in *in flower* – ~**less** *adj*

²**flower** *v* **1** to produce flowers; blossom **2** to reach a peak condition; flourish

'**flower,pot** /-,pot/ *n* a pot, typically the shape of a small bucket, in which to grow plants

flowery /'flowəri/ *adj* **1** of or resembling flowers **2** containing or using highly ornate language

flown /flohn/ *past part of* **fly**

flu /flooh/ *n* influenza

fluctuate /'fluktyoo,ayt, -choo,ayt/ *v* **1** to rise and fall; swing back and forth **2** to change continually and irregularly; waver – **-ation** *n*

flue /flooh/ *n* **1** a channel in a chimney for flame and smoke **2** a pipe for conveying heat (e g to water in a steam boiler)

fluent /'flooh-ənt/ *adj* able to speak or write with facility; *also* spoken or written in this way **2** effortlessly smooth and rapid; polished – **-ency** *n* – ~**ly** *adv*

¹**fluff** /fluf/ *n* **1a** small loose bits of waste material (e g hairs and threads) that stick to clothes, carpets, etc **b** soft light fur, down, etc **2** a blunder; *esp* an actor's lapse of memory – chiefly infml – ~**y** *adj* – ~**iness** *n*

²**fluff** *v* **1** to make or become fluffy – often + *out* or *up* **2** to make a mistake, esp in a performance

¹**fluid** /'flooh-id/ *adj* **1a** able to flow **b** likely or tending to change or move; not fixed **2** characterized by or employing a smooth easy style **3** easily converted into cash – ~**ity** *n*

²**fluid** *n* sthg capable of flowing to conform to the outline of its container; *specif* a liquid or gas

'**fluid 'ounce**, *NAm* **fluidounce** /,flooh-i'downs/ *n* a British unit of liquid capacity equal to ¹/₂₀ imperial pt 28.41cm³)

¹**fluke** /floohk/ *n* **1** a flatfish **2** a liver fluke or related parasitic worm

²**fluke** *n* **1** the part of an anchor that digs into the sea, river, etc bottom **2** a barbed end (e g of a harpoon)

³**fluke** *n* **1** an accidentally successful stroke or action **2** a stroke of luck – **-ky**, **-key** *adj*

flummox /'fluməks/ *v* to bewilder or confuse completely

flung /flung/ *past of* **fling**

flunk /flungk/ *v, chiefly NAm* **1** to fail, esp in an examination or course **2** to be turned *out* of a school or college for failure

flunky, flunkey /'flungki/ *n* **1** a liveried servant **2** a person performing menial duties

fluorescent /flooə'res(ə)nt/ *adj* **1** emitting light when subjected to electromagnetic radiation **2** bright and glowing – **-escence** *n*

fluoridate /'flooəri,dayt/ *v* to add a fluoride to (e g drinking water)

fluoride /'flooəried/ *n* a compound of fluorine

fluorine /'flooəreen/ *n* a nonmetallic element that is normally a pale yellowish toxic gas

¹**flurry** /'fluri/ *n* **1a** a gust of wind **b** a brief light fall of snow **2** a state of nervous excitement or bustle **3** a short-lived outburst of trading activity

²**flurry** *v* to (cause to) become agitated and confused

¹**flush** /flush/ *v* to expose or chase from a place of concealment – often + *out*

²**flush** n 1 (a cleansing with) a sudden flow, esp of water 2 a surge of emotion 3 a a tinge of red, esp in the cheeks; a blush b a fresh and vigorous state 4 a transitory sensation of extreme heat

³**flush** v 1 a to glow brightly with a ruddy colour b to blush 2 to inflame, excite – usu pass 3 to pour liquid over or through; esp to cleanse or dispose of (the contents of a toilet) with a rush of liquid

⁴**flush** adj 1 a having or forming a continuous edge or plane surface; not indented, recessed, or projecting b arranged edge to edge so as to fit snugly 2 having a plentiful supply of money – infml

⁵**flush** adv 1 so as to form a level or even surface or edge 2 squarely

⁶**flush** n a hand of playing cards, esp in a gambling game, all of the same suit

fluster /'flustə/ v to make or become agitated, nervous, or confused – **fluster** n

flute /flooht/ n 1 a keyed woodwind instrument consisting of a cylindrical tube stopped at one end that is played by blowing air across a side hole 2 a a grooved pleat b any of the vertical parallel grooves on the shaft of a classical column

¹**flutter** /'flutə/ v 1 to flap the wings rapidly 2 a to move with quick wavering or flapping motions b to beat or vibrate in irregular spasms 3 to move about or behave in an agitated aimless manner

²**flutter** n 1 a state of (nervous) confusion, excitement, or commotion 2 chiefly Br a small gamble or bet

flux /fluks/ n 1 a continuous flow or flowing 2 a an influx b continual change; fluctuation 3 a substance used to promote fusion of metals (e g in soldering)

¹**fly** /flie/ v **flew** /flooh/; **flown** /flohn/ 1 a to move in or through the air by means of wings b to float, wave, or soar in the air 2 to take flight; flee 3 a to move, act, or pass swiftly b to move or pass suddenly and violently into a specified state 4 to operate or travel in an aircraft or spacecraft 5 to depart in haste; dash – chiefly infml — **fly at/on, fly out at** to assail suddenly and violently — **fly in the face/teeth of** to act in open defiance or disobedience of — **fly off the handle** to lose one's temper, esp suddenly

²**fly** n 1 pl the space over a stage where scenery and equipment can be hung 2 a (garment) opening concealed by a fold of cloth extending over the fastener; esp, pl such an opening in the front of a pair of trousers

³**fly** adj, chiefly Br keen, artful – infml

⁴**fly** n 1 a winged insect – often in combination (e g mayfly) 2 a natural or artificial fly attached to a fishhook for use as bait — **fly in the ointment** a detracting factor or element

flyaway /'flie-ə₁way/ adj 1 lacking practical sense; flighty 2 esp of the hair tending not to stay in place

¹**fly₁blown** /-₁blohn/ adj 1 infested with maggots 2 impure, tainted; also not new; used

¹**fly-by-₁night** n 1 one who seeks to evade responsibilities or debts by flight 2 a shaky business enterprise USE chiefly infml

²**fly-by-₁night** adj 1 given to making a quick profit, usu by disreputable or irresponsible acts; broadly untrustworthy 2 transitory, passing USE chiefly infml

flyer /'flie-ə/ n a flier

¹**fly-₁fishing** n fishing (e g for salmon or trout) using artificial flies as bait

¹**fly-₁half** n a position in rugby between the scrum and the three-quarters

¹**flying** /'flie-ing/ adj 1 a (capable of) moving in the air b rapidly moving c very brief; hasty 2 intended for ready movement or action 3 of (the operation of) or using an aircraft 4 (to be) traversed after a flying start — **with flying colours** with complete or eminent success

₁flying 'saucer n any of various unidentified flying objects reported as being saucer- or disc-shaped

¹**flying ₁squad** n, often cap F&S a standby group of people, esp police, ready to move or act swiftly in an emergency

₁flying 'start n a privileged or successful beginning

¹**fly₁over** /-₁ohvə/ n, Br (the upper level of) a crossing of 2 roads, railways, etc at different levels

¹**fly₁paper** /-₁paypə/ n paper coated with a sticky, often poisonous, substance for killing flies

¹**fly₁past** /-₁pahst/ n, Br a ceremonial usu low-altitude flight by (an) aircraft over a person or public gathering

¹**fly ₁sheet** n 1 a small pamphlet or circular 2 an outer protective sheet covering a tent

¹**fly₁weight** /-₁wayt/ n a boxer who weighs not more than 8st (50.8kg) if professional or more than 48kg (about 7st 7lb) but not more than 51kg (about 8st) if amateur

¹**fly₁wheel** /-₁weel/ n a wheel with a heavy rim that when revolving can either reduce speed fluctuations in the rotation of an engine or store energy

FM /₁ef 'em/ adj of or being a broadcasting or receiving system using frequency modulation and usu noted for lack of interference

¹**foal** /fohl/ n a young animal of the horse family

²**foal** v to give birth to (a foal)

¹**foam** /fohm/ n 1 a (a substance in the form of) a light frothy mass of fine bubbles formed in or on the surface of a liquid (e g by agitation or fermentation) b a frothy mass formed in salivating or sweating c a chemical froth discharged from fire extinguishers 2 a material in a lightweight cellular form resulting from introduction of gas bubbles during manufacture — **foamy** adj

²**foam** v 1 a to produce or form foam b to froth at the mouth, esp in anger; broadly to be angry 2 to gush out in foam 3 to become covered (as if) with foam 4 to cause air bubbles to form in

fob /fob/ *n* **1** a small pocket on or near the waistband of a man's trousers, orig for holding a watch **2** a short strap or chain attached to a watch carried in a fob or a waistcoat pocket

fob off *v* **-bb- 1** to put off with a trick or excuse – usu + *with* **2** to pass or offer (sthg spurious or inferior) as genuine or perfect – usu + *on*

focal length *n* the distance between the optical centre of a lens or mirror and the focal point

fo'c'sle /'fohks(ə)l/ *n* a forecastle

¹**focus** /'fohkəs/ *n, pl* **focuses, foci** /'fohkie, -sie/ **1a** a point at which rays (e g of light, heat, or sound) converge or from which they (appear to) diverge after reflection or refraction **b** the point at which an object must be placed for an image formed by a lens or mirror to be sharp **2a** the distance between a lens and the point at which it forms a focus **b** adjustment (e g of the eye) necessary for distinct vision **c** a state in which sthg must be placed in order to be clearly perceived **3** a centre of activity or attention **4** the place of origin of an earthquake – **focal** *adj* — **out of/in focus** not/having or giving the proper sharpness of outline due to good focussing

²**focus** *v* **-ss-, -s- 1** to bring or come to a focus; converge **2** to cause to be concentrated **3** to adjust the focus of **4** to bring one's eyes or a camera to a focus

fodder /'fodə/ *n* **1** (coarse) food for cattle, horses, sheep, or other domestic animals **2** sthg used to supply a constant demand

foe /foh/ *n* an enemy, adversary

foetus, fetus /'feetəs/ *n* an unborn or unhatched vertebrate; *specif* a developing human from usu 3 months after conception to birth – **foetal** *adj*

¹**fog** /fog/ *n* **1** a (murky condition of the atmosphere caused esp by) fine particles, specif of water, suspended in the lower atmosphere **2a** a state of confusion or bewilderment **b** sthg that confuses or obscures

²**fog** *v* **1** to envelop or suffuse (as if) with fog **2** to make confused or confusing **3** to produce fog on (e g a photographic film) during development

'**fog,bound** /-₁bownd/ *adj* **1** covered with or surrounded by fog **2** unable to move because of fog

fogey, fogy /'fohgi/ *n* a person with old-fashioned ideas

foggy /'fogi/ *adj* **1a** thick with fog **b** covered or made opaque by moisture or grime **2** blurred, obscured – **-ggily** *adv* – **-gginess** *n*

'**fog,horn** /-₁hawn/ *n* **1** a horn (e g on a ship) sounded in a fog to give warning **2** a loud hoarse voice – *infml*

foible /'foybl/ *n* a minor weakness or shortcoming in personal character or behaviour; *also* a quirk

¹**foil** /foyl/ *v* to prevent from attaining an end; frustrate, defeat

²**foil** *n* (fencing with) a light fencing sword with a circular guard and a flexible blade tapering to a blunted point

³**foil** *n* **1** any of several arcs that enclose a complex design **2** very thin sheet metal **3** sby or sthg that serves as a contrast to another **4** a hydrofoil

⁴**foil** *v* to back or cover with foil

foist /foyst/ *v* **1a** to introduce or insert surreptitiously or without warrant – + *in* or *into* **b** to force another to accept or tolerate, esp by stealth or deceit **2** to pass off as genuine or worthy *USE* (1b&2) usu + *off on, on,* or *upon*

¹**fold** /fohld/ *n* **1** an enclosure for sheep; *also* a flock of sheep **2** *sing* or *pl in constr* a group of people adhering to a common faith, belief, or enthusiasm

²**fold** *v* to pen (e g sheep) in a fold

³**fold** *v* **1** to lay one part of over another part **2** to reduce the length or bulk of by doubling over – often + *up* **3a** to clasp together; entwine **b** to bring (limbs) to rest close to the body **4a** to clasp closely; embrace **b** to wrap, envelop **5** to gently incorporate (a food ingredient) into a mixture without thorough stirring or beating – usu + *in* **6** to become or be capable of being folded **7** to fail completely; *esp* to stop production or operation because of lack of business or capital – often + *up; chiefly infml*

⁴**fold** *n* **1** (a crease made by) a doubling or folding over **2** a part doubled or laid over another part; a pleat **3** (a hollow inside) sthg that is folded or that enfolds **4** *chiefly Br* an undulation in the landscape

'**fold,away** /-ə,way/ *adj* designed to fold out of the way or out of sight

folder /'fohldə/ *n* a folded cover or large envelope for holding or filing loose papers

foliage /'fohli·ij/ *n* **1** the leaves of a plant or clump of plants **2** (an ornamental representation of) a cluster of leaves, branches, etc

¹**folk** /fohk/ *n* **1** *pl in constr* the great proportion of a people that tends to preserve its customs, superstitions, etc **2** *pl in constr* a specified kind or class of people – often *pl* with *sing.* meaning **3** simple music, usu song, of traditional origin or style **4** *pl in constr* people generally – *infml*; often *pl* with *sing.* meaning **5** *pl* the members of one's own family; relatives – *infml*

²**folk** *adj* **1** originating or traditional with the common people **2** of (the study of) the common people

'**folk,lore** /-,law/ *n* **1** traditional customs and beliefs of a people preserved by oral tradition **2** the study of the life and spirit of a people through their folklore – **-lorist** *n*

follicle /'folikl/ *n* **1** a small anatomical cavity or deep narrow depression **2** a dry 1-celled many-seeded fruit

follow /'foloh/ *v* 1 to go, proceed, or come after 2 to pursue, esp in an effort to overtake 3a to accept as a guide or leader b to obey or act in accordance with 4 to copy, imitate 5a to walk or proceed along b to engage in as a calling or way of life; pursue (e g a course of action) 6 to come or take place after in time or order 7 to come into existence or take place as a result or consequence of 8a to attend closely to; keep abreast of b to understand the logic of (e g an argument) 9 to go or come after sby or sthg in place, time, or sequence 10 to result or occur as a consequence or inference — **follow one's nose** to go in a straight or obvious course — **follow suit** 1 to play a card of the same suit as the card led 2 to follow an example set

follower /'foloh-ə/ *n* 1a one who follows the opinions or teachings of another b one who imitates another 2 a fan

¹**following** /-ing/ *adj* 1 next after; succeeding 2 now to be stated 3 *of a wind* blowing in the direction in which sthg is travelling

²**following** *n pl* (1) **following**, (2) **followings** 1 sthg that comes immediately after or below in writing or speech 2 *sing or pl in constr* a group of followers, adherents, or partisans

³**following** *prep* subsequent to

follow on *v, of a side in cricket* to bat a second time immediately after making a score that is less, by more than a predetermined limit, than that of the opposing team in its first innings – **follow-on** *n*

follow through *v* 1 to pursue (an activity or process), esp to a conclusion 2 to continue the movement of a stroke after a cricket, golf, etc ball has been struck

follow up *v* 1a to follow with sthg similar, related, or supplementary b to take appropriate action about 2 to maintain contact with or reexamine (a person) at usu prescribed intervals in order to evaluate a diagnosis or treatment – **follow-up** *n, adj*

folly /'foli/ *n* 1 lack of good sense or prudence 2 a foolish act or idea 3 (criminally or tragically) foolish actions or conduct 4 a usu fanciful structure (e g a summerhouse) built esp for scenic effect or to satisfy a whim

foment /foh'ment/ *v* to promote the growth or development of; incite – ~ **ation** *n*

fond /fond/ *adj* 1 foolish, silly 2 having an affection or liking for sthg specified – + *of* 3a foolishly tender; indulgent b affectionate, loving 4 doted on; cherished – ~ **ly** *adv* – ~ **ness** *n*

fondant /'fondə/ (*Fr* fɔ̃dã) *n* (a sweet made from) a soft creamy preparation of flavoured sugar and water

fondle /'fondl/ *v* **fondling** /'fondling/ to handle tenderly, affectionately, or lingeringly

fondue /'fond(y)ooh (*Fr* fɔ̃dy)/ *n* a dish consisting of a hot liquid (e g oil or a thick sauce) into which pieces of food are dipped for cooking or coating; *esp* one made with melted cheese and white wine

font /font/ *n* 1 a receptacle for holy water; *esp* one used in baptism 2 a receptacle for oil in a lamp

food /foohd/ *n* **1a** (minerals, vitamins, etc together with) material consisting essentially of protein, carbohydrate, and fat taken into the body of a living organism and used to provide energy and sustain processes (e g growth and repair) essential for life b inorganic substances absorbed (e g in gaseous form or in solution) by plants 2 nutriment in solid form 3 sthg that sustains or supplies

'food,stuff /-,stuf/ *n* a substance with food value; *esp* the raw material of food before or after processing

¹**fool** /foohl/ *n* 1 a person lacking in prudence, common sense, or understanding **2a** a jester b a person who is victimized or made to appear foolish; a dupe 3 a cold dessert of fruit puree mixed with whipped cream or custard

²**fool** *v* **1a** to act or spend time idly or aimlessly b to meddle, play, or trifle *with* 2 to play or improvise a comic role; *specif* to joke 3 to make a fool of; deceive

'fool,hardy /-,hahdi/ *adj* rash – **-diness** *n*

foolish /'foohlish/ *adj* 1 marked by or proceeding from folly 2 absurd, ridiculous – ~ **ly** *adv* – ~ **ness** *n*

'fool,proof /-,proohf/ *adj* so simple or reliable as to leave no opportunity for error, misuse, or failure

foolscap /'foohlskap, 'fool-/ *n* a size of paper usu 17 × 13¹/₂in (432 × 343mm)

,fool's 'paradise *n* a state of illusory happiness

¹**foot** /foot/ *n, pl* **feet** /feet/, (3) **feet** *also* **foot** 1 the end part of the vertebrate leg on which an animal stands 2 an organ of locomotion or attachment of an invertebrate animal, esp a mollusc 3 a unit of length equal to ¹/₃yd (0.305m) 4 the basic unit of verse metre consisting of any of various fixed combinations of stressed and unstressed or long and short syllables 5 manner or motion of walking or running; step **6a** the lower end of the leg of a chair, table, etc b the piece on a sewing machine that presses the cloth against the feed 7 the lower edge or lowest part; the bottom **8a** the end that is opposite the head or top or nearest to the human feet b the part (e g of a stocking) that covers the human foot — **my foot** my eye — *infml* — **on foot** by walking or running — **on one's feet** 1 standing 2 in a recovered condition (e g from illness) 3 in an impromptu manner

²**foot** *v* 1 to walk, run, or dance on, over, or through 2 to pay or stand credit for — **foot it** 1 to dance 2 to travel on foot

footage /'footij/ n 1 length or quantity expressed in feet 2 (the length in feet of) exposed film

'foot,ball /-,bawl/ n (the inflated round or oval ball used in) any of several games, esp soccer, that are played between 2 teams on a usu rectangular field having goalposts at each end and whose object is to get the ball over a goal line or between goalposts by running, passing, or kicking

'football ,pools n pl a form of organized gambling based on forecasting the results of football matches

'foot,board /-,bawd/ n 1 a narrow platform on which to stand or brace the feet 2 a board forming the foot of a bed

'foot,bridge /-,brij/ n a bridge for pedestrians

'foot,fall /-,fawl/ n the sound of a footstep

'foot,hill /-,hil/ n a hill at the foot of mountains

'foot,hold /-,hohld/ n 1 a footing 2 an (established) position or basis from which to progress

footing /'footing/ n 1 a stable position or placing of or for the feet 2 a (condition of a) surface with respect to its suitability for walking or running on 3 a an established position or rank in relation to others

footle /'foohtl/ v **footling** /'foohtling/ to mess or potter *around* or *about*; *also* to waste time – infml

'foot,lights /-,liets/ n pl a row of lights set across the front of a stage floor

footling /'foohtling/ adj 1 bungling, inept 2 unimportant, trivial; *also* pettily fussy *USE* infml

'foot,loose /-,loohs/ adj having no ties; free to go or do as one pleases

footman /-man/ n a servant in livery hired chiefly to wait, receive visitors, etc

footnote /-,noht/ n 1 a note of reference, explanation, or comment typically placed at the bottom of a printed page 2 sthg subordinately related to a larger event or work

'foot,path /-,pahth/ n a narrow path for pedestrians; *also* a pavement

'foot,plate /-,playt/ n, Br the platform on which the crew stand in a locomotive

'foot,print /-,print/ n an impression left by the foot

'foot,slog /-,slog/ v **-gg-** to march or tramp laboriously – infml – ~ger n – ~ging n

'foot,step /-,step/ n 1 the sound of a step or tread 2 distance covered by a step

'foot,wear /-,wea/ n articles (eg shoes or boots) worn on the feet

'foot,work /-,wuhk/ n 1 the control and placing of the feet, esp in sport (eg in boxing or batting) 2 the activity of moving from place to place on foot

fop /fop/ n a dandy – ~pish adj

¹for /fə; strong faw/ prep **1a** – used to indicate purpose (eg a grant *for* studying medicine), goal or direction (eg left *for* home), or that which is to be had or gained (eg run *for* your life) **b** to belong to (eg the flowers are *for* you) **2** as being or

constituting (eg ate it *for* breakfast) **3** because of (eg cried *for* joy) **4a** in place of (eg change *for* a pound) **b** on behalf of; representing (eg acting *for* my client) **c** in support of; in favour of (eg he played *for* England) **5** considered as; considering (eg tall *for* her age) **6** with respect to; concerning (eg famous *for* its scenery) **7** – used to indicate cost, payment, equivalence, or correlation (eg £7 *for* a hat) **8** – used to indicate duration of time or extent of space (eg *for* 10 miles; gone *for* months) **9** on the occasion or at the time of (eg came home *for* Christmas) — **for all 1** in spite of **2** to the extent that **3** considering how little — **for all one is worth** with all one's might — **for it** chiefly Br likely to get into trouble – infml — **for what it is worth** without guarantee of wisdom or accuracy

²for conj **1** and the reason is that **2** because

³for adj being in favour of a motion or measure

¹forage /'forij/ n **1** food for animals, esp when taken by browsing or grazing **2** a foraging for provisions; broadly a search

²forage v **1** to collect or take provisions or forage from **2** to wander in search of forage or food **3** to make a search *for*; rummage

¹foray /'foray/ v to make a raid or incursion

²foray n **1** a sudden invasion, attack, or raid **2** a brief excursion or attempt, esp outside one's accustomed sphere

¹forbear /faw'bea/ v **forbore** /faw'baw/; **forborne** /faw'bawn/ to hold oneself back from, esp with an effort of self-restraint

²forbear /'faw,bea/ n a forebear

forbearance /faw'beərəns/ n **1** a refraining from the enforcement of sthg (eg a debt, right, or obligation) that is due **2** patience **3** leniency, mercifulness

forbid /fə'bid/ v **forbidding**; **forbade** /fə'bad, -'bayd, -'bed/, **forbad**; **forbidden** /fə'bid(ə)n/ **1a** to refuse (eg by authority) to allow; command against **b** to refuse access to or use of **2** to make impracticable; hinder, prevent – **-bidden** adj

forbidding /fə'biding/ adj **1** having a menacing or dangerous appearance **2** unfriendly – ~ly adv

¹force /faws/ n **1a** strength or energy exerted or brought to bear; active power **b** moral or mental strength **c** capacity to persuade or convince **d** (legal) validity; operative effect **2a** pl the armed services of a nation or commander **b** a body of people or things fulfilling an often specified function **c** an individual or group having the power of effective action **3** violence, compulsion, or constraint exerted on or against a person or thing **4a** (the intensity of) an agency that if applied to a free body results chiefly in an acceleration of the body and sometimes in elastic deformation and other effects **b** an agency or influence analogous to a physical force **5** cap a measure of wind strength as expressed by a number on the Beaufort scale — **in force 1** in great numbers **2** valid, operative

²**force** v 1 to compel by physical, moral, or intellectual means 2 to make or cause through natural or logical necessity 3a to press, drive, or effect against resistance or inertia b to impose or thrust urgently, importunately, or inexorably 4 to break open or through 5a to raise or accelerate to the utmost b to produce only with unnatural or unwilling effort 6 to hasten the growth, onset of maturity, or rate of progress of — **force someone's hand** to cause sby to act precipitately or reveal his/her purpose or intention

'**forceful** /-f(ə)l/ adj possessing or filled with force; effective – ~**ly** adv – ~**ness** n

'**force,meat** /-,meet/ n a savoury highly seasoned stuffing, esp of breadcrumbs and meat

forceps /'fawsips, -seps/ n, pl **forceps** an instrument used (e g in surgery and watchmaking) for grasping, holding firmly, or pulling – usu pl with sing. meaning

forcible /'fawsəbl/ adj 1 effected by force used against opposition or resistance 2 powerful, forceful – -**bly** adv

'**ford** /fawd/ n a shallow part of a river or other body of water that can be crossed by wading, in a vehicle, etc

²**ford** v to cross (a river, stream, etc) at a ford

'**fore** /faw/ adj or adv (situated) in, towards, or adjacent to the front

²**fore** n sthg that occupies a forward position — **to the fore** in or into a position of prominence

³**fore** interj – used by a golfer to warn anyone in the probable line of flight of his/her ball

,**fore-and-'aft** /ahft/ adj lying, running, or acting in the general line of the length of a ship or other construction

,**fore and 'aft** adv from stem to stern

'**forearm** /'faw'rahm, faw'ahm/ v to arm in advance; prepare

²**forearm** /'faw,rahm/ n (the part in other vertebrates corresponding to) the human arm between the elbow and the wrist

forebear, forbear /'faw,beə/ n an ancestor, forefather

forebode /faw'bohd, fə-/ v 1 to foretell, portend 2 to have a premonition of (evil, misfortune, etc)

fore'boding /-'bohding/ n an omen, prediction, or presentiment, esp of impending evil

'**forecast** /'faw,kahst/ v **forecast, forecasted** 1 to estimate or predict (some future event or condition), esp as a result of rational study and analysis of available pertinent data 2 to serve as a forecast of; presage 3 to calculate or predict the future

²**forecast** n a prophecy, estimate, or prediction of a future happening or condition; esp a weather forecast

forecastle, fo'c's'le /'fohks(ə)l/ n 1 a short raised deck at the bow of a ship 2 a forward part of a merchant ship having the living quarters

'**fore,court** /-,kawt/ n an open or paved area in front of a building; esp that part of a petrol station where the petrol pumps are situated

'**fore,father** /-,fahdhə/ n 1 an ancestor 2 a person of an earlier period and common heritage

'**fore,finger** /-,fing-gə/ n the finger next to the thumb

'**fore,front** /-,frunt/ n the foremost part or place; the vanguard

forego /fə'goh, faw-/ v **foregoes; foregoing; forewent** /faw'went/; **foregone** /faw'gon/ to forgo

foregoing /'faw,goh·ing/ adj going before; that immediately precedes

'**fore,ground** /-,grownd/ n 1 the part of a picture or view nearest to and in front of the spectator 2 the forefront

'**fore,hand** /-,hand/ n a forehand stroke in tennis, squash, etc; also the side or part of the court on which such strokes are made

²**forehand** adj or adv (made) with the palm of the hand turned in the direction of movement

forehead /'faw,hed, 'forid/ n the part of the face above the eyes

foreign /'forən; also 'forin/ adj 1 (situated) outside a place or country; esp (situated) outside one's own country 2 born in, belonging to, or characteristic of some place or country other than the one under consideration 3 alien in character; not connected or pertinent to 4 of, concerned with, or dealing with other nations 5 occurring in an abnormal situation in the living body and commonly introduced from outside

'**foreigner** /-nə/ n 1 a person belonging to or owing allegiance to a foreign country; an alien 2 chiefly dial a stranger; esp a person not native to a community

'**fore,limb** /-,lim/ n a front leg or similar limb

'**fore,lock** /-,lok/ n a lock of hair growing just above the forehead

'**foreman** /-mən/, fem '**fore,woman** n pl **foremen** /-mən/ 1 the chairman and spokesman of a jury 2 a person, often a chief worker, who supervises a group of workers, a particular operation, or a section of a plant

'**fore,most** /-,mohst, -məst/ adj 1 first in a series or progression 2 of first rank or position; preeminent

²**foremost** adv most importantly

'**fore,name** /-,naym/ n a name that precedes a person's surname

'**fore,noon** /-,noohn/ n the morning – fml

forensic /fə'renzik/ adj of or being the scientific investigation of crime

,**foreor'dain** /-aw'dayn/ v to settle, arrange, or appoint in advance; predestine

'**fore,part** /-,paht/ n the front part of sthg

'**fore,runner** /-,runə/ n 1 a warning sign or symptom 2a a predecessor, forefather b a prototype

'fore,sail /-,sayl/ n 1 the lowest square sail on the foremast of a square-rigged ship 2 the principal fore-and-aft sail set on a schooner's foremast

foresee /faw'see/ v foreseeing; foresaw /-'saw/; foreseen /-'seen/ to be aware of (e g a development) beforehand – ~able adj

fore'shadow /-'shadoh/ v to represent or typify beforehand; suggest

'fore,shore /-,shaw/ n the part of a seashore between high-tide and low-tide marks

fore'shorten /-'shawt(ə)n/ v 1 to shorten (a detail in a drawing or painting) so as to create an illusion of depth 2 to make more compact

'fore,sight /-,siet/ n 1 foreseeing; insight into the future 2 provident care; prudence 3 the sight nearest the muzzle on a firearm

'fore,skin /-,skin/ n a fold of skin that covers the head of the penis

'forest /'forist/ n 1 a tract of wooded land in Britain formerly owned by the sovereign and used for hunting game 2 a dense growth of trees and underbrush covering a large tract of land 3 sthg resembling a profusion of trees

'forest v to cover with trees or forest

fore'stall /-'stawl/ v 1 to exclude, hinder, or prevent by prior measures 2 to get ahead of; anticipate

forester /'foristə/ n 1 a person trained in forestry 2 a person, animal, etc that inhabits forest land

forestry /'foristri/ n 1 forest land 2 the scientific cultivation or management of forests

foretaste /'faw,tayst/ n 1 an advance indication or warning 2 a small anticipatory sample

fore'tell /-'tel/ v foretold /-'tohld/ to tell beforehand; predict

'fore,thought /-,thawt/ n 1 a thinking or planning out in advance; premeditation 2 consideration for the future

forever /fə'revə/ adv 1 for all future time; indefinitely 2 persistently, incessantly

fore'warn /-'wawn/ v to warn in advance

'fore,word /-,wuhd/ n a preface; esp one written by sby other than the author of the text

'forfeit /'fawfit/ n 1 sthg lost, taken away, or imposed as a penalty 2 the loss or forfeiting of sthg, esp of civil rights 3a an article deposited or a task performed in the game of forfeits b pl but sing or pl in constr a game in which articles are deposited (e g for making a mistake) and then redeemed by performing a silly task – forfeit adj

'forfeit v 1 to lose the right to by some error, offence, or crime 2 to subject to confiscation as a forfeit – ~ure n

'forge /fawj/ n (a workshop with) an open furnace where metal, esp iron, is heated and wrought

'forge v 1 to shape (metal or a metal object) by heating and hammering or with a press 2 to form or bring into being, esp by an expenditure of effort 3 to counterfeit (esp a signature, document, or bank note) 4 to commit forgery – ~r n

'forge v 1 to move forwards slowly and steadily but with effort 2 to move with a sudden increase of speed and power

forgery /'fawjəri/ n 1 (the crime of) forging 2 a forged document, bank note, etc

forget /fə'get/ v forgetting; forgot /-'got/; forgotten /-'got(ə)n/, archaic or NAm forgot 1 to fail to remember 2 to fail to give attention to; disregard 3 to disregard intentionally — forget oneself to lose one's dignity, temper, or self-control; act unsuitably or unworthily

for'getful /-f(ə)l/ adj 1 likely or apt to forget 2 characterized by negligent failure to remember; neglectful – usu + of – ~ly adv – ~ness n

for'get-me-,not n any of a genus of small plants of the borage family with white or bright blue flowers

forgive /fə'giv/ v forgave /-'gayv/; forgiven /-giv(ə)n/ 1 to cease to resent 2 to pardon – -vable adj – -ving adj

for'giveness /-nis/ n forgiving or being forgiven; pardon

forgo, forego /fə'goh, faw-/ v forgoes; forgoing; forwent /faw'went/; forgone /faw'gon/ to abstain or refrain from

'fork /fawk/ n 1 a tool or implement with 2 or more prongs set on the end of a handle: e g 1a an agricultural or gardening tool for digging, carrying, etc b a small implement for eating or serving food 2a a forked part, or piece of equipment b a forked support for a cycle wheel – often pl with sing. meaning 3 (a part containing) a division into branches 4 any of the branches into which sthg forks

'fork v 1 to divide into 2 or more branches 2 to make a turn into one of the branches of a fork 3 to pay, contribute – + out, over, or up

forked adj having one end divided into 2 or more branches or points

'fork,lift, ,forklift 'truck n a vehicle for hoisting and transporting heavy objects by means of steel prongs inserted under the load

forlorn /fə'lawn/ adj 1a bereft or forsaken of b sad and lonely because of isolation or desertion; desolate 2 in poor condition; miserable, wretched 3 nearly hopeless – ~ly adv – ~ness n

'form /fawm/ n 1 the shape and structure of sthg as distinguished from its material 2 the essential nature of a thing as distinguished from the matter in which it is embodied 3a established or correct method of proceeding or behaving b a prescribed and set order of words 4 a printed or typed document; esp one with blank spaces for insertion of required or requested information 5 conduct regulated by external controls (e g custom or etiquette); ceremony **6a** the bed or nest of a hare **b** a long seat; a bench **7** sthg (e g shuttering) that holds, supports, and determines shape **8a** the way in which sthg is arranged, exists, or shows itself **b** a kind, variety **9** the structural element, plan, or design of a work of art **10** *sing or pl in constr* a class organized for the work of a particular year, esp in a British school **11a** the past performances of a competitor considered as a guide to its future performance **b** known ability to perform **c** condition suitable for performing, esp in sports – often + *in*, *out of*, or *off* **12** *Br* a criminal record – slang – ~ **less** *adj*

²**form** *v* **1** to give form, shape, or existence to **2a** to give a particular shape to; shape or mould into a certain state or after a particular model **b** to model or train by instruction and discipline **3** to develop, acquire **4** to serve to make up or constitute; be a usu essential or basic element of

formal /'fawml/ *adj* **1a** pertaining to or being the essential constitution or structure **b** of, concerned with, or being the (outward) form of sthg as distinguished from its content **2a** following or based on conventional forms and rules **b** characterized by punctilious respect for correct procedure **3** having the appearance without the substance; ostensible – ~ **ly** *adv*

formaldehyde /faw'maldi,hied/ *n* a pungent irritating gas used chiefly as a disinfectant and preservative and in chemical synthesis

formality /faw'malǝti/ *n* **1** compliance with or observance of formal or conventional rules **2** an established form that is required or conventional

format /'fawmat/ *n* **1** the shape, size, and general make-up (e g of a book) **2** the general plan of organization or arrangement

formation /faw'maysh(ǝ)n/ *n* **1** giving form or shape to sthg or taking form; development **2** sthg formed **3** the manner in which a thing is formed; structure **4** an arrangement of a group of people or things in some prescribed manner or for a particular purpose

formative /'fawmǝtiv/ *adj* **1** (capable of) giving form; constructive **2** capable of alteration by growth and development **3** of or characterized by formative effects or formation

¹**former** /'fawmǝ/ *adj* **1** of or occurring in the past **2** preceding in time or order **3** first of 2 things (understood to have been) mentioned

²**former** *n*, *pl* **former** the first mentioned; first

formerly /'fawmǝli/ *adv* at an earlier time; previously

Formica /faw'miekǝ/ *trademark* – used for any of various laminated plastics used for surfaces, esp on wood

formidable /'fawmidǝbl/; *also* fǝ'midǝbl/ *adj* **1** difficult to overcome; discouraging approach **2** tending to inspire respect or awe – ~ **bly** *adv*

formula /'fawmyoolǝ/ *n*, *pl* **formulas, formulae** /-lee, -lie/ **1a** a set form of words for use in a ceremony or ritual **b** (a conventionalized statement intended to express) a truth, principle, or procedure, esp as a basis for negotiation or action **2** (a list of ingredients used in) a recipe **3a** a fact, rule, or principle expressed in symbols **b** a symbolic expression of the chemical composition of a substance **4** a prescribed or set form or method (e g of writing); an established rule or custom **5** a classification of racing cars specifying esp size, weight, and engine capacity

formulate /'fawmyoolayt/ *v* **1** to state in or reduce to a formula **2** to devise or develop – **-ation** *n*

fornicate /'fawnikayt/ *v* to have sexual relations outside marriage – **-cation** *n*

forsake /fǝ'sayk/ *v* **forsook** /fǝ'sook/; **forsaken** /fǝ'saykǝn/ **1** to renounce (e g sthg once cherished) without intent to recover or resume **2** to desert, abandon

forswear /,faw'sw:eǝ/ *v* **forswear; forsworn** /-'swawn/ to (solemnly) renounce

forsythia /faw'siethi-ǝ, -thyǝ/ *n* any of a genus of ornamental shrubs with bright yellow bell-shaped flowers

fort /fawt/ *n* a strong or fortified place

¹**forte** /fawt/ *esp sense* ' /'fawtay/ *n* the area or skill in which a person excels

²**forte** /'fawti, -tay/ *n, adv, or adj* (a note or passage played) in a loud and often forceful manner

forth /fawth/ *adv* **1** onwards in time, place, or order; forwards (e g from this day *forth*) **2** out into notice or view (e g put *forth* leaves) **3** away from a centre; abroad (e g went *forth* to preach)

forth'coming /-'kuming/ *adj* **1** approaching **2a** made available **b** willing to give information; responsive

'**forth,right** /-,riet/ *adj* going straight to the point without ambiguity or hesitation – ~ **ness** *n*

forth'with /-'widh/ *adv* immediately

fortification /,fawtifi'kaysh(ǝ)n/ *n* sthg that fortifies, defends, or strengthens; *esp* works erected to defend a place or position

fortify /'fawtifie/ *v* **1** to give strength, courage, or endurance to; strengthen **2** to erect fortifications – **-fiable** *adj* – **-fier** *n*

fortissimo /faw'tisimoh/ *adv or adj* very loud

fortitude /'fawtityoohd, -choohd/ *n* patient courage in pain or adversity

fortnight /'fawt,niet/ *n, chiefly Br* two weeks

¹**fort,nightly** /-li/ *adj* occurring or appearing once a fortnight – **fortnightly** *adv*

²**fortnightly** *n* a publication issued fortnightly

fortress /'fawtris/ *n* a fortified place; *esp* a large and permanent fortification, sometimes including a town

fortuitous /faw'tyooh·itəs, -'chooh-/ *adj* **1** occurring by chance **2** fortunate, lucky – **~ly** *adv* – **~ness** *n*

fortunate /'fawch(ə)nət/ *adj* **1** unexpectedly bringing some good; auspicious **2** lucky

fortune /'fawchoohn, -chən/ *n* **1** *often cap* a supposed (personified) power that unpredictably determines events and issues **2a** (prosperity attained partly through) luck **b** *pl* the favourable or unfavourable events that accompany the progress of an individual or thing **3** destiny, fate **4** material possessions or wealth

'fortune ˌhunter *n* a person who seeks wealth, esp by marriage

'fortune-ˌteller *n* a person who claims to foretell future events

forty /'fawti/ *n* **1** the number 40 **2** *pl* the numbers 40 to 49; *specif* a range of temperatures, ages, or dates in a century characterized by those numbers – **-tieth** *adj, n, pron, adv*

forum /'fawrəm/ *n, pl* **forums** *also* **fora** /-rə/ **1** the marketplace or public place of an ancient Roman city forming the public centre **2** a public meeting place or medium for open discussion (e g on radio or television)

¹forward /'faw·wood, *sense* 1 *also* 'forəd *when referring to ships and aeroplanes*/ *adj* **1a** located at or directed towards the front **b** situated in advance **2a** eager, ready **b** lacking modesty or reserve; pert **3** advanced in development; precocious **4** moving, tending, or leading towards a position in (or at the) front **5** of or getting ready for the future (e g *forward* planning) – **~ly** *adv* – **~ness** *n*

²forward *adv* **1** to or towards what is ahead or in front **2** to or towards an earlier time (e g bring *forward* the date of the meeting) **3** into prominence

³forward /'faw·wood/ *n* a mainly attacking player in hockey, soccer, etc stationed at or near the front of his/her side or team

⁴forward *v* **1** to help onwards; promote **2a** to send (forwards) **b** to send onwards from an intermediate point in transit – **~ing** *n*

¹fossil /'fosl/ *n* **1** a relic of an animal or plant of a past geological age, preserved in the earth's crust **2a** a person with outmoded views **b** sthg that has become rigidly fixed – **~ize** *v*

²fossil *adj* **1** preserved in a petrified form from a past geological age **2** outmoded

¹foster /'fostə/ *adj* giving, receiving, or sharing parental care though not related by blood

²foster *v* **1** to give parental care to; nurture **2** to promote the growth or development of

fought /fawt/ *past of* **fight**

¹foul /fowl/ *adj* **1** dirty, stained **2** notably offensive, unpleasant, or distressing **3** obscene, abusive **4a** treacherous, dishonourable **b** constituting a foul in a game or sport **5** polluted **6** entangled – *adv* – **~ness** *n*

²foul *n* **1** an entanglement or collision in angling, sailing, etc **2** an infringement of the rules in a game or sport

³foul *v* **1** to commit a foul in a sport or game **2** to pollute **3** to become entangled with **4** to obstruct, block **5** to dishonour, discredit

ˌfoul 'play *n* violence; *esp* murder

¹found /fownd/ *past of* **find**

²found *adj* having all usual, standard, or reasonably expected equipment

³found *v* **1** to set or ground on sthg solid – often + *on* or *upon* **2** to establish (e g a city or institution)

foundation /fown'daysh(ə)n/ *n* **1** the act of founding **2** the basis on which sthg stands or is supported **3** an organization or institution established by endowment with provision for future maintenance **4** an underlying natural or prepared base or support; *esp* the whole masonry substructure on which a building rests **5** a cream, lotion, etc applied as a base for other facial make-up

foun'dation ˌstone *n* a stone in the foundation of a building, esp when laid with public ceremony

founder /'fowndə/ *v* **1** to go lame **2** to collapse; give way **3** to sink **4** to come to grief; fail

foundry /'fowndri/ *n* (a place for) casting metals

¹fountain /'fowntən/ *n* **1** a spring of water issuing from the earth **2** a source **3** (the structure providing) an artificially produced jet of water

²fountain *v* to (cause to) flow or spout like a fountain

'fountain ˌhead /-ˌhed/ *n* a principal source

'fountain ˌpen *n* a pen containing a reservoir that automatically feeds the nib with ink

four /faw/ *n* **1** the number 4 **2** the fourth in a set or series **3** sthg having 4 parts or members or a denomination of 4; *esp* (the crew of) a 4-person racing rowing boat **4** a shot in cricket that crosses the boundary after having hit the ground and scores 4 runs

ˌfour'square /-'skwee/ *adj* forthright

²foursquare *adv* **1** in a solidly based and steady way **2** resolutely

fourteen /faw'teen/ *n* the number 14 – **~th** *adj, n, pron, adv*

fourth /fawth/ *n* **1** number four in a countable series **2** (the combination of 2 notes at) a musical interval of 4 diatonic degrees **3** the 4th and usu highest forward gear or speed of a motor vehicle – **fourth** *adj* – **fourthly** *adv*

fourth dimension *n* sthg outside the range of ordinary experience

fowl /fowl/ *n pl* **fowls**, *esp collectively* **fowl 1** a bird **2** a domestic fowl; *esp* an adult hen **3** the flesh of birds used as food

fox

[^1]**fox** /foks/ *n pl* **foxes**, *esp collectively* **fox 1** (the fur of) a red fox or related flesh-eating mammal of the dog family with a pointed muzzle, large erect ears, and a long bushy tail **2** a clever crafty person

[^2]**fox** *v* **1** to outwit **2** to baffle

'fox,glove /-,gluv/ *n* a common tall European plant that has showy white or purple tubular flowers

'fox,hound /-,hownd/ *n* any of various large swift powerful hounds of great endurance used in hunting foxes

fox-trot *v or n* (to dance) a ballroom dance that includes slow walking and quick running steps

foxy /'foksi/ *adj* **1** cunningly shrewd in conniving and contriving **2** warmly reddish brown **3** *NAm* physically attractive

foyer /'foy,ay, -a (*Fr* fwaje)/ *n* a lobby (e g of a theatre); *also* an entrance hallway

fracas /'frakah/ *n, pl* **fracas** /-ah(z)/, *NAm* **fracases** /-siz/ a noisy quarrel; a brawl

fraction /'fraksh(ə)n/ *n* **1a** a number (e g $3/4$, $5/8$, 0.234) that is expressed as the quotient of 2 numbers **b** a (small) portion or section **2** an act of breaking up **3** a tiny bit; a little **4** any of several separate portions separable by distillation

fractional /'fraksh(ə)nl/ *adj* **1** of or being a fraction **2** relatively tiny or brief **3** of or being a process for separating components of a mixture through differences in physical or chemical properties

'fractionally /-li/ *adv* to a very small extent

fractious /'frakshəs/ *adj* irritable and restless; hard to control – **~ly** *adv* – **~ness** *n*

[^1]**fracture** /'frakchə/ *n* a break or breaking, esp of hard tissue (e g bone)

[^2]**fracture** *v* **1** to cause or undergo fracture **2** to damage or destroy as if by breaking apart; break up

fragile /'frajiel/ *adj* **1** easily shattered **2** lacking in strength; delicate – **-gility** *n*

[^1]**fragment** /'fragmənt/ *n* an incomplete, broken off, or detached part

[^2]**fragment** /frag'ment/ *v* to break up or apart into fragments

fragmentary /'fragmənt(ə)ri/ *adj* consisting of fragments; incomplete

fragrant /'fraygrənt/ *adj* sweet or pleasant smelling – **-ance** *n* – **~ly** *adv*

frail /frayl/ *adj* **1** morally or physically weak **2** easily broken or destroyed **3** slight, insubstantial

frailty /'fraylti/ *n* a (moral) fault due to weakness

[^1]**frame** /fraym/ *v* **1** to plan, shape **2** to fit or adjust for a purpose **3a** to contrive evidence against (an innocent person) **b** to prearrange the outcome of (e g a contest)

[^2]**frame** *n* **1** the physical structure of a human body **2** a structure that gives shape or strength (e g to a building) **3a** an open case or structure made for admitting, enclosing, or supporting sthg **b** the

rigid part of a bicycle **c** the outer structure of a pair of glasses that holds the lenses **4a** an enclosing border **b** the matter or area enclosed in such a border: e g **b(1)** a single picture of the series on a length of film **b(2)** a single complete television picture made up of lines **c** a limiting, typical, or esp appropriate set of circumstances; a framework **5** one round of play in snooker, bowling, etc

,frame of 'mind *n* a particular mental or emotional state

'frame-,up *n* a conspiracy to frame sby or sthg – *infml*

'frame,work /-,wuhk/ *n* **1** a skeletal, openwork, or structural frame **2** a basic structure (e g of ideas)

franc /frangk/ *n* (a note or coin representing) the basic money unit of France, Belgium, Switzerland, and certain other French-speaking countries

[^1]**franchise** /'frahnchiez/, 'fran-/ *n* **1** a right or privilege; *specif* the right to vote **2** the right granted to an individual or group to market a company's goods or services in a particular territory; *also* the territory involved in such a right

[^2]**franchise** *v* to grant a franchise to

Franciscan /fran'siskən/ *n* a member of the Order of missionary friars founded by St Francis of Assisi in 1209

[^1]**frank** /frangk/ *adj* marked by free, forthright, and sincere expression – **~ness** *n* – **~ly** *adv*

[^2]**frank** *n* a mark or stamp on a piece of mail indicating postage paid – **frank** *v*

frankfurter /'frangk,fuhtə/ *n* a cured cooked, usu beef and pork, sausage

frankincense /'frangkin,sens/ *n* a fragrant gum resin chiefly from E African or Arabian trees that is burnt as incense

frantic /'frantik/ *adj* **1** emotionally out of control **2** marked by fast and nervous, disordered, or anxiety-driven activity – **~ally** *adv*

fraternal /frə'tuhnl/ *adj* **1a** of or involving brothers **b** of or being a fraternity or society **2** friendly, brotherly – **~ly** *adv* – **-nize** *v*

fraternity /frə'tuhnəti/ *n* **1** *sing or pl in constr* a group of people associated or formally organized for a common purpose, interest, or pleasure **2** brotherliness **3** *sing or pl in constr* men of the same usu specified class, profession, character, or tastes

fratricide /'fratri,sied, 'fray-/ *n* (the act of) sby who kills his/her brother or sister – **-cidal** *adj*

fraud /frawd/ *n* **1a** deception, esp for unlawful gain **b** a trick **2a** a person who is not what he/she pretends to be **b** sthg that is not what it seems or is represented to be

fraught /frawt/ *adj* **1** filled or charged *with* sthg specified **2** *Br* characterized by anxieties and tensions

[^1]**fray** /fray/ *n* a brawl, fight

[^2]**fray** *v* to wear out or into shreds

¹**freak** /freek/ *n* **1** a person or animal with a physical oddity who appears in a circus, funfair, etc **2** a person seen as being highly unconventional, esp in dress or ideas **3** an ardent enthusiast **4a** a sexual pervert **b** someone addicted to a specified drug – slang – **freak** *adj*

²**freak** *v* to freak out – slang

freakish /ˈfreekish/ *adj* whimsical, capricious – ~**ly** *adv* – ~**ness** *n*

freak out *v* **1** to experience hallucinations or withdraw from reality, esp by taking drugs **2** to behave in an irrational, uncontrolled, or unconventional manner (as if) under the influence of drugs *USE* slang – **freak-out** *n*

freckle /ˈfrekl/ *n* any of the small brownish spots on the skin, esp of white people, that increase in number and intensity on exposure to sunlight – **freckle** *v*

¹**free** /free/ *adj* **1a** enjoying civil and political liberty **b** not subject to the control or domination of another **2a** not determined by external influences **b** voluntary, spontaneous **3a** exempt, released, or released, esp from an unpleasant or unwanted condition or obligation – often in combination **b** not bound, confined, or detained by force **4a** having no trade restrictions **b** not subject to government regulation **5** having or taken up with no obligations or commitments **6** having an unrestricted scope **7a** not obstructed or impeded **b** not being used or occupied **8** not fastened **9a** lavish, unrestrained **b** outspoken **c** too familiar or forward **10** not costing or charging anything **11** not (permanently) united with, attached to, or combined with sthg else; separate **12a** not literal or exact **b** not restricted by or conforming to conventional forms – ~**ly** *adv*

²**free** *adv* **1** in a free manner **2** without charge

³**free** *v* **1** to cause to be free **2** to relieve or rid of sthg that restrains, confines, restricts, or embarrasses **3** to disentangle, clear

'**free,booter** /-ˌbootə/ *n* a pirate, plunderer

'**free,born** /-ˌbawn/ *adj* not born in slavery

Free Church *n*, *chiefly Br* a British Nonconformist church

'**freed,man** /-man/, *fem* '**freed,woman** *n* sby freed from slavery

freedom /ˈfreedəm/ *n* **1a** the absence of necessity or constraint in choice or action **b** liberation from slavery or restraint **c** being exempt or released *from* sthg (onerous) **2a** ease, facility **b** being frank, open, or outspoken **c** improper familiarity **3** boldness of conception or execution **4** unrestricted use *of*

free enterprise *n* an economic system based on private business operating competitively for profit

'**free-,fall** *n* **1** (the condition of) unrestrained motion in a gravitational field **2** the part of a parachute jump before the parachute opens

'**free-for-,all** *n* **1** a fight or competition open to all comers and usu with no rules **2** an often vociferous quarrel or argument involving several participants

'**free,hand** /-ˌhand/ *adj* done without the aid of drawing or measuring instruments – **freehand** *adv*

,**free'handed** /-ˈhandid/ *adj* openhanded, generous

'**free,hold** /-ˌhohld/ *n* a tenure in absolute possession; *also* a property held by such tenure – ~**er** *n*

'**free ,house** *n* a public house in Britain that is entitled to sell drinks supplied by more than 1 brewery

,**free 'kick** *n* an unhindered kick in soccer, rugby, etc awarded because of a breach of the rules by an opponent

¹'**free,lance** /-ˌlahns/ *n* a person who pursues a profession without long-term contractual commitments to any one employer – **freelance** *adj*

²**freelance** *v* to act as a freelance – **-lancer** *n*

'**free,man** /-man/ *n* **1** sby enjoying civil or political liberty **2** sby who has the full rights of a citizen

'**Free,mason** /-ˌmays(ə)n/ *n* a member of an ancient and widespread secret fraternity called Free and Accepted Masons

'**free,masonry** /-ˌmays(ə)nri/ *n* **1** *cap* the principles, institutions, or practices of Freemasons **2** natural or instinctive fellowship or sympathy

,**free-'range** *adj* of, being, or produced by poultry reared in the open air rather than in a battery

,**free'standing** /-ˈstanding/ *adj* standing without lateral support or attachment

'**free,style** /-ˌstiel/ *n* **1** (a style used in) a competition in which a contestant uses a style (e g of swimming) of his/her choice **2** a style of wrestling in which any kind of hold is allowed

,**free,thinker** /-ˈthingkə/ *n* a person who forms opinions on the basis of reason; *esp* one who rejects religious dogma – **-thinking** *adj*

free verse *n* verse without fixed metrical form

,**free 'will** *n* the power of choosing without the constraint of divine necessity or causal law

¹**freeze** /freez/ *v* **froze** /frohz/; **frozen** /ˈfrohz(ə)n/ **1** to convert from a liquid to a solid by cold **2a** to make extremely cold **b** to anaesthetize (as if) by cold **3a** to become clogged with ice **b** to become fixed or motionless; *esp* to abruptly cease acting or speaking **4** to immobilize the expenditure, withdrawal, or exchange of (foreign-owned bank balances) by government regulation **5** to preserve (e g food) by freezing

²**freeze** *n* **1** freezing cold weather **2** an act or period of freezing sthg, esp wages or prices at a certain level

freeze-dry *v* to dehydrate (sthg) while in a frozen state in a vacuum, esp for preservation

freezer /'freezə/ n an apparatus that freezes or keeps cool; *esp* an insulated cabinet or room for storing frozen food or for freezing food rapidly

freight /frayt/ n 1 the charge made for transporting goods 2 a cargo 3 a goods train

freighter /'fraytə/ n a ship or aircraft used chiefly to carry freight

¹**French** /french/ adj of France, its people, or their language

²**French** n 1 the Romance language of the people of France and of parts of Belgium, Switzerland, and Canada 2 pl in constr the people of France

,French 'bean n (the seed or pod of) a common bean often cultivated for its slender edible green pods

,French 'dressing n a salad dressing of oil, vinegar, and seasonings

,french 'fry n, chiefly NAm a chip – usu pl

,French 'horn n a circular valved brass instrument

,French 'leave n leave taken without permission

,French 'letter n, Br a condom – infml

,French 'polish n a solution of shellac used as a wood polish – **French-polish** v

,French 'windows n pl a pair of doors with full length glazing

frenetic /frə'netik/ adj frenzied, frantic – ∼**ally** adv

frenzy /'frenzi/ n 1 a temporary madness 2 (a spell of) wild, compulsive, or agitated behaviour – **-zied** adj – **-ziedly** adv

frequency /'freekwənsi/ n 1 the fact or condition of occurring frequently 2a the number of complete alternations per second of an alternating current b the number of sound waves per second produced by a sounding body c the number of complete oscillations per second of an electromagnetic wave

¹**frequent** /'freekwənt/ adj 1 often repeated or occurring 2 habitual, persistent – ∼**ly** adv

²**frequent** /fri'kwent/ v to be in or visit often or habitually

fresco /'freskoh/ n, pl **frescoes**, **frescos** (a painting made by) the application of water colours to moist plaster

¹**fresh** /fresh/ adj 1a not salt b free from taint; clean c of weather cool and windy 2a of food not preserved b not stale, sour, or decayed 3a (different or alternative and) new b newly or just come or arrived 4 too forward with a person of the opposite sex – infml – ∼**ness** n – ∼**ly** adv – ∼**en** v

²**fresh** adv 1 just recently; newly 2 chiefly NAm as of a very short time ago

freshen up v to make (oneself) fresher or more comfortable, esp by washing, changing one's clothes, etc

¹**fret** /fret/ v **-tt-** 1 to torment with anxiety or worry; vex 2a to eat or gnaw into; corrode b to rub, chafe 3 to agitate, ripple

²**fret** n a state of (querulous) mental agitation or irritation

³**fret** v **-tt-** 1 to decorate with interlaced designs 2 to decorate (e g a ceiling) with embossed or carved patterns

⁴**fret** n any of a series of ridges fixed across the fingerboard of a stringed musical instrument (e g a guitar)

fretful /-f(ə)l/ adj 1 tending to fret; in a fret 2 of water having the surface agitated – ∼**ly** adv – ∼**ness** n

fretsaw /'fret,saw/ n a narrow-bladed fine-toothed saw held under tension in a frame and used for cutting intricate patterns in thin wood

'fret,work /-,wuhk/ n ornamental openwork, esp in thin wood; also ornamental work in relief

Freudian slip n a slip of the tongue that is held to reveal some unconscious aspect of the speaker's mind

friar /'frie-ə/ n a member of a religious order combining monastic life with outside religious activity

friary /'frie-əri/ n (a building housing) a community of friars

fricassee /'frikə,see, ,--'-/ n a dish of small pieces of stewed chicken, rabbit, etc served in a white sauce

friction /'friksh(ə)n/ n 1a the rubbing of one body against another b resistance to relative motion between 2 bodies in contact 2 disagreement between 2 people or parties of opposing views

Friday /'frieday, -di/ n the day of the week following Thursday

fridge /frij/ n, chiefly Br a refrigerator

friend /frend/ n 1a a person whose company, interests, and attitudes one finds sympathetic and to whom one is not closely related b an acquaintance 2a sby or sthg not hostile b sby or sthg that favours or encourages sthg (e g a charity) 3 cap a Quaker

¹'**friendly** /-li/ adj 1a having the relationship of friends b not hostile c inclined to be favourable – usu + to 2 cheerful, comforting – **-liness** n

²**friendly** n, chiefly Br a match played for practice or pleasure and not as part of a competition

,friendly so'ciety n, often cap F&S, Br a mutual insurance association providing its subscribers with benefits during sickness, unemployment, and old age

,friendship /-ship/ n being friends or being friendly

frieze /freez/ n a sculptured or ornamented band (e g on a building)

frigate /'frigət/ n 1 a square-rigged 3-masted warship 2 a general-purpose naval escort vessel

fright /friet/ n 1 fear excited by sudden danger or shock 2 sthg unsightly, strange, ugly, or shocking – infml – **fright** v

frighten /'friet(ə)n/ v 1 to make afraid; scare 2 to force by frightening – ~**ingly** adv

'frightful /-f(ə)l/ adj 1 causing intense fear, shock, or horror 2 unpleasant, difficult – infml – ~**ness** n – ~**ly** adv

frigid /'frijid/ adj 1a intensely cold b lacking warmth or intensity of feeling 2 esp of a woman abnormally averse to sexual contact, esp intercourse – ~**ly** adv – ~**ity** n

frill /fril/ n 1 a gathered or pleated fabric edging used on clothing 2 a ruff of hair or feathers round the neck of an animal 3a an affectation, air b sthg decorative but not essential USE (3) usu pl

'fringe /frinj/ n 1 an ornamental border (e g on a curtain or garment) consisting of straight or twisted threads or tassels 2 the hair that falls over the forehead 3a sthg marginal, additional, or secondary b sing or pl in constr a group with marginal or extremist views c often cap theatre featuring small-scale avant-garde productions

'fringe v 1 to provide or decorate with a fringe 2 to serve as a fringe for

fringe benefit n a benefit (e g a pension) granted by an employer to an employee that involves a money cost without affecting basic wage rates

frippery /'fripəri/ n 1 nonessential ornamentation, esp of a showy or tawdry kind 2 affected elegance – **frippery** adj

'frisk /frisk/ v 1 to leap, skip, or dance in a lively or playful way 2 to search (a person) for sthg, esp a hidden weapon, by passing the hands over his/her body – infml

'frisk n 1 a gambol, romp 2 an act of frisking

frisky /'friski/ adj lively, playful – ~**kily** adv – ~**kiness** n

fritter /'fritə/ n a piece of fried batter often containing fruit, meat, etc

fritter away v to waste bit by bit

frivolous /'frivələs/ adj 1 lacking in seriousness 2 lacking practicality or serious purpose; unimportant – ~**ly** adv – ~**ness** n – **-volity** n

frizz /friz/ n (hair in) a mass of small tight curls

frizzle /'frizl/ v **frizzling** /'frizling/ 1 to fry (e g bacon) until crisp and curled 2 to burn, scorch

fro /froh/ prep, dial form

frock /frok/ n a woman's dress

frog /frog/ n 1 any of various tailless smooth-skinned web-footed largely aquatic leaping amphibians 2 the triangular horny pad in the middle of the sole of a horse's foot 3 a usu ornamental fastening for the front of a garment consisting of a button and a loop 4 often cap a French person – chiefly derog; infml

'frogman /-mən/ n a person equipped with face mask, flippers, rubber suit, etc and an air supply for swimming underwater for extended periods

'frog,march /-ˌmahch/ v 1 to carry (a person) face downwards by the arms and legs 2 to force (a person) to move forwards with the arms held firmly behind

'frolic /'frolik/ v **-ck-** 1 to play and run about happily 2 to make merry

'frolic n 1 (a) playful expression of high spirits; gaiety 2 a lighthearted entertainment or game

from /frəm; strong from/ prep 1 – used to indicate a starting point: e g 1a a place where a physical movement, or an action or condition suggestive of movement, begins (e g came here from the city) b a starting point in measuring or reckoning or in a statement of extent or limits (e g lives 5 miles from the coast) c a point in time after which a period is reckoned (e g a week from today) d a viewpoint 2 – used to indicate separation: e g 2a physical separation (e g absent from school) b removal, refraining, exclusion, release, or differentiation (e g relief from pain; don't know one from the other) 3 – used to indicate the source, cause, agent, or basis (e g a call from my lawyer; made from flour)

frond /frond/ n (a shoot resembling) a leaf, esp of a palm or fern

'front /frunt/ n 1 (feigned) demeanour or bearing, esp in the face of a challenge, danger, etc 2 often cap a zone of conflict between armies 3a a sphere of activity b a movement linking divergent elements to achieve certain common objectives; esp a political coalition 4a the (main) face of a building b the forward part or surface: e g 4b(1) the part of the human body opposite to the back b(2) the part of a garment covering the chest c the beach promenade at a seaside resort 5 the boundary between 2 dissimilar air masses 6a a position ahead of a person or of the foremost part of a thing b a position of importance, leadership, or advantage 7 a person, group, or thing used to mask the identity or true character of the actual controlling agent; also a poorly nominal head — **in front of** 1 directly ahead of 2 in the presence of — **out front** in the audience

'front v 1 to face – often + on or onto 2 to serve as a front – often + for

'front adj of or situated at the front

frontage /'fruntij/ n 1 the land between the front of a building and the street 2 (the width of) the front face of a building

frontal /'fruntl/ adj 1 of or adjacent to the forehead 2a of, situated at, or showing the front b direct 3 of a meteorological front

front bench n either of 2 rows of benches in Parliament on which party leaders sit

frontier /'frun'tiə/ n 1 a border between 2 countries 2 the boundary between the known and the unknown – often pl with sing. meaning 3 NAm a region that forms the margin of settled or developed territory

frontispiece /'fruntis,pees/ n an illustration preceding and usu facing the title page of a book or magazine

,front-'page adj very newsworthy

'front-,runner n 1 a contestant who runs best when in the lead 2 a leading contestant in a competition

¹**frost** /frost/ n 1a (the temperature that causes) freezing b a covering of minute ice crystals on a cold surface 2 coldness of attitude or manner

²**frost** v 1 to freeze – often + over 2a to produce a fine-grained slightly roughened surface on (metal, glass, etc) b to cover (e g a cake or grapes) with sugar; also, chiefly NAm to ice (a cake)

'frost,bite /-,biet/ n (gangrene or other local effect of a partial) freezing of some part of the body – **-bitten** adj

frosty /'frosti/ adj 1 marked by or producing frost 2 (appearing as if) covered with frost 3 marked by coolness or extreme reserve in manner – **-tily** adv – **-tiness** n

¹**froth** /froth/ n 1a a mass of bubbles formed on or in a liquid b a foamy saliva sometimes accompanying disease or exhaustion 2 sthg insubstantial or of little value – ~y adj – ~ily adv – ~iness n

²**froth** v to cause to foam – often + up

¹**frown** /frown/ v 1 to contract the brow 2 to give evidence of displeasure or disapproval – often + on or upon – ~ingly adv

²**frown** n 1 a wrinkling of the brow in displeasure, concentration, or puzzlement 2 an expression of displeasure

frowsy, frowzy /'frowzi/ adj 1 having a slovenly uncared-for appearance 2 musty, stale

froze /frohz/ past of **freeze**

frozen /'frohz(ə)n/ adj 1a treated, affected, solidified, or crusted over by freezing b subject to long and severe cold 2a drained or incapable of emotion b incapable of being changed, moved, or undone c not available for present use

frugal /'froohg(ə)l/ adj economical in the expenditure of resources – ~ly adv – ~ity n

fruit /frooht/ n 1a a product of plant growth (e g grain or vegetables) b a succulent edible plant part used chiefly in a dessert or sweet dish c the ripened fertilized ovary of a flowering plant together with its contents 2 offspring, progeny 3 a (favourable) product or result – often pl with sing. meaning – **fruit** v

fruiterer /'froohtərə/ n one who deals in fruit

fruitful /'froohtf(ə)l/ adj 1 (conducive to) yielding or producing (abundant) fruit 2 abundantly productive – ~ly adv – ~ness n

fruition /frooh'ish(ə)n/ n 1 bearing fruit 2 realization, fulfilment

fruitless /'froohtlis/ adj 1 lacking or not bearing fruit 2 useless, unsuccessful – ~ly adv – ~ness n

'fruit ma,chine n, Br a coin-operated gambling machine that pays out according to different combinations of symbols (e g different types of fruit) visible on wheels

fruity /'froohti/ adj 1 having the flavour of the unfermented fruit 2 of a voice marked by richness and depth 3 amusing in a sexually suggestive way – infml

frump /frump/ n a dowdy unattractive girl or woman – ~ish adj – ~y adj

frustrate /fru'strayt/ v 1a to balk or defeat in an endeavour; foil b to induce feelings of discouragement and vexation in 2 to make ineffectual; nullify – **-ation** n

¹**fry** /frie/ v to cook in hot fat

²**fry** n, pl **fry** 1a recently hatched or very small (adult) fishes b the young of other animals, esp when occurring in large numbers 2 a member of a group or class; esp a person

'frying ,pan n a shallow metal pan with a handle that is used for frying foods – **out of the frying pan into the fire** clear of one difficulty only to fall into a greater one

fuchsia /'fyoohshə/ n any of a genus of decorative shrubs with showy nodding flowers

fuck /fuk/ v 1 to have sexual intercourse (with) 2 to mess about or around USE vulg – **fuck** n

fuddle /'fudl/ v 1 to make drunk 2 to make confused – **fuddle** n

fuddy-duddy /'fudi ,dudi/ n a person who is old-fashioned, pompous, unimaginative, or concerned about trifles – infml

¹**fudge** /fuj/ v 1 to devise or put together roughly or without adequate basis 2 to fail to come to grips with; dodge

²**fudge** n a soft (creamy) sweet made typically of sugar, milk, butter, and flavouring

¹**fuel** /'fyooh-əl/ n 1a a material used to produce heat or power by combustion b nutritive material 2 a source of sustenance, strength, or encouragement

²**fuel** v -ll- (NAm -l-, -ll-) 1 to provide with fuel 2 to support, stimulate

fug /fug/ n the stuffy atmosphere of a poorly ventilated space – chiefly infml – ~gy adj

¹**fugitive** /'fyoohjətiv/ adj 1 running away or trying to escape 2a elusive b likely to change, fade, or disappear

²**fugitive** n a person who flees or tries to escape, esp from danger, justice, or oppression

fugue /fyoohg/ n a musical composition in which 1 or 2 themes are repeated or imitated by successively entering voices and are developed in a continuous interweaving of the voice parts

führer, fuehrer /'fyoorər (əer fyrə)/ n the leader of a totalitarian party or state

fulcrum /'fulkrəm, 'fool-/ n, pl **fulcrums, fulcra** /-krə/ the support about which a lever turns

fulfil, *NAm chiefly* **fulfill** /fool'fil/ *v* **-ll- 1a** to cause to happen as appointed or predicted – usu pass **b** to put into effect **c** to measure up to; satisfy **2** to develop the full potential of – ~ **ment** *n*

¹**full** /fool/ *adj* **1** possessing or containing a great amount or as much or as many as is possible or normal **2a** complete, esp in detail, number, or duration **b** lacking restraint, check, or qualification **3** at the highest or greatest degree; maximum **4** rounded in outline; *also* well filled out or plump **5a** having an abundance of material (e g in the form of gathers or folds) **b** rich in experience **6** satisfied, esp with food or drink, often to the point of discomfort – usu + *up* **7** filled with excited anticipation or pleasure **8** possessing a rich or pronounced quality – ~ **ness, fulness** *n* — **full of oneself** bumptiously self-centred or conceited

²**full** *adv* exactly, squarely

³**full** *n* **1** the highest or fullest state, extent, or degree **2** the requisite or complete amount – chiefly in *in full*

⁴**full** *v* to cleanse and finish (woollen cloth) by moistening, heating, and pressing – ~ **er** *n*

'**full back** /-ˌbak/ *n* a primarily defensive player in soccer, rugby, etc, usu stationed nearest the defended goal

,**full-'blooded** *adj* **1** of unmixed ancestry; purebred **2** forceful, vigorous – ~ **ness** *n*

,**full-'blown** *adj* **1** at the height of bloom **2** fully developed or mature

,**fuller's 'earth** /'foolaz/ *n* a clayey substance used in fulling cloth and as a catalyst

,**full 'house** *n* a poker hand containing **3** of a kind and a pair

,**full-'length** *adj* **1** showing or adapted to the entire length, esp of the human figure **2** having a normal or standard length; unabridged

,**full-'scale** *adj* **1** identical to an original in proportion and size **2** involving full use of available resources

,**full 'stop** *n* a punctuation mark . used to mark the end (e g of a sentence or abbreviation)

,**full-'time** *adj* employed for or involving full time

,**full 'time** *n* **1** the amount of time considered the normal or standard amount for working during a given period, esp a week **2** the end of a sports, esp soccer, match

,**full 'toss** *n* a throw, esp a bowled ball in cricket, that has not hit the ground by the time it arrives at the point at which it was aimed

fully /'fooli/ *adv* **1** completely **2** at least

,**fully-'fledged**, *NAm* **full-'fledged** *adj* having attained complete status

'**fulminate** /'foolminayt/ *v* to thunder forth censure or invective – usu + *against* or *at* – **-ation** *n*

fulsome /'fools(ə)m/ *adj* **1** overabundant, copious **2a** unnecessarily effusive **b** obsequious – ~ **ly** *adv* – ~ **ness** *n*

fumble /'fumbl/ *v* **fumbling** /'fumbling/ **1a** to grope for or handle sthg clumsily or awkwardly **b** to make awkward attempts to do or find sthg **2** to feel one's way or move awkwardly – ~ **r** *n* – **fumble** *n* – **-lingly** *adv*

¹**fume** /fyoohm/ *n* **1** an (irritating or offensive) smoke, vapour, or gas – often pl with sing. meaning **2** a state of unreasonable excited irritation or anger

²**fume** *v* **1** to emit fumes **2** to be in a state of excited irritation or anger

fumigate /'fyoohmigayt/ *v* to apply smoke, vapour, or gas to, esp in order to disinfect or destroy pests – **-gation** *n*

¹**fun** /fun/ *n* **1** (a cause of) amusement or enjoyment **2** derisive jest; ridicule **3** violent or excited activity or argument

²**fun** *adj* providing entertainment, amusement, or enjoyment – infml

¹**function** /'fungksh(ə)n/ *n* **1** an occupational duty **2** the action characteristic of a person or thing or for which a thing exists **3** an impressive, elaborate, or formal ceremony or social gathering **4** a quality, trait, or fact dependent on and varying with another

²**function** *v* **1** to have a function; serve **2** to operate

functional /'fungksh(ə)nl/ *adj* **1** of, connected with, or being a function **2** designed or developed for practical use without ornamentation – ~ **ly** *adv*

functionary /'fungksh(ə)nəri/ *n* **1** sby who serves in a certain function **2** sby holding office

¹**fund** /fund/ *n* **1** an available quantity of material or intangible resources **2** (an organization administering) a resource, esp a sum of money, whose principal or interest is set apart for a specific objective **3** *pl* an available supply of money

²**fund** *v* **1** to make provision of resources for discharging the interest or principal of **2** to provide funds for

¹**fundamental** /ˌfundə'mentl/ *adj* **1** serving as a basis to support existence or to determine essential structure or function – often + *to* **2** of essential structure, function, or facts **3** of, being, or produced by the lowest component of a complex vibration **4** of central importance; principal

²**fundamental** *n* **1** a minimum constituent without which a thing or system would not be what it is **2** the prime tone of a harmonic series **3** the harmonic component of a complex wave that has the lowest frequency

,**funda'mentalism** /-iz(ə)m/ *n* (adherence to) a belief in the literal truth of the Bible – **-ist** *n*, *adj*

funeral /'fyoohn(ə)rəl/ *n* (a procession connected with) a formal and ceremonial disposing of dead body, esp by burial or cremation

funerary /'fyoohnərəri/ *adj* of, used for, or associated with burial

funereal /fyooh'niəri·əl/ *adj* 1 of a funeral 2 gloomy, solemn – **~ly** *adv*

¹fun .fair *n, chiefly Br* a usu outdoor show offering amusements (e g sideshows, rides, or games of skill)

fungicide /'funjisied/ *n* a substance used for destroying or preventing fungus

fungus /'fung·gəs/ *n, pl* **fungi** /-gie, -gi/ *also* **funguses** any of a major group of often parasitic organisms lacking chlorophyll and including moulds, rusts, mildews, smuts, mushrooms, and toadstools – **-goid** *adj* – **-gal** *adj* – **-gous** *adj*

¹funk /fungk/ *n* **1a** a state of paralysing fear **b** a fit of inability to face difficulty 2 a coward *USE* infml

²funk *v* to avoid doing or facing (sthg) because of lack of determination *USE* infml

³funk *n* funky music – slang

funky /'fungki/ *adj* 1 having an earthy unsophisticated style and feeling (as in the blues) 2 – used to approve sthg or sby, esp in pop culture *USE* slang

¹funnel /'funl/ *n* 1 a utensil usu having the shape of a hollow cone with a tube extending from the smaller end, designed to direct liquids or powders into a small opening 2 a shaft, stack, or flue for ventilation or the escape of smoke or steam

²funnel *v* **-ll-** (*NAm* **-l-, -ll-**) *pres part* /'funl·ing/ 1 to pass (as if) through a funnel 2 to move to a focal point or into a central channel

funny /'funi/ *adj* 1 causing mirth and laughter; seeking or intended to amuse 2 peculiar, strange, or odd 3 involving trickery, deception, or dishonesty – **funnily** *adv* – **funniness** *n*

¹funny .bone *n* the place at the back of the elbow where the nerve supplying the hand and forearm rests against the bone

¹fur /fuh/ *v* **-rr-** to (cause to) become coated or clogged (as if) with fur – often + *up*

²fur *n* 1 the hairy coat of a mammal, esp when fine, soft, and thick; *also* such a coat with the skin 2 an article of clothing made of or with fur 3 a coating resembling fur: e g **3a** a coating of dead cells on the tongue of sby who is unwell **b** the thick pile of a fabric **c** a coating formed in vessels (e g kettles or pipes) by deposition of scale from hard water

furbish /'fuhbish/ *v* 1 to polish 2 to renovate – often + *up*

furious /'fyooəri·əs/ *adj* 1 exhibiting or goaded by uncontrollable anger 2 giving a stormy or turbulent appearance 3 marked by (violent) noise, excitement, or activity – **~ness** *n* – **~ly** *adv*

furl /fuhl/ *v* to fold or roll (e g a sail or umbrella) close to or round sthg

furlong /'fuhlong/ *n* a unit of length equal to 220yd (about 0.201km)

furlough /'fuhloh/ *n* leave of absence from duty granted esp to a soldier

furnace /'fuhnis/ *n* an enclosed apparatus in which heat is produced (e g for heating a building or reducing ore)

furnish /'fuhnish/ *v* to provide or supply (with what is needed); *esp* to equip with furniture – **~ings** *n pl*

furniture /'fuhnichə/ *n* necessary, useful, or desirable equipment: e g **a** the movable articles (e g tables, chairs, and beds) that make an area suitable for living in or use **b** accessories **c** the whole movable equipment of a ship (e g rigging, sails, anchors, and boats)

furore /fyoo'rawri/ *n* an outburst of general excitement or indignation

furrier /'furi·ə/ *n* a fur dealer

¹furrow /'furoh/ *n* 1 a trench in the earth made by a plough 2 a groove

²furrow *v* to make or form furrows, grooves, lines, etc (in)

furry /'fuhri/ *adj* like, made of, or covered with fur

¹further /'fuhdhə/ *adv* 1 farther 2 moreover 3 to a greater degree or extent (e g *further* annoyed by a second interruption)

²further *adj* 1 farther 2 extending beyond what exists or has happened; additional (e g *further* volumes) 3 coming after the one referred to

³further *v* to help forward

further.more /-'maw/ *adv* in addition to what precedes; moreover

¹further.most /-.mohst/ *adj* most distant

¹further to *prep* following up

furthest /'fuhdhist/ *adv or adj* farthest

furtive /'fuhtiv/ *adj* expressing or done by stealth – **~ly** *adv* – **~ness** *n*

fury /'fyooəri/ *n* 1 intense, disordered, and often destructive rage 2 *cap* any of the 3 avenging deities who in Greek mythology punished crimes 3 wild disordered force or activity

furze /fuhz/ *n* gorse

¹fuse /fyoohz/ *n* the detonating device for setting off the charge in a projectile, bomb, etc

²fuse, *NAm also* **fuze** *v* 1 to become fluid with heat 2 to become blended (as if) by melting together 3 to fail because of the melting of a fuse

³fuse *n* (a device that includes) a wire or strip of fusible metal that melts and interrupts the circuit when the current exceeds a particular value

fuselage /'fyoohzi.lahzh/ *n* the central body portion of an aeroplane

fusillade /.fyoohzə'layd/ *n* 1 a number of shots fired simultaneously or in rapid succession 2 a spirited outburst, esp of criticism

fusion /'fyoohzh(ə)n/ *n* 1 fusing or rendering plastic by heat 2 a union (as if) by melting: e g **2a** a merging of diverse elements into a unified whole **b** the union of light atomic nuclei to form heavier nuclei resulting in the release of enormous quantities of energy

¹**fuss** /fus/ *n* **1a** needless or useless bustle or excitement **b** a show of (affectionate) attention – often in *make a fuss of* **2a** a state of agitation, esp over a trivial matter **b** an objection, protest

²**fuss** *v* **1a** to create or be in a state of restless activity; *specif* to shower affectionate attentions **b** to pay close or undue attention to small details **2** to become upset; worry

'**fuss,pot** /-,pot/ *n* a person who fusses about trifles – infml

fussy /'fusi/ *adj* **1** nervous and excitable (about small matters) **2a** showing too much concern over details **b** fastidious **3** having too much or too detailed ornamentation – **-ssily** *adv* – **-ssiness** *n*

fusty /'fusti/ *adj* **1** stale or musty **2** out-of-date **3** rigidly old-fashioned or reactionary – **-tiness** *n*

futile /'fyoohtiel/ *adj* **1** completely ineffective **2** *of a person* ineffectual – **-lity** *n*

¹**future** /'fyoohchə/ *adj* **1** that is to be; *specif* existing after death **2** of or constituting the future tense

²**future** *n* **1a** time that is to come **b** that which is going to occur **2** sthg (e g a bulk commodity) bought for future acceptance or sold for future delivery – usu pl **3** (a verb form in) a tense indicating the future

futuristic /,fyoohchə'ristik/ *adj* bearing no relation to known or traditional forms – ~ **ally** *adv*

¹**fuzz** /fuz/ *n* fine light particles or fibres (e g of down or fluff)

²**fuzz** *n sing or pl in constr* the police – slang

fuzzy /'fuzi/ *adj* **1** marked by or giving a suggestion of fuzz **2** not clear; indistinct – **-zzily** *adv* – **-zziness** *n*

G

g /jee/ *n*, *pl* **g's**, **gs** *often cap* **1** (a graphic representation or device for reproducing) the 7th letter of the English alphabet **2** a speech counterpart of written g

gabardine /,gabə'deen, '-,-/ *n* **1** gaberdine **2a** a firm durable fabric (e g of wool or rayon) with diagonal ribs on the right side; *also* a waterproof coat made of this

gabble /'gabl/ *v* **gabbling** /'gabl-ing, 'gabling/ to talk or utter rapidly or unintelligibly

gaberdine /'gabə,deen, ,--'-/ *n* **1** a coarse long coat or smock worn chiefly by Jews in medieval times **2** gabardine

gable /'gaybl/ *n* the vertical triangular section of wall between 2 slopes of a pitched roof – ~ **d** *adj*

gad /gad/ *v* **-dd-** to go or travel in an aimless or restless manner or in search of pleasure – usu + *about* – **gadabout** *n*

gadget /'gajit/ *n* a usu small and often novel device, esp on a piece of machinery – ~ **ry** *n*

Gaelic /'gaylik, *Scots* 'gahlik, *Irish* 'galik/ *adj* of or being the Celts in Ireland, the Isle of Man, and the Scottish highlands

¹**gaff** /gaf/ *n* **1a** a spear or spearhead for killing fish or turtles **b** a pole with a hook for holding or landing heavy fish **2** a spar on which the head of a fore-and-aft sail is extended

²**gaff** *v* to strike or secure (e g a fish) with a gaff

gaffe /gaf/ *n* a social blunder

gaffer /'gafə/ *n* **1** the chief lighting electrician in a film or television studio **2** *Br* a foreman or overseer **3** *dial* an old man

¹**gag** /gag/ *v* **-gg- 1** to apply a gag to or put a gag in the mouth of (to prevent speech) **2** to (cause to) retch **3** to prevent from having free speech or expression – chiefly *journ*

²**gag** *n* **1** sthg thrust into the mouth to keep it open or prevent speech or outcry **2** a joke or trick

gaggle /'gagl/ *n* **1** a flock of geese **2** *sing or pl in constr* a typically noisy or talkative group or cluster – chiefly *infml*

gaiety /'gayəti/ *n* **1** merrymaking; *also* festive activity **2** gay quality, spirits, manner, or appearance

¹**gain** /gayn/ *n* **1** resources or advantage acquired or increased; a profit **2** the obtaining of profit or possessions **3** an increase in amount, magnitude, or degree

²**gain** *v* **1a(1)** to get possession of or win, usu by industry, merit, or craft **a(2)** to increase a lead over or catch up a rival by (esp time or distance) **b** to acquire **2** to increase, specif in weight **3** *of a timepiece* to run fast — **gain ground** to make progress

'**gainful** /-f(ə)l/ *adj* profitable – ~ **ly** *adv*

gait /gayt/ *n* **1** a manner of walking or moving on foot **2** a sequence of foot movements (e g a walk, trot, or canter) by which a horse moves forwards

gaiter /'gaytə/ *n* a cloth or leather covering reaching from the instep to ankle, mid-calf, or knee

gala /'gahlə/ *n* a festive gathering (that constitutes or marks a special occasion)

galactic /gə'laktik/ *adj* of a galaxy, esp the Milky Way

galaxy /'galəksi/ *n* **1** *often cap* the Milky Way **2** any of many independent systems in the universe, composed chiefly of stars, dust, and gases

gale /gayl/ *n* **1** a strong wind **2** a noisy outburst

¹**gall** /gawl/ *n* **1a** bile **b** sthg bitter to endure **c** rancour **2** brazen and insolent audacity or cheek

²**gall** *n* a skin sore caused by rubbing

³**gall** *v* **1** to become sore or worn by rubbing **2** to cause feelings of dismay and irritation in; vex acutely

gal

⁴**gall** *n* a diseased swelling of plant tissue produced by infection with fungi, insect parasites, etc

¹**gallant** /'galənt, gə'lahnt, gə'lant/ *n* a (young) man of fashion (who is particularly attentive to women)

²**gallant** /*sense* ' 'galənt; *sense* 2 'galənt, gə'lahnt, gə'lan t/ *adj* **1a** splendid, stately **b** nobly chivalrous and brave **2** courteously and elaborately attentive, esp to ladies

gallantry /'galəntri/ *n* **1** (an act of) courteous attention, esp to a lady **2** spirited and conspicuous bravery

'**gall ,bladder** *n* a muscular sac in which bile from the liver is stored

galleon /'gali·ən/ *n* a heavy square-rigged sailing ship of the 15th to early 18th c

gallery /'galəri/ *n* **1** a covered passage for walking; a colonnade **2** an outdoor balcony **3a** a long and narrow passage, room, or corridor **b** a horizontal subterranean passage in a cave or (military) mining system **4a** a room or building devoted to the exhibition of works of art **b** an institution or business exhibiting or dealing in works of art **5** *sing or pl in constr* **5a** (the occupants of) a balcony projecting from 1 or more interior walls of a hall, auditorium, or church, to accommodate additional people, or reserved for musicians, singers, etc **b** the undiscriminating general public **c** the spectators at a tennis, golf, etc match

galley /'gali/ *n* **1** a large low usu single-decked ship propelled by oars and sails **2** a kitchen on a ship or aircraft **3** a long oblong tray with upright sides for holding set type **b galley, galley proof** a proof in the form of a long sheet (taken from type on a galley)

Gallic /'galik/ *adj* (characteristic) of Gaul or France

gallivant /'galivant/ *v* to gad

gallon /'galən/ *n* a unit of liquid capacity equal to 8pt

¹**gallop** /'galəp/ *n* **1** a fast bounding gait of a quadruped; *specif* the fastest natural 4-beat gait of the horse **2** a ride or run at a gallop **3** a rapid or hasty progression

²**gallop** *v* to progress or ride at a gallop

gallows /'galohz/ *v pl* **gallows** *also* **gallowses 1** a frame, usu of 2 upright posts and a crosspiece, for hanging criminals **2** *the* punishment of hanging

gallstone /'gawl,stohn/ *n* a stone formed in the gall bladder or bile ducts

'**Gallup ,poll** /'galəp/ *n* a survey of public opinion frequently used as a means of forecasting sthg (e g an election result)

galore /gə'law/ *adj* abundant, plentiful – used after a noun

galosh /gə'losh/ *n* a rubber overshoe

galvanism /'galvən,iz(ə)m/ *n* **1** (the therapeutic use of) direct electric current produced by chemical action **2** vital or forceful activity

'**galvan·ize, -ise** /-iez/ *v* **1** to subject to or stimulate, rouse, or excite (as if) by the action of an electric current **2** to coat (iron or steel) with zinc as a protection from rust

gambit /'gambit/ *n* **1** a chess opening, esp in which a player risks (several) minor pieces to gain an advantage **2a** a remark intended to start a conversation or make a telling point **b** a calculated move; a stratagem

¹**gamble** /'gambl/ *v* **gambling** /'gambling/ **1a** to play a game (of chance) for money or property **b** to bet or risk sthg on an uncertain outcome **2** to speculate in business – **-bler** *n*

²**gamble** *n* (sthg involving) an element of risk

gambol /'gambl/ *v or n* **-ll-** (*NAm* **-l-, -ll-**); **gam-bolling** /'gambl·ing, 'gambling/ (to engage in) skipping or leaping about in play

¹**game** /gaym/ *n* **1a** activity engaged in for diversion or amusement; play **b** often derisive or mocking jesting **2a** a course or plan consisting of (secret) manoeuvres directed towards some end **b** a specified type of activity seen as competitive or governed by rules (and pursued for financial gain) **3a(1)** a physical or mental competition conducted according to rules with the participants in direct opposition to each other; a match **a(2)** a division of a larger contest **b** *pl* organized sports, esp athletics **4a** animals under pursuit or taken in hunting; *specif* the (edible flesh of) certain wild mammals, birds, and fish (e g deer and pheasant), hunted for sport or food **b** an object of ridicule or attack – often in *fair game*

²**game** *adj* **1** having a resolute unyielding spirit **2** ready to take risks or try sthg new – ~**ly** *adv*

³**game** *adj* injured, crippled, or lame

'**game,keeper** /-,keepə/ *n* one who has charge of the breeding and protection of game animals or birds on a private preserve

gamesmanship /'gaymzmən,ship/ *n* the art or practice of winning games by means other than superior skill without actually violating the rules

gamete /'gameet, gə'meet/ *n* a mature cell with a single set of chromosomes capable of fusing with another gamete of the other sex to form a zygote from which a new organism develops

gamma /'gamə/ *n* **1** the 3rd letter of the Greek alphabet **2** a mediocre mark or rating

'**gamma ,ray** *n* electromagnetic radiation of shorter wavelength than X rays emitted in some radioactive decay processes

gammon /'gamən/ *n* (the meat of) the lower end including the hind leg of a side of bacon removed from the carcass after curing with salt

gammy /'gami/ *adj, of a limb* game, lame

gamut /'gamət/ *n* **1** the whole series of recognized musical notes **2** an entire range or series

gamy, gamey /'gaymi/ *adj* having the strong flavour or smell of game (that has been hung until high) – **-miness** *n*

¹**gander** /'gandə/ *n* an adult male goose

²**gander** *n* a look, glance – slang

gang /gang/ *n* **1** a combination of similar implements or devices arranged to act together **2** *sing or pl in constr* a group of people **2a** associating for criminal, disreputable, etc ends; *esp* a group of adolescents who (disreputably) spend leisure time together **b** that have informal and usu close social relations **c** that have informal and usu close social relations

gangling /'gang-gling/, **gangly** /-gli/ *adj* tall, thin, and awkward in movement

ganglion /'gang-glion, -ən/ *n, pl* **ganglia** /-gli-ə/ *also* **ganglions** a mass of nerve cells outside the brain or spinal cord

gangplank /'gang,plangk/ *n* a movable board, plank, etc used to board a ship from a quay or another ship

gangrene /'gang,green/ *n* **1** local death of the body's soft tissues due to loss of blood supply **2** a pervasive moral evil – **-grenous** *adj*

gangster /'gangstə/ *n* a member of a criminal gang

gang up *v* **1** to combine as a group for a specific (disreputable) purpose **2** to make a joint assault *on*

'**gang,way** /-,way/ *n* **1** a (temporary) passageway (constructed of planks) **2a** the opening in a ship's side or rail through which it is boarded **b** a gangplank **3** a clear passage through a crowd – often used interjectionally **4** *Br* a narrow passage between sections of seats in a theatre, storage bays in a warehouse, etc

gannet /'ganit/ *n* any of several related large fish-eating seabirds

gantry /'gantri/ *n* **1** a frame for supporting barrels **2** a frame structure raised on side supports that spans over or round sthg and is used for railway signals, as a travelling crane, for servicing a rocket before launching, etc

gaol /jayəl/ *v or n, chiefly Br* (to) jail – **~er** *n*

gap /gap/ *n* **1** a break in a barrier (e g a wall or hedge) **2a** a mountain pass **b** a ravine **3** an empty space between 2 objects or 2 parts of an object **4** a break in continuity **5** a disparity or difference

gape /gayp/ *v* **1a** to open the mouth wide **b** to open or part widely **2** to gaze stupidly or in open-mouthed surprise or wonder

garage /'garahzh, 'garij/ *n* **1** a building for the shelter of motor vehicles **2** an establishment for providing essential services (e g the supply of petrol or repair work) to motor vehicles

garb /gahb/ *n* **1** a style of clothing; dress **2** an outward form; appearance – **garb** *v*

garbage /'gahbij/ *n* **1** worthless writing or speech **2** *chiefly NAm* domestic rubbish

garble /'gahbl/ *v* **garbling** /'gahbling/ to distort or confuse, giving a false impression of the facts

¹**garden** /'gahd(ə)n/ *n* **1** a plot of ground where herbs, fruits, vegetables, or typically flowers are cultivated **2** a public recreation area or park

²**garden** *v* to work in, cultivate, or lay out a garden – **~er** *n* – **~ing** *n*

³**garden** *adj* of a cultivated as distinguished from a wild kind grown in the open

garden city *n* a planned town with spacious residential areas including public parks and considerable garden space

gargantuan /gah'gantyoo-ən/ *adj* gigantic, colossal

¹**gargle** /'gahgl/ *v* **gargling** /'gahgling, 'gahgl·ing/ **1** to blow air from the lungs through (a liquid) held in the mouth or throat **2** to cleanse (the mouth or throat) in this manner

²**gargle** *n* **1** a liquid used in gargling **2** a bubbling liquid sound produced by gargling

gargoyle /'gah,goyl/ *n* a spout in the form of a grotesque human or animal figure projecting from a roof gutter to throw rainwater clear of a building

garish /'geərish/ *adj* **1** excessively and gaudily bright or vivid **2** tastelessly showy – **~ly** *adv*, **~ness** *n*

¹**garland** /'gahlənd/ *n* a wreath of flowers or leaves worn as an ornament or sign of distinction

²**garland** *v* to form into or deck with a garland

garlic /'gahlik/ *n* (the pungent compound bulb, much used as a flavouring in cookery, of) a plant of the onion family

garment /'gahmənt/ *n* an article of clothing

garnet /'gahnit/ *n* **1** a hard brittle mineral used as an abrasive and in its transparent deep red form as a gem **2** a dark red

¹**garnish** /'gahnish/ *v* **1** to decorate, embellish **2** to add decorative or savoury touches to (food)

²**garnish** *n* **1** an embellishment, ornament **2** an edible savoury or decorative addition (e g watercress) to a dish

garret /'garit/ *n* a small room just under the roof of a house

garrison /'garis(ə)n/ *n* **1a** a (fortified) town or place in which troops are stationed **2** *sing or pl in constr* the troops stationed at a garrison – **garrison** *v*

¹**garrotte, garotte**, *chiefly NAm* **garrote** /gə'rot/ *n* (a Spanish method of execution using) an iron collar for strangling sby

²**garrotte, garotte**, *chiefly NAm* **garrote** *v* **1** to execute with a garrotte **2** to strangle and rob

garrulous /'gar(y)ooləs/ *adj* excessively talkative – **~ly** *adv* *adv* – **-lity** *n* – **~ness** *n*

garter /'gahtə/ *n* **1** a band, usu of elastic, worn to hold up a stocking or sock **2** *cap* (the blue velvet garter that is the badge of) the Order of the Garter; *also* membership of the Order

gas /gas/ *n pl* **-s-** *also* **-ss- 1** a fluid (e g air) that has neither independent shape nor volume and tends to expand indefinitely **2a** a gas or gaseous mixture used to produce general anaesthesia, as a fuel, etc **b** a substance (e g tear gas or mustard gas) that can be used to produce a poisonous, choking, or irritant atmosphere **3** *NAm* petrol **4** empty talk – chiefly infml – ~**eous** *adj*

²**gas** *v* -**ss**- **1** to poison or otherwise affect adversely with gas **2** to talk idly – chiefly infml

'**gas ,chamber** *n* a chamber in which prisoners are executed by poison gas

gash /gash/ *vt or n* (to injure with) a deep long cut or cleft, esp in flesh

gasholder /'gas,hohldə/ *n* a gasometer

gasify /'gasifie, 'gay-/ *v* to change into gas – -**fication** *n*

gasket /'gaskit/ *v* (a specially shaped piece of) sealing material for ensuring that a joint, esp between metal surfaces, does not leak liquid or gas

gasoline, gasolene /,gasə'leen, '--,-/ *n*, *NAm* petrol

gasometer /ga'somitə/ *a* (large cylindrical storage) container for gas

gasp /gahsp/ *v* **1** to catch the breath suddenly and audibly (e g with shock) **2** to utter with gasps – usu + *out* – **gasp** *n*

'**gas ,ring** *n* a hollow metal perforated ring through which jets of gas issue and over which food is cooked

gassy /'gasi/ *adj* full of, containing, or like gas – **gassiness** *n*

gastric /'gastrik/ *adj* of the stomach

gastroenteritis /,gastroh,entə'rietəs/ inflammation of the lining of the stomach and the intestines, usu causing painful diarrhoea

gastronomy /ga'stronəmi/ *n* the art of science of good eating – -**nomic** *adj*, -**nomically** *adv*

'**gas ,works** /-,wuhks/ *n pl* **gasworks** a plant for manufacturing gas

¹**gate** /gayt/ *n* **1** (the usu hinged frame or door that closes) an opening in a wall, fence, etc **2a** a space between 2 markers through which a skier, canoeist, etc must pass in a slalom race **b** a mechanically operated barrier used as a starting device for a race **c** either of a pair of barriers that **c**(1) let water in and out of a lock **c**(2) close a road at a level crossing **3** an (electronic) device (e g in a computer) that produces a signal when specified input conditions are met **4** the total admission receipts or the number of spectators at a sporting event

²**gate** *v*, *Br* to punish by confinement to the premises of a school or college

gateau /'gatoh/ *n*, *pl* **gateaus, gateaux** /-tohz/ any of various rich often filled elaborate (cream) cakes

'**gate-,crash** *v* to enter, attend, or participate without a ticket or invitation – ~**er** *n*

'**gate,post** /-,pohst/ *n* the post on which a gate is hung or against which it closes

¹**gather** /'gadhə/ *v* **1** to bring together; collect (*up*) **2** to pick, harvest **3a** to summon up **b** to accumulate **4a** to bring together the parts of **b** to draw about or close to sthg **c** to pull (fabric) together, esp along a line of stitching, to create small tucks **5** to reach a conclusion (intuitively from hints or through inferences)

²**gather** *n* a tuck in cloth made by gathering

'**gathering** /-ring/ *n* **1** an assembly, meeting **2** an abscess **3** a gather or series of gathers in cloth

gauche /gohsh/ *adj* lacking social experience or grace – ~**rie** *n*

gaudy /'gawdi/ *adj* ostentatiously or tastelessly (and brightly) ornamented – -**dily** *adv*, -**diness** *n*

¹**gauge**, *NAm also* **gage** /gayj/ *n* **1** measurement according to some standard or system **2** an instrument for or a means of measuring or testing sthg (e g a dimension or quantity) **3** relative position of a ship with reference to another ship and the wind **4** the distance between the rails of a railway, wheels on an axle, etc **5a** the thickness of a thin sheet of metal, plastic, etc **b** the diameter of wire, a screw, etc **c** (a measure of) the fineness of a knitted fabric

²**gauge**, *NAm also* **gage** *v* **1** to measure (exactly) the size, dimensions, capacity, or contents of **2** to estimate, judge

gaunt /gawnt/ *adj* **1** excessively thin and angular as if from suffering **2** barren, desolate – ~**ness** *n*

¹**gauntlet** /'gawntlit/ *n* **1** a glove to protect the hand, worn with medieval armour **2** a strong protective glove with a wide extension above the wrist, used esp for sports and in industry **3** a challenge to combat – esp in *take up/throw down the gauntlet*

²**gauntlet** *n* a double file of men armed with weapons with which to strike at sby made to run between them; *broadly* criticism or an ordeal or test – usu in *run the gauntlet*

gauze /gawz/ *n* **1a** a thin often transparent fabric used chiefly for clothing or draperies **b** a loosely woven cotton surgical dressing **c** a fine mesh of metal or plastic filaments **2** a thin haze or mist – -**zy** *adj*

gave /gayv/ *past of* **give**

gavel /'gavl/ *n* a small mallet with which a chairman, judge, or auctioneer commands attention or confirms a vote, sale, etc

gavotte /gə'vot/ *n* **1** an 18th-c dance **2** a composition or movement of music in moderately quick ⁴/₄ time

¹**gawk** /gawk/ *v* to gawp – infml

²**gawk** *n* a clumsy awkward person

gawky /'gawki/ *adj* awkward and lanky – -**kiness** *n*

gawp /gawp/ *v* to gape or stare stupidly – infml

gay /gay/ *adj* **1** happily excited **2** bright, attractive **3** given to social pleasures **4** homosexual

gaze /gayz/ v or n (to fix the eyes in) a steady and intent look – **-er** n

gazebo /gə'zeeboh/ n pl **gazebos** a freestanding structure placed to command a view; also a summer house

gazelle /gə'zel/ n any of numerous small, graceful, and swift African and Asian antelopes

¹**gazette** /gə'zet/ n 1 a newspaper –usu in newspaper titles 2 an official journal containing announcements of honours and government appointments

²**gazette** v to announce (the appointment or status of) in an official gazette

gazetteer /ˌgazə'tiə/ n a dictionary of place names

gazump /gə'zump/ v to thwart (a would-be house purchaser) by raising the price after agreeing to sell at a certain price

G clef /jee/ n the treble clef

¹**gear** /giə/ n **1a** clothing, garments **b** movable property; goods 2 a set of equipment usu for a particular purpose **3a(1)** a mechanism that performs a specific function in a complete machine **a(2)** a toothed wheel (that is one of a set of interlocking wheels) **b** any of 2 or more adjustments of a transmission (e g of a bicycle or motor vehicle) that determine direction of travel or ratio of engine speed to vehicle speed

²**gear** v **1a** to provide with or connect by gearing **b** to put into gear 2 to adjust to so as to match, blend with, or satisfy bhg

gear box /-ˌboks/ n (a protective casing enclosing) a set of (car) gears

gear up v to make ready for effective operation; also to put (e g oneself) into a state of anxious excitement or nervous anticipation

gee-gee /'jee-jee/ n a horse – used esp by or to children or in racing slang

geese /gees/ pl of **goose**

geezer /'geezə/ n a man (who is thought a little odd or peculiar)

Geiger counter /'geigə/ n an electronic instrument for detecting the presence and intensity of radiation from a radioactive substance

geisha /'gayshə/, **geisha girl** n, pl **geisha, geishas** a Japanese girl who is trained to provide entertaining and lighthearted company

¹**gel** /jel/ n a substance in a state between solid and liquid; a jelly

²**gel, geld** chiefly NAm **jell** v **-ll-** 1 to change (from a sol) into a gel 2 to (cause to) take shape or become definite

gelatin, gelatine /'jelətin, -teen/ n 1 a glutinous material obtained from animal tissues by boiling; esp a protein used esp in food (e g to set jellies) and photography 2 a thin coloured transparent sheet used to colour a stage light – **-nous** adj

geld /geld/ v to castrate (a male animal)

gelding /'gelding/ n a castrated male horse

gelignite /'jelignīet/ n a dynamite in which the absorbent base is a mixture of potassium or sodium nitrate usu with wood pulp

gem /jem/ n 1 a precious stone, esp when cut and polished for use in jewellery 2 sby or sthg highly prized or much beloved

Gemini /'jemini, -nie/ n (sby born under) the 3rd sign of the zodiac in astrology, which is pictured as twins

gen /jen/ n the correct or complete information – infml

gendarme /'zhon,dahm/ (Fr ʒãdarm) n a member of a corps of armed police, esp in France

gender /'jendə/ n 1 sex 2 a system of subdivision within a grammatical class of a language (e g noun or verb), partly based on sexual characteristics, that determines agreement with and selection of other words or grammatical forms

gene /jeen/ n a unit of inheritance that is carried on a chromosome and controls the transmission of hereditary characteristics

genealogy /ˌjeeni'alɒji/ n 1 (an account of) the descent of a person, family, or group from an ancestor or from older forms 2 the study of family pedigrees – **-gist** n, **-logical** adj

genera /'jenərə/ pl of **genus**

¹**general** /'jen(ə)rəl/ adj 1 involving or applicable to the whole 2 of, involving, or applicable to (what is common to) every member of a class, kind, or group **3a** applicable to or characteristic of the majority of individuals involved; prevalent **b** concerned or dealing with universal rather than particular aspects 4 approximate rather than strictly accurate 5 holding superior rank or taking precedence over others similarly titled — **in general** usually; for the most part

²**general** n a high-ranking officer in the armed forces; esp one in command of an army

general election n an election in which candidates are elected in all constituencies of a nation or state

generality /ˌjenə'raləti/ n 1 total applicability 2 generalization 3 the greatest part; the bulk

generalize, -ise /'jen(ə)rə,līez/ v 1 to give a general form to 2 to derive or induce (a general conception or principle) from particulars 3 to give general applicability to 4 to make vague or indefinite statements – **-ization** n

generally /'jen(ə)rəli/ adv 1 without regard to specific instances 2 usually; as a rule 3 collectively; as a whole

general practitioner n a medical doctor who treats all types of disease and is usu the first doctor consulted by a patient

general staff n a group of officers who aid a commander in administration, training, supply, etc

general strike n a strike in all or many of the industries of a region or country

generate /'jenə,rayt/ v 1 to bring into existence or originate produce 2 to define (a linguistic, mathematical, etc structure (e g a curve or surface)) by the application of 1 or more rules or operations to given quantities

generation /,jenə'raysh(ə)n/ n 1 sing or pl in constr 1a a group of living organisms constituting a single step in the line of descent from an ancestor b a group of individuals born and living at the same time c a type or class of objects usu developed from an earlier type 2 the average time between the birth of parents and that of their offspring 3 the process of coming or bringing into being

generative /'jen(ə)rətiv/ adj having the power or function of generating, originating, producing, reproducing, etc

generator /'jenə,raytə/ n 1 an apparatus for producing a vapour or gas 2 a machine for generating electricity; esp a dynamo

generic /ji'nerik/ adj 1 (characteristic) of or applied to (members of) a whole group or class 2 (having the rank) of a biological genus – ~ally adv

generous /'jen(ə)rəs/ adj 1 magnanimous, kindly 2 liberal in giving (e g of money or help) 3 marked by abundance, ample proportions, or richness – -rosity n – ~ly adv

genesis /'jenəsis/ n pl geneses /-,seez/ the origin or coming into being of sthg

genetic /jə'netik/ adj 1 of or determined by the origin or development of sthg 2 of or involving genes or genetics – ~ally adv

ge'netics n pl but sing in constr 1 the biology of (the mechanisms and structures involved in) the heredity and variation of organisms 2 the genetic make-up of an organism, type, group, or condition – -icist n

genial /'jeenyəl, ni·əl/ 1 favourable to growth or comfort; mild 2 cheerfully good-tempered; kindly – -ally adv, ~ity n

genie /'jeeni/ n pl genies also genii /-ni,ie/, a spirit, often in human form, which in Muslim legends serves whoever summons it

genitals /'jenitlz/ n pl the (external) reproductive and sexual organs – genital adj

genitive /'jenitiv/ adj or n (of or in) a grammatical case expressing typically a relationship of possessor or source; also sthg in this case

genius /'jeenyəs, -ni·əs/ n pl (1a) genii /-ni,ie/, (1b & 3) genii also geniuses, (4) geniuses also genii 1 an attendant spirit of a person or place 2a a peculiar, distinctive, or identifying character or spirit b the associations and traditions of a place 3 a spirit or genie 4a a single strongly marked capacity or aptitude b (a person endowed with) extraordinary intellectual power (as manifested in creative activity)

genocide /'jenə,sied/ n the deliberate murder of a racial or cultural group

genre /'zhonh·rə (Fr ʒɑ:r)/ n 1 a sort, type 2 a category of artistic, musical, or literary composition characterized by a particular style, form, or content

genteel /jen'teel/ adj 1 free from vulgarity or rudeness; polite 2a maintaining or striving to maintain the appearance of superior social status or respectability b marked by false delicacy, prudery, or affectation – -teelly adv, -tility n

gentile /'jentiel/ adj or n, often cap (of) a non-Jewish person

gentle /'jentl/ adj 1a honourable, distinguished; specif of or belonging to a gentleman b kind, amiable 2 free from harshness, sternness, or violence; mild, soft; also tractable 3 soft, moderate – ~ness n, -ly adv

'gentle,folk /-,fohk/ also gentlefolks n pl people of good family and breeding

gentleman /'jentlmən/ n pl gentlemen /-~/ 1a a man belonging to the landed gentry or nobility; also a man of independent wealth b a man who is chivalrous, well-mannered, and honourable 2 a valet – usu in gentleman's gentleman 3 a man of social class or condition – ~ly adj

gentleman's agreement gentlemen's agreement n an unwritten agreement secured only by the honour of the participants

gentry /'jentri/ n, sing or pl in constr 1 the upper class 2 a class whose members are (landed proprietors) entitled to bear a coat of arms though not of noble rank

gents /jents/ n, pl gents often cap, Br a public lavatory for men – chiefly infml

genuflect /'jenyoo,flekt/ v to bend the knee, esp in worship or as a gesture of respect (to sacred objects) – -tion n

genuine /'jenyooin/ adj 1 actually produced by or proceeding from the alleged source or author or having the reputed qualities of character 2 free from pretence; sincere – ~ly adv, ~ness n

genus /'jeenəs/ n, pl genera /'jenərə/ 1 a category in the classification of living things ranking between the family and the species 2 a class divided into several subordinate classes

geography /ji'ogrəfi/ n a science that deals with the earth and its life; esp the description of land, sea, air, and the distribution of plant and animal life including human beings and their industries 2 the geographical features of an area – -pher n, -phical adj

geology /ji'oləji/ n 1 a science that deals with the history of the earth's crust, esp as recorded in rocks 2 the geological features of an area – -gical adj

253   **get**

geometric /ji-ə'metrik/, **geometrical** /-kl/ *adj* **1a** of or according to (the laws of) geometry **b** increasing in a geometric progression **2** using, being, or decorated with patterns formed from straight and curved lines

geometric progression *n* a sequence (e g 2,4,8) in which the ratio of any term to its predecessor is constant

geometry /ji'omətri/ *n* **1** a branch of mathematics that deals with the measurement, properties, and relationships of points, lines, angles, surfaces, and solids **2** (surface) shape **3** an arrangement of objects or parts that suggests geometrical figures

geophysics /-'fiziks/ *n pl but sing or pl in constr* the physics of the earth including meteorology, oceanography, seismology, etc – **ical** *adj*

¹Georgian /'jawj(ə)n/ *n or adj* (a native or inhabitant of the language) of Georgia

²Georgian *adj* **1** (characteristic) of (the time of) the reigns of the first 4 Georges (1714 to 1830) **2** (characteristic) of the reign of George V (1910 to 1936)

geranium /jə'raynyəm, -nyi-əm/ *n* any of a widely distributed genus of plants having radially symmetrical flowers; *esp* a garden variety with showy red flowers

gerbil *also* **gerbille** /'juh,bil/ *n* any of numerous Old World mouselike desert rodents

geriatrics /,jeri'atriks/ *n pl but sing in constr* a branch of medicine that deals with (the diseases of) old age – **geriatric** *adj*

germ /juhm/ *n* **1a** a small mass of cells capable of developing into (a part of) an organism **b** the embryo of a cereal grain that is usu separated from the starchy parts during milling **2** sthg that serves as an origin **3** a (disease-causing) microorganism

german /'juhmən/ *adj* having the same parents, or the same grandparents, on either the maternal or paternal side –usu in comb

¹German /'juhmən/ *n* **1a** a native or inhabitant of Germany **b** one (e g a Swiss German) who speaks German as his/her native language outside Germany **2** the language of the people of Germany, Austria, and parts of Switzerland – **~ic** *adj*

²German *adj* (characteristic) of Germany, the Germans, or German

germane /juh'mayn/ *adj* both relevant and appropriate

German 'measles *n pl but sing or pl in constr* a virus disease that is milder than typical measles

germicide /'juhmi,sied/ *n* sthg that kills germs

germinal /'juhminl/ *adj* **1** in the earliest stage of development **2** creative, seminal

germinate /'juhminayt/ *v* **1** to begin to grow; sprout **2** to come into being

gerrymander /'jeri,mandə/ *v* to divide (an area) into election districts to give one political party an electoral advantage

gerund /'jerənd/ a verbal noun esp in Latin

gestapo /gə's(h)tahpoh/ *n pl* **gestapos** a secret-police organization operating esp against suspected traitors; *specif, cap* that of Nazi Germany

gestation /je'staysh(ə)n/ *n* **1** the carrying of young in the uterus; pregnancy **2** conception and development, esp in the mind

gesticulate /je'stikyoo,layt/ *v* to make expressive gestures, esp when speaking – **lation** *n*

¹gesture /'jeschə/ *n* **1** a movement, usu of the body or limbs, that expresses or emphasizes an idea, sentiment, or attitude **2** sthg said or done for its effect on the attitudes of others or to convey a feeling (e g friendliness)

²gesture *v* to make or express (by) a gesture

get /get/ *v* **-tt-; got; got; got** /got/, *NAm also* **gotten** /'gotn/; *nonstandard pres pl & 1 & 2 sing* **got 1** to gain possession of **2a** to receive as a reward; earn **b** to become affected by; catch **c** to be subjected to **3a** to cause to come, go, or move **b** to prevail on; induce **4** to make ready; prepare **5a** to have – used in the present perfect tense form with present meaning **b** to have as an obligation or necessity –used in the present perfect tense form with present meaning; + *to* and an understood or expressed infinitive (e g in he's *got* to go) **6a** to puzzle **b** to irritate **7** to affect emotionally **8** to reach or enter into the specified condition or activity (e g in *get* drunk) **9** to contrive by effort, luck, or permission – + *to* and an infinitive

get across *v* to make or become clear or convincing

get along *v* **1** to move away; leave for another destination **2** to manage **3** to be or remain on congenial terms

getaway /'getə,way/ *n* a departure, escape

get by *v* **1** to manage, survive **2** to succeed by a narrow margin; be just about acceptable

get down *v* **1** to leave (the table) or descend (from a vehicle) **2** to depress **3** to swallow **4** to record in writing **5** to apply serious attention or consideration — **get down to** to apply serious attention or consideration to; concentrate one's efforts on

get off *v* **1** to start, leave **2** to escape from a dangerous situation or from punishment **3** to leave work with permission **4** *Br* to start an amorous or sexual relationship – often + *with*

get on *v* **1** to be friends **2** to become late or old **3** to come near; approach – + *for* **4** to hurry

get out *v* **1** to emerge, escape **2a** to become known **b** to bring before the public; *esp* to publish

get round *v* **1** to circumvent, evade **2** to cajole, persuade — **get round to** to give esp overdue attention or consideration

'get-to,gether *n* an (informal social) gathering or meeting

get together *v* **1** to come together; assemble **2** to unite in discussion or promotion of a project

getup /'get,up/ n an outfit, clothing

get up v **1a** to arise from bed **b** to rise to one's feet **2** to go ahead or faster – used in the imperative as a command, esp to driven animals **3** to organize **4** to arrange the external appearance of; dress **5** to acquire a knowledge of **6** to create in oneself

geyser /'geeza; *sense* ' *also* 'gieza/ n **1** a spring that intermittently throws out jets of heated water and steam **2** *Br* an apparatus with a boiler in which water (e g for a bath) is rapidly heated by a gas flame

ghastly /'gahstli/ **1a** (terrifyingly) horrible **b** intensely unpleasant, disagreeable, or objectionable **2** pale, wan – **-liness** n

gherkin /'guhkin/ n (a slender annual climbing plant of the cucumber family that bears) a small prickly fruit used for pickling

ghetto /'getoh/ n pl **ghettos, ghettoes 1** part of a city in which Jews formerly lived **2** an often slum area of a city in which a minority group live, esp because of social, legal, or economic pressures

¹**ghost** /gohst/ n **1** a disembodied soul; *esp* the soul of a dead person haunting the living **2a** a faint shadowy trace **b** the least bit **3** a false image in a photographic negative or on a television screen – **~ly** adj – **~liness** n

²**ghost** v to write something to appear under another person's name

ghoul /goohl/ n **1** a evil being of Arabic legend that robs graves and feeds on corpses **2** one who enjoys the macabre – **~ish** adj – **~ishness** n

¹**GI** /jee 'ie/ adj (characteristic) of US military personnel or equipment

²**GI** n, pl **GI's, GIs** a member of the US army, esp a private

¹**giant** /'jie·ant/ n **1** *fem* **giantess** a legendary human being of great stature and strength **2** sby or sthg extraordinarily large **3** a person of extraordinary powers

²**giant** adj extremely large

,**giant 'panda** n the black and white Chinese panda

gibber /'jiba/ v to make rapid, inarticulate, and usu incomprehensible utterances

gibberish /'jiborish/ n meaningless language

gibbet /'jibit/ v or n **1** (to execute or expose on) an upright post with an arm for hanging the bodies of executed criminals

gibbon /'gib(a)n/ n any of several tailless Asian anthropoid tree-dwelling apes

gibe, jibe /jieb/ v to jeer at – **gibe** n

giblets /'jiblits/ n pl a fowl's heart, liver, or other edible internal organs

giddy /'gidi/ adj **1** lightheartedly frivolous **2a** feeling, or causing to feel, a sensation of unsteadiness and lack of balance as if everything is whirling round **b** whirling rapidly

gift /gift/ n **1** a natural capacity or talent **2** sthg freely given by one person to another **3** the act, right, or power of giving — **gift of the gab** the ability to talk glibly and persuasively – *infml*

'**gifted** adj **1** having or revealing great natural ability **2** highly intelligent

¹**gig** /gig/ n **1** a long light ship's boat propelled by oars, sails, etc **2** a light 2-wheeled one-horse carriage

²**gig** n a musician's engagement for a specified time; *esp* such an engagement for 1 performance

gigantic /jie'gantik/ adj unusually great or enormous – **~ally** adv

¹**giggle** /'gigl/ v **giggling** /'gig·ling, 'gigling/ to laugh with repeated short catches of the breath (and in a silly manner)

²**giggle** n **1** an act or instance of giggling **2** *chiefly Br* sthg that amuses or diverts

gigolo /'zhigaloh/ n pl **gigolos 1** a man paid by a usu older woman for companionship or sex **2** a professional dancing partner or male escort

¹**gild** /gild/ v **gilded, gilt** /gilt/ **1** to overlay (as if) with a thin covering of gold **2** to give an attractive but often deceptive appearance to — **gild the lily** to add unnecessary ornamentation to sthg beautiful in its own right

²**gild** n a guild

¹**gill** /jil/ n a measure equal to ¹/₄ pint or 0.142 litre

²**gill** /gil/ n **1** an organ, esp of a fish, for oxygenating blood using the oxygen dissolved in water **2** the flesh under or about the chin or jaws – usu pl with sing. meaning **3** any of the radiating plates forming the undersurface of the cap of some fungi (e g mushrooms)

³**gill, ghyll** /gil/ n, *Br* **1** a ravine **2** a narrow mountain stream

gillie, gilly, ghillie /'gili/ n an attendant to sby who is hunting or fishing in Scotland

¹**gilt** /gilt/ adj covered with gold or gilt; of the colour of gold

²**gilt** n **1** (sthg that resembles) gold laid on a surface **2** superficial brilliance; surface attraction **3** a gilt-edged security – usu pl

,**gilt-'edged, gilt-edge** adj **1** of the highest quality or reliability **2** *of government securities* having a guaranteed fixed interest rate and redeemable at face value

¹**gimlet** /'gimlit/ n a tool for boring small holes in wood, usu consisting of a crosswise handle fitted to a tapered screw

²**gimlet** adj, *of eyes* piercing, penetrating

gimmick /'gimik/ n a scheme, device, or object devised to gain attention or publicity – **~y** adj

¹**gin** /jin/ n any of various tools or mechanical devices: e g **a** a snare or trap for game **b** a device for removing the seeds from cotton

²**gin** n a spirit made by distilling a mash of grain with juniper berries

ginger /'jinjə/ n **1a** (any of several cultivated tropical plants with) a thickened pungent aromatic underground stem used (dried and ground) as a spice, or candied as a sweet **b** the spice usu prepared by drying and grinding ginger **2** a strong brown colour

'ginger,bread /-,bred/ n a thick biscuit or cake made with treacle or syrup and flavoured with ginger

gingerly /'jinjəli/ adj very cautious or careful

ginger up v to stir to activity; vitalize

gipsy, NAm **gypsy** /'jipsi/ **1** often cap a member of a dark Caucasian people coming orig from India to Europe in the 14th or 15th c and leading a migratory way of life **2** a person who moves from place to place; a wanderer

giraffe /ji'raf, ji'rahf/ n pl **giraffes,** esp collectively **giraffe** a large African ruminant mammal with a very long neck and a beige coat marked with brown or black patches

gird /guhd/ v **girded, girt** /guht/ **1a** to encircle or bind with a flexible band (e g a belt) **b** to surround **2** to prepare (oneself) for action — **gird one's loins, gird up one's loins** to prepare for action; muster one's resources

girder /'guhdə/ n a horizontal main supporting beam

¹girdle /'guhdl/ n **1a** a belt or cord encircling the body, usu at the waist **b** a woman's tightly fitting undergarment that extends from the waist to below the hips **2** a ring made by the removal of the bark and cambium round a plant stem or tree trunk

²girdle v **girdling** /'guhdling/ **1** to encircle (as if) with a girdle **2** to cut a girdle round (esp a tree), usu in order to kill

³girdle n, Scot & dial Eng a griddle

girl /guhl/ n **1a** a female child **b** a young unmarried woman **2a** a sweetheart, girlfriend **b** a daughter **3** a woman – chiefly infml

'girl,friend /-,frend/ n **1** a frequent or regular female companion of a boy or man; esp one with whom he is romantically involved **2** a female friend

girlie, girly /'guhli/ adj, of a magazine featuring nude or semi-nude photos of women

giro /'jie(ə)roh/ n a computerized low-cost system of money transfer comparable to a current account that is one of the national post office services in many European countries

girt /guht/ v to gird

girth /guhth/ n **1** a strap that passes under the body of a horse or other animal to fasten esp a saddle on its back **2** a measurement of thickness round a body

gist /jist/ n the main point of a matter; the essence

¹give /giv/ v **gave** /gayv/; **given** /'giv(ə)n/ **1** to make a present of **2** to grant, bestow, or allot (by formal action) **3a** to administer **b** to commit to another

as a trust or responsibility **c** to convey or express to another **4a** to proffer, present (for another to use or act on) **b** to surrender (oneself) to a partner in sexual intercourse **5** to present to view or observation **6a** to present for, or provide by way of, entertainment **b** to present, perform, or deliver in public **7** to attribute, ascribe **8** to yield as a product or effect **9** to yield possession of by way of exchange; pay **10** to make, execute, or deliver (e g by some bodily action) **11** to cause to undergo; impose **12** to award by formal verdict **13** to offer for consideration, acceptance, or use **14a** to cause to have or receive **b** to cause to catch or contract **15** to apply freely or fully; devote **16** to allow, concede **17** to care to the extent of **18** to yield or collapse in response to pressure — **given** n — **give a dog a bad name** to implant prejudice by slander — **give a good account of** to acquit (oneself) well — **give a miss** chiefly Br to avoid, bypass — **give as good as one gets** to counterattack with equal vigour — **give birth to 1** to bring forth as a mother **2** to be the cause or origin of — **give chase** to go in pursuit — **give ground** to withdraw before superior force; retreat — **give me I prefer** — **give or take** allowing for a specified imprecision — **give place** to yield by way of being superseded — **give someone a wide berth** to stay at a safe distance from sby — **give someone best** Br to acknowledge sby's superiority — **give someone/something his/her/its head 1** to give sby or sthg greater freedom and responsibility **2** to allow (a horse) to gallop — **give someone rope** to give sby free scope — **give the lie to** to belie — **give way 1a** to retreat; give ground **b** to yield the right of way **2** to yield oneself without restraint or control **3a** to yield (as if) to physical stress **b** to yield to entreaty or insistence **4** give place

²give n the capacity or tendency to yield to pressure; resilience, elasticity

,give-and-'take n **1** the practice of making mutual concessions **2** the good-natured exchange of ideas or words

'give,away /-ə,way/ n **1** an unintentional revelation or betrayal **2** sthg given free or at a reduced price

give away v **1** to make a present of **2** to hand over (a bride) to the bridegroom at a wedding **3a** to betray **b** to disclose, reveal – esp in **give the game/show away**

given /'giv(ə)n/ adj **1** prone, disposed **2a** fixed, specified **b** assumed as actual or hypothetical

give off v to emit

give out v **1** to declare, publish **2** to emit **3** to issue, distribute **4** to come to an end; fail

give over v **1** to set apart for a particular purpose or use **2** to deliver to sby's care **3** to bring an activity to an end – infml

give up *v* 1 to surrender, esp as a prisoner 2 to stop trying 3 to renounce 4 to abandon (oneself) *to* sthg 5 to declare incurable or insoluble 6 to stop having a relationship with — **give up the ghost** to die

gizzard /'gizǝd/ *n* a muscular enlargement of the alimentary canal of birds that immediately follows the crop and has a tough horny lining for grinding food; *also* a similar anatomical part in other animals

glacé /'glasay/ *adj* 1 made or finished so as to have a smooth glossy surface 2 coated with a glaze; candied

glacial /'glays(h)ǝl/ *adj* 1 extremely cold 2 of or produced by glaciers 3 resembling ice in appearance, esp when frozen

glacier /'glasi-ǝ, 'glay-/ *n* a large body of ice moving slowly down a slope or spreading outwards on a land surface

glad /glad/ *adj* **-dd-** 1 expressing or experiencing pleasure, joy, or delight 2 very willing 3 causing happiness and joy

glade /glayd/ *n* an open space within a wood or forest

gladiator /'gladi,aytǝ/ *n* 1 sby trained to fight in the arena for the entertainment of ancient Romans 2 sby engaging in a public fight or controversy — **~ial** *adj*

gladiolus /gladi'ohlǝs/ *n*, *pl* **gladioli** /-lie/ any of a genus of (African) plants of the iris family with spikes of brilliantly coloured irregular flowers

'glad ,rags *n pl* smart clothes – infml

glamour, *NAm also* **glamor** /'glamǝ/ *n* a romantic, exciting, and often illusory attractiveness; *esp* alluring or fascinating personal attraction — **-orize** *v* – **-orous** *adj*

¹glance /glahns/ *v* 1 to strike a surface obliquely so as to go off at an angle – often + *off* 2 to touch on a subject or refer to it briefly or indirectly 3a *of the eyes* to move swiftly from one thing to another b to take a quick look at sthg

²glance *n* 1 a quick intermittent flash or gleam 2 a deflected impact or blow 3a a swift movement of the eyes b a quick or cursory look

glancing /'glahnsing/ *adj* having a slanting direction – **~ly** *adv*

gland /gland/ *n* 1 an organ that selectively removes materials from the blood, alters them, and secretes them esp for further use in the body or for elimination 2 any of various secreting organs of plants

¹glare /gleǝ/ *v* 1 to shine with a harsh uncomfortably brilliant light 2 to express hostility by staring fiercely

²glare *n* 1 a harsh uncomfortably bright light; *specif* painfully bright sunlight 2 an angry or fierce stare

glaring /'gleǝring/ *adj* painfully and obtrusively evident – **~ly** *adv*

glass /glahs/ *n* 1a a hard brittle usu transparent substance formed by fusing silica sand and other ingredients b a substance resembling glass, esp in hardness and transparency 2a sthg made of glass: e g 2a(1) a glass drinking vessel (e g a tumbler or wineglass) a(2) a mirror a(3) a barometer b(1) an optical instrument (e g a magnifying glass) for viewing objects not readily seen b(2) *pl* a pair of lenses together with a frame to hold them in place for correcting defects of vision or protecting the eyes

,glass 'fibre *n* fibreglass

'glass,house /-,hows/ *n*, *chiefly Br* 1 a greenhouse 2 a military prison – slang

'glass,paper /-,paypǝ/ *n* paper to which a thin layer of powdered glass has been glued for use as an abrasive

'glass,ware /-,weǝ/ *n* articles made of glass

glassy /'glahsi/ *adj* dull, lifeless

¹glaze /glayz/ *v* 1 to provide or fit with glass 2 to coat (as if) with a glaze 3 to give a smooth glossy surface to

²glaze *n* 1a a liquid preparation that gives a glossy coating to food b a preparation applied to the surface of ceramic wares as decoration and to make them nonporous 2 a glassy film (e g of ice)

glazier /'glayzi-ǝ, -zyǝ/ *n* one who fits glass, esp into windows, as an occupation

¹gleam /gleem/ *n* 1a a transient appearance of subdued or partly obscured light b a glint 2a a brief or faint appearance or occurrence

²gleam *v* 1 to shine with subdued steady light or moderate brightness 2 to appear briefly or faintly

glean /gleen/ *v* 1 to gather produce, esp grain, left by reapers 2 to gather material (e g information) bit by bit – **~er** *n*

gleanings /'gleenings/ *n pl* things acquired by gleaning

glee /glee/ *n* 1 a feeling of merry high-spirited joy or delight 2 an unaccompanied song for 3 or more usu male solo voices – **~ful** *adj*

glen /glen/ *n* a secluded narrow valley

glib /glib/ *adj* **-bb-** 1 showing little forethought or preparation; lacking depth and substance 2 marked by (superficial or dishonest) ease and fluency in speaking or writing – **~ly** *adv* – **~ness** *n*

glide /glied/ *v* 1 to move noiselessly in a smooth, continuous, and effortless manner 2 to pass gradually and imperceptibly 3 *of an aircraft* to fly without the use of engines

glider /'gliedǝ/ *n* an aircraft similar to an aeroplane but without an engine

¹glimmer /'glimǝ/ *v* 1 to shine faintly or unsteadily 2 to appear indistinctly with a faintly luminous quality

²glimmer *n* 1 a feeble or unsteady light 2a a dim perception or faint idea b a small sign or amount

¹glimpse /glimps/ *v* to get a brief look at

²glimpse *n* a brief fleeting view or look

¹glint /glint/ *v* to shine with tiny bright flashes; sparkle or glitter, esp by reflection

²glint *n* **1** a tiny bright flash of light; a sparkle **2** a brief or faint manifestation

glisten /'glis(ə)n/ *v* to shine, usu by reflection, with a sparkling radiance or with the lustre of a wet or oiled surface – ~**ing** *adj* – ~**ingly** *adv*

¹glitter /'glitə/ *v* **1** to shine by reflection with a brilliant or metallic lustre **2** to be brilliantly attractive in a superficial or deceptive way

²glitter *n* **1** sparkling brilliance, showiness, or attractiveness **2** small glittering particles used for ornamentation

gloat /gloht/ *v* to observe or think about sthg with great and often malicious satisfaction, gratification, or relish

global /'glohbl/ *adj* **1** spherical **2** of or involving the entire world **3** general, comprehensive – **globally** *adv*

globe /glohb/ *n* sthg spherical or rounded: e g **a** a spherical representation of the earth, a heavenly body, or the heavens **b** the earth

globe artichoke *n* an artichoke with an edible flower-head

'globe-,trotter *n* one who travels widely

globular /'globyoolə/ *adj* **1** globe- or globule-shaped **2** having or consisting of globules

globule /'globyoohl/ *n* a tiny globe or ball

gloom /gloohm/ *n* **1** partial or total darkness **2a** lowness of spirits **b** an atmosphere of despondency – ~**y** *adj*

glorify /'glawri,fie/ *v* **1** to make glorious by bestowing honour, praise, or admiration **2** to shed radiance or splendour on **3** to cause to appear better, more appealing, or more important than in reality **4** to give glory to (e g in worship) – **-fication** *n*

glorious /'glawri-əs/ *adj* **1a** possessing or deserving glory **b** conferring glory **2** marked by great beauty or splendour **3** delightful, wonderful – ~**ly** *adv*

¹glory /'glawri/ *n* **1** (sthg that secures) praise or renown **2** a (most) commendable asset **3a** (sthg marked by) resplendence or magnificence **b** the splendour, blessedness, and happiness of heaven; eternity **4** a state of great gratification or exaltation

²glory *v* to rejoice proudly

¹gloss /glos/ *n* **1** (sthg that gives) surface lustre or brightness **2** a deceptively attractive outer appearance **3** paint to which varnish has been added to give a gloss finish

²gloss *n* **1** a brief explanation (e g in the margin of a text) of a difficult word or expression **2a** a glossary **b** an interlinear translation **c** a continuous commentary accompanying a text – **gloss** *v*

glossary /'glosəri/ *n* a list of terms (e g those used in a particular text or in a specialized field), usu with their meanings

gloss over *v* **1** to make appear right and acceptable **2** to veil or hide by treating rapidly or superficially

¹glossy /'glosi/ *adj* **1** having a surface lustre or brightness **2** attractive in an artificially opulent, sophisticated, or smoothly captivating manner

²glossy *n*, *chiefly Br* a magazine expensively produced on glossy paper and often having a fashionable or sophisticated content

glottis /'glotis/ *n*, *pl* **glottises, glottides** /-ti,deez/ (the structures surrounding) the elongated space between the vocal cords

glove /gluv/ *n* a covering for the hand having separate sections for each of the fingers and the thumb and often extending part way up the arm

'glove com,partment *n* a small storage compartment in the dashboard of a motor vehicle

¹glow /gloh/ *v* **1** to shine (as if) with an intense heat **2a** to experience a sensation (as if) of heat; show a ruddy colour (as if) from being too warm **b** to show satisfaction or elation

²glow *n* **1** brightness or warmth of colour **2a** warmth of feeling or emotion **b** a sensation of warmth **3** light (as if) from sthg burning without flames or smoke

glower /'glowə/ *v* to look or stare with sullen annoyance or anger – ~**ingly** *adv*

'glow,worm /-,wuhm/ *n* a larva or wingless female of a firefly that emits light from the abdomen

glucose /'gloohkohz, -kohs/ *n* a sugar that occurs widely in nature and is the usual form in which carbohydrate is assimilated by animals

¹glue /glooh/ *n* any of various strong adhesives; *also* a solution of glue used for sticking things together – ~**y** *adj*

²glue *v* **gluing** *also* **glueing** **1** to cause to stick tightly with glue **2** to fix (e g the eyes) on an object steadily or with deep concentration

glum /glum/ *adj* **-mm- 1** broodingly morose **2** dreary, gloomy – ~**ly** *adv* – ~**ness** *n*

¹glut /glut/ *v* **-tt- 1** to fill, esp with food, to beyond capacity **2** to flood (the market) with goods so that supply exceeds demand

²glut *n* an excessive supply (e g of a harvested crop) which exceeds market demand

glutinous /'gloohtinəs/ *adj* (thick and) sticky; gummy

glutton /'glut(ə)n/ *n* **1** one given habitually to greedy and voracious eating and drinking **2** one who has a great capacity for accepting or enduring sthg – ~**ous** *adj* – ~**ously** *adv* – ~**y** *n*

glycerine /'glisəreen/, **glycerin** /'gliserin/ *n* a sticky colourless liquid, made from fats, used in the manufacture of soap and explosives

gnarled /nahld/ *adj* **1** full of or covered with knots or protuberances **2** crabbed in disposition, aspect, or character

gnash /nash/ *v* to strike or grind (esp the teeth) together

gnat /nat/ *n* any of various small usu biting 2-winged flies

gnaw /naw/ *v* **1** to bite or chew on with the teeth; *esp* to wear away by persistent biting or nibbling **2** to affect as if by continuous eating away; plague **3** to erode, corrode

gnome /nohm/ *n* a dwarf of folklore who lives under the earth and guards treasure

gnu /nooh/ *n pl* **gnus,** *esp collectively* **gnu** any of several large horned African antelopes with an oxlike head, a short mane, and a long tail

¹**go** /goh/ *v* went /went/; **gone** /gon/ **1** to proceed on a course **2a** to move out of or away from a place; leave **b** to make an expedition for a specified activity **3** to be, esp habitually **4a** to become lost, consumed, or spent **b** to die **c** to elapse **d** to be got rid of (e g by sale or removal) **e** to fail **f** to succumb; give way **5a** to happen, progress – often + *on* **b** to be in general or on an average **c** to turn out (well) **6** to put or subject oneself **7a** to begin an action, motion, or process **b** to maintain or perform an action or motion **c** to function in a proper or specified way **d** to make a characteristic noise **e** to perform a demonstrated action **8a** to be known or identified as specified **b** to be performed or delivered in a specified manner **9a** to act or occur in accordance or harmony **b** to contribute to a total or result **10** to be about, intending, or destined – + *to* and an infinitive (e g is it *going* to rain) **11a** to come or arrive at a specified state or condition **b** to join a specified institution professionally or attend it habitually **c** to come to be; turn **d(1)** to become voluntarily **d(2)** to change to a specified system or tendency **e** to continue to be; remain **12** to be compatible *with*, harmonize **13a** to be capable of passing, extending, or being contained or inserted **b** to belong **14a** to carry authority **b** to be acceptable, satisfactory, or adequate **c** to be the case; be valid — **go about** to undertake; set about — **go after** to seek, pursue — **go against 1** to act in opposition to; offend **2** to turn out unfavourably to — **go ahead 1** to begin **2** to continue, advance — **go all the way 1** to enter into complete agreement **2** to engage in actual sexual intercourse — **go along with 1** to occur as a natural accompaniment of **2** to agree with; support — **go ape** to run amok; lose control — **go at 1** to attack, assail **2** to undertake energetically — **go back on 1** to fail to keep (e g a promise) **2** to be disloyal to; betray — **go begging** to be available but in little demand — **go by the board** to be discarded — **go crook** *Aust & NZ* to lose one's temper — **go for 1** to serve or be accounted as **2** to try to secure **3a** to favour, accept **b** to have an interest in or liking for **4** to attack, assail — **go for a burton** *Br* to get lost, broken, or killed — *slang* — **go great guns** to achieve great success — **go hang** to cease to be of interest or concern — **go into 1** to be contained in **2** to investigate **3** to explain in depth — **go it 1** to behave in a reckless, excited, or impromptu manner **2** to proceed rapidly or furiously **3** to conduct one's affairs; act — **go missing** *chiefly Br* to disappear — **go off the deep end 1** to enter recklessly on a course of action **2** to become very excited or perturbed — **go on** to be enthusiastic about — **go through** — **go one better** to outdo or surpass another — **go out of one's way** to take extra trouble — **go over 1** to examine **2a** to repeat **b** to study, revise — **go phut** *chiefly Br* to stop functioning — *infml* — **go places** to be on the way to success — **go slow** to hold a go-slow — **go steady** to be the constant and exclusive boyfriend or girl friend of another or each other — **go straight** to abandon a life of crime — **go the way of all flesh** to die — **go through 1** to subject to thorough examination, study, or discussion; GO OVER **2** to experience, undergo **3** to perform — **go to bed with** to have sexual intercourse with — **go to one's head 1** to make one confused, excited, or dizzy **2** to make one conceited or overconfident — **go to pieces** to become shattered (e g in nerves or health) — **go to pot** to deteriorate, collapse — *infml* — **go to sleep** to lose sensation; become numb — **go to town 1** to work or act rapidly or efficiently **2** to indulge oneself ostentatiously — **go walkabout 1** *Austr* to go on a walkabout **2** *Br* to meet and hold a conversation informally with members of the public during an official engagement or tour — **go west** to die or become destroyed or expended — humor

²**go** *n, pl* **goes 1** energy, vigour **2a** a turn in an activity (e g a game) **b** an attempt, try **3** a spell of activity **4** a success — **on the go** constantly or restlessly active — infml

³**go** *adj* functioning properly

⁴**go** *n* an Oriental board game of capture and territorial domination

go about *v* to change tack when sailing

¹**goad** /gohd/ *n* **1** a pointed rod used to urge on an animal **2** sthg that pricks, urges, or stimulates (into action)

²**goad** *v* to incite or rouse by nagging or persistent annoyance

¹**go-a'head** *adj* energetic and progressive

²**go-a,head** *n* a sign, signal, or authority to proceed

goal /gohl/ *n* **1** an end towards which effort is directed **2a** an area or object through or into which players in various games attempt to put a ball or puck against the defence of the opposing side **b** (the points gained by) the act of putting a ball or puck through or into a goal

'**goal,keeper** /-,keepə/ n a player who defends the goal in soccer, hockey, lacrosse, etc

'**goal ,line** n a line at either end and usu running the width of a playing area on which a goal or goal post is situated

'**goal,mouth** /-,mowth/ n the area of a playing field directly in front of the goal

go along v **1** to move along; proceed **2** to go or travel as a companion **3** to agree, cooperate

'**goal,post** /-,pohst/ n either of usu 2 vertical posts that with or without a crossbar constitute the goal in soccer, rugby, etc

goat /goht/ n **1** any of various long-legged (horned) ruminant mammals smaller than cattle and related to the sheep **2** a lecherous man **3** a foolish person

goatee /'goh,tee/ n a small pointed beard

₁**gob** /gob/ n a shapeless or sticky lump

²**gob** n, Br a mouth – slang

¹**gobble** /'gobl/ v **gobbling** /'gobling, 'gobl·ing/ **1** to swallow or eat greedily or noisily **2** to take, accept, or read eagerly – often + up

²**gobble** v to make the guttural sound of a male turkey or a similar sound

gobbledygook, gobbledegook /'gobldi,goohk/ n wordy unintelligible jargon

'**go-be,tween** n an intermediate agent

goblet /'goblit/ n a drinking vessel that has a usu rounded bowl, a foot, and a stem and is used esp for wine

goblin /'goblin/ n a grotesque mischievous elf

go-by /'goh ,bie/ n an act of avoidance; a miss

go by v to pass

god /god/ n **1** cap the being perfect in power, wisdom, and goodness whom human beings worship as creator and ruler of the universe **2** a being or object believed to have more than natural attributes and powers and to require human beings' worship **3** pl the highest gallery in a theatre, usu with the cheapest seats

'**god,child** /-,chield/ n sby for whom sby else becomes sponsor at baptism

'**godfor,saken** /-fə,saykən/ adj **1** remote, desolate **2** neglected, dismal

'**godless** /-lis/ adj not acknowledging a deity; impious – ~**ly** adv – ~**ness** n

'**godly** /-li/ adj pious, devout

go down v **1a** to fall (as if) to the ground **b** to sink (below the horizon) **2** to be capable of being swallowed **3** to undergo defeat **4a** to find acceptance **b** to come to be remembered, esp by posterity **5a** to undergo a decline or decrease **b** esp of a computer system or program to crash **6** to become ill – usu + with **7** Br to leave a university **8** to be sent to prison – slang

'**god,parent** /-,peərənt/ n a sponsor at baptism

godsend /'god,send/ n a desirable or needed thing or event that comes unexpectedly

,**go-'getter** n an aggressively enterprising person

goggle /'gogl/ v **goggling** /'gogling/ to stare with wide or protuberant eyes

'**goggle- ,box** n, Br a television set – infml

goggles /'goglz/ n pl protective glasses set in a flexible frame that fits snugly against the face

go-go /'goh ,goh/ adj of or being the music or a style of dance performed or a dancer performing at a disco

go in v **1** to enter **2** of the sun, moon, etc to be hidden by cloud **3** to form a union with — **go in for 1** to engage in, esp as a hobby or for enjoyment **2** to enter and compete in (e g a test or race)

¹**going** /'goh·ing/ n **1** an act or instance of going – often in combination **2** the condition of the ground (e g for horse racing) **3** advance, progress

²**going** adj **1** current, prevailing **2** profitable, thriving — **going for** favourable to

,**going-'over** n pl **goings-over 1** a thorough examination or investigation **2** a severe scolding; also a beating

,**goings-'on** n pl **1** actions, events **2** reprehensible happenings or conduct

go-kart /'goh ,kaht/ n a tiny racing car with small wheels

gold /gohld/ n **1** a heavy ductile yellow metallic element that occurs chiefly free and is used esp in coins and jewellery **2** a gold medal **3** a deep metallic yellow colour

golden /'gohld(ə)n/ adj **1** consisting of, relating to, or containing gold **2** of the colour of gold **3** prosperous, flourishing **4** favourable, advantageous **5** of or marking a 50th anniversary

'**golden ,age** n a period of great happiness, prosperity, and achievement

,**golden 'hand,shake** n a large money payment given by a company to an employee, esp on retirement

,**golden 'syrup** n the pale yellow syrup derived from cane sugar refining and used in cooking

'**gold,finch** /-,finch/ n a small red, black, yellow, and white European finch

'**gold,fish** /-,fish/ n a small (golden yellow) fish related to the carps and widely kept in aquariums and ponds

'**gold ,mine** n a rich source of sthg desired (e g information)

'**gold ,rush** n a rush to newly discovered goldfields in pursuit of riches

'**gold,smith** /-,smith/ n one who works in gold or deals in articles of gold

golf /golf/ n a game in which a player using special clubs attempts to hit a ball into each of the 9 or 18 successive holes on a course with as few strokes as possible – ~**er** n

gollywog, golliwog /'goliwog/ n a child's black-faced doll, usu made of fabric

gonad /'gohnad; also 'go-/ n any of the primary sex glands (e g the ovaries or testes)

gondola /'gondələ/ n 1 a long narrow flat-bottomed boat used on the canals of Venice 2 a cabin suspended from a cable and used for transporting passengers (e g up a ski slope)

gondolier /ˌgondə'liə/ n a boatman who propels a gondola

¹**gone** /gon/ adj 1a involved, absorbed b pregnant by a specified length of time c infatuated - often + on; infml 2 dead - euph

²**gone** adv, Br past, turned (a certain age)

goner /'gonə/ n one whose case or state is hopeless or lost - infml

gong /gong/ n 1 a disc-shaped percussion instrument that produces a resounding tone when struck with a usu padded hammer 2 a flat saucer-shaped bell 3 a medal or decoration - slang

gonorrhoea, chiefly NAm **gonorrhea** /ˌgonə'riə/ n a venereal disease

goo /gooh/ n 1 sticky matter 2 cloying sentimentality USE infml

¹**good** /good/ adj better /'betə/; best /best/ 1a(1) of a favourable character or tendency a(2) bountiful, fertile a(3) handsome, attractive b(1) suitable, fit b(2) free from injury or disease; whole c(1) agreeable, pleasant; specif amusing c(2) beneficial to the health or character c(3) not rotten; fresh d ample, full e(1) well-founded, true e(2) deserving of respect; honourable e(3) legally valid 2a(1) morally commendable; virtuous a(2) correct; specif well-behaved a(3) kind, benevolent b reputable; specif wellborn c competent, skilful d loyal – ~ness n — as good as virtually; in effect — as good as gold extremely well-behaved — good and very, entirely – infml — in someone's good books in sby's favour

²**good** n 1 prosperity, benefit 2a sthg that has economic utility or satisfies an economic want – usu pl b pl personal property having intrinsic value but usu excluding money, securities, and negotiable instruments c pl wares, merchandise 3 pl but sing or pl in constr the desired or necessary article – infml — for good forever, permanently — to the good 1 for the best; beneficial 2 in a position of net gain or profit

³**good** adv well – infml

good-for-ˌnothing adj of no value; worthless; also idle

ˌ**Good 'Friday** n the Friday before Easter, observed in churches as the anniversary of the crucifixion of Christ

ˌ**good-'humoured** adj good-natured – ~ly adv

ˌ**good-'natured** adj of a cheerful and cooperative disposition – ~ly adv

ˌ**good'will** /-'wil/ n 1 a kindly feeling of approval and support; benevolent interest or concern 2 the favour or prestige that a business has acquired beyond the mere value of what it sells

goody, goodie /'goodi/ n 1 sthg particularly attractive, pleasurable, or desirable 2 a good person or hero USE infml

ˌ**goody-,goody** n or adj (sby) affectedly or ingratiatingly prim or virtuous – infml

¹**goof** /goohf/ n 1 a ridiculous stupid person 2 chiefly NAm a blunder USE infml

²**goof** v to make a mess of; bungle – often + up

go off v 1 to explode 2 to go forth or away; depart 3 of food or drink to become rotten or sour 4 to follow a specified course; proceed 5 to make a characteristic noise; sound

goofy /'goohfi/ adj silly, daft – infml – **goofiness** n

googly /'goohgli/ n a delivery by a right-handed bowler in cricket that is an off break as viewed by a right-handed batsman although apparently delivered with a leg-break action

goon /goohn/ n 1 NAm a man hired to terrorize opponents 2 an idiot, dope – slang

go on v 1 to continue 2a to proceed (as if) by a logical step b of time to pass 3 to take place; happen 4a to talk, esp in an effusive manner b to criticize constantly; nag 5 to come into operation, action, or production

¹**goose** /goohs/ n, pl (1 & 2) **geese** /gees/, (3) **gooses** 1 (the female of) any of numerous large long-necked web-footed waterfowl 2 a simpleton, dolt

²**goose** v to poke between the buttocks

gooseberry /'goozb(ə)ri/ n 1 (the shrub that bears) an edible acid usu prickly green or yellow fruit 2 an unwanted companion to 2 lovers – chiefly in to play gooseberry

ˌ**goose,flesh** /-ˌflesh/ n a bristling roughness of the skin usu from cold or fear

ˌ**goose ,step** n a straight-legged marching step

go out v 1 to leave a room, house, country, etc 2a to become extinguished b to become obsolete or unfashionable 3 to spend time regularly with sby of esp the opposite sex 4 to be broadcast

¹**gore** /gaw/ n (clotted) blood

²**gore** n a tapering or triangular piece of material used to give shape to sthg – **gored** adj

³**gore** v to pierce or wound with a horn or tusk

¹**gorge** /gawj/ n 1 the throat 2 a narrow steep-walled valley, often with a stream flowing through it

²**gorge** v 1 to eat greedily or until full 2 to fill completely or to the point of being distended

gorgeous /'gawjəs/ adj 1 splendidly beautiful or magnificent 2 very fine; pleasant – ~ly adv – ~ness n

gorgon /'gawgən/ n 1 cap any of 3 sisters in Greek mythology who had live snakes in place of hair and whose glance turned the beholder to stone 2 an ugly or repulsive woman

Gorgonzola /ˌgawgən'zohlə/ n a blue-veined strongly flavoured cheese of Italian origin

gorilla /gəˈrilə/ n an anthropoid ape of western equatorial Africa

gormless /ˈgawmlis/ adj, Br stupid – infml – ~ly adv

go round v 1 to spread, circulate 2 to satisfy demand; meet the need

gorse /gaws/ n a spiny yellow-flowered evergreen leguminous European shrub

gory /ˈgawri/ adj 1 covered with gore; blood-stained 2 full of violence; bloodcurdling

gosling /ˈgozling/ n a young goose

go-ˈslow n, Br a deliberate slowing down of production by workers as a form of industrial action

¹**gospel** /ˈgospl/ n 1 often cap the message of the life, death, and resurrection of Jesus Christ; esp any of the first 4 books of the New Testament 2 the message or teachings of a usu religious teacher or movement

²**gospel** adj 1 of the Christian gospel; evangelical 2 of or being usu evangelistic religious songs of American origin

gossamer /ˈgosəmə/ n 1 a film of cobwebs floating in air in calm clear weather 2 sthg light, insubstantial, or tenuous

gossip /ˈgosip/ n 1 sby who habitually reveals usu sensational facts concerning other people's actions or lives 2a (rumour or report of) the facts related by a gossip b a chatty talk – **gossip** v

got /got/ 1 past of **get** 2 pres pl & 1&2 sing of **get** – nonstandard

¹**Gothic** /ˈgothik/ adj 1 of the Goths, their culture, or Gothic 2 of a style of architecture prevalent from the middle of the 12th c to the early 16th c characterized by vaulting and pointed arches

²**Gothic** n 1 the E Germanic language of the Goths 2 Gothic architectural style

go through v 1 to continue firmly or obstinately to the end – often + with 2 to receive approval or sanction

Gouda /ˈgowdə/ n a mild cheese of Dutch origin

¹**gouge** /gowj/ n a chisel with a curved cross section and bevel on the concave side of the blade

²**gouge** v 1 to scoop out (as if) with a gouge 2 to force out (an eye), esp with the thumb

goulash /ˈgoohlash/ n a meat stew highly seasoned with paprika

go under v 1 to be destroyed or defeated; fail

go up v, Br to enter or return to a university

gourmand /ˈgawmənd, ˈgooə- (Fr gurmã)/ n one who is excessively fond of or heartily interested in food and drink

gourmet /ˈgawmay, ˈgooə- (Fr gurme)/ n a connoisseur of food and drink

gout /gowt/ n 1 painful inflammation of the joints, esp that of the big toe, resulting from a disorder of the blood 2 a sticky blob – ~y adj

govern /ˈguv(ə)n/ v 1 to exercise continuous sovereign authority over 2a to control, determine, or strongly influence b to hold in check; restrain

governess /ˈguv(ə)nis/ n a woman entrusted with the private teaching and often supervision of a child

government /ˈguv(ə)nmənt, ˈguvəmənt/ n 1 the office, authority, or function of governing 2 policy making as distinguished from administration 3 the machinery through which political authority is exercised 4 sing or pl in constr the body of people that constitutes a governing authority – ~al adj

governor /ˈguv(ə)nə/ n 1a a ruler, chief executive, or nominal head of a political unit b the managing director and usu the principal officer of an institution or organization c a member of a group (e g the governing body of a school) that controls an institution 2 sby (e g a father, guardian, or employer) looked on as governing – slang – ~ship n

,**governor-ˈgeneral** n, pl governors-general, governor-generals a governor of high rank; esp one representing the Crown in a Commonwealth country

gown /gown/ n 1a a loose flowing robe worn esp by a professional or academic person when acting in an official capacity 2 a woman's dress, esp one that is elegant or for formal wear

grab /grab/ v -bb- 1 to take or seize hastily; snatch 2 to obtain unscrupulously 3 to forcefully engage the attention of – infml – **grab** n

¹**grace** /grays/ n 1a divine assistance given to human beings b a state of being pleasing to God 2 a short prayer at a meal asking a blessing or giving thanks 3 disposition to or an act or instance of kindness or clemency 4a a charming trait or accomplishment b an elegant appearance or effect; charm c ease and suppleness of movement or bearing 5 – used as a title for a duke, duchess, or archbishop 6 consideration, decency – **with bad/good grace** (un)willingly or (un)happily

²**grace** v 1 to confer dignity or honour on 2 to adorn, embellish

graceful /ˈgraysf(ə)l/ adj displaying grace in form, action, or movement – **-fully** adv

'**grace ,note** n a musical note added as an ornament

Graces /ˈgraysiz/ n pl the 3 beautiful sister goddesses in Greek mythology who are the givers of charm and beauty

gracious /ˈgrayshəs/ adj 1a marked by kindness and courtesy b having those qualities (e g comfort, elegance, and freedom from hard work) made possible by wealth 2 merciful, compassionate – used conventionally of royalty and high nobility – ~ly adv – ~ness n

gradation /grə'daysh(ə)n/ n 1 (a step or place in) a series forming successive stages 2 a gradual passing from one tint or shade to another (e g in a painting)

¹**grade** /grayd/ n 1 a position in a scale of ranks or qualities 2 a class of things of the same stage or degree 3 NAm a school form; a class 4 NAm a mark indicating a degree of accomplishment at school

²**grade** v 1 to arrange in grades; sort 2 to arrange in a scale or series 3 NAm to assign a mark to

gradient /'graydi·ənt, -dyənt/ n the degree of inclination of a road or slope; also a sloping road or railway

gradual /'gradyoooəl, -joool, -jəl/ adj proceeding or happening by steps or degrees – **-ually** adv – **~ness** n

¹**graduate** /'gradyoo·ət, -joo-/ n 1 the holder of an academic degree 2 chiefly NAm one who has completed a course of study

²**graduate** /'gradyoo,ayt, -joo-/ v 1 to mark with degrees of measurement 2 to divide into grades or intervals 3 to receive an academic degree 4 to move up to a usu higher stage of experience, proficiency, or prestige

graduation /,gradyoo'aysh(ə)n, -joo-/ n 1 a mark (e g on an instrument or vessel) indicating degrees or quantity 2 the award of an academic degree

¹**graft** /grahft/ v 1 to cause (a plant scion) to unite with a stock; also to unite (plants or scion and stock) to form a graft 2 to attach, add 3 to implant (living tissue) surgically 4 NAm to practise graft

²**graft** n 1a a grafted plant b (the point of insertion upon a stock of) a scion 2 (living tissue used in) grafting 3 the improper use of one's position (e g public office) to one's private, esp financial, advantage

³**graft** v, Br to work hard – slang

grain /grayn/ n 1 a seed or fruit of a cereal grass; also (the seeds or fruits collectively of) the cereal grasses or similar food plants 2a a discrete (small hard) particle or crystal (e g of sand, salt, or a metal) b the least amount possible 3 a granular surface, nature, or appearance 4 a small unit of weight, used for medicines (¹/₇₀₀₀ of a pound or 0.0648 gram) 5a the arrangement of the fibres in wood b the direction, alignment, or texture of the constituent particles, fibres, or threads 6 natural disposition or character; temper — **against the grain** counter to one's inclination, disposition, or feeling

gram, gramme /gram/ n a metric unit of weight equal to about 0.04 oz

¹**grammar** /'gramə/ n 1 the study of the classes of words, their inflections, and their functions and relations in the sentence 2 the characteristic system of inflections and syntax of a language 3 a grammar textbook 4 the principles or rules of an art, science, or technique

²**grammar** adj of the type of education provided at a grammar school

'**grammar ,school** n, Br a secondary school providing an academic type of education from the age of 11 to 18

grammatical /grə'matikl/ adj (conforming to the rules) of grammar – **~ly** adv

gramophone /'graməfohn/ n a device for reproducing sounds from the vibrations of a stylus resting in a spiral groove on a rotating disc; a record player

gran /gran/ n, chiefly Br a grandmother – infml

granary /'granəri/ n 1 a storehouse for threshed grain 2 a region producing grain in abundance

¹**grand** /grand/ adj 1 having more importance than others; foremost 2 complete, comprehensive 3 main, principal 4 large and striking in size, extent, or conception 5a lavish, sumptuous b marked by regal form and dignity; imposing c lofty, sublime 6 intended to impress 7 very good; wonderful – infml – **~ly** adv – **~ness** n

²**grand** n 1 a grand piano 2a Br a thousand pounds b NAm a thousand dollars USE (2) slang

grandad, granddad /'gran,dad/ n a grandfather – infml

grandchild /'gran,chield/ n a child of one's son or daughter

granddaughter /'gran,dawtə/ n a daughter of one's son or daughter

grandeur /'granjə, -dyə/ n 1 the quality of being large or impressive; magnificence 2 personal greatness marked by nobility, dignity, or power

grandfather /'gran(d),fahdhə/ n the father of one's father or mother; broadly a male ancestor

,**grand,father 'clock** n a tall pendulum clock standing directly on the floor

grandiose /'grandiohs, -ohz/ adj 1 impressive because of uncommon largeness, scope, or grandeur 2 characterized by affectation of grandeur or by absurd exaggeration

grandmother /'gran,mudhə, 'grand-, 'gram-/ n the mother of one's father or mother; broadly a female ancestor

grandparent /'gran(d),peərənt/ n the parent of one's father or mother

,**grand pi'ano** n a piano with horizontal frame and strings

,**grand 'slam** n the winning of all the tricks in 1 hand of a card game, specif bridge

grandson /'gran(d),sun/ n a son of one's son or daughter

'**grand,stand** /-,stand/ n a usu roofed stand for spectators at a racecourse, stadium, etc

grange /graynj/ n a farm; esp a farmhouse with outbuildings

granite /'granit/ n 1 a very hard granular igneous rock formed of quartz, feldspar, and mica and used esp for building 2 unyielding firmness or endurance

granny, grannie /'grani/ a grandmother – infml

¹**grant** /grahnt/ v **1a** to consent to carry out or fulfil (e g a wish or request) **b** to permit as a right, privilege, or favour **2** to bestow or transfer formally **3a** to be willing to concede **b** to assume to be true

²**grant** n **1** sthg granted; esp a gift for a particular purpose **2a** transfer of property; also the property so transferred

granulate /'granyoo,layt/ v to form or crystallize into grains or granules

granule /'granyoohl/ n a small grain – **-lar** adj

grape /grayp/ n (any of a genus of widely cultivated woody vines that bear, in clusters,) a smooth-skinned juicy greenish white to deep red or purple berry eaten as a fruit or fermented to produce wine

'**grape,fruit** /-,frooht/ n (a small tree that bears) a large round citrus fruit with a bitter yellow rind and a somewhat acid juicy pulp

'**grape,vine** /-,vien/ n a secret or unofficial means of circulating information or gossip

graph /grahf, graf/ n a diagram (e g a series of points, a line, a curve, or an area) expressing a relation between quantities or variables

¹**graphic** /'grafik/ also **graphical** /-kl/ adj **1** formed by writing, drawing, or engraving **2** marked by clear and vivid description; sharply outlined **3a** of the pictorial arts **b** of or employing engraving, etching, lithography, photography, or other methods of reproducing material in the graphic arts **4** of or represented by a graph **5** of writing

²**graphic** n **1** a product of graphic art **2** a picture, map, or graph used for illustration or demonstration **3** a graphic representation displayed by a computer (e g on a VDU)

graphite /'grafiet/ n a soft black lustrous form of carbon that conducts electricity and is used esp in lead pencils and as a lubricant

grapnel /'grapnol/ n an instrument with several claws that is hurled with a line attached in order to hook onto a ship, the top of a wall, etc

¹**grapple** /'grapl/ n **1** a grapnel **2** a hand-to-hand struggle

²**grapple** v **grappling** /'grapling, 'grapl·ing/ to come to grips with

¹**grasp** /grahsp/ v **1** to take, seize, or clasp eagerly (as if) with the fingers or arms **2** to succeed in understanding; comprehend

²**grasp** n **1** a firm hold **2** control, power **3** the power of seizing and holding or attaining **4** comprehension

grasping /'grahsping/ adj eager for material possessions; avaricious – **~ly** adv

¹**grass** /grahs/ n **1** pasture **2** any of a large family of plants with slender leaves and flowers in small spikes or clusters, that includes bamboo, wheat, rye, corn, etc **3** land on which grass is grown; esp a lawn **4** cannabis; specif marijuana – slang **5** Br a police informer – slang — **put/send out to grass** to cause (sby) to enter usu enforced retirement

²**grass** v **1** to cover or seed with grass – often + down **2**, Br to inform the police; esp to betray sby to the police – slang

'**grass,hopper** /-,hopo/ n any of numerous plant-eating insects with hind legs adapted for leaping

,**grass 'roots** n pl but sing or pl in constr **1** society at the local level as distinguished from the centres of political leadership **2** the fundamental level or source

grassy /'grahsi/ adj **1** consisting of or covered with grass **2** (having a smell) like grass

¹**grate** /grayt/ n **1** a frame or bed of metal bars to hold the fuel in a fireplace, stove, or furnace **2** a fireplace

²**grate** v **1** to reduce to small particles by rubbing on sthg rough **2a** to gnash or grind noisily **b** to cause to make a rasping sound **3** to cause irritation; jar

grateful /'graytf(o)l/ adj **1** feeling or expressing thanks **2** pleasing, comforting – **~ly** adv – **~ness** n

gratify /'grati,fie/ v **1** to be a source of or give pleasure or satisfaction to **2** to give in to; satisfy – **-fication** n – **~ing** adj – **~ingly** adv

grating /'grayting/ n **1** a partition, covering, or frame of parallel bars or crossbars **2** a lattice used to close or filter any of various openings

gratis /'gratis, 'grah-, 'gray-/ adv or adj without charge or recompense; free

gratitude /'grati,tyoohd/ n the state or feeling of being grateful; thankfulness

gratuitous /gro'tyooh·itos/ adj **1a** costing nothing; free **b** not involving a return benefit or compensation **2** not called for by the circumstances; unwarranted – **~ly** adv – **~ness** n

gratuity /gro'tyooh·oti/ n sthg given voluntarily, usu in return for or in anticipation of some service; esp a tip

¹**grave** /grayv/ n an excavation for burial of a body; broadly a tomb

²**grave** adj **1a** requiring serious consideration; important **b** likely to produce great harm or danger **2** serious, dignified **3** drab in colour; sombre – **~ly** adv

³**grave** /grahv/ adj or n (being or marked with) an accent ` used in various languages

gravel /'gravl/ n **1** (a stratum or surface of) loose rounded fragments of rock mixed with sand **2** a sandy deposit of small stones in the kidneys and urinary bladder

gravelly /'gravl·i/ adj **1** of, containing, or covered with gravel **2** harsh, grating

'**grave,stone** /-,stohn/ n a stone over or at one end of a grave, usu inscribed with the name and details of the dead person

'grave,yard /-,yahd/ *n* a cemetery

gravitate /'gravitayt/ *v* to move or be drawn *towards*

gravitation /,gravi'taysh(ə)n/ *n* (movement resulting from) the natural force of mutual attraction between bodies or particles – ~**al** *adj*

gravity /'gravati/ *n* **1a** dignity or sobriety of bearing **b** significance; *esp* seriousness **2** (the quality of having) weight **3** (the attraction of a celestial body for bodies at or near its surface resulting from) gravitation

gravy /'grayvi/ *n* the (thickened and seasoned) fat and juices from cooked meat used as a sauce

¹graze /grayz/ *v* **1** to feed on the grass of (e g a pasture) **2** to put to graze

²graze *v* **1** to touch (sthg) lightly in passing **2** to abrade, scratch

³graze *n* (an abrasion, esp of the skin, made by) a scraping along a surface

¹grease /grees/ *n* **1** melted down animal fat **2** oily matter **3** a thick lubricant — **in the grease** *of wool or fur* in the natural uncleaned condition

²grease *v* **1** to smear, lubricate, or soil with grease **2** to hasten or ease the process or progress of — **grease the palm of** to bribe

'grease,paint /-,paynt/ *n* theatrical make-up

greasy /'greesi/ *adj* **1a** smeared or soiled with grease **b** oily in appearance, texture, or manner **c** slippery **2** containing an unusual amount of grease – **-sily** *adv* – **-siness** *n*

¹great /grayt/ *adj* **1a** notably large in size or number **b** of a relatively large kind – in plant and animal names **c** elaborate, ample **2a** extreme in amount, degree, or effectiveness **b** of importance; significant **3** eminent, distinguished **4** main, principal **5** removed in a family relationship by at least 3 stages directly or 2 stages indirectly – chiefly in combination **6** markedly superior in character or quality; *esp* noble **7a** remarkably skilled **b** enthusiastic, keen **8** – used as a generalized term of approval; *infml* – **~ly** *adv* – **~ness** *n* – **no great shakes** not very good, skilful, effective, etc

²great *n pl* **great, greats** one who is great – usu pl

'great,coat /-,koht/ *n* a heavy overcoat

,Great 'Dane /dayn/ *n* any of a breed of massive powerful smooth-coated dogs

grebe /greeb/ *n* any of a family of swimming and diving birds that have unwebbed feet

Grecian /'greesh(ə)n/ *adj* Greek

greed /greed/ *n* **1** excessive acquisitiveness; avarice **2** excessive desire for or consumption of food – ~**y** *adj* – ~**ily** *adv* – ~**iness** *n*

¹Greek /greek/ *n* **1** a native or inhabitant of Greece **2** the Indo-European language used by the Greeks **3** *not cap* sthg unintelligible – *infml*

²Greek *adj* **1** of Greece, the Greeks, or Greek **2** **Greek, Greek Orthodox** of an Eastern church, esp the established Orthodox church of Greece using the Byzantine rite in Greek

¹green /green/ *adj* **1** of the colour green **2a** covered by green growth or foliage **b** consisting of green (edible) plants **3a** youthful, vigorous **b** not ripened or matured; immature **c** fresh, new **4** appearing pale, sickly, or nauseated **5** affected by intense envy or jealousy **6** not aged; unseasoned **7** deficient in training, knowledge, or experience – ~**ness** *n* – ~**ish** *adj*

²green *n* **1** a colour whose hue resembles that of growing fresh grass or the emerald and lies between blue and yellow in the spectrum **2** sthg of a green colour **3** *pl* green leafy vegetables (e g spinach and cabbage) the leaves and stems of which are often cooked **4a** a common or park in the centre of a town or village **b** a smooth area of grass for a special purpose (e g bowling or putting)

greenery /'greenəri/ *n* green foliage or plants

,green 'fingers *n pl* an unusual ability to make plants grow

'green,fly /-,flie/ *n, pl* green**flies**, *esp collectively* greenfly *Br* (an infestation by) any of various green aphids that are destructive to plants

'green,gage /-,gayj/ *n* any of several small rounded greenish cultivated plums

'green,grocer /-,grohsə/n, *chiefly Br* a retailer of fresh vegetables and fruit

'green,horn /-,hawn/ *n* an inexperienced or unsophisticated (easily cheated) person

'green,house /-,hows/ *n* a glassed enclosure for the cultivation or protection of tender plants

green pepper *n* a sweet pepper

Greenwich Mean Time /'grenich, 'grinij, -nich/ *n* the mean solar time of the meridian of Greenwich used as the primary point of reference for standard time throughout the world

¹greet /greet/ *v*, **1** to welcome with gestures or words **2** to meet or react to in a specified manner

²greet *v* **grat** /grat/; **grutten** /'grutn/ *Scot* to weep, lament

greeting /'greeting/ *n* **1** a salutation at meeting **2** an expression of good wishes; regards – usu pl with sing. meaning

gregarious /gri'geari-əs/ *adj* **1a** tending to associate with others of the same kind **b** marked by or indicating a liking for companionship; sociable **c** of a crowd, flock, or other group of people, animals, etc **2** *of a plant* growing in a cluster or a colony – ~**ly** *adv* – ~**ness** *n*

Gregorian calendar /gri'gawri-ən/ *n* a revision of the Julian Calendar now in general use, that restricts leap years to every 4th year except for those centenary years not divisible by 400

Gregorian chant *n* a rhythmically free liturgical chant in unison practised in the Roman Catholic church

gremlin /'gremlin/ *n* a mischievous creature said to cause malfunctioning of machinery or equipment

grenade /grə'nayd/ *n* **1** a small missile that contains explosive, gas, incendiary chemicals, etc and is thrown by hand or launcher **2** a glass container of chemicals that bursts when thrown, releasing a fire extinguishing agent, tear gas, etc

grenadier /ˌgrenə'diə/ *n* a member of a regiment or corps formerly specially trained in the use of grenades

grenadine /ˌgrenə'deen, '---/ *n* a syrup flavoured with pomegranates and used in mixed drinks

grew /grooh/ *past of* **grow**

¹**grey, NAm chiefly gray** /gray/ *adj* **1** of the colour grey **2** dull in colour **3a** lacking cheer or brightness; dismal **b** intermediate or unclear in position, condition, or character – ~ness *n* – ~ish *adj*

²**grey, NAm chiefly gray** *n* **1** any of a series of neutral colours ranging between black and white **2** sthg grey; *esp* grey clothes, paint, or horses

greyhound /-hownd/ *n* (any of) a tall slender smooth-coated breed of dogs characterized by swiftness and keen sight

grey matter *n* **1** brownish-grey nerve tissue, esp in the brain and spinal cord, containing nerve-cell bodies as well as nerve fibres **2** brains, intellect – infml

grid /grid/ *n* **1** a grating **2a** a network of conductors for distribution of electric power **b** (sthg resembling) a network of uniformly spaced horizontal and perpendicular lines for locating points on a map **3** the starting positions of vehicles on a racetrack

griddle /'gridl/ *n* a flat metal surface on which food is cooked by dry heat

grief /greef/ *n* (a cause of) deep and poignant distress (e g due to bereavement)

grievance /'greev(ə)ns/ *n* **1** a cause of distress (e g unsatisfactory working conditions) felt to afford reason for complaint or resistance **2** the formal expression of a grievance; a complaint

¹**grieve** /greev/ *v* to (cause to) suffer grief

²**grieve** *n, Scot* a farm or estate manager

grievous /'greevəs/ *adj* causing or characterized by severe pain, suffering, or sorrow **2** serious, grave – ~ly *adv* – ~ness *n*

griffin /'grifin/, **griffon, gryphon** /-fən/ *n* a mythical animal with the head and wings of an eagle and the body of a lion

¹**grill** /gril/ *v* **1** to cook on or under a grill by radiant heat **2** to subject to intense and usu long periods of questioning – infml

²**grill** *n* **1** a cooking utensil of parallel bars on which food is exposed to heat (e g from burning charcoal) **2** an article or dish of grilled food **3** grill, **grillroom** a usu informal restaurant or dining room, esp in a hotel **4** *Br* an apparatus on a cooker under which food is cooked or browned by radiant heat

grille, grill /gril/ *n* (an opening covered with) a grating forming a barrier or screen; *specif* an ornamental metal one at the front end of a motor vehicle

grim /grim/ *adj* **-mm- 1** fierce or forbidding in disposition, action, or appearance **2** unflinching, unyielding **3** ghastly or sinister in character **4** unpleasant, nasty – infml – ~ly *adv* – ~ness *n*

grimace /'griməs, gri'mays/ *n* a distorted facial expression, usu of disgust, anger, or pain – **grimace** *v*

grime /grīm/ *n* soot or dirt, esp when sticking to or embedded in a surface – **grimy** *adj*

grin /grin/ *v* **-nn-** to smile so as to show the teeth

¹**grind** /grīnd/ *v* **ground** /grownd/ **1** to reduce to powder or small fragments by crushing between hard surfaces **2** to wear down, polish, or sharpen by friction; whet **3a** to rub, press, or twist harshly **b** to press together with a rotating motion **4** to operate or produce by turning a crank **5** to become pulverized, polished, or sharpened by friction **6** to move with difficulty or friction, esp so as to make a grating noise **7** to work monotonously; *esp* to study hard **8** to rotate the hips in an erotic manner — **grind into** to instil (knowledge, facts, etc) into (sby) with great difficulty

²**grind** *n* **1** dreary monotonous labour or routine **2** the result of grinding; *esp* material obtained by grinding to a particular degree of fineness **3a** the act of rotating the hips in an erotic manner **b** *Br* an act of sexual intercourse – vulg

grind down *v* to oppress, harass

¹**grindstone** /-ˌstohn/ *n* **1** a millstone **2** a flat circular stone that revolves on an axle and is used for grinding, shaping, etc

¹**grip** /grip/ *v* **-pp- 1** to seize or hold firmly **2** to attract and hold the interest of

²**grip** *n* **1a** a strong or tenacious grasp **b** manner or style of gripping **2a** control, mastery, power **b** (power of) understanding or doing **3** a part or device that grips **4** a part by which sthg is grasped; *esp* a handle **5** one who handles scenery, properties, lighting, or camera equipment in a theatre or film or television studio **6** a travelling bag

¹**gripe** /grīp/ *v* **1** to cause or experience intestinal gripes (in) **2** to complain persistently – infml

²**gripe** *n* **1** a stabbing spasmodic intestinal pain – usu pl **2** a grievance, complaint – infml

grisly /'grizli/ *adj* inspiring horror, intense fear, or disgust; forbidding

grist /grist/ *n* **1** (a batch of) grain for grinding **2** the product obtained from grinding grain — **grist to the mill** sthg that can be put to use or profit

gristle /'grisl/ *n* cartilage; *broadly* tough cartilaginous or fibrous matter, esp in cooked meat – **-tly** *adj*

¹grit /grit/ n **1** a hard sharp granule (e g of sand or stone); *also* material composed of such granules **2** the structure or texture of a stone that adapts it to grinding **3** firmness of mind or spirit; unyielding courage – infml – **gritty** adj

²grit v **-tt- 1** to cover or spread with grit **2** to cause (esp one's teeth) to grind or grate

grizzle /'grizl/ v, **grizzling** /'grizling, 'grizl·ing/ Br **1** *of a child* to cry quietly and fretfully **2** to complain in a self-pitying way – often + *about USE* infml

¹grizzled adj sprinkled or streaked with grey

¹grizzly /-li/ adj grizzled

²grizzly, grizzly bear n a very large typically brownish yellow bear that lives in the highlands of Western N America

groan /grohn/ v **1** to utter a deep moan **2** to creak under strain

¹groat /groht/ n hulled grain (broken into fragments larger than grits) – usu pl with sing. meaning but sing. or pl in constr

²groat n a former British coin worth 4 old pence

grocer /'grohsə/ n a dealer in (packaged or tinned) staple foodstuffs, household supplies, and usu fruit, vegetables, and dairy products

grocery /'grohs(ə)ri/ n **1** pl commodities sold by a grocer **2** a grocer's shop

grog /grog/ n alcoholic drink; *specif* spirits (e g rum) mixed with water

groggy /'grogi/ adj weak and dazed, esp owing to illness or tiredness – **-ggily** adv

groin /groyn/ n **1a** the fold marking the join between the lower abdomen and the inner part of the thigh **b** the male genitals – euph **2** the line along which 2 intersecting vaults meet

¹groom /groohm/ n **1** one who is in charge of the feeding, care, and stabling of horses **2** a bridegroom

²groom v **1** to clean and care for (e g a horse) **2** to make neat or attractive **3** to get into readiness for a specific objective; prepare

¹groove /groohv/ n **1a** a long narrow channel or depression **b** the continuous spiral track on a gramophone record whose irregularities correspond to the recorded sounds **2** a fixed routine; a rut **3** top form – infml **4** an enjoyable or exciting experience – infml; no longer in vogue

²groove v **1** to make or form a groove (in) **2** to excite pleasurably – infml; no longer in vogue **3** to enjoy oneself intensely; *also* to get on well – infml; no longer in vogue

groovy /'groohvi/ adj fashionably attractive or exciting – infml; no longer in vogue

grope /grohp/ v **1** to feel about or search blindly or uncertainly *for* **2** to touch or fondle the body of (a person) for sexual pleasure – **grope** n – **-pingly** adv

¹gross /grohs/ adj **1** glaringly noticeable, usu because excessively bad or objectionable; flagrant **2a** big, bulky; *esp* excessively fat **b** *of vegetation* dense, luxuriant **3** consisting of an overall total before deductions (e g for taxes) are made **4** made up of material or perceptible elements; corporal **5** coarse in nature or behaviour; *specif* crudely vulgar – ~**ly** adv – ~**ness** n

²gross n an overall total exclusive of deductions

³gross v to earn or bring in (an overall total) exclusive of deductions

⁴gross n, pl **gross** a group of 12 dozen things

¹grotesque /groh'tesk/ n a style of decorative art in which incongruous or fantastic human and animal forms are interwoven with natural motifs (e g foliage)

²grotesque adj (having the characteristics) of the grotesque: e g **a** fanciful, bizarre **b** absurdly incongruous **c** departing markedly from the natural, expected, or typical

grotto /'grotoh/ n, pl **grottoes** *also* **grottos 1** an esp picturesque cave **2** an excavation or structure made to resemble a natural cave

grotty /'groti/ adj, Br nasty, unpleasant – slang – **-ttiness** n

grouch /growch/ n **1** a bad-tempered complaint **2** a habitually irritable or complaining person; a grumbler – **grouch** v – ~**y** adj

¹ground /grownd/ n **1a** the bottom of a body of water **b** pl **1(1)** sediment **b(2)** ground coffee beans after brewing **2** a basis for belief, action, or argument – often pl with sing. meaning **3a** a surrounding area; a background **b** (material that serves as) a substratum or foundation **4a** the surface of the earth **b** an area used for a particular purpose **c** pl the area round and belonging to a house or other building **d** an area to be won or defended (as if) in battle **5** soil – **off the ground** started and in progress – **to ground** into hiding

²ground v **1** to bring to or place on the ground **2a** to provide a reason or justification for **b** to instruct in fundamentals (e g of a subject) **3** to restrict (e g a pilot or aircraft) to the ground **4** to run aground

³ground past of **grind**

grounding /'grownding/ n fundamental training in a field of knowledge

groundless /-lis/ adj having no foundation – ~**ly** adv – ~**ness** n

groundnut /-,nut/ n **1** (a N American leguminous plant with) an edible root **2** chiefly Br the peanut

groundsel /'grown(d)zl, -sl/ n a (plant related to a) European composite plant that is a common weed and has small yellow flower heads

groundsheet /-,sheet/ n a waterproof sheet placed on the ground (e g in a tent)

groundsman /-mən/ n sby who tends a playing field, esp a cricket pitch

'ground,work /-,wuhk/ n (work done to provide) a foundation or basis

¹group /groohp/ n 1 two or more figures or objects forming a complete unit in a composition 2 *sing or pl in constr* 2a a number of individuals or objects assembled together or having some unifying relationship b an operational and administrative unit belonging to a command of an air force

²group v 1 to combine in a group 2 to assign to a group; classify 3 to form or belong to a group

group captain n a middle-ranking officer in the Royal Air Force, equal to a captain in the navy or a colonel in the army

grouping /'groohping/ n a set of individuals or objects combined in a group

¹grouse /grows/ n, pl **grouse** any of several (important game) birds with a plump body and strong feathered legs

²grouse v or n (to) grumble – infml

grove /grohv/ n a small wood, group, or planting of trees

grovel /'grovl/ v -ll- (NAm l-, -ll-) /'grovl·ing/ 1 to lie or creep with the body prostrate in token of submission or abasement 2 to abase or humble oneself – ~ler n

grow /groh/ v grew /grooh/; **grown** /grohn/ 1a to spring up and develop to maturity (in a specified place or situation) b to assume some relation (as if) through a process of natural growth 2a to increase in size by addition of material (e g by assimilation into a living organism or by crystallization) b to increase, expand 3 to develop from a parent source 4 to become gradually 5 to cause to grow; produce 6 to develop — **grow on** to have an increasing influence on; *esp* to become more pleasing to

'growing ,pains n pl the early problems attending a new project or development

¹growl /growl/ v 1 to rumble 2 to utter a growl

²growl n a deep guttural inarticulate sound

grown /grohn/ adj 1 fully grown; mature 2 overgrown or covered (*with*)

'grown-,up n or adj (an) adult

growth /grohth/ n 1a (a stage in the process of) growing b progressive development c an increase, expansion 2a sthg that grows or has grown b a tumour or other abnormal growth of tissue 3 the result of growth; a product

grow up v 1 of a person to develop towards or arrive at a mature state 2 to arise and develop

¹grub /grub/ v -bb- 1 to clear by digging up roots and stumps 2 to dig *up* or *out* (as if) by the roots 3 to dig in the ground, esp for sthg that is difficult to find or extract 4 to search about; rummage

²grub n 1 a soft thick wormlike larva of an insect 2 food – infml

grubby /'grubi/ adj dirty, grimy

grudge /gruj/ v to be unwilling or reluctant to give or admit; begrudge

²grudge n a feeling of deep-seated resentment or ill will

grudging /'grujing/ adj unwilling, reluctant – ~ly adv

gruel /'grooh·əl/ n a thin porridge

gruelling, NAm chiefly grueling /'grooh·əling/ adj trying or taxing to the point of causing exhaustion; punishing – ~ly adv

gruesome /'groohs(ə)m/ adj inspiring horror or repulsion; – ~ly adv – – ~ness n

gruff /gruf/ adj 1 brusque or stern in manner, speech, or aspect 2 deep and harsh – ~ly adv – ~ness n

grumble /'grumbl/ v **grumbling** /'grumbling/ 1 to mutter in discontent 2 to rumble

grumbling /'grumbling/ adj causing intermittent pain or discomfort

grumpy /'grumpi/ adj moodily cross; surly – -pily adv – -piness n

¹grunt /grunt/ v to utter (with) a grunt

²grunt n the deep short guttural sound of a pig; *also* a similar sound

Gruyère /'grooh·yeə (Fr gryjɛːr)/ n a Swiss cheese with smaller holes and a slightly fuller flavour than Emmenthal

gryphon /'grifən/ n a griffin

'G-,string n a small piece of cloth covering the genitals and held in place by thongs, elastic, etc

¹guarantee /,garən'tee/ n 1 one who guarantees 2 a (written) undertaking to answer for the payment of a debt or the performance of a duty of another in case of the other's default 3 an assurance of the quality of or of the length of use to be expected from a product offered for sale, accompanied by a promise to replace it or pay the customer back 4 sthg given as security; a pledge

²guarantee v **guaranteed; guaranteeing** 1 to undertake to answer for the debt or default of 2a to undertake to do or secure (sthg) b to engage for the existence, permanence, or nature of 3 to give security to

guarantor /,garən'taw/ n 1 one who guarantees 2 one who makes or gives a guarantee

guaranty /'garənti/ n a guarantee

¹guard /gahd/ n 1 a defensive position in boxing, fencing, etc 2 the act or duty of protecting or defending 3a a person or group whose duty is to protect a place, people, etc b pl troops part of whose duties are to guard a sovereign 4 a protective or safety device; *esp* a device on a machine for protecting against injury 5 Br the person in charge of a railway train

²guard v 1 to protect from danger, esp by watchful attention; make secure 2 to watch over so as to prevent escape, entry, theft, etc; *also* to keep in check — **guard against** to attempt to prevent (sthg) by taking precautions

guarded /'gahdid/ adj marked by caution – ~ly adv

guardian /'gahdi·ən, -dyən/ n **1** one who or that which guards or protects **2** sby who has the care of the person or property of another; *specif* sby entrusted by law with the care of sby who is of unsound mind, not of age, etc – ~**ship** n

'guard,rail /-,rayl/ n a railing for guarding against danger or trespass

'guardsman /-mən/ n a member of a military body called *guard* or *guards*

'guard's ,van n, Br a railway wagon or carriage attached usu at the rear of a train for the use of the guard

guava /'gwahvə/ n (the sweet acid yellow edible fruit of) a shrubby tropical American tree

guerrilla, guerilla /gə'rilə/ n a member of an irregular, usu politically motivated fighting unit often engaged in harassing stronger regular units

¹**guess** /ges/ v **1** to form an opinion of with little or no consideration of the facts **2** to arrive at a correct conclusion about by conjecture, chance, or intuition **3** *chiefly NAm* to believe, suppose – *infml* **4** to make a guess

²**guess** n a surmise, estimate

'guess,work /-,wuhk/ n (judgment based on) the act of guessing

guest /gest/ n **1a** a person entertained in one's home **b** a person taken out, entertained, and paid for by another **c** a person who pays for the services of an establishment (e g a hotel) **2** one who is present by invitation

'guest,house /-,hows/ n a private house used to accommodate paying guests

guffaw /'gufaw, gə'faw/ v or n (to utter) a loud or boisterous laugh

guidance /'gied(ə)ns/ n help, advice

¹**guide** /gied/ n **1a** one who leads or directs another **b** one who shows and explains places of interest to travellers, tourists, etc **c** sthg, esp a guidebook, that provides sby with information about a place, activity, etc **d** sthg or sby that directs a person in his/her conduct or course of life **2** a bar, rod, etc for steadying or directing the motion of sthg **3** *often cap, chiefly Br* a member of a worldwide movement of girls and young women founded with the aim of forming character and teaching good citizenship through outdoor activities and domestic skills

²**guide** v **1** to act as a guide (to); direct in a way or course **2** to direct or supervise, usu to a particular end; *also* to supervise the training of

guild /gild/ n *sing or pl in constr* an association of people with similar interests or pursuits; *esp* a medieval association of merchants or craftsmen

,guild'hall /-'hawl/ n a hall where a guild or corporation usu assembles; *esp* a town hall

guile /giel/ n deceitful cunning; duplicity – ~**ful** *adj* – ~**fully** *adv* – ~**fulness** n

guillemot /'gili,mot/ n pl **guillemots**, *esp collectively* **guillemot** any of several narrow-billed auks of northern seas

guillotine /'giləteen/ n **1** a machine for beheading consisting of a heavy blade that slides down between grooved posts **2** an instrument (e g a paper cutter) that works like a guillotine **3** the placing of a time limit on the discussion of legislative business

guilt /gilt/ n **1** the fact of having committed a breach of conduct, esp one that violates law **2a** responsibility for a criminal or other offence **b** feelings of being at fault or to blame, esp for imagined offences or from a sense of inadequacy – ~**less** *adj* – ~**lessly** *adv* – ~**lessness** n

guilty /'gilti/ *adj* **1** justly answerable for an offence **2a** suggesting or involving guilt **b** feeling guilt – **-tily** *adv* – **-tiness** n

guinea /'gini/ n **1** a former British gold coin worth 21 shillings **2** a money unit worth £1 and 5 new pence

'guinea ,fowl /'gini/ n a W African bird with white-speckled slate-grey plumage

'guinea ,pig n **1** a small stout-bodied short-eared nearly tailless rodent often kept as a pet **2** sby or sthg used as a subject of (scientific) research or experimentation

guise /giez/ n **1** external appearance; aspect **2** assumed appearance; semblance — **in the guise of** masquerading as

guitar /gi'tah/ n a flat-bodied stringed instrument with a long fretted neck

gulden /'goold(ə)n/ n, pl **guldens, gulden** the major unit of currency of the Netherlands

gulf /gulf/ n **1** a partially landlocked part of the sea, usu larger than a bay **2** a deep chasm; an abyss **3** an unbridgeable gap

¹**gull** /gul/ n any of numerous related long-winged web-footed largely white, grey, or black aquatic birds

²**gull** v to trick, cheat, or deceive

gullet /'gulit/ n the throat; the windpipe

gullible /'gulibl/ *adj* easily deceived or cheated – **-bility** n – **-bly** *adv*

gully *also* **gulley** /'guli/ n **1** a deep trench worn by running water **2** a deep gutter or drain

gulp /gulp/ **1** to swallow hurriedly, greedily, or in 1 swallow – often + *down* **2** to make a sudden swallowing movement as if surprised or nervous

¹**gum** /gum/ n (the tissue that surrounds the teeth and covers) the parts of the jaws from which the teeth grow

²**gum** n **1** any of various substances (e g gum resin) that exude from plants **2** a substance or deposit resembling a plant gum (e g in adhesive quality)

³**gum** v **-mm- 1** to smear or stick (as if) with gum **2** to exude or form gum

gumboil /'gum,boyl/ n an abscess in the gum

'**gum,boot** /-,booht/ *n* a strong waterproof rubber boot reaching usu to the knee

gumption /'gumpsh(ə)n/ *n* **1** shrewd practical common sense **2** initiative; *specif* boldness

¹**gun** /gun/ *n* **1a** a rifle, pistol, etc **b** a device that throws a projectile **2** a discharge of a gun **3** sby who carries a gun in a shooting party

²**gun** *v* **-nn-** **1** to shoot – often + *down* **2** to search *for* **~** to attack

'**gun,boat** /-,boht/ *n* a relatively heavily armed ship of shallow draught

'**gun,dog** /-,dog/ *n* a dog trained to locate or retrieve game for hunters

'**gun,fire** /-,fie-ə/ *n* the (noise of) firing of guns

gunge /gunj/ *n, Br* an unpleasant, dirty, or sticky substance – slang

'**gunman** /-mən/ *n* a man armed with a gun; *esp* a professional killer

'**gun,metal** /-,metl/ *n* (a metal treated to imitate) a bronze formerly used for cannon

gunner /'gunə/ *n* **1** a soldier or airman who operates a gun; *specif* a private in the Royal Artillery **2** sby who hunts with a gun **3** a warrant officer who supervises naval ordnance and ordnance stores

'**gun,powder** /-,powdə/ *n* an explosive mixture of potassium nitrate, charcoal, and sulphur used in gunnery and blasting

'**gun,runner** /-,runə/ *n* one who carries or deals in contraband arms and ammunition – **-running** *n*

'**gun,shot** /-,shot/ *n* **1** a shot or projectile fired from a gun **2** the range of a gun

'**gun,smith** /-,smith/ *n* sby who designs, makes, or repairs firearms

gunwale, gunnel /'gunl/ *n* the upper edge of a boat's side

gurgle /guhgl/ *v* **gurgling** /'guhgling/ to make the sound (as if) of unevenly flowing water; *also* to flow or move with such a sound – **gurgle** *n*

guru /'goohrooh, 'goo-/ *n pl* **gurus** **1** a personal religious teacher and spiritual guide (e g in Hinduism) **2** an acknowledged leader or chief proponent (e g of a cult or idea) – infml

¹**gush** /gush/ *v* **1** to issue copiously or violently **2** to emit (in) a sudden copious flow **3** to make an effusive often affected display of sentiment or enthusiasm – **~ing** *adj* – **~ingly** *adv*

²**gush** *n* **1** (sthg emitted in) a sudden outpouring **2** an effusive and usu affected display of sentiment or enthusiasm

gusset /'gusit/ *n* **1** a piece of material inserted in a seam (e g the crotch of an undergarment) to provide expansion or reinforcement **2** a plate or bracket for strengthening an angle in framework

¹**gust** /gust/ *n* **1** a sudden brief rush of (rain carried by the) wind **2** a sudden outburst; a surge

²**gust** *v* to blow in gusts

gusto /'gustoh/ *n* enthusiastic and vigorous enjoyment or vitality

¹**gut** /gut/ *n* **1a** the basic emotionally or instinctively responding part of a person **b** (a part of) the alimentary canal **c** the belly or abdomen **d** catgut **2** *pl* the inner essential parts – infml **3** *pl* courage, determination – infml

²**gut** *v* **-tt-** **1** to eviscerate, disembowel **2** to destroy the inside of **3** to extract the essentials of

³**gut** *adj* arising from or concerning one's strongest emotions or instincts

gutless /-lis/ *adj* lacking courage; cowardly – infml – **~ness** *n*

gutta-percha /,gutə 'puhchə/ *n* a tough plastic substance obtained from the latex of several Malaysian trees and used esp for electrical insulation

¹**gutter** /'gutə/ *n* **1** a trough just below the eaves or at the side of a street to catch and carry off rainwater, surface water, etc **2** the lowest or most vulgar level or condition of human life

²**gutter** *v, of a flame* to burn fitfully or feebly; be on the point of going out

³**gutter** *adj* (characteristic) of the gutter; *esp* marked by extreme vulgarity or cheapness

'**gutter,snipe** /-,sniep/ *n* a deprived child living in poverty and usu dressed in ragged clothes

guttural /'gut(ə)rəl/ *adj* **1** of the throat **2** formed or pronounced in the throat

¹**guy** /gie/ *v or n* (to steady or reinforce with) a rope, chain, rod, etc attached to sthg as a brace or guide

²**guy** *n* **1** *often cap* a humorous effigy of a man burnt in Britain on Guy Fawkes Night **2** a man, fellow – infml

³**guy** *v* to make fun of; ridicule

'**Guy ,Fawkes ,Night** /,gie 'fawks/ *n* November 5 observed in Britain with fireworks and bonfires in commemoration of the arrest of Guy Fawkes in 1605 for attempting to blow up the Houses of Parliament

guzzle /'guzl/ *v* **guzzling** /'guzling, 'guzl-ing/ to consume (sthg) greedily, continually, or habitually

gym /jim/ *n* **1** a gymnasium **2** development of the body by games, exercises, etc, esp in school

gymkhana /jim'kahnə/ *n* a sporting event featuring competitions and displays; *specif* a meeting involving competition in horse riding and carriage driving

gymnasium /jim'nayzi-əm, -zyəm/ *n, pl* **gymnasiums, gymnasia** /-zi-ə/ a large room or separate building used for indoor sports and gymnastic activities

gymnast /'jimnast/ *n* sby trained in gymnastics – **~ic** *adj* – **~ically** *adv*

gymnastics /jim'nastiks/ *n pl but sing or pl in constr* **1** physical exercises developing or displaying bodily strength and coordination, often performed in competition **2** an exercise in intellectual or physical dexterity

gym

gymslip /'jim,slip/ *n, chiefly Br* a girl's tunic or pinafore dress that is worn usu with a belt as part of a school uniform

gynaecology /,gienə'koləji, jie-/ *n* a branch of medicine that deals with diseases and disorders (of the reproductive system) of women – **-logical** *adj* – **-logist** *n*

¹gyp /jip/ *n* a fraud, swindle

²gyp *v* **-pp-** to cheat – *infml*

³gyp *n* sharp pain – chiefly in *give one gyp*; *infml*

gypsum /'jipsəm/ *n* a mineral used to make plaster of paris

gypsy /'jipsi/ *n, chiefly NAm* a gipsy

gyrate /jie'rayt, ji/ *v* **1** to revolve round a point or axis **2** to (cause to) move with a circular or spiral motion – **-tion** *n*

'gyro,scope /-,skohp/ *n* a wheel that is mounted to spin rapidly about an axis and is free to turn in various directions but that maintains constant orientation while spinning in the absence of applied forces – **-scopic** *adj*

H

h /aych/ *n, pl* **h's, hs** *often cap* **1** (a graphic representation of or device for reproducing) the 8th letter of the English alphabet **2** a speech counterpart of written *h*

habeas corpus /,haybi·əs 'kawpəs, -byəs/ *n* a judicial writ requiring a detained person to be brought before a court so that the legality of his/her detention may be examined

haberdasher /'habə,dashə/ *n, Br* a dealer in buttons, thread, ribbon, etc used in making clothes

'haber,dashery /-ri/ *n* **1** goods sold by a haberdasher **2** a haberdasher's shop

habit /'habit/ *n* **1** a costume characteristic of a calling, rank, or function **2** bodily or mental make-up **3a** a settled tendency or usual manner of behaviour **b** an acquired pattern or mode of behaviour **4** addiction

habitable /'habitəbl/ *adj* capable of being lived in

habitat /'habitat/ *n* the (type of) place where a plant or animal naturally grows or lives

habitation /,habi'taysh(ə)n/ *n* **1** the act of inhabiting; occupancy **2** a dwelling place; a residence, home

habitual /hə'bityooəl, -chooəl/ *adj* **1** having the nature of a habit **2** by force of habit **3** in accordance with habit; customary – **~ly** *adv*

habituate /hə'bityooayt, -choo-/ *v* to make used to

¹hack /hak/ *v* **1** to cut or sever (as if) with repeated (irregular or unskilful) blows **2** to clear by cutting away vegetation **3** to kick (an opposing player or the ball in football) **4** to cough in a short dry manner

²hack *n* **1** a mattock, pick, etc **2** a hacking blow

³hack *n* **1** a light easily saddle horse **2** an act of hacking; a ride **3** one who produces mediocre work for financial gain; *esp* a commercial writer

⁴hack *adj* **1** performed by, suited to, or characteristic of a hack **2** hackneyed, trite

⁵hack *v* to ride (a horse) at an ordinary pace, esp over roads

hackneyed /'haknid/ *adj* lacking in freshness or originality; meaningless because used or done too often

hacksaw /'hak,saw/ *n* a fine-toothed saw, esp for cutting metal

had /d, əd, had/ *strong* had/ *past of* **have**

haddock /'hadək/ *n* an important Atlantic food fish, usu smaller than the related common cod

Hades /'haydeez/ *n* **1** the underground abode of the dead in Greek mythology **2** *often not cap* hell – *euph*

,haemo'globin /-'glohbin/ *n* an iron-containing protein that occurs in the red blood cells of vertebrates and is the means of oxygen transport from the lungs to the body tissues

haemophilia /,heemoh'fili·ə, -mə-/ *n* delayed clotting of the blood with consequent difficulty in controlling bleeding even after minor injuries, occurring as a hereditary defect, usu in males – **-philiac** *n, adj*

haemorrhage /'hemərij/ *n* a (copious) loss of blood from the blood vessels

haemorrhoid /'heməroyd/ *n* a mass of swollen veins round or near the anus – usu *pl* with sing. meaning

haft /hahft/ *n* the handle of a weapon or tool

hag /hag/ *n* **1** a witch **2** an ugly and usu ill-natured old woman

haggard /'hagəd/ *adj* having a worn or emaciated appearance, esp through anxiety or lack of sleep

haggis /'hagis/ *n* a traditionally Scottish dish that consists of the heart, liver, and lungs of a sheep, calf, etc minced with suet, oatmeal, and seasonings

haggle /'hagl/ *v* **haggling** /'hagling/ to bargain, wrangle

¹ha-ha /hah 'hah 'hah/ *interj* – used to express or represent laughter or derision

²ha-ha /'hah ,hah/ *n* a fence or retaining wall sunk into a ditch and used as a boundary (e g of a park or grounds) so as to give an uninterrupted view

¹hail /hayl/ *n* **1** (precipitation in the form of) small particles of clear ice or compacted snow **2** a group of things directed at sby or sthg and intended to cause pain, damage, or distress

²hail *v* 1 to precipitate hail 2 to pour down or strike like hail

³hail *interj* 1 – used to express acclamation 2 *archaic* – used as a salutation

⁴hail *v* 1a to salute, greet **b** to greet with enthusiastic approval; acclaim *as* 2 to greet or summon by calling 3 to come *from*, be a native of

⁵hail *n* 1 a call to attract attention 2 hearing distance

'hail,stone /-,stohn/ *n* a pellet of hail

hair /heə/ *n* 1 (a structure resembling) a slender threadlike outgrowth on the surface of an animal; *esp* (any of) the many usu coloured hairs that form the characteristic coat of a mammal 2 the coating of hairs, esp on the human head or other body part

'hair,cut /-,kut/ *n* (the result of) cutting and shaping of the hair

'hair,do /-,dooh/ *n pl* **hairdos** a hairstyle

'hair,dresser /-,dresə/ *n* sby whose occupation is cutting, dressing, and styling the hair – **-sing** *n*

'hair,grip /-,grip/ *n*, *Br* a flat hairpin with prongs that close together

'hair,line /-,lien/ *n* 1 a very slender line; *esp* a tiny line or crack on a surface 2 the line above the forehead beyond which hair grows

'hair,piece /-,pees/ *n* a section of false hair worn to enhance a hairstyle or make a person's natural hair seem thicker or more plentiful

¹'hair,pin /-,pin/ *n* 1 a 2-pronged U-shaped pin of thin wire for holding the hair in place 2 a sharp bend in a road

²hairpin *adj* having the shape of a hairpin

'hair-,raising *adj* causing terror or astonishment

'hair's ,breadth *n* a very small distance or margin

'hair-,slide *n*, *Br* a (decorative) clip for the hair

'hair,splitting /-,spliting/ *n* argument over unimportant differences and points of detail; quibbling

'hair,spring /-,spring/ *n* a slender spiral spring that regulates the motion of the balance wheel of a timepiece

'hair,style /-,stiel/ *n* a way of wearing or arranging the hair – **-styling** *n* – **-stylist** *n*

hairy /'heəri/ *adj* 1 covered with (material like) hair 2 made of or resembling hair 3 frighteningly dangerous – *infml* – **-riness** *n*

hake /hayk/ *n pl* **hakes**, *esp collectively* **hake** any of several marine food fishes related to the common Atlantic cod

halcyon /'halsi-ən/ *adj* calm, peaceful – esp in *halcyon days*

hale /hayl/ *adj* free from defect, disease, or infirmity; sound

¹half /hahf/ *n*, *pl* **halves** /hahvz/ 1a either of 2 equal parts into which sthg is divisible; *also* a part of a thing approximately equal to a half **b** half an hour – used in designation of time 2 either of a pair: e g

2a a partner **b** a school term – used esp at some British public schools 3 half the value or quantity: e g **3a** half a pint **b** a child's ticket — **and a half** of remarkable quality — *infml* — **by half** by a great deal — **by halves** half heartedly — **in half** into 2 (nearly) equal parts

²half *adj* 1a being one of 2 equal parts **b(1)** amounting to approximately half **b(2)** falling short of the full or complete thing (e g a *half* smile) 2 extending over or covering only half (e g *half* sleeves) 3 *Br* half past

³half *adv* 1 in an equal part or degree (e g she was *half* laughing, *half* crying) 2 nearly but not completely (e g *half* cooked) — **half as much again** one-and-a-half times as much

'half,back /-,bak/ *n* a player in rugby, soccer, hockey, etc positioned immediately behind the forward line

,half-'baked *adj* marked by or showing a lack of forethought or judgment; foolish

,half-,breed *n* the offspring of parents of different races

half brother *n* a brother related through 1 parent only

half cock *n* 1 the position of the hammer of a firearm when about half retracted and held by the safety catch so that it cannot be operated by a pull on the trigger 2 a state of inadequate preparation – esp in *go off at half cock*

,half'hearted /-'hahtid/ *adj* lacking enthusiasm or effort

,half-'holiday *n* a holiday of half a day, esp an afternoon

,half-,mast *n* the position of a flag lowered halfway down the staff as a mark of mourning

halfpenny /'haypni/ *n* 1 (a British bronze coin representing) one half of a penny 2 a small amount

half sister *n* a sister related through 1 parent only

,half 'term *n*, *chiefly Br* (a short holiday taken at) a period about halfway through a school term

,half'time /-'tiem/ *n* (an intermission marking) the completion of half of a game or contest

'half,tone /-,tohn/ *n* any of the shades of grey between the darkest and the lightest parts of a photographic image

,half-'volley *n* 1 a shot in tennis made at a ball just after it has bounced 2 an easily-hit delivery of the ball in cricket that bounces closer than intended to the batsman

'half,way /-'way/ *adj or adv* 1 midway between 2 points 2 (done or formed) partially

'half-,wit *n* a foolish or mentally deficient person – derog – ~ **ted** *adj* – ~ **tedly** *adv*

halibut /'halibət/ *n* a large marine food flatfish

halitosis /,hali'tohsis/ *n* (a condition of having) offensively smelling breath

hall /hawl/ n 1 the house of a medieval king or noble 2 the manor house of a landed proprietor 3 the entrance room or passage of a building 4 a large room for public assembly or entertainment

¹**hallmark** /'hawl,mahk/ n 1 an official mark stamped on gold and silver articles in Britain after an assay test to testify to their purity 2 a distinguishing characteristic or object

²**hallmark** v to stamp with a hallmark

hallow /'haloh/ v 1 to make holy or set apart for holy use 2 to respect and honour greatly; venerate

Halloween, Hallowe'en /,haloh'een/ n October 31, the eve of All Saints' Day, observed by dressing up in disguise, party turns, etc

hallstand /'hawl,stand/ n a piece of furniture with pegs for holding coats, hats, and umbrellas

hallucinate /ha'loohsinayt/ v 1 to perceive or experience as a hallucination 2 to have hallucinations

hallucination /ha,loohsi'naysh(a)n/ n 1 the perception of sthg apparently real to the perceiver but which has no objective reality, also the image, object, etc perceived 2 a completely unfounded or mistaken impression or belief – **-atory** adj

¹**halo** /'hayloh/ n, pl **halos, haloes** 1 a circle of light appearing to surround the sun or moon and resulting from refraction or reflection of light by ice particles in the earth's atmosphere 2 a nimbus 3 the aura of glory or veneration surrounding an idealized person or thing

²**halo** v **haloing; haloed** to form into or surround with a halo

¹**halt** /hawlt/ v 1 to hesitate between alternative courses; waver 2 to display weakness or imperfection (e g in speech or reasoning); falter

²**halt** n 1 a (temporary) stop or interruption 2 Br a railway stopping place, without normal station facilities, for local trains

³**halt** v 1 to come to a halt 2 to bring to a stop 3 to cause to stop; end

halter /'hawlta/ n 1 a rope or strap for leading or tying an animal 2 a noose for hanging criminals

halting /'hawlting/ adj hesitant, faltering – **~ly** adv

halve /hahv/ v 1a to divide into 2 equal parts b to reduce to a half 2 to play (e g a hole or match in golf) in the same number of strokes as one's opponent

¹**halves** /hahvz/ pl of **half**

²**halves** adv with equal half shares

halyard, halliard /'halyad/ n a rope or tackle for hoisting or lowering

¹**ham** /ham/ n 1 a buttock with its associated thigh – usu pl 2 (the meat of) the rear end of a bacon pig, esp the thigh, when removed from the carcass before curing with salt 3a an inexpert but showy performer; also an actor performing in an exaggerated theatrical style b an operator of an amateur radio station

²**ham** v **-mm-** to execute with exaggerated speech or gestures; overact

hamburger /'hambuhga/ n a round flat cake of minced beef; also a sandwich of a fried hamburger in a bread roll

,**ham-'fisted** adj, chiefly Br lacking dexterity with the hands; clumsy – infml

hamlet /'hamlit/ n a small village

¹**hammer** /'hama/ n 1a a hand tool that consists of a solid head set crosswise on a handle and is used to strike a blow (e g to drive in a nail) b a power tool that substitutes a metal block or a drill for the hammerhead 2a a lever with a striking head for ringing a bell or striking a gong b the part of the mechanism of a modern gun whose action ignites the cartridge c one of the three bones of the middle ear d(1) a padded mallet in a piano action for striking a string d(2) a hand mallet for playing various percussion instruments 3 (an athletic field event using) a metal sphere weighing 16lb (about 7.3kg) attached by a wire to a handle and thrown for distance — **under the hammer** for sale at auction

²**hammer** v 1 to strike blows, esp repeatedly, (as if) with a hammer; pound 2 to make repeated efforts at; esp to reiterate an opinion or attitude 3 to beat, drive, or shape (as if) with repeated blows of a hammer 4 to force as if by hitting repeatedly 5 to beat decisively – infml — **hammer into** to cause (sby) to learn or remember (sthg) by continual repetition

,**hammer and 'sickle** n an emblem consisting of a crossed hammer and sickle used chiefly as a symbol of Communism

hammer out v to produce or bring about through lengthy discussion

hammock /'hamak/ n a hanging bed, usu made of netting or canvas and suspended by cords at each end

¹**hamper** /'hampa/ v 1 to restrict the movement or operation of by bonds or obstacles; hinder 2 to interfere with; encumber

²**hamper** n a large basket with a cover for packing, storing, or transporting crockery, food, etc

hamster /'hamsta/ n any of numerous small Old World rodents with very large cheek pouches

¹**hamstring** /'ham,string/ n 1 either of 2 groups of tendons at the back of the human knee 2 a large tendon above and behind the hock of a quadruped

²**hamstring** v **hamstring** /-strung/ 1 to cripple by cutting the leg tendons 2 to make ineffective or powerless; cripple

¹**hand** /hand/ n 1a (the segment of the forelimb of vertebrate animals corresponding to) the end of the forelimb of human beings, monkeys, etc when modified as a grasping organ b a stylized figure of a hand used as a pointer or marker c a forehock of pork d an indicator or pointer on a dial 2 either of

2 sides or aspects of an issue or argument 3 a pledge, esp of betrothal or marriage 4 handwriting 5 a unit of measure equal to 4in (about 102mm) used esp for the height of a horse 6a assistance or aid, esp when involving physical effort b a round of applause 7a (the cards or pieces held by) a player in a card or board game b a single round in a game c the force or solidity of one's position (e g in negotiations) d a turn to serve in a game (e g squash) in which only the server may score points and which lasts as long as the server can win points 8a a worker, employee ; *esp* one employed at manual labour or general tasks b a member of a ship's crew c one skilled in a particular action or pursuit 9a handiwork b style of execution; workmanship — **at hand** near in time or place — **at the hands of, at the hand of** by the act or instrumentality of — **by hand** with the hands, usu as opposed to mechanically — **in hand** 1 not used up or lost and at one's disposal 2 *of a horse* being led rather than being ridden 3 under way — **off one's hands** out of one's care or charge — **on hand** 1 ready to use 2 in attendance; present — **on one's hands** in one's possession, care, or management — **out of hand** 1 without delay; without reflection or consideration 2 out of control — **to hand** available and ready for use; *esp* within reach

²**hand** v 1 to lead or assist with the hand 2 to give or pass (as if) with the hand — **hand it to** to give credit to

handbag /'hand,bag/ n a bag designed for carrying small personal articles and money, carried usu by women

'**hand,bill** n a small printed sheet to be distributed (e g for advertising) by hand

'**hand,book** n a short reference book, esp on a particular subject

handcuff /'hand,kuf/ v to apply handcuffs to; manacle

handcuffs n pl a pair of metal rings, usu connected by a chain or bar, for locking round prisoners' wrists

hand down v 1 to transmit in succession (e g from father to son); bequeath 2 to give (an outgrown article of clothing) to a younger member of one's family 3 to deliver in court

handful /'handf(ə)l/ n, pl **handfuls** also **handsful** /' handzf(ə)l/ 1 as much or as many as the hand will grasp 2 a small quantity or number 3 sby or sthg (e g a child or animal) that is difficult to control – infml

¹**handicap** /'handi,kap/ n 1 (a race or contest with) an artificial advantage or disadvantage given to contestants so that all have an equal chance of winning 2 a (physical) disability or disadvantage that makes achievement unusually difficult

²**handicap** v -pp- 1 to assign handicaps to; impose handicaps on 2 to put at a disadvantage

handicraft /'handi,krahft/ n 1 (an occupation requiring) manual skill 2 articles fashioned by handicraft

handiwork /'handi,wuhk/ n 1 (the product of) work done by the hands 2 work done personally

handkerchief /'hangkə,cheef, -chif/ n, pl **handkerchiefs** also **handkerchieves** /-,cheevz/ a small piece of cloth used for various usu personal purposes (e g blowing the nose or wiping the eyes) or as a clothing accessory

¹**handle** /'handl/ n 1 a part that is designed to be grasped by the hand 2 the feel of a textile 3 a title; *also* an esp aristocratic or double-barrelled name – infml — **off the handle** into a state of sudden and violent anger

²**handle** v **handling** /'handling, 'handl·ing/ 1a to try or examine (e g by touching or moving) with the hand b to manage with the hands 2a to deal with (e g a subject or idea) in speech or writing, or as a work of art b to manage, direct 3 to deal with, act on, or dispose of 4 to engage in the buying, selling, or distributing of (a commodity) 5 to respond to controlling movements in a specified way – ~**able** adj

handler /'handlə/ n one who is in immediate physical charge of an animal

,**hand'made** adj made by hand rather than by machine

'**hand,maiden** n a personal maid or female servant

'**hand,out** n 1 sthg (e g food, clothing, or money) distributed free, esp to people in need 2 a folder or circular of information for free distribution

hand out v 1 to give freely or without charge 2 to administer

hand over v to yield control or possession (of)

,**hand'pick** v 1 to pick by hand rather than by machine 2 to select personally and carefully

'**hand,rail** n a narrow rail for grasping with the hand as a support, esp near stairs

'**hand,shake** n a clasping and shaking of each other's usu right hand by 2 people (e g in greeting or farewell)

handsome /'hansəm/ adj 1 considerable, sizable 2 marked by graciousness or generosity; liberal 3a *of a man* having a pleasing appearance; good-looking b *of a woman* attractive in a dignified statuesque way – ~**ly** adv

,**hand-to-'hand** adj involving physical contact; very close – **hand to hand** adv

,**hand-to-'mouth** adj having or providing only just enough to live on; precarious – **hand to mouth** adv

'**hand,writing** n writing done by hand; *esp* the style of writing peculiar to a particular person

handy /'handi/ *adj* **1** convenient for use; useful **2** clever in a variety of ways, esp in a variety of practical ways **3** conveniently near – *infml* – **-dily** *adv* – **-diness** *n*

'handyman /-mən, -,man/ *n* **1** sby who does odd jobs **2** sby competent in a variety of skills or repair work

¹hang /hang/ *v* **hung** /hung/, (1b) **hanged 1a** to fasten to some elevated point by the top so that the lower part is free; suspend **b** to suspend by the neck until dead **c** to fasten on a point of suspension so as to allow free motion within given limits **d** to suspend (meat, esp game) before cooking to make the flesh tender and develop the flavour **2** to decorate, furnish, or cover by hanging sthg up (e g flags or bunting) **3** to hold or bear in a suspended or inclined position **4** to fasten (sthg, esp wallpaper) to a wall (e g with paste) **5** to display (pictures) in a gallery **6** to remain fastened at the top so that the lower part is free; dangle **7** to remain poised or stationary in the air **8** to stay on; persist **9** to fall or droop from a usu tense or taut position **10** to depend **11** to lean, incline, or jut over or downwards — **hang fire 1** to be slow in the explosion of a charge after its primer has been discharged **2** to be delayed or held up — **hang in the balance** to be uncertain or at stake — **hang on 1** to pay close attention to **2** to depend on **3** to be burdensome or oppressive

²hang *n* **1** the manner in which a thing hangs **2** a downward slope; *also* a droop **3** the special method of doing, using, or dealing with sthg; the knack – chiefly in *get the hang of*

hang about *v*, *Br* **1** to wait or stay, usu without purpose or activity **2** to delay or move slowly *USE infml*

hangar /'hangə/ *n* a shed; *esp* a large shed for housing aircraft

hang back *v* to be reluctant to move or act; hesitate

hangdog /'hang,dog/ *adj* ashamed; *also* abject

hanger /'hangə/ *n* a device (e g a loop or strap) by which or to which sthg is hung or hangs; *esp* a hook and crosspiece to fit inside the shoulders of a dress, coat, etc to keep the shape of the garment when hung up

,hanger-'on *n pl* **hangers-on** one who attempts to associate with a person, group, etc, esp for personal gain; a dependant

'hang-,glider *n* (sby who flies) a glider resembling a kite that is controlled by the body movements of the person harnessed beneath it – **hang-glide** *v* – **hang-gliding** *n*

¹hanging /'hang·ing/ *n* **1** (an) execution by suspension from a noose **2a** a curtain **b** a covering (e g a tapestry) for a wall

²hanging *adj* **1** situated or lying on steeply sloping ground **2** jutting out; overhanging **3** adapted for sustaining a hanging object **4** deserving or liable to inflict hanging

'hangman /-mən/ *n* one who hangs a condemned person; a public executioner

hangnail /'hang,nayl/ *n* a bit of skin hanging loose at the side or root of a fingernail

hang on *v* **1** to keep hold; hold onto sthg **2** to persist tenaciously **3** to wait for a short time **4** to remain on the telephone — **hang on to** to hold or keep tenaciously

'hang,out *n* a place where one is often to be seen – *slang*

hang out *v* **1** to protrude, esp downwards **2** to live or spend much time – *slang*

hangover /'hang·ohvə/ *n* **1** sthg (e g a custom) that remains from the past **2** the disagreeable physical effects following heavy consumption of alcohol or use of other drugs

'hang-,up *n* a source of mental or emotional difficulty – *infml*

hang up *v* to terminate a telephone conversation, often abruptly

hank /hangk/ *n* **1** a coil, loop; *specif* a coiled or looped bundle (e g of yarn, rope, or wire) usu containing a definite length **2** a ring attaching a jib or staysail to a stay

hanker /'hangkə/ *v* to desire strongly or persistently – usu + *after* or *for* – ~**ing** *n*

hankie, hanky /'hangki/ *n* a handkerchief

,hanky-'panky /'pangki/ *n* mildly improper or deceitful behaviour – *infml*

hansom /'hansəm/, **hansom cab** *n* a light 2-wheeled covered carriage

haphazard /hap'hazəd/ *adj* random – ~**ly** *adv*

hapless /'haplis/ *adj* having no luck; unfortunate

happen /'hapn/ *v* **happening** /'hapn·ing, 'hapn·ing/ **1** to occur by chance **2** to come into being as an event; occur **3** to have the luck or fortune *to*; chance — **happen on/upon** to see or meet (sthg or sby) by chance

happening /'hapn·ing, 'hapning/ *n* **1** sthg that happens; an occurrence **2a** the creation or presentation of a nonobjective work of art (e g an action painting) **b** a usu unscripted or improvised public performance in which the audience participates

happy /'hapi/ *adj* **1** favoured by luck or fortune; fortunate **2** well adapted or fitting; felicitous **3a** enjoying or expressing pleasure and contentment **b** glad, pleased **4** characterized by a dazed irresponsible state – usu in combination **5** impulsively quick or overinclined to use sthg – usu in combination **6** having or marked by an atmosphere of good fellowship; friendly – **-pily** *adv* – **-piness** *n*

'happy-go-'lucky *adj* blithely unconcerned; carefree

hara-kiri /ˌharə ˈkiriˌ/ n suicide by ritual disembowelment practised by the Japanese samurai

[1]**harangue** /həˈrangˌ/ n 1 a speech addressed to a public assembly 2 a lengthy, ranting, speech or piece of writing

[2]**harangue** v to make or address in a harangue

harass /ˈharəsˌ/ v 1 toˉworry and impede by repeated raids 2 to annoy or worry persistently – **harasser** n – **harassment** n

harbinger /ˈhahbinjəˌ/ n 1 a precursor 2 sthg that presages or foreshadows what is to come

[1]**harbour**, NAm chiefly **harbor** /ˈhahbəˌ/ n 1 a place of security and comfort; a refuge 2 a part of a body of water providing protection and anchorage for ships

[2]**harbour**, NAm chiefly **harbor** v 1 to give shelter or refuge to 2 to be the home or habitat of; contain 3 to have or keep (e g thoughts or feelings) in the mind – **~er** n

[1]**hard** /hahd/ adj 1 not easily penetrated or yielding to pressure; firm **2a** of alcoholic drink having a high percentage of alcohol **b** of water containing salts of calcium, magnesium, etc that inhibit lathering with soap **3a** not speculative or conjectural; factual **b** close, searching **4a(1)** difficult to endure **a(2)** oppressive, inequitable **b** lacking consideration or compassion **c(1)** harsh, severe **c(2)** resentful **d** not warm or mild **e(1)** forceful, violent **e(2)** demanding energy or stamina **e(3)** using or performing with great energy or effort **5a** difficult to do, understand, or explain **b** having difficulty in doing sthg **6a** of a drug addictive and gravely detrimental to health **b** of pornography hard-core – **~ness** n

[2]**hard** adv **1a** with great or maximum effort or energy; strenuously **b** in a violent manner; fiercely **c** to the full extent – used in nautical directions **d** in a searching or concentrated manner **2a** in such a manner as to cause hardship, difficulty, or pain; severely **b** with bitterness or grief **3** in a firm manner; tightly **4** to the point of hardness **5** close in time or space — **hard done by** unfairly treated

hard-and-'fast adj fixed, strict

hard back n a book bound in stiff covers

hard-'bitten adj steeled by difficult experience; tough

hard board n (a) composition board made by compressing shredded wood chips

hard-'boiled adj devoid of sentimentality; tough

hard core n, Br compacted rubble or clinker used esp as a foundation for roads, paving, or floors

hard-'core adj 1 of or constituting a hard core 2 of pornography extremely explicit

hard core n sing or pl in constr the unyielding or uncompromising members that form the nucleus of a group

harden /ˈhahdnˌ/ v 1 to make or become hard or harder 2 to confirm or become confirmed in disposition, feelings, or action; esp to make callous **3a** to toughen, inure to **b** to inure (e g plants) to cold or other unfavourable environmental conditions – often + off **4** to assume an appearance of harshness **5** of currency, prices, etc to become higher or less subject to fluctuations downwards

hard-'headed adj 1 stubborn 2 sober, realistic

hard-'hearted adj lacking in sympathetic understanding; unfeeling

hardly /ˈhahdliˌ/ adv 1 in a severe manner; harshly 2 with difficulty; painfully 3 only just; barely 4 scarcely

hard-of-'hearing adj partially deaf

hardship /ˈhahdshipˌ/ n (an instance of) suffering, privation

hard 'shoulder n either of 2 surfaced strips of land along a road, esp a motorway, on which stopping is allowed only in an emergency

hard 'up adj short of sthg, esp money – infml

hard ware n 1 items sold by an ironmonger 2 the physical components (e g electronic and electrical devices) of a vehicle (e g a spacecraft) or an apparatus (e g a computer) 3 tape recorders, closed-circuit television, etc used as instructional equipment

hard-'wearing adj durable

hard wood n (the wood of) a broad-leaved as distinguished from a coniferous tree

hardy /ˈhahdiˌ/ adj 1 bold, audacious **2a** inured to fatigue or hardships; robust **b** capable of withstanding adverse conditions; esp capable of living outdoors over winter without artificial protection – **~diness** n

[1]**hare** /heəˌ/ n pl **hares**, esp collectively **hare** 1 any of various swift timid long-eared mammals like large rabbits with long hind legs 2 a figure of a hare moved mechanically along a dog track for the dogs to chase

[2]**hare** v to run fast – infml

hare bell n a slender plant with blue bell-shaped flowers that grows on heaths or in open woodland

hare brained adj flighty, foolish

hare lip n a split in the upper lip like that of a hare occurring as a congenital deformity – **-lipped** adj

harem /ˈheerəmˌ, hahˈreemˌ/ n **1a** a usu secluded (part of a) house allotted to women in a Muslim household **b** sing or pl in constr the women occupying a harem 2 a group of females associated with 1 male – used with reference to polygamous animals

haricot /ˈharikohˌ/, **haricot 'bean** n a French bean

hark /hahk/ v to listen closely

hark back v to return to an earlier topic or circumstance

harlequin /ˈhahlikwinˌ/ n 1 cap a stock character in comedy and pantomime 2 a buffoon

harlot /'hahlət/ *n, archaic* a woman prostitute – ~ **ry** *n*

¹**harm** /hahm/ *n* **1** physical or mental damage; injury **2** mischief, wrong – ~ **ful** *adj* – ~ **fully** *adv* – ~ **fulness** *n* — **out of harm's way** safe from danger

²**harm** *v* to cause harm to

harmless /'hahmlis/ *adj* **1** free from harm, liability, or loss **2** lacking capacity or intent to injure – ~ **ly** *adv* – ~ **ness** *n*

¹**harmonic** /hah'monik/ *adj* **1** of musical harmony, a harmonic, or harmonics **2** pleasing to the ear; harmonious

²**harmonic** *n* a tone in a harmonic series

harmonica /hah'monikə/ *n* a small rectangular wind instrument

harmonium /hah'mohni·əm, -nyəm/ *n* a reed organ in which pedals operate a bellows

harmony /'hahmoni/ *n* **1a** the (pleasant-sounding) combination of simultaneous musical notes in a chord **b** (the science of) the structure of music with respect to the composition and progression of chords **2a** pleasing or congruent arrangement of parts **b** agreement, accord – **-nious** *adj* – **-niously** *adv* – **-niousness** *n* – **-nize** *v*

¹**harness** /'hahnis/ *n* **1** the gear of a draught animal other than a yoke **2** sthg that resembles a harness (e g in holding or fastening sthg) — **in harness 1** in one's usual work, surroundings, or routine **2** in close association

²**harness** *v* **1a** to put a harness on (e g a horse) **b** to attach (e g a wagon) by means of a harness **2** to tie together; yoke **3** to utilize; *esp* to convert a (natural force) into energy

harp /hahp/ *n* a musical instrument that has strings stretched across an open triangular frame, plucked with the fingers

harp on *v* to dwell on or return to (a subject) tediously or repeatedly

harpoon /hah'poohn/ *n* a barbed spear used esp in hunting large fish or whales

harpsichord /'hahpsi,kawd/ *n* a keyboard instrument having a horizontal frame and strings and producing notes by the action of quills or leather points plucking the strings

harpy /'hahpi/ *n* **1** *cap* a rapacious creature of Greek mythology with the head of a woman and the body of a bird **2** a predatory person; *esp* a rapacious woman – *derog*

harridan /'harid(ə)n/ *n* an ill-tempered unpleasant woman

¹**harrier** /'hari·ə/ *n* **1** a hunting dog resembling a small foxhound and used esp for hunting hares **2** a runner in a cross-country team

²**harrier** *n* any of various slender hawks with long angled wings

,**Harris 'tweed** /'haris/ *trademark* – used for a loosely woven tweed made in the Outer Hebrides

¹**harrow** /'haroh/ *n* a cultivating implement set with spikes, spring teeth, or discs and drawn over the ground esp to pulverize and smooth the soil

²**harrow** *v* **1** to cultivate (ground or land) with a harrow **2** to cause distress to; agonize

harry /'hari/ *v* **1** to make a destructive raid on; ravage **2** to torment (as if) by constant attack; harass

harsh /hahsh/ *adj* **1** having a coarse uneven surface; rough **2** disagreeable or painful to the senses **3** unduly exacting; severe – ~ **ly** *adv* – ~ **ness** *n*

hart /haht/ *n, chiefly Br* the male of the (red) deer, esp when over 5 years old

harum-scarum /,hearəm 'skearəm/ *adj* reckless, irresponsible – *infml*

¹**harvest** /'hahvist/ *n* **1** (the season for) the gathering in of agricultural crops **2** (the yield of) a mature crop of grain, fruit, etc **3** the product or reward of exertion

²**harvest** *v* to gather in (a crop); reap

has /haz/ *pres 3rd sing of* **have**

'**has-,been** *n* sby or sthg that has passed the peak of effectiveness, success, or popularity – *infml*

¹**hash** /hash/ *n* **1** (a dish consisting chiefly of reheated cooked) chopped food, esp meat **2** a rehash **3** a muddle, mess *USE*(2 & 3) *infml*

²**hash** *n* hashish – *infml*

hashish /'hashish, -sheesh/ *n* the resin from the flowering tops of the female hemp plant that is smoked, chewed, etc for its intoxicating effect

hasp /hahsp/ *n* a device for fastening; *esp* a hinged metal strap that fits over a staple and is secured by a pin or padlock

¹**hassle** /'hasl/ *n* **1** a heated often protracted argument; a wrangle **2** a trying problem; a struggle *USE infml*

²**hassle** *v* **hassling** /'hasling/ **1** to argue, fight **2** to subject to usu persistent harassment *USE infml*

hast /hast/ *archaic pres 2 sing of* **have**

¹**haste** /hayst/ *n* **1** rapidity of motion; swiftness **2** rash or headlong action; precipitateness — **make haste** to act quickly; hasten

²**haste** *v* to move or act swiftly – *fml*

hasten /'hays(ə)n/ *v* **1** to cause to hurry **2** to accelerate **3** to move or act quickly; hurry

hasty /'haysti/ *adj* **1** done or made in a hurry **2** precipitate, rash – **-tily** *adv* – **-tiness** *n*

hat /hat/ *n* a covering for the head usu having a shaped crown and brim

¹**hatch** /hach/ *n* **1** a small door or opening (e g in a wall or aircraft) **2a** (the covering for) an opening in the deck of a ship or in the floor or roof of a building **b** a hatchway

²**hatch** *v* **1** to emerge from an egg or pupa **2** to incubate eggs; brood **3** to give forth young **4** to produce (young) from an egg by applying heat **5** to devise, esp secretly; originate

³**hatch** *v* to mark (e g a drawing, map, or engraving) with fine closely spaced parallel lines

'hatch,back *n* (a usu small motor car with) an upward-opening hatch giving entry to the luggage and passenger compartment

hatchet /'hachit/ *n* a short-handled axe

¹**hate** /hayt/ *n* 1 intense hostility or dislike; loathing 2 an object of hatred – *infml*

²**hate** *v* to feel extreme enmity or aversion (towards) — **hate someone's guts** to hate sby with great intensity

'**hateful** /-f(ə)l/ *adj* 1 full of hate; malicious 2 deserving of or arousing hate – ~**ly** *adv* – ~**ness** *n*

hath /hath/ *archaic pres* 3 *sing of* **have**

hatred /'haytrid/ *n* hate

'**hat ,trick** *n* three successes by 1 person or side in a usu sporting activity

haughty /'hawti/ *adj* disdainfully proud; arrogant – **-tily** *adv* **-tiness** *n*

¹**haul** /hawl/ *v* 1a to pull with effort; drag b to transport in a vehicle, esp a cart 2 to bring *up* (e g before an authority for judgment) – *infml*

²**haul** *n* 1 the act or process of hauling 2 an amount gathered or acquired; a take 3a transport by hauling or the load transported b the distance or route over which a load is transported

haulier /'hawli-ə/, *NAm* **hauler** /'hawlə/ *n* a person or commercial establishment whose business is transport by lorry 2 *Br* an individual plant stem

haunch /hawnch/ *n* 1 a hip 2 the hind legs (and adjoining parts) of a quadruped – usu pl 3 the lower half of either of the sides of an arch — **on one's haunches** in a squatting position

¹**haunt** /hawnt/ *v* 1 to visit often; frequent 2a to recur constantly and spontaneously to b to reappear continually in; pervade 3 to visit or inhabit as a ghost 4 to stay around or persist; linger

²**haunt** *n* a place habitually frequented

hauteur /oh'tuh, *Fr* otœːr)/ *n* arrogance, haughtiness

Havana /hə'vanə/ *n* (a cigar made in Cuba or from) tobacco (of the type) grown in Cuba

¹**have** /v, əv, həv; *strong* hav/ *v* **has** /s, z, əz, həz; *strong* haz/; **had** /d, əd, həd; *strong* had/ 1a to hold in one's possession or at one's disposal b to contain as a constituent or be characterized by 2 to own as an obligation or necessity – + *to* and an expressed or understood infinitive (e g you don't *have* if you don't want to) 3 to stand in relationship to (e g have 2 sisters) 4a to get, obtain b to receive (e g *had* news) c to accept; *specif* to accept in marriage d to have sexual intercourse with (a woman or passive partner) 5a to experience, esp by undergoing or suffering (e g *have* a cold) b to undertake and make or perform (e g *have* a look at that) c to entertain in the mind (e g *have* an opinion) d to engage in; carry on 6a to cause to by persuasive or forceful means (e g so he would *have* us believe) b to cause to be (brought into a specified condition) (e g *have* it finished) c to invite as a

guest 7 to allow, permit 8a to hold in a position of disadvantage or certain defeat (e g we *have* him now) b to perplex, floor (e g you *have* me there) 9a to be pregnant with or be the prospective parents of b to give birth to 10 to partake of; consume 11 to take advantage of; fool (e g been *had* by his partner) – infml 12 – used with the past participle to form perfect tenses (e g we *have* had); used with *got* to express obligation or necessity (e g *have* got to go) 13 would (e g I *had* as soon not) — **have an ear to the ground** to be in receipt of information not generally known — **have a way with** to be good at dealing with — **have a way with one** to be charming, esp persuasively — **have coming** to deserve or merit what one gets, benefits by, or suffers — **have done with** to bring to an end; have no further concern with — **have had it** 1 to have had and missed one's chance – infml 2 to have passed one's prime; be obsolete, smashed, or dead – infml — **have it both ways** to exploit or profit from each of a pair of contradictory positions, circumstances, etc; *also* to maintain 2 contradictory views simultaneously — **have it in for** to intend to do harm to — **have it out** to settle a matter of contention by discussion or a fight — **have one's head screwed on** to be sensible, practical, or provident — **have one's work cut out** to be hard put to it — **have taped** to have the measure of; be in command or control of — **have to do with** 1 to deal with 2 to have in the way of connection or relation with or effect on — compare to DO WITH — **have up one's sleeve** to have as an undeclared resource — **not have a clue** to know nothing; not to know — **what have you** any of various other things that might also be mentioned

²**have** *n* a wealthy person – usu pl; esp in *the haves and have-nots*

haven /'hayv(ə)n/ *n* 1 a harbour, port 2 a place of safety or refuge

,**have 'on** *v* 1 to be wearing 2 to have plans for 3 *chiefly Br* to deceive, tease – infml

haversack /'havə,sak/ *n* a knapsack

,**have 'up** *v* to bring before the authorities – infml

havoc /'havək/ *n* 1 widespread destruction; devastation 2 great confusion and disorder

haw /haw/ *n* (a berry of) hawthorn

¹**hawk** /hawk/ *n* 1 any of numerous medium-sized birds of prey that have (short) rounded wings and long tails 2 one who takes a militant attitude; a supporter of a warlike policy – ~**ish** *adj* – ~**ishness** *n*

²**hawk** *v* to hunt game with a trained hawk – ~**er** *n*

³**hawk** *v* to offer for sale in the street

⁴**hawk** *v* to utter a harsh guttural sound (as if) in clearing the throat

hawser /'hawzə/ *n* a large rope

hawthorn /'haw,thawn/ *n* any of a genus of spring-flowering spiny shrubs of the rose family with white or pink flowers and small red fruits

hay /hay/ *n* herbage, esp grass, mowed and cured for fodder

'hay ,fever *n* nasal catarrh and swollen eyes occurring usu in the spring and summer through allergy to pollen

'hay,stack *n* a relatively large sometimes thatched outdoor pile of hay

'hay,wire *adj* 1 out of order 2 emotionally or mentally upset; crazy *USE* infml

¹hazard /'hazəd/ *n* 1 a game of chance played with 2 dice 2a a risk, peril b a source of danger 3 a golf-course obstacle (e g a bunker)

²hazard *v* 1 to expose to danger 2 to venture, risk

hazardous /'hazədəs/ *adj* 1 depending on hazard or chance 2 involving or exposing one to risk – ~**ly** *adv* – ~**ness** *n*

haze /hayz/ *n* 1 vapour, dust, smoke, etc causing a slight decrease in the air's transparency 2 vagueness or confusion of mental perception

hazel /'hayzl/ *n* 1 (the wood or nut of) any of a genus of shrubs or small trees bearing nuts 2 a yellowish light to strong brown colour

hazy /'hayzi/ *adj* 1 obscured, cloudy 2 vague, indefinite – -**zily** *adv* – -**ziness** *n*

'H-,bomb *n* a hydrogen bomb

¹he /(h)i, ee; *strong* hee/ *pron* 1 that male person or creature who is neither speaker nor hearer – + cap in reference to God 2 – used in a generic sense or when the sex of the person is unspecified

²he *n* 1 a male person or creature 2 the player in a children's game who must catch others; it

¹head /hed/ *n*, *pl* **heads**, (4b) **head** 1 the upper or foremost division of the body containing the brain, the chief sense organs, and the mouth 2a the seat of the intellect; the mind b natural aptitude or talent c mental or emotional control; composure 3 the obverse of a coin – usu pl with sing. meaning 4a a person, individual b a single individual (domestic animal) out of a number – usu pl 5a the end that is upper, higher, or opposite the foot b the source of a stream, river, etc 6 a director, leader 6a a school principal b one in charge of a department in an institution 7 the part of a plant bearing a compact mass of leaves, fruits, flowers, etc 8 the leading part of a military column, procession, etc 9a the uppermost extremity or projecting part of an object; the top b the striking part of a weapon, tool, implement, etc 10 a mass of water in motion 11 (the pressure resulting from) the difference in height between 2 points in a body of liquid 12a (parts adjacent to) the bow of a ship b a (ship's) toilet – usu pl with sing. meaning in British English 13 a measure of length equivalent to a head 14 the place of leadership, honour, or command 15a a word often in larger letters placed above a passage in order to introduce or categorize b a separate part or topic 16 the foam or froth that rises on a fermenting or effervescing liquid 17a the part of a boil, pimple, etc at which it is likely to break b a culminating point; a crisis – esp in *come to a head* 18a a part of a machine or machine tool containing a device (e g a cutter or drill); *also* the part of an apparatus that performs the function of a particular device b any of at least 2 electromagnetic components which bear on the magnetic tape in a tape recorder, such that one can erase recorded material if desired and another may either record or play back — **off one's head** crazy, mad — **over someone's head** 1 beyond sby's comprehension 2 so as to pass over sby's superior standing or authority

²head *adj* 1 principal, chief 2 situated at the head

³head *v* 1 to cut back or off the upper growth of (a plant) 2a to provide with or form a head b to form the head or top of 3 to be at the head of; lead 4a to put sthg at the head of (e g a list); *also* to provide with a heading b to stand as the first or leading member of 5 (e g a soccer ball) with the head 6 to point or proceed in a specified direction

headache /'hedayk/ *n* 1 pain in the head 2 a difficult situation or problem – -**achy** *adj*

'head,band *n* a band worn round the head, esp to keep hair out of the eyes

'head,board *n* a board forming the head (e g of a bed)

'head,dress *n* an often elaborate covering for the head

header /'hedə/ *n* 1 a brick or stone laid in a wall with its end towards the face of the wall 2 a headfirst fall or dive 3 a shot or pass in soccer made by heading the ball

,head'first *adv* with the head foremost; headlong

heading /'heding/ *n* 1 the compass direction in which a ship or aircraft points 2 an inscription, headline, or title standing at the top or beginning (e g of a letter or chapter)

headland /'hedland/ *n* 1 unploughed land near an edge of a field 2 a point of usu high land jutting out into a body of water

'head,light *n* (the beam cast by) the main light mounted on the front of a motor vehicle

'head,line *n* a title printed in large type above a newspaper story or article; *also*, *pl*, *Br* a summary given at the beginning or end of a news broadcast

'head,long *adv* or *adj* 1 headfirst 2 without thought or deliberation 3 without pause or delay

'headman /-mən/ *n* a chief of a primitive community

,head'master, *fem* **,head'mistress** *n* one who heads the staff of a school

head off *v* to stop the progress of or turn aside by taking preventive action; block

,head-'on *adv* or *adj* 1 with the head or front making the initial contact 2 in direct opposition

'head,phone *n* an earphone held over the ear by a band worn on the head – usu pl

,head'quarters *n, pl* **headquarters** **1** a place from which a commander exercises command *USE* often pl with sing. meaning

'head,rest *n* a support for the head; *esp* a cushioned pad supporting the head in a vehicle

'headroom /-,room, -roohm/ *n* vertical space (e g beneath a bridge) sufficient to allow passage or unrestricted movement

'headship /-ship/ *n* the position or office of a head (e g a headmaster); leadership

'head,strong *adj* wilful, obstinate

'head,way /-,way/ *n* (rate of) motion in a forward direction **a** advance, progress **2** headroom

'head,wind /-,wind/ *n* a wind blowing in a direction opposite to a course, esp of a ship or aircraft

heady /'hedi/ *adj* **1** violent, impetuous **2** (tending to make) giddy or exhilarated; intoxicating

heal /heel/ *v* **1a** to make sound or whole **b** to restore to health **2** to restore to a sound or normal state; mend – ~**er** *n*

health /helth/ *n* **1a** soundness of body, mind, or spirit **b** the general condition of the body **2** condition; *esp* a sound or flourishing condition; well-being

'healthful /-f(ə)l/ *adj* beneficial to health of body or mind

healthy /'helthi/ *adj* **1** enjoying or showing health and vigour of body, mind, or spirit **2** conducive to good health **3** prosperous, flourishing – **healthily** *adv* – **healthiness** *n*

¹heap /heep/ *n* **1** a collection of things lying one on top of another; a pile **2** a great number or large quantity; a lot – infml; often pl with sing. meaning

²heap *v* **1a** to throw or lay in a heap; pile *up* **b** to form or round into a heap **2** to supply abundantly *with*; *also* to bestow lavishly or in large quantities *upon*

hear /hiə/ *v* **heard** /huhd/ **1** to perceive or have the capacity of perceiving (sound) with the ear **2** to learn or gain information (by hearing) **3** to listen to with attention; heed **4** to give a legal hearing to — **hear from** to receive a communication from — **hear of** to entertain the idea of — usu neg

hearing /'hiəring/ *n* **1a** the one of the 5 basic physical senses by which waves received by the ear are interpreted by the brain as sounds varying in pitch, intensity, and timbre **b** earshot **2a** an opportunity to be heard **b** a trial in court

hearken /'hahkən/ *v* to listen *to*; *also* to heed – poetic

hearsay /'hiə,say/ *n* sthg heard from another; rumour

hearse /huhs/ *n* a vehicle for transporting a dead body in its coffin

heart /haht/ *n* **1a** a hollow muscular organ that by its rhythmic contraction acts as a force pump maintaining the circulation of the blood **b** the breast, bosom **c** sthg resembling a heart in shape; *specif* a conventionalized representation of a heart **2a** a playing card marked with l or more red heart-shaped figures **b** pl *but sing or pl in constr* the suit comprising cards identified by this figure **3a** humane disposition; compassion **b** love, affections **c** courage, spirit **4** one's innermost character or feelings **5a** the central or innermost part (of a lettuce, cabbage, etc) **b** the essential or most vital part — **by heart** by rote or from memory

'heart,ache *n* mental anguish; sorrow

'heart at,tack *n* an instance of abnormal functioning of the heart; *esp* coronary thrombosis

'heart,beat *n* a single complete pulse of the heart

'heart,break *n* intense grief or distress

'heart,breaking *adj* **1** causing intense sorrow or distress **2** extremely trying or difficult – ~**ly** *adv*

'heart,broken *adj* overcome by sorrow

'heart,burn *n* a burning pain behind the lower part of the breastbone usu resulting from spasm of the stomach or throat muscles

hearten /'hahtn/ *v* to cheer, encourage

'heart,felt *adj* deeply felt; earnest

hearth /hahth/ *n* **1** a brick, stone, or cement area in front of the floor of a fireplace **2** home, fireside

'heartless /-lis/ *adj* unfeeling, cruel – ~**ly** *adv* – ~**ness** *n*

'heart,rending *adj* heartbreaking – ~**ly** *adv*

'heart,sick *adj* very despondent; depressed

'heart,strings *n pl* the deepest emotions or affections

'heart,throb *n* one who is the object of or arouses infatuation

¹heart-to-'heart *adj* sincere and intimate

²heart-to-heart *n* a frank or intimate talk – infml

'heart,warming *adj* inspiring sympathetic feeling; cheering – ~**ly** *adv*

'heart,wood *n* the older harder nonliving central wood in a tree

hearty /'hahti/ *adj* **1a** jovial **b** unrestrained, vigorous **2a** robustly healthy **b** substantial, abundant

¹heat /heet/ *v* to make or become warm or hot – often + *up*

²heat *n* **1a** the condition of being hot; warmth; *also* a marked degree of this **b** excessively high bodily temperature **c** any of a series of degrees of heating **2a** intensity of feeling or reaction **b** the height or stress of an action or condition **c** readiness for sexual intercourse in a female animal – usu in *on heat* or (*chiefly NAm*) *in heat* **3** pungency of flavour **4a** a single round of a contest that has 2 or more rounds for each contestant **b** any of several preliminary contests whose winners go into the final **5** pressure, coercion – slang

heated /'heetid/ *adj* marked by anger – ~**ly** *adv*

heater /'heetə/ n a device that gives off heat or holds sthg to be heated

heath /heeth/ n 1 any of various related evergreen plants that thrive on barren usu acid soil, with whorls of needlelike leaves and clusters of small flowers 2a a tract of wasteland b a large area of level uncultivated land usu with poor peaty soil and bad drainage

heathen /'heedh(9)n/ n pl **heathens, heathen** 1 an unconverted member of a people or nation that does not acknowledge the God of the Bible – often pl + the 2 an uncivilized or irreligious person – ~**ish** adj – ~**dom** n

heather /'hedhə/ n a (common usu purplish-pink flowered northern) heath

'heat ,rash n prickly heat

'heat ,wave n a period of unusually hot weather

¹**heave** /heev/ v **heaved, hove** /hohv/ 1 to lift upwards or forwards, esp with effort 2 to throw, cast 3 to utter with obvious effort 4 to cause to swell or rise 5 to haul, draw 6 to rise and fall rhythmically 7 to vomit 8 to pull — **heave in/into sight** to come into view

²**heave** n 1a an effort to heave or raise b a throw, cast 2 an upward motion; esp a rhythmical rising

heaven /'hev(ə)n/ n 1 (any of the spheres of) the expanse of space that surrounds the earth like a dome; the firmament – usu pl with sing. meaning 2 often cap the dwelling place of God, his angels, and the spirits of those who have received salvation; Paradise 3 a place or condition of utmost happiness

'heavenly /-li/ adj 1 of heaven or the heavens; celestial 2a suggesting the blessed state of heaven; divine b delightful – infml

heaven-'sent adj providential

heave 'to v to bring (a ship) to a stop with head to wind

¹**heavy** /'hevi/ adj 1 having great weight in proportion to size 2 hard to bear; specif grievous 3 of weighty import; serious 4 emotionally intense; profound 5 oppressed; burdened 6 lacking sparkle or vivacity; slow, dull 7 dulled with weariness; drowsy 8a of an unusually large amount b of great force c overcast d of ground or soil full of clay and inclined to hold water; impeding motion e loud and deep f laborious, difficult g of large capacity or output h consuming in large quantities – usu + on 9a digested with difficulty, usu because of excessive richness b esp of bread not sufficiently raised or leavened 10 producing heavy usu large goods (e g coal, steel, or machinery) often used in the production of other goods 11a of the larger variety b heavily armoured, armed, or equipped 12 of rock music loud and strongly rhythmic – slang – ~**ily** adv – ~**viness** n — **with a heavy hand** 1 with little mercy; sternly 2 without grace; clumsily

²**heavy** adv in a heavy manner; heavily

³**heavy** n 1 pl units (e g of bombers, artillery, or cavalry) of the heavy sort 2a (an actor playing) a villain b sby of importance or significance – infml 3 one hired to compel or deter by means of threats or physical violence – slang

,heavy-'duty adj able or designed to withstand unusual strain or wear

,heavy-'handed adj 1 clumsy, awkward 2 oppressive, harsh – ~**ly** adv – ~**ness** n

,heavy'hearted adj despondent, melancholy

'heavy,weight n 1 sby or sthg above average weight 2 one in the usu heaviest class of contestants; specif a boxer whose weight is not limited if he is professional or is more than 81kg (about 12st 10lb) if he is amateur 3 an important or influential person

Hebraic /hi'brayik/, **Hebraistic** /,heebray'istik/ adj of the Hebrews, their culture, or Hebrew

Hebrew /'heebrooh/ n 1 a member or descendant of any of a group of N Semitic peoples including the Israelites; esp an Israelite 2 the Semitic language of the ancient Hebrews; also a later form of Hebrew

heck /hek/ n hell – used as an interjection or intensive

heckle /'hekl/ v **heckling** /'hekling/ to harass and try to disconcert (e g a speaker) with questions, challenges, or gibes – ~**r** n

hectare /'hektah/ n (a measure of land which equals) 10,000 square metres

hectic /'hektik/ adj filled with excitement or feverish activity – ~**ally** adv

hedge /hej/ n 1a a boundary formed by a dense row of shrubs or low trees b a barrier, limit 2 a means of protection or defence (e g against financial loss) 3 a calculatedly noncommittal or evasive statement

²**hedge** v 1 to enclose or protect (as if) with a hedge 2 to hem in or obstruct (as if) with a barrier; hinder 3 to protect oneself against losing (e g a bet), esp by making counterbalancing transactions 4 to plant, form, or trim a hedge 5 to avoid committing oneself to a definite course of action, esp by making evasive statements

hedgehog /'hej,hog/ n any of a genus of small Old World spine-covered insect-eating mammals that are active at night

'hedge,hop v **-pp-** to fly an aircraft close to the ground and rise over obstacles as they appear – ~**per** n

'hedge,row /-,roh/ n a row of shrubs or trees surrounding a field

hedonism /'heda,niz(a)m, 'hee-/ n (conduct based on) the doctrine that personal pleasure is the sole or chief good – **-ist** n – **-istic** adj

heebie-jeebies /,heebi 'jeebiz/ n pl the jitters, willies – infml

¹**heed** /heed/ v to pay attention (to)

²**heed** n attention, notice – ~**ful(ly)** adj (adv) – ~ **fulness** n – ~**less(ly)** adj (adv)

¹**heel** /'heel/ n **1** (the back part of the hind limb of a vertebrate corresponding to) the back of the human foot below the ankle and behind the arch or an anatomical structure resembling this **2** either of the crusty ends of a loaf of bread **3** the part of a garment or an article of footwear that covers or supports the human heel **4a** the lower end of a mast **b** the base of a tuber or cutting of a plant used for propagation **5** a backward kick with the heel in rugby, esp from a set scrum **6** a contemptible person – slang — **down a/the heel** in or into a run-down or shabby condition — **on the heels of** immediately following; closely behind — **to heel 1** close behind – usu used in training a dog **2** into agreement or line; under control

²**heel** v **1** to supply with a heel; esp to renew the heel of **2** to exert pressure on, propel, or strike (as if) with the heel; specif to kick (a rugby ball) with the heel, esp out of a scrum

³**heel** v to tilt to one side

⁴**heel** n (the extent of) a tilt to one side

hefty /'heftí/ adj **1** large or bulky and usu heavy **2** powerful, mighty **3** impressively large — **heftily** adv

hegemony /hi'gemǝni/ n domination by one nation, group, etc over others

heifer /'hefǝ/ n a young cow (that has at most 1 calf)

heigh-ho /'hay ,hoh/ interj – used to express boredom, weariness, or sadness

height /hiet/ n **1** the highest or most extreme point; the zenith **2a** the distance from the bottom to the top of sthg standing upright **b** the elevation above a level **3** the condition of being tall or high **4a** a piece of land (e g a hill or plateau) rising to a considerable degree above the surrounding country – usu pl with sing. meaning **b** a high point or position

heighten /'hiet(ǝ)n/ v **1a** to increase the amount or degree of; augment **b** to deepen, intensify **2** to raise high or higher; elevate **3** to become great or greater in amount, degree, or extent

heinous /'haynǝs, 'heenǝs/ adj abominable – ~ **ly** adj – ~ **ness** n

heir /eǝ/ n **1** sby who inherits or is entitled to succeed to an estate or rank **2** sby who receives or is entitled to receive some position, role, or quality passed on from a parent or predecessor

heir ap'parent n, pl **heirs apparent** one whose succession, esp to a position or role, appears certain under existing circumstances

'**heir,loom** /-loohm/ n **1** a piece of valuable property handed down within a family for generations **2** sthg of special value handed on from one generation to another

held /held/ past of **hold**

helicopter /'heli,koptǝ/ n an aircraft which derives both lift and propulsive power from a set of horizontally rotating rotors or vanes and is capable of vertical takeoff and landing

heliport /'heli,pawt/ n a place for helicopters to take off and land

helium /'heeli-ǝm, -lyǝm/ n a noble gaseous element found in natural gases and used esp for inflating balloons and in low-temperature research

helix /'heeliks/ n, pl **helices** /'heli,seez/ also **helixes 1** sthg spiral in form (e g a coil formed by winding wire round a uniform tube) **2** the rim curved inwards of the external ear

hell /hel/ n **1a** the nether world (e g Hades or Sheol) inhabited by the spirits of the dead **b** the nether realm of the devil in which the souls of those excluded from Paradise undergo perpetual torment **2** a place or state of torment, misery, chaos, or wickedness — **for the hell of it** for the intrinsic amusement or satisfaction of an activity — **hell to pay** serious trouble — **like hell 1** very hard or much **2** — used to intensify denial of a statement; slang — **what the hell** it doesn't matter

hell-'bent adj stubbornly and often recklessly determined

Hellene /'heleen/ n Greek

Hellenic /he'lenik, -'leenik, hǝ-/ adj of Greece, its people, or its language

¹**hellish** /'helish/ adj of, resembling, or befitting hell; diabolical

²**hellish** adv extremely, damnably

hello /he'loh, 'heloh, hǝ-/ n, pl **hellos** an expression or gesture of greeting

¹**helm** /helm/ n **1** a tiller or wheel controlling the steering of a ship **2** the position of control; the head

²**helm** v to steer (as if) with a helm

helmet /'helmit/ n **1** a covering or enclosing headpiece of ancient or medieval armour **2** any of various protective head coverings, esp made of a hard material to resist impact **3** sthg, esp a hood-shaped petal or sepal, resembling a helmet

helmsman /'helmzmǝn/ n the person at the helm

helot /'helǝt/ n **1** cap a serf in ancient Sparta **2** a serf, slave

¹**help** /help/ v **1** to give assistance or support to **2** to remedy, relieve **3a** to be of use to; benefit **b** to further the advancement of; promote **4a** to keep from occurring; prevent **b** to restrain (oneself) from taking action **5** to serve with food or drink, esp at a meal **6** to appropriate sthg for (oneself), esp dishonestly **7** to be of use or benefit — **help somebody on/off with** to help sby take off/put on (an article of clothing)

²**help** n **1** aid, assistance **2** remedy, relief **3a** sby, esp a woman, hired to do work, esp housework **b** the services of a paid worker; also, chiefly NAm the workers providing such services

'helpful /-f(ə)l/ *adj* of service or assistance; useful – **~ly** *adv* – **~ness** *n*

helping /'helping/ *n* a serving of food

'helpless /-lis/ *adj* **1** lacking protection or support; defenceless **2** lacking strength or effectiveness; powerless – **~ly** *adv* – **~ness** *n*

'help,mate *n* one who is a companion and helper; *esp* a spouse

help out *v* to give assistance or aid (to), esp when in great difficulty

¹helter-skelter /,heltə 'skeltə/ *adj or adv* (done) in a hurried and disorderly manner

²helter-'skelter *n* a spiral slide at a fairground

¹hem /hem/ *n* **1** the border of a cloth article when turned back and stitched down; *esp* the bottom edge of a garment finished in this manner **2** a similar border on an article of plastic, leather, etc

²hem *v* **-mm- 1a** to finish (e g a skirt) with a hem **b** to border, edge **2** to enclose, confine – usu + *in* or *about* **3** to make a hem in sewing

'he-,man /'hee/ *n* a strong virile man – *infml*

hemisphere /'hemi,sfiə/ *n* **1a** a half of the celestial sphere when divided into 2 halves by the horizon, the celestial equator, or the ecliptic **b** the northern or southern half of the earth divided by the equator or the eastern or western half divided by a meridian **2** either of the 2 half spheres formed by a plane that passes through the sphere's centre

hemline /'hem,lien/ *n* the line formed by the lower hemmed edge of a garment, esp a dress

hemlock /'hemlok/ *n* **1** (a poison obtained from) a very tall plant of the carrot family or a related very poisonous plant **2** (the soft light wood of) any of a genus of evergreen coniferous trees of the pine family

hemp /hemp/ *n* **1** (marijuana, hashish, or a similar drug obtained from) a tall widely cultivated plant from which a tough fibre used esp for making rope is prepared **2** the fibre of hemp or (a plant yielding) a similar fibre (e g jute)

¹hen /hen/ *n* **1a** a female bird, specif a domestic fowl (over a year old) **b** a female lobster, crab, fish, or other aquatic animal **2** an esp fussy woman – *infml* **3** *chiefly Scot* dear – used to girls and women

²hen *adj* relating to or intended for women only

hence /hens/ *adv* **1** from this time; later than now **2** because of a preceding fact or premise **3** from here; away – *fml*; sometimes + *from*; sometimes used as an interjection

,hence'forth *adv* from this time or point on

henchman /'henchmən/ *n* a trusted follower; a right-hand man

¹henna /'henə/ *n* **1** an Old World tropical shrub or small tree with fragrant white flowers **2** a reddish brown dye obtained from the leaves of the henna plant and used esp on hair

henpecked /'hen,pekt/ *adj* cowed by persistent nagging

hepatic /hi'patik/ *adj* of or resembling the liver

hepatitis /,hepə'tietəs/ *n pl* **hepatitides** /-'titdeez/ (a condition marked by) inflammation of the liver

¹her /hə, ə; *strong* huh/ *adj* of her or herself, esp as possessor, agent, or object of an action – used in titles of females (e g *her* Majesty)

²her *pron, objective case of* **she** (e g older than *her*; that's *her*)

herald /'herəld/ *n* **1a** an officer whose original duties of officiating at tournaments gave rise to other duties (e g recording names, pedigrees, and coats of arms or tracing genealogies) **b** an official messenger between leaders, esp in war **2a** an official crier or messenger **b** sby or sthg that conveys news or proclaims **3** a harbinger, forerunner

heraldry /'herəldri/ *n* **1** the system of identifying individuals by hereditary insignia **2** the study of the history, display, and description of heraldry and heraldic insignia **3** pageantry – **-dic** *adj*

herb /huhb/ *n* **1** a seed plant that does not develop permanent woody tissue and dies down at the end of a growing season **2** a plant (part) valued for its medicinal, savoury, or aromatic qualities

herbaceous /huh'bayshəs/ *adj* of, being, or having the characteristics of a (part of a) herb

'herbalist /-ist/ *n* sby who grows or sells herbs, esp for medicines

herbivore /'huhbivaw/ *n* a plant-eating animal – **-vorous** *adj*

herculean /,huhkyoo'lee-ən/ *adj* of extraordinary strength, size, or difficulty

¹herd /huhd/ *n* **1** a number of animals of 1 kind kept together or living as a group **2a** *sing or pl in constr* a group of people usu having a common bond – often derog **b** *the* masses – derog

²herd *v* **1** to keep or move (animals) together **2** to gather, lead, or drive as if in a herd

'herdsman /-mən/ *n* a manager, breeder, or tender of livestock

¹here /hiə/ *adv* **1** in or at this place – often interjectional, esp in answering a roll call **2** at or in this point or particular (e g here we agree) **3** to this place or position (e g come *here*) **4** – used when introducing, offering, or drawing attention (e g *here* she comes) **5** – used interjectionally to attract attention — **here goes** – used to express resolution at the outset of a bold act; *infml* — **here's to** — used when drinking a toast — **here, there, and everywhere** scattered lavishly about — **here we go again** the same distressing events are repeating themselves — **here you are 1** here is what you wanted **2** you have arrived — **neither here nor there** of no consequence; irrelevant

²here *adj* **1** – used for emphasis, esp after a demonstrative (e g this book *here*) **2** – used for emphasis between a demonstrative and the following noun; substandard (e g this *here* book)

³here *n* this place or point

'herea,bouts /-ə‚bowts/ *adv* in this vicinity

¹here'after /-'ahftə/ *adv* 1 after this 2 in some future time or state

²here'after *n, often cap* 1 the future 2 an existence beyond earthly life

hereby /hiə'bie, 'hiə-/ *adv* by this means or pronouncement

hereditary /hi'redit(ə)ri/ *adj* 1a genetically transmitted or transmissible from parent to offspring b characteristic of one's predecessors; ancestral 2a received or passing by inheritance b having title through inheritance 3 traditional 4 of inheritance or heredity – **-rily** *adv*

heredity /hi'rediti/ *n* 1 the sum of the qualities and potentialities genetically derived from one's ancestors 2 the transmission of qualities from ancestor to descendant through a mechanism lying primarily in the chromosomes

heresy /'herəsi/ *n* 1 (adherence to) a religious belief or doctrine contrary to or incompatible with an explicit church dogma 2 an opinion or doctrine contrary to generally accepted belief

heretic /'herətik/ *n* 1 a dissenter from established church dogma; *esp* a baptized member of the Roman Catholic church who disavows a revealed truth 2 one who dissents from an accepted belief or doctrine – **~al** *adj* – **~ally** *adv*

herewith /hiə'widh/ *adv* 1 hereby 2 with this; enclosed in this – *fml*

heritable /'heritəbl/ *adj* 1 capable of being inherited 2 hereditary

heritage /'heritij/ *n* 1 sthg transmitted by or acquired from a predecessor; a legacy 2 a birthright

hermaphrodite /huh'mafrədiet/ *n* 1 an animal or plant having both male and female reproductive organs 2 sthg that is a combination of 2 usu opposing elements – **-ditic** *adj*

hermetic /huh'metik/ *also* hermetical /-kl/ *adj* 1a airtight b impervious to external influences 2 *often cap* abstruse, obscure – *infml* – **~ally** *adv*

hermit /'huhmit/ *n* 1 one who retires from society and lives in solitude, esp for religious reasons 2 a recluse

'hermitage /-tij/ *n* 1 the habitation of one or more hermits 2 a secluded place or private retreat; a hideaway

hernia /'huhni-ə, -nyə/ *n, pl* hernias, herniae /-ni,ee/ a protrusion of (part of) an organ through a wall of its enclosing cavity (e g the abdomen)

hero /'hiəroh/ *n, pl* heroes 1a a mythological or legendary figure often of divine descent endowed with great strength or ability b an illustrious warrior c a person, esp a man, admired for noble achievements and qualities (e g courage) 2 the principal (male) character in a literary or dramatic work

heroic /hi'roh·ik/ *also* heroical /-kl/ *adj* 1 of or befitting heroes 2a showing or marked by courage b grand, noble – **~ally** *adv*

heroics *n pl* extravagantly grand behaviour or language

heroin /'heroh·in/ *n* a strongly physiologically addictive narcotic made from, but more potent than, morphine

heroism /'heroh,iz(ə)m/ *n* heroic conduct or qualities; *esp* extreme courage

heron /'herən/ *n, pl* herons, *esp collectively* heron any of various long-necked long-legged wading birds with a long tapering bill, large wings, and soft plumage

herpes /'huhpeez/ *n* an inflammatory virus disease of the skin and esp the genitals

herring /'hering/ *n,* a N Atlantic food fish that is preserved in the adult state by smoking or salting

¹'herring,bone /-,bohn/ *n* 1 (sthg arranged in) a pattern made up of rows of parallel lines with any 2 adjacent rows slanting in opposite directions; *esp* a twilled fabric decorated with this pattern

²herringbone *v* 1 to make a herringbone pattern on 2 to ascend a (snow) slope by pointing the toes of the skis out

hers /huhz/ *pron, pl* hers that which or the one who belongs to her – used without a following noun as a pronoun equivalent in meaning to the adjective *her* (e g the car is *hers*)

herself /hə'self; *medially often* ə-/ *pron* 1 that identical female person or creature used reflexively, for emphasis, or in absolute constructions (e g *herself* an orphan, she understood the situation) 2 her normal self (e g isn't quite *herself*)

hertz /huhts/ *n, pl* hertz the SI unit of frequency equal to 1 cycle per second

hesitant /'hezit(ə)nt/ *adj* tending to hesitate; irresolute – **~ly** *adv*

hesitate /'hezitayt/ *v* 1 to hold back, esp in doubt or indecision 2 to be reluctant or unwilling *to* 3 to stammer – **-tating** *adj* – **-tion** *n*

hessian /'hesi·ən/ *n* 1 a coarse heavy plain-weave fabric, usu of jute or hemp, used esp for sacking 2 a lightweight material resembling hessian and used chiefly in interior decoration

heterogeneous /,hetərə'jeeni·əs, -nyəs/ *adj* consisting of dissimilar ingredients or constituents; disparate – **~ly** *adv* – **-neity** *n*

hetero'sexual /-'seksyoo(ə)l, -sh(ə)l/ *adj or n* (of or being) sby having a sexual preference for members of the opposite sex – **~ly** *adv* – **~ity** *n*

het 'up *adj* highly excited; upset – *infml*

hew /hyooh/ *v* hewed; hewed, hewn /hyoohn/ 1 to strike, chop, or esp fell with blows of a heavy cutting instrument 2 to give form or shape to (as if) with heavy cutting blows – often + *out*

hexagon /'heksəgən/ *n* a polygon of 6 angles and 6 sides – **~al** *adj*

hey /hay/ *interj* – used esp to call attention or to express inquiry, surprise, or exultation

heyday /'hay,day/ *n* the period of one's greatest vigour, prosperity, or fame

hey presto /,hay 'presto/ *interj* – used as an expression of triumph or satisfaction on completing or demonstrating sthg; *esp* used by conjurers about to reveal the outcome of a trick

hi /hie/ *interj* – used esp to attract attention or, esp in the USA, as a greeting

¹**hiatus** /hie'aytəs/ *n* **1a** a break, gap **b** an (abnormal) anatomical gap or passage **2** a lapse in continuity

²**hiatus** *adj* **1** involving a hiatus **2** *of a hernia* protruding upwards through the diaphragm

hibernate /'hiebənayt/ *v* **1** to pass the winter in a torpid or resting state **2** to be or become inactive or dormant – **-nation** *n*

hiccup *also* **hiccough** /'hikup/ *n* **1** an involuntary spasmodic intake of breath with a characteristic sound **2** a snag, hitch – **hiccup** *v*

hickory /'hikəri/ *n* (the usu tough pale wood of) any of a genus of N American hardwood trees of the walnut family that often have sweet edible nuts

¹**hide** /hied/ *v* **hid** /hid/, **hidden** /hid(ə)n/, **hid 1** to put out of sight; conceal **2** to keep secret **3** to screen from view **4** to conceal oneself **5** to remain out of sight – often + *out*

²**hide** *n*, *chiefly Br* a camouflaged hut or other shelter used for observation, esp of wildlife or game

³**hide** *n* the raw or dressed skin of an animal – used esp with reference to large heavy skins

'**hide-and-,seek** *n* a children's game in which one player covers his/her eyes and then hunts for the other players who have hidden themselves

'**hide,bound** /-,bownd/ *adj* narrow or inflexible in character

hideous /'hidi·əs/ *adj* **1** exceedingly ugly **2** morally offensive; shocking – ~**ly** *adv* – ~**ness** *n*

'**hiding** /'hieding/ *n* a state or place of concealment

²**hiding** *n* a beating, thrashing; also a severe defeat – *infml*

hie /hie/ *v* **hying, hieing** *archaic* to hurry

hierarchy /'hie·ərahki, 'hiə-/ *n* **1** (church government by) a body of clergy organized according to rank, specif the bishops of a province or nation **2** a graded or ranked series – **-chical** *adj* – **-chically** *adv*

hieroglyph /'hie·ərə,glif, 'hiərə-/ *n* a pictorial character used in some writing systems (e g by the ancient Egyptians) – ~**ic** *adj* – ~**ics** *n*

hi-fi /'hie ,fie, ,hie 'fie/ *n* **1** high fidelity **2** equipment for the high-fidelity reproduction of sound *USE* infml

higgledy-piggledy /,higldi 'pigldi/ *adv* in confusion; topsy-turvy – *infml*

¹**high** /hie/ *adj* **1a** extending upwards for a considerable or above average distance **b** situated at a considerable height above a base (e g the ground) **c** *of physical activity* extending to or from, or taking place at a considerable height above, a base (e g the ground or water) **d** having a specified elevation; tall – often in combination **2** at the period of culmination or fullest development **3** elevated in pitch **4** relatively far from the equator **5** *of meat, esp game* slightly decomposed or tainted **6a** exalted in character; noble **b** good, favourable **7** of greater degree, amount, cost, value, or content than average **8a** foremost in rank, dignity, or standing **b** critical, climactic **c** marked by sublime or heroic events or subject matter **9** forcible, strong **10a** showing elation or excitement **b** intoxicated by alcohol or a drug **11** *of a gear* designed for fast speed — **on one's high horse** stubbornly or disdainfully proud

²**high** *adv* at or to a high place, altitude, or degree

³**high** *n* **1** a region of high atmospheric pressure **2** a high point or level; a height — **on high** in or to a high place, esp heaven

,**high-and-'mighty** *adj* arrogant, imperious

,**high'born** /-'bawn/ *adj* of noble birth

'**high,brow** /-,brow/ *adj* dealing with, possessing, or having pretensions to superior intellectual and cultural interests or activities

'**high ,chair** *n* a child's chair with long legs, a footrest, and usu a feeding tray

,**high-'class** *adj* superior, first-class

,**high com'missioner** *n* a principal commissioner; *esp* an ambassadorial representative of one Commonwealth country stationed in another

,**High 'Court** *n* the lower branch of the Supreme Court of Judicature of England and Wales

,**higher edu'cation** *n* education beyond the secondary level, at a college or university

,**highfa'lutin** /-fə'loohtin/ *adj* pretentious, pompous – *infml*

high fidelity *n* the faithful reproduction of sound

,**high-'flier, high-flyer** *n* a person of extreme ambition or outstanding promise

,**high-'handed** *adj* overbearingly arbitrary – ~**ly** *adv* – ~**ness** *n*

'**high ,jump** *n* (an athletic field event consisting of) a jump for height over a bar suspended between uprights — **for the high jump** about to receive a severe reprimand or punishment

highland /'hielənd/ *n* high or mountainous land – usu pl with sing. meaning

Highland *adj* relating to or being a member of a shaggy long-haired breed of hardy beef cattle

,**high-'level** *adj* **1** occurring, done, or placed at a high level **2** of high importance or rank

'**high ,life** *n* luxurious living associated with the rich

hi

¹**high light** /-ˌliet/ n **1** the lightest spot or area (e g in a painting or photograph) **2** an event or detail of special significance or interest **3** a contrasting brighter part in the hair or on the face that reflects or gives the appearance of reflecting light

²**high light** v **1** to focus attention on; emphasize **2** to emphasize (e g a figure) with light tones in painting, photography, etc

highly /'hieli/ adv **1** to a high degree; extremely **2** with approval; favourably

ˌhighly-'strung, high-strung adj extremely nervous or sensitive

ˌhigh-'minded adj having or marked by elevated principles and feelings – ~ly adv – ~ness n

Highness /'hienis/ n – used as a title for a person of exalted rank (e g a king or prince)

ˌhigh-'powered also high-power adj having great drive, energy, or capacity; dynamic

ˌhigh-'pressure adj **1** having or involving a (comparatively) high pressure, esp greatly exceeding that of the atmosphere **2a** using, involving, or being aggressive and insistent sales techniques **b** imposing or involving severe strain or tension

ˌhigh 'priest n **1** a chief priest, esp of the ancient Jewish priesthood **2** the head or chief exponent of a movement

ˌhigh-'rise adj (situated in a building) constructed with a large number of storeys

'high road /-ˌrohd/ n, chiefly Br a main road

'high school n, chiefly Br a secondary school; esp a grammar school – now chiefly in names

ˌhigh-'spirited adj characterized by a bold or lively spirit; also highly-strung

'high street n, Br a main or principal street, esp containing shops

ˌhigh 'tea n, Br a fairly substantial early evening meal (at which tea is served)

high technology n technology using or producing the most advanced devices (e g in microelectronics)

ˌhigh-'water ˌmark n **1** a mark showing the highest level reached by the surface of a body of water **2** the highest point or stage

'high way /-ˌway/ n a public way; esp a main direct road

ˌhighway 'code n, often cap H&C, Br the official code of rules and advice for the safe use of roads

'highwayman /-mən/ n a (mounted) robber of travellers on a road, esp in former times

hijack, high-jack /'hiejak/ v **1a** to stop and steal from (a vehicle in transit) **b** to seize control of, and often divert, (a means of transport) by force **2** to steal, rob, or kidnap as if by hijacking – **hijack** n – ~er n – ~ing n

¹**hike** /hiek/ v to go on a hike – **hiker** n – **hiking** n

²**hike** n **1** a long walk in the country, esp for pleasure or exercise **2** chiefly NAm an increase or rise

hilarious /hi'leəri-əs/ adj marked by or causing hilarity – ~ly adv – ~ness n

hilarity /hi'laroti/ n mirth, merriment

¹**hill** /hil/ n **1** a usu rounded natural rise of land lower than a mountain **2** an artificial heap or mound (e g of earth) **3** an esp steep slope — **over the hill** past one's prime; too old

²**hill** v to draw earth round the roots or base of (plants)

hillbilly /'hil,bili/ n, chiefly NAm a person from a remote or culturally unsophisticated area

hillock /'hilək/ n a small hill

hilt /hilt/ n a handle, esp of a sword or dagger — **to the hilt** completely

him /him/ pron, objective case of **he** (e g threw it at him, it's him)

himself /him'self; medially often im-/ pron **1a** that identical male person or creature used reflexively, for emphasis, or in absolute constructions (e g himself a rich man, he knew the pitfalls) **b** – used reflexively when the sex of the antecedent is unspecified (e g everyone must fend for himself) **2** his normal self (e g isn't quite himself)

¹**hind** /hiend/ n, pl **hinds** also **hind** a female (red) deer

²**hind** adj situated at the back or behind; rear

¹**hinder** /'hində/ vt **1** to retard or obstruct the progress of; hamper **2** to restrain, prevent – often + from

²**hinder** /'hiendə/ adj situated behind or at the rear; posterior

hindmost /'hiend,mohst/ adj furthest to the rear; last

hindrance /'hindrəns/ n **1** the action of hindering **2** an impediment, obstacle

hindsight /'hiend,siet/ n the grasp or picture of a situation that one has after it has occurred

Hindu, archaic **Hindoo** /'hindooh, hin'dooh/ n an adherent of Hinduism

'**Hindu ism** /-ˌiz(ə)m/ n the dominant religion of India which involves belief in the illusory nature of the physical universe and in cycles of reincarnation, and is associated with a caste system of social organization

¹**hinge** /hinj/ n **1a** a jointed or flexible device on which a swinging part (e g a door or lid) turns **b** a flexible joint in which bones are held together by ligaments **c** a small piece of thin gummed paper used in fastening a postage stamp in an album **2** a point or principle on which sthg turns or depends

²**hinge** v **1** to attach to or provide with hinges **2** to hang or turn (as if) on a hinge **3** to depend or turn on a single consideration or point

¹**hint** /hint/ n **1** a brief practical suggestion or piece of advice **2** an indirect or veiled statement; an insinuation **3** a slight indication or trace; a suggestion – usu + of

²**hint** v **1** to indicate indirectly or by allusion **2** to give a hint — **hint at** to imply or allude to (sthg)

hin

hinterland /'hintə,land/ *n* **1** a region lying inland from a coast **2** a region remote from urban or cultural centres

¹hip /hip/ *n* the ripened fruit of a rose

²hip *n* **1** the projecting region at each side of the lower or rear part of the mammalian trunk formed by the pelvis and upper part of the thigh; *also* the joint or socket where the thighbone articulates with the pelvis **2** an external angle formed by 2 adjacent sloping sides of a roof

³hip *adj* keenly aware of or interested in the newest developments; *broadly* trendy – infml

'hip ,flask *n* a flat flask, usu for holding spirits, carried in a hip pocket

hippie, hippy /'hipi/ *n* a usu long-haired unconventionally dressed young person esp of anti-establishment and non-violent views

Hippocratic oath /,hipə'kratik/ *n* an oath embodying a code of medical ethics

hippopotamus /,hipə'potəməs/ *n, pl* **hippopotamuses, hippopotami** /-mie/ any of several large plant-eating 4-toed chiefly aquatic mammals

¹hire /hiɛ-ə/ *n* **1** payment for the temporary use of sthg **2** hiring or being hired

²hire *v* **1a** to engage the services of for a set sum **b** to engage the temporary use of for an agreed sum **2** to grant the services of or temporary use of for a fixed sum

'hireling /-ling/ *n* a person who works for payment, esp for purely mercenary motives – derog

,hire 'purchase *n, chiefly Br* a system of paying for goods by instalments

hirsute /huh'syooht/ *adj* covered with (coarse stiff) hairs

¹his /iz; *strong* hiz/ *adj* **1** of him or himself, esp as possessor, agent, or object of an action – used in titles of males (e g *his* Majesty)

²his /hiz/ *pron, pl* **his** that which or the one who belongs to him – used without a following noun as a pronoun equivalent in meaning to the adjective *his* (e g the house is *his*)

hiss /his/ *v* **1** to make a sharp voiceless sound like a prolonged *s*, esp in disapproval **2** to show disapproval of by hissing – **hiss** *n*

histology /hi'stolǝji/ *n* (anatomy that deals with) the organization and microscopic structure of animal and plant tissues

historian /hi'stawri-ən/ *n* a student or writer of history

historic /hi'storik/ *adj* **1** (likely to be) famous or important in history **2** *of a tense* expressive of past time

history /'histəri/ *n* **1** (a chronological record of) significant past events **2a** a treatise presenting systematically related natural phenomena **b** an account of sby's medical, sociological, etc background **3** a branch of knowledge that records the

past **4a** past events **b** an unusual or interesting past **c** previous treatment, handling, or experience – **-rical** *adj* – **-rically** *adv*

histrionic /,histri'onik/ *adj* **1** of actors, acting, or the theatre **2** deliberately affected; theatrical – **-ics** *n* – **-ally** *adv*

¹hit /hit/ *v* **-tt-; hit 1a** to reach (as if) with a blow; strike (a blow) **b** to make forceful contact with **2a** to bring or come into contact (with) **b** to deliver, inflict **3** to have a usu detrimental effect or impact on **4** to discover or meet, esp by chance **5a** to reach, attain **b** to cause a propelled object to strike (e g a target), esp for a score in a contest **c** *of a batsman* to score (runs) in cricket; *also* to score runs off a ball bowled by (a bowler) **6** to indulge in, esp excessively **7** to arrive at or in **8** to rob – infml **9** *chiefly NAm* to kill – slang **10a** to attack **b** to happen or arrive, esp with sudden or destructive force **11** to come, esp by chance; arrive at or find sthg – + *on* or *upon* — **hit it off** to get along well – infml — **hit the jackpot** to be or become notably and unexpectedly successful — **hit the nail on the head** to be exactly right — **hit the road** to start on a journey — infml — **hit the roof** to give vent to a burst of anger or angry protest — infml

²hit *n* **1** a blow; *esp* one that strikes its target **2a** a stroke of luck **b** sthg (e g a popular tune) that enjoys great success **3** a telling remark **4** a robbery **5** *chiefly NAm* an act of murder *USE* (4 & 5) slang

,hit-and-'run *adj* **1** being or involving a driver who does not stop after causing damage or injury **2** involving rapid action and immediate withdrawal

¹hitch /hich/ *v* **1** to move by jerks **2** to catch or fasten (as if) by a hook or knot – often + *up* **3** to solicit and obtain (a free lift) in a passing vehicle

²hitch *n* **1** a sudden movement or pull; a jerk **2** a sudden halt or obstruction; a stoppage **3** a knot used for a temporary fastening

'hitch,hike /-,hiek/ *v* to travel by obtaining free lifts in passing vehicles – **-hiker** *n*

¹hither /'hidhə/ *adv* to or towards this place – fml

²hither *adj* being the closer of 2 or the left-hand member of a pair – fml

,hither'to /-'tooh/ *adv* up to this time; until now – fml

hit off *v* to represent or imitate accurately

,hit-or-'miss *adj* showing a lack of planning or forethought; haphazard

'hit pa,rade *n* a group or listing of popular songs ranked in order of the number of records of each sold

¹hive /hiev/ *n* **1** (a structure for housing) a colony of bees **2** a place full of busy occupants

²hive *v* **1** to collect into a hive **2** *of bees* to enter and take possession of a hive

hive off *v* to separate or become separated from a group; form a separate or subsidiary unit

¹**hoard** /hawd/ *n* **1** an often secret supply (e g of money or food) stored up for preservation or future use **2** a cache of valuable archaeological remains

²**hoard** *v* to lay up a hoard (of) – ~ er *n*

hoarding /'hawding/ *n* **1** a temporary fence put round a building site **2** *Br* a large board designed to carry outdoor advertising

'hoar,frost /-,frost/ *n* a white frost

hoarse /haws/ *adj* **1** rough or harsh in sound; grating **2** having a hoarse voice – ~ **ly** *adv* – ~ **ness** *n*

hoary /'hawri/ *adj* **1a** grey or white with age; *also* grey-haired **b** having greyish or whitish hair, down, or leaves **2** impressively or venerably old; ancient **3** hackneyed – **hoariness** *n*

¹**hoax** /hohks/ *v* to play a trick on; deceive

²**hoax** *n* an act of deception; a trick – ~ **er** *n*

¹**hob** /hob/ *n, dial Br* a goblin, elf

²**hob** *n* **1** a ledge near a fireplace on which sthg may be kept warm **2** a horizontal surface either on a cooker or installed as a separate unit that contains heating areas on which pans are placed

hobble /'hobl/ *v* **1** to move along unsteadily or with difficulty; *esp* to limp **2** to fasten together the legs of (e g a horse) to prevent straying; fetter

¹**hobby** /'hobi/ *n* a leisure activity or pastime engaged in for interest or recreation

²**hobby** *n* a small Old World falcon that catches small birds while in flight

'hobby,horse /-,haws/ *n* **1** a figure of a horse fastened round the waist of a performer in a morris dance **2a** a toy consisting of an imitation horse's head attached to one end of a stick on which a child can pretend to ride **b** a rocking horse **3** a topic to which one constantly returns

hobgoblin /,hob'goblin/ *n* **1** a goblin **2** a bugbear or bogey

hobnail /'hob,nayl/ *n* a short large-headed nail for studding shoe soles – ~ **ed** *adj*

hobnob /'hob,nob/ *v* **-bb- 1** to associate familiarly **2** to talk informally *USE* usu + *with*; infml

hobo /'hoh,boh/ *n, pl* **hoboes** *also* **hobos 1** *chiefly NAm* a migratory worker **2** *NAm* a tramp

Hobson's choice /'hobs(ə)nz/ *n* an apparently free choice which offers no real alternative

¹**hock** /hok/ *n* the joint of the hind limb of a horse or related quadruped that corresponds to the ankle in human beings

²**hock** *n, often cap, chiefly Br* a dry to medium-dry or sometimes sweet white table wine produced in the Rhine valley

³**hock** *n* **1** pawn **2** debt *USE* infml; usu + *in*

⁴**hock** *v* to pawn – infml

hockey /'hoki/ *n* **1** a game played on grass between 2 teams of usu 11 players whose object is to direct a ball into the opponents' goal with a stick that has a flat-faced blade **2** *NAm* ice hockey

hocus-'pocus /'pohkəs/ *n* **1** sleight of hand **2** pointless activity or words, usu intended to obscure or deceive

hod /hod/ *n* **1** a trough mounted on a pole handle for carrying mortar, bricks, etc **2** a coal scuttle; *specif* a tall one used to shovel fuel directly onto a fire

¹**hoe** /hoh/ *n* any of various implements, esp one with a long handle and flat blade, used for tilling, weeding, etc

²**hoe** *v* **1** to weed or cultivate (land or a crop) with a hoe **2** to remove (weeds) by hoeing

¹**hog** /hog/ *n* **1** a young unshorn sheep **2** a warthog or other wild pig **3** *Br* a castrated male pig raised for slaughter **4** a selfish, gluttonous, or filthy person – slang

²**hog** *v* **-gg-** to appropriate a selfish or excessive share of; monopolize – infml

Hogmanay /'hogmənay, ,hogmə'nay/ *n, Scot* the eve of New Year's Day

'hogs,head /-,hed/ *n* **1** a large cask or barrel **2** any of several measures of capacity; *esp* a measure of 52¹/₂ imperial gallons (about 238l)

'hog,wash /-,wosh/ *n* **1** swill, slop **2** sthg worthless; *specif* meaningless talk – slang

hoi polloi /,hoy pə'loy/ *n pl* the common people; *the* masses

¹**hoist** /hoyst/ *v* to raise into position (as if) by means of tackle; *broadly* to raise

²**hoist** *n* an apparatus for hoisting

hoity-toity /,hoyti 'toyti/ *adj* having an air of assumed importance; haughty – infml

¹**hold** /hohld/ *v* **held** /held/ **1a** to have in one's keeping; possess **b** to retain by force **c** to keep by way of threat or coercion **2a** to keep under control; check **b** to stop the action of temporarily; delay **c** to keep from advancing or from attacking successfully **d** to restrict, limit **e** to bind legally or morally **3a** to have, keep, or support in the hands or arms; grasp **b** to keep in a specified situation, position, or state **c** to support, sustain **d** to retain **e** to keep in custody **f** to set aside; reserve **4** to bear, carry **5a** to keep up without interruption; continue **b** to keep the uninterrupted interest or attention of **6a** to contain or be capable of containing **b** to have in store **7a** to consider to be true; believe **b** to have in regard **8a** to engage in with sby else or with others **b** to cause to be conducted; convene **9a** to occupy as a result of appointment or election **b** to have earned or been awarded **10a** to maintain position **b** to continue unchanged; last **11** to withstand strain without breaking or giving way **12** to bear or carry oneself **13** to be or remain valid; apply **14** to maintain a course; continue — **hold a brief for** to be retained as counsel for — **hold forth** to speak at great length — **hold good** to be true or valid — **hold one's own** to maintain one's ground, position, or strength in the face of competition or adversity — **hold the**

fort to cope with problems for or look after the work of sby who is absent — **hold to 1** to remain steadfast or faithful to; abide by **2** to cause to hold to — **hold water** to stand up under criticism or analysis — **not hold a candle to** to be much inferior to; not qualify for comparison with

²**hold** n **1a** a manner of grasping an opponent in wrestling **b** influence, control **c** possession **2** sthg that may be grasped as a support

³**hold** n **1** a space below a ship's deck in which cargo is stored **2** the cargo compartment of a plane

'**hold,all** /-,awl/ n a bag or case for miscellaneous articles

hold back v **1** to hinder the progress of; restrain **2** to keep oneself in check

hold down v to hold and keep (a position of responsibility)

holder /'hohldǝ/ n **1** a device that holds an often specified object **2a** an owner **b** a tenant **c** a person in possession of and legally entitled to receive payment of a bill, note, or cheque

holding /'hohlding/ n **1** land held **2** property (e g land or securities) owned – usu pl with sing. meaning

'**holding ,company** n a company whose primary business is holding a controlling interest in the shares of other companies

hold off v **1** to resist successfully; withstand **2** to defer action; delay

hold on v **1** to persevere in difficult circumstances **2** to wait; hang on — **hold on to** to keep possession of

hold out v **1** to last **2** to refuse to yield or give way — **hold out for** to insist on as the price for an agreement — **hold out on** to withhold sthg (e g information) from – infml

hold over v **1** to postpone **2** to prolong the engagement or tenure of

'**hold,up** /-,up/ n **1** an armed robbery **2** a delay

hold up v **1** to delay, impede **2** to rob at gunpoint **3** to present, esp as an example **4** to endure a test

¹**hole** /hohl/ n **1** an opening into or through a thing **2a** a hollow place; esp a pit or cavity **b** a deep place in a body of water **3** an animal's burrow **4** a serious flaw (e g in an argument) **5a** the unit of play from the tee to the hole in golf **b** a cavity in a putting green into which the ball is to be played in golf **6** a dirty or dingy place **7** an awkward position; a fix USE (6 & 7) infml

²**hole** v **1** to make a hole in **2** to drive into a hole **3** to make a hole in sthg

hole up v to take refuge or shelter in USE infml

¹**holiday** /'holiday, -di/ n **1** a day, often in commemoration of some event, on which no paid employment is carried out **2** a period of relaxation or recreation spent away from home or work – often pl with sing. meaning

²**holiday** v to take or spend a holiday

'**holiday,maker** /-,maykǝ/ n a person who is on holiday

holiness /'hohlinis/ n **1** cap – used as a title for various high religious dignitaries **2** sacredness

holler /'holǝ/ v, chiefly NAm to call out or shout (sthg) – **holler** n

¹**hollow** /'holoh/ adj **1a** having a recessed surface; sunken **b** curved inwards; concave **2** having a cavity within **3** echoing like a sound made in or by beating on an empty container; muffled **4a** deceptively lacking in real value or significance **b** lacking in truth or substance; deceitful – ~**ly** adv – ~**ness** n

²**hollow** v to make or become hollow

³**hollow** n **1** a depressed or hollow part of a surface; esp a small valley or basin **2** an unfilled space; a cavity

⁴**hollow** adv **1** in a hollow manner **2** completely, totally – infml

holly /'holi/ n (the foliage of) any of a genus of trees and shrubs with thick glossy spiny-edged leaves and usu bright red berries

hollyhock /'holi,hok/ n a tall plant of the mallow family with spikes of showy flowers

holocaust /'holǝ,kawst/ n **1** a sacrificial offering consumed by fire **2** an instance of wholesale destruction or loss of life **3** often cap the genocidal persecution of the European Jews by Hitler and the Nazi party during WW II

holster /'hohlstǝ, 'hol-/ n a usu leather holder for a pistol

holy /'hohli/ adj **1** set apart to the service of God or a god; sacred **2a** characterized by perfection and transcendence; commanding absolute adoration and reverence **b** spiritually pure; godly **3** terrible, awful – used as an intensive

,**Holy Com'munion** n the sacrament of Communion

,**Holy 'Spirit** n the 3rd person of the Trinity

'**Holy ,Week** n the week before Easter during which the last days of Christ's life are commemorated

homage /'homij/ n **1a** a ceremony by which a man acknowledges himself the vassal of a lord **b** an act done or payment made by a vassal **2a** a reverential regard; deference **b** flattering attention; tribute

homburg /'hombuhg/ n a felt hat with a stiff curled brim and a high crown creased lengthways

¹**home** /hohm/ n **1a** a family's place of residence; a domicile **b** a house **2** the social unit formed by a family living together **3a** a congenial environment **b** a habitat **4a** a place of origin; also one's native country **b** the place where sthg originates or is based **5** an establishment providing residence and often care for children, convalescents, etc – ~**less** adj – ~**lessness** n — **at home 1** relaxed and comfortable **2** on familiar ground; knowledgeable

²home adv **1** to or at home **2** to a final, closed, or standard position (e g drive a nail *home*) **3** to an ultimate objective (e g a finishing line) **4** to a vital sensitive core (e g the truth struck *home*)

³home adj **1** of or being a home, place of origin, or base of operations **2** prepared, carried out, or designed for use in the home **3** operating or occurring in a home area

⁴home v **1** to go or return home **2** *of an animal* to return accurately to one's home or birthplace from a distance **3** to be directed *in on* a target

'home ,brew n an alcoholic drink (e g beer) made at home – ~**ed** adj

'home,coming /-,kuming/ n a returning home

,home'grown /-'grohn/ adj produced in, coming from, or characteristic of the home country or region

'homeland /-land/ n **1** one's native land **2** a tribal state in South Africa

'homely /-li/ adj **1** commonplace, familiar **2** of a sympathetic character; kindly **3** simple, unpretentious **4** not good-looking; plain – **-liness** n

,home'made /-'mayd/ adj made in the home, on the premises, or by one's own efforts

'home ,office n, *often cap* H&O *the* government office concerned with internal affairs

Homeric /hoh'merik/ adj **1** (characteristic) of Homer, his age, or his writings **2** of epic proportions; heroic

,home 'rule n limited self-government by the people of a dependent political unit

'home,sick /-,sik/ adj longing for home and family while absent from them – **~ness** n

'home,spun /-,spun/ adj lacking sophistication; simple

'homestead /-stid/ n a house and adjoining land occupied by a family

,home 'truth n an unpleasant but true fact about a person's character or situation – *often pl*

'homeward /-wood/ adj being or going towards home

'homewards, *chiefly NAm* **homeward** adv towards home

'home,work /-,wuhk/ n **1** work done in one's own home for pay **2** an assignment given to a pupil to be completed esp away from school **3** preparatory reading or research (e g for a discussion)

homicide /'homisied/ n (the act of) sby who kills another

'homing ,pigeon /'hohming/ n a domesticated pigeon trained to return home

homoeopathy /,homi'opəthi/ n a system of disease treatment relying on the administration of minute doses of a substance that in larger doses produces symptoms like those of the disease – **-path** n

homogeneous /,homə'jeenyəs, -ni·əs/ adj **1** of the same or a similar kind or nature **2** of uniform structure or composition throughout – **-neity** n – **~ly** adv – **-nize** v

Homo sapiens /,hohmoh 'sapi·enz, 'homoh-/ n mankind

homosexual /,homə'seksyooəl, -'seksh(ə)l/ adj or n (of, for, or being) sby having a sexual preference for members of his/her own sex

hone /hohn/ v or n (to sharpen or make more keen or effective with or as if with) a stone for sharpening a cutting tool

honest /'onist/ adj **1** free from fraud or deception; legitimate, truthful **2** respectable or worthy **3a** marked by integrity **b** frank, sincere – **~y** n

'honestly /-li/ adv to speak in an honest way

honey /'huni/ n **1** (a pale golden colour like that typical of) a sweet viscous sticky liquid formed from the nectar of flowers in the honey sac of various bees **2** sthg sweet or agreeable; sweetness **3** a superlative example – *chiefly infml*

'honey ,bee /-,bee/ n (a social honey-producing bee related to) a European bee kept for its honey and wax

¹'honey,comb /-,kohm/ n (sthg resembling in shape or structure) a mass of 6-sided wax cells built by honeybees in their nest to contain their brood and stores of honey

²honeycomb v **1** to cause to be chequered or full of cavities like a honeycomb **2** to penetrate into every part; riddle

'honey,dew /-,dyooh/ n a sweet deposit secreted on the leaves of plants usu by aphids

honeyed *also* **honied** /'hunid/ adj sweetened (as if) with honey

'honey,moon /-,moohn/ n **1** the period immediately following marriage, esp when taken as a holiday by the married couple **2** a period of unusual harmony following the establishment of a new relationship

'honey,suckle /-,sukl/ n any of a genus of (climbing) shrubs usu with showy sweet-smelling flowers rich in nectar

¹honk /hongk/ n (a sound made by a car's electric horn like) the short loud unmusical tone that is the characteristic cry of the goose

²honk v to (cause to) make a honk

honorary /'on(ə)rəri/ adj **1a** conferred or elected in recognition of achievement, without the usual obligations b unpaid, voluntary **2** depending on honour for fulfilment

¹honour, *NAm chiefly* **honor** /'onə/ n **1a** good name or public esteem **b** outward respect; recognition **2** a privilege **3** *cap* a person of superior social standing – now used esp as a title for a holder of high office (e g a judge in court) **4** one who brings respect or fame **5** a mark or symbol of distinction: e g **5a** an exalted title or rank **b** a ceremonial rite or observance – *usu pl* **6** *pl* a course of study for a university degree more exacting and specialized than that leading to a pass degree **7** (a woman's) chastity or purity **8a** a high standard of ethical conduct; integrity **b** one's word given as a pledge

²honour, *NAm chiefly* **honor** *v* **1a** to regard or treat with honour or respect **b** to confer honour on **2a** to live up to or fulfil the terms of **b** to accept and pay when due

honourable, *NAm chiefly* **honorable** /'on(ə)rəbl/ *adj* **1** worthy of honour **2** performed or accompanied with marks of honour or respect **3** entitled to honour – used as a title for the children of certain British noblemen and for various government officials **4a** bringing credit to the possessor or doer **b** consistent with blameless reputation **5** characterized by (moral) integrity **– bly** *adv*

hooch /hoohch/ *n* spirits, esp when inferior or illicitly made or obtained – slang

¹hood /hood/ *n* **1a** a loose often protective covering for the top and back of the head and neck that is usu attached to the neckline of a garment **b** a usu leather covering for a hawk's head and eyes **2a** an ornamental scarf worn over an academic gown that indicates by its colour the wearer's university and degree **b** a hoodlike marking, crest, or expansion on the head of an animal (e g a cobra or seal) **3a** a folding waterproof top cover for an open car, pram, etc **b** a cover or canopy for carrying off fumes, smoke, etc

²hood *n* a hoodlum or gangster – infml

¹hooded *adj* **1** covered (as if) by a hood **2** shaped like a hood

hoodlum /'hoohdlam/ *n* **1 a** (violent) thug **2 a** young rowdy

hoodwink /'hood,wingk/ *v* to deceive, delude – chiefly infml

hooey /'hooh·i/ *n* nonsense – slang

hoof /hoohf, hoof/ *n, pl* **hooves** /hoohvz/, **hoofs** (a foot which) a curved horny casing that protects the ends of the digits of a horse, cow, or similar mammal and that corresponds to a nail or claw — **on the hoof** *of a meat animal* before being butchered; while still alive

²hoof *v* **1** to kick **2** to go on foot – usu + *it USE* infml

hoo-ha /'hooh ˌhah/ *n* a fuss, to-do – chiefly infml

¹hook /hook/ *n* **1** a curved or bent device for catching, holding, or pulling **2a** (a flight of) a ball in golf that deviates from a straight course in a direction opposite to the dominant hand of the player propelling it **b** an attacking stroke in cricket played with a horizontal bat aimed at a ball of higher than waist height and intended to send the ball on the leg side **3** a short blow delivered in boxing with a circular motion while the elbow remains bent and rigid — **by hook or by crook** by any possible means — **hook, line, and sinker** completely

²hook *v* **1** to form (into a) hook (shape) **2** to seize, make fast, or connect (as if) by a hook **3** to hit or throw (a ball) so that a hook results **4** to become hooked

hookah /'hookə, -kah/ *n* a water pipe

hooked *adj* **1** (shaped) like or provided with a hook **2a** addicted to drugs – slang **b** very enthusiastic or compulsively attached (to sthg specified) – infml

hooker /'hookə/ *n* **1** (the position of) a player in rugby stationed in the middle of the front row of the scrum **2** a woman prostitute – slang

hooky, hookey /'hooki/ *n* truant – usu in *play hooky*

hooligan /'hoohligən/ *n* a young ruffian or hoodlum – **~ism** *n*

¹hoop /hoohp/ *n* **1** a large (rigid) circular strip used esp for holding together the staves of containers, as a child's toy, or to expand a woman's skirt **2** a circular figure or object **3** an arch through which balls must be hit in croquet

²hoop *v* to bind or fasten (as if) with a hoop

hoop-la /'hoohp ˌlah/ *n* a (fairground) game in which prizes are won by tossing rings over them

hooray /hoo'ray/ *interj* hurray

¹hoot /hooht/ *v* **1** to utter a loud shout, usu in contempt **2a** to make (a sound similar to) the long-drawn-out throat noise of an owl **b** to sound the horn, whistle, etc of a motor car or other vehicle **3** to laugh loudly – infml

²hoot *n* **1** a sound of hooting **2** a damn **3** a source of laughter or amusement *USE* (2, 3) infml

hooter /'hoohtə/ *n, chiefly Br* **1** a device (e g the horn of a car) for producing a loud hooting noise **2** the nose – infml

hoover /'hoohvə/ *v* to clean using a vacuum cleaner

Hoover *trademark* – used for a vacuum cleaner

¹hop /hop/ *v* **-pp-** **1** to move by a quick springy leap or in a series of leaps; *esp* to jump on 1 foot **2** to make a quick trip, esp by air **3** to board or leave a vehicle **4** to jump over — **hop it** *Br* go away! – infml

²hop *n* **1a** a short leap, esp on 1 leg **b** a bounce, a rebound **2** a short or long flight between 2 landings **3** a dance – infml

³hop *n* **1** a climbing plant of the hemp family with inconspicuous green flowers of which the female ones are in cone-shaped catkins **2** *pl* the ripe dried catkins of a hop used esp to impart a bitter flavour to beer

¹hope /hohp/ *v* **1** to wish or long for with expectation of fulfilment **2** to expect with desire; trust — **hope against hope** to hope without any basis for expecting fulfilment

²hope *n* **1** trust, reliance **2a** desire accompanied by expectation of or belief in fulfilment **b** sby or sthg on which hopes are centred **c** sthg hoped for

¹**hopeful** /-f(ə)l/ *adj* **1** full of hope **2** inspiring hope – ~**ness** *n*

²**hopeful** *n* a person who aspires to or is likely to succeed

'**hopefully** /-f(ə)l·i/ *adv* **1** in a hopeful manner **2** it is hoped – disapproved of by some speakers

'**hopeless** /-lis/ *adj* **1** having no expectation of success **2a** giving no grounds for hope **b** incapable of solution, management, or accomplishment **3** incompetent, useless – chiefly *infml* – ~**ly** *adv* – ~**ness** *n*

hopper /'hopə/ *n* **1a** (a funnel-shaped) receptacle for the discharging or temporary storage of grain, coal, etc **2** a goods wagon with a floor through which bulk materials may be discharged

'**hop,scotch** /-,skoch/ *n* a children's game in which a player tosses an object (e g a stone) into areas of a figure outlined on the ground and hops through the figure and back to regain the object

horde /hawd/ *n* **1** a (Mongolian) nomadic people or tribe **2** a crowd, swarm

horizon /hə'rīz(ə)n/ *n* **1a** the apparent junction of earth and sky **b(1)** the plane that is tangent to the earth's surface at an observer's position **b(2)** (the great circle formed by the intersection with the celestial sphere of) the plane parallel to such a plane but passing through the earth's centre **2** range of perception, experience, or knowledge

horizontal /,hori'zontl/ *adj* **1a** near the horizon **b** in the plane of or (operating in a plane) parallel to the horizon or a base line; level **2** of or concerning relationships between people of the same rank in different hierarchies – ~**ly** *adv*

hormone /'hawmohn/ *n* (a synthetic substance with the action of) a product of living cells that usu circulates in body liquids (e g the blood or sap) and produces a specific effect on the activity of cells remote from its point of origin

horn /hawn/ *n* **1a(1)** any of the usu paired bony projecting parts on the head of cattle, giraffes, deer, and similar hoofed mammals and some extinct mammals and reptiles **a(2)** a permanent solid pointed part attached to the nasal bone of a rhinoceros **b** a natural projection from an animal (e g a snail or owl) resembling or suggestive of a horn **c** the tough fibrous material consisting chiefly of keratin that covers or forms the horns and hooves of cattle and related animals, or other hard parts (e g claws or nails) **d** a hollow horn used as a container **2** sthg resembling or suggestive of a horn; *esp* either of the curved ends of a crescent **3a** an animal's horn used as a wind instrument **b(1)** a hunting horn **b(2)** a French horn **c** a wind instrument used in a jazz band; *esp* a trumpet **d** a device (e g on a motor car) for making loud warning noises – ~**like**, – ~**ed** *adj*

hornet /'hawnit/ *n* a large wasp with a black and yellow banded abdomen and a powerful sting

'**hornet's ,nest** *n* an angry or hostile reaction – esp in *stir up a hornet's nest*

'**horn,pipe** /-,piep/ *n* (a piece of music for) a lively British folk dance typically associated with sailors

horny /'hawni/ *adj* **1** (made) of horn **2** sexually aroused – slang

horology /ho'rolǝji/ *n* **1** the science of measuring time **2** the art of constructing instruments for indicating time

horoscope /'horǝ,skohp/ *n* (an astrological forecast based on) a diagram of the relative positions of planets and signs of the zodiac at a specific time, esp sby's birth, used by astrologers to infer individual character and personality traits and to foretell events in a person's life

horrendous /hǝ'rendǝs/ *adj* dreadful, horrible – ~**ly** *adv*

horrible /'horǝbl/ *adj* **1** marked by or arousing horror **2** extremely unpleasant or disagreeable – chiefly *infml* –**bly** *adv*

horrid /'horid/ *adj* **1** horrible, shocking **2** repulsive, nasty – ~**ly** *adv* – ~**ness** *n*

horrify /'horifie/ *v* **1** to cause to feel horror **2** to fill with distaste; shock – ~**ingly**, **-fically** *adv* – **-fic** *adj*

horror /'horǝ/ *n* **1a** intense fear, dread, or dismay **b** intense aversion or repugnance **2** (sby or sthg that has) the quality of inspiring horror

hors de combat /,aw dǝ 'kombah (*Fr* ɔːr dǝ kõba)/ *adv or adj* out of the fight; disabled

hors d'oeuvre /,aw 'duhv (*Fr* ɔːr dœvr)/ *n, pl* **hors d'oeuvres** *also* **hors d'oeuvre** /'duhv(z) (*Fr* ~)/ any of various savoury foods usu served as appetizers

horse /haws/ *n pl* **horses**, (3) **horse 1a(1)** a large solid-hoofed plant-eating quadruped mammal domesticated by humans since prehistoric times and used as a beast of burden, a draught animal, or for riding **a(2)** a racehorse **b** a male horse; a stallion or gelding **2a** a usu 4-legged frame for supporting sthg (e g planks) **b** a padded obstacle for vaulting over **3** *sing or pl in constr* the cavalry **4** heroin – slang — **from the horse's mouth** from the original source

'**horse,box** /-,boks/ *n* a lorry or closed trailer for transporting horses

,**horse 'chestnut** *n* (the large glossy brown seed of) a large tree with 5-lobed leaves and erect conical clusters of showy flowers

'**horse,fly** /-,flie/ *n* any of a family of swift usu large flies with bloodsucking females

'**horse,laugh** /-,lahf/ *n* a loud boisterous laugh

'**horseman** /-mǝn/, *fem* '**horse,woman** *n* **1** a rider on horseback **2** a (skilled) breeder, tender, or manager of horses – ~**ship** *n*

'**horse,play** /-,play/ *n* rough or boisterous play

'**horse,power** /-,powǝ/ *n* an imperial unit of power equal to about 746W

hor

'horse,radish /-,radish/ n 1 a tall coarse
white-flowered plant of the mustard family 2 (a
condiment prepared from) the pungent root of
the horseradish

'horse,shoe /-,shooh/ n (sthg with a shape resembling) a shoe for horses, usu consisting of a narrow U-shaped plate of iron fitting the rim of the
hoof

'horse,whip /-,wip/ v to flog (as if) with a whip
for horses

hortative /'hawtativ/, hortatory /'hawtət(ə)ri/
adj giving encouragement – fml

horticulture /'hawti,kulchə/ n the science and
art of growing fruits, vegetables, and flowers
– -tural adj – -turalist n

hosanna /hoh'zanə/ interj or n (used as) a cry of
acclamation and adoration

¹hose /hohz/ n pl (1) hose, (2) hoses 1 a leg covering
that sometimes covers the foot 2 a flexible tube for
conveying fluids (e g from a tap or in a car engine)

²hose v to spray, water, or wash with a hose

hosiery /'hohzyəri/ n socks, stockings, and tights
in general

hospice /'hospis/ n 1 a place of shelter for travellers or the destitute (run by a religious order) 2 Br
a nursing home, esp for terminally ill patients

hospitable /ho'spitəbl, 'hos-/ adj 1a offering a
generous and cordial welcome (to guests or strangers) b offering a pleasant or sustaining environment 2 readily receptive – -bly adv

hospital /'hospitl/ n an institution where the sick
or injured are given medical care – ~ize v

hospitality /,hospi'taləti/ n hospitable treatment
or reception

¹host /hohst/ n 1 a very large number; a multitude
2 an army – chiefly poetic or archaic

²host n 1a an innkeeper b one who receives or
entertains guests socially or officially c sby or sthg
that provides facilities for an event or function 2a
a living animal or plant on or in which a parasite
or smaller organism lives b an individual into
which a tissue or part is transplanted from
another

³host v to act as host at or of

⁴host n, often cap the bread consecrated in the
Eucharist

hostage /'hostij/ n a person held by one party as a
pledge that promises will be kept or terms met by
another party

hostel /'hostl/ n 1 chiefly Br a supervised residential home: e g 1a an establishment providing
accommodation for nurses, students, etc b an
institution for junior offenders, ex-offenders, etc,
encouraging social adaptation 2a Youth Hostel 3
an inn – chiefly poetic or archaic

'hostelry /-ri/ n an inn, hotel

hostess /hoh'stes/ n 1 a woman who entertains
socially or acts as host 2a a female employee on a
ship, aeroplane, etc who manages the provisioning of food and attends to the needs of passengers
b a woman who acts as a companion to male
patrons, esp in a nightclub; also a prostitute

hostile /'hostiel/ adj 1 of or constituting an enemy
2 antagonistic, unfriendly 3 not hospitable

hostility /ho'stiləti/ n 1 pl overt acts of warfare 2
antagonism, opposition, or resistance

¹hot /hot/ adj -tt- 1a having a relatively high temperature b capable of giving a sensation of heat or
of burning, searing, or scalding c having a temperature higher than normal body temperature
2a vehement, fiery b sexually excited; also sexually arousing c eager, enthusiastic d of or being an
exciting style of jazz with strong rhythms 3 severe,
stringent – usu + on 4 having or causing the
sensation of an uncomfortable degree of body
heat 5a very recent; fresh b close to sthg sought 6a
suggestive of heat or of burning objects b pungent, peppery 7a of intense and immediate interest; sensational b performing well or strongly
fancied to win (e g in a sport) c currently popular;
selling very well d very good – used as a generalized term of approval 9a recently and illegally
obtained b wanted by the police USE
(2b, 2c, & 7d) infml, (9) slang

²hot adv hotly

hot 'air n empty talk – chiefly infml

'hot,bed /-,bed/ n 1 a bed of soil heated esp by
fermenting manure and used for forcing or raising seedlings 2 an environment that favours rapid
growth or development, esp of sthg specified

,hot-'blooded adj excitable, ardent

hotchpotch /'hoch,poch/ n a mixture composed
of many usu unrelated parts; a jumble

,hot ,cross 'bun n a yeast-leavened spicy bun
marked with a cross and eaten esp on Good
Friday

'hot ,dog n a frankfurter or other sausage (heated
and served in a bread roll)

hotel /(h)oh'tel/ n a usu large establishment that
provides meals and (temporary) accommodation
for the public, esp for people travelling away from
home

hotelier /(h)oh'telyə, -yay/ n a proprietor or manager of a hotel

'hot,foot /-,foot/ v or adv (to go) in haste – hot-
foot adv

'hot,head /-,hed/ n a fiery and impetuous person
– ~ed adj – ~edly adv

¹hot,house /-,hows/ n a heated greenhouse, esp
for tropical plants

²hothouse adj delicate, overprotected

'hot ,line n a direct telephone line kept in constant
readiness for immediate communication (e g
between heads of state)

'hotly /-li/ adv in a hot or fiery manner

'hot ,plate *n* a metal plate or spiral, usu on an electric cooker, on which food can be heated and cooked

'hot ,pot *n* a (mutton, lamb, or beef and potato) stew cooked esp in a covered pot

'hot ,seat *n* a position involving risk, embarrassment, or responsibility for decision-making – infml

Hottentot /'hot(ə)n,tot/ *n* a member, or the language, of a people of southern Africa

,hot 'water *n* a distressing predicament (likely to lead to punishment); trouble – infml

,hot-'water ,bottle *n* a usu flat rubber container that is filled with hot water and used esp to warm a (person in) bed

'hound /hownd/ *n* **1** a dog; *esp* one of any of various hunting breeds typically with large drooping ears and a deep bark that track their prey by scent **2** a mean or despicable person **3** one who is devoted to the pursuit of sthg specified

'hound *v* **1** to pursue (as if) with hounds **2** to harass persistently

hour /owə/ *n* **1** (any of the 7 times of day set aside for) a daily liturgical devotion **2** the 24th part of a day; a period of 60 minutes **3a** *the* time of day reckoned in hours and minutes by the clock; *esp* the beginning of each full hour measured by the clock **b** *pl* the time reckoned in one 24-hour period from midnight to midnight **4a** a fixed or customary period of time set aside for a usu specified purpose – often *pl* **b** a particular, usu momentous, period or point of time **c** *the* present **5** the work done or distance travelled at normal rate in an hour

'hour,glass /-,glahs/ *n* a glass or perspex instrument for measuring time consisting of 2 bulbs joined by a narrow neck from the uppermost of which a quantity of sand, water, etc runs into the lower in the space of an hour

'hourglass *adj* shapely with a narrow waist

'hourly /'owəli/ *adv* **1** at or during every hour; *also* continually **2** by the hour

'hourly *adj* **1** occurring or done every hour; *also* continual **2** reckoned by the hour

'house /hows/ *n*, *pl* **houses** /'howziz/ **1** a building designed for people to live in **2a** an animal's shelter or refuge (e g a nest or den) **b** a building in which sthg is housed or stored **c** a building used for a particular purpose, esp eating, drinking, or entertainment **3** any of the 12 equal sectors into which the celestial sphere is divided in astrology **4a** *sing or pl in constr* the occupants of a house **b** a family including ancestors, descendants, and kindred **5a** (a residence of) a religious community **b** any of several groups into which a British school may be divided for social purposes or games **6** (the chamber of) a legislative or deliberative assembly; *esp* a division of a body consisting of 2

chambers **7** a business organization or establishment **8** (the audience in) a theatre or concert hall — **on the house** at the expense of an establishment or its management

'house /howz/ *v* **1** to provide with accommodation or storage space **2** to serve as shelter for; contain

'house ar,rest *n* confinement to one's place of residence instead of prison

'house,boat /-,boht/ *n* an often permanently moored boat that is fitted out as a home

'house,bound /-,bownd/ *adj* confined to the house (e g because of illness)

'house,coat /-,koht/ *n* a woman's light dressing gown for wear round the house; *also* a short overall

'house,craft /-,krahft/ *n* **1** domestic science **2** skill in running a household

'house,fly /-,flie/ *n* a fly found in most parts of the world that frequents houses and carries disease

'house,hold /-,hohld/ *n sing or pl in constr* all the people who live together in a dwelling

'household *adj* **1** domestic **2** familiar, common

'house,holder /-,hohldə/ *n* a person who occupies a dwelling as owner or tenant

'house,keeper /-,keepə/ *n* sby, esp a woman, employed to take charge of the running of a house

'house,keeping /-,keeping/ *n* **1** (money used for) the day-to-day running of a house and household affairs **2** the general management of an organization which ensures its smooth running (e g the provision of equipment, keeping of records, etc)

'house,maid /-,mayd/ *n* a female servant employed to do housework

house,maid's knee *n* a swelling over the knee due to an enlargement of the tissues between the kneecap and the knee

'houseman /-mən/ *n* (one holding) the most junior grade of British hospital doctor

'house ,martin *n* a European martin with blue-black plumage and white rump that nests on cliffs and under the eaves of houses

'house,master /-,mahstə/, *fem* **'house,mistress** *n* a teacher in charge of a school house

,House of 'Commons *n* the lower house of the British and Canadian parliaments

,House of 'Lords *n* **1** the upper house of Parliament **2** the body of Law Lords that constitutes the highest British court of appeal

'house ,party *n* a party lasting for a day or more held at a large, usu country, house

'house-,proud *adj* (excessively) careful about the management and appearance of one's house

'house ,sparrow *n* a brown Eurasian sparrow that lives esp in or near human settlements

,house-to-'house *adj* door-to-door

'house,warming /-,wawming/ *n* a party to celebrate moving into a new house or premises

housewife /'hows,wief/ *sense 2* 'huzif/ *n* **1** a usu married woman who runs a house **2** a small container for needlework articles (e g thread) – **~ly** *adj*

'house,work /-,wuhk/ *n* the work (e g cleaning) involved in maintaining a house

housing /'howzing/ *n* **1** (the provision of) houses or dwelling-places collectively **2** a protective cover for machinery, sensitive instruments, etc

hove /hohv/ *past of* **heave**

hovel /'hovl/ *n* a small, wretched, and often dirty house or abode

hover /'hovə/ *v* **1** to hang in the air or on the wing **2a** to linger or wait restlessly around a place **b** to be in a state of uncertainty, indecision, or suspense

'hover,craft /-,krahft/ *n, pl* **hovercraft** a vehicle supported on a cushion of air provided by fans and designed to travel over both land and sea

¹**how** /how/ *adv* **1a** in what manner or way (e g how do you spell it?) **b** with what meaning; to what effect (e g how can you explain it?) **c** for what reason; why (e g how could you do it?) **2** by what measure or quantity (e g how much does it cost) – often used in an exclamation as an intensive (e g how nice of you!) **3** in what state or condition (e g of health) (e g how are you?) — **how about** what do you say to or think of — **how come** how does it happen; why is it — *infml* — **how do you do** — used as a formal greeting between people meeting for the first time — **how's that 1** — used to call attention to and invite comment on sthg **2** please repeat **3** — used in cricket as an appeal to the umpire to give the batsman out

²**how** *conj* **1a** the way, manner, or state in which (e g remember how they fought?) **b** that (e g do you remember how he arrived right at the end?) **2** however, as (e g do it how you like)

³**how** *n* the manner in which sthg is done

,how-do-you-'do, how d'ye do /dyə/ *n* a confused or embarrassing situation – *infml*

¹**however** /how'evə/ *conj* in whatever manner or way (e g can go *however* he likes)

²**however** *adv* **1** to whatever degree or extent; no matter how (e g *however* hard I try) **2** in spite of that; nevertheless (e g would like to; *however*, I'd better not) **3** how in the world (e g *however* did you manage it?) – *infml*

howitzer /'how·itzə/ *n* a short cannon usu with a medium muzzle velocity and a relatively high trajectory

howl /howl/ *v* **1a** *esp of dogs, wolves, etc* to make a loud sustained doleful cry **b** *of wind* to make a sustained wailing sound **2** to cry loudly and without restraint (e g with pain or laughter) **3** to utter with a loud sustained cry – **howl** *n*

howl down *v* to express one's disapproval of (e g a speaker or his/her views), esp by shouting in order to prevent from being heard

howler /'howlə/ *n* a stupid and comic blunder – *infml*

howling /'howling/ *adj* very great, extreme, or severe – *infml*

hoyden /'hoydn/ *n* a boisterous girl – **~ish** *adj*

hub /hub/ *n* **1** the central part of a wheel, propeller, or fan through which the axle passes **2** the centre of activity or importance

hubbub /'hubub/ *n* a noisy confusion; uproar

hubby /'hubi/ *n* a husband – *infml*

hubcap /'hub,kap/ *n* a removable metal cap placed over the hub of a wheel

hubris /'hyoohbris/ *n* overweening pride, usu leading to retribution

¹**huddle** /'hudl/ *v* **huddling**, 'hudl·ing/ **1** to crowd together **2** to draw or curl (oneself) up

²**huddle** *n* **1** a closely-packed group; a bunch **2** a secretive or conspiratorial meeting

hue /hyooh/ *n* **1** a complexion, aspect **2** the attribute of colours that permits them to be classed as red, yellow, green, blue, or an intermediate between any adjacent pair of these colours; *also* a colour having this attribute

,hue and 'cry *n* a clamour of alarm or protest

huff /huf/ *v* **1** to emit loud puffs (e g of breath or steam) **2** to make empty threats

¹**hug** /hug/ *v* **-gg- 1** to hold or press tightly, esp in the arms **2a** to feel very pleased with (oneself) **b** to cling to; cherish **3** to stay close to

²**hug** *n* a tight clasp or embrace

huge /hyoohj/ *adj* great in size, scale, degree, or scope; enormous – **~ness** *n*

'hugely /-li/ *adv* very much; enormously

hulk /hulk/ *n* **1a** the hull of a ship that is no longer seaworthy and is used as a storehouse or, esp formerly, as a prison **b** an abandoned wreck or shell, esp of a vessel **2** a person, creature, or thing that is bulky or unwieldy

hulking /'hulking/ *adj* bulky, massive

¹**hull** /hul/ *n* **1a** the outer covering of a fruit or seed **b** the calyx that surrounds some fruits (e g the strawberry) **2** the main frame or body of a ship, flying boat, airship, etc **3** a covering, casing

²**hull** *v* to remove the hulls of

hullabaloo /,hulabə'looh/ *n pl* **hullabaloos** a confused noise; uproar – *infml*

hullo /hu'loh/ *interj or n, chiefly Br* hello

hum /hum/ *v* **-mm- 1a** to utter a prolonged /m/ sound **b** to make the characteristic droning noise of an insect in motion or a similar sound **2** to be lively or active – *infml* **3** to have an offensive smell – *slang* **4** to sing with the lips closed and without articulation – **hum** *n* — **hum and ha** *also* **hum and haw** to equivocate

¹**human** /'hyoohmən/ *adj* **1** (characteristic) of humans **2** consisting of men and women **3a** having the esp good attributes (e g kindness and compassion) thought to be characteristic of

humans **b** having, showing, or concerned with qualities or feelings characteristic of mankind – ~**ize** v

²**human**, ,human 'being n a man, woman, or child; a person

humane /hyooh'mayn/ adj **1a** marked by compassion or consideration for other human beings or animals **b** causing the minimum pain possible **2** characterized by broad humanistic culture; liberal

humanism /'hyoohmə,niz(ə)m/ n **1** a cultural movement dominant during the Renaissance that was characterized by a revival of classical learning and a shift of emphasis from religious to secular concerns; broadly literary culture **2** humanitarianism **3** a doctrine, attitude, or way of life based on human interests or values; esp a philosophy that asserts the intrinsic worth of man and that usu rejects religious belief – **-ist** n, adj – **-istic** adj

humanitarian /hyooh,mani'teəri-ən/ n one who promotes human welfare and social reform; a philanthropist

humanity /hyooh'manəti/ n **1** the quality of being humane **2** the quality or state of being human **3** pl the cultural branches of learning **4** mankind

,human'kind /-'kiend/ n sing or pl in constr human beings collectively

'**humanly** /-li/ adv **1a** from a human viewpoint **b** within the range of human capacity **2a** in a manner characteristic of humans, esp in showing emotion or weakness **b** with humaneness

¹**humble** /'humbl/ adj **1** having a low opinion of oneself; unassertive **2** marked by deference or submission **3a** ranking low in a hierarchy or scale **b** modest, unpretentious – **-bly** adv

²**humble** v **1** to make humble in spirit or manner; humiliate **2** to destroy the power, independence, or prestige of

¹**humbug** /'hum,bug/ n **1a** sthg designed to deceive and mislead **b** an impostor, sham **2** drivel, nonsense **3** a hard usu peppermint-flavoured striped sweet made from boiled sugar

²**humbug** v **-gg-** to deceive with a hoax

humdinger /'hum,dingə/ n an excellent or remarkable person or thing – infml

humdrum /'hum,drum/ adj monotonous, dull

humerus /'hyoohmərəs/ n, pl **humeri** /-,rie/ the long bone of the upper arm or forelimb extending from the shoulder to the elbow

humid /'hyoohmid/ adj containing or characterized by perceptible moisture

humidity /hyooh'midəti/ n (the degree of) moisture or dampness, esp in the atmosphere

humiliate /hyooh'miliayt/ v to cause to feel humble; lower the dignity or self-respect of – **-ation** n

humility /hyooh'miləti/ n the quality or state of being humble

hummingbird /'huming,buhd/ n any of numerous tiny brightly coloured usu tropical American birds

humorist /'hyoohmərist/ n a person specializing in or noted for humour in speech, writing, or acting

humorous /'hyoohmərəs/ adj full of, characterized by, or expressing humour – ~**ly** adv

¹**humour**, NAm chiefly **humor** /'hyoohmə/ n **1** any of the 4 fluids of the body (blood, phlegm, and yellow and black bile) formerly held to determine, by their relative proportions, a person's health and temperament **2** characteristic or habitual disposition **3** a state of mind; a mood **4** a sudden inclination; a caprice **5a** (sthg having) the quality of causing amusement **b** the faculty of expressing or appreciating what is comic or amusing — **out of humour** in a bad temper

²**humour**, NAm chiefly **humor** v to comply with the mood or wishes of; indulge

¹**hump** /hump/ n **1** a rounded protuberance: e g **1a** a humped or crooked back **b** a fleshy protuberance on the back of a camel, bison, etc **2** a difficult, trying, or critical phase **3** Br a fit of depression or sulking – infml; + the

²**hump** v **1** to form or curve into a hump **2** chiefly Br to carry with difficulty **3** to have sexual intercourse (with) – slang

'**hump,back** /-,bak/ n **1** a hunchback **2** also **humpback whale** a large whale with very long flippers – ~**ed** adj

humph /hum(p)f/ interj a grunt used to express doubt or contempt

humus /'hyoohməs/ n a brown or black organic soil material resulting from partial decomposition of plant or animal matter

Hun /hun/ n pl **Huns** (2b) **Huns,** esp collectively **Hun 1** a member of a nomadic Mongolian people who overran a large part of central and E Europe under Attila during the 4th and 5th c AD **2a** often not cap a person who is wantonly destructive **b** a German; esp a German soldier in WW I or II – derog

¹**hunch** /hunch/ v **1** to assume a bent or crooked posture **2** to bend into a hump or arch

²**hunch** n a strong intuitive feeling

'**hunch,back** /-,bak/ n (sby with) a humped back – ~**ed** adj

hundred /'hundrəd/ n, pl **hundreds, hundred 1** the number 100 **2** the number occupying the position 3 to the left of the decimal point in Arabic notation; also, pl this position **3** 100 units or digits; specif £100 **4** pl the numbers 100 to 999 **5** a score of 100 or more runs made by a batsman in cricket **6** pl the 100 years of a specified century **7** a historical subdivision of a county **8** an indefinitely large number – infml; often pl with sing. meaning – ~**th** adj, n, pron, adv

'hundred,weight /-,wayt/ *n, pl* **hundredweight,
hundredweights** a British unit of weight equal to
112lb (about 50.80kg)

hung /hung/ *past of* **hang**

'hunger /'hung·ga/ *n* **1a** (a weakened condition or
unpleasant sensation arising from) a craving or
urgent need for food **2** a strong desire; a craving

'hunger *v* to have an eager desire – *usu* + *for or
after n*

hungry /'hung·gri/ *adj* **1a** feeling hunger **b** characterized by or indicating hunger or appetite **2**
eager, avid – **-grily** *adv*

hunk /hungk/ *n* **1** a large lump or piece **2** a usu
muscular sexually attractive man – *infml*

'hunt /hunt/ *v* **1a** to pursue for food or enjoyment
b to use (e g hounds) in the search for game **2a** to
pursue with intent to capture **b** to search out; seek
3 to persecute or chase, esp by harrying **4** to take
part in a hunt, esp regularly **5** to attempt to find
sthg

'hunt *n* **1** the act, the practice, or an instance of
hunting **2** *sing or pl in constr* a group of usu
mounted hunters and their hounds

hunter /'hunta/, *fem* (1a&2) **huntress** /-tris/ *n* **1a**
sby who hunts game, esp with hounds **b** a usu fast
strong horse used in hunting **2** a person who
hunts or seeks sthg, esp overeagerly **3** a watch
with a hinged metal cover to protect it

hunting /'hunting/ *n* the pursuit of game on
horseback with hounds

'huntsman /-man/ *n* someone who hunts with
hounds; *also* sby who looks after the hounds
belonging to a hunt

'hurdle /'huhdl/ *n* **1a** a portable framework, usu of
interlaced branches and stakes, used esp for
enclosing land or livestock **b** a frame formerly
used for dragging traitors to execution **2a** a light
barrier jumped by men, horses, dogs, etc in certain races **b** *pl* any of various races over hurdles **3**
a barrier, obstacle

'hurdle *v* **hurdling** /'huhdling/ **1** to jump over, esp
while running **2** to overcome, surmount **3** to run
in hurdle races – **~r** *n*

hurdy-gurdy /,huhdi 'guhdi/ *n* a musical instrument in which the sound is produced by turning a
crank; *esp* a barrel organ

hurl /huhl/ *v* **1** to drive or thrust violently **2** to
throw forcefully **3** to utter or shout violently

hurly-burly /,huhli 'buhli/ *n* (an) uproar,
commotion

hurray /hoo'ray/ *interj* – used to express joy,
approval, etc

hurricane /'hurikan/ *n* (a usu tropical cyclone
with) a wind of a velocity greater than 117km/h
(73 to 136mph)

hurried /'hurid/ *adj* done in a hurry – **~ly** *adv*

'hurry /'huri/ *v* **1a** to transport or cause to go with
haste; rush **b** to cause to move or act with (greater)
haste **2** to hasten the progress or completion of **3**
to move or act with haste – often + *up*

'hurry *n* **1** flurried and often bustling haste **2** a need
for haste; urgency – **in a hurry 1** without delay;
hastily **2** eager **3** without difficulty; easily – *infml*

'hurt /huht/ *v* **hurt 1a** to afflict with physical pain;
wound **b** to cause mental distress to; offend **2** to be
detrimental to **3** to feel pain; suffer **4** to cause
damage, distress, or pain

'hurt *n* **1** (a cause of) mental distress **2** wrong, harm

hurtle /'huhtl/ *v* **hurtling** /'huhtling/ **1** to move
rapidly or precipitately **2** to hurl, fling

'husband /'huzband/ *n* a married man, esp in
relation to his wife

'husband *v* to make the most economical use of;
conserve

husbandry /'huzbandri/ *n* **1** the judicious management of resources **2** farming, esp of domestic
animals

'hush /hush/ *v* to make or become quiet or calm

'hush *n* a silence or calm, esp following noise

,hush-'hush *adj* secret, confidential – *infml*

'hush ,money *n* money paid secretly to prevent
disclosure of damaging information

hush up *v* to keep secret; suppress – **hush-up** *n*

'husk /husk/ *n* **1** a dry or membranous outer covering (e g a shell or pod) of a seed or fruit **2** a useless
outer layer of sthg

'husk *v* to strip the husk from

'husky /'huski/ *adj* of, resembling, or containing
husks

'husky *adj* hoarse, breathy – **-kily** *adv* – **-kiness** *n*

'husky *adj* burly, hefty – *infml*

'husky *n* (any of) a breed of sledge dogs native to
Greenland

hussar /hoo'zah/ *n* **1** a Hungarian horseman of
the 15th c **2** *often cap* a member of any of various
European cavalry regiments

hussy /'husi/ *n* an impudent or promiscuous
woman or girl

hustings /'hustingz/ *n pl but sing or pl in constr* **1** a
raised platform used until 1872 for the nomina-
tion of candidates for Parliament and for election
speeches **2** a place where election speeches are
made **3** the proceedings of an election campaign

hustle /'husl/ *v* **hustling** /'husling/ **1a** to push or
convey roughly, forcibly, or hurriedly **b** to impel,
force **2** to swindle, cheat *out of* – *infml* **3** *chiefly
NAm* to make strenuous, often dishonest, efforts
to secure money or business **4** *chiefly NAm* to
engage in prostitution; solicit – **hustle** *n*

hut /hut/ *n* a small often temporary dwelling of
simple construction

hutch /huch/ *n* **1** a pen or cage for a small animal
(e g a rabbit) **2** a shack, shanty – *infml; derog*

hyacinth /'hie-ə‚sinth/ n 1 a common garden plant with fragrant usu blue, pink, or white flowers that grow in spikes 2 a colour varying from light violet to mid-purple

hyaena n a hyena

hybrid /'hiebrid/ n 1 an offspring of 2 animals or plants of different races, breeds, varieties, etc 2 a person of mixed cultural background 3 sthg heterogeneous in origin or composition – ~ize v

hydrangea /hie'draynjə/ n any of a genus of shrubs which produce large clusters of white, pink, or pale blue flowers

hydrant /'hiedrənt/ n a discharge pipe with a valve and nozzle from which water may be drawn from a main

hydraulic /hie'drolik/ adj 1 operated, moved, or effected by means of liquid, esp liquid moving through pipes 2 of hydraulics 3 hardening or setting under water – ~ally adv

hy'draulics n pl but sing in constr a branch of physics that deals with the practical applications of liquid in motion

hydrocarbon /‚hiedroh'kahb(ə)n/ n an organic compound (e g benzene) containing only carbon and hydrogen

hydroe'lectric /-i'lektrik/ adj of or being the production of electricity by waterpower – ~ally adv

hydrofoil /'hiedrə‚foyl/ n (a ship or boat fitted with) a device that, when attached to a ship, lifts the hull out of the water at speed

hydrogen /'hiedrəj(ə)n/ n the simplest and lightest of the elements that is normally a highly inflammable gas

'hydrogen ‚bomb n a bomb whose violent explosive power is due to the sudden release of atomic energy resulting from the nuclear fusion of hydrogen initiated by the explosion of an atom bomb

hydrolysis /hie'droləsis/ n chemical breakdown involving splitting of a bond and addition of the elements of water

hydrophobia /‚hiedrə'fohbi-ə/ n 1 abnormal dread of water 2 rabies

hydroplane /'hiedroh‚playn, -drə-/ n 1 a speedboat fitted with hydrofoils or a stepped bottom so that the hull is raised wholly or partly out of the water when moving at speed 2 a horizontal surface on a submarine's hull, used to control movement upwards or downwards

hyena, hyaena /hie'eenə/ n any of several large nocturnal Old World mammals that usu feed as scavengers

hygiene /'hie‚jeen/ n (conditions or practices, esp cleanliness, conducive to) the establishment and maintenance of health

hymen /'hiemən/ n a fold of mucous membrane partly closing the opening of the vagina in virgins

hymn /him/ n 1 a song of praise to God; esp a metrical composition that can be included in a religious service 2 a song of praise or joy

hyperbole /hie'puhbəli/ n a figure of speech based on extravagant exaggeration

hyperbolic /‚hiepə'bolik/ also **hyperbolical** /-kl/ adj of, characterized by, or given to hyperbole

'hyper‚market /-‚mahkit/ n a very large self-service retail store selling a wide range of household and consumer goods

‚hyper'sensitive /-'sensətiv/ adj abnormally susceptible (e g to a drug or antigen) – **-tivity** n any of the threads that make up the mycelium of a fungus

hyphen /'hief(ə)n/ n a punctuation mark - used to divide or to join together words, word elements, or numbers

hypnosis /hip'nohsis/ n pl **hypnoses** /-seez/ any of various conditions that (superficially) resemble sleep; specif one induced by a person to whose suggestions the subject is then markedly susceptible – **-notic** adj – **-notically** adv

hypnotism /'hipnə‚tiz(ə)m/ n 1 the induction of hypnosis 2 hypnosis – **-tist** n – **-ize** v

‚hypo'chondria /-'kondri-ə/ also **hypochondriasis** /-kond'rie-əsis/ n morbid concern about one's health – ~ **c** n, adj

hypocrisy /hi'pokrəsi/ n the feigning of virtues, beliefs, or standards, esp in matters of religion or morality

hypocrite /'hipəkrit/ n one given to hypocrisy – **-critical** adj

¹hypo'dermic /-'duhmik/ adj of the parts beneath the skin – ~ally adv

²hypodermic n 1 a hypodermic injection 2 a hypodermic syringe

hypodermic syringe n a small syringe used with a hollow needle for injection or withdrawal of material beneath the skin

hypotenuse /hie'pot(ə)n‚yoohz/ n the side of a right-angled triangle that is opposite the right angle

hypothermia /‚hiepoh'thuhmi-ə/ n abnormally low body temperature

hypothesis /hie'pothəsis/ n, pl **hypotheses** /-seez/ a provisional assumption made in order to investigate its consequences or for the sake of argument

hypothetical /‚hiepə'thetikl/ adj of or depending on supposition; conjectural

hysterectomy /‚histə'rektəmi/ n surgical removal of the uterus

hysteria /hi'stiəri-ə/ n 1 a mental disorder marked by emotional excitability and disturbances (e g paralysis) of the normal bodily processes 2 unmanageable emotional excess – **-ric** n – **-rical** adj

hysterics /hi'steriks/ n pl but sing or pl in constr a fit of uncontrollable laughter or crying; hysteria

i /ie/ *n, pl* **i's, is** *often cap* **1** (a graphic representation of or device for reproducing) the 9th letter of the English alphabet **2** one

I /ie/ *pron* the one who is speaking or writing

iamb /'ie·am(b)/ *n* a metrical foot consisting of 1 short or unstressed syllable followed by 1 long or stressed syllable – ~**ic** *adj, n*

Iberian /ie'biəri·ən/ *n* a native or inhabitant of Spain or Portugal – **-Iberian** *adj*

ibidem /i'biedem/ *adv* in the same book, chapter, passage, etc as previously mentioned

ibis /'iebis/ *n* any of several wading birds related to the herons

¹**ice** /ies/ *n* **1a** frozen water **b** a sheet or stretch of ice **2** a substance reduced to the solid state by cold **3** (a serving of) a frozen dessert: e g **3a** an ice cream **b** a water ice **4** *NAm* diamonds – *slang* — **on ice** in abeyance; in reserve for later use

²**ice** *v* **1a** to coat with or convert into ice **b** to supply or chill with ice **2** to cover (as if) with icing **3** to become ice-cold **4** to become covered or clogged with ice

ice age *n* a time of widespread glaciation; *esp* that occurring in the Pleistocene epoch

iceberg /-,buhg/ *n* **1** a large floating mass of ice detached from a glacier **2** an emotionally cold person

ice cap /-,kap/ *n* a lasting (extensive) cover of ice

ice cream /,ies 'kreem, 'ies ,kreem/ *n* a sweet flavoured frozen food containing cream (substitute) and often eggs

ice hockey *n* a game played on an ice rink by 2 teams of 6 players on skates whose object is to drive a puck into the opponent's goal with a hockey stick

¹**Icelandic** /ies'landik/ *adj* (characteristic) of Iceland

²**Icelandic** *n* the N Germanic language of the Icelandic people

ice lolly /,ies 'loli, 'ies ,loli/ *n* an ice cream or esp a flavoured piece of ice on a stick

icicle /'iesikl/ *n* a hanging tapering mass of ice formed by the freezing of dripping water

icing /'iesing/ *n* a sweet (creamy) coating for cakes or other baked goods

icon, ikon /'iekon/ *n* **1** a usu pictorial image **2** a conventional religious image, usu painted on a small wooden panel, used in worship in the Eastern Church

i'cono,clast /-,klast/ *n* **1** a person who destroys religious images or opposes their veneration **2** one who attacks established beliefs or institutions – ~**ic** *adj*

icy /'iesi/ *adj* **1a** covered with, full of, or consisting of ice **b** intensely cold **2** characterized by personal coldness – **icily** *adv* – **iciness** *n*

id /id/ *n* the one of the 3 divisions of the mind in psychoanalytic theory that is completely unconscious and is the source of psychic energy derived from instinctual needs and drives

idea /ie'diə/ *n* **1** an indefinite or vague impression **2** sthg (e g a thought, concept, or image) actually or potentially present in the mind **3** a formulated thought or opinion **4** whatever is known or supposed about sthg **5** an individual's conception of the perfect or typical example of sthg specified **6** the central meaning or aim of a particular action or situation

¹**ideal** /ie'deel/ *adj* **1a** existing only in the mind; *broadly* lacking practicality **b** relating to or constituting mental images, ideas, or conceptions **2** of or embodying an ideal; perfect – ~**ly** *adv*

²**ideal** *n* **1** a standard of perfection, beauty, or excellence **2** one looked up to as embodying an ideal or as a model for imitation **3** an ultimate object or aim – ~**ize** *v*

idealism /ie'dee,liz(ə)m/ *n* **1a** a theory that the essential nature of reality lies in consciousness or reason **b** a theory that only what is immediately perceived (e g sensations or ideas) is real **2** the practice of living according to one's ideals

i'dealist /-list/ *n* **1** one who advocates or practises idealism **2** sby guided by ideals; *esp* one who places ideals before practical considerations – ~**ic** *adj* – ~**ically** *adv*

idem /'idem, 'iedem/ *pron* the same as previously mentioned

identical /ie'dentikl/ *adj* **1** being the same **2** being very similar or exactly alike **3** of *twins, triplets, etc* derived from a single egg

identification /ie,dentifi'kaysh(ə)n/ *n* **1a** identifying or being identified **b** evidence of identity **2a** the putting of oneself mentally in the position of another

identification parade *n, chiefly Br* a line-up of people arranged by the police to allow a witness to identify a suspect

identify /ie'dentifie/ *v* **1a** to cause to be or become identical **b** to associate or link closely **2** to establish the identity of

¹**identikit** /ie'dentikit/ *n, often cap a* set of alternative facial characteristics used by the police to build up a likeness, esp of a suspect; *also* a likeness constructed in this way

²**identikit** *adj, often cap* **1** of or produced by identikit **2** like many others of the same type

identity /ie'dentəti/ *n* **1** the condition of being exactly alike **2** the distinguishing character or personality of an individual **3** the condition of being the same as sthg known or supposed to exist **4** *Austr & NZ* a person, character

ideogram /'idi·ə,gram/ *n* a stylized picture or symbol used instead of a word or sound to represent a thing or idea

ideology /,iedi'oləji/ *n* **1** a systematic body of concepts **2** a manner of thinking characteristic of an individual, group, or culture **3** the ideas behind a social, political, or cultural programme – **ogical** *adj* – **ogist** *n*

ides /iedz/ *n pl but sing or pl in constr* (the week preceding) the 15th day of March, May, July, or October or the 13th day of any other month in the ancient Roman calendar

idiocy /'idi·əsi/ *n* **1** extreme mental deficiency **2** sthg notably stupid or foolish

idiom /'idi·əm/ *n* **1a** the language peculiar to a people or to a district, community, or class **b** the syntactic, grammatical, or structural form peculiar to a language **2** an expression in the usage of a language that has a meaning that cannot be derived from the sum of the meanings of its elements **3** a characteristic style or form of artistic expression

idiomatic /,idi·ə'matik/ *adj* of or conforming to idiom – ~ **ally** *adv*

idiosyncrasy /,idioh'singkrəsi/ *n* **1** characteristic peculiarity of habit or structure **2** a characteristic of thought or behaviour peculiar to an individual or group; *esp* an eccentricity

idiot /'idi·ət/ *n* **1** a person suffering from acute mental deficiency, esp from birth **2** a silly or foolish person – ~ **ic** *adj* – ~ **ically** *adv*

¹idle /'iedl/ *adj* **1** having no particular purpose or value **2** groundless **3** not occupied or employed: e g **3a** not in use or operation **b** not turned to appropriate use **4** lazy – ~ **ness** *n* – **idly** *adv*

²idle *v* **idling** /'iedling/ **1a** to spend time in idleness **b** to move idly **2** *esp of an engine* to run without being connected to the part (e g the wheels of a car) that is driven, so that no useful work is done

idol /'iedl/ *n* **1** an image or symbol used as an object of worship; *broadly* a false god **2** an object of passionate or excessive devotion – ~ **ize** *v*

idolater /ie'dolətə/ *n* **1** a worshipper of idols **2** a passionate and often uncritical admirer – **-trous** *adj* – **-trously** *adv* – **-try** *n*

idyll, idyl /'idil/ *n* (a work in poetry or prose describing) a scene or episode of peaceful country life – ~ **ic** *adj*

¹if /if/ *conj* **1a** in the event that (e g *if* she should call, let me know) **b** supposing *(e g if* you'd listened, you'd know) **c** on condition that **2** whether (e g asked *if* the mail had come) **3** – used to introduce an exclamation expressing a wish (e g *if* only it would rain) **4** even if; although (e g an interesting

if irrelevant point) **5** that – used after expressions of emotion (e g I don't care *if* she's cross) — **if anything** on the contrary even; perhaps even

²if *n* **1** a condition, stipulation **2** a supposition

igloo /'iglooh/ *n pl* **igloos** an Eskimo dwelling, usu made of snow blocks and in the shape of a dome

igneous /'igni·əs/ *adj* **1** fiery **2** relating to or formed by the flow or solidification of molten rock from the earth's core

ignite /ig'niet/ *v* **1a** to set fire to; *also* to kindle **b** to cause (a fuel mixture) to burn **c** to catch fire **2** to spark off; excite, esp suddenly

ignition /ig'nish(ə)n/ *n* **1** the act or action of igniting **2** the process or means (e g an electric spark) of igniting a fuel mixture

ignoble /ig'nohbl/ *adj* **1** of low birth or humble origin **2** base, dishonourable

ignominious /,ignə'mini·əs/ *adj* **1** marked by or causing disgrace or discredit **2** humiliating, degrading

ignominy /'ignəmini/ *n* **1** deep personal humiliation and disgrace **2** disgraceful or dishonourable conduct or quality

ignoramus /,ignə'rayməs, -'rahməs/ *n* an ignorant person

ignorance /'ignərəns/ *n* the state of being ignorant

ignorant /'ignərənt/ *adj* **1** lacking knowledge, education, or comprehension (of sthg specified) **2** caused by or showing lack of knowledge **3** lacking social training; impolite – chiefly *infml*

ignore /ig'naw/ *v* to refuse to take notice of; disregard

iguana /i,igyoo'ahnə, i'gwahnə/ *n* any of various large lizards; *esp* a plant-eating (dark-coloured) tropical American lizard with a serrated crest on its back

ikon /'iekon/ *n* an icon

¹ilk /ilk/ *pron, chiefly Scot* that same – esp in the names of landed families

²ilk *n* sort, kind

¹ill /il/ *adj* **worse** /wuhs/; **worst** /wuhst/ **1** bad: e g **1a** morally evil **b** malevolent, hostile **c** attributing evil or an objectionable quality **2a** causing discomfort or inconvenience; disagreeable **b(1)** not normal or sound **b(2)** not in good health; *also* nauseated **3** unlucky, disadvantageous **4** socially improper **5a** unfriendly, hostile **b** harsh

²ill *adv* **worse**; **worst 1a** with displeasure or hostility **b** in a harsh manner **c** so as to reflect unfavourably **2** in a reprehensible, harsh, or deficient manner **3** hardly, scarcely (e g can *ill* afford it) **4a** in an unfortunate manner; badly, unluckily **b** in a faulty, imperfect, or unpleasant manner *USE* often in combination

³ill *n* **1** the opposite of good; evil **2a** (a) misfortune, trouble **b(1)** an ailment **b(2)** sthg that disturbs or afflicts **3** sthg that reflects unfavourably

,ill-ad'vised adj showing lack of proper consideration or sound advice

,ill-'bred adj having or showing bad upbringing; impolite

illegal /i'leegl/ adj not authorized by law – ~ity n – ~ly adv

illegible /i'lejəbl/ adj not legible – -bility n – -bly adv

illegitimate /,ili'jitimət/ adj 1 not recognized as lawful offspring; specif born out of wedlock 2 wrongly deduced or inferred 3 departing from the regular; abnormal 4 illegal – -macy n

,ill-'favoured adj 1 unattractive in physical appearance 2 offensive, objectionable

,ill-'gotten adj acquired by illicit or improper means – esp in ill-gotten gains

illiberal /,i'librəl/ adj not liberal: e g a lacking culture and refinement b not broad-minded; bigoted c opposed to liberalism – ~ity n

illicit /i'lisit/ adj not permitted; unlawful

illiterate /i'lit(ə)rət/ adj 1 unable to read or write 2 showing lack of education – -racy n

,ill-'natured adj having a disagreeable disposition; surly

illness /'ilnis/ n an unhealthy condition of body or mind

illogical /i'lojikl/ adj 1 contrary to the principles of logic 2 devoid of logic; senseless

,ill-'timed adj badly timed; esp inopportune

,ill-'treat v to treat cruelly or improperly – ~ment n

illuminate /i'l(y)oohminayt/ v 1a(1) to cast light on; fill with light a(2) to brighten b to enlighten spiritually or intellectually 2 to elucidate 3 to decorate (a manuscript) with elaborate initial letters or marginal designs in gold, silver, and brilliant colours – -ation n

illusion /i'l(y)oohzh(ə)n/ n 1 a false impression or notion 2a(1) a misleading image presented to the vision a(2) sthg that deceives or misleads intellectually b perception of an object in such a way that it presents a misleading image

illusory /i'l(y)oohsəri, -zəri/ adj deceptive, unreal

illustrate /'iləstrayt/ v 1a to clarify (by giving or serving as an example or instance) b to provide (e g a book) with visual material 2 to show clearly; demonstrate – -tive adj – -tively adv

illustration /,ilə'straysh(ə)n/ n 1 illustrating or being illustrated 2 sthg that serves to illustrate: e g 2a an example that explains or clarifies sthg b a picture or diagram that helps to make sthg clear or attractive

illustrious /i'lustri-əs/ adj marked by distinction or renown

image /'imij/ n 1 a reproduction (e g a portrait or statue) of the form of a person or thing 2a the optical counterpart of an object produced by a lens, mirror, etc or an electronic device b a likeness of an object produced on a photographic

material 3a exact likeness b a person who strikingly resembles another specified person 4 a typical example or embodiment (e g of a quality) 5a a mental picture of sthg (not actually present) b an idea, concept 6 a figure of speech, esp a metaphor or simile

imagery /'imij(ə)ri/ n 1 (the art of making) images 2 figurative language 3 mental images; esp the products of imagination

imaginable /i'majinəbl/ adj capable of being imagined

imaginary /i'majin(ə)ri/ adj existing only in imagination; lacking factual reality

imagination /i,maji'naysh(ə)n/ n 1 the act or power of forming a mental image of sthg not present to the senses or never before wholly perceived in reality 2 creative ability 3 a fanciful or empty notion

imaginative /i'maj(i)nətiv/ adj 1 of or characterized by imagination 2 given to imagining; having a lively imagination 3 of images; esp showing a command of imagery

imagine /i'maj(ə)n/ v 1 to form a mental image of (sthg not present) 2 to suppose, think 3 to believe without sufficient basis 4 to use the imagination

imbalance /im'baləns/ n lack of balance

imbecile /'imbəseel, -siel/ n 1 a mental defective 2 a fool, idiot – -ility n

imbibe /im'bieb/ v 1 to drink (habitually or to excess) 2 to take in or up; absorb, assimilate

imbroglio /im'brohlioh/ n pl imbroglios 1 a confused mass 2 an intricate or complicated situation or misunderstanding

imbue /im'byooh/ v to cause to become permeated with

imitate /'imitayt/ v 1 to follow as a pattern, model, or example 2 to reproduce 3 to resemble 4 to mimic – -ation, -ativeness n – -ative adj

immaculate /i'makyoolət/ adj 1 without blemish; pure 2 free from flaw or error 3 spotlessly clean

immaterial /,imə'tiəri-əl/ adj 1 not consisting of matter; incorporeal 2 unimportant

immature /,imə'tyooə/ adj 1 lacking complete growth, differentiation, or development 2a not having arrived at a definitive form or state b exhibiting less than an expected degree of maturity – -turity n

immeasurable /i'mezh(ə)rəbl/ adj indefinitely extensive – -bly adv

immediacy /i'meedi-əsi/ n 1 the quality or state of being immediate 2 sthg requiring immediate attention – usu pl

immediate /i'meedi-ət, -dyət/ adj 1 acting or being without any intervening agency or factor 2 next in line or relationship 3 occurring at once or very shortly 4 in close or direct physical proximity 5 directly touching or concerning a person or thing

imp

¹**im'mediately** /-li/ *adv* **1** in direct relation or proximity; directly **2** without delay

²**immediately** *conj* as soon as

immemorial /ˌimi'mawri:əl/ *adj* extending beyond the reach of memory, record, or tradition

immense /i'mens/ *adj* very great, esp in size, degree, or extent – **-ensity** *n*

immerse /i'muhs/ *v* **1** to plunge into sthg, esp a fluid, that surrounds or covers **2** to baptize by complete submergence **3** to engross, absorb – **-sion** *n*

immigrate /'imigrayt/ *v* to come into a country of which one is not a native for permanent residence – **-gration** *n* – **-grant** *n*

imminent /'iminənt/ *adj* about to take place; *esp* impending, threatening – **-ence, -ency** *n*

immobile /i'mohbiel/ *adj* **1** incapable of being moved **2** motionless – **-bility** *n*, **-bilize** *v*

immoderate /i'mod(ə)rət/ *adj* lacking in moderation; excessive – **-racy** *n*

immodest /i'modist/ *adj* not conforming to standards of sexual propriety – **~y** *n*

immolate /'imohlayt/ *v* to kill (as a sacrificial victim) – **-lation** *n*

immoral /i'morəl/ *adj* not conforming to conventional moral standards, esp in sexual matters – **~ity** *n*

¹**immortal** /i'mawtl/ *adj* **1** exempt from death **2** enduring forever; imperishable – **~ity** *n*

²**immortal** *n* **1a** one exempt from death **b** *pl, often cap* the gods of classical antiquity **2** a person of lasting fame

immovable /i'moohvəbl/ *adj* **1** not moving or not intended to be moved **2a** steadfast, unyielding **b** incapable of being moved emotionally

immune /i'myoohn/ *adj* **1** free, exempt **2** having a high degree of resistance to a disease **3a** having or producing antibodies to a corresponding antigen **b** concerned with or involving immunity – **immunity** *n* – **immunize** *v*

immure /i'myooə/ *v* **1** to enclose (as if) within walls; imprison **2** to build into, or esp entomb in, a wall

immutable /i'myoohtəbl/ *adj* not capable of or susceptible to change – **-bility** *n*

imp /imp/ *n* **1** a small demon **2** a mischievous child; a scamp

¹**impact** /im'pakt/ *v* **1** to fix or press firmly (as if) by packing or wedging **2** to impinge or make contact, esp forcefully

²**impact** /'impakt/ *n* **1a** an impinging or striking, esp of one body against another **b** (the impetus produced by or as if by) a violent contact or collision **2** a strong or powerful effect or impression

impair /im'peə/ *v* to diminish in quality, strength, or amount – **~ment** *n*

impale /im'payl/ *v* to pierce (as if) with sthg pointed; *esp* to torture or kill by fixing on a stake

impalpable /im'palpəbl/ *adj* **1** incapable of being sensed by the touch; intangible **2** not easily discerned or grasped by the mind

impart /im'paht/ *v* **1** to convey, transmit **2** to make known; disclose

impartial /im'pahsh(ə)l/ *adj* not biased – **~ity** *n*

impassable /im'pahsəbl/ *adj* incapable of being passed, traversed, or surmounted

impasse /'am,pas (Fr ɛpɑːs)/ *n* **1** a predicament from which there is no obvious escape **2** a deadlock

impassive /im'pasiv/ *adj* **1** incapable of or not susceptible to emotion **2** showing no feeling or emotion – **-sivity** *n* – **~ly** *adv*

impatient /im'paysh(ə)nt/ *adj* **1a** restless or quickly roused to anger or exasperation **b** intolerant **2** showing or caused by a lack of patience **3** eagerly desirous; anxious – **-ience** *n* – **~ly** *adv*

impeach /im'peech/ *v* **1a** to bring an accusation against **b** to charge with a usu serious crime; *specif, chiefly NAm* to charge (a public official) with misconduct in office **2** to cast doubt on; *esp* to challenge the credibility or validity of – **~ment** *n* – **~able** *adj*

impeccable /im'pekəbl/ *adj* **1** incapable of sinning **2** free from fault or blame; flawless

impecunious /ˌimpi'kyoohnyəs, -ni:əs/ *adj* having very little or no money – chiefly *fml* – **~ness** *n*

impedance /im'peed(ə)ns/ *n* sthg that impedes; *esp* the opposition in an electrical circuit to the flow of an alternating current that is analogous to the opposition of an electrical resistance to the flow of a direct current

impede /im'peed/ *v* to interfere with or retard the progress of – **-diment** *n*

impel /im'pel/ *v* **-ll- 1** to urge forward or force into action **2** to propel

impenetrable im'penitrəbl/ *adj* **1a** incapable of being penetrated or pierced **b** inaccessible to intellectual influences or ideas **2** incapable of being comprehended

¹**imperative** /im'perətiv/ *adj* **1a** of or being the grammatical mood that expresses command **b** expressive of a command, entreaty, or exhortation **c** having power to restrain, control, and direct **2** urgent

²**imperative** *n* **1** (a verb form expressing) the imperative mood **2** sthg imperative: e g **2a** a command, order **b** an obligatory act or duty **c** an imperative judgment or proposition

imperceptible /impə'septəbl/ *adj* **1** not perceptible by the mind or senses **2** extremely slight, gradual, or subtle – **-bility** *n* – **-bly** *adv*

¹**imperfect** /im'puhfikt/ *adj* **1** not perfect: e g **1a** defective **b** not having the stamens and carpels in the same flower **2** of or being a verb tense expressing a continuing state or an incomplete action, esp in the past – **~ion** *n* – **~ly** *adv*

²**imperfect** *n* (a verb form expressing) the imperfect tense

imperial /im'piəri·əl/ *adj* **1a** of or befitting an empire, emperor, or empress **b** of the British Empire **2a** sovereign, royal **b** regal, imperious **3** belonging to an official nonmetric British series of weights and measures

imperialism /im'piəri·ə‚liz(ə)m/ *n* **1** government by an emperor **2** the policy, practice, or advocacy of extending the power and dominion of a nation, esp by territorial acquisition – **~ist** *adj*, *n* – **‑istic** *adj*

imperil /im'perəl/ *v* **‑ll‑** (*NAm* **‑l‑**, **‑ll‑**) to endanger

imperious /im'piəri·əs/ *adj* marked by arrogant assurance; domineering – **~ness** *n*

imperishable /im'perishəbl/ *adj* **1** not perishable or subject to decay **2** enduring permanently

impermanent /im'puhmənənt/ *adj* transient – **‑nence** *n*

impermeable /im'puhmi·əbl/ *adj* not permitting passage, esp of a fluid

impersonal /‑'puhs(ə)nl/ *adj* **1a** denoting verbal action with no expressed subject (e g *methinks*) or with a merely formal subject (e g *rained* in *it rained*) **b** of a *pronoun* indefinite **2a** having no personal reference or connection; objective **b** not involving or reflecting the human personality or emotions **c** not having personality

impersonate /im'puhsənayt/ *v* to assume or act the character of – **‑nation** *n* – **‑nator** *n*

impertinent /im'puhtinənt/ *adj* **1** not restrained within due or proper bounds; *also* rude, insolent **2** irrelevant – chiefly *fml* – **‑nence** *n*

imperturbable /‚impə'tuhbəbl, ‑puh‑/ *adj* marked by extreme calm and composure – **‑bility** *n*

impervious /im'puhvi·əs/ *adj* **1** impenetrable **2** not capable of being affected or disturbed *USE* usu + *to*

impetuous /im'petyoo·əs/ *adj* **1** marked by impulsive vehemence **2** marked by forceful and violent movement – chiefly poetic – **‑osity** *n*

impetus /'impitəs/ *n* **1a** a driving force **b** an incentive, stimulus **2** the energy possessed by a moving body

impiety /im'pie·əti/ *n* (an act showing) a lack of reverence – **impious** *adj*

impinge /im'pinj/ *v* **1** to make an impression **2** to encroach, infringe *USE* usu + *on* or *upon*

impish /'impish/ *adj* mischievous – **~ness** *n*

implacable /im'plakəbl/ *adj* not capable of being appeased or pacified

¹**implant** /im'plahnt/ *v* **1** to fix or set securely or deeply **2** to insert in the tissue of a living organism

²**implant** /'im‚plahnt/ *n* sthg (e g a graft or hormone pellet) implanted in tissue

¹**implement** /'implimənt/ *n* **1** an article serving to equip **2** (sby or sthg that serves as) a utensil or tool

²**implement** /'impliment, ‑mənt/ *v* to carry out; *esp* to give practical effect to

implicate /'implikayt/ *v* **1** to involve as a consequence, corollary, or inference; imply **2a** to bring into (incriminating) connection with sthg **b** to involve in the nature or operation of sthg; affect

implication /‚impli'kaysh(ə)n/ *n* **1a** implicating or being implicated **b** incriminating involvement **2a** implying or being implied **b** a logical relation between 2 propositions such that if the first is true the second must be true **3** sthg implied

implicit /im'plisit/ *adj* **1a** implied rather than directly stated **b** potentially present though not realized or visible **2** unquestioning, absolute

implode /im'plohd/ *v* to collapse inwards suddenly – **implosion** *n*

implore /im'plaw/ *v* **1** to call on in supplication; beseech **2** to call or beg for earnestly; entreat

imply /im'plie/ *v* **1** to involve or indicate as a necessary or potential though not expressly stated consequence **2** to express indirectly; hint at

impolite /‚impə'liet/ *adj* not polite; rude – **~ness** *n*

impolitic /im'polətik/ *adj* unwise, ill-advised – chiefly *fml*

imponderable /im'pond(ə)rəbl/ *n or adj* (sthg) incapable of being precisely weighed or evaluated

¹**import** /im'pawt/ *v* **1** to bring from a foreign or external source; *esp* to bring (e g merchandise) into a place or country from another country **2** to convey as meaning or portent; signify – chiefly *fml* – **~er** *n*

²**import** /'impawt/ *n* **1** sthg imported **2** importing, esp of merchandise **3** purport, meaning **4** (relative) importance *USE* (3 & 4) *fml*

important /im'pawt(ə)nt/ *adj* of considerable significance or consequence – **‑ance** *n* – **~ly** *adj*

importunate /im'pawtyoonət, ‑chənət/ *adj* troublesomely persistent in request or demand – chiefly *fml* – **‑nity** *n*

importune /im'pawtyoohn, ‑choohn/ *v* **1** to press or urge with repeated requests **2** to solicit for purposes of prostitution *USE* chiefly *fml*

impose /im'pohz/ *v* **1a** to establish or apply as compulsory **b** to establish or make prevail by force **2** to force into the company or on the attention of another **3** to take unwarranted advantage; *also* to be an excessive requirement or burden – **‑sition** *n*

imposing /im'pohzing/ *adj* impressive because of size, bearing, dignity, or grandeur

impossible /im'posibl/ *adj* **1a** incapable of being or occurring; not possible **b** seemingly incapable of being done, attained, or fulfilled; insuperably difficult **c** difficult to believe **2** extremely undesirable or difficult to put up with – **‑bility** *n*

impostor, imposter /im'postə/ *n* one who assumes a false identity or title for fraudulent purposes

impotent /'impət(ə)nt/ *adj* 1 lacking in efficacy, strength, or vigour 2a unable to copulate through an inability to maintain an erection of the penis b *of a male* sterile – not used technically – **-tence** *n*

impound /im'pownd/ *v* 1a to shut up (as if) in a pound; confine b to take and hold in legal custody 2 to collect and confine (water) (as if) in a reservoir

impoverish /im'pov(ə)rish/ *v* 1 to make poor 2 to deprive of strength, richness, or fertility

impracticable /im'praktikəbl/ *adj* 1 incapable of being put into effect or carried out 2 impassable – **-bility** *n*

impractical /im'praktikl/ *adj* not practical: e g a incapable of dealing sensibly with practical matters b impracticable – **~ity** *n*

impregnable /im'pregnəbl/ *adj* 1 incapable of being taken by assault 2 beyond criticism or question – **-bility** *n*

impregnate /'impregnayt/ *v* 1a to introduce sperm cells into b to make pregnant; fertilize 2a to cause to be imbued, permeated, or saturated b to permeate thoroughly

impresario /,impri'sahrioh/ *n pl* **impresarios** one who organizes, puts on, or sponsors a public entertainment

¹**impress** /im'pres/ *v* 1a to apply with pressure so as to imprint b to mark (as if) by pressure or stamping 2a to fix strongly or deeply (e g in the mind or memory) b to produce a deep and usu favourable impression (on) 3 to transmit (force or motion) by pressure

²**impress** /'impres/ *n* 1 the act of impressing 2 a mark made by pressure 3 an impression, effect

³**im'press** *v* to procure or enlist by forcible persuasion

impression /im'presh(ə)n/ *n* 1 the act or process of impressing 2 the effect produced by impressing: e g 2a a stamp, form, or figure produced by physical contact b a (marked) influence or effect on the mind or senses; *esp* a favourable impression 3a an effect of alteration or improvement b a telling image impressed on the mind or senses 4a (a print or copy made from) the contact of a printing surface and the material being printed b all the copies of a publication (e g a book) printed in 1 continuous operation 5 a usu indistinct or imprecise notion or recollection 6 an imitation or representation of salient features in an artistic or theatrical medium; *esp* an imitation in caricature of a noted personality as a form of theatrical entertainment

im'pressionable /-əbl/ *adj* 1 easily influenced 2 easily moulded – **-bly** *adv* – **-bility** *n*

impressionism /-iz(ə)m/ *n* 1 *often cap* an art movement, esp in late 19th-c France, that tries to convey the effects of actual reflected light on natural usu outdoor subjects 2 literary depiction that seeks to convey a general subjective impression rather than a detailed re-creation of reality – **-ist** *adj*, *n*

im,pression'istic /-'istik/ *adj* 1 of or being impressionism 2 based on or involving subjective impression as distinct from knowledge, fact, or systematic thought – **~ally** *adv*

impressive /im'presiv/ *adj* making a marked impression; stirring deep feelings, esp of awe or admiration – **~ly** *adv* – **~ness** *n*

¹**imprint** /im'print/ *v* 1 to mark (as if) by pressure 2 to fix indelibly or permanently (e g on the memory)

²**imprint** /'imprint/ *n* 1 a mark or depression made by pressure 2 a publisher's name printed at the foot of a title-page 3 an indelible distinguishing effect or influence

imprison /im'priz(ə)n/ *v* to put (as if) in prison – **~ment** *n*

improbable /im'probəbl/ *adj* unlikely to be true or to occur – **-bility** *n* – **-bly** *adv*

¹**impromptu** /im'promptyooh/ *adj* made, done, composed, or uttered (as if) on the spur of the moment

²**impromptu** *n* 1 sthg impromptu 2 a musical composition suggesting improvisation

improper /im'propə/ *adj* 1 not in accordance with fact, truth, or correct procedure 2 not suitable or appropriate 3 not in accordance with propriety or modesty; indecent – **-priety** *n*

improve /im'proohv/ *v* 1 to enhance in value or quality; make better 2 to use to good purpose 3 to advance or make progress in what is desirable 4 to make useful additions or amendments – **~ment** *n*

improvident /im'provid(ə)nt/ *adj* lacking foresight; not providing for the future – **-dence** *n*

improvise /'imprəviez/ *v* 1 to compose, recite, or perform impromptu or without a set script, musical score, etc 2 to make, devise, or provide (sthg) without preparation (from what is conveniently to hand) – **-visation** *n*

imprudent /im'proohd(ə)nt/ *adj* lacking discretion or caution – **-dence** *n*

impudent /'impyood(ə)nt/ *adj* insolent – **-dence** *n*

impugn /im'pyoohn/ *v* to assail by words or arguments; call into question the validity or integrity of

impulse /'impuls/ *n* 1a (motion produced by) the act of driving onwards with sudden force b a wave of excitation transmitted through a nerve that results in physiological (e g muscular) activity or inhibition 2a a force so communicated as to produce motion suddenly b impulsion, stimulus 3a a sudden spontaneous inclination or incitement to some usu unpremeditated action b a propensity or natural tendency, usu other than rational

impulsion /im'pulsh(ə)n/ *n* 1 impelling or being impelled 2 an impelling force 3 an impetus

impulsive /im'pulsiv/ *adj* **1** having the power of driving or impelling **2** actuated by or prone to act on impulse – ~**ness** *n*

impunity /im'pyoohnəti/ *n* exemption or freedom from punishment, harm, or loss

impure /im'pyooə/ *adj* not pure: e **a** not chaste **b** containing sthg unclean **c** ritually unclean **d** mixed; *esp* adulterated – **rity** *n*

impute /im'pyooht/ *v* to attribute unjustly *to*; blame

¹**in** /in/ *prep* **1a**(1) – used to indicate location within or inside sthg three-dimensional (e g swimming *in* the lake) **a**(2) – used to indicate location within or not beyond limits (e g *in* sight) **a**(3) at – used with the names of cities, countries, and seas (e g *in* London) **a**(4) during (e g *in* the summer) **a**(5) by or before the end of (e g will come *in* an hour) **b** into (e g come *in* the kitchen and get warm) **2a** – used to indicate means, instrumentality, or medium of expression (e g written *in* French) **b** – used to describe costume (e g a girl *in* red) **3a** – used to indicate qualification, manner, circumstance, or condition (e g *in* fun; *in* a hurry) **b** – used to indicate occupation or membership (e g a job *in* insurance) **4a** as regards (e g equal *in* distance) **b** by way of (e g said *in* reply) **5a** – used to indicate division, arrangement, or quantity (e g standing *in* a circle) **b** – used to indicate the larger member of a ratio (e g one *in* six is eligible) — **in** *it* of advantage (e g between competitors or alternatives)

²**in** *adv* **1a** to or towards the inside or centre (e g come *in* out of the rain) **b** so as to incorporate (e g mix *in* the flour) **c** to or towards home, the shore, or one's destination (e g 3 ships came sailing *in*) **d** at a particular place, esp at one's home or business (e g be *in* for lunch) **e** into concealment (e g the sun went *in*) **2a** so as to be added or included (e g fit a piece *in*) **b** in or into political power (e g voted them *in*) **c**(1) on good terms (e g *in* with the boss) **c**(2) in a position of assured success **c**(3) into a state of efficiency or proficiency (e g work a horse *in*) **d** in or into vogue or fashion **e** in or into a centre, esp a central point of control (e g letters pouring *in*) — **in for** certain to experience — **in** on having a share in

³**in** *adj* **1a** located inside **b** being in operation or power (e g the fire's still *in*) **c** shared by a select group (e g an *in* joke) **2** extremely fashionable

inability /,inə'biləti/ *n* lack of sufficient power, resources, or capacity

inaccurate /in'akyoorət/ *adj* faulty – **racy** *n*

inaction /in'aksh(ə)n/ *n* lack of action or activity – **tive** *adj* – **tivity** *n*

inadequate /in'adikwət/ *adj* not adequate: e g **a** insufficient **b** characteristically unable to cope – **acy** *n*

inadvertent /,inəd'vuht(ə)nt/ *adj* **1** heedless, inattentive **2** unintentional – **tence** *n*

inalienable /in'aylyənəbl/ *adj* incapable of being alienated

inane /i'nayn/ *adj* lacking significance, meaning, or point – **nity** *n*

inanimate /in'animət/ *adj* **1** not endowed with life or spirit **2** lacking consciousness or power of motion – ~**ness** *n*

inappropriate *adj* not suitable or fitting

inapt /in'apt/ *adj* not suitable or appropriate – ~**ness** *n*

inaptitude /in'aptityoohd/ *n* lack of aptitude

inarticulate /,inah'tikyoolət/ *adj* **1a** not understandable as spoken words **b** incapable of (being expressed by) speech, esp under stress of emotion **2a** not giving or not able to give coherent, clear, or effective expression to one's ideas or feelings **b** not coherently, clearly, or effectively expressed **3** not jointed or hinged – ~**ness** *n*

inasmuch as /inəz'much az/ *conj* **1** insofar as **2** in view of the fact that; because

inattention /,inə'tensh(ə)n/ *n* failure to pay attention; disregard – **tive** *adj* – **tiveness** *n*

inaugurate /in'awgyoorayt/ *v* **1** to induct ceremonially into office **2** to observe formally, or bring about, the beginning of – **tion** *n* – **ral** *adj*

in'born /-'bawn/ *adj* **1** born in or with one; forming part of one's natural make-up **2** hereditary, inherited

,in'bred /-'bred/ *adj* **1** rooted and deeply ingrained in one's nature **2** subjected to or produced by inbreeding

'in,breeding /-,breeding/ *n* **1** the interbreeding of closely related individuals, esp to preserve and fix desirable characters **2** confinement to a narrow range or a local or limited field of choice

incalculable /in'kalkyoolabl/ *adj* **1** too large or numerous to be calculated **2** unpredictable, uncertain – **bly** *adv*

incandescent /,inkan'des(ə)nt/ *adj* **1a** white, glowing, or luminous with intense heat **b** strikingly bright, radiant, or clear **2** of or being visible light produced by a (white) hot body – ~**ence** *n*

incantation /,inkan'taysh(ə)n/ *n* the use of spoken or sung spells in magic ritual; *also* a formula so used

incapable /in'kaypəbl/ *adj* lacking capacity, ability, or qualification for the purpose or end in view: e g **a** not in a state or of a kind to admit *of* **b** not able or fit for the doing or performance *of* – **bility** *n* – **bly** *adv*

incapacitate /,inkə'pasitayt/ *v* **1** to deprive of capacity or natural power; disable **2** to disqualify legally – **pacity** *n*

incarcerate /in'kahsərayt/ *v* to imprison, confine – **ration** *n*

¹**incarnate** /in'kahnət, -nayt/ *adj* **1** invested with bodily, esp human, nature and form **2** that is the essence of; typified

²**incarnate** /'inkah,nayt/ *v* to make incarnate

incarnation /ˌinkah'naysh(ə)n/ *n* 1 making or being incarnate 2a(1) the embodiment of a deity or spirit in an earthly form a(2) *cap* Christ's human manifestation b a quality or concept typified or made concrete, esp in a person 3 any of several successive bodily manifestations or lives

¹**incendiary** /in'sendyəri/ *n* 1a one who deliberately sets fire to property b an incendiary agent (e g a bomb) 2 one who inflames or stirs up factions, quarrels, or sedition

²**incendiary** *adj* 1 of the deliberate burning of property 2 tending to inflame or stir up trouble 3 (of, being, or involving the use of) a missile containing a chemical) that ignites spontaneously on contact

¹**incense** /'insens/ *n* 1 material used to produce a fragrant smell when burned 2 the perfume given off by some spices and gums when burned; *broadly* a pleasing scent

²**incense** /in'sens/ *v* to arouse the extreme anger or indignation of

incentive /in'sentiv/ *n* sthg that motivates or spurs one on

inception /in'sepsh(ə)n/ *n* a beginning

incessant /in'ses(ə)nt/ *adj* continuing without interruption – ~**ly** *adv*

incest /'insest/ *n* sexual intercourse between people so closely related that they are forbidden by law to marry – ~**uous** *adj*

¹**inch** /inch/ *n* 1 a unit of length equal to ¹/₃₆yd (about 25.4mm) 2 a small amount, distance, or degree — **every inch** to the utmost degree — **within an inch of one's life** very thoroughly; soundly

²**inch** *v* to move by small degrees

inchoate /'inkoh-ayt/ *adj* only partly in existence or operation; *esp* imperfectly formed or formulated – *fml*

incidence /'insid(ə)ns/ *n* 1 an occurrence 2 the rate of occurrence or influence

¹**incident** /'insid(ə)nt/ *n* 1 an occurrence of an action or situation that is a separate unit of experience 2 an occurrence that is a cause of conflict or disagreement 3 an event occurring as part of a series or as dependent on or subordinate to sthg else

²**incident** *adj* 1 that is a usual accompaniment or consequence 2 dependent on another thing in law

¹**incidental** /ˌinsi'dentl/ *adj* 1 occurring merely by chance 2 likely to ensue as a chance or minor consequence

²**incidental** *n* 1 sthg incidental 2 *pl* minor items (e g of expenses)

incidentally /ˌinsi'dentl·i/ *adv* 1 by chance 2 by the way

incinerate /in'sinərayt/ *v* to cause to burn to ashes – **-ration** *n*

incinerator /in'sinəraytə/ *n* a furnace or container for incinerating waste materials

incipient /in'sipi-ənt/ *adj* beginning to come into being or to become apparent – **-ience, -iency** *n*

incise /in'siez/ *v* 1 to cut into 2 to engrave – **-cision** *n*

incisive /in'siesiv/ *adj* impressively direct and decisive (e g in manner or presentation)

incisor /in'siezə/ *n* a cutting tooth; *specif* any of the cutting teeth in mammals in front of the canines

incite /in'siet/ *v* to move to action; stir up – ~**ment** *n*

¹**incline** /in'klien/ *v* 1 to (cause to) lean, tend, or become drawn towards an opinion or course of conduct 2 to (cause to) deviate or move from a line, direction, or course – **-nation** *n*

²**incline** /'inklien/ *n* an inclined surface; a slope

inclose /in'klohz/ *v* to enclose

include /in'kloohd/ *v* 1 to contain, enclose 2 to take in or comprise as a part of a larger group, set, or principle – **-ding** *prep* – ~**d** *adj* – **-usion** *n*

inclusive /in'kloohsiv, -ziv/ *adj* 1a broad in orientation or scope b covering or intended to cover all or the specified items, costs, or services 2 including the stated limits or extremes

incognito /ˌinkog'neetoh/ *adv or adj* with one's identity concealed

incoherent /ˌinkoh'hiərənt/ *adj* lacking in logical connection or clarity of expression; unintelligible – **-ence** *n*

incombustible /ˌinkəm'bustəbl/ *adj* incapable of being ignited or burned

income /'inkum, 'inkəm/ *n* (the amount of) a usu periodic gain or recurrent benefit usu measured in money that derives from one's work, property, or investment

'income ˌtax *n* a tax on income

¹**incoming** /'inˌkuming/ *n* 1 a coming in, arrival 2 *pl* income

²**incoming** *adj* 1 arriving or coming in 2 just starting, beginning, or succeeding

incommensurable /ˌinkə'mensh(ə)rəbl/ *adj* incapable of being compared

incommensurate /ˌinkə'menshərət/ *adj* not adequate (in proportion)

incommode /ˌinkə'mohd/ *v* to inconvenience, trouble – *fml* – **-dious** *adj*

incommunicado /ˌinkəˌmyoohni'kahdoh/ *adv or adj* without means of communication; *also* in solitary confinement

incomparable /in'komp(ə)rəbl/ *adj* 1 matchless 2 not suitable for comparison – **-bility** *n* – **-bly** *adv*

incompatible /ˌinkəm'patəbl/ *adj* 1 (incapable of association because) incongruous, discordant, or disagreeing 2 unsuitable for use together because of undesirable chemical or physiological effects – **-bility** *n* – **-bly** *adv*

incompetent /in'kompit(ə)nt/ adj 1 lacking the qualities needed for effective action 2 not legally qualified 3 inadequate to or unsuitable for a particular purpose – **-ence, -ency** n

incomplete /ˌinkəm'pleet/ adj 1 unfinished 2 lacking a part – ~ness n

incomprehensible /ˌinkompri'hensəbl, -ˌ--'---/ adj impossible to comprehend or understand – **-bility** n – **-bly** adv

incomprehension /inkompri'hensh(ə)n/ n lack of comprehension or understanding

inconceivable /ˌinkən'seevəbl/ adj 1 beyond comprehension; unimaginable 2 unbelievable – **-bility** n

inconclusive /ˌinkən'klooshiv/ adj leading to no conclusion or definite result – ~ness n

incongruous /in'kong·groo·əs/ adj out of place; discordant or disagreeing – ~ness n; -**uity** n

inconsequential /ˌinkonsi'kwensh(ə)l/ adj 1 irrelevant 2 of no significance – ~**ity** n

inconsiderable /ˌinkən'sid(ə)rəbl/ adj trivial

inconsiderate /ˌinkən'sid(ə)rət/ adj careless of the rights or feelings of others; thoughtless – ~ness n

inconsistent /ˌinkən'sist(ə)nt/ adj 1 not compatible; containing incompatible elements 2 not consistent or logical in thought or actions – **-ency** n

inconsolable /ˌinkən'sohləbl/ adj incapable of being consoled; brokenhearted – **-bly** adv

incon'spicuous /ˌinkən'spikyoo·əs/ adj not readily noticeable – **-bility** n – ~ness n

inconstant /in'konst(ə)nt/ adj 1 likely to change frequently without apparent reason 2 unfaithful – **-stancy** n

incontestable /ˌinkən'testəbl/ adj not contestable; indisputable – **-bility** n – **-bly** adv

incontinent /in'kontinənt/ adj 1 lacking self-restraint (eg in sexual appetite) 2 suffering from lack of control of urination or defecation 3 not under control or restraint – **-nence** n

incontrovertible /ˌinkontrə'vuhtəbl, inˌkon-/ adj indisputable – **-bly** adv

inconvenience /ˌinkən'veenyəns, -ni·əns/ v or n (to subject to) difficulty or discomfort or sthg that is inconvenient

inconvenient /ˌinkən'veenyənt, -ni·ənt/ adj not convenient, esp in causing difficulty, discomfort, or annoyance – ~**ly** adv

incorporate /in'kawpərayt/ v 1a to unite thoroughly with or work indistinguishably into sthg **b** to admit to membership in a corporate body 2a to combine thoroughly to form a consistent whole **b** to form into a legal corporation 3 to unite in or as 1 body – **-ration** n

incorrect /ˌinkə'rekt/ adj 1 inaccurate; factually wrong 2 not in accordance with an established norm; improper – ~**ly** adv – ~ness n

incorrigible /in'korijəbl/ adj 1 incapable of being corrected or amended; esp incurably bad 2 unwilling or unlikely to change – **-bility** n – **-bly** adv

incorruptible /ˌinkə'ruptəbl/ adj 1 not subject to decay or dissolution 2 incapable of being bribed or morally corrupted – **-bility** n – **-bly** adv

¹**increase** /in'krees/ v 1 to make or become (progressively) greater (eg in size, amount, quality, number, or intensity) 2 to multiply by the production of young

²**increase** /'inkrees/ n 1 (an) addition or enlargement in size, extent, quantity, etc 2 sthg (eg offspring, produce, or profit) added to an original stock by addition or growth – **-singly** adv

incredible /in'kredəbl/ adj 1 too extraordinary and improbable to be believed; also hard to believe 2 – used as a generalized term of approval – **-bility** n – **-bly** adv

incredulous /in'kredyooləs/ adj 1 unwilling to admit or accept what is offered as true 2 expressing disbelief – **-ulity** n – ~**ly** adv

increment /'ingkrimənt, in-/ n 1 (the amount of) an increase, esp in quantity or value 2 any of a series of regular consecutive additions 3 a regular increase in pay resulting from an additional year's service – ~**al** adj – ~**ally** adv

incriminate /in'kriminayt/ v to involve in or demonstrate involvement in a crime or fault – **-nation** n

incrustation /ˌinkru'staysh(ə)n/ n 1 encrusting or being encrusted 2 (a growth or accumulation resembling) a crust or hard coating

incubate /'ingkyoobayt, 'in-/ v 1 to sit on so as to hatch (eggs) by the warmth of the body; also to maintain (eg an embryo or a chemically active system) under conditions favourable for hatching, development, or reaction 2 to cause (eg an idea) to develop 3 to undergo incubation

incubation /ˌingkyoo'baysh(ə)n, ˌin-/ n 1 incubating 2 the period between infection by a disease-causing agent and the manifestation of the disease

incubator /'ingkyooˌbaytə, 'in-/ n 1 an apparatus in which eggs are hatched artificially 2 an apparatus that maintains controlled conditions, esp for the housing of premature or sick babies or the cultivation of microorganisms

incubus /'ingkyoobəs, 'in-/ n, pl **incubuses, incubi** /-ˌbie/ 1 a male demon believed to have sexual intercourse with women in their sleep 2 (one who or that which oppresses or burdens like) a nightmare

incumbency /in'kumb(ə)nsi/ n the sphere of action or period of office of an incumbent

¹**incumbent** /in'kumb(ə)nt/ n the holder of an office or Anglican benefice

²**incumbent** adj 1 imposed as a duty or obligation – usu + on or upon 2 occupying a specified office

incur /in'kuh/ v -rr- to become liable or subject to; bring upon oneself

incursion /in'kuhsh(ə)n/ n an unexpected or sudden usu brief invasion or entrance, esp into another's territory

indebted /in'detid/ adj 1 owing money 2 owing gratitude or recognition to another – ~ness n

in'decent /in'dees(ə)nt/ adj 1 hardly suitable; unseemly 2 morally offensive – ~ly adv – -cency n

indecent assault n a sexual assault exclusive of rape

indecent exposure n intentional public exposure of part of one's body (e g the genitals) in violation of generally accepted standards of decency

indecision /,indi'sizh(ə)n/ n a wavering between 2 or more possible courses of action

indecisive /,indi'siesiv/ adj 1 giving an uncertain result 2 marked by or prone to indecision – ~ly adv – ~ness n

indeed /in'deed/ adv 1 without any question; truly – often used in agreement 2 – used for emphasis after very and an adjective or adverb 3 in point of fact; actually 4 – expressing irony, disbelief, or surprise

indefatigable /,indi'fatigəbl/ adj tireless

inde'fensible /-di'fensəbl/ adj incapable of being defended or justified

in'definite /-'definət/ adj 1 designating an unidentified or not immediately identifiable person or thing 2 not precise; vague 3 having no exact limits – ~ness n – ~ly adv

indelible /in'deləbl/ adj (making marks difficult to remove or) incapable of being removed or erased – -bly adv

indelicate /in'delikət/ adj offensive to good manners or refined taste – ~ly adv – -cacy n

indemnify /in'demnifie/ v 1 to secure against harm, loss, or damage 2 to make compensation to for incurred harm, loss, or damage – -fication n

indemnity /in'demnəti/ n security against harm, loss, or damage

¹**indent** /in'dent/ v 1a to cut or divide (a document) to produce sections with edges that can be matched for authentication b to draw up (e g a deed) in 2 or more exact copies 2 to notch the edge of 3 to set (e g a line of a paragraph) in from the margin 4 chiefly Br to requisition officially 5 to form an indentation

²**indent** /'indent/ n 1 an indenture 2 an indention 3 chiefly Br an official requisition

³**indent** /-'-/ v (to force inwards so as) to form a depression in

indentation /,inden'taysh(ə)n/ n 1a an angular cut in an edge b a usu deep recess {e g in a coastline} 2 indention

indention /in'densh(ə)n/ n 1 indenting or being indented 2 the blank space produced by indenting

¹**indenture** /in'denchə/ n 1a an indented document b a contract binding sby to work for another – usu pl with sing. meaning 2a a formal certificate (e g an inventory or voucher) prepared for purposes of control b a document stating the terms under which a security (e g a bond) is issued

²**indenture** v to bind (e g an apprentice) by indentures

¹**independent** /,indi'pend(ə)nt/ adj 1 not dependent: e g 1a(1) self-governing a(2) not affiliated with a larger controlling unit b(1) not relying on sthg else b(2) not committed to a political party c(1) not requiring or relying on, or allowing oneself to be controlled by, others (e g for guidance or care) c(2) having or providing enough money to live on, esp without working 2 of a clause able to stand alone as a complete statement – -ence n – ~ly adv

²**independent** n, often cap sby not bound by a political party

indescribable /,indi'skriebəbl/ adj 1 that cannot be described 2 surpassing description – -bly adv

indeterminable /,indi'tuhminəbl/ adj incapable of being definitely decided or ascertained – -bly adv

indeterminate /,indi'tuhminət/ adj not definitely or precisely determined or fixed – -nacy n

¹**index** /'indeks/ n, pl **indexes, indices** /'indiseez/ 1 a guide or list to aid reference; e g esp an alphabetical list of items (e g topics or names) treated in a printed work that gives with each item the page number where it appears 2 sthg that points towards or demonstrates a particular state of affairs 3 a list of restricted or prohibited material; specif, cap the list of books banned by the Roman Catholic church

²**index** v 1 to provide with or list in an index 2 to serve as an index of

¹**index finger** n the forefinger

Indian /'indi·ən/ n 1 a native or inhabitant of India 2a a member of any of the indigenous peoples of N, Central, or S America excluding the Eskimos b any of the native languages of American Indians

¹**Indian file** n single file

,**indian 'ink** n, often cap 1st I, Br (an ink made from) a solid black pigment used in drawing and lettering

,**Indian 'summer** n 1 a period of warm weather in late autumn or early winter 2 a happy or flourishing period occurring towards the end of sthg, esp of a person's life

,**india 'rubber** n, often cap I a rubber; an eraser

indicate /'indikayt/ v 1a(1) to point to; point out a(2) to show or demonstrate as or by means of a sign or pointer b to be a sign or symptom of c to demonstrate or suggest the necessity or advisability of – chiefly pass 2 to state or express briefly; suggest – -ation n

indicative /in'dikətiv/ adj serving to indicate – **-ly** adv

indicator /'indikaytə/ n **1a** a hand or needle on an instrument (e g a dial) **b** an instrument for giving visual readings attached to a machine or apparatus **c** a device (e g a flashing light) on a vehicle that indicates an intention to change direction **2a** a substance (e g litmus) that shows, esp by change of colour, the condition (e g acidity or alkalinity) of a solution **b** a chemical tracer (e g an isotope) **3** a statistic (e g the level of industrial production) that gives an indication of the state of a national economy

indices /'indiseez/ pl of **index**

indict /in'diet/ v **1** to charge with an offence **2** to charge with a crime – **~ment** n – **~able** adj

indifferent /in'difrənt/ adj **1** that does not matter one way or the other **2** not interested in or concerned about sthg **3a** neither good nor bad; mediocre **b** not very good; inferior – **~ly** adv – **-ence** n

indigenous /in'dij(ə)nəs/ adj **1** originating, growing, or living naturally in a particular region or environment **2** innate, inborn – **~ly** adv

indigent /'indij(ə)nt/ adj needy, poor – fml – **-gence** n

indigestible /,indi'jestəbl/ adj not (easily) digested – **-bility** n, **-bly** adv

indigestion /,indi'jeschən/ n (pain in the digestive system usu resulting from) difficulty in digesting sthg

indignant /in'dignənt/ adj angry because of sthg judged unjust, mean, etc – often + at – **~ly** adv

indignity /in'dignəti/ n **1** an act that offends against a person's dignity or self-respect **2** humiliating treatment

indigo /'indigoh/ n **1** (any of several dyes related to) a blue dye with a coppery lustre **2** a dark greyish blue colour whose hue lies between violet and blue in the spectrum

indirect /,indi'rekt, -die-/ adj **1a** deviating from a direct line or course **b** not going straight to the point **2** not straightforward or open **3** not directly aimed at **4** stating what a real or supposed original speaker said but with changes of tense, person, etc – **~ly** adv – **~ness** n

indirect object n a grammatical object representing the secondary goal of the action of its verb (e g her in I gave her the book)

indiscernible /,indi'suhnəbl/ adj **1** that cannot be perceived or recognized **2** not recognizable as separate or distinct

indiscipline /in'disiplin/ n lack of discipline

indiscreet /,indi'skreet/ adj not discreet; imprudent – **-cretion** n – **~ly** adv

indiscriminate /,indi-di'skriminət/ adj **1** not marked by careful distinction; lacking in discrimination and discernment **2** not differentiated; confused – **~ly** adv

indispensable /,indi-di'spensəbl/ adj that cannot be done without – **-bility** n – **-bly** adv

indisposed adj **1** slightly ill **2** averse – **-position** n

indisputable /,indi-di'spyoohtəbl/ adj incontestable – **-bly** adv

indistinct /,indi-di'stingkt/ adj not distinct: e g **a** not sharply outlined or separable; not clearly seen **b** not clearly recognizable or understandable – **~ly** adv – **~ness** n

indistinguishable /,indi-di'sting·gwishəbl/ adj incapable of being **a** clearly perceived **b** discriminated – **-bly** adv

¹individual /,indi'vidyooəl, -jəl/ adj **1a** of or being an individual **b** intended for 1 person **2** existing as a distinct entity; separate **3** having marked individuality – **~ly** adv

²individual n **1** a particular person, being, or thing (as distinguished from a class, species, or collection) **2** a person

individualism /,indi'vidyoo·ə,liz(ə)m, -jəliz(ə)m/ n (conduct guided by) **a** a doctrine that bases morality on the interests of the individual **b** a theory maintaining the independence of the individual and stressing individual initiative – **-ist** n, adj – **-istic** adj

individuality /,individyoo·a'ləti, -joo-/ n **1** the total character peculiar to and distinguishing an individual from others **2** the tendency to pursue one's course with marked independence or self-reliance

individual·ize, -ise /,indi'vidyooə,liez, -jəliez/ v **1** to make individual in character **2** to treat individually **3** to adapt to suit a particular individual – **-ization** n

indoctrinate /in'doktrinayt/ v to imbue with a usu partisan or sectarian opinion, point of view, or ideology – **-nation** n

Indo-Euro'pean adj or n (of or belonging to) a family of languages spoken in most of Europe, Asia as far east as N India, and N and S America

indolent /'indələnt/ adj lazy – **~ly** adv – **-lence** n

indomitable /in'domitəbl/ adj incapable of being subdued – **-bly** adv

indoor /in'daw/ adj **1** of the interior of a building **2** done, living, or belonging indoors

indoors /in'dawz/ adv in or into a building

indrawn /in'drawn/ adj **1** drawn in **2** aloof, reserved

indubitable /in'dyoohbitəbl/ adj too evident to be doubted – **-bly** adv

induce /in'dyoohs/ v **1** to lead on to do sthg; move by persuasion or influence **2a** to cause to appear or to happen; bring on; specif to cause (labour) to begin by the use of drugs **b** to cause the formation of **3** to establish by logical induction; specif to infer from particulars

in'ducement /-mənt/ n sthg that induces; *esp* a motive or consideration that encourages one to do sthg

inductance /in'duktəns/ n a property of an electric circuit by which an electromotive force is induced in it by a variation of current either in the circuit itself or in a neighbouring circuit

induction /in'duksh(ə)n/ n **1a** the act or process of inducting (e g into office) **b** an initial experience; an initiation **2** the act or an instance of reasoning from particular premises to a general conclusion; *also* a conclusion reached by such reasoning **3a** the act of causing or bringing on or about **b** the drawing of the fuel-air mixture from the carburettor into the combustion chamber of an internal-combustion engine

inductive /in'duktiv/ adj **1** of or employing mathematical or logical induction **2** of inductance or electrical induction **3** introductory – **~ly** adv

inductor /in'duktə/ n a component that is included in an electrical circuit to provide inductance and that usu consists of a coiled conductor

indulge /in'dulj/ v **1a** to give free rein to (e g a taste) **b** to allow (oneself) to do sthg pleasurable or gratifying **2** to treat with great or excessive leniency, generosity, or consideration – **~nt** adj – **~ntly** adv

indulgence /in'duljəns/ n **1** a remission of (part of) the purgatorial atonement for confessed sin in the Roman Catholic church **2** indulging or being indulgent **3** an indulgent act **4** sthg indulged in

industrial /in'dustri-əl/ adj **1** of, involved in, or derived from industry **2** characterized by highly developed industries **3** used in industry

industrialism /in'dustri-ə,liz(ə)m/ n social organization in which industries, esp large-scale industries, are dominant

industrialist /in'dustri-əlist/ n one who is engaged in the management of an industry

in,dustrial revo'lution n a rapid major development of an economy (e g in England in the late 18th c) marked by the general introduction of mechanized techniques and large-scale production

industrious /in'dustri-əs/ adj **1** persistently diligent **2** constantly, regularly, or habitually occupied – **~ly** adv – **~ness** n

industry /'indəstri/ n **1** diligence in an employment or pursuit **2a** systematic work, esp for the creation of value **b(1)** a usu specified group of productive or profit-making enterprises **b(2)** an organized field of activity regarded in its commercial aspects **c** manufacturing activity as a whole – **~rialize** v

inebriate /in'eebriayt/ v to intoxicate

inedible /in'edəbl/ adj not fit to be eaten – **-bility** n – **-bly** adv

ineffable /in'efəbl/ adj **1** unutterable **2** not to be uttered; taboo – **-bility** n – **-bly** adv

ineffective /,ini'fektiv/ adj **1** not producing an intended effect **2** not capable of performing efficiently or achieving results – **~ly** adv – **~ness** n

ineffectual /,ini'fektyooəl, -chooəl/ adj **1** not producing or not able to give the proper or intended effect **2** unable to get things done; weak in character

inefficient /,ini'fish(ə)nt/ adj not producing the effect intended or desired, esp in a capable or economical way – **~ly** adv – **-ciency** n

inelegant /in'eligənt/ adj lacking in refinement, grace, or good taste – **~ly** adv – **-gance** n

ineligible /in'elijəbl/ adj not qualified or not worthy to be chosen or preferred – **-bility** n

inept /i'nept/ adj **1** not suitable or apt to the time, place, or occasion **2** lacking sense or reason **3** generally incompetent – **~ly** adv – **~itude**, **~ness** n

inequality /,ini'kwoləti/ n **1a** social disparity **b** disparity of distribution or opportunity **2** an instance of being unequal

inequitable /in'ekwitəbl/ adj unfair – **-bly** adv

inequity /in'ekwiti/ n (an instance of) injustice or unfairness

ineradicable /,ini'radikəbl/ adj incapable of being eradicated – **-bly** adv

inert /i'nuht/ adj **1** lacking the power to move **2** deficient in active (chemical or biological) properties **3** not moving; inactive, indolent – **~ly** adv – **~ness** n

inertia /i'nuhshə/ n **1** a property of matter by which it remains at rest or in uniform motion in the same straight line unless acted on by some external force **2** indisposition to motion, exertion, or change

inescapable /,ini'skaypəbl/ adj unavoidable

inessential /,ini'sensh(ə)l/ n or adj (sthg) that is not essential

inestimable /in'estiməbl/ adj **1** too great to be estimated **2** too valuable or excellent to be measured – **-bly** adv

inevitable /in'evitəbl/ adj incapable of being avoided or evaded; bound to happen or to confront one – **-bility** n – **-bly** adv

inexact /,inig'zakt/ adj not precisely correct or true – **~itude**, **~ness** n

inexcusable /,iniks'kyoohzəbl/ adj without excuse or justification – **-bly** adv

inexhaustible /,inig'zawstəbl/ adj incapable of being used up or worn out – **-bly** adv

inexorable /in'eks(ə)rəbl/ adj **1** not to be persuaded or moved by entreaty **2** continuing inevitably; that cannot be averted – **-bly** adv – **-bility** n

inexpensive /,inik'spensiv/ adj reasonable in price; cheap – **~ly** adv

inexperience /,inik'spiəri-əns/ n **1** lack of (the skill gained from) experience **2** lack of knowledge of the ways of the world – **~d** adj

inexpert /in'ekspuht/ adj unskilled – **~ly** adv

ine

inexplicable /,inik'splikəbl, in'eksplikəbl/ *adj* incapable of being explained, interpreted, or accounted for – **-bility** *n* – **-bly** *adv*

inexpressible /,inik'spresəbl/ *adj* beyond one's power to express – **-bly** *adv*

inextinguishable /,inik'sting·gwishəbl/ *adj* unquenchable

inextricable /in'ekstrikəbl/ *adj* 1 from which one cannot extricate oneself 2 incapable of being disentangled or untied – **-bly** *adv*

infallible /in'falabl/ *adj* 1 incapable of error; *esp, of the Pope* incapable of error in defining dogma 2 not liable to fail – **-bility** *n*

infamy /'infəmi/ *n* 1 evil reputation brought about by sthg grossly criminal, shocking, or brutal 2 an extreme and publicly known criminal or evil act – **-mous** *adj*

infancy /'inf(ə)nsi/ *n* 1 early childhood 2 a beginning or early period of existence 3 the legal status of an infant

¹**infant** /'inf(ə)nt/ *n* 1 a child in the first period of life 2 a minor

²**infant** *adj* 1 in an early stage of development 2 concerned with or intended for young children, esp those aged from 5 to 7 or 8

infanticide /in'fantisied/ *n* (the act of) sby who kills an infant

infantile /'inf(ə)ntiel/ *adj* (suggestive) of infants or infancy

infantry /'inf(ə)ntri/ *n sing or pl in constr* (a branch of an army containing) soldiers trained, armed, and equipped to fight on foot – **~man** *n*

'**infant ,school** *n, Br* a school for children aged from 5 to 7 or 8

infect /in'fekt/ *v* 1 to contaminate (e g air or food) with a disease-causing agent 2a to pass on a disease or a disease-causing agent to b to invade (an individual or organ), usu by penetration – used with reference to a disease-causing organism 3 to transmit or pass on sthg (e g an emotion) to

infection /in'feksh(ə)n/ *n* 1 infecting 2 (an agent that causes) a contagious or infectious disease 3 the communication of emotions or qualities through example or contact

infectious /in'fekshəs/ *adj* 1 **1a** infectious, infective capable of causing infection b communicable by infection 2 readily spread or communicated to others – **~ly** *adj* – **~ness** *n*

infelicitous /,infə'lisitəs/ *adj* not apt; not suitably chosen for the occasion – **-licity** *n*

infer /in'fuh/ *v* **-rr-** 1 to derive as a conclusion from facts or premises 2 to suggest, imply – disapproved of by some speakers – **~ence** *n* – **~ential** *adj* – **entially** *adv*

inferior /in'fiəri·ə/ *adj* 1 situated lower down 2 of low or lower degree or rank 3 of little or less importance, value, or merit – **~ity** *n*

inferi'ority ,complex *n* a sense of personal inferiority often resulting either in timidity or, through overcompensation, in exaggerated aggressiveness

infernal /in'fuhnl/ *adj* 1 of hell 2 hellish, diabolical 3 damned – infml – **~ly** *adv*

inferno /in'fuhnoh/ *n pl* **infernos** a place or a state that resembles or suggests hell, esp in intense heat or raging fire

infertile /in'fuhtiel/ *adj* not fertile or productive – **-tility** *n*

infest /in'fest/ *v* 1 to spread or swarm in or over in a troublesome manner 2 to live in or on as a parasite – **~ation** *n*

infidel /'infidl/ *n* **1a** an unbeliever in or opponent of a particular religion, esp of Christianity or Islam b sby who acknowledges no religious belief 2 a disbeliever in sthg specified or understood

infidelity /,infi'deləti/ *n* 1 lack of belief in a religion 2a unfaithfulness, disloyalty b marital unfaithfulness

infighting /'in,fieting/ *n* 1 fighting or boxing at close quarters 2 prolonged and often bitter dissension among members of a group or organization

infiltrate /'infiltrayt/ *v* 1 to cause (e g a liquid) to permeate sthg e g by penetrating its pores or interstices) 2 to pass into or through (a substance) by filtering or permeating 3 to enter or become established in gradually or unobtrusively – **-trator** *n* – **-tion** *n*

¹**infinite** /'infinət/ *adj* 1 subject to no limitation or external determination 2 extending indefinitely 3 immeasurably or inconceivably great or extensive **4a** extending beyond, lying beyond, or being greater than any arbitrarily chosen finite value, however large b extending to infinity – **~ly** *adv*

²**infinite** *n* 1 diviness, sublimity – + *the* 2 an infinite quantity or magnitude

infinitesimal /,infini'tesiml/ *adj* immeasurably or incalculably small – **~ly** *adv*

infinitive /in'finətiv/ *adj or n* (using) a verb form that performs some functions of a noun and that in English is used with *to* (e g *go* in *I asked him to go*) except with auxiliary and various other verbs (e g *go* in *I must go*)

infinity /in'finəti/ *n* **1a** the quality of being infinite b unlimited extent of time, space, or quantity 2 an indefinitely great number or amount

infirm /in'fuhm/ *adj* 1 physically feeble, esp from age 2 weak in mind, will, or character – **~ity** *n*

infirmary /in'fuhməri/ *n* a hospital

inflame /in'flaym/ *v* 1 to set on fire 2a to excite or arouse passion or excessive action or feeling in b to make more heated or violent 3 to cause to redden or grow hot 4 to cause or become affected with inflammation in (bodily tissue) 5 to burst into flame

inflammable /in'flaməbl/ *adj* **1** capable of being easily ignited and of burning rapidly **2** easily inflamed, excited, or angered

inflammation /,inflə'maysh(ə)n/ *n* swelling, soreness, etc in a body part

inflammatory /in'flamət(ə)ri/ *adj* **1** tending to inflame **2** accompanied by or tending to cause inflammation

inflate /in'flayt/ *v* **1** to swell or distend (with air or gas) **2** to increase (a price level) or cause (a volume of credit or the economy) to expand **3** to become inflated – **-atable** *adj*

in'flated *adj* **1** bombastic, exaggerated **2** expanded to an abnormal or unjustifiable volume or level **3** swelled out; distended

inflation /in'flaysh(ə)n/ *n* inflating or being inflated; *esp* a substantial and continuing rise in the general level of prices, caused by or causing an increase in the volume of money and credit or an expansion of the economy

inflect /in'flekt/ *v* **1** to vary (a word) by inflection **2** to change or vary the pitch of (a voice or note) **3** to become modified by inflection

inflection, *Br also* **inflexion** /in'fleksh(ə)n/ *n* **1** change in pitch or loudness of the voice **2** (an element showing) the change in the form of a word to mark case, gender, number, tense, etc

inflexible /in'fleksəbl/ *adj* rigidly firm: e g **a** lacking or deficient in suppleness **b** unyielding **c** incapable of change – **-bility** *n* – **-bly** *adv*

inflict /in'flikt/ *v* to force or impose (sthg damaging or painful) *on* sby – ~**er**, ~**or** *n* – ~**ion** *n*

¹**influence** /'infloo-əns/ *n* **1** the power to achieve sthg desired by using wealth or position **2** the act, power, or capacity of causing or producing an effect in indirect or intangible ways **3** sby or sthg that exerts influence; *esp* sby or sthg that tends to produce a mental or immoral effect on another – **-ential** *adj* **-entially** *adv* — **under the influence** affected by alcohol; drunk

²**influence** *v* to affect, alter, or modify by indirect or intangible means

influenza /,infloo'enzə/ *n* **1** a highly infectious virus disease characterized by sudden onset, fever, severe aches and pains, and inflammation of the respiratory mucous membranes **2** any of numerous feverish usu virus diseases of domestic animals marked by respiratory symptoms

influx /'influks/ *n* a usu sudden increase in flowing in; the arrival of large amounts

info /'infoh/ *n* information – *infml*

inform /in'fawm/ *v* **1** to impart an essential quality or character to **2** to communicate knowledge to **3** to give information or knowledge **4** to act as an informer *against* or *on* – ~**ant** *n* – ~**ative** *adj* – ~**atively** *adv*

informal /in'fawml/ *adj* marked by an absence of formality or ceremony; everyday – ~**ity** *n* – ~**ly** *adv*

information /,infə'maysh(ə)n/ *n* **1** the communication or reception of facts or ideas **2a** knowledge obtained from investigation, study, or instruction **b** news **c** (significant) facts or data **3** a formal accusation presented to a magistrate

informed /in'fawmd/ *adj* **1** possessing or based on possession of information **2** knowledgeable about matters of contemporary interest

informer /in'fawmə/ *n* one who informs against another, esp to the police for a financial reward

infraction /in'fraksh(ə)n/ *n* a violation, infringement

infra 'dig *adj* beneath one's dignity – *infml*

infrared /,infrə'red/ *adj or n* (being, using, producing, or sensitive to) electromagnetic radiation with a wavelength between the red end of the visible spectrum and microwaves, that is commonly perceived as heat

'infra,structure /-,strukchə/ *n* **1** an underlying foundation or basic framework **2** the permanent installations required for military purposes

infrequent /in'freekwənt/ *adj* **1** rare **2** not habitual or persistent – ~**ly** *adv* – **-quency** *n*

infringe /in'frinj/ *v* to encroach on; violate – ~**ment** *n*

infuriate /in'fyooəriayt/ *v* to make furious

infuse /in'fyoohz/ *v* **1** to inspire, imbue **2** to steep in liquid without boiling so as to extract the soluble properties or constituents

infusion /in'fyoohzh(ə)n/ *n* **1** infusing **2** the continuous slow introduction of a solution, esp into a vein **3** an extract obtained by infusing

ingenious /in'jeeni-əs/ *adj* marked by originality, resourcefulness, and cleverness – ~**ly** *adv* – **ingenuity** *n*

ingenuous /in'jenyoo-əs/ *adj* showing innocent or childlike simplicity; frank, candid – ~**ly** *adv* – ~**ness** *n*

ingest /in'jest/ *v* to take in (as if) for digestion; absorb – ~**ion** *n*

inglenook /'ing-gl,nook/ *n* (a seat in) an alcove by a large open fireplace

inglorious /in'glawri-əs/ *adj* shameful, ignominious – ~**ly** *adv*

ingot /'ing-gət/ *n* a (bar-shaped) mass of cast metal

'in,grained *adj* firmly and deeply implanted; deep-rooted

ingratiate /in'grayshi,ayt/ *v* to gain favour for (e g oneself) by deliberate effort – **-ting** *adj* – **-tingly** *adv*

ingratitude /in'gratityoohd/ *n* forgetfulness or scant recognition of kindness received

ingredient /in'greedi-ənt/ *n* sthg that forms a component part of a compound, combination, or mixture

inhabit /in'habit/ *v* to occupy or be present in – ~**able** *adj* – **-ant** *n*

inhale /in'hayl/ *v* to breathe in – **-lation** *n*

inhaler /in'haylə/ *n* a device used for inhaling a medication

inharmonious /,inhah'mohnyəs, -ni·əs/ *adj* 1 not harmonious 2 not congenial or compatible – ~ **ly** *adv* – ~ **ness** *n*

inherent /in'herənt, -'hiə-/ *adj* intrinsic to the constitution or essence of sthg – ~ **ly** *adv* – **-ence** *n*

inherit /in'herit/ *v* 1 to receive, either by right or from an ancestor at his/her death 2 to receive by genetic transmission – ~ **ance** *n*

inhibit /in'hibit/ *v* 1 to prohibit *from* doing sthg 2a to restrain b to discourage from free or spontaneous activity, esp by psychological or social controls – ~ **ion** *n*

inhospitable /,inho'spitəbl/ *adj* 1 not friendly or welcoming 2 providing no shelter or means of support – **-bly** *adv*

inhuman /in'hyoohmən/ *adj* 1a inhumane b failing to conform to basic human needs 2 being other than human

inhumane /,inhyooh'mayn/ *adj* lacking in kindness or compassion – ~ **ly** *adv*

inhumanity /,inhyooh'manəti/ *n* 1 being pitiless or cruel 2 a cruel or barbarous act

inimical /i'nimik(ə)l/ *adj* 1 hostile or indicating hostility 2 adverse in tendency, influence, or effects

inimitable /i'nimitəbl/ *adj* defying imitation – **-bly** *adv*

iniquity /i'nikwəti/ *n* 1 gross injustice 2 a sin – **-tous** *adj* – **-tously** *adv*

¹**initial** /i'nish(ə)l/ *adj* 1 of the beginning 2 first

²**initial** *n* 1 the first letter of a name 2 *pl* the first letter of each word in a full name

³**initial** *v* **-ll-** (*NAm* **-l, -ll-**) to put initials (indicating ownership or authorization) on

¹**initiate** /i'nishiayt/ *v* 1 to cause or enable the beginning of; start 2 to instil with rudiments or principles (of sthg complex or obscure) 3 to induct into membership (as if) by formal rites

²**initiate** /i'nishi·ət/ *n* 1 sby who is undergoing or has undergone initiation 2 sby who is instructed or proficient in a complex or specialized field

initiation /i,nishi'aysh(ə)n/ *n* 1 initiating or being initiated 2 the ceremony or formal procedure with which sby is made a member of a sect or society

¹**initiative** /i'nish(y)ətiv/ *adj* introductory, preliminary

²**initiative** *n* 1 a first step, esp in the attainment of an end or goal 2 energy or resourcefulness displayed in initiation of action 3 a procedure enabling voters to propose a law by petition — **on one's own initiative** without being prompted; independently of outside influence or control

inject /in'jekt/ *v* 1a to throw, drive, or force into sthg b to force a fluid into 2 to introduce as an element or factor

injection /in'jeksh(ə)n/ *n* 1 injecting sthg (e g a medication) that is injected

injudicious /,injooh'dishəs/ *adj* indiscreet, unwise – ~ **ly** *adv* – ~ **ness** *n*

injunction /in'jungksh(ə)n/ *n* 1 an order, warning 2 a writ requiring sby to do or refrain from doing a particular act

injure /'injə/ *v* 1 to do injustice to 2a to inflict bodily hurt on b to impair the soundness of c to inflict damage or loss on – **-rious** *adj* – **-riously** *adv*

injury /'injəri/ *n* 1 a wrong 2 hurt, damage, or loss sustained

injustice /in'justis/ *n* (an act or state of) unfairness

¹**ink** /ingk/ *n* 1 a coloured liquid used for writing and printing 2 the black secretion of a squid, octopus, etc that hides it from a predator or prey

²**ink** *v* to apply ink to

inkling /'ingkling/ *n* 1 a faint indication 2 a slight knowledge or vague idea

'ink,well /-,wel/ *n* a container (e g in a school desk) for ink

inlaid /in'layd/ *adj* 1 set into a surface in a decorative design 2 decorated with a design or material set into a surface

¹**inland** /'in,land, -lənd/ *adv or n* (into or towards) the interior part of a country

²**inland** /'inlənd/ *adj* 1 of the interior of a country 2 *chiefly Br* not foreign; domestic

,Inland 'Revenue *n* the government department responsible for collecting taxes in Britain

¹**inlay** /in'lay/ *v* **inlaid** /-'layd/ 1 to set into a surface or ground material for decoration or reinforcement 2 to decorate with inlaid material

²**inlay** /'inlay/ *n* inlaid work or a decorative inlaid pattern

inlet /'inlet, -lit/ *n* 1 a (long and narrow) recess in a shoreline or a water passage between 2 land areas 2 a means of entry; *esp* an opening for intake

inmate /'inmayt/ *n* any of a group occupying a place of residence, esp a prison or hospital

in memoriam /,in mi'mawri·əm, -am/ *prep* in memory of

inmost /'inmohst/ *adj* 1 furthest within 2 most intimate

inn /in/ *n* 1a an establishment (e g a small hotel) providing lodging and food, esp for travellers b a public house 2 a residence formerly provided for students in London

innards /'inədz/ *n pl* 1 the internal organs of a human being or animal; *esp* the viscera 2 the internal parts of a structure or mechanism *USE* infml

innate /i'nayt/ *adj* 1 existing in or belonging to an individual from birth 2 inherent 3 originating in the intellect – ~ **ly** *adv*

inner /'inə/ *adj* 1a situated within; internal b situated near to a centre, esp of influence 2 of the mind or soul

'innings *n pl* innings 1a any of the alternating divisions of a cricket match during which one side bats and the other bowls b (the (runs scored in or quality of the) turn of 1 player to bat 2a a period in which sby has opportunity for action or achievements b *chiefly Br* the duration of sby's life

innocent /'inəs(ə)nt/ *adj* 1a free from guilt or sin; pure b harmless in effect or intention c free from legal guilt 2 lacking or deprived of sthg 3a artless, ingenuous b ignorant, unaware – **-ence, -ency** *n* – innocent *n* – **~ly** *adv*

innocuous /i'nokyoo·əs/ *adj* 1 having no harmful effects 2 inoffensive, insipid – **~ly** *adv* – **~ness** *n*

innovate /'inəvayt/ *v* to make changes; introduce sthg new – **-vator** *n* – **-vatory** *adj* – **-vation** *n*

innuendo /,inyoo'endoh/ *n, pl* innuendos, innuendoes an oblique allusion; *esp* a veiled slight on sby's character or reputation

innumerable /i'nyoohmərəbl/ *adj* countless – **-bly** *adv*

inoculate /i'nokyoolayt/ *v* 1a to introduce a microorganism into b to introduce (e g a microorganism) into a culture, animal, etc for growth 2 to vaccinate – **-lation** *n*

inoffensive /,inə'fensiv/ *adj* 1 not causing any harm; innocuous 2 not objectionable to the senses – **~ly** *adv* – **~ness** *n*

inoperable /in'op(ə)rəbl/ *adj* impracticable

inoperative /in'op(ə)rətiv/ *adj* not functioning; having no effect

inopportune /,inopə'tyoohn/ *adj* inconvenient, unseasonable – **~ly** *adv* – **~ness** *n*

inordinate /in'awdinət/ *adj* exceeding reasonable limits – **~ly** *adv*

inorganic /,inaw'ganik/ *adj* 1a being or composed of matter other than plant or animal; mineral b of, being, or dealt with by a branch of chemistry concerned with inorganic substances 2 not arising through natural growth – **~ally** *adv*

input /'inpoot/ *n* 1a an amount coming or put in b sthg (e g energy, material, or data) supplied to a machine or system c a component of production (e g land, labour, or raw materials) 2 the point at which an input (e g of energy, material, or data) is made

inquest /'in(g)kwest/ *n* 1 a judicial inquiry, esp by a coroner, into the cause of a death 2 an inquiry or investigation, esp into sthg that has failed

inquietude /in'kwie·ətyoohd/ *n* uneasiness, restlessness

inquire /in'kwie·ə/ *v* to seek information; ask about — inquire after to ask about the health of

inquiry /in'kwie·əri/ *n* 1 a request for information 2 a thorough or systematic investigation

inquisition /,inkwi'zish(ə)n/ *n* 1 the act of inquiring 2 a judicial or official inquiry 3a *cap* a former Roman Catholic tribunal for the discovery and punishment of heresy b a ruthless investigation or examination – **-tor** *n* – **-torial** *adj* – **-torially** *adv*

inquisitive /in'kwizətiv/ *adj* 1 eager for knowledge or understanding 2 fond of making inquiries; *esp* unduly curious about the affairs of others – **~ly** *adv* – **~ness** *n*

inroad /'in,rohd/ *n* 1 a raid 2 a serious or forcible encroachment or advance

insane /in'sayn/ *adj* 1 mentally disordered; exhibiting insanity 2 typical of or intended for insane people 3 utterly absurd – **~ly** *adv* – **-anity** *n*

insanitary /in'sanit(ə)ri/ *adj* unclean enough to endanger health; filthy, contaminated

insatiable /in'saysh(y)əbl/ *adj* incapable of being satisfied – **-bly** *adv*

inscribe /in'skrieb/ *v* 1a to write, engrave, or print (as a lasting record) b to enter on a list; enrol 2 to address or dedicate to sby, esp by a handwritten note

inscription /in'skripsh(ə)n/ *n* 1a a title, superscription b words engraved or stamped (e g on a coin) 2 a handwritten dedication in a book or on a work of art 3a the act of inscribing b the enrolment of a name (as if) on a list

inscrutable /in'skroohtəbl/ *adj* hard to interpret or understand; enigmatic – **-bility** *n* – **-bly** *adv*

insect /'insekt/ *n* 1 any of a class of arthropods with a well-defined head, thorax, and abdomen, only 3 pairs of legs, and typically 1 or 2 pairs of wings 2 any of various small invertebrate animals (e g woodlice and spiders) – not used technically

insecticide /in'sektisied/ *n* sthg that destroys insects – **-cidal** *adj*

insecure /,insi'kyooə/ *adj* 1 lacking adequate protection or guarantee 2 not firmly fixed or supported 3a not stable or well-adjusted b deficient in assurance; beset by fear and anxiety – **-curity** *n* – **~ly** *adv*

inseminate /in'seminayt/ *v* to introduce semen into the genital tract of (a female) – **-ation** *n*

insensible /in'sensəbl/ *adj* 1 incapable or bereft of feeling or sensation: e g 1a having lost consciousness b lacking or deprived of sensory perception 2 incapable of being felt or sensed 3 lacking concern or awareness

insensitive /in'sensətiv/ *adj* 1 lacking the ability to respond to or sympathize with the needs or feelings of others 2 not physically or chemically sensitive – **~ly** *adv* – **-tivity** *n* – **~ly** *adv*

inseparable /in'sep(ə)rəbl/ *adj* incapable of being separated – **-bility** *n* – **-bly** *adv*

¹insert /in'zuht, -'suht/ *v* 1 to put or thrust in 2 to put or introduce into the body of sthg 3 to set in and make fast; *esp* to insert by sewing between 2 cut edges – **~ion** *n*

²insert /'--/ *n* sthg (esp written or printed) inserted

inset /'inset/ *n* sthg set in; *esp* a piece of cloth set into a garment for decoration, shaping, etc

inshore /in'shaw/ *adj or adv* (near or moving) towards the shore

¹**inside** /in'sied/ *n* **1** an inner side or surface **2a** an interior or internal part **b** inward nature, thoughts, or feeling **c** viscera, entrails – usu pl with sing. meaning **3** a position of confidence or of access to confidential information **4** the middle portion of a playing area

²**inside** *adj* **1** of, on, near, or towards the inside of **2** of or being the inner side of a curve or being near the side of the road nearest the kerb or hard shoulder

³**inside** *prep* **1a** in or into the interior of **b** on the inner side of **2** within (e g *inside* an hour)

⁴**inside** *adv* **1** to or on the inner side **2** in or into the interior **3** indoors **4** *chiefly Br* in or into prison – slang

insidious /in'sidi-əs/ *adj* **1** harmful but enticing **2a** acting gradually and imperceptibly but with grave consequences – ~ly *adv* – ~ness *n*

insight /in,siet/ *n* the power of or an act or result of discerning the true or underlying nature of sthg

insignia /in'signi-ə/ *n pl* badges of authority or honour

insignificant /,insig'nifikənt/ *adj* **1** lacking meaning or import; inconsequential **2** very small in size, amount, or number – -cance *n* – ~ly *adv*

insincere /,insin'siə/ *adj* hypocritical – ~ly *adv* – -cerity *n*

insinuate /in'sinyoo,ayt/ *v* **1** to introduce (an idea) or suggest (sthg unpleasant) in a subtle or oblique manner **2** to gain acceptance for (e g oneself) by craft or stealth – -ation *n*

insipid /in'sipid/ *adj* **1** devoid of any definite flavour **2** devoid of interesting or stimulating qualities – ~ly *adv* – ~ness *n* – ~ity *n*

insist /in'sist/ *v* **1** to take a resolute stand **2** to place great emphasis or importance *on* sthg **3** to maintain persistently – ~ence, ~ency *n*

insistent /in'sist(ə)nt/ *adj* **1** insisting forcefully or repeatedly; emphatic **2** demanding attention – ~ly *adv*

in situ /in 'sityooh/ *adv or adj* in the natural or original position

,**inso'far as** /insə'fah, insoh'fah/ *conj* to the extent or degree that

insolent /'insələnt/ *adj* showing disrespectful rudeness – ~ly *adv* – -solence *n*

insoluble /in'solyoobl/ *adj* **1** having or admitting of no solution or explanation **2** (practically) incapable of being dissolved in liquid – -bly *adv* – -bility *n*

insolvent /in'solvənt/ *adj* **1** unable to pay debts as they fall due; *specif* having liabilities in excess of the value of assets held **2** relating to or for the relief of insolvents – -vency *n*

insomnia /in'somni-ə/ *n* prolonged (abnormal) inability to obtain adequate sleep – ~c *n, adj*

insouciance /in'soohsyəns (*Fr* ɛ̃suːsjɑ̃ːs)/ *n* light-hearted unconcern – -ant *adj*

inspect /in'spekt/ *v* **1** to examine closely and critically; scrutinize **2** to view or examine officially – ~ion *n*

inspector /in'spektə/ *n* a police officer ranking immediately above a sergeant; *also*, an official who inspects – ~ate, ~ship *n*

inspiration /,inspi'raysh(ə)n/ *n* **1a** a divine influence or action on a person which qualifies him/her to receive and communicate sacred revelation **b** the action or power of stimulating the intellect or emotions **2** an inspired idea **3** an inspiring agent or influence – ~al *adj*

inspire /in'spie-ə/ *v* **1** to influence or guide by divine inspiration **2** to exert an animating or exalting influence on **3** to act as a stimulus for **4** to affect – usu + *with*

in'spired *adj* outstanding or brilliant in a way that suggests divine inspiration

instability /,instə'biləti/ *n* lack of (emotional or mental) stability

install, instal /in'stawl/ *v* **1** to induct into an office, rank, or order, esp with ceremonies or formalities **2** to establish in a specified place, condition, or status **3** to place in usu permanent position for use or service

installation /,instə'laysh(ə)n/ *n* **1** a device, apparatus, or piece of machinery fixed or fitted in place to perform some specified function **2** a military base or establishment

instalment, *NAm chiefly* **installment** /in'stawlmənt/ *n* **1** any of the parts into which a debt is divided when payment is made at intervals **2** any of several parts (e g of a publication) presented at intervals

¹**instance** /'inst(ə)ns/ *n* **1** an example cited as an illustration or proof **2** the institution of a legal action **3** a situation viewed as 1 stage in a process or series of events — **for instance** as an example

²**instance** *v* to put forward as a case or example; cite

¹**instant** /'inst(ə)nt/ *n* **1** an infinitesimal space of time; *esp* a point in time separating 2 states **2** the present or current month

²**instant** *adj* **1a** present, current **b** of or occurring in the present month – used in commercial communications **2** immediate **3a(1)** premixed or precooked for easy final preparation **a(2)** appearing (as if) in ready-to-use form **b** immediately soluble in water **4** demanding, urgent – *fml* – ~ly *adv* – ~aneous *adj* – ~aneously *adv* – ~aneousness *n*

instead /in'sted/ *adv* as a substitute or alternative (e g sent his son *instead*)

instep /'in,step/ *n* **1** (the upper surface of) the arched middle portion of the human foot **2** the part of a shoe or stocking over the instep

instigate /'instigayt/ *v* **1** to goad or urge forwards; provoke, incite **2** to initiate (a course of action or procedure, e g a legal investigation) – **-gation** *n* – **-gator** *n*

instil, *NAm chiefly* **instill** /in'stil/ *v* **-ll- 1** to cause to enter drop by drop **2** to impart gradually – + *in* or *into* – ~**lation** *n*

instinct /'instingkt/ *n* **1** a natural or inherent aptitude, impulse, or capacity **2** (a largely inheritable tendency of an organism to make a complex and specific) response to environmental stimuli without involving reason – ~**ive** *adj* – ~**ively** *adv* – ~**ual** *adj*

¹**institute** /'instityooht/ *v* to originate and establish; inaugurate

²**institute** *n* **1** (the premises used by) an organization for the promotion of a cause **2** an educational institution

institution /,insti'tyoohsh(ə)n/ *n* **1** an established practice in a culture; *also* a familiar object **2** an established organization or (public) body (e g a university or hospital) – ~**al** *adj*

instruct /in'strukt/ *v* **1** to teach **2a** to direct authoritatively **b** to command **3** to engage (a lawyer, specif a barrister) for a case – ~**or** *n*

instruction /in'struksh(ə)n/ *n* **1a** an order, a command – often pl with sing. meaning **b** *pl* an outline or manual of technical procedure **2** teaching – ~**al** *adj*

instructive /in'struktiv/ *adj* carrying a lesson; enlightening – ~**ly** *adv*

¹**instrument** /'instrəmənt/ *n* **1a** a means whereby sthg is achieved, performed, or furthered **b** a dupe; a tool of another **2** an implement, tool, or device designed esp for delicate work or measurement **3** a device used to produce music **4** a formal legal document **5** an electrical or mechanical device used in navigating an aircraft

²**instrument** *v* to orchestrate

¹**instrumental** /,instrə'mentl/ *adj* **1a** serving as an instrument, means, agent, or tool **b** of or done with an instrument or tool **2** relating to, composed for, or performed on a musical instrument

²**instrumental** *n* a musical composition or passage for instruments but not voice

instrumentalist /,instrə'mentl,ist/ *n* a player on a musical instrument

instrumentation /,instrəmən'taysh(ə)n, -men-/ *n* the arrangement or composition of music for instruments

insubordinate /,insə'bawdinət/ *adj* unwilling to submit to authority – **-nation** *n*

insubstantial /,insəb'stansh(ə)l/ *adj* **1** lacking substance or material nature; unreal **2** lacking firmness or solidity; flimsy

insufferable /in'suf(ə)rəbl/ *adj* intolerable – **-bly** *adv*

insufficient /,insə'fish(ə)nt/ *adj* deficient in power, capacity, or competence – ~**ly** *adv* – **-ciency** *n*

insular /'insyoolə/ *adj* **1** of or being an island **2a** of island people **b** that results (as if) from lack of contact with other peoples or cultures; narrow-minded – ~**ity** *n*

insulate /'insyoolayt/ *v* to place in a detached situation; *esp* to separate from conducting bodies by means of nonconductors so as to prevent transfer of electricity, heat, or sound

insulation /,insyoo'laysh(ə)n/ *n* **1** insulating or being insulated **2** material used in insulating

insulator /'insyoo,laytə/ *n* (a device made from) a material that is a poor conductor of electricity and is used for separating or supporting conductors to prevent undesired flow of electricity

insulin /'insyoo,lin/ *n* a hormone produced in the pancreas that is essential esp for the metabolism of carbohydrates and is used in the treatment of diabetes

¹**insult** /in'sult/ *v* to treat with insolence, indignity, or contempt; *also* to cause offence or damage to

²**insult** /'insult/ *n* an act of insulting; sthg that insults

insuperable /in's(y)oohprəbl/ *adj* incapable of being surmounted, overcome, or passed over – **-bly** *adv*

insupportable /,insə'pawtəbl/ *adj* **1** unendurable **2** incapable of being sustained

insurance /in'shooərəns, -'shaw-/ *n* **1** insuring or being insured **2a** the business of insuring people or property **b** (the protection offered by) a contract whereby one party undertakes to indemnify or guarantee another against loss by a particular contingency or risk **c**(1) the premium demanded under such a contract **c**(2) the sum for which sthg is insured

insure /in'shooə, in'shaw/ *v* **1** to give, take, or procure insurance on or for **2** to contract to give or take insurance; *specif* to underwrite

in'sured *n pl* **insured** sby whose life or property is insured

insurgent /in'suhj(ə)nt/ *n* a rebel – **-ence, ency** *n* – **insurgent** *adj*

insurmountable /,insə'mowntəbl/ *adj* insuperable

insurrection /,insə'reksh(ə)n/ *n* (a) revolt against civil authority or established government – ~**ist** *n*

intact /in'takt/ *adj* untouched, esp by anything that harms or diminishes; whole, uninjured – ~**ness** *n*

intaglio /in'tahlioh/ *n pl* **intaglios 1a** (the act or process of producing) an incised or engraved design made in hard material, esp stone, and sunk below the surface of the material **b** printing done from a plate engraved in intaglio **2** sthg (e g a gem) carved in intaglio

intake /'in,tayk/ n 1 an opening through which liquid or gas enters an enclosure or system 2a a taking in b(1) *sing or pl in constr* an amount or number taken in b(2) sthg taken in

intangible /in'tanjəbl/ n or adj (sthg) not tangible – **-bility** n – **-bly** adv

integer /'intijə/ n the number 1 or any number (e g 6, 0, -23) obtainable by once or repeatedly adding 1 to or subtracting 1 from the number 1

integral /'intigrəl; *esp in maths* in'tegrəl/ adj 1a essential to completeness; constituent – chiefly in *integral part* b formed as a unit with another part 2 composed of integral parts 3 lacking nothing essential; whole

integrate /'intigrayt/ v 1 to form or blend into a whole 2a to combine together or with sthg else b to incorporate into a larger unit – usu + *into* 3 to end the segregation of or in 4 to become integrated – **-gration** n – **-d** adj

integrated 'circuit n an electronic circuit formed in or on a single tiny slice of semiconductor material (e g silicon)

integrity /in'tegrəti/ n 1 an unimpaired condition 2 uncompromising adherence to a code of esp moral or artistic values 3 the quality or state of being complete or undivided

intellect /'int(ə)lekt/ n the capacity for intelligent thought, esp when highly developed

¹**intellectual** /,int(ə)l'ektyoo·əl, -chəl/ adj 1a of the intellect b developed or chiefly guided by the intellect rather than by emotion or experience 2 given to or requiring the use of the intellect – **~ly** adv

²**intellectual** n an intellectual person

intelligence /in'telij(ə)ns/ n 1 the ability to learn, apply knowledge, or think abstractly, esp in allowing one to deal with new or trying situations; *also* the skilled use of intelligence or reason 2 the act of understanding 3a news; information b (a group of people who gather) information concerning an enemy – **-gent** adj – **-gently** adv

intelligible /in'telijəbl/ adj 1 capable of being understood 2 able to be apprehended by the intellect only – **-bility** n – **-bly** adv

intemperate /in'temp(ə)rət/ adj not temperate; *esp* going beyond the bounds of reasonable behaviour – **-ance** n – **~ly** adv

intend /in'tend/ v 1 to mean, signify 2a to have in mind as a purpose or goal b to design for a specified use or future

intense /in'tens/ adj 1a existing or occurring in an extreme degree b having or showing a usual characteristic in extreme degree 2 intensive 3a feeling emotion deeply, esp by nature or temperament b deeply felt – **~ly** adv – **-sity** n

intensify /in'tensi,fie/ v to make or become (more) intense – **-fication** n

intensive /in'tensiv/ adj of or marked by intensity or intensification: e g a highly concentrated b constituting or relating to a method designed to increase productivity by the expenditure of more capital and labour rather than by increase in the land or raw materials used

¹**intent** /in'tent/ n 1a the act or fact of intending b the state of mind with which an act is done 2 criminal intention 3 meaning, significance — **to all intents and purposes** in every practical or important respect; virtually

²**intent** adj 1 directed with strained or eager attention; concentrated 2 having the mind, attention, or will concentrated *on* sthg or some end or purpose – **~ly** adv – **~ness** n

intention /in'tensh(ə)n/ n 1 a determination to act in a certain way; a resolve 2 pl purpose with respect to proposal of marriage 3a what one intends to do or bring about; an aim b the object for which religious devotion is offered 4 a concept

intentional /in'tensh(ə)nl/ adj done by intention or design – **~ly** adv

interact /,intə'rakt/ v to act upon each other – **~ion** n – **~ive** adj

inter'breed /-'breed/ v interbred /-'bred/ 1 to crossbreed 2 to breed within a closed population 3 to cause to interbreed

intercede /,intə'seed/ v to beg or plead on behalf of another with a view to reconciling differences – **-cession** n

¹**inter'cept** /-'sept/ v to stop, seize, or interrupt in progress, course, or movement, esp from one place to another – **~ion** n

²**inter,cept** n an interception

¹**inter'change** /-'chaynj/ v 1 to put each of (2 things) in the place of the other 2 to exchange 3 to change places reciprocally

²**inter,change** n 1 (an) interchanging 2 a junction of 2 or more roads having a system of separate levels that permit traffic to pass from one to another without the crossing of traffic streams

'inter,com /-,kom/ n a local communication system (e g in a ship or building) with a microphone and loudspeaker at each station

,inter,conti'nental /-,konti'nentl/ adj extending among continents; *also* carried on or (capable of) travelling between continents

'inter,course /-,kaws/ n 1 connection or dealings between people or groups 2 exchange, esp of thoughts or feelings 3 physical sexual contact between individuals; *esp* sexual intercourse

¹**inter,dict** /-,dikt/ n 1 a Roman Catholic disciplinary measure withdrawing most sacraments and Christian burial from a person or district 2 a prohibition

²**inter'dict** v to forbid in a usu formal or authoritative manner – **~ion** n – **~ory** adj

¹**interest** /'int(ə)rest, -rəst/ n **1a(1)** right, title, or legal share in sthg **a(2)** participation in advantage and responsibility **b** a business in which one has an interest **2** benefit; advantage; *specif* self-interest **3a** a charge for borrowed money, generally a percentage of the amount borrowed **b** sthg added above what is due **4** a financially interested group **5a** readiness to be concerned with, moved by, or have one's attention attracted by sthg; curiosity **b** (the quality in) a thing that arouses interest

²**interest** v **1** to induce or persuade to participate or engage, esp in an enterprise **2** to concern or engage (sby, esp oneself) in an activity or cause **3** to engage the attention or arouse the interest of – ~ **ing** adj – ~ **ingly** adv

'**interested** adj **1** having the interest aroused or attention engaged **2** affected or involved; not impartial

'**inter,face** /-,fays/ n **1** a surface forming a common boundary of 2 bodies, regions, or phases **2** the place at which independent systems meet and act on or communicate with each other – **interface** v

'**inter,facing** /-,faysing/ n stiffening material attached between 2 layers of fabric

,**inter'fere** /-'fiə/ v **1** to get in the way of, hinder, or impede another – + with **2** to enter into or take a part in matters that do not concern one **3** to hinder illegally an attempt of a player to catch or hit a ball or puck – usu + with

,**inter'ference** /-'fiərəns/ n **1** the phenomenon resulting from the meeting of 2 wave trains (e g of light or sound) with an increase in intensity at some points and a decrease at others **2** the illegal hindering of an opponent in hockey, ice hockey, etc **3** (sthg that produces) the confusion of received radio signals by unwanted signals or noise

¹**interim** /'intərim/ n an intervening time

²**interim** adj temporary, provisional

¹**interior** /in'tiəri-ə/ adj **1** lying, occurring, or functioning within the limits or interior **2** away from the border or shore **3** of the mind or soul

²**interior** n **1** the internal or inner part of a thing; *also* the inland **2** internal affairs **3** a representation of the interior of a building or room

interject /,intə'jekt/ v to throw in (e g a remark) abruptly among or between other things

,**inter'jection** /-'jeksh(ə)n/ n an ejaculatory word (e g *Wonderful*) or utterance (e g *ah* or *good heavens*) usu expressing emotion – ~**ally** adv

,**inter'lace** /-'lays/ v **1** to unite (as if) by lacing together **2** to mingle, blend, or intersperse **3** to cross one another intricately

,**inter'lock** /-'lok/ v **1** to become engaged, interrelated, or interlocked **2** to lock together

'**inter,loper** /-,lohpə/ n sby who interferes or encroaches; an intruder

'**inter,lude** /-,loohd/ n **1** an intervening or interruptive period, space, or event, esp of a contrasting character; an interval **2** a musical composition inserted between the parts of a longer composition, a drama, or a religious service

,**inter'marry** /-'mari/ v **1** to marry each other or sby from the same group **2** to become connected by marriage with another group or with each other – **riage** n

,**inter'mediary** /-'meedi-əri/ n or adj (sby or sthg) acting as a mediator or go-between

,**inter'mediate** /-'meedi-ət/ adj being or occurring at or near the middle place, stage, or degree or between 2 others or extremes

intermezzo /,intə'metsoh/ n pl **intermezzi** /-see,/, **intermezzos** **1** a movement coming between the major sections of an extended musical work (e g an opera) **2** a short independent instrumental composition

interminable /in'tuhminəbl/ adj having or seeming to have no end; esp wearisomely long – **bly** adv

,**inter'mingle** /-'ming-gl/ v to mix or mingle together or with sthg else

,**inter'mission** /-'mish(ə)n/ n **1** intermitting or being intermitted **2** an intervening period of time (e g between acts of a performance or attacks of a disease)

,**inter'mit** /-'mit/ v -tt- to (cause to) cease for a time or at intervals

,**inter'mittent** /-'mit(ə)nt/ adj coming and going at intervals; not continuous – ~**ly** adv

intern /in'tuhn/ v to confine, esp during a war

internal /in'tuhnl/ adj **1** existing or situated within the limits or surface of sthg **2** of or existing within the mind **3** depending only on the properties of the thing under consideration without reference to things outside it **4** (present or arising) within (a part of) the body or an organism **5** within a state – ~**ize** v – ~**ly** adv

in,ternal-com'bustion ,engine n a heat engine in which the combustion that generates the heat energy takes place inside the engine (e g in a cylinder)

¹,**inter'national** /-'nash(ə)nl/ adj **1** affecting or involving 2 or more nations **2** known, recognized, or renowned in more than 1 country – ~**ize** v

²**international** n **1** (sby who plays or has played in) a sports, games, etc match between 2 national teams **2** *also* **internationale** often cap any of several socialist or communist organizations of international scope

,**inter'national,ism** /-,iz(ə)m/ n **1** international character, interests, or outlook **2** (an attitude favouring) cooperation among nations – **ist** n

internecine /,intə'neesien/ adj **1** mutually destructive **2** of or involving conflict within a group

,inter'planetary /-'planit(ə)ri/ *adj* existing, carried on, or operating between planets

'inter,play /-,play/ *n* interaction

'Inter,pol /-,pol/ *n* an international police organization for liaison between national police forces

interpolate /in'tuhpəlayt/ *v* 1 to alter or corrupt (e g a text) by inserting new or foreign matter 2 to insert between other things or parts; *esp* to insert (words) into a text or conversation – **-lation** *n*

interpose /,intə'pohz/ *v* 1 to place between 2 things or in an intervening position 2 to put forth by way of interference or intervention 3 to interrupt 4 to be or come in an intervening position – **-position** *n*

interpret /in'tuhprit/ *v* 1 to expound the meaning of 2 to conceive of in the light of one's beliefs, judgments, or circumstances; construe 3 to represent by means of art; bring to realization by performance 4 to act as an interpreter – ~**er** *n* – ~**ative,** ~**ive** *adj*

interpretation /in,tuhpri'taysh(ə)n/ *n* an instance of artistic interpreting in performance or adaptation

interregnum /,intə'regnəm/ *n, pl* **interregnums, interregna** /-'regnə/ 1 the time during which 1a a throne is vacant between reigns b the normal functions of government are suspended 2 a lapse or pause in a continuous series

,interre'late /-ri'layt/ *v* to bring into or be in a relationship where each one depends upon or is acting upon the other – **-lation, -lationship** *n*

interrogate /in'terəgayt/ *v* to question formally – **-gation** *n* – **-gator** *n*

¹interrogative /,intə'rogətiv/, **interrogatory** /-t(ə)ri/ *adj* 1a of or being the grammatical mood that expresses a question b used in a question 2 questioning – ~**ly** *adv*

²interrogative *n* 1 an interrogative utterance 2 a word, esp a pronoun, used in asking questions 3 the interrogative mood of a language

interrupt /,intə'rupt/ *v* 1 to break the flow or action of (a speaker or speech) 2 to break the uniformity or continuity of (sthg) 3 to interrupt an action; *esp* to interrupt another's utterance with one's own – ~**ion** *n*

,inter'sect /-'sekt/ *v* 1 to pierce or divide (e g a line or area) by passing through or across 2 to meet and cross at a point

intersection /'intə,seksh(ə)n, ,--'--/ *n* a place where 2 or more things (e g streets) intersect

,inter'sperse /-'spuhs/ *v* 1 to insert at intervals among other things 2 to diversify or vary with scattered things

,inter'stellar /-'stelə/ *adj* located or taking place among the stars

interstice /in'tuhstis/ *n* a small space between adjacent things – *fml*

,inter'twine /-'twien/ *v* to twine together

interval /'intəv(ə)l/ *n* 1 an intervening space: e g 1a a time between events or states; a pause b a distance or gap between objects, units, or states c the difference in pitch between 2 notes 2 *Br* a break in the presentation of an entertainment (e g a play)

,inter'vene /-'veen/ *v* 1 to enter or appear as sthg irrelevant or extraneous 2 to occur or come between 2 things, esp points of time or events 3 to come in or between so as to hinder or modify 4a to enter a lawsuit as a third party b to interfere in another nation's internal affairs – **-vention** *n*

'inter,view /-'vyooh/ *n* 1 a formal consultation usu to evaluate qualifications (e g of a prospective student or employee) 2 (a report of) a meeting at which information is obtained (e g by a journalist) from sby – **interview** *v* – ~**er** *n* – ~**ee** *n*

,inter'weave /-'weev/ *v* **interwove** /-'wohv/ *also* **interweaved; interwoven** /-'wohv(ə)n/ *also* **interweaved** 1 to weave together 2 to intermingle, blend

intestate /in'testayt, -tət/ *adj* having made no valid will

intestine /in'testin/ *n* the tubular part of the alimentary canal that extends from the stomach to the anus – **-inal** *adj*

¹intimate /'intimayt/ *v* to make known: e g **a** to announce **b** to hint; imply – **-mation** *n*

²intimate /'intimət/ *adj* 1a intrinsic, essential b belonging to or characterizing one's deepest nature 2 marked by very close association, contact, or familiarity 3 suggesting informal warmth or privacy 4 of a very personal or private nature 5 involved in a sexual relationship; *specif* engaging in an act of sexual intercourse – euph – ~**ly** *adv* – **-macy** *n*

³intimate *n* a close friend or confidant

intimidate /in'timidayt/ *v* to frighten; *esp* to compel or deter (as if) by threats – **-dation** *n*

into /'intə before consonants; otherwise 'intooh/ *prep* 1a so as to be inside (e g come *into* the house) b so as to be (e g grow *into* a woman) c so as to be in (a state) (e g shocked *into* silence) d so as to be expressed in, dressed in, engaged in, or a member of (e g translate *into* French; enter *into* an alliance) e – used in division as the inverse of *by* or *divided by* (e g divide 35 *into* 70) 2 – used to indicate a partly elapsed period of time or a partly traversed extent of space (e g far *into* the night; deep *into* the jungle) 3 in the direction of; *esp* towards the centre of (e g look *into* the sun) 4 to a position of contact with; against (e g ran *into* the wall) 5 involved with; *esp* keen on (e g are you *into* meditation?) – infml

intolerable /in'tol(ə)rəbl/ *adj* unbearable – **-bly** *adv*

inv

in'tolerant /-'tolərənt/ adj **1** unable or unwilling to endure **2** unwilling to grant or share social, professional, political, or religious rights; bigoted – ~**ly** adv – **-rance** n

intonation /ˌintə'naysh(ə)n/ n **1** performance of music with respect to correctness of pitch and harmony **2** the rise and fall in pitch of the voice in speech

intone /in'tohn/ v to utter (sthg) in musical or prolonged tones; recite in singing tones or in a monotone

in toto /in 'tohtoh/ adv totally, entirely

intoxicate /in'toksikayt/ v **1** to poison **2a** to excite or stupefy by alcohol or a drug, esp to the point where physical and mental control is markedly diminished **b** to cause to lose self-control through excitement or elation – **-cant** adj, n – **-cation** n

intractable /in'traktəbl/ adj **1** not easily managed or directed; obstinate **2** not easily manipulated, wrought, or solved – **-bility** n – **-bly** adv

intransigent /in'transij(ə)nt, -'tranzi-/ adj uncompromising – **-gence** n – ~**ly** adv

in'transitive /-'transitiv, -'trahn-, -'tranh-, -zitiv/ adj characterized by not having a direct object – ~**ly** adv

intrauterine device, intrauterine contraceptive device n a device inserted and left in the uterus to prevent conception

intra'venous /-'veenas/ adj situated or occurring in, or entering by way of a vein; also used in intravenous procedures – ~**ly** adv

intrench /in'trench/ v to entrench

intrepid /in'trepid/ adj fearless, bold, and resolute – ~**ly** adv – ~**ity** n

intricate /'intrikat/ adj **1** having many complexly interrelating parts or elements **2** difficult to resolve or analyse – ~**ly** adv – **-cacy** n

¹**intrigue** /in'treeg/ v **1** to arouse the interest or curiosity of **2** to captivate; fascinate **3** to carry on an intrigue; esp to plot, scheme

²**intrigue** /'intreeg, -'-/ n **1** a secret scheme or plot **2** a clandestine love affair

intrinsic /in'trinzik/ adj **1** belonging to the essential nature or constitution of sthg **2** originating or situated within the body – ~**ally** adv

introduce /ˌintrə'dyoohs/ v **1** to lead or bring in, esp for the first time **2a** to bring into play **b** to bring into practice or use; institute **3** to lead to or make known by a formal act, announcement, or recommendation **3a** to cause to be acquainted; make (oneself or sby) known to another **b** to make preliminary explanatory or laudatory remarks about (e g a speaker) **4** to place, insert **5** to bring to a knowledge or discovery of sthg – **-ductory** adj

introduction /ˌintrə'duksh(ə)n/ n **1a** a preliminary treatise or course of study **b** a short introductory musical passage **2** sthg introduced; specif a plant or animal new to an area

¹**intro'vert** /-'vuht/ v to turn inwards or in on itself or oneself

²**intro,vert** n one whose attention and interests are directed towards his/her own mental life

intrude /in'troohd/ v to thrust or force in or on, esp without permission, welcome, or suitable reason – ~**r, -usion** n

intrusive /in'troohsiv, -ziv/ adj characterized by (a tendency to) intrusion

intuition /ˌintyooh'ish(ə)n/ n **1a** (knowledge gained by) immediate apprehension or cognition **b** the power of attaining direct knowledge without evident rational thought and the drawing of conclusions from evidence available **2** quick and ready insight – **-tive** adj – **-tively** adv

inundate /'inundayt/ v to cover or overwhelm (as if) with a flood – **-dation** n

inure /i'nyooə/ v to accustom to sthg undesirable

invade /in'vayd/ v **1** to enter (e g a country) for hostile purposes **2** to encroach on **3** to spread over or into as if invading – ~**r** n

¹**invalid** /in'valid/ adj **1** without legal force **2** logically inconsistent – ~**ly** adv – ~**ity** n

²**invalid** /'invalid; also -,leed/ adj **1** suffering from disease or disability **2** of or suited to an invalid – ~**ism** n

³**invalid** /'invalid/ n one who is sickly or disabled

⁴**invalid** /'invalid, ,invə'leed/ v to remove from active duty by reason of sickness or disability

invalidate /in'validayt/ v to make invalid; esp to weaken or destroy the convincingness of (e g an argument or claim) – **-dation** n

invaluable /in'valyooəbl/ adj valuable beyond estimation; priceless

invariable /in'veəri·əbl/ adj not (capable of) changing; constant – **-bly** adv – **-bility** n

invasion /in'vayzh(ə)n/ n **1** an invading, esp by an army **2** the incoming or spread of sthg usu harmful – **-ive** adj

invective /in'vektiv/ n abusive or insulting (use of) language; denunciation

inveigh /in'vay/ v to speak or protest bitterly against

inveigle /in'vaygl/ v **inveigling** /in'vaygling/ to talk sby into sthg by ingenuity or flattery

invent /in'vent/ v **1** to think up **2** to produce (e g sthg useful) for the first time – ~**or** n

invention /in'vensh(ə)n/ n **1** productive imagination; inventiveness **2a** a (misleading) product of the imagination **b** a contrivance or process devised after study and experiment

inventive /in'ventiv/ adj **1** creative **2** characterized by invention – ~**ly** adv – ~**ness** n

¹**inventory** /'invəntri/ n 1 an itemized list (e g of the property of an individual or estate) 2 the items listed in an inventory 3 the taking of an inventory

²**inventory** v to make an inventory of; catalogue

¹**inverse** /in'vuhs, '-/ adj 1 opposite in order, direction, nature, or effect 2 of a mathematical function expressing the same relationship as another function but from the opposite viewpoint

²**inverse** n a direct opposite – ~ly adv

invert /in'vuht/ v 1a to turn inside out or upside down b to turn (e g a foot) inwards 2a to reverse in position, order, or relationship b to subject to musical inversion

invertebrate /in'vuhtibrət, -brayt/ n or adj (an animal) lacking a spinal column

in,verted 'comma n, chiefly Br a quotation mark

¹**invest** /in'vest/ v 1 to confer (the symbols of) authority, office, or rank on 2 to clothe, endow, or cover (as if) with sthg

²**invest** v 1 to commit (money) to a particular use (e g buying shares or new capital outlay) in order to earn a financial return 2 to devote (e g time or effort) to sthg for future advantages 3 to make an investment

investigate /in'vestigayt/ v 1 to make a systematic examination or study (of) 2 to conduct an official inquiry (into) – -gator n – -gation n

investiture /in'vestichə/ n a formal ceremony conferring an office or honour on sby

investment /in'vestmənt/ n a (sum of) money invested for income or profit; also the asset (e g property) purchased

inveterate /in'vet(ə)rət/ adj 1 firmly, obstinately, and persistently established 2 habitual

invidious /in'vidi·əs/ adj 1 tending to cause discontent, ill will, or envy 2 of an unpleasant or objectionable nature; of a kind causing or likely to cause harm or resentment – ~ly adv – ~ness n

invigilate /in'vijilayt/ v to keep watch (over); specif, Br to supervise (candidates) at (an examination) – -lator n – -lation n

invigorate /in'vigərayt/ v to give fresh life and energy to

invincible /in'vinsəbl/ adj incapable of being conquered or subdued – -bility n – -bly adj

inviolable /in'vie·əbbl/ adj (to be kept) secure from violation, profanation, or assault – -bility n

invisible /in'vizəbl/ adj 1 incapable (by nature or circumstances) of being seen 2a not appearing in published financial statements b not reflected in statistics 3 too small or unobtrusive to be seen or noticed; inconspicuous – -bly adv – -bility n

invitation /,invi'taysh(ə)n/ n 1 an often formal request to be present or participate 2 an incentive, inducement

invite /in'viet/ v 1a to offer an incentive or inducement to b to (unintentionally) increase the likelihood of 2 to request (the presence of) formally or politely

inviting /in'vieting/ adj attractive, tempting – ~ly adv

¹**invoice** /'invoys/ n 1 a bill; specif an itemized list of goods shipped, usu specifying the price and the terms of sale 2 a consignment of merchandise

²**invoice** v to submit an invoice for or to

invoke /in'vohk/ v 1 to appeal to or cite as an authority 2 to call forth (e g a spirit) by uttering a spell or magical formula 3 to put into effect – -vocation n

involuntary /in'volənt(ə)ri/ adj 1 done contrary to or without choice 2 not subject to conscious control; reflex – -tarily adv – -tariness n

involve /in'volv/ v 1a to cause to be associated or take part b to occupy (oneself) absorbingly; esp to commit (oneself) emotionally 2 to relate closely 3a to have within or as part of itself b to require as a necessary accompaniment – ~ment n

in'volved adj 1 (needlessly or excessively) complex 2 taking part in

invulnerable /in'vulnərəbl/ adj 1 incapable of being injured or harmed 2 immune to or proof against attack – -bility n – -bly adv

inward /'inwood/ adj 1 situated within or directed towards the inside 2 of or relating to the mind or spirit (e g struggled to achieve inward peace) – ~ly adv

¹**inwards, NAm chiefly inward** adv 1 towards the inside, centre, or interior 2 towards the inner being

iodine /'ie·ə,deen/ n a chemical element used in photography, and in solution as a disinfectant for wounds, grazes, etc

ion /'ie·ən/ n 1 an atom or group of atoms that carries a positive or negative electric charge as a result of having lost or gained 1 or more electrons 2 a free electron or other charged subatomic particle – ~ize v – ~ization n

ionosphere /ie'onə,sfiə/ n the part of the earth's atmosphere that extends from an altitude above that of the stratosphere out to at least 480km (about 300mi)

iota /ie'ohtə/ n 1 the 9th letter of the Greek alphabet 2 an infinitesimal amount

IOU /,ie oh 'yooh/ n (a written acknowledgment of) a debt

irascible /i'rasibl/ adj having an easily provoked temper – -bility n – -bly adv

irate /ie'rayt/ adj roused to or arising from anger – ~ly adv – ~ness n

ire /ie·ə/ n intense anger – ~ful adj

iridium /i'ridi·əm/ n a silver-white hard brittle very heavy metallic element of the platinum group

iris /'ieris/ n, pl (1) **irises, irides** /'ierideez/, (2) **irises, irides**, esp collectively **iris** 1 the opaque contractile diaphragm perforated by the pupil that forms the coloured portion of the eye 2 any of a large genus of plants with long straight leaves and large showy flowers

¹**Irish** /'ierish/ adj 1 of Ireland or the Irish (language) 2 amusingly illogical

²**Irish** n 1 pl in constr the people of Ireland 2 **Irish, Irish Gaelic** the Celtic language of Ireland, esp as used since the end of the medieval period

irk /uhk/ v to make weary, irritated, or bored

¹**irksome** /-s(ə)m/ adj troublesome, annoying

¹**iron** /'ie·ən/ n 1 a heavy malleable ductile magnetic silver-white metallic element that readily rusts in moist air, occurs in most igneous rocks, and is vital to biological processes 2a stng used to bind or restrain – usu pl b a heated metal implement used for branding or cauterizing c a metal implement with a smooth flat typically triangular base that is heated (e g by electricity) and used to smooth or press clothing d a stirrup e any of a numbered series of usu 9 golf clubs with metal heads of varying angles for hitting the ball to various heights and lengths — **iron in the fire** a prospective course of action; a plan not yet realized

²**iron** adj 1 (made) of iron 2 resembling iron (e g in appearance, strength, solidity, or durability)

³**iron** v to smooth (as if) with a heated iron

Iron Age n the period of human culture characterized by the widespread use of iron for making tools and weapons and dating from before 1000 BC

,**iron 'curtain** n, often cap I&C an esp political and ideological barrier between the Communist countries of E Europe and the non-Communist countries of (and those friendly to) W Europe

ironic /ie'ronik/, **ironical** /-kl/ adj 1 of, containing, or constituting irony 2 given to irony – ~ **ally** adv

'**iron,monger** /-,mung·gə/ n, Br a dealer in esp household hardware – ~ **y** n

iron out v to put right or correct (e g a problem or defect); resolve (e g difficulties)

'**iron,works** /-,wuhks/ n pl **ironworks** a mill or building where iron or steel is smelted or heavy iron or steel products are made – often pl with sing. meaning

irony /'ierəni/ n 1 the use of words to express a meaning other than and esp the opposite of the literal meaning 2 (an event or situation showing) incongruity between actual circumstances and the normal, appropriate, or expected result 3 an attitude of detached awareness of incongruity

irradiate /i'raydiayt/ v 1a to cast rays (of light) upon b to give intellectual or spiritual insight to c to affect or treat by (exposure to) radiant energy (e g heat) 2 to emit like rays (of light); radiate – ~ **ation** n

¹**irrational** /i'rash(ə)nl/ adj not rational; not governed by or according to reason – ~ **ly** adv – ~ **ity**

²**irrational, irrational number** n a number (e g p) that cannot be expressed as the result of dividing 1 integer by another

¹**irreconcilable** /i'rekən,sieləbl/ adj impossible to reconcile: e g a resolutely opposed b incompatible – **-bly** adv

²**irreconcilable** n an opponent of compromise or collaboration

irrecoverable /,iri'kuv(ə)rəbl/ adj not capable of being recovered or retrieved – **-bly** adv

irredeemable /,iri'deeməbl/ adj not redeemable; esp beyond remedy; hopeless – **-bly** adv

irreducible /,iri'dyoohsəbl/ adj impossible to bring into a desired, normal, or simpler state – **-bly** adv

irrefutable /,iri'fyoohtəbl, i'refyootəbl/ adj incontrovertible – **-bly** adv

irregular /i'regyoolə/ adj 1a contrary to rule, custom, or moral principles b not inflected in the normal manner c inadequate because of failure to conform 2 lacking symmetry or evenness 3 lacking continuity or regularity, esp of occurrence or activity – ~ **ly** adv

irregularity /i,regyoo'larəti/ n stng irregular (e g contrary to accepted professional or ethical standards)

irrelevant /i'reliv(ə)nt/ adj not relevant; inapplicable – ~ **ly** adv – **-vance, -vancy** n

irreparable /i'rep(ə)rəbl/ adj not able to be restored to a previous condition – **-bly** adv

irreplaceable /,iri'playsəbl/ adj having no adequate substitute

irrepressible /,iri'presəbl/ adj impossible to restrain or control – **-bly** adv

irreproachable /,iri'prohchəbl/ adj offering no foundation for blame or criticism – **-bly** adv

irresistible /,iri'zistəbl/ adj impossible to resist successfully; highly attractive or enticing – **-bly** adv

irresolute /i'rezəl(y)ooht/ adj lacking decision or a firm aim and purpose – **-lution** n

,**irre'spective** /,iri'spektiv/ prep without regard or reference to; in spite of

irresponsible /,iri'sponsəbl/ 1 showing no regard for the consequences of one's actions 2 unable to bear responsibility – **-bility** n – **-bly** adv

irreversible /,iri'vuhsəbl/ adj unable to be changed back into a previous state or condition – **-bly** adv

irrevocable /i'revəkəbl/ adj incapable of being revoked or altered – **-bly** adv

irrigate /'irigayt/ *v* **1** to supply (e g land) with water by artificial means **2** to flush (e g an eye or wound) with a stream of liquid – **-gable** *adj* – **-gation** *n*

irritable /'iritəbl/ *adj* capable of being irritated: e g **a** easily exasperated or excited **b** (excessively) responsive to stimuli – **-bility** *n* – **-bly** *adv*

irritate /'iritayt/ *v* **1** to excite impatience, anger, or displeasure (in) **2** to induce a response to a stimulus in or of – **-tant** *n* – **-tation** *n*

is /z; *strong* iz/ *pres 3 sing of* **be**, *dial pres 1 &2 sing of* **be**, *substandard pres pl of* **be**

Islam /'izlahm, -lam/ *n* **1** the religious faith of Muslims including belief in Allah as the sole deity and in Muhammad as his prophet **2** the civilization or culture accompanying Islamic faith – **~ic** *adj*

island /'iełənd/ *n* **1** an area of land surrounded by water and smaller than a continent **2** sthg like an island (e g in being isolated or surrounded) **3** a traffic island **4** an isolated superstructure on the deck of a ship, esp an aircraft carrier

isle /iel/ *n* a (small) island – used in some names

islet /'ielit/ *n* a little island

isobar /'iesohbah, 'iesə-/ *n* a line on a chart connecting places where the atmospheric pressure is the same

isolate /'ies(ə)layt/ *v* **1** to set apart from others; *also* to quarantine **2** to separate from another substance so as to obtain in a pure form **3** to insulate – **-lation** *n*

isolationism /,iesə'layshən,iz(ə)m/ *n* a policy of national isolation by refraining from engaging in international relations – **-ist** *n*, *adj*

isotope /'iesə,tohp/ *n* any of 2 or more species of atoms of a chemical element that have the same atomic number and nearly identical chemical behaviour but differ in atomic mass or mass number and physical properties

Israeli /iz'rayli/ *adj* (characteristic) of modern Israel

Israelite /'izrəliet/ *n* any of the descendants of the Hebrew patriarch Jacob; *specif* a member of any of the 10 Hebrew tribes occupying northern Palestine in biblical times

¹issue /'ish(y)ooh, 'isyooh/ *n* **1** the action of going, coming, or flowing out **2** a means or place of going out **3** offspring **4** an outcome that usu resolves or decides a problem **5** a matter that is in dispute between 2 or more parties; a controversial topic **6** sthg coming out from a usu specified source **7a** the act of publishing, giving out, or making available **b** the thing or the whole quantity of things given out, published, or distributed at 1 time — **at issue** under discussion or consideration; in dispute — **join/take issue** to take an opposing or conflicting stand; disagree or engage in argument on a point of dispute

²issue *v* **1a** to go, come, or flow out **b** to emerge **2** to appear or become available through being given out, published, or distributed **3a** to give out, distribute, or provide officially **b** to send out for sale or circulation

isthmus /'isməs; *also* 'isthməs/ *n* a narrow strip of land connecting 2 larger land areas

¹it /it/ *pron* **1a** that thing, creature, or group – used as subject or object; (e g noticed that *it* was old; had a baby but lost *it*) **b** the person in question **2** – used as subject of an impersonal verb (e g *it's* raining) **3a** – used to highlight part of a sentence (e g *it* was yesterday that he arrived) **b** – used with many verbs and prepositions as a meaningless object (e g run for *it*) **4** – used to refer to an explicit or implicit state of affairs (e g how's *it* going?) **5** that which is available, important, or appropriate (e g one boiled egg and that's *it*; a bit brighter, that's *it*)

²it *n* **1** the player in a usu children's game who performs a unique role (e g trying to catch others in a game of tag) **2** sex appeal; *also* sexual intercourse – *infml*

Italian /i'tali·ən/ *n* **1** a native or inhabitant of Italy **2** the Romance language of the Italians

¹itch /ich/ *v* **1** to have or produce an itch **2** to have a restless desire – *infml*

²itch *n* **1a** an irritating sensation in the upper surface of the skin that makes one want to scratch **b** a skin disorder characterized by such a sensation **2** a restless desire – *infml*

item /'ietəm/ *n* **1** a separate unit in an account or series **2** a separate piece of news or information – **~ize** *v*

i'tinerary /ie'tinərəri, i'ti-/ *n* **1** the (proposed) route of a journey **2** a travel diary **3** a traveller's guidebook

its /its/ *adj* relating to it or itself, esp as possessor, agent, or object of an action

itself /it'self/ *pron* **1** that identical thing, creature, or group **2** its normal self — **in itself** intrinsically considered

IUD *n* an intrauterine device

ivory /'ievəri/ *n* **1** the hard creamy-white form of dentine of which the tusks of elephants and other tusked mammals are made **2** a creamy slightly yellowish white colour **3** *pl* things (e g dice or piano keys) made of (sthg resembling) ivory – *infml*

,ivory 'tower *n* aloofness from practical concerns; *also* a place encouraging such an attitude

ivy /'ievi/ *n* a very common and widely cultivated Eurasian woody climbing plant with evergreen leaves, small yellowish flowers, and black berries

J

j /jay/ *n, pl* **j's, js** *often cap* (a graphic representation of or device for reproducing) the 10th letter of the English alphabet

¹**jab** /jab/ *v* **-bb- 1a** to pierce (as if) with a sharp object **b** to poke quickly or abruptly **2** to strike (sby) with a short straight blow **3** to make quick or abrupt thrusts (as if) with a pointed or sharp object

²**jab** *n* a hypodermic injection – *infml*

jabber /'jabə/ *v or n* (to engage in) rapid or unintelligible talk or chatter

¹**jack** /jak/ *n* **1** any of various portable mechanisms for exerting pressure or lifting a heavy object a short distance **2a** a small white target ball in lawn bowling **b(1)** *pl but sing in constr* a game in which players toss and pick up small bone or metal objects in a variety of shapes in between throws of a ball **b(2)** a small 6-pointed metal object used in the game of jacks **3** a playing card carrying the figure of a soldier or servant and ranking usu below the queen **4** a single-pronged electric plug

²**jack** *v* **1** to move or lift (as if) by a jack **2** to raise the level or quality of **3** give up – usu + *in*; *infml USE* (1&2) usu + *up*

jackal /'jakl/ *v or n* any of several Old World wild dogs smaller than the related wolves

jackass /'jak,as/ *n* **1** a male ass **2** a fool

¹**jack,boot** /-,booht/ *n* a laceless military boot reaching to the calf

jackdaw /'jak,daw/ *n* a common black and grey Eurasian bird that is related to but smaller than the common crow

¹**jacket** /'jakit/ *n* **1** an outer garment for the upper body opening down the full length of the centre front **2** the skin of a (baked) potato **3a** a thermally insulating cover (e g for a hot water tank) **b(1)** a dust jacket **b(2)** the cover of a paperback book

²**jacket** *v* to put a jacket on; enclose in or with a jacket

Jack 'Frost *n* frost or frosty weather personified

jack-in-the-,box *n, pl* **jack-in-the-boxes, jacks-in-the-box** a toy consisting of a small box out of which a figure springs when the lid is raised

¹**jack,knife** /-,nief/ *n* **1** a large clasp knife for the pocket **2** a dive in which the diver bends from the waist, touches the ankles with straight knees, and straightens out before hitting the water

²**jackknife** *v* **1** to (cause to) double up like a jackknife **2** *esp of an articulated lorry* to turn or rise and form an angle of 90 degrees or less

jack-of-'all-,trades *n* a handy versatile person – sometimes *derog*

'**jack,pot** /-,pot/ *n,* **1** (a combination that wins) a top prize on a fruit machine **2** a large prize (e g in a lottery), often made up of several accumulated prizes that have not been previously won

Jacobean /,jakə'bee·ən/ *adj* of (the age of) James I

Jacobite /'jakəbiet/ *n* a supporter of James II or of the Stuarts after 1688

¹**jade** /jayd/ *n* **1** a vicious or worn-out old horse **2** *archaic* a flirtatious or disreputable woman

²**jade** *n* either of 2 typically green hard gemstones

'**jaded** *adj* fatigued (as if) by overwork or dissipation

¹**jag** /jag/ *v* **-gg- 1** to cut or tear unevenly or raggedly **2** to cut indentations into

²**jag** *n* a sharp projecting part

³**jag** *n* a period of indulgence; *esp* a drinking bout – *slang*

jagged /'jagid/ *adj* having a sharply uneven edge or surface – ~ **ly** *adv*

jaguar /'jagyoo·ə/ *n* a big cat of tropical America that is typically brownish yellow or buff with black spots

¹**jail**, *Br also* **gaol** /jayl/ *n* a prison

²**jail**, *Br also* **gaol** *v* to confine (as if) in a jail

'**jail,bird** /-,buhd/ *n* a person who has been (habitually) confined in jail

'**jail,break** /-,brayk/ *n* an escape from jail

jailer, jailor /'jaylə/ *n* a keeper of a jail

jalopy /jə'lopi/ *n* a dilapidated old vehicle or aircraft – *infml*

¹**jam** /jam/ *v* **-mm- 1a** to press, squeeze, or crush into a close or tight position **b** to (cause to) become wedged or blocked so as to be unworkable **c** to block passage of or along **d** to fill (to excess) **2** to crush; *also* to bruise by crushing **3** to send out interfering signals or cause reflections so as to make unintelligible

²**jam** *n* **1** a crowded mass that impedes or blocks **2** the pressure or congestion of a crowd **3** a difficult state of affairs – *infml*

³**jam** *n* a preserve made by boiling fruit and sugar to a thick consistency

jamb /jam/ *n* a straight vertical member or surface forming the side of an opening for a door, window, etc

jamboree /,jambə'ree/ *n* **1** a large festive gathering **2** a large gathering of scouts or guides in a camp

jammy /'jami/ *adj, Br* **1** lucky **2** easy *USE infml*

'**jam ,session** *n* an impromptu jazz performance that features group improvisation

jangle /'jang·gl/ v 1 *of the nerves* to be in a state of tense irritation 2 to make a harsh or discordant often ringing noise

janissary /'janisəri/ n 1 *often cap* a soldier of a former élite corps of Turkish troops 2 a loyal or subservient official or supporter

janitor /'janitə/, *fem* **janitress** /-tris/ n 1 a doorkeeper; a porter 2 a caretaker

January /'janyoo(ə)ri/ n the 1st month of the Gregorian calendar

japan /jə'pan/ n 1 a varnish giving a hard brilliant finish 2 work (e g lacquer ware) finished and decorated in the Japanese manner

Japanese /,japə'neez/ n, pl **Japanese** 1 a native or inhabitant of Japan 2 the language of the Japanese – **Japanese** adj

japonica /jə'ponikə/ n a hardy ornamental shrub of the rose family with clusters of scarlet, white, or pink flowers

¹**jar** /jah/ v **-rr- 1a** to make a harsh or discordant noise **b** to have a harshly disagreeable effect – + *on* or *upon* 2 to vibrate 3 to cause to jar, esp by shaking or causing a shock to

²**jar** n 1 a jarring noise 2a a sudden or unexpected shake **b** an unsettling shock (e g to nerves or feelings)

³**jar** n 1 a usu cylindrical short-necked and wide-mouthed container, made esp of glass 2 the contents of or quantity contained in a jar

jargon /'jahgən/ n 1 the terminology or idiom of a particular activity or group 2 obscure and often pretentious language

jasmine /'jasmin, 'jaz-/ n 1 any of numerous often climbing shrubs that usu have extremely fragrant flowers; *esp* a high-climbing half-evergreen Asian shrub with fragrant white flowers 2 a light yellow colour

jaundice /'jawndis/ n 1 an abnormal condition marked by yellowish pigmentation of the skin, tissues, and body fluids caused by the deposition of bile pigments 2 a state of prejudice inspired by bitterness, envy, or disillusionment

jaundiced adj mistrustful or prejudiced, esp because of bitterness, envy, or disillusionment

jaunt /jawnt/ v or n (to make) a short journey for pleasure

jaunty /'jawnti/ adj having or showing airy self-confidence; sprightly – **-tily** adv – **-tiness** n

javelin /'jav(ə)lin/ n a light spear thrown as a weapon or in an athletic field event

¹**jaw** /jaw/ n 1 either of 2 cartilaginous or bony structures that in most vertebrates form a framework above and below the mouth in which the teeth are set 2 pl **2a** the entrance of a narrow pass or channel **b** the 2 parts of a machine, tool, etc between which sthg may be clamped or crushed **c** a position or situation of imminent danger

²**jaw** v to talk or gossip for a long time or long-windedly – *infml*

jay /jay/ n an Old World bird of the crow family with a dull pink body, black, white, and blue wings, and a black-and-white crest

'**jay,walk** /-,wawk/ v to cross a street carelessly so as to be endangered by traffic – ~ **er** n

jazz /jaz/ n 1 music developed esp from ragtime and blues and characterized by syncopated rhythms and individual or group improvisation around a basic theme or melody 2 similar but unspecified things – *infml*

jazz up v to enliven – *infml*

jazzy /'jazi/ adj 1 having the characteristics of jazz 2 garish, gaudy – *infml* – **jazzily** adv

jealous /'jeləs/ adj **1a** intolerant of rivalry or unfaithfulness **b** apprehensive of and hostile towards a (supposed) rival 2 resentful, envious of 3 vigilant in guarding a possession, right, etc – ~ **ly** adv – ~ **y** n

jeans /jeenz/ n pl in constr, pl **jeans** casual usu close-fitting trousers, made esp of blue denim

jeep /jeep/ n a small rugged general-purpose motor vehicle with 4-wheel drive, used esp by the armed forces

jeer /jiə/ v to laugh mockingly or scoff (at) – **jeer** n

Jehovah /ji'hohvə/ n God; esp the God of the Old Testament

Je,hovah's 'Witness n a member of a fundamentalist sect practising personal evangelism, rejecting the authority of the secular state, and preaching that the end of the present world is imminent

¹**jelly** /'jeli/ n **1a** a soft fruit-flavoured transparent dessert set with gelatin **b** a savoury food product of similar consistency, made esp from meat stock and gelatin 2 a clear fruit preserve made by boiling sugar and the juice of fruit 3 a substance resembling jelly in consistency

²**jelly** v 1 to bring to the consistency of jelly; cause to set 2 to set in a jelly

'**jelly,fish** /-,fish/ n a free-swimming marine animal that has a nearly transparent saucer-shaped body and extendable tentacles covered with stinging cells

jemmy /'jemi/ v or n, Br (to force open with) a steel crowbar, used esp by burglars

jeopardy /'jepədi/ n exposure to or risk of death, loss, injury, etc; danger – **-dize** v

¹**jerk** /juhk/ v 1 to give a quick suddenly arrested push, pull, twist, or jolt to 2 to propel with short abrupt motions 3 to utter in an abrupt or snappy manner 4 to make a sudden spasmodic motion 5 to move in short abrupt motions

²**jerk** n 1 a single quick motion (e g a pull, twist, or jolt) 2 an involuntary spasmodic muscular movement due to reflex action 3 chiefly NAm a stupid, foolish, or naive person – *infml*

jerkin /'juhkin/ n a sleeveless jacket, usu hip-length and close-fitting

jin

jerky /'juhki/ adj marked by abrupt or awkward movements or changes – **-kily** adv – **-kiness** n

Jerry /'jeri/ n, chiefly Br a German; esp a German soldier or the German armed forces in WW II

jersey /'juhzi/ n 1 a plain weft-knitted fabric made of wool, nylon, etc and used esp for clothing 2 a jumper 3 often cap any of a breed of small short-horned cattle noted for their rich milk

Jerusalem artichoke /jə'roohsələm/ n (an edible sweet-tasting tuber of) a perennial N American sunflower

¹**jest** /jest/ n 1 a joke 2 a frivolous mood or manner

²**jest** v 1 to speak or act without seriousness 2 to make a witty remark

jester /'jestə/ n a retainer formerly kept in great households to provide casual amusement and commonly dressed in a brightly coloured costume

Jesuit /'jezyoo·it/ n a member of the Society of Jesus, a Roman Catholic order which is devoted to missionary and educational work educational work

¹**jet** /jet/ n 1 a hard black form of coal that is often polished and used for jewellery 2 an intense black

²**jet** v -tt- 1 to emit in a jet or jets 2 to direct a jet of liquid or gas at

³**jet** n 1a a forceful stream of fluid discharged from a narrow opening or a nozzle b a nozzle or other narrow opening for emitting a jet of fluid 2 (an aircraft powered by) a jet engine

⁴**jet** v -tt- 2 to travel by jet aircraft

jet-'black adj of a very dark black

¹**jet ,engine** n an engine that produces motion in one direction as a result of the discharge of a jet of fluid in the opposite direction; specif an aircraft engine that discharges the hot air and gases produced by the combustion of a fuel to produce propulsion or lift

¹**jet ,lag** n a temporary disruption of normal bodily rhythms after a long flight, esp due to differences in local time

jetsam /'jetsəm/ n 1 goods thrown overboard to lighten a ship in distress; esp such goods when washed ashore 2 odds and ends; rubbish

¹**jet ,set** n sing or pl in constr an international wealthy élite who frequent fashionable resorts

¹**jettison** /'jetis(ə)n/ n 1 the act of jettisoning cargo 2 abandonment

²**jettison** v 1 to throw (e g goods or cargo) overboard to lighten the load of a ship in distress 2 to cast off as superfluous or encumbering; abandon 3 to drop (e g unwanted material) from an aircraft or spacecraft in flight

jetty /'jeti/ n 1 a structure (e g a pier or breakwater) extending into a sea, lake, or river to influence the current or tide or to protect a harbour 2 a small landing pier

Jew, fem **Jewess** /-'es, -is/ n 1 a member of a Semitic people existing as a nation in Palestine from the 6th c BC to the 1st c AD, some of whom now live in Israel and others in various countries throughout the world 2 a person whose religion is Judaism 3 sby given to hard financial bargaining – derog – **~ish** adj

jewel /'jooh·əl/ n 1 an ornament of precious metal often set with stones and worn as an accessory 2 sby or sthg highly esteemed 3 a precious stone 4 a bearing for a pivot (e g in a watch or compass) made of crystal, precious stone, or glass

jeweller, NAm chiefly **jeweler** /'jooh·ələ/ n sby who deals in, makes, or repairs jewellery and often watches, silverware, etc

'jewellery, NAm chiefly **jewelry** /-ri/ n jewels, esp as worn for personal adornment

¹**jib** /jib/ n a triangular sail set on a stay extending from the top of the foremast to the bow or the bowsprit

²**jib** n the projecting arm of a crane

³**jib** v, esp of a horse to refuse to proceed further

jibe /jieb/ v to gibe

jiffy /'jifi/ n a moment, instant – infml

¹**jig** /jig/ n 1 (a piece of music for) any of several lively springy dances in triple time 2a any of several fishing lures that jerk up and down in the water b a device used to hold a piece of work in position (e g during machining or assembly) and to guide the tools working on it

²**jig** v -gg- 1 to dance (in the rapid lively manner of) a jig 2 to (cause to) make a rapid jerky movement 3 to catch (a fish) with a jig 4 to work with or machine by using a jig

jiggered /'jigəd/ adj 1 blowed, damned – infml 2 N Eng tired out; exhausted

jiggery-pokery /jigəri 'pohkəri/ n, Br dishonest underhand dealings or scheming – infml

jiggle /'jigl/ v jiggling /'jigl·ing, 'jigling/ to (cause to) move with quick short jerks – infml – **jiggle** n – **-gly** adj

jigsaw /'jig,saw/ n 1 a power-driven fretsaw 2 **jigsaw, jigsaw puzzle** a puzzle consisting of small irregularly cut pieces, esp of wood or card, that are fitted together to form a picture for amusement; broadly sthg composed of many disparate parts or elements

jihad /ji'had/ n 1 a holy war waged on behalf of Islam as a religious duty 2 a crusade for a principle or belief

jilt /jilt/ v to cast off (e g one's lover) capriciously or unfeelingly

¹**jingle** /'jing·gl/ v jingling /'jing·gling, 'jing·gl·ing/ to (cause to) make a light clinking or tinkling sound

²**jingle** n 1 a light, esp metallic clinking or tinkling sound 2 a short catchy song or rhyme characterized by repetition of phrases and used esp in advertising

'jingo,ism /'jing·goh,iz(ə)m/ n belligerent patriotism; chauvinism – **-ist(ic)** adj

jinx /jingks/ *n* sby or sthg (e g a force or curse) which brings bad luck – *infml*

jitter /'jitə/ *v* to be nervous or anxious – ~**s** *n pl* – **y** *adj*

¹**jive** /jiev/ *n* (dancing or *the* energetic dance performed to) swing music

²**jive** *v* to dance to or play jive

¹**job** /job/ *n* **1a** a piece of work; *esp* a small piece of work undertaken at a stated rate **b** sthg produced by work **2a(1)** a task **a(2)** sthg requiring unusual exertion **b** a specific duty, role, or function **c** a regular paid position or occupation **d** *chiefly Br* a state of affairs – + *bad* or *good* **3** an object of a usu specified type **4a** a plan or scheme designed or carried out for private advantage **b** a crime; *specif* a robbery *USE* (3&4) *infml*

²**job** *v* **-bb-** **1** to do odd or occasional pieces of work, usu at a stated rate **2** to carry on public business for private gain **3a** to carry on the business of a middleman or wholesaler **b** to work as a stockjobber **4** to buy and sell (e g shares) for profit

jobber /'jobə/ *n* a stockjobber

job 'lot *n* a miscellaneous collection of goods sold as a lot; *broadly* any miscellaneous collection of articles

¹**jockey** /'joki/ *n* sby who rides a horse, esp as a professional in races

²**jockey** *v* **1** to manoeuvre or manipulate by adroit or devious means **2** to act as a jockey

jockstrap /'jok,strap/ *n* a support for the genitals worn by men taking part in strenuous esp sporting activities

jocular /'jokyoolə/ *adj* **1** habitually jolly **2** characterized by joking – ~**ly** *adv* – ~**ity** *n*

jodhpurs /'jodpəz/ *n pl in constr, pl* **jodhpurs** riding trousers cut full at the hips and close-fitting from knee to ankle

¹**jog** /jog/ *v* **-gg-** **1** to give a slight shake or push to; nudge **2** to rouse (the memory) **3** to move up and down or about with a short heavy motion **4** to run or ride at a slow trot – ~**ger** *n*

²**jog** *n* **1** a slight shake **2a** a jogging movement or pace **b** a slow trot

John 'Bull /jon'bool/ *n* a typical Englishman, esp regarded as truculently insular

johnny /'joni/ *n, often cap* a fellow, guy – *infml*

¹**join** /joyn/ *v* **1a** to put or bring together so as to form a unit **b** to connect (e g points) by a line **c** to adjoin; meet **2** to put, bring, or come into close association or relationship **3a** to come into the company of **b** to become a member of (a group) **4** to come together so as to be connected **5** to take part in a collective activity – usu + *in* — **join battle** to engage in battle or conflict

²**join** *n* a joint

joiner /'joynə/ *n* **1** one who constructs or repairs wooden articles, esp furniture or fittings **2** a gregarious person who joins many organizations – *infml*

joinery /'joynəri/ *n* **1** the craft or trade of a joiner **2** woodwork done or made by a joiner

¹**joint** /joynt/ *n* **1a(1)** a point of contact between 2 or more bones of an animal skeleton together with the parts that surround and support it **b** a part or space included between 2 articulations, knots, or nodes **c** a large piece of meat (for roasting) cut from a carcass **2a** a place where 2 things or parts are joined **b** an area at which 2 ends, surfaces, or edges are attached **3** a shabby or disreputable place of entertainment – *infml* **4** a marijuana cigarette – *slang* — **out of joint 1** *of a bone* dislocated **2** disordered, disorganized

²**joint** *adj* **1** united, combined **2** common to 2 or more: e g **2a** involving the united activity of 2 or more **b** held by, shared by, or affecting 2 or more 3 sharing with another – ~**ly** *adv*

³**joint** *v* **1** to fit together **2** to provide with a joint **3** to prepare (e g a board) for joining by planing the edge **4** to separate the joints of (e g meat)

join up *v* to enlist in an armed service

joist /joyst/ *n* any of the parallel small timbers or metal beams that support a floor or ceiling

¹**joke** /johk/ *n* **1a** sthg said or done to provoke laughter; *esp* a brief oral narrative with a humorous twist **b** the humorous or ridiculous element in sthg **c** an instance of joking or making fun **d** a laughingstock **2** a trifling matter

²**joke** *v* to make jokes – **jokingly** *adv*

joker /'johkə/ *n* **1** sby given to joking **2** a playing card added to a pack usu as a wild card **3** a fellow; *esp* an insignificant, obnoxious, or incompetent person – *infml*

¹**jolly** /'joli/ *adj* **1a** full of high spirits **b** given to conviviality **c** expressing, suggesting, or inspiring gaiety **2** extremely pleasant or agreeable – *infml* – **jollity, jolliness** *n*

²**jolly** *adv* very – *infml*

³**jolly** *v* **1** to (try to) put in good humour, esp to gain an end – usu + *along* **2** to make cheerful or bright – + *up*; *infml*

Jolly 'Roger /'rojə/ *n* a pirate's black flag with a white skull and crossbones

¹**jolt** /johlt/ *v* **1** to (cause to) move with a sudden jerky motion **2** to give a (sudden) knock or blow to **3** to abruptly disturb the composure of

²**jolt** *n* an unsettling blow, movement, or shock

joss /jos/ *n* a Chinese idol or cult image

'joss ,stick *n* a slender stick of incense (e g for burning in front of a joss)

jostle /'josl/ *v* **jostling** /'josling, 'josl·ing/ **1a** to come in contact or into collision (with) **b** to make (one's way) by pushing **2** to vie (with) in gaining an objective

¹**jot** /jot/ *n* the least bit

²**jot** *v* **-tt-** to write briefly or hurriedly

joule /joohl/ *n* the SI unit of work or energy equal to the work done when a force of 1 newton moves its point of application through a distance of 1m

journal /'juhnl/ *n* **1a** an account of day-to-day events **b** a private record of experiences, ideas, or reflections kept regularly **c** a record of the transactions of a public body, learned society, etc **2a** a daily newspaper **b** a periodical dealing esp with matters of current interest or specialist subjects

'journal,ism /-,iz(ə)m/ *n* **1** (the profession of) the collecting and editing of material of current interest for presentation through news media **2a** writing designed for publication in a newspaper or popular magazine **b** writing characterized by a direct presentation of facts or description of events without an attempt at interpretation – **-ist** *n* – **-istic** *adj*

journey /'juhni/ *n* travel from one place to another, esp by land and over a considerable distance

'journeyman /-mən/ *n* **1** a worker who has learned a trade and is employed by another person, usu by the day **2** an experienced reliable worker or performer, as distinguished from one who is outstanding

¹joust /jowst/ *v* to fight in a joust or tournament

²joust *n* a combat on horseback between 2 knights or men-at-arms with lances

jovial /'johvi-əl/ *adj* markedly good-humoured – **~ity** *n*

¹jowl /jowl/ *n* **1** the jaw; *esp* a mandible **2** a cheek

²jowl *n* usu slack flesh associated with the lower jaw or throat – often pl with sing. meaning

joy /joy/ *n* **1** (the expression of) an emotion or state of great happiness, pleasure, or delight **2** a source or cause of delight **3** *Br* success, satisfaction – infml

'joyful /-f(ə)l/ *adj* filled with, causing, or expressing joy – **~ly** *adv* – **~ness** *n*

'joyous /-əs/ *adj* joyful – **~ly** *adv* – **~ness** *n*

'joy,ride /-,ried/ *n* **1** a ride in a motor car taken for pleasure and often without the owner's consent **2** a short pleasure flight in an aircraft

'joy,stick /-,stik/ *n* **1** a hand-operated lever that controls an aeroplane's elevators and ailerons **2** a control for any of various devices that resembles an aeroplane's joystick

jubilant /'joohbilənt/ *adj* filled with or expressing great joy – **~ly** *adv*

jubilation /,joohbi'laysh(ə)n/ *n* being jubilant; rejoicing

jubilee /,joohbi'lee, '--,-/ *n* **1** (a celebration of) a special anniversary (e g of a sovereign's accession) **2** a season or occasion of celebration

Judaism /'joohday,iz(ə)m/ *n* **1** a religion developed among the ancient Hebrews and characterized by belief in one transcendent God and by a religious life in accordance with Scriptures and traditions **2** (conformity with) the cultural, social, and religious beliefs and practices of the Jews

Judas /'joohdəs/ *n* **1** one who betrays, esp under the guise of friendship **2 judas, judas hole** a peephole in a door

judder /'judə/ *v, chiefly Br* to vibrate jerkily

¹judge /juj/ *v* **1** to form an opinion about through careful weighing of evidence **2** to sit in judgment on **3** to determine or pronounce after deliberation **4** to decide the result of (a competition or contest) **5** to act as a judge

²judge *n* sby who judges: e g **a** a public official authorized to decide questions brought before a court **b** sby appointed to decide in a competition or (sporting) contest **c** sby who gives an (authoritative) opinion

judgment, judgement /'jujmənt/ *n* **1** a formal decision by a court **2** (the process of forming) an opinion or evaluation based on discerning and comparing **3** the capacity for judging **4 Judgment, Judgment Day** *the* final judging of mankind by God

judicature /'joohdikəchə/ *n* **1** the administration of justice **2** the judiciary

judicial /jooh'dish(ə)l/ *adj* **1** of a judgment, judging, justice, or the judiciary **2** ordered by a court **3** of, characterized by, or expressing judgment; critical – **~ly** *adv*

judiciary /jooh'dishəri/ *n* **1a** a system of courts of law **b** the judges of these courts **2** a judicial branch of the US government

judicious /jooh'dishəs/ *adj* having or showing sound judgment – **~ly** *adv* – **~ness** *n*

judo /'joohdoh/ *n* a Japanese martial art emphasizing the use of quick movement and leverage to throw an opponent

¹jug /jug/ *n* **1a** *chiefly Br* a vessel for holding and pouring liquids that typically has a handle and a lip or spout **b** the contents of or quantity contained in a jug; a jugful **2** prison – infml

²jug *v* **-gg-** to stew (e g a hare) in an earthenware vessel

juggernaut /'jugə,nawt/ *n* **1** an inexorable force or object that crushes anything in its path **2** *chiefly Br* a very large, usu articulated, lorry

juggle /'jugl/ *v* **juggling** /'jugling/ **1** to perform the tricks of a juggler **2** to manipulate, esp in order to achieve a desired end **3** to hold or balance precariously

juggler /'juglə/ *n* one skilled in keeping several objects in motion in the air at the same time by alternately tossing and catching them

jugular vein, jugular /'jugyoolə/ *n* any of several veins of each side of the neck that return blood from the head

juice /joohs/ *n* **1** the extractable fluid contents of cells or tissues **2a** *pl* the natural fluids of an animal body **b** the liquid or moisture contained in sthg **2** the inherent quality of sthg; *esp* the basic force or strength of sthg **4** a medium (e g electricity or petrol) that supplies power – infml

juicy /'joohsi/ *adj* **1** succulent **2** financially rewarding or profitable – infml **3** rich in interest; *esp* interesting because of titillating content – infml – **-ciness** *n*

jujitsu, jiu-jitsu /, jooh 'jitsooh/ *n* a Japanese martial art employing holds, throws, and paralysing blows to subdue an opponent

jukebox /'joohk ,boks/ *n* a coin-operated record player that automatically plays records chosen from a restricted list

Julian calendar /'joohlyən, -li-ən/ *n* a calendar introduced in Rome in 46 BC establishing the 12-month year of 365 days with an extra day every fourth year

July /joo'lie/ *n* the 7th month of the Gregorian calendar

¹**jumble** /'jumbl/ *v* **jumbling** /'jumbling/ to mix *up* in a confused or disordered mass

²**jumble** *n* **1** a mass of things mingled together without order or plan **2** *Br* articles for a jumble sale

'**jumble ,sale** *n, Br* a sale of donated secondhand articles, usu conducted to raise money for some charitable purpose

jumbo /'jumboh/ *n pl* **jumbos** a very large specimen of its kind

¹**jump** /jump/ *v* **1a** to spring into the air, esp using the muscular power of feet and legs **b** to move suddenly or involuntarily from shock, surprise, etc **c** to move quickly or energetically (as if) with a jump; *also* to act with alacrity **2** to pass rapidly, suddenly, or abruptly (as if) over some intervening thing: e g **2a** to skip **b** to rise suddenly in rank or status **c** to make a mental leap **d** to come to or arrive at a position or judgment without due deliberation **e** to undergo a sudden sharp increase **3** to make a sudden verbal or physical attack – usu + *on* or *upon* **4a** to (cause to) leap over **b** to pass over, esp to a point beyond; skip, bypass **c** to act, move, or begin before (e g a signal) **5a** to escape or run away from **b** to leave hastily or in violation of an undertaking **c** to depart from (a normal course) – infml **d** to accept eagerly — **jump the gun 1** to start in a race before the starting signal **2** to act, move, or begin sth before the proper time — **jump the queue 1** to move in front of others in a queue **2** to obtain an unfair advantage over others who have been waiting longer — **jump to it 1** to make an enthusiastic start **2** to hurry

²**jump** *n* **1a(1)** an act of jumping; a leap **a(2)** a sports contest (e g the long jump) including a jump **a(3)** a space, height, or distance cleared by a jump **a(4)** an obstacle to be jumped over (e g in a horse race) **b** a sudden involuntary movement; a start **2a** a sharp sudden increase (e g in amount, price, or value) **b** a sudden change or transition; *esp* one that leaves a break in continuity **c** any of a series of moves from one position or place to another

jumped-'up *adj* recently risen in wealth, rank, or status – derog

¹**jumper** /'jumpə/ *n* a jumping animal; *esp* a horse trained to jump obstacles

²**jumper** *n, Br* a knitted or crocheted garment worn on the upper body

jumpy /'jumpi/ *adj* **1** having jumps or sudden variations **2** nervous, jittery – **-pily** *adv* – **-piness** *n*

junction /'jungksh(ə)n/ *n* **1** joining or being joined **2a** a place of meeting **b** an intersection of roads, esp where 1 terminates **3** sthg that joins

juncture /'jungkchə/ *n* **1** an instance or place of joining; a connection or joining part **2** a point of time (made critical by a concurrence of circumstances)

June /joohn/ *n* the 6th month of the Gregorian calendar

jungle /'jung-gl/ *n* **1** an area overgrown with thickets or masses of (tropical) trees and other vegetation **2a** a confused, disordered, or complex mass **b** a place of ruthless struggle for survival

¹**junior** /'joohnyə/ *n* **1** a person who is younger than another **2a** a person holding a lower or subordinate position in a hierarchy of ranks **b** a member of a younger form in a school **3** *NAm* a male child; a son – infml

²**junior** *adj* **1** younger – used, esp in the USA, to distinguish a son with the same name as his father **2** lower in standing or rank **3** for children aged from 7 to 11

juniper /'joohnipə/ *n* any of several evergreen shrubs or trees of the cypress family

¹**junk** /jungk/ *n* **1a** secondhand or discarded articles or material; *broadly* rubbish **b** sthg of little value or inferior quality **2** narcotics; *esp* heroin – slang

²**junk** *n* a sailing ship used in the Far East with a high poop, overhanging stem, and little or no keel

¹**junket** /'jungkit/ *n* **1** a dessert of sweetened flavoured milk curdled with rennet **2** a festive social affair (at public or a firm's expense) – chiefly infml

²**junket** *v* to feast, banquet – infml

junkie, junky /'jungki/ *n* a drug addict – infml

Junoesque /, joohnoh'esk/ *adj, of a woman* having stately beauty

junta /'juntə, 'hoontə/ *n sing or pl in constr* a political council or committee; *esp* a group controlling a government after a revolution

Jupiter /'joohpitə/ *n* the largest of the planets and 5th in order from the sun

juris'diction /, jooəris'diksh(ə)n/ *n* **1** the power, right, or authority to apply the law **2** the authority of a sovereign power **3** the limits within which authority may be exercised

juris'prudence /-'proohd(ə)ns/ *n* (the science or philosophy of) a body or branch of law

jurist /'jooərist/ *n* sby with a thorough knowledge of law

juror /'jooərə/ n 1 a member of a jury 2 one who takes an oath

jury /'jooəri/ n 1 a body of usu 12 people who hear evidence in court and are sworn to give an honest verdict based on this evidence 2 a committee for judging a contest or exhibition

¹**just** /just/ adj 1a conforming (rigidly) to fact or reason b conforming to a standard of correctness; proper 2a(1) acting or being in conformity with what is morally upright or equitable a(2) being what is merited; deserved b legally correct – ~ly adv – ~ness n

²**just** adv 1a exactly, precisely – not following not (e g just right) b at this moment and not sooner (e g he's only just arrived) – sometimes used with the past tense c only at this moment and not later (e g I'm just coming) 2a by a very small margin; immediately, barely (e g only just possible) b only, simply (e g just a short note) 3 quite (e g not just yet) 4 perhaps, possibly (e g it might just snow) — **just about** 1 almost 2 not more than — **just in case** as a precaution — **just now** 1 at this moment 2 a moment ago — **just on** almost exactly – used with reference to numbers and quantities — **just so** 1 tidily arranged 2 — used to express agreement — **just the same** nevertheless; even so

justice /'justis/ n 1a the maintenance or administration of what is just b the administration of law 2a the quality of being just, impartial, or fair b (conformity) to the principle or ideal of just dealing or right action 3 conformity to truth, fact, or reason 4 Br – used as a title for a judge

,**justice of the 'peace** n a lay magistrate empowered chiefly to administer summary justice in minor cases and to commit for trial

justify /'justifie/ v 1 to prove or show to be just, right, or reasonable 2 to space out (e g a line of printed text) so as to be flush with a margin – ~fiable adj – ~fiably adv – ~fication n

jut /jut/ v -tt- to stick out; project

jute /jooht/ n the glossy fibre of either of 2 E Indian plants used chiefly for sacking, twine, etc

¹**juvenile** /'joovəniel/ adj 1 immature or undeveloped 2 of or suitable for children or young people

²**juvenile** n 1 a young person 2 a young individual resembling an adult of its kind except in size and reproductive activity 3 an actor who plays youthful parts

juxtapose /,jukstə'pohz/ v to place side by side – ~**position** n

K

k /kay/ n, pl **k's**, **ks**, often cap (a graphic representation of or device for reproducing) the 11th letter of the English alphabet

kaftan /'kaf,tan/ n a caftan

kaiser /'kiezə/ n an emperor of Germany during the period 1871 to 1918

kaleidoscope /kə'liedə,skohp/ n 1 a tubular instrument containing loose chips of coloured glass between mirrors so placed that an endless variety of symmetrical patterns is produced as the instrument is rotated 2 sthg that is continually changing; variegated changing pattern, scene, or succession of events – **-scopic** adj – **-scopically** adv

kangaroo /,kang·gə'rooh/ n pl **kangaroos** any of various plant-eating marsupial mammals of Australia, New Guinea, and adjacent islands that hop on their long powerful hind legs

kaolin /'kayəlin/ n a fine usu white clay used esp in ceramics

kapok /'kaypok/ n a mass of silky fibres that surround the seeds of a tropical tree and are used esp as a soft (insulating) filling for mattresses

kaput /kə'poot/ adj broken, exhausted – infml

karate /kə'rahti/ n a martial art in which opponents use their hands and feet to deliver crippling blows

kayak /'kie(y)ak/ n an Eskimo canoe made of a frame covered with skins; also a similar canvas-covered or fibreglass canoe

kebab /ki'bab/ n (cubes of) meat cooked on a skewer

kedgeree /,kejə'ree, '—/ n a dish containing rice, flaked fish, and chopped hard-boiled eggs

¹**keel** /keel/ n a flat-bottomed ship; esp a barge used on the river Tyne to carry coal

²**keel** n 1a a timber or plate which extends along the centre of the bottom of a vessel and usu projects somewhat from the bottom b the main load-bearing member (e g in an airship) 2 a projection (e g the breastbone of a bird) suggesting a keel

³**keel** v 1 to (cause to) turn over 2 to fall over (as if) in a faint

'**keel,haul** /-,hawl/ v 1 to drag (a person) under the keel of a ship as punishment 2 to rebuke severely

¹**keen** /keen/ adj 1a having or being a fine edge or point; sharp b affecting one as if by cutting or piercing 2a enthusiastic, eager b of emotion or feeling intense 3a intellectually alert; also shrewdly astute b sharply contested; competitive;

specif, Br, of prices low in order to be competitive
c extremely sensitive in perception – ~**ly** *adv*
– **keenness** *n* — **keen on** interested in; attracted to

²**keen** *v or n* (to utter) a loud wailing lamentation
for the dead, typically at Irish funerals

¹**keep** /keep/ *v* kept /kept/ **1a** to take notice of by
appropriate conduct; fulfil (the obligations of) **b**
to act fittingly in relation to (a feast or ceremony)
c to conform to in habits or conduct **d** to stay in
accord with (a beat) **2a** to watch over and defend;
guard **b(1)** to take care of, esp as an owner; tend
b(2) to support **b(3)** to maintain in a specified
condition – often in combination **c** to continue to
maintain **d(1)** to cause to remain in a specified
place, situation, or condition **d(2)** to store habitually for use **d(3)** to preserve (food) in an unspoilt
condition **e** to have or maintain in one's service,
employment, or possession or at one's disposal –
often + *on* **f** to record by entries in a book **g** to
have customarily in stock for sale **3a** to delay,
detain **b** to hold back; restrain **c** to save, reserve **d**
to refrain from revealing or releasing **4** to retain
possession or control of **5a** to continue to follow **b**
to stay or remain on or in, often against opposition **6** to manage, run **7a** to maintain a course **b** to
continue, usu without interruption **c** to persist in a
practice **8a** to stay or remain in a specified
desired place, situation, or condition **b** to remain
in good condition **c** to be or remain with regard to
health **d** to call for no immediate action **9** to act as
wicketkeeper or goalkeeper – *infml* — **keep
an/one's eye on** to watch over — **keep at** to
persist in doing or concerning oneself with —
keep cave *Br* to act as a lookout at school — **keep
company** to provide with companionship — **keep
from** to refrain from; help — **keep one's eye in**
chiefly Br to keep in practice; *specif* to retain
ability to judge the speed and direction of a moving ball — **keep one's eyes open/peeled,** *Br* **keep
one's eyes skinned** to be on the alert; be watchful
— **keep one's feet** to avoid overbalancing — **keep
one's fingers crossed** to hope for the best — **keep
one's hand in** to remain in practice — **keep one's
head above water** to remain solvent; *broadly* to
stay out of difficulty — **keep one's nose clean** to
keep one's record untarnished by playing safe —
keep one's shirt on, *Br* **keep one's hair on** to
remain calm; keep one's temper — *infml* — **keep
the ball rolling** to play one's part (e g in conversation) — **keep to 1** to stay in or on **2** not to deviate
from; abide by — **keep to oneself 1** to keep secret
2 *also* **keep oneself to oneself** to remain solitary or
apart from other people — **keep warm** to occupy
(a position) temporarily for another

²**keep** *n* **1** a castle, fortress, or fortified tower **2** the
means (e g food) by which one is kept – *infml* —
for keeps 1 with the provision that one keeps as
one's own what one wins or receives – *infml* **2** for
good

keeper /'keepə/ *n* **1a** a protector, guardian, or
custodian **b** a gamekeeper **c** a curator **2** any of
various devices (e g a latch or guard ring) for
keeping sthg in position **3a** a goalkeeper **b** a
wicketkeeper

keeping /'keeping/ *n* custody, care — **out of/in
keeping** not/conforming or agreeing with sthg
implied or specified — usu + *with*

keep on *v* to talk continuously; *esp* to nag

'keep,sake /'sayk/ *n* sthg (given, to be) kept as a
memento, esp of the giver

keep up *v* **1** to persist or persevere in; continue **2**
to preserve from decline **3** to maintain an equal
pace or level of activity, progress, or knowledge
(e g with another) **4** to continue without
interruption

keg /keg/ *n, Br* a small barrel having a capacity of
(less than) 10gal (about 45.5l); *specif* a metal beer
barrel from which beer is pumped by pressurized
gas

kelvin /'kelvin/ *n* the SI unit of temperature
defined by the Kelvin scale

Kelvin *adj* of, conforming to, or being a scale of
temperature on which absolute zero is at 0 and
water freezes at 273.16K under standard
conditions

¹**ken** /ken/ *v,* **-nn-** *chiefly Scot* to have knowledge
(of); know

²**ken** *n* the range of perception, understanding, or
knowledge – usu + *beyond, outside*

¹**kennel** /'kenl/ *n* **1** a shelter for a dog **2** an establishment for the breeding or boarding of dogs –
often pl with sing. meaning but sing. or pl in
constr

²**kennel** *v* **-ll-** (*NAm* **-l-, -ll-**), /'kenl·ing/ to put or
keep (as if) in a kennel

kept /kept/ *past of* **keep**

kerb /kuhb/ *n, Br* the edging, esp of stone, to a
pavement, path, etc

kerchief /'kuhchif/ *n, pl* **kerchiefs** /-chivz/ *also*
kerchieves /~, -cheevz/ **1** a square or triangle of
cloth used as a head covering or worn as a scarf
around the neck **2** a handkerchief

kerfuffle /kə'fufl/ *n, chiefly Br* a fuss, commotion
– *infml*

kernel /'kuhnl/ *n* **1** the inner softer often edible
part of a seed, fruit stone, or nut **2** a whole seed of
a cereal **3** a central or essential part; core

kestrel /'kestrəl/ *n* a small common Eurasian and
N African falcon that is noted for its habit of
hovering

ketchup /'kechap, -up/, *NAm chiefly* **catchup** /~,
'kachap/ *n* any of several sauces made with vinegar and seasonings and used as a relish; *esp* a
sauce made from seasoned tomato puree

kettle /'ketl/ *n* a metal vessel used esp for boiling
liquids; *esp* one with a lid, handle, and spout that
is used to boil water

'**kettle,drum** /-,drum/ *n* a percussion instrument that consists of a hollow brass or copper hemisphere with a parchment head

¹**key** /kee/ *n* **1a** a usu metal instrument by which the bolt of a lock is turned **b** sthg having the form or function of such a key **2a** a means of gaining or preventing entrance, possession, or control **b** an instrumental or deciding factor **3a** sthg that gives an explanation or identification or provides a solution **b** a list of words or phrases explaining symbols or abbreviations **4a** any of the levers of a keyboard musical instrument that is pressed by a finger or foot to actuate the mechanism and produce the notes **b** a lever that controls a vent in the side of a woodwind instrument or a valve in a brass instrument **c** a small button or knob on a keyboard (e g of a typewriter) designed to be pushed down by the fingers **5** a dry usu single-seeded fruit (e g of an ash or elm tree) **6** a particular system of 7 musical notes forming a scale

²**key** *v* **1** to roughen (a surface) to improve adhesion of plaster, paint, etc **2** to bring into harmony or conformity; make appropriate **3** to make nervous, tense, or excited – usu + *up* **4** to keyboard

³**key** *adj* of basic importance; fundamental

⁴**key** *n* a low island or reef, esp in the Caribbean area

¹**key,board** /-,bawd/ *n* **1a** a bank of keys on a musical instrument (e g a piano) typically having 7 usu white and 5 raised usu black keys to the octave **b** any instrument having such a keyboard **2** a set of systematically arranged keys by which a machine is operated

²**keyboard** *v* **1** to operate a machine (e g for typesetting) by means of a keyboard **2** to capture or set (e g data or text) by means of a keyboard

'**key ,money** *n* a payment made by a tenant to secure occupancy of a rented property

keynote /'key,noht/ *n* **1** the first and harmonically fundamental note of a scale **2** the fundamental or central fact, principle, idea, or mood

key signature *n* the sharps or flats placed on the musical staff to indicate the key

'**key,stone** /-,stohn/ *n* **1** the wedge-shaped piece at the apex of an arch that locks the other pieces in place **2** sthg on which associated things depend for support

khaki /'kahki/ *n* **1** a dull yellowish brown colour **2** a khaki-coloured cloth used esp for military uniforms

kibbutz /ki'boots/ *n, pl* **kibbutzim** /-'tseem/ a collective farm or settlement in Israel

¹**kick** /kik/ *v* **1a** to strike (out) with the foot or feet **b** to make a kick in football **2** to show opposition; rebel **3** *of a firearm* to recoil when fired – infml — **kick oneself** to reprove oneself for some stupidity or omission — **kick one's heels 1** to be kept waiting

2 to be idle — **kick over the traces** to cast off restraint, authority, or control — **kick the bucket** to die — infml, humor — **kick upstairs** to promote to a higher but less desirable position

²**kick** *n* **1a** a blow or sudden forceful thrust with the foot **b** the power to kick **c** a repeated motion of the legs used in swimming **d** a sudden burst of speed, esp in a footrace **2** the recoil of a gun **3a** a stimulating effect or quality **b** a stimulating or pleasurable experience or feeling – often *pl* **c** an absorbing or obsessive new interest

'**kick,back** /-,bak/ *n* **1** a sharp violent reaction **2** a money return received usu because of help or favours given

'**kick,off** /-,of/ *n* **1** a kick that puts the ball into play in soccer, rugby, etc **2** an act or instance of starting or beginning

kick off *v* **1** to start or resume play with a kickoff **2** to start or begin proceedings – infml

¹**kid** /kid/ *n* **1** the young of a goat or related animal **2** the flesh, fur, or skin of a kid **3** a child; *also* a young person (e g a teenager) – infml — **with kid gloves** with special consideration

²**kid** *v* **-dd- 1a** to mislead as a joke **b** to convince (oneself) of sthg untrue or improbable **2** to make fun of **3** to engage in good-humoured fooling

kiddie, kiddy /kidi/ a small child – infml

kid-'glove *adj* using or involving extreme tact

kidnap /'kidnap/ *v* **-pp-, -p-** to seize and detain (a person) by force and often for ransom – **kidnap** *n* – **napper** *n*

kidney /'kidni/ *n* **1a** either of a pair of organs situated in the body cavity near the spinal column that excrete waste products of metabolism in the form of urine **b** an excretory organ of an invertebrate **2** the kidney of an animal eaten as food **3** sort, kind, or type, esp with regard to temperament

'**kidney ,bean** *n* (any of the kidney-shaped seeds of) the French bean

¹**kill** /kil/ *v* **1** to deprive of or destroy life **2a** to put an end to **b** to defeat, veto **3a** to destroy the vital, active, or essential quality of **b** to spoil, subdue, or neutralize the effect of **4** to cause (time) to pass (e g while waiting) — **to kill** to the nines

²**kill** *n* **1** a killing or being killed **2** sthg killed: e g **2a** animals killed in a shoot, hunt, season, or particular period of time **b** an enemy aircraft, submarine, etc destroyed by military action

'**killer ,whale** /'kilə/ *n* a flesh-eating gregarious black-and-white toothed whale found in most seas of the world

¹**killing** /'kiling/ *n* a sudden notable gain or profit – infml

²**killing** *adj* **1** extremely exhausting or difficult to endure **2** highly amusing *USE* infml

'**kill,joy** /-,joy/ *n* one who spoils the pleasure of others

kiln /kiln/ n an oven, furnace, or heated enclosure used for processing a substance by burning, firing, or drying

'kilo,calorie /-,kaləri/ n the quantity of heat required to raise the temperature of 1kg of water 1°C under standard conditions

'kilo,gram /-,gram/ n 1 the SI unit of mass and weight equal to the mass of a platinum-iridium cylinder kept near Paris, and approximately equal to the weight of a litre of water (about 2.205lb) 2 a unit of force equal to the weight of a kilogram mass under the earth's gravitational attraction

'kilo,hertz /-,huhts/ n a unit of frequency equal to 1000 hertz

kilometre /'kilə,meetə, ki'lomitə/ n 1000 metres

'kilo,watt /-,wot/ n 1000 watts

kilt /kilt/ n a skirt traditionally worn by Scotsmen that is formed usu from a length of tartan, is pleated at the back and sides, and is wrapped round the body and fastened at the front

kimono /ki'mohnoh/ n pl kimonos a loose robe with wide sleeves and a broad sash traditionally worn by the Japanese

¹kin /kin/ n 1 a group of people of common ancestry 2 sing or pl in constr one's relatives 3 archaic kinship

²kin adj kindred, related

¹kind /kiend/ n 1 fundamental nature or quality 2a a group united by common traits or interests b a specific or recognized variety – often in combination — in kind 1 in goods, commodities, or natural produce as distinguished from money 2 in a similar way or with the equivalent of what has been offered or received

²kind adj 1 disposed to be helpful and benevolent 2 forbearing, considerate, or compassionate 3 cordial, friendly 4 not harmful; mild, gentle – ~ness n

kindergarten /'kində,gahtn/ n a school or class for small children

kindle /'kindl/ v kindling /'kindling/ 1 to set (a fire, wood, etc) burning 2 to stir up (e g emotion) 3 to catch fire

kindling /'kindling/ n material (e g dry wood and leaves) for starting a fire

¹kindly /'kiendli/ adj 1 agreeable, beneficial 2 sympathetic, generous – -liness n

²kindly adv 1 in an appreciative or sincere manner 2 – used (1) to add politeness or emphasis to a request (2) to convey irritation or anger in a command

¹kindred /'kindrid/ n 1 sing or pl in constr (one's) relatives 2 family relationship

²kindred adj similar in nature or character

kinetic /ki'netik/ adj of motion – ~ally adv

kinetic energy n energy that a body or system has by virtue of its motion

ki'netics n pl but sing or pl in constr science that deals with the effects of forces on the motions of material bodies or with changes in a physical or chemical system

king /king/ n 1 a male monarch of a major territorial unit; esp one who inherits his position and rules for life 2 the holder of a preeminent position 3 the principal piece of each colour in a set of chessmen that has the power to move 1 square in any direction and must be protected against check 4 a playing card marked with a stylized figure of a king and ranking usu below the ace 5 a draughtsman that has reached the opposite side of the board and is empowered to move both forwards and backwards – ~ly adj – ~ship n

'kingdom /-d(ə)m/ n 1 a territorial unit with a monarchical form of government 2 often cap the eternal kingship of God 3 an area or sphere in which sby or sthg holds a preeminent position

'king,fisher /-,fishə/ n any of numerous small brightly-coloured fish-eating birds with a short tail and a long stout sharp bill

'king,maker /-,maykə/ n sby having influence over the choice of candidates for office

'king,pin /-,pin/ n the key person or thing in a group or undertaking

King's 'English n standard or correct S British English speech or usage – used when the monarch is a man

kink /kingk/ n 1 a short tight twist or curl caused by sthg doubling or winding on itself 2 an eccentricity or mental peculiarity; esp such eccentricity in sexual behaviour or preferences – ~y adj

kinsfolk /'kinz,fohk/ n pl relatives

kinship /'kinship/ n 1 blood relationship 2 similarity

kiosk /'kee,osk/ n 1 an open summerhouse or pavilion common in Turkey or Iran 2 a small stall or stand used esp for the sale of newspapers, cigarettes, and sweets 3 Br a public telephone box

¹kip /kip/ n, chiefly Br 1 a place to sleep 2 a period of sleep USE infml

²kip v, chiefly Br to (lie down to) sleep USE infml

¹kipper /'kipə/ n a kippered fish, esp a herring

²kipper v to cure (split dressed fish) by salting and drying, usu by smoking

kirk /kuhk/ n 1 cap the national Church of Scotland as distinguished from the Church of England or the Episcopal Church in Scotland 2 chiefly Scot a church

¹kiss /kis/ v 1 to touch with the lips, esp as a mark of affection or greeting 2 to touch gently or lightly – ~able adj

²kiss n an act or instance of kissing

¹kit /kit/ n 1 a set of tools or implements 2 a set of parts ready to be assembled 3 a set of clothes and equipment for use in a specified situation; esp the equipment carried by a member of the armed forces

²**kit** v, -**tt**- chiefly Br to equip, outfit; esp to clothe – usu + out or up

kitchen /'kichin/ n a place (e g a room in a house or hotel) where food is prepared

kitchenette /,kichi'net/ n a small kitchen or alcove containing cooking facilities

kite /kiet/ n **1** any of various hawks with long narrow wings, a deeply forked tail, and feet adapted for taking insects and small reptiles as prey **2** a light frame covered with thin material (e g paper or cloth), designed to be flown in the air at the end of a long string

kitsch /kich/ n artistic or literary material that is pretentious or inferior and is usu designed to appeal to popular or sentimental taste – ~**y** adj

¹**kitten** /'kitn/ n the young of a cat or other small mammal

²**kitten** v to give birth to kittens

kitty /'kiti/ n a jointly held fund of money (e g for household expenses)

kiwi /'keewi/ n **1** a flightless New Zealand bird with hairlike plumage **2** cap a New Zealander

Klaxon /'klaks(ə)n/ trademark – used for a powerful electrically operated horn or warning signal

Kleenex /'kleeneks/ trademark – used for a paper handkerchief

kleptomania /,kleptə'maynyə/ n an irresistible desire to steal – ~**c** n

knack /nak/ n a special ability, capacity, or skill that enables sthg, esp of a difficult or unusual nature, to be done with ease

¹**knacker** /'nakə/ n, Br sby who buys and slaughters worn-out horses for use esp as animal food or fertilizer **2** a buyer of old ships, houses, or other structures for their constituent materials

²**knacker** v, chiefly Br to exhaust – infml

knave /nayv/ n **1** an unprincipled deceitful fellow **2** a jack in a pack of cards – **knavish** adj – **knavishly** adv – **knavishness**, **knavery** n

knead /need/ v to work and press into a mass (as if) with the hands

¹**knee** /nee/ n **1** (the part of the leg that includes) a joint in the middle part of the human leg that is the articulation between the femur, tibia, and kneecap **2** a corresponding joint in an animal, bird, or insect

²**knee** v to strike with the knee

¹**kneecap** /'nee,kap/ n a thick flat triangular movable bone that forms the front point of the knee

²**kneecap** v to smash the kneecap of, as a punishment or torture

kneel /neel/ v **knelt** /nelt/, **kneeled** to fall or rest on the knee or knees

knell /nel/ n **1** (the sound of) a bell rung slowly (e g for a funeral or disaster) **2** an indication of the end or failure of sthg

knew /nyooh/ past of **know**

'**knicker,bockers** n pl short baggy trousers gathered on a band at the knee

knickers /'nikəz/ n pl, Br women's pants

'**knick-,knack** /'nik,nak/ n a trivial ornament or trinket

¹**knife** /nief/ n, pl **knives** /nievz/ **1** a cutting implement consisting of a more or less sharp blade fastened to a handle **2** a sharp cutting blade or tool in a machine — **at knifepoint** under a threat of death by being knifed

²**knife** v **1** to cut, slash, or wound with a knife **2** to cut, mark, or spread with a knife

'**knife-,edge** n **1** sthg sharp and narrow (e g a ridge of rock) resembling the edge of a knife **2** an uncertain or precarious position or condition

¹**knight** /niet/ n **1a** a mounted man-at-arms serving a feudal superior **b** a man honoured by a sovereign for merit, ranking below a baronet **2** either of 2 pieces of each colour in a set of chessmen that move from 1 corner to the diagonally opposite corner of a rectangle of 3 by 2 squares over squares that may be occupied – ~**hood** n – ~**ly** adj

²**knight** v to make a knight of

¹**knit** /nit/ v **knit, knitted; -tt- 1a** to link firmly or closely **b** to unite intimately **2a** to (cause to) grow together **b** to contract into wrinkles **3** to form (e g a fabric, garment, or design) by working 1 or more yarns into a series of interlocking loops using 2 or more needles or a knitting machine **4** to make knitted fabrics or articles

²**knit, knit stitch** n a basic knitting stitch that produces a raised pattern on the front of the work

knitting /'niting/ n work that has been or is being knitted

knob /nob/ n **1a** a rounded protuberance **b** a small rounded ornament, handle, or control (for pushing, pulling, or turning) **2** a small piece or lump (e g of coal or butter) – ~**bly** adj — **with knobs on** to an even greater degree – infml

¹**knock** /nok/ v **1** to strike sthg with a sharp (audible) blow; esp to strike a door seeking admittance **2** to (cause to) collide with sthg **3** to be in a place, often without any clearly defined aim or purpose – usu + about or around **4a** to make a sharp pounding noise **b** of an internal-combustion engine to make a series of sharp popping noises because of faulty combustion of the fuel-air mixture **5** to find fault (with) **6a(1)** to strike sharply **a(2)** to drive, force, make, or take (as if) by so striking **7** to set forcibly in motion with a blow — **knock together** to make or assemble, esp hurriedly or shoddily

²**knock** n **1a** (the sound of) a knocking or a sharp blow or rap **b** a piece of bad luck or misfortune **2** a harsh and often petty criticism

knockabout /'nokə,bowt/ adj **1** suitable for rough use **2** (characterized by antics that are) boisterous

knock back *v, chiefly Br* **1** to drink (an alcoholic beverage) rapidly **2** to cost; set back **3** to surprise, disconcert *USE* infml

'knock,down /-,down/ *adj* **1** having such force as to strike down or overwhelm **2** easily assembled or dismantled **3** *of a price* very low or substantially reduced

knock down *v* **1** to dispose of (an item for sale at an auction) *to* a bidder **2** to take apart; disassemble

knocker /'nokə/ *n* a metal ring, bar, or hammer hinged to a door for use in knocking

knock off *v* **1** to stop doing sthg, esp one's work **2** to do hurriedly or routinely **3** to deduct **4** to kill; *esp* to murder **5** to steal *USE* (4&5) infml

'knock-,on *n* (an instance of) the knocking of the ball forwards on the ground with the hand or arm in rugby in violation of the rules

knockout, knock-out /'nok,owt/ *n* **1** a blow that knocks out an opponent (or knocks him down for longer than a particular time, usu 10s, and results in the termination of a boxing match) **2** a competition or tournament with successive rounds in which losing competitors are eliminated until a winner emerges in the final **3** sby or sthg that is sensationally striking or attractive – infml

knock out *v* **1a** to defeat (a boxing opponent) by a knockout **b** to make unconscious **2** to tire out; exhaust **3** to eliminate (an opponent) from a knockout competition **4** to overwhelm with amazement or pleasure – infml

knock up *v* **1** to make, prepare, or arrange hastily **2** to achieve a total of **3** *Br* to rouse, awaken **4** to make pregnant – infml **5** to practise informally before a tennis, squash, etc match

¹knot /not/ *n* **1a** an interlacing of (parts of) 1 or more strings, threads, etc that forms a lump or knob **b** a piece of ribbon, braid etc tied as an ornament **c** a (sense of) tight constriction **2** sthg hard to solve **3** a bond of union; *esp* the marriage bond **4a** a protuberant lump or swelling in tissue **b** (a rounded cross-section in timber of) the base of a woody branch enclosed in the stem from which it arises **5** a cluster of people or things **6** a speed of 1 nautical mile per hour

²knot *v* **-tt-** **1** to tie in or with a knot **2** to unite closely or intricately **3** to form a knot or knots

knotty /'noti/ *adj* complicated or difficult (to solve)

¹know /noh/ *v* knew /nyooh/; known /nohn/ **1a(1)** to perceive directly **a(2)** to have understanding of **a(3)** to recognize or identify **b(1)** to be acquainted or familiar with **b(2)** to have experience of **2a** to be aware of the truth or factual nature of; be convinced or certain of **b** to have a practical understanding of **3** (to come) to have knowledge (of sthg) — **be to know** to be expected to discern;

have any knowledge of — **not know someone from Adam** have no idea who sby is — **you know** — used for adding emphasis to a statement

²know *n* — **in the know** in possession of confidential or otherwise exclusive knowledge or information

'know-,all *n* one who behaves as if he knows everything

'know-,how *n* (practical) expertise

knowing /'noh·ing/ *adj* **1** having or reflecting knowledge, information, or intelligence **2** shrewd or astute; *esp* implying (that one has) knowledge of a secret **3** deliberate, conscious

knowledge /'nolij/ *n* **1a** the fact or condition of knowing sthg or sby through experience or association **b** acquaintance with, or understanding or awareness of, sthg **2** the range of a person's information, perception, or understanding **3** the sum of what is known

knowledgeable /'nolijəbl/ *adj* having or exhibiting knowledge or intelligence; well-informed – **-bly** *adv*

known /nohn/ *adj* generally recognized

knuckle /'nukl/ *n* **1** the rounded prominence formed by the ends of the 2 bones at a joint; *specif* any of the joints between the hand and the fingers or the finger joints closest to these **2** a cut of meat consisting of the lowest leg joint of a pig, sheep, etc with the adjoining flesh — **near the knuckle** almost improper or indecent

knuckle down *v* to apply oneself earnestly

'knuckle-,duster *n* a metal device worn over the front of the doubled fist for protection and use as a weapon

knuckle under *v* to give in, submit

koala /koh'ahlə/, **ko,ala 'bear** *n* an Australian tree-dwelling marsupial mammal that has large hairy ears, grey fur, and sharp claws

kohl /kohl/ *n* (a cosmetic preparation made with) a black powder used to darken the eyelids

kola /'kohlə/ *n* cola

kookaburra /'kookə,burə/ *n* a large Australian kingfisher that has a call resembling loud laughter

kopeck, copeck *also* **kopek** /'kohpek/ *n* (a Russian coin worth) $1/100$ of a rouble

Koran, Qur'an /kaw'rahn/ *n* the book composed of writings accepted by Muslims as revelations made to Muhammad by Allah through the angel Gabriel – **~ic** *adj*

kosher /'kohshə/ *adj* **1a** *of food* prepared according to Jewish law **b** selling kosher food **2** proper, legitimate – infml

kowtow /kow,tow, 'koh-/ *n* a (Chinese) gesture of deep respect in which one kneels and touches the ground with one's forehead

²kowtow /,-'-/ *v* **1** to make a kowtow **2** to show obsequious deference

kraal /krahl/ *n* **1** a village of S African tribesmen **2** an enclosure for domestic animals in S Africa

kremlin /'kremlin/ *n* **1** a citadel within a Russian town or city **2** *cap the* the government of the USSR

kudos /'k(y)oohdos/ *n* fame and renown, esp resulting from an act or achievement

Ku Klux Klan /ˌk(y)ooh ˌkluks 'klan/ *n* a secret political organization in the USA that confines its membership to American-born Protestant whites and is hostile to blacks

kung fu /ˌkung 'fooh, ˌkoong/ *n* a Chinese martial art resembling karate

L

l /el/ *n*, *pl* **l's, ls** *often cap* **1a** (a graphic representation of or device for reproducing) the 12th letter of the English alphabet **b** sthg shaped like the letter L **2** fifty

la /lah/ *n* the 6th note of the diatonic scale in solmization

lab /lab/ *n* a laboratory

¹**label** /'laybl/ *n* **1** a slip (e g of paper or cloth), inscribed and fastened to sthg to give information (e g identification or directions) **2** a descriptive or identifying word or phrase: e g **2a** an epithet **b** a word or phrase used with a dictionary definition to provide additional information (e g level of usage) **3** an adhesive stamp **4** a trade name; *specif* a name used by a company producing commercial recordings

²**label** *v* **-ll-** (*NAm* **-l-, -ll-**), /'laybl·ing/ **1** to fasten a label to **2** to describe or categorize (as if) with a label

laboratory /lə'borətri/ *n* a place equipped for scientific experiment, testing, or analysis; *broadly* a place providing opportunity for research in a field of study

laborious /lə'bawri·əs/ *adj* involving or characterized by effort – **~ly** *adv* – **~ness** *n*

¹**labour**, *NAm chiefly* **labor** /'laybə/ *n* **1a** expenditure of effort, esp when difficult or compulsory; toil **b** human activity that provides the goods or services in an economy **c** (the period of) the physical activities involved in the birth of young **2** an act or process requiring labour; a task **3** workers **4** *sing or pl in constr, cap* the Labour party

²**labour**, *NAm chiefly* **labor** *v* **1** to exert one's powers of body or mind, esp with great effort; work, strive **2** to move with great effort **3** to be in labour when giving birth **4** to suffer from some disadvantage or distress **5** to treat in laborious detail

Labour *adj* of or being a political party, specif one in the UK, advocating a planned socialist economy and associated with working-class interests – **~ite** *n*

labourer /'layb(ə)rə/ *n* one who does unskilled manual work, esp outdoors

¹**labour exˌchange** *n*, *often cap L&E* a government office that seeks to match unemployed people and vacant jobs and that is responsible for paying out unemployment benefit

labrador /'labrədaw/ *n*, *often cap* a dog used esp for retrieving game, characterized by a dense black or golden coat

laburnum /lə'buhnəm/ *n* any of a small genus of Eurasian leguminous shrubs and trees with bright yellow flowers and poisonous seeds

labyrinth /'labərinth/ *n* **1** a place that is a network of intricate passageways, tunnels, blind alleys, etc **2** sthg perplexingly complex or tortuous in structure, arrangement, or character **3** (the tortuous anatomical structure in) the ear or its bony or membranous part – **~ine** *adj*

¹**lace** /lays/ *n* **1** a cord or string used for drawing together 2 edges (e g of a garment or shoe) **2** an ornamental braid for trimming coats or uniforms **3** an openwork usu figured fabric made of thread, yarn, etc, used for trimmings, household furnishings, garments, etc

²**lace** *v* **1** to draw together the edges of (as if) by means of a lace passed through eyelets **2** to draw or pass (e g a lace) through sthg **3** to confine or compress by tightening laces, esp of a corset **4a** to add a dash of an alcoholic drink to **b** to give savour or variety to

lacerate /'lasəˌrayt/ *v* **1** to tear or rend roughly **2** to cause sharp mental or emotional pain to – **-ration** *n*

lachrymal, lacrimal /'lakriməl/ *adj* **1** of or constituting the glands that produce tears **2** of or marked by tears

¹**lack** /lak/ *v* **1** to be deficient or missing **2** to be short or have need of sthg – usu + *for*

²**lack** *n* **1** the fact or state of being wanting or deficient **2** sthg lacking

lackadaisical /ˌlakə'dayzikl/ *adj* lacking life or zest; *also* (reprehensibly) casual or negligent – **~ly** *adv*

lackey /'laki/ *n* **1** a usu liveried retainer **2** a servile follower

¹**lackˌlustre** /-ˌlustə/ *adj* lacking in sheen, radiance, or vitality; dull

laconic /lə'konik/ *adj* using a minimum of words – **~ally** *adv*

¹**lacquer** /'lakə/ *n* **1** a clear or coloured varnish obtained by dissolving a substance (e g shellac) in a solvent (e g alcohol) **2** a durable natural varnish; *esp* one obtained from an Asian shrub

²**lacquer** *v* to coat with lacquer

lacrosse /lə'kros/ *n* a game played on grass by 2 teams of 10 players, whose object is to throw a ball into the opponents' goal, using a long-handled stick that has a triangular head with a loose mesh pouch for catching and carrying the ball

lactose /'laktohz, -tohs/ *n* a sugar that is present in milk

lacy /'laysi/ *adj* resembling or consisting of lace

lad /lad/ *n* 1 a male person between early boyhood and maturity 2 a fellow, chap 3 *Br* a stable lad

ladder /'ladə/ *n* 1 a structure for climbing up or down that has 2 long sidepieces of metal, wood, rope, etc joined at intervals by crosspieces on which one may step 2a sthg that resembles or suggests a ladder in form or use b *chiefly Br* a vertical line in hosiery or knitting caused by stitches becoming unravelled 3 a series of ascending steps or stages

laddie /'ladi/ *n* a (young) lad

laden /'laydn/ *adj* 1 heavily loaded 2 weighed down; deeply troubled

la-di-da, lah-di-dah /ˌlah di 'dah/ *adj* affectedly refined in voice or manner

ladies /'laydiz/ *n* a public lavatory for women – infml

¹ladle /'laydl/ *n* a deep-bowled long-handled spoon used esp for taking up and conveying liquids or semiliquid foods (e g soup)

²ladle *v* **ladling** /'laydl·ing/ to take up and convey (as if) in a ladle

lady /'laydi/ *n* 1a a woman with authority, esp as a feudal superior b a woman receiving the homage or devotion of a knight or lover 2a a woman of refinement or superior social position b a woman – often in courteous reference or usu pl in address 3 a wife 4a *cap* any of various titled women in Britain – used as a title b *cap* a female member of an order of knighthood

'lady,bird /-ˌbuhd/ *n* any of numerous small beetles of temperate and tropical regions; *esp* any of several ladybirds that have red wing cases with black spots

ˌlady-in-'waiting *n, pl* **ladies-in-waiting** a lady of a queen's or princess's household appointed to wait on her

'lady-ˌkiller *n* a man who captivates women

'lady,like /-ˌliek/ *adj* 1 resembling a lady, esp in manners; well-bred 2 becoming or suitable to a lady

'ladyship /-ship/ *n* – used as a title for a woman having the rank of lady

¹lag /lag/ *v* **-gg-** to stay or fall behind; fail to keep pace – often + *behind*

²lag *n* 1 the act or an instance of lagging 2 an interval between related events; *specif* a time lag

³lag *n* a convict or an ex-convict

⁴lag *v* **-gg-** to cover or provide with lagging

lager /'lahgə/ *n* a light beer brewed by slow fermentation

lagging /'laging/ *n* material for thermal insulation (e g wrapped round a boiler or laid in a roof)

lagoon /lə'goohn/ *n* a shallow channel or pool usu separated from a larger body of water by a sand bank, reef, etc

laid /layd/ *past of* **lay**

lain /layn/ *past part of* **lie**

lair /leə/ *n* 1 the resting or living place of a wild animal 2 a refuge or place for hiding

laird /leəd/ *n, Scot* a member of the landed gentry

laissez-faire, *Br also* **laisser-faire** /ˌlesay 'feə/ (*Fr* lese fɛːr)/ *n* a doctrine opposing government regulation of economic affairs – **laissez-faire** *adj*

laity /'layəti/ *n sing or pl in constr* 1 the people of a religion other than its clergy 2 the mass of the people as distinguished from those of a particular profession

¹lake /layk/ *n* a large inland body of water; *also* a pool of oil, pitch, or other liquid

²lake *n* a deep purplish red pigment

lam /lam/ *v* **-mm-** to beat soundly

lama /'lahmə/ *n* a Buddhist monk of Tibet

¹lamb /lam/ *n* 1a a young sheep, esp one that is less than a year old b the young of various animals (e g the smaller antelopes) other than sheep 2 a gentle, meek, or innocent person 3 the flesh of a lamb used as food

²lamb *v* to give birth to a lamb

lambaste, lambast /lam'bast/ *v* 1 to beat, thrash 2 to attack verbally; censure

lambskin /'lam,skin/ *n* 1 (leather made from) the skin of a lamb or small sheep 2 the skin of a lamb dressed with the wool on

¹lame /laym/ *adj* 1 having a body part, esp a leg, so disabled as to impair freedom of movement; *esp* having a limp caused by a disabled leg 2 weak, unconvincing – ~**ly** *adv* – ~**ness** *n*

²lame *v* to make lame

lamé /'lahmay/ *n* a brocaded clothing fabric made from any of various fibres combined with tinsel weft threads often of gold or silver

ˌlame 'duck *n* sby or sthg (e g a person or business) that is weak or incapable

¹lament /lə'ment/ *v* to feel or express grief or deep regret; mourn aloud – often + *for* or *over* – ~**ation** *n*

²lament *n* 1 an expression of grief 2 a dirge, elegy

lamentable /'lamentəbl/ *adj* that is to be regretted; deplorable – **bly** *adv*

¹laminate /'lami,nayt/ *v* 1 to roll or compress (e g metal) into a thin plate or plates 2 to separate into thin layers 3 to make by uniting superimposed layers of 1 or more materials 4 to overlay with a thin sheet or sheets of material (e g metal or plastic)

²laminate /'laminət, -nayt/ *adj* covered with or consisting of thin layers

lamp /lamp/ n 1 any of various devices for producing visible light: e g **1a** a vessel containing an inflammable substance (e g oil or gas) that is burnt to give out artificial light **b** a usu portable electric device containing a light bulb **2** any of various light-emitting devices (e g a sunlamp) which produce electromagnetic radiation (e g heat radiation)

lampoon /lam'poohn/ v or n (to make the subject of) a harsh satire – ~**ist** n

lamprey /'lampri/ n any of several eel-like aquatic vertebrates that have a large sucking mouth with no jaws

'lamp,shade /-,shayd/ n a decorative translucent cover placed round an electric light bulb to reduce glare

¹**lance** /lahns/ n 1 a weapon having a long shaft with a sharp steel head carried by horsemen for use when charging **2** a lancet

²**lance** v 1 to pierce (as if) with a lance **2** to open (as if) with a lancet

,**lance 'corporal** n a noncommissioned officer of the lowest rank in the British army or US marines

lancer /'lahnsə/ n 1 a member of a light-cavalry unit (formerly) armed with lances **2** pl but sing in constr (the music for) a set of 5 quadrilles each in a different metre

lancet /'lahnsit/ n a small surgical knife

¹**land** /land/ n **1a** the solid part of the surface of a celestial body, esp the earth **b** ground or soil of a specified situation, nature, or quality **2** (the way of life in) the rural and esp agricultural regions of a country **3** (the people of) a country, region, etc **4** a realm, domain **5** ground owned as property – often pl with sing. meaning

²**land** v 1 to set or put on shore from a ship **2a** to set down (e g passengers or goods) after conveying **b** to bring to or cause to reach a specified place, position, or condition **c** to bring (e g an aeroplane) to a surface from the air **3a** to catch and bring in (e g a fish) **b** to gain, secure – infml **4** to strike, hit – infml **5** to present or burden with sthg unwanted – infml **6a** to go ashore from a ship; disembark **b** of a boat, ship, etc to come to shore; also to arrive on shore in a boat, ship, etc **7a** to end up – usu + up **b** to strike or come to rest on a surface (e g after a fall) **c** of an aircraft, spacecraft, etc to alight on a surface; also to arrive in an aircraft, spacecraft, etc which has alighted on a surface

landed /'landid/ adj 1 owning land **2** consisting of land

'land,fall /-,fawl/ n an act or instance of sighting or reaching land after a voyage or flight

landing /'landing/ n 1 the act of going or bringing to a surface from the air or to shore from the water **2** a place for discharging and taking on passengers and cargo **3** a level space at the end of a flight of stairs or between 2 flights of stairs

'landing ,stage n a sometimes floating platform for landing passengers or cargo

'land,lady /-,laydi/ n 1 a female landlord **2** the female proprietor of a guesthouse or lodging house

'land,locked /-,lokt/ adj (nearly) enclosed by land

'land,lord /-,lawd/ n 1 sby who owns land, buildings, or accommodation for lease or rent **2** sby who owns or keeps an inn; an innkeeper

'land,lubber /-,lubə/ n a person unacquainted with the sea or seamanship

'land,mark /-,mahk/ n **1a** an object (e g a stone) that marks a boundary **b** a conspicuous object that can be used to identify a locality **2** an event that marks a turning point or new development

¹**'land,scape** /-,skayp/ n 1 natural, esp inland scenery **2a** a picture, drawing, etc of landscape **b** the art of depicting landscape

²**landscape** v to improve or modify the natural beauties of

'land,slide /-,slied/ n 1 a usu rapid movement of rock, earth, etc down a slope; also the moving mass **2** an overwhelming victory, esp in an election

lane /layn/ n 1 a narrow passageway, road, or street **2a** a fixed ocean route used by ships **b** a strip of road for a single line of vehicles **c** any of several marked parallel courses to which a competitor must keep during a race (e g in running or swimming) **d** a narrow hardwood surface down which the ball is sent towards the pins in tenpin bowling

language /'lang·gwij/ n **1a** those words, their pronunciation, and the methods of combining them used by a particular people, nation, etc **b(1)** (the faculty of making and using) audible articulate meaningful sound **b(2)** a systematic means of communicating using conventionalized signs, sounds, gestures, or marks **b(3)** the suggestion by objects, actions, or conditions of associated ideas or feelings **2a** a particular style or manner of verbal expression **b** the specialized vocabulary and phraseology belonging to a particular group or profession

languid /'lang·gwid/ adj 1 drooping or flagging (as if) from exhaustion; weak **2** spiritless or apathetic in character **3** lacking force or quickness, esp of movement; sluggish – ~**ly** adv

languish /'lang·gwish/ v 1 to be or become feeble or enervated **2a** to become dispirited or depressed; pine – often + for **b** to lose intensity or urgency **c** to suffer hardship or neglect **3** to assume an expression of emotion appealing for sympathy

languor /'lang·gə/ n 1 weakness or weariness of body or mind **2** a feeling or mood of wistfulness or dreaminess **3** heavy or soporific stillness – ~**ous** adj – ~**ously** adv

lan

lank /langk/ *adj* **1** lean, gaunt **2** straight, limp, and usu greasy – **~ly** *adv* – **~ness** *n*

lanky /'langki/ *adj* ungracefully tall and thin – **lankily** *adv* – **lankiness** *n*

lanolin, lanoline /'lanəlin/ *n* wool grease, esp when refined for use in ointments and cosmetics

lantern /'lantən/ *n* **1** a portable protective case with transparent windows that houses a light (e g a candle) **2a** the chamber in a lighthouse containing the light **b** a structure above an opening in a roof which has glazed or open sides for light or ventilation

lanyard /'lanyəd/ *n* **1** a piece of rope or line for fastening sthg on board ship **2** a cord worn round the neck as a decoration or to hold sthg (e g a knife) **3** a cord used in firing certain types of cannon

¹**lap** /lap/ *n* (the clothing covering) the front part of the lower trunk and thighs of a seated person — **drop/land (sthg) in someone's lap** to (cause to) become sby's responsibility — **in the lap of luxury** in an environment of great ease, comfort, and wealth — **in the lap of the gods** beyond human influence or control

²**lap** *v* **-pp- 1** to fold or wrap over or round **2a** to place or lie so as to (partly) cover (one another) **b** to unite (e g beams or timbers) so as to preserve the same breadth and depth throughout **3a** to overtake and thereby lead or increase the lead over (another contestant) by a full circuit of a racetrack **b** to complete a circuit of (a racetrack)

³**lap** *n* **1** the amount by which one object overlaps another **2a** (the distance covered during) the act or an instance of moving once round a closed course or track **b** one stage or segment of a larger unit (e g a journey) **c** one complete turn (e g of a rope round a drum)

⁴**lap** *v* **-pp- 1** to take in (liquid) with the tongue **2** to move in little waves, usu making a gentle splashing sound **3** to take in eagerly or quickly – usu + *up*

⁵**lap** *n* **1** an act or instance of lapping **2** a gentle splashing sound

lapdog /'lap,dog/ *n* a small dog that may be held in the lap

lapel /lə'pel/ *n* a fold of the top front edge of a coat or jacket that is continuous with the collar

lapidary /'lapidəri/ *adj* **1** sculptured in or engraved on stone **2** of or relating to (the cutting of) gems

lapis lazuli /,lapis 'lazyoolie, -li/ *n* (the colour of) a rich blue semiprecious stone

¹**lapse** /laps/ *n* **1** a slight error (e g of memory or in manners) **2a** a drop; *specif* a drop in temperature, humidity, or pressure with increasing height **b** an esp moral fall or decline **3a(1)** the legal termination of a right or privilege through failure to exercise it **a(2)** the termination of insurance coverage for nonpayment of premiums **b** a decline into disuse **4** an abandonment of religious faith **5** a continuous passage or elapsed period

²**lapse** *v* **1a** to fall or depart from an attained or accepted standard or level (e g of morals) – usu + *from* **b** to sink or slip gradually **2** to go out of existence or use **3** to pass to another proprietor by omission or negligence **4** *of time* to run its course; pass

lapwing /'lap,wing/ *n* a crested Old World plover noted for its shrill wailing cry

larceny /'lahsəni/ *n* theft

larch /lahch/ *n* (the wood of) any of a genus of trees of the pine family with short deciduous leaves

¹**lard** /lahd/ *v* **1** to dress (e g meat) for cooking by inserting or covering with fat, bacon, etc **2** to intersperse or embellish (e g speech or writing) *with* sthg

²**lard** *n* a soft white solid fat obtained by rendering the esp abdominal fat of a pig

larder /'lahdə/ *n* a place where food is stored; a pantry

¹**large** /lahj/ *adj* **1** having more than usual power, capacity, or scope **2** exceeding most other things of like kind (in quantity or size) **3** dealing in great numbers or quantities; operating on an extensive scale

²**large** *n* — **at large 1** without restraint or confinement; at liberty **2** as a whole

large intestine *n* the rear division of the vertebrate intestine that is divided into caecum, colon, and rectum, and concerned esp with the resorption of water and formation of faeces

largely /'lahjli/ *adv* to a large extent

largo /'lahgoh/ *n, adv,* or *adj, pl* **largos** (a movement to be) played in a very slow and broad manner – used in music

¹**lark** /lahk/ *n* any of numerous brown singing birds mostly of Europe, Asia, and northern Africa; *esp* a skylark

²**lark** *v* to have fun – usu + *about* or *around*

³**lark** *n* **1** a lighthearted adventure; *also* a prank **2** *Br* a type of activity; *esp* a business, job *USE* infml

larva /'lahvə/ *n, pl* **larvae** /-vi/ **1** the immature, wingless, and often wormlike feeding form that hatches from the egg of many insects and is transformed into a pupa or chrysalis from which the adult emerges **2** the early form (e g a tadpole) of an animal (e g a frog) that undergoes metamorphosis before becoming an adult – **~l** *adj*

laryngitis /,larin'jietəs/ *n* inflammation of the larynx

larynx /'laringks/ *n, pl* **larynges** /lə'rin,jeez/, **larynxes** the modified upper part of the trachea of air-breathing vertebrates that contains the vocal cords in most mammals – **laryngeal** *adj*

lascivious /lə'sivi·əs/ *adj* inclined or inciting to lechery or lewdness – ~**ly** *adv* – ~**ness** *n*

laser /'layzə/ *n* a device that generates an intense beam of light or other electromagnetic radiation of a single wavelength by using the natural oscillations of atoms or molecules

¹**lash** /lash/ *v* 1 to move violently or suddenly 2 to beat, pour 3 to attack physically or verbally, (as if) with a whip – often + *at*, *against*, or *out* 4 to strike quickly and forcibly (as if) with a lash 5 to drive (as if) with a whip; rouse

²**lash** *n* 1a(1) a stroke (as if) with a whip a(2) (the flexible part of) a whip b a sudden swinging movement or blow 2 violent beating 3 an eyelash

³**lash** *v* to bind or fasten with a cord, rope, etc

¹**lashing** /'lashing/ *n* a physical or verbal beating

²**lashing** *n* stng used for binding, wrapping, or fastening

'**lashings** *n pl* an abundance – usu + *of*; infml

lash out *v* 1 to make a sudden violent physical or verbal attack – usu + *at* or *against* 2 *Br* to spend unrestrainedly – often + *on*; infml

lass /las/, **lassie** /'lasi/ *n* a young woman; a girl

lasso /la'sooh, 'lasoh/ *n, pl* **lassos, lassoes** a rope or long thong of leather with a running noose that is used esp for catching horses and cattle

²**lasso** *v* **lassos, lassoes; lassoed; lassoing** to catch (as if) with a lasso

¹**last** /lahst/ *v* 1 to continue in time 2a to remain in good or adequate condition, use, or effectiveness b to manage to continue (e g in a course of action) 3 to continue in existence or action as long as or longer than – often + *out* 4 to be enough for the needs of

²**last** *adj* 1 following all the rest: e g 1a final, latest b being the only remaining 2 of the final stage of life (e g *last* rites) 3 next before the present; most recent 4a lowest in rank or standing; *also* worst b least suitable or likely (e g the *last* person you'd think of) 5a conclusive, definitive (e g the *last* word) b single – used as an intensive (e g ate every *last* scrap) — **last but one** 1 second most recent 2 penultimate

³**last** *adv* 1 after all others; at the end 2 on the most recent occasion 3 in conclusion; lastly

⁴**last** *n* sby or stng last — **at last/at long last** after everything; finally; *esp* after much delay — **to the last** till the end

⁵**last** *n* a form (e g of metal) shaped like the human foot, over which a shoe is shaped or repaired

,**last 'straw** *n* the last of a series (e g of events or indignities) stretching one's patience beyond its limit

,**last 'word** *n* the most up-to-date or fashionable example of its kind

¹**latch** /lach/ *v* 1 to attach oneself 2 to gain understanding or comprehension *USE* + *on* or *onto*

²**latch** *n* a fastener (e g for a door)

¹**late** /layt/ *adj* 1a occurring or arriving after the expected time b of the end of a specified time span 2a (recently) deceased – used with reference to names, positions or specified relationships b just prior to the present, esp as the most recent of a succession 3 far on in the day or night

²**late** *adv* 1a after the usual or proper time b at or near the end of a period of time or of a process – often + *on* 2 until lately – ~**ness** — **of late** in the period shortly or immediately before; recently

lately /'laytli/ *adv* recently; of late

latent /'layt(ə)nt/ *adj* present but not manifest – **-tency** *n*

,**latent 'heat** *n* heat given off or absorbed in a change of phase without a change in temperature

lateral /'lat(ə)ral/ *adj* of the side; situated on, directed towards, or coming from the side

latest /'laytist/ *n* 1 the most recent or currently fashionable style or development 2 the latest acceptable time

latex /'layteks/ *n pl* **latices** /'latə,seez/, **latexes** 1 a milky usu white fluid that is produced by various flowering plants (e g of the spurge and poppy families) and is the source of rubber, gutta-percha, etc 2 a water emulsion of a synthetic rubber or plastic

lath /lahth/ *n, pl* **laths** /lahths, lahdhz/ **lath** a thin narrow strip of wood, esp for nailing to woodwork (e g rafters or studding) as a support (e g for tiles or plaster)

lathe /laydh/ *n* a machine in which work is rotated about a horizontal axis and shaped by a fixed tool

¹**lather** /'lahdhə/ *n* 1a a foam or froth formed when a detergent (e g soap) is agitated in water b foam or froth from profuse sweating (e g on a horse) 2 an agitated or overwrought state – ~**y** *adj*

²**lather** *v* 1 to spread lather over 2 to form a (froth like) lather

¹**Latin** /'latin/ *adj* 1 of Latium or the Latins 2a of or composed in Latin b Romance 3 of the part of the Christian church using a Latin liturgy; *broadly* Roman Catholic 4 of the peoples or countries using Romance languages 5 *chiefly NAm* of the peoples or countries of Latin America

²**Latin** *n* 1 the language of ancient Latium and of Rome 2 a member of the people of ancient Latium 3 a member of any of the Latin peoples 4 *chiefly NAm* a native or inhabitant of Latin America

latitude /'latityoohd/ *n* 1a the angular distance of a point on the surface of a celestial body, esp the earth, measured N or S from the equator b the angular distance of a celestial body from the ecliptic 2a region as marked by its latitude – often pl with sing. meaning 3 (permitted) freedom of action or choice

latrine /lə'treen/ *n* a small pit used as a toilet, esp in a military camp, barracks, etc; *broadly* a toilet

¹**latter** /'latə/ *adj* **1** of the end; later, final **2** recent, present (e g in *latter* years) **3** second of 2 things, or last of several things mentioned or understood

²**latter** *n, pl* **latter** the second or last mentioned
'**latterly** /-li/ *adv* **1** towards the end or latter part of a period **2** lately

lattice /'latis/ *n* **1** (a window, door, etc having) a framework or structure of crossed wooden or metal strips with open spaces between **2** a network or design like a lattice **3** a regular geometrical arrangement of points or objects over an area or in space

laudable /'lawdəbl/ *adj* worthy of praise; commendable – **-bility** *n* – **-bly** *adv*

laudatory /'lawdət(ə)ri/, **laudative** /-dətiv/ *adj* of or expressing praise

¹**laugh** /lahf/ *v* **1a** to make the explosive vocal sounds characteristically expressing amusement, mirth, joy, or derision **b** to experience amusement, mirth, joy, or derision **2** to dismiss as trivial – + *off* or *away* — **laugh up one's sleeve** to be secretly amused

²**laugh** *n* **1** the act or sound of laughing **2** an expression of mirth or scorn **3** a means of entertainment; a diversion – often pl with sing. meaning **4** a cause for derision or merriment; a joke – *infml*

laughable /'lahfəbl/ *adj* of a kind to provoke laughter or derision; ridiculous – **-bly** *adv*
'**laughing ,gas** *n* nitrous oxide
'**laughing ,stock** /-,stok/ *n* an object of ridicule

laughter /'lahftə/ *n* **1** a sound (as if) of laughing **2** the action of laughing

¹**launch** /lawnch/ *v* **1a** to throw forward; hurl **b** to release or send off (e g a self-propelled object) **2a** to set (an esp newly built boat or ship) afloat **b** to start or set in motion (e g on a course or career) **c** to introduce (a new product) onto the market **3** to throw oneself energetically – + *into* or *out into* **4** to make a start – usu + *out* or *forth*

²**launch** *n* an act or instance of launching

³**launch** *n* **1** the largest boat carried by a warship **2** a large open or half-decked motorboat

launder /'lawndə/ *v* **1** to wash (e g clothes) in water **2** to give (sthg, esp money, obtained illegally) the appearance of being respectable or legal

launderette /,lawnd(ə)'ret/ *n* a self-service laundry

laundry /'lawndri/ *n* **1** clothes or cloth articles that have been or are to be laundered, esp by being sent to a laundry **2** a place where laundering is done; *esp* a commercial laundering establishment

laurel /'lorəl/ *n* **1** any of a genus of trees or shrubs that have alternate entire leaves, small flowers, and fruits that are ovoid berries **2** a tree or shrub that resembles the true laurel **3** a crown of laurel awarded as a token of victory or preeminence; distinction, honour – usu pl with sing. meaning

lava /'lahvə/ *n* (solidified) molten rock that issues from a volcano

lavatory /'lavətri/ *n* a toilet

lavender /'lavində/ *n* **1** a Mediterranean plant of the mint family widely cultivated for its narrow aromatic leaves and spikes of lilac-purple flowers which are dried and used in perfume sachets **2** a pale purple colour

¹**lavish** /'lavish/ *adj* **1** expending or bestowing profusely **2** expended, bestowed, or produced in abundance – **-ly** *adv*

²**lavish** *v* to expend or bestow *on* with profusion

law /law/ *n* **1a**(1) a rule of conduct formally recognized as binding or enforced by authority **a**(2) the whole body of such rules **a**(3) common law **b** the control brought about by such law – esp in *law and order* **c** litigation **2a** a rule one should observe **b** control, authority **3** *often cap* the revelation of the will of God set out in the Old Testament **4** a rule of action, construction, or procedure **5** the law relating to one subject **6** *often cap the* legal profession **7a** a statement of an order or relation of natural phenomena **b** a necessary relation between mathematical or logical expressions **8** *sing or pl in constr, often cap the* police – *infml* — **in/at law** according to the law — **law unto him-/her-/itself** sby or sthg that does not follow accepted conventions

lawful /'lawf(ə)l/ *adj* **1** allowed by law **2** rightful – **-ly** *adv* – **-ness** *n*

lawless /'lawlis/ *adj* **1** not regulated by or based on law **2** not restrained or controlled by law – **-ly** *adv* – **-ness** *n*

¹**lawn** /lawn/ *n* a fine sheer linen or cotton fabric of plain weave that is thinner than cambric

²**lawn** *n* an area of ground (e g around a house or in a garden or park) that is covered with grass and is kept mowed

lawn 'tennis *n* tennis played on a grass court
'**law ,suit** /-,s(y)ooht/ *n* a noncriminal case in a court of law

lawyer /'lawyə, 'loyə/ *n* sby whose profession is to conduct lawsuits or to advise on legal matters

lax /laks/ *adj* **1** not strict or stringent; negligent; *also* deficient in firmness or precision **2a** not tense, firm, or rigid; slack **b** not compact or exhibiting close cohesion; loose – **-ly** *adv* – **-ness**, – **-ity** *n*

laxative /'laksətiv/ *n or adj* (a usu mild purgative) having a tendency to loosen or relax the bowels (to relieve constipation)

¹**lay** /lay/ *v* **laid** /layd/ **1** to beat or strike down with force **2a** to put or set down **b** to place for rest or sleep; *esp* to bury **3** *of a bird* to produce (an egg) **4** to calm, allay **5** to bet, wager **6a** to dispose or spread over or on a surface **b** to set in order or position **7** to put or impose (as a tax, burden, or punishment – esp + *on* or *upon* **8** to prepare, contrive **9a** to bring into position or against or into contact with sthg **b** to prepare or position for

action or operation **10** to bring to a specified condition **11a** to assert, allege **b** to submit for examination and judgment **12** to put aside for future use; store, reserve – + *aside, by, in,* or *up* **13** to put out of use or consideration – + *aside* or *by* **14** to copulate with – slang — **lay about one** to deal blows indiscriminately; lash out on all sides — **lay hands on** **1** to seize forcibly **2** to find — **lay into** to attack with words or blows — **lay it on 1** to exaggerate, esp in order to flatter or impress **2** to charge an exorbitant price — **lay on the table** to make public; disclose — **lay low 1** to knock or bring down; *esp* destroy **2** to cause to be ill or physically weakened — **lay open** to expose: e g a to cut **b** to explain or make known — **lay siege to 1** to besiege militarily **2** to attempt to conquer or persuade diligently or persistently

²**lay** *past of* lie

³**lay** *n* a simple narrative poem intended to be sung; a ballad

⁴**lay** *adj* **1** of or performed by the laity **2** of domestic or manual workers in a religious community **3** not belonging to a particular profession

layabout /'layǝbowt/ *n, chiefly Br* a lazy shiftless person

'**lay-,by** *n, pl* **lay-bys** *Br* a branch from or widening of a road to permit vehicles to stop without obstructing traffic

¹**layer** /'layǝ/ *n* **1a** a single thickness of some substance spread or lying over or under another **b** any of a series of gradations or depths **2** a branch or shoot of a plant treated to induce rooting while still attached to the parent plant

²**layer** *v* **1** to propagate (a plant) by means of layers **2** to arrange or form (as if) in layers **3** to form out of or with layers

layman /'laymǝn/, *fem* '**lay,woman** *n* **1** a person not of the clergy **2** a person without special (e g professional) knowledge of some field

'**lay,off** /-,of/ *n* **1** the laying off of an employee or work force **2** a period of unemployment, inactivity, or idleness

lay off *v* **1** to cease to employ (a worker), usu temporarily **2** to stop or desist, specif from an activity causing annoyance – infml

lay on *v* to supply; organize

'**lay,out** /-,owt/ *n* the plan, design, or arrangement of sthg (e g rooms in a building or matter to be printed) laid out

lay out *v* **1** to prepare (a corpse) for a funeral **2** to arrange according to a plan **3** to knock flat or unconscious

lay up *v* **1** to store up; have or keep for future use **2** to disable or confine with illness or injury **3** to take out of active service

laze /layz/ *v* to pass (time) *away* in idleness or relaxation

lazy /'layzi/ *adj* **1a** disinclined or averse to activity; indolent; *also* not energetic or vigorous **b** encouraging inactivity or indolence **2** moving slowly – -**zily** *adv* – -**ziness** *n*

leach /leech/ *v* to separate the soluble components from (a mixture) or remove (sthg soluble) by the action of a percolating liquid

¹**lead** /leed/ *v* **led** /led/ **1a(1)** to guide on a way, esp by going in advance **a(2)** to cause to go with one (under duress) **b** to direct or guide on a course or to a state or condition; influence **c** to serve as a channel or route for **d(1)** to lie or run in a specified place or direction **d(2)** to serve as an entrance or passage **2** to go through; live **3a** to direct the operations, activity, or performance of; have charge of **b** to go or be at the head or ahead of **c** to be first or ahead **4a** to begin, open – usu + *off* **b** to play the first card of a trick, round, or game **5** to tend or be directed towards a specified result **6** to direct the first of a series of blows at an opponent in boxing (*with* the right or left hand) — **lead up to** to prepare the way for, esp by using a gradual or indirect approach — **lead someone a dance** to cause sby a lot of trouble

²**lead** /leed/ *n* **1a(1)** position at the front or ahead **a(2)** the act or privilege of leading in cards; *also* the card or suit led **b** guidance, direction; (an) example **c** a margin or position of advantage or superiority **2a** an indication, clue **b** (one who plays) a principal role in a dramatic production **c** a line or strap for leading or restraining an animal (e g a dog) **d** news story of chief importance **3** an insulated electrical conductor

³**lead** /led/ *n* **1** a heavy soft malleable bluish-white metallic element used esp in pipes, cable sheaths, batteries, solder, type metal, and shields against radioactivity **2** the (lead) weight on a sounding line **3** a thin stick of graphite or crayon in or for a pencil **4** *pl, Br* (a usu flat roof covered with) thin lead sheets

leaden /'led(ǝ)n/ *adj* **1a** made of lead **b** dull grey **2a** oppressively heavy **b** lacking spirit or animation; sluggish

leader /'leedǝ/ *n* **1a** a main or end shoot of a plant **b** a blank section at the beginning or end of a reel of film or recorded tape **2** sby or sthg that ranks first, precedes others, or holds a principal position **3** *chiefly Br* a newspaper editorial **4** *Br* the principal first violinist and usu assistant conductor of an orchestra – ~**ship** *n*

leading /'leeding/ *adj* coming or ranking first; foremost, principal

,**leading 'question** *n* a question so phrased as to suggest the expected answer

lead on *v* **1** to entice or induce to proceed in a (mistaken or unwise) course **2** to cause to believe sthg that is untrue

¹leaf /leef/ *n, pl* **leaves** /leevz/ **1a** any of the usu green flat and typically broad-bladed outgrowths from the stem of a plant that function primarily in food manufacture by photosynthesis **b** (the state of having) foliage **2a** a part of a book or folded sheet of paper containing a page on each side **b** a part (e g of a window shutter, folding door, or table) that slides or is hinged **c** metal (e g gold or silver) in sheets, usu thinner than foil

²leaf *v* **1** to shoot out or produce leaves **2** to glance quickly *through* a book, magazine, etc

leaflet /'leeflit/ *n* **1** a small or young foliage leaf **2** a single sheet of paper or small loose-leaf pamphlet containing printed matter (e g advertising)

leafy /'leefi/ *adj* **1** having or thick with leaves **2** consisting chiefly of leaves

¹league /leeg/ *n* any of various units of distance of about 3mi (5km)

²league *n* **1a** an association of nations, groups, or people for a common purpose or to promote a common interest **b** (a competition for an overall title, in which each person or team plays all the others at least once, held by) an association of people or sports clubs **2** a class, category — **in league** in alliance

¹leak /leek/ *v* **1** to (let a substance) enter or escape through a crack or hole **2** to become known despite efforts at concealment – often + *out* **3** to give out (information) surreptitiously

²leak *n* **1a** a crack or hole through which sthg (e g a fluid) is admitted or escapes, usu by mistake **b** a means by which sthg (e g secret information) is admitted or escapes, usu with prejudicial effect **2a** a leaking or that which is leaked; *esp* a disclosure **3** an act of urinating – slang

leaky /'leeki/ *adj* permitting fluid, information, etc to leak in or out; *broadly* not watertight – **-kily** *adv* **-kiness** *n*

¹lean /leen/ *v* **leant**, **leaned** /leend, lent/ **1a** to incline or bend from a vertical position **b** to rest supported *on*/*against* sthg **2** to rely for support or inspiration – + *on* or *upon* **3** to incline in opinion, taste, etc **4** to exert pressure; use coercion – + *on*; infml

²lean *adj* **1a** lacking or deficient in flesh or bulk **b** *of meat* containing little or no fat **2** *esp of a fuel mixture* low in the combustible component – **~ness** *n*

³lean *n* the part of meat that consists principally of fat-free muscular tissue

leaning /'leening/ *n* a definite but weak attraction, tendency, or partiality

'lean-,to *n pl* **lean-tos** a small building having a roof that rests on the side of a larger building or wall

¹leap /leep/ *v* **leapt** /lept/, **leaped** /leept, lept/ **1** to jump **2a** to pass abruptly from one state or topic to another; *esp* to rise quickly **b** to seize eagerly *at* an opportunity, offer, etc

²leap *n* **1a** (the distance covered by) a jump **b** a place leapt over or from **2** a sudden transition, esp a rise or increase

'leap,frog /-,frog/ *n* a game in which one player bends down and another leaps over him/her

²leapfrog *v* **-gg- 1** to leap (over) (as if) in leapfrog **2** to go ahead of (each other) in turn

'leap ,year *n* a year with an extra day added to make it coincide with the solar year

learn /luhn/ *v* **learnt** /luhnt/, **learned** /luhnd, luhnt/ **1a** to gain knowledge of or skill in **b** to memorize **2** to come to be able – + infinitive **3** to come to realize or know – **~ er** *n*

learned /'luhnid; *sense* 2 luhnd/ *adj* characterized by or associated with learning; erudite – **~ly** *adv*

learning /'luhning/ *n* **1** acquired knowledge or skill **2** modification of a behavioural tendency by experience (e g exposure to conditioning)

¹lease /lees/ *n* **1** a contract putting the land or property of one party at the disposal of another, usu for a stated period and rent **2** a (prospect of) continuance – chiefly in *lease of life*

²lease *v* to grant by or hold under lease

'lease,hold /-,hohld/ *n* tenure by or property held by lease – **~ er** *n*

leash /leesh/ *n* **1a** a (dog's) lead **b** a restraint, check **2** a set of 3 animals (e g greyhounds, foxes, or hares)

¹least /leest/ *adj* **1** lowest in rank, degree, or importance **2a** smallest in quantity or extent **b** smallest possible; slightest — **at least 1** at a minimum; if not more **2** if nothing else; in any case

²least *n* the smallest quantity, number, or amount — **least of all** especially not

³least *adv* to the smallest degree or extent

¹leather /'ledhə/ *n* **1** animal skin dressed for use **2** sthg wholly or partly made of leather; *esp* a piece of chamois, used esp for polishing metal or glass

²leather *v* to beat with a strap; thrash

leathery /'ledhəri/ *adj* resembling leather in appearance or consistency; *esp* tough

¹leave /leev/ *v* **left** /left/ **1a** to bequeath **b** to cause to remain as an aftereffect **2a** to cause or allow to be or remain in a specified or unaltered condition **b** to fail to include, use, or take along – sometimes + *off* or *out* **c** to have remaining or as a remainder **d** to allow to do or continue sthg without interference **3a** to go away from; *also* set out *for* **b** to desert, abandon **c** to withdraw from **4** to put, station, deposit, or deliver, esp before departing — **leave alone/be** to let alone/be — **leave go** to let go — **leave well alone** to avoid meddling

²leave *n* **1** permission to do sthg **2** authorized (extended) absence (e g from employment)

¹leaven /'lev(ə)n/ *n* a substance (e g yeast) used to produce fermentation or a gas in dough, batter, etc to lighten it; *esp* a mass of fermenting dough reserved for this purpose

²**leaven** v to raise or make lighter (as if) with a leaven

leaves /leevs/ pl of leaf

'**leave-,taking** n a departure, farewell

lecher /'lecha/ n a sexually promiscuous man – ~**ous** adj – ~**ously** adv – ~**y**, ~**ousness** n

lectern /'lek,tuhn/ n a reading desk; esp one from which the Bible is read in church

¹**lecture** /'lekcha/ n 1 a discourse given to an audience, esp for instruction 2 a reproof delivered at length; a reprimand

²**lecture** v to deliver a lecture or series of lectures; specif to work as a teacher at a university or college – ~**r** n

led /led/ past of **lead**

LED /,el ,ee 'dee; also led/ n a diode that emits light when an electric current is passed through it and that is used esp to display numbers, symbols, etc on a screen (e g in a pocket calculator)

ledge /lej/ n 1 a (narrow) horizontal surface that projects from a vertical or steep surface (e g a wall or rock face) 2 an underwater ridge or reef

ledger /'leja/ n 1 a book containing the (complete record of all) accounts 2 a horizontal piece of timber secured to the uprights of scaffolding

lee /lee/ n 1 protecting shelter 2 **lee, lee side** the side (e g of a ship) sheltered from the wind

¹**leech** /leech/ n 1 any of numerous flesh-eating or bloodsucking usu freshwater worms 2 one who gains or seeks to gain profit or advantage from another, esp by clinging persistently

²**leech** n 1 either vertical edge of a square sail 2 the rear edge of a fore-and-aft sail

leek /leek/ n an onion-like vegetable with a white cylindrical edible bulb

leer /lia/ v or n (to give) a lascivious, knowing, or sly look

lees /leez/ n pl the sediment of a liquor (e g wine) during fermentation and aging

leeward /'leewood; naut 'looh-ad/ adj or adv in or facing the direction towards which the wind is blowing

'**lee,way** /-,way/ n 1 off-course sideways movement of a ship in the direction of the wind 2 an allowable margin of freedom or variation; tolerance

¹**left** /left/ adj 1 a of, situated on, or being the side of the body in which most of the heart is located b located nearer to the left hand than to the right; esp located on the left hand when facing in the same direction as an observer 2 often cap of the Left in politics

²**left** n 1 a (a blow struck with) the left hand b the location or direction of the left side c the part on the left side 2 sing or pl in constr, cap those professing socialist or radical political views

³**left** past of **leave**

,**left-'hand** adj 1 situated on the left 2 left-handed

,**left-'handed** adj 1 using the left hand habitually or more easily than the right 2 of, designed for, or done with the left hand 3 clumsy, awkward 4 ambiguous, double-edged – ~**ly** adv – ~**ness** n

,**left 'wing** n sing or pl in constr, often cap L&W the more socialist division of a group or party – **left-winger** n

¹**leg** /leg/ n 1 a limb of an animal used esp for supporting the body and for walking: e g 1a (an artificial replacement for) either of the lower limbs of a human b a (hind) leg of a meat animal, esp above the hock c any of the appendages on each segment of an arthropod (e g an insect or spider) used in walking and crawling 2 a pole or bar serving as a support (e g for a table) 3 the part of a garment that covers (part of) the leg 4 the side of a cricket pitch to the left of a right-handed batsmen or to the right of a left-handed one 5a the course and distance sailed on a single tack b a portion of a trip; a stage c the part of a relay race run by 1 competitor d any of a set of events or games that must all be won to decide a competition — **a leg to stand on** the least support or basis for one's position, esp in a controversy — **on one's last legs** at or near the end of one's resources; on the verge of failure, exhaustion, or ruin

²**leg** adj **-gg-** in, on, through, or towards the leg side of a cricket field

legacy /'legasi/ n 1 a gift by will; a bequest 2 sthg passed on or remaining from an ancestor or predecessor or from the past

legal /'leegl/ adj 1 of law 2a deriving authority from law b established by or having a formal status derived from law 3 permitted by law – ~**ly** adv – ~**ity** n – ~**ize** v

,**legal 'aid** n payments from public funds to those who cannot afford legal advice or representation

,**legal 'tender** n currency which a creditor is bound by law to accept as payment of a money debt

legate /'legat/ n an official delegate or representative

legation /li'gaysh(a)n/ n (the official residence of) a diplomatic mission in a foreign country headed by a minister

legato /li'gahtoh/ n, adv, or adj, pl **legatos** (a manner of performing or passage of music performed) in a smooth and connected manner

'**leg ,bye** n a run scored in cricket after the ball has touched a part of the batsman's body but not his bat or hands

legend /'lej(a)nd/ n 1a a story coming down from the past; esp one popularly regarded as historical b a person, act, or thing that inspires legends 2a an inscription or title on an object (e g a coin) b a caption c the key to a map, chart, etc – ~**ary** adj

legging /'leging/ *n* a closely-fitting covering (e g of leather) reaching from the ankle to the knee or thigh

legible /'lejəbl/ *adj* capable of being read or deciphered – **-bility** *n* – **-bly** *adv*

¹**legion** /'leej(ə)n/ *n sing or pl in constr* 1 the principal unit of the ancient Roman army comprising 3000 to 6000 foot soldiers with cavalry 2 a very large number; a multitude 3 a national association of ex-servicemen

²**legion** *adj* many, numerous

legislate /'lejə,slayt/ *v* to make or enact laws – **-tor** *n* – **-ture** *n*

legislation /,leji'slaysh(ə)n/ *n* (the making of) laws – **-tive** *adj*

¹**legitimate** /lə'jitimət/ *adj* 1 lawfully begotten; *specif* born in wedlock 2 neither spurious nor false; genuine 3a in accordance with law b ruling by or based on the strict principle of hereditary right 4 conforming to recognized principles or accepted rules and standards

²**legitimate** /lə'jitimayt/, **legitimatize, -ise** /lə'jitimə,teiz/ **legitimize, -ise** /-,meiz/ *v* 1a to give legal status to b to justify 2 to give (an illegitimate child) the legal status of one legitimately born

legume /'legyoohm/ *n* 1 the (edible) pod or seed of a leguminous plant 2 any of a large family of plants, shrubs, and trees having pods containing 1 or many seeds and including important food and forage plants (e g peas, beans, or clovers) **-minous** *adj*

leisure /'lezhə/ *n* 1 freedom provided by the cessation of activities; *esp* time free from work or duties 2 unhurried ease – **~d** *adj* — **at leisure, at one's leisure** 1 at an unhurried pace 2 at one's convenience

¹**leisurely** /-li/ *adv* without haste; deliberately

²**leisurely** *adj* characterized by leisure; unhurried

lemming /'leming/ *n* any of several small short-tailed furry-footed northern voles; *esp* one of northern mountains that undergoes recurrent mass migrations

lemon /'lemən/ *n* 1 (a stout thorny tree that bears) an oval yellow acid citrus fruit 2 a pale yellow colour 3 one who or that which is unsatisfactory or worthless; a dud - infml

lemonade /,lemə'nayd/ *n* a (carbonated) soft drink made or flavoured with lemon

lemur /'leemə/ *n* any of numerous tree-dwelling chiefly nocturnal mammals, esp of Madagascar, typically having a muzzle like a fox, large eyes, very soft woolly fur, and a long furry tail

lend /lend/ *v* **lent** /lent/ **1a** to give for temporary use on condition that the same or its equivalent be returned **b** to let out (money) for temporary use on condition of repayment with interest 2 to give the assistance or support of; afford, contribute – **~er** *n*

length /leng(k)th/ *n* **1a(1)** the longer or longest dimension of an object **a(2)** the extent from end to end **b** a measured distance or dimension **c** the quality or state of being long 2 duration or extent in or with regard to time 3 distance or extent in space 4 the degree to which sthg (e g a course of action or a line of thought) is carried; a limit, extreme – often pl with sing. meaning **5a** a long expanse or stretch **b** a piece, esp of a certain length (being or usable as part of a whole or of a connected series) 6 the vertical extent of sthg (e g an article of clothing), esp with reference to the position it reaches on the body – usu in combination — **at length 1** fully, comprehensively 2 for a long time 3 finally; at last

lengthen /'length(ə)n, 'lengkth(ə)n/ *v* to make or become longer

¹**length,ways** /-,wayz/, **lengthwise** /-,wiez/ *adv* in the direction of the length

lengthy /'leng(k)thi/ *adj* of great or unusual length; long; *also* excessively or tediously protracted – **-thily** *adv* – **-thiness** *n*

lenient /'leenyənt, 'leeni-ənt/ *adj* of a mild or merciful nature; not severe – **-ience** *n* – **~ly** *adv*

lens /lenz/ *n* 1 a piece of glass or other transparent material with 2 opposite regular surfaces, at least 1 of which is curved, that is used either singly or combined in an optical instrument to form an image by focussing rays of light 2 a device for directing or focussing radiation other than light (e g sound waves or electrons)

Lent /lent/ *n* the 40 weekdays from Ash Wednesday to Easter observed by Christians as a period of penitence and fasting

lentil /'lentl/ *n* (the small round edible seed of) a widely cultivated Eurasian leguminous plant

lento /'lentoh/ *adv or adj* in a slow manner – used in music

Leo /'lee·oh/ *n* (sby born under) the 5th sign of the zodiac in astrology, pictured as a lion

leopard /'lepəd/, *fem* **leopardess** /-'des/ *n* a big cat of southern Asia and Africa that is usu tawny or buff with black spots arranged in broken rings or rosettes

leotard /'lee·ə,tahd/ *n* a close-fitting one-piece garment worn by dancers or others performing physical exercises

leper /'lepə/ *n* 1 sby suffering from leprosy 2 a person shunned for moral or social reasons; an outcast

leprechaun /'leprik(h)awn/ *n* a mischievous elf of Irish folklore

leprosy /'leprəsi/ *n* a long-lasting bacterial disease characterized by loss of sensation with eventual paralysis, wasting of muscle, and production of deformities and mutilations

lesbian /'lezbi-ən/ *n, often cap* a female homosexual – **~ism** *n*

,lese 'majesty /leez. lez/, lèse majesté /(Fr lez maʒeste)/ n **1a** a crime (e g treason) committed against a sovereign power **b** an offence violating the dignity of a ruler **2** an affront to dignity or importance

lesion /'leezh(ə)n/ n **1** injury. harm **2** abnormal change in the structure of an organ or part due to injury or disease

¹less /les/ adj **1** fewer (e g *less* than 3) — disapproved of by some speakers **2** lower in rank. degree, or importance (e g no *less* a person than the President himself(**3** smaller in quantity or extent (e g of *less* importance)

²less adv to a lesser degree or extent — **less and less** to a progressively smaller size or extent — **less than** by no means; not at all

³less prep diminished by; minus (e g £100 *less* tax)

⁴less n, pl less a smaller portion or quantity

lessee /le'see/ n sby who holds property under a lease

lessen /'les(ə)n/ v to reduce in size, extent, etc; diminish, decrease

lesser /'lesə/ adj or adv less in size, quality, or significance

lesson /'les(ə)n/ n **1** a passage from sacred writings read in a service of worship **2a** a reading or exercise to be studied **b** a period of instruction **3** sthg, esp a piece of wisdom, learned by study or experience

lessor /'lesaw, -'-/ n sby who conveys property by lease

lest /lest/ conj so that not; for fear that (e g obeyed her *lest* she should be angry)

¹let /let/ n **1** a serve or rally in tennis, squash, etc that does not count and must be replayed **2** sthg that impedes; an obstruction fml

²let v let; -tt- **1** to offer or grant for rent or lease **2** to give opportunity to, whether by positive action or by failure to prevent; allow to **3** used in the imperative to introduce a request or proposal, a challenge, or a command — **let alone/be** to stop or refrain from molesting, disturbing, or interrupting — **let fall/drop** to mention casually as if by accident — **let fly** to aim a blow — **let go** to stop holding — **let in for** to involve (sby, esp oneself) in sthg undesirable — **let into** to insert into (a surface) — **let loose on** to give freedom of access to or of action with respect to — **let oneself go 1** to behave with relaxed ease or abandonment **2** to allow one's appearance to deteriorate — **let rip** to proceed with abandon infml — **let slip 1** to let fall **2** to fail to take — **let up on** to become less severe towards

³let n, Br **1** an act or period of letting premises (e g a flat or bed-sitter) **2** premises rented or for rent

'let,down /-,down/ n a disappointment, disillusionment infml

let down v **1** to make (a garment) longer **2** to fail in loyalty or support; disappoint

lethal /'leeth(ə)l/ adj relating to or (capable of) causing death

lethargy /'lethəji/ n **1** abnormal drowsiness **2** lack of energy or interest — **-gic** adj

let off v **1** to cause to explode **2** to excuse from punishment

let on v to reveal or admit sthg; esp to divulge secret information

'let-,out n sthg (e g an exclusion clause in a contract) that provides an opportunity to escape or be released from an obligation infml

let out v **1** to make (a garment) wider (e g by inserting an inset) **2** chiefly Br to express publicly; esp to blab

letter /'letə/ n **1** a symbol, usu written or printed, representing a speech sound and constituting a unit of an alphabet **2** a written or printed message addressed to a person or organization and usu sent through the post **3** pl but sing or pl in constr **3a** literature; writing **b** learning; esp scholarly knowledge of or achievement in literature **4** the precise wording; the strict or literal meaning

'letter ,box n a hole or box (e g in a door) to receive material delivered by post

'letter,head /-,hed/ n stationery printed with a heading; also the heading itself

lettering /'letəring/ n the letters used in an inscription, esp as regards their style or quality

lettuce /'letis/ n a common garden vegetable whose succulent edible leaves are used esp in salads

leucocyte /'l(y)oohkə,siet/ n a white blood cell

leukaemia /l(y)ooh'keemyə, -mi·ə/ n any of several usu fatal types of cancer that are characterized by an abnormal increase in the number of white blood cells in the blood

¹level /'levəl/ n **1** a device (e g a spirit level) for establishing a horizontal line or plane **2a** a horizontal state or condition **b** an (approximately) horizontal line, plane, or surface **3a** a position of height in relation to the ground; height **b** a practically horizontal or flat area, esp of land **4** a position or place in a scale or rank (e g of value or importance) **5** the (often measurable) size or amount of sthg specified

²level v -ll- (NAm -l-, -ll-), /'levl·ing/ **1a** to make (a line or surface) horizontal; make level, even, or uniform **b** to raise or lower to the same height often + up **c** to attain or come to a level usu + out or off **2** to aim, direct + at or against **3** to bring to a common level, plane, or standard; equalize **4** to lay level with the ground; raze

³level adj **1a** having no part higher than another **b** parallel with the plane of the horizon **2a** even, unvarying **b** equal in advantage, progression, or standing **c** steady, unwavering — **level best** very best

,level 'crossing n the crossing of railway and road or 2 railways on the same level

¹**lever** /'leevə/ *n* **1** a bar used for prizing up or dislodging sthg **2a** a rigid bar used to exert a pressure or sustain a weight at one end by applying force at the other and turning it on a fulcrum **b** a projecting part by which a mechanism is operated or adjusted

²**lever** *v* to prize, raise, or move *up* (as if) with a lever – ~ **age** *n*

leveret /'lev(ə)rit/ *n* a hare in its first year

leviathan /lə'vie·əthən/ *n* **1** *often cap* a biblical sea monster **2** sthg large or formidable

levitate /'levi,tayt/ *v* to (cause to) rise or float in the air, esp in apparent defiance of gravity – ~**ation** *n*

levity /'levəti/ *n* lack of seriousness; *esp* excessive or unseemly frivolity

¹**levy** /'levi/ *n* **1** the imposing or collection of a tax, fine, etc **2a** the enlistment or conscription of men for military service **b** *sing or pl in constr* troops raised by levy

²**levy** *v* **1** to impose, collect, or demand by legal authority **2** to enlist or conscript for military service

lewd /l(y)oohd/ *adj* **1** sexually coarse or suggestive **2** obscene, salacious – ~**ly** *adv* – ~**ness** *n*

lexical /'leksikl/ *adj* **1** of words or the vocabulary of a language as distinguished from its grammar and construction **2** of a lexicon – ~**ly** *adv*

lexicography /,leksi'kografi/ *n* (the principles of) the editing or making of a dictionary

lexicon /'leksikən/ *n, pl* **lexica** /-kə/, **lexicons** **1** a dictionary, esp of Greek, Latin, or Hebrew **2** the vocabulary of a language, individual, or subject

liable /'lie·əbl/ *adj* **1a** legally responsible **2** exposed or subject *to* **3** habitually likely *to* – -**bility** *n*

liaise /lee'ayz/ *v* to establish a connection and cooperate *with* – ~**son** *n*

liar /'lie·ə/ *n* one who (habitually) tells lies

lib /lib/ *n, often cap* **1a** liberation – *infml* – ~**ber** *n*

libation /lie'baysh(ə)n/ *n* **1** (an act of pouring) a liquid used in a sacrifice to a god **2** an act or instance of drinking

¹**libel** /'liebl/ *n* **1** (a) defamation of sby by published writing or pictorial representation as distinguished from spoken words or gestures **2** a false insulting statement

²**libel** *v* **-ll-** (*NAm* **-l-, -ll-**), /'liebl·ing/ to make or publish a libel (against) – ~**lous** *adj* – ~**lously** *adv*

¹**liberal** /'librəl/ *adj* **1a** generous, openhanded **b** abundant, ample **2** broad-minded, tolerant; *esp* not bound by authoritarianism, orthodoxy, or tradition **3** *cap* of a political party in the UK advocating economic freedom and moderate reform – ~**ize** *v*, ~**ly** *adv*

²**liberal** *n* **1** one who is not strict in the observance of orthodox ways (e g in politics or religion) **2** *cap* a supporter of a Liberal party – ~**ism** *n*

liberate /'libə,rayt/ *v* **1** to set free; *specif* to free (e g a country) from foreign domination **2** to steal – *euph or humor* – ~**rator** *n*

liberation /,libə'raysh(ə)n/ *n* the seeking of equal rights and status; *also* a movement dedicated to seeking these for a specified group

liberty /'libəti/ *n* **1a** freedom from physical restraint or dictatorial control **b** the power of choice **2** a right or immunity awarded or granted; a privilege **3** a breach of etiquette or propriety — **at liberty 1** free **2** at leisure; unoccupied

Libra /'leebrə, 'lie-/ *n* (sby born under) the 7th sign of the zodiac in astrology, pictured as a pair of scales

librarian /lie'breəri·ən/ *n* sby who manages or assists in a library – ~**ship** *n*

library /'librəri/ *n* **1** a place in which books, recordings, films, etc are kept for reference or for borrowing by the public **2** a collection of such books, recordings, etc

libretto /li'bretoh/ *n, pl* **librettos, libretti** /-ti/ (the book containing) the text of a work (e g an opera) that is both theatrical and musical

lice /'lies/ *pl of* **louse**

licence, *NAm chiefly* **license** /'lies(ə)ns/ *n* **1** (a certificate giving evidence of) permission granted by authority to engage in an otherwise unlawful activity, esp the sale of alcoholic drink **2a** freedom that allows or is used with irresponsibility **b** disregard for rules of propriety or personal conduct

license, licence /'lies(ə)ns/ *v* to give official permission to or for (esp the sale of alcholic drinks)

licensee /,lies(ə)n'see/ *n, Br* a publican

lichen /'liekən, 'lichin/ *n* any of numerous complex plants made up of an alga and a fungus growing in symbiotic association on a solid surface (e g a rock or tree trunk)

¹**lick** /lik/ *v* **1** to lap up (as if) with the tongue; *also* to dart like a tongue **2** to get the better of; overcome – ~**ing** *n* — **lick into shape** to put into proper form or condition

²**lick** *n* **1** a small amount; a touch **2** a stroke or blow **3** a place to which animals regularly go to lick a salt deposit **4** speed, pace – *infml*

licorice /'likərish, -ris/ *n* liquorice

lid /lid/ *n* a hinged or detachable cover (for a receptacle)

lido /'leedoh, 'lee-/ *n pl* **lidos 1** a fashionable beach resort **2** a public open-air swimming pool

¹**lie** /lie/ *v* **lying; lay** /lay/; **lain** /layn/ **1a** to be or to stay at rest in a horizontal position; rest, recline **b** to assume a horizontal position – often + *down* **2a** *of sthg inanimate* to be or remain in a flat or horizontal position on a surface **b** *of snow* to remain on the ground without melting **3** to have as a direction **4a** to occupy a specified place or position **b** *of an action, claim, etc in a court of law*

to be sustainable or admissible — **lie low 1** to stay in hiding; strive to avoid notice **2** to bide one's time

²**lie** *n* **1** the way, position, or situation in which sthg lies **2** a haunt of an animal or fish

³**lie** *v* **lying** /'lie·ing/ **1** to make an untrue statement with intent to deceive; speak falsely **2** to create a false or misleading impression

⁴**lie** *n* **1** an untrue or false statement, esp when made with intent to deceive **2** sthg that misleads or deceives

liege /leej/ *n* **1a** a feudal vassal **b** a loyal subject **2** a feudal superior

lieutenant /lef'tenant; *Royal Navy* lə'tenant; *NAm* looh'tenant/ *n* **1** an official empowered to act for a higher official; a deputy or representative **2** a low-ranking officer in the navy, British army, etc

¹**life** /lief/ *n, pl* **lives** /lievz/ **1** the quality that distinguishes a vital and functional being from a dead body **b** a state of matter (e g a cell or an organism) characterized by capacity for metabolism, growth, reaction to stimuli, and reproduction **2** an aspect of the process of living **3** a biography **4** a state or condition of existence; a manner of living **5a** the period from birth to death or to the present time **b** the period from an event or the present time until death **c** a sentence of imprisonment for life **6** the period of usefulness, effectiveness, or functioning of sthg inanimate **7** living beings (e g of a specified kind or environment) **8** any of several chances to participate given to a contestant in some games, 1 of which is forfeited each time he/she loses

²**life** *adj* **1** using a living model **2** of, being, or provided by life insurance

'**life ,belt** *n* a buoyant belt for keeping a person afloat

'**life ,boat** /-,boht/ *n* a robust buoyant boat for use in saving lives at sea

'**life ,buoy** /boy/ *n* a buoyant often ring-shaped float to which a person may cling in the water

'**life ,cycle** *n* the series of stages in form and functional activity through which an organism, group, culture, etc passes during its lifetime

'**life,guard** /-,gahd/ *n* a usu expert swimmer employed to safeguard other swimmers

'**life ,jacket** *n* a buoyant device that is designed to keep a person afloat and can be worn continuously as a precaution against drowning

'**lifeless** /-lis/ *adj* **1** dead **b** inanimate **2** having no living beings **3** lacking qualities expressive of life and vigour; dull – ~**ly** *adv* – ~**ness** *n*

'**life,like** /-,liek/ *adj* accurately reproducing or imitating (the appearance of objects) in real life

'**life,line** /-,lien/ *n* **1a** a rope for saving or safeguarding life: e g **1a(1)** one stretched along the deck of a ship in rough weather **a(2)** one fired to a ship in distress by means of a rocket **b** the line by which a diver is lowered and raised **2** sthg, esp the sole means of communication, regarded as indispensable for the maintenance or protection of life

'**life ,long** /-,long/ *adj* lasting or continuing throughout life

,**life 'peer**, *fem* **life peeress** /'piəris/ *n* a British peer whose title is not hereditary

lifer /'liefə/ *n* one sentenced to life imprisonment – infml

¹**lift** /lift/ *v* **1** to raise from a lower to a higher position; elevate **2** to put an end to (a blockade or siege) by withdrawing the surrounding forces **3** to revoke, rescind **4a** to copy without acknowledgement **b** to take out of normal setting **5** *of bad weather* to cease temporarily **6** to steal – infml

²**lift** *n* **1** (a device for) lifting or (the amount) being lifted **2** a usu free ride as a passenger in a motor vehicle **3** a slight rise or elevation of ground **4** the distance or extent to which sthg (e g water in a canal lock) rises **5** a usu temporary feeling of cheerfulness, pleasure, or encouragement **6** any of the ropes by which the yard is suspended from the mast on a square-rigged ship **7** *chiefly Br* a device for conveying people or objects from one level to another, esp in a building

'**lift-,off** *n* a vertical takeoff by an aircraft, rocket vehicle, or missile

ligament /'ligəmənt/ *n* a tough band of connective tissue forming the capsule round a joint or supporting an organ (e g the womb)

¹**light** /liet/ *n* **1** an electromagnetic radiation in the wavelength range including infrared, visible, ultraviolet, and X rays; *specif* the part of this range that is visible to the human eye **2** daylight **3** an electric light **4a** spiritual illumination **b** understanding, knowledge **c** the truth **5a** public knowledge **b** a particular aspect or appearance in which sthg is viewed **6** a medium (e g a window) through which light is admitted **7** *pl* a set of principles, standards, or opinions **8** the representation in art of the effect of light on objects or scenes **9** a flame or spark for lighting sthg (e g a cigarette) — **in the light of** with the insight provided by

²**light** *adj* **1** having plenty of light; bright **2a** pale in colour or colouring **b** *of colours* medium in saturation and high in lightness

³**light** *v* **lit** /lit/, **lighted** /'lietid/ **1** to set fire to **2** to conduct (sby) along with a light; guide

⁴**light** *adj* **1a** having little weight; not heavy **b** designed to carry a comparatively small load **c** (made of materials) having relatively little weight in proportion to bulk **d** containing less than the legal, standard, or usual weight **2a** of little importance; trivial **b** not abundant **3a** *of sleep or a sleeper* easily disturbed **b** exerting a minimum of force or pressure; gentle, soft **c** faint **4a** easily endurable **b** requiring little effort **5** nimble **6** lacking seriousness; frivolous **7** free from care; cheerful **8** intending or intended chiefly to entertain **9** of

a drink having a comparatively low alcoholic content or a mild flavour **10** easily digested **11** producing light usu small goods often for direct consumption – **~ness** *n* – **~ly** *adv*

⁵**light** *adv* **1** lightly **2** with the minimum of luggage

⁶**light** *v* **lighted, lit** /lit/ **1** to settle, alight **2** to arrive by chance; happen

¹**lighten** /'liet(ə)n/ *v* **1** to make (more) light or clear; illuminate **2** to make (e g a colour) lighter **3** to discharge flashes of lightning

²**lighten** *v* **1** to reduce the weight of **2** to relieve (partly) of a burden **3** to make less wearisome; alleviate; *broadly* to cheer, gladden

¹**lighter** /'lietə/ *n* a large usu flat-bottomed barge used esp in unloading or loading ships

²**lighter** *n* a device for lighting (a cigar, cigarette, etc)

,**light'hearted** /-'hahtid/ *adj* free from care or worry; cheerful

'**light,house** /-,hows/ *n* a tower, mast, etc equipped with a powerful light to warn or guide shipping at sea

lighting /'lieting/ *n* (the apparatus providing) an artificial supply of light

¹**lightning** /'lietning/ *n* (the brilliant light flash resulting from) an electric discharge between 2 clouds or between a cloud and the earth

²**lightning** *adj* very quick, short, or sudden

'**lightning con,ductor** *n* a metal rod fixed to the highest point of a building or mast and connected to the earth or water below as a protection against lightning

lights /liets/ *n pl* the lungs, esp of a slaughtered sheep, pig, etc

'**light,weight** /-,wayt/ *n or adj* **1** (a boxer) weighing not more than about 9¹/₂st **2** (sby) of little ability or importance

'**light-,year** *n* a unit of length in astronomy equal to the distance that light travels in 1 year in a vacuum; 9,460 thousand million km (about 5,878 thousand million mi)

¹**like** /liek/ *v* **1a** to find agreeable, acceptable, or pleasant; enjoy **b** to feel towards; regard **2** to wish or choose to have, be, or do; want – **kable** *adj* – **king** *n* – **if you like** so to speak

²**like** *adj* **1a** alike in appearance, character, or quantity (e g suits of *like* design) **b** bearing a close resemblance; *esp* faithful (e g his portrait is very *like*) **2** likely

³**like** *prep* **1a** having the characteristics of; similar to **b** typical of **2a** in the manner of; similarly to **b** to the same degree as (e g fits *like* a glove) **c** close to (e g cost something *like* £5) **3** appearing to be, threaten, or promise (e g you seem *like* a sensible man) **4** – used to introduce an example (e g a subject *like* physics) – **like that 1** in that way **2** without demur or hesitation — **like anything/crazy** — used to emphasize a verb; infml

⁴**like** *n* one who or that which is like another, esp in high value; a counterpart — **the like** similar things

⁵**like** *adv* **1** likely, probably (e g he'll come *like* as not) **2** so to speak (e g went up to her casually, *like*) – nonstandard

⁶**like** *conj* **1** in the same way as (e g if she can sing *like* she can dance) **2** *chiefly NAm* as if (e g acts *like* he knows what he's doing)

likelihood /'liekli,hood/ *n* probability

¹**likely** /'liekli/ *adj* **1** having a high probability of being or occurring **2** reliable, credible **3** seeming appropriate; suitable **4** promising

²**likely** *adv* probably – often in *most/very/more/quite likely*

'**likeness** /-nis/ *n* **1** resemblance **2** a copy, portrait

'**like,wise** /-,wiez/ *adv* **1** in like manner; similarly **2** moreover; in addition **3** similarly so with me

lilac /'lielək, -lak/ *n* **1** a shrub with large clusters of fragrant white or (pale pinkish) purple flowers **2** a pale pinkish purple colour

¹**lilt** /lilt/ *v* to sing or speak rhythmically and with varying pitch

²**lilt** *n* **1** (a song or tune with) a rhythmic swing, flow, or rising and falling inflection **2** a light springy motion

lily /'lili/ *n* **1** any of a genus of plants that grow from bulbs and are widely cultivated for their variously coloured showy flowers **2** a water lily

,**lily of the 'valley** *n* a low perennial plant of the lily family that has usu 2 large leaves and a stalk of fragrant drooping bell-shaped white flowers

¹**limb** /lim/ *n* **1** any of the projecting paired appendages of an animal body used esp for movement and grasping but sometimes modified into sensory or sexual organs; *esp* a leg or arm of a human being **2** a large primary branch of a tree **3** an extension, branch; *specif* any of the 4 branches or arms of a cross — **out on a limb** in an exposed and unsupported position

²**limb** *n* **1** the outer edge of the apparent disc of a celestial body **2** the broad flat part of a petal or sepal furthest from its base

limber up *v* to (cause to) become supple, flexible, or prepared for physical action

¹**limbo** /'limboh/ *n pl* **limbos 1** *often cap* an abode of souls that are according to Roman Catholic theology barred from heaven because of not having received Christian baptism **2a** a place or state of restraint or confinement, or of neglect or oblivion **b** an intermediate or transitional place or state

²**limbo** *n, pl* **limbos** a W Indian acrobatic dance that involves bending over backwards and passing under a low horizontal pole

¹**lime** /liem/ *n* **1** a caustic solid consisting of calcium (and some magnesium) oxide, obtained by heating calcium carbonate (e g in the form of shells or limestone) to a high temperature, and used in

building (e g in plaster) and in agriculture **2** calcium hydroxide (occurring as a dry white powder), made by treating caustic lime with water

²**lime** *v* to treat or cover with lime

³**lime** *n* (the light fine-grained wood of) any of a genus of widely planted (ornamental) trees that usu have heart-shaped leaves

⁴**lime** *n* (spiny tropical citrus tree cultivated for its) small spherical greenish-yellow fruit

'**lime,light** /-,liet/ *n* **1** (the white light produced by) a stage lighting instrument producing illumination by means of an intense flame directed on a cylinder of lime **2** *the* centre of public attention

limerick /'limǝrik/ *n* a humorous and often epigrammatic or indecent verse form of 5 lines with a rhyme scheme of aabba

'**lime,stone** /-,stohn/ *n* a widely-occurring rock consisting mainly of calcium carbonate

limey /'liemi/ *n, often cap, NAm* a British person, esp a sailor – slang

¹**limit** /'limit/ *n* **1a** a boundary **b** *pl* the place enclosed within a boundary **2a** sthg that bounds, restrains, or confines **b** a line or point that cannot or should not be passed **3** a prescribed maximum or minimum amount, quantity, or number **4** sby or sthg exasperating or intolerable – + *the*; infml

²**limit** *v* **1** to restrict to specific bounds or limits **2** to curtail or reduce in quantity or extent; curb – ~**ation** *n*

limited /'limitid/ *adj* **1** confined within limits; restricted **2** restricted as to the scope of powers **3** lacking the ability to grow or do better

limousine /,limǝ'zeen, '---/ *n* a luxurious motor car

¹**limp** /limp/ *v* **1** to walk in a manner that avoids putting the full weight of the body on 1 (injured) leg **2** to proceed slowly or with difficulty – **limp** *n*

²**limp** *adj* **1a** lacking firmness and body; drooping or shapeless **b** not stiff or rigid **2** lacking energy – ~**ly** *adv*, – ~**ness** *n*

limpet /'limpit/ *n* **1** a shellfish with a low conical shell broadly open beneath, that clings very tightly to rock when disturbed **2** sby or sthg that clings tenaciously **3** an explosive device designed to cling to the hull of a ship, tank, etc

limpid /'limpid/ *adj* **1** transparent, pellucid **2** clear and simple in style – ~**ly** *adv* – ~**ity** *n*

linctus /'lingktǝs/ *n* any of various syrupy usu medicated liquids used to relieve throat irritation and coughing

linden /'lind(ǝ)n/ *n* a lime tree

¹**line** /lien/ *v* **1** to cover the inner surface of; provide with a lining **2** to fill

²**line** *n* **1a** a cord or rope; *esp* one on a ship **b** a device for catching fish consisting of a usu single-filament cord with hooks, floats, a reel, etc **c** a length of material (e g cord) used in measuring and levelling **d** piping for conveying a fluid (e g steam or compressed air) **e(1)** (a connection for communication by means of) a set of wires connecting one telephone or telegraph (exchange) with another **e(2)** the principal circuits of an electric power distribution system **2a** a horizontal row of written or printed characters **b** a single row of words in a poem **c** a short letter; a note **d** a short sequence of words spoken by an actor playing a particular role; *also, pl* all of the sequences making up a particular role **3a** sthg (e g a ridge, seam, or crease) that is distinct, elongated, and narrow **b** a wrinkle (e g on the face) **c** the course or direction of sthg in motion **d** (a single set of rails forming) a railway track **4a** a course of conduct, action, or thought **b** a field of activity or interest **5a** a related series of people or things coming one after the other in time; a family, lineage **b** a linked series of trenches and fortifications, esp facing the enemy – usu pl with sing. meaning **c** the regular and numbered infantry regiments of the army as opposed to auxiliary forces or household troops **d** a rank of objects of 1 kind; a row **e** (the company owning or operating) a group of vehicles, ships, aeroplanes, etc carrying passengers or goods regularly over a route **f** an arrangement of operations in manufacturing allowing ordered occurrence of various stages of production **6** a narrow elongated mark drawn, projected, or imagined (e g on a map): e g **6a** a boundary, contour, circle of latitude or longitude, etc **b** the equator **c** a mark (e g in pencil) that forms part of the formal design of a picture; *also* an artist's use of such lines **d** a limit or farthest edge with reference to which the playing of some game or sport is regulated – usu in combination **7** a straight or curved geometric element, generated by a moving point (continually satisfying a particular condition), that has length but no breadth **8** merchandise or services of the same general class for sale or regularly available **9** *pl, Br* a (specified) number of lines of writing, esp to be copied as a school punishment — **between the lines 1** by concealed implication **2** by way of inference — **in line for** due or in a position to receive — **into line** into a state of agreement or obedience — **on the line** at risk

³**line** *v* **1** to mark or cover with a line or lines **2** to place or form a line along **3** to form *up* into a line or lines

lineage /'lini·ij/ *n* a line of descent from a common ancestor or source – **lineal** *adj* – **lineally** *adv*

linear /'lini·ǝ/ *adj* **1a** of, being, or resembling a line **b** involving a single dimension **2** characterized by an emphasis on line; *esp* having clearly defined outlines

linen /'linin/ *n* **1** cloth or yarn made from flax **2** clothing or household articles (e g sheets and tablecloths) made of a usu washable cloth, esp linen

'line-,out *n* (a method in Rugby Union of returning the ball to play after it has crossed a touchline which involves throwing it in between) a line of forwards from each team

'line ,printer *n* a high-speed printing device (e g for a computer) that prints each line as a unit rather than character by character

¹liner /'liənə/ *n* a passenger ship belonging to a shipping company and usu sailing scheduled routes

²liner *n* a replaceable (metal) lining (for reducing the wear of a mechanism)

linesman /'lienzmən/ *n* an official who assists the referee or umpire in various games, esp in determining if a ball or player is out of the prescribed playing area

'line,up /-,up/ *n* (a list of) the players playing for usu 1 side in a game

'line-,up *n* **1** a line of people arranged esp for inspection or as a means of identifying a suspect **2** a group of people or items assembled for a particular purpose

line up 1 to put into alignment **2** to assemble or organize **3** to assume an orderly arrangement in a line a large food fish of shallow seas off Greenland and Europe

linger /'ling·gə/ *v* **1a** to delay going; tarry **b** to dwell on a subject – usu + *over, on,* or *upon* **2** to continue unduly or unhappily in a failing or moribund state – often + *on* **3** to be slow to act; procrastinate **4** to be slow in disappearing – **~er** *n* – **~ing** *adj* – **~ingly** *adv*

lingerie /'lonh·zhəri, 'lan(h)-/ *(Fr lɛ̃ʒri)/ n* women's underwear and nightclothes

lingo /'ling·goh/ *n, pl* **lingoes 1** a foreign language **2** jargon

lingua franca /,ling·gwə 'frangkə/ *n, pl* **lingua francas, linguae francae** /-,gwie 'frangkie/ a language used as a common or commercial tongue among people not speaking the same native language

linguist /'ling·gwist/ *n* **1** sby accomplished in languages; *esp* a polyglot **2** sby who specializes in linguistics

linguistic /ling'gwistik/ *adj* of language or linguistics – **~ally** *adv*

linguistics /ling'gwistiks/ *n pl but sing in constr* the study of human language with regard to its nature, structure, and modification

liniment /'linimənt/ *n* a liquid preparation that is applied to the skin, esp to allay pain or irritation

lining /'liening/ *n* **1** (a piece of) material used to line sthg (e g a garment) **2** providing sthg with a lining

¹link /lingk/ *n* **1** a connecting structure: e g **1a** a single ring or division of a chain **b** the fusible part of an electrical fuse **2** sthg analogous to a link of chain; a connecting element

²link *v* **1** to join, connect **2** to become connected by a link – often + *up* – **~age** *n*

links /lingks/ *n pl* **1** a golf course – often pl with sing. meaning **2** *Scot* sand hills, esp along the seashore

linnet /'linit/ *n* a common small Old World finch having variable reddish brown plumage

linoleum /li'nohli·əm/ *n* a floor covering with a canvas back and a coloured or patterned surface of hardened linseed oil and a filler (e g cork dust)

linseed /'linseed/ *n* the seed of flax used esp as a source of linseed oil

'linseed ,oil *n* a yellowish drying oil obtained from flaxseed and used esp in paint, varnish, printing ink, and linoleum and for conditioning wood

lint /lint/ *n* a soft absorbent material with a fleecy surface that is made from linen and is used chiefly for surgical dressings

lintel /'lintl/ *n* a horizontal architectural member spanning and usu carrying the load above an opening

lion /'lie·ən/, *fem* **lioness** /'lie·ənes/ *n pl* **lions**, (1a) **lions**, *esp collectively* **lion 1a** a flesh-eating big cat of open or rocky areas of Africa and formerly southern Asia that has a tawny body with a tufted tail and in the male a shaggy blackish or dark brown mane **b** *cap* Leo **2** a person of interest or importance

lion'hearted /-'hahtid/ *adj* courageous, brave

lion·ize, -ise /'lie·ə,niez/ *v* to treat as an object of great interest or importance

lip /lip/ *n* **1** either of the 2 fleshy folds that surround the mouth **2** a fleshy fold surrounding some other body opening (e g the vagina) **3** the edge of a hollow vessel or cavity; *esp* one shaped to make pouring easy **4** impudent or insolent talk, esp in reply – *slang*

'lip ,gloss *n* a cosmetic for giving a gloss to the lips

'lip ,service *n* support in words but not in deeds

lipstick /'lip,stik/ *n* (a cased stick of) a waxy solid cosmetic for colouring the lips

liquefy *also* **liquify** /'likwifie/ *v* **1** to reduce to a liquid state **2** to become liquid

liqueur /li'kyooə/ *n* any of several usu sweetened alcoholic drinks variously flavoured (e g with fruit or aromatic herbs)

liquid /'likwid/ *adj* **1** flowing freely like water **2** neither solid nor gaseous **3a** shining and clear **b** *of a sound* flowing, pure, and free of harshness **c** smooth and unconstrained in movement **4** consisting of or capable of ready conversion into cash – **liquid** *n*

liquidate /'likwidayt/ *v* **1a** to settle (a debt), esp by payment **b** to settle the accounts of (e g a business) and use the assets towards paying off the debts **2** to get rid of; *specif* to kill **3** to convert (assets) into cash – **-ation** *n*

liquidator /'likwi‚dayta/ *n* a person appointed by law to liquidate a company

liquid·ize, -ise /'likwidiez/ *v* to cause to be liquid; *esp* to pulverize (e g fruit or vegetables) into a liquid

liquid·izer, -iser /'likwidieza/ *n*, *chiefly Br* a domestic electric appliance for grinding, puréeing, liquidizing, or blending foods

liquor /'lika/ *n* a liquid substance: e g **a** a solution of a drug in water **b** a liquid, esp water, in which food has been cooked **c** *chiefly NAm* a usu distilled rather than fermented alcoholic drink

liquorice /'likarish, -ris/ *n* a sweet, black highly-flavoured plant-extract used in brewing, medicine and confectionery

lira /'liara/ *n*, *pl* (1) **lire** *also* **liras**, (2) **liras** *also* **lire** **1** the major unit of currency of Italy **2** the major unit of currency of Turkey

lisp /lisp/ *v* to pronounce /s/ and /z/ imperfectly, esp by giving them the sounds of /th/ and /dh/ – **lisp** *n* – **ingly** *adv*

¹**list** /list/ *n*, *pl but sing or pl in constr* **1** (the fence surrounding) a court or yard for jousting **2** a scene of competition

²**list** *n* a roll or catalogue of words or numbers (e g representing people or objects belonging to a class), usu arranged in order so as to be easily found

³**list** *v* **1** to make a list of **2** to include on a list; *specif*, *Br* to include (a building) in an official list as being of architectural or historical importance and hence protected from demolition

⁴**list** *v* to (cause to) lean to one side

listen /'lis(a)n/ *v* **1** to pay attention to sound **2** to hear or consider with thoughtful attention; heed **3** to be alert to catch an expected sound

listen in *v* to tune in to or monitor a broadcast

listless /'listlis/ *adj* characterized by indifference, lack of energy, and disinclination for exertion; languid – **ly** *adv* – **ness** *n*

lit /lit/ *past of* **light**

literacy /'lit(a)rasi/ *n* the quality or state of being literate

¹**literal** /'lit(a)ral/ *adj* **1a** according with the exact letter of a written text **b** having the factual or ordinary construction or primary meaning of a term or expression **c** characterized by a lack of imagination **2** of or expressed in letters **3** reproduced word for word; exact, verbatim – **ly** *adv*

²**literal** *n* a misprint involving a single letter

literary /'lit(a)rari/ *adj* **1a** of, being, or concerning literature **b** characteristic of or being in a formal, rather than colloquial, style **2a** well-read **b** producing, well versed in, or connected with literature

literate /'lit(a)rat/ *adj* **1a** educated, cultured **b** able to read and write **2** versed in literature or creative writing

literature /'lit(a)racha/ *n* **1** writings in prose or verse; *esp* writings having artistic value or expression and expressing ideas of permanent or universal interest **2** the body of writings on a particular subject **3** printed matter (e g leaflets or circulars)

lithe /liedh/ *adj* flexible, supple – **ly** *adv*

lithium /'lithi-am/ *n* a soft silver-white element of the alkali metal group that is the lightest metal known

lithograph /'litha‚grahf, -‚graf/ *v or n* (to produce or copy in the form of) a print made on a prepared stone slab or metal plate – **ic** *adj* – **y** *n*

litigate /'litigayt/ *v* to carry on a lawsuit – **-gant** *n* – **-gation** *n*

litmus /'litmas/ *n* a colouring matter from lichens that turns red in acid solutions and blue in alkaline solutions and is used as an acid-alkali indicator

litre, *NAm chiefly* **liter** /'leeta/ *n* a metric unit of capacity equal to 1.000 028dm³ (about 0.220gal)

¹**litter** /'lita/ *n* **1a** a covered and curtained couch carried by people or animals **b** a stretcher or other device for carrying a sick or injured person **2a** material used as bedding for animals **b** the uppermost slightly decayed layer of organic matter on the forest floor **3** a group of offspring of an animal, born at 1 birth **4a** rubbish or waste products, esp in a public place **b** an untidy accumulation of objects (e g papers)

²**litter** *v* **1** to give birth to a litter **2** to strew with litter **3** to scatter about in disorder

¹**little** /'litl/ *adj* **littler** /'litlə/, **less** /les/, **lesser** /'lesə/; **littlest** /'litlist/, **least** /leest/ **1a** amounting to only a small quantity **b** *of a plant or animal* small in comparison with related forms – used in vernacular names **c** small in condition, distinction, or scope **2** not much: e g **2a** existing only in a small amount or to a slight degree **b** short in duration; brief **c** existing to an appreciable though not extensive degree or amount – + a **3** small in importance or interest; trivial

²**little** *adv* **less** /les/; **least** /leest/ **1** to no great degree or extent; not much (e g *little*-known) **2** not at all (e g cared *little* for his neighbours)

³**little** *n* **1a** only a small portion or quantity; not much **b** at least some, though not much – + a (e g have a *little* of this cake) **2** a short time or distance – **a little** somewhat, rather

little 'finger *n* the fourth and smallest finger of the hand counting the index finger as the first

'little ‚people *n pl* imaginary beings (e g fairies, elves, etc) of folklore – + *the*

¹**littoral** /'litaral/ *adj* of or occurring on or near a (sea) shore

²**littoral** *n* a coastal region; *esp* the region between high and low tides

liturgy /'litʃji/ *n* **1** *often cap* the form of service used in the celebration of Communion, esp in the Orthodox church **2** a prescribed form of public worship – **-gical** *adj* – **-gically** *adv*

livable *also* **liveable** /'livəbl/ *adj* **1** suitable for living in or with **2** endurable

¹**live** /liv/ *v* **1** to be alive; have the life of an animal or plant **2** to continue alive **3** to maintain oneself; subsist **4** to conduct or pass one's life **5** to occupy a home; dwell — **live in sin** to cohabit — **live it up** to enjoy an exciting or extravagant social life or social occasion — **live up to** to act or be in accordance with (esp a standard expected by sby)

²**live** /liev/ *adj* **1** having life **2** containing living organisms **3** exerting force or containing energy: e g **3a** glowing **b** connected to electric power **c** of ammunition, bombs, *etc* unexploded, unfired **4** of continuing or current interest

³**live** /liev/ *adv* during, from, or at a live production

livelihood /'lievli,hood/ *n* a means of support or sustenance

livelong /'liv,long/ *adj* whole, entire – chiefly poetic

lively /'lievli/ *adj* **1** briskly alert and energetic; vigorous, animated **2** quick to rebound; resilient **3** full of life, movement, or incident – **-liness** *n*

¹**liver** /'livə/ *n* **1a** a large organ of vertebrates that secretes bile and causes changes in the blood (e g by acting upon blood sugar) **b** any of various large digestive glands of invertebrates **2** the liver of an animal (e g a calf or pig) eaten as food **3** a greyish reddish brown colour

²**liver** *n* one who lives, esp in a specified way

liverish /'livərish/ *adj* **1** suffering from liver disorder; bilious **2** peevish, irascible; *also* glum

livery /'livəri/ *n* **1** the uniform of servants employed by an individual or a single household **2** distinctive colouring or marking; *also* distinctive dress **3** a distinctive colour scheme (e g on aircraft) distinguishing an organization or group

lives /lievz/ *pl of* **life**

¹**live,stock** /-,stok/ *n* farm animals

livid /'livid/ *adj* **1** discoloured by bruising **2** ashen, pallid **3** reddish **4** very angry; enraged – **~ly** *adv*

¹**living** /'living/ *adj* **1a** having life; alive **b** existing in use **2** true to life; exact – esp in *the living image of* **3** – used as an intensive **4** *of feelings, ideas, etc* full of power and force

²**living** *n* **1** the condition of being alive **2** a manner of life **3** means of subsistence; a livelihood

living ,room *n* a room in a residence used for everyday activities

lizard /'lizəd/ *n* any of a suborder of reptiles distinguished from the snakes by 2 pairs of well differentiated functional limbs (which may be lacking in burrowing forms), external ears, and eyes with movable lids

llama /'lahmə/ *n* any of several wild and domesticated S American ruminant mammals related to the camels but smaller and without a hump

¹**load** /lohd/ *n* **1a** an amount, esp large or heavy, that is (to be) carried, supported, or borne **b** the quantity that can be carried at 1 time by a specified means – often in combination **2** the forces to which a structure is subjected **3** a burden of responsibility, anxiety, *etc* **4** external resistance overcome by a machine or other source of power **5** power output (e g of a power plant) **6** the amount of work to be performed by a person, machine, *etc* **7** a large quantity or amount; a lot – usu pl with sing. meaning; infml — **get a load of** to pay attention to (sth surprising) – slang

²**load** *v* **1a** to put a load in or on **b** to place in or on a means of conveyance **2** to encumber or oppress with sth heavy, laborious, or disheartening; burden **3a** to weight or shape (dice) to fall unfairly **b** to charge with hidden implications; *also* to bias **4** to put a load or charge in a device or piece of equipment; esp to insert the charge in a firearm

¹**loaded** *adj* having a large amount of money – infml

¹**load,stone** /-,stohn/ *n* (a) lodestone

¹**loaf** /lohf/ *n, pl* **loaves** /lohvz/ **1** a mass of bread often having a regular shape and standard weight **2** a shaped or moulded often symmetrical mass of food (e g sugar or chopped cooked meat) **3** *Br* head, brains – slang; esp in *use one's loaf*

²**loaf** *v* to spend time in idleness – **~er** *n*

loam /lohm/ *n* crumbly soil consisting of a mixture of clay, silt, and sand – **~y** *adj*

¹**loan** /lohn/ *n* **1a** money lent at interest **b** sth lent, usu for the borrower's temporary use **2** the grant of temporary use

²**loan** *v* to lend

¹**loan,word** /-,wuhd/ *n* a word taken from another language and at least partly naturalized

loath, loth /lohth/ *also* **loathe** /lohdh/ unwilling, reluctant

loathe /lohdh/ *v* to dislike greatly, often with disgust or intolerance – **-thing** *n*

loathsome /'lohdhs(ə)m, 'lohth-/ *adj* giving rise to loathing; disgusting – **~ly** *adv* – **~ness** *n*

loaves /lohvz/ *pl of* **loaf**

¹**lob** /lob/ *v* **-bb-** to hit a ball easily in a high arc, esp in tennis, squash, *etc*

²**lob** *n* a lobbed ball

¹**lobby** /'lobi/ *n* **1** a porch or small entrance hall **2** an anteroom of a legislative chamber to which members go to vote during a division **3** *sing or pl in constr* a group of people engaged in lobbying

²**lobby** *v* to try to influence (e g a member of a legislative body) towards an action

lobe /lohb/ *n* a curved or rounded projection or division; *esp* such a projection or division of a bodily organ or part – **~d** *adj*

353   log

lobster /'lobstə/ *n pl* **lobsters**, *esp collectively* **lobster** any of a family of large edible 10-legged marine crustaceans that have stalked eyes, a pair of large claws, and a long abdomen

lobster ,pot *n* (a basket used as) a trap for catching lobsters

¹**local** /'lohk(ə)l/ *adj* **1** (characteristic) of or belonging to a particular place; not general or widespread **2a** primarily serving the needs of a particular limited district **b** *of a public conveyance* making all the stops on a route – ~ **ize** *v* – ~ **ly** *adv*

²**local** *n, Br* the neighbourhood pub

locality /loh'kaləti/ *n* **1** the fact or condition of having a location in space or time **2** a particular place, situation, or location

locate /loh'kayt/ *v* **1** to determine or indicate the place, site, or limits of **2** to set or establish in a particular spot – ~ **d** *adj*

location /loh'kaysh(ə)n/ *n* **1** a particular place or position **2a** place outside a studio where a (part of a) picture is filmed

loch /lohh/ *n* a lake or (nearly landlocked) arm of the sea in Scotland

loci /'lohsi; *also* lohki/ *pl of* **locus**

¹**lock** /lok/ *n* a curl, tuft, etc of hair

²**lock** *n* **1** a fastening that can be opened and often closed only by means of a particular key or combination **2** an enclosed section of waterway (e g a canal) which has gates at each end and in which the water level can be raised or lowered to move boats from one level to another **3** a hold in wrestling secured on a usu specified body part **4** *chiefly Br* the maximum extent to which the front wheels of a vehicle can be turned

³**lock** *v* **1a** to fasten the lock of **b** to make fast (as if) with a lock **2a** to shut in or out or make secure or inaccessible (as if) by means of locks **b** to hold fast or inactive; fix in a particular situation or method of operation **3a** to make fast by the interlacing or interlocking of parts **b** to grapple in combat; *also* to bind closely – often pass – ~ **able** *adj*

locker /'lokə/ *n* **1** a cupboard or compartment that may be closed with a lock; *esp* one for individual storage use **2** a chest or compartment on board ship

locket /'lokit/ *n* a small case usu of precious metal that has space for a memento (e g a small picture) and is usu worn on a chain round the neck

lockjaw /'lok,jaw/ *n* an early symptom of tetanus characterized by spasm of the jaw muscles and inability to open the jaws

'**lock,nut** /-,nut/ *n* **1** a nut screwed hard up against another to prevent either of them from moving **2** a nut so constructed that it locks itself when screwed up tight

'**lock,out** /-,owt/ *n* a whole or partial closing of a business by an employer in order to gain concessions from or resist demands of employees

'**lock,smith** /-,smith/ *n* sby who makes or mends locks as an occupation

'**lock,stitch** /-,stich/ *n* a sewing machine stitch formed by the looping together of 2 threads, 1 on each side of the material being sewn

locomotion /,lohkə'mohsh(ə)n/ *n* **1** an act or the power of moving from place to place **2** travel

locomotive /,lohkə'mohtiv/ *n* an engine that moves under its own power; *esp* one that moves railway carriages and wagons

locum /'lohkəm/ *n* sby filling an office for a time or temporarily taking the place of another

locus /'lohkəs, 'lokəs/ *n, pl* **loci** /'lohsie, 'lohsi; *also* 'lohkie, 'lohki/ *also* **locuses 1** a place, locality **2** the set of all points whose location is determined by stated conditions

locust /'lohkəst/ *n* **1** a migratory grasshopper that often travels in vast swarms stripping the areas passed of all vegetation **2** any of various hard-wooded leguminous trees

lode /lohd/ *n* an ore deposit

'**lode,stone, loadstone** /-,stohn/ a piece of magnetized rock; *broadly* a magnet

¹**lodge** /loj/ *v* **1a** to provide temporary, esp rented, accommodation for **b** to establish or settle in a place **2** to serve as a receptacle for; contain, house **3** to fix in place **4** to deposit for safeguard or preservation **5** to place or vest (e g power), esp in a source, means, or agent **6** to lay (e g a complaint) before authority

²**lodge** *n* **1** the meeting place of a branch of an esp fraternal organization **2** a house set apart for residence in a particular season (e g the hunting season) **3a** a house orig for the use of a gamekeeper, caretaker, porter, etc **b** a porter's room (e g at the entrance to a college, block of flats, etc) **c** the house where the head of a university college lives, esp in Cambridge **4** a den or lair of an animal or a group of animals (e g beavers or otters)

lodger /'lojə/ *n* one who occupies a rented room in another's house

lodging /'lojing/ *n* **1** a place to live; a dwelling **2a** a temporary place to stay **b** a rented room or rooms for residing in, usu in a private house rather than a hotel – usu pl with sing. meaning

¹**loft** /loft/ *n* **1** an attic **2a** a gallery in a church or hall **b** an upper floor in a barn or warehouse used for storage – sometimes in combination

²**loft** *v* to propel through the air or into space – ~ **ed** *adj*

lofty /'lofti/ *adj* **1** having a haughty overbearing manner; supercilious **2a** elevated in character and spirit; noble **b** elevated in position; superior **3** impressively high – **-tily** *adv* – **-tiness** *n*

¹**log** /log/ *n* **1** a usu bulky piece or length of unshaped timber (ready for sawing or for use as firewood) **2** an apparatus for measuring the rate

of a ship's motion through the water **3a** the full nautical record of a ship's voyage **b** the full record of a flight by an aircraft

²**log** *v* -**gg-** **1** to cut trees for timber **2** to enter details of or about in a log **3a** to move or attain (e g an indicated distance, speed, or time) as noted in a log **b** to have (an indicated record) to one's credit; achieve

³**log** *n* a logarithm

loganberry /'lohgənb(ə)ri, -ˌberi/ *n* (the red sweet edible berry of) an upright-growing raspberry hybrid

logarithm /'logəˌridh(ə)m/ *n* the exponent that indicates the power to which a number is raised to produce a given number – ~**ic** *adj* – ~**ically** *adv*

'**log ˌbook** /-ˌbook/ *n Br* a document held with a motor vehicle that gives the vehicle's registration number, make, engine size, etc and a list of its owners – not now used technically

logger /'logə/ *n*, *NAm* a lumberjack

logic /'lojik/ *n* **1a** a science that deals with the formal principles and structure of thought and reasoning **b** a particular mode of reasoning viewed as valid or faulty **2** the interrelation or sequence of facts or events when seen as inevitable or predictable – ~**al** *adj* – ~**ally** *adv*

logistics /lo'jistiks, lə-/ *n pl but sing or pl in constr* **1** the aspect of military science dealing with the transportation, quartering, and supplying of troops in military operations **2** the handling of the details of an operation – **logistic** *adj* – **-cally** *adv*

loin /loyn/ *n* **1a** the part of a human being or quadruped on each side of the spinal column between the hipbone and the lower ribs **b** a cut of meat comprising this part of one or both sides of a carcass with the adjoining half of the vertebrae included **2** *pl* the pubic region; *also* the genitals

'**loin ˌcloth** /-ˌkloth/ *n* a cloth worn about the hips and covering the genitals

loiter /'loytə/ *v* **1** to remain in an area for no obvious reason **2** to dawdle – ~**er** *n*

loll /lol/ *v* **1** to hang down loosely **2** to recline, lean, or move in a lazy or excessively relaxed manner; lounge

lollipop, lollypop /'loliˌpop/ *n* a large often round flat sweet of boiled sugar on the end of a stick

'**lollipop ˌman**, *fem* '**lollipop ˌlady** *n*, *Br* sby controlling traffic to allow (school) children to cross busy roads

lollop /'loləp/ *v* to move or proceed with an ungainly loping motion

lolly /'loli/ *n* **1** a lollipop or ice lolly **2** *Br* money – *infml*

lone /lohn/ *adj* **1** only, sole **2** situated alone or separately; isolated **3** having no company; solitary – *fml*

lonely /'lohnli/ *adj* **1** cut off from others; solitary **2** not frequented by people; desolate **3** sad from being alone or without friends – **-liness** *n*

loner /'lohnə/ *n* a person or animal that prefers solitude

lonesome /'lohns(ə)m/ *adj* **1** lonely **2** isolated

¹**long** /long/ *adj* **1a** extending for a considerable distance **b** having greater length than usual **2** having a specified length **3** extending over a considerable or specified time **4** containing a large or specified number of items or units **5** reaching or extending a considerable distance **6** *of betting odds* greatly differing in the amounts wagered on each side – **before long** in a short time; soon — **in the long run** in the course of sufficiently prolonged time, trial, or experience — **long in the tooth** past one's best days; old — **not by a long chalk** not at all

²**long** *adv* **1** for or during a long or specified time **2** at a point of time far before or after a specified moment or event **3** after or beyond a specified time — **so long** goodbye – *infml*

³**long** *v* to feel a strong desire or craving, esp *for* sthg not likely to be attained – ~**ing** *n*, *adj* – ~**ingly** *adv*

'**long ˌboat** /-ˌboht/ *n* the largest boat carried by a sailing vessel

'**long ˌbow** /-ˌboh/ *n* a long wooden bow for shooting arrows

ˌ**long di'vision** *n* arithmetical division in which the calculations corresponding to the division of parts of the dividend by the divisor are written out

longevity /lon'jevəti; *also* long'gevəti/ *n* (great) length of life

'**long ˌhand** /-ˌhand/ *n* ordinary writing; handwriting

'**long ˌhop** *n* an easily hit short-pitched delivery of a cricket ball

longitude /'lonjityoohd; *also* 'long·giˌtyoohd/ *n* the (time difference corresponding to) angular distance of a point on the surface of a celestial body, esp the earth, measured E or W from a prime meridian (e g that of Greenwich)

ˌ**longi'tudinal** /-'tyoohdinl/ *adj* **1** of length or the lengthways dimension **2** placed or running lengthways – ~**ly** *adv*

'**long ˌjohns** /ˌjonz/ *n pl* underpants with legs extending usu down to the ankles – *infml*

'**long ˌjump** *n* (an athletic field event consisting of) a jump for distance from a running start

ˌ**long-'range** *adj* involving or taking into account a long period of time

'**long ˌshot** *n* **1** (a bet at long odds on) a competitor given little chance of winning **2** a venture that involves considerable risk and has little chance of success — **by a long shot** by a great deal

ˌ**long 'sighted** /-'sietid/ *adj* able to see distant objects better than close ones

ˌ**long-'standing** *adj* of long duration

ˌ**long-'suffering** *n or adj* (the quality of) patiently enduring pain, difficulty, or provocation

,long-'term *adj* occurring over or involving a relatively long period of time

'long ,wave *n* a band of radio waves typically used for sound broadcasting and covering wavelengths of 1000m or more

,long-'winded /-'windid/ *adj* tediously long in speaking or writing

¹**loo** /looh/ *n* (money staked at) an old card game in which the winner of each trick takes a portion of the pool while losing players have to contribute to the next pool

²**loo** *n, chiefly Br* a toilet – *infml*

loofah /'loohfə/ *n* a dried seed-pod of any of several plants of the cucumber family, used as a rough bath sponge

¹**look** /look/ *v* **1a** to use the power of sight; *esp* to make a visual search *for* **b** to direct one's attention **c** to direct the eyes **2** to have the appearance of being; appear, seem **3** to have a specified outlook — **look after** to take care of — **look sharp** to be quick; hurry

²**look** *n* **1a** the act of looking **b** a glance **2a** a facial expression **b** (attractive) physical appearance – usu pl with sing. meaning **3** the state or form in which sthg appears

'look-a,like *n or adj* (sby or sthg) looking like another

look back *v* **1** to remember – often + *to, on* **2** to fail to make successful progress – in *never look back*

'look-,in *n* a chance to take part; *also* a chance of success – *infml*

look in *v, Br* to pay a short visit

'looking ,glass *n* /'looking/ *n* a mirror

'look,out /-,owt/ *n* **1** one engaged in keeping watch **2** a place or structure affording a wide view for observation **3** a careful looking or watching **4** a matter of care or concern **5** *chiefly Br* a future possibility; a prospect

look out *v* **1** to take care – often imper **2** to keep watching

look up *v* **1** to search for (as if) in a reference work **2** to pay a usu short visit to **3** to improve in prospects or conditions

¹**loom** /loohm/ *n* a frame or machine for weaving together yarns or threads into cloth

²**loom** *v* **1** to come into sight indistinctly, in enlarged or distorted and menacing form, often as a result of atmospheric conditions **2** to appear in an impressively great or exaggerated form

loony, looney /'loohni/ *adj* crazy, foolish – *infml*

'loony ,bin *n* a mental hospital – *humor*

¹**loop** /loohp/ *n* **1a** a (partially) closed figure that has a curved outline surrounding a central opening **2** a zigzag-shaped intrauterine contraceptive device **3** a ring or curved piece used to form a fastening or handle **4** a piece of film or magnetic tape whose ends are spliced together so as to reproduce the same content continuously

²**loop** *v* **1a** to make a loop in, on, or about **b** to fasten with a loop **2** to form a loop with — **loop the loop** to perform a loop in an aircraft

loophole /'loohp,hohl/ *n* **1** a small opening through which missiles, firearms, etc may be discharged or light and air admitted **2** a means of escape; *esp* an ambiguity or omission in a text through which its intent may be evaded

¹**loose** /loohs/ *adj* **1a** not rigidly fastened or securely attached **b** having worked partly free from attachments **c** not tight-fitting **2a** free from a state of confinement, restraint, or obligation **b** not brought together in a bundle, container, or binding **3** not dense, close, or compact in structure or arrangement **4a** lacking in (power of) restraint **b** dissolute, promiscuous **5** not tightly drawn or stretched; slack **6a** lacking in precision, exactness, or care **b** permitting freedom of interpretation – ~**ly** *adv* – ~**n** *v* – ~**ness** *n*

²**loose** *v* **1a** to let loose; release **b** to free from restraint **2** to make loose; untie **3** to cast loose; detach **4** to let fly; discharge (e g a bullet)

³**loose** *adv* in a loose manner; loosely

¹**loot** /looht/ *n* **1** goods, usu of considerable value, taken in war; spoils **2** sthg taken illegally (e g by force or deception)

²**loot** *v* to seize and carry away (sthg) by force or illegally, esp in war or public disturbance – ~**er** *n*

¹**lop** /lop/ *n* small branches and twigs cut from a tree

²**lop** *v* -**pp**- **1** to cut off branches or twigs from **2** to remove or do away with as unnecessary or undesirable – usu + *off or away*

lope /lohp/ *n* an easy bounding gait capable of being sustained for a long time – **lope** *v*

lopsided /,lop'siedid/ *adj* **1** having one side heavier or lower than the other **2** lacking in balance, symmetry, or proportion

loquacious /lə'kwayshəs/ *adj* talkative – *fml* – ~**ly** *adv* – -**city** *n*

¹**lord** /lawd/ *n* **1** one having power and authority over others **2** *cap* **2a** God **b** Jesus – often + *Our* **3** a man of rank or high position: e g **3a** a feudal tenant holding land directly from the king **b** a British nobleman **4** *pl* the House of Lords

²**lord** *v* to act like a lord; *esp* to put on airs – usu + *it*

,lord 'chancellor *n, often cap L & C* an officer of state who presides over the House of Lords, serves as head of the judiciary, and is usu a member of the cabinet

lordly /'lawdli/ *adj* **1a** dignified **b** grand, noble **2** disdainful and arrogant – -**liness** *n*

,Lord's 'Prayer *n* the prayer taught by Jesus beginning 'Our Father'

lore /law/ *n* a specified body of knowledge or tradition

lorgnette /law'nyet/ (*Fr* lɔrnɛt)/ *n* a pair of glasses or opera glasses with a handle

lorry /'lori/ *n, Br* a large motor vehicle for carrying loads by road

lose /loohz/ *v* **lost** /lost/ **1** to miss from one's possession or from a customary or supposed place; *also* to fail to find **2** to suffer deprivation of; part with, esp in an unforeseen or accidental manner **3** to suffer loss through the death of or final separation from (sby) **4a** to fail to use; let slip by **b** to be defeated in (a contest for) **c** to fail to catch with the senses or the mind **5** to fail to keep or maintain **6** to fail to keep in sight or in mind **7** to free oneself from; get rid of **8** to run slow by the amount of – used with reference to a timepiece — **lose one's head** to lose self-control (e g in anger or panic)

lose out *v* **1** to make a loss **2** to be the loser, esp unluckily *USE* often + *on*

loser /'loohzə/ *n* **1** one who loses, esp consistently **2** one who does poorly; a failure

loss /los/ *n* **1a** the act or an instance of losing possession **b** the harm or privation resulting from loss or separation **2** a person, thing, or amount lost; *esp, pl* killed, wounded, or captured soldiers **3a** failure to gain, win, obtain, or use sthg **b** amount by which cost exceeds revenue **4** decrease in amount, size, or degree **5** destruction, ruin — **at a loss** uncertain, puzzled

loss leader *n* an article sold at a loss in order to draw customers

lost /lost/ *adj* **1a** unable to find the way **b** bewildered, helpless **2** ruined or destroyed physically or morally **3a** no longer possessed **b** no longer known **4** rapt, absorbed

lot /lot/ *n* **1** an object used as a counter in deciding a question by chance **2** (the use of lots as a means of making) a choice **3a** sthg that falls to sby by lot; a share **b** one's way of life or worldly fate; fortune **4** a film studio and its adjoining property **5** an article or a number of articles offered as 1 item (e g in an auction sale) **6a** *sing or pl in constr* a number of associated people; a set (e g you *lot*) **b** a kind, sort – chiefly in *a bad lot* **7** a considerable amount or number – often *pl* with sing. meaning **8** *chiefly Br* the whole amount or number (e g ate up the whole *lot*) *USE* (6a&8) *infml* — **a lot 1** lots **2** often, frequently

lotion /'lohsh(ə)n/ *n* a medicinal or cosmetic liquid for external use

lottery /'lot(ə)ri/ *n* **1** (a way of raising money by the sale or) the distribution of numbered tickets some of which are later randomly selected to entitle the holder to a prize **2** an event or affair whose outcome is (apparently) decided by chance

lotus /'lohtəs/ *n* **1** a fruit considered in Greek legend to cause indolence and dreamy contentment **2** any of various water lilies

'lotus-,eater *n* sby who lives in dreamy indolence

loud /lowd/ *adj* **1** marked by or producing a high volume of sound **2** clamorous, noisy **3** obtrusive or offensive in appearance; flashy – ~**ly** *adv*

loud-'hailer *n* a megaphone

'loud,mouth /-,mowth/ *n* a person given to much loud offensive talk – *infml* – ~**ed** *adj*

loudspeaker /,lowd'speekə/ *n* an electromechanical device that converts electrical energy into acoustic energy and that is used to reproduce audible sounds

¹lounge /lownj/ *v* to act or move idly or lazily; loll – ~**r** *n*

²lounge *n* **1** a room in a private house for sitting in **2** a room in a public building providing comfortable seating; *also* a waiting room (e g at an airport)

'lounge ,suit *n* a man's suit for wear during the day

lour /'lowə/ *v* **1** to look sullen; frown **2** to become dark, gloomy and threatening – **lour** *n*

louse /lows/ *n, pl* **lice**, /lies/; *sense 2* **louses 1** any of various small wingless insects parasitic on warm-blooded animals **2** a contemptible person – *infml*

lousy /'lowzi/ *adj* **1** infested with lice **2a** very mean; despicable **b** very bad, unpleasant, useless, etc

lout /lowt/ *n* a rough ill-mannered man or youth – ~**ish** *adj*

louvre, louver /'loohvə/ *n* an opening provided with 1 or more slanted fixed or movable strips of metal, wood, glass, etc to allow flow of air but to exclude rain or sun

¹love /luv/ *n* **1a** strong affection for another **b** attraction based on sexual desire **2** warm interest in, enjoyment of, or attraction to sthg **3a** the object of interest and enjoyment **b** a person who is loved; a dear (one) **4** unselfish loyal and benevolent concern for the good of another **5** a god or personification of love **6** an amorous episode; a love affair **7** a score of zero in tennis, squash, etc **8** sexual intercourse – *euph* — **for love or money** in any possible way — usu neg

²love *v* **1** to hold dear; cherish **2a** to feel a lover's passion, devotion, or tenderness for **b** to have sexual intercourse with **3** to like or desire actively; take pleasure in **4** to thrive in – **-vable** *adj*

'loveless /-lis/ *adj* **1** without love **2** unloving **3** unloved

'love,lorn /-,lawn/ *adj* sad because of unrequited love

¹lovely /'luvli/ *adj* **1** delicately or delightfully beautiful **2** very pleasing; fine – **-liness** *n*

²lovely *n* a beautiful woman – *infml*

lover /'luvə/ *n* **1a** a person in love **b** a man with whom a woman has sexual relations, esp outside marriage **c** *pl* 2 people in love with each other; *esp* **2** people who habitually have sexual relations **2a** a devotee

'love,sick /-,sik/ *adj* languishing with love

loving /'luving/ *adj* feeling or showing love; affectionate – ~**ly** *adv*

¹**low** /loh/ *v or n* (to make) the deep sustained throat sound characteristic of esp a cow

²**low** *adj* 1 not measuring much from the base to the top; not high **2a** situated or passing below the normal level or below the base of measurement **b** marking a nadir or bottom **3** *of sound* not shrill or loud; soft **4** near the horizon **5** humble in character or status **6a** weak **b** depressed **7** of less than usual degree, size, amount, or value **8a** lacking dignity or formality **b** morally reprehensible **c** coarse, vulgar **9** unfavourable, disparaging **10** *of a gear* designed for slow speed – ~**ness** *n*

³**low** *n* sthg low: e g **a** a depth, nadir **b** a region of low atmospheric pressure

⁴**low** *adv* at or to a low place, altitude, or degree

low'born /-'bawn/ *adj* born to parents of low social rank

low,brow /-,brow/ *adj* dealing with or having unsophisticated or unintellectual tastes, esp in the arts – often derog

low'down /-,down/ *n* inside information – usu + *the*; infml

low-'down *adj* contemptible, base – infml

¹**lower** /'lohə/ *adj* 1 relatively low in position, rank, or order **2** less advanced in the scale of evolutionary development **3** constituting the popular, more representative, and often (e g in Britain) more powerful branch of a legislative body consisting of 2 houses **4a** beneath the earth's surface **b** *often cap* being an earlier division of the named geological period or series

²**lower** *v* **1a** to cause to descend **b** to reduce the height of **2a** to reduce in value, amount, degree, strength, or pitch **b** to degrade; *also* to humble

lower-'case *adj, of a letter* or conforming to the series (e g a, b, c rather than A, B, C) typically used elsewhere than at the beginning of sentences or proper names

low-'key *also* **low-keyed** /keed/ *adj* of low intensity; restrained

Lowland /'lohland/ *adj* of the Lowlands of Scotland

¹**lowly** /'lohli/ *adv* **1** in a humble or meek manner **2** in a low position, manner, or degree

²**lowly** *adj* **1** humble and modest in manner or spirit **2** low in the scale of biological or cultural evolution **3** ranking low in a social or economic hierarchy – **liness** *n*

low 'profile *n* an inconspicuous mode of operation or behaviour (intended to attract little attention)

low technology *n* technology using old-established resources and devices, usu to produce staple items

loyal /'loyəl/ *adj* unswerving in allegiance (e g to a person, country, or cause) – ~**ly** *adv*, *adv*, n – ~**ty** *n*

loyalist /'loyəlist/ *n* sby loyal to a government or sovereign, esp in time of revolt

lozenge /'lozinj/ *n* **1** (sthg shaped like) a figure with 4 equal sides and 2 acute and 2 obtuse angles **2** a small often medicated sweet

LP /,el 'pee/ *n* a gramophone record designed to be played at 33¹/₃ revolutions per minute and typically having a diameter of 12in (30.5cm) and a playing time of 20–25min

LSD /,el es 'dee/ *n* a drug taken illegally for its potent action in producing hallucinations and altered perceptions

lubricant /'loohbrikənt/ *n* **1** a substance (e g oil) capable of reducing friction and wear when introduced as a film between solid surfaces **2** sthg that lessens or prevents difficulty

lubricate /'loohbrikayt/ *v* **1** to make smooth or slippery **2** to act as a lubricant – **-cation** – **-cator** *n*

lucerne *also* **lucern** /looh'suhn/ *n, chiefly Br* a deep-rooted European leguminous plant widely grown for fodder

lucid /'loohsid/ *adj* **1** having full use of one's faculties; sane **2** clear to the understanding; plain – ~**ly** *adv* – ~**ity** *n*

luck /luk/ *n* **1** whatever good or bad events happen to a person by chance **2** the tendency for a person to be consistently fortunate or unfortunate **3** success as a result of good fortune

lucky /'luki/ *adj* having, resulting from, or bringing good luck – **-kily** *adv* – **-kiness** *n*

lucky 'dip *n* an attraction (e g at a fair) in which articles can be drawn unseen from a receptacle

lucrative /'loohkrativ/ *adj* producing wealth; profitable – ~**ly** *adv*

lucre /'loohkə/ *n* financial gain; profit; *also* money – esp in *filthy lucre*

ludicrous /'loohdikrəs/ *adj* **1** amusing because of obvious absurdity or incongruity **2** meriting derision – ~**ly** *adv* – ~**ness** *n*

ludo /'loohdoh/ *n* a simple game played with counters and dice on a square board

¹**luff** /luf/ *n* the forward edge of a fore-and-aft sail

²**luff** *v* to sail nearer the wind – often + *up*

¹**lug** /lug/ *v* -**gg**- to drag, pull, or carry with great effort – infml

²**lug** *n* **1** sthg (e g a handle) that projects like an ear **2** an ear – chiefly dial or humor

luggage /'lugij/ *n* (cases, bags, etc containing) the belongings that accompany a traveller

lugger /'lugə/ *n* a small fishing or coasting boat that carries 1 or more lugsails

lugsail /'lug,sayl, -səl/ *n* a 4-sided fore-and-aft sail set to an obliquely hanging yard

lugubrious /looh'goohbri‐əs, lə‐/ *adj* (exaggeratedly or affectedly) mournful – ~**ly** *adv* – ~**ness** *n*

lugworm /'lug,wuhm/ *n* any of a genus of marine worms that are used for bait

lukewarm /ˌloohk'wawm/ adj 1 moderately warm; tepid 2 lacking conviction; indifferent

¹**lull** /lul/ v 1 to cause to sleep or rest; soothe 2 to cause to relax vigilance, esp by deception

²**lull** n a temporary pause or decline in activity

lullaby /'lulabie/ n a song to quieten children or lull them to sleep

lumbago /lum'baygoh/ n muscular pain of the lumbar region of the back

lumbar /'lumbə/ adj of or constituting the loins or the vertebrae to lower back

¹**lumber** /'lumbə/ v to move heavily or clumsily

²**lumber** n 1 surplus or disused articles (e g furniture) that are stored away 2 NAm timber or logs, esp when dressed for use

³**lumber** v to clutter, encumber

'**lumberjack** /-jak/ n a person engaged in logging

luminous /'loohminəs/ adj 1 emitting or full of light; bright 2 easily understood; also explaining clearly – ~ly adv – -nosity n

¹**lump** /lump/ n 1 a usu compact piece or mass of indefinite size and shape 2 an abnormal swelling 3 a heavy thickset person 4 Br the whole group of casual nonunion building workers

²**lump** v to group without discrimination

³**lump** adj not divided into parts; entire

⁴**lump** v to put up with – chiefly in like it or lump it

lumpy /'lumpi/ adj 1a filled or covered with lumps b characterized by choppy waves 2 having a thickset clumsy appearance

lunacy /'loohnəsi/ n 1 insanity (amounting to lack of capability or responsibility in law) 2 wild foolishness; extravagant folly

lunar /'loohnə/ adj 1a of the moon b designed for use on the moon 2 **lunar**, **lunate** shaped like a crescent 3 measured by the moon's revolution

lunar month n the period of time, averaging $29^1/_2$ days, between 2 successive new moons

lunatic /'loohnətik/ adj 1a insane b of or designed for the care of insane people 2 wildly foolish

lunch /lunch/ n a midday meal – **lunch** v

'**luncheon** ˌmeat n a precooked mixture of meat (e g pork) and cereal shaped in a loaf

lung /lung/ n 1 either of the usu paired organs in the chest that constitute the basic respiratory organ of air-breathing vertebrates 2 any of various respiratory organs of invertebrates

¹**lunge** /lunj/ v to make a lunge (with)

²**lunge** n 1 a sudden thrust or forceful forward movement 2 the act of plunging forward

³**lunge** n a long rein used to hold and guide a horse in breaking and training

'**lung**ˌfish /-ˌfish/ n any of various fishes that breathe by a modified air bladder as well as gills

lupin also **lupine** /'loohpin/ n any of a genus of leguminous plants some of which are cultivated for fertilizer, fodder, their edible seeds, or their long spikes of variously coloured flowers

lurch /luhch/ v 1 to roll or tip abruptly; pitch 2 to stagger – **lurch** n

¹**lure** /lyooə, looə/ n 1 a bunch of feathers and often meat attached to a long cord and used by a falconer to recall his/her bird 2a sby or sthg used to entice or decoy b the power to appeal or attract 3 a decoy for attracting animals to capture

²**lure** v to tempt with a promise of pleasure or gain

lurid /'l(y)ooərid/ adj 1 wan and ghastly pale in appearance 2a causing horror or revulsion; gruesome b sensational c highly coloured; gaudy – ~ly adv – ~ness n

lurk /luhk/ v 1 to lie hidden, esp with evil intent 2 to move furtively or inconspicuously

luscious /'lushəs/ adj 1 having a delicious taste or smell 2 richly luxurious or appealing to the senses; also excessively ornate – ~ly adv – ~ness n

¹**lush** /lush/ adj 1 producing or covered by luxuriant growth 2 opulent, sumptuous

²**lush** n, chiefly NAm a heavy drinker; an alcoholic

¹**lust** /lust/ n 1 strong sexual desire, esp as opposed to love 2 an intense longing; a craving

²**lust** v to have an intense (sexual) desire or craving

lustre, NAm chiefly **luster** /'lustə/ n 1 (the quality of) the glow of reflected light from a surface (e g of a mineral) 2a a glow of light (as if) from within b radiant beauty 3 glory, distinction 4 a glass pendant used esp to ornament a chandelier

lustrous /'lustrəs/ adj evenly shining – ~ly adv

lusty /'lusti/ adj 1 full of vitality; healthy 2 full of strength; vigorous – -tily adv – -tiness n

lute /looht/ n a stringed instrument with a large pear-shaped body, a neck with a fretted fingerboard, and pairs of strings tuned in unison – -tanist, -tenist n

luxuriant /lug'zhooəri·ənt/ adj 1 characterized by abundant growth 2a exuberantly rich and varied; prolific b richly or excessively ornamented – ~ly adv – -ance n

luxuriate /lug'zhooəriayt/ v to revel in

luxurious /lug'zhooəri·əs/ adj 1 fond of luxury or self-indulgence; also voluptuous 2 characterized by opulence and rich abundance – ~ly adv

luxury /'lukshəri/ n 1 great ease or comfort based on habitual or liberal use of expensive items without regard to cost 2a sthg desirable but costly or difficult to obtain b sthg relatively expensive adding to pleasure or comfort but not indispensable

lychee /'liechi/ n (a Chinese tree that bears) an oval fruit that has a hard scaly outer covering, sweet white perfumed flesh, and a small hard seed

'**lych-**ˌgate /lich/ n a roofed gate in a churchyard

lymph /limf/ n a pale fluid resembling blood plasma – ~atic adj

lynch /linch/ v to put to death illegally by mob action

lynx /lingks/ *n pl* **lynx, lynxes** any of various wildcats with relatively long legs, a short stubby tail, mottled coat, and often tufted ears

lyre /'lie·ə/ *n* a stringed instrument of the harp family used by the ancient Greeks esp to accompany song and recitation

¹**lyric** /'lirik/ *adj* 1 suitable for being set to music and sung 2 expressing direct personal emotion

²**lyric** *n* 1 a lyric poem 2 *pl* the words of a popular song

'**lyrical** /'lirikl/ *adj* 1 lyric 2 full of admiration or enthusiasm – esp in *wax lyrical* – ~**ly** *adv*

lyricism /'lirisiz(ə)m/ *n* 1 a directly personal and intense style or quality in an art 2 great enthusiasm or exuberance

M

m /em/ *n, pl* **m's, ms** *often cap* 1 (a graphic representation of or device for reproducing) the 13th letter of the English alphabet 2 one thousand

ma /mah/ *n* mother – chiefly as a term of address; *infml*

ma'am /mam, mahm; *unstressed* məm/ *n* madam – used widely in the USA and in Britain, esp by servants and when addressing the Queen or a royal princess

mac, mack /mak/ *n, Br* a raincoat – *infml*

macabre /mə'kahb(r)ə/ *adj* 1 dwelling on the gruesome 2 tending to produce horror in an onlooker

macadam /mə'kadəm/ *n* small broken stones compacted into a solid layer as a method of road construction – ~**ize** *v*

macaroni /,makə'rohni/ *n* pasta made from hard wheat and shaped in hollow tubes

macaroon /,makə'roohn/ *n* a small cake or biscuit composed chiefly of egg whites, sugar, and ground almonds

macaw /mə'kaw/ *n* any of numerous parrots including some of the largest and showiest

¹**mace** /mays/ *n* an ornamental staff used as a symbol of authority

²**mace** *n* an aromatic spice consisting of the dried external fibrous covering of a nutmeg

macerate /'masərayt/ *v* to cause to become soft or separated into constituent elements (as if) by steeping in fluid – **-ation** *n*

machete /mə'sheti, -'chayti/ *n* a large heavy knife used for cutting vegetation and as a weapon

machination /,maki'naysh(ə)n/ *n* a scheming or crafty action or plan intended to accomplish some usu evil end

¹**machine** /mə'sheen/ *n* 1a a combination of parts that transmit forces, motion, and energy one to another in a predetermined manner b an instrument (e g a lever or pulley) designed to transmit or modify the application of power, force, or motion c a combination of mechanically, electrically, or electronically operated parts for performing a task 2 a person or organization that acts like a machine

²**machine** *v* 1 to shape, finish, or operate on by a machine 2 to act on, produce, or perform a particular operation or activity on, using a machine; *esp* to sew using a sewing machine

ma'chine ,gun *n* an automatic gun for rapid continuous fire

machinery /mə'sheen(ə)ri/ *n* 1a machines in general or as a functioning unit b the working parts of a machine 2 the means by which sthg is kept in action or a desired result is obtained 3 the system or organization by which an activity or process is controlled

ma'chine ,tool *n* a usu power-driven machine designed for cutting or shaping wood, metal, etc

machinist /mə'sheenist/ *n* 1 a craftsman skilled in the use of machine tools 2 one who operates a machine, esp a sewing machine

machismo /mə'kiznoh, -'chiz-/ *n* an exaggerated awareness and assertion of masculinity

macho /'machoh, 'makoh/ *adj* aggressively virile

mackerel /'mak(ə)rəl/ *n* a fish of the N Atlantic that is green with dark blue bars above and silvery below and is one of the most important food fishes

mackintosh *also* **macintosh** /'makintosh/ *n, chiefly Br* a raincoat

macrobiotic /,makrəbie'otik, -kroh-/ *adj* of or being a diet consisting chiefly of whole grains or whole grains and vegetables

macrocosm /'makrə,koz(ə)m/ *n* 1 the universe 2 a complex that is a large-scale reproduction of 1 of its constituents

mad /mad/ *adj* 1 mentally disordered; insane 2 utterly foolish; senseless 3 carried away by intense anger 4 carried away by enthusiasm or desire 5 intensely excited or distraught; frantic 6 marked by intense and often chaotic hectic activity — **like mad** very hard, fast, loud, etc

madam /'madəm/ *n pl* **madams, (1) mesdames** /' may,dam/ *n* 1 a lady – without a name as a form of respectful or polite address to a woman 2 a female brothel keeper 3 a conceited pert young lady or girl

madame /'madəm;/ *n, pl* **mesdames** /'may,dam/, (2) **madames** – used as a title equivalent to *Mrs* preceding the name of a married woman not of English-speaking nationality or used without a name as a generalized term of direct address

madcap /'mad,kap/ *adj* marked by impulsiveness or recklessness – **madcap** *n*

madden /'madn/ *v* 1 to drive mad; craze 2 to exasperate, enrage

made /mayd/ *adj* 1 assembled or prepared, esp by putting together various ingredients 2 assured of success – *infml*

Madeira /mə'diərə/ *n* any of several fortified wines from Madeira

madeira cake *n* a very rich sponge cake

mademoiselle /,madmwə'zel/ *n, pl* **mademoiselles, mesdemoiselles** /,maydmwə'zel/ 1 an unmarried French-speaking girl or woman – used as a title equivalent to *Miss* for an unmarried woman not of English-speaking nationality 2 a French governess or female language teacher

made-to-'measure *adj, of a garment* made according to an individual's measurements in order to achieve a good fit

madhouse /'mad,hows/ *n* 1 a lunatic asylum 2 a place of uproar or confusion

'**madly** /-li/ *adv* to a degree suggestive of madness: e g **a** with great energy; frantically **b** without restraint; passionately

'**madness** /-nis/ *n* 1 insanity 2 extreme folly

Madonna /mə'donə/ *n the* Virgin Mary

madrigal /'madrig(ə)l/ *n* an unaccompanied and often complex song for several voices

maelstrom /'maylstrohm/ *n* 1 a powerful whirlpool 2 sthg resembling a maelstrom in turbulence and violence

maestro /'miestroh/ *n pl* **maestros, maestri** /-tri/ a master in an art; *esp* an eminent composer, conductor, or teacher of music

Mafia /'mafi-ə/ *n sing or pl in constr* 1 a secret society of Sicilian political terrorists 2 an organized secret body originating in Sicily and prevalent esp in the USA that controls illicit activities (e g vice and narcotics) 3 *often not cap* an excessively influential group or clique of a usu specified kind

magazine /,magə'zeen, '---/ *n* 1 a storeroom for arms, ammunition, or explosives 2a a usu illustrated periodical, bound in paper covers, containing miscellaneous pieces by different authors **b** a television or radio programme containing a number of usu topical items, often without a common theme 3 a supply chamber: e g 3a a holder from which cartridges can be fed into a gun chamber automatically **b** a lightproof chamber for films or plates in a camera or for film in a film projector

magenta /mə'jentə/ *n* a deep purplish red (dye)

maggot /'magət/ *n* a soft-bodied legless grub that is the larva of a 2-winged fly (e g the housefly) – **~y** *adj*

magi /'mayjie/ *pl of* **magus**

¹**magic** /'majik/ *n* 1 (rites, incantations, etc used in) the art of invoking supernatural powers to control natural forces by means of charms, spells, etc 2a an extraordinary power or influence producing results which defy explanation **b** sthg that seems to cast a spell 3 the art of producing illusions by sleight of hand – **~al** *adj*

²**magic** *adj* 1 of, being, or used in magic 2 having seemingly supernatural qualities 3 – used as a general term of approval; *infml*

³**magic** *v* **-ck-** to affect, influence, or take *away* (as if) by magic

magician /mə'jish(ə)n/ *n* 1 one skilled in magic 2 a conjurer

magisterial /,maji'stiəri·əl/ *adj* 1a of, being, or like a master or teacher **b** having masterly skill 2 of a magistrate

magistrate /'majistrayt, -strət/ *n* a civil legislative or executive official: e g **a** a principal official exercising governmental powers **b** a paid or unpaid local judicial officer who presides in a magistrates' court – **~acy** *n* – **~ature** *n*

magma /'magmə/ *n* molten rock material within the earth from which an igneous rock results by cooling

magnate /'magnayt/ *n* a person of wealth or influence

magnesium /mag'neezyəm/ *n* a silver-white metallic element that burns with an intense white light

magnet /'magnit/ *n* 1 a body (of iron, steel, etc) that has an (artificially imparted) magnetic field external to itself and attracts iron 2 sthg that attracts – **~ic** *adj* – **~ically** *adv* – **~ism** *n* – **~ize** *v*

magnetic pole *n* either of 2 small nonstationary regions in the N and S geographical polar areas of the earth towards which a magnetic needle points from any direction

magnetic tape *n* a ribbon of thin paper or plastic with a magnetizable coating for use in recording sound, video, etc signals

magnification /,magnifi'kaysh(ə)n/ *n* 1 a magnifying or being magnified 2 the apparent enlargement of an object by a microscope, telescope, etc

magnificent /mag'nifis(ə)nt/ *adj* 1 marked by stately grandeur and splendour 2a sumptuous in structure and adornment **b** strikingly beautiful or impressive 3 sublime 4 exceptionally fine or excellent – **~cence** *n* – **~ly** *adv*

magnify /'magnifie/ *v* 1 to have the power of causing objects to appear larger than they are 2 to enlarge in fact or in appearance – **~fier** *n*

'**magnifying ,glass** *n* a single optical lens for magnifying

magnitude /'magnityoohd/ *n* **1a** (great) size or extent **b** a quantity, number **2** the importance or quality of sthg

magnolia /mag'nohli·ə, -lyə/ *n* any of a genus of shrubs and trees with evergreen or deciduous leaves and usu large white, yellow, rose, or purple flowers

magnum /'magnəm/ *n* a wine bottle holding twice the usual amount (about 1.5l)

magpie /'magpie/ *n* **1** any of numerous birds of the crow family with a very long tail and black-and-white plumage **2** one who chatters noisily **3** one who collects objects in a random fashion

magus /'maygəs/ *n, pl* **magi** /-jie/ **1a** a member of a Zoroastrian hereditary priestly class in ancient Persia **b** *often cap* any of the traditionally 3 wise men from the East who paid homage to the infant Jesus **2** a magician, sorcerer

maharajah, maharaja /,mah·hah'rahjə/ *n* an Indian prince ranking above a rajah

mahogany /mə'hog(ə)ni/ *n* **1** (any of various tropical, esp W Indian, trees that yield) a durable usu reddish-brown moderately hard and heavy wood, widely used for fine cabinetwork **2** the reddish-brown colour of mahogany

maid /mayd/ *n* **1** an unmarried girl or woman; *also* a female virgin **2** a female servant

¹**maiden** /'mayd(ə)n/ *n* **1** an unmarried girl or woman **2 maiden, maiden over** an over in cricket in which no runs are credited to the batsman

²**maiden** *adj* **1a(1)** not married **a(2)** virgin **b** *of a female animal* never having borne young or been mated **c** that has not been altered from its original state **2** being the first or earliest of its kind

'**maiden,head** /-,hed/ *n* **1** virginity **2** the hymen

'**maiden ,name** *n* the surname of a woman prior to marriage

¹**mail** /mayl/ *n* **1** the postal matter that makes up 1 particular consignment **2** a conveyance that transports mail **3** a postal system

²**mail** *v* to post

³**mail** *n* **1** armour made of interlocking metal rings, chains, or sometimes plates **2** a hard enclosing covering of an animal

⁴**mail** *v* to clothe (as if) with mail

'**mail ,order** *n* an order for goods that is received and fulfilled by post

maim /maym/ *v* to mutilate, disfigure, or wound seriously; cripple

¹**main** /mayn/ *n* **1** physical strength – in *with might and main* **2** the chief or essential part – chiefly in *in the main* **3** the chief pipe, duct, or cable of a public service (e g gas, electricity, or water) – often pl with sing. meaning **4** the high sea

²**main** *adj* chief, principal **2** fully exerted **3** connected with or located near the mainmast or mainsail

'**main,frame** /-,fraym/ *n* a large computer that can run several independent programs independently or is connected to other smaller computers

'**mainland** /-lənd/ *n* the largest land area of a continent, country, etc, considered in relation to smaller offshore islands

'**main,line** /-,lien/ *v* to inject (a narcotic or other drug of abuse) into a vein – slang

'**mainly** /-li/ *adv* in most cases or for the most part; chiefly

'**main,mast** /-,mahst; *naut* -məst/ *n* (the lowest section of) a sailing vessel's principal mast

mains /maynz/ *adj* of or (suitable to be) powered by electricity from the mains

'**main,sail** /-,sayl; *naut* -s(ə)l/ *n* **1** the lowest square sail on the mainmast of a square-rigged ship **2** the principal fore-and-aft sail on the mainmast of a fore-and-aft rigged ship

'**main,spring** /-,spring/ *n* the chief motive, agent, or cause

'**main,stay** /-,stay/ *n* **1** a rope that stretches forwards from the top of a sailing ship's mainmast, usu to the foot of the foremast, and provides the chief support of the mainmast **2** a chief support

'**main,stream** /-,streem/ *n* a prevailing current or direction of activity or influence

maintain /mayn'tayn/ *v* **1** to keep in an existing state (e g of operation, repair, efficiency, or validity) **2** to sustain against opposition or danger **3** to continue or persevere in **4** to support, sustain, or provide for **5** to affirm (as if) in argument – ~**able** *adj*

maintenance /'mayntinəns/ *n* **1** maintaining or being maintained **2** (payment for) the upkeep of property or equipment **3** payments for the support of one spouse by another, esp of a woman by a man, pending or following legal separation or divorce

maisonette /,mays(ə)n'et/ *n* a part of a house, usu on two floors, let or sold separately

maize /mayz/ *n* (the ears or edible seeds of) a tall widely cultivated cereal grass bearing seeds on elongated ears

majesty /'majəsti/ *n* **1** sovereign power **2a** impressive bearing or aspect **b** greatness or splendour of quality or character – ~**tic** *adj* – ~**tically** *adv*

¹**major** /'mayjə/ *adj* **1a** greater in importance, size, rank, or degree **b** of considerable importance **2** notable or conspicuous in effect or scope **3** involving serious risk to life; serious **4** *esp of a scale* having semitones between the third and fourth and the seventh and eighth notes

²**major** *n* **1** a major musical interval, scale, key, or mode **2** a middle-ranking officer in the army

majority /mə'jorəti/ *n* **1** the (status of one who has attained the) age at which full legal rights and responsibilities are acquired **2** a number greater than half of a total **3** the greatest in number of 2 or more groups constituting a whole; *specif* (the excess of votes over its rival obtained by) a group having sufficient votes to obtain control **4** the military office, rank, or commission of a major

¹**make** /mayk/ *v* **made** /mayd/ **1a** to create or produce (for someone) by work or action **b** to cause; bring about **2** to formulate in the mind **3** to put together from ingredients or components – often + *up* **4** to compute or estimate to be **5a** to assemble and set alight the materials for (a fire) **b** to renew or straighten the bedclothes on (a bed) **6a** to cause to be or become **b** to cause (sthg) to appear or seem to; represent as **c(1)** to change, transform **c(2)** to produce as an end product **7a** to enact, establish **b** to draft or produce a version of **8** to perform; carry out **9** to put forward for acceptance **10** to cause to act in a specified way; compel **11a** to amount to; count as **b** to combine to form **12** to be capable of becoming or of serving as **13** to reach, attain – often + *it* **14** to gain (e g money) by working, trading, dealing, etc **15a** to act so as to acquire **b** to score (points, runs, etc) in a game or sport — **make a meal of** *Br* to make more of than is necessary or tactful — **make an exhibition of oneself *** to behave foolishly in public — **make believe** to pretend, feign — **make bold** to venture, dare — **make do** to get along or manage with the means at hand — **make ends meet** to live within one's income — **make eyes to** ogle — + *at* — **make fast** to tie or attach firmly — **make for** to be conducive to — **make free with** to take excessive or disrespectful liberties with — **make fun of** to make an object of amusement or ridicule — **make head or tail of** to understand in the least — **make it 1** to be successful — *infml* **2** to achieve sexual intercourse — *slang* — **make love 1** to woo, court; *also* to pet, neck **2** to engage in sexual intercourse — **make no bones** to have no hesitation or shame — **make of 1** to attribute a specified degree of significance to **2** to understand by; conclude as to the meaning of — **make oneself scarce** to hide or avoid sby or sthg unobtrusively — **make public** to disclose — **make tracks** to leave — *infml* — **make water** to urinate — *euph* — **make way** to give room

²**make** *n* **1a** the manner or style in which sthg is constructed **b** a place or origin of manufacture; a brand **2** the physical, mental, or moral constitution of a person — **on the make 1** rising or attempting to rise to a higher social or financial status **2** *NAm* in search of a sexual partner or sexual adventure

'**make-be,lieve** *n or adj* (sthg) imaginary or pretended

make off *v* to leave in haste — **make off with** to take away; steal

make out *v* **1** to complete (e g a printed form or document) by writing information in appropriate spaces **2** to find or grasp the meaning of **3** to claim or pretend to be true **4** to identify (e g by sight or hearing) with difficulty or effort

make over *v* to transfer the title of (property)

'**make,shift** /-,shift/ *adj or n* (being) a crude and temporary expedient

'**make-,up** *n* **1** the way in which the parts of sthg are put together **2a** cosmetics (e g lipstick and mascara) applied, esp to the face, to give colour or emphasis **b** materials (e g wigs and cosmetics) used for special costuming (e g for a play)

make up *v* **1** to invent (e g a story), esp in order to deceive **2** to arrange typeset matter into (columns or pages) for printing **3** to wrap or fasten up **4** to become reconciled; *also* to attempt to ingratiate **5** to compensate *for* **6** to put on costumes or make-up (e g for a play)

making /'mayking/ *n* **1** a process or means of advancement or success **2** the essential qualities for becoming – often pl with sing. meaning — **in the making** in the process of becoming, forming, or developing

maladjusted /,mala'justid/ *adj* poorly or inadequately adjusted, specif to one's social environment and conditions of life — **-justment** *n*

maladministration /,maladmini'straysh(ə)n/ *n* incompetent or corrupt administration, esp in public office

maladroit /,mala'droyt/ *adj* clumsy, inept – **~ly** *adv* – **~ness** *n*

malady /'maladi/ *n* a disease or disorder

malaise /ma'lez, -'layz/ *n* **1** an indeterminate feeling of debility or lack of health, often accompanying the start of an illness **2** a vague sense of mental or moral unease

malapropism /'malapro,piz(ə)m/ *n* (an instance of) an incongruous misapplication of a word (e g in 'a table with contemptible legs')

malaria /mə'leari-ə/ *n* a disease transmitted by the bite of mosquitoes, and characterized by periodic attacks of chills and fever – **~l** *adj*

'**malcontent** /,malkan'tent/ *n* a discontented person; *esp* sby violently opposed to a government or regime

²**malcontent, malcontented** *adj* dissatisfied with the existing state of affairs

'**male** /mayl/ *adj* **1a(1)** of or being the sex that produces sperm or spermatozoa by which the eggs of a female are made fertile **a(2)** *of a plant or flower* having stamens but no ovaries **b(1)** (characteristic) of the male sex **b(2)** made up of male individuals **2** designed for fitting into a corresponding hollow part

²**male** *n* a male person, animal, or plant

malediction /,mali'diksh(ə)n/ *n* a curse – *fml*

malefactor /'mali,fakta/ *n* **1** a criminal; *esp* a felon **2** one who does evil – *fml*

malevolent /mə'levələnt/ *adj* having, showing, or arising from an often intense desire to do harm – **-lence** *n* – **-ly** *adv*

mal'function /-'fungksh(ə)n/ *v* to fail to operate in the normal manner

malice /'malis/ *n* conscious desire to harm; *esp* a premeditated desire to commit a crime – **-cious** *adj*

¹**malign** /mə'lien/ *adj* 1 harmful in nature, influence, or effect 2 bearing or showing (vicious) ill will or hostility – **-ity** *n*

²**malign** *v* to utter injuriously (false) reports about; speak ill of

malignant /mə'lignənt/ *adj* 1 harmful in nature, influence, or effect 2 *of a disease* very severe or deadly; *specif, of a tumour* tending to cause death – **-nancy** *n* – **-ly** *adv*

malinger /mə'ling·gə/ *v* to pretend illness or incapacity so as to avoid duty or work – **~er** *n*

mall /mawl, mal/ *n* 1 a public promenade, often bordered by trees 2 *NAm* a shopping precinct, usu with associated parking space

mallard /'malahd, -ləd/ *n pl* **mallards**, *esp collectively* **mallard** a common large wild duck that is the ancestor of the domestic ducks

malleable /'mali·əbl/ *adj* 1 *esp of metals* capable of being beaten or rolled into a desired shape 2 easily shaped by outside forces or influences – **-bility** *n*

mallet /'malit/ *n* 1 a hammer with a usu large head of wood, plastic, etc 2 an implement with a large usu cylindrical wooden head for striking the ball in croquet, polo, etc 3 a light hammer with a small rounded or spherical usu padded head used in playing certain musical instruments (e g a vibraphone)

mallow /'maloh/ *n* any of various related plants with usu deeply cut lobed leaves and showy flowers

malnutrition /,malnyooh'trish(ə)n/ *n* faulty or inadequate nutrition

mal'odorous /-'ohd(ə)rəs/ *adj* smelling bad – *fml*

malpractice /mal'praktis/ *n* failure to exercise due professional skill or care

malt /mawlt/ *n* 1 grain softened in water, allowed to germinate, then roasted and used esp in brewing and distilling 2 unblended malt whisky produced in a particular area

Maltese /mawl'teez/ *n, pl* **Maltese** (the language of) a native or inhabitant of Malta

Maltese 'cross *n* a cross consisting of 4 equal arms that widen out from the centre and have their outer ends indented by a V

maltreat /,mal'treet/ *v* to treat cruelly or roughly – **~ment** *n*

mama, mamma /mə'mah/ *n* mummy – used informally and by children

mamba /'mambə/ *n* any of several (tropical) African venomous snakes related to the cobras but with no hood

mammal /'maml/ *n* any of a class of higher vertebrates comprising humans and all other animals that have mammary glands and nourish their young with milk

mammary /'maməri/ *adj* of, lying near, or affecting the breasts

¹**mammoth** /'maməth/ *n* any of numerous extinct large hairy elephants

²**mammoth** *adj* of very great size

¹**man** /man/ *n, pl* **men** /men/ **1a**(1) a human being; *esp* an adult male as distinguished from a woman or child **a**(2) a husband – esp in *man and wife* **b** the human race **c** any ancestor of modern man **d** one possessing the qualities associated with manhood (e g courage and strength) **e** a fellow, chap – used interjectionally **2a** *pl* the members of (the ranks of) a military force **b** *pl* the working force as distinguished from the employer and usu the management **3** any of the pieces moved by each player in chess, draughts, etc – **~like** *adj* – **~ly** *adj* – **~liness** *n* — **to a man** without exception

²**man** *v* **-nn-** 1 to supply with the men or men necessary 2 to take up station by (e g in *'man the pumps!')*

manacle /'manəkl/ *n* 1 a shackle or handcuff 2 a restraint *USE* usu pl – **manacle** *v*

manage /'manij/ *v* **1a** to make and keep submissive **b** to use (e g money) economically 2 to succeed in handling (e g a difficult situation or person) 3 to succeed in accomplishing 4 to conduct the running of (esp a business); *also* to have charge of (e g a sports team or athlete)

management /-mənt/ *n* 1 the act or art of managing 2 *sing or pl in constr* the collective body of those who manage or direct an enterprise

manager /'manijə/, *fem* **manageress** /-jə,res/ *n* 1 one who conducts business affairs 2 sby who directs a sports team, player, entertainer, etc

man-at-'arms *n, pl* **men-at-arms** a (heavily armed and usu mounted) soldier

mandarin /'mandərin, ,--'-/ *n* **1a** a public official in the Chinese Empire **b** a person of position and influence, esp in literary or bureaucratic circles; *esp* an elder and often reactionary member of such a circle 2 *cap* the chief dialect of Chinese that has a standard variety spoken in the Peking area 3 **mandarin, mandarin orange** (a small spiny Chinese orange tree that bears) a yellow to reddish orange fruit

mandate /'mandayt, -dət/ *n* 1 an authorization to act on the behalf of another; *specif* the political authority given by electors to parliament 2 an order granted by the League of Nations to a member nation for the establishment of a responsible government over a conquered territory

mandatory /'mandət(ə)ri/ *adj* **1** containing or constituting a command **2** compulsory, obligatory

mandible /'mandibl/ *n* **1a** a lower jaw together with its surrounding soft parts **b** the upper or lower part of a bird's bill **2** any of various mouth parts in insects or other invertebrates for holding or biting food

mandolin *also* mandoline /,mandə'lin/ *n* a musical instrument of the lute family with a fretted neck

mandrill /'mandril/ *n* a large gregarious baboon found in W Africa, the male of which has red and blue striped cheeks

mane /mayn/ *n* **1** long thick hair growing about the neck of a horse, male lion, etc **2** long thick hair on a person's head

'man-,eater *n* a person or animal that eats human flesh – man-eating *adj*

manful /'manf(ə)l/ *adj* having courage and resolution – ~ly *adv*

manganese /,mang-gə'neez/ *n* a hard greyish white metallic element

mange /manj, maynj/ *n* any of various contagious skin diseases affecting domestic animals or sometimes human beings, marked by inflammation and loss of hair and caused by a minute parasitic mite

mangel-wurzel /'mang-gl ,wuhzl/, mangel *n* a large yellow to orange type of beet grown as food for livestock

manger /'maynjə/ *n* a trough or open box in a stable for holding feed

¹mangle /'mang-gl/ *v* **1** to hack or crush (as if) by repeated blows **2** to spoil by poor work, errors, etc

²mangle *v* or *n* (to pass through) a machine with rollers for squeezing water from and pressing laundry

mango /'mang-goh/ *n, pl* mangoes, mangos (a tropical evergreen tree that bears) a yellowish red fruit with a firm skin, large stone, and juicy edible slightly acid pulp

mangrove /'mang,grohv/ *n* any of a genus of tropical maritime trees or shrubs with prop roots that form dense masses

mangy /'manji, 'maynji/ *adj* **1** suffering or resulting from mange **2** having many worn or bare spots – ~gily *adv*

manhandle /'man'handl, '-,--/ *v* **1** to move or manage by human force **2** to handle roughly

manhole /'man,hohl/ *n* a covered opening through which a person may go, esp to gain access to an underground or enclosed structure (e g a sewer)

'manhood /-hood/ *n* **1** manly qualities **2** the condition of being an adult male as distinguished from a child or female

'man-,hour *n* a unit of 1 hour's work by 1 person, used esp as a basis for cost accounting and wage calculation

mania /'maynyə/ *n* **1** abnormal excitement and euphoria marked by mental and physical hyperactivity and disorganization of behaviour **2** excessive or unreasonable enthusiasm – often in combination

maniac /'mayniak/ *n* one who is or acts as if (violently) insane; a lunatic – ~al *adj* – ~ally *adv*

manic /'manik/ *adj* affected by, relating to, or resembling mania

,manic-de'pressive *adj* of or affected by a mental disorder characterized by alternating mania and (extreme) depression

¹manicure /'manikyooə/ *n* (a) treatment for the care of the hands and fingernails

²manicure *v* to trim closely and evenly

¹manifest /'manifest/ *adj* readily perceived by the senses (e g sight) or mind; obvious – ~ly *adv*

²manifest *v* **1** to make evident by showing **2** *of a spirit, ghost, etc* to appear in visible form

³manifest *n* a list of passengers or an invoice of cargo, esp for a ship

manifestation /,manife'staysh(ə)n/ *n* a sign (e g materialization) of the presence of a spirit

manifesto /,mani'festoh/ *n, pl* manifestos, manifestoes a public declaration of intentions, esp by a political party before an election

¹manifold /'manifohld/ *adj* many and varied

²manifold *n* **1** a whole that unites or consists of many diverse elements **2** a hollow fitting (e g connecting the cylinders of an internal combustion engine with the exhaust pipe) with several outlets or inlets for connecting 1 pipe with several other pipes

manikin, mannikin /'manikin/ *n* **1** a mannequin **2** a little man

manipulate /mə'nipyoolayt/ *v* **1** to handle or operate, esp skilfully **2a** to manage or use skilfully **b** to control or influence by artful, unfair, or insidious means, esp to one's own advantage **3** to examine and treat (a fracture, sprain, etc) by moving bones into the proper position manually – -lative *adj* – -lation *n*

mankind /man'kiend/ *n sing but sing or pl in constr* the human race

,man-'made *adj* made or produced by human beings rather than by nature; *also* synthetic

manna /'manə/ *n* **1** food miraculously supplied to the Israelites in their journey through the wilderness **2** a sudden source of benefit

manned /mand/ *adj* equipped or carrying men

mannequin /'manikin/ *n* **1** an artist's, tailor's, or dressmaker's model of the human figure; *also* such a model used esp for displaying clothes **2** a woman who models clothing

manner /'manə/ n 1 a kind, sort; *also* sorts 2a the mode or method in which sthg is done or happens b a method of artistic execution; a style 3 *pl* social behaviour evaluated as to politeness; *esp* conduct indicating good background 4 characteristic or distinctive bearing, air, or deportment

mannered /'manəd/ *adj* 1 having manners of a specified kind – usu in combination 2 having an artificial or stilted character

mannerism /'manə,riz(ə)m/ n 1 exaggerated or affected adherence to a particular style in art or literature 2 a characteristic (unconscious) gesture or trait; an idiosyncrasy

mannish /'manish/ *adj* resembling, befitting, or typical of a man rather than a woman – ~ly *adv* – ~ness n

¹**manoeuvre**, *NAm chiefly* **maneuver** /mə'noohvə/ n 1a a military or naval movement b a (large-scale) training exercise for the armed forces 2 an intended and controlled deviation from a straight and level flight path in the operation of an aircraft 3 a skilful or dexterous movement 4 an adroit and clever management of affairs, often using deception

²**manoeuvre**, *NAm chiefly* **maneuver** v 1 to perform a military or naval manoeuvre (to secure an advantage) 2 to perform a manoeuvre 3 to cause (e g troops) to execute manoeuvres 4 to manipulate with adroitness – **-vrer** n

man-of-'war n, *pl* **men-of-war** /men/ a warship (of the days of sail)

manor /'manə/ n 1 a landed estate 2a a medieval estate under a lord who held a variety of rights over land and tenants, including the right to hold court b **manor, manor house** the house of the lord of a manor 3 a district of police administration – slang – ~**ial** *adj*

'**man,power** /-,powə/ n the total supply of people available for work or service

manse /mans/ n the residence of an esp Presbyterian or Baptist clergyman

manservant /'man,suhv(ə)nt/ n *pl* **manservants** a male servant, esp a valet

mansion /'mansh(ə)n/ n 1a the house of the lord of a manor b a large imposing residence 2 a separate apartment in a large structure

manslaughter /'man,slawtə/ n the unlawful killing of sby without malicious intent

mantelpiece /'mantl,pees/, **mantel** n an ornamental structure round a fireplace

mantle /'mantl/ n 1 a loose sleeveless garment worn over other clothes; a cloak 2 sthg that covers, envelops, or conceals 3 a lacelike sheath of some material that gives light by becoming white-hot when placed over a flame 4 the part of the earth or a similar planet that lies between the crust and central core

man-to-'man *adj* 1 characterized by frankness and honesty 2 of or being a defensive system in soccer, basketball, etc in which each player marks 1 specific opponent

¹**manual** /'manyooəl/ *adj* 1 of or involving the hands 2 requiring or using physical skill and energy 3 worked or done by hand and not by machine or automatically – ~ly *adv*

²**manual** n 1 a book of instructions; a handbook 2 a keyboard for the hands; *specif* any of the several keyboards of an organ that control separate divisions of the instrument

¹**manufacture** /,manyoo'fakchə/ n 1 the esp large-scale making of wares by hand or by machinery 2 the act or process of producing sthg

²**manufacture** v 1 to make (materials) into a product suitable for use 2 to make (wares) from raw materials by hand or by machinery, esp on a large scale 3 to invent, fabricate

manure /mə'nyooə/ n material that fertilizes land; *esp* the faeces of domestic animals

manuscript /'manyoo,skript/ n or *adj* (a composition or document) written by hand or typed as distinguished from a printed copy

¹**Manx** /mangks/ *adj* (characteristic) of the Isle of Man

²**Manx** n *pl in constr* the people of the Isle of Man

,**Manx 'cat** n (any of) a breed of short-haired domestic cats some of which have no external tail

¹**many** /'meni/ *adj more* /maw/; *most* /mohst/ 1 consisting of or amounting to a large but unspecified number 2 being one of a large number (e g *many* a man) — **as many** the same in number

²**many** *pron pl in constr* a large number of people or things

³**many** n *pl in constr* 1 a large but indefinite number 2 *the* great majority

⁴**many** *adv* to a considerable degree or amount; far – with plurals

,**many-'sided** *adj* 1 having many sides or aspects 2 having many interests or aptitudes – ~**ness** n

Maori /'mowri, 'mahri/ n 1 a member of the indigenous people of New Zealand 2 the Austronesian language of the Maori

¹**map** /map/ n 1 a representation, usu on a flat surface, of (part of) the earth's surface, the celestial sphere, etc 2 sthg that represents with a clarity suggestive of a map

²**map** v **-pp-** 1 to make a map of 2 to survey in order to make a map 3 to plan in detail – often + *out*

maple /'maypl/ n (the hard light-coloured close-grained wood, used esp for furniture, of) any of a genus of widely planted trees or shrubs

mar /mah/ v **-rr-** to detract from the perfection or wholeness of

marathon /'marəth(ə)n/ n 1 a long-distance race; *specif* a foot race of 26mi 385yd (about 42.2km) that is contested on an open course in major athletics championships **2a** an endurance contest **b** an event or activity characterized by great length or concentrated effort

maraud /mə'rawd/ *v* to roam about in search of plunder

¹**marble** /'mahbl/ *n* **1a** (more or less) crystallized limestone that can be highly polished and is used esp in building and sculpture **b** a sculpture or carving made of marble **2** a little ball made of a hard substance, esp glass, and used in children's games **3** *pl* elements of common sense; *esp* sanity – infml

²**marble** *v* **marbling** /'mahbl·ing, 'mahbling/ to give a veined or mottled appearance to (e g the edges of a book)

'**marbled** *adj* **1** made of or veneered with marble **2** *of meat* marked by a mixture of fat and lean

¹**march** /mahch/ *n, often cap* a border region; *esp* a tract of land between 2 countries whose ownership is disputed – usu pl

²**march** *v* **1** to move along steadily, usu in step with others **2a** to move in a direct purposeful manner **b** to make steady progress **3** to cause to march **4** to cover by marching – ~ **er** *n*

³**march** *n* **1a** the action of marching **b** the distance covered within a specified period of time by marching **c** a regular measured stride or rhythmic step used in marching **d** steady forward movement **2** a musical composition with a strongly accentuated beat and is designed or suitable to accompany marching

March *n* the 3rd month of the Gregorian calendar

'**marching orders** /'mahching/ *n pl* notice of dismissal

marchioness /,mahshə'nes, 'mahshənis/ *n* **1** the wife or widow of a marquis **2** a woman having in her own right the rank of a marquis

Mardi Gras /,mahdi 'grah/ *n* (a carnival period culminating on) Shrove Tuesday often observed (e g in New Orleans) with parades and festivities

mare /meə/ *n* a female equine animal, esp when fully mature or of breeding age; *esp* a female horse

margarine /,mahjə'reen; *also* ,mahgə'reen, '---/ *n* a substitute for butter made usu from vegetable oils churned with ripened skimmed milk to a smooth emulsion

¹**margin** /'mahjin/ *n* **1** the part of a page outside the main body of printed or written text **2** the outside limit and adjoining surface of sthg **3a** a spare amount or measure or degree allowed (e g in case of error) **b**(1) a bare minimum below which or an extreme limit beyond which sthg becomes impossible or is no longer desirable **b**(2) the limit below which economic activity cannot be continued under normal conditions **4** the difference between net sales and the cost of merchandise sold **5** measure or degree of difference

²**margin** *v* to provide with a border

marginal /'mahjinl/ *adj* **1** written or printed in the margin **2** of or situated at a margin or border **3** close to the lower limit of qualification, acceptability, or function **4** of or providing a nominal profit margin **5** being a constituency where the Member of Parliament was elected with only a small majority

marigold /'marigohld/ *n* any of a genus of composite plants with showy yellow or red flower heads

marijuana, marihuana /,marə'(h)wahnə, -yoo'ahnə/ *n* a usu mild form of cannabis

marina /mə'reenə/ *n* a dock or basin providing secure moorings for motorboats, yachts, etc

marinade /,mari'nayd/ *v or n* (to soak in) a blend of oil, wine or vinegar, herbs, and spices in which meat, fish, etc is soaked, esp to enrich its flavour

marinate /'marinayt/ *v* to marinade

¹**marine** /mə'reen/ *adj* **1** of (living) in the sea **2** of or used in the navigation or commerce of the sea

²**marine** *n* **1** seagoing ships (of a specified nationality or class) **2a** any of a class of soldiers serving on shipboard or in close association with a naval force **b** a soldier who serves on a naval ship or in the navy

mariner /'marinə/ *n* a seaman, sailor

marionette /,mari·ə'net/ *n* a small-scale usu wooden figure with jointed limbs that is moved from above by attached strings or wires

marital /'maritl/ *adj* of marriage – ~ **ly** *adv*

maritime /'mari,tiem/ *adj* **1** marine **2** of or bordering on the sea

marjoram /'mahjəram, -ram/ *n* any of various plants of the mint family used as herbs

¹**mark** /mahk/ *n* **1a** sthg (e g a line, notch, or fixed object) designed to record position **b** a target **c** the starting line or position in a track event **d** a goal or desired object **2a**(1) a sign or token **a**(2) an impression on the surface of sthg; *esp* a scratch, stain, etc that spoils the appearance of a surface **a**(3) a distinguishing characteristic **b** a symbol used for identification or indication of ownership **c** a written or printed symbol **d** *cap* – used with a numeral to designate a particular model of a weapon or machine **e** a point or level (reached) **3** an assessment of (educational) merits **4** an object of attack; *specif* a victim of a swindle – infml

²**mark** *v* **1a**(1) to fix or trace *out* the limits of **a**(2) to plot the course of **b** to set apart (as if) by a line or boundary – usu + *off* **2a**(1) to designate, identify or indicate (as if) by a mark **a**(2) to make or leave a mark on **a**(3) to add appropriate symbols, characters, or other marks to or on – usu + *up* **b**(1) to register, record **b**(2) to evaluate by marks **c**(1) to characterize, distinguish **c**(2) to be the occasion of (sthg notable); to indicate as a particular time **3** to take notice of **4** *Br* to stay close to (an opposing player) in hockey, soccer, etc so as to hinder the getting or play of the ball **5** to become or make

sthg stained, scratched, etc **6** to evaluate sthg by marks – ~ **er** *n* – **mark time 1** to keep the time of a marching step by moving the feet alternately without advancing **2** to function listlessly or unproductively while waiting to progress or advance

³**mark** *n often cap* (a note or coin representing) the basic money unit of either East or West Germany

'**mark,down** /-ˌdown/ *n* (the amount of) a reduction in price

marked /mahkt/ *adj* **1a** having natural marks (of a specified type) **b** made identifiable by marking **2** having a distinctive or emphasized character **3** being an object of attack, suspicion, or vengeance – ~ **ly** *adv*

¹**market** /'mahkit/ *n* **1a** a meeting together of people for the purpose of trade, by private purchase and sale **b** an open space, building, etc where a market (e g for trading in provisions or livestock) is held **2a** (a geographical area or section of the community in which there is) demand for commodities **b** commercial activity; extent of trading **c** an opportunity for selling **d** the area of economic activity in which the supply and demand affect prices — **in the market** interested in buying — **on the market** available for purchase

²**market** *v* **1** to deal in a market **2** to sell – ~ **able** *adj* – ~ **ability** *n* – ~ **er**, ~ **eer** *n*

,**market 'garden** *n* a plot in which vegetables are grown for market – ~ **er** *n* – ~ **ing** *n*

marketing /'mahkiting/ *n* the skills and functions, including packaging, promotion, and distribution, involved in selling goods

'**market,place** /-ˌplays/ *n* **1** an open place in a town where markets are held **2** somewhere where there is a demand for commodities

,**market 'research** *n* research (e g the collection and analysis of information about consumer preferences) dealing with the patterns or state of demand (for a particular product) in a market

marking /'mahking/ *n* **1** (the giving of) a mark or marks **2** arrangement, pattern, or disposition of marks

marksman /'mahksmən/, *fem* **marks,woman** *n pl* **marksmen**, *fem* **markswomen** a person skilled in hitting a mark or target – ~ **ship** *n*

'**mark,up** /-ˌup/ *n* (the amount of) an increase in price

'**marline,spike, marlinspike** /-ˌspiek/ *n* a pointed steel tool used to separate strands of rope or wire

¹**marmalade** /'mahməˌlayd/ *n* a clear sweetened preserve made from oranges, lemons, etc and usu containing pieces of fruit peel

²**marmalade** *adj, esp of cats* brownish orange

marmoreal /mah'mawri-əl/, *also* **marmorean** /-ri-ən/ *adj* of or like marble or a marble statue – chiefly poetic

marmoset /'mahmə,zet/ *n* any of numerous soft-furred S and Central American monkeys

¹**maroon** /mə'roohn/ *v* **1** to abandon on a desolate island or coast **2** to isolate in a helpless state

²**maroon** *n* **1** a dark brownish red colour **2** an explosive rocket used esp as a distress signal

marquee /mah'kee/ *n* a large tent (e g for an outdoor party or exhibition)

marquetry *also* **marqueterie** /'mahkətri/ *n* decorative work of pieces of wood, ivory, etc inlaid in a wood veneer that is then applied to a surface (e g of a piece of furniture)

marquis, marquess /'mahkwis/ *n* a member of the British peerage ranking below a duke and above an earl

marriage /'marij/ *n* **1a** the state of being or mutual relation of husband and wife **b** the institution whereby a man and a woman are joined in a special kind of social and legal dependence **2** an act or the rite of marrying; *esp* the wedding ceremony **3** an intimate or close union

married /'marid/ *adj* **1a** joined in marriage **b** of married people **2** united, joined

marrow /'maroh/ *n* **1a** a soft tissue that fills the cavities and porous part of most bones and contains many blood vessels **b** the substance of the spinal cord **2** the inmost, best, or essential part; the core **3** *chiefly Br* a vegetable marrow

marry /'mari/ *v* **1a** to give in marriage **b** to take as spouse **c** to perform the ceremony of marriage for **d** to obtain by marriage **2** to bring together closely, harmoniously, and usu permanently **3a** to take a spouse **b** to become husband and wife — **marry into** to become a member of or obtain by marriage

Mars /mahz/ *n* the planet 4th in order from the sun and conspicuous for its red colour

marsh /mahsh/ *n* (an area of) soft wet land usu covered with sedges, rushes, etc

¹**marshal** /'mahsh(ə)l/ *n* **1a** one who arranges and directs a ceremony **b** one who arranges the procedure at races **2a** a field marshal **b** an officer of the highest military rank **3** a chief officer in the USA responsible for court processes in a district

²**marshal** *v* **-ll-** (*NAm* **-l-, -ll-**), /'mahshl·ing/ **1** to place in proper rank or position **2** to bring together and order in an effective way **3** to lead ceremoniously or solicitously; usher

'**marshalling ,yard** *n, chiefly Br* a place where railway vehicles are shunted and assembled into trains

'**marsh ,gas** *n* methane

marshmallow /,mahsh'maloh/ *n* **1** a pink-flowered Eurasian marsh plant of the mallow family **2** a light spongy confection made from the root of the marshmallow or from sugar, albumen, and gelatin

marsupial /mah'syoohpi-əl, -'sooh-/ n any of an order of lower mammals including the kangaroos, wombats, and opossums that have a pouch on the abdomen of the female for carrying young, and do not develop a placenta

mart /maht/ n a place of trade (e g an auction room or market)

marten /'mahtin/ n pl **martens**, esp collectively **marten** any of several slender-bodied flesh-eating tree-dwelling mammals larger than the related weasels

martial /'mahsh(ə)l/ adj of or suited to war or a warrior; also warlike

martial 'law n the law administered by military forces in occupied territory or in an emergency

Martian /'mahsh(ə)n/ adj of or coming from the planet Mars

martin /'mahtin/ n any of various birds of the swallow family

martinet /,mahti'net/ n a strict disciplinarian

martini /mah'teeni/ n a cocktail made of gin and dry vermouth

¹**martyr** /'mahtə/ n 1 one who is put to death for adherence to a cause, esp a religion 2 a victim, esp of constant (self-inflicted) suffering

²**martyr** v 1 to put to death as a martyr 2 to inflict agonizing pain on

¹**marvel** /'mahv(ə)l/ n one who or that which is marvellous

²**marvel** v -ll- (NAm -l-, -ll-), /'mahvl·ing/ to become filled with surprise, wonder, or amazed curiosity

marvellous, NAm chiefly **marvelous** /'mahvl·əs/ adj 1 causing wonder 2 of the highest kind or quality – ~ly adv

Marxism /'mahksiz(ə)m/ n the political and economic principles and policies advocated by Karl Marx, that stress the importance of human labour in determining economic value, the struggle between classes as an instrument of social change, and dictatorship of the proletariat – **-ist** n, adj

marzipan /'mahzi,pan/ n a paste made from ground almonds, sugar, and egg whites, used for coating cakes or shaped into small sweets

mascara /ma'skahrə/ n a cosmetic for colouring, esp darkening, the eyelashes

mascot /'maskot, -kat/ n a person, animal, or object adopted as a (good luck) symbol

masculine /'maskyoolin/ adj 1a male b having qualities appropriate to a man 2 of, belonging to, or being the gender that normally includes most words or grammatical forms referring to males 3 having or occurring in a stressed final syllable

¹**mash** /mash/ n 1 crushed malt or grain meal steeped and stirred in hot water to ferment 2 a mixture of bran or similar feeds and hot water for livestock 3 a soft pulpy mass 4 Br mashed potatoes – infml

²**mash** v to crush, pound, etc to a soft pulpy state

¹**mask** /mahsk/ n 1a a (partial) cover for the face used for disguise or protection **b(1)** a figure of a head worn on the stage in ancient times to identify the character **b(2)** a grotesque false face worn at carnivals or in rituals c a copy of a face made by sculpting or by means of a mould 2a sthg that disguises or conceals; esp a pretence, facade b a translucent or opaque screen to cover part of the sensitive surface in taking or printing a photograph 3 a device covering the mouth and nose used 3a to promote breathing (e g by connection to an oxygen supply) b to remove noxious gas from air c to prevent breathing out of infective material (e g during surgery) 4 the head or face of a fox, dog, etc – ~ed adj

²**mask** v 1 to provide, cover, or conceal (as if) with a mask: e g 1a to make indistinct or imperceptible b to cover up 2 to cover for protection 3 to modify the shape of (e g a photograph) by means of a mask

masochism /'masə,kiz(ə)m/ n 1 a sexual perversion in which pleasure is experienced from being physically or mentally abused 2 pleasure from sthg tiresome or painful – not used technically – **-chist** n – **-chistic** adj

mason /'mays(ə)n/ n 1 a skilled worker with stone 2 cap a freemason – ~ic adj

masonry /'mays(ə)nri/n 1 work done with or sthg constructed of stone; also a brick construction 2 cap freemasonry

masque /mahsk/ n 1 a masquerade 2 a short allegorical dramatic entertainment of the 16th and 17th c performed by masked actors

¹**masquerade** /,maskə'rayd/ n a social gathering of people wearing masks and often fantastic costumes

²**masquerade** v 1 to disguise oneself; also to wear a disguise 2 to assume the appearance of sthg that one is not – usu + as – **-rader** n

¹**mass** /mas/ n 1 cap the liturgy or a celebration of the Eucharist, esp in Roman Catholic and Anglo-Catholic churches 2 a musical setting of the Mass

²**mass** n 1a a quantity of matter or the form of matter that holds together in 1 body **b(1)** an (unbroken) expanse **b(2)** the principal part or main body c the property of a body that is a measure of its inertia, causes it to have weight in a gravitational field, and is commonly taken as a measure of the amount of material it contains 2 a large quantity, amount, or number – often pl with sing. meaning 3 pl the body of ordinary people as contrasted with the élite

³**mass** v to assemble in or collect into a mass

⁴**mass** adj 1a of, designed for, or consisting of the mass of the people b participated in by or affecting a large number of individuals c large scale 2 viewed as a whole; total

¹**massacre** /'masəkə/ v 1 to kill (as if) in a massacre 2 to defeat severely – infml

²**massacre** n 1 the ruthless and indiscriminate killing of large numbers 2 complete defeat or destruction

massage /'masahj, -sahzh/ n (an act of) kneading, rubbing, etc of the body in order to relieve aches, tone muscles, give relaxation, etc – **massage** v

masseur /ma'suh/, fem **masseuse** /mas'suhz/ n one who practises massage and physiotherapy

massive /'masiv/ adj 1 large, solid, or heavy b impressively large or ponderous 2 large or impressive in scope or degree – **~ly** adv – **~ness** n

,**mass 'media** n pl broadcasting, newspapers, and other means of communication designed to reach large numbers of people

,**mass-pro'duce** /prə'dyoohs/ v to produce (goods) in large quantities by standardized mechanical processes – **-duction** n

¹**mast** /mahst/ n 1 a tall pole or structure rising from the keel or deck of a ship, esp for carrying sails 2 a vertical pole or lattice supporting a radio or television aerial — **before the mast** as an ordinary sailor, not an officer

²**mast** n beechnuts, acorns, etc accumulated on the forest floor and often serving as food for animals (e g pigs)

mastectomy /ma'stektəmi/ n amputation of a breast

¹**master** /'mahstə/ n 1a(1) a male teacher a(2) a person holding an academic degree higher than a bachelor's but lower than a doctor's b a workman qualified to teach apprentices c an artist, performer, player, etc of consummate skill 2a one having control or authority over another b one who or that which conquers or masters c a person qualified to command a merchant ship d an owner, esp of a slave or animal e an employer 3 cap a youth or boy too young to be called mister – used as a title 4 a presiding officer in an institution or society (e g a Masonic lodge) or at a function 5 an original from which copies (e g of film or gramophone records) can be made – **~y** n

²**master** v 1 to become master of; overcome 2a to become skilled or proficient in the use of b to gain a thorough understanding of

³**master** adj 1 having chief authority; controlling 2 principal, main

'**masterful** /-f(ə)l/ adj 1 inclined to take control and dominate 2 having or showing the technical, artistic, or intellectual skill of a master – **~ly** adv

'**masterly** /-li/ adj showing superior knowledge or skill – **-liness** n

'**master,mind** /-,miend/ v to be the intellectual force behind (a project) – **mastermind** n

,**master of 'ceremonies,** fem ,**mistress of 'ceremonies** /'mistris/ n 1 one who determines the procedure to be observed on a state or public occasion 2 one who acts as host, esp by introducing speakers, performers, etc, at an event

'**master,piece** /-,pees/ n a work done with extraordinary skill; esp the supreme creation of a type, period, or person

'**master,stroke** /-,strohk/ n a masterly performance or move

masthead /'mahst,hed/ n 1 the top of a mast 2 the name of a newspaper displayed on the top of the first page

masticate /'mastikayt/ v to chew – **-cation** n

mastiff /'mastif/ n any of a breed of very large powerful deep-chested smooth-coated dogs used chiefly as guard dogs

mastitis /ma'stietəs/ n inflammation of the breast or udder, usu caused by infection

mastoid /'mastoyd/ adj or n (of, near, or being) a somewhat conical part of the temporal bone lying behind the ear

¹**mat** /mat/ n 1a a piece of coarse usu woven, felted, or plaited fabric (e g of rushes or rope) used esp as a floor covering b a doormat c an often decorative piece of material used to protect a surface from heat, moisture, etc used by an object placed on it 2 sthg made up of many intertwined or tangled strands

²**mat** v -tt- to become tangled or intertwined

³**mat** v, adj, or n -tt- (to) matt

matador /'matədaw/ n one who has the principal role and who kills the bull in a bullfight

¹**match** /mach/ n 1a one who or that which is equal to or able to contend with another b a person or thing exactly like another 2 two people, animals, or things that go well together 3 a contest between 2 or more teams or individuals 4a a marriage union b a prospective partner in marriage

²**match** v 1 to be a counterpart or equal 2 to harmonize

³**match** n a short slender piece of wood, cardboard, etc tipped with a mixture that ignites when subjected to friction

'**matchless** /-lis/ adj having no equal – **~ly** adv

matchmaker /'mach,maykə/ n one who arranges marriages; also one who derives vicarious pleasure from contriving to arrange marriages – **making** n

'**match ,point** n a situation in tennis, badminton, etc in which a player will win the match by winning the next point

matchwood /'mach,wood/ n wood suitable for matches; also wood splinters

¹**mate** /mayt/ v or n (to) checkmate

²**mate** n 1a an associate, companion – usu in combination b an assistant to a more skilled workman 2 a deck officer on a merchant ship ranking below

the captain **3a** either of a pair: e g **3a(1)** either member of a breeding pair of animals **a(2)** either of 2 matched objects **b** a marriage partner

³**mate** v **1** to join or fit together **2** to copulate

¹**material** /mə'tiəri·əl/ adj **1a(1)** of, derived from, or consisting of matter; esp physical **a(2)** bodily **b** of matter rather than form **2** important, significant **3** of or concerned with physical rather than spiritual things – ~**ly** adv

²**material** n **1a** the elements, constituents, or substances of which sthg is composed or can be made **b(1)** data that may be worked into a more finished form **b(2)** a person considered with a view to his/her potential for successful training **c** cloth **2** pl materials necessary for doing or making sthg

ma'teria,lism /-,liz(ə)m/ n **1a** a theory that only physical matter is real and that all processes and phenomena can be explained by reference to matter **b** a doctrine that the highest values lie in material well-being and material progress **2** a preoccupation with or stress on material rather than spiritual things – **-ist** n, adj – **-istic** adj – **-isti-cally** adv

materialize, -ise /mə'tiəri·ə,liez/ v **1** to (cause to) have existence **2** to (cause to) appear in or assume bodily form

maternal /mə'tuhnl/ adj **1** (characteristic) of a mother **2** related through a mother – ~**ly** adv

¹**maternity** /mə'tuhnəti/ n **1a** motherhood **b** motherliness **2** a hospital department for the care of women before and during childbirth

²**maternity** adj designed for wear during pregnancy

¹**matey** /'mayti/ n, chiefly Br mate – chiefly in familiar address

²**matey** adj, chiefly Br friendly – infml

mathematics /,mathə'matiks/ n pl but sing or pl in constr the science of numbers and their operations, interrelations, and combinations and of space configurations and their structure, measurement, etc – **-ical** adj – **-ically** adv – **-ician** n

matinée, matinee /'matinay/ n a musical or dramatic performance during the day, esp the afternoon

matins /'matinz/ n pl but sing or pl in constr, often cap morning prayer

matri,archy /-ki/ n a (system of) social organization in which the female is the head of the family, and descent and inheritance are traced through the female line – **matriarch** n – **-archal** adj

matricide /'maytri,sied/ n (the act of) one who kills his/her mother

matriculate /mə'trikyoolayt/ v to enrol as a member of a body, esp a college or university – **-lation** n

matrilineal /,matri'lini·əl, ,maytri-/ adj of or tracing descent through the maternal line

matrimony /'matriməni/ n marriage – **-monial** adj

matrix /'maytriks/ n, pl **matrices** /-,seez/, **matrixes 1** a substance, environment, etc within which sthg else originates or develops **2** a mould in which sthg is cast or from which a surface in relief (e g a piece of type) is made by pouring or pressing

matron /'maytrən/ n **1a** a (dignified mature) married woman **b** a woman in charge of living arrangements in a school, residential home, etc **2** Br a woman in charge of the nursing in a hospital – not now used technically

¹**matt, mat, matte** /mat/ v to make (e g metal or colour) matt

²**matt, mat, matte** adj lacking lustre or gloss; esp having an even surface free from shine or highlights

³**matt, mat, matte** n **1** a border round a picture between the picture and frame or serving as the frame **2** a dull or roughened finish (e g on gilt or paint)

¹**matter** /'matə/ n **1a** a subject of interest or concern or which merits attention **b** an affair, concern **c** material (for treatment) in thought, discourse, or writing **d** a condition (unfavourably) affecting a person or thing **2a** the substance of which a physical object is composed **b** material substance that occupies space and has mass **c** sthg of a specified kind or for a specified purpose **d** material discharged by suppuration; pus — **as a matter of fact** as it happens; actually — often used in correcting a misapprehension — **for that matter** so far as that is concerned — **no matter** it does not matter; irrespective of

²**matter** v to be of importance

,**matter of 'course** n sthg routine or to be expected as a natural consequence – **matter-of-course** adj

,**matter-of-'fact** adj keeping to or concerned with fact; esp not fanciful or imaginative

matting /'mating/ n material (e g hemp) for mats

mattock /'matək/ n a digging tool with a head like that of a pick and often a blade like that of an axe or adze

mattress /'matris/ n a fabric casing filled with resilient material (e g foam rubber or an arrangement of coiled springs) used esp on a bed

¹**mature** /mə'tyooə/ adj **1** based on careful consideration **2a** having completed natural growth and development; adult **b** having attained a final or desired state **3** older or more experienced than others of his/her kind – **-rity** n – ~**ly** adv

²**mature** v **1** to bring to full development or completion **2** to become due for payment – **-ration** n

maudlin /'mawdlin/ adj **1** weakly and effusively sentimental **2** drunk enough to be emotionally silly

¹**maul** /mawl/ v **1** esp of an animal to attack and tear the flesh of **2** to handle roughly

²**maul** n 1 a situation in Rugby Union in which 1 or more players from each team close round the player carrying the ball who tries to get the ball out to his own team 2 a confused and noisy struggle

maunder /'mawndə/ v 1 to act or wander idly 2 to speak in a rambling or indistinct manner; *also, Br* to grumble

Maundy 'Thursday n the Thursday before Easter observed in commemoration of the Last Supper

mausoleum /ˌmawsə'lee-əm/ n, pl **mausoleums** *also* **mausolea** /-'lee-ə/ a large and elaborate tomb

mauve /mohv/ n or adj bluish purple

maverick /'mav(ə)rik/ n 1 an independent and nonconformist individual 2 NAm an unbranded range animal; *esp* a motherless calf

mawkish /'mawkish/ adj sickly or feebly sentimental – ~ly adv – ~ness n

maxi /'maksi/ n, pl **maxis** a floor-length woman's coat, skirt, etc

maxim /'maksim/ n (a succinct expression of) a general truth, fundamental principle, or rule of conduct

maximal /'maksiml/ adj greatest; most comprehensive – ~ly adv

maximum /'maksiməm/ n, pl **maxima** /-mə/, **maximums** 1 the greatest quantity or value attainable or attained 2 the period of highest or most extreme development – **-mize** v

may /may/ verbal auxiliary, pres sing & pl **may**; past **might** /miet/ **1a** have permission to; have liberty to **b** be in some degree likely to 2 – used to express a wish or desire, esp in prayer, curse, or benediction (e g long may he reign) 3 – used to express purpose or expectation (e g sit here so I may you better) contingency (e g he'll do his duty come what may); or concession (e g he may be slow, but he's thorough); used in questions to emphasize ironic uncertainty (e g and who may you be?)

May n 1 the 5th month of the Gregorian calendar 2 not cap (the blossom of) hawthorn

maybe /'may,bee/ adv perhaps

'**May ,Day** n May 1 celebrated as a springtime festival and in many countries as a public holiday in honour of working people

'**may,fly** /-ˌflie/ n any of an order of insects with an aquatic nymph and a short-lived fragile adult with membranous wings

mayhem /'mayhem/ n 1 needless or wilful damage 2 a state of great confusion or disorder

mayonnaise /ˌmayə'nayz/ n a thick dressing (e g for salad) made with egg yolks, vegetable oil, and vinegar or lemon juice

mayor /mea/ n the chief executive or nominal head of a city or borough – ~al adj

mayoress /'mearis/ n 1 the wife or hostess of a mayor 2 a female mayor

maypole /'may,pohl/ n a tall ribbon-wreathed pole forming a centre for dances, esp on May Day

maze /mayz/ n 1 (a drawn representation of) a network of paths designed to confuse and puzzle those who attempt to walk through it 2 sthg intricately or confusingly complicated

mazurka *also* **mazourka** /mə'zuhkə/ n (music for, or in the rhythm of) a Polish folk dance in moderate triple time

¹**me** /mee/ pron, objective case of **I** (e g fatter than me; it's me)

²**me** n sthg suitable for me (e g that dress isn't really me)

³**me** n the 3rd note of the diatonic scale in solmization

¹**mead** /meed/ n a fermented alcoholic drink made of water, honey, malt, and yeast

²**mead** n a meadow – archaic or poetic

meadow /'medoh/ n (an area of moist low-lying usu level) grassland

meagre, NAm chiefly **meager** /'meegə/ adj 1 having little flesh 2 deficient in quality or quantity – ~ly adv – ~ness n

¹**meal** /meel, miəl/ n 1 the portion of food taken or provided at 1 time to satisfy appetite 2 (the time of) eating a meal

²**meal** n (a product resembling, esp in texture) the usu coarsely ground seeds of a cereal grass or pulse

mealy /'meeli/ adj 1 soft, dry, and crumbly 2 containing meal 3 covered with meal or fine granules

,**mealy-'mouthed** adj unwilling to speak plainly or directly, esp when this may offend

¹**mean** /meen/ adj 1 lacking distinction or eminence; merely ordinary or inferior 2 of poor shabby inferior quality or status 3 not honourable or worthy; base; *esp* small-minded **4a** not generous **b** characterized by petty malice; spiteful **c** chiefly NAm particularly bad-tempered, unpleasant, or disagreeable – ~ly adv – ~ness n

²**mean** v **meant** /ment/ 1 to have in mind as a purpose; intend 2 to serve or intend to convey, produce, or indicate; signify 3 to intend for a particular use or purpose 4 to have significance or importance to the extent or degree of — **I mean**— used to introduce and emphasize a clause or sentence or when hesitating — **mean business** to be in earnest

³**mean** n **1a** a middle point between extremes **b** a value that lies within a range of values and is computed according to a prescribed law; *esp* an average 2 pl but sing or pl in constr that which enables a desired purpose to be achieved; *also* the method used to attain an end 3 pl resources available for disposal; *esp* wealth

⁴**mean** adj 1 occupying a middle position; intermediate in space, order, time, kind, or degree 2 being the mean of a set of values

¹**meander** /mi'andə/ *n* a turn or winding of a stream – usu pl

²**meander** *v* to wander aimlessly without urgent destination

¹**meaning** /'meening/ *n* 1 that which is conveyed or which one intends to convey, esp by language 2 significant quality; value 3 implication of a hidden or special significance – ~less *adj*

²**meaning** *adj* significant, expressive

'**means** ,test *n* an examination into sby's financial state to determine whether he/she should receive public assistance, a student grant, etc

meant /ment/ *adj, past of* **mean** *Br* expected, supposed

¹**meantime** /'meen,tiem/ *n* the intervening time

²**meantime** *adv* meanwhile

'**mean** ,time *n* time that is based on the motion of the mean sun and that has the mean solar second as its unit

¹**meanwhile** /'meen,wiel/ *n* the meantime

²**meanwhile** *adv* 1 during the intervening time 2 during the same period (e g *meanwhile*, down on the farm)

measles /'meezlz/ *n pl but sing or pl in constr* an infectious virus disease marked by a rash of distinct red circular spots

measly /'meezli/ *adj* contemptibly small; *also* worthless – *infml* – **liness** *n*

¹**measure** /'mezhə/ *n* 1a1(1) an appropriate or due portion **a**(2) a (moderate) extent, amount, or degree **a**(3) a fixed, suitable, or conceivable limit **b**(1) the dimensions, capacity, or amount of sthg ascertained by measuring **b**(2) the character, nature, or capacity of sby or sthg ascertained by assessment – esp in *get the measure of* **c** a measured quantity **2a** an instrument or utensil for measuring **b** a standard or unit of measurement **3a** a (slow and stately) dance **b**(1) poetic rhythm measured by quantity or accent **b**(2) musical time **c**(1) the notes and rests that form a bar of music **c**(2) a metrical unit; a foot **4** a basis or standard of comparison **5a** a step planned or taken to achieve an end **b** a proposed legislative act

²**measure** *v* 1 to take or allot in measured amounts – usu + *out* 2 to mark off by making measurements – often + *off* 3 to ascertain the measurements of 4 to estimate or appraise by a criterion – usu + *against* or *by*

'**measured** *adj* 1 rhythmical; *esp* slow and regular 2 carefully thought out

'**measureless** /-lis/ *adj* having no observable limit; immeasurable

'**measurement** /-mənt/ *n* 1 measuring 2 a figure, extent, or amount obtained by measuring

measure up *v* to have necessary or fitting qualifications – often + *to*

meat /meet/ *n* 1 food; *esp* solid food as distinguished from drink 2 animal tissue used as food 3 the core or essence of sthg

meaty /'meeti/ *adj* 1 full of meat; fleshy 2 rich in matter for thought 3 of or like meat – **meatiness** *n*

mecca /'mekə/ *n, often cap* a place regarded as a goal (by a specified group of people)

mechanic /mi'kanik/ *n* a skilled worker who repairs or maintains machinery

me'chanical /-kl/ *adj* 1a of or using machinery **b** made, operated by, or being a machine or machinery 2 done as if by machine; lacking in spontaneity 3 of, dealing with, or in accordance with (the principles of) mechanics – ~ly *adv*

mechanics /mi'kaniks/ *n pl but sing or pl in constr* 1 the physics and mathematics of (the effect on moving and stationary bodies of) energy and forces 2 the practical application of mechanics to the design, construction, or operation of machines or tools

mechanism /'mekəniz(ə)m/ *n* 1 a piece of machinery 2 mechanical operation or action 3 a theory that all natural processes are mechanically determined and can be explained by the laws of physics and chemistry – **-istic** *adj* – **-istically** *adv* – **-ize** *v*

medal /'medl/ *n* a piece of metal with a (stamped) design, emblem, inscription, etc that commemorates a person or event or is awarded for excellence or achievement

medallion /mi'dalyən/ *n* 1 a large medal 2 a decorative tablet, panel, etc, often bearing a figure or portrait in relief

meddle /'medl/ *v* **meddling** /'medling, 'medl·ing/ to interest oneself in what is not one's concern; interfere unduly – usu + *in* or *with* – ~r *n* – ~some *adj*

media /'meedi·ə/ *n pl* 1 *pl of* **medium** 2 mass media

medial /'meedi·əl/ *adj* being, occurring in, or extending towards the middle; median – ~ly *adv*

¹**median** /'meedi·ən/ *n* a value in a series above and below which there are an equal number of values

²**median** *adj* 1 in the middle or in an intermediate position 2 lying in the plane that divides an animal into right and left halves

¹**mediate** /'meedi·ət/ *adj* acting through an intervening agent or agency

²**mediate** /'meedi,ayt/ *v* 1 to intervene between parties in order to reconcile them 2 to transmit or effect by acting as an intermediate mechanism or agency

medic /'medik/ *n* a medical doctor or student – infml

¹**medical** /'medikl/ *adj* 1 of or concerned with physicians or the practice of medicine 2 requiring or devoted to medical treatment – ~ly *adv*

²**medical** /'medikl/, **medical examination** *n* an examination to determine sby's physical fitness

medicament /mi'dikəmənt/ *n* a medicine

medicate /'medikayt/ *v* to impregnate with a medicinal substance – **-tion** *n*

medicinal /mə'dis(ə)nl/ *n or adj* (a substance) tending or used to cure disease or relieve pain – **~ly** *adv*

medicine /'medsin/ *n* **1** a substance or preparation used (as if) in treating disease **2** the science and art of the maintenance of health and the prevention and treatment of disease (using nonsurgical methods)

'medicine ,ball *n* a heavy ball that is usu thrown between people for exercise

'medicine ,man *n* a healer or sorcerer, esp among the N American Indians

medieval, mediaeval /,medi'eevl/ *adj* of or like the Middle Ages

mediocre /,meedi'ohkə/ *adj* **1** neither good nor bad; indifferent; *esp* conspicuously lacking distinction or imagination **2** not good enough; fairly bad – **-crity** *n*

meditate /'meditayt/ *v* **1** to engage in deep or serious reflection **2** to empty the mind of thoughts and fix the attention on 1 matter, esp as a religious exercise – **-tion** *n* – **-tive** *adj* – **-tively** *adv*

Mediterranean /,meditə'raynyən, -ni-ən/ *adj* of or characteristic of (the region round) the Mediterranean sea

¹**medium** /'meedi-əm/ *n, pl* **mediums, media** /-di-ə/, (*2b*(2)) **media**, (*2e*) **mediums**, (*3b*) **media** *also* **mediums 1** (sthg in) a middle position or state **2** a means of effecting or conveying sthg: e g **2a**(1) a substance regarded as the means of transmission of a force or effect **a**(2) a surrounding or enveloping substance **b** a mode of artistic expression or communication **c** one through whom others seek to communicate with the spirits of the dead **3a** a condition or environment in which sthg may function or flourish **b** a nutrient for the artificial cultivation of bacteria and other (single-celled) organisms **c** a liquid with which dry pigment can be mixed

²**medium** *adj* intermediate in amount, quality, position, or degree

'medium ,wave *n* a band of radio waves, typically used for sound broadcasting, covering wavelengths about 180m and 600m – sometimes pl with sing. meaning

medley /'medli/ *n* **1** a (confused) mixture **2** a musical composition made up of a series of songs or short musical pieces

meek /meek/ *adj* **1** patient and without resentment **2** lacking spirit and courage; timid – **~ly** *adv* – **~ness** *n*

¹**meet** /meet/ *v* **meet** /met/ **1a** to come into the presence of by accident or design **b** to be present to greet the arrival of **c** to come into contact or conjunction with **2** to encounter as antagonist or foe **3** to answer, esp in opposition **4** to conform to, esp exactly and precisely; satisfy **5** to pay fully **6** to

become acquainted with **7** to experience during the course of sthg — **meet someone halfway** to make concessions to; compromise with

²**meet** *n* the assembling of participants for a hunt or for competitive sports

³**meet** *adj* suitable, proper – *fml*

meeting /'meeting/ *n* **1** a coming together: e g **1a** an assembly of people for a common purpose **b** a session of horse or greyhound racing **2** a permanent organizational unit of the Quakers **3** an intersection, junction

'mega,hertz /-,huhts/ *n* a unit of frequency equal to 1,000,000 hertz

megalith /'megalith/ *n* a huge undressed block of stone used in prehistoric monuments

megalomania /,meg(ə)lə'maynyə/ *n* **1** a mania for grandiose things **2** feelings of personal omnipotence and grandeur occurring as a delusional mental disorder – **~ c** *n*

megaphone /'mega,fohn/ *n* a hand-held device used to amplify or direct the voice

'mega,ton /-tun/ *n* an explosive force (of an atom or hydrogen bomb) equivalent to that of 1,000,000 tons of TNT

¹**melancholy** /'melənkəli, -koli/ *n* **1** (a tendency to) bad temper or depression; melancholia **2a** depression of mind or spirits **b** a sad pensive mood – **-olic** *adj*

²**melancholy** *adj* **1** depressed in spirits; dejected **2** causing, tending to cause, or expressing sadness or depression

mélange /'maylonhzh (*Fr* melɑ̃ːɜ)/ *n* a mixture (of incongruous elements)

mêlée, melee /'melay/ *n* a confused or riotous struggle; *esp* a general hand-to-hand fight

mellifluous /mə'liflooəs/, **mellifluent** /-ənt/ *adj* smoothly or sweetly flowing

mellow /'meloh/ *adj* **1** of a fruit tender and sweet because ripe **2a** made gentle by age or experience **b** rich and full but free from harshness **c** pleasantly intoxicated

melodious /mə'lohdi-əs/ *adj* of or producing a (pleasing) melody – **~ly** *adv* – **~ness** *n*

melodrama /'melə,drahmə/ *n* **1a** a work (e g a film or play) characterized by crude emotional appeal and by the predominance of plot and action over characterization **b** the dramatic genre comprising such works **2** sensational or sensationalized events or behaviour

melody /'melədi/ *n* **1** an agreeable succession or arrangement of sounds **2a** a rhythmic succession of single notes organized as an aesthetic whole **b** the chief part in a harmonic composition – **-dic** *adj*

melon /'melən/ *n* (any of various plants of the cucumber family having) a fruit (e g a watermelon) containing sweet edible flesh and usu eaten raw

mel

374

¹**melt** /melt/ *v* 1 to become altered from a solid to a liquid state, usu by heating 2a to dissolve, disintegrate b to disappear as if by dissolving 3 to be or become mild, tender, or gentle

²**melt** *n* the spleen, esp when used as food

member /'membə/ *n* 1 a part or organ of the body: e g 1a a limb b the penis – euph 2a an individual or unit belonging to or forming part of a group or organization b *often cap* one who is entitled to sit in a legislative body; *esp* a member of Parliament 3a a constituent part of a whole b a beam or similar (load-bearing) structure, esp in a building

'**membership** /-ship/ *n sing or pl in constr* the body of members

membrane /'membrayn/ *n* a thin pliable sheet or layer, esp in an animal or plant – **-anous** *adj*

memento /mə'mentoh/ *n pl* **mementos, mementoes** sthg (e g a souvenir) that serves as a reminder of past events, people, etc

memo /'memoh/ *n pl* **memos** a memorandum

memoir /'memwah/ *n* 1a a narrative written from personal experience b an autobiography – usu pl with sing. meaning c a biography 2 a learned essay on a particular topic *USE* (1a&1c) often pl with sing. meaning

memorable /'mem(ə)rəbl/ *adj* worth remembering; notable – **-bly** *adv*

memorandum /,memə'randəm/ *n, pl* **memorandums, memoranda** /-də/ 1 an often unsigned informal record or communication; *also* a written reminder 2 a document recording the terms of an agreement, the formation of a company, etc 3 a usu brief communication for internal circulation (e g within an office)

¹**memorial** /mə'mawri-əl/ *adj* serving to commemorate a person or event

²**memorial** *n* sthg, esp a monument, that commemorates a person or event

memory /'mem(ə)ri/ *n* 1 (the power or process of recalling or realizing) the store of things learned and retained from an organism's experience 2 commemorative remembrance 3a (the object of) recall or recollection b the time within which past events can be or are remembered 4 (the capacity of) a device in which information, esp for a computer, can be inserted and stored, and from which it may be extracted when wanted – **-orize** *v*

men /men/ *pl of* **man**

¹**menace** /'menis/ *n* 1 a threat 2a a source of danger b a person who causes annoyance

²**menace** *v* to threaten or show intent to harm – **-acingly** *adv*

,**ménage à 'trois** /ah trwah/ *n* a relationship in which 3 people, esp a married couple and the lover of 1, live together

menagerie /mə'najəri/ *n* a place where animals are kept and trained, esp for exhibition; *also* a zoo

¹**mend** /mend/ *v* 1 to improve or rectify 2 to restore to sound condition or working order; repair – **~er** *n*

²**mend** *n* a mended place or part — **on the mend** improving, esp in health

mendicant /'mendikənt/ *n* a beggar

menfolk /'men,fohk/ *n pl in constr* 1 men in general 2 the men of a family or community

¹**menial** /'meenyəl, -ni-əl/ *adj* 1 of servants; lowly 2a degrading; *also* servile b lacking in interest or status – **~ly** *adv*

²**menial** *n* a domestic servant or retainer

meningitis /,menin'jietəs/ *n* inflammation of the membrane enclosing the brain and spinal cord

meniscus /mə'niskəs/ *n, pl* **menisci** /-'nisie/ *also* **meniscuses** the curved concave or convex upper surface of a column of liquid

menopause /'menə,pawz/ *n* (the time of) the natural cessation of menstruation occurring usu between the ages of 45 and 50

menses /'menseez/ *n pl but sing or pl in constr* menstrual flow

menstruation /,menstroo'aysh(ə)n/ *n* the monthly discharging of blood and tissue debris from the uterus in nonpregnant females – **-truate** *v* – **-trual** *adj*

mensuration /,menshə'raysh(ə)n/ *n* geometry applied to the computation of lengths, areas, or volumes

mental /'mentl/ *adj* 1a of the mind or its activity b of intellectual as contrasted with emotional or physical activity c (performed or experienced) in the mind 2 of, being, or (intended for the care of people) suffering from a psychiatric disorder 3 crazy; *also* stupid – *infml* – **~ly** *adv*

mentality /men'taliti/ *n* 1 mental power or capacity; intelligence 2 a mode of thought; mental disposition or outlook

menthol /'menthol/ *n* an alcohol that occurs esp in mint oils and has the smell and cooling properties of peppermint – **~ated** *adj*

¹**mention** /'mensh(ə)n/ *n* 1a a brief reference to sthg 2 a formal citation for outstanding achievement

²**mention** *v* to make mention of; refer to

mentor /'mentaw/ *n* a wise and trusted adviser

menu /'menyooh/ *n pl* **menus** (a list of) the dishes that may be ordered (e g in a restaurant) or that are to be served (e g at a banquet)

Mephistopheles /,mefis'tofəleez/ *n* a devilish or fiendish person – **~lean** *adj*

mercantile /'muhkəntiel/ *adj* of or concerned with merchants or trading

¹**mercenary** /'muhs(ə)nri/ *n* a hired soldier in foreign service

²**mercenary** *adj* 1 serving merely for (financial) reward 2 hired for service in the army of a foreign country

merchandise /'muhchən,dies/ *n* 1 the commodities that are bought and sold in commerce 2 wares for sale

[1]**merchant** /'muhchənt/ *n* 1 a wholesaler; *also, chiefly NAm* a shopkeeper 2 a person who is given to a specified activity – chiefly derog

[2]**merchant** *adj* of or used in commerce; *esp* of a merchant navy

merchantman /-mən/ *n pl* **merchantmen** /-mən/ a ship used in commerce

merchant 'navy *n, Br* (the personnel of) the privately or publicly owned commercial ships of a nation

mercury /'muhkyoori/ *n* a heavy silver-white poisonous metallic element that is liquid at ordinary temperatures and used in thermometers, barometers, etc 2 *cap* the planet nearest the sun

mercy /'muhsi/ *n* 1 compassion or forbearance shown esp to an offender 2a an act of divine compassion; a blessing b a fortunate circumstance – **merciful** *adj* — **at the mercy of** wholly in the power of; with no way to protect oneself against

[1]**mere** /miə/ *n* a (small) lake

[2]**mere** *adj* being what is specified and nothing else; nothing more than – ~**ly** *adv*

meretricious /,merə'trishəs/ *adj* 1 tawdrily and falsely attractive 2 based on pretence or insincerity – ~**ly** *adv* – ~**ness** *n*

merge /muhj/ *v* 1 to (cause to) combine or unite 2 to blend or (cause to) come together gradually without abrupt change

merger /'muhjə/ *n* a combining or combination, esp of 2 organizations (e g business concerns)

meridian /mə'ridi·ən/ *n* 1 a great circle passing through the poles of the celestial sphere and the zenith of a given place 2 a high point, esp of success or greatness

meringue /mə'rang/ *n* (a small cake, cream-filled shell, etc made with) a mixture of stiffly beaten egg whites and sugar baked until crisp

[1]**merit** /'merit/ *n* 1a the quality of deserving well or ill b a praiseworthy feature; virtue c worth, excellence 2 *pl* the intrinsic rights and wrongs of a (legal) case

[2]**merit** *v* to be worthy of or entitled to

meritocracy /,meri'tokrəsi/ *n* (a social system based on) leadership by the talented

meritorious /,meri'tawri·əs/ *adj* deserving of reward or honour – ~**ly** *adv*

mermaid /'muh,mayd/, *masc* **merman** /-,man/ *n pl masc* **mermen** /-,men/ a mythical sea creature usu represented with a woman's body to the waist and a fish's tail

merriment /'merimənt/ *n* lighthearted gaiety or fun

merry /'meri/ *adj* 1 full of gaiety or high spirits 2 marked by festivity 3 slightly drunk; tipsy – infml – ~**rily** *adv* – ~**riness** *n*

'**merry-go-,round** *n* a fairground machine with seats, often shaped like horses, that revolve about a fixed centre

'**merry,making** *n* gay or festive activity – **-maker** *n*

[1]**mesh** /mesh/ *n* 1 an open space in a net, network, etc 2a the cords, wires, etc that make up a net b a woven, knitted, or knotted fabric with evenly spaced small holes 3a an interlocking or intertwining arrangement or construction b a web, snare – usu pl with sing. meaning 4 working contact (e g of the teeth of gears)

[2]**mesh** *v* 1 to catch or entangle (as if) in the openings of a net 2 to cause to engage 3 to fit or work together properly or successfully

mesmerize, -ise /'mezməriez/ *v* 1 to hypnotize 2 to fascinate

[1]**mess** /mes/ *n* 1 a prepared dish of soft or liquid food; *also* a usu unappetizing mixture of ingredients eaten together 2 *sing or pl in constr* a group of people (e g servicemen or servicewomen) who regularly take their meals together 3a a confused, dirty, or offensive state or condition b a disordered situation resulting from misunderstanding, blundering, or misconduct

[2]**mess** *v* 1 to take meals with a mess 2 to make a mess 3a to dabble, potter b to handle or play *with* sthg, esp carelessly c to interfere, meddle *USE* (3) often + *about* or *around*

mess about *v* 1 to waste time 2a to conduct an affair *with* b to treat roughly or without due consideration

message /'mesij/ *n* 1 a communication in writing, in speech, or by signals 2 a central theme or idea intended to inspire, urge, warn, enlighten, advise, etc

messenger /'mesinjə/ *n* one who bears a message or does an errand

messiah /mə'sie·ə/ *n* 1 *often cap* 1a *the* expected king and deliverer of the Jews b Jesus 2 a professed leader of some cause – **-ianic** *adj*

Messrs /'mesəz/ *pl of* **Mr**

messy /'mesi/ *adj* 1 marked by confusion, disorder, or dirt 2 lacking neatness or precision; slovenly 3 unpleasantly or tryingly difficult to conclude – **messily** *adv* – **messiness** *n*

[1]**met** /met/ *past of* **meet**

[2]**met** *adj* meteorological

metabolism /mə'tabl,iz(ə)m/ *n* the chemical changes in living cells by which energy is provided and new material is assimilated – **-ic** *adj*

metal /'metl/ *n* any of various opaque, fusible, ductile, and typically lustrous substances (e g iron, copper, or mercury), esp chemical elements, that are good conductors of electricity and heat

metallic /mi'talik/ *adj* 1 of, containing, like, or being (a) metal 2 yielding metal 3 having an acrid quality

metallurgy /mə'taləji, 'metl,uhji/ n the science and technology of metals – **-gical** adj – **-gist** n

'**metal,work** /-,wuhk/ n the craft or product of shaping things out of metal – **~er** n

,**meta'morphosis** /-'mawfəsis/ n, pl **metamorphoses** /-seez/ **1a** change of form, structure, or substance, esp by supernatural means **b** a striking alteration (e g in appearance or character) **2** a marked (abrupt) change in the form or structure of a butterfly, frog, etc occurring in the course of development

metaphor /'metəfə, -,faw/ n a figure of speech in which a word or phrase literally denoting one kind of object or idea is applied to another to suggest a likeness or analogy between them (e g in *the ship ploughs the sea*) – **~ical** adj

,**meta'physical** /-'fizikl/ adj **1** of metaphysics **2** *often cap* of or being poetry, esp of the early 17th c, marked by elaborate subtleties of thought and expression – **~ly** adv

,**meta'physics** n pl but sing in constr **1** a division of philosophy concerned with ultimate causes and the underlying nature of things **2** pure or speculative philosophy

meteor /'meeti-ə, -,aw/ n (the streak of light produced by the passage of) any of many small particles of matter in the solar system observable only when heated by friction so that they glow as they fall into the earth's atmosphere

meteoric /,meeti'orik/ adj resembling a meteor in speed or in sudden and temporary brilliance – **~ally** adv

meteorite /'meeti-ə,riet/ n a meteor that reaches the surface of the earth without being completely vaporized

meteoroid /'meeti-ə,royd/ n a particle in orbit round the sun that becomes a meteor when it meets the earth's atmosphere

meteorology /,meeti-ə'roləji/ n the science of the atmosphere and its phenomena, esp weather and weather forecasting – **-gical** adj – **-gist** n

'**meter** /'meetə/ n, NAm a metre

²**meter** n an instrument for measuring (and recording) the amount of sthg (e g gas, electricity, or parking time) used

³**meter** v **1** to measure by means of a meter **2** to supply in a measured or regulated amount

methane /'mee,thayn/ n an inflammable hydrocarbon gas used as a fuel and as a raw material in chemical synthesis

method /'methəd/ n **1a** a systematic procedure for doing sthg **b** a regular way of doing sthg **2a** an orderly arrangement or system **b** the habitual practice of orderliness and regularity

methodical /mə'thodikl/, NAm also **methodic** adj **1** arranged, characterized by, or performed with method or order **2** habitually proceeding according to method; systematic – **~ly** adv

Methodism /'methədiz(ə)m/ n (the doctrines and practice of) the churches derived from the teachings of John Wesley – **-dist** adj, n

methodology /,methə'doləji/ n (the analysis of) the body of methods and rules employed by a science or discipline – **-gical** adj – **-gically** adv

meths /meths/ n pl but sing in constr, Br methylated spirits – infml

,**methylated 'spirits** n pl but sing or pl in constr alcohol mixed with a substance that makes it undrinkable so that it can be sold exempt from duty

meticulous /mə'tikyooləs/ adj marked by extreme or excessive care over detail – **~ly** adv – **~ness** n

métier /'maytyay/ n one's trade; also sthg (e g an activity) in which one is expert or successful

¹**metre**, NAm chiefly **meter** /'meetə/ n the SI unit of length equal to a certain number of wavelengths of a specific radiation of the krypton isotope $_{36}Kr^{86}$ (about 1.094yd)

²**metre**, NAm chiefly **meter** n **1** systematically arranged and measured rhythm in verse **2** a basic recurrent rhythmical pattern of accents and beats per bar in music

metric /'metrik/ adj (using or being units) based on the metre, litre, and kilogram as standard of measurement – **~ize** v

metrical /'metrikl/, **metric** adj **1** of or composed in metre **2** of measurement – **~ly** adv

metric ton n a tonne

metro /'metroh/ n pl **metros** an underground railway system in a city

metronome /'metrə,nohm/ n an instrument designed to mark exact time by a regularly repeated tick

metropolis /mi'tropəlis/ n **1** the chief city of a country, state, or region **2** a centre of a usu specified activity – **-itan** adj

mettle /'metl/ n **1** strength of spirit or temperament **2** staying quality; stamina — **on one's mettle** aroused to do one's best

'**mettlesome** /-s(ə)m/ adj spirited

mews /myoohz/ n pl but sing or pl in constr, pl **mews** chiefly Br (living accommodation adapted from) stables built round an open courtyard

mezzanine /'mezəneen/ n a low-ceilinged storey between 2 main storeys, esp the ground and first floors, of a building

mezzo /'metsoh/, **mezzo-soprano** n a woman's voice with a range between that of the soprano and contralto

mi /mee/ n the 3rd note of the diatonic scale in solmization

miaow, meow /mi'ow, myow/ v or n (to make) the characteristic cry of a cat

miasma /mɪ'azmə/ n, pl **miasmas** also **miasmata** /-mətə/ **1** a heavy vapour (e g from a swamp) formerly believed to cause disease; broadly any heavy or malodorous vapour **2** a pervasive influence that tends to weaken or corrupt – ~1 adj

mica /'miekə/ n any of various coloured or transparent silicate materials occurring as crystals that readily separate into very thin flexible leaves

mice /mies/ pl of **mouse**

Michaelmas /'mik(ə)lməs/ n September 29 celebrated as the feast of St Michael the Archangel

Michaelmas daisy n any of several (Autumn-blooming) asters widely grown as garden plants

micro /'miekroh/ n a microprocessor

microbe /'miekrohb/ n a microorganism, germ

microbiology /ˌmiekrəbie'olǝji, -kroh-/ n the biology of bacteria and other microscopic forms of life – -gical adj – -gist n

'microcom,puter /-kəm,pyoohtə/ n a microprocessor

microcosm /'miekrə,koz(ə)m/ n **1** a little world; esp an individual human being or human nature seen as an epitome of the world or universe **2** a whole (e g a community) that is an epitome of a larger whole

microfilm /'miekrə,film/ n a film bearing a photographic record on a reduced scale of graphic matter (e g printing)

micrometer /mie'kromitə/ n a gauge for making precise measurements of length by means of a spindle moved by a finely threaded screw

micro'organism /-'awgəniz(ə)m/ n a very small, usu single celled, living creature

microphone /'miekrə,fohn/ n a device that converts sounds into electrical signals, esp for transmission or recording

micro'processor /-'prohsesə/ n a very small computer composed of 1 or more integrated circuits functioning as a unit

microscope /'miekrə,skohp/ n an instrument consisting of (a combination of) lenses for making enlarged images of minute objects using light or other radiations – -py n

micro'scopic /-'skopik/ also **microscopical** /-kl/ adj **1** of or conducted with the microscope or microscopy **2a** invisible or indistinguishable without the use of a microscope **b** very small, fine, or precise – ~ally adv

microwave /'miekrə,wayv/ n a band of very short electromagnetic waves of between 1m and 0.1m in wavelength

¹mid /mid/ adj **1** being the part in the middle or midst – often in combination **2** occupying a middle position

²mid prep amid – poetic

'mid,day /-'day/ n the middle part of the day; noon

midden /'mid(ə)n/ n **1** a dunghill **2** a heap or stratum of domestic rubbish found on the site of an ancient settlement

¹middle /'midl/ adj **1** equally distant from the extremes; central **2** at neither extreme

²middle n **1** a middle part, point, or position **2** the waist **3** the position of being among or in the midst of sthg **4** sthg intermediate between extremes; a mean

,middle 'age n the period of life from about 40 to about 60

'Middle ,Ages n pl the period of European history from about AD 500 to about 1500

'middle,brow /-,brow/ adj dealing with or having conventional intellectual and cultural interests and activities – often derog

,middle 'class n a class occupying a position between upper and lower; esp a fluid heterogeneous grouping of business and professional people, bureaucrats, and some farmers and skilled workers – often pl with sing. meaning

middle ear n a cavity through which sound waves are transmitted by a chain of tiny bones from the eardrum to the inner ear

'middle,man /-,man/ n an intermediary between 2 parties; esp a dealer intermediate between the producer of goods and the retailer or consumer

middle school n (part of) a school for pupils aged 8–12 or 9–13

'middle,weight /-,wayt/ n a boxer who weighs not more than about 11st 6lb

middling /'midling/ adj **1** of middle or moderate size, degree, or quality **2** mediocre, second-rate

midfield /'mid,feeld, -'-/ n (the players who normally play in) the part of a pitch or playing field midway between the goals

midge /mij/ n a tiny two-winged fly

midget /'mijit/ n **1** a very small person; a dwarf **2** sthg (e g an animal) much smaller than usual

midi /'midi/ n a woman's garment that extends to the mid-calf

midland /'midlənd/ n, often cap the central region of a country – usu pl with sing. meaning

midnight /'mid,niet/ n the middle of the night; specif 12 o'clock at night

,mid-'off n a fielding position in cricket near the bowler on the off side of the pitch

,mid-'on n a fielding position in cricket near the bowler on the leg side of the pitch

midriff /'midrif/ n **1** the diaphragm **2** the middle part of the human torso

midshipman /'mid,shipmən/ n (the rank of) a young person training to become a naval officer

midst /midst/ n **1** the inner or central part or point; the middle **2** a position near to the members of a group **3** the condition of being surrounded or beset (e g by problems) **4** a period of time about the middle of a continuing act or state

,mid'summer /-'sumə/ n the summer solstice

mid·way /-'way/ *adv* halfway

mid·week /-'week/ *n* the middle of the week

mid-'wicket *n* a fielding position in cricket on the leg side equidistant from each wicket

midwife /'mid,wief/ *n* **1** a woman who assists other women in childbirth **2** sby or sthg that helps to produce or bring forth sthg – ~**ry** *n*

mien /meen/ *n* air or bearing, esp as expressive of mood or personality – fml

¹**might** /miet/ *past of* **may** – used to express permission or liberty in the past (e g asked whether he *might* come), a past or present possibility contrary to fact (e g I *might* well have been killed) purpose or expectation in the past (e g wrote it down so that I *might* not forget it), less probability or possibility than may (e g *might* get there before it rains), a polite request (e g you *might* post this letter for me), or as a polite or ironic alternative to *may* (e g who *might* you be?) or to *ought* or *should* (e g you *might* at least apologize)

²**might** *n* **1** power, authority, or resources wielded individually or collectively **2a** physical strength **b** all the power or effort one is capable of

mightily /'miet(ə)li/ *adv* very much

¹**mighty** /'mieti/ *adj* **1** powerful **2** accomplished or characterized by might **3** imposingly great

²**mighty** *adv* to a great degree; extremely

migraine /'meegrayn/ *n* recurrent severe headache usu associated with disturbances of vision, sensation, and movement often on only side of the body

migrant /'miegrənt/ *n* **1** a person who moves regularly in order to find work, esp in harvesting crops **2** an animal that moves from one habitat to another

migrate /mie'grayt/ *v* **1** to move from one country or locality to another **2** *of an animal* to pass usu periodically from one region or climate to another for feeding or breeding – **-ory** *adj*

mikado /mi'kahdoh/ *n, pl* **mikados** – formerly used as a title for the emperor of Japan

mike /miek/ *n* a microphone – infml

¹**mild** /mield/ *adj* **1** gentle in nature or manner **2a** not strong in flavour or effect **b** not being or involving what is extreme **3** not severe; temperate – ~**ly** *adv* – ~**ness** *n*

²**mild** *n, Br* a dark-coloured beer not flavoured with hops

¹**mildew** /'mildyooh/ *n* (a fungus producing) a usu whitish growth on the surface of organic matter (e g paper or leather) or living plants – ~**y** *adj*

²**mildew** *v* to affect or become affected (as if) with mildew

mile /miel/ *n* **1** any of various units of distance: e g **1a** a unit equal to 1760yd (about 1.61km) **b** a nautical mile **2** a large distance or amount – often pl with sing. meaning — **miles from nowhere** in an extremely remote place

mileage /'mielij/ *n* **1** an allowance for travelling expenses at a certain rate per mile **2** total length or distance in miles: e g **2a** the number of miles travelled (over a period of time) **b** the average distance in miles a vehicle will travel for an amount of fuel

milestone /'miel,stohn/ *n* **1** a stone serving as a milepost **2** a crucial stage in sthg's development

milieu /'meelyuh (*Fr* milj ∅)/ *n, pl* **milieus, milieux** /-lyuh(z) (*Fr* ∼)/ *an* environment, setting

militant /'milit(ə)nt/ *adj* **1** engaged in warfare or combat **2** aggressively active (e g in a cause); combative

militarism /'milita,riz(ə)m/ *n* **1** exaltation of military virtues and ideals **2** a policy of aggressive military preparedness – **-rist** *n* – **-ristic** *adj* – **-ristically** *adv*

¹**military** /'milit(ə)ri/ *adj* **1** (characteristic) of soldiers, arms, or war **2** carried on or supported by armed force **3** of the army or armed forces

²**military** *n* **1** *pl in constr* soldiers **2** *sing or pl in constr* the army (as opposed to civilians or police)

militate /'militayt/ *v* to have significant weight or effect – usu + *against*

militia /mi'lish(y)ə/ *n sing or pl in constr* a body of citizens with some military training who are called on to fight only in an emergency

¹**milk** /milk/ *n* **1a** (a white or creamy) liquid secreted by the mammary glands of females for the nourishment of their young (and used as a food by humans) **2a** a milklike liquid: e g **2a** the latex of a plant **b** the juice of a coconut **c** a cosmetic lotion, esp a cleanser

²**milk** *v* **1** to draw milk from the breasts or udder of **2** to draw sthg from as if by milking: e g **2a** to induce (a snake) to eject venom **b** to compel or persuade to yield illicit or excessive profit or advantage

'**milk ,float** *n, Br* a light usu electrically-propelled vehicle for carrying esp milk for domestic delivery

'**milk,maid** /-,mayd/ *n* a female who works in a dairy

'**milkman** /-mən/ *n* one who sells or delivers milk

'**milk ,run** *n* a regular journey or course

milk shake *n* a thoroughly shaken or blended beverage made of milk and a flavouring syrup

milk tooth *n* a tooth of a mammal, esp a child, that is replaced later in life

Milky Way /'milki/ *n* a broad irregular band of faint light that stretches completely round the celestial sphere and is caused by the light of the many stars forming the galaxy of which the sun and the solar system are a part

¹**mill** /mil/ *n* **1** a building provided with machinery for grinding grain into flour **2a** a machine or apparatus for grinding grain **b** a machine or hand-operated device for crushing or grinding a

solid substance (e g coffee beans or peppercorns) **3** a building or collection of buildings with machinery for manufacturing

²**mill** v **1a** to grind into flour, meal, or powder **b** to shape or dress by means of a rotary cutter **2** to give a raised rim or a ridged edge to (a coin) **3** to move in a confused swirling mass – usu + *about* or *around*

millennium /mi'leni·əm/ n, pl **millennia** /-ni·ə/, **millenniums 1** a period of 1000 years **2a** *the* thousand years mentioned in Revelation 20 during which holiness is to prevail and Christ is to reign on earth **b** a (future) golden age

miller /'milə/ n sby who owns or works a mill, esp for corn

millet /'milit/ n (the seed of) any of various small-seeded annual cereal and forage grasses cultivated for their grain, used as food

milligram /'mili,gram/ n one thousandth of a gram (about 0.015 grain)

millilitre n a thousandth of a litre (.002pt)

millimetre /'mili,meetə/ n one thousandth of a metre (about 0.039in)

milliner /'milinə/ n sby who designs, makes, trims, or sells women's hats – ~ **y** n

million /'milyən/ n pl **millions, million 1** the number 1,000,000 **2** an indefinitely large number – infml; often pl with sing. meaning – ~ **th** adj, n, pron, adv

millionaire /,milyə'neə/ n sby whose wealth is estimated at a million or more money units

millipede, millepede /'mili,peed/ n an insect-like creature with a many-segmented body and 2 pairs of legs on each segment

'**mill,race** /-,rays/ n (the current in) a channel in which water flows to and from a mill wheel

'**mill,stone** /-,stohn/ n **1** either of a pair of circular stones that rotate against each other and are used for grinding (grain) **2** a heavy or crushing burden

milt /milt/ n the male reproductive glands of fishes when filled with secretion

'**mime** /miem/ n **1** an ancient dramatic entertainment representing scenes from life usu in a ridiculous manner **2** the art of portraying a character or telling a story by body movement **3** sby who performs the art of mime

²**mime** v to act a part with mimic gesture and action, usu without words

mimetic /mi'metik/ adj **1** imitative **2** relating to, characterized by, or exhibiting mimicry

'**mimic** /'mimik/ adj **1** imitation, mock **2** of mime or mimicry

²**mimic** v **-ck- 1** to imitate slavishly; ape **2** to ridicule by imitation **3** to simulate

mimicry /'mimikri/ n **1** the act or an instance of mimicking **2** resemblance of one organism to another that secures it an advantage (e g protection from predation)

minaret /,minə'ret/ n a slender tower attached to a mosque and surrounded by 1 or more projecting balconies from which the summons to prayer is made

'**mince** /mins/ v **1** to cut or chop into very small pieces **2** to walk with short affected steps

²**mince** n minced meat

'**mince,meat** /-,meet/ n a finely chopped mixture of raisins, apples, suet, spices, etc (with brandy) which traditionally used to contain meat

,**mince 'pie** n a sweet usu small and round pie filled with mincemeat

'**mind** /miend/ n **1** the (capabilities of the) organized conscious and unconscious mental processes of an organism that result in reasoning, thinking, perceiving, etc **2a** recollection, memory **b** attention, concentration **3** the normal condition of the mental faculties **4** a disposition, mood **5** the mental attributes of a usu specified group **6a** the intellect and rational faculties as contrasted with the emotions **b** the human spirit and intellect as opposed to the body and the material world — **bear/keep in mind** to think of, esp at the appropriate time; not forget — **on one's mind** as a preoccupation; troubling one's thoughts

²**mind** v **1** to pay attention to or follow (advice, instructions, or orders) **2a** to be concerned about; care **b** to object to **3a** to be careful **b** to be attentive or wary – often + *out* **4** to give protective care to; look after — **mind you** take this fact into account; notice this

'**mind-,blowing** adj **1** of or causing a psychic state similar to that produced by a psychedelic drug **2** mentally or emotionally exhilarating *USE* infml

'**minded** adj having a (specified kind of) mind – usu in combination

'**mindful** /-f(ə)l/ adj keeping in mind; aware *of* – ~ **ness** n

'**mindless** /-lis/ adj **1** devoid of thought or intelligence; senseless **2** involving or requiring little thought or concentration **3** inattentive, heedless – usu + *of* – ~ **ly** adv – ~ **ness** n

,**mind's 'eye** n the faculty of visual memory or imagination

'**mine** /mien/ pron, that which or the one who belongs to me – used without a following noun as a pronoun equivalent in meaning to the adjective *my* (e g children younger than *mine*; that brother of *mine*)

²**mine** n **1** an excavation from which mineral substances are taken **2** an encased explosive designed to destroy enemy personnel, vehicles, or ships **3** a rich source *of* — **me and mine** I and my family and possessions

³**mine** v **1** to dig an underground passage to gain access to or cause the collapse of (an enemy position) **2** to place military mines in, on, or under **3** to dig into for ore, coal, etc

mineral /'min(ə)rəl/ n 1 any of various naturally occurring substances (e g stone, coal, and petroleum) obtained by drilling, mining, etc 2 sthg neither animal nor vegetable

'mineral ‚water n water naturally or artificially impregnated with mineral salts or gases (e g carbon dioxide); *broadly* any effervescent nonalcoholic beverage

minestrone /‚mini'strohni/ n a rich thick vegetable soup usu containing pasta (e g macaroni)

minesweeper /'mien‚sweepə/ n a ship designed for removing or neutralizing mines – **-sweeping** n

mingle /'ming·gl/ v **mingling** /'ming·gling/ 1 to bring or mix together or with sthg else 2 to mix with or go among a group of people

mingy /'minji/ adj mean, stingy – infml

mini /'mini/ n, pl **minis** 1 sthg small of its kind (e g a motor car) 2 a woman's skirt or dress with the hemline several inches above the knee

¹miniature /'minəchə/ n **1a** a copy or representation on a much reduced scale **b** sthg small of its kind 2 a very small painting (e g a portrait on ivory or metal)

²miniature adj (represented) on a small or reduced scale

minibus /'mini‚bus/ n a small bus for carrying usu between 5 and 10 passengers

minim /'minim/ n a musical note with the time value of 2 crotchets or ¹/₂ of a semibreve

minimal /'miniml/ adj of or being a minimum; constituting the least possible – **-ly** adv

minimum /'miniməm/ n, pl **minima** /-mə/, **minimums** 1 the least quantity or value assignable, admissible, or possible 2 the lowest degree or amount reached or recorded – **-mize** v

minion /'minyən/ n 1 a servile attendant 2 a minor official – derog

¹minister /'ministə/ n 1 an agent 2 a clergyman, esp of a Protestant or nonconformist church 3 a high officer of state managing a division of government 4 a diplomatic representative accredited to a foreign state – **~ial** adj – **~ially** adv

²minister v 1 to perform the functions of a minister of religion 2 to give aid or service

ministration /‚mini'straysh(ə)n/ n the act or process of ministering, esp in religious matters – **-trant** n

ministry /'ministri/ n 1 service, ministration 2 the office, duties, or functions of a minister 3 the body of ministers of religion or government 4 the period of service or office of a minister or ministry 5 a government department presided over by a minister

mink /mingk/ n 1 any of several semiaquatic flesh-eating mammals that resemble weasels 2 the soft fur or pelt of the mink

minnow /'minoh/ n pl **minnows**, esp collectively **minnow** 1 a small dark-coloured freshwater fish or any of various small fishes 2 sthg small or insignificant of its kind

¹minor /'mienə/ adj **1a** inferior in importance, size, rank, or degree **b** comparatively unimportant 2 not having attained majority **3a** *esp of a scale or mode* having semitones between the second and third, fifth and sixth, and sometimes seventh and eighth steps **b** being or based on a (specified) minor scale 4 not serious or involving risk to life

²minor n 1 sby who has not attained majority 2 a minor musical interval, scale, key, or mode

minority /mie'norəti, mi-/ n **1a** the period before attainment of majority **b** the state of being a legal minor 2 the smaller of 2 groups constituting a whole; *specif* a group with less than the number of votes necessary for control 3 *sing or pl in constr* a group of people who share common characteristics or interests differing from those of the majority of a population

minster /'minstə/ n a large or important church often having cathedral status

minstrel /'minstrəl/ n 1 a medieval singer, poet, or musical entertainer 2 any of a troupe of performers usu with blackened faces giving a performance of supposedly Negro singing, jokes, dancing, etc

¹mint /mint/ n 1 a place where money is made 2 a vast sum or amount – infml

²mint v 1 to make (e g coins) by stamping metal 2 to fabricate, invent

³mint adj unspoilt as if fresh from a mint; pristine

⁴mint n 1 any of a genus of plants that have leaves with a characteristic strong taste and smell, used esp as a flavouring 2 a sweet, chocolate, etc flavoured with mint

minuet /‚minyoo'et/ n (music for or in the rhythm of) a slow graceful dance in ³₄ time

¹minus /'mienəs/ prep 1 diminished by 2 without

²minus n 1 a negative quantity 2 a deficiency, defect

³minus adj 1 negative 2 having negative qualities; *esp* involving a disadvantage

minuscule /'minə‚skyoohl/ adj very small

¹minute /'minit/ n 1 the 60th part of an hour or of a degree 2 a short space of time; a moment **3a** a memorandum **b** pl the official record of the proceedings of a meeting

²minute v to make notes or a brief summary (of)

³minute /mie'nyooht/ adj 1 extremely small 2 of minor importance; petty 3 marked by painstaking attention to detail – **~ness** n

minutia /mi'nyoohshyə, mie-/ n, pl **minutiae** /-shi‚ee/ a minor detail – usu pl

minx /mingks/ n a flirtatious girl

miracle /'mirəkl/ n 1 an extraordinary event manifesting divine intervention in human affairs 2 an astonishing or unusual event, thing, or accomplishment 3 a person or thing that is a remarkable example or instance of sthg

'**miracle** ,**play** n a medieval drama based on episodes from the Bible or the life of a saint

miraculous /mi'rakyoolas/ adj 1 of the nature of a miracle; supernatural 2 evoking wonder like a miracle; marvellous – ~ly adv

mirage /'mirahzh/ n 1 an optical illusion appearing esp as a pool of water or as the reflection of distant objects caused by the reflection of rays of light by a layer of heated air (near the ground) 2 sthg illusory and unattainable

¹**mire** /'mie-ə/ n 1 a tract of soft waterlogged ground; a marsh, bog 2 (deep) mud or slush

²**mire** v to cause to stick fast (as if) in mire

¹**mirror** /'mirə/ n 1 a smooth surface (e g of metal or silvered glass) that forms images by reflection 2 sthg that gives a true representation

²**mirror** v to reflect (as if) in a mirror

mirth /muhth/ n happiness or amusement accompanied with laughter – ~**ful** adj – ~**fully** adv – ~**less** adj

misadventure /,misəd'venchə/ n a misfortune, mishap

misal'liance /-ə'lie-əns/ n an improper or unsuitable alliance

misanthrope /'miz(ə)n,throhp/, **misanthropist** /mi'zanthrəpist/ n one who hates or distrusts people – -**thropy** n – -**thropic** adj – -**thropically** adv

misapply /,misə'plie/ v to apply wrongly – -**lication** n

misappre'hend /-apri'hend/ v to misunderstand

misap'propriate /-ə'prohpriayt/ v to appropriate wrongly (e g by theft or embezzlement) – -**ation** n

misbe'gotten /-bi'gotn/ adj 1 having a disreputable or improper origin 2 wretched, contemptible

misbe'have /-bi'hayv/ v to behave badly – ~**d** adj – -**viour** n

mis'calculate /-'kalkyoolayt/ v to calculate wrongly – -**lation** n

'**mis,carriage** /-,karij/ n 1 a failure in administration 2 the expulsion of a human foetus before it is viable, esp after the 12th week of gestation

mis'carry /-'kari/ v 1 to suffer miscarriage of a foetus 2 to fail to achieve an intended purpose

mis'cast /-'kahst/ v **miscast** to cast in an unsuitable role

miscellaneous /-nyəs, -ni-əs/ adj 1 consisting of diverse items or members 2 having various characteristics or capabilities – ~**ly** adv – ~**ness** n

miscellany /mi'selani/ n a mixture of various things

mischance /,mis'chahns/ n (a piece of) bad luck

mischief /'mischif/ n 1 sthg or esp sby that causes harm or annoyance 2 often playful action that annoys or irritates, usu without causing or intending serious harm

mischievous /'mischivəs/ adj 1 harmful, malicious 2 able or tending to cause annoyance, unrest, or minor injury 3a playfully provocative; arch b disruptively playful – ~**ly** adv – ~**ness** n

misconceive /,miskən'seev/ v to interpret wrongly; misunderstand – -**ception** n

mis'conduct /-'kondukt/ n 1 mismanagement of responsibilities 2 adultery

miscon'strue /-kən'strooh/ v to construe wrongly; misinterpret

mis'count /-'kownt/ v to count wrongly; esp to make a wrong count – **miscount** n

miscreant /'miskri-ənt/ adj or n (of) one who behaves criminally or maliciously

mis'date /-'dayt/ v to date (e g a letter) wrongly

mis'deal /-'deel/ v to deal (cards) incorrectly – **misdeal** n

mis'deed /-'deed/ n a wrong deed; an offence

misde'meanour /-di'meenə/ n 1 a minor crime 2 a misdeed

misdi'rect /-di'rekt, -die-/ v 1 to give a wrong direction to 2 to address (mail) wrongly – ~**ion** n

miser /'miezə/ n a mean grasping person; esp one who hoards wealth – ~**ly** adv – ~**liness** n

miserable /'miz(ə)rəbl/ adj **1a** wretchedly inadequate or meagre **b** causing extreme discomfort or unhappiness **2** in a pitiable state of distress or unhappiness **3** shameful, contemptible – **bly** adv

misery /'mizəri/ n 1 (a cause of) physical or mental suffering or discomfort 2 great unhappiness and distress 3 chiefly Br a grumpy or querulous person; esp a killjoy – infml

mis'fire /-'fie-ə/ v 1 of an engine, rocket etc to have the explosive or propulsive charge fail to ignite at the proper time 2 esp of a firearm to fail to fire 3 to fail to have an intended effect – **misfire** n

'**mis,fit** /-,fit/ n 1 sthg that fits badly 2 a person poorly adjusted to his/her environment

mis'fortune /-'fawchoohn, -chən/ n 1 bad luck 2 a distressing or unfortunate incident or event

mis'giving /-'giving/ n a feeling of doubt, suspicion, or apprehension, esp concerning a future event

mis'govern /-'guvən/ v to govern badly – ~**ment** n

mis'guide /-'gied/ v to lead astray – ~**d** adj – ~**dly** adv

mis'handle /-'handl/ v 1 to treat roughly; maltreat 2 to mismanage (a situation, crisis, etc)

mishap /'mis,hap/ n an unfortunate accident

mis'hear /-'hiə/ v **misheard** /-'huhd/ to hear wrongly

mishmash /'mish,mash/ n a hotchpotch, jumble – infml

mis

misinform /ˌmisin'fawm/ *v* to give untrue or mis-leading information to

misin'terpret /-in'tuhprit/ *v* to understand or explain wrongly – **~ation** *n*

mis'judge /-'juj/ *v* **1** to estimate wrongly **2** to have an unjust opinion of – **~ment** *n*

mislay /mis'lay/ *v* **mislaid** /-'layd/ to leave in an unremembered place

mis'lead /-'leed/ *v* **misled** /-'led/ to lead in a wrong direction or into a mistaken action or belief – **~ingly** *adv*

mis'manage /-'manij/ *v* to manage wrongly or incompetently – **~ment** *n*

mis'match /-'mach/ *v* to match incorrectly or unsuitably, esp in marriage – **mismatch** *n*

mis'nomer /-'nohmə/ *n* (a use of) a wrong name or designation

misogynist /mi'soj(ə)n·ist, mie-/ *n* one who hates women – **-gyny** *n*

misplace /mis'plays/ *v* **1a** to put in the wrong place **b** to mislay **2** to fail to suit to the occasion – **~ment** *n*

mis'print /-'print/ *v* to print wrongly

mispro'nounce /-prə'nowns/ *v* to pronounce wrongly – **-nunciation** *n*

mis'quote /-'kwoht/ *v* to quote incorrectly – **-quotation** *n*

mis'read /-'reed/ *v* **misread** /-'red/ to read or interpret incorrectly

misre'port /-ri'pawt/ *v* to report falsely

misrepre'sent /-repri'zent/ *v* to represent falsely; give an untrue or misleading account of – **~ation** *n*

¹**mis'rule** /-'roohl/ *v* to rule incompetently

²**mis'rule** *n* disorder, anarchy

¹**miss** /mis/ *v* **1** to fail to hit, reach, contact, or attain **2** to discover or feel the absence of, esp with regret **3** to escape, avoid **4** to leave out; omit – often + *out* **5** to fail to perform or attend **6** to fail to take advantage of — **miss out on** to lose or not to have had (a good opportunity) — **miss the boat** to fail to take advantage of an opportunity

²**miss** *n* **1** a failure to hit **2** a failure to attain a desired result **3** a deliberate avoidance or omission of sthg

³**miss** *n* **1** – used as a title preceding the name of an unmarried woman or girl **2** a young unmarried woman or girl – chiefly infml

missal /'misl/ *n* a book containing the order of service of the mass for the whole year

missile /'misiel/ *NAm* 'misl/ *n* an object thrown or projected, usu so as to strike sthg at a distance; *also* a self-propelled weapon that travels through the air

missing /'mising/ *adj* absent; *also* lost

missing 'link *n* a supposed intermediate form between man and his anthropoid ancestors

mission /'mish(ə)n/ *n* **1a** a ministry commissioned by a religious organization to propagate its faith or carry on humanitarian work, usu abroad **b** a mission establishment **c** a campaign to increase church membership or strengthen Christian faith **2a** a group sent to a foreign country to negotiate, advise, etc **b** a permanent embassy or legation **3** a specific task with which a person or group is charged **4** a definite military, naval, or aerospace task

¹**missionary** /'mishən(ə)ri/ *adj* **1** relating to, engaged in, or devoted to missions **2** characteristic of a missionary

²**missionary** *n* a person undertaking a mission; *esp* one in charge of a religious mission in some remote part of the world

missive /'misiv/ *n* a written communication; a letter – *fml*

misspell /ˌmis'spel/ *v* **misspelt**, *Nam chiefly* **misspelled** to spell incorrectly – **~ing** *n*

mis'spend /-'spend/ *v* **misspent** /-'spent/ to spend wrongly or foolishly; squander

mis'state /-'stayt/ *v* to state incorrectly; give a false account of – **~ment** *n*

mist /mist/ *n* **1** water in the form of diffuse particles in the atmosphere, esp near the earth's surface **2** sthg that dims or obscures **3** a film, esp of tears, before the eyes

¹**mistake** /mi'stayk/ *v* **mistook** /mi'stook/; **mistaken** /mi'staykən/ **1** to choose wrongly **2a** to misunderstand the meaning, intention, or significance of **b** to estimate wrongly **3** to identify wrongly; confuse with another

²**mistake** *n* **1** a misunderstanding of the meaning or significance of sthg **2** a wrong action or statement arising from faulty judgment, inadequate knowledge, or carelessness

mistaken /mi'staykən/ *adj* **1** *of a person* wrong in opinion **2** *of an action, idea, etc* based on wrong thinking; incorrect – **~ly** *adv*

mister /'mistə/ *n* – used sometimes in writing instead of the usual *Mr*

mistime /ˌmis'tiem/ *v* to time badly

mistletoe /'misl,toh/ *n* a European shrub that grows as a parasite on the branches of trees and has thick leaves and waxy white glutinous berries

mistress /'mistris/ *n* **1a** a woman in a position of power or authority **b** the female head of a household **2** a woman who has achieved mastery of a subject or skill **3** a woman with whom a man has a continuing sexual relationship outside marriage **4** *chiefly Br* a schoolmistress

mis'trust /-'trust/ *v* **1** to have little trust in; be suspicious of **2** to doubt the reliability or effectiveness of – **mistrust** *n*

misty /'misti/ *adj* **1** obscured by mist **2** not clear to the mind or understanding; indistinct – **-tily** *adv* – **-tiness** *n*

misunderstand /,misundə'stand/ v **1** to fail to understand **2** to interpret incorrectly

,misunder'standing /-'standing/ n **1** a failure to understand; a misinterpretation **2** a disagreement, dispute

,mis'use /-'yoohz/ v **1** to put to wrong or improper use **2** to abuse or maltreat – **misuse** n

mite /miet/ n **1** any of numerous (extremely) small arachnids that often infest animals, plants, and stored foods **2** a small coin or sum of money **3** a very small object or creature; esp a small child — **a mite** to a small extent — infml

mitigate /'mitigayt/ v **1** to cause to become less harsh or hostile **2a** to make less severe or painful; alleviate **b** to extenuate – **-gation** n

¹**mitre**, NAm chiefly **miter** /'mietə/ n **1** a tall pointed divided headdress with 2 bands hanging down at the back worn by bishops and abbots on ceremonial occasions **2** mitre, mitre joint a joint made by cutting the ends of 2 pieces of wood at an oblique angle so that they form a right angle when fitted together

²**mitre**, NAm chiefly **miter** v **1** to bevel the ends of to make a mitre joint **2** to match or fit together in a mitre joint

mitt /mit/ n **1a** a glove that leaves the (ends of the) fingers uncovered **b** a mitten **2** a hand or paw; specif a person's hand – infml

mitten /'mit(ə)n/ n a glove that is divided into one part covering the fingers and another part covering the thumb

¹**mix** /miks/ v **1a(1)** to combine or blend into a mass **a(2)** to combine with another – often + in **b** to bring into close association **2** to prepare by mixing different components or ingredients **3** to control the balance of (various sounds), esp during the recording of a film, broadcast, record, etc **4** to seek or enjoy the society of others — **mix it** to fight, brawl — infml

²**mix** n an act or process of mixing **2** a product of mixing; specif a commercially prepared mixture of food ingredients **3** a combination **4** a combination in definite proportions of 2 or more recordings (e g of a singer and an accompaniment)

mixed /mikst/ adj **1** combining diverse elements **2** made up of or involving people of different races, national origins, religions, classes, or sexes **3** including or accompanied by conflicting or dissimilar elements

,mixed 'metaphor n a combination of incongruous metaphors (e g in iron out bottlenecks)

,mixed-'up adj marked by perplexity, uncertainty, or disorder; confused – infml

mixer /'miksə/ n a person considered with respect to his/her ability to mix well in company

mixture /'mikschə/ n **1a** mixing or being mixed **b** the relative proportions of constituents; specif the proportion of fuel to air produced in a carburettor **2a** (a portion of) matter consisting of 2 or more components in varying proportions that retain their own properties **b** a combination of several different kinds; a blend

¹**'mix-,up** n a state or instance of confusion

mix up v **1** to make untidy or disordered **2** to mistake or confuse – **mix-up** n

mizzen, **mizen** /'miz(ə)n/ n (the sail set on) the mast behind the mainsail

mnemonic /ni'monik, nee-/ adj **1** assisting or intended to assist the memory **2** of memory — **mnemonic** n

mo, mo' /moh/ n, chiefly Br a very short space of time; a moment – infml; often in half a mo

¹**moan** /mohn/ n a low prolonged sound of pain or grief

²**moan** v **1** to produce (a sound like) a moan **2** to complain, grumble – **~er** n

moat /moht/ n a deep wide trench round a castle, fortified home, etc that is usu filled with water

¹**mob** /mob/ n **1** the masses, populace **2a** a disorderly riotous crowd **3** a criminal gang **4** chiefly Austr a flock, drove, or herd of animals **5** sing or pl in constr, chiefly Br a crowd, bunch – infml – **mob** adj

²**mob** v -bb- **1** to attack in a large crowd or group **2** to crowd round, esp out of curiosity or admiration

¹**mobile** /'mohbiel/ adj **1** capable of moving or being moved **2** changing quickly in expression or mood **3** (capable of) undergoing movement into a different social class – **-ility** n

²**mobile** n a structure (e g of cardboard or metal) with usu suspended parts that are moved in different planes by air currents or machinery

mobil·ize, **-ise** /'mohbiliez/ v **1** to put into movement or circulation **2a** to call up troops for active service **b** to marshal resources ready for action – **-ization** n

mobster /'mobstə/ n, chiefly NAm a member of a criminal gang

moccasin /'mokəsin/ n a soft leather heelless shoe with the sole brought up the sides of the foot and joined to the upper by a puckered seam

mocha /'mokə, 'mohkə/ n **1** a coffee of superior quality, specif grown in Arabia **2** a flavouring obtained from a (mixture of cocoa or chocolate with) a strong coffee infusion

¹**mock** /mok/ v **1** to treat with contempt or ridicule **2** to disappoint the hopes of **3** to mimic in fun or derision – **~er** n – **~ingly** adv

²**mock** n a school examination used as a rehearsal for an official one

³**mock** adj (having the character) of an imitation or simulation

⁴**mock** adv in an insincere or pretended manner – usu in combination

mockery /'mokəri/ *n* **1** jeering or contemptuous behaviour or words **2** an object of laughter or derision **3** a deceitful or contemptible imitation; a travesty

mockingbird /'moking,buhd/ *n* a common bird of esp the southern USA that imitates the calls of other birds

'mock-,up *n* a full-sized structural model built accurately to scale

modal /'mohdl/ *adj* **1** of or being (in) a mode (e g in music); *specif* being in one of the church modes rather than a major or minor key **2** of general form or structure as opposed to particular substance or content – **~ly** *adv*

modal auxiliary *n* an auxiliary verb (e g *can*, *must*, *may*) expressing a distinction of mood

mod con /ˌmod 'kon/ *n, Br* a modern convenience; *esp* a household fitting or device designed to increase comfort or save time – *infml*

¹mode /mohd/ *n* **1** an arrangement of the 8 diatonic musical notes of an octave in any of several fixed schemes which use different patterns of whole tones and semitones between successive notes **2a** a particular form or variety of sthg **b** a form or manner of expression; a style **3** a way of doing or carrying out sthg

²mode *n* a prevailing fashion or style (e g of dress or behaviour) – fml

¹model /'modl/ *n* **1** structural design **2** a replica of sthg in relief or 3 dimensions; *also* a representation of sthg to be constructed **3** an example worthy of imitation or emulation **4** sby or sthg that serves as a pattern for an artist; *esp* one who poses for an artist **5** one who is employed to wear merchandise, esp clothing, in order to display it **6** a type or design of an article or product (e g a garment or car)

²model *v* **-ll-** (*NAm* **-l-**, **-ll-**), /'modl·ing/ **1** to plan or form after a pattern **2** to shape in a mouldable material; *broadly* to produce a representation or simulation of **3** to construct or fashion in imitation of a particular model **4** to display, esp by wearing

³model *adj* **1** (worthy of) being a pattern for others **2** being a miniature representation of sthg

¹moderate /'mod(ə)rət/ *adj* **1a** avoiding extremes of behaviour or expression **b** not violent; temperate **2** being (somewhat less than) average in quality, amount, or degree – **-tion** *n* – **~ly** *adv*

²moderate /'modərayt/ *v* **1** to lessen the intensity or extremeness of **2** to preside over

³moderate /'mod(ə)rət/ *n* one who holds moderate views or favours a moderate course

moderato /ˌmodə'rahtoh/ *adv or adj* in a moderate tempo – used in music

moderator /'modəraytə/ *n* **1** a mediator **2** the presiding officer of a Presbyterian governing body

modern /'modən/ *adj* **1a** (characteristic) of a period extending from a particular point in the past to the present time **b** (characteristic) of the present or the immediate past; contemporary **2** involving recent techniques, styles, or ideas – **~ize** *v*

modernism /'modəniz(ə)m/ *n* **1** a practice, usage, or expression characteristic of modern times **2** the theory and practices of modern art; *esp* a search for new forms of expression involving a deliberate break with the past – **-ist** *adj*, *n*

modest /'modist/ *adj* **1** having a moderate estimate of one's abilities or worth; not boastful or self-assertive **2** (characteristic) of a modest nature **3** carefully observant of proprieties of dress and behaviour **4** small or limited in size, amount, or aim – **~ly** *adv* – **~y** *n*

modicum /'modikəm/ *n* a small or limited amount

modify /'modifie/ *v* **1** to make less extreme **2** to undergo change **3a** to make minor changes in **b** to make basic changes in, often for a specific purpose – **-fication** *n*

modish /'mohdish/ *adj* fashionable, stylish – **~ly** *adv*

modulate /'modyoolayt/ *v* **1** to vary in tone; make tuneful **2** to adjust to or keep in proper measure or proportion **3** to vary the amplitude, frequency, or phase of (a carrier wave or signal) by combining with a wave of a different frequency, so as to transmit a radio, television, etc signal **4** to pass by regular chord or melodic progression from one musical key or tonality into another – **-ation** *n*

module /'modyoohl/ *n* a standardized or independent unit used in construction (e g of buildings, electronic systems, or spacecraft) – **modular** *adj*

mogul /'mohg(ə)l/ *n* **1 Mogul, Moghul** a member of a Muslim dynasty of Turkish and Mongolian origin ruling India from the 16th to the 18th c **2** a great or prominent (business) person

mohair /'moh,heə/ *n* a fabric or yarn made (partly) from the long silky hair of the Angora goat

Mohammedan /mə'hamid(ə)n/ *adj* Muhammadan – **~ism** *n*

moiré /'mwahray (*Fr* mware)/, **moire** /'mwahray; *also* mwah/ *n* an irregular wavy sheen on a fabric or metal

moist /moyst/ *adj* **1** slightly wet; damp **2** highly humid – **~en** *v* – **~ly** *adv* – **~ness** *n*

moisture /'moyschə/ *n* liquid diffused, condensed, or absorbed in relatively small amounts

¹molar /'mohlə/ *n* a grinding tooth with a rounded or flattened surface; *specif* one lying behind the incisors and canines of a mammal

²**molar** *adj* **1** of a mass of matter as distinguished from the properties of individual molecules or atoms **2** of or containing 1 gram molecule (of dissolved substance) in 1 litre of solution

molasses /mə'lasiz/ *n* the darkest most viscous syrup remaining after all sugar that can be separated by crystallization has been removed during the refining of raw sugar

¹**mole** /mohl/ *n* a dark spot, mark, or lump on the human body

²**mole** *n* **1** any of numerous small burrowing insect-eating mammals with minute eyes, concealed ears, and soft fur **2** one who works subversively within an organization, esp to secretly further the interests of a rival organization or government

³**mole** *n* (a harbour formed by) a massive work of masonry, large stones, etc laid in the sea as a pier or breakwater

⁴**mole** *n* the basic SI unit of substance; the amount of substance that contains the same number of atoms, molecules, ions, etc as there are atoms in 0.012kg of carbon-12

molecule /'molikyoohl/ *n* the smallest particle of a substance that retains its characteristic properties, consisting of 1 or more atoms – **~ular** *adj*

'**mole,hill** /-,hil/ *n* a mound of earth thrown up by a burrowing mole

molest /mə'lest/ *v* to annoy, disturb, or attack; *specif* to annoy or attack (esp a child or woman) sexually – **~ation** *n* – **~er** *n*

moll /mol/ *n* a gangster's girl friend *USE* infml

mollify /'molifie/ *v* **1** to lessen the anger or hostility of **2** to reduce in intensity – **-fication** *n*

mollusc , *NAm chiefly* **mollusk** /'moləsk/ *n* any of a large phylum of invertebrate animals with soft bodies not divided into segments and usu enclosed in a shell, including the snails, shellfish, octopuses, and squids

mollycoddle /'moli,kodl/ *v* **mollycoddling** /'moli,kodling, -,kodl·ing/ to treat with excessive indulgence and attention – **mollycoddle** *n*

,**Molotov 'cocktail** /'molətof/ *n* a crude hand grenade made from a bottle filled with petrol or other inflammable liquid with usu a saturated rag for a wick

molten /'mohlt(ə)n/ *adj* melted by heat

molybdenum /mə'libdənəm/ *n* a metallic element resembling chromium and tungsten and used esp in strengthening and hardening steel

moment /'mohmənt/ *n* **1** a very brief interval or point of time **2a** present time **b** a time of excellence or prominence **3** importance in influence or effect **4** a stage in historical or logical development **5** (a measure of) the tendency of a force to produce turning motion

momentary /'mohmənt(ə)ri/ *adj* lasting a very short time – **-rily** *adv*

momentous /mə'mentəs, moh-/ *adj* of great consequence or significance

momentum /mə'mentəm, moh-/ *n pl* **momenta** /-tə/, **momentums** the product of the mass of a body and its velocity

monarch /'monək/ *n* **1** sby who reigns over a kingdom or empire **2** sby or sthg occupying a commanding or preeminent position – **~ic**, **~ical** *adj*

monarchism /'monə,kiz(ə)m/ *n* government by or the principles of monarchy – **-chist** *n, adj*

monarchy /'monəki/ *n* (a government or state with) undivided rule by a monarch

monastery /'monəst(ə)ri/ *n* a residence occupied by a religious community, esp of monks

monastic /mə'nastik/ *adj* of or being monasteries, monks, or nuns – **~ism** *n* – **~ally** *adv*

Monday /'munday, -di/ *n* the day of the week following Sunday

monetary /'munit(ə)ri/ *adj* of money or its behaviour in an economy

money /'muni/ *n, pl* **moneys, monies 1** sthg generally accepted as a means of payment; *esp* officially printed, coined, or stamped currency **2** a form or denomination of coin or paper money – **~less** *adj*

'**money ,grubber** *n* a person sordidly bent on accumulating money – infml

'**money,lender** /-,lendə/ *n* one whose business is lending money and charging interest on it

'**money-,maker** *n* a product or enterprise that produces much profit

'**money-,spinner** *n, chiefly Br* a money-maker – infml

Mongol /'mong,gol, 'mong·gl/ *n* **1** a member of any of the chiefly pastoral peoples of Mongolia **2** *often not cap* a sufferer from Down's syndrome

mongolism /'mong·g(ə)l,iz(ə)m/ *n* Down's syndrome

mongoose /'mong,goohs/ *n pl* **mongooses** *also* **mongeese** /-,gees/ an agile ferret-sized Indian mammal that feeds on snakes and rodents

mongrel /'mong·grəl, 'mung-/ *n* a dog or other individual (of unknown ancestry) resulting from the interbreeding of diverse breeds

¹**monitor** /'monitə/, *fem* **monitress** /'monitris/ *n* **1** a pupil appointed to help a teacher **2** any of various large tropical Old World lizards closely related to the iguanas

²**monitor** *v* **1** to keep (a broadcast) under surveillance by means of a receiver, in order to check the quality or fidelity to a frequency or to investigate the content (e g for political significance) **2** to observe or inspect, esp for a special purpose **3** to regulate or control the operation of (e g a machine or process)

monk /mungk/ *n* a male member of a religious order, living apart from the world under vows of poverty, chastity, etc – **~ish** *adj*

¹**monkey** /'mungki/ *n* **1** any small long-tailed primate mammal **2a** a mischievous child; a scamp **b** a ludicrous figure; a fool *USE* (2) infml

²**monkey** *v* **1** to act in an absurd or mischievous manner **2** to mess around *with USE* infml; often + *about* or *around*

'**monkey** ,**business** *n* mischievous or underhand activity – infml

'**monkey** ,**nut** *n* a peanut

mono /'monoh/ *adj* or *n* monophonic (sound reproduction)

monochrome /'monə,krohm/ *adj* or *n* (of, using, or being) reproduction or execution in 1 colour, black and white, or shades of grey

monocle /'monəkl/ *n* an eyeglass for 1 eye

monogamy /mə'nogami/ *n* the state or custom of being married to 1 person at a time – **-mous** *adj* – **-mously** *adv*

monogram /'monə,gram/ *v* or *n* (to mark with) a character usu formed of the interwoven initials of a name – ~**med** *adj*

monograph /'monə,grahf, -,graf/ *n* a treatise on a small area of learning

monolith /'monə,lith/ *n* **1** a single large block of stone, often in the form of an obelisk or column **2** a massive structure **3** an organized whole that acts as a single powerful force

monolithic /,monə'lithik/ *adj* constituting a massive uniform whole – ~**ally** *adv*

monologue, *NAm also* **monolog** /'monə,log/ *n* **1** a dramatic or literary soliloquy; *also* a dramatic sketch performed by 1 speaker **2** a long speech monopolizing conversation

monomania /,monoh'maynyə/ *n* obsessional concentration on a single object or idea – ~**c** *n*

monophonic /,monə'fonik/ *adj* of or being a system for sound reproduction in which the sound signal is not split into 2 or more different channels between the source and the point of use

monoplane /'monə,playn/ *n* an aeroplane with only 1 main pair of wings

monopol·ize, -ise /mə'nopoliez/ *v* to assume complete possession or control of

monopoly /mə'nopoli/ *n* **1** (a person or group having) exclusive ownership or control (through legal privilege, command of the supply of a commodity, concerted action, etc) **2** sthg, esp a commodity, controlled by one party

monorail /'monoh,rayl/ *n* (a vehicle running on) a single rail serving as a track for a wheeled vehicle

monosodium glutamate /,monə,sohdi·əm 'gloohtəmayt/ *n* an artificially produced white powder used for seasoning foods

monosyllable /'monə,siləbl/ *n* a word of 1 syllable; *specif* one used by sby intending to be pointedly brief in answering or commenting – **-syllabic** *adj*

monotheism /'monohthee,iz(ə)m/ *n* the doctrine or belief that there is only 1 God – **-ist** *n* – **-istic** *adj*

¹**monotone** /'monə,tohn/ *n* **1** a succession of speech sounds in 1 unvarying pitch **2** a single unvaried musical note **3** a tedious sameness or repetition

²**monotone** *adj* having a uniform colour

monotonous /mə'not(ə)nəs/ *adj* **1** uttered or sounded in 1 unvarying tone **2** tediously uniform or repetitive – **-ny**, ~**ness** *n* – ~**ly** *adv*

monsieur /mə'syuh/ *n, pl* **messieurs** /me'syuh, mə'syuhz/ – used by or to a French-speaking man as a title equivalent to Mr or without a name as a term of direct address

monsignor /mon'seenyaw/ *n, pl* **monsignors, monsignori** /-'ri/ – used as a title for certain Roman Catholic prelates and officers of the papal court

monsoon /mon'soohn/ *n* **1** a seasonal wind of S Asia blowing from the SW in summer and the NE in winter **2** the season of the SW monsoon, marked by very heavy rains

monster /'monstə/ *n* **1a** an animal or plant of (grotesquely) abnormal form or structure **b** an (imaginary) animal of incredible shape or form that is usu dangerous or horrifying **2** one exceptionally large for its kind **3** sthg monstrous; *esp* a person of appalling ugliness, wickedness, or cruelty

monstrosity /mon'strosəti/ *n* **1** a monstrous plant or animal **2** (the quality or state of being) sthg monstrous

monstrous /'monstrəs/ *adj* **1** having the qualities or appearance of a monster; extraordinarily large **2a** extraordinarily ugly or vicious **b** outrageously wrong or ridiculous – ~**ly** *adv*

montage /monh'tahzh/ *n* **1** a picture made by combining or overlapping several separate pictures **2** (a film sequence using) a method of film editing in which the chronological sequence of events is interrupted by juxtaposed or rapidly succeeding shots

month /munth/ *n* **1a** any of the 12 divisions of the year in the Julian or Gregorian calendars corresponding roughly with the period of the moon's rotation; *also* any similar division of the year in other calendars **b** 28 days or 4 weeks; *also* the interval between the same date in adjacent months **2** *pl* an indefinite usu protracted period of time – ~**ly** *adj* or *adv*

'**monthly** /-li/ *n* **1** a monthly periodical **2** *pl* a menstrual period – infml

monument /'monyoomənt/ *n* **1a** a lasting evidence or reminder of sby or sthg notable or influential **b** a memorial stone, sculpture, or structure erected to commemorate a person or event **2** a structure or site of historical or archaeological importance

monumental /,monyoo'mentl/ *adj* **1** of, serving as, or resembling a monument **b** occurring or used on a monument **2** very great in degree; imposing, outstanding

moo /mooh/ *v or n* (to) low

¹**mood** /moohd/ *n* **1a** (the evocation, esp in art or literature, of) a predominant emotion, feeling, or frame of mind **b** the right frame of mind **2** a fit of often silent anger or bad temper

²**mood** *n* a distinct form or set of inflectional forms of a verb indicating whether the action or state it denotes is considered a fact, wish, possibility, etc

moody /'moohdi/ *adj* **1** sullen or gloomy **2** temperamental – **moodily** *adv* – **moodiness** *n*

¹**moon** /moohn/ *n* **1** the earth's natural satellite that shines by reflecting the sun's light **2** a satellite – **over the moon** absolutely delighted

²**moon** *v* **1** to move about listlessly **2** to spend time in idle gazing or daydreaming *USE* often + *around* or *about*; infml

'**moon,beam** /-,beem/ *n* a ray of light from the moon

'**moon,light** /-,liet/ *v* **moonlighted** to hold a second job in addition to a regular one

'**moon,shine** /-,shien/ *n* **1** the light of the moon **2** empty talk; nonsense **3** (illegally distilled) spirits, esp whisky – infml

'**moon,struck** /-,struk/ *adj* affected (as if) by the moon; *specif* mentally unbalanced

¹**moor** /maw, mooə/ *n, chiefly Br* an expanse of open peaty infertile usu heath-covered upland

²**moor** *v* to make (e g a boat or buoy) fast with cables, lines, or anchors

Moor *n* a member of the mixed Arab and Berber people that conquered Spain in the 8th c AD

moorhen /'maw,hen, 'mooə-/ *n* a common red-billed blackish bird of the rail family that nests near fresh water

moose /moohs/ *n, pl* **moose** a large N American ruminant mammal of the deer family with very large flattened antlers

¹**moot** /mooht/ *n* **1** an early English assembly to decide points of community and political interest **2** a mock court in which law students argue hypothetical cases

²**moot** *v* to put forward for discussion

³**moot** *adj* open to question; debatable – usu in *moot point*

¹**mop** /mop/ *n* **1** an implement consisting of a head made of absorbent material fastened to a long handle and used esp for cleaning floors **2** a shock of untidy hair

²**mop** *v* **-pp-** **1** to clean (a floor or other surface) with a mop **2** to wipe (as if) with a mop

mope /mohp/ *v* to give oneself up to brooding; become listless or dejected

moped /'mohped/ *n* a low-powered motorcycle whose engine can be pedal-assisted (e g for starting)

moppet /'mopit/ *n* a young child; *esp* a little girl – chiefly infml; apprec

moraine /mo'rayn/ *n* an accumulation of earth and stones carried and deposited by a glacier

¹**moral** /'morəl/ *adj* **1a** of or being principles of right and wrong in conduct; ethical **b** conforming to a standard of right conduct **c** capable of distinguishing right and wrong **2** of, occurring in, or acting on the mind, emotions, or will – **~ly** *adv*

²**moral** *n* **1** (a concluding passage pointing out) the moral significance or practical lesson **2** *pl* **2a** standards of esp sexual conduct **b** ethics

morale /mo'rahl/ *n* the mental and emotional condition (e g of enthusiasm or loyalty) of an individual or group with regard to the function or tasks at hand

moralist /'morəlist/ *n* one concerned with regulating the morals of others – often derog

morality /mo'raləti/ *n* **1** a system or sphere of moral conduct **2** (degree of conformity to standards of) right conduct or moral correctness

mo'rality ,play *n* a form of allegorical drama popular esp in the 15th and 16th c in which the characters personify moral or abstract qualities (e g pride or youth)

moral·ize, -ise /'morəliez/ *v* to make (unnecessary) moral judgments or reflections

morass /mo'ras/ *n* **1** a marsh, swamp **2** sthg that ensnares, confuses, or impedes

moratorium /,morə'tawri·əm/ *n, pl* **moratoriums, moratoria** /-ri·ə/ a suspension of (a specified) activity – usu + *on*

morbid /'mawbid/ *adj* **1** of, affected with, induced by, or characteristic of disease **2** abnormally susceptible to or characterized by gloomy feelings; *esp* having an unnatural preoccupation with death **3** grisly, gruesome – ~**ity** *n* – ~**ly** *adv*

¹**mordant** /'mawd(ə)nt/ *adj* **1** caustic or sharply critical in thought, manner, or style **2** burning, pungent

²**mordant** *n* a chemical that fixes a dye by combining with it to form an insoluble compound

¹**more** /maw/ *adj* **1** greater in quantity or number **2** additional, further – **neither/nothing more or/nor less than** simply, plainly

²**more** *adv* **1a** as an additional amount **b** moreover, again **2** to a greater degree or extent – often used with an adjective or adverb to form the comparative (e g much *more* even) – **more often than not** at most times; usually

³**more** *n, pl* **more 1** a greater or additional quantity, amount, or part **2** *pl* additional ones – **more of** nearer to being (sthg specified)

moreover /maw'rohvə/ *adv* in addition to what has been said – used to introduce new matter

mores /'mawreez/ *n pl* (the morally binding) customs or conventions of a particular group

morgue /mawg/ *n* **1** a mortuary **2** a collection of reference works and files in a newspaper office

mor

moribund /'mori,bund/ *adj* dying

Mormon /'mawmən/ *n* a member of the Church of Jesus Christ of Latter-Day Saints, founded in 1830 in the USA by Joseph Smith, and following precepts contained in the Book of Mormon, a sacred text that he discovered – ~**ism** *n*

morn /mawn/ *n* the morning – chiefly poetic

morning /'mawning/ *n* **1a** the dawn **b** the time from midnight or sunrise to noon **2** an early period (e g of time or life); the beginning — **in the morning** tomorrow morning

'**morning dress** *n* men's dress for formal occasions (e g a wedding) during the day

'**morning sickness** *n* nausea and vomiting occurring esp in the morning during the earlier months of a woman's pregnancy

morocco /mə'rokoh/ *n* a fine leather made from goatskin

moron /'mawron/ *n* **1** a mental defective **2** a very stupid person – *infml* – ~**ic** *adj*

morose /mə'rohs/ *adj* (having a disposition) marked by or expressive of gloom – ~**ly** *adv* – ~**ness** *n*

morphine /'mawfeen/ *n* the principal alkaloid of opium that is an addictive narcotic drug used esp as a powerful painkiller

'**morris dance** /'moris/ *n* any of several traditional English dances that are performed by groups of people wearing costumes to which small bells are attached

morrow /'moroh/ *n* the next day – *fml*

morsel /'mawsl/ *n* **1** a small piece of food **2** a small quantity; a scrap

'**mortal** /'mawtl/ *adj* **1** causing or about to cause death; fatal **2** not living forever; subject to death **3** marked by relentless hostility **4** of or connected with death – *infml*

²**mortal** *n* **1** a human being **2** a person of a specified kind

mortality /maw'taləti/ *n* **1** being mortal **2** the death of large numbers of people, animals, etc; *also* the number of deaths in a given time or place **3** the human race

mortally /'mawtl·i/ *adv* **1** in a deadly or fatal manner **2** to an extreme degree; intensely

'**mortar** /'mawtə/ *n* **1** a strong usu bowl-shaped vessel (e g of stone) in which substances are pounded or ground with a pestle **2** a usu muzzle-loading artillery gun having a tube short in relation to its calibre, a low muzzle velocity, and a high trajectory

²**mortar** *n* a mixture of cement, lime, gypsum plaster, etc with sand and water, that hardens and is used to join bricks, stones etc or for plastering

'**mortar board** /-,bawd/ *n* an academic cap consisting of a close-fitting crown with a stiff flat square attached on top

'**mortgage** /'mawgij/ *n* a transfer of the ownership of property (e g for security or a loan) on condition that the transfer becomes void on payment

²**mortgage** *v* **1** to transfer the ownership of (property) by a mortgage **2** to make subject to a claim or obligation

mortify /'mawtifie/ *v* **1** to subdue (e g bodily needs and desires), esp by abstinence or self-inflicted suffering **2** to subject to feelings of shame or acute embarrassment **3** to become decaying infected with gangrene – **-fication** *n*

mortise *also* **mortice** /'mawtis/ *n* a usu rectangular cavity cut into a piece of material (e g wood) to receive a protrusion, esp a tenon, of another piece – **mortise** *v*

'**mortuary** /'mawtyoori, -chəri/ *n* a room or building in which dead bodies are kept before burial or cremation

²**mortuary** *adj* of death or the burial of the dead

mosaic /mə'zayik, moh-/ *n* **1** (a piece of) decorative work made from small pieces of different coloured material (e g glass or stone) inlaid to form pictures or patterns **2** a virus disease of plants (e g tobacco) characterized esp by diffuse yellow and green mottling of the foliage

Mosaic *adj* of Moses or the institutions or writings attributed to him

Moslem /'moozlim/ *n or adj* (a) Muslim

mosque /mosk/ *n* a building used for public worship by Muslims

mosquito /mo'skeetoh/ *n*, *pl* **mosquitoes** *also* **mosquitos** any of numerous 2-winged flies with females that suck the blood of animals and often transmit diseases (e g malaria) to them

moss /mos/ *n* **1** any of a class of primitive plants with small leafy stems bearing sex organs at the tip; *also* many of these plants growing together and covering a surface **2** *chiefly Scot* a (peat) bog – ~**y** *adj*

'**most** /mohst/ *adj* **1** the majority of **2** greatest in quantity or extent

²**most** *adv* **1** to the greatest degree or extent – often used with an adjective or adverb to form the superlative (e g the *most* challenging job he ever had) **2** very (e g shall *most* certainly come)

³**most** *n*, *pl* **most** the greatest quantity, number, or amount — **at most, at the most 1** as a maximum limit **2** at best

⁴**most** *adv*, *archaic*, *dial*, *or NAm* almost

mostly /'mohstli/ *adv* for the greatest part; mainly; *also* in most cases; usually

mot /moh/ *n*, *pl* **mots** /moh(z)/ a pithy or witty saying

MOT *also* **MoT** *n* a compulsory annual roadworthiness test in Britain for motor vehicles older than a certain age

mote /moht/ *n* a small particle; *esp* a particle of dust suspended in the air

motel /'moh'tel/ n an establishment which provides accommodation and parking

motet /'moh'tet/ n a choral composition on a sacred text

moth /moth/ n 1 a clothes moth 2 a usu night-flying insect with feathery antennae and a stouter body and duller colouring than the butterflies

'moth,ball /-,bawl/ n 1 a naphthalene or (formerly) camphor ball used to keep moths from clothing 2 pl a state of indefinitely long protective storage; also a state of having been rejected as of no further use or interest

'moth-,eaten adj 1 very worn-out or shabby in appearance 2 antiquated, outmoded

¹mother /'mudhə/ n 1 a a female parent b an old or elderly woman 2 a source, origin – ~less adj

²mother adj 1 a of or being a mother b bearing the relation of a mother 2 derived (as if) from one's mother 3 acting as or providing a parental stock – used without reference to sex

³mother v 1 a to give birth to b to give rise to; initiate, produce 2 to care for or protect like a mother – often derog

'mother-in-,law n, pl **mothers-in-law** the mother of one's spouse

'motherly /-li/ adj 1 (characteristic) of a mother 2 like a mother; maternal – **liness** n

,mother-of-'pearl n the hard pearly iridescent substance forming the inner layer of a mollusc shell

,mother su'perior n, often cap M&S the head of a religious community of women

motif /moh'teef/ n 1 a recurring element forming a theme in a work of art or literature; esp a dominant idea or central theme 2 a single or repeated design or colour

¹motion /'mohsh(ə)n/ n 1 a a formal proposal made in a deliberative assembly b an application to a court or judge for an order, ruling, or direction 2 a an act, process, or instance of changing position; movement b an active or functioning state or condition 3 a an act or instance of moving the body or its parts; a gesture b pl actions, movements; esp merely simulated or mechanical actions – often in go through the motions 4 an evacuation of the bowels – usu pl with sing. meaning – ~less adj

²motion v to direct by a gesture

'motion ,picture n, chiefly NAm a film, movie

motivate /'mohtivayt/ v to provide with a motive or incentive; impel – **-ation** n

¹motive /'mohtiv/ n 1 a need, desire, etc that causes sby to act 2 a recurrent phrase or figure that is developed through the course of a musical composition – ~**less** adj

²motive adj 1 moving or tending to move action 2 of (the causing of) motion

¹motley /'motli/ adj 1 multicoloured 2 composed of varied (disreputable or unsightly) elements

²motley n a haphazard mixture (of incompatible elements)

moto-cross /'mohtoh ,kros/ n the sport of racing motorcycles across country on a rugged usu hilly closed course

¹motor /'mohtə/ n 1 sthg or sby that imparts motion 2 a an internal-combustion engine b a rotating machine that transforms electrical energy into mechanical energy 3 a motor vehicle; esp a motor car

²motor adj 1 a causing or imparting motion b of or involving muscular movement 2 a equipped with or driven by a motor b of or involving motor vehicles

³motor v to travel by motor car; esp to drive – ~**ist** n

'motor ,bike n a motorcycle – infml

'motor,boat /-,boht/ n a usu small boat propelled by a motor

'motor,cade /-,kayd/ n a procession of motor vehicles

'motor ,car n a usu 4-wheeled motor vehicle designed for transporting a small number of people and typically propelled by an internal-combustion engine

'motor,cycle /-,siekl/ n a 2-wheeled motor vehicle that can carry 1 or sometimes 2 people astride the engine – **-clist** n

'motor ,scooter n a usu 2-wheeled motor vehicle having a seat so that the driver sits in front of rather than astride the engine

'motor ,vehicle also **motor** n a self-propelled vehicle not operated on rails; esp one with rubber tyres for use on roads

'motor,way /-,way/ n, Br a major road designed for high-speed traffic

mottled /'motld/ adj having irregular spots or markings; dappled

motto /'motoh/ n, pl **mottoes** also **mottos** 1 a sentence, phrase, or word inscribed on sthg as appropriate to or indicative of its character or use 2 a short expression of a guiding principle; a maxim 3 (a piece of paper printed with) a usu humorous or sentimental saying

¹mould, NAm chiefly **mold** /mohld/ n crumbling soft (humus-rich) soil suited to plant growth

²mould, NAm chiefly **mold** n 1 the frame on or round which an object is constructed 2 a cavity or form in which a substance (e g a jelly or a metal casting) is shaped 3 a fixed pattern or form

³mould, NAm chiefly **mold** v 1 to give shape to 2 to form in a mould 3 to exert a steady formative influence on 4 to fit closely to the contours of

⁴mould, NAm chiefly **mold** n (a fungus producing) an often woolly growth on the surface of damp or decaying organic matter

moulder, *NAm chiefly* **molder** /'mohldə/ *v* to crumble into dust or decayed fragments, esp gradually

moulding /'mohlding/ *n* a decorative band or strip used for ornamentation or finishing (e g on a cornice)

mouldy /'mohldi/ *adj* 1 of, resembling, or covered with a mould-producing fungus 2 old and mouldering; fusty, crumbling 3a miserable, nasty b stingy *USE* (3) infml – **mouldiness** *n*

moult, *NAm chiefly* **molt** /mohlt/ *v* to shed or cast off (hair, feathers, shell, horns, or an outer layer) periodically – **moult** *n*

mound /mownd/ *n* 1a an artificial bank of earth or stones b a small hill 2 a heap, pile

¹**mount** /mownt/ *n* a high hill; a mountain – usu before a name

²**mount** *v* 1 to increase in amount, extent, or degree 2 to rise, ascend 3a to get up on or into sthg above ground level; *esp* to seat oneself (e g on a horse) for riding b to go up; climb c *of a male animal* to copulate with (a female animal) 4 to initiate and carry out (e g an assault or strike) 5 to station for defence or observation or as an escort 6a to attach to a support b to arrange or assemble for use or display 7a to prepare (e g a specimen) for examination or display b to organize and present for public viewing or performance; stage

³**mount** *n* 1a the material (e g cardboard) on which a picture is mounted b a jewellery setting c a hinge, card, etc for mounting a stamp in a stamp collection 2 a horse for riding

mountain /'mownt(ə)n, -tayn/ *n* 1 a landmass that projects conspicuously above its surroundings and is higher than a hill 2a a vast amount or quantity – often pl with sing. meaning b a supply, esp of a specified usu agricultural commodity, in excess of demand

,**mountain 'ash** *n* a rowan or related tree usu with small red fruits

mountaineering /,mowntə'niəring/ *n* the pastime or technique of climbing mountains and rock faces – **mountaineer** *n*

mountainous /'mownt(ə)nəs/ *adj* 1 containing many mountains 2 resembling a mountain; huge

mountebank /'mownti,bangk/ *n* 1 sby who sells quack medicines from a platform 2 a charlatan

Mountie /'mownti/ *n* a member of the Royal Canadian Mounted Police

mourn /mawn/ *v* to feel or express (e g in a conventional manner) grief or sorrow, esp for a death – **mourner** *n*

'**mournful** /-f(ə)l/ *adj* expressing, causing, or filled with sorrow – **~ly** *adv* – **~ness** *n*

mourning /'mawning/ *n* 1 the act or state of one who mourns 2a an outward sign (e g black clothes or an armband) of grief for a person's death b a period of time during which signs of grief are shown

¹**mouse** /mows/ *n, pl* **mice** /mies/ 1 any of numerous small rodents with a pointed snout, rather small ears, and slender tail 2 a timid person

²**mouse** *v* 1 to hunt for mice 2 *chiefly NAm* to search for carefully – usu + *out*

'**mouse,trap** /-,trap/ *n* a trap for mice

moussaka, mousaka /mooh'sahkə/ *n* a Greek dish consisting of layers of minced meat (e g lamb), aubergine or potato, tomato, and cheese with cheese or savoury custard topping

mousse /moohs/ *n* a light sweet or savoury cold dish usu containing cream, gelatin, and whipped egg whites

moustache, *NAm chiefly* **mustache** /mə'stahsh, mə'stash/ *n* the hair growing or allowed to grow on sby's upper lip

mousy, mousey /'mowsi/ *adj* 1 of or resembling a mouse: e g 1a quiet, stealthy b timid; *also* colourless 2 *of hair* light greyish brown – **mousiness** *n*

¹**mouth** /mowth/ *n, pl* **mouths** /mowdhz/ 1a the opening through which food passes into an animal's body; *also* the cavity in the head of the typical vertebrate animal bounded externally by the lips that encloses the tongue, gums, and teeth b an individual, esp a child, requiring food 2 sthg like a mouth, esp in affording entrance or exit: e g 2a the place where a river enters a sea, lake, etc b the opening of a cave, volcano, etc c the opening of a container 3 a tendency to talk too much — **down in the mouth** dejected, sulky

²**mouth** /mowdh/ *v* 1 to utter pompously 2 to repeat without comprehension or sincerity 3 to form (words) soundlessly with the lips

mouthful /'mowthf(ə)l/ *n* 1 a quantity that fills the mouth 2 a small quantity 3 a word or phrase that is very long or difficult to pronounce

'**mouth ,organ** *n* a harmonica

'**mouth,piece** /-,pees/ *n* 1 sthg placed at or forming a mouth 2 a part (e g of a musical instrument or a telephone) that goes in the mouth or is put next to the mouth 3 sby or sthg that expresses or interprets another's views

'**mouth-,watering** *adj* stimulating or appealing to the appetite; appetizing

movable, moveable /'moohvəbl/ *n or adj* (property) able to be removed – often used to distinguish personal property from land, buildings, etc; usu pl

¹**move** /moohv/ *v* 1a(1) to go or pass with a continuous motion a(2) to proceed or progress towards a (specified) place or condition – often + *on* b to change the place or position of c(1) to transfer a piece in a board game (e g in chess) from one position to another c(2) *of a piece in board games* to travel or be capable of travelling to another position d to change one's residence 2 to pass one's life in a specified environment 3 to (cause to) change position or posture 4a to take action; act b to prompt to action 5a to make a formal request,

application, or appeal **b** to propose formally in a deliberative assembly **6** to affect in such a way as to lead to a show of emotion or of a specified emotion **7** of the bowels to evacuate **8a** to (cause to) operate or function, esp mechanically **b** to show marked activity or speed – infml – **~ r** n

²move /mmoov/ n **1a** the act of moving a piece (e g in chess) **b** the turn of a player to move **2a** a step taken so as to gain an objective **b** a movement **c** a change of residence or official location — **on the move 1** in a state of moving about from place to place **2** in a state of moving ahead or making progress

'movement /-mənt/ n **1a** the act or process of moving; esp change of place, position, or posture **b** an action, activity – usu pl with sing. meaning **2a** a trend, specif in prices **b** an organized effort to promote an end **3** the moving parts of a mechanism that transmit motion **4** a unit or division having its own key, rhythmic structure, and themes and forming a separate part of an extended musical composition

movie /'moohvi/ n a film

moving /'moohving/ adj **1a** marked by or capable of movement **b** of a change of residence **2a** producing or transferring motion or action **b** evoking a deep emotional response – **~ly** adv

'mow /mow/ n the part of a barn where hay or straw is stored

²mow /moh/ v **mowed; mowed, mown** /mohn/ **1** to cut down a crop, esp grass **2** to cut down the standing herbage, esp grass, of (e g a field) – **~er** n

Mr /'mistə/ n pl **Messrs** /'mesəz/ **1** – used as a conventional title of courtesy before a man's surname where no other title is appropriate **2** – used in direct address before a man's title of office

Mrs /'misiz/ n pl **Mesdames** /may'dahm/ **1** – used as a conventional title of courtesy before a married woman's surname where no other title is appropriate **2** a wife – infml

Ms /məz, miz/ n – used instead of Mrs or Miss, esp when marital status is unknown or irrelevant

'much /much/ adj **more** /maw/; **most** /mohst/ **1** great in quantity or extent (e g how much milk is there?) **2** excessive, immoderate (e g it's a bit much) — **too much 1** wonderful, exciting **2** terrible, awful

²much adv **more; most 1a(1)** to a great degree or extent; considerably (e g was much happier) **a(2)** very – with verbal adjectives (e g was much amused) **b** frequently, often (e g much married) **c** by far (e g much the fatter) **2** nearly, approximately (e g looks much the same) — **as much 1** the same quantity **2** that, so — **much less** and certainly not

³much n **1** a great quantity, amount, or part **2** sthg considerable or impressive (e g wasn't much to look at) **3** a relative quantity or part (e g I'll say this much for him) — **too much for 1** more than a match for **2** beyond the endurance of

muck /muk/ n **1** soft moist farmyard manure **2** slimy dirt or filth **3** mire, mud **4a** a worthless or useless thing; rubbish – infml **b** Br – used in Lord Muck and Lady Muck to designate an arrogantly patronizing person

muck about v, chiefly Br to mess about

muck in v, chiefly Br to share or join in esp a task; also to share sleeping accommodation

muck out v to remove manure or filth, esp from an animal's quarters

'muck₁rake /-₁rayk/ v to search out and publicly expose real or apparent misconduct of prominent individuals – **~ r** n – **-raking** n

muck up v, chiefly Br to bungle, spoil

mucous /'myoohkəs/ adj of, like, secreting, or covered (as if) with mucus

₁mucous 'membrane /'membrayn/ n a membrane rich in mucous glands, specif lining body passages and cavities (e g the mouth) with openings to the exterior

mucus /'myoohkəs/ n a thick slippery secretion produced by mucous membranes (e g in the nose) which it moistens and protects

mud /mud/ n **1** (a sticky mixture of a solid and a liquid resembling) soft wet earth **2** abusive and malicious remarks or charges

'muddle /'mudl/ v **muddling** /'mudling, mudl·ing/ **1** to stupefy, esp with alcohol **2** to mix confusedly in one's mind – often – up **3** to proceed or get along in a confused aimless way – + along or on

²muddle n **1** a state of (mental) confusion **2** a confused mess

muddle'headed /-'hedid/ adj **1** mentally confused **2** inept, bungling

'muddy /'mudi/ adj **1** lacking in clarity or brightness **2** obscure in meaning; muddled, confused

²muddy v to make cloudy, dull, or confused

'mud₁guard /-₁gahd/ n a metal or plastic guard over the wheel of a bicycle, motorcycle, etc to deflect or catch mud

muesli /'m(y)oohzli, 'mwayzli/ n a (breakfast) dish of Swiss origin consisting of rolled oats, dried fruit, nuts, grated apple, etc

'muff /muf/ n a warm cylindrical wrap in which both hands are placed

²muff n **1** a failure to hold a ball in attempting a catch **2** a timid awkward person, esp in sports – infml

³muff v **1** to handle awkwardly; bungle **2** to fail to hold (a ball) when attempting a catch

muffin /'mufin/ n a light round yeast-leavened bun usu served hot

muffle /'mufl/ v **muffling** /'mufling/ **1** to wrap up so as to conceal or protect **2a** to wrap or pad with sthg to dull the sound **b** to deaden the sound of **3** to keep down; suppress

muffler /'muflə/ n a warm scarf worn round the neck

mufti /'mufti/ *n* civilian or ordinary clothes worn by one who is usually in uniform

mug /mug/ *n* **1** a large usu cylindrical drinking cup **2** the face or mouth of sby **3** *Br* sby easily deceived; a sucker *USE* (2 & 3) infml

mug *v* **-gg-** to assault, esp in the street with intent to rob – **mugger** *n* – **mugging** *n*

muggins /'muginz/ *n, pl* **mugginses, muggins** a fool, simpleton – slang; often used in address

muggy /'mugi/ *adj, of weather* warm, damp, and close – **-giness** *n*

'mug's ˌgame *n, chiefly Br* a profitless activity – infml

mug up *v, Br* to study hard – infml

mulatto /myooh'latoh/ *n pl* **mulattoes, mulattos** the first-generation offspring of a Negro and a white person

mulberry /'mulb(ə)ri/*n* (any of a genus of trees of the fig family bearing) an edible usu purple multiple fruit

mulch /mulch/ *v or n* (to spread) a protective covering (e g of compost) spread on the ground to control weeds, enrich the soil, etc

¹**mule** /myoohl/ *n* **1** the offspring of a mating between a (female) horse and an ass **2** a very stubborn person **3** a machine for simultaneously drawing and twisting fibre into yarn or thread and winding it onto spindles

²**mule** *n* a backless shoe or slipper

muleteer /,myoohli'tia/ *n* sby who drives mules

mulish /'myoohlish/ *adj* unreasonably and inflexibly obstinate – **~ly** *adv* – **~ness** *n*

¹**mull** /mul/ *v* to heat, sweeten, and flavour (e g wine or beer) with spices

²**mull** *n* a headland or peninsula in Scotland

mullet /'mulit/ *n* any of a family of **a** food fishes with elongated bodies **b** red or golden fishes with 2 barbels on the chin

mulligatawny /,muligə'tawni/ *n* a rich meat soup of Indian origin seasoned with curry

mullion /'muli·ən/ *n* a slender vertical bar placed esp between panes or panels (e g of windows or doors) – **~ed** *adj*

mull over *v* to consider at length

multi'farious /-'feəri·əs/ *adj* having or occurring in great variety; diverse – **~ly** *adv* – **~ness** *n*

'multiˌform /-ˌfawm/ *adj* having many forms or appearances

multiˌlateral /-'lat(ə)rəl/ *adj* **1** having many sides **2** participated in by more than 2 parties – **~ly** *adv*

multiˌlingual /-'ling·gwəl/ *adj* using or able to use several languages

¹**multiple** /'multipl/ *adj* **1** consisting of, including, or involving more than 1 **2** many, manifold **3** shared by many

²**multiple** *n* **1** the product of a quantity by an integer **2** **multiple, multiple store** a chain store

multiple scle'rosis *n* progressively developing paralysis and jerking muscle tremor resulting from the formation of patches of hardened tissue in nerves of the brain and spinal cord

multiplex /'multiˌpleks/ *adj* manifold, multiple

multiplication /,multipli'kaysh(ə)n/ *n* **1** multiplying or being multiplied **2** a mathematical operation that at its simplest is an abbreviated process of adding an integer to itself a specified number of times

multiplicity /,multi'plisəti/ *n* **1** the quality or state of being multiple or various **2** a great number

multiply /'multiplie/ *v* **1a** to become greater in number; spread **b** to breed or propagate **2** to perform multiplication

multiˌracial /-'raysh(ə)l/ *adj* composed of, involving, or representing various races

multiˌstorey /-'stawri/ *n or adj* (a building, esp a car park) having several storeys

multitude /'multityoohd/ *n* **1** a great number; a host **2** a crowd – chiefly fml **3** *the* populace, masses

multitudinous /,multi'tyoohdinəs/ *adj* **1** comprising a multitude of individuals; populous **2** existing in or consisting of innumerable elements or aspects *USE* fml – **~ly** *adv* – **~ness** *n*

¹**mum** /mum/ *adj* silent – infml

²**mum** *n, chiefly Br* mother

mumble /'mumbl/ *v* (**mumbling** /'mumbling, ' mumbl·ing/ to say (words) in an inarticulate usu subdued voice

mumbo jumbo /,mumboh 'jumboh/ *n* **1** elaborate but meaningless ritual **2** involved activity or language that obscures and confuses

mummify /'mumifie/ *v* to embalm and dry (the body of an animal or human being) – **-fication** *n*

mumming /'muming/ *n* **1** the practice of performing in a traditional pantomime **2** the custom of going about merrymaking in disguise during festivals – **mummer** *n*

¹**mummy** /'mumi/ *n* a body embalmed for burial in the manner of the ancient Egyptians

²**mummy** *n* mother

mumps /mumps/ *n pl but sing or pl in constr* an infectious virus disease marked by gross swelling of esp the glands of the neck and face

munch /munch/ *v* to chew (food) with a crunching sound and visible movement of the jaws

mundane /mun'dayn/ *adj* **1** (characteristic) of this world in contrast to heaven **2** practical and ordinary, esp to the point of dull familiarity – **~ly** *adv*

municipal /myooh'nisipl/ *adj* **1a** of a municipality **b** having local self-government **2** restricted to 1 locality – **~ly** *adv*

municipality /myooh,nisi'palǝti/ *n* (the governing body of) a primarily urban political unit having corporate status and some self-government

¹**mural** /'myooǝrǝl/ *adj* of, resembling, or applied to a wall

²**mural** *n* a mural work of art (e g a painting)

¹**murder** /'muhdǝ/ *n* the crime of unlawfully and intentionally killing sby

²**murder** *v* 1 to kill (sby) unlawfully and intentionally 2 to slaughter brutally 3 to mutilate, mangle – ~**er** *n* – ~**ess** *n*

murderous /'muhd(ǝ)rǝs/ *adj* 1 having the purpose or capability of murder 2 characterized by or causing murder or bloodshed – ~**ly** *adv* – ~**ness** *n*

murk /muhk/ *n* gloom, darkness; *also* fog

murky /'muhki/ *adj* dark and gloomy – **murkily** *adv*

¹**murmur** /'muhmǝ/ *n* 1 a half-suppressed or muttered complaint 2a a low indistinct (continuous) sound b a subdued or gentle utterance

²**murmur** *v* 1 to make a murmur 2 to complain, grumble – ~**ing** *n*

muscle /'musl/ *n* 1 (an organ that moves a body part, consisting of) a tissue made of modified elongated cells that contract when stimulated to produce motion 2 muscular strength; brawn – ~**d** *adj*

'muscle-,bound /-,bownd/ *adj* 1 having enlarged muscles with impaired elasticity, often as a result of excessive exercise 2 lacking flexibility; rigid

muscle in *v* **muscling** /'musl·ing, 'musling/ to interfere forcibly – *infml*; often + *on*

muscular /'muskyoolǝ/ *adj* 1a of, constituting, or performed by muscle or the muscles b having well-developed muscles 2 having strength of expression or character; vigorous – ~**ly** *adv*

muscular 'dystrophy *n* progressive wasting of muscles occurring as a hereditary disease

¹**muse** /myoohz/ *v* to become absorbed in thought; *esp* to engage in daydreaming – **musingly** *adv*

²**muse** *n* 1 *cap* any of the 9 sister goddesses in Greek mythology who were the patrons of the arts and sciences 2 a source of inspiration; *esp* a woman who influences a creative artist

museum /myooh'zee·am/ *n* an institution devoted to the acquiring, care, study, and display of objects of interest or value; *also* a place exhibiting such objects

mush /mush/ *n* 1 a soft mass of semiliquid material 2 mawkish sentimentality

¹**mushroom** /'mushroohm, -room/ *n* the enlarged, esp edible, fleshy fruiting body of a fungus, consisting typically of a stem bearing a flattened cap

²**mushroom** *v* 1 to spring up suddenly or multiply rapidly 2 to flatten at the end on impact 3 to pick wild mushrooms

mushy /'mushi/ *adj* 1 having the consistency of mush 2 mawkishly sentimental

music /'myoohzik/ *n* 1 vocal, instrumental, or mechanical sounds having rhythm, melody, or harmony 2 an agreeable sound 3 the score of a musical composition set down on paper

¹**musical** /'myoohzikl/ *adj* 1 having the pleasing harmonious qualities of music 2 having an interest in or talent for music 3 set to or accompanied by music 4 of music, musicians, or music lovers – ~**ly** *adv*

²**musical** *n* a film or theatrical production containing songs, dances, and dialogue

'musical ,box, *chiefly NAm* **music box** *n* a container enclosing an apparatus that reproduces music mechanically when activated

,musical 'chairs *n pl but sing in constr* a game in which players march to music round a row of chairs numbering 1 less than the players and scramble for seats when the music stops

'music ,centre *n, Br* a record player, a radio, and a cassette tape recorder in a single unit

'music ,hall *n* (a theatre formerly presenting) entertainments consisting of a variety of unrelated acts (e g acrobats, comedians, or singers)

musician /myooh'zish(ǝ)n/ *n* a composer, conductor, or performer of music; *esp* an instrumentalist

musk /musk/ *n* 1 a substance with a penetrating persistent smell that is obtained from a gland of the male musk deer and used as a perfume fixative 2 any of various plants with musky smells – ~**y** *adj*

musket /'muskit/ *n* a heavy large-calibre shoulder firearm with a smooth bore

musketeer /,muskǝ'tiǝ/ *n* a soldier armed with a musket

'musk,rat /-,rat/ *n pl* **muskrats**, *esp collectively* **muskrat** an aquatic rodent of N America with a long scaly tail and webbed hind feet

Muslim /'moozlim, 'muz-/ *n* an adherent of Islam

muslin /'muzlin/ *n* a plain-woven sheer to coarse cotton fabric

mussel /'musl/ *n* 1 a marine bivalve mollusc with a dark elongated shell 2 a freshwater bivalve mollusc whose shell has a lustrous mother-of-pearl lining

¹**must** /mǝs(t); *strong* must/ *verbal auxiliary, pres & past all persons* **must** 1a be commanded or requested to (e g you *must* stop) b certainly should; ought by all means to (e g I *must* read that book) 2 be compelled by physical, social, or legal necessity to (e g man *must* eat to live); be required by need or purpose to (e g we *must* hurry if we want to catch the bus) – past often replaced by *had to* except in reported speech; used in the negative

to express the idea of prohibition (e g we *must* not park here) **3** be unreasonably or perversely compelled to (e g why *must* you be so stubborn?) **4** be logically inferred or supposed to (e g it *must* be time) **5** was presumably certain to; was or were bound to (e g if he really was there, I *must* have seen him)

²**must** /must/ *n* an essential or prerequisite

³**must** /must/ *n* grape juice before and during fermentation

mustang /'mustang/ *n* the small hardy naturalized horse of the western plains of the USA

mustard /'mustəd/ *n* a pungent yellow powder used as a condiment or in medicine, esp as an emetic; *also* any of several related plants with lobed leaves, yellow flowers, and straight pods that produce seeds from which mustard is prepared

¹**muster** /'mustə/ *v* **1** to assemble, convene **2** to summon in response to a need

²**muster** *n* **1a** assembling (for military inspection) **b** an assembled group; a collection **2** a critical examination

musty /'musti/ *adj* **1** affected by mould, damp, or mildew **2** tasting or smelling of decay and decay – **mustiness** *n*

mutable /'myoohtəbl/ *adj* **1** capable of or liable to change or alteration **2** capable of or subject to mutation – **-bility** *n*

mutation /myooh'taysh(ə)n/ *n* **1** (a) significant and fundamental alteration **2** (an individual or strain differing from others of its type and resulting from) a relatively permanent change in an organism's hereditary material

¹**mute** /myooht/ *adj* **1** unable to speak; dumb **2** felt but not expressed – **~ly** *adv* – **~ness** *n*

²**mute** *n* **1** one who cannot or does not speak **2** a device attached to a musical instrument to reduce, soften, or muffle its tone

³**mute** *v* **1** to muffle or reduce the sound of **2** to tone down (a colour) – **muted** *adj*

mutilate /'myoohtilayt/ *v* **1** to cut off or permanently destroy or damage a limb or essential part of **2** to damage or deface – **-tion** *n*

mutiny /'myoohtini/ *n* concerted revolt (e g of a naval crew) against discipline or a superior officer – **-inous** *adj* – **-inously** *adv* – **mutiny** *v*

mutt /mut/ *n* **1** a dull or stupid person **2** a (mongrel) dog

mutter /'mutə/ *v* to utter, esp in a low or indistinct voice – **mutter** *n* – **~er** *n*

mutton /'mutn/ *n* the flesh of a mature sheep used as food

mutual /'myoohtyooəl, -chəl/ *adj* **1a** directed by each towards the other **b** having the same specified feeling for each other **2** shared by 2 or more in common – **~ity** *n* – **~ly** *adv*

Muzak /'myoohzak/ *trademark* – used for recorded background music played in public places

¹**muzzle** /'muzl/ *n* **1a** the projecting jaws and nose of a dog or other animal **b** a covering for the mouth of an animal used to prevent biting, barking, etc **2** the discharging end of a pistol, rifle, etc

²**muzzle** *v* **muzzling** /'muzl-ing, 'muzling/ **1** to restrain from free expression; gag

muzzy /'muzi/ *adj* mentally confused; befuddled – **-zily** *adv* – **-ziness** *n*

my /mie/ *adj* **1** of me or myself, esp as possessor, agent, or object of an action – sometimes used with vocatives (e g *my* lord) **2** – used interjectionally to express surprise, in certain fixed exclamations (e g *my* God!), and with names of certain parts of the body to express doubt or disapproval (e g *my* foot!)

myoelium /mie'seelyəm/ *n*, *pl* **mycelia** /-lyə/ the mass of interwoven threads that forms the body of a fungus

mycology /mie'koləji/ *n* (the biology of) fungal life or fungi

myopia /mie'ohpi·ə/ *n* defective vision of distant objects resulting from the focussing of the visual images in front of the retina; shortsightedness – **-pic** *adj* – **-pically** *adv*

¹**myriad** /'miri·əd/ *n* an indefinitely large number – often pl with sing. meaning

²**myriad** *adj* innumerable, countless

myrrh /muh/ *n* a brown bitter aromatic gum resin obtained from any of several African and Asian trees

myself /mie'self/ *pron* **1** that identical one that is I – used reflexively, for emphasis, or in absolute constructions (e g *myself* a tourist, I nevertheless avoided other tourists) **2** my normal self (e g I'm not quite *myself* today)

mysterious /mi'stiəri·əs/ *adj* **1** difficult to comprehend **2** containing, suggesting, or implying mystery – **~ly** *adv* – **~ness** *n*

mystery /'mist(ə)ri/ *n* **1a** a religious truth disclosed by revelation alone **b** a secret religious rite **2a** sthg not understood or beyond understanding **b** a fictional work dealing usu with the solution of a mysterious crime **3** an enigmatic or secretive quality

'**mystery ,play, mystery** *n* a medieval religious drama based on episodes from the Scriptures

mystic /'mistik/ *n* a person who believes that God or ultimate reality can only be apprehended by direct personal experience

mystical /'mistikl/, **mystic** *adj* **1** having a sacred or spiritual meaning not given by normal modes of thought or feeling **2** of mysteries or esoteric rites **3** of mysticism or mystics **4a** mysterious, incomprehensible **b** obscure, esoteric

mystify /'mistifie/ *v* **1** to perplex, bewilder **2** to cause to appear mysterious or obscure – **-fication** *n*

mystique /mi'steek/ *n* **1** a mystical reverential atmosphere or quality associated with a person or thing **2** an esoteric skill peculiar to an occupation or activity

myth /mith/ *n* **1** a traditional story that embodies popular beliefs or explains a practice, belief, or natural phenomenon **2** a parable, allegory **3a** a person or thing having a fictitious existence **b** a belief subscribed to uncritically by an (interested) group – ~**ical** *adj*

mythological /,mithə'lojikl/ *adj* **1** of or dealt with in mythology or myths **2** lacking factual or historical basis

mythology /mi'tholəji/ *n* **1** a body of myths, esp those dealing with the gods and heroes of a particular people **2** a body of beliefs, usu with little factual foundation, lending glamour or mystique to sby or sthg

myxomatosis /,miksəmə'tohsis/ *n* a severe flea-transmitted virus disease of rabbits

N

n /en/ *n, pl* **n's, ns** *often cap* **1** (a graphic representation of or device for reproducing) the 14th letter of the English alphabet **2** an indefinite number 'n' *also* **'n** /(ə)n/ *conj* and

Naafi /'nafi/ *n* the organization which runs shops and canteens in British military establishments

nab /nab/ *v* **-bb-** **1** to arrest **2** to grab *USE* infml

nabob /'naybob/ *n* **1** a provincial governor of the Mogul empire in India **2** a man of great wealth – used orig of an Englishman grown rich in India

nadir /'naydia, 'nah-/ *n* **1** the point of the celestial sphere that is directly opposite the zenith and vertically downwards from the observer **2** the lowest point

¹**nag** /nag/ *n* a horse; *esp* one that is old or in poor condition

²**nag** /nag/ *v* **-gg-** **1** to subject to constant scolding or urging **2** to be a persistent source of annoyance or discomfort – ~**ger** *n*

³**nag** *n* a person, esp a woman, who nags habitually

naiad /'niead/ *n, pl* **naiads, naiades** /'nie-ə,deez/ **1** *often cap* a nymph in classical mythology living in lakes, rivers, etc **2** the aquatic larva of a mayfly, dragonfly, etc

¹**nail** /nayl/ *n* **1** a horny sheath protecting the upper end of each finger and toe of human beings and other primates **2** a slender usu pointed and headed spike designed to be driven in, esp with a hammer, to join materials, act as a support, etc

²**nail** *v* **1** to fasten (as if) with a nail **2** to fix steadily **3** to catch, trap **4** to detect and expose (e g a lie or scandal) so as to discredit

naive, naïve /nah'eev, nie-/ *adj* **1** ingenuous, unsophisticated **2** lacking worldly wisdom or experience; *esp* credulous – ~**ty** *n*

naked /'naykid/ *adj* **1** having no clothes on **2a** *of a knife or sword* not enclosed in a sheath or scabbard **b** exposed to the air or to full view **3** without furnishings or ornamentation **4** unarmed, defenceless **5** not concealed or disguised **6** unaided by any optical device – ~**ly** *adv* – ~**ness** *n*

¹**name** /naym/ *n* **1** a word or phrase designating an individual person or thing **2** a descriptive usu disparaging epithet **3a** reputation **b** a famous or notorious person or thing — **one's name is mud** one is in disgrace

²**name** *v* **1** to give a name to; call **2** to identify by name **3** to nominate, appoint **4** to decide on; choose **5** to mention explicitly; specify

'**nameless** /-lis/ *adj* **1** obscure, undistinguished **2** not known by name; anonymous **3** having no legal right to a name; illegitimate **4a** having no name **b** left purposely unnamed **5** too terrible or distressing to describe

'**namely** /-li/ *adv* that is to say

'**name,sake** /-,sayk/ *n* sby or sthg that has the same name as another

nanny *also* **nannie** /'nani/ *n* a child's nurse; a nursemaid

'**nanny ,goat** *n* a female domestic goat – infml

¹**nap** /nap/ *v* **-pp-** **1** to take a short sleep, esp during the day **2** to be off one's guard

²**nap** *n* a short sleep, esp during the day

³**nap** *n* a hairy or downy surface (e g on a woven fabric); a pile – ~**ped** *adj*

⁴**nap** *v* **-pp-** to recommend (a horse) as a possible winner – **nap** *n*

napalm /'nay,pahm/ *n* petrol thickened with a jelly and used esp in incendiary bombs and flamethrowers

nape /nayp/ *n* the back of the neck

napkin /'napkin/ *n* **1** a usu square piece of material (e g linen or paper) used at table to wipe the lips or fingers and protect the clothes **2** a nappy

nappy /'napi/ *n, chiefly Br* a square piece of cloth or paper worn by babies to absorb and retain excreta and usu drawn up between the legs and fastened at the waist

narcissism /'nahsi,siz(ə)m/ *n* love of or sexual desire for one's self or one's own body – **-sist** *n* – **-sistic** *adj* – **-sistically** *adv*

narcissus /nah'sisəs/ n a daffodil; esp one whose flowers are borne separately and have a short corona

¹**narcotic** /nah'kotik/ n a usu addictive drug, esp (a derivative of) morphine, that dulls the senses, induces prolonged sleep, and relieves pain

²**narcotic** adj 1 like, being, or yielding a narcotic 2 inducing mental lethargy; soporific

¹**nark** /nahk/ n, Br a police informer

²**nark** v 1 to act as an informer – slang; often + on 2 to offend, affront – infml

narrate /nə'rayt/ v to recite the details of (a story) – **-ator** n

narration /nə'raysh(ə)n/ n 1 (a) narrating 2 a story, narrative

narrative /'narətiv/ n 1 sthg (e g a story) that is narrated 2 the art or practice of narration

¹**narrow** /'naroh/ adj 1 of little width, esp in comparison with height or length 2 limited in size or scope; restricted 3 inflexible, hidebound 4 only just sufficient or successful – ~**ness** n – **~ly** adv

²**narrow** n a narrow part or (water) passage – usu pl with sing. meaning

³**narrow** v to make or become narrow or narrower

'**narrow ,boat** n a canal barge

narrow-'minded /-'miendid/ adj lacking tolerance or breadth of vision; bigoted – ~**ness** n

nasal /'nayzl/ adj 1 of the nose 2a uttered through the nose with the mouth passage closed (as in English /m, n, ng/) b characterized by resonance produced through the nose

nascent /'nas(ə)nt, 'nay-/ adj in the process of being born; just beginning to develop – fml

nasturtium /nə'stuhsh(ə)m/ n (any of a genus of plants related to) a widely cultivated plant with showy spurred flowers and pungent seeds

nasty /'nahsti/ adj 1 repugnant, esp to smell or taste 2 obscene, indecent 3 mean, tawdry 4a harmful, dangerous b disagreeable, dirty 5 giving cause for concern or anxiety 6 spiteful, vicious – **-tily** adv – **-tiness** n

natal /'naytl/ adj of, present at, or associated with (one's) birth

nation /'naysh(ə)n/ n 1 a people with a common origin, tradition, and language (capable of) constituting a nation-state 2 a community of people possessing a more or less defined territory and government

¹**national** /'nash(ə)nl/ adj 1 of a nation 2 belonging to or maintained by the central government 3 of or being a coalition government – ~**ally** adv

²**national** n 1 a citizen of a specified nation 2 a competition that is national in scope – usu pl

,**national 'debt** n the amount of money owed by the government of a country

,**National 'Front** n an extreme right-wing political party of Britain asserting the racial superiority of the indigenous British population over immigrants (e g blacks)

,**National 'Health ,Service, National Health** n the British system of medical care, started in 1948, by which every person receives free or subsidized medical treatment paid for by taxation

,**national in'surance** n, often cap N&I a compulsory social-security scheme in Britain funded by contributions from employers, employees, and the government which insures the individual against sickness, retirement, and unemployment

nationalism /'nash(ə)nl,iz(ə)m/ n loyalty and devotion to a nation; esp the exalting of one nation above all others – **-list** n, adj – **-listic** adj – **-listically** adv

nationality /,nash(ə)n'aləti/ n 1 national character 2 national status 3 citizenship of a particular nation 4 existence as a separate nation

national·ize, -ise /'nash(ə)nl,iez/ v to invest control or ownership of in the national government

,**national 'service** n conscripted service in the British armed forces

¹**native** /'naytiv/ adj 1 inborn, innate 2 belonging to a particular place 3a belonging to or being the place of one's birth b of or being one's first language or sby using his/her first language 4 living (naturally), grown, or produced in a particular place; indigenous 5 found in nature, esp in a pure form

²**native** n 1 one born or reared in a particular place 2a an original or indigenous (non-European) inhabitant b a plant, animal, etc indigenous to a particular locality 3 a local resident

nativity /nə'tivəti/ n 1 birth; specif, cap the birth of Jesus 2 a horoscope

natter /'natə/ v or n (to) chatter, gossip – infml

natty /'nati/ adj neat and trim; spruce – **-tily** adv

¹**natural** /'nachərəl/ adj 1 based on an inherent moral sense 2 in accordance with or determined by nature 3 related by blood rather than by adoption 4 innate, inherent 5 of nature as an object of study 6 having a specified character or attribute by nature 7 happening in accordance with the ordinary course of nature 8 normal or expected 9 of the physical as opposed to the spiritual world 10a true to nature; lifelike b free from affectation or constraint c not disguised or altered in appearance or form 11 (containing only notes that are) neither sharp nor flat – ~**ness** n

²**natural** n 1 (a note affected by) a sign placed on the musical staff to nullify the effect of a preceding sharp or flat 2 one having natural skills or talents

,**natural 'history** n the usu amateur study, esp in the field, of natural objects (e g plants and animals), often in a particular area

naturalist /'nachərə,list/ n a student of natural history

natural·ize, -ise /'nachərə,liez/ v 1 to cause a plant to become established as if native 2 to grant citizenship to

'naturally /-li/ *adv* 1 by nature 2 as might be expected 3 in a natural manner

,natural re'sources *n pl* industrial materials and capacities (e g mineral deposits and waterpower) supplied by nature

,natural se'lection *n* a natural process that tends to result in the survival of organisms best adapted to their environment and the elimination of organisms carrying undesirable traits

nature /'naychə/ *n* 1 the inherent character or constitution of a person or thing 2 a creative and controlling force in the universe 3 the physical constitution of an organism 4 the external world in its entirety 5 natural scenery

naturism /'naychə,riz(ə)m/ *n* nudism – **-ist** *n*

naught /nawt/ *n* 1 nothing 2 nought

naughty /'nawti/ *adj* 1 badly behaved; wicked 2 slightly improper – euph or humor – **-tily** *adv* – **-tiness** *n*

nausea /'nawzi-ə/ *n* 1 a feeling of discomfort in the stomach accompanied by a distaste for food and an urge to vomit 2 extreme disgust

nauseate /'nawzi,ayt/ *v* to (cause to) become affected with nausea or disgust

nauseous /'nawzi-əs/ *adj* causing or affected with nausea or disgust – **~ly** *adv* – **~ness** *n*

nautical /'nawtikl/ *adj* of or associated with seamen, navigation, or ships – **~ly** *adv*

,nautical 'mile *n* any of various units of distance used for sea and air navigation based on the length of a minute of arc of a great circle of the earth; *esp* a British unit equal to 6080ft (about 1853.18m)

naval /'nayvl/ *adj* 1 of a navy 2 consisting of or involving warships

'nave /nayv/ *n* the hub of a wheel

'nave *n* the main body of a church lying to the west of the chancel; *esp* the long central space flanked by aisles

navel /'nayvl/ *n* a depression in the middle of the abdomen marking the point of former attachment of the umbilical cord

navigable /'navigəbl/ *adj* 1 suitable for ships to pass through or along 2 capable of being steered – **-gability** *n*

navigate /'navigayt/ *v* 1 to steer a course through a medium (e g water) 2 to perform the activities (e g taking sightings and making calculations) involved in navigation 3a to steer or manage (a boat) in sailing b to operate or direct the course of (e g an aircraft) – **-ation** *n* – **-ational** *adj* – **-ator** *n*

navvy /'navi/ *n, Br* an unskilled labourer

navy /'nayvi/ *n* 1 a nation's ships of war and support vessels together with the organization needed for maintenance 2 *sing or pl in constr* the personnel manning a navy 3 navy blue

navy 'blue *adj or n* deep dark blue

'nay /nay/ *adv* 1 not merely this but also 2 *N Eng or archaic* no

'nay *n* 1 denial, refusal 2 a vote or voter against

nazi /'nahtsi/ *n, often cap* a member of the German fascist party controlling Germany from 1933 to 1945

NCO *n* a noncommissioned officer

neap tide *n* a tide of minimum height occurring at the 1st and the 3rd quarters of the moon

'near /niə/ *adv* 1 in or into a near position or manner (e g came *near* to tears) 2 closely approximating; nearly (e g a *near*-perfect performance)

'near *prep* near to (e g went too *near* the edge)

'near *adj* 1 intimately connected or associated 2a not far distant in time, space, or degree b close, narrow (e g a *near* miss) 3a being the closer of 2 (e g the *near* side) b being the left-hand one of a pair (e g the *near* wheel of a cart) – **~ness** *n*

'near *v* to approach

,near'by /-'bie/ *adv or adj* close at hand

nearly /'niəli/ *adv* 1 in a close manner or relationship (e g *nearly* related) 2 almost but not quite

,near'side /-'sied/ *n, Br* the left-hand side (e g of a vehicle or road)

'neat /neet/ *adj* 1 without addition or dilution 2 elegantly simple 3a precise, well-defined b skilful, adroit 4 (habitually) tidy and orderly 5 *chiefly NAm* fine, excellent – *infml*

'neat *adv* without addition or dilution; neatly

nebula /'nebyoolə/ *n, pl* **nebulas, nebulae** /-li/ 1 any of many immense bodies of highly rarefied gas or dust in interstellar space 2 a galaxy – **~r** *adj*

nebulous /'nebyooləs/ *adj* 1 indistinct, vague 2 of or resembling a nebula; nebular – **-losity** *n* – **~ly** *adv* – **~ness** *n*

necessarily /'nesəs(ə)rəli, ,nesə'serəli/ *adv* as a necessary consequence; inevitably

'necessary /'nesəs(ə)ri, 'nesə,seri/ *n* an indispensable item; an essential

'necessary *adj* 1a inevitable, inescapable b logically unavoidable 2 essential, indispensable

necessitate /nə'sesitayt/ *v* to make necessary or unavoidable

necessitous /nə'sesitəs/ *adj* needy, impoverished – fml – **~ly** *adv*

necessity /nə'sesəti/ *n* 1 the quality of being necessary, indispensable, or unavoidable 2 impossibility of a contrary order or condition 3 poverty, want 4a sthg necessary or indispensable b a pressing need or desire – **of necessity** necessarily

'neck /nek/ *n* 1a the part of an animal that connects the head with the body; *also* a cut of meat taken from this part b the part of a garment that covers the neck; *also* the neckline 2a a narrow part, esp shaped like a neck b the part of a stringed musical instrument extending from the body and supporting the fingerboard and strings – **neck of the woods** area or district in which one lives; locality

'neck *v* to kiss and caress in sexual play – *infml*

neckerchief /'nekə,cheef, -,chif/ *n, pl* **neckerchiefs** *also* **neckerchies** /-cheevz/ a square of fabric folded and worn round the neck

necklace /'neklis/ *n* a string of jewels, beads, etc worn round the neck as an ornament

'neck,line /-,lien/ *n* the upper edge of a garment that forms the opening for the neck and head

necromancy /'nekrə,mansi/ *n* 1 the conjuring up of the spirits of the dead in order to predict or influence the future 2 magic, sorcery – **-ancer** *n*

nectar /'nektə/ *n* 1 the drink of the gods in classical mythology; *broadly* a delicious drink 2 a sweet liquid secreted by the flowers of many plants that is the chief raw material of honey

nectarine /'nektərin, -reen/ *n* (a tree that bears) a smooth-skinned peach

née, nee /nay/ *adj* – used to identify a woman by her maiden name

'need /need/ *n* 1a a lack of sthg necessary, desirable, or useful b a physiological or psychological requirement for the well-being of an organism 2 a condition requiring supply or relief 3 poverty, want

'need *v* 1 to be in need of; require 2 to be constrained (e g I'll *need* to work hard) 3 to be under necessity or obligation to

'needful /-f(ə)l/ *adj* necessary, requisite – **-ly** *adv*

'needle /'needl/ *n* 1a a small slender usu steel instrument with an eye for thread at one end and a sharp point at the other, used for sewing b any of various similar larger instruments without an eye, used for carrying thread and making stitches (e g in crocheting or knitting) c the slender hollow pointed end of a hypodermic syringe for injecting or removing material 2 a slender, usu sharp-pointed, indicator on a dial; *esp* a magnetic needle 3 a needle-shaped leaf, esp of a conifer 4 *Br* a feeling of enmity or ill will – *infml*

'needle *v* to provoke by persistent teasing or gibes

needless /'needlis/ *adj* not needed; unnecessary – **-ly** *adv*

'needle,woman /-,woomən/ *n* a woman who does needlework

'needle,work /-,wuhk/ *n* sewing; *esp* fancy work (e g embroidery)

needs /needz/ *adv* necessarily (e g must *needs* be recognized)

needy /'needi/ *adj* in want, impoverished – **neediness** *n*

'ne'er-do-,well *n* an idle worthless person

nefarious /ni'feari·əs/ *adj* evil, wicked – **-ly** *adv* – **-ness** *n*

negate /ni'gayt/ *v* 1 to deny the existence or truth of 2 to make ineffective or invalid – **-gation** *n*

'negative /'negativ/ *adj* 1a marked by denial, prohibition, or refusal b expressing negation 2 lacking positive or agreeable features 3 less than zero and opposite in sign to a positive number that when added to the given number yields zero 4 having lower electric potential and constituting the part towards which the current flows from the external circuit 5 having the light and dark parts in approximately inverse order to those of the original photographic subject – **-ly** *adv*

'negative *n* 1 a negative reply 2 sthg that is the negation or opposite of sthg else 3 an expression (e g the word *no*) of negation or denial 4 the side that upholds the contradictory proposition in a debate 5 the plate of an electric cell that is at the lower potential 6 a negative photographic image on transparent material used for printing positive pictures

'neglect /ni'glekt/ *v* 1 to pay insufficient attention to; disregard 2 to leave undone or unattended to

'neglect *n* neglecting or being neglected

ne'glectful /-f(ə)l/ *adj* careless, forgetful – **-ly** *adv* – **-ness** *n*

negligee, negligé /'neglizhay/ *n* a woman's light decorative housecoat, often designed to be worn with a matching nightdress

negligent /'neglij(ə)nt/ *adj* 1 (habitually or culpably) neglectful 2 pleasantly casual in manner – **-ly** *adv* – **-gence** *n*

negligible /'neglijəbl/ *adj* trifling, insignificant – **-bly** *adv*

negotiable /ni'gohsh(i)əbl/ *adj* 1 capable of being passed along or through 2 capable of being dealt with or settled through discussion

negotiate /ni'gohshiayt/ *v* 1 to confer with another in order to reach an agreement 2a to transfer (e g a bill of exchange) to another by delivery or endorsement b to convert into cash or the equivalent value 3a to travel successfully along or over b to complete or deal with successfully – **-ation** *n* – **-ator** *n*

Negress /'neegris/ *n* a female Negro – chiefly derog

Negro /'neegroh/ *n, pl* **Negroes** a member of the esp African branch of the black race of mankind

neigh /nay/ *v* to make the loud prolonged cry characteristic of a horse

'neighbour, *NAm chiefly* **neighbor** /'naybə/ *n* 1 one living or situated near another 2 a fellow human being

'neighbour, *NAm chiefly* **neighbor** *v* to adjoin or lie near to

'neighbour,hood /-,hood/ *n* 1 an adjacent or surrounding region 2 an approximate amount, extent, or degree 3 (the inhabitants of) a district of a town, city etc, forming a distinct community

neighbouring /'nayb(ə)ring/ *adj* nearby, adjacent

'neighbourly /-li/ *adj* characteristic of congenial neighbours; *esp* friendly – **-liness** *n*

'neither /'niedhə; *or* 'needhə/ *pron* not the one or the other (e g *neither* of us)

²**neither** *conj* **1** not either (e g *neither* here nor there) **2** also not; nor (e g he didn't go and *neither* did I)

³**neither** *adj* not either (e g *neither* hand)

⁴**neither** *adv* **1** similarly not; also not (e g I can't swim. *Neither* can I) **2** *chiefly dial* either

nemesis /'nemasis/ *n, pl* **nemeses** /-seez/ **1** (an agent of) retribution or vengeance **2** downfall, undoing

Neolithic /,nee·ə'lithik/ *adj* of the last period of the Stone Age characterized by polished stone implements

neologism /ni'olajiz(ə)m/ *n* (the use of) a new word, usage, or expression

neon /'neeon/ *n* a gaseous element used esp in electric lamps

neophyte /'nee·ə,fiet/ *n* **1** a new convert **2** a beginner

nephew /'nefyooh/ *n* a son of one's brother or sister or of one's brother-in-law or sister-in-law

nepotism /'nepə,tiz(ə)m/ *n* favouritism shown to a relative (e g by appointment to office)

Neptune /'neptyoohn/ *n* **1** the ocean personified **2** the planet 8th in order from the sun

nerd /nuhd/ *n* an unpleasant or foolish person – *infml*

¹**nerve** /nuhv/ *n* **1** any of the filaments of nervous tissue that conduct nervous impulses to and from the nervous system **2** fortitude, tenacity **3** (disrespectful) assurance or boldness **4a** a sore or sensitive subject – esp in *hit/touch a nerve* **b** *pl* acute nervousness or anxiety

²**nerve** *v* **1** to give strength and courage to **2** to prepare (oneself) psychologically *for* – often + *up*

'**nerveless** /-lis/ *adj* **1** lacking strength or vigour **2** not agitated or afraid; cool – ~**ly** *adv* – ~**ness** *n*

'**nerve-,racking**, '**nerve-,wracking** *adj* placing great strain on the nerves

nervous /'nuhvəs/ *adj* **1** of, affected by, or composed of (the) nerves or neurons **2a** easily excited or agitated **b** timid, apprehensive – ~**ly** *adv* – ~**ness** *n*

,**nervous 'break,down** *n* (an occurrence of) a disorder in which worrying, depression, severe tiredness, etc prevent one from coping with one's responsibilities

'**nervous ,system** *n* the brain, spinal cord, or other nerves and nervous tissue together forming a system for interpreting stimuli from the sense organs and transmitting impulses to muscles, glands, etc

nervy /'nuhvi/ *adj* **1** suffering from nervousness or anxiety **2** brash, imprudent – *infml*

¹**nest** /nest/ *n* **1a** a bed or receptacle prepared by a bird for its eggs and young **b** a place or structure in which animals live, esp in their immature stages **2a** a place of rest, retreat, or lodging **b** a den or haunt **3** a series of objects made to fit close together or one inside another

²**nest** *v* **1** to build or occupy a nest **2** to fit compactly together

'**nest ,egg** *n* an amount of money saved up as a reserve

nestle /'nesl/ *v* **nestling** /'nesling, 'nesl·ing/ **1** to settle snugly or comfortably together **2** to lie in a sheltered position

nestling /'nes(t)ling/ *n* a young bird that has not abandoned the nest

¹**net** /net/ *n* **1** an open meshed fabric twisted, knotted, or woven together at regular intervals and used for a variety of purposes, e g fishing or as a barrier in various games **2** (the fabric that encloses the sides and back of) a soccer, hockey, etc goal **3a** a practice cricket pitch surrounded by nets – usu *pl* **b** a period of practice in such a net

²**net** *v* -**tt**- **1** to cover or enclose (as if) with a net **2** to hit (a ball) into the net for the loss of a point in a game

³**net**, *chiefly Br* **nett** *adj* **1** remaining after all deductions (e g for taxes, outlay, or loss) **2** final, ultimate

⁴**net**, *chiefly Br* **nett** *v* -**tt**- **1** to make by way of profit **2** to get possession of

'**net,ball** /-,bawl/ *n* a game, usu for women, between 2 sides of 7 players each who score goals by tossing an inflated ball through a high horizontal ring on a post at each end of a hard court

nether /'nedhə/ *adj* lower, under – *fml*

netting /'neting/ *n* network

¹**nettle** /'netl/ *n* any of a genus of widely distributed green-flowered plants covered with (stinging) hairs

²**nettle** *v* **nettling** /'netl·ing/ **1** to strike or sting (as if) with nettles **2** to arouse to annoyance or anger

'**nettle ,rash** *n* a skin rash resembling nettle stings

'**net,work** /-,wuhk/ *n* **1** a fabric or structure of cords or wires that cross at regular intervals and are knotted or secured at the crossings **2** a system of crisscrossing lines or channels **3** an interconnected chain, group, or system **4a** a group of radio or television stations linked together so that they can broadcast the same programmes if desired **b** a radio or television company that produces programmes for broadcast over such a network

neural /'nyooərəl/ *adj* **1** of or affecting a nerve or the nervous system **2** dorsal

neuralgia /nyoo(ə)'raljə/ *n* intense paroxysms of pain radiating along the course of a nerve without apparent cause – **-gic** *adj*

neurology /nyoo(ə)'roləji/ *n* the study of (diseases of) the nervous system – **-gist** *n*

neuron /'nyooəron/ *n* any of the many specialized cells that form the impulse-transmitting units of the nervous system – ~**al** *adj*

neurosis /nyoo(ə)'rohsis/ *n, pl* **neuroses** /-,seez/ a nervous disorder in which phobias, compulsions, anxiety, and obsessions make normal life difficult

neurotic /nyoo(ə)'rotik/ *n* one who is emotionally unstable or is affected with a neurosis

¹**neuter** /'nyoohtə/ *adj* 1 of or belonging to the gender that is neither masculine nor feminine 2 lacking generative organs or having nonfunctional ones – **neuter** *n*

²**neuter** *v* to castrate

¹**neutral** /'nyoohtrəl/ *adj* 1 (of or being a country, person, etc) not engaged on either side of a war, dispute, etc 2a indifferent, indefinite b without colour c neither acid nor alkaline d not electrically charged or positive or negative; not live – ~**ity** *n* – ~**ly** *adv*

²**neutral** *n* 1 a neutral country, person, etc 2 a neutral colour 3 a position (of a gear lever) in which gears are disengaged

neutral·ize, -ise /'nyoohtrə,liez/ *v* 1 to make (chemically, politically, etc) neutral 2 to nullify or counteract the effect of sthg with an opposing action, force, etc – ~**r** *n*

neutron /'nyooh,tron/ *n* an uncharged elementary particle with a mass about that of the proton, present in the nuclei of all atoms except those of normal hydrogen

never /'nevə/ *adv* 1 not ever; at no time 2 not in any degree; not under any condition (e g this will *never* do) 3 surely not (e g you're *never* 18!) – chiefly *infml* — **I never** 1 — used to express amazement; chiefly *infml* 2 I didn't do it — nonstandard

never·more *adv* never again

never-'never *n, Br* hire purchase – + *the*; *infml*

never-'never ,land *n* an ideal or imaginary place

nevertheless /,nevədhə'les/ *adv* in spite of that; yet

¹**new** /nyooh/ *adj* 1 not old; not used previously; recent 2a only recently discovered, recognized, or in use; novel b different from or replacing a former one of the same kind 3 having been in the specified condition or relationship for only a short time; unaccustomed 4 *cap* modern; *esp* in use after medieval times

²**new** *adv* newly, recently – usu in combination

new·comer /-,kumə/ *n* 1 a recent arrival 2 a beginner, novice

newel /'nyooh·əl/ *n* 1 an upright post about which the steps of a spiral staircase wind 2 *also* **newel post** a principal post supporting either end of a staircase handrail

new·fangled /-'fang·gld/ *adj* modern and unnecessarily complicated or gimmicky – *derog or humor* – ~**ness** *n*

newly /'nyoohli/ *adv* 1 lately, recently 2 anew

newly·wed /-,wed/ *n or adj* (one who is) recently married

news /nyoohz/ *n pl but sing in constr* 1 (a report or series of reports of) recent (notable) events; new information about sthg 2a news reported in a newspaper, a periodical, or a broadcast b material that is newsworthy 3 a radio or television broadcast of news

'news,agent /-,ayjənt/ *n, chiefly Br* a retailer of newspapers and magazines

'news,boy /-,boy/, *fem* **'news,girl** *n* a paperboy

'news,cast /-,kahst/ *n* a news broadcast

'news,letter /-,letə/ *n* a printed pamphlet containing news or information of interest chiefly to a special group

newspaper /'nyoohs,paypə/ *n* (an organization that publishes) a paper printed and distributed usu daily or weekly and containing news, articles of opinion, features, and advertising

'news,print /nyoohz,print/ *n* cheap paper made chiefly from wood pulp and used mostly for newspapers

'news,reel /-,reel/ *n* a short film dealing with current events

'news,room /-,room, -,roohm/ *n* a place (e g an office) where news is prepared for publication or broadcast

'news,stand /-,stand/ *n* a stall where newspapers and periodicals are sold

'news,worthy /-,wuhdhi/ *adj* sufficiently interesting to warrant reporting

newt /nyooht/ *n* any of various small semiaquatic salamanders

,New 'Testament *n* the second part of the Christian Bible comprising the canonical Gospels and Epistles, the books of Acts, and the book of Revelation

newton /'nyooht(ə)n/ *n* the SI unit of force equal to the force that when acting for 1s on a free mass of 1kg will give it a velocity of 1m/s

,New 'World *n* the W hemisphere; *esp* the continental landmass of N and S America

,New 'Year *n* the first day or days of a year

,New ,Year's 'Day *n* January 1 observed as a public holiday in many countries

¹**next** /nekst/ *adj* 1 immediately adjacent or following (e g in place or order) 2 immediately after the present or a specified time

²**next** *adv* 1 in the time, place, or order nearest or immediately succeeding 2 on the first occasion to come (e g when we *next* meet)

³**next** *prep* nearest or adjacent to (e g wear wool *next* to the skin)

⁴**next** *n* the next occurrence, item, or issue of a kind

,next-'door *adj* situated or living in the next building, room, etc

next door *adv* in or to the next building, room, etc – **next-door** *adj*

,next of 'kin *n, pl* **next of kin** the person most closely related to another person

nexus /'neksəs/ *n, pl* **nexuses, nexus** 1 a connection or link 2 a connected group or series

nib /nib/ *n* 1 a bill or beak 2 the writing point of a pen 3 a small pointed or projecting part or article

¹**nibble** /'nibl/ *v* **nibbling** /'nibling/ **1** to take gentle, small, or cautious bites **2** to show cautious or qualified interest *USE* often + *at*

²**nibble** *n* **1** an act of nibbling **2** a very small amount (e g of food) *USE* infml

nice /nies/ *adj* **1** showing or requiring fine discrimination or treatment **2a** pleasant, agreeable **b** well done; well-executed **3** inappropriate or unpleasant – usu ironic **4a** socially acceptable; well-bred **b** decent, proper – ~ **ly** *adv* – ~ **ness** *n* — **nice and** to a satisfactory degree

nicety /'niesəti/ *n* **1** an elegant or refined feature **2** a fine point or distinction **3** (the showing or requiring of) delicacy, discernment, or careful attention to details — **to a nicety** to the point at which sthg is at its best

niche /neesh, nich/ *n* **1** a recess in a wall, esp for a statue **2a** a place or activity for which a person is best suited **b** the ecological role of an organism in a community, esp in regard to food consumption

¹**nick** /nik/ *n* **1** a small notch or groove **2** *Br* state of health or repair – infml; esp in *in good/bad nick* **3** *Br* a prison or police station – slang — **in the nick of time** at the final critical moment; just before it would be too late

²**nick** *v* **1** to cut into or wound slightly **2** *Br* **2a** to steal **b** to arrest

nickel /'nik(ə)l/ *n* **1** a hard metallic element with magnetic properties like those of iron **2** (a US coin containing 1 part of nickel to 3 of copper and worth) the sum of 5 cents

nickname /'nik,naym/ *n* **1** a name used in place of or in addition to a proper name **2** a familiar form of a proper name, esp of a person

nicotine /'nikəteen/ *n* an alkaloid that is the chief drug in tobacco

niece /nees/ *n* a daughter of one's brother or sister or of one's brother-in-law or sister-in-law

nifty /'nifti/ *adj* very good or effective; *esp* cleverly conceived or executed – infml

niggard /'nigəd/ *n* a mean and stingy person – ~ **ly** *adj* – ~ **liness** *n*

niggle /'nigl/ *v* **niggling** /'nigling/ **1** to waste time or effort on minor details **2** to find fault constantly in a petty way **3** to cause slight irritation to; bother – ~ **r** *n*

niggling /'nigling/ *adj* **1** petty **2** persistently annoying

nigh /nie/ *adv, adj, or prep* near (in place, time, or relation)

night /niet/ *n* **1** the period of darkness from dusk to dawn caused by the earth's daily rotation **2** an evening characterized by a specified event or activity **3a** darkness **b** a state of affliction, ignorance, or obscurity

'**night,cap** /-,kap/ *n* **1** a cloth cap worn in bed **2** a drink taken at bedtime

'**night,club** /-,klub/ *n* a place of entertainment open at night that has a floor show, provides music and space for dancing, and usu serves drinks and food

'**night,dress** /-,dres/ *n* a woman's or girl's nightgown

'**night,fall** /-,fawl/ *n* dusk

'**night,gown** /-,gown/ *n* a loose garment for sleeping in

nightingale /'nieting,gayl/ *n* any of several Old World thrushes noted for the sweet usu nocturnal song of the male

'**night,life** /-,lief/ *n* late evening entertainment or social life

'**nightly** /-li/ *adj or adv* (of, occurring, taken, or done) at or by night or every night

'**night,mare** /-,meə/ *n* **1** a frightening dream that usu awakens the sleeper **2** an experience, situation, or object that causes acute anxiety or terror – **-marish** *adj* – **-marishly** *adv* – **-marishness** *n*

nightshade /'niet,shayd/ *n* any of various related usu poisonous plants: e g deadly nightshade

'**night,shirt** /-,shuht/ *n* a long loose shirt for sleeping in

nihilism /'nie-ə,liz(ə)m, 'ni-/ *n* **1** a view that rejects all values and beliefs as meaningless or unfounded **2a** *often cap* the doctrine that social conditions are so bad as to make destruction desirable for its own sake, adhered to specif by a 19th-c Russian terrorist revolutionary party **b** terrorism – **-ist** *n* – **-istic** *adj*

nil /nil/ *n* nothing, zero

nimble /'nimbl/ *adj* **1** quick, light, and easy in movement **2** quick and clever in thought and understanding – ~ **ness** *n* – **-bly** *adv*

nimbus /'nimbəs/ *n, pl* **nimbi** /-,bie, -bi/, **nimbuses** **1** a luminous circle about the head of a representation of a god, saint, or sovereign **2** a cloud from which rain is falling

nincompoop /'ningkəm,poohp/ *n* a silly or foolish person

nine /nien/ *n* **1** the number 9 **2** the ninth in a set or series **3** sthg having 9 parts or members or a denomination of 9 **4** the first or last 9 holes of an 18-hole golf course — **to the nines** elaborately in special, formal, or party clothes

nineteen /nien'teen/ *n* the number 19 – ~ **th** *adj, adv, n, pron* — **nineteen to the dozen** very fast and volubly

ninety /'nienti/ *n* **1** the number 90 **2** *pl* (a range of temperatures, ages, or dates within a century characterized by) the numbers 90 to 99 – **-tieth** *adj, n, adv, pron*

ninny /'nini/ *n* a silly or foolish person – humor; infml

ninth /nienth/ n 1 number nine in a countable series 2a (a chord containing) a musical interval of an octave and a second b the note separated by this interval from a lower note – **ninth** adj – ~ly adv

¹**nip** /nip/ v **-pp-** 1 to catch hold of and squeeze sharply; pinch 2 to sever (as if) by pinching sharply – often + off 3 to injure or make numb with cold 4 to go quickly or briefly; hurry – infml

²**nip** n 1 a sharp stinging cold 2 (an instance of) nipping; a pinch

³**nip** n a small measure or drink of spirits

Nip n a Japanese – derog

nipper /'nipə/ n 1 any of various devices (e g pincers) for gripping or cutting – usu pl with sing. meaning 2 chiefly Br a child; esp a small boy – infml

nipple /'nipl/ n 1 the small protuberance of a breast from which milk is drawn in the female 2 an artificial teat through which a bottle-fed infant feeds 3 a small projection through which oil or grease is injected into machinery

nippy /'nipi/ adj 1 nimble and lively; snappy 2 chilly – **-piness** n

nirvana /niə'vahnə, nuh-/ n, often cap 1 a Hindu and Buddhist state of final bliss and freedom from the cycle of rebirth, attainable through the extinction of desire and individual consciousness 2 a place or state of relief from pain or anxiety

nisi /'niesie, 'neezi/ adj taking effect at a specified time unless previously modified or avoided

¹**nit** /nit/ n (the egg of) a parasitic insect (e g a louse)

²**nit** n, chiefly Br a nitwit – infml

'**nit-**,picking n petty and usu unjustified criticism

¹**nitrate** /'nietrayt/ n 1 a salt or ester of nitric acid 2 sodium or potassium nitrate used as a fertilizer

²**nitrate** v to treat or combine with nitric acid or a nitrate

nitric /'nietrik/ adj of or containing nitrogen (with a relatively high valency)

,**nitric 'acid** n a corrosive inorganic liquid acid used esp as an oxidizing agent and in making fertilizers, dyes, etc

nitrogen /'nietrəj(ə)n/ n a gaseous chemical element that constitutes about 78 per cent by volume of the atmosphere and is found in combined form as a constituent of all living things

nitroglycerine /,nietroh'glisəreen, -rin/ n an oily highly explosive liquid used chiefly to make dynamite

nitrous /'nietrəs/ adj of or containing a potassium nitrate b nitrogen (with a relatively low valency)

nitwit /'nit,wit/ n a scatterbrained or stupid person – infml

¹**no** /noh/ adv 1 – used to negate an alternative choice 2 in no respect or degree – in comparisons 3 – used in answers expressing negation, dissent, denial, or refusal; contrasted with yes 4 – used like

a question demanding assent to the preceding statement 5 nay 6 – used as an interjection to express incredulity 7 chiefly Scot nay

²**no** adj 1a not any (e g no money) b hardly any; very little (e g I'll be finished in no time) 2a not a; quite other than a (e g he's no expert) b – used before a noun phrase to give force to an opposite meaning (e g in no uncertain terms)

³**no** n, pl noes, nos a negative reply or vote

¹**nob** /nob/ n a person's head – infml

²**nob** n a wealthy or influential person – infml

,**no-'ball** interj or n – (used as a call by an umpire to indicate) an illegal delivery of the ball in cricket

nobble /'nobl/ v **nobbling** /'nobling, 'nobl·ing/ 1 to incapacitate (esp a racehorse), esp by drugging 2a to win over to one's side, esp by dishonest means b to get hold of, esp dishonestly c to swindle, cheat USE infml

,**Nobel 'prize** /noh'bel/ n any of various annual prizes for the encouragement of people who work for the interests of humanity (e g in the fields of peace, literature, medicine, and physics)

nobility /noh'bil**ə**ti/ n 1 being noble 2 sing or pl in constr the people making up a noble class

¹**noble** /'nohbl/ adj 1a gracious and dignified in character or bearing b famous, notable 2 of or being high birth or exalted rank 3 imposing, stately 4 having or showing a magnanimous character or high ideals – **nobly** adv

²**noble** n a person of noble rank or birth

noblesse oblige /,nohbles o'bleezh, no-/ n the obligation of honourable and responsible behaviour associated with high rank

¹**nobody** /'nohbədi, -,bodi/ pron not anybody

²**nobody** n a person of no influence or consequence

nocturnal /nok'tuhnl/ adj 1 of or occurring in the night 2 active at night – ~ly adv

nocturne /'noktuhn/ n a work of art dealing with evening or night; esp a dreamy pensive composition for the piano

¹**nod** /nod/ v **-dd-** 1 to make a short downward movement of the head (e g in assent or greeting) 2 to become drowsy or sleepy 3 to make a slip or error in a moment of inattention

²**nod** n 1 (an instance of) nodding 2 an unconsidered indication of agreement, approval, etc – infml

node /nohd/ n a point on a stem at which 1 or more leaves are attached – **-dal** adj

nodule /'nodyohl/ n 1 a small rounded mass 2 a swelling on the root of a leguminous plant (e g clover) containing bacteria that convert atmospheric nitrogen into a form in which it can be used by the plant

Noel, Noël /noh'el/ n the Christmas season

noes /nohz/ pl of no

noggin /'nogin/ n 1 a small mug or cup 2 a small measure of spirits, usu 0.142 litres ($^1/_4$pt) 3 a person's head – infml

¹**noise** /noyz/ n 1 loud confused shouting or outcry 2a a (harsh or unwanted) sound b unwanted signals or fluctuations in an electrical circuit

²**noise** v to spread by gossip or hearsay – usu + *about* or *abroad*

noisome /'noys(ə)m/ adj repellent, offensive – fml

noisy /'noyzi/ adj 1 making noise 2 full of or characterized by noise – **noisily** adv – **noisiness** n

nomad /'nohmad/ n 1 a member of a people that wanders from place to place, usu seasonally 2 one who wanders aimlessly from place to place – ~**ic** adj – ~**ically** adv

'no-,man's-,land n 1a an area of waste or unclaimed land b an unoccupied area between opposing armies 2 an area of anomalous, ambiguous, or indefinite character

nom de plume /,nom de 'ploohm/ n, pl **noms de plume** /~/ a pseudonym under which an author writes

nomenclature /no'menkləchə/ n 1 a name, designation 2 (an instance of) naming, esp within a particular system 3 a system of terms used in a particular science, discipline, or art

nominal /'nomin(ə)l/ adj 1 of or constituting a name 2a being sthg in name only b negligible, insignificant – ~**ly** adv

nominate /'nominayt/ v 1 to designate, specify 2a to appoint or recommend for appointment b to propose for an honour, award, or as a candidate – **tion** n

nominative /'nominətiv/ adj of or being the grammatical case expressing the subject of a verb

nonagenarian /,nohnaji'neəri·ən, ,nonə-/ n a person between 90 and 99 years old

nonaligned /,nonə'liend/ adj not allied with other nations, esp any of the great powers – **lignment** n

nonce /nons/ n the present occasion, time, or purpose

nonchalant /'nonshələnt/ adj giving an impression of easy unconcern or indifference – **lance** n – ~**ly** adv

noncombatant /non'kombət(ə)nt, -kəm'bat(ə)nt/ n a civilian, army chaplain, etc who does not engage in combat

,noncom'missioned 'officer /-nonkə'mish(ə)nd/ n a subordinate officer (e g a sergeant) in the armed forces appointed from among the personnel who do not hold a commission

,noncom'mittal /-kə'mitl/ adj giving no clear indication of attitude or feeling – ~**ly** adv

,noncon'formist /-kən'fawmist/ n 1 often cap a member of a Protestant body separated from the Church of England 2 one who does not conform to a generally accepted pattern of thought or behaviour

,noncon'formity /-kən'fawməti/ n 1 refusal to conform to an established creed, rule, or practice 2 absence of correspondence or agreement

nondescript /'nondiskript/ adj 1 (apparently) belonging to no particular class or kind 2 lacking distinctive or interesting qualities; dull

¹**none** /nun/ pron, pl **none** 1 not any; no part or thing 2 not one person; nobody (e g it's *none* other than Tom) 3 not any such thing or person

²**none** adv 1 by no means; not at all 2 in no way; to no extent

nonentity /no'nentiti/ n sby or sthg of little importance or interest

nonesuch also **nonsuch** /'nun,such/ n a person or thing without an equal; a paragon

nonetheless /,nundhə'les/ adv nevertheless

,non'flammable /-'flaməbl/ adj difficult or impossible to set alight

nonpareil /'nonparel, ,nonpə'rayl/ n or adj (sby or sthg) having no equal

nonplus /,non'plus/ v **-ss-** (NAm **-s-, -ss-**) to perplex or disconcert

nonsense /'nonsəns/ n 1a meaningless words or language b foolish or absurd language, conduct, or thought 2 frivolous or insolent behaviour 3 – used interjectionally to express forceful disagreement

non sequitur /,non 'sekwitə/ n 1 a conclusion that does not follow from the premises 2 a statement that does not follow logically from anything previously said

,non'standard /standəd/ adj not conforming in pronunciation, grammatical construction, idiom, or word choice to accepted usage

,non'starter /-'stahtə/ n sby or sthg that is sure to fail or prove impracticable

,non'stick /-'stik/ adj having or being a surface that prevents adherence of food during cooking

,non'stop /-'stop/ adj done or made without a stop – **nonstop** adv

,non-'U /-'yooh/ adj not characteristic of the upper classes

,non'union /-'yoohnyən/ adj not belonging to or connected with a trade union

,non'violence /-'vie·ələns/ n 1 refraining from violence on moral grounds 2 passive resistance or peaceful demonstration for political ends – **nt** adj

,non'white /-'wiet/ n or adj (one who is) not Caucasian

¹**noodle** /'noohdl/ n a silly or foolish person – humor

²**noodle** n a narrow flat ribbon of pasta made with egg

nook /nook/ n a small secluded or sheltered place or part

noon /noohn/ n 1 noon, **noonday** the middle of the day; midday 2 the highest or culminating point

'no ,one pron nobody

noose /noohs/ *n* a loop with a running knot that tightens as the rope is pulled – **noose** *v*

nor /naw/ *conj* **1** – used to join 2 sentence elements of the same class or function (e g not done by you *nor* me) **2** also not; neither (e g it didn't seem hard, *nor* was it)

Nordic /'nawdik/ *adj* **1** of a tall, fair, longheaded, blue-eyed physical type characteristic of the Germanic peoples of N Europe, esp Scandinavia **2** of competitive ski events consisting of ski jumping and cross-country racing

norm /nawm/ *n* **1** an authoritative standard; a model **2** a principle of correctness that is binding upon the members of a group, and serves to regulate action and judgment **3** a pattern typical of a social group

normal /'nawml/ *adj* **1** conforming to or constituting a norm, rule, or principle; not odd or unusual **2** occurring naturally **3a** having average intelligence or development **b** free from mental disorder – ~ **ize** *v* – ~ **ly** *adv* – ~ **ity** *n*

Norman /'nawmən/ *n* **1** a (former) native or inhabitant of Normandy; *esp* any of the Norman-French conquerors of England in 1066 **2** a style of architecture characterized, esp in its English form, by semicircular arches and heavy pillars

¹**north** /nawth/ *adj or adv* towards, at, belonging to, or coming from the north

²**north** *n* **1** (the compass point corresponding to) the direction of the north terrestrial pole **2** *often cap* regions or countries lying to the north of a specified or implied point of orientation

¹**north'east** /-'eest/ *adj or adv* towards, at, belonging to, or coming from the northeast

²**north'east** *n* **1** (the general direction corresponding to) the compass point midway between north and east **2** *often cap* regions or countries lying to the northeast of a specified or implied point of orientation

¹**northeasterly** /-'eestəli/ *adj or adv* northeast

²**northeasterly**, **north'easter** /-'eestə/ *n* a wind from the northeast

north'eastern /-'eest(ə)n/ *adj* **1** *often cap* (characteristic) of a region conventionally designated Northeast **2** northeast

¹**northerly** /'nawdhəli/ *adj or adv* north

²**northerly** *n* a wind from the north

northern /'nawdhən/ *adj* **1** *often cap* (characteristic) of a region conventionally designated North **2** north

Northerner /'nawdhənə/ *n* a native or inhabitant of the North

north 'pole *n* **1a** *often cap N&P* the northernmost point of the rotational axis of the earth **b** the northernmost point on the celestial sphere, about which the stars seem to revolve **2** the northward-pointing pole of a magnet

¹**north'west** /-'west/ *adj or adv* towards, at, belonging to, or coming from the northwest

²**north'west** *n* **1** (the general direction corresponding to) the compass point midway between north and west **2** *often cap* regions or countries lying to the northwest of a specified or implied point of orientation

¹**north'westerly** /-'westəli/ *adj or adv* northwest

²**north'westerly**, **northwester** /-'westə/ *n* a wind from the northwest

north'western /-'west(ə)n/ *adj* **1** *often cap* (characteristic) of a region conventionally designated Northwest **2** northwest

Norwegian /naw'weejən/ *n or adj* (a native or inhabitant or the language) of Norway

¹**nose** /nohz/ *n* **1a** the part of the face that bears the nostrils and covers the front part of the nasal cavity **b** a snout, muzzle **2a** the sense or (vertebrate) organ of smell **b** aroma, bouquet **3** the projecting part or front end of sthg **4a** the nose as a symbol of undue curiosity or interference **b** a knack for detecting what is latent or concealed — **through the nose** at an exorbitant rate

²**nose** *v* **1** to use the nose in examining, smelling, etc; to sniff or nuzzle **2a** to pry – often + *into* **b** to search or look inquisitively – usu + *about* or *around* **3** to move ahead slowly or cautiously

¹**nose 'dive** *n* a sudden dramatic drop

²**nose,gay** /-,gay/ *n* a small bunch of flowers; a posy

¹**nosh** /nosh/ *v* to eat – *infml* – ~ **er** *n*

²**nosh** *n* food; a meal – *infml*

'nosh-,up *n*, a large meal – *infml*

nostalgia /no'staljə/ *n* **1** homesickness **2** a wistful or excessively sentimental yearning for sthg past or irrecoverable – **gic** *adj* – **gically** *adv*

nostril /'nostril, nostrəl/ *n* the opening of the nose to the outside

nosy, **nosey** /'nohzi/ *adj* prying, snooping – *infml*

nosy 'parker /'pahkə/ *n*, *Br* a busybody – *infml*

not /not/ *adv* **1** – used to negate a (preceding) word or word group (e g *not* thirsty; will it rain? I hope *not*) **2** – used to give force to an opposite meaning (e g *not* without – reason) — **not a** not even one — **not at all** — used in answer to thanks or to an apology — **not half 1** *chiefly Br* not nearly **2** very much; totally — slang

¹**notable** /'nohtəbl/ *adj* **1** worthy of note; remarkable **2** distinguished, prominent – **bly** *adv* – **bility** *n*

²**notable** *n* **1** a prominent person **2** *pl*, *often cap* a group of people summoned, esp in France when it was a monarchy, to act as a deliberative body

notary /'nohtəri/, **notary public** *n*, *pl* **notaries, notaries public, notary publics** a public officer appointed to administer oaths and draw up and authenticate documents

notation /noh'taysh(ə)n/ *n* (a representation of sthg by) a system or set of marks, signs, symbols, figures, characters, or abbreviated expressions (e g to express technical facts or quantities)

¹**notch** /noch/ *n* 1 a V-shaped indentation 2 a degree, step

²**notch** *v* 1 to make a notch in 2 to score or achieve – usu + *up*

¹**note** /noht/ *v* 1a to take due or special notice of b to record in writing 2 to make special mention of; remark

²**note** *n* 1a(1) a sound having a definite pitch a(2) a call, esp of a bird b a written symbol used to indicate duration and pitch of a tone by its shape and position on the staff 2a a characteristic feature of smell, flavour, etc b a mood or quality 3a a memorandum b a brief comment or explanation c a piece of paper money d(1) a short informal letter d(2) a formal diplomatic communication 4a distinction, reputation b observation, notice

'**note,book** /-,book/ *n* a book for notes or memoranda

noted /'nohtid/ *adj* well-known, famous

'**note,worthy** /-,wuhdhi/ *adj* worthy of or attracting attention; notable

¹**nothing** /'nuthing/ *pron* 1 not any thing; no thing 2 sthg of no consequence 3 no truth or value (e g there's *nothing* in this rumour) — **like nothing on earth** 1 severely indisposed or embarrassed 2 grotesque, outlandish

²**nothing** *adv* not at all; in no degree

³**nothing** *n* 1 sthg that does not exist 2 sby or sthg of no or slight value or size

'**nothingness** /-nis/ *n* 1a nonexistence b utter insignificance 2 a void, emptiness

¹**notice** /'nohtis/ *n* 1a warning of a future occurrence b notification of intention of terminating an agreement at a particular time 2 attention, heed 3 a written or printed announcement 4 a review (e g of a play)

²**notice** *v* 1 to comment upon; refer to 2 to take notice of; mark

noticeable /'nohtisəbl/ *adj* 1 worthy of notice 2 capable of being noticed; perceptible – **-ably** *adv*

notification /,nohtifi'kaysh(ə)n/ *n* 1 (an instance of) notifying 2 sthg written that gives notice

notify /'nohti,fie/ *v* 1 to give (official) notice to 2 to make known

notion /'nohsh(ə)n/ *n* 1a a broad general concept b a conception, impression 2 a whim or fancy

notional /'nohsh(ə)nl/ *adj* 1 theoretical, speculative 2 existing only in the mind; imaginary

notoriety /,nohtə'rie əti/ *n* the quality or state of being notorious

notorious /noh'tawri əs/ *adj* well-known, esp for a specified (unfavourable) quality or trait – **~ly** *adv*

¹**notwithstanding** /,notwidh'standing, -with-/ *prep* in spite of

²**notwithstanding** *adv* nevertheless

³**notwithstanding** *conj* although

nougat /'nugət, 'nooh,gah/ *n* a sweetmeat of nuts or fruit pieces in a semisolid sugar paste

nought /nawt/ *n* 1 naught; nothing 2 the arithmetical symbol 0; zero

noun /nown/ *n* a word that is the name of a person, place, thing, substance, or state and that belongs to 1 of the major form classes in grammar

nourish /'nurish/ *v* 1 to nourish, rear 2 to encourage the growth of; foster 3 to provide or sustain with nutriment; feed – **~ment** *n*

nouveau riche /,noohvoh 'reesh/ *n*, *pl* **nouveaux riches** /~ / sby who has recently become rich (and shows it)

nova /'nohvə/ *n*, *pl* **novas**, **novae** /-vi, -vay/ a previously faint star that becomes suddenly very bright and then fades away

¹**novel** /'novl/ *adj* 1 new and unlike anything previously known 2 original and striking, esp in conception or style

²**novel** *n* an invented prose narrative that deals esp with human experience and social behaviour – **~ist** *n*

novelette /,novl'et/ *n* a short novel or long short story, often of a sentimental nature

novelty /'nov(ə)lti/ *n* 1 sthg new and unusual 2 a small manufactured often cheap article for personal or household adornment

November /noh'vembə/ *n* the 11th month of the Gregorian calendar

novice /'novis/ *n* 1 a person admitted to probationary membership of a religious community 2 a beginner

¹**now** /now/ *adv* 1a at the present time b in the immediate past c in the time immediately to follow; forthwith 2 – used with the sense of present time weakened or lost 2a to introduce an important point or indicate a transition (e g *now* if we turn to the next aspect of the problem) b to express command, request, or warning (e g *now*, don't squabble) 3 sometimes – linking 2 or more coordinate words or phrases (e g *now* one and *now* another) 4 under the changed or unchanged circumstances (e g he'll never believe me *now*) 5 at the time referred to (e g *now* the trouble began) 6 up to the present or to the time referred to (e g haven't been for years *now*)

²**now** *conj* in view of the fact that; since

³**now** *n* 1 the present time 2 the time referred to

nowadays /'nowə,dayz/ *adv* in these modern times; today

noway /'noh,way/, **noways** *adv* in no way whatever; not at all – fml

¹**nowhere** /'noh,weə/ *adv* 1 not anywhere 2 to no purpose or result

²**nowhere** *n* a nonexistent place

noxious /'nokshəs/ *adj* **1** harmful to living things **2** having a harmful moral influence; unwholesome – ~**ly** *adv* – ~**ness** *n*

nozzle /'nozl/ *n* a projecting part with an opening that usu serves as an outlet; *esp* a short tube with a taper or constriction used on a hose, pipe, etc to speed up or direct a flow of fluid

nuance /'nyooh,onhs √/ *n* a subtle distinction or gradation; a shade

nub /nub/ *n* **1** a knob, lump **2** *the* gist or crux

nubile /'n(y)ooh,biel/ *adj*, *of a girl* of marriageable age; *esp* young and sexually attractive – often humor

nuclear /'nyoohkli·ə/ *adj* **1** of or constituting a nucleus **2** of, using, or being the atomic nucleus, atomic energy, the atom bomb, or atomic power

nuclear-free zone *n* an area in which the use, storage, and transport of all nuclear materials are officially declared prohibited

nuclear winter *n* a state of extreme coldness on earth, caused by clouds of smoke blocking sunlight, which is thought likely to follow a nuclear war

nucleus /'nyoohkli·əs/ *n*, *pl* **nuclei** /-kli,ie, -kli·i/ *also* **nucleuses** a central point, mass, etc about which gathering, concentration, etc takes place: e g a **a** usu round membrane-surrounded cell part that contains the chromosomes **b** the positively charged central part of an atom that accounts for nearly all of the atomic mass and consists of protons and usu neutrons

¹**nude** /n(y)oohd/ *adj* without clothing or covering; naked, bare – **nudity** *n*

²**nude** *n* **1 a** a representation of a nude human figure **b** a nude person **2** the state of being nude

nudge /nuj/ *v* **1** to touch or push gently; *esp* to catch the attention of by a push of the elbow **2** to move (as if) by pushing gently or slowly – **nudge** *n*

nudism /'nooh,diz(ə)m, 'nyooh-/ *n* the cult or practice of going nude as much as possible – **-ist** *adj*, *n*

nugatory /'nyoohgət(ə)ri/ *adj* **1** trifling, inconsequential **2** inoperative *USE* fml

nugget /'nugət/ *n* a solid lump, esp of a precious metal in its natural state

nuisance /'nyoohs(ə)ns/ *n* **1** (legally actionable) harm or injury **2** an annoying or troublesome person or thing

¹**null** /nul/ *adj* amounting to nothing; nil

²**null** *n* zero, nought

null and 'void *adj* completely invalid

nullify /'nulifie/ *v* **1** to make (legally) null or invalid **2** to make worthless, unimportant, or ineffective – **-ification** *n*

numb /num/ *adj* **1** devoid of sensation, esp as a result of cold or anaesthesia **2** devoid of emotion

¹**number** /'numbə/ *n* **1 a(1)** *sing or pl in constr* an indefinite, usu large, total **a(2)** *pl* a numerous group; many; *also* an instance of numerical superiority **b(1)** any of an ordered set of standard names or symbols (e g 2, 5, 27th) used in counting or in assigning a position in an order **b(2)** an element (e g 6, -3, ⁵/₈, √7) belonging to an arithmetical system based on or analogous to the numbers used in counting and subject to specific rules of addition, subtraction, and multiplication **2a** a word, symbol, letter, or combination of symbols representing a number **b** one or more numerals or digits used to identify or designate **3** a group of individuals **4a** sthg viewed in terms of the advantage or enjoyment obtained from it **b** an article of esp women's clothing **c** a person or individual, esp an attractive girl **5** insight into a person's motives or character — **without number** innumerable

²**number** *v* **1** to include as part of a whole or total **2** to assign a number to **3** to comprise in number; total

number 'one *n* **1** sthg that is first in rank, order, or importance **2** one's own interests or welfare – infml

'number plate /-,playt/ *n*, *chiefly Br* a rectangular identifying plate fastened to a vehicle and bearing the vehicle's registration number

numeral /'nyoohm(ə)rəl/ *n* a conventional symbol that represents a natural number or zero

numerate /'nyoohm(ə)rət/ *adj* having an understanding of mathematics, esp arithmetic – **-racy** *n*

numerator /'nyoohmə,raytə/ *n* the part of a fraction that is above the line and signifies the number of parts of the denominator that is shown by the fraction

numerical /nyooh'merikl/, **numeric** *adj* of, expressed in, or involving numbers or a number system – **ly** *adv*

numerous /'nyoohm(ə)rəs/ *adj* consisting of many units or individuals – **ly** *adv* – **ness** *n*

numismatics /,nyoohmiz'matiks/ *n pl but sing in constr* the study or collection of coinage, coins, paper money, medals, tokens, etc – **numismatic** *adj* – **-tist** *n*

numskull, numbskull /'num,skul/ *n* a dull or stupid person

nun /nun/ *n* a female member of a religious order living in a convent and often engaged in educational or nursing work

nunnery /'nunəri/ *n* a convent of nuns

¹**nuptial** /'nupsh(ə)l/ *adj* **1** of marriage **2** characteristic of or occurring in the breeding season

²**nuptial** *n* a wedding – usu pl

¹**nurse** /nuhs/ *n* **1** a woman employed to take care of a young child **2** sby skilled or trained in caring for the sick or infirm, esp under the supervision of a physician

²**nurse** v 1 to suckle an offspring 2 to encourage the development of; nurture **3a** to attempt to cure (e g an illness or injury) by appropriate treatment **b** to care for and wait on (e g a sick person) 4 to hold in one's mind; harbour 5 to hold (e g a baby) lovingly or caressingly

nursery /'nuhs(ə)ri/ n 1 a child's bedroom or playroom 2 a place where small children are looked after in their parents' absence 3 an area where plants, trees, etc are grown for propagation, sale, or transplanting

'**nurseryman** /-mən, -ˌman/ n one whose occupation is the cultivation of plants, usu for sale

'**nursery ˌrhyme** n a short traditional story in rhyme for children

'**nursery ˌschool** n a school for children aged usu from 2 to 5

¹**nurture** /'nuhchə/ n 1 training, upbringing 2 food, nourishment 3 all the environmental influences that affect the innate genetic potentialities of an organism

²**nurture** v 1 to give care and nourishment to 2 to educate or develop

nut /nut/ n 1 (the often edible kernel of) a dry fruit or seed with a hard separable rind or shell 2 a difficult person, problem, or undertaking 3 a typically hexagonal usu metal block with an internal screw thread cut on it that can be screwed onto a bolt to tighten or secure sthg 4 a small piece or lump 5 a person's head 6a an insane or wildly eccentric person **b** an ardent enthusiast

'**nut ˌcase** /-ˌkays/ n a lunatic – infml

'**nut ˌhouse** /-ˌhows/ n a madhouse – slang

nutmeg /'nutmeg/ n (an Indonesian tree that produces) an aromatic seed used as a spice

nutrient /'nyoohtri·ənt/ n or adj (sthg) that provides nourishment

nutriment /'nyoohtrimənt/ n sthg that nourishes or promotes growth

nutrition /nyooh'trish(ə)n/ n all the processes by which an organism takes in and uses food

nutritious /nyooh'trishəs/ adj nourishing – ~ly adv – ~tive adj

nuts /nuts/ adj 1 passionately keen or enthusiastic 2 crazy, mad USE infml

'**nut ˌshell** /-ˌshel/ n the hard outside covering enclosing the kernel of a nut — **in a nutshell** in a brief accurate account

nutty /'nuti/ adj 1 having a flavour like that of nuts 2 eccentric, silly; also nuts – infml – **-tiness** n

nuzzle /'nuzl/ v nuzzling /'nuzling/ 1 to push or rub sthg with the nose 2 to lie close or snug; nestle

nylon /'nielon/ n 1 any of numerous strong tough elastic synthetic fibres used esp in textiles and plastics 2 pl stockings made of nylon

nymph /nimf/ n 1 any of the minor female divinities of nature in classical mythology 2 any of various immature insects; esp a larva of a dragonfly or other insect with incomplete metamorphosis

O

o /oh/ n, pl **o's, os** often cap 1 (a graphic representation of or device for reproducing) the 15th letter of the English alphabet 2 sthg shaped like the letter O; esp zero

O /oh/ interj or n oh

o' also **o** /ə/ prep 1 of 2 chiefly dial on

oaf /ohf/ n a clumsy slow-witted person – ~ish adj – ~ishly adv – ~ishness n

oak /ohk/ n, pl **oaks, oak** (the tough hard durable wood of) any of various trees or shrubs of the beech family

'**oak ˌapple** n a large round gall produced on oak stems or leaves by a gall wasp

oakum /'ohkəm/ n hemp or jute fibre impregnated with tar and used in packing joints and stopping up gaps between the planks of a ship

oar /aw/ n a long usu wooden shaft with a broad blade at one end used for propelling or steering a boat

oarsman /'awzmən/ n one who rows a boat, esp in a racing crew

oasis /oh'aysis/ n, pl **oases** /-seez/ a fertile or green area in a dry region

'**oast ˌhouse** /ohst/ n a usu circular building housing a kiln for drying hops or making malt from barley

oath /ohth/ n pl **oaths** /ohdhz/ 1 a solemn calling upon God or a revered person or thing to witness to the true or binding nature of one's declaration 2 an irreverent use of a sacred name; declaration broadly a swearword — **on/under oath** bound by a solemn promise to tell the truth

'**oat ˌmeal** /-ˌmeel, -ˌmial/ n 1 meal made from oats, used esp in porridge 2 a greyish beige colour

oats /ohts/ n pl a widely cultivated cereal grass that does not form a tight head like wheat or barley

¹**obbligato** /ˌobli'gahtoh/ adj not to be omitted – used in music

²**obbligato** n, pl **obbligatos** also **obbligati** /-ti/ an elaborate, esp melodic, accompaniment, usu played by a single instrument

obdurate /'obdyoorət, -joo-/ adj stubbornly persistent – ~ly adv – **-racy** n

obedient /ə'beedi·ənt, oh-/ *adj* willing to obey – ~ly *adv* – -ence *n*

obeisance /oh'bay(i)səns, -'bee-/ *n* 1 a movement or gesture made as a sign of respect or submission 2 deference, homage

obelisk /'obolisk/ *n* an upright 4-sided pillar that gradually tapers towards the top

obese /oh'bees/ *adj* excessively fat – **obesity** *n*

obey /ə'bay, oh'bay/ *v* 1 to submit to the commands or guidance of 2 to comply with; execute

obfuscate /'obfus·kayt/ *v* 1 to make obscure or difficult to understand 2 to confuse, bewilder – -cation *n*

obituary /ə'bityoo(ə)ri/ *n* a notice of a person's death, usu with a short biography

¹**object** /'objekt/ *n* 1 sthg that is (capable of) being sensed physically or examined mentally 2 sthg or sby that arouses an emotion or provokes a reaction or response 3 an end towards which effort, action, etc is directed; a goal 4 a noun or noun equivalent appearing in a prepositional phrase or representing the goal or the result of the action of its verb (e g *house* in *we built a house*)

²**object** /əb'jekt/ *v* 1 to oppose sthg with words or arguments 2 to feel dislike or disapproval – ~ion *n* – ~or *n*

objectionable /əb'jcksh(ə)nəbl/ *adj* unpleasant or offensive – -bly *adv*

¹**objective** /əb'jektiv/ *adj* 1a constituting an object; *specif* belonging to the external world and observable or verifiable b concerned with or expressing the nature of external reality rather than personal feelings or beliefs 2 dealing with facts without distortion by personal feelings or prejudices – ~ly *adv* – -tivity *n*

²**objective** *n* 1 sthg towards which efforts are directed; a goal 2 sthg to be attained or achieved by a military operation 3 a lens or system of lenses that forms an image of an object

obligation /,obli'gaysh(ə)n/ *n* 1 sthg (e g a contract or promise) that binds one to a course of action 2 (the amount of) a financial commitment 3 sthg one is bound to do; a duty

obligatory /ə'bligət(ə)ri/ *adj* 1 binding in law or conscience 2 relating to or enforcing an obligation 3 compulsory

oblige /ə'bliej/ *v* 1 to constrain by force or circumstance 2 to do sthg as a favour; be of service to

obliging /ə'bliejing/ *adj* eager to help; accommodating – ~ly *adv*

oblique /ə'bleek/ *adj* 1a neither perpendicular nor parallel; inclined b *of an angle* greater than but not a multiple of 90° 2 not straightforward or explicit; indirect – ~ly *adv*

obliterate /ə'blitərayt/ *v* 1 to make illegible or imperceptible 2 to destroy all trace or indication of – -ation *n*

oblivion /ə'blivi·ən/ *n* 1 the state of forgetting or being oblivious 2 the state of being forgotten

oblivious /ə'blivi·əs/ *adj* lacking conscious knowledge; completely unaware – usu + *of* or *to* – ~ly *adv* – ~ness *n*

oblong /'oblong/ *adj* rectangular with adjacent sides unequal – **oblong** *n*

obnoxious /əb'nokshəs/ *adj* highly offensive or repugnant – ~ly *adv* – ~ness *n*

oboe /'oh,boh/ *n* a double-reed woodwind instrument – **oboist** *n*

obscene /əb'seen/ *adj* 1 offending standards of sexual propriety or decency 2 (morally) repugnant – ~ly *adv* – ~nity *n*

¹**obscure** /əb'skyooə/ *adj* 1 hard to understand; abstruse 2 not well-known or widely acclaimed 3 faint, indistinct – ~ly *adv* – -rity *n*

²**obscure** *v* 1 to conceal (as if) by covering 2 to make indistinct or unintelligible

obsequious /əb'seekwi·əs/ *adj* showing a servile willingness to oblige

observance /əb'zuhv(ə)ns/ *n* 1 a customary practice, rite, or ceremony – often *pl* 2 an act of complying with a custom, rule, or law

observatory /əb'zuhvət(ə)ri/ *n* a building or institution for (the interpretation of) astronomical observation

observe /əb'zuhv/ *v* 1a to act in due conformity with b to celebrate or perform (e g a ceremony or festival) 2 to perceive or take note of, esp for scientific purposes 3 to utter as a comment – -vable *adj* – -vably *adv* – -vant *adj* – -vation *n* – ~r *n*

obsess /əb'ses/ *v* to preoccupy intensely or abnormally

obsession /əb'sesh(ə)n/ *n* a persistent (disturbing) preoccupation with an often unreasonable idea – -ive *adj*

obsolescent /,obsə'les(ə)nt/ *adj* becoming obsolete – -cence *n*

obsolete /'obsəleet/ *adj* 1 no longer in use 2 outdated, outmoded

obstacle /'obstəkl/ *n* sthg that hinders or obstructs

ob'stetrics *n pl but sing or pl in constr* a branch of medicine dealing with the care and treatment of women before, during, and after childbirth – -ric(al) *adj* – -rician *n*

obstinate /'obstinət/ *adj* clinging stubbornly to an opinion or course of action – ~ly *adv* – -nacy *n*

obstreperous /əb'strep(ə)rəs/ *adj* 1 aggressively noisy 2 unruly – ~ly *adv* – ~ness *n*

obstruct /əb'strukt/ *v* 1 to block or close up by an obstacle 2 to hinder, impede – ~ion *n* – ~ive *adj* – ~ively *adv*

obtain /əb'tayn/ *v* 1 to acquire or attain 2 to be generally accepted or practised – *fml* – ~able *adj*

obtrude /əb'troohd/ *v* 1 to thrust out 2 to assert without warrant or request – -usion *n*

obtrusive /əb'troohsiv, -ziv/ *adj* **1** forward in manner; pushing **2** unduly noticeable – ~**ly** *adv* – ~**ness** *n*

obtuse /əb'tyoohs/ *adj* **1** lacking sensitivity or mental alertness **2a** being or forming an angle greater than 90° but less than 180° **b** not pointed or acute – ~**ly** *adv* – ~**ness** *n*

¹**obverse** /'obvuhs/ *adj* **1** facing the observer or opponent **2** constituting a counterpart or complement

²**obverse** *n* **1a** the side of a coin, medal, or currency note that bears the principal device and lettering **b** the more conspicuous of 2 possible sides or aspects **2** a counterpart to a fact or truth

obviate /'obviayt/ *v* **1** to anticipate and dispose of in advance **2** to make unnecessary

obvious /'obvi·əs/ *adj* **1** evident to the senses or understanding **2** unsubtle – ~**ly** *adv* – ~**ness** *n*

ocarina /ˌokə'reenə/ *n* a simple wind instrument with an oval body

¹**occasion** /ə'kayzh(ə)n/ *n* **1** a suitable opportunity or circumstance **2** a state of affairs that provides a reason or grounds **3** the immediate or incidental cause **4** a time at which sthg occurs **5** a special event or ceremony — **on occasion** from time to time

²**occasion** *v* to bring about; cause – *fml*

occasional /ə'kayzh(ə)nl/ *adj* **1** of a particular occasion **2** composed for a particular occasion **3** occurring at irregular or infrequent intervals **4** acting in a specified capacity from time to time **5** designed for use as the occasion demands – ~**ly** *adv*

Occident /'oksid(ə)nt/ *n* the west – ~**al** *n, adj*

occult /'okult, -'-/ *adj* **1** secret; *esp* esoteric **2** not easily understood; abstruse **3** involving (secret knowledge of) supernatural powers

occupation /ˌokyoo'paysh(ə)n/ *n* **1** an activity in which one engages, esp to earn a living **2a** the occupancy of land **b** tenure **3** taking possession or the holding and control of a place or area, esp by a foreign military force – ~**al** *adj*

occupy /'okyoopie/ *v* **1** to engage the attention or energies of **2** to fill up (a portion of space or time) **3** to take or maintain possession of **4** to reside in or use as an owner or tenant – **-pant** *n* – **-pancy** *n*

occur /ə'kuh/ *v* **-rr-** **1** to be found; exist **2** to become the case; happen **3** to come to mind

occurrence /ə'kurəns/ *n* sthg that takes place; an event

ocean /'ohsh(ə)n/ *n* **1** (any of the large expanses that together constitute) the whole body of salt water that covers nearly ³/₄ of the surface of the globe **2** a huge amount – *infml* – ~**ic** *adj*

oceanography /ˌohsh(ə)n'ogrəfi/ *n* the science dealing with oceans and their form, biology, and resources – **-pher** *n*

ocelot /'osəˌlot/ *n* a medium-sized American wildcat with a yellow or greyish coat dotted with black

oche /'oki/ *n* the line on the floor behind which a player must stand when throwing darts at a dartboard

ochre, *NAm chiefly* **ocher** /'ohkə/ *n* **1** the colour of esp yellow ochre **2** an earthy usu red or yellow (impure) iron ore used as a pigment

ocker /'okə/ *n, Austr & NZ* an Australian; *specif* one who boorishly asserts Australian nationality

o'clock /ə'klok/ *adv* according to the clock – used in specifying the exact hour

octagon /'oktəgon, -gən/ *n* a polygon of 8 angles and 8 sides – ~**al** *adj*

octave /'oktiv, 'oktayv/ *n* **1** a group of 8 lines of verse, esp the first 8 of a sonnet **2a** (the combination of 2 notes at) a musical interval of 8 diatonic degrees **b** a note separated from a lower note by this interval **c** the whole series of notes or piano, organ, etc keys within this interval that form the unit of the modern scale

octet /ok'tet/ *n* (a musical composition for) 8 instruments, voices, or performers

October /ok'tohbə/ *n* the 10th month of the Gregorian calendar

octogenarian /ˌoktəjə'neəri·ən/ *n* a person between 80 and 89 years old

octopus /'oktəpəs/ *n, pl* **octopuses, octopi** /-pie/ any of a genus of molluscs related to the squids and cuttlefishes with 8 muscular arms equipped with 2 rows of suckers

ocular /'okyoolə/ *adj* **1** performed or perceived with the eyes **2** of the eye

oculist /'okyoolist/ *n* an ophthalmologist or optician

odd /od/ *adj* **1a** left over when others are paired or grouped **b** not matching **2** not divisible by 2 without leaving a remainder **3** somewhat more than the specified number – usu in combination **4** not regular or planned; casual, occasional **5** different from the usual or conventional; strange – ~**ly** *adv* – ~**ness** *n*

odd·ball /-ˌbawl/ *n* an eccentric or peculiar person – *infml*

oddity /'odəti/ *n* **1** an odd person, thing, event, or trait **2** oddness, strangeness

oddment /'odmənt/ *n* **1** sthg left over; a remnant **2** *pl* odds and ends

odds /odz/ *n pl but sing or pl in constr* **1** the probability (expressed as a ratio) that one thing will happen rather than another **2** disagreement, variance **3** the ratio between the amount to be paid off for a winning bet and the amount of the bet

odds and 'ends *n pl* miscellaneous items or remnants

odds-'on *adj* **1** (viewed as) having a better than even chance to win **2** not involving much risk

ode /ohd/ *n* a lyric poem, often addressed to a particular subject, marked by a usu exalted tone

odious /'ohdi·əs/ *adj* arousing hatred or revulsion – ~**ly** *adv*

odium /'ohdi·əm/ *n* general condemnation or disgrace associated with a despicable act – *fml*

odour, *NAm chiefly* **odor** /'ohdə/ *n* **1** (the sensation resulting from) a quality of sthg that stimulates the sense of smell **2** repute, favour – *fml* **3** a characteristic quality; a savour – chiefly *derog* – ~**less** *adj* – **odorous** *adj*

odyssey /'odəsi/ *n* a long wandering or quest

o'er /aw, 'oh·ə/ *adv or prep* over – *poetic*

oesophagus /ee'sofəgəs/ *n pl* **oesophagi** /-,gie/ the muscular tube leading from the back of the mouth to the stomach

oestrogen /'eestrəj(ə)n, 'estrə-/ *n* a sex hormone that stimulates the development of female secondary sex characteristics

of /əv; *strong* ov/ *prep* **1a** – used to indicate origin or derivation (e g a man *of* noble birth) **b** – used to indicate cause, motive, or reason (e g died *of* pneumonia) **c** proceeding from; on the part of (e g very kind *of* him) **d** by (e g the plays *of* Shaw) **2a**(1) composed or made from (e g a crown *of* gold) **b** containing (e g a cup *of* water) **c** – used to indicate the mass noun or class that includes the part denoted by the previous word (e g an inch *of* rain; a blade *of* grass) **d** from among (e g one *of* his poems) **3a** belonging to; related to (e g the leg *of* the chair) **b** that is or are – used before possessive forms (e g a friend *of* John's) **c** characterized by; with, having (e g a man *of* courage) **d** connected with (e g a teacher *of* French) **e** existing or happening in or on (e g the battle *of* Blenheim; my letter *of* the 19th) **4a** relating to (a topic); concerning (e g stories *of* his travels) **b** in respect to (e g slow *of* speech) **c** directed towards (e g love *of* nature) **d** – used to show separation or removal (e g eased *of* pain) **e** – used as a function word to indicate a whole or quantity from which a part is removed or expended **5** – used to indicate apposition (e g the art *of* painting) **6** in, during (e g go there *of* an evening) – *infml* — **of a** -like — used after expressions of strong feeling

¹**off** /of/ *adv* **1a**(1) from a place or position; *specif* away from land (e g the ship stood *off* to sea) **a**(2) away in space or ahead in time (e g Christmas is a week *off*) **b** from a course; aside; (e g turned *off* into a lay-by) *specif* away from the wind **c** into sleep or unconsciousness (e g dozed *off*) **2a** so as to be not supported, not in close contact, or not attached (e g the hands came *off*; took his coat *off*) **b** so as to be divided (e g a corner screened *off*) **3a** to or in a state of discontinuance or suspension (e g the radio is *off*) **b** so as to be completely finished or no longer existent (e g kill them *off*) **c** in or into a state of putrefaction (e g the cream's

gone *off*) **d** (as if) by heart (e g knew it *off* pat) **4** away from an activity or function (e g the night shift went *off*) **5** offstage (e g noises *off*) **6** to a sexual climax (e g brought him *off*) – *slang*

²**off** *prep* **1a** – used to indicate physical separation or distance from (e g take it *off* the table) **b** to seaward of (e g 2 miles *off* shore) **c** lying or turning aside from; adjacent to (e g a shop just *off* the high street) **d** (slightly) away from – often in combination (e g a week *off* work; *off*-target) **2** – used to indicate the source from which sthg derives or is obtained (e g bought it *off* a friend) **3a** not occupied in (e g *off* duty) **b** tired of; no longer interested in or using (e g he's *off* drugs) **c** below the usual standard or level of (e g *off* his game)

³**off** *adj* **1a** being the most distant of 2 **b** seaward **c** being the right-hand one of a pair (e g the *off* wheel of a cart) **c** situated to one side; adjoining (e g bedroom with dressing room *off*) **2a** started on the way (e g *off* on a spree) **b** not taking place or staying in effect; cancelled (e g the match is *off*) **c** *of a dish on a menu* no longer being served **3a** not up to standard; unsatisfactory in terms of achievement (e g an *off* day) **b** slack (e g *off* season) **4** affected (as if) with putrefaction **5** provided (e g how are you *off* for socks?) **6a** in, on, through, or towards the *off* side of a cricket field **b** *esp of a ball bowled in cricket* moving or tending to move in the direction of the leg side **7** *of behaviour* not what one has a right to expect; *esp* rather unkind or dishonest – *infml*

⁴**off** *n* the start or outset; *also* a starting signal

offal /'ofl/ *n* **1** the liver, heart, kidney, etc of a butchered animal used as food **2** refuse

,**off'beat** /-'beet/ *adj* unusual; *esp* unconventional – *infml*

,**off-'colour** *adj* **1** unwell **2** somewhat indecent; risqué

offence, *NAm chiefly* **offense** /ə'fens/ *n* **1** sthg that occasions a sense of outrage **2** (an) attack, assault **3** displeasure, resentment **4a** a sin or misdeed **b** an illegal act; a crime

offend /ə'fend/ *v* **1** to break a moral or divine law – often + *against* **2** to cause displeasure, difficulty, or discomfort to – ~**er** *n*

¹**offensive** /ə'fensiv/ *adj* **1** of or designed for aggression or attack **2** arousing physical disgust; repellent **3** causing indignation or outrage – ~**ly** *adv* – ~**ness** *n*

²**offensive** *n* **1** the position or attitude of an attacking party **2** an esp military attack on a large scale

¹**offer** /'ofə/ *v* **1** to present (e g a prayer or sacrifice) in an act of worship – often + *up* **2** to present (e g for acceptance, rejection, or consideration) **3** to declare one's willingness **4** to make available **5** to present (goods) for sale **6** to tender as payment; bid

²**offer** *n* **1a** a proposal; *specif* a proposal of marriage **b** an undertaking to do or give sthg on a specific condition **2** a price named by a prospective buyer — **on offer** being offered; *specif* for sale, esp at a reduced price — **under offer** sold subject to the signing of contracts — used in connection with sales of real estate

offering /'of(ə)riŋ/ *n* **1** the act of one who offers **2** sthg offered; *esp* a sacrifice ceremonially offered as a part of worship **3** a contribution to the support of a church or other religious organization

offhand /ˌof'hand/ *adv or adj* **1** without forethought or preparation **2** without proper attention or respect – ~**edly** *adv* – ~**edness** *n*

office /'ofis/ *n* **1** an esp beneficial service or action carried out for another **2** a position with special (public) duties or responsibilities **3** a prescribed form or service of worship **4a** a place, esp a large building, where the business of a particular organization is carried out **b** (a group of people sharing) a room in which the administrative, clerical, or professional work of an organization is performed

officer /'ofisə/ *n* **1** a policeman **2** one who holds a position with special duties or responsibilities (e g in a government or business) **3a** one who holds a position of authority or command in the armed forces; *specif* a commissioned officer **b** a master or any of the mates of a merchant or passenger ship – **officer** *v*

¹**official** /ə'fish(ə)l/ *n* one who holds an esp public office – ~**dom** *n*

²**official** *adj* **1** of an office and its duties **2** holding an office **3** authoritative, authorized **4** suitable for or characteristic of a person in office; formal – ~**ly** *adv*

officiate /ə'fishiayt/ *v* **1** to perform an esp religious ceremony, function, or duty **2** to act as an official or in an official capacity

officious /ə'fishəs/ *adj* given to or marked by overzealousness in exercising authority or carrying out duties – ~**ly** *adv* – ~**ness** *n*

¹**off-ˈlicence** *n*, *Br* a shop, part of a public house, etc licensed to sell alcoholic drinks to be consumed off the premises

off-ˈload *v* to unload

ˌoff-ˈpeak *adj* (used) at a time of less than the maximum demand or activity

ˈoff-ˌprint /-ˌprint/ *n* a separately printed excerpt (e g an article from a magazine)

ˌoff-ˈputting *adj* disagreeable, disconcerting – *infml*

¹**off-set** /-ˌset/ *n* **1** an abrupt bend in an object by which one part is turned aside out of line **2** sthg that serves to compensate for sthg else **3** a printing process in which an inked impression from a plate is first made on a rubber surface and then transferred to paper

²**off-set** *v* **-tt-; offset 1** to balance **2** to compensate or make up for

ˌoff-ˈside /-ˈsied/ *adv or adj* illegally in advance of the ball or puck in a team game

¹**off-ˌside** *n* **1** the part of a cricket field on the opposite side of a line joining the middle stumps to that in which the batsman stands when playing a ball **2** *chiefly Br* the right side of a horse, vehicle, etc

ˈoff-spring /-ˌspring/ *n pl* **offspring** the progeny of a person, animal, or plant; young

ˌoff-the-ˈrecord *adj or adv* (given or made) unofficially or in confidence

ˌoff-ˈwhite *n or adj* (a) yellowish or greyish white

oft /oft/ *adv* often – *poetic*

often /'of(t)ən/ *adv* **1** (at) many times **2** in many cases

ogle /'ohgl/ *v* **ogling** /'ohgliŋ/ to glance or stare with esp sexual interest (at) – **ogle** *n* – ~**r** *n*

ogre /'ohgə/, *fem* **ogress** /'ohgris/ *n* **1** a hideous giant of folklore believed to feed on human beings **2** a dreaded person or thing – **ogreish** *adj* – **ogreishly** *adv*

¹**oh, O** /oh/ *interj* – used to express surprise, pain, disappointment, etc

²**oh, O** *n* nought

ohm /ohm/ *n* the derived SI unit of electrical resistance equal to the resistance between 2 points of a conductor when a constant potential difference of 1 volt applied to these points produces a current of 1 ampere

¹**oil** /oyl/ *n* **1** any of numerous smooth greasy combustible liquids or low melting-point solids that are insoluble in water but dissolve in organic solvents **2a** *pl* oil paint **b** an oil painting **3** petroleum – **oily** *adj*

²**oil** *v* to treat or lubricate with oil — **oil the wheels** to help things run smoothly

ˈoil-ˌcloth /-ˌkloth/ *n* cloth treated with oil or paint and used for table and shelf coverings

ˈoil ˌpaint *n* paint consisting of ground pigment mixed with oil

ˈoil-ˌskin /-ˌskin/ *n* **1** an oiled waterproof cloth used for coverings and garments **2** an oilskin or plastic raincoat **3** *pl* an oilskin or plastic suit of coat and trousers

ˈoil ˌslick *n* a film of oil floating on water

ointment /'oyntmənt/ *n* a soothing or healing salve for application to the skin

¹**OK, okay** /oh'kay, '-,-/ *adv, adj, or interj* all right

²**OK, okay** /oh'kay/ *v or n* **OK's; OK'ing; OK'd** (to give) approval or authorization (of), sanction

¹**old** /ohld/ *adj* **1a** dating from the esp remote past **b** persisting from an earlier time **c** of long standing **2** having existed for a specified period of time **3** advanced in years or age **4** former **5a** made long ago; *esp* worn with time or use **b** no longer in use; discarded **6** long familiar

²old *n* **1** old or earlier time **2** one of a specified age – usu in combination

,**old 'boy**, *fem* ,**old 'girl** *n*, *chiefly Br* **1** a former pupil of a particular, esp public, school **2** a fellow or friend – often used as an informal term of address

,**old 'boy ,network** *n*, *chiefly Br the* system of favouritism operating among people of a similar privileged background, esp among former pupils of public schools

olden /'ohldn/ *adj* of a bygone era

olde-worlde /,ohld 'wuhld; *often* ,ohldi 'wuhldi/ *adj* (excessively) of an old or mock old style

,**old-'fashioned** *adj* **1** (characteristic) of a past era; outdated **2** clinging to customs of a past era

,**old 'guard** *n sing or pl in constr, often cap O&G* the (original) conservative members of a group or party

,**old 'hand** *n* a very experienced person

,**old 'hat** *adj* **1** old-fashioned **2** hackneyed, trite

,**old 'lady** *n* one's wife or mother – *infml*

,**old 'maid** *n* **1** a spinster **2** a prim fussy person – *infml*

,**old 'man** *n* **1** one's husband or father **2** one in authority (e g one's employer, manager, or commander) – + *the USE infml*

,**old 'master** *n* (a work by) a distinguished European painter of the 16th to early 18th c

,**old 'school** *n* adherents of traditional ideas and practices

,**old ,school 'tie** *n* the conservatism and upper-class solidarity traditionally attributed to former members of British public schools

,**old 'stager** /'stayjə/ *n* a veteran

,**Old 'Testament** *n* a collection of writings forming the Jewish canon of Scripture and the first part of the Christian Bible

,**old-'timer** *n* **1** an old hand **2** *chiefly NAm* an old man

,**old 'wives' ,tale** *n* a traditional superstitious notion

,**old 'woman** *n* **1** one's wife or mother **2** a timid, prim, or fussy person, esp a man – *derog USE infml*

,**old-'world** *adj* **1** of the E hemisphere **2** reminiscent of a past age; *esp* quaintly charming

,**Old 'World** *n* the E Hemisphere; *specif* Europe, Asia, and Africa

oleaginous /,ohli'ajinəs/ *adj* oily

oligarchy /'oligahki/ *n* **1** government by a small group **2** a state or organization in which a small group exercises control, esp for its own interests **3** a small group exercising such control

¹olive /'oliv/ *n* **1** (an Old World evergreen tree that grows esp around the Mediterranean and bears) a small stone fruit used as a food and a source of oil **2** olive, olive green a dull yellowish green colour resembling that of an unripe olive

²olive ,**olive 'green** *adj* of the colour olive

'**olive ,branch** *n* an offer or gesture of peace or goodwill

olympiad /ə'limpi,ad/ *n*, *often cap* an olympic games

¹Olympian /ə'limpi-ən/ *adj* of the ancient Greek region of Olympia

²Olympian *adj* lofty, detached

³Olympian *n* **1** an inhabitant of the ancient Greek region of Olympia **2** any of the ancient Greek deities dwelling on Olympus **3** a loftily detached or superior person

Olympic /ə'limpik/ *adj* of or executed in the Olympic Games

O,lympic 'Games *n pl pl* **Olympic Games** an international sports meeting held once every 4 years in a different host country

ombudsman /'ombоodzmən/ *n* a government official appointed to investigate complaints made by individuals against government or public bodies

omega /'ohmigə/ *n* **1** the 24th and last letter of the Greek alphabet **2** the last one in a series, order, etc

omelette, omelet /'omlit/ *n* a mixture of beaten eggs cooked until set in a shallow pan

omen /'ohmən/ *n* an event or phenomenon believed to be a sign of some future occurrence

ominous /'ominəs/ *adj* portentous; *esp* foreboding evil or disaster – ~ly *adv*

omit /oh'mit, ə-/ *v* -tt- **1** to leave out or unmentioned **2** to fail to do or perform – **omission** *n*

¹omnibus /'omnibəs/ *n* **1** a book containing reprints of a number of works, usu by 1 author **2** a bus

²omnibus *adj* of, containing, or providing for many things at once

omnipotent /om'nipət(ə)nt/ *adj* having unlimited or very great power or influence – **-ence** *n*

omnipresent /,omni'prez(ə)nt/ *adj* present in all places at all times – **-ence** *n*

omniscient /om'nisi-ənt, om'nish(ə)nt/ *adj* **1** having infinite awareness or understanding **2** possessed of complete knowledge; all-knowing – **-ence** *n*

omnivorous /om'nivərəs/ *adj* **1** feeding on both animal and vegetable substances **2** avidly taking in, and esp reading, everything – ~**ly** *adv* – ~**ness** *n*

¹on /on/ *prep* **1a**(1) in contact with or supported from below by (e g sat on the table) **a**(2) attached or fastened to (e g a dog on a lead) **a**(3) carried on the person of (e g have you a match on you?) **a**(4) very near to, esp along an edge or border (e g towns on the frontier) **a**(5) within the limits of a usu specified area (e g on page 17) **b** at the usual standard or level of (e g on form) **c**(1) in the direction of (e g on the right) **c**(2) into contact with (e g jumped on the horse) **c**(3) with regard to; concerning (e g keen on sports) **c**(4) with a specified person or thing as object (e g try it out on her) **c**(5) having as a topic;

about (e g a book *on* India) c(6) staked on the success of (e g put £5 *on* a horse) c(7) doing or carrying out a specified action or activity (e g here *on* business) c(8) working for, supporting, or belonging to (e g *on* a committee) c(9) working at; in charge of (e g the man *on* the gate) **2a** having as a basis or source (e g of knowledge or comparison) (e g have it *on* good authority) **b** at the expense of (e g drinks are *on* the house) **3a** in the state or process of (e g *on* strike) **b** in the specified manner (e g *on* the cheap) **c** using as a medium (e g played it *on* the clarinet); *esp* over **4b** (e g talking *on* the telephone) **d** using by way of transport (e g arrived *on* foot) **e** sustained or powered by (e g car runs *on* petrol) **f** regularly taking (e g *on* valium) **4** through contact with (e g cut himself *on* a piece of glass) **5a** at the time of (e g every hour *on* the hour) **b** on the occasion of or immediately after and usu in consequence of (e g fainted *on* hearing the news) **c** in the course of (e g *on* a journey) **d** after (e g blow *on* blow)

²**on** *adv* **1** so as to be supported from below, in close contact, or attached (e g put the top *on*) **2a** ahead or forwards in space or time (e g do it later *on*) **b** with the specified part forward (e g cars crashed head *on*) **c** without interruption (e g chattered *on*) **d** in continuance or succession **3a** in or into (a state permitting) operation (e g put a record *on*) **b** in or into an activity or function (e g the night shift came *on*)

³**on** *adj* **1a** *cricket* leg (e g *on* drive) **b** taking place (e g the game is *on*) **c** performing or broadcasting (e g we're *on* in 10 minutes) **d** intended, planned (e g has nothing *on* for tonight) **e** worn as clothing (e g just a cardigan *on*) **2a** committed to a bet **b** in favour of a win (e g the odds are 2 to 1 *on*) **3** *chiefly Br* possible, practicable – usu neg (e g it's just not *on*) **4a** *chiefly Br* nagging (e g always *on* at him) **b** talking dully, excessively, or incomprehensibly (e g what's he *on* about) *USE* (3&4) infml

¹**once** /wuns/ *adv* **1** one time and no more **2** even 1 time; ever (e g if *once* we lose the key) **3** at some indefinite time in the past; formerly **4** by 1 degree of relationship (e g second cousin *once* removed) — **once again/more 1** now again as before **2** for 1 more time

²**once** *n* one single time — **all at once 1** all at the same time **2** all of a sudden — **at once 1** at the same time; simultaneously **2** IMMEDIATELY 2 — **once and for all, once for all** for the final or only time; conclusively

³**once** *conj* from the moment when; as soon as

'once-,over *n* a swift appraising glance – infml

oncoming /'on,kuming/ *adj* coming nearer in time or space; advancing

¹**one** /wun/ *adj* **1a** being a single unit or thing **b** being the first – used after the noun modified (e g on page *one*) **2** being a particular but unspecified instance (e g saw her *one* morning) **3a(1)** the same; identical (e g both of *one* mind) **a(2)** constituting a unified entity (e g all shouted with *one* voice) **b** being in a state of agreement; united **4** being some unspecified instance – used esp of future time (e g we might try it *one* weekend) **5a** being a particular object or person (e g close first *one* eye, then the other) **b** being the only individual of an indicated or implied kind (e g the *one* and only person she wanted) — **one and the same** the very same

²**one** *pron, pl* **ones 1** a single member or specimen of a usu specified class or group **2** an indefinitely indicated person; anybody at all (e g has a duty to one's public) **3** – used to refer to a noun or noun phrase previously mentioned or understood (e g 2 grey shirts and 3 red ones) *USE* used as a subject or object; no pl for sense 2

³**one** *n* **1** the number 1 **2** the number denoting unity **3** the first in a set or series (e g takes a *one* in shoes) **4a** a single person or thing **b** a unified entity (e g is secretary and treasurer in *one*) **c** a particular example or instance (e g *one* of the coldest nights this year) **d** a certain specified person (e g *one* George Hopkins) **5a** a person with a liking or interest for a specified thing; an enthusiast (e g he's rather a *one* for bikes) **b** a bold, amusing, or remarkable character (e g oh! you are a *one*) **6a** a blow, stroke **7** sthg having a denomination of 1 (e g I'll take the money in *ones*) — **for one** even if alone; not to mention others — **one by one** singly, successively

,**one a'nother** *pron* each other

,**one-armed 'bandit** *n* a fruit machine

onerous /'ohnərəs, 'on-/ *adj* burdensome, troublesome – **~ly** *adv* – **~ness** *n*

oneself /wun'self/ *pron* **1** a person's self; one's own self – used reflexively (e g one should wash *oneself*) or for emphasis (e g to do it *oneself*) **2** one's normal self (e g not feeling quite *oneself*)

,**one-'sided** *adj* **1a** having or occurring on 1 side only **b** having 1 side prominent or more developed **2** partial, biased – **~ly** *adv* – **~ness** *n*

'one,time /-,tiem/ *adj* former, sometime

,**one-'upmanship** /'upmanship/ *n* the art of gaining a psychological advantage over others by professing social or professional superiority

,**one-'way** *adj* **1** that moves in or allows movement in only 1 direction **2** one-sided, unilateral

onion /'unyən/ *n* (a plant with) a pungent usu white bulb much used in cooking

onlooker /'on,lookə/ *n* a passive spectator

¹**only** /'ohnli/ *adj* **1** unquestionably the best **2** alone in its class or kind; sole

²**only** *adv* **1a** nothing more than; merely **b** solely, exclusively **2** nothing other than (e g it was *only* too true) **3a** in the final outcome (e g will *only*

make you sick) **b** with nevertheless the final result (e g won the battle, *only* to lose the war) **4** no earlier than (e g *only* last week)

³**only** *conj* **1** but, however (e g they look very nice, *only* we can't use them) **2** were it not for the fact that *USE* infml

onomatopoeia /ˌonəˌmatəˈpeeˈə/ *n* the formation or use of words intended to be a vocal imitation of the sound associated with the thing or action designated (e g in *buzz, cuckoo*) – **-poeic** *adj*

onrush /ˈonˌrush/ *n* a forceful rushing forwards – ~**ing** *adj*

onset /ˈonˌset/ *n* **1** an attack, assault **2** a beginning, commencement

on·side /ˈ-ˈsied/ *adv or adj* not offside

onslaught /ˈonˌslawt/ *n* a fierce attack

onto, on to /ˈontə; *strong* ˈontooh/ *prep* **1** to a position on **2** in or into a state of awareness about (e g put the police *onto* him) **3** *chiefly Br* in or into contact with (e g been *onto* him about the drains); *esp* on at; nagging

onus /ˈohnəs/ *n* **1a** duty, responsibility **b** blame **2** burden of proof

onward /ˈonwood/ *adj* directed or moving onwards; forward

onwards, onward *adv* towards or at a point lying ahead in space or time; forwards

onyx /ˈoniks/ *n* a translucent variety of quartz with layers of different colours

oodles /ˈoohdlz/ *n pl but sing or pl in constr* a great quantity; a lot – infml

oops /oops, oohps/ *interj* – used to express apology or surprise

¹**ooze** /oohz/ *n* a soft deposit of mud, slime, debris, etc on the bottom of a body of water – **oozy** *adj*

²**ooze** *v* **1a** to pass or flow slowly through small openings **b** to diminish gradually; dwindle *away* **2** to display in abundance

op /op/ *n* an operation – infml

opal /ˈohp(ə)l/ *n* a transparent to translucent mineral used in its opalescent forms as a gem

opalescent /ˌohplˈes(ə)nt, ˌohpəˈles(ə)nt/ *adj* reflecting a warm milky light – **-cence** *n*

opaque /ohˈpayk/ *adj* **1** not transmitting radiant energy, esp light; not transparent **2** hard to understand – **-acity** *n* – **ly** *adv* – ~**ness** *n*

¹**open** /ˈohp(ə)n/ *adj* **1** having no enclosing or confining barrier **2** allowing passage; not shut or locked **3a** exposed to general view or knowledge; public **b** vulnerable to attack or question **4a** not covered or protected **b** not fastened or sealed **5** not restricted to a particular category of participants; *specif* contested by both amateurs and professionals **6** presenting no obstacle to passage or view **7** having the parts or surfaces spread out or unfolded **8a** not finally decided or settled **b** available for a qualified applicant; vacant **c**

remaining available for use or filling until cancelled **9** willing to consider new ideas; unprejudiced **10** candid, frank **11** in operation; *esp* ready for business or use **12** *Br, of a cheque* payable in cash to the person, organization, etc named on it; not crossed – ~**ly** *adv* – ~**ness** *n*

²**open** *v* **1a** to change or move from a closed position **b** to permit entry *into* or *onto* **c** to gain access to the contents of **2a** to make available for or active in a particular use or function; *specif* to establish **b** to declare available for use, esp ceremonially **c** to make the necessary arrangements for (e g a bank account), esp by depositing money **3** to disclose, reveal – often + *up* **4** to make 1 or more openings in **5** to unfold; spread *out* **6** to begin, commence

³**open** *n* **1** outdoors **2** *often cap* an open contest, competition, or tournament — **bring into/be in the open** to (cause) to be generally known

open-·air *adj* outdoor

open-·ended *adj* without any definite limits or restrictions (e g of time or purpose) set in advance

opener /ˈohp(ə)nə/ *n* **1a** an instrument that opens sthg – usu in combination **b** one who opens; *specif* an opening batsman **2** the first item or event in a series

open·handed /-ˈhandid/ *adj* generous in giving

open·hearted /-ˈhahtid/ *adj* **1** candidly straightforward **2** kind, generous – ~**ly** *adv* – ~**ness** *n*

opening /ˈohp(ə)ning/ *n* **1** an act of making or becoming open **2** a breach, aperture **3a** an often standard series of moves made at the beginning of a game of chess or draughts **b** a first performance **4a** a favourable opportunity; a chance **b** an opportunity for employment; a vacancy

open out *v* to speak more freely and confidently

open ˈseason *n* a period during which it is legal to kill or catch game or fish protected at other times by law

open ˈverdict *n* a verdict at an inquest that records a death but does not state its cause

¹**opera** /ˈop(ə)rə/ *pl of* **opus**

²**opera** /ˈoprə/ *n* **1** (the performance of or score for) a drama set to music and made up of vocal pieces with orchestral accompaniment and usu other orchestral music (e g an overture) **2** the branch of the arts concerned with such works **3** a company performing operas – ~**tic** *adj*

operable /ˈop(ə)rəbl/ *adj* suitable for surgical treatment – **-bly** *adv*

operate /ˈopərayt/ *v* **1** to exert power or influence; act **2** to produce a desired effect **3a** to work; (cause to) function **b** to perform surgery – usu + *on* **c** to carry on a military or naval action or mission **4** to be in action; *specif* to carry out trade or business

operation /ˌopəˈraysh(ə)n/ *n* **1** the act, method, or process of operating **b** sthg (to be) done; an activity **2** the state of being functional or operative **3** a surgical procedure carried out on a living body for the repair of damage or the restoration of health 4 any of various mathematical or logical processes (e g addition) carried out to derive one expression from others according to a rule 5 a usu military action, mission, or manoeuvre and its planning 6 a business or financial transaction

operational /ˌopəˈraysh(ə)nl/ adj 1 of or based on operations 2a of, involved in, or used for the execution of commercial, military, or naval operations b (capable of) functioning – **~ly** adv

¹**operative** /ˈop(ə)rətiv/ adj 1a producing an appropriate effect; efficacious b significant, relevant 2 in force or operation

²**operative** n an operator; esp a workman

operator /ˈopəˌraytə/ n 1a one who operates a machine or device b one who owns or runs a business, organization, etc c one who is in charge of a telephone switchboard 2 a shrewd and skilful manipulator – infml

operetta /ˌopəˈretə/ n a usu romantic comic opera that often includes dancing

ophthalmic /ofˈthalmik; also op-/ adj of (the medical treatment of) the eye

ophthalmology /ˌofthalˈmoləji; also op-/ n the branch of medical science dealing with the structure, functions, diseases of the eye – **-ogist** n

opiate /ˈohpi-ət, -ˌayt/ n 1 a preparation or derivative of opium; broadly a narcotic 2 sthg that induces inaction or calm

opine /oh'pien/ v to state as an opinion – fml

opinion /əˈpinyən/ n 1 a view or judgment formed about a particular matter 2 a generally held view 3 a formal expression by an expert of his/her professional judgment or advice; esp a barrister's written advice to a client

opinionated /əˈpinyəˌnaytid/ adj stubbornly sticking to one's own opinions

opium /ˈohpi-əm/ n the dried juice of the unripe seed capsules of the opium poppy, containing morphine and other addictive narcotics

opossum /əˈposəm/ n pl **opossums** also esp collectively **opossum** any of various American or Australian marsupial mammals

opponent /əˈpohnənt/ n one who takes the opposite side in a contest, conflict, etc

opportune /ˌopəˈtyoohn, '--,-/ adj 1 suitable or convenient for a particular occurrence 2 occurring at an appropriate time – **~ly** adv

opportunism /ˌopəˈtyoohˌniz(ə)m/ n the taking advantage of opportunities or circumstances, esp with little regard for principles or consequences – **-ist** n or adj

opportunity /ˌopəˈtyoohnəti/ n 1 a favourable set of circumstances 2 a chance for advancement or progress

oppose /əˈpohz/ v 1 to place opposite or against sthg so as to provide counterbalance, contrast, etc 2 to offer resistance to

¹**opposite** /ˈopəzit/ n sthg or sby opposed or contrary

²**opposite** adj 1 set over against sthg that is at the other end or side of an intervening line or space 2a occupying an opposing position b diametrically different; contrary 3 being the other of a matching or contrasting pair

³**opposite** adv on or to an opposite side

⁴**opposite** 1 across from and usu facing 2 in a role complementary to

opposition /ˌopəˈzish(ə)n/ n 1 placing opposite or being so placed 2 hostile or contrary action 3 sing of pl in constr 3a the body of people opposing sthg b often cap a political party opposing the party in power

oppress /əˈpres/ v 1 to crush by harsh or authoritarian rule 2 to weigh heavily on the mind or spirit of – **~ion** n – **~ive** adj – **~ively** adv – **~iveness** n – **~or** n

opt /opt/ v to decide in favour of sthg

optic /ˈoptik/ adj of vision or the eye

optician /opˈtish(ə)n/ n one who prescribes spectacles for eye defects or supplies lenses for spectacles on prescription

optics /ˈoptiks/ n pl but sing or pl in constr 1 the science of the nature, properties, and uses of (radiation or particles that behave like) light 2 optical properties or components

optimism /ˈoptiˌmiz(ə)m/ n a tendency to emphasize favourable aspects of situations or events or to expect the best possible outcome – **-mist** n – **-mistic** adj – **-mistically** adv

optimum /ˈoptiməm/ n, pl **optima** /-mə/ also **optimums** (the amount or degree of) sthg that is most favourable to a particular end

option /ˈopsh(ə)n/ n 1 an act of choosing 2 (a contract conveying) a right to buy or sell designated securities or commodities at a specified price during a stipulated period 3a an alternative course of action b an item offered in addition to or in place of standard equipment

optional /ˈopsh(ə)nl/ adj not compulsory; available as a choice – **~ly** adv

opt out v to choose not to participate in sthg – often + of

opulent /ˈopyoolənt/ adj 1 wealthy, rich 2 abundant, profuse – **-ence** n – **~ly** adv

opus /ˈohpəs/ n, pl **opera** /ˈop(ə)rə/ also **opuses** a musical composition or set of compositions

¹**or** /ə; strong aw/ conj 1a – used to join 2 sentence elements of the same class or function and often introduced by either to indicate that what immediately follows is another or a final alternative b – used before the second and later of several suggestions to indicate approximation or uncertainty (e g 5 or 6 days) 2 and not – used after a neg (e g never drinks or smokes) 3 that is – used to indicate equivalence or elucidate meaning (e g a heifer or a young cow) 4 – used to indicate the result of

rejecting a preceding choice (e g hurry *or* you'll be late) — **or so** – used to indicate an approximation or conjecture

²**or** /aw/ *n* a gold colour; *also* yellow – used in heraldry

oracle /'orəkl/ *n* 1 an often cryptic answer to some question, usu regarding the future, purporting to come from a deity 2 (a shrine housing) a priest or priestess who delivers oracles – **-cular** *adj*

¹**oral** /'awrəl, 'o-/ *adj* 1 uttered in words; spoken 2 of, given through, or affecting the mouth

²**oral** *n* an oral examination

¹**orange** /'orinj/ *n* 1 a spherical fruit with a reddish yellow leathery aromatic rind and sweet juicy edible pulp; *also* the tree that bears this 2 a colour whose hue resembles that of the orange and lies between red and yellow in the spectrum

²**orange** *adj* of the colour orange

Orange *adj* of Orangemen

¹**Orangeman** /-mən/ *n pl* **Orangemen** /~/ a member of a Protestant loyalist society in the north of Ireland; *broadly* an Ulsterman

oration /aw'raysh(ə)n/ *n* a speech delivered in a formal and dignified manner

orator /'orətə/ *n* a public speaker

oratorio /,orə'tawrioh/ *n*, *pl* **oratorios** a choral work based usu on a religious subject

¹**oratory** /'orət(ə)ri/ *n* a place of prayer; *esp* a private or institutional chapel

²**oratory** *n* 1 the art of public speaking 2 public speaking characterized by (excessive) eloquence – **-orical** *adj* – **-orically** *adv*

orb /awb/ *n* 1 a spherical body; *esp* a celestial sphere 2 a sphere surmounted by a cross symbolizing royal power and justice

¹**orbit** /'awbit/ *n* 1 the bony socket of the eye 2 a path described by one body in its revolution round another (e g that of the earth round the sun) 3 a sphere of influence – **~al** *adj*

²**orbit** *v* to revolve in an orbit round

orchard /'awchad/ *n* a usu enclosed area in which fruit trees are planted

orchestra /'awkistrə/ *n* 1 the space in front of the stage in a modern theatre that is used by an orchestra 2 a group of musicians including esp string players organized to perform ensemble music – **~l** *adj*

orchestrate /'awki,strayt/ *v* to compose or arrange (music) for an orchestra – **-tration** *n*

orchid /'awkid/ *n* a plant or flower of a large family of plants related to the lilies usu having striking 3-petalled flowers

ordain /aw'dayn/ *v* 1 to make a priest of 2 to order by appointment, decree, or law **b** to destine, foreordain

ordeal /aw'deel/ *n* a severe or testing experience

¹**order** /'awdə/ *n* 1a a religious body or community often required to take vows of renunciation of earthly things **b** a military decoration 2 *pl* the

office of a person in the Christian ministry 3a a rank or group in a community **b** a category in the classification of living things ranking above the family and below the class 4a a rank, level, or category **b** arrangement of objects or events according to sequence in space, time, value, etc 5a (a rank in) a social or political system **b** regular or harmonious arrangement 6 customary procedure, esp in debate 7 the rule of law or proper authority 8 a proper, orderly, or functioning condition 9a a direction to purchase, sell, or supply goods or to carry out work **b** goods bought or sold — **in order that** – used to introduce a subordinate clause expressing purpose — **in order to** for the purpose of — **in the order of** about as much or as many as; approximately — **on order** having been ordered — **to order** according to the specifications of an order

²**order** *v* 1 to put in order; arrange 2a to give an order to; command **b** to place an order for

¹**ordered** *adj* 1 well regulated or ordered 2a having elements succeeding or arranged according to rule

¹**orderly** /'awdəli/ *adj* 1a arranged in order; neat, tidy **b** liking or exhibiting order; methodical 2 well behaved; peaceful – **-liness** *n*

²**orderly** *n* 1 a soldier assigned to carry messages, relay orders, etc for a superior officer 2 a hospital attendant who does routine or heavy work

ordinal /'awdinl/ *adj* of a specified order or rank in a series

ordinance /'awdinəns/ *n* 1 an authoritative decree; *esp* a municipal regulation 2 a prescribed usage, practice, or ceremony

ordinary /'awdn(ə)ri, 'awd(ə)nri/ *adj* 1 routine, usual 2 not exceptional; commonplace – **-rily** *adv* – **-riness** *n*

,**ordinary 'seaman** *n* (a sailor with) the lowest rank on a ship

ordination /,awdi'naysh(ə)n/ *n* (an) ordaining; being ordained

ordnance /'awdnəns/ *n* 1 (a branch of government service dealing with) military supplies 2 cannon, artillery

,**Ordnance 'Survey** *n* (a British or Irish government organization that produces) a survey of Great Britain or Ireland published as a series of detailed maps

ordure /'awdyooə/ *n* excrement

ore /aw/ *n* a mineral containing a metal or other valuable constituent for which it is mined

oregano /ori'gahnoh, ə'regənoh/ *n* a bushy plant of the mint family whose leaves are used as a herb in cooking

organ /'awgən/ *n* 1 a wind instrument consisting of sets of pipes made to sound by compressed air and controlled by keyboards; *also* an electronic keyboard instrument producing a sound approximating to that of an organ 2 a differentiated structure (e g the heart or a leaf) consisting of cells and tissues and performing some specific function in an organism **3** a periodical

'organ-,grinder *n* a street musician who operates a barrel organ

organic /aw'ganik/ *adj* **1a** of or arising in a bodily organ **b** affecting the structure of the organism **2a** of or derived from living organisms **b** of or being food produced using fertilizer solely of plant or animal origin without the aid of chemical fertilizers, pesticides, etc **3a** forming an integral element of a whole **b** having coordinated organization of parts **c** containing carbon compounds, esp those occurring in living organisms; *also* of or being the branch of chemistry dealing with these – ~ally *adv*

organism /'awgə,niz(ə)m/ *n* **1** a complex structure of interdependent and subordinate elements **2** a living being

organ·ization, -isation /,awgənie'zaysh(ə)n/ *n* **1** the arrangement of parts so as to form an effective whole **2a** an association, society **b** an administrative and functional body

organ·ize, -ise /'awgə,niez/ *v* **1** to arrange into a functioning whole **2a** to set up an administrative structure for **b** to cause to form an association, esp a trade union **3** to arrange by systematic planning and effort

orgasm /'aw,gaz(ə)m/ *n* (an instance of) the climax of sexual excitement, occurring as the culmination of sexual intercourse – ~ic *adj*

orgy /'awji/ *n* **1a** a drunken revelry **b** an instance (e g a party) of wild sexual activity **2** an excessive or frantic indulgence in a specified activity – **-giastic** *adj*

'orient /'awri-ənt, 'o-/ *n cap* the East

²orient *v* **1** to set in a definite position, esp in relation to the points of the compass **2a** to adjust to an environment or a situation **b** to acquaint (oneself) with the existing situation or environment

orientate /'awri-ən,tayt, 'o-/ *v, chiefly Br* to orient – **-ation** *n*

orifice /'orifis/ *n* an opening (e g a vent or mouth) through which sthg may pass

origin /'orijin/ *n* **1** ancestry, parentage **2** a source or starting-point

'original /ə'rijinl/ *n* **1** that from which a copy, reproduction, or translation is made **2** an eccentric person

²original *adj* **1** initial, earliest; not secondary or derivative **2** being the first instance or source of a copy, reproduction, or translation **3** inventive, creative – ~**ly** *adv* – ~**ity** *n*

o,riginal 'sin *n* (the doctrine of) man's innate sinfulness resulting from Adam's fall

originate /ə'rijə,nayt/ *v* to (cause to) begin or come into existence – **-nator** *n*

oriole /'awri,ohl, -əl/ *n* any of a family of birds with black and either orange or yellow plumage

'ornament /'awnəmənt/ *n* **1** sthg that lends grace or beauty; (a) decoration or embellishment **2** an embellishing note not belonging to the essential harmony or melody – ~**al** *adj* – ~**ally** *adv*

²ornament /'awnə,ment/ *v* to add ornament to; embellish – **-ation** *n*

ornate /aw'nayt/ *adj* **1** rhetorical or florid in style **2** elaborately or excessively decorated – ~**ly** *adv* – ~**ness** *n*

ornithology /,awnə'tholəji/ *n* a branch of zoology dealing with birds – **-gist** *n* – **-gical** *adj*

orotund /'orətund, 'oroh-/ *adj* **1** sonorous **2** pompous, bombastic

'orphan /'awf(ə)n/ *n* a child **1** or both of whose parents are dead

²orphan *v* to cause to be an orphan

orphanage /'awf(ə)n·ij/ *n* an institution for the care of orphans

orthodox /'awthə,doks/ *adj* **1a** conforming to established, dominant, or official doctrine (e g in religion) **b** conventional **2** *cap* (consisting) of the Eastern churches headed by the patriarch of Constantinople which separated from the Western church in the 9th c – ~**y** *n*

orthography /aw'thogrəfi/ *n* correct spelling – **-phic(al)** *adj* – **-phically** *adv*

orthopaedics, NAm chiefly orthopedics /,awthə'peediks/ *n pl* the prevention or correction of skeletal and muscular deformities, esp by surgery

Oscar /'oskə/ *n* an award made annually by a US professional organization for outstanding achievement in the cinema

oscillate /'osi,layt/ *v* to swing backwards and forwards like a pendulum – **-ation** *n*

oscillator /'osi,laytə/ *n* a device for producing alternating current; *esp* a radio-frequency or audio-frequency signal generator

osier /'ohzhə/ *n* **1** any of various willows whose pliable twigs are used for furniture and basketry **2** a willow rod used in basketry

osmosis /oz'mohsis, os-/ *n* movement of a solvent through a membrane (e g of a living cell) into a solution of higher concentration that tends to equalize the concentrations on the 2 sides of the membrane

osprey /'ospray, -pri/ *n* a large fish-eating hawk with dark brown and white plumage

ossify /'osi,fie/ *v* **1** to become bone **2** to become unfeeling, unimaginative, or rigid

ostensible /o'stensəbl/ *adj* being such in appearance rather than reality; professed, declared – **-bly** *adv*

ostentation /,osten'taysh(ə)n/ *n* unnecessary display of wealth, knowledge, etc designed to impress or attract attention – **-tious** *adj* – **-tiously** *adv*

osteopathy /ˌosti'opəthi/ n a system of treatment of diseases based on the theory that they can be cured by manipulation of bones – **osteopath** n

ostler, *chiefly NAm* **hostler** /'oslə/ n a groom or stableman at an inn

ostracize, -ise /'ostrə.siez/ v to refuse to have social contact with; exclude from membership of a group – **cism** n

ostrich /'ostrich, *also* 'ostrij/ n **1** a swift-footed 2-toed flightless bird that has valuable wing and tail plumes and is the largest of existing birds **2** one who refuses to face up to unpleasant realities

¹**other** /'udhə/ adj **1a** being the 1 left of 2 or more (e g held on with one hand and waved with the *other*) **b** being the ones distinct from that or those first mentioned (e g taller than the *other* boys) **c** second (e g every *other* day) **2a** not the same; different (e g schools *other* than hers) **b** far, opposite (e g lives on the *other* side of town) **3** additional, further (e g John and 2 *other* boys) **4** recently past (e g the *other* evening)

²**other** pron, pl **others** *also* **other 1** the remaining or opposite one (e g went from one side to the *other*) **2** a different or additional one (e g some film or *other*)

³**other** adv otherwise – + *than*

¹**other,wise** /-,wiez/ adv **1** in a different way **2** in different circumstances **3** in other respects **4** if not; or else **5** not – used to express the opposite (e g mothers, whether married or *otherwise*) **6** alias

²**otherwise** adj of a different kind (e g how can I be *otherwise* than grateful?)

,**other'worldly** adj concerned with spiritual or intellectual matters rather than the material world

otter /'otə/ n pl **otters**, *esp collectively* **otter** (the dark brown fur or pelt of) any of several aquatic fish-eating mammals with webbed and clawed feet, related to the weasels

ottoman /'otəmən/ n **1** cap a Turk **2a** a usu heavily upholstered box or seat without a back or arms **b** a cushioned stool for the feet

Ottoman adj Turkish

ouch /owch/ interj – used esp to express sudden sharp pain

ought /awt/ verbal auxiliary – used to express moral obligation (e g *ought* to pay your debts), advisability (e g *ought* to be boiled for 10 minutes), enthusiastic recommendation (e g you *ought* to hear her sing), natural expectation (e g *ought* to have arrived by now) or logical consequence (e g the result *ought* to be infinity); used in the negative to express moral condemnation of an action (e g you *ought* not to treat him like that)

ounce /owns/ n ¹/₁₆ of a pound avoirdupois or ¹/₁₂ of a pound troy weight

our /'owə, ah/ adj of us, ourself, or ourselves, esp as possessors or possessor, agents or agent, or objects or object of an action; of ourself

ours /'owəz, ahz/ pron, pl **ours** that which or the one who belongs to us – used without a following noun as a pronoun equivalent in meaning to the adjective *our*

our'selves /-'selvz/ pron, pl in constr **1** those identical people that are we – used reflexively (e g we're doing it for *ourselves*) or for emphasis (e g we *ourselves* will never go) **2** our normal selves (e g not feeling quite *ourselves*)

oust /owst/ v **1** to remove from or dispossess of property or position **2** to take the place of; supplant

¹**out** /owt/ adv **1a** away from the inside or centre (e g went *out* into the garden) **b** from among other things (e g separate *out* the bad apples) **c** away from the shore, the city, or one's homeland (e g live *out* in the country) **d** away from a particular place, esp of one's home or business (e g move *out* into lodgings) **e(1)** clearly in or into view (e g when the sun's *out*) **e(2)** of a flower in or into full bloom **2a(1)** out of the proper place (e g left a word *out*) **a(2)** amiss in reckoning **b** in all directions from a central point of control (e g lent *out* money) **c** from political power (e g voted them *out*) **d** into shares or portions **e** out of vogue or fashion **3a** to or in a state of extinction or exhaustion (e g before the year is *out*) **b** to the fullest extent or degree; completely (e g hear me *out*) **c** in or into a state of determined effort (e g *out* to fight pollution) **4a** aloud **b** in existence; ever – with a superlative; infml (e g the funniest thing *out*) **5** so as to be put out of a game **6** – used on a 2-way radio circuit to indicate that a message is complete and no reply is expected

²**out** v to become publicly known

³**out** adj **1** located outside; external **2** located at a distance; outlying **3** not being in operation or power **4** directed or serving to direct outwards (e g the *out* tray) **5** not allowed to continue batting **6** out of the question

⁴**out** n a way of escaping from an embarrassing or difficult situation

'**out,back** /-,bak/ n isolated rural (Australian) country

,**out'balance** /-'balans/ v to outweigh in value or importance

,**out'bid** /-'bid/ v **outbid; -dd-** to make a higher bid than

'**out,break** /-,brayk/ n **1a** a sudden or violent breaking out **b** a sudden increase in numbers of a harmful organism or in sufferers from a disease within a particular area **2** an insurrection, revolt

'**out,building** /-,bilding/ n a smaller building (e g a stable or a woodshed) separate from but belonging to a main building '**out,burst** /-/ n **1** a violent expression of feeling **2** a surge of activity or growth

'**out,cast** /-,kahst/ n one who is cast out by society

'**out,caste** /-,kahst/ n a Hindu who has been ejected from his/her caste

,**out'class** /-'klahs/ v to excel, surpass

,**out'come** /-,kum/ n a result, consequence

'**out,crop** /-,krop/ n **1** (the emergence of) the part of a rock formation that appears at the surface of the ground **2** an outbreak – **outcrop** v

'**out,cry** /-,krie/ n **1** a loud cry; clamour **2** a public expression of anger or disapproval

,**out'dated** /-'daytid/ adj outmoded

,**out'distance** /-'dist(ə)ns/ v to go far ahead of (e g in a race)

,**out'do** /-'dooh/ v **outdoes** /-'duz/; **outdid** /-'did/; **outdone** /-'dun/ v to surpass in action or performance

'**out,door** /-,daw/ also ,**out'doors** adj **1** of or performed outdoors **2** not enclosed; without a roof

¹,**out'doors** adv outside a building; in or into the open air

²,**out'doors** n pl but sing in constr **1** the open air **2** the world remote from human habitation

outer /'owtə/ adj **1** existing independently of the mind; objective **2a** situated farther out **b** away from a centre **c** situated or belonging on the outside

,**out'face** /-'fays/ v **1** to cause to waver or submit (as if) by staring **2** to confront unflinchingly; defy

'**out,field** /-,feeld/ n the part of a cricket field beyond the prepared section on which wickets are laid out – **~er** n

'**out,fit** /-,fit/ n **1a** a complete set of equipment needed for a particular purpose **b** a set of garments worn together, often for a specified occasion or activity **2** sing or pl in constr a group that works as a team – infml – **outfit** v

,**out'flank** /-'flangk/ v **1** to go round or extend beyond the flank of (an opposing force) **2** to gain an advantage over by doing sthg unexpected

'**out,going** /-,goh-ing/ adj **1** going away; departing **b** retiring or withdrawing from a position **2** friendly, sociable

'**out,goings** n pl expenditures; esp overheads

,**out'grow** /-'groh/ v **outgrew** /-'grooh/; **outgrown** /-'grohn/ **1** to grow or increase faster than **2** to grow too large or too old for

'**out,house** /-,hows/ n an outbuilding

outing /'owting/ n a short pleasure trip

outlandish /owt'landish/ adj strikingly unusual; bizarre – **~ly** adv – **~ness** n

,**out'last** /-'lahst/ v to last longer than

¹'**out,law** /-,law/ n a fugitive from the law

²'**out,law** v **1** to deprive of the protection of law **2** to make illegal

'**out,lay** /-/ n expenditure, payment

outlet /'owtlit, -,let/ n **1a** an exit or vent **b** a means of release or satisfaction for an emotion or drive **2** an agency (e g a shop or dealer) through which a product is marketed

¹'**out,line** /-,lien/ n **1** a line bounding the outer limits of sthg; shape **2** (a) drawing with no shading **3** a condensed treatment or summary **4** a preliminary account of a project

²**outline** /'-,-, ,-'-/ v **1** to draw the outline of **2** to indicate the principal features of

,**out'live** /-'liv/ v **1** to live longer than **2** to survive the effects of

'**out,look** /-,look/ n **1** an attitude; point of view **2** a prospect for the future

'**out,lying** /-,lie-ing/ adj remote from a centre or main point

,**outma'noeuvre**, NAm **outmaneuver** /-mə' noohvə/ v to defeat by more skilful manoeuvring

,**out'match** /-'mach/ v to surpass, outdo

,**out'moded** /-'mohdid/ adj **1** no longer in fashion **2** no longer acceptable or usable; obsolete

,**out'play** /-'play/ v to defeat or play better than in a game

'**out,post** /-,pohst/ n **1** a post or detachment established at a distance from a main body of troops, esp to protect it from surprise attack **2** an outlying or frontier settlement

output /-,poot/ n **1** mineral, agricultural, or industrial production **2** mental or artistic production **3** the amount produced by sby in a given time **4** sthg (e g energy, material, or data) produced by a machine or system

¹'**out,rage** /-,rayj/ n **1** an act of violence or brutality **2** an act that violates accepted standards of behaviour or taste

²'**out,rage** v to violate the standards or principles of

outrageous /owt'rayjəs/ adj **1** not conventional or moderate; extravagant **2** going beyond all standards of propriety, decency, or taste; shocking, offensive – **~ly** adv

'**out,rider** /-,riedə/ n a mounted attendant or motorcyclist who rides ahead of or beside a carriage or car as an escort

¹,**out'right** /-'riet/ adv **1** completely **2** instantaneously

²'**out,right** adj being completely or exactly what is stated

,**out'run** /-'run/ v **outran** /-'ran/; **outrun**; **-nn-** **1** to run faster than **2** to exceed, surpass

,**out'sell** /-'sel/ v **outsold** /-'sohld/ to surpass in selling, salesmanship, or numbers sold

outset /-,set/ n the beginning, start

¹'**out,side** /,owt'sied, '-,-/ n **1a** an external part; the region beyond a boundary **b** the area farthest from a point of reference: eg **1a** the section of a playing area towards the sidelines; also a corner **b(2)** the side of a pavement nearer the traffic **2** an

outer side or surface **3** an outer manifestation; an appearance **4** the extreme limit of an estimation or guess; a maximum

²**out,side** _adj_ **1a** of or being on, near, or towards the outside **b** of or being the outer side of a curve or near the middle of the road **2** maximum **3a** originating elsewhere (e g an _outside_ broadcast) **b** not belonging to one's regular occupation or duties **4** barely possible; remote

³**out'side** _adv_ **1** on or to the outside **2** outdoors **3** _chiefly Br_ not in prison – slang

⁴**outside** /'-,-, ,-'-/ _prep_ **1** on or to the outside of **2** beyond the limits of **3** except, besides (e g few interests _outside_ her children)

outsider /owt'siedə/ _n_ **1** sby who does not belong to a particular group **2** a competitor who has only an outside chance of winning

outsize /'owt,siez/ _adj or n_ (of) an unusual or above standard size

,**out'smart** /-'smaht/ _v_ to get the better of; outwit

,**out'spoken** /-'spohkən/ _adj_ direct and open in speech or expression; frank – ~**ly** _adv_ – ~**ness** _n_

,**out'standing** /-'standing/ _adj_ **1a** unpaid **b** continuing, unresolved **2a** standing out from a group; conspicuous **b** marked by eminence and distinction – ~**ly** _adv_

,**out'stay** /-'stay/ _v_ **1** to overstay **2** to surpass in staying power

,**out'strip** /-'strip/ _v_ **-pp-** **1** to go faster or farther than **2** to get ahead of; leave behind

outward /-wood/ _adj_ **1a** situated at or directed towards the outside **b** being or going away from home **2** of the body or external appearances

outwardly /-li/ _adv_ in outward appearance; superficially

outwards _adv_ towards the outside

,**out'weigh** /-'way/ _v_ to exceed in weight, value, or importance

,**out'wit** /-'wit/ _v_ **-tt-** to get the better of by superior cleverness

,**out,work** /-,wuhk/ _n_ **1** a minor defensive position constructed outside a fortified area **2** work done for a business or organization off its premises as usu by employees based at home – ~**er** _n_

ova /'ohvə/ _pl of_ **ovum**

¹**oval** /'ohvl/ _adj_ having the shape of an egg; _also_ elliptical

²**oval** _n_ an oval figure or object

ovary /'ohvəri/ _n_ **1** the typically paired female reproductive organ that produces eggs and female sex hormones **2** the enlarged rounded female part of a flowering plant that bears the ovules and consists of 1 or more carpels – **-arian** _adj_

ovation /oh'vaysh(ə)n/ _n_ an expression of popular acclaim

oven /'uv(ə)n/ _n_ a chamber used for baking, heating, or drying

¹**over** /'ohvə/ _adv_ **1a** across a barrier **b** across an intervening space **c** downwards from an upright position (e g fell _over_) **d** across the brim or brink (e g the soup boiled _over_) **e** so as to bring the underside up **f** so as to be reversed or folded **g** from one person or side to another **h** across (e g got his point _over_) **2a(1)** beyond some quantity or limit **a(2)** excessively, inordinately – often in combination **a(3)** in excess; remaining **b** till a later time (e g stay _over_ till Monday) **3** so as to cover the whole surface (e g windows boarded _over_) **4a** at an end **b** – used on a two-way radio circuit to indicate that a message is complete and a reply is expected **5** – used to show repetition (e g told you _over_ and _over_)

²**over** _prep_ **1a** higher than; above **b** vertically above but not touching **c** – used to indicate movement down upon (e g hit him _over_ the head) or down across the edge of (e g fell _over_ the cliff) **d** across (e g climbed _over_ the gate) **e** so as to cover **f** divided by (e g 6 _over_ 2 is 3) **2a** with authority, power, or jurisdiction in relation to **b** – used to indicate superiority, advantage, or preference (e g a big lead _over_ the others) **3** more than **4a** all through or throughout (e g showed me all _over_ the house) **b** by means of (a medium or channel of communication) (e g _over_ the radio) **5a** in the course of; during **b** until the end of (stay _over_ Sunday) **c** past, beyond **6** – used to indicate an object of occupation or activity or reference (e g sitting _over_ their wine, laughed _over_ the incident)

³**over** _adj_ **1** upper, higher (e g overlord) **2** outer, covering (e g overcoat) **3** excessive (e g overconfident) _USE_ often in combination

⁴**over** _n_ any of the divisions of an innings in cricket during which 1 bowler bowls 6 or 8 balls from the same end of the pitch

over'act /-'akt/ _v_ to perform (a part) with undue exaggeration

¹**overall** /,ohvə'rawl/ _adv_ **1** as a whole **2** from end to end, esp of a ship

²**overall** /'ohvə,rawl/ _n_ **1** _pl_ a protective garment resembling a boiler suit or dungarees **2** _chiefly Br_ a usu loose-fitting protective coat worn over other clothing

³**overall** _adj_ including everything

overarm /'ohvə,rahm/ _adj or adv_ overhand

,**over'awe** /-'aw/ _v_ to fill with respect or fear

,**over'balance** /-'baləns/ _v_ (to cause) to lose one's balance

,**over'bearing** /-'beəring/ _adj_ harshly masterful or domineering – ~**ly** _adv_

¹**over'blown** /-'blohn/ _adj_ inflated, pretentious

²**overblown** _adj_ past the prime of bloom

'**over,board** /-,bawd/ _adv_ **1** over the side of a ship or boat into the water **2** to extremes of enthusiasm

overcast /'ohvə,kahst, ,--'-/ _adj_ being, having, or characterized by a cloudy sky

,over'charge /-'chahj/ v to make an excessive charge – **overcharge** n

'over,coat /-,koht/ n 1 a warm usu thick coat for wearing outdoors over other clothing 2 a protective coat (e g of paint)

,over'come /-'kum/ v overcame /-'kaym/; overcome 1 to get the better of; surmount 2 to overpower, overwhelm

,over'crowd /-'krowd/ v to (cause to) be too crowded

,over'do /-'dooh/ v overdoes /-'duz/; overdid /-'did/; overdone /-'dun/ 1a to do or use in excess b to exaggerate 2 to cook too much

overdose /'ohvə,dohs/ vb /-,-, ,--'-/ v or n (to give or take) too great a dose of drugs, medicine, etc

'over,draft /-,drahft/ n an act of overdrawing at a bank; the state of being overdrawn; also the sum overdrawn

,over'draw /-'draw/ v overdrew /-'drooh/; overdrawn /-'drawn/ to draw cheques on (a bank account) for more than the balance – ~n adj

'over,drive /-,driev/ n a transmission gear in a motor vehicle that provides a ratio higher than the normal top gear

,over'due /-'dyooh/ adj 1a unpaid when due b delayed beyond an appointed time 2 more than ready or ripe

,over'estimate /-'estimayt/ v 1 to estimate as being more than the actual amount or size 2 to place too high a value on; overrate

¹,over'flow /-'floh/ v to flow over or beyond a brim, edge, or limit

²'over,flow n 1 a flowing over; an inundation 2 sthg that flows over; also, sing or pl in constr the excess members of a group 3 an outlet or receptacle for surplus liquid

,over'grown /-'grohn/ adj 1 grown over or choked with vegetation 2 grown too large – ~**growth** n

'over,hand /-,hand/ adj or adv with the hand brought forwards and down from above shoulder level

¹,over'hang /-'hang/ v overhung /-'hung/ 1 to project over 2 to threaten

²'over,hang n 1 sthg that overhangs; also the extent by which sthg overhangs 2 a projection of the roof or upper storey of a building beyond the wall of the lower part

,over'haul /-'hawl/ v 1 to examine thoroughly and carry out necessary repairs 2 to overtake

¹,over'head /-'hed/ adv above one's head

²'over,head adj 1 operating, lying, or coming from above 2 of overhead expenses

³'over,head n 1 a business expense (e g rent, insurance, or heating) not chargeable to a particular part of the work or product 2 a stroke in squash, tennis, etc made above head height

,over'hear /-'hiə/ v overheard /-'huhd/ to hear (sby or sthg) without the speaker's knowledge or intention

,over'joyed /-'joyd/ adj extremely pleased; elated

¹,over'kill /-'kil/ v to obliterate (a target) with more (nuclear) force than required

²'over,kill n 1 the capability of destroying an enemy or target with a force, esp nuclear, larger than is required 2 an excess of sthg beyond what is required or suitable for a particular purpose

'over,land /-,land/ adv or adj by, upon, or across land rather than sea or air

,over'lap /-'lap/ v -pp- to extend over and cover a part of; partly coincide

,over'lay /-'lay/ v overlaid /-'layd/ to cover usu thinly

,over'leaf /-'leef/ adv on the other side of the page

,over'look /-'look/ v 1a to look or provide a view of from above 2a to fail to notice; miss b to ignore c to excuse

'overly /-li/ adv to an excessive degree

,over'man /-'man/ v -nn- to have or provide too many workers for – ~**ning** n

,over'master /-'mahstə/ v to overpower, subdue

,over'much /-'much/ adj or adv too much

,over'night /-'niet/ adv 1 during or throughout the evening or night 2 suddenly – **overnight** adj

'over,pass /-,pahs/ n a flyover

,over'play /-'play/ v 1 to exaggerate (e g a dramatic role) 2 to give too much emphasis to — **overplay one's hand** to overestimate one's capacities

,over'power /-'powə/ v 1 to overcome by superior force 2 to overwhelm – ~**ing** adj – ~**ingly** adv

,over'rate /-'rayt/ v to rate too highly

,over'reach /-'reech/ v to defeat (oneself) by trying to do or gain too much

¹,over'ride /-'ried/ v overrode /-'rohd/; overridden /-'rid(ə)n/ 1a to prevail over; dominate b to set aside or annul; also to neutralize the action of (e g an automatic control) 2 to overlap

²'over,ride n a device or system used to override a control

,over'rule /-'roohl/ v to rule against or set aside, esp by virtue of superior authority

,over'run /-'run/ v overran /-'ran/; -nn- 1a to defeat decisively and occupy the positions of b to swarm over; infest 2 to run or go beyond or past 3 to flow over

¹,over'seas /-'seez/, oversea /-'see/ adv beyond or across the seas

²'over,seas, oversea adj 1 of transport across the seas 2 of, from, or in (foreign) places across the seas

,over'see /-'see/ v oversaw /-'saw/; overseen /-'seen/ to supervise – **seer** n

,over'sell /-'sel/ v oversold /-'sohld/ 1 to sell too much of 2 to make excessive claims for

,over'sexed /-'sekst/ *adj* with an abnormally strong sexual drive

,over'shadow /-'shadoh/ *v* 1 to cast a shadow over 2 to exceed in importance; outweigh

'over,shoe /-,shooh/ *n* a usu rubber shoe worn over another as protection (e g from rain or snow)

,over'shoot /-'shooht/ *or* overshot /-'shot/ to shoot or pass over or beyond, esp so as to miss

'over,sight /-,siet/ *n* 1 supervision 2 an inadvertent omission or error

,over'simpli,fy /-'simpli,fie/ *v* to simplify (sthg) to such an extent as to cause distortion or error – ~fication *n*

,over'sleep /-'sleep/ *v* overslept /-'slept/ to sleep beyond the intended time

'over,spill /-,spil/ *n* people who have moved away from crowded urban areas

,over'state /-'stayt/ *v* to state in too strong terms; exaggerate – ~ment *n*

,over'step /-'step/ *v* -pp- to exceed, transgress – esp in *overstep the mark*

,over'strung /-'strung/ *adj* too highly strung; too sensitive

overt /'ohvuht, ,-'-/ *adj* public, manifest – ~ly *adv*

,over'take /-'tayk/ *v* overtook /-'took/; overtaken /-'taykən/ 1 to catch up with (and pass beyond), esp a motor vehicle 2 to come upon suddenly

,over'tax /-'taks/ *v* 1 to tax too heavily 2 to put too great a burden or strain on

¹,over'throw /-'throh/ *v* overthrew /-'throoh/; overthrown /-'throhn/ 1 to overturn, upset 2 to cause the downfall of; defeat

²'over,throw *n* (a run scored from) a return of the ball from a fielder in cricket that goes past the wicket

'over,time /-,tiem/ *n* 1 time in excess of a set limit; *esp* working time in excess of a standard working day or week 2 the wage paid for overtime

overture /'ohvatyooə, -chə/ *n* 1 an initiative towards agreement or action – often pl with sing. meaning 2a the orchestral introduction to a musical dramatic work b an orchestral concert piece written esp as a single movement

,over'turn /-'tuhn/ *v* 1 to cause to turn over; upset 2 to overthrow

,over'weening /-'weening/ *adj* 1 arrogant, presumptuous 2 immoderate, exaggerated – ~ly *adv*

,over'weight *adj* exceeding the expected, normal, or proper (bodily) weight

,over'whelm /-'welm/ *v* 1 to cover over completely; submerge 2 to overcome by superior force or numbers 3 to overpower with emotion – ~ing *adj* – ~ingly *adv*

,over'work /-'wuhk/ *v* 1 (to cause) to work too hard or too long 2 to make excessive use of – overwork *n*

,over'wrought /-'rawt/ *adj* extremely excited; agitated

oviduct /'ohvi,dukt/ *n* the tube that serves for the passage of eggs from an ovary, esp before laying

ovoid /'ohvoyd/, ovoidal /oh'voydl/ *adj* shaped like an egg

ovulate /'ovyoo,layt/ *v* to produce eggs or discharge them from an ovary – -ation *n*

ovule /'ovyoohl, 'oh-/ *n* an outgrowth of the ovary of a seed plant that develops into a seed after fertilization of the egg cell it contains

ovum /'ohvəm/ *n*, *pl* ova /'ohvə/ an animal's female gamete that when fertilized can develop into a new individual

owe /oh/ *v* 1a to be under obligation to pay or render b to be indebted to 2 to have or enjoy as a result of the action or existence of sthg or sby else

'owing to /'oh·ing/ *prep* because of

owl /owl/ *n* any of an order of chiefly nocturnal birds of prey with large head and eyes and a short hooked bill – ~ish *adj* – ~ishly *adv*

¹own /ohn/ *adj* belonging to, for, or relating to oneself or itself – usu after a possessive pronoun (e g cooked his *own* dinner)

²own *v* 1 to have or hold as property; possess 2 to acknowledge, admit – often + *to* – ~er *n* – ~ership *n*

³own *pron*, *pl* own one belonging to oneself or itself – usu after a possessive pronoun — on one's own 1 in solitude; alone 2 without assistance or control

own up *v* to confess a fault frankly

ox /oks/ *n*, *pl* oxen /'oks(ə)n/ *also* ox 1 a (domestic species of) bovine mammal 2 an adult castrated male domestic ox

Oxbridge /'oks,brij/ *adj or n* (of) the universities of Oxford and Cambridge

oxide /'oksied/ *n* a compound of oxygen with an element or radical

oxid·ize, -ise /'oksi,diez/ *v* 1 to combine with oxygen 2 to remove hydrogen or 1 or more electrons from an atom, ion, or molecule

oxtail /'oks,tayl/ *n* the tail of cattle (skinned and used for food, esp in soup)

oxyacetylene /,oksi·ə'set(ə)lin, -leen/ *adj* of or using a mixture of oxygen and acetylene, esp for producing a hot flame

oxygen /'oksij(ə)n/ *n* a gaseous chemical element that forms about 21 per cent by volume of the atmosphere and is essential for the life of all plants and animals

oyez /oh'yay, -yes/ *v* *imper* – uttered by a court official or public crier to gain attention

oyster /'oystə/ *n* 1 any of various (edible) marine bivalve molluscs with a rough irregular shell 2 a small mass of muscle on each side of the back of a fowl

ozone /'oh,zohn/ *n* 1 a form of oxygen with 3 atoms in each molecule 2 pure and refreshing air

P

p /pee/ *n, pl* **p's, ps** *often cap* (a graphic representation of or device for reproducing) the 16th letter of the English alphabet

pa /pah/ *n* father – *infml*

¹**pace** /pays/ *n* **1** rate of movement or activity **2** a manner of walking **3** the distance covered by a single step in walking, usu taken to be about 0.75m (about 30in) **4a** a gait; *esp* a fast 2-beat gait of a horse in which the legs move in lateral pairs **b** *pl* an exhibition of skills or abilities

²**pace** *v* **1** to walk with a slow or measured tread **2** to measure by pacing – often + *out* or *off* **3** to set or regulate the pace of; *specif* to go ahead of (e g a runner) as a pacemaker

³**pace** /'paysi/ *prep* with due respect to

'**pace ,maker** /-,maykə/ *n* **1** sby or sthg that sets the pace for another (e g in a race) **2** (a device for applying regular electric shocks to the heart that reproduces the function of) a part of the heart that maintains rhythmic (coordinated) contractions

pachyderm /'pakiduhm/ *n* an elephant, rhinoceros, pig, or other usu thick-skinned (hoofed) mammal that does not chew the cud

pacific /pə'sifik/ *adj* **1** having a mild peaceable nature **2** *cap* of (the region round) the Pacific ocean – ~ **ally** *adv*

pacifism /'pasifiz(ə)m/ *n* opposition to war as a means of settling disputes; *specif* refusal to bear arms on moral or religious grounds

pacify /'pasifie/ *v* **1** to allay the anger or agitation of **2a** to restore to a peaceful state; subdue **b** to reduce to submission – **-fication, -fier** *n*

¹**pack** /pak/ *n* **1** a bundle or bag of things carried on the shoulders or back **2a** a large amount or number **b** a full set of playing cards **3** an organized troop (e g of cub scouts) **4** *sing or pl in constr* the forwards in a rugby team, esp when acting together **5** *sing or pl in constr* **5a** a group of domesticated animals trained to hunt or run together **b** a group of (predatory) animals of the same kind **6** wet absorbent material for application to the body as treatment (e g for a bruise)

²**pack** *v* **1a** to stow (as if) in a container, esp for transport or storage – often + *up* **b** to cover, fill, or surround with protective material **2a** to crowd together so as to fill; cram **b** to force into a smaller volume; compress **3** to bring to an end; finish – + *up* or *in* **4** to gather into a pack **5** to cover or surround with a pack

³**pack** *v* to influence the composition of (e g a jury) so as to bring about a desired result

package /'pakij/ *n* **1a** a small or medium-sized pack; a parcel **b** sthg wrapped or sealed **2** a wrapper or container in which sthg is packed **3** **package, package holiday** a holiday, booked through a single agent, including transport, accommodation and (some) meals at an all-in price – **package** *v*

'**package ,deal** *n* an offer or agreement involving a number of related items and making acceptance of one item dependent on the acceptance of all

packed /pakt/ *adj* **1a** that is crowded or stuffed – often in combination **b** compressed **2** filled to capacity

packet /'pakit/ *n* **1** a small pack or parcel **2** a passenger boat carrying mail and cargo on a regular schedule **3** *Br* a large sum of money – *infml*

'**pack ,ice** *n* sea ice crushed together into a large floating mass

pack up *v* **1** to finish work **2** to cease to function

pact /pakt/ *n* an agreement, treaty

¹**pad** /pad/ *n* **1** a thin flat mat or cushion: e g **1a** padding used to shape an article of clothing **b** a padded guard worn to shield body parts, esp the legs of a batsman, against impact **c** a piece of absorbent material used as a surgical dressing or protective covering **2** (the cushioned thickening of the underside of) the foot of an animal **3** a number of sheets of paper (e g for writing or drawing on) fastened together at 1 edge **4** a flat surface for a vertical takeoff or landing **5** living quarters – *infml*

²**pad** *v* **-dd-** **1** to provide with a pad or padding **2** to expand or fill out (speech or writing) with superfluous matter – often + *out*

³**pad** *v* **-dd-** to walk with a muffled step

padding /'pading/ *n* material used to pad

¹**paddle** /'padl/ *n* **1a** a usu wooden implement similar to but smaller than an oar, used to propel and steer a small craft (e g a canoe) **b** an implement with a short handle and broad flat blade used for stirring, mixing, hitting, etc **2** any of the broad boards at the circumference of a paddle wheel or waterwheel

²**paddle** *v* **paddling** /'padling/ to go on or through water (as if) by means of paddling a craft

³**paddle** *v* to walk, play, or wade in shallow water

'**paddle ,wheel** *n* a power-driven wheel with paddles, floats, or boards round its circumference used to propel a boat

paddock /'padək/ *n* **1** a small usu enclosed field, esp for pasturing or exercising animals **2** an area at a motor-racing track where cars, motorcycles, etc are parked and worked on before a race

paddy /'padi/ n 1 (threshed unmilled) rice 2 a paddyfield

Paddy n an Irishman – chiefly derog

'paddy,field /-,feeld/ n a field of wet land in which rice is grown

padlock /'padlok/ n a portable lock with a shackle that can be passed through a staple or link and then secured

padre /'pahdri/ n 1 a Christian priest 2 a military chaplain

paediatrics /,peedi'atriks/ n pl but sing or pl in constr medicine dealing with the development, care, and diseases of children – **-trician** n

paella /pie'ela/ n a saffron-flavoured Spanish dish containing rice, meat, seafood, and vegetables

pagan /'paygən/ n 1 sby worshipping several gods 2 an irreligious person – **pagan** adj – **~ism** n

¹page /payj/ n 1a a youth attending on a person of rank; esp one in the personal service of a knight b a boy serving as an honorary attendant at a formal function (e g a wedding) 2 sby employed to deliver messages or run errands

²page v to summon esp by repeatedly calling out the name of (e g over a public-address system)

³page n (a single side of) a leaf of a book, magazine, etc

pageant /'paj(ə)nt/ n 1 an ostentatious display 2 a show, exhibition; esp a colourful spectacle with a series of tableaux, dramatic presentations, or a procession, expressing a common theme

pageantry /'paj(ə)ntri/ n 1 pageants and the presentation of pageants 2 colourful or splendid display; spectacle

pagoda /pə'gohdə/ n a many-storied usu polygonal tower erected as a temple or memorial in the Far East

paid /payd/ past of **pay**

,paid-'up adj having paid the necessary fees to be a full member of a group or organization; broadly showing the characteristic attitudes and behaviour of a specified group to a marked degree

pail /payl/ n (the contents of or quantity contained in) an esp wooden or metal bucket

¹pain /payn/ n 1a a basic bodily sensation induced by a noxious stimulus or physical disorder and characterized by physical discomfort (e g pricking, throbbing, or aching) b acute mental or emotional distress 2 pl trouble or care taken 3 sby or sthg that annoys or is a nuisance – infml — **on/under pain of** subject to penalty or punishment of — **pain in the neck** a source of annoyance; a nuisance — infml

²pain v to make suffer or cause distress to; hurt

painful /'paynf(ə)l/ adj **-ll- 1a** feeling or giving pain b irksome, annoying 2 requiring effort or exertion – **~ly** adv – **~ness** n

painstaking /'payn,stayking/ adj showing diligent care and effort – **~ly** adv

¹paint /paynt/ v 1 to apply colour, pigment, etc to 2a to represent in colours on a surface by applying pigments b to decorate by painting 3 to depict as having specified or implied characteristics

²paint n a mixture of a pigment and a suitable liquid which forms a closely adherent coating when spread on a surface

'paint,brush /-,brush/ n a brush for applying paint

¹painter /'payntə/ n 1 an artist who paints 2 sby who applies paint (e g to a building), esp as an occupation

²painter n a line used for securing or towing a boat

painting /'paynting/ n 1 a product of painting; esp a painted work of art 2 the art or occupation of painting

'paint,work /-,wuhk/ n paint that has been applied to a surface

¹pair /peə/ n sing or pl in constr pl **pairs** also **pair** **1a**(1) two corresponding things usu used together **a**(2) two corresponding bodily parts b a single thing made up of 2 connected corresponding pieces **2a** two similar or associated things: e g **2a**(1) a couple in love, engaged, or married **a**(2) two playing cards of the same value in a hand **a**(3) two horses harnessed side by side **a**(4) two mated animals b a partnership between 2 people, esp in a contest against another partnership

²pair v to arrange in pairs

paisley /'payzli/ adj, often cap of a fabric or garment made usu of soft wool and woven or printed with colourful abstract teardrop-shaped figures

Pakistani /,paki'stahni, ,pah-/ n 1 a native or inhabitant of Pakistan 2 a descendant of Pakistanis

pal /pal/ n a close friend – used as a familiar form of address, esp to a stranger USE infml – **~ly** adj

¹palace /'palis/ n 1 the official residence of a ruler (e g a sovereign or bishop) **2a** a large public building **b** a large and often ornate place of public entertainment

²palace adj 1 of a palace 2 of or involving the intimates of a chief executive

palais /'palay, 'pali/, **palais de dance** /~ də ' donhs/ n a public dance hall – chiefly infml

palatable /'palətəbl/ adj 1 pleasant to the taste 2 acceptable to the mind – **-bly** adv

palate /'palət/ n 1 the roof of the mouth, separating it from the nasal cavity **2a** the sense of taste b a usu intellectual taste or liking – **palatal** adj

palatial /pə'laysh(ə)l/ adj 1 of or being a palace 2 suitable to a palace; magnificent – **~ly** adv

palaver /pə'lahvə/ n 1 a long parley or discussion 2 idle talk

¹pale /payl/ adj 1 deficient in (intensity of) colour 2 not bright or brilliant; dim 3 feeble, faint – **~ly** adv – **~ness** n

pan

²**pale** *n* **1** a slat in a fence **2** a territory under a particular jurisdiction — **beyond the pale**, in violation of good manners, social convention etc

paleface /'payl,fays/ *n* a white person, esp as distinguished from an American Indian

palette /'palit/ *n* **1** a thin board held in the hand on which an artist mixes pigments **2** a particular range, quality, or use of colour; *esp* that of an individual artist

'**palette knife** *n* a knife with a flexible steel blade and no cutting edge, used esp in cooking or by artists for mixing and applying paints

palindrome /'palindrohm/ *n* a word, sentence, etc that reads the same backwards or forwards

¹**palisade** /,pali'sayd/ *n* a long strong stake pointed at the top and set close with others as a defence

²**palisade** *v* to surround or fortify with palisades

¹**pall** /pawl/ *n* **1** a square of linen used to cover the chalice containing the wine used at Communion **2** a heavy cloth draped over a coffin or tomb **3** sthg heavy or dark that covers or conceals

²**pall** *v* to cease to be interesting or attractive

pallbearer /'pawl,beərə/ *n* a person who helps to carry the coffin at a funeral or is part of its immediate escort

¹**pallet** /'palit/ *n* **1** a straw-filled mattress **2** a small hard often makeshift bed

²**pallet** *n* **1** a flat-bladed wooden tool used esp by potters for shaping clay **2** a portable platform intended for handling, storing, or moving materials and packages

palliate /'paliayt/ *v* **1** to lessen the unpleasantness of (e g a disease) without removing the cause **2** to disguise the gravity of (a fault or offence) by excuses or apologies; extenuate **3** to moderate the intensity of — **-ation** *n* — **-ative** *n*, *adj*

pallid /'palid/ *adj* **1** lacking colour; wan **2** lacking sparkle or liveliness; dull — **-ly** *adv* — ~**ness** *n*

pallor /'palə/ *n* deficiency of (facial) colour; paleness

¹**palm** /pahm; *NAm* pah(l)m/ *n* **1** any of a family of tropical or subtropical trees, shrubs, etc usu having a simple stem and a crown of large leaves **2** (a leaf of the palm as) a symbol of victory, distinction, or rejoicing

²**palm** *n* the concave part of the human hand between the bases of the fingers and the wrist

³**palm** *v* **1a** to conceal in or with the hand **b** to pick up stealthily **2** to impose by fraud

palm off *v* to get rid of (sthg unwanted or inferior) by deceiving sby into taking it – often + *on*

Palm 'Sunday *n* the Sunday before Easter celebrated in commemoration of Christ's triumphal entry into Jerusalem

palmy /'pahmi, 'pahlmi/ *adj* marked by prosperity; flourishing

palpable /'palpəbl/ *adj* **1** capable of being touched or felt; tangible **2** easily perceptible by the mind; manifest — **-bly** *adv*

palpitate /'palpitayt/ *v* to beat rapidly and strongly; throb – **-tation** *n*

palsy /'pawlzi, 'polzi/ *n* paralysis or uncontrollable tremor of (a part of) the body

paltry /'pawltri/ *adj* **1** mean, despicable **2** trivial

pamper /'pampə/ *v* to treat with extreme or excessive care and attention

pamphlet /'pamflit/ *n* a usu small unbound printed publication with a paper cover, often dealing with topical matters

pamphleteer /,pamfli'tiə/ *n* a writer of (political) pamphlets attacking sthg or urging a cause

¹**pan** /pan/ *n* **1a** any of various usu broad shallow open receptacles: e g **1a(1)** a dustpan **a(2)** a round metal container or vessel usu with a long handle, used to heat or cook food **2** a hollow or depression in land **3** *chiefly Br* the bowl of a toilet **4** *chiefly NAm* a baking tin

²**pan** *v* **-nn-** **1** to wash earth, gravel, etc in search of metal (e g gold) **2** to separate (e g gold) by panning **3** to criticize severely – *infml*

³**pan** /pahn/ *n* (a substance for chewing consisting of betel nut and various spices etc wrapped in) a betel leaf

⁴**pan** /pan/ *v* **-nn-** to rotate a film or television camera so as to keep a moving object in view

⁵**pan** /pan/ *n* the act or process of panning a camera; the movement of the camera in a panning shot

panacea /,panə'see-ə/ *n* a remedy for all ills or difficulties

panache /pə'nash, pa-/ *n* dash or flamboyance in style and action; verve

panama /,panə'mah/ *n*, *often cap* a lightweight hat of plaited straw

panatela, panatella /,panə'telə/ *n* a long thin cigar

pancake /'pan,kayk/ *n* **1** a flat cake made from thin batter and cooked on both sides usu in a frying pan **2** make-up compressed into a flat cake or stick form

pancreas /'pangkri-əs/ *n* a large compound gland in vertebrates that secretes digestive enzymes into the intestines and hormones (e g insulin) into the blood

panda /'pandə/ *n* **1** a long-tailed Himalayan flesh-eating mammal resembling the American racoon and having long chestnut fur spotted with black **2** a large black-and-white plant-eating mammal of western China resembling a bear but related to the racoons

'**panda car** *n*, *Br* a small car used by police patrols, esp in urban areas

pandemonium /,pandi'mohnyəm, -ni-əm/ *n* a wild uproar; a tumult

pander /'pandə/ *v* to provide gratification for other's desires – usu + *to*

pane /payn/ *n* **1** a framed sheet of glass in a window or door **2** any of the sections into which a sheet of postage stamps is cut for distribution

panegyric /,pani'jirik/ *n* a oration or piece of writing in praise of sby

¹**panel** /'panl/ *n* **1a** a list of persons summoned for jury service **b** a group of people selected to perform some service (e g investigation or arbitration), or to discuss or compete on radio or television programme **2** a separate or distinct part of a surface: e g **2a** a thin usu rectangular board set in a frame (e g in a door) **b** a vertical section of fabric **3** a thin flat piece of wood on which a picture is painted **4a** a flat often insulated support (e g for parts of an electrical device) usu with controls on 1 face **b** a usu vertical mount for controls or dials (e g in a car or aircraft)

²**panel** *v* -ll- (*NAm* -l-, -ll-), /'panl·ing/ to furnish or decorate with panels

panellist /'panl·ist/ *n* a member of a discussion or advisory panel or of a radio or television panel

pang /pang/ *n* **1** a brief piercing spasm of pain **2** a sharp attack of mental anguish

¹**panic** /'panik/ *n* a sudden overpowering fright; *esp* a sudden unreasoning terror that spreads rapidly through a group **2** a sudden widespread fright concerning financial affairs and resulting in a depression in values – ~**ky** *adj*

²**panic** *v* -ck- to (cause to) be affected with panic

panic-stricken *adj* overcome with panic

pannier, panier /'panyə, 'pani·ə/ *n* **1** a large basket; *esp* either of a pair carried on the back of an animal **2** *chiefly Br* either of a pair of bags or boxes fixed on either side of the rear wheel of a bicycle or motorcycle

panoply /'panəpli/ *n* **1** ceremonial dress **2** a magnificent or impressive array – **plied** *adj*

panorama /,panə'rahmə/ *n* **1a** a large pictorial representation encircling the spectator **b** a picture exhibited by being unrolled before the spectator **2a** an unobstructed or complete view of a landscape or area **b** a comprehensive presentation or survey of a series of events – **-mic** *adj* – **-mically** *adv*

pansy /'panzi/ *n* **1** (a flower of) a garden plant derived from wild violets **2** an effeminate male or male homosexual – *derog*

¹**pant** /pant/ *v* **1a** to breathe quickly, spasmodically, or in a laboured manner **b** to make a puffing sound **2** to long eagerly; yearn – ~**ingly** *adv*

²**pant** *n* **1** a panting breath **2** a puffing sound

pantaloon /,pantə'loohn/ *n* **1** a stock character in pantomime who is usu a skinny old man wearing pantaloons **2** *pl* any of several kinds of men's breeches or trousers; *esp* close-fitting trousers fastened under the calf or instep and worn in the 18th and 19th c

pantheism /'panthee·iz(ə)m/ *n* **1** a doctrine that equates God with the forces and laws of nature **2** the indiscriminate worship of all the gods of different religions and cults – **-ist** *n* – **-istic** *adj*

pantheon /'panthi·ən, pan'thee·ən/ *n* **1** a building serving as the burial place of or containing memorials to famous dead **2** the gods of a people; *esp* the officially recognized gods

panther /'panthə/ *n pl* **panthers** *also esp collectively* **panther** **1** a leopard, esp of the black colour phase **2** *NAm* a puma

panties /'pantiz/ *n pl* pants for women or children; *also* knickers

pantile /'pan,tiel/ *n* a roofing tile whose transverse section is a flattened S-shape

pantomime /'pantə,miem/ *n* **1a** any of various dramatic or dancing performances in which a story is told by bodily or facial movements **b** a British theatrical and musical entertainment of the Christmas season based on a nursery tale with stock roles and topical jokes **2** mime

pantry /'pantri/ *n* **1** a room or cupboard used for storing provisions or tableware **2** a room (e g in a hotel or hospital) for preparation of cold foods to order

pants /pants/ *n pl* **1** *chiefly Br* an undergarment that covers the crotch and hips and that may extend to the waist and partly down each leg **2** *chiefly NAm* trousers

pap /pap/ *n* **1** a soft food for infants or invalids **2** sthg lacking solid value or substance

¹**papa** /pə'pah/ *n*, *chiefly Br* father – formerly used formally, esp in address

²**papa** /'papə/ *n* daddy – used informally and by children

papacy /'paypəsi/ *n* the (term of) office of pope

papal /'paypl/ *adj* of a pope or the Roman Catholic church

¹**paper** /'paypə/ *n* **1** a sheet of closely compacted vegetable fibres (e g of wood or cloth) **2a** a piece of paper containing a written or printed statement; a document; *specif* a document carried as proof of identity or status – often *pl* **b** a piece of paper containing writing or print **c** the question set or answers written in an examination in 1 subject **3** a paper container or wrapper **4** a newspaper **5** wallpaper — **on paper** in theory; hypothetically

²**paper** *v* to cover or line with paper; *esp* to apply wallpaper to

³**paper** *adj* **1a** made of paper, thin cardboard, or papier-mâché **b** papery **2** of clerical work or written communication **3** existing only in theory; nominal

paperback /-,bak/ *n* a book with a flexible paper binding

paperboy /-,boy/, *fem* **papergirl** *n* a boy who delivers or sells newspapers 'paper,weight /-,wayt/ n a usu small heavy object used to hold down loose papers (e g on a desk)

'paper,work /-,wuhk/ n routine clerical or record-keeping work, often incidental to a more important task

papery /'paypə(ə)ri/ adj resembling paper in thinness or consistency

papier-mâché /,papyay 'mashay, mə'shay, ' paypə/ n a light strong moulding material made of paper pulped with glue that is used for making boxes, trays, etc

papist /'paypist/ n, often cap a Roman Catholic – chiefly derog

papoose /pə'poohs/ n a young N American Indian child

paprika /'paprikə, pa'preekə/ n (a mild to hot red condiment consisting of the finely ground dried pods of) any of various cultivated sweet peppers

papyrus /pə'pie-ərəs/ n, pl papyruses, papyri /-'rie/ 1 a tall sedge of the Nile valley 2 the pith of the papyrus plant, esp when made into a material for writing on 3 a usu ancient manuscript written on papyrus

par /pah/ n 1 the money value assigned to each share of stock in the charter of a company 2 a common level; equality – esp in on a par with 3 an amount taken as an average or norm b an accepted standard; specif a usual standard of physical condition or health 4 the standard score (of a good player) for each hole of a golf course

parable /'parəbl/ n a usu short allegorical story illustrating a moral or religious principle

parachute /'parə,shooht/ n a folding device of light fabric used esp for ensuring a safe descent of a person or object from a great height (e g from a aeroplane) – -chutist n

¹parade /pə'rayd/ n 1 an ostentatious show 2 the (ceremonial) ordered assembly of a body of troops before a superior officer 3 a public procession 4 chiefly Br a row of shops, esp with a service road

²parade v 1 to march in a procession 2 to promenade 3 to show off

paradise /'parə,dies/ n 1 often cap 1a the garden of Eden b Heaven 2 a place of bliss, felicity, or delight

paradox /'parə,doks/ n 1 a tenet contrary to received opinion 2 a statement that is apparently contradictory or absurd and yet might be true 3 sthg (e g a person, condition, or act) with seemingly contradictory qualities or phases – ~ical adj – -ically adv

paraffin /'parəfin, ,--'-/ n 1 a usu waxy inflammable mixture of hydrocarbons used chiefly in candles, cosmetics, and in making other chemicals 2 an inflammable liquid hydrocarbon obtained by distillation of petroleum and used esp as a fuel

paragon /'parəgən/ n a model of excellence or perfection

paragraph /'parə,grahf, -,graf/ n a usu indented division of a written composition that develops a single point or idea

parakeet, NAm also parrakeet /,parə'keet, '--,-/ n any of numerous usu small slender long-tailed parrots

¹parallel /'parəlel/ adj 1a extending in the same direction, everywhere equidistant, and not meeting b everywhere equally distant 2 analogous, comparable

²parallel n 1 a parallel line, curve, or surface 2 sby or sthg equal or similar in all essential particulars; a counterpart, analogue 3 a comparison to show resemblance 4 the arrangement of 2-terminal electrical devices in which one terminal of each device is joined to one conductor and the others are joined to another conductor

³parallel v 1 to compare 2a to equal, match b to correspond to

,parallel 'bars n pl (a men's gymnastic event using) a pair of bars supported horizontally 1.7m (5ft 7in) above the floor usu by a common base

parallelogram /,parə'lelə,gram/ n a quadrilateral with opposite sides parallel and equal

paralysis /pə'ralasis/ n pl paralyses /-seez/ loss of function or the ability to move – -yse v

¹paralytic /,parə'litik/ adj 1 of, resembling, or affected with paralysis 2 chiefly Br very drunk – infml

²paralytic n one suffering from paralysis

parameter /pə'ramitə/ n a characteristic, factor

paramilitary /,parə'milit(ə)ri/ adj formed on a military pattern (as a potential auxiliary military force)

paramount /'paramownt/ adj superior to all others; supreme – ~cy n

paramour /'parəmooə/ n an illicit lover; esp a mistress

paranoia /,parə'noyə/ n 1 a mental disorder characterized by delusions of persecution or grandeur 2 a tendency towards excessive or irrational suspiciousness and distrustfulness of others

parapet /'parəpit, -pet/ n 1 a wall, rampart, or elevation of earth or stone to protect soldiers 2 a low wall or balustrade to protect the edge of a platform, roof, or bridge

paraphernalia /,parəfə'naylyə/ n 1 personal belongings 2a articles of equipment b accessory items

¹paraphrase /'parə,frayz/ n a restatement of a text, passage, or work giving the meaning in another form

²paraphrase v to make a paraphrase (of)

paraplegia /,parə'pleejə/ n paralysis of the lower half of the body including the legs – -gic adj, n – -gically adv

parasite /'parəsiet/ *n* **1** an organism living in or on another organism to its own benefit **2** sthg or sby depending on sthg or sby else for existence or support without making a useful or adequate return – **-sitic, -sitical** *adj* – **-sitically** *adv* – **-sitism** *n*

parasol /'parəsol/ *n* a lightweight umbrella used, esp by women, as a protection from the sun

paratroops /'parə,troohps/ *n pl* troops trained and equipped to parachute from an aeroplane – **-trooper** *n*

parboil /'pah,boyl/ *v* to boil briefly as a preliminary or incomplete cooking procedure

¹**parcel** /'pahsl/ *n* a wrapped bundle; a package

²**parcel** *v* **-ll-** (*NAm* **-l-, -ll-**), /'pahsl·ing/ **1** to divide into parts; distribute – often + *out* **2** to make up into a parcel; wrap – often + *up*

parch /pahch/ *v* to make or become dry or scorched

parchment /'pahchmənt/ *n* **1** the skin of an animal, esp of a sheep or goat, prepared for writing on **2** a parchment manuscript

¹**pardon** /'pahdn/ *n* **1** a release from legal penalties **2** excuse or forgiveness for a fault, offence, or discourtesy

²**pardon** *v* **1** to absolve from the consequences of a fault or crime **2** to allow (an offence) to pass without punishment

pare /peə/ *v* **1** to cut or shave off (an outer surface) **2** to diminish gradually (as if) by paring – **parer** *n*

¹**parent** /'peərənt/ *n* **1** sby who begets or brings forth offspring; a father or mother **2a** an animal or plant regarded in relation to its offspring **b** the material or source from which sthg is derived – **~al** *adj*

²**parent** *v* to be or act as the parent of

parentage /'peərəntij/ *n* descent from parents or ancestors; lineage

parenthesis /pə'renthəsis/ *n*, *pl* **parentheses** /-, seez/ **1** an amplifying or explanatory word or phrase inserted in a passage from which, in writing, it is usu set off by punctuation **2** an interlude, interval

parent-teacher association *n sing or pl in constr* an organization of teachers at a school and the parents of their pupils, that works for the improvement of the school

par excellence /pah 'reks(ə)lons/ *adj* being the best example of a kind; without equal

pariah /pə'rie·ə, 'pari·ə/ *n* **1** a member of a low caste of S India and Burma **2** an outcast

parish /'parish/ *n* **1** the subdivision of a diocese served by a single church or clergyman **2** a unit of local government in rural England

parishioner /pə'rish(ə)nə/ *n* a member or inhabitant of a parish

parity /'parəti/ *n* the quality or state of being equal or equivalent

¹**park** /pahk/ *n* **1** an area of land for recreation in or near a city or town **2** an area maintained in its natural state as a public property **3** an assigned space for military animals, vehicles, or materials

²**park** *v* **1** to leave or place (a vehicle) for a time, esp at the roadside or in a car park or garage **2** to set and leave temporarily

parka /'pahkə/ *n* **1** a hooded fur garment for wearing in the arctic **2** an anorak

parkin /'pahkin/ *n* a thick heavy ginger cake made with oatmeal and treacle

'**parking ,meter** *n* a coin-operated device which registers the payment and shows the time allowed for parking a motor vehicle

,**Parkinson's di,sease** /'pahkins(ə)nz/ *n* tremor, weakness of resting muscles, and a peculiar gait occurring in later life as a progressive nervous disease

Parkinson's Law *n* an observation in office organization: work expands so as to fill the time available for its completion

parky /'pahki/ *adj*, *Br* chilly – *infml*

¹**parley** /'pahli/ *v* to speak with another; confer; *specif* to discuss terms with an enemy

²**parley** *n* a conference for discussion of points in dispute; *specif* a conference under truce to discuss terms with an enemy

parliament /'pahləmənt, *also* -lyə-/ *n* **1** a formal conference for the discussion of public affairs **2** *often cap* the supreme legislative body of the UK that consists of the House of Commons and the House of Lords; *also* a similar body in another nation or state – **~ary** *adj*

parliamentarian /,pahləmən'teəri·ən, -men-, *also* -lyə-/ *n* **1** *often cap* an adherent of the parliament during the Civil War **2** an expert in parliamentary rules and practice

¹**parlour**, *NAm* **parlor** /'pahlə/ *n* **1a** a room in a private house for the entertainment of guests **b** a room in an inn, hotel, or club for conversation or semiprivate uses **2** any of various business places **3** a place for milking cows

²**parlour** *adj* fostered or advocated in comfortable seclusion without consequent action or application to affairs

'**parlour ,game** *n* an indoor word game, board game, etc

parlous /'pahləs/ *adj* full of uncertainty and danger – fml or humor

Parmesan /,pahmi'zan, '—'/ *n* a very hard dry strongly flavoured cheese that is often used grated

parochial /pə'rohki·əl/ *adj* **1** of a (church) parish **2** limited in range or scope (e g to a narrow area or region); provincial, narrow – **~ly** *adv* – **~ism** *n*

¹**parody** /'parədi/ *n* **1** a literary or musical work in which the style of an author is imitated for comic or satirical effect **2** a feeble or ridiculous imitation

²**parody** *v* to compose a parody on – **-dist** *n*

¹**parole** /pə'rohl/ *n* 1 a pledge of one's honour; *esp* the promise of a prisoner of war to fulfil stated conditions in consideration of release or the granting of privileges 2 a password given only to officers of the guard and of the day 3 a conditional release of a prisoner

²**parole** *v* to put on parole

paroxysm /'parək,siz(ə)m/ *n* 1 a fit, attack, or sudden increase or recurrence of (disease) symptoms; a convulsion 2 a sudden violent emotion or action

parquet /'pahkay, -ki/ *n* **parqueted** /'pahkayd/; **parqueting** /'pahkaying/ a floor made of wooden blocks

parricide /'parisied/ *n* (the act of) sby who murders his/her father, mother, or a close relative

¹**parrot** /'parət/ *n* 1 any of numerous chiefly tropical birds that have a distinctive stout hooked bill, are often crested and brightly coloured, and are excellent mimics 2 a person who parrots another's words

²**parrot** *v* to repeat or imitate (e g another's words) without understanding or thought

parry /'pari/ *v* 1 to ward off a weapon or blow 2 to evade, esp by an adroit answer – **parry** *n*

parse /pahz/ *v* to resolve (e g a sentence) into component parts of speech and describe them grammatically

parsec /'pah,sek/ *n* a unit of distance for use in astronomy equal to about 3¹/₄ light-years

Parsi, Parsee /,pah'see, '-,-/ *n* an Indian member of an ancient Persian religious group

parsimonious /,pahsi'mohnəs/ *adj* frugal to the point of stinginess; niggardly – **~ly** *adv* – **~ness** *n*

parsimony /'pahsiməni/ *n* thrift; *also* stinginess

parsley /'pahsli/ *n* an orig S European plant of the carrot family widely cultivated for its leaves used as a herb or garnish in cooking

parsnip /'pahsnip/ *n* (the long edible tapering root of) a European plant of the carrot family with large leaves and yellow flowers

parson /'pahs(ə)n/ *n* 1 the incumbent of a parish 2 a clergyman

parsonage /'pahsənij/ *n* the house provided by a church for its parson

¹**part** /paht/ *n* **1a** any of the often indefinite or unequal subdivisions into which sthg is (regarded as) divided and which together constitute the whole **b** an amount equal to another amount **c** an organ, member, or other constituent element of a plant or animal body **d** a division of a literary work **e** a vocal or instrumental line or melody in music or harmony **f** a constituent member of an apparatus (e g a machine); *also* a spare part 2 sthg falling to one in a division or apportionment; a share 3 any of the opposing sides in a conflict or dispute 4 a function or course of action performed 5a an actor's lines in a play **b** a role — **for**

the most part in most cases or respects; mainly — in part in some degree; partly — **on the part of** with regard to the one specified

²**part** *v* 1 to separate from or take leave of sby 2 to become separated, detached, or broken 3 to separate (the hair) by combing on each side of a line

³**part** *adv* partly

⁴**part** *adj* partial

partake /pah'tayk/ *v* **partook** /-'took/; **partaken** /-'taykən/ to take a part or share; participate – usu + *in* or *of*; *fml*

partial /'pahsh(ə)l/ *adj* 1 inclined to favour one party more than the other; biased 2 markedly fond of sby or sthg – + *to* 3 of a part rather than the whole; not general or total – **~ly** *adv*

partiality /,pahshi'aləti/ *n* 1 a bias 2 a special taste or liking

participate /pah'tisipayt/ *v* 1 to take part 2 to have a part or share in sthg – **-pant** *n* – **-pation** *n*

participle /'pahti,sipl, pah'tisipl/ *n* a verbal form (e g *singing* or *sung*) that has the function of an adjective and at the same time can be used in compound verb forms

particle /'pahtikl/ *n* 1 a minute subdivision of matter (e g an electron, atom or molecule) 2 a minute quantity or fragment 3 a minor unit of speech including all uninflected words or all words except nouns and verbs; *esp* a function word

¹**particular** /pə'tikyoolə/ *adj* 1 of or being a single person or thing; specific 2 detailed, exact 3 worthy of notice; special, unusual **4a** concerned over or attentive to details; meticulous **b** hard to please; exacting – **~ity** *n* – **~ly** *adv*

²**particular** *n* an individual fact, point, circumstance, or detail — **in particular** particularly, especially

particular-ize, -ise /pə'tikyoolariez/ *v* to go into details; specify

¹**parting** /'pahting/ *n* 1 a place or point where a division or separation occurs 2 the line where the hair is parted

²**parting** *adj* given, taken, or performed at parting

partisan, partizan /,pahtizan/ *n* 1 an over-zealous adherent to a party, faction, or cause 2 a guerrilla

¹**partition** /pah'tish(ə)n/ *n* 1 division into parts 2 sthg that divides; *esp* a light interior dividing wall

²**partition** *v* 1 to divide into parts or shares 2 to divide or separate *off* by a partition

partly /'pahtli/ *adv* in some measure or degree; partially

¹**partner** /'pahtnə/ *n* **1a** either of a couple who dance together **b** sby who plays with 1 or more others in a game against an opposing side **c** a person with whom one is having a sexual relationship; a spouse, lover, etc 2 any of the principal members of a joint business – **~ship** *n*

²**partner** *v* to act as a partner to

,part of 'speech *n* a class of words distinguished according to the kind of idea denoted and the function performed in a sentence

partridge /'pahtrij/ *n pl* partridges, *esp collectively* partridge any of various typically medium-sized stout-bodied Old World game birds

,part-'time *adj* involving or working less than customary or standard hours

parturition /,pahtyoo'rish(ə)n/ *n* the action or process of giving birth

party /'pahti/ *n* 1a a person or group taking 1 side of a question, dispute, or contest b *sing or pl constr* a group of people organized to carry out an activity or fulfil a function together 2 *sing or pl in constr* a group organized for political involvement 3 one who is involved; a participant – usu + *to* 4 a (festive) social gathering

party line *n* 1 a single telephone line connecting 2 or more subscribers with an exchange 2 the official principles of a political party

paschal /'paskl/ *adj* 1 of the Passover 2 of or appropriate to Easter

¹pass /pahs/ *v* 1 to move, proceed 2a to go away – often + *off* b to die – often + *on* or *away*; euph 3a to go by; move past; *also* surpass b *of time* to elapse c to overtake another vehicle 4a to go across, over, or through b to emit or discharge from a bodily part, esp the bowels or bladder c to go uncensured or unchallenged 5 to go from one quality, state, or form to another 6a to pronounce a judgment b to utter – esp in *pass a comment, pass a remark* 7 to go from the control or possession of one person or group to that of another 8 to take place as a mutual exchange or transaction 9a to become approved by a body (e g a legislature) b to undergo an inspection, test, or examination successfully 10a to be accepted or regarded as adequate or fitting b to resemble or act the part of so well as to be accepted – usu + *for* 11 to kick, throw, or hit a ball or puck to a teammate 12 to decline to bid, bet, or play in a card game — in passing as a relevant digression; parenthetically — pass muster to be found adequate, esp in passing an inspection or examination — pass the buck to shift a responsibility to sby else — pass the time of day to give or exchange friendly greetings — pass water to urinate – euph

²pass *n* a narrow passage over low ground in a mountain range

³pass *n* 1 a usu distressing or bad state of affairs – often in *come to a pretty pass* 2a a written leave of absence from a military post or station for a brief period b a permit or ticket allowing free transport or free admission 3 the passing of an examination 4a an act of passing in cards, soccer, rugby, etc; *also* a ball or puck passed b a ball hit to the side

and out of reach of an opponent, esp in tennis 5 a sexually inviting gesture or approach – usu in *make a pass at*

passable /'pahsəbl/ *adj* 1 capable of being passed, crossed, or travelled on 2 barely good enough; tolerable

passage /'pasij/ *n* 1 the action or process of passing from one place or condition to another 2a a way of exit or entrance; a road, path, channel, or course by which sthg passes b passage, passageway a corridor or lobby giving access to the different rooms or parts of a building or apartment 3a a specified act of travelling or passing, esp by sea or air b the passing of a legislative measure 4 a right, liberty, or permission to pass 5a a brief noteworthy portion of a written work or speech b a phrase or short section of a musical composition

pass away *v* 1 to go out of existence 2 to die – euph

passé /'pahsay, 'pasay/ *adj* 1 outmoded 2 behind the times

passenger /'pasinjə, -s(ə)n-/ *n* 1 sby who travels in, but does not operate, a public or private conveyance 2 *chiefly Br* a member of a group who contributes little or nothing to the functioning or productivity of the group

passerby /,pahsə'bie/ *n pl* passersby /,pahsəz-/ a person who happens by chance to pass by a particular place

passing /'pahsing/ *adj* 1 going by or past 2 having a brief duration 3 superficial

passion /'pash(ə)n/ *n* 1 *often cap* 1a the sufferings of Christ between the night of the Last Supper and his death b a musical setting of a gospel account of the Passion story 2a intense, driving, or uncontrollable feeling b an outbreak of anger 3 ardent affection; *also* strong sexual desire b (the object of) a strong liking, feeling, or interest – ~less *adj* – ~lessly *adv*

passionate /'pash(ə)nət/ *adj* 1 easily aroused to anger 2a capable of, affected by, or expressing intense feeling, esp love, hatred, or anger b extremely enthusiastic; keen – ~ly *adv*

'passion,flower /-,flowə/ *n* any of a genus of chiefly tropical plants with usu showy flowers and pulpy often edible berries

'passion ,play *n, often cap 1st P* a dramatic representation of the passion and crucifixion of Christ

passive /'pasiv/ *adj* 1a acted on, receptive to, or influenced by external forces or impressions b *of a verb form or voice* expressing an action that is done to the grammatical subject of a sentence (e g *was hit* in 'the ball was hit') c *of a person* lacking in energy, will, or initiative; meekly accepting 2a not active or operative; inert b of or characterized by chemical inactivity 3 offering no resistance; submissive – ~ly *adv*

passive resistance *n* resistance characterized by nonviolent noncooperation

pass off *v* **1** to present with intent to deceive **2** to give a false identity or character to **3** to take place and be completed

pass out *v* **1** to lose consciousness **2** *chiefly Br* to finish a period of (military) training

Passover /'pahsohvə/ *n* the Jewish celebration of the liberation of the Hebrews from slavery in Egypt

pass over *v* **1** to ignore in passing **2** to pay no attention to the claims of; disregard

passport /'pahs,pawt/ *n* **1** an official document issued by a government as proof of identity and nationality to one of its citizens for use when leaving or reentering the country **2a** a permission or authorization to go somewhere **b** sthg that secures admission or acceptance

pass up *v* to decline, reject

'pass,word /-,wuhd/ *n* **1** a word or phrase that must be spoken by a person before being allowed to pass a guard **2** a watchword

¹**past** /pahst/ *adj* **1a** just gone or elapsed **b** having gone by; earlier **2** finished, ended **3** of or constituting the past tense expressing elapsed time **4** preceding, former

²**past** *prep* **1a** beyond the age of or for **b** subsequent to in time (e g half *past* 2) **2a** at the farther side of; beyond **b** up to and then beyond (e g drove *past* the house) **3** beyond the capacity, range, or sphere of — **past it** no longer effective or in one's prime — *infml*

³**past** *n* **1a** a time gone by **b** sthg that happened or was done in the past **2** a past life, history, or course of action; *esp* one that is kept secret

⁴**past** *adv* so as to pass by the speaker (e g children ran *past*)

pasta /'pastə/ *n* any of several (egg or oil enriched) flour and water doughs that are usu shaped and used fresh or dried (e g as spaghetti)

¹**paste** /payst/ *n* **1a** a fat-enriched dough used esp for pastry **b** a usu sweet doughy confection **c** a smooth preparation of meat, fish, etc used as a spread **2a** a preparation of flour or starch and water used as an adhesive **b** clay or a clay mixture used in making pottery or porcelain **3** a brilliant glass used in making imitation gems

²**paste** *v* **1** to stick with paste **2** to cover with sthg pasted on

¹**'paste,board** /-,bawd/ *n* board made by pasting together sheets of paper

²**pasteboard** *adj* **1** made of pasteboard **2** sham, insubstantial

¹**pastel** /'pastl; *NAm* pas'tel/ *n* **1** (a crayon made of) a paste of powdered pigment mixed with gum **2** a drawing in pastel

²**pastel** *adj* pale and light in colour

pastern /'pastuhn/ *n* a part of a horse's foot extending from the fetlock to the hoof

pasteur·ize, -ise /'pahstyoo-,riez/ *v* to sterilize a liquid by heating for a short period – **-ization** *n*

pastiche /pa'steesh/ *n* a literary, artistic, or musical work that imitates the style of a previous work

pastille *also* **pastil** /'past(ə)l, -stil, -steel/ *n* **1** a small cone of aromatic paste, burned to fumigate or scent a room **2** an aromatic or medicated lozenge

pastime /'pahs,tiem/ *n* sthg (e g a hobby, game, etc) that amuses and serves to make time pass agreeably

,**past 'master** *n* one who is expert or experienced (in a particular activity)

pastor /'pahstə/ *n* one having responsibility for the spiritual welfare of a group (e g a congregation)

pastoral /'pahst(ə)rəl/ *adj* **1a(1)** (composed of) shepherds or herdsmen **a(2)** used for or based on livestock rearing **b** of the countryside; not urban **c** portraying rural life, esp in an idealized and conventionalized manner; *also* idyllic **2** of or providing spiritual care or guidance, esp of a church congregation

past participle *n* a participle with past, perfect, or passive meaning

past perfect *adj* of or being a verb tense (e g *had finished*) that expresses completion of an action at or before a past time

pastry /'paystri/ *n* **1** a dough containing fat esp when baked (e g for piecrust) **2** (an article of) usu sweet food made with pastry

pasturage /'pastyoorij, 'pahschərij/ *n* pasture

pasture /'pahschə/ *n* **1** plants (e g grass) grown for feeding (grazing) animals **2** (a plot of) land used for grazing **3** the feeding of livestock; grazing – **pasture** *v*

¹**pasty** /'pasti/ *n* a small filled usu savoury pie or pastry case baked without a container

²**pasty** /'paysti/ *adj* resembling paste; *esp* pallid and unhealthy in appearance

¹**pat** /pat/ *n* **1** a light tap, esp with the hand or a flat instrument **2** a small mass of sthg (e g butter) shaped (as if) by patting

²**pat** *v* **-tt- 1** to strike lightly with the open hand or some other flat surface **2** to flatten, smooth, or put into place or shape with light blows **3** to tap or stroke gently with the hand to soothe, caress, or show approval

³**pat** *adv* in a pat manner; aptly, promptly

⁴**pat** *adj* **1** prompt, immediate **2** suspiciously appropriate; contrived **3** learned, mastered, or memorized exactly

¹**patch** /pach/ *n* **1** a piece of material used to mend or cover a hole or reinforce a weak spot **2** a tiny piece of black silk worn on the face, esp by women in the 17th and 18th c, to set off the complexion **3a** a small piece; a scrap **b** a small piece of land usu used for growing vegetables **4** *chiefly Br* a usu specified period **5** *chiefly Br* an area for which a

pat

particular individual or unit (e g of police) has responsibility — **not a patch on** not nearly as good as

²**patch** v 1 to mend or cover (a hole) with a patch 2 to mend or put together, esp in a hasty or shabby fashion – usu + *up*

patch up v to bring (a quarrel, dispute, etc) to an end

¹**patch,work** /-,wuhk/ n 1 sthg composed of miscellaneous or incongruous parts 2 work consisting of pieces of cloth of various colours and shapes sewn together

patchy /'pachi/ adj 1 uneven in quality; incomplete 2 of certain types of weather appearing in patches – **-chily** adv – **-chiness** n

pate /payt/ n (the crown of) the head

pâté /'patay/ n a rich savoury paste of seasoned and spiced meat, fish, etc

patella /pə'telə/ n, pl **patellae** /-li/, **patellas** the kneecap

¹**patent** /'payt(ə)nt, 'pat(ə)nt; sense 5 'payt(ə)nt/ adj 1 secured by or made under a patent **b** proprietary 2 made of patent leather 3 readily visible or intelligible; not hidden or obscure

²**patent** /'payt(ə)nt, 'pat(ə)nt/ n 1 (a formal document securing to an inventor) the exclusive right to make or sell an invention 2 a patented invention 3 a privilege, licence

³**patent** v to obtain a patent for (an invention)

,**patent 'leather** /'payt(ə)nt/ n a leather with a hard smooth glossy surface

paternal /pə'tuhnl/ adj 1 fatherly 2 received or inherited from one's male parent 3 related through one's father – **~ly** adv

pa'ternal,ism /-,iz(ə)m/ n a system under which a government or organization deals with its subjects or employees in an authoritarian but benevolent way – **-ist** n – **-istic** adj – **-istically** adv

paternity /pə'tuhnəti/ n 1 being a father 2 origin or descent from a father

path /pahth/ n, pl **paths** /pahdhz/ 1 a track formed by the frequent passage of people or animals 2 a course, route 3 a way of life, conduct, or thought – **~less** adj

pathetic /pə'thetik/ adj 1 pitiful 2 marked by sorrow or melancholy; sad – **-ically** adv

pathfinder /'pahth,fiendə/ n 1 sby or sthg that explores unexplored regions to mark out a new route 2 sby who discovers new ways of doing things

pathology /pə'tholəji/ n 1 the study of (the structure and functional changes produced by) diseases 2 the anatomical and physiological abnormalities that constitute or characterize a (particular) disease – **-gist** n – **-gical** adj – **-gically** adv

pathos /'paythos/ n 1 a quality in experience or in artistic representation evoking pity or compassion 2 an emotion of sympathetic pity

patience /'paysh(ə)ns/ n 1 the capacity, habit, or fact of being patient 2 chiefly Br any of various card games that can be played by 1 person and usu involve the arranging of cards into a prescribed pattern

¹**patient** /'paysh(ə)nt/ adj 1 bearing pains or trials calmly or without complaint 2 not hasty or impetuous 3 steadfast despite opposition, difficulty, or adversity – **~ly** adv

²**patient** n an individual awaiting or under medical care

patina /'patinə/ n, pl **patinas, patinae** /-ni/ 1 a usu green film formed on copper and bronze by weathering 2 a surface appearance of sthg (e g polished wood) that has grown more beautiful esp with age or use

patio /'pati-oh/ n, pl **patios** a usu paved area adjoining a dwelling

patisserie /pə'teesəri, -'ti-/ n 1 sweet cakes and pastry 2 an establishment where patisserie is made and sold

patois /'patwah/ n, pl **patois** /'patwahz/ a provincial dialect other than the standard or literary dialect

patrial /'paytri-əl/ n sby who has a legal right to reside in the UK because one of his/her parents or grandparents was born there

patriarch /'paytri,ahk, 'pat-/ n 1**a** any of the biblical fathers of the human race or of the Hebrew people **b** a man who is father or founder (e g of a race, science, religion, or class of people) **c** a venerable old man 2 the head or bishop of any of various Eastern churches – **~al** adj

patriarchy /'paytri,ahki, 'patri-/ n social organization marked by the supremacy of the father in the clan or family and the reckoning of descent and inheritance in the male line

patrician /pə'trish(ə)n/ n 1 a member of any of the original citizen families of ancient Rome 2 sby of high birth; an aristocrat – **patrician** adj

patricide /'patri,sied/ n (the act of) sby who kills his/her father

patriot /'paytri-ət, 'patri-/ n one who loves and zealously supports his/her country – **~ism** n – **~ic** adj – **~ically** adv

¹**patrol** /pə'trohl/ n 1**a** traversing a district or beat or going the rounds of a garrison or camp for observation or the maintenance of security **b** sing or pl in constr a detachment of men employed for reconnaissance, security, or combat 2 sing or pl in constr a subdivision of a scout troop or guide company that has 6 to 8 members

²**patrol** v -ll- to carry out a patrol (of)

patron /'paytrən; sense 4 pa'tronh/, fem **patroness** /'paytrənəs, -'nes/ n 1 a wealthy or influential supporter of an artist or writer 2 sby who uses his/her wealth or influence to help an individual, institution, or cause 3 a customer 4 the proprietor of an establishment (e g an inn), esp in France

patronage /'patrənij/ n 1 the support or influence of a patron 2 the granting of favours in a condescending way 3 business or activity provided by patrons 4 the power to appoint to government jobs

patron·ize, -ise /'patrəniez/ v 1 to be or act as a patron of 2 to adopt an air of condescension towards

patron 'saint n a saint regarded as having a particular person, group, church, etc under his/her special care and protection

¹**patter** /'patə/ n 1 the sales talk of a street hawker 2 empty chattering talk 3 the talk with which an entertainer accompanies his/her routine

²**patter** v 1 to strike or tap rapidly and repeatedly 2 to run with quick light-sounding steps

¹**pattern** /'patən/ n 1 a form or model proposed for imitation; an example 2 a design, model, or set of instructions for making things 3 a specimen, sample 4 a usu repeated decorative design (e g on fabric) 5 a (natural or chance) configuration

²**pattern** v 1 to make or model according to a pattern 2 to decorate with a design

paunch /pawnch/ n 1 the belly 2 a potbelly – ∼y adj – ∼iness n

pauper /'pawpə/ n a very poor person

¹**pause** /pawz/ n 1 a temporary stop 2 temporary inaction, esp as caused by uncertainty; hesitation

²**pause** v 1 to stop temporarily 2 to linger for a time

pave /payv/ v 1 to lay or cover with material (e g stone or concrete) to form a firm level surface for walking or travelling on 2 to serve as a covering or pavement of — **pave the way** to prepare a smooth easy way; facilitate development

pavement /'payvmənt/ n a paved surface for pedestrians at the side of a road

pavilion /pə'vilyən, -li·ən/ n 1 a large often sumptuous tent 2 a light sometimes ornamental structure in a garden, park, etc 3 *chiefly Br* a permanent building on a sports ground, specif a cricket ground, containing changing rooms and often also seats for spectators

¹**paw** /paw/ n 1 the (clawed) foot of a lion, dog, or other (quadruped) animal 2 a human hand – infml; chiefly humor

²**paw** v 1 to feel or touch clumsily, rudely, or indecently 2 to touch or strike at with a paw 3 to scrape or strike (as if) with a hoof

pawky /'pawki/ adj, *chiefly Br* artfully shrewd, esp in a humorous way; canny – **-kily** adv – **-kiness** n

¹**pawn** /pawn/ n 1 sthg delivered to or deposited with another as a pledge or security (e g for a loan) 2 the state of being pledged – usu + *in*

²**pawn** v to deposit in pledge or as security

³**pawn** n 1 any of the 8 chessmen of each colour of least value that have the power to move only forwards usu 1 square at a time 2 sby or sthg that can be used to further the purposes of another

'**pawn,broker** /-,brohkə/ n one who lends money on the security of personal property pledged in his/her keeping

'**pawn,shop** /-,shop/ n a pawnbroker's shop

pawpaw /'paw,paw/ n an edible yellow tropical fruit

¹**pay** /pay/ v **paid**, (7) **paid** *also* **payed** /payd/ 1 to make due return to or for services done or property received 2a to give in return for goods or service b to discharge indebtedness for 3 to give or forfeit in reparation or retribution 4 to requite according to what is deserved 5 to give, offer, or make willingly or as fitting 6 to be profitable to; be worth the expense or effort to 7 to slacken (e g a rope) and allow to run out – usu + *out* – ∼**er** n

²**pay** n 1 the status of being paid by an employer; employ 2 sthg paid as a salary or wage

³**pay** adj 1 equipped with a coin slot for receiving a fee for use 2 requiring payment

payable /'payəbl/ adj that may, can, or must be paid

'**pay,day** /-,day/ n a regular day on which wages are paid

'**pay,load** /-,lohd/ n 1 the revenue-producing load that a vehicle of transport can carry 2 the explosive charge carried in the warhead of a missile 3 the load (e g instruments) carried in a spacecraft relating directly to the purpose of the flight as opposed to the load (e g fuel) necessary for operation

'**pay,master** /-,mahstə/ n an officer or agent whose duty it is to pay salaries or wages

,**paymaster 'general** n, *often cap P&G* a British government minister who is often made a member of the cabinet and entrusted with special functions

'**payment** /-mənt/ n 1 the act of paying 2 sthg that is paid 3 a recompense (e g a reward or punishment)

'**pay,off** /-,of/ n 1 a profit or reward, esp received by a player in a game 2 a decisive fact or factor resolving a situation or bringing about a definitive conclusion 3 the climax of an incident or chain of events; the denouement – infml

pay off v 1 to pay in full and discharge (an employee) 2 to pay (a debt or a creditor) in full 3 to yield returns

'**pay-,out** n (the act of making) a usu large payment of money – infml

'**pay-,packet** n, *Br* (an envelope containing) sby's wages

'**pay,roll** /-,rohl/ n 1 a list of those entitled to be paid and of the amounts due to them 2 the sum necessary to pay those on a payroll

pay up v to pay in full

pea /pee/ *n pl* **peas** *also* **pease** /peez; *also* **pees**/ **1** (a leguminous climbing plant that bears) an edible rounded protein-rich green seed **2** any of various leguminous plants related to or resembling the pea – usu with a qualifying term

peace /pees/ *n* **1** a state of tranquillity or quiet **2** freedom from disquieting or oppressive thoughts or emotions **3** harmony in personal relations **4a** mutual concord between countries **b** an agreement to end hostilities — **at peace** in a state of concord or tranquillity

peaceable /'peesəbl/ *adj* **1a** disposed to peace; not inclined to dispute or quarrel **b** quietly behaved **2** free from strife or disorder – **bly** *adv*

¹peaceful /-f(ə)l/ *adj* **1** peaceable **2** untroubled by conflict, agitation, or commotion; quiet, tranquil **3** of a state or time of peace – **~ly** *adv* – **~ness** *n*

'peace,time /-,tiem/ *n* a time when a nation is not at war

¹peach /peech/ *n* **1** (a low spreading tree that bears) an edible fruit with a large stone, thin downy skin, and sweet white or yellow flesh **2** a light yellowish pink colour **3** a particularly excellent person or thing; *specif* an unusually attractive girl or young woman – *infml*

²peach *v* to turn informer *on*

peacock /'peekok/ *n* a bird the male of which has very large tail feathers that are usu tipped with eyelike spots and can be erected and spread in a fan shimmering with iridescent colour

,peacock 'blue *n* lustrous greenish blue

¹peak /peek/ *v* to grow thin or sickly

²peak *n* **1** a projecting part on the front of a cap or hood **2** a sharp or pointed end **3** (the top of) a hill or mountain ending in a point **4** the upper aftermost corner of a 4-cornered fore-and-aft sail **5** the highest level or greatest degree, esp as represented on a graph

³peak *v* to reach a maximum

⁴peak *adj* at or reaching the maximum of capacity, value, or activity

¹peaked /peekt/ *adj* having a peak; pointed

²peaked *adj* peaky

peaky /'peeki/ *adj* looking pale and wan; sickly

peal /peel/ *n* **1a** a complete set of changes on a given number of bells **b** a set of bells tuned to the notes of the major scale for change ringing **2** a loud prolonged sound – **peal** *v*

peanut /'peenut/ *n* **1** (the pod or oily edible seed of) a low-branching widely cultivated leguminous plant with showy yellow flowers and pods containing 1 to 3 seeds that ripen in the earth **2** *pl* a trifling amount – *infml*

pear /peə/ *n* (a tree that bears) a large fleshy edible fruit wider at the end furthest from the stalk

¹pearl /puhl/ *n* **1** a dense usu milky white lustrous mass of mother-of-pearl layers, formed as an abnormal growth in the shell of some molluscs, esp oysters, and used as a gem **2** sby or sthg very rare or precious

²pearl *adj* **1a** of or resembling pearl **b** made of or adorned with pearls **2** having medium-sized grains

¹pearly /'puhli/ *adj* resembling, containing, or decorated with pearls or mother-of-pearl

²pearly *n*, *Br* **1** a button made of mother-of-pearl **2** a member of certain cockney families who are traditionally costermongers and entitled to wear a special costume covered with pearlies

peasant /'pez(ə)nt/ *n* **1** a small landowner or farm labourer **2** a usu uneducated person of low social status

'pea,shooter /-,shoohtə/ *n* a toy blowpipe for shooting peas

,pea-'souper /'soohpə/ *also* **pea soup** *n* a heavy fog

peat /peet/ *n* partially carbonized vegetable tissue found in large bogs and used esp as a fuel for domestic heating and as a fertilizer – **~y** *adj*

pebble /'pebl/ *n* a small usu rounded stone, often worn smooth by the action of water

'pebble,dash /-,dash/ *n* a finish for exterior walls consisting of small pebbles embedded in a stucco base

peccadillo /,pekə'diloh/ *n, pl* **peccadilloes, peccadillos** a slight or trifling offence

¹peck /pek/ *n* a unit of volume or capacity equal to 2gall (about 9.1l)

²peck *v* **1** to strike or pierce (repeatedly) with the beak or a pointed tool **b** to kiss perfunctorily **2** to eat reluctantly and in small bites

³peck *v, of a horse* to stumble on landing from a jump

pecker /'pekə/ *n* **1** *chiefly Br* courage – in **keep one's pecker up**; *infml* **2** *NAm* a penis – *vulg*

'pecking ,order /'peking-, **peck order** *n* the natural hierarchy within a flock of birds, esp poultry, in which each bird pecks another lower in the scale without fear of retaliation

peckish /'pekish/ *adj*, *chiefly Br* agreeably hungry – *infml*

pectin /'pektin/ *n* any of various water-soluble substances that yield a gel which acts as a setting agent in jams and fruit jellies

pectoral /'pekt(ə)rəl/ *adj* of, situated in or on, or worn on the chest

peculate /'pekyoolayt/ *v* to embezzle – **-lation** *n*

peculiar /pi'kyoohli-ə, -lyə/ *adj* **1** belonging exclusively to 1 person or group **2** distinctive **3** different from the usual or normal; strange, curious

peculiarity /pi,kyoohli'arəti/ *n* a distinguishing characteristic

pecuniary /pi'kyoohnyəri/ *adj* of or measured in money – *fml* – **-rily** *adv*

pedagogue /'pedəgog/ *n* a teacher, schoolmaster – now chiefly derog

pedagogy /'pedəgoji, -gogi, -goh-/ *n* the science of teaching – **-gic** *adj* – **-gical** *adj* – **-gically** *adv*

¹**pedal** /'pedl/ *n* 1 a lever pressed by the foot in playing a musical instrument 2 a foot lever or treadle by which a part is activated in a mechanism

²**pedal** *adj* of the foot

³**pedal** *v* **-ll-** (*NAm* **-l-** *also* **-ll-**), /'pedl·ing, 'pedling/ 1 to use or work a pedal or pedals 2 to ride a bicycle

pedant /'ped(ə)nt/ *n* one who is unimaginative or unnecessarily concerned with detail, esp in academic matters – **~ic** *adj* – **~ically** *adv*

peddle /'pedl/ *v* **peddling** /'pedling, 'pedl·ing/ 1 to sell goods as a pedlar 2 to deal out or seek to disseminate (e g ideas or opinions)

pedestal /'pedistl/ *n* 1 a base supporting a column, statue, etc 2 a position of esteem or idealized respect

¹**pedestrian** /pi'destri·ən/ *adj* 1 commonplace, unimaginative or 2a going or performed on foot b of or designed for walking

²**pedestrian** *n* sby going on foot; a walker

pedicure /'pedikyoo/ *n* (a) treatment for the care of the feet and toenails – **-curist** *n*

pedigree /'pedigree/ *n* 1 a register recording a line of ancestors 2a an esp distinguished ancestral line; a lineage b the origin and history of sthg 3 the recorded purity of breed of an individual or strain – **pedigree** *adj*

pedlar, *NAm chiefly* **peddler** /'pedlə/ *n* 1 one who travels about offering small wares for sale 2 one who deals in or promotes sthg intangible

¹**pee** /pee/ *v* to urinate – *euph* – *infml*

²**pee** *n* 1 an act of urinating 2 urine *USE infml*

peek /peek/ *v* 1 to look furtively – often + *in* or *out* 2 to take a brief look; glance – **peek** *n*

¹**peel** /peel/ *v* 1 to strip off an outer layer 2a to come off in sheets or scales b to lose an outer layer (e g of skin) 3 to take off one's clothes – usu + *off*; *infml*

²**peel** *n* the skin or rind of a fruit

peeler /'peelə/ *n*, *archaic Br* a policeman

peel off *v* to veer away from an aircraft formation, esp when diving or landing 2 to break away from a group or formation (e g of marchers or ships in a convoy)

¹**peep** /peep/ *v* 1 to utter a feeble shrill sound characteristic of a newly hatched bird; cheep 2 to utter a slight sound

²**peep** *n* 1 a cheep 2 a slight sound, esp spoken – *infml*

³**peep** *v* 1 to look cautiously or slyly, esp through an aperture 2 to begin to emerge (as if) from concealment; show slightly

⁴**peep** *n* 1 the first faint appearance 2 a brief or furtive look; a glance

'**peep hole** /-, hohl/ *n* a hole or crevice to peep through

¹**peer** /piə/ *n* 1 sby who is of equal standing with another 2 a duke, marquess, earl, viscount, or baron of the British peerage

²**peer** *adj* belonging to the same age, grade, or status group

³**peer** *v* to look narrowly or curiously; *esp* to look searchingly at sthg difficult to discern

peerage /'piərij/ *n* **1** *sing or pl in constr* the body of peers **2** the rank or dignity of a peer

peeress /'piəris/ *n* 1 the wife or widow of a peer 2 a woman having a rank in her own right the rank of a peer

'**peerless** /-lis/ *adj* matchless, incomparable

peevish /'peevish/ *adj* querulous in temperament or mood; fretful – **~ly** *adv* – **~ness** *n*

peewit, pewit /'peewit/ *n* a lapwing

¹**peg** /peg/ *n* 1 a small usu cylindrical pointed or tapered piece of wood, metal, or plastic used to pin down or fasten things or to fit into or close holes; a pin 2a a projecting piece used to hold or support b sthg (e g a fact or opinion) used as a support, pretext, or reason 3a any of the wooden pins set in the head of a stringed instrument and turned to regulate the pitch of the strings b a step or degree, esp in estimation – esp in *take sby down a peg (or two)* — **off the peg** mass-produced; ready-made

²**peg** *v* **-gg-** 1 to put a peg into 2 to pin down; restrict 3 to fix or hold (e g prices) at a predetermined level 4 *Br* to fasten (e g washing) to a clothesline with a clothes peg – often + *out*

peg away *v* to work hard and steadily – often + *at*

peg out *v* 1 to mark by pegs 2 *chiefly Br* to die – *infml*

pejorative /pə'jorətiv, *also* 'peej(ə)rətiv/ *adj* rude or belittling, disparaging – **~ly** *adv*

Pekinese, Pekingese /,peeki'neez/ *n* (any of) a breed of small short-legged dogs with a broad flat face and a long coat

pekoe /'peekoh/ *n* a black tea of superior quality

pelf /pelf/ *n* money, riches

pelican /'pelikən/ *n* any of a genus of large web-footed birds with a very large bill containing a pouch in which fish are kept

,**pelican 'crossing** *n* a crossing in the UK at which the movement of vehicles and pedestrians is controlled by pedestrian-operated traffic lights

pellet /'pelit/ *n* 1 a usu small rounded or spherical body (e g of food or medicine) 2 a piece of small shot

pell-mell /,pel 'mel/ *adv* 1 in confusion or disorder 2 in confused haste – **pell-mell** *adj*

pellucid /pi'l(y)oohsid/ *adj* 1 transparent 2 easy to understand *USE fml* or *poetic* – **~ly** *adv*

pelmet /'pelmit/ *n, chiefly Br* a length of board or fabric placed above a window to conceal curtain fixtures

[1]**pelt** /pelt/ *n* **1** a usu undressed skin with its hair, wool, or fur **2** a skin stripped of hair or wool before tanning

[2]**pelt** *v* **1** *of rain* to fall heavily and continuously **2** to move rapidly and vigorously; hurry **3** to hurl, throw **4** to strike with a succession of blows or missiles

[3]**pelt** *n* — **at full pelt** as fast as possible

pelvis /'pelvis/ *n, pl* **pelvises, pelves** /-veez/ a basin-shaped structure of bones at the base of the backbone in many vertebrate animals – **pelvic** *adj*

pemmican *also* **pemican** /'pemikən/ *n* a concentrated food of lean dried meat

[1]**pen** /pen/ *n* **1** a small enclosure for animals **2** a small place of confinement or storage

[2]**pen** *v* **-nn-** to shut in a pen

[3]**pen** *n* **1** an implement for writing or drawing with fluid (e g ink) **2a** a writing instrument as a means of expression **b** a writer – *fml*

[4]**pen** *v* **-nn-** to write – *fml*

[5]**pen** *n* a female swan

penal /'peenl/ *adj* **1** of punishment **2** liable to punishment – **penally** *adv*

penal·ize, -ise /'peenl·iez/ *v* **1** to inflict a penalty on **2** to put at a serious disadvantage

penalty /'pen(ə)lti/ *n* **1** a punishment legally imposed or incurred **2** a forfeiture to which a person agrees to be subject if conditions are not fulfilled **3a** disadvantage, loss, or suffering due to some action **b** a disadvantage imposed for violation of the rules of a sport

'penalty ,area *n* a rectangular area 44yd (about 40m) wide and 18yd (about 16m) deep in front of each goal on a soccer pitch

penance /'penəns/ *n* an act of self-abasement or devotion performed to show repentance for sin

pence /pens/ *pl of* **penny**

penchant /'penchant, 'pon(h)shonh (*Fr* pãʃã)/ *n* a strong leaning; a liking

[1]**pencil** /'pensl/ *n* **1** an implement for writing, drawing, or marking consisting of or containing a slender cylinder or strip of a solid marking substance (e g graphite) **2** a set of light rays, esp when diverging from or converging to a point **3** sthg long and thin like a pencil

[2]**pencil** *v* **-ll-** (*NAm* **-l-, -ll-,**) /'pensl·ing/ to draw, write, or mark with a pencil

pendant *also* **pendent** /'pend(ə)nt/ *n* a hanging ornament; *esp* one worn round the neck

pendent, pendant /'pend(ə)nt/ *adj* **1** suspended **2** jutting or leaning over; overhanging **3** remaining undetermined; pending

[1]**pending** /'pending/ *prep* until – *fml*

[2]**pending** *adj* **1** not yet decided or dealt with **2** imminent, impending

pendulous /'pendyooləs/ *adj* suspended, inclined, or hanging downwards – **~ly** *adv*

pendulum /'pendyooləm/ *n* a body suspended from a fixed point so as to swing freely periodically under the action of gravity and commonly used to regulate movements (e g of clockwork)

penetrate /'penitrayt/ *v* **1a** to pass into or through **b** to enter, esp by overcoming resistance; pierce **2** to see into or through; discern **3** to be absorbed by the mind; be understood – **-tration** *n* – **-trable, -trative** *adj* – **-trability** *n*

penetrating /'penitrayting/ *adj* **1** having the power of entering, piercing, or pervading **2** acute, discerning – **~ly** *adv*

'pen·,friend *n* a person, esp one in another country, with whom a friendship is made through correspondence

penguin /'peng·gwin/ *n* any of various erect short-legged flightless aquatic birds of the southern hemisphere

penicillin /,peni'silin/ *n* any of several antibiotics or antibacterial drugs orig obtained from moulds

peninsula /pə'ninsyoolə/ *n* a piece of land jutting out into or almost surrounded by water; *esp* one connected to the mainland by an isthmus – **~r** *adj*

penis /'peenis/ *n, pl* **penes** /-neez/, **penises** the male sexual organ by means of which semen is introduced into the female during coitus

penitent /'penit(ə)nt/ *adj* feeling or expressing sorrow for sins or offences – **penitent** *n* – **~ly** *adv* – **-tence** *n*

penitential /,peni'tensh(ə)l/ *adj* of penitence or penance – **~ly** *adv*

penitentiary /,peni'tensh(ə)ri/ *n* a prison in the USA

penknife /'pen,nief/ *n* a small pocketknife

'pen ,name *n* an author's pseudonym

pennant /'penənt/ *n* a flag that tapers to a point or has a swallowtail

penniless /'penilis/ *adj* lacking money; poor

pennon /'penən/ *n* a long usu triangular or swallow-tailed streamer typically attached to the head of a lance as a knight's personal flag

penny /'peni/ *n, pl* **pennies, pence** /pens/, **(2) pennies 1a** (a usu bronze coin representing) (1) a former British money unit worth £$^1/_{240}$ (2) a British money unit in use since 1971 that is worth £$^1/_{100}$ **b** a unit of currency of the Irish Republic, Gibraltar and the Falkland Islands **2** *NAm* a cent — **the penny drops** the true meaning finally dawns

penny-'farthing *n, Br* an early type of bicycle having 1 small and 1 large wheel

penology /pee'noləji/ *n* criminology dealing with prison management and the treatment of offenders

'pen ,pusher *n* one whose work involves usu boring or repetitive writing at a desk

¹**pension** /'pensh(ə)n; pãsjɔ̃/ n a fixed sum paid regularly to a person (e g following retirement or as compensation for a wage-earner's death) – ~**able** adj

²**pension** /'ponhsyonh/ n (bed and board provided by) a hotel or boardinghouse, esp in continental Europe

pensioner /'pensh(ə)nə/ n one who receives or lives on an esp old-age pension

pension off v 1 to dismiss or retire from service with a pension 2 to set aside or dispense with after long use – infml

pensive /'pensiv/ adj sadly or dreamily thoughtful – ~**ly** adv – ~**ness** n

pentagon /'pentəgon, -,gon/ n a polygon of 5 angles and 5 sides – ~**al** adj

Pentagon n sing or pl in constr the US military establishment

pentagram /'pentə,gram/ n a 5-pointed star used as a magical symbol

pentathlon /pen'tathlon/ n a contest in which each competitor competes in 5 events

Pentecost /'pentikost/ n (a Christian festival on the 7th Sunday after Easter commemorating the descent of the Holy Spirit on the apostles at) the Jewish festival of Shabuoth

penthouse /'pent,hows/ n 1 a structure (e g a shed or roof) attached to and sloping from a wall or building 2 a structure or dwelling built on the roof of a (tall) building

,pent-'up /pent/ adj confined, held in check

penultimate /pi'nultimət, pe-/ adj next to the last

penumbra /pi'numbrə/ n, pl penumbrae /-bri/, **penumbras** 1 a region of partial darkness (e g in an eclipse) 2 a less dark region surrounding the dark centre of a sunspot

penury /'penyoori/ n severe poverty – fml – **-rious** adj

peony, paeony /'pee-əni/ n any of various garden plants with large usu double red, pink, or white flowers

¹**people** /'peepl/ n 1 human beings in general 2 a group of persons considered collectively 3 the members of a family or kinship 4 the mass of a community 5 a body of persons that are united by a common culture and that often constitute a politically organized group — **of all people** — used to show surprise

²**people** v 1 to supply or fill with people 2 to dwell in; inhabit

pep /pep/ v or n -**pp**- (to liven up or instil with) brisk energy or initiative and high spirits

¹**pepper** /'pepə/ n 1a any of a genus of tropical mostly climbing shrubs with aromatic leaves; esp one with red berries from which black pepper and white pepper are prepared b a condiment made from ground dried pepper berries 2 any of various products similar to pepper; esp a pungent condiment obtained from capsicums – used with a qualifying term 3 (the usu red or green fruit of) a capsicum whose fruits are hot peppers or sweet peppers

²**pepper** v 1a to sprinkle, season, or cover (as if) with pepper b to shower with shot or other missiles 2 to sprinkle

'pepper,corn /-,kawn/ n a dried berry of the pepper plant

'pepper,mint /-,mint/ n 1 (an aromatic essential oil obtained from) a mint with dark green tapering leaves and whorls of small pink flowers 2 a sweet flavoured with peppermint oil

peppery /'pep(ə)ri/ adj 1 hot, pungent 2 hot-tempered, touchy 3 fiery, stinging

'pep ,pill n a tablet of a stimulant drug

'pep ,talk n a usu brief, high-pressure, and emotional talk designed esp to encourage

peptic /'peptik/ adj connected with or resulting from the action of digestive juices

per /pə; strong puh/ prep 1 by the means or agency of; through 2 with respect to every; for each 3 according to (e g per list price)

peradventure /pərəd'venchə, ,puh-/ adv, archaic perhaps, possibly

perambulate /pə'rambyoolayt/ v to stroll (through) USE fml – **-lation** n

perambulator /pə'rambyoolaytə/ n a pram

per 'annum /pər 'anəm/ adv in or for each year

per 'capita /'kapitə/ adv or adj per unit of population; by or for each person

perceive /pə'seev/ v 1 to understand, realize 2 to become aware of through the senses; esp to see, observe – **-ceivable** adj

¹**per cent** /pə 'sent/ adv in or for each 100

²**per cent** n, pl per cent 1 one part in a 100 2 a percentage

³**per cent** adj reckoned on the basis of a whole divided into 100 parts

percentage /pə'sentij/ n 1 a proportion (expressed as per cent of a whole) 2 a share of winnings or profits 3 an advantage, profit – infml

perceptible /pə'septəbl/ adj capable of being perceived, esp by the senses – **-bly** adv – **-bility** n

perception /pə'sepsh(ə)n/ n 1a a result of perceiving; an observation b a mental image; a concept 2 the mental interpretation of physical sensations produced by stimuli from the external world 3 intuitive discernment; insight, understanding

perceptive /pə'septiv/ adj 1 capable of or exhibiting (keen) perception; observant, discerning 2 characterized by sympathetic understanding or insight – **-ly** adv – ~**ness** n – **-tivity** n

¹**perch** /puhch/ n 1 a roost for a bird 2 chiefly Br a unit of length equal to 5¹⁄₂ yds; a rod 3a a resting place or vantage point; a seat b a prominent position USE (3) infml

²**perch** v to alight, settle, or rest, esp briefly or precariously

³**perch** *n* a small European freshwater spiny-finned fish

perchance /pə'chahns/ *adv* perhaps, possibly – usu poetic or humor

percipient /pə'sipi·ənt/ *adj* perceptive, discerning – *fml* **-ence** *n*

percolate /'puhkəlayt/ *v* **1a** to ooze or filter through a substance; seep **b** to prepare coffee in a percolator **2** to become diffused – **-lation** *n*

percolator /'puhkəlaytə/ *n* a coffee pot in which boiling water rising through a tube is repeatedly deflected downwards through a perforated basket containing ground coffee beans

percussion /pə'kush(ə)n/ *n* **1a** the beating or striking of a musical instrument **b** the tapping of the surface of a body part (e g the chest) to learn the condition of the parts beneath (e g the lungs) by the resultant sound **3** *sing or pl in constr* percussion instruments that form a section of a band or orchestra – **-sive** *adj*

percussionist /pə'kush(ə)nist/ *n* one who plays percussion instruments

perdition /pə'dish(ə)n/ *n* eternal damnation; Hell

peregrination /,perigri'naysh(ə)n/ *n* a long and wandering journey, esp in a foreign country – humor

peremptory /pə'rempt(ə)ri/ *adj* **1** admitting no contradiction or refusal **2** expressive of urgency or command **3** (having an attitude or nature) characterized by imperious or arrogant self-assurance – **-rily** *adv*

perennial /pə'renyəl, -ni·əl/ *adj* **1** present at all seasons of the year **2** *of a plant* living for several years, usu with new herbaceous growth each year **3** lasting for a long time or forever; constant – **~ly** *adv*

¹**perfect** /'puhfikt/ *adj* **1a** entirely without fault or defect; flawless **b** corresponding to an ideal standard or abstract concept **2a** accurate, exact **b** lacking in no essential detail; complete **c** absolute, utter **3** of or constituting a verb tense or form that expresses an action or state completed at the time of speaking or at a time spoken of

²**perfect** /pə'fekt/ *v* **1** to make perfect; improve, refine **2** to bring to final form – **~ible** *adj* – **~ibility** *n*

perfection /pə'feksh(ə)n/ *n* **1a** making or being perfect **b** freedom from (moral) fault or defect **c** full development; maturity **2** (an example of) unsurpassable accuracy or excellence

perfectly /'puhfiktli/ *adv* to an adequate extent; quite

perfidy /'puhfidi/ *n* treachery – **-dious** *adj* – **-diously** *adv*

perforate /'puhfə,rayt/ *v* to make a hole through; *specif* to make a line of holes in or between (e g rows of postage stamps in a sheet) to make separation easier

perforce /pə'faws/ *adv* by force of circumstances – *fml*

perform /pə'fawm/ *v* **1** to do; carry out **2a** to do in a formal manner or according to prescribed ritual **b** to give a rendering of; present – **~er** *n*

performance /pə'fawməns/ *n* **1a** the execution of an action **b** sthg accomplished; a deed, feat **2** the fulfilment of a claim, promise, etc **3a** a presentation to an audience of (a character in a) play, a piece of music, etc **4** the ability to perform or work (efficiently or well) **5a** a lengthy or troublesome process or activity **b** a display of bad behaviour

¹**perfume** /'puhfyoohm/ *n* **1** a sweet or pleasant smell; a fragrance **2** a pleasant-smelling (liquid) preparation (e g of floral essences)

²**perfume** /pə'fyoohm, 'puhfyoohm/ *v* to fill or imbue with a sweet smell

perfunctory /pə'fungkt(ə)ri/ *adj* cursory – **-rily** *adv* – **-riness** *n*

pergola /'puhgələ/ *n* (an arbour made by training plants over) a support for climbing plants

perhaps /pə'haps, p(ə)raps/ *adv* possibly but not certainly; maybe

peril /'perəl, -ril/ *n* **1** exposure to the risk of being injured, destroyed, or lost; danger **2** sthg that imperils; a risk

perimeter /pə'rimitə/ *n* **1** (the length of) the boundary of a closed plane figure **2** a line, strip, fence, etc bounding or protecting an area **3** the outer edge or limits of sthg

¹**period** /'piəri·əd/ *n* **1a** a complete sentence **b** the full pause at the end of a sentence; *also, chiefly NAm* a full stop **c** a stop, end **2a** a portion of time **b** the (interval of) time that elapses before a cyclic motion or phenomenon begins to repeat itself; the reciprocal of the frequency **c** (a single cyclic occurrence of) menstruation **3** a chronological division; a stage (of history) **4** any of the divisions of the school day

²**period** *adj* of, representing, or typical of a particular historical period

periodic /,piəri'odik/ *adj* **1** recurring at regular intervals **2** consisting of or containing a series of repeated stages – **~ally** *adv*

¹**periodical** /,piəri'odikl/ *adj* **1** periodic **2** *of a magazine or journal* published at fixed intervals (e g weekly or quarterly)

²**periodical** *n* a periodical publication

periodic table *n* an arrangement of chemical elements in the order of their atomic numbers

¹**peripatetic** /,peripə'tetik/ *n* sby, esp a teacher unattached to a particular school, or sthg that travels about from place to place (on business)

²**peripatetic** *adj* itinerant

peripheral /pə'rif(ə)rəl/ *adj* **1** of, involving, or forming a periphery; *also* of minor significance **2** located away from a centre or central portion; external **3** of, using, or being the outer part of the field of vision

periphery /pə'rif(ə)ri/ n 1 the perimeter of a closed curve (e g a circle or polygon) 2 an outer edge

periphrasis /pə'rifrəsis/ n, pl **periphrases** /-seez/ (a) circumlocution

periscope /'peri,skohp/ n a tubular optical instrument containing lenses, mirrors, or prisms for seeing objects not in the direct line of sight

perish /'perish/ v 1a to be destroyed or ruined b to die, esp in a terrible or sudden way – poetic or journ f *chiefly Br* to deteriorate, spoil

perishable /'perishəbl/ n or adj (sthg, esp food) liable to spoil or decay

perisher /'perishə/ n, *Br* an annoying or troublesome person or thing – infml

perishing /'perishing/ adj 1 freezingly cold 2 damnable, confounded

peritonitis /,peritə'nietəs/ n inflammation of the inside wall of the abdomen

perjure /'puhjə/ v to make (oneself) guilty of perjury – ~ r n

perjury /'puhj(ə)ri/ n the voluntary violation of an oath, esp by a witness

perk up v to (cause to) recover one's vigour or cheerfulness, esp after a period of weakness or depression

perky /'puhki/ adj 1 briskly self-assured; cocky 2 jaunty – **-kily** adv – **-kiness** n

¹**perm** /puhm/ n a long-lasting wave set in the hair by chemicals

²**perm** v to give a perm to

³**perm** v, *Br* to permute; *specif* to pick out and combine (a specified number of teams in a football pool) in all the possible permutations

¹**permanent** /'puhmənənt/ adj 1 continuing or enduring without fundamental or marked change; lasting, stable 2 not subject to replacement according to political circumstances – ~ly adv – **-ence, -ency** n

permeate /'puhmi,ayt/ v to diffuse through or penetrate sthg – **-ation, -ability** n

permissible /pə'misəbl/ adj allowable – **-bly** adv

permission /pə'mish(ə)n/ n formal consent; authorization

permissive /pə'misiv/ adj 1 tolerant; *esp* accepting a relaxed social or sexual morality 2 allowing (but not enforcing) – ~ly adv – ~ness n

¹**permit** /pə'mit/ v -tt- 1 to consent to, usu expressly or formally 2 to give leave; authorize 3 to make possible

²**permit** /'puhmit/ n a written warrant allowing the holder to do or keep sthg

permutation /,puhmyoo'taysh(ə)n/ n 1 a variation or change (e g in character or condition) brought about by rearrangement of existing elements 2 (the changing from one to another of) any of the various possible ordered arrangements of a set of objects, numbers, letters, etc

permute /pə'myooht/ v to change the order or arrangement of; *esp* to arrange successively in all possible ways

pernicious /pə'nishəs, puh-/ adj highly injurious or destructive; deadly – ~ly adv – ~ness n

pernickety /pə'nikəti/ adj 1 fussy about small details; fastidious 2 requiring precision and care

peroration /,perə'raysh(ə)n/ n 1 the concluding part of a discourse, in which the main points are summed up 2 a highly rhetorical speech

peroxide /pə'roksied/ v to bleach (hair) with the chemical compound hydrogen peroxide

¹**perpendicular** /,puhpən'dikyoolə/ adj 1 being or standing at right angles to the plane of the horizon or a given line or plane 2 *cap* of, being, or built in a late Gothic style of architecture prevalent in England from the 15th to the 16th c characterized by large windows, fan vaults, and an emphasis on vertical lines – ~ly adv

²**perpendicular** n a line, plane, or surface at right angles to the plane of the horizon or to another line or surface

perpetrate /'puhpi,trayt/ v to be guilty of performing or doing; commit – **-tration** n – **-trator** n

perpetual /pə'petyoo(ə)l, -choo(ə)l/ adj 1a everlasting b holding sthg (e g an office) for life or for an unlimited time 2 occurring continually; constant 3 *of a plant* blooming continuously throughout the season – ~ly adv

perpetuate /pə'petyoo,ayt, -choo,ayt/ v to make perpetual; cause to last indefinitely – **-ation** n

perpetuity /,puhpi'tyooh-əti/ n (the quality or state of) sthg that is perpetual; eternity

perplex /pə'pleks/ v 1 to puzzle, confuse 2 to complicate

perplexity /pə'pleksəti/ n (sthg that causes) the state of being perplexed or bewildered

perquisite /'puhkwizit/ n 1 sthg held or claimed as an exclusive right or possession 2 a perk – fml

perry /'peri/ n an alcoholic drink made from fermented pear juice

per se /pə 'say/ adv by, of, or in itself; intrinsically

persecute /'puhsi,kyooht/ v 1 to cause to suffer because of race, religion, political beliefs, etc 2 to pester – **-cution** n – **-cutor** n

persevere /,puhsi'viə/ v to persist in a state, enterprise, or undertaking in spite of adverse influences, opposition, or discouragement – **-verance** n

Persian /'puhsh(ə)n, *also* -zh(ə)n/ n or adj (a native, inhabitant, or language) of ancient Persia or modern Iran

persist /pə'sist/ v 1 to go on resolutely or stubbornly in spite of opposition or warning 2 to be insistent in the repetition or pressing of an utterance (e g a question or opinion) 3 to continue to exist, esp past a usual, expected, or normal time

persistent /pə'sist(ə)nt/ *adj* **1** continuing to exist in spite of interference or treatment **2** remaining **2a** beyond the usual period **b** without change in function or structure – ~ly *adv* – **-tence** *n*

person /'puhs(ə)n/ *n* **1** a human being (considered as being different from all others) **2** any of the 3 modes of being in the Trinity as understood by Christians **3** a living human body or its outward appearance — **in person** in one's own bodily presence

personable /'puhs(ə)nəbl/ *adj* pleasing in person; attractive – **-bly** *adv*

personage /'puhs(ə)nij/ *n* **1** a person of rank, note, or distinction **2** a dramatic, fictional, or historical character

personal /'puhs(ə)nl/ *adj* **1** of or affecting a person; private **2a** done in person without the intervention of another **b** carried on between individuals directly **3** of the person or body **4** of or referring to (the character, conduct, motives, or private affairs of) an individual, often in an offensive manner

personality /,puhs(ə)n'aləti/ *n* **1** the totality of an individual's behavioural and emotional tendencies; *broadly* a distinguishing complex of individual or group characteristics **2a** (sby having) distinction or excellence of personal and social traits **b** a person of importance, prominence, renown, or notoriety

personally /'puhs(ə)nli/ *adv* **1** in person **2** as a person; in personality **3** for oneself; as far as oneself is concerned **4** as directed against oneself in a personal way

personal pronoun *n* a pronoun (e g *I*, *you*, or *they*) that expresses a distinction of person

persona non grata /puh,sohnə non 'grahtə/ *adj* personally unacceptable or unwelcome

personification /pə,sonifi'kaysh(ə)n/ *n* **1** the personifying of an abstract quality or thing **2** an embodiment, incarnation

personify /pə'sonifie/ *v* **1** to conceive of or represent as having human qualities or form **2** to be the embodiment of in human form

personnel /,puhsə'nel/ *n* **1** *sing or pl in constr* a body of people employed (e g in a factory, office, or organization) or engaged on a project **2** a division of an organization concerned with the employees and their welfare at work

[1]**perspective** /pə'spektiv/ *adj* of, using, or seen in perspective

[2]**perspective** *n* **1a** the visual appearance of solid objects with respect to their relative distance and position **b** a technique for representing this, esp by showing parallel lines as converging **2** the aspect of an object of thought from a particular standpoint

Perspex /'puh,speks/ *trademark* – used for a transparent plastic

perspicacious /,puhspi'kayshəs/ *adj* of acute mental vision or discernment – *fml* – ~ly *adv* – **-city** *n*

perspiration /,puhspi'raysh(ə)n/ *n* **1** sweating **2** sweat

perspire /pə'spie-ə/ *v* to sweat

persuade /pə'swayd/ *v* **1** to move by argument, reasoning, or entreaty to a belief, position, or course of action **2** to get (sthg) with difficulty *out* of or *from*

persuasion /pə'swayzh(ə)n/ *n* **1a** persuading or being persuaded **b** persuasiveness **2a** an opinion held with complete assurance **b** (a group adhering to) a particular system of religious beliefs

persuasive /pə'swaysiv, -ziv/ *adj* tending or able to persuade – ~ly *adv* – ~ness *n*

pert /puht/ *adj* **1** impudent and forward; saucy **2** trim and chic; jaunty – ~ly *adv* – ~ness *n*

pertain /pə'tayn/ *v* to belong *to*; be about, or appropriate *to*

pertinacious /,puhti'nayshəs/ *adj* clinging resolutely or stubbornly to an opinion, purpose, or design – *fml* – ~ly *adv* – **-city** *n*

pertinent /'puhtinənt/ *adj* clearly relevant (to the matter in hand) – ~ly *adv* – **-nence** *n*

perturb /pə'tuhb, puh-/ *v* **1** to disturb greatly in mind; disquiet **2** to throw into confusion; disorder – ~**ation** *n*

peruse /pə'roohz/ *v* **1** to study – *fml* **2** to look over the contents of (e g a book) – **perusal** *n*

pervade /pə'vayd, puh-/ *v* to become diffused throughout every part of

perverse /pə'vuhs, puh-/ *adj* **1a** obstinate in opposing what is right, reasonable, or accepted; wrongheaded **b** arising from or indicative of stubbornness or obstinacy **2** unreasonably opposed to the wishes of others; uncooperative, contrary – ~ly *adv* – ~ness *n* – **-sity** *n*

perversion /pə'vuhsh(ə)n, puh-/ *n* **1** perverting or being perverted **2** abnormal sexual behaviour

[1]**pervert** /pə'vuht/ *v* **1** to cause to turn aside or away from what is good, true, or morally right; corrupt **2a** to divert to a wrong end or purpose; misuse **b** to twist the meaning or sense of; misinterpret

[2]**pervert** /'puhvuht/ *n* a person given to some form of sexual perversion

peseta /pə'seetə, pə'saytə/ *n* the basic unit of currency of Spain

pessary /'pesəri/ *n* **1** a vaginal suppository **2** a device worn in the vagina to support the uterus or prevent conception

pessimism /'pesi,miz(ə)m/ *n* a tendency to stress the adverse aspects of a situation or event or to expect the worst possible outcome – **-mist** *n* – **-mistic** *adj* – **-mistically** *adv*

pest /pest/ *n* **1** a plant or animal capable of causing damage or carrying disease **2** sby or sthg that pesters or annoys; a nuisance

pester /'pestə/ *v* to harass with petty irritations; annoy

pesticide /'pestisied/ *n* a chemical used to destroy insects and other pests of crops, domestic animals, etc

pestilence /'pestiləns/ *n* a virulent and devastating epidemic disease

pestilent /'pestilənt/ *adj* **1** destructive of life; deadly **2** morally harmful; pernicious

pestle /'pesl/ *n* **1** a usu club-shaped implement for pounding substances in a mortar **2** any of various devices for pounding, stamping, or pressing

¹**pet** /pet/ *n* **1** a domesticated animal kept for companionship rather than work or food **2** sby who is treated with unusual kindness or consideration; a favourite **3** *chiefly Br* darling – used chiefly by women as an affectionate form of address

²**pet** *adj* **1a** kept or treated as a pet **b** for pet animals **2** expressing fondness or endearment **3** favourite

³**pet** *v* **-tt- 1** to treat with unusual kindness and consideration; pamper **2** to engage in amorous embracing, caressing, etc

⁴**pet** *n* a fit of peevishness, sulkiness, or anger

petal /'petl/ *n* any of the modified often brightly coloured leaves making up the flower head of a plant

petard /pe'tahd, pi-/ *n* a case containing an explosive for military demolitions

petit bourgeois /,peti 'booəzh·wah (*Fr* pəti burʒwa)/ *n, pl* **petits bourgeois** /∼/ a member of the lower middle class

petite /pə'teet/ *adj, esp of a woman* having a small trim figure

¹**petition** /pi'tish(ə)n/ *n* **1** an earnest request; an entreaty **2** (a document embodying) a formal written request to a superior – **∼er** *n*

²**petition** *v* to make an esp formal written request (to or for)

petrel /'petrəl/ *n* any of the smaller long-winged seabirds (e g a storm petrel) that fly far from land

petrify /'petrifie/ *v* **1** to convert (as if) into stone or a stony substance **2** to confound with fear, amazement, or awe; paralyse – **-faction** *n*

petrochemical /,petroh'kemikl, -trə-/ *n* a chemical obtained from petroleum or natural gas

petrol /'petrəl/ *n, chiefly Br* a volatile inflammable liquid used as a fuel for internal-combustion engines

petroleum /pə'trohli·əm, -lyəm/ *n* an oily inflammable usu dark liquid widely occurring in the upper strata of the earth that is refined to produce petrol and other products

pe,troleum 'jelly *n* a semisolid obtained from petroleum and used esp as the basis of ointments

petrology /pe'troləji/ *n* a science that deals with the origin, structure, composition, etc of rocks – **-gist** *n*

¹**petticoat** /'peti,koht/ *n* a skirt designed to be worn as an undergarment

²**petticoat** *adj* of or exercised by women; female – chiefly humor or derog

petty /'peti/ *adj* **1** having secondary rank or importance; *also* trivial **2** small-minded – **-tily** *adv* **-tiness** *n*

,**petty 'cash** *n* cash kept on hand for payment of minor items

petty officer *n* a non-commissioned naval officer

petulant /'petyoolənt/ *adj* ill humoured; peevish – **∼ly** *adv* **-lance** *n*

petunia /pi'tyoohnyə, -ni·ə/ *n* any of a genus of plants with large brightly coloured funnel-shaped flowers

pew /pyooh/ *n* **1** a bench fixed in a row for the use of the congregation in a church **2** *Br* a seat – infml

pewter /'pyoohtə/ *n* (utensils, vessels, etc made of) an alloy of tin and lead

pfennig /'(p)fenig, -nikh (əer 'pfenic)/ *n, pl* **pfennigs, pfennige** /-nigə (*Ger* -nigə)/ *often cap* a unit of currency of the Federal Republic of Germany and the German Democratic Republic

PG *n or adj* (a film that is) certified in Britain as suitable for all ages although parental guidance is recommended for children under 15

pH /,pee 'aych/ *n* a measure of the acidity or alkalinity of a solution, on a scale of 0 to 14 with 7 representing neutrality

phagocyte /'fagə,siet/ *n* a cell, esp white blood cell, that engulfs foreign material (e g bacteria) and consumes debris (e g from tissue injury)

phalanx /'falangks/ *n, pl* **phalanges** /fə'lanjeez/, **phalanxes** *sing or pl in constr* **1** a body of troops, esp those of ancient Greece, in close array **2** a massed arrangement of people, animals, or things

phallus /'faləs/ *n, pl* **phalli** /-lie/ **phalluses** (a symbol or representation of) the penis – **phallic** *adj*

phantasmagoria /,fantazmə'gawri·ə/ *n* a constantly shifting, confused succession of things seen or imagined (e g in a dreaming or feverish state) – **-goric** *adj* **-gorical** *adj*

¹**phantasy** /'fantasi/ *v or n* (to) fantasy

¹**phantom** /'fantəm/ *n* **1** sthg (e g a ghost) apparent to the senses but with no substantial existence **2** sthg existing only in the imagination

²**phantom** *adj* **1** of or being a phantom **2** fictitious, dummy

pharaoh /'feəroh/ *n, often cap* a ruler of ancient Egypt

pharisaic /,fari'say·ik/, **pharisaical** /-kl/ *adj* **1** *cap* of the Pharisees **2** marked by hypocritical self-righteousness – **-ism** *n*

pharisee /'farisee/ *n* **1** *cap* a member of a Jewish party noted for strict adherence to (their own oral traditions interpreting) the Torah **2** a pharisaic person

¹**pharmaceutical** /,fahmə'syoohtikl/ *also* **pharmaceutic** *adj* of or engaged in pharmacy or in the manufacture of medicinal substances

²**pharmaceutical** *n* a medicinal drug

pharmacology /,fahmə'koləji/ *n* the science of drugs and their effect on living things – **-gist** *n*

pharmacopoeia /,fahməkə'pee-ə/ *n* an (official) book describing drugs, chemicals, and medicinal preparations

pharmacy /'fahməsi/ *n* 1 the preparation, compounding, and dispensing of drugs 2 a place where medicines are compounded or dispensed – **pharmacist** *n*

¹**phase** /fayz/ *n* 1a a discernible part or stage in a course, development, or cycle b an aspect or part (e g of a problem) under consideration 2 a stage of a regularly recurring motion or cyclic process (e g an alternating electric current) with respect to a starting point or standard position

²**phase** *v* 1 to conduct or carry out by planned phases 2 to schedule (e g operations) or contract for (e g goods or services) to be performed or supplied as required

pheasant /'fez(ə)nt/ *n pl* **pheasants**, *esp collectively* **pheasant** any of numerous large often long-tailed and brightly coloured Old World (game) birds

phenomenal /fi'nominl/ *adj* extraordinary, remarkable – **-ly** *adv*

phenomenon /fi'nominən/ *n, pl* **phenomena** /-nə/ *also* **phenomenons** 1 an object of sense perception rather than of thought or intuition 2 a fact or event that can be scientifically described and explained 3 a rare, exceptional, unusual, or abnormal person, thing, or event

phial /'fie-əl/ *n* a small closed or closable vessel, esp for holding liquid medicine

philander /fi'landə/ *v* to have many casual love affairs – **-er** *n*

philanthropy /fi'lanthrəpi/ *n* 1 active effort to promote the welfare of others 2 a philanthropic act or gift – **-pic** *adj* – **-pically** *adv*

philately /fi'latəli/ *n* the study and collection of (postage) stamps – **-list** *n* – **-lic** *adj*

philistine /'filistien/ *n* 1 *cap* a native or inhabitant of ancient Philistia 2 *often cap* a person who professes indifference or opposition to intellectual or aesthetic values – **-tinism** *n*

philology /fi'loləji/ *n* (historical and comparative) linguistics – **-logical** *adj* – **-logist** *n*

philosopher /fi'losəfə/ *n* 1 a specialist in philosophy 2 a person whose philosophical viewpoint enables him/her to meet trouble with equanimity

philosophical /,filə'sofikl/ *adj* 1 of philosophers or philosophy 2 calm in the face of trouble – **~ly** *adv*

philosoph·ize, -ise /fi'losəfiez/ *v* 1 to engage in philosophical reasoning 2 to expound a trite philosophy

philosophy /fi'losəfi/ *n* 1 the study of the nature of knowledge and existence and the principles of moral and aesthetic value 2 the philosophical principles, teachings, or beliefs of a specified individual, group, or period 3 equanimity in the face of trouble or stress

philtre, *NAm chiefly* **philter** /'filtə/ *n* a potion or drug reputed to have the power to arouse sexual passion

phlegm /flem/ *n* 1 thick mucus secreted in abnormal quantities in the respiratory passages 2a dull or apathetic coldness or indifference b intrepid coolness; composure

phlegmatic /fleg'matik/ *adj* having or showing a slow and stolid temperament – **~ally** *adv*

phloem /'floh·em/ *n* a complex vascular tissue of higher plants that functions chiefly in the conduction of soluble food substances (e g sugars)

phlox /floks/ *n pl* **phlox**, *esp for different types* **phloxes** any of a genus of American plants with red, purple, white, or variegated flowers

phobia /'fohbi·ə, -byə/ *n* an exaggerated and illogical fear of sthg – **phobic** *n, adj*

phoenix /'feeniks/ *n* a mythical bird believed to live for 500 years, burn itself on a pyre, and rise alive from the ashes to live another cycle

¹**phone** /fohn/ *n* a telephone

²**phone** *v* to telephone – often + *up*

'**phone-,in** *n* a broadcast programme in which viewers or listeners can participate by telephone

phonetic /fə'netik/, **phonetical** /-kl/ *adj* 1a of spoken language or speech sounds b of the study of phonetics 2 representing speech sounds by symbols that each have 1 value only – **~ally** *adv*

pho'netics *n pl* 1 *sing in constr* the study and classification of speech sounds 2 *sing or pl in constr* the system of speech sounds of a language

phoney, *NAm chiefly* **phony** /'fohni/ *adj* not genuine or real: e g a counterfeit; false, sham b *of a person* pretentious – **phoney** *n*

phosphate /'fosfayt/ *n* a salt or ester of a phosphoric acid; esp one used as a fertilizer

phosphorescence /,fosfə'res(ə)ns/ *n* emission of light without noticeable heat – **-cent** *adj*

phosphorus /'fosf(ə)rəs/ *n* a nonmetallic element of the nitrogen family that occurs widely, esp as phosphates, 1 form of which ignites readily in warm moist air – **-ric** *adj*

¹**photo** /'fohtoh/ *v or n* **photos; photoing; photoed;** *pl* **photos** (to) photograph

²**photo** *adj* photographic

¹**photocopy** /'fohtə,kopi, -toh-/ *n* a photographic reproduction of graphic matter

²**photocopy** *v* to make a photocopy (of) – **-pier** *n*

photoelectric /,fohtoh·i'lektrik/ *adj* involving, relating to, or using any of various electrical effects caused by the interaction of radiation (e g light) with matter

photoelectric cell *n* a cell whose electrical properties are modified by the action of light

photo finish n 1 a race finish so close that the winner is only revealed (as if) by a photograph of the contestants as they cross the finishing line 2 a close contest

photogenic /ˌfohtə'jenik, -'jeenik/ adj suitable for being photographed

[1]**photograph** /'fohtə,grahf, -,graf/ n a picture or likeness obtained by photography

[2]**photograph** v to take a photograph – ~er n – ~ic adj – ~ically adv

photography /fə'togrəfi/ n the art or process of producing images on a sensitized surface (e g a film) by the action of radiant energy, esp light

photosynthesis /ˌfohtoh'sinthəsis/ n the formation of carbohydrates from carbon dioxide in the chlorophyll-containing tissues of plants exposed to light

[1]**phrase** /frayz/ n 1 a brief usu idiomatic or pithy expression; esp a catchphrase 2 a group of musical notes forming a natural unit of melody 3 a group of 2 or more grammatically related words that do not form a clause

[2]**phrase** v 1 to express in words or in appropriate or telling terms 2 to divide into melodic phrases

phrenology /fri'nolaji/ n the study of the shape and esp irregularities of the skull as a supposed indicator of mental faculties and character

phylloxera /ˌfilok'siərə/ n any of various plant lice that are destructive to many plants (e g grapevines)

phylum /'filəm/ n, pl **phyla** /-lə/ a major group of related species in the classification of plants and animals

physical /'fizikl/ adj 1 having material existence; perceptible, esp through the senses, and subject to the laws of nature 2 of natural science or physics 3 of the body, esp as opposed to the spirit – ~ly adv

physical 'jerks n bodily exercises – infml

physician /fi'zish(ə)n/ n a person skilled in the art of healing

physics /'fiziks/ n pl but sing or pl in constr 1 a science that deals with (the properties and interactions of) matter and energy in such fields as mechanics, heat, electricity, magnetism, atomic structure, etc 2 the physical properties and phenomena of a particular system

physiology /ˌfizi'olaji/ n 1 biology that deals with the functions and activities of life or of living matter (e g organs, tissues, or cells) and the physical and chemical phenomena involved 2 the physiological activities of (part of) an organism or a particular bodily function – **-gist** n – **-gical** adj

physiotherapy /ˌfizi-oh'therəpi/ n the treatment of disease by physical and mechanical means (e g massage and regulated exercise) – **-pist** n

physique /fi'zeek/ n the form or structure of a person's body

[1]**pi** /pie/ n, pl **pis** /piez/ 1 the 16th letter of the Greek alphabet 2 (the symbol p denoting) the ratio of the circumference of a circle to its diameter with a value, to 8 decimal places, of 3.14159265

[2]**pi** adj, Br pious – derog

pianissimo /ˌpee-ə'nisimoh/ adv or adj very soft

pianist /'pee-ənist/ n a performer on the piano

[1]**piano** /pi'ahnoh, 'pyah-/ adv or adj in a soft or quiet manner

[2]**piano** /pi'anoh/ n, pl **pianos** a stringed instrument having steel wire strings that sound when struck by felt-covered hammers operated from a keyboard

picador /'pikə,daw/ n, pl **picadors, picadores** /-daw,rayz/ a horseman who in a bullfight prods the bull with a lance to weaken its neck and shoulder muscles

picaresque /ˌpikə'resk/ adj of or being fiction narrating in loosely linked episodes the adventures of a rogue

piccalilli /ˌpikə'lili/ n a hot relish of chopped vegetables, mustard, and spices

piccolo /'pikə,loh/ n, pl **piccolos** a flute with a range an octave higher than an ordinary flute's

[1]**pick** /pik/ v 1a to remove bit by bit b to remove covering or clinging matter from 2a to gather by plucking b to choose, select 3 to provoke 4a to dig into, esp in order to remove unwanted matter; probe b to pluck with a plectrum or with the fingers 5 to unlock with a device (e g a wire) other than the key 6 to make (one's way) carefully on foot — **pick and choose** to select with care and deliberation — **pick at 1** to find fault with, esp in a petty way 2 to eat sparingly and with little interest; toy with — **pick on 1** to single out for unpleasant treatment or an unpleasant task 2 to single out for a particular purpose or for special attention — **pick someone's brains** to obtain ideas or information from sby — **pick someone/something to pieces** to subject to systematic adverse criticism

[2]**pick** n 1 the act or privilege of choosing or selecting; a choice 2 sing or pl in constr the best or choicest

[3]**pick** n 1 pick, pickaxe a heavy wooden-handled tool with a head that is pointed at one or both ends 2 a plectrum

picker /'pikə/ n a person or machine that picks crops

[1]**picket** /'pikit/ n 1 a pointed or sharpened stake, post, or pale 2 sing or pl in constr a small body of troops detached to guard an army from surprise attack 3 a person posted by a trade union at a place of work to enforce a strike

[2]**picket** v 1 to enclose, fence, or fortify with pickets 2 to tether 3a to post pickets at b to walk or stand in front of as a picket – ~er n

pickle /'pikl/ *n* **1** a brine or vinegar solution in which meat, fish, vegetables, etc are preserved **2** (an article of) food preserved in a pickle; *also* chutney – often *pl* **3** a difficult situation – *infml* – **pickle** *v*

¹**'pick,pocket** /-,pokit/ *n* one who steals from pockets or bags

pickup /-,up/ *n* **1** sby or sthg picked up: e g **1a** a hitchhiker who is given a lift **b** a casual acquaintance made with the intention of having sex **2** a device (e g on a record player) that converts mechanical movements into electrical signals **3** a light motor truck having an open body with low sides and tailboard

pick up *v* **b** to gather together; collect; *also* tidy **2** to take (passengers or freight) into a vehicle **3a** to acquire casually or by chance **b** to acquire by study or experience; learn **4** to enter informally into conversation or companionship with (a previously unknown person), usu with the intention of having sex **5** to bring within range of sight, hearing, or a sensor **6** to revive or improve **7** to resume after a break; continue

¹**picnic** /'piknik/ *n* **1** (the food eaten at) an outing that includes an informal meal, usu lunch, eaten in the open **2** a pleasant or amusingly carefree experience; *also* an easily accomplished task or feat – *infml*

²**picnic** *v* **-ck-** to go on a picnic – **picnicker** *n*

pictorial /pik'tawri‧əl/ *adj* **1** of (a) painting or drawing **2** consisting of or illustrated by pictures – **~ly** *adv*

¹**picture** /'pikchə/ *n* **1** a design or representation made by painting, drawing, etc **2a** a description so vivid or graphic as to suggest a mental image or give an accurate idea of sthg **b** a presentation of the relevant or characteristic facts concerning a problem or situation **3a** a film **b** *pl, chiefly Br* the cinema — **in the picture** fully informed and up to date

²**picture** *v* **1** to paint or draw a representation, image, or visual conception of; depict **2** to describe graphically in words **3** to form a mental image of; imagine

picturesque /,pikchə'resk/ *adj* **1** pleasing to the eye **2** quaint, charming **3** vivid – **~ly** *adv* – **~ness** *n*

¹**piddle** /'pidl/ *v* **piddling** /'pidling/ **1** to act or work in an idle or trifling manner **2** to urinate *USE* infml

²**piddle** *n* **1** urine **2** an act of urinating *USE* infml

pidgin /'pijin/ *n* a language based on 2 or more languages and used esp for trade between people with different native languages

¹**pie** /pie/ *n* **1** a magpie **2** a variegated animal

²**pie** *n* a dish consisting of a sweet or savoury filling covered or encased by pastry and baked in a container

piebald /'pie,bawld/ *adj* **1** *esp of a horse* of different colours; *specif* spotted or blotched with different colours, esp black and white **2** composed of incongruous parts; heterogeneous

¹**piece** /pees/ *n* **1** a part of a whole; *esp* a part detached, cut, etc from a whole **2** an object or individual regarded as a unit of a kind or class **3** a standard quantity (e g of length, weight, or size) in which sthg is made or sold **4a** a literary, artistic, dramatic, or musical work **b** a passage to be recited **5** a man used in playing a board game; *esp* a chessman of rank superior to a pawn — **piece of one's mind** a severe scolding — **of a piece** alike, consistent — **to pieces 1** into fragments **2** out of control

²**piece** *v* **1** to repair, renew, or complete by adding pieces; patch – often + *up* **2** to join into a whole – *together*

¹**'piece,meal** /-meel/ *adv* **1** one piece at a time; gradually **2** in pieces or fragments; apart

²**piecemeal** *adj* done, made, or accomplished piece by piece or in a fragmentary way

'piece,work /-,wuhk/ *n* work that is paid for at a set rate per unit

pied /pied/ *adj* having patches of 2 or more colours

,pie-'eyed *adj* drunk – *infml*

pier /piə/ *n* **1** an intermediate support for the adjacent ends of 2 bridge spans **2** a structure extending into navigable water for use as a landing place, promenade, etc

pierce /'piəs/ *v* **1** to enter or thrust into sharply or painfully **2** to make a hole in or through **3** to penetrate with the eye or mind **4** to move or affect the emotions, esp sharply or painfully

piercing /'piəsing/ *adj* penetrating: e g **a** loud, shrill **b** perceptive **c** penetratingly cold; biting **d** cutting, incisive – **~ly** *adv*

piety /'pie‧əti/ *n* **1** devoutness **2** dutifulness, esp to parents

¹**pig** /pig/ *n* **1** *chiefly Br* any of various (domesticated) stout-bodied short-legged omnivorous mammals with a thick bristly skin and a long mobile snout **2** sby like or suggestive of a pig in habits or behaviour (e g in dirtiness, greed, or selfishness) **3** a policeman – slang; derog

²**pig** *v* **-gg- 1** to live like a pig – + *it* **2a** to eat (food) greedily **b** to overindulge (oneself)

pigeon /'pij(ə)n/ *n* any of a family of birds with a stout body and smooth and compact plumage, many of which are domesticated or live in urban areas

¹**'pigeon,hole** /-,hohl/ *n* **1** a small open compartment (e g in a desk or cabinet) for letters or documents **2** a neat category which usu fails to reflect actual complexities

²**pigeonhole** *v* **1a** to place (as if) in the pigeonhole of a desk **b** to lay aside; shelve **2** to assign to a category; classify

¹'piggy,back /-,bak/ *adv* up on the back and shoulders

²piggyback *n* a ride on the back and shoulders of another

pigheaded /pig'hedid/ *adj* obstinate, stubborn – ~**ly** *adv* – ~**ness** *n*

'pig ,iron *n* crude iron from the blast furnace before refining

pigment /'pigmənt/ *n* **1** a substance that colours other materials **2** any of various colouring matters in animals and plants – **pigment** *v*

pigmentation /,pigmən'taysh(ə)n/ *n* **1** (excessive) coloration with, or deposition of, (bodily) pigment

pigmy /'pigmi/ *n* **1** a member of a people of equatorial Africa who are under 5ft in height **2** a dwarf; *also* sby markedly inferior or insignificant in a particular area

pignut /'pig,nut/ *n* a common plant of the carrot family

'pig,sty /-,stie/ *n* **1** an enclosure with a covered shed for pigs **2** a dirty, untidy, or neglected place

'pig,tail /-,tayl/ *n* **1** a tight plait of hair, esp at the back of the head **2** either of 2 bunches of hair worn loose or plaited at either side of the head by young girls – ~**ed** *adj*

¹pike /piek/ *n* a large long-snouted fish-eating bony fish widely distributed in cooler parts of the N hemisphere

²pike *n* a weapon consisting of a long wooden shaft with a pointed steel head that was used by foot soldiers until superseded by the bayonet

pilaster /pi'lastə/ *n* an upright rectangular column that is usu embedded in a wall

pilau /'pilow, 'pee,low/ *n* (a dish of) seasoned rice often with meat or vegetables

pilchard /'pilchəd/ *n* a fish of the herring family that occurs in great schools along the coasts of Europe

¹pile /piel/ *n* a beam of timber, steel, reinforced concrete, etc driven into the ground to carry a vertical load

²pile *n* **1a** a quantity of things heaped together **b** a large quantity, number, or amount **2** a large building or group of buildings **3** a great amount of money; a fortune **4** an atomic reactor

³pile *v* **1** to lay or place in a pile; stack – often + *up* **2** to move or press forwards (as if) in a mass; crowd — **pile it on** to exaggerate

⁴pile *n* a soft raised surface on a fabric or carpet consisting of cut threads or loops

⁵pile *n* a haemorrhoid – usu pl

'pile,up /-,up/ *n* a collision involving usu several motor vehicles and causing damage or injury

pile up *v* to accumulate

pilfer /'pilfə/ *v* to steal stealthily in small amounts or to small value – ~**er** *n* – ~**age** *n*

pilgrim /'pilgrim/ *n* a person making a pilgrimage

pilgrimage /'pilgrimij/ *n* a journey to a shrine or sacred place as an act of devotion, in order to acquire spiritual merit, or as a penance

,Pilgrim 'Fathers *n pl* the English colonists who settled at Plymouth, Massachusetts, in 1620

pill /pil/ *n* **1a** a small rounded solid mass of medicine to be swallowed whole **b** an oral contraceptive taken daily by a woman over a monthly cycle – + *the* **2** sthg repugnant or unpleasant that must be accepted or endured

pillage /'pilij/ *v* to plunder ruthlessly; loot – **pillage** *n*

pillar /'pilə/ *n* **1a** a firm upright support for a superstructure **b** a usu ornamental column or shaft **2** a chief supporter; a prop — **from pillar to post** from one place or one situation to another

'pillar ,box *n* a red pillar-shaped public letter box

pillbox /'pil,boks/ *n* **1** a box for pills; *esp* a shallow round box made of pasteboard **2** a small low concrete weapon emplacement **3** a small round brimless hat with a flat crown and straight sides

¹pillion /'pilyən/ *n* a saddle or seat for a passenger on a motorcycle or motor scooter

²pillion *adv* (as if) on a pillion

pillory /'piləri/ *n* **1** a device for publicly punishing offenders consisting of a wooden frame with holes for the head and hands **2** a means for exposing one to public scorn or ridicule – **pillory** *v*

¹pillow /'piloh/ *n* a usu rectangular cloth bag (e g of cotton) filled with soft material (e g down) and used to support the head of a reclining person

²pillow *v* **1** to rest or lay (as if) on a pillow **2** to serve as a pillow for

'pillow,case /-,kays/ *n* a removable washable cover for a pillow

¹pilot /'pielət/ *n* **1** sby qualified and usu licensed to conduct a ship into and out of a port or in specified waters **2** a guide, leader **3** sby who handles or is qualified to handle the controls of an aircraft or spacecraft

²pilot *v* **1** to act as a guide to; lead or conduct over a usu difficult course **2a** to direct the course of **b** to act as pilot of

³pilot *adj* serving as a guide, activator, or trial

'pilot ,light *n* a small permanent flame used to ignite gas at a burner

pimp /pimp/ *n* a man who solicits clients for a prostitute or brothel

pimpernel /'pimpə,nel/ *n* any of several plants of the primrose family: e g **a** the scarlet pimpernel, having usu red flowers that close in cloudy weather **b** the yellow pimpernel, having bright yellow flowers

pimple /'pimpl/ *n* a small solid inflamed (pus-containing) swelling – **-ply** *adj* – ~**d** *adj*

¹pin /pin/ *n* **1** a piece of solid material (e g wood or metal) used esp for fastening separate articles together or as a support **2a** a small thin pointed piece of metal with a head used esp for fastening cloth, paper, etc **b** sthg of small value; a trifle **3** a projecting metal bar on a plug which is inserted into a socket **4** a leg – infml; usu pl

²**pin** v **-nn- 1a** to fasten, join, or secure with a pin **b** to hold fast or immobile **2a** to attach, hang **b** to assign the blame or responsibility for

pinafore /'pinə,faw/ n **1** an apron, usu with a bib **2** *also* **pinafore dress** a sleeveless usu low-necked dress designed to be worn over another garment (e g a blouse)

pinball /'pin,bawl/ n a game in which a ball is propelled across a sloping surface at pins and targets that score points if hit

pince-nez /'pans ,nay, 'pins- (*Fr* pɛs ne)/ n, pl **pince-nez** /~/ glasses clipped to the nose by a spring

pincer /'pinsə/ n **1a** pl an instrument having 2 short handles and 2 grasping jaws working on a pivot and used for gripping things **b** a claw (e g of a lobster) resembling a pair of pincers **2** either part of a double military envelopment of an enemy position

¹**pinch** /pinch/ v **1a** to squeeze or compress painfully (e g between the finger and thumb) **b** to prune the tip of (a plant or shoot), usu to induce branching – + *out* or *back* **2** to subject to strict economy or want **3a** to steal – slang **b** to arrest – slang – ~ **ed** adj

²**pinch** n **1a** a critical juncture; an emergency **b(1)** pressure, stress **b(2)** hardship, privation **2a** an act of pinching **b** as much as may be taken between the finger and thumb — **at a pinch** in an emergency — **with a pinch of salt** with reservations as to the validity of sthg

pincushion /'pin,koosh(ə)n/ n a small cushion in which pins are stuck ready for use, esp in sewing

pin down v **1** to force (sby) to state his/her position or make a decision **2** to define precisely **3** to fasten down; prevent from moving

¹**pine** /pien/ v **1** to lose vigour or health (e g through grief) – often + *away* **2** to yearn intensely and persistently, esp for sthg unattainable

²**pine** n **1** (any of various trees related to) any of a genus of coniferous evergreen trees which have slender elongated needles **2** the straight-grained white or yellow usu durable and resinous wood of a pine

pineapple /'pienapl/ n **1** (the large oval edible succulent yellow-fleshed fruit of) a tropical plant with rigid spiny leaves and a dense head of small flowers

ping /ping/ v *or* n (to make) a sharp ringing sound

Ping-Pong /'ping ,pong/ n *trademark* – used for table tennis

¹**pinion** /'pinyən/ n **1** (the end section of) a bird's wing **2** a bird's feather

²**pinion** v **1** to restrain (a bird) from flight, esp by cutting off the pinion of a wing **2** to disable or restrain by binding the arms

³**pinion** n a gear with a small number of teeth designed to mesh with a larger gear wheel or rack

¹**pink** /pingk/ v to cut a zigzag or saw-toothed edge on

²**pink** n any of a genus of plants related to the carnation and widely grown for their white, pink, red, or variegated flowers

³**pink** adj **1** of the colour pink **2** holding moderately radical political views — **in the pink** in the best of health — infml

⁴**pink** n **1** any of various shades of pale red **2** (the scarlet colour of) a fox hunter's coat

⁵**pink** v, *Br, of an internal-combustion engine* to make a series of sharp popping noises because of faulty combustion of the fuel-air mixture

'**pin ,money** n **1a** extra money earned by sby, esp a married woman (e g in a part-time job) **b** money set aside for the purchase of incidentals **2** a trivial amount of money

pinnacle /'pinəkl/ n **1** an architectural ornament resembling a small spire and used esp to crown a buttress **2** a lofty mountain **3** the highest point of development or achievement

pinnate /'pinayt, -nət/ adj resembling a feather

pinny /'pini/ n a pinafore – infml

¹**pinpoint** /'pin,poynt/ v **1** to fix, determine, or identify with precision **2** to cause to stand out conspicuously; highlight

²**pinpoint** adj **1** extremely small, fine, or precise **2** located, fixed, or directed with extreme precision

³**pinpoint** n a very small point or area

,**pins and 'needles** n pl a pricking tingling sensation in a limb recovering from numbness

'**pin ,stripe** /-,striep/ n **1** a very thin stripe, esp on a fabric **2** a suit or trousers with pinstripes – often pl with sing. meaning

pint /pient/ n **1** a unit of liquid capacity equal to ¹/₈gal **2** a pint of liquid, esp milk or beer

pinup /'pin,up/ n (a person whose glamorous qualities make him/her a suitable subject of) a photograph pinned up on an admirer's wall

¹**pioneer** /,pie-ə'niə/ n **1** a member of a military unit (e g engineers) engaging in light construction and defensive works **2a** a person or group that originates or helps open up a new line of thought or activity or a new method or technical development **b** any of the first people to settle in a territory

²**pioneer** adj **1** original, earliest **2** (characteristic) of early settlers or their time

³**pioneer** v **1** to open or prepare for others to follow; esp to settle **2** to originate or take part in the development of

pious /'pie-əs/ adj **1** devout **2** sacred or devotional as distinct from the profane or secular **3** dutiful **4** sanctimonious – ~**ly** adv – ~**ness** n

¹**pip** /pip/ n a fit of irritation, low spirits, or disgust – chiefly infml; esp in *to give one the pip*

²**pip** n 1 any of the dots on dice and dominoes that indicate numerical value 2 a star worn, esp on the shoulder, to indicate an army officer's rank

³**pip** v -**pp**- to beat by a narrow margin – infml — **pip at the post** to beat at the very last minute (e g in a race or competition)

⁴**pip** n a small fruit seed of an apple, orange, etc

⁵**pip** n -**pp**- a short high-pitched tone, esp broadcast in a series as a time signal

¹**pipe** /piep/ n **1a** a tubular wind instrument **b** a bagpipe – usu pl with sing. meaning 2 a long tube or hollow body for conducting a liquid, gas, etc **3a** a tubular or cylindrical object, part, or passage 4 a large cask used esp for wine (e g port) 5 a wood, clay, etc tube with a mouthpiece at one end, and at the other a small bowl in which tobacco is burned for smoking

²**pipe** v 1 to play on a pipe **2a** to speak in a high or shrill voice **b** to make a shrill sound **3a** to trim with piping **b** to force (e g cream or icing) through a piping tube or nozzle in order to achieve a decorative effect

'**pipe ,dream** n an illusory or fantastic plan, hope, or story

'**pipe ,line** /-,lien/ n **1** the processes through which supplies pass from source to user 2 sthg considered as a continuous set of processes which the individual must go through or be subjected to

piper /'piepə/ n one who plays on a pipe

pipette, NAm pipet /pi'pet/ n a narrow tube into which fluid is drawn (e g for dispensing or measuring) by suction and retained by closing the upper end

piping /'pieping/ n **1a** the music of a pipe **b** a sound, note, or call like that of a pipe 2 a quantity or system of pipes **3a** a narrow trimming consisting of a folded strip of cloth often enclosing a cord, used to decorate upholstery, garments, etc **b** a thin cordlike line of icing piped onto a cake

pipit /'pipit/ n any of various small birds resembling larks

'**pip- ,squeak** n a small or insignificant person – infml

piquant /'peekənt/ adj agreeably stimulating to the palate or mind – **-ly** adv – **-quancy** n

¹**pique** /peek/ n resentment resulting from wounded vanity

²**pique** v 1 to offend by slighting 2 to excite or arouse by a provocation, challenge, or rebuff

piracy /'pie·ərəsi/ n **1** robbery or illegal violence at sea; also a similar act against an aircraft in flight 2 the infringement of a copyright, patent, etc

piranha /pi'rahn(y)ə/ n a small S American fish capable of attacking and (fatally) wounding human beings and large animals

¹**pirate** /'pie·ərət/ n **1** sby who commits piracy 2 an unauthorized radio station; esp one located on a ship in international waters – **-ratical** adj – **-ratically** adv

²**pirate** v **1** to commit piracy on 2 to take or appropriate by piracy 3 to reproduce without authorization

pirouette /,piroo'et/ n a rapid whirling about of the body; specif a full turn on the toe or ball of one foot in ballet

Pisces /'pieseez/ n pl but sing in constr (sby born under) the 12th sign of the zodiac in astrology, which is pictured as 2 fishes

¹**piss** /pis/ v **1** to urinate 2 to discharge (as if) as urine 3 to rain heavily USE vulg

²**piss** n **1** urine 2 an act of urinating USE vulg

pissed adj, Br drunk – slang

piss off v, Br **1** to go away 2 to cause to be annoyed or fed up USE vulg

pistachio /pi'stahshi·oh/ n pl **pistachios** 1 a small green much-prized nut; also the tree on which it grows 2 the vivid green colour of the pistachio nut

pistil /'pistil/ n a carpel

pistol /'pistl/ n a short firearm intended to be aimed and fired with 1 hand

piston /'pist(ə)n/ n **1** a sliding disc or short cylinder fitting within a cylindrical vessel along which it moves back and forth by or against fluid pressure 2 a sliding valve in a cylinder in a brass instrument that is used to lower its pitch

¹**pit** /pit/ n **1a** a hole, shaft, or cavity in the ground **b** a mine 2 an area often sunken or depressed below the adjacent floor area; esp one in a theatre housing an orchestra 3 a hollow or indentation, esp in the surface of a living plant or animal; esp a natural hollow in the surface of the body 4 any of the areas alongside a motor-racing track used for refuelling and repairing the vehicles during a race – usu pl with sing. meaning; + **the**

²**pit** v -**tt**- **1** to make pits in; esp to scar or mark with pits 2 to set into opposition or rivalry; oppose – often + **against**

³**pit** n, NAm a fruit stone

¹**pitch** /pich/ n **1** a black or dark viscous substance obtained as a residue in the distillation of tar 2 resin obtained from various conifers

²**pitch** v **1** to erect and fix firmly in place 2 to throw, fling **3a(1)** to cause to be at a particular level or of a particular quality **a(2)** to set in a particular musical pitch or key **b** to cause to be set at a particular angle; slope **4a** to fall precipitately or headlong **b** of a ship to move so that the bow is alternately rising and falling 5 of a ball to bounce

³**pitch** n **1** pitching; esp an up-and-down movement 2a a slope; also the degree of slope **b** distance from any point on the thread of a screw to the corresponding point on an adjacent thread measured parallel to the axis **c** the distance advanced by a propeller in 1 revolution **d** the number of teeth on a gear or of threads on a screw per unit distance **3a** the relative level, intensity, or extent of some quality or state **b(1)** the property of a sound, esp a musical note, that is determined by

the frequency of the waves producing it; highness or lowness of sound **b(2)** a standard frequency for tuning instruments **4** an often high-pressure sales talk or advertisement **5** a wicket **6** *chiefly Br* **6a** a usu specially marked area used for playing soccer, rugby, hockey, etc **b** an area or place, esp in a street, to which a person lays unofficial claim for carrying out business or activities

,pitch-'black *adj* intensely dark or black – ~ness *n*

pitchblende /'pich,blend/ *n* a radium-containing uranium oxide occurring as a brown to black lustrous mineral

,pitched 'battle *n* an intense battle; *specif* one fought on previously chosen ground

pitcher /'pichə/ *n* a large deep usu earthenware vessel with a wide lip and a handle or 2 ear-shaped handles, for holding and pouring liquids; *broadly* a large jug

¹pitchfork /'pich,fawk/ *n* a long-handled fork with 2 or 3 long curved prongs used esp for hay

²pitchfork *v* **1** to lift and toss (as if) with a pitchfork **2** to thrust (sby) into a position, office, etc suddenly or without preparation

piteous /'pitiəs/ *adj* causing or deserving pity or compassion – ~ly *adv* – ~ness *n*

pitfall /'pit,fawl/ *n* **1** a trap or snare; *specif* a camouflaged pit used to capture animals **2** a hidden or not easily recognized danger or difficulty

¹pith /pith/ *n* **1a** a (continuous) central area of spongy tissue in the stems of most vascular plants **b** the white tissue surrounding the flesh and directly below the skin of a citrus fruit **2** the essential part; the core

²pith *v* to remove the pith from (a plant part)

pithy /'pithi/ *adj* **1** consisting of or having much pith **2** tersely cogent – **-thily** *adv* – **-thiness** *n*

pitiable /'pitiəbl/ *adj* deserving or exciting pity or contempt, esp because of inadequacy – **-bly** *adv*

pitiful /'pitif(ə)l/ *adj* **1** deserving or arousing pity or sympathy **2** exciting pitying contempt (e g by meanness or inadequacy) – ~ly *adv* – ~ness *n*

pitiless /'pitilis/ *adj* devoid of pity; merciless – ~ly *adv* – ~ness *n*

piton /pi'ton(h) *(Fr* pit5)/ *n* a spike or peg that is driven into a rock or ice surface as a support, esp for a rope, in mountaineering

pittance /'pit(ə)ns/ *n* a small amount or allowance; *specif* a meagre wage or remuneration

pituitary /pi'tyooh-it(ə)ri/ *adj or n* (of) the gland attached to the brain that secretes hormones regulating growth, metabolism, etc

¹pity /'piti/ *n* **1a** (the capacity to feel) sympathetic sorrow for one suffering, distressed, or unhappy **b** a contemptuous feeling of regret aroused by the inferiority or inadequacy of another **2** sthg to be regretted

²pity *v* to feel pity (for)

¹pivot /'pivət/ *n* **1** a shaft or pin on which sthg turns **2a** a person, thing, or factor having a major or central role, function, or effect **b** a key player or position – ~al *adj*

²pivot *v* to turn (as if) on a pivot

pixie, pixy /'piksi/ *n* a (mischievous) fairy

pizza /'peetsə/ *n* a round thin cake of baked bread dough spread with a mixture of tomatoes, cheese, herbs, etc

pizzicato /,pitsi'kahtoh/ *n, adv, or adj, pl* pizzicati /-ti/ (a note or passage played) by means of plucking instead of bowing

placard /'plakahd/ *n* a notice for display or advertising purposes, usu printed on or fixed to a stiff backing material

placate /plə'kayt/ *v* to soothe or mollify, esp by concessions – **-catory** *adj*

¹place /plays/ *n* **1a** physical environment; a space **b** physical surroundings; atmosphere **2** an indefinite region or expanse; an area **3** a particular region or centre of population **4** a particular part of a surface or body; a spot **5** relative position in a scale or series: e g **5a** a particular part in a piece of writing; *esp* the point at which a reader has temporarily stopped **b** an important or valued position **c** degree of prestige **6** a leading place, esp second or third, in a competition **7a** a proper or designated niche **b** an appropriate moment or point **8** an available seat or accommodation **9a** employment; a job; *esp* public office **b** prestige accorded to one of high rank; status **10** a public square — **in place** of so as to replace

²place *v* **1** to distribute in an orderly manner **2a** to put in, direct to, or assign to a particular place **b** to put in a particular state **3** to appoint to a position **4** to find employment or a home for **5a** to assign to a position in a series or category **b** to identify by connecting with an associated context **c** to put, lay **6** to give (an order) to a supplier

placebo /plə'seeboh/ *n, pl* placebos **1a** a medication that has no physiological effect and is prescribed more for the mental relief of the patient **b** an inert substance against which an active substance (e g a drug) is tested in a controlled trial **2** sthg tending to soothe or gratify

placed *adj* in a leading place, esp second or third, at the end of a competition, horse race, etc

'place,kick /-,kik/ *v or n* (to kick or score by means of) a kick at a ball (e g in rugby) placed or held in a stationary position on the ground

placenta /plə'sentə/ *n, pl* placentas, placentae /-ti/ the organ in all higher mammals that unites the foetus to the maternal uterus and provides for the nourishment of the foetus and the elimination of waste

placid /'plasid/ *adj* serenely free of interruption or disturbance – ~ly *adv* – ~ity *n*

plagiar·ize, -ise /'playj(y)ə,riez/ *v* to copy the ideas or words of another and pass them off as one's own – **-izer, -ist** *n* – **-ism** *n*

¹**plague** /playg/ *n* **1a** a disastrous evil or affliction; a calamity **b** a large destructive influx **2** any of several epidemic virulent diseases that cause many deaths **3** a cause of irritation; a nuisance

²**plague** *v* **1** to cause worry or distress to **2** to disturb or annoy persistently

plaice /plays/ *n, pl* **plaice** any of various flatfishes; a flounder

plaid /plad/ *n* **1** a rectangular length of tartan worn over the left shoulder as part of Highland dress **2** a usu twilled woollen fabric with a tartan pattern

¹**plain** /playn/ *n* **1** an extensive area of level or rolling treeless country **2** a broad unbroken expanse

²**plain** *adj* **1** lacking ornament; undecorated **2** free of added substances; pure **3a** evident to the mind or senses; obvious **b** clear **4** free from deceitfulness or subtlety; candid **5** lacking special distinction; ordinary **6a** not complicated **b** not rich or elaborately prepared or decorated **7** unremarkable either for physical beauty or for ugliness **8** *of flour* not containing a raising agent

³**plain** *adv* in a plain manner; clearly, simply; *also* totally, utterly

,**plain 'clothes** *n* ordinary civilian dress as opposed to (police) uniform

'**plain,song** /-,song/ *n* **1** the music of the medieval church **2** a liturgical chant of any of various Christian rites

plaint /playnt/ *n* a protest

plaintiff /'playntif/ *n* sby who commences a civil legal action

plaintive /'playntiv/ *adj* expressive of suffering or woe; melancholy, mournful – **~ly** *adv* – **~ness** *n*

¹**plait** *also* **plat** /plat/ *n* a length of plaited material, esp hair

²**plait,** *also* **plat** /plat/ *v* **1** to interweave the strands of **2** to make by plaiting

¹**plan** /plan/ *n* **1** a drawing or diagram: e g **1a** a top or horizontal view of an object **b** a large-scale map of a small area **2a** a method for achieving an end **b** a customary method of doing sthg **c** a detailed formulation of a programme of action

²**plan** *v* **-nn-** **1** to design **2** to arrange in advance **3** to have in mind; intend – **~ner** *n*

¹**plane** /playn/ *v* **1** to make flat or even with a plane **2** to remove by planing – often **+ away** or **down**

²**plane,** '**plane ,tree** *n* any of a genus of trees with large deeply cut lobed leaves and flowers in spherical heads

³**plane** *n* a tool with a sharp blade protruding from the base of a flat metal or wooden stock for smoothing or shaping a wood surface

⁴**plane** *n* **1** a surface such that any 2 included points can be joined by a straight line lying wholly within the surface **2** a level of existence, consciousness, or development **3** an aeroplane; *also* any of the surfaces that support it in flight

⁵**plane** *adj* **1** having no elevations or depressions; flat **2a** of or dealing with geometric planes **b** lying in a plane

planet /'planit/ *n* **1** any of the bodies, except a comet, meteor, or satellite, that revolve round a star, esp the sun in our solar system **2** a star held to have astrological significance – **~ary** *adj*

planetarium /,plani'teəri·əm/ *n pl* **planetariums, planetaria** /-ri·ə/ **1** a model of the solar system **2** (a building or room housing) an optical projector for projecting images of celestial bodies and effects as seen in the night sky

¹**plank** /plangk/ *n* **1** a long flat piece of wood **2** a (principal) item of a political policy or programme

²**plank** *v* to cover or floor with planks

plankton /'plangktən/ *n* the floating or weakly swimming minute animal and plant organisms of a body of water

¹**plant** /plahnt/ *v* **1a** to put in the ground, soil, etc for growth **b** to set or sow (land) with seeds or plants **2** to establish, institute **3** to place firmly or forcibly **4** to position secretly; *specif* to conceal in order to observe or deceive

²**plant** *n* **1** any of a kingdom of living things (e g a green alga, moss, fern, conifer, or flowering plant) typically lacking locomotive movement or obvious nervous or sensory organs **2a** the buildings, machinery, etc employed in carrying on a trade or an industrial business **b** a factory or workshop for the manufacture of a particular product

¹**plantain** /'plantayn, -tin/ *n* any of a genus of short-stemmed plants bearing dense spikes of minute greenish or brownish flowers

²**plantain** *n* (the angular greenish starchy fruit of) a type of banana plant

plantation /plahn'taysh(ə)n, plan-/ *n* **1** (a place with) a usu large group of plants, esp trees, under cultivation **2** a settlement in a new country or region; a colony **3** an agricultural estate, usu worked by resident labour

planter /'plahntə/ *n* **1** one who owns or operates a plantation **2** one who settles or founds a new colony

plaque /plak, plahk/ *n* **1** a commemorative or decorative inscribed tablet of ceramic, wood, metal, etc **2** a film of mucus on a tooth that harbours bacteria

plasma /'plazmə/ *n* the fluid part of blood, lymph, or milk as distinguished from suspended material

¹**plaster** /'plahstə/ *n* **1** a medicated or protective dressing **2** a pastelike mixture (e g of lime, water, and sand) that hardens on drying and is used esp

for coating walls, ceilings, and partitions **3** plaster, **plaster cast** a rigid dressing of gauze impregnated with plaster of paris for immobilizing a diseased or broken body part

²**plaster** *v* **1** to overlay or cover with (a) plaster **2a** to cover over or conceal as if with a coat of plaster **b** to smear (sthg) thickly (on); coat **3** to fasten (sthg) (to) or place (sthg) (on), esp conspicuously or in quantity **4** to inflict heavy damage, injury, or casualties on, esp by a concentrated or unremitting attack – *infml*

'**plaster,board** /-,bawd/ *n* a board with a plaster core used esp as a substitute for plaster on walls

'**plastered** *adj* drunk – *infml*

,**plaster of 'paris** /'paris/ *n, often cap 2nd P* a white powdery plaster made from gypsum that when mixed with water forms a quicksetting paste used chiefly for casts and moulds

¹**plastic** /'plastik; *also* 'plahstik/ *adj* **1** capable of being moulded or modelled **2** supple, pliant **3** sculptural **4** made or consisting of a plastic **5** formed by or adapted to an artificial or conventional standard; synthetic – *chiefly derog* – ~ **ally** *adv* – ~ **ity** *n*

²**plastic** *n* any of numerous (synthetic) organic polymers that can be moulded, cast, extruded, etc into objects, films, or filaments

Plasticine /'plasti,seen; *also* 'plahs-/ *trademark* – used for a modelling substance that remains plastic for a long period

,**plastic 'surgery** *n* surgery concerned with the repair or cosmetic improvement of parts of the body chiefly by the grafting of tissue

¹**plate** /playt/ *n* **1a** a smooth flat thin usu rigid piece of material **b** an (external) scale or rigid layer of bone, horn, etc forming part of an animal body **2a** domestic utensils and tableware made of or plated with gold, silver, or base metals **b** a shallow usu circular vessel, made esp of china, from which food is eaten or served **3a** a prepared surface from which printing is done **b** a sheet of material (e g glass) coated with a light-sensitive photographic emulsion **c** an electrode in an accumulator **4** a horizontal structural member (e g a timber) that provides bearing and anchorage, esp for rafters or joists **5** the part of a denture that fits to the mouth **6** a full-page book illustration — **on a plate** so as not to require effort – *infml*

²**plate** *v* to cover permanently with an adherent layer, esp of metal; *also* to deposit (e g a layer) on a surface – **plating** *n*

plateau /'platoh/ *n, pl* **plateaus, plateaux** /-tohz/ **1** a usu extensive relatively flat land area raised sharply above adjacent land on at least 1 side **2** a relatively stable level, period, or condition

,**plate 'glass** *n* rolled, ground, and polished sheet glass – **plate-glass** *adj*

platform /'platfawm/ *n* **1** a declaration of (political) principles and policies **2a** a raised surface at a railway station to facilitate access to trains **b** a raised flooring (e g for speakers) **3** a place or opportunity for public discussion **4** *chiefly Br* the area next to the entrance or exit of a bus

platinum /'platinam/ *n* a heavy precious greyish white noncorroding metallic element used esp as a catalyst and for jewellery

,**platinum 'blonde** *n* (sby having hair of) a pale silvery blond colour usu produced in human hair by bleach and bluish rinse

platitude /'platityoohd/ *n* a banal, trite, or stale remark, esp when presented as if it were original and significant – **-tudinous** *adj*

platonic /pla'tonik/ *adj* of or being a close relationship between 2 people in which sexual desire is absent or has been repressed or sublimated – ~ **ally** *adv*

platoon /pla'toohn/ *n* a subdivision of a military company normally consisting of 2 or more sections or squads

platter /'plata/ *n* a large often oval plate used esp for serving meat

platypus /'platipas/ *n, pl* **platypuses** *also* **platypi** /-pie/ a small aquatic Australian and Tasmanian primitive mammal that lays eggs and has a fleshy bill resembling that of a duck, webbed feet, and a broad flattened tail

plausible /'plawzabl/ *adj* **1** apparently fair, reasonable, or valid but often specious **2** *of a person* persuasive but deceptive – **-bly** *adv* – **-bility** *n*

¹**play** /play/ *n* **1** the conduct, course, or (a particular) action in or of a game **2a** (children's spontaneous) recreational activity **b** the absence of serious or harmful intent; jest **3a** operation, activity **b** light, quick, transitory, or fitful movement **c** free or unimpeded motion **4a** the dramatized representation of an action or story on stage **b** a dramatic composition (for presentation in a theatre) — **in/into play 1** in/into condition or position to be legitimately played **2** in/into operation or consideration — **out of play** not in play

²**play** *v* **1a** to engage in sport or recreation **b(1)** to deal or behave frivolously, mockingly, or playfully – often + *around* or *about* **b(2)** to make use of double meaning or of the similarity of sound of 2 words for stylistic or humorous effect – usu in *play on words* **c(1)** to deal with, handle, or manage – often + *it* **c(2)** to exploit, manipulate **d** to pretend to engage in **e(1)** to perform or execute for amusement or to deceive or mock **e(2)** to wreak **2a** to take advantage **b** to move or operate in a lively, irregular, or intermittent manner **c** to move or function freely within prescribed limits **d** to discharge repeatedly or in a stream **3** to act with special consideration so as to gain favour, approval, or sympathy – usu + *up to* **4a** to put on a performance of (a play) **b** to act or perform in or

as **5a(1)** to contend against in a game **a(2)** to perform the duties associated with (a certain position) **b(1)** to make bets on **b(2)** to operate on the basis of **c** to put into action in a game **d** to direct the course of (e g a ball); hit **6a** to perform music on an instrument **b** to perform music on **c** to perform music of a specified composer **d** to reproduce sounds, esp music, on (an apparatus) **7** to have (promiscuous or illicit) sexual relations – euph; usin *play around* – ~ **er** — **play ball** to cooperate — **play by ear** to deal with from moment to moment rather than making plans in advance — **play fast and loose** to act in a reckless, irresponsible, or craftily deceitful way — **play into the hands of** to act so as to prove advantageous to (an opponent) — **play second fiddle** to take a subordinate position — **play the field** to have a number of boyfriends or girl friends rather than committing oneself exclusively to one person — **play the game** to act according to a code or set of standards — **play with oneself** to masturbate — **to play with** at one's disposal

'play,back /-,bak/ n (a ̄ vice that provides for) the reproduction of recorded sound or pictures

play back v to listen to or look at material on (a usu recently recorded disc or tape)

'play,boy /-,boy/ n a man who lives a life devoted chiefly to the pursuit of pleasure

'play ,down v to cause to seem less important; minimize

'playful /-f(ə)l/ adj **1** full of fun; frolicsome **2** humorous, lighthearted – ~ **fully** adv – ~ **ness** n

'play,ground /-,grownd/ n a piece of land for children to play on

'play,group /-,groohp/ n, chiefly Br a supervised group of children below school age who play together regularly

'play,house /-,hows/ n a theatre

'play,mate /-,mayt/ n a companion in play

'play-,off n a final contest to determine a winner

play off v **1** to decide the winner of (a competition) or break (a tie) by a play-off **2** to set in opposition for one's own gain

'play,pen /-,pen/ n a portable usu collapsible enclosure within which a baby or young child may play

'play,thing /-,thing/ n a toy

play up v **1** to give special emphasis or prominence to **2** to cause pain or distress to **3** to behave in a disobedient or annoying manner

'play,wright /-,riet/ n one who writes plays

plaza /'plahzə/ n a public square in a city or town

plea /plee/ n **1** an accused person's answer to an indictment **2** sthg offered by way of excuse or justification **3** an earnest entreaty; an appeal

plead /pleed/ v **pleaded, pled** /pled/ **1** to make or answer an allegation in a legal proceeding **2** to make a specified plea **3a** to urge reasons for or against sthg **b** to entreat or appeal earnestly; implore – ~ **ing** n

pleasant /'plez(ə)nt/ adj **1** having qualities that tend to give pleasure; agreeable **2** of a person likable, friendly – ~ **ly** adv

pleasantry /'plez(ə)ntri/ n **1** an agreeable remark (made in order to be polite) **2** a humorous act or remark; a joke

please /pleez/ v **1** to afford or give pleasure or satisfaction **2** to like, wish **3** to be willing – usu used in the imperative (1) to express a polite request (e g please come in) (2) to turn an apparent question into a request (e g can you shut it, please?) **4** to be the will or pleasure of – fml

pleasure /'plezh-ə/ n **1** (a state of) gratification **2** enjoyment, recreation **3** a source of delight or joy **4** a wish, desire – fml – **pleasure** v – **-rable** adj – **-rably** adv

¹pleat /pleet/ v to fold; esp to arrange in pleats

²pleat n a fold in cloth made by doubling material over on itself

¹plebeian /pli'bee-ən/ n a member of the (Roman) common people

²plebeian adj **1** of plebeians **2** crude or coarse in manner or style; common

plebiscite /'plebi,siet/ n a vote by the people of an entire country or district for or against a proposal

plectrum /'plektrəm/ n, pl **plectra** /-trə/, **plectrums** a small thin piece of plastic, metal, etc used to pluck the strings of a musical instrument

¹pledge /plej/ n **1** sthg delivered as security for an obligation (e g a debt) **2** the state of being held as a security **3** a token, sign, or earnest of sthg else **4** a binding promise to do or forbear

²pledge v **1** to deposit as security for fulfilment of a contract or obligation **2** to drink the health of **3** to bind by a pledge **4** to give a promise of

plenary /'pleenəri/ adj **1** absolute, unqualified **2** attended by all entitled to be present

plenipotentiary /,plenipə'tensh(ə)ri/ n or adj (sby, esp a diplomatic agent) invested with full power to transact business

¹plenty /'plenti/ n **1a** sing or pl in constr a full or more than adequate amount or supply **b** a large number or amount **2** copiousness, plentifulness – **-tiful** adj

²plenty adv **1** quite, abundantly **2** chiefly NAm to a considerable or extreme degree; very (e g plenty hungry) USE infml

pleurisy /'plooərəsi/ n inflammation of the membrane surrounding the lungs, usu with fever and painful breathing

pliable /'plie-əbl/ adj **1** easily bent without breaking; flexible **2** yielding readily to others; compliant – **-bility** n

pliant /'plie-ənt/ adj pliable

pli

pliers /'plie-əz/ *n pl pl* **pliers** a pair of pincers with long jaws for holding small objects or for bending and cutting wire

¹**plight** /pliet/ *v* to put or give in pledge; engage

²**plight** *n* an (unpleasant or difficult) state; a predicament

plimsoll /'plims(ə)l, -sol, -sohl/ *n*, *Br* a shoe with a rubber sole and canvas top worn esp for sports

Plimsoll line *n* a set of markings indicating the draught levels to which a vessel may legally be loaded in various seasons and waters

plod /plod/ *v* **-dd- 1** to tread slowly or heavily along or over **2** to work laboriously and monotonously

¹**plonk** /plongk/ *v* to set down suddenly

²**plonk** *n*, *chiefly Br* cheap or inferior wine – *infml*

plop /plop/ *v* **-pp- 1** to drop or move suddenly with a sound suggestive of sthg dropping into water **2** to allow (the body) to drop heavily – **plop** *n*

¹**plot** /plot/ *n* **1** a small piece of land, esp one used or designated for a specific purpose **2** the plan or main story of a literary work **3** a secret plan for accomplishing a usu evil or unlawful end; an intrigue

²**plot** *v* **-tt- 1** to make a plot, map, or plan of **2** to draw (a curve) by means of plotted points **3** to plan or contrive, esp secretly **4** to invent or devise the plot of (a literary work) – **~ter** *n*

¹**plough**, *NAm* **plow** /plow/ *n* **1** an implement used to cut, lift, and turn over soil, esp in preparing ground for sowing **2** ploughed land

²**plough**, *NAm* **plow** *v* **1** to make or work with a plough **2** to cut into, open, or make furrows or ridges in (as if) with a plough – often + *up* **3** to force a way, esp violently **4** to proceed steadily and laboriously; plod **5** to fail an exam

plough back *v* to reinvest (profits) in an industry

,ploughman's 'lunch /-mənz/ *n* a cold lunch of bread, cheese, and usu pickled onions

'plough,share /-,sheə/ *n* the part of a plough that cuts the furrow

plover /'pluvə/ *n pl* **plovers**, *esp collectively* **plover** any of numerous wading birds with a short beak and usu a stout compact build

ploy /ploy/ *n* sthg devised or contrived, esp to embarrass or frustrate an opponent

¹**pluck** /pluk/ *v* **1** to pull or pick off or out **2** to pick, pull, or grasp at; *also* to play (an instrument) in this manner

²**pluck** *n* **1** an act or instance of plucking or pulling **2** courage and determination

plucky /'pluki/ *adj* marked by courage; spirited – **-kily** *adv* – **-kiness** *n*

¹**plug** /plug/ *n* **1** a stopper **2** a flat compressed cake of (chewing) tobacco **3** a small core or segment removed from a larger object **4** a device having usu 3 pins projecting from an insulated case for

making electrical connection with a suitable socket; *also* the electrical socket **5** a piece of favourable publicity (e g for a commercial product) usu incorporated in general matter – *infml*

²**plug** *v* **-gg- 1** to block, close, etc (as if) by inserting a plug **2** to hit with a bullet **3** to advertise or publicize insistently **4** to work doggedly and persistently *on*

plug in *v* to attach or connect to a power point

plum /plum/ *n* **1** (any of numerous trees that bear) an edible globular to oval smooth-skinned fruit with an oblong seed **2** sthg excellent or superior; *esp* an opportunity or position offering exceptional advantages **3** a dark reddish purple colour

plumage /'ploohmij/ *n* the entire covering of feathers of a bird

¹**plumb** /plum/ *n* **1** a lead weight attached to a cord and used to indicate a vertical line **2** any of various weights (e g a sinker for a fishing line or a lead for sounding)

²**plumb** *adv* **1** straight down or up; vertically **2** exactly, precisely

³**plumb** *v* **1** to examine minutely and critically, esp so as to achieve complete understanding **2** to adjust, measure, or test by a plumb line **3** to supply with or install as plumbing – often + *in*

⁴**plumb** *adj* **1** exactly vertical or true **2** downright, complete – *infml*

plumber /'plumə/ *n* sby who installs, repairs, and maintains water piping and fittings

plumbing /'pluming/ *n* the apparatus (e g pipes and fixtures) concerned in the distribution and use of water in a building

plume /ploohm/ *n* **1** a usu large feather or cluster of feathers esp worn as an ornament **2** sthg resembling a feather (e g in shape, appearance, or lightness): e g **2a** a feathery or feather-like animal or plant part; *esp* a full bushy tail **b** a trail of smoke, blowing snow, etc – **~d** *adj*

plummet /'plumit/ *v* to fall sharply and abruptly

¹**plump** /plump/ *v* to drop or sink suddenly or heavily — **plump for** to decide on out of several choices or courses of action

²**plump** *adj* having a full rounded form; slightly fat

plump up *v* to cause to fill or swell out

¹**plunder** /'plundə/ *v* **1** to pillage, sack **2** to take, esp by force (e g in war); steal – **~er** *n*

²**plunder** *n* sthg taken by force, theft, or fraud; loot

¹**plunge** /plunj/ *v* **1** to thrust or cast oneself (as if) into water **2** to cause to penetrate quickly and forcibly **3a** to be thrown headlong or violently forwards and downwards; *also* to move oneself in such a manner **b** to act with reckless haste; enter suddenly or unexpectedly **4** to descend or dip suddenly

²**plunge** *n* a dive; *also* a swim

plunger /'plunjə/ *n* **1** a device (e g a piston in a pump) that acts with a plunging or thrusting motion **2** a rubber suction cup on a handle used to free plumbing from blockages

pluperfect /plooh'puhfikt/ *adj* past perfect

plural /'plooərəl/ *adj* **1** of or being a word form (e g *we, houses, cattle*) denoting more than 1, or in some languages more than 2 or 3, persons, things, or instances **2** consisting of or containing more than 1 (kind or class) – ~ly *adv* – ~ize *v* – ~ism *n* – ~ity *n*

¹**plus** /plus/ *prep* **1** increased by; with the addition of 2 and also

²**plus** *n pl* **-s-** *also* **-ss- 1** an added quantity **2** a positive factor, quantity, or quality

³**plus** *adj* **1** algebraically or electrically positive **2** additional and welcome **3** greater than that specified

⁴**plus** *conj* and moreover

,**plus 'fours** *n pl* loose wide trousers gathered on a band and finishing just below the knee

¹**plush** /plush/ *n* a fabric with an even pile longer and less dense than that of velvet

²**plush** *adj* luxurious, showy

Pluto /'ploohtoh/ *n* the planet furthest from the sun

plutocracy /plooh'tokrəsi/ *n* (government by) a controlling class of wealthy people

plutonium /plooh'tonyəm, -ni-əm/ *n* a radioactive metallic element similar to uranium that is formed in atomic reactors

¹**ply** /plie/ *n* **1a** a strand in a yarn, wool, etc **b** any of several layers (e g of cloth) usu sewn or laminated together **2** (any of the veneer sheets forming) plywood

²**ply** *v* **1** to apply oneself steadily **2** *of a boatman, taxi driver, etc* to wait regularly in a particular place for custom – esp in *ply for hire* **3** to go or travel regularly

plywood /'plie,wood/ *n* a light structural material of thin sheets of wood glued or cemented together

pneumatic /nyooh'matik/ *adj* **1** moved or worked by air pressure **2** adapted for holding or inflated with compressed air – ~ally *adv*

pneumonia /nyooh'mohnyə, -ni-ə/ *n* localized or widespread inflammation of the lungs with change from an air-filled to a solid consistency, caused by infection or irritants

¹**poach** /pohch/ *v* to cook (e g fish or an egg) in simmering liquid

²**poach** *v* **1** to take game or fish illegally **2** to trespass on or upon – ~er *n*

pock /pok/ *n* a spot or blister caused by a disease (e g smallpox)

¹**pocket** /'pokit/ *n* **1** a small bag that is sewn or inserted in a garment so that it is open at the top or side **2** any of several openings at the corners or sides of a billiard table into which balls are propelled **3** a small isolated area or group — **in pocket** in the position of having made a profit — **out of pocket** having suffered a financial loss

²**pocket** *v* **1** to appropriate to one's own use; steal **2** to accept; put up with **3** to drive (a ball) into a pocket of a billiard table

³**pocket** *adj* small, miniature

¹**pocket,knife** /-,nief/ *n* a knife that has 1 or more blades that fold into the handle so that it can be carried in the pocket

¹**pocket ,money** *n* money for small personal expenses, esp as given to a child

pockmark /'pok,mahk/ *n* a mark or pit (like that) caused by smallpox – ~ed *adj*

¹**pod** /pod/ *n* **1** a long seed vessel or fruit, esp of the pea, bean, or other leguminous plant **2** an egg case of a locust or similar insect

²**pod** *v* **-dd-** to remove (e g peas) from the pod

podgy /'poji/ *adj* short and plump; chubby – **-giness** *n*

poem /'poh·im/ *n* **1** an individual work of poetry **2** a creation, experience, or object suggesting a poem

poet /'poh·it/, *fem* **poetess** /'poh·ites, ,poh·i'tes/ *n* **1** one who writes poetry **2** a creative artist with special sensitivity to his/her medium – ~ical *adj* – ~ic *adj* – ~ically *adv*

poetic justice *n* an outcome in which vice is punished and virtue rewarded in an (ironically) appropriate manner

,**poet 'laureate** *n pl* **poets laureate, poet laureates** a poet appointed for life by the sovereign as a member of the British royal household and expected to compose poems for state occasions

poetry /'poh·itri/ *n* **1a** metrical writing; verse **b** a poet's compositions; poems **2** writing that is arranged to formulate a concentrated imaginative awareness of experience through meaning, sound, and rhythm **3** a quality of beauty, grace, and great feeling

¹**pogo ,stick** /'pohgoh/ *n* a pole with a spring at the bottom and 2 footrests on which sby stands and can move along with a series of jumps

pogrom /'pogrəm/ *n* an organized massacre, esp of Jews

poignant /'poynyənt/ *adj* **1a** painfully affecting the feelings; distressing **b** deeply affecting; touching **2** designed to make an impression; cutting – ~ly *adv* – -nancy *n*

¹**point** /poynt/ *n* **1a** an individual detail; an item **b** the most important essential in a discussion or matter **2** an end or object to be achieved; a purpose **3a** a geometric element that has a position but no extent or magnitude **b** a precisely indicated position **c** an exact moment; *esp the* moment before sthg **d** a particular step, stage, or degree in development **4a** the sharp or narrowly rounded end of sthg; a tip **b** the tip of the toes – used in

ballet; *usu pl* **5a** a projecting usu tapering piece of land **b(1)** the tip of a projecting body part **b(2)** a tine **6a** a very small mark **b(1)** a punctuation mark; *esp* full stop **b(2)** a decimal point **7** any of the 32 evenly spaced compass directions; *also* the 11° 15' interval between 2 successive points **8** a unit of counting in the scoring of a game or contest **9** a fielding position in cricket near to the batsman on the off side **10** *pl, Br* a device made of usu 2 movable rails and necessary connections and designed to turn a locomotive or train from one track to another — **beside the point** irrelevant — **to the point** relevant, pertinent

²**point** *v* **1** to give added force, emphasis, or piquancy to **2** to scratch out the old mortar from the joints of (e g a brick wall) and fill in with new material **3a** to indicate the position or direction of sthg, esp by extending a finger **b** *of a gundog* to indicate the presence and place of (game) for a hunter **4** to lie extended, aimed, or turned in a particular direction

,**point-'blank** *adj* **1** so close to a target that a missile fired will travel in a straight line to the mark **2** direct, blunt

'**point-'duty** *n* traffic regulation carried out usu by a policeman stationed at a particular point

pointed /'poyntid/ *adj* **1** having a point **2a** pertinent **b** aimed at a particular person or group **3** conspicuous, marked – ~**ly** *adv*

pointer /'poyntə/ *n* **1** a rod used to direct attention **2** a large strong slender smooth-haired gundog that hunts by scent and indicates the presence of game by pointing **3** a useful suggestion or hint; a tip

pointless /-lis/ *adj* devoid of meaning, relevance, or purpose; senseless – ~**ly** *adv* – ~**ness** *n*

,**point of 'order** *n* a question relating to procedure in an official meeting

,**point of 'view** *n* a position from which sthg is considered or evaluated

point out *v* to direct sby's attention to

pointsman /'poyntsmən/ *n* a person in charge of railway points

,**point-to-'point** *n* a usu cross-country steeplechase for amateur riders

'**poise** /poyz/ *v* **1** to hold supported or suspended without motion in a steady position **2** to put into readiness; brace

²**poise** *n* **1** easy self-possessed assurance of manner **2** a particular way of carrying oneself

poised /poyzd/ *adj* **1** marked by balance or equilibrium or by easy composure of manner **2** in readiness

'**poison** /'poyz(ə)n/ *n* a substance that through its chemical action kills, injures, or impairs an organism

²**poison** *v* **1** to injure, kill, treat, etc with poison **2** to exert a harmful influence on; corrupt – ~**er** *n*

poisonous /'poyz(ə)nəs/ *adj* having the properties or effects of poison – ~**ly** *adv*

'**poke** /pohk/ *n, chiefly dial NAm* a bag, sack

²**poke** *v* **1a** to prod, jab **b** to stir the coals or logs of (a fire) so as to promote burning **2a** to look *about* or *through* sthg without system; rummage **b** to meddle **3** to become stuck out or forwards; protrude **4** *of a man* to have sexual intercourse with – *vulg* — **poke fun at** to mock — **poke one's nose into** to meddle in or interfere with (esp sthg that does not concern one)

³**poke** *n* **1** a quick thrust; a jab **2** a punch – *infml* **3** an act of sexual intercourse – *vulg*

'**poker** /'pohkə/ *n* a metal rod for poking a fire

²**poker** *n* any of several card games in which a player bets that the value of his/her hand is greater than that of the hands held by others

'**poker ,face** *n* an inscrutable face that reveals no hint of a person's thoughts or feelings – **-faced** *adj*

poky *also* **pokey** /'pohki/ *adj* small and cramped – *infml* – **pokiness** *n*

polar /'pohlə/ *adj* **1a** of, coming from, or characteristic of (the region round) a geographical pole **b** *esp of an orbit* passing over a planet's N and S poles **2** of 1 or more poles (e g of a magnet) **3** resembling a pole or axis round which all else revolves; pivotal

,**polar 'bear** *n* a large creamy-white bear that inhabits arctic regions

polarity /pə'larəti, poh-/ *n* **1** the quality or condition of a body that has opposite or contrasted properties or powers in opposite directions **2** attraction towards a particular object or in a specific direction **3** the particular electrical state of being either positive or negative **4** (an instance of) total opposition – **-ize** *v*

'**pole** /pohl/ *n* **1a** a long slender usu cylindrical object (e g a length of wood) **b** a shaft which extends from the front axle of a wagon between the draught animals **2** a unit of length equal to 5¹/₂yd (about 5m) **3** the most favourable front-row position on the starting line of a (motor) race

²**pole** *v* to push or propel (e g a boat) with poles

³**pole** *n* **1** either extremity of an axis of (a body, esp the earth, resembling) a sphere **2a** either of 2 related opposites **b** a point of guidance or attraction **3a** either of the 2 terminals of an electric cell, battery, or dynamo **b** any of 2 or more regions in a magnetized body at which the magnetic flux density is concentrated

Pole *n* a native or inhabitant of Poland

'**poleaxe** /'pohl,aks/ *n* **1** a battle-axe with a short handle and often a hook or spike opposite the blade **2** an axe used, esp formerly, in slaughtering cattle

²**poleaxe** *v* to attack, strike, or fell (as if) with a poleaxe

pol

polecat /'pohl‚kat/ *n pl* **polecats,** *esp collectively* **polecat** 1 a European flesh-eating mammal of which the ferret is considered a domesticated variety 2 *NAm* a skunk

polestar /'pohl‚stah/ *n* 1 a directing principle; a guide 2 a centre of attraction

Pole Star *n* the star in the constellation Ursa Minor that lies very close to the N celestial pole

'**pole ‚vault** *n* (an athletic field event consisting of) a jump for height over a crossbar with the aid of a pole

police /pə'lees/ *n* 1 the department of government concerned with maintenance of public order and enforcement of laws 2a *sing or pl in constr* a police force **b** *pl in constr* policemen – **police** *v*

po'liceman /-mən/, *fem* **po'lice‚woman** *n* a member of a police force

police state *n* a political unit characterized by repressive governmental control of political, economic, and social life, usu enforced by (secret) police

'**policy** /'polisi/ *n* 1 a definite course of action selected from among alternatives to guide and determine present and future decisions 2 an overall plan embracing general goals and procedures, esp of a governmental body

²**policy** *n* (a document embodying) a contract of insurance

polio /'pohli‑oh/, **poliomyelitis** /‚pohlioh‚mie´-lietis/ *n* an infectious virus disease, esp of children, characterized by motor paralysis and atrophy of skeletal muscles often leading to permanent disability or deformity

'**polish** /'polish/ *v* 1 to make smooth and glossy, usu by friction 2 to refine in manners or condition 3 to bring to a highly developed, finished, or refined state; perfect – often + *up* – ~**er** *n*

²**polish** *n* 1a a smooth glossy surface **b** freedom from rudeness or coarseness 2 a preparation used to produce a gloss and often a colour for the protection and decoration of a surface

'**Polish** /'pohlish/ *adj* (characteristic) of Poland

²**Polish** *n* the language of the Poles

polish off *v* to dispose of rapidly or completely

politburo /'polit‚byoooaroh, -'-,--/ *n* the principal committee of a Communist party

polite /pə'liet/ *adj* showing or characterized by correct social usage; refined 2 marked by consideration and deference; courteous – ~**ly** *adv* – ~**ness** *n*

politic /'politik/ *adj* 1 *of a person* shrewd and sagacious in managing, contriving, or dealing 2 *of a policy* expedient

political economy *n* a social science dealing with the interrelationship of political and economic processes – **‑mist** *n*

politician /‚poli'tish(ə)n/ *n* a person experienced or engaged in politics

politics /'politiks/ *n pl but sing or pl in constr* 1 the art or science of government 2a political affairs; *specif* competition between interest groups in a government **b** political life as a profession **c** sby's political sympathies

polka /'polkə/ *n* (music for or in the rhythm of) a vivacious dance of Bohemian origin in duple time

'**polka ‚dot** *n* any of many regularly distributed dots in a textile design

'**poll** /pohl/ *n* 1 (the hairy top or back of) the head 2 the broad or flat end of the head of a striking tool (e g a hammer) 3a the casting of votes **b** the place where votes are cast – usu *pl* with sing. meaning **c** the number of votes recorded 4 a survey conducted by the questioning of people selected at random or by quota

²**poll** *v* 1 to cut off or cut short the horns of (a cow) 2 to pollard (a tree) 3 to receive and record the votes of; *also* to cast one's vote 4 to question in a poll

³**poll** *n* a polled animal

pollard /'poləd/ *n* a tree cut back to the main stem to promote the growth of a dense head of foliage – **pollard** *v*

pollen /'polən/ *n* (a fine dust of) the minute granular spores discharged from the anther of the flower of a flowering plant that serve to fertilize the ovules

pollinate /'polə‚nayt/ *v* to fertilize with pollen – **‑nation** *n*

pollute /pə'looht/ *v* 1 to make morally impure; defile 2 to make physically impure or unclean; *esp* to contaminate (an environment), esp with man-made waste – **‑tion** *n*

polo /'pohloh/ *n* a game played by teams of usu 4 players on ponies using mallets with long flexible handles to drive a wooden ball into the opponent's goal

polo neck *n, chiefly Br* (a jumper with) a very high closely fitting collar worn folded over

polony /pə'lohni/ *n* a dry sausage of partly cooked meat, esp pork

poltergeist /'poltə‚giest/ *n* a noisy mischievous ghost believed to be responsible for unexplained noises and physical damage

poly /'poli/ *n, pl* **polys** *Br* a polytechnic – *infml*

polyandry /'poli‚andri/ *n* having more than 1 husband at a time – **‑rous** *adj*

‚**poly'ester** /-'estə/ *n* a polymer containing ester groups used esp in making fibres, resins, or plastics

‚**poly'ethylene** /-'ethi‚leen/ *n* polythene

polygamy /pə'ligami/ *n* being married to more than 1 person at a time; *esp* marriage to more than 1 wife – **‑mous** *adj*

'‚**poly'glot** /-‚glot/ *n* 1 one who is polyglot 2 a mixture or confusion of languages

polyglot adj 1 multilingual 2 containing matter in several languages

polygon /'poligən, -gon/ n a closed plane figure bounded by straight lines – ~**al** adj

polyhedron /,poli'heedrən/ n, pl **polyhedrons, polyhedra** /-drə/ a solid formed by plane faces – -**ral** adj

polymer /'polimə/ n a chemical compound or mixture of compounds containing repeating structural units and formed by chemical combination of many small molecules

polyp /'polip/ n 1 a primitive animal with a hollow cylindrical body attached at one end and having a central mouth surrounded by tentacles at the other 2 a projecting mass of tissue (e g a tumour) – ~**ous** adj

polyphony /pə'lifəni/ n a style of musical composition in which 2 or more independent but organically related voice parts sound against one another – -**nic** adj

poly'styrene /-'stie-əreen/ n a rigid plastic used esp in moulded products, foams, and sheet materials

[1]**poly'technic** /-'teknik/ adj relating to or devoted to instruction in many technical arts or applied sciences

[2]**polytechnic** n any of a number of British institutions offering full-time, sandwich, and part-time courses in various subjects but with a bias towards the vocational

'polythe,ism /-thi,iz(ə)m/ n belief in or worship of 2 or more gods

'polythene /-theen/ n any of various lightweight plastics used esp for packaging and bowls, buckets, etc

pomander /po'mandə, pə-/ n a mixture of aromatic substances enclosed in a perforated bag or box and used to scent clothes or linen

pomegranate /'pomi,granət/ n (an Old World tree that bears) a thick-skinned reddish fruit about the size of an orange

pommel /'puməl, 'po-/ n 1 the knob on the hilt of a sword 2 the protuberance at the front and top of a saddle

Pommy, Pommie /'pomi/ n, often not cap, Austr & NZ a British person; esp a British immigrant

pomp /pomp/ n 1 a show of magnificence; splendour 2 ostentatious or specious display

[1]**pom-pom** /'pom ,pom/ n an automatic gun mounted on ships in pairs, fours, or eights

[2]**pom-pom** n an ornamental ball or tuft used esp on clothing, hats, etc

pompous /'pompəs/ adj 1 self-important, pretentious 2 excessively elevated or ornate – ~**ly** adv – -**posity,** ~**ness** n

[1]**ponce** /pons/ n, Br 1 a pimp 2 a man who behaves in an effeminate manner – infml

[2]**ponce** v 1 to pimp 2 to act in a frivolous, showy, or effeminate manner – usu + around or about

poncho /'ponchoh/ n pl **ponchos** a cloak resembling a blanket with a slit in the middle for the head

pond /pond/ n a body of (fresh) water usu smaller than a lake

ponder /'pondə/ v 1 to weigh in the mind; assess 2 to review mentally; think over

ponderous /'pond(ə)rəs/ adj 1 unwieldy or clumsy because of weight and size 2 oppressively or unpleasantly dull; pedestrian – ~**ly** adv – ~**ness** n

pong /pong/ v or n, Br (to emit) an unpleasant smell; stink – infml – ~**y** adj

poniard /'ponyəd/ n a small dagger

pontiff /'pontif/ n a bishop; specif the pope

pontifical /pon'tifikl/ adj 1 of a pontiff 2 pretentiously dogmatic

[1]**pontificate** /pon'tifikət/ n the state, office, or term of office of the pope

[2]**pontificate** /pon'tifikayt/ v to deliver dogmatic opinions

[1]**pontoon** /pon'toohn/ n a flat-bottomed boat or portable float (used in building a floating temporary bridge)

[2]**pontoon** n a gambling card game

pony /'pohni/ n a small horse; esp a member of any of several breeds of very small stocky horses under 14·2 hands in height

'pony,tail /-,tayl/ n a hairstyle in which the hair is drawn back tightly and tied high at the back of the head

poodle /'poohdl/ n (any of) a breed of active intelligent dogs with a thick curly coat which is of 1 colour only

poof, pouf /poohf, poof/ n an effeminate or homosexual man

,pooh-'pooh v to express contempt (for)

[1]**pool** /poohl/ n 1 a small and relatively deep body of usu fresh water (e g a still place in a stream or river) 2 a small body of standing liquid; a puddle

[2]**pool** n 1 an aggregate stake to which each player of a game has contributed 2 any of various games played on a billiard table with 6 pockets and often 15 numbered balls 3 a facility, service, or group of people providing a service for a number of people (e g the members of a business organization) 4 pl the football pools

[3]**pool** v to contribute to a common stock (e g of resources or effort)

[1]**poop** /poohp/ n an enclosed superstructure at the stern of a ship above the main deck

[2]**poop** v, chiefly NAm to put out of breath; also to tire out

poor /pooə, paw/ adj 1 lacking material possessions 2 less than adequate; meagre 3 exciting pity 4 inferior in quality, value, or workmanship 5 humble, unpretentious – ~**ly** adv – ~**ness** n

'poor ,law n a law that in former times provided for the relief of the poor

poorly /'pooəli/ adj somewhat ill

¹**pop** /pop/ v -pp- 1 to push, put, or thrust *out* suddenly 2 to cause to explode or burst open 3 to protrude from the sockets 4 *Br* to pawn — **pop the question** to propose marriage — infml

²**pop** n 1 a popping sound 2 a flavoured fizzy drink

³**pop** adv like or with a pop; suddenly – infml

⁴**pop** n, chiefly NAm a father – infml

⁵**pop** adj popular: eg a of pop music b of or constituting a mass culture widely disseminated through the mass media

⁶**pop** n pop music

pop art n, often cap P&A art that incorporates everyday objects from popular culture and the mass media (eg comic strips)

'**pop,corn** /-,kawn/ n (the popped kernels of) a maize whose kernels burst open when heated to form a white starchy mass

pope /pohp/ n 1 often cap the prelate who as bishop of Rome is the head of the Roman Catholic church 2 a priest of an Eastern church

'**pop-,eyed** adj having staring or bulging eyes (eg as a result of surprise or excitement)

'**pop,gun** /-,gun/ n a toy gun that shoots a cork or pellet and produces a popping sound; *also* an inadequate or inefficient firearm

poplar /'poplə/ n (the wood of) any of a genus of slender quick-growing trees (eg an aspen) of the willow family

poplin /'poplin/ n a strong usu cotton fabric in plain weave with crosswise ribs

pop music n modern commercially promoted popular music that is usu short and simple and has a strong beat

pop off v 1 to leave suddenly 2 to die unexpectedly USE infml

popper /'popə/ n, chiefly Br a press-stud

poppet /'popit/ n a lovable or enchanting person or animal – infml

'**popping ,crease** /'poping/ n either of the lines behind which the foot or bat of a batsman must be grounded in cricket to avoid being run out or stumped

poppy /'popi/ n any of several genera of plants with showy flowers and capsular fruits including the opium poppy and several other plants cultivated for their ornamental value

'**poppy,cock** /-,kok/ n empty talk; nonsense – infml

populace /'popyoolas/ n sing or pl in constr the (common) people; the masses

popular /'popyoolə/ adj 1 (suited to the needs, means, tastes, or understanding) of the general public 2 having general currency 3 commonly liked or approved – **~ity** n – **~ize** v – **~ly** adv

populate /'popyoolayt/ v 1 to have a place in; occupy, inhabit 3 to supply or provide with inhabitants; people

population /,popyoo'laysh(ə)n/ n 1 sing or pl in constr the whole number of people or inhabitants in a country or region 2 sing or pl in constr a body of people or individuals having a quality or characteristic in common 3 a set (eg of individual people or items) from which samples are taken for statistical measurement

populist /'popyoolist/ n 1 a member of a political party claiming to represent the common people 2 a believer in the rights, wisdom, or virtues of the common people

populous /'popyoolas/ adj densely populated – **~ness** n

porcelain /'paws(ə)lin/ n a type of hard translucent ceramic ware

porch /pawch/ n 1 a covered usu projecting entrance to a building 2 NAm a veranda

porcupine /'pawkyoopien/ n any of various large rodents with stiff sharp erectile bristles

¹**pore** /paw/ v 1 to study closely or attentively 2 to reflect or meditate steadily USE usu + on, over, or upon

²**pore** n a minute opening; esp one (eg in a membrane, esp the skin, or between soil particles) through which fluids pass or are absorbed

pork /pawk/ n the flesh of a pig used as food

porker /'pawkə/ n a young pig fattened for food

porky /'pawki/ adj fat, fleshy – infml

porn /pawn/ n pornography – infml

pornography /paw'nografi/ n (books, photographs, films, etc containing) the depiction of erotic behaviour intended to cause sexual excitement – **-pher** n – **-phic** adj – **-phically** adv

porous /'pawrəs/ adj 1 having or full of pores or spaces 2 allowing liquids to pass through – **~ness** n

porpoise /'pawpəs/ n a blunt-snouted usu largely black whale about 2m (6ft) long

porridge /'porij/ n 1 a soft food made by boiling oatmeal in milk or water until thick 2 Br time spent in prison – slang

porringer /'porinjə/ n a small bowl from which esp soft or liquid foods (eg porridge) are eaten

¹**port** /pawt/ n a town or city with a harbour where ships may take on or discharge cargo or passengers

²**port** n 1 an opening (eg in machinery) for intake or exhaust of a fluid 2 an opening in a ship's side to admit light or air or to load cargo 3 a hole in an armoured vehicle or fortification through which guns may be fired

³**port** adj or n (of or at) the left side of a ship or aircraft looking forwards

⁴**port** v to turn or put (a helm) to the left – used chiefly as a command

⁵**port** n a fortified sweet wine of rich taste and aroma made in Portugal

portable /'portəbl/ n or adj (sthg) capable of being carried or moved about – **-bility** n

portage /'pawtij/ *n* **1** the carrying of boats or goods overland from one body of water to another **2** the route followed in portage; *also* a place where such a transfer is necessary – **portage** *v*

portal /'pawtl/ *n* a (grand or imposing) door or entrance

portcullis /pawt'kulis/ *n* a usu iron or wood grating that can prevent entry to a fortified place by being lowered into a gateway

portend /paw'tend/ *v* **1** to give an omen or fore warning sign of; bode **2** to indicate, signify

portent /'pawt(ə)nt, -tent/ *n* **1** sthg foreshadowing a coming event; an omen **2** prophetic indication or significance

portentous /paw'tentəs/ *adj* **1** eliciting amazement or wonder; prodigious **2** self-consciously weighty; pompous – **~ly** *adv*

¹**porter** /'pawtə/, *fem* **portress** /-tris/ *n* a gatekeeper or doorkeeper, esp of a large building, who usu regulates entry and answers enquiries

²**porter** *n* **1** sby who carries burdens; *specif* sby employed to carry luggage **2** a heavy dark brown beer – **~age** *n*

'**porter,house** /-,hows/ *n* a large steak cut from the back end of the sirloin above the ribs

portfolio /pawt'fohli·oh/ *n pl* **portfolios 1** a hinged cover or flexible case for carrying loose papers, pictures, etc **2** the office of a government minister or member of a cabinet **3** the securities held by an investor

porthole /'pawt,hohl/ *n* a usu glazed opening, esp in the side of a ship or aircraft

portico /'pawtikoh/ *n pl* **porticoes, porticos** a colonnade or covered veranda, usu at the entrance of a building and characteristic of classical architecture

¹**portion** /'pawsh(ə)n/ *n* **1** a part or share of sthg; *esp* a helping of food **2** an individual's lot or fate

²**portion** *v* to divide into portions; distribute – often + *out*

,**portly** /'pawtli/ *adj* rotund, stout – **-liness** *n*

¹**portmanteau** /pawt'mantoh/ *n*, *pl* **portmanteaus, portmanteaux** /-tohz/ a trunk for a traveller's belongings that opens into 2 equal parts

²**portmanteau** *adj* combining more than 1 use or quality

portmanteau word *n* a word (e g *brunch*) formed by combining other (parts of) words

,**port of 'call** *n* **1** a port where ships customarily stop during a voyage **2** a stop included in an itinerary

portrait /'pawtrit, -trayt/ *n* **1** a pictorial likeness of a person **2** a verbal portrayal or representation

portray /paw'tray/ *v* **1** to make a picture of; depict **2a** to describe in words **b** to play the role of – **~al** *n*

Portuguese /,pawchoo'geez, ,pawtyoo'geez/ *n pl* **Portuguese 1** a native or inhabitant of Portugal **2** the language of esp Portugal and Brazil

Portuguese man-of-war *n* any of several large floating jellyfishes with very long stinging tentacles

¹**pose** /pohz/ *v* **1** to assume a posture or attitude, usu for artistic purposes **2** to affect an attitude or character; posture – usu + *as* **3** to present for attention or consideration

²**pose** *n* **1** a sustained posture; *esp* one assumed for artistic purposes **2** an assumed attitude of mind or mode of behaviour

¹**poser** /'pohzə/ *n* a puzzling or baffling question

²**poser** *n* an affected or insincere person

posh /posh/ *adj* **1** very fine; splendid **2** socially exclusive or fashionable – often derog *USE* infml

¹**position** /pə'zish(ə)n/ *n* **1** an opinion; point of view **2** a market commitment in securities or commodities **3** the place occupied by sby or sthg; *also* the proper place **4a** a condition, situation **b** social or official rank or status **5** a post, job – fml

²**position** *v* to put in a proper or specified position

positional /pə'zish(ə)nl/ *adj* of or fixed by position

positive /'pozətiv/ *adj* **1** fully assured; confident **2** incontestable **3** utter **4** real, active **5a** capable of being constructively applied; helpful **b** concentrating on what is good or beneficial **6** having or expressing actual existence or quality as distinguished from deficiency **7** having the light and dark parts similar in tone to those of the original photographic subject **8** in a direction arbitrarily or customarily taken as that of increase or progression **9** numerically greater than zero **10a** charged with electricity **b** having higher electric potential and constituting the part from which the current flows to the external circuit **11** marked by or indicating acceptance, approval, or affirmation – **positive** *n* – **~ly** *adv*

positron /'pozitron/ *n* an elementary particle that has the same mass as the electron but the opposite electrical charge

posse /'posi/ *n sing or pl in constr* a body of people summoned by a sheriff, esp in N America, to assist in preserving the public peace, usu in an emergency

possess /pə'zes/ *v* **1** to make the owner or holder – + *of* or *with* **2a** to have and hold as property; own **b** to have as an attribute, knowledge, or skill **3** to influence so strongly as to direct the actions; *also*, *of a demon, evil spirit, etc* to enter into and control – **~or** *n*

pos'sessed *adj* **1** influenced or controlled by sthg (e g an evil spirit or a passion) **2** mad, crazed

possession /pə'zesh(ə)n/ *n* **1a** having or taking into control **b** ownership **2a** sthg owned, occupied, or controlled **b** *pl* wealth, property **3** domination by sthg (e g an evil spirit or passion)

¹possessive /pəˈzesiv/ *adj* **1** manifesting possession or the desire to own or dominate **2** of or being the grammatical possessive – **~ly** *adv* – **~ness** *n*

²possessive *n* (a form in) a grammatical case expressing ownership or a similar relation

possibility /ˌposəˈbiləti/ *n* **1** the condition or fact of being possible **2** sthg possible **3** potential or prospective value – usu pl with sing. meaning

possible /ˈposəbl/ *adj* **1** within the limits of ability, capacity, or realization **2** capable of being done or occurring according to nature, custom, or manners **3** that may or may not occur – **possible** *n*

possibly /ˈposəbli/ *adv* **1** it is possible that; maybe **2** – used as an intensifier with *can* or *could*

possum /ˈposəm/ *n* an opossum

¹post /pohst/ *n* **1** a piece of timber, metal, etc fixed firmly in an upright position, esp as a stay or support **2** a stake marking the starting or finishing point of a horse race **3** a goalpost

²post *v* **1** to fasten to a wall, board, etc in order to make public – often + *up* **2** to publish, announce, or advertise (as if) by use of a placard

³post *n* **1** (a single despatch or delivery of) the mail handled by a postal system **2** *chiefly Br* a postal system or means of posting

⁴post *v* **1** to send by post **2** to provide with the latest news; inform

⁵post *n* **1a** the place at which a soldier or body of troops is stationed **b** a station or task to which one is assigned **2** an office or position to which a person is appointed **3** a trading post, settlement **4** *Br* either of 2 bugle calls giving notice of the hour for retiring at night

⁶post *v* to station

postage /ˈpohstij/ *n* (markings or stamps representing) the fee for a postal service

postal /ˈpohstl/ *adj* **1** of or being a system for the conveyance of written material, parcels, etc between a large number of users **2** conducted by post

'postal ˌorder *n*, *Br* an order issued by a post office for payment of a specified sum of money usu at another post office

'postˌbox /-ˌboks/ *n* a secure receptacle for the posting of outgoing mail

'postˌcard /-ˌkahd/ *n* a card that can be posted without an enclosing envelope

'postˌcode /-ˌkohd/ *n* a combination of letters and numbers that is used in the postal address of a place in the UK to assist sorting

ˌpost'date /-ˈdayt/ *v* **1** to date with a date later than that of execution **2** to assign (an event) to a date subsequent to that of actual occurrence

poster /ˈpohstə/ *n* a (decorative) bill or placard for display often in a public place

poste restante /ˌpohst ˈrestont/ *n*, *chiefly Br* mail that is intended for collection from a post office

¹posterior /poˈstiəri·ə/ *adj* **1** situated behind or towards the back: e g **2a** of an animal part near the tail **b** of the human body or its parts dorsal **3** of a plant part (on the side) facing towards the stem or axis

²posterior *n* the buttocks

posterity /poˈsterəti/ *n* all future generations

postern /ˈpostuhn, ˈpoh-/ *n* a back door or gate

'poster ˌpaint *n* an opaque watercolour paint containing gum

ˌpost'graduate /-ˈgradyoo·ət/ *n* a student continuing higher education after completing a first degree

ˌpost'haste /-ˈhayst/ *adv* with all possible speed

'post ˌhorn *n* a simple wind instrument with cupped mouthpiece used esp in the 18th and 19th c by stage coaches

posthumous /ˈpostyooməs/ *adj* following, occurring, published, etc after death – **~ly** *adv*

'postman /-mən/, *fem* **'post,woman** *n* sby who delivers the post

'postˌmark /-ˌmahk/ *v or n* (to mark with) a cancellation mark showing the post office and date of posting of a piece of mail

'postˌmaster /-ˌmahstə/, *fem* **'post,mistress** *n* sby who has charge of a post office

ˌpostmaster 'general *n pl* **postmasters general** an official in charge of a national post office

ˌpost me'ridiem /məˈridi·əm/ *adj* being after noon – abbr **pm**

ˌpost'mortem /-ˈmawtəm/ *adj* occurring after death

²postmortem *n* **1** an examination of a body after death for determining the cause of death or the character and extent of changes produced by disease **2** an examination of a plan or event that failed, in order to discover the cause of failure

'post ˌoffice *n* **1** a national usu governmental organization that runs a postal system **2** a local branch of a national post office

postpone /pəˈspohn, ˌpohs(t)ˈpohn/ *v* to hold back to a later time; defer – **~ment** *n*

postscript /ˈpohs(t)ˌskript/ *n* **1** a note or series of notes appended to a completed article, a book, or esp a letter **2** a subordinate or supplementary part

¹postulate /ˈpostyoo·layt/ *v* **1** to assume or claim as true **2** to assume as a postulate or axiom

²postulate /ˈpostyoolət/ *n* **1** a hypothesis advanced as a premise in a train of reasoning **2** an axiom

¹posture /ˈposchə/ *n* **1** the position or bearing of (relative parts of) the body **2** a frame of mind; an attitude

²posture *v* **1** to assume a posture; *esp* to strike a pose for effect **2** to assume an artificial or insincere attitude; attitudinize

posy /ˈpohzi/ *n* a small bouquet of flowers; a nosegay

¹**pot** /pot/ n 1 any of various usu rounded vessels (e g of metal or earthenware) used for holding liquids or solids, esp in cooking 2 an enclosed framework for catching fish or lobsters 3 a drinking vessel (e g of pewter) used esp for beer 4 the total of the bets at stake at 1 time 5 *Br* a shot in billiards or snooker in which an object ball is pocketed 6 *NAm* the common fund of a group 7 a large amount (of money) – usu pl with sing. meaning; infml 8 a potbelly – infml 9 cannabis; *specif* marijuana – slang

²**pot** v -tt- 1 to preserve in a sealed pot, jar, or can 2 to make or shape (earthenware) as a potter

potash /'potash/ n potassium or a potassium compound, esp as used in agriculture or industry

potassium /po'tasyəm, -si-əm/ n a soft light metallic element

potation /poh'taysh(ə)n/ n an act or instance of drinking; *also* a usu alcoholic drink – fml or humor

potato /po'taytoh/ n, pl **potatoes** 1 a sweet potato, yam 2 a plant widely cultivated in temperate regions for its edible starchy tubers; *also* a potato tuber eaten as a vegetable

,**pot'belly** /-'beli/ n an enlarged, swollen, or protruding abdomen

'**pot,boiler** /-,boylə/ n a usu inferior work (e g of art or literature) produced chiefly to make money

'**pot-,bound** adj, *of a potted plant* having roots so densely matted as to allow little or no space for further growth

poteen, potheen /po'cheen, po'teen/ n Irish whiskey illicitly distilled

potent /'pot(ə)nt/ adj 1 powerful 2 achieving or bringing about a particular result; effective 3 producing an esp unexpectedly powerful reaction; strong 4 *of a male* able to have sexual intercourse – **potency** n – ~**ly** adv

potentate /'pot(ə)n,tayt/ n one who wields controlling power

¹**potential** /po'tensh(ə)l/ adj existing in possibility; capable of being made real – ~**ly** adv

²**potential** n 1 sthg that can develop or become actual; possible capacity or value 2 the difference between the voltages at 2 points (e g in an electrical circuit or in an electrical field)

potential energy n the energy that sthg has because of its position or because of the arrangement of parts

potentiality /po,tenshi'aləti/ n potential

pother /'podhə/ n needless agitation over a trivial matter; fuss

¹**pot,hole** /-,hohl/ n 1 a circular hole worn in the rocky bed of a river by stones or gravel whirled round by the water 2 a natural vertically descending hole in the ground or in the floor of a cave; *also* a system of these usu linked by caves 3 an unwanted hole in a road surface

²**pothole** v to explore pothole systems – ~**er** n

potion /'pohsh(ə)n/ n a mixed drink, esp of medicine, often intended to produce a specified effect

,**pot'luck** /-'luk/ n 1 food that is available without special preparations being made 2 whatever luck or chance brings – esp in *take potluck*

potpourri /,pohpo'ree, poh'poori/ n 1 a mixture of dried flowers, herbs, and spices, usu kept in a jar for its fragrance 2 a miscellaneous collection; a medley

'**pot ,roast** n a joint of meat cooked by braising, usu on the top of a cooker

'**pot,sherd** /-,shuhd/ n a pottery fragment

'**pot,shot** /-,shot/ n 1 a shot taken in a casual manner or at an easy target 2 a critical remark made in a careless manner

potted /'potid/ adj 1 planted or grown in a pot 2 *chiefly Br* abridged or summarized, usu in a simplified or popular form

¹**potter** /'potə/ n one who makes pottery

²**potter** v 1 to spend time in aimless or unproductive activity – often + *around* or *about* 2 to move or travel in a leisurely or random fashion – **potter** n

pottery /'pot(ə)ri/ n 1 a place where ceramic ware is made and fired 2 articles of fired clay; *esp* coarse or hand-made ceramic ware

¹**potty** /'poti/ adj, *chiefly Br* 1 slightly crazy 2 foolish, silly USE infml – **pottiness** n

²**potty** n a chamber pot, esp for a small child

pouch /powch/ n 1 a small drawstring bag carried on the person 2 a lockable bag for mail or diplomatic dispatches 3 an anatomical structure resembling a pouch: e g 3a a pocket of skin in the abdomen of marsupials for carrying their young b a pocket of skin in the cheeks of some rodents used for storing food

poulterer /'pohlt(ə)rə/ n one who deals in poultry, poultry products, or game

poultice /'pohltis/ n a soft usu heated and sometimes medicated mass spread on cloth and applied to inflamed or injured parts (e g sores)

poultry /'pohltri/ n domesticated birds (e g chickens) kept for eggs or meat

pounce /powns/ v 1 to swoop on and seize sthg (as if) with talons 2 to make a sudden assault or approach – **pounce** n

¹**pound** /pownd/ n pl **pounds** also **pound** 1 a unit of mass and weight equal to 16oz avoirdupois (about 0.453kg) 2 the basic money unit of the UK and many other countries

²**pound** v 1 to reduce to powder or pulp by beating or crushing 2 to strike heavily or repeatedly 3 to move or run along with heavy steps

³**pound** n 1 an enclosure for animals; *esp* a public enclosure for stray or unlicensed animals 2 a place for holding personal property until redeemed by the owner

pour /paw/ v **1** (to cause) to flow in a stream **2** to dispense (a drink) into a container **3** to supply or produce freely or copiously **4** to rain hard – often + *down* – **pour cold water on** to be critical or unenthusiastic about – **pour oil on troubled waters** to calm or defuse a heated situation

pout /powt/ v **1a** to show displeasure by thrusting out the lips or wearing a sullen expression **b** to sulk **2** *of lips* to protrude – **pout** n

poverty /'povəti/ n **1** the lack of sufficient money or material possessions **2** the condition of lacking desirable qualities; deficiency, death

'poverty-,stricken adj very poor; destitute

¹powder /'powdə'/ n **1** matter reduced to a state of dry loose particles (e g by crushing or grinding) **2** a preparation in the form of fine particles, esp for medicinal or cosmetic use **3** any of various solid explosives used chiefly in gunnery and blasting

²powder v **1** to sprinkle or cover (as if) with powder **2** to reduce or convert to powder

'powder ,keg n an explosive place or situation

'powder ,room n a public toilet for women in a hotel, department store, etc

¹power /'pow-ə/ n **1a** possession of control, authority, or influence over others **b** a sovereign state **c** a controlling group – often in *the powers that be* **2** ability to act or produce or undergo an effect **3a** physical might **b** mental or moral efficacy; vigour **c** political control or influence **4** the number of times, as indicated by an exponent, that a number has to be multiplied by itself **5a** electricity the rate at which work is done or energy emitted or transferred **6** magnification **7** a large amount *of* – infml

²power v **1** to supply with esp motive power **2** to make (one's way) in a powerful and vigorous manner

³power adj driven by a motor

'powerful /-f(ə)l/ adj having great power, prestige, or influence – **~ly** adv

'powerless /-lis/ adj **1** devoid of strength or resources; helpless **2** lacking the authority or capacity to act – **~ly** adv – **~ness** n

power of attorney n a legal document authorizing one to act as sby's agent

'power ,station n an electricity generating station

powwow /'pow,wow/ n **1** a N American Indian ceremony **2** a meeting for discussion – infml

²powwow v to hold a powwow

practicable /'praktikəbl/ adj **1** capable of being carried out; feasible **2** usable – **-bly** adv – **-bility** n

¹practical /'praktikl/ adj **1a** of or manifested in practice or action **b** being such in practice or effect; virtual **2** capable of being put to use or account; useful **3** suitable for use **4** disposed to or capable of positive action as opposed to speculation; *also* prosaic – **~ity** n

²practical n a practical examination or lesson

,practical 'joke n a trick or prank played on sby to derive amusement from his/her discomfort

practically /'praktikli/ adv almost, nearly

practice, *NAm also* **practise** /'praktis/ n **1a** actual performance or application **b** a repeated or customary action; a habit **c** the usual way of doing sthg **d** dealings, conduct – esp in *sharp practice* **2** (an instance of) regular or repeated exercise in order to acquire proficiency; *also* proficiency or experience gained in this way **3** a professional business

practise, *NAm chiefly* **practice** /'praktis/ v **1** to perform or work at repeatedly so as to become proficient **2** to be professionally engaged in

'practised, *NAm chiefly* **practiced** adj **1** experienced, skilled **2** learned by practice – often derog

practitioner /prak'tish(ə)nə/ n **1** one who practises a profession, esp law or medicine **2** one who practises a skill or art

pragmatic /prag'matik/ adj concerned with practicalities or expediency rather than theory or dogma; realistic – **~ally** adv

pragmatism /'pragmə,tiz(ə)m/ n **1** a practical approach to problems and affairs **2** a philosophical movement asserting that the meaning or truth of a concept depends on its practical consequences – **-tist** n

prairie /'preəri/ n an extensive area of level or rolling (practically) treeless grassland, esp in N America

¹praise /prayz/ v **1** to express a favourable judgment of; commend **2** to glorify or extol (e g God or a god)

²praise n **1** expression of approval; commendation **2** worship

'praise,worthy /-,wuhdhi/ adj laudable, commendable – **-thily** adv – **-thiness** n

pram, praam /pram, prahm/ n a small lightweight nearly flat-bottomed boat with a broad transom and usu squared-off bow

²pram /pram/ n a usu 4-wheeled carriage for babies that is pushed by a person on foot

prance /prahns/ v to walk or move in a gay, lively, or haughty manner – **prance** n

prank /prangk/ n a mildly mischievous act; a trick

prankster /'prangkstə/ n one who plays pranks

prate /prayt/ v to talk foolishly and excessively *about*; chatter

¹prattle /'pratl/ v **prattling** /'pratling/ to chatter in an artless or childish manner – **~r** n

²prattle n idle or childish talk

prawn /prawn/ n any of numerous widely distributed edible 10-legged crustaceans that resemble large shrimps

pray /pray/ v **1** to request earnestly or humbly **2** to address prayers to God or a god

prayer /preə/ *n* **1a** an address to God or a god in word or thought, with a petition, confession, thanksgiving, etc **b** an earnest request **2** the act or practice of praying **3** a religious service consisting chiefly of prayers – often *pl* with sing. meaning

,**praying 'mantis** /'praying/ *n* a (large green) mantis

preach /preech/ *v* **1** to deliver a sermon **2** to urge acceptance or abandonment of an idea or course of action, esp in an officious manner – ~**er** *n*

preamble /'pree,ambl/ *n* **1** an introductory statement; *specif* that of a constitution or statute **2** an introductory or preliminary fact or circumstance

,**prear'range** /-ə'raynj/ *v* to arrange beforehand – ~**ment** *n*

precarious /pri'keəri-əs/ *adj* **1** dependent on chance or uncertain circumstances; doubtful **2** characterized by a lack of security or stability; dangerous – ~**ly** *adv* – ~**ness** *n*

precast /,pree'kahst/ *adj* being concrete that is cast in the form of a panel, beam, etc before being placed in final position

precaution /pri'kawsh(ə)n/ *n* **1** care taken in advance; foresight **2** a measure taken beforehand to avoid possible harmful consequences; a safeguard – ~**ary** *adj*

precede /pri'seed/ *v* **1** to surpass in rank, dignity, or importance **2** to be, go, or come before, ahead, or in front of

precedence /'presid(ə)ns/ *also* **precedency** /-d(ə)nsi/ *n* **1** the right to superior honour on a ceremonial or formal occasion **2** priority of importance; preference

precedent /'presid(ə)nt/ *n* **1** an earlier occurrence of sthg similar **2** a judicial decision that serves as a rule for subsequent similar cases

precept /'preesept/ *n* a command or principle intended as a general rule of conduct – ~**ive** *adj*

precinct /'preesingkt/ *n* **1** *pl* the region immediately surrounding a place; environs **2** an area of a town or city containing a shopping centre and not allowing access to traffic **3** *NAm* an administrative district for election purposes or police control

¹**precious** /'preshəs/ *adj* **1** of great value or high price **2** highly esteemed or cherished; dear **3** excessively refined; affected – ~**ly** *adv* – ~**ness** *n*

²**precious** *adv* very, extremely

³**precious** *n* a dear one; darling

precipice /'presipis/ *n* **1** a very steep, perpendicular, or overhanging surface (e g of a rock or mountain) **2** the brink of disaster

¹**precipitate** /pri'sipitayt/ *v* **1** to throw violently; hurl **2** to bring about suddenly, unexpectedly, or too soon **3a** to separate from solution or suspension **b** to fall as rain, snow, etc

²**precipitate** /pri'sipitət/ *n* a substance separated from a solution or suspension by chemical or physical change, often as crystals

³**precipitate** /pri'sipitət/ *adj* **1** exhibiting violent or undue haste **2** lacking due care or consideration; rash – ~**ly** *adv*

precipitation /pri,sipi'taysh(ə)n/ *n* (the amount of) a deposit of rain, snow, hail, etc on the earth

precipitous /pri'sipitəs/ *adj* **1** precipitate **2** dangerously steep or perpendicular – ~**ly** *adv* – ~**ness** *n*

précis /'praysee/ *n*, *pl* **précis** a concise summary of essential points, facts, etc – **précis** *v*

precise /pri'sies/ *adj* **1** exactly or sharply defined or stated **2** highly exact **3** strictly conforming to a rule, convention, etc; punctilious **4** distinguished from every other; very – ~**ly** *adv* – ~**ness** *n*

¹**precision** /pri'sizh(ə)n/ *n* **1** being precise; exactness **2** the degree of refinement with which an operation is performed or a measurement stated

²**precision** *adj* **1** adapted for extremely accurate measurement or operation **2** marked by precision of execution

preclude /pri'kloohd/ *v* **1** to exclude **2** to prevent – ~**clusion** *n*

precocious /pri'kohshəs/ *adj* exhibiting mature qualities at an unusually early age – ~**ly** *adv* – ~**ness** *n* – ~**city** *n*

precognition /,preekog'nish(ə)n/ *n* clairvoyance of a future event

precursor /pri'kuhsə/ *n* **1** sby or sthg that precedes and signals the approach of sby or sthg else **2** a predecessor

predatory /'predət(ə)ri/ *adj* **1a** of or carrying out plunder or robbery **b** injuring or exploiting others for one's own gain **2** feeding by killing and eating other animals – ~**ation** *n* – ~**ator** *n*

predecessor /'preedi,sesə/ *n* **1** the previous occupant of a position or office to which another has succeeded **2** an ancestor

,**predesti'nation** /-desti'naysh(ə)n/ *n* the doctrine that salvation or damnation is foreordained

,**pre'destine** /-'destin/ *v* to destine or determine (e g damnation or salvation) beforehand

,**prede'termine** /-di'tuhmin/ *v* **1** to determine or arrange beforehand **2** to impose a direction or tendency on beforehand – ~**mination** *n*

predicament /pri'dikəmənt/ *n* a (difficult, perplexing, or trying) situation

¹**predicate** /'predikət/ *n* **1** sthg that is stated or denied of the subject in a logical proposition **2** the part of a sentence or clause that expresses what is said of the subject

²**predicate** /'predikayt/ *v* **1** to affirm, declare **2** to assert to be a quality or property **3** *chiefly NAm* to base – usu + *on* or *upon* USE *chiefly fml*

predicative /pri'dikətiv/ *adj* **1** of a predicate **2** joined to a modified noun by a linking verb (e g *red* in *the dress is red*) – ~**ly** *adv*

predict /pri'dikt/ *v* to foretell (sthg) on the basis of observation, experience, or scientific reason

prediction /pri'diksh(ə)n/ *n* sthg that is predicted; a forecast – **-tive** *adj* – **-tively** *adv*

predilection /preedi'leksh(ə)n, pre-/ *n* a liking, preference

,predi'spose /-di'spohz/ *v* 1 to incline, esp in advance 2 to make susceptible *to* – **-sition** *n*

predominate /pri'dominayt/ *v* 1 to exert controlling power or influence; prevail 2 to hold advantage in numbers or quantity – **-ance** *n* – **-ant** *adj* – **-antly** *adv*

preeminent /pri'eminənt/ *adj* excelling all others; paramount – **-nence** *n*

preempt /pri'empt/ *v* to invalidate or render useless by taking action or appearing in advance – ~**or** *n*

preemption /pri'empsh(ə)n/ *n* 1 the right of purchasing before others 2 a prior seizure or appropriation

preemptive /pri'emptiv/ *adj* 1 (capable of) preemption 2 carried out in order to forestall intended action by others

preen /preen/ *v* 1 to smarten oneself, esp in a vain way 2 to pride or congratulate oneself *on*; gloat 3 *of a bird* to trim and arrange the feathers

prefab /'preefab/ *n* a prefabricated structure or building

prefabricate /pri'fabrikayt/ *v* to fabricate the parts of (e g a building) at a factory ready for assembly elsewhere – **-cation** *n* – ~**d** *adj*

¹**preface** /'prefəs/ *n* 1 an introduction to a book, speech, etc 2 sthg that precedes or heralds; a preliminary

²**preface** *v* to introduce *by* or provide *with* a preface – **-atory** *adj*

prefect /'preefekt/ *n* 1 a chief officer or chief magistrate (e g in France or Italy) 2 a monitor in a secondary school, usu with some authority over other pupils

prefecture /'preefekchə/ *n* the office or official residence of a prefect – **-tural** *adj*

prefer /pri'fuh/ *v* **-rr-** 1 to choose or esteem above another; like better 2 to bring (a charge) against sby

preference /'pref(ə)rəns/ *n* 1 the power or opportunity of choosing 2 sby or sthg preferred; a choice 3 priority in the settlement of an obligation – **-ential** *adj* – **-entially** *adv* — **for preference** as being the more desirable; preferably

¹**prefix** /'preefiks/ *v* to add to the beginning

²**prefix** *n* 1 an affix (e g *un* in *unhappy*) placed at the beginning of a word or before a root 2 a title used before a person's name

pregnancy /'pregnənsi/ *n* 1 the condition or quality of being pregnant 2 fertility of mind; inventiveness

pregnant /'pregnənt/ *adj* 1 full of ideas or resourcefulness; inventive 2 containing unborn young within the body 3 showing signs of the future; portentous 4 full, teeming – usu + *with* – ~**ly** *adv*

prehensile /pri'hensiel, ,pree-/ *adj* adapted for seizing or grasping, esp by wrapping round

prehistoric /,preehi'storik/, **prehistorical** /-kl/ *adj* of or existing in times antedating written history – ~**ally** *adv*

,pre'history /-'histəri/ *n* (the study of) the prehistoric period of human beings' evolution

,pre'judge /-'juj/ *v* to pass judgment on prematurely or before a full and proper examination – **-judgment, -judgement** *n*

¹**prejudice** /'prejoodis, -jə-/ *n* 1 (an instance of) a preconceived judgment or opinion; *esp* a biased and unfavourable one formed without sufficient reason or knowledge 2 an irrational attitude of hostility directed against an individual, group, or race

²**prejudice** *v* 1 to injure by some judgment or action 2 to cause (sby) to have an unreasonable bias

'**prejudiced** *adj* having a prejudice or bias esp against

prejudicial /prejə'dish(ə)l/, **prejudicious** /-'dishəs/ *adj* 1 detrimental 2 leading to prejudiced judgments – **-ly** *adv*

prelate /'prelət/ *n* a clergyman (e g a bishop or abbot) of high rank

prelim /'preelim/ *n* a preliminary

¹**preliminary** /pri'limin(ə)ri/ *n* sthg that precedes or is introductory or preparatory: e g **a** a preliminary scholastic examination **b** *pl*, *Br* matter (e g a list of contents) preceding the main text of a book

²**preliminary** *adj* preceding and preparing for what is to follow

preliterate /,pree'litərət/ *adj* not yet employing writing

prelude /'prelyoohd/ *n* 1 an introductory or preliminary performance, action, or event; an introduction 2**a** a musical section or movement introducing the theme or chief subject or serving as an introduction (e g to an opera) **b** a short separate concert piece, usu for piano or orchestra – **prelude** *v*

premature /'premchə, ,premə'tyooə, 'premə,tyoo ə/ *adj* happening, arriving, existing, or performed before the proper or usual time; *esp*, *of a human* born after a gestation period of less than 37 weeks – ~**ly** *adv*

premeditate /pri'meditayt, ,pree-/ *v* to think over and plan beforehand – **-tation** *n* – ~**d** *adj*

¹**premier** /'premyə, 'premi-ə/ *adj* 1 first in position, rank, or importance; principal 2 first in time; earliest

²**premier** *n* a prime minister – ~**ship** *n*

premiere /'premi,eə, 'premi·ə/ *n* a first public showing (e g of a play or film)

premise *also* **premiss** /'premis/ *n* a proposition taken as the basis for argument or inference

premises /'premisiz/ *n pl* a piece of land with the buildings on it; *also* (part of) a building

¹**premium** /'preemyəm, -mi·əm/ *n* **1 a** a sum above a fixed price or wage, paid chiefly as an incentive **b** a sum in advance of or in addition to the nominal value of sthg **2** the sum paid for a contract of insurance **3** a high value or a value in excess of that normally expected — **at a premium** valuable because rare or difficult to obtain

²**premium** *adj* of exceptional quality

premium bond *n* a government bond which instead of earning interest is entered into a monthly draw for money prizes

premolar /,pree'mohlə/ *n or adj* (a tooth) situated in front of the true molar teeth

premonition /,premə'nish(ə)n, ,pree-/ *n* an anticipation of an event without conscious reason – **-tory** *adj*

preoccupation /pri,okyoo'paysh(ə)n, ,pree-/ *n* (sthg that causes) complete mental absorption

,**pre'occupy** /-'okyoopie/ *v* to engage or engross the attention of to the exclusion of other things – **-pied** *adj*

,**preor'dain** /-aw'dayn/ *v* to decree or determine in advance – **-dination** *n* – **~ment** *n*

prep /prep/ *n* homework done at or away from school

preparation /,prepə'raysh(ə)n/ *n* **1** preparing **2** a state of being prepared; readiness **3** a preparatory act or measure – usu pl **4** sthg prepared; *esp* a medicine

¹**preparatory** /pri'parət(ə)ri/, **preparative** /-tiv/ *adj* preparing or serving to prepare for sthg; introductory

²**preparatory** *adv* by way of preparation; in a preparatory manner – usu + *to*

pre'paratory ,school *n* a private school preparing pupils for public schools

prepare /pri'peə/ *v* **1 a** to make ready beforehand for some purpose, use, or activity **b** to put into a suitable frame of mind for sthg **2** to work out the details of; plan in advance **3** to draw up in written form

pre'pared *adj* subjected to a special process or treatment

preparedness /pri'peə(ri)dnis/ *n* adequate preparation (in case of war)

preponderant /pri'pond(ə)rənt/ *also* **preponderate** /-rət/ *adj* **1** having superior weight, force, or influence **2** occurring in greater number or quantity – **-ance** *n* – **~ly** *adv*

preponderate /pri'pondərayt/ *v* to predominate

preposition /,prepə'zish(ə)n/ *n* a linguistic form (e g *by, of, for*) that combines with a noun, pronoun, etc to form a phrase – **~al** *adj* – **~ally** *adv*

,**prepos'sessing** /-pə'zesing/ *adj* tending to create a favourable impression; attractive

,**prepos'session** /-pə'zesh(ə)n/ *n* **1** an opinion or impression formed beforehand; a prejudice **2** a preoccupation

preposterous /pri'post(ə)rəs/ *adj* contrary to nature or reason; absurd; *also* ridiculous – **~ly** *adv* – **~ness** *n*

'**prep ,school** /prep/ *n* a preparatory school

prepuce /'pree,pyoohs/ *n* the foreskin; *also* a similar fold surrounding the clitoris

prerequisite /pri'rekwizit/ *n* a requirement that must be satisfied in advance

prerogative /pri'rogətiv/ *n* **1** an exclusive or special right or privilege belonging esp to a person or group of people by virtue of rank or status **2** the discretionary power of the Crown

presage /'presij, pri'sayj/ *v* **1** to portend **2** to forecast, predict **3** to have a presentiment of – **presage** *n*

presbyter /'prezbitə/ *n* a member of the governing body of an early Christian or nonconformist church

Presbyterian /,prezbi'tiəri·ən/ *adj* of or constituting a Christian church governed by elected representative bodies and traditionally Calvinistic in doctrine – **Presbyterian** *n*

presbytery /'prezbit(ə)ri/ *n* **1** the part of a church (e g the E end of the chancel) reserved for the officiating clergy **2** a local ruling body in Presbyterian churches **3** the house of a Roman Catholic parish priest

preschool /,pree'skoohl/ *adj* of the period from infancy to first attendance at primary school

prescribe /pri'skrieb/ *v* **1** to lay down a rule; dictate **2** to designate or order the use of as a remedy

prescription /pri'skripsh(ə)n/ *n* **1** the action of laying down authoritative rules or directions **2** a written direction or order for the preparation and use of a medicine; *also* the medicine prescribed

presence /'prez(ə)ns/ *n* **1** the fact or condition of being present **2** the immediate vicinity of a (specified) person **3** sby or sthg present; *also* a spirit felt to be present **4** a quality of poise or distinction that enables a person, esp a performer, to impress, or have a strong effect on, others

presence of mind *n* self-possession

¹**present** /'prez(ə)nt/ *n* sthg presented; a gift

²**present** /pri'zent/ *v* **1 a** to introduce (sby) esp to another of higher rank **b** to bring (e g a play) before the public **2** to make a gift (to) **3** to give or bestow formally **4** to lay (e g a charge) before a court **5 a** to offer for show; exhibit **b** to offer for approval or consideration

³**present** /'prez(ə)nt/ *adj* **1** now existing or in progress **2a** in or at a usu specified place **b** existing in sthg mentioned or understood **c** vividly felt,

remembered, or imagined – usu + *to* or *in* 3 of or being a verb tense that expresses present time or the time of speaking

⁴**present** /'prez(ə)nt/ *n* 1 (a verb form in) the present tense of a language 2 the present time

presentable /pri'zentəbl/ *adj* 1 fit to be seen or inspected 2 fit (e g in dress or manners) to appear in company – **-bly** *adv*

presentation /,prezən'taysh(ə)n/ *n* 1a a thing offered or given; a gift b a descriptive or persuasive account (e g by a salesman of a product) 2 the manner in which sthg is set forth, laid out, or presented

present-'day /'prez(ə)nt/ *adj* now existing or occurring

presentiment /pri'zentimənt/ *n* a premonition

presently /'prez(ə)ntli/ *adv* 1 before long; soon 2 *chiefly NAm & Scot* at the present time; now

present participle /'prez(ə)nt/ *n* a participle (e g *dancing*, *being*) with present or active meaning

preservative /pri'zuhvətiv/ *n or adj* (sthg) that preserves or has the power to preserve; *specif* (sthg) used to protect esp food against decay, discoloration, etc

¹**preserve** /pri'zuhv/ *v* 1 to keep safe from harm or destruction; protect 2a to keep alive, intact, or free from decay b to maintain 3a to keep or save from decomposition b to can, pickle, or similarly prepare (a perishable food) for future use c to make a preserve of (fruit) – **-servable** *adj*

²**preserve** *n* 1 a preparation (e g a jam or jelly) consisting of fruit preserved by cooking with sugar 2 an area restricted for the preservation of natural resources (e g animals or trees); *esp* one used for regulated hunting or fishing 3 (e g a sphere of activity) reserved for certain people

preset /,pree'set/ *v* **-tt-**; **preset** to set beforehand

preside /pri'zied/ *v* 1 to occupy the place of authority 2 to exercise guidance, authority, or control *over*

presidency /'prezid(ə)nsi/ *n* 1 the office of president 2 the term during which a president holds office

president /'prezid(ə)nt/ *n* 1 an elected head of state in a republic 2 *chiefly NAm* the chief officer of an organization (e g a business corporation or university) – **~ial** *adj*

¹**press** /pres/ *n* 1 a crowd of people; a throng; *also* crowding 2 an apparatus or machine by which pressure is applied (e g for shaping material, extracting liquid, or compressing sthg) 3 a cupboard; *esp* one for books or clothes 4 an action of pressing or pushing; pressure 5a a printing press; *also* a publishing house b the act or process of printing 6a *sing or pl in constr, often cap* 6a(1) the newspapers and magazines collectively a(2) the journalists collectively b comment or notice in newspapers and magazines

²**press** *v* 1 to push firmly and steadily against 2a to squeeze out the juice or contents of (e g citrus fruits) b to iron (clothes) 3a to exert influence on; constrain b to try hard to persuade; entreat 4 to follow through (a course of action) 5 to clasp in affection or courtesy 6 to require haste or speed in action

³**press** *v* 1 to force into military service, esp in an army or navy 2 to take by authority, esp for public use; commandeer

'press-,gang *n sing or pl in constr* a detachment empowered to press men into military or naval service

press gang *v* to force into service (as if) by a press-gang

¹**pressing** /'presing/ *adj* 1 very important; critical 2 earnest, insistent – **~ly** *adv*

²**pressing** *n* one or more gramophone records produced from a single matrix

press on *v* 1 to continue on one's way 2 to proceed in an urgent or resolute manner

'press-,stud *n, Br* a metal fastener consisting of 2 parts joined by pressing

'press-,up *n* an exercise performed in a prone position by raising and lowering the body with the arms while supporting it only on the hands and toes

¹**pressure** /'preshə/ *n* 1 the burden of physical or mental distress 2 the application of force to sthg by sthg else in direct contact with it; compression 3 the force or thrust exerted over a surface divided by its area 4 the stress of urgent matters 5a influence or compulsion directed towards achieving a particular end b repeated persistent attack; harassment – **-rize** *v*

²**pressure** *v* 1 to apply pressure to 2 *chiefly NAm* to cook in a pressure cooker

'pressure ,cooker *n* a metal vessel with an airtight lid in which steam under pressure produces a very high temperature so that food can be cooked very quickly

'pressure ,group *n* an interest group organized to influence public, esp governmental, policy

prestige /pre'steezh, -'steej/ *n* high standing or esteem in the eyes of others

prestigious /pre'stijəs/ *adj* having or conferring prestige

presto /'prestoh/ *n, adv, or adj pl* **prestos** (a musical passage or movement played) at a rapid tempo – used in music

presume /pri'zyoohm/ *v* 1 to suppose or assume, esp with some degree of certainty 2 to take sthg for granted 3 to take liberties 4 to take advantage, esp in an unscrupulous manner – usu + *on* or *upon* – **-mable** *adj* – **-mably** *adv*

presumption /pri'zumsh(ə)n, pri'zumsh(ə)n/ *n* 1 presumptuous attitude or conduct; effrontery 2 an attitude or belief based on reasonable evidence or grounds; an assumption

presumptive /pri'zum(p)tiv/ *adj* 1 giving grounds for reasonable opinion or belief 2 based on probability or presumption – **~ly** *adv*

presumptuous /pri'zum(p)choo·əs, -tyoo·əs/ *adj* overstepping due bounds; forward – **~ly** *adv*

presuppose /,preesə'pohz/ *v* 1 to suppose beforehand 2 to require as an antecedent in logic or fact – **-position** *n*

pretence, *NAm chiefly* **pretense** /pri'tens/ *n* 1 a claim made or implied; *esp* one not supported by fact 2 a false or feigning act or assertion 3 an outward and often insincere or inadequate show; a semblance 4 a professed rather than a real intention or purpose; a pretext – *esp in false pretences*

¹**pretend** /pri'tend/ *v* 1 to give a false appearance of; feign 2 to claim or assert falsely; profess

²**pretend** *adj* make-believe – used esp by children

pretender /pri'tendə/ *n* 1 sby who lays claim to sthg; *specif* a (false) claimant to a throne 2 sby who makes a false or hypocritical show

pretension /pri'tensh(ə)n/ *n* vanity, pretentiousness

pretentious /pri'tenshəs/ *adj* making usu unjustified or excessive claims (e g of value or standing) – **~ness** *n* – **~ly** *adv*

preternatural /,preetə'nachərəl/ *adj* 1 exceeding what is natural or regular; extraordinary 2 lying beyond or outside normal experience *USE fml* – **~ly** *adv*

pretext /'preetekst/ *n* a false reason given to disguise the real one; an excuse

¹**pretty** /'priti/ *adj* 1a attractive or aesthetically pleasing, esp because of delicacy or grace, but less than beautiful b outwardly pleasant but lacking strength, purpose, or intensity 2 miserable, terrible 3 moderately large; considerable – **-tily** *adv* – **-tiness** *n*

²**pretty** *adv* 1a in some degree; *esp* somewhat b very – used to emphasize *much* or *nearly* 2 in a pretty manner; prettily – *infml*

,**pretty-'pretty** *adj* excessively pretty, esp in an insipid or inappropriate way

prevail /pri'vayl/ *v* 1 to gain ascendancy through strength or superiority; triumph – often + *against* or *over* 2 to persuade successfully – + *on*, *upon*, or *with* 3 to be frequent; *also* to persist

prevalent /'prevələnt/ *adj* generally or widely occurring or existing; widespread – **~ly** *adv* – **-lence** *n*

prevaricate /pri'varikayt/ *v* to speak or act evasively so as to hide the truth – **-cation** *n* – **-cator** *n*

prevent /pri'vent/ *v* 1 to keep from happening or existing 2 to hold or keep back; stop – often + *from* – **~able** *adj* – **~ion** *n*

preventive /pri'ventiv/, **preventative** /-tətiv/ *adj* 1 intended or serving to prevent; precautionary 2 undertaken to forestall anticipated hostile action

¹**preview** /'pree,vyooh/ *v* to see beforehand; *specif* to view or show in advance of public presentation

²**preview** *n* 1 an advance showing or performance (e g of a film or play) 2 a brief view or foretaste of sthg that is to come

previous /'preevyəs, -vi·əs/ *adj* 1 going before in time or order 2 acting too soon; premature – **~ly** *adv*

prevision /,pree'vizh(ə)n/ *n* 1 foreknowledge, prescience 2 a forecast, prophecy

¹**prey** /pray/ *n* 1 an animal taken by a predator as food 2 sby or sthg helpless or unable to resist attack; a victim

²**prey** *v* 1 to seize and devour prey – often + *on* or *upon* 2 to live by extortion, deceit, or exerting undue influence 3 to have continuously oppressive or distressing effect

price /pries/ *n* 1 the money, or amount of goods or services, that is exchanged or demanded in barter or sale 2 the terms for the sake of which sthg is done or undertaken: e g 2a an amount sufficient to bribe sby b a reward for the catching or killing of sby 3 the cost at which sthg is done or obtained – **price** *v* – **~y** *adj*

¹**priceless** /-lis/ *adj* 1 having a worth beyond any price; invaluable 2 particularly amusing or absurd – *infml*

¹**prick** /prik/ *n* 1 a mark or shallow hole made by a pointed instrument 2a a nagging or sharp feeling of sorrow or remorse b a sharp localized pain 3 the penis – *infml* 4 a disagreeable person – *infml*

²**prick** *v* 1 to pierce slightly with a sharp point 2 to trace or outline with punctures 3 to cause to be or stand erect – often + *up* — **prick up one's ears** to start to listen intently

¹**prickle** /'prikl/ *n* 1 a sharp pointed spike arising from the skin or bark of a plant 2 a prickling sensation

²**prickle** *v* **prickling** /'prikling, 'prikl·ing/ to cause or feel a stinging sensation; tingle

prickly /'prik(ə)li/ *adj* 1 full of or covered with prickles 2 prickling, stinging 3a troublesome, vexatious b easily irritated – **-liness** *n*

prickly pear *n* any of a genus of cacti having yellow flowers and bearing spines or prickly hairs

prick out *v* to transplant (seedlings) from the place of germination to a more permanent position (e g in a flower bed)

¹**pride** /pried/ *n* 1a inordinate self-esteem; conceit b a reasonable or justifiable self-respect c delight or satisfaction arising from some act, possession, or relationship 2 *sing or pl in constr* a group of lions

²**pride** *v* to be proud of (oneself) – + *on* or *upon*

priest /preest/ *n* a person authorized to perform the sacred rites of a religion – **~hood** *n* – **~ly** *adj* – **~liness** *n*

prig /prig/ n one who is excessively self-righteous or affectedly precise about the observance of proprieties – ~**gish** adj – ~**gishly** adv – ~**gishness** n

prim /prim/ adj -**mm**- 1 stiffly formal and proper; decorous 2 prudish – ~**ly** adv – ~**ness** n

prima ballerina /'preemə/ n the principal female dancer in a ballet

primacy /'priemasi/ n 1 the office or rank of an ecclesiastical primate 2 the state of being first (e g in importance, order, or rank); preeminence – fml

prima donna /,preema 'donə/ n, pl **prima donnas** 1 a principal female singer (e g in an opera company) 2 an extremely sensitive or temperamental person

primaeval /prie'meevl/ adj, chiefly Br primeval

¹**prima facie** /,priemə 'fayshi/ adv at first view; on the first appearance

²**prima facie** adj true, valid, or sufficient at first impression; apparent

primal /'priem(ə)l/ adj 1 original, primitive 2 first in importance; fundamental

primarily /'priem(ə)rəli, prie'merəli/ adv 1 for the most part, chiefly 2 in the first place; originally

¹**primary** /'priem(ə)ri/ adj 1a of first rank, importance, or value; principal b basic, fundamental 2a direct, firsthand b not derivable from other colours, odours, or tastes c of or at a primary school 3 of or being an industry that produces raw materials

²**primary** n 1 sthg that stands first in rank, importance, or value; a fundamental – usu pl 2 any of the usu 9 or 10 strong feathers on the joint of a bird's wing furthest from the body 3 a primary colour 4 a caucus 5 a primary school

primary colour n 1 any of the 3 bands of the spectrum: red, green, and bluish violet, from which all other colours can be obtained by suitable combinations 2 any of the 3 coloured pigments red, yellow, and blue that cannot be matched by mixing other pigments

'**primary** ,**school** n a school for pupils from 5 to 11

primate /'priemayt or (esp in sense ') -mət/ n 1 often cap a bishop having precedence (e g in a nation) 2 any of an order of mammals including human beings, the apes, monkeys, etc

¹**prime** /priem/ n 1 the most active, thriving, or successful stage or period 2 the chief or best individual or part; the pick 3 **prime**, **prime number** a positive integer that has no factor except itself and 1

²**prime** adj 1 having no factor except itself and 1 2 first in rank, authority, or significance; principal 3 of meat of the highest grade or best quality 4 not deriving from sthg else; primary

³**prime** v 1 to fill, load; esp to fill or ply (a person) with liquor 2 to prepare (a firearm or charge) for firing by supplying with priming or a primer 3 to apply a first coat (e g of paint or oil) to (a surface) 4 to put into working order by filling or charging with sthg, esp a liquid 5 to instruct beforehand; prepare

,**prime 'minister** n the chief executive of a parliamentary government – ~**ship** n

¹**primer** /'priemə/ n a small book for teaching children to read

²**primer** n 1 a device (e g a percussion cap) used for igniting a charge 2 material used in priming a surface

primeval /prie'meevl/ adj 1 of the earliest age or period 2 existing in or persisting from the beginning

priming /'prieming/ n the explosive used for igniting a charge

¹**primitive** /'primitiv/ adj 1 original, primary 2a of the earliest age or period; primeval b belonging to or characteristic of an early stage of development or evolution 3a of or produced by a relatively simple people or culture b lacking in sophistication or subtlety; crude; also uncivilized – ~**ly** adv – ~**ness** n

²**primitive** n 1a a primitive concept, term, or proposition 2a an artist of an early, esp pre-Renaissance, period b an artist, esp self-taught, whose work is marked by directness and naiveté 3 a member of a primitive people

primordial /prie'mawdyəl/ adj 1 existing from or at the beginning; primeval 2 fundamental, primary – ~**ly** adv

primrose /'primrohz/ n 1 any of a genus of perennial plants with showy, esp yellow, flowers 2 a pale yellow colour

primula /'primyoolə/ n a primrose

Primus /'priemas/ trademark – used for a portable oil-burning stove used chiefly for cooking (e g when camping)

¹**prince** /prins/ n 1 a sovereign ruler, esp of a principality 2 a foreign nobleman of varying rank and status

,**prince 'consort** n pl **princes consort** the husband of a reigning female sovereign

¹**princely** /-li/ adj 1 befitting a prince; noble 2 magnificent, lavish

princess /,prin'ses as an ordinary word, usu ' prinses or 'prinsəs before a name/ n 1 a female member of a royal family; esp a daughter of a sovereign 2 the wife or widow of a prince 3 a woman having in her own right the rank of a prince

¹**principal** /'prinsipl/ adj most important, consequential, or influential; chief – ~**ly** adv

²**principal** n 1 a person who has controlling authority or is in a leading position: e g 1a the head of an educational institution b one who employs another to act for him/her c a leading performer 2 a capital sum placed at interest, due as a debt, or used as a fund

principality /ˌprinsi'paləti/ n the office or territory of a prince

principle /'prinsipl/ n **1a** a universal and fundamental law, doctrine, or assumption **b** a rule or code of conduct **c** the laws or facts of nature underlying the working of an artificial device **2** a primary source; a fundamental element **3** an underlying faculty or endowment — **in principle** with respect to fundamentals

'principled adj exhibiting, based on, or characterized by principle – often used in combination

¹**print** /print/ n **1a** a mark made by pressure **b** sthg impressed with a print or formed in a mould **2** printed state or form **3** printed matter or letters **4a(1)** a copy made by printing (e g from a photographic negative) **a(2)** a reproduction of an original work of art (e g a painting) **a(3)** an original work of art (e g a woodcut or lithograph) intended from) graphic reproduction **b** (an article made from) cloth with a pattern applied by printing **c** a photographic copy, esp from a negative — **in print** obtainable from the publisher — **out of print** not obtainable from the publisher

²**print** v **1** to stamp (e g a mark or design) in or on sthg **2a** to make a copy of by impressing paper against an inked printing surface **b** to impress with a design or pattern **c** to publish in print **3** to write each letter of separately, not joined together **4** to make (a positive picture) on sensitized photographic surface from a negative or a positive

printable /'printǝbl/ adj **1** capable of being printed or of being printed from or on **2** considered fit to publish

ˌ**printed 'circuit** n a circuit for electronic apparatus consisting of conductive material in thin continuous paths from terminal to terminal on an insulating surface

printer /'printǝ/ n **1** a person engaged in printing **2** a machine for printing from photographic negatives **3** a device (e g a line printer) that produces printout

printing /'printing/ n **1** reproduction in printed form **2** the art, practice, or business of a printer

ˈ**print,out** /-ˌowt/ n a printed record produced automatically (e g by a computer)

¹**prior** /'prie·ǝ/ n the head (of a house) of any of various religious communities

²**prior** adj **1** earlier in time or order **2** taking precedence (e g in importance)

priority /prie'orǝti/ n **1a** being prior **b** superiority in rank **2** sthg meriting prior attention

ˈ**prior to** prep before in time; in advance of – fml

priory /'prie·ǝri/ n (the church of) a religious house under a prior or prioress

prise /priez/ vt, chiefly Br to prize up or open

prism /'priz(ǝ)m/ n a transparent body that is bounded in part by 2 nonparallel plane faces and is used to deviate or disperse a beam of light

prismatic /priz'matik/ adj **1** of, like, or being a prism **2** formed, dispersed, or refracted (as if) by a prism

prison /'priz(ǝ)n/ n a place of enforced confinement; specif a building in which people are confined for safe custody when on trial or for punishment after conviction

prisoner /'priz(ǝ)nǝ/ n sby kept under involuntary confinement; esp sby on trial or in prison

prissy /'prisi/ adj prim and over-precise; finicky – **prissily** adv – **prissiness** n

pristine /'pristeen, -tien/ adj **1** belonging to the earliest period or state **2** free from impurity or decay; fresh and clean as if new

privacy /'prievǝsi, pri-/ n **1** seclusion **2** freedom from undesirable intrusions and esp publicity

¹**private** /'privit/ adj **1a** intended for or restricted to the use of a particular person, group, etc **b** belonging to or concerning an individual person, company, or interest **2** not related to one's official position; personal **3a** withdrawn from company or observation **b** not (intended to be) known publicly; secret – ~**ly** adv

²**private** n a soldier of the lowest rank

private enterprise n an economic system based on private businesses operating competitively for profit

privateer /ˌprievǝ'tiǝ/ n an armed private ship commissioned to cruise against the commerce or warships of an enemy

private school n an independent school that is not a British public school

privation /prie'vaysh(ǝ)n/ n **1** an act or instance of depriving; deprivation **2** being deprived; esp lack of the usual necessities of life

privet /'privit/ n an ornamental shrub with half-evergreen leaves widely planted for hedges

privilege /'priv(i)lij/ n a right, immunity, or advantage granted exclusively to a particular person, class, or group; a prerogative; esp such an advantage attached to a position or office

¹**privy** /'privi/ adj **1** sharing in a secret – + to **2** secret, private

²**privy** n (a small building containing a bench with a hole in it used as) a toilet

Privy Council n an advisory council nominally chosen by the British monarch and usu functioning through its committees – **-cillor** n

¹**prize** /priez/ n **1** sthg offered or striven for in competition or in a contest of chance **2** sthg exceptionally desirable or precious

²**prize** adj **1a** awarded or worthy of a prize **b** awarded as a prize **2** outstanding of a kind

³**prize** v **1** to estimate the value of; rate **2** to value highly; esteem

⁴**prize** n property or shipping lawfully captured at sea in time of war

⁵**prize**, *Br also* **prise** /priez/ *v* **1** to press, force, or move with a lever **2** to open, obtain, or remove with difficulty

¹**pro** /proh/ *n, pl* **pros** an argument or piece of evidence in favour of a particular proposition or view

²**pro** *adv* in favour or affirmation

³**pro** *prep* for; in favour of

⁴**pro** *n or adj, pl* **pros** (a) professional – *infml*

pro-am /,proh 'am/,*proh* an esp golf competition in which amateurs play professionals

probability /,probǝ'bilǝti/ *n* **1** being probable **2** sthg (e g an occurrence or circumstance) probable **3** a measure of the likelihood that a given event will occur, usu expressed as the ratio of the number of times it occurs in a test series to the total number of trials in the series

¹**probable** /'probǝbl/ *adj* **1** supported by evidence strong enough to establish likelihood but not proof **2** likely to be or become true or real

²**probable** *n* sby or sthg probable; *esp* sby who will probably be selected

probate /'prohbayt, -bǝt/ *n* the judicial determination of the validity of a will

probation /prǝ'baysh(ǝ)n, proh-/ *n* **1** subjection of an individual to a period of testing to ascertain fitness **2** a method of dealing with (young) offenders by which sentence is suspended subject to regular supervision by a probation officer – ~ **ary** *adj*

probationer /prǝ'baysh(ǝ)nǝ/ *n* **1** one (e g a newly admitted student nurse) whose fitness for a post is being tested during a trial period **2** an offender on probation

¹**probe** /prohb/ *n* **1** a slender surgical instrument for examining a cavity **2** a device used to investigate or send back information, esp from interplanetary space **3a** a tentative exploratory survey **b** a penetrating or critical investigation; an inquiry – *journ*

²**probe** *v* **1** to investigate thoroughly – *journ* **2** to make an exploratory investigation – **probing** *adj* – **probingly** *adv*

probity /'prohbǝti/ *n* adherence to the highest principles and ideals; uprightness – *fml*

¹**problem** /'problǝm/ *n* **1a** a question raised for inquiry, consideration, or solution **b** a proposition in mathematics or physics stating sthg to be done **2a** a situation or question that is difficult to understand or resolve **b** sby who is difficult to deal with or understand

²**problem** *adj* difficult to deal with; presenting a problem

problematic /,problǝ'matik/, **problematical** /-kl/ *adj* **1** difficult to solve or decide; puzzling **2** open to question or debate; questionable – ~ **ally** *adv*

proboscis /prǝ'bosis/ *n, pl* **proboscises** *also* **proboscides** /-,deez/ **1** a long flexible snout (e g the trunk of an elephant) **2** any of various elongated or extendable tubular parts (e g the sucking organ of a mosquito) of an invertebrate

procedural /prǝ'seej(ǝ)rǝl, -dooǝrǝl, -dǝ-/ *adj* of procedure

procedure /prǝ'seejǝ, proh-/ *n* **1** a particular way of acting or accomplishing sthg **2** an established method of doing things

proceed /prǝ'seed, proh-/ *v* **1** to arise from a source; originate **2** to continue after a pause or interruption **3** to begin and carry on an action, process, or movement **4** to move along a course; advance

proceeding /prǝ'seeding, proh-/ *n* **1** a procedure **2** *pl* events, goings-on **3** *pl* legal action **4** *pl* an official record of things said or done

proceeds /'prohseedz/ *n pl* **1** the total amount brought in **2** the net amount received

¹**process** /'prohses/ *n* **1** sthg going on; a proceeding **2a** a natural phenomenon marked by gradual changes that lead towards a particular result **b** a series of actions or operations designed to achieve an end; *esp* a continuous operation or treatment (e g in manufacture) **3** a whole course of legal proceedings **4** a prominent or projecting part of a living organism or an anatomical structure

²**process** *v* **1** to subject to a special process or treatment (e g in the course of manufacture) **2** to take appropriate action on

³**process** *v* to move in a procession

procession /prǝ'sesh(ǝ)n/ *n* **1** a group of individuals moving along in an orderly way, esp as part of a ceremony or demonstration **2** a succession, sequence

¹**processional** /prǝ'sesh(ǝ)nl/ *n* a musical composition (e g a hymn) designed for a procession

²**processional** *adj* of or moving in a procession

proclaim /prǝ'klaym, proh-/ *v* **1** to declare publicly and usu officially; announce **2** to give outward indication of; show

proclamation /,proklǝ'maysh(ǝ)n/ *n* **1** proclaiming or being proclaimed **2** an official public announcement

proclivity /prǝ'klivǝti, proh-/ *n* an inclination or predisposition towards sthg

proconsul /,proh'konsl/ *n* a governor or military commander of an ancient Roman province – ~ **ar** *adj* – ~ **ate** *n*

procrastinate /proh'krastinayt, prǝ-/ *v* to delay intentionally and reprehensibly in doing sthg necessary – *fml* – **-nation** *n*

procreate /'prohkri'ayt/ *v* to beget or bring forth (young) – **-ation** *n*

,**procurator-'fiscal** *n, often cap P&F* a local public prosecutor in Scotland

procure /prə'kyooə/ v 1 to get and provide (esp women) to act as prostitutes 2 to obtain, esp by particular care and effort 3 to achieve – **~curable** adj – **~ment** n – **~r** n

¹**prod** /prod/ v **-dd-** 1 to poke or jab (as if) with a pointed instrument, esp repeatedly 2 to incite to action; stir

²**prod** n 1 a prodding action; a jab 2 an incitement to act

¹**prodigal** /'prodigl/ adj 1 recklessly extravagant or wasteful 2 yielding abundantly; lavish – fml

²**prodigal** n 1 a repentant sinner or reformed wastrel 2 one who spends or gives lavishly and foolishly

prodigious /prə'dijəs/ adj 1 exciting amazement or wonder 2 extraordinary in bulk, quantity, or degree; enormous – **~ly** adv

prodigy /'prodiji/ n 1 sthg extraordinary, inexplicable, or marvellous 2 a person, esp a child, with extraordinary talents

¹**produce** /prə'dyooս/ v 1 to give birth or rise to 2 to act as a producer of 3 to give being, form, or shape to; make; esp to manufacture 4 to (cause to) accumulate

²**produce** /'prodyooս/ n agricultural products; esp fresh fruits and vegetables as distinguished from grain and other staple crops

producer /prə'dyoosə/ n 1 an individual or entity that grows agricultural products or manufactures articles 2a sby who has responsibility for the administrative aspects of the production of a film (e g casting, schedules, and esp finance) b Br a theatre producer

product /'prodakt, -dukt/ n 1 the result of the multiplying together of 2 or more numbers or expressions 2 sthg produced by a natural or artificial process; esp a marketable commodity

production /prə'duksh(ə)n/ n 1a a literary or artistic work b a work presented on the stage or screen or over the air 2 the making of goods available for human wants 3 total output, esp of a commodity or an industry

productive /prə'duktiv/ adj 1 having the quality or power of producing, esp in abundance 2 effective in bringing about; being the cause of 3a yielding or furnishing results or benefits b yielding or devoted to the satisfaction of wants or the creation of utilities – **~ly** adv – **~ness** n

prof /prof/ n a professor – slang

¹**profane** /prə'fayn/ v 1 to treat (sthg sacred) with abuse, irreverence, or contempt; desecrate 2 to debase by an unworthy or improper use – **-fana-tion** n

²**profane** adj 1 not concerned with religion or religious purposes 2 debasing or defiling what is holy; irreverent 3 not possessing esoteric or expert knowledge – **~ly** adv – **-fanity** n

profess /prə'fes/ v 1 to declare or admit openly or freely; affirm 2 to declare falsely; pretend 3 to confess one's faith in or allegiance to

pro'fessed adj 1 openly and freely admitted or declared 2 pretended, feigned

profession /prə'fesh(ə)n/ n 1 an act of openly declaring or claiming a faith, opinion, etc 2 an avowed religious faith 3 a calling requiring specialized knowledge and often long and intensive academic preparation

¹**professional** /prə'fesh(ə)nl/ adj **1a** (characteristic) of a profession **b** engaged in 1 of the learned professions **c**(1) characterized by or conforming to the technical or ethical standards of a profession **c**(2) characterized by conscientious workmanship 2 engaging for gain or livelihood in an activity or field of endeavour often engaged in by amateurs 3 following a line of conduct as though it were a profession – derog 4 of a breaking of rules, esp in sport intentional – euph – **~ly** adv

²**professional** n 1 one who engages in a pursuit or activity professionally 2 one with sufficient experience or skill in an occupation or activity to resemble a professional – infml

pro'fessionalism /-iz(ə)m/ n 1 the esp high and consistent conduct, aims, or qualities that characterize a profession or a professional person 2 the following for gain or livelihood of an activity often engaged in by amateurs

professor /prə'fesə/ n a staff member of the highest academic rank at a university; esp the head of a university department – **~ial** adj – **~ially** adv – **~ship** n

proffer /'profə/ v to present for acceptance; tender

proficient /prə'fish(ə)nt/ adj well advanced or expert in an art, skill, branch of knowledge, etc – **~ly** adv – **-ciency** n

profile /'prohfiel/ n 1 a side view, esp of the human face 2 an outline seen or represented in sharp relief; a contour 3 a side or sectional elevation 4 a concise written or spoken biographical sketch – **profile** v

¹**profit** /'profit/ n 1 a valuable return; a gain 2 the excess of returns over expenditure – **~able** adj – **~ably** adv – **~less** adj – **~lessly** adv

²**profit** v to derive benefit; gain – usu + from or by

profiteer /,profi'tiə/ n one who makes an unreasonable profit, esp on the sale of scarce and essential goods – **profiteer** v

¹**profligate** /'profligət/ adj 1 utterly dissolute; immoral 2 wildly extravagant; prodigal – **-gacy** n

²**profligate** n a person given to wildly extravagant and usu grossly self-indulgent expenditure

profound /prə'fownd/ adj **1a** having intellectual depth and insight **b** difficult to fathom or understand 2 coming from, reaching to, or situated at a depth; deep-seated **3a** characterized by intensity of feeling or quality **b** all encompassing; complete – **~ly** *adv*

profundity /prəˈfunditi/ *n* **1a** intellectual depth **b** sthg profound or abstruse **2** being profound or deep

profuse /prəˈfyoohs/ *adj* **1** liberal, extravagant **2** greatly abundant; bountiful – **~ly** *adv* – **~ness** *n*

profusion /prəˈfyoohzh(ə)n/ *n* **1** being profuse **2** a large or lavish amount

progenitor /ˌprohˈjenitə/ *n* **1a** a direct ancestor; a forefather **b** a biologically ancestral form **2** a precursor, originator

progeny /ˈprojini/ *n* **1** descendants, children **2** offspring of animals or plants

prognosis /progˈnohsis/ *n, pl* **prognoses** /-seez/ **1** the prospect of recovery as anticipated from the usual course of disease or peculiarities of a particular case **2** a forecast, prognostication – *fml*

prognostic /progˈnostik/ *n* **1** sthg that foretells; a portent **2** prognostication, prophecy *USE fml*

prognosticate /progˈnosti.kayt/ *v* to foretell from signs or symptoms; predict – **-cation** *n* – **-cator** *n*

¹**program** /ˈprohgram/ *n* **1** a sequence of coded instructions that can be inserted into a mechanism (e g a computer) or that is part of an organism **2** *chiefly NAm* a programme

²**program** *v* **-mm-** (*NAm* **-mm-**, **-m-**) to work out a sequence of operations to be performed by (a computer or similar mechanism); provide with a program

¹**programme, *NAm chiefly* program** /ˈprohgram/ *n* **1** a brief usu printed (pamphlet containing a) list of the features to be presented, the people participating, etc (e g in a public performance or entertainment) by a radio or television broadcast characterized by some feature (e g a presenter, a purpose, or a theme) giving it coherence and continuity **2a** systematic plan of action **3** a curriculum **4** a prospectus, syllabus

²**programme, *NAm chiefly* program** *v* to cause to conform to a pattern (e g of thought or behaviour); condition

programme music *n* music intended to suggest a sequence of images or incidents

¹**progress** /ˈprohgres/ *n* **1** a ceremonial journey; *esp* a monarch's tour of his/her dominions **2** a forward or onward movement (e g to an objective or goal); an advance **3** gradual improvement; *esp* the progressive development of mankind — **in progress** occurring; going on

²**progress** /prəˈgres/ *v* **1** to move forwards; proceed **2** to develop to a higher, better, or more advanced stage

progression /prəˈgresh(ə)n/ *n* **1a** progressing, advance **b** a continuous and connected series; a sequence **2** succession of musical notes or chords

¹**progressive** /prəˈgresiv/ *adj* **1a** making use of or interested in new ideas, findings, or opportunities **b** of or being an educational theory marked by emphasis on the individual, informality, and self-expression **2** moving forwards continuously or in stages; advancing – **~ly** *adv*

²**progressive** *n* **1** sby or sthg progressive **2** sby believing in moderate political change, esp social improvement

prohibit /prəˈhibit, proh-/ *v* **1** to forbid by authority **2** to prevent from doing sthg

prohibition /ˌprohˈhibish(ə)n/ *n* **1** the act of prohibiting by authority **2** an order to restrain or stop **3** *often cap* the forbidding by law of the manufacture and sale of alcohol

prohibitive /prəˈhibətiv, proh-/, **prohibitory** /-t(ə)ri/ *adj* **1** tending to prohibit or restrain **2** tending to preclude the use or acquisition of sthg – **~ly** *adv*

¹**project** /ˈprojekt; *also* proh-/ *n* **1** a specific plan or design; a scheme **2a** a large undertaking, esp a public works scheme **b** a task or problem engaged in usu by a group of pupils, esp to supplement and apply classroom studies

²**project** /prəˈjekt/ *v* **1** to plan, figure, or estimate for the future **2** to throw forwards or upwards, esp by mechanical means **3** to present or transport in imagination **4** to cause to protrude **5** to cause (light or an image) to fall into space or on a surface **6a** to cause (one's voice) to be heard at a distance **b** to communicate vividly, esp to an audience **7** to attribute (sthg in one's own mind) to a person, group, or object

projectile /prəˈjektiel/ *n* a body projected by external force and continuing in motion by its own inertia; *esp* a missile (e g a bullet, shell, or grenade) fired from a weapon

projection /prəˈjeksh(ə)n/ *n* **1** a systematic representation on a flat surface of latitude and longitude from the curved surface of the earth, celestial sphere, etc **2** the act of throwing or shooting forward; ejection **3** a part that juts out **4** the attribution of one's own ideas, feelings, or attitudes to other people or to objects, esp as a defence against feelings of guilt or inadequacy **5** the display of films or slides by projecting an image from them onto a screen **6** an estimate of future possibilities based on a current trend

projectionist /prəˈjekch(ə)nist/ *n* the operator of a film projector

projector /prəˈjektə/ *n* an apparatus for projecting films or pictures onto a surface

proletarian /ˌprohliˈteəri·ən *n or adj* (a member) of the proletariat

proletariat /ˌprohliˈteəri·at/ *n* **1** the lowest class of a community **2** those workers who lack their own means of production and hence sell their labour to live

proliferate /prə'lifərayt/ v to grow or increase (as if) by rapid production of new parts, cells, buds, etc – **-ation** n

prolific /prə'lifik/ adj 1 producing young or fruit (freely) 2 marked by abundant inventiveness or productivity – ~**ally** adv

prologue, NAm also **prolog** /'prohlog/ n 1 the preface or introduction to a literary work 2 (the actor delivering) a speech, often in verse, addressed to the audience at the beginning of a play 3 an introductory or preceding event or development

prolong /prə'long/ v to lengthen – ~**ation** n

prom /prom/ n 1 a promenade concert 2 Br a seaside promenade

¹**promenade** /'promə,nahd/, ,–'-/ n 1 a leisurely stroll or ride taken for pleasure, usu in a public place and often as a social custom 2 a paved walk along the seafront at a resort

²**promenade** v 1 to walk about in or on 2 to display (as if) by promenading around

promenade concert n a concert at which some of the audience stand or can walk about

prominence /'prominəns/ n 1 being prominent or conspicuous 2 sthg prominent; a projection

prominent /'prominənt/ adj 1 projecting beyond a surface or line; protuberant 2a readily noticeable; conspicuous b widely and popularly known; leading – ~**ly** adv

promiscuous /prə'miskyoo·əs/ adj 1 not restricted to 1 class or person; indiscriminate; esp not restricted to 1 sexual partner 2 casual, irregular – ~**cuity**, ~**ness** n – ~**ly** adv

¹**promise** /'promis/ n 1 a declaration that one will do or refrain from doing sthg specified 2 grounds for expectation usu of success, improvement, or excellence 3 sthg promised

²**promise** v 1 to pledge oneself to do, bring about, or provide (sthg for) 2 to assure 3 to suggest beforehand; indicate

promised land n a place or condition believed to promise final satisfaction or realization of hopes

promising /'promising/ adj likely to succeed or to yield good results – ~**ly** adv

promissory note n a written promise to pay, either on demand or at a fixed future time, a sum of money to a specified individual or to the bearer

promontory /'promənt(ə)ri/ n a headland

promote /prə'moht/ v 1 to advance in station, rank, or honour; raise 2a to contribute to the growth or prosperity of; further b to help bring (e g an enterprise) into being; launch c to present (e g merchandise) for public acceptance through advertising and publicity – ~**r** n

promotion /prə'mohsh(ə)n/ n 1 being raised in position or rank 2a the act of furthering the growth or development of sthg, esp sales or public

awareness b sthg (e g a price reduction or free sample) intended to promote esp sales of merchandise – ~**al** adj

¹**prompt** /'prompt/ v 1 to move to action; incite 2 to assist (sby acting or reciting) by saying the next words of sthg forgotten or imperfectly learnt

²**prompt** adj of or for prompting actors – ~**ly** adv – ~**ness** n

³**prompt** adj 1a ready and quick to act as occasion demands b punctual 2 performed readily or immediately

⁴**prompt** n the act or an instance of prompting; a reminder

promulgate /'prom(ə)l,gayt/ v to make known by open declaration – fml – **-gation** n – **-gator** n

prone /prohn/ adj 1 having a tendency or inclination; disposed to 2 having the front or ventral surface downwards; prostrate – ~**ness** n

prong /prong/ n 1 any of the slender sharp-pointed parts of a fork 2a subdivision of an argument, attacking force, etc

pronoun /'prohnown/ n a word used as a substitute for a noun or noun equivalent and referring to a previously named or understood person or thing

pronounce /prə'nowns/ v 1 to pass judgment; declare one's opinion definitely or authoritatively – often + on or upon 2 to produce speech sounds; also to say correctly

pro'nounced adj strongly marked; decided – ~**ly** adv

pro'nouncement /-mənt/ n 1 a usu formal declaration of opinion 2 an authoritative announcement

pronto /'prontoh/ adv without delay; quickly – infml

pronunciation /prə,nunsi'aysh(ə)n/ n the act or manner of pronouncing sthg

¹**proof** /proohf/ n 1 the cogency of evidence that compels acceptance of a truth or a fact 2 an act, effort, or operation designed to establish or discover a fact or the truth; a test 3a an impression (e g from type) taken for examination or correction b a proof impression of an engraving, lithograph, etc 4 the alcoholic content of a beverage compared with the standard for proof spirit

²**proof** adj 1 designed for or successful in resisting or repelling; impervious – often in combination 2 used in proving or testing or as a standard of comparison 3 of standard strength or quality or alcoholic content

³**proof** v 1 to make or take a proof of 2 to give a resistant quality to; make (sthg) proof against

¹**proof,read** /-,reed/ v to read and mark corrections on (a proof) – ~**er** n

proof spirit n a mixture of alcohol and water containing a standard amount of alcohol, in Britain 57.1% by volume

¹**prop** /prop/ *n* **1** a rigid usu auxiliary vertical support (e g a pole) **2** a source of strength or support

²**prop** *v* **-pp- 1** to support by placing sthg under or against **2** to support by placing against sthg *USE* often + *up*

³**prop** /prop/ *n* any article or object used in a play or film other than painted scenery or costumes

propaganda /ˌpropəˈgandə/ *n* (the usu organized spreading of) ideas, information, or rumour designed to promote or damage an institution, movement, person, etc

propagate /ˈpropəˌgayt/ *v* **1** to reproduce or increase by sexual or asexual reproduction **2** to increase, extend – **-gation** *n* – **-gator** *n*

propane /ˈprohpayn/ *n* a hydrocarbon used as a fuel

propel /prəˈpel/ *v* **-ll- 1** to drive forwards by means of a force that imparts motion **2** to urge on; motivate – **~lant** *adj or n*

pro'peller *also* **propellor** /prəˈpelə/ *n* a device consisting of a central hub with radiating blades that is used to propel a ship, aeroplane, etc

propeller shaft *n* a shaft that transmits mechanical power, esp from an engine

propelling pencil /prəˈpeling/ *n, Br* a usu metal or plastic pencil whose lead can be extended by a screw device

propensity /prəˈpensəti/ *n* a natural inclination or tendency

¹**proper** /ˈpropə/ *adj* **1** suitable, appropriate **2** belonging to one; own **3** belonging strictly, specifically *to* a species or individual; peculiar **4** being strictly so-called **5** strictly decorous; genteel **6** *chiefly Br* thorough, complete

²**proper** *adv, chiefly dial* in a thorough manner; completely

proper fraction *n* a fraction in which the numerator is less or of lower degree than the denominator

¹**properly** /-li/ *adv* **1** in a fit manner; suitably **2** strictly in accordance with fact; correctly **3** *chiefly Br* to the full extent; completely

proper noun *n* a noun that designates a particular being or thing and is usu capitalized (e g *Janet, London*)

propertied /ˈpropətid/ *adj* possessing property, esp land

property /ˈpropəti/ *n* **1a** a quality, attribute, or power inherent in sthg **b** an attribute common to all members of a class **2a** sthg owned or possessed; *specif* a piece of real estate **b** sthg to which a person has a legal title **3** a prop

prophecy /ˈprofisi/ *n* **1** (the capacity to utter) an inspired declaration of divine will and purpose **2** a prediction of an event

prophesy /ˈprofisie/ *v* **1** to speak as if divinely inspired **2** to make a prediction

prophet /ˈprofit/, *fem* **prophetess** /-tes, -ˈtes/ *n* **1** a person who utters divinely inspired revelations **2** one who foretells future events; a predictor **3** a spokesman for a doctrine, movement, etc – ~**ic**, ~**ical** *adj* – ~**ically** *adv*

prophylactic /ˌprofiˈlaktik/ *adj* **1** guarding or protecting from or preventing disease **2** tending to prevent or ward off; preventive – *fml* – **prophylactic** *n* – ~**ally** *adv*

prophylaxis /ˌprofiˈlaksis/ *n pl* **prophylaxes** /-ˈlak,seez/ measures designed to preserve health and prevent the spread of disease

propinquity /prəˈpingkwəti/ *n* **1** nearness of blood; kinship **2** nearness in place or time; proximity *USE* fml

propitiate /prəˈpishiˌayt/ *v* to gain or regain the favour or goodwill of; appease – **-ation** *n* – **-atory** *adj*

propitious /prəˈpishəs/ *adj* **1** boding well; auspicious **2** tending to favour; opportune – ~**ly** *adv*

proponent /prəˈpohnənt/ *n* one who argues in favour of sthg; an advocate

¹**proportion** /prəˈpawsh(ə)n/ *n* **1** the relation of one part to another or to the whole with respect to magnitude, quantity, or degree **2** harmonious relation of parts to each other or to the whole; balance **3a** proper or equal share **b** a quota, percentage **4** *pl* size, dimension

²**proportion** *v* **1** to adjust (a part or thing) in proportion to other parts or things **2** to make the parts of harmonious or symmetrical

proportional /prəˈpawsh(ə)nl/ *adj* **1a** proportionate – usu + *to* **b** having the same or a constant ratio **2** regulated or determined in proportionate amount or degree

proportional representation *n* an electoral system designed to represent in a legislative body each political group in proportion to its voting strength in the electorate

proportionate /prəˈpawsh(ə)nət/ *adj* being in due proportion – **proportionate** *v*

proposal /prəˈpohzl/ *n* **1** an act of putting forward or stating sthg for consideration **2a** a proposed idea or plan of action; a suggestion **b** an offer of marriage **3** an application for insurance

propose /prəˈpohz/ *v* **1** to present for consideration or adoption **2** to make an offer of marriage **3a** to recommend to fill a place or vacancy; nominate **b** to offer as a toast – ~**r** *n*

¹**proposition** /ˌpropəˈzish(ə)n/ *n* **1** sthg offered for consideration or acceptance; *specif* a proposal of sexual intercourse **2** an expression, in language or signs, of sthg that can be either true or false **3** a project, situation, or individual requiring to be dealt with

²**proposition** *v* to make a proposal to; *specif* to propose sexual intercourse to

propound /prəˈpownd/ *v* to offer for discussion or consideration – fml

proprietary /prə'prie-ət(ə)ri/ *adj* **1** (characteristic) of a proprietor **2** made and marketed under a patent, trademark, etc **3** privately owned and managed

proprietor /prə'prie-ətə/, *fem* **proprietress** /-tris/ *n* an owner

propriety /prə'prie-əti/ *n* **1** the quality or state of being proper; fitness **2** the standard of what is socially or morally acceptable in conduct or speech, esp between the sexes; decorum

propulsion /prə'pulsh(ə)n/ *n* the action or process of propelling – **-sive** *adj*

pro rata /,proh 'rahtə/ *adv* proportionately according to an exactly calculable factor

prorogue /prə'rohg, ,proh-/ *v* to suspend a legislative session of – **-gation** *n*

prosaic /proh'zayik, prə-/ *adj* **1a** characteristic of prose as distinguished from poetry **b** dull, unimaginative **2** belonging to the everyday world; commonplace – ~ **ally** *adv*

proscenium /proh'seenyəm, prə-, -ni-əm/ *n* **1** the stage of an ancient Greek or Roman theatre **2 proscenium arch, proscenium** the space occupied by a theatre curtain when lowered

proscribe /proh'skrieb/ *v* **1** to outlaw, exile **2** to condemn or forbid as harmful; prohibit – **-scription** *n*

prose /prohz/ *n* **1** ordinary unrhymed language **2** a literary medium distinguished from poetry esp by its closer correspondence to the patterns of everyday speech

prosecute /'prosikyooht/ *v* **1** to institute legal proceedings **2** to follow through, pursue

prosecution /prosi'kyoohsh(ə)n/ *n* **1** prosecuting; *specif* the formal institution of a criminal charge **2** *sing or pl in constr* the party by whom criminal proceedings are instituted or conducted

prosecutor /'prosikyoohtə/ *n* sby who institutes or conducts an official prosecution

proselyte /'prosiliet/ *n* a new convert, esp to Judaism – **-tize** *v*

prosody /'prosədi/ *n* the study of verse forms and esp of metrical structure – **-dic** *adj* – **-dically** *adv*

[1]**prospect** /'prospekt/ *n* **1** an extensive view; a scene **2** *pl* **2a** financial and social expectations **b** chances, esp of success **3** a potential client, candidate, etc

[2]**prospect** /prə'spekt/ *v* to explore (an area), esp for mineral deposits – ~ **or** *n*

prospective /prə'spektiv/ *adj* **1** likely to come about; expected **2** likely to be or become

prospectus /prə'spektəs/ *n* a printed statement, brochure, etc describing an organization or enterprise and distributed to prospective buyers, investors, or participants

prosper /'prospə/ *v* to succeed, thrive; *specif* to achieve economic success

prosperous /'prosp(ə)rəs/ *adj* marked by esp financial success – ~ **ly** *adv* – **-rity** *n*

prostate /'prostayt/, **prostate gland** *n* a partly muscular, partly glandular body situated around the base of the male mammalian urethra that secretes a major constituent of the ejaculatory fluid

prosthesis /'prosthəsis; *sense* ' *or* -'thee-/ *n*, *pl* **prostheses** /-,seez/ an artificial device to replace a missing part of the body

[1]**prostitute** /'prosti,tyooht/ *v* to devote to corrupt or unworthy purposes; debase

[2]**prostitute** *n* a person, esp a woman, who engages in sex for money – **-tion** *n*

[1]**prostrate** /'prostrayt/ *adj* **1** lying full-length face downwards **2a** physically and emotionally weak; overcome **b** physically exhausted **3** *of a plant* trailing on the ground – **-tration** *n*

[2]**prostrate** /pro'strayt/ *v* **1** to put (oneself) in a humble and submissive posture **2** to reduce to submission, helplessness, or exhaustion

prosy /'prohzi/ *adj* dull, commonplace; *esp* tedious in speech or manner – **-sily** *adv* – **-siness** *n*

protagonist /proh'tagənist, prə-/ *n* **1** one who takes the leading part in a drama, novel, or story **2** a leader or notable supporter of a cause

protect /prə'tekt/ *v* **1** to cover or shield *from* injury or destruction; guard *against* **2** to shield or foster (a home industry) by a protective tariff – ~ **ive** *adj*

protection /prə'teksh(ə)n/ *n* **1** protecting or being protected **2** sthg that protects **3** the shielding of the producers of a country from foreign competition by import tariffs **4a** immunity from threatened violence, often purchased under duress **b** money extorted by racketeers posing as a protective association

pro'tector /prə'tektə/, *fem* **protectress** /-tris/ *n* **1a** a guardian **b** a device used to prevent injury; a guard **2** *often cap* the executive head of the Commonwealth from 1653 to 1659

protectorate /prə'tekt(ə)rət/ *n* **1a** government by a protector **b** *often cap* the government of the Commonwealth from 1653 to 1659 **2** the relationship of one state over another dependent state which it partly controls but has not annexed **b** the dependent political unit in such a relationship

protégé, *fem* **protégée** /'protə,zhay, 'proh-, -tay-/ (*Fr* prɔteʒe) *n* a person under the protection, guidance, or patronage of sby influential

protein /'prohteen/ *n* any of numerous extremely complex combinations of amino acids that are essential constituents of all living cells and are an essential part of the diet of animals and humans

[1]**protest** /'prohtest/ *n* **1** a formal declaration of disapproval **2** protesting; *esp* an organized public demonstration of disapproval **3** an objection or display of unwillingness

[2]**protest** /prə'test/ *v* **1** to make formal or solemn declaration or affirmation of **2** to enter a protest – ~ **er**, ~ **or** *n*

Protestant /'protistənt/ n a Christian who denies the universal authority of the pope and affirms the principles of the Reformation – **Protestant** adj – ~**ism** n

protestation /ˌprote'staysh(ə)n, proh-, -ti-/ n 1 an act of protesting 2 a solemn declaration or avowal

protocol /'prohtəkol/ n 1 an original draft or record of a document or transaction 2 a code of correct etiquette and precedence

proton /'prohton/ n an elementary particle identical with the nucleus of the hydrogen atom, that carries a positive charge

protoplasm /'prohtə,plaz(ə)m/ n 1 the organized complex of organic and inorganic substances (e g proteins and salts in solution) that constitutes the living nucleus and contents of the cell 2 cytoplasm

prototype /'prohtə,tiep, -toh-/ n 1 sby or sthg that exemplifies the essential or typical features of a type 2 a first full-scale and usu operational form of a new type or design of a construction (e g an aeroplane)

protozoan /ˌprohtə'zoh·ən/ n any of a subkingdom of minute single-celled animals which have varied structure and physiology and often complex life cycles

protozoon /ˌprohtə'zoh·on/ n, pl **protozoa** /-'zoh·ə/ a protozoan

protract /prə'trakt/ v to prolong in time or space – ~**ion** n

protractor /prə'traktə/ n 1 a muscle that extends a body part 2 an instrument that is used for marking out or measuring angles in drawing

protrude /prə'troohd/ v to (cause to) jut out – **-trusion** n

protuberant /prə'tyoohb(ə)rənt/ adj thrusting or projecting out from a surrounding or adjacent surface – **-nce** n – ~**ly** adv

proud /prowd/ adj 1a having or displaying excessive self-esteem b much pleased; exultant 2a stately, magnificent b giving reason for pride; glorious 3 projecting slightly from a surrounding surface

prove /proohv/ v **proved, proven** /'proohv(ə)n/ 1a to test the quality of; try out b to subject to a testing process 2 to establish the truth or validity of by evidence or demonstration 3 to turn out, esp after trial 4 to allow (bread dough) to rise and become light before baking – **-vable** adj – **-vably** adv

proverb /'provuhb/ n a brief popular epigram or maxim; an adage

proverbial /prə'vuhbyəl, -bi·əl/ adj 1 of or like a proverb 2 that has become a proverb or byword; commonly spoken of – ~**ly** adv

provide /prə'vied/ v 1 to furnish, equip with 2 to supply what is needed for sustenance or support 3 to stipulate

pro'vided conj on condition; if and only if

providence /'provid(ə)ns/ n often cap God conceived as the power sustaining and guiding human destiny

provident /'provid(ə)nt/ adj making provision for the future, esp by saving – ~**ly** adv

providential /ˌprovi'densh(ə)l/ adj of or determined (as if) by Providence; lucky – ~**ly** adv

provider /prə'viedə/ n one who provides for his/her family

province /'provins/ n 1a an administrative district of a country b pl all of a country except the metropolis – usu + the 2 a field of knowledge or activity; sphere

[1]**provincial** /prə'vinsh(ə)l/ n 1 one living in or coming from a province 2 a person with a narrow or unrefined outlook

[2]**provincial** adj 1 of or coming from a province 2a limited in outlook; narrow b lacking polish; unsophisticated

'**proving ground** /'proohving/ n a place where sthg new is tried out

[1]**provision** /prə'vizh(ə)n/ n 1a providing b a measure taken beforehand; a preparation 2 pl a stock of food or other necessary goods 3 a proviso, stipulation

[2]**provision** v to supply with provisions

provisional /prə'vizh(ə)nl/ adj serving for the time being; specif requiring later confirmation – ~**ly** adv

Provisional adj of or being the secret terrorist wing of the IRA

proviso /prə'viezoh/ n pl **provisos, provisoes** 1 a clause that introduces a condition 2 a conditional stipulation

provocation /ˌprovə'kaysh(ə)n/ n 1 an act of provoking; incitement 2 sthg that provokes or arouses

provocative /prə'vokətiv/ adj serving or tending to provoke or arouse to indignation, sexual desire, etc – ~**ly** adv

provoke /prə'vohk/ v 1 to incite to anger; incense 2a to call forth; evoke b to stir up on purpose; induce

provoking /prə'vohking/ adj causing mild anger; annoying – ~**ly** adv

provost /'provəst/ n 1 the head of a collegiate or cathedral chapter 2 the chief magistrate of a Scottish burgh 3 the head of certain colleges at Oxford, Cambridge, etc

prow /prow/ n 1 the bow of a ship 2 a pointed projecting front part

prowess /'prowis/ n 1 outstanding (military) valour and skill 2 outstanding ability

[1]**prowl** /prowl/ v to move about (in) or roam (over) in a stealthy or predatory manner

[2]**prowl** n an act or instance of prowling

proximal /'proksim(ə)l/ adj, esp of an anatomical part next to or nearest the point of attachment or origin – ~**ly** adv

proximate /'proksimət/ adj **1a** very near; close **b** forthcoming; imminent **2** next preceding or following USE fml – ~**ly** adv

proximity /prok'siməti/ n being close in space, time, or association; esp nearness

proxy /'proksi/ n **1** (the agency, function, or office of) a deputy authorized to act as a substitute for another **2** (a document giving) authority to act or vote for another

prude /proohd/ n one who shows or affects extreme modesty or propriety, esp in sexual matters – **-dish** adj – **-dishly** adv – **-dishness** n

prudence /'proohd(ə)ns/ n **1** discretion or shrewdness **2** caution or circumspection with regard to danger – **-ent** adj – **-ently** adv

prudential /prooh'densh(ə)l/ adj **1** of or proceeding from prudence **2** exercising prudence, esp in business matters – ~**ly** adv

prudery /'proohd(ə)ri/ n **1** the quality of being a prude **2** a prudish act or remark

¹**prune** /proohn/ n a plum dried or capable of drying without fermentation

²**prune** v to cut off the dead or unwanted parts of (a usu woody plant or shrub)

prurient /'prooəri-ənt/ adj inclined to, having, or arousing an excessive or unhealthy interest in sexual matters – **-ence** n – ~**ly** adv

Prussian blue /'prush(ə)n/ n **1** any of numerous blue iron pigments **2** a strong greenish blue colour

pry /prie/ v **1** to inquire in an overinquisitive or impertinent manner into **2** to look closely or inquisitively at sby's possessions, actions, etc – ~**ly** adv

psalm /sahm/ n, often cap any of the sacred songs attributed to King David and collected in the Book of Psalms of the Old Testament

Psalter /'sawltə/ n a book containing a collection of Psalms for liturgical or devotional use

pseudonym /'s(y)oohdə,nim/ n a fictitious name; esp one used by an author – ~**ous** adj

psyche /'sieki/ n **1** the soul, self **2** the mind

psychedelic /,siekə'delik/ adj **1** of drugs capable of producing altered states of consciousness that involve changed mental and sensory awareness, hallucinations, etc **2** of colours fluorescent

psychiatry /sie'kie-ətri/ n a branch of medicine that deals with mental, emotional, or behavioural disorders – **-trist** n – **-tric** adj – **-trically** adv

¹**psychic** /'siekik/ also **psychical** /-kl/ adj **1** lying outside the sphere of physical science or knowledge **2** of a person sensitive to nonphysical or supernatural forces and influences – ~**ally** adv

²**psychic** n **1** a psychic person **2** a medium

psycho /'siekoh/ n, pl **psychos** a psychopath, psychotic – infml

psychoanalysis /,siekoh-ə'naləsis/ n a method of analysing unconscious mental processes and treating mental disorders, esp by allowing the patient to talk freely about early childhood experiences, dreams, etc – **-lyst** n – **-lytic** adj – **-lytically** adv

psychological /,siekə'lojikl/ adj **1a** of psychology **b** mental **2** directed towards or intended to affect the will or mind – ~**ly** adv

psychology /sie'kolaji/ n the science or study of mind and behaviour – **-logist** n

psychopath /'siekəpath/ n a person suffering from a severe emotional and behavioural disorder characterized by the pursuit of immediate gratification through often violent acts; broadly a dangerously violent mentally ill person – ~**ic** adj – ~**ically** adv

psychosis /sie'kohsis/ n, pl **psychoses** /-,seez/ severe mental derangement (e g schizophrenia) that results in the impairment or loss of contact with reality – **-otic** adj

psychosomatic /,siekohsə-'matik/ adj of or resulting from the interaction of psychological and bodily factors, esp in the production of physical symptoms by mental processes – ~**ally** adv

psychotherapy /-'therəpi/ n treatment by psychological methods for mental, emotional, or psychosomatic disorders – **-pist** n

ptarmigan /'tahmigən/ n pl **ptarmigans**, esp collectively **ptarmigan** any of various grouse of northern regions whose plumage turns white in winter

pterodactyl /,terə'daktil/ n any of an order of extinct flying reptiles without feathers

Ptolemaic system /,tolə'mayik/ n the system of planetary motions according to which the sun, moon, and planets revolve round a stationary earth

pub /pub/ n an establishment where alcoholic beverages are sold and consumed

puberty /'pyoohbəti/ n the condition of being or the period of becoming capable of reproducing sexually

pubic /'pyoohbik/ adj of or situated in or near the region of the bone above the genitals

¹**public** /'publik/ adj **1** of or being in the service of the community **2** general, popular **3** of national or community concerns as opposed to private affairs **4** accessible to or shared by all members of the community **5a** exposed to general view; open **b** well-known, prominent – ~**ly** adv

²**public** n **1** the people as a whole; the populace **2** a group or section of people having common interests or characteristics — **in public** in the presence, sight, or hearing of strangers

publican /'publikən/ n, chiefly Br the licensee of a public house

publication /,publi'kaysh(ə)n/ n **1** the act or process of publishing **2** a published work

public bar n, Br a plainly furnished and often relatively cheap bar in a public house

,public 'company n a company whose shares are offered to the general public

,public con'venience n, Br public toilet facilities provided by local government

,public 'house n, chiefly Br an establishment where alcoholic beverages are sold to be drunk on the premises

publicist /'publisist/ n an expert or commentator on public affairs

publicity /pu'blisti/ n 1a paid advertising b the dissemination of information or promotional material 2 public attention or acclaim – -cize v

,public 'prosecutor n an official who conducts criminal prosecutions on behalf of the state

,public re'lations n pl but usu sing in constr the business of inducing the public to have understanding for and goodwill towards a person, organization, or institution

,public 'school n an endowed independent usu single-sex school in Britain, typically a large boarding school preparing pupils for higher education

,public 'servant n a government employee

publish /'publish/ v 1 to make generally known 2a to produce or release for publication; specif to print b to issue the work of (an author) – ~ er n

puce /pyoohs/ adj or n brownish purple

puck /puk/ n a hard rubber disc used in ice hockey

¹pucker /'puka/ v to (cause to) become wrinkled or irregularly creased

²pucker n a crease or wrinkle in a normally even surface

puckish /'pukish/ adj impish, whimsical – ~ly adv

pud /pood/ n, Br a pudding – infml

pudding /'pooding/ n 1 a sausage 2 any of various sweet or savoury dishes of a soft to spongy or fairly firm consistency that are made from rice, tapioca, flour, etc and are cooked by boiling, steaming, or baking 3 dessert

¹puddle /'pudl/ n a small pool of liquid; esp one of usu muddy rainwater

²puddle v puddling /'pudling, 'pudl·ing/ to work (a wet mixture of earth or concrete) into a dense impervious mass

pudendum /pyooh'dendam/ n, pl pudenda /-da/ the external genital organs of a (female) human being – usu pl with sing. meaning

puerile /'pyooariel/ adj 1 juvenile 2 not befitting an adult; childish – -ility n

puerperal /pyooh'uhp(a)ral/ adj of or occurring during the (period immediately following) childbirth

¹puff /puf/ v 1a(1) to blow in short gusts b(2) to exhale or blow forcibly b to breathe hard and quickly; pant c to draw on (a pipe, cigarette, etc) with intermittent exhalations of smoke 2a to become distended; swell b to distend (as if) with air or gas; inflate c to make proud or conceited – USE (2) usu + up

²puff n 1a an act or instance of puffing b a small cloud (e g of smoke) emitted in a puff 2 a light round hollow pastry made of puff paste 3 a highly favourable notice or review, esp one that publicizes sthg or sby 4 chiefly Br a breath of wind – infml

'puff ,adder n a large venomous African viper that inflates its body and hisses loudly when disturbed

'puff ,ball /-,bawl/ n any of various spherical and often edible fungi

puffin /'pufin/ n any of several seabirds that have a short neck and a deep grooved multicoloured bill

puff out v 1 to extinguish by blowing 2 to cause to enlarge, esp by filling or inflating with air

puff pastry n a light flaky pastry made with a rich dough containing a large quantity of butter

pug /pug/ n a small sturdy compact dog with a tightly curled tail and broad wrinkled face

pugilism /'pyoohji,liz(a)m/ n boxing – fml – pugilist n – -istic adj

pugnacious /pug'nayshas/ adj inclined to fight or quarrel; belligerent – -ity, ~ness n – ~ly adv

puissance /'pyooh·is(a)ns, 'pwis(a)ns, pyoo(h)'is(a)ns; in showjumping 'pweesahnhs   n 1 a showjumping competition which tests the horse's power to jump high obstacles 2 strength, power – fml or poetic

puke /pyoohk/ v to vomit – infml – puke n

pukka /'puka/ adj 1 genuine, authentic; also first-class 2 chiefly Br stiffly formal or proper

pulchritude /'pulkri,tyoohd/ n physical beauty – fml – -dinous adj

pule /pyoohl/ v to whine, whimper

¹pull /pool/ v 1a to exert force upon so as to (tend to) cause motion towards the force; tug at b to move, esp through the exercise of mechanical energy 2 to strain (a muscle) 3 to hit (e g a ball in cricket or golf) towards the left from a right-handed swing or towards the right from a left-handed swing 4 to draw apart; tear 5 to print (e g a proof) by impression 6 to bring out (a weapon) ready for use 7 to draw from the barrel, esp by pulling a pump handle 8a to carry out, esp with daring and imagination – usu + off b to do, perform, or say with a deceptive intent 9 to draw or inhale hard in smoking — pull a fast one to perpetrate a trick or fraud — infml — pull oneself together to regain one's self-possession or self-control — pull one's punches to refrain from using all the force at one's disposal — pull one's weight to do one's full share of the work — pull out all the stops to do everything possible to achieve an effect or action — pull rank on somebody to assert one's authority in order to get sthg

pleasant — **pull someone's leg** to deceive sby playfully; hoax — **pull strings** to exert (secret) personal influence — **pull the wool over someone's eyes** to blind sby to the true situation; hoodwink sby — **pull together** to work in harmony towards a common goal; cooperate

²**pull** n **1a** the act or an instance of pulling **b(1)** a draught of liquid **b(2)** an inhalation of smoke (e g from a cigarette) **2** (special influence exerted to obtain) an advantage **3** a force that attracts, compels, or influences

pull away v **1** to draw oneself back or away; withdraw **2** to move off or ahead

pull down v **1** to demolish, destroy

pullet /'poolit/ n a young female domestic fowl less than a year old

pulley /'pooli/ n **1** a wheel with a grooved rim that is used with a rope or chain to change the direction and point of application of a pulling force **2** a wheel used to transmit power or motion by means of a belt, rope, or chain passing over its rim

'**pull-, in** n, chiefly Br a place where vehicles may pull in and stop; also a roadside café

pull in v **1** to arrest **2** to acquire as payment or profit – infml **3** of a vehicle or driver to move to the side or off the road in order to stop

Pullman /'poolmən/ n a railway passenger carriage with extra-comfortable furnishings, esp for night travel

pull off v to carry out or accomplish despite difficulties

'**pull,out** /-,owt/ n **1** a larger leaf in a book or magazine that when folded is the same size as the ordinary pages **2** a removable section of a magazine, newspaper, or book

pull out v **1** esp of a train or road vehicle to leave, depart **2a** to withdraw from a military position **b** to withdraw from a joint enterprise or agreement **3** of a motor vehicle **3a** to move into a stream of traffic **b** to move out from behind a vehicle (e g when preparing to overtake)

'**pull,over** /-,ohvə/ n a garment for the upper body, esp a jumper, put on by being pulled over the head

pull over v, of a driver or vehicle to move towards the side of the road, esp in order to stop

pull through v to (cause to) survive a dangerous or difficult situation (e g illness)

pull up v **1** to bring to a stop; halt **2** to reprimand, rebuke **3** to draw even with or gain on others (e g in a race) — **pull one's socks up** or **pull up one's socks** to make an effort to show greater application or improve one's performance

pulmonary /'poolmən(ə)ri, 'pul-/, **pulmonic** /-'monik/ adj of, associated with, or carried on by the lungs

'**pulp** /pulp/ n **1a** the soft juicy or fleshy part of a fruit or vegetable **b** a material prepared by chemical or mechanical means from rags, wood, etc

that is used in making paper **2** a soft shapeless mass, esp produced by crushing or beating **3** a magazine or book cheaply produced on rough paper and containing sensational material – ∼y adj

²**pulp** v **1** to reduce to pulp **2** to remove the pulp from

pulpit /'poolpit/ n a raised platform or high reading desk in church from which a sermon is preached

pulsar /'pulsah/ n a celestial source, prob a rotating neutron star, of uniformly pulsating radio waves

pulsate /pul'sayt/ v **1** to beat with a pulse **2** to throb or move rhythmically; vibrate – **-sation** n

'**pulse** /puls/ n the edible seeds of any of various leguminous crops (e g peas, beans, or lentils); also the plant yielding these

²**pulse** /puls/ n **1** a regular throbbing caused in the arteries by the contractions of the heart; also a single movement of such throbbing **2a** (an indication of) underlying sentiment or opinion **b** a feeling of liveliness; vitality **3a** rhythmical vibrating or sounding **b** a single beat or throb

³**pulse** v to pulsate, throb

pulver·ize, -ise /'pulvəriez/ v **1** to reduce (e g by crushing or grinding) to very small particles **2** to annihilate, demolish

puma /'pyoohmə/ n pl **pumas,** esp collectively **puma** a powerful tawny big cat

pumice /'pumis/ n a light porous volcanic rock used esp as an abrasive and for polishing

pummel /'puml/ v -ll- (NAm -l-, -ll-), /'puml·ing/ to pound or strike repeatedly, esp with the fists

'**pump** /pump/ n a device that raises, transfers, or compresses fluids or that reduces the density of gases, esp by suction or pressure or both

²**pump** v **1a** to raise (e g water) with a pump **b** to draw fluid from with a pump – often + out **2** to question persistently **3** to move (sthg) rapidly up and down as if working a pump handle **4** to inflate by means of a pump or bellows – usu + up

³**pump** n **1** a low shoe without fastenings that grips the foot chiefly at the toe and heel **2** Br a plimsoll

pumpernickel /'pumpə,nikl, 'poompə-/ n a dark coarse slightly sour-tasting bread made from wholemeal rye

pumpkin /'pum(p)kin/ n (a usu hairy prickly plant that bears) a very large usu round fruit with a deep yellow to orange rind and edible flesh

'**pun** /pun/ n a humorous use of a word with more than 1 meaning or of words with (nearly) the same sound but different meanings

²**pun** v -nn- to make puns

'**punch** /punch/ v **1** to strike, esp with a hard and quick thrust of the fist **2** to drive or push forcibly (as if) by a punch **3** to emboss, cut, or make (as if) with a punch – ∼er n

²**punch** *n* **1** a blow (as if) with the fist **2** effective energy or forcefulness

³**punch** *n* **1** a tool, usu in the form of a short steel rod, used esp for perforating, embossing, cutting, or driving the heads of nails below a surface **2** a device for cutting holes or notches in paper or cardboard

⁴**punch** *n* a hot or cold drink usu made from wine or spirits mixed with fruit, spices, water, and occas tea

'**punch-drunk** *adj* **1** suffering brain damage as a result of repeated punches or blows to the head **2** behaving as if punch-drunk; dazed

,**punched 'card**, '**punch ,card** *n* a card used in data processing in which a pattern of holes or notches has been cut to represent information or instructions

'**punch ,line** *n* a sentence or phrase, esp a joke, that forms the climax to a speech or dialogue

'**punch-,up** *n*, *chiefly Br* a usu spontaneous fight, esp with the bare fists – *infml*

punctilious /pung(k)'tili·əs/ *adj* strict or precise in observing codes of conduct or conventions – ~**ly** *adv* – ~**ness** *adv*

punctual /'pung(k)chooəl, -tyoo-/ *adj* (habitually) arriving, happening, performing, etc at the exact or agreed time – ~**ity** *n* – ~**ly** *adv*

punctuate /'pung(k)choo,ayt, -tyoo-/ *v* **1** to mark or divide with punctuation marks **2** to break into or interrupt at intervals

punctuation /,pung(k)choo'aysh(ə)n, -tyoo-/ *n* the dividing of writing with marks to clarify meaning; *also* a system of punctuation

'**puncture** /'pung(k)chə/ *n* a hole, narrow wound, etc made by puncturing; *esp* a small hole made accidentally in a pneumatic tyre

²**puncture** *v* **1** to pierce with a pointed instrument or object **2** to make useless or deflate as if by a puncture

pundit /'pundit/ *n* **1** a learned man or teacher **2** one who gives opinions in an authoritative manner; an authority

pungent /'punj(ə)nt/ *adj* **1** marked by a sharp incisive quality; caustic **2** to the point; highly expressive **3** having a strong sharp smell or taste; *esp* acrid – ~**ly** *adv* – ~**gency** *n*

punish /'punish/ *v* **1** to impose a penalty on (an offender) or for (an offence) **2** to treat roughly or damagingly – *infml*

'**punishment** /-mənt/ *n* **1a** punishing or being punished **b** a judicial penalty **2** rough or damaging treatment – *infml*

punitive /'pyoohnətiv/ *adj* inflicting or intended to inflict punishment – ~**ly** *adv*

'**punk** /pungk/ *n* **1** sby following punk styles in music, dress, etc **2** *chiefly NAm* sby considered worthless or inferior; *esp* a petty criminal

²**punk** *adj* **1** of or being a movement among young people of the 1970s and 1980s in Britain characterized by a violent rejection of established society **2** *chiefly NAm* of very poor quality; inferior – *slang*

³**punk** *n* a dry spongy substance prepared from fungi and used to ignite fuses

punnet /'punit/ *n*, *chiefly Br* a small basket of wood, plastic, etc, esp for soft fruit or vegetables

'**punt** /punt/ *n* a long narrow flat-bottomed boat with square ends, usu propelled with a pole

²**punt** *v* to propel (e g a punt) with a pole – ~**er** *n*

³**punt** *v*, *Br* to gamble – ~**er** *n*

⁴**punt** *n* kicking a football with the top or tip of the foot after it is dropped from the hands and before it hits the ground – **punt** *v*

⁵**punt** *n* the basic currency unit of the Irish Republic

puny /'pyoohni/ *adj* slight or inferior in power, size, or importance; weak – **nily** *adv* – **niness** *n*

'**pup** /pup/ *n* a young dog; *also* a young seal, rat, etc

²**pup** *v* **-pp-** to give birth to pups

pupa /'pyoohpə/ *n*, *pl* **pupae** /-pi/, **pupas** the intermediate usu inactive form of an insect (e g a bee, moth, or beetle) that occurs between the larva and the final adult stage – ~**l** *adj*

pupate /pyooh'payt/ *v* to become a pupa – **-pation** *n*

'**pupil** /'pyoohpl/ *n* **1** a child or young person at school or receiving tuition **2** one who has been taught or influenced by a distinguished person

²**pupil** *n* the contractile usu round dark opening in the iris of the eye

puppet /'pupit/ *n* **1a** a small-scale toy figure (e g of a person or animal) usu with a cloth body and hollow head that fits over and is moved by the hand **b** a marionette **2** one whose acts are controlled by an outside force or influence

puppy /'pupi/ *n* **1** a young dog (less than a year old) **2** a conceited or ill-mannered young man

'**puppy ,fat** *n* temporary plumpness in children and adolescents

'**puppy ,love** *n* short-lived romantic affection felt by an adolescent for sby of the opposite sex

'**purchase** /'puhchəs/ *v* **1** to obtain by paying money or its equivalent; buy **2** to obtain by labour, danger, or sacrifice – **-chasable** *adj* – ~**r** *n*

²**purchase** *n* **1** sthg obtained by payment of money or its equivalent **2a** a mechanical hold or advantage (e g that applied through a pulley or lever); *broadly* an advantage used in applying power or influence **b** a means, esp a mechanical device, by which one gains such an advantage

pure /pyooə/ *adj* **1a(1)** unmixed with any other matter **a(2)** free from contamination **a(3)** free from moral fault **b** *of a musical sound* being in tune and free from harshness **2a** sheer, unmitigated **b** abstract, theoretical **3a** free from anything that vitiates or weakens **b** containing nothing that does not properly belong **4a** chaste **b** ritually clean

¹**puree, purée** /'pyooəray/ *n* a thick pulp (e g of fruit or vegetable) usu produced by rubbing cooked food through a sieve or blending in a liquidizer

²**puree, purée** *v* to reduce to a puree

purely /'pyoooli/ *adv* **1** simply, merely **2** in a chaste or innocent manner **3** wholly, completely

purgative /'puhgətiv/ *n or adj* (a medicine) causing evacuation of the bowels

purgatory /'puhgət(ə)ri/ *n* **1** a place or state of punishment in which, according to Roman Catholic doctrine, souls may make amends for past sins and so become fit for heaven **2** a place or state of temporary suffering or misery – *infml* – **-rial** *adj*

¹**purge** /puhj/ *v* **1a** to clear of guilt or to free from moral or physical impurity **2a** to cause evacuation from (e g the bowels) **b** to rid (e g a nation or party) of unwanted or undesirable members, often summarily or by force – **-gation** *n*

²**purge** *n* **1** an (esp political) act of purging **2** a purgative

purify /'pyooərifi/ *v* **1** to free of physical or moral impurity or imperfection **2** to free from undesirable elements – **-fication** *n*

purist /'pyooərist/ *n* one who keeps strictly and often excessively to established or traditional usage, esp in language – **-ism** *n*

puritan /'pyooərit(ə)n/ *n* **1** *cap* a member of a 16th- and 17th-c mainly Calvinist Protestant group in England and New England **2** one who practises or preaches a rigorous or severe moral code – **~ism** *n* – **~ical** *adj* – **~ically** *adv*

purity /'pyooərəti/ *n* **1** pureness **2** saturation of a colour

¹**purl** /puhl/ *n* **1** a thread of twisted gold or silver wire used for embroidering or edging **2 purl, purl stitch** a basic knitting stitch made by inserting the needle into the back of a stitch that produces a raised pattern on the back of the work

²**purl** *v* to knit in purl stitch

purlieus /'puhlyoohz/ *n pl* **1** environs, neighbourhood **2** confines, bounds – *fml*

purloin /puh'loyn, pə-/ *v* to take dishonestly; steal – *fml*

¹**purple** /'puhpl/ *adj* **1** of the colour purple **2** highly rhetorical; ornate – **purplish** *adj*

²**purple** *n* **1** a colour falling about midway between red and blue in hue **2** imperial, regal, or very high rank

¹**purport** /'puhpawt, -pət/ *n* professed or implied meaning; import; *also* substance – *fml*

²**purport** /pə'pawt, puh'pawt, 'puhpət/ *v* to (be intended to) seem; profess

¹**purpose** /'puhpəs/ *n* **1** the object for which sthg exists or is done; the intention **2** resolution, determination — **on purpose** with intent; intentionally

²**purpose** *v* to have as one's intention – *fml*

,**purpose-'built** *adj* designed to meet a specific need

'**purposeful** /-f(ə)l/ *adj* **1** full of determination **2** having a purpose or aim – **~ly** *adv*

'**purposely** /-li/ *adv* with a deliberate or express purpose

purr /puh/ *v* to make the low vibratory murmur of a contented cat – **purr** *n*

¹**purse** /puhs/ *n* **1** a small flattish bag for money; *esp* a wallet with a compartment for holding change **2** a sum of money offered as a prize or present; *also* the total amount of money offered in prizes for a given event **3** *NAm* a handbag

²**purse** *v* to pucker, knit

purser /'puhsə/ *n* an officer on a ship responsible for documents and accounts and on a passenger ship also for the comfort and welfare of passengers

'**purse ,strings** *n pl* control over expenditure

pursuance /pə'syooh·əns/ *n* a carrying out or into effect (e g of a plan or order)

pursue /pə'syooh/ *v* **1** to follow in order to overtake, capture, kill, or defeat **2** to find or employ measures to obtain or accomplish **3a** to engage in **b** to follow up **4** to continue to afflict; haunt – **~r** *n*

pursuit /pə'syooht/ *n* **1** an act of pursuing **2** an activity that one regularly engages in (e g as a pastime or profession)

purulent /'pyooərələnt/ *adj* **1** containing, consisting of, or being pus **2** accompanied by suppuration – **-lence** *n* – **~ly** *adv*

purvey /pə'vay, puh-/ *v* to supply (e g provisions), esp in the course of business – **~ance, ~or** *n*

pus /pus/ *n* thick opaque usu yellowish white fluid matter formed by suppuration (e g in an abscess)

¹**push** /poosh/ *v* **1** to apply a force to (sthg) in order to cause movement away from the person or thing applying the force **2a** to develop (e g an idea or argument), esp to an extreme degree **b** to urge or press the advancement, adoption, or practice of; *specif* to make aggressive efforts to sell **c** to press or urge (sby) to sthg; pressurize **3** to press forwards energetically against obstacles or opposition **4** to exert oneself continuously or vigorously to achieve an end **5** to approach in age or number – *infml* **6** to engage in the illicit sale of (drugs) – slang **7** to press against sthg with steady force (as if) in order to move it away – **push one's luck** to take an increasing risk

²**push** *n* **1** a vigorous effort to attain an end; a drive **2a** an act or action of pushing **b** vigorous enterprise or energy **3a** an exertion of influence to promote another's interests **b** stimulation to

activity; an impetus **4** *Br* dismissal – esp in *get/give the push* — **at a push** *chiefly Br* if really necessary; if forced by special conditions
push around *v* to order about; bully
'push-,bike *n*, *Br* a pedal bicycle
'push-,button *adj* **1** operated by means of a push button **2** characterized by the use of long-range weapons rather than physical combat
'push ,button *n* a button or knob that, when pushed, operates or triggers sthg
'push,chair /-,cheə/ *n*, *Br* a light folding chair on wheels in which young children may be pushed
pushed /poosht/ *adj* having difficulty in finding enough time, money, etc – infml
pusher /'pooshə/ *n* **1** a utensil used by a child for pushing food onto a spoon or fork **2** one who sells drugs illegally – slang
push in *v* to join a queue at a point in front of others already waiting, esp by pushing or jostling
push off *v* to go away, esp hastily or abruptly – infml
push on *v* to continue on one's way, esp despite obstacles or difficulties
'push,over /-,ohvə/ *n* **1** an opponent who is easy to defeat or a victim who is incapable of effective resistance **2** sby unable to resist a usu specified attraction; a sucker **3** sthg accomplished without difficulty *USE* infml
pushy /'pooshi/ *adj* self-assertive often to an objectionable degree; forward – infml – **-hily** *adv* – **-hiness** *n*
pusillanimous /,pyoohsi'laniməs/ *adj* timid – fml – **-ly** *adv* – **-mity** *n*
puss /poos/ *n* a cat – used chiefly as a pet name or calling name *USE* infml
pussy /'poosi/ *n* **1** a catkin of the pussy willow **2** a cat – infml; used chiefly as a pet name
'pussy,foot /-,foot/ *v* **1** to tread or move warily or stealthily **2** to avoid committing oneself (e g to a course of action)
,pussy 'willow *n* any of various willows having grey silky catkins
pustule /'pustyoohl/ *n* a small raised spot on the skin filled with pus; *also* a blister, pimple
¹put /poot/ *v put; -tt-* **1a** to place in or move into a specified position or relationship **b** to bring into a specified condition **2a** to cause to endure or undergo; subject **b** to impose, establish **3a** to formulate for judgment or decision **b** to express, state **4a** to turn into language or literary form **b** to adapt, set **5a** to devote, apply **b** to impel, incite **6a** to repose, rest **b** to invest **7** to give as an estimate; *also* to imagine as being **8** to write, inscribe **9** to bet, wager — **put a foot wrong** to make the slightest mistake — **put a good/bold face on** to represent (a matter) or confront (an ordeal) as if all were well — **put a sock in it** *Br* to stop talking; shut up – slang — **put a spoke in someone's wheel** to thwart sby's plans — **put forth 1a** to

assert, propose **b** to make public; issue **2** to bring into action; exert **3** to produce or send out by growth — **put in mind** to remind – often + of — **put it across someone** *Br* to deceive sby into believing or doing sthg — **put it past someone** to think sby at all incapable or unlikely — **put it there** – used as an invitation to shake hands — **put one's best foot forward** to make every effort — **put one's finger on** to identify — **put one's foot down** to take a firm stand — **put one's foot in it** to make an embarrassing blunder — **put one's shirt on** to risk all one's money on — **put one's shoulder to the wheel** to make an effort, esp a cooperative effort — **put on the map** to cause to be considered important — **put paid to** *Br* to ruin; bring to an end — **put someone's nose out of joint** to supplant sby distressingly — **put the lid on** *chiefly Br* to be the culminating misfortune of (a series) — **put the wind up** *Br* to scare, frighten – infml — **put to bed** to make the final preparations for printing (e g a newspaper) — **put together** to create as a united whole; construct — **put to it** to give difficulty to; press hard — **put to shame** to disgrace by comparison — **put two and two together** to draw the proper conclusion from given premises — **put wise** to inform, enlighten – infml
²put *n* a throw made with an overhand pushing motion; *specif* the act or an instance of putting the shot
³put *adj* in the same position, condition, or situation – in *stay put*
put about *v*, *of a ship* to change direction
put across *v* to convey (the meaning or significance of sthg) effectively
putative /'pyoohtətiv/ *adj* **1** commonly accepted or supposed **2** assumed to exist or to have existed *USE* fml
put away *v* **1** to discard, renounce **2a** to place for storage when not in use **b** to save (money) for future use **3** to confine, esp in an asylum
put by *v* to save or store up
'put-,down *n* a humiliating remark; a snub
put down *v* **1** to bring to an end; suppress **2** to kill (e g a sick or injured animal) painlessly **3a** to put in writing **b** to enter in a list (e g of subscribers) **4** to pay as a deposit **5** to attribute **6** to store or set aside (e g bottles of wine) for future use **7** to disparage, humiliate **8**, *of an aircraft* to land
put forward *v* **1** to propose (e g a theory) **2** to bring into prominence
put in *v* **1** to spend (time) at an occupation or job **2** to make an application, request, or offer *for*
put off *v* **1** to disconcert, distract **2a** to postpone **b** to get rid of or persuade to wait, esp by means of excuses or evasions
¹'put-,on *adj* pretended, assumed
²put-on *n* an instance of deliberately misleading sby; *also*, *chiefly NAm* a parody, spoof

put on *v* **1a** to dress oneself in; don **b** to feign, assume **2** to cause to act or operate; apply **3** to come to have an increased amount of **4** to stage, produce (e g a play) **5** to bet (a sum of money)

put out *v* **1** to extinguish **2** to publish, issue **3** to produce for sale **4a** to disconcert, confuse **b** to annoy, irritate **c** to inconvenience **5** to give or offer (a job of work) to be done by another outside the premises **6** to set out from shore

put over *v* to put across

putrefaction /ˌpyoohtriˈfaksh(ə)n/ *n* the decomposition of organic matter; *esp* the breakdown of proteins by bacteria and fungi, typically in the absence of oxygen, with the formation of foul-smelling products

putrefy /ˈpyoohtrifie/ *v* to make or become putrid – **-rescent** *adj* **-rescence** *n*

putrid /ˈpyoohtrid/ *adj* **1** in a state of putrefaction **2** foul-smelling – ~**ity** *n*

putsch /pooch/ *n* a secretly plotted and suddenly executed attempt to overthrow a government

putt /put/ *n* a gentle golf stroke made to roll the ball towards or into the hole on a putting green – **putt** *v*

puttee /ˈputi, puˈtee/ *n* a long cloth strip wrapped spirally round the leg from ankle to knee

putter /ˈputə/ *n* a golf club used for putting

put through *v* **1** to carry into effect or to a successful conclusion **2** to obtain a connection for (a telephone call)

¹**putty** /ˈputi/ *n* a dough-like cement, usu made of whiting and boiled linseed oil, used esp in fixing glass in sashes and stopping crevices in woodwork

²**putty** *v* to use putty on or apply putty to

²**put-up** *adj* contrived secretly beforehand – infml

put up *v* **1** to nominate for election – often + *for* **2** to offer for public sale **3** to give food and shelter to; accommodate **4** to build, erect **5** to offer as a prize or stake **6** to increase the amount of; raise — **put someone's back up** to annoy or irritate sby — **put up to** to urge on, instigate — **put up with** to endure or tolerate without complaint or protest

²**put-u‚pon** *adj* imposed upon; taken advantage of

¹**puzzle** /ˈpuzl/ *v* **puzzling** /ˈpuzling, ˈpuzl·ing/ to offer or represent a problem difficult to solve or a situation difficult to resolve; perplex; *also* to exert (e g oneself) *over* or *about* such a problem or situation – **puzzled** *adj* – **puzzler** *n*

²**puzzle** *n* a problem, contrivance, etc designed for testing one's ingenuity – ~**ment** *n*

pygmy /ˈpigmi/ *n* **1** a member of a very small people of equatorial Africa **2** an insignificant or worthless person in a specified sphere

pyjamas /pəˈjahməz/ *n pl* **1** loose lightweight trousers traditionally worn in the East **2** a suit of loose lightweight jacket and trousers for sleeping in

pylon /ˈpielon, -lən/ *n* a tower for supporting either end of a wire, esp electricity power cables, over a long span

pyramid /ˈpiramid/ *n* **1** an ancient massive structure having typically a square ground plan and tapering smoothly or stepped walls that meet at the top **2** a polyhedron having for its base a polygon and for faces triangles with a common vertex **3** a nonphysical structure or system (e g a social or organizational hierarchy) having a broad supporting base and narrowing gradually to an apex

pyre /ˈpie·ə/ *n* a heap of combustible material for burning a dead body as part of a funeral rite

pyromania /ˌpierəˈmaynyə, -ni·ə/ *n* a compulsive urge to start fires – ~**c** *n*

pyrotechnics /ˌpierəˈteknikz/ *n pl* **1** fireworks **2** a brilliant or spectacular display (e g of oratory)

ˌ**Pyrrhic ˈvictory** *n* a victory won at excessive cost

python /ˈpieth(ə)n/ *n* a large boa or other constrictor; *esp* any of a genus that includes the largest living snakes

Q

q /kyooh/ *n*, *pl* **q's, qs** *often cap* (a graphic representation or device for reproducing) the 17th letter of the English alphabet

¹**quack** /kwak/ *v* or *n* (to make) the characteristic cry of a duck

²**quack** *n* **1** one who has or pretends to have medical skill **2** a charlatan *USE* infml – ~**ery** *n*

¹**quad** /kwod/ *n* a quadrangle

²**quad** *n* a quadruplet

Quadragesima /ˌkwodrəˈjesimə/ *n* the first Sunday in Lent

quadrant /ˈkwodrənt/ *n* **1** an instrument for measuring angles, consisting commonly of a graduated arc of 90° **2** (the area of 1 quarter of a circle that is bounded by) an arc of a circle containing an angle of 90° **3** any of the 4 quarters into which sthg is divided by 2 lines that intersect at right angles

quadrilateral /ˌkwodriˈlat(ə)rəl/ *n or adj* (a polygon) having 4 sides

quadrille /kwəˈdril/ *n* (the music for) a square dance for 4 couples made up of 5 or 6 figures

quadruped /ˈkwodrooˌped/ *n* an animal having 4 feet

¹**quadruple** /ˈkwodroopl, kwoˈdroohpl/ *v* to make or become 4 times as great or as many

²**quadruple** *adj* **1** having 4 units or members **2** being 4 times as great or as many **3** marked by 4 beats per bar – **-ply** *adv*

quadruplet /'kwodrooplit, kwo'droohplit/ *n* **1** any of 4 offspring born at 1 birth **2** a combination of 4 of a kind **3** a group of 4 musical notes performed in the time of 3 notes of the same value

quaff /kwof, kwahf/ *v* to drink (a beverage) deeply in long draughts

quagmire /'kwag‚mie·ə, 'kwog-/ *n* **1** soft miry land that shakes or yields under the foot **2** a predicament from which it is difficult to extricate oneself

¹**quail** /kwayl/ *n* **1** a migratory Old World game bird **2** any of various small American game birds

²**quail** *v* to shrink back in fear; cower

quaint /kwaynt/ *adj* **1** unusual or different in character or appearance; odd **2** pleasingly or strikingly old-fashioned or unfamiliar – **~ly** *adv* – **~ness** *n*

¹**quake** /kwayk/ *v* **1** to shake or vibrate, usu from shock or instability **2** to tremble or shudder, esp inwardly from fear

²**quake** *n* **1** a quaking **2** an earthquake – *infml*

Quaker /'kwaykə/ *n* a member of a pacifist Christian sect that stresses Inner Light and rejects sacraments and an ordained ministry

qualification /‚kwolifi'kaysh(ə)n/ *n* **1** a restriction in meaning or application **2a** a quality or skill that fits a person (e g for a particular task or appointment) **b** a condition that must be complied with (e g for the attainment of a privilege)

qualified /'kwolified/ *adj* **1a** fitted (e g by training or experience) for a usu specified purpose; competent **b** complying with the specific requirements or conditions (e g for appointment to an office); eligible **2** limited or modified in some way

qualify /'kwolifie/ *v* **1a** to reduce from a general to a particular or restricted form; modify **b** to make less harsh or strict; moderate **2** to reach an accredited level of competence **3** to exhibit a required degree of ability or achievement in a preliminary contest

qualitative /'kwolitətiv/ *adj* of or involving quality or kind – **~ly** *adv*

¹**quality** /'kwoləti/ *n* **1a** peculiar and essential character; nature **b** an inherent feature; a property **2a** degree of excellence; grade **b** superiority in kind **3** a distinguishing attribute; a characteristic

²**quality** *adj* **1** concerned with or displaying excellence **2** of a *newspaper* aiming to appeal to an educated readership

qualm /kwahm, kwawm/ *n* **1** a sudden and brief attack of illness, faintness, or nausea **2** a sudden feeling of anxiety or apprehension **3** a scruple or feeling of uneasiness

quandary /'kwond(ə)ri/ *n* a state of perplexity or doubt

quango /'kwang·goh/ *n, pl* **quangos** *Br* an autonomous body (e g the Race Relations Board) set up by the British government and having statutory powers in a specific field

quantify /'kwontifie/ *v* to determine, express, or measure the quantity of – **-fiable** *adj* – **-fication** *n*

quantitative /'kwontitətiv/ *adj* **1** (expressible in terms) of quantity **2** of or involving the measurement of quantity or amount – **~ly** *adv*

quantity /'kwontəti/ *n* **1** an indefinite amount or number **2** a known, measured or estimated amount **3** the total amount or number

quantity surveyor *n* sby who estimates or measures quantities (e g for builders)

quantum /'kwontəm/ *n, pl* **quanta** /-tə/ **1a** a quantity, amount **b** a portion, part **2** any of the very small parcels or parts into which many forms of energy are subdivided and which cannot be further subdivided

¹**quarantine** /'kworən‚teen/ *n* **1** (the period of) a restraint on the activities or communication of people or the transport of goods or animals, designed to prevent the spread of disease or pests **2** a state of enforced isolation

²**quarantine** *v* **1** to detain in or exclude by quarantine **2** to isolate from normal relations or communication

quark /kwahk/ *n* a hypothetical particle that carries a fractional electric charge and is held to be a constituent of known elementary particles

¹**quarrel** /'kworəl/ *n* **1** a reason for dispute or complaint **2** a usu verbal conflict between antagonists

²**quarrel** *v* **-ll- 1** to find fault *with* **2** to contend or dispute actively; argue

¹**quarrelsome** /-səm/ *adj* inclined or quick to quarrel

¹**quarry** /'kwori/ *n* the prey or game of a predator or of a hunter

²**quarry** *n* **1** an open excavation from which building materials (e g stone, slate, and sand) are obtained **2** a source from which useful material, esp information, may be extracted – **quarry** *v*

quart /kwawt/ *n* a unit of liquid capacity equal to 2pt

¹**quarter** /'kwawtə/ *n* **1** any of 4 equal parts into which sthg is divisible **2** any of various units equal to or derived from a fourth of some larger unit **3** a fourth of a measure of time: e g **3a** any of 4 3-month divisions of a year **b** a quarter of an hour – used in designation of time **4** (a coin worth) a quarter of a (US) dollar **5** a hindquarter, rump **6** (the direction of or region round) a (cardinal) compass point **7** *pl* living accommodation; lodgings; *esp* accommodation for military personnel or their families **8** merciful consideration of an opponent; *specif* the clemency of not killing a defeated enemy **9** the part of a ship's side towards the stern

²quarter *v* 1 to divide into 4 (almost) equal parts 2 to provide with lodgings or shelter; *esp* to assign (a member of the armed forces) to accommodation 3 to crisscross (an area) in many directions

³quarter *adj* consisting of or equal to a quarter

'quarter ,day *n* a day which begins a quarter of the year and on which a quarterly payment often falls due

'quarter ,deck /-ˌdek/ *n* 1 the stern area of a ship's upper deck 2 *chiefly Br* the officers of a ship or navy

'quarter,final /-ˌfienl/ *n* a match whose winner goes through to the semifinals of a knockout tournament

'quarterly /ˈkwawtəli/ *n* a periodical published at 3-monthly intervals

²quarterly *adj* 1 computed for or payable at 3-monthly intervals 2 recurring, issued, or spaced at 3-monthly intervals

'quarter,master /-ˌmahstə/ *n* 1 a petty officer or seaman who attends to a ship's compass, tiller or wheel, and signals 2 an army officer who provides clothing, subsistence, and quarters for a body of troops

'quarter,staff /-ˌstahf/ *n, pl* **quarterstaves** /-ˌstayvz, -ˌstahvz/ a long stout staff formerly used as a weapon

quartet *also* **quartette** /kwaw'tet/ *n* (a musical composition for) a group of four performers

'quartz /kwawts/ *n* a mineral occurring in transparent hexagonal crystals or in crystalline masses

²quartz *adj* controlled by the oscillations of a quartz crystal

quasar /ˈkwaysah/ *n* any of various unusually bright very distant star-like celestial objects

quash /kwosh/ *v* 1a to nullify (by judicial action) b to reject (a legal document) as invalid 2 to suppress or extinguish summarily and completely

quatrain /ˈkwotrayn/ *n* a stanza of 4 lines

'quaver /ˈkwayvə/ *v esp of the voice* to tremble, shake 2 to speak or sing in a trembling voice – ~y *adj*

²quaver *n* 1 a musical note with the time value of ¹/₂ that of a crotchet 2 a tremulous sound

quay /kee/ *n* an artificial landing place beside navigable water for loading and unloading ships

queasy *also* **queazy** /ˈkweezi/ *adj* causing or suffering from nausea or uneasiness – **-sily** *adv* – **-siness** *n*

queen /kween/ *n* 1 the wife or widow of a king 2 a female monarch 3 the most powerful piece of each colour in a set of chessmen, which has the power to move any number of squares in any direction 4 a playing card marked with a stylized figure of a queen and ranking usu below the king 5 the fertile fully developed female in a colony of bees, ants, or termites

,queen 'mother *n* a woman who is the widow of a king and the mother of the reigning sovereign

,Queen's 'Counsel *n* a barrister who has been appointed by the Crown to senior rank with special privileges – used when the British monarch is a queen

'queer /kwiə/ *adj* 1a eccentric, unconventional b mildly insane 2 questionable, suspicious 3 not quite well; queasy – infml 4 homosexual – derog

²queer *v* to spoil the effect or success of — **queer someone's pitch** to prejudice or ruin sby's chances in advance

quell /kwel/ *v* 1 to overwhelm thoroughly and reduce to submission or passivity 2 to quiet, pacify

quench /kwench/ *v* 1 to put out (the light or fire of) 2a to terminate (as if) by destroying; eliminate b to relieve or satisfy with liquid

querulous /ˈkwer(y)oolas/ *adj* habitually complaining – **~ly** *adv* – **~ness** *n*

'query /ˈkwiəri/ *n* a question, esp expressing doubt or uncertainty

²query *v* 1 to put as a question 2 to question the accuracy of (a statement)

'quest /kwest/ *n* 1 (the object of) a pursuit or search 2 an adventurous journey undertaken by a knight in medieval romance

²quest *v* to search for – *chiefly poetic*

'question /ˈkwesch(ə)n/ *n* 1a an interrogative expression used to elicit information or test knowledge b an interrogative sentence or clause 2 an act or instance of asking; an inquiry 3a a subject or concern that is uncertain or in dispute b the specific point at issue 4a (room for) doubt or objection b chance, possibility — **in question** under discussion — **out of the question** preposterous, impossible

²question *v* 1a to ask a question of b to interrogate 2 to doubt, dispute – **~able** *adj* – **~ingly** *adv* – **~er** *n*

questionable /ˈkweschənəbl/ *adj* 1 open to doubt or challenge 2 of doubtful morality or propriety – **-bly** *adv*

'question ,mark *n* a punctuation mark ? used in writing and printing at the end of a sentence to indicate a direct question

questionnaire /ˌkwescha'neə; *also* ˌkes-/ *n* (a form having) a set of questions to be asked of a number of people to obtain information

'queue /kyooh/ *n* 1 a pigtail 2 a waiting line, esp of people or vehicles

²queue *v* **queuing, queueing** to line up or wait in a queue

'quibble /ˈkwibl/ *n* a minor objection or criticism

²quibble *v* **quibbling** /ˈkwibl-ing, ˈkwibling/ 1 to equivocate 2 to bicker – **~r** *n* – **-ling** *adj*

quiche /keesh/ *n* a pastry shell filled with a rich savoury custard and various other ingredients

'quick /kwik/ *adj* 1a fast in understanding, thinking, or learning; mentally agile b reacting with speed and keen sensitivity 2a fast in development or occurrence **b** done or taking place with rapidity **c** inclined to hastiness (e g in action or response) **d** capable of being easily and speedily prepared – ~ly *adv* – ~ness *n*

²**quick** *adv* in a quick manner

³**quick** *n* 1 painfully sensitive flesh, esp under a fingernail, toenail, etc **2** the inmost sensibilities

quicken /'kwikən/ *v* **1** to enliven, stimulate **2** to make more rapid; accelerate **3** to come to life

quickie /'kwiki/ *n* sthg done or made in a hurry – infml

'**quick,sand** /'kwik'sand/ -,sand/ *n* (a deep mass of) loose sand, esp mixed with water, into which heavy objects readily sink

'**quick,silver** /-,silvə/ *n* mercury

'**quick,step** /-,step/ *n* a fast foxtrot characterized by a combination of short rapid steps

'**quid** /kwid/ *n*, *pl* **quid** *also* **quids** *Br* the sum of £1 – infml — **quids in** in the state of having made a usu large profit — infml

²**quid** *n* a wad of sthg, esp tobacco, for chewing

quiescent /kwi'es(ə)nt/ *adj* **1** causing no trouble **2** at rest; inactive — **-cence** *n* – ~**ly** *adv*

'**quiet** /'kwiə-ət/ *n* being quiet; tranquillity — **on the quiet** without telling anyone; discreetly, secretly

²**quiet** *adj* **1a** marked by little or no motion or activity; calm **b** free from noise or uproar; still **c** secluded **2a** gentle, reserved **b** unobtrusive, conservative **3** private, discreet – ~**ly** *adv* – ~**ness** *n*

³**quiet** *adv* in a quiet manner

⁴**quiet** *v* to calm, soothe

quieten /'kwiə-ətn/ *v* to make or become quiet – often + *down*

quietude /'kwiə-ətyoohd/ *n* being quiet; repose – fml

quiff /kwif/ *n*, *Br* a lock of hair brushed so as to stand up over the forehead

quill /kwil/ *n* **1a** the hollow horny barrel of a feather **b** any of the large stiff feathers of a bird's wing or tail **c** any of the hollow sharp spines of a porcupine, hedgehog, etc **2** sthg made from or resembling the quill of a feather; *esp* a pen for writing

'**quilt** /kwilt/ *n* **1** a thick warm top cover for a bed consisting of padding held in place between 2 layers of cloth by lines of stitching **2** a bedspread

²**quilt** *v* to stitch or sew together in layers with padding in between

quince /kwins/ *n* (a central Asian tree that bears) a fruit resembling a hard-fleshed yellow apple

quinine /'kwineen, -'-/ *n* a drug obtained from cinchona bark formerly used as the major treatment of malaria

quintessence /kwin'tes(ə)ns/ *n* **1** the pure and concentrated essence of sthg **2** the most typical example or representative (e g of a quality or class) – **-sential** *adj* – **-sentially** *adv*

quintet *also* **quintette** /kwin'tet/ *n* (a musical composition for) a group of 5 performers

quintuplet /'kwintyooplit, kwin'tyoohplit/ *n* **1** a combination of 5 of a kind **2** any of 5 offspring born at 1 birth

quip /kwip/ *v or n* (to make) a clever, witty, or sarcastic observation or response

quirk /kwuhk/ *n* **1** an odd or peculiar trait; an idiosyncrasy **2** an accident, vagary

quisling /'kwizling/ *n* a traitor who collaborates with invaders

'**quit** /kwit/ *adj* released from obligation, charge, or penalty – + *of*

²**quit** *v* **-tt-;** **quitted** (*NAm chiefly* **quit**) **1** to cease doing sthg; *specif* to give up one's job **2** of a tenant to vacate occupied premises **3** to admit defeat; give up

quite /kwiet/ *adv or adj* **1a** wholly, completely **b** positively, certainly **2** more than usually; rather **3** *chiefly Br* to only a moderate degree — **quite so** – used to express agreement

quits /kwits/ *adj* on even terms as a result of repaying a debt or retaliating for an injury

quitter /'kwitə/ *n* one who gives up too easily; a defeatist

'**quiver** /'kwivə/ *n* a case for carrying or holding arrows

²**quiver** *v* to shake or move with a slight trembling motion

quixotic /kwik'sotik/, **quixotical** /-kl/ *adj* idealistic or chivalrous in a rash or impractical way – ~**ally** *adv*

'**quiz** /kwiz/ *n* **-zz-** a public test of (general) knowledge, esp as a television or radio entertainment

²**quiz** *v* **-zz-** to question closely – journ

quizzical /'kwizikl/ *adj* **1** gently mocking; teasing **2** questioning – ~**ly** *adv*

quorum /'kwawrəm/ *n* the number of members of a body that when duly assembled is constitutionally competent to transact business

quota /'kwohtə/ *n* **1** a proportional part or share; *esp* the share or proportion to be either contributed or received by an individual or body **2** a numerical limit set on some class of people or things

quotable /'kwohtəbl/ *adj* **1** fit for or worth quoting **2** made with permission for publication (e g in a newspaper) – **-bility** *n*

quotation /kwoh'taysh(ə)n/ *n* **1** sthg quoted; *esp* a passage or phrase quoted from printed literature **2** quoting **3a** current bids and offers for or prices of shares, securities, commodities, etc **b** an estimate

quo'tation ,mark *n* either of a pair of punctuation marks ' ' or " " used to the beginning and end of a direct quotation

'**quote** /kwoht/ *v* **1** to repeat a passage or phrase previously said or written, esp by another in writing or speech, esp in substantiation or illustration

2 to cite in illustration **3** to make an estimate of or give exact information on (e g the price of a commodity or service)

²quote *n* **1** a quotation **2** quotation mark

quoth /kwohth/ *v past, archaic* said – chiefly in the 1st and 3rd persons with a subject following

quotient /'kwohsh(ə)nt/ *n* **1** the result of the division of one number or expression by another **2** the ratio, usu multiplied by 100, between a test score and a measurement on which that score might be expected to depend

R

r /ah/ *n, pl* **r's, rs** *often cap* (a graphic representation of or device for reproducing) the 18th letter of the English alphabet

rabbi /'rabie/ *n* a Jew trained and ordained for professional religious leadership; *specif* the official leader of a Jewish congregation – ~ **nical** *adj*

¹rabbit /'rabit/ *n pl* **rabbits,** (1) *esp collectively* **rabbit 1** (the fur of) a small long-eared mammal that is related to the hares but differs from them in producing naked young and in its burrowing habits **2** *Br* an unskilful player (e g in golf, cricket, or tennis)

²rabbit *v, Br* to talk aimlessly or inconsequentially – *infml; often* + *on*

rabble /'rabl/ *n* a disorganized or disorderly crowd of people; *also the* mob

rabid /'rabid; *sense 2 also* 'raybid/ *adj* **1** unreasoning or fanatical in an opinion or feeling **2** affected with rabies

rabies /'raybeez, -biz/ *n pl* **rabies** a fatal short-lasting disease of the nervous system transmitted esp through the bite of an affected animal and characterized by extreme fear of water and convulsions

¹race /rays/ *n* **1a** a strong or rapid current of water in the sea, a river, etc **b** a watercourse used to turn the wheel of a mill **2a** a contest of speed (e g in running or riding) **b** *pl* a meeting in which several races (e g for horses) are run

²race *v* **1** to compete in a race **2** to go or move at top speed or out of control **3** of a *motor, engine, etc* to revolve too fast under a diminished load – ~ **r** *n*

³race *n* **1** a family, tribe, people, or nation belonging to the same stock **2** an actually or potentially interbreeding group within a species **3a** a division of mankind having traits that are sufficient to characterize it as a distinct human type **b** human beings collectively – **race, racial** *adj* – **racially** *adv*

'race,course /-,kaws/ *n* a place where or the track on which races, esp horse races, are held

racialism /'raysha,liz(ə)m/ *n* **1** racial prejudice or discrimination **2** the belief that racial differences produce an inherent superiority for a particular race – **racialist, racist** *adj, n*

¹rack /rak/ *n* **1** an instrument of torture on which the victim's body is stretched – usu + *the* **2a** a framework, stand, or grating on or in which articles are placed

²rack *v* **1** to torture on the rack **2** to cause to suffer torture, pain, or anguish **3** to raise (rents) oppressively **4** to place in a rack

³rack *v* to draw off (e g wine) from the lees

⁴rack *n* the front rib section of lamb used for chops or as a roast

⁵rack *n* destruction – chiefly in *rack and ruin*

¹racket *also* **racquet** /'rakit/ *n* **1** a lightweight implement consisting of netting stretched in an open frame with a handle attached that is used for striking the ball, shuttle, etc in various games **2** *pl, but sing in constr* a game for 2 or 4 players play on a 4-walled court

²racket *n* **1** a loud and confused noise **2a** a fraudulent enterprise made workable by bribery or intimidation **b** an easy and lucrative occupation or line of business – *infml*

racketeer /,raki'tiə/ *n* one who extorts money or advantages by threats, blackmail, etc

raconteur /,rakon'tuh/ *n* one who excels in telling anecdotes

racoon /rə'koohn/ *n* (the fur of) a small flesh-eating mammal of N America that has a bushy ringed tail

racy /'raysi/ *adj* **1** full of zest or vigour **2** having a strongly marked quality; piquant **3** risqué, suggestive – **racily** *adv* – **raciness** *n*

radar /'raydah/ *n* an electronic device that generates high-frequency radio waves and locates objects in the vicinity by analysis of the radio waves reflected back from them

¹radial /'raydyəl/ *adj* **1** (having parts) arranged like rays or radii from a central point or axis **2** characterized by divergence from a centre – ~ **ly** *adv*

²radial *n* **1** any line in a system of radial lines **2 radial, radial tyre** a pneumatic tyre in which the ply cords are laid at a right angle to the centre line of the tread

radiant /'raydyənt/ *adj* **1** radiating rays or reflecting beams of light **b** vividly bright and shining; glowing **2** of or emitting radiant heat

radiate /'raydi,ayt/ *v* **1** to send out rays of light, heat, or any other form of radiation **2** to proceed in a direct line from or towards a centre **3** to show or display clearly

radiation /,raydi'aysh(ə)n/ n 1 the action or process of radiating; esp the process of emitting radiant energy in the form of waves or particles 2 electromagnetic radiation (e g light) or emission from radioactive sources (e g alpha rays)

radiator /'raydi,aytə/ n 1 a room heater through which hot water or steam circulates as part of a central-heating system 2 a device with a large surface area used for cooling an internal-combustion engine by means of water circulating through it

¹**radical** /'radikl/ adj 1a of or growing from the root or the base of a stem b designed to remove the root of a disease or all diseased tissue 2 essential, fundamental 3a departing from the usual or traditional; extreme b of or constituting a political group advocating extreme measures – ~**ly** adv – ~**ness** n

²**radical** n sby who is a member of a radical party or who holds radical views

radicle /'radikl/ n 1 the lower part of the axis of a plant embryo or seedling, including the embryonic root 2 the rootlike beginning of an anatomical vessel or part

radii /'raydi,ie/ pl of **radius**

¹**radio** /'raydi,oh/ n pl **radios** 1 the system of wireless transmission and reception of signals by means of electromagnetic waves 2 a radio receiver 3a a radio transmitter (e g in an aircraft) b a radio broadcasting organization or station c the radio broadcasting industry

²**radio** v to send or communicate sthg by radio

radioac'tivity /,raydioh·ak'tivəti/ n the property possessed by some elements (e g uranium) of spontaneously emitting alpha or beta rays and sometimes also gamma rays by the disintegration of the nuclei of atoms – **-tive** adj

radiogram /'raydi·ə,gram, -dioh-/ n 1 a radiograph 2 Br a combined radio receiver and record player

radiograph /'raydi·ə,grahf, -,graf, -dioh-/ n a picture produced on a sensitive surface by a form of radiation other than light; specif an X-ray or gamma-ray photograph

radiology /,raydi'oləji/ n the use of radiant energy (e g X rays and gamma rays) in the diagnosis and treatment of disease – **-gist** n

radiotelegraphy /,raydiohtə'legrəfi/ n telegraphy carried out by means of radio waves – **-graphic** adj

radio 'telephone /-'telifohn/ n an apparatus for enabling telephone messages to be sent by radio (e g from a moving vehicle) – **-phony** n

radio 'telescope n a radio receiver connected to a large often dish-shaped aerial for recording and measuring radio waves from celestial bodies

radish /'radish/ n (a plant of the mustard family with) a pungent fleshy typically dark red root, eaten raw as a salad vegetable

radium /'raydyəm/ n an intensely radioactive metallic element that occurs naturally and is used chiefly in luminous materials and in the treatment of cancer

radius /'raydi·əs/ n, pl **radii** /-di,ie/ also **radiuses** 1 a straight line extending from the centre of a circle or sphere to the circumference or surface 2 a bounded or circumscribed area

raffia, raphia /'rafi·ə/ n the fibre of a palm tree used esp for making baskets, hats, and table mats

raffish /'rafish/ adj marked by careless unconventionality; rakish – ~**ly** adv – ~**ness** n

raffle /'rafl/ v or n **raffling** /'rafling, 'rafl·ing/ (to dispose of by means of) a lottery in which the prizes are usually goods

raft /rahft/ n 1 a flat usu wooden structure designed to float on water and used as a platform or vessel 2 a foundation slab for a building, usu made of reinforced concrete – **raft** v

rafter /'rahftə/ n any of the parallel beams that form the framework of a roof

¹**rag** /rag/ n 1a (a waste piece of) worn cloth b pl clothes, esp when in poor or ragged condition 2 a usu sensational or poorly written newspaper

²**rag** v to torment, tease; also to engage in horseplay

³**rag** n, **-gg-** chiefly Br 1 an outburst of boisterous fun; a prank 2 a series of processions and stunts organized by students to raise money for charity

⁴**rag** n (a composition or dance in) ragtime

ragamuffin /'ragə,mufin/ n a ragged often disreputable person, esp a child

ragbag /'rag,bag/ n 1 a dishevelled or slovenly person 2 a miscellaneous collection USE infml

¹**rage** /rayj/ n 1a (a fit or bout of) violent and uncontrolled anger 2 (an object of) fashionable and temporary enthusiasm

²**rage** v 1 to be in a rage 2 to be unchecked in violence or effect

ragged /'ragid/ adj 1 having an irregular edge or outline 2 torn or worn to tatters 3 straggly – ~**ly** adv – ~**ness** n

raglan /'raglən/ adj having sleeves that extend to the neckline with slanted seams from the underarm to the neck

ragout /'ragooh, -'-/ n a well-seasoned stew, esp of meat and vegetables, cooked in a thick sauce

ragtime /'rag,tiem/ n (music having) rhythm characterized by strong syncopation in the melody with a regularly accented accompaniment

¹**rag 'trade** n the clothing trade – infml

¹**raid** /rayd/ n 1a a usu hostile incursion made in order to seize sby or sthg b a surprise attack by a small force 2 a sudden invasion by the police (e g in search of criminals or stolen goods)

²**raid** v to make or take part in a raid

¹**rail** /rayl/ n 1 an esp horizontal bar, usu supported by posts, which may serve as a barrier (e g across a balcony) or as a support on or from which sthg (e g a curtain) may be hung 2a a railing b either of

the fences on each side of a horse-racing track – usu pl with sing. meaning **3a** either of a pair of lengths of rolled steel forming a guide and running surface (e g a railway) for wheeled vehicles **b** the railway – **off the rails 1** away from the proper or normal course; awry **2** mad, crazy

²**rail** *v* to enclose or separate with a rail or rails – often + *off*

³**rail** *n pl* **rails**, *esp collectively* **rail** any of numerous wading birds of small or medium size, usu having very long toes which enable them to run on soft wet ground

⁴**rail** *v* to utter angry complaints or abuse – often + *against* or *at*

railhead /'rayl,hed/ *n* the farthest point reached by a railway

railing /'rayling/ *n* **1** a usu vertical rail in a fence or similar barrier **2** (material for making) rails

raillery /'rayl(ə)ri/ *n* (a piece of) good-humoured teasing

¹**railroad** /'rayl,rohd/ *n*, *NAm* (a) railway

²**railroad** *v* **1** to push through hastily or without due consideration **2** to hustle into taking action or making a decision

railway /'rayl,way/ *n*, *chiefly Br* **1** a line of track usu having 2 parallel lines or rails fixed to sleepers on which vehicles run to transport goods and passengers **2** an organization which runs a railway network

raiment /'raymant/ *n* garments, clothing – poetic

¹**rain** /rayn/ *n* **1** (a descent of) water falling in drops condensed from vapour in the atmosphere **2** *pl* the rainy season **3** a dense flow or fall of sthg – ~**less** *adj*

²**rain** *v* **1** *of rain* to fall in drops from the clouds **2** to cause to fall; pour or send down **3** to bestow abundantly – **rain cats and dogs** to rain heavily

rainbow /'raynboh/ *n* **1** an arch in the sky consisting of a series of concentric arcs of the colours red, orange, yellow, green, blue, indigo, and violet, formed esp opposite the sun by the refraction, reflection, and interference of light rays in raindrops, spray, etc **2** an array of bright colours

,**rainbow 'trout** *n* a large stout-bodied trout of Europe and western N America

'**rain,coat** /-,koht/ *n* a coat made from waterproof or water-resistant material

'**rain,fall** /-,fawl/ *n* **1** a fall of rain; a shower **2** the amount of rain that has fallen in a given area during a given time, usu measured by depth

rain off *v* to interrupt or prevent (e g a sporting fixture) by rain

rainy /'rayni/ *adj* **1** having or characterized by heavy rainfall **2** wet with rain

¹**raise** /rayz/ *v* **1** to cause or help to rise to an upright or standing position **2** to stir up; incite **3** to lift up **4a** to levy, obtain **b** to assemble, collect **5a** to grow, cultivate **b** to rear (e g a child) **6** to give rise to; provoke **7** to bring up for consideration or debate **8** to increase the strength, intensity, degree, or pitch of — **raise Cain/hell/the roof** to create a usu angry and noisy disturbance; *esp* to complain vehemently — *infml* — **raise an eyebrow/eyebrows** to cause surprise, doubt, or disapproval

²**raise** *n* **1** an act of raising or lifting **2** an increase of a bet or bid

raisin /'rayz(ə)n/ *n* a dried grape

raison d'être /,rayzon(h) 'detrə, (*Fr* rezɔ̃ detr)/ *n* a reason or justification for existence

raj /rahj/ *n* rule; *specif*, *cap* British rule in India

rajah, raja /'rahjə/ *n* an Indian, esp Hindu, prince or ruler

¹**rake** /rayk/ *n* **1** a long-handled implement with a head on which a row of projecting prongs is fixed for gathering hay, grass, etc or for loosening or levelling the surface of the ground **2** a mechanical implement, usu with rotating pronged wheels, used for gathering hay

²**rake** *v* **1** to gather, loosen, or level (as if) with a rake **2** to search through, esp in a haphazard manner – often + *through* or *among* **3** to sweep the length of, esp with gunfire

³**rake** *v* to (cause to) incline from the perpendicular

⁴**rake** *n* **1** the overhang of a ship's bow or stern **2** the angle of inclination or slope, esp of a stage in a theatre

⁵**rake** *n* a dissolute man, esp in fashionable society – **rakish** *adj* – **rakishly** *adv*

'**rake-,off** *n* a share of usu dishonestly gained profits – infml

rake up *v* **1** to uncover, revive **2** to find or collect, esp with difficulty

¹**rally** /'rali/ *v* **1** to bring together for a common cause **2a** to come together again to renew an effort **b** to arouse for or recall to order or action **3** to recover, revive

²**rally** *n* **1a** a mustering of scattered forces to renew an effort **b** a recovery of strength or courage after weakness or dejection **c** an increase in price after a decline **2** a mass meeting of people sharing a common interest or supporting a common, usu political, cause **3** a series of strokes interchanged between players (e g in tennis) before a point is won **4** *also* **rallye** a motor race, usu over public roads, designed to test both speed and navigational skills

¹**ram** /ram/ *n* **1** an uncastrated male sheep **2a** a battering ram **b** a heavy beak on the prow of a warship for piercing enemy vessels

²**ram** *v* **-mm-** to strike against violently and usu head-on — **ram something down someone's throat** to force sby to accept or listen to sthg, esp by constant repetition

¹**ramble** /'rambl/ *v* **rambling** /'rambling, 'rambl·ing/ **1** to walk for pleasure, esp without a planned route **2** to talk or write in a disconnected long-winded fashion **3** to grow or extend irregularly

²**ramble** *n* a leisurely walk taken for pleasure and often without a planned route – ~**r** *n*

rambunctious /ram'bungkshəs/ *adj*, *NAm* rumbustious, unruly – *infml* – ~**ly** *adv* – ~**ness** *n*

ramification /,ramifi'kaysh(ə)n/ *n* **1** a branching out **2** a branched structure **3** a usu extended or complicated consequence

ramify /'ramifie/ *v* to (cause to) separate or split up into branches, divisions, or constituent parts

ramp /ramp/ *n* **1** a sloping floor, walk, or roadway leading from one level to another **2** a stairway for entering or leaving an aircraft

rampage /ram'payj/ *v* to rush about wildly or violently – **rampage** *n*

rampant /'rampant/ *adj* **1** *of a heraldic animal* rearing upon the hind legs with forelegs extended – used after a noun **2** characterized by wildness or absence of restraint – ~**ly** *adv*

rampart /'rampaht/ *n* **1** a broad embankment raised as a fortification (e g around a fort or city) and usu surmounted by a parapet **2** a protective barrier; a bulwark

ramrod /'ram,rod/ *n* **1** a rod for ramming home the charge in a muzzle-loading firearm **2** a rod for cleaning the barrels of rifles and other small arms

ramshackle /'ramshakl/ *adj* badly constructed or needing repair; rickety

ran /ran/ *past of* **run**

ranch /rahnch/ *n* **1** a large farm for raising livestock esp in N America and Australia **2** *chiefly NAm* a farm or area devoted to raising a particular crop or animal

rancid /'ransid/ *adj* (smelling or tasting) rank – ~**ity** *n*

rancour, *NAm* **rancor** /'rangkə/ *n* bitter and deep-seated ill will or hatred

rand /rand/ *n*, *pl* **rand** the basic unit of currency of South Africa

random /'randəm/ *adj* **1** lacking a definite plan, purpose, or pattern **2** (of, consisting of, or being events, parts, etc) having or relating to a probability of occurring equal to that of all similar parts, events, etc – ~**ly** *adv* – ~**ness** *n*

randy /'randi/ *adj* sexually aroused; lustful – *infml* – **randiness** *n*

rang /rang/ *past of* **ring**

¹**range** /raynj/ *n* **1a** a series of mountains **b** a number of objects or products forming a distinct class or series **c** a variety, cross-section **2** a usu solid-fuel fired cooking stove with 1 or more ovens, a flat metal top, and 1 or more areas for heating pans **3a** an open region over which livestock may roam and feed, esp in N America **b** the

region throughout which a kind of living organism or ecological community naturally lives or occurs **4a(1)** the distance to which a projectile can be propelled **a(2)** the distance between a weapon and the target **b** the maximum distance a vehicle can travel without refuelling **c** a place where shooting (e g with guns or missiles) is practised **5a** the space or extent included, covered, or used **b** the extent of pitch within a melody or within the capacity of a voice or instrument **6a** a sequence, series, or scale between limits **b** (the difference between) the least and greatest values of an attribute or series

²**range** *v* **1** to set in a row or in the proper order **2** to roam over or through **3** to determine or give the elevation necessary for (a gun) to propel a projectile to a given distance **4** to extend in a usu specified direction **5** to change or differ within limits

'**range ,finder** *n* a device for indicating or measuring the distance between a gun and a target or a camera and an object

ranger /'raynjə/ *n* **1** the keeper of a park or forest **2** a soldier in the US army specially trained in close-range fighting and raiding tactics **3** *often cap* a private in an Irish line regiment **4** *cap* a senior member of the British Guide movement aged from 14 to 19

rani, **ranee** /rah'nee, '–/ *n* a Hindu queen or princess; *esp* the wife of a rajah

¹**rank** /rangk/ *adj* **1** excessively vigorous and often coarse in growth **2** offensively gross or coarse **3a** shockingly conspicuous; flagrant **b** complete – used as an intensive **4** offensive in odour or flavour – ~**ly** *adv* – ~**ness** *n*

²**rank** *n* **1a** a row, line, or series of people or things **b(1)** *sing or pl in constr* a line of soldiers ranged side by side in close order **b(2)** *pl* rank and file **c** any of the 8 rows of squares that extend across a chessboard perpendicular to the files **2** an esp military formation – often pl with sing. meaning **3a** a degree or position in a hierarchy or order; *specif* an official position in the armed forces **b** (high) social position **4** *Br* a place where taxis wait to pick up passengers

³**rank** *v* **1** to take or have a position in relation to others **2** to determine the relative position of; rate

,**rank and 'file** *n sing or pl in constr* **1** the body of members of an armed force as distinguished from the officers **2** the individuals constituting the body of an organization as distinguished from the leading or principal members

ranking /'rangking/ *adj* having a high or the highest position

rankle /'rangkl/ *v* **rankling** /'rangkling, 'rangkl·ing/ to cause continuing anger, irritation, or bitterness

ransack /'ransak/ *v* **1** to search in a disordered but thorough manner **2** to rob, plunder

¹ransom /'ransəm/ *n* a price paid or demanded for the release of a captured or kidnapped person

²ransom *v* to free from captivity or punishment by paying a ransom – **~er** *n*

¹rant /rant/ *v* to talk in a noisy, excited, or declamatory manner

²rant *n* (a) bombastic extravagant speech

¹rap /rap/ *n* 1 (the sound made by) a sharp blow or knock 2 blame, punishment – *infml*

²rap *v* **-pp-** 1 to strike with a sharp blow 2 to utter (e g a command) abruptly and forcibly – usu + *out* 3 to criticize sharply – *journ* — **(a) rap over the knuckles** (to give) a scolding

³rap *n* the least bit (e g of care or consideration) – *infml*

⁴rap *n, chiefly NAm* talk, conversation – *slang* – **rap** *v*

rapacious /rə'payshəs/ *adj* 1 excessively grasping or covetous 2 *of an animal* living on prey – **-city** *n* – **~ly** *adv* – **~ness** *n*

¹rape /rayp/ *n* a European plant of the mustard family grown as a forage crop and for its oil-producing seeds

²rape *v* 1 to despoil 2 to commit rape on – **rapist** *n*

³rape *n* 1 an act or instance of robbing, despoiling, or violating 2 the crime of forcing a woman to have sexual intercourse against her will 3 an outrageous violation

¹rapid /'rapid/ *adj* moving, acting, or occurring with speed; swift – **~ity** *n* – **~ly** *adv*

²rapid *n* a part of a river where the water flows swiftly over a steep usu rocky slope in the river bed – usu pl with sing. meaning

rapier /'raypi-ə/ *n* a straight 2-edged sword with a narrow pointed blade

rapine /'rapien/ *n* pillage, plunder

rapport /ra'paw/ *n* a sympathetic or harmonious relationship

rapprochement /ra'proshmonh/ *n* the reestablishment of cordial relations, esp between nations

rapscallion /rap'skalyən/ *n* a rascal

rapt /rapt/ *adj* 1 enraptured 2 wholly absorbed – **~ly** *adv* – **~ness** *n*

rapture /'rapchə/ *n* 1 a state or experience of being carried away by overwhelming emotion 2 an expression or manifestation of ecstasy or extreme delight – **-rous** *adj* – **-rously** *adv*

¹rare /reə/ *adj, of meat* cooked so that the inside is still red

²rare *adj* 1 lacking in density; thin 2 marked by unusual quality, merit, or appeal 3 seldom occurring or found – **~ness** *n*

rarefied *also* **rarified** /'reərified/ *adj* esoteric, abstruse

rarefy *also* **rarify** /'reərifie/ *v* 1 to make or become rare, porous, or less dense 2 to make more spiritual, refined, or abstruse

rarity /'reərəti/ *n* 1 the quality, state, or fact of being rare 2 sby or sthg rare

rascal /'rahsk(ə)l/ *n* 1 an unprincipled or dishonest person 2 a mischievous person or animal – usu humor *or* affectionate

¹rash /rash/ *adj* acting with, characterized by, or proceeding from undue haste or impetuosity – **~ly** *adv* – **~ness** *n*

²rash *n* 1 an outbreak of spots on the body 2 a large number of instances of a specified thing during a short period

rasher /'rashə/ *n* a thin slice of bacon or ham

¹rasp /rahsp/ *v* 1 to rub with sthg rough 2 to grate upon; irritate 3 to utter in a grating tone – **~ingly** *adv*

²rasp *n* a coarse file with rows of cutting teeth

raspberry /'rahzb(ə)ri/ *n* 1 (a widely grown shrub that bears) any of various usu red edible berries 2 a rude sound made by sticking the tongue out and blowing noisily – *slang*

¹rat /rat/ *n* 1 any of numerous rodents that are considerably larger than the related mice 2 a contemptible or wretched person; *specif* one who betrays or deserts his party, friends, or associates

²rat *v* **-tt-** to betray, desert, or inform on one's associates – usu + *on*

ratchet /'rachit/ *n* a mechanism that consists of a bar or wheel having inclined teeth into which a bar or lever drops so that motion is allowed in 1 direction only

¹rate /rayt/ *n* 1 valuation 2a a fixed ratio between 2 things **b** a charge, payment, or price fixed according to a ratio, scale, or standard **c** *Br* a tax levied by a local authority – usu pl with sing. meaning 3 a quantity, amount, or degree of sthg measured per unit of sthg else — **at any rate** in any case; anyway

²rate *v* 1 to consider to be; value as 2 to determine or assign the relative rank or class of 3 to be worthy of; deserve 4 to think highly of; consider to be good – *infml*

rate-capping *n, Br* restriction by central government legislation of the level of rates which a local authority can levy – **rate-cap** *v*

rather /'rahdhə/ *adv or adj* 1 more readily or willingly; sooner 2 more properly, reasonably, or truly 3 to some degree; somewhat; *esp* somewhat excessively 4 on the contrary

ratify /'ratifie/ *v* to approve or confirm formally

rating /'rayting/ *n* 1 a classification according to grade 2 relative estimate or evaluation 3 *pl* any of various indexes which list television programmes, new records, etc in order of popularity – usu + *the* 4 *chiefly Br* an ordinary seaman

ratio /'rayshioh/ *n, pl* **ratios** 1 the indicated division of one mathematical expression by another 2 the relationship in quantity, number, or degree between things or between one thing and another thing

¹ration /'rash(ə)n/ n a share or amount (e g of food) which one permits oneself or which one is permitted

²ration v 1 to distribute or divide (e g commodities in short supply) in fixed quantities – often + *out* 2 to use sparingly

rational /'rash(ə)nl/ adj 1 having, based on, or compatible with reason; reasonable 2 of, involving, or being (a mathematical expression containing) 1 or more rational numbers – **~ly** adv – **~ity** n

rationale /,rashə'nahl/ n an underlying reason; basis

rationalism /'rash(ə)nə,liz(ə)m/ n a theory that reason is a source of knowledge superior to and independent of sense perception – **-list** n

rational·ize, -ise /'rash(ə)nəliez/ v 1 to provide plausible reasons for one's behaviour, opinions, etc 2 to increase the efficiency of (e g an industry) by more effective organization – **-zation** n

,rational 'number n a number (e g 2, ⁵/₂, - ¹/₂) that can be expressed as the result of dividing one integer by another

'rat ,race n the struggle to maintain one's position in a career or survive the pressures of modern urban life

¹rattle /'ratl/ v **rattling** /'ratling, 'ratl·ing/ 1 to (cause to) make a rapid succession of short sharp sounds 2 to chatter incessantly and aimlessly – often + *on* 3 to say or perform in a brisk lively fashion – often + *off* 4 to upset to the point of loss of poise and composure

²rattle n 1 a rattling sound 2a a child's toy consisting of loose pellets in a hollow container that rattles when shaken **b** a device that consists of a springy tongue in contact with a revolving ratchet wheel which is rotated or shaken to produce a loud noise 3 a throat noise caused by air passing through mucus and heard esp at the approach of death

'rattle,snake /-,snayk/ n any of various American poisonous snakes with horny interlocking joints at the end of the tail that rattle when shaken

ratty /'rati/ adj irritable – infml

raucous /'rawkəs/ adj disagreeably harsh or strident; noisy – **~ly** adv – **~ness** n

¹ravage /'ravij/ n damage resulting from ravaging – usu pl

²ravage v to wreak havoc (on); cause (violent) destruction (to)

¹rave /rayv/ v 1 to talk irrationally (as if) in delirium; *broadly* to rage, storm 2 to talk with extreme or passionate enthusiasm

²rave n 1 a raving 2 an extravagantly favourable review

¹ravel /'ravl/ v **-ll-** (*NAm* **-l-, -ll-**), 'ravling, ' ravl·ing/ 1 to unravel, disentangle – usu + *out* 2 to entangle, confuse

²ravel n a tangle or tangled mass

raven /'rayv(ə)n/ n a very large glossy black bird of the crow family

ravenous /'rav(ə)nəs/ adj 1 urgently seeking satisfaction, gratification, etc; grasping, insatiable 2 fiercely eager for food; famished – **~ly** adv

raver /'rayvə/ n, *chiefly Br* an energetic and uninhibited person who enjoys a hectic social life; *also* a sexually uninhibited or promiscuous person – slang

'rave-,up n, *chiefly Br* a wild party – slang

ravine /rə'veen/ n a narrow steep-sided valley smaller than a canyon and usu worn by running water

¹raving /'rayving/ n irrational, incoherent, wild, or extravagant utterance or declamation – usu pl with sing. meaning

²raving adj extreme, marked – infml

ravioli /,ravi'ohli/ n little cases of pasta containing meat, cheese, etc

ravish /'ravish/ v 1 to overcome with joy, delight, etc 2 to rape, violate

ravishing /'ravishing/ adj unusually attractive or pleasing – **~ly** adv

raw /raw/ adj 1 not cooked 2 not processed or purified 3 having the surface abraded or chafed 4 lacking experience, training, etc; new 5 disagreeably damp or cold – **~ness** n

'raw,hide /-,hied/ n (a whip of) untanned hide

¹ray /ray/ n any of numerous fishes having the eyes on the upper surface of a flattened body and a long narrow tail

²ray n 1a any of the lines of light that appear to radiate from a bright object **b** a narrow beam of radiant energy (e g light or X rays) **c** a stream of (radioactive) particles travelling in the same line 2 any of a group of lines diverging from a common centre 3a any of the bony rods that support the fin of a fish **b** any of the radiating parts of the body of a radially symmetrical animal (e g a starfish) 4 a slight manifestation or trace (e g of intelligence or hope)

rayon /'rayon, -ən/ n (a fabric made from) a yarn or fibre produced by drawing and forcing cellulose through minute holes

raze, rase /rayz/ v to lay (e g a town or building) level with the ground

razor /'rayzə/ n a sharp-edged cutting implement for shaving or cutting (facial) hair

razzle /'razl/ n a spree, binge

¹re /ray, ree/ n the 2nd note of the diatonic scale in solmization

²re /ree/ prep with regard to; concerning

¹reach /reech/ v 1 to stretch out 2a to touch or grasp by extending a part of the body (e g a hand) or an object **b** to pick up and draw towards one; pass **c**(1) to extend to **c**(2) to get up to or as far as; arrive at **d** to contact or communicate with

rea

²**reach** *n* **1a** the action or an act of reaching **b** the distance or extent of reaching or of ability to reach **c** a range; *specif* comprehension **2** a straight uninterrupted portion of a river or canal **3** the tack sailed by a vessel with the wind blowing more or less from the side

react /ri'akt/ *v* **1** to exert a reciprocal or counteracting force or influence – often + *on* or *upon* **2** to respond to a stimulus **3** to act in opposition to a force or influence – usu + *against* **4** to undergo chemical reaction

reaction /ri'aksh(ə)n/ *n* **1a** a reacting **b** tendency towards a former and usu outmoded (political or social) order or policy **2** bodily response to or activity aroused by a stimulus: e g **2a** the response of tissues to a foreign substance (e g an antigen or infective agent) **b** a mental or emotional response to circumstances **3** the force that sthg subjected to the action of a force exerts equally in the opposite direction **4a** a chemical transformation or change; an action between atoms, molecules, etc to form new substances **b** a process involving change in atomic nuclei resulting from interaction with a particle or another nucleus

reactionary /ri'akshən(ə)ri/ *also* **reactionist** *n or adj* (a person) opposing radical social change or favouring a return to a former (political) order

reactivate /ri'aktivayt/ *v* to make or become active again

reactive /ri'aktiv/ *adj* **1** of or marked by reaction or reacting **2** tending to or liable to react – ~ly *adv* – ~ness *n*

reactor /ri'aktə/ *n* an apparatus in which a chain reaction of fissile material (e g uranium or plutonium) is started and controlled, esp for the production of nuclear power or elementary particles

¹**read** /reed/ *v* **read** /red/ **1a(1)** to look at or otherwise sense (e g letters, symbols, or words) with mental assimilation of the communication represented **a(2)** to utter aloud (interpretatively) the printed or written words of – often + *out* **b** to study (a subject), esp for a degree **2a** to understand, comprehend **b** to interpret the meaning or significance of

²**read** /reed/ *n* **1** sthg to read with reference to the interest, enjoyment, etc it provides **2** *chiefly Br* a period of reading

³**read** /red/ *adj* instructed by or informed through reading

readable /'reedəbl/ *adj* **1** legible **2** pleasurable or interesting to read – **-bility** *n*

reader /'reedə/ *n* **1a** one who reads and corrects proofs **b** one who evaluates manuscripts **2** a member of a British university staff between the ranks of lecturer and professor **3** a usu instructive (introductory) book or anthology

readership /'reedə,ship/ *n, sing or pl in constr* a collective body of readers; *esp* the readers of a particular publication or author

readily /'redəli/ *adv* **1** without hesitating **2** without much difficulty

reading /'reeding/ *n* **1a** material read or for reading **b** the extent to which a person has read **c** an event at which a play, poetry, etc is read to an audience **d** an act of formally reading a bill that constitutes any of 3 successive stages of approval by a legislature, *specif* Parliament **2a** a form or version of a particular (passage in a) text **b** the value indicated or data produced by an instrument **3** a particular interpretation

'**read out** /-,owt/ *n* the removal of information from storage (e g in a computer memory or on magnetic tape) for display in an understandable form (e g as a printout)

¹**ready** /'redi/ *adj* **1a** prepared mentally or physically for some experience or action **b** prepared or available for immediate use **2a(1)** willingly disposed **a(2)** likely or about to do the specified thing **b** spontaneously prompt – **ready** *adv* – **-diness** *n*

²**ready** *v* to make ready

³**ready** *n* (ready) money

⁴**ready** *adv* in advance

,**ready-'made** *adj* **1** made beforehand, esp for general sale or use rather than to individual specifications **2** lacking originality or individuality

reafforest /,ree-ə'forəst/ *v* to renew the forest cover by seeding or planting – ~**ation** *n*

reagent /ri'ayj(ə)nt/ *n* a substance that takes part in or brings about a particular chemical reaction, used esp to detect sthg

real /reel, riəl/ *adj* **1a** not artificial, fraudulent, illusory, fictional, etc; *also* being precisely what the name implies; genuine **b** of practical or everyday concerns or activities **2** measured by purchasing power rather than the paper value of money **3** complete, great – used chiefly for emphasis

'**real e,state** *n* property in buildings and land

realign /,ree-ə'lien/ *v* to reorganize or make new groupings of – ~**ment** *n*

realism /'ree,liz(ə)m, 'riə-/ *n* **1** concern for fact or reality and rejection of the impractical and visionary **2** the belief that objects of sense perception have real existence independent of the mind **3** fidelity in art, literature, etc to nature and to accurate representation without idealization – **-list** *n*

realistic /,riə'listik/ *adj* **1** not impractical or over optimistic; sober **2** of realism

reality /ri'aləti/ *n* **1** being real **2a** a real event, entity, or state of affairs **b** the totality of real things and events — **in reality** as a matter of fact

real·ize, -ise /'reeliez, 'riə-/ *v* **1** to accomplish **2** to bring or get by sale, investment or effort **3** to be fully aware of – **-zation** *n*

really /'reeli, 'riəli/ *adv* **1a** in reality, actually **b** without question; thoroughly **2** more correctly – used to give force to an injunction (e g you *really* should have asked me first) **3** – expressing surprise or indignation

realm /relm/ *n* **1** a kingdom **2** a sphere, domain – often pl with sing. meaning

,real 'tennis *n* a game played with a racket and ball in an irregularly-shaped indoor court divided by a net

¹**ream** /reem/ *n* **1** a quantity of paper equal to 20 quires or variously 480, 500, or 516 sheets **2** a great amount (e g of sthg written or printed) – usu pl with sing. meaning

²**ream** *v* to enlarge or widen a hole – ~**er** *n*

reap /reep/ *v* **1** to cut a crop; *also* to harvest **2** to obtain or win, esp as the reward for effort – ~**er** *n*

¹**rear** /riə/ *v* **1a** to breed and tend (an animal) or grow (e g a crop) for use or sale **b** to bring up **2** to rise to a height **3** *of a horse* to rise up on the hind legs

²**rear** *n* **1** the back part of sthg: e g **1a** the part (e g of an army) away from the enemy **b** the part of sthg located opposite its front **c** the buttocks **2** the space or position at the back

³**rear** *adj* at the back

'rear ,guard *n* a military detachment for guarding the rear of a force, esp during a retreat

rearm /,ree'ahm/ *v* to arm (e g a nation or military force) again, esp with new or better weapons – ~**ament** *n*

¹'rear,ward /-,wood/ *n* the rear; *esp* the rear division (e g of an army)

²'rear,ward /-wood/ *adj* located at or directed towards the rear

¹**reason** /'reez(ə)n/ *n* **1a** (a statement offered as) an explanation or justification **b** a rational ground or motive **2a** proper exercise of the mind; *also* the intelligence **b** sanity — **within reason** within reasonable limits — **with reason** with good cause

²**reason** *v* **1** to use the faculty of reason so as to arrive at conclusions **2** to talk or argue *with* another so as to influence his/her actions or opinions **3** to formulate, assume, analyse, or conclude by the use of reason – often + *out* – ~**er** *n*

reasonable /'reez(ə)nəbl/ *adj* **1a** in accord with reason **b** not extreme or excessive **c** moderate, fair **d** inexpensive **2a** having the faculty of reason; rational **b** sensible – ~**bleness** *n* – ~**bly** *adv*

reasoning /'reez(ə)ning/ *n* the drawing of inferences or conclusions through the use of reason

reassure /,ree-ə'shooə, -'shaw/ *v* to restore confidence to – ~**surance** *n* – ~**suringly** *adv*

¹**rebate** /'reebayt/ *n* **1** a return of part of a payment **2** a deduction from a sum before payment; a discount

¹**rebel** /'rebl/ *adj* **1** in rebellion **2** of rebels

²**rebel** *n* one who rebels against a government, authority, convention, etc

³**rebel** /ri'bel/ *v* **-ll- 1** to oppose or disobey (one in) authority or control, esp a government **2** to act in or show opposition

rebellion /ri'belyən/ *n* **1** opposition to (one in) authority or dominance **2** (an instance of) open armed resistance to an established government

rebellious /ri'belyəs/ *adj* **1a** in rebellion **b** (characteristic) of or inclined towards rebellion **2** refractory – ~**ly** *adv* – ~**ness** *n*

rebirth /,ree'buhth/ *n* **1a** a new or second birth **b** spiritual regeneration **2** a renaissance, revival

reborn /,ree'bawn/ *adj* born again; regenerated

¹**rebound** /ri'bownd/ *v* **1** to spring back (as if) on collision or impact with another body **2** to return with an adverse effect to a source or starting point

²**rebound** /'ree,bownd; *also* ri'bownd/ *n* **1** a rebounding, recoil **2** a recovery — **on the rebound** (whilst) in an unsettled or emotional state resulting from setback, frustration, or crisis

rebuff /ri'buf/ *v or n* (to) snub

rebuke /ri'byoohk/ *v or n* (to) reprimand

rebus /'reebəs/ *n* (a riddle using) a representation of words or syllables by pictures that suggest the same sound

rebut /ri'but/ *v* **-tt- 1** to drive back; repel **2** to disprove or expose the falsity of; refute – **rebuttal** *n*

recalcitrant /ri'kalsitrənt/ *adj* **1** obstinately defiant of authority or restraint **2** difficult to handle or control – **trance** *n*

¹**recall** /ri'kawl/ *v* **1a** to call or summon back **b** to bring back to mind **2** to cancel, revoke – ~**able** *adj*

²**recall** /ri'kawl, 'ree,kawl/ *n* **1** a call or summons to return **2** remembrance of what has been learned or experienced **3** the act of revoking or the possibility of being revoked

recant /ri'kant/ *v* to make an open confession of error; *esp* to disavow a religious belief or withdraw a statement – ~**ation** *n*

recap /'ree,kap/ *v* **-pp-** to recapitulate

recapitulate /,reekə'pityoolayt/ *v* to repeat the principal points or stages of (e g an argument or discourse) in summing up – **lation** *n*

recapture /,ree'kapchə/ *v* **1** to capture again **2** to experience again

recede /ri'seed/ *v* **1a** to move back or away; withdraw **b** to slant backwards **2** to grow less, smaller, or more distant; diminish

receipt /ri'seet/ *n* **1** the act or process of receiving **2** sthg (e g goods or money) received – usu pl with sing. meaning **3** a written acknowledgment of having received goods or money

receive /ri'seev/ *v* **1** to (willingly) come into possession of or be provided with **2a** to act as a receptacle or container for; *also* to take (an impression, mark, etc) **b** to assimilate through the mind or senses **3** to welcome; greet; *also* to entertain **4a** to take the force or pressure of **b** to suffer the hurt or injury of

re·ceiver /ri'seevə/ *n* **1** a person appointed to hold in trust and administer property of a bankrupt or insane person or property under litigation **2** one who receives stolen goods **3a** a radio, television, or other part of a communications system that receives the signal **b** the part of a telephone that contains the mouthpiece and earpiece

recent /'rees(ə)nt/ *adj* **1** of a time not long past **2** having lately come into existence – ~**ly** *adv*

receptacle /ri'septəkl/ *n* **1** an object that receives and contains sthg **2** the end of the flower stalk of a flowering plant upon which the floral organs are borne

reception /ri'sepsh(ə)n/ *n* **1** receiving or being received: e g **1a** an admission **b** a response, reaction **c** the receiving of a radio or television broadcast **2** a formal social gathering during which guests are received **3** *Br* an office or desk where visitors or clients (e g to an office, factory, or hotel) are received on arrival

receptionist /ri'sepshənist/ *n* one employed to greet and assist callers or clients

receptive /ri'septiv/ *adj* open and responsive to ideas, impressions, or suggestions – ~**ly** *adv* – ~**ness** *n* – **-tivity** *n*

¹recess /ri'ses, 'reeses/ *n* **1** a hidden, secret, or secluded place – usu pl **2** an alcove **3** a suspension of business or activity, usu for a period of rest or relaxation

²recess /ri'ses/ *v* **1** to put in a recess **2** to make a recess in **3** to interrupt for a recess

recession /ri'sesh(ə)n/ *n* **1** a withdrawal **2** a period of reduced economic activity

recessional /ri'sesh(ə)nl/ *n* a hymn or musical piece at the conclusion of a church service

recessive /ri'sesiv/ *adj* **1** receding or tending to recede **2** being the one of a pair of (genes determining) contrasting inherited characteristics that is suppressed if a dominant gene is present

recharge /,ree'chahj/ *v* to charge again; *esp* to renew the active materials in (a storage battery)

recherché /rə'sheəshay (*Fr* rəʃerʃe)/ *adj* **1** exotic, rare **2** precious, affected

recidivist /ri'sidivist/ *n* one who relapses, specif into criminal behaviour – **-vism** *n*

recipe /'resipi/ *n* **1** a list of ingredients and instructions for making sthg, specif a food dish **2** a procedure for doing or attaining sthg

recipient /ri'sipi·ənt/ *n* sby who or sthg that receives

¹reciprocal /ri'siprəkl/ *adj* **1** shared, felt, or shown by both sides **2** consisting of or functioning as a return in kind **3** mutually corresponding; equivalent

²reciprocal *n* **1** either of a pair of numbers (e g $^2/_3$, $^3/_2$) that when multiplied together equal 1 **2** the inverse of a number under multiplication – ~**ly** *adv*

reciprocate /ri'siprə,kayt/ *v* **1** to give and take mutually **2** to return in kind or degree – **-cation** *n*

recital /ri'sietl/ *n* **1** a reciting **2** a concert or public performance given by a musician, small group of musicians, or dancer

recitative /,resitə'teev/ *n* (a passage delivered in) a rhythmically free declamatory style for singing a narrative text

recite /ri'siet/ *v* **1** to repeat from memory or read aloud, esp before an audience **2** to relate in detail; enumerate – **-tation** *n* – ~**r** *n*

reckless /'reklis/ *adj* marked by lack of proper caution; careless of consequences – ~**ly** *adv* – ~**ness** *n*

reckon /'rekən/ *v* **1a** to count – usu + *up* **b** to estimate, compute **2** to consider or think of in a specified way **3** to suppose, think **4** to esteem highly – infml **5** to place reliance *on* **6** to take into account – + *with* – ~**er** *n*

reckoning /'rekəning/ *n* **1a** a calculation or counting **b** an account, bill **2** a settling of accounts **3** an appraisal

reclaim /ri'klaym/ *v* **1** to rescue or convert from an undesirable state; reform **2** to make available for human use by changing natural conditions **3** to obtain from a waste product – **reclamation** *n*

recline /ri'klien/ *v* **1** (to cause or permit) to incline backwards **2** to place or be in a recumbent position; lean, repose

recluse /ri'kloohs/ *n or adj* (sby) leading a secluded or solitary life

recognition /,rekəg'nish(ə)n/ *n* **1** recognizing or being recognized **2** special notice or attention

recog·ize, -ise /'rekəgniez/ *v* **1** to perceive to be something already known **2** to show appreciation of **3** to admit as being of a particular status or having validity

¹recoil /ri'koyl/ *v* **1** to shrink back physically or emotionally (e g in horror, fear, or disgust) **2** to spring back; rebound

²recoil /'ree,koyl, ri'koyl/ *n* recoiling; *esp* the backwards movement of a gun on firing

recollect /,rekə'lekt/ *v* **1** to bring back to the level of conscious awareness; remember, recall **2** to bring (oneself) back to a state of composure or concentration – ~**ion** *n*

recommend /,rekə'mend/ *v* **1** to endorse as fit, worthy, or competent **2** to advise – ~**ation** *n*

¹recompense /'rekəmpens/ *v* **1** to give sthg to by way of compensation **2** to make or amount to an equivalent or compensation for

²recompense *n* an equivalent or a return for sthg done, suffered, or given

reconcile /'rekənsiel/ *v* **1** to restore to friendship or harmony **2** to make consistent or congruous **3** to cause to submit to or accept – **-cilable** *adj*

recondition /,reekən'dish(ə)n/ *v* to restore to good (working) condition (e g by replacing parts)

reconnaissance /ri'konəs(ə)ns/ *n* a preliminary survey to gain information; *esp* an exploratory military survey of enemy territory or positions

reconnoitre, *NAm* **reconnoiter** /,rekə'noytə/ *v* to make a reconnaissance (of)

reconsider /,reekən'sidə/ *v* to consider (sthg) again with a view to change, revision, or revocation – ~**ation** *n*

reconstitute /ree'konstityooht, -chooht/ *v* to constitute again or anew; *esp* to restore to a former condition by adding water

reconstruct /,reekən'strukt/ *v* **1a** to restore to a previous condition **b** to recreate **2** to build up a mental image or physical representation of (e g a crime or a battle) from the available evidence – ~**ion** *n*

¹**record** /ri'kawd/ *v* **1a** to commit to writing so as to supply written evidence **b** to register by mechanical or other means **2** to give evidence of; show **3** to convert (e g sound) into a permanent form fit for reproduction

²**record** /'rekawd, 'rekəd/ *n* **1a** sthg recorded or on which information, evidence, etc has been registered **b** sthg that recalls, relates, or commemorates past events or feats **c** an authentic official document **2a(1)** a body of known or recorded facts regarding sthg or sby **a(2)** a list of previous criminal convictions **b** the best recorded performance in a competitive sport **3** a flat usu plastic disc with a spiral groove whose undulations represent recorded sound for reproduction on a gramophone — **off the record** not for publication — **on record** in or into the status of being known, published, or documented

recorder /ri'kawdə/ *n* **1** *often cap* a magistrate formerly presiding over the court of quarter sessions **2** any of a group of wind instruments consisting of a slightly tapering tube with usu 8 finger holes and a mouthpiece like a whistle

recording /ri'kawding/ *n* sthg (e g sound or a television programme) that has been recorded electronically

¹**recount** /ri'kownt/ *v* to relate in detail

²**recount** /,ree'kownt/ *n* a recounting, esp of votes

recoup /ri'koohp/ *v* **1** to get an equivalent for (e g losses) **2** to regain

recourse /ri'kaws/ *n* (a turning or resorting to) a source of help, strength, or protection

recover /ri'kuvə/ *v* **1a** to get back **b** to regain a normal or stable position or condition (e g of health) **2** to obtain by legal action – ~**able** *adj*

recovery /ri'kuv(ə)ri/ *n* a recovering: e g **a** a return to normal health **b** a regaining of balance or control (e g after a stumble or mistake) **c** an economic upturn (e g after a depression)

recreate /,reekri'ayt/ *v* to create again: e g **a** to reproduce so as to resemble exactly **b** to visualize or create again in the imagination

recreation /,rekri'aysh(ə)n/ *n* (a means of) pleasurable activity, diversion, etc

recriminate /ri'krimi,nayt/ *v* to indulge in bitter mutual accusations – **-natory** *adj*

¹**recruit** /ri'krooht/ *n* a newcomer to a field or activity; *specif* a newly enlisted member of the armed forces

²**recruit** *v* **1** to enlist recruits **2** to secure the services of; hire – ~**ment** *n*

rectangle /'rektang-gl/ *n* a parallelogram all of whose angles are right angles; *esp* one that is not a square – **-gular** *adj*

rectify /'rekti,fie/ *v* **1** to set right; remedy **2** to correct by removing errors

rectilinear /,rekti'lini-ə/ *adj* **1** (moving) in or forming a straight line **2** characterized by straight lines

rectitude /'rekti,tyoohd/ *n* **1** moral integrity **2** correctness in judgment or procedure

rector /'rektə/ *n* **1** a clergyman in charge of a parish **2** the head of a university or college

rectory /'rekt(ə)ri/ *n* a rector's residence or benefice

rectum /'rektəm/ *n pl* **rectums, recta** /-tə/ the last part of the intestine of a vertebrate, ending at the anus – **-tal** *adj*

recumbent /ri'kumbənt/ *adj* **1** in an attitude suggestive of repose **2** lying down

recuperate /ri'k(y)oohpə,rayt/ *v* to regain a former (healthy) state or condition – **-ration** *n*

recur /ri'kuh/ *v* **-rr-** to occur again, esp repeatedly or after an interval: e g **a** to come up again for consideration **b** to come again to mind – ~**rence** *n*

recurrent /ri'kurənt/ *adj* returning or happening repeatedly or periodically – ~**ly** *adv*

recycle /,ree'siekl/ *v* to process (sewage, waste paper, glass, etc) for conversion back into a useful product

¹**red** /red/ *adj* **-dd-** **1** of the colour red **2a** flushed, esp with anger or embarrassment **b** tinged with or rather red **3** failing to show a profit **4** *often cap* communist – infml – ~**ness** *n* – ~**dish** *adj*

²**red** *n* **1** a colour whose hue resembles that of blood or of the ruby or is that of the long-wave extreme of the visible spectrum **2** the condition of being financially in debt or of showing a loss – usu in *in/out of the red* **3** a red traffic light meaning 'stop' **4** *cap* a communist *USE* (4) chiefly derog

,red '**admiral** *n* a common N American and European butterfly that has broad orange-red bands on the fore wings

,red-'**blooded** *adj* full of vigour; virile

red

'**red brick** /-ˌbrik/ *n or adj* (an English university) founded between 1800 and WW II

ˌ**red·currant** /-ˈkʌrənt/ *n* (the small red edible fruit of) a widely cultivated European currant bush

redden /ˈred(ə)n/ *v* to make or become red; *esp* to blush

redeem /riˈdeem/ *v* 1 to release from blame or debt 2 to free from the consequences of sin 3a to eliminate another's right to (sthg) by payment of a debt; *esp* to repurchase a pawned item b to convert (trading stamps, tokens, etc) into money or goods c to make good; fulfil 4a to atone for b to make worthwhile; retrieve – ~able *adj* – ~er *n*

redemption /riˈdempsh(ə)n/, -ˈdemsh(ə)n/ *n* redeeming or being redeemed; *also* sthg that redeems

redeploy /ˌreediˈploy/ *v* to transfer (e g troops or workers) from one area or activity to another – ~ment *n*

ˌ**red-ˈhanded** *adv or adj* in the act of committing a crime or misdeed

'**red head** /-ˌhed/ *n* a person with red hair

ˌ**red-ˈhot** *adj* 1 glowing with heat; extremely hot 2a ardent, passionate b sensational; *specif* salacious 3 new, topical

ˌ**Red ˈIndian** *n* a N American Indian

ˌ**red-ˈlight district** *n* a district having many brothels

ˌ**red ˈmeat** *n* dark-coloured meat (e g beef or lamb)

redo /ˌreeˈdooh/ *v* redoes; redoing; redid; redone 1 to do over again 2 to decorate (a room or interior of a building) anew

redolent /ˈredələnt/ *adj* 1 full of a specified fragrance 2 evocative, suggestive – **-lence** *n*

redouble /riˈdubl/, *sense* 2 ˌree-/ *v* redoubling /-ˈdubl·ing, -ˈdubling/ to make or become greater, more numerous, or more intense

redoubtable /riˈdowtəbl/ *adj* 1 formidable 2 inspiring or worthy of awe or reverence

'**redress** /riˈdres/ *v* 1 to set right 2 to make or exact reparation for

²**redress** *n* 1 compensation for wrong or loss 2 the (means or possibility of) putting right what is wrong

'**red skin** /-ˌskin/ *n* a N American Indian – chiefly derog

ˌ**red ˈsquirrel** *n* a reddish brown Eurasian squirrel native to British woodlands

ˌ**red ˈtape** *n* excessively complex bureaucratic routine that results in delay

reduce /riˈdyoohs/ *v* 1 to diminish in size, amount, extent, or number; *also* to lose weight by dieting 2 to bring or force to a specified state or condition 3 to force to capitulate 4 to bring to a systematic form or character 5 to lower in grade, rank, status, or condition 6a to diminish in strength, density, or value b to lower the price of – **reducible** *adj*

reductio ad absurdum /riˌdukti·oh ad abˈsuhdəm/ *n* proof of the falsity of a proposition by revealing the absurdity of its logical consequences

reduction /riˈduksh(ə)n/ *n* 1 a reducing or being reduced 2a sthg made by reducing; *esp* a reproduction (e g of a picture) in a smaller size b the amount by which sthg is reduced

redundancy /riˈdundənsi/ *n* dismissal from a job

redundant /riˈdundənt/ *adj* 1a superfluous b excessively verbose 2 *chiefly Br* unnecessary, unfit, or no longer required for a job – ~ly *adv*

'**red wing** /-ˌwing/ *n* a Eurasian thrush with red patches beneath its wings

'**red wood** /-ˌwood/ *n* (the wood of) a commercially important Californian timber tree of the pine family

reed /reed/ *n* 1 (the slender, often prominently jointed, stem of) any of various tall grasses that grow esp in wet areas 2 a growth or mass of reeds; *specif* reeds for thatching 3a a thin elastic tongue or flattened tube (e g of cane) fastened over an air opening in a musical instrument (e g an organ or clarinet) and set in vibration by an air current b a woodwind instrument having a reed

reeducate /ˌreeˈedyookayt, -ˈejoo-/ *v* to rehabilitate through education – **-cation** *n*

reedy /ˈreedi/ *adj* 1 full of, covered with, or made of reeds 2 slender, frail 3 having the tonal quality of a reed instrument; *esp* thin and high – **reediness** *n*

'**reef** /reef/ *n* a part of a sail taken in or let out to regulate the area exposed to the wind

²**reef** *v* to reduce the area of (a sail) exposed to the wind by rolling up or taking in a portion

³**reef** *n* a ridge of rocks or sand at or near the surface of water

'**reefer** /ˈreefə/, '**reefer jacket** *n* a close-fitting usu double-breasted jacket of thick cloth

²**reefer** *n* a cigarette containing cannabis

'**reef ˌknot** *n* a symmetrical knot made of 2 half-knots tied in opposite directions and commonly used for joining 2 pieces of material

'**reek** /reek/ *n* 1 a strong or disagreeable smell 2 *chiefly Scot & N Eng* smoke, vapour

²**reek** *v* 1 to give off or become permeated with a strong or offensive smell 2 to give a strong impression (of some usu undesirable quality or feature) – + *of* or *with*

'**reel** /reel, riəl/ *n* a revolvable device on which sthg flexible is wound: e g a a small wheel at the butt of a fishing rod for winding the line b a flanged spool for photographic film, magnetic tape, etc c *chiefly Br* a small spool for sewing thread – **reel** *v*

²reel *v* 1 to be giddy; be in a whirl 2 to waver or fall back (e g from a blow) 3 to move unsteadily (e g from dizziness or intoxication)

³reel *n* (the music for) a lively esp Scottish-Highland or Irish dance in which 2 or more couples perform a series of circular figures and winding movements

reel off *v* 1 to tell or repeat readily and without pause 2 to chalk up, usu as a series

reentry /,ree'entri/ *n* 1 the retaking of possession 2 the return to and entry of the earth's atmosphere by a space vehicle

¹reeve /reev/ *n* a medieval English manor officer

²reeve *v* rove /rohv/, reeved 1 to pass a rope through a hole or opening 2 to fasten by passing through a hole or round sthg

ref /ref/ *n* a referee – infml

refectory /ri'fekt(ə)ri/ *n* a dining hall in an institution (e g a monastery or college)

refer /ri'fuh/ *v* -rr- 1 to explain in terms of a general cause 2 to send or direct for information, aid, treatment, etc 3 to relate *to* sthg; *also* allude *to* 4 to have recourse; glance briefly for information

¹referee /,refə'ree/ *n* 1a one to whom a legal matter is referred for investigation or settlement b a (character) reference 2 an official who supervises the play and enforces the laws in any of several sports (e g football and boxing)

²referee *v* to act as a referee (in or for)

¹reference /'ref(ə)rəns/ *n* 1 referring or consulting 2 (a) bearing on or connection with a matter – often in *in/with reference to* 3a an allusion, mention b sthg that refers a reader to another source of information (e g a book or passage); *also* the other source of information 4a a person to whom inquiries as to character or ability can be made b a statement of the qualifications of a person seeking employment or appointment given by sby familiar with him/her c a standard for measuring, evaluating, etc

²reference *v* to provide (e g a book) with references to authorities and sources of information

'reference ,book *n* a book (e g a dictionary, encyclopedia, or atlas) intended primarily for consultation rather than for consecutive reading

referendum /,refə'rendəm/ *n*, *pl* **referendums** *also* **referenda** /-də/ the submitting to popular vote of a measure proposed by a legislative body or by popular initiative

refill /'ree,fil/ *n* a fresh or replacement supply (for a device)

refine /ri'fien/ *v* 1 to free from impurities 2 to improve or perfect by pruning or polishing 3 to free from imperfection, esp from what is coarse, vulgar, or uncouth

re'fined *adj* 1 fastidious, cultivated 2 *esp of food* processed to the extent that desirable ingredients may be lost in addition to impurities or imperfections

re'finement /-mənt/ *n* 1 refining or being refined 2a a (highly) refined feature, method, or distinction b a contrivance or device intended to improve or perfect

refinery /ri'fien(ə)ri/ *n* a plant where raw materials (e g oil or sugar) are refined or purified

refit /,ree'fit/ *v* -tt- to fit out or supply again; *esp* to renovate and modernize (e g a ship)

reflation /,ree'flaysh(ə)n/ *n* an expansion in the volume of available money and credit or in the economy, esp as a result of government policy

reflect /ri'flekt/ *v* 1 to send or throw (light, sound, etc) back or at an angle 2 to show as an image or likeness; mirror 3 to make manifest or apparent 4 to consider 5 to tend to bring reproach or discredit – usu + *on* or *upon*

reflection, *Br also* **reflexion** /ri'fleksh(ə)n/ *n* 1 a reflecting of light, sound, etc 2a an image given back (as if) by a reflecting surface b an effect produced by or related to a specified influence or cause 3 an often obscure or indirect criticism 4 consideration of some subject matter, idea, or purpose

reflective /ri'flektiv/ *adj* 1 capable of reflecting light, images, or sound waves 2 thoughtful, deliberative 3 of or caused by reflection

reflector /ri'flektə/ *n* 1 a polished surface for reflecting radiation, esp light 2 a telescope in which the principal focussing element is a mirror

¹reflex /'reefleks/ *n* 1 an automatic response to a stimulus that does not reach the level of consciousness 2 *pl* the power of acting or responding with adequate speed 3 an (automatic) way of behaving or responding

²reflex *adj* 1 bent, turned, or directed back 2 occurring as an (automatic) response 3 *of an angle* greater than 180° but less than 360°

reflexive /ri'fleksiv/ *adj* 1 directed or turned back on itself 2 of, denoting, or being an action (e g in *he perjured himself*) directed back upon the agent or the grammatical subject – **-ly** *adv*

¹reform /ri'fawm/ *v* 1 to amend or alter for the better 2 to put an end to (an evil) by enforcing or introducing a better method or course of action 3 to induce or cause to abandon evil ways – **~ er** *n*

²reform *n* 1 amendment of what is defective or corrupt 2 (a measure intended to effect) a removal or correction of an abuse, a wrong, or errors

reformation /,refə'maysh(ə)n/ *n* 1 reforming or being reformed 2 *cap the* 16th-c religious movement marked by the rejection of papal authority and the establishment of the Protestant churches

reformatory /ri'fawmət(ə)ri/ *n*, *chiefly NAm* a penal institution to which young or first offenders or women are sent for reform

refract /ri'frakt/ v to deflect (light or another wave motion) from one straight path to another when passing from one medium (e g glass) to another (e g air) in which the velocity is different – ~**ion** n

refractory /ri'frakt(ə)ri/ adj 1 resisting control or authority; stubborn, unmanageable 2 resistant to treatment or cure 3 difficult to fuse, corrode, or draw out; esp capable of enduring high temperatures

¹**refrain** /ri'frayn/ v to keep oneself from doing, feeling, or indulging in sthg, esp from following a passing impulse – usu + from

²**refrain** n (the musical setting of) a regularly recurring phrase or verse, esp at the end of each stanza or division of a poem or song; a chorus

refresh /ri'fresh/ v 1 to restore strength and vigour to; revive (e g by food or rest) 2 to arouse, stimulate (e g the memory)

refreshing /ri'freshing/ adj agreeably stimulating because of freshness or newness – ~**ly** adv

re'freshment /-mənt/ n 1 refreshing or being refreshed 2 assorted foods, esp for a light meal – usu pl with sing. meaning

refrigerate /ri'frijərayt/ v to freeze or chill (e g food) or remain frozen for preservation – -**rant** n – -**ration** n

refrigerator /ri'frijəraytə/ n an insulated cabinet or room for keeping food, drink, etc cool

refuge /'refyoohj/ n 1 (a place that provides) shelter or protection from danger or distress 2 a person, thing, or course of action that offers protection or is resorted to in difficulties

refugee /,refyoo'jee/ n one who flees for safety, esp to a foreign country to escape danger or persecution

¹**refund** /ri'fund/ v to return (money) in restitution, repayment, or balancing of accounts

²**refund** /'ree,fund/ n 1 a refunding 2 a sum refunded

³**refund** /,ree'fund/ v to fund (a debt) again

refurbish /,ree'fuhbish/ v to renovate

refusal /ri'fyoohzl/ n 1 a refusing, denying, or being refused 2 the right or option of refusing or accepting sthg before others

¹**refuse** /ri'fyoohz/ v 1 to express oneself as unwilling to accept 2a to show or express unwillingness to do or comply with b of a horse to decline to jump a fence, wall, etc

²**refuse** /'refyoohs/ n worthless or useless stuff; rubbish, garbage

refute /ri'fyooht/ v 1 to prove wrong by argument or evidence 2 to deny the truth or accuracy of

regain /ri'gayn, ,ree-/ v to gain or reach again; recover

regal /'reegl/ adj 1 of or suitable for a king or queen 2 stately, splendid – ~**ly** adv

regalia /ri'gaylyə/ n pl but sing or pl in constr 1 (the) ceremonial emblems or symbols indicative of royalty 2 special dress; esp official finery

¹**regard** /ri'gahd/ n 1 a gaze, look 2 attention, consideration 3a a feeling of respect and affection b pl friendly greetings — **in/with regard to** with reference to; on the subject of

²**regard** v 1 to pay attention to; take into consideration or account 2 to look steadily at 3 to consider and appraise in a specified way or from a specified point of view — **as regards** with regard to

regarding /ri'gahding/ prep with regard to

¹**re'gardless** /-lis/ adj heedless, careless

²**regardless** adv despite everything

regatta /ri'gatə/ n a series of rowing, speedboat, or sailing races

regency /'reej(ə)nsi/ n the office, period of rule, or government of a regent or regents

¹**regenerate** /ri'jen(ə)rət/ adj 1 spiritually reborn or converted 2 restored to a better, higher, or more worthy state

²**regenerate** /ri'jenərayt/ v 1 to change radically and for the better 2 to generate or produce anew; esp to replace (a body part) by a new growth of tissue

regent /'reej(ə)nt/ n one who governs a kingdom in the minority, absence, or disability of the sovereign

reggae /'regay/ n popular music of West Indian origin that is characterized by a strongly accented subsidiary beat

regicide /'reji,sied/ n (the act of) one who kills a king

regime also **régime** /ray'zheem/ n 1 a regimen 2a a form of management or government b a government in power

regimen /'rejimən/ n a systematic plan (e g of diet, exercise, or medical treatment) adopted esp to achieve some end

¹**regiment** /'rejimənt/ n sing or pl in constr 1 a permanent military unit consisting usu of a number of companies, troops, batteries, or sometimes battalions 2 a large number or group – ~**al** adj

²**regiment** /'reji,ment/ v to subject to strict and stultifying organization or control – ~**ation** n

regimentals /,reji'mentlz/ n pl 1 the uniform of a regiment 2 military dress

region /'reej(ə)n/ n 1 an administrative area 2 an indefinite area of the world or universe; esp an area with broadly uniform features 3 an indefinite area surrounding a specified body part 4 a sphere of activity or interest – ~**al** adj – ~**ally** adv — **in the region of** approximating to; more or less

¹**register** /'rejistə/ n 1 a written record containing (official) entries of items, names, transactions, etc 2a a roster of qualified or available individuals b a school attendance record 3 (a part of) the range of a human voice or a musical instrument 4 a device registering a number or a quantity 5 a condition

of correct alignment or proper relative position (e g of the plates used in colour printing) – often in *in/out of register*

²**register** *v* **1a** to enrol formally **b** to record automatically; indicate **c** to make a (mental) record of; note **2** to secure special protection (for a piece of mail) by prepayment of a fee **3** to convey an impression of **4** to achieve, win

registrar /,reji'strah, '--,-/ *n* **1** an official recorder or keeper of records: e g **1a** a senior administrative officer of a university **b** an official responsible for recording births, marriages and deaths in an area and for conducting civil marriages **2** a British hospital doctor in training

registration /,reji'straysh(ə)n/ *n* **1** registering or being registered **2** an entry in a register

registry /'rejistri/ *n* a place where births, marriages and deaths are recorded and civil marriages conducted

regnant /'regnənt/ *adj* reigning

¹**regress** /'ree,gres/ *n* **1** a trend to a lower, less perfect, or earlier condition **2** an act of going or coming back

²**regress** /ri'gres/ *v* to undergo or exhibit backwards movement, esp to an earlier state – ~**ion** *n*

¹**regret** /ri'gret/ *v* -**tt**- to be very sorry about

²**regret** *n* **1** grief or sorrow tinged esp with disappointment, longing, or remorse **2** *pl* a conventional expression of disappointment, esp on declining an invitation – ~**ful** *adj* – ~**fully** *adv* – ~**fulness** *n*

¹**regular** /'regyoolə/ *adj* **1a** formed, built, arranged, or ordered according to some rule, principle, or type **b(1)** with equilateral and equiangular **b(2)** having faces that are identical regular polygons with identical angles between them **c** perfectly (radially) symmetrical or even **2a** steady or uniform in course, practice, or occurrence; habitual, usual, or constant **b** recurring or functioning at fixed or uniform intervals **3** constituted, conducted, or done in conformity with established or prescribed usages, rules, or discipline **4** of or being a permanent standing army – infml – ~**ity** *n* – ~**ize** *v* – ~**ly** *adv*

²**regular** *n* **1** a soldier in a regular army **2** one who is usu present or participating; *esp* one who habitually visits a particular place

regulate /'regyoo,layt/ *v* **1** to govern or direct according to rule **2** to bring order, method, or uniformity to **3** to fix or adjust the time, amount, degree, or rate of

¹**regulation** /,regyoo'laysh(ə)n/ *n* **1** regulating or being regulated **2** an authoritative rule or order

²**regulation** *adj* conforming to regulations; official

regulo /'regyooloh/ *n, chiefly Br* the temperature in a gas oven expressed as a specified number

regurgitate /ri'guhji,tayt/ *v* to vomit or pour back or out (as if) from a cavity – -**tation** *n*

rehabilitate /,ree(h)ə'bilitayt/ *v* **1** to reestablish the good name of **2** to restore to a condition of health or useful and constructive activity (e g after illness or imprisonment) – -**tation** *n*

¹**rehash** /ree'hash/ *v* to present or use again in another form without substantial change or improvement

²**rehash** /'ree,hash, ,-'-/ *n* sthg presented in a new form without change of substance

rehearsal /ri'huhsl/ *n* a practice session, esp of a play, concert, etc preparatory to a public appearance

rehearse /ri'huhs/ *v* **1** to present an account of (again) **2** to give a rehearsal of; practise

rehouse /,ree'howz, -'hows/ *v* to establish in new or better-quality housing

¹**reign** /rayn/ *n* the time during which sby or sthg reigns

²**reign** *v* **1** to hold office as head of state; rule **2** to be predominant or prevalent

reimburse /,ree-im'buhs/ *v* to pay back – ~**ment** *n*

¹**rein** /rayn/ *n* **1** a long line fastened usu to both sides of a bit, by which a rider or driver controls an animal **2** controlling or guiding power – usu pl

²**rein** *v* to check or stop (as if) by pulling on reins – often + *in*

reincarnate /,ree'inkahnayt, ,--'-/ *v* to give a new form or fresh embodiment to – -**nation** *n*

reindeer /'rayn,diə/ *n* any of several deer that inhabit N Europe, Asia, and America, have antlers in both sexes, and are often domesticated

reinforce /,ree-in'faws/ *v* **1** to make stronger or more pronounced **2** to strengthen or increase (e g an army) by fresh additions – ~**ment** *n*

reinforced concrete /,ree-in'fawst, '--,-/ *n* concrete in which metal is embedded for strengthening

reinstate /,ree-in'stayt/ *v* to restore to a previous state or condition – ~**ment** *n*

reiterate /,ree'itərayt/ *v* to say or do over again or repeatedly – -**ration** *n*

¹**reject** /ri'jekt/ *v* **1a** to refuse to accept, consider, submit to, or use **b** to refuse to accept or admit **2** to fail to accept (e g a skin graft or transplanted organ) as part of the organism because of immunological differences – ~**ion** *n*

²**reject** /'reejekt/ *n* a rejected person or thing; *esp* a substandard article of merchandise

rejoice /ri'joys/ *v* to feel or express joy or great delight

rejoin /ri'joyn/ *v* to say (sharply or critically) in response

rejoinder /ri'joyndə/ *n* (an answer to) a reply

rejuvenate /,ree'joohvə,nayt, ri-/ *v* to make young or youthful again – -**nation** *n*

¹**relapse** /ri'laps, 'ree,laps/ *n* a relapsing or backsliding; *esp* a recurrence of symptoms of a disease after a period of improvement

rel

²relapse /ri'laps/ v **1** to slip or fall back into a former worse state **2** to sink, subside

relate /ri'layt/ v **1** to give an account of; tell **2** to show or establish logical or causal connection between **3** to respond, esp favourably – often + to

re'lated adj **1** connected by reason of an established or discoverable relation **2** connected by common ancestry or sometimes by marriage – ~ness n

relation /ri'laysh(ə)n/ n **1** the act of telling or recounting **2** an aspect or quality (e g resemblance) that connects 2 or more things as belonging or working together or as being of the same kind **3** a relative **4** reference, respect, or connection **5** the interaction between 2 or more people or groups – usu pl with sing. meaning **6** pl **6a** dealings, affairs **b** communication, contact

re'lationship /-ship/ n **1** the state or character of being related or interrelated **2** (a specific instance or type of) kinship **3** a state of affairs existing between those having relations or dealings

¹relative /'relətiv/ n **1** a word referring grammatically to an antecedent **2a** a person connected with another by blood relationship or marriage **b** an animal or plant related to another by common descent

²relative adj **1** introducing a subordinate clause qualifying an expressed or implied antecedent; also introduced by such a connective **2a** not absolute or independent; comparative **b** expressing, having, or existing in connection with or with reference to sthg else (e g a standard) adv

relativity /,relə'tivəti/ n **1** being relative **2a** also **special theory of relativity** a theory (based on the 2 postulates (1) that the speed of light in a vacuum is constant and independent of the source or observer and (2) that all motion is relative) that leads to the assertion that mass and energy are equivalent and that mass, dimension, and time will change with increased velocity **b** also **general theory of relativity** an extension of this theory to include gravitation and related acceleration phenomena

relax /ri'laks/ v **1** to make less tense, rigid or severe **2** to cast off inhibition, nervous tension, or anxiety **3** to seek rest or recreation

relaxation /,reelak'saysh(ə)n/ n **1** relaxing or being relaxed **2** a relaxing or recreational state, activity, or pastime

¹relay /'ree,lay/ n **1** a number of people who relieve others in some work **2** a race between teams in which each team member successively covers a specified portion of the course **3** the act of passing sthg along by stages; also such a stage

²relay /'ree,lay, ri'lay/ v **1** to provide with relays **2** to pass along by relays

¹release /ri'lees/ v **1** to set free from restraint, confinement, or servitude **2** to relieve from sthg that confines, burdens, or oppresses **3** to relinquish (e g a claim or right) in favour of another **4** to give permission for publication, performance, exhibition, or sale of, on but not before a specified date; also to publish, issue

²release n **1** relief or deliverance from sorrow, suffering, or trouble **2** discharge from obligation or responsibility **3** freeing or being freed; liberation (e g from jail) **4a** (the act of permitting) performance or publication **b(1)** a statement prepared for the press **b(2)** a (newly issued) gramophone record

relegate /'relə,gayt/ v **1** to assign to a place of insignificance or oblivion; put out of sight or mind; specif to demote to a lower division of a sporting competition (e g a football league) **2** to submit or refer to sby or sthg for appropriate action – **-gation** n

relent /ri'lent/ v **1** to become less severe, harsh, or strict, usu from reasons of humanity **2** to slacken; let up

re'lentless /-lis/ adj persistent, unrelenting – ~**ly** adv – ~**ness** n

relevant /'reliv(ə)nt/ adj **1** having significant and demonstrable bearing on the matter at hand **2** having practical application, esp to the real world – ~**ly** adv –**vance**, **-vancy** n

reliable /ri'lie-əbl/ adj suitable or fit to be relied on; dependable – **-bly** adv

reliance /ri'lie-əns/ n the act of relying; the condition or attitude of one who relies

relic /'relik/ n **1** a part of the body of or some object associated with a saint or martyr, that is preserved as an object of reverence **2** sthg left behind after decay, disintegration, or disappearance; also an outmoded custom, belief, or practice

relict /'relikt/ n **1a** (a type of) plant or animal that is a remnant of an otherwise extinct flora, fauna, or kind of organism **2** a geological or geographical feature (e g a lake or mountain) or a rock remaining after other parts have disappeared or substantially altered

relief /ri'leef/ n **1a** removal or lightening of sthg oppressive, painful, or distressing **b** aid in the form of money or necessities, esp for the poor **c** military assistance to an endangered or surrounded post or force **d** a means of breaking or avoiding monotony or boredom **2** (release from a post or duty by) one who takes over the post or duty of another **3** (a method of) sculpture in which the design stands out from the surrounding surface **4** sharpness of outline due to contrast **5** the differences in elevation of a land surface

relieve /ri'leev/ v **1a** to free from a burden; give aid or help to **b** to set free from an obligation, condition, or restriction – often + of **2** to bring about the removal or alleviation of **3** to release from a post, station, or duty **4** to remove or lessen the monotony of **5** to give relief to (oneself) by urinating or defecating

re'lieved *adj* experiencing or showing relief, esp from anxiety or pent-up emotions

religion /ri'lij(ə)n/ *n* **1a** the (organized) service and worship of a god, gods, or the supernatural **b** personal commitment or devotion to religious faith or observance **2** a cause, principle, or system of beliefs held to with ardour and faith; sthg considered to be of supreme importance

religious /ri'lijəs/ *adj* **1** of or manifesting faithful devotion to an acknowledged ultimate reality or deity **2** of, being, or devoted to the beliefs or observances of a religion **3** scrupulously and conscientiously faithful

relinquish /ri'lingkwish/ *v* **1** to renounce or abandon **2** to give over possession or control of

¹**relish** /'relish/ *n* **1** characteristic, pleasing, or piquant flavour or quality **2** enjoyment of or delight in sthg (that satisfies one's tastes, inclinations, or desires) **3** sthg that adds an appetizing or savoury flavour; *esp* a highly seasoned sauce (e g of pickles or mustard) eaten with plainer food

²**relish** *v* to enjoy; have pleasure from

relive /,ree'liv/ *v* to live over again; *esp* to experience again in the imagination

reluctance /ri'luktəns/ *n* being reluctant

reluctant /ri'luktənt/ *adj* holding back; unwilling – ~**ly** *adv*

rely /ri'lie/ *v* **1** to have confidence based on experience **2** to be dependent *USE* + *on* or *upon*

remain /ri'mayn/ *v* **1** to be sthg or a part not destroyed, taken, or used up **2** to stay behind (with) **3** to continue to be

remainder /ri'mayndə/ *n* **1a** a remaining group, part, or trace **b(1)** the number left after a subtraction **b(2)** the final undivided part after division, that is less than the divisor **2** a book sold at a reduced price by the publisher after sales have fallen off

remains /ri'maynz/ *n* **1** a remaining part or trace **2** a dead body

¹**remake** /,ree'mayk/ *v* **remade** to make anew or in a different form

²**re,make** *n* a new version of a film

remand /ri'mahnd/ *v* to return to custody, esp pending further enquiries – **remand** *n*

¹**remark** /ri'mahk/ *v* to notice sthg and make a comment or observation *on* or *upon*

²**remark** *n* **1** mention or notice of that which deserves attention **2** a casual expression of an opinion or judgment

remarkable /ri'mahkəbl/ *adj* worthy of being or likely to be noticed, esp as being uncommon or extraordinary – **-bly** *adv*

remedial /ri'meedi·əl, -dyəl/ *adj* **1** intended as a remedy **2** concerned with the correction of faulty study habits – ~**ly** *adv*

¹**remedy** /'remədi/ *n* **1** a medicine, application, or treatment that relieves or cures a disease **2** sthg that corrects or counteracts an evil or deficiency

²**remedy** *v* to provide or serve as a remedy for

remember /ri'membə/ *v* **1** to bring to mind or think of again (for attention or consideration) **2** to retain in the memory **3** to convey greetings from

remembrance /ri'membrəns/ *n* **1** the period over which one's memory extends **2** an act of recalling to mind **3** a memory of a person, thing, or event **4** sthg that serves to keep in or bring to mind

remind /ri'miend/ *v* to cause to remember – ~**er** *n*

reminisce /,reminis/ *v* to indulge in reminiscence

reminiscence /,remi'nis(ə)ns/ *n* **1** the process or practice of thinking or telling about past experiences **2** an account of a memorable experience – often *pl*

reminiscent /,remi'nis(ə)nt/ *adj* tending to remind one (e g of sthg seen or known before)

remiss /ri'mis/ *adj* **1** negligent in the performance of work or duty **2** showing neglect or inattention – ~**ness** *n*

remission /ri'mish(ə)n/ *n* **1** the act or process of remitting **2** reduction of a prison sentence

¹**remit** /ri'mit/ *v* **-tt-** **1** to refer for consideration; *specif* to return (a case) to a lower court **2** to postpone, defer **3** to send (money) to a person or place **4** to moderate

²**remit** *n* **1** an act of remitting **2** sthg remitted to another person or authority for consideration or judgment

remittance /ri'mit(ə)ns/ *n* a transmittal of money

remittent /ri'mit(ə)nt/ *adj, of a disease* marked by alternating periods of abatement and increase of symptoms

remnant /'remnənt/ *n* **1a** a usu small part or trace remaining **b** a small surviving group – often *pl* **2** an unsold or unused end of fabric

remodel /,ree'modl/ *v* to reconstruct

remonstrate /'remən,strayt, ri'mon-/ *v* to present and urge reasons in opposition – often + *with* – **-strance** *n*

remorse /ri'maws/ *n* a deep and bitter distress arising from a sense of guilt for past wrongs – ~**ful** *adj* – ~**fully** *adv* – ~**fulness** *n* – ~**less** *adj* – ~**lessly** *adv* – ~**lessness** *n*

remote /ri'moht/ *adj* **1** far removed in space, time, or relation **2** out-of-the-way, secluded **3** small in degree **4** distant in manner – ~**ly** *adv* – ~**ness** *n*

re,mote con'trol *n* control over an operation (e g of a machine or weapon) exercised from a distance usu by means of an electrical circuit or radio waves

¹**remould** /,ree'mohld/ *v* to refashion the tread of (a worn tyre)

²remould /'ree,mohld/ *n* a remoulded tyre

remount /,ree'mownt/ *v* **1** to mount again **2** to provide (e g a unit of cavalry) with fresh horses

removal /ri'moohvl/ *n* **1** *Br* the moving of household goods from one residence to another **2** removing or being removed

¹remove /ri'moohv/ *v* **1** to change the location, position, station, or residence of **2** to move by lifting, pushing aside, or taking away or off **3** to get rid of – **removable** *adj*

²remove *n* **1a** a distance or interval separating one person or thing from another **b** a degree or stage of separation **2** a form intermediate between **2** others in some British schools

remunerate /ri'myoohnǝ,rayt/ *v* **1** to pay an equivalent for **2** to recompense – **-ation** *n* – **-ative** *adj*

renaissance /ri'nays(ǝ)ns, ri'nesonhs/ *n* **1** *cap the* (period of the) humanistic revival of classical influence in Europe from the 14th c to the 17th c, expressed in a flowering of the arts and literature and by the beginnings of modern science **2** a rebirth, revival, esp of artistic or intellectual activity

renal /'reenl/ *adj* relating to or located in the region of the kidneys

rend /rend/ *v* **rent** /rent/ **1** to wrest, split, or tear apart or in pieces (as if) by violence **2** to tear (the hair or clothing) as a sign of anger, grief, or despair **3** to pierce with sound

render /'rendǝ/ *v* **1** to melt down; extract by melting **2a** to yield; give up **b** to deliver for consideration, approval, or information **3a** to give in return or retribution **b** to restore; give back **4a** to cause to be or become **b** to reproduce or represent by artistic or verbal means **5** to apply a coat of plaster or cement directly to

rendering /'rend(ǝ)ring/ *n* a covering material, usu of cement, sand, and a small percentage of lime, applied to exterior walls

rendezvous /'rondi,vooh, -day-, 'ronh-/ *n, pl* **rendezvous 1** a place (appointed) for assembling or meeting **2** a meeting at an appointed place and time

rendition /ren'dish(ǝ)n/ *n* **1** a translation **2** a performance, interpretation

renegade /'reni,gayd/ *n* **1** a deserter from one faith, cause, or allegiance to another **2** an individual who rejects lawful or conventional behaviour

renew /ri'nyooh/ *v* **1** to restore to freshness, vigour, or perfection **2** to revive **3** to make changes in; rebuild **4** to make or do again **5** to begin again; resume **6** to replace, replenish **7** to grant or obtain an extension of or on (e g a subscription, lease, or licence) – **~able** *adj* – **~al** *n*

rennet /'renit/ *n* a preparation used for curdling milk

renounce /ri'nowns/ *v* **1** to give up, refuse, or resign, usu by formal declaration **2** to refuse to follow, obey, or recognize any further – **renunciation** *n*

renovate /'renǝ,vayt/ *v* to restore to a former or improved state (e g by cleaning, repairing, or rebuilding) – **-vation** *n*

renown /ri'nown/ *n* a state of being widely acclaimed; fame – **~ed** *adj*

¹rent /rent/ *n* **1** a usu fixed periodical payment made by a tenant or occupant of property or user of goods to the owner for the possession and use thereof **2** the portion of the income of an economy (e g of a nation) attributable to land as a factor of production in addition to capital and labour

²rent *v* **1** to take and hold under an agreement to pay rent **2** to grant the possession and use of for rent – **~able** *adj*

³rent *past of* **rend**

⁴rent *n* **1** an opening or split made (as if) by rending **2** an act or instance of rending

¹rental /'rentl/ *n* **1** an amount paid or collected as rent **2** an act of renting

²rental *adj* of or relating to rent or renting

rep, repp /rep/ *n* a plain-weave fabric with raised crosswise ribs

²rep *n* a (sales) representative – *infml*

³rep *n* repertory

¹repair /ri'peǝ/ *v* to go; take oneself off *to* – *fml*

²repair *v* **1** to restore by replacing a part or putting together what is torn or broken **2** to restore to a sound or healthy state – **~able** *adj* – **~er** *n*

³repair *n* **1** an instance or the act or process of repairing **2** relative condition with respect to soundness or need of repairing

reparable /'rep(ǝ)rǝbl/ *adj* capable of being repaired

reparation /,repǝ'raysh(ǝ)n/ *n* **1** the act of making amends, offering expiation, or giving satisfaction for a wrong or injury **2** damages; *specif* compensation payable by a defeated nation for war damages – usu pl with sing. meaning

repartee /,repah'tee/ *n* **1** a quick and witty reply **2** (skill in) amusing and usu light sparring with words

repast /ri'pahst/ *n* a meal – *fml*

repatriate /,ree'patri,ayt, ri-, -'pay-/ *v* to restore to the country of origin – **-ation** *n*

repay /ri'pay, ,ree-/ *v* **repaid** /-'payd/ **1a** to pay back **b** to give or inflict in return or requital **2** to compensate, require **3** to recompense – **~able** *adj* – **~ment** *n*

repeal /ri'peel/ *v* to revoke (a law) – **repeal** *n*

¹repeat /ri'peet/ *v* **1a** to say or state again **b** to say through from memory **c** to say after another **2** to make, do, perform, present, or broadcast again **3** to express or present (oneself or itself) again in the same words, terms, or form – **~ed** *adj* – **~edly** *adv*

²repeat n 1 the act of repeating 2a a television or radio programme that has previously been broadcast at least once b (a sign placed before or after) a musical passage to be repeated in performance

repel /ri'pel/ v -ll- 1 to drive back; repulse 2a to be incapable of sticking to, mixing with, taking up, or holding b to (tend to) force away or apart by mutual action at a distance 3 to cause aversion in; disgust

¹repellent also **repellant** /ri'pelənt/ adj 1 serving or tending to drive away or ward off 2 repulsive

²repellent also **repellant** n sthg that repels; esp a substance used to prevent insect attacks

repent /ri'pent/ v to feel sorrow, regret, or contrition for – ~ance n – ~ant adj

repercussion /,reepə'kush(ə)n/ n 1 an echo, reverberation 2 a widespread, indirect, or unforeseen effect of an act, action, or event

repertoire /'repə,twah/ n 1a a list or supply of dramas, operas, pieces, or parts that a company or person is prepared to perform b a range of skills, techniques, or expedients 2 a list or stock of capabilities

repertory /'repət(ə)ri/ n 1 a repertoire 2 (a theatre housing) a company that presents several different plays in the course of a season at one theatre

repetition /,repi'tish(ə)n/ n 1 repeating or being repeated 2 a reproduction, copy – **-tive** adj – **-tively** adv

repetitious /,repi'tishəs/ adj tediously repeating – ~ness n – ~ly adv

replace /ri'plays/ v 1 to restore to a former place or position 2 to take the place of, esp as a substitute or successor 3 to put sthg new in the place of – ~able adj

re'placement /-mənt/ n 1 replacing or being replaced 2 sthg or sby that replaces another

¹replay /,ree'play/ v to play again

²replay /'reeplay/ n 1a an act or instance of replaying b the playing of a tape (e g a videotape) 2 a match played to resolve a tie in an earlier match

replenish /ri'plenish/ v to stock or fill up again – ~ment n

replete /ri'pleet/ adj 1 fully or abundantly provided or filled 2 abundantly fed; sated – **repletion** n

replica /'replikə/ n a copy, duplicate

replicate /'repli,kayt/ v to duplicate, repeat

¹reply /ri'plie/ v 1 to respond in words or writing 2 to do sthg in response 3 to give as an answer

²reply n sthg said, written, or done in answer or response

¹report /ri'pawt/ n 1 (an account spread by) common talk 2a a usu detailed account or statement b a usu formal record of the proceedings of a meeting or inquiry c a statement of a pupil's performance at school usu issued every term to the pupil's parents or guardian 3 a loud explosive noise

²report v 1 to give information about; relate 2a to convey news of b to make a written record or summary of c to present the newsworthy aspects or developments of in writing or for broadcasting 3a to make known to the relevant authorities b to make a charge of misconduct against

reportedly /ri'pawtidli/ adv reputedly

reporter /ri'pawtə/ n sby who or sthg that reports: e g a one who makes a shorthand record of a proceeding b a journalist who writes news stories c one who gathers and broadcasts news

¹repose /ri'pohz/ v 1a to lie resting b to lie dead 2 to take rest 3 to rest for support – chiefly fml

²repose n 1 a place or state of rest or resting; esp rest in sleep 2a calm, tranquillity b a restful effect (e g of a painting or colour scheme) 3 cessation of activity, movement, or animation – ~ful adj

repository /ri'pozət(ə)ri/ n 1 a place, room, or container where sthg is deposited or stored 2 sby who or sthg that holds or stores sthg nonmaterial (e g knowledge)

repossess /,reepə'zes/ v 1 to regain possession of 2 to resume possession of in default of the payment of instalments due – ~ion n

reprehend /,repri'hend/ v to voice disapproval of; censure

reprehensible /,repri'hensəbl/ adj deserving censure; culpable – **-bly** adv

represent /,repri'zent/ v 1 to convey a mental impression of 2 to serve as a sign or symbol of 3 to portray or exhibit in art; depict 4a to take the place of in some respect; stand in for b to serve, esp in a legislative body, by delegated authority 5 to serve as a specimen, exemplar, or instance of

representation /,reprizen'taysh(ə)n/ n 1a an artistic likeness or image b a usu formal protest 2 representing or being represented on or in some formal, esp legislative, body

representational /,reprizen'taysh(ə)nl/ adj 1 of representation 2 of realistic depiction of esp physical objects or appearances in the graphic or plastic arts

¹representative /,repri'zentətiv/ adj 1 serving to represent 2a standing or acting for another, esp through delegated authority b of or based on representation of the people in government by election 3 serving as a typical or characteristic example

²representative n 1 a typical example of a group, class, or quality 2a(1) one who represents a constituency a(2) a member of a House of Representatives or of a US state legislature b a deputy, delegate c one who represents a business organization

repress /ri'pres/ v 1a to curb b to put down by force 2a to hold in or prevent the expression of, by self-control b to exclude (e g a feeling) from consciousness – ~ive adj – ~ively adv

repression /ri'presh(ə)n/ *n* **1** repressing or being repressed **2** an instance of repressing

¹reprieve /ri'preev/ *v* **1** to delay or remit the punishment of (e g a condemned prisoner) **2** to give temporary relief or rest to

²reprieve *n* **1a** reprieving or being reprieved **b** (a warrant for) a suspension or remission of a (death) sentence **2** a temporary remission (e g from pain or trouble)

¹reprimand /'repri,mahnd/ *n* a severe (and formal) reproof

²reprimand /'--,-, ,--'-/ *v* to criticize sharply or formally censure

reprint /'ree,print/ *n* **1** a subsequent impression of a book previously published in the same form **2** matter (e g an article) that has appeared in print before

reprisal /ri'priezl/ *n* **1** (a) retaliation by force short of war **2** a retaliatory act

¹reproach /ri'prohch/ *n* **1** (a cause or occasion of) discredit or disgrace **3** an expression of rebuke or disapproval – ~ **ful** *adj* – ~ **fully** *adv*

²reproach *v* to express disappointment and displeasure with (a person) for conduct that is blameworthy or in need of amendment

¹reprobate /'reprə,bayt/ *v* to condemn strongly as unworthy, unacceptable, or evil

²reprobate /'reprəbayt/ *adj* morally dissolute; unprincipled

reproduce /,reeprə'dyoohs/ *v* **1** to produce (new living things of the same kind) by a sexual or asexual process **2** to imitate closely **3** to make an image or copy of – **-ducible** *adj*

reproduction /,reeprə'duksh(ə)n/ *n* **1** the sexual or asexual process by which plants and animals give rise to offspring **2** sthg (e g a painting) that is reproduced – **-tive** *adj*

reproof /ri'proohf/ *n* criticism for a fault

reprove /ri'proohv/ *v* **1** to call attention to the remissness of **2** to express disapproval of; censure

reptile /'reptiel/ *n* **1** any of a class of vertebrates that include the alligators and crocodiles, lizards, snakes, turtles, and extinct related forms (e g the dinosaurs) and have a bony skeleton and a body usu covered with scales or bony plates **2** a grovelling or despicable person – **-tilian** *adj, n*

republic /ri'publik/ *n* **1** a state in which supreme power resides in the people and is exercised by their elected representatives governing according to law **2** a body of people freely and equally engaged in a common activity

¹republican /ri'publikən/ *adj* **1a** of or like a republic **b** advocating a republic **2** *cap* of or constituting a political party of the USA that is usu primarily associated with business, financial, and some agricultural interests and is held to favour a restricted governmental role in social and economic life

²republican *n* **1** one who favours republican government **2** *cap* a member of the US Republican party

repudiate /ri'pyoohdi,ayt/ *v* **1** to refuse to have anything to do with **2a** to refuse to accept **b** to reject as untrue or unjust – **-ation** *n*

repugnance /ri'pugnəns/ *n* **1** the quality or fact or an instance of being contradictory or incompatible **2** strong dislike, aversion, or antipathy – **-nant** *adj*

¹repulse /ri'puls/ *v* **1** to drive or beat back **2** to repel by discourtesy, coldness, or denial

²repulse *n* **1** a rebuff, rejection **2** repelling an assailant or being repelled

repulsion /ri'pulsh(ə)n/ *n* **1** repulsing or being repulsed **2** a force (e g between like electric charges or like magnetic poles) tending to produce separation **3** a feeling of strong aversion – **-sive** *adj* – **-sively** *adv* – **-siveness** *n*

reputable /'repyootəbl/ *adj* held in good repute; well regarded – **-bly** *adv*

reputation /,repyoo'taysh(ə)n/ *n* **1** overall quality or character as seen or judged by others **2** a place in public esteem or regard; good name

repute /ri'pyooht/ *n* **1** the character, quality, or status commonly ascribed **2** the state of being favourably known or spoken of

re'puted *adj* being such according to general or popular belief – ~ **ly** *adv*

¹request /ri'kwest/ *n* **1** the act or an instance of asking for sthg **2** sthg asked for

²request *v* **1** to make a request to or of **2** to ask as a favour or privilege **3** to ask for

requiem /'rekwi-əm, -,em/ *n, often cap* (a musical setting of) the mass for the dead

require /ri'kwie-ə/ *v* **1a** to call for as suitable or appropriate **b** to call for as necessary or essential; have a compelling need for **2** to impose an obligation or command on; compel – ~ **ment** *n*

requisite /'rekwizit/ *adj* necessary, required

requisition /,rekwi'zish(ə)n/ *n* **1** the act of requiring sthg to be supplied **2** a formal and authoritative (written) demand or application

requite /ri'kwiet/ *v* **1** to make suitable return to (for a benefit or service) **2** to compensate sufficiently for (an injury) – **requital** *n*

rescind /ri'sind/ *v* **1** to annul **2** to repeal, revoke (e g a law, custom, etc)

rescue /'reskyooh/ *v* to free from confinement, danger, or evil – **rescue** *n* – ~ **r** *n*

¹research /ri'suhch, 'reesuhch/ *n* scientific or scholarly inquiry; *esp* study or experiment aimed at the discovery, interpretation, reinterpretation, or application of (new) facts, theories, or laws

²research *v* **1** to search or investigate thoroughly **2** to engage in research on or for – ~ **er** *n*

resemble /ri'zembl/ *v* resembling /ri'zembling, -'zembl·ing/ to be like or similar to – **-blance** *n*

res

resent /ri'zent/ v to harbour or express ill will or bitterness at – ~**ful** adj – ~**fully** adv – ~**fulness** n – ~**ment** n

reservation /,reza'vaysh(a)n/ n 1 an act of reserving sthg; esp (a promise, guarantee, or record of) an arrangement to have sthg (e g a hotel room) held for one's use 2 a tract of land set aside; specif one designated for the use of American Indians by treaty 3 a specific doubt or objection 4 a strip of land separating carriageways 5 chiefly NAm an area in which hunting is not permitted; esp one set aside as a secure breeding place

¹**reserve** /ri'zuhv/ v to hold in reserve; keep back

²**reserve** n 1 sthg retained for future use or need 2 sthg reserved or set aside for a particular use or reason: e g 2a(1) a military force withheld from action for later use – usu pl with sing. meaning a(2) the military forces of a country not part of the regular services; also a reservist b chiefly Br a tract (e g of public land) set apart for the conservation of natural resources or (rare) flora and fauna 3 restraint, closeness, or caution in one's words and actions 4 money, gold, foreign exchange, etc kept in hand or set apart usu to meet liabilities – often pl with sing. meaning 5 a player or participant who has been selected to substitute for another if the need should arise — **in reserve** held back ready for use if needed

re'served adj 1 restrained in speech and behaviour 2 kept or set apart or aside for future or special use

reservoir /'reza,vwah/ n 1a an artificial lake where water is collected and kept in quantity for use b a part of an apparatus in which a liquid is held 2 an available but unused extra source or supply

reshuffle /,ree'shufl/ v to reorganize by the redistribution of (existing) elements – **reshuffle** n

reside /ri'zied/ v 1a to dwell permanently or continuously; occupy a place as one's legal domicile b to make one's home for a time 2 to be present as an element or quality

residence /'rezid(a)ns/ n 1 the act or fact of dwelling in a place 2 a (large or impressive) dwelling 3 the period of abode in a place — **in residence** 1 serving in a regular capacity 2 actually living in a usu specified place

¹**resident** /'rezid(a)nt/ adj 1 living in a place, esp for some length of time 2 of an animal not migratory

²**resident** n one who resides in a place

residential /,rezi'densh(a)l/ adj 1a used as a residence or by residents b entailing residence 2 given over to private housing as distinct from industry or commerce

residual /ri'zidyooal/ adj of or constituting a residue

residue /'rezidyooh/ n sthg that remains after a part is taken, separated, or designated; a remnant, remainder

resign /ri'zien/ v 1 to give up one's office or position 2 to reconcile, consign; esp to give (oneself) over without resistance

resignation /,rezig'naysh(a)n/ n an act or instance of resigning sthg b a formal notification of resigning 2 the quality or state of being resigned

re'signed adj marked by or expressing submission to sthg regarded as inevitable – ~**ly** adv

resilient /ri'zilyant/ adj 1 capable of withstanding shock without permanent deformation or rupture 2 able to recover quickly from or adjust easily to misfortune, change, etc – ~**ly** adv – ~**ence, -ency** n

resin /'rezin/ n (a synthetic plastic with some of the characteristics of) any of various solid or semi-solid yellowish to brown inflammable natural plant secretions (e g amber) that are insoluble in water and are used esp in varnishes, sizes, inks, and plastics – ~**ous** adj

resist /ri'zist/ v 1a to withstand the force or effect of b to exert force in opposition 2 to refrain from

resistance /ri'zist(a)ns/ n 1 an act or instance of resisting 2 the ability to resist 3 an opposing or retarding force 4 the opposition offered to the passage of a steady electric current through a substance, usu measured in ohms 5 often cap an underground organization of a conquered country engaging in sabotage – ~**tant** adj

resistor /ri'zista/ n a component included in an electrical circuit to provide resistance

resolute /'rezal(y)ooht/ adj 1 firmly resolved; determined 2 bold, unwavering – ~**ly** adv – ~**ness** n

resolution /,reza'loohsh(a)n, -'lyoohsh(a)n/ n 1a the act of making a firm decision b the act of finding out sthg (e g the answer to a problem); solving c the process or capability (e g of a microscope) of making individual parts or closely adjacent images distinguishable 2a sthg that is resolved b firmness of resolve 3 a formal expression of opinion, will, or intent voted by a body or group

¹**resolve** /ri'zolv/ v 1 to break up or separate into constituent parts 2 to cause or produce the resolution of 3a to deal with successfully b to find an answer to 4 to reach a firm decision about

²**resolve** n 1 sthg that is resolved 2 fixity of purpose

resonance /'rezanans/ n 1 strong vibration caused by the stimulus of a relatively small vibration of (nearly) the same frequency as the natural frequency of the system 2 the enrichment of musical tone resulting from supplementary vibration

resonant /'rezənənt/ *adj* 1 continuing to sound 2a capable of inducing resonance b relating to or exhibiting resonance 3 intensified and enriched by resonance – ~ly *adv*

resonate /'rezə,nayt/ *v* to produce or exhibit resonance (in)

¹**resort** /ri'zawt/ *n* 1 sby who or sthg that is looked to for help 2 a frequently visited place (e g a village or town), esp providing accommodation and recreation for holidaymakers

²**resort** *v* 1 to go, esp frequently or in large numbers 2 to have recourse *to*

resound /ri'zownd/ *v* 1 to become filled with sound 2 to produce a sonorous or echoing sound 3 to become renowned

resounding /ri'zownding/ *adj* 1a resonating b impressively sonorous 2 vigorously emphatic; unequivocal – ~ly *adv*

resource /ri'zaws, ri'saws/ *n* 1a a natural source of wealth or revenue b a source of information or expertise 2 a means of occupying one's spare time 3 the ability to deal with a difficult situation

re'sourceful /-f(ə)l/ *adj* skilful in handling situations; capable of devising expedients – ~ly *adv* – ~ness *n*

¹**respect** /ri'spekt/ *n* 1 a relation to or concern with sthg usu specified; reference – in *with/in respect to* 2a high or special regard; esteem b *pl* expressions of respect or deference 3 an aspect; detail – **in respect of** 1 from the point of view of 2 in payment of

²**respect** *v* 1a to consider worthy of high regard b to refrain from interfering with 2 to have reference to

respectable /ri'spektəbl/ *adj* 1 decent or conventional in character or conduct 2a acceptable in size or quantity b fairly good; tolerable 3 presentable – **-bly** *adv* – ~ness *n* – **-ability** *n*

re'spectful /-f(ə)l/ *adj* marked by or showing respect or deference – ~ly *adv* – ~ness *n*

respecting /ri'spekting/ *prep* with regard to; concerning

respective /ri'spektiv/ *adj* of or relating to each; particular, separate

re'spectively /-li/ *adv* 1 in particular; separately 2 in the order given

respiration /,respi'raysh(ə)n/ *n* the processes by which an organism supplies its cells with the oxygen needed for and removes the carbon dioxide formed in energy-producing reactions; breathing – **respire** *v* – **-tory** *adj*

respirator /'respi,raytə/ *n* 1 a device worn over the mouth or nose to prevent the breathing of poisonous gases, harmful dusts, etc 2 a device for maintaining artificial respiration

respite /'respiet, 'respit/ *n* 1 a period of temporary delay 2 an interval of rest or relief

resplendent /ri'splend(ə)nt/ *adj* characterized by splendour – ~ly *adv* – **-dence, -dency** *n*

respond /ri'spond/ *v* 1 to write or speak in reply; make an answer 2 to show a (favourable) reaction

¹**respondent** /ri'spond(ə)nt/ *n* 1 a defendant, esp in an appeal or divorce case 2 a person who replies to a poll

²**respondent** *adj* making response

response /ri'spons/ *n* 1 an act of responding 2a sthg (e g a verse) sung or said by the people or choir after or in reply to the officiant in a liturgical service b a change in the behaviour of an organism resulting from stimulation

responsibility /ri,sponsə'biləti/ *n* 1a moral or legal obligation b reliability, trustworthiness 2 sthg or sby that one is responsible for

responsible /ri'sponsəbl/ *adj* 1a liable to be required to justify b being the reason or cause 2a able to answer for one's own conduct b able to discriminate between right and wrong – **-ibly** *adv*

responsive /ri'sponsiv/ *adj* 1 giving response; constituting a response 2 quick to respond or react appropriately or sympathetically – ~ly *adv* – ~ness *n*

¹**rest** /rest/ *n* 1 repose, sleep 2a freedom or a break from activity or labour b a state of motionlessness or inactivity 3 peace of mind or spirit 4 a silence in music of a specified duration 5 sthg (e g an armrest) used for support — **at rest** resting or reposing, esp in sleep or death

²**rest** *v* 1a to relax by lying down; *esp* to sleep b to lie dead 2 to cease from action or motion; desist from labour or exertion 3 to be free from anxiety or disturbance 4 to be set or lie fixed or supported 5 to be based or founded 6 to depend for action or accomplishment 7 to stop introducing evidence in a law case

³**rest** *n* a collection or quantity that remains over

restate /,ree'stayt/ *v* to state again or in a different way (e g more emphatically) – ~ment *n*

restaurant /'rest(ə)ronh, -ront, -rənt/ *n* a place where refreshments, esp meals, are sold usu to be eaten on the premises

restaurateur /,rest(ə)rə'tuh, ,resto-/ *n* the manager or proprietor of a restaurant

restful /'restf(ə)l/ *adj* 1 marked by, affording, or suggesting rest and repose 2 quiet, tranquil – ~ly *adv* – ~ness *n*

restitution /,resti'tyoohsh(ə)n/ *n* 1a the returning of sthg (e g property) to its rightful owner b the making good of or giving a compensation for an injury 2 a legal action serving to cause restoration of a previous state

restive /'restiv/ *adj* 1 stubbornly resisting control 2 restless, uneasy – ~ly *adv* – ~ness *n*

¹**restless** /-lis/ *adj* 1 affording no rest 2 continuously agitated 3 characterized by or manifesting unrest, esp of mind; *also* changeful, discontented – ~ly *adv* – ~ness *n*

restoration /ˌrestəˈraysh(ə)n/ *n* **1** restoring or being restored: e g **1a** a reinstatement **b** a handing back of sthg **2** a representation or reconstruction of the original form (e g of a fossil or building) **3** *cap* the reestablishment of the monarchy in England in 1660 under Charles II; *also* the reign of Charles II

restorative /riˈstawrətiv, -ˈsto-/ *n or adj* (sthg capable of) restoring esp health or vigour

restore /riˈstaw/ *v* **1** to give back **2** to bring back into existence or use **3** to bring back to or put back into a former or original (unimpaired) state

restrain /riˈstrayn/ *v* **1** to prevent *from* doing sthg **2** to limit, repress, or keep under control

re'strained *adj* characterized by restraint; being without excess or extravagance

restraint /riˈstraynt/ *n* **1a** restraining or being restrained **b** a means of restraining; a restraining force or influence **2** moderation of one's behaviour; self-restraint

restrict /riˈstrikt/ *v* to regulate or limit as to use or distribution – **~ed** *adj* – **~ion** *n*

restrictive /riˈstriktiv/ *adj* restricting or tending to restrict – **~ly** *adv* – **~ness** *n*

restructure /ˌreeˈstrukchə/ *v* to change the make-up, organization, or pattern of

¹**result** /riˈzult/ *v* **1** to proceed or arise as a consequence, effect, or conclusion **2** to have a usu specified outcome or end

²**result** *n* **1** sthg that results as a (hoped for or required) consequence, outcome, or conclusion **2** sthg obtained by calculation or investigation

resultant /riˈzult(ə)nt/ *adj* derived or resulting from sthg else, esp as the total effect of many causes

resume /riˈzyoohm/ *v* **1** to take or assume again **2** to return to or begin again after interruption – **resumption** *n*

résumé, resumé *also* **resume** /ˈrezyooˌmay/ *n* a summing up of sthg (e g a speech or narrative)

resurgence /riˈsuhj(ə)ns/ *n* a rising again into life, activity, or influence – **-gent** *adj*

resurrect /ˌrezəˈrekt/ *v* **1** to bring back to life from the dead **2** to bring back into use or view

resurrection /ˌrezəˈreksh(ə)n/ *n* **1a** *cap* the rising of Christ from the dead **b** *often cap* the rising again to life of all the human dead before the last judgment **2** a resurgence, revival, or restoration

resuscitate /riˈsusəˌtayt/ *v* to revive from apparent death or from unconsciousness; *also* to revitalize – **-tation** *n*

¹**retail** /ˈree,tayl; *sense* 2 *often* riˈtayl/ *v* to sell (goods) in carrying on a retail business

²**retail** /ˈreetayl/ *adj, adv, or n* (of, being, or concerned with) the sale of commodities or goods in small quantities to final consumers who will not resell them

retain /riˈtayn/ *v* **1a** to keep in possession or use **b** to engage by paying a retainer **c** to keep in mind or memory **2** to hold secure or intact; contain in place – **retention** *n* – **retentive** *adj* – **retentively** *adv*

¹**retainer** /riˈtaynə/ *n* a fee paid to a lawyer or professional adviser for services

²**retainer** *n* an old and trusted domestic servant

retaliate /riˈtaliˌayt/ *v* to return like for like; *esp* to get revenge – **-ation** *n* – **-atory, -ative** *adj*

retard /riˈtahd/ *v* to slow down or delay, esp by preventing or hindering advance or accomplishment – **~ation** *n*

retarded /riˈtahdid/ *adj* slow in intellectual or emotional development or academic progress

retch /rech/ *v* to (make an effort to) vomit

rethink /ˌreeˈthingk/ *v* **rethought** /ˌreeˈthawt/ to think (about) again; *esp* to reconsider (a plan, attitude, etc) with a view to changing

reticent /ˈretis(ə)nt/ *adj* **1** inclined to be silent or reluctant to speak **2** restrained in expression, presentation, or appearance – **~ly** *adv* – **-cence** *n*

reticule /ˈretikyoohl/ *n* a decorative drawstring bag used as a handbag by women in the 18th and 19th c

retina /ˈretinə/ *n pl* **retinas, retinae** /-ni/ the sensory membrane at the back of the eye that receives the image formed by the lens and is connected with the brain by the optic nerve

retinue /ˈretiˌnyooh/ *n* a group of retainers or attendants accompanying an important personage

retire /riˈtie-ə/ *v* **1** to withdraw **1a** from action or danger **b** for rest or seclusion; go to bed **2** to recede; fall back **3** to give up one's position or occupation; conclude one's working or professional career

re'tired *adj* **1** remote from the world; secluded **2** having concluded one's career **3** received or due in retirement – **-rement** *n*

retiring /riˈtie-əring/ *adj* reserved, shy

¹**retort** /riˈtawt/ *v* **1** to say or exclaim in reply or as a counter argument **2** to answer (e g an argument) by a counter argument

²**retort** *n* a terse, witty, or cutting reply; *esp* one that turns the first speaker's words against him/her

³**retort** *v or n* (to treat by heating in) a vessel in which substances are distilled or decomposed by heat

retouch /ˌreeˈtuch/ *v* **1** to touch up a painting **2** to alter (e g a photographic negative) to produce a more acceptable appearance

retrace /ˌreeˈtrays/ *v* to trace again or back

retract /riˈtrakt/ *v* **1** to draw back or in **2** to withdraw; take back – **~ion** *n* – **~able** *adj*

retractile /riˈtraktiel/ *adj* capable of being retracted

¹**retread** /ˌree'tred/ *v* to replace the tread of (a worn tyre)

²**retread** /'ree,tred/ *n* (a tyre with) a new tread

¹**retreat** /ri'treet/ *n* 1 an act or process of withdrawing, esp from what is difficult, dangerous, or disagreeable; *specif* (a signal for) the forced withdrawal of troops from an enemy or position 2 a place of privacy or safety; a refuge 3 a period of usu group withdrawal for prayer, meditation, and study

²**retreat** *v* 1 to make a retreat; withdraw 2 to recede

retrench /ri'trench/ *v* to make reductions, esp in expenses – ~ment *n*

retribution /ˌretri'byoohsh(ə)n/ *n* 1 requital for an insult or injury 2 (the dispensing or receiving of reward or) punishment – used esp with reference to divine judgment – **-tive** *adj*

retrieve /ri'treev/ *v* 1a to get back again; recover (and bring back) b to rescue, save 2 to remedy the ill effects of 3 to recover (e g information) from storage, esp in a computer memory 4 *esp of a dog* to retrieve game; *also* to bring back an object thrown by a person – **-vable** *adj* – **-val** *n*

retriever /ri'treevə/ *n* a medium-sized dog with water-resistant coat used esp for retrieving game

retroactive /-'aktiv/ *adj* extending in scope or effect to a prior time – ~ly *adv*

retrogress /ˌretrə'gres/ *v* to regress, or decline from a better to a worse state – **-ion** *n* – **-ive** *adj* – ~**ively** *adv*

retrospect /'retrəspekt/ *n* a survey or consideration of past events —**in retrospect** in considering the past or a past event

retrospection /ˌretrə'speksh(ə)n/ *n* the act or process or an instance of surveying the past

retrospective /ˌretrə'spektiv/ *adj* 1 of, being, or given to retrospection 2 relating to or affecting things past; retroactive

retsina /ret'seenə/ *n* a resin-flavoured Greek wine

¹**return** /ri'tuhn/ *v* 1a to go back or come back again b to go back in thought, conversation, or practice 2 to pass back to an earlier possessor 3 to reply, retort – *fml* 4a to elect a candidate b to bring in (a verdict) 5 to restore to a former or proper place, position, or state 6 to bring in (e g a profit) 7 to give or send back, esp to an owner

²**return** *n* 1 the act or process of coming back to or from a place or condition 2a (a financial) account or formal report b a report or declaration of the results of an election – usu pl with sing. meaning 3 the profit from labour, investment, or business – often pl with sing. meaning 4 the act of returning sthg, esp to a former place, condition, or owner 5 *Br* a ticket bought for a trip to a place and back again — **by return (of post)** by the next returning post — **in return** in compensation or repayment

³**return** *adj* 1 doubled back on itself 2 played, delivered, or given in return; taking place for the second time 3 used or followed on returning 4 permitting return 5 of or causing a return to a place or condition

returning officer /ri'tuhning/ *n*, *Br* an official who presides over an election count and declares the result

reunion /ree'yoohnyən/ *n* 1 reuniting or being reunited 2 a gathering of people (e g relatives or associates) after a period of separation

reunite /ˌreeyoo'niet/ *v* to come or bring together again

reuse /ˌree'yoohz/ *v* to use again, esp after reclaiming or reprocessing – **reusable** *adj*

¹**rev** /rev/ *n* a revolution of a motor

²**rev** *v* -**vv**- to increase the number of revolutions per minute of (esp an engine) – often + *up*

revalue /ˌree'valyooh/ *v* 1 to change, specif to increase, the exchange rate of (a currency) 2 to reappraise – **-uation** *n*

revamp /ˌree'vamp/ *v* 1 to renovate, reconstruct 2 to revise without fundamental alteration

¹**reveal** /ri'veel/ *v* 1 to make known (sthg secret or hidden) 2 to open up to view

²**reveal** *n* the side of an opening (e g for a window) between a frame and the outer surface of a wall; *also* a jamb

reveille /ri'vali, -'ve-/ *n* a call or signal to get up in the morning; *specif* a military bugle call

¹**revel** /'revl/ *v* -**ll**- (*NAm* -**l**-, -**ll**-), **revelling** /'revl·ing/ 1 to take part in a revel 2 to take intense satisfaction *in*

²**revel** *n* a usu riotous party or celebration – often pl with sing. meaning

revelation /ˌrevə'laysh(ə)n/ *n* 1 *cap* a prophetic book of the New Testament – often pl with sing. meaning but sing. in constr 2 a revealing or sthg revealed; *esp* a sudden and illuminating disclosure

revelry /'revlri/ *n* exuberant festivity or merrymaking

¹**revenge** /ri'venj/ *v* 1 to inflict injury in return for (an insult, slight, etc) 2 to avenge (e g oneself) usu by retaliating in kind or degree

²**revenge** *n* 1 (a desire for) retaliating in order to get even 2 an opportunity for getting satisfaction or requital – ~**ful** *adj* – ~**fully** *adv* – ~**fulness** *n*

revenue /'revənyooh/ *n* 1 the total yield of income; *esp* the income of a national treasury 2 a government department concerned with the collection of revenue

reverberate /ri'vuhbə,rayt/ *v* 1a to be reflected b to continue (as if) in a series of echoes 2 to produce a continuing strong effect – **-ration** *n* – **-rant** *adj*

revere /ri'viə/ *v* to regard with deep and devoted or esp religious respect

reverence /'rev(ə)rəns/ n 1 honour or respect felt or shown; esp profound respect accorded to sthg sacred 2 a gesture (e g a bow) denoting respect 3 being revered 4 – used as a title for a clergyman

reverence v to regard or treat with reverence

reverend /'rev(ə)rənd/ adj 1 revered 2 cap being a member of the clergy – used as a title, usu preceded by the

reverie, revery /'revəri/ n 1 a daydream 2 the condition of being lost in thought or dreamlike fantasy

revers /ri'viə/ n, pl **revers** /ri'viəz/ a wide turned-back or applied facing along each of the front edges of a garment

reverse /ri'vuhs/ adj 1a (acting, operating, or arranged in a manner) opposite or contrary to a previous, normal, or usual condition b having the front turned away from an observer or opponent 2 effecting reverse movement

reverse v 1a to turn or change completely about in position or direction b to turn upside down 2a to overthrow (a legal decision) b to change (e g a policy) to the contrary 3 to cause (e g a motor car) to go backwards or in the opposite direction – **reversal** n – **reversible** adj – **reversibility** n – **reverse the charges** Br to arrange for the recipient of a telephone call to pay for it

reverse n 1 the opposite of sthg 2 reversing or being reversed 3 a misfortune 4a the side of a coin, medal, or currency note that does not bear the principal device b the back part of sthg; esp the back cover of a book 5 a gear that reverses sthg — **in reverse** backwards

reversion /ri'vuhsh(ə)n/ n 1 the right of future possession or enjoyment 2 (an organism showing) a return to an ancestral type or reappearance of an ancestral character

revert /ri'vuht/ v 1 to return, esp to a lower, worse or more primitive condition or ancestral type 2 to go back in thought or conversation

review /ri'vyooh/ n 1 a revision 2 a formal military or naval inspection 3 a general survey (e g of current affairs) 4 an act of inspecting or examining 5 judicial reexamination of a case 6a a critical evaluation of a book, play, etc b (a part of) a magazine or newspaper devoted chiefly to reviews and essays

review v 1a to go over (again) or examine critically or thoughtfully b to give a review of (a book, play, etc) 2 to hold a review of (troops, ships, etc)

reviewer /ri'vyooh-ə/ n a writer of critical reviews

revile /ri'viel/ v to subject to harsh verbal abuse – **reviler** n

revise /ri'viez/ v 1 to look over again in order to correct or improve 2 to make an amended, improved, or up-to-date version of 3 Br to refresh knowledge of (e g a subject), esp before an exam – **reviser** n – **revision** n

revitalize, -ise /,ree'vietl,iez/ v to impart new life or vigour to

revival /ri'vievl/ n 1 renewed attention to or interest in sthg 2 a new presentation or production (e g of a play) 3 an often emotional evangelistic meeting or series of meetings 4 restoration of an earlier fashion, style, or practice

revive /ri'viev/ v to return to consciousness, life, health, (vigorous) activity, or current use

revoke /ri'vohk/ v to annul, rescind, or withdraw

revolt /ri'vohlt/ v 1 to renounce allegiance or subjection to a government; rebel 2 to experience or recoil from disgust or abhorrence

revolt n 1 a (determined armed) rebellion 2 a movement or expression of vigorous opposition

revolting /ri'vohlting/ adj extremely offensive; nauseating – **~ly** adv

revolution /,revə'loohsh(ə)n/ n 1a the action of or time taken by a celestial body in going round in an orbit b the motion of a figure or object about a centre or axis 2a a sudden or far-reaching change b the overthrow of one government and the substitution of another by the governed

revolutionary /,revə'loohshən(ə)ri/ adj 1a of or being a revolution b promoting or engaging in revolution; also extremist 2 completely new and different

revolutionary n sby who advocates or is engaged in a revolution

revolutionize, -ise /-iez/ v to cause a revolution in; change utterly or fundamentally

revolve /ri'volv/ v 1 to move in a curved path round (and round) a centre or axis; turn round (as if) on an axis 2 to be centred on a specified theme or main point

revolver /ri'volvə/ n a handgun with a revolving cylinder of several chambers each holding 1 cartridge and allowing several shots to be fired without reloading

revue /ri'vyooh/ n a theatrical production consisting typically of brief loosely connected often satirical sketches, songs, and dances

revulsion /ri'vulsh(ə)n/ n a feeling of utter distaste or repugnance

reward /ri'wawd/ v 1 to give a reward to or for 2 to recompense

reward n sthg that is given in return for good or evil done or received; esp sthg offered or given for some service, effort, or achievement

rewarding /ri'wawding/ adj yielding a reward; personally satisfying

rewire /,ree'wie-ə/ v to provide (e g a house) with new electric wiring

reword /,ree'wuhd/ v to alter the wording of; also to restate in different words

rewrite /,ree'riet/ v rewrote /,ree'roht/; rewritten /,ree'ritn/ to revise (sthg previously written)

rhapsodize, -ise /'rapsədiez/ v to over-enthuse

rhapsody /'rapsədi/ n **1** a highly rapturous or emotional utterance or literary composition **2** a musical composition of irregular form suggesting improvisation

'**rhesus ,factor** /'reesəs/ n any of several substances in red blood cells that can induce intense allergic reactions

rhetoric /'retərik/ n **1** the art of speaking or writing effectively; specif (the study of) the principles and rules of composition **2** insincere or exaggerated language (that is calculated to produce an effect) – ~ **al** adj – ~**ally** adv – ~**ian** n

rhe,torical 'question n a question asked merely for effect with no answer expected

rheumatic /rooh'matik, roo-/ adj of, being, characteristic of, or suffering from rheumatism

rheu,matic 'fever n rheumatism – not used technically

rheumatism /'roohmə,tiz(ə)m/ n any of various conditions characterized by inflammation and pain in muscles, joints, or fibrous tissue

rheumatoid /'roohmə,toyd/ adj characteristic of or affected with rheumatism

'**rhine,stone** /-,stohn/ n a lustrous imitation gem made of glass, paste, quartz, etc

rhinoceros /rie'nos(ə)rəs/ n pl **rhinoceroses** /-siz/, esp collectively **rhinoceros** any of various large plant-eating very thick-skinned hoofed African or Asian mammals with 1 or 2 horns on the snout

rhizome /'riezohm/ n an elongated (thickened and horizontal) underground plant stem

rhododendron /,rohdə'dendrən/ n any of a genus of showy-flowered shrubs and trees of the heath family

rhomboid /'romboyd/ n a parallelogram that is neither a rhombus nor a square – **rhomboid,** ~**al** adj

rhombus /'rombəs/ n pl **rhombuses, rhombi** /-bie/ a parallelogram with equal sides but unequal angles; a diamond-shaped figure

rhubarb /'roohbahb/ n **1** (the thick succulent stems, edible when cooked, of) any of several plants of the dock family **2** chiefly Br – used by actors to suggest the sound of (many) people talking in the background

'**rhyme** /riem/ n **1a** correspondence in the sound of (the last syllable of) words, esp those at the end of lines of verse **b** a word that provides a rhyme for another **2** (a) rhyming verse

²**rhyme** v **1** to compose rhyming verse **2a** of a word or (line of) verse to end in syllables that rhyme

rhyming slang n slang in which the word actually meant is replaced by a rhyming phrase of which only the first element is usu pronounced (e g 'head' becomes 'loaf of bread' and then 'loaf')

rhythm /'ridh(ə)m/ n **1** the pattern of recurrent alternation of strong and weak elements in the flow of sound and silence in speech **2a** (the aspect of music concerning) the regular recurrence of a pattern of stress and length of notes **b** a characteristic rhythmic pattern **c rhythm, rhythm section** sing or pl in constr the group of instruments in a band (e g the drums, piano, and bass) supplying the rhythm **3** movement or fluctuation marked by a regular recurrence of elements (e g pauses or emphases) **4** a regularly recurrent change in a biological process or state (e g with night and day) **5 rhythm, rhythm method** birth control by abstinence from sexual intercourse during the period when ovulation is most likely to occur – ~**ic, ~ical** adj – ~**ically** adv

¹**rib** /rib/ n **1** any of the paired curved rods of bone or cartilage that stiffen the body walls of most vertebrates and protect the heart, lungs, etc **2a** a transverse member of the frame of a ship that runs from keel to deck **b** any of the stiff strips supporting an umbrella's fabric **c** an arched support or ornamental band in Romanesque and Gothic vaulting **3a** a vein of a leaf or insect's wing **b** any of the ridges in a knitted or woven fabric; also ribbing – ~**bed** adj

²**rib** v **-bb-** to form a pattern of vertical ridges in by alternating knit stitches and purl stitches

³**rib** v **-bb-** to tease – infml

ribald /'rib(ə)ld, 'rie,bawld/ adj **1** crude, offensive **2** characterized by coarse or indecent humour – ~**ry** n

ribbing /'ribing/ n an arrangement of ribs; esp a knitted pattern of ribs

ribbon /'ribən/ n **1a** a (length of a) narrow band of decorative fabric used for ornamentation (e g of hair), fastening, tying parcels, etc **b** a piece of usu multicoloured ribbon worn as a military decoration or in place of a medal **2** pl tatters, shreds

'**rib ,cage** n the enclosing wall of the chest consisting chiefly of the ribs and their connections

rice /ries/ n (the seed, important as a food, of) a cereal grass widely cultivated in warm climates

'**rice ,paper** n a very thin edible paper made from the pith of an oriental tree

rich /rich/ adj **1** having abundant possessions, esp material and financial wealth **2** well supplied or endowed – often + in **3** sumptuous **4a** vivid and deep in colour **b** full and mellow in tone and quality **5** highly productive or remunerative; giving a high yield **6a** (of food that is) highly seasoned, fatty, oily, or sweet **b** esp of mixtures of fuel with air containing more petrol than normal **7** highly amusing; also laughable – infml – ~**ly** adv – ~**ness** n

riches /'richiz/ n pl (great) wealth

¹**rick** /rik/ n a stack (e g of hay) in the open air

²**rick** v to wrench or sprain (e g one's neck)

rickets /'rikits/ n pl but sing in constr soft and deformed bones in children normally due to a lack of sunlight or vitamin D

rickety /'rikiti/ *adj* 1 suffering from rickets 2 shaky, unsound

rickshaw, ricksha /'rik,shaw/ *n* a small covered 2-wheeled vehicle pulled by usu 1 person

¹**ricochet** /'rikashay; *also* -shet/ *n* the glancing rebound of a projectile (e g a bullet) off a hard or flat surface

²**ricochet** *v* **ricocheting** /-'shaying/, **ricocheted** /-, shayd/; **ricochetting** /-,sheting/, **ricochetted** /-, shetid/ to proceed (as if) with glancing rebounds

rid /rid/ *v* **-dd-; rid** *also* **ridded** to relieve, disencumber

riddance /'rid(ə)ns/ *n* deliverance, relief – often in *good riddance*

¹**riddle** /'ridl/ *n* 1 a short and esp humorous verbal puzzle 2 sthg or sby mystifying or difficult to understand

²**riddle** *v* **riddling** /'ridl·ing/ to speak in or propound riddles

³**riddle** *n* a coarse sieve (e g for sifting grain or gravel)

⁴**riddle** *v* 1 to separate (e g grain from chaff) with a riddle; sift 2 to cover *with* holes 3 to spread through, esp as an affliction

¹**ride** /ried/ *v* **rode** /rohd/; **ridden** /'rid(ə)n/ **1a** to sit and travel mounted on or in a vehicle **2a** to lie moored or anchored **b** to appear to float **3** to be contingent; depend *on* **4** to work *up* or *down* the body **5** to survive without great damage or loss; last *out* **6** to obsess, oppress **7** to give with (a punch) to soften the impact — **ride high** to experience success — **ride roughshod over** to disregard in a high-handed or arrogant way

²**ride** *n* 1 a trip on horseback or by vehicle 2 a usu straight road or path in a wood, forest, etc used for riding, access, or as a firebreak 3 *chiefly NAm* a trip on which gangsters take a victim to murder him/her – *euph*

rider /'riedə/ *n* 1 sby who rides; *specif* sby who rides a horse 2 sthg added by way of qualification or amendment 3 sthg used to overlie another or to move along on another piece

ridge /rij/ *n* **1a** a range of hills or mountains **b** an elongated elevation of land 2 the line along which 2 upward-sloping surfaces meet; *specif* the top of a roof 3 an elongated part that is raised above a surrounding surface (e g the raised part between furrows on ploughed ground)

¹**ridicule** /'ridikyoohl/ *n* exposure to laughter

²**ridicule** *v* to mock; make fun of

ridiculous /ri'dikyoolas/ *adj* arousing or deserving ridicule – ~**ly** *adv* – ~**ness** *n*

riding /'rieding/ *n* any of the 3 former administrative jurisdictions of Yorkshire

rife /rief/ *adj* 1 prevalent, esp to a rapidly increasing degree 2 abundant, common 3 abundantly supplied – usu + *with*

riff /rif/ *n* (a piece based on) a constantly repeated phrase in jazz or rock music, typically played as a background to a solo improvisation

riffraff /'rif,raf/ *n sing or pl in constr* 1 disreputable people 2 rabble

¹**rifle** /'riefl/ *v* **rifling** /'riefling, 'riefl·ing/ to search through, esp in order to steal and carry away sthg

²**rifle** *v* to cut spiral grooves into the bore of (a rifle, cannon, etc)

³**rifle** *n* 1 a shoulder weapon with a rifled bore 2 *pl* a body of soldiers armed with rifles

¹**rift** /rift/ *n* 1 a fissure or crack, esp in the earth 2 an estrangement

²**rift** *v* to tear apart; split

rift valley *n* a valley formed by the subsidence of the earth's crust between at least 2 faults

¹**rig** /rig/ *v* **-gg-** 1 to fit out (e g a ship) with rigging 2 to clothe, dress up – usu + *out* 3 to supply with special gear 4 to put together, esp for temporary use – usu + *up*

²**rig** *n* 1 the distinctive shape, number, and arrangement of sails and masts of a ship 2 an outfit of clothing worn for an often specified occasion or activity 3 tackle, equipment, or machinery fitted for a specified purpose

³**rig** *v* **-gg-** to manipulate, influence, or control for dishonest purposes

rigging /'riging/ *n* lines and chains used aboard a ship, esp for controlling sails and supporting masts and spars

¹**right** /riet/ *adj* 1 in accordance with what is morally good, just, or proper 2 conforming to facts or truth 3 suitable, appropriate 4 straight 5a of, situated on, or being the side of the body that is away from the heart b located on the right hand when facing in the same direction as an observer c being the side of a fabric that should show or be seen when made up 6 having its axis perpendicular to the base 7 acting or judging in accordance with truth or fact; not mistaken 8 in a correct, proper, or healthy state 9 *often cap* of the Right, esp in politics 10 *chiefly Br* real, utter – *infml*

²**right** *n* 1 qualities (e g adherence to duty) that together constitute the ideal of moral conduct or merit moral approval 2a a power, privilege, interest, etc to which one has a just claim b a property interest in sthg – often pl with sing. meaning 3 sthg one may legitimately claim as due 4 the cause of truth or justice 5 the quality or state of being factually or morally correct 6a *sing or pl in constr, cap* those professing conservative political views b *often cap* a conservative position — **by rights** with reason or justice; properly — **in one's own right** by virtue of one's own qualifications or properties — **to rights** into proper order

³**right** *adv* 1 in a right, proper, or correct manner 2 in the exact location or position 3 in a direct line or course; straight 4 all the way; completely 5a

without delay; straight **b** immediately **6** to the full (e g entertained *right* royally) – often in British titles **7** on or to the right – ~**ness** *n*

⁴**right** *v* **1** to avenge **2a** to adjust or restore to the proper state or condition; correct **b** to bring or restore (e g a boat) to an upright position

'**right ,angle** *n* the angle bounded by 2 lines perpendicular to each other; an angle of 90° – **right-angled** *adj*

,**right a'way** *adv* without delay or hesitation

righteous /'riechəs/ *adj* **1** acting in accord with divine or moral law; free from guilt or sin **2a** morally right or justified **b** arising from an outraged sense of justice – ~**ly** *adv* – ~**ness** *n*

rightful /'rietf(ə)l/ *adj* **1** just, equitable **2a** having a just claim **b** held by right – ~**ly** *adv* – ~**ness** *n*

,**right-'hand** *adj* **1** situated on the right **2** chiefly or constantly relied on

,**right 'hand** *n* **1** a reliable or indispensable person **2a** the right side **b** a place of honour

,**right-'handed** *adj* **1** using the right hand habitually or more easily than the left **2** relating to, designed for, or done with the right hand **3** clockwise – used of a twist, rotary motion, or spiral curve as viewed from a given direction with respect to the axis of rotation – ~**ly** *adv* – ~**ness** *n*

rightly /'rietli/ *adv* **1** in accordance with right conduct; fairly **2** in the right manner; properly **3** according to truth or fact **4** with certainty

,**right-'minded** *adj* thinking and acting by just or honest principles – ~**ness** *n*

,**right of 'way** *n pl* **rights of way 1** a legal right of passage over another person's property **2** the strip of land over which a public road is built **3** a precedence in passing accorded to one vehicle over another by custom, decision, or statute

rightward /'rietwood/ *adj* being towards or on the right – ~**s** *adv*

,**right 'wing** *n often cap R&W* the more conservative division of a group or party – ~**er** *n*

rigid /'rijid/ *adj* **1** deficient in or devoid of flexibility **2a** inflexibly set in opinions or habits **b** strictly maintained **3** precise and accurate in procedure – ~**ly** *adv* – ~**ity** *n*

rigmarole /'rigmə,rohl/ *n* **1** confused or nonsensical talk **2** an absurd and complex procedure

,**rigor 'mortis** /'mawtis/ *n* the temporary rigidity of muscles that occurs after death

rigour /'rigə/ *n* **1a(1)** harsh inflexibility **a(2)** severity of life; austerity **b** an act or instance of strictness or severity – often *pl* **2** a condition that makes life difficult, challenging, or painful; *esp* extremity of cold – often *pl* **3** strict precision – **rigorous** *adj*

rigout /'rigowt/ *n* a complete outfit of clothing – infml

rile /riel/ *v* to make angry or resentful

rim /rim/ *n* **1** an outer usu curved edge or border **2** the outer ring of a wheel not including the tyre – ~**less** *adj*

¹**rime** /riem/ *n* **1** frost **2** an accumulation of granular ice tufts on the windward sides of exposed objects at low temperatures

²**rime** *v* to cover (as if) with rime

rind /riend/ *n* **1** the bark of a tree **2** a usu hard or tough outer layer of fruit, cheese, bacon, etc

¹**ring** /ring/ *n* **1** a circular band for holding, connecting, hanging, moving, fastening, etc or for identification **2** a circlet usu of precious metal, worn on the finger **3a** a circular line, figure, or object **b** an encircling arrangement **4a** an often circular space, esp for exhibitions or competitions; *esp* such a space at a circus **b** a square enclosure in which boxers or wrestlers contest **5** any of the concentric bands that revolve round some planets (e g Saturn or Uranus) **6** an electric element or gas burner in the shape of a circle, set into the top of a cooker, stove, etc, which provides a source of heat for cooking

²**ring** *v* **ringed 1** to place or form a ring round; encircle **2** to attach a ring to

³**ring** *v* **rang** /rang/; **rung** /rung/ **1** to sound resonantly **2a** to sound a bell as a summons **b** to announce (as if) by ringing – often + *in* or *out* **3a** to be filled with talk or report **b** to sound repeatedly **4** *chiefly Br* to telephone – often + *up* — **ring a bell** to sound familiar — **ring the changes** to run through the range of possible variations — **ring true** to appear to be true or authentic

⁴**ring** *n* **1** a set of bells **2** a clear resonant sound made by vibrating metal **3** resonant tone **4** a loud sound continued, repeated, or reverberated **5** a sound or character suggestive of a particular quality or feeling **6** a telephone call – usu in *give somebody a ring*

'**ring,leader** /-,leedə/ *n* a leader of a group that engages in objectionable activities

ringlet /'ringlit/ *n* a long lock of hair curled in a spiral

'**ring,master** /-,mahstə/ *n* one in charge of performances in a ring (e g of a circus)

'**ring ,road** *n, Br* a road round a town or town centre designed to relieve traffic congestion

ring up *v* **1** to record by means of a cash register **2** to record, achieve **3** to telephone

ringworm /'ring,wuhm/ *n* any of several fungous diseases of the skin or hair in which ring-shaped blistered patches form on the skin

rink /ringk/ *n* **1a** (a building containing) a surface of ice for ice-skating **b** an enclosure for roller-skating **2** part of a bowling green being used for a match

¹**rinse** /rins/ *v* **1** to cleanse (e g from soap) with liquid (e g clean water) – often + *out* **2** to remove (dirt or impurities) by washing lightly

²**rinse** *n* **1** (a) rinsing **2a** liquid used for rinsing **b** a solution that temporarily tints the hair

riot /'rie-ət/ *n* **1** unrestrained revelry **2 (a)** violent public disorder **3** a profuse and random display **4** sby or sthg wildly funny – **riot** *v* – **~er** *n*

riotous /'rie-ətəs/ *adj* **1** participating in a riot **2a** wild and disorderly **b** exciting, exuberant – **~ly** *adv* – **~ness** *n*

¹**rip** /rip/ *v* **-pp- 1a** to tear or split apart, esp in a violent manner **b** to saw or split (wood) along the grain **2** to rush along **3** to remove by force – + *out* or *off*

²**rip** *n* a rough or violent tear

³**rip** *n* a body of rough water formed **a** by the meeting of opposing currents, winds, etc **b** by passing over ridges

⁴**rip** *n* a mischievous usu young person

'**rip ,cord** *n* a cord or wire for releasing a parachute from its pack

ripe /riep/ *adj* **1** fully grown and developed; mature **2** mature in knowledge, understanding, or judgment **3** of advanced years **4** fully prepared; ready *for* **5** brought by aging to full flavour or the best state; mellow – **~ly** *adv* – **~n** *v* – **~ness** *n*

'**rip-,off** *n* **1** an act or instance of stealing **2** an instance of financial exploitation; *esp* the charging of an exorbitant price *USE* infml

rip off *v* **1** to rob; *also* to steal **2** to defraud *USE* infml

riposte /ri'pohst, -post/ *n* **1** a piece of retaliatory banter **2** a usu rapid retaliatory manoeuvre or measure

'**ripple** /'ripl/ *v* **rippling** /'ripling, 'ripl-ing/ **1** to cover with small waves **2a** to proceed with an undulating motion (so as to cause ripples) **b** to impart a wavy motion or appearance to **3** to spread irregularly outwards, esp from a central point

²**ripple** *n* **1** a small wave or succession of small waves **2** a sound like that of rippling water

'**rip-,roaring** *adj* noisily excited or exciting; exuberant

ripsaw /'rip,saw/ *n* a coarse-toothed saw that is designed to cut wood in the direction of the grain

riptide /'rip,tied/ *n* a strong surface current flowing outwards from a shore

'**rise** /riez/ *v* **rose** /rohz/; **risen** /'riz(ə)n/ **1a** to assume an upright position, esp from lying, kneeling, or sitting **b** to get up from sleep or from one's bed **2** to take up arms **3** to respond warmly or readily; applaud – usu + *to* **4** to respond to nasty words or behaviour, esp by annoyance or anger **5** to appear above the horizon **6a** to move upwards; ascend **b** to increase in height or volume **7** to extend above other objects or people **8** to increase in fervour or intensity **9** to attain a higher office or rank **10** to increase in amount or number **11** to come into being; originate **12** to show oneself equal to a challenge

²**rise** *n* **1a** a movement upwards **b** emergence (e g of the sun) above the horizon **c** the upward movement of a fish to seize food or bait **2** origin **3** the vertical height of sthg, esp a step **4a** an increase, esp in amount, number, or intensity **b** an increase in pay **5a** an upward slope or gradient **b** a spot higher than surrounding ground — **get/take a rise out of** to provoke to annoyance by teasing

riser /'riezə/ *n* the upright part between 2 consecutive stair treads

risible /'rizəbl/ *adj* arousing or provoking laughter

'**rising** /'riezing/ *n* an insurrection, uprising

²**rising** *adv* approaching a specified age

'**risk** /risk/ *n* **1** possibility of loss, injury, or damage **2** a dangerous element or factor; hazard **3** the chance of loss or the dangers to that which is insured in an insurance contract – **~y** *adj* – **~iness** *n* — **at risk** in danger (e g of infection or of behaving in ways which are considered antisocial) — **on risk** *of an insurer* having assumed and accepting liability for a risk

²**risk** *v* **1** to expose to hazard or danger **2** to incur the risk or danger of

risotto /ri'zotoh, -'so-/ *n pl* **risottos** an Italian dish of rice cooked in meat stock

risqué /'reeskay, 'ri-/ *adj* verging on impropriety or indecency

rissole /'risohl/ *n* a small fried cake or ball of cooked minced food, esp meat

rite /riet/ *n* **1** (a prescribed form of words or actions for) a ceremonial act or action **2** the characteristic liturgy of a church or group of churches

'**ritual** /'richooəl, -tyoo-/ *adj* according to religious law or social custom – **~ly** *adv*

²**ritual** *n* **1** the form or order of words prescribed for a religious ceremony **2 (a)** ritual observance; *broadly* any formal and customary act or series of acts

'**rival** /'rievl/ *n* **1a** any of 2 or more competing for a single goal **b** sby who tries to compete with and be superior to another **2** sby who or sthg that equals another in desirable qualities – **~ry** *n*

²**rival** *adj* having comparable pretensions or claims

³**rival** *v* **-ll-** (*NAm* **-l, -ll-**), /'rievl-ing/ **1** to be in competition with; contend with **2** to strive to equal or excel **3** to possess qualities that approach or equal (those of another)

river /'rivə/ *n* **1** a natural stream of water of considerable volume **2** a copious or overwhelming quantity – often *pl*

'**rivet** /'rivit/ *n* a headed metal pin used to unite 2 or more pieces by passing the shank through a hole in each piece and then beating or pressing down the plain end so as to make a second head – **~er** *n*

²**rivet** *v* **1** to hammer or flatten the end or point of (e g a metal pin, rod, or bolt) so as to form a head **2** to fix firmly **3** to attract and hold (e g the attention) completely

RNA *n* any of various acids in the nuclei of cells similar to DNA that are associated with the control of cellular chemical activities

¹**roach** /rohch/ *n pl* **roach** *also* **roaches** a silver-white European freshwater fish of the carp family

²**roach** *n, NAm* **1** a cockroach **2** the butt of a marijuana cigarette – slang

road /rohd/ *n* **1** a relatively sheltered stretch of water near the shore where ships may ride at anchor – often pl with sing. meaning **2** an open usu paved way for the passage of vehicles, people, and animals **3** a route or path – ~**less** *adj* — **off the road** *of a vehicle* not roadworthy — **on the road** travelling or touring on business

'road,block /-,blok/ *n* **1** a road barricade set up by an army, the police, etc **2** an obstruction in a road

'road ,hog *n* a driver of a motor vehicle who obstructs or intimidates others

'road,house /-,hows/ *n* an inn situated usu on a main road

'road,worthy /-,wuhdhi/ *adj, of a vehicle* in a fit condition to be used on the roads; in proper working order – **-thiness** *n*

roam /rohm/ *v* **1** to go aimlessly from place to place; wander **2** to travel unhindered through a wide area – ~**er** *n*

roan /rohn/ *adj, esp of horses and cattle* having a coat of a usu reddish brown base colour that is muted and lightened by some white hairs – **roan** *n*

¹**roar** /'raw/ *v* **1** to give a roar **2** to laugh loudly and deeply **3** to be boisterous or disorderly – usu + *about*

²**roar** *n* **1** the deep prolonged cry characteristic of a wild animal **2** a loud cry, call, etc (e g of pain, anger, or laughter) **3** a loud continuous confused sound

¹**roaring** /'rawring/ *adj* **1** making or characterized by a sound resembling a roar **2** marked by energetic or successful activity

²**roaring** *adv* extremely, thoroughly – infml

¹**roast** /rohst/ *v* **1a** to cook by exposing to dry heat (e g in an oven) **b** to dry and brown slightly by exposure to heat **2** to heat to excess **3** *chiefly NAm* to criticize severely

²**roast** *n* a piece of meat roasted or suitable for roasting

³**roast** *adj* roasted

rob /rob/ *v* **-bb-** **1** to steal sthg from (a person or place), esp by violence or threat **2** to deprive of sthg due, expected, or desired – ~**ber** *n*

robbery /'robəri/ *n* theft accompanied by violence or threat

robe /rohb/ *n* **1** a long flowing outer garment; *esp* one used for ceremonial occasions or as a symbol of office or profession **2** *NAm* a woman's dressing gown – **robe** *v*

robin /'robin/, **robin 'red,breast** /'red,brest/ *n* a small brownish European thrush having an orange-red throat and breast; *also* a larger but similarly coloured N American bird

robot /'rohbot/ *n* **1a** a (fictional) humanoid machine that walks and talks **b** sby efficient or clever who lacks human warmth or sensitivity **2** an automatic apparatus or device that performs functions ordinarily performed by human beings **3** sthg guided by automatic controls

robust /roh'bust, '–'/ *adj* **1a** having or exhibiting vigorous health or stamina **b** firm in purpose or outlook **c** strongly formed or constructed **2** earthy, rude – ~**ly** *adv* – ~**ness** *n*

¹**rock** /rok/ *v* **1** to become moved rapidly or violently backwards and forwards (e g under impact) **2a** to move rhythmically back and forth **b(1)** to daze or stun **b(2)** to disturb, upset — **rock the boat** to disturb the equilibrium of a situation

²**rock, rock and roll, rock 'n' roll** /,rok (ə)n 'rohl/ *n* music usu played on electronically amplified instruments, with a persistent heavily accented beat and often country, folk, and blues elements

³**rock** *n* **1** a large mass of stone forming a cliff, promontory, or peak **2** a large mass of stony material **3** a firm or solid foundation or support **4** a coloured and flavoured sweet produced in the form of a usu cylindrical stick — **on the rocks 1** in or into a state of destruction or wreckage **2** on ice cubes

,rock-'bottom *adj* being the lowest possible

,rock 'bottom *n* the lowest or most fundamental part or level

rock crystal *n* transparent colourless quartz

rocker /'rokə/ *n* **1a** either of the 2 curved pieces of wood or metal on which an object (e g a cradle) rocks **b** sthg mounted on rockers **2** a device that works with a rocking motion **3** a member of a group of aggressive leather-jacketed young British motorcyclists in the 1960s — **off one's rocker** crazy, mad — infml

rockery /'rokəri/ *n* a bank of rocks and earth where rock plants are grown

¹**rocket** /'rokit/ *n* any of numerous plants of the mustard family

²**rocket** *n* **1a** a firework consisting of a long case filled with a combustible material fastened to a guiding stick and projected through the air by the rearward discharge of gases released in combustion **b** such a device used as an incendiary weapon or as a propelling unit (e g for a lifesaving line or whaling harpoon) **2a** a jet engine that carries with it everything necessary for its operation and is thus

independent of the oxygen in the air **3** a rocket-propelled bomb, missile, or projectile **4** *chiefly Br* a sharp reprimand – *infml*

³**rocket** *v* **1** to rise or increase rapidly or spectacularly **2** to travel with the speed of a rocket

rocketry /'rokitri/ *n* the study of, experimentation with, or use of rockets

'**rocking ,horse** *n* a toy horse mounted on rockers

rock 'n' roll /,rok (ə)n 'rohl/ *n* rock music

'**rock ,salt** *n* common salt occurring as a solid mineral

¹**rocky** /'roki/ *adj* **1** full of or consisting of rocks **2** filled with obstacles; difficult

²**rocky** *adj* unsteady, tottering

¹**rococo** /ro'kohkoh, rə-/ *adj* **1a** (typical) of a style of architecture and decoration in 18th-c Europe characterized by elaborate curved forms and shell motifs **b** of an 18th-c musical style marked by light gay ornamentation **2** excessively ornate or florid

²**rococo** *n* rococo work or style *n* rococo work or style

¹**rod** /rod/ *n* **1a(1)** a straight slender stick **a(2)** (a stick or bundle of twigs used for) punishment **a(3)** a pole with a line for fishing **b** a slender bar (e g of wood or metal) **2** a unit of length equal to 5¹/₂yd (about 5m) **3** any of the relatively long rod-shaped light receptors in the retina that are sensitive to faint light

rode /rohd/ *past of* **ride**

rodent /'rohd(ə)nt/ *n* any of an order of relatively small gnawing mammals including the mice, rats, and squirrels

rodeo /'roh'dayoh, 'rohdi,oh/ *n pl* **rodeos** **1** a roundup **2** a public performance featuring the riding skills of cowboys

roe /roh/ *n* **1** the eggs of a female fish, esp when still enclosed in a membrane, or the corresponding part of a male fish **2** the eggs or ovaries of an invertebrate (e g a lobster)

'**roe ,deer** *n* a small Eurasian deer with erect cylindrical antlers that is noted for its nimbleness and grace

¹**rogue** /rohg/ *n* **1** a wilfully dishonest or corrupt person **2** a mischievous person; a scamp

²**rogue** *adj*, **roguing**, **rogueing** *of an animal* (roaming alone and) vicious and destructive

roguery /'rohg(ə)ri/ *n* an act characteristic of a rogue

roister /'roystə/ *v* to engage in noisy revelry

role, rôle /rohl/ *n* **1a** a socially expected behaviour pattern, usu determined by an individual's status in a particular society **b** a part played by an actor or singer **2** a function

¹**roll** /rohl/ *n* **1a** a written document that may be rolled up; *specif* one bearing an official or formal record **b** a list of names or related items; a catalogue **c** an official list of people (e g members of a school or of a legislative body) **2a** a quantity (e g of fabric or paper) rolled up to form a single package **b** any of various food preparations rolled up for cooking or serving; *esp* a small piece of baked yeast dough

²**roll** *v* **1a** to propel forwards by causing to turn over and over on a surface **b** to cause to move in a circular manner; turn over and over **c** to form into a mass by revolving and compressing **d** to carry forwards with an easy continuous motion **2** to move onwards in a regular cycle or succession **3** to flow with an undulating motion **4a** to become carried on a stream **b** to move on wheels **5a** to take the form of a cylinder or ball – often + *up* **b** to wrap round on itself; shape into a ball or roll – often + *up* **6** to press, spread, or level with a roller; make thin, even, or compact **7** to luxuriate *in* an abundant supply; wallow **8a** to make a deep reverberating sound **b** to utter with a trill **9a** to rock from side to side **b** to walk with a swinging gait **c** to move so as to reduce the impact of a blow – + *with* **10a** to begin to move or operate **b** to move forwards; develop and maintain impetus **11** *NAm* to rob (sby sleeping or unconscious) – *infml*

³**roll** *n* **1a** a sound produced by rapid strokes on a drum **b** a reverberating sound **2a** a swaying movement of the body (e g in walking or dancing) **b** a side-to-side movement (e g of a ship) **c** a flight manoeuvre in which a complete revolution about the longitudinal axis of an aircraft is made with the horizontal direction of flight being approximately maintained

'**roll ,call** *n* the calling out of a list of names (e g for checking attendance)

roller /'rohlə/ *n* **1a(1)** a revolving cylinder over or on which sthg is moved or which is used to press, shape, or apply sthg **a(2)** a hair curler **b** a cylinder or rod on which sthg (e g a blind) is rolled up **2** a long heavy wave

'**roller ,coaster** *n* an elevated railway (e g in a funfair) constructed with curves and inclines on which the cars roll

'**roller ,skate** *n* (a shoe fitted with) a metal frame holding usu 4 small wheels that allows the wearer to glide over hard surfaces

rollicking /'roliking/ *adj* boisterously carefree

'**rolling ,pin** *n* a long usu wooden cylinder for rolling out dough

'**rolling ,stock** *n* the vehicles owned and used by a railway

,**rolling 'stone** *n* one who leads a wandering or unsettled life

,**rolltop 'desk** /'rohl,top/ *n* a writing desk with a sliding cover often of parallel slats fastened to a flexible backing

'**roll-,up** *n*, *Br* a hand-rolled cigarette – *infml*

roll up *v* **1** to arrive in a vehicle **2** to turn up at a destination, esp unhurriedly

¹ **roly-poly** /ˌrohli 'pohli/ n a dish, esp a pudding, consisting of pastry spread with a filling (e g jam), rolled, and baked or steamed

² **roly-'poly** adj short and plump – infml

¹ **Roman** /'rohmən/ n 1 a native or inhabitant of (ancient) Rome 2 a Roman Catholic 3 not cap roman letters or type

² **Roman** adj 1 (characteristic) of Rome or the (ancient) Romans 2 not cap, of numbers and letters not slanted; perpendicular 3 of the see of Rome or the Roman Catholic church

¹ **Roman 'Catholic** n a member of the Roman Catholic church

² **Roman Catholic** adj of the body of Christians headed by the pope, with a liturgy centred on the Mass and a body of dogma formulated by the church as the infallible interpreter of revealed truth

¹ **romance** /roh'mans, rə-/ n 1a a medieval usu verse tale dealing with courtly love and adventure b a prose narrative dealing with imaginary characters involved in usu heroic, adventurous, or mysterious events that are remote in time or place; broadly a love story 2 sthg lacking any basis in fact 3 an emotional aura attaching to an enthralling era, adventure, or pursuit 4 a love affair

² **romance** v 1 to exaggerate or invent detail or incident 2 to entertain romantic thoughts or ideas

³ **romance** n a short instrumental piece of music in ballad style

Romance adj of or constituting the languages developed from Latin

Romanesque /ˌrohmə'nesk/ adj of a style of architecture developed in Italy and western Europe after 1000 AD and using typically the round arch and vault and elaborate mouldings

Roman 'numeral n a numeral in a system of notation based on the ancient Roman system using the symbols I, V, X, L, C, D, M

¹ **romantic** /rə'mantik, roh-/ adj 1 consisting of or like a romance 2 having no basis in real life 3 impractical or fantastic in conception or plan 4a marked by the imaginative appeal of the heroic, remote, or mysterious b often cap of romanticism c of or being (a composer of) 19th-c music characterized by an emphasis on subjective emotional qualities and freedom of form 5a having an inclination for romance b marked by or constituting strong feeling, esp love – ~ally adv – ~ize v

² **romantic** n 1 a romantic person 2 cap a romantic writer, artist, or composer

romanticism /roh'manti,siz(ə)m, rə-/ n, often cap a chiefly late 18th- and early 19th-c literary, artistic, and philosophical movement that reacted against neoclassicism by emphasizing individual aspirations, nature, the emotions, and the remote and exotic – **-cist** n

Romany /'rohməni/ n 1 a gipsy 2 the Indic language of the Gipsies

¹ **romp** /romp/ n 1 boisterous or bawdy entertainment or play 2 an effortless winning pace

² **romp** v 1 to play in a boisterous manner 2 to win easily

rondo /'rondoh/ n, pl **rondos** an instrumental composition, esp a movement in a concerto or sonata, typically having a recurring theme

¹ **roof** /roohf/ n pl **roofs** also **rooves** /roohvz/ **1a** the upper usu rigid cover of a building **b** a dwelling, home 2 the highest point or level 3 the vaulted or covering part of the mouth, skull, etc

² **roof** v 1 to cover (as if) with a roof 2 to serve as a roof over

rook /rook/ n a common Old World social bird similar to the related carrion crow but having a bare grey face

² **rook** n either of 2 pieces of each colour in a set of chessmen having the power to move along the ranks or files across any number of consecutive unoccupied squares

rookery /'rookəri/ n 1a (the nests, usu built in the upper branches of trees, of) a colony of rooks b (a breeding ground or haunt of) a colony of penguins, seals, etc 2 a crowded dilapidated tenement or maze of dwellings

rookie /'rooki/ n a recruit; also a novice

room /roohm, room/ n 1 an extent of space occupied by, or sufficient or available for, sthg 2a a partitioned part of the inside of a building b such a part used as a separate lodging – often pl 3 suitable or fit occasion; opportunity + for

roommate /'roohm,mayt, 'room-/ n any of 2 or more people sharing the same room (e g in a university hall)

'**room ,service** n the facility by which a hotel guest can have food, drinks, etc brought to his/her room

roomy /'roohmi/ adj spacious – **roominess** n

¹ **roost** /roohst/ n 1 a support or place where birds roost 2 a group of birds roosting together

² **roost** v, esp of a bird to settle down for rest or sleep; perch

rooster /'roohstə/ n, chiefly NAm a cock

¹ **root** /rooht/ n 1a the (underground) part of a flowering plant that usu anchors and supports it and absorbs and stores food b (a fleshy and edible) root, bulb, tuber, or other underground plant part 2 the part of a tooth, hair, the tongue, etc by which it is attached to the body 3a sthg that is an underlying cause or basis b pl a feeling of belonging established through close familiarity or family ties with a particular place 4 a number which produces a given number when taken an indicated number of times as a factor 5 the basis from which a word is derived

² **root** v 1 to grow roots or take root 2 to have an origin or base

³root v 1 *esp of a pig* to dig with the snout 2 to poke or dig about *in*; search (unsystematically) for sthg

⁴root v to lend vociferous or enthusiastic support to sby or sthg – + *for*

'root ,crop n a crop (e g turnips or sugar beet) grown for its enlarged roots

root out v 1 to discover or cause to emerge by rooting 2 to get rid of or destroy completely

¹rope /rohp/ n 1 a strong thick cord composed of strands of fibres or wire twisted or braided together 2 a row or string consisting of things united (as if) by braiding, twining, or threading 3 *pl* special methods or procedures

²rope v 1 to bind, fasten, or tie with a rope 2 to enlist (sby reluctant) *in* a group or activity

ropy, ropey /'rohpi/ adj 1 like rope, esp in being able to be drawn out in a thread 2a of poor quality; shoddy b somewhat unwell

rosary /'rohz(ə)ri/ n a string of beads used in counting prayers

¹rose /rohz/ *past of* rise

²rose n 1 (the showy often double flower of) any of a genus of widely cultivated usu prickly shrubs 2a a compass card b a perforated outlet for water (e g from a shower or watering can) c an electrical fitting that anchors the flex of a suspended light bulb to a ceiling 3 a pale to dark pinkish colour – **rose** adj

rosé /roh'zay, '--/ n a light pink table wine made from red grapes by removing the skins after fermentation has begun

rosebud /'rohz,bud/ n the bud of a rose

rosemary /'rohzməri/ n a fragrant shrubby Eurasian plant used as a cooking herb

rosette /roh'zet, rə-/ n 1 an ornament usu made of material gathered so as to resemble a rose and worn as a badge, trophy, or trimming 2 a cluster of leaves in crowded circles or spirals (e g in the dandelion)

'rose,wood /-,wood/ n (any of various esp leguminous tropical trees yielding) a valuable dark red or purplish wood, streaked and variegated with black

roster /'rostə/ n 1 a list or register giving the order in which personnel are to perform a duty, go on leave, etc 2 an itemized list

rostrum /'rostrəm/ n pl **rostrums, rostra** /'rostrə/ 1 a stage for public speaking 2 a raised platform (on a stage)

rosy /'rohzi/ adj 1 a rose b having a rosy complexion – often in combination 2 characterized by or encouraging optimism – **rosiness** n

¹rot /rot/ v -**tt**- 1a to undergo decomposition, esp from the action of bacteria or fungi – often + *down* b to become unsound or weak (e g from chemical or water action) 2 to go to ruin

²rot n 1 (sthg) rotting or being rotten; decay 2 any of several plant or animal diseases, esp of sheep, with breakdown and death of tissues 3 nonsense, rubbish – often used interjectionally

rota /'rohtə/ n a list specifying a fixed order of rotation (e g of people or duties)

rotary /'roht(ə)ri/ adj 1 a turning on an axis like a wheel b proceeding about an axis 2 having a principal part that turns on an axis 3 characterized by rotation

rotate /'rohtayt/ v 1 to turn about an axis or a centre; revolve 2a to take turns at performing an act or operation b to perform an ordered series of actions or functions

rotation /roh'taysh(ə)n/ n 1a a rotating or being rotated (as if) on an axis or centre b one complete turn 2a recurrence in a regular series b the growing of different crops in succession in 1 field, usu in a regular sequence

rote /roht/ n the mechanical use of the memory

rotgut /'rot,gut/ n spirits of low quality – infml

rotor /'rohtə/ n 1 a part that revolves in a machine 2 a complete system of more or less horizontal blades that supplies (nearly) all the force supporting an aircraft (e g a helicopter) in flight

rotten /'rot(ə)n/ adj 1 having rotted; putrid 2 morally or politically corrupt 3 extremely unpleasant or inferior 4 marked by illness, discomfort, or unsoundness *USE* (3, 4) infml – ~**ly** adv – ~**ness** n

rotter /'rotə/ n a thoroughly objectionable person – often humor

rotund /roh'tund/ adj 1 rounded 2 high-flown or sonorous 3 markedly plump – ~**ity** n – ~**ly** adv

rotunda /roh'tundə/ n a round building covered by a dome

rouble, ruble /'roohbl/ n the major monetary unit of the USSR

rouge /roohzh/ n a red cosmetic, esp for the cheeks

¹rough /ruf/ adj 1a not smooth b covered with or made up of coarse hair c covered with boulders, bushes, etc 2a turbulent, stormy b(1) harsh, violent b(2) requiring strenuous effort b(3) unfortunate and hard to bear – often + *on* 3a harsh to the ear b crude in style or expression c ill-mannered, uncouth 4a crude, unfinished b executed hastily or approximately 5 *Br* poorly or exhausted, esp through lack of sleep or heavy drinking – infml

²rough n 1 uneven ground bordering a golf fairway 2 the rugged or disagreeable side or aspect 3a sthg, esp written or illustrated, in a crude or preliminary state b broad outline c a quick preliminary drawing or layout

³rough adv, *chiefly Br* in want of material comforts; without proper lodging – esp in *live/sleep rough*

roughage /'rufij/ *n* coarse bulky food (e g bran) that is relatively high in fibre and low in digestible nutrients and that by its bulk stimulates the passage of matter through the intestines

,**rough-and-'tumble** *n* disorderly unrestrained fighting or struggling

roughcast /'ruf,kahst/ *n* a plaster of lime mixed with shells or pebbles used for covering buildings – **roughcast** *v*

roughen /'ruf(ə)n/ *v* to make or become (more) rough

,**rough-'hewn** /-/ *adj* **1** in a rough or unfinished state **2** lacking refinement

roughhouse /'ruf,hows/ *n* an instance of brawling or excessively boisterous play – *infml*

roughly /'rufli/ *adv* **1a** with insolence or violence or in primitive fashion; crudely **2** without claim to completeness or exactness

rough out *v* **1** to shape or plan in a preliminary way **2** to outline

roughshod /'ruf,shod, ,-'-/ *adv* forcefully and without justice or consideration

'**rough ,stuff** *n* violent behaviour; violence – *infml*

roulette /rooh'let, roo-/ *n* a gambling game in which players bet on which compartment of a revolving wheel a small ball will come to rest in

¹**round** /rownd/ *adj* **1a** having every part of the surface or circumference equidistant from the centre **b** cylindrical **2** well filled out; plump **3a** complete, full **b** approximately correct; *esp* exact only to a specific decimal **c** substantial in amount **4** direct in expression **5a** moving in or forming a ring or circle **b** following a roughly circular route **6** presented with lifelike fullness **7** having full resonance or tone – ~ **ness** *n*

²**round** *adv* **1a** in a circular or curved path **b** with revolving or rotating motion **c** in circumference **d** in, along, or through a circuitous or indirect route **e** in an encircling position **2a** in close from all sides so as to surround (e g the children crowded *round*) **b** near, about **c** here and there in various places **3a** in rotation or recurrence **b** from beginning to end; through (e g all year *round*) **c(1)** in or to the other or a specified direction (e g turn *round*) **c(2)** to (e g came *round* after fainting) **c(3)** in the specified order or relationship (e g got the story the wrong way *round*) **4** about, approximately **5** to a particular person or place (e g invite them *round* for drinks) — **round and round 1** approximately; more or less **2** in a ring round; on all sides of

³**round** *prep* **1a** so as to revolve or progress about (a centre) **b** so as to encircle or enclose **c** so as to avoid or get past; beyond the obstacle of **d** near to; about **2a** in all directions outwards from (e g he looked *round* her) **b** here and there in or throughout (e g travel *round* Europe) **3** so as to have a

centre or basis in (e g a movement organized *round* the idea of service) **4** continuously during; throughout

⁴**round** *n* **1a** sthg round (e g a circle, curve, or ring) **b** a circle of people or things **2** a musical canon sung in unison in which each part is continuously repeated **3a** a circling or circuitous path or course **b** a route or assigned territory habitually traversed (e g by a milkman or policeman) **c** a series of visits made by **c(1)** a general practitioner to patients in their homes **c(2)** a hospital doctor to the patients under his/her care **4** a set of usu alcoholic drinks served at 1 time to each person in a group **5** a unit of ammunition consisting of the parts necessary to fire 1 shot **6** a division of a tournament in which each contestant plays 1 other **7** a prolonged burst (e g of applause) **8** a single slice of bread or toast; *also* a sandwich made with 2 whole slices of bread — **in the round 1** in full sculptured form unattached to a background **2** with a centre stage surrounded by an audience

⁵**round** *v* **1** to make round or rounded **2** to go round (e g a bend, corner) **3** to bring to completion or perfection – often + *off* or *out* **4** to express as a round number – often + *off*, *up*, or *down* **5** to turn *on* suddenly and attack

¹**roundabout** /'rownda,bowt/ *n, Br* **1** a merry-go-round **2** a road junction formed round a central island about which traffic moves in 1 direction only

²**roundabout** *adj* circuitous, indirect

Roundhead /'rownd,hed/ *n* an adherent of Parliament in its contest with Charles I

roundly /'rowndli/ *adv* **1** in a round or circular form or manner **2** in a blunt or severe manner

,**round-'shouldered** *adj* having stooping or rounded shoulders

roundsman /'rowndzman/ *n* sby (e g a milkman) who takes, orders, sells, or delivers goods on an assigned route

,**round 'table** *n* a meeting or conference of several people on equal terms

,**round-the-'clock** *adj* lasting or continuing 24 hours a day; constant

'**round ,up** /-,up/ *n* **1a** the collecting in of cattle by riding round them and driving them **b** a gathering in of scattered people or things **2** a summary of information (e g from news bulletins)

round up *v* **1** to collect (cattle) by a roundup **2** to gather in or bring together from various quarters

rouse /rowz/ *v* **1** to stir up; provoke **2** to arouse from sleep or apathy

rousing /'rowzing/ *adj* giving rise to enthusiasm; stirring

¹**rout** /rowt/ *n* a disorderly crowd of people; a mob

²**rout** *n* **1** a state of wild confusion; *specif* a confused retreat; headlong flight **2a** a disastrous defeat

519   **rub**

³**rout** *v* **1** to disorganize completely; wreak havoc among **2** to put to headlong flight **3** to defeat decisively or disastrously

¹**route** /rooht/ *n* **1a** a regularly travelled way **b** a means of access **2** a line of travel **3** an itinerary

²**route** *v* to send by a selected route; direct

'**route** '**march** *n* a usu long and tiring march, esp as military training

¹**routine** /rooh'teen/ *n* **1a** a regular course of procedure **b** habitual or mechanical performance of an established procedure **2** a fixed piece of entertainment often repeated

²**routine** *adj* **1** commonplace or repetitious in character **2** of or in accordance with established procedure – ~**ly** *adv*

roux /rooh/ *n, pl* **roux** /rooh(z)/ a cooked mixture of fat and flour used as a thickening agent in a sauce

¹**rove** /rohv/ *v* to wander aimlessly or idly (through or over) – ~**r** *n*

²**rove** *past of* **reeve**

³**rove** *v* to join (textile fibres) with a slight twist and draw out

¹**row** /roh/ *v* **1** to propel a boat by means of oars **2** to occupy a specified position in a rowing crew – ~**er** *n* – ~**ing** *adj*

²**row** /roh/ *n* an act of rowing a boat

³**row** /roh/ *n* **1** a number of objects arranged in a (straight) line; *also* the line along which such objects are arranged **2** a way, street — **in a row** one after another; successively

⁴**row** /row/ *n* **1** a noisy quarrel or stormy dispute **2** excessive or unpleasant noise

⁵**row** /row/ *v* to engage in quarrelling

rowan /'roh·ən/ *n* (the red berry of) a small Eurasian tree that bears flat clusters of white flowers and red berries; a mountain ash

rowdy /'rowdi/ *n or adj* (sby) coarse or boisterous – **rowdily** *adv* – **rowdiness, rowdyism** *n*

rowlock /'rolək; *also* (*not tech*) 'roh,lok/ *n* a device for holding an oar in place and providing a fulcrum for its action

royal /'roy(ə)l/ *adj* **1a** of monarchical ancestry **b** of the crown **c** in the crown's service **2** of superior size, magnitude, or quality **3** of or being a part of the rigging of a sailing ship next above the topgallant – ~**ly** *adv*

royalist /'royalist/ *n, often cap* a supporter of a king or of monarchical government

'**royal** '**jelly** *n* a highly nutritious secretion of the honeybee that is fed to the very young larvae and to all larvae that will develop into queens

'**royal** pre'**rogative** *n* the constitutional rights of the monarch

royalty /'royalti/ *n* **1** royal sovereignty **2** people of royal blood **3** a share of the product or profit reserved by one who grants esp an oil or mining lease **4** a payment made to an author, composer, or inventor for each copy or example of his/her work sold

¹**rub** /rub/ *v* **-bb- 1** to subject to pressure and friction, esp with a back-and-forth motion **2a** to cause (a body) to move with pressure and friction along a surface **b** to treat in any of various ways by rubbing — **rub shoulders** to associate closely; mingle socially — **rub the wrong way** to arouse the antagonism or displeasure of; irritate

²**rub** *n* **1a** an obstacle, difficulty – usu + *the* **b** sthg grating to the feelings (e g a gibe or harsh criticism) **2** the application of friction and pressure

rub along *v* **1** to continue coping in a trying situation **2** to remain on friendly terms

¹**rubber** /'rubə/ *n* **1a** an instrument or object used in rubbing, polishing, or cleaning **b** *Br* a small piece of rubber or plastic used for rubbing out esp pencil marks on paper, card, etc **2** (any of various synthetic substances like) an elastic substance obtained by coagulating the milky juice of the rubber tree or other plant that is used, esp when toughened by chemical treatment, in car tyres, waterproof materials, etc

²**rubber** *n* a contest consisting of an odd number of games won by the side that takes a majority

'**rubber** ,**plant** *n* a tall Asian tree of the fig family frequently dwarfed and grown as an ornamental plant

,**rubber-**'**stamp** *v* **1** to imprint with a rubber stamp **2** to approve, endorse, or dispose of as a matter of routine or at the dictate of another

,**rubber** '**stamp** *n* **1** a stamp of rubber for making imprints **2** sby who unthinkingly assents to the actions or policies of others **3** a routine endorsement or approval

'**rubber** ,**tree** *n* a S American tree that is cultivated in plantations and is the chief source of rubber

rubbing /'rubing/ *n* an image of a raised surface obtained by placing paper over it and rubbing the paper with charcoal, chalk, etc

¹**rubbish** /'rubish/ *n* **1** worthless or rejected articles; trash **2** sthg worthless; nonsense – often used interjectionally – ~**y** *adj*

²**rubbish** *v* **1** to condemn as rubbish **2** to litter with rubbish

rubble /'rubl/ *n* **1** broken fragments of building material (e g brick, or stone) **2** rough stone from the quarry

rubella /rooh'belə/ *n* German measles

Rubicon /'roohbikən/ *n* a bounding or limiting line; *esp* one that when crossed commits sby irrevocably

rub in *v* to harp on (e g sthg unpleasant or embarrassing)

rubric /'roohbrik/ *n* 1 a heading under which sthg is classed 2 an authoritative rule; *esp* a rule for the conduct of church ceremonial 3 an explanatory or introductory commentary

rub up *v* to revive or refresh knowledge of; revise – **rub-up** *n*

¹**ruby** /'roohbi/ *n* 1 a red corundum used as a gem 2 the dark red colour of the ruby

²**ruby** *adj* of or marking a 40th anniversary

¹**ruck** /ruk/ *n* 1a an indistinguishable mass b *the* usual run of people or things 2 a situation in Rugby Union in which 1 or more players from each team close round the ball when it is on the ground and try to kick the ball out to their own team

²**ruck** *v* to wrinkle, crease – often + *up*

rucksack /'ruk,sak/ *n* a lightweight bag carried on the back and fastened by straps over the shoulders, used esp by walkers and climbers

rudder /'rudə/ *n* 1 a flat piece or structure of wood or metal hinged vertically to a ship's stern for changing course with 2 a movable auxiliary aerofoil, usu attached to the fin, that serves to control direction of flight of an aircraft in the horizontal plane – **less** *adj*

ruddy /'rudi/ *adj* 1 having a healthy reddish colour 2 red, reddish 3 *Br* bloody

rude /roohd/ *adj* 1a in a rough or unfinished state b primitive, undeveloped 2a discourteous b vulgar, indecent c ignorant, unlearned 3 showing or suggesting lack of training or skill 4 robust, vigorous – esp in *rude health* 5 sudden and unpleasant; abrupt – **ly** *adv* – **ness** *n*

rudiment /'roohdimənt/ *n* 1 a basic principle or element or a fundamental skill 2a sthg as yet unformed or undeveloped b a deficiently developed body part or organ

rudimentary /,roohdi'ment(ə)ri/ *adj* 1 basic, fundamental 2 of a primitive kind; crude 3 very poorly developed or represented only by a vestige

¹**rue** /rooh/ *v* to feel penitence or bitter regret for – **ful** *adj* – **fully** *adv*

²**rue** *n* a strong-scented woody plant with bitter leaves formerly used in medicine

¹**ruff**, **ruffe** /ruf/ *n* a small freshwater European perch

²**ruff** *n* 1 a broad starched collar of fluted linen or muslin worn in the late 16th and early 17th c 2 a fringe or frill of long hairs or feathers growing round the neck 3 *fem* **reeve** a Eurasian sandpiper the male of which has a large ruff of erectable feathers during the breeding season

³**ruff** *v* to trump

ruffian /'rufi·ən/ *n* a brutal and lawless person – **ly** *adj*

¹**ruffle** /'rufl/ *v* **ruffling** /'rufling, 'rufl·ing/ 1a to disturb the smoothness of b to trouble, vex 2 to erect (e g feathers) (as if) in a ruff 3 to make into a ruffle

²**ruffle** *n* 1 a disturbance of surface evenness (e g a ripple or crumple) 2a a strip of fabric gathered or pleated on 1 edge b a ruff

rug /rug/ *n* 1 a heavy mat, usu smaller than a carpet and with a thick pile, which is used as a floor covering 2a a woollen blanket, often with fringes on 2 opposite edges, used as a wrap esp when travelling b a blanket for an animal (e g a horse)

rugby /'rugbi/ *n, often cap* a football game that is played with an oval football, that features kicking, lateral hand-to-hand passing, and tackling

rugged /'rugid/ *adj* 1 having a rough uneven surface or outline 2 seamed with wrinkles and furrows 3 austere, stern; *also* uncompromising 4 strongly built or constituted; sturdy – **ly** *adv* – **ness** *n*

¹**ruin** /'roohin/ *n* 1 physical, moral, economic, or social collapse 2a the state of being wrecked or decayed b the remains of sthg destroyed – usu pl with sing. meaning 3 (a cause of) destruction or downfall 4 a ruined person or structure – **ation** *n*

²**ruin** *v* 1 to reduce to ruins 2a to damage irreparably; spoil b to reduce to financial ruin

ruinous /'roohi·nəs/ *adj* 1 dilapidated, ruined 2 causing (the likelihood of) ruin – **ly** *adv*

¹**rule** /roohl/ *n* 1a a prescriptive specification of conduct or action b an established procedure, custom, or habit 2a a usu valid generalization b a standard of judgment c a regulating principle, esp of a system 3 the exercise or a period of dominion 4 a strip or set of jointed strips of material marked off in units and used for measuring or marking off lengths — **as a rule** generally; for the most part

²**rule** *v* 1a to exercise power or firm authority over b to be preeminent in; dominate 2 to lay down authoritatively, esp judicially 3 to mark with lines drawn (as if) along the straight edge of a ruler

rule out *v* 1a to exclude, eliminate b to deny the possibility of 2 to make impossible; prevent

ruler /'roohlə/ *n* 1 sby, specif a sovereign, who rules 2 a smooth-edged strip of material that is usu marked off in units (e g centimetres) and is used for guiding a pen or pencil in drawing lines, for measuring, or for marking off lengths

¹**ruling** /'roohling/ *n* an official or authoritative decision

²**ruling** *adj* 1 exerting power or authority 2 chief, predominant

¹**rum** /rum/ *adj*, **-mm-** *chiefly Br* queer, strange – infml

²**rum** *n* a spirit distilled from a fermented cane product (e g molasses)

rumba, rhumba /'rumbə/ *n* (the music for) a ballroom dance of Cuban Negro origin

¹**rumble** /'rumbl/ *v* **rumbling** /'rumbling, 'rumbl·ing/ 1 to make a low heavy rolling sound 2 to reveal or discover the true character of – infml

²rumble *n* **1** a rumbling sound **2** *NAm* a street fight, esp between gangs – *infml*

rumbustious /rum'buschas/ *adj*, *chiefly Br* irrepressibly or coarsely exuberant

¹ruminant /'roohminant/ *n* a ruminant mammal

²ruminant *adj* **1** of or being (a member of) a group of hoofed mammals including the cattle, sheep, giraffes, and camels that chew the cud and have a complex 3- or 4-chambered stomach **2** meditative

ruminate /'roohmi,nayt/ *v* **1** to chew again (what has been chewed slightly and swallowed) **2** to engage in contemplation (of) – **-nation** *n*

¹rummage /'rumij/ *n* a thorough search, esp among a jumbled assortment of objects

²rummage *v* **1** to make a thorough search of (an untidy or congested place) **2** to uncover by searching – usu + *out*

rummy /'rumi/ *n* any of several card games for 2 or more players in which each player tries to assemble combinations of 3 or more related cards

¹rumour, *NAm chiefly* **rumor** /'roohma/ *n* **1** a statement or report circulated without confirmation of its truth **2** talk or opinion widely disseminated but with no identifiable source

²rumour, *NAm chiefly* **rumor** *v* to tell or spread by rumour

rump /rump/ *n* **1** the rear part of a quadruped mammal, bird, etc; the buttocks **2** a cut of beef between the loin and round **3** a small or inferior remnant of a larger group (e g a parliament)

¹rumple /'rumpl/ *n* a fold, wrinkle

²rumple *v* **rumpling** /'rumpl·ing/ **1** to wrinkle, crumple **2** to make unkempt; tousle

rumpus /'rumpas/ *n* a usu noisy commotion

¹run /run/ *v* **-nn-; ran** /ran/; **run 1a** to go faster than a walk; *specif* to go steadily by springing steps so that both feet leave the ground for an instant in each step **b** to flee, escape **2a** to contend in a race; *also* to finish a race in the specified place **b** to put forward as a candidate for office **3a** to move (as if) on wheels **b** to pass or slide freely or cursorily **4a** to slip through or past **b** to smuggle **5** to sing or play quickly **6a** to go back and forth; ply **b** *of fish* to ascend a river to spawn **7a** to function, operate **b** to carry on, manage, or control **8** to own and drive **9** to continue in force **10** to pass, esp by negligence or indulgence, into a specified state **11a(1)** to flow **a(2)** to be full of; flow with **b** to discharge liquid **c** to melt **d** to spread, dissolve **12** to have a tendency; be prone **13a** to lie or extend in a specified position, direction, or relation to sthg **b** to extend in a continuous range **14** to occur persistently **15** to make oneself liable to **16** to carry in a printed medium; print **17** to spread quickly from point to point **18** to ladder — **run across** to meet with or discover by chance — **run after** to pursue, chase; *esp* to seek the company of — **run a temperature** to be feverish — **run foul of 1** to collide with **2** to come into conflict with —

run into 1a to merge with **b** to mount up to **2a** to collide with **b** to encounter, meet — **run into the ground** to tire out or use up with heavy work — **run it fine** to leave only the irreducible margin — **run on** to be concerned with; dwell on — **run rings round** to show marked superiority over; defeat decisively — **run riot 1** to act or function wildly or without restraint **2** to grow or occur in profusion — **run short 1** to become insufficient **2** to come near the end of available supplies — **run somebody off his/her feet 1** to tire sby out with running **2** to keep sby very busy **1** to squander **2a** to perform, esp for practice or instruction **b** to deal with rapidly and usu perfunctorily — **run to 1** to extend to **2a** to afford **b** *of money* to be enough for — **run to earth/ground** to find after protracted search

²run *n* **1a** an act or the activity of running; continued rapid movement **b** the gait of a runner **c** (a school of fish) migrating or ascending a river to spawn **2a** the direction in which sthg (e g a vein of ore or the grain of wood) lies **b** general tendency or direction **3** a continuous series or unbroken course, esp of identical or similar things: e g **3a** a rapid passage up or down a musical scale **b** an unbroken course of performances or showings **c** a persistent and heavy commercial or financial demand **4** the quantity of work turned out in a continuous operation **5** the average or prevailing kind or class **6a** the distance covered in a period of continuous journeying **b** a short excursion in a car **c** freedom of movement in or access to a place **7** an enclosure for domestic animals where they may feed or exercise **8a** an inclined course (e g for skiing) **b** a support or channel (e g a track, pipe, or trough) along which sthg runs **9** a unit of scoring in cricket made typically by each batsman running the full length of the wicket **10** a ladder (e g in a stocking) — **on the run 1** in haste; without pausing **2** in hiding or running away, esp from lawful authority — **run for one's money** the profit or enjoyment to which one is legitimately entitled

runaround /'runa,rownd/ *n* delaying action, esp in response to a request

¹runaway /'runa,way/ *n* a fugitive

²runaway *adj* **1** fugitive **2** won by a long lead; decisive **3** out of control

run away *v* **1** to take to flight **2** to flee from home; *esp* to elope — **run away with 1** to take away in haste or secretly; *esp* to steal **2** to believe too easily **3** to carry beyond reasonable limits

rundown /'run,down/ *n* an item-by-item report; a résumé

run-'down *adj* **1** in a state of disrepair **2** in poor health

run down *v* **1** to knock down, esp with a motor vehicle **2a** to chase to exhaustion or until captured **b** to find by searching **3** to disparage **4** to

run

allow the gradual decline or closure of **5** to cease to operate because of the exhaustion of motive power **6** to decline in physical condition

rune /roohn/ *n* **1** any of the characters of an alphabet used in medieval times, esp in carved inscriptions, by the Germanic peoples **2** a magical or cryptic utterance or inscription – **runic** *adj*

¹**rung** /rung/ *past part of* **ring**

²**rung** *n* **1a** a rounded part placed as a crosspiece between the legs of a chair **b** any of the crosspieces of a ladder **2** a level or stage in sthg that can be ascended

run in *v* **1** to use (e g a motor car) cautiously for an initial period **2** to arrest, esp for a minor offence – *infml*

runnel /'runl/ *n* a small stream; a brook

runner /'runə/ *n* **1** an entrant for a race who actually competes in it **2** sby who smuggles or distributes illicit or contraband goods – usu in combination **3** a straight piece on which sthg slides: e g **3a** a longitudinal piece on which a sledge or ice skate slides **b** a groove or bar along which sthg (e g a drawer or sliding door) slides **4a** a long narrow carpet (e g for a hall or staircase) **b** a narrow decorative cloth for a table or dresser top

runner 'bean *n, chiefly Br* (the long green edible pod of) a widely cultivated orig tropical American high-climbing bean with large usu bright red flowers

runner-'up *n pl* **runners-up** *also* **runner-ups** a competitor other than the outright winner whose attainment still merits a prize

¹**running** /'runing/ *n* **1** the state of competing, esp with a good chance of winning – in *in*/*out of the running* **2** management, operation

²**running** *adj* **1** runny **2a** having stages that follow in rapid succession **b** made during the course of a process or activity **3** being part of a continuous length **4** cursive, flowing

³**running** *adv* in succession

runny /'runi/ *adj* tending to run

runoff /'run,of/ *n* a final decisive race, contest, or election

run off *v* **1a** to compose rapidly or glibly **b** to produce with a printing press or copier **c** to decide (e g a race) by a runoff **2** to drain off (a liquid) **3** to run away; elope

run-of-the-'mill *adj* average, commonplace

run out *v* **1a** to come to an end **b** to become exhausted or used up **2** to dismiss a batsman who is outside his crease and attempting a run by breaking the wicket with the ball **3** *chiefly NAm* to compel to leave — **run out of** to use up the available supply of — **run out on** to leave, abandon

runt /runt/ *n* **1** an animal unusually small of its kind; *esp* the smallest of a litter of pigs **2** a puny person

'**run-,through** *n* **1** a cursory reading, summary, or rehearsal **2** a sequence of actions performed for practice

run through *v* **1** to pierce with a weapon (e g a sword) **2** to perform, esp for practice or instruction

'**run-,up** *n* **1** (the track or area provided for) an approach run to provide momentum (e g for a jump or throw) **2** *Br* a period that immediately precedes an action or event

run up *v* **1** to make (esp a garment) quickly **2a** to erect hastily **b** to hoist (a flag) **3** to accumulate or incur (debts) — **run up against** to encounter (e g a difficulty)

runway /'run,way/ *n* an artificially surfaced strip of ground on an airfield for the landing and take-off of aeroplanes

rupee /rooh'pee/ *n* (a note or coin representing) the basic money unit of various countries of the Indian subcontinent and the Indian Ocean (e g India, Pakistan, Seychelles, and Sri Lanka)

¹**rupture** /'rupchə/ *n* **1** breach of peace or concord; *specif* open hostility between nations **2a** the tearing apart of a tissue, esp muscle **b** a hernia **3** a breaking apart or bursting

²**rupture** *v* **1a** to part by violence; break, burst **b** to create a breach of **2** to produce a rupture in

rural /'rooərəl/ *adj* of the country, country people or life, or agriculture – ~**ly** *adv*

ruse /roohz/ *n* a wily subterfuge

¹**rush** /rush/ *n* any of various often tufted marsh plants with cylindrical (hollow) leaves, used for the seats of chairs and for plaiting mats – **rushy** *adj*

²**rush** *v* **1** to push or impel forwards with speed or violence **2** to perform or finish in a short time or without adequate preparation **3** to run against in attack, often with an element of surprise

³**rush** *n* **1a** a rapid and violent forward motion **b** a sudden onset of emotion **2** a surge of activity; *also* busy or hurried activity **3** a great movement of people, esp in search of wealth **4** the unedited print of a film scene processed directly after shooting – usu pl

⁴**rush** *adj* requiring or marked by special speed or urgency

'**rush ,hour** *n* a period of the day when traffic is at a peak

rusk /rusk/ *n* (a light dry biscuit similar to) a piece of sliced bread baked again until dry and crisp

russet /'rusit/ *n* **1** a reddish to yellowish brown colour **2** any of various russet-coloured winter eating apples

Russian /'rush(ə)n/ *n* **1** a native or inhabitant of Russia; *broadly* a native or inhabitant of the USSR **2** a Slavonic language of the Russians

,**Russian rou'lette** n an act of bravado consisting of spinning the cylinder of a revolver loaded with 1 cartridge, pointing the muzzle at one's own head, and pulling the trigger

¹**rust** /rust/ n **1** a brittle reddish coating on iron, esp iron chemically attacked by moist air **2** corrosive or injurious influence or effect **3** (a fungus causing) any of numerous destructive diseases of plants in which reddish brown blisters form **4** a reddish brown to orange colour

²**rust** v **1** to form rust; become oxidized **2** to degenerate, esp through lack of use or advancing age **3** to become reddish brown as if with rust

¹**rustic** /'rustik/ adj of or suitable for the country or country people – ~**ity** n

²**rustic** n an unsophisticated rural person

rusticate /'rusti,kayt/ v **1** to suspend (a student) from college or university **2** to bevel or cut a groove, channel etc in (e g the edges of stone blocks) to make the joints conspicuous **3** to impart a rustic character to

¹**rustle** /'rusl/ v **rustling** /'rusling, 'rusl·ing/ **1a** to make or cause a rustle **b** to move with a rustling sound **2** chiefly NAm to steal cattle or horses – ~**r** n

²**rustle** n a quick succession or confusion of faint sounds

rusty /'rusti/ adj **1** affected (as if) by rust; esp stiff (as if) with rust **2** inept and slow through lack of practice or advanced age **3a** of the colour rust **b** dulled in colour by age and use; shabby – **rustiness** n

¹**rut** /rut/ n an annually recurrent state of readiness to copulate, in the male deer or other mammal

²**rut** n **1** a track worn by habitual passage, esp of wheels on soft or uneven ground **2** an established practice; esp a tedious routine

ruthless /'roohthlis/ adj showing no pity or compassion – ~**ly** adv – ~**ness** n

rye /rie/ n (the seeds, from which a wholemeal flour is made, of) a hardy grass widely grown for grain

S

s /es/ n, pl **s's, ss** /'esiz/ often cap (a graphic representation of or device for reproducing) the 19th letter of the English alphabet

sabbath /'sabəth/ n **1** often cap the 7th day of the week observed from Friday evening to Saturday evening as a day of rest and worship by Jews **2** often cap Sunday observed among Christians as a day of rest and worship

¹**sabbatical** /sə'batikl/, **sabbatic** adj **1** of the sabbath **2** of or being a sabbatical

²**sabbatical** n a leave, often with pay, granted usu every 7th year (e g to a university teacher)

sable /'saybl/ n **1** (the valuable dark brown fur of) a N Asian and European flesh-eating mammal **2** black – poetic or used technically in heraldry

sabot /'saboh/ n a wooden shoe

¹**sabotage** /'sabə,tahzh/ n **1** destructive or obstructive action carried on by a civilian or enemy agent, intended to hinder military activity **2** deliberate subversion (e g of a plan or project)

²**sabotage** v to practise sabotage on – ~**teur** n

sabre, NAm chiefly **saber** /'saybə/ n **1** a cavalry sword with a curved blade, thick back, and guard **2** a light fencing or duelling sword

,**sabre-toothed 'tiger** n an extinct big cat with long curved upper canines

sac /sak/ n a (fluid-filled) pouch within an animal or plant

saccharin /'sak(ə)rin/ n a compound containing no calories that is several hundred times sweeter than cane sugar and is used as a sugar substitute (e g in low-calorie diets)

saccharine /'sak(ə)rin, -reen/ adj **1** of, like, or containing sugar **2** excessively sweet; mawkish

sachet /'sashay/ n **1** a small usu plastic bag or packet; esp one holding just enough of sthg (e g shampoo or sugar) for use at 1 time **2** a small bag containing a perfumed powder used to scent clothes and linens

¹**sack** /sak/ n **1** a usu rectangular large bag (e g of paper or canvas) **2** a garment without shaping; esp a loosely fitting dress **3** dismissal from employment – usu + get or give + the; infml

²**sack** v to dismiss from a job – infml

³**sack** n any of various dry white wines formerly imported to England from S Europe

⁴**sack** n the plundering of a place captured in war

⁵**sack** v **1** to plunder (e g a town) after capture **2** to strip (a place) of valuables

sacrament /'sakrəmənt/ n **1** a formal religious act (e g baptism) functioning as a sign or symbol of a spiritual reality **2** cap the bread and wine used at Communion; specif the consecrated Host – ~**al** adj

sacred /'saykrid/ adj **1** dedicated or set apart for the service or worship of a god or gods **2a** worthy of religious veneration **b** commanding reverence and respect **3** of religion; not secular or profane – ~**ly** adv – ~**ness** n

,**sacred 'cow** n sby or sthg granted unreasonable immunity from criticism

¹**sacrifice** /'sakrifīs/ n 1 an act of offering to a deity; esp the killing of a victim on an altar 2a destruction or surrender of one thing for the sake of another of greater worth or importance b sthg given up or lost – **-ficial** adj

²**sacrifice** v 1 to offer as a sacrifice 2 to give up or lose for the sake of an ideal or end

sacrilege /'sakrilij/ n 1 a violation of what is sacred 2 gross irreverence toward sby or sthg sacred – **-legious** adj – **-legiously** adv

sacristy /'sakristi/ n a room in a church where sacred vessels and vestments are kept and where the clergy put on their vestments

sacrosanct /'sakrasangkt/ adj accorded the highest reverence and respect; also regarded with unwarranted reverence

sad /sad/ adj **-dd- 1a** affected with or expressing unhappiness b deplorable, regrettable 2 of a dull sombre colour 3 of baked goods heavy – **~ly** adv – **~ness** n

sadden /'sadn/ v to make or become sad

¹**saddle** /'sadl/ n **1a** a usu padded and leather-covered seat secured to the back of a horse, donkey, etc for the rider to sit on b a seat in certain types of vehicles (e g a bicycle or agricultural tractor) 2 a ridge connecting 2 peaks 3 a large cut of meat from a sheep, hare, rabbit, deer, etc consisting of both sides of the unsplit back including both loins — **in the saddle** in control

²**saddle** v **saddling** /'sadl·ing/ to encumber

saddler /'sadlə/ n one who makes, repairs, or sells furnishings (e g saddles) for horses

saddlery /'sadləri/ n 1 the trade, articles of trade, or shop of a saddler 2 a set of the equipment used for sitting on and controlling a riding horse

sadism /'saydiz(ə)m/ n a sexual perversion in which pleasure is obtained by inflicting physical or mental pain on others; broadly delight in inflicting pain – **sadist** n – **sadistic** adj – **sadistically** adv

sae /,es,ay'ee/ n a stamped addressed envelope

¹**safari** /sə'fahri/ n (the caravan and equipment of) a hunting or scientific expedition, esp in E Africa

²**safari** adj made of lightweight material, esp cotton, and typically having 2 breast pockets and a belt

sa'fari ,park n a park stocked with usu big game animals (e g lions) so that visitors can observe them in natural-appearing surroundings

¹**safe** /sayf/ adj 1 freed from harm or risk 2 secure from threat of danger, harm, or loss 3 affording safety from danger **4a** not threatening or entailing danger b unlikely to cause controversy **5a** not liable to take risks b trustworthy, reliable – **~ly** adv – **~ness** n

²**safe** n 1 a room or receptacle for the safe storage of valuables 2 a receptacle, esp a cupboard, for the temporary storage of fresh and cooked foods

that typically has at least 1 side of wire mesh to allow ventilation while preventing flies from entering

,**safe-'conduct** n (a document authorizing) protection given to a person passing through a military zone or occupied area

¹**safe,guard** /-,gahd/ n a precautionary measure or stipulation

²**safeguard** v to make safe; protect

,**safe'keeping** /-'keeping/ n keeping safe or being kept safe

safety /'sayfti/ n the condition of being safe from causing or suffering hurt, injury, or loss

'**safety ,match** n a match capable of being ignited only on a specially prepared surface

'**safety ,pin** n a pin in the form of a clasp with a guard covering its point when fastened

'**safety ,valve** n 1 an automatic escape or relief valve (e g for a steam boiler) 2 an outlet for pent-up energy or emotion

saffron /'safron, 'safrən/ n 1 (the deep orange aromatic pungent dried stigmas, used to colour and flavour foods, of) a purple-flowered crocus 2 an orange-yellow colour

¹**sag** /sag/ v **-gg- 1** to droop, sink, or settle (as if) from weight, pressure, or loss of tautness 2 to lose firmness or vigour 3 to fail to stimulate or retain interest

²**sag** n 1 a sagging part 2 an instance or amount of sagging

saga /'sahgə/ n 1 a medieval Icelandic narrative dealing with historic or legendary figures and events 2 a long detailed account

sagacious /sə'gayshəs/ adj of keen and farsighted judgment – **-city** n – **~ly** adv

¹**sage** /sayj/ adj having or indicating wisdom and sound judgment – **~ly** adv

²**sage** n 1 sby (e g a great philosopher) renowned for wise teachings 2 a venerable man of sound judgment

³**sage** n a plant of the mint family whose greyish green aromatic leaves are used esp in flavouring meat

Sagittarius /,saji'teəri·əs/ n (sby born under) the 9th sign of the zodiac in astrology, pictured as a centaur shooting an arrow

sago /'saygoh/ n, pl **sagos** a dry powdered starch prepared from the pith of a palmtree and used esp as a food (e g in a milk pudding)

sahib /'sah-(h)ib/ n sir, master – used, esp among Hindus and Muslims in colonial India, when addressing or speaking of a European of some social or official status

said /sed/ adj aforementioned

¹**sail** /sayl/ n 1 an expanse of fabric which is spread to catch or deflect the wind as a means of propelling a ship, sand yacht, etc 2 a voyage by ship — **under sail** in motion with sails set

²**sail** v **1** to travel in a boat or ship **2a** to travel on water, esp by the action of wind on sails **b** to move without visible effort or in a stately manner **3** to begin a journey by water — **sail into** to attack vigorously or sharply — **sail close to the wind 1** to sail as nearly as possible against the main force of the wind **2** to be near to dishonesty or improper behaviour

sailor /'sayla/ n **1a** a seaman, mariner **b** a member of a ship's crew other than an officer **2** a traveller by water; esp one considered with reference to any tendency to seasickness

saint /saynt/ n; before a name usu s(ə)nt/ n **1** a person officially recognized through canonization as being outstandingly holy and so worthy of veneration **2** any of the spirits of the departed in heaven **b** an angel **3** a person of outstanding piety or virtue – ~ **ly** adj – ~ **liness** n

'**saint's ,day** /'saynts/ n a day in a church calendar on which a saint is commemorated

¹**sake** /sayk/ n **1** the purpose of – in for the sake of **2** interest, benefit or advantage – in for someone's/something's sake – **for the sake of, for someone's/something's sake 1** for the purpose of **2** so as to get, keep, or improve **3** so as to help, please, or honour – **for God's/goodness/Heaven's/pity's sake** — used in protest or supplication

²**sake, saki** /'sahki/ n a Japanese alcoholic drink of fermented rice

salaam /sə'lahm/ n **1** a ceremonial greeting in E countries **2** an obeisance made by bowing low and placing the right palm on the forehead – **salaam** v

salacious /sə'layshəs/ adj **1** arousing or appealing to sexual desire **2** lecherous, lustful – ~ **ly** adv – ~ **ness** n

salad /'saləd/ n **1a** (mixed) raw vegetables (e g lettuce, watercress, or tomato) often served with a dressing **b** a dish of raw or (cold) cooked foods often cut into small pieces and combined with a dressing **2** a vegetable or herb eaten raw (in salad); esp lettuce

'**salad ,days** n pl time of youthful inexperience or indiscretion

salamander /'salə,mandə, ,--'--/ n **1** a mythical animal with the power to endure fire without harm **2** any of numerous scaleless amphibians superficially resembling lizards

salami /sə'lahmi/ n a highly seasoned, esp pork, sausage

salary /'saləri/ n a fixed usu monthly payment for regular services, esp of a nonmanual kind

sale /sayl/ n **1** the act or an instance of selling **2** quantity sold - often pl with sing. meaning **3** an event at which goods are offered for sale **4** public disposal to the highest bidder **5** a selling of goods at bargain prices **6a** pl operations and activities involved in promoting and selling goods or services **b** gross receipts obtained from selling — **on/for sale** available for purchase

saleroom /'saylroohm, -room/ n, chiefly Br a place where goods are displayed for sale, esp by auction

sales /saylz/ adj of, engaged in, or used in selling

¹**salient** /'saylyənt, -li·ənt/ adj **1** pointing upwards or outwards **2a** projecting beyond a line or level **b** standing out conspicuously

²**salient** n an outwardly projecting part of a fortification, trench system, or line of defence

saline /'say,lien/ adj (consisting) of, containing, or resembling (a) salt

saliva /sə'lievə/ n a liquid secreted into the mouth by glands that lubricates ingested food and often begins the breakdown of starches – **-vary** adj

salivate /'salivayt/ v to have an (excessive) flow of saliva – **-vation** n

¹**sallow** /'saloh/ n any of various Old World broad-leaved willows

²**sallow** adj of a sickly yellowish colour

¹**sally** n **1** a rushing forth; esp a sortie of troops from a besieged position **2** a witty or penetrating remark **3** a short excursion; a jaunt

²**sally** v **1** to rush out or issue forth suddenly **2** to set out (e g on a journey) – usu + forth

salmon /'samən/ n **1** (any of various fishes related to) a large soft-finned game and food fish of the N Atlantic that is highly valued for its pink flesh **2** an orangy-pink colour

salmonella /,salmə'nelə/ n pl **salmonellae** /-li/, **salmonellas, salmonella** any of a genus of bacteria that cause food poisoning

salon /'salonh/ n **1** an elegant reception room or living room **2** a gathering of literary figures, statesmen, etc held at the home of a prominent person and common in the 17th and 18th c **3** cap an exhibition, esp in France, of works of art by living artists

saloon /sə'loohn/ n **1** a public apartment or hall (e g a ballroom, exhibition room, or shipboard social area) **2** Br an enclosed motor car having no partition between the driver and passengers **3** NAm a room or establishment in which alcoholic beverages are sold and consumed

sa'loon ,bar n, Br a comfortable, well-furnished, and often relatively expensive bar in a public house

salsify /'salsifie, -fi/ n a long tapering root-vegetable

¹**salt** /sawlt, solt/ n **1a** sodium chloride, occurring naturally esp as a mineral deposit and dissolved in sea water, and used esp for seasoning or preserving **b** any of numerous compounds resulting from replacement of (part of) the hydrogen ion of an acid by a (radical acting like a) metal **c** pl c(1) a mixture of the salts of alkali metals or magnesium (e g Epsom salts) used as a purgative c(2) smelling

salts **2a** an ingredient that imparts savour, piquancy, or zest **b** sharpness of wit **3** an experienced sailor — **above/below the salt** placed, esp seated, in a socially advantageous/disadvantageous position — **worth one's salt** worthy of respect; competent, effective

²**salt** v **1** to treat, provide, season, or preserve with common salt or brine **2** to give flavour or piquancy to (e g a story)

³**salt** adj **1a** saline, salty **b** being or inducing a taste similar to that of common salt that is one of the 4 basic taste sensations **2** cured or seasoned with salt; salted **3** containing, overflowed by, or growing in salt water **4** sharp, pungent – ~ness n

salt away v to put by in reserve; save

¹**salt,cellar** /-,selə/ n a cruet for salt

,**salt'petre**, NAm **saltpeter** /-'peetə/ n potassium nitrate, esp as used in gunpowder and in curing meat

salty /'sawlti, 'solti/ adj **1** of, seasoned with, or containing salt **2** having a taste of (too much) salt **3a** piquant, witty **b** earthy, coarse – **saltiness** n

salubrious /sə'l(y)oohbri·əs/ adj **1** favourable to health or well-being **2** respectable – ~ness, -brity n

salutary /'salyoot(ə)ri/ adj having a beneficial or edifying effect

salutation /,salyoo'taysh(ə)n/ n **1** an expression of greeting or courtesy by word or gesture **2** pl regards

¹**salute** /sə'l(y)ooht/ v **1** to address with expressions of greeting, goodwill, or respect **2a** to honour by a conventional military or naval ceremony **b** to show respect and recognition to (a military superior) by assuming a prescribed position

²**salute** n **1** a greeting, salutation **2a** a sign or ceremony expressing goodwill or respect **b** an act of saluting a military superior; also the position (e g of the hand or weapon) or the entire attitude of a person saluting a superior

¹**salvage** /'salvij/ n **1a** compensation paid to those who save property from loss or damage; esp compensation paid for saving a ship from wreckage or capture **b** the act of saving or rescuing a ship or its cargo **c** the act of saving or rescuing property in danger (e g from fire) **2a** property saved from a calamity (e g a wreck or fire) **b** sthg of use or value extracted from waste material

²**salvage** v to rescue or save (e g from wreckage or ruin)

salvation /sal'vaysh(ə)n/ n **1** deliverance from the power and effects of sin **2** deliverance from danger, difficulty, or destruction

Sal,vation 'Army n an international Christian group organized on military lines for evangelizing and performing social work among the poor – **salvationist** n

¹**salve** /salv, sahv/ n **1** an ointment for application to wounds or sores **2** a soothing influence or agency

²**salve** v to ease

salver /'salvə/ n a tray; esp an ornamental tray (e g of silver) on which food or beverages are served or letters and visiting cards are presented

salvo /'salvoh/ n pl **salvos, salvoes 1a** a simultaneous discharge of 2 or more guns or missiles in military or naval action or as a salute **b** the release at one moment of several bombs or missiles from an aircraft **2** a sudden or emphatic burst (e g of cheering or approbation)

Samaritan /sə'marit(ə)n/ n **1** a native or inhabitant of ancient Samaria **2a** often not cap one who selflessly gives aid to those in distress **b** a member of an organization that offers help to those in despair

samba /'sambə/ n (the music for) a Brazilian dance of African origin

¹**same** /saym/ adj **1** being 1 single thing, person, or group; identical – often as an intensive (e g born in this very same house) **2** being the specified one or ones – + as or that **3** corresponding so closely as to be indistinguishable — **at the same time** for all that; nevertheless

²**same** pron, pl **same 1** the same thing, person, or group (e g do the same for you) **2** sthg previously mentioned (e g ordered a drink and refused to pay for same)

³**same** adv in the same manner – + the

sameness /'saymnis/ n **1** identity, similarity **2** monotony, uniformity

samovar /'samovah, ,--'-/ n a metal urn with a tap at its base and an interior heating tube, that is used, esp in Russia, to boil water for tea

sampan /'sam,pan/ n a small flat-bottomed boat used in rivers and harbours in the Far East

¹**sample** /'sahmpl/ n **1** an item serving to show the character or quality of a larger whole or group **2** a part of a statistical population whose properties are studied to gain information about the whole

²**sample** v **sampling** /'sahmpl·ing, 'sahmpling/ to take a sample of or from; esp to test the quality of by a sample

³**sample** adj intended as an example

sampler /'sahmplə/ n a decorative piece of needlework

samurai /'sam(y)oo,rie/ n, pl **samurai 1** a military retainer of a Japanese feudal baron **2** the warrior aristocracy of Japan

sanatorium /,sanə'tawri·əm/ n pl **sanatoriums, sanatoria** /-ri·ə/ an establishment that provides therapy, rest, or recuperation for convalescents, the chronically ill, etc

sanctify /'sangkti,fie/ v **1** to set apart for a sacred purpose or for religious use **2** to give moral or social sanction to – **-fication** n

sanctimonious /ˌsangkti'mohnyəs, -ni·əs/ *adj* self-righteous – ~**ly** *adv* – ~**ness** *n*

¹**sanction** /'sangksh(ə)n/ *n* **1** a penalty annexed to an offence **2a** a consideration that determines moral action or judgment **b** a mechanism of social control (e g shame) for enforcing a society's standards **c** official permission or authoritative ratification **3** an economic or military coercive measure adopted to force a nation to conform to international law

²**sanction** *v* **1** to make valid; ratify **2** to give authoritative consent to

sanctity /'sangktəti/ *n* **1** holiness of life and character **2** the quality or state of being holy or sacred

sanctuary /'sangktyoo(ə)ri, -chəri/ *n* **1** a consecrated place: e g **1a** the ancient temple at Jerusalem or its holy of holies **b** the part of a Christian church in which the altar is placed **2a** a place of refuge and protection **b** a refuge for (endangered) wildlife where predators are controlled and hunting is illegal

sanctum /'sangktəm/ *n pl* **sanctums** *also* **sancta** /-tə/ a place of total privacy and security (e g a study)

¹**sand** /sand/ *n* **1** loose granular particles smaller than gravel and coarser than silt that result from the disintegration of (silica-rich) rocks **2** an area of sand; a beach – usu pl with sing. meaning **3** moments of time measured (as if) with an hourglass – usu pl with sing. meaning **4** a yellowish grey colour

²**sand** *v* **1** to sprinkle (as if) with sand **2** to cover or choke with sand – usu + *up* **3** to smooth or dress by grinding or rubbing with an abrasive (e g sandpaper) – often + *down*

sandal /'sandl/ *n* a shoe consisting of a sole held on to the foot by straps or thongs

'**sandal,wood** /-ˌwood/ *n* (the compact close-grained fragrant yellowish heartwood, used in ornamental carving and cabinetwork, of) an Indo-Malayan tree

sandbag /'sand,bag/ *n* a bag filled with sand and used in usu temporary fortifications or constructions, as ballast, or as a weapon

'**sand,bank** /-ˌbangk/ *n* a large deposit of sand, esp in a river or coastal waters

'**sand,bar** /-ˌbah/ *n* a sandbank

'**sand,blast** /-ˌblahst/ *v* *or* *n* (to treat with) a high-speed jet of sand propelled by air or steam (e g for cutting or cleaning glass or stone)

'**sand,castle** /-ˌkahsl/ *n* a model of a castle made in damp sand, esp at the seaside

¹**sand,paper** /-ˌpaypə/ *n* paper to which a thin layer of sand has been glued for use as an abrasive; *broadly* any abrasive paper (e g glasspaper)

²**sandpaper** *v* to rub (as if) with sandpaper

'**sand,piper** /-ˌpiepə/ *n* any of numerous small wading birds with longer bills than the plovers

'**sand,pit** /-ˌpit/ *n* an enclosure containing sand for children to play in

'**sand,stone** /-ˌstohn/ *n* a sedimentary rock consisting of cemented (quartz) sand

'**sand,storm** /-ˌstawm/ *n* a storm driving clouds of sand, esp in a desert

¹**sandwich** /'san(d)wij, -wich/ *n* **1a** two slices of usu buttered bread containing a layer of filling **b** a sponge cake containing a filling **2** sthg like a sandwich in having a layered or banded arrangement

²**sandwich** *v* **1** to insert *between* 2 things of a different quality or character **2** to create room or time for – often + *in* or *between*

³**sandwich** *adj* **1** of or used for sandwiches **2** *Br* of a sandwich course

'**sandwich ,board** *n* either of 2 boards hung at the front of and behind the body by straps from the shoulders and used esp for advertising

'**sandwich ,course** *n* a British vocational course consisting of alternate periods of some months' duration in college and in employment

sandy /'sandi/ *adj* **1** consisting of, containing, or sprinkled with sand **2** resembling sand in colour or texture – **sandiness** *n*

sane /sayn/ *adj* mentally sound – ~**ly** *adv* – ~**nity** *n*

sang /sang/ *past of* **sing**

sangfroid /ˌsong'frwah/ *n* imperturbability, esp under strain

sanguine /'sang·gwin/ *adj* **1** confident, optimistic **2** ruddy – ~**guinity** *n*

sanitary /'sanit(ə)ri/ *adj* **1** of or promoting health **2** free from danger to health

'**sanitary ,towel** *n* a disposable absorbent pad worn after childbirth or during menstruation to absorb the flow from the womb

sanitation /ˌsani'taysh(ə)n/ *n* (the promotion of hygiene and prevention of disease by) maintenance or improvement of sanitary conditions

sank /sangk/ *past of* **sink**

Sanskrit /'sanskrit/ *n* an ancient sacred Indic language of India and of Hinduism

Santa Claus /'santə ˌklawz, ˌ-- ˈ-/ *n* Father Christmas

¹**sap** /sap/ *n* **1a** a watery solution that circulates through a plant's vascular system **b** (the vital essential to life or) bodily health and vigour **2** a foolish gullible person – *infml*

²**sap** *n* **-pp-** the extension of a trench from within the trench itself to a point near an enemy's fortifications

³**sap** *v* **1** to destroy (as if) by undermining **2** to weaken or exhaust gradually **3** to operate against or pierce by a sap

sapling /'sapling/ *n* a young tree

sapper /'sapə/ *n* a (private) soldier of the Royal Engineers

sapphire /'safie·ə/ n 1 a semitransparent mineral of a colour other than red, used as a gem; esp a transparent rich blue sapphire 2 a deep purplish blue colour

sapwood /'sap,wood/ n the younger softer usu lighter-coloured living outer part of wood that lies between the bark and the heartwood

sarcasm /'sahkaz(ə)m/ n (the use of) caustic and often ironic language to express contempt or bitterness – **-castic** adj – **-castically** adv

sarcophagus /sah'kofəgəs/ n, pl **sarcophagi** /-gie/ also **sarcophaguses** a stone coffin

sardine /sah'deen/ n pl **sardines** also **sardine** the young of the European pilchard, or another small or immature fish, when of a size suitable for preserving for food

sardonic /sah'donik/ adj disdainfully or cynically humorous; derisively mocking – **-ally** adv

sarge /sahj/ n a sergeant – infml

sari also **saree** /'sahri/ n a garment worn by Hindu women that consists of a length of lightweight cloth draped so that one end forms a skirt and the other a head or shoulder covering

sarong /sə'rong, 'sahrong/ n a loose skirt made of a long strip of cloth wrapped round the body and traditionally worn by men and women in Malaysia and the Pacific islands

sartorial /sah'tawri·əl/ adj with regard to clothing – fml; used esp with reference to men – **~ly** adv

¹**sash** /sash/ n a band of cloth worn round the waist or over 1 shoulder as a dress accessory or as the emblem of an honorary or military order

²**sash** n, pl **sash** also **sashes** the framework in which panes of glass are set in a window or door; also such a framework forming a sliding part of a window

sat /sat/ past of **sit**

Satan /'sayt(ə)n/ n the adversary of God and lord of evil in Judaism and Christianity

satanic /sə'tanik/ adj 1 (characteristic) of Satan or satanism 2 extremely cruel or malevolent – **~ally** adv

satanism /'sayt(ə)niz(ə)m/ n, often cap 1 diabolism 2 the worship of Satan marked by the travesty of Christian rites

satchel /'sachəl/ n a usu stiff bag often with a shoulder strap; esp one carried by schoolchildren

sate /sayt/ v 1 to surfeit with sthg 2 to satisfy (e g a thirst) by indulging to the full

satellite /'satl·iet/ n 1 an obsequious follower 2a a celestial body orbiting another of larger size **b** a man-made object or vehicle intended to orbit a celestial body 3 a country subject to another more powerful country 4 an urban community that is physically separate from an adjacent city but dependent on it

satiate /'sayshi,ayt/ v to satisfy (e g a need or desire) to the point of excess – **-iety** n – **-iable** adj – **-iation** n

¹**satin** /'satin/ n a fabric (e g of silk) with lustrous face and dull back

²**satin** adj 1 made of satin 2 like satin, esp in lustrous appearance or smoothness

satire /'satie·ə/ n 1 a literary work holding up human vices and follies to ridicule or scorn 2 biting wit, irony, or sarcasm intended to expose foolishness or vice – **-ric, -rical** adj – **-rize** v

satisfaction /,satis'faksh(ə)n/ n 1a fulfilment of a need or want **b** being satisfied **c** a source of pleasure or fulfilment 2a compensation for a loss, insult, or injury **b** vindication of one's honour, esp through a duel 3 full assurance or certainty

satisfactory /,satis'fakt(ə)ri/ adj satisfying needs or requirements; adequate – **-rily** adv

satisfy /'satis,fie/ v 1a to discharge; carry out 2a to make content **b** to meet the requirements of 3 to convince 4 to conform to (e g criteria) – **~ing** adj

satsuma /sat'soohmə/ n a sweet seedless type of mandarin orange

saturate /'sachoorayt/ v 1 to treat or provide with sthg to the point where no more can be absorbed, dissolved, or retained 2 to cause to combine chemically until there is no further tendency to combine

saturation /,satchoo'raysh(ə)n/ n 1 the chromatic purity of a colour; freedom from dilution with white 2 the point at which a market is supplied with all the goods it will absorb 3 an overwhelming concentration of military forces or firepower

Saturday /'satəday, -di/ n the day of the week following Friday

Saturn /'satən, 'sa,tuhn/ n the planet 6th in order from the sun and conspicuous for its rings

saturnine /'satə,nien/ adj 1 gloomy 2 sullen

satyr /'satə/ n a Greek minor woodland deity having certain characteristics of a horse or goat and associated with revelry

¹**sauce** /saws/ n 1 a liquid or soft preparation used as a relish, dressing, or accompaniment to food 2 sthg adding zest or piquancy 3 cheek – infml

²**sauce** v to be impudent to – infml

saucepan /'sawspən/ n a deep usu cylindrical cooking pan typically having a long handle and a lid

saucer /'sawsə/ n a small usu circular shallow dish with a central depression in which a cup is set 2 a flying saucer

saucy /'sawsi/ adj 1a disrespectfully bold and impudent **b** engagingly forward and flippant 2 smart, trim – **saucily** adv – **sauciness** n

sauerkraut /'sowə,krowt/ n finely cut cabbage fermented in a brine made from its juice

sauna /'sawnə/ n a Finnish steam bath in which water is thrown on hot stones

saunter /'sawntə/ v to walk about in a casual manner

saurian /'sawri·ən/ *n* any of a group of reptiles including the lizards and formerly the crocodiles and dinosaurs

sausage /'sosij; *NAm* 'saw-/ *n* (sthg shaped like) a cylindrical mass of seasoned minced meat often mixed with a filler (e g bread) and enclosed in a casing usu of prepared animal intestine

sauté /'sawtay, 'soh-/ *v* **sautéing; sautéed, sautéd** /-tayd/ to fry in a small amount of fat – **sauté** *adj*

¹**savage** /'savij/ *adj* **1** not domesticated or under human control; untamed **2** rugged, rough **3** boorish, rude **4** lacking a developed culture – now usu taken to be offensive – ~**ly** *adv* – ~**ness**, ~**ry** *n*

²**savage** *n* **1** a member of a primitive society **2** a brutal, rude, or unmannerly person

³**savage** *v* to attack or treat brutally; *esp* to maul

savant /'sav(ə)nt/ *n* one who has exceptional knowledge of a particular field (e g science or literature)

¹**save** /sayv/ *v* **1** to rescue from danger or harm **2a** to put aside as a store or for a particular use – usu + *up* **b** to economize in the use of; conserve **3a** to make unnecessary **b** to prevent an opponent from scoring, winning, or scoring with – ~**r** *n*

²**save** *prep* except – chiefly fml

³**save** *conj* were it not; only – chiefly fml

¹**saving** /'sayving/ *n* **1** preservation from danger or destruction **2** sthg saved **3a** *pl* money put by over a period of time **b** the excess of income over expenditures – often *pl*

²**saving** *prep* **1** except, save **2** without disrespect to

saviour, *NAm chiefly* **savior** /'sayvyə/ *n* **1** one who brings salvation; *specif, cap* Jesus **2** one who saves sby or sthg from danger or destruction

savoir faire /,savwah 'feə/ *n* polished self-assurance in social behaviour

¹**savour,** *NAm chiefly* **savor** /'sayvə/ *n* **1** the characteristic taste or smell of sthg **2** a particular flavour or smell **3** a (pleasantly stimulating) distinctive quality

²**savour,** *NAm chiefly* **savor** *v* **1** to taste or smell with pleasure; relish **2** to delight in; enjoy

¹**savoury,** *NAm chiefly* **savory** /'sayv(ə)ri/ *adj* salty, spicy, meaty, etc, rather than sweet

²**savoury,** *NAm chiefly* **savory** *n* a dish of piquant or stimulating flavour served usu at the end of a main meal

¹**savvy** /'savi/ *v* to know, understand – slang

²**savvy** *n* practical know-how; shrewd judgment – slang

¹**saw** /saw/ *past of* **see**

²**saw** *n* a hand or power tool with a toothed part (e g a blade or disc) used to cut wood, metal, bone, etc

³**saw** *v* **sawed, sawn** /sawn/ **1** to cut or shape with a saw **2** to make motions as though using a saw

⁴**saw** *n* a maxim, proverb

'saw,dust /-,dust/ *n* fine particles of wood produced in sawing

'saw,mill /-,mil/ *n* a factory or machine that cuts wood

saxifrage /'saksifrij, -,frayj/ *n* any of a genus of usu showy-flowered plants often with tufted leaves

saxophone /'saksə,fohn/ *n* any of a group of single-reed woodwind instruments having a conical metal tube and finger keys – ~**nist** *n*

¹**say** /say/ *v* **says** /sez/; **said** /sed/ **1a** to state in spoken words **b** to form an opinion as to **2** to utter, pronounce **3a** to indicate, show **b** to give expression to; communicate **4a** to suppose, assume **b** to allege – usu pass – **I say** *chiefly Br* – used as a weak expression of surprise or to attract attention – **not to say** and indeed; or perhaps even – **say boo to a goose** to brave even trivial dangers – usu neg – **say fairer** *Br* to express oneself any more generously – **say when** to tell sby when to stop, esp when pouring a drink – **that is to say 1** in other words; in effect **2** or at least – **to say nothing of** without even considering; not to mention

²**say** *n* **1** an expression of opinion – esp in *have one's say* **2** a right or power to influence action or decisions; *esp* the authority to make final decisions

³**say** *adv* **1** at a rough estimate **2** for example

saying *n* a maxim, proverb

'say-,so *n* **1** one's unsupported assertion **2** the right of final decision

scab /skab/ *n* **1** scabies of domestic animals **2** a crust of hardened blood and serum over a wound **3** a blackleg **4** any of various plant diseases characterized by crusted spots; *also* any of these spots

scabbard /'skabəd/ *n* a sheath for a sword, dagger, or bayonet

scabies /'skaybiz/ *n, pl* **scabies** a skin disease, esp contagious itch or mange, caused by a parasitic mite and usu characterized by oozing scabs

scabious /'skaybi·əs/ *n* any of a genus of plants with flowers in dense heads at the end of usu long stalks

scabrous /'skaybrəs/ *adj* **1** rough to the touch with scales, scabs, raised patches, etc **2** dealing with indecent or offensive themes – fml

scaffold /'skafohld, -f(ə)ld/ *n* a platform on which a criminal is executed

scaffolding /'skafəlding/ *n* **1** a supporting framework **2** a temporary platform for workmen working above the ground

¹**scalar** /'skaylə/ *adj* **1** having a continuous series of steps **2** capable of being represented by a point on a scale

²**scalar** *n* **1** a real number rather than a vector **2** a quantity (e g mass or time) that has a magnitude describable by a real number, and no direction

¹**scald** /skawld/ *v* **1** to burn (as if) with hot liquid or steam **2a** to subject to boiling water or steam **b** to heat to just short of boiling

²**scald** n an injury to the body caused by scalding

scalding /'skawlding/ adj 1 boiling hot 2 biting, scathing

¹**scale** /skayl/ n 1a either pan of a balance b a beam that is supported freely in the centre and has 2 pans of equal weight suspended from its ends 2 an instrument or machine for weighing *USE* (1b, 2) usu pl with sing. meaning

²**scale** n 1 (a small thin plate resembling) a small flattened rigid plate forming part of the external body covering of a fish, reptile, etc 2 a small thin dry flake shed from the skin 3 a thin coating, layer, or incrustation; esp a hard incrustation usu of calcium sulphate or carbonate that is deposited on the inside of a kettle, boiler, etc by the evaporation or constant passage of hard water 4 a usu thin, membranous, chaffy, or woody modified leaf

³**scale** v 1 to cover with scale 2 to shed or separate or come off in scales; flake

⁴**scale** n 1 a graduated series of musical notes ascending or descending in order of pitch according to a specified scheme of their intervals 2 sthg graduated, esp when used as a measure or rule: e g 2a a linear region divided by lines into a series of spaces and used to register or record sthg (e g the height of mercury in a barometer) b a graduated line on a map or chart indicating the length used to represent a larger unit of measure c an instrument having a scale for measuring or marking off distances or dimensions a graduated system 4 a proportion between 2 sets of dimensions (e g between those of a drawing and its original) 5 a graded series of tests

⁵**scale** v 1 to climb up or reach (as if) by means of a ladder 2a to change the scale of b to pattern, make, regulate, set, or estimate according to some rate or standard *USE* (2) often + up or down — **to scale** according to the proportions of an established scale of measurement

scalene /'skayleen/ adj, of a triangle having the 3 sides of unequal length

scallion /'skalyən/ n 1 a leek 2 a spring onion 3 chiefly NAm a shallot

scallop /'skoləp/ n 1 a shellfish having 2 wavy-edged halves 2 one of a row of small curves forming a patterned edge

scallywag /'skali,wag/, NAm chiefly **scalawag** /'skalawag/ n a rascal

¹**scalp** /skalp/ n 1 the skin of the human head, usu covered with hair in both sexes 2a a part of the human scalp with attached hair cut or torn from an enemy as a trophy, esp formerly by N American Indian warriors b a trophy of victory

²**scalp** v 1 to remove the scalp of 2 NAm 2a to buy and sell to make small quick profits b to obtain speculatively and resell at greatly increased prices *USE* (2) infml

scalpel /'skalpl/ n a small very sharp straight thin-bladed knife used esp in surgery

scaly /'skayli/ adj flaky – **scaliness** n

¹**scamp** /skamp/ n an impish or playful young person

²**scamp** v to perform in a hasty, careless, or haphazard manner

¹**scamper** /'skampə/ v to run about nimbly and playfully

²**scamper** n a playful scurry

scampi /'skampi/ n, pl **scampi** a (large) prawn (often prepared with a batter coating)

¹**scan** /skan/ v **-nn-** 1 to check or read hastily or casually 2a to traverse (a region) with a controlled beam (e g radar) b to make a detailed examination of (e g the human body) using any of a variety of sensing devices (e g ones using ultrasonics, thermal radiation, X-rays, or radiation from radioactive materials) 3 of verse to conform to a metrical pattern

²**scan** n 1 a scanning 2 a radar or television trace

scandal /'skandl/ n 1 a circumstance or action that causes general offence or indignation or that disgraces those associated with it 2 malicious or defamatory gossip 3 indignation, chagrin, or bewilderment brought about by a flagrant violation of propriety or religious opinion – ~**ize** v

scandalous /'skandl-əs/ adj 1 libellous, defamatory 2 offensive to propriety – ~**ly** adv

Scandinavian /,skandi'nayvyən, -vi-ən/ n (a language of) a native or inhabitant of Scandinavia – **Scandinavian** adj

scanner /'skanə/ n 1 a device that automatically monitors a system or process 2 a device for sensing recorded data 3 the rotating aerial of a radar set

scansion /'skansh(ə)n/ n the way in which a piece of verse scans

¹**scant** /skant/ adj 1a barely sufficient; inadequate b lacking in quantity 2 having a small or insufficient supply

²**scant** v to restrict or withhold the supply of

scanty /'skanti/ adj scant; esp deficient in coverage – -**tily** adv – -**tiness** n

¹**scape,goat** /-,goht/ n sby or sthg made to bear the blame for others' faults

scapula /'skapyoolə/ n, pl **scapulae** /-li/, **scapulas** a large flat triangular bone at the upper part of each side of the back; the shoulder blade

¹**scar** /skah/ n a steep rocky place on a mountainside

²**scar** n 1 a mark left (e g on the skin) by the healing of injured tissue 2 a mark left on a stem after the fall of a leaf 3 a mark of damage or wear 4 a lasting moral or emotional injury

³**scar** v **-rr-** 1 to mark with or form a scar 2 to do lasting injury to

scarab /'skarəb/ n a representation of a beetle, usu made of stone or glazed earthenware, used in ancient Egypt esp as a talisman

scarce /skeəs/ adj 1 not plentiful or abundant 2 few in number; rare – ~ **ness, scarcity** n

scarcely /-li/ adv **1a** by a narrow margin; only just **b** almost not **2** not without unpleasantness or discourtesy

¹scare /skeə/ v **1** to frighten suddenly **2** to drive off by frightening – ~ **d** adj

²scare n **1** a sudden or unwarranted fright **2** a widespread state of alarm or panic

scarecrow /-,kroh/ n **1** an object usu suggesting a human figure, set up to frighten birds away from crops **2** a skinny or ragged person – infml

¹scarf /skahf/ n, pl **scarves** /skahvz/, **scarfs** a strip or square of cloth worn round the shoulders or neck or over the head for decoration or warmth

²scarf n, pl **scarfs 1** either of the bevelled or cut away ends that fit together to form a scarf joint **2 scarf, scarf joint** a joint made by bevelling, halving, or notching 2 pieces to correspond and lapping and bolting them

³scarf, scarph /skahf/ v **1** to unite by a scarf joint **2** to form a scarf on

scarify /'skeərifie, 'skari-/ v **1** to make scratches or small cuts in (e g the skin) **2** to wound the feelings of (e g by harsh criticism) **3** to break up and loosen the surface of (e g a field or road)

scarlet /'skahlət/ adj or n (of) a vivid red colour tinged with orange

scarlet fever n an infectious fever caused by a bacterium in which there is a red rash and inflammation of the nose, throat, and mouth

scarlet woman n a prostitute – euph

scarp /skahp/ n **1** the inner side of a ditch below the parapet of a fortification **2** a steep slope, esp a cliff face, produced by faulting or erosion

scarper /'skahpə/ v, Br to run away (e g from creditors) – infml

¹scat /skat/ v **-tt-** to depart rapidly – infml

²scat n jazz singing with nonsense syllables

scathing /'skaydhing/ adj bitterly severe – ~ **ly** adv

scatter /'skatə/ v **1** to cause (a group or collection) to separate widely **2a** to distribute in irregular intervals **b** to distribute recklessly and at random **3** to sow (seed) by casting in all directions **4** to reflect or disperse (e g a beam of radiation or particles) irregularly and diffusely – **scatter** n

scatterbrain /-,brayn/ n sby incapable of concentration – ~ **ed** adj

scatty /'skati/ adj, Br scatterbrained – infml – ~ **iness** n

scavenge /'skavinj/ v **1** to salvage from discarded or refuse material; also to salvage usable material from 2 to feed on (carrion or refuse) – ~ **r** n

scenario /si'nahri·oh, -'neə-/ n pl **scenarios 1** an outline or synopsis of a dramatic work **2a** a screenplay **b** a shooting script **3** an account or synopsis of a projected course of action

scene /seen/ n **1** any of the smaller subdivisions of a dramatic work: e g **1a** a division of an act presenting continuous action in 1 place **b** an episode, sequence, or unit of dialogue in a play, film, or television programme **2** a vista suggesting a stage setting **3** the place of an occurrence or action **4** an exhibition of unrestrained feeling **5** a sphere of activity or interest – slang — **behind the scenes** out of the public view; in secret

scenery /'seen(ə)ri/ n **1** the painted scenes or hangings and accessories used on a theatre stage **2** landscape, esp when considered attractive

scenic /'seenik/ also **scenical** /-kl/ adj **1** of the stage, a stage setting, or stage representation **2** of or displaying (fine) natural scenery – ~ **ally** adv

¹scent /sent/ v **1** to get or have an inkling of **2** to fill with a usu pleasant smell

²scent n **1** odour: e g **1a** a smell left by an animal on a surface it passes over **b** a characteristic or particular, esp agreeable, smell **c** a perfume **2a** power of smelling; the sense of smell **b** power of detection; a nose **3** a course of pursuit or discovery **4** a hint, suggestion – ~ **less** adj

sceptic /'skeptik/ n a person disposed to scepticism, esp regarding religion or religious principles

sceptical /'skeptikl/ adj of scepticism – ~ **ly** adv

scepticism /'skepti,siz(ə)m/ n **1** doubt concerning basic religious principles (e g immortality, providence, or revelation) **2** the doctrine that certain knowledge is unattainable either generally or in a particular sphere **3** an attitude of doubt, esp associated with implied criticism

sceptre, NAm chiefly scepter /'septə/ n **1** a staff borne by a ruler as an emblem of sovereignty **2** royal or imperial authority

¹schedule /'shedyool, -jəl; also, esp NAm ' skedyool, -jəl/ n **1** a statement of supplementary details appended to a document **2** a list, catalogue, or inventory **3** (the times fixed in) a timetable **4** a programme, proposal **5** a body of items to be dealt with

²schedule v **1a** to place on a schedule **b** to make a schedule of **2** to appoint or designate for a fixed time **3** Br to place on a list of buildings or historical remains protected by state legislation

schema /'skeemə/ n, pl **schemata** /-mətə/ a diagrammatic representation; a plan

schematic /ski'matik/ adj of a scheme or schema; diagrammatic – ~ **ally** adv

schematize, -ise /'skeemə,tiez/ v **1** to form into a systematic arrangement **2** to express or depict schematically

¹**scheme** /skeem/ *n* 1 a concise statement or table 2 a plan or programme of action; a project 3 a crafty or secret strategy 4 a systematic arrangement of parts or elements

²**scheme** *v* to make plans; *also* to plot, intrigue – **schemer** *n*

scherzo /'skeətsoh/ *n*, *pl* **scherzos, scherzi** /-tsi/ a lively instrumental musical composition or movement

schism /'siz(ə)m, 'skiz(ə)m/ *n* 1 separation into opposed factions 2 formal division in or separation from a religious body

¹**schismatic** /siz'matik, skiz-/ *n* a person who creates or takes part in schism

²**schismatic** *also* **schismatical** /-kl/ *adj* 1 (having the character) of schism 2 guilty of schism

schist /shist/ *n* a metamorphic crystalline rock composed of thin layers of minerals

schizoid /'skitsoyd/ *adj* of schizophrenia

schizophrenia /,skitsə'freenyə/ *n* a mental disorder characterized by loss of contact with reality and disintegration of personality, usu with hallucinations and disorder of feeling, behaviour, etc – **-nic** *n*, *adj* – **-nically** *adv*

schnapps /shnaps/ *n*, *pl* **schnapps** strong gin as orig made in the Netherlands

scholar /'skolə/ *n* 1 one who attends a school or studies under a teacher 2 one who has done advanced study 3 the holder of a scholarship

scholarly /-li/ *adj* learned, academic

scholarship /-ship/ *n* 1 a grant of money to a student 2 the character, methods, or attainments of a scholar; learning 3 a fund of knowledge and learning

scholastic /skə'lastik/ *adj* 1 suggestive or characteristic of a scholar or pedant, esp in specious subtlety or dryness 2 of schools or scholars

¹**school** /skoohl/ *n* 1a an institution for the teaching of children b a part of a university c an establishment offering specialized instruction 2 d *NAm* a college, university 2a a session of a school b a school building 3a people with a common doctrine or teacher (e g in philosophy or theology) b a group of artists under a common stylistic influence 4 a body of people with similar opinions

²**school** *v* 1 to educate in an institution of learning 2a to teach or drill in a specific knowledge or skill b to discipline or habituate to sthg

³**school** *n* a large number of fish or aquatic animals of 1 kind swimming together

'**school,boy** /-,boy/, *fem* '**school,girl** *n* a child still at school

'**school,house** /-,hows/ *n* a building used as a school; *esp* a country primary school

schooling /'skoohling/ *n* 1a instruction in school b training or guidance from practical experience 2 the cost of instruction and maintenance at school 3 the training of a horse to service

'**school,marm, schoolma'am** /-,mahm/ *n* 1 a prim censorious woman 2 *chiefly NAm* a female schoolteacher; *esp* a rural or small-town schoolmistress

'**school,master** /-,mahstə/, *fem* '**school,mistress** *n* a schoolteacher

'**school,teacher** /-,teechə/ *n* a person who teaches in a school

schooner /'skoohnə/ *n* 1 a fore-and-aft rigged sailing vessel having 2 or more masts 2 a relatively tall narrow glass

sciatic /sie'atik/ *adj* 1 of or situated near the hip 2 of or caused by sciatica

sciatica /sie'atikə/ *n* pain in the back of the thigh, buttocks, and lower back

science /'sie-əns/ *n* 1a a department of systematized knowledge b sthg (e g a skill) that may be learned systematically c any of the natural sciences 2a coordinated knowledge of the operation of general laws, esp as obtained and tested through scientific method b such knowledge of the physical world and its phenomena; natural science 3 a system or method (purporting to be) based on scientific principles – **scientist** *n*

,**science 'fiction** *n* fiction of a type orig set in the future and dealing principally with the impact of science on society or individuals, but now including also works of literary fantasy

scientific /,sie-ən'tifik/ *adj* of or exhibiting the methods of science – **-ally** *adv*

scimitar /'simitə, -tah/ *n* a chiefly Middle Eastern sword having a curved blade which narrows towards the hilt and is sharpened on the convex side

scintillate /'sinti,layt/ *v* 1 to emit sparks 2 to emit flashes as if throwing off sparks; *also* to sparkle, twinkle 3 to be brilliant or animated – **-lation** *n*

scion /'sie-ən/ *n* 1 a detached living part of a plant joined to a stock in grafting and usu supplying parts above ground of the resulting graft 2 a (male) descendant or offspring

scissors /'sizəz/ *n pl* a cutting instrument with 2 blades pivoted so that their cutting edges slide past each other

sclerosis /sklə'rohsis/ *n* (a disease characterized by) abnormal hardening of tissue, esp from overgrowth of fibrous tissue

¹**scoff** /skof/ *n* an expression of scorn, derision, or contempt – **~er** *n*

²**scoff** *v* to show contempt by derisive acts or language – often + *at*

³**scoff** *v*, *chiefly Br* to eat, esp greedily, rapidly, or in an ill-mannered way – *infml*

¹**scold** /skohld/ *n* a woman who habitually nags or quarrels

²**scold** *v* 1 to find fault noisily and at length 2 to reprove sharply – **~ing** *n*

scollop /'skoləp/ *n* a scallop

scone /skohn; *or* skon/ *n* any of several small light cakes made from a dough or batter containing a raising agent and baked in a hot oven or on a griddle

¹**scoop** /skoohp/ *n* **1a** a large ladle for taking up or skimming liquids **b** a deep shovel for lifting and moving granular material (e g corn or sand) **c** a handled utensil of shovel shape or with a hemispherical bowl for spooning out soft food (e g ice cream) **2a** an act or the action of scooping **b** the amount held by a scoop **3** a cavity **4** material for publication or broadcast, esp when obtained ahead or to the exclusion of competitors

²**scoop** *v* **1** to take out or up (as if) with a scoop **2** to empty by scooping **3** to make hollow; dig out **4** to obtain a news story in advance or to the exclusion of (a competitor)

scoot /skooht/ *v* to go suddenly and swiftly – *infml*

scooter /'skoohtə/ *n* **1** a child's foot-operated vehicle consisting of a narrow board with usu 1 wheel at each end and an upright steering handle **2** a motor scooter

¹**scope** /skohp/ *n* **1** space or opportunity for unhampered action, thought, or development **2a** extent of treatment, activity, or influence **b** extent of understanding or perception

²**scope** *n* a periscope, telescope, or other optical instrument – *infml*

¹**scorch** /skawch/ *v* **1** to burn so as to produce a change in colour and texture **2a** to parch (as if) with intense heat **b** to criticize or deride bitterly **3** to devastate completely, esp before abandoning – used in *scorched earth*, of property of possible use to an enemy **4** to travel at (excessive) speed

²**scorch** *n* a mark resulting from scorching

scorcher /'skawchə/ *n* a very hot day – *infml*

¹**score** /skaw/ *n pl* **scores**, (1a, b) **scores**, **score 1a** twenty **b** a group of 20 things – used in combination with a cardinal number **c** *pl* an indefinite large number **2** a line (e g a scratch or incision) made (as if) with a sharp instrument **3** an account of debts **4** a grudge **5a** a reason, ground **b** a subject, topic **6a** the copy of a musical composition in written or printed notation **b** the music for a film or theatrical production **7a** a number that expresses accomplishment (e g in a game or test) **b** an act (e g a goal, run, or try) in any of various games or contests that increases such a number **8** the inescapable facts of a situation

²**score** *v* **1a** to enter (a debt) in an account – usu + *to* or *against* **b** to cancel or strike out (e g record of a debt) with a line or notch – often + *out* **2** to mark with grooves, scratches, or notches **3a(1)** to gain (e g points) in a game or contest **a(2)** to have as a value in a game or contest **b** to gain, win **c** to gain or have an advantage or a success **d** to obtain illicit drugs – *slang* **e** to achieve a sexual success –

slang **4** to write or arrange (music) for specific voice or instrumental parts — **score off someone** *Br* to get the better of sby in debate or argument

'**score,board** /-,bawd/ *n* a usu large board for displaying the state of play (e g the score) in a game or match

¹**scorn** /skawn/ *n* disdain or derision – ~**ful** *adj* – ~**fully** *adv*

²**scorn** *v* to reject with outspoken contempt

Scorpio /'skawpioh/ *n* (sby born under) the 8th sign of the zodiac in astrology, which is pictured as a scorpion

scorpion /'skawpyən/ *n* any of an order of arachnids having an elongated body and a narrow tail bearing a venomous sting at the tip

scotch /skoch/ *v* **1** to stamp out; crush **2** to hinder, thwart

¹**Scotch** *adj* Scottish

²**Scotch** *n pl in constr* the Scots **2** *often not cap* Scotch whisky *n*

,**Scotch 'broth** *n* soup made from beef or mutton, vegetables, and barley

,**Scotch 'egg** *n* a hard-boiled egg covered with sausage meat, coated with breadcrumbs, and deep-fried

,**scot-'free** *adj* without any penalty, payment, or injury

,**Scotland 'Yard** /'skotlənd/ *n sing or pl in constr* the criminal investigation department of the London metropolitan police force

Scottish /'skotish/ *adj* (characteristic) of Scotland

,**Scottish 'terrier** *n* (any of) a Scottish breed of terrier with short legs and a very wiry coat of usu black hair

scoundrel /'skowndrəl/ *n* a wicked or dishonest fellow

¹**scour** /'skowə/ *v* **1** to move through or range over usu swiftly **2** to make a rapid but thorough search of

²**scour** *v* **1** to rub vigorously in order to cleanse **2** to clear, excavate, or remove (as if) by a powerful current of water

¹**scourge** /skuhj/ *n* **1a** a whip **b** a means of vengeance or criticism **2** a cause of affliction

²**scourge** *v* **1** to whip **2** to punish severely

¹**scout** /skowt/ *v* **1** to observe or explore in order to obtain information **2** to find by making a search – often + *out* or *up*

²**scout** *n* **1** sby or sthg sent to obtain (military) information **2** *often cap* a member of a worldwide movement of boys and young men that was founded with the aim of developing leadership and comradeship and that lays stress on outdoor activities

'**scout,master** /-,mahstə/ *n* the adult leader of a troop of scouts – no longer used technically

¹**scowl** /skowl/ *v* **1** to frown or wrinkle the brows in expression of displeasure **2** to exhibit a gloomy or threatening aspect

²**scowl** *n* an angry frown

¹**scrabble** /'skrabl/ *v* **scrabbling** /'skrabling/ **1** to scratch or scrape about **2a** to scramble, clamber **b** to struggle frantically *USE* infml

²**scrabble** *n* **1** a persistent scratching or clawing **2** a scramble *USE* infml

Scrabble *trademark* – used for a board game of word-building from individual letters

¹**scrag** /skrag/ *n* **1** a scraggy person or animal **2** a neck of mutton or veal

²**scrag** *v* **-gg-** **1** to kill or execute by hanging, garrotting, or wringing the neck of **2** to attack in anger – infml

scraggy /'skragi/ *adj* lean and lanky in growth or build

scram /skram/ *v* **-mm-** to go away at once – infml

¹**scramble** /'skrambl/ *v* **scrambling** /'skrambling/ **1a** to move or climb using hands and feet, esp hastily **b** to move with urgency or panic **2** to struggle eagerly or chaotically for possession of sthg **3a** to toss or mix together **b** to prepare (eggs) in a pan by stirring during cooking **4** *esp of an aircraft or its crew* to take off quickly in response to an alert **5** to collect by scrambling – + *up* or *together* **6** to encode (the elements of a telecommunications transmission) in order to make unintelligible on unmodified receivers

²**scramble** *n* **1** a scrambling movement or struggle **2** a disordered mess; a jumble **3** a rapid emergency takeoff of aircraft **4** a motorcycle race over very rough ground

¹**scrap** /skrap/ *n* **1** *pl* fragments of leftover food **2a** a small detached fragment **b** the smallest piece **3a** the residue from a manufacturing process **b** manufactured articles or parts, esp of metal, rejected or discarded and useful only for reprocessing

²**scrap** *v* **-pp-** **1** to convert into scrap **2** to abandon or get rid of, as without further use

³**scrap** *v or n* **-pp-** (to engage in) a minor fight or dispute – infml

'**scrap,book** /-ˌbook/ *n* a blank book in which miscellaneous items (e g newspaper cuttings or postcards) may be pasted

¹**scrape** /skrayp/ *v* **1a** to remove (clinging matter) from a surface by usu repeated strokes of an edged instrument **b** to make (a surface) smooth or clean with strokes of an edged or rough instrument **2** to grate harshly over or against **3** to collect or procure (as if) by scraping – often + *up* or *together* **4** to get by with difficulty or succeed by a narrow margin – often + *in*, *through*, or *by*

²**scrape** *n* **1a** an act, process, or result of scraping **b** the sound of scraping **2** a disagreeable predicament, esp as a result of foolish behaviour – infml

scrappy /'skrapi/ *adj* consisting of scraps

¹**scratch** /skrach/ *v* **1** to use the claws or nails in digging, tearing, or wounding **2** to scrape or rub oneself (e g to relieve itching) **3** to acquire money by hard work and saving **4** to make a thin grating sound **5** to withdraw (an entry) from competition

²**scratch** *n* **1** a mark, injury, or slight wound (produced by scratching) **2** the sound of scratching **3** the most rudimentary beginning – in *from scratch* **4** standard or satisfactory condition or performance

³**scratch** *adj* **1** arranged or put together haphazardly or hastily **2** without handicap or allowance

scratchy /'skrachi/ *adj* **1** tending to scratch or irritate **2** making a scratching noise **3** uneven in quality **4** irritable, fractious – **scratchiness** *n*

scrawl /skrawl/ *v* to write or draw awkwardly, hastily, or carelessly – **scrawl** *n*

scrawny /'skrawni/ *adj* exceptionally thin and slight

¹**scream** /skreem/ *v* **1a** to voice a sudden piercing cry, esp in alarm or pain **b** to move with or make a shrill noise like a scream **2** to produce a vivid or startling effect

²**scream** *n* **1** a shrill penetrating cry or noise **2** sby or sthg that provokes screams of laughter – infml

screamingly /'skreemingli/ *adv* extremely

scree /skree/ *n* (a mountain slope covered with) loose stones or rocky debris

¹**screech** /skreech/ *v* **1** to utter a shrill piercing cry; cry out, esp in terror or pain **2** to make a sound like a screech

²**screech** *n* a shrill sound or cry

screed /skreed/ *n* **1** an overlong usu dull piece of writing **2** a strip (e g of plaster) serving as a guide to the thickness of a subsequent coat

¹**screen** /skreen/ *n* **1** a usu movable piece of furniture that gives protection from heat or draughts or is used as an ornament **2a** sthg that shelters, protects, or conceals **b** a shield for secret usu illicit practices **3** a frame holding a netting used esp in a window or door to exclude mosquitoes and other pests **4a** a surface on which images are projected or reflected **b** the surface on which the image appears in a television or radar receiver **5a** the film industry; films

²**screen** *v* **1** to guard from injury, danger, or punishment **2** to examine systematically so as to separate into different groups **3** to show or broadcast a film or television programme

'**screen,play** /-ˌplay/ *n* the script of a film including description of characters, details of scenes and settings, dialogue, and stage directions

¹**screw** /skrooh/ *n* **1a** a usu pointed tapering metal rod having a raised thread along all or part of its length and a usu slotted head which may be driven into a body by rotating (e g with a screwdriver) **b** a screw-bolt that can be turned by a screwdriver **2** sthg like a screw in form or function; a spiral **3** a propeller **4** *chiefly Br* a small

twisted paper packet (e g of tobacco) **5** sby who drives a hard bargain – slang **6** a prison guard – slang **7** an act of sexual intercourse – vulg

²**screw** v **1a** to attach, close, operate, adjust, etc by means of a screw **b** to unite or separate by means of a screw or a twisting motion **2a** to contort (the face) or narrow (the eyes) (e g with effort or an emotion) – often + up **b** to crush into irregular folds – usu + up **3** to increase the intensity, quantity, or effectiveness of – usu + up **4a** to make oppressive demands on **b** to extract by pressure or threat – usu + from or out of **5** to copulate with – vulg

screw,driver /-,drievə/ n a tool for turning screws

screw top n (an opening designed to take) a cover secured by twisting

screw up v **1** to bungle, botch **2** to cause to become anxious or neurotic USE slang

screwy /'skrooh·i/ adj crazily absurd, eccentric, or unusual; also mad – infml

scribble /'skribl/ v **scribbling** /'skribling/ to write or draw without regard for legibility or coherence – **scribble** n

scribbler /'skriblə/ n a minor or worthless author

¹**scribe** /skrieb/ n **1** a member of a learned class of lay jurists in ancient Israel up to New Testament times **2** a copier of manuscripts **3** an author; specif a journalist – chiefly humor

²**scribe** v **1** to mark a line on by scoring with a pointed instrument **2** to make (e g a line) by scratching or gouging

scrimmage /'skrimij/ v or n (to take part in) a confused fight or minor battle; a mêlée

scrimp /skrimp/ v to be frugal or niggardly – esp in scrimp and save

¹**script** /skript/ n **1a** sthg written; text **b** an original document **c** the written text of a stage play, film, or broadcast (used in production or performance) **2a** (printed lettering resembling) handwriting **b** the characters used in the alphabet of a particular language

²**script** v to prepare a script for or from

scripture /'skripchə/ n **1a** often cap the sacred writings of a religion; esp the Bible – often pl with sing. meaning **b** a passage from the Bible **2** an authoritative body of writings – **-ral** adj

scroll /skrohl/ n **1** a written document in the form of a roll **2** a stylized ornamental design imitating the spiral curves of a scroll

scrooge /skroohj/ n, often cap a miserly person – infml

scrotum /'skrohtəm/ n, pl **scrota** /-tə/, **scrotums** the external pouch of most male mammals that contains the testes

¹**scrounge** /skrownj/ v **1** to hunt around **2** to wheedle, beg

²**scrounge** n — **on the scrounge** attempting to obtain sthg by wheedling or cajoling

¹**scrub** /skrub/ n (an area covered with) vegetation consisting chiefly of stunted trees or shrubs

²**scrub** v **-bb- 1** to clean by rubbing, esp with a stiff brush **2** to abolish; do away with; also to cancel – infml

scrubber /'skrubə/ n **1** Br a girl who is readily available for casual sex; also a prostitute **2** Br a coarse or unattractive person USE slang

scrubby /'skrubi/ adj **1** inferior in size or quality; stunted **2** lacking distinction; trashy – infml

¹**scruff** /skruf/ n the back of the neck; the nape

²**scruff** n an untidily dressed or grubby person – infml

scruffy /'skrufi/ adj **1** seedy, disreputable **2** slovenly and untidy, esp in appearance

scrum /skrum/ n **1** a set piece in rugby in which the forwards of each side crouch in a tight formation with the 2 front rows of each team meeting shoulder to shoulder so that the ball can be put in play between them **2** a disorderly struggle

scrum-'half n the player in rugby who puts the ball into the scrum

scrummage /'skrumij/ v or n (to take part in) a scrum

scrumptious /'skrum(p)shəs/ adj, esp of food delicious – infml

scrumpy /'skrumpi/ n, Br dry rough cider

scrunch /skrunch/ v **1** to crunch, crush **2** to crumple – often + up – **scrunch** n

scruple /'skroohpl/ n a unit of weight equal to 20 grains, $\frac{1}{3}$ drachm, or $\frac{1}{24}$ ounce, usu used by apothecaries

²**scruple** n a moral consideration that inhibits action

³**scruple** v to be reluctant on grounds of conscience

scrupulous /'skroohpyooləs/ adj **1** inclined to have moral scruples **2** painstakingly exact – **~ly** adv – **~ness** n

scrutineer /,skroohti'niə/ n, Br sby who examines or observes sthg, esp the counting of votes at an election

scrutiny /'skroohtini/ n **1** a searching study, inquiry, or inspection **2** a searching or critical look **3** close watch – **-nize** v

scuba /'sk(y)oohbə/ n an aqualung

¹**scud** /skud/ v **-dd- 1** to move or run swiftly, esp as if swept along **2** of a ship to run before a gale

²**scud** n **1** ocean spray or loose vaporizing clouds driven swiftly by the wind **2** a gust of wind

scuff /skuf/ v **1** to slouch along without lifting the feet **2** to become scratched or roughened by wear – **scuff** n

¹**scuffle** /'skufl/ v **scuffling** /'skufling/ **1** to struggle confusedly and at close quarters **2** to move (hurriedly) about with a shuffling gait

²**scuffle** n a confused impromptu usu brief fight

scu 536

¹**scull** /skul/ *n* **1** an oar worked to and fro over the stern of a boat as a means of propulsion **2** either of a pair of light oars used by a single rower

²**scull** *v* to propel a boat by sculls or by a large oar worked to and fro over the stern – ~**er** *n*

scullery /'skul(ə)ri/ *n* a room for menial kitchen work (e g washing dishes and preparing vegetables)

scullion /'skulyən/ *n, archaic* a kitchen servant

sculptor /'skulptə/, *fem* **sculptress** /-tris/ *n* an artist who sculptures

¹**sculpture** /'skulpchə/ *n* **1** the art of creating three-dimensional works of art out of mouldable or hard materials by carving, modelling, casting, etc **2** (a piece of) work produced by sculpture – ~**ral** *adj*

²**sculpture** *v* **1a** to represent in sculpture **b** to form (e g wood or stone) into a sculpture **2** to shape (as if) by carving or moulding

scum /skum/ *n* **1** pollutants or impurities risen to or collected on the surface of a liquid **2** *pl in constr* the lowest class; the dregs

¹**scupper** /'skupə/ *n* an opening in a ship's side for draining water from the deck

²**scupper** *v, Br* to wreck; put paid to – *infml*

scurf /skuhf/ *n* dandruff – ~**y** *adj*

scurrilous /'skuriləs/ *adj* **1** wicked and unscrupulous in behaviour **2** containing obscenities or coarse abuse – ~**ly** *adv* – ~**ness, -ility** *n*

scurry /'skuri/ *v* to move briskly, esp with short hurried steps, and often in some agitation or confusion; scamper

¹**scurvy** /'skuhvi/ *adj* disgustingly mean or contemptible – **scurvily** *adv*

²**scurvy** *n* a disease caused by lack of vitamin C and marked by loosening of the teeth, and bleeding under the skin

scut /skut/ *n* a short erect tail (e g of a hare)

¹**scuttle** /'skutl/ *n* a vessel that resembles a bucket and is used for storing and carrying coal

²**scuttle** *v* **1** to sink (a ship) by making holes in the hull or opening the sea-cocks **2** to destroy, wreck

³**scuttle** *v* **scuttling** /'skutling/ to scurry, scamper

⁴**scuttle** *n* **1** a quick shuffling pace **2** a short swift dash; *esp* a swift departure

scythe /siedh/ *n* a long curving blade fastened at an angle to a long handle for cutting standing plants, esp grass – **scythe** *v*

sea /see/ *n* **1** an ocean; *broadly* the waters of the earth as distinguished from the land and air **2** sthg vast or overwhelming likened to the sea **3** the seafaring life **4** any of several dark areas on the surface of the moon or Mars — **at sea 1** on the sea; *specif* on a sea voyage **2** unable to understand; bewildered

'**sea ,nemone** *n* any of numerous brightly coloured polyps with a cluster of tentacles superficially resembling a flower

'**sea,board** /-,bawd/ *n* (the land near) a seashore

'**sea,borne** /-,bawn/ *adj* conveyed on or over the sea

'**sea ,change** *n* a complete transformation

'**sea,faring** /-,fering/ *n* travel by sea; *esp* the occupation of a sailor

'**sea,food** /-,foohd/ *n* edible marine fish, shellfish, crustaceans, etc

'**sea,front** /-,frunt/ *n* the waterfront of a seaside town

'**sea,girt** /-,guht/ *adj* surrounded by the sea – poetic

'**sea ,gull** *n* any of various sea birds

'**sea ,horse** *n* any of numerous small fishes whose head and body are shaped like the head and neck of a horse

¹**seal** /seel/ *n* any of numerous marine flesh-eating mammals chiefly of cold regions with limbs modified into webbed flippers for swimming

²**seal** *n* **1a** an emblem or word impressed or stamped on a document as a mark of authenticity **b** an article used to impress such a word or emblem (e g on wax); *also* a disc, esp of wax, bearing such an impression **2a** a closure (e g a wax seal on a document or a strip of paper over the cork of a bottle) that must be broken in order to give access, and so guarantees that the item so closed has not been tampered with **b** a tight and effective closure (e g against gas or liquid)

³**seal** *v* **1** to confirm or make secure (as if) by a seal **2** to attach an authenticating seal to; *also* to authenticate, ratify **3** to close or make secure against access, leakage, or passage by a fastening or coating; *esp* to make airtight **4** to determine irrevocably

'**sea ,legs** *n pl* bodily adjustment to the motion of a ship, indicated esp by ability to walk steadily and by freedom from seasickness

sealer /'seelə/ *n* a coat (e g of size) applied to prevent subsequent coats of paint or varnish from being too readily absorbed

'**sealing ,wax** /'seeling/ *n* a resinous composition that becomes soft when heated and is used for sealing letters, parcels, etc

'**sea ,lion** *n* any of several large Pacific seals

¹**seam** /seem/ *n* **1** a line of stitching joining 2 separate pieces of fabric, esp along their edges **2** a line, groove, or ridge formed at the meeting of 2 edges **3** a layer or stratum of coal, rock, etc – ~**less** *adj*

²**seam** *v* **1** to join (as if) by sewing **2** to mark with a seam, furrow, or scar

seaman /'seemən/ *n* **1** a sailor, mariner **2** a member of the navy holding any of the lowest group of ranks below Petty Officer

seamstress /'seemstris/ *n* a woman whose occupation is sewing

seamy /'seemi/ *adj* unpleasant, sordid – **seaminess** *n*

séance /'say·on(h)s/ *n* a meeting at which spiritualists attempt to communicate with the dead

¹**sear** /siə/ *adj* shrivelled, withered

²**sear** *v* 1 to make withered and dried up 2 to burn, scorch, or injure (as if) with a sudden application of intense heat

³**sear** *n* a mark or scar left by searing

¹**search** /suhch/ *v* 1a to look through or over carefully or thoroughly in order to find or discover sthg b to examine (a person) for concealed articles (e g weapons or drugs) c to scrutinize, esp in order to discover intention or nature 2 to uncover or ascertain by investigation – usu + *out* – **~er** *n* — **search me** — used to express ignorance of an answer

²**search** *n* 1 an act or process of searching; *esp* an organized act of searching 2 an exercise of the right of search

searching /'suhching/ *adj* piercing, penetrating – **~ly** *adv*

'**search,light** /-,liet/ *n* (an apparatus for projecting) a movable beam of light

'**sea,shell** /-,shel/ *n* the shell of a sea animal, esp a mollusc

,**sea'shore** /-'shaw/ *n* land (between high and low water marks) next to the sea

'**sea,sick** /-,sik/ *adj* suffering from the motion sickness associated with travelling by boat or hovercraft – **~ness** *n*

'**sea,side** /-,sied/ *n* (a holiday resort or beach on) land bordering the sea

¹**season** /'seez(ə)n/ *n* 1 any of the 4 quarters into which the year is commonly divided 2 a period characterized by a particular kind of weather 3 the time of year when a place is most frequented — **in season** 1 *of food* readily available and in the best condition for eating 2 *of game* legally available to be hunted or caught 3 *of an animal* on heat 4 *esp of advice* given when most needed or most welcome — **out of season** not in season

²**season** *v* 1 to give (food) more flavour by adding seasoning or savoury ingredients 2a to treat or expose (e g timber) over a period so as to prepare for use b to make fit or expert by experience

seasonable /'seez(ə)nnəbl/ *adj* 1 occurring in good or proper time; opportune 2 suitable to the season or circumstances – **-bly** *adv*

seasonal /'seez(ə)nl/ *adj* 1 of, occurring, or produced at a particular season 2 determined by seasonal need or availability

seasoning /'seez(ə)ning/ *n* a condiment, spice, herb, etc added to food primarily for the savour that it imparts

'**season ,ticket** *n, Br* a ticket sold, usu at a reduced price, for an unlimited number of trips over the same route during a limited period

¹**seat** /seet/ *n* 1a a piece of furniture (e g a chair, stool, or bench) for sitting in or on b the part of sthg on which one rests when sitting; *also* the

buttocks 2a a special chair (e g a throne) of sby in authority; *also* the status symbolized by it b a large country mansion 3a a place where sthg is established or practised b a place from which authority is exercised 4 a bodily part in which a particular function, disease, etc is centred 5 posture in or a way of sitting on horseback

²**seat** *v* 1a to cause to sit or assist in finding a seat b to put (e g oneself) in a sitting position 2 to fit to or with a seat 3, *of a garment* to become baggy in the area covering the buttocks

'**seat ,belt** *n* an arrangement of straps designed to secure a person in a seat in an aeroplane, vehicle, etc

seating /'seeting/ *n* 1a the act of providing with seats b the arrangement of seats (e g in a theatre) 2a material for upholstering seats b a base on or in which sthg rests

'**sea ,urchin** *n* any of a class of echinoderms usu with a thin shell covered with movable spines

'**sea,way** /-,way/ *n* 1 a ship's headway 2 the sea as a route for travel 3 a deep inland waterway that admits ocean shipping

'**sea,weed** /-,weed/ *n* (an abundant growth of) a plant, specif an alga, growing in the sea, typically having thick slimy fronds

'**sea,worthy** /-,wuhdhi/ *adj* fit or safe for a sea voyage

sebaceous /si'bayshəs/ *adj* of, producing, or being fatty material secreted from the skin

sec /sek/ *n, Br* a second, moment – *infml*

secede /si'seed/ *v* to withdraw from an organization (e g a church or federation) – **secession, secessionist** *n*

seclude /si'kloohd/ *v* to remove or separate from contact with others

se'cluded *adj* 1 screened or hidden from view 2 living in isolation – **-usion** *n*

¹**second** /'sekənd/ *adj* 1a next to the first in place or time b(1) next to the first in value, quality, or degree b(2) inferior, subordinate c standing next below the top in authority or importance 2 alternate, other 3 resembling or suggesting a prototype 4 being the forward gear or speed 1 higher than first in a motor vehicle — **at second hand** from or through an intermediary

²**second** *n* 1a a number two in a countable series b sthg that is next after the first in rank, position, authority, or precedence 2 sby who aids, supports, or stands in for another; *esp* the assistant of a duellist or boxer 3 a slightly flawed or inferior article (e g of merchandise) 4a a place next below the first in a contest b *also* **second class** *often cap* the second level of British honours degree 5 the second forward gear or speed of a motor vehicle 6 *pl* a second helping of food – *infml*

³**second** *n* 1 a 60th part of a minute of time or of a minute of angular measure 2 a moment

⁴second *v* **1** to give support or encouragement to **2** to endorse (a motion or nomination) – ~**er** *n* – ~**ment** *n*

⁵second /si'kond/ *v* to release (e g a teacher, businessman, or military officer) from a regularly assigned position for temporary duty with another organization

secondary /'sekənd(ə)ri/ *adj* **1** of second rank or importance **2** immediately derived from sthg primary or basic; derivative **3a** not first in order of occurrence or development **b** of the second order or stage in a series or sequence

secondary modern, secondary modern school *n* a secondary school formerly providing a practical rather than academic type of education

,second-'best *adj* next after the best

second 'childhood *n* dotage

¹second-'class *adj* **1** of a second class **2** inferior, mediocre; *also* socially, politically, or economically deprived

²second-class *adv* **1** in accommodation next below the best **2** by second-class mail

second class *n* the second and usu next to highest group in a classification

Second Coming *n* the return of Christ to judge the world on the last day

¹second'hand /-'hand/ *adj* **1** not original; derivative **2** acquired after being owned by another

²secondhand *adv* indirectly; at second hand

second lieutenant *n* an army officer of the lowest rank

,second 'nature *n* an action or ability that practice has made instinctive

second person *n* (any of) a set of linguistic forms referring to the person or thing addressed (e g 'you')

,second-'rate *adj* of inferior quality or value

,second 'sight *n* clairvoyance, precognition

secrecy /'seekrəsi/ *n* **1** the habit or practice of keeping secrets or maintaining privacy or concealment **2** the condition of being hidden or concealed

¹secret /'seekrit/ *adj* **1a** kept or hidden from knowledge or view **b** conducted in secret **2** revealed only to the initiated; esoteric **3** containing information whose unauthorized disclosure could endanger national security – ~**ly** *adv*

²secret *n* **1** sthg kept hidden or unexplained **2** a fact concealed from others or shared confidentially with a few — **in secret** in a private place or manner; in secrecy

secret agent *n* a spy

secretariat /,sekrə'teəri·ət/ *n* **1** the office of secretary **2** the clerical staff of an organization **3** a government administrative department

secretary /'sekrətri, -,teri/ *n* **1** sby employed to handle correspondence and manage routine work for a superior **2** an officer of an organization or

society responsible for its records and correspondence **3** an officer of state who superintends a government administrative department – **-rial** *adj*

'secretary ,bird *n* a large long-legged African bird of prey that feeds largely on reptiles

,secretary-'general *n pl* **secretaries-general** a principal administrative officer (e g of the United Nations)

¹secrete /si'kreet/ *v* to form and give off (a secretion)

²secrete *v* to deposit in a hidden place

secretion /si'kreesh(ə)n/ *n* **1** (a product formed by) the bodily process of making and releasing some material either functionally specialized (e g a hormone, saliva, latex, or resin) or isolated for excretion (e g urine) **2** the act of hiding sthg

secretive /'seekrətiv/ *adj* inclined to secrecy; not open or outgoing in speech or behaviour – ~**ly** *adv* – ~**ness** *n*

secret service *n* a (secret) governmental agency concerned with national security or intelligence gathering

sect /sekt/ *n* **1** a (heretical) dissenting or schismatic religious body **2a** a group maintaining strict allegiance to a doctrine or leader **b** a party; *esp* a faction

¹sectarian /sek'teəri·ən/ *n* **1** a (fanatical) adherent of a sect **2** a bigoted person

²sectarian *adj* **1** (characteristic) of a sect or sectarian **2** limited in character or scope; parochial

¹section /'seksh(ə)n/ *n* **1** the action or an instance of (separating by) cutting; *esp* the action of dividing sthg (e g tissues) surgically **2** a distinct part or portion of sthg written; *esp* a subdivision of a chapter **3** the profile of sthg as it would appear if cut through by an intersecting plane **4** a distinct part of an area, community, or group **5** *sing or pl in constr* a subdivision of a platoon, troop, or battery that is the smallest tactical military unit **6** any of several component parts that may be separated and reassembled **7** a division of an orchestra composed of 1 class of instruments

²section *v* **1** to cut or separate into sections **2** to represent in sections (e g by a drawing)

sectional /'seksh(ə)nl/ *adj* **1** restricted to a particular group or locality **2** composed of or divided into sections

sectionalism /'seksh(ə)nl,iz(ə)m/ *n* an excessive concern for the interests of a region or group

sector /'sektə/ *n* **1** a portion of a military area of operation **2** a part of a field or activity, esp of business, trade, etc

secular /'sekyoolə/ *adj* **1a** of this world rather than the heavenly or spiritual **b** not overtly or specifically religious **2** taking place once in an age or a century

secularism /'sekyooǝ,riz(ǝ)m/ n disregard for or rejection of religious beliefs and practices – **-ist** n, adj

¹**secure** /si'kyooǝ/ adj **1a** free from danger **b** free from risk of loss **c** firm, dependable; esp firmly fastened **2** assured, certain – **~ly** adv

²**secure** v **1a** to make safe from risk or danger **b** to guarantee against loss **c** to give pledge of payment to (a creditor) or of (an obligation) **2** to make fast; shut tightly **3** to obtain or bring about, esp as the result of effort

security /si'kyooǝrǝti/ n **1a** freedom from danger, fear, or anxiety **b** stability, dependability **2** sthg pledged to guarantee the fulfilment of an obligation **3** an evidence of debt or of ownership (e g a stock certificate) **4a** protection **b** measures taken to protect against esp espionage or sabotage

Security Council n a permanent council of the United Nations responsible for the maintenance of peace and security

sedan chair n a portable often enclosed chair, esp of the 17th and 18th c, designed to seat 1 person and be carried on poles by 2 people

¹**sedate** /si'dayt/ adj calm and even in temper or pace – **~ly** adv – **~ness** n

²**sedate** v to give a sedative to – **-ation** n

sedative /'sedǝtiv/ n or adj (sthg, esp a drug) tending to calm or to tranquillize nervousness or excitement

sedentary /'sed(ǝ)ntri/ adj **1** esp of birds not migratory **2** doing or involving much sitting

sedge /sej/ n any of a family of usu tufted marsh plants differing from grasses in having solid stems – **sedgy** adj

sediment /'sedimǝnt/ n **1** the matter that settles to the bottom of a liquid **2** material deposited by water, wind, or glaciers

sedimentary /,sedi'ment(ǝ)ri/ adj **1** of or containing sediment **2** formed by or from deposits of sediment

sedimentation /,sedimen'taysh(ǝ)n/ n the forming or depositing of sediment

sedition /si'dish(ǝ)n/ n incitement to defy or rise up against lawful authority – **-ious** adj – **-iously** adv – **-iousness** n

seduce /si'dyoohs/ v **1** to incite to disobedience or disloyalty **2** to lead astray, esp by false promises **3** to effect the physical seduction of – **seducer** n

seduction /si'duksh(ǝ)n/ n **1** the act of seducing; specif enticement to sexual intercourse **2** a thing or quality that attracts by its charm

seductive /si'duktiv/ adj tending to seduce; alluring – **~ly** adv – **~ness** n

sedulous /'sedyoolǝs/ adj **1** involving or accomplished with steady perseverance **2** diligent in application or pursuit USE fml – **~ly** adv

¹**see** /see/ v saw /saw/; seen /seen/ **1a** to perceive by the eye **b** to look at; inspect **2a** to have experience of; undergo **b** to (try to) find out or determine **3** to

form a mental picture of; imagine, envisage **4** to perceive the meaning or importance of; understand **5a** to observe, watch **b** to be a witness of **6** to ensure; make certain **7** of a period of time to be marked by **8a** to call on; visit **b** to keep company with **c** to grant an interview to **9** to meet (a bet) in poker or equal the bet of (a player) — **see about 1** to deal with **2** to consider further — **see eye to eye** to have a common viewpoint; agree — **see fit** to consider proper or advisable — **see one's way to** to feel capable of — **see red** to become suddenly enraged — **see someone right** to protect and reward (a protégé) — **see someone through** to provide for, support, or help sby until the end of (a time of difficulty) — **see the light 1a** to be born **b** to be published **2** to undergo conversion — **see the wood for the trees** to grasp the total picture without being confused by detail — **see through** to grasp the true nature of; penetrate — **see to** to attend to; care for

²**see** n a bishopric

¹**seed** /seed/ n pl seeds, esp collectively seed **1a** the grains or ripened ovules of plants used for sowing **b** the fertilized ripened ovule of a (flowering) plant that contains an embryo and is capable of germination to produce a new plant **c** semen or milt **2** a source of development or growth **3** a competitor who has been seeded in a tournament – **~less** adj — **go/run to seed 1** to develop seed **2** to decay; also to become unattractive by being shabby or careless about appearance

²**seed** v **1** to sow seed **2** of a plant to produce or shed seeds **3** to extract the seeds from (e g raisins) **4** to schedule (tournament players or teams) so that superior ones will not meet in early rounds

seed,bed /-,bed/ n a place where sthg specified develops

seedling /'seedling/ n **1** a plant grown from seed rather than from a cutting **2** a young plant; esp a nursery plant before permanent transplantation

seedy /'seedi/ adj **1** containing or full of seeds **2a** shabby, grubby **b** somewhat disreputable; run-down **c** slightly unwell – infml – **seedily** adv – **seediness** n

seek /seek/ v sought /sawt/ **1a** to go in search of – often + out **b** to try to discover **2** to ask for **3** to try to acquire or gain **4** to make an effort; aim – + infinitive – **~er** n

seem /seem/ v **1** to give the impression of being **2** to appear to the observation or understanding **3** to give evidence of existing

seeming /'seeming/ adj apparent rather than real

seemingly /-li/ adv **1** so far as can be seen or judged **2** to outward appearance only

seemly /'seemli/ adj in accord with good taste or propriety – **seemliness** n

see off v **1** to be present at the departure of **2** to avert, repel

see out *v* 1 to escort to the outside (e g of a room, office, or house) 2 to last until the end of

seep /seep/ *v* to pass slowly (as if) through fine pores or small openings – ~**age** *n*

seer /sia/ *n* 1 sby who predicts future events 2 sby credited with exceptional moral and spiritual insight

seersucker /'sia,suka/ *n* a light slightly puckered fabric of linen, cotton, or rayon

¹**seesaw** /'see,saw/ *n* 1 an alternating up-and-down or backwards-and-forwards movement; *also* anything (e g a process or movement) that alternates 2 (a game in which 2 or more children ride on opposite ends of) a plank balanced in the middle so that one end goes up as the other goes down

²**seesaw** *v* 1a to move backwards and forwards or up and down b to play as seesaw 2a to alternate b to vacillate

seethe /seedh/ *v* 1 to be in a state of agitated usu confused movement 2 to churn or foam as if boiling

'**see-, through** *adj* transparent

see through *v* to undergo or endure to the end

¹**segment** /'segmant/ *n* 1a a separated piece of sthg b any of the constituent parts into which a body, entity, or quantity is divided or marked off 2 a portion cut off from a geometrical figure by 1 or more points, lines, or planes

²**segment** /seg'ment/ *v* to separate into segments

segregate /'segri,gayt/ *v* 1 to separate or set apart 2 to cause or force separation of (e g criminals from society) or in (e g a community) – ~**d** *adj*

segregation /,segri'gaysh(a)n/ *n* the separation or isolation of a race, class, or ethnic group

seigneur /say'nyuh/ *n* a feudal lord

seismic /'siezmik/, **seismal** /-ml/ *adj* of or caused by an earth vibration, specif an earthquake

'**seismo,graph** /-,grahf, -,graf/ *n* an apparatus to measure and record earth tremors

seismology /seiz'molaji/ *n* a science that deals with earth vibrations, esp earthquakes – **-gist** *n*

seize /seez/ *v* 1a to confiscate, esp by legal authority b to lay hold of sthg suddenly, forcibly, or eagerly – usu + *on* or *upon* 2a to take possession of by force b to take prisoner 3 to take hold of abruptly or eagerly 4 to attack or afflict physically or mentally 5 (of brakes, pistons, *etc* to become jammed through excessive pressure, temperature, or friction – often + *up*

seizure /'seezhə/ *n* 1 the taking possession of sby or sthg by legal process 2 a sudden attack (e g of disease)

¹**seldom** /'seldam/ *adv* in few instances; rarely, infrequently

²**seldom** *adj* rare, infrequent

¹**select** /si'lekt/ *adj* 1 picked out in preference to others 2a of special value or quality b exclusively or fastidiously chosen, esp on the basis of social characteristics 3 judicious in choice

²**select** *v* to take according to preference from among a number; pick out – ~**or** *n*

select committee *n* a temporary committee of a legislative body, established to examine 1 particular matter

selection /si'leksh(ə)n/ *n* 1 sby or sthg selected; *also* a collection of selected items 2 a range of things from which to choose

selective /si'lektiv/ *adj* of or characterized by selection; selecting or tending to select – ~**ly** *adv* – ~**ness** *n* – **-tivity** *n*

¹**self** /self/ *pron* myself, himself, herself

²**self** *adj* identical throughout, esp in colour

³**self** *n*, *pl* **selves** /selvz/ 1 the entire being of an individual 2 a (part or aspect of a) person's individual character 3 the body, emotions, thoughts, sensations, *etc* that constitute the individuality and identity of a person 4 personal interest, advantage, or welfare

,**self-ad'dressed** *adj* addressed for return to the sender

,**self-as'sertion** *n* the act of asserting oneself or one's own rights, claims, or opinions, esp aggressively or conceitedly – **-tive** *adj* – **-tiveness** *n*

,**self-as'surance** *n* self-confidence – **-red** *adj*

,**self-'centred** *adj* concerned excessively with one's own desires or needs – ~**ness** *n*

,**self-con'fessed** *adj* openly acknowledged

,**self-'confidence** *n* confidence in oneself and one's powers and abilities – **-dent** *adj*

,**self-'conscious** *adj* 1a conscious of oneself as a possessor of mental states and originator of actions b intensely aware of oneself 2 uncomfortably conscious of oneself as an object of notice; ill at ease – ~**ly** *adv* – ~**ness** *n*

,**self-con'tained** *adj* 1 complete in itself 2a showing self-possession b formal and reserved in manner

,**self-con'trol** *n* restraint of one's own impulses or emotions – **-trolled** *adj*

,**self-de'fence** *n* 1 the act of defending or justifying oneself 2 the legal right to defend oneself with reasonable force

,**self-de'nial** *n* the restraint or limitation of one's desires or their gratification – **self-denying** *adj*

,**self-determi'nation** *n* 1 free choice of one's own actions or states without outside influence 2 determination by a territorial unit of its own political status

,**self-'discipline** *n* the act of disciplining or power to discipline one's thoughts and actions, usu for the sake of improvement

self-drive *adj*, *of a hired vehicle* intended to be driven by the hirer

,self-em'ployed *adj* earning income directly from one's own business, trade, or profession rather than as salary or wages from an employer

,self-e'steem *n* 1 confidence and satisfaction in oneself; self-respect 2 vanity

,self-'evident *adj* requiring no proof; obvious

,self-exami'nation *n* the analysis of one's conduct, motives, etc

,self-ex'planatory *adj* capable of being understood without explanation

,self-'government *n* control of one's own (political) affairs – self-governing *adj*

,self-'help *n* the bettering or helping of oneself without dependence on others

,self-im'portance *n* 1 an exaggerated sense of one's own importance 2 arrogant or pompous behaviour – -ant *adj* – -antly *adv*

,self-in'dulgence *n* excessive or unrestrained gratification of one's own appetites, desires, or whims – -ent *adj* – -ently *adv*

,self-'interest *n* (a concern for) one's own advantage and well-being – ~ ed *adj*

selfish /'selfish/ *adj* concerned with or directed towards one's own advantage, pleasure, or well-being without regard for others – ~ ly *adv* – ~ ness *n*

'selfless /-lis/ *adj* having no concern for self; unselfish – ~ ly *adv* – ~ ness *n*

,self-'made *adj* raised from poverty or obscurity by one's own efforts

,self-o'pinionated *adj* 1 conceited 2 stubbornly holding to one's own opinion; opinionated

,self-'pity *n* a self-indulgent dwelling on one's own sorrows or misfortunes

,self-pos'session *n* control of one's emotions or behaviour, esp when under stress; composure – -sed *adj*

,self-preser'vation *n* an instinctive tendency to act so as to safeguard one's own existence

,self-'raising ,flour *n* a commercially prepared mixture of flour containing a raising agent

,self-re'liance *n* reliance on one's own efforts and abilities; independence – -ant *adj*

,self-re'spect *n* a proper respect for one's human dignity

,self-re'specting *adj* having or characterized by self-respect or integrity

,self-'righteous *adj* assured of one's own righteousness, esp in contrast with the actions and beliefs of others; narrow-mindedly moralistic – ~ ly *adv* – ~ ness *n*

,self-'sacrifice *n* sacrifice of oneself or one's well-being for the sake of an ideal or for the benefit of others – -icing *adj*

'self,same *adj* precisely the same; identical

,self-satis'faction *n* a smug satisfaction with oneself or one's position or achievements – -fied *adj*

,self-'seeking *adj* seeking only to safeguard or further one's own interests – -seeker *n*

,self-'service *n* the serving of oneself (e g in a cafeteria or supermarket) with things to be paid for at a cashier's desk, usu upon leaving

,self-'starter *n* an electric motor used to start an internal-combustion engine

,self-'styled *adj* called by oneself, esp without justification

,self-suf'ficient *adj* 1 able to maintain oneself or itself without outside aid; capable of providing for one's own needs 2 having unwarranted assurance of one's own ability or worth – -ency *n*

,self-sup'porting *adj* 1 meeting one's needs by one's own labour or income 2 supporting itself or its own weight

,self-'will *n* stubborn or wilful adherence to one's own desires or ideas; obstinacy – ~ ed *adj*

¹sell /sel/ *v* sold /sohld/ 1 to deliver or give up in violation of duty, trust, or loyalty; betray – often + out 2a to give up (property) in exchange, esp for money b to give up or dispose of foolishly or dishonourably (in return for sthg else) 3 to cause or promote the sale of 4a to make acceptable, believable, or desirable by persuasion b to persuade to accept or enjoy sthg – usu + on; infml — sell down the river to betray the faith of

²sell *n* 1 the act or an instance of selling 2 a deliberate deception; a hoax – infml

seller /'selə/ *n* a product offered for sale and selling well, to a specified extent, or in a specified manner

sellotape /'selə,tayp/ *v* to fix (as if) with Sellotape

Sellotape *trademark* – used as usu transparent adhesive tape

'sell-,out *n* 1 a performance, exhibition, or contest for which all tickets or seats are sold 2 a betrayal – infml

sell out *v* to betray or be unfaithful to (e g one's cause or associates), esp for the sake of money

sell up *v* to sell (e g one's house or business) in a conclusive or forced transaction

selves /selvz/ *pl of* self

se'mantics *n pl but sing or pl in constr* the branch of linguistics concerned with meaning; *also* the study of the relation between signs and the objects they refer to – semantic *adj*

semaphore /'semə,faw/ *n* 1 an apparatus for conveying information by visual signals (e g by the position of 1 or more pivoted arms) 2 a system of visual signalling by 2 flags held 1 in each hand – semaphore *v*

semblance /'sembləns/ *n* outward and often deceptive appearance; a show

semen /'seemən/ *n* a suspension of spermatozoa produced by the male reproductive glands that is conveyed to the female reproductive tract during coitus

semester /si'mestə/ n an academic term lasting half a year, esp in America and Germany

'semi,breve /-,breev/ n a musical note with the time value of 2 minims or 4 crotchets

'semi,circle /-,suhkl/ n (an object or arrangement in the form of) a half circle – **-cular** adj

,semi'colon /-'kohlən/ n a punctuation mark #; used chiefly to coordinate major sentence elements where there is no conjunction

,semicon'ductor /-kən'duktə/ n a substance (e g silicon) whose electrical conductivity at room temperature is between that of a conductor and that of an insulator

,semide'tached /-di'tacht/ adj forming 1 of a pair of residences joined into 1 building by a common wall – **semidetached** n

¹,semi'final /-'fienl/ adj 1 next to the last in a knockout competition 2 of or participating in a semifinal

²semifinal /,--'--, '--,--/ n a semifinal match or round – often pl with sing. meaning

seminal /'seminl/ adj 1 (consisting of, storing, or conveying seed or semen 2 containing or contributing the seeds of future development; original and influential

seminar /'semi,nah/ n 1 an advanced or graduate class often featuring informality and discussion 2 a meeting for exchanging and discussing information

seminary /'semin(ə)ri/ n an institution for the training of candidates for the (Roman Catholic) priesthood – **-rist** n

,semi'precious /-'preshəs/ adj, of a gemstone of less commercial value than a precious stone

'semi,quaver /-,kwayvə/ n a musical note with time value of ₂ of a quaver

Semitic /si'mitik/ adj 1 of or characteristic of the Semites; specif Jewish 2 of a branch of the Afro-Asiatic language family that includes Hebrew, Aramaic, Arabic, and Ethiopic

'semi,tone /-,tohn/ n the musical interval (e g E–F or F–F #) equal to the interval between 2 adjacent keys on a keyboard instrument

,semi'weekly /-'weekli/ adj or adv appearing or taking place twice a week

semolina /,semə'leenə/ n the purified hard parts left after milling of (hard) wheat used for pasta and in milk puddings

senate /'senit/ n sing or pl in constr 1a the supreme council of the ancient Roman republic and empire b the 2nd chamber in some legislatures that consist of 2 houses 2 the governing body of some universities

senator /'senatə/ n a member of a senate

send /send/ v sent /sent/ 1 of God, fate, etc to cause to be; grant; bring about 2 to dispatch by a means of communication 3a to cause, direct, order, or request to go b to dismiss 4 to cause to assume a specified state 5a to pour out; discharge b to emit (e g radio signals) c to grow out (parts) in the course of development 6 to consign to a destination (e g death or a place of imprisonment) — **send for** to request by message to come; summon — **send packing** to dismiss roughly or in disgrace

send down v, Br 1 to suspend or expel from a university 2 to send to jail – infml

'send-,off n a usu enthusiastic demonstration of goodwill at the beginning of a venture (e g a trip)

send off v to attend to the departure of

'send-,up n, Br a satirical imitation, esp on stage or television; a parody

send up v, chiefly Br to make an object of mockery or laughter; ridicule

senile /'seeniel/ adj of, exhibiting, or characteristic of (the mental or physical weakness associated with) old age – **-lity** n

¹**senior** /'seenyə, 'seeni-ə/ n 1 sby who is older than another 2 sby of higher standing or rank

²**senior** adj 1 elder – used, chiefly in the USA, to distinguish a father with the same name as his son 2 higher in standing or rank

,senior 'citizen n sby beyond the usual age of retirement – euph

senor, señor /se'nyaw/ n, pl **senors, señores** /-rays/ a Spanish-speaking man – used as a title equivalent to Mr or as a generalized term of direct address

senora, señora /se'nyawrə/ n a married Spanish-speaking woman – used as a title equivalent to Mrs or as a generalized term of direct address

senorita, señorita /,senyə'reetə/ n an unmarried Spanish-speaking girl or woman – used as a title equivalent to Miss

sensation /sen'saysh(ə)n/ n 1a a mental process (e g seeing or hearing) resulting from stimulation of a sense organ b a state of awareness of a usu specified type resulting from internal bodily conditions or external factors; a feeling or sense 2a a surge of intense interest or excitement b a cause of such excitement; esp sby or sthg in some respect remarkable or outstanding

sensational /sen'saysh(ə)nl/ adj 1 arousing an immediate, intense, and usu superficial interest or emotional reaction 2 exceptionally or unexpectedly excellent or impressive – infml – **~ly** adv

sen'sational,ism /-,iz(ə)m/ n the use of sensational subject matter or style, esp in journalism – **-ist** n

¹**sense** /sens/ n 1 a meaning conveyed or intended; esp any of a range of meanings a word or phrase may bear, esp as isolated in a dictionary entry 2 any of the senses of feeling, hearing, sight, smell, taste, etc 3 soundness of mind or judgment – usu pl with sing. meaning 4a an ability to use the senses for a specified purpose b a definite but

often vague awareness or impression **c** an awareness that motivates action or judgment **d** a capacity for discernment and appreciation **5** an ability to put the mind to effective use; practical intelligence

²**sense** /sens/ *v* **1a** to perceive by the senses **b** to be or become conscious of **2** to grasp, comprehend

¹**senseless** /-lis/ *adj* deprived of, deficient in, or contrary to sense: e g **a** unconscious **b** foolish, stupid **c** meaningless, purposeless – ~**ly** *adv* – ~**ness** *n*

sensibility /ˌsensə'biləti/ *n* **1** heightened susceptibility to feelings of pleasure or pain (e g in response to praise or blame) – often *pl* with sing. meaning **2** the ability to discern and respond freely to sthg (e g emotion in another)

sensible /'sensəbl/ *adj* **1** having, containing, or indicative of good sense or sound reason **2a** perceptible to the senses or to understanding **b** large enough to be observed or noticed; considerable – **bly** *adv*

sensitive /'sensətiv/ *adj* **1** capable of being stimulated or excited by external agents (e g light, gravity, or contact) **2** highly responsive or susceptible: e g **2a(1)** easily provoked or hurt emotionally **a(2)** finely aware of the attitudes and feelings of others or of the subtleties of a work of art **b** capable of registering minute differences; delicate **3** concerned with highly classified information – ~**ly** *adv* – ~**tivity** *n*

sensit·ize, -ise /'sensətiez/ *v* to make or become sensitive

sensor /'sensə, -saw/ *n* a device that responds to heat, light, sound, pressure, magnetism, etc and transmits a resulting impulse (e g for measurement or operating a control)

sensory /'sens(ə)ri/ *adj* of sensation or the senses

sensual /'sensyoo-əl, -shoo-/ *adj* **1** sensory **2** relating to or consisting in the gratification of the senses or the indulgence of appetites **3a** devoted to or preoccupied with the senses or appetites **b** voluptuous – ~**ly** *adv*

sensuous /'sensyoo-əs, -shoo-əs/ *adj* **1a** (of objects perceived by) the senses **b** providing or characterized by gratification of the senses; appealing strongly to the senses **2** suggesting or producing rich imagery or sense impressions – ~**ly** *adv* – ~**ness** *n*

sent /sent/ *past of* **send**

¹**sentence** /'sentəns/ *n* **1a** a judgment formally pronounced by a court and specifying a punishment **b** the punishment so imposed **2a** a grammatically self-contained speech unit that expresses an assertion, a question, a command, a wish, or an exclamation and is usu shown in writing with a capital letter at the beginning and with appropriate punctuation at the end

²**sentence** /-/ *v* **1** to impose a judicial sentence on **2** to consign to a usu unpleasant fate

sententious /sen'tenshəs/ *adj* **1** terse, pithy **2a** full of terse or pithy sayings **b** pompous, moralizing – ~**ly** *adv* – ~**ness** *n*

sentient /'sensh(ə)nt/ *adj* **1** capable of perceiving through the senses; conscious **2** keenly sensitive in perception or feeling *USE* chiefly *fml*

sentiment /'sentimənt/ *n* **1a** (an attitude, thought, or judgment prompted by or coloured by) feeling or emotion **b** a specific view or attitude; an opinion – usu *pl* with sing. meaning **2** indulgently romantic or nostalgic feeling

sentimental /ˌsenti'mentl/ *adj* **1** resulting from feeling rather than reason **2** having an excess of superficial sentiment – ~**ly** *adv* – ~**ism**, ~**ity**, ~**ist** *n* – ~**ize** *v*

sentry /'sentri/ *n* a guard, watch; *esp* a soldier standing guard at a gate, door, etc

sepal /'sepl/ *n* any of the modified leaves comprising the calyx of a flower

separable /ˌsep(ə)rəbl/ *adj* capable of being separated or dissociated – **bly** *adv* – **bility** *n*

¹**separate** /'sepərayt/ *v* **1a** to set or keep apart; detach, divide **b** to make a distinction between; distinguish **c** to disperse in space or time; scatter **2a** to isolate from a mixture or compound – often + *out* **b** to divide into constituent parts or types **3** to cease to live together as man and wife, esp by formal arrangement **4** to go in different directions

²**separate** /'sep(ə)rət/ *adj* **1** set or kept apart; detached, separated **2** not shared with another; individual **3a** existing independently; autonomous **b** different in kind; distinct – ~**ness** *n* – ~**ly** *adv*

separation /ˌsepə'raysh(ə)n/ *n* **1a** a point, line, or means of division **b** an intervening space; a gap, break **2** cessation of cohabitation between husband and wife by mutual agreement or judicial decree

separatism /'sep(ə)rə,tiz(ə)m/ *n* a belief or movement advocating separation (e g schism, secession, or segregation) – **-ist** *n*

¹**sepia** /'seepyə/ *n* **1** the inky secretion of cuttlefishes; *also* a pigment prepared from this **2** a rich dark brown colour

²**sepia** *adj* **1** of the colour sepia **2** made of or done in sepia

sepsis /'sepsis/ *n*, *pl* **sepses** /-seez/ the spread of bacteria from a focus of infection

September /sep'tembə, səp-/ *n* the 9th month of the Gregorian calendar

septet /sep'tet/ *n* **1** a musical composition for 7 instruments, voices, or performers **2** *sing or pl in constr* a group or set of 7; *esp* the performers of a septet

septic /'septik/ *adj* relating to, involving, or characteristic of sepsis

ˌ**septic 'tank** *n* a tank in which the solid matter of continuously flowing sewage is disintegrated by bacteria

septuagenarian /,sepchooǝji'neǝri·ǝn, ,septwǝ-/ *n* sby between 70 and 79 years old

septum /'septǝm/ *n, pl* **septa** /-tǝ/ a dividing wall or membrane, esp between bodily spaces or masses of soft tissue

sepulchral /si'pulkrǝl/ *adj* **1** of the burial of the dead **2** suited to or suggestive of a tomb; funereal

sepulchre, *NAm chiefly* **sepulcher** /'sep(ǝ)lkǝ/ *n* **1** a place of burial; a tomb **2** a receptacle (in an altar) for religious relics

sequel /'seekwǝl/ *n* **1** a consequence, result **2a** subsequent development or course of events **b** a play, film, or literary work continuing the course of a narrative begun in a preceding one

sequence /'seekwǝns/ *n* **1** a continuous or connected series **2** an episode, esp in a film **3** order of succession **4** a continuous progression – **sequence** *v* – **-ential** *adj* – **-entially** *adv*

sequin /'seekwin/ *n* a very small disc of shining metal or plastic used for ornamentation, esp on clothing – ~**ed** *adj*

seraglio /se'rahli·oh, -lyoh/ *n, pl* **seraglios** a harem

¹**serenade** /,serǝ'nayd/ *n* **1** a complimentary vocal or instrumental performance (given outdoors at night for a woman) **2** an instrumental composition in several movements written for a small ensemble

²**serenade** *v* to perform a serenade (in honour of)

serendipity /,serǝn'dipǝti/ *n* the faculty of discovering pleasing or valuable things by chance

serene /sǝ'reen/ *adj* **1** free of storms or adverse changes; clear, fine **2** having or showing tranquillity and peace of mind – ~**ly** *adv* – **serenity** *n*

serf /suhf/ *n* a member of a class of agricultural labourers in a feudal society, bound in service to a lord, and esp transferred with the land they worked if its ownership changed hands – ~**dom** *n*

serge /suhj/ *n* a durable twilled fabric having a smooth clear face and a pronounced diagonal rib on the front and the back

sergeant /'sahj(ǝ)nt/ *n* **1** a police officer ranking in Britain between constable and inspector **2** a non-commissioned officer of upper rank in the army, airforce, or marines

sergeant 'major *n pl* **sergeant majors, sergeants major** a warrant officer in the British army or Royal Marines

¹**serial** /'siǝri·ǝl/ *adj* **1** of or constituting a series, rank, or row **2** appearing in successive instalments **3** of or being music based on a series of notes in an arbitrary but fixed order without regard for traditional tonality – ~**ly** *adv*

²**serial** *n* a work appearing (e g in a magazine or on television) in parts at usu regular intervals **2** a publication issued as **1** of a consecutively numbered continuing series

series /'siǝriz, -reez/ *n pl* **series 1** a number of things or events of the same kind following one another in spatial or temporal succession **2** a usu infinite mathematical sequence whose terms are to be added together **3** a succession of issues of volumes published with continuous numbering or usu related subjects or authors and format **4** a division of rock formations that comprises the rocks deposited during an epoch **5** an arrangement of devices in an electrical circuit in which the whole current passes through each device

serious /'siǝri·ǝs/ *adj* **1** grave or thoughtful in appearance or manner; sober **2a** requiring careful attention and concentration **b** of or relating to a weighty or important matter **3** not jesting or deceiving; in earnest **4** having important or dangerous consequences; critical – ~**ly** *adv* – ~**ness** *n*

sermon /'suhmǝn/ *n* **1** a religious discourse delivered in public, usu by a clergyman as a part of a religious service **2** a speech on conduct or duty; *esp* one that is unduly long or tedious

serpent /'suhpǝnt/ *n* **1** a (large) snake **2** *the* Devil **3** a wily treacherous person

¹**serpentine** /'suhpǝn,tien/ *adj* **1** of or like a serpent (e g in form or movement) **2** subtly tempting; wily, artful **3** winding or turning one way and another

²**serpentine** *n* a usu dull green mottled mineral

serried /'serid/ *adj* crowded or pressed together; compact

serum /'siǝrǝm/ *n, pl* **serums, sera** /'siǝrǝ/ the watery part of an animal liquid (remaining after coagulation): **a** blood serum, esp when containing specific antibodies **b** whey

servant /'suhv(ǝ)nt/ *n* sby who or sthg that serves others; *specif* sby employed to perform personal or domestic duties for another

¹**serve** /suhv/ *v* **1a** to act as a servant **b** to do military or naval service **c** to undergo a term of imprisonment **2a** to be of use; fulfil a specified purpose – often + *as* **b** to be favourable, opportune, or convenient **c** to hold a post or office; discharge a duty **3** to prove adequate or satisfactory; suffice **4** to distribute drinks or helpings of food **5** to attend to customers in a shop **6** to put the ball or shuttle in play in any of various games (e g tennis or volleyball) — **serve someone right** to be a deserved punishment for sby

²**serve** *n* the act of putting the ball or shuttle in play in any of various games (e g volleyball, badminton, or tennis)

server /'suhvǝ/ *n* **1** sby who serves food or drink **2** the player who serves (e g in tennis) **3** sthg (e g tongs) used in serving food or drink

¹**service** /'suhvis/ *n* **1a** work or duty performed for sby **b** employment as a servant **2a** the function performed by sby who or sthg that serves **b** help, use, benefit **c** disposal for use or assistance **3a** a form followed in a religious ceremony **b** a meeting

for worship **4a** a helpful act; a favour **b** a piece of useful work that does not produce a tangible commodity – usu pl with sing. meaning **c** a serve **5** a set of articles for a particular use; *specif* a set of matching tableware **6** any of a nation's military forces (e g the army or navy) **7a(1)** a facility supplying some public demand **a(2)** *pl* utilities (e g gas, water sewage, or electricity) available or connected to a building **b** the usu routine repair and maintenance of a machine or motor vehicle **c** a facility providing broadcast programmes **8** the bringing of a legal writ, process, or summons to notice as prescribed

²**service** *adj* **1** of the armed services **2** used in serving or delivering **3** providing services

³**service** *v* to perform services for: e g **a** to repair or provide maintenance for **b** to meet interest and sinking fund payments on (e g government debt) **c** to perform any of the business functions auxiliary to production or distribution of **d** *of a male animal* to copulate with

⁴**service, 'service ,tree** *n* an Old World tree resembling the related mountain ashes but with larger flowers and smaller edible fruits

serviceable /'suhvisǝbl/ *adj* **1** fit to use; suited for a purpose **2** wearing well in use; durable – **-bility** *n* – **~ness** *n* – **-bly** *adv*

'service ,charge *n* a proportion of a bill added onto the total bill to pay for service, usu instead of tips

'serviceman /-mǝn/, *fem* **'service ,woman** *n* a member of the armed forces

'service ,station *n* a retail station for servicing motor vehicles, esp with oil and petrol

serviette /,suhvi'et/, *chiefly Br* a table napkin

servile /'suhviel/ *adj* **1** of or befitting a slave or a menial position **2** slavishly or unctuously submissive; abject, obsequious – **-vility** *n* – **~ly** *adv*

serving /'suhving/ *n* a single portion of food or drink; a helping

servitude /'suhvityoohd/ *n* lack of liberty; bondage

sesame /'sesǝmi/ *n* (an E Indian plant with) small flattish seeds used as a source of oil and as a flavouring agent

session /'sesh(ǝ)n/ *n* **1** a meeting or series of meetings of a body (e g a court or council) for the transaction of business; a sitting **2** a period devoted to a particular activity, esp by a group of people

sestet /ses'tet/ *n* a poem or stanza of 6 lines; *specif* the last 6 lines of an Italian sonnet

¹**set** /set/ *v* **-tt-; set 1** to cause to sit; place in or on a seat **2a** to place with care or deliberate purpose and with relative stability **b** to transplant **3** to cause to assume a specified condition **4a** to appoint or assign to an office or duty **b** to post, station **5a** to place in a specified relation or position **b** to place in a specified setting **6a** to fasten **b**

to apply **7** to fix or decide on as a time, limit, or regulation; prescribe **8a** to establish as the most extreme, esp the highest, level **b** to provide as a pattern or model **c** to allot as or compose for a task **9a** to adjust (a device, esp a measuring device) to a desired position **b** to restore to normal position or connection after dislocation or fracturing **c** to spread to the wind **10** to divide (an age-group of pupils) into sets **11a** to make ready for use **b** to provide music or instrumentation for (a text) **c** to arrange (type) for printing **12a** to put a fine edge on by grinding or honing **b** to bend slightly the alternate teeth of (a saw) in opposite directions **13** to fix in a desired position **14** to fix (the hair) in a desired style by waving, curling, or arranging, usu while wet **15** to fix a gem in a metal setting **16a** to fix at a specified amount **b** to value, rate **17** to place in relation for comparison; *also* to offset **18a** to put into activity or motion **b** to incite to attack or antagonism **c** to make an attack – + *on* or *upon* **19** to fix firmly; give rigid form to **20** to cause to become firm or solid **21** to cause fruit to develop **22** to pass below the horizon; go down **23** – used as an interjection to command runners to put themselves into the starting position before a race — **set about 1** to begin to do **2** to attack — **set foot** to pass over the threshold; enter – + *in, on,* or *inside* — **set in motion** to get (sthg) started; initiate — **set on** to cause to attack or pursue — **set one's face against** to oppose staunchly — **set one's hand to** to become engaged in — **set one's heart** to resolve; *also* to want (sthg) very much — + *on* or *upon* — **set one's house in order** to introduce necessary reforms — **set one's sights** to focus one's concentration or intentions; aim — **set one's teeth on edge** to give one an unpleasant sensation (e g that caused by an acid flavour or squeaky noise) — **set sail** to begin a voyage — **set store by** to consider valuable, trustworthy, or worthwhile, esp to the specified degree — **set the scene** to provide necessary background information — **set to work** to apply oneself; begin

²**set** *adj* **1** intent, determined **2** fixed by authority or binding decision; prescribed, specified **3** *of a meal* consisting of a specified combination of dishes available at a fixed price **4** reluctant to change; fixed by habit **5** immovable, rigid **6** ready, prepared

³**set** *n* **1** setting or being set **2** a mental inclination, tendency, or habit **3** a number of things, usu of the same kind, that belong or are used together or that form a unit **4** the arrangement of the hair by curling or waving **5** a young plant, rooted cutting, etc ready for transplanting **6** an artificial setting for a scene of a theatrical or film production **7** a division of a tennis match won by the side that wins at least 6 games beating the opponent by 2 games or that wins a tie breaker **8** *sing or pl in constr* a group of people associated by common

interests **9** a collection of mathematical elements (e g numbers or points) **10** an apparatus of electronic components assembled so as to function as a unit **11** *sing or pl in constr* a group of pupils of roughly equal ability in a particular subject who are taught together **12** a sett

set aside *v* **1** to reserve for a particular purpose; save **2** to reject from consideration **3** to annul or overrule (a sentence, verdict, etc)

'**set**,**back** /-ˌbak/ *n* **1** an arresting of or hindrance in progress **2** a defeat, reverse

set back *v* **1** to prevent or hinder the progress of; impede, delay **2** to cost – *infml*

set down *v* **1** to cause or allow (a passenger) to alight from a vehicle **2** to land (an aircraft) on the ground or water **3** to put in writing **4** to attribute, ascribe

set in *v* **1a** to become established **2** to insert; *esp* to stitch (a small part) into a larger article

'**set**-,**off** *n* **1a 1** a decoration, adornment **b** a counterbalance, compensation **2** the discharge of a debt by setting against it a sum owed by the creditor to the debtor

set off *v* **1a** to put in relief; show up by contrast **b** to make distinct or outstanding; enhance **2** to treat as a compensating item **3a** to set in motion; cause to begin **b** to cause to explode; detonate **4** to start out on a course or journey

set piece *n* **1** (a part of) a work of art, literature, etc with a formal pattern or style **2** any of various moves in soccer or rugby (e g a corner kick or free kick) by which the ball is put back into play after a stoppage

'**set**,**screw** /-ˌskrooh/ *n* a screw that serves to adjust a machine

set square *n*, *chiefly Br* a flat triangular instrument with 1 right angle and 2 other precisely known angles, used to mark out or test angles

sett, set /set/ *n* **1** the burrow of badger **2** a block of usu stone used for paving streets

settee /se'tee/ *n* a long often upholstered seat with a back and usu arms for seating more than 1 person; *broadly* a sofa

setter /'setə/ *n* a large gundog trained to point on finding game

setting /'seting/ *n* **1** the manner, position, or direction in which sthg (e g a dial) is set **2** the (style of) frame in which a gem is mounted **3a** the background, surroundings **b** the time and place of the action of a literary, dramatic, or cinematic work **4** the music composed for a text (e g a poem)

'**settle** /'setl/ *n* a wooden bench with arms, a high solid back, and an enclosed base which can be used as a chest

²**settle** *v* settling /'setling/ **1** to place firmly or comfortably **2a** to establish in residence **b** to supply with inhabitants; colonize **3a** to cause to sink and become compacted **b** to clarify by causing the sediment to sink **4** to come to rest **5** to free

from pain, discomfort, disorder, or disturbance **6** to fix or resolve conclusively **7** to bestow legally for life – *usu + on* **8a** to become calm or orderly – often + *down* **b** to adopt an ordered or stable life-style – *usu + down* **9a** to adjust differences or accounts; pay – often + *with or up* **b** to end a legal dispute by the agreement of both parties, without court action — **settle for** to be content with; accept

'**settlement** /-mənt/ *n* **1** settling **2** an estate, income, etc legally bestowed on sby **3a** a newly settled place or region **b** a small, esp isolated, village **4** an agreement resolving differences

settler /'setlə/ *n* one who settles sthg (e g a new region)

'**set**-,**to** *n pl* **set-tos** a usu brief and vigorous conflict – *chiefly infml*

set to *v* **1** to make an eager or determined start on a job or activity **2** to begin fighting

'**set**-,**up** *n* **1** an arrangement; *also* an organization **2** a task or contest with a prearranged or artificially easy course – *chiefly infml*

set up *v* **1** to put forward (e g a theory) for acceptance; propound **2** to assemble and prepare for use or operation **3** to give voice to, esp loudly; raise **4** to claim (oneself) to be a specified thing **5** to found, institute **6** to provide with what is necessary or useful – *usu + with or for* — **set up shop** to establish one's business

seven /'sev(ə)n/ *n* **1** the number 7 **2** the seventh in a set or series **3** sthg having 7 parts or members or a denomination of 7 – ~**th** *adj, n, pron, adv*

seventeen /ˌsev(ə)n'teen/ *n* the number 17 – ~**th** *adj, n, pron, adv*

,**seventh** '**heaven** *n* a state of supreme rapture or bliss

seventy /'sev(ə)nti/ *n* **1** the number 70 **2** *pl* the numbers 70 to 79; *specif* a range of temperatures, ages, or dates within a century characterized by those numbers – **-tieth** *adj, n, pron, adv*

sever /'sevə/ *v* **1** to put or keep apart; separate; *esp* to remove (a major part or portion) (as if) by cutting **2** to break off; terminate – ~**ance** *n*

'**several** /'sev(ə)rəl/ *adj* **1** more than 2 but fewer than many **2** separate or distinct from one another; respective – *chiefly fml*

²**several** *pron, pl in constr* an indefinite number more than 2 and fewer than many

severally /'sev(ə)rəli/ *adv* each by itself or him-/herself; separately – *chiefly fml*

severe /si'viə/ *adj* **1** having a stern expression or character; austere **2** rigorous in judgment, requirements, or punishment; stringent **3** strongly critical or condemnatory; censorious **4** sober or restrained in decoration or manner; plain **5** marked by harsh or extreme conditions **6** serious, grave – ~**ly** *adv* – **-rity** *n*

sew /soh/ *v* **sewed** /sohd/; **sewn** /sohn/, **sewed 1** to unite, fasten, or attach by stitches made with a needle and thread **2** to close or enclose by sewing **3** to make or mend by sewing – **~er** *n*

sewage /'s(y)ooh·ij, 's(y)oo·ij/ *n* waste matter carried off by sewers

sewer /'s(y)ooə/ *n* an artificial usu underground conduit used to carry off waste matter, esp excrement, from houses, towns, schools, towns, etc and surface water from roads and paved areas

sewerage /'s(y)ooərij/ *n* **1** sewage **2** the removal and disposal of surface water by sewers **3** a system of sewers

sewing /'soh·ing/ *n* **1** the act, action, or work of one who sews **2** work that has been or is to be sewn

sew up *v* to bring to a successful or satisfactory conclusion – chiefly *infml*

sex /seks/ *n* **1** either of 2 divisions of organisms distinguished as male or female **2** the structural, functional, and behavioural characteristics that are involved in reproduction and that distinguish males and females **3** sexual intercourse – **sex, sexual** *adj* – **~ually** *adv*

sexagenarian /ˌseksəji'neəri·ən/ *n* a person between 60 and 69 years old

sexism /'sek,siz(ə)m/ *n* **1** a belief that sex determines intrinsic capacities and role in society and that sexual differences produce an inherent superiority of one sex, usu the male **2** discrimination on the basis of sex; *esp* prejudice against women on the part of men – **-ist** *adj*, *n*

sexless /-lis/ *adj* **1** lacking sexuality or sexual intercourse **2** lacking sex appeal

sextant /'sekstənt/ *n* an instrument for measuring angles that is used, esp in navigation, to observe the altitudes of celestial bodies and so determine the observer's position on the earth's surface

sextet /sek'stet/ *n* (a musical composition for) a group of 6 instruments, voices, or performers

sexton /'sekstən/ *n* a church officer who takes care of the church property and is often also the gravedigger

sextuplet /'sekstyooplit/ *n* **1** a combination of 6 of a kind **2** a group of 6 equal musical notes performed in the time ordinarily given to 4 of the same value

sexual intercourse *n* intercourse with genital contact **a** involving penetration of the vagina by the penis; coitus **b** other than penetration of the vagina by the penis

sexy /'seksi/ *adj* sexually suggestive or stimulating; erotic – **sexily** *adv* – **sexiness** *n*

sh /sh/ *interj* – used often in prolonged or reduplicated form to urge or command silence

shabby /'shabi/ *v* **1a** threadbare or faded from wear **b** dilapidated, run-down **2** dressed in worn or grubby clothes; seedy **3** shameful, despicable – **-bily** *adv* – **-biness** *n*

shack /shak/ *n* a small crudely built dwelling or shelter

¹shackle /'shakl/ *n* **1** (a metal ring like) a manacle or handcuff **2** sthg that restricts or prevents free action or expression – usu pl with sing. meaning **3** a U-shaped piece of metal with a pin or bolt to close the opening

²shackle *v* **1** to bind or make fast with shackles **2** to deprive of freedom of thought or action by means of restrictions or handicaps

shack up *v* to live with and have a sexual relationship with sby; *also* to spend the night as a partner in sexual intercourse – usu + *together* or *with*

¹shade /shayd/ *n* **1a** partial darkness caused by the interception of rays of light **b** relative obscurity or insignificance **2a** a transitory or illusory appearance **b** a ghost **3** sthg that intercepts or diffuses light or heat; e g **3a** a lampshade **b** *chiefly NAm pl* sunglasses – *infml* **4** a particular level of depth or brightness of a colour **5** a minute difference or amount — **a shade** a tiny bit; somewhat — **shades of** — used interjectionally to indicate that one is reminded of or struck by a resemblance to a specified person or thing

²shade *v* **1** to shelter or screen by intercepting radiated light or heat **2** to darken or obscure (as if) with a shadow **3** to mark with shading or gradations of colour **4** to pass by slight changes or imperceptible degrees – usu + *into* or *off into*

shading /'shayding/ *n* an area of filled-in outlines to suggest three-dimensionality, shadow, or degrees of light and dark in a picture

¹shadow /'shadoh/ *n* **1** partial darkness caused by an opaque body interposed so as to cut off rays from a light source **2** a faint representation or suggestion; an imitation **3** a dark figure cast on a surface by a body intercepting light rays **4** a phantom **5** *pl* darkness **6** a shaded or darker portion of a picture **7a** an inseparable companion or follower **b** one (e g a spy or detective) who shadows **8** a small degree or portion; a trace **9** a source of gloom or disquiet

²shadow *v* **1** to cast a shadow over **2** to follow (a person) secretly; keep under surveillance **3** to shade

³shadow *adj* **1** identical with another in form but without the other's power or status; *specif* of or constituting the probable cabinet when the opposition party is returned to power **2** shown by throwing the shadows of performers or puppets on a screen

shadow-·box *v* to box with an imaginary opponent, esp as a form of training

shadowy /'shadoh·i/ *adj* **1a** of the nature of or resembling a shadow, insubstantial **b** scarcely perceptible; indistinct **2** lying in or obscured by shadow

sha

shady /'shaydi/ *adj* **1** sheltered from the direct heat or light of the sun **2** of doubtful integrity; disreputable – chiefly *infml*

shaft /shahft/ *n* **1a** (the long handle of) a spear, lance, or similar weapon **b** either of 2 poles between which a horse is hitched to a vehicle **2** a sharply delineated beam of light shining from an opening **3a** the trunk of a tree **b** the cylindrical pillar between the capital and the base of a column **c** the handle of a tool or implement (e g a hammer or golf club) **d** a usu cylindrical bar used to support rotating pieces or to transmit power or motion by rotation **e** a man-made vertical or inclined opening leading underground to a mine, well, etc **f** a vertical opening or passage through the floors of a building **4** a scornful, satirical, or pithily critical remark; a barb

¹**shag** /shag/ *n* **1a** an unkempt or uneven tangled mass or covering (e g of hair) **b** long coarse or matted fibre or nap **2** a strong coarse tobacco cut into fine shreds **3** a European bird smaller than the closely related cormorant – ~**gy** *adj*

²**shag** *v* **-gg-** **1** to fuck, screw – *vulg* **2** *Br* to make utterly exhausted – usu + *out*; *slang*

³**shag** *n* an act of sexual intercourse – *vulg*

shaggy-dog story /'shagi/ *n* a protracted and inconsequential funny story whose humour lies in the pointlessness or irrelevance of the conclusion

shah /shah/ *n*, *often cap* a sovereign of Iran

¹**shake** /shayk/ *v* **shook** /shook/; **shaken** /'shaykən/ **1a** to move to and fro with rapid usu irregular motion **b** to brandish, wave, or flourish, esp in a threatening manner **2** to vibrate, esp from the impact of a blow or shock **3a** to tremble as a result of physical or emotional disturbance **b** to cause to quake, quiver, or tremble **4** to cause to waver; weaken **5** to clasp (hands) in greeting or farewell or to convey goodwill or agreement **6** to agitate the feelings of; upset — **shake a leg** to hurry up; hasten — *infml* — **shake one's head** to move one's head from side to side to indicate disagreement, denial, disapproval, etc

²**shake** *n* **1** an act of shaking **2** *pl* a condition of trembling (e g from chill or fever); *specif* delirium tremens **3** a wavering, vibrating, or alternating motion caused by a blow or shock **4** a trill **5** *chiefly NAm* a milk shake **6** a moment – (6) *infml*

shake down *v* **1** to stay the night or sleep, esp in a makeshift bed **2** to become comfortably established, esp in a new place or occupation

shaker /'shaykə/ *n* **1** a container or utensil used to sprinkle or mix a substance by shaking **2** *cap* a member of an American sect practising celibacy and a self-denying communal life, and looking forward to the millennium

'**shake-,up** *n* an act or instance of shaking up; *specif* an extensive and often drastic reorganization (e g of a company) – *infml*

shake up *v* **1** to jar (as if) by a physical shock **2** to reorganize by extensive and often drastic measures – *infml*

shaky /'shayki/ *adj* **1a** lacking stability; precarious **b** lacking in firmness (e g of beliefs or principals) **2** unsound in health; poorly **3** likely to give way or break down; rickety – **shakily** *adv* – **shakiness** *n*

shale /shayl/ *n* a finely stratified or laminated rock formed by the consolidation of clay

shale oil *n* a crude dark oil obtained from oil shale by heating

shall /shəl; *strong* shal/ *verbal auxiliary pres sing & pl* **shall**; *past* **should** /shəd; *strong* shood/ **1** – used to urge or command or denote what is legally mandatory **2a** – used to express what is inevitable or seems likely to happen in the future **b** – used in the question form to express simple futurity or with the force of an offer or suggestion **3** – used to express determination

shallot /shə'lot/ *n* (any of the small clusters of bulbs, used esp for pickling and in seasoning, produced by) a plant that resembles an onion

¹**shallow** /'shaloh/ *adj* **1** having little depth **2** superficial in knowledge, thought, or feeling **3** not marked or accentuated – ~**ly** *adv* – ~**ness** *n*

²**shallow** *n* a shallow place in a body of water – usu pl with sing. meaning but sing. or pl in constr

shalom /shə'lohm, shə'lom/ *interj* – used as a Jewish greeting and farewell

shalt /shalt/ *archaic pres* 2 *sing of* **shall**

¹**sham** /sham/ *n* **1** cheap falseness; hypocrisy **2** an imitation or counterfeit purporting to be genuine **3** a person who shams

²**sham** *v* **-mm-** to act so as to counterfeit; *also* to give a deliberately false impression

¹**shamble** /'shambl/ *v* **shambling** /'shambling/ to walk awkwardly with dragging feet; shuffle

²**shamble** *n* a shambling gait

shambles /'shamblz/ *n pl* **shambles** **1** a slaughterhouse **2a** a place of carnage **b** a scene or a state of chaos or confusion; a mess

¹**shame** /shaym/ *n* **1** a painful emotion caused by consciousness of guilt, shortcomings, impropriety, or disgrace **2** humiliating disgrace or disrepute; ignominy **3** sthg bringing regret or disgrace

²**shame** *v* **1** to bring shame to; disgrace **2** to put to shame by outdoing **3** to fill with a sense of shame **4** to compel by causing to feel guilty

'**shame,faced** /-'fayst/ *adj* **1** showing modesty; bashful **2** showing shame; ashamed

'**shameful** /-f(ə)l/ *adj* **1** bringing disrepute or ignominy; disgraceful **2** arousing the feeling of shame – ~**ly** *adv* – ~**ness** *n*

'**shameless** /-lis/ *adj* **1** insensible to disgrace **2** showing lack of shame; disgraceful – ~**ly** *adv* – ~**ness** *n*

¹**shampoo** /sham'pooh/ *v* **shampoos; shampooing; shampooed** **1** to clean (esp the hair or a carpet) with shampoo **2** to wash the hair of

²**shampoo** *n pl* **shampoos** **1** a washing of the hair esp by a hairdresser **2** a soap, detergent, etc used for shampooing

shamrock /'sham,rok/ *n* any of several plants (e g a wood sorrel or some clovers) whose leaves have 3 leaflets and are used as a floral emblem by the Irish

shandy /'shandi/ *n* a drink consisting of beer mixed with lemonade or ginger beer

shanghai /,shang'hie/ *n* **shanghais; shanghaiing; shanghaied** /-'hied/ **1** to compel to join a ship's crew, esp by the help of drink or drugs **2** to put into an awkward or unpleasant position by trickery

Shangri-la /,shang-gri'lah/ *n* a remote imaginary place where life approaches perfection

shank /shangk/ *n* **1a** a leg; *specif* the part of the leg between the knee and the ankle **b** a cut of beef, veal, mutton, or lamb from the upper of the lower part of the leg **2** a straight na̱᷄ ᷄w usu vital part of an object; e g **2a** the straight part of a nail or pin **b** the part of an anchor between the ring and the crown **c** the part of a fishhook between the eye and the bend **d** the part of a key between the handle and the bit **3** a part of an object by which it can be attached to sthg else: e g **3a** a projection on the back of a solid button **b** the end (e g of a drill bit) that is gripped in a chuck

,shanks's 'pony *n* one's own feet or legs considered as a means of transport

¹**shanty** /'shanti/ *n* a small crudely built or dilapidated dwelling or shelter; a shack

²**shanty** *n* a song sung by sailors in rhythm with their work

'shanty ,town /-,town/ *n* (part of) a town consisting mainly of shanties

¹**shape** /shayp/ *v* **1** to form, create; *esp* to give a particular form or shape to **2** to adapt in shape so as to fit neatly and closely **3** to guide or mould into a particular state or condition **4** to determine or direct the course of (e g a person's life)

²**shape** *n* **1a** the visible or tactile form of a particular (kind of) item **b** spatial form **2** the contour of the body, esp of the trunk; the figure **3** an assumed appearance; a guise **4** definite form (e g in thought or words) **5** a general structure or plan **6** sthg made in a particular form **7** the condition of a person or thing, esp at a particular time – **shapeless** *adj* – ~**lessly** *adv* – ~**lessness** *n*

'shapely /-li/ *adj* having a pleasing shape; well-proportioned – **-liness** *n*

shape up *v* to (begin to) behave or perform satisfactorily

shard /shahd/ *n* a piece or fragment of sthg brittle (e g earthenware)

¹**share** /sheə/ *n* **1a** a portion belonging to, due to, or contributed by an individual **b** a full or fair portion **2a** the part allotted or belonging to any of a number owning property or interest together **b** any of the equal portions into which property or invested capital is divided **c** *pl, chiefly Br* the proprietorship element in a company, usu represented by transferable certificates

²**share** *v* **1** to divide and distribute in shares; apportion – usu + *out* **2** to partake of, use, experience, or enjoy with others **3** to have a share or part – often + *in*

³**share** *n* a ploughshare

'share,holder /-,hohldə/ *n* the holder or owner of a share in property

shark /shahk/ *n* **1** any of numerous mostly large typically grey marine fishes that are mostly active, voracious, and predators **2** a greedy unscrupulous person who exploits others by usury, extortion, or trickery

¹**sharp** /shahp/ *adj* **1** (adapted to) cutting or piercing: e g **1a** having a thin keen edge or fine point **b** bitingly cold; icy **2a** keen in intellect, perception, attention, etc **b** paying shrewd usu selfish attention to personal gain **3a** brisk, vigorous **b** capable of acting or reacting strongly; *esp* caustic **4a** marked by irritability or anger; fiery **b** causing intense usu sudden anguish **5** affecting the senses or sense organs intensely; e g **5a(1)** pungent, tart, or acid, esp in flavour **a(2)** acrid **b** shrill, piercing **6a** characterized by hard lines and angles **b** involving an abrupt change in direction **c** clear in outline or detail; distinct **7** of a musical note raised a semitone in pitch **8** stylish, dressy – *infml* – ~**ly** *adv* – ~**ness** *n*

²**sharp** *adv* **1** in an abrupt manner **2** exactly, precisely **3** above the proper musical pitch

³**sharp** *n* a musical note **1** semitone higher than another indicated or previously specified note **2** a relatively long needle with a sharp point and a small rounded eye for use in general sewing **3** *chiefly NAm* a swindler, sharper

sharpen /'shahpən/ *v* to make or become sharp or sharper – ~**er** *n*

'sharp,shooter /-,shoohtə/ *n* a good marksman

shatter /'shatə/ *v* **1** to break suddenly apart; disintegrate **2** to have a forceful or violent effect on the feelings of **3** to cause to be utterly exhausted

¹**shave** /shayv/ *v* **shaved, shaven** /'shayv(ə)n/ **1a** to remove in thin layers or shreds – often + *off* **b** to cut or trim closely **2** to cut off (hair or beard) close to the skin **3** to come very close to or brush against in passing

²**shave** *n* a tool or machine for shaving **2** an act or process of shaving

shaver /'shayvə/ *n* **1** an electric-powered razor **2** a boy, youngster – *infml*

shaving /'shayving/ *n* sthg shaved off – usu pl

shawl /shawl/ *n* a usu decorative square, oblong, or triangular piece of fabric that is worn to cover the head or shoulders

¹**she** /shi; *strong* shee/ *pron* **1** that female person or creature who is neither speaker nor hearer – used to refer to stg (e g a ship) regarded as feminine

²**she** /shee/ *n* a female person or creature – often in combination

sheaf /sheef/ *n, pl* **sheaves** /sheevz/ **1** a quantity of plant material, esp the stalks and ears of a cereal grass, bound together **2** a collection of items laid or tied together

¹**shear** /shia/ *v* **sheared, shorn** /shawn/ **1** to cut or clip (hair, wool, a fleece, etc) from sby or sthg; *also* to cut sthg from **2** to cut with sthg sharp **3** to deprive of sthg as if by cutting off – usu passive + *of* **4** to become divided or separated under the action of a shear force

²**shear** *n* **1a** a cutting implement similar to a pair of scissors but typically larger **b** any of various cutting tools or machines operating by the action of opposed cutting edges of metal **2** an action or force that causes or tends to cause 2 parts of a body to slide on each other in a direction parallel to their plane of contact – (*1a, b*) usu pl with sing. meaning

sheath /sheeth/ *n, pl* **sheaths** /sheedhz/ **1** a case or cover for a blade (e g of a knife or sword) **2** a cover or case of (a part of a) plant or animal body **3** a condom

sheathe /sheedh/ *v* **1** to put into or provide with a sheath **2** to withdraw (a claw) into a sheath **3** to encase or cover with sthg protective (e g thin boards or sheets of metal)

¹**shed** /shed/ *v* **-dd-; shed 1** to be incapable of holding or absorbing; repel **2a** to cause (blood) to flow by wounding or killing **b** to pour forth; let flow **3** to cast off hairs, threads etc; moult

²**shed** *n* a usu single-storied building for shelter, storage, etc

she'd /shid; *strong* sheed/ she had; she would

sheen /sheen/ *n* **1** a bright or shining quality or condition; brightness, lustre **2** a subdued shininess or glitter of a surface **3** a lustrous quality imparted to textiles through finishing processes or use of shiny yarns

sheep /sheep/ *n, pl* **sheep 1** any of numerous ruminant mammals related to the goats but stockier and lacking a beard in the male; *specif* one domesticated, esp for its flesh and wool **2** an inane or docile person; *esp* one easily influenced or led

'**sheep-,dip** *n* a liquid preparation into which sheep are plunged, esp to destroy parasites

'**sheep,dog** /-,dog/ *n* a dog used to tend, drive, or guard sheep; *esp* a collie

sheepish /'sheepish/ *adj* embarrassed by consciousness of a fault – ~**ly** *adv* – ~**ness** *n*

'**sheep,skin** /-,skin/ *n* **1** (leather from) the skin of a sheep **2** the skin of a sheep dressed with the wool on

¹**sheer** /shiə/ *adj* **1** transparently fine; diaphanous **2a** unqualified, utter **b** not mixed or mingled with anything else; pure, unadulterated **3** marked by great and unbroken steepness; precipitous

²**sheer** *adv* **1** altogether, completely **2** straight up or down without a break

³**sheer** *v* to (cause to) deviate from a course

⁴**sheer** *n* a turn, deviation, or change in a course (e g of a ship)

¹**sheet** /sheet/ *n* **1** a broad piece of cloth; *specif* a rectangle of cloth (e g of linen or cotton) used as an article of bed linen **2a** a usu rectangular piece of paper **b** a printed section for a book, esp before it has been folded, cut, or bound – usu pl **3** a broad usu flat expanse **4** a suspended or moving expanse **5** a piece of sthg that is thin in comparison to its length and breadth

²**sheet** *v* **1** to form into, provide with, or cover with a sheet or sheets **2** to come down in sheets

³**sheet** *adj* rolled into or spread out in a sheet

⁴**sheet** *n* **1** a rope that regulates the angle at which a sail is set in relation to the wind **2** *pl* the spaces at either end of an open boat

sheet anchor *n* **1** an emergency anchor formerly carried in the broadest part of a ship **2a** a principal support or dependence, esp in danger; a mainstay

sheeting /'sheeting/ *n* (material suitable for making into) sheets

sheet lightning *n* lightning in diffused or sheet form due to reflection and diffusion by clouds

sheikh, sheik /shayk, sheek/ **1** an Arab chief **2** **sheik, sheikh** a romantically attractive or dashing man

sheila, sheilah /'sheelə/ *n, Austr, NZ, & SAfr* a young woman; a girl – *infml*

shekel /'shekl/ *n* **1** the standard currency of Israel **2** *pl* money – *infml*

shelduck /'shelduk/ *n* a common mostly black and white duck slightly larger than the mallard

shelf /shelf/ *n, pl* **shelves** /shelvz/ **1** a thin flat usu long and narrow piece of material (e g wood) fastened horizontally (e g on a wall or in a cupboard, bookcase, etc) at a distance from the floor to hold objects **2a** (a partially submerged) sandbank or ledge of rocks **b** a flat projecting layer of rock — **off the shelf 1** available from stock **2** off the peg — **on the shelf 1** in a state of inactivity or uselessness **2** *of a single woman* considered as unlikely to marry, esp because too old

¹**shell** /shel/ *n* **1a** a hard rigid often largely calcium-containing covering of a (sea) animal **b** the hard or tough outer covering of an egg, esp a bird's egg **2** the covering or outside part of a fruit or seed, esp when hard or fibrous **3a** a framework or exterior structure; *esp* the outer frame of a building that is unfinished or has been destroyed

(e g by fire) **b** a hollow form devoid of substance **c** an edible case for holding a filling **4** a cold and reserved attitude that conceals the presence or absence of feeling **5a** a projectile for a cannon containing an explosive bursting charge **b** a metal or paper case which holds the charge in cartridges, fireworks, etc

²**shell** v **1** to take out of a natural enclosing cover, esp a pod **2** to fire shells at, on, or into

she'll /shil; *strong* sheel/ she will; she shall

shellac /'shelak/ n the purified form of a resin produced by various insects, usu obtained as yellow or orange flakes; *also* a solution of this in alcohol used esp in making varnish

'**shell,fish** /-,fish/ n an aquatic invertebrate animal with a shell; *esp* an edible mollusc or crustacean

shell out v to pay (money) – infml

'**shell ,shock** n a mental disorder characterized by neurotic and often hysterical symptoms that occurs under conditions (e g wartime combat) that cause intense stress

¹**shelter** /'sheltə/ n **1** sthg. esp a structure, affording cover or protection **2** the state of being covered and protected; refuge

²**shelter** v **1** to take shelter **2** to keep concealed or protected

shelve /shelv/ v **1** to provide with shelves **2** to put off or aside **3** to slope gently

shelving /'shelving/ n (material for constructing) shelves

shenanigan /shi'nanigən/ n **1** deliberate deception; trickery **2** boisterous mischief; high jinks – usu pl with sing. meaning *USE* infml

¹**shepherd** /'shepəd/ n **1** *fem* **shepherdess** one who tends sheep **2** a pastor

²**shepherd** v **1** to tend as a shepherd **2** to guide, marshal, or conduct (people) like sheep

,**shepherd's 'pie** n hot dish of minced meat, esp lamb, with a mashed potato topping

sherbet /'shuhbət/ n **1** (a drink made with) a sweet powder that effervesces in liquid and is eaten dry or used to make fizzy drinks **2** a water ice with egg white, gelatin, or sometimes milk added

sherd /shuhd, shahd/ n **1** a shard **2** fragments of pottery vessels

sheriff /'sherif/ n **1** the honorary chief executive officer of the Crown in each English county who has mainly judicial and ceremonial duties **2** the chief judge of a Scottish county or district **3** a county law enforcement officer in the USA

Sherpa /'shuhpə/ n a member of a Tibetan people living on the high southern slopes of the Himalayas

sherry /'sheri/ n a blended fortified wine that varies in colour from very light to dark brown

she's /shiz; *strong* sheez/ she is; she has

,**Shetland 'pony** n (any of) a breed of small stocky shaggy hardy ponies

shibboleth /'shibə,leth/ n **1a** a catchword, slogan **b** a use of language that distinguishes a group of people **c** a commonplace belief or saying **2** a custom that characterizes members of a particular group

¹**shield** /sheeld/ n **1** a piece of armour (e g of wood, metal, or leather) carried on the arm or in the hand and used esp for warding off blows **2** sby or sthg that protects or shelters; a defence **3** a piece of material or a pad attached inside a garment (e g a dress) at the armpit to protect the garment from perspiration **4** sthg designed to protect people from injury from moving parts of machinery, live electrical conductors, etc **5** the Precambrian central rock mass of a continent

²**shield** v **1** to protect (as if) with a shield; provide with a protective cover or shelter **2** to cut off from observation; hide

¹**shift** /shift/ v **1** to exchange for or replace by another; change **2** to change the place, position, or direction of; move **3** to get rid of; dispose of **4** to assume responsibility for

²**shift** n **1** a loose unfitted slip or dress **2a** a change in direction **b** a change in emphasis, judgment, or attitude **3** *sing or pl in constr* a group who work (e g in a factory) in alternation with other groups **4** a change in place or position

'**shiftless** /-lis/ adj **1** lacking resourcefulness; inefficient **2** lacking ambition or motivation; lazy

'**shifty** /-ti/ adj **1** given to deception, evasion, or fraud; slippery **2** indicative of a fickle or devious nature – **-tily** adv – **-tiness** n

shilling /'shiling/ n **1** (a coin representing) a former money unit of the UK worth 12 old pence or £¹/₂₀ **2** a money unit equal to £¹/₂₀ of any of various other countries (formerly) in the Commonwealth

shilly-shally /'shili ,shali/ v to show hesitation or lack of decisiveness

¹**shimmer** /'shimə/ v **1** to shine with a softly tremulous or wavering light; glimmer **2** to (cause sthg to) appear in a fluctuating wavy form

²**shimmer** n **1** a shimmering light **2** a wavering and distortion of the visual image of a far object usu resulting from heat-induced changes in atmospheric refraction

¹**shin** /shin/ the front part of the leg of a vertebrate animal below the knee; *also* a cut of meat from this part, esp from the front leg

²**shin** v **-nn-** to climb by gripping with the hands or arms and the legs and hauling oneself up or lowering oneself down

'**shin,bone** /-,bohn/ n the tibia

shindy /'shindi/ n pl **shindys, shindies** a quarrel, brawl – infml

¹**shine** /shien/ v **shone** /shon/, (vt 2) **shined 1** to emit light **2** to be bright with reflected light **3** to be outstanding or distinguished **4** to make bright by polishing **5** to direct the light of

[2]**shine** n 1 brightness caused by the emission or reflection of light 2 brilliance, splendour 3 fine weather; sunshine 4 an act of polishing shoes 5 a fancy, crush –esp in *take a shine to*; infml

[1]**shingle** /'shing·gl/ n 1 a small piece of building material for laying in overlapping rows as a covering for the roof or sides of a building 2 a woman's short haircut in which the hair is shaped into the nape of the neck

[2]**shingle** v 1 to cover (as if) with shingles 2 to cut (hair) in a shingle

[3]**shingle** n (a place, esp a seashore, strewn with) small rounded pebbles.

shingles /'shing·glz/ n pl but sing in constr severe short-lasting inflammation of certain nerves that leave the brain and spinal cord, caused by a virus and associated with a rash of blisters and often intense neuralgic pain

shiny /'shieni/ adj 1 bright or glossy in appearance; lustrous, polished 2 of material, clothes, etc rubbed or worn to a smooth surface that reflects light

[1]**ship** /ship/ n 1 a large seagoing vessel 2 a boat (propelled by power or sail) 3 sing or pl in constr a ship's crew 4 an airship, aircraft, or spacecraft — **when one's ship comes in** when one becomes rich

[2]**ship** v -pp- 1 to place or receive on board a ship for transportation 2 to put in place for use 3 to take into a ship or boat 4 to engage for service on a ship 5 to cause to be transported or sent

'**ship,board** /-,bawd/ adj existing or taking place on board a ship

'**shipment** /-mənt/ n 1 the act or process of shipping 2 the quantity of goods shipped

shipper /'shipə/ n a person or company that ships goods

shipping /'shiping/ n 1 ships (in 1 place or belonging to 1 port or country) 2 the act or business of a shipper

'**ship,shape** /-,shayp/ trim, tidy

[1]'**ship,wreck** /-,rek/ n 1 a wrecked ship or its remains 2 the destruction or loss of a ship 3 an irrevocable collapse or destruction

[2]**shipwreck** v 1 to cause to undergo shipwreck 2 to ruin

'**ship,wright** /-,riet/ n a carpenter skilled in ship construction and repair

shire /shie·ə/ n 1a an administrative subdivision; specif an English county, esp with a name ending in -shire b pl the English fox-hunting district consisting chiefly of Leicestershire and Northamptonshire 2 any of a British breed of large heavy draught horses

shirk /shuhk/ v to evade or dodge a duty, responsibility, etc

shirring /'shuhring/ n a decorative gathering, esp in cloth, made by drawing up the material along 2 or more parallel lines of stitching or by stitching in rows of elastic thread or an elastic webbing

shirt /shuht/ n an (esp man's) garment for the upper body; esp one that opens the full length of the centre front and has sleeves and a collar

shirting /'shuhting/ n fabric suitable for shirts

'**shirt-,sleeve** also **shirt-sleeves, shirt-sleeved** adj 1 (having members) without a jacket 2 marked by informality and directness

shirty /'shuhti/ bad-tempered, fractious

shish kebab /,shish ki'bab/ n kebab cooked on skewers

shit /shit/ n -tt-; **shitted, shit, shat** /shat/ 1 faeces 2 an act of defecation 3a nonsense, foolishness b a despicable person USE vulg

shitty /'shiti/ adj nasty, unpleasant – vulg

[1]**shiver** /'shivə/ n any of the small pieces that result from the shattering of sthg brittle

[2]**shiver** v to break into many small fragments; shatter

[3]**shiver** v to tremble, esp with cold or fever

[4]**shiver** n an instance of shivering; a tremor

[1]**shoal** /shohl/ n 1 a shallow 2 an underwater sandbank; esp one exposed at low tide

[2]**shoal** v to become shallow or less deep

[3]**shoal** n a large group (e g of fish)

[1]**shock** /shok/ n a pile of sheaves of grain or stalks of maize set upright in a field

[2]**shock** n 1 a violent shaking or jarring 2a a disturbance in the equilibrium or permanence of sthg (e g a system) b a sudden or violent disturbance of thoughts or emotions 3 a state of serious depression of most bodily functions associated with reduced blood volume and pressure and caused usu by severe injuries, bleeding, or burns 4 sudden stimulation of the nerves and convulsive contraction of the muscles caused by the passage of electricity through the body

[3]**shock** v 1a to cause to feel sudden surprise, terror, horror, or offence b to cause to undergo a physical or nervous shock 2 to cause (e g an animal) to experience an electric shock

[4]**shock** n a thick bushy mass, usu of hair

'**shock ab,sorber** n any of various devices for absorbing the energy of sudden impulses or shocks in machinery, vehicles, etc

shocking /'shoking/ adj 1 giving cause for indignation or offence 2 very bad – infml

'**shock,proof** /-,proohf/ adj resistant to shock; constructed so as to absorb shock without damage

'**shock ,troops** n pl troops trained and selected for assault

shod /shod/ adj 1a wearing shoes, boots, etc b equipped with (a specified type or) tyres 2 furnished or equipped with a shoe

[1]**shoddy** /'shodi/ n a fabric often of inferior quality manufactured wholly or partly from reclaimed wool

²shoddy *adj* 1 made wholly or partly of shoddy **2a** cheaply imitative; vulgarly pretentious **b** hastily or poorly done; inferior **c** shabby

¹shoe /shooh/ *n* **1a** an outer covering for the human foot that does not extend above the ankle and has a thick or stiff sole and often an attached heel **b** a metal plate or rim for the hoof of an animal **2** sthg resembling a shoe in shape or function **3** *pl* a situation, position; *also* a predicament **4** the part of a vehicle braking system that presses on the brake drum

²shoe *v* shoeing; shod /shod/ *also* shoed /shoohd/ **1** to fit (e g a horse) with a shoe **2** to protect or reinforce with a usu metal shoe

'shoe,horn /-,hawn/ *n* a curved piece of metal, plastic, etc used to ease the heel into the back of a shoe

'shoe-,horn *v* to force into a limited space

'shoe,lace /-,lays/ *n* a lace or string for fastening a shoe

¹'shoe,string /-,string/ *n* **1** a shoelace **2** an amount of money inadequate or barely adequate to meet one's needs

²shoestring *adj* operating on, accomplished with, or consisting of a small amount of money

shone /shon/ *past of* shine

¹shoo /shooh/ *interj* – used in frightening away an (esp domestic) animal

²shoo to drive away (as if) by crying 'shoo'

shook /shook/ *past & chiefly dial past part of* shake

¹shoot /shooht/ *v* shot /shot/ **1a** to eject or impel by a sudden release of tension (e g of a bowstring or by a flick of a finger) **b** to drive forth **b(1)** by an explosion (e g of a powder charge in a firearm or of ignited fuel in a rocket) **b(2)** by a sudden release of gas or air **c** to drive the ball or puck in football, hockey, etc towards a goal **d** to send forth with suddenness or intensity **2** to wound or kill with a bullet, arrow, shell, etc shot from a gun, bow, etc **3a** to push or slide (a bolt) in order to fasten or unfasten a door **b** to pass (a shuttle) through the warp threads in weaving **c** to push or thrust forwards; stick out –usu + out **d** to put forth in growing – usu + out **4** to score by shooting **5** to hunt over with a firearm or bow **6** to cause to move suddenly or swiftly forwards **7** to pass swiftly by, over, or along **8** to take a picture or series of pictures or television images of; film; *also* to make (a film, videotape, etc) — **shoot a line** to invent romantic or boastful detail — *infml* — **shoot one's bolt** to exhaust one's capabilities and resources — **shoot one's mouth off** to talk foolishly or indiscreetly

²shoot *n* **1** a stem or branch with its leaves, buds, etc, esp when not yet mature **2a** a shooting trip or party **b** (land over which is held) the right to shoot game **3** (a rush of water down) a descent in a stream

,shooting 'star *n* a meteor appearing as a temporary streak of light in the night sky

'shooting ,stick *n* a spiked stick with a handle that opens out into a seat

'shoot-,out *n* a usu decisive battle fought with handguns or rifles

¹shop /shop/ *n* **1** a building or room for the retail sale of merchandise or for the sale of services **2** a place or part of a factory where a particular manufacturing or repair process takes place **3** the jargon or subject matter peculiar to an occupation or sphere of interest – chiefly in *talk shop*

²shop *v* **-pp-** **1** to visit a shop with intent to purchase goods **2** to make a search; hunt **3** to inform on; betray

shop around *v* to investigate a market or situation in search of the best buy or alternative

'shop ,assistant *n*, *Br* one employed to sell goods in a retail shop

,shop'floor /-'flaw/ *n* the area in which machinery or workbenches are located in a factory or mill, esp considered as a place or work; *also*, *sing or pl in constr* the workers in an establishment as distinct from the management

'shop,lift /-,lift/ *v* to steal from a shop – ~ing *n*

'shopping ,centre *n* a group of retail shops and service establishments of different types, often designed to serve a community or neighbourhood

'shop,soiled /-,soyld/ *adj*, *chiefly Br* **1** deteriorated (e g soiled or faded) through excessive handling or display in a shop **2** no longer fresh or effective; clichéd

,shop 'steward *n* a union member elected to represent usu manual workers

¹shore /shaw/ *n* **1** the land bordering the sea or another (large) body of water **2** land as distinguished from the sea

²shore *v* **1** to support with shores; prop **2** to give support to; brace, sustain – usu + up

³shore *n* a prop for preventing sinking or sagging

shorn /shawn/ *past part of* shear

¹short /shawt/ *adj* **1** having little or insufficient length or height **2a** not extended in time; brief **b** *of the memory* not retentive **c** quick, expeditious **d** seeming to pass quickly **3a** *of a speech sound* having a relatively short duration **b** *of a syllable in prosody* unstressed **4** limited in distance **5a** not coming up to a measure or requirement **b** insufficiently supplied **6a** abrupt, curt **b** quickly provoked **7** *of pastry, biscuits, etc* crisp and easily broken owing to the presence of fat **8** made briefer; abbreviated **9** being or relating to a sale of securities or commodities that the seller does not possess at the time of the sale — **by the short hairs, by the short and curlies** totally at one's mercy — **in the short run** for the immediate future

²short *adv* **1** curtly **2** for or during a brief time **3** in an abrupt manner; suddenly **4** at a point or degree before a specified or intended goal or limit — **be taken/caught short** *Br* to feel a sudden embarrassing need to defecate or urinate

³short *n* **1** *pl* knee-length or less than knee-length trousers **2** *pl* short-term bonds **3** a short circuit **4** a brief often documentary or educational film **5** *Br* a drink of spirits — **for short** as an abbreviation — **in short** by way of summary; briefly

⁴short *v* to short-circuit

shortage /'shawtij/ *n* a lack, deficit

ˌshort'bread /-ˌbred/ *n* a thick biscuit made from flour, sugar, and fat

ˌshort'change /-'chaynj/ *v* **1** to give less than the correct amount of change to **2** to cheat – *infml*

ˌshort-'circuit *v* **1** to apply a short circuit to or cause a short circuit in (so as to render inoperative) **2** to bypass, circumvent

ˌshort 'circuit *n* the accidental or deliberate joining by a conductor of 2 parts of an electric circuit

ˈshort,coming /-ˌkuming/ *n* a deficiency, defect

ˈshort,cut /-ˌkut/ *n* a route or procedure quicker and more direct than one customarily followed

shorten /'shawt(ə)n/ *v* **1** to make short or shorter **2** to add fat to (e g pastry dough) **3** to reduce the area or amount of (sail that is set)

shortening /'shawt(ə)n·ing/ *n* an edible fat (e g butter or lard) used to shorten pastry, biscuits, etc

ˈshortˌfall /-ˌfawl/ *n* (the degree or amount of) a deficit

ˈshortˌhand /-ˌhand/ *n* **1** a method of rapid writing that substitutes symbols and abbreviations for letters, words, or phrases **2** a system or instance of rapid or abbreviated communication

ˌshort'handed /-'handid/ *adj* short of the usual or requisite number of staff; undermanned

ˌshorthand 'typist *n* sby who takes shorthand notes, esp from dictation, then transcribes them using a typewriter

ˈshort ˌlist *n*, *Br* a list of selected candidates (e g for a job) from whom a final choice must be made

ˌshort-'lived *adj* not living or lasting long

ˈshortly /-li/ *adv* **1a** in a few words; briefly **b** in an abrupt manner **2a** in a short time **b** at a short interval

ˌshort-'range *adj* **1** short-term **2** relating to, suitable for, or capable of travelling (only) short distances

short shrift *n* **1** a brief respite for confession before execution **2** summary or inconsiderable treatment

ˌshort'sighted /-'sietid/ *adj* **1** able to see near objects more clearly than distant objects **2** lacking foresight – **~ness** *n*

ˌshort 'story *n* a piece of prose fiction usu dealing with a few characters and often concentrating on mood rather than plot

ˌshort-'term *adj* **1** involving a relatively short period of time **2** of or constituting a financial operation or obligation based on a short term, esp one of less than a year

'short,wave /-ˌwayv/ *n* a band of radio waves having wavelengths between about 120m and 20m and typically used for amateur transmissions or long-range broadcasting – often *pl* with sing. meaning

ˌshort-'winded *adj* **1** affected with or characterized by shortness of breath **2** brief or concise in speaking or writing

¹shot /shot/ *n* **1a** an action of shooting **b** a directed propelling of a missile; *specif* a directed discharge of a firearm **c** a stroke or throw in a game (e g tennis, cricket, or basketball); *also* an attempt to kick the ball into the goal in soccer **d** a hypodermic injection **2a(1)** small lead or steel pellets (for a shotgun) **a(2)** a single (nonexplosive) projectile for a gun or cannon **b** a metal sphere that is thrown for distance as an athletic field event **3** one who shoots; *esp* a marksman **4a** an attempt, try **b** a guess, conjecture **5a** a single photographic exposure **b** an image or series of images in a film or a television programme shot by a camera from 1 angle without interruption **6** a small amount applied at one time; a dose — **like a shot** very rapidly — **shot in the arm** a stimulus, boost — **shot in the dark** a wild guess

²shot *adj* **1a** of a fabric having contrasting and changeable colour effects; iridescent **b** infused or permeated *with* a quality or element **2** utterly exhausted or ruined — **be/get shot of** *chiefly Br* get rid of — *infml*

¹shot,gun /-ˌgun/ *n* an often double-barrelled smoothbore shoulder weapon for firing quantities of metal shot at short ranges

²shotgun *adj* enforced

ˈshot ˌput /poot/ *n* the athletic event of throwing the shot

should /shəd; *strong* shood/ *past of* **shall 1** – used (e g in the main clause of a conditional sentence) to introduce a contingent fact, possibility, or presumption **2** ought to **3** used in reported speech to represent *shall* or *will* **4** will probably **5** –used to soften a direct statement

¹shoulder /'shohldə/ *n* **1** the part of the human body formed of bones, joints, and muscles that connects the arm to the trunk; *also* a corresponding part of another animal **2** *pl* **2a** the 2 shoulders and the upper part of the back **b** capacity for bearing a burden (e g of blame or responsibility) **3** a cut of meat including the upper joint of the foreleg and adjacent parts **4** an area adjacent to a higher, more prominent, or more important part; e g **4a(1)** the slope of a mountain near the top **a(2)** a lateral protrusion of a mountain **b** that part of a road to the side of the surface on which vehicles travel **5** a rounded or sloping part (e g of a stringed instrument or a bottle) where the neck joins the body

²**shoulder** *v* **1** to push or thrust (as if) with the shoulder **2a** to place or carry on the shoulder **b** to assume the burden or responsibility

'**shoulder ,blade** *n* the scapula

shouldest /shoodist/, **shouldst** /shoodst/ *archaic past* **2** *sing of* **shall**

¹**shout** /showt/ *v* **1** to utter a sudden loud cry or in a loud voice **2** to buy a round of drinks

²**shout** *n* **1** a loud cry or call **2** a round of drinks

shove /shuv/ *v* **1** to push along with steady force **2** to push in a rough, careless, or hasty manner; thrust **3** to force a way forwards – **shove** *n*

¹**shovel** /'shuvl/ *n* **1** an implement consisting of a broad scoop or a dished blade with a handle, used to lift and throw loose material **2** (a similar part on) a digging or earth-moving machine

²**shovel** *v* **-ll-** (*NAm* **-l-**, **-ll-**), /'shuvl·ing, 'shuvling/ **1** to dig, clear, or shift with a shovel **2** to convey clumsily or in a mass as if with a shovel

shove off *v* to go away; leave – *infml*

¹**show** /shoh/ *v* **shown** /shohn/, **showed** **1a** to cause or permit to be seen; exhibit **b** to be or come in view **c** to appear in a specified way **2** to present as a public spectacle **3** to reveal by one's condition **4** to demonstrate by one's achievements **5a** to point out to sby **b** to conduct, usher **6** to make evident; indicate **7a** to establish or make clear by argument or reasoning **b** to inform, instruct — **show one's hand** to declare one's intentions or reveal one's resources — **show one's true colours** to show one's real nature or opinions — **show over** *chiefly Br* to take on a tour or inspection of — **show someone the door** to tell sby to get out

²**show** *n* **1** a display – often + *on* **2a** a false semblance; a pretence **b** a more or less true appearance of sthg **c** an impressive display **d** ostentation **3a** a large display or exhibition arranged to arouse interest or stimulate sales **b** a competitive exhibition of animals, plants, etc to demonstrate quality in breeding, growing, etc **4a** a theatrical presentation **b** a radio or television programme **5** an enterprise, affair

'**show ,biz** /biz/ *n* show business – *infml*

'**show ,business** *n* the arts, occupations, and businesses (e g theatre, films, and television) that comprise the entertainment industry

'**show,down** /-,down/ *n* the final settlement of a contested issue or the confrontation by which it is settled

¹**shower** /'showə/ *n* **1** a fall of rain, snow, etc of short duration **2** sthg like a rain shower **3** an apparatus that provides a stream of water for spraying on the body; *also* an act of washing oneself using such an apparatus **4** *sing or pl in constr*, *Br* a motley or inferior collection of people – *infml*

²**shower** *v* **1a** to wet copiously (e g with water) in a spray, fine stream, or drops **b** to descend (as if) in a shower **c** to cause to fall in a shower **2** to bestow or present in abundance **3** to take a shower

showing /'shoh·ing/ *n* **1** an act of putting sthg on view; a display, exhibition **2** performance in competition

'**show,jumping** /-,jumping/ *n* the competitive riding of horses **1** at a time over a set course of obstacles

'**showman** /-mən/ *n* **1** one who presents a theatrical show; *also* the manager of a circus or fairground **2** a person with a flair for dramatically effective presentation

show off *v* **1** to exhibit proudly **2** to seek attention or admiration by conspicuous behaviour – **show-off** *n*

'**show,piece** /-,pees/ *n* a prime or outstanding example used for exhibition

'**show,place** /-,plays/ *n* a place (e g an estate or building) regarded as an example of beauty or excellence

'**show,room** /-,roohm/ *n* a room where (samples of) goods for sale are displayed

show up *v* **1a** to be plainly evident; stand out **b** to appear in a specified light or manner **2** to expose (e g a defect, deception, or impostor) **3** to embarrass **4** to arrive

showy /'shoh·i/ *adj* **1** making an attractive show; striking **2** given to or marked by pretentious display; gaudy – **-wily** *adv* – **-winess** *n*

shrank /shrangk/ *past of* **shrink**

shrapnel /'shrapnəl/ *n pl* **shrapnel** **1** a hollow projectile that contains bullets or pieces of metal and that is exploded by a bursting charge to produce a shower of fragments **2** bomb, mine, or shell fragments thrown out during explosion

¹**shred** /shred/ *n* a narrow strip cut or torn off; *also* a fragment, scrap

²**shred** *v* **-dd-** to cut or tear into shreds – **~der** *n*

shrew /shrooh/ *n* **1** any of numerous small chiefly nocturnal mammals having a long pointed snout, very small eyes, and velvety fur **2** an ill-tempered nagging woman; a scold

shrewd /shroohd/ *adj* **1** marked by keen discernment and hardheaded practicality **2** wily, artful – **~ly** *adv* – **~ness** *n*

shrewish /'shrooh-ish/ *adj* ill-tempered, intractable

¹**shriek** /shreek/ *v* **1** to utter or make a shrill piercing cry; screech **2** to utter with a shriek or sharply and shrilly – often + *out*

²**shriek** *n* (a sound similar to) a shrill usu wild cry

shrike /shriek/ *n* any of numerous usu largely grey or brownish birds that often impale their (insect) prey on thorns

¹**shrill** /shril/ *v* to utter or emit a high-pitched piercing sound

²shrill *adj* having, making, or being a sharp high-pitched sound

¹shrimp /shrimp/ *n pl* **shrimps**, (1) **shrimps**, *esp collectively* **shrimp 1** any of numerous mostly small marine 10-legged crustacean animals with a long slender body, compressed abdomen, and long legs **2** a very small or puny person – infml; humor

²shrimp *v* to fish for or catch shrimps – usu in *go shrimping*

shrine /shrien/ *n* **1a** a receptacle for sacred relics **b** a place in which devotion is paid to a saint or deity **2** a place or object hallowed by its history or associations

¹shrink /shringk/ *v* **shrank** /shrangk/ *also* **shrunk** /shrungk/; **shrunk, shrunken** /'shrungkən/ **1** to draw back or cower away (e g from sthg painful or horrible) **2** to contract to a smaller volume or extent (e g as a result of heat or moisture) **3** to show reluctance (e g before a difficult or unpleasant duty); recoil

²shrink *n* **1** shrinkage **2** a psychoanalyst or psychiatrist – humor

shrivel /'shrivl/ *v* **-ll-** (*NAm* **-l-, -ll-**), /'shrivl·ing/ to (cause to) contract into wrinkles, esp through loss of moisture

¹shroud /shrowd/ *n* **1** a burial garment (e g a winding sheet) **2** sthg that covers, conceals, or guards **3** any of the ropes or wires giving support, usu in pairs, to a ship's mast

²shroud *v* **1** to envelop and conceal **2** to obscure, disguise

Shrove 'Tuesday *n* the Tuesday before Ash Wednesday; pancake day

shrub /shrub/ *n* a low-growing usu several-stemmed woody plant – ~**by** *adj*

shrubbery /'shrub(ə)ri/ *n* a planting or growth of shrubs, esp in a garden

shrug /shrug/ *v* **-gg-** to lift and contract (the shoulders), esp to express aloofness, aversion, or doubt – **shrug** *n*

shrug off *v* to brush aside; disregard, belittle

shrunk /shrungk/ *past & past part of* **shrink**

shrunken /'shrungkən/ *past part of* **shrink**

¹shuck /shuk/ *n* **1** a pod, husk **2** *pl* – used interjectionally to express mild annoyance or disappointment; infml

²shuck *v, NAm* to remove or dispose of like a shuck – often + *off*

shudder /'shudə/ *v* **1** to tremble with a sudden brief convulsive movement **2** to quiver, vibrate – **shudder** *n*

¹shuffle /'shufl/ *v* **shuffling** /'shufling, 'shuf·ling/ **1** to rearrange (e g playing cards or dominoes) to produce a random order **2** to move or walk by sliding or dragging the feet – ~**r** *n*

²shuffle *n* **1a** shuffling (of cards) **b** a right or turn to shuffle **2** (a dance characterized by) a dragging sliding movement

shun /shun/ *v* **-nn-** to avoid deliberately, esp habitually

¹shunt /shunt/ *v* **1** to move a train from one track to another **2** to travel back and forth

²shunt *n* **1** a means or mechanism for turning or thrusting aside **2** a usu minor collision of motor vehicles – infml

¹shush /sh, shush/ *n* **1** – used interjectionally to demand silence **2** peace and quiet; silence – infml

²shush *v* to tell to be quiet, esp by saying 'Shush!' – infml

shut /shut/ *v* **-tt-; shut 1** to place in position to close an opening **2** to confine (as if) by enclosure **3** to fasten with a lock or bolt **4** to close by bringing enclosing or covering parts together **5** to cause to cease or suspend operation – usu + *down*

'shut,down /-,down/ *n* the cessation or suspension of an activity (e g work in a mine or factory)

'shut-,eye *n* sleep – infml

¹shutter /'shutə/ *n* **1** a usu hinged outside cover for a window, often fitted as one of a pair **2** a device that opens and closes the lens aperture of a camera

²shutter *v* to provide or close with shutters

¹shuttle /'shutl/ *n* **1a** a usu spindle-shaped device that holds a bobbin and is used in weaving for passing the thread of the weft between the threads of the warp **b** a sliding thread holder that carries the lower thread in a sewing machine through a loop of the upper thread to make a stitch **2** a lightweight conical object with a rounded nose that is hit as the object of play in badminton and consists of (a moulded plastic imitation of) a cork with feathers stuck in it **3a** (a route or vehicle for) a regular going back and forth over a usu short route **b** a reusable space vehicle for use esp between earth and outer space

²shuttle *v* **shuttling** /'shutl·ing, 'shutling/ **1** to (cause to) move to and fro rapidly **2** to transport or be transported (as if) in or by a shuttle

'shuttle,cock /-,kok/ *n* a badminton shuttle

shut up *v* to become silent; *esp* to stop talking USE infml

¹shy /shie/ *adj* **shier, shyer; shiest, shyest 1** easily alarmed; timid, distrustful – often in combination **2** wary of **3** sensitively reserved or retiring; bashful; *also* expressive of such a state or nature – ~**ly** *adv* – ~**ness** *n*

²shy *v* **1** to start suddenly aside in fright or alarm; recoil **2** to move or dodge to evade a person or thing – usu + *away* or *from*

³shy *v* to throw with a jerking movement; fling

⁴shy *n* **1** a toss, throw **2** a verbal sally **3** a stall (e g at a fairground) in which people throw balls at targets (e g coconuts) in order to knock them down **4** an attempt

shyster /'shiestə/ *n, chiefly NAm* sby (esp a lawyer) who is professionally unscrupulous

SI *n* a system of units whose basic units are the metre, kilogram, second, ampere, kelvin, candela, and mole and which uses prefixes (e g micro-, kilo-, and mega-) to indicate multiples or fractions of 10

,**Siamese 'twin** *n* either of a pair of congenitally joined twins

sibilant /'sibilənt/ *adj* having, containing, or producing a hissing sound (e g sh,zh, s, z/) – **sibilant** *n*

sibling /'sibling/ *n* any of 2 or more individuals having common parents

sibyl /'sibil/ *n, often cap* any of several female prophets credited to widely separate parts of the ancient world; *broadly* any female prophet – ~ **ine** *adj*

sic /sik/ *adv* intentionally so written – used after a printed word or passage to indicate that it is intended exactly as printed or that it exactly reproduces an original

¹**sick** /sik/ *adj* **1a** ill, ailing **b** queasy, nauseated; likely to vomit – often in combination **2a** disgusted or weary, esp because of surfeit **b** distressed and longing for sthg that one has lost or been parted from **3** mentally or emotionally disturbed; *also* macabre – ~ **en** *v* — **be sick** *chiefly Br* to vomit

²**sick** *n, Br* vomit

'**sick ,bay** *n* a compartment or room (e g in a ship) used as a dispensary and hospital

sicken /'sikən/ *v* **1** to become ill; show signs of illness **2** to drive to the point of despair or loathing

sickening /'sikəning/ *adj* very horrible or repugnant – ~ **ly** *adv*

¹**sickle** /'sikl/ *n* **1** an agricultural implement for cutting plants or hedges, consisting of a curved metal blade with a short handle **2** a cutting mechanism (e g of a combine harvester) consisting of a bar with a series of cutting parts

²**sickle** *adj* having a curve resembling that of a sickle blade

sickly /'sikli/ *adj* **1** somewhat unwell; *also* habitually ailing **2** feeble, weak **3** mawkish, saccharine – ~ **liness** *n*

'**sickness** /-nis/ *n* **1** ill health **2** a specific disease **3** nausea, queasiness

¹**side** /sied/ *n* **1a** the right or left part of the wall or trunk of the body **b** the right or left half of the animal body or of a meat carcass **2** a location, region, or direction considered in relation to a centre or line of division **3** a surface forming a border or face of an object **4** a slope of a hill, ridge, etc **5** a bounding line or surface of a geometrical figure **6a** *sing or pl in constr* a person or group in competition or dispute with another **b** the attitude or activity of such a person or group; a part **7** a line of descent traced through a parent **8** an aspect or part of sthg viewed in contrast with some other aspect or part — **on the side 1** in addition to a principal occupation; *specif* as a dishonest or illegal secondary activity **2** *NAm* in addition to the main portion

²**side** *adj* **1** at, from, towards, etc the side **2a** incidental, subordinate **b** made on the side, esp in secret **c** additional to the main part or portion

³**side** *v* to take sides; join or form sides

'**side ,arm** *n* a weapon (e g a sword, revolver, or bayonet) worn at the side or in the belt

'**side ,board** /-,bawd/ *n* **1** a usu flat-topped piece of dining-room furniture having compartments and shelves for holding articles of table service **2** *pl, Br* whiskers on the side of the face that extend from the hairline to below the ears

'**side ,car** /-,kah/ *n* a car attached to the side of a motorcycle or motor scooter for 1 or more passengers

'**side ,light** /-,liet/ *n* **1** incidental or additional information **2a** the red port light or the green starboard light carried by ships travelling at night **b** a light at the side of a (motor) vehicle

'**side ,line** /-,lien/ *n* **1** a line at right angles to a goal line or end line and marking a side of a court or field of play **2a** a line of goods manufactured or esp sold in addition to one's principal line **b** a business or activity pursued in addition to a full-time occupation

¹**side ,long** /-,long/ *adv* towards the side; obliquely

²**sidelong** *adj* **1** inclining or directed to one side **2** indirect rather than straightforward

sidereal /sie'diəri·əl/ *adj* of or expressed in relation to stars or constellations

sidesaddle /'sied,sadl/ *n* a saddle for women in which the rider sits with both legs on the same side of the horse

'**side ,show** /-,shoh/ *n* **1** a fairground booth or counter offering a game of luck or skill **2** an incidental diversion

sidesman /'siedzmən/ *n* any of a group of people in an Anglican church who assist the churchwardens, esp in taking the collection in services

'**side ,splitting** /-,spliting/ *adj* causing raucous laughter

'**side ,step** /-,step/ *v* **-pp-** **1** to step sideways or to one side **2** to evade an issue or decision

'**side ,street** *n* a minor street branching off a main thoroughfare

¹**side ,track** /-,trak/ *n* an unimportant line of thinking that is followed instead of a more important one

²**sidetrack** *v* to divert from a course or purpose; distract

'**sidewards** /-woodz/, *NAm chiefly* **sideward** *adv* towards one side

'side,ways /-ˌwayz/, *NAm also* **sideway** /-ˌway/ *adv or adj* **1** to or from the side; *also* askance **2** with 1 side forward (e g turn it *sideways*) **3** to a position of equivalent rank (e g he was promoted *sideways*)

siding /'sieding/ *n* a short railway track connected with the main track

sidle /'siedl/ *v* **sidling** /'siedling/ **1** to move obliquely **2** to walk timidly or hesitantly; edge along – usu + *up*

siege /seej/ *n* a military blockade of a city or fortified place to compel it to surrender — **lay siege to 1** to besiege militarily **2** to pursue diligently or persistently

sienna /si'enə/ *n* an earthy substance that is brownish yellow when raw and orange red or reddish brown when burnt and is used as a pigment

sierra /si'eərə/ *n* a range of mountains, esp with a serrated or irregular outline

siesta /si'estə/ *n* an afternoon nap or rest

'sieve /siv/ *n* a device with a meshed or perforated bottom that will allow the passage of liquids or fine solids while retaining coarser material or solids

'sieve *v* to sift

sift /sift/ *v* **1a** to put through a sieve **b** to separate (out) (as if) by passing through a sieve **2** to scatter (as if) with a sieve — **sift through** to make a close examination of (things in a mass or group)

sifter /'siftə/ *n* a castor for strewing sugar, flour, etc

'sigh /sie/ *v* **1** to take a long deep audible breath (e g in weariness or grief) **2** *esp of the wind* to make a sound like sighing **3** to grieve, yearn – usu + *for*

'sigh *n* an act of sighing, esp when expressing an emotion or feeling (e g weariness or relief)

'sight /siet/ *n* **1** thing seen; *esp* a spectacle **2a** a thing (e g an impressive or historic building) regarded as worth seeing – often pl **b** sthg ridiculous or displeasing in appearance **3** the process, power, or function of seeing **4** a view, glimpse **5** the range of vision **6a** a device for guiding the eye (e g in aiming a firearm or bomb) **b** a device with a small aperture through which objects are to be seen and by which their direction is ascertained **7** a great deal; a lot – *infml* — **at first sight** when viewed without proper investigation — **at/on sight** as soon as presented to view — **out of sight 1** beyond all expectation or reason **2** *chiefly NAm* marvellous, wonderful – *infml*; no longer in vogue — **sight for sore eyes** sby or sthg whose appearance or arrival is an occasion for joy or relief

'sight *v* **1** to get or catch sight of **2** to aim (e g a weapon) by means of sights – ~ing *n*

'sighted *adj* having sight, esp of a specified kind – often in combination

'sightly /-li/ *adj* pleasing to the eye; attractive – ~liness *n*

'sight-,read /reed/ *v* **sight-read** /red/ to read at sight; *esp* to perform music at sight – ~er *n* – ~ing *n*

sight screen *n* a screen placed on the boundary of a cricket field behind the bowler to improve the batsman's view of the ball

'sight,seeing /-see-ing/ *n* the act or pastime of touring interesting or attractive sights – often in **go sightseeing** – **seer** *n*

'sign /sien/ *n* **1a** a motion or gesture by which a thought, command, or wish is made known **b** a signal **2** a mark with a conventional meaning, used to replace or supplement words **3** a character (e g ÷) indicating a mathematical operation; *also* either of 2 characters + and – that form part of the symbol of a number and characterize it as positive or negative **4** a board or notice bearing information or advertising matter or giving warning, command, or identification **5a** sthg serving to indicate the presence or existence of sby or sthg **b** a presage, portent

'sign *v* **1** to indicate, represent, or express by a sign **2** to put one's signature to **3** to engage by securing the signature of on a contract of employment – often + *on* or *up*

'signal /'signəl/ *n* **1** sthg that occasions action **2** a conventional sign (e g a siren or flashing light) made to give warning or command **3** an object used to transmit or convey information beyond the range of human voice **4** the sound or image conveyed in telegraphy, telephony, radio, radar, or television

'signal *v* -ll- (*NAm* -l-, -ll-) **1** to warn, order, or request by a signal **2** to communicate by signals **3** to be a sign of; mark

'signal *adj* **1** used in signalling **2** distinguished from the ordinary; conspicuous – *chiefly fml*

'signal,box /-ˌboks/ *n*, *Br* a raised building above a railway line from which signals and points are worked

signally /'signəli/ *adv* in a signal manner; remarkably – *chiefly fml*

'signalman /-mən/ *n pl* **signalmen** /-mən/ sby employed to operate signals (e g for a railway)

signatory /'signət(ə)ri/ *n* a signer with another or others; *esp* a government bound with others by a signed convention

signature /'signəchə/ *n* **1** the name of a person written with his/her own hand **2** a letter or figure placed usu at the bottom of the first page on each sheet of printed pages (e g of a book) as a direction to the binder in gathering the sheets

'signature ,tune *n* a melody, passage, or song used to identify a programme, entertainer, etc

signet /'signit/ *n* **1** a personal seal used officially in place of signature **2** a small intaglio seal (e g in a finger ring)

significance /sig'nifikəns/ n 1 sthg conveyed as a meaning, often latently or indirectly 2 the quality of being important; consequence

significant /sig'nifikənt/ adj 1 having meaning; esp expressive 2 suggesting or containing a veiled or special meaning 3a having or likely to have influence or effect; important b probably caused by sthg other than chance – ~ly adv

signify /'signifie/ v 1 to mean, denote 2 to show, esp by a conventional token (e g a word, signal, or gesture)

sign off v 1 to announce the end of a message, programme, or broadcast and finish broadcasting 2 to end a letter (e g with a signature)

sign on v 1 to commit oneself to a job by signature or agreement 2 Br to register as unemployed, esp at an employment exchange

signor /'seen,yaw, -,-'-/ n, pl signors, signori /-ri/ an Italian man – used as a title equivalent to Mr

signora /seen'yawrə/ n, pl signoras, signore /-ray/ an Italian married woman – used as a title equivalent to Mrs or as a generalized term of direct address

signorina /,seenyaw'reenə/ n, pl signorinas, signorine /-nay/ an unmarried Italian girl or woman – used as a title equivalent to Miss

¹**sign post** /-,pohst/ n a post (e g at a road junction) with signs on it to direct travellers

²**signpost** v 1 to provide with signposts or guides 2 to indicate, mark, esp conspicuously

sign up v to join an organization or accept an obligation by signing a contract; esp to enlist in the armed services

Sikh /seek/ n or adj (an adherent) of a monotheistic religion of India marked by rejection of idolatry and caste

silage /'sielij/ n fodder converted, esp in a silo, into succulent feed for livestock

¹**silence** /'sieləns/ n 1 forbearance from speech or noise; muteness 2 absence of sound or noise; stillness 3 failure to mention a particular thing 4a oblivion, obscurity b secrecy

²**silence** v 1 to put or reduce to silence; still 2 to restrain from expression; suppress 3 to cause (a gun, mortar, etc) to cease firing by return fire, bombing, etc

silencer /'sielənsə/ n 1 a silencing device for a small firearm 2 chiefly Br a device for deadening the noise of the exhaust gas release of an internal-combustion engine

silent /'sielənt/ adj 1 mute, speechless; also not talkative 2 free from sound or noise; also without spoken dialogue 3a endured without utterance b conveyed by refraining from reaction or comment; tacit – ~ly adv

silhouette /,silooh'et/ n 1 a portrait in profile cut from dark material and mounted on a light background 2 the shape of a body as it appears against a lighter background – silhouette v

silica /'silikə/ n silicon dioxide occurring in many rocks and minerals (e g quartz, opal, and sand)

silicate /'silikət, -kayt/ n any of numerous insoluble often complex compounds that contain silicon and oxygen, constitute the largest class of minerals, and are used in building materials (e g cement, bricks, and glass)

silicon /'silikən/ n a nonmetallic element that occurs, in combination with other elements, as the most abundant element next to oxygen in the earth's crust and is used esp in alloys

silk /silk/ n 1 a fibre produced by various insect larvae, usu for cocoons; esp a lustrous tough elastic fibre produced by silkworms and used for textiles 2 thread, yarn, or fabric made from silk filaments

silken /'silkən/ adj 1 made of silk 2 resembling silk, esp in softness or lustre

silk screen, silk-screen printing n a stencil process in which paint or ink is forced onto the material to be printed, through the meshes of a prepared silk screen

'**silk,worm** /-,wuhm/ n a moth whose larva spins a large amount of strong silk in constructing its cocoon

silky /'silki/ adj 1 silken 2 having or covered with fine soft hairs, plumes, or scales – silkiness n

sill /sil/ n a horizontal piece (e g a timber) that forms the lowest member or one of the lowest members of a framework or supporting structure (e g a window frame or door frame)

silly /'sili/ adj 1a showing a lack of common sense or sound judgment b trifling, frivolous 2 stunned, dazed – silliness n

silo /'sieloh/ n pl silos 1 a trench, pit, or esp a tall cylinder (e g of wood or concrete) usu sealed to exclude air and used for making and storing silage 2 an underground structure for housing a guided missile

¹**silt** /silt/ n a deposit of sediment (e g at the bottom of a river)

²**silt** v to make or become choked or obstructed with silt – often + up

¹**silver** /'silvə/ n 1 a white ductile and malleable metallic element that takes a very high degree of polish and has the highest thermal and electrical conductivity of any substance 2 coins made of silver or cupro-nickel 3 articles, esp tableware, made of or plated with silver; also cutlery made of other metals 4 a whitish grey colour 5 a silver medal for second place in a competition

²**silver** adj 1 made of silver 2 resembling silver, esp in having a white lustrous sheen 3 consisting of or yielding silver 4 of or marking a 25th anniversary

,**silver 'birch** n a common Eurasian birch with a silvery-white trunk

'silver₁fish /-₁fish/ n any of various small wingless insects; esp one found in houses and sometimes injurious to sized paper (e g wallpaper) or starched fabrics

'silver₁smith /-₁smith/ n sby who works in silver

silvery /'silv(ə)ri/ adj 1 having a soft clear musical tone 2 having the lustre or whiteness of silver

similar /'similə/ adj 1 marked by correspondence or resemblance, esp of a general kind 2 alike in 1 or more essential aspects – ~ity n – ~ly adv

simile /'simili/ n a figure of speech explicitly comparing 2 unlike things (e g in *cheeks like roses*)

simmer /'simə/ v 1 to bubble gently below or just at the boiling point 2 to be agitated by suppressed emotion – **simmer** n

¹simper /'simpə/ v to smile in a foolish self-conscious manner

²simper n a foolish self-conscious smile

simple /'simpl/ adj 1a free from guile or vanity; unassuming b free from elaboration or showiness; unpretentious 2a lacking intelligence; esp mentally retarded b naive 3a sheer, unqualified b composed essentially of 1 substance 4 not subdivided 5 readily understood or performed; straightforward

simple interest n interest paid or calculated on only the original capital sum of a loan

₁simple'minded /-'miendid/ adj devoid of subtlety; unsophisticated; *also* mentally retarded

simplicity /sim'plisiti/ n 1 the state or quality of being simple 2 naivety 3 freedom from affectation or guile 4a directness of expression; clarity b restraint in ornamentation

simplify /'simplifie/ v to make or become simple or simpler – **-fication** n

simply /'simpli/ adv 1a without ambiguity; clearly b without ornamentation or show c without affectation or subterfuge; candidly 2a solely, merely b without any question

simulate /'simyoo₁layt/ v 1 to assume the outward qualities or appearance of, usu with the intent to deceive 2 to make a functioning model of (a system, device, or process) (e g by using a computer) – ~d adj – -ator n – -ation n

simultaneous /₁siml'taynyəs, -ni-əs/ adj existing, occurring, or functioning at the same time – ~ly adv – -neity, ~ness n

¹sin /sin/ n 1 an offence against moral or religious law or divine commandments 2 an action considered highly reprehensible

²sin v -nn- to commit a sin or an offence – often + *against* – ~ner n

¹since /sins/ adv 1 continuously from then until now (e g has stayed here ever *since*) 2 before now; ago (e g should have done it long *since*) 3 between then and now; subsequently (e g has *since* become rich) USE + tenses formed with *to have*

²since prep in the period between (a specified past time) and now (e g haven't met *since* 1973); from (a specified past time) until now (e g it's a long time *since* breakfast) – + present tenses and tenses formed with *to have*

³since conj 1 between now and the past time when (e g has held 2 jobs *since* he left school); continuously from the past time when (e g ever *since* he was a child) 2 in view of the fact that; because (e g more interesting, *since* rarer)

sincere /sin'siə/ adj free from deceit or hypocrisy; honest, genuine – ~ly adv – -rity n

sine /sien/ n the trigonometric function that for an acute angle in a right-angled triangle is the ratio between the side opposite the angle and the hypotenuse

sinecure /'sinikyooə, 'sie-/ n an office or position that provides an income while requiring little or no work

sinew /'sinfooh/ n 1 a tendon 2a solid resilient strength; vigour b the chief means of support; mainstay

sinful /'sinf(ə)l/ adj tainted with, marked by, or full of sin; wicked – ~ly adv – ~ness n

sing /sing/ v sang /sang/, sung /sung/; sung 1a to produce musical sounds by means of the voice b to utter words in musical notes and with musical inflections and modulations 2 to make a loud clear sound or utterance 3a to relate or celebrate in verse b to express vividly or enthusiastically 4 to give information or evidence – slang – ~able adj – ~er n

singe /sinj/ v singeing; singed to burn superficially or slightly; scorch – **singe** n

¹single /'sing-gl/ adj 1 not married 2 not accompanied by others; sole 3 consisting of or having only 1 part or feature 4 consisting of a separate unique whole; individual 5 of *combat* involving only 2 people

²single n 1 a single person, thing or amount 2 a single run scored in cricket 3 a gramophone record, esp of popular music, with a single short track on each side 4 *Br* a ticket bought for a trip to a place but not back again

³single v to select or distinguish from a number or group – usu + *out*

₁single-'breasted adj having a centre fastening with 1 row of buttons

₁single 'file n a line (e g of people) moving one behind the other

₁single-'handed adj 1 performed or achieved by 1 person or with 1 on a side 2 working or managing alone or unassisted by others

₁single-'minded adj having a single overriding purpose – ~ly adv – ~ness n

'singles n pl singles a game (e g of tennis) with 1 player on each side

singlet /'sing-glit/ n, chiefly Br a vest

singsong /'sing,song/ n 1 a voice delivery characterized by a monotonous cadence or rhythm or rising and falling inflection 2 Br a session of group singing

¹**singular** /'sing·gyoolə/ adj 1a of a separate person or thing; individual b of or being a word form denoting 1 person, thing, or instance 2 distinguished by superiority; exceptional 3 not general 4 very unusual or strange; peculiar

²**singular** n the singular number, the inflectional form denoting it, or a word in that form

Sinhalese /,sinhə'leez/ n, pl **Sinhalese** 1 a member of the predominant people that inhabit Sri Lanka 2 the Indic language of the Sinhalese

sinister /'sinistə/ adj 1 (darkly or insidiously) evil or productive of vice 2 threatening evil or ill fortune; ominous 3 of or situated on the left side or to the left of sthg, esp in heraldry

¹**sink** /sip/ v **sank** /sangk/, **sunk** /sungk/; **sunk 1a** to go down below a surface (e g of water or a soft substance) **b** to cause sthg to penetrate **2a** to fall or drop to a lower place or level **b** to disappear from view **c** to take on a hollow appearance **3** to be or become deeply absorbed in 4 to dig or bore (a well or shaft) in the earth **5** to invest — ~ **able** adj

²**sink** n 1 a basin, esp in a kitchen, connected to a drain and usu a water supply for washing up **2** a place of vice or corruption **3** a depression in which water (e g from a river) collects and becomes absorbed or evaporated

sink in v 1 to enter a solid through the surface **2** to become understood

sinuous /'sinyoo·əs/ adj 1a of or having a serpentine or wavy form; winding **b** lithe, supple **2** intricate, tortuous — **-osity**, ~ **ness** n

sinus /'sinəs/ n a cavity, hollow: esp any of several cavities in the skull that usu communicate with the nostrils and contain air

¹**sip** /sip/ v **-pp-** to drink (sthg) delicately or a little at a time

²**sip** n (a small quantity imbibed by) sipping

¹**siphon, syphon** /'siefən/ n 1 a tube by which a liquid can be transferred up over the wall of a container to a lower level by using atmospheric pressure **2** a bottle for holding carbonated water in which the pressure of the gas is used to drive the contents out when a valve is opened

²**siphon, syphon** v to draw off, empty, etc, (as if) using a siphon

¹**sir** /sə; strong suh/ n 1 a man entitled to be addressed as sir – used as a title before the Christian name of a knight or baronet **2a** – used as a usu respectful form of address to a male **b** cap – used as a conventional form of address at the beginning of a letter

¹**sire** /sie·ə/ n 1 the male parent of a (domestic) animal **2** archaic **2a** a father **b** a male ancestor **3** a man of rank or authority; esp a lord – used formerly as a title and form of address

²**sire** v 1 to beget – esp with reference to a male domestic animal **2** to bring into being; originate

siren /'sierən/ n 1 often cap any of a group of mythological partly human female creatures that lured mariners to destruction by their singing **2** a dangerously alluring or seductive woman; a temptress **3** a usu electrically operated device for producing a penetrating warning sound

sirloin /'suh,loyn/ n a cut of beef from the upper part of the hind loin just in front of the rump

sirocco /si'rokoh/ n pl **siroccos 1** a hot dust-laden wind from the Libyan deserts that blows onto the N Mediterranean coast **2** a warm moist oppressive southeasterly wind in the same regions

sisal /'siesl/ n (a W Indian plant whose leaves yield) a strong white fibre used esp for ropes and twine

¹**sister** /'sistə/ n 1a a female having the same parents as another person **b** a half sister **2** often cap (the title given to) a Roman Catholic nun **3** a woman related to another person by a common tie or interest (e g adherence to feminist principles) **4** chiefly Br a female nurse; esp one who is next in rank below a nursing officer and is in charge of a ward or a small department — ~ **hood** n

²**sister** adj related (as if) by sisterhood; essentially similar

'sister-in-,law n, pl **sisters-in-law 1** the sister of one's spouse **2** the wife of one's brother

sit /sit/ v **-tt-; sat** /sat/ **1a** to rest on the buttocks or haunches **b** to perch, roost **2** to occupy a place as a member of an official body **3** to be in session for official business **4** to cover eggs for hatching **5a** to take up a position for being photographed or painted **b** to act as a model **6** to lie or hang relative to a wearer **7** to take a examination — **sit on 1** to repress, squash **2** to delay action or decision concerning — **sit on one's hands** to fail to take action — **sit on the fence** to adopt a position of neutrality or indecision

sitar /si'tah/ n an Indian lute with a long neck and a varying number of strings

¹**site** /siet/ n 1 an area of ground that was, is, or will be occupied by a structure or set of structures (e g a building, town, or monument) **2** the place, scene, or point of sthg

²**site** v to place on a site or in position; locate

'sit-,in n a continuous occupation of a building by a body of people as a protest and means towards forcing compliance with demands

sit in v to participate as a visitor or observer – usu + on

sit out v 1 to remain until the end of or the departure of **2** to refrain from participating in

sitter /'sitə/ n 1 sby who sits (e g as an artist's model) **2** a baby-sitter

¹**sitting** /'siting/ n 1 a single occasion of continuous sitting (e g for a portrait or meal) **2** a session

²**sitting** *adj* **1** that is sitting **2** in office or actual possession — **sitting pretty** in a highly favourable or satisfying position

,**sitting 'duck** *n* an easy or defenceless target for attack, criticism, or exploitation

situated /'sityoo,aytid, 'sichoo-/ *adj* **1** located **2** supplied to the specified extent with money or possessions **3** being in the specified situation

,**situ'ation** /,sityoo'aysh(ə)n, ,sichoo-/ *n* **1a** the way in which sthg is placed in relation to its surroundings **b** a locality **2** position with respect to conditions and circumstances **3** the circumstances at a particular moment; *esp* a critical or problematic state of affairs **4** a position of employment; a post – *chiefly fml*

sit up *v* **1** to show interest, alertness, or surprise **2** to stay up after the usual time for going to bed

six /siks/ *n* **1** the number 6 **2** the sixth in a set or series **3** sthg having 6 parts or members or a denomination of 6: e g **3a** a shot in cricket that crosses the boundary before it bounces and so scores 6 runs **b** *pl in constr, cap* the Common Market countries before 1973 – ~ **th** *adj, n, pron, adv* — **at sixes and sevens** in disorder, confused, or in a muddle — **for six** so as to be totally wrecked or defeated

sixteen /,sik'steen/ *n* the number 16 – ~ **th** *adj, n, pron, adv*

,**sixth 'sense** *n* a keen intuitive power viewed as analogous to the 5 physical senses

sixty /'siksti/ *n* **1** the number 60 **2** *pl* the numbers 60-69; *specif* a range of temperatures, ages, or dates in a century characterized by those numbers – **-tieth** *adj, n, pron, adv*

sizable, sizeable /'siezəbl/ *adj* of a good size, fairly large

¹**size** /siez/ *n* **1a** physical magnitude, extent, or bulk **b** relative amount or number **c** bigness **2** any of a series of graduated measures, esp of manufactured articles (e g of clothing), conventionally identified by numbers or letters

²**size** *v* to arrange or grade according to size or bulk

³**size** *n* any of various thick and sticky materials used for filling the pores in surfaces (e g of paper, textiles, leather, or plaster) or for applying colour or metal leaf (e g to book edges or covers)

⁴**size** *v* to cover, stiffen, or glaze (as if) with size

size up *v* to form a judgment of

sizzle /'sizl/ *v* **sizzling** /'sizling, 'sizl·ing/ to make a hissing sound (as if) in frying

¹**skate** /skayt/ *n, pl* **skate**, *esp for different types* **skates** any of numerous rays that have greatly developed pectoral fins and many of which are important food fishes

²**skate** *n* **1** a roller skate **2** an ice skate

³**skate** *v* **1** to glide along on skates propelled by the alternate action of the legs **2** to glide or slide as if on skates **3** to proceed in a superficial manner – ~**r** *n*

'**skate,board** /-,bawd/ *n* a narrow board about 60cm (2ft) long mounted on roller-skate wheels

skedaddle /ski'dadl/ *v* **skedaddling** /ski'dadling, -'dadl·ing/ to run away – *infml*

skein /skayn/ *n* **1** a loosely coiled length of yarn or thread **2** a flock of geese in flight

skeleton /'skelitn/ *n* **1** a supportive or protective usu rigid structure or framework of an organism; *esp* the bony or more or less cartilaginous framework supporting the soft tissues and protecting the internal organs of a fish or mammal **2** sthg reduced to its bare essentials **3** an emaciated person or animal **4** a secret cause of shame, esp in a family – often in *skeleton in the cupboard*

skeleton key *n* a key that is able to open many simple locks

¹**sketch** /skech/ *n* **1** a preliminary study or draft; *esp* a rough often preliminary drawing representing the chief features of an object or scene **2** a brief description or outline **3** a short theatrical piece having a single scene; *esp* a comic variety act

²**sketch** *v* to make a sketch, rough draft, or outline of – ~**er** *n*

sketchy /'skechi/ *adj* lacking completeness, clarity, or substance; superficial, scanty – **sketchily** *adv* – **sketchiness** *n*

¹**skew** /skyooh/ *v* **1** to take an oblique course; twist **2** to distort from a true value or symmetrical curve

²**skew** *adj* **1** set, placed, or running obliquely **2** more developed on one side or in one direction than another; not symmetrical

³**skew** *n* a deviation from a symmetrical or symmetrical curve

'**skew,bald** /-,bawld/ *n or adj* (an animal) marked with spots and patches of white,and another colour, esp not black

¹**skewer** /'skyooh·ə/ *n* a long pin of wood or metal used chiefly to fasten a piece of meat together while roasting or to hold small pieces of meat for grilling (e g for a kebab)

²**skewer** *v* to fasten or pierce (as if) with a skewer

¹**ski** /skee/ *n, pl* **skis 1a** a long narrow strip usu of wood, metal, or plastic that curves upwards in front and is typically one of a pair used esp for gliding over snow **b** a water ski **2** a runner on a vehicle – **ski** *v* – ~**er** *n*

¹**skid** /skid/ *n* **1** a device placed under a wheel to prevent its turning or used as a drag **2** the act of skidding; a slide

²**skid** *v, -dd- of a vehicle, wheel, driver, etc* to slip or slide, esp out of control

'**skid,pan** /-,pan/ *n* a slippery surface on which vehicle drivers may practise the control of skids

,**skid 'row** /roh/ *n, chiefly NAm* a district frequented by down-and-outs and alcoholics

skiff /skif/ *n* a light rowing or sailing boat

skiffle /'skifl/ n jazz or folk music played by a group and using washboards or noisemakers (e g washboards or Jew's harps)

skilful, NAm chiefly **skillful** /'skilf(ə)l/ adj possessing or displaying skill; expert – ~ly adv

'**ski** ,**lift** n a power-driven conveyor for transporting skiers or sightseers up and down a long slope or mountainside

skill /skil/ n 1 the ability to utilize one's knowledge effectively and readily 2 a developed aptitude or ability in a particular field – ~ed adj

skim /skim/ v -mm- 1a to remove (e g film or scum) from the surface of a liquid b to remove cream from (milk) c to remove (the choicest part or members) from sthg; cream 2 to glance through (e g a book) for the chief ideas or the plot 3 to glide lightly or smoothly along or just above a surface

skimp /skimp/ v 1 to give insufficient or barely sufficient attention or effort to or money for 2 to save (as if) by skimping sthg – ~y adj – ~ily adv – ~iness n

¹**skin** /skin/ n 1a the external covering of an animal (e g a fur-bearing mammal or a bird) separated from the body, usu with its hair or feathers; pelt b(1) the pelt of an animal prepared for use as a trimming or in a garment b(2) a container (e g for wine or water) made of animal skin 2a the external limiting layer of an animal body, esp when forming a tough but flexible cover b any of various outer or surface layers (e g a rind, husk, or film) 3 the life or welfare of a person – esp in save one's skin 4 a sheathing or casing forming the outside surface of a ship, aircraft, etc – ~less adj — **by the skin of one's teeth** by a very narrow margin — **under the skin** beneath apparent or surface differences; fundamentally

²**skin** v -nn- 1a to strip, scrape, or peel away an outer covering (e g the skin or rind) of b to cut, graze, or damage the surface of 2 to strip of money or property; fleece – infml

,**skin-'deep** adj 1 as deep as the skin 2 superficial

'**skin,flint** /-,flint/ n a miser, niggard

skinny /'skini/ adj very thin; lean, emaciated – infml

skint /skint/ adj, Br penniless – infml

,**skin'tight** /-'tiet/ adj extremely closely fitted to the body

¹**skip** /skip/ v -pp- 1a to gambol b to swing a rope round the body from head to toe, making a small jump each time it passes beneath the feet c to rebound from one point or thing after another; ricochet 2 to leave hurriedly or secretly; abscond 3 to leave out (a step in a progression or series); omit 4 to fail to attend

²**skip** n 1 a light bounding step or gait 2 an act of omission (e g in reading)

³**skip** n¹1 a bucket or cage for carrying men and materials (e g in mining or quarrying) 2 a large open container for waste or rubble

¹**skipper** /'skipə/ n any of numerous small butterflies

²**skipper** n 1 the master of a fishing, small trading, or pleasure boat 2 the captain or first pilot of an aircraft 3 Br the captain of a sports team USE (2&3) infml

¹**skirmish** /'skuhmish/ n 1 a minor or irregular fight in war 2 a brief preliminary conflict; broadly any minor or petty dispute

²**skirmish** v to engage in a skirmish – ~er n

¹**skirt** /skuht/ n 1a(1) a free-hanging part of a garment (e g a coat) extending from the waist down a(2) a garment or undergarment worn by women and girls that hangs from and fits closely round the waist b either of 2 usu leather flaps on a saddle covering the bars on which the stirrups are hung 2 the borders or outer edge of an area or group – often pl with sing. meaning

²**skirt** v 1 to extend along or form the border or edge of; border 2 to go or pass round; specif to avoid through fear of difficulty, danger, or dispute

'**skirting ,board** n, Br a board, esp with decorative moulding, that is fixed to the base of a wall and that covers the joint of the wall and floor

skit /skit/ n a satirical or humorous story or sketch

skitter /'skitə/ v 1 to glide or skip lightly or swiftly 2 to skim along a surface

skittish /'skitish/ adj 1a lively or frisky in behaviour; capricious b variable, fickle 2 easily frightened; restive – ~ly adv – ~ness n

skittle /'skitl/ n 1 pl but sing in constr any of various bowling games played with 9 pins and wooden balls or discs 2 a pin used in skittles

skive /skiev/ v, Br to evade one's work or duty, esp out of laziness; shirk – often + off; infml – ~r n

¹**skivvy** /'skivi/ n, Br a female domestic servant

²**skivvy** v, Br to perform menial domestic tasks; act as a skivvy

skua /'skyooh-ə/ n any of several large dark-coloured seabirds of northern and southern seas

skulk /skulk/ v 1 to move in a stealthy or furtive manner 2 to hide or conceal oneself, esp out of cowardice or fear or from a sinister purpose – ~er n

skull /skul/ n the skeleton of the head of a vertebrate animal forming a bony or cartilaginous case that encloses and protects the brain and chief sense organs and supports the jaws

,**skull and 'crossbones** /'kros,bohnz/ n, pl **skulls and crossbones** a representation of a human skull over crossbones, usu used as a warning of danger to life

'**skull ,cap** /-,kap/ n a closely fitting cap; esp a light brimless cap for indoor wear

skunk /skungk/ n pl **skunks**, *esp collectively* **skunk**
1a any of various common black-and-white New
World mammals that have a pair of anal glands
from which a foul-smelling secretion is ejected **b**
the fur of a skunk **2** a thoroughly obnoxious
person – infml

¹sky /skie/ n **1** the upper atmosphere when seen as
an apparent great vault over the earth **2** weather
as manifested by the condition of the sky

²sky v, **skied, skyed** *chiefly Br* to throw, toss, or hit
(e g a ball) high in the air

ˌsky 'blue *adj or n* (of) the light blue colour of the
sky on a clear day

'sky¸diving /-¸dieving/ n jumping from an aeroplane and executing body manoeuvres while in
free-fall before pulling the rip cord of a parachute
– **skydiver** n

ˌsky-'high *adv or adj* **1a** very high **b** to a high level
or degree **2** to bits; apart – in *blow sthg sky-high*

¹sky¸lark /-¸lahk/ n a common largely brown Old
World lark noted for its song, esp as uttered in
vertical flight or while hovering

²skylark v to frolic

'sky¸light /-¸liet/ n a window or group of windows
in a roof or ceiling

'sky¸line /-¸lien/ n **1** the horizon **2** an outline (e g of
buildings or a mountain range) against the back-
ground of the sky

'sky¸scraper /-¸skraypə/ n a many-storeyed
building

slab /slab/ n a thick flat usu large plate or slice (e g
of stone, wood, or bread)

¹slack /slak/ *adj* **1** insufficiently prompt, diligent,
or careful; negligent **2a** characterized by slowness, indolence, or languor **b** *of tide* flowing
slowly; sluggish **3a** not taut; relaxed **b** lacking in
usual or normal firmness and steadiness – **~ly**
adv – **~ness** n

²slack v **1** to be or become slack **2** to shirk or evade
work or duty

³slack n **1** cessation in movement or flow **2** a part of
sthg (e g a sail or a rope) that hangs loose without
strain **3** pl trousers, esp for casual wear **4** a lull or
decrease in activity

⁴slack n the finest particles of coal produced at a
mine

slacken /'slakən/ v **1** to make or become less
active, rapid, or intense – often + *off* **2** to make or
become slack

slag /slag/ n **1** waste matter from the smelting of
metal ores **2** the rough cindery lava from a volcano **3** *Br* a dirty slovenly (immoral) woman –
slang

slain /slayn/ *past part of* **slay**

slake /slayk/ v **1** to satisfy, quench **2** to cause (e g
lime) to heat and crumble by treatment with
water

slalom /'slahləm/ n a skiing or canoeing race
against time on a zigzag or wavy course between
obstacles

¹slam /slam/ n a banging noise; *esp* one made by a
door

²slam -mm- v **1** to shut forcibly and noisily; bang **2**
to put or throw down noisily and violently **3** to
criticize harshly – infml

³slam n grand slam

¹slander /'slahndə/ n the utterance of false charges
which do damage to another's reputation

²slander v to utter slander against – **~er** n – **~ous**
adj – **~ously** *adv*

slang /slang/ n **1** language peculiar to a particular
group **2** informal usu spoken vocabulary – **~y** *adj*
– **~iness** n

¹slant /slahnt/ v **1** to turn or incline from a horizontal or vertical line or a level **2** to take a diagonal
course, direction, or path **3** to interpret or present
with a bias – **~ingly** *adv*

²slant n **1** a slanting direction, line, or plane; a
slope **2a** a particular or personal point of view,
attitude, or opinion **b** an unfair bias or distortion
(e g in a piece of writing)

¹slap /slap/ n a quick sharp blow, esp with the open
hand — **slap in the face** a rebuff, insult

²slap v **-pp-** **1** to strike sharply (as if) with the open
hand **2** to put, place, or throw with careless haste
or force

³slap *adv* directly, smack

ˌslap-'bang *adv* **1** in a highly abrupt or forceful
manner **2** precisely USE infml

'slap¸dash /-¸dash/ *adj* haphazard, slipshod

'slap¸happy /-¸hapi/ *adj* **1** punch-drunk **2** irresponsibly casual; happy-go-lucky

'slap¸stick /-¸stik/ n comedy stressing farce and
horseplay; knockabout comedy

'slap-¸up *adj, chiefly Br* marked by lavish consumption or luxury – infml

¹slash /slash/ v **1** to cut with violent usu random
sweeping strokes **2** to lash **3** to cut slits in (e g a
garment) so as to reveal an underlying fabric or
colour **4** to criticize cuttingly **5** to reduce
drastically

²slash n **1** the act of slashing; *also* a long cut or
stroke made (as if) by slashing **2** an ornamental
slit in a garment **3** *chiefly Br* an act of urinating –
vulg

slat /slat/ n a thin narrow flat strip, esp of wood or
metal

¹slate /slayt/ n **1** a piece of slate rock used as
roofing material **2** a fine-grained rock consisting
of compressed clay, shale, etc and easily split into
(thin) layers **3** a tablet of material, esp slate, used
for writing on **4** a dark bluish or greenish grey
colour

²slate v, *chiefly Br* to criticize or censure severely –
infml

slattern /'slatən/ n a slut – **~ly** *adj*

¹**slaughter** /'slawtə/ n 1 the act of killing; *specif* the butchering of livestock for market 2 killing of many people (e g in battle); carnage

²**slaughter** v 1 to kill (animals) for food 2 to kill violently or in large numbers

'**slaughter,house** /-,hows/ n an establishment where animals are killed for food

Slav /slahv/ n a speaker of a group of E European languages including Russian, Polish, Czech, and Serbo-Croat

¹**slave** /slayv/ n 1 sby held in servitude as the property of another 2 sby who is dominated by a specified thing or person 3 a drudge

²**slave** v to work like a slave; toil

'**slave ,driver** n a harsh taskmaster

¹**slaver** /'slavə/ v to drool, slobber

²**slaver** /'slayvə/ n 1 sby engaged in the slave trade 2 a ship used in the slave trade

slavery /'slayv(ə)ri/ n 1 drudgery, toil 2a being a slave b owning slaves

Slavic /'slahvik, 'slavik/ adj of or related to the Slavs or their language

slavish /'slayvish/ adj 1 abjectly servile 2 obsequiously imitative; devoid of originality – ~ly adv

Slavonic /slə'vonik/ adj Slavic

slay /slay/ v slew /slooh/; slain /slayn/ 1 to kill violently or with great bloodshed; slaughter 2 to affect overpoweringly (e g with awe or delight) – infml – ~er n

sleazy /'sleezi/ adj squalid and disreputable – **-ziness** n

¹**sledge** /slej/ n a sledgehammer

²**sledge** n a vehicle with runners that is pulled by reindeer, horses, dogs, etc and is used esp over snow or ice; *also* a toboggan

'**sledge,hammer** /-,hamə/ n a large heavy hammer that is wielded with both hands

¹**sleek** /sleek/ v to slick

²**sleek** adj 1a smooth and glossy as if polished b well-groomed c having a well fed or flourishing appearance 2 elegant, stylish – ~ly adv – ~ness n

¹**sleep** /sleep/ n 1 the natural periodic suspension of consciousness that is essential for the physical and mental well-being of higher animals 2 a sleeplike state: e g 2a a state marked by a diminution of feeling followed by tingling b the state of an animal during hibernation c death – euph 3 a period spent sleeping

²**sleep** v slept /slept/ 1 to rest in a state of sleep 2 to have sexual relations – + with or together — **sleep on** to consider (sthg) fully before discussing again the next day

sleeper /'sleepə/ n 1 a timber, concrete, or steel transverse support to which railway rails are fixed 2 a railway carriage containing bunks or beds 3 a ring or stud worn in a pierced ear to keep the hole open

sleep in v to sleep late, either intentionally or accidentally

'**sleeping ,car** n a railway carriage divided into compartments having berths for sleeping

,**sleeping 'partner** n a partner who takes no active part in the running of a firm's business

'**sleeping ,sickness** n a serious disease prevalent in much of tropical Africa that is transmitted by tsetse flies

'**sleepless** /-lis/ adj 1 not able to sleep 2 unceasingly active – ~ly adv – ~ness n

sleepy /'sleepi/ adj 1 ready to fall asleep 2 lacking alertness; sluggish, lethargic 3 sleep-inducing – **sleepily** adv – **sleepiness** n

'**sleepy,head** /-,hed/ n a sleepy person – humor

¹**sleet** /sleet/ n partly frozen rain, or snow and rain falling together – ~y adj

²**sleet** v to send down sleet

sleeve /sleev/ n 1 a part of a garment covering the arm 2 a paper or cardboard covering that protects a gramophone record when not in use – **less** adj — **up one's sleeve** held secretly in reserve

¹**sleigh** /slay/ n a sledge

²**sleigh** v to drive or travel in a sleigh

,**sleight of 'hand** n 1 manual skill and dexterity in conjuring or juggling 2 adroitness in deception

slender /'slendə/ adj 1a gracefully slim b small or narrow in circumference or width in proportion to length or height 2a flimsy, tenuous b limited or inadequate in amount; meagre – ~ly adv – ~ness n

sleuth /sloohth/ v or n (to act as) a detective – infml

¹**slew** /slooh/ past of slay

²**slew** v 1 to turn, twist, or swing about 2 to skid

¹**slice** /slies/ n 1a a thin broad flat piece cut from a usu larger whole b a wedge-shaped piece (e g of pie or cake) 2 an implement with a broad blade used for lifting, turning, or serving food 3 a portion, share

²**slice** v 1 to cut through (as if) with a knife 2 to cut into slices

¹**slick** /slik/ v to make sleek or smooth

²**slick** adj 1 superficially plausible; glib 2a characterized by suave or wily cleverness b deft, skilful 3 of a tyre having no tread – ~ly adv – ~ness n

³**slick** n (a patch of water covered with) a smooth film of crude oil

slicker /'slikə/ n, NAm an artful crook; a swindler – infml

¹**slide** /slied/ v slid /slid/ 1a to move in continuous contact with a smooth surface b to glide over snow or ice 2 to pass quietly and unobtrusively; steal 3 to pass by smooth or imperceptible gradations

²**slide** n 1 an act or instance of sliding 2 a sliding part or mechanism: e g 2a a U-shaped section of tube in the trombone that is pushed out and in to produce notes of different pitch b a moving piece of a mechanism that is guided by a part along which it slides 3a(1) a track or slope suitable for

sliding or tobogganing **a(2)** a chute with a slippery surface down which children slide in play **b** a channel or track down or along which sthg is slid **4a** a flat piece of glass on which an object is mounted for examination using a microscope **b** a photographic transparency on a small plate or film suitably mounted for projection

'**slide** ,**rule** *n* an instrument for calculating numbers, consisting in its simple form of a ruler with a central slide

sliding scale /ˈslieding/ *n* a flexible scale (e g of fees or subsidies) adjusted to the needs or income of individuals

¹**slight** /sliet/ *adj* **1a** having a slim or frail build **b** lacking strength or bulk; flimsy **c** trivial; minor **2** scanty, meagre – ~**ly** *adv* – ~**ness** *n*

²**slight** *v* **1** to treat as slight or unimportant **2** to treat with disdain or pointed indifference; snub – ~**ingly** *adv*

³**slight** *n* **1** an act of slighting **2** a humiliating affront

¹**slim** /slim/ *adj* -**mm**- **1** of small or narrow circumference or width, esp in proportion to length or height **2** slender in build **3** scanty, slight – ~**ly** *adv* – ~**ness** *n*

²**slim** *v* -**mm**- to become thinner (e g by dieting) – ~**mer** *n* – ~**ming** *n*

slime /sliem/ *n* **1** soft moist soil or clay; *esp* viscous mud **2** mucus or a mucus-like substance secreted by slugs, catfish, etc

slimy /ˈsliemi/ *adj* **1** of or resembling slime; viscous; *also* covered with or yielding slime **2** characterized by obsequious flattery – **sliminess** *n*

¹**sling** /sling/ *v* **slung** /slung/ **1** to cast with a careless and usu sweeping or swirling motion; fling **2** *Br* to cast forcibly and usu abruptly – infml – ~**er** *n*

²**sling** *n* an act of slinging or hurling a stone or other missile

³**sling** *n* **1** a device that gives extra force to a stone or other missile thrown by hand and usu consists of a short strap that is looped round the missile, whirled round, and then released at 1 end **2a** a usu looped line used to hoist, lower, or carry sthg (e g a rifle); *esp* a bandage suspended from the neck to support an arm or hand **b** a device (e g a rope net) for enclosing material to be hoisted by a tackle or crane

slink /slingk/ *v* **slunk** /slungk/ *also* **slinked 1** to go or move stealthily or furtively (e g in fear or shame); steal **2** to move in a graceful provocative manner

¹**slip** /slip/ *v* -**pp**- **1a** to move with a smooth sliding motion **b** to move quietly and cautiously; steal **2** *of time* to elapse, pass **3a** to slide out of place or away from a support or one's grasp **b** to slide on or down a slippery surface **4** to get speedily *into* or *out of* clothing **5** to fall off from a standard or accustomed level by degrees **6** to escape from (one's memory or notice) **7a** to cause to slip open;

release, undo **b** to let go of **8a** to insert, place, or pass quietly or secretly **b** to give or pay on the sly **9** to dislocate

²**slip** *n* **1** a sloping ramp extending out into the water to serve as a place for landing, repairing, or building ships **2** *the* act or an instance of eluding or evading **3a** a mistake in judgment, policy, or procedure; a blunder **b** an inadvertent and trivial fault or error **4** (a movement producing) a small geological fault **5** a fall from some level or standard **6** a women's sleeveless undergarment with shoulder straps that resembles a light dress **7** any of several fielding positions in cricket that are close to the batsman and just to the (off) side of the wicketkeeper

³**slip** *n* **1** a long narrow strip of material (e g paper or wood) **2** a slim and slender person

⁴**slip** *n* -**pp**- a semifluid mixture of clay and water used by potters (e g for coating or decorating ware)

'**slip** ,**knot** /-ˌnot/ *n* a knot that can be untied by pulling

,**slipped** '**disc** /slipt/ *n* a protrusion of 1 of the cartilage discs that normally separate the spinal vertebrae

slipper /ˈslipə/ *n* a light shoe that is easily slipped on the foot; *esp* a flat-heeled shoe that is worn while resting at home

slippery /ˈslip(ə)ri/ *adj* **1a** causing or tending to cause sthg to slide or fall **b** tending to slip from the grasp **2** not to be trusted; shifty – -**eriness** *n*

slipshod /ˈslip,shod/ *adj* careless, slovenly

'**slip** ,**stream** /-ˌstreem/ *n* **1** an area of reduced air pressure and forward suction immediately behind a rapidly moving vehicle **2** sthg that sweeps one along in its course

²**slipstream** *v* to drive or ride in a slipstream and so gain the advantage of reduced air resistance (e g in a bicycle' race)

'**slip**-,**up** *n* a mistake, oversight

slip up *v* to make a mistake; blunder

'**slip** ,**way** /-ˌway/ *n* a slip on which ships are built

¹**slit** /slit/ *v* -**tt**-; **slit 1** to make a slit in **2** to cut or tear into long narrow strips

²**slit** *n* a long narrow cut or opening

slither /ˈslidhə/ *v* **1** to slide unsteadily, esp (as if) on a slippery surface **2** to slip or slide like a snake – ~**y** *adj*

¹**sliver** /ˈslivə/ *n* a small slender piece cut, torn, or broken; a splinter

²**sliver** *v* to become split into slivers; splinter

slob /slob/ *n* a slovenly or uncouth person – infml

¹**slobber** /ˈslobə/ *v* **1** to let saliva dribble from the mouth; drool **2** to express emotion effusively and esp oversentimentally – often + *over*

²**slobber** *n* **1** saliva drooled from the mouth **2** oversentimental language or conduct

sloe /sloh/ *n* (the small dark spherical astringent fruit of) the blackthorn

¹slog /slog/ *v* **-gg-** **1** to hit (e g a cricket ball or an opponent in boxing) hard and often wildly **2** to plod (one's way) with determination, esp in the face of difficulty

²slog *n* **1** a hard and often wild blow **2** persistent hard work **3** an arduous march or tramp

slogan /'slohgən/ *n* **1** a phrase used to express and esp make public a particular view, position, or aim **2** a brief catchy phrase used in advertising or promotion

sloop /sloohp/ *n* a fore-and-aft rigged sailing vessel with 1 mast and a single foresail

¹slop /slop/ *n* **1** thin tasteless drink or liquid food; *also, pl* waste food or a thin gruel fed to animals **2** *pl* liquid household refuse (e g dirty water or urine) **3** mawkish sentiment in speech or writing; gush

²slop *v* **-pp-** **1a** to cause (a liquid) to spill over the side of a container **b** to splash or spill liquid on **2** to serve messily **3** to slouch, flop

¹slope /slohp/ *v* to lie at a slant; incline

²slope *n* **1** a piece of inclined ground **2** upward or downward inclination or (degree of) slant

slope off *v* to go away, esp furtively; sneak off – *infml*

slop out *v, of a prisoner* to empty slops from a chamber pot

sloppy /'slopi/ *adj* **1a** wet so as to splash; slushy **b** wet or smeared (as if) with sthg slopped over **2** slovenly, careless **3** disagreeably effusive – **-pily** *adv* – **-piness** *n*

¹slosh /slosh/ *n* **1** slush **2** the slap or splash of liquid **3** *chiefly Br* a heavy blow; a bash – *infml*

²slosh *v* **1** to flounder or splash through water, mud, etc **2** to splash (a liquid) about, on, or into sthg **3** *chiefly Br* to hit, beat – *infml*

sloshed /slosht/ *adj* drunk – *infml*

¹slot /slot/ *n* **1** a narrow opening, groove, or passage; a slit **2** a place or position in an organization or sequence; a niche

²slot *v* **-tt-** **1** to cut a slot in **2** to place in or assign to a slot – often + *in* or *into*

sloth /slohth/ *n* **1** disinclination to action or work; indolence **2** any of several slow-moving tree-dwelling mammals that inhabit tropical forests of S and Central America, hang face upwards from the branches, and feed on leaves, shoots, and fruits

'slot ma,chine *n* a machine (e g for selling cigarettes, chocolate, etc or for gambling) whose operation is begun by dropping a coin or disc into a slot

¹slouch /slowch/ *n* a gait or posture characterized by stooping or excessive relaxation of body muscles

²slouch *v* **1** to sit, stand, or walk with a slouch **2** to cause to droop; *specif* to turn down one side of (a hat brim) – **~ingly** *adv*

¹slough /slow/ *n* **1a** a place of deep mud or mire **b** a swamp **2** a state of dejection

²slough *also* **sluff** /sluf/ *n* the cast-off skin of a snake

³slough *also* **sluff** /sluf/ *v* **1** to cast off (e g a skin or shell) **2** to get rid of or discard as irksome or objectionable – usu + *off*

sloven /'sluvn/ *n* one habitually negligent of neatness or cleanliness, esp in personal appearance – **~ly** *adj* – **~liness** *n*

¹slow /sloh/ *adj* **1a** lacking in intelligence; dull **b** naturally inert or sluggish **2a** lacking in readiness, promptness, or willingness **b** not quickly aroused or excited **3a** flowing or proceeding with little or less than usual speed **b** exhibiting or marked by retarded speed **c** low, feeble **4** requiring a long time; gradual **5a** having qualities that hinder or prevent rapid movement **b** (designed) for slow movement **6** registering a time earlier than the correct one **7** lacking in liveliness or variety; boring – **~ly** *adj* – **~ness** *n*

²slow *adv* in a slow manner; slowly

³slow *v* to make or become slow or slower – often + *down* or *up*

slowcoach /'sloh,kohch/ *n* one who thinks or acts slowly

,slow 'motion *n* a technique in filming which allows an action to be shown as if it is taking place unnaturally slowly

'slow,worm /-,wuhm/ *n* a legless European lizard popularly believed to be blind

sludge /sluj/ *n* **1** (a deposit of) mud or ooze **2a** a slimy or slushy mass, deposit, or sediment **b** precipitated solid matter produced by water and sewage treatment processes

¹slug /slug/ *n* any of numerous slimy elongated chiefly ground-living gastropod molluscs that are found in most damp parts of the world and have no shell

²slug *n* **1** a lump, disc, or cylinder of material (e g plastic or metal): e g **1a** a bullet – slang **b** *NAm* a disc for insertion in a slot machine; *esp* one used illegally instead of a coin *chiefly NAm* a quantity of spirits that can be swallowed at a single gulp – slang

³slug *n* a heavy blow, esp with the fist – *infml*

⁴slug *v* **-gg-** to hit hard (as if) with the fist – *infml*

sluggish /'slugish/ *adj* **1** indolent **2** slow to respond (e g to stimulation or treatment) **3** markedly slow in movement, flow, or growth – **~ly** *adv* – **~ness** *n*

¹sluice /sloohs/ *n* **1** an artificial passage for water (e g in a millstream) fitted with a gate for stopping or regulating flow **2** a dock gate **3** a long inclined trough (e g for washing ores or gold-bearing earth)

²sluice *v* **1** to wash with or in water running through or from a sluice **2** to drench with a sudden vigorous flow; flush

¹**slum** /slum/ *n* **1** a poor overcrowded run-down area, esp in a city – often pl with sing. meaning **2** a squalid disagreeable place to live – ~**my** *adj*

²**slum** *v* -**mm**- **1** to live in squalor or on very slender means – often + *it* **2** to amuse oneself by visiting a place on a much lower social level; *also* to affect the characteristics of a lower social class

¹**slumber** /'slumbə/ *v* **1** to sleep **2** to lie dormant or latent

²**slumber** *n* sleep – often pl with sing. meaning

¹**slump** /slump/ *v* **1a** to fall or sink abruptly **b** to drop down suddenly and heavily; collapse **2** to assume a drooping posture or carriage; slouch

²**slump** *n* a marked or sustained decline, esp in economic activity or prices

slung /slung/ *past of* **sling**

slunk /slungk/ *past of* **slink**

¹**slur** /sluh/ *v* -**rr**- **1** to pass *over* without due mention, consideration, or emphasis **2** to run together, omit, or pronounce unclearly (words, sounds, etc)

²**slur** *n* **1** (a curved line connecting) notes to be sung to the same syllable or performed without a break **2** a slurring manner of speech

³**slur** *v* -**rr**- **1** to cast aspersions on; disparage

⁴**slur** *n* **1a** an insulting or disparaging remark **b** a shaming or degrading effect **2** a blurred spot in printed matter

slurp /sluhp/ *v* to eat or drink noisily or with a sucking sound

slurry /'sluri/ *n* a watery mixture of insoluble matter (e g mud, manure, or lime)

slush /slush/ *n* **1** partly melted or watery snow **2** liquid mud; mire **3** worthless and usu oversentimental material (e g literature) – **slushy** *adj*

slut /slut/ *n* **1** a dirty slovenly woman **2** an immoral woman; *esp* a prostitute – ~**tish** *adj*

sly /slie/ *adj* **slier** *also* **slyer**; **sliest** *also* **slyest 1a** clever in concealing one's ends or intentions; furtive **b** lacking in integrity and candour; crafty **2** humorously mischievous; roguish – ~**ly** *adv* – ~**ness** *n* —**on the sly** in a manner intended to avoid notice; secretly

¹**smack** /smak/ *n* (a slight hint of) a characteristic taste, flavour, or aura

²**smack** *v* **1** to slap smartly, esp in punishment **2** to open (the lips) with a sudden sharp sound, esp in anticipation of food or drink — **smack of** to have a trace or suggestion of

³**smack** *n* **1** a sharp blow, esp from sthg flat; a slap **2** a noisy parting of the lips **3** a loud kiss **4** *chiefly NAm* heroin – slang

⁴**smack** *adv* squarely and with force; directly – infml

⁵**smack** *n* a small inshore fishing vessel

¹**small** /smawl/ *adj* **1a** having relatively little size or dimensions **b** immature, young **2a** little in quantity, value, amount, etc **b** made up of few individuals or units **3** lower-case **4** lacking in strength **5a** operating on a limited scale **b** minor in power, influence, etc **c** limited in degree **6** of little consequence; trivial **7a** mean, petty **b** reduced to a humiliating position – ~**ness** *n*

²**small** *adv* **1** in or into small pieces **2** in a small manner or size

³**small** *n* **1** a part smaller and esp narrower than the remainder; *specif* the narrowest part of the back **2** *pl*, *Br* small articles of underwear – infml

'small .ad /ad/ *n*, *Br* a classified advertisement

,small 'change *n* coins of low denomination

'small ,fry *n pl in constr* young or insignificant people or things

'small,holding /-,hohlding/ *n*, *chiefly Br* a small agricultural farm – **smallholder** *n*

,small in'testine *n* the part of the intestine that lies between the stomach and colon

,small-'minded *adj* **1** having narrow interests or outlook; narrow-minded **2** characterized by petty meanness – ~**ness** *n*

smallpox /'smawl,poks/ *n* an acute infectious feverish virus disease characterized by skin eruption with pustules and scar formation

'small ,talk *n* light or casual conversation; chitchat

,small-'time *adj* insignificant in operation and status; petty – ~**timer** *n*

smarmy /'smahmi/ *adj* marked by flattery or smugness; unctuous – infml

¹**smart** /smaht/ *v* **1** to be (the cause or seat of) a sharp pain **2** to feel or endure mental distress

²**smart** *adj* **1** making one smart; causing a sharp stinging **2** forceful, vigorous **3** brisk, spirited **4a** mentally alert; bright **b** clever, shrewd **5** witty, persuasive **6a** neat or stylish in dress or appearance **b** characteristic of or frequented by fashionable society – ~**ly** *adv* – ~**ness** *n*

³**smart** *adv* in a smart manner; smartly

⁴**smart** *n* **1** a smarting pain; *esp* a stinging local pain **2** poignant grief or remorse

¹**smash** /smash/ *v* **1** to break in pieces by violence; shatter **2a** to drive, throw, or hit violently, esp causing breaking or shattering **b** to hit (e g a ball) with a forceful stroke, *specif* a smash **3** to destroy utterly; wreck – often + *up* **4** to crash *into*; collide

²**smash** *n* **1a(1)** a smashing blow, attack, or collision **a(2)** the result of smashing; *esp* a wreck due to collision **b** a forceful overhand stroke (e g in tennis or badminton) **2** utter collapse; ruin; *esp* bankruptcy

³**smash** *adv* with a resounding crash

,smash-and-'grab *n or adj*, *chiefly Br* (a robbery) committed by smashing a shop window and snatching the goods on display

smashed *adj* extremely drunk – infml

smashing /'smashing/ *adj* extremely good; excellent – infml

'smash-,up *n* a serious accident; a crash

smattering /'smat(ə)ring/ n a piecemeal or superficial knowledge *of*

¹**smear** /smiə/ n 1 a mark or blemish made (as if) by smearing a substance 2 material taken or prepared for microscopic examination by smearing on a slide 3 a usu unsubstantiated accusation

²**smear** v 1 to spread with sthg sticky, greasy, or viscous 2a to stain or dirty (as if) by smearing b to sully, besmirch; *specif* to blacken the reputation of

¹**smell** /smel/ v **smelled**, **smelt** /smelt/ 1a to have a usu specified smell b to have a characteristic aura; be suggestive *of* c to have an offensive smell; stink 2 to perceive the odour of (as if) by use of the sense of smell 3 to detect or become aware of by instinct
— **smell a rat** to have a suspicion of sthg wrong

²**smell** n 1 the one of the 5 basic physical senses by which the qualities of gaseous or volatile substances in contact with certain sensitive areas in the nose are interpreted by the brain as characteristic odours 2 an odour 3 a pervading quality; an aura

'**smelling ,salts** /'smeling/ n pl but sing or pl in constr a usu scented preparation of ammonium carbonate and ammonia water sniffed as a stimulant to relieve faintness

smelly /'smeli/ adj having an esp unpleasant smell – **smelliness** n

¹**smelt** /smelt/ n any of various small fishes that closely resemble the trouts

²**smelt** v 1 to melt (ore) to separate the metal 2 to separate (metal) by smelting

¹**smile** /smiel/ v 1 to have or assume a smile 2a to look with amusement or scorn b to bestow approval c to appear pleasant or agreeable – **smilingly** adv

²**smile** n 1 a change of facial expression in which the corners of the mouth curve slightly upwards and which expresses esp amusement, pleasure, approval, or sometimes scorn 2 a pleasant or encouraging appearance

smirch /smuhch/ v 1 to make dirty or stained, esp by smearing 2 to bring discredit or disgrace on – **smirch** n

smirk /smuhk/ v to smile in a fatuous or scornful manner – **smirk** n

smite /smiet/ v **smote** /smoht/; **smitten** /'smit(ə)n/, **smote** 1 to strike sharply or heavily, esp with (an implement held in) the hand 2 to kill, injure, or damage by smiting 3 to have a sudden powerful effect on; afflict; *specif* to attract strongly

smith /smith/ n 1 a worker in metals; *specif* a blacksmith 2 a maker – often in combination

smithereens /,smidhə'reenz, '-,-/ n pl fragments, bits

smithy /'smidhi/ n the workshop of a smith

¹**smock** /smok/ n a light loose garment esp with a yoke

²**smock** v to ornament (e g a garment) with smocking

smocking /'smoking/ n a decorative embroidery or shirring made by gathering cloth in regularly spaced round or diamond-shaped tucks held in place with ornamental stitching

smog /smog/ n a fog made heavier and darker by smoke and chemical fumes

¹**smoke** /smohk/ n 1 the gaseous products of burning carbon-containing materials made visible by the presence of small particles of carbon 2 fumes or vapour resembling smoke 3 an act or spell of smoking esp tobacco – **less** adj

²**smoke** v 1 to emit smoke 2 to (habitually) inhale and exhale the fumes of burning tobacco 3a to fumigate b to drive *out* or away by smoke 4 to colour or darken (as if) with smoke 5 to cure (e g meat or fish) by exposure to smoke, traditionally from green wood or peat

smoker /'smohkə/ n 1 sby who regularly or habitually smokes tobacco 2 a carriage or compartment in which smoking is allowed

'**smoke ,screen** n 1 a screen of smoke to hinder observation 2 sthg designed to conceal, confuse, or deceive

'**smoke,stack** /-,stak/ n a chimney or funnel through which smoke and gases are discharged, esp from a locomotive or steamship

smoky also **smokey** /'smohki/ adj 1 emitting smoke, esp in large quantities 2 suggestive of smoke, esp in flavour, smell, or colour 3a filled with smoke b made black or grimy by smoke – **smokiness** n

smooch /smoohch/ v to kiss, caress – infml – **smooch** n – **er** n

¹**smooth** /smoohdh/ adj 1a having a continuous even surface b free from hair or hairlike projections c of liquid of an even consistency; free from lumps d giving no resistance to sliding; frictionless 2 free from difficulties or obstructions 3 even and uninterrupted in movement or flow 4a urbane, courteous b excessively and often artfully suave; ingratiating 5 not sharp or acid – **ly** adv – **ness** n

²**smooth** v 1 to make smooth 2 to free from what is harsh or disagreeable 3 to dispel or alleviate (e g enmity or perplexity) – often + away or over 4 to free from obstruction or difficulty 5 to press flat – often + out 6 to cause to lie evenly and in order – often + down

smorgasbord /'smawgəs,bawd, 'smuh-/ n a luncheon or supper buffet offering a variety of foods and dishes

smote /smoht/ past of **smite**

¹**smother** /'smudhə/ n a confused mass of things; a welter

²**smother** v **1** to overcome or kill with smoke or fumes **2** to overcome or discomfort (as if) through lack of air **3a** to suppress expression or knowledge of; conceal **b** to prevent the growth and development of; suppress **4a** to cover thickly; blanket **b** to overwhelm

smoulder, *NAm chiefly* **smolder** /'smohldə/ v **1** to burn feebly with little flame and often much smoke **2** to exist in a state of suppressed ferment

¹**smudge** /smuj/ v **1** to soil (as if) with a smudge **2a** to smear, daub **b** to make indistinct; blur

²**smudge** n **1** a blurry spot or streak **2** an indistinct mass; a blur

smug /smug/ adj -gg- highly self-satisfied and complacent – ~ **ly** adv – ~ **ness** n

smuggle /'smugl/ v **smuggling** /'smugling/ **1** to import or export secretly contrary to the law, esp without paying duties **2** to convey or introduce surreptitiously – **-gler** n – **-gling** n

¹**smut** /smut/ v **-tt- 1** to stain or taint with smut **2** to affect (a crop or plant) with smut

²**smut** n **1** matter, esp a particle of soot, that soils or blackens **2** any of various destructive fungous diseases, esp of cereal grasses, marked by transformation of plant organs into dark masses of spores **3** obscene language or matter

snack /snak/ n a light meal; food eaten between regular meals

¹**snaffle** /'snafl/ n a simple usu jointed bit for a bridle

²**snaffle** v **snaffling** /'snafling/ to appropriate, esp by devious means; pinch – infml

snag /snag/ n **1** a sharp or jagged projecting part **2** a concealed or unexpected difficulty or obstacle **3** an irregular tear or flaw made (as if) by catching on a snag

snail /snayl/ n **1** a gastropod mollusc; esp one that has an external enclosing spiral shell **2** a slow-moving or sluggish person or thing

¹**snake** /snayk/ n **1** any of numerous limbless scaly reptiles with a long tapering body and with salivary glands often modified to produce venom which is injected through grooved or tubular fangs **2** a sly treacherous person

²**snake** v to wind in the manner of a snake – **snaky** adj

¹**snap** /snap/ v **-pp- 1** to grasp or snatch at sthg eagerly **2** to utter sharp biting words; give an irritable retort **3a** to break suddenly, esp with a sharp cracking sound **b** to close or fit in place with an abrupt movement or sharp sound **4** to take possession or advantage of suddenly or eagerly – usu + up **5** to photograph – **snap out of it** to free oneself from sthg (e g a mood) by an effort of will – infml

²**snap** n **1** an abrupt closing (e g of the mouth in biting or of scissors in cutting) **2** an act or instance of seizing abruptly; a sudden snatch or bite **3** a brief usu curt retort **4a** a sound made by snapping **b** a sudden sharp breaking of sthg thin or brittle **5** a sudden spell of harsh weather **6** a thin brittle biscuit **7** a snapshot **8** a card game in which each player tries to be the first to shout '*snap*' when 2 cards of identical value are laid successively

³**snap** interj, *Br* – used to draw attention to an identity or similarity

⁴**snap** adv with (the sound of) a snap

⁵**snap** adj performed suddenly, unexpectedly, or without deliberation

snapdragon /'snap,drag(ə)n/ n any of several garden plants having showy white, red, or yellow 2-lipped flowers

snappish /'snapish/ adj **1a** given to curt irritable speech **b** bad-tempered, testy **2** inclined to snap or bite – ~ **ly** adv – ~ **ness** n

snappy /'snapi/ adj **1** snappish **2a** brisk, quick **b** lively, animated **c** stylish, smart – **-pily** adv – **-piness** n

snapshot /'snap,shot/ n a casual photograph made typically by an amateur with a small hand-held camera

¹**snare** /sneə/ n **1a** a trap often consisting of a noose for catching animals **b** sthg by which one is trapped or deceived **2** any of the catgut strings or metal spirals of a snare drum which produce a rattling sound

²**snare** v **1** to procure by artful or skilful actions **2** to entangle or hold as if in a snare

'**snare ,drum** n a small double-headed drum with 1 or more snares stretched across its lower head

¹**snarl** /snahl/ n **1** a tangle, esp of hair or thread; a knot **2** a confused or complicated situation

²**snarl** v **1** to cause to become knotted and intertwined; tangle **2** to make excessively confused or complicated *USE* often + up

³**snarl** v **1** to growl with bared teeth **2** to speak in a vicious or bad-tempered manner – **snarl** n

'**snarl-,up** n an instance of confusion, disorder, or obstruction; specif a traffic jam

¹**snatch** /snach/ v to attempt to seize sthg suddenly – often + at – ~ **er** n

²**snatch** n **1** a snatching at or of sthg **2a** a brief period of time or activity **b** sthg fragmentary or hurried **3** a robbery – infml

snazzy /'snazi/ adj stylishly or flashily attractive – infml

¹**sneak** /sneek/ v **sneaked**, *NAm also* **snuck** /snuk/ **1** to go or leave stealthily or furtively; slink **2** to behave in a furtive or servile manner **3** *Br* to tell tales – infml – **sneak up on** to approach or act on stealthily

²**sneak** n **1** a person who acts in a stealthy or furtive manner **2** the act or an instance of sneaking **3** *Br* a person, esp a schoolchild, who tells tales against others – infml

sneaker /'sneekə/ n, chiefly *NAm* a plimsoll – usu pl

sneaking /'sneeking/ *adj* **1** furtive, underhand **2** mean, contemptible **3** instinctively felt but unverified

¹**sneer** /sniə/ *v* **1** to smile or laugh with a curl of the lips to express scorn or contempt **2** to speak or write in a scornfully jeering manner – ~**er** *n* – ~**ingly** *adv*

²**sneer** *n* a sneering expression or remark

sneeze /sneez/ *v or n* (to make) a sudden violent involuntary audible expiration of breath — **sneeze at** to make light of

snick /snik/ *v* **1** to cut slightly; nick **2** to edge (a ball)

snide /snied/ *adj* **1** slyly disparaging; insinuating **2** *chiefly NAm* mean, low – ~**ly** *adv* – ~**ness** *n*

¹**sniff** /snif/ *v* **1** to draw air audibly up the nose, esp for smelling **2** to show or express disdain or scorn *at* **3** to detect or become aware of (as if) by smelling – ~**er** *n*

²**sniff** *n* **1** an act or sound of sniffing **2** a quantity that is sniffed

¹**sniffle** /'snifl/ *v* **sniffling** /'snifling, 'snifl·ing/ to sniff repeatedly – ~**r** *n*

²**sniffle** *n* **1** an act or sound of sniffling **2** *often pl* a head cold marked by nasal discharge

snifter /'sniftə/ *n* a small drink of spirits – *infml*

snigger /'snigə/ *v* to laugh in a partly suppressed often derisive manner – **snigger** *n*

¹**snip** /snip/ *n* **1a** a small piece snipped off; *also* a fragment, bit **b** a cut or notch made by snipping **2** *pl but sing or pl in constr* shears used esp for cutting sheet metal by hand **3** *Br* a bargain

²**snip** *v* **-pp-** to cut (as if) with shears or scissors, esp with short rapid strokes

¹**snipe** /sniep/ *n* any of several game birds that occur esp in marshy areas

²**snipe** *v* **1** to shoot *at* exposed individuals usu from in hiding at long range **2** to aim a snide or obliquely critical attack *at* – **sniper** *n*

snippet /'snipit/ *n* a small part, piece, or item; *esp* a fragment of writing or conversation

¹**snitch** /snich/ *v* to pilfer, pinch – infml

²**snitch** *n* an esp petty theft – infml

snivel /'snivl/ *v* **-ll-** (*NAm* **-l-, -ll-**), /'snivl·ing/ **1** to sniff mucus up the nose audibly **2** to whine, snuffle **3** to speak or act in a whining, tearful, cringing, or weakly emotional manner – ~**ler** *n*

snob /snob/ *n* **1** one who blatantly attempts to cultivate or imitate those he/she admires as social superiors **2** one who has an air of smug superiority in matters of knowledge or taste – ~**bish** *adj* – ~**bishly** *adv* – ~**bishness** *n*

snobbery /'snob(ə)ri/ *n* (an instance of) snobbishness

snog /snog/ *v*, **-gg-** *Br* to kiss and cuddle – slang – **snog** *n*

¹**snooker** /'snoohkə/ *n* **1** a game played with a white ball, 15 red balls and 6 variously coloured balls on a table with side cushions and pockets in which the object is to use a cue to hit the white ball in such a manner as to drive a coloured ball into a pocket **2** a position of the balls in snooker in which a direct shot would lose points

²**snooker** *v* **1** to prevent (an opponent) from making a direct shot in snooker by playing the cue ball so that another ball rests between it and the object ball **2** to present an obstacle to; thwart – infml

snoop /snoohp/ *v* to look or pry in a sneaking or interfering manner – ~**er** *n*

snooty /'snoohti/ *adj* **1** haughty, disdainful **2** characterized by snobbish attitudes *USE* infml – **snootily** *adv* – **snootiness** *n*

snooze /snoohz/ *v or n* (to take) a nap – infml

snore /snaw/ *v or n* (to breathe with) a rough hoarse noise due to vibration of the soft palate during sleep

snorkel /'snawkl/ *n* **1** a tube housing an air intake and exhaust pipes that can be extended above the surface of the water from a submerged submarine **2** a J-shaped tube allowing a skin diver to breathe while face down in the water

¹**snort** /snawt/ *v* **1** to force air violently through the nose with a rough harsh sound **2** to express scorn, anger, or surprise by a snort **3** to take in (a drug) by inhalation – infml

²**snort** *n* an act or sound of snorting **2** a snifter – infml

snot /snot/ *n* **1** nasal mucus **2** a snotty person – slang

snotty /'snoti/ *adj* **1** soiled with nasal mucus – infml **2** arrogantly or snobbishly unpleasant

snout /snowt/ *n* **1** a long projecting nose (e g of a pig) **2** a forward prolongation of the head of various animals

¹**snow** /snoh/ *n* **1a** (a descent of) water falling in the form of white flakes consisting of small ice crystals formed directly from vapour in the atmosphere **b** fallen snow **2** cocaine – slang

²**snow** *v* **1** to fall in or as snow **2** to cover, shut in, or block (as if) with snow – usu + *in* or *up*

¹**'snow,ball** /-,bawl/ *n* a round mass of snow pressed or rolled together for throwing

²**snowball** *v* **1** to throw snowballs at **2** to increase or expand at a rapidly accelerating rate

'snow ,blindness *n* inflammation and painful sensitivity to light caused by exposure of the eyes to ultraviolet rays reflected from snow or ice – **snow-blind** *adj*

'snow,bound /-,bownd/ *adj* confined or surrounded by snow

'snow,drift /-,drift/ *n* a bank of drifted snow

'snow,drop /-,drop/ *n* a bulbous European plant of the daffodil family bearing nodding white flowers in spring

'snow,fall /-,fawl/ *n* the amount of snow falling at one time or in a given period

'snow,flake /-,flayk/ *n* a flake or crystal of snow

snow line *n* the lower margin of a permanent expanse of snow

'snow‚man /-‚man/ *n* a pile of snow shaped to resemble a human figure

'snow‚plough /-‚plow/ *n* any of various vehicles or devices used for clearing snow

'snow‚shoe /-‚shooh/ *n* a light oval wooden frame that is strung with thongs and attached to the foot to enable a person to walk on soft snow without sinking

snow under *v* to overwhelm, esp in excess of capacity to handle or absorb sthg

snowy /'snoh·i/ *adj* **1a** composed of (melted) snow **b** characterized by or covered with snow **2** snow-white – **snowiness** *n*

¹snub /snub/ *v* **-bb- 1** to check or interrupt with a cutting retort; rebuke **2** to treat with contempt, esp by deliberately ignoring

²snub *n* an act or an instance of snubbing; *esp a* slight

³snub *adj* short and stubby

¹snuff /snuf/ *v* **1** to trim or put out a candle by pinching or by the use of snuffers **2** to make extinct; put an end to – usu + *out* – **snuff it** to die – *infml*

²snuff *n* a preparation of pulverized often scented tobacco inhaled usu through the nostrils

snuffer /'snufǝ/ *n* **1** an instrument resembling a pair of scissors for trimming the wick of a candle – usu pl but sing. or pl in constr **2** an instrument consisting of a small hollow cone attached to a handle, used to extinguish candles

snuffle /'snufl/ *v* **snuffling** /'snufling, 'snufl·ing/ **1a** to sniff, usu audibly and repeatedly **b** to draw air through an obstructed nose with a sniffing sound **2** to speak (as if) through the nose

¹snug /snug/ *adj* **-gg- 1** fitting closely and comfortably **2a** enjoying or affording warm secure comfortable shelter **b** marked by relaxation and cordiality **3** affording a degree of comfort and ease – **~ly** *adv*

²snug *v* **-gg-** to snuggle

³snug *n, Br* a small private room or compartment in a pub

snuggle /'snugl/ *v* **snuggling** /'snugling/ to curl up comfortably or cosily; nestle – *infml*

¹so /soh; *also (occasional weak form)* sǝ/ *adv* **1a(1)** in this way; thus – often used as a substitute for a preceding word or word group (e g do you really think *so?*) **a(2)** most certainly; indeed (e g I hope to win and *so* I shall) **b(1)** in the same way; also – used after *as* to introduce a parallel (e g as the French drink wine, *so* the British love their beer) **b(2)** as an accompaniment – after *as* **c** in such a way – used esp before *as* or *that*, to introduce a result or to introduce the idea of purpose **2a** to such an extreme degree – used before *as* to introduce a comparison, esp in the negative (e g not *so*

fast as mine), or, esp before *as* or *that*, to introduce a result (e g *so* tired that I went to bed) **b** very **c** to a definite but unspecified extent or degree (e g can only do *so* much in a day) **3** therefore, consequently **4** then, subsequently **5** *chiefly dial & NAm* – used, esp by children, to counter a negative charge

²so /soh/ *conj* **1** with the result that **2** in order that **3a** for that reason; therefore **b(1)** – used as an introductory particle (e g *so* here we are) often to belittle a point under discussion (e g *so* what?)

³so /soh/ *adj* **1** conforming with actual facts; true **2** disposed in a definite order (e g his books were always exactly *so*)

⁴so /soh/ *pron* such as has been specified or suggested; the same — **or so** — used to indicate an approximation or conjecture

⁵so, soh /soh/ *n* the musical note sol

¹soak /sohk/ *v* **1** to lie immersed in liquid (e g water), esp so as to become saturated or softened **2** to become fully felt or appreciated – usu + *in* or *into* **3** to intoxicate (oneself) with alcohol – *infml* **4** to charge an excessive amount of money – *infml* – **~ed** *adj* – **~ing** *adj*

²soak *n* **1a** soaking or being soaked **b** that (e g liquid) in which sthg is soaked **2** a drunkard – *infml*

'so-and-‚so *n, pl* **so-and-sos, so-and-so's 1** an unnamed or unspecified person or thing **2** a disliked or unpleasant person – *euph*

¹soap /sohp/ *n* a cleansing and emulsifying agent that lathers when rubbed in water – **soapy** *adj*

²soap *v* **1** to rub soap over or into **2** to flatter – often + *up*; *infml*

'soap‚box /-‚boks/ *n* an improvised platform used by an informal orator

'soap ‚opera *n* a radio or television drama characterized by stock domestic situations and melodramatic or sentimental treatment

¹soar /saw/ *v* **1a** to fly high in the air **b** to sail or hover in the air, often at a great height **2** to rise rapidly or to a very high level **3** to be of imposing height or stature; tower

²soar *n* (the range, distance, or height attained in) soaring

¹sob /sob/ *v* **-bb- 1** to weep with convulsive catching of the breath **2** to make a sound like that of a sob or sobbing

²sob *n* an act or sound of sobbing; *also* a similar sound

¹sober /'sohbǝ/ *adj* **1** not drunk or addicted to drink **2** gravely or earnestly thoughtful **3** calmly self-controlled; sedate **4a** well balanced; realistic **b** sane, rational **5** subdued in tone or colour – **~ly** *adv*

²sober *v* to make or become sober – usu + *up*

sobriety /sǝ'brie·ǝti/ *n* being sober – *fml*

'sob ‚story *n* a sentimental story or account intended chiefly to elicit sympathy – *infml*

,so-'called *adj* 1 commonly named; popularly so termed 2 falsely or improperly so named

soccer /'sokə/ *n* a football game that is played with a round ball between teams of 11 players each, that features the kicking and heading of the ball, and in which use of the hands and arms is prohibited except to the goalkeepers

sociable /'sohsh(i)əbl/ *adj* 1 inclined to seek or enjoy companionship; companionable 2 conducive to friendliness or cordial social relations – **-bility** *n* – **-bly** *adv*

¹social /'sohsh(ə)l/ *adj* 1 of promoting companionship or friendly relations 2a tending to form cooperative relationships; gregarious b living and breeding in more or less organized communities 3 of human society – ~**ly** *adv*

²social *n* a social gathering, usu connected with a church or club

,social 'climber *n* one who strives to gain a higher social position or acceptance in fashionable society – *derog*

,social de'mocracy *n* a political movement advocating a gradual and democratic transition to socialism

socialism /'sohsh(ə)l,iz(ə)m/ *n* an economic and political theory advocating, or a system based on, collective or state ownership and administration of the means of production and distribution of goods

¹socialist /-ist/ *n* 1 one who advocates or practises socialism 2 *cap* a member of a socialist party or group

²socialist *adj* 1 of socialism 2 *cap* of or constituting a party advocating socialism

socialite /'sohsh(ə)liet/ *n* a socially active or prominent person

social-ize, -ise /'sohsh(ə)l,iez/ *v* 1 to fit or train for life in society; learn to get on with others 2 to adapt to the needs or take into the ownership of society 3 to act in a sociable manner

,social 'science *n* 1 the scientific study of human society and the relationships between its members 2 a science (e g economics or politics) dealing with a particular aspect of human society

,social se'curity *n* 1 provision by the state through pensions, unemployment benefit, sickness benefit, etc for its citizens' economic security and social welfare 2 supplementary benefit

,social 'service *n* activity designed to promote social welfare; *esp* an organized service (e g education or housing) provided by the state

'social ,work *n* any of various professional activities concerned with the aid of the needy and socially maladjusted – ~**er** *n*

¹society /sə'sie-əti/ *n* 1 companionship or association with others; company 2a *often cap* the human race considered in terms of its structure of social institutions b(1) a community having common traditions, institutions, and collective interests b(2) an organized group working together or periodically meeting because of common interests, beliefs, or profession 3 a fashionable leisure class

²society *adj* (characteristic) of fashionable society

sociology /,sohs(h)i'oləji/ *n* the science of social institutions and relationships; *specif* the study of the behaviour of organized human groups – **-gical** *adj* – **-gically** *adv* – **-gist** *n*

¹sock /sok/ *n pl* socks, *NAm also* sox a knitted or woven covering for the foot usu extending above the ankle and sometimes to the knee

²sock *v* to hit or apply forcefully – *infml* — **sock it to** to subject to vigorous or powerful attack — *infml*

³sock *n* a vigorous or forceful blow; a punch – *infml*

socket /'sokit/ *n* an opening or hollow that forms a holder for sthg; *also* an electrical plug

¹sod /sod/ *n* 1 turf; *also* the grass-covered surface of the ground 2 one's native land – *infml*

²sod *n, Br* an objectionable person, esp male USE slang

³sod *v*, **-dd-** *Br* to damn – usu used as an oath or in the present participle as a meaningless intensive; slang

soda /'sohdə/ *n* (2b) *pl* sodas 1 any of various compounds of sodium 2a soda water b *chiefly NAm* a sweet drink consisting of soda water, flavouring, and often ice cream

'soda ,water *n* a beverage consisting of water highly charged with carbonic acid gas

sodden /'sod(ə)n/ *adj* 1 full of moisture or water; saturated 2 heavy, damp, or doughy because of imperfect cooking 3 dull or expressionless, esp from habitual drunkenness

sodium /'sohdi-əm, 'sohdyəm/ *n* a silver white soft ductile element that occurs abundantly in nature in combined form and is very active chemically

,sodium 'chloride *n* common salt

sodomite /'sodəmiet/ *n* one who engages in sodomy

sodomy /'sodəmi/ *n* 1 anal intercourse 2 sexual relations between a human being and an animal

sofa /'sohfə/ *n* a long upholstered seat with a back and 2 arms or raised ends that typically seats 2 to 4 people

¹soft /soft/ *adj* 1a yielding to physical pressure b of a consistency that may be shaped, moulded, spread, or easily cut c lacking in hardness 2a pleasing or agreeable to the senses; bringing ease or quiet b having a bland or mellow taste c not bright or glaring; subdued d(1) quiet in pitch or volume; not harsh d(2) *of c and g* pronounced /s/ and /j/ respectively (e g in *acid* and *age*) – not used technically e(1) *of the eyes* having a liquid or gentle appearance e(2) having a gently curved outline f smooth or delicate in texture falling or

blowing with slight force or impact **3a** marked by a kindness, lenience, or moderation: e g **b** mild, low-key; *specif* not of the most extreme or harmful kind **4a** lacking resilience or strength, esp as a result of having led a life of ease **b** mentally deficient; feebleminded **5** amorously attracted, esp covertly – + *on*

²**soft** *n* a soft object, material, or part

³**soft** *adv* in a soft or gentle manner; softly

soften /'sof(ə)n/ *v* **1** to make soft or softer **2a** to weaken the military resistance or the morale of **b** to impair the strength or resistance of *USE* (2) often + *up*

,**soft'hearted** /-'hahtid/ *adj* kind, compassionate
– ~ **ness** *n*

,**soft-'pedal** *v* **-ll-** (*NAm* **-l-, -ll-**) to attempt to minimize the importance of (sthg), esp by talking cleverly or evasively

soft pedal *n* a foot pedal on a piano that reduces the volume of sound

,**soft-'soap** *v* to persuade or mollify with flattery or smooth talk – *infml*

soft soap *n* flattery – *infml*

soft spot *n* a sentimental weakness

'**soft,ware** /-,weə/ *n* **1** the entire set of programs and procedures associated with a system, esp a computer system **2** sthg contrasted with hardware; *esp* materials for use with audiovisual equipment

'**soft,wood** /-,wood/ *n* the wood of a coniferous tree

soggy /'sogi/ *adj* **1a** waterlogged, soaked **b** sodden **2** heavily dull – **-gily** *adv* – **-giness** *n*

¹**soil** /soyl/ *v* **1** to stain or make unclean, esp superficially; dirty **2** to defile morally; corrupt **3** to blacken or tarnish (e g a person's reputation)

²**soil** *n* **1** firm land; earth **2** the upper layer of earth that may be dug or ploughed and in which plants grow **3** country, land **4** refuse or sewage **5** a medium in which sthg takes hold and develops

sojourn /'sojən, 'su-/ *v or n* (to make) a temporary stay – *fml*

sol /sol/ *n* the 5th note of the diatonic scale in solmization

¹**solace** /'soləs/ *n* (a source of) consolation or comfort in grief or anxiety

²**solace** *v* **1** to give solace to; console **2** to alleviate, relieve

solar /'sohlə/ *adj* **1** of or derived from the sun, esp as affecting the earth **2** (of or reckoned by time) measured by the earth's course in relation to the sun **3** produced or operated by the action of the sun's light or heat; *also* using the sun's rays

solarium /sə'leəri·əm/ *n, pl* **solaria** /-ri·ə/ *also* **solariums** a room exposed to the sun (e g for relaxation or treatment of illness); *also* an establishment offering facilities for producing a sun tan, usu artificially

,**solar 'plexus** /'pleksəs/ *n* the pit of the stomach

'**solar ,system** *n* the sun together with the group of celestial bodies that are held by its attraction and revolve round it

sold /sohld/ *past of* **sell**

¹**solder** /'sohldə, 'soldə/ *n* an alloy, esp of tin and lead, used when melted to join metallic surfaces

²**solder** *v* **1** to unite or make whole (as if) by solder **2** to hold or join together; unite

'**soldering ,iron** /'sohld(ə)ring, 'sol-/ *n* a usu electrically heated device that is used for melting and applying solder

¹**soldier** /'sohljə/ *n* **1** sby engaged in military service, esp in the army **2** any of a caste of ants or wingless termites having a large head and jaws

²**soldier** *v* **1** to serve as a soldier **2** to press doggedly forward – usu + *on*

soldier of fortune *n* sby who seeks an adventurous, esp military, life wherever chance allows

¹**sole** /sohl/ *n* **1a** the undersurface of a foot **b** the part of a garment or article of footwear on which the sole rests **2** the usu flat bottom or lower part of sthg or the base on which sthg rests

²**sole** *v* to provide with a (new) sole

³**sole** *n* any of several flatfish including some valued as superior food fishes

⁴**sole** *adj* **1** being the only one; only **2** belonging or relating exclusively to 1 individual or group – ~ **ly** *adv*

solecism /'soli,siz(ə)m/ *n* **1** a minor blunder in speech or writing **2** a breach of etiquette or decorum

solemn /'soləm/ *adj* **1** performed so as to be legally binding **2** celebrated with full liturgical ceremony **3a** conveying a deep sense of reverence or exaltation; sublime **b** marked by seriousness and sobriety **c** sombre, gloomy – ~ **ly** *adv* – ~ **ness** *n*

solemnity /sə'lemnəti/ *n* **1** formal or ceremonious observance of an occasion or event **2** a solemn event or occasion **3** solemn character or state – **-nize** *v*

solenoid /'solənoyd/, 'soh-/ *n* a coil of wire commonly in the form of a long cylinder that when carrying a current produces a magnetic field and draws in a movable usu ferrous core

sol-fa /'sol ,fah/ *n* the system of using syllables *do, re, mi,* etc for the notes of the scale

solicit /sə'lisit/ *v* **1** to make a formal or earnest appeal or request to; entreat **2a** to attempt to lure or entice, esp into evil **b** *of a prostitute* to proposition publicly **3** to try to obtain by usu urgent requests or pleas – ~ **ation** *n*

solicitor /sə'lisitə/ *n* a qualified lawyer who advises clients, represents them in the lower courts, and prepares cases for barristers to try in higher courts

so,licitor 'general *n pl* **solicitors general** *often cap S&G* a Crown law officer ranking after the attorney general in England

solicitous /sə'lisitəs/ *adj* **1** showing consideration or anxiety; concerned **2** desirous *of*; eager *to* – fml – ~**ly** *adv* – ~**ness** *n*

solicitude /sə'lisityoohd/ *n* being solicitous; concern; *also* excessive care or attention

¹solid /'solid/ *adj* **1a** without an internal cavity **b** having no opening or division **2** of uniformly close and coherent texture; compact **3** of good substantial quality or kind: e g **3a** well constructed from durable materials **b** sound, cogent **4a** having, involving, or dealing with 3 dimensions or with solids **b** neither gaseous nor liquid **5** without interruption; full **6** of a single substance or character: e g **6a** (almost) entirely of 1 metal **b** of uniform colour or tone **7** reliable, reputable, or acceptable – ~**ity** *n* – ~**ly** *adv* – ~**ness** *n* – ~**ify** *v* – ~**ification** *n*

²solid *adv* in a solid manner; *also* unanimously

³solid *n* **1** a substance that does not flow perceptibly under moderate stress **2** sthg solid; *esp* a solid colour

solidarity /,soli'darəti/ *n* unity based on shared interests and standards

soliloquy /sə'liləkwi/ *n* a dramatic monologue that gives the illusion of being a series of unspoken reflections – **quize** *v*

solitaire /'soli,teə, ,--'-/ *n* **1** a gem, esp a diamond, set by itself **2** a game played by 1 person in which a number of pieces are removed from a cross-shaped pattern according to certain rules **3** *chiefly NAm* (a card-game similar to) patience

¹solitary /'solit(ə)ri/ *adj* **1a** (fond of) being or living alone or without companions **b** lonely **2** taken, spent, or performed without companions **3** being the only one; sole **4** unfrequented, remote

²solitary *n* one who habitually seeks solitude

solitude /'solityoohd/ *n* **1** being alone or remote from society; seclusion **2** a lonely place; a fastness

solmization /,solmie'zaysh(ə)n/ *n* the use of sol-fa syllables in or for singing

¹solo /'sohloh/ *n pl* **solos 1** a (musical composition for) performance by a single voice or instrument with or without accompaniment **2** a flight by 1 person alone in an aircraft; *esp* a person's first solo flight

²solo *adv* without a companion; alone

solstice /'solstis/ *n* either of the times when the sun's distance from the celestial equator is greatest and which occurs about June 22nd and December 22nd each year

soluble /'solyoobl/ *adj* **1** capable of being dissolved (as if) in a liquid **2** capable of being solved or explained – **bility** *n*

solution /sə'loohsh(ə)n/ *n* **1a** an act or the process by which a solid, liquid, or gaseous substance is uniformly mixed with a liquid or sometimes a gas or solid **b** a typically liquid uniform mixture

formed by this process **c** a liquid containing a dissolved substance **2a** an action or process of solving a problem **b** an answer to a problem

solve /solv/ *v* to find a solution for sthg – **solvable** *adj* – **solver** *n*

¹solvent /'solvant/ *adj* **1** able to pay all legal debts; *also* in credit **2** that dissolves or can dissolve – **-vency** *n*

²solvent *n* a usu liquid substance capable of dissolving or dispersing 1 or more other substances

sombre, *NAm chiefly* **somber** /'sombə/ *adj* **1** dark, gloomy **2** of a dull, dark, or heavy shade or colour **3a** serious, grave **b** depressing, melancholy – ~**ly** *adv* – ~**ness** *n*

sombrero /som'breəroh/ *n pl* **sombreros** a high-crowned hat of felt or straw with a very wide brim, worn esp in Mexico

¹some /sum/, *senses* ³*c and* ⁴*d* səm; *strong* sum/ *adj* **1a** being an unknown, undetermined, or unspecified unit or thing (e g *some* film or other) **b** being an unspecified member of a group or part of a class (e g *some* gems are hard) **c** being an appreciable number, part, or amount of (e g have *some* consideration for others) **d** being of an unspecified amount or number (e g give me *some* water) – used as an indefinite pl of **a** (e g have *some* apples) **2a** important, striking, or excellent (e g that was *some* party) – chiefly infml **b** no kind of (e g *some* friend you are) – chiefly infml

²some /sum/ *pron* **1** *sing or pl in constr* some part, quantity, or number but not all **2** *chiefly NAm* an indefinite additional amount (e g ran a mile and then *some*)

³some /sum/ *adv* **1** about (e g *some* 80 houses) **2** somewhat – used in Br English in *some more* and more widely in NAm — **some little** a fair amount of — **some few** quite a number

¹somebody /'sumbədi/ *pron* some indefinite or unspecified person

²somebody *n* a person of position or importance

somehow /'sum,how/ *adv* **1a** by some means not known or designated **b** no matter how **2** for some mysterious reason

someone /'sumwən, -,wun/ *pron* somebody

somersault /'sumə,sawlt/ *n* a leaping or rolling movement in which a person turns forwards or backwards in a complete revolution bringing the feet over the head and finally landing on the feet

¹something /'sumthing/ *pron* **1a** some indeterminate or unspecified thing – used to replace forgotten matter or to express vagueness (e g he's *something* or other in the Foreign Office) **b** some part; a certain amount (e g seen *something* of her work) **2a** a person or thing of consequence (e g their daughter is quite *something*) **b** some truth or value (e g there's *something* in what you say) — **something of a** a fairly notable

²**something** adv 1 in some degree; somewhat – also used to suggest approximation (e g *something* like 1,000 people) 2 to an extreme degree (e g swears *something* awful) – infml

¹**sometime** /'sum,tiem/ adv 1 at some unspecified future time 2 at some point of time in a specified period

²**sometime** adj having been formerly; late (e g the *sometime* chairman)

'**some,times** adv at intervals; occasionally; now and again

somewhat /'sumwot/ adv to some degree; slightly

¹**somewhere** /'sum,weə/ adv 1 in, at, or to some unknown or unspecified place 2 to a place or state symbolizing positive accomplishment or progress (e g at last we're getting *somewhere*) 3 in the vicinity of; approximately

²**somewhere** n an undetermined or unnamed place

somnolent /'somnələnt/ adj 1 inclined to or heavy with sleep 2 tending to induce sleep – ~ly adv – ~ence n

son /sun/ n 1a a male offspring, esp of human beings b a male adopted child c a male descendant – often pl 2 cap the second person of the Trinity; Christ

sonar /'sohnə/ n an apparatus that detects the presence and location of a submerged object

sonata /sə'nahtə/ n an instrumental musical composition typically for 1 or 2 players and of 3 or 4 movements in contrasting forms and keys

son et lumière /,son ay looh'myeə/ n an entertainment held at night at a historical site (e g a cathedral or stately home) that uses lighting and recorded sound to present the place's history

song /song/ n 1 the act, art, or product of singing 2 poetry 3 (the melody of) a short musical composition usu with words 4 a very small sum

songster /'songstə/, fem **songstress** /-stris/ n a skilled singer

sonic /'sonik/ adj 1 of waves and vibrations having a frequency within the audibility range of the human ear 2 using, produced by, or relating to sound waves 3 of or being the speed of sound in air at sea level (about 340 m/s or 741 mph)

,**sonic 'boom** n a sound resembling an explosion produced when a shock wave formed at the nose of an aircraft travelling at supersonic speed reaches the ground

'**son-in-,law** n, pl **sons-in-law** the husband of one's daughter

sonnet /'sonit/ n (a poem in) a fixed verse form with any of various rhyming schemes, consisting typically of 14 lines of 10 syllables each

sonny /'suni/ n a young boy – usu used in address; infml

sonorous /'sonərəs, 'soh-/ adj 1 giving out sound (e g when struck) 2 pleasantly loud 3 impressive in effect or style – ~ly adv – -rity n

soon /soohn/ adv 1 before long; without undue time lapse 2 in a prompt manner; speedily 3 in agreement with one's preference; willingly – in comparisons (e g I'd *sooner* walk than drive) — **no sooner . . . than** at the very moment that

²**soon** adj advanced in time; early

soot /soot/ n a fine black powder that consists chiefly of carbon and is formed by combustion, or separated from fuel during combustion – ~y adj – ~iness n

soothe /soohdh/ v 1 to calm (as if) by showing attention or concern; placate 2 to relieve, alleviate 3 to bring comfort or reassurance to– **soothingly** adv

sop /sop/ n 1 a piece of food, esp bread, dipped, steeped, or for dipping in a liquid (e g soup) 2 sthg offered as a concession, appeasement, or bribe

sophisticated /sə'fisti,kaytid/ adj 1a highly complicated or developed; complex b worldly-wise, knowing 2 intellectually subtle or refined – -**cation** n

sophistry /'sofistri/ n speciously subtle reasoning or argument – **sophist** n

soporific /,sopə'rifik/ adj 1 causing or tending to cause sleep 2 of or marked by sleepiness or lethargy – ~ally adv

¹**sopping** /'soping/ adj wet through; soaking

²**sopping** adv to an extreme degree of wetness

soppy /'sopi/ adj 1 weakly sentimental; mawkish 2 chiefly Br silly, inane USE infml

soprano /sə'prahnoh/ n pl **sopranos** 1 the highest part in 4-part harmony 2 (a person with) the highest singing voice of women or boys 3 a member of a family of instruments having the highest range

sorbet /'sawbit/ n a water ice; also a sherbet

sorcerer /'saws(ə)rə/, fem **sorceress** /-ris/ n a person who uses magical power, esp with the aid of evil spirits; a wizard

sorcery /'saws(ə)ri/ n the arts and practices of a sorcerer

sordid /'sawdid/ adj 1a dirty, filthy b wretched, squalid 2 base, vile 3 meanly avaricious; niggardly – ~ly adv – ~ness n

¹**sore** /saw/ adj 1a causing pain or distress b painfully sensitive or inflamed so as to be or seem painful 2a causing irritation or offence b causing great difficulty or anxiety; desperate 3 chiefly NAm angry, vexed – ~ness n

²**sore** n 1 a localized sore spot on the body 2 a source of pain or vexation; an affliction

sorely /'sawli/ adv 1 painfully, grievously 2 much, extremely

¹**sorrel** /'sorəl/ n 1 a brownish orange to light brown colour 2 a sorrel-coloured animal; esp a sorrel-coloured horse

²**sorrel** *n* any of various plants similar to the dock

¹**sorrow** /'soroh/ *n* **1** deep distress and regret (e g over the loss of sthg precious) **2** a cause or display of grief or sadness – ~ **ful** *adj* – ~**fully** *adv* – ~**fulness** *n*

²**sorrow** *v* to feel or express sorrow

sorry /'sori/ *adj* **1** feeling regret, penitence, or pity **2** inspiring sorrow, pity, or scorn

¹**sort** /sawt/ *n* **1 a** a group constituted on the basis of any common characteristic; a class, kind **b** an instance of a kind **2** nature, disposition **3** a person, individual – *infml* — **of sorts/of a sort** of an inconsequential or mediocre quality — **out of sorts 1** somewhat ill **2** grouchy, irritable

²**sort** *v* **1** to put in a rank or particular place according to kind, class, or quality – often + *through* **2** *chiefly Scot* to put in working order; mend – ~**er** *n* — **sort with** to correspond to; agree with — *fml*

sortie /'sawti/ *n* **1** a sudden issuing of troops from a defensive position **2** a single mission or attack by 1 aircraft

'**sort of** *adv* **1** to a moderate degree; rather **2** kind of *USE* infml

SOS /,es oh 'es/ *n* **1** an internationally recognized signal of distress which is rendered in Morse code as ··· ––– ··· **2** a call or request for help or rescue

¹**so-so** /'soh ,soh/ *adv* moderately well; tolerably

²**so-so** *adj* neither very good nor very bad; middling

sou /sooh/ *n, pl* **sous** /sooh(z)/ **1** any of various former French coins of low value **2** the smallest amount of money

¹**soufflé** /'soohflay/ *n* a light fluffy baked or chilled dish made with a thick sauce into which stiffly beaten egg whites are incorporated

²**soufflé, souffléed** /'soohflayd/ *adj* puffed or made light by or in cooking

sought /sawt/ *past of* **seek**

'**sought-,after** *adj* greatly desired or courted

¹**soul** /sohl/ *n* **1** the immaterial essence or animating principle of an individual life **2** all that constitutes a person's self **3a** an active or essential part **b** a moving spirit; a leader **4** a person **5** exemplification, personification **6a** a strong positive feeling esp of intense sensitivity and emotional fervour conveyed esp by American Negro performers **b** music that originated in American Negro gospel singing, is closely related to rhythm and blues, and is characterized by intensity of feeling and earthiness

²**soul** *adj* (characteristic) of American Negroes or their culture

'**soul-de,stroying** *adj* giving no chance for the mind to work; very uninteresting

'**soulful** /-f(ə)l/ *adj* full of or expressing esp intense or excessive feeling – ~**ly** *adv* – ~**ness** *n*

'**soulless** /-lis/ *adj* **1** having no soul or no warmth of feeling **2** bleak, uninviting – ~**ly** *adv* – ~**ness** *n*

'**soul-,searching** *n* scrutiny of one's mind and conscience, esp with regard to aims and motives

¹**sound** /sownd/ *adj* **1** healthy **b** free from defect or decay **2** solid, firm; *also* stable **3a** free from error, fallacy, or misapprehension **b** exhibiting or grounded in thorough knowledge and experience **c** conforming to accepted views; orthodox **4a** deep and undisturbed **b** thorough, severe – ~**ly** *adv* – ~**ness** *n*

²**sound** *adv* fully, thoroughly

³**sound** *n* **1a** the sensation perceived by the sense of hearing **b** energy that is transmitted by longitudinal pressure waves in a material medium (e g air) and is the objective cause of hearing **2** a speech sound **3** a characteristic musical style **4** radio broadcasting as opposed to television – ~**less** *adj* – ~**lessly** *adv*

⁴**sound** *v* **1a** to make a sound **b** to resound **c** to give a summons by sound **2** to have a specified import when heard; seem

⁵**sound** *n* **1** a long broad sea inlet **2** a long passage of water connecting 2 larger bodies or separating a mainland and an island

⁶**sound** *v* **1** to determine the depth of water, esp with a sounding line **2** *of a fish or whale* to dive down suddenly

'**sound ,barrier** *n* a sudden large increase in aerodynamic drag that occurs as an aircraft nears the speed of sound

'**sounding ,board** *n* **1a(1)** a structure behind or over a pulpit, rostrum, or platform to direct sound forwards **a(2)** a thin board placed so as to increase the resonance of a musical instrument **b** a device or agency that helps disseminate opinions or ideas **2** sby or sthg used to test reaction to new ideas, plans, etc

sound out *v* to attempt to find out the views or intentions of

¹'**sound,proof** /-,proohf/ *adj* impervious to sound

²**soundproof** *v* to insulate so as to obstruct the passage of sound

'**sound ,track** *n* the area on a film that carries the sound recording; *also* the recorded music accompanying a film

soup /soohp/ *n* **1** a liquid food typically having a meat, fish, or vegetable stock as a base and often thickened and containing pieces of solid food **2** an awkward or embarrassing predicament – *infml*

'**soup ,kitchen** *n* an establishment dispensing minimum food (e g soup and bread) to the needy

soup up *v* **1** to increase the power of (an engine or car) **2** to make more attractive, interesting, etc *USE* infml

¹**sour** /sowə/ *adj* **1** being or inducing the one of the 4 basic taste sensations that is produced chiefly by acids **2a** having the acid taste or smell (as if) of

fermentation **b** smelling or tasting of decay; rotten **c** wrong, awry **3a** unpleasant, distasteful **b** morose, bitter – ~**ly** *adv* – ~**ness** *n*

²**sour** *n* the primary taste sensation produced by sthg sour

source /saws/ *n* **1** the point of origin of a stream of water **2a(1)** a generative force; a cause **a(2)** a means of supply **b(1)** a place of origin; a beginning **b(2)** sby or sthg that initiates **b(3)** a person, publication, etc that supplies information, esp at firsthand

'**sour puss** /-,poos/ *n* a habitually gloomy or bitter person – *infml*

sousaphone /'soohzə,fohn/ *n* a large tuba that has a flared adjustable bell

souse /sows/ *v* **1** to pickle **2** to drench, saturate; *also* immerse **3** to make drunk; inebriate – *infml*

¹**south** /sowth; *also* sowdh (*in names*) *before words beginning with a vowel*/ *adj or adv* towards, at, belonging to, or coming from the south

²**south** *n* **1** (the compass point corresponding to) the direction of the south terrestrial pole **2** *often cap* regions or countries lying to the south of a specified or implied point of orientation

¹**south'east** /-'eest/ *adj or adv* towards, at, belonging to, or coming from the southeast

²**southeast** *n* **1** (the general direction corresponding to) the compass point midway between south and east **2** *often cap* regions or countries lying to the southeast of a specified or implied point of orientation

¹**south'easterly** /-'eestəli/ *adj or adv* southeast

²**southeasterly, southeaster** *n* a wind from the SE

,**south'eastern** /-'eestən/ *adj* **1** *often cap* (characteristic) of a region conventionally designated Southeast **2** southeast

¹**southerly** /'sudhəli/ *adj or adv* south

²**southerly** *n* a wind from the S

southern /'sudhən/ *adj* **1** *often cap* (characteristic) of a region conventionally designated South **2** south

Southerner /'sudhənə/ *n* a native or inhabitant of the South

'**south paw** /-,paw/ *n* a left-hander; *specif* a boxer who leads with the right hand and guards with the left

,**south 'pole** *n* **1a** *often cap S&P* the southernmost point of the rotational axis of the earth or another celestial body **b** the southernmost point on the celestial sphere, about which the stars seem to revolve **2** the southward-pointing pole of a magnet

¹**southwest** /,sowth'west; *esp tech* ,sow'west/ *adj or adv* towards, at, belonging to, or coming from the southwest

²**southwest** *n* **1** (the general direction corresponding to) the compass point midway between south and west **2** *often cap* regions or countries lying to the southwest of a specified or implied point of orientation

¹,**south'westerly** /-li/ *adj or adv* southwest

²**southwesterly, southwester** *n* a wind from the SW

,**south'western** /-'westən/ *adj* **1** *often cap* (characteristic) of a region conventionally designated Southwest **2** southwest

souvenir /,soohvə'niə/ *n* sthg that serves as a reminder (e g of a place or past event); a memento

sou'wester /,sow'westə/ *n* **1** a southwesterly **2a** a long usu oilskin waterproof coat worn esp at sea during stormy weather **b** a waterproof hat with a wide slanting brim longer at the back than in front

¹**sovereign** /'sovrin/ *n* **1** a ruler **2** a former British gold coin worth 1 pound

²**sovereign** *adj* **1a** possessing supreme (political) power **b** unlimited in extent; absolute **c** enjoying political autonomy **2a** of outstanding excellence or importance **b** of an unqualified nature; utmost **3** (characteristic) of or befitting a sovereign – ~**ty** *n*

soviet /'sohvyət, 'so-/ *n* **1** an elected council in a Communist country **2** *pl, cap* the people, esp the leaders, of the USSR

¹**sow** /sow/ *n* an adult female pig; *also* the adult female of various other animals (e g the grizzly bear)

²**sow** /soh/ *v* **sowed**; **sown** /sohn/, **sowed 1a** to scatter (e g seed) on the earth for growth **b** to strew (as if) with seed **2** to implant, initiate – ~**er** *n* — **sow one's wild oats** to indulge in youthful wildness and dissipation, usu before settling down to a steady way of life

soya bean *n* (the edible oil-rich and protein-rich seeds of) an annual Asiatic leguminous plant

sozzled /'soz(ə)ld/ *adj, chiefly Br* drunk – *slang*; often humor

spa /spah/ *n* **1** a usu fashionable resort with mineral springs **2** a spring of mineral water

¹**space** /spays/ *n* **1** (the duration of) a period of time **2a** a limited extent in 1, 2, or 3 dimensions; distance, area, or volume **b** an amount of room set apart or available **3a** a boundless 3-dimensional extent in which objects and events occur and have relative position and direction **b** physical space independent of what occupies it **4** the region beyond the earth's atmosphere **5** (a piece of type giving) a blank area separating words or lines (e g on a page)

²**space** *v* to place at intervals or arrange with space between

'**space craft** /-,krahft/ *n* a device designed to travel beyond the earth's atmosphere

,spaced-'out *adj* dazed or stupefied (as if) by a narcotic substance – slang

'space,ship /-,ship/ *n* a manned spacecraft

'space ,shuttle *n* a vehicle that has usu 2 stages and is designed to serve as a reusable transport between the earth and an orbiting space station

spacing /'spaysing/ *n* 1 a the act of providing with spaces or placing at intervals b an arrangement in space 2 the distance between any 2 objects in a usu regularly arranged series

spacious /'spayshas/ *adj* 1 containing ample space; roomy 2a broad or vast in area b large in scale or space; expansive – ~**ly** *adv* – ~**ness** *n*

¹spade /spayd/ *n* a digging implement that can be pushed into the ground with the foot

²spade *n* 1a a playing card marked with 1 or more black figures shaped like a spearhead b *pl but sing or pl in constr* the suit comprising cards identified by these figures 2 a Negro – derog

'spade,work /-,wuhk/ *n* the routine preparatory work for an undertaking

spaghetti /spo'geti/ *n* pasta in the form of thin often solid strings

spake /spayk/ *archaic past of* **speak**

Spam /spam/ *trademark* – used for a tinned pork luncheon meat

¹span /span/ *archaic past of* **spin**

²span *n* 1 the distance from the end of the thumb to the end of the little finger of a spread hand 2 an extent, distance, or spread between 2 limits: e g 2a a limited stretch (e g of time); *esp* an individual's lifetime b the full reach or extent c the distance or extent between supports (e g of a bridge); *also* a part of a bridge between supports d a wingspan

³span *v* **-nn-** 1 to extend across 2 to form an arch over

¹spangle /'spang·gl/ *n* 1 a sequin 2 a small glittering object or particle

²spangle *v* **spangling** /'spang·gling/ to set or sprinkle (as if) with spangles

spaniel /'spanyal/ *n* 1 any of several breeds of small or medium-sized mostly short-legged dogs usu having long wavy hair, feathered legs and tail, and large drooping ears 2 a fawning servile person

Spanish /'spanish/ *n* 1 the official Romance language of Spain and of the countries colonized by Spaniards 2 *pl in constr* the people of Spain

¹spank /spangk/ *v* to strike, esp on the buttocks, (as if) with the open hand – **spank** *n* – ~**ing** *n*

²spank *v* to move quickly or spiritedly

spanner /'spana/ *n, chiefly Br* a tool with 1 or 2 ends shaped for holding or turning nuts or bolts with nut-shaped heads — **(put) a spanner in the works** (to cause) obstruction or hindrance (e g to a plan or operation) – infml

¹spar /spah/ *n* 1 a stout pole 2 a mast, boom, gaff, yard, etc used to support or control a sail

²spar *v* **-rr-** 1 to engage in (a practice bout of) boxing 2 to skirmish, wrangle

¹spare /spea/ *v* 1 to refrain from destroying, punishing, or harming 2 to relieve of the necessity of doing, undergoing, or learning sthg 3 to refrain from; avoid 4 to use or dispense frugally – chiefly neg 5 to give up as surplus to requirements

²spare *adj* 1 not in use; *esp* reserved for use in emergency 2a in excess of what is required; surplus b not taken up with work or duties; free 3 healthily lean; wiry 4 not abundant; meagre – infml 5 *Br* extremely angry or distraught – infml

³spare *n* a spare or duplicate item or part; *specif* a spare part for a motor vehicle

,spare 'tyre *n* a roll of fat at the waist – infml

sparing /'spearing/ *adj* 1 frugal 2 meagre, scant – ~**ly** *adv*

¹spark /spahk/ *n* 1a a small particle of a burning substance thrown out by a body in combustion or remaining when combustion is nearly completed b a hot glowing particle struck from a larger mass 2 a luminous disruptive electrical discharge of very short duration between 2 conductors of opposite high potential separated by a gas (e g air) 3 a sparkle, flash 4 sthg that sets off or stimulates an event, development, etc

²spark *v* 1 to produce or give off sparks 2 to cause to be suddenly active; precipitate – usu + *off*

³spark *n* a lively and usu witty person – esp in **bright spark**

'sparking ,plug /'spahking/ *n* a part that fits into the cylinder head of an internal-combustion engine and produces the spark which ignites the explosive mixture

¹sparkle /'spahkl/ *v* **sparkling** /'spahkling/ 1 to give off or reflect glittering points of light 2 to effervesce 3 to show brilliance or animation

²sparkle *n* 1 a little spark 2 sparkling 3a vivacity, gaiety b effervescence

sparkler /'spahkla/ *n* 1 a firework that throws off brilliant sparks on burning 2 a (cut and polished) diamond – infml

sparrow /'sparoh/ *n* any of several small dull-coloured songbirds related to the finches

sparse /spahs/ *adj* of few and scattered elements; *esp* not thickly grown or settled – ~**ly** *adv* – ~**ness, sparsity** *n*

¹Spartan /'spaht(a)n/ *n* 1 a native or inhabitant of ancient Sparta 2 a person of great courage and endurance

²Spartan *adj* 1 of Sparta in ancient Greece 2a rigorously strict; austere b having or showing courage and endurance

spasm /'spaz(a)m/ *n* 1 an involuntary and abnormal muscular contraction 2 a sudden violent and brief effort or emotion

spasmodic /spaz'modik/ *adj* **1a** relating to, being, or affected or characterized by spasm **b** resembling a spasm, esp in sudden violence **2** acting or proceeding fitfully; intermittent – ~ **ally** *adv*

¹**spastic** /'spastik/ *adj* **1** of or characterized by spasm **2** suffering from a form of paralysis marked by involuntary jerks and twitches

²**spastic** *n* **1** one who is suffering from spastic paralysis **2** an ineffectual person – used esp by children

¹**spat** /spat/ *past of* **spit**

²**spat** *n pl* **spats**, *esp collectively* **spat** a cloth or leather gaiter covering the instep and ankle

³**spat** *n* **1** *NAm* a light splash **2** a petty argument – *infml*

spate /spayt/ *n* **1** flood **2a** a large number or amount, esp occurring in a short space of time **b** a sudden or strong outburst; a rush

spatial /'spaysh(ə)l/ *adj* relating to, occupying, or occurring in space – ~ **ly** *adv*

¹**spatter** /'spatə/ *v* to splash or sprinkle (as if) with drops of liquid; *also* to soil in this way

²**spatter** *n* **1** (the sound of) spattering **2** a drop spattered on sthg or a stain due to spattering

spatula /'spatyoolə, -chələ/ *n* a flat thin usu metal implement used esp for spreading, mixing, etc soft substances or powders

¹**spawn** /spawn/ *v* **1** *of an aquatic animal* to produce or deposit (eggs) **2** to bring forth, esp abundantly

²**spawn** *n* **1** the large number of eggs of frogs, oysters, fish, etc **2** material for propagating mushrooms

spay /spay/ *v* to remove the ovaries of

speak /speek/ *v* **spoke** /spohk/; **spoken** /'spohkən/ **1a** to utter words with the ordinary voice; talk **b(1)** to give voice to thoughts or feelings **b(2)** to be on speaking terms **c** to address a group **2** to act as spokesman *for* **3** to make a claim *for*; reserve **4** to make a characteristic or natural sound **5** to be indicative or suggestive — **so to speak** — used as an apologetic qualification for an imprecise, unusual, ambiguous, or unclear phrase — **to speak of** worth mentioning — usu *neg*

speakeasy /'speek,eezi/ *n* a place where alcoholic drinks were illegally sold during Prohibition in the USA in the 1920's and 30's

speaker /'speekə/ *n* **1a** one who speaks, esp at public functions **b** one who speaks a specified language **2** the presiding officer of a deliberative or legislative assembly **3** a loudspeaker

speak out *v* **1** to speak loudly enough to be heard **2** to speak boldly; express an opinion frankly

speak up *v* **1** to speak more loudly – often *imper* **2** to express an opinion boldly

¹**spear** /spiə/ *n* a thrusting or throwing weapon with long shaft and sharp head or blade

²**spear** *v* to pierce, strike, or take hold of (as if) with a spear

³**spear** *n* a usu young blade, shoot, or sprout (e g of asparagus or grass)

¹**spear,head** /-,hed/ *n* **1** the sharp-pointed head of a spear **2** a leading element or force in a development, course of action, etc

²**spearhead** *v* to serve as leader or leading force of

spear,mint /-,mint/ *n* a common mint grown esp for its aromatic oil

spec /spek/ *n* a speculation – *infml* — **on spec** *Br* as a risk or speculation; *also* as a risk in the hope of finding or obtaining sthg desired — *infml*

¹**special** /'spesh(ə)l/ *adj* **1** distinguished from others of the same category, esp because in some way superior **2** held in particular esteem **3** specific **4** other than or in addition to the usual **5** designed, undertaken, or used for a particular purpose or need – ~ **ly** *adv*

²**special** *n* **1** sthg that is not part of a series **2** sby or sthg reserved or produced for a particular use or occasion

specialist /'spesh(ə)list/ *n* **1** one who devotes him-/herself to a special occupation or branch of knowledge **2** a medical practitioner limiting his/her practice to a specific group of complaints – ~ **ist** *adj* – ~ **ism** *n*

speciality /,speshi'aləti/ *n* **1** (the state of having) a distinctive mark or quality **2** a product or object of particular quality **3a** a special aptitude or skill **b** a particular occupation or branch of knowledge

special-ize, -ise /'spesh(ə)liez/ *v* to apply or direct to a specific end or use; *esp* to concentrate one's efforts in a special or limited activity or field

species /'speeshiz/ *n pl* **species 1a** a class of individuals having common attributes and designated by a common name **b** a category in the biological classification of living things that ranks immediately below a genus, and comprises related organisms or populations potentially capable of interbreeding **2** a kind, sort – *chiefly derog*

¹**specific** /spə'sifik/ *adj* **1** being or relating to those properties of sthg that allow it to be assigned to a particular category **2** confined to a particular individual, group, or circumstance **3** free from ambiguity; explicit **4** of or constituting a (biological) species

²**specific** *n* **1** a characteristic quality or trait **2** *pl*, *chiefly NAm* particulars

specification /,spesifi'kaysh(ə)n/ *n* **1** specifying **2a** a detailed description of sthg (e g a building or car), esp in the form of a plan – usu *pl* with *sing*. meaning **b** a written description of an invention for which a patent is sought

spe,cific 'gravity *n* the ratio of the density of a substance to the density of a substance (e g pure water or hydrogen) taken as a standard when both densities are obtained by weighing in air

specify /'spesifie/ *v* 1 to name or state explicitly or in detail 2 to include as an item in a specification

specimen /'spesimin/ *n* 1 an item, part, or individual typical of a group or category; an example 2 a person, individual – chiefly derog

specious /'speesh(y)əs/ *adj* 1 having deceptive attraction or fascination 2 superficially sound or genuine but fallacious – ~**ly** *adv* – ~**ness** *n*

¹**speck** /spek/ *n* 1 a small spot or blemish, esp from stain or decay 2 a small particle

²**speck** *v* to mark with specks

¹**speckle** /'spekl/ *n* a little speck (e g of colour)

²**speckle** *v* **speckling** /'spekling, 'spekl·ing/ to mark (as if) with speckles

spectacle /'spektəkl/ *n* 1a sthg exhibited as unusual, noteworthy, or entertaining b an object of scorn or ridicule, esp due to odd appearance or behaviour 2 *pl* glasses

'**spectacled** *adj* having (markings suggesting) a pair of spectacles

¹**spectacular** /spek'takyoolə/ *adj* of or being a spectacle; sensational – ~**ly** *adv*

²**spectacular** *n* sthg (e g a stage show) that is spectacular

spectator /spek'taytə/ *n* 1 one who attends an event or activity in order to watch 2 one who looks on without participating; an onlooker

spectre, *NAm chiefly* **specter** /'spektə/ *n* 1 a visible ghost 2 sthg that haunts or perturbs the mind; a phantasm – **-tral** *adj*

spectrum /'spektrəm/ *n, pl* **spectra** /-trə/, **spectrums** 1a a series of images formed when a beam of radiant energy is subjected to dispersion and brought to focus so that the component waves are arranged in the order of their wavelengths (e g when a beam of sunlight is refracted and dispersed by a prism forms a display of colours) b the range of frequencies of electromagnetic or sound waves 2 a sequence, range

speculate /'spekyoolayt/ *v* 1 to meditate *on* or ponder *about* sthg; reflect 2 to buy or sell in expectation of profiting from market fluctuations – **-lation** *n* – **-lator** *n*

speculative /'spekyoolətiv/ *adj* 1 involving, based on, or constituting speculation; *also* theoretical rather than demonstrable 2 questioning, inquiring – ~**ly** *adv*

speech /speech/ *n* 1a the communication or expression of thoughts in spoken words b conversation 2 a public discourse; an address 3 a language, dialect

'**speechless** /-lis/ *adj* 1a unable to speak; dumb b deprived of speech (e g through horror or rage) 2 refraining from speech; silent 3 incapable of being expressed in words – ~**ly** *adv* – ~**ness** *n*

¹**speed** /speed/ *n* 1a moving swiftly; swiftness b rate of motion 2 rate of performance or execution 3a the sensitivity of a photographic film, plate, or paper expressed numerically b the duration of a photographic exposure 4 an amphetamine drug – slang — **at speed** at a fast speed; while travelling rapidly

²**speed** *v* **sped** /sped/, **speeded** 1 to move or go quickly 2 to travel at excessive or illegal speed 3 to promote the success or development of

speedometer /spee'domitə, spi-/ *n* 1 an instrument for indicating speed 2 an instrument for indicating distance travelled as well as speed

'**speed,way** /-,way/ *n* 1 a usu oval racecourse for motorcycles 2 the sport of racing motorcycles usu belonging to professional teams on closed cinder or dirt tracks

'**speed,well** /-,wel/ *n* any of a genus of plants that mostly have slender stems and small blue or whitish flowers

speedy /'speedi/ *adj* swift, quick – **speedily** *adv* – **speediness** *n*

¹**spell** /spel/ *n* 1a a spoken word or form of words held to have magic power b a state of enchantment 2 a compelling influence or attraction

²**spell** *v* **spelt** /spelt/, *NAm chiefly* **spelled** 1 to name or write the letters of (e g a word) in order; *also, of letters* to form (e g a word) 2 to amount to; mean – chiefly journ – ~**er** *n*

³**spell** *v* **spelled** 1 to give a brief rest to 2 to relieve for a time; stand in for

⁴**spell** *n* 1 a period spent in a job or occupation 2 a short or indefinite period or phase

spelling /'speling/ *n* 1 the forming of or ability to form words from letters 2 the sequence of letters that make up a particular word

spell out *v* 1 to read slowly and haltingly 2 to come to understand; discern 3 to explain clearly and in detail

spend /spend/ *v* **spent** /spent/ 1 to use up or pay out; expend 2 to wear out, exhaust 3 to cause or permit to elapse; pass — **spend a penny** *Br* to urinate – euph

'**spend,thrift** /-,thrift/ *n* one who spends carelessly or wastefully

spent /spent/ *adj* 1a used up; consumed b exhausted of useful components or qualities 2 drained of energy; exhausted

sperm /spuhm/ *n pl* **sperms**, *esp collectively* **sperm** 1a the male fertilizing fluid; semen b a male gamete 2 oil and other products from the sperm whale

'**sperm ,whale** *n* a large toothed whale that has a vast blunt head in the front part of which is a cavity containing a fluid mixture of oil and other waxy substances used in cosmetics

spew /spyooh/ *v* 1 to vomit 2 to come forth in a flood or gush

sphagnum /'sfagnəm, 'spagnəm/ *n* any of a large genus of atypical mosses that grow only in wet acid areas (e g bogs) where their remains become compacted with other plant debris to form peat

sphere /sfiə/ *n* **1a** a globular body; a ball **b** (a space or solid enclosed by) a surface, all points of which are equidistant from the centre **2** natural or proper place; *esp* social position or class **3** a field of action, existence, or influence

spherical /'sferikl/ *adj* **1** having the form of (a segment of) a sphere **2** relating to or dealing with (the properties of) a sphere

spheroid /'sfiəroyd/ *n* a figure resembling a sphere

sphinx /sfinks/ *n, pl* **sphinxes, sphinges** /-jeez/ **1a** *cap* a female monster in Greek mythology, with a lion's body and a human head, that killed those who failed to answer a riddle she asked **b** an enigmatic or mysterious person **2** an ancient Egyptian image in the form of a recumbent lion, usu with a human head

¹**spice** /spies/ *n* **1** any of various aromatic vegetable products (e g pepper, ginger, or nutmeg) used to season or flavour foods **2** sthg that adds zest or relish **3** a pungent or aromatic smell

²**spice** *v* **1** to season with spice **2** to add zest or relish to

spick-and-span, spic-and-span /,spik ən 'span/ *adj* spotlessly clean and tidy; spruce

spicy /'spiesi/ *adj* **1** lively, spirited **2** piquant, zestful **3** somewhat scandalous; risqué – **spicily** *adv* – **-ciness** *n*

spider /'spiedə/ *n* any of an order of arachnids having a body with 2 main divisions, 4 pairs of walking legs, and 2 or more pairs of abdominal glands for spinning threads of silk used for cocoons, nests, or webs

spidery /'spied(ə)ri/ *adj* resembling a spider in form or manner; *specif* long, thin, and sharply angular like the legs of a spider

¹**spiel** /s(h)peel/ *v, chiefly NAm* to utter or express volubly or extravagantly – usu + *off USE* infml

²**spiel** *n, chiefly NAm* a voluble talk designed to influence or persuade; patter – infml

spigot /'spigət/ *n* **1** a small plug used to stop up the vent of a cask **2** the part of a tap, esp on a barrel, which controls the flow

¹**spike** /spiek/ *n* **1** a very large nail **2a** any of a row of pointed iron pieces (e g on the top of a wall or fence) **b(1)** any of several metal projections set in the sole and heel of a shoe to improve traction **b(2)** *pl* a pair of (athletics) shoes having spikes attached

²**spike** *v* **1** to fasten or provide with spikes **2** to disable (a muzzle-loading cannon) by driving a spike into the vent **3** to pierce with or impale on a spike; *specif* to reject (newspaper copy), orig by impaling on a spike **4** to add spirits to (a nonalcoholic drink) — **spike someone's guns** to frustrate sby's opposition; foil an opponent

³**spike** *n* **1** an ear of grain **2** an elongated flower head with the flowers stalkless on a single main axis

¹**spill** /spil/ *v* **spilt** /spilt/, *NAm chiefly* **spilled** **1** to cause or allow to fall or flow out so as to be lost or wasted, esp accidentally **2** to spread profusely or beyond limits — **spill the beans** to divulge information indiscreetly — infml

²**spill** *n* **1** a fall from a horse or vehicle **2** a quantity spilt

³**spill** *n* a thin twist of paper or sliver of wood used esp for lighting a fire

¹**spin** /spin/ *v* **-nn-; spun** /spun/ **1** to draw out and twist fibre into yarn or thread **2** *esp of a spider or insect* to form a thread by forcing out a sticky rapidly hardening fluid **3a** to revolve rapidly; whirl **b** to have the sensation of spinning; reel **4** to move swiftly, esp on wheels or in a vehicle **5** to compose and tell (a usu involved or fictitious story)

²**spin** *n* **1a** the act or an instance of spinning sthg **b** the whirling motion imparted (e g to a cricket ball) by spinning **c** a short excursion, esp in or on a motor vehicle **2** a state of mental confusion; a panic – infml

spina bifida /,spienə 'bifidə/ *n* a congenital condition in which there is a defect in the formation of the spine so that the spinal cord is uncovered

spinach /'spinij, -nich/ *n* a plant cultivated for its edible leaves

spinal /'spienəl/ *adj* **1** of or situated near the backbone **2** of or affecting the spinal cord

spinal cord *n* the cord of nervous tissue that extends from the brain lengthways along the back in the spinal canal, carries impulses to and from the brain, and serves as a centre for initiating and coordinating many reflex actions

spindle /'spindl/ *n* **1a** a round stick with tapered ends used to form and twist the yarn in hand spinning **b** the long slender pin by which the thread is twisted in a spinning wheel **c** any of various rods or pins holding a bobbin in a textile machine (e g a spinning frame) **2a** a turned often decorative piece (e g on a piece of furniture) **b** a newel **c** a pin or axis about which sthg turns

spindly /'spindli/ *adj* having an unnaturally tall or slender appearance, esp suggestive of physical weakness

spin-'dry *v* to remove water from (wet laundry) by placing in a rapidly revolving drum

spine /spien/ *n* **1a** the spinal column **b** the back of a book, usu lettered with the title and author's name **2** a stiff pointed plant part **3** a sharp rigid part of an animal or fish

spineless /'spienlis/ *adj* **1** free from spines, thorns, or prickles **2a** having no spinal column; invertebrate **b** lacking strength of character – **~ly** *adv* – **~ness** *n*

spinet /'spinit, spi'net/ *n* a small harpsichord having the strings at an angle to the keyboard

spinnaker /'spinəkə/ *n* a large triangular sail set forward of a yacht's mast on a long light pole

spinner /'spinə/ n 1 a fisherman's lure consisting of a spoon, blade, or set of wings that revolves when drawn through the water 2 a bowler of spin bowling

spinney /'spini/ n, Br a small wood with undergrowth

spinning 'jenny /'jeni/ n an early multiple-spindle machine for spinning wool or cotton

'spinning ,wheel n a small domestic machine for spinning yarn or thread by means of a spindle driven by a hand- or foot-operated wheel

'spin-,off n a by-product; also sthg which is a further development of some idea or product

spinster /'spinstə/ n an unmarried woman; esp a woman who is past the usual age for marrying or who seems unlikely to marry – **~hood** n

spiny /'spieni/ adj 1 covered or armed with spines; broadly bearing spines, prickles, or thorns 2 full of difficulties or annoyances; thorny

¹spiral /'spie-ərəl/ adj 1 a winding round a centre or pole and gradually approaching or receding from it **b** helical 2 of the advancement to higher levels through a series of cyclical movements

²spiral n 1a the path of a point in a plane moving round a central point while continuously receding from or approaching it **b** a 3-dimensional curve (e g a helix) with 1 or more turns about an axis 2 a single turn or coil in a spiral object 3 a continuously expanding and accelerating increase or decrease – **spiral** v

spire /spie-ə/ n a tall tapering roof or other construction on top of a tower

¹spirit /'spirit/ n 1 a supernatural being or essence: e g **1a** cap the Holy Spirit **b** the soul **c** a ghost **d** a malevolent being that enters and possesses a human being 2 temper or state of mind – often pl with sing. meaning 3 the immaterial intelligent or conscious part of a person 4 the attitude or intention characterizing or influencing sthg 5 liveliness, energy; also courage **6** a person of a specified kind or character 7 distilled liquor of high alcoholic content – usu pl with sing. meaning 8a prevailing characteristic **b** the true meaning of sthg (e g a rule or instruction) in contrast to its verbal expression – **in spirits** in a cheerful or lively frame of mind – **out of spirits** in a gloomy or depressed frame of mind

²spirit v to carry off, esp secretly or mysteriously – usu + away or off

'spirited adj 1 full of energy, animation, or courage 2 having a specified frame of mind – often in combination

'spirit ,level n a level that uses the position of a bubble in a curved transparent tube of liquid to indicate whether a surface is level

¹spiritual /'spirichooəl/ adj 1 (consisting of) spirit; incorporeal 2 ecclesiastical rather than lay or temporal 3 concerned with religious values 4 of supernatural beings or phenomena – **~ly** adv

²spiritual n a usu emotional religious song of a kind developed esp among Negroes in the southern USA

spiritualism /'spirichooə,liz(ə)m/ n a belief that spirits of the dead communicate with the living, esp through a medium or at a séance – **-ist** n – **-istic** adj

spirituality /,spirichoo'aləti/ n 1 sensitivity or attachment to religious values 2 a practice of personal devotion and prayer

¹spit /spit/ n 1 a slender pointed rod for holding meat over a source of heat (e g an open fire) 2 a small point of land, esp of sand or gravel, running into a river mouth, bay, etc

²spit v **-tt-** to fix (as if) on a spit; impale

³spit v **-tt-; spat** /spat/, **spit** 1 to eject saliva from the mouth (as an expression of aversion or contempt); also to get rid of something in the mouth by ejecting it with some force 2 to express (hostile or malicious feelings) (as if) by spitting 3 to rain or snow slightly or in flurries 4 to sputter – **spit it out** to utter promptly what is in the mind

⁴spit n **1a** spittle, saliva **b** the act or an instance of spitting 2 a frothy secretion exuded by some insects

,spit and 'polish n extreme attention to cleanliness, orderliness, and ceremonial

¹spite /spiet/ n petty ill will or malice – **~ful** adj – **~fully** adv – **~fulness** n — **in spite of** in defiance or contempt of

²spite v to treat vindictively or annoy out of spite

spitting image n perfect likeness

spittle /'spitl/ n saliva

spittoon /spi'toohn/ n a receptacle for spit

splash /splash/ v **1a** to strike and move about a liquid **b** to move through or into a liquid and cause it to spatter **2a** to dash a liquid or semiliquid substance on or against **b** to soil or stain with splashed liquid; spatter **3a** to spread or scatter in the manner of splashed liquid **b** to flow, fall, or strike with a splashing sound 4 chiefly Br to spend money liberally; splurge – usu + out

²splash n **1a** a spot or daub (as if) from splashed liquid **b** a usu vivid patch of colour or of sthg coloured **2a** (the sound of) splashing **b** a short plunge 3 (a vivid impression created esp by) an ostentatious display 4 a small amount, esp of a mixer added to an alcoholic drink; a dash

'splash,down /-,down/ n the landing of a spacecraft in the ocean

splatter /'splatə/ v 1 to spatter 2 to scatter or fall (as if) in heavy drops

¹splay /splay/ v 1 to spread out 2 to make (e g the edges of an opening) slanting

²splay adj turned outwards

spleen /spleen/ *n* 1 an organ near the stomach or intestine of most vertebrates that is concerned with final destruction of blood cells, storage of blood, and production of white blood cells 2 bad temper; spite 3 *archaic* melancholy

splendid /'splendid/ *adj* 1 magnificent, sumptuous 2 illustrious, distinguished 3 of the best or most enjoyable kind; excellent – ~**ly** *adv*

splendour, *NAm chiefly* **splendor** /'splendə/ *n* 1a great brightness or lustre; brilliance b grandeur, pomp 2 sthg splendid

¹**splice** /splies/ *v* 1a to join (e g ropes) by interweaving the strands b to unite (e g film, magnetic tape, or timber) by overlapping the ends or binding with adhesive tape 2 *Br* to unite in marriage; marry – *infml*

²**splice** *n* a joining or joint made by splicing

splint /splint/ *n* material or a device used to protect and immobilize a body part (e g a broken arm)

¹**splinter** /'splintə/ *n* 1 a sharp thin piece, esp of wood or glass, split or broken off lengthways 2 a small group or faction broken away from a parent body

²**splinter** *v* 1 to split or rend into long thin pieces; shatter 2 to split into fragments, parts, or factions

¹**split** /split/ *v* **-tt-;** **split** 1a to divide, esp lengthways or into layers b to break apart; burst 2 to subject (an atom or atomic nucleus) to artificial disintegration, esp by fission 3 to divide into parts or portions: e g 3a to divide between people; share b to divide into opposing factions, parties, etc 4 to sever relations or connections – often + *up* 5 to share sthg (e g loot or profits) with others – often + *with* 6 to let out a secret; act as an informer – often + *on* 7 to leave, esp hurriedly; depart – *infml* — **split hairs** to make oversubtle or trivial distinctions — **split one's sides** to laugh heartily — **split the difference** to compromise by taking the average of 2 amounts

²**split** *n* 1 a narrow break made (as if) by splitting 2 a piece broken off by splitting 3 a division into divergent groups or elements; a breach 4a splitting b *pl but sing in constr* the act of lowering oneself to the floor or leaping into the air with legs extended at right angles to the trunk 5 a wine bottle holding a quarter of the usual amount; *also* a small bottle of mineral water, tonic water, etc 6 a sweet dish composed of sliced fruit, esp a banana, ice cream, syrup, and often nuts and whipped cream

³**split** *adj* 1 divided, fractured 2 prepared for use by splitting

,**split-'level** *adj* divided so that the floor level in one part is less than a full storey higher than an adjoining part

split pea *n* a dried pea in which the cotyledons are usu split apart

,**split 'second** *n* a fractional part of a second; a flash – **split-second** *adj*

splutter /'splutə/ *v* to utter hastily and confusedly

¹**spoil** /spoyl/ *n* plunder taken from an enemy in war or a victim in robbery; loot – often *pl* with sing. meaning

²**spoil** *v* **spoilt,** **spoiled** /spoylt/, **spoiled** 1a to damage seriously; ruin b to impair the enjoyment of; mar 2a to impair the character of by overindulgence or excessive praise b to treat indulgently; pamper 3 to lose good or useful qualities, usu as a result of decay 4 to have an eager desire *for* – esp in *spoiling for a fight* – ~**er** *n*

'**spoil,sport** /-,spawt/ *n* one who spoils the fun of others – *infml*

¹**spoke** /spohk/ *past & archaic past part of* **speak**

²**spoke** *n* 1 any of the small radiating bars inserted in the hub of a wheel to support the rim 2 a rung of a ladder

spoken /'spohkən/ *adj* 1a delivered by word of mouth; oral b used in speaking or conversation; uttered 2 characterized by speaking in a specified manner – in combination

'**spoke,shave** /-,shayv/ *n* a plane having a blade set between 2 handles and used for shaping curved surfaces

spokesman /'spohksmən/, *fem* '**spokes,woman** *n* one who speaks on behalf of another or others

spoliation /,spohli'aysh(ə)n/ *n* 1a the act of plundering b the state of being plundered, esp in war 2 the act of damaging or injuring, esp irreparably

spondee /'spondee/ *n* a metrical foot consisting of 2 long or stressed syllables – **-daic** *adj*

¹**sponge** /spunj, spunzh/ *n* 1a(1) an elastic porous mass of interlacing horny fibres that forms the internal skeleton of various marine animals and is able when wetted to absorb water a(2) a porous rubber or cellulose product used similarly to a sponge b any of a group of aquatic lower invertebrate animals that are essentially double-walled cell colonies and permanently attached as adults 2 a sponger 3 a cake or sweet steamed pudding made from a light-textured mixture

²**sponge** *v* 1 to cleanse, wipe, or moisten (as if) with a sponge 2 to obtain esp financial assistance by exploiting natural generosity or organized welfare facilities – usu + *on* – ~**r** *n*

'**sponge ,bag** *n, Br* a small waterproof usu plastic bag for holding toilet articles

spongy /'spunji/ *adj* 1 resembling a sponge, esp in being soft, porous, absorbent, or moist – **-giness** *n*

¹**sponsor** /'sponsə/ *n* 1 sby who presents a candidate for baptism or confirmation and undertakes responsibility for his/her religious education or spiritual welfare 2 sby who assumes responsibility for some other person or thing 3 sby who or sthg that pays for a project or activity – ~**ship** *n*

²**sponsor** *v* to be or stand as sponsor for

spontaneous /spon'taynyəs, -ni·əs/ *adj* **1** proceeding from natural feeling or innate tendency without external constraint **2** springing from a sudden impulse **3** controlled and directed internally **4** developing without apparent external influence, force, cause, or treatment – ~**ly** *adv* – ~**ness**, **-neity** *n*

¹spoof /spoohf/ *v* **1** to deceive, hoax **2** to make good-natured fun of; lampoon *USE* infml

²spoof *n* **1** a hoax, deception **2** a light, humorous, but usu telling parody *USE* infml

spook /spoohk/ *n* a ghost, spectre – chiefly infml

spooky /'spoohki/ *adj* eerie – chiefly infml

¹spool /spoohl/ *n* **1** a cylindrical device on which wire, yarn, film, etc is wound **2** (the amount of) material wound on a spool

²spool *v* to wind on a spool

¹spoon /spoohn/ *n* an eating, cooking, or serving implement consisting of a small shallow round or oval bowl with a handle

²spoon *v* **1** to take up and usu transfer (as if) in a spoon **2** to propel (a ball) weakly upwards **3** to indulge in caressing and amorous talk – not now in vogue

spoonerism /'spoohnə,riz(ə)m/ *n* a transposition of usu initial sounds of 2 or more words (e g in *tons of soil* for *sons of toil*)

'spoon-,feed *v* to present (e g information or entertainment) in an easily assimilable form that precludes independent thought or critical judgment

'spoonful /-f(ə)l/ *n*, *pl* **spoonfuls** *also* **spoonsful** as much as a spoon will hold

spoor /spooə, spaw/ *n* a track, a trail, or droppings, esp of a wild animal

sporadic /spə'radik, spaw-/ *adj* occurring occasionally or in scattered instances – ~**ally** *adv*

spore /spaw/ *n* a primitive usu single-celled hardy reproductive type produced by plants, protozoans, bacteria, etc and capable of development into a new individual either on its own or after fusion with another spore

sporran /'sporən/ *n* a pouch of animal skin with the hair or fur on that is worn in front of the kilt with traditional Highland dress

¹sport /spawt/ *v* **1** to exhibit for all to see; show off **2** to play about happily; frolic **3** to speak or act in jest; trifle

²sport *n* **1a** a source of diversion or recreation; a pastime **b** physical activity engaged in for recreation **2a** pleasantry, jest **b** mockery, derision **3** sby who is fair, generous, and esp a good loser **4** an individual exhibiting a sudden deviation from type beyond the normal limits of individual variation

sporting /'spawting/ *adj* **1** concerned with, used for, or suitable for sport **2** marked by or calling for sportsmanship **3** involving such risk as a sports competitor might take or encounter **4** fond of or taking part in sports – ~**ly** *adv*

sportive /'spawtiv/ *adj* frolicsome, playful – ~**ly** *adv* – ~**ness** *n*

sports /spawts/, *NAm chiefly* **sport** *adj* of or suitable for sports; *esp* styled in a manner suitable for casual or informal wear

'sports ,car *n* a low fast usu 2-passenger motor car

'sportsman /-mən/, *fem* **'sports,woman** *n* **1** sby who engages in sports, esp blood sports **2** sby who is fair, a good loser, and a gracious winner – ~**like** *adj*

'sportsmanship /-ship/ *n* conduct becoming to a sportsman

sporty /'spawti/ *adj* **1** fond of sport **2a** notably loose or dissipated; fast **b** flashy, showy – **sportiness** *n*

¹spot /spot/ *n* **1** a blemish on character or reputation; a stain **2a** a small usu round area different (e g in colour or texture) from the surrounding surface **b(1)** an area marred or marked (e g by dirt) **b(2)** a pimple **c** a conventionalized design used on playing cards to distinguish suits and indicate values **3a** a small amount; a bit **4** a particular place or area **5** a place on an entertainment programme **6** a spotlight **7** a usu difficult or embarrassing position; a fix — **on the spot 1** in one place; without travelling away **2** at the place of action; available at the appropriate place and time **3** in an awkward or embarrassing position

²spot *v* **-tt- 1** to mark or mar (as if) with spots **2a** to single out; identify **b** to detect, notice **c** to watch for and record the sighting of **3** *chiefly Br* to fall lightly in scattered drops

³spot *adj* **1a** available for immediate delivery after sale **b** involving immediate cash payment **2** given on the spot or restricted to a few random places or instances; *also* selected at random or as a sample

,spot-'check *v* to make a quick or random sampling or investigation of

'spotless /-lis/ *adj* **1** free from dirt or stains; immaculate **2** pure, unblemished – ~**ly** *adv* – ~**ness** *n*

'spot,light /-,liet/ *n* **1a** a projected spot of light used for brilliant illumination of a person or object on a stage **b** a light designed to direct a narrow intense beam on a small area full public attention – **spotlight** *v*

spot-'on *adj*, *Br* **1** absolutely correct or accurate **2** exactly right *USE* infml

spotted /'spotid/ *adj* **1** marked with spots **2** sullied, tarnished

,spotted 'dick /dik/ *n*, *Br* a steamed or boiled sweet suet pudding containing currants

spotter /'spotə/ n sby or sthg that keeps watch or observes; *esp* a person who watches for and notes down vehicles (e g aircraft or trains)

spotty /'spoti/ *adj* **1a** marked with spots **b** having spots, esp on the face **2** lacking evenness or regularity, esp in quality

spouse /spows, spowz/ n a married person; a husband or wife

¹**spout** /spowt/ v **1** to eject (e g liquid) in a copious stream **2** to speak or utter in a strident, pompous, or hackneyed manner; declaim – *infml* – **~er** n

²**spout** n **1** a projecting tube or lip through which liquid issues from a teapot, roof, kettle, etc **2** a discharge or jet of liquid (as if) from a pipe — **up the spout 1** beyond hope of improvement; ruined — *infml* **2** pregnant – *slang*

sprain /sprayn/ n a sudden or violent twist or wrench of a joint with stretching or tearing of ligaments – **sprain** v

sprang /sprang/ *past of* **spring**

sprat /sprat/ n a small or young herring

¹**sprawl** /sprawl/ v **1** to lie or sit with arms and legs spread out carelessly or awkwardly **2** to spread or develop irregularly

²**sprawl** n **1** a sprawling position **2** an irregular spreading mass or group

¹**spray** /spray/ n **1** a usu flowering branch or shoot **2** a decorative arrangement of flowers and foliage (e g on a dress)

²**spray** n **1** fine droplets of water blown or falling through the air **2a** a jet of vapour or finely divided liquid **b** a device (e g an atomizer or sprayer) by which a spray is dispersed or applied

³**spray** v **1** to discharge, disperse, or apply as a spray **2** to direct a spray on – **~er** n

¹**spread** /spred/ v **spread 1a** to open or extend over a larger area – often + *out* **b** to stretch out; extend **2a** to distribute over an area **b** to distribute over a period or among a group **c** to apply as a layer or covering **3a** to make widely known **b** to extend the range or incidence of **4** to force apart – **~able** *adj*

²**spread** n **1** (extent of) spreading **2** sthg spread out: e g **2a** a surface area; an expanse **b** (the matter occupying) **2** facing pages, usu with printed matter running across the fold **3a** a food product suitable for spreading **b** a sumptuous meal; a feast **c** a cloth cover; *esp* a bedspread

'**spread-,eagle** v to (cause to) stand or lie with arms and legs stretched out wide; (cause to) sprawl

'**spread,sheet** n a software system in which large groups of numerical data can be displayed on a VDU in set format (e g in rows and columns) and rapid automatic calculations can be made

spree /spree/ n a bout of unrestrained indulgence in an activity; *esp* a binge

¹**sprig** /sprig/ n **1** a small shoot or twig **2** a small headless nail **3** a young offspring; *specif* a youth – *infml*

²**sprig** v **-gg-** to decorate with a representation of plant sprigs

sprightly /'sprietli/ *adj* marked by vitality and liveliness; spirited – **-liness** n

¹**spring** /spring/ v **sprang** /sprang/, **sprung** /sprung/; **sprung 1a(1)** to dart, shoot **a(2)** to be resilient or elastic; *also* to move by elastic force **b** to become warped **2** to issue suddenly and copiously; pour out **3a** to issue by birth or descent **b** to come into being; arise **4a** to make a leap or leaps **b** to rise or jump up suddenly **5** to produce or disclose suddenly or unexpectedly **6** to release from prison – *infml*

²**spring** n **1a** a source of supply; *esp* an issue of water from the ground **b** an ultimate source, esp of thought or action **2** a time or season of growth or development; *specif* the season between winter and summer comprising, in the northern hemisphere, the months of March, April, and May **3** a mechanical part that recovers its original shape when released after deformation **4a** the act or an instance of leaping up or forward; a bound **b(1)** capacity for springing; resilience **b(2)** bounce, energy – **~less** *adj*

'**spring,board** /-,bawd/ n **1** a flexible board secured at one end that a diver or gymnast jumps off to gain extra height **2** sthg that provides an initial stimulus or impetus

springbok /'springbok/ n pl **springboks**, (1) **springboks**, *esp collectively* **springbok 1** a swift and graceful southern African gazelle noted for its habit of springing lightly and suddenly into the air **2** *often cap* a sportsman or sportswoman representing S Africa in an international match or tour abroad

,**spring-'clean** v **1** to give a thorough cleaning to (e g a house or furnishings) **2** to put into a proper or more satisfactory order – **spring-clean**, **~ing** n

,**spring 'onion** n an onion with a small mild-flavoured thin-skinned bulb and long shoots that is chiefly eaten raw in salads

,**spring 'tide** n a tide of maximum height occurring at new and full moon

springy /'spring-i/ *adj* having an elastic or bouncy quality; resilient

¹**sprinkle** /'springkl/ v **sprinkling** /'springkling/ **1** to scatter in fine drops or particles **2a** to distribute (sthg) at intervals (as if) by scattering **b** to occur at (random) intervals on; dot **c** to wet lightly

²**sprinkle** n **1** an instance of sprinkling; *specif* a light fall of rain **2** a sprinkling

sprinkler /'springklə/ n a device for spraying a liquid, esp water: e g **a** a fire extinguishing system that works automatically on detection of smoke or a high temperature **b** an apparatus for watering a lawn

sprinkling /'springkling/ n a small quantity or number, esp falling in scattered drops or particles or distributed randomly

¹sprint /sprint/ *v* to run or ride a bicycle at top speed, esp for a short distance – ~**er** *n*

²sprint *n* **1** (an instance of) sprinting **2a** a short fast running, swimming, or bicycle race **b** a burst of speed

sprite /spriet/ *n* a (playful graceful) fairy

sprocket /'sprokit/ *n* **1** a tooth or projection on the rim of a wheel, shaped so as to engage the links of a chain **2** *also* **sprocket wheel** a wheel or cylinder having sprockets (e g to engage a bicycle chain)

¹sprout /sprowt/ *v* **1** to grow, spring up, or come forth as (if) a shoot **2** to send out shoots or new growth

²sprout *n* **1** a (young) shoot (e g from a seed or root) **2** a Brussels sprout

¹spruce /sproohs/ *n* any of a genus of evergreen coniferous trees with a conical head of dense foliage and soft light wood

²spruce *adj* neat or smart in dress or appearance; trim – ~**ly** *adv* – ~**ness** *n*

³spruce *v* to make (oneself) spruce – *USE* usu + *up*

sprung /sprung/ *adj*, **1** *past of* **spring 2** equipped with springs

spry /sprie/ *adj* **sprier, spryer; spriest, spryest** vigorously active; nimble – ~**ly** *adv* – ~**ness** *n*

spud /spud/ *n* **1** a small narrow spade **2** a potato – infml

spume /spyoohm/ *v or n* (to) froth, foam

spun /spun/ *past of* **spin**

spunk /spungk/ *n* **1** any of various fungi used to make tinder **2** spirit, pluck **3** *Br* semen – vulg – ~**y**

¹spur /spuh/ *n* **1a** a pointed device secured to a rider's heel and used to urge on a horse **b** *pl* recognition and reward for achievement **2** a goad to action; a stimulus **3a** a stiff sharp spine (e g on the wings or legs of a bird or insect); *esp* one on a cock's leg **b** a hollow projection from a plant's petals or sepals (e g in larkspur or columbine) **4** a lateral projection (e g a ridge) of a mountain (range) — **on the spur of the moment** on impulse; suddenly

²spur *v* **-rr-** to incite to usu faster action or greater effort; stimulate – usu + *on*

spurious /'spyooari·əs/ *adj* **1** having a superficial usu deceptive resemblance or correspondence; false **2a** of deliberately falsified or mistakenly attributed origin; forged **b** based on mistaken ideas – ~**ly** *adv* – ~**ness** *n*

spurn /spuhn/ *v* to reject with disdain or contempt; scorn

¹spurt /spuht/ *v or n* (to make) a sudden brief burst of increased effort, activity, or speed

²spurt *v* to (cause to) gush out in a jet

³spurt *n* a sudden forceful gush; a jet

sputnik /'sputnik, 'spootnik/ *n* a Russian artificial satellite

¹sputter /'sputə/ *v* **1** to utter hastily or explosively in confusion, anger, or excitement; splutter **2** to make explosive popping sounds

²sputter *n* **1** confused and excited speech **2** (the sound of) sputtering

sputum /'spyoohtəm/ *n pl* **sputa** /-tə/ matter, made up of discharges from the respiratory passages and saliva, that is coughed up

¹spy /spie/ *v* **1** to catch sight of; see **2** to watch secretly; act as a spy – often + *on*

²spy *n* **1** one who keeps secret watch on sby or sthg **2** one who attempts to gain information secretly from a country, company, etc and communicate it to another

'spy,glass /-,glahs/ *n* a small telescope

squabble /'skwobl/ *v or n* **squabbling** /'skwobling/ (to engage in) a noisy or heated quarrel, esp over trifles

squad /skwod/ *n* **1** a small group of military personnel assembled for a purpose **2** a small group working as a team

squadron /'skwodrən/ *n* a unit of military organization: **a** a unit of cavalry or of an armoured regiment, usu consisting of 3 or more troops **b** a variable naval unit consisting of a number of warships on a particular operation **c** a unit of an air force consisting of between 10 and 18 aircraft

squalid /'skwolid/ *adj* **1** filthy and degraded from neglect or poverty **2** sordid – ~**ly** *adv*

¹squall /skwawl/ *v* to cry out raucously; scream – **squall, ~er** *n*

²squall *n* **1** a sudden violent wind, often with rain or snow **2** a short-lived commotion – **squally** *adj*

squalor /'skwolə/ *n* the quality or state of being squalid

squander /'skwondə/ *v* to spend extravagantly, foolishly, or wastefully; dissipate – ~**er** *n*

¹square /skweə/ *n* **1** an instrument (e g a set square or T square) with at least 1 right angle and 2 straight edges, used to draw or test right angles or parallel lines **2** a rectangle with all 4 sides equal **3a** a square scarf **b** an area of ground for a particular purpose (e g military drill) **4** any of the rectangular, square, etc spaces marked out on a board used for playing games **5** the product of a number multiplied by itself **6** an open space in a town, city, etc formed across the meeting of 2 or more streets, and often laid out with grass and trees **7** one who is excessively conventional or conservative in tastes or outlook – infml; no longer in vogue — **out of square** not at an exact right angle

²square *adj* **1a** having 4 equal sides and 4 right angles **b** forming a right angle **2a** approximating to a cube **b** of a shape or build suggesting strength and solidity; broad in relation to length or height **c** square in cross section **3** *of a unit of length* denoting the area equal to that of a square whose edges are of the specified length **4a** exactly adjusted, arranged, or aligned; neat and orderly **b** fair, honest, or straightforward **c** leaving no balance; settled **d** even, tied **5** excessively conservative; dully conventional – *infml*; no longer in vogue – ~**ly** *adv* – ~**ness** *n*

³square *v* **1a** to make square or rectangular **b** to test for deviation from a right angle, straight line, or plane surface **2a** to multiply (a number) by the same number; to raise to the second power **3a** to balance, settle *up; esp* to pay the bill **b** to even the score of (a contest) **4** to mark *off* into squares or rectangles **5a** to bring into agreement *with;* match **b** to bribe – *infml* — **square up to 1** to prepare oneself to meet (a challenge) **2** to take a fighting stance towards (an opponent)

⁴square *adv* **1** in a straightforward or honest manner **2a** so as to face or be face to face **b** at right angles

'square ,dance *n* a dance for 4 couples who form a hollow square

square-rigged *adj, of a ship* having square sails hanging from horizontal yards

,square 'root *n* a (positive) number whose square is a usu specified number

¹squash /skwosh/ *v* **1a** to press or beat into a pulp or a flat mass; crush **b** to apply pressure to by pushing or squeezing **2** to reduce to silence or inactivity

²squash *n* **1** the act or soft dull sound of squashing **2** a crushed mass; *esp* a mass of people crowded into a restricted space **3** *also* **squash rackets** a game played in a 4-walled court with long-handled rackets and a rubber ball that can be played off any number of walls **4** *Br* a beverage made from sweetened and often concentrated citrus fruit juice, usu drunk diluted

³squash *n, pl* **squashes, squash** any of various (plants of the cucumber family bearing) fruits widely cultivated as vegetables

¹squat /skwot/ *v* **-tt- 1** to crouch close to the ground as if to escape detection **2** to assume or maintain a position in which the body is supported on the feet and the knees are bent, so that the haunches rest on or near the heels **3** to occupy property as a squatter

²squat *n* **1** squatting **b** the posture of sby or sthg that squats **2** an empty building occupied by or available to squatters – *infml*

³squat *adj* **-tt- 1** with the heels drawn up under the haunches **2** disproportionately short or low and broad

squatter /'skwotə/ *n* **1** one who occupies usu otherwise empty property without rights of ownership or payment of rent **2** *Austr* one who owns large tracks of grazing land

squaw /skwaw/ *n* a N American Indian (married) woman

squawk /skwawk/ *v or n* **1** (to utter) a harsh abrupt scream **2** (to make) a loud or vehement protest – ~**er** *n*

¹squeak /skweek/ *v* to utter or make a squeak – ~**er** *n*

²squeak *n* **1** a short shrill cry or noise **2** an escape – usu *in a narrow squeak; infml* – ~**y** *adj*

¹squeal /skweel/ *v* **1** to utter or make a squeal **2a** to turn informer – *infml* **b** to complain, protest – *infml* – ~**er** *n*

²squeal *n* a shrill sharp cry or noise

squeamish /'skweemish/ *adj* **1** easily nauseated **2a** excessively fastidious in manners, scruples, or convictions **b** easily shocked or offended – ~**ly** *adv* – ~**ness** *n*

¹squeeze /skweez/ *v* **1a** to apply physical pressure to; compress **b** to extract or discharge under pressure **c** to force one's way **2a** to obtain by force or extortion **b** to cause (economic) hardship to **3** to fit into a limited time span or schedule – usu + *in* or *into* **4** to pass, win, or get by narrowly

²squeeze *n* **1a** a squeezing or compressing **b** a handshake; *also* an embrace **2** a condition of being crowded together; a crush **3a** a financial pressure caused by narrowing margins or by shortages **b** pressure brought to bear on sby – chiefly in *put the squeeze on; infml*

squelch /skwelch/ *v* **1** to emit a sucking sound like that of an object being withdrawn from mud **2** to walk or move, esp through slush, mud, etc, making a squelching noise – **squelch** *n*

squib /skwib/ *n* **1** a small firework that burns with a fizz and finishes with a small explosion **2** a short witty or satirical speech or piece of writing

squid /skwid/ *n pl* **squids,** *esp collectively* **squid** any of numerous 10-armed marine creatures, related to the octopus and cuttlefish, that have a long tapered body and a tail fin on each side

squidgy /'skwiji/ *adj, chiefly Br* soft and squashy – *infml*

squiffy /'skwifi/ *adj* slightly drunk, tipsy – *infml*

squiggle /'skwigl/ *v or n* (to draw) a short wavy twist or line, esp in handwriting or drawing – -**gly** *adj*

¹squint /skwint/ *adj* having a squint; squinting

²squint *v* **1** to look or look with a squint **2** to look or peer with eyes partly closed

³squint *n* **1** an inability to direct both eyes to the same object because of imbalance of the muscles of the eyeball **2** a glance, look – esp in *have/take a squint at; infml*

¹squire /skwie-ə/ *n* **1** a shield-bearer or armour-bearer of a knight **2** an owner of a country estate; *esp* the principal local landowner

²squire *v* to attend on or escort (a woman)

squirearchy, squirarchy /'skwie-ə,rahki/ *n* the gentry or landed-proprietor class

squirm /skwuhm/ v **1** to twist about like a worm; wriggle **2** to feel or show acute discomfort at sthg embarrassing, shameful, or unpleasant – **squirm** n

squirrel /'skwirəl/ n (the usu grey or red fur of) any of various New or Old World small to medium-size tree-dwelling rodents that have a long bushy tail and strong hind legs

¹**squirt** /skwuht/ v **1** to issue in a sudden forceful stream from a narrow opening **2** to direct a jet or stream of liquid at

²**squirt** n **1** a small rapid stream of liquid; a jet **2** a small or insignificant (impudent) person – infml

SS /,es 'es/ n sing or pl in constr Hitler's bodyguard and special police force

¹**stab** /stab/ n **1** a wound produced by a pointed weapon **2a** a thrust (as if) with a pointed weapon **b(1)** a sharp spasm of pain **b(2)** a pang of intense emotion **3** an attempt, try – infml

²**stab** v **-bb- 1** to pierce or wound (as if) with a pointed weapon **2** to thrust, jab – ~ **ber** n

stabilize /'staybl,iez/ v to make stable

¹**stable** /'staybl/ n **1** a building in which domestic animals, esp horses, are sheltered and fed – often pl with sing. meaning **2** sing or pl in constr **2a** the racehorses or racing cars owned by one person or organization **b** a group of athletes (e g boxers) or performers under one management

²**stable** v to put or keep in a stable

³**stable** adj **1a** securely established; fixed **b** not subject to change or fluctuation; unvarying **2** not subject to feelings of mental or emotional insecurity **3a** placed or constructed so as to resist forces tending to cause (change of) motion **b** able to resist alteration in chemical, physical, or biological properties – **-bility** n – **-bly** adv

stabling /'staybling/ n indoor accommodation for animals

staccato /stə'kahtoh/ n, adv, or adj, pl **staccatos** (a manner of speaking or performing, or a piece of music performed) in a sharp, disconnected, or abrupt way

¹**stack** /stak/ n **1** a large usu circular or square pile of hay, straw, etc **2** an (orderly) pile or heap **3** a chimney stack **4** a high pillar of rock rising out of the sea, that was detached from the mainland by the erosive action of waves **5** a large quantity or number – often pl with sing. meaning; infml

²**stack** v **1** to arrange in a stack; pile **2** to arrange (cards) secretly for cheating **3** to assign (an aircraft) to a particular altitude and position within a group of aircraft circling before landing

stadium /'staydi·əm/ n, pl **stadiums** also **stadia** /-di·ə/ a sports ground surrounded by a large usu unroofed building with tiers of seats for spectators

¹**staff** /stahf/ n, pl **staffs, staves** /stayvz/, (5) **staffs 1a** a long stick carried in the hand for use in walking or as a weapon **b** sthg which gives strength or sustains **2** a rod carried as a symbol of office or authority **3** a set of usu 5 parallel horizontal lines on which music is written **4** sing or pl in constr **4a** the body of people in charge of the internal operations of an institution, business, etc **b** a group of officers appointed to assist a military commander **c** the teachers at a school or university

²**staff** v **1** to supply with a staff or with workers **2** to serve as a staff member of

staff sergeant n a sergeant of the highest rank in the British army

¹**stag** /stag/ n pl **stags,** (1) **stags,** esp collectively **stag** an adult male red deer; broadly the male of any of various deer

²**stag** adj of or intended for men only

¹**stage** /stayj/ n **1a** a raised platform **b(1)** the area of a theatre where the acting takes place, including the wings and storage space **b(2)** the acting profession; also the theatre as an occupation or activity **2** a centre of attention or scene of action **3a** a place of rest formerly provided for those travelling by stagecoach **b** the distance between 2 stopping places on a road **c** a stagecoach **4** a period or step in a progress, activity, or development **5** any of the divisions (e g 1 day's riding or driving between predetermined points) of a race or rally that is spread over several days

²**stage** v **1** to produce (e g a play) on a stage **2** to produce and organize, esp for public view

¹**stage,coach** /-,kohch/ n a horse-drawn passenger and mail coach that in former times ran on a regular schedule between established stops

¹**stage di,rection** n a description (e g of a character or setting) or direction (e g to indicate sound effects or the movement or positioning of actors) provided in the text of a play

¹**stage- manage** v to arrange or direct, esp from behind the scenes, so as to achieve a desired result

,**stage 'manager** n one who is in charge of the stage during a performance and supervises related matters beforehand

¹**stage,struck** /-'struk/ adj fascinated by the stage; esp having an ardent desire to become an actor or actress

stage whisper n **1** a loud whisper by an actor, audible to the audience, but supposedly inaudible to others on stage **2** a whisper that is deliberately made audible

stagger /'stagə/ v **1** to reel from side to side (while moving); totter **2** to dumbfound, astonish **3** to arrange in any of various alternating or overlapping positions or times – **stagger** n

staggering /'stag(ə)ring/ adj astonishing, overwhelming – ~ **ly** adv

stagnant /'stagnənt/ adj **1a** not flowing in a current or stream; motionless **b** stale **2** dull, inactive – ~ **ly** adv

stagnate /stag'nayt/ v to become or remain stagnant – **-nation** n

stagy, stagey /'stayji/ adj marked by showy pretence or artificiality; theatrical – **stagily** adv – **staginess** n

staid /stayd/ adj sedate and often primly self-restrained; sober – **~ly** adv – **~ness** n

¹stain /stayn/ v 1 to discolour, soil 2 to taint with guilt, vice, corruption, etc; bring dishonour to

²stain n 1 a soiled or discoloured spot 2 a moral taint or blemish 3a a preparation (e g of dye or pigment) used in staining; esp one capable of penetrating the pores of wood b a dye or mixture of dyes used in microscopy to make minute and transparent structures visible, to differentiate tissue elements, or to produce specific chemical reactions

'stainless /-lis/ adj 1 free from stain or stigma 2 (made from materials) resistant to stain, specif rust

stair /steə/ n 1 a series of (flights of) steps for passing from one level to another – usu pl with sing. meaning 2 any step of a stairway

'stair,case /-,kays/ n 1 the structure or part of a building containing a stairway 2 a flight of stairs with the supporting framework, casing, and balusters

'stair,well /-,wel/ n a vertical shaft in which stairs are located

¹stake /stayk/ n 1 a pointed piece of material (e g wood) for driving into the ground as a marker or support 2a a post to which sby was bound for execution by burning b execution by burning at a stake – + the 3a sthg, esp money, staked for gain or loss b the prize in a contest, esp a horse race – often pl with sing. meaning c an interest or share in an undertaking (e g a commercial venture) — **at stake** in jeopardy; at issue

²stake v 1 to mark the limits of (as if) by stakes – often + off or out 2 to tether to a stake 3 to bet, hazard 4 to fasten up or support (e g plants) with stakes — **stake a/one's claim** to state that sthg is one's by right

stalactite /'stalək,tiet/ n an icicle-like deposit of calcium carbonate hanging from the roof or sides of a cavern

stalagmite /'staləgmiet/ n a deposit of calcium carbonate like an inverted stalactite formed on the floor of a cavern

stale /stayl/ adj 1a tasteless or unpalatable from age b of air musty, foul 2 tedious from familiarity 3 impaired in vigour or effectiveness, esp from overexertion – **stale** v – **~ly** adv – **~ness** n

stalemate /'stayl,mayt/ v or n (to bring into) a a drawing position in chess in which only the king can move and although not in check can move only into check b a deadlock

¹stalk /stawk/ v 1 to pursue or approach quarry or prey stealthily 2 to walk stiffly or haughtily – **~er** n

²stalk n 1 the stalking of quarry or prey 2 a stiff or haughty walk

³stalk n 1 the main stem of a herbaceous plant, often with its attached parts 2 a slender upright supporting or connecting (animal) structure

¹stall /stawl/ n 1 any of usu several compartments for domestic animals in a stable or barn 2a a wholly or partly enclosed seat in the chancel of a church b a church pew 3a a booth, stand, or counter at which articles are displayed or offered for sale b a sideshow 4 Br a seat on the main floor of an auditorium (e g in a theatre)

²stall v 1 to put or keep in a stall 2a to bring to a standstill; block b to cause (e g a car engine) to stop, usu inadvertently

³stall n the condition of an aerofoil or aircraft when the airflow is so obstructed (e g from moving forwards too slowly) that lift is lost

⁴stall v to play for time; delay

'stall,holder /-,hohldə/ n one who runs a (market) stall

stallion /'stalyən/ n an uncastrated male horse; esp one kept for breeding

¹stalwart /'stawlwət/ adj 1 strong in body, mind, or spirit 2 dependable, staunch – **~ly** adv – **~ness** n

²stalwart n a stalwart person; specif a staunch supporter

stamen /'staymən/ n the organ of a flower that produces pollen, and consists of an anther and a filament

stamina /'staminə/ n (capacity for) endurance

stammer /'stamə/ v to speak or utter with involuntary spasms and repetitions

¹stamp /stamp/ v 1 to bring down the foot forcibly 2a to impress, imprint b(1) to attach a (postage) stamp to b(2) to mark with an (official) impression, device, etc 3 to provide with a distinctive character

²stamp n 1 a device or instrument for stamping 2 the impression or mark made by stamping or imprinting 3a a distinctive feature, indication, or mark b a lasting imprint 4 a printed or stamped piece of paper that for some restricted purpose is used as a token of credit or occasionally of debit: e g 4a a postage stamp b a stamp used as evidence that tax has been paid

¹stampede /stam'peed/ n 1 a wild headlong rush or flight of frightened animals 2 a sudden mass movement of people

²stampede v to (cause to) run away or rush in panic or on impulse

'stamping ,ground /'stamping/ n a favourite or habitual haunt

stamp out v to eradicate, destroy

591 sta

stance /stahns, stans/ *n* **1a** a way of standing or being placed **b** intellectual or emotional attitude **2** the position of body or feet from which a sportsman (e g a batsman or golfer) plays

stanchion /'stahnsh(ə)n/ *v or n* (to provide with) an upright bar, post, or support (e g for a roof)

¹**stand** /stand/ *v* **stood** /stood/ **1a** to support oneself on the feet in an erect position **b** to rise to or maintain an erect or upright position **2** to take up or maintain a specified position or posture **3** to be in a specified state or situation **4** to be in a position to gain or lose because of an action taken or a commitment made **5** to occupy a place or location **6** to remain stationary or inactive **7** to agree, accord – chiefly in *it stands to reason* **8a** to exist in a definite (written or printed) form **b** to remain valid or effective **9** *chiefly Br* to be a candidate in an election **10a** to endure or undergo **b** to tolerate, bear; put up with **11** to remain firm in the face of **12** to pay the cost of; pay for – infml – ~ **er** *n* — **stand a chance** to have a chance — **stand by** to remain loyal or faithful to — **stand for 1** to be a symbol for; represent **2** to permit; put up with — **stand on** to insist on — **stand one in good stead** to be of advantage or service to one — **stand one's ground** to remain firm and unyielding in the face of opposition — **stand on one's own feet** to think or act independently

²**stand** *n* **1** an act, position, or place of standing **2a** a usu relative effort of some length or success **b** a stop made by a touring theatrical company, rock group, etc to give a performance **3** a strongly or aggressively held position, esp on a debatable issue **4a** a structure of tiered seats for spectators – often pl with sing. meaning **b** a raised platform serving as a point of vantage or display (e g for a speaker or exhibit) **5** a small usu temporary and open-air stall where goods are sold or displayed **6** a place where a passenger vehicle awaits hire **7** a frame on or in which sthg may be placed for support **8** a group of plants or trees growing in a continuous area **9** *NAm the* witness-box

¹**standard** /'standad/ *n* **1** a (long narrow tapering) flag **2a** sthg established by authority, custom, or general consent as a model or example; a criterion **b** a (prescribed) degree of quality or worth **3** *pl* moral integrity; principles **4** sthg set up and established by authority as a rule for the measure of quantity, weight, value, or quality **5** the basis of value in a money system **6** a shrub or herbaceous plant grown with an erect main stem so that it forms or resembles a tree

²**standard** *adj* **1a** being or conforming to a standard, esp as established by law or custom **b** sound and usable but not of top quality **2a** regularly and widely used, available, or supplied **b** well established and familiar **3** having recognized and permanent value – ~**ize** *v*

'**standard ,lamp** *n* a lamp with a tall support that stands on the floor

,**standard of 'living** *n* a level of welfare or subsistence maintained by an individual, group, or community and shown esp by the level of consumption of necessities, comforts, and luxuries

¹**standby** /'stand,bie/ *n pl* **standbys** /-,biez/ one who or that which is held in reserve and can be relied on, made, or used in case of necessity

²**standby** *adj* **1** held near at hand and ready for use **2** relating to the act or condition of standing by

stand by *v* **1** to be present but remain aloof or inactive **2** to wait in a state of readiness

stand down *v* **1** to leave the witness-box **2** *chiefly Br* to relinquish (candidature for) an office or position **3** *chiefly Br* to send (soldiers) off duty; *broadly* to dismiss (workers); lay off

'**stand-,in** *n* **1** one who is employed to occupy an actor's place while lights and camera are made ready **2** a substitute

¹**standing** /'standing/ *adj* **1** used or designed for standing in **2** not yet cut or harvested **3** not flowing; stagnant **4** continuing in existence or use indefinitely **5** established by law or custom **6** done from a standing position

²**standing** *n* **1a** length of service or experience, esp as determining rank, pay, or privilege **b** position, status, or condition, esp in relation to a group or other individuals in a similar field; *esp* good reputation **2** maintenance of position or condition; duration

,**standing 'order** *n* **1** a rule governing the procedure of an organization, which remains in force until specifically changed **2** an instruction (e g to a banker or newsagent) in force until specifically changed

standoffish /,stand'ofish/ *adj* reserved, aloof – ~**ly** *adv* – ~**ness** *n*

stand out *v* **1a** to appear (as if) in relief; project **b** to be prominent or conspicuous **2** to be stubborn in resolution or resistance

'**stand,pipe** /-,piep/ *n* a pipe fitted with a tap and used for outdoor water supply

'**stand,point** /-,poynt/ *n* a position from which objects or principles are viewed and according to which they are compared and judged

'**stand,still** /-,stil/ *n* a state in which motion or progress is absent; a stop

'**stand-,up** *adj* **1** stiffened to stay upright without folding over **2** performed in or requiring a standing position **3** (having an act) consisting of jokes usu performed solo standing before an audience

stand up *v* **1** to remain sound and intact under stress, attack, or close scrutiny **2** to fail to keep an appointment with — **stand up for** to defend against attack or criticism — **stand up to 1** to withstand efficiently or unimpaired **2** to face boldly

stank /stangk/ *past of* **stink**

stanza /'stanzə/ *n* a division of a poem consisting of a series of lines arranged together in a usu recurring pattern of metre and rhyme

¹**staple** /'staypl/ *v or n* (to provide with or secure by) **a** a U-shaped metal loop both ends of which can be driven into a surface (e g to secure sthg) **b** a small piece of wire with ends bent at right angles which can be driven through thin sheets of material, esp paper, and clinched to secure the items

²**staple** *n* **1** a chief commodity or production of a place **2** a raw material

³**staple** *adj* **1** used, needed, or enjoyed constantly, usu by many individuals **2** produced regularly or in large quantities **3** principal, chief

stapler /'stayplə/ *n* a small usu hand-operated device for inserting wire staples

¹**star** /stah/ *n* **1** any natural luminous body visible in the sky, esp at night **2a** a planet or a configuration of the planets that is held in astrology to influence a person's destiny – often pl **b** a waxing or waning fortune or fame **3a** an often star-shaped ornament or medal worn as a badge of honour, authority, or rank or as the insignia of an order **b** any of a group of stylized stars used to place sthg in a scale of value or quality – often in combination **4a** a (highly publicized) performer in the cinema or theatre who plays leading roles **b** an outstandingly talented performer – ~**ry**, ~**less** *adj*

²**star** *v* -**rr**- to play the most prominent or important role

³**star** *adj* of, being, or appropriate to a star

¹**starboard** /'stahbəd/ *adj or n* (of or at) the right side of a ship or aircraft looking forwards

²**starboard** *v* to turn or put (a helm or rudder) to the right

¹**starch** /stahch/ *v* to stiffen (as if) with starch

²**starch** *n* **1** an odourless tasteless complex carbohydrate that is the chief storage form of carbohydrate in plants, is an important foodstuff, and is used also in adhesives and sizes, in laundering, and in pharmacy and medicine **2** a stiff formal manner; formality

starchy /'stahchi/ *adj* marked by formality or stiffness

'**star-,crossed** *adj* not favoured by the stars; ill-fated

'**stardom** /-d(ə)m/ *n* the status or position of a celebrity or star

¹**stare** /steə/ *v* to look fixedly, often with wide-open eyes

²**stare** *n* a staring look

starfish /'stah,fish/ *n* any of a class of sea animals that have a body consisting of a central disc surrounded by 5 equally spaced arms

'**star,gazer** /-,gayzə/ *n* **1** an astrologer **2** an astronomer *USE* chiefly humor

¹**stark** /stahk/ *adj* **1** sheer, utter **2a(1)** barren, desolate **a(2)** having few or no ornaments; bare **b** harsh, blunt **3** sharply delineated – ~**ly** *adv* – ~**ness** *n*

²**stark** *adv* to an absolute or complete degree; wholly

starkers /'stahkəz/ *adj*, *Br* completely naked – used predicatively; slang

starlet /'stahlit/ *n* a young film actress being coached and publicized for starring roles

starling /'stahling/ *n* a dark brown (or in summer, glossy greenish black) European bird that lives in large social groups

,**starry-'eyed** *adj* given to thinking in a dreamy, impractical, or overoptimistic manner

Stars and Stripes *n pl but sing in constr* the flag of the USA

¹**start** /staht/ *v* **1** to react with a sudden brief involuntary movement **2** to come into being, activity, or operation **3a** to begin a course or journey **b** to range from a specified initial point **4** to begin an activity or undertaking; *esp* to begin work **5a** to cause to move, act, operate, or do sthg specified **b** to cause to enter or begin a game, contest, or business activity; *broadly* to put in a starting position **6** to perform or undergo the first stages or actions of; begin — **start something** to cause trouble — **to start with 1** at the beginning; initially **2** taking the first point to be considered

²**start** *n* **1** a sudden involuntary bodily movement or reaction (e g from surprise or alarm) **2** a beginning of movement, activity, or development **3a** a lead conceded at the start of a race or competition **b** an advantage, lead; a head start **4** a place of beginning

starter /'stahtə/ *n* **1** one who initiates or sets going; *esp* one who gives the signal to start a race **2a** one who is in the starting lineup of a race or competition **b** one who begins to engage in an activity or process **3** an electric motor used to start a petrol engine **4a** sthg that is the beginning of a process, activity, or series **b** *chiefly Br* the first course of a meal – often pl with sing. meaning

startle /'stahtl/ *v* **startling** /'stahtling/ to (cause to) be suddenly frightened or surprised and usu to (cause to) make a sudden brief movement – **-lingly** *adv*

starve /stahv/ *v* **1** to suffer or feel extreme hunger **2** to suffer or perish from deprivation

starveling /'stahvling/ *n* a person or animal that is thin (as if) from lack of food

¹**stash** /stash/ *v* to store in a usu secret place for future use – often + *away*

²**stash** *n*, *chiefly NAm* **1** a hiding place; a cache **2** sthg stored or hidden away

¹**state** /stayt/ *n* **1a** a mode or condition of being (with regard to circumstances, health, temperament, etc) **b** a condition of abnormal tension or excitement **2** a condition or stage in the physical

being of sthg **3a** luxurious style of living **b** formal dignity; pomp – usu + *in* **4** a politically organized (sovereign) body, usu occupying a definite territory; *also* its political organization **5** the operations of the government **6** *often cap* a constituent unit of a nation having a federal government

²**state** *v* **1** to set, esp by regulation or authority; specify **2** to express the particulars of, esp in words; *broadly* to express in words

'**stateless** /-lis/ *adj* having no nationality – ~**ness** *n*

'**stately** /-li/ *adj* **1** imposing, dignified **2** impressive in size or proportions – **-liness** *n*

statement /'staytmənt/ *n* **1** stating orally or on paper **2** sthg stated: e g **2a** a report of facts or opinions **b** a single declaration or remark; an assertion **3** a proposition (e g in logic) **4** the presentation of a theme in a musical composition **5** a summary of a financial account **6** an outward expression of thought, feeling, etc made without words

,**state-of-the'art** *adj* being or using the latest available resources, esp technology

'**stateroom** /-,roohm, -room/ *n* **1** a large room in a palace or similar building for use on ceremonial occasions **2** a (large and comfortable) private cabin in a ship

'**statesman** /-mən/, *fem* '**states,woman** *n pl* **statesmen** /-mən/, *fem* **stateswomen 1** one versed in or esp engaged in the business of a government **2** one who exercises political leadership wisely and without narrow partisanship – ~**ship** *n*

¹**static** /'statik/ *also* **statical** /-kl/ *adj* **1** exerting force by reason of weight alone without motion **2** of or concerned with bodies at rest or forces in equilibrium **3** characterized by a lack of movement, animation, progression, or change **4** of, producing, or being stationary charges of electricity

²**static** *n* (the electrical disturbances causing) unwanted signals in a radio or television system; atmospherics

statics /'statiks/ *n pl but sing or pl in constr* a branch of mechanics dealing with the relations of forces that produce equilibrium among solid bodies

¹**station** /'staysh(ə)n/ *n* **1** the place or position in which sthg or sby stands or is assigned to stand or remain a stopping place; *esp* (the buildings at) a regular or major stopping place for trains, buses, etc **3a** a post or sphere of (naval or military) duty or occupation **b** a stock farm or ranch in Australia or New Zealand **4** standing, rank **5** a place for specialized observation and study of scientific phenomena **6** a place established to provide a public service; *esp* a police station **7** an establishment equipped for radio or television transmission or reception

²**station** *v* to assign to or set in a station or position; post

stationary /'stayshən(ə)ri/ *adj* **1a** having a fixed position; immobile **2** unchanging in condition

stationer /'stayshənə/ *n* one who deals in stationery

stationery /'stayshən(ə)ri/ *n* materials (e g paper) for writing or typing

'**station,master** /-,mahstə/ *n* an official in charge of a railway station

statistics /stə'tistiks/ *n pl but sing or pl in constr* **1** a branch of mathematics dealing with the collection, analysis, interpretation, and presentation of masses of numerical data **2** a collection of quantitative data – **-tical** *adj* – **-tically** *adv* – **-tician** *n*

¹**statuary** /'statyooəri/ *n* statues collectively

²**statuary** *adj* of or suitable for statues

statue /'statyooh, -chooh/ *n* a likeness (e g of a person or animal) sculptured, cast, or modelled in a solid material (e g bronze or stone)

,**statu'esque** /-'esk/ *adj* resembling a statue, esp in dignity, shapeliness, or formal beauty

stature /'stachə/ *n* **1** natural height (e g of a person) in an upright position **2** quality or status gained by growth, development, or achievement

status /'staytəs/ *n* **1** the condition of sby or sthg (in the eyes of the law) **2** (high) position or rank in relation to others or in a hierarchy

,**status 'quo** /'kwoh/ *n* the existing state of affairs

statute /'statyooht/ *n* **1** a law passed by a legislative body and recorded **2** a rule made by a corporation or its founder, intended as permanent

statute book *n* the whole body of legislation of a given jurisdiction

statutory /'statyoot(ə)ri/, **statutable** /-təbl/ *adj* established, regulated, or imposed by or in conformity to statute

¹**staunch** /stawnch/ *v* to stop the flow of, esp blood

²**staunch** *adj* steadfast in loyalty or principle – ~**ly** *adv* – ~**ness** *n*

¹**stave** /stayv/ *n* **1** the musical staff **2** any of the narrow strips of wood or iron placed edge to edge to form the sides, covering, or lining of a vessel (e g a barrel) or structure **3** a supporting bar **4** a stanza

²**stave** *v* **staved**, **stove** /stohv/ to crush or break inwards – usu + *in*

stave off *v* to ward or fend off, esp temporarily

staves *pl of* **staff**

¹**stay** /stay/ *n* a strong rope, now usu of wire, used to support a ship's mast or similar tall structure (e g a flagstaff)

²**stay** *v* to support (e g a chimney) (as if) with stays

³**stay** *v* **1** to continue in a place or condition; remain **2** to take up temporary residence; lodge **3** *of a racehorse* to run well over long distances **4** to stop

or delay the proceeding, advance, or course of; halt — **stay put** to be firmly fixed, attached, or established

⁴**stay** /stay/ n **1a** stopping or being stopped **b** a suspension of judicial procedure **2** a residence or sojourn in a place

⁵**stay** n **1** sby who or sthg that serves as a prop; a support **2** a corset stiffened with bones – usu pl with sing. meaning

'**stay-at-,home** n or adj (one) preferring to remain in his/her own home, locality, or country

stayer /'staya/ n a racehorse that habitually stays the course

stead /sted/ n the office, place, or function ordinarily occupied or carried out by sby or sthg else

steadfast /'sted,fahst, -fəst/ adj **1a** firmly fixed in place or position **b** not subject to change **2** firm in belief, determination, or adherence; loyal – ~**ly** adv – ~**ness** n

¹**steady** /'stedi/ adj **1a** firm in position; not shaking, rocking, etc **b** direct or sure; unfaltering **2** showing or continuing with little variation or fluctuation **3a** not easily moved or upset; calm **b** dependable, constant **c** not given to dissipation; sober – **steadily** adv – **steadiness** n

²**steady** v to make, keep, or become steady

³**steady** adv in a steady manner; steadily

⁴**steady** n a regular boy/girl friend

steady state theory n a theory in cosmology: the universe has always existed and has always been expanding with matter being created continuously

steak /stayk/ n **1a** a slice of meat from a fleshy part (e g the rump) of a (beef) carcass and suitable for grilling or frying **b** a poorer-quality less tender beef cut, usu from the neck and shoulder, suitable for braising or stewing **2** a cross-sectional slice from between the centre and tail of a large fish

steal /steel/ v **stole** /stohl/; **stolen** /'stohlən/ **1** to take (the property of another) **2** to come or go secretly or unobtrusively — **steal a march** to gain an advantage unobserved – usu + on — **steal someone's thunder** to appropriate or adapt sthg devised by another in order to take the credit due to him/her

stealth /stelth/ n **1** the act or action of proceeding furtively or unobtrusively **2** the state of being furtive or unobtrusive – ~**y** adj – ~**ily** adv

¹**steam** /steem/ n **1a** vapour given off by a heated substance; esp the vapour into which water is converted when heated to its boiling point **2a** energy or power generated (as if) by steam under pressure **b** driving force; power – infml — **let/blow off steam** to release pent-up emotions

²**steam** v **1** to give off steam or vapour **2** to apply steam to; esp to expose to the action of steam (e g for softening or cooking) **3** to proceed quickly **4** to be angry; boil **5** to become covered up or over with steam or condensation

steamer /'steemə/ n **1** a device in which articles are steamed; esp a vessel in which food is cooked by steam **2a** a ship propelled by steam **b** an engine, machine, or vehicle operated or propelled by steam

¹'**steam,roller** /-,rohlə/ n **1** a machine equipped with wide heavy rollers for compacting the surfaces of roads, pavements, etc **2** a crushing force, esp when ruthlessly applied to overcome opposition

²**steamroller** also **steamroll** v to force to a specified state or condition by the use of overwhelming pressure

steam up v to make angry or excited; arouse

steed /steed/ n a horse; esp a spirited horse for state or war – chiefly poetic

¹**steel** /steel/ n **1** commercial iron distinguished from cast iron by its malleability and lower carbon content **2a** a fluted round steel rod with a handle for sharpening knives **b** a piece of steel for striking sparks from flint **3** a quality (e g of mind or spirit) that suggests steel, esp in strength or hardness

²**steel** v **1** to make unfeeling; harden **2** to fill with resolution or determination

steel band n a band that plays tuned percussion instruments cut out of oil drums, developed orig in Trinidad

steely /'steeli/ adj of or like (the hardness, strength, or colour of) steel

¹**steep** /steep/ adj **1** making a large angle with the plane of the horizon; almost vertical **2** being or characterized by a rapid and severe decline or increase **3** difficult to accept, comply with, or carry out; excessive – infml – ~**ly** adv – ~**ness** n

²**steep** v **1** to cover with or plunge into a liquid (e g in rinsing, bleaching or soaking) **2** to imbue with or subject thoroughly to – usu + in

steeple /'steepl/ n (a tower with) a tall spire on a church

'**steeple,chase** /-,chays/ n **1** a horse race across country or over jumps **2** a middle-distance running race over obstacles

'**steeple,jack** /-,jak/ n one who climbs chimneys, towers, etc to paint, repair, or demolish them

¹**steer** /stiə/ n a male bovine animal castrated before sexual maturity

²**steer** v **1** to direct the course of; esp to guide a ship by means of a rudder **2** to set and hold to (a course) — **steer clear** to keep entirely away — often + of

steerage /'stiərij/ n **1** the act or practice of steering; broadly direction **2a** a large section in a passenger ship for passengers paying the lowest fares

steersman /'stiəzmən/ n a helmsman

stegosaurus /,stegə'sawrəs/ n any of a genus of large armoured dinosaurs

stellar /'stelə/ adj of or composed of (the) stars

¹**stem** /stem/ *n* **1a** the main trunk of a plant **b** a branch or other plant part that supports a leaf, fruit, etc **2** the bow or prow of a vessel **3** a line of ancestry; *esp* a fundamental line from which others have arisen **4** that part of a word which has unchanged spelling when the word is inflected **5a** the tubular part of a tobacco pipe from the bowl outwards, through which smoke is drawn **b** the often slender and cylindrical upright support between the base and bowl of a wineglass

²**stem** *v* **-mm- 1** to make headway against (e g an adverse tide, current, or wind) **2** to check or go counter to (sthg adverse)

³**stem** *v* **-mm-** to originate – usu + *from*

⁴**stem** *v* **-mm-** to stop or check (as if) by damming

stench /stench/ *n* a stink

stencil /'stens(ə)l/ *n* **1** (a printing process using, or a design, pattern, etc produced by means of) an impervious material perforated with a design or lettering through which ink or paint is forced onto the surface below **2** a sheet of strong tissue paper impregnated or coated (e g with paraffin or wax) for use esp in typing a stencil

stenography /ste'nografi/ *n* the writing and transcription of shorthand – **-pher** *n*

stentorian /sten'tawri·ən/ *adj, esp of a voice* extremely loud

¹**step** /step/ *n* **1** a rest for the foot in ascending or descending: e g **1a** a single tread and riser on a stairway; a stair **b** a ladder rung **2a(1)** an advance or movement made by raising the foot and bringing it down at another point **a(2)** a combination of foot (and body) movements constituting a unit or a repeated pattern **b** the sound of a footstep **3a** a short distance **4** *pl* a course, way **5a** a degree, grade, or rank in a scale **b** a stage in a process **c** an action, proceeding, or measure often occurring as 1 in a series – often pl with sing. meaning **6** *pl* a stepladder — **in step 1** with each foot moving to the same time as the corresponding foot of others or in time to music **2** in harmony or agreement — **out of step** not in step

²**step** *v* **-pp- 1** to move by raising the foot and bringing it down at another point or by moving each foot in succession **2a** to go on foot; walk **b** to be on one's way; leave – often + *along* **3** to press down *on* sthg with the foot **4** to measure by steps – usu + *off* or *out* — **step into** to attain or adopt (sthg) with ease — **step on it/the gas** to increase one's speed; hurry up – infml

'**step,brother** /-,brudhə/ *n* a son of one's stepparent by a former marriage

'**step,child** /-,chield/ *n pl* **stepchildren** /-,childrən/ a child of one's wife or husband by a former marriage

step down *v* **1** to lower (the voltage at which an alternating current is operating) by means of a transformer **2** to retire, resign

'**step,ladder** /-,ladə/ *n* a portable set of steps with a hinged frame

'**step,parent** /-,peərənt/ *n* the husband or wife of one's parent by a subsequent marriage

steppe /step/ *n* a vast usu level and treeless plain, esp in SE Europe or Asia

'**stepping-,stone** *n* **1** a stone on which to step (e g in crossing a stream) **2** a means of progress or advancement

'**step,sister** /-,sistə/ *n* a daughter of one's stepparent by a former marriage

stereo /'sterioh, 'stiərioh/ *n pl* **stereos** a device (e g a record player) for reproducing sound in which the sound is split into and reproduced by 2 different channels to give a special effect – **stereo** *adj*

stereophonic /,steri·ə'fonik, ,stiəri-, -rioh-/ *adj* stereo

stereoscope /'steri·ə,skohp, 'stiəri·ə-/ *n* an optical instrument with 2 eyepieces through which the observer views 2 pictures taken from points of view a little way apart to get the effect of a single three-dimensional picture – **-pic** *adj*

¹**stereo,type** /'steri·ə,tiep, 'stiəri-/ *n* sby who or sthg that conforms to a fixed or general pattern; *esp* a standardized, usu oversimplified, mental picture or attitude held in common by members of a group

²**stereotype** *v* to repeat without variation; make hackneyed

sterile /'steriel/ *adj* **1** failing or not able to produce or bear fruit, crops, or offspring **2a** deficient in ideas or originality **b** free from living organisms, esp microorganisms **3** bringing no rewards or results; not productive – **-lization** *n* – **-lize** *v*

¹**sterling** /'stuhling/ *n* British money

²**sterling** *adj* **1** of or calculated in terms of British sterling **2a** *of silver* having a fixed standard of purity; *specif* 92.5 per cent pure **3** conforming to the highest standard

¹**stern** /stuhn/ *adj* **1a** hard or severe in nature or manner; austere **b** expressive of severe displeasure; harsh **2** forbidding or gloomy in appearance **3** inexorable, relentless – **~ly** *adv* – **~ness** *n*

²**stern** *n* **1** the rear end of a ship or boat **2** a back or rear part; the last or latter part

sternum /'stuhnəm/ *n pl* **sternums, sterna** /-nə/ a bone or cartilage at the front of the body that connects the ribs, both sides of the shoulder girdle, or both; the breastbone

steroid /'steroyd, 'stiə-/ *n* any of numerous compounds of similar to fats which effect the body's metabolism in various ways

stertorous /'stuhtərəs/ *adj* characterized by a harsh snoring or gasping sound – **~ly** *adv*

stet /stet/ *v* **-tt-** to direct retention of (a word or passage previously ordered to be deleted or omitted) by annotating, usu with the word *stet*

stethoscope /'steθə,skohp/ *n* an instrument used to detect and study sounds produced in the body

stetson /'stets(ə)n/ *n* a broad-brimmed high-crowned felt hat

stevedore /'steevədaw/ *n* a docker

¹**stew** /styooh/ *n* **1a** a savoury dish, usu of meat and vegetables stewed and served in the same liquid **b** a mixture composed of many usu unrelated parts **2** a state of excitement, worry, or confusion – *infml*

²**stew** *v* to cook (e g meat or fruit) slowly by boiling gently or simmering in liquid

¹**steward** /'styooh-əd/ *n* **1** one employed to look after a large household or estate **2a** one who manages the provisioning of food and attends to the needs of passengers (e g on an airliner, ship, or train) **b** one who supervises the provision and distribution of food and drink in a club, college, etc **3** an official who actively directs affairs (e g at a race meeting)

²**steward** *v* to act as a steward (for)

stewardess /'styooh-ədis, ,styooh-ə'des/ *n* a woman who performs the duties of a steward

stewed /styoohd/ *adj* drunk – *infml*

¹**stick** /stik/ *n* **1** a (dry and dead) cut or broken branch or twig **2a** a walking stick **b** an implement used for striking an object in a game (e g hockey) **3** sthg prepared (e g by cutting, moulding, or rolling) in a relatively long and slender often cylindrical form **4** a person of a specified type **5** a stick-shaped plant stalk (e g of rhubarb or celery) **6** several bombs, parachutists, etc released from an aircraft in quick succession **7** *pl the* wooded or rural and usu backward districts

²**stick** *v* **stuck** /stuk/ **1** to fasten in position (as if) by piercing **2** to push, thrust **3** to attach (as if) by causing to adhere to a surface **4** to become blocked, wedged, or jammed **5** to project, protrude – often + *out* or *up* **6a** to halt the movement or action of **b** to baffle, stump **7** to put or set in a specified place or position **8** to saddle with sthg disadvantageous or disagreeable **9** *chiefly Br* to bear, stand — **stick by** to continue to support — **stick one's neck out** to take a risk (e g by saying sthg unpopular) and make oneself vulnerable — *infml* — **stuck on** infatuated with – *infml*

³**stick** *n* adhesive quality or substance

stick around *v* to stay or wait about; linger – *infml*

sticker /'stikə/ *n* **1** sby who or sthg that sticks or causes sticking **2** a slip of paper with gummed back that, when moistened, sticks to a surface

sticking plaster *n* an adhesive plaster, esp for covering superficial wounds

'stick-in-the-,mud *n* one who dislikes and avoids change

stickleback /'stikl,bak/ *n* any of numerous small scaleless fishes that have 2 or more spines in front of the dorsal fin

stickler /'stiklə/ *n* one who insists on exactness or completeness in the observance of sthg

stick out *v* **1** to be prominent or conspicuous – often in *stick out a mile*, *stick out like a sore thumb* **2** to be persistent (e g in a demand or an opinion) – usu + *for* **3** to endure to the end – often + *it*

stick up *v* to rob at gunpoint – *infml* – **stick-up** *n* — **stick up for** to speak or act in defence of; support

sticky /'stiki/ *adj* **1a** adhesive **b** viscous, gluey **2** humid, muggy; *also* clammy **3a** disagreeable, unpleasant **b** awkward, stiff **c** difficult, problematic – **stickily** *adv* – **stickiness** *n*

,sticky 'wicket *n* a difficult situation – *infml*

stiff /stif/ *adj* **1a** not easily bent; rigid **b** lacking in suppleness and often painful **2a** firm, unyielding **b(1)** marked by reserve or decorum; formal **b(2)** lacking in ease or grace; stilted **3** hard fought **4** exerting great force; forceful **5** of a dense or glutinous consistency; thick **6a** harsh, severe **b** arduous **7** expensive, steep – **~en** *v* – **~ly** *adv* – **~ness** *n*

²**stiff** *adv* in a stiff manner; stiffly

³**stiff** *n* a corpse – slang

,stiff-'necked *adj* haughty, stubborn

stifle /'stiefl/ *v* **1a** to overcome or kill by depriving of oxygen; suffocate, smother **b** to muffle **2a** to cut off (e g the voice or breath) **b** to prevent the development or expression of; check, suppress

stigma /'stigmə/ *n*, *pl* **stigmata** /stig'mahtə, 'stigmətə/, **stigmas**, (2) **stigmata 1** a mark of shame or discredit **2** *pl* marks resembling the wounds of the crucified Christ, believed to be impressed on the bodies of holy or saintly people **3** the portion of the female part of a flower which receives the pollen grains and on which they germinate

stigmat·ize, -ise /'stigmətiez/ *v* to describe or identify in disparaging or abusive terms

stile /stiel/ *n* **1** a step or set of steps for passing over a fence or wall **2** a turnstile

stiletto /sti'letoh/ *n*, *pl* **stilettos, stilettoes 1** a slender rodlike dagger **2** a pointed instrument for piercing holes (e g for eyelets) in leather, cloth, etc **3** *Br* an extremely narrow tapering high heel on a woman's shoe

¹**still** /stil/ *adj* **1a** devoid of or abstaining from motion **b** having no effervescence; not carbonated **2** uttering no sound; quiet **3a** calm, tranquil **b** free from noise or turbulence – **~ness** *n*

²**still** *v* **1a** to allay, calm **b** to put an end to; settle **2** to arrest the motion or noise of; quiet

³**still** *adv* **1** as before; even at this or that time **2** in spite of that; nevertheless **3a** even (e g a *still* more difficult problem) **b** yet

⁴**still** *n* **1** a still photograph; *specif* a photograph of actors or of a scene from a film **2** quiet, silence – chiefly poetic

⁵**still** *n* an apparatus used in distillation, esp of spirits, consisting of either the chamber in which the vaporization is carried out or the entire equipment

'**still birth** /-,buhth/ *n* the birth of a dead infant

,**still born** /-'bawn/ *adj* **1** dead at birth **2** failing from the start; abortive

,**still 'life** *n pl* **still lifes** a picture showing an arrangement of inanimate objects (e g fruit or flowers)

stilt /stilt/ *n pl* **stilts,** (2) **stilts,** *esp collectively* **stilt 1a** either of 2 poles each with a rest or strap for the foot, that enable the user to walk along above the ground **b** any of a set of piles, posts, etc that support a building above ground or water level **2** any of various notably long-legged 3-toed wading birds related to the avocets

stilted /'stiltid/ *adj* stiffly formal and often pompous – ~ **ly** *adv*

Stilton /'stilt(ə)n/ *n* a cream-enriched white cheese that has a wrinkled rind and is often blue-veined

stimulant /'stimyoolənt/ *n* sthg (e g a drug) that produces a temporary increase in the functional activity or efficiency of (a part of) an organism

stimulate /'stimyoo,layt/ *v* to excite to (greater) activity – **lation** *n*

stimulus /'stimyooləs/ *n, pl* **stimuli** /-li, -lie/ **1** sthg that rouses or incites to activity; an incentive **2** sthg (e g light) that directly influences the activity of living organisms (e g by exciting a sensory organ or evoking muscular contraction or glandular secretion)

'**sting** /sting/ *v* **stung** /stung/ **1a** to give an irritating or poisonous wound to, esp with a sting **b** to affect with sharp quick pain **2** to cause to suffer acute mental pain; *also* to incite or goad thus **3** to overcharge, cheat – *infml*

²**sting** *n* **1a** a stinging; *specif* the thrust of a sting into the flesh **b** a wound or pain caused (as if) by stinging **2** *also* **stinger** a sharp organ of a bee, scorpion, etc that is usu connected with a poison gland or otherwise adapted to wound by piercing and injecting a poisonous secretion

stingy /'stinji/ *adj* **1** mean or ungenerous in giving or spending **2** meanly scanty or small – **gily** *adv* – **giness** *n*

stink /stingk/ *v* **stank** /stangk/, **stunk** /stungk/; **stunk 1** to emit a strong offensive smell **2** to be offensive; *also* to be in bad repute or of bad quality **3** to possess sthg to an offensive degree – usu + *with USE (except* 1) *infml*

²**stink** *n* **1** a strong offensive smell; a stench **2** a public outcry against sthg offensive – *infml*

'**stinking** /'stingking/ *adj* severe and unpleasant – *infml*

²**stinking** *adv* to an extreme degree – *infml*

'**stint** /stint/ *v* to restrict to a small share or allowance; be frugal with

²**stint** *n* **1** restraint, limitation **2** a definite quantity or period of work assigned

stipend /'stiepend/ *n* a fixed sum of money paid periodically (e g to a clergyman) as a salary or to meet expenses – ~ **iary** *adj*

'**stipple** /'stipl/ *v* **stippling** /'stipling, 'stipl·ing/ to speckle, fleck

²**stipple** *n* (the effect produced by) a method of painting using small points, dots, or strokes to represent degrees of light and shade

stipulate /'stipyoo,layt/ *v* **1** to specify as a condition or requirement of an agreement or offer **2** to give a guarantee of in making an agreement – **-ation** *n* — **stipulate for** to demand as an express term in an agreement

'**stir** /stuh/ *v* **-rr- 1a** to make or cause a slight movement or change of position **b** to disturb the quiet of; agitate **2a** to disturb the relative position of the particles or parts of (a fluid or semifluid), esp by a continued circular movement in order to make the composition homogeneous **b** to mix (as if) by stirring **3** to bestir, exert **4a** to rouse to activity; produce strong feelings in **b** to provoke – often + *up*

²**stir** *n* **1a** a state of disturbance, agitation, or brisk activity **b** widespread notice and discussion **2** a slight movement or a stirring movement

stirring /'stuhring/ *adj* rousing, inspiring – ~ **ly** *adv*

stirrup /'stirəp/ *n* either of a pair of D-shaped metal frames attached by a strap to a saddle to support the feet of a rider

'**stirrup ,cup** *n* a farewell usu alcoholic drink; *specif* one taken on horseback

'**stitch** /stich/ *n* **1** a local sharp and sudden pain, esp in the side **2a** a single in-and-out movement of a threaded needle in sewing, embroidering, or closing (surgical) wounds **b** a portion of thread left in the material after 1 stitch **3** a single loop of thread or yarn round a stitching implement (e g a knitting needle) **4** the least scrap of clothing – usu neg; *infml* — **in stitches** in a state of uncontrollable laughter

²**stitch** *v* **1** to fasten, join, or close (as if) with stitches; sew **2** to work on or decorate (as if) with stitches

stoat /stoht/ *n pl* **stoats,** *esp collectively* **stoat** a European weasel with a long black-tipped tail

'**stock** /stok/ *n* **1a** *pl* a wooden frame with holes for the feet (and hands) in which offenders are held for public punishment **b** the part to which the barrel and firing mechanism of a gun are attached **2a** the main stem of a plant or tree **b**(1) (part) consisting of roots and lower trunk onto which a graft is made **b**(2) a plant from which cuttings are taken **3a** the original (e g a man, race, or language) from which others derive; a source **b** the descendants of an individual; family, lineage **4a** *sing or pl in constr* livestock **b** a store or supply accumulated (e g of raw materials or finished goods) **5a** a debt or fund due (e g from a government) for money loaned at interest; *also, Br* capital or a debt or fund which continues to bear interest but is not usually redeemable as far as the original sum is concerned **b** (preference) shares – often **pl 6** any of a genus of plants with usu sweet-scented flowers **7** a wide band or scarf worn round the neck, esp by some clergymen **8** the liquid in which meat, fish, or vegetables have been simmered that is used as a basis for soup, gravy, etc **9a** an estimate or appraisal of sthg **b** the estimation in which sby or sthg is held — **in stock** in the shop and ready for delivery — **out of stock** having no more on hand; sold out

²**stock** *v* **1** to provide with (a) stock; supply **2** to procure or keep a stock of **3** to take in a stock – often *+ up*

³**stock** *adj* **1a** kept in stock regularly **b** regularly and widely available or supplied **2** used for (breeding and rearing) livestock **3** commonly used or brought forward; standard – chiefly derog

¹**stockade** /sto'kayd/ *n* **1** a line of stout posts set vertically to form a defence **2** an enclosure or pen made with posts and stakes

²**stockade** *v* to fortify or surround with a stockade

stockbreeder /'stok,breedə/ *n* one who breeds livestock

'**stock,broker** /-,brohkə/ *n* a broker who buys and sells securities

'**stock ,car** *n* a racing car having the chassis of a commercially produced assembly-line model

'**stock ex,change** *n* (a building occupied by) an association of people organized to provide an auction market among themselves for the purchase and sale of securities

stocking /'stoking/ *n* a usu knitted close-fitting often nylon covering for the foot and leg

,**stock-in-'trade** *n* **1** the equipment necessary to or used in a trade or business **2** sthg like the standard equipment of a tradesman or business

stockist /'stokist/ *n, Br* one (e g a retailer) who stocks goods, esp of a particular kind or brand

'**stock,jobber** /-,jobə/ *n* a stock-exchange member who deals only with brokers or other jobbers

'**stockman** /-mən/ *n* one who owns or takes care of livestock

'**stock,pile** /-,piel/ *n* an accumulated store; *esp* a reserve supply of sthg essential accumulated for use during a shortage – **stockpile** *v*

,**stock-'still** *adj* completely motionless

'**stock,taking** /-,tayking/ *n* **1** the checking or taking of an inventory of goods or supplies on hand (e g in a shop) **2** estimating a situation at a given moment (e g by considering past progress and resources)

stocky /'stoki/ *adj* short, sturdy, and relatively thick in build – **stockily** *adv* – **stockiness** *n*

'**stock,yard** /-,yahd/ *n* a yard in which cattle, pigs, horses, etc are kept temporarily for slaughter, market, or shipping

stodge /stoj/ *n* **1** filling (starchy) food **2** turgid and unimaginative writing – *infml*

stodgy /'stoji/ *adj* **1** *of food* heavy and filling **2** dull, boring – *infml* – **stodginess** *n*

¹**stoic** /'stoh-ik/ *n* **1** *cap* a member of an ancient Greek or Roman school of philosophy equating happiness with knowledge and holding that wisdom consists in self-mastery and submission to natural law **2** sby apparently or professedly indifferent to pleasure or pain

²**stoic, stoical** /-kl/ *adj* not affected by or showing passion or feeling; *esp* firmly restraining response to pain or distress

stoke /stohk/ *v* **1** to poke or stir up (e g a fire); *also* to supply with fuel **2** to feed abundantly

stoker /'stohkə/ *n* one employed to tend a furnace, esp on a ship

¹**stole** /stohl/ *past of* **steal**

²**stole** *n* **1** a long usu silk band worn traditionally over both shoulders and hanging down in front by priests **2** a long wide strip of material worn by women usu across the shoulders, esp with evening dress

stolen /'stohlən/ *past part of* **steal**

stolid /'stolid/ *adj* difficult to arouse emotionally or mentally; unemotional – **~ly** *adv* – **~ness**, **~ity** *n*

¹**stomach** /'stumək/ *n* **1a** (a cavity in an invertebrate animal analogous to) a saclike organ formed by a widening of the alimentary canal of a vertebrate, that is between the oesophagus at the top and the duodenum at the bottom and in which the first stages of digestion occur **b** that part of the body that contains the stomach; belly, abdomen **2a** desire for food; appetite **b** inclination, desire – usu neg

²**stomach** *v* **1** to find palatable or digestible **2** to bear without protest or resentment *USE* usu neg

'**stomach ,pump** *n* a suction pump with a flexible tube for removing liquids from the stomach or injecting liquids into it

¹**stomp** /stomp/ *v* to walk or dance with a heavy step – *infml*

²**stomp** *n* a jazz dance characterized by heavy stamping

¹**stone** /stohn/ *n pl* **stones**, (3) **stone** *also* **stones 1** a concretion of earthy or mineral matter: **1a(1)** a piece of this, esp one smaller than a boulder **a(2)** rock **b(1)** a building or paving block **b(2)** a gem **b(3)** a sharpening stone **2** the hard central portion of a fruit (e g a peach or date) **3** an imperial unit of weight equal to 14lb (about 6.35kg)

²stone *v* **1** to hurl stones at; *esp* to kill by pelting with stones **2** to face, pave, or fortify with stones **3** to remove the stones or seeds of (a fruit)

³stone *adj* (made) of

'Stone ,Age *n* the first known period of prehistoric human culture characterized by the use of stone tools and weapons

stoned *adj* intoxicated by alcohol or a drug (e g marijuana) – *infml*

'stone's ,throw *n* a short distance

stony *also* **stoney** /'stohni/ *adj* **1** containing many stones or having the nature of stone **2a** insensitive to pity or human feeling **b** showing no movement or reaction; dumb, expressionless – **stonily** *adv*

,stony-'broke *adj*, *Br* completely without funds; broke – *infml*

stood /stood/ *past of* **stand**

¹stooge /stoohj/ *n* **1** one who usu speaks the feed lines in a comedy duo **2** one who plays a subordinate or compliant role to another

²stooge *v* **1** to act as a stooge – usu + *for* **2** to move, esp fly, aimlessly to and fro or at leisure – usu + *around* or *about* *USE* infml

stool /stoohl/ *n* **1a** a seat usu without back or arms supported by 3 or 4 legs or a central pedestal **b** a low bench or portable support for the feet or for kneeling on **2** a discharge of faecal matter

'stool ,pigeon *n, chiefly NAm* sby acting as a decoy; *esp* a police informer

¹stoop /stoohp/ *v* **1a** to bend the body forwards and downwards, sometimes simultaneously bending the knees **b** to stand or walk with a temporary or habitual forward inclination of the head, body, or shoulders **2a** to condescend **b** to lower oneself morally **3** *of a bird* to fly or dive down swiftly, usu to attack prey

²stoop *n* **1a** an act of bending the body forwards **b** a temporary or habitual forward bend of the back and shoulders **2** the descent of a bird, esp on its prey

³stoop *n, chiefly NAm* a porch, platform, entrance stairway, or small veranda at a house door

¹stop /stop/ *v* **-pp- 1a** to close by filling or obstructing **b** to hinder or prevent the passage of **2a** to restrain, prevent **b** to withhold **3a** to cause to cease; check, suppress **b** to discontinue; come to an end **4** to instruct one's bank not to honour or pay **5a** to arrest the progress or motion of; cause to halt **b** to cease to move on; halt **c** to pause, hesitate **6a** to break one's journey – often + *off* **b** *chiefly Br* to remain **c** *chiefly NAm* to make a brief call; drop in – usu + *by* **7** to get in the way of, esp so as to be wounded or killed – *infml* – ~**pable** *adj*

²stop *n* **1** a cessation, end **2** a graduated set of organ pipes of similar design and tone quality **3a** sthg that impedes, obstructs, or brings to a halt; an impediment, obstacle **b** (any of a series of

markings, esp f-numbers, for setting the size of) the circular opening of an optical system (e g a camera lens) **4** a device for arresting or limiting motion **5** stopping or being stopped **6a** a halt in a journey **b** a stopping place **7** *chiefly Br* any of several punctuation marks; *specif* full stop

'stop,cock /-,kok/ *n* a cock for stopping or regulating flow (e g of fluid through a pipe)

stopgap /'stop,gap/ *n* sthg that serves as a temporary expedient; a makeshift

,stop-'go *adj* alternately active and inactive

'stop-,off *n* a stopover

'stop,over /-,ohvə/ *n* a stop at an intermediate point in a journey

stoppage /'stopij/ *n* **1** a deduction from pay **2** a concerted cessation of work by a group of employees that is usu more spontaneous and less serious than a strike

stopper /'stopə/ *n* sby or sthg that closes, shuts, or fills up; *specif* sthg (e g a bung or cork) used to plug an opening

,stop 'press *n* (space reserved for) late news added to a newspaper after printing has begun

'stop,watch /-,woch/ *n* a watch that can be started and stopped at will for exact timing

storage /'stawrij/ *n* **1** (a) space for storing **2a** storing or being stored (e g in a warehouse) **b** the price charged for keeping goods in storage

¹store /staw/ *v* **1** to collect as a reserve supply – often + *up* or *away* **2** to place or leave in a location (e g a warehouse, library, or computer memory) for preservation or later use or disposal **3** to provide storage room for; hold

²store *n* **1a** sthg stored or kept for future use **b** *pl* articles accumulated for some specific object and drawn on as needed **c** a source from which things may be drawn as needed; a reserve fund **2** storage – usu + *in* **3** a large quantity, supply, or number **4** a warehouse **5** a large shop – **in store** about to happen; imminent

'store,house /-,hows/ *n* **1** a warehouse **2** an abundant supply or source

'store,room /-,roohm, -,room/ *n* a place for the storing of goods or supplies

storey, *NAm chiefly* **story** /'stawri/ *n* (a set of rooms occupying) a horizontal division of a building

stork /stawk/ *n* any of various large mostly Old World wading birds that have long stout bills and are related to the ibises and herons

¹storm /stawm/ *n* **1** a violent disturbance of the weather marked by high winds, thunder and lightning, rain or snow, etc **2** a disturbed or agitated state; a sudden or violent commotion **3** a tumultuous outburst **4** a violent assault on a defended position — **by storm** (as if) by using a bold frontal movement to capture quickly

²**storm** v **1a** *of wind* to blow with violence **b** to rain, hail, snow, or sleet **2** to be in or to exhibit a violent passion; rage **3** to rush about or move impetuously, violently, or angrily **4** to attack or take (e g a fortified place) by storm

'**storm ,trooper** n **1** a member of a Nazi party militia **2** a member of a force of shock troops

stormy /'stawmi/ adj marked by turmoil or fury – **stormily** adv – **storminess** n

stormy petrel n **1** a small black and white sea bird of the N Atlantic **2** sby fond of strife

story /'stawri/ n **1a** an account of incidents or events **b** a statement of the facts of a situation in question e an anecdote; *esp* an amusing one **2a** a short fictional narrative **b** the plot of a literary work **3** a widely circulated rumour **4** a lie **5** a news article or broadcast

'**story,book** /-,book/ adj fairy-tale

'**story,teller** /-,telə/ n **1** a teller of tales or anecdotes; a narrator **2** a liar

¹**stout** /stowt/ adj **1** firm, resolute **2** physically or materially strong: **2a** sturdy, vigorous **b** staunch, enduring **3** corpulent, fat – ~**ly** adv – ~**ness** n

²**stout** n a dark sweet heavy-bodied beer

stout,hearted /-'hahtid/ adj courageous

stove /stohv/ n **1** an enclosed appliance that burns fuel or uses electricity to provide heat chiefly for domestic purposes **2** a cooker

²**stove** *past of* **stave**

stow /stoh/ v **1a** to pack away in an orderly fashion in an enclosed space **b** to fill (e g a ship's hold) with cargo **2** to stop, desist – slang; esp in *stow it*

stowage /'stowij/ n **1** goods in storage or to be stowed **2** storage capacity **3** the state of being stored

¹**stowaway** /'stoh·ə,way/ n sby who stows away

²**stowaway** adj designed to be dismantled or folded for storage

stow away v to hide oneself aboard a vehicle, esp a ship, as a means of travelling without payment or escaping from a place undetected

straddle /'stradl/ v **straddling** /'stradling, 'stradl·ing/ **1** to stand or esp sit with the legs wide apart **2** to bracket (a target) with missiles (e g shells or bombs)

strafe /strahf, strayf/ v to rake (e g ground troops) with fire at close range, esp with machine-gun fire from low-flying aircraft

straggle /'stragl/ v **straggling** /'stragling, 'stragl·ing/ **1** to lag behind or stray away from the main body of sthg, esp from a line of march **2** to move or spread untidily away from the main body of sthg – **gler** n

straggly /'stragli/ adj loosely spread out or scattered irregularly

¹**straight** /strayt/ adj **1a** free from curves, bends, angles, or irregularities **b** generated by a point moving continuously in the same direction **2** direct, uninterrupted: e g **2a** holding to a direct or proper course or method **b** candid, frank e coming directly from a trustworthy source **3a** honest, fair **b** properly ordered or arranged (e g with regard to finance) **c** correct **4** unmixed **5a** not deviating from the general norm or prescribed pattern **b** accepted as usual, normal, or proper **6a** conventional in opinions, habits, appearance etc **b** heterosexual *USE* (6) infml – ~**ness** n

²**straight** adv **1** in a straight manner **2** without delay or hesitation; immediately

³**straight** n **1** sthg straight: e g **1a** a straight line or arrangement **b** a straight part of sthg; *esp* a home straight **2** a poker hand containing 5 cards in sequence but not of the same suit **3a** a conventional person **b** a heterosexual *USE* (3) infml

,**straight'way** /-ə'way/ adv without hesitation or delay; immediately

straighten /'strayt(ə)n/ v to make or become straight – usu + *up* or *out*

,**straight'forward** /-'faw·wəd/ adj **1** free from evasiveness or ambiguity; direct, candid **2** presenting no hidden difficulties **3** clear-cut, precise – ~**ly** adv – ~**ness** n

,**straight 'up** adv, Br truly, honestly – infml; used esp in asking or replying to a question

¹**strain** /strayn/ n **1a** a lineage, ancestry **b** a kind, sort **2** a passage of verbal or musical expression – usu pl with sing. meaning

²**strain** v **1** to stretch to maximum extension and tautness **2a** to exert (e g oneself) to the utmost **b** to injure by overuse, misuse, or excessive pressure **3** to cause to pass through a strainer; filter **4** to stretch beyond a proper limit

³**strain** n straining or being strained: e g **a** (a force, influence, or factor causing) physical or mental tension **b** excessive or difficult exertion or labour **c** a wrench, twist, or similar bodily injury resulting esp from excessive stretching of muscles or ligaments

strained adj **1** done or produced with excessive effort **2** subjected to considerable tension

strainer /'straynə/ n a device (e g a sieve) to retain solid pieces while a liquid passes through

strait /strayt/ n **1** a narrow passageway connecting 2 large bodies of water – often pl with sing. meaning but sing. or pl in constr **2** a situation of perplexity or distress – usu pl with sing. meaning

'**strait,jacket, straightjacket** /-,jakit/ n a cover or outer garment of strong material used to bind the body and esp the arms closely, in restraining a violent prisoner or patient

,**strait'laced**, NAm also **straightlaced** /-'layst/ adj excessively strict in manners or morals

¹**strand** /strand/ n a shore, beach

²**strand** v to leave in a strange or unfavourable place, esp without funds or means to depart

³**strand** n **1** any of the threads, strings, or wires twisted or laid parallel to make a cord, rope, etc **2** an elongated or twisted and plaited body resembling a rope **3** any of the elements interwoven in a complex whole

strange /straynj/ adj **1** not native to or naturally belonging in a place; of external origin, kind, or character **2a** not known, heard, or seen before **b** exciting wonder or surprise **3** lacking experience or acquaintance; unaccustomed to – ~**ly** adv – ~**ness** n

stranger /straynjə/ n **1a** a foreigner, alien **b** sby who is unknown or with whom one is unacquainted **2** one ignorant of or unacquainted with sby or sthg

strangle /strangl/ v **strangling** /ˈstrang-gling, ˈstrang-gl-ing/ **1** to choke (to death) by compressing the throat; throttle **2** to suppress or hinder the rise, expression, or growth of

'**strangle,hold** /-,hohld/ n a force or influence that prevents free movement or expression

¹**strap** /strap/ n **1** a strip of metal or a flexible material, esp leather, for holding objects together or in position **2** (the use of, or punishment with) a strip of leather for flogging

²**strap** v **-pp- 1a** to secure with or attach by means of a strap **b** to support (e g a sprained joint) with adhesive plaster **2** to beat with a strap

strapping /ˈstraping/ adj big, strong, and sturdy in build

stratagem /ˈstratəjəm/ n **1** an artifice or trick for deceiving and outwitting the enemy **2** a cleverly contrived trick or scheme

strategy /ˈstratiji/ n **1** the science and art of military command exercised to meet the enemy in combat under advantageous conditions **2a** a clever plan or method **b** the art of employing plans towards achieving a goal – **gic** adj – **gically** adv – **gist** n

stratify /ˈstratifie/ v to form, deposit, or arrange in layers – **fication** n

stratosphere /ˈstratə,sfiə/ n the upper part of the atmosphere above about 11 km (7mi) in which the temperature changes little and clouds are rare

stratum /ˈstrahtəm, ˈstraytəm/ n, pl **strata** /-tə/ **1** a horizontal layer or series of layers of any homogeneous material: e g **1a** a sheetlike mass of rock or earth deposited between beds of other rock **b** a layer of the sea or atmosphere **c** a layer in which archaeological remains are found on excavation **2** a socioeconomic level of society

¹**straw** /straw/ n **1** dry stalky plant residue, specif stalks of grain after threshing, used for bedding, thatching, fodder, making hats, etc **2a** a dry coarse stem, esp of a cereal grass **3** sthg of small value or importance **4** a tube of paper, plastic, etc for sucking up a drink — **straw in the wind** a hint or apparently insignificant fact that is an indication of a coming event

²**straw** adj of or resembling (the colour of) straw

strawberry /ˈstrawb(ə)ri/ n (the juicy edible usu red fruit of) any of several white-flowered creeping plants

strawberry mark n a usu red and elevated birthmark composed of small blood vessels

straw poll n an assessment made by an unofficial vote

¹**stray** /stray/ v **1** to wander from a proper place, course, or line of conduct or argument **2** to roam about without fixed direction or purpose

²**stray** n a domestic animal wandering at large or lost

³**stray** adj **1** having strayed; wandering, lost **2** occurring at random or sporadically

¹**streak** /streek/ n **1** a line or band of a different colour from the background **2** an inherent quality; esp one which is only occasionally manifested

²**streak** v **1** to make streaks on or in **2** to move swiftly **3** to run through a public place while naked

streaky /ˈstreeki/ adj **1** marked with streaks **2** of meat, esp bacon having lines of fat and lean **3** of a shot in cricket hit off the edge of the bat – **kily** adv – **kiness** n

¹**stream** /streem/ n **1** a body of running water, esp one smaller than a river **2a** a steady succession of words, events, etc **b** a continuous moving procession **3** an unbroken flow (e g of gas or particles of matter) **4** a prevailing attitude or direction of opinion – esp in *go against/with the stream* **5** Br a group of pupils of the same general academic ability

²**stream** v **1** to flow (as if) in a stream **2** to run with a fluid **3** to trail out at full length **4** to pour in large numbers in the same direction **5** Br to practise the division of pupils into streams –

streamer /ˈstreemə/ n **1a** a pennant **b** a strip of coloured paper used as a party decoration **2** a long extension of the sun's corona visible only during a total eclipse

¹**stream,line** /-,lien/ n a contour given to a car, aeroplane, etc so as to minimize resistance to motion through a fluid (e g air)

²**streamline** v to make simpler, more efficient, or better integrated

street /street/ n **1** a thoroughfare, esp in a town or village, with buildings on either side **2** the part of a street reserved for vehicles — **on the street** idle, homeless, or out of a job — **on the streets** earning a living as a prostitute — **up/down one's street** suited to one's abilities or tastes

'**street,wise** adj familiar with the (disreputable or criminal) life of city streets; *broadly* able to survive and prosper in modern urban conditions

strength /streng(k)th/ n **1** the quality of being strong; capacity for exertion or endurance **2** solidity, toughness **3a** legal, logical, or moral force **b** a strong quality or inherent asset **4a**

degree of potency of effect or of concentration **b** intensity of light, colour, sound, or smell **5** force as measured in members **6** a basis – chiefly in *on the strength of* – **from strength to strength** with continuing success and progress

strengthen /'streng(k)than/ *v* to make or become stronger

strenuous /'strenyoo-əs/ *adj* **1** vigorously active **2** requiring effort or stamina – ~**ly** *adv* – ~**ness** *n*

¹**stress** /stres/ *n* **1a** the force per unit area producing or tending to produce deformation of a body; *also* the state of a body under such stress **b** (a physical or emotional factor that causes) bodily or mental tension **c** strain, pressure **2** emphasis, weight **3** intensity of utterance given to a speech sound, syllable, or word so as to produce relative loudness

²**stress** *v* **1** to subject to physical or mental stress **2** to lay stress on; emphasize

¹**stretch** /strech/ *v* **1** to extend in a reclining position – often + *out* **2** to extend to full length **3** to extend (oneself or one's limbs), esp so as to relieve muscular stiffness **4** to pull taut **5** to strain **6** to cause to reach (e g from one point to another or across a space) **7** to fell (as if) with a blow – often + *out*; infml – ~**able** *adj* — **stretch a point** to go beyond what is strictly warranted in making a claim or concession — **stretch one's legs** to take a walk in order to relieve stiffness caused by prolonged sitting

²**stretch** *n* **1** the extent to which sthg may be stretched **2** stretching or being stretched **3** a continuous expanse of time or space **4** elasticity **5** a term of imprisonment – infml

stretcher /'strechə/ *n* **1** a brick or stone laid with its length parallel to the face of the wall **2** a device, consisting of a sheet of canvas or other material stretched between 2 poles, for carrying a sick, injured, or dead person **3** a rod or bar extending between 2 legs of a chair or table

strew /strooh/ *v* **strewed, strewn** /stroohn/ **1** to spread by scattering **2** to become dispersed over

stricken /'strikən/ *adj* afflicted or overwhelmed (as if) by disease, misfortune, or sorrow

strict /strikt/ *adj* **1a** stringent in requirement or control **b** severe in discipline **2a** inflexibly maintained or kept to; complete **b** rigorously conforming to rules or standards **3** exact, precise – ~**ly** *adv* – ~**ness** *n*

stricture /'strikchə/ *n* **1** an abnormal narrowing of a bodily passage **2** sthg that closely restrains or limits; a restriction **3** an unfavourable criticism; a censure *USE* (2&3) usu pl with sing. meaning

¹**stride** /stried/ *v* **strode** /strohd/; **stridden** /'stridən/ to walk (as if) with long steps

²**stride** *n* **1** a long step **2** an advance – often pl with sing. meaning **3** (the distance covered in) an act of movement completed when the feet regain the initial relative positions **4** a striding gait — **in one's stride** without becoming upset

strident /'stried(ə)nt/ *adj* characterized by harsh and discordant sound; *also* loud and obtrusive – ~**ly** *adv* – **-dency** *n*

stridulate /'stridyoolayt/ *v*, *esp of crickets, grasshoppers, etc* to make a shrill creaking noise by rubbing together special bodily structures – **-lation** *n*

strife /strief/ *n* bitter conflict or dissension

¹**strike** /striek/ *v* **struck** /struk/; **struck** *also* **stricken** /'strikən/ **1a** to aim a blow at; hit **b** to make an attack **2a** to haul down **b** to take down the tents of a camp **3a** to collide forcefully **b** to afflict suddenly **4** to delete, cancel **5** to penetrate painfully **6** *of the time* to be indicated by the sounding of a clock, bell, etc **7a** *of light* to fall on **b** *of a sound* to become audible to **8** to cause suddenly to become **9** to cause (a match) to ignite **10a** to make a mental impact on **b** to occur suddenly to **11** to make and ratify (a bargain) **12** *of a fish* to snatch at (bait) **13** to arrive at (a balance) by computation **14** to assume (a pose) **15** to place (a plant cutting) in a medium for rooting **16** to engage in a strike *against*

²**strike** *n* **1** a work stoppage by a body of workers, made as a protest or to force an employer to comply with demands **2** a success in finding or hitting sthg; *esp* a discovery of a valuable mineral deposit **3** the opportunity to receive the bowling by virtue of being the batsman at the wicket towards which the bowling is being directed **4** an (air) attack on a target

'**strike,breaker** /-,braykə/ *n* one hired to replace a striking worker – **-king** *n*

strike out *v* **1** to delete **2** to set out vigorously

striker /'striekə/ *n* **1** a games player who strikes; *esp* a soccer player whose main duty is to score goals **2** a worker on strike

strike up *v* **1** to begin to sing or play **2** to cause to begin

striking /'strieking/ *adj* attracting attention, esp because of unusual or impressive qualities – ~**ly** *adv*

¹**string** /string/ *n* **1** a narrow cord used to bind, fasten, or tie **2a** the gut or wire cord of a musical instrument **b** a stringed instrument of an orchestra – usu pl **3a** a group of objects threaded on a string **b** (a set of things arranged in) a sequence **c** a group of usu scattered business concerns **d** the animals, esp horses, belonging to or used by sby **4** pl conditions or obligations attached to sthg

²**string** *v* **strung** /strung/ **1** to equip with strings **2a** to thread (as if) on a string **b** to tie, hang, or fasten with string **3** to remove the strings of

³string *adj* made with wide meshes and usu of string

string along *v* **1** to accompany sby, esp reluctantly **2** to agree; go along – usu + *with* **3** to deceive, fool *USE* infml

stringent /'strinj(ə)nt/ *adj* **1** rigorous or strict, esp with regard to rules or standards **2** marked by money scarcity and credit strictness – **~ly** *adv* – **-gency** *n*

string up *v* to hang; *specif* to kill by hanging

stringy /'string-i/ *adj* **1a** containing or resembling fibrous matter or string **b** sinewy, wiry **2** capable of being drawn out to form a string – **stringiness** *n*

¹strip /strip/ *v* **-pp- 1a(1)** to remove clothing, covering, or surface or extraneous matter from; *esp* to undress **a(2)** to perform a striptease **b** to deprive of possessions, privileges, or rank **2** to remove furniture, equipment, or accessories from **3** to damage the thread or teeth of (a screw, cog, etc)

²strip *n* **1a** a long narrow piece of material **b** a long narrow area of land or water **2** *Br* clothes worn by a rugby or soccer team

stripe /striep/ *n* **1** a line or narrow band differing in colour or texture from the adjoining parts **2** a bar, chevron, etc of braid or embroidery worn usu on the sleeve of a uniform to indicate rank or length of service

stripling /'stripling/ *n* an adolescent boy

stripper /'stripə/ *n* **1** sby who performs a striptease **2** a tool or solvent for removing sthg, esp paint

striptease /-'teez/ *n* an act or entertainment in which a performer, esp a woman, undresses gradually in view of the audience

stripy /'striepi/ *adj* striped

strive /striev/ *v* **strove** /strohv/ *also* **strived; striven** /striv(ə)n/, **strived 1** to struggle in opposition; contend **2** to endeavour; try hard – **~r** *n*

strode /strohd/ *past of* **stride**

¹stroke /strohk/ *v* to pass the hand over gently in 1 direction

²stroke *n* **1** the act of striking; *esp* a blow with a weapon or implement **2** a single unbroken movement; *esp* one that is repeated **3** a striking of the ball in a game (e g cricket or tennis); *specif* an (attempted) striking of the ball that constitutes the scoring unit in golf **4** an unexpected occurrence **5** (an attack of) sudden usu complete loss of consciousness, sensation, and voluntary motion caused by rupture, thrombosis, etc of a brain artery **6a** the technique or mode used for) a propelling beat or movement against a resisting medium **b** an oarsman who sits at the stern of a racing rowing boat and sets the pace for the rest of the crew **7** (the distance of) the movement in either direction of a reciprocating mechanical part (e g a piston rod) **8** the sound of a striking

clock **9** a mark or dash made by a single movement of an implement — **at a stroke** by a single action — **off one's stroke** in a situation where one performs below a usual standard

stroll /strohl/ *v* to walk in a leisurely or idle manner – **stroll** *n* – **~er** *n*

strong /strong/ *adj* **1** having or marked by great physical power **2** having moral or intellectual power **3** of a specified number **4a** striking or superior of its kind **b** effective or efficient, esp in a specified area **5** forceful, cogent **6a** rich in a colour active agent (e g a flavour or extract) **b** *of a colour* intense **7** moving with vigour or force **8** ardent, zealous **9** well established; firm **10** having a pungent or offensive smell or flavour **11** of or being a verb that forms inflections by internal vowel change (e g *drink, drank, drunk*) – **~ly** *adv*

'strong ,arm /-,ahm/ *adj* using or involving undue force

'strong,box /-,boks/ *n* a strongly made chest for money or valuables

'strong,hold /-,hohld/ *n* **1** a fortified place **2a** a place of refuge or safety **b** a place dominated by a specified group

,strong-'minded *adj* marked by firmness and independence of judgment – **~ly** *adv* – **~ness** *n*

'strong ,point *n* sthg in which one excels

'strong ,room *n* a (fireproof and burglarproof) room for money and valuables

strontium /'strontyəm/ *n* a soft metallic element chemically similar to calcium

,strontium '90 *n* a hazardous radioactive isotope of strontium present in the fallout from nuclear explosions

strop /strop/ *n* sthg, esp a leather band, for sharpening a razor – **strop** *v*

stroppy /'stropi/ *adj*, *Br* quarrelsome, obstreperous – infml

strove /strohv/ *past of* **strive**

¹structure /'strukchə/ *n* **1a** sthg (e g a building) that is constructed **b** sthg organized in a definite pattern **2a** the arrangement of particles or parts in a substance or body **b** arrangement or interrelation of elements – **-ral** *adj* – **-rally** *adv*

²structure *v* to form into a structure

strudel /'stroohdl/ *n* a pastry made from a thin sheet of dough rolled up with filling and baked

¹struggle /'strugl/ *v* **struggling** /'strugling, 'strugl-ing/ **1** to make violent or strenuous efforts against opposition **2** to proceed with difficulty or great effort

²struggle *n* **1** a violent effort; a determined attempt in adverse circumstances **2** a hard-fought contest

strum /strum/ *v* **-mm- 1** to brush the fingers lightly over the strings of (a musical instrument) in playing **2** to play (music) on a guitar

strumpet /'strumpit/ *n* a prostitute

strung /strung/ *past of* **string**

¹**strut** /strut/ *v* -tt- 1 to walk with a proud or erect gait 2 to walk with a pompous air; swagger

²**strut** *n* 1 a structural piece designed to resist pressure in the direction of its length 2 a pompous step or walk

strychnine /'strikneen/ *n* a plant product used as a poison (e g for rodents) and medicinally as a stimulant to the central nervous system

¹**stub** /stub/ *n* 1 a short blunt part of a pencil, cigarette, etc left after a larger part has been broken off or used up 2a a small part of a leaf or page (e g of a chequebook) left on the spine as a record of the contents of the part torn away **b** the part of a ticket returned to the user after inspection

²**stub** *v* -bb- 1 to extinguish (e g a cigarette) by crushing – usu + *out* 2 to strike (one's foot or toe) against an object

stubble /'stubl/ *n* 1 the stalky remnants of plants, esp cereal grasses, which remain rooted in the soil after harvest 2 a rough growth (e g of beard) resembling stubble – **-bly** *adv*

stubborn /'stubən/ *adj* 1 (unreasonably) unyielding or determined 2 refractory, intractable – ~**ly** *adv* – ~**ness** *n*

stubby /'stubi/ *adj* short and thick like a stub

stucco /'stukoh/ *n pl* **stuccos, stuccoes** a cement or fine plaster used in the covering and decoration of walls – **stucco** *v*

stuck /stuk/ *past of* **stick**

stuck-'up *adj* superciliously self-important or conceited – infml

¹**stud** /stud/ *n* 1 *sing or pl in constr* a group of animals, esp horses, kept primarily for breeding 2a a male animal, esp a stallion, kept for breeding **b** a sexually active man – vulg — **at stud** for breeding as a stud

²**stud** *n* 1 any of the smaller upright posts in the walls of a building to which panelling or laths are fastened 2a a rivet or nail with a large head used for ornament or protection **b** a solid button with a shank or eye on the back inserted through an eyelet in a garment as a fastener or ornament 3a a piece (e g a rod or pin) projecting from a machine and serving chiefly as a support or axis **b** a projecting piece of metal inserted in a horseshoe or snow tyre to increase grip

³**stud** *v* -dd- to set thickly with a number of prominent objects

student /'styood(ə)nt/ *n* 1 a scholar, learner; *esp* one who attends a college or university 2 an attentive and systematic observer

studied /'studid/ *adj* 1 carefully considered or prepared 2 deliberate, premeditated

studio /'styoohdi-oh/ *n pl* **studios** 1a the workroom of a painter, sculptor, or photographer **b** a place for the study of an art (e g dancing, singing, or acting) 2 a place where films are made; *also, sing or pl in constr* a film production company including its premises and employees 3 a room equipped for the production of radio or television programmes

studious /'styoohdi-əs/ *adj* 1 of, concerned with, or given to study 2a earnest **b** studied, deliberate – ~**ly** *adv* – ~**ness** *n*

¹**study** /'studi/ *n* 1a the application of the mind to acquiring (specific) knowledge **b** a careful examination or analysis of a subject 2 a room devoted to study 3 a branch of learning 4 a literary or artistic work intended as a preliminary or experimental interpretation

²**study** *v* 1 to engage in the study of 2 to consider attentively or in detail

¹**stuff** /stuf/ *n* 1a materials, supplies, or equipment used in various activities **b** personal property; possessions 2 a finished textile suitable for clothing; *esp* wool or worsted material 3 an unspecified material substance 4 the essence of a usu abstract thing 5 subject matter

²**stuff** *v* 1a to fill (as if) by packing things in; cram **b** to gorge (oneself) with food **c** to fill (e g meat or vegetables) with a stuffing **d** to fill with stuffing or padding **e** to fill out the skin of (an animal) for mounting 2 to choke or block *up* (the nasal passages) 3 to force into a limited space; thrust

,**stuffed 'shirt** *n* a smug, pompous, and usu reactionary person

stuffing /'stufing/ *n* material used to stuff sthg; *esp* a seasoned mixture used to stuff meat, eggs, etc

stuffy /'stufi/ *adj* 1a badly ventilated; close **b** stuffed up 2 stodgy, dull 3 prim, straitlaced – **stuffily** *adv* – **stuffiness** *n*

stultify /'stultifie/ *v* to make futile or absurd – **-fication** *n*

stumble /'stumbl/ *v* **stumbling** /'stumbling/ 1 to trip in walking or running 2a to walk unsteadily or clumsily **b** to speak or act in a hesitant or faltering manner 3 to come unexpectedly or by chance – + *upon, on,* or *across* – **stumble** *n*

'**stumbling ,block** /'stumbling/ *n* an obstacle to progress or understanding

¹**stump** /stump/ *n* 1 the part of an arm, leg, etc remaining attached to the trunk after the rest is removed 2 the part of a plant, esp a tree, remaining in the ground attached to the root after the stem is cut 3 any of the 3 upright wooden rods that together with the bails form the wicket in cricket

²**stump** *v* 1 to walk heavily or noisily 2 *of a wicket-keeper* to dismiss (a batsman who is outside his popping crease but not attempting to run) by breaking the wicket with the ball before it has touched another fieldsman 3 to baffle, bewilder – infml

stumpy /'stumpi/ *adj* short and thick; stubby

stun /stun/ *v* -nn- 1 to make dazed or dizzy (as if) by a blow 2 to overcome, esp with astonishment or disbelief

stung /stung/ *past of* **sting**

stunk /stunk/ *past of* **stink**

stunner /'stunə/ *n* an unusually beautiful or attractive person or thing – *infml*

stunning /'stuning/ *adj* strikingly beautiful or attractive – *infml* – ~**ly** *adv*

¹**stunt** /stunt/ *v* to hinder or arrest the growth or development of

²**stunt** *n* an unusual or difficult feat performed to gain publicity

'**stunt ,man**, *fem* '**stunt ,woman** *n* sby employed, esp as a substitute for an actor, to perform dangerous feats

stupefy /'st(y)oohpifie/ *v* 1 to make groggy or insensible 2 to astonish – **-faction** *n*

stupendous /styooh'pendəs/ *adj* of astonishing size or greatness; amazing, astounding – ~**ly** *adv*

stupid /'styoohpid/ *adj* 1 slow-witted, obtuse 2 dulled in feeling or perception; torpid 3 annoying, exasperating – *infml* – ~**ity** *n* – ~**ly** *adv*

stupor /'styoohpə/ *n* a state of extreme apathy, torpor, or reduced sense or feeling (e g resulting from shock or intoxication)

sturdy /'stuhdi/ *adj* 1 strongly built or constituted; stout, hardy 2a having physical strength or vigour; robust **b** firm, resolute – **sturdily** *adv* – **sturdiness** *n*

sturgeon /'stuhj(ə)n/ *n* any of various usu large edible fishes whose roe is made into caviar

stutter /'stutə/ *v* to speak with involuntary disruption or blocking of speech (e g by spasmodic repetition or prolongation of vocal sounds) – **stutter** *n*

¹**sty** /stie/ *n*, *pl* **sties** *also* **styes** a pigsty

²**sty, stye** /~/ *n*, *pl* **sties, styes** an inflamed swelling of a sebaceous gland at the margin of an eyelid

stygian /'stiji·ən/ *adj*, *often cap* extremely dark or gloomy – *fml*

¹**style** /stiel/ *n* 1 a prolongation of a plant ovary bearing a stigma at the top 2a a manner of expressing thought in language, esp when characteristic of an individual, period, etc **b** the custom or plan followed in spelling, capitalization, punctuation, and typographic arrangement and display 3 mode of address; a title 4a a distinctive or characteristic manner of doing sthg **b** excellence or distinction in social behaviour, manners, or appearance – ~**less** *adj*

²**style** *v* 1 to designate by an identifying term; name 2 to fashion according to a particular mode

stylish /'stielish/ *adj* fashionably elegant – ~**ly** *adv* – ~**ness** *n*

stylistic /stie'listik/ *adj* of esp literary or artistic style

styl·ize, -ise /'stieliez/ *v* to make (e g a work of art) conform to a conventional style rather than to nature

stylus /'stieləs/ *n*, *pl* **styli** /-lie/, **styluses** an instrument for writing, marking, incising, or following a groove: e g **a** an instrument used by ancients for writing on clay or waxed tablets **b** a tiny piece of material (e g diamond) with a rounded tip used in a gramophone to follow the groove on a record

stymie /'stiemi/ *v* to present an obstacle to; thwart

styptic /'stiptik/ *adj* tending to contract, bind, or check bleeding; astringent – **styptic** *n*

suave /swahv/ *adj* smoothly though often superficially affable and polite – **suavity** *n* – ~**ly** *adv*

¹**sub** /sub/ *n* a substitute – *infml*

²**sub** *v* **-bb-** 1 to act as a substitute 2 to subedit

³**sub** *n* a submarine – *infml*

⁴**sub** *n*, *Br* 1 a small loan or advance 2 a subscription *USE infml*

⁵**sub** *n* a subeditor – *infml*

'**subcom,mittee** /-kə,miti/ *n* a subdivision of a committee usu organized for a specific purpose

,**sub'conscious** /-'konshəs/ *adj* existing in the mind but not immediately available to consciousness – ~**ly** *adv* – **subconscious**, ~**ness** *n*

,**sub'continent** /-'kontinənt/ *n* a vast subdivision of a continent; *specif*, *often cap the* Indian subcontinent

¹**subcon'tract** /-kən'trakt/ *v* 1 to engage a third party to perform under a subcontract all or part of (work included in an original contract) 2 to undertake (work) under a subcontract

²**sub'contract** /-'kontrakt/ *n* a contract between a party to an original contract and a third party; *esp* one to provide all or a specified part of the work or materials required in the original contract

,**subcu'taneous** /-kyooh'taynyəs, -ni·əs/ *adj* being, living, used, or made under the skin – ~**ly** *adv*

subdue /səb'dyooh/ *v* 1 to conquer and bring into subjection 2 to bring under control; curb 3 to reduce the intensity or degree of (e g colour)

sub'dued *adj* 1 brought under control (as if) by military conquest 2 reduced or lacking in force, intensity, or strength

,**sub'editor** /-'editə/ *n* 1 an assistant editor 2 *chiefly Br* one who edits sthg (e g newspaper copy) in preparation for printing

,**sub'human** /-'hyoohmən/ *adj* less than human: e g **a** below the level expected of or suited to normal human beings **b** of animals lower than humans; *esp* anthropoid

¹**subject** /'subjikt/ *n* 1a sby subject to a ruler and governed by his/her law **b** sby who enjoys the protection of and owes allegiance to a sovereign power or state 2a that of which a quality, attribute, or relation may be stated **b** the entity (e g the mind or ego) that sustains or assumes the form of thought or consciousness 3a a department of knowledge or learning **b** an individual whose reactions are studied **c**(1) sthg concerning which

sthg is said or done **c(2)** sby or sthg represented in a work of art **d(1)** the term of a logical proposition denoting that of which sthg is stated, denied, or predicated **d(2)** the word or phrase in a sentence or clause denoting that of which sthg is predicated or asserted **e** the principal melodic phrase on which a musical composition or movement is based

²**subject** *adj* **1** owing obedience or allegiance to another **2a** liable or exposed to **b** having a tendency or inclination; prone to **3** dependent or conditional on sthg *USE* usu + *to*

³**subject** /sǝb'jekt/ *v* **1** to bring under control or rule **2** to make liable; expose **3** to cause to undergo sthg *USE* usu + *to* – ~**ion** *n*

subjective /sǝb'jektiv/ *adj* **1** of or being a grammatical subject **2a** relating to, determined by, or arising from the mind or self **b** characteristic of or belonging to reality as perceived rather than as independent of mind; phenomenal **3a** peculiar to a particular individual; personal **b** lacking in reality or substance; illusory – ~**ly** *adv* – -**tivity** *n*

¹**subject to** *prep* depending on; conditionally upon

,**sub 'judice** /'joohdisi/ *adv* before a court; not yet judicially decided

subjugate /'subjoogayt/ *v* to conquer and hold in subjection – -**gation** *n*

subjunctive /sǝb'jungktiv/ *adj* of or being a grammatical mood that represents the denoted act or state not as fact but as contingent or possible or viewed emotionally (e g with doubt or desire)

,**sub 'let** /-'let/ *v* -tt-; **sublet** to lease or rent (all or part of a property) to a subtenant

,**sublieu 'tenant** /-lef'tenant; *NAm* -looh'tenant/ *n* an officer of the lowest rank in the British navy

sublimate /'sublimayt/ *v* **1** to sublime **2** to divert the expression of (an instinctual desire or impulse) from a primitive form to a socially or culturally acceptable one – -**ation** *n*

¹**sublime** /sǝ'bliem/ *v* to pass directly from the solid to the vapour state

²**sublime** *adj* **1** lofty, noble, or exalted in thought, expression, or manner **2** tending to inspire awe, usu because of elevated quality

subliminal /,sub'liminl/ *adj* existing, functioning, or having effects below the level of conscious awareness – ~**ly** *adv*

¹,**subma 'rine** /-mǝ'reen/ *adj* being, acting, or growing under water, esp in the sea

²**submarine** /'submǝ,reen, ,--'-/ *n* a vessel designed for undersea operations; *esp* a submarine warship that is typically armed with torpedoes or missiles and uses diesel, electric, diesel, or nuclear propulsion

submerge /sǝb'muhj/ *v* **1** to go or put under water **2** to cover (as if) with water; inundate – ~**nce** *n*

¹**submersible** /sǝb'muhsǝbl/ *adj* capable of going under water

²**submersible** *n* a vessel used for undersea exploration and construction work

submission /sǝb'mish(ǝ)n/ *n* **1** an act of submitting sthg for consideration, inspection, etc **2** the state of being submissive, humble, or compliant **3** an act of submitting to the authority or control of another

submissive /sǝb'misiv/ *adj* willing to submit to others – ~**ly** *adv* – ~**ness** *n*

submit /sǝb'mit/ *v* -tt- **1a** to yield to the authority or will of another **b** to subject to a process or practice **2a** to send or commit to another for consideration, inspection, etc **b** to put forward as an opinion; suggest

,**sub 'normal** /-'nawmǝl/ *adj* **1** lower or smaller than normal **2** having less of sthg, esp intelligence, than is normal

¹**subordinate** /sǝ'bawd(ǝ)nǝt/ *adj* **1** occupying a lower class or rank; inferior **2** subject to or controlled by authority **3** *of a clause* functioning as a noun, adjective, or adverb in a complex sentence (e g the clause 'when he heard' in 'he laughed when he heard') – ~**ly** *adv*

²**subordinate** /sǝ'bawd(ǝ)nayt/ *v* **1** to place in a lower order or class **2** to make subject or subservient; subdue – -**ation** *n* – -**ative** *adj*

suborn /sǝ'bawn/ *v* to induce to commit perjury or another illegal act

'**sub ,plot** /-,plot/ *n* a subordinate plot in fiction or drama

¹**subpoena** /sǝ(b)'peenǝ/ *n* a writ commanding sby to appear in court

²**subpoena** *v* **subpoenaing; subpoenaed** to serve with a subpoena

subscribe /sǝb'skrieb/ *v* **1a** to give consent or approval to sthg written by signing **b** to give money (e g to charity) **c** to pay regularly in order to receive a periodical or service **2** to feel favourably disposed *USE* usu + *to*

subscriber /sǝb'skriebǝ/ *n* sby who subscribes; *specif* the owner of a telephone who pays rental and call charges

subscription /sǝb'skripsh(ǝ)n/ *n* **1** a sum subscribed **2a** a purchase by prepayment for a certain number of issues (e g of a periodical) **b** *Br* membership fees paid regularly

subsequent /'subsikwǝnt/ *adj* following in time or order; succeeding – ~**ly** *adv*

subservient /sǝb'suhvi·ǝnt/ *adj* obsequiously submissive – ~**ly** *adv* – -**ience** *n*

subside /sǝb'sied/ *v* **1** to sink or fall to the bottom; settle **2a** to descend; *esp* to sink so as to form a depression **b** *of ground* to cave in; collapse **3** to become quiet; abate – ~**nce** *n*

¹**subsidiary** /sǝb'sidyǝri, -'sij(ǝ)ri/ *adj* **1** serving to assist or supplement; auxiliary **2** of secondary importance

²**subsidiary** *n* sby or sthg subsidiary; *esp* a company wholly controlled by another

subsidy /'subsidi/ *n* a grant or gift of money (e g by a government to a person or organization, to assist an enterprise deemed advantageous to the public) – **-dize** *v*

subsist /səb'sist/ *v* to have the bare necessities of life; be kept alive – ~**ence** *n*

subsoil /'sub,soyl/ *n* the layer of weathered material that underlies the surface soil

,**sub'sonic** /-'sonik/ *adj* of or relating to (objects moving at) less than the speed of sound

substance /'substəns/ *n* **1a** a fundamental or essential part **b** correspondence with reality **2** ultimate underlying reality **3a** (a) physical material from which sthg is made **b** matter of particular or definite chemical constitution **4** material possessions; property — **in substance** in respect to essentials

,**sub'standard** /-'standəd/ *adj* deviating from or falling short of a standard or norm (e g of quality or correctness)

substantial /səb'stansh(ə)l/ *adj* **1a** having material existence; real **b** important, essential **2** ample to satisfy and nourish **3a** well-to-do, prosperous **b** considerable in quantity **4** firmly constructed; solid

substantiate /səb'stanshi-ayt/ *v* to establish (e g a statement or claim) by proof or evidence; verify – **-ation** *n* – **-ative** *adj*

¹**substitute** /'substityooht/ *n* sby or sthg that takes the place of another

²**substitute** *v* **1** to exchange for another **2** to take the place of; *also* to introduce a substitute for – **-tution** *n*

subtenant /'sub,tenənt/ *n* sby who rents from a tenant

subterfuge /'subtə,fyoohj/ *n* **1** deception or trickery used as a means of concealment or evasion **2** a trick or ruse

,**subter'ranean** /-tə'raynyən, -ni-ən/, **subterraneous** /-nyəs, -ni-əs/ *adj* **1** being or operating under the surface of the earth **2** hidden or out of sight

subtitle /,sub'tietl/ *n* **1** a secondary or explanatory title **2** a printed explanation that appears on the screen during a film

subtle /'sutl/ *adj* **1** delicate, elusive **2** cleverly contrived; ingenious **3** artful, cunning – **-tly** *adv*

subtlety /'sutl-ti/ *n* **1** the quality of being subtle **2** sthg subtle; *esp* a fine distinction

subtract /səb'trakt/ *v* to take away (a quantity or amount) from another – **-ion** *n*

suburb /'subuhb/ *n* an outlying part of a city or large town

suburbia /sə'buhbyə/ *n* (the inhabitants of) the suburbs of a city

subvert /səb'vuht/ *v* to overthrow or undermine the power of – **-version** *n* – **-versive** *adj*

subway /'sub,way/ *n* **a** an underground way: e g **a** a passage under a street (e g for pedestrians, power cables, or water or gas mains) **b** *chiefly NAm* an underground railway

succeed /sək'seed/ *v* **1a** to inherit sthg, esp sovereignty, rank, or title **b** to follow after another in order **2** to have a favourable or desired result

success /sək'ses/ *n* **1** a favourable outcome to an undertaking **2** the attainment of wealth or fame **3** sby or sthg that succeeds – ~**ful** *adj* – ~**fully** *adv*

succession /sək'sesh(ə)n/ *n* **1** the order or right of succeeding to a property, title, or throne **2a** the act of following in order; a sequence **b** the act or process of becoming entitled to a deceased person's property or title

successive /sək'sesiv/ *adj* following one after the other in succession – ~**ly** *adv*

successor /sək'sesə/ *n* sby or sthg that follows another; *esp* a person who succeeds to throne, title, or office

succinct /sək'singkt/ *adj* clearly expressed in few words; concise – ~**ly** *adv* – ~**ness** *n*

¹**succour**, *NAm chiefly* **succor** /'sukə/ *n* relief; *also* aid, help

²**succour**, *NAm chiefly* **succor** *v* to go to the aid of (sby in need or distress)

succubus /'sukyoobəs/ *n*, *pl* **succubi** /-,bie/ a female demon believed to have sexual intercourse with men in their sleep

succulent /'sukyoolənt/ *adj* **1** full of juice; juicy **2** *of a plant* having juicy fleshy tissues – **-lence** *n*

succumb /sə'kum/ *v* to yield or give in *to*

¹**such** /such; *also* (*occasional weak form*) səch/ *adj* *or adv* **1a** of the kind, quality, or extent – used before *as* to introduce an example or comparison **b** of the same sort **2** of so extreme a degree or extraordinary a nature – used before *as* to suggest that a name is unmerited (e g we forced down the soup, *such* as it was)

²**such** *pron*, *pl* **such 1** *pl* such people; those **2** that thing, fact, or action (e g *such* was the result) **3** *pl* similar people or things (e g tin and glass and *such*) — **as such** intrinsically considered; in him-/herself, itself, or themselves

¹**'such,like** /-,liek/ *adj* of like kind; similar

²**suchlike** *pron pl* **suchlike** a similar person or thing

¹**suck** /suk/ *v* **1** to draw sthg into esp the mouth by suction; *esp* to draw milk from a breast or udder with the mouth **2** to act in an obsequious manner – *infml*; usu + *up*

²**suck** *n* **1** the act of sucking **2** a sucking movement

sucker /'sukə/ *n* **1a** a mouth (e g of a leech) or other animal organ adapted for sucking or sticking **b** a device, esp of rubber, that can cling to a surface by suction **2** a shoot from the roots or lower part of the stem of a plant **3a** a gullible person – *infml* **b** a person irresistibly attracted by sthg specified – *infml*

suckle /'sukl/ *v* **suckling** /'sukling, 'sukl·ing/ to give milk to from the breast or udder; *also* to receive milk from the udder or breast of

suckling /'sukling/ *n* a young unweaned animal

sucrose /'s(y)oohkrohs, -krohz/ *n* the sugar obtained from sugarcane and sugar beet and occurring in most plants

suction /'suksh(ə)n/ *n* **1** the act of sucking **2** the action of exerting a force on a solid, liquid, or gaseous body by means of reduced air pressure over part of its surface

sudden /'sud(ə)n/ *adj* **1a** happening or coming unexpectedly **b** abrupt, steep **2** marked by or showing haste – ~**ly** *adv* – ~**ness** *n*

suds /sudz/ *n pl but sing or pl in constr* (the lather on) soapy water – **sudsy** *adj*

sue /s(y)ooh/ *v* **1** to bring a legal action against **2** to make a request or application – usu + *for* or *to*

suede, suède /swayd/ *n* leather with a napped surface

suet /'s(y)ooh·it/ *n* the hard fat round the kidneys in beef and mutton esp as used in cooking – ~**y** *adj*

suffer /'sufə/ *v* **1** to submit to or be forced to endure pain, distress, etc **2** to allow, permit **3** to sustain loss or damage **4** to be handicapped or at a disadvantage

sufferance /'suf(ə)rəns/ *n* tacit permission

suffering /'suf(ə)ring/ *n* the state of one who suffers

suffice /sə'fies/ *v* to be enough (for)

sufficiency /sə'fish(ə)nsi/ *n* **1** sufficient means to meet one's needs **2** the quality of being sufficient; adequacy

sufficient /sə'fish(ə)nt/ *adj* enough to meet the needs of a situation – ~**ly** *adv*

suffix /'sufiks/ *n* an affix (e g -*ness* in *happiness*) appearing at the end of a word or phrase or following a root

suffocate /'sufə,kayt/ *v* **1** to stop the breathing of (e g by asphyxiation) **2** to make uncomfortable by want of cool fresh air – ~**cation** *n*

suffrage /'sufrij/ *n* the right of voting

suffragette /,sufrə'jet/ *n* a woman who advocates suffrage for her sex

suffuse /sə'fyoohz/ *v* to spread over or through, esp with a liquid or colour; permeate – ~**fusion** *n*

¹**sugar** /'shoogə/ *n* any of a class of water-soluble carbohydrates that are of varying sweetness and include glucose, ribose, and sucrose; *specif* a sweet crystallizable material that consists of sucrose, is colourless or white when pure tending to brown when less refined, is obtained commercially esp from sugarcane or sugar beet, and is used as a sweetener and preservative of other foods – ~**less** *adj*

²**sugar** *v* to make palatable or attractive

'**sugar ,beet** *n* a white-rooted beet grown for the sugar in its root

'**sugar ,cane** *n* a stout tall grass widely grown in warm regions as a source of sugar

'**sugar ,daddy** *n* a usu elderly man who lavishes gifts and money on a young woman in return for sex or companionship

sugary /'shoog(ə)ri/ *adj* **1** containing, resembling, or tasting of sugar **2** exaggeratedly or cloyingly sweet

suggest /sə'jest/ *v* **1** to put forward as a possibility or for consideration **2a** to call to mind by thought or association; evoke **b** to indicate the presence of

suggestible /sə'jestəbl/ *adj* easily influenced by suggestion

suggestion /sə'jesch(ə)n/ *n* **1** sthg suggested; a proposal **2a** indirect means (e g the natural association of ideas) to evoke ideas or feeling **b** the impressing of an idea, attitude, desired action, etc on the mind of another **3** a slight indication; a trace

suggestive /sə'jestiv/ *adj* **1a** indicative **b** evocative **2** suggesting sthg improper or indecent – ~**ly** *adv*

suicidal /,s(y)ooh·i'siedl/ *adj* **1** dangerous, esp to life **2** harmful to one's own interests – ~**ly** *adv*

suicide /'s(y)ooh·i,sied/ *n* **1a** (an) act of taking one's own life intentionally **b** ruin of one's own interests **2** one who commits or attempts suicide

¹**suit** /s(y)ooht/ *n* **1** a legal action **2** a petition or appeal; *specif* courtship **3** a group of things forming a unit or constituting a collection – used chiefly with reference to sails **4a** an outer costume of 2 or more matching pieces that are designed to be worn together **b** a costume to be worn for a specified purpose **5** all the playing cards in a pack bearing the same symbol (i e hearts, clubs, diamonds, or spades)

²**suit** *v* **1** to be appropriate or satisfactory **2a** to be good for the health or well-being of **b** to be becoming to; look right with **3** to satisfy, please — **suit someone down to the ground** to suit sby extremely well

suitable /'s(y)oohtəbl/ *adj* appropriate, fitting – ~**bility** *n* – ~**ness** *n* – ~**bly** *adv*

suitcase /-,kays/ *n* a rectangular usu rigid case with a hinged lid and a handle, used for carrying articles (e g clothes)

suite /sweet/ *n* **1** *sing or pl in constr* a retinue; *esp* the personal staff accompanying an official or dignitary on business **2a** a group of rooms occupied as a unit **b** a musical work consisting of several loosely connected instrumental pieces **c** a set of matching furniture (e g a settee and 2 armchairs) for a room

suitor /'s(y)oohtə/ *n* one who courts a woman with a view to marriage

¹**sulk** /sulk/ *v* to be moodily silent

²**sulk** *n* a fit of sulking – usu pl with sing meaning

sullen /'sulən/ *adj* **1** silently gloomy or resentful; ill-humoured and unsociable **2** dismal, gloomy – **~ly** *adv* – **~ness** *n*

sully /'suli/ *v* to mar the purity of; tarnish

sulphate /'sulfayt/ *n* a salt or ester of sulphuric acid

sulphide /'sulfied/ *n* a compound of sulphur, usu with a more electropositive element

sulphur /'sulfə/ *n* **1** a nonmetallic element chemically resembling oxygen that occurs esp as yellow crystals **2** a pale greenish yellow colour

sul,phuric 'acid *n* a corrosive oily strong acid that is a vigorous oxidizing and dehydrating agent

sultan /'sult(ə)n/ *n* a sovereign of a Muslim state

sultana /səl'tahnə/ *n* **1** a sultan's wife **2** (the raisin of) a pale yellow seedless grape

sultry /'sultri/ *adj* **1** oppressively hot and humid **2** (capable of) exciting strong sexual desire; sensual – **trily** *adv* – **triness** *n*

sum /sum/ *n* **1** a (specified) amount of money **2** the whole amount; the total **3a** the result of adding numbers **b** numbers to be added; *broadly* a problem in arithmetic – **sum** *v* – **in sum** briefly

¹**summary** /'suməri/ *adj* **1** concise but comprehensive **2a** done quickly without delay or formality **b** of or using a summary proceeding; *specif* tried or triable in a magistrates' court – **-rily** *adv*

²**summary** *n* a brief account covering the main points of sthg – **-arize** *v*

summation /su'maysh(ə)n/ *n* **1** the act or process of forming a sum **2** a total **3** (a) summing up of an argument

¹**summer** /'sumə/ *n* **1** the season between spring and autumn comprising in the northern hemisphere the months of June, July, and August **2** a period of maturity **3** a year – *chiefly poetic*

²**summer** *adj* sown in the spring and harvested in the same year as sown

'**summer ,house** /-,hows/ *n* a small building in a garden designed to provide a shady place in summer

'**summer ,school** *n* a course of teaching held during the summer vacation, esp on university premises

summery /'sum(ə)ri/ *adj* of, suggesting, or suitable for summer

,**summing-'up** /'suming/ *n* **1** a concluding summary **2** a survey of evidence given by a judge to the jury before it considers its verdict

summit /'sumit/ *n* **1** a top; *esp* the highest point or peak **2** the topmost level attainable; the pinnacle **3** a conference of highest-level officials

summon /'sumən/ *v* **1** to command by a summons to appear in court **2** to call upon to come; send for

summons /'sumənz/ *n, pl* **summonses** a written notification warning sby to appear in court

sump /sump/ *n* **1a** a cesspool **b** *chiefly Br* the lower section of the crankcase used as a lubricating-oil reservoir in an internal-combustion engine **2** the lowest part of a mine shaft, into which water drains

sumptuous /'sum(p)choo·əs, -tyoo-/ *adj* lavishly rich, costly, or luxurious – **~ly** *adv* – **~ness** *n*

sum up *v* **1** to summarize **2** to form or express a rapid appraisal of

¹**sun** /sun/ *n* **1a** the star nearest to the earth, round which the earth and other planets revolve **b** a star or other celestial body that emits its own light **2** the heat or light radiated from the sun — **under the sun** in the world; on earth

²**sun** *v* **-nn-** to expose oneself to the rays of the sun

'**sun,baked** /-,baykt/ *adj* baked hard by exposure to sunshine

'**sun,bathe** /-,baydh/ *v* to expose the body to the rays of the sun or a sunlamp – **~r** *n*

'**sun,beam** /-,beem/ *n* a ray of light from the sun

'**sun,blind** /-,bliend/ *n* an awning or a shade on a window (e g a venetian blind) that gives protection from the sun's rays

'**sun,burn** /-,buhn/ *v* **sunburnt** /-,buhnt/, **sunburned** to burn or tan by exposure to sunlight – **sunburn** *n*

sundae /'sunday/ *n* an ice cream served with a topping of fruit, nuts, syrup, etc

¹**Sunday** /'sunday, -di/ *n* **1** the day of the week falling between Saturday and Monday, observed by Christians as a day of worship **2** a newspaper published on Sundays

²**Sunday** *adj* **1** of or associated with Sunday **2** amateur – *derog*

,**Sunday 'best** *n sing or pl in constr* one's best clothes – *infml*

'**Sunday ,school** *n* a class usu of religious instruction held, esp for children, on Sundays

sunder /'sundə/ *v* to break apart or in two; sever

'**sun,dial** /-,die·əl/ *n* an instrument to show the time of day by the shadow of a pointer on a graduated plate

'**sun,down** /-,down/ *n* sunset

'**sun,drenched** /-,drencht/ *adj* exposed to much hot sunshine

¹**sundry** /'sundri/ *adj* miscellaneous, various

²**sundry** *pron pl in constr* an indeterminate number – *chiefly in* all and sundry

³**sundry** *n* **1** *pl* miscellaneous small articles or items **2** *Austr* a run in cricket that is not credited to a batsman; an extra

'**sun,flower** /-,flowə/ *n* any of a genus of composite plants with large yellow-rayed flower heads bearing edible seeds

sung /sung/ *past of* **sing**

'**sun,glasses** /-,glahsiz/ *n pl* glasses to protect the eyes from the sun

sunk /sungk/ *past of* **sink**

sunken /'sungkən/ *adj* **1** submerged; *esp* lying at the bottom of a body of water **2a** hollow, recessed **b** lying or constructed below the surrounding or normal level

'**sun,light** /-,liet/ *n* sunshine

sunny /'suni/ *adj* **1** bright with sunshine **2** cheerful, optimistic **3** exposed to or warmed by the sun – – **nily** *adv* – – **niness** *n*

'**sun,rise** /-,riez/ *n* (the time of) the rising of the topmost part of the sun above the horizon as a result of the rotation of the earth

'**sun,roof** /-,roohf/ *n* a motor-car roof having an opening or removable panel

sunset /'sunsit, -,set/ *n* (the time of) the descent of the topmost part of the sun below the horizon as a result of the rotation of the earth

'**sun,shade** /-,shayd/ *n* **1** a parasol **2** an awning

'**sun,shine** /-,shien/ *n* the sun's light or direct rays

'**sun,spot** /-,spot/ *n* a transient dark marking on the visible surface of the sun caused by a relatively cooler area

'**sun,stroke** /-,strohk/ *n* heatstroke caused by direct exposure to the sun

'**sun,tan** /-,tan/ *n* a browning of the skin from exposure to the sun – – **ned** *adj*

'**sun,trap** /-,trap/ *n* a sheltered place that receives a large amount of sunshine

¹**sup** /sup/ *v*, **-pp-** *chiefly dial* to drink (liquid) in small mouthfuls – **sup** *n*

²**sup** *v* **1** to eat the evening meal **2** to make one's supper – + **on** or **off**

¹**super** /'s(y)oohpə/ *n* **1** a superfine grade or extra large size **2** a police or other superintendent – infml

²**super** *adj* – used as a general term of approval; infml

superb /s(y)ooh'puhb/ *adj* **1** marked by grandeur or magnificence **2** of excellent quality – ~**ly** *adv*

'**super,charger** *n* a device supplying fuel or air to an internal-combustion engine at a pressure higher than normal for greater efficiency

,**super'cilious** /-'sili-əs/ *adj* coolly disdainful – ~**ly** *adv* – ~**ness** *n*

,**super,conduc'tivity** /-,konduk'tivəti/ *n* a complete disappearance of electrical resistance in various metals and alloys at temperatures near absolute zero

,**super'ficial** /-'fish(ə)l/ *adj* **1** not penetrating below the surface **2a** not thorough or profound; shallow **b** apparent rather than real – ~**ity** *n* – ~**ly** *adv*

superfluous /s(y)ooh'puhfloo-əs/ *adj* exceeding what is sufficient or necessary – ~**ly** *adv* – ~**ness, -fluity** *n*

,**super'human** /-'hyoohmən/ *adj* **1** being above the human; divine **2** exceeding normal human power, size, or capability

,**superim'pose** /-im'pohz/ *v* to place or lay over or above sthg

,**superin'tend** /-in'tend/ *v* to be in charge of; direct

,**superin'tendent** /-in'tend(ə)nt/ *n* **1** one who supervises or manages sthg **2** a British police officer ranking next above a chief inspector

¹**superior** /s(y)ooh'piəri-ə/ *adj* **1** situated higher up; upper **2** of higher rank or status **3a** greater in quality, amount, or worth **b** excellent of its kind **4** *of an animal or plant part* situated above or at the top of another (corresponding) part **5** thinking oneself better than others; supercilious – ~**ity** *n*

²**superior** *n* **1** a person who is above another in rank or office **2** sby or sthg that surpasses another in quality or merit

¹**superlative** /s(y)ooh'puhlətiv/ *adj* **1** of or constituting the degree of grammatical comparison expressing an extreme or unsurpassed level or extent **2** surpassing all others; of the highest degree

²**superlative** *n* an exaggerated expression, esp of praise

'**superman** /-man/ *n* a person of extraordinary power or achievements – infml

'**super,market** /-,mahkit/ *n* a usu large self-service retail shop selling foods and household merchandise

,**super'natural** /-'nach(ə)rəl/ *adj* **1** of an order of existence or an agency (e g a god or spirit) not bound by normal laws of cause and effect **2a** departing from what is usual or normal, esp in nature **b** attributed to an invisible agent (e g a ghost or spirit) – ~**ly** *adv*

,**super'nova** /-'nohvə/ *n* any of the rarely observed nova outbursts in which the luminosity reaches 100 million times that of the sun

super'scription /-'skripsh(ə)n/ *n* words written on the surface of, outside, or above sthg else; an inscription

,**super'sede** /-'seed/ *v* **1** to take the place of (esp sthg inferior or outmoded) **2** to displace in favour of another; supplant – **session** *n*

,**super'sonic** /-'sonik/ *adj* **1** (using, produced by, or relating to waves or vibrations) having a frequency above the upper threshold of human hearing of about 20,000 Hz **2** of, being, or using speeds from 1 to 5 times the speed of sound in air

,**super'stition** /-'stish(ə)n/ *n* **1** a belief or practice resulting from ignorance, fear of the unknown, trust in magic or chance, or a false conception of causation **2** an irrational abject attitude of mind towards the supernatural, nature, or God resulting from superstition – **-tious** *adj* – **-tiously** *adv*

'**super,structure** /-,strukchə/ *n* **1a** the part of a building above the ground **b** the structural part of a ship above the main deck **2** an entity or complex based on a more fundamental one

'**super,tax** /-,taks/ *n* a tax paid in addition to normal tax by people with high incomes

,super'vene /-'veen/ v to happen in a way that interrupts some plan or process – fml

supervise /'s(y)oohpə,viez/ v to superintend, oversee – **-vision** n – **-visor** n – **-visory** adj

supine /'s(y)ooh,pien, ,-'-/ adj 1 lying on the back or with the face upwards 2 mentally or morally lazy; lethargic

supper /'supə/ n (the food for) a usu light evening meal or snack – ~less n

supplant /sə'plahnt/ v to take the place of (another), esp by force or treachery – ~er n

supple /'supl/ adj 1 capable of easily being bent or folded; pliant 2 able to perform bending or twisting movements with ease and grace; lithe

supplement /'supliment/ n 1 sthg that completes, adds, or makes good a deficiency, or makes an addition 2 a part issued to update or extend a book or periodical – **supplement** v

supplementary /,supli'ment(ə)ri/ adj additional

supplementary benefit n British social-security benefit paid to those who do not qualify for unemployment benefit

supplicant /'suplikant/ adj humbly imploring or entreating – **supplicant** n

¹supply /sə'plie/ v 1 to provide for; satisfy 2 to provide, furnish – **supply** n

²supply n 1a the quantity or amount needed or available b provisions, stores – usu pl with sing. meaning 2 the quantities of goods and services offered for sale at a particular time or at one price 3 **supply, supply teacher** Br a teacher who fills a temporary vacancy

¹support /sə'pawt/ v 1 to bear, tolerate 2a(1) to promote the interests of; encourage a(2) to argue or vote for b to assist, help 3 to provide livelihood or subsistence for 4 to hold up or serve as a foundation or prop for – ~ive adj

²support n 1 supporting or being supported 2 maintenance, sustenance 3 a device that supports sthg 4 sing or pl in constr a body of supporters

supporter /sə'pawtə/ n 1 an adherent or advocate 2 either of 2 figures (e g of men or animals) placed one on each side of a heraldic shield as if holding or guarding it

suppose /sə'pohz/ v 1a to lay down tentatively as a hypothesis, assumption, or proposal b(1) to hold as an opinion; believe b(2) to conjecture, think 2 to devise for a purpose; intend 3 to presuppose 4 to allow, permit – used negatively 5 to expect because of moral, legal, or other obligations USE (2, 4, & 5) chiefly in be supposed to

sup'posed adj believed or imagined to be such – ~ly adv

supposition /,supo'zish(ə)n/ n a hypothesis

suppository /sə'pozot(ə)ri/ n a readily meltable cone or cylinder of medicated material for insertion into a bodily passage or cavity (e g the rectum)

suppress /sə'pres/ v 1 to put down by authority or force 2 to stop the publication or revelation of 3 to hold back, check 4 to inhibit the growth or development of – ~ion n

suppressor /sə'presə/ n an electrical component (e g a capacitor) added to a circuit to suppress oscillations that would otherwise cause radio interference

suppurate /'supyoo,rayt/ v to form or discharge pus – **-ration** n

su'premacy /s(y)ooh'premasi/ n the state of being supreme; supreme authority, power, or position

supreme /s(y)ooh'preem/ adj 1 highest in rank or authority 2 highest in degree or quality – ~ly adv

Supreme Court n the highest judicial tribunal in a nation or state

¹surcharge /'suh,chahj/ v to subject to an additional or excessive charge

²surcharge n 1 an additional tax or cost 2 an extra fare

surd /suhd/ n an irrational root (e g √2); also an algebraic expression containing irrational roots

¹sure /shooə, shaw/ adj 1 firm, secure 2 reliable, trustworthy 3 assured, confident 4 bound, certain – ~ness n — **for sure** as a certainty — **to be sure** it must be acknowledged; admittedly

²sure adv, chiefly NAm surely, certainly – infml

,sure'fire /-'fie-ə/ adj certain to succeed – infml

,sure'footed /-'footid/ adj not liable to stumble or fall – ~ly adv – ~ness n

'surely /-li/ adv 1 without doubt; certainly 2 it is to be believed, hoped, or expected that

surety /'shooərti/ n 1 a guarantee 2 sby who assumes legal liability for the debt, default, or failure in duty (e g appearance in court) of another

¹surf /suhf/ n the foam and swell of waves breaking on the shore

²surf v to ride as a sport on breaking waves, esp while standing or lying on a surfboard

¹surface /'suhfis/ n 1 the external or upper boundary or layer of an object or body 2 (a portion of) the boundary of a three-dimensional object 3 the external or superficial aspect of sthg — **on the surface** to all outward appearances; superficially

²surface v 1 to come to the surface; emerge 2 to wake up; also get up – infml

³surface adj 1 situated or employed on the surface, esp of the earth or sea 2 lacking depth; superficial

surfboard /'suhf,bawd/ n a usu long narrow buoyant board used in surfing

¹surfeit /'suhfit/ n 1 an excessive amount 2 excessive indulgence in food, drink, etc

²surfeit v to fill to excess; satiate

¹surge /suhj/ v to rise and move (as if) in waves or billows

²surge n the motion of swelling, rolling, or sweeping forwards like a wave

surgeon /'suhj(ə)n/ n a medical specialist who practises surgery

surgery /'suhjəri/ n 1 medicine that deals with diseases and conditions requiring or amenable to operative or manual procedures 2 a surgical operation 3 Br (the hours of opening of) a doctor's, dentist's, etc room where patients are advised or treated 4 Br a session at which an elected representative (e g an MP) is available for usu informal consultation

surgical /'suhjikl/ adj of surgeons or surgery – **~ly** adv

surly /'suhli/ adj irritably sullen and churlish

¹surmise /suh'miez/ v to infer on scanty evidence; guess

²surmise /suh'miez, 'suhmiez/ n a conjecture or guess – fml

surmount /suh'mownt/ v 1 to overcome, conquer 2 to get over or above – **~able** adj

surname /'suhnaym/ n the name shared in common by members of a family

surpass /suh'pahs/ v 1 to go beyond in quality, degree, or performance; exceed 2 to transcend the reach, capacity, or powers of – **~ing** adj – **~ingly** adv

surplice /'suhplis/ n a loose white outer ecclesiastical vestment usu of knee length with large open sleeves – **~d** adj

surplus /'suhpləs/ n 1 the amount in excess of what is used or needed 2 an excess of receipts over disbursements

¹surprise /sə'priez/ n 1 an act of taking unawares 2 sthg unexpected or surprising 3 the feeling caused by an unexpected event; astonishment

²surprise v 1 to take unawares 2 to fill with wonder or amazement

surprising /sə'priezing/ adj causing surprise; unexpected – **~ly** adv

surrealism /sə'riə,liz(ə)m/ n, often cap a 20th-c movement in art and literature seeking to use the incongruous images formed by the unconscious to transcend reality as perceived by the conscious mind; also surrealistic practices or atmosphere – **-ist** adj, n – **-istic** adj

¹surrender /sə'rendə/ 1a to give oneself up into the power of another; yield b to relinquish; give up 2 to abandon (oneself) to sthg unrestrainedly

²surrender n 1 the act or an instance of surrendering oneself or sthg 2 the voluntary cancellation of an insurance policy by the party insured in return for a payment

surreptitious /,surəp'tishəs/ adj done, made, or acquired by stealth – **~ly** adv – **~ness** n

surrogate /'surəgət/ n 1 a deputy 2 sthg that serves as a substitute

¹surround /sə'rownd/ v 1a to enclose on all sides b to be part of the environment of; be present round 2 to form a ring round; encircle – **~ing** adj

²surround n a border or edging

surroundings /sə'rowndingz/ n pl the circumstances, conditions, or objects by which one is surrounded

surtax /'suhtaks/ n an additional tax; esp a supertax formerly imposed in the UK

surveillance /suh'vaylons, sə-/ n close watch kept over sby or sthg

¹survey /suh'vay, '--/ v 1a to look over and examine closely b to examine the condition of and often give a value for (a building) 2 to determine and portray the form, extent, and position of (e g a tract of land) 3 to view as a whole or from a height

²survey /'suhvay/ n a surveying or being surveyed; also sthg surveyed

surveyor /sə'vay-ə/ n sby whose occupation is surveying land

survival /sə'vievl/ n 1a the condition of living or continuing b the continuation of life or existence 2 sby or sthg that survives, esp after others of its kind have disappeared

survive /sə'viev/ v to remain alive or in existence; live on – **-vivor** n

susceptible /sə'septəbl/ adj 1 capable of submitting to an action, process, or operation 2 open, subject, or unresistant to some stimulus, influence, or agency 3 easily moved or emotionally affected; impressionable – **-bility** n

¹suspect /'suspekt/ adj (deserving to be) regarded with suspicion

²suspect n sby who is suspected

³suspect /sə'spekt/ v 1 to be suspicious of; distrust 2 to believe to be guilty without conclusive proof 3 to imagine to be true, likely, or probable

suspend /sə'spend/ v 1 to debar temporarily from a privilege, office, membership, or employment 2 to make temporarily inoperative 3 to defer till later on certain conditions 4 to hang, esp so as to be free on all sides

suspender /sə'spendə/ n 1 an elasticated band with a fastening device for holding up a sock 2 Br any of the fastening devices on a suspender belt 3 pl, NAm braces

su'spender ,belt n, Br a garment consisting of 2 pairs of short straps hanging from a girdle to which are attached fastening devices for holding up a woman's stockings

suspense /sə'spens/ n a state of uncertain expectation as to a decision or outcome

suspension /sə'spensh(ə)n/ n 1a temporary removal from office or privileges b temporary withholding or postponement c temporary abolishing of a law or rule 2a hanging or being hung b a solid that is dispersed, but not dissolved, in a solid, liquid, or gas **3** the system of devices supporting the upper part of a vehicle on the axles

suspicion /sə'spish(ə)n/ *n* **1a** suspecting or being suspected **b** a feeling of doubt or mistrust **2** a slight touch or trace

suspicious /sə'spishəs/ *adj* **1** tending to arouse suspicion; dubious **2** inclined to suspect; distrustful – ~ly *adv* – ~ness *n*

sustain /sə'stayn/ *v* **1** to give support or relief to **2** to cause to continue; prolong **3** to buoy up the spirits of **4** to suffer, undergo

sustenance /'sustinəns/ *n* **1** food, provisions; *also* nourishment **2** sustaining

suttee /,su'tee, '-,-/ *n* the custom of a Hindu widow being cremated on the funeral pile of her husband; *also* such a widow

suture /'soohchə/ *n* **1a** the sewing together of parts of the living body **b** a stitch made in a suture **2** the solid join between 2 bones (e g of the skull)

suzerain /'soohz(ə)rayn/ *n* **1a** a feudal overlord **2** a dominant state controlling the foreign relations of an internally autonomous vassal state – ~ty *n*

svelte /sfelt, svelt/ *adj* slender, lithe

¹**swab** /swob/ *n* a wad of absorbent material used for applying medication, cleaning wounds, taking bacterial specimens, etc

²**swab** *v* **-bb- 1** to clean (a wound) with a swab **2** to clean (a surface, esp a deck) by washing (e g with a mop) – often + *down*

swaddle /'swodl/ *v* **swaddling** /'swodling/ **1** to wrap an infant tightly in narrow strips of cloth **2** to swathe, envelop

swag /swag/ *n* **1a** an arrangement of fabric hanging in a heavy curve or fold **b** a suspended cluster (e g of flowers) **2** *chiefly Austr* a pack or roll of personal belongings **3** goods acquired, esp by unlawful means; loot – *infml*

¹**swagger** /'swagə/ *v* to behave or esp walk in an arrogant or pompous manner – ~er *n* – ~ingly *adv*

²**swagger** *n* an act or instance of swaggering **2** arrogant or conceitedly self-assured behaviour

swain /swayn/ *n* **1** a male admirer or suitor **2** a peasant; *specif* a shepherd – chiefly poetic

¹**swallow** /'swoloh/ *n* any of numerous small long-winged migratory birds noted for their graceful flight

²**swallow** *v* **1** to take through the mouth into the stomach **2** to envelop, engulf **3** to accept without question or protest; *also* to believe naively **4** to refrain from expressing or showing – ~er *n*

³**swallow** *n* an amount that can be swallowed at one time

swam /swam/ *past of* **swim**

¹**swamp** /swomp/ *n* (an area of) wet spongy land sometimes covered with water – ~y *adj*

²**swamp** *v* **1** to inundate, submerge **2** to overwhelm by an excess of work, difficulties, etc

¹**swan** /swon/ *n* any of various heavy-bodied long-necked mostly pure white aquatic birds

²**swan** *v* **-nn-** to wander or travel aimlessly – infml

¹**swank** /swangk/ *v* to swagger; show off – infml

²**swank** *n* (one given to) pretentiousness or swagger – infml – ~y *adj* – ~iness *n*

swan ,song *n* a farewell appearance or final work or pronouncement

swap /swop/ *n* **1** an act of exchanging one thing for another **2** sthg so exchanged – **swap, swop** *v*

¹**swarm** /swawm/ *n* **1** a colony of honeybees, esp when emigrating from a hive with a queen bee to start a new colony elsewhere **2** *sing or pl in constr* a group of animate or inanimate things, esp when massing together

²**swarm** *v* **1** to collect together and depart from a hive **2** to move or assemble in a crowd **3** to contain a swarm; teem

³**swarm** *v* to climb, esp with the hands and feet – usu + *up*

swarthy /'swawdhi/ *adj* of a dark colour, complexion, or cast

¹**swash ,buckler** /-,buklə/ *n* a swaggering adventurer or daredevil – **-ling** *adj*

swastika /'swostikə/ *n* an ancient symbol in the shape of a cross with the ends of the arms extended at right angles in a clockwise or anticlockwise direction

¹**swat** /swot/ *v* **-tt-** to hit with a sharp slapping blow; *esp* to kill (an insect) with such a blow – ~ter *n*

²**swat** *n* **1** a quick crushing blow **2** a swatter

swatch /swoch/ *n* a sample piece (e g of fabric)

swath /swawth/ *n* **1a** a row of cut grain or grass left by a scythe or mowing machine **b** the path cut in 1 passage (e g of a mower) **2** a long broad strip

¹**swathe** /swaydh/ *v* **1** to bind or wrap (as if) with a bandage **2** to envelop

²**swathe** *n* a swath

¹**sway** /sway/ *v* **1** to swing slowly and rhythmically back and forth **2** to fluctuate or alternate between one attitude or position and another **3** to change the opinions of, esp by eloquence or argument

²**sway** *n* **1** swaying or being swayed **2a** controlling influence or power **b** rule, dominion

swear /sweə/ *v* **swore** /swaw/; **sworn** /swawn/ **1** to utter or take (an oath) solemnly **2** to promise emphatically or earnestly **3** to use profane or obscene language – ~er *n* — **swear by** to place great confidence in — **swear to** to have any positive conviction of

swear in *v* to induct into office by administration of an oath

¹**sweat** /swet/ *v* **sweated**, *NAm chiefly* **sweat 1** to excrete sweat in visible quantities **2a** to emit or exude moisture **b** to gather surface moisture as a result of condensation **3** to undergo anxiety or

tension 4 to exact work from under sweatshop conditions — **sweat blood** to work or worry intensely

²**sweat** n 1 the fluid excreted from the sweat glands of the skin; perspiration 2 moisture gathering in drops on a surface 3 hard work; drudgery 4 a state of anxiety or impatience *USE* (3&4) infml – ~y *adj* – **no sweat** not a problem or difficulty – infml

'sweat‚band /-‚band/ n a band of material worn round the head or wrist or inserted in a hat or cap to absorb sweat

sweater /'sweta/ n a pullover

sweat out v to endure or wait through the course of

'sweat ‚shirt n a loose collarless pullover of heavy cotton jersey

'sweat‚shop /-‚shop/ n a place of work in which workers are employed for long hours at low wages and under unhealthy conditions

swede /sweed/ n 1 cap a native or inhabitant of Sweden 2 a large type of turnip with edible yellow flesh

Swedish /'sweedish/ n the N Germanic language spoken in Sweden and part of Finland – **Swedish** *adj*

¹**sweep** /sweep/ v **swept** /swept/ **1a** to remove or clean (as if) by brushing **b** to destroy completely – usu + *away* **c** to drive or carry along with irresistible force 2 to move through or along with overwhelming speed or violence 3 to go with stately or sweeping movements 4 to cover the entire range of 5 to move or extend in a wide curve — **sweep someone off his/her feet** to gain immediate and unquestioning support, approval, or acceptance by sby; *esp* to cause sby to fall in love with one — **sweep the board** to win convincingly; win everything (e g in a contest)

²**sweep** n **1a** a long oar **b** a windmill sail 2 a clearing out or away (as if) with a broom **3a** a curving course or line **b** a broad extent 4 a sweepstake

sweeper /'sweepa/ n a defensive player in soccer who plays behind the backs as a last line of defence before the goalkeeper

sweeping /'sweeping/ adj 1 extending in a wide curve or over a wide area **2a** extensive, wide-ranging **b** marked by wholesale and indiscriminate inclusion – ~**ly** *adv*

'sweep‚stake /-‚stayk/ n a lottery *USE* often pl with sing. meaning but sing. or pl in constr

¹**sweet** /sweet/ adj **1a** being or inducing the one of the 4 basic taste sensations that is typically induced by sugar **b** *of a beverage* containing a sweetening ingredient; not dry **2a** delightful, charming **b** marked by gentle good humour or kindliness **c** fragrant **d** pleasing to the ear or eye 3 much loved **4a** not sour, rancid, decaying, or stale **b** not salt or salted; fresh – ~**ly** *adv* – ~**ness** n – ~**ish** adj

²**sweet** n 1 a darling or sweetheart 2 Br 2a dessert **b** a toffee, truffle, or other small piece of confectionery prepared with (flavoured or filled) chocolate or sugar; *esp* one made chiefly of (boiled and crystallized) sugar

'sweet‚bread /-‚bred/ n the pancreas of a young animal (e g a calf) used for food

'sweet ‚corn n (the young kernels of) a maize with kernels that contain a high percentage of sugar and are eaten as a vegetable when young and milky

sweeten /'sweet(ə)n/ v 1 to make (more) sweet 2 to soften the mood or attitude of 3 to make less painful or trying – ~**er** *n*

'sweet‚heart /-‚haht/ n a darling, lover

'sweet‚meat /-‚meet/ n a crystallized fruit, sugar-coated nut, or other sweet or delicacy rich in sugar

sweet pea n a leguminous garden plant with slender climbing stems and large fragrant flowers

sweet pepper n a large mild thick-walled capsicum fruit

sweet tooth n a craving or fondness for sweet food

¹**swell** /swel/ v **swollen** /'swohlən/, **swelled 1a** to expand gradually beyond a normal or original limit **b** to be distended or puffed up **c** to curve outwards or upwards; bulge 2 to become charged with emotion

²**swell** n 1 a rounded protuberance or bulge 2 a (massive) surge of water, often continuing beyond or after its cause (e g a gale) 3 a gradual increase and decrease of the loudness of a musical sound 4 a person of fashion or high social position – infml

³**swell** adj, chiefly NAm excellent

swelling /'sweling/ n an abnormal bodily protuberance or enlargement

¹**swelter** /'sweltə/ v to suffer, sweat, or be faint from heat

²**swelter** n a state of oppressive heat

sweltering /'swelt(ə)ring/ adj oppressively hot

swerve /swuhv/ v to (cause to) turn aside abruptly from a straight line or course

¹**swift** /swift/ adj 1 (capable of) moving at great speed 2 occurring suddenly or within a very short time 3 quick to respond; ready – ~**ly** *adv* – ~**ness** n

²**swift** n any of numerous dark-coloured birds that resemble swallows and are noted for their fast darting flight in pursuit of insects

¹**swig** /swig/ n a quantity drunk in 1 draught – infml

²**swig** v -gg- to drink (sthg) in long draughts – infml

¹swill /swil/ *v* **1** to wash, esp by flushing with water **2** to drink greedily

²swill *n* a semiliquid food for animals (e g pigs) composed of edible refuse mixed with water or skimmed or sour milk

¹swim /swim/ *v* **-mm-; swam** /swam/; **swum** /swum/ **1** to propel oneself in water by bodily movements (e g of the limbs, fins, or tail) **2** to surmount difficulties; not go under **3** to have a floating or dizzy effect or sensation – ~ **mer** *n* — **swim against the tide** to move counter to the prevailing or popular trend

²swim *n* **1** an act or period of swimming **2** the main current of events

swimming /'swiming/ *adj* capable of, adapted to, or used in or for swimming

'**swimmingly** /-li/ *adv* very well; splendidly – infml

¹swindle /'swindl/ *v* **swindling** /'swindling/ to obtain property or take property from by fraud – ~ **r** *n*

²swindle *n* a fraud, deceit

swine /swien/ *n, pl* **swine 1** a pig – used esp technically or in literature **2** a contemptible person **3** sthg unpleasant *USE* (2 & 3) infml – **-nish** *adj*

'**swine,herd** /-,huhd/ *n* sby who tends pigs

¹swing /swing/ *v* **swung** /swung/ **1** to move freely to and fro, esp when hanging from an overhead support **2** to turn (as if) on a hinge or pivot **3a** to influence decisively **b** to manage; bring about **4** to play or sing with a lively compelling rhythm; *specif* to play swing music **5** to shift or fluctuate between 2 moods, opinions, etc **6a** to move along rhythmically **b** to start up in a smooth rapid manner **7** to engage freely in sex, specif wife-swapping – slang

²swing *n* **1a** a sweeping or rhythmic movement of the body or a bodily part **b** the regular movement of a freely suspended object to and fro along an arc **c** a steady vigorous rhythm or action **2** the progression of an activity; course **3** the arc or range through which sthg swings **4** a suspended seat on which one may swing to and fro **5** jazz played usu by a large dance band and characterized by a steady lively rhythm, simple harmony, and a basic melody often submerged in improvisation

swingeing, swinging /'swinjing/ *adj, chiefly Br* severe, drastic

swinging /'swing·ing/ *adj* lively and up-to-date – infml – ~ **ly** *adv*

¹swipe /swiep/ *n* a strong sweeping blow – infml

²swipe *v* **1** to strike or hit out with a sweeping motion **2** to steal, pilfer *USE* infml

¹swirl /swuhl/ *n* **1** a whirling mass or motion **2** a twisting shape, mark, or pattern

²swirl *v* to move in eddies or whirls

¹swish /swish/ *v* to move with (the sound of) a swish

²swish *n* **1a** a sound as of a whip cutting the air **b** a light sweeping or brushing sound **2** a swishing movement

³swish *adj* smart, fashionable – infml

Swiss /swis/ *n, pl* **Swiss** a native or inhabitant of Switzerland – **Swiss** *adj*

,**Swiss 'roll** *n* a thin sheet of sponge cake spread with jam and rolled up

¹switch /swich/ *n* **1** a slender flexible twig or rod **2** a shift or change from one to another **3** a tuft of long hairs at the end of the tail of an animal (e g a cow) **4** a device for making, breaking, or changing the connections in an electrical circuit

²switch *v* **1** to shift, change **2a** to shift to another electrical circuit by means of a switch **b** to operate an electrical switch so as to turn *off* or *on* **3** to lash from side to side – ~ **able** *adj*

'**switch,back** /-,bak/ *n* **1** a zigzag road or railway in a mountainous region **2** *chiefly Br* any of various amusement rides; *esp* a roller coaster

'**switch,board** /-,bawd/ *n* an apparatus consisting of a panel or frame on which switching devices are mounted; *specif* an arrangement for the manual switching of telephone calls

'**switch,over** /-,ohvə/ *n* a conversion to a different system or method

¹swivel /'swivl/ *n* a device joining 2 parts so that the moving part can pivot freely

²swivel *v* **-ll-** (*NAm* **-l-, -ll-**), /'swivl·ing/ to turn (as if) on a swivel

swiz /swiz/ *n, pl* **-zz-** *Br* sthg that does not live up to one's hopes or expectations – infml

'**swizzle ,stick** /'swizl/ *n* a thin rod used to stir mixed drinks

swollen /'swohlən/ *past part of* **swell**

swoon /swoohn/ *v* to faint – **swoon** *n*

¹swoop /swoohp/ *v* **1** to make a sudden attack or downward sweep **2** to carry off abruptly; snatch – ~ **er** *n*

²swoop *n* an act of swooping

swop /swop/ *n or v* **-pp-** (to) swap

sword /sawd/ *n* **1** a cutting or thrusting weapon having a long usu sharp-pointed and sharp-edged blade **2** death caused (as if) by a sword – usu + *the* – ~ **sman** *n* ~ **smanship** *n*

'**sword ,dance** *n* a Scottish-Highland solo dance usu performed in the angles formed by 2 swords crossed on the ground – **sword dancer** *n*

'**sword,fish** /-,fish/ *n* a very large oceanic food fish that has a long swordlike beak formed by the bones of the upper jaw

'**sword,stick** /-,stik/ *n* a walking stick in which a sword blade is concealed

swore /swaw/ *past of* **swear**

sworn /swawn/ *past part of* **swear**

¹swot /swot/ *n, Br* one who studies hard or excessively – infml

²**swot** v, **-tt-** Br **1** to study hard **2** to study a subject intensively – usu + *up USE* infml – ~**ter** n

swum /swum/ *past part of* **swim**

swung /swung/ *past of* **swing**

sybarite /'sibəriet/ n, *often cap* a voluptuary, sensualist – **-itic** adj

sycamore /'sikə,maw/ n a Eurasian maple widely planted as a shade tree

sycophant /'sikə,fant/ n a self-seeking flatterer; a toady – ~**ic** adj

syllable /'siləbl/ n (a letter or symbol representing) an uninterruptible unit of spoken language that usu consists of 1 vowel sound either alone or with a consonant sound preceding or following – **-abic** adj

syllabub, sillabub /'siləbub/ n a cold dessert usu made by curdling sweetened cream or milk with wine, cider, etc

syllabus /'siləbəs/ n pl **syllabi** /-bie/, **syllabuses** a summary of a course of study or of examination requirements

sylph /silf/ n a slender graceful woman or girl – ~**like** adj

symbiosis /ˌsimbi'ohsis, -bie-/ n, pl **symbioses** /-seez/ the living together of 2 dissimilar organisms in intimate association (to their mutual benefit) – **-otic** adj

symbol /'simbl/ n **1** sthg that stands for or suggests sthg else by reason of association, convention, etc **2** a sign used in writing or printing to represent operations, quantities, elements, relations, or qualities in a particular field (e g chemistry or music) – ~**ic**, **-ical** adj – ~**ically** adv – ~**ize** v

symbolism /'simbə,liz(ə)m/ n **1** *often cap* an artistic movement, esp in 19th-c France, making much use of symbols rather than using direct expressions or representations **2** a system of symbols – **-list** adj, n

symmetry /'simitri/ n **1** (beauty of form arising from) balanced proportions **2** the property of being symmetrical; *esp* correspondence in size, shape, and relative position of parts on opposite sides of a dividing line or about a centre or axis – **-trical**, **-tric** adj – **-trically** adv

sympathetic /ˌsimpə'thetik/ adj **1** appropriate to one's mood or temperament; congenial **2** given to or arising from compassion and sensitivity to others' feelings **3** favourably inclined – ~**ally** adv

sympathy /'simpəthi/ n **1a** relationship between people or things in which each is simultaneously affected in a similar way **b** unity or harmony in action or effect **2a** inclination to think or feel alike **b** tendency to favour or support – often pl with sing. meaning **3** (the expression of) pity or compassion – **-thize** v

symphony /'simfəni/ n **1** a usu long and complex sonata for symphony orchestra **2** sthg of great harmonic complexity or variety – **-onic** adj

symposium /sim'pohzyəm, -zi·əm/ n, pl **symposia** /-zyə, -zi·ə/, **symposiums 1** a party (e g after a banquet in ancient Greece) with music and conversation **2** a formal meeting at which several specialists deliver short addresses on a topic

symptom /'simptəm/ n **1** sthg giving (subjective) evidence or indication of disease or physical disturbance **2** sthg that indicates the existence of sthg else – ~**atic** adj – ~**atically** adv

synagogue /'sinəgog/ n (the house of worship and communal centre of) a Jewish congregation

sync *also* **synch** /singk/ n synchronization – infml

synchron·ize, -ise /'singkrə,niez/ v **1** to happen at the same time; *esp* to make sound and image coincide (e g with a film) **2** to make synchronous in operation; *esp* to set clocks or watches to the same time – **-ization** n

syncopate /'singkə,payt/ v to change the rhythm of music by altering the note on which the beat falls – **-ation** n

syndicalism /'sindikl,iz(ə)m/ n **1** a revolutionary doctrine according to which workers should seize control of the economy and the government by direct means (e g a general strike) **2** a system of economic organization in which industries are owned and managed by the workers – **-list** adj, n

¹**syndicate** /'sindikət/ n **1** *sing or pl in constr* a group of people or concerns who combine to carry out a particular transaction (e g buying or renting property) or to promote some common interest **2** a business concern that supplies material for simultaneous publication in many newspapers or periodicals

²**syndicate** /'sindi,kayt/ v **1** to form into or manage as a syndicate **2** to sell (e g a cartoon) to a syndicate for simultaneous publication in many newspapers or periodicals – **-cation** n

syndrome /'sindrohm/ n a group of signs and symptoms that occur together and characterize a particular (medical) abnormality

synod /'sinəd, 'sinod/ n **1** a formal meeting to decide ecclesiastical matters **2** a church governing or advisory council

synonym /'sinənim/ n any of 2 or more words or expressions in a language that are used with (nearly) the same meaning – ~**ous** adj – ~**ously** adv

synopsis /si'nopsis/ n, pl **synopses** /-seez/ a condensed statement or outline (e g of a narrative)

syntax /'sintaks/ n (the part of grammar dealing with) the way in which words are put together to form phrases, clauses, or sentences

synthes·ize, ise /'sinthəsiez/ v to make, esp by combining parts or in imitation of a natural product

synthetic /sin'thetik/ *also* **synthetical** /-kl/ adj **1** asserting of a subject a predicate that is not part of the meaning of that subject **2** produced artificially; man-made – ~**ally** adv

syphilis /'sifəlis/ n a contagious usu venereal and often congenital disease caused by a bacterium – -**itic** adj

syphon /'siefən/ v or n (to) siphon

syringe /sə'rinj/ n a device used to inject fluids into or withdraw them from sthg (e g the body or its cavities); esp one that consists of a hollow barrel fitted with a plunger and a hollow needle

syrup /'sirəp/ n **1a** a thick sticky solution of (flavoured, medicated, etc) sugar and water **b** the raw sugar juice obtained from crushed sugarcane after evaporation and before crystallization in sugar manufacture **2** cloying sweetness or sentimentality – ~**y** adj

system /'sistəm/ n **1a** a group of body organs that together perform 1 or more usu specified functions **b** a group of interrelated and interdependent objects or units **c** a form of social, economic, or political organization **2** an organized set of doctrines or principles usu intended to explain the arrangement or working of a systematic whole **3** a manner of classifying, symbolizing, or formalizing **4** orderly methods

systematic /ˌsistə'matik/ also **systematical** /-kl/ adj **1** relating to, consisting of, or presented as a system **2** methodical in procedure or plan; thorough **3** of or concerned with classification; specif taxonomic – ~**ally** adv – -**tize** v

T

t /tee/ n, pl **t's**, **ts** often cap (a graphic representation of or device for reproducing) the 20th letter of the English alphabet — **to a T** to perfection; exactly *'t* definite article, NEng dial the pron it

¹**tab** /tab/ n **1** a flap, loop, etc fixed to or projecting from sthg and used for gripping or suspending or to aid identification **2** close surveillance; watch – usu pl with sing. meaning **3** chiefly NAm a statement of money owed; a bill – infml

²**tab** v -**bb**- to provide or decorate with tabs

tabard /'tabəd/ n a short loosely fitting sleeveless or short-sleeved coat or cape

tabby /'tabi/, **'tabby ˌcat** n **1** a domestic cat with a usu buff and black striped and mottled coat **2** a female domestic cat

tabernacle /'tabəˌnakl/ n a receptacle for the consecrated bread and wine used at Communion, often forming part of an altar

¹**table** /'taybl/ n **1** a piece of furniture consisting of a smooth flat slab (e g of wood) fixed on legs **2** a systematic arrangement of data usu in rows and columns **3** sthg having a flat level surface — **on the table** chiefly Br under or put forward for discussion — **under the table 1** into a stupor **2** not aboveboard

²**table** v **1** to enter in a table **2a** Br to place on the agenda **b** NAm to postpone consideration of

tableau /'tabloh/ n, pl **tableaux** also **tableaus** /'tabloh(z)/ **1** a graphic representation of a group or scene **2** a depiction of a scene usu presented on a stage by silent and motionless costumed participants

'table ˌcloth /-ˌkloth/ n an often decorative cloth spread over a dining table before the places are set

table d'hôte /ˌtahblə 'doht/ n a meal often of several prearranged courses served to all guests at a fixed price

tableland /'taybl ˌland/ n a broad level area elevated on all sides

'table ˌmat /-ˌmat/ n a small often decorative mat placed under a hot dish to protect the surface of a table from heat

'table ˌspoon /-ˌspoohn/ n a large spoon used for serving – ~**ful** n

tablet /'tablit/ n **1** a flat slab or plaque suitable for or bearing an inscription **2a** a compressed block of a solid material **b** a small solid shaped mass or capsule of medicinal material

table tennis n a game resembling lawn tennis that is played on a tabletop with bats and a small hollow plastic ball

'table ˌware /-ˌweə/ n utensils (e g glasses, dishes, plates, and cutlery) for table use

tabloid /'tabloyd/ n a newspaper of which 2 pages make up 1 printing plate and which contains much photographic matter

¹**taboo** also **tabu** /tə'booh/ adj **1a** too sacred or evil to be touched, named, or used **b** set apart as unclean or accursed **2** forbidden, esp on grounds of morality, tradition, or social usage

²**taboo** also **tabu** n pl **taboos** also **tabus 1** a prohibition against touching, saying, or doing sthg for fear of harm from a supernatural force **2** a prohibition imposed by social custom

³**taboo** also **tabu** v **1** to set apart as taboo **2** to avoid or ban as taboo

tabor also **tabour** /'taybə/ n a small drum used to accompany a pipe or fife played by the same person

tabular /'tabyoolə/ adj **1** having a broad flat surface **2** arranged in the form of a table

tabulate /'tabyoolayt/ v to arrange in tabular form – -**lation** n

tabulator /'tabyoo ˌlaytə/ n **1** a business machine that sorts and selects information from marked or perforated cards **2** an attachment to a typewriter that is used for arranging data in columns

tacit /'tasit/ adj implied or understood but not actually expressed – ~**ly** adv

taciturn /'tasi,tuhn/ *adj* not communicative or talkative – ~**ity** *n* – ~**ly** *adv*

¹**tack** /tak/ *n* **1** a small short sharp-pointed nail, usu with a broad flat head **2** the lower forward corner of a fore-and-aft sail **3a** the direction of a sailing vessel with respect to the direction of the wind **b** a change of course from one tack to another **c** a course of action **4** a long loose straight stitch usu used to hold 2 or more layers of fabric together temporarily **5** saddlery

²**tack** *v* **1a** to fasten or attach with tacks **b** to sew with long loose stitches in order to join or hold in place temporarily before fine or machine sewing **2** to add as a supplement **3a** to change the course of (a close-hauled sailing vessel) from one tack to the other by turning the bow to windward **b** to follow a zigzag course **c** to change one's policy or attitude abruptly

¹**tackle** /'takl/ *n* **1** a set of equipment used in a particular activity **2** an assembly of ropes and pulleys arranged to gain mechanical advantage for hoisting and pulling **3** an act of tackling

²**tackle** *v* **tackling** /'takling, 'takl·ing/ **1a** to take hold of or grapple with, esp in an attempt to stop or restrain **b(1)** to (attempt to) take the ball from (an opposing player) in hockey or soccer **b(2)** to seize and pull down or stop (an opposing player with the ball) in rugby or American football **2** to set about dealing with

¹**tacky** /'taki/ *adj* slightly sticky to the touch

²**tacky** *adj, chiefly NAm* shabby, shoddy – *slang*

tact /takt/ *n* a keen sense of how to handle people or affairs so as to avoid friction or giving offence – ~**ful** *adj* – ~**fully** *adv* – ~**less** *adj* – ~**lessly** *adv* – ~**lessness** *n*

tactic /'taktik/ *n* **1** a method of employing forces in combat **2** a device for achieving an end

tactician /tak'tish(a)n/ *n* sby skilled in tactics

tactics /'taktiks/ *n pl but sing or pl in constr* **1** the science and art of disposing and manoeuvring forces in combat **2** the art or skill of employing available means to accomplish an end – **-tical** *adj* – **-tically** *adv*

tactile /'taktiel/ *adj* of or perceptible by (the sense of) touch

tadpole /'tad,pohl/ *n* a frog or toad larva with a rounded body, a long tail, and external gills

taffeta /'tafita/ *n* a crisp plain-woven lustrous fabric of various fibres used esp for women's clothing

taffrail /'taf,rayl, 'tafrəl/ *n* a rail round the stern of a ship

¹**tag** /tag/ *n* **1** a loose hanging piece of torn cloth **2** a rigid binding on an end of a shoelace **3** a piece of hanging or attached material; *specif* a flap on a garment that carries information (e g washing instructions) **4** a trite quotation used for rhetorical effect **5** a marker of plastic, metal, etc used for identification or classification

²**tag** *v* **-gg-** **1a** to provide with an identifying marker **b** to label, brand **2** to attach, append

³**tag** *n* a game in which one player chases others and tries to make one of them it by touching him/her

¹**tail** /tayl/ *n* **1** (an extension or prolongation of) the rear end of the body of an animal **2** sthg resembling an animal's tail in shape or position **3** *pl* a tailcoat; *broadly* formal evening dress for men including a tailcoat and a white bow tie **4** the last, rear, or lower part of sthg **5** the reverse of a coin – usu *pl* with sing. meaning **6** the stabilizing assembly (e g fin, rudder, and tailplane) at the rear of an aircraft **7** sby who follows or keeps watch on sby – *infml* – ~**less** *adj*

²**tail** *v* **1** to remove the stalk of (e g a gooseberry) **2** to diminish gradually in strength, volume, quantity, etc – usu + *off* or *away* **3a** to follow for purposes of surveillance – *infml* **b** to follow closely

'**tail,back** /-,bak/ *n* a long queue of motor vehicles, esp when caused by an obstruction that blocks the road

'**tail,coat** /-,koht/ *n* a coat with tails; *esp* a man's formal evening coat with 2 long tapering skirts at the back

tail end *n* **1** the back or rear end of sthg **2** the concluding period

'**tail,gate** /-,gayt/ *v* to drive dangerously close behind another vehicle

¹**tailor** /'taylə/, *fem* **tailoress** /,taylə'res, '--,-/ *n* sby whose occupation is making or altering esp men's garments

²**tailor** *v* **1** to make or fashion as the work of a tailor; *specif* to cut and stitch (a garment) so that it will hang and fit well **2** to make or adapt to suit a special need or purpose

,**tailor-'made** *adj* made or fitted for a particular use or purpose

¹**taint** /taynt/ *v* **1** to touch or affect slightly with sthg bad **2** to affect with putrefaction; spoil **3** to contaminate morally; corrupt

²**taint** *n* a contaminating mark or influence

¹**take** /tayk/ *v* **took** /took/; **taken** /'taykən/ **1** to seize or capture physically **2** to grasp, grip **3a** to catch or attack through a sudden effect **b** to surprise; come upon suddenly **c** to attract, delight **4a** to receive into one's body, esp through the mouth **b** to eat or drink habitually **5** to bring or receive into a relationship or connection **6a** to acquire, borrow, or use without authority or right **b** to pay to have (e g by contract or subscription) **7a** to assume **b** to perform or conduct (e g a lesson) as a duty, task, or job **c** to commit oneself to **d** to involve oneself in **e** to consider or adopt as a point of view **f** to claim as rightfully one's own **8** to obtain by competition **9** to pick out; choose **10** to adopt or avail oneself of for use: e g **10a** to have recourse to as an instrument for doing sthg **b** to use as a means of transport or progression **11a** to

derive, draw **b(1)** to obtain or ascertain by testing, measuring, etc **b(2)** to record in writing **b(3)** to get or record by photography **12a** to receive or accept either willingly or reluctantly **b** to have the natural or intended effect or reaction **c** to begin to grow; strike root **13a** to accommodate **b** to be affected injuriously by (e g a disease) **14a** to apprehend, understand **b** to look upon; consider **c** to feel, experience **15a** to lead, carry, or remove with one to another place **b** to require or cause to go **16a** to obtain by removing **b** to subtract **17** to undertake and make, do, or perform **18a** to deal with **b** to consider or view in a specified relation **c** to apply oneself to the study of or undergo examination in – ~ **r n** — **take account of** take into account — **take action 1** to begin to act **2** to begin legal proceedings — **take advantage of 1** to use to advantage; profit by **2** to impose upon; exploit — **take after** to resemble (an older relative) in appearance, character, or aptitudes — **take against** *chiefly Br* to take sides ..gainst; come to dislike — **take apart 1** to disassemble, dismantle **2** to analyse, dissect **3** to treat roughly or harshly — *infml* — **take as read** to accept as axiomatic — **take a toss** to fall off a horse — **take care** to be careful; exercise caution or prudence; be watchful — **take care of** to attend to or provide for the needs, operation, or treatment of — **take charge** to assume care, custody, command, or control — **take effect 1** to become operative **2** to produce a result — **take exception** to object, demur — **take five** to take a brief intermission — *infml* — **take for** to suppose, esp mistakenly, to be — **take for a ride** to deceive wilfully; hoodwink — *infml* — **take for granted 1** to assume as true, real, or certain to occur **2** to value too lightly — **take from** to detract from — **take heart** to gain courage or confidence — **take hold 1** to grasp, grip, seize **2** to become attached or established; TAKE EFFECT — **take in good part** to accept without offence — **take in hand** to embark on the control or reform of — **take into account** to make allowances for — **take into consideration** take into account; *specif* to take account of (additional offences admitted by a defendant) so that the sentence to be imposed will preclude any chance of subsequent prosecution — **take into one's head** to conceive as a sudden notion or resolve — **take in vain** to use (a name) profanely or without proper respect — **take it upon oneself** to venture, presume — **take offence** to be offended — **take on board** *Br* to apprehend fully; grasp — *infml* — **take one all one's time** *Br* to be the utmost one can manage — **take one's leave** to bid farewell — often + *of* — **take one's time** to be leisurely about doing sthg — **take part** to join, participate, share — **take place** to happen; come about — **take root 1** to become rooted **2** to become fixed or

established — **take silk** to become a Queen's or King's Counsel — **take someone at his/her word** to believe sby literally — **take someone out of him-/herself** to provide sby with needful diversion — **take someone to task** to rebuke or scold sby — **take stock 1** to make an inventory **2** to make an assessment — **take the biscuit** *Br* to be the most astonishing or preposterous thing heard of or seen, esp concerning a particular issue — *infml* — **take the field 1** to go onto the playing field **2** to enter on a military campaign — **take the floor 1** to rise (e g in a meeting) to make a formal address **2** to begin dancing — **take the gilt off the gingerbread** to take away the part that makes the whole attractive — **take the law into one's own hands** to seek redress by force — **take the mickey** to behave disrespectfully; mock — *infml* — **take the wind out of someone's sails** to frustrate sby by anticipating or forestalling him/her — **take the words out of someone's mouth** to utter the exact words about to be used by sby — **take to 1** to betake oneself to, esp for refuge **2** to apply or devote oneself to (e g a practice, habit or occupation) **3** to adapt oneself to; respond to **4** to conceive a liking or affectionate concern for — **take to heart** to be deeply affected by — **take to one's heels** to run away; flee — **take to task** to call to account for a shortcoming — **take to the cleaners 1** to rob, defraud — *infml* **2** to criticize harshly — *infml* — **take turns, take it in turns** to act by turns — **what it takes** the qualities or resources needed for success or for attainment of a goal

²**take** *n* **1** the uninterrupted recording, filming, or televising of sthg (e g a gramophone record or film sequence); *also* the recording or scene produced **2** proceeds, takings

takeaway /'taykə,way/ *n*, *Br* **1** a cooked meal that is eaten away from the premises from which it was bought **2** a shop or restaurant that sells takeaways

take back *v* to retract, withdraw

take in *v* **1a** to furl **b** to make (a garment) smaller (e g by altering the positions of the seams or making tucks) **2** to offer accommodation or shelter to **3** to include **4** to perceive, understand **5** to deceive, trick — *infml*

¹**take off** /-,of/ *n* **1** an imitation; *esp* a caricature **2** an act of leaving or a rise from a surface (e g in making a jump, dive, or flight or in the launching of a rocket) **3** a starting point

take off *v* **1a** to deduct **b** to remove (e g clothing) **2** to take or spend (a period of time) as a holiday, rest, etc **3** to mimic **4** to start off or away **5** to begin a leap or spring **6** to leave the surface; begin flight

take on *v* **1a** to agree to undertake **b** to contend with as an opponent **2** to engage, hire **3** to assume or acquire (e g an appearance or quality) **4** to become emotional or distraught – *infml*

tak

take out *v* **1a** to extract **b** to give vent to – usu + *on* **2** to escort or accompany in public **3a** to obtain officially or formally **b** to acquire (insurance) by making the necessary payment — **take it out on** to vent anger, vexation, or frustration on — **take it out of 1** take it out on **2** to fatigue, exhaust

'take,over /-,ohvə/ *n* an act of gaining control of a business company by buying a majority of the shares

take over *v* to assume control or possession (of) or responsibility (for)

take up *v* **1** to remove by lifting or pulling up **2** to receive internally or on the surface and hold **3a** to begin to engage in or study **b** to raise (a matter) for consideration **4** to occupy (e g space or time) entirely or exclusively **5** to shorten (e g a garment) **6** to respond favourably to a bet, challenge, or proposal made by **7** to begin again; resume — **take up the cudgels** to engage vigorously in a defence — **take up with** to begin to associate with; consort with

taking /'tayking/ *adj* attractive, captivating

takings /'taykingz/ *n pl* receipts, esp of money

talc /talk/ *n* **1** a soft usu greenish or greyish mineral consisting of a magnesium silicate **2** talcum powder

'talcum ,powder /'talkəm/ *n* a powder for toilet use consisting of perfumed talc

tale /tayl/ *n* **1** a series of events or facts told or presented; an account **2a** a usu fictitious narrative; a story **b** a lie, a falsehood

'tale,bearer /-,beərə/ *n* a telltale; gossip

talent /'talənt/ *n* **1a** any of several ancient units of weight **b** a unit of money equal to the value of a talent of gold or silver **2a** a special often creative or artistic aptitude **b** general ability or intelligence **3** sexually attractive members of the opposite sex – *slang* – **~ed** *adj*

talisman /'talizmən/ *n, pl* **talismans 1** an engraved object believed to act as a charm **2** sthg believed to produce magical or miraculous effects

'talk /tawk/ *v* **1** to express or exchange ideas verbally or by other means **2** to use speech; speak **3** to use a particular, esp foreign language for conversing or communicating **4a** to gossip **b** to reveal secret or confidential information — **talk shop** to talk about one's job, esp outside working hours — **talk through one's hat** to voice irrational, or erroneous ideas, esp in attempting to appear knowledgeable — **talk turkey** *chiefly NAm* to speak frankly or bluntly

'talk *n* **1** a verbal exchange of thoughts or opinions; a conversation **2** meaningless speech; verbiage **3** a formal discussion or exchange of views – often pl with sing. meaning **4** an often informal address or lecture

talkative /'tawkətiv/ *adj* given to talking – **~ness** *n*

talk down *v* **1** to defeat or silence by argument or by loud talking **2** to radio instructions to (a pilot) to enable him/her to land when conditions are difficult **3** to speak in a condescending or oversimplified fashion *to*

talkie /'tawki/ *n* a film with a synchronized sound track

talking point *n* a subject of conversation or argument

talk out *v* to clarify or settle by discussion

talk over *v* to review or consider in conversation

tall /tawl/ *adj* **1a** of above average height **b** of a specified height **2** *of a plant* of a higher growing variety or species **3** highly exaggerated; incredible – **~ish** *adj* – **~ness** *n*

tallboy /'tawl,boy/ *n* **1** a tall chest of drawers supported on a low legged base **2** a double chest of drawers usu with the upper section slightly smaller than the lower

tallow /'taloh/ *n* the solid white rendered fat of cattle and sheep used chiefly in soap, candles, and lubricants

'tally /'tali/ *n* **1** a record or account (e g of items or charges) **2** a record of the score (e g in a game)

'tally *v* **1** to make a count of **2** to correspond, match

tally-ho /,tali 'hoh/ *n* a call of a huntsman at the sight of a fox

tallyman /'taliman/ *n* **1** one who checks or keeps an account or record (e g of receipt of goods) **2** *Br* one who sells goods on credit; *also* one who calls to collect hire purchase payments

Talmud /'talmood, 'tahl-/ *n* the authoritative body of Jewish traditional lore

talon /'talən/ *n* a claw of an animal, esp a bird of prey

tamarisk /'tamərisk/ *n* any of a genus of chiefly tropical or Mediterranean shrubs and trees

tambourine /,tambə'reen/ *n* a shallow one-headed drum with loose metallic discs at the sides

'tame /taym/ *adj* **1** changed from a state of native wildness, esp so as to be trainable and useful to human beings **2** made docile and submissive **3** lacking spirit, zest, or interest – **~ly** *adv* – **~ness** *n*

'tame *v* **1** to make tame; domesticate **2** to deprive of spirit; subdue – **tamable** *or* **tameable** *adj* – **tamer** *n*

tam-o'-shanter /,tam ə 'shantə/ *n* a round flat woollen or cloth cap of Scottish origin

tamp /tamp/ *v* to drive in or down by a succession of light or medium blows – often + *down*

tamper /'tampə/ *v* to interfere or meddle *with* without permission

tampon /'tampon/ *v or n* (to plug with) an absorbent plug put into a cavity (e g the vagina) to absorb secretions, arrest bleeding, etc

tap

¹**tan** /tan/ *v* **-nn- 1** to convert (hide) into leather, esp by treatment with an infusion of tannin-rich bark **2** to make (skin) tan-coloured, esp by exposure to the sun **3** to thrash, beat - *infml* — **tan someone's hide** *or* **tan the hide off someone** to beat sby severely; thrash — *infml*

²**tan** *n* **1** a brown colour given to the skin by exposure to sun or wind **2 (a)** light yellowish brown colour — **tan** *adj*

¹**tandem** /'tandəm/ *n* **1** a (2-seat carriage drawn by) horses harnessed one before the other **2** a bicycle or tricycle having 2 or more seats one behind the other — **in tandem 1** in a tandem arrangement **2** in partnership or conjunction

²**tandem** *adv* one behind the other

tandoori /tan'dawri/ *n* (food cooked by) a N Indian method of cooking in a large clay oven

¹**tang** /tang/ *n* **1** a projecting shank or tongue (e g on a knife, file, or sword) that connects with and is enclosed by a handle **2a** a sharp distinctive flavour **b** a pungent or distinctive smell

²**tang** *n* any of various large coarse seaweeds

¹**tangent** /'tangənt/ *adj* **1** touching a curve or surface at only 1 point **2** having a common tangent at a point

²**tangent** *n* **1** the trigonometric function that for an acute angle in a right-angled triangle is the ratio between the shorter sides opposite and adjacent to the angle **2** a straight line tangent to a curve — **fly/go off at/on a tangent** to change suddenly from one subject, course of action, etc, to another

tangential /tan'jensh(ə)l/ *adj* **1** divergent, digressive **2** incidental, peripheral

tangerine /tanjə'reen/ *n* **1** (a tree that produces) any of various mandarin oranges with deep orange skin and pulp **2 (a)** bright reddish orange colour

tangible /'tanjəbl/ *adj* **1a** capable of being perceived, esp by the sense of touch **b** substantially real; material **2** capable of being appraised at an actual or approximate value — **-bility** *n* — **-bly** *adv*

¹**tangle** /'tang·gl/ *v* **tangling** /'tang·gling, 'tang·gl·ing/ **1** to involve so as to be trapped or hampered **2** to bring together or intertwine in disordered confusion **3** to engage in conflict or argument – *usu* + *with*; *infml*

²**tangle** *n* **1** a confused twisted mass **2** a complicated or confused state

tango /'tang·goh/ *n*, *pl* **tangos** (the music for) a ballroom dance of Latin-American origin

tank /tangk/ *n* **1** a large receptacle for holding, transporting, or storing liquids or gas **2** an enclosed heavily armed and armoured combat vehicle that moves on caterpillar tracks

tankard /'tangkəd/ *n* a silver or pewter mug

tanker /'tangkə/ *n* a ship, aircraft, or road or rail vehicle designed to carry fluid, esp liquid, in bulk (e g an aircraft used for transporting fuel and usu capable of refuelling other aircraft in flight)

tanner /'tanə/ *n*, *Br* a coin worth 6 old pence – *infml*

tannin /'tanin/ *n* any of various acidic substances of plant origin used esp in tanning, dyeing, and making ink

Tannoy /'tanoy/ *trademark* – used for a loudspeaker apparatus that broadcasts to the public

tantal·ize, -ise /'tantəliez/ *v* to tease or frustrate by offering sthg just out of reach

tantamount /'tantə,mownt/ *adj* equivalent in value, significance, or effect *to*

tantrum /'tantrəm/ *n* a fit of childish bad temper

¹**tap** /tap/ *n* **1a** a plug designed to fit an opening, esp in a barrel **b** a device consisting of a spout and valve attached to a pipe, bowl, etc to control the flow of a fluid **2** a tool for forming an internal screw thread **3** the act or an instance of tapping a telephone, telegraph, etc; *also* an electronic listening device used to do this — **on tap 1** *of beer* on draught **2** readily available

²**tap** *v* **-pp- 1** to let out or cause to flow by piercing or by drawing a plug from the containing vessel **2a** to pierce so as to let out or draw off a fluid (e g from a body cavity) **b** to draw from or upon **c** to connect an electronic listening device to (e g a telegraph or telephone wire), esp in order to acquire secret information **3** to form an internal screw thread in (e g a nut) by means of a special tool **4** to get money from as a loan or gift – *infml*

³**tap** *v* **-pp- 1** to strike lightly, esp with a slight sound **2** to produce by striking in this manner – often + *out*

⁴**tap** *n* (the sound of) a light blow

¹**tape** /tayp/ *n* **1** a narrow band of woven fabric **2** *the* string stretched above the finishing line of a race **3** a narrow flexible strip or band; *esp* magnetic tape **4** a tape recording

²**tape** *v* **1** to fasten, tie, or bind with tape **2** to record on tape, esp magnetic tape — **have someone/something taped** to have fully understood or learnt how to deal with sby or sthg — *infml*

'**tape ,deck** *n* a mechanism or self-contained unit that causes magnetic tape to move past the heads of a magnetic recording device in order to generate electrical signals or to make a recording

'**tape ,measure** *n* a narrow strip (e g of a limp cloth or steel tape) marked off in units for measuring

¹**taper** /'taypə/ *n* **1a** a slender candle **b** a long waxed wick used esp for lighting candles, fires, etc **2** gradual diminution of thickness, diameter, or width

²**taper** *v* to decrease gradually in thickness, diameter, or width towards one end; *broadly* to diminish gradually

tape recorder *n* a device for recording on magnetic tape

tapestry /'tapostri/ *n* 1 a heavy handwoven textile used for hangings, curtains, and upholstery, characterized by complicated pictorial designs 2 a machine-made imitation of tapestry used chiefly for upholstery – **-tried** *adj*

tapeworm /'tayp,wuhm/ *n* any of numerous worms, which when adult are parasitic in the intestine of human beings or other vertebrates

tapioca /,tapi'ohkə/ *n* (a milk pudding made with) a usu granular preparation of starch produced from the cassava root

tapir /'taypə/ *n* any of several large chiefly nocturnal hoofed mammals with long snouts found in tropical America and Asia

tappet /'tapit/ *n* a lever or projection moved by or moving some other piece (e g a cam)

'tap,root /-,rooht/ *n* a main root of a plant that grows vertically downwards and gives off small side roots

¹tar /tah/ *n* **1a** a dark bituminous usu strong-smelling viscous liquid obtained by heating and distilling wood, coal, peat, etc **b** a residue present in smoke from burning tobacco that contains resins, acids, phenols, etc **2** a sailor – infml

²tar *v* **-rr-** to smear with tar — **tar and feather** to smear (a person) with tar and cover with feathers as a punishment or humiliation — **tarred with the same brush** having the same faults

tarantella /,tarən'telə/ *n* (music suitable for) a vivacious folk dance of southern Italy

tarantula /tə'ranchoolə/ *n pl* **tarantulas** *also* **tarantulae** /-li/ any of various large hairy spiders

tardy /'tahdi/ *adj* **1** moving or progressing slowly; sluggish **2** delayed beyond the expected time; late – **tardily** *adv* – **tardiness** *n*

¹tare /teə/ *n* **1** any of several vetches **2** *pl* a weed found in cornfields – used in the Bible

²tare *n* **1** a deduction from the gross weight of a substance and its container made in allowance for the weight of the container **2** the weight of an unloaded goods vehicle

target /'tahgit/ *n* **1** a small round shield **2a** an object to fire at in practice or competition; *esp* one consisting of a series of concentric circles with a bull's-eye at the centre **b** sthg (e g an aircraft or installation) fired at or attacked **3a** an object of ridicule, criticism, etc **b** a goal, objective

tariff /'tarif/ *n* **1** a duty or schedule of duties imposed by a government on imported or in some countries exported goods **2** a schedule of rates or prices

tarmac /'tahmak/ *n* **1** stone chippings bonded with tar to produce a road surface **2** a runway, apron, or road made of tarmac

tarn /tahn/ *n* a small mountain lake

tarnish /'tahnish/ *v* **1** to dull the lustre of (as if) by dirt, air, etc **2a** to mar, spoil **b** to bring discredit on – **tarnish** *n*

tarot /'taroh/ *n* any of a set of 78 pictorial playing cards used esp for fortune-telling

tarpaulin /tah'pawlin/ *n* (a piece of) heavy waterproof usu tarred canvas material used for protecting objects or ground exposed to the elements

tarragon /'tarogən/ *n* (a small European herb with) pungent aromatic leaves used as a flavouring

tarry /'tari/ *v* **1** to delay or be slow in acting or doing **2** to stay in or at a place

tarsus /'tahsəs/ *n, pl* **tarsi** /-sie/ **1** (the small bones that support) the back part of the foot of a vertebrate that includes the ankle and heel **2** the part of the limb of an arthropod furthest from the body – **-sal** *adj*

¹tart /taht/ *adj* **1** agreeably sharp or acid to the taste **2** caustic, cutting – ~**ly** *adv* – ~**ness** *n*

²tart *n* **1** a pastry shell or shallow pie containing a usu sweet filling (e g jam or fruit) **2** a sexually promiscuous girl or woman; *also* a prostitute – infml

tartan /'taht(ə)n/ *n* (a usu twilled woollen fabric with) a plaid textile design of Scottish origin consisting of checks of varying width and colour usu patterned to designate a distinctive clan

¹tartar /'tahtə/ *n* **1** a substance derived from the juice of grapes deposited in wine casks as a reddish crust or sediment **2** an incrustation on the teeth consisting esp of calcium salts

²tartar *n* **1** *cap, NAm chiefly* **Tatar** a member of a group of people found mainly in the Tatar Republic of the USSR, the north Caucasus, Crimea, and parts of Siberia **2** an irritable, formidable, or exacting person

tartaric acid /tah'tarik/ *n* a strong acid from plants that is usu obtained from tartar, and is used esp in food and medicines

task /tahsk/ *n* **1** an assigned piece of work; a duty **2** sthg hard or unpleasant that has to be done; a chore

'task ,force *n* a temporary grouping under 1 leader for the purpose of accomplishing a definite objective

'task,master /-,mahstə/ *n* one who assigns tasks

tassel /'tasl/ *n* **1** a dangling ornament (e g for a curtain or bedspread) consisting of a bunch of cords or threads usu of even length fastened at 1 end **2** the tassel-like flower clusters of some plants, esp maize

¹taste /tayst/ *v* **1** to test the flavour of sthg by taking a little into the mouth **2** to have perception, experience, or enjoyment – usu + *of* **3** to eat or drink, esp in small quantities **4** to have a specified flavour – often + *of*

²**taste** n **1a** the act of tasting **b** a small amount tasted **c** a first acquaintance or experience of sthg **2** (the quality of a dissolved substance as perceived by) the basic physical sense by which the qualities of dissolved substances in contact with taste buds on the tongue are interpreted by the brain as a sensation of sweet, bitter, sour, or salt **3** individual preference; inclination **4** (a manner or quality indicative of) critical judgment or discernment esp in aesthetic or social matters

'**taste ,bud** n any of the small organs, esp on the surface of the tongue, that receive and transmit the sensation of taste

'**tasteful** /-f(ə)l/ adj showing or conforming to good taste – ~**ly** adv – ~**ness** n

'**tasteless** /-lis/ adj **1** having no taste; insipid **2** showing poor taste – ~**ly** adv – ~**ness** n

taster /'taystə/ n sby who tests food or drink by tasting, esp in order to assess quality

tasty /'taysti/ adj having an appetizing flavour – **tastily** adv – **tastiness** n

tatter /'tatə/ n **1** an irregular torn shred, esp of material **2** pl tattered clothing; rags — **in tatters 1** torn in pieces; ragged **2** in disarray; useless

tattered /'tatəd/ adj (dressed in clothes which are) old and torn

tatting /'tating/ n (the act or art of making) a delicate handmade lace formed usu by making loops and knots using a single thread and a small shuttle

tattle /'tatl/ v **tattling** /'tatling, 'tatl·ing/ to chatter, gossip – **tattle** n

¹**tattoo** /ta'tooh/ n pl **tattoos 1a** an evening drum or bugle call sounded as notice to soldiers to return to quarters **b** an outdoor military display given by troops as a usu evening entertainment **2** a rapid rhythmic beating or rapping

²**tattoo** n pl **tattoos** (an indelible mark made by) tattooing

³**tattoo** v to mark (the body) by inserting pigments under the skin – ~**ist** n

tatty /'tati/ adj shabby, dilapidated – infml – **-tily** adv – **-tiness** n

taught /'tawt/ past & past part of **teach**

¹**taunt** /'tawnt/ v to provoke in a mocking way; jeer at – ~**ingly** adv

²**taunt** n a sarcastic provocation or insult

Taurus /'tawrəs/ n (sby born under) the 2nd sign of the zodiac in astrology which is pictured as a bull

taut /'tawt/ adj **1** tightly drawn; tensely stretched **2** showing anxiety; tense – ~**ly** adv – ~**ness** n

tautology /taw'toləji/ n (an instance of) needless repetition of an idea, statement, or word – **-gical** adj

tavern /'tavən/ n an inn

tawdry /'tawdri/ adj cheap and tastelessly showy in appearance – **-drily** adv – **-driness** n

tawny /'tawni/ adj of a warm sandy or brownish orange colour like that of well-tanned skin

¹**tax** /taks/ v **1** to levy a tax on **2** to charge, accuse – with **3** to make strenuous demands on – ~**ability** n – ~**able** adj

²**tax** n a charge, usu of money, imposed by a government on individuals, organizations, or property, esp to raise revenue

taxation /tak'saysh(ə)n/ n **1** the action of taxing; esp the imposition of taxes **2** revenue obtained from taxes **3** the amount assessed as a tax

'**tax ,haven** n a country with a relatively low level of taxation, esp on incomes

¹**taxi** /'taksi/ n, pl **taxis** also **taxies** a motor car that may be hired to carry passengers short distances, esp in towns

²**taxi** v, **taxis**, **taxies**, **taxiing**, **taxying**; **taxied** of an aircraft to go at low speed along the surface of the ground or water

taxidermy /'taksi,duhmi/ n the art of preparing, stuffing, and mounting the skins of animals – **-mist** n

taxonomy /tak'sonəmi/ n (the study of the principles of) classification, specif of plants and animals according to their presumed natural relationships

TB n tuberculosis

'**T-,bone, T-bone steak** n a thick steak from the thin end of a beef sirloin containing a T-shaped bone

tea /tee/ n **1a** a shrub cultivated esp in China, Japan, and the E Indies **b** the leaves of a tea plant prepared for the market **2** an aromatic beverage prepared from tea leaves by infusion with boiling water **3a** refreshments including tea with sandwiches, cakes, etc served in the late afternoon **b** a late-afternoon or early-evening meal that is usu less substantial than the midday meal

tea cake n a round yeast-leavened (sweet) bread bun that often contains currants

teach /teech/ v **taught** /tawt/ **1** to provide instruction in **2** to guide the studies of **3** to impart the knowledge of **4** to instruct by precept, example, or experience

teacher /'teechə/ n sby whose occupation is teaching

'**teach-,in** n **1** an informally structured conference on a usu topical issue **2** an extended meeting for lectures, demonstrations, and discussions on a topic

teaching /'teeching/ n **1** the profession of a teacher **2** sthg taught; esp a doctrine

teaching hospital n a hospital that is affiliated to a medical school and provides medical students with the opportunity of gaining practical experience under supervision

teak /teek/ n (a tall E Indian tree with) hard yellowish brown wood used for furniture and shipbuilding

teal /teel/ *n pl* **teals**, *esp collectively* **teal** (any of several ducks related to) a small Old World dabbling duck the male of which has a distinctive green and chestnut head

¹**team** /teem/ *n* **1** two or more draught animals harnessed together **2** *sing or pl in constr* a group formed for work or activity: e g **2a** a group on 1 side (e g in a sporting contest or debate) **b** a crew, gang

²**team** *v* **1** to come together (as if) in a team – often + *up* **2** to form a harmonizing combination

'**team,work** /-,wuhk/ *n* mutual cooperation in a group enterprise

teapot /'tee,pot/ *n* a usu round pot with a lid, spout, and handle in which tea is brewed and from which it is served

¹**tear** /tia/ *n* **1** a drop of clear salty fluid secreted by the lachrymal gland that lubricates the eye and eyelids and is often shed as a result of grief or other emotion **2** a transparent drop of (hardened) fluid (e g resin) — **in tears** crying, weeping

²**tear** /tea/ *v* **tore** /taw/; **torn** /tawn/ **1a** to pull apart by force **b** to wound by tearing; lacerate **2** to move or act with violence, haste, or force — **tear a strip off** to rebuke angrily – *infml* — **tear into** to attack physically or verbally without restraint or caution — **tear one's hair** to experience or express grief, rage, desperation, or anxiety

³**tear** /tea/ *n* **1** damage from being torn – chiefly in *wear and tear* **2** a hole or flaw made by tearing

tearaway /'teara,way/ *n*, *Br* an unruly and reckless young person – *infml*

tear away *v* to remove (oneself or another) reluctantly

teardrop /'tia,drop/ *n* a tear

'**tearful** /-f(ə)l/ *adj* **1** flowing with or accompanied by tears **2** causing tears **3** inclined or about to cry – ~**ly** *adv* – ~**ness** *n*

tearoom /'tee,roohm/ *n* a restaurant where light refreshments are served

tear up /tea/ *v* **1** to tear into pieces **2** to cancel or annul, usu unilaterally

¹**tease** /teez/ *v* **1** to disentangle and straighten by combing or carding **2a** (to attempt to) disturb or annoy by persistently irritating or provoking **b** to persuade to acquiesce, esp by persistent small efforts; coax; *also* to obtain by repeated coaxing

²**tease** *n* sby or sthg that teases

teaser /'teezə/ *n* **1** a frustratingly difficult problem **2** sby who derives malicious pleasure from teasing

teaspoon /'tee,spoohn/ *n* a small spoon used esp for eating soft foods and stirring beverages – ~**ful** *n*

teat /teet/ *n* **1** a nipple **2** a small projection or a nib (e g on a mechanical part); *specif* a rubber mouthpiece with usu 2 or more holes in it, attached to the top of a baby's feeding bottle

'**tea ,towel** *n* a cloth for drying the dishes

tech /tek/ *n*, *Br* a technical school or college – *infml*

technical /'teknikl/ *adj* **1a** having special and usu practical knowledge, esp of a mechanical or scientific subject **b** marked by or characteristic of specialization **2** of a particular subject; *esp* of a practical subject organized on scientific principles – ~**ly** *adv*

technicality /,tekni'kaləti/ *n* sthg technical; *esp* a detail meaningful only to a specialist

technician /tek'nish(ə)n/ *n* **1** a specialist in the technical details of a subject or occupation **2** sby who has acquired the technique of an area of specialization (e g an art)

technique /tek'neek/ *n* **1** the manner in which an artist, performer, or athlete displays or manages the formal aspect of his/her skill **2a** a body of technical methods (e g in a craft or in scientific research) **b** a method of accomplishing a desired aim

technocracy /tek'nokrəsi/ *n* (management of society by) a body of technical experts; *also* a society so managed – chiefly *derog*

technology /tek'noləji/ *n* **1** (the theory and practice of) applied science **2** the totality of the means and knowledge used to provide objects necessary for human sustenance and comfort – **-gical** *adj* – **-gically** *adv* – **-gist** *n*

tec'tonics *n pl but sing or pl in constr* **1** the science or art of construction (e g of a building) **2** (a branch of geology concerned with) structural features, esp those connected with folding and faulting

'**teddy ,bear** *n* a stuffed toy bear

Te Deum /,tay 'dayəm, ,tee 'dee-/ *n pl* **Te Deums** a liturgical Christian hymn of praise to God

tedious /'teedi·əs/ *adj* tiresome because of length or dullness – ~**ly** *adv* – ~**ness** *n*

tedium /'teedi·əm/ *n* tediousness; *also* boredom

¹**tee** /tee/ *n* **1** sthg shaped like a capital T **2** a mark aimed at in various games (e g curling)

²**tee** *n* **1** a peg or a small mound used to raise a golf ball into position for striking at the beginning of play on a hole **2** the area from which a golf ball is struck at the beginning of play on a hole

³**tee** *v* to place (a ball) on a tee – often + *up*

¹**teem** /teem/ *v* **1** to abound in **2** to be present in large quantities

²**teem** *v* to rain hard

teenage /'teenayj/, **teenaged** /'teenayjd/ *adj* of or being people in their teens

teens /teenz/ *n pl* the numbers 13 to 19 inclusive; *specif* the years 13 to 19 in a lifetime

tee off /tee/ *v* to drive a golf ball from a tee; *broadly* to start

'**tee ,shirt** *n* a short-sleeved vest worn in place of a shirt

teeter /'teetə/ *v* to move unsteadily; wobble, waver

teeth /teeth/ *pl of* **tooth**

teethe /teedh/ *v* to cut sby one's teeth; grow teeth

'teething ,troubles *n pl* temporary problems occurring with new machinery or during the initial stages of an activity

teetotal /'tee'tohtl/ *adj* practising complete abstinence from alcoholic drinks – **~ler** *n*

telegram /'teligram/ *n* a message sent by telegraph and delivered as a written or typed note

'telegraph /'teligrahf, -graf/ *n* an apparatus or system for communicating at a distance, esp by making and breaking an electric circuit

²telegraph *v* 1 to send or communicate (as if) by telegraph 2 to make known by signs, esp unknowingly and in advance

telegraphese /,teligrah'feez, -gra-/ *n* the terse and abbreviated language characteristic of telegrams

telegraphic /,teli'grafik/ *adj* concise, terse – **~ally** *adv*

telepathy /tə'lepəthi/ *n* communication directly from one mind to another without use of the known senses – **-thic** *adj* – **-thically** *adv*

'telephone /'telifohn/ *n* 1 a device for reproducing sounds at a distance; *specif* one for converting sounds into electrical impulses for transmission, usu by wire, to a particular receiver 2 the system of communications that uses telephones

²telephone *v* to make a telephone call

telephonist /tə'lefənist/ *n, Br* a telephone switchboard operator

telephoto /'teli,fohtoh/ *adj* being a lens (system) designed to give enlarged images of distant objects

telephotography /,telifə'togrəfi/ *n* the photography of distant objects – **-phic** *adj*

teleprinter /'teli,printə/ *n* a typewriter keyboard that transmits telegraphic signals, a typewriting device activated by telegraphic signals, or a machine that combines both these functions

'telescope /'teliskohp/ *n* 1 a usu tubular optical instrument for viewing distant objects by means of the refraction of light rays through a lens or the reflection of light rays by a concave mirror 2 a radio telescope

²telescope *v* 1 to slide one part within another like the cylindrical sections of a hand telescope 2 to become compressed under impact 3 to become condensed or shortened

telescopic /,teli'skopik/ *adj* 1 suitable for seeing or magnifying distant objects 2 able to discern objects at a distance 3 having parts that telescope

televise /'teliviez/ *v* to broadcast (an event or film) by television

television /'telivizh(ə)n, –'--/ *n* 1 an electronic system of transmitting changing images together with sound by converting the images and sounds

into electrical signals 2 a television receiving set 3a the television broadcasting industry b a television broadcasting organization or station

telex /'teleks/ *n* a communications service involving teleprinters connected by wire through automatic exchanges; *also* a message by telex

tell /tel/ *v* told /tohld/ 1a to relate in detail; narrate b to give utterance to; express in words 2 to make known; divulge 3a to report to; inform; *also* to inform *on* b to assure emphatically 4 to order 5a to ascertain by observing b to distinguish, discriminate 6 to take effect 7 to serve as evidence or indication

teller /'telə/ *n* 1 sby who relates or communicates 2 sby who counts: e g 2a sby appointed to count votes b a member of a bank's staff concerned with the direct handling of money received or paid out

telling /'teling/ *adj* carrying great weight and producing a marked effect – **~ly** *adv*

tell off *v* 1 to number and set apart; *esp* to assign to a special duty 2 to reprimand

telltale /'tel,tayl/ *n* sby who spreads gossip or rumours; *esp* an informer

telly /'teli/ *n, chiefly Br* (a) television – *infml*

temerity /tə'merəti/ *n* unreasonable disregard for danger or opposition; *broadly* cheek, nerve

temp /temp/ *n* sby (e g a typist or secretary) employed temporarily – *infml* – **temp** *v*

'temper /'tempə/ *v* 1 to moderate (sthg harsh) *with* the addition of sthg less severe 2 to bring (esp steel) to the right degree of hardness by reheating (and quenching) after cooling 3 to strengthen the character of through hardship

²temper *n* 1 the state of a substance with respect to certain desired qualities (e g the degree of hardness or resilience given to steel by tempering) 2a a characteristic cast of mind or state of feeling b composure, equanimity c (proneness to displays of) an uncontrolled and often disproportionate rage

tempera /'tempərə/ *n* (a work produced by) a method of painting using pigment ground and mixed with an emulsion (e g of egg yolk and water)

temperament /'temprəmənt/ *n* 1a a person's peculiar or distinguishing mental or physical character b excessive sensitiveness or irritability 2 the modification of the musical intervals of the pure scale to produce a set of 12 fixed notes to the octave which enables a keyboard instrument to play in more than 1 key

temperamental /,temprə'mentl/ *adj* 1 of or arising from individual character or constitution 2a easily upset or irritated; liable to sudden changes of mood b unpredictable in behaviour or performance – **~ly** *adv*

temperance /'tempərəns/ *n* 1 moderation, self-restraint 2 abstinence from the use of alcoholic drink

temperate /'tempərət/ *adj* 1 moderate: e g **1a** not extreme or excessive **2a** abstemious in the consumption of alcohol **2a** having a moderate climate **b** found in or associated with a temperate climate

temperature /'temprəchə/ *n* **1a** degree of hotness or coldness as measured on an arbitrary scale (e g in degrees Celsius) **b** the degree of heat natural to the body of a living being **2** an abnormally high body heat

tempest /'tempist/ *n* **1** a violent storm **2a** tumult, uproar

tempestuous /tem'peschoo·əs/ *adj* turbulent, stormy – **~ly** *adv*

¹**temple** /'templ/ *n* **1** a building dedicated to worship among any of various ancient civilizations (e g the Egyptians, the Greeks, and the Romans) and present-day non-Christian religions (e g Hinduism and Buddhism) **2** a place devoted or dedicated to a specified purpose

²**temple** *n* the flattened space on either side of the forehead of some mammals (e g human beings)

tempo /'tempoh/ *n, pl* **tempi** /-pi/, **tempos** **1** the speed of a musical piece or passage indicated by any of a series of directions and often by an exact metronome marking **2** rate of motion or activity

temporal /'temp(ə)rəl/ *adj* **1** of time as opposed to eternity or space; *esp* transitory **2** of earthly life **3** of lay or secular concerns

¹**temporary** /'temp(ə)rəri, 'tempə,reri/ *adj* lasting for a limited time – **-arily** *adv* – **-ariness** *n*

²**temporary** *n* a temp

tempt /tempt/ *v* **1** to entice, esp to evil, by promise of pleasure or gain **2** to risk provoking the disfavour of **3a** to induce to do sthg **b** to cause to be strongly inclined **c** to appeal to; entice – **~er** *n* – **~ingly** *adv*

temptation /temp'taysh(ə)n/ *n* **1** tempting or being tempted, esp to evil **2** sthg tempting

ten /ten/ *n* **1** the number 10 **2** the tenth in a set or series **3** sthg having 10 parts or members or a denomination of 10 **4** the number occupying the position 2 to the left of the decimal point in the Arabic notation; *also, pl* this position – **tenth** *adj, n, pron, adv*

tenacious /tə'nayshəs/ *adj* **1** tending to stick or cling, esp to another substance **2a** persistent in maintaining or keeping to sthg valued as habitual **b** retentive – **~ly** *adv* – **~ness** *n* – **-city** *n*

tenant /'tenənt/ *n* **1** an occupant of lands or property of another; *specif* sby who rents or leases a house or flat from a landlord **2** an occupant, dweller – **tenant** *v*

¹**tend** /tend/ *v* to have charge of; take care of

²**tend** *v* **1** to move, direct, or develop one's course in a specified direction **2** to show an inclination or tendency – **+** *to, towards*, or *to* and an infinitive

tendency /'tendənsi/ *n* **1** a general trend or movement **2** an inclination or predisposition to some particular end, or towards a particular kind of thought or action

¹**tender** /'tendə/ *adj* **1** having a soft or yielding texture; easily broken, cut, or damaged **2a** physically weak **b** immature, young **3** fond, loving **4a** showing care **b** highly susceptible to impressions or emotions **5** gentle, mild **6a** sensitive to touch **b** sensitive to injury or insult – **~ly** *adv* – **~ness** *n*

²**tender** *n* **1a** a ship employed to attend other ships (e g to supply provisions) **b** a boat or small steamer for communication between shore and a larger ship **2** a vehicle attached to a locomotive for carrying a supply of fuel and water

³**tender** *v* **1** to make a bid **2** to present for acceptance

⁴**tender** *n* **1a** a formal esp written offer or bid for a contract **b** a public expression of willingness to buy not less than a specified number of shares at a fixed price from shareholders **2** sthg that may be offered in payment; *specif* money

'**tender,foot** /-,foot/ *n pl* **tenderfeet** /-,feet/ *also* **tenderfoots** an inexperienced beginner

,**tender'hearted** /-'hahtid/ *adj* easily moved to love, pity, or sorrow – **~ly** *adv* – **~ness** *n*

tenderloin /'tendə,loyn/ *n* a pork or beef fillet

tendon /'tendən/ *n* a tough cord or band of dense white fibrous connective tissue that connects a muscle with a bone or other part and transmits the force exerted by the muscle

tendril /'tendrəl/ *n* a slender spirally coiling sensitive organ that attaches a plant to its support

tenement /'tenəmənt/ *n* (a flat in) a large building; *esp* one meeting minimum standards and typically found in the poorer parts of a city

tenet /'tenət/ *n* a principle, belief, or doctrine; *esp* one held in common by members of an organization or group

tenner /'tenə/ *n, Br* a £10 note; *also* the sum of £10 – *infml*

tennis /'tenis/ *n* a singles or doubles game that is played with rackets and a light elastic ball on a flat court divided by a low net

tennis elbow *n* inflammation and pain of the elbow, usu resulting from excessive twisting movements of the hand

¹**tenon** /'tenən/ *n* a projecting part of a piece of material (e g wood) for insertion into a mortise

²**tenon** *v* **1** to unite by a tenon **2** to cut or fit for insertion in a mortise

'**tenon ,saw** *n* a woodworking saw that has a reinforced blade and is used for making fine cuts

tenor /'tenə/ *n* **1** the course of thought of sthg spoken or written **2a** (sby with) the highest natural adult male singing voice **b** a member of a family of instruments having a range next lower than that of the alto **3** a continuance in a course or activity

,tenpin 'bowling *n* an indoor bowling game using 10 pins and a large ball

¹**tense** /tens/ *n* (a member of) a set of inflectional forms of a verb that express distinctions of time

²**tense** *adj* 1 stretched tight; made taut 2a feeling or showing nervous tension **b** marked by strain or suspense – ~ly *adv* – ~ness *n*

³**tense** *v* to make or become tense – often + *up*

tensile /'tensiel/ *adj* 1 ductile 2 of or involving tension

¹**tension** /'tenshən/ *n* 1a stretching or being stretched to stiffness **b** stress 2 either of 2 balancing forces causing or tending to cause extension 3a inner striving, unrest, or imbalance, often with physiological indication of emotion **b** latent hostility **c** a balance maintained in an artistic work between opposing forces or elements

²**tension** *v* to tighten to a desired or appropriate degree

tent /tent/ *n* 1 a collapsible shelter (e g of canvas) stretched and supported by poles 2 a canopy or enclosure placed over the head and shoulders to retain vapours or oxygen during medical treatment

tentacle /'tentəkl/ *n* any of various elongated flexible animal parts, chiefly on the head or about the mouth, used for feeling, grasping, etc

tentative /'tentətiv/ *adj* 1 not fully worked out or developed 2 hesitant, uncertain – ~ly *adv* – ~ness *n*

tenuous /'tenyoo·əs/ *adj* 1 not dense in consistency 2 not thick 3 having little substance or strength – ~ly *adv* – ~ness *n*

tenure /'tenyə/ *n* 1 the holding of property, an office, etc 2 freedom from summary dismissal, esp from a teaching post

tepee /'tee,pee/ *n* a N American Indian conical tent, usu made of skins

tepid /'tepid/ *adj* 1 moderately warm 2 not enthusiastic – ~ity *n* – ~ly *adv* – ~ness *n*

¹**term** /tuhm/ *n* 1a an end, termination; *also* a time assigned for sthg (e g payment) **b** the time at which a pregnancy of normal length ends 2a a limited or definite extent of time; *esp* the time for which sthg lasts **b** any one of the periods of the year during which the courts are in session **c** any of the usu 3 periods of instruction into which an academic year is divided 3 an expression that forms part of a fraction or proportion or of a series or sequence 4 a word or expression with a precise meaning; *esp* one peculiar to a restricted field 5 *pl* provisions relating to an agreement; *also* agreement on such provisions 6 *pl* mutual relationship — **in terms** expressly, explicitly — **in terms of** in relation to; concerning

²**term** *v* to apply a term to; call

termagant /'tuhməgənt/ *n* an overbearing or nagging woman

¹**terminal** /'tuhminl/ *adj* 1a of or being an end, extremity, boundary, or terminus **b** growing at the end of a branch or stem 2a of or occurring in a term or each term **b** occurring at or causing the end of life 3 occurring at or being the end of a period or series – ~ly *adv*

²**terminal** *n* 1a a device attached to the end of a wire or cable or to an electrical apparatus for convenience in making connections 2 the end of a carrier line (e g shipping line or airline) with its associated buildings and facilities 3 a device (e g a teleprinter) through which a user can communicate with a computer

terminate /'tuhminayt/ *v* 1 to bring to an end; form the conclusion of 2 to come to an end in time; form an ending or outcome – often + *in* or *with* – -**ation** *n*

terminology /,tuhmi'noləji/ *n* the technical terms used in a particular subject – -**ogical** *adj* – -**ogically** *adv*

terminus /'tuhminəs/ *n, pl* **termini** /-nie/, **terminuses** 1 a finishing point; an end 2 a post or stone marking a boundary 3 (the station, town, or city at) the end of a transport line or travel route

termite /'tuh,miet/ *n* any of numerous often destructive pale-coloured soft-bodied insects that live in colonies and feed on wood

tern /tuhn/ *n* any of numerous water birds that are smaller than the related gulls

terrace /'teris/ *n* 1 a relatively level paved or planted area adjoining a building 2 a raised embankment with a level top 3a a row of houses or flats on raised ground or a sloping site **b** a row of similar houses joined into 1 building by common walls

terracotta /,terə'kotə/ *n* 1 an unglazed brownish red fired clay used esp for statuettes and vases and as a building material 2 brownish orange

,terra 'firma /'fuhmə/ *n* dry land; solid ground

terrain /tə'rayn/ *n* 1 (the physical features of) an area of land 2 an environment, milieu

terrapin /'terəpin/ *n* any of several small edible freshwater reptiles of the same order as, and similar to, tortoises but adapted for swimming

terrestrial /tə'restri·əl/ *adj* 1a of the earth or its inhabitants **b** mundane, prosaic 2a of land as distinct from air or water **b** *of organisms* living on or in land or soil – ~ly *adv*

terrible /'terəbl/ *adj* 1a exciting intense fear; terrifying **b** formidable in nature **c** requiring great fortitude; *also* severe 2 extreme, great 3 of very poor quality; awful; *also* highly unpleasant *USE* (2&3) *infml*

terribly /'terəbli/ *adv* very – *infml*

terrier /'teri·ə/ *n* (a member of) any of various breeds of usu small dogs, orig used by hunters to drive out small furred game from underground

terrific /tə'rifik/ adj 1 exciting fear or awe 2 extraordinarily great or intense 3 unusually fine – ~ally adv USE (2&3) infml

terrify /'terifie/ v 1 to fill with terror or apprehension 2 to drive or impel by menacing; scare, deter – ~ingly adv

territorial /,teri'tawri-əl/ adj 1a of territory or land b of private property 2 of or restricted to a particular area or district

terri,torial 'army n a voluntary force organized by a locality to provide a trained army reserve that can be mobilized in an emergency

terri,torial 'waters n pl the waters under the sovereign jurisdiction of a nation

territory /'territ(ə)ri/ n 1a a geographical area under the jurisdiction of a government b an administrative subdivision of a country 2a a geographical area; esp one having a specified characteristic b a field of knowledge or interest 3a an assigned area; esp one in which an agent or distributor operates b an area, often including a nesting site or den, occupied and defended by an animal or group of animals

terror /'terə/ n 1 a state of intense fear 2 sby or sthg that inspires fear 3 revolutionary violence (e g the planting of bombs) 4 an appalling person or thing; esp a brat – infml

terrorism /'terə,riz(ə)m/ n the systematic use of terror, esp as a means of coercion – **-ist** adj, n – **-ize** v

'terror-,stricken adj overcome with an uncontrollable terror

terse /tuhs/ adj concise; also brusque, curt – ~ly adv – ~ness n

tertiary /'tuhshəri/ adj 1a of third rank, importance, or value b of higher education c of or being a service industry 2 occurring in or being a third stage

tessellated /'tesə,laytid/ adj chequered

'test /test/ n 1a a critical examination, observation, or evaluation b a basis for evaluation 2a a procedure used to identify a substance b a series of questions or exercises for measuring the knowledge, intelligence, etc of an individual or group c a test match

'test v 1 to put to the test; try 2 to apply a test as a means of analysis or diagnosis – often + for – ~er n

'test n an external hard or firm covering (e g a shell) of an invertebrate (e g a mollusc)

testa /'testə/ n, pl testae /'testi/ the hard external coat of a seed

testament /'testəmənt/ n 1 cap either of the 2 main divisions of the Bible 2 a tangible proof or tribute 3 a will – ~ary adj

testate /'testayt/ adj having made a valid will

testator /te'staytə/, fem testatrix /te'staytriks/ n sby who leaves a will

'test ,ban n a self-imposed ban on the atmospheric testing of nuclear weapons

'test ,case n a representative case whose outcome is likely to serve as a precedent

testicle /'testikl/ n a testis, esp of a mammal and usu with its enclosing structures (e g the scrotum)

testify /'testifie/ v 1a to make a statement based on personal knowledge or belief b to serve as evidence or proof 2a to make a solemn declaration under oath b to make known (a personal conviction)

'testimonial /,testi'mohnyəl, -ni-əl/ adj 1 of or constituting testimony 2 expressive of appreciation, gratitude, or esteem

'testimonial n 1 a letter of recommendation 2 an expression of appreciation or esteem (e g in the form of a gift)

testimony /'testiməni/ n 1a firsthand authentication of a fact b an outward sign; evidence c a sworn statement by a witness 2 a public declaration of religious experience

testis /'testis/ n, pl testes /'testeez/ a male reproductive gland

'test ,match n any of a series of international (cricket) matches

'test ,pilot n a pilot who specializes in putting new or experimental aircraft through manoeuvres designed to test them

'test-,tube adj, of a baby conceived by artificial insemination, esp outside the mother's body

'test ,tube n a thin glass tube closed at 1 end and used in chemistry, biology, etc

testy /'testi/ adj impatient, ill-humoured – **-tily** adv – **-tiness** n

tetanus /'tet(ə)nəs/ n (the bacterium, usu introduced through a wound, that causes) an infectious disease characterized by spasm of voluntary muscles, esp of the jaw

'tête-à-tête /,tet ah 'tet, tayt ah atayt/ adv or adj (in) private

'tête-à-tête n 1 a private conversation between 2 people 2 a seat (e g a sofa) designed for 2 people to sit facing each other

'tether /'tedhə/ n 1 a rope, chain, etc by which an animal is fastened so that it can move only within a set radius 2 the limit of one's strength or resources – chiefly in the end of one's tether

'tether v to fasten or restrain (as if) by a tether

tetrahedron /,tetrə'heedrən/ n, pl tetrahedrons, tetrahedra /-drə/ a polyhedron of 4 faces

Teutonic /tyooh'tonik/ n or adj Germanic

text /tekst/ n 1 (a work containing) the original written or printed words and form of a literary composition 2 the main body of printed or written matter, esp on a page or in a book 3a a passage of Scripture chosen esp for the subject of a sermon or in authoritative support of a doctrine b a passage from an authoritative source providing a theme (e g for a speech)

¹**'text,book** /-,book/ *n* a book used in the study of a subject; *specif* one containing a presentation of the principles of a subject and used by students

²**textbook** *adj* conforming to the principles or descriptions in textbooks: e g a **ideal** b typical

textile /'tekstiel/ *n* 1 a (woven or knitted) cloth 2 a fibre, filament, or yarn used in making cloth

¹**texture** /'tekschə/ *n* 1 identifying quality; character 2a the size or organization of the constituent particles of a body or substance b the visual or tactile surface characteristics of sthg, esp fabric 3 the distinctive or identifying part or quality

²**texture** *v* to give a particular texture to

thalidomide /thə'lidəmied/ *adj or n* (of or affected by) a sedative and hypnotic drug found to cause malformation of infants born to mothers using it during pregnancy

¹**than** /dhan; *strong* dhan/ *conj* 1a – used with comparatives to indicate the second member or the member taken as the point of departure in a comparison (e g older *than* I am) b – used to indicate difference of kind, manner, or degree (e g would starve rather *than* beg) 2 rather than – usu only after *prefer, preferable* 3 other than; but (e g no alternative *than* to sack) 4 *chiefly NAm* from – usu only after *different, differently*

²**than** *prep* in comparison with

thane *also* **thegn** /thayn/ *n* 1 a free retainer of an Anglo-Saxon lord; *esp* one holding lands in exchange for military service 2 a Scottish feudal lord

thank /thangk/ *v* 1 to express gratitude to – used in *thank you*, usu without a subject, to express gratitude politely; used in such phrases as *thank God, thank heaven*, usu without a subject, to express the speaker's or writer's pleasure or satisfaction in sthg 2 to hold responsible

thankful /'thangkf(ə)l/ *adj* 1 conscious of benefit received; grateful 2 feeling or expressing thanks 3 well pleased; glad – ~**ly** *adv* – ~**ness** *n*

thankless /'thangklis/ *adj* 1 not expressing or feeling gratitude 2 not likely to obtain thanks; unappreciated; *also* unprofitable, futile – ~**ly** *adv* – ~**ness** *n*

thanks *n pl* 1 kindly or grateful thoughts; gratitude 2 an expression of gratitude – often in an utterance containing no verb and serving as a courteous and somewhat informal expression of gratitude — **no thanks to** not as a result of any benefit conferred by — **thanks to 1** with the help of 2 owing to

thanksgiving /thangks'giving, '—/ *n* an expression of gratefulness, esp to God

'thank-,you *n* a polite expression of one's gratitude

¹**that** /dhat/ *pron, pl* **those** /dhohz/ 1a the thing or idea just mentioned (e g after *that* we went to bed) b a relatively distant person or thing introduced for observation or discussion (e g who's *that?*) c the thing or state of affairs there (e g look at *that*) – sometimes used disparagingly of a person d the kind or thing specified as follows (e g the purest water is *that* produced by distillation) e what is understood from the context (e g take *that!*) 2 one of such a group; such (e g *that's* life) 3 – used to indicate emphatic repetition of an idea previously presented (e g is he capable? He is *that*) 4 *pl* the people; such (e g *those* who think the time has come)

²**that** *adj, pl* **those** 1 being the person, thing, or idea specified, mentioned, or understood (e g *that* cake we bought) 2 the farther away or less immediately under observation (e g this chair or *that* one)

³**that** /dhət; *strong* dhat/ *conj* 1 – used to introduce a noun clause as subject, object, or complement (e g said *that* we he afraid; the fact *that* you're here) 2 – used to introduce a subordinate clause expressing (1) purpose, (2) reason, or (3) result (e g worked harder *that* he might win; glad *that* you are free of it)

⁴**that** /dhət; *strong* dhat/ *pron* 1 – used to introduce some relative clauses (e g it was George *that* told me; the house *that* Jack built) or as object of a verb or of a following preposition 2a at, in, on, by, with, for, or to which (e g the reason *that* he came; the way *that* he spoke) b according to what; to the extent of what – used after a negative (e g has never been there *that* I know of)

⁵**that** /dhat/ *adv* 1 to the extent indicated or understood (e g a nail about *that* long) 2 very, extremely – usu with the negative (e g not really *that* expensive) 3 *dial Br* to such an extreme degree (e g I'm *that* hungry I could eat a horse)

¹**thatch** /thach/ *v* to cover (as if) with thatch

²**thatch** *n* 1 plant material (e g straw) used as a roof covering 2 the hair of one's head; *broadly* anything resembling the thatch of a house

¹**thaw** /thaw/ *v* 1a to go from a frozen to a liquid state b to become free of the effect (e g stiffness, numbness, or hardness) of cold as a result of exposure to warmth – often + *out* 2 to be warm enough to melt ice and snow – used in reference to the weather 3 to become less hostile 4 to become less aloof, cold, or reserved

²**thaw** *n* 1 the action, fact, or process of thawing 2 a period of weather warm enough to thaw ice

¹**the** /*before consonants* dhə; *strong and before vowels* dhee/ *definite article* 1 – used before nouns when the referent has been previously specified by context or circumstance (e g put *the* cat out; ordered bread and cheese, but didn't eat *the* cheese) b – indicating that a following noun is unique or universally recognized (e g *the* Pope; *the* south) c – used before certain proper names (e g *the* Rhine; *the* MacDonald) d – designating 1 of a class as the best or most worth singling out (e g you can't be *the* Elvis Presley) e – used before the pl form of a number that is a multiple of 10 to

denote a particular decade of a century or of a person's life (e g life *in the* twenties) **2** – used before a singular noun to indicate generic use (e g a history *of the* novel) **3a** that which is (e g nothing but *the* best) **b** those who are (e g *the* élite) **c** he or she who is (e g *the* accused stands before you) **4** – used after *how, what, where, who,* and *why* to introduce various expletives (e g who *the* devil are you?)

²the *adv* **1** than before; than otherwise – with comparatives (e g so much *the* worse) **2a** to what extent (e g *the* sooner the better) **b** to that extent (e g *the* sooner the better) **3** beyond all others – with superlatives (e g likes this *the* best)

³the *prep* per (e g 50p *the* dozen)

theatre, *NAm chiefly* **theater** /'thiatə/ *n* **1** a building for dramatic performances **2** a room with rising tiers of seats (e g for lectures) **3** a place of enactment of significant events or action **4** *the* theatrical world **5** *Br* an operating theatre

theatrical /thi'atrikl/ *adj* **1** of the theatre or the presentation of plays **2** marked by artificiality (e g of emotion) **3** marked by exhibitionism; histrionic – ~**ly** *adv*

the'atricals *n pl* the performance of plays

thee /dhee/ *pron, archaic or dial* **1a** *objective case of* **thou 2** thyself

theft /theft/ *n* the act of stealing; *specif* dishonest appropriation of property with the intention of keeping it

their /dhə; *strong* dhea/ *adj* **1** of them or themselves, esp as possessors, agents, or objects of an action **2** his or her; his, her, its *USE* used attributively

theirs /dheaz/ *pron, pl* **theirs 1** that which or the one who belongs to them – used without a following noun as a pronoun equivalent in meaning to the adjective *their* **2** his or hers; his, hers

theism /'thee,iz(ə)m/ *n* belief in the existence of a creator god everywhere in the universe but transcending it – **-ist** *n* – **-istic** *adj* – **-istically** *adv*

¹them /dhəm; *strong* dhem/ *pron, objective case of* **they**

²them /dhem/ *adj* those – nonstandard

theme /theem/ *n* **1** a subject of artistic representation or a topic of discourse **2** a melodic subject of a musical composition or movement

themselves /dhəm'selvz/ *pron pl in constr* **1a** those identical people, creatures, or things that are they – used reflexively or for emphasis **b** himself or herself; himself, herself (e g hoped nobody would hurt *themselves*) **2** their normal selves (e g soon be *themselves* again)

¹then /dhen/ *adv* **1** at that time **2a** soon after that; next in order (of time) **b** besides; in addition **3a** in that case **b** as may be inferred (e g your mind is made up *then*?) **c** accordingly, so – indicating casual connection in speech or writing (e g our hero, *then*, was greatly relieved) **d** as a necessary consequence **e** – used after *but* to offset a preceding statement (e g he lost the race, but *then* he never expected to win)

²then *n* that time

³then *adj* existing or acting at that time (e g the *then* secretary of state)

thence /dhens/ *adv* **1** from there **2** from that preceding fact or premise – chiefly fml

thence'forth /-'fawth/ *adv* from that time or point on – chiefly fml

theocracy /thi'okrəsi/ *n* (a state having) government by immediate divine guidance or by officials regarded as divinely guided – **-cratic** *adj*

theodolite /thi'od(ə)l,iet/ *n* a surveyor's instrument for measuring horizontal and usu also vertical angles

theology /thi'oləji/ *n* **1** the study of God, esp by analysis of the origins and teachings of an organized religion **2** a theological theory, system, or body of opinion – **-ogical** *adj* – **-ogically** *adv* – **-ogian** *n*

theorem /'thiərəm, 'thee-ərəm/ *n* **1** a proposition in mathematics or logic deducible from other more basic propositions **2** an idea proposed as a demonstrable truth, often as a part of a general theory; a proposition

theoretical /thiə'retikl, ,thee-ə-/ *also* **theoretic** /thiə'retik, ,thee-ə-/ *adj* **1a** relating to or having the character of theory; abstract **b** confined to theory or speculation; speculative **2** existing only in theory; hypothetical – ~**ly** *adv*

theorist /'thiərist, 'thee-ə-/ *n* a theoretician

theory /'thiəri, 'thee-ə-/ *n* **1a** a belief, policy, or procedure forming the basis for action **b** an ideal or supposed set of facts, principles, or circumstances – often in *in theory* **2** the general or abstract principles of a subject **3** a scientifically acceptable body of principles offered to explain a phenomenon **4a** a hypothesis assumed for the sake of argument or investigation **b** an unproved assumption; a conjecture – **-rize** *v*

therapeutic /therə'pyoohtik/ *adj* of the treatment of disease or disorders by remedial agents or methods – ~**ally** *adv*

therapist /'therəpist/ *n* sby trained in methods of treatment and rehabilitation other than the use of drugs or surgery

therapy /'therəpi/ *n* therapeutic treatment of bodily, mental, or social disorders

¹there /dhea/ *adv* **1** in or at that place – often used to draw attention or to replace a name **2** thither **3a** now (e g *there* goes the hooter) **b** at or in that point or particular (e g *there* is where I disagree with you) **4** – used interjectionally to express satisfaction, approval, encouragement, or defiance — **there and back** for a round trip — **there it is** such is the unfortunate fact — **there's a** — used when urging a course of action — **there you are 1** here you are **2** I told you so

²there *pron* – used to introduce a sentence or clause expressing the idea of existence (e g *there* shall come a time)

³there *n* that place or point

⁴there *adj* – used for emphasis, esp after a demonstrative (e g those men *there* can tell you)

thereabouts /ˌdheərə'bowts/, *NAm also* **therea'bout** *adv* **1** in that vicinity **2** near that time, number, degree, or quantity

thereafter /dheə'rahftə/ *adv* after that

thereby /dheə'bie/ *adv* **1** by that means; resulting from which **2** in which connection (e g thereby hangs a tale)

therefore /'-,-; *also* ,-'-/ *adv* **1** for that reason; to that end **2** by virtue of that; consequently (e g I was tired and *therefore* irritable) **3** as this proves (e g I think *therefore* I exist)

therein /dheə'rin/ *adv* in that; *esp* in that respect – fml

therm /thuhm/ *n* a quantity of heat equal to 100,000Btu (about 105,506MJ)

¹thermal /'thuhml/ *adj* **1 thermal, thermic** of or caused by heat **2** designed (e g with insulating air spaces) to prevent the dissipation of body heat

²thermal *n* a rising body of warm air

thermodynamics /ˌthuhmohdie'namiks, -di-/ *n pl but sing or pl in constr* (physics that deals with) the mechanical action of, or relations between, heat and other forms of energy

thermometer /thə'momitə/ *n* an instrument for determining temperature; *esp* a glass bulb attached to a fine graduated tube of glass and containing a liquid (e g mercury) that rises and falls with changes of temperature

thermonuclear /ˌthuhmoh'nyoohkli·ə/ *adj* of, using, or being (weapons using) transformations occurring in the nucleus of low atomic weight atoms (e g hydrogen) at very high temperatures

Thermos *trademark* – used for an insulated flask used for keeping liquids, etc hot or cold

thermostat /'thuhmə,stat/ *n* an automatic device for regulating temperature

thesaurus /thi'sawrəs, 'thesərəs/ *n, pl* **thesauri** /-rie, -ri/, **thesauruses** a book of words or of information about a particular field or set of concepts; *esp* a book of words and their synonyms

these /dheez/ *pl of* this

thesis /'theesis/ *n, pl* **theses** /-,seez/ **1** a proposition to be proved or one advanced without proof; a hypothesis **2** the first stage of a reasoned argument presenting the case **3** a dissertation embodying the results of original research; *specif* one submitted for a doctorate in Britain

they /dhay/ *pron pl in constr* **1a** those people, creatures, or things; *also, chiefly Br* that group **b** he (e g if anyone have found it, *they* will hand it in) **2a** people (e g *they* say that there's no truth in it) **b** the authorities

they'd /dhayd/ they had; they would

¹thick /thik/ *adj* **1a** having or being of relatively great depth or extent between opposite surfaces **b** of comparatively large diameter in relation to length **2a** closely-packed; dense **b** great in number **c** viscous in consistency **d** foggy or misty **3a** imperfectly articulated **b** plainly apparent; marked **4a** sluggish, dull **b** obtuse, stupid **5** on close terms; intimate **6** unreasonable, unfair *USE* (4, 5, & 6) infml – ~**ly** *adv*

²thick *n* **1** the most crowded or active part **2** the part of greatest thickness

thicket /'thikit/ *n* a dense growth of shrubbery or small trees

thickness /'thiknis/ *n* **1** the smallest of the 3 dimensions of a solid object **2** the thick part of sthg **3** a layer, ply

thickset /thik'set/ *adj* **1** closely placed; *also* growing thickly **2** heavily built; burly

thick-skinned *adj* callous, insensitive

thief /theef/ *n, pl* **thieves** /theevz/ sby who steals, esp secretly and without violence

thieve /theev/ *v* to steal, rob – ~**ving** *n, adj* – ~**vish** *adj* – ~**vishly** *adv* – ~**vishness** *n*

thigh /thie/ *n* the segment of the vertebrate hind limb nearest the body that extends from the hip to the knee and is supported by a single large bone

thimble /'thimbl/ *n* **1** a pitted metal or plastic cap or cover worn to protect the finger and to push the needle in sewing **2** a movable ring, tube, or lining in a hole

¹thin /thin/ *adj* -**nn-** **1a** having little depth between opposite surfaces **b** measuring little in cross section **2** not dense or closely-packed **3** without much flesh; lean **4a** more rarefied than normal **b** few in number **5** lacking substance or strength **6** flimsy, unconvincing **7** somewhat feeble and lacking in resonance **8** lacking in intensity or brilliance **9** disappointingly poor or hard – ~**ly** *adv* – ~**ness** *n* — **thin end of the wedge** sthg apparently insignificant that is the forerunner of a more important development

²thin *v* -**nn-** **1** to reduce in thickness or depth; attenuate **2** to reduce in strength or density **3** to reduce in number or bulk

¹thine /dhien/ *adj, archaic* thy – used esp before a vowel or *h*

²thine *pron, pl* **thine** *archaic or dial* that which belongs to thee – used without a following noun as a pronoun equivalent in meaning to the adjective *thy*

thing /thing/ *n* **1a** a matter, affair, concern **b** an event, circumstance **2a(1)** a deed, act, achievement **a(2)** an activity, action **b** a product of work or activity **c** the aim of effort or activity **d** sthg necessary or desirable **3a** a separate and distinct object of thought (e g a quality, fact, or idea) **b** an inanimate object as distinguished from a living being **c** *pl* imaginary objects or entities **4a** *pl* possessions, effects **b** an article of clothing **c** *pl* equipment or utensils, esp for a particular purpose **5** an object or entity not (capable of being) precisely designated **6** *the* proper or fashionable way of behaving, talking, or dressing **7a** a preoccupation (e g a mild obsession or phobia) of a specified type **b** an intimate relationship; *esp* a love affair

¹**think** /thingk/ *v* **thought** /thawt/ **1a** to exercise the powers of judgment, conception, or inference **b** to have in mind or call to mind a thought or idea – usu + *of* **2** to have as an opinion; consider **3a** to reflect on – often + *over* **b** to determine by reflecting – often + *out* **c** to have the mind engaged in reflection – usu + *of* or *about* **4** to call to mind; remember **5** to devise by thinking – usu + *up* **6** to have as an expectation **7** to subject to the processes of logical thought – usu + *out* or *through* – ~**er** *n*

²**think** *n* an act of thinking – infml

¹**thinking** /'thingking/ *n* **1** the action of using one's mind to produce thoughts **2** opinion that is characteristic (e g of a period, group, or individual) — **put/have on one's thinking cap** to ponder or reflect on sthg

²**thinking** *adj* marked by use of the intellect

'**think ,tank** *n sing or pl in constr* a group of people formed as a consultative body to evolve new ideas and offer expert advice

thinner /'thinə/ *n* liquid (e g turpentine) used esp to thin paint

,**thin-'skinned** *adj* unduly susceptible to criticism or insult

¹**third** /thuhd/ *adj* **1a** next after the second in place or time **b** ranking next to second in authority or precedence **2a** being any of 3 equal parts into which sthg is divisible **b** being the last in each group of 3 in a series

²**third** *n* **1a** number three in a countable series **b** sthg or sby that is next after second in rank, position, authority, or precedence **c third, third class** *often cap* the third and usu lowest level of British honours degree **2** any of 3 equal parts of sthg **3** (the combination of 2 notes at) a musical interval of 3 diatonic degrees

,**third de'gree** *n* the subjection of a prisoner to torture to obtain information

,**third-'party** *adj* of insurance covering loss or damage sustained by sby other than the insured

,**third 'party** *n* sby other than the principals

,**third 'person** *n* a set of linguistic forms (e g verb forms or pronouns) referring neither to the speaker or writer of the utterance in which they occur nor to the one to whom that utterance is addressed

,**third-'rate** *adj* third in quality or value; *broadly* of extremely poor quality

,**third 'world** *n, often cap T&W, sing or pl in constr* **1** a group of nations, esp in Africa and Asia, that are not aligned with either the communist or the capitalist blocs **2** the underdeveloped nations of the world

¹**thirst** /thuhst/ *n* **1** (the sensation of dryness in the mouth and throat associated with) a desire or need to drink **2** an ardent desire; a craving

²**thirst** *v* **1** to feel thirsty **2** to crave eagerly

thirsty /'thuhsti/ *adj* **1a** feeling thirst **b** deficient in moisture; parched **2** having a strong desire; avid – **thirstily** *adv*

thirteen /thuh'teen/ *n* the number 13 – ~**th** *adj, pron, adv*

thirty /'thuhti/ *n* **1** the number 30 **2** *pl* the numbers 30 to 39; *specif* a range of temperatures, ages, or dates in a century characterized by these numbers – **-tieth** *adj, n, pron, adv*

¹**this** /dhis/ *pron, pl* **these** /dheez/ **1a** the thing or idea that has just been mentioned **b** what is to be shown or stated (e g do it like *this*) **c** this time or place **2a** a nearby person or thing introduced for observation or discussion **b** the thing or state of affairs here (e g what's all *this*?; please carry *this*)

²**this** *adj, pl* **these 1a** being the person, thing, or idea that is present or near in time or thought (e g early *this* morning; who's *this* Mrs Fogg anyway?) **b** the nearer at hand or more immediately under observation (e g *this* chair or that one) **c** constituting the immediate past or future period (e g have lived here *these* 10 years) **d** constituting what is to be shown or stated (e g have you heard *this* one?) **2** a certain (e g there was *this* Irishman ...)

³**this** *adv* **1** to this extent (e g known her since she was *this* high) **2** to this extreme degree – usu + the negative (e g didn't expect to wait *this* long)

thistle /'thisl/ *n* any of various prickly composite plants with (showy) heads of mostly tubular flowers – **thistly** *adv*

thistledown /'thisl,down/ *n* the fluffy hairs from the ripe flower head of a thistle

thither /'dhidhə/ *adv* to or towards that place – chiefly *fml*

thong /thong/ *n* a narrow strip, esp of leather

thorax /'thaw,raks/ *n, pl* **thoraxes, thoraces** /'thawrə,seez/ (a division of the body of an insect, spider, etc corresponding to) the part of the mammalian body between the neck and the abdomen; *also* its cavity in which the heart and lungs lie

thorn /thawn/ *n* **1** a woody plant (of the rose family) bearing sharp prickles of thorns **2** a short hard sharp-pointed plant part, *specif* a leafless branch **3** sby or sthg that causes irritation

thorny /'thawni/ *adj* **1** full of or covered in thorns **2** full of difficulties or controversial points – **thorniness** *n*

thorough /'thurə/ *adj* **1** marked by full detail **2** painstaking **3** being fully and without qualification as specified – ~**ly** *adv*

¹'thorough,bred /-,bred/ *adj* having the characteristics associated with good breeding or pedigree

²thoroughbred *n cap* any of an English breed of horses kept chiefly for racing

'thorough,fare /-,fea/ *n* **1** a public way (e g a road, street, or path); *esp* a main road **2** passage, transit

'thorough,going /-,goh·ing/ *adj* **1** extremely thorough or zealous **2** absolute, utter

those /dhohz/ *pl of* ¹,²**that**

¹thou /dhow/ *pron, archaic or dial* the one being addressed; you

²thou /thow/ *n, pl* **thou, thous 1** a thousand (of sthg, esp money) **2** a unit of length equal to $\frac{1}{1000}$in (about 0.0254mm)

¹though *also* **tho** /dhoh/ *adv* however, nevertheless

²though *also* **tho** *conj* **1** in spite of the fact that; while **2** in spite of the possibility that; even if **3** and yet; but

¹thought /thawt/ *past of* **think**

²thought *n* **1a** thinking **b** serious consideration **2** reasoning or conceptual power **3a** an idea, opinion, concept, or intention **b** the intellectual product or the organized views of a period, place, group, or individual

'thoughtful /-f(ə)l/ *adj* **1a** having thoughts; absorbed in thought **b** showing careful reasoned thinking **2** showing concern for others – ~**ly** *adv* – ~**ness** *n*

'thoughtless /-lis/ *adj* **1** lacking forethought; rash **2** lacking concern for others – ~**ly** *adv* – ~**ness** *n*

thousand /'thowz(ə)nd/ *n, pl* **thousands, thousand 1** the number 1,000 **2** the number occupying the position **4** to the left of the decimal point in the Arabic notation; *also, pl* this position **3** an indefinitely large number – often *pl with sing. meaning* – ~**th** *adj, n, pron, adv*

thrall /thrawl/ *n* a state of complete absorption or enslavement – **thralldom** *n*

¹thrash /thrash/ *v* **1** to thresh **2a** to beat soundly (as if) with a stick or whip **b** to defeat heavily or decisively **3** to move or stir about violently; toss about – usu + *around* or *about*

²thrash *n* **1** an act of thrashing, esp in swimming **2** a wild party – *infml*

thrash out *v* to discuss (e g a problem) exhaustively with a view to finding a solution; *also* to arrive at (e g a decision) in this way

thread /thred/ *n* **1** a filament, group of filaments twisted together, or continuous strand (formed by spinning and twisting together short textile fibres) **2a** sthg (e g a thin stream of liquid) like a thread in length and narrowness **b** a projecting spiral ridge (e g on a bolt or pipe) by which parts

can be screwed together **3** sthg continuous or drawn out: e g **3a** a train of thought **b** a pervasive recurring element **4** a precarious or weak support

²thread *v* **1a** to pass a thread through the eye of (a needle) **b** to arrange a thread, yarn, or lead-in piece in working position for use in (a machine) **2a(1)** to pass sthg through the entire length of **a(2)** to pass (e g a tape or film) into or through sthg **b** to make one's way cautiously through or between **3** to string together (as if) on a thread

threadbare /'thred,bea/ *adj* **1** having the nap worn off so that the threads show; worn, shabby **2** hackneyed

threat /thret/ *n* **1** an indication of sthg, usu unpleasant, to come **2** an expression of intention to inflict punishment, injury, or damage **3** sthg that is a source of imminent danger or harm

threaten /'thret(ə)n/ *v* **1** to utter threats against **2a** to give ominous signs of **b** to be a source of harm or danger to **3** to announce as intended or possible – ~**ingly** *adv*

three /three/ *n* **1** the number 3 **2** the third in a set or series **3** sthg having 3 parts or members or a denomination of 3

,three-di'mensional *adj* **1** having 3 dimensions **2** giving the illusion of depth – used of an image or pictorial representation, esp when this illusion is enhanced by stereoscopic means

three-line whip *n* an instruction from a party to its Members of Parliament that they must attend a debate and vote in the specified way

,three-'quarter *adj* **1** consisting of 3 fourths of the whole **2** *esp of a view of a rectangular object* including 1 side and 1 end

,three 'R's *n pl* the fundamentals taught in primary school; *esp* reading, writing, and arithmetic

threnody /'threnadi, 'three-/ *n* a song of lamentation, esp for the dead

thresh /thresh/ *v* **1** to separate the seeds from (a harvested plant) by (mechanical) beating **2** to strike repeatedly – ~**er** *n*

threshold /'thresh,hohld, 'thresh·ohld/ *n* **1a** the doorway or entrance to a building **b** the point of entering or beginning **2** a level, point, or value above which sthg is true or will take place

threw /throoh/ *past of* **throw**

thrice /thries/ *adv* **1** three times **2** in a threefold manner or degree

thrift /thrift/ *n* **1** careful management, esp of money; frugality **2** any of a genus of tufted herbaceous plants – ~**y** *adj* – ~**ily** *adv*

thrill /thril/ *v* **1** to (cause to) experience a sudden tremor of excitement or emotion **2** to tingle, throb

thriller /'thrilə/ *n* a work of fiction or drama characterized by a high degree of intrigue or suspense

thrive /thriev/ *v* **throve** /throhv/, **thrived; thriven** /'thriv(ə)n/ *also* **thrived 1** to grow vigorously **2** to gain in wealth or possessions

throat /throht/ *n* **1a** the part of the neck in front of the spinal column **b** the passage through the neck to the stomach and lungs **2** sthg throatlike, esp in being a constricted passageway

throaty /'throhti/ uttered or produced low in the throat; hoarse, guttural – **throatily** *adv* – **throatiness** *n*

¹**throb** /throb/ *v* **-bb-** **1** to pulsate with unusual force or rapidity **2** to (come in waves that seem to) beat or vibrate rhythmically

²**throb** *n* a beat, pulse

thrombosis /throm'bohsis/ *n, pl* **thromboses** /-seez/ the formation or presence of a blood clot within a blood vessel during life

throne /throhn/ *n* **1** the chair of state of a sovereign or bishop **2** sovereignty

¹**throng** /throng/ *n sing or pl in constr* **1** a multitude of assembled people, esp when crowded together **2** a large number

²**throng** *v* **1** to crowd upon (esp a person) **2** to crowd into

¹**throttle** /'throtl/ *v* **throttling** /'throtling, throtl·ing/ **1a** to compress the throat of; *also* to kill in this way **b** to suppress **2** to regulate, esp reduce the speed of (e g an engine), by means of a throttle – usu + *back* or *down*

²**throttle** *n* **1** the windpipe **2** (the lever or pedal controlling) a valve for regulating the supply of a fluid (e g fuel) to an engine

¹**through** *also* **thro**, *NAm also* **thru** /throoh/ *prep* **1a(1)** into at one side or point and out at the other **a(2)** past (e g saw *through* the deception) **b** – used to indicate passage into and out of a treatment, handling, or process (e g flashed *through* my mind) **2** – used to indicate means, agency, or intermediacy: e g **2a** by means of; by the agency of **b** because of (e g failed *through* ignorance) **c** by common descent from or relationship with (e g related *through* their grandfather) **3a** over the whole surface or extent of (e g homes scattered *through* the valley) **b** – used to indicate movement within a large expanse (e g flew *through* the air) **c** among or between the parts or single members of (e g search *through* my papers) **4** during the entire period of (e g all *through* her life) **5a** – used to indicate completion, exhaustion, or accomplishment (e g got *through* the book) **b** – used to indicate acceptance or approval, esp by an official body (e g got the bill *through* Parliament) **6** *chiefly NAm* up till and including (e g Saturday *through* Sunday)

²**through**, *NAm also* **thru** *adv* **1** from one end or side to the other **2a** all the way from beginning to end **b** to a favourable or successful conclusion (e g see it *through*) **3** to the core; completely (e g wet *through*) **4** into the open; out (e g break *through*) **5** *chiefly Br* in or into connection by telephone (e g put me *through* to him)

³**through**, *NAm also* **thru** *adj* **1a** extending from one surface to the other (e g a *through* beam) **b** direct (e g a *through* road) **2a** allowing a continuous journey from point of origin to destination without change or further payment (e g a *through* train) **b** starting at and destined for points outside a local zone (e g *through* traffic) **3** arrived at completion, cessation, or dismissal; finished (e g I'm *through* with man)

¹**through'out** /-'owt/ *adv* **1** in or to every part; everywhere (e g of 1 colour *throughout*) **2** during the whole time or action; from beginning to end

²**throughout** *prep* **1** in or to every part of **2** during the entire period of

'**through,put** /-,poot/ *n* the amount of material put through a process

¹**throw** /throh/ *v* **threw** /throoh/, **thrown** /throhn/ **1** to propel through the air in some manner, esp by a forward motion of the hand and arm **2** to cause to fall **3a** to fling (oneself) abruptly **b** to hurl violently **4** to put *on* or *off* hastily or carelessly **5** to shape by hand on a potter's wheel **6** to deliver (a punch) **7** to send forth; cast, direct **8** to commit (oneself) for help, support, or protection **9** to bring forth; produce **10** to move (a lever or switch) so as to connect or disconnect parts of a mechanism **11** to project (the voice) **12** to give by way of entertainment **13** to disconcert – infml – ~ **er** *n* — **throw one's weight about/around** to exercise influence or authority, esp to an excessive degree or in an objectionable manner — infml — **throw together 1** knock together **2** to bring into casual association

²**throw** *n* **1a** an act of throwing **b** a method or instance of throwing an opponent in wrestling or judo **2** (the distance of) the extent of movement of a cam, crank, or other pivoted or reciprocating piece

¹'**throwa,way** /-ə,way/ *n* a line of dialogue (e g in a play) made to sound incidental by casual delivery

²**throwaway** *adj* written or spoken (e g in a play) with deliberate casualness

throw away *v* **1** to get rid of as worthless or unnecessary **2** to use in a foolish or wasteful manner

'**throw,back** /-,bak/ *n* (an individual exhibiting) reversion to an earlier genetic type or phase

throw back *v* **1** to delay the progress or advance of **2** to cause to rely; make dependent – + *on* or *upon*; usu pass

'**throw-,in** *n* a throw made from the touchline in soccer to put the ball back in play after it has gone over the touchline

throw in *v* **1** to add as a gratuity or supplement **2** to introduce or interject in the course of sthg — **throw in the sponge/towel** to abandon a struggle or contest; acknowledge defeat

throw out *v* **1** to remove from a place or from employment, usu in a sudden or unexpected manner **2** to refuse to accept or consider **3** to confuse, disconcert

throw over *v* to forsake or abandon (esp a lover)

throw up *v* **1** to raise quickly **2** to give up **3** to vomit

thrum /thrum/ *v* **-mm- 1** to play or pluck a stringed instrument idly **2** to drum or tap idly **3** to sound with a monotonous hum

¹**thrush** /thrush/ *n* any of numerous small or medium-sized mostly drab-coloured birds many of which are excellent singers

²**thrush** *n* **1** a whitish intensely irritating fungal growth occurring on mucous membranes, esp in the mouth or vagina **2** a disorder of the feet in various animals, esp horses

¹**thrust** /thrust/ *v* **thrust 1** to force an entrance or passage – often + *into* or *through* **2** to stab, pierce **3** to put (an unwilling person) into a course of action or position **4** to press, force, or impose the acceptance of *on* or *upon* sby

²**thrust** *n* **1a** a push or lunge with a pointed weapon **b(1)** a verbal attack **b(2)** a concerted military attack **2a** a strong continued pressure **b** the force exerted by a propeller, jet engine, etc to give forward motion **3a** a forward or upward push **b** a movement (e g by a group of people) in a specified direction

¹**thud** /thud/ *v* **-dd-** to move or strike with a thud

²**thud** *n* **1** a blow **2** a dull thump

thug /thug/ *n* **1** *often cap* a member of a former religious sect in India given to robbery and murder **2** a violent criminal – ~**gery** *n*

¹**thumb** /thum/ *n* the short thick digit of the hand that is next to the forefinger; *also* the part of a glove, etc that covers this — **all thumbs** extremely awkward or clumsy — **under someone's thumb** under sby's control; in a state of subservience to sby

²**thumb** *v* **1** to leaf through pages **2** to request or obtain a lift in a passing vehicle; hitchhike

'**thumb,screw** /-,skrooh/ *n* an instrument of torture for squeezing the thumb

¹**thump** /thump/ *v* **1** to strike or knock with a thump **2** to thrash **3** to produce (music) mechanically or in a mechanical manner

²**thump** *n* (a sound of) a blow or knock (as if) with sthg blunt or heavy

³**thump** *adv* with a thump

thumping /'thumping/ *adv, Br* very – chiefly in *thumping great* and *thumping good*; infml

¹**thunder** /'thundə/ *n* **1** the low loud sound that follows a flash of lightning and is caused by sudden expansion of the air in the path of the electrical discharge **2** a loud reverberating noise

²**thunder** *v* **1a** to give forth thunder – usu impersonally **b** to make a sound like thunder **2** to roar, shout – ~**er** *n*

'**thunder,bolt** /-,bohlt/ *n* **1** a single discharge of lightning with the accompanying thunder **2** sthg like lightning in suddenness, effectiveness, or destructive power

'**thunder,clap** /-,klap/ *n* (sthg loud or sudden like) a clap of thunder

'**thunder,cloud** /-,klowd/ *n* a cloud charged with electricity and producing lightning and thunder

thundering /'thund(ə)ring/ *adv, Br* very, thumping – infml

'**thunder,storm** /-,stawm/ *n* a storm accompanied by lightning and thunder

'**thunder,struck** /-,struk/ *adj* dumbfounded, astonished

thundery /'thund(ə)ri/ *adj* producing or presaging thunder

Thursday /'thuhzday, -di/ *n* the day of the week following Wednesday

thus /dhus/ *adv* **1** in the manner indicated; in this way **2** to this degree or extent; so **3** because of this preceding fact or premise; consequently **4** as an example

¹**thwart** /thwawt/ *v* to defeat the hopes or aspirations of

²**thwart** *n* a seat extending across a boat

thy /dhie/ *adj, archaic or dial* of thee or thyself

thyme /tiem/ *n* any of a genus of plants of the mint family with small pungent aromatic leaves; *esp* a garden plant used in cooking as a seasoning

¹**thyroid** /'thieroyd/ *also* **thyroidal** /thie'roydl/ *adj* of or being (an artery, nerve, etc associated with) **a** the thyroid gland **b** the chief cartilage of the larynx

²**thyroid** *n* a large endocrine gland that lies at the base of the neck and produces hormones (e g thyroxine) that increase the metabolic rate and influence growth and development

thyself /dhie'self/ *pron, archaic or dial* that identical person that is thou; yourself

ti /tee/ *n* the 7th note of the diatonic scale in tonic sol-fa

tiara /ti'ahrə/ *n* **1** the 3-tiered crown worn by the pope **2** a decorative usu jewelled band worn on the head by women on formal occasions

tibia /'tibiə/ *n, pl* **tibiae** /'tibi,ee/ *also* **tibias 1** the inner and usu larger of the 2 bones of the vertebrate hind limb between the knee and ankle; the shinbone **2** the 4th joint of the leg of an insect between the femur and tarsus

tic /tik/ *n* **1** (a) local and habitual spasmodic motion of particular muscles, esp of the face; twitching **2** a persistent trait of character or behaviour

¹**tick** /tik/ *n* **1** any of numerous related bloodsucking arachnids that feed on warm-blooded animals and often transmit infectious diseases **2** any of various usu wingless parasitic insects

tic

636

²**tick** *n* 1 a light rhythmic audible tap or beat; *also* a series of such sounds 2 a small spot or mark, typically √; *esp* one used to mark sthg as correct, to draw attention to sthg, to check an item on a list, or to represent a point on a scale 3 *Br* a moment, second – *infml*

³**tick** *v* 1 to make the sound of a tick 2 to function or behave characteristically 3 to mark or count (as if) by ticks – usu + *off*

⁴**tick** *n* credit, trust – *infml*

ticker /'tikə/ *n* sthg that produces a ticking sound: e g a a watch b the heart – *infml*

'**ticker ,tape** *n* a paper tape on which a certain type of telegraphic receiving instrument prints out its information

ticket /'tikit/ *n* 1a a mariner's or pilot's certificate b a tag, label 2 an official notification issued to sby who has violated a traffic regulation 3 a usu printed card or piece of paper entitling its holder to the use of certain services (e g a library), showing that a fare or admission has been paid, etc 4 *Br* a certificate of discharge from the armed forces 5 *chiefly NAm* a list of candidates for nomination or election 6 the correct, proper, or desirable thing – *infml*

ticking /'tikiŋ/ *n* a strong linen or cotton fabric used esp for a case for a mattress or pillow

tickle /'tikl/ *v* **tickling** /'tikliŋ, 'tikl·iŋ/ 1 to provoke to laughter 2 to touch (e g a body part) lightly and repeatedly so as to excite the surface nerves and cause uneasiness, laughter, or spasmodic movements – **tickle** *n*

ticklish /'tiklish/ *adj* 1 sensitive to tickling 2 easily upset 3 requiring delicate handling – ~**ly** *adv* – ~**ness** *n*

tick off *v* to scold, rebuke

tick over *v* to operate at a normal or reduced rate of activity

tidal /'tiedl/ *adj* of, caused by, or having tides

'**tidal ,wave** *n* 1 an unusually high sea wave that sometimes follows an earthquake 2 an unexpected, intense, and often widespread reaction (e g a sweeping majority vote or an overwhelming impulse)

tiddler /'tidlə/ *n*, *Br* sby or sthg small in comparison to others of the same kind; *esp* a minnow, stickleback, or other small fish

tiddly /'tidli/ *adj* 1 slightly drunk 2 very small

¹**tide** /tied/ *n* 1a (a current of water resulting from) the periodic rise and fall of the surface of a body of water, specif the sea, that occurs twice a day and is caused by the gravitational attraction of the sun and moon b the level or position of water on a shore with respect to the tide; *also* the water at its highest level 2 a flowing stream; a current

'**tide ,mark** /-,mahk/ *n* a mark left on a bath that shows the level reached by the water; *also* a mark left on the body showing the limit of washing – *chiefly infml*

tide over *v* to enable to surmount or withstand a difficulty

¹**tidy** /'tiedi/ *adj* 1a neat and orderly in appearance or habits; well ordered and cared for b methodical, precise 2 large, substantial – *infml* – **-dily** *adv* – **-diness** *n*

²**tidy** *v* to put (things) in order; make (things) neat or tidy

³**tidy** *n* a receptacle for odds and ends (e g kitchen scraps)

¹**tie** /tie/ *n* 1a a line, ribbon, or cord used for fastening or drawing sthg together b a structural element (e g a rod or angle iron) holding 2 pieces together 2a a moral or legal obligation to sby or sthg that restricts freedom of action b a bond of kinship or affection 3 a curved line that joins 2 musical notes of the same pitch to denote a single sustained note with the time value of the 2 4a a match or game between 2 teams, players, etc b (a contest that ends in) a draw or dead heat 5 a narrow length of material designed to be worn round the neck and tied in a knot in the front

²**tie** *v* **tying, tieing** 1a to fasten, attach, or close by knotting b to form a knot or bow in 2a to unite in marriage b to unite (musical notes) by a tie 3 to restrain from independence or from freedom of action or choice; constrain (as if) by authority or obligation – often + *down* 4a to even the score in a game or contest

tied cottage /tied/ *n*, *Br* a house owned by an employer (e g a farmer) and reserved for occupancy by an employee

tied house *n* a public house in Britain that is bound to sell only the products of the brewery that owns or rents it out

¹**tier** /tiə/ *n* any of a series of levels (e g in an administration)

²**tier** *v* to place, arrange, or rise in tiers

'**tie-,up** *n* a connection, association

tie up *v* 1 to attach, fasten, or bind securely; *also* to wrap up and fasten 2 to place or invest in such a manner as to make unavailable for other purposes 3 to keep busy 4 to dock

tiff /tif/ *n* or *v* (to have) a petty quarrel

tiger /'tiegə/, *fem* **tigress** /'tiegris/ *n pl* **tigers**, (1) **tigers**, *esp collectively* **tiger** 1 a very large Asiatic cat having a tawny coat transversely striped with black 2 a fierce and often bloodthirsty person

¹**tight** /tiet/ *adj* 1 so close or solid in structure as to prevent passage (e g of a liquid or gas) – often in combination 2a fixed very firmly in place b firmly stretched, drawn, or set c fitting (too) closely 3 set close together 4 difficult to get through or out of 5 evenly contested 6 packed, compressed or condensed to (near) the limit 7 stingy, miserly 8 intoxicated, drunk *USE* (7&8) *infml* – ~**en** *v* – ~**ly** *adv* – ~**ness** *n*

²**tight** *adv* 1 fast, tightly 2 in a sound manner

tighten /'tiet(ə)n/ *v* to make or become tight or tighter or more firm or severe – often + *up*

tighten up *v* to enforce regulations more stringently – usu + *on*

'tight'fisted /-'fistid/ *adj* reluctant to part with money – ~**ness** *n*

'tight-'lipped *adj* **1** having the lips compressed (e g in determination) **2** reluctant to speak; taciturn

'tight'rope /-,rohp/ *n* **1** a rope or wire stretched taut for acrobats to perform on **2** a dangerously precarious situation

tights /tiets/ *n pl* a skintight garment covering each leg (and foot) and reaching to the waist

tigress /'tiegris/ *n* a female tiger; *also* a tigerish woman

¹tile /tiel/ *n* **1** a thin slab of fired clay, stone, or concrete shaped according to use: e g **1a** a flat or curved slab for use on roofs **b** a flat and often ornamented slab for floors, walls, or surrounds **2** a thin piece of resilient material (e g cork or linoleum) used esp for covering floors or walls —**on the tiles** enjoying oneself socially, esp in an intemperate or wild manner

²tile *v* to cover with tiles – **tiler** *n*

¹till /til, tl/ *prep* until

²till *conj* until

³till /til/ *v* to work (e g land) by ploughing, sowing, and raising crops

⁴till *n* **1a** a receptacle (e g a drawer or tray) in which money is kept in a shop or bank **b** a cash register **2** the money contained in a till

tiller /'tilə/ *n* a lever used to turn the rudder of a boat from side to side

¹tilt /tilt/ *v* **1** to cause to slope **2** to point or thrust (as if) in a joust

²tilt *n* **1** a military exercise in which a mounted person charges at an opponent or mark **2** speed – in *at full tilt* **3** a written or verbal attack – *at* **4** a sloping surface

¹timber /'timbə/ *n* **1** growing trees or their wood **2** wood suitable for carpentry or woodwork **3** material, stuff; *esp* personal character or quality

²timber *v* to frame, cover, or support with timbers

timbered /'timbəd/ *adj* having walls framed by exposed timbers

'timber,line /-,lien/ *n* the tree line

timbre /'tambə, 'timbə, 'tahmbə/ (*Fr* tĕ:br)/ *also* **timber** /'timbə/ *n* the quality given to a sound by its overtones; *esp* the quality of tone distinctive of a particular singing voice or musical instrument

¹time /tiem/ *n* **1a** the measurable period during which an action, process, or condition exists or continues **b** a continuum in which events succeed one another **2a** the point or period when sthg occurs **b** the period required for an action **3a** a period set aside or suitable for an activity or event **b** an appointed, fixed, or customary period for sthg to happen, begin, or end; *esp, Br* closing time

in a public house as fixed by law **4a** a historical period – often pl with sing. meaning **b** conditions or circumstances prevalent during a period – usu pl with sing. meaning **5** a term of imprisonment – infml **6** a season **7a** a tempo **b** the grouping of the beats of music; a rhythm, metre **8** a moment, hour, day, or year as measured or indicated by a clock or calendar **9a** any of a series of recurring instances or repeated actions **b** pl **b(1)** multiplied instances **b(2)** equal fractional parts of which a specified number equal a comparatively greater quantity (e g **7** *times* smaller) **10** the end of the playing time of (a section of a) game – often used as an interjection — **at times** at intervals; occasionally — **behind the times** old-fashioned — **for the time being** for the present — **from time to time** at irregular intervals — **in time 1** sufficiently early **2** eventually **3** in correct tempo — **on time** at the appointed time — **time and (time) again** frequently, repeatedly

²time *v* **1** to arrange or set the time of **2** to regulate the moment, speed, or duration of, esp to achieve the desired effect **3** to determine or record the time, duration, or speed of

³time *adj* (able to be) set to function at a specific moment

'time-,honoured *adj* sanctioned by custom or tradition

'timeless /-lis/ *adj* **1a** unending, eternal **b** not restricted to a particular time or date **2** not affected by time; ageless – ~**ly** *adv* – ~**ness** *n*

'timely /-li/ *adv or adj* at an appropriate time – **liness** *n*

times /tiemz/ *prep* multiplied by

'time-,sharing *n* **1** simultaneous access to a computer by many users **2** a method of sharing holiday accommodation whereby each of a number of people buys a share of a lease in a property, entitling him/her to spend a proportionate amount of time there each year

time signature *n* a sign placed on a musical staff being usu a fraction whose denominator indicates the kind of note taken as the time unit for the beat (e g **4** for a crotchet or **8** for a quaver) and whose numerator indicates the number of beats per bar

¹time,table /-,taybl/ *n* **1** a table of departure and arrival times of public transport **2** a schedule showing a planned order or sequence of events, esp of classes (e g in a school)

²timetable *v* to arrange or provide for in a timetable

'time,zone *n* a geographical region within which the same standard time is used

timid /'timid/ *adj* lacking in courage, boldness, or self-confidence – ~**ity** *n* – ~**ly** *adv* – ~**ness** *n*

timing /'tieming/ *n* selection for maximum effect of the precise moment for doing sthg

timorous /'tim(ə)rəs/ *adj* timid – ~**ly** *adv* – ~**ness** *n*

timpani /'timpəni/ *n pl but sing or pl in constr* a set of 2 or 3 kettledrums played by 1 performer (e g in an orchestra) – ~**st** *n*

¹**tin** /tin/ *n* 1 a soft lustrous metallic element that is malleable and ductile at ordinary temperatures and is used as a protective coating, in tinfoil, and in soft solders and alloys 2 a box, can, pan, vessel, or sheet made of tinplate: e g 2a a hermetically sealed tinplate container for preserving foods b any of various usu tinplate or aluminium containers of different shapes and sizes in which food is cooked, esp in an oven

²**tin** *v*, **-nn-** *chiefly Br* to can

¹**tincture** /'tiŋ(k)chə/ *n* 1 **1a** a substance that colours or stains **b** a colour, hue 2 a slight addition; a trace 3 a solution of a substance in alcohol for medicinal use

²**tincture** *v* to tint or stain with a colour

tinder /'tində/ *n* any combustible substance suitable for use as kindling

'**tinder,box** /-,boks/ *n* 1 a metal box for holding tinder and usu a flint and steel for striking a spark 2 a potentially unstable place, situation, or person

tine /tien/ *n* 1 a prong (e g of a fork) 2 a pointed branch of an antler

tinfoil /,tin'foyl/ *-,-/ n* a thin metal sheeting of tin, aluminium, or a tin alloy

¹**tinge** /tinj/ *v* **tingeing, tinging** 1 to colour with a slight shade 2 to impart a slight smell, taste, or other quality to

²**tinge** *n* 1 a slight staining or suffusing colour 2 a slight modifying quality; a trace

tingle /'ting·gl/ *v or n* **tingling** /'ting·gling, 'ting·gling/ (to feel or cause) a stinging, prickling, or thrilling sensation

tin god *n* 1 a pompous and self-important person 2 sby unjustifiably esteemed or venerated *USE infml*

¹**tinker** /'tingkə/ *n* 1 a usu itinerant mender of household utensils 2 *chiefly Scot & Irish* a gipsy

²**tinker** *v* to repair, adjust, or work with sthg in an unskilled or experimental manner – usu + *at* or *with*

¹**tinkle** /'tingkl/ *v* **tinkling** /'tingkling, 'tingkl·ing/ to make (a sound suggestive of) a tinkle

²**tinkle** *n* 1 a series of short light ringing or tinkling sounds 2 a jingling effect in verse or prose 3 *Br* a telephone call – infml

tinny /'tini/ *adj* 1 of, containing, or yielding tin 2a having the taste, smell, or appearance of tin **b** not solid or durable; shoddy 3 having a thin metallic sound – **-niness** *n*

¹**tinsel** /'tins(ə)l/ *-,-/ n* 1 a thread, strip, or sheet of metal, plastic, or paper used to produce a glittering and sparkling effect (e g in fabrics or decorations) 2 sthg superficial, showy, or glamorous

²**tinsel** *adj* cheaply gaudy; tawdry

¹**tint** /tint/ *n* 1 a usu slight or pale coloration; a hue 2 any of various lighter or darker shades of a colour; *esp* one produced by adding white

²**tint** *v* to apply a tint to – ~**er** *n*

tiny /'tieni/ *adj* very small or diminutive

¹**tip** /tip/ *n* 1 the usu pointed end of sthg 2 a small piece or part serving as an end, cap, or point – **tip** *v* — **on the tip of one's tongue** about to be uttered

²**tip** *v v* **-pp-** 1 to overturn, upset – usu + *over* 2 to cant, tilt 3 to deposit or transfer by tilting 1 to overturn, upset – usu + *over* 2 to cant, tilt 3 to deposit or transfer by tilting

³**tip** *n* a place for tipping sthg (e g rubbish or coal); a dump – ~**per** *n* a place for tipping sthg (e g rubbish or coal); a dump – ~**per** *n*

⁴**tip** *v* to strike lightly *v* to strike lightly

⁵**tip** *v or n v or n* **-pp-** (to give or present with) a sum of money in appreciation of a service performed (to give or present with) a sum of money in appreciation of a service performed

⁶**tip** *n n* **-pp-** 1 a piece of useful or expert information 2 a piece of inside information which, acted upon, may bring financial gain (e g by betting or investment) – **tip** *v* 1 a piece of useful or expert information 2 a piece of inside information which, acted upon, may bring financial gain (e g by betting or investment) – **tip** *v*

'**tip-,off** *n* a tip given usu as a warning – **tip off** *v*

¹**tipple** /'tipl/ *v* **tippling** /'tipl·ing, 'tipling/ to drink (esp spirits), esp continuously in small amounts

²**tipple** *n* a drink; *esp* the drink one usually takes – infml

tipstaff /'tip,stahf/ *n pl* **tipstaves** /-,stayvz/ an officer in certain lawcourts

tipster /'tipstə/ *n* one who gives or sells tips, esp for gambling or speculation

tipsy /'tipsi/ *adj* 1 unsteady, staggering, or foolish from the effects of alcoholic drink 2 askew – **-sily** *adv* – **-siness** *n*

'**tip,toe** /-,toh/ *n* the tip of a toe; *also* the ends of the toes

²**tiptoe** *adv* (as if) on tiptoe

³**tiptoe** *adj* 1 standing or walking (as if) on tiptoe 2 cautious, stealthy

⁴**tiptoe** *v* **tiptoeing** 1 to stand, walk, or raise oneself on tiptoe 2 to walk silently or stealthily as if on tiptoe

,**tip-'top** *adj* excellent, first-rate – infml – **tip-top** *adv*

tirade /tie'rayd/ *n* a long vehement speech or denunciation

¹**tire** /tie·ə/ *v* 1 to fatigue 2 to wear out the patience of

²**tire** *n*, *chiefly NAm* a tyre

tired /tie·əd/ *adj* 1 weary, fatigued 2 exasperated; fed up 3a trite, hackneyed **b** lacking freshness – ~**ly** *adv* – ~**ness** *n*

tireless /'tie·əlis/ *adj* indefatigable, untiring – ~**ly** *adv*

tiresome /'tie-əsəm/ adj wearisome, tedious – **~ly** adv

tissue /'tishooh; also 'tisyooh/ n **1a** a fine gauzy often sheer fabric **b** a mesh, web **2** a paper handkerchief **3** a cluster of cells, usu of a particular kind, together with their intercellular substance that form any of the structural materials of a plant or animal

¹**tit** /tit/ n **1** a teat or nipple **2** a woman's breast – infml

²**tit** n any of various small tree-dwelling insect-eating birds (e g a blue tit)

titan /'tiet(ə)n/, fem **titaness** /,tiet(ə)n'es, '---/ n sby or sthg very large or strong; also sby notable for outstanding achievement – **~ic** adj

titanium /tiʰtaynyəm, -niʰəm, tie-/ n a light strong metallic element used esp in alloys

titbit /'tit,bit/, chiefly N Am **tidbit** /'tid-/ n a choice or pleasing piece (e g of food or news)

tithe /tiedh/ n a tax or contribution of a 10th part of sthg (e g income) for the support of a religious establishment; esp such a tax formerly due in an English parish to support its church

titillate /'titi,layt/ v to excite pleasurably; arouse by stimulation – **-lation** n

titivate, tittivate /'titivayt/ v to smarten up (oneself or another)

¹**title** /'tietl/ n **1** (a document giving proof of) legal ownership **2** an alleged or recognized right **3a** a descriptive or general heading (e g of a chapter in a book) **b** a title page and the printed matter on it **c** written material introduced into a film or television programme to represent credits, dialogue, or fragments of narrative – usu pl with sing. meaning **4** the distinguishing name of a work of art (e g a book, picture or musical composition) **5** a descriptive name **6** designation as champion **7** a hereditary or acquired appellation given to a person or family as a mark of rank, office, or attainment

²**title** v **1** to provide a title for **2** to designate or call by a title

titled adj having a title, esp of nobility

title deed n the deed constituting evidence of ownership

titrate /'tietrayt/ v to determine the amount of a substance in (a solution) by reaction with another substance of known composition – **-tion** n

titter /'titə/ v to giggle, snigger – **titter** n

'**tittle-tattle** /'tatl/ v or n (to) gossip, prattle

titular /'tityoolə/ adj **1** in title only; nominal **2** of or constituting a title

tizzy /'tizi/ n a highly excited and confused state of mind – infml

TNT n trinitrotoluene: a type of powerful explosive

¹**to** /,tooh; unstressed preceeding vowels too; unstressed preceeding consonants tə/ prep **1** – used to indicate a terminal point or destination: e g **1a** a place where a physical movement or an action or condition suggestive of movement ends (e g drive to the city) **b** a direction (e g turned his back to the door) **c** a terminal point in measuring or reckoning or in a statement of extent or limits (e g 10 miles to the nearest town; not to my knowledge) **d** a point in time before which a period is reckoned (e g how long to dinner?) **e** a point of contact or proximity (e g pinned it to my coat) **f** a purpose, intention, tendency, result, or end (e g a temple to Mars; held them to ransom; broken to pieces) **g** the one to or for which sthg exists or is done or directed (e g kind to animals) **2** – used to indicate addition, attachment, connection, belonging, or possession (e g add 17 to 20; the key to the door) **3** – used to indicate relationship or conformity: e g **3a** relative position (e g next door to me) **b** proportion or composition (e g 400 to the box; won by 17 points to 11) **c** correspondence to a standard (e g second to none) **4a** – used to indicate that the following verb is an infinitive (e g wants to go); often used by itself at the end of a clause in place of an infinitive suggested by the preceding context (e g knows more than he seems to) **b** for the purpose of (e g did it to annoy)

²**to** adv **1a** – used to indicate direction towards; chiefly in to and fro close to the wind (e g the ship hove to) **2** of a door or window into contact, esp with the frame **3** – used to indicate application or attention **4** back into consciousness or awareness **5** at hand (e g saw her close to)

toad /tohd/ n **1** any of numerous tailless leaping amphibians that differ from the related frogs by living more on land and in having a shorter squatter body with a rough, dry, and warty skin **2** a loathsome and contemptible person or thing

toad-in-the-'hole n a dish of sausages baked in a thick Yorkshire-pudding batter

toady /'tohdi/ v or adj (to behave as) a sycophant

to-and-'fro n or adj (activity involving alternating movement) forwards and backwards

to and fro adv from one place to another; back and forth

¹**toast** /tohst/ v **1** to make (e g bread) crisp, hot, and brown by heat **2** to warm thoroughly (e g at a fire)

²**toast** n **1** sliced bread browned on both sides by heat **2** sthg in honour of which people drink **3** an act of drinking in honour of sby or sthg

³**toast** v to drink to as a toast

toaster /'tohstə/ n an electrical appliance for toasting esp bread

'**toasting fork** /'tohsting/ n a long-handled fork on which bread is held for toasting in front of or over a fire

'**toast,master** /-,mahstə/, fem '**toast,mistress** n sby who presides at a banquet, proposes toasts, and introduces after-dinner speakers

tobacco /tə'bakoh/ *n pl* **tobaccos 1** a tall erect annual S American herb cultivated for its leaves **2** the leaves of cultivated tobacco prepared for use in smoking or chewing or as snuff; *also* cigars, cigarettes, or other manufactured products of tobacco

tobacconist /tə'bakənist/ *n* a seller of tobacco, esp in a shop

toboggan /tə'bogən/ *v or n* (to ride on) a long light sledge, usu curved up at the front and used esp for gliding downhill over snow or ice

today /tə'day/ *adv or n* **1** (on) this day **2** (at) the present time or age

toddle /'todl/ *v* **toddling** /'todling, 'todl·ing/ **1** to walk haltingly in the manner of a young child **2a** to take a stroll; saunter **b** *Br* to depart *USE* (2) infml

toddler /'todlə/ *n* a young child

toddy /'todi/ *n* a usu hot drink consisting of spirits mixed with water, sugar, and spices

to-'do *n, pl* **to-dos** bustle, fuss – infml

toe /toh/ *n* **1a** any of the digits at the end of a vertebrate's foot **b** the fore end of a foot or hoof **2** the front of sthg worn on the foot – **toe** *v*

'toe ,cap *n* a piece of material (e g steel or leather) attached to the toe of a shoe or boot to reinforce or decorate it

toffee, toffy /'tofi/ *n* a sweet with a texture from chewy to brittle, made by boiling sugar, water, and often butter

toga /'tohgə/ *n* a loose outer garment worn in public by citizens of ancient Rome

together /tə'gedhə/ *adv* **1a** in or into 1 place, mass, collection, or group **b** in joint agreement or cooperation; as a group **2a** in or into contact (e g connection, collision, or union) (e g mix the ingredients *together*) **b** in or into association, relationship, or harmony (e g colours that go well *together*) **3a** at one time; simultaneously **b** in succession; without intermission (e g was depressed for days *together*) **4** *of a single unit* in or into an integrated whole (e g pull yourself *together*) **5a** to or with each other **b** considered as a unit; collectively (e g these arguments taken *together* make a convincing case) — **together with** with the addition of

to'getherness /-nis/ *n* the feeling of belonging together

toggle /'tog(ə)l/ *n* a piece or device for holding or securing; *esp* a crosspiece attached to the end of or to a loop in a chain, rope, line, etc, usu to prevent slipping, to serve as a fastening, or as a grip for tightening

togs /togz/ *n pl* clothes – infml

'toil /'toyl/ *n* long strenuous fatiguing labour

'toil *v* **1** to work hard and long **2** to proceed with laborious effort

'toil *n* sthg by or with which one is held fast or inextricably involved – usu pl with sing. meaning

toilet /'toylit/ *n* **1** the act or process of dressing and grooming oneself **2a** a fixture or arrangement for receiving and disposing of faeces and urine **b** a room or compartment containing a toilet and sometimes a washbasin **3** formal or fashionable (style of) dress – fml

'toilet ,paper *n* a thin usu absorbent paper for sanitary use after defecation or urination

'toilet ,water *n* (a) liquid containing a high percentage of alcohol used esp as a light perfume

'token /'tohkən/ *n* **1** an outward sign or expression (e g of an emotion) **2** a characteristic mark or feature **3a** a souvenir, keepsake **b** sthg given or shown as a guarantee (e g of authority, right, or identity) **4** a coinlike object used in place of money (e g to pay a milkman) **5** a certified statement redeemable for a usu specified form of merchandise to the amount stated thereon — **by the same token** furthermore and for the same reason

'token *adj* **1** done or given as a token, esp in partial fulfilment of an obligation or engagement **2** done or given merely for show

told /tohld/ *past of* **tell**

tolerable /'tol(ə)rəbl/ *adj* **1** capable of being borne or endured **2** moderately good or agreeable

tolerance /'tolərəns/ *n* **1a** indulgence for beliefs or practices differing from one's own **b** the act of allowing sthg; toleration **2** an allowable variation from a standard dimension

tolerant /'tolərənt/ *adj* inclined to tolerate; *esp* marked by forbearance or endurance – ~**ly** *adv*

tolerate /'tolərayt/ *v* to allow to be (done) without prohibition, hindrance, or contradiction

toleration /tolə'raysh(ə)n/ *n* a government policy of permitting forms of religious belief and worship not officially established

'toll /tol, tohl/ *n* **1** a fee paid for some right or privilege (e g of passing over a highway or bridge) or for services rendered **2** a grievous or ruinous price; *esp* cost in life or health

'toll /tohl/ *v* **1** to sound (a bell) by pulling the rope **2** to signal, announce, or summon (as if) by means of a tolled bell

tollgate /'tol,gayt, tohl-/ *n* a barrier across a road to prevent passage until a toll is paid

tomahawk /'toma,hawk/ *n* a light axe used by N American Indians as a throwing or hand weapon

tomato /tə'mahtoh/ *n, pl* **tomatoes 1** any of a genus of S American plants of the nightshade family; *esp* one widely cultivated for its edible fruits **2** the usu large and rounded red, yellow, or green pulpy fruit of a tomato

tomb /toohm/ *n* **1** an excavation in which a corpse is buried **2** a chamber or vault for the dead, built either above or below ground and usu serving as a memorial

tombola /tom'bohlə/ *n* a lottery in which people buy tickets which may entitle them to a prize

tomboy /'tom,boy/ *n* a girl who behaves in a manner conventionally thought of as typical of a boy – ~**ish** *adj*

tombstone /'toohm,stohn/ *n* a gravestone

tomcat /'tom,kat/ *n* a male cat

tome /tohm/ *n* a (large scholarly) book

tomfoolery /,tom'foohləri/ *n* foolish trifling; nonsense

tomorrow /tə'moroh/ *adv or n* **1** (on) the day after today **2** (in) the future

'**tom-,tom** /tom/ *n* a usu long and narrow small-headed drum commonly beaten with the hands

ton /tun/ *n pl* **tons** *also* **ton 1** any of various units of weight; *esp* one equal to 2,240 lbs **2a** a great quantity – often *pl* with sing. meaning **b** a great weight **3** a group, score, or speed of 100 *USE* (2&3) *infml*

tonal /'tohn(ə)l/ *adj* **1** of tone, tonality, or tonicity **2** having tonality

tonality /toh'naləti/ *n* **1** tonal quality **2a** musical key **b** the organization of all the notes and chords of a piece of music in relation to a tonic

'**tone** /tohn/ *n* **1** a vocal or musical sound; *esp* one of a specified quality **2** a sound of a definite frequency with relatively weak overtones **3** an accent or inflection of the voice expressive of a mood or emotion **4** (a change in) the pitch of a word often used to express differences of meaning **5** style or manner of verbal expression **6** the colour that appreciably modifies a hue or white or black **7** the general effect of light, shade, and colour in a picture **8** the state of (an organ or part of) a living body in which the functions are healthy and performed with due vigour **9** prevailing character, quality, or trend (e g of morals)

²**tone** *v* to blend or harmonize in colour

,**tone-'deaf** *adj* relatively insensitive to differences in musical pitch

toneless /'tohnlis/ *adj* lacking in expression – ~**ly** *adv*

tongs /tongz/ *n pl also* any of various grasping devices consisting commonly of 2 pieces joined at 1 end by a pivot or hinged like scissors

'**tongue** /tung/ *n* **1a** a fleshy muscular movable organ of the floor of the mouth in most vertebrates that bears sensory end organs and small glands and functions esp in tasting and swallowing food and in human beings as a speech organ **b** a part of various invertebrate animals that is analogous to the tongue of vertebrates **2** the tongue of an ox, sheep, etc used as food **3** the power of communication through speech **4a** a (spoken) language **b** the cry (as if) of a hound pursuing or in sight of game – esp in *give tongue* **6** sthg like an animal's tongue (e g elongated and fastened at 1 end only):e g **6a** a piece of metal suspended inside a bell so as to strike against the sides as the bell is swung **b** the flap under the

lacing or buckles on the front of a shoe or boot **7** the rib on one edge of a board that fits into a corresponding groove in an edge of another board to make a flush joint

²**tongue** *v* **1** to touch or lick (as if) with the tongue **2** to articulate notes on a wind instrument by successively interrupting the stream of wind with the action of the tongue

'**tongue-,tied** *adj* unable to speak freely (e g because of shyness)

'**tongue ,twister** *n* a word or phrase difficult to articulate because of several similar consonantal sounds (e g 'she sells seashells on the seashore')

'**tonic** /'tonik/ *adj* **1** increasing or restoring physical or mental tone **2** of or based on the first note of a scale

²**tonic** *n* **1a** sthg that invigorates, refreshes, or stimulates **b tonic, tonic water** a carbonated drink flavoured with a small amount of quinine, lemon, and lime **2** the first note of a diatonic scale

,**tonic 'sol-fa** *n* a system of solmization that replaces the normal notation with sol-fa syllables

tonight /tə'niet/ *adv or n* (on) this night or the night following today

tonnage /'tunij/ *n* **1** ships considered in terms of the total number of tons registered or carried or of their carrying capacity **2** the carrying capacity of a merchant ship in units of 100ft³ (about 2.83m³) **3** total weight in tons shipped, carried, or produced

tonne /tun/ *n* a metric unit of weight equal to 1000kg

tonsil /'tons(ə)l/ *n* either of a pair of prominent oval masses of spongy tissue that lie **1** on each side of the throat at the back of the mouth – ~**litis** *n*

'**ton-,up** *adj, Br* of or being sby who has achieved a score, speed, etc of 100 – *infml*

too /tooh/ *adv* **1** also; in addition **2a** to a regrettable degree; excessively **b** to a higher degree than meets a standard **3** indeed, so – used to counter a negative charge (e g he did *too*!)

took /took/ *past of* **take**

'**tool** /toohl/ *n* **1a** an implement that is used, esp by hand, to carry out work of a mechanical nature (e g cutting, levering, or digging) – not usu used with reference to kitchen utensils or cutlery **b** (the cutting or shaping part in) a machine tool **2** sthg (e g an instrument or apparatus) used in performing an operation, or necessary for the practice of a vocation or profession **3** sby who is used or manipulated by another **4** a penis – *vulg*

²**tool** *v* **1** to work, shape, or finish with a tool; *esp* to letter or ornament (e g leather) by means of hand tools **2** to equip (e g a plant or industry) with tools, machines, and instruments for production – often + *up*

toot /tooht/ *v* to produce a short blast or similar sound – **toot** *n*

too

642

tooth /toohth/ *n, pl* **teeth** /teeth/ **1a** any of the hard bony structures that are borne esp on the jaws of vertebrates and serve esp for the seizing and chewing of food and as weapons **b** any of various usu hard and sharp projecting parts about the mouth of an invertebrate **2** a taste, liking **3** any of the regular projections on the rim of a cogwheel **4** *pl* effective means of enforcement — **in the teeth of** in direct opposition to

'**tooth,ache** /-,ayk/ *n* pain in or about a tooth

toothy /'toohthi/ *adj* having or showing prominent teeth

tootle /'toohtl/ *v* **tootling** /'toohtling/ **1** to toot gently or continuously **2** to drive or move along in a leisurely manner – *infml* – **tootle** *n*

¹**top** /top/ *n* **1a(1)** the highest point, level, or part of sthg **a(2)** the (top of the) head – esp in *top to toe* **a(3)** the head of a plant, esp one with edible roots **a(4)** a garment worn on the upper body **b(1)** the highest or uppermost region or part **b(2)** the upper end, edge, or surface **2** a fitted or attached part serving as an upper piece, lid, or covering **3** the highest degree or pitch conceivable or attained **4** (sby or sthg in) the highest position (e g in rank or achievement) **5** *Br* the transmission gear of a motor vehicle giving the highest ratio of propeller-shaft to engine-shaft speed and hence the highest speed of travel — **off the top of one's head** in an impromptu manner — **on top of 1a** in control of **b** informed about **2** in sudden and unexpected proximity to **3** in addition to — **on top of the world** in high spirits; in a state of exhilaration and well-being

²**top** *v* **-pp- 1a** to cut the top off **b** to shorten or remove the top of (a plant); *also* to remove the calyx of (e g a strawberry) **2a** to cover with a top or on the top; provide, form, or serve as a top for **b** to complete the basic structure of (e g a high-rise building) by putting on a cap or uppermost section – usu + *out or off* **3** to be or become higher than; overtop **4** to go over the top of; clear, surmount

³**top** *adj* **1** of or at the top **2** foremost, leading **3** of the highest quality, amount, or degree

⁴**top** *n* a child's toy that has a tapering point on which it is made to spin

topaz /'tohpaz/ *n* a yellow sapphire or quartz

'**top,coat** /-,koht/ *n* **1a** (lightweight) overcoat **2** a final coat of paint

,**top 'dog** *n* a person in a position of authority, esp through victory in a hard-fought competition – *infml*

,**top-'flight** *adj* of the highest grade or quality; best

top hat *n* a man's tall-crowned hat

,**top-'heavy** *adj* **1** having the top part too heavy for or disproportionate to the lower part **2** capitalized beyond what is prudent

topiary /'tohpyari/ *adj or n* (of or being) the practice or art of training, cutting, and trimming trees or shrubs into odd or ornamental shapes

topic /'topik/ *n* **1a** a heading in an outlined argument or exposition **b** the subject of (a section of a) discourse **2** a subject for discussion or consideration

topical /'topikl/ *adj* **1** of a place **2a** of or arranged by topics **b** referring to the topics of the day; current interest – ~**ly** *adv* – ~**ity** *n*

'**top,knot** /-,not/ *n* an arrangement or growth of hair or feathers on top of the head

topless /'toplis/ *adj* **1** nude above the waist; *esp* having the breasts exposed **2** featuring topless waitresses or entertainers

topmast /'top,mahst/ *n* a mast that is next above the lowest mast

topmost /'topmohst/ *adj* highest of all

,**top-'notch** *adj* of the highest quality – *infml*

topography /to'pografi/ *n* **1** (the mapping or charting of) the configuration of a land surface, including its relief and the position of its natural and man-made features **2** the physical or natural features of an object or entity and their structural relationships – **-phical** *adj* – **-phically** *adv*

topology /to'polaji/ *n* a branch of mathematics that deals with geometric properties which are unaltered by elastic deformation (e g stretching or twisting)

topper /'topə/ *n* **1** a top hat **2** sthg (e g a joke) that caps everything preceding – *infml*

'**topping** /'toping/ *n* sthg that forms a top; *esp* a garnish or edible decoration on top of a food

²**topping** *adj, chiefly Br* excellent – not now in vogue

topple /'topl/ *v* **toppling** /'topling, 'topl·ing/ **1** to fall (as if) from being top-heavy **2** to overthrow

topside /'top,sied/ *n* **1** *pl* the sides of a ship above the waterline **2** a lean boneless cut of beef from the inner part of a round

topsoil /'top,soyl/ *n* surface soil, usu including the organic layer in which plants form roots and which is turned over in ploughing

topspin *n* a rotary motion imparted to a ball that causes it to rotate forwards in the direction of its travel

topsy-turvy /,topsi 'tuhvi/ *adj or adv* **1** upside down **2** in utter confusion or disorder

top up *v* to make up to the full quantity, capacity, or amount

tor /taw/ *n* a high rock or rocky mound

torch /tawch/ *n* **1** a burning stick of resinous wood or twist of tow used to give light **2** *Br* a small portable electric lamp powered by batteries

tore /taw/ *past of* **tear**

toreador /'tori·ə,daw/ *n* a bullfighter

¹**torment** /'tawment/ *n* **1** extreme pain or anguish of body or mind **2** a source of vexation or pain

²**torment** /taw'ment/ *v* to cause severe usu persistent distress of body or mind to – ∼ **or** *n*

torn /tawn/ *past part of* **tear**

tornado /taw'naydoh/ *n pl* **tornadoes, tornados** a violent or destructive whirlwind

¹**torpedo** /taw'peedoh/ *n, pl* **torpedoes** 1 an electric ray 2 a self-propelling cigar-shaped submarine explosive projectile used for attacking ships

²**torpedo** *v* **torpedoing; torpedoed** 1 to hit or destroy by torpedo 2 to destroy or nullify (e g a plan) – infml

torpid /'tawpid/ *adj* 1a having temporarily lost the power of movement or feeling (e g in hibernation) b sluggish in functioning or acting 2 lacking in energy or vigour – ∼**ity**, – ∼**ness** *n* – ∼**ly** *adv*

torpor /'tawpə/ *n* 1a a state of mental and motor inactivity with partial or total insensibility b extreme sluggishness of action or function 2 apathy

¹**torque** /tawk/ *n* a twisted metal collar or neck chain worn by the ancient Gauls, Germans, and Britons

²**torque** *n* a turning or twisting force

torrent /'torənt/ *n* 1 a violent stream of water, lava, etc 2 a raging tumultuous flow – ∼**ial** *adj*

torrid /'torid/ *adj* 1a parched with heat, esp of the sun b giving off intense heat 2 ardent, passionate – ∼**ly** *adv*

torsion /'tawsh(ə)n/ *n* 1 the act or process of twisting or turning sthg, esp by forces exerted on one end while the other is fixed or twisted in the opposite direction 2 the state of being twisted

torso /'tawsoh/ *n, pl* **torsos, torsi** /'tawsi/ 1 (a sculptured representation of) the human trunk 2 sthg (e g a piece of writing) that is mutilated or left unfinished

tortilla /taw'teeyə/ *n* a round thin cake of unleavened maize bread, usu eaten hot with a topping or filling of minced meat or cheese

tortoise /'tawtəs, 'taw,toys/ *n* 1 any of an order of land and freshwater (and marine) reptiles with a toothless horny beak and a bony shell which encloses the trunk 2 sby or sthg slow or laggard

¹**tortoiseshell** /'tawtəs,shel/ *n* 1 the mottled horny substance of the shell of some marine turtles used in inlaying and in making various ornamental articles 2 any of several butterflies with striking orange, yellow, brown, and black coloration

²**tortoiseshell** *adj* mottled black, brown, and yellow

tortuous /'tawtyooəs/ *adj* 1 marked by repeated twists, bends, or turns 2a marked by devious or indirect tactics b circuitous, involved – ∼**ly** *adv* – ∼**ness** *n*

¹**torture** /'tawchə/ *n* 1 the infliction of intense physical or mental suffering as a means of punishment, coercion, or sadistic gratification 2 (sthg causing) anguish of body or mind

²**torture** *v* 1 to subject to torture 2 to cause intense suffering to 3 to twist or wrench out of shape; *also* to pervert (e g the meaning of a word) – ∼**r** *n*

Tory /'tawri/ *n* 1 a member of a major British political group of the 18th and early 19th c favouring at first the Stuarts and later royal authority and the established church and seeking to preserve the traditional political structure and defeat parliamentary reform 2 a Conservative – ∼**ism** *n*

¹**toss** /tos/ *v* 1 to fling or heave repeatedly about; *also* to bandy 2a to throw with a quick, light, or careless motion b to throw up in the air c to flip (a coin) to decide an issue 3 to lift with a sudden jerking motion

²**toss** *n* 1 a fall, esp from a horse – chiefly in *take a toss* 2a an abrupt tilting or upward fling b an act or instance of deciding by chance, esp by tossing a coin c a throw

toss off *v* 1 to perform or write quickly and easily 2 to consume quickly; *esp* to drink in a single draught 3 *Br* to masturbate – infml

'**toss-,up** *n* 1 a toss of a coin 2 an even chance or choice – infml

tot /tot/ *n* 1 a small child; a toddler 2 a small amount or allowance of alcoholic drink

¹**total** /'tohtl/ *adj* 1 comprising or constituting a whole; entire 2 complete 3 concentrating all available personnel and resources on a single objective – ∼**ly** *adv*

²**total** *n* 1 a product of addition 2 an entire quantity

³**total** *v* **-ll-** (*NAm* **-l-, -ll-**) /'tohtl-ing/ to amount to

totalitarian /,tohtali'teəri-ən/ *adj* 1 authoritarian, dictatorial 2 of or constituting a political regime based on subordination of the individual to the state and strict control over all aspects of the life and productive capacity of the nation – ∼**ism** *n*

totality /toh'taləti/ *n* 1 an entire amount; a whole 2 wholeness

¹**tote** /toht/ *v* 1 to carry by hand or on the person 2 to transport, convey *USE* infml

²**tote** *n* a system of horse-race betting

totem /'tohtəm/ *n* 1 a natural object serving as the emblem of a family or clan; *also* a carved or painted representation of this 2 sthg that serves as an emblem or revered symbol

¹**totter** /'totə/ *v* 1a to tremble or rock as if about to fall b to become unstable; threaten to collapse 2 to move unsteadily; stagger

²**totter** *n* an unsteady gait

tot up *v* to add together; *also* to increase by additions

toucan /'tooh,kan/ *n* any of a family of fruit-eating birds of tropical America with brilliant colouring and a very large but light beak

¹**touch** /tuch/ *v* 1 to bring a bodily part into contact with, esp so as to perceive through the sense of feeling; feel 2 to strike or push lightly, esp with

the hand or foot or an implement **3** to take into the hands or mouth **4** to put hands on in any way or degree; *esp* to commit violence against **5** to concern oneself with **6** to cause to be briefly in contact with sthg **7** to affect the interest of; concern **8** to move to esp sympathetic feeling **9** to speak or tell of, esp in passing **10** to rival **11** to induce to give or lend – ~**able** *adj* – ~**er** *n* — **touch wood 1** with a certain amount of luck **2** *Br* to touch a wooden surface as a gesture to bring luck

²**touch** *n* **1** a light stroke, tap, or push **2** the act or fact of touching **3** the sense of feeling, esp as exercised deliberately with the hands, feet, or lips **4** mental or moral sensitivity, responsiveness, or tact **5** sthg slight of its kind: e g **5a** a light attack **b** a small amount; a trace **6a** a manner or method of touching or striking esp the keys of a keyboard instrument **b** the relative resistance to pressure of the keys of a keyboard (e g of a piano or typewriter) **7** an effective and appropriate detail; *esp* one used in an artistic composition **8** a distinctive or characteristic manner, trait, or quality **9** the state or fact of being in contact or communication **10** the area outside the touchlines in soccer or outside and including the touchlines in rugby **11** sby who can be easily induced to part with money – chiefly in *a soft/easy touch*

,**touch and 'go** *n* a highly uncertain or precarious situation

'**touch,down** /-,down/ *n* **1** the act of touching down a football **2** (the moment of) touching down (e g of an aeroplane or spacecraft)

touch down *v* **1** to place (the ball in rugby) by hand on the ground either positioned on or over an opponent's goal line in scoring a try, or behind one's own goal line as a defensive measure **2** to reach the ground

touché /tooh'shay/ *interj* – used to acknowledge a hit in fencing or the success of an argument, accusation, or witty point

touched /tucht/ *adj* **1** emotionally moved (e g with gratitude) **2** slightly unbalanced mentally – *infml*

'**touch,line** /-,lien/ *n* either of the lines that bound the sides of the field of play in rugby and soccer

touch off *v* to cause to explode (as if) by touching with a naked flame

'**touch,stone** /-,stohn/ *n* **1** a black flintlike stone that when rubbed by gold or silver showed a streak of colour and was formerly used to test the purity of these metals **2** a test or criterion for determining the genuineness of sthg

touch up *v* **1** to improve or perfect by small alterations; make good the minor defects of **2** to make often unwelcome physical advances to; touch with a view to arousing sexually – slang

touchy /'tuchi/ *adj* **1** ready to take offence on slight provocation **2** calling for tact, care, or caution – **touchily** *adv* – **touchiness** *n*

¹**tough** /tuf/ *adj* **1a** strong and flexible; not brittle or liable to cut, break, or tear **b** not easily chewed **2** capable of enduring great hardship or exertion **3** very hard to influence **4** extremely difficult or testing **5** aggressive or threatening in behaviour **6** without softness or sentimentality **7** unfortunate, unpleasant – *infml* – ~**ly** *adv* – ~**ness** *n*

²**tough** *n* a tough person; *esp* sby aggressively violent

³**tough** *adv* in a tough manner

toughen /'tuf(ə)n/ *v* to make or become tough

toupee /'tooh,pay/ *n* a wig or hairpiece worn to cover a bald spot

¹**tour** /tooə/ *n* **1** a period during which an individual or unit is engaged on a specific duty, esp in 1 place **2a** a journey (e g for business or pleasure) in which one returns to the starting point **b** a visit (e g to a historic site or factory) for pleasure or instruction **c** a series of professional engagements involving travel

²**tour** *v* **1** to make a tour of **2** to present (e g a theatrical production or concert) on a tour

tour de force /,tooə də 'faws/ (*Fr* tuːr də fɔrs)/ *n*, *pl* **tours de force** /~/ a feat of strength, skill, or ingenuity

tourism /'tooə,riz(ə)m/ *n* **1** the practice of travelling for recreation **2** the organizing of tours for commercial purposes **3** the provision of services (e g accommodation) for tourists

tourist /'tooərist/ *n* **1** sby who makes a tour for recreation or culture **2** a member of a sports team that is visiting another country to play usu international matches

tournament /'tooənəmənt, 'taw-/ *n* **1** a contest between 2 parties of mounted knights armed with usu blunted lances or swords **2** a series of games or contests for a championship

tourniquet /'tooəni,kay, 'taw-/ *n* a bandage or other device for applying pressure to check bleeding or blood flow

tousle /'towzl/ *v* to dishevel, rumple

¹**tout** /towt/ *v* to solicit for customers

²**tout** *n* **1** sby who solicits custom, usu importunately **2** *Br* sby who offers tickets for a sold-out entertainment (e g a concert or football match) at vastly inflated prices

¹**tow** /toh/ *v* to draw or pull along behind, esp by a rope or chain

²**tow** *n* **1** a rope or chain for towing **2** towing or being towed **3** sthg towed (e g a boat or car) — **in tow 1** being towed **2a** under guidance or protection **b** in the position of a dependent or devoted follower or admirer

³**tow** *n* short or broken fibre (e g of flax or hemp) prepared for spinning

towards /tə'wawdz/ *prep* **1** moving or situated in the direction of **2a** along a course leading to **b** in relation to (e g an attitude *towards* life) **3** turned in the direction of **4** not long before (e g *towards* evening) **5** for the partial financing of (e g gave her £5 *towards* a new dress)

¹**towel** /'towəl/ *n* an absorbent cloth or paper for wiping or drying sthg (e g crockery or the body) after washing

²**towel** *v* -ll- (*NAm* -l-, -ll-) to rub or dry (e g the body) with a towel

¹**tower** /'towə/ *n* **1** a building or structure typically higher than its diameter and high relative to its surroundings that may stand apart or be attached to a larger structure and that may be fully walled in or of skeleton framework **2 tower block, tower** a tall multi-storey building, often containing offices

²**tower** *v* to reach or rise to a great height

towering /'towəring/ *adj* **1** impressively high or great **2** reaching a high point of intensity **3** going beyond proper bounds

town /town/ *n* **1a** a compactly settled area as distinguished from surrounding rural territory; *esp* one larger than a village but smaller than a city **b** a city **2** the city or urban life as contrasted with the country or rural life — **on the town** in usu carefree pursuit of entertainment or amusement (e g city nightlife)

town clerk *n* the chief official of a British town

town crier /'krie-ə/ *n* a town officer who makes public proclamations

town hall *n* the chief administrative building of a town

township /'township/ *n* **1** an ancient unit of administration in England identical in area with or being a division of a parish **2** an urban area inhabited by nonwhite citizens in S Africa

'towns,people /-,peepl/ *n pl* the inhabitants of a town or city

toxic /'toksik/ *adj* **1** of or caused by a poison or toxin **2** poisonous — ~**ity** *n*

toxin /'toksin/ *n* an often extremely poisonous protein produced by a living organism (e g a bacterium), esp in the body of a host

¹**toy** /toy/ *n* **1** a trinket, bauble **2a** sthg for a child to play with **b** sthg designed for amusement or diversion rather than practical use **3** an animal of a breed or variety of exceptionally small size

²**toy** *v* to act or deal *with* sthg without purpose or conviction

³**toy** *adj* **1** designed or made for use as a toy **2** toylike, esp in being small

¹**trace** /trays/ *n* **1** a mark or line left by sthg that has passed **2** a vestige of some past thing **3** sthg traced or drawn (e g the graphic record made by a seismograph) **4** a minute and often barely detectable amount or indication, esp of a chemical

²**trace** *v* **1a** to delineate, sketch **b** to copy (e g a drawing) by following the lines or letters as seen through a semitransparent superimposed sheet **2a** to follow back or study in detail or step by step **b** to discover signs, evidence, or remains of — ~**able** *adj*

³**trace** *n* either of 2 straps, chains, or lines of a harness for attaching a vehicle to a horse

tracery /'traysəri/ *n* ornamental stone openwork in architecture, esp in the head of a Gothic window

trachea /trə'kee-ə/ *n, pl* **tracheae** *also* **tracheas 1** the main trunk of the system of tubes by which air passes to and from the lungs in vertebrates; the windpipe **2** any of the small tubes carrying air in most insects and many other arthropods

tracing /'traysing/ *n* a copy (e g of a design or map) made on a superimposed semitransparent sheet

¹**track** /trak/ *n* **1a** detectable evidence (e g a line of footprints or a wheel rut) that sthg has passed **b** a path beaten (as if) by feet **c** a specially laid-out course, esp for racing **d(1)** the parallel rails of a railway **d(2)** a rail or length of railing along which sthg, esp a curtain, moves or is pulled **e** a more or less independent sequence of recording (e g a single song) visible as a distinct band on a gramophone record **2** a footprint **3** the course along which sthg moves **4** the condition of being aware of a fact or development **5a** the width of a wheeled vehicle from wheel to wheel, usu from the outside of the rims **b** either of 2 endless usu metal belts on which a tracklaying vehicle travels — **in one's tracks** where one stands or is at the moment

²**track** *v* **1** to follow the tracks or traces of **2** to observe or plot the course of (e g a spacecraft) instrumentally **3** to move a film or television camera towards, beside, or away from a subject while shooting a scene — ~**er** *n*

track suit *n* a warm loose-fitting suit worn by athletes when training

¹**tract** /trakt/ *n* a short practical treatise; *esp* a pamphlet of religious propaganda

²**tract** *n* **1** a region or area of land of indefinite extent **2** a system of body parts or organs that collectively serve some often specified purpose

tractable /'traktəbl/ *adj* **1** easily taught or controlled **2** easily handled or wrought — **ability** *n*

traction /'traksh(ə)n/ *n* **1** pulling or being pulled; *also* the force exerted in pulling **2** the drawing of a vehicle by motive power **3a** the adhesive friction of a body on a surface on which it moves **b** a pulling force exerted on a skeletal structure (e g in treating a fracture) by means of a special device

traction engine *n* a large steam- or diesel-powered vehicle used to draw other vehicles or equipment over roads or fields and sometimes to provide power (e g for sawing or ploughing)

tractor /'traktə/ n 1 a 4-wheeled or tracklaying vehicle used esp for pulling or using farm machinery 2 a truck with a short chassis and no body except a driver's cab, used to haul a large trailer or trailers

¹trad /trad/ adj, chiefly Br traditional – infml

²trad n traditional jazz

¹trade /trayd/ n 1a the business or work in which one engages regularly b an occupation requiring manual or mechanical skill; a craft c the people engaged in an occupation, business, or industry 2a the business of buying and selling or bartering commodities b business, market 3 sing or pl in constr the people or group of firms engaged in a particular business or industry

²trade v to give in exchange for another commodity; also to make an exchange of – ~ r n — **trade on** to take often unscrupulous advantage of

³trade adj 1 of or used in trade 2 intended for or limited to people in a business or industry

trade gap n the value by which a country's imports exceed its exports

'trade-,in n an item of merchandise (e g a car or refrigerator) that is traded in

trade in v to give as payment or part payment for a purchase or bill

'trade,mark /-,mahk/ n 1 a name or distinctive symbol or device attached to goods produced by a particular firm or individual and legally reserved to the exclusive use of the owner of the mark as maker or seller 2 a distinguishing feature firmly associated with sby or sthg

tradesman /'traydzmən/ n 1 a shopkeeper 2 one who delivers goods to private houses

trade union also **trades union** n an organization of workers formed for the purpose of advancing its members' interests – ~ism n – ~ist n

tradition /trə'dish(ə)n/ n 1 the handing down of information, beliefs, and customs by word of mouth or by example from one generation to another 2a an inherited practice or opinion b conventions associated with a group or period 3 cultural continuity in attitudes and institutions – ~al adj – ~ally adv

traduce /trə'dyoohs/ v to (attempt to) damage the reputation or standing of, esp by misrepresentation – fml – ~r n

traffic /'trafik/ n 1a the business of bartering or buying and selling b illegal or disreputable trade 2a the movement (e g of vehicles or pedestrians) through an area or along a route b the vehicles, pedestrians, ships, or aircraft moving along a route 3 dealings between individuals or groups – fml

tragedy /'trajədi/ n 1 (a) serious drama in which destructive circumstances result in adversity for and usu the deaths of the main characters 2 a disastrous event; a calamity 3 tragic quality or element

tragic /'trajik/ also **tragical** /-kl/ adj 1 (expressive) of tragedy 2 of, appropriate to, dealing with, or treated in tragedy 3 deplorable, lamentable – ~ally adv

tragicomedy /,traji'komədi/ n a literary work in which tragic and comic elements are mixed in a usu ironic way; also a situation or event of such a character

¹trail /trayl/ v 1 to hang down so as to sweep the ground 2a to walk or proceed draggingly or wearily – usu + along b to lag behind; do poorly in relation to others 3 to dwindle 4 to follow a trail; track game

²trail n 1a sthg that follows as if being drawn behind b the streak of light produced by a meteor 2a a trace or mark left by sby or sthg that has passed or is being followed b(1) a track made by passage, esp through a wilderness b(2) a marked path through a forest or mountainous region

trailer /'traylə/ n 1 a trailing plant 2 a wheeled vehicle designed to be towed (e g by a lorry or car) 3 a set of short excerpts from a film shown in advance for publicity purposes

¹train /trayn/ n 1 a part of a gown that trails behind the wearer 2a a retinue, suite b a moving file of people, vehicles, or animals 3 the vehicles, men, and sometimes animals that accompany an army with baggage, supplies, ammunition, or siege artillery 4 a connected series of ideas, actions, or events 5 a connected line of railway carriages or wagons with or without a locomotive

²train v 1 to direct the growth of (a plant), usu by bending, pruning, etc 2a to form by instruction, discipline, or drill b to teach so as to make fit or proficient 3 to prepare (e g by exercise) for a test of skill 4 to aim at an object or objective – ~able adj

trainee /,tray'nee/ n one who is being trained for a job

trainer /'traynə/ n 1 sby who or sthg which trains (e g a person who trains the members of a sports team) 2 a sports shoe used esp for running, jogging, or casual wear

training /'trayning/ n 1 the bringing of a person or animal to a desired degree of proficiency in some activity or skill 2 the condition of being trained, esp for a contest

traipse /trayps/ v to walk or trudge about, often to little purpose

trait /trayt, tray/ n a distinguishing (personal) quality or characteristic

traitor /'traytə/, fem **traitress** /'traytris/ n 1 sby who betrays another's trust 2 sby who commits treason

trajectory /trə'jektəri/ n 1 the curve that a planet, projectile, etc follows 2 a path, progression, or line of development like a physical trajectory

tram /tram/ *n, chiefly Br* a passenger vehicle running on rails and typically operating on urban streets

'**tram,line** /-,lien/ *n, Br pl* (the area between) either of the 2 pairs of sidelines on a tennis court that mark off the area used in doubles play

¹**trammel** /'traml/ *n* sthg that impedes freedom of action – usu pl with sing. meaning

²**trammel** *v* -**ll-** (*NAm* -**l-**, -**ll-**), /'traml·ing/ to impede the free play of

¹**tramp** /tramp/ *v* 1 to walk or tread, esp heavily 2a to travel about on foot **b** to journey as a tramp

²**tramp** *n* 1 a wandering vagrant who survives by taking the occasional job or by begging or stealing money and food 2 a usu long and tiring walk 3 the heavy rhythmic tread of feet 4 a merchant vessel that does not work a regular route but carries general cargo to any port as required

trample /'trampl/ *v* **trampling** /'trampling/ 1 to tread heavily so as to bruise, crush, or injure 2 to treat destructively with ruthlessness or contempt – usu ~ *on, over,* or *upon*

trampoline /,trampo'leen/ *n* a resilient sheet or web supported by springs in a frame and used as a springboard in tumbling

trance /trahns/ *n* 1 a state of semiconsciousness or unconsciousness with reduced or absent sensitivity to external stimulation 2 a state of profound abstraction or absorption

tranny /'trani/ *n, chiefly Br* a transistor radio – infml

tranquil /'trangkwil/ *adj* free from mental agitation or from disturbance or commotion – ~**lity** *n* – ~**ly** *adv* – ~**lize** *v*

tranquill·izer, -**iser**, *NAm chiefly* **tranquilizer** /'trangkwi,liezə/ *n* a drug used to reduce tension, anxiety, etc

transact /tran'zakt/ *v* to perform; carry out; *esp* to conduct – ~**ion** *n*

transatlantic /,tranzat'lantik, ,trahn-/ *adj* 1 crossing or extending across the Atlantic ocean 2 situated beyond the Atlantic ocean 3 (characteristic) of people or places situated beyond the Atlantic ocean; *specif, chiefly Br* American

transcend /tran'send, trahn-/ *v* to rise above or extend notably beyond ordinary limits

transcendent /tran'send(ə)nt; *also* trahn-/ *adj* 1a exceeding usual limits; surpassing **b** beyond the limits of ordinary experience 2 transcending the universe or material existence – ~**ly** *adv* – -**ence,** -**ency** *n*

transcendental /,transen'dentl; *also* trahn-/ *adj* 1 of or employing the basic categories (e g space and time) presupposed by knowledge and experience 2a supernatural **b** abstruse, abstract – ~**ly** *adv*

transcontinental /,tranz,konti'nentl, trahnz-/ *adj* crossing or extending across a continent

transcribe /tran'skrieb; *also* trahn-/ *v* 1a to make a written copy or version of (e g sthg written or printed) **b** to write in a different medium; transliterate 2 to make a musical transcription of – -**scription** *n*

transcript /'transkript, 'trahn-/ *n* 1 a written, printed, or typed copy, esp of dictated or recorded material 2 an official written copy

transept /'transept/ *n* (either of the projecting arms of) the part of a cross-shaped church that crosses the E end of the nave at right angles

¹**transfer** /trans'fuh, trahns-/ *v* -**rr-** 1a to convey or cause to pass from one person, place, or situation to another **b** to move or send to another location; *specif* to move (a professional soccer player) to another football club 2 to make over the possession or control of – ~**ability** *n* – ~**able** *adj* – ~**ence** *n*

²**transfer** /'transfuh, 'trahns-/ *n* 1 conveyance of right, title, or interest in property 2 transferring

transfiguration /,trans,figə'raysh(ə)n, ,trahns-/ *n* 1a a change in form or appearance; a metamorphosis **b** an exalting, glorifying, or spiritual change 2 *cap* August 6 observed as a Christian festival in commemoration of the transfiguration of Christ

transfigure /trans'figə, trahns-/ *v* to give a new appearance to; transform outwardly and usu for the better

transfix /trans'fiks, trahns-/ *v* 1 to pierce through (as if) with a pointed weapon 2 to hold motionless (as if) by piercing

transform /trans'fawm, trahns-/ *v* 1 to change radically (e g in structure, appearance, or character) 2 to subject to mathematical transformation 3 to change (a current) in potential (e g from high voltage to low) or in type (e g from alternating to direct)

transformation /,transfaw'maysh(ə)n, ,trahns-/ *n* the operation of changing one configuration or expression into another in accordance with a mathematical rule – ~**al** *adj*

transformer /trans'fawmə, trahns-/ *n* an electrical device making use of the principle of mutual induction to convert variations of current in a primary circuit into variations of voltage and current in a secondary circuit

transfuse /trans'fyoohz, trahns-/ *v* 1 to diffuse into or through; *broadly* to spread across 2 to transfer (e g blood) into a vein – -**fusion** *n*

transgress /trans'gres, trahns-/ *v* 1 to go beyond limits set or prescribed by 2 to violate a command or law – ~**ion** *n* – ~**or** *n*

¹**transient** /'tranzi·ənt/ *adj* 1 passing quickly away; transitory 2 making only a brief stay

²**transient** *n* a transient guest or worker

transistor /tran'zistə, trahn-/ *n* any of several semiconductor devices that have usu 3 electrodes and make use of a small current to control a larger one; *also* a radio using using such devices

transit /'transit, -zit/ *n* **1a** passing or conveying through or over **b** a change, transition **2** passage of a smaller celestial body across the disc of a larger one – ~**ory** *adj* — **in transit** in passage

transition /tran'zish(ə)n, trahn-/ *n* **1a** passage from one state or stage to another **b** a movement, development, or evolution from one form, stage, or style to another **2** a musical passage leading from one section of a piece to another – ~**al** *adj* – ~**ally** *adv*

transitive /'transitiv, 'trahn-, -zitiv/ *adj* having or containing a direct object

translate /trans'layt, trahns-/ *v* **1a** to bear, remove, or change from one place, state, form, or appearance to another **b** to transfer (a bishop) from one see to another **2a** to turn into another language **b** to express in different or more comprehensible terms – **latable** *adj* – **lator** *n*

translation /trans'laysh(ə)n, trahns-/ *n* **1** (a version produced by) a rendering from one language into another **2** a change to a different substance or form

transliterate /tranz'litərayt, trahnz-, trans-, trahns-/ *v* to represent or spell in the characters of another alphabet – **ation** *n*

translucent /tranz'loohs(ə)nt, trahnz-/ *adj* **1** transparent **2** transmitting and diffusing light so that objects beyond cannot be seen clearly – **cence, -cency** *n*

transmission /tranz'mish(ə)n, trahns-, tranz-, trahnz-/ *n* **1** transmitting; *esp* transmitting by radio waves or over a wire **2** the assembly by which the power is transmitted from a motor vehicle engine to the axle

transmit /tranz'mit, trahns-, tranz-, trahnz-/ *v* **-tt- 1a** to send or transfer from one person or place to another **b** to convey (as if) by inheritance or heredity **2a** to cause (e g light or force) to pass or be conveyed through a medium **b** to send out (a signal) either by radio waves or over a wire

trans'mitter /-tə/ *n* **1** the portion of a telegraphic or telephonic instrument that sends the signals **2** a radio or television transmitting station or set

transmogrify /tranz'mogrifie/ *v* to transform, often with grotesque or humorous effect – **-fica-tion** *n*

transmute /tranz'myooht, trahnz-/ *v* to change in form, substance, or characteristics – **-mutable** *adj* – **-mutation** *n*

transom /'transəm/ *n* a transverse piece in a structure: e g **a** a lintel **b** a horizontal crossbar in a window, over a door, or between a door and window or fanlight above it **c** any of several transverse timbers or beams secured to the stern-post of a boat

transparency /tran'sparənsi, trahn-/ *n* **1** a picture or design on glass, film, etc viewed by a light shining through it from behind; *esp* a colour photograph for projecting onto a screen; a slide **2** a framework covered with thin cloth or paper bearing a device for public display (e g for advertisement) and lit from within

transparent /tran'sparənt, trahn-/ *adj* **1a(1)** transmitting light without appreciable scattering so that bodies lying beyond are entirely visible **a(2)** penetrable by a specified form of radiation (e g X rays or ultraviolet) **b** fine or sheer enough to be seen through **2a** free from pretence or deceit **b** easily detected or seen through **c** readily understood – ~**ly** *adv*

transpire /tran'spie-ə, trahn-/ *v* **1** to give off a vapour; *specif* to give off or exude water vapour, esp from the surfaces of leaves **2** to become known; come to light **3** to occur; take place – **-piration** *n*

¹**transplant** /trans'plahnt, trahns-/ *v* **1** to lift and reset (a plant) in another soil or place **2** to remove from one place and settle or introduce elsewhere **3** to transfer (an organ or tissue) from one part or individual to another – ~**ation** *n*

²**transplant** /'trans,plahnt, 'trahns-/ *n* **1** transplanting **2** sthg transplanted

¹**transport** /tran'spawt, trahn-/ *v* **1** to transfer or convey from one place to another **2** to carry away with strong and often pleasurable emotion **3** to send to a penal colony overseas – ~**able** *adj*

²**transport** /'transpawt, 'trahn-/ *n* **1** the conveying of goods or people from one place to another **2** strong and often pleasurable emotion – often pl with sing. meaning **3** a ship or aircraft for carrying soldiers or military equipment **4** a mechanism for moving a tape, esp a magnetic tape, or disk past a sensing or recording head

transportation /ˌtranspaw'taysh(ə)n, trahn-/ *n* **1** the act of transporting **2** banishment to a penal colony **3** means of conveyance or travel from one place to another

transport café *n, Br* an inexpensive roadside cafeteria catering mainly for long-distance lorry drivers

transporter /tran'spawtə, trahn-/ *n* a vehicle for transporting large or heavy loads

transpose /tran'spohz, trahn-/ *v* **1** to transfer from one place or period to another **2** to change the relative position of **3** to alter the sequence of **3** to write or perform (music) in a different key

transship, tranship /tranz'ship, trahnz-/ *v* to transfer from one ship or conveyance to another for further transportation – ~**ment** *n*

transub'stanti'ation /-shi'aysh(ə)n/ *n* the miraculous change by which, according to Roman Catholic and Eastern Orthodox dogma, bread and wine used at communion become the body and blood of Christ when they are consecrated, although their appearance remains unchanged

transverse /tranz'vuhs, trahnz-, '--/ *adj* lying or being across; set or made crosswise – ~**ly** *adv*

¹**trap** /trap/ *n* **1** a device for taking animals; *esp* one that holds by springing shut suddenly **2a** sthg designed to catch sby unawares **b** a situation from which it is impossible to escape; *also* a plan to trick a person into such a situation **3a** a trapdoor **b** a device from which a greyhound is released at the start of a race **4** a light usu 1-horse carriage with springs **5** the mouth – *slang*

²**trap** *v* **-pp-** **1** to catch or take (as if) in a trap **2** to provide or set (a place) with traps **3** to stop, retain

trap'door /-'daw/ *n* a lifting or sliding door covering an opening in a floor, ceiling, etc

trapeze /trə'peez/ *n* a gymnastic or acrobatic apparatus consisting of a short horizontal bar suspended by 2 parallel ropes

trapezium /trə'peezi·əm/ *n, pl* **trapeziums, trapezia** /-zi·ə/ *Br* a quadrilateral having only 2 sides parallel

trappings /'trapingz/ *n pl* outward decoration or dress; *also* outward signs and accessories

Trappist /'trapist/ *n* a member of a reformed branch of the Roman Catholic Cistercian Order noted for its vow of silence

trash /trash/ *n* **1** sthg of little or no value: e g **1a** junk, rubbish **b** inferior literary or artistic work **2** a worthless person; *also, sing or pl in constr* such people as a group – *infml*

trashy /'trashi/ *adj* of inferior quality or worth – **-shiness** *n*

trauma /'trawmə/ *n, pl* **traumata** /-mətə/, **traumas** a disordered mental or behavioural state resulting from mental or emotional stress or shock – **-tic** *adj*

¹**travel** /'travl/ *v* **-ll-** (*NAm* **-l-, -ll-**), /'travl·ing/ **1a** to go (as if) on a tour **b** to go as if by travelling **c** to go from place to place as a sales representative **2a** to move or be transmitted from one place to another **b** *esp of machinery* to move along a specified direction or path **c** to move at high speed – *infml* — **travel light** to travel with a minimum of equipment or baggage

²**travel** *n* **1** a journey, esp to a distant or unfamiliar place – often *pl* **2** movement, progression

'travel ˌagent *n* sby engaged in selling and arranging personal transport, tours, or trips for travellers

'travelled, NAm chiefly travelled *adj* **1** experienced in travel **2** used by travellers

traveller, NAm chiefly traveler /'travlə, 'travl·ə/ *n* **1** a sales representative **2** any of various devices for handling sthg that is being moved laterally **3** *dial Br* a gipsy

'traveller's ˌcheque, NAm traveler's check *n* a cheque that is purchased from a bank and that may be exchanged abroad for foreign currency

travelogue, NAm also travelog /'travə,log/ *n* **1** a film or illustrated talk or lecture on some usu exotic or remote place **2** a narrated documentary film about travel

¹**traverse** /'travuhs, -'-/ *n* **1** sthg that crosses or lies across **2** a route or way across or over: e g **2a** a curving or zigzag way up a steep slope **b** the course followed in traversing **3** (a) traversing **4** the lateral movement of a gun to change direction of fire

²**traverse** /trə'vuhs, 'travuhs/ *v* **1** to pass or travel across, over, or through **2** to lie or extend across **3a** to move to and fro over or along **b** to ascend, descend, or cross (a slope or gap) at an angle **c** to move (a gun) to right or left

³**traverse** /'travuhs, -'-/ *adj* lying across

¹**travesty** /'travəsti/ *n* **1** a crude or grotesque literary or artistic parody **2** a debased, distorted, or grossly inferior imitation

²**travesty** *v* to make a travesty of

¹**trawl** /trawl/ *v* to fish (for or in) with a trawl

²**trawl** *n* a large conical net dragged along the sea bottom to catch fish

trawler /'trawlə/ *n* a boat used in trawling

tray /tray/ *n* an open receptacle with a flat bottom and a low rim for holding, carrying, or exhibiting articles

treacherous /'trech(ə)rəs/ *adj* **1** characterized by treachery; perfidious **2a** of uncertain reliability **b** marked by hidden dangers or hazards – ~**ly** *adv*

treachery /'trech(ə)ri/ *n* (an act of) violation of allegiance; (a) betrayal of trust

treacle /'treekl/ *n, chiefly Br* **1** any of the edible grades of molasses that are obtained in the early stages of sugar refining **2** golden syrup

¹**tread** /tred/ *v* **trod** /trod/ *also* **treaded; trodden** /'trod(ə)n/, **trod 1a** to step or walk on or over **b** to walk along **2** to beat or press with the feet **3** *of a male bird* to copulate with **4** to execute by stepping or dancing — **tread on someone's toes/corns** to give offence or hurt sby's feelings, esp by encroaching on his/her rights — **tread water** to keep the body nearly upright in the water and the head above water by a treading motion of the feet, usu aided by the hands

²**tread** *n* **1** an imprint made (as if) by treading **2** the sound or manner of treading **3a** the part of a wheel or tyre that makes contact with a road or rail **b** the pattern of ridges or grooves made or cut in the face of a tyre **4** (the width of) the upper horizontal part of a step

treadle /'tredl/ *n* a lever pressed by the foot to drive a machine

treadmill /'tred,mil/ n 1a a mill used formerly in prison punishment that was worked by people treading on steps inside a wide wheel with a horizontal axis b a mill worked by an animal treading an endless belt 2 a wearisome or monotonous routine

treason /'treez(ə)n/ n 1 the betrayal of a trust 2 the offence of violating the duty of allegiance owed to one's crown or government – ~able adj – ~ably adv

¹**treasure** /'trezhə/ n 1 wealth, esp in a form which can be accumulated or hoarded 2 sthg of great worth or value; also sby highly valued or prized

²**treasure** v to hold or preserve as precious

treasurer /'trezh(ə)rə/ n the financial officer of an organization (e g a society)

treasure trove /'trohv/ n treasure that anyone finds; specif gold or silver money, plate, or bullion which is found hidden and whose ownership is not known

treasury /'trezh(ə)ri/ n 1a a place in which stores of wealth are kept b the place where esp public funds that have been collected are deposited and disbursed 2 often cap a government department in charge of finances, esp the collection, management, and expenditure of public revenues

¹**treat** /treet/ v 1 to deal with 2a to behave oneself towards b to regard and deal with in a specified manner – usu + as 3 to provide with free food, drink, entertainment, etc – usu + to 4 to care for or deal with medically or surgically 5 to act on with some agent, esp so as to improve or alter – ~able adj – ~er n

²**treat** n 1 an entertainment given free of charge to those invited 2 a source of pleasure or amusement; esp an unexpected one — **a treat** very well or successfully — infml

treatise /'treetiz/ n a formal written exposition on a subject

treatment /'treetmənt/ n 1a treating sby or sthg b the actions customarily applied in a particular situation 2 a substance or technique used in treating

treaty /'treeti/ n (a document setting down) an agreement or contract made by negotiation (e g between states)

¹**treble** /'trebl/ n 1a the highest voice part in harmonic music; also sby, esp a boy, who performs this part b a member of a family of instruments having the highest range c the upper half of the whole vocal or instrumental tonal range 2 sthg treble in construction, uses, amount, number, or value: e g 2a a type of bet in which the winnings and stake from a previous race are bet on the next of 3 races b (a throw landing on) the middle narrow ring on a dart board counting treble the stated score

²**treble** adj 1a having 3 parts or uses b triple 2a relating to or having the range or part of a treble b high-pitched, shrill

treble clef n a clef that places the note G above middle C on the second line of the staff

tree /tree/ n 1 a tall woody perennial plant having a single usu long and erect main stem, generally with few or no branches on its lower part 2 a device for inserting in a boot or shoe to preserve its shape when not being worn 3 a diagram or graph that branches, usu from a single stem

trefoil /'trefoyl, 'tree-/ n 1a (a) clover; broadly any of several leguminous plants having leaves of 3 leaflets b a leaf consisting of 3 leaflets 2 a stylized figure or ornament in the form of a 3-lobed leaf or flower

trek /trek/ v or n -kk- (to make) 1 a journey; esp an arduous one 2 chiefly SAfr a journey by ox wagon

¹**trellis** /'trelis/ n a frame of latticework used as a screen or as a support for climbing plants

²**trellis** v to provide with a trellis; esp to train (e g a vine) on a trellis

¹**tremble** /'trembl/ v trembling /'trembling/ 1 to shake involuntarily (e g with fear or cold) 2 to be affected with fear or apprehension – -blingly adv

²**tremble** n 1 a fit or spell of involuntary shaking or quivering 2 a tremor or series of tremors

tremendous /trə'mendəs/ adj 1 such as to arouse awe or fear 2 of extraordinary size, degree, or excellence – ~ly adv

tremolo /'tremʌloh/ n pl tremolos 1a the rapid reiteration of a musical note or of alternating notes to produce a tremulous effect b a perceptible rapid variation of pitch in the (singing) voice; vibrato 2 a mechanical device in an organ for causing a tremulous effect

tremor /'tremə/ n 1 a trembling or shaking, usu from physical weakness, emotional stress, or disease 2 a (slight) quivering or vibratory motion, esp of the earth 3 a thrill, quiver

tremulous /'tremyooləs/ adj 1 characterized by or affected with trembling or tremors 2 uncertain, wavering – ~ly adv – ~ness n

¹**trench** /trench/ n a deep narrow excavation (e g for the laying of underground pipes); esp one used for military defence

²**trench** v to dig a trench (in)

trenchant /'trenchənt/ adj 1 keen, sharp 2 vigorously effective and articulate 3a incisive, penetrating b clear-cut, distinct – ~ly adv – -ancy n

'**trench coat** n a double-breasted raincoat with deep pockets, a belt, and epaulettes

¹**trend** /trend/ v 1 to show a general tendency to move or extend in a specified direction 2 to deviate, shift

²**trend** n 1 a line of general direction 2a a prevailing tendency or inclination b a general movement, esp in taste or fashion

¹**trendy** /'trendi/ *adj, chiefly Br* characterized by uncritical adherence to the latest fashions or progressive ideas – *infml* – **trendiness** *n*

²**trendy** *n, chiefly Br* sby trendy – chiefly *derog*

trepidation /ˌtrepi'daysh(ə)n/ *n* nervous agitation or apprehension

¹**trespass** /'trespəs/ *n* 1 a violation of moral or social ethics; *esp* a sin 2 any unlawful act that causes harm to the person, property, or rights of another; *esp* wrongful entry on another's land

²**trespass** *v* 1a to err, sin b to make an unwarranted or uninvited intrusion *on* 2 to commit a trespass; *esp* to enter sby's property unlawfully

trestle /'tresl/ *n* 1 a (braced) frame serving as a support (e g for a table top) 2 a braced framework of timbers, piles, or girders for carrying a road or railway over a depression

trews /troohz/ *n pl in constr, pl* **trews** trousers; *specif* tartan trousers

¹**trial** /'trie·əl/ *n* 1 trying or testing 2 the formal examination and determination by a competent tribunal of the matter at issue in a civil or criminal cause 3 a test of faith, patience, or stamina by suffering or temptation; *broadly* a source of vexation or annoyance 4 an experiment to test quality, value, or usefulness 5 an attempt, effort

²**trial** *adj* 1 of a trial 2 made or done as, or used or tried out in, a test or experiment

triangle /'trie·ang·gl/ *n* 1 a polygon of 3 sides and 3 angles 2 a percussion instrument consisting of a steel rod bent into the form of a triangle open at 1 angle and sounded by striking with a small metal rod

triangular /trie'ang·gyoolə/ *adj* 1 (having the form) of a triangle 2 between or involving 3 elements, things, or people

tribalism /'triebl,iz(ə)m/ *n* 1 tribal consciousness and loyalty 2 strong loyalty or attachment to a group

tribe /trieb/ *n sing or pl in constr* 1 a social group comprising numerous families, clans, or generations together with slaves, dependants, or adopted strangers 2 a group of people having a common character or interest 3 a category in the classification of living things ranking above a genus and below a family – **tribal** *adj*

tribesman /'triebzmən/, *fem* **tribeswoman** /-, woomən/ *n* a member of a tribe

tribulation /ˌtribyoo'laysh(ə)n/ *n* distress or suffering resulting from oppression

tribunal /trie'byoohnl/ *n* a court of justice; *specif* a board appointed to decide disputes of a specified kind

tribune /'tribyoohn/ *n* 1 an official of ancient Rome with the function of protecting the plebeian citizens from arbitrary action by the patrician magistrates 2 an unofficial defender of the rights of the individual

¹**tributary** /'tribyoot(ə)ri/ *adj* 1 paying tribute to another; subject 2 paid or owed as tribute 3 providing with material or supplies

²**tributary** *n* 1 a tributary ruler or state 2 a stream feeding a larger stream or a lake

tribute /'tribyooht/ *n* 1 a payment by one ruler or nation to another in acknowledgement of submission or as the price of protection 2a sthg (e g a gift or formal declaration) given or spoken as a testimonial of respect, gratitude, or affection b evidence of the worth or effectiveness of sthg specified – chiefly in *a tribute to*

trice /tries/ *n* a brief space of time – chiefly in *in a trice*

¹**trick** /trik/ *n* 1a a crafty practice or stratagem meant to deceive or defraud b a mischievous act c a deceptive, dexterous, or ingenious feat designed to puzzle or amuse 2a a habitual peculiarity of behaviour or manner b a deceptive appearance, esp when caused by art or sleight of hand 3a a quick or effective way of getting a result b a technical device or contrivance (e g of an art or craft) 4 the cards played in 1 round of a card game, often used as a scoring unit – ~ **ery** *n*

²**trick** *adj* 1 of or involving tricks or trickery 2 skilled in or used for tricks

³**trick** *v* 1 to deceive by cunning or artifice – often + *into, out of* 2 to dress or embellish showily – usu + *out* or *up*

¹**trickle** /'trikl/ *v* **trickling** /'trikling, 'trikl·ing/ 1 to flow in drops or a thin slow stream 2 to move or go gradually or one by one

²**trickle** *n* a thin slow stream or movement

trickster /'trikstə/ *n* a person who defrauds others by trickery

tricky /'triki/ *adj* 1 inclined to or marked by trickery 2 containing concealed difficulties or hazards 3 requiring skill, adroitness, or caution (e g in doing or handling) – **trickiness** *n*

¹**tricolour**, *NAm* **tricolor** /'trie,kulə/ *n* a flag of 3 colours

²**tricolour**, **tricoloured**, *NAm* **tricolor**, **tricolored** *adj* having or using 3 colours

tricycle /'triesikl/ *n* a 3-wheeled pedal-driven vehicle

¹**trident** /'tried(ə)nt/ *n* a 3-pronged (fish) spear **a** serving as the attribute of a sea god **b** used by ancient Roman gladiators

²**trident** *adj* having 3 prongs or points

tried /tried/ *adj* 1 found to be good or trustworthy through experience or testing 2 subjected to trials or severe provocation – often in combination

triennial /trie'enyəl, -ni·əl/ *adj* 1 consisting of or lasting for 3 years 2 occurring every 3 years

trier /'trie·ə/ *n* 1 sby who makes an effort or perseveres 2 an implement (e g a tapered hollow tube) used in obtaining samples of bulk material, esp foodstuffs, for examination and testing

¹**trifle** /'triefl/ *n* **1** sthg of little value or importance; *esp* an insignificant amount (e g of money) **2** *chiefly Br* a dessert typically consisting of sponge cake soaked in wine (e g sherry), spread with jam or jelly, and topped with custard and whipped cream — **a trifle** to some small degree

²**trifle** *v* **trifling** /'triefling/ **1** to act heedlessly or frivolously – often + *with* **2** to handle sthg idly **3** to spend or waste in trifling or on trifles

trifling /'triefling/ *adj* lacking in significance or solid worth: e g **a** frivolous **b** trivial, insignificant

¹**trigger** /'trigə/ *n* a device (e g a lever) connected with a catch as a means of release; *esp* the tongue of metal in a firearm which when pressed allows the gun to fire

²**trigger** *v* **1a** to release, activate, or fire by means of a trigger **b** to cause the explosion of **2** to initiate or set off as if by pulling a trigger – often + *off*

'trigger-happy *adj* **1** irresponsible in the use of firearms **b** aggressively belligerent **b** too prompt in one's response

trigonometry /,trigə'nomətri/ *n* the study of the properties of triangles and trigonometric functions and of their applications – **-ric, -rical** *adj*

trilateral /,trie'lat(ə)rəl/ *adj* having 3 sides – ~ly *adv*

trilby /'trilbi/ *n*, *chiefly Br* a soft felt hat with an indented crown

trilingual /,trie'ling·gwəl/ *adj* **1** of, containing, or expressed in 3 languages **2** using or able to use 3 languages, esp with the fluency of a native – ~ly *adv*

trill /tril/ *n* **1** the alternation of 2 musical notes 2 semitones apart **2** a sound resembling a musical trill – **trill** *v*

trillion /'trilyən/ *n* **1a** *Br* a million million millions (10^{18}) **b** *chiefly NAm* a million millions (10^{12})

trilogy /'triləji/ *n* a group of 3 closely related works (e g novels)

¹**trim** /trim/ *v* **-mm- 1** to decorate (e g clothes) with ribbons, lace, or ornaments; adorn **2** to make trim and neat, esp by cutting or clipping **3a** to cause (e g a ship, aircraft, or submarine) to assume a desired position by arrangement of ballast, cargo, passengers, etc **b** to adjust (e g a sail) to a desired position **4** to maintain a neutral attitude towards opposing parties or favour each equally

²**trim** *adj* **-mm-** appearing neat or in good order; compact or clean-cut in outline or structure – ~ly *adv*

³**trim** *n* **1** the readiness or fitness of a person or thing for action or use; *esp* physical fitness **2a** material used for decoration or trimming **b** the decorative accessories of a motor vehicle **3a** the position of a ship or boat, esp with reference to the horizontal **b** the inclination of an aircraft or spacecraft in flight with reference to a fixed point (e g the horizon), esp with the controls in some neutral position

trimaran /'triemə,ran/ *n* a sailing vessel used for cruising or racing that has 3 hulls side by side

trimming /'triming/ *n* **1** *pl* pieces cut off in trimming sthg; scraps **2a** a decorative accessory or additional item (e g on the border of a garment) that serves to finish or complete **b** an additional garnish or accompaniment to a main item – usu *pl*

Trinity /'trinəti/ *n* **1** the unity of Father, Son, and Holy Spirit as 3 persons in 1 Godhead according to Christian theology **2** the Sunday after Whitsunday observed as a festival in honour of the Trinity

trinket /'tringkit/ *n* a small (trifling) article; *esp* an ornament or piece of (cheap) jewellery

trio /'tree·oh/ *n pl* **trios 1a** (a musical composition for) 3 instruments, voices, or performers **b** the secondary division of a minuet, scherzo, etc **2** *sing or pl in constr* a group or set of 3

¹**trip** /trip/ *v* **-pp- 1a** to dance, skip, or walk with light quick steps **b** to proceed smoothly, lightly, and easily; flow **2a** to catch the foot against sthg so as to stumble **b** to detect in a fault or blunder; catch out – usu + *up* **3** to stumble in articulation when speaking **4** to make a journey **5** to release or operate (a device or mechanism), esp by releasing a catch or producing an electrical signal **6** to get high on a psychedelic drug (e g LSD) – slang

²**trip** *n* **1a** a voyage, journey, or excursion **b** a single round or tour (e g on a business errand) **2** an error, mistake **3** a quick light step **4** a faltering step caused by stumbling **5** a device (e g a catch) for tripping a mechanism **6** an intense, often visionary experience undergone by sby who has taken a psychedelic drug (e g LSD) **7** a self-indulgent or absorbing course of action, way of behaving, or frame of mind *USE* (6&7) infml

tripartite /trie'pahtiet/ *adj* made between or involving 3 parties

tripe /triep/ *n* **1** the stomach tissue of an ox, cow, etc for use as food **2** sthg inferior, worthless, or offensive – infml

¹**triple** /'tripl/ *v* **tripling, tripling, 'tripl·ing/** to make or become 3 times as great or as many

²**triple** *n* **1** a triple sum, quantity, or number **2** a combination, group, or series of 3

³**triple** *adj* **1** having 3 units or members **2** being 3 times as great or as many **3** marked by 3 beats per bar of music **4** having units of 3 components

triple jump *n* an athletic field event consisting of a jump for distance combining a hop, a step, and a jump in succession

triplet /'triplit/ *n* **1** a unit of 3 lines of verse **2** a combination, set, or group of 3 **3** any of 3 children or animals born at 1 birth

triplex /'tripleks, 'trie-/ *adj* threefold, triple

triplicate /'triplikət/ *n* **1** any of 3 things exactly alike; *specif* any of 3 identical copies **2** three copies all alike – + *in* – **triplicate** *v*

tripod /'trie,pod/ *n* 1 a stool, table, or vessel (e g a cauldron) with 3 legs 2 a 3-legged stand (e g for a camera)

tripos /'triepos/ *n* either part of the honours examination for the Cambridge BA degree

tripper /'tripə/ *n, chiefly Br* one who goes on an outing or pleasure trip, esp one lasting only 1 day – often used disparagingly

triptych /'trip,tik/ *n* a picture or carving on 3 panels side by side

trireme /'trie,reem/ *n* a galley with 3 banks of oars

trite /triet/ *adj* hackneyed from much use – ~ly *adv* – ~ness *n*

¹**triumph** /'trie,um(p)f/ *n* 1 the joy or exultation of victory or success 2 a notable success, victory, or achievement – ~al *adj*

²**triumph** *v* 1 to celebrate victory or success boastfully or exultantly 2 to obtain victory – often + *over*

triumphant /trie'um(p)fənt/ *adj* 1 victorious, conquering 2 rejoicing in or celebrating victory – ~ly *adv*

triumvirate /trie'umvirət/ *n* a group of 3; *esp* a group of 3 ruling a country

trivet /'trivit/ *n* 1 a three-legged (iron) stand for holding cooking vessels over or by a fire; *also* a bracket that hooks onto a grate for this purpose 2 a (metal) stand with 3 feet for holding a hot dish at table

trivia /'trivi·ə/ *n pl but sing or pl in constr* unimportant matters or details

trivial /'trivi·əl/ *adj* 1 commonplace, ordinary 2 of little worth or importance; insignificant – ~ly *adv* – ~ity *n* – ~ize *v*

trochee /'troh,kee/ *n* a metrical foot consisting of 1 long or stressed syllable followed by 1 short or unstressed syllable (e g in *apple*) – **trochaic** *adj*

trod /trod/ *past of* **tread**

trodden /'trod(ə)n/ *past part of* **tread**

troglodyte /'troglədiet/ *n* 1 a cave dweller 2 a person resembling a troglodyte, esp in being solitary or unsocial or in having primitive or outmoded ideas

Trojan /'trohj(ə)n/ *n* 1 a native of Troy 2 one who shows qualities (e g pluck or endurance) attributed to the defenders of ancient Troy – chiefly in *work like a Trojan*

¹**troll** /trohl, trol/ *v* 1 to sing or play an instrument in a jovial manner 2 to fish, esp by drawing a hook through the water

²**troll** *n* (a line with) a lure used in trolling

³**troll** *n* a dwarf or giant of Germanic folklore inhabiting caves or hills

trolley *also* **trolly** /'troli/ *n* 1 a device (e g a grooved wheel or skid) attached to a pole that collects current from an overhead electric wire for powering an electric vehicle 2 *chiefly Br* 2a a shelved stand mounted on castors for conveying sthg (e g food or books) b a basket on wheels that is pushed or pulled by hand and used for carrying goods (e g purchases in a supermarket)

trollop /'troləp/ *n* a slovenly or immoral woman

trombone /trom'bohn/ *n* a brass instrument consisting of a long cylindrical metal tube with a movable slide for varying the pitch – ~**ist** *n*

¹**troop** /troohp/ *n* 1 *sing or pl in constr* 1a a military subunit (e g of cavalry) corresponding to an infantry platoon b a collection of people or things c a unit of scouts under a leader 2 *pl* the armed forces

²**troop** *v* to move in a group, esp in a way that suggests regimentation

trooper /'troohpə/ *n* 1a a cavalry soldier; *esp* a private soldier in a cavalry or armoured regiment b the horse of a cavalry soldier 2 *chiefly NAm & Austr* a mounted policeman

trophy /'trohfi/ *n* sthg gained or awarded in victory or conquest, esp when preserved as a memorial

tropic /'tropik/ *n* 1 either of the 2 small circles of the celestial sphere on each side of and parallel to the equator at a distance of $23\frac{1}{2}$ degrees, which the sun reaches at its greatest declination N or S 2 *pl, often cap* the region between the 2 terrestrial tropics

tropical /'tropikl/ *adj* 1 *also* **tropic** of, occurring in, or characteristic of the tropics 2 *of a sign of the zodiac* beginning at either of the tropics – ~ly *adv*

tropism /'trohpiz(ə)m/ *n* (an) involuntary orientation by (a part of) an organism, esp a plant, that involves turning or curving in response to a source of stimulation (e g light)

¹**trot** /trot/ *n* 1 a moderately fast gait of a horse or other quadruped in which the legs move in diagonal pairs 2 *pl but sing or pl in constr* diarrhoea – usu + *the*; *humor* — **on the trot** in succession — *infml*

²**trot** *v* **-tt-** 1 to ride, drive, or proceed at a trot 2 to proceed briskly

troth /trohth/ *n, archaic* one's pledged word; *also* betrothal – chiefly in *plight one's troth*

Trotskyism /'trotski,iz(ə)m/ *n* the political, economic, and social principles advocated by Trotsky; *esp* adherence to the concept of permanent worldwide revolution – **-ist, -ite** *n, adj*

trotter /'trotə/ *n* the foot of an animal, esp a pig, used as food

troubadour /'troohbədaw, -dooə/ *n* any of a class of lyric poets and poet-musicians, chiefly in France in the 11th to 13th c, whose major theme was courtly love

¹**trouble** /'trubl/ *v* **troubling** /'trubling/ 1a to agitate mentally or spiritually; worry b to produce physical disorder or discomfort in c to put to exertion or inconvenience 2 to make (e g the surface of water) turbulent

²**trouble** *n* **1a** being troubled **b** an instance of distress, annoyance, or disturbance **2** a cause of disturbance, annoyance, or distress: e g **2a** public unrest or demonstrations of dissatisfaction – often *pl* with sing. meaning **b** effort made; exertion **3** a problem, snag

'**trouble,shooter** /-,shoohtə/ *n* **1** a skilled workman employed to locate faults and make repairs in machinery and technical equipment **2** one who specializes or is expert in resolving disputes

'**troublesome** /-s(ə)m/ *adj* giving trouble or anxiety; annoying or burdensome

trough /trof/ *n* **1** a long shallow receptacle for the drinking water or feed of farm animals **2** a long narrow or shallow trench between waves, ridges, etc **3a** the (region round the) lowest point of a regularly recurring cycle of a varying quantity (e g a sine wave) **b** an elongated area of low atmospheric pressure

trounce /trowns/ *v* **1** to thrash or punish severely **2** to defeat decisively

troupe /troohp/ *n* a company or troop (of theatrical performers)

trouper /'troohpə/ *n* a loyal or dependable person

trousers /'trowzəz/ *n pl*, *pl* **trousers** a 2-legged outer garment extending from the waist to the ankle or sometimes only to the knee – **trouser** *adj*

trousseau /'troohsoh/ *n pl* **trousseaux, trousseaus** /-sohz/ the personal outfit of a bride including clothes, accessories, etc

trout /trowt/ *n* **1** any of various food and sport fishes of the salmon family restricted to cool clear fresh waters; *esp* any of various Old World or New World fishes some of which ascend rivers from the sea to breed **2** an ugly unpleasant old woman – slang

trove /trohv/ *n* a treasure trove

trowel /'trowəl/ *n* any of various smooth-bladed hand tools used to apply, spread, shape, or smooth loose or soft material; *also* a scoop-shaped or flat-bladed garden tool for taking up and setting small plants

'**troy ,weight** *n* the series of units of weight based on the pound of 12oz and the ounce of 20 pennyweights or 480 grains

truant /'trooh-ənt/ *n* one who shirks duty; *esp* one who stays away from school without permission – **-ancy** *n*

truce /troohs/ *n* a (temporary) suspension of fighting by agreement of opposing forces

'**truck** /truk/ *n* **1** close association; dealings – chiefly in *have no truck with* **2** payment of wages in goods instead of cash

²**truck** *n* **1a** a usu 4- or 6-wheeled vehicle for moving heavy loads; a lorry **b** a usu 2- or 4-wheeled cart for carrying heavy articles (e g luggage at railway stations) **2** *Br* an open railway goods wagon – **truck** *v*

'**truckle ,bed** *n* a low bed, usu on castors, that can be slid under a higher bed

truculent /'trukyoolənt/ *adj* aggressively self-assertive; belligerent – **-ly** *adv* – **-ence, -ency** *n*

'**trudge** /truj/ *v* to walk steadily and laboriously (along or over)

²**trudge** *n* a long tiring walk

'**true** /trooh/ *adj* **1** steadfast, loyal **2a** in accordance with fact or reality **b** being that which is the case rather than what is claimed or assumed **c** consistent, conforming **3** genuine, real **4a** accurately fitted, adjusted, balanced, or formed **b** exact, accurate

²**true** *n* the state of being accurate (e g in alignment or adjustment) – chiefly in *in/out of true*

³**true** *adv* **1** truly **2a** without deviation; straight **b** without variation from type

,**true-'blue** *adj* staunchly loyal; *specif, Br* being a staunch supporter of the Conservative party

truffle /'trufl/ *n* **1** (any of several fungi (any of several Old World fungi with) a usu dark and wrinkled edible fruiting body that grows under the ground and is eaten as a delicacy **2** a rich soft creamy sweet made with chocolate

trug /trug/ *n*, *Br* a shallow rectangular wooden basket for carrying garden produce

truism /'trooh,iz(ə)m/ *n* an undoubted or self-evident truth

truly /'troohli/ *adv* **1** in accordance with fact or reality; truthfully **2** accurately, exactly **3a** indeed **b** genuinely, sincerely **4** properly, duly

'**trump** /trump/ *n* a trumpet (call) – chiefly poetic

²**trump** *n* **1a** a card (of a suit any of whose cards will win over a card that is not of this suit **b** *pl* the suit whose cards are trumps for a particular hand **2** a worthy and dependable person – *infml* — **come/turn up trumps** to prove unexpectedly helpful or generous

³**trump** *v* to play a trump on (a card or trick) when another suit was led

trumpery /'trumpəri/ *adj* **1** worthless, useless **2** cheap, tawdry

'**trumpet** /'trumpit/ *n* **1** a wind instrument consisting of a usu metal tube, a cup-shaped mouthpiece, and a flared bell; *specif* a valved brass instrument having a cylindrical tube and a usual range from F sharp below middle C upwards for 2¹/₂ octaves **2** sthg that resembles (the flared bell or loud penetrating sound of) a trumpet; *esp* the loud cry of an elephant

²**trumpet** *v* to sound or proclaim loudly (as if) on a trumpet – **-er** *n*

trump up *v* to concoct, fabricate

'**truncate** /'trungkayt, -'-/ *v* to shorten (as if) by cutting off a part

²·**truncate** *adj* having the end square or even

truncheon /'trunchən/ *n* **1** a staff of office or authority **2** a short club carried esp by policemen

trundle /'trundl/ *v* **trundling** /'trundling/ to move heavily or pull along (as if) on wheels

trunk /trungk/ *n* **1a** the main stem of a tree as distinguished from branches and roots **b** the human or animal body apart from the head and limbs **2** a large rigid box used usu for transporting clothing and personal articles **3** the long muscular proboscis of the elephant **4** *pl* men's usu close-fitting shorts worn chiefly for swimming or sports

'**trunk ,call** *n* a long distance telephone call

'**trunk ,road** *n* a road of primary importance, esp for long distance travel

¹**truss** /trus/ *v* **1** to secure tightly; bind – often + *up* **2** to bind the wings or legs of (a fowl) closely in preparation for cooking **2** to support or stiffen (e g a bridge) with a truss

²**truss** *n* **1** a usu triangular assemblage of members (e g beams) forming a rigid framework (e g in a roof or bridge) **2** a device worn to reduce a hernia by pressure **3** a compact flower or fruit cluster (e g of tomatoes)

¹**trust** /trust/ *n* **1** confident belief in or reliance on (the ability, character, honesty, etc of) sby or sthg **2a** a property interest held by one person for the benefit of another **b** a combination of companies formed by a legal agreement **3a** responsible charge or office **b** care, custody — **in trust** in the care or possession of a trustee

²**trust** *v* **1** to place confidence in; rely on **2** to expect or hope, esp confidently

trustee /tru'stee/ *n* **1** a country charged with the supervision of a trust territory **2a** a natural or legal person appointed to administer property in trust for a beneficiary **b** any of a body of people administering the affairs of a company or institution and occupying a position of trust

'**trust,worthy** /-,wuhdhi/ *adj* dependable, reliable – **-thiness** *n*

¹**trusty** /'trusti/ *adj* trustworthy

²**trusty** *n* a trusted person; *specif* a convict considered trustworthy and allowed special privileges

truth /troohth/ *n pl* **truths** /troohdhz, troohths/ **1** sincerity, honesty **2a(1)** the state or quality of being true or factual **a(2)** reality, actuality **b** a judgment, proposition, idea, or body of statements that is (accepted as) true **3** conformity to an original or to a standard

¹**try** /trie/ *v* **1a** to investigate judicially **b** to conduct the trial of **2a** to test by experiment or trial – often + *out* **b** to subject to sthg that tests the patience or endurance **3** to make an attempt at — **try for size** to test for appropriateness or fittingness — **try one's hand** to make an attempt for the first time

²**try** *n* **1** an experimental trial; an attempt **2** a score in rugby that is made by touching down the ball behind the opponent's goal line

try on *v* **1** to put on (a garment) in order to examine the fit or appearance **2** *Br* to attempt to impose on sby – *infml*

tsar, czar, tzar /zah/ *n* a male ruler of Russia

tsetse /'tetsi/ *n* an African fly responsible for the transmission of various diseases including sleeping sickness

'**T-,shirt** /tee/ *n* a vest-like garment worn casually as a shirt

'**T ,square** *n* a ruler with a crosspiece or head at 1 end used in making parallel lines

tub /tub/ *n* **1a** any of various wide low often round vessels typically made of wood, metal, or plastic, and used industrially or domestically (e g for washing clothes or holding soil for shrubs) **b** a small round (plastic) container in which cream, ice cream, etc may be bought **2** a bath **3** an old or slow boat – *infml*

tuba /'tyoohbə/ *n* a large brass instrument having valves, a conical tube, and a cup-shaped mouthpiece

tubby /'tubi/ *adj* podgy, fat

tube /tyoohb/ *n* **1a** a hollow elongated cylinder; *esp* one to convey fluids **2** any of various usu cylindrical structures or devices: e g **2a** a small cylindrical container of soft metal or plastic sealed at one end, and fitted with a cap at the other, from which a paste is dispensed by squeezing **b** the basically cylindrical section between the mouthpiece and bell of a wind instrument **3** *Br* (a train running in) an underground railway – **-bular** *adj*

'**tubeless** /-lis/ *adj* being a pneumatic tyre that does not depend on an inner tube to be airtight

tuber /'tyoohbə/ *n* (a root resembling) a short fleshy usu underground stem (e g a potato) that is potentially able to produce a new plant

tuberculosis /tyoo,buhkyoo'lohsis, tə-/ *n* a serious infectious disease of human beings and other vertebrates and characterized by fever and the formation of abnormal lumps in the body – **-lar** *adj*

tubing /'tyoohbing/ *n* **1** (a length of) material in the form of a tube **2** a series or system of tubes

tub-thumper /'tub ,thumpə/ *n* an impassioned or ranting public speaker

¹**tuck** /tuk/ *v* **1** to draw into a fold or folded position **2** to place in a snug often concealed or isolated spot **3a** to push in the loose end or ends of so as to make secure or tidy **b** to cover snugly by tucking in bedclothes **4a** to eat – usu + *away* **b** to eat heartily – usu + *in* or *into*

²**tuck** *n* **1** a (narrow) fold stitched into cloth to shorten, decorate, or reduce fullness **2** (an act of) tucking **3** *Br* food, esp chocolate, pastries, etc, as eaten by schoolchildren – *infml*

'**tuck-,in** *n, chiefly Br* a hearty meal – *infml*

Tuesday /'tyoohzday, -di/ *n* the day of the week following Monday

tuf

¹tuft /tuft/ *n* **1** a small cluster of long flexible hairs, feathers, grasses, etc attached or close together at the base **2** a clump, cluster

²tuft *v* **1** to adorn with a tuft or tufts **2** to make (e g a mattress) firm by stitching at intervals and sewing on tufts

¹tug /tug/ *v* **-gg-** to pull hard (at)

²tug *n* **1a** a hard pull or jerk **b** a strong pulling force **2** a struggle between 2 people or opposite forces **3a** **tug, tugboat** a strongly built powerful boat used for towing or pushing large ships (e g in and out of dock) **b** an aircraft that tows a glider

tug-of-'war *n pl* **tugs-of-war 1** a struggle for supremacy **2** a contest in which teams pulling at opposite ends of a rope attempt to pull each other across a line marked between them

tuition /tyooh'ish(ə)n/ *n* teaching, instruction

tulip /'tyoohlip/ *n* (the flower of) any of a genus of Eurasian bulbous plants widely grown for their showy flowers

¹tumble /'tumbl/ *v* **tumbling** /'tumbling/, **tumbl·ing 1** to turn end over end in falling or flight **2a** to fall suddenly and helplessly **b** to suffer a sudden overthrow or defeat **c** to decline suddenly and sharply **3** to roll over and over, to and fro, or around **4** to realize suddenly – often + *to*; infml

²tumble *n* **1** a confused heap **2** an act of tumbling; *specif* a fall

'tumble,down /-,down/ *adj* dilapidated, ramshackle

tumbler /'tumblə/ *n* **1a** an acrobat **b** any of various domestic pigeons that tumble or somersault backwards in flight or on the ground **2** a relatively large drinking glass without a foot, stem, or handle

tumescent /tyooh'mes(ə)nt/ *adj* somewhat swollen; *esp, of the penis or clitoris* engorged with blood in response to sexual stimulation – **-cence** *n*

tummy /'tumi/ *n* the stomach – infml

tumour, *NAm chiefly* **tumor** /'tyoohmə/ *n* an abnormal mass of tissue that arises without obvious cause from cells of existing tissue

tumult /'tyoohmult/ *n* **1a** commotion, uproar (e g of a crowd) **b** a turbulent uprising; a riot **2** violent mental or emotional agitation

tumultuous /tyooh'multyoo-əs, -choo-əs/ *adj* **1** marked by commotion; riotous **2** marked by violent turbulence or upheaval – **-ly** *adv*

tumulus /'tyoohmyooləs/ *n, pl* **tumuli** /-lie/ an ancient grave; a barrow

tun /tun/ *n* a large cask, esp for wine

tuna /'tyoohnə/ *n* any of numerous large vigorous food and sport fishes related to the mackerels

tundra /'tundrə/ *n* a level or undulating treeless plain with a permanently frozen subsoil that is characteristic of arctic and subarctic regions

¹tune /tyoohn/ *n* **1a** a pleasing succession of musical notes; a melody **b** the dominant tune in a musical composition **2** correct musical pitch (with another instrument, voice, etc) **3a** accord, harmony **b** general attitude; approach

²tune *v* **1** to bring a musical instrument or instruments into tune, esp with a standard pitch – usu + *up* **2** to adjust for optimum performance – often + *up* **3** to adjust a receiver for the reception of a particular broadcast or station – + *in* or *to*

tungsten /'tungstən/ *n* a hard metallic element with a high melting point that is used esp for electrical purposes and in hard alloys (e g steel)

tunic /'tyoohnik/ *n* **1** a simple (hip- or knee-length) slip-on garment usu belted or gathered at the waist **2** a close-fitting jacket with a high collar worn esp as part of a uniform

'tuning ,fork /'tyoohning/ *n* a 2-pronged metal implement that gives a fixed tone when struck and is useful for tuning musical instruments and setting pitches for singing

¹tunnel /'tunl/ *n* **1** a hollow conduit or recess (e g for a propeller shaft) **2a** a man-made horizontal passageway through or under an obstruction **b** a subterranean passage (e g in a mine)

²tunnel *v* **-ll-** (*NAm* **-l-, -ll-**), /'tunl·ing/ **1** to make a passage through or under **2** to make (e g one's way) by excavating a tunnel – **~ler** *n*

tunny /'tuni/ *n pl* **tunnies**, *esp collectively* **tunny** tuna

tuppence /'tup(ə)ns/ *n* (a) twopence

turban /'tuhbən/ *n* (a headdress, esp for a lady, resembling) a headdress worn esp by Muslims and Sikhs and made of a long cloth wound round a cap or directly round the head – **~ed** *adj*

turbid /'tuhbid/ *adj* **1a** opaque (as if) with disturbed sediment; cloudy **b** thick with smoke or mist **2** (mentally or emotionally) confused – **~ness**, **~ity** *n*

turbine /'tuhbien/ *n* a rotary engine whose central driving shaft is fitted with vanes whirled round by the pressure of water, steam, exhaust gases, etc

'turbo,prop /-,prop/ *n* (an aircraft powered by) an engine that has a turbine-driven propeller for providing the main thrust

turbot /'tuhbət/ *n pl* **turbot**, *esp for different types* **turbots** a large European flatfish highly valued as food

turbulence /'tuhbyooləns/ *n* **1** wild commotion or agitation **2** irregular atmospheric motion, esp when characterized by strong currents of rising and falling air

turbulent /'tuhbyoolənt/ *adj* **1** causing unrest, violence, or disturbance **2** agitated, stormy, or tempestuous **3** exhibiting physical turbulence

turd /tuhd/ *n* **1** a piece of excrement **2** a despicable person *USE* vulg

tureen /tyoo'reen, tə-/ *n* a deep (covered) dish from which a food, esp soup, is served at table

¹**turf** /tuhf/ n, pl **turfs, turves** /tuhvz/ 1 the upper layer of soil bound by grass and plant roots into a thick mat 2 (a piece of dried) peat 3 the sport or business of horse racing or the course on which horse races are run

²**turf** v to cover with turf

'**turf ac,countant** n, Br a bookmaker

turf out v to dismiss or throw out forcibly – infml

turgid /'tuhjid/ adj 1 distended, swollen 2 in a pompous inflated style; laboured – ~ ity n – ~ ly adv

turkey /'tuhki/ n pl **turkeys**, esp collectively **turkey** (the flesh of) a large orig American bird that is farmed for its meat in most parts of the world

¹**Turkish** /'tuhkish/ adj (characteristic) of Turkey or the Turks

²**Turkish** n the Turkic language of the Republic of Turkey

,**Turkish 'bath** n a steam bath followed by a rubdown, massage, and cold shower

,**Turkish de'light** n a jellylike confection, usu cut in cubes and dusted with sugar

turmoil /'tuhmoyl/ n an extremely confused or agitated state

¹**turn** /tuhn/ v 1a(1) to (make) rotate or revolve a(2) to alter the functioning of (as if) by turning a knob b to perform by rotating or revolving c(1) to become giddy or dizzy c(2) of the stomach to feel nauseated d to centre or hinge on sthg 2a(1) to dig or plough so as to bring the lower soil to the surface a(2) to renew (e g a garment) by reversing the material and resewing b to cause to change or reverse direction c to direct one's course 3a to change position so as to face another way b to change one's attitude to one of hostility c to make a sudden violent physical or verbal assault – usu + on or upon 4a to direct, present, or point (e g the face) in a specified direction b to aim, train c to direct, induce, or influence in a specified direction, esp towards or away from sthg or sthg d to apply, devote; also resort, have recourse to e to direct into or out of a receptacle (as if) by inverting 5a to become changed, altered, or transformed: e g 5a(1) to change colour a(2) to become acid or sour b to become by change 6a to give a rounded form to b to fashion elegantly or neatly 7 to fold, bend 8 to gain in the course of business – esp in turn an honest penny — **turn a blind eye** to refuse to see; be oblivious — **turn a deaf ear** to refuse to listen — **turn a hair** to show any reaction (e g of surprise or alarm) — **turn back the clock** to revert to an earlier or past state or condition — **turn colour** to change colour; esp to grow pale or red — **turn in one's grave** to be disturbed at goings-on that would have shocked one when alive — said of a dead person — **turn King's/Queen's evidence** Br, of an accomplice to testify for the prosecution in court — **turn one's**

back on to reject, deny — **turn one's hand** to apply oneself; set to work — **turn someone's head** to cause sby to become infatuated or to harbour extravagant notions of conceit — **turn someone's stomach** 1 to disgust sby completely 2 to sicken, nauseate — **turn tail** to run away; flee — **turn the other cheek** to respond to injury or unkindness with patience; forgo retaliation — **turn the scale/scales** 1 to register a usu specified weight 2 to prove decisive — **turn the tables** to bring about a reversal of the relative conditions or fortunes of 2 contending parties — **turn turtle** to capsize, overturn

²**turn** n **1a** a turning about a centre or axis; (a) rotation **b** any of various rotating or pivoting movements (in dancing) **2a** a change or reversal of direction, stance, position, or course **b** a deflection, deviation **3** a short trip out and back or round about **4** an act or deed of a specified kind **5a** a place, time, or opportunity granted in succession or rotation **b** a period of duty, action, or activity **6a** an alteration, change **b** a point of change in time **7** a style of expression **8** a single coil (e g of rope wound round an object) **9** a bent, inclination **10a** a spell or attack of illness, faintness, etc **b** a nervous start or shock — **at every turn** on every occasion; constantly, continually — **by turns** one after another in regular succession — **in turn** in due order of succession; alternately — **on the turn** at the point of turning — **out of turn** 1 not in due order of succession 2 at a wrong time or place — **to a turn** to perfection — **turn and turn about** by turns

turnabout /'tuhnə,bowt/ n a change or reversal of direction, trend, etc

'**turn,coat** /-,koht/ n one who switches to an opposing side or party; a traitor

'**turn,down** /-,down/ adj worn turned down

turn down v 1 to reduce the intensity, volume, etc of (as if) by turning a control 2 to decline to accept; reject

turner /'tuhnə/ n one who forms articles on a lathe

turn in v 1 to deliver, hand over; esp to deliver up to an authority 2 to give, execute 3 to go to bed – infml

turning /'tuhning/ n 1 a place of turning, turning off, or turning back, esp on a road 2a a forming or being formed by use of a lathe b pl waste produced in turning sthg on a lathe 3 the width of cloth that is folded under for a seam or hem

'**turning ,point** n a point at which a significant change occurs

turnip /'tuhnip/ n (a plant of the mustard family with) a thick white-fleshed root eaten as a vegetable or fed to stock

turnkey /'tuhn,kee/ n a prison warden

'**turn,off** /-,of/ n a turning off

turn off v 1 to stop the flow or operation of (as if) by turning a control 2 to deviate from a straight course or from a main road 3 to cause to lose (sexual) interest – infml

turn on v 1 to cause to flow or operate (as if) by turning a control 2 to excite or interest pleasurably and esp sexually – infml

'turn,out /-,owt/ n 1 people in attendance (e g at a meeting) 2 manner of dress; getup

turn out v 1 to empty the contents of, esp for cleaning 2 to produce often rapidly or regularly (as if) by machine 3 to equip or dress in a specified way 4 to put out (esp a light) by turning a switch 5 to leave one's home for a meeting, public event, etc 6 to get out of bed – infml

'turn,over /-,ohvə/ n 1 a small semicircular filled pastry made by folding half of the crust over the other half 2a the total sales revenue of a business b the ratio of sales to average stock for a stated period 3 (the rate of) movement (e g of goods or people) into, through, and out of a place

turn over v 1 to think over; meditate on 2 of an internal combustion engine to revolve at low speed 3 of merchandise to be stocked and disposed of —

turn over a new leaf to make a change for the better, esp in one's way of living

'turn,stile /-,stiel/ n a gate with arms pivoted on the top that turns to admit 1 person at a time

'turn,table /-,taybl/ n 1 a circular platform for turning wheeled vehicles, esp railway engines 2 the platform on which a gramophone record is rotated while being played

turn to v to apply oneself to work

'turn-,up n 1 chiefly Br a turned-up hem, esp on a pair of trousers 2 an unexpected or surprising event – esp in turn-up for the book; infml

turn up v 1 to increase the intensity, volume, etc of (as if) by turning a control 2 to find, discover 3 to come to light unexpectedly; also to happen unexpectedly 4 to appear, arrive — **turn up one's nose** to show scorn or disdain

turpentine /'tuhpən,tien/ n 1 a resinous substance obtained from various trees 2 an essential oil obtained from turpentines by distillation and used esp as a solvent and paint thinner

turquoise /'tuhkwoyz, -kwoyz/ n 1 a sky blue to greenish mineral used as a gem 2 a light greenish blue colour

turret /'turit/ n 1 a little tower, often at the corner of a larger building 2 a rotatable holder (e g for a tool or die) in a lathe, milling machine, etc 3 a usu revolving armoured structure on warships, forts, tanks, aircraft, etc in which guns are mounted

turtle /'tuhtl/ n any of several marine reptiles of the same order as and similar to tortoises but adapted for swimming

'turtle,dove /-,duv/ n any of several small wild pigeons noted for plaintive cooing

'turtle,neck /-,nek/ n a high close-fitting neckline, esp of a sweater

tusk /tusk/ n a long greatly enlarged tooth of an elephant, boar, walrus, etc, that projects when the mouth is closed and serves for digging food or as a weapon

tussle /'tusl/ n a (physical) contest or struggle – **tussle** v

tussock /'tusək/ n a compact tuft of grass, sedge, etc

tut /tut; or clicked t []/, **tut-tut** interj – used to express disapproval or impatience – **tut** v

tutelage /'tyoohtilij/ n 1 guardianship 2 the state or period of being under a guardian or tutor

'tutor /'tyoohtə/ n 1 a private teacher 2 a British university teacher who 2a gives instruction to students, esp individually b is in charge of the social and moral welfare of a group of students 3 Br an instruction book

'tutor v to teach or guide usu individually; coach

'tutorial /tyooh'tawri-əl/ adj of or involving (individual tuition by) a tutor

'tutorial n a class conducted by a tutor for 1 student or a small number of students

tutti-frutti /,toohti 'froohti/ n (a confection, esp an ice cream, containing) a mixture of chopped, dried, or candied fruits

tutu /'tooh,tooh/ n a very short projecting stiff skirt worn by a ballerina

tuxedo /tuk'seedoh/ n, pl **tuxedos, tuxedoes** NAm a dinner jacket

TV /,tee 'vee/ n television

twaddle /'twodl/ n **twaddling** /'twodl·ing, 'twodling/ rubbish or drivel – **twaddle** v

twain /twayn/ n, adj, or pron, archaic two

'twang /twang/ n a harsh quick ringing sound like that of a plucked bowstring

'twang v to pluck the string of

tweak /tweek/ v to pinch and pull with a sudden jerk and twist – **tweak** n

twee /twee/ adj excessively sentimental, pretty, or coy

tweed /tweed/ n 1 a rough woollen fabric made usu in twill weaves and used esp for suits and coats 2 pl tweed clothing; specif a tweed suit

tweet /tweet/ v or n (to) chirp

tweeter /'tweetə/ n a small loudspeaker that responds mainly to the higher frequencies

tweezers /'tweezəz/ n pl pl **tweezers** a small metal instrument that is usu held between thumb and forefinger, is used for plucking, holding, or manipulating, and consists of 2 prongs joined at 1 end

twelfth /twelf(f)th/ n 1 number twelve in a countable series 2 often cap, Br the twelfth of August on which the grouse-shooting season begins – **twelfth** adj – **~ly** adv

twelve /twelv/ n 1 the number 12 2 the twelfth in a set or series 3 sthg having 12 parts or members or a denomination of 12

twenty /'twenti/ n 1 the number 20 2 pl the numbers 20 to 29; specif a range of temperatures, ages, or dates in a century characterized by those numbers 3 sthg (e g a bank note) having a denomination of 20 – **-tieth** n, adj, adv

twenty-'one n 1 the number 21 2 pontoon

twerp also **twirp** /twuhp/ n a silly fool

twice /twies/ adv 1 on 2 occasions 2 two times; in doubled quantity or degree

¹**twiddle** /'twidl/ v **twiddling** /'twidling, 'twidl·ing/ to play negligently with sthg

²**twiddle** n a turn, twist

¹**twig** /twig/ n a small woody shoot or branch, usu without its leaves – **twiggy** adj

²**twig** v -gg- to catch on; understand – infml

twilight /'twie,liet/ n 1a the light from the sky between full night and sunrise or esp between sunset and full night b the period between sunset and full night 2a a shadowy indeterminate state b a period or state of decline

twill /twil/ n (a fabric with) a textile weave in which the weft threads pass over 1 and under 2 or more warp threads to give an appearance of diagonal lines – **-ed** adj

¹**twin** /twin/ adj 1 born with one other or as a pair at 1 birth 2 having or made up of 2 similar, related, or identical units or parts

²**twin** n 1 either of 2 offspring produced at 1 birth 2 either of 2 people or things closely related to or resembling each other

³**twin** v -nn- 1 to become paired or closely associated 2 to give birth to twins

twin 'bed n either of 2 matching single beds

¹**twine** /twien/ n a strong string of 2 or more strands twisted together

²**twine** v 1 to twist together 2 to twist or coil round sthg

twinge /twinj/ v or n **twinging, twingeing** (to feel) 1 a sudden sharp stab of pain 2 an emotional pang

¹**twinkle** /'twingkl/ v **twinkling** /'twingkling, 'twingkl·ing/ 1 to shine with a flickering or sparkling light 2 to appear bright with gaiety or amusement

²**twinkle** n 1 an instant, twinkling 2 an (intermittent) sparkle or gleam

twinkling /'twingkling/ n a very short time; a moment

'**twin ,set** n a jumper and cardigan designed to be worn together, usu by a woman

¹**twirl** /twuhl/ v to revolve rapidly – ~ **er** n

²**twirl** n 1 an act of twirling 2 a coil, whorl – ~ **y** adj

twirp /twuhp/ n a twerp

¹**twist** /twist/ v 1 to join together by winding 2 to wind or coil round sthg 3a to wring or wrench so as to dislocate or distort b to distort the meaning

of; pervert c to pull off, turn, or break by a turning force d to warp 4 to follow a winding course; snake — **twist someone's arm** to bring strong pressure to bear on sby

²**twist** n 1 sthg formed by twisting: e g 1a a thread, yarn, or cord formed by twisting 2 or more strands together b a screw of paper used as a container 2a a twisting or being twisted b a dance popular esp in the 1960s and performed with gyrations, esp of the hips c a spiral turn or curve 3a a turning off a straight course; a bend b a distortion of meaning or sense 4 an unexpected turn or development – **twisty** adj

twister /'twista/ n a dishonest person; a swindler – infml

¹**twit** /twit/ v -tt- to tease, taunt

²**twit** n, Br an absurd or silly person

¹**twitch** /twich/ v 1 to pull, pluck 2 to move jerkily or involuntarily – ~ **er** n

²**twitch** n 1 a short sudden pull or jerk 2 a physical or mental pang 3 a tic

¹**twitter** /'twita/ v 1 to utter twitters 2 to talk in a nervous chattering fashion 3 to tremble with agitation; flutter – ~ **er** n

²**twitter** n 1 a nervous agitation – esp in all of a twitter 2 a small tremulous intermittent sound characteristic of birds – ~ **y** adj

¹**two** /tooh/ pron, pl in constr 1 two unspecified countable individuals 2 a small approximate number of indicated things

²**two** n, pl **twos** 1 the number 2 2 the second in a set or series 3 sthg having 2 parts or members or a denomination of 2

two-'edged adj double-edged

two-'faced adj double-dealing, hypocritical

two-'handed adj 1 used with both hands 2 requiring 2 people 3 ambidextrous

twosome /'toohs(ə)m/ n a group of 2 people or things

'**two-,step** n (a piece of music for) a ballroom dance in either ²/₄ or ⁴/₄ time

two-'time v to be unfaithful to (a spouse or lover) by having a secret relationship with another – **two-timer** n

two-'way adj 1 moving or allowing movement or use in 2 (opposite) directions 2 involving mutual responsibility or a reciprocal relationship 3 involving 2 participants

tycoon /tie'koohn/ n a businessman of exceptional wealth and power

tying /'tie·ing/ pres part of **tie**

tyke, tike /tiek/ n 1 a (mongrel) dog 2 Br a boorish churlish person 3 a small child

tympanum /'timpənəm/ n, pl **tympana** /-nə/, **tympanums** 1a the eardrum b a thin tense membrane covering the hearing-organ of an insect 2 the space within an arch and above a lintel (e g in a medieval doorway)

¹type /tiep/ *n* **1** a model, exemplar, or characteristic specimen **2a** (any of) a collection of usu rectangular blocks or characters bearing a relief from which an inked print can be made **b** printed letters **3a** a person of a specified nature **b** a particular kind, class, or group with distinct characteristics **c** sthg distinguishable **as** a variety; a sort

²type *v* to write with a typewriter; *also* to keyboard

'type,cast /-,kahst/ *v* **typecast** to cast an actor repeatedly in the same type of role; *broadly* to stereotype

'type,face /-,fays/ *n* (the appearance of) a single design of printing type

'type,script /-,skript/ *n* a typewritten manuscript (e g for use as printer's copy)

'type,writer /-,rietə/ *n* a machine with a keyboard for writing in characters resembling type – **typewrite** *v*

typhoid /'tiefoyd/, **typhoid fever** *n* a serious communicable human disease caused by a bacterium and marked esp by fever and intestinal inflammation

typhoon /tie'foohn/ *n* a tropical cyclone occurring in the Philippines or the China sea

typhus /'tiefəs/ *n* a serious human disease transmitted esp by body lice

typical /'tipikl/ *adj* **1** being or having the nature of a type; symbolic, representative **2a** having or showing the essential characteristics of a type **b** showing or according with the usual or expected (unfavourable) traits – **~ly** *adv*

typify /'tipifie/ *v* **1** to constitute a typical instance of **2** to embody the essential characteristics of

typist /'tiepist/ *n* one who uses a typewriter, esp as an occupation

typography /tie'pogrəfi/ *n* the style, arrangement, or appearance of printed matter – **-pher** *n* – **-phic** *adj* – **-phically** *adv*

tyranny /'tirəni/ *n* **1** a government in which absolute power is vested in a single ruler **2** oppressive power (exerted by a tyrant) **3** sthg severe, oppressive, or inexorable in effect – **-nical** *adj* – **-nically** *adv* – **-nize** *v*

tyrant /'tie(ə)rənt/ *n* **1** a ruler who exercises absolute power, esp oppressively or brutally **2** one who exercises authority harshly or unjustly

tyre, *NAm chiefly* **tire** /tie·ə/ *n* a continuous solid or inflated hollow rubber cushion set round a wheel to absorb shock

U

u /yooh/ *n, pl* **u's**, **us** *often cap* (a graphic representation of or device for reproducing) the 21st letter of the English alphabet

¹U *adj, chiefly Br* upper-class

²U *n or adj* (a film that is) certified in Britain as suitable for all age groups

ubiquitous /yooh'bikwitəs/ *adj* being everywhere at the same time

'U-,boat *n* a German submarine

udder /'udə/ *n* a large pendulous organ consisting of 2 or more mammary glands enclosed in a common envelope and each having a single nipple

UFO /'yoohfoh, ,yooh ef 'oh/ *n, pl* **UFO's**, **UFOs** an unidentified flying object; *esp* a flying saucer

ugh /ookh, uh/ *interj* – used to express disgust or horror

ugly /'ugli/ *adj* **1** frightful, horrible **2** offensive or displeasing to any of the senses, esp to the sight **3** morally offensive or objectionable **4a** ominous, threatening **b** surly, quarrelsome – **-liness** *n*

,ugly 'duckling *n* sby who or sthg that appears unpromising but turns out successful

ukulele /,yoohkə'layli/ *n* a small guitar

ulcer /'ulsə/ *n* **1** a persistent open sore in skin **2** sthg that festers and corrupts – **~ous** *adj*

ulcerate /'ulsə,rayt/ *v* to (cause to) become affected (as if) with an ulcer – **-ation** *n*

ulna /'ulnə/ *n* the bone of the human forearm on the little-finger side

ulterior /ul'tiəri·ə/ *adj* going beyond what is openly said or shown

¹ultimate /'ultimət/ *adj* **1a** last in a progression or series **b** eventual **2a** fundamental, basic **b** incapable of further analysis, division, or separation **3** maximum, greatest

²ultimate *n* sthg ultimate; *the* highest point

'ultimately /-li/ *adv* finally; at last

ultimatum /,ulti'maytəm/ *n, pl* **ultimatums**, **ultimata** /-tə/ a final proposition or demand; *esp* one whose rejection will end negotiations and cause a resort to direct action

ultrahigh frequency /,ultrə'hie/ *n* a radio frequency in the range between 300 megahertz and 3000 megahertz

ultramarine /,ultrəmə'reen/ *n* a deep blue

,ultra'sonic /-'sonik/ *adj, of waves and vibrations* having a frequency above about 20,000Hz

,ultra'violet /-'vie·ələt/ *n* electromagnetic radiation having a wavelength between the violet end of the visible spectrum and X rays – **ultraviolet** *adj*

umber /'umbə/ *n* **1** a brown earth used as a pigment **2** a dark or yellowish brown colour

umbilical cord *n* a cord arising from the navel that connects the foetus with the placenta

umbrage /'umbrij/ *n* a feeling of pique or resentment

umbrella /um'brelə/ *n* a collapsible shade for protection against weather, consisting of fabric stretched over hinged ribs radiating from a central pole

¹**umpire** /'umpiə-ə/ *n* 1 one having authority to settle a controversy or question between parties 2 a referee in any of several sports (e g cricket)

²**umpire** *v* to act as or supervise (e g a match) as umpire

umpteen /,ump'teen/ *adj* very many; indefinitely numerous – *infml* – ~ **th** *n, adj*

unable /un'ayb(ə)l/ *adj* not able; incapable: **a** unqualified, incompetent **b** impotent, helpless

unaccountable /,unə'kowntəbl/ *adj* 1 inexplicable, strange 2 not to be called to account; not responsible – **-bly** *adv*

unaccustomed /,unə'kustəmd/ *adj* 1 not customary 2 not used *to*

unadulterated /,unə'dultəraytid/ *adj* unmixed; pure

unaffected /,unə'fektid/ *adj* 1 not influenced or changed 2 free from affectation; genuine – ~ **ly** *adv*

unanimous /yoo'nanimas/ *adj* 1 being of one mind; agreeing 2 characterized by the agreement and consent of all – ~ **ly** *adv* – **-mity** *n*

unassuming /,unə'syoohming/ *adj* modest – ~ **ly** *adv*

unawares /,unə'weaz/ *adv* 1 without noticing or intending 2 suddenly, unexpectedly

unbalance /un'baləns/ *v* to put out of balance; *esp* to derange mentally

unbearable /un'beərəbl/ *adj* not endurable; intolerable – **-ly** *adv*

unbeknown /,unbi'nohn/ *adj* happening without one's knowledge – usu + *to*

unbelievable /,unbi'leevəbl/ *adj* incredible – **-bly** *adv*

unbeliever /,unbi'leevə/ *n* one who does not believe, esp in a particular religion

unbend /un'bend/ *v* **unbent** /,un'bent/ 1 to become more relaxed, informal, or outgoing in manner 2 to become straight

unbending /un'bending/ *adj* 1 unyielding, inflexible 2 aloof or unsociable in manner

unborn /,un'bawn/ *adj* still to appear; future

unbosom /un'boozəm/ *v* to disclose the thoughts or feelings of (oneself)

unbounded /un'bowndid/ *adj* having no limits or constraints

unbowed /un'bowd/ *adj* not bowed down; *esp* not subdued

un'bridled *adj* unrestrained, ungoverned

unbuckle /un'bukl/ *v* to unfasten

unburden /un'buhd(ə)n/ *v* to free or relieve from anxiety, cares, etc

uncalled-for /un'kawld faw/ *adj* 1 unnecessary 2 offered without provocation or justification; gratuitous

uncanny /un'kani/ *adj* 1 eerie, mysterious 2 beyond what is normal or expected – **-nily** *adv*

unceremonious /,unserə'mohnyəs/ *adj* abrupt, rude – ~ **ly** *adv* – ~ **ness** *n*

uncertain /un'suhtn/ *adj* 1 not reliable or trustworthy 2a not definitely known; undecided, unpredictable **b** not confident or sure; doubtful 3 variable, changeable – ~ **ly** *adv* – ~ **ness** *n* – ~ **ty** *n*

uncharitable /un'charitəbl/ *adj* severe in judging others; harsh – **-bly** *adv*

unchristian /un'kristi-ən/ *adj* barbarous, uncivilized

uncle /'ungkl/ *n* **1a** the brother of one's father or mother **b** the husband of one's aunt 2 a man who is a very close friend of a young child or its parents

unclean /un'kleen/ *adj* 1 morally or spiritually impure 2 ritually unclean as food – ~ **ness** *n*

Uncle 'Sam /sam/ *n* the American nation, people, or government

uncomfortable /un'kumftəbl/ *adj* feeling discomfort; ill at ease – **-bly** *adv*

uncommitted /,unkə'mitid/ *adj* not pledged to a particular belief, allegiance, or course of action

uncompromising /un'komprəmiezing/ *adj* not making or accepting a compromise; unyielding – ~ **ly** *adv*

unconcerned /,unkən'suhnd/ *adj* 1 not involved or interested 2 not anxious or worried – ~ **ly** *adv*

unconditional /,unkən'dish(ə)nl/ *adj* absolute, unqualified – ~ **ly** *adv*

unconscionable /un'konsh(ə)nəbl/ *adj* 1 unscrupulous, unprincipled 2 excessive, unreasonable – **-bly** *adv*

¹**unconscious** /un'konshəs/ *adj* 1 not knowing or perceiving **2a** not possessing mind or having lost consciousness **b** not marked by or resulting from conscious thought, sensation, or feeling 3 not intentional or deliberate – ~ **ly** *adv* – ~ **ness** *n*

²**unconscious** *n* the part of the mind that does not ordinarily enter a person's awareness but nevertheless influences behaviour and may be manifested in dreams or slips of the tongue

unconsidered /,unkən'sidəd/ *adj* 1 disregarded, unnoticed 2 not carefully thought out

uncork /,un'kawk/ *v* to release from a pent-up state; unleash

uncouple /,un'kupl/ *v* to detach, disconnect

uncouth /un'koohth/ *adj* awkward and uncultivated in speech or manner; boorish – ~ **ly** *adv* – ~ **ness** *n*

uncover /un'kuvə/ *v* to disclose, reveal

uncritical /un'kritikl/ *adj* lacking in discrimination or critical analysis

uncrowned /ʌnˈkrownd/ *adj* having a specified status in fact but not in name

unctuous /ˈʌngktyoo·əs/ *adj* marked by ingratiating smoothness and false sincerity – **~ly** *adv* – **~ness** *n*

uncut /ʌnˈkut/ *adj* **1** not cut down or into **2** *of a book* not having the folds of the leaves trimmed off **3** not abridged or curtailed

undaunted /ʌnˈdawntid/ *adj* not discouraged by danger or difficulty

undecided /ˌundiˈsiedid/ *adj* **1** in doubt **2** without a result – **~ly** *adv* – **~ness** *n*

undeniable /ˌundiˈnie·əbl/ *adj* **1** plainly true; incontestable **2** unquestionably excellent or genuine – **-bly** *adv*

¹under /ˈundə/ *adv* **1** in or to a position below or beneath sthg **2a** in or to a lower rank or number (e g £10 or *under*) **b** to a subnormal degree; deficiently – often in combination (e g *under*-financed) **3** in or into a condition of subjection, subordination, or unconsciousness **4** so as to be covered, buried, or sheltered

²under *prep* **1a** below or beneath so as to be overhung, surmounted, covered, protected, or hidden **b** using as a pseudonym or alias **2a(1)** subject to the authority, control, guidance, or instruction of **a(2)** during the rule or control of **b** receiving or undergoing the action or effect of (e g *under* treatment) **3** within the group or designation of (e g *under* this heading) **4** less than or inferior to; *esp* falling short of (a standard or required degree)

³under *adj* **1a** lying or placed below, beneath, or on the lower side **b** facing or pointing downwards **2** lower in rank or authority; subordinate **3** lower than usual, proper, or desired in amount or degree *USE* often in combination

under·act /-ˈakt/ *v* **1** to perform (a dramatic part) without adequate force or skill **2** to perform with restraint for greater dramatic impact or personal force

¹under·arm /-ˌahm/ *adj* **1** under or on the underside of the arm **2** made with the arm brought forwards and up from below shoulder level

²underarm *v or adv* (to throw) with an underarm motion

under·carriage /-ˌkarij/ *n* the part of an aircraft's structure that supports its weight, when in contact with the land or water

under·charge /-ˈchahj/ *v* to charge (e g a person) too little

under·clothes /-ˌklohdhz/ *n pl* underwear

under·coat /-ˌkoht/ *n* **1** a growth of short hair or fur partly concealed by a longer growth **2** a coat (e g of paint) applied as a base for another coat

under·cover /-ˈkuvə/ *adj* acting or done in secret; *specif* engaged in spying

under·current /-ˌkurənt/ *n* a hidden opinion, feeling, or tendency

under·cut /-ˈkut/ *v* **-tt-**; **undercut 1** to cut away material from the underside of so as to leave a portion overhanging **2** to offer sthg at lower prices than or work for lower wages than (a competitor)

¹under·dog /-ˌdog/ *n* a victim of injustice or persecution

under·done /-ˈdun/ *adj* not thoroughly cooked

under·estimate /-ˈestimayt/ *v* **1** to estimate as being less than the actual size, quantity, etc **2** to place too low a value on; underrate

under·felt /-ˌfelt/ *n* a thick felt underlay placed under a carpet

under·foot /-ˈfoot/ *adv* under the feet, esp against the ground

under·garment /-ˌgahmənt/ *n* a garment to be worn under another

under·go /-ˈgoh/ *v* **underwent** /-ˈwent/; **undergone** /-ˈgon/ to be subjected to; experience

under·graduate /-ˌgradyoo·ət/ *n* a college or university student who has not taken a first degree

¹under·ground /-ˈgrownd/ *adv* **1** beneath the surface of the earth **2** in or hiding or secret operation

²underground *adj* **1** growing, operating, or situated below the surface of the ground **2a** conducted in hiding or in secret **b** existing or operated outside the establishment, esp by the avant-garde

³under·ground *n* **1** *sing or pl in constr* **1a** a secret movement or group esp in an occupied country, for concerted resistive action **b** a usu avant-garde group or movement that functions outside the establishment **2** *Br* a usu electric underground urban railway; *also* a train running in an underground

under·growth /-ˌgrohth/ *n* shrub, bushes, saplings, etc growing under larger trees in a wood or forest

¹underhand /ˌundəˈhand; *sense 2* ˈ--,-/ *adv* **1** in an underhand manner; secretly **2** underarm

²underhand *adj* not honest and aboveboard; sly

¹under·lay /-ˈlay/ *v*, **under·laid** /-ˈlayd/ to cover or line the bottom of; give support to the underside of or below

²under·lay *n* sthg that is (designed to be) laid under sthg else

under·lie /-ˈlie/ *v* **underlying** /-ˈlie·ing/; **underlay** /-ˈlay/; **underlain** /-ˈlayn/ **1** to lie or be situated under **2** to form the basis or foundation of **3** to be concealed beneath the exterior of

under·line /-ˈlien/ *v* to emphasize, stress

underling /-ling/ *n* a subordinate or inferior

under·mentioned /-ˌmensh(ə)nd/ *adj*, *Br* referred to at a later point in a text

under·mine /-ˈmien/ *v* to weaken or destroy gradually or insidiously

underneath /ˌundəˈneeth/ *prep* directly below; close under

²under'neath *adv* **1** under or below an object or a surface; beneath **2** on the lower side

'under,pants /-,pants/ *n pl* men's pants

'under,pass /-,pahs/ *n* a tunnel or passage taking a road and pavement under another road or a railway

under'pin /-,pin/ *v* **-nn-** to form part of, strengthen, or replace the foundation of

,under'play /-'play/ *v* **1** to underact (a role) **2** to play down the importance of

,under'privileged /-'priv(i)lijd/ *adj* deprived of some of the fundamental social or economic rights of a civilized society

,under'rate /-'rayt/ *v* to rate too low; undervalue

,under'score /-'skaw/ *v* to underline

,under'sell /-'sel/ *v*, **under'sold** /-'sohld/ **1** to be sold cheaper than **2** to make little of the merits of; *esp* to promote or publicize in a (deliberately) low-key manner

'under,signed /-,siend/ *n pl* **undersigned** the one who signs his/her name at the end of a document

understand /,undə'stand/ *v* **understood** /-'stood/ **1a** to grasp the meaning of; comprehend **b** to have a thorough knowledge of or expertise in **2** to assume, suppose **3** to interpret in one of a number of possible ways **4** to show a sympathetic or tolerant attitude – ~**able** *adj* – ~**ably** *adv*

¹,under'standing /-'standing/ *n* **1** a mental grasp; comprehension **2** the power of comprehending; intelligence **3a** a friendly or harmonious relationship **b** an informal mutual agreement

²understanding *adj* tolerant, sympathetic

,under'state /-'stayt/ *v* **1** to state as being less than is the case **2** to present with restraint, esp for greater effect – ~**ment** *n*

¹,under'study /,undə'studi, '--,--/ *v* to study another actor's part in order to take it over in an emergency

²'under,study *n* one who is prepared to act another's part or take over another's duties

,under'take /-'tayk/ *v*, **under'took** /-'took/; **under'taken** /-'taykən/ **1** to take upon oneself as a task **2** to put oneself under obligation to do; contract **3** to guarantee, promise

'under,taker /-,taykə/ *n* sby whose business is preparing the dead for burial and arranging and managing funerals

'under,taking /-,tayking/ *n* **1** an enterprise **2** a pledge, guarantee

'under,tone /-,tohn/ *n* **1** a subdued utterance **2** an underlying quality (e g of emotion)

'under,tow /-,toh/ *n* **1** an undercurrent that flows in a different direction from the surface current, esp out to sea **2** a hidden tendency often contrary to the one that is plainly apparent

,under'water /-'wawtə/ *adj* **1** situated, used, or designed to operate below the surface of the water **2** being below the waterline of a ship

'under,wear /-,weə/ *n* clothing worn next to the skin and under other clothing

underweight /,undə'wayt/ *noun* '--,-/ *adj or n* (of a) weight below average or normal

'under,world /-,wuhld/ *n* **1** the place of departed souls; Hades **2** the world of organized crime

,under'write /-'riet/ *v* **underwrote** /-'roht/; **underwritten** /-'ritn/ **1** to set one's signature to (an insurance policy) thereby assuming liability in case of specified loss or damage; *also* to assume (a sum or risk) by way of insurance **2** to subscribe to; agree to **3** to guarantee financial support of

'under,writer /-,rietə/ *n* **1** one who underwrites sthg, esp an insurance policy **2** one who selects risks to be solicited or rates the acceptability of risks solicited

undesirable /,undi'zie-ərəbl/ *n or adj* (sby or sthg) unwanted or objectionable

undo /un'dooh/ *v* **undid** /un'did/; **undone** /un'dun/ **1** to open or loosen by releasing a fastening **2** to reverse or cancel out the effects of **3** to destroy the standing, reputation, hopes, etc of

undoing /un'dooh-ing/ *n* (a cause of) ruin or downfall

¹undone /un'dun/ *past part of* **undo**

²undone *adj* not performed or finished

undoubted /un'dowtid/ *adj* not disputed; genuine – ~**ly** *adv*

¹undress /un'dres/ *v* to take off (one's) clothes

²undress *n* a state of having little or no clothing on

un'dressed *adj* partially or completely unclothed

undue /un'dyooh/ *adj* **1** not yet due **2** excessive, immoderate

¹undulate /'undyoo,layt/, **undulated** /-,laytid/ *adj* having a wavy surface, edge, or markings

²undulate *v* **1** to rise and fall in waves; fluctuate **2** to have a wavy form or appearance

undulation /,undyoo'laysh(ə)n/ *n* **1** a wavelike motion; *also* a single wave or gentle rise **2** a wavy appearance, outline, or form

unduly /un'dyoohli/ *adv* excessively

undying /un'die-ing/ *adj* eternal, perpetual

unearth /un'uhth/ *v* **1** to dig up out of the ground **2** to make known or public

unearthly /un'uhthli/ *adj* **1** exceeding what is normal or natural; supernatural **2** weird, eerie **3** unreasonable, preposterous – **-liness** *n*

uneasy /un'eezi/ *adj* **1** uncomfortable, awkward **2** apprehensive, worried **3** precarious, unstable – **-sily** *adv* – **-siness** *n*

uneconomic /,unekə'nomik, -eekə-/ *also* **uneconomical** /-kl/ *adj* not economically practicable – ~**ally** *adv*

unemployed /,unim'ployd/ *adj* **1** not engaged in a job **2** not invested

unemployment /,unim'ploymənt/ *n* the state of being unemployed; lack of available employment

unequal /un'eekwəl/ adj **1a** not of the same measurement, quantity, or number as another **b** not like in quality, nature, or status **c** not the same for every member of a group, class, or society **2** badly balanced or matched **3** incapable of meeting the requirements of sthg – + to – ~ly adv – ~ness n

un'equalled adj not equalled; unparalleled

unequivocal /,uni'kwivəkl/ adj clear, unambiguous – ~ly adv

unerring /un'uhring/ adj faultless, unfailing – ~ly adv

uneven /un'eev(ə)n/ adj **1a** not level, smooth, or uniform **b** irregular, inconsistent **c** varying in quality **2** unequal – ~ly adv – ~ness n

uneventful /,uni'ventf(ə)l/ adj without any noteworthy or untoward incidents – ~ly adv – ~ness n

unexceptionable /,unik'sepsh(ə)nəbl/ adj beyond reproach or criticism; unimpeachable – -bly adv

unfailing /un'fayling/ adj that can be relied on; constant – ~ly adv

unfaithful /un'faythf(ə)l/ adj **1** disloyal, faithless **2** not faithful to a marriage partner, lover, etc, esp in having sexual relations with another person – ~ly adv – ~ness n

unfaltering /un'fawltəring/ adj not wavering or hesitating; firm – ~ly adv

unfavourable /un'fayv(ə)rəbl/ adj **1** expressing disapproval; negative **2** disadvantageous, adverse – -bly adv

unfeeling /un'feeling/ adj not kind or sympathetic; hardhearted – ~ly adv

unfit /un'fit/ adj **1** unsuitable, inappropriate **2** incapable, incompetent **3** physically or mentally unsound

unflagging /un'flaging/ adj never flagging; tireless – ~ly adv

unflappable /un'flapəbl/ adj remaining calm and composed – -bly adv

unflinching /un'flinching/ adj steadfast – ~ly adv

unfold /un'fohld/ v **1** to open from a folded state **2** to open out gradually to the mind or eye

unforgettable /,unfə'getəbl/ adj incapable of being forgotten; memorable – -bly adv

1unfortunate /un'fawch(ə)nət/ adj **1a** unsuccessful, unlucky **b** accompanied by or resulting in misfortune **2** unsuitable, inappropriate

2unfortunate n an unfortunate person

un'fortunately /-li/ adv **1** in an unfortunate manner **2** as is unfortunate

unfounded /un'fowndid/ adj lacking a sound basis; groundless

unfrequented /,unfri'kwentid, -'freekwəntid/ adj not often visited or travelled over

ungainly /un'gaynli/ adj lacking in grace; clumsy – -liness n

ungenerous /un'jen(ə)rəs/ adj **1** petty, uncharitable **2** stingy, mean – ~ly adv

ungodly /un'godli/ adj **1** sinful, wicked **2** indecent, outrageous

ungovernable /un'guv(ə)nəbl/ adj not capable of being controlled or restrained

ungracious /un'grayshəs/ adj rude, impolite – ~ly adv

ungrateful /un'graytf(ə)l/ adj **1** showing no gratitude **2** disagreeable, unpleasant – ~ly adv – ~ness n

unguarded /un'gahdid/ adj **1** vulnerable to attack **2** showing lack of forethought or calculation; imprudent

unguent /'ung-gwənt/ n a soothing or healing salve; ointment

unhappy /un'hapi/ adj **1** not fortunate; unlucky **2** sad, miserable **3** unsuitable, inappropriate – -piness n – -pily adv

unhealthy /un'helthi/ adj **1** not in or conducive to good health **2** morbid – -thily adv – -thiness n

unheard /un'huhd/ adj **1** not perceived by the ear **2** not given a hearing

un'heard-of adj previously unknown; unprecedented

unhinge /un'hinj/ v to make (mentally) unstable; unsettle

unholy /un'hohli/ adj **1** wicked, reprehensible **2** terrible, awful – infml – -liness n

unicorn /'yoohni,kawn/ n a mythical animal usu depicted as a white horse with a single horn in the middle of the forehead

1uniform /'yoohni,fawm/ adj **1** not varying in character, appearance, quantity, etc **2** conforming to a rule, pattern, or practice; consonant – ~ity n – ~ly adv

2uniform n dress of a distinctive design or fashion worn by members of a particular group and serving as a means of identification – ~ed adj

unify /'yoohni,fie/ v to make into a unit or a coherent whole; unite – fication n

uni'lateral /-'lat(ə)rəl/ adj **1a** done or undertaken by 1 person or party **b** of or affecting 1 side **2** produced or arranged on or directed towards 1 side – ~ly adv

unimpeachable /,unim'peechəbl/ adj **1** not to be doubted; beyond question **2** irreproachable, blameless – -bly adv

uninhibited /,unin'hibitid/ adj acting spontaneously without constraint or regard for what others might think – ~ly adv

1union /'yoohnyən/ n **1a(1)** the formation of a single political unit from 2 or more separate and independent units **a(2)** a uniting in marriage; also sexual intercourse **b** combination, junction **2a** an association of independent individuals (e g nations) for some common purpose **b** a trade union

2union adj of, dealing with, or constituting a union

unionism /'yoohnyə,niz(ə)m/ *n* **1** adherence to the principles of trade unions **2** *cap* a political movement giving support for the continued union of Great Britain and Ireland – **-ist** *n, adj*

,Union 'Jack /jak/ *n* the national flag of the UK combining crosses representing England, Scotland, and N Ireland

unique /yooh'neek, yoo-/ *adj* **1** sole, only **2** without a like or equal; unequalled **3** very rare or unusual – disapproved of by some speakers – **~ly** *adv* – **~ness** *n*

unisex /'yoohni,seks/ *adj* suitable for both sexes

unison /'yoohnis(ə)n, -z(ə)n/ *n* **1** the writing, playing, or singing of parts in a musical passage at the same pitch or in octaves **2** harmonious agreement or union

unit /'yoohnit/ *n* **1a**(1) the first and lowest natural number; one **a**(2) a single quantity regarded as a whole in calculation **b** the number occupying the position immediately to the left of the decimal point in the Arabic notation; *also, pl* this position **2** a determinate quantity (e g of length, time, heat, value, or housing) adopted as a standard of measurement **3** a part of a military establishment that has a prescribed organization (e g of personnel and supplies)

unite /yoo'niet, yooh-/ *v* **1** to join together to form a single unit **2** to link by a legal or moral bond **3** to act in concert

u'nited *adj* **1** combined, joined **2** relating to or produced by joint action **3** in agreement; harmonious – **~ly** *adv*

unit trust *n* an investment company that minimizes the risk to investors by collective purchase of shares in many different enterprises

unity /'yoohnəti/ *n* **1a** the state of being **1** or united **b** a definite amount taken as 1 or for which 1 is made to stand in calculation **2a** concord, harmony **b** continuity and agreement in aims and interests

univalent /,yoohni'vaylənt/ *adj* having a valency of 1

¹**universal** /,yoohni'vuhs(ə)l/ *adj* **1** including or covering all or a whole without limit or exception **2** present or occurring everywhere or under all conditions

²**universal** *n* a general concept or term

universe /'yoohni,vuhs/ *n* **1a** all things that exist; the cosmos **b** a galaxy **2** the whole world; everyone

university /,yoohni'vuhsəti/ *n* (the premises of) an institution of higher learning that provides facilities for full-time teaching and research and is authorized to grant academic degrees

unjust /un'just/ *adj* unfair; without showing, giving, etc justice

unkempt /un'kempt/ *adj* **1** not combed; dishevelled **2** not neat or tidy

unkind /un'kiend/ *adj* **1** not pleasing or mild **2** lacking in kindness or sympathy; harsh – **~ly** *adv*

unknowing /un'noh·ing/ *adj* not knowing – **~ly** *adv*

¹**unknown** /un'nohn/ *adj* not known; *also* having an unknown value

²**unknown** *n* a person who is little known (e g to the public)

unlawful /un'lawf(ə)l/ *adj* **1** illegal **2** not morally right or conventional – **~ly** *adv*

unleash /un'leesh/ *v* to loose from restraint or control

unless /ən'les/ *conj* **1** except on the condition that **2** without the necessary accompaniment that; except when

¹**unlike** /,un'liek/ *prep* **1** different from **2** not characteristic of **3** in a different manner from

²**unlike** *adj* **1** marked by dissimilarity; different **2** unequal

un'likely /-li/ *adj* **1** having a low probability of being or occurring **2** not believable; improbable **3** likely to fail; unpromising **4** not foreseen (e g the *unlikely* result) – **-liness, -lihood** *n*

unload /un'lohd/ *v* **1a** to take (cargo) off or out **b** to give vent to; pour forth **2** to relieve of sthg burdensome **3** to draw the charge from – **~er** *n*

unlock /un'lok/ *v* **1** to unfasten the lock of **2** to open, release

unmannerly /un'manəli/ *adj* discourteous, rude

unmask /un'mahsk/ *v* to reveal the true nature of; expose

unmentionable /un'mensh(ə)nəbl/ *adj* not fit to be mentioned; unspeakable

unmistakable /,unmi'staykəbl/ *adj* clear, obvious – **-bly** *adv*

unmitigated /un'mitigaytid/ *adj* **1** not diminished in severity, intensity, etc **2** out-and-out, downright – **~ly** *adv*

unnatural /un'nachərəl/ *adj* **1** not in accordance with nature or a normal course of events **2a** not in accordance with normal feelings or behaviour; perverse **b** artificial or contrived in manner – **~ly** *adv*

unnerve /un'nuhv/ *v* to deprive of nerve, courage, or the power to act

unnumbered /,un'numbəd/ *adj* innumerable

unobtrusive /,unəb'troohsiv, -ziv/ *adj* not too easily seen or noticed; inconspicuous – **~ly** *adv* – **~ness** *n*

unorthodox /un'awthədoks/ *adj* not conventional in behaviour, beliefs, doctrine, etc

unpack /un'pak/ *v* **1** to remove the contents of **2** to remove or undo from packing or a container

unparalleled /un'parəleld/ *adj* having no equal or match; unique

unparliamentary /,unpahlə'mentəri; *also* -lyə-/ *adj* not in accordance with parliamentary practice

unpick /un'pik/ *v* to undo (e g sewing) by taking out stitches

unpleasant /un'plez(ə)nt/ adj not pleasant or agreeable; displeasing – ~**ly** adv – ~**ness** n

unprecedented /un'presidntid/ adj having no precedent; novel – ~**ly** adv

unprejudiced /un'prejoodist, -jə-/ adj impartial, fair

unpretentious /,unpri'tenshəs/ adj not seeking to impress others by means of wealth, standing, etc; not affected or ostentatious – ~**ly** adv – ~**ness** n

unprincipled /un'prinsip(ə)ld/ adj without moral principles; unscrupulous

unprintable /un'printəbl/ adj unfit to be printed

unqualified /un'kwolified/ adj 1 not having the necessary qualifications 2 not modified or restricted by reservations

unquestionable /un'kwesch(ə)nəbl/ adj not able to be called in question; indisputable – -**bly** adv

unquestioning /un'kwesch(ə)ning/ adj not expressing doubt or hesitation

unquote /,un'kwoht/ n – used orally to indicate the end of a direct quotation

unravel /un'rav(ə)l/ v -**ll**- (NAm -**l**-, -**ll**-), /un'ravling, -'ravl·ing/ 1 to disentangle 2 to clear up or solve (sthg intricate or obscure)

unreasonable /un'reez(ə)nəbl/ adj 1 not governed by or acting according to reason 2 excessive, immoderate – -**bly** adv – ~**ness** n

unreasoning /un'reezəning/ adj not moderated or controlled by reason

unrelenting /,unri'lenting/ adj 1 not weakening in determination; stern 2 not letting up in vigour, pace, etc – ~**ly** adv

unremitting /,unri'miting/ adj constant, incessant – ~**ly** adv

unreserved /,unri'zuhvd/ adj 1 entire, unqualified 2 frank and open in manner – ~**ly** adv

unrest /un'rest/ n agitation, turmoil

unrestrained /unri'straynd/ adj not held in check; uncontrolled

unrivalled, NAm chiefly **unrivaled** /un'rievld/ adj unequalled, unparalleled

unroll /un'rohl/ v to open out; uncoil

unruffled /un'rufld/ adj 1 poised, serene 2 smooth, calm

unruly /un'roohli/ adj difficult to discipline or manage – -**liness** n

unsaid /un'sed/ adj not said or spoken

unsavoury /un'sayvəri/ adj disagreeable, distasteful; esp morally offensive

unscathed /un'skaydhd/ adj entirely unharmed or uninjured

unschooled /un'skoohld/ adj untaught, untrained

unscramble /,un'skrambl/ v 1 to separate into original components 2 to restore (scrambled communication) to intelligible form

unscrew /un'skrooh/ v to loosen or withdraw by turning

unscrupulous /un'skroohpyooləs/ adj without moral scruples; unprincipled – ~**ly** adv – ~**ness** n

unseat /,un'seet/ v to remove from a (political) position

unseemly /un'seemli/ adj not conforming to established standards of good behaviour or taste – -**liness** n

¹**unseen** /,un'seen/ adj done without previous preparation

²**unseen** n, chiefly Br a passage of unprepared translation

unsettle /un'setl/ v to perturb or agitate

unsettled /un'setld/ adj 1a not calm or tranquil; disturbed b variable, changeable 2 not resolved or worked out; undecided 3 not inhabited or populated 4 not paid or discharged

unsightly /un'sietli/ adj not pleasing to the eye; ugly – -**liness** n

unskilled /,un'skild/ adj 1 of, being, or requiring workers who are not skilled in any particular branch of work 2 showing a lack of skill

unsociable /un'sohsh(i)əbl/ adj not liking social activity; reserved, solitary

unsocial /un'sohsh(ə)l/ adj 1 marked by or showing a dislike for social interaction 2 Br worked at a time that falls outside the normal working day and precludes participation in normal social activities

unsound /,un'sownd/ adj 1 not healthy or whole 2 mentally abnormal 3 not firmly made, placed, or fixed 4 not valid or true; specious

unsparing /,un'speəring/ adj 1 not merciful; hard, ruthless 2 liberal, generous – ~**ly** adv

unspeakable /un'speekəbl/ adj 1 incapable of being expressed in words 2 too terrible or shocking to be expressed – -**bly** adv

unstable /un'staybl/ adj not stable; not firm or fixed; not constant: e g a apt to move, sway, or fall; unsteady b characterized by inability to control the emotions

unstop /,un'stop/ v -**pp**- to free from an obstruction

unstudied /un'studid/ adj 1 not acquired by study 2 not done or planned for effect

unsung /,un'sung/ adj not celebrated or praised (e g in song or verse)

unswerving /un'swuhving/ adj not deviating; constant

untangle /un'tang-gl/ v to loose from tangles or entanglement; unravel

untapped /un'tapt/ adj 1 not yet tapped 2 not drawn on or exploited

untenable /un'tenəbl/ adj not able to be defended

unthinkable /un'thingkəbl/ adj contrary to what is acceptable or probable; out of the question

unthinking /un'thingking/ adj not taking thought; heedless, unmindful – ~**ly** adv

untie /un'tie/ v 1 to free from sthg that fastens or restrains **2a** to separate out the knotted parts of **b** to disentangle, resolve

¹**until** /un'til, ən-/ *prep* 1 up to as late as 2 up to as far as

²**until** *conj* up to the time that; until such time as

untimely /un'tiemli/ *adj* 1 occurring before the natural or proper time; premature 2 inopportune, unseasonable – **-liness** *n*

unto /'untoo, -tə/ *prep, archaic* to

untold /un'tohld/ *adj* 1 incalculable, vast 2 not told or related

¹**untouchable** /un'tuchəbl/ *adj* 1 that may not be touched 2 lying beyond reach

²**untouchable** *n* sby or sthg untouchable; *specif, often cap* a member of a large formerly segregated hereditary group in India who in traditional Hindu belief can defile a member of a higher caste by contact or proximity

untoward /,untə'wawd/ *adj* not favourable; adverse, unfortunate – **~ly** *adv* – **~ness** *n*

untruth /,un'troohth/ *n* 1 lack of truthfulness 2 sthg untrue; a falsehood

untruthful /un'troohthf(ə)l/ *adj* not telling the truth; false, lying – **~ly** *adv*

unused /un'yoohst; *senses 2a and 2b* -'yoohzd/ *adj* 1 unaccustomed – usu + *to* 2a fresh, new **b** not used up

unusual /un'yoohzhoool, -zhəl/ *adj* 1 uncommon, rare 2 different, unique – **~ly** *adv*

unutterable /un'ut(ə)rəbl/ *adj* 1 beyond the powers of description; inexpressible 2 out-and-out, downright – **-bly** *adv*

unvarnished /,un'vahnisht/ *adj* not adorned or glossed; plain

unveil /un'vayl/ v to make public; divulge

unwarranted /un'worəntid/ *adj* not justified; (done) without good reason

unwell /un'wel/ *adj* in poor health

unwieldy /un'weeldi/ *adj* difficult to move or handle; cumbersome – **-diness** *n*

unwind /un'wiend/ v **unwound** /-'wownd/ 1 to uncoil; unroll 2 to become less tense; relax

unwitting /un'witing/ *adj* not intended; inadvertent – **~ly** *adv*

unzip /un'zip/ v **-pp-** to open (as if) by means of a zip

¹**up** /up/ *adv* **1a** at or towards a relatively high level **b** from beneath the ground or water to the surface **c** above the horizon **d** upstream **e** in or to a raised or upright position; *specif* out of bed **f** off or out of the ground or a surface (e g pull *up* a daisy) **g** to the top; *esp* so as to be full **2a** into a state of, or with, greater intensity or activity (e g speak *up*) **b** into a faster pace or higher gear **3a** in or into a relatively high condition or status – sometimes used interjectionally as an expression of approval (e g *up* BBC2!) **b** above a normal or former level: e g **b(1)** upwards **b(2)** higher in price **c** ahead of an opponent (e g we're 3 points *up*) **4a(1)** in or into existence, evidence, prominence, or prevalence (e g new houses haven't been *up* long) **a(2)** in or into operation or full power (e g get *up* steam) **b** under consideration or attention; *esp* before a court **5** so as to be together (e g add *up* the figures) **6a** entirely, completely (e g eat *up* your spinach) **b** so as to be firmly closed, joined, or fastened **c** so as to be fully inflated **7** in or into storage **8** in a direction conventionally the opposite of down: **8a(1)** to windward **a(2)** with rudder to leeward – used with reference to a ship's helm **b** in or towards the north **c** so as to arrive or approach (e g walked *up* to her) **d** to or at the rear of a theatrical stage **e** *chiefly Br* to or in the capital of a country or a university city (e g *up* in London) **9** in or into parts (e g chop *up*) **10** to a stop – usu + *draw*, *bring*, *fetch*, or *pull*

²**up** *adj* 1 moving, inclining, bound, or directed upwards or *up* 2 ready, prepared (e g dinner's *up*) 3 going on, taking place; *esp* being the matter (e g what's *up*?) 4 at an end; *esp* hopeless (e g it's all *up* with him now) 5 well informed 6 *of a road* being repaired; having a broken surface 7 ahead of an opponent 8 *of a ball in court games* having bounced only once on the ground or floor after being hit by one's opponent and therefore playable 9 *Br, of a train* travelling towards a large town; *specif* travelling towards London — **up against** faced with; confronting — **up against it** in great difficulties

³**up** v **-pp-** 1 – used with *and* and another verb to indicate that the action of the following verb is either surprisingly or abruptly initiated (e g he *upped* and married) 2 to increase

⁴**up** *prep* **1a** up along, round, through, towards, in, into, or on **b** at the top of (e g the office is *up* those stairs) 2 *Br* (up) to (e g going *up* the West End) – nonstandard

⁵**up** *n* 1 (sthg in) a high position or an upward incline 2 a period or state of prosperity or success

,**up-and-'coming** *adj* likely to advance or succeed

,**up-and-'up** *n, chiefly Br* a potentially or increasingly successful course – chiefly in *on the up-and-up*

¹**upbeat** /'up,beet/ *n* an unaccented (e g the last) beat in a musical bar

²**upbeat** *adj, chiefly NAm* optimistic, cheerful – *infml*

upbraid /up'brayd/ v to scold or reproach severely

upbringing /'up,bring-ing/ *n* a particular way of bringing up a child

,**up-'country** *adj* 1 (characteristic) of an inland, upland, or outlying region 2 not socially or culturally sophisticated

update /,up'dayt/ v to bring up to date – **update** *n*

upend /ˌup'end/ v 1 to cause to stand on end 2 to knock down

upgrade /ˌup'grayd/ v to advance to a job requiring a higher level of skill, esp as part of a training programme

upheaval /up'heevl/ n (an instance of) extreme agitation or radical change

¹**uphill** /ˌup'hil/ adv upwards on a hill or incline

²**up'hill** adj 1 situated on elevated ground 2 going up; ascending 3 difficult, laborious

uphold /up'hohld/ v upheld /-'held/ 1 to give support to; maintain 2 to support against an opponent or challenge – ~ er n

upholster /up'hohlstə, -'hol-/ v to provide with upholstery – ~ er n

up'holstery /-ri/ n materials (e g fabric, padding, and springs) used to make a soft covering, esp for a seat

upkeep /'up,keep/ n (the cost of) maintaining or being maintained in good condition

¹**uplift** /up'lift/ v 1 to raise, elevate 2 to improve the spiritual, social, or intellectual condition of

²**up,lift** n 1 a moral or social improvement 2 influences intended to uplift

upon /ə'pon/ prep on – chiefly fml

¹**upper** /'upə/ adj 1a higher in physical position, rank, or order b farther inland 2 being the branch of a legislature consisting of 2 houses that is usu more restricted in membership, is in many cases less powerful, and possesses greater traditional prestige than the lower house

²**upper** n the parts of a shoe or boot above the sole — **on one's uppers** at the end of one's means

³**upper** n a stimulant drug; esp amphetamine – infml

upper case n capital letters – **upper-case** adj

ˌ**upper 'class** n the class occupying the highest position in a society; esp the wealthy or the aristocracy

ˌ**upper 'crust** n sing or pl in constr the highest social class – infml

uppercut /'upə,kut/ n a swinging blow directed upwards with a bent arm

ˌ**upper 'hand** n mastery, advantage – + the

uppermost /'upə,mohst/ adv in or into the highest or most prominent position

uppish /'upish/ adj hit up and travelling far in the air 2 conceited – infml – ~ly adv – ~ness n

¹**upright** /'up,riet/ adj 1a perpendicular, vertical b erect in carriage or posture 2 marked by strong moral rectitude – ~ly adv – ~ness n

²**upright** adv in an upright or vertical position

³**upright** n 1 sthg that stands upright 2 **upright, upright piano** a piano with vertical frame and strings

uprising /'up,riezing/ n a usu localized rebellion

uproar /'up,raw/ n a state of commotion or violent disturbance

uproarious /ˌup'rawri·əs/ adj 1 marked by noise and disorder 2 extremely funny – ~ly adv

uproot /up'rooht/ v 1 to remove by pulling up by the roots 2 to displace from a country or traditional habitat or environment

¹**upset** /up'set/ v -tt-; **upset** 1 to overturn, knock over 2a to trouble mentally or emotionally b to throw into disorder 3 to make somewhat ill

²**up,set** n 1 a minor physical disorder 2 an emotional disturbance 3 an unexpected defeat (e g in politics)

upshot /'up,shot/ n the final result; the outcome

ˌ**upside 'down** /ˌup,sied/ adv 1 with the upper and the lower parts reversed 2 in or into great disorder or confusion

¹**upstage** /ˌup'stayj/ adv at the rear of a theatrical stage; also away from the audience or film or television camera

²**upstage** adj 1 of or at the rear of a stage 2 haughty, aloof

³**up,stage** n the part of a stage that is farthest from the audience or camera

⁴**upstage** v to steal attention from

¹**upstairs** /ˌup'steəz/ adv 1 up the stairs; to or on a higher floor 2 to or at a higher position

²**upstairs** adj situated above the stairs, esp on an upper floor

³**upstairs** /'-,-, ,-'-/ n pl but sing or pl in constr the part of a building above the ground floor

upstanding /up'standing/ adj 1 erect, upright 2 marked by integrity; honest

upstart /'up,staht/ n one who has risen suddenly (e g from a low position to wealth or power); esp one who claims more personal importance than he/she warrants

upstream /ˌup'streem/ adv or adj in the direction opposite to the flow of a stream

upsurge /'up,suhj/ n a rapid or sudden rise

upswing /'up,swing/ n 1 an upward swing 2 a marked increase or rise

uptake /'up,tayk/ n understanding, comprehension – infml

uptight /ˌup'tiet/ adj 1 tense, nervous, or uneasy 2 angry, indignant USE infml

'**up to** prep 1 – used to indicate an upward limit or boundary 2 as far as; until 3a equal to b good enough for 4 engaged in (a suspect activity) (e g what's he up to?) 5 being the responsibility of (e g it's up to me)

ˌ**up-to-'date** adj 1 including the latest information 2 abreast of the times; modern

¹**upturn** /ˌup'tuhn/ v 1 to turn up or over 2 to direct upwards

²**up,turn** n an upward turn, esp towards better conditions or higher prices

upward /'upwood/ adj moving or extending upwards; ascending

upwards *adv* **1a** from a lower to a higher place, condition, or level; in the opposite direction from down **b** so as to expose a particular surface (e g turned the cards *upwards*) **2** to an indefinitely greater amount, price, figure, age, or rank (e g from £5 *upwards*)

uranium /yoo(ə)'raynyəm, -ni-əm/ *n* a heavy radioactive element

Uranus /yoo(ə)'raynəs, 'yooərənəs/ *n* the planet 7th in order from the sun

urban /'uhbən/ *adj* (characteristic) of or constituting a city or town

urbane /uh'bayn/ *adj* notably polite or smooth in manner; suave – **~ly** *adv* – **-banity** *n*

urchin /'uhchin/ *n* a mischievous and impudent young boy, esp one who is scruffy

¹**urge** /uhj/ *v* **1** to advocate or demand earnestly or pressingly **2** to try to persuade **3** to force or impel in a specified direction or to greater speed

²**urge** *n* a force or impulse that urges

urgent /'uhjənt/ *adj* **1** calling for immediate attention; pressing **2** conveying a sense of urgency – **~ly** *adv* – **-gency** *n*

urinal /yoo(ə)'rienl/ *n* a fixture used for urinating into, esp by men; *also* a room, building, etc containing a urinal

urinary /'yooərin(ə)ri/ *adj* relating to (or occurring in or constituting the organs concerned with the formation and discharge of) urine

urinate /'yooəri,nayt/ *v* to discharge urine – **-nation** *n*

urine /'yooərin/ *n* waste material that is secreted by the kidney in vertebrates and forms a clear amber and usu slightly acid fluid

urn /uhn/ *n* **1** an ornamental vase on a pedestal used esp for preserving the ashes of the dead after cremation **2** a large closed container, usu with a tap at its base, in which large quantities of tea, coffee, etc may be heated or served

us /əs; *strong us/ pron* **1** *objective case of* **we 2** *chiefly Br* me – nonstandard

usage /'yoohsij, -zij/ *n* **1** (an instance of) established and generally accepted practice or procedure **2** (an instance of) the way in which words and phrases are actually used in a language

¹**use** /yoohs/ *n* **1a** using or being used **b** a way of using sthg **2** habitual or customary usage **3a** the right or benefit of using sthg **b** the ability or power to use sthg (e g a limb) **4a** a purpose or end **b** practical worth or application

²**use** /yoohz/ *v* **used** / *vt* yoohzd; *vi* yoohst/ **1** to put into action or service **2** to carry out sthg by means of **3** to expend or consume **4** to treat in a specified manner **5** – used in the past with *to* to indicate a former fact or state – **user** *n* – **usable** *adj*

used /*senses* ¹ *and* 2 yoohzd; *sense* 3 yoohst/ *adj* **1** employed in accomplishing sthg **2** that has endured use; *specif* secondhand **3** accustomed

useful /'yoohsf(ə)l/ *adj* **1** having utility, esp practical worth or applicability; *also* helpful **2** of highly satisfactory quality – **~ly** *adv* – **~ness** *n*

useless /'yoohslis/ *adj* **1** having or being of no use **2** inept – *infml* – **~ly** *adv* – **~ness** *n*

user-friendly *adj* **1** *of a computer system* designed for easy operation by guiding users along a series of simple steps **2** easy to operate or understand

¹**usher** /'ushə/ *n* **1** an officer or servant who acts as a doorkeeper (e g in a court of law) **2** *fem* **usherette** one who shows people to their seats (e g in a theatre)

²**usher** *v* **1** to conduct to a place **2** to inaugurate, introduce – usu + *in*

usual /'yoohzhooəl, -zhəl/ *adj* **1** in accordance with usage, custom, or habit; normal **2** commonly or ordinarily used – **~ly** *adv* – **as usual** in the accustomed or habitual way

usurer /'yoohzhərə/ *n* one who lends money, esp at an exorbitant rate

usurp /yooh'suhp, -'zuhp/ *v* to seize and possess by force or without right – **~ation** *n* – **~er** *n*

usury /'yoohzyəri, -zhəri/ *n* **1** the lending of money at (exorbitant) interest **2** an exorbitant or illegal rate or amount of interest – **-rious** *adj* – **-riousness** *n*

utensil /yooh'tens(i)l/ *n* **1** an implement, vessel, or device used in the household, esp the kitchen **2** a useful tool or implement

uterus /'yoohtərəs/ *n, pl* **uteri** /-,rie, -ri/ *also* **uteruses** an organ of the female mammal for containing and usu for nourishing the young during development before birth – **-rine** *adj*

utilitarian /yooh,tili'teəri-ən/ *adj* **1** marked by utilitarian views or practices **2** made for or aiming at practical use rather than beautiful appearance – **utilitarian** *n*

u,tili'tarianism /-niz(ə)m/ *n* a doctrine that the criterion for correct conduct should be the usefulness of its consequences; *specif* a theory that the aim of action should be the greatest happiness of the greatest number

¹**utility** /yooh'tiləti/ *n* **1** fitness for some purpose; usefulness **2** sthg useful or designed for use **3** a business organization performing a public service

²**utility** *adj* **1** capable of serving as a substitute in various roles or positions **2** designed or adapted for general use – **-ize** *v*

¹**utmost** /'ut,mohst/ *adj* **1** situated at the farthest or most distant point; extreme **2** of the greatest or highest degree

²**utmost** *n* **1** the highest point or degree **2** the best of one's abilities, powers, etc

utopia /yooh'tohpi-ə/ *n* **1** *often cap* a place or state of ideal (political and social) perfection **2** an impractical scheme for social or political improvement

utopian /yooh'tohpi·ən/ *adj* **1** impossibly ideal, esp in social and political organization **2** proposing impractically ideal social and political schemes – **utopian** *n*

¹utter /'utə/ *adj* absolute, total – ~**ly** *adv*

²utter *v* **1** to emit as a sound **2** to give (verbal) expression to – ~**ance** *n*

'U-,turn /yooh/ *n* **1** a turn executed by a motor vehicle without reversing that takes it back along the direction from which it has come **2** a total reversal of policy

V

v /vee/ *n*, *pl* **v's** *or* **vs** *often cap* **1** (a graphic representation of or device for reproducing) the 22nd letter of the English alphabet **2** five

vac /vak/ *n*, *Br* a vacation, esp from college or university – *infml*

vacancy /'vaykənsi/ *n* **1** physical or mental inactivity; idleness **2** a vacant office, post, or room **3** an empty space

vacant /'vaykənt/ *adj* **1** without an occupant **2** free from activity or work **3a** stupid, foolish **b** expressionless – ~**ly** *adv*

vacate /və'kayt/ *v* to give up the possession or occupancy of

¹vacation /vay'kash(ə)n, və-/ *n* **1** a scheduled period during which activity (e g of a university) is suspended **2** *chiefly NAm* a holiday

²vacation *v*, *chiefly NAm* to take or spend a holiday

vaccinate /'vaksinayt/ *v* to administer a vaccine to, usu by injection – **-ation** *n*

vaccine /'vak,seen, -sin/ *n* material (e g a preparation of killed or modified virus or bacteria) used in vaccinating to produce an immunity

vacillate /'vasə,layt/ *v* **1** to sway; *also* to fluctuate, oscillate **2** to hesitate or waver in choosing – **-lation** *n*

vacuous /'vakyoo·əs/ *adj* **1** empty **2** stupid, inane **3** idle, aimless – ~**ly** *adv* – ~**ness** *n*

¹vacuum /'vakyoohm, 'vakyooəm, 'vakyoom/ *n pl* **vacuums, vacua** /'vakyooh·ə/ **1a** a space absolutely devoid of matter **b** an air pressure below atmospheric pressure **2a** a vacant space; a void **b** a state of isolation from outside influences **3** a vacuum cleaner

²vacuum *v* to clean using a vacuum cleaner

'vacuum ,cleaner *n* an (electrical) appliance for removing dust and dirt (e g from carpets or upholstery) by suction

¹vagabond /'vagə,bond/ *adj* **1** (characteristic) of a wanderer **2** leading an unsettled, irresponsible, or disreputable life

²vagabond *n* a wanderer; *esp* a tramp

vagary /'vaygəri/ *n* an erratic, unpredictable, or extravagant idea, act, etc

vagina /və'jienə/ *n pl* **vaginae** /-ni/, **vaginas** a canal in a female mammal that leads from the uterus to the external orifice of the genital canal – ~**l** *adj*

¹vagrant /'vaygrənt/ *n* **1** one who has no established residence or lawful means of support **2** a wanderer, vagabond – **-rancy** *n*

²vagrant *adj* **1** wandering about from place to place, usu with no means of support **2** having no fixed course; random

vague /vayg/ *adj* **1a** not clearly defined, expressed, or understood; indistinct **b** not clearly felt or sensed **2** not thinking or expressing one's thoughts clearly – ~**ly** *adv* – ~**ness** *n*

vain /vayn/ *adj* **1** unsuccessful, ineffectual **2** having or showing excessive pride in one's appearance, ability, etc; conceited – ~**ly** *adv* — **in vain** to no end; without success or result

valance /'vayləns, 'va-/ *n* **1** a piece of drapery hung as a border, esp along the edge of a bed, canopy, or shelf **2** a pelmet

vale /vayl/ *n* a valley – poetic or in place-names

valediction /,valə'diksh(ə)n/ *n* **1** an act of bidding farewell **2** an address or statement of farewell or leave-taking *USE* fml – **-tory** *n*

valency /'vay.lənsi/, *NAm chiefly* **valence** /'vayləns/ *n* the degree of combining power of an element or radical as shown by the number of atomic weights of a univalent element (e g hydrogen) with which the atomic weight of the element will combine or for which it can be substituted or with which it can be compared

valentine /'valəntien/ *n* **1** a sweetheart chosen on St Valentine's Day **2** a gift or greeting card sent or given, esp to a sweetheart, on St Valentine's Day

valet /'valay/ *n* a gentleman's male servant who performs personal services (e g taking care of clothing)

valiant /'vali·ənt/ *adj* characterized by or showing valour; courageous – ~**ly** *adv*

valid /'valid/ *adj* **1** having legal efficacy; *esp* executed according to the proper formalities **2** well-grounded or justifiable; relevant and meaningful – ~**ity** *n* – ~**ly** *adv*

valley /'vali/ *n* **1** an elongated depression of the earth's surface, usu between hills or mountains **2** a hollow, depression

valour, *NAm chiefly* **valor** /'valə/ *n* strength of mind or spirit that enables sby to encounter danger with firmness; personal bravery

¹valuable /'valyoo(ə)bl/ *adj* **1** having (high) money value **2** of great use or worth

²**valuable** *n* a usu personal possession of relatively great money value – usu pl

¹**value** /'valyooh/ *n* 1 a fair return or equivalent for sthg exchanged 2 the worth in money or commodities of sthg 3 relative worth, utility, or importance 4 a numerical quantity assigned or computed 5 sthg (e g a principle or quality) intrinsically valuable or desirable – ~**less** *adj*

²**value** *v* 1a to estimate the worth of in terms of money b to rate in terms of usefulness, importance, etc 2 to consider or rate highly; esteem – **-uation** *n*

,**value-'added ,tax** *n*, *often cap V, A, & T* a tax levied at each stage of the production and distribution of a commodity and passed on to the consumer as a form of purchase tax

valve /valv/ *n* 1 a structure, esp in the heart or a vein, that closes temporarily to obstruct passage of material or permits movement of fluid in 1 direction only 2a any of numerous mechanical devices by which the flow of liquid, gas, or loose material in bulk may be controlled, usu to allow movement in 1 direction only b a device in a brass musical instrument for quickly varying the tube length in order to change the fundamental tone by a definite interval 3 any of the separate joined pieces that make up the shell of an (invertebrate) animal; *specif* either of the 2 halves of the shell of a bivalve mollusc 4 *chiefly Br* a vacuum- or gas-filled device for the regulation of electric current by the control of free electrons or ions

valvular /'valvyoolə/ *adj* resembling or functioning as a valve; *also* opening by valves

vamoose /va'moohs/ *v*, *chiefly NAm* to depart quickly – slang

¹**vamp** /vamp/ *n* 1 the part of a shoe or boot covering the front of the foot 2 a simple improvised musical accompaniment – **vamp** *v*

²**vamp** *n* a woman who uses her charm to seduce and exploit men

vampire /'vampie·ə/ *n* 1 a dead person believed to come from the grave at night and suck the blood of sleeping people 2 any of various S American bats that feed on blood

¹**van** /van/ *n* the vanguard

²**van** *n* 1 an enclosed motor vehicle used for transport of goods, animals, furniture, etc 2 *chiefly Br* an enclosed railway goods wagon

vanadium /və'naydi·əm/ *n* a metallic element found combined in minerals and used esp to form alloys

vandal /'vandl/ *n* one who wilfully or ignorantly destroys or defaces (public) property

'**vandal,ism** /-,iz(ə)m/ *n* wilful destruction or defacement of property – **-ize** *v*

vane /vayn/ *n* 1 a weather vane 2 a thin flat or curved object that is rotated about an axis by wind or water; *also* a device revolving in a similar manner and moving in water or air 3 the flat expanded part of a feather

vanguard /'vangahd/ *n* 1 *sing or pl in constr* the troops moving at the head of an army 2 the forefront of an action or movement

vanilla /və'nilə/ *n* 1 any of a genus of tropical American climbing orchids whose long capsular fruit-pods yield an important flavouring 2 a commercially important extract of the vanilla pod that is used esp as a flavouring

vanish /'vanish/ 1 to pass quickly from sight; disappear 2 to cease to exist

'**vanishing ,cream** /'vanishing/ *n* a light cosmetic cream used chiefly as a foundation for face powder

vanity /'vanəti/ *n* 1 worthlessness 2 excessive pride in oneself; conceit

vanquish /'vangkwish, 'van-/ *v* 1 to overcome, conquer 2 to gain mastery over (an emotion, passion, etc)

vapid /'vapid/ *adj* insipid – ~**ly** *adv* – ~**ness** *n* – ~**ity** *n*

vapour, *NAm chiefly* **vapor** /'vaypə/ *n* 1 smoke, fog, etc suspended floating in the air and impairing its transparency 2 a substance in the gaseous state; *esp* such a substance that is liquid under normal conditions – **vaporize** *v* – **vaporous** *adj*

¹**variable** /'veəri·əbl/ *adj* 1 subject to variation or changes 2 having the characteristics of a variable – **-bly** *adv* – ~**ness** *n*

²**variable** *n* 1 sthg (e g a variable star) that is variable 2 (a symbol representing) a quantity that may assume any of a set of values

¹**variant** /'veəri·ənt/ *adj* varying (slightly) from the standard form

²**variant** *n* any of 2 or more people or things displaying usu slight differences; *esp* sthg that shows variation from a type or norm

variation /,veəri'aysh(ə)n/ *n* 1a varying or being varied b an instance of varying c the extent to which or the range in which a thing varies 2 the repetition of a musical theme with modifications in rhythm, tune, harmony, or key 3 divergence in characteristics of an organism from those typical or usual of its group 4 a solo dance in ballet

varicoloured /'veəri,kuləd/ *adj* having various colours

varicose /'varikəs, -kohs/ *also* **varicosed** *adj* abnormally swollen or dilated

varied /'veərid/ *adj* 1 having numerous forms or types; diverse 2 variegated

variegated /'veəri·ə,gaytid/ *adj* having patches of different colours; dappled – **-ation** *n*

variety /vəˈrie-əti/ n 1 the state of having different forms or types; diversity 2 an assortment of different things, esp of a particular class 3a sthg differing from others of the same general kind; a sort b any of various groups of plants or animals ranking below a species 4 theatrical entertainment consisting of separate performances (e g of songs, skits, acrobatics, etc)

various /ˈveəri-əs/ adj 1a of differing kinds; diverse b dissimilar in nature or form; unlike 2 having a number of different aspects or characteristics 3 more than one; several

variously /-li/ adv in various ways; at various times

¹varnish /ˈvahnish/ n 1 a liquid preparation that forms a hard shiny transparent coating on drying 2 outside show

²varnish v 1 to apply varnish to 2 to gloss over

varsity /ˈvahsiti/ n, Br university – now chiefly humor

vary /ˈveəri/ v 1 to exhibit or undergo change 2 to deviate

vascular /ˈvaskyoolə/ adj of or being a channel or system of channels conducting blood, sap, etc in a plant or animal; also supplied with or made up of such channels, esp blood vessels

vascular bundle n a single strand of the vascular system of a plant

vase /vahz/ n an ornamental vessel usu of greater depth than width, used esp for holding flowers

vasectomy /vəˈsektəmi, va-/ n surgical cutting out of a section of the tube conducting sperm from the testes usu to induce permanent sterility

Vaseline /ˈvas(ə)leen/ trademark – used for petroleum jelly

vassal /ˈvas(ə)l/ n 1 sby under the protection of another who is his/her feudal lord 2 sby in a subservient or subordinate position

vast /vahst/ adj very great in amount, degree, intensity, or esp in extent or range

¹vat /vat/ n a tub, barrel, or other large vessel, esp for holding liquids undergoing chemical change or preparations for dyeing or tanning

²vat n, often cap value-added tax

Vatican /ˈvatikan/ n the official residence of the Pope and the administrative centre of Roman Catholicism

vaudeville /ˈvawdə.vil/ n a light often comic theatrical piece frequently combining pantomime, dialogue, dancing, and song

¹vault /vawlt, volt/ n 1 an arched structure of masonry, usu forming a ceiling or roof 2a an underground passage, room, or storage compartment b a room or compartment for the safekeeping of valuables 3 a burial chamber, esp beneath a church or in a cemetery

²vault v to form or cover (as if) with a vault

³vault v to bound vigorously (over); esp to execute a leap (over) using the hands or a pole – ~er n

⁴vault n an act of vaulting

VD /ˌvee ˈdee/ n venereal disease

VDU /ˌvee dee ˈyooh/ n a screen for displaying information from a computer visually

veal /veel/ n the flesh of a young calf used as food

vector /ˈvektə/ n a quantity (e g velocity or force) that has magnitude and direction and that is commonly represented by a directed line segment whose length represents the magnitude and whose orientation in space represents the direction

veer /viə/ 1 to change direction, position, or inclination 2 of the wind to shift in a clockwise direction – veer n

veg /vej/ n, pl veg Br a vegetable – infml

¹vegetable /ˈvej(i)təbl/ adj 1a of, constituting, or growing like plants b consisting of plants 2 made or obtained from plants or plant products

²vegetable n 1 a plant 2 a plant (e g the cabbage, bean, or potato) grown for an edible part which is usu eaten with the principal course of a meal; also this part of the plant 3 a person whose physical and esp mental capacities are severely impaired by illness or injury

vegetable marrow n (any of various large smooth-skinned elongated fruits, used as a vegetable, of) a cultivated variety of a climbing plant of the cucumber family

¹vegetarian /ˌvejiˈteəri-ən/ n one who practises vegetarianism

²vegetarian adj 1 of vegetarians or vegetarianism 2 consisting wholly of vegetables

vegetarianism /-ˌniz(ə)m/ n the theory or practice of living on a diet that excludes the flesh of animals and often other animal products

vegetate /ˈveji.tayt/ v 1 to grow in the manner of a plant 2 to lead a passive monotonous existence

vegetation /ˌvejiˈtaysh(ə)n/ n plant life or total plant cover (e g of an area)

vehement /ˈvee-əmənt/ adj 1 intensely felt; impassioned 2 forcibly expressed – ~ly adv – ~mence n

vehicle /ˈvee-ik(ə)l/ n 1 any of various usu liquid media acting esp as solvents, carriers, or binders for active ingredients (e g drugs) or pigments 2 a means of transmission; a carrier 3 a medium through which sthg is expressed or communicated 4 a motor vehicle

vehicular /veeˈikyoolə/ adj of or designed for vehicles, esp motor vehicles

¹veil /vayl/ n 1a a length of cloth worn by women as a covering for the head and shoulders and often, esp in eastern countries, the face b a piece of sheer fabric attached for protection or ornament to a hat or headdress 2 the cloistered life of a nun 3 a concealing curtain or cover of cloth 4 a disguise, pretext – ~ed adj

²veil v to cover, provide, or conceal (as if) with a veil

¹**vein** /vayn/ n **1** a deposit of ore, coal, etc, esp in a rock fissure **2** any of the tubular converging vessels that carry blood from the capillaries towards the heart **3a** any of the vascular bundles forming the framework of a leaf **b** any of the ribs that serve to stiffen the wings of an insect **4** a streak or marking suggesting a vein (e g in marble) **5** a distinctive element or quality; a strain

²**vein** v to pattern (as if) with veins

veld, veldt /velt, felt/ n shrubby grassland, esp in S Africa

vellum /'veləm/ n a fine-grained skin (e g calf) prepared esp for writing on or binding books

velocity /və'losəti/ n **1** speed, esp of inanimate things **2** speed in a given direction

velvet /'velvit/ n **1** a fabric (e g of silk, rayon, or cotton) characterized by a short soft dense pile **2** sthg suggesting velvet in softness, smoothness, etc – ~**y** adj

velveteen /velvi,teen/ n a fabric made with a short close weft pile in imitation of velvet

venal /'veenl/ adj open to corrupt influence, esp bribery – ~**ity** n – ~**ly** adv

vend /vend/ v to sell, esp by means of a vending machine – ~**or** n

vendetta /ven'detə/ n **1** a blood feud arising from the murder or injury of a member of one family by a member of another **2** a prolonged bitter feud

'**vending ma,chine** /'vending/ n a coin-operated machine for selling merchandise

¹**veneer** /və'niə/ n **1** a thin layer of wood of superior appearance or hardness used esp to give a decorative finish (e g to joinery) **2** a protective or ornamental facing (e g of brick or stone) **3** a superficial or deceptively attractive appearance

²**veneer** v **1** to overlay (e g a common wood) with veneer; broadly to face with a material giving a superior surface **2** to conceal under a superficial and deceptive attractiveness

venerable /'ven(ə)rəbl/ adj **1** – used as a title for an Anglican archdeacon, or for a Roman Catholic who has been accorded the lowest of 3 degrees of recognition for sanctity **2** made sacred, esp by religious or historical association **3a** commanding respect through age, character, and attainments **b** impressive by reason of age

venerate /'venərayt/ v to regard with reverence or admiring deference – -**ration** n

venereal /və'niəri·əl/ adj **1** of sexual desire or sexual intercourse **2** resulting from or contracted during sexual intercourse

ve'nereal di,sease n a contagious disease (e g gonorrhoea or syphilis) that is typically acquired during sexual intercourse

ve,netian 'blind /və'neesh(ə)n/ n a blind (e g for a window) made of horizontal slats that may be adjusted so as to vary the amount of light admitted

vengeance /'venj(ə)ns/ n punishment inflicted in retaliation for injury or offence — **with a vengeance 1** with great force or vehemence **2** to an extreme or excessive degree

venial /'veenyəl, -ni·əl/ adj forgivable, pardonable

venison /'venis(ə)n/ n the flesh of a deer as food

venom /'venəm/ n **1** poisonous matter normally secreted by snakes, scorpions, bees, etc and transmitted chiefly by biting or stinging **2** ill will, malevolence

venomous /'venəməs/ adj **1a** poisonous **b** spiteful, malevolent **2** able to inflict a poisoned wound – ~**ly** adv

venous /'veenəs/ adj, of blood containing carbon dioxide rather than oxygen

¹**vent** /vent/ v to give (vigorous) expression to

²**vent** n **1** a means of escape or release; an outlet – chiefly in give vent to **2a** the anus of a bird or reptile **b** an outlet of a volcano **c** a hole at the breech of a gun through which the powder is ignited

³**vent** n a slit in a garment; specif an opening in the lower part of a seam (e g of a jacket or skirt)

ventilate /'ventilayt/ v **1** to examine freely and openly; expose publicly **2** to cause fresh air to circulate through – -**lation** n

ventilator /'venti,laytə/ n an apparatus or aperture for introducing fresh air or expelling stagnant air

ventral /'ventrəl/ adj **1a** abdominal **b** relating to or situated near or on the front or lower surface of an animal or aircraft opposite the back **2** being or located on the lower or inner surface of a plant structure – ~**ly** adv

ventricle /'ventrikl/ n a chamber of the heart which receives blood from a corresponding atrium and from which blood is pumped to the arteries

ventriloquism /ven'trilə,kwiz(ə)m/ n the production of the voice in such a manner that the sound appears to come from a source other than the vocal organs of the speaker – -**ist** n

¹**venture** /'venchə/ v **1** to proceed despite danger; dare to go or do **2** to offer at the risk of opposition or censure

²**venture** n **1** an undertaking involving chance, risk, or danger, esp in business **2** sthg (e g money or property) at risk in a speculative venture – ~**r** n

'**venturesome** /-s(ə)m/ adj **1** ready to take risks; daring **2** involving risk; hazardous – ~**ness** n

venue /'venyooh/ n the place where a gathering takes place

Venus /'veenəs/ n the planet second in order from the sun

veracious /və'rayshəs/ adj true, accurate; also truthful – -**city** n

veranda, verandah /və'randə/ n a usu roofed open structure attached to the outside of a building

verb /vuhb/ n any of a class of words that characteristically are the grammatical centre of a predicate and express an act, occurrence, or mode of being

¹**verbal** /'vuhbl/ adj 1 of, involving, or expressed in words 2 of or formed from a verb 3 spoken rather than written; oral 4 verbatim, word-for-word

²**verbal** n, Br a spoken statement; esp one made to the police admitting or implying guilt and used in evidence

verbatim /vuh'baytim/ adv or adj in the exact words

verbiage /'vuhbi·ij/ n wordiness, verbosity

verbose /vuh'bohs/ adj 1 containing more words than necessary 2 given to wordiness – ~ly adv – ~sity, ~ness n

verdant /'vuhd(ə)nt/ adj green in tint or colour; esp green with growing plants – -dancy n

verdict /'vuhdikt/ n 1 the decision of a jury on the matter submitted to them 2 an opinion, judgment

verdigris /'vuhdigris; also -,gree/ n a green or bluish deposit formed on copper, brass, or bronze surfaces

¹**verge** /vuhj/ n 1 an outer margin of an object or structural part 2 the brink, threshold 3 Br a surfaced or planted strip of land at the side of a road

²**verge** v m verge on to be near to; border on

³**verge** v to move or extend towards a specified condition

verger /'vuhjə/ n a church official who keeps order during services or serves as an usher or sacristan

verify /'verifie/ v 1 to ascertain the truth, accuracy, or reality of 2 to bear out, fulfil – -fiable adj – -fication n

verily /'verəli/ adv, archaic 1 indeed, certainly 2 truly, confidently

veritable /'veritəbl/ adj being in fact the thing named and not false or imaginary – often used to stress the aptness of a metaphor – -bly adv

verity /'veriti/ n 1 the quality or state of being true or real 2 sthg (e g a statement) that is true; esp a permanently true value or principle

vermiform /'vuhmi,fawm/ adj resembling a worm in shape

vermilion, vermillion /və'milyən/ adj or n (of the brilliant red colour of) mercuric sulphide used as a pigment

vermin /'vuhmin/ n pl vermin 1 pl lice, rats, or other common harmful or objectionable animals 2 an offensive person – ~ous adj

vermouth /'vuhməth/ n a dry or sweet alcoholic drink that has a white wine base and is flavoured with aromatic herbs

¹**vernacular** /və'nakyoolə/ adj 1 expressed or written in a language or dialect native to a region or country rather than a literary, learned, or foreign language 2 of or being the common building style of a period or place

²**vernacular** n the mode of expression of a group or class

vernal /'vuhnl/ adj 1 of or occurring in the spring 2 fresh, youthful

verruca /və'roohkə/ n pl verrucas also verruccae /-ki/ 1 a wart or warty skin growth 2 a warty prominence on a plant or animal

versatile /'vuhsətiel/ adj 1 embracing a variety of subjects, fields, or skills; also turning with ease from one thing to another 2 having many uses or applications – -tility n

verse /vuhs/ n 1 a line of metrical writing 2 poetry; esp undistinguished poetry 3 a stanza 4 any of the short divisions into which a chapter of the Bible is traditionally divided

versed adj possessing a thorough knowledge (of) or skill in

versify /'vuhsifie/ v to compose verses – -fier n – -fication n

version /'vuhsh(ə)n, -zh(ə)n/ n 1 an account or description from a particular point of view, esp as contrasted with another account 2 an adaptation of a work of art into another medium 3 a form or variant of a type or original

versus /'vuhsəs/ prep 1 against 2 in contrast to or as the alternative of

vertebra /'vuhtibrə/ n, pl vertebrae /-bri/, vertebras any of the bony or cartilaginous segments composing the spinal column – ~l adj

¹**vertebrate** /'vuhtibrət, -brayt/ adj 1 having a spinal column 2 of the vertebrates

²**vertebrate** n any of a large group of animals (e g mammals, birds, reptiles, amphibians, and fishes) with a segmented backbone

vertex /'vuhteks/ n, pl vertices /'vuhtiseez/ also vertexes 1a the point opposite to and farthest from the base in a figure b the zenith 2 the highest point; the summit

vertical /'vuhtikl/ adj 1 situated at the highest point; directly overhead or in the zenith 2 perpendicular to the plane of the horizon 3 of or concerning the relationships between people of different rank in a hierarchy – ~ly adv

vertigo /'vuhtigoh/ n a disordered state in which the individual loses balance and the surroundings seem to whirl dizzily – -ginous adj

verve /vuhv/ n 1 the spirit and enthusiasm animating artistic work 2 energy, vitality

¹**very** /'veri/ adj 1 properly so called; actual, genuine 2 absolute (e g the very thing for the purpose) 3 being no more than; mere (e g the very thought terrified me) USE used attributively

²**very** adv 1 to a high degree; exceedingly 2 – used as an intensive to emphasize same, own, or the superlative degree

,**very ,high 'frequency** n a radio frequency in the range between 30MHz and 300MHz

vesicle /'vesikl/ n 1 a membranous usu fluid-filled pouch (e g a cyst, vacuole, or cell) in a plant or animal 2 a pocket of embryonic tissue from which an organ develops – **-cular** adj

vespers /'vespəz/ n pl but sing or pl in constr, a service of evening worship

vessel /'vesl/ n 1 a hollow utensil (e g a jug, cup, or bowl) for holding esp liquid 2 a large hollow structure designed to float on and move through water carrying a crew, passengers, or cargo 3a a tube or canal (e g an artery) in which a body fluid is contained and conveyed or circulated b a conducting tube in a plant

¹**vest** /vest/ v 1 to endow with a particular authority, right, or property 2 to robe in ecclesiastical vestments

²**vest** n 1 chiefly Br a usu sleeveless undergarment for the upper body 2 chiefly NAm a waistcoat

vested 'interest /'vestid/ n an interest (e g in an existing political or social arrangement) in which the holder has a strong personal commitment

vestibule /'vestibyoohl/ n 1 a lobby or chamber between the outer door and the interior of a building 2 any of various bodily cavities, esp when serving as or resembling an entrance to some other cavity or space

vestige /'vestij/ n 1a a trace or visible sign left by sthg vanished or lost b a minute remaining amount 2 a small or imperfectly formed body part or organ that remains from one more fully developed in an earlier stage of the individual, in a past generation, or in closely related forms – **-gial** adj

vestment /'vestmənt/ n any of the ceremonial garments and insignia worn by ecclesiastical officiants and assistants as appropriate to their rank and to the rite being celebrated

vestry /'vestri/ n 1a a sacristy b a room used for church meetings and classes 2 the business meeting of an English parish

¹**vet** /vet/ n sby qualified and authorized to treat diseases and injuries of animals

²**vet** v, **-tt-** chiefly Br to subject to careful and thorough appraisal

vetch /vech/ n any of a genus of climbing or twining leguminous plants including valuable fodder and soil-improving plants

veteran /'vet(ə)rən/ n 1 sby who has had long experience of an occupation, skill, or (military) service 2 **veteran, veteran car** Br an old motor car; specif one built before 1916 3 NAm a former serviceman

veterinary /'vet(ə)rinəri/ adj of or being the medical care of animals, esp domestic animals

¹**veto** /'veetoh/ n pl **vetoes** 1 a right to declare inoperative decisions made by others; esp a power vested in a chief executive to prevent permanently or temporarily the enactment of measures passed by a legislature

²**veto** v **vetoing; vetoed** to subject to a veto – **vetoer** n

vex /veks/ v **vexed** also **vext** 1a to bring distress, discomfort, or agitation to b to irritate or annoy by petty provocations; harass 2 to puzzle, baffle – **~ation** n – **~atious** adj – **~atiously** adv

via /'vie-ə/ prep 1 passing through or calling at (a place) on the way 2 through the medium of; also by means of

viable /'vie-əbl/ adj 1 (born alive and developed enough to be) capable of living 2 capable of working; practicable – **-bility** n – **-bly** adv

viaduct /'vie-ə,dukt/ n a usu long bridge, esp on a series of arches, that carries a road, railway, canal, etc over a deep valley

vibrant /'viebrənt/ adj 1a oscillating or pulsating rapidly b pulsating with life, vigour, or activity 2 sounding as a result of vibration; resonant – **~ly** adv – **-ancy** n

vibraphone /'viebrə,fohn/ n a percussion instrument resembling the xylophone but having metal bars

vibrate /vie'brayt/ v 1 to move to and fro; oscillate 2 to have an effect as of vibration; throb 3 to be in a state of vibration; quiver 4 to emit (e g sound) (as if) with a vibratory motion

vibration /vie'braysh(ə)n/ n 1a a periodic motion of the particles of an elastic body or medium in alternately opposite directions from a position of equilibrium b an oscillation or quivering 2 a distinctive usu emotional atmosphere capable of being sensed – usu pl with sing. meaning – **-tory** adj

vibrato /vi'brahtoh/ n pl **vibratos** a slightly tremulous effect imparted to musical tone to add expressiveness, by slight and rapid variations in pitch

vicar /'vikə/ n a Church of England incumbent receiving a stipend but formerly not the tithes of a parish

vicarage /'vikərij/ n the benefice or house of a vicar

vicarious /vie'keəri·əs, vi-/ adj 1 performed or suffered by one person as a substitute for, or to the benefit of, another 2 experienced through imaginative participation in the experience of another – **~ly** adv – **~ness** n

¹**vice** /vies/ n 1a moral depravity or corruption; wickedness b a habitual and usu minor fault or shortcoming 2 sexual immorality; esp prostitution

²**vice**, NAm chiefly **vise** /vies/ n any of various tools, usu attached to a workbench, that have 2 jaws that close for holding work by operation of a screw, lever, or cam

vice-'chancellor n an officer ranking next below a chancellor; esp the administrative head of a British university

vic

viceroy /'viesroy/ *n* the governor of a country or province who rules as the representative of his sovereign – **viceregal** *adj*

vice versa /ˌviesi 'vuhsə, ˌvieso, ˌvies/ *adv* with the order changed and relations reversed; conversely

vicinity /vi'sinəti/ *n* 1 a surrounding area or district 2 being near; proximity – *fml*

vicious /'vishəs/ *adj* 1 having the nature or quality of vice; depraved 2 unpleasantly fierce, malignant, or severe 3 malicious, spiteful – ~**ly** *adv* – ~**ness** *n*

ˌvicious 'circle *n* 1 a chain of events in which the apparent solution of 1 difficulty creates a new problem that makes the original difficulty worse 2 the logical fallacy of using 1 argument or definition to prove or define a second on which the first depends

victim /'viktim/ *n* sby or sthg that is adversely affected by a force or agent: e g **a** one who or that which is injured, destroyed, or subjected to oppression or mistreatment **b** a dupe, prey – ~**ize** *v*

victor /'viktə/ *n* a person, country, etc that defeats an enemy or opponent; a winner

Vicˌtoria 'Cross *n* a bronze Maltese cross that is the highest British military decoration

¹**Victorian** /vik'tawri·ən/ *adj* 1 (characteristic) of the reign of Queen Victoria or the art, letters, or taste of her time 2 typical of the moral standards or conduct of the age of Queen Victoria, esp in being prudish or hypocritical

²**Victorian** *n* sby living during Queen Victoria's reign

victorious /vik'tawri·əs/ *adj* 1a having won a victory **b** (characteristic) of victory 2 successful, triumphant – ~**ly** *adv*

victory /'vikt(ə)ri/ *n* 1 the overcoming of an enemy or antagonist 2 achievement of mastery or success in a struggle or endeavour

victualler, *NAm also* **victualer** /'vitl·ə/ *n* 1 a publican 2 sby who or sthg that provisions an army, a navy, or a ship with food

vide /'viedi/ *v imper* see – used to direct a reader to another item

¹**video** /'vidioh/ *adj* of a form of magnetic recording for reproduction on a television screen

²**video** *n* a machine for videotaping

video nasty *n* a video film of (allegedly) sensational nature, usu including scenes of explicit sex, violence, and horror

videotape /'vidioh·tayp/ *v* to make a recording of (e g sthg that is televised) on magnetic tape

vie /vie/ *v* **vying**; **vied** to strive for superiority; contend

¹**view** /vyooh/ *n* 1 the act of seeing or examining; inspection; *also* a survey 2 a way of regarding sthg; an opinion 3 a scene, prospect; *also* an aspect 4 extent or range of vision; sight 5 an intention, object 6 a pictorial representation — **in**

view of 1 taking the specified feature into consideration 2 able to be seen by or from — **on view** open to public inspection

²**view** *v* 1a to see, watch; *also* to watch television **b** to look on in a specified way; regard 2 to look at attentively; inspect

viewer /'vyooh·ə/ *n* 1 an optical device used in viewing 2 sby who watches television

viewfinder /'vyooh·fiendə/ *n* a device on a camera for showing what will be included in the picture

¹**view·point** /-ˌpoynt/ *n* a standpoint; point of view

vigil /'vijil/ *n* 1 a devotional watch formerly kept on the night before a religious festival 2 the act of keeping awake at times when sleep is customary; *also* a period of wakefulness 3 an act or period of watching or surveillance; watch

vigilant /'vijilənt/ *adj* alert and watchful – ~**ly** *adv* – -**ance** *n*

vigilante /ˌviji'lanti/ *n* sby who seeks to keep order and punish crime without recourse to the established processes of law

vigorous /'vigərəs/ *adj* 1 possessing or showing vigour; full of active strength 2 done with vigour; carried out forcefully and energetically – ~**ly** *adv*

vigour, *NAm* **vigor** /'vigə/ *n* 1 active physical or mental strength or force 2 active healthy well-balanced growth, esp of plants 3 intensity of action or effect; force

Viking /'vieking/ *n* 1 a Norse trader and warrior of the 8th to 10th c 2 a Scandinavian

vile /viel/ *adj* 1 morally despicable or abhorrent **b** physically repulsive; foul 2 tending to degrade 3 disgustingly or utterly bad; contemptible – ~**ly** *adv* – ~**ness** *n*

vilify /'vilifie/ *v* to utter slanderous and abusive statements against; defame – -**fication** *n*

villa /'vilə/ *n* 1 a country mansion 2 an ancient Roman mansion and the surrounding agricultural estate 3 *Br* a detached or semidetached suburban house, usu having a garden and built before WW I

village /'vilij/ *n* a group of dwellings in the country, larger than a hamlet and smaller than a town

villain /'vilən/ *n* 1 a scoundrel, rascal; *also* a criminal 2 a character in a story or play whose evil actions affect the plot – ~**ous** *adj*

villainy /'viləni/ *n* 1 villainous conduct; *also* a villainous act 2 depravity

vim /vim/ *n* robust energy and enthusiasm – *infml*

vindicate /'vindikayt/ *v* 1a to exonerate, absolve **b** to provide justification for; justify 2 to maintain the existence of; uphold – -**cation** *n*

vindictive /vin'diktiv/ *adj* 1a disposed to seek revenge; vengeful **b** intended as revenge 2 intended to cause anguish; spiteful – ~**ly** *adv* – ~**ness** *n*

vine /vien/ *n* 1 the climbing plant that bears grapes 2 (a plant with) a stem that requires support and that climbs by tendrils or twining

vinegar /'vinigə/ *n* a sour liquid obtained esp by acetic fermentation of wine, cider, etc and used as a condiment or preservative – ~y *adj*

vineyard /'vinyahd, -yəd/ *n* a plantation of grapevines

vinous /'vienəs/ *adj* 1 of or made with wine 2 (showing the effects of being) addicted to wine

¹vintage /'vintij/ *n* 1 a wine, specif one of a particular type, region, and year and usu of superior quality that is dated and allowed to mature **b** a collection of contemporary and similar people or things; a crop 2 the act or time of harvesting grapes or making wine

²vintage *adj* 1 of a vintage; *esp* being a product of 1 particular year rather than a blend of wines from different years 2 of the best and most characteristic; classic 3 *Br, of a motor vehicle* built between 1917 and 1930

vintner /'vintnə/ *n* a wine merchant

vinyl /'vienl/ *n* a plastic derived from ethylene

viol /'vie-əl/ *n* any of a family of bowed stringed instruments chiefly of the 16th and 17th c with usu 6 strings and a fretted fingerboard, played resting on or between the player's knees

¹viola /vi'ohlə/ *n* a musical instrument of the violin family that is intermediate in size and range between the violin and cello and is tuned a 5th below the violin

²viola /'vie-ələ, vie'ohlə/ *n* a violet; *esp* any of various cultivated violets with (variegated) flowers resembling pansies

violate /'vie-əlayt/ *v* 1 to fail to comply with; infringe 2 to do harm to; *specif* to rape – **-lation** *n*

violence /'vie-ələns/ *n* 1 (an instance of) exertion of physical force so as to injure or abuse 2 unjust or unwarranted distortion; outrage **3a** intense or turbulent action or force **b** (an instance of) vehement feeling or expression; fervour

violent /'vie-ələnt/ *adj* 1 marked by extreme force or sudden intense activity 2 notably furious or vehement; *also* excited or mentally disordered to the point of loss of self-control – **~ly** *adv*

violet /'vie-əlet/ *n* 1 any of a genus of plants with often sweet-scented flowers, usu of all 1 colour **2** a bluish purple colour

violin /,vie-ə'lin/ *n* a bowed stringed instrument having a fingerboard with no frets and 4 strings – **~ist** *n*

violoncello /,vie-ələn'cheloh/ *n pl* **violoncellos** a cello

VIP *n, pl* **VIPs** a person of great influence or prestige

viper /'viepə/ *n* 1 (any of various snakes related to) the adder 2 a malignant or treacherous person

virago /vi'rahgoh/ *n pl* **viragoes, viragos** 1 a termagant 2 *archaic* a woman of great stature, strength, and courage

¹virgin /'vuhjin/ *n* a person, esp a girl, who has not had sexual intercourse – **~ity** *n*

²virgin *adj* 1 free of impurity or stain; unsullied 2 being a virgin 3 characteristic of or befitting a virgin; modest 4 untouched, unexploited; *specif* not altered by human activity

¹virginal /'vuhjinl/ *adj* 1 (characteristic) of a virgin or virginity; *esp* pure, chaste 2 fresh, untouched, uncorrupted

²virginal *n* a small rectangular harpsichord popular in the 16th and 17th c – often *pl* with sing. meaning

Virgo /'vuhgoh/ *n* (sby born under) the 6th sign of the zodiac in astrology, which is pictured as a woman holding an ear of corn

virile /'viriel/ *adj* 1 having the nature, properties, or qualities (often thought of as typical) of a man; *specif* capable of functioning as a male in copulation 2 vigorous, forceful – **-ility** *n*

virology /vie-ə'roləji/ *n* a branch of science that deals with viruses – **-gist** *n*

virtual /'vuhchooal/ *adj* that is such in essence or effect though not formally recognized or admitted

virtually /'vuhchəli, -chooəli/ *adv* almost entirely; for all practical purposes

virtue /'vuhtyooh, -chooh/ *n* **1a** conformity to a standard of right; morality **b** a particular moral excellence 2 a beneficial or commendable quality 3 a capacity to act; potency 4 chastity, esp in a woman — **by virtue of** 1 through the force of; having as a right 2 as a result of; because of

virtuoso /,vuhtyooh'ohsoh, -zoh/ *n, pl* **virtuosos, virtuosi** /-si, -zi/ one who excels in the technique of an art, esp in musical performance – **virtuoso** *adj*

virtuous /'vuhchoo-əs/ *adj* 1 having or exhibiting virtue; *esp* morally excellent; righteous 2 chaste – **~ly** *adv*

virulent /'viryoolənt, -rə-/ *adj* 1 *of a disease* severe and developing rapidly 2 extremely poisonous or venomous 3 full of malice; malignant – **~ly** *adv* – **-ence, -ency** *n*

virus /'vie-ərəs/ *n* (a disease caused by) any of a large group of submicroscopic often disease-causing agents

visa /'veezə/ *n* an endorsement made on a passport by the proper authorities (e g of a country at entrance or exit) denoting that the bearer may proceed

visage /'vizij/ *n* a face, countenance; *also* an aspect – *fml or poetic*

vis-à-vis /,vee zah 'vee/ *prep* 1 face to face with; opposite 2 in relation to

viscera /'visərə/ *n pl* the internal body organs collectively – **~l** *adj*

viscosity /vis'kosəti/ *n* **1** being viscous **2** (a measure of the force needed to overcome) the property of a liquid, gas, or semifluid that enables it to offer resistance to flow

viscount /'viekownt/ *n* a member of the peerage in Britain ranking below an earl and above a baron – ~**cy** *n*

viscountess /,viekown'tes, 'viekowntis/ *n* **1** the wife or widow of a viscount **2** a woman having the rank of a viscount

viscous /'viskəs/ *adj* **1** sticky, adhesive **2** having or characterized by (high) viscosity

visibility /,vizə'biləti/ *n* **1** being visible **2** the clearness of the atmosphere as revealed by the greatest distance at which prominent objects can be identified visually with the naked eye

visible /'vizəbl/ *adj* **1** capable of being seen **2** exposed to view **3** capable of being perceived; noticeable **4** of or being trade in goods rather than services

vision /'vizh(ə)n/ *n* **1** sthg (revelatory) seen in a dream, trance, or ecstasy **2** discernment, foresight **3a** the act or power of seeing; sight **b** the sense by which the qualities of an object (e g colour, luminosity, shape, and size) constituting its appearance are perceived and which acts through the eye **4** a lovely or charming sight

[1]**visionary** /'vizh(ə)nri, -əri/ *adj* **1a** able or likely to see visions **b** disposed to daydreaming or imagining; dreamy **2** impracticable, utopian

[2]**visionary** *n* **1** one who sees visions; a seer **2** one whose ideas or projects are impractical; a dreamer

[1]**visit** /'vizit/ *v* **1a** to afflict **b** to inflict punishment for **2a** to pay a call on for reasons of kindness, friendship, ceremony, or business **b** to go or come to look at or stay at (e g for business or sightseeing)

[2]**visit** *n* **1a** an act of visiting; a call **b** an extended but temporary stay **2** an official or professional call; a visitation

visitation /,vizi'taysh(ə)n/ *n* **1** the act or an instance of visiting; *esp* an official visit (e g for inspection) **2a** a special dispensation of divine favour or wrath **b** a severe trial; an affliction

visiting card /'viziting/ *n* a small card of introduction bearing the name and sometimes the address and profession of the owner

visitor /'vizitə/ *n* sby who or sthg that makes (formal) visits

visor, vizor /'viezə/ *n* **1** the (movable) part of a helmet that covers the face **2** a usu movable flat sunshade attached at the top of a vehicle windscreen **3** *chiefly NAm* a peak on a cap

vista /'vistə/ *n* **1** a distant view esp through or along an avenue or opening; a prospect **2** an extensive mental view (e g over a stretch of time or a series of events)

visual /'viz(h)oool/ *adj* **1** visible **2** producing mental images; vivid **3** done or executed by sight only

visual display unit *n* a VDU

visual·ize, -ise /'vizhooə,liez/ *v* to see or form a mental picture of

vital /'vietl/ *adj* **1** concerned with or necessary to the maintenance of life **2** full of life and vigour; animated **3** of the utmost importance; essential to continued worth or well-being – ~**ly** *adv*

vitality /vie'taləti/ *n* **1a** the quality which distinguishes the living from the dead or inanimate **b** capacity to live and develop; *also* physical or mental liveliness **2** power of enduring

vitals /'vietlz/ *n pl* **1** the vital organs (e g the heart, liver, or brain) **2** essential parts

vital statistics *n pl* **1** statistics relating to births, deaths, health, etc **2** facts considered to be interesting or important; *specif* a woman's bust, waist, and hip measurements

vitamin /'vitamin, 'vie-/ *n* any of various organic compounds that are essential in minute quantities to the nutrition of most animals and regulate metabolic processes

vitiate /'vishiayt/ *v* **1** to make faulty or defective; debase **2** to invalidate – ~**ation** *n*

vitreous /'vitri·əs/ *adj* resembling glass in colour, composition, brittleness, etc

vituperate /vi'tyoohpərayt/ *v* to use harsh condemnatory language of – ~**ation** *n* – ~**ative** *adj*

vivacious /vi'vayshəs/ *adj* lively in temper or conduct; sprightly – ~**ly** *adv* – ~**vivacity** *n* – ~**ness** *n*

vivarium /vie'veari·əm/ *n pl* **vivaria** /-ri·ə/, **vivariums** an enclosure for keeping and observing plants or esp terrestrial animals indoors

viva voce /,vievə 'vohsi, ,veevə 'vohchi/ *n, adj, or adv* (an examination conducted) by word of mouth

vivid /'vivid/ *adj* **1** *of a colour* very intense **2** producing a strong or clear impression on the senses; *specif* producing distinct mental images – ~**ly** *adv* – ~**ness** *n*

viviparous /vi'vipərəs/ *adj* producing living young, instead of eggs, from within the body in the manner of nearly all mammals, many reptiles, and a few fishes

vivisect /'vivisekt, --'-/ *v* to perform an operation on (a living animal), esp for experimental purposes – ~**ion** *n* – ~**ionist** *n*

vixen /'viks(ə)n/ *n* **1** a female fox **2** a scolding ill-tempered woman

vizier /vi'ziə/ *n* a high executive officer of various Muslim countries, esp of the former Ottoman Empire

vocabulary /voh'kabyooləri, və-/ *n* **1** a list of words, and sometimes phrases, usu arranged alphabetically and defined or translated **2** the words employed by a language, group, or individual or in a field of work or knowledge

¹**vocal** /'vohkl/ *adj* **1** uttered by the voice; oral **2** of, composed or arranged for, or sung by the human voice **3a** having or exercising the power of producing voice, speech, or sound **b** given to strident or insistent expression; outspoken – ~**ly** *adv*

²**vocal** *n* **1** a vocal sound **2** a usu accompanied musical composition or passage for the voice

vocalist /'vohkl·ist/ *n* a singer

vocation /voh'kaysh(ə)n, və-/ *n* **1** a summons or strong inclination to a particular state or course of action; *esp* a divine call to the religious life **2** the work in which a person is regularly employed; a career

vocational /voh'kaysh(ə)nl, və-/ *adj* of or being training in a skill or trade to be pursued as a career

vocative /'vokətiv/ *n* (a form in) a grammatical case expressing the one addressed

vociferate /voh'sifərayt, və-/ *v* to cry out or utter loudly; clamour, shout – **-ation** *n*

vociferous /voh'sif(ə)rəs, və-/ *adj* marked by or given to vehement insistent outcry – ~**ly** *adv* – ~**ness** *n*

vodka /'vodkə/ *n* a colourless and unaged neutral spirit distilled from a mash (e g of rye or wheat)

vogue /vohg/ *n* **1** the prevailing, esp temporary, fashion **2** popular acceptance or favour; popularity

¹**voice** /voys/ *n* **1a** sound produced by humans, birds, etc by forcing air from the lungs through the vocal organs **b(1)** (the use, esp in singing or acting, of) musical production of the vocal cords and resonated by the cavities of the head, throat, lungs, etc **b(2)** any of the melodic parts in a vocal or instrumental composition **c** the faculty of utterance; speech **2a** the expressed wish or opinion **b** right of expression; say **3** distinction of form or a particular system of inflections of a verb to indicate whether it is the subject of the verb that acts

²**voice** *v* **1** to express (a feeling or opinion) in words; utter **2** to adjust (e g an organ pipe) in manufacture, for producing the proper musical sounds

'**voice ,box** *n* the larynx

¹**void** /voyd/ *adj* **1** containing nothing; unoccupied **2a** devoid **b** having no members or examples; *specif, of a suit* having no cards represented in a particular hand **3** vain, useless **4** of no legal effect

²**void** *n* **1a** empty space; vacuum **b** an opening, gap **2** a feeling of lack, want, or emptiness

³**void** *v* **1** to make empty or vacant; clear **2** to discharge or emit

voile /voyl/ *n* a fine soft sheer fabric used esp for women's summer clothing or curtains

volatile /'volə,tiel/ *adj* **1** capable of being readily vaporized at a relatively low temperature **2a** lighthearted, lively **b** dangerously unstable; explosive **3a** frivolously changeable; fickle **b** characterized by rapid change

vol-au-vent /,vol oh 'vonh, '- -,-/ *n* a round case of puff pastry filled with a mixture of meat, poultry, or fish in a thick sauce

volcanic /vol'kanik/ *adj* explosively violent; volatile

volcano /vol'kaynoh/ *n, pl* **volcanoes, volcanos 1** (a hill or mountain surrounding) an outlet in a planet's crust from which molten or hot rock and steam issue **2** a dynamic or violently creative person; *also* a situation liable to become violent

vole /vohl/ *n* any of various small plant-eating rodents usu with a stout body, blunt nose, and short ears

volition /və'lish(ə)n/ *n* **1** (an act of making) a free choice or decision **2** the power of choosing or determining; will – ~**al** *adj*

¹**volley** /'voli/ *n* **1a** a simultaneous discharge of a number of missile weapons **b** a return or succession of returns made by hitting a ball, shuttle, etc before it touches the ground **2** a burst or emission of many things at once or in rapid succession

²**volley** *v* **volleying; volleyed 1** to discharge (as if) in a volley **2** to propel (an object that has not yet hit the ground), esp with an implement or the hand or foot

'**volley ball** /-,bawl/ *n* a game between 2 teams of usu 6 players who volley a ball over a high net in the centre of a court

volt /vohlt, volt/ *n* the derived SI unit of electrical potential difference and electromotive force equal to the difference of potential between 2 points in a conducting wire carrying a constant current of 1 ampere when the power dissipated between these 2 points is equal to 1 watt

voltage /'vohltij, 'voltij/ *n* an electric potential difference; electromotive force

volte-face /,volt 'fahs, fas/ *n* a sudden reversal of attitude or policy; an about-face

voltmeter /'volt,meetə, 'vohlt-/ *n* an instrument for measuring in volts the differences of potential between different points of an electrical circuit

voluble /'volyoobl/ *adj* characterized by ready or rapid speech; talkative – **-bility** *n* – **-bly** *adv*

volume /'volyoohm, 'volyoom/ *n* **1a** a series of printed sheets bound typically in book form; a book **b** a series of issues of a periodical **2** space occupied as measured in cubic units (e g litres); cubic capacity **3a** an amount; *also* a bulk, mass **b** (the representation of) mass in art or architecture **c** a considerable quantity; a great deal – often *pl* with sing. meaning; esp in *speak volumes for* **4** the degree of loudness or the intensity of a sound

voluminous /və'lyoohminəs/ *adj* **1** having or containing a large volume; *specif, of a garment* very full **2** writing much or at great length – ~**ly** *adv* – ~**ness** *n*

¹**voluntary** /'volənt(ə)ri/ *adj* **1** proceeding from free choice or consent **2** intentional **3** provided or supported by voluntary action – **-tarily** *adv*

²**voluntary** n an organ piece played before or after a religious service

¹**volunteer** /ˌvolənˈtiə/ n one who undertakes a service of his/her own free will; esp sby who enters into military service voluntarily

²**volunteer** adj being, consisting of, or engaged in by volunteers

³**volunteer** v 1 to communicate voluntarily; say 2 to offer oneself as a volunteer

voluptuary /vəˈluptyoo(ə)ri/ n one whose chief interest is luxury and sensual pleasure

voluptuous /vəˈluptyoo-əs/ adj 1 causing delight or pleasure to the senses; conducive to, occupied with, or arising from sensual gratification 2 suggestive of sensual pleasure; broadly sexually attractive, esp owing to shapeliness – ~ly adv – ~ness n

¹**vomit** /ˈvomit/ n a vomiting; also the vomited matter

²**vomit** v 1 to disgorge (the contents of the stomach) through the mouth 2 to eject (sthg) violently or abundantly; spew

¹**voodoo** /ˈvoohdooh/ n pl voodoos a set of magical beliefs and practices, mainly of W African origin, practised chiefly in Haiti and characterized by communication by trance with deities

²**voodoo** v voodoos; voodooing; voodooed to bewitch (as if) by means of voodoo

voracious /vəˈrayshəs/ adj 1 having a huge appetite; ravenous 2 excessively eager; insatiable – ~ly adv

vortex /ˈvawteks/ n, pl vortices /ˈvawtiseez/ also vortexes 1 a mass of whirling water, air, etc that tends to form a cavity or vacuum in the centre of the circle into which material is drawn; esp a whirlpool or whirlwind 2 sthg that resembles a whirlpool in violent activity or in engulfing or overwhelming

¹**vote** /voht/ n 1 a ballot 2 the collective verdict of a body of people expressed by voting 3 the franchise

²**vote** v 1 to cast one's vote; esp to exercise a politicaI franchise 2a to judge by general agreement; declare b to offer as a suggestion; propose

vouch /vowch/ v 1 to give or act as a guarantee for 2 to supply supporting evidence or personal assurance for

voucher /ˈvowchə/ n, Br a ticket that can be exchanged for specific goods or services

vouchsafe /vowchˈsayf/ v 1 to grant as a special privilege or in a gracious or condescending manner 2 to condescend, deign to do sthg

¹**vow** /vow/ n a solemn and often religiously binding promise or assertion; specif one by which a person binds him-/herself to an act, service, or condition

²**vow** v 1 to promise solemnly; swear 2 to resolve to bring about

vowel /ˈvowl/ n (a letter, in English usu a, e, i, o, u, and sometimes y, representing) any of a class of speech sounds characterized by lack of closure in the breath channel or lack of audible friction

vox populi /ˌvoks ˈpopyoolie, -li/ n the opinion of the general public

¹**voyage** /ˈvoyij/ n a considerable course or period of travelling by other than land routes; broadly a journey

²**voyage** v to make a voyage (across) – ~r n

voyeur /vwahˈyuh/ n 1 one who gains sexual satisfaction by looking, esp at sexual acts, organs, etc 2 a prying observer who is usu seeking the sordid or scandalous

'V ,sign /vee/ n a gesture made by raising the index and middle fingers in a V a with the palm outwards signifying victory b with the palm inwards signifying insult or contempt

vulcan-ize /ˈvulkaniez/ v to treat rubber so as to make more suitable for certain purposes (e g making tyres)

vulgar /ˈvulgə/ adj 1 generally used, applied, or accepted 2a of or being the common people; plebeian b generally current; public 3a lacking in cultivation, breeding, or taste; coarse b ostentatious or excessive in expenditure or display; pretentious 4 lewdly or profanely indecent; obscene – ~ize v – ~ly adv – ~ity n

,vulgar 'fraction n a fraction in which both the denominator and numerator are explicitly present and are separated by a horizontal or slanted line

vulgarian /vulˈgeəri-ən/ n a vulgar and esp rich person

vulgarism /ˈvulgəˌriz(ə)m/ n 1 a word or expression originated or used chiefly by illiterate people 2 vulgarity

vulnerable /ˈvuln(ə)rəbl/ adj 1 capable of being physically or mentally wounded 2 open to attack or damage; assailable – -bility n – -bly adv

vulture /ˈvulchə/ n any of various large usu bald-headed birds of prey that are related to the hawks, eagles, and falcons and feed on carrion

vulva /ˈvulvə/ n pl vulvas, vulvae /-vi/ the (opening between the projecting) external parts of the female genital organs

vying /ˈvie-ing/ pres part of vie

W

w /'dubl,yooh/ *n, pl* **w's, ws** *often cap* (a graphic representation of, or device for reproducing,) the 23rd letter of the English alphabet

wacky /'waki/ *adj, chiefly NAm* absurdly or amusingly eccentric or irrational; crazy – *infml* – **wackiness** *n*

¹**wad** /wod/ *n* **1a** a soft mass, esp of a loose fibrous material, variously used (e g to stop an aperture or pad a garment) **b** a soft plug used to retain a powder charge, esp in a muzzle-loading cannon or gun **2** a roll of paper money

²**wad** *v* **-dd-** **1** to form into a wad or wadding **2** to stuff, pad, or line with some soft substance

wadding /'woding/ *n* stuffing or padding in the form of a soft mass or sheet of short loose fibres

¹**waddle** /'wodl/ *v* **waddling** /'wadl·ing, 'wodling/ **1** to walk with short steps swinging the forepart of the body from side to side **2** to move clumsily in a manner suggesting a waddle – **waggle** *n*

²**waddle** *n* an awkward clumsy swaying gait

¹**wade** /wayd/ *v* **1** to walk through water **2** to proceed with difficulty or effort **3** to attack with determination or vigour – + *in* or *into*

²**wade** *n* an act of wading

wader /'wayda/ *n* **1** *pl* high waterproof boots used for walking **2** any of many long-legged birds (e g sandpipers and snipes) that wade in water in search of food

wadge /woj/ *n, Br* a thick bundle; a wad – *infml*

wafer /'wayfa/ *n* **1a** a thin crisp biscuit; *also* a biscuit consisting of layers of wafer sometimes sandwiched with a filling **b** a round piece of thin unleavened bread used in the celebration of the Eucharist **2** an adhesive disc of dried paste used, esp formerly, as a seal

¹**waffle** /'wofl/ *n* a cake of batter that is baked in a waffle iron and has a crisp dimpled surface

²**waffle** *v* **waffling** /'wofl·ing, 'wofling/ to talk or write foolishly

³**waffle** *n* empty or pretentious words – *infml*

'**waffle ,iron** *n* a cooking utensil with 2 hinged metal parts that shut on each other and impress surface projections on the waffle being cooked

¹**waft** /woft/ *v* to convey or be conveyed lightly (as if) by the impulse of wind or waves

²**waft** *n* **1** sthg (e g a smell) that is wafted; a whiff **2** a slight breeze; a puff

¹**wag** /wag/ *v* **-gg-** **1** to move to and fro, esp with quick jerky motions **2** to move in chatter or gossip

²**wag** *n* an act of wagging; a shake

³**wag** *n* a wit, joker

¹**wage** /wayj/ *v* to engage in or carry on (a war, conflict, etc)

²**wage** *n* **1a** a payment for services, esp of a manual kind, usu according to contract and on an hourly, daily, weekly, or piecework basis – usu pl with sing. meaning **b** *pl* the share of the national product attributable to labour as a factor in production **2** a recompense, reward

¹**wager** /'wayja/ *n* **1** sthg (e g a sum of money) risked on an uncertain event **2** sthg on which bets are laid

²**wager** *v* to lay as or make a bet

waggish /'wagish/ *adj* befitting or characteristic of a wag; humorous – ~**ly** *adv* – ~**ness** *n*

waggle /'wagl/ *v* **waggling** /'wagling, 'wagl·ing/ to (cause to) sway or move repeatedly from side to side; wag – **waggle** *n*

waggon /wagǝn/ *n* **1** a usu 4-wheeled vehicle for carrying bulky or heavy loads; *esp* one drawn by horses **2** a railway goods vehicle

wagtail /'wag,tayl/ *n* any of numerous birds with trim slender bodies and very long tails that they habitually jerk up and down

waif /wayf/ *n* a stray helpless person or animal; *esp* a homeless child

¹**wail** /wayl/ *v* **1** to express sorrow by uttering mournful cries; lament **2** to express dissatisfaction plaintively; complain

²**wail** *n* **1** a usu loud prolonged high-pitched cry expressing grief or pain **2** a sound suggestive of wailing

¹**wainscot** /'waynskǝt/ *n* **1** a usu panelled wooden lining of an interior wall **2** the lower part of an interior wall when finished differently from the remainder of the wall

²**wainscot** *v* **-t-, -tt-** to line (as if) with boards or panelling

waist /wayst/ *n* **1a** the (narrow) part of the body between the chest and hips **b** the greatly constricted part of the abdomen of a wasp, fly, etc **2** the part of sthg corresponding to or resembling the human waist; *esp* the middle part of a sailing ship between foremast and mainmast **3** the part of a garment covering the body at the waist or waistline

'**waist,coat** /-,koht/ *n, chiefly Br* a sleeveless upper garment that fastens down the centre front and usu has a V-neck;

'**waist,line** /-,lien/ *n* **1** an imaginary line encircling the narrowest part of the waist; *also* the part of a garment corresponding to this line or to the place where fashion dictates this should be **2** body circumference at the waist

¹**wait** /wayt/ *v* **1a** to remain stationary in readiness or expectation **b** to pause for another to catch up **2a** to look forward expectantly **b** to hold back expectantly **3** to serve at meals – usu in *wait at table* **4** to be ready and available – **wait on/upon 1** to act as an attendant on; serve **2** to await **3** *archaic* to make a formal call on

²**wait** n 1 any of a group who serenade for gratuities, esp at the Christmas season 2 an act or period of waiting

waiter /'wayta/ n one who waits at table (e g in a restaurant), esp as a regular job

waive /wayv/ v 1 to refrain from demanding or enforcing; relinquish, forgo 2 to put off from immediate consideration; postpone

waiver /'wayva/ n (a document giving proof of) the relinquishing of a right

¹**wake** /wayk/ v **waked, woke** /wohk/; **waked, woken** /'wohkan/, **woke** 1 to rouse (as if) from sleep; awake – often + *up* 2 to arouse, evoke 3 to arouse conscious interest in; alert – usu + *to*

²**wake** n 1 a watch held over the body of a dead person prior to burial and sometimes accompanied by festivity; *broadly* any festive leavetaking 2 *Br* an annual holiday in northern England – usu pl but sing. or pl in constr

³**wake** n the track left by a ship

'**wakeful** /-f(a)l/ *adj* 1 not sleeping or able to sleep 2 spent without sleep – ~**ly** *adv* – ~**ness** n

waken /'waykan/ v to awake – often + *up*

¹**walk** /wawk/ **1a** to move along on foot; advance by steps, in such a way that at least 1 foot is always in contact with the ground **b** to go on foot for exercise or pleasure 2 to take (an animal) for a walk 3 to follow on foot for the purposes of examining, measuring, etc – ~ **er** n — **walk off with 1a** to steal and take away **b** to take away unintentionally 2 to win or gain, esp by outdoing one's competitors without difficulty — **walk over** to treat contemptuously — **walk tall** to bear oneself proudly — **walk the plank** to be forced to walk, esp blindfold, along a board laid over the side of a ship until one falls into the sea

²**walk** n 1 an act or instance of going on foot, esp for exercise or pleasure 2 a route for walking 3 a railed or colonnaded platform 4 distance to be walked **5a** the gait of a 2-legged animal in which the feet are lifted alternately with 1 foot always (partially) on the ground **b** the slow 4-beat gait of a quadruped, specif a horse, in which there are always at least 2 feet on the ground **c** a low rate of speed 6 a route regularly traversed by a person (e g a postman or policeman) in the performance of a particular activity 7 an occupation, calling – chiefly in *walk of life*

walkabout /'wawka,bowt/ n 1 a short period of wandering bush life engaged in occasionally by an Australian aborigine for ceremonial reasons 2 an informal walk among the crowds by a public figure

walkie-talkie /,wawki 'tawki/ n a compact battery-operated transmitter/receiver

walking /'wawking/ *adj* **1a** animate; *esp* human **b** able to walk **2a** used for or in walking **b** characterized by or consisting of walking

'**walk-on** n (sby who has) a small usu nonspeaking part in a dramatic production

'**walk,out** /-,owt/ n 1 a strike 2 the action of leaving a meeting or organization as an expression of protest

walk out v 1 to go on strike 2 to depart suddenly, often as an expression of protest — **walk out on** to leave in the lurch; abandon

'**walk,over** /-,ohva/ n an easily won contest; *also* an advance from one round of a competition to the next without contest, due to the withdrawal or absence of other entrants

¹**wall** /wawl/ n 1 a usu upright and solid structure, esp of masonry or concrete, having considerable height and length in relation to width and serving esp to divide, enclose, retain, or support: e g **1a** a structure bounding a garden, park, or estate **b** any of the upright enclosing structures of a room or house 2 a material layer enclosing space **3a** an almost vertical rock surface **b** sthg that acts as a barrier or defence — **to the wall** into a hopeless position — **up the wall** *Br* into a state of exasperation – *infml*

²**wall** v 1 to protect or surround (as if) with a wall **b** to separate or shut out (as if) by a wall **2a** to immure **b** to close (an opening) (as if) with a wall *USE* (2) usu + *up*

wallaby /'wolabi/ n pl **wallabies** *also esp collectively* **wallaby** any of various small or medium-sized kangaroos

wallet /'wolit/ n 1 a holder for paper money, usu with compartments for other items (e g credit cards and stamps) 2 a flat case or folder

'**wall,flower** /-,flowə/ n 1 any of several Old World perennial plants of the mustard family; *esp* a hardy erect plant with showy fragrant flowers 2 a woman who fails to get partners at a dance – infml

¹**wallop** /'wolap/ n 1 a powerful body blow – sometimes used interjectionally; infml 2 emotional or psychological force; impact – infml 3 *Br* beer – slang

²**wallop** v 1 to hit with force; thrash 2 to beat by a wide margin; trounce *USE* infml

¹**wallow** /'woloh/ v 1 to roll or lie around lazily or luxuriously 2 to indulge oneself immoderately; revel *in* 3 of a ship to struggle laboriously in or through rough water; *broadly* to pitch

²**wallow** n 1 an act or instance of wallowing 2 a muddy or dusty area used by animals for wallowing

¹'**wall,paper** /-,paypə/ n decorative paper for the walls of a room

²**wallpaper** v to apply wallpaper to (the walls of a room)

'**Wall ,Street** n the influential financial interests of the US economy

walnut /'wawl,nut/ *n* (an edible nut or the wood of) any of a genus of trees with richly grained wood used for cabinetmaking and veneers

walrus /'wawlrəs/ *n pl* **walruses**, *esp collectively* **walrus** either of 2 large sea mammals of northern seas, related to the seals

¹**waltz** /wawlts/ *n* (music for or in the tempo of) a ballroom dance in ³₄ time with strong accent on the first beat

²**waltz** *v* 1 to dance a waltz 2 to move *along* in a lively or confident manner 3 to grab and lead (e g a person) unceremoniously; march

wampum /'wompəm/ *n* beads of polished shells strung together and used by N American Indians as money and ornaments

wan /won/ *adj* **-nn-** 1a suggestive of poor health; pallid b lacking vitality; feeble 2 *of light* dim, faint – ~**ly** *adv* – ~**ness** *n*

wand /wond/ *n* a slender rod a carried as a sign of office b used by conjurers and magicians

wander /'wondə/ *v* 1 to go or travel idly or aimlessly 2 to follow or extend along a winding course; meander 3a to deviate (as if) from a course; stray b to lose concentration; stray in thought c to think or speak incoherently or illogically

¹**wandering** /'wondəring/ *n* 1 a going about from place to place 2 movement away from the proper or usual course or place *USE* often pl with sing. meaning

²**wandering** *adj* 1 winding, meandering 2 not keeping a rational or sensible course 3 nomadic

wanderlust /'wondə,lust/ *n* eager longing for or impulse towards travelling

¹**wane** /wayn/ *v* 1 to decrease in size or extent; dwindle 2 to fall gradually from power, prosperity, or influence; decline

²**wane** *n* 1 the act or process of waning 2 a time of waning; *specif* the period from full phase of the moon to the new moon — **on the wane** in a state of decline; waning

wangle /'wang·gl/ *v* **wangling** /'wang·gling/ 1 to adjust or manipulate for personal or fraudulent ends 2 to bring about or get by devious means *USE infml*

¹**want** /wont/ *v* 1 to fail to possess, esp in customary or required amount; lack 2a to have a desire for b to have an inclination to; like 3a to have need of; require b to suffer from the lack of; need 4 to wish or demand the presence of 5 ought – + *to* and infinitive

²**want** *n* 1a the quality or state of lacking sthg required or usual b extreme poverty 2 sthg wanted; a need

wanting /'wonting/ *adj* 1 not present or in evidence; absent 2a not up to the required standard or expectation b lacking in the specified ability or capacity; deficient

¹**wanton** /'wont(ə)n/ *adj* 1 sexually unbridled; promiscuous 2 having no just foundation or provocation; malicious 3 uncontrolled, unbridled – ~**ly** *adv* – ~**ness** *n*

²**wanton** *n* a wanton person; *esp* a lewd or lascivious woman

¹**war** /waw/ *n* 1 a state or period of usu open and declared armed hostile conflict between states or nations 2 a struggle between opposing forces or for a particular end

²**war** *v* **-rr-** 1 to engage in warfare 2 to be in active or vigorous conflict

¹**warble** /'wawbl/ *v* **warbling** /'wawbling, 'wawbl·ing/ to sing or sound in a trilling manner or with many turns and variations

²**warble** *n* (a swelling under the hide of cattle, horses, etc caused by) the maggot of a fly

warbler /'wawblə/ *n* any of numerous small Old World birds (e g a whitethroat) which are related to the thrushes and many of which are noted songsters

ward /wawd/ *n* 1 a division of a prison or hospital 2 a division of a city or town for electoral or administrative purposes 3 a person under guard, protection, or surveillance; *esp* one under the care or control of a legal guardian

warden /'wawd(ə)n/ *n* 1 one having care or charge of sthg; a guardian 2 the governor of a town, district, or fortress 3 an official charged with special supervisory duties or with the enforcement of specified laws or regulations 4 any of various British college officials

warder /'wawdə/, *fem* **wardress** /'wawdris/ *n* a prison guard

ward off *v* to deflect, avert

wardrobe /'waw,drohb/ *n* 1 a room or (movable) cupboard, esp fitted with shelves and a rail or pegs, where clothes are kept 2a a collection of clothes (e g belonging to 1 person) b a collection of stage costumes and accessories

ware /weə/ *n* 1a manufactured articles; goods – usu in combination b *pl* goods for sale 2 pottery or china, esp of a specified kind or make

warehouse /'weə,hows/ *v or n* (to deposit, store, or stock in) a structure or room for the storage of merchandise or commodities

warfare /'waw,feə/ *n* 1 hostilities, war 2 struggle, conflict

warhead /'waw,hed/ *n* the section of a missile containing the explosive, chemical, or incendiary charge

¹**war·like** /-,liek/ *adj* 1 fond of war 2 of or useful in war 3 hostile

warlock /'wawlok/ *n* a man practising black magic

warlord /'waw,lawd/ *n* a supreme military leader

¹**warm** /wawm/ *adj* 1a having or giving out heat to a moderate or adequate degree; *also* experiencing heat to this degree b feeling or causing sensations

of heat brought about by strenuous exertion **2a** marked by enthusiasm; cordial **b** marked by excitement, disagreement, or anger **3** affectionate and outgoing in temperament **4** dangerous, hostile **5** *of a colour* producing an impression of being warm; *specif* in the range yellow to red **6** near to a goal, object, or solution sought – chiefly in children's games – ~**ish** *adj* – ~**ly** *adv* – ~**ness** *n*

²**warm** *v* **1** to make warm **2** to become filled with interest, enthusiasm, or affection – + *to* or *towards* **3** to reheat (cooked food) for eating – often + *up* — **warm the cockles of one's heart** to make one happy; cheer, encourage

,warm-'blooded *adj* **1** having a relatively high and constant body temperature more or less independent of the environment **2** fervent or ardent in spirit – ~**ly** *adv* – ~**ness** *n*

'**warming ,pan** /'wawming/ *n* a usu long-handled flat covered pan (e g of brass) filled with hot coals, formerly used to warm a bed

warmonger /'waw,mung·gə/ *n* one who attempts to stir up war

warmth /wawmth/ *n* the quality or state of being warm **a** in temperature **b** in feeling

'**warm-,up** *n* the act or an instance of warming up; *also* a procedure (e g a set of exercises) used in warming up

warm up *v* **1** to engage in exercise or practice, esp before entering a game or contest; *broadly* to get ready **2** to put (an audience) into a receptive mood (e g before a show), esp by telling jokes, singing, etc

warn /wawn/ *v* **1a** to give notice to beforehand, esp of danger or evil **b** to give admonishing advice to; counsel **2** to order to go or stay away – often + *off* or *away*

warning /'wawning/ *n* sthg that warns; *also* a notice

¹**warp** /wawp/ *n* **1** a series of yarns extended lengthways in a loom and crossed by the weft **2** a rope for warping a ship or boat **3a** a twist or curve that has developed in sthg formerly flat or straight **b** a mental twist or aberration

²**warp** *v* **1a** to turn or twist (e g planks) out of shape, esp out of a plane **b** to cause to think or act wrongly; pervert **2** to manoeuvre (e g a ship) by hauling on a line attached to a fixed object

'**war ,paint** *n* **1** paint put on the body by N American Indians as a sign of going to war **2** cosmetics – infml

warpath /'waw,pahth/ *n* the route taken by a war party of N American Indians — **on the warpath** pursuing an angry or hostile course; taking or starting to take action in a struggle or conflict

¹**warrant** /'worənt/ *n* **1** a sanction, authorization; *also* evidence for or token of authorization **b** a guarantee, security **c** a ground, justification; *also* proof **2a** a document authorizing an officer to

make an arrest, a search, etc **b** an official certificate of appointment issued to a noncommissioned officer

²**warrant** *v* **1** to declare or maintain with certainty **2** to guarantee to be as represented **3** to give sanction to **4a** to prove or declare the authenticity or truth of **b** to give assurance of the nature of or for the undertaking of; guarantee **5** to serve as or give adequate ground or reason for

'**warrant ,officer** *n* a member of the British army, airforce, or Royal Marines with a rank between non-commissioned officer and commissioned officer

warranty /'worənti/ *n* a usu written guarantee of the soundness of a product and of the maker's responsibility for repair or replacement

warren /'worən/ *n* **1** an area of ground (or a structure) where rabbits breed **2** a crowded tenement or district

warrior /'wori·ə/ *n* a man engaged or experienced in warfare

warship /'waw,ship/ *n* an (armed) ship for use in warfare

wart /wawt/ *n* **1** a horny projection on the skin, usu of the hands or feet, caused by a virus; *also* a protuberance, esp on a plant, resembling this **2** an ugly or objectionable man or boy – chiefly Br schoolboy slang – ~**y** *adj*

warthog /'wawt,hog/ *n* any of a genus of African wild pigs with 2 pairs of rough warty lumps on the face and large protruding tusks

wartime /'waw,tiem/ *n* a period during which a war is in progress

wary /'weəri/ *adj* marked by caution and watchful prudence in detecting and escaping danger – **warily** *adv* – **wariness** *n*

was /wəz; *strong* woz/ *past* 1 & 3 *sing of* **be**

¹**wash** /wosh/ *v* **1a** to cleanse (as if) by the action of liquid (e g water) **b** to remove (e g dirt) by applying liquid **c** to wash articles; do the washing **2** *of an animal* to cleanse (fur or a furry part) by licking or by rubbing with a paw moistened with saliva **3** to suffuse with light **4** to flow along, over, or against **5** to move, carry, or deposit (as if) by the force of water in motion **6** to cover or daub lightly with a thin coating (e g of paint or varnish) **7** to gain acceptance; inspire belief – infml — **wash one's hands of** to disclaim interest in, responsibility for, or further connection with

²**wash** *n* **1a** (an instance of) washing or being washed **b** articles for washing **2** the surging action of waves **3a** a thin coat of paint (e g watercolour) **4** a lotion

washable /'woshəbl/ *adj* capable of being washed without damage

'**wash ,basin** /-,bays(ə)n/ *n* a basin or sink usu connected to a water supply for washing the hands and face 'wash,board /-,bawd/ *n* a corrugated board for scrubbing clothes on when washing

wash down *v* 1 to facilitate the swallowing of (food) by taking gulps of liquid 2 to wash the whole surface of

,washed-'out *adj* 1 faded in colour 2 listless, exhausted – *infml*

,washed-'up *adj* no longer successful or useful; finished – *infml*

washer /'wosho/ *n* 1 a washing machine 2 a thin flat ring (e g of metal or leather) used to ensure tightness or prevent friction in joints and assemblies

'washerwoman /-woomon/, *masc* 'washerman /-mon/ *n* a woman who takes in washing

washing /'woshing/ *n* articles, esp clothes, that have been or are to be washed

,washing-'up *n, chiefly Br* the act or process of washing dishes and kitchen utensils; *also* the dishes and utensils to be washed

'wash-,leather *n* a soft leather similar to chamois

'wash,out /-,owt/ *n* 1 the washing out or away of a road, railway line, etc by a large amount of water 2 a failure, fiasco

wash out *v* to become depleted in colour or vitality; fade

'wash,room /-,roohm, -room/ *n, NAm* the toilet – *euph*

'wash,stand /-,stand/ *n* a piece of furniture used, esp formerly, to hold a basin, jug, etc needed for washing one's face and hands

wash up *v* 1 to bring into the shore 2 *Br* to wash (the dishes and utensils) after a meal

wasp /wosp/ *n* any of numerous largely flesh-eating slender narrow-waisted insects many of which have an extremely painful sting; *esp* one with black and yellow stripes

WASP, Wasp /wosp/ *n* an American of N European, esp British, stock and of Protestant background; *esp* one in North America considered to be a member of the dominant and most privileged class

waspish /'wospish/ *adj* resembling a wasp in behaviour; *esp* snappish – ~**ly** *adv* – ~**ness** *n*

'wassail /'wosayl/ *n* 1 a toast to sby's health made in England in former times 2 *archaic* revelry, carousing

'wassail *vi v* 1 to carouse 2 *dial Eng* to sing carols from house to house at Christmas

wast /wost/ *archaic past* 2 *sing of* be

wastage /'waystij/ *n* 1a loss, decrease, or destruction of sthg (e g by use, decay, or leakage); *esp* wasteful or avoidable loss of sthg valuable b waste, refuse 2 reduction or loss in numbers (e g of employees or students), usu caused by individuals leaving or retiring voluntarily – esp in *natural wastage*

'waste /wayst/ *n* 1a uncultivated land b a broad and empty expanse (e g of water) 2 wasting or being wasted 3 gradual loss or decrease by use, wear, or decay 4 material rejected during a textile manufacturing process and used usu for wiping away dirt and oil 5 human or animal refuse

'waste *v* 1 to lose weight, strength, or vitality – often + *away* 2 to spend or use carelessly or inefficiently; squander — **waste one's breath** to accomplish nothing by speaking

'waste *adj* 1a uninhabited, desolate b not cultivated or used; not productive 2 discarded as refuse 3 serving to conduct or hold refuse material; *specif* carrying off superfluous fluid

'wasteful /-f(o)l/ *adj* given to or marked by waste; prodigal – ~**ly** *adv* – ~**ness** *n*

waste product *n* 1 debris resulting from a process (e g of manufacture) that is of no further use to the system producing it 2 material (e g faeces) discharged from, or stored in an inert form in, a living body as a by-product of metabolic processes

waster /'waysto/ *n* 1 one who spends or consumes extravagantly without thought for the future 2 a good-for-nothing, idler

wastrel /'waystrol/ *n* 1 a vagabond, waif 2 a waster

'watch /woch/ *v* 1 to remain awake during the night, esp in order to keep vigil 2a to be attentive or vigilant; wait *for* b to keep guard 3a to observe closely, esp in order to check on action or change b to look at (an event or moving scene) 4a to take care of; tend b to be careful of c to take care that 5 to be on the alert for – ~**er** *n* — **watch it** to be careful; look out — **watch one's step** to proceed with extreme care; act or talk warily — **watch over** to have charge of; superintend

'watch *n* 1a the act of keeping awake or alert to guard, protect, or attend b a state of alert and continuous attention; lookout 2 a watchman; *also, sing or pl in constr* a body of watchmen, *specif* those formerly assigned to patrol the streets of a town at night 3a a period of keeping guard b(1) a period of time during which a part of a ship's company is on duty while another part rests b(2) *sing or pl in constr* the part of a ship's company on duty during a particular watch 4 a small portable timepiece powered esp by a spring or battery and usu worn on a wrist — **on the watch** on the alert

'watch,dog /-,dog/ *n* 1 a dog kept to guard property 2 a person or group (e g a committee) that guards against inefficiency, undesirable practices, etc

'watchful /-f(o)l/ *adj* carefully observant or attentive – ~**ly** *adv* – ~**ness** *n*

'watchman /-mon/ *n, pl* watchmen sby who keeps watch; a guard

'watch,tower /-,towə/ n a tower from which a
lookout can keep watch

'watch,word /-,wuhd/ n 1 a word or phrase used
as a sign of recognition among members of the
same group 2 a motto that embodies a guiding
principle

¹water /'wawtə/ n 1a the colourless odourless liquid that descends from the clouds as rain, forms
streams, lakes, and seas, is a major constituent of
all living matter, and is an oxide of hydrogen
which freezes at 0°C and boils at 100°C 2a(1) pl
the water occupying or flowing in a particular bed
a(2) chiefly Br a body of water (e g a river or lake)
b(1) pl a stretch of sea surrounding and controlled
by a country b(2) the sea of a specified part of the
earth – often pl with. meaning c a water
supply 3 the level of water at a specified state of
the tide 4 liquid containing or resembling water;
esp a pharmaceutical or cosmetic preparation 5 a
wavy lustrous pattern (e g of a textile) — water
under the bridge past events which it is futile to
attempt to alter

²water v 1a to moisten, sprinkle, or soak with
water b to form or secrete water or watery matter
(e g tears or saliva) 2a to supply with water for
drink b to supply water to 3 to be a source of
water for 4 to impart a lustrous appearance and
wavy pattern to (cloth) by calendering 5 to dilute
(as if) by the addition of water – often + down

'water ,closet n (a room or structure containing)
a toilet with a bowl that can be flushed with water

'water,colour /-,kulə/ n 1 a paint made from
pigment mixed with water rather than oil 2 (a
work produced by) the art of painting with
watercolours

'water,course /-,kaws/ n (a natural or
man-made channel for) a stream of water

'water,cress /-,kres/ n any of several cresses of
wet places widely grown for use in salads

'water,fall /-,fawl/ n a vertical or steep descent of
the water of a river or stream

'water,front /-,frunt/ n land or a section of a
town fronting or bordering on a body of water

'water ,hen n any of various birds (e g a coot or
moorhen) related to the rails

'water ,ice n a frozen dessert of water, sugar, and
flavouring

'watering ,can /'wawt(ə)ring/ n a vessel having a
handle and a long spout often fitted with a rose,
used for watering plants

'watering ,place n a health or recreational
resort featuring mineral springs or bathing; esp a
spa

'water ,lily n any of a family of aquatic plants
with floating leaves and usu showy colourful
flowers

'water,line /-,lien/ n the level on the hull of a
vessel to which the surface of the water comes
when it is afloat; also any of several lines marked
on the hull to correspond with this level

'water,logged /-,logd/ adj filled or soaked with
water; specif, of a vessel so filled with water as to
be (almost) unable to float

waterloo /,wawtə'looh/ n pl waterloos often cap
a decisive defeat

'waterman /-mən/ n a man who works on or near
water or who engages in water recreations; esp a
boatman whose boat and services are available
for hire

'water,mark /-,mahk/ n 1 a mark indicating the
height to which water has risen 2 (the design or
the metal pattern producing) a marking in paper
visible when the paper is held up to the light

'water ,meadow n a meadow kept fertile by a
regular influx of water (e g from the flooding of a
bordering river)

'water,melon /-,melən/ n (an African climbing
plant of the cucumber family that bears) a large
oblong or roundish fruit with a hard green often
striped or variegated rind, a sweet watery pink
pulp, and many seeds

'water ,polo n a game played in water by teams of
7 swimmers using a ball that is thrown or dribbled
with the object of putting it into a goal

¹'water,proof /-,proohf/ adj impervious to
water; esp covered or treated with a material to
prevent passage of water

²waterproof n (a garment made of) waterproof
fabric

³waterproof v to make waterproof

'water,shed /-,shed/ n 1 a dividing ridge between
2 drainage areas 2 a crucial turning point

'water-,skiing n the sport of planing and jumping on water skis

'water ,table n the level below which the ground
is wholly saturated with water

'water,tight /-,tiet/ adj 1 of such tight construction or fit as to be impermeable to water 2 esp of
an argument impossible to disprove; without
loopholes

'water ,tower n a tower supporting a raised
water tank to provide the necessary steady pressure to distribute water

'water ,vole n a common large vole of W Europe
that inhabits river banks and often digs extensive
tunnels

'water,wheel /-,weel/ n 1 a wheel made to rotate
by direct action of water, and used esp to drive
machinery 2 a wheel for raising water

'water ,wings n pl a pair of usu air-filled floats
worn to give support to the body of sby learning
to swim

'water,works /-,wuhks/ n pl waterworks 1 the
reservoirs, mains, building, and pumping and
purifying equipment by which a water supply is

obtained and distributed (e g to a city) – often pl with sing. meaning **2** *chiefly Br* the urinary system – euph or humor **3** (the shedding of) tears – infml

watery /'wawt(ə)ri/ *adj* **1a** consisting of or filled with water **b** containing, sodden with, or yielding water or a thin liquid **c** containing too much water **2a** pale, faint **b** vapid, wishy-washy

watt /wot/ *n* the SI unit of power equal to the power that in 1s gives rise to an energy of 1J

wattage /'wotij/ *n* amount of power expressed in watts

¹**wattle** /'wotl/ *n* **1** (material for) a framework of poles interwoven with slender branches or reeds and used, esp formerly, in building **2** a fleshy protuberance usu near or on the head or neck, esp of a bird

²**wattle** *v* **wattling** /'wotling, 'wotl·ing/ **1** to form or build of or with wattle **2** to unite or make solid by interweaving light flexible material

¹**wave** /wayv/ *v* **1** to flutter or sway to and fro **2** to direct by waving; signal **3** to move (the hand or an object) to and fro in greeting, farewell, or homage **4** to brandish, flourish — **wave aside** to dismiss or put out of mind; disregard

²**wave** *n* **1** a moving ridge or swell on the surface of a liquid (e g the sea) **2a** a shape or outline having successive curves **b** a waviness of the hair **c** an undulating line or streak **3** stg that swells and dies away: e g **3a** a surge of sensation or emotion **b** a movement involving large numbers of people in a common activity **4** a sweep of the hand or arm or of some object held in the hand, used as a signal or greeting **5** a rolling or undulatory movement or any of a series of such movements passing along a surface or through the air **6** a movement like that of an ocean wave: e g **6a** a surging movement; an influx **b** *sing or pl in constr* a line of attacking or advancing troops, aircraft, etc **7** (a complete cycle of) a periodic variation of pressure, electrical or magnetic intensity, electric potential, etc by which energy is transferred progressively from point to point without a corresponding transfer of a medium

'**wave ,band** *n* a band of radio frequency waves

'**wave,length** /-,leng(k)th/ *n* the distance in the line of advance of a wave from any 1 point to the next point of corresponding phase (e g from 1 peak to the next) — **be on somebody's the same wavelength** to have the same outlook, views, etc as sby else

waver /'wayvə/ *v* **1** to vacillate between choices; fluctuate **2a** to sway unsteadily to and fro **b** to hesitate as if about to give way; falter **3** to make a tremulous sound; quaver — **~er** *n* – **~ingly** *adv*

wavy /'wayvi/ *adj* **1** having waves **2** having a wavelike form or outline – **waviness** *n*

¹**wax** /waks/ *n* **1** beeswax **2a** any of numerous plant or animal substances that are harder, more brittle, and less greasy than fats **b** a pliable or liquid composition used esp for sealing, taking impressions, or polishing

²**wax** *v* **1** to increase in size and strength **2** *archaic* to assume a specified quality or state; become

³**wax** *n* a fit of temper – infml

waxen /'waks(ə)n/ *adj* **1** made of or covered with wax **2** resembling wax, esp in being pliable, smooth, or pallid

waxy /'waksi/ *adj* **1** made of, full of, or covered with wax **2** resembling wax, esp in smooth whiteness or pliability – **waxiness** *n*

¹**way** /way/ *n* **1a** a thoroughfare for travel or transport from place to place **b** an opening for passage **c** space or room, esp for forward movement **2** the course to be travelled from one place to another; a route **3a** a course leading in a direction or towards an objective **b** what one desires, or wants to do **4a** the manner in which sthg is done or happens **b** a method of doing or accomplishing; a means **c** a characteristic, regular, or habitual manner or mode of being, behaving, or happening **5** the distance to be travelled in order to reach a place or point **6a** a direction – often in combination **b** (the direction of) the area in which one lives **7** a state of affairs; a condition **8** motion or speed of a ship or boat through the water — **by the way** incidentally — usu used to introduce or to comment on the introduction of a new subject — **by way of 1** to be considered as; as a sort of **2** by the route through; via **3** in the form of — **in a way** from one point of view; to some extent — **in the way of** in the form of — **no way** under no circumstances – infml — **on one's way** on the way — **on the way 1** while moving along a course; in the course of travelling **2** coming, approaching; *specif* conceived but not yet born — **on the way out** about to disappear or die — **out of the way 1** unusual, remarkable **2** in or to a secluded or remote place **3** done, completed — **under way** in progress; started

²**way** *adv* **1** away **2** *chiefly NAm* all the way — **way back** long ago

waylay /way'lay/ *v* **waylaid** /way'layd/ **1** to attack from ambush **2** to accost

,**way-'out** *adj* far-out – infml

,**ways and 'means** *n pl, often cap W&M* methods and resources for raising revenue for the use of government

'**way,side** /-,sied/ *n* the side of or land adjacent to a road

¹**wayward** /-wood/ *adj* **1** following one's own capricious or wanton inclinations; ungovernable **2** following no clear principle or law; unpredictable

we /wi; *strong* wee/ *pron pl in constr* **1** I and one or more other people **2** I – used, esp formerly, by sovereigns; used by writers to maintain an impersonal character

weak /week/ *adj* **1a** deficient in physical vigour; feeble **b** not able to sustain or exert much weight, pressure, or strain **c** not able to resist external force or withstand attack **2a** lacking determination or decisiveness; ineffectual **b** unable to withstand temptation or persuasion **3** not factually grounded or logically presented **4a** unable to function properly **b** lacking skill or proficiency **5a** deficient in a specified quality or ingredient **b** lacking normal intensity or potency **c** mentally or intellectually deficient **d** deficient in strength or flavour; dilute **6** not having or exerting authority or political power **7** of or constituting a verb (conjugation) that in English forms inflections by adding the suffix *-ed* or *-d* or *-t* – **~ly** *adv* – **~en** *v*

weak-'kneed *adj* lacking in resolution; easily intimidated

weakling /'weekling/ *n* a person or animal weak in body, character, or mind

weakness /'weeknis/ *n* **1** a fault, defect **2** (an object of) a special desire or fondness

weal, wheal /weel/ *n* a welt, scar

wealth /welth/ *n* **1** the state of being rich **2** abundance of money and valuable material possessions **3** abundant supply; a profusion – **~y** *adj*

wean /ween/ *v* **1** to accustom (a child or other young mammal) to take food other than mother's milk **2** to cause to abandon a state of usu unwholesome dependence or preoccupation **3** to cause to become acquainted with an idea, writer, etc at an early age; bring up *on*

weapon /'wepon/ *n* an instrument of offensive or defensive combat – **~less** *adj* – **~ry** *n*

¹wear /wee/ *v* **wore** /waw/; **worn** /wawn/ **1a** to have or carry on the body as clothing or adornment **b** to dress in (a particular manner, colour, or garment), esp habitually **2** to have or show on the face **3** to impair, damage, or diminish by use or friction **4** to produce gradually by friction or attrition **5** to exhaust or lessen the strength of; weary **8** *chiefly Br* to find (a claim, proposal etc) acceptable – *infml* – **~able** *adj* – **~er** *n* — **wear the trousers** to have the controlling authority in a household — **wear thin 1** to become weak or ready to give way **2** to become trite, unconvincing, or out-of-date

²wear *n* **1** clothing, usu of a specified kind **2** capacity to withstand use; durability **3** minor damage or deterioration through use

wear and 'tear *n* the normal deterioration or depreciation which sthg suffers in the course of use

wearing /'weering/ *adj* causing fatigue; tiring

wearisome /'wiaris(a)m/ *adj* causing weariness; tiresome

¹weary /'wiari/ *adj* **1** exhausted, tired **2** having one's patience, tolerance, or pleasure exhausted – + *of* **3** wearisome – **wearily** *adv* – **weariness** *n*

²weary *v* to make or become weary

weasel /'weezl/ *n pl* **weasels**, *esp collectively* **weasel** any of various small slender flesh-eating mammals with reddish brown fur which, in northern forms, turns white in winter

¹weather /'wedha/ *n* the prevailing (bad) atmospheric conditions, esp with regard to heat or cold, wetness or dryness, calm or storm, and clearness or cloudiness — **under the weather** mildly ill or depressed; not fully well — *infml*

²weather *v* **1** to expose or subject to atmospheric conditions **2** to bear up against and come safely through

'weather-,beaten *adj* **1** worn or damaged by exposure to weather **2** toughened or tanned by the weather

'weather,cock /-,kok/ *n* a weather vane; *esp* one in the figure of a cockerel

'weather,proof /-,proohf/ *adj* able to withstand exposure to weather without damage or loss of function

'weather ,station *n* a station for taking, recording, and reporting meteorological observations

¹weave /weev/ *v* **wove** /wove/, **weaved**; **woven** /'wohv(a)n/, **weaved 1a** to form (cloth) by interlacing strands (e g of yarn), esp on a loom **b** to interlace (e g threads) into a fabric, design, etc **c** to make (e g a basket) by intertwining **2a** to produce by elaborately combining elements into a coherent whole **b** to introduce; work in – usu + *in* or *into* – **weave** *n*

²weave *v* to direct (e g the body or one's way) in a winding or zigzag course, esp to avoid obstacles

weaver /'weeva/ *n* **1** sby who weaves, esp as an occupation **2 weaver, weaverbird** any of numerous Old World birds that resemble finches and usu construct elaborate nests of interlaced vegetation

¹web /web/ *n* **1** a woven fabric; *esp* a length of fabric still on the loom **2** a spider's web; *also* a similar network spun by various insects **3** a tissue or membrane; *esp* that uniting fingers or toes either at their bases (e g in human beings) or for most of their length (e g in many water birds) **4** an intricate structure suggestive of sthg woven; a network **5** a continuous sheet of paper for use in a printing press – **webbed** *adj*

²web *v* **-bb-** to entangle, ensnare

webbing /'webing/ *n* a strong narrow closely woven tape used esp for straps, upholstery, or harnesses

wed /wed/ *v* **-dd-**; **wedded** *also* **wed** to marry

wedded /'wedid/ *adj* **1** joined in marriage **2** conjugal, connubial **3** strongly emotionally attached; committed *to*

wedding /'weding/ n 1 a marriage ceremony, usu with its accompanying festivities 2 a joining in close association 3 a wedding anniversary or its celebration – usu in combination

'**wedding ,ring** n a ring usu of plain metal (e g gold) given by 1 marriage partner to the other during the wedding ceremony and worn thereafter to signify marital status

¹**wedge** /wej/ n 1 a piece of wood, metal, etc tapered to a thin edge and used esp for splitting wood or raising heavy objects 2a (a shoe with) a wedge-shaped sole raised at the heel and tapering towards the toe b an iron golf club with a broad face angled for maximum loft 3 sthg causing a breach or separation

²**wedge** v 1 to fasten or tighten by driving in a wedge 2 to force or press into a narrow space; cram – usu + in or into

Wedgwood /'wejwood/ trademark – used for pottery made by Josiah Wedgwood and his successors and typically decorated with a classical cameo-like design in white relief

wedlock /'wedlok/ n the state of being married; marriage — **out of wedlock** with the natural parents not legally married to each other

Wednesday /'wenzday, -di, 'wednz-/ n the day of the week following Tuesday

¹**wee** /wee/ adj very small; diminutive

²**wee** n (an act of passing) urine – used esp by or to children

¹**weed** /weed/ n 1 an unwanted wild plant which often overgrows or chokes out more desirable plants 2 an obnoxious growth or thing 3 Br a weedy person – infml

²**weed** v 1 to clear of weeds 2 to remove the undesirable parts of

weed out v to get rid of (sby or sthg harmful or unwanted); remove

weeds /weedz/ n pl mourning garments

weedy /'weedi/ adj 1 covered with or consisting of weeds 2 noticeably weak, thin, and ineffectual – infml – **weediness** n

week /week/ n 1a any of several 7-day cycles used in various calendars b a week beginning with a specified day or containing a specified event 2 a period of 7 consecutive days — **week in, week out** for an indefinite or seemingly endless number of weeks

'**weekday** /-day/ n any day of the week except (Saturday and) Sunday

¹**weekend** /,week'end, '-,-/ n the end of the week; specif the period from Friday night to Sunday night

'**week'end** v to spend the weekend (e g at a place)

¹**weekly** /'weekli/ adv every week; once a week; by the week

²**weekly** adj 1 occurring, appearing, or done weekly 2 calculated by the week

³**weekly** n a weekly newspaper or periodical

¹**weep** /weep/ v **wept** /wept/ **1a** to express deep sorrow for, usu by shedding tears; bewail **b** to mourn for sby or sthg **2** to pour forth (tears) from the eyes **3** to exude (a fluid) slowly; ooze

²**weep** n a fit of weeping

weeping /'weeping/ adj, of a tree (being a variety) having slender drooping branches

weevil /'weevl/ n any of numerous usu small beetles with a long snout bearing jaws at the tip, many of which are injurious, esp as larvae, to grain, fruit, etc

weft /weft/ n the thread or yarn that interlaces the warp in a fabric; the crosswise yarn in weaving

weigh /way/ v **1** to ascertain the weight of (as if) on a scale **2** to have weight or a specified weight **3** to consider carefully; evaluate – often + up **4** to measure (a definite quantity) (as if) on a scale – often + out **5** to be a burden or cause of anxiety to – often + on or upon — **weigh anchor** to pull up an anchor preparatory to sailing

weigh down v **1** to make heavy **2** to oppress, burden

weigh in v to have oneself or one's possessions (e g luggage) weighed; esp to be weighed after a horse race or before a boxing or wrestling match

¹**weight** /wayt/ n **1a** the amount that a quantity or body weighs, esp as measured on a particular scale **b** any of the classes into which contestants in certain sports (e g boxing and wrestling) are divided according to body weight **2a** a quantity weighing a certain amount **b** a heavy object thrown or lifted as an athletic exercise or contest **3a** a system of units of weight **b** any of the units of weight used in such a system **c** a piece of material (e g metal) of known weight for use in weighing articles **4a** sthg heavy; a load **b** a heavy object to hold or press sthg down or to counterbalance **5a** a burden, pressure **b** corpulence **6** relative heaviness **7a** relative importance, authority, or influence **b** the main force or strength

²**weight** v **1** to load or make heavy (as if) with a weight **2** to oppress with a burden **3** to arrange in such a way as to create a bias

weighting /'wayting/ n, Br an additional sum paid on top of wages; esp one paid to offset the higher cost of living in a particular area

'**weightless** /-lis/ adj having little weight; lacking apparent gravitational pull – **~ly** adv – **~ness** n

weighty /'wayti/ adj **1** of much importance, influence, or consequence; momentous **2** heavy, esp in proportion to bulk **3** burdensome, onerous – **weightily** adv – **weightiness** n

weir /wia/ n a dam in a stream to raise the water level or control its flow

weird /wiad/ adj of a strange or extraordinary character; odd – infml – **~ly** adv – **~ness** n

welch /welch/ v to welsh

Welch /welsh/ adj Welsh – now only in names

¹welcome /'welkəm/ *interj* – used to express a greeting to a guest or newcomer on his/her arrival

²welcome *v* 1 to greet hospitably and with courtesy 2 to greet or receive in the specified, esp unpleasant, way 3 to receive or accept with pleasure — **welcome with open arms** to greet or accept with great cordiality or pleasure

³welcome *adj* 1 received gladly into one's presence or companionship 2 giving pleasure; received with gladness, esp because fulfilling a need

⁴welcome *n* 1 a greeting or reception on arrival or first appearance 2 the hospitable treatment that a guest may expect

¹weld /weld/ *v* 1a to fuse (metallic parts) together by heating and allowing the metals to flow together or by hammering or compressing with or without previous heating **b** to unite (plastics) in a similar manner by heating or by using a chemical solvent 2 to unite closely or inseparably – ~**er** *n*

²weld *n* a welded joint

welfare /'welfeə/ *n* 1 well-being 2 organized efforts to improve the living conditions of the poor, elderly, etc

welfare 'state *n* (a country operating) a social system based on the assumption by the state of responsibility for the individual and social welfare of its citizens

welkin /'welkin/ *n* the sky, firmament –poetic

¹well /wel/ *n* 1 (a pool fed by) a spring of water 2 a pit or hole sunk into the earth to reach a supply of water 3 a shaft or hole sunk in the earth to reach a natural deposit (e g oil or gas) 4 an open space extending vertically through floors of a structure 5 a source from which sthg springs 6 *Br* the open space in front of the judge in a law court

²well *v* 1 to rise to the surface and usu flow forth 2 to rise to the surface like a flood of liquid

³well *adv* **better** /'betə/; **best** /best/ 1 in a good or proper manner; rightly 2 in a way appropriate to the circumstances; satisfactory, skilfully 3 in a kind or friendly manner; favourably 4 in a prosperous manner (e g he lives *well*) 5a to an extent approaching completeness; thoroughly (e g after being *well* dried with a towel) **b** on a close personal level; intimately 6a easily, fully (e g *well* worth the price) **b** much, considerably (e g *well* over a million) **c** in all likelihood; indeed (e g may *well* be true) — **as well** 1 also; in addition 2 to the same extent or degree 3 with equivalent or preferable effect 4 advisable, desirable — **as well as** in addition to — **well and truly** totally, completely — **well away** 1 making good progress 2 (almost) drunk –infml — **well out of** lucky to be free from

⁴well *interj* 1 – used to express surprise, indignation, or resignation 2 – used to indicate a pause in talking or to introduce a remark

⁵well *adj* 1 satisfactory, pleasing 2 advisable, desirable 3 prosperous, well-off 4 healthy 5 being a cause for thankfulness; fortunate (e g it is *well* that this has happened)

well-ad'vised *adj* 1 acting with wisdom; prudent 2 resulting from or showing wisdom

well-ap'pointed *adj* having good and complete facilities, furniture, etc

well-'being *n* the state of being happy, healthy, or prosperous

well-'bred *adj* 1 having or indicating good breeding; refined 2 of good pedigree

well-con'nected *adj* having useful social or family contacts

well-di'sposed *adj* having a favourable or sympathetic disposition

well-'done *adj* cooked thoroughly

well-'favoured *adj* good-looking; handsome – not now in vogue

well-'founded *adj* based on good grounds or reasoning

well-'groomed *adj* well dressed and scrupulously neat

well-'grounded *adj* 1 having a good basic knowledge 2 well-founded

well-in'formed *adj* 1 having a good knowledge of a wide variety of subjects 2 having reliable information on a usu specified topic, event, etc

well-in'tentioned *adj* well-meaning

well-'knit *adj* well constructed; *esp* having a compact usu muscular physique

well-'known *adj* fully or widely known; *specif* famous

well-'meaning *adj* having or based on good intentions though often failing

well-'meant *adj* based on good intentions

well-'nigh *adv* almost, nearly

well-'off *adj* 1 well-to-do, rich 2 in a favourable or fortunate situation 3 well supplied

well-'read /red/ *adj* well-informed through much and varied reading

well-'spoken *adj* 1 speaking clearly, courteously, and usu with a refined accent 2 spoken in a pleasing or fitting manner

well-'timed *adj* said or done at an opportune moment; timely

well-to-'do *adj* moderately rich; prosperous

well-,wisher *n* one who feels goodwill towards a person, cause, etc

well-'worn *adj* 1 having been much used or worn 2 made trite by overuse; hackneyed

welsh /welsh/ *v* 1 to evade an obligation, esp payment of a debt 2 to break one's word – ~**er** *n*

Welsh *adj* of Wales, its people, or its language

¹welt /welt/ *n* 1 a strip, usu of leather, between a shoe sole and upper through which they are fastened together 2 a doubled edge, strip, insert, or seam (e g on a garment) for ornament or reinforcement 3 (a ridge or lump raised on the body usu by) a heavy blow

²**welt** v to hit hard

¹**welter** /'weltə/ v 1 to writhe, toss; also to wallow 2 to become soaked, sunk, or involved in sthg

²**welter** n 1 a state of wild disorder; a turmoil 2 a chaotic mass or jumble

'**welter,weight** /-,wayt/ n a boxer who weighs not more than 10st 7lb

¹**wench** /wench/ n 1 a female servant or rustic working girl 2 a young woman; a girl – now chiefly humor or dial

²**wench** v to have sexual relations habitually with women, esp prostitutes

wend /wend/ v to proceed on (one's way)

Wensleydale /'wenzli,dayl/ n a crumbly mild-flavoured English cheese

went /went/ past of **go**

were /wə; strong wuh/ past 2 sing, past pl, substandard past 1 & 3 sing, or past subjunctive of **be**

werewolf /'weə,woolf, 'wiə-/ n pl **werewolves** /-woolvz/ a person transformed into a wolf or capable of assuming a wolf's form

¹**west** /west/ adj or adv towards, at, belonging to, or coming from the west

²**west** n 1 (the compass point corresponding to) the direction 90° to the left of north that is the general direction of sunset 2 often cap regions or countries lying to the west of a specified or implied point of orientation; esp the non-Communist countries of Europe and America 3 European civilization in contrast with that of the Orient

West 'End n the western part of central London where the main shopping centres, theatres, etc are located

¹**westerly** /'westəli/ adj or adv west

²**westerly** n a wind from the west

¹**western** /'westən/ adj 1 often cap (characteristic) of a region conventionally designated West: e g **1a** of or stemming from European traditions in contrast with those of the Orient **b** of the non-Communist countries of Europe and America 2 west

²**western** n, often cap a novel, film, etc dealing with cowboys, frontier life, etc in the W USA, esp during the latter half of the 19th c

West 'Indian n 1 a native or inhabitant of the W Indies 2 a descendant of W Indians

¹**wet** /wet/ adj -tt- 1 consisting of, containing, or covered or soaked with liquid (e g water) 2 rainy 3 still moist enough to smudge or smear 4 involving the use or presence of liquid 5 chiefly Br feebly ineffectual or dull; also, of a politician moderate – infml – ~ **ly** adv – ~ **ness** n — **wet behind the ears** immature, inexperienced — infml

wet n 1 moisture, wetness 2 rainy weather; rain 3 chiefly Br a wet person; a drip – infml

³**wet** v -tt-; (2) **wet** 1 to make wet 2 to urinate in or on — **wet one's whistle** to take an esp alcoholic drink — infml

,**wet 'blanket** n one who quenches or dampens enthusiasm or pleasure

,**wet 'dream** n an erotic dream culminating in orgasm

wet-nurse /'-,-, ,-'-/ v 1 to act as wet nurse to 2 to give constant and often excessive care to

'**wet ,nurse** n a woman who cares for and suckles another's children

'**wet ,suit** n a close-fitting suit made of material, usu rubber, that admits water but retains body heat so as to insulate its wearer (e g a skin diver), esp in cold water

¹**whack** /wak/ vt 1 to strike with a smart or resounding blow 2 to get the better of; defeat USE infml

²**whack** n 1 (the sound of) a smart resounding blow 2 a portion, share 3 an attempt, go USE infml

whacked /wakt/ adj completely exhausted – infml

¹**whacking** /'waking/ adj extremely big; whopping – infml

²**whacking** adv very, extremely – infml

whale /wayl/ n any of an order of often enormous aquatic mammals that superficially resemble large fish, have tails modified as paddles, and are frequently hunted for oil, flesh, or whalebone — **whale of a time** an exceptionally enjoyable time

'**whale,bone** /-,bohn/ n a horny substance found in 2 rows of plates up to 4m (about 12ft) long attached along the upper jaw of whalebone whales and used for stiffening things

whaler /'waylə/ n a person or ship engaged in whaling

whaling /'wayling/ n the occupation of catching and processing whales for oil, food, etc

¹**wham** /wam/ n (the sound made by) a forceful blow – infml

²**wham** interj – used to express the noise of a forceful blow or impact; infml

³**wham** v -mm- to throw or strike with a loud impact – infml

wharf /wawf/ n, pl **wharves** /wawvz/ also **wharfs** a structure built along or out from the shore of navigable water so that ships may load and unload

¹**what** /wot/ pron **1a(1)** – used as an interrogative expressing inquiry about the identity, nature, purpose, or value of sthg or sby (e g what is this?) **a(2)** – used to ask for repetition of sthg not properly heard or understood **b** – used as an exclamation expressing surprise or excitement and frequently introducing a clause **c** chiefly Br – used in demanding assent (e g a clever play, what?); not now in vogue 2 that which; the one that (e g no income but what he gets from his

writing) **3a** anything or everything that; whatever **b** how much – used in exclamations (e g *what* it must cost!) — **or what** – used at the end of a question to express inquiry about additional possibilities — **what about 1** what news or plans have you concerning **2** *also* **what do you say to, what's wrong with** let's; how about — **what for 1** for what purpose or reason; why – usu used with the other words of a question between *what* and *for* except when used alone **2** punishment, esp by blows or by a sharp reprimand — **what have you** any of various other things that might also be mentioned — **what if 1** what will or would be the result if **2** what does it matter if — **what it takes** the qualities or resources needed for success or for attainment of a usu specified goal — **what not** what have you — **what of 1** what is the situation with respect to **2** what importance can be assigned to — **what of it** what does it matter — **what's what** the true state of things

²**what** *adv* in what respect?; how much?

³**what** *adj* **1a** which **b** how remarkable or striking – used esp in exclamatory utterances and dependent clauses (e g *what* a suggestion!) **2** the . . . that; as much or as many . . . as (e g told him *what* little I knew)

¹**whatever** /wot'evə/ *pron* **1a** anything or everything that **b** no matter what **2** what in the world? – infml — **or whatever** or anything else at all – infml

²**whatever** *adj* **1a** any . . . that; all . . . that (e g buy peace on *whatever* possible terms) **b** no matter what **2** of any kind at all – used after a noun with *any* or with a negative

whatnot /'wot,not/ *n* **1** a lightweight open set of shelves for bric-a-brac **2** other usu related goods, objects, etc **3** sthg whose name is unknown or (temporarily) forgotten *USE* (2&3) infml

wheat /weet/ *n* (any of various grasses cultivated in most temperate areas for) a cereal grain that yields a fine white flour and is used for making bread and pasta, and in animal feeds

wheaten /'weet(ə)n/ *adj* made of (the grain, meal, or flour of) wheat

wheat ,germ *n* the embryo of the wheat kernel separated in milling and used esp as a source of vitamins

wheedle /'weedl/ *v* **wheedling** /'weedling, 'weedl·ing/ **1** to influence or entice by soft words or flattery **2** to cause to part with sthg by wheedling – + *out of*

¹**wheel** /weel/ *n* **1** a circular frame of hard material that may be (partly) solid or spoked and that is capable of turning on an axle **2** a contrivance or apparatus having as its principal part a wheel; *esp* a chiefly medieval instrument of torture to which the victim was tied while his/her limbs were broken by a metal bar **3** sthg resembling a wheel in shape or motion; *esp* a catherine wheel **4a** a curving or circular movement **b** a rotation or turn, usu about an axis or centre; *specif* a turning movement of troops or ships in line in which the units preserve alignment and relative positions **5** *pl* the workings or controlling forces of sthg **6** *pl* a motor vehicle, esp a motor car *USE* (6) infml

²**wheel** *v* **1** to turn (as if) on an axis; revolve **2** to change direction as if revolving on a pivot **3** to move or extend in a circle or curve **4** to alter or reverse one's opinion – often + *about* or *round* **5** to convey or move (as if) on wheels; *esp* to push (a wheeled vehicle or its occupant) — **wheel and deal** to pursue one's own usu commercial interests, esp in a shrewd or unscrupulous manner

wheel,barrow /-,baroh/ *n* a load-carrying device that consists of a shallow box supported at 1 end by usu 1 wheel and at the other by a stand when at rest or by handles when being pushed

wheel,base /-,bays/ *n* the distance between the front and rear axles of a vehicle

wheel,chair /-,chea/ *n* an invalid's chair mounted on wheels

wheel,wright /-,riet/ *n* sby who makes or repairs wheels, esp wooden ones for carts

¹**wheeze** /weez/ *v* **1** to breathe with difficulty, usu with a whistling sound **2** to make a sound like that of wheezing – **-zy** *adj* – **-zily** *adv* – **-ziness** *n*

²**wheeze** *n* **1** a sound of wheezing **2** a cunning trick or expedient – infml

whelk /welk/ *n* any of numerous large marine snails; *esp* one much used as food in Europe

¹**whelp** /welp/ *n* **1** any of the young of various flesh-eating mammals, esp a dog **2** a disagreeable or impudent child or youth

²**whelp** *v* to give birth to (esp a puppy)

¹**when** /wen/ *adv* **1** at what time? **2a** at or during which time **b** and then; whereupon

²**when** *conj* **1a** at or during the time that **b** as soon as **c** whenever **2** in the event that; if **3a** considering that (e g why smoke *when* you know it's bad for you?) **b** in spite of the fact that; although (e g he gave up politics *when* he might have done well)

³**when** *pron* what or which time (e g since *when* have you known that?)

⁴**when** *n* a date, time

whence /wens/ *adv* or *conj* **1a** from where?; from which place, source, or cause? **b** from which place, source, or cause **2** to the place from which *USE* chiefly fml

¹**whenever** /wen'evə/ *conj* **1** at every or whatever time **2** in any circumstance — **or whenever** or at any similar time – infml

²**whenever** *adv* when in the world? – infml

¹**where** /wea/ *adv* **1a** at, in, or to what place? (e g *where* is the house?) **b** at, in, or to what situation, direction, circumstances, or respect? (e g *where* does this plan lead?) **2** at, in, or to which (place) (e g the town *where* he lives)

²**where** *conj* **1a** at, in, or to the place at which (e g stay *where* you are) **b** wherever **c** in a case, situation, or respect in which (e g outstanding *where* endurance is called for) **2** whereas, while — **where it's at** the real scene of the action — *slang*

¹**where** *n* **1** what place or point? **2** a place, point – *infml*

¹**whereabouts** /ˌweərə'bowts/ *also* **whereabout** *adv or conj* in what vicinity

²**whereabouts** /ˌweərə'bowts/ *n pl but sing or pl in constr* the place or general locality where a person or thing is

whereas /weə'raz/ *conj* **1** in view of the fact that; since – used, esp formally, to introduce a preamble **2** while on the contrary; although

whereby /weə'bie/ *conj* **1** in accordance with which (e g a law *whereby* children receive cheap milk) **2** by which means – chiefly fml

¹**wherefore** /'weəfaw, -'-'-/ *adv* **1** for what reason; why **2** for that reason; therefore *USE* chiefly fml

²**wherefore** *n* a reason, cause – chiefly in *the whys and wherefores*

¹**wherein** /weə'rin/ *adv* in what; how (e g showed him *wherein* he was wrong) – chiefly fml

²**wherein** *conj* in which; where – chiefly fml

whereupon /ˌweərə'pon/ *adv or conj* closely following and in consequence of which – chiefly fml

¹**wherever** /weə'revə/ *adv* where in the world? – chiefly infml — **or wherever** or anywhere else at all – chiefly infml

²**wherever** *conj* at, in, or to every or whatever place

wherewithal /'weəwiˌdhawl/ *n* means, resources; *specif* money

whet /wet/ *v* **-tt-** **1** to sharpen by rubbing on or with sthg (e g a stone) **2** to make keen or more acute; stimulate

whether /'wedhə/ *conj* – used usu with correlative *or* or with *or whether* to indicate **a** an indirect question involving alternatives (e g decide *whether* he should protest) **b** indifference between alternatives (e g seated him next to her, *whether* by accident or design)

whetstone /'wetˌstohn/ *n* **1** a stone for sharpening an edge (e g of a chisel) **2** sthg that stimulates or makes keen

whey /way/ *n* the watery part of milk separated from the curd, esp in cheese-making, and rich in lactose, minerals, and vitamins

¹**which** /wich/ *adj* **1** being what one or ones out of a known or limited group? (e g which tie should I wear?) **2** whichever **3** – used to introduce a relative clause by modifying the noun which refers either to a preceding word or phrase or to a whole previous clause (e g he may come, in *which* case I'll ask him)

²**which** *pron, pl* **which 1** what one out of a known or specified group? (e g *which* of those houses do you live in?) **2** whichever **3** – used to introduce a relative clause (e g the office in *which* I work)

¹**whichever** /wi'chevə/ *pron, pl* **whichever 1** whatever one out of a group **2** no matter which **3** which in the world? – chiefly infml

²**whichever** *adj* being whatever one or ones out of a group; no matter which

¹**whiff** /wif/ *n* **1** a quick puff, slight gust, or inhalation, esp of air, a smell, smoke, or gas **2** a slight trace

²**whiff** *v* to smell unpleasant – ~**y** *adj*

Whig /wig/ *n or adj* (a member) of a major British political group of the 18th and early 19th c seeking to limit royal authority and increase parliamentary power

¹**while** /wiel/ *n* **1** a period of time, esp when short and marked by the occurrence of an action or condition; a time (e g stay here for a *while*) **2** the time and effort used; trouble (e g it's worth your *while*)

²**while** *conj* **1a** during the time that **b** providing that; as long as **2a** when; on the other hand; whereas **b** in spite of the fact that; although (e g *while* respected, he is not liked)

³**while** *prep, archaic or dial* until

while away *v* to pass (time) in a leisurely, often pleasant manner

whim /wim/ *n* a sudden, capricious, or eccentric idea or impulse; a fancy

whimper /'wimpə/ *v or n* **1** (to make) a low plaintive whining sound **2** (to make) a petulant complaint or protest

whimsical /'wimzikl/ *adj* **1** full of whims; capricious **2** resulting from or suggesting mild affectation; *esp* quizzical, playful – ~**ly** *adv*

¹**whine** /wien/ *v* to utter or make a whine

²**whine** *n* **1** (a sound like) a prolonged high-pitched cry, usu expressive of distress or pain **2** a querulous or peevish complaint

whinny /'wini/ *v or n* (to make or utter with or as if with) a low gentle neigh or similar sound

¹**whip** /wip/ *v* **-pp-** **1** to take, pull, jerk, or move very quickly **2a** to strike with a whip or similar slender flexible implement, esp as a punishment; *also* to spank **b** to drive or urge on (as if) by using a whip **3** to bind or wrap (e g a rope or rod) with cord for protection and strength **4** to beat (e g eggs or cream) into a froth with a whisk, fork, etc **5** to overcome decisively; defeat – *infml* **6** to snatch suddenly; *esp* to steal – *slang* — **whip into shape** to bring (sby or sthg) into a desired state, esp by hard work or practice

²**whip** *n* **1** an instrument consisting usu of a lash attached to a handle, used for driving and controlling animals and for punishment **2** a dessert made by whipping some of the ingredients **3** a light hoisting apparatus consisting of a single

pulley, a block, and a rope **4a** a member of Parliament or other legislative body appointed by a political party to enforce discipline and to secure the attendance and votes of party members **b** *often cap* an instruction (e g a three-line whip or a two-line whip) to each member of a political party in Parliament to be in attendance for voting **c** (the privileges and duties of) membership of the official parliamentary representation of a political party

,whip 'hand *n* a controlling position; *the advantage*

'whip,lash /-,lash/ *n* **1** the lash of a whip **2 whiplash, whiplash injury** injury to the neck resulting from a sudden sharp whipping movement of the neck and head (e g in a car collision)

whippersnapper /'wipə,snapə/ *n* an insignificant but impudent person, esp a child

whippet /'wipit/ *n* (any of) a breed of small swift slender dogs related to greyhounds

'whipping ,boy *n* a scapegoat

whippy /'wipi/ *adj* unusually resilient; springy

'whip-,round *n*, *chiefly Br* a collection of money made usu for a benevolent purpose – infml

whip up *v* **1** to stir up; stimulate **2** to produce in a hurry

¹whirl /wuhl/ *v* **1** to move along a curving or circling course, esp with force or speed **2** to turn abruptly or rapidly round (and round) on an axis; rotate, wheel **3** to pass, move, or go quickly **4** to become giddy or dizzy; reel

²whirl *n* **1** (sthg undergoing or having a form suggestive of) a rapid rotating or circling movement **2a** a confused tumult; a bustle **b** a confused or disturbed mental state; a turmoil **3** an experimental or brief attempt; a try – infml

whirlpool /'wuhl,poohl/ *n* (sthg resembling, esp in attracting or engulfing power) a circular eddy of rapidly moving water with a central depression into which floating objects may be drawn

'whirl,wind /-,wind/ *n* **1** a small rapidly rotating windstorm of limited extent marked by an inward and upward spiral motion of the lower air round a core of low pressure **2** a confused rush; a whirl

whirr, whir /wuh/ *v or n* -rr- (to make or revolve or move with) a continuous buzzing or vibrating sound made by sthg in rapid motion

¹whisk /wisk/ *n* **1** a quick light brushing or whipping motion **2a** any of various small usu hand-held kitchen utensils used for whisking food **b** a small bunch of flexible strands (e g twigs, feathers, or straw) attached to a handle for use as a brush

²whisk *v* **1** to convey briskly **2** to mix or fluff up (as if) by beating with a whisk **3** to brandish lightly; flick

whisker /'wiskə/ *n* **1a** a hair of the beard or sideboards **b** a hair's breadth **2** any of the long projecting hairs or bristles growing near the mouth of an animal (e g a cat)

whisky /'wiski/ *n* a spirit distilled from fermented mash of rye, corn, wheat, or esp barley

¹whisper /'wispə/ *v* **1** to speak softly with little or no vibration of the vocal cords **2** to make a hissing or rustling sound like whispered speech **3** to report or suggest confidentially – ~ er *n*

²whisper *n* **1a** whispering; *esp* speech without vibration of the vocal cords **b** a hissing or rustling sound like whispered speech **2a** a rumour; a hint, trace

¹whist /wist/ *v*, *dial Br* to be silent; hush – often used as an interjection to call for silence

²whist *n* (any of various card games similar to) a card game for 4 players in 2 partnerships in which each trick made in excess of 6 tricks scores 1 point

'whist ,drive *n*, *Br* an evening of whist playing with a periodic change of partners, usu with prizes at the finish

¹whistle /'wisl/ *n* **1** a device (e g a small wind instrument) in which the forcible passage of air, steam, the breath, etc through a slit or against a thin edge in a short tube produces a loud sound **2** (a sound like) a shrill clear sound produced by whistling or by a whistle

²whistle *v* whistling /'wisling/ **1** to utter a (sound like a) whistle (by blowing or drawing air through the puckered lips) **2** to make a whistle by rapid movement; *also* to move rapidly (as if) with such a sound **3** to blow or sound a whistle — **whistle for** to demand or request in vain

whit *n* /wit/ the smallest part imaginable; a bit

Whit *n* Whitsuntide

¹white /wiet/ *adj* **1a** free from colour **b** of the colour white **c** light or pallid in colour **d** *of wine* light yellow or amber in colour **e** *Br*, *of coffee* served with milk or cream **2** of a group or race characterized by reduced pigmentation **3** *of magic* not intended to cause harm **4a** dressed in white **b** accompanied by snow **5** reactionary, counterrevolutionary – ~ ness *n*

²white *n* **1** the neutral colour that belongs to objects that reflect diffusely nearly all incident light **2** a white or light-coloured part of sthg: e g **2a** the mass of albumin-containing material surrounding the yolk of an egg **b** the white part of the ball of the eye **c** (the player playing) the light-coloured pieces in a two-handed board game **3a** *pl* white (sports) clothing **b** a white animal (e g a butterfly or pig) **4** sby belonging to a light-skinned race

whitebait /'wiet,bayt/ *n* (any of various small food fishes similar to) the young of any of several European herrings (e g the common herring or the sprat) eaten whole

,white-'collar *adj* of or being the class of non-manual employees whose duties do not call for the wearing of work clothes or protective clothing

,white 'dwarf *n* a small whitish star of high surface temperature, low brightness, and high density

,white 'elephant *n* **1** a property requiring much care and expense and yielding little profit **2** sthg that is no longer of value (to its owner)

,white 'feather *n* a mark or symbol of cowardice

,white 'flag *n* a flag of plain white used as a flag of truce or as a token of surrender

Whitehall /'wiet,hawl, ,-'-/ *n* the British government

,white 'heat *n* a temperature higher than red heat, at which a body emits white light

,white 'hope *n* a person expected to bring fame and glory to his/her group, country, etc

'White ,House *n* the executive branch of the US government

,white 'lead /led/ *n* any of several white lead-containing pigments

,white 'magic *n* magic used for good purposes (e g to cure disease)

whiten /'wiet(ə)n/ *v* to make or become white or whiter; bleach

,white 'paper *n*, *often cap W&P* a (British) government report

,white 'pepper *n* a condiment prepared from the husked dried berries of an E Indian plant used either whole or ground

,white 'sauce *n* a sauce made with milk, cream, or a chicken, veal, or fish stock

,white 'spirit *n* an inflammable liquid distilled from petroleum used esp as a solvent and thinner for paints

,white-'tie *adj* characterized by or requiring the wearing of formal evening dress by men

¹'white,wash /-,wosh/ *v* **1** to apply whitewash to **2a** to gloss over or cover up (e g vices or crimes) **b** to exonerate by concealment or through biased presentation of data **3** to defeat overwhelmingly in a contest or game – *infml*

²whitewash *n* **1** a liquid mixture (e g of lime and water or whiting, size, and water) for whitening outside walls or similar surfaces **2** a whitewashing

whither /'widhə/ *adv or conj* **1** to or towards what place? – also used in rhetorical questions without a verb **2** to the place at, in, or to which **3** to which place *USE chiefly fml*

whiting /'wieting/ *n* any of various marine food fishes; *esp* one related to the cod

Whitsun /'wits(ə)n/ *adj or n* (of, being, or observed on or at) Whitsuntide or Whitsuntide

Whitsunday /wit'sunday, -di/ *n* a Christian feast on the 7th Sunday after Easter commemorating the descent of the Holy Spirit at Pentecost

Whitsuntide /'wits(ə)n,tied/ *n* Whitsunday and the following Monday and/or the days of public holiday celebrated with or in place of these days

whittle /'witl/ *v* whittling /'witling, 'witl·ing/ **1a** to pare or cut off chips from the surface of (wood) with a knife **b** to shape or form by so paring or cutting **2** to reduce, remove, or destroy gradually as if by cutting off bits with a knife; pare – usu + *down or away*

whiz, whizz /wiz/ *v* -zz- **1** to move (through the air) with a buzz or whirr **2** to move swiftly

'whiz ,kid, whizz kid *n* sby unusually successful or clever, esp at an early age

who /hoo; *strong* hooh/ *pron, pl* who **1** what or which person or people? **2** – used to introduce a relative clause (e g my father, *who* was a lawyer) *USE* often used as object of a verb or of a following preposition though still disapproved of by some — who is/was who the identity of or the noteworthy facts about each of a number of people

whoa /'woh·ə, woh/ *interj* – used as a command (e g to a draught animal) to stand still

whodunit *also* whodunnit /,hooh'dunit/ *n* a play, film, or story dealing with the detection of crime or criminals

whoever /hooh'evə/ *pron* **1** whatever person **2** no matter who **3** who in the world? – *chiefly infml USE* (1&2) used in any grammatical relation except that of a possessive

¹whole /hohl/ *adj* **1a** free of wound, injury, defect, or impairment; intact, unhurt, or healthy **b** restored **2** having all its proper constituents; unmodified **3** each or all of; entire **4a** constituting an undivided unit; unbroken **b** directed to (the accomplishment of) 1 end or aim **5** very great – in *a whole lot*

²whole *n* **1** a complete amount or sum; sthg lacking no part, member, or element **2** sthg constituting a complex unity; a coherent system or organization of parts — as a whole considered all together as a body rather than as individuals — on the whole **1** in view of all the circumstances **2** in most instances; typically

,whole'hearted /-'hahtid/ *adj* earnestly committed or devoted; free from all reserve or hesitation

'whole,meal /-,meel/ *adj* made with (flour from) ground entire wheat kernels

¹'whole,sale /-,sayl/ *n* the sale of commodities in large quantities usu for resale (by a retailer) – ~r *n*

²wholesale *adj or adv* **1** (sold or selling) at wholesale **2** (performed) on a large scale, esp without discrimination

'whole,some /-s(ə)m/ *adj* **1** promoting health or well-being of mind or spirit **2** promoting health of body; *also* healthy – ~ness *n*

wholly /'hohl·li/ *adv* **1** to the full or entire extent; completely **2** to the exclusion of other things; solely

whom /hoohm/ *pron*, *objective case of* **who** – used as an interrogative or relative; used as object of a preceding preposition (e g for *whom* the bell tolls); or less frequently as object of a verb or of a following preposition (e g the man *whom* you wrote to)

whoop /woohp/ *n* **1** a loud yell expressive of eagerness, exuberance, or jubilation **2** the hoot of an owl, crane, etc – **whoop** *v* — **whoop it up** to celebrate riotously; carouse – infml

¹**whoopee** /'woo'pee/ *interj* – used to express exuberance

²**whoopee** /'woopi/ *n* boisterous convivial fun – in *make whoopee*; infml

'**whooping ,cough** /'hoohping/ *n* an infectious bacterial disease, esp of children, marked by a convulsive spasmodic cough sometimes followed by a crowing intake of breath

whoosh /woosh, woohsh/ *v or n* (to move quickly with) a swift or explosive rushing sound

whop /wop/ *v* **-pp- 1** to beat, strike **2** to defeat totally *USE* infml

whopper /'wopə/ *n* **1** sthg unusually large or otherwise extreme of its kind **2** an extravagant or monstrous lie *USE* infml

¹**whopping** /'woping/ *adj* extremely big – infml

²**whopping** *adv* very, extremely – infml

¹**whore** /haw/ *n* a prostitute

²**whore** *v* **1** to have sexual intercourse outside marriage, esp with a prostitute **2** to pursue an unworthy or idolatrous desire

whorl /wuhl, wawl/ *n* **1** an arrangement of similar anatomical parts (e g leaves) in a circle round a point on an axis (e g a stem) **2** sthg spiral in form or movement; a swirl **3** a single turn of a spiral (shape) **4** a fingerprint in which the central ridges turn through at least 1 complete circle

¹**whose** /hoohz/ *adj* of whom or which, esp as possessor agent or object of an action (e g *whose* hat is this; the factory in *whose* construction they were involved)

²**whose** *pron*, *pl* **whose** that which belongs to whom – used without a following noun as a pronoun equivalent in meaning to the adjective *whose* (e g tell me *whose* it was)

whosoever /,hoohsoh'evə/ *pron*, *archaic* whoever

¹**why** /wie/ *adv* for what cause, reason, or purpose? — **why not** — used in making a suggestion

²**why** *conj* the cause, reason, or purpose for which **2** on which grounds

³**why** *n*, *pl* **whys** a reason, cause – chiefly in *the whys and wherefores*

⁴**why** *interj* – used to express mild surprise, hesitation, approval, disapproval, or impatience

wick /wik/ *n* a cord, strip, or cylinder of loosely woven material through which a liquid (e g paraffin, oil, or melted wax) is drawn by capillary action to the top in a candle, lamp, oil stove, etc for burning

wicked /'wikid/ *adj* **1** morally bad; evil **2** disposed to mischief; roguish **3** very unpleasant, vicious, or dangerous – infml – **~ly** *adv* – **~ness** *n*

wicker /'wikə/ *adj or n* (made of) interlaced osiers, twigs, canes, or rods

'**wicker,work** /-,wuhk/ *n* (work consisting of) wicker

wicket /'wikit/ *n* **1** a small gate or door; *esp* one forming part of or placed near a larger one **2a** either of the 2 sets of stumps set 22yd (20.12m) apart, at which the ball is bowled and which the batsman defends in cricket **b** the area 12ft (3.66m) wide bounded by these wickets **c** a partnership between 2 batsmen who are in at the same time

'**wicket,keeper** /-,keepə/ *n* the fieldsman in cricket who is stationed behind the batsman's wicket

¹**wide** /wied/ *adj* **1a** having great horizontal extent; vast **b** embracing much; comprehensive **2a** having a specified width **b** having much extent between the sides; broad **3a** extending or fluctuating over a considerable range **b** distant or deviating from sthg specified **4** *Br* shrewd, astute – slang – **~ly** *adv*

²**wide** *adv* **1** over a great distance or extent; widely **2a** so as to leave much space or distance between **b** so as to miss or clear a point by a considerable distance **3** to the fullest extent; completely – often as an intensive + *open*

³**wide** *n* a ball bowled in cricket that is out of reach of the batsman in his normal position and counts as 1 run to his side

,**wide-'angle** *adj* (having or using a camera with a lens) that has an angle of view wider than the ordinary

,**wide-a'wake** *adj* **1** fully awake **2** alertly watchful, esp for advantages or opportunities

'**wide,spread** /-,spred/ *adj* **1** widely extended or spread out **2** widely diffused or prevalent

widgeon *also* **wigeon** /'wijin/ *n pl* **widgeons**, *esp collectively* **widgeon** an Old World freshwater dabbling duck the male of which has a chestnut head

¹**widow** /'widoh/ *n* **1** a woman whose husband has died (and who has not remarried) **2** a woman whose husband spends much time away from her pursuing a specified (sporting) activity

²**widow** *v* **1** to cause to become a widow **2** to deprive of sthg greatly valued or needed

widower /'widoh·ə/ *n* a man whose wife has died (and who has not remarried)

width /wit·th, width/ *n* **1** the measurement taken at right angles to the length **2** largeness of extent or scope

wield /weeld/ *v* **1** to handle (e g a tool) effectively **2** to exert, exercise – **~er** *n*

wife /wief/ *n, pl* **wives** /wievz/ a married woman, esp in relation to her husband

wig /wig/ *n* a manufactured covering of natural or synthetic hair for the (bald part of a) head

wigging /'wiging/ *n* a severe scolding – infml

¹wiggle /'wigl/ *v* **wiggling** /'wigling, 'wigl·ing/ to (cause to) move with quick jerky or turning motions or smoothly from side to side

²wiggle *n* **1** a wiggling movement **2** a wavy line; a squiggle

wigwam /'wig,wam/ *n* a N American Indian hut having a framework of poles covered with bark, rush mats, or hides

¹wild /wield/ *adj* **1a 1a** (of organisms) living in a natural state and not (ordinarily) tame, domesticated, or cultivated **b** growing or produced without the aid and care of humans **2** not (amenable to being) inhabited or cultivated **3a**(1) free from restraint or regulation; uncontrolled **a**(2) emotionally overcome; *also* passionately eager or enthusiastic **a**(3) very angry; infuriated **b** marked by great agitation; *also* stormy **c** going beyond reasonable or conventional bounds; fantastic **4** uncivilized, barbaric **5a** deviating from the intended or regular ·course **b** having no logical basis; random **6** *of a playing card* able to represent any card designated by the holder – **~ly** *adv* – **~ness** *n*

²wild *n* **1** the wilderness **2** a wild, free, or natural state or existence

³wild *adv* in a wild manner: e g **a** without regulation or control **b** off an intended or expected course

wild 'boar *n* an Old World wild pig from which most domestic pigs have derived

¹wild,cat /-,kat/ *n pl* **wildcats**, (**1b**) **wildcats**, *esp collectively* **wildcat 1a** either of 2 cats that resemble but are heavier in build than the domestic cat and are usu held to be among its ancestors **b** any of various small or medium-sized cats (e g the lynx or ocelot) **2** a savage quick-tempered person

²wildcat *adj* **1** operating, produced, or carried on outside the bounds of standard or legitimate business practices **2** of or being an oil or gas well drilled in territory not known to be productive **3** initiated by a group of workers without formal union approval or in violation of a contract

wildcat *v* **-tt-** to prospect and drill an experimental oil or gas well

wildebeest /'wildi,beest, 'vil-/ *n pl* **wildebeests**, *esp collectively* **wildebeest** a gnu

wilderness /'wildənis/ *n* **1a** a (barren) region or area that is (essentially) uncultivated and uninhabited by human beings **b** an empty or pathless area or region **c** a part of a garden or nature reserve devoted to wild growth **2** a confusing multitude or mass **3** *the* state of exclusion from office or power

'wild,fire /-,fie·ə/ *n* sthg that spreads very rapidly – usu in *like wildfire*

'wild,fowl /-,fowl/ *n* a wild duck, goose, or other game bird, esp a waterfowl

,wild-'goose ,chase *n* a hopeless pursuit after sthg unattainable

'wild,life /-,lief/ *n* wild animals

wiles /wielz/ *n pl* deceitful or beguiling tricks, esp used to persuade

wilful, *NAm chiefly* **willful** /'wilf(ə)l/ *adj* **1** obstinately and often perversely self-willed **2** done deliberately; intentional – **~ly** *adv* – **~ness** *n*

¹will /wil/ *v, pres sing & pl* **will**; *pres neg* **won't** /wohnt/; *past* **would** /wəd/; *strong* **wood**/ **1** – used to express choice, willingness, or consent or in negative constructions refusal (e g can find no one who *will* take the job); used in the question form with the force of a request or of an offer or suggestion (e g *will* you have some tea) **2** – used to express custom or inevitable tendency (e g accidents *will* happen); used with emphatic stress to express exasperation (e g he *will* drink his tea from a saucer) **3** – used to express futurity (e g tomorrow I will get up early) **4** *can* (e g the back seat *will* hold 3 passengers) **5** – used to express logical probability (e g that *will* be the milkman) **6** – used to express determination or command or urge (e g you *will* do as I say at once) **7** to wish, desire (e g whether we *will* or no)

²will *n* **1** a desire, wish: e g **1a** a resolute intention **b** an inclination **c** a choice, wish **2** what is wished or ordained by the specified agent **3a** a mental power by which one (apparently) controls one's wishes, intentions, etc **b** an inclination to act according to principles or ends **c** a specified attitude towards others **4** willpower, self-control **5** a (written) legal declaration of the manner in which sby would have his/her property disposed of after his/her death — **at will** as one wishes; as or when it pleases or suits oneself

³will *v* **1** to bequeath **2a** to determine deliberately; purpose **b** to (attempt to) cause by exercise of the will

willies /'wiliz/ *n pl* nervousness, jitters – + *the*; infml

¹willing /'wiling/ *adj* **1** inclined or favourably disposed in mind; ready **2** prompt to act or respond **3** done, borne, or given without reluctance – **~ly** *adv* – **~ness** *n*

²willing *n* cheerful alacrity – in *show willing*

will-o'-the-wisp /,wil ə dhə 'wisp/ *n* **1** a phosphorescent light sometimes seen over marshy ground and often caused by the combustion of gas from decomposed organic matter **2** an enticing but elusive goal

willow /'wiloh/ n 1 any of a genus of trees and shrubs bearing catkins of petal-less flowers 2 an object made of willow wood; *esp* a cricket bat – infml

'**willow ,pattern** n china tableware decorated with a usu blue-and-white story-telling design of oriental style

willowy /'wiloh·i/ adj 1 full of willows 2a supple, pliant b gracefully tall and slender

'**will,power** /-,powə/ n self-control, resoluteness

willy-nilly /,wili 'nili/ adv or adj 1 by compulsion; without choice 2 (carried out or occurring) in a haphazard or random manner

¹**wilt** /wilt/ archaic pres 2 sing of **will**

²**wilt** v 1 of a plant to lose freshness and become flaccid; droop 2 to grow weak or faint; languish

³**wilt** n a disease of plants marked by wilting period and by some nuns

wily /'wieli/ adj full of wiles; crafty

wimple /'wimpl/ n wimpling /'wimpl·ing/ a cloth covering worn over the head and round the neck and chin, esp by women in the late medieval period and by some nuns

¹**win** /win/ v -nn-; won /wun/ 1a to gain the victory in a contest; succeed b to be right in an argument, dispute, etc; also to have one's way 2a to get possession of by qualities or fortune b to obtain by effort; earn 3a to solicit and gain the favour of; also to persuade – usu + over or round b to induce (a woman) to accept oneself in marriage 4 to reach by expenditure of effort

²**win** n 1 a victory or success, esp in a game or sporting contest 2 first place at the finish, esp of a horse race

wince /wins/ v to shrink back involuntarily (e g from pain); flinch

winceyette /,winsi'et/ n a lightweight usu cotton fabric napped on 1 or both sides

winch /winch/ n any of various machines or instruments for hoisting or pulling; a windlass – **winch** v

¹**wind** /wind/ n 1 a (natural) movement of air, esp horizontally 2 a force or agency that carries along or influences; a trend 3 breath 4 gas generated in the stomach or the intestines 5a musical wind instruments collectively, esp as distinguished from stringed and percussion instruments b sing or pl in constr the group of players of such instruments — **before the wind** in the same direction as the main force of the wind — **close to the wind 1** as nearly as possible against the main force of the wind 2 close to a point of danger; near the permissible limit — **have the wind up** to be scared or frightened — **in the wind** about to happen; astir, afoot — **off the wind** away from the direction from which the wind is blowing — **on the wind** towards the direction from which the wind is blowing — **put the wind up** to scare, frighten — **under the wind 1** to leeward 2 in a place protected from the wind; under the lee

²**wind** /wind/ v 1 to make short of breath 2 to rest (e g a horse) in order to allow the breath to be recovered

³**wind** /wiend/ v winded, wound /wownd/ to sound (e g a call or note) on a horn

⁴**wind** /wiend/ v wound /wownd/ also winded 1 to have a curving course; extend or proceed in curves 2 to coil, twine 3a to surround or wrap with sthg pliable b to tighten the spring of 4 to raise to a high level (e g of excitement or tension) – usu + up

⁵**wind** /wiend/ n a coil, turn

windbag /'wind,bag/ n an excessively talkative person – infml

windbreak /'wind,brayk/ n sthg (e g a growth of trees or a fence) that breaks the force of the wind

'**wind ,cheater** /-,cheetə/ n, chiefly Br a weatherproof or windproof coat or jacket; an anorak

windfall /'wind,fawl/ n 1 sthg, esp a fruit, blown down by the wind 2 an unexpected gain or advantage; esp a legacy

'**winding-,sheet** /'wiending/ n a sheet in which a corpse is wrapped for burial

'**wind ,instrument** /wind/ n a musical instrument (e g a trumpet, clarinet, or recorder) sounded by the player's breath

windjammer /'wind,jamə/ n 1 a large fast square-rigged sailing vessel 2 Br a windcheater

windlass /'windlas/ n any of various machines for hoisting or hauling: e g a a horizontal drum supported on vertical posts and turned by a crank so that the hoisting rope is wound round the drum b a steam, electric, etc winch with a horizontal or vertical shaft and 2 drums, used to raise a ship's anchor

windmill /'wind,mil/ n 1 a mill operated by vanes that are turned by the wind 2 a toy consisting of lightweight vanes that revolve at the end of a stick

window /'windoh/ n 1 an opening, esp in the wall of a building, for admission of light and air that is usu fitted with a frame containing glass and capable of being opened and shut 2 a pane (e g of glass) in a window 3 an interval of time within which a rocket or spacecraft must be launched to accomplish a particular mission

'**window ,box** n a box for growing plants on the (outside) sill of a window

'**window ,dressing** n the display of merchandise in a shop window

windpipe /'wind,piep/ n the trachea

windscreen /'wind,skreen/ n, Br a transparent screen, esp of glass, at the front of a (motor) vehicle

'**wind-,sock** /wind/ n a truncated cloth cone that is open at both ends and mounted on a pole and is used to indicate the direction of the wind, esp at airfields

'wind-,surfing *n* the sport of sailing on a flat buoyant board equipped with a sail, retractable stabilizer, and rudder – **surfer** *n*

windswept /'wind,swept/ *adj* dishevelled (as if) from being exposed to the wind

'wind ,tunnel /wind/ *n* a tunnel-like apparatus through which air is blown at a known velocity to determine the effects of wind pressure on an object placed in the apparatus

wind up /wiend/ *v* **1** to bring to a conclusion; *specif* to bring (a business) to an end by liquidation **2** to put in order; settle

windward /'windwood/ *adj, adv, or n* (in or facing) the direction from which the wind is blowing

windy /'windi/ *adj* **1a** windswept **b** marked by strong or stormy wind **2** *chiefly Br* frightened, nervous – *infml* – **windily** *adv* – **windiness** *n*

'wine /wien/ *n* **1** fermented grape juice containing varying percentages of alcohol together with ethers and esters that give it bouquet and flavour **2** the usu fermented juice of a plant or fruit used as a drink **3** the colour of red wine

'wine *v* to entertain with or drink wine – usu in *wine and dine*

'wine,glass /-,glahs/ *n* any of several variously shaped and sized drinking glasses for wine, that usu have a rounded bowl and are mounted on a stem and foot

'wing /wing/ *n* **1a** (a part of a nonflying bird or insect corresponding to) any of the movable feathered or membranous paired appendages by means of which a bird, bat, or insect flies **b** any of various body parts (e g of a flying fish or flying lemur) providing means of limited flight **2** an appendage or part resembling a wing in shape, appearance, or position: e g **2a** a sidepiece at the top of a high-backed armchair **b** any of the aerofoils that develop a major part of the lift which supports a heavier-than-air aircraft **c** *Br* a mudguard, esp when forming an integral part of the body of a motor vehicle **3** a means of flight – usu pl with sing. meaning **4** a part of a building projecting from the main or central part **5** *pl* the area at the side of the stage out of sight of the audience **6a** a left or right flank of an army or fleet **b** any of the attacking positions or players on either side of a centre position in certain team sports **7** *sing or pl in constr* a group or faction holding distinct opinions or policies within an organized body (e g a political party) **8** an operational and administrative unit of an air force – **~less** *adj* — **in the wings** in the background; in readiness to act — **on the wing** in flight; flying — **under one's wing** under one's protection; in one's care

'wing *v* **1** to (enable to) fly or move swiftly **2** to wound (e g with a bullet) without killing

wing commander *n* a middle-ranking officer in the Royal Air Force

winger /'wing-ə/ *n, chiefly Br* a player (e g in soccer) in a wing position

'wing ,nut *n* a nut that has projecting wings or flanges so that it may be turned by finger and thumb

'wing,span /-,span/ *n* the distance from the tip of one of a pair of wings to that of the other

'wink /wingk/ *v* **1** to shut 1 eye briefly as a signal or in teasing; *also, of an eye* to shut briefly **2** to avoid seeing or noting sthg – usu + *at* **3** to gleam or flash intermittently; twinkle

'wink *n* **1** a brief period of sleep; a nap **2** an act of winking **3** the time of a wink; an instant **4** a hint or sign given by winking

winkle /'wingkl/ *n* a small edible marine snail

winkle out *v*, **winkling** /'wingkling, 'wingkl·ing/ *chiefly Br* to displace or extract from a position; *also* to discover or identify with difficulty

winner /'winə/ *n* sthg (expected to be) successful – *infml*

winnow /'winoh/ *v* **1a** to get rid of (sthg undesirable or unwanted); remove – often + *out* **b** to separ :e, sift **2** to remove waste matter from (e g grain) by exposure to a current of air

winsome /'wins(ə)m/ *adj* pleasing and engaging, often because of a childlike charm and innocence – **~ly** *adv* – **~ness** *n*

'winter /'wintə/ *n* **1** the season between autumn and spring comprising in the N hemisphere the months December, January, and February **2** the colder part of the year **3** *a year* – usu pl **4** a period of inactivity or decay – **-try**, **~y** *adj*

'winter *adj* **1** of, during, or suitable for winter **2** sown in autumn and harvested the following spring or summer

'winter *v* to keep or feed (e g livestock) during the winter

win through *v* to reach a desired or satisfactory end, esp after overcoming difficulties

'wipe /wiep/ *v* **1a** to clean or dry by rubbing, esp with or on sthg soft **b** to draw or pass for rubbing or cleaning **2a** to remove (as if) by rubbing **b** to erase completely; obliterate **3** to spread (as if) by wiping — **wipe the floor with** to defeat decisively

'wipe *n* **1** an act or instance of wiping **2** power or capacity to wipe

wipe out *v* to destroy completely annihilate

'wire /wie-əliz/ *n* **1** metal in the form of a usu very flexible thread or slender rod **2a** a line of wire for conducting electrical current **b** a telephone or telegraph wire or system **c** a telegram **3** a barrier or fence of usu barbed wire

'wire *v* to send or send word to by telegraph

'wireless /'wie-əlis/ *adj, chiefly Br* of radiotelegraphy, radiotelephony, or radio

'wireless *n, chiefly Br* (a) radio

,wire 'netting *n* a network of coarse woven wire

,wire 'wool n an abrasive material consisting of fine wire strands woven into a mass and used for scouring esp kitchen utensils (e g pans)

'wire,worm /-,wuhm/ n the slender hard-coated larva of various click beetles, destructive esp to plant roots

wiry /'wie-əri/ adj 1 resembling wire, esp in form and flexibility 2 lean and vigorous; sinewy – wiriness n

wisdom /'wizd(ə)m/ n 1a accumulated learning; knowledge b the thoughtful application of learning; insight 2 good sense; judgment

'wisdom ,tooth n any of the 4 molar teeth in humans which are the last to erupt on each side at the back of each jaw

¹wise /wiez/ n manner, way

²wise adj 1a characterized by or showing wisdom; marked by understanding, discernment, and a capacity for sound judgment b judicious, prudent 2 well-informed 3 possessing inside knowledge; shrewdly cognizant – often + to

wisecrack /'wiez,krak/ v or n (to make) a sophisticated or knowing witticism – infml

'wise ,guy n a conceited and self-assertive person – infml

¹wish /wish/ v 1 to express the hope that sby will have or attain (sthg); esp to bid 2a to give form to (a wish) b to feel or express a wish for; want c to request in the form of a wish; order 3 to make a wish — wish on/upon 1 to hope or will that (sby else) should have to suffer (a difficult person or situation) 2 to confer or foist (sthg unwanted) on (sby)

²wish n 1a an act or instance of wishing or desire; a want b an object of desire; a goal 2a an expressed will or desire b an expressed greeting – usu pl 3 a ritual act of wishing

'wish,bone /-,bohn/ n a forked bone in front of the breastbone of a bird consisting chiefly of the 2 clavicles fused at their lower ends

wishy-washy /'wishi ,woshi/ adj 1 lacking in strength or flavour 2 lacking in character or determination; ineffectual USE infml

wisp /wisp/ n 1a a thin separate streak or piece b sthg frail, slight, or fleeting 2 a flock of birds (e g snipe) – ~ y adj

wisteria /wi'stiəri·ə, -'steə-/, wistaria /wi'steəri·ə/ n any of a genus of chiefly Asiatic climbing plants with showy flowers

wistful /'wistf(ə)l/ adj 1 full of unfulfilled desire; yearning 2 musingly sad; pensive – ~ly adv – ~ness n

wit /wit/ n 1 reasoning power; intelligence 2a mental soundness; sanity b mental resourcefulness; ingenuity 3a the ability to relate seemingly disparate things so as to illuminate or amuse b a talent for banter or raillery 4 a witty individual 5 pl senses

witch /wich/ n 1 one who is credited with supernatural powers; esp a woman practising witchcraft 2 an ugly old woman; a hag – ~ ery n

'witch ,craft /-,krahft/ n (the use of) sorcery or magic

'witch ,doctor n a professional sorcerer, esp in a primitive tribal society

'witch-,hunt n the searching out and harassment of those with unpopular views – witch-hunting n

with /widh/ prep 1a in opposition to; against (e g had a fight with his brother) b so as to be separated or detached from (e g I disagree with you) 2a in relation to (e g the frontier with Yugoslavia) b – used to indicate the object of attention, behaviour, or feeling (e g in love with her) c in respect to; so far as concerns (e g the trouble with this machine) – sometimes used redundantly (e g get it finished with) 3a – used to indicate accompaniment or association b – used to indicate one to whom a usu reciprocal communication is made (e g talking with a friend) c – used to express agreement or sympathy (e g forced to conclude with him that it is a forgery) d able to follow the reasoning of 4a on the side of; for b employed by 5a – used to indicate the object of a statement of comparison, equality, or harmony (e g dress doesn't go with her shoes) b as well as c in addition to – used to indicate combination d inclusive of (e g costs £5 with tax) 6a by means of; using b through the effect of (e g pale with anger) b – used to indicate an attendant or contributory circumstance (e g stood there with his hat on) c in the possession or care of (e g the decision rests with you) 8a – used to indicate a close association in time e g with the outbreak of war, they went home) b in proportion to (e g the pressure varies with the depth) 9a notwithstanding; in spite of (e g love her with all her faults) b except for (e g similar, with 1 important difference)

withdraw /widh'draw/ v withdrew /-'drooh/, withdrawn /-'drawn/ 1a to go back or away; retire from participation b to retreat c to remove money from a place of deposit 2 to become socially or emotionally detached 3 to retract – ~al n

withdrawn /widh'drawn/ adj 1 secluded, isolated 2 socially detached and unresponsive; also shy

wither /'widhə/ v 1 to become dry and shrivel (as if) from loss of bodily moisture 2 to lose vitality, force, or freshness 3 to make speechless or incapable of action; stun – ~ing adj – ~ingly adv

withers /'widhəz/ n pl the ridge between the shoulder bones of a horse or other quadruped

withhold /widh'hohld/ v withheld /-'held/ 1 to hold back from action; check 2 to refrain from granting or giving

¹within /wi'dhin/ adv 1 in or into the interior; inside 2 in one's inner thought, mood, or character

²**within** *prep* **1** inside – used to indicate enclosure or containment, esp in sthg large **2** – used to indicate situation or circumstance in the limits or compass of: e g **2a(1)** before the end of (e g gone *within* a week) **a(2)** since the beginning of (e g been there *within* the last week) **b(1)** not beyond the quantity, degree, or limitations of (e g was *within* his income) **b(2)** in or into the scope or sphere of (e g *within* his rights) **b(3)** in or into the range of (e g *within* reach) **b(4)** – used to indicate a specific difference or margin (e g *within* a mile of the town) **3** to the inside of; into

³**within** *n* an inner place or area

¹**without** /wi'dhowt/ *prep* **1** – used to indicate the absence or lack of or freedom from sthg **2** outside – now chiefly poetic

²**without** *adv* **1** with sthg lacking or absent **2** on or to the exterior; outside – now chiefly poetic

³**without** *conj, chiefly dial* unless

⁴**without** *n* an outer place or area

withstand /widh'stand/ *v* **withstood** /-'stood/ **1** to resist with determination; *esp* to stand up against successfully **2** to be proof against

witless /'witlis/ *adj* **1** lacking wit or understanding; foolish **2** crazy – ~**ly** *adv* – ~**ness** *n*

¹**witness** /'witnis/ *n* **1** sby who gives evidence, specif before a tribunal **2** sby asked to be present at a transaction so as to be able to testify to its having taken place **3** sby who personally sees or hears an event take place **4** public affirmation by word or example of usu religious faith or conviction

²**witness** *v* **1** to testify to **2** to act as legal witness of (e g by signing one's name) **3** to give proof of; betoken – often in the subjunctive **4** to observe personally or directly; see for oneself **5** to be the scene or time of

'**witness-,box** *n, chiefly Br* an enclosure in which a witness testifies in court

witticism /'witi,siz(ə)m/ *n* a witty and often ironic remark

witty /'witi/ *adj* **1** amusingly or ingeniously clever **2** having or showing wit **3** quick to see or express illuminating or amusing relationships or insights

wives /wievz/ *pl of* **wife**

¹**wizard** /'wizəd/ *n* **1** a man skilled in magic **2** one who is very clever or skilful, esp in a specified field – *infml*

²**wizard** *adj, chiefly Br* great, excellent – *infml*

woad /wohd/ *n* (a European plant of the mustard family formerly grown for) the blue dyestuff yielded by its leaves

¹**wobble** /'wobl/ *v* **wobbling** /'wobl·ing, 'wobling/ **1a** to proceed with an irregular swerving or staggering motion **b** to rock unsteadily from side to side **2** to waver, vacillate

²**wobble** *n* **1** an unequal rocking motion **2** an act or instance of vacillating or fluctuating – **wobbly** *adj*

¹**woe** /woh/ *interj* – used to express grief, regret, or distress

²**woe** *n* **1** great sorrow or suffering caused by misfortune, grief, etc **2** a calamity, affliction – usu pl

woebegone /'wohbi,gon/ *adj* expressive of great sorrow or misery

woeful *also* **woful** /'wohf(ə)l/ *adj* **1** feeling or expressing woe **2** inspiring woe; grievous – ~**ly** *adv*

woke /wohk/ *past of* **wake**

woken /'wohkən/ *past part of* **wake**

wold /wohld/ *n* an upland area of open country

¹**wolf** /woolf/ *n, pl* **wolves** /woolvz/ **1** (the fur of) any of various large predatory flesh-eating mammals that resemble the related dogs, prey on livestock, and usu hunt in packs **2** a fiercely rapacious person **3** a man who pursues women in an aggressive way – *infml* – ~**ish** *adj* – **keep the wolf from the door** to avoid or prevent starvation or want — **wolf in sheep's clothing** one who cloaks a hostile intention with a friendly manner

²**wolf** *v* to eat greedily; devour – often + *down*

'**wolf ,whistle** *n* a distinctive whistle sounded by a man to express sexual admiration for a woman

woman /'woomən/ *n, pl* **women** /'wimin/ **1a** an adult female human as distinguished from a man or child **b** a woman belonging to a particular category (e g by birth, residence, membership, or occupation) – usu in combination **2** womankind **3** distinctively feminine nature; womanliness **4** a personal maid, esp in former times – ~**ly** *adj*

'**womanhood** /-hood/ *n* **1a** the condition of being an adult female as distinguished from a child or male **b** the distinguishing character or qualities of a woman or of womankind **2** women, womankind

womanish /'woomanish/ *adj* unsuitable to a man or to a strong character of either sex; effeminate

woman-ize, -ise /'woomaniez/ *v* to spend much time with, or chase after women, esp for sex

,**woman'kind** /-'kiend/ *n sing or pl in constr* female human beings; women as a whole, esp as distinguished from men

womb /woohm/ *n* **1** the uterus **2** a place where sthg is generated

wombat /'wombat/ *n* any of several stocky Australian marsupial mammals resembling small bears

won /wun/ *past of* **win**

¹**wonder** /'wundə/ *n* **1a** a cause of astonishment or admiration; a marvel **b** a miracle **2** rapt attention or astonishment at sthg unexpected, strange, new to one's experience, etc

²**wonder** *adj* noted for outstanding success or achievement

³**wonder** *v* **1a** to be in a state of wonder; marvel *at* **b** to feel surprise **2** to feel curiosity or doubt; speculate – ~**ingly** *adv*

'wonderful /-f(ə)l/ *adj* **1** exciting wonder; astonishing **2** unusually good; admirable – **~ly** *adv infml*

'wonder,land /-,land/ *n* **1** a fairylike imaginary place **2** a place that excites admiration or wonder

'wonderment /-mənt/ *n* **1** astonishment, marvelling **2** a cause of or occasion for wonder **3** curiosity

wondrous /'wundrəs/ *adj* wonderful – *poetic*

wonky /'wongki/ *adj*, *Br* awry, crooked; *also* shaky, unsteady – *infml*

¹wont /wohnt/ *adj* **1** accustomed, used **2** inclined, apt *USE* + *to* and infm; *fml*

²wont *n* customary practice – *fml*

woo /wooh/ *v* to try to win the affection of and a commitment of marriage from (a woman); court – **~er** *n*

¹wood /wood/ *n* **1** a dense growth of trees, usu greater in extent than a copse and smaller than a forest – often pl with sing. meaning **2a** a hard fibrous plant tissue that makes up the greater part of the stems and branches of trees or shrubs beneath the bark **b** wood suitable or prepared for some use (e g burning or building) **3a** a golf club with a wooden head **b** a wooden cask **c** any of the large wooden bowls used in the sport of bowling — **not see the wood for the trees** to be unable to see broad outlines because of a mass of detail — **out of the wood** *Br* escaped from peril or difficulty

²wood *adj* **1** wooden **2** suitable for cutting, storing, or carrying wood

¹'wood,block /-,blok/ *n* a woodcut

²woodblock *adj*, *of a floor* made of parquet

'wood,cock /-,kok/ *n pl* **woodcocks**, *esp collectively* **woodcock** an Old World long-billed wading bird of wooded regions that is related to the sandpipers and shot as game

'wood,craft /-,krahft/ *n* **1** skill and practice in anything relating to woods or forests, esp in surviving, travelling, and hunting **2** skill in shaping or making things from wood

'wood,cut /-,kut/ *n* (a print taken from) a relief-printing surface consisting of a wooden block with a design cut esp in the direction of the grain

wooded /'woodid/ *adj* covered with growing trees

wooden /'wood(ə)n/ *adj* **1** made of consisting of or derived from wood **2** lacking ease or flexibility; awkwardly stiff

'woodland /-lənd/ *n* land covered with trees, scrub, etc – often pl with sing. meaning

'wood,louse /-,lows/ *n pl* **woodlice** /-,lies/ a small ground-living crustacean with a flattened elliptical body often capable of rolling into a ball in defence

'wood,pecker /-,pekə/ *n* any of numerous usu multicoloured birds with very hard bills used to drill holes in the bark or wood of trees to find insect food or to dig out nesting cavities

'wood,shed /-,shed/ *n* a shed for storing wood, esp firewood

woodsman /'woodzmən/ *n* one who lives in, frequents, or works in the woods

'wood,wind /-,wind/ *n* **1** any of a group of wind instruments (e g a clarinet, flute, or saxophone) that is characterized by a cylindrical or conical tube of wood or metal, usu with finger holes or keys, that produces notes by the vibration of a single or double reed or by the passing of air over a mouth hole **2** *sing or pl in constr* the woodwind section of a band or orchestra – often pl with sing. meaning

'wood,work /-,wuhk/ *n* **1** wooden interior fittings (e g mouldings or stairways) **2** the craft of constructing things from wood

'wood,worm /-,wuhm/ *n* an insect larva, esp that of the furniture beetle, that bores in dead wood; *also* an infestation of woodworm

woody /'woodi/ *adj* **1** overgrown with or having many woods **2a** of or containing (much) wood or wood fibres **b** *of a plant stem* tough and fibrous

¹woof /woohf/ *n* **1** the weft **2** a basic or essential element or material

²woof /woof/ *v or n* (to make) the low gruff sound characteristic of a dog

woofer /'woohfə/ *n* a loudspeaker that responds mainly to low frequencies

wool /wool/ *n* **1** the soft wavy coat of various hairy mammals, esp the sheep **2** a dense felted hairy covering, esp on a plant **3** a wiry or fibrous mass (e g of steel or glass) – usu in combination – **~len** *adj*

¹woolly, *NAm also* **wooly** /'wooli/ *adj* **1** (made) of or resembling wool; *also* bearing (sthg like) wool **2a** lacking in clearness or sharpness of outline **b** marked by mental vagueness or confusion **3** boisterously rough – chiefly in *wild and woolly* – **-liness** *n*

²woolly, **woolie**, *NAm also* **wooly** *n*, *chiefly Br* a woollen jumper or cardigan

'wool,sack /-,sak/ *n* the official seat of the Lord Chancellor in the House of Lords

woozy /'woohzi/ *adj* **1** mentally unclear or hazy **2** dizzy or slightly nauseous *USE* infml

¹word /wuhd/ *n* **1a** sthg that is said **b** *pl* talk, discourse **c** a short remark, statement, or conversation **2** a meaningful unit of spoken language that can stand alone as an utterance and is not divisible into similar units; *also* a written or printed representation of a spoken word that is usu set off by spaces on either side **3** an order, command **4** the expressed or manifested mind and will of God; *esp* the Gospel **5a** news, information **b** rumour **6** the act of speaking or of making verbal communication **7** a promise **8** *pl* a quarrelsome utterance or conversation **9** a verbal signal; a password **10** *the* most appropriate description – **~less** *adj* – **~lessly** *adv* – **~lessness** *n* — **from**

the word **go** from the beginning — **in a word** in short — **in so many words** in exactly those terms — **my word** — used to express surprise or astonishment — **of one's word** that can be relied on to keep a promise — used only after *man* or *woman*

²**word** v to express in words; phrase

word-for-'word adj, of a report or translation in or following the exact words; verbatim

wording /'wuhding/ n the act or manner of expressing in words

word-'perfect adj having memorized sthg perfectly

wordy /'wuhdi/ adj using or containing (too) many words – **wordily** adv – **wordiness** n

wore /waw/ past of **wear**

¹**work** /wuhk/ n **1a** sustained physical or mental effort to achieve a result **b** the activities that afford one's accustomed means of livelihood **c** a specific task, duty, function, or assignment **2a** (the result of) expenditure of energy by natural phenomena **b** the transference of energy that is produced by the motion of the point of application of a force and is measured by the product of the force and the distance moved along the line of action **3a** (the result of) a specified method of working – often in combination **b** sthg made from a specified material – often in combination **b** pl structures in engineering (e g docks, bridges, or embankments) or mining (e g shafts or tunnels) **5** pl but sing or pl in constr a place where industrial activity is carried out; a factory – often in combination **6** pl the working or moving parts of a mechanism **7** an artistic production or creation **8a** effective operation; an effect, result **b** activity, behaviour, or experience of the specified kind **9** pl **9a** everything possessed, available, or belonging – infml; + *the* **b** subjection to all possible abuse – infml; usu + *get* or *give* — **at work 1** engaged in working; busy — **2** engaged in one's regular occupation **2** at one's place of work — **in the works** in process of preparation, development, or completion — **one's work cut out** as much as one can do — **out of work** without regular employment; unemployed

²**work** adj **1** suitable for wear while working **2** used for work

³**work** /wuhk/ v **worked, wrought** /rawt/ **1** to bring to pass; effect **2a** to fashion or create sthg by expending labour on; forge, shape **b** to make or decorate with needlework; embroider **3** to prepare or form into a desired state for use by kneading, hammering, etc **4** to operate **5** to solve (a problem) by reasoning or calculation – usu + *out* **6** to carry on an operation in (a place or area) **7a** to manoeuvre (oneself or an object) gradually or with difficulty into or out of a specified condition or position **b** to contrive, arrange — **work on** to strive to influence

or persuade; affect — **work to rule** to obey the rules of one's work precisely and so reduce efficiency, esp as a form of industrial action

workable /'wuhkəbl/ adj **1** capable of being worked **2** practicable, feasible – ~**ness** n

workaday /'wuhkəday/ adj **1** of or suited for working days **2** prosaic, ordinary

'**work,basket** /-,bahskit/ n a basket for needlework implements and materials

'**work,bench** /-,bench/ n a bench on which work, esp of mechanics or carpenters, is performed

'**work,book** /-,book/ n an exercise book of problems to be solved directly on the pages

,**worked 'up** adj emotionally aroused; excited

worker /'wuhkə/ n **1a** one who works, esp at manual or industrial work or with a particular material – often in combination **b** a member of the working class **2** any of the sexually underdeveloped usu sterile members of a colony of ants, bees, etc that perform most of the labour and protective duties of the colony

workforce /'wuhk,faws/ n sing or pl in constr the workers engaged in a specific activity or potentially available

'**work,house** /-,hows/ n Br an institution formerly maintained at public expense to house paupers

'**work-,in** n a continuous occupation of a place of employment by employees continuing to work normally as a protest, usu against the threat of factory closure

work in v **1** to cause to penetrate by persistent effort **2** to insinuate unobtrusively; also to find room for

¹**working** /'wuhking/ adj **1a** that functions or performs labour **b** of a domestic animal trained or bred for useful work **2** adequate to permit effective work to be done **3** serving as a basis for further work **4** during which one works; also during which one discusses business or policy

²**working** n **1** (a part of) a mine, quarry, or similar excavation **2** the fact or manner of functioning or operating – usu pl with sing. meaning

,**working 'class** n sing or pl in constr the class of people who work (manually) for wages – often pl with sing. meaning

,**working ,party** n, chiefly Br a committee set up (e g by a government) to investigate and report on a particular problem

'**workman** /-mən/, fem '**work,woman** n an artisan

'**workman,like** /-,liek/ also **workmanly** /-li/ adj worthy of a good workman: **a** skilful **b** efficient in appearance

'**workman,ship** /-,ship/ n the relative art or skill of a workman; craftsmanship; also the quality or finish exhibited by a thing

work off v to dispose of or get rid of by work or activity '**work-out** /-,owt/ *n* a practice or exercise to test or improve fitness, ability, or performance, esp for sporting competition

work out *v* **1a** to find out by calculation **b** to amount to a total or calculated figure – often + *at* or *to* **2** to devise by resolving difficulties **3** to elaborate in detail

work over *v* **1** to subject to thorough examination, study, or treatment **2** to beat up thoroughly; manhandle – *infml*

works /wuhks/ *adj* of a place of industrial labour

'**work-shop** /-,shop/ *n* **1** a room or place (e g in a factory) in which manufacture or repair work is carried out **2** a brief intensive educational programme for a relatively small group of people in a given field that emphasizes participation

'**work-shy** /-,shie/ *adj* disliking work; lazy

'**work-top** /-,top/ *n* a flat surface (e g of Formica) on a piece of esp kitchen furniture (e g a cupboard or dresser) suitable for working on

,**work-to-'rule** *n* an instance of industrial action designed to reduce output by deliberately keeping very rigidly to rules and regulations

'**world** /wuhld/ *n* **1** the earth with its inhabitants and all things on it **2** the course of human affairs **3** the human race **4** the concerns of earthly existence or secular affairs as distinguished from heaven and the life to come or religious and ecclesiastical matters **5** the system of created things; the universe **6** a distinctive class of people or their sphere of interest **7a** human society as a whole; *also* the public **b** fashionable or respectable people; public opinion **8** a part or section of the earth that is a separate independent unit **9a** one's personal environment in the sphere of one's life or work **b** a particular aspect of one's life **10** an indefinite multitude or a great quantity or amount **11** a planet; *esp* one that is inhabited *USE (except* 10 & 11) + *the* — **best of both worlds** the benefit of the advantages of 2 alternatives, esp without their disadvantages — **for all the world** in every way; exactly — **for the world** in any circumstances; for anything — **in the world** among innumerable possibilities; ever — **out of this world** of extraordinary excellence; superb

²**world** *adj* **1** of the whole world **2** extending or found throughout the world; worldwide

worldly /'wuhldli/ *adj* of or devoted to this world and its pursuits rather than to religion or spiritual affairs – **-liness** *n*

,**worldly-'wise** *adj* possessing a practical and often shrewd and materialistic understanding of human affairs; sophisticated

,**world 'war** *n* a war engaged in by (most of) the principal nations of the world; *esp, cap both W*s either of 2 such wars of the first half of the 20th c

,**world-'weary** *adj* bored with the life of the world and its material pleasures – **-riness** *n*

,**world'wide** /-'wied/ *adj* extended throughout or involving the entire world

'**worm** /wuhm/ *n* **1a** an earthworm **b** any of numerous relatively small elongated soft-bodied invertebrate animals **2** a human being who is an object of contempt, loathing, or pity; a wretch **3** infestation with or disease caused by parasitic worms – usu pl with sing. meaning but sing. or pl in constr **4** the thread of a screw

²**worm** *v* **1a** to cause to move or proceed (as if) in the manner of a worm **b** to insinuate or introduce (oneself) by devious or subtle means **2** to obtain or extract by artful or insidious questioning or by pleading, asking, or persuading – usu + *out of*

'**worm-,eaten** *adj* **1** eaten or burrowed into (as if) by worms **2** worn-out, antiquated

worn /wawn/ *past part of* **wear**

,**worn-'out** *adj* exhausted or used up (as if) by wear

worrisome /'wuris(ə)m/ *adj* **1** causing distress or worry **2** inclined to worry or fret

'**worry** /'wuri/ *v* **1** to shake or pull at with the teeth **2** to work at sthg difficult **3a** to feel or experience concern or anxiety; fret **b** to subject to persistent or nagging attention or effort **4** to afflict with mental distress or agitation; make anxious – **~ingly** *adv* — **not to worry** *Br* do not worry; do not feel anxious, dispirited, or troubled – *infml*

²**worry** *n* **1** mental distress or agitation resulting from concern, usu for sthg impending or anticipated; anxiety **2** a cause of worry; a trouble, difficulty – **-ried** *adj* – **-riedly** *adv*

'**worse** /wuhs/ *adj, comparative of* BAD *or* ILL **1** of lower quality **2** in poorer health — **the worse for** harmed by

²**worse** *n, pl* **worse** sthg worse

³**worse** *adv, comparative of* BAD, BADLY, *or* ILL in a worse manner; to a worse extent or degree

'**worship** /'wuhship/ *n* **1** (an act of) reverence offered to a divine being or supernatural power **2** a form of religious practice with its creed and ritual **3** extravagant admiration for or devotion to an object of esteem **4** *chiefly Br* a person of importance – used as a title for various officials (e g magistrates and some mayors)

²**worship** *v* **-pp-** (*NAm* **-p-, -pp-**) **1** to honour or reverence as a divine being or supernatural power **2** to regard with great, even extravagant respect, honour, or devotion – **~ per** *n*

'**worst** /wuhst/ *adj, superlative of* BAD *or* ILL **1** most productive of evil **2** most wanting in quality

²**worst** *n, pl* **worst 1** the worst state or part **2** sby or sthg that is worst **3** the utmost harm of which one is capable (e g do your *worst*) — **at worst, at the worst** under the worst circumstances; seen in the worst light — **if the worst comes to the worst** if the very worst thing happens

³**worst** *adv, superlative of* BAD, BADLY, *or* ILL in the worst manner; to the worst extent or degree

wre

⁴**worst** *v* to get the better of; defeat

worsted /'woostid/ *n* a smooth compact yarn from long wool fibres used esp for firm napless fabrics, carpeting, or knitting

¹**worth** /wuhth/ *prep* **1a** equal in value to **b** having property equal to (e g he's *worth* £1,000,000) **2** deserving of — **worth it** worthwhile

²**worth** *n* **1a** (money) value **b** the equivalent of a specified amount or figure (e g 3 quids*worth* of petrol) **2** moral or personal merit, esp high merit – ~**less** *adj* – ~**lessly** *adv* – ~**lessness** *n*

,**worth'while** /-'wiel/ *adj* worth the time or effort spent

¹**worthy** /'wuhdhi/ *adj* **1a** having moral worth or value **b** honourable, meritorious **2** important enough; deserving – **-thily** *adv* – **-thiness** *n*

²**worthy** *n* a worthy or prominent person – often humor

would /wad; *strong* wood/ *past of* WILL **1a** to desire, wish **b** – used in auxiliary function to express preference **2a** – used in auxiliary function to express wish, desire, or intent (e g those who *would* forbid gambling); used in the question form with the force of a polite request or of an offer or suggestion (e g *would* you like some tea?) **b** – used in auxiliary function in reported speech or writing to represent *shall* or *will* (e g said he *would* come) **3a** used to (e g we *would* meet often for lunch) – used with emphatic stress to express exasperation **b** – used in auxiliary function with emphatic stress as a comment on the annoyingly typical (e g you *would* say that) **4** – used in auxiliary function to introduce a contingent fact, possibility, or presumption (e g it *would* break if you dropped it) or after a verb expressing desire, request, or advice (e g wish he *would* go) **5** could (e g door *wouldn't* open) **6** – used in auxiliary function to soften direct statement (e g that *would* be the milkman)

,**would-be** *adj* desiring or intended to be

¹**wound** /woohnd/ *n* **1** an injury to the body or to a plant (e g from violence or accident) that involves tearing or breaking of a membrane (e g the skin) and usu damage to underlying tissues **2** a mental or emotional hurt or blow

²**wound** *v* to cause a wound to or in

³**wound** /wownd/ *past of* **wind**

wove /wohv/ *past of* **weave**

woven /'wohv(ə)n/ *past part of* **weave**

¹**wow** /wow/ *interj* – used to express strong feeling (e g pleasure or surprise); slang

²**wow** *n* a striking success; a hit – slang

³**wow** *v* to excite to enthusiastic admiration or approval – slang

⁴**wow** *n* a distortion in reproduced sound that is heard as a slow rise and fall in the pitch of the reproducing system

¹**wrack** /rak/ *n* **1** destruction **2** (a remnant of) sthg destroyed

²**wrack** *n* (dried) marine vegetation

wraith /rayth/ *n pl* **wraiths** /rayths; *also* raydhz/ an apparition of a living person in his/her exact likeness seen before or after death

¹**wrangle** /'rang·gl/ *v* **wrangling** /'rang·gling/ to dispute angrily or peevishly; bicker

²**wrangle** *n* an angry, noisy, or prolonged dispute or quarrel

wrangler /'rang·glə/ *n* **1** a bickering disputant **2** the holder of a Cambridge first in mathematics

¹**wrap** /rap/ *v* **-pp- 1a** to envelop, pack, or enfold in sthg flexible **b** to fold round sthg specified **2** to involve completely; engross – usu + *up*

²**wrap** *n* **1** a wrapping; *specif* a waterproof wrapping placed round food to be frozen, esp in a domestic freezer **2** an article of clothing that may be wrapped round a person; *esp* an outer garment (e g a shawl) — **under wraps** secret

wrapper /'rapə/ *n* that in which sthg is wrapped: e g **a a** fine quality tobacco leaf used for the covering of a cigar **b** a dust jacket on a book

wrapping /'raping/ *n* material used to wrap an object

wrap up *v* **1** to bring to a usu successful conclusion; end – infml **2** to protect oneself with outer garments

wrath /roth/ *n* **1** strong vengeful anger or indignation **2** retributory, esp divine, chastisement – ~**ful** *adj* – ~**fully** *adv*

wreak /reek/ *v* **1** to give free play to (malevolent feeling); inflict **2** to cause or create (havoc or destruction)

wreath /reeth/ *n pl* **wreaths** /reedhz/ **1** sthg intertwined into a circular shape; *esp* a garland **2** a drifting and coiling whorl

wreathe /reedh/ *v* **1** to cause (the face) to take on a happy joyful expression – usu pass **2a** to shape (e g flowers) into a wreath **b** to coil about sthg

¹**wreck** /rek/ *n* **1** sthg cast up on the land by the sea, esp after a shipwreck **2a** (a) shipwreck **b** destruction **3a** the broken remains of sthg (e g a building or vehicle) wrecked or ruined **b** a person or animal of broken constitution, health, or spirits

²**wreck** *v* **1** to cast ashore **2a** to reduce to a ruinous state by violence **b** to cause (a vessel) to be shipwrecked **c** to involve in disaster or ruin

wreckage /'rekij/ *n* **1** wrecking or being wrecked **2** broken and disordered parts or material from a wrecked structure

wrecker /'rekə/ *n* **1** sby who wrecks ships (e g by false lights) for plunder **2** sby whose work is the demolition of buildings

wren /ren/ *n* a very small European bird that has a short erect tail

Wren *n* a woman serving in the Women's Royal Naval Service

¹**wrench** /rench/ *v* **1** to pull or twist violently **2** to injure or disable by a violent twisting or straining **3** to distort, pervert **4** to snatch forcibly; wrest

²**wrench** *n* **1a** a violent twisting or a sideways pull **b** (a sharp twist or sudden jerk causing) a strain to a muscle, ligament, etc (e g of a joint) **2** a spanner with jaws adjustable for holding nuts of different sizes

wrest /rest/ *v* **1** to obtain or take away by violent wringing or twisting **2** to obtain with difficulty or force or determined labour

wrestle /'resl/ *v* **wrestling** /'resling, 'resl·ing/ **1** to fight hand-to-hand without hitting with the aim of throwing or immobilizing an opponent **2** to push, pull, or manhandle by force – **-tling** *n* ~ **r** *n*

wretch /rech/ *n* **1** a profoundly unhappy or unfortunate person **2** a base, despicable, or vile person or animal – ~ **ed** *adj* – ~ **edly** *adv* – ~ **edness** *n*

¹**wriggle** /'rigl/ *v* **wriggling** /'rigling, 'rigl·ing/ **1** to move the body or a bodily part to and fro with short writhing motions; squirm **2** to move or advance by twisting and turning **3** to extricate or insinuate oneself by manoeuvring, equivocation, evasion, etc

²**wriggle** *n* a short or quick writhing motion or contortion

wring /ring/ *v* **wrung** /rung/ **1** to twist or compress, esp so as to extract liquid **2** to exact or extort by coercion or with difficulty **3** to twist together (one's clasped hands) as a sign of anguish **4** to distress, torment **5** to shake (sby's hand) vigorously in greeting

wringer /'ring·ə/ *n* a mangle

¹**wrinkle** /'ringkl/ *n* **1** a small ridge, crease, or furrow formed esp in the skin due to aging or stress or on a previously smooth surface (e g by shrinkage or contraction) **2** a valuable trick or dodge for effecting a result – infml – **-kly** *adj*

²**wrinkle** *v* **wrinkling** /'ringkling, 'ringkl·ing/ to contract into wrinkles

wrist /rist/ *n* **1** (a part of a lower animal corresponding to) (the region of the) joint between the human hand and the arm **2** the part of a garment or glove covering the wrist

'**wrist band** /-,band/ *n* a band (e g on the sleeve of a garment) encircling the wrist

'**wrist watch** /-,woch/ *n* a small watch attached to a bracelet or strap and worn round the wrist

writ /rit/ *n* **1** an order in writing issued under seal in the name of the sovereign or of a court or judicial officer commanding or forbidding an act specified in it **2** a written order constituting a symbol of the power and authority of the issuer

write /riet/ *v* **wrote** /roht/; **written** /'ritn/ *also* **writ** /rit/ **1a** to form (legible characters, symbols, or words) on a surface, esp with an instrument **b** to

spell in writing **c** to cover, fill, or fill in by writing **2** to set down in writing: e g **2a** to be the author of; compose **b** to use (a specific script or language) in writing

'**write-off** *n* sthg written off as a total loss

write off *v* **1** to cancel **2** to concede to be irreparably lost, useless, or dead

writer /'rietə/ *n* one who writes as an occupation; an author

,**writer's 'cramp** *n* a painful spasmodic cramp of the hand or finger muscles brought on by excessive writing

'**write-up** *n* a written, esp flattering, account

write up *v* **1** to put into finished written form **2** to bring up to date the writing of (e g a diary)

writhe /riedh/ *v* **1** to proceed with twists and turns **2** to twist (as if) from pain or struggling **3** to suffer keenly

writing /'rieting/ *n* **1** the act, practice, or occupation of literary composition **2a** written letters or words; *esp* handwriting **b** a written composition — **writing on the wall** an omen of one's unpleasant fate

¹**wrong** /rong/ *n* **1** an injurious, unfair, or unjust act; action or conduct inflicting harm without due provocation or just cause **2** what is wrong, immoral, or unethical **3a** the state of being mistaken or incorrect **b** the state of being or appearing to be the offender

²**wrong** *adj* **1** against moral standards; evil **2** not right or proper according to a code, standard, or convention; improper **3** not according to truth or facts; incorrect; *also* in error; mistaken **4** not satisfactory (e g in condition, results, health, or temper) **5** not in accordance with one's needs, intent, or expectations **6** of or being the side of sthg not meant to be used or exposed or thought the less desirable – ~ **ly** *adv*

³**wrong** *adv* **1** without accuracy; incorrectly **2** without regard for what is proper **3** on a mistaken course; astray **4** out of proper working order

⁴**wrong** *v* **1** to do wrong to; injure, harm **2** to mistakenly impute a base motive to; misrepresent

'**wrongful** /-f(ə)l/ *adj* **1** wrong, unjust **2** unlawful – ~ **ly** *n*

wrong headed /-'hedid/ *adj* stubborn in adherence to wrong opinion or principles; perverse – ~ **ly** *adv* – ~ **ness** *n*

wrote /roht/ *past of* **write**

wrought /rawt/ *adj* **1** worked into shape by artistry or effort **2** processed for use; manufactured **3** *of metals* beaten into shape by tools **4** deeply stirred; excited – usu + *up*

wrought 'iron *n* a tough malleable iron containing very little carbon and 1 or 2 per cent slag

wrung /rung/ *past of* **wring**

wry /rie/ *adj* **1** bent or twisted, esp to one side **2** ironically or grimly humorous – ~ **ly** *adv*

X

x /eks/ *n, pl* **x's, xs** *often cap* **1** (a graphic representation of or device for reproducing) the 24th letter of the English alphabet **2** ten **3** sby or sthg whose identity is unknown or withheld

X *n or adj*, (a film that is) certified in Britain as suitable only for people over 18 – no longer used technically

xerox /'zeroks, 'ziəroks/ *v, often cap* to photocopy

Xerox *trademark* – used for a photocopying machine

Xmas /'eksməs/ *n* Christmas

x-ray /'eksray/ *v, often cap* x to examine, treat, or photograph with X rays

X ray /'eks ray/ *n* **1** an electromagnetic radiation of extremely short wavelength that has the properties of ionizing a gas when passing through it and of penetrating various thicknesses of all solids **2** an examination or photograph made by means of X rays

xylem /'zieləm, 'zielem/ *n* a complex vascular tissue of higher plants that functions chiefly in the conduction of water, gives support, and forms the woody part of many plants

xylophone /'zielə,fohn/ *n* a percussion instrument that has a series of wooden bars graduated in length and sounded by striking with 2 small wooden hammers

Y

y /wie/ *n, pl* **y's, ys** *often cap* (a graphic representation of or device for reproducing) the 25th letter of the English alphabet

¹yacht /yot/ *n* any of various relatively small sailing or powered vessels that are used for pleasure cruising or racing

²yacht *v* to race or cruise in a yacht

¹yak /yak/ *n pl* **yaks**, *esp collectively* **yak** a large long-haired wild or domesticated ox of Tibet and nearby mountainous regions

²yak, yack /yak/ *n* persistent or voluble talk – slang

³yak, yack *v* **-kk-** to talk persistently; chatter – slang

yam /yam/ *n* **1** (any of various related plants with) an edible starchy tuberous root used as a staple food in tropical areas **2** *NAm* a moist-fleshed usu orange sweet potato

yank /yangk/ *v* to pull or extract (sthg) with a quick vigorous movement – infml

Yankee /'yangki/ *n* a native or inhabitant of **a** *chiefly Br* the USA **b** *chiefly NAm* the N USA **c** *NAm* New England

¹yap /yap/ *v* **-pp-** **1** to bark snappishly; yelp **2** to talk in a shrill insistent querulous way; scold – infml

²yap *n* a quick sharp bark; a yelp **2** (foolish) chatter – infml

¹yard /yahd/ *n* **1a** a unit of length equal to 3ft (about 0.914m) **b** a unit of volume equal to 1yd³ (about 0.765m³) **2** a long spar tapered towards the ends to support and spread a sail

²yard *n* **1a** a small usu walled and often paved area open to the sky and adjacent to a building; a courtyard **b** the grounds of a specified building or group of buildings – in combination **2a** an area with its buildings and facilities set aside for a specified business or activity – often in combination **b** a system of tracks for the storage and maintenance of railway carriages and wagons and the making up of trains **3** *cap, Br* Scotland Yard – + *the* **4** *NAm* a garden of a house

³yard *v* to drive into or confine in a restricted area; herd, pen

yardarm /'yahd,ahm/ *n* either end of the yard of a square-rigged ship

'yard,stick /-,stik/ *n* a standard basis of calculation or judgment; a criterion

¹yarn /yahn/ *n* **1** thread; *esp* a spun thread (e g of wool, cotton, or hemp) as prepared and used for weaving, knitting, and rope-making **2a** a narrative of adventures; *esp* a tall tale **b** a conversation, chat *USE* (2) infml

²yarn *v* to tell a yarn; *also* to chat garrulously – infml

yarrow /'yaroh/ *n* a strong-scented Eurasian composite plant with dense heads of small usu white flowers

yashmak /'yashmak/ *also* **yasmak** /~, 'yas-/ *n* a veil worn over the face by Muslim women, so that only the eyes remain exposed

yaw /yaw/ *v* **1** to deviate erratically from a course **2** *of an aircraft, spacecraft, or projectile* to deviate from a straight course by esp side-to-side movement

yawl /yawl/ *n* a fore-and-aft rigged sailing vessel with 2 masts

¹yawn /yawn/ *v* **1** to open wide; gape **2** to open the mouth wide and inhale, usu in reaction to fatigue or boredom

yaw

---

²yawn n 1 a deep usu involuntary intake of breath through the wide open mouth 2 a boring thing or person – slang

¹ye /yee/ pron, archaic or dial the ones being addressed; you

²ye /dhee, yee/ definite article, archaic the

¹yea /yay/ adv 1 more than this; indeed 2 archaic yes

²yea n 1 affirmation, assent 2 chiefly NAm (a person casting) an affirmative vote

year /yiə/ n 1 the period of about 365¼ solar days required for 1 revolution of the earth round the sun 2a a cycle in the Gregorian calendar of 365 or 366 days divided into 12 months beginning with January and ending with December b a period of time equal to 1 year of the Gregorian calendar but beginning at a different time 3 a calendar year specified usu by a number 4 pl age; also old age — **year in, year out** for an indefinite or seemingly endless number of successive years

'year,book /-,book/ n a book published yearly as a report or summary of statistics or facts

yearling /'yiəling/ n sby or sthg 1 year old: e g a an animal 1 year old or in its second year b a racehorse between January 1st of the year following its birth and the next January 1st

yearly /'yiəli/ adj 1 reckoned by the year 2 done or occurring once every year; annual

yearn /yuhn/ v 1 to long persistently, wistfully, or sadly 2 to feel tenderness or compassion – ~**ing** n

yeast /yeest/ n 1 a (a commercial preparation of) yellowish surface froth or sediment that consists largely of fungal cells, occurs esp in sweet liquids in which it promotes alcoholic fermentation, and is used esp in making alcoholic drinks and as a leaven in baking 2 a minute fungus that is present and functionally active in yeast, usu has little or no mycelium, and reproduces by budding – -**y** adj

¹yell /yel/ v to utter a sharp loud cry, scream, or shout

²yell n a scream, shout

¹yellow /'yeloh/ adj 1a of the colour yellow b yellowish through age, disease, or discoloration; sallow 2a featuring sensational or scandalous items or ordinary news sensationally distorted b dishonourable, cowardly – infml

²yellow v to make or become yellow – ~**ish** adj

³yellow n 1 a colour whose hue resembles that of ripe lemons or dandelions and lies between green and orange in the spectrum 2 sthg yellow: esp the yolk of an egg

,yellow 'fever n an often fatal infectious disease of warm regions caused by a mosquito-transmitted virus

yelp /yelp/ v or n (to utter) a sharp quick shrill cry

¹yen /yen/ n pl **yen** the basic unit of currency of Japan

²yen n a strong desire or propensity; a longing – infml

yeoman /'yohmən/ n pl **yeomen** 1 a petty officer who carries out visual signalling in the British navy 2 a small farmer who cultivates his own land

'yeomanry /-ri/ n sing or pl in constr 1 the body of small landed proprietors 2 a British volunteer cavalry force created from yeomen in 1761 as a home defence force and reorganized in 1907 as part of the territorial force

¹yes /yes/ adv 1 – used in answers expressing affirmation, agreement, or willingness; contrasted with no 2 – used in answers correcting or contradicting a negative assertion or direction

²yes n an affirmative reply or vote; an aye

'yes-,man n one who endorses or supports everything said to him, esp by a superior; a sycophant – infml

¹yesterday /'yestəday, -di/ adv on the day before today

²yesterday n 1 the day before today 2 recent time; time not long past

¹yet /yet/ adv 1a again; in addition b – used to emphasize the comparative degree (e g a yet higher speed) 2a up to this or that time; so far – not in affirmative statements b still (e g while it was yet dark) c at some future time and despite present appearances (e g we may win yet) 3 nevertheless (e g strange and yet true) — **yet again** still 1 more time

²yet conj but nevertheless

yeti /'yeti/ n an abominable snowman

yew /yooh/ n (the wood of) any of a genus of evergreen coniferous trees and shrubs with stiff straight leaves and red fruits

Yiddish /'yidish/ n a High German language containing elements of Hebrew and Slavonic that is spoken by Jews chiefly in or from E Europe

¹yield /yeeld/ v 1 to give or render as fitting, rightfully owed, or required 2 to give up possession of on claim or demand: e g 2a to surrender or submit (oneself) to another b to give (oneself) up to an inclination, temptation, or habit 3a to bear or bring forth as a natural product b to give as a return or in result of expended effort c to produce as revenue 4 to give way under physical force (e g bending, stretching, or breaking) 5 to give place or precedence; acknowledge the superiority of another

²yield n the capacity of yielding produce; also the produce yielded

yielding /'yeelding/ adj lacking rigidity or stiffness; flexible

yobbo /'yoboh/ n, Br a rough idle youth; a slob

¹yodel /'yohdl/ v -ll- (NAm -l, -ll-), /'yohdling, ᵗyohdl·ing/ to sing, shout, or call (a tune) by suddenly changing from a natural voice to a falsetto and back

²yodel n a yodelled song, shout, or cry

yoga /'yohgǝ/ n 1 cap a Hindu philosophy teaching the suppression of all activity of body, mind, and will so that the self may attain liberation from them 2 a system of exercises for attaining bodily or mental control and well-being

yoghurt, yoghourts, yogurt /yogǝt/ n a slightly acid semisolid preparation of fermented milk eaten as a dessert or used in cooking

yogi /'yohgi/ n 1 sby who practises or is a master of yoga 2 cap an adherent of Yoga philosophy

¹**yoke** /yohk/ n 1a a bar or frame by which 2 draught animals (e g oxen) are joined at the heads or necks for working together b a frame fitted to sby's shoulders to carry a load in 2 equal portions 2 sing or pl in constr 2 animals yoked or worked together 3a an oppressive agency b a tie, link; esp marriage 4 a fitted or shaped piece at the top of a garment from which the rest hangs

²**yoke** v 1 to attach (a draught animal) to (sthg) 2 to join (as if) by a yoke

yokel /'yohkl/ n a naive or gullible rustic; a country bumpkin

yolk also **yoke** /yohk/ n the usu yellow round mass of stored food that forms the inner portion of the egg of a bird or reptile

yonder /'yondǝ/ adj or adv over there

yore /yaw/ n time (long) past – usu in of yore

yorker /'yawkǝ/ n a ball bowled in cricket that is aimed to bounce on the popping crease and so pass under the bat

Yorkshire 'pudding n a savoury baked pudding made from a batter

you /yoo; strong yooh/ pron, pl you 1 the one being addressed – used as subject or object 2 a person; one — you get there is or are

¹**young** /yung/ adj younger /'yung·gǝ/; youngest /'yung·gist/ 1 in the first or an early stage of life, growth, or development 2 recently come into being; new 3 of or having the characteristics (e g vigour or gaiety) of young people – ~ish adj

²**young** n pl 1 young people; youth 2 immature offspring, esp of an animal — with young of a female animal pregnant

youngster /'yungstǝ/ n 1 a young person or creature 2 a young child, baby

your /yǝ; strong yaw/ adj 1 of you or yourself or yourselves, esp as possessor, agent or object of an action –used with certain titles in the vocative (e g your Eminence) 2 of one or oneself (e g when you face north, east is on your right) 3 – used for indicating sthg well-known and characteristic; infml (e g your typical commuter) USE used attributively

yours /yawz/ pron, pl yours that which or the one who belongs to you – used without a following noun as a pronoun equivalent in meaning to the adjective your

yourself /yǝ'self, yaw'self/ pron, pl yourselves /-'selvz/ 1a that identical person or creature that is you – used reflexively, for emphasis, or in absolute constructions (e g yourself a man of learning, you will know what I mean) b your normal self (e g you'll soon be yourself again) 2 oneself

youth /yoohth/ n pl youths /yoohdhz/ 1 the time of life when one is young; esp adolescence 2a a young male adolescent b young people – often pl in constr 3 the quality of being youthful – ~ful adj – ~fully adv – ~fulness n

'youth ,hostel n a lodging typically providing inexpensive bed and breakfast accommodation for esp young travellers or hikers

yowl /yowl/ v or n (to utter) the loud long wail of a cat or dog in pain or distress

yo-yo /'yoh ,yoh/ n,pl yo-yos a toy that consists of 2 discs separated by a deep groove in which a string is attached and wound and that is made to fall and rise when held by the string

Z

z /zed/ n, pl z's, zs often cap (a graphic representation of or device for reproducing) the 26th letter of the English alphabet

¹**zany** /'zayni/ n one who acts the buffoon to amuse others

²**zany** adj fantastically or absurdly ludicrous – zanily adv – zaniness n

zeal /zeel/ n eagerness and ardent interest in pursuit of sthg; keenness

zealot /'zelǝt/ n a zealous person; esp a fanatical partisan

zealous /'zelǝs/ adj filled with or characterized by zeal – ~ly adv – ~ness n

zebra /'zebrǝ, 'zeebrǝ/ n pl zebras, esp collectively zebra any of several black and white striped fast-running African mammals related to the horse

,zebra 'crossing n a crossing in Britain marked by a series of broad white stripes to indicate that pedestrians have the right of way across a road

zed /zed/ n, chiefly Br the letter z

Zen /zen/ n a Japanese sect of Buddhism that aims at enlightenment by direct intuition through meditation (e g on paradoxes)

zenith /'zenith/ n 1 the point of the celestial sphere that is directly opposite the nadir and vertically above the observer 2 the highest point reached in the heavens by a celestial body 3 the culminating point or stage

zephyr /'zefə/ n a gentle breeze, esp from the west

zeppelin /'zep(ə)lin/ n, often cap a large rigid cigar-shaped airship of a type built in Germany in the early 20th c; broadly an airship

¹**zero** /'ziəroh/ n, pl **zeros** also **zeroes** 1 the arithmetical symbol 0 or ∅ denoting the absence of all magnitude or quantity 2 the number 0 3 the point of departure in reckoning; specif the point from which the graduation of a scale begins 4a nothing b the lowest point

²**zero** adj having no magnitude or quantity

³**zero** v to move near to or focus attention as if on a target; close – usu + in on

'**zero** ,**hour** n the time at which an event is scheduled to take place

zest /zest/ n 1 the outer peel of a citrus fruit used as flavouring 2 piquancy, spice 3 keen enjoyment; gusto – ~**ful**, ~**y** adj

¹**zigzag** /'zig,zag/ n a line, course, or pattern consisting of a series of sharp alternate turns or angles

²**zigzag** adj forming or going in a zigzag; consisting of zigzags

³**zigzag** v -**gg**- to proceed along or consist of a zigzag course

zinc /zingk/ n a bluish white metallic element that is used esp as a protective coating for iron and steel

Zionism /'zie·ə,niz(ə)m/ n a movement for setting up a Jewish homeland in Palestine – **-ist** adj, n

¹**zip** /zip/ v -**pp**- 1 to move with speed and vigour 2 to become open, closed, or attached by means of a zip 3 to travel (as if) with a sharp hissing or humming sound 4 to add zest or life to – often + up

²**zip** n 1 a light sharp hissing sound 2 energy, liveliness 3 chiefly Br a fastener that joins 2 edges of fabric by means of 2 flexible spirals or rows of teeth brought together by a sliding clip

zither /'zidhə/ n a stringed instrument having usu 30 to 40 strings over a shallow horizontal soundboard

zodiac /'zohdiak/ n an imaginary belt in the heavens that is divided into 12 constellations or signs each taken for astrological purposes to extend 30 degrees of longitude – ~ **al** adj

zombie, NAm also **zombi** /'zombi/ n 1 a human in W Indies voodooism who is held to have died and have been reanimated 2 a person resembling the walking dead; a shambling automaton

¹**zone** /zohn/ n 1 any of 5 great divisions of the earth's surface with respect to latitude and temperature 2 a distinctive layer of rock or other earth materials 3 an area distinct from adjoining parts 4 any of the sections into which an area is divided for a particular purpose – **-nal** adj

²**zone** v 1 to arrange in, mark off, or partition into zones 2 to assign to a zone

zoo /zooh/ n, pl **zoos** a collection of living animals usu open to the public

zoology /zooh'oləji, zoh-/ n (biology that deals with) animals and animal life, usu excluding human beings – **-gical** adj – **-gist** n

¹**zoom** /zoohm/ v 1 to move with a loud low hum or buzz 2 to rise sharply

²**zoom** n 1 an act or process of zooming 2 a photographic lens that can be used to move quickly from a distant shot into close-up

Zulu /'zoohlooh/ n 1 a member of a Bantu-speaking people of Natal 2 a Bantu language of the Zulus

zygote /'ziegoht, 'zigoht/ n (the developing individual produced from) a cell formed by the union of 2 gametes

Common Abbreviations

A

a 1 acceleration 2 acre 3 answer 4 are – a metric unit of area 5 area

A 1 ampere 2 Associate

AA 1 Alcoholics Anonymous 2 antiaircraft 3 Automobile Association

AAA 1 Amateur Athletic Association 2 American Automobile Association

A and M ancient and modern – used of hymns

AB 1 able seaman; able-bodied seaman 2 *NAm* bachelor of arts

ABA Amateur Boxing Association

ABC 1 American Broadcasting Company 2 Australian Broadcasting Commission

ABM antiballistic missile

AC 1 alternating current 2 appellation contrôlée 3 athletic club

a/c account

ACA Associate of the Institute of Chartered Accountants

ACAS Advisory Conciliation and Arbitration Service

acc 1 according to 2 account 3 accusative

ACV air-cushion vehicle

ACW aircraftwoman

ADAS Agricultural Development and Advisory Service

ADC 1 aide-de-camp 2 amateur dramatic club

ad inf ad infinitum

adj 1 adjective 2 adjustment – used in banking 3 adjutant

Adm admiral

adv 1 adverb; adverbial 2 against

AEA Atomic Energy Authority

AERE Atomic Energy Research Establishment

aet, aetat of the specified age; aged

AEU Amalgamated Engineering Union – now AUEW

AEW airborne early warning

AF 1 Anglo-French 2 audio frequency

AFM Air Force Medal

Afr Africa; African

AG 1 adjutant general 2 attorney general 3 joint-stock company

AGM *chiefly Br* annual general meeting

AGR advanced gas-cooled reactor

AI artificial insemination

AIA Associate of the Institute of Actuaries

AIB Associate of the Institute of Bankers

AID 1 Agency for International Development – a US agency 2 artificial insemination by donor

AIH artificial insemination by husband

AKA also known as

ALA Associate of the Library Association

ald alderman

alt 1 alternate 2 altitude 3 alto

AM 1 Albert Medal 2 amplitude modulation 3 associate member 4 *NAm* master of arts

AMDG to the greater glory of God

anon anonymous

aob any other business

AOC Air Officer Commanding

AP Associated Press

APEX Association of Professional, Executive, Clerical, and Computer Staff

app 1 apparent; apparently 2 appendix 3 appointed

Apr April

APT Advanced Passenger Train

ARA Associate of the Royal Academy

ARAM Associate of the Royal Academy of Music

ARC Agricultural Research Council

ARCA Associate of the Royal College of Art

ARCM Associate of the Royal College of Music

ARCS Associate of the Royal College of Science

ARIBA Associate of the Royal Institute of British Architects

ARP air-raid precautions

arr 1 arranged by – used in music 2 arrival; arrives

art 1 article 2 artificial 3 artillery

AS 1 airspeed 2 Anglo-Saxon 3 antisubmarine

asap as soon as possible

ASLEF Associated Society of Locomotive Engineers and Firemen

assoc association

ASSR Autonomous Soviet Socialist Republic

ASTMS Association of Scientific, Technical, and Managerial Staffs
ATC 1 air traffic control 2 Air Training Corps
attn for the attention of
ATV Associated Television
AUEW Amalgamated Union of Engineering Workers
Aug August
AUT Association of University Teachers
av 1 average 2 avoirdupois
AV 1 ad valorem 2 audiovisual 3 Authorized Version (of the Bible)
avdp avoirdupois
AVM Air Vice Marshal

B

b 1 born 2 bowled by – used in cricket 3 breadth 4 bye – used in cricket
B 1 bachelor 2 bishop – used in chess 3 black – used esp on lead pencils
BA 1 Bachelor of Arts 2 British Academy 3 British Airways 4 British Association
BAOR British Army of the Rhine
Bart baronet
BB 1 Boys' Brigade 2 double black – used on lead pencils
BBBC British Boxing Board of Control
BBC British Broadcasting Corporation
BC 1 before Christ 2 British Columbia 3 British Council
BCh Bachelor of Surgery
BCom Bachelor of Commerce
BD 1 Bachelor of Divinity 2 bank draft 3 barrels per day
BDA British Dental Association
BDS Bachelor of Dental Surgery
BEA British European Airways – now BA
BEd Bachelor of Education
Beds Bedfordshire
BEF British Expeditionary Force
BEM British Empire Medal
BEng Bachelor of Engineering
Berks Berkshire
BeV billion electron volts
BFPO British Forces Post Office
BL 1 Bachelor of Law 2 bill of lading 3 British Legion 4 British Leyland 5 British Library
BLitt Bachelor of Letters
BM 1 Bachelor of Medicine 2 bench mark 3 British Medal 4 British Museum
BMA British Medical Association
BMC British Medical Council
BMJ British Medical Journal
BMus Bachelor of Music
BOAC British Overseas Airways Corporation – now BA

BOC British Oxygen Company
BOSS Bureau of State Security – a SAfr organization
BOT Board of Trade
BOTB British Overseas Trade Board
BP 1 boiling point 2 British Petroleum 3 British Pharmacopoeia
BPC British Pharmaceutical Codex
BPhil Bachelor of Philosophy
BR British Rail
Brig brigade; brigadier
Brig-Gen brigadier-general
Brit Britain; British
bros, Bros brothers
BRS British Road Services
BS 1 Bachelor of Surgery 2 balance sheet 3 bill of sale 4 British Standard 5 *NAm* Bachelor of Science
BSA Building Societies Association
BSc Bachelor of Science
BSC 1 British Steel Corporation 2 British Sugar Corporation
BSI 1 British Standards Institution 2 Building Societies Institute
BST British Standard Time; British Summer Time
Bt Baronet
BTh Bachelor of Theology
Btu British thermal unit
Bucks Buckinghamshire
BUPA British United Provident Association

C

c 1 canine – used in dentistry 2 carat 3 caught by – used in cricket 4 centi- 5 century 6 chapter 7 circa 8 cloudy 9 cold 10 college 11 colt 12 copyright 13 cubic
C 1 calorie 2 castle – used in chess 3 Catholic 4 Celsius 5 centigrade 6 *Br* Conservative 7 corps
ca circa
CA 1 California 2 chartered accountant 3 chief accountant 4 Consumers' Association 5 current account
CAA Civil Aviation Authority
CAB Citizens' Advice Bureau
cal 1 calibre 2 (small) calorie
Cal 1 California 2 (large) calorie
Cambs Cambridgeshire
Can Canada; Canadian
C and G City and Guilds
C and W country and western
Cantab of Cambridge – used with academic awards <MA ~ >
Cantuar of Canterbury – used chiefly in the signature of the Archbishop of Canterbury
caps 1 capital letters 2 capsule
Capt captain

Card cardinal
CAT 1 College of Advanced Technology **2** computerized axial tomography
CB 1 Citizens' Band **2** Companion of the (Order of the) Bath
CBC Canadian Broadcasting Corporation
CBE Commander of the (Order of the) British Empire
CBI Confederation of British Industry
CBS Columbia Broadcasting System
cc 1 carbon copy **2** chapters **3** cubic centimetre
CC 1 Chamber of Commerce **2** County Council **3** Cricket Club
CD 1 civil defence **2** diplomatic corps
Cdr Commander
Cdre Commander
CE 1 Church of England **2** civil engineer **3** Council of Europe
CEGB Central Electricity Generating Board
CENTO Central Treaty Organization
cf compare
CFE College of Further Education
ch 1 chain – a unit of length **2** central heating **3** chapter **4** check – used in chess **5** child; children **6** church
CH 1 clubhouse **2** Companion of Honour
chap 1 chaplain **2** chapter
ChB Bachelor of Surgery
Ches Cheshire
ChM Master of Surgery
CI Channel Islands
CIA Central Intelligence Agency
CID Criminal Investigation Department
C in C Commander in Chief
cl 1 centilitre **2** clerk
Cllr *Br* councillor
Clo close – used in street names
cm centimetre
Cmdr Commander
Cmdre Commodore
CMG Companion of (the Order of) St Michael and St George
CND Campaign for Nuclear Disarmament
CO 1 commanding officer **2** Commonwealth Office **3** conscientious objector
c/o 1 care of **2** carried over
COD 1 cash on delivery **2** Concise Oxford Dictionary
C of E 1 Church of England **2** Council of Europe
C of S Church of Scotland
COHSE Confederation of Health Service Employees
COI Central Office of Information
col 1 colour; coloured **2** column
Col 1 Colonel **2** Colorado
coll 1 college **2** colloquial

Com, Comm 1 Commander **2** Commodore **3** Commonwealth **4** Communist
Comdr Commander
Comdt Commandant
Con, Cons Conservative
cont 1 containing **2** contents **3** continent; continental **4** continued
contd continued
Corp 1 Corporal **2** corporation
CP 1 Communist Party **2** Country Party – an Australian political party
Cpl Corporal
CPR Canadian Pacific Railway
CPRE Council for the Preservation of Rural England
cresc, cres 1 crescendo **2** *often cap* crescent – used esp in street names
CRO 1 cathode ray oscilloscope **2** Criminal Records Office
CRT cathode-ray tube
CS 1 chartered surveyor **2** Civil Service **3** Court of Session – the supreme civil court of Scotland
CSE Certificate of Secondary Education
CSM Company Sergeant Major
CSO 1 Central Statistical Office **2** Community Service Order
cu cubic
Cumb Cumbria
CV curriculum vitae
CVO Commander of the (Royal) Victorian Order
CWS Cooperative Wholesale Society
cwt hundredweight

D

d 1 date **2** daughter **3** day **4** deca- **5** deci- **6** delete **7** penny; pence – used before introduction of decimal currency **8** density **9** departs **10** diameter **11** died **12** dose **13** drizzle
DA 1 deposit account **2** *NAm* district attorney
D & C dilatation and curettage
dB decibel
DBE Dame Commander of the (Order of the) British Empire
DC 1 from the beginning **2** Detective Constable **3** direct current **4** District of Columbia **5** District Commissioner
DCB Dame Commander of the (Order of the) Bath
DCh Doctor of Surgery
DCL 1 Distillers Company Limited **2** Doctor of Civil Law
DCM Distinguished Conduct Medal
DCMG Dame Commander of (the Order of) St Michael and St George

DCVO Dame Commander of the (Royal) Victorian Order
DD 1 direct debit **2** Doctor of Divinity
DDS Doctor of Dental Surgery
DE 1 Delaware **2** Department of Employment
dec 1 deceased **2** declared – used esp in cricket **3** declension **4** declination **5** decrease **6** decrescendo
Dec December
dep 1 departs; departure **2** deposed **3** deposit **4** depot **5** deputy
dept department
DES Department of Education and Science
det detached; detachment
Det Detective
DF Defender of the Faith
DFC Distinguished Flying Cross
DFM Distinguished Flying Medal
DG 1 by the grace of God **2** director general
DHSS Department of Health and Social Security
DI Detective Inspector
Dip Diploma
Dip Ed Diploma in Education
Dip HE Diploma in Higher Education
div 1 divergence **2** divide; divided **3** dividend **4** division **5** divorced
DIY do-it-yourself
DLitt Doctor of Letters
DM Doctor of Medicine
DMus Doctor of Music
do ditto
DOA dead on arrival – used chiefly in hospitals
DOE Department of the Environment
DoT Department of Trade
doz dozen
DP 1 data processing **2** displaced person
dpc damp proof course
DPhil Doctor of Philosophy
DPP Director of Public Prosecutions
dr 1 debtor **2** drachm **3** dram **4** drawer
Dr 1 doctor **2** Drive – used in street names
DS 1 from the sign **2** Detective Sergeant
DSc Doctor of Science
DSC Distinguished Service Cross
DSM Distinguished Service Medal
DSO Distinguished Service Order
dsp 1 died without issue **2** dessertspoon; dessertspoonful
DST daylight saving time
DTh, DTheol Doctor of Theology
DVLC Driver and Vehicle Licensing Centre
dz dozen

E

E 1 Earl **2** earth – used esp on electrical plugs **3** East; Easterly; Eastern **4** energy **5** English

E and OE errors and omissions excepted
ECG electrocardiogram; electrocardiograph
ECT electroconvulsive therapy
ed, edit edited; edition; editor
EDP electronic data processing
EEC European Economic Community
EEG electroencephalogram; electroencephalograph
EFL English as a foreign language
EFTA European Free Trade Association
eg for example
EHF extremely high frequency
EHT extremely high tension
ELF extremely low frequency
ELT English language teaching
EMI Electrical and Musical Industries
Emp Emperor; Empress
ENE east-northeast
ENEA European Nuclear Energy Agency
Eng England; English
ENSA Entertainments National Service Association
ENT ear, nose, and throat
EO Executive Officer
EOC Equal Opportunities Commission
ep en passant
EPNS electroplated nickel silver
eq equal
equiv equivalent
ER 1 Eastern Region **2** King Edward **3** Queen Elizabeth
ESA European Space Agency
ESE east-southeast
ESL English as a second language
ESN educationally subnormal
Esq *also* **Esqr** esquire
est 1 established **2** estate **3** estimate; estimated
EST 1 Eastern Standard Time **2** electro-shock treatment
ETA estimated time of arrival
ETD estimated time of departure
et seq 1 and the following one **2** and the following ones
ETU Electrical Trades Union
EVA extravehicular activity
ex 1 examined **2** example **3** except **4** exchange

F

f 1 fathom **2** female **3** femto- **4** force **5** forte **6** frequency **7** focal length **8** folio **9** following (e g page) **10** foot
F 1 Fahrenheit **2** false **3** farad **4** Fellow **5** filial generation **6** fine – used esp on lead pencils **7** forward **8** French
FA Football Association

Fahr Fahrenheit
F and F fixtures and fittings
FBI Federal Bureau of Investigation
FBR fast breeder reactor
FC 1 Football Club **2** Forestry Commission
FCA Fellow of the (Institute of) Chartered Accountants
FCII Fellow of the Chartered Insurance Institute
FCIS Fellow of the Chartered Institute of Secretaries
FCO Foreign and Commonwealth Office
FCS Fellow of the Chemical Society
FD Defender of the Faith
Feb February
ff 1 folios **2** following (e g pages) **3** fortissimo
FIFA International Football Federation
fig 1 figurative; figuratively **2** figure
fl 1 floor **2** flourished – used to indicate a period of renown of sby whose dates of birth and death are unknown **3** fluid
FL 1 Florida **2** focal length
fl oz fluid ounce
Flt Lt Flight Lieutenant
Flt Off Flight Officer
Flt Sgt Flight Sergeant
fm fathom
FM Field Marshal
fo, fol folio
FO 1 Field Officer **2** Flying Officer **3** Foreign Office
FOC Father of the Chapel (in a Trade Union)
FOE Friends of the Earth
Fr 1 Father **2** French **3** Friar
FRCM Fellow of the Royal College of Music
FRCOG Fellow of the Royal College of Obstetricians and Gynaecologists
FRCP Fellow of the Royal College of Physicians
FRCS Fellow of the Royal College of Surgeons
FRCVS Fellow of the Royal College of Veterinary Surgeons
Fri Friday
FRIBA Fellow of the Royal Institute of British Architects
FRIC Fellow of the Royal Institute of Chemistry
FRICS Fellow of the Royal Institution of Chartered Surveyors
FRS Fellow of the Royal Society
FSA Fellow of the Society of Actuaries
ft 1 feet; foot **2** fort
FT Financial Times
FWD 1 four-wheel drive **2** front-wheel drive

G

g 1 gauge **2** giga- **3** good **4** gram
G acceleration due to gravity
GB Great Britain
GBE Knight/Dame Grand Cross of the (Order of the) British Empire
GBH *Br* grievous bodily harm
GC George Cross
GCB Knight/Dame Grand Cross of the (Order of the) Bath
GCE General Certificate of Education
GCHQ Government Communications Headquarters
GCMG Knight/Dame Grand Cross of (the Order of) St Michael and St George
GCVO Knight/Dame Grand Cross of the (Royal) Victorian Order
Gdns Gardens – used esp in street names
GDP gross domestic product
GDR German Democratic Republic
GHQ general headquarters
gi gill
Gib Gibraltar
Glam Glamorgan
GLC Greater London Council
Glos Gloucestershire
gm gram
GM 1 general manager **2** George Medal **3** guided missile
GMC 1 General Medical Council **2** general management committee
GMT Greenwich Mean Time
GMWU General and Municipal Workers Union
GNP gross national product
GOC General Officer Commanding
gov 1 government **2** governor
govt government
GP 1 general practitioner **2** Grand Prix
Gp Capt Group Captain
GPI general paralysis of the insane
GPO general post office
GQ general quarters
gr 1 grade **2** grain **3** gram **4** gravity **5** gross
GR King George
gro gross
Gro Grove – used in street names
gt great
GT grand tourer

H

h 1 hect-; hecto **2** height **3** high **4** hot **5** hour **6** husband
H 1 harbour **2** hard – used esp on lead pencils **3** hardness
ha hectare
h and c hot and cold (water)
Hants Hampshire

HB hard black – used on lead pencils
HBM His/Her Britannic Majesty
HCF highest common factor
HE 1 high explosive 2 His Eminence 3 His/Her Excellency
HEO Higher Executive Officer
Here, Heref Herefordshire
Herts Hertfordshire
HF high frequency
HG 1 His/Her Grace 2 Home Guard
HGV *Br* heavy goods vehicle
HH 1 double hard – used on lead pencils 2 His/Her Highness 3 His Holiness
HIH His/Her Imperial Highness
HIM His/Her Imperial Majesty
HM 1 headmaster 2 headmistress 3 His/Her Majesty
HMF His/Her Majesty's Forces
HMG His/Her Majesty's Government
HMI His/Her Majesty's Inspector (of Schools)
HMS His/Her Majesty's Ship
HMSO His/Her Majesty's Stationery Office
HMV His Master's Voice
HNC Higher National Certificate
HND Higher National Diploma
HO Home Office
Hon (the) Honourable
Hons *Br* honours
Hon Sec *Br* Honorary Secretary
HP 1 high pressure 2 hire purchase 3 horsepower 4 Houses of Parliament
HQ headquarters
HRH His/Her Royal Highness
HSO Higher Scientific Officer
HST high speed train
ht height
HT 1 high-tension 2 under this title
HV 1 high velocity 2 high-voltage
HW 1 high water 2 hot water
Hz hertz

I

I 1 inductance 2 island; isle
IAEA International Atomic Energy Agency
IAM Institute of Advanced Motorists
IATA International Air Transport Association
ib ibidem
IBA Independent Broadcasting Authority
ibid ibidem
IBM International Business Machines
IC integrated circuit
ICA Institute of Contemporary Arts
ICBM intercontinental ballistic missile
ICC International Cricket Conference
ICE 1 Institute of Civil Engineers 2 internal-combustion engine

ICI Imperial Chemical Industries
ICL International Computers Limited
id idem
ID 1 Idaho 2 (proof of) identification 3 inner diameter 4 intelligence department
IDA International Development Association
i e that is
IHS Jesus
ILEA Inner London Education Authority
ILO 1 International Labour Organization 2 International Labour Office
ILP Independent Labour Party
IMF International Monetary Fund
imp 1 Emperor; Empress 2 imperative 3 imperfect 4 imperial
in inch
inc 1 increase 2 *chiefly NAm* incorporated
incl included; including; inclusive
ind 1 independent 2 indicative 3 industrial; industry
INRI Jesus of Nazareth, King of the Jews
inst 1 instant 2 institute; institution
int 1 integral 2 interior 3 intermediate 4 internal 5 international 6 interpreter 7 intransitive
I/O input/output
IOC International Olympic Committee
IOM Isle of Man
IOW Isle of Wight
IPA International Phonetic Alphabet
IPC International Publishing Corporation
IPM 1 inches per minute 2 Institute of Personnel Management
IPS inches per second
IR 1 information retrieval 2 infrared 3 Inland Revenue
IRA Irish Republican Army
IRBM intermediate range ballistic missile
IRO 1 Inland Revenue Office 2 International Refugee Organization
ISBN International Standard Book Number
ISD international subscriber dialling
ISO 1 Imperial Service Order 2 International Standardization Organization
ita initial teaching alphabet
ITA Independent Television Authority – now IBA
ital italic; italicized
ITN Independent Television News
ITT International Telephone and Telegraph (Corporation)
ITU International Telecommunications Union
ITV Independent Television
IU international unit
IUD intrauterine device
IVR International Vehicle Registration
IWW Industrial Workers of the World

J

J 1 joule 2 Judge 3 Justice
Jan January
JC 1 Jesus Christ 2 Julius Caesar
JCD 1 Doctor of Canon Law 2 Doctor of Civil Law
JCR Junior Common Room
jnr junior
JP Justice of the Peace
Jr junior
Jul July
Jun June

K

k 1 carat 2 kilo- 3 kitchen 4 knot 5 kosher
K 1 kelvin 2 king – used in chess 3 knit
KB 1 King's Bench 2 Knight Bachelor
KBE Knight (Commander of the Order of the) British Empire
KC 1 Kennel Club 2 King's Counsel
KCB Knight Commander of the (Order of the) Bath
KCIE Knight Commander of the (Order of the) Indian Empire
KCMG Knight Commander of (the Order of) St Michael and St George
KCSI Knight Commander of the (Order of the) Star of India
KCVO Knight Commander of the (Royal) Victorian Order
kg 1 keg 2 kilogram
KG Knight of the (Order of the) Garter
KGB (Soviet) State Security Committee
kHz kilohertz
KKK Ku Klux Klan
kl kilolitre
km kilometre
kn knot
kph kilometres per hour
kt karat
KT 1 knight – used in chess 2 Knight Templar 3 Knight of the (Order of the) Thistle
kV kilovolt
kW kilowatt
kWh, kwh kilowatt-hour

L

l 1 Lady 2 lake 3 large 4 left 5 length 6 Liberal 7 pound 8 lightning 9 line 10 litre 11 little 12 long 13 last 14 lower
L 1 Latin 2 live – used esp on electrical plugs 3 *Br* learner (driver)
La lane – used esp in street names 2 Louisiana
LA 1 law agent 2 Library Association 3 *Br* local authority 4 Los Angeles 5 Louisiana

Lab 1 Labour 2 Labrador
Lancs Lancashire
lat latitude
lb 1 pound 2 leg bye
LBC London Broadcasting Company
LCC London County Council
lcd 1 liquid crystal display 2 lowest (*or* least) common denominator
LCM lowest (*or* least) common multiple
LCpl lance corporal
Ld Lord
LDS Licentiate in Dental Surgery
LEA Local Education Authority
led light emitting diode
Leics Leicestershire
LEM lunar excursion module
LF low frequency
LHA Local Health Authority
LHD Doctor of Letters; Doctor of Humanities
Lieut Lieutenant
Lincs Lincolnshire
lit 1 litre 2 literature
Litt D doctor of letters; doctor of literature
LLB Bachelor of Laws
LLD Doctor of Laws
LLM Master of Laws
LOB Location of Offices Bureau
loc cit in the place cited
long longitude
LPG liquefied petroleum gas
LPO London Philharmonic Orchestra
LRAM Licentiate of the Royal Academy of Music
LSE London School of Economics
LSO London Symphony Orchestra
LT 1 lieutenant 2 low-tension
LTA Lawn Tennis Association
Lt Cdr Lieutenant Commander
Lt Col Lieutenant Colonel
Ltd limited
Lt Gen Lieutenant General
LV 1 low velocity 2 low voltage 3 *Br* luncheon voucher
LVT 1 landing vehicle, tracked 2 landing vehicle (tank)
LW 1 long wave 2 low water
LWR light water reactor
LWT London Weekend Television

M

m 1 maiden (over) – used in cricket 2 male 3 married 4 masculine 5 mass 6 metre 7 middle 8 mile 9 thousand 10 milli- 11 million 12 minute – used for the unit of time 13 molar 14 month
M 1 Mach 2 Master 3 mega- 4 Member 5 Monsieur 6 motorway

MA 1 Massachusetts **2** Master of Arts **3** Middle Ages **4** Military Academy

MAFF Ministry of Agriculture, Fisheries, and Food

Maj Major

Maj Gen Major General

Mar March

MASH *NAm* mobile army surgical hospital

max maximum

MB Bachelor of Medicine

MBE Member of the (Order of the) British Empire

MC 1 Master of Ceremonies **2** Member of Congress **3** Military Cross

MCC Marylebone Cricket Club

mcg microgram

MCh, MChir Master of Surgery

MD 1 Managing Director **2** Doctor of Medicine **3** right hand – used in music

MDS Master of Dental Surgery

MEP Member of the European Parliament ·

met 1 meteorological; meteorology **2** metropolitan

mf 1 medium frequency **2** mezzo forte

MFH Master of Foxhounds

mg milligram

Mgr 1 Monseigneur **2** Monsignor

MHz megahertz

mi mile; mileage

MI 1 Michigan **2** military intelligence

Middx Middlesex

min 1 minimum **2** minor **3** minute – used for the unit of time

Min Minister; Ministry

misc miscellaneous; miscellany

ml 1 mile **2** millilitre

MLitt Master of Letters

Mlle mademoiselle

MLR minimum lending rate

mm millimetre

MM 1 Maelzel's metronome **2** messieurs **3** Military Medal

Mme madame

Mmes mesdames

MN 1 Merchant Navy **2** Minnesota

MO 1 Medical Officer **2** Missouri **3** modus operandi **4** money order

mod 1 moderate **2** moderato **3** modern **4** modulus

MoD Ministry of Defence

MOH Medical Officer of Health

mol 1 molecular; molecule **2** mole

Mon Monday

MP 1 Member of Parliament **2** Metropolitan Police **3** Military Police; Military Policeman

mpg miles per gallon

mph miles per hour

MPhil Master of Philosophy

MRCP Member of the Royal College of Physicians

MRCS Member of the Royal College of Surgeons

MRCVS Member of the Royal College of Veterinary Surgeons

MS 1 left hand – used in music **2** manuscript **3** Mississippi **4** multiple sclerosis

MSc Master of Science

Msgr *chiefly NAm* Monseigneur; Monsignor

MSS manuscripts

Mt 1 Matthew **2** Mount

MW 1 medium wave **2** megawatt

mW milliwatt

N

n 1 name **2** nano- **3** born **4** net **5** new **6** neuter **7** nominative **8** noon **9** noun **10** numerical aperture

N 1 knight – used in chess **2** newton **3** North; Northerly; Northern **4** neutral – used esp on electric plugs

NA 1 North America **2** not applicable

NAAFI Navy, Army, and Air Force Institutes

NALGO National and Local Government Officers Association

NAm North America; North American

NASA National Aeronautics and Space Administration – a US government organization

NATO North Atlantic Treaty Organization

NATSOPA National Society of Operative Printers, Graphical and Media Personnel

NB 1 Nebraska **2** New Brunswick **3** note well

NCB National Coal Board

NCC Nature Conservancy Council

NCO non-commissioned officer

NCP National Car Parks

NCR National Cash Register (Company)

NE 1 modern English [*New English*] **2** New England **3** Northeast; Northeastern

NEB 1 National Enterprise Board **2** New English Bible

NEC National Executive Committee

NEDC National Economic Development Council

NERC Natural Environment Research Council

NF 1 National Front **2** Newfoundland **3** no funds

NFU National Farmers' Union

NFWI National Federation of Women's Institutes

NGA National Graphical Association

NHS National Health Service

NI 1 National Insurance **2** Northern Ireland

NLF National Liberation Front

NNE north-northeast

NNW north-northwest
Norf Norfolk
Northants Northamptonshire
Northumb Northumberland
Notts Nottinghamshire
Nov November
NSB National Savings Bank
NSPCC National Society for the Prevention of Cruelty to Children
NSW New South Wales
NT 1 National Trust **2** New Testament **3** no trumps
NUJ National Union of Journalists
NUM National Union of Mineworkers
NUPE National Union of Public Employees
NUR National Union of Railwaymen
NUS 1 National Union of Seamen **2** National Union of Students
NUT National Union of Teachers
NW Northwest; Northwestern
NY New York
NYC New York City
NZ New Zealand

O

o 1 ohm **2** old
OAP Br old-age pensioner
OBE Officer of the (Order of the) British Empire
Oct October
OCTU Officer Cadets Training Unit
OECD Organization for Economic Cooperation and Development
OHMS On His/Her Majesty's Service
OM Order of Merit
ONC Ordinary National Certificate
OND Ordinary National Diploma
ono or near offer – used with prices of goods for sale
op cit in the work cited
OPEC Organization of Petroleum Exporting Countries
orig original; originally; originator
OT 1 occupational therapy; Occupational Therapist **2** Old Testament **3** overtime
OTC Officers' Training Corps
OU Open University
OXFAM Oxford Committee for Famine Relief
Oxon 1 Oxfordshire **2** of Oxford – used chiefly with academic awards <MA ~>
oz ounce; ounces

P

p 1 page **2** participle **3** past **4** pence; penny **5** per **6** piano – used as an instruction in music **7** pico- **8** pint **9** power **10** premolar **11** pressure

pa per annum
Pa 1 Pennsylvania **2** pascal
PA 1 Pennsylvania **2** personal assistant **3** press agent **4** public address (system) **5** purchasing agent
P & O Peninsular and Oriental (Steamship Company)
p & p Br postage and packing
PAX Br private automatic (telephone) exchange
PAYE pay as you earn
PBX private branch (telephone) exchange
PC 1 police constable **2** Privy Councillor
PDSA People's Dispensary for Sick Animals
PE physical education
PEP Br Political and Economic Planning
PER Professional Employment Register
PGA Professional Golfers' Association
PhB Bachelor of Philosophy
PhD Doctor of Philosophy
plc public limited company
PLO Palestine Liberation Organization
PLP Parliamentary Labour Party
PLR Public Lending Right
PM 1 postmortem **2** Prime Minister **3** Provost Marshal
PO 1 Petty Officer **2** Pilot Officer **3** postal order **4** Post Office
POB Post Office box
POE 1 port of embarkation **2** port of entry
pop population
POP Br Post Office Preferred
POW prisoner of war
pp 1 pages **2** past participle **3** by proxy **4** pianissimo
PPE Philosophy, Politics, and Economics
PPS 1 Parliamentary Private Secretary **2** further postscript
PR 1 proportional representation **2** public relations **3** Puerto Rico
Pres President
PRO 1 Public Records Office **2** public relations officer
Prof Professor
PROM programmable read-only memory
PS 1 Police Sergeant **2** postscript **3** Private Secretary **4** prompt side – used to designate part of the theatrical stage
pseud pseudonym; pseudonymous
psi pounds per square inch
PSV Br public service vehicle
pt 1 part **2** pint **3** point **4** port
PT 1 Pacific time **2** physical training
PTA Parent-Teacher Association
Pte Private
PTO please turn over
Pty chiefly Austr, NZ, & SAfr Proprietary
PVC polyvinyl chloride
Pvt chiefly NAm Private
pw per week

PW *Br* policewoman
PX post exchange

Q

q 1 quarto 2 quintal 3 quire
QB Queen's Bench
QC Queen's Counsel
QED which was to be demonstrated
QM quartermaster
QMG Quartermaster General
QMS Quartermaster Sergeant
QPR Queen's Park Rangers
qqv which (*pl*) see
QSO quasi-stellar object
qt quart
qto quarto
qty quantity

R

r 1 radius 2 railway 3 recto 4 resistance 5
right 6 runs – used in cricket
R 1 rabbi 2 radical – used in chemistry 3
rain 4 Reaumur 5 rector 6 queen 7
registered (as a trademark) 8 king 9 ring
road 10 river 11 röntgen 12 rook – used in
chess 13 Royal
RA 1 Rear Admiral 2 Royal Academician;
Royal Academy 3 Royal Artillery
RAAF Royal Australian Air Force
RAC 1 Royal Armoured Corps 2 Royal
Automobile Club
RADA Royal Academy of Dramatic Art
RAF Royal Air Force
RAM 1 random access memory 2 Royal
Academy of Music
RAMC Royal Army Medical Corps
R and A Royal and Ancient – used as the
title of St Andrews Golf Club
RAOC Royal Army Ordnance Corps
RC 1 Red Cross 2 reinforced concrete 3
Roman Catholic
RCAF Royal Canadian Air Force
RCM Royal College of Music
RCMP Royal Canadian Mounted Police
RCN 1 Royal Canadian Navy 2 Royal
College of Nursing
RDC Rural District Council
RE 1 religious education 2 Royal Engineers
reg 1 regiment 2 register; registered 3
registrar; registry 4 regulation 5 regulo
regd registered
regt regiment
Rev 1 Revelation – used for the book of the
Bible 2 Reverend
Revd Reverend
RF 1 radio frequency 2 Rugby Football
RFC 1 Royal Flying Corps 2 Rugby Football
Club

RFU Rugby Football Union
RH Royal Highness
RHS 1 Royal Historical Society 2 Royal
Horticultural Society 3 Royal Humane
Society
RIBA Royal Institute of British Architects
RIC Royal Institute of Chemistry
RICS Royal Institution of Chartered
Surveyors
RIP 1 may he rest in peace 2 may they rest
in peace
RL Rugby League
RM 1 Royal Mail 2 Royal Marines
RMA Royal Military Academy (Sandhurst)
RN Royal Navy
RNAS Royal Naval Air Service
RNIB Royal National Institute for the Blind
RNLI Royal National Lifeboat Institution
RNR Royal Naval Reserve
RNVR Royal Naval Volunteer Reserve
ROC Royal Observer Corps
RoSPA Royal Society for the Prevention of
Accidents
RPI *Br* retail price index
rpm 1 *Br, often cap* retail price
maintenance 2 revolutions per minute
rps revolutions per second
rpt 1 repeat 2 report
RS 1 right side 2 Royal Society
RSC Royal Shakespeare Company
RSM 1 Regimental Sergeant Major 2 Royal
Society of Medicine
RSPB Royal Society for the Protection of
Birds
RSPCA Royal Society for the Prevention of
Cruelty to Animals
RSV Revised Standard Version (of the
Bible)
RSVP please answer
Rt Hon Right Honourable
Rt Rev, Rt Revd Right Reverend
RU Rugby Union
RUC Royal Ulster Constabulary
RV Revised Version (of the Bible)

S

S 1 saint 2 sea 3 siemens 4 Signor 5
society 6 South; Southerly; Southern 7 sun
SA 1 Salvation Army 2 sex appeal 3 small
arms 4 limited liability company 5 Society
of Actuaries 6 South Africa 7 South
America
sae stamped addressed envelope
SALT Strategic Arms Limitation Talks
SAM surface-to-air missile
SAS Special Air Service
Sat Saturday
SATB soprano, alto, tenor, bass
SAYE save-as-you-earn

SBN Standard Book Number
Sc Scots
ScD Doctor of Science
SCE Scottish Certificate of Education
SCF Save the Children Fund
SDLP Social Democratic and Labour Party
SDP Social Democratic Party
SE southeast; southeastern
SEATO Southeast Asia Treaty Organization
sec 1 second; secondary 2 secretary 3 section 4 according to 5 secant
SEN State Enrolled Nurse
Sep, Sept September
seq the following
Serg, Sergt Sergeant
SG 1 Solicitor General 2 *often not cap* specific gravity
Sgt Sergeant
Sgt Maj Sergeant Major
SHAPE Supreme Headquarters Allied Powers Europe
SI International System of Units
Sig Signor
SIS Secret Intelligence Service
SJ Society of Jesus
SLADE Society of Lithographic Artists, Designers and Etchers
SLP Scottish Labour Party
SM Sergeant Major
SNP Scottish National Party
snr senior
So south
soc society
SOGAT Society of Graphical and Allied Trades
Som Somerset
sop soprano
SPCK Society for Promoting Christian Knowledge
SPQR the Senate and the people of Rome
sq square
Sqn Ldr Squadron Leader
Sr 1 senior 2 Senor 3 Sir 4 Sister
SRC Science Research Council
SRN State Registered Nurse
SS 1 saints 2 steamship 3 Sunday School
SSE south-southeast
SSM surface-to-surface missile
SSR Soviet Socialist Republic
SSRC Social Science Research Council
SSW south-southwest
St 1 Saint 2 street
Staffs Staffordshire
STD 1 doctor of sacred theology 2 subscriber trunk dialling
sth south
STP standard temperature and pressure
STUC Scottish Trades Union Congress
Sun Sunday
supp, suppl supplement; supplementary

supt superintendent
SW 1 shortwave 2 southwest; southwestern
SWALK sealed with a loving kiss
SWAPO South-West Africa People's Organization
Sx Sussex

T

T temperature
TA Territorial Army
T & AVR Territorial and Army Volunteer Reserve
TASS the official news agency of the Soviet Union
TB tubercle bacillus
tbs, tbsp tablespoon; tablespoonful
TCCB Test and County Cricket Board
tech 1 technical; technically; technician 2 technological; technology
temp 1 temperature 2 temporary 3 in the time of
Terr, Terr 1 terrace – used esp in street names 2 territory
TGWU Transport and General Workers' Union
Th Thursday
Thur, Thurs Thursday
TIR International Road Transport
TM 1 trademark 2 transcendental meditation
TOPS Training Opportunities Scheme
trans 1 transitive 2 translated; translation; translator
transl translated; translation
trs transpose
TSB Trustee Savings Bank
tsp teaspoon; teaspoonful
TT 1 teetotal; teetotaller 2 Tourist Trophy 3 tuberculin tested
Tue, Tues Tuesday
TU trade union
TUC Trades Union Congress
TV television
TWA Trans-World Airlines

U

u 1 unit 2 upper
UAE United Arab Emirates
UAR United Arab Republic
UAU Universities Athletic Union
UCCA Universities Central Council on Admissions
UCL University College, London
UDA Ulster Defence Association
UDI unilateral declaration of independence
UDR Ulster Defence Regiment
UEFA Union of European Football Associations

UHF ultrahigh frequency
UHT ultrahigh temperature
UK United Kingdom
UKAEA United Kingdom Atomic Energy Authority
ult 1 ultimate 2 ultimo
UN United Nations
UNA United Nations Association
UNESCO United Nations Educational, Scientific, and Cultural Organization
UNICEF United Nations Children's Fund
UNO United Nations Organization
US United States
USA 1 United States Army 2 United States of America
USAF United States Air Force
USN United States Navy
USS United States Ship
USSR Union of Soviet Socialist Republics
UU Ulster Unionist
UV ultraviolet
UVF Ulster Volunteer Force

V

v 1 vector 2 verb 3 verse 4 versus 5 very 6 verso 7 vice 8 vide 9 von – used in German personal names
V 1 velocity 2 volt; voltage 3 volume
V & A Victoria and Albert Museum
var 1 variable 2 variant 3 variation 4 variety 5 various
VAT value-added tax
VC 1 Vice Chairman 2 Vice Chancellor 3 Vice Consul 4 Victoria Cross
VCR video cassette recorder
VD venereal disease
VDT visual display terminal
VDU visual display unit
VE Victory in Europe
Ven Venerable
Vet MB Bachelor of Veterinary Medicine
VG 1 very good 2 Vicar General
VHF very high frequency
vi 1 verb intransitive 2 see below
VLF very low frequency
vol 1 volume 2 volunteer
VR 1 Queen Victoria 2 Volunteer Reserve
VSO Voluntary Service Overseas ·
VSOP Very Special Old Pale – a type of brandy

W

W 1 Watt 2 West; Westerly; Western
WAAC 1 Women's Army Auxiliary Corps – the women's component of the British army from 1914 to 1918 2 Women's Army Auxiliary Corps – the women's component of the US army from 1942 to 1948

WAAF Women's Auxiliary Air Force – the women's component of the RAF
WAC Women's Army Corps – the women's component of the US army
WAF Women in the Air Force – the women's component of the USAF
War, Warw, Warwks Warwickshire
WBA World Boxing Association
WBC 1 white blood cells; white blood count 2 World Boxing Council
wf wrong fount
WHO World Health Organization
WI 1 West Indies 2 Wisconsin 3 Women's Institute
Wilts Wiltshire
wk 1 week 2 work
wkly weekly
Wlk walk – used in street names
Wm William
WNP Welsh National Party
WNW west-northwest
w/o without
WO Warrant Officer
Worcs Worcestershire
WOW War on Want
WPC Woman Police Constable
wpm words per minute
WPS Woman Police Sergeant
WR Western Region
WRAC Women's Royal Army Corps
WRAF Women's Royal Air Force
WRNS Women's Royal Naval Service
WRVS Women's Royal Voluntary Service
WSW west-southwest
WW World War

X

X Christ
XL extra large
XT Christ

Y

y year
yd yard
YHA Youth Hostels Association
YMCA Young Men's Christian Association
YMHA Young Men's Hebrew Association
Yorks Yorkshire
yr 1 year 2 younger 3 your
YWCA Young Women's Christian Association
YWHA Young Women's Hebrew Association

Z

ZANU Zimbabwe African National Union
ZAPU Zimbabwe African People's Union